Prepublication Prai~~se~~ *through* Literature *by Judith* ~~Ferster~~

Arguing through Literature: A Thematic Anthology and Guide

JUDITH FERSTER

North Carolina State University

Boston   Burr Ridge, IL   Dubuque, IA   Madison, WI   New York
San Francisco   St. Louis   Bangkok   Bogotá   Caracas   Kuala Lumpur
Lisbon   London   Madrid   Mexico City   Milan   Montreal   New Delhi
Santiago   Seoul   Singapore   Sydney   Taipei   Toronto

The McGraw·Hill Companies

Mc Graw Hill Higher Education

ARGUING THROUGH LITERATURE: A THEMATIC ANTHOLOGY AND GUIDE
Published by McGraw-Hill, a business unit of The McGraw-Hill Companies, Inc., 1221
Avenue of the Americas, New York, NY, 10020. Copyright © 2005 by The McGraw-Hill
Companies, Inc. All rights reserved. No part of this publication may be reproduced or distributed in any form or by any means, or stored in a database or retrieval system, without the
prior written consent of The McGraw-Hill Companies, Inc., including, but not limited to, in
any network or other electronic storage or transmission, or broadcast for distance learning.
Some ancillaries, including electronic and print components, may not be available to
customers outside the United States.

This book is printed on acid-free paper.

4 5 6 7 8 9 0 DOC/DOC 0 9 8 7 6

ISBN-13: 978-0-07-234946-7
ISBN-10: 0-07-234946-8

President of McGraw-Hill Humanities/Social Sciences: *Steve Debow*
Publisher: *Lisa Moore*
Senior sponsoring editor: *Alexis Walker*
Editorial coordinator: *Bennett Morrison*
Marketing manager: *Lori DeShazo*
Senior media producer: *Todd Vaccaro*
Senior project manager: *Rebecca Komro*
Associate production supervisor: *Jason I. Huls*
Designer: *Laurie Entringer*
Associate media project manager: *Meghan Durko*
Photo research coordinator: *Natalia C. Peschiera*
Photo researcher: *Robin Sand*
Permissions editor: *Marty Granahan*
Interior and cover design: *Ellen Pettengell Design*
Cover image: Homage to Cézanne, *Marko Duricic. Ackland Art Museum, Gift of Jonathan P.
Sher in loving memory of his son, Matthew Adam Sher, 95.12. Permission granted
by Jan De Maere, Galerie Jan De Maere, Brussels.*
Typeface: *10/12 Minion*
Compositor: *Interactive Composition Corporation*
Printer: *R.R. Donnelley and Sons Inc.*

Library of Congress Cataloging-in-Publication Data

Ferster, Judith, 1947-
    Arguing through literature : a thematic anthology and guide / Judith Ferster.
      p. cm.
    Includes Index.
    ISBN 0-07-234946-8 (pbk. : acid-free paper)
      1. English language—Rhetoric—Problems, exercises, etc. 2.
    Criticism—Authorship—Problems, exercises, etc. 3. Literature—History and
    criticism—Theory, etc. 4. College readers. I. Title.
    PE1479.C7F47 2005
    808'.0668—dc22   2004055204

www.mhhe.com

Preface

Ⓒ

Arguing through Literature: A Thematic Anthology and Guide to Academic Writing has two goals. First and foremost, it serves as a guide to literature; its apparatus helps students to think, speak, and write knowledgeably about poems, short stories, plays, and essays. Second, it serves as a guide to argument, encouraging students to read and analyze arguments in a number of disciplines and to construct their own arguments about the literature that they read.

More specifically, *Arguing through Literature* uses secondary sources from academic disciplines as "frameworks" to help students analyze, interpret, and write about literature. The core metaphor of frameworks suggests that the way a scene is framed changes the way we see it. The window we look through determines our perspective and so determines what is central and what is peripheral. If we approach a piece of literature through New Criticism, for instance, its concepts help us decide which features of the work are salient, which features "count" as clues to its meaning. Other approaches highlight other features as keys to other kinds of meaning.

Like researchers in other fields, literary critics regularly borrow frameworks from other disciplines in order to look at their subject in new ways. Marxist, Freudian, and feminist "readings" of texts are only a few of the many different schools of literary criticism produced by such borrowings. But instead of giving students examples of those schools of criticism, this book provides them with both primary and secondary sources—literary works and cross-disciplinary writing—they can use to construct their own critiques. Students will work with a variety of disciplinary genres and come to understand how different disciplines accomplish similar tasks in different ways. When, for assignments in the later chapters, they are asked to find their own frameworks, they learn research methods and gain experience doing work that can explore new ground.

This is not a *writing* across the curriculum approach, but rather a *reading* (and thinking) across the curriculum approach. It doesn't ask a student to produce a sociology paper, but rather it asks a student to look at sociology texts to understand how sociologists communicate, and to consider what a sociological idea might contribute to the understanding of literature. The book thus helps students to prepare for the reading they will do in other courses, in other disciplines, throughout their academic careers.

In sum, working with this book will enable students to:

- **understand** the relationships between literary and nonliterary writing, recognizing the features that they share and the features that they don't;

- **analyze** arguments, especially academic arguments;
- **generate** sound academic arguments;
- **analyze and interpret** literary works by reading them closely; and
- **analyze and interpret** literary works by contextualizing them using concepts garnered from various academic disciplines.

NOTABLE FEATURES

Arguing through Literature helps instructors and students to achieve these goals with features that include:

- **A wealth of prompts for writing activities,** in class and out, that make any classroom a student-centered environment for active learning and that offer choices and opportunities for professors with individualized teaching goals;
- **Detailed explanation of the elements of language,** like diction and syntax, that provides tools for analyzing texts and writing well;
- **Detailed pedagogy on the features and strategies of argument,** especially academic argument, demystifying the disciplines and revealing further links between analyzing texts and generating ideas for one's own writing;
- **A wide range of engaging selections** by authors both contemporary and classic, from the United States and abroad;
- **A section of full-color reproductions of works of art** to facilitate comparison of visual and verbal modes of representation; and
- **Sample student papers,** some in multiple drafts so that students can watch the revision process.

ORGANIZATION

Arguing through Literature's two major sections are indicated by its subtitle: *A Thematic Anthology and Guide to Academic Writing.* The guide is a three-part section of pedagogical chapters that offer students guidance on reading and writing different kinds of texts, teach them the key elements of literature, and explain argument, research, and the concept of disciplinary frameworks. The guide is followed by the thematically organized anthology of poetry, fiction, drama, and nonfiction prose. In addition, four appendices at the end of the book offer support for the activities prompted in the text.

Parts I, II, and III: The "Guide"

In **Part I: An Introduction to Reading and Writing,** students learn how to identify civic argument, academic argument, and imaginative literature by recognizing and interpreting key features of each. **Chapter 1: On Reading and Writing** introduces students to the concepts of genre, audience, and the purposes for writing, and **Chapter 2: The Writing Process** provides a step-by-step guide to the writing process, illustrated by a sample student paper. **Chapter 3: Kinds of Writing** develops the definitions of the major genres and shows how the different kinds of writing can speak to each other, introducing the idea of interpretive frameworks.

Part II: The Elements of Literature offers students tools for close reading and encourages them to try them out, providing multiple activities and a diverse set of exemplary texts, using "literature" in the widest sense of the word. Among the examples are poetry by Donne, Frost, and Michael Stipe of the rock group R.E.M.; fiction by Borges; and a medical abstract.

Part III: Argument, Research, and Literature: Conversations among Different Kinds of Writing introduces students to the principles of effective argument and shows them how to use those principles to interpret literature. **Chapter 8: Argument** introduces students to the basic elements of argument: claims, reasons, and assumptions. This chapter draws on the terms set forth in previous chapters to show how the different elements of argument and different kinds of claims appear in arguments from different fields. It examines not only argument, but also the way academic texts situate themselves in relation to previous research in the field, the ways they are structured, and some of their stylistic features.

In **Chapter 9: Exploring Literature through Other Disciplines** and **Chapter 10: Using Research to Write about Literature,** students learn how to use academic arguments as conceptual frameworks for interpreting literature, thus practicing the valuable skill of applying information from one context to material in another, an important goal of intellectual development. As they work through these chapters, they have opportunities to see the way close reading and contextualizing enrich each other and to search for conceptual frameworks on their own.

Part IV: The "Thematic Anthology"

Part IV: A Thematic Anthology presents literature and disciplinary arguments arranged into eight thematic groupings. Many of the selections and some of the themes are favorites of teachers and students, but some of the works are less frequently anthologized. In addition, some of the favorites appear under uncommon headings to encourage fresh views of them.

The thematic anthology and the prompts for writing and discussion were developed to provide instructors with enough flexibility to adapt learning to individual goals. Each genre of literature, including nonfiction prose, is represented in each thematic chapter, and the selections range from classic to contemporary. For example, **Chapter 11: Body** has poems from Emily Dickinson, John Donne, and William Shakespeare but also from newer poets Lucille Clifton, Galway Kinnell, and Sharon Olds. Nonfiction prose writers include a pharmacologist, an academic writing civic discourse, and a memoir writer.

The Appendices

Four helpful appendices round out the text. **Appendix A: Critical Approaches** gives students an overview of the important schools of criticism. **Appendix B: Glossary of Terms** provides students with definitions of important literary and rhetorical terms. **Appendix C: Reading Non-literary Texts** gives students guidance for comprehending and responding to nonfiction prose. **Appendix D** offers a guide to MLA and APA documentation styles.

SUPPLEMENTARY RESOURCES

Arguing through Literature provides a host of supplemental resources for instructors and students.

- The Instructor's Resource CD-ROM contains potential responses to class activities and suggestions for teaching.
- The Online Learning Center, located at **www.mhhe.com/ferster,** has a student side that includes casebooks for featured authors and portions of the texts connected to the sample student papers in Chapters 8 and 10. It also has a chart outlining a brief history of the English language and an exercise helping students to distinguish between civic and academic discourse. For easy reference, OLC icons appear in the margin next to authors included in the Online Learning Center author casebooks. The instructor side includes the instructor's manual.
- ARIEL (A Resource for the Interactive Exploration of Literature), McGraw-Hill English's fully interactive CD-ROM, is an exciting new tool that introduces students to the pleasures of studying literature. The CD features nearly thirty casebooks on authors ranging from Sophocles to Rita Dove. Each casebook offers a rich array of resources, including hyperlinked texts, video and audio clips, critical essays, a biography, bibliography, and webliography, essay questions, quizzes, and visuals. To make the text-CD connections as seamless as possible, ARIEL icons appear in the margins next to authors featured in ARIEL. Among numerous other resources are a robust glossary and a visual timeline.

Acknowledgments

The idea for this book came out of the goals set for the first-year writing program of North Carolina State University when I was the director of the program. The teachers of the program, including graduate teaching assistants who had responsibility for their own sections, responded to those goals with great ingenuity and imagination. Many talked with me about teaching, used drafts of chapters of this book in classes, let me observe classes, and shared their students' writing. Some of them helped with the study questions for selections in the anthology. In addition, several graduate students served as research assistants. Other members of the English Department faculty responded generously to my requests for help with ideas and selections for the anthology. Several are rhetoricians who, along with writing teachers, served on the advisory council of the program and taught me more than I knew about teaching writing. Several members of the administrative staff introduced me to new genres of popular music. They all helped me learn a great deal while trying to make this book grow and certainly helped me have fun doing it. They include: Prof. Chris Anson, Ms. Evelyn Audi, David Baker, Prof. John Balaban, David L. P. Carter, Prof. Michael P. Carter, Prof. Christopher Cobb, Alyssa Fountain, Dr. Meredith Fosque, Prof. Charlotte Gross, Mr. Phil Lisi, Ms. Rachel Lutwick-Deaner, Amy Sue Martin, Justin Marks, Prof. David Herman, Mr. Larry Johnson, Prof. John Kessel, Prof. Antony Harrison, Prof. Deborah Hooker, Prof. Steven B. Katz, Dr. Cathy Leaker, Mr. Steven Luyendyk, Mr. Eugene Melton, Dr. Kevin McGowin, Prof. Carolyn Miller, Twila Mills, Veronica Norris, Prof. Nancy Penrose, Prof. Joyce Pettis, Mr. Matt Porter, Ms. Laura Prewitt, Prof. Kirsten Shepherd-Barr, Prof. Judy Jo Small (Emerita), Mr. Roy Stamper, Prof. Jon Thompson, Dr. Anjel Tozcu, Mr. Tom Wallis, Prof. Walt Wolfram, and Prof. Robert Young.

I would also like to thank faculty members from other departments of North Carolina State University and other institutions for answering my questions about ideas and sources in their disciplines. From North Carolina State, William Adler, Religion; Maxine Atkinson, Sociology; Dennis Boos, Statistics; Fred Gorelick, Theatre; Robert Hambourger, Philosophy; Jane McCoubrie, Communications; Samuel (Bob) Pond, Psychology; and David Zonderman, History.

From other institutions: Dr. Joe Alessi, Psychiatry, University of Buffalo School of Medicine; Louise Antony, Philosophy, Ohio State University; Dr. Helen Aronoff, Psychiatry, University of Buffalo School of Medicine; Joe Levine, Philosophy, Ohio State University; David Ferster, Neurobiology,

XII *Acknowledgments*

Northwestern; Peter Filene, History, University of North Carolina; John Kasson, History, University of North Carolina; Geoffrey Gault Harpham, President and Director, National Humanities Center; Gregory Meyerson, North Carolina A&T State University; Andrew Scott, Political Science, University of North Carolina (Emeritus); Anne Scott, History, Duke (Emerita); Edward Shannon, Ramapo College; Laurie Shannon, English, Duke University; and Mohan Srinivasarao, Textile and Fiber Engineering, Georgia Institute of Technology.

I also appreciate the help of the following individuals, who tutored me in diverse subjects ranging from the Supreme Court to computers and hip-hop: Paul Antony-Levine; Rachel Antony-Levine; Dr. Larry Aronoff; Hon. Joan B. Gottschall, United States District Court, Northern District, Illinois; John Prioli; Rajaie Qubain; Erica Rothman, M.S.W.; and Rabbi Alan Sokobin, D.D., Th.D., J.D.

My parents Paul Ferster and Dorothy Ferster provided remarkable material support so that my house wouldn't fall apart while I was absorbed in writing. They also brought the research, editorial, and production skills they had developed while working on their own publications into the late drafts, especially of the anthology. The usual "sine qua non" is more than usually true in the case of their extraordinary gifts to this project. They didn't have to.

Lisa Moore of McGraw-Hill memorably helped me translate pedagogy into written form in the earliest drafts. McGraw-Hill editors Sarah Touborg, Alexis Walker, and Bennett Morrison attended to form and content at every level of the project and helped to keep me on track, as well. Katharine Glynn helped give the anthology substance and shape.

The following reviewers read drafts and responded meticulously and helpfully: Susan Al-Jarrah, Southwestern Oklahoma State University; Regina Alston, North Carolina Central University; Michael Anzelone, Nassau Community College; Scott Ash, Nassau Community College; Kathyrn Benzel, University of Nebraska–Kearney; Brenda Boudreau, McKendree College; Sharon Buzzard, Quincy University; Sean Chapman, University of Arkansas; Maryanne Cole, Truckee Meadows Community College; Laurie Coleman, San Antonio College; Tamera Davis, Pratt Community College; Dallas Dillon, Merced College; Sascha Feinstein, Lycoming College; Jason Fichtel, University of New Mexico; Meredith Fosque, North Carolina State University; Scott Gilbert, Winthrop University; George Gopen, Duke University; Laura Gray, University of Arkansas; Ann Hawkins, Austin Peay State University; Jeff Henderson, Kalamazoo Valley Community College; Douglas Hesse, Illinois State University; Lesa Hildebrand, Triton College; Michael Hogan, Southeast Missouri State University; Matthew Jockers, Stanford University; Alan Johnson, Idaho State University; Kimberlie Johnson, Eastern Washington University; Susanne Johnston, University of Wisconsin–Stout; Timothy Kiogora, Eastern Kentucky University; Benjamin Kostival, University of Alaska Fairbanks; Catherine Kroll, Sonoma State University; Wallis Leslie, De Anza

DEDICATION

To Paul Ferster, Dorothy Ferster, and David Ferster,
My family of origin—I couldn't have chosen better.

And to the teachers and students of the freshman writing program
at North Carolina State University—
The community of choice that inspired this book

College; Michael Levy, University of Wisconsin–Stout; Simon Lewis, College of Charleston; Alfred Guy Litton, Texas Woman's University; Zhanshu Liu, Nassau Community College; Kelley Logan, Southwestern Oklahoma State University; E. David Morgan, Longwood College; Ann Moser, Radford University; Trudi Muro, University of Texas–Arlington; E. Suzanne Owens, Lorain County Community College; Mike Pennell, Purdue University; Dennis Quinn, Worcester State College; Shelley Rees, University of North Texas; Cecelia Robinson, William Jewell College; Melissa Root, University of Denver; Elizabeth Roth, Southwest Texas State University; Marie Sagues, Sonoma State University; Lynn Severson, Bismarck State College; Cynthia Sheard, University of Kentucky; Lori Spillane, Indiana University–Purdue University Indianapolis; David Stevens, Seton Hall University; J. Don Vann, University of North Texas; Ted Wadley, Georgia Perimeter College; Stephanie Wardrop, Colorado State University; Angela Jane Weisl, Seton Hall University; Joseph Wilferth, State University of West Georgia; Debbie Williams, Abilene Christian University; Margaret Whitt, University of Denver; Bernadette Wilkowski, Seton Hall University; Greg Winston, Lincoln University; Kenneth Womack, Penn State Altoona; Randal Woodland, University of Michigan–Dearborn; Teresa Young, Philander Smith College.

All of the people listed here have been my teachers. I hope my responses to their comments and suggestions are worthy of their patience and generosity, for which I am deeply grateful.

The following pages illustrate how this book works. Spending a few minutes getting to know the features of *Arguing through Literature* will help you get the most out of the text.

▶ Examples of **student writing** throughout the first three parts show you how other students accomplished the writing tasks that you will face in this course.

Digging

SEAMUS HEANEY (1939–), born in Castledawson, County Derry, Northern Ireland, won the Nobel Prize for Literature in 1995.

Whoa! Is he angry at someone? I thought the pen was resting. How did it turn into a weapon?

Not a very dignified position. Is this supposed to be funny?

What's a potato drill? The dictionary has a "drill" meaning a trench or furrow for planting seeds—that must be it, not an instrument for boring holes or the German cotton or the W. African baboon.

Between my finger and my thumb
The <u>squat</u> pen <u>rests</u>; <u>snug</u> as a <u>gun</u>.

Under my window, a clean <u>rasping</u> sound
When the spade sinks into gravelly ground.
My father, digging. I look down

Till his straining rump among the flowerbeds
Bends low, comes up twenty years away
Stooping in rhythm through potato drills
Where he was digging.

[1]Of course, this advice pertains only if you have "writing rights" over a text. If you need to be actively engaged with something from a library, photocopy it so that you can respond fully without intruding on the experience of later readers.

Clearly, there are significant differences between Belluck's account for the readers of the *New York Times* and Snowdon's scientific article. The activity below will help you articulate them.

ACTIVITY 5: *Comparing Belluck and Snowdon*

What differences do you see between Belluck's article for the *New York Times* and the abstract of the scientists' report for the New York Academy of Sciences?

* Compare the length of the abstract's single paragraph with the length of the paragraphs of the *New York Times*.
* What kinds of vocabulary does each piece use? How many words in each of them are you unfamiliar with?
* Who is speaking in each piece?
* What other differences between the two pieces do you see? How do you account for them?

◀ **Activity prompts** throughout the first three parts give you the opportunity to write in response to literature using the skills presented in the text.

Checklist for Improving Drafts

____Does the draft fulfill the assignment? Does it accomplish goals that the major verbs of the assignment call for?
____What is the thesis? How can it be made clearer?
____Does the introduction predict what happens in the draft without stealing its own thunder?
____Does the conclusion recapitulate without being boring?
____How does the conclusion offer something new without going off on an irrelevant tangent?
____Does the draft divide its material into appropriate categories and subcategories?
____Does it put them in a logical order with appropriate transitions between them?
____Does the draft offer enough relevant evidence to support its thesis? What further evidence could be added? What contradictory evidence does it ignore?
____Does it use references, paraphrases, and quotations to gather evidence?
____How could its style be improved?
____How can its grammar and mechanical errors be corrected?

◀ **Checklists,** located throughout Part I, ask you questions that will help you review important principles.

▶ **Part IV: A Thematic Anthology**
presents literature and academic writing
arranged into eight thematic chapters:
Body; Spirit; Acting and Authenticity;
Gender, Sex, and Love; Race and
Ethnicity; Ethical Questions; Nature;
and Sight and Insight.

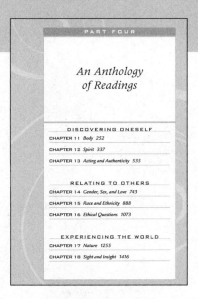

1. What is the structure of the poem? The important features of its language?
2. Who is speaking? To whom? What is narrator's argument in the poem?
   What argumentative tactics does the narrator use to try to get his way?
   Compare it to the argument in "To His Coy Mistress" (see Chapter 13).
   What other poems in this section can this poem be compared to?
3. What disciplines could shed light on this poem?

⟨ FRAMEWORKS ⟩

Looking at Shakespeare through Medicine

SHAKESPEARE, *Sonnets 65, 72, 73*

HOBART WALLING, "Life's Brief Candle: A Shakespearean Guide to Death and Dying for
Compassionate Physicians"

WILLIAM SHAKESPEARE

WILLIAM SHAKESPEARE (1564–1616) was born at Stratford-on-Avon to a middle
class family. Many of the theories that someone else wrote his plays are motivated by
the fact that little is known about his education. He seems to have been educated
at the free-grammar school in Stratford and to have been, possibly, a schoolmaster
there, but there is no record of any time at a university. Some find it hard to explain
how a person without university training could have had as much knowledge about
the natural world, the arts and sciences, the practical arts, and classical literature as
is revealed in the works. But the plays and poems show not only learning, but also a
keen ear for language, great wit, and deep insights into the complexities of human
character. Shakespeare invented words and developed the genres of Renaissance
tragedy and the blank verse line in agile and inventive ways. After marrying Anne
Hathaway, and possibly having a pair of twins named Hamnet and Judith, he
moved to London, where he became an actor in a very successful acting company and
a shareholder in the Globe Theatre. There he wrote, produced, and acted in a stream
of plays that are cherished around the world and have been given continuously in
every possible medium. When he died in Stratford, he bequeathed his second-best
bed to his wife. To the world, he bequeathed poems, including the "Sonnets," "Venus
and Adonis," and "The Rape of Lucrece" and a trove of comedies, tragedies, and
histories that have influenced writers all over the world.

Shakespeare, Sonnets 65, 72, 73

A number of Renaissance poets produced sequences of sonnets, including Sir Philip
Sidney ("Astrophel and Stella"), Edmund Spenser ("Amoretti"), and Shakespeare,
whose 154 sonnets consider themes of love, life, death, and art.

◀ Each thematic chapter in the anthology has a **Frameworks** section that offers
a literary selection paired with relevant
academic writing that you can use to
interpret the literary selection.

▶ A selection of **full-color reproductions**
of works of art let you compare visual
representations to the written representations elsewhere in the text.

FIGURE I-B *Pieter Brueghel, the Elder (Flemish 1525?–69), Landscape with the
Fall of Icarus. Oil on canvas, 29 × 44 in. (73.5 × 112 cm). 1558. Royal Museum of
Fine Arts, Brussels, Belgium.*
See W.H. Auden, "Musée des Beaux Arts," p. 127.
See William Carlos Williams, "Landscape with the Fall of Icarus," p. 1437.

JOHN DONNE

(For biographical notes, see p. 256.)

Song

Go, and catch a falling star,
    Get with child° a mandrake root,°
Tell me, where all past years are,
    Or who cleft the devil's foot,
5 Teach me to hear mermaids singing
Or to keep off envy's stinging,
        And find
        What wind
Serves to advance an honest mind.

◀ **ARIEL icons** in the margin of
the book indicate authors about
whom you will find additional
resources in the ARIEL CD-ROM
that accompanies the text.

Contents

EXPERIENCING THE WORLD

An Introduction
to Reading and Writing

Reading Texts

We swim in a sea of written language. As students and teachers, in particular, we are textual beings, constantly reading, and then writing in response to what we read. If your mailboxes—physical and digital—are anything like mine, they are awash in texts: notes, announcements, invitations, forms, advertisements, surveys, newspapers, newsletters, magazines, and more.

We can classify these different kinds of writing in different ways by concentrating on what they intend to do, whom they intend to address, or what they look like. If we put the emphasis on *purpose*, or what texts are intended to *do*, we can identify three broad categories of writing:

- **Exposition** explains; that is, it offers to expose the truth about something. Expository writing is informative.
- **Argument** attempts to persuade someone to think or do something. It makes claims—assertions that something is true—and defends them.
- **Expressive writing** conveys thoughts and feelings.

In contrast, if we concentrate on the audience texts mean to address, we will group them differently, perhaps distinguishing between these two kinds:

- **Civic writing,** which speaks to communities of any membership and size, addressing readers as citizens or members of the group;
- **Academic writing,** which speaks to students or experts in colleges and universities on subjects of study in academic disciplines.

For instance, after the smoky summer of 2002, the United States Department of the Interior issued a press release on President George W. Bush's recommendations for a forest policy aimed at preventing wildfires: entitled "President Bush Announces Initiative to Restore Forest Health and Prevent Catastrophic Wildfires,"[1] this example of civic writing addressed the whole nation. Environmental groups' websites and e-mail distribution lists speak to address a worldwide virtual community. Newspaper reports in Oregon, where Bush announced his new policy, are likewise examples of civic writing, but addressed to a more local audience.[2]

In contrast, writing done by researchers in the field of forestry addresses students and other experts in the field. "Introducing Wildfire into Forest Management Planning: Towards a Conceptual Approach" addresses the more specialized audience that reads the academic journal *Forest Ecology and Management*, in which it appeared. You would expect to find that journal in a college or university collection, not the local branch of a county library.[3] Some issues are available online, but with access limited to subscribers.

 ACTIVITY 1: *Describing Three Kinds of Writing*

We can examine the different categories of writing in a chart like this one that makes room for both kinds of writing and the different audiences they address. Fill out a chart like the one below. Under "Examples," list kinds of writing meant to inform, persuade, or express. Under "Audience," list the readers that writers might be addressing. Whom do they want to read their writing? Under "Features," list anything distinctive about each kind or genre of writing. For instance, how do they look different from each other?

---

[1]U.S. Department of the Interior, "President Bush Announces Initiative to Restore Forest Health and Prevent Catastrophic Wildfires," 22 August 2002, http://www.doi.gov/news/020822b.htm.

[2]Tim Hearden, "Bush Urges Forest Thinning: Plan Would Prevent Many Fires, He Says," *Record Searchlight*, 23 August 2002, http://www.redding.com/redd/home/.

[3]K.D. Kalabokidis, S. Gatzojannis, and S. Galatsidas, "Introducing Wildfire into Forest Management Planning: Towards a Conceptual Approach," *Forest Ecology and Management* 158 (2002): 41–50.

Are they printed or handwritten? Short or long? Do they include pictures or not? Graphs and tables? Under "Response Called For," list the thought or actions the writers want to elicit from their audiences. Do they want us to think something? Do something?

Kind of Writing	Examples	Audience	Features	Response Called For
Expository Writing				
Argumentative Writing				
Expressive Writing				

THE COMMUNICATIONS TRIANGLE

All of the elements we have so far discussed make up the social, or **rhetorical,** context of communication, which is often depicted as a triangle in which the corners, representing the message, its sender, and its receiver, all center on a common subject matter:

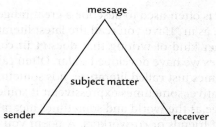

FIGURE 1 *The Communications Triangle*

Because the points of the triangle are interdependent, changes at one point affect the others. For example, imagine describing your instructor to your best friend after class. Now imagine describing this same instructor on an official evaluation form to be submitted to your school. The messages you send to these different receivers (friend, school) about the same subject (your instructor) will likely be very different in terms of format, word choice, tone, etc. Now imagine another faculty member (different sender) describing your instructor (same subject matter) to your best friend (same receiver). How similar is that description likely to be to yours?

Understanding the social context of a message, also called its **rhetorical situation,** is absolutely critical in interpreting its meaning. We will be returning again and again to this concept in the chapters that follow.

ACTIVITY 2: *Tugging at the Corners of the Communications Triangle*

Write a short letter or memo. Label it according to the elements in the diagram of the communications triangle in Figure 1: subject matter, message (what kind of message is it?), sender, receiver. Then write another version of your message having changed your definition of the audience. For instance, you might write two versions of a letter of support for a friend applying for a job. Assume that the job supervisor has asked for insights into candidates' strengths and weaknesses. One version of the letter should be written for the eyes of the supervisor only. The other should be written as though the friend will read it, too. Then write a few sentences about the difference between the two versions. Does your letter change when you know that your friend will have access to it? If having a double audience makes writing the letter more difficult, say how.

KINDS OF WRITING:
PURPOSE, AUDIENCE, AND FORM

The word *literature* is often used to describe a great range of texts, including academic research, as in "Have you read the latest literature on wild fires?" But there is another kind of writing that doesn't fit comfortably into any one of the categories we have developed so far. Often called imaginative literature but sometimes just called literature, it is sometimes argumentative, sometimes informative, sometimes expressive; it is sometimes addressed to an audience as large as the world and sometimes meant only for the writer or a small group of friends or co-workers. A poem you write in your journal and show to no one, the latest bestseller, a Shakespeare play, and the lyrics of rock songs are all examples of imaginative literature. Consisting primarily of stories, novels, poems, plays, and the recently named "creative nonfiction," this type of writing will be our main concern here. The book will help you to read, interpret, and write about imaginative literature, partly by examining its features and how they work and partly by comparing it to other kinds of writing.

Let's now look in more depth at the different types of writing we've introduced thus far.

Addressing the Public: Civic Writing

Civic writing can address communities of every conceivable size—as small as a city block or neighborhood or as large as "the people of the world." It can be commercial and aim to make a profit, nonprofit and aim to improve public welfare, or voluntary and be written for and by people donating their time out of interest or conviction. It can therefore take many forms.

A reader can determine which particular audience a piece of civic writing has in mind, and what its purpose is, by looking at its title, the kinds of sources it uses and how it treats them, and the kinds of language it uses, among other factors. Since most advertisements have to fight for attention among the chaotic flow of texts in our lives, they rely heavily on short, memorable phrases and visuals. Legal contracts, by contrast, are notoriously dense and full of jargon, since they must be precise; few people read them unless they have an important stake in doing so.

Most newspapers and newsletters include writing with different (not strictly informational) purposes. These different purposes are expressed in different *genres*, or kinds of writing, within the larger category of civic writing. Even the simplest organizational newsletter might include a report on the budget *informing* members of the group's finances, a letter from the president *arguing* that dues should be raised, a memoir *expressing* a member's feelings about a fundraiser the organization sponsored, and a (paid) ad for a local restaurant *inviting* readers to hold meetings there.

Here is an example of one genre of civic writing—a *New York Times* article reporting on current research on the brain.

From *Nuns Offer Clues to Alzheimer's and Aging*[4]

PAM BELLUCK

ANKATO, Minn., May 2—A spiraling road slopes gently up to Good Counsel Hill, where the convent of the School Sisters of Notre Dame perches peacefully. Within its thick red brick walls are bright paintings of nuns and children. Organ hymns waft from a circular chapel, and nuns attend Mass and murmur rosaries under a white vaulted dome.

But this crucible of faith is also the site of an extraordinary scientific experiment. For 15 years, elderly Catholic nuns here have had their genes analyzed and balance and strength measured. They have been tested on how many words they can remember minutes after reading them on flashcards, how many animals they can name in a minute and whether they can count coins correctly.

The autobiographical essays they wrote for their order in their 20's, when they took their vows, have been scrutinized, their words plumbed for meaning.

---

[4]Pam Belluck, "Nuns Offer Clues to Alzheimer's and Aging," *New York Times*, 7 May 2001, http://www.nytimes.com/.

And as they have died, their brains have been removed and shipped in plastic tubs to a laboratory where they are analyzed and stored in jars.

The experiment, called the Nun Study, is considered by experts on aging to be one of the most innovative efforts to answer questions about who gets Alzheimer's disease and why. And now in a new report it is offering insight on a different subject—whether a positive emotional outlook early in life can help people live longer.

5   "The Nun Study has certainly been pioneering," said Dr. Richard Suzman, chief of demography and population epidemiology at the National Institute on Aging. "It's helped change the paradigm about how people think about aging and Alzheimer's disease."

By studying 678 nuns—at this convent and six others in the order, in Connecticut, Maryland, Texas, Wisconsin, Missouri and Illinois—Dr. David A. Snowdon, an epidemiologist at the University of Kentucky, and colleagues have come up with tantalizing clues and provocative theories over the years.

Their research has shown that folic acid may help stave off Alzheimer's disease; that small, barely perceptible strokes may trigger some dementia; and, in an especially striking finding, that early language ability may be linked to lower risk of Alzheimer's because nuns who packed more ideas into the sentences of their early autobiographies were less likely to get Alzheimer's disease six decades later.

The new report, being published on Monday in *The Journal of Personality and Social Psychology*, says that nuns who expressed more positive emotions in their autobiographies lived significantly longer—in some cases 10 years longer—than those expressing fewer positive emotions.

"It's an important finding," Dr. Suzman said, "and I think it will lead to lots of additional studies."

10   The nuns are ideal for scientific study because their stable, relatively similar lives preclude certain factors from contributing to illness. They do not smoke, hardly drink and do not experience physical changes related to pregnancy. The School Sisters are white and eat in convent cafeterias, and most were teachers in Catholic schools.

The study is also considered powerful because it has information from several stages in its subjects' lives, including when they were too young to manifest Alzheimer's or other diseases related to aging.

"I think the Nun Study is very important because it uses information obtained about people before the period of illness," said Dr. Robert P. Friedland, professor of neurology at Case Western Reserve University and author of a study showing that people with Alzheimer's were, as young adults, less mentally and physically active outside their jobs than people without the disease. "So we know from the Nun Study and others that Alzheimer's disease takes several decades to develop, and the disease has many important effects on all aspects of a person's life."

All this has given Dr. Snowdon, author of a new book on the study called "Aging With Grace" (Bantam), a rare window through which to examine why some nuns thrive and others deteriorate so much they lose speech, mobility and much of their memory. The differences show up even in nuns with virtually identical backgrounds, even those who are biologically related.

At 93, Sister Nicolette Welter still reads avidly, recently finishing a biography of Bishop James Patrick Shannon. She knits, crochets, plays rousing card games and, until a recent fall, was walking several miles a day with no cane or walker.

But a younger sibling, Sister Mary Ursula, 92, shows clear Alzheimer's symptoms, Dr. Snowdon said. Several times a day, Sister Nicolette feeds and reads prayers to Sister Mary Ursula, who uses a wheelchair and can hardly lift her head or gnarled hands.

The other day, Sister Nicolette prompted Sister Mary Ursula to remember her age and birth date, but when Sister Nicolette asked if she recalled when "Sister Julia told you to pick up the Kleenex people used after Mass and you didn't want to," Sister Mary Ursula's eyes glazed, showing no hint of recognition.

Another Welter sister, 87-year-old Sister Claverine, is still active and clear-headed. A fourth sibling, Sister Mary Stella, died in 1996 at 80.

"I wouldn't have any idea why this happened to Mary Ursula," said Sister Nicolette, "but I just feel like I'll keep my mental faculties." . . .

Dr. Snowdon, 48, has become unusually close to his subjects. He says that when he was in Catholic school as a child, the nuns were more rigid and strict than the warm, good humored School Sisters he sees almost as grandmothers. That relationship has made him acutely aware of sensitive ethical issues, like how forthright to be with nuns who show slight signs of Alzheimer's.

"Do we really want to tell these dear women who are having memory loss that they are in the early phases of Alzheimer's, that they should start taking something?" he asked.

Dr. Snowdon is quick to agree with other experts who say his conclusions need to be corroborated by other studies. There are limitations to the autobiographies, for instance, since the nuns knew a mother superior would see their writing and therefore may not have been totally candid.

"He's pointed us in some directions," said Dr. Bill Thies, vice president for medical and scientific affairs at the Alzheimer's Association, based in Chicago, "but I think it's going to take a fair amount of work before we start making public health recommendations about behaviors that will prevent Alzheimer's."

Still, Dr. Snowdon hopes his study will encourage people to do things to ward off the disease, like quit smoking and other stroke-causing behaviors, and read to children to stimulate language development. His current project involves analyzing old photographs of nuns for personality clues in their face muscles to see if personality correlates to Alzheimer's or longevity.

And, although he cannot prove it scientifically, he contends the nuns' spirituality and community living helps them too.

"You don't necessarily have to join a church or join a convent," Dr. Snowdon said. "But that love of other people, that caring, how good they are to each other and patient, that's something all of us can do."

Several nuns agree.

45 "The science is important," Sister Miriam said. "But the science is dictated by providence anyway." [May 7, 2001]

ACTIVITY 3: *Analyzing the* New York Times *Article*

Use the following questions as a guide to exploring "Nuns Offer Clues to Alzheimer's and Aging":

- What kind of an audience does Belluck seem to address in her article? How do you know? What kinds of things does she expect us to know about her subject? Which does she explain to us?
- What do you think Belluck's background is? Is she a scientist herself? How do you know? What kind of research on the topic does Belluck seem to have done before writing the article?
- Where in the article do you find out what its main subject is?
- What happens in the article before the main subject is introduced?
- Can you tell whether Belluck believes that Dr. David Snowdon's research is valid and his conclusions correct?
- If you wanted to learn more about the Nun Study, does this article contain information that would allow you to find it?
- Which of the features you have identified above are specific to civic writing?

Of course, not all civic writing looks like newspaper articles. The following exercise is an opportunity for you to think about different kinds of civic writing.

ACTIVITY 4 (GROUP WORK): *Describing Public Language*

This activity can be done in one large or several small groups. Groups should brainstorm together to make a list of different kinds of writing that make up our public language environment.

Designate a recorder to write down suggestions as group members think of them. On a piece of paper, the recorder should make a chart like the one below. Group members should work together to fill in the columns. For "Features," list anything distinctive about this kind of writing. For instance, how do these different types of writing look different from each other? How densely are they printed? Do they include pictures? Under "Response Called For," list the thought or actions the writers want to elicit from their audiences. The recorder should be prepared to report the results of the group's brainstorming to the class as a whole.

ACTIVITY 4 (GROUP WORK): *(Continued)*

Types of Public Language: Sample Entry

Genre	Purpose	Audience	Features	Response Called For
Letter to the editor	To make one's views known on a topic; to publicly correct or contend with a previously published statement	Readers of the newspaper (or other publication)	Short; fairly formal; refers to previously published piece; usually signed, often with place of residence and/or occupation listed	Agreement with the writer's argument; taking an action such as voting a particular way or lobbying a congressional representative

Addressing Experts and Students: Academic Writing

Academic writing takes place in colleges and universities. Its chief purposes are to inform and to argue, and it is chiefly meant to be read by scholars and students. Researchers investigate problems and questions and then write reports in which they announce their results; their purpose is to try to persuade other researchers that their results are valid and significant. Researchers typically publish their reports as articles in scholarly journals or books published by university presses. Unlike most civic writing, scholarly writing does not get published until it is reviewed and approved by panels of experts in the field. But like civic writing, it is governed by conventions that determine its form, length, and style. Each journal or press establishes guidelines for what its publications will look like.

Academic writing sometimes expresses purposes we normally associate with civic writing and expressive writing. Although expressive writing figures the least in academic journals, academic writers occasionally reveal how they feel about their work. For instance, in one of his essays historian J.G.A. Pocock says that upon discovering a particularly hard-to-find kind of evidence, "you get up and dance around the room." The reference is to a general "you," but we assume that he would not write about the exhilaration of discovery without having experienced it. He follows this description with the wry warning, "This does not happen very often."[5] Still, the passage gives us a glimpse into what it feels like to do academic research.

The great majority of writing by the professors in colleges and universities is a combination of exposition and argument, with an emphasis on

[5]J.G.A. Pocock, "Texts and Events: Reflections on the History of Political Thought," in *Politics of Discourse: The Literature and History of Seventeenth-Century England,* ed. Kevin Sharp and Steven N. Zwicker (Berkeley: University of California Press, 1987), 28.

argument. Much of it consists of accounts of original research in which the writer explains the methods of investigation and the results obtained (exposition) and then interprets the meaning and importance of the results (argument). Some academic writing gathers and analyzes the published work of others—review articles and some student research papers, for example, have this purpose. The presentation of the work is exposition, while the analysis and interpretation of it is argument.

As an example of academic writing, look at the **abstract** of one of the primary research reports that Pam Belluck talks about in the *New York Times* article we looked at earlier in the chapter. (An abstract is a short summary describing a longer work and giving its main arguments.)

◎◎◎

Linguistic Ability in Early Life and the Neuropathology of Alzheimer's Disease and Cerebrovascular Disease: Findings from the Nun Study[6]

DAVID A. SNOWDON, LYDIA H. GREINER, WILLIAM R. MARKESBERY

Findings from the Nun Study indicate that low linguistic ability in early life has a strong association with dementia and premature death in late life. In the present study, we investigated the relationship of linguistic ability in early life to the neuropathology of Alzheimer's disease and cerebrovascular disease. The analyses were done on a subset of 74 participants in the Nun Study for whom we had handwritten autobiographies completed some time between the ages of 19 and 37 (mean = 23). An average of 62 years after writing the autobiographies, when the participants were 78 to 97 years old, they died and their brains were removed for our neuropathologic studies. Linguistic ability in early life was measured by the idea (proposition) density of the autobiographies, i.e., a standard measure of the content of ideas in text samples. Idea density scores from early life had strong inverse correlations with the severity of Alzheimer's disease pathology in the neocortex: Correlation between idea density scores and neurofibrillary tangle counts were -0.59 for the frontal lobe, -0.48 for the temporal lobe, and -0.49 for the parietal lobe (all p-values < 0.0001). Idea density scores were unrelated to the severity of atherosclerosis of the major arteries at the base of the brain and to the presence of lacunar and large brain infarcts. Low linguistic ability in early life may reflect suboptimal neurological and cognitive development which might increase susceptibility to the development of Alzheimer's disease pathology in late life.   [2000]

[6]David A. Snowdon, Lydia H. Greiner, and William R. Markesbery, "Linguistic Ability in Early Life and the Neuropathology of Alzheimer's Disease and Cerebrovascular Disease: Findings from the Nun Study," *Annals of the New York Academy of Sciences* 903 (2000): 34–38.

Clearly, there are significant differences between Belluck's account for the readers of the *New York Times* and Snowdon's scientific article. The activity below will help you articulate them.

ACTIVITY 5: *Comparing Belluck and Snowdon*

What differences do you see between Belluck's article for the *New York Times* and the abstract of the scientists' report for the New York Academy of Sciences?

- Compare the length of the abstract's single paragraph with the length of the paragraphs of the *New York Times*.
- What kinds of vocabulary does each piece use? How many words in each of them are you unfamiliar with?
- Who is speaking in each piece?
- What other differences between the two pieces do you see? How do you account for them?

We are discovering that writing with different purposes for different audiences creates different genres. We could chart our findings as follows:

Some Genres of Civic and Academic Writing

	Civic Writing	Academic Writing
Exposition	Newspaper reports	Summaries and syntheses of work in a particular field
Argument	Editorials, op-ed pieces, letters to the editors, proposals	Primary research reports that make claims about the significance of experimental results; editorials about research policies
Expressive Writing	Memoirs; poems in publications of commercial, nonprofit, and volunteer organizations; poems in the obituary section of newspapers	Rare glimpses into the personal lives and feelings of the researchers

Addressing Self and World: Imaginative Literature

Imaginative literature is sometimes private, meant for the writer only, and occasionally it is occasional—that is, it is written for a specific community at a specific time or event: It may be silly poems written to entertain employees at an office party or tease a couple at the dinner after their wedding rehearsal, or grand poems written for the inauguration of a United States president.

But imaginative literature is usually not aimed at specific communities united by specific interests. Like much civic writing, imaginative literature addresses the public. If it is published, it is available to anyone who can read the language in which it is written, and it addresses them not so much as citizens, friends, residents of a place, or members of a club, but as human beings, individuals with private as well as public lives.

Imaginative literature therefore isn't shaped and limited by the kinds of formal rules that govern letters to the editor and lab reports. It might be shorter than a limerick or longer than Tolstoy's *War and Peace*. Although much of what we call imaginative literature takes the form of poetry, plays, and prose fiction, it can violate the normal rules of genre and still find its place among the creative arts. It may express the feelings of the author and may make an argument, although those are not always its chief aims. As long as it has some integrity, some beauty, or some message that makes it meaningful to someone, it may find an audience. It may even change the way many people see the world.

While it sometimes claims to portray literal truth, even when it doesn't, imaginative literature offers a version of reality with some insight into human life. Like civic and academic writing, it can make use of exposition and argument. Exposition is especially important because much imaginative literature describes the world and people's experiences in it. Because descriptions are not exact copies, writers always have to select some elements and leave out others. For this reason, describing the world is not merely passive imitation. To describe a world is to create it and take an attitude toward it. Consider the **haiku** below:[7]

Haiku

BASHO (1644–94) *is the pseudonym of Matsuo Munefusa. He was born to be a Japanese samurai but studied philosophy and Zen Buddhism, traveled, and became a poet, writing many* haiku *as well as* haibun, *brief travelogues in poetry and prose.*

A crow is perched
Upon a leafless withered bough—
The autumn dusk.   [Late seventeenth century]

Basho gives us a scene with no action—there is just an observation. Nothing happens and there is not even an observer. We do not know who is watching, but the poem says, "This is how it is now."

 ACTIVITY 6: *Reflecting on Basho*

> What is there in the poem besides pure presentation? Does the poet have an attitude toward the scene? If so, where does it come from?

---

[7]A haiku is an unrhymed Japanese poem with a fixed structure. Seventeen syllables are arranged in lines of five syllables in the first and last line, with seven in the middle line. Translators may or may not follow the exact arrangement of syllables in lines, but they always try to capture the poems' careful observations of nature in a particular season.

Like Basho's haiku, most works that present a central figure place it in a scene. To understand the central figure, we need to understand its relationship to the scene, as in this poem:

Cut

SYLVIA PLATH *(For biographical notes, see p. 551.)*

What a thrill——
My thumb instead of an onion.
The top quite gone
Except for a sort of hinge

Of skin,   5
A flap like a hat,
Dead white.
Then that red plush.

Little pilgrim,
The Indian's axed your scalp.   10
Your turkey wattle
Carpet rolls

Straight from the heart.
I step on it,
Clutching my bottle of pink fizz.   15

A cerebration, this is.
Out of a gap
A million soldiers run,
Redcoats, every one.

Whose side are they on?   20
O my
Homunculus,
I am ill.
I have taken a pill to kill

The thin   25
Papery feeling.
Saboteur,
Kamikaze man——

The stain on your
Gauze Ku Klux Klan   30
Babushka
Darkens and tarnishes and when

The balled
Pulp of your heart
Confronts its small   35
Mill of silence

How you jump——
Trepanned veteran,
Dirty girl,
40 Thumb stump.   [1966]

 ACTIVITY 7: *Reflecting on "Cut"*

Write a few paragraphs on the poem.
- What or who is the main subject of this poem?
- What is the scene? What action has just taken place?
- Do we have a speaker/observer? Who is it?
- What is the speaker's attitude to the main subject?
- What can we learn from the other experiences to which the narrator compares the cut thumb?

In recording her observations, Plath is giving us a careful description of what it is like to live in a physical body. However, writers can also put themselves into nature so that the observing self is defined in relationship to the larger physical world. Here, for example, is James Wright's poem, "Lying in a Hammock at William Duffy's Farm in Pine Island, Minnesota."

Lying in a Hammock at William Duffy's Farm in Pine Island, Minnesota

JAMES WRIGHT (1927–80) *studied at Kenyon College and the University of Washington. He taught at the University of Minnesota, Macalester College, and Hunter College and received a Rockefeller Foundation grant and the Pulitzer Prize for Poetry.*

Over my head, I see the bronze butterfly,
Asleep on the black trunk,
Blowing like a leaf in green shadow.
Down the ravine behind the empty house,
5 The cowbells follow one another
Into the distances of the afternoon.
To my right,
In a field of sunlight between two pines,
The droppings of last year's horses
10 Blaze up into golden stones.
I lean back, as the evening darkens and comes on.
A chicken hawk floats over, looking for home.
I have wasted my life.   [1963]

Compare Wright's poem to Basho's haiku, using the following questions as a guide:

- What are the important elements in each scene?
- Which details convey information about how the speaker values the scene?
- What is the speaker trying to tell us in the last line of each of the poems?

Besides helping us explore what it's like to be in a physical body and what it's like to define a self in relation to the natural world, another thing that imaginative literature can do is help us understand what it's like to define a self in relation to a social world. Here's a story about a boy with a fractured family who is called upon to forge a relationship with his father.

Powder

TOBIAS WOLFF, *who teaches at Stanford University, has published story collections, including* In the Garden of North American Martyrs, Back in the World, *and* The Night in Question *(which contains "Powder"); the novel* The Barracks Thief; *and two memoirs,* This Boy's Life *and* In Pharaoh's Army. *Though "Powder" is not autobiography, the figure of the father has kinship with Wolff's own father, who was characterized by what Wolff calls "outlaw charm and maddening, tragic irresponsibility."*

Just before Christmas my father took me skiing at Mount Baker. He'd had to fight for the privilege of my company, because my mother was still angry with him for sneaking me into a nightclub during our last visit, to see Thelonious Monk.

He wouldn't give up. He promised, hand on heart, to take good care of me and have me home for dinner on Christmas Eve, and she relented. But as we were checking out of the lodge that morning it began to snow, and in this snow he observed some quality that made it necessary for us to get in one last run. We got in several last runs. He was indifferent to my fretting. Snow whirled around us in bitter, blinding squalls, hissing like sand, and still we skied. As the lift bore us to the peak yet again, my father looked at his watch and said, "Criminey. This'll have to be a fast one."

By now I couldn't see the trail. There was no point in trying. I stuck to him like white on rice and did what he did and somehow made it to the bottom without sailing off a cliff. We returned our skis and my father put chains on the Austin-Healy while I swayed from foot to foot, clapping my mittens and wishing I were home. I could see everything. The green tablecloth, the plates with the holly pattern, the red candles waiting to be lit.

We passed a diner on our way out. "You want some soup?" my father asked. I shook my head. "Buck up," he said, "I'll get you there. Right, doctor?"

5   I was supposed to say, "Right, doctor," but I didn't say anything.

A state trooper waved us down outside the resort. A pair of sawhorses were blocking the road. The trooper came up to our car and bent down to my father's window. His face was bleached by the cold. Snowflakes clung to his eyebrows and to the fur trim of his jacket and cap.

"Don't tell me," my father said.

The trooper told him. The road was closed. It might get cleared, it might not. Storm took everyone by surprise. So much, so fast. Hard to get people moving. Christmas Eve. What can you do?

My father said, "Look. We're talking about four, five inches. I've taken this car through worse than that."

10   The trooper straightened up, boots creaking. His face was out of sight but I could hear him. "The road is closed."

My father sat with both hands on the wheel, rubbing the wood with his thumbs. He looked at the barricade for a long time. He seemed to be trying to master the idea of it. Then he thanked the trooper, and with a weird, old-maidy show of caution turned the car around. "Your mother will never forgive me for this," he said.

"We should have left before," I said. "Doctor."

He didn't speak to me again until we were both in a booth at the diner, waiting for our burgers. "She won't forgive me," he said. "Do you understand? Never."

"I guess," I said, but no guesswork was required; she wouldn't forgive him.

15   "I can't let that happen." He bent toward me. "I'll tell you what I want. I want us to be together again. Is that what you want?"

I wasn't sure, but I said, "Yes, sir."

He bumped my chin with his knuckles. "That's all I needed to hear."

When we finished eating he went to the pay phone in the back of the diner, then joined me in the booth again. I figured he'd called my mother, but he didn't give a report. He sipped at his coffee and stared out the window at the empty road. "Come on!" When the trooper's car went past, lights flashing, he got up and dropped some money on the check. "Okay. *Vamanos.*"°

The wind had died. The snow was falling straight down, less of it now; lighter. We drove away from the resort, right up to the barricade. "Move it," my father told me. When I looked at him he said, "What are you waiting for?" I got out and dragged one of the sawhorses aside, then pushed it back after he drove through. When I got inside the car he said, "Now you're an accomplice. We go down together." He put the car in gear and looked at me. "Joke, doctor."

20   "Funny, doctor."

Down the first long stretch I watched the road behind us, to see if the trooper was on our tail. The barricade vanished. Then there was nothing but snow: snow on the road, snow kicking up from the chains, snow on the trees, snow in

---

¹⁸***Vamanos*** [sic] *Vamonos* means "Let's go" in Spanish.

the sky; and our trail in the snow. I faced around and had a shock. The lie of the road behind us had been marked by our own tracks, but there were no tracks ahead of us. My father was breaking virgin snow between a line of tall trees. He was humming "Stars Fell on Alabama." I felt snow brush along the floorboards under my feet. To keep my hands from shaking I clamped them between my knees.

My father grunted in a thoughtful way and said, "Don't ever try this yourself."

"I won't."

"That's what you say now, but someday you'll get your license and then you'll think you can do anything. Only you won't be able to do this. You need, I don't know—a certain instinct."

"Maybe I have it."

"You don't. You have your strong points, but not . . . you know. I only mention it because I don't want you to get the idea this is something just anybody can do. I'm a great driver. That's not a virtue, okay? It's just a fact, and one you should be aware of. Of course you have to give the old heap some credit, too—there aren't many cars I'd try this with. Listen!"

I listened. I heard the slap of the chains, the stiff, jerky rasp of the wipers, the purr of the engine. It really did purr. The car was almost new. My father couldn't afford it, and kept promising to sell it, but here it was.

I said, "Where do you think that policeman went to?"

"Are you warm enough?" He reached over and cranked up the blower. Then he turned off the wipers. We didn't need them. The clouds had brightened. A few sparse, feathery flakes drifted into our slipstream and were swept away. We left the trees and entered a broad field of snow that ran level for a while and then tilted sharply downward. Orange stakes had been planted at intervals in two parallel lines and my father ran a course between them, though they were far enough apart to leave considerable doubt in my mind as to where exactly the road lay. He was humming again, doing little scat riffs around the melody.

"Okay then. What are my strong points?"

"Don't get me started," he said. "It'd take all day."

"Oh, right. Name one."

"Easy. You always think ahead."

True. I always thought ahead. I was a boy who kept his clothes on numbered hangers to ensure proper rotation. I bothered my teachers for homework assignments far ahead of their due dates so I could make up schedules. I thought ahead, and that was why I knew that there would be other troopers waiting for us at the end of our ride, if we got there. What I did not know was that my father would wheedle and plead his way past them—he didn't sing "O Tannenbaum" but just about—and get me home for dinner, buying a little more time before my mother decided to make the split final. I knew we'd get caught; I was resigned to it. And maybe for this reason I stopped moping and began to enjoy myself.

Why not? This was one for the books. Like being in a speedboat, only better. You can't go downhill in a boat. And it was all ours. And it kept coming, the laden trees, the unbroken surface of snow, the sudden white vistas. Here and there I saw hints of the road, ditches, fences, stakes, but not so many that I could have found my way. But then I didn't have to. My father in his forty-eighth year, rumpled, kind, bankrupt of honor, flushed with certainty. He was a great driver. All persuasion, no coercion. Such subtlety at the wheel, such tactful pedalwork. I actually trusted him. And the best was yet to come—switchbacks and hairpins impossible to describe. Except maybe to say this: If you haven't driven fresh powder, you haven't driven.   [1996]

ACTIVITY 9: *Exploring "Powder"*

- What is the narrator's opinion of his father at the start of the story? How do you know?
- Does the narrator's opinion of his father change? Why? Is it a good or bad thing for him to see his father in a new light?
- Is there an argument embedded in the story? What are its claims?

Why Read Imaginative Literature?

In these few pieces of imaginative literature, we have just skimmed the surface of what fiction, poems, and plays can do. Occasionally, world events remind us of how people reach for literature, reach for each other, and reach for each other *through* literature. Very shortly after the destruction of the World Trade Center towers and part of the Pentagon on September 11, 2001, many people turned to poetry. Remembered poems along with new poems and stories written in response to the events were posted on the Internet and on sidewalk memorials, read at memorial services and on the radio, and published in newspapers.[8] Dickinson, Blake, and Yeats all made appearances, as did the part of "Song of Myself" in which nineteenth-century American poet Walt Whitman describes New York firemen rescuing people from a burning building.[9] "September 1, 1939," the poem that W.H. Auden wrote after Hitler started World War II by invading Poland, was widely circulated and was read on National Public Radio.[10] Poet Laureate Billy Collins and his immediate predecessor Robert Pinsky were asked what to read and why it mattered. (Both later wrote their own poems reflecting

---

[8]Margery Snyder, "Poems After the Attack: A Contemporary Anthology," http://poetry.about.com/ (accessed 20 May 2004); Mary Schmich, "Poetry Soothes the Soul in These Painful Days," http://poetry.about.com/ (accessed 16 November 2001); Academy of American Poets, "Post-9/11 Poetry Resources," http://www.poets.org/sept11.cfm (accessed 24 May 2004); People's Poetry Gathering, "Poems Found in NYC Streets Post 9/11," http://www.peoplespoetry.org/ (accessed 24 May 2004).

[9]David Remnick, "Many Voices," *New Yorker*, 15 October 2001.

[10]W.H. Auden, *Another Time* (New York: Random House, 1940).

on the events of the day.)[11] And media pundits tried to figure out why poetry suddenly seemed so important.[12]

The crisis of 9/11 only made visible what is always true—we use language to shape and know our worlds, both through the media (newspapers, magazines, television, etc.) and through imaginative literature (poetry, fiction, etc.). Even without national crises, human beings clearly crave stories and descriptions both of their own world and of unfamiliar worlds—we dream, we gossip, we go to the movies, we write diaries, memoirs, and autobiographies, and we narrate our lives out loud to our friends and relatives and mentally to ourselves.

Imaginative literature creates worlds and invites us into them so that we can see how they work. If the people and situations are like us, we can identify with them and learn about ourselves; if they are not, we can learn about those who are different from us. We can see what happens without living through the events they depict. Art can help us celebrate, commemorate, grieve, analyze, argue, and play.

THE PLAN OF THE BOOK

This book juxtaposes imaginative literature with other kinds of writing in order to help you explore how they all work while improving your own. Chapter 2 surveys a number of the steps leading from a writing assignment to the finished essay it prompts. Chapter 3 surveys several different kinds (genres) of writing. Chapters 4–7 examine the features of writing in those genres to show how writers of all kinds (including student writers) can deploy the resources of language. They provide the tools for close reading, which can turn readers into writers by providing them with things to say. But since one of the chief ways to interpret writing is to read it through the concepts offered by the disciplines, or methodologies, practiced in universities and colleges, Chapter 8 concentrates on techniques for reading academic argument to help you know what to look for when you encounter the writing from the disciplines. Chapter 9 then puts the two kinds of texts together, demonstrating how ideas from the disciplines can help interpreters to notice new aspects of the characters and dilemmas in imaginative literature. The chapter shows how the two genres can illuminate each other, producing new insights and interpretations. Chapter 10 will help you do the research to find interpretive frameworks on your own.

---

[11]Billy Collins, "The Names," http://www.loc.gov/poetry/names.html (accessed 20 May 2004); Robert Pinsky, "9/11," http://www.alumni.rutgers.edu/attack/pinsky911b.html (accessed 20 May 2004).

[12]For instance, Christopher Knight, "What Exactly Can Art Heal?" *Los Angeles Times,* 4 November 2001. There is an excerpt in Chapter 3 (see "The Essay").

The Writing Process

ACTIVE READING

Reading both literary and nonliterary texts for pleasure can be blissful trips away from everyday reality. Reading for school can also be absorbing but is designed to accomplish a purpose; teachers have something in mind when they assign reading. Sometimes they want you to absorb information and make it your own thoroughly enough that you can use it elsewhere, and sometimes they want you to analyze or interpret it. Often, the purpose of reading imaginative literature is to determine not only what a work says but also how it says it.

To fulfill each of these purposes, reading must be active and critical. The key is to engage the text dynamically, joining the conversation of which it is part. One of the best ways to do this is to read with a pen in hand.[1] While highlighters are very popular for marking important passages and can be helpful (and fun to use), pointing is all they do: they don't say *why* something is important. For that, you need a pen or pencil. Use it to make the piece your own in these ways:

1. **Write in the margins:**

   - Note how the work looks physically. What is its format? Mark any unusual features.
   - Note the subject under discussion in each section or even in each paragraph, depending on the density of the ideas. If the text is non-literary, note what it is trying to do: does it want readers to believe something? Do something? If so, what?
   - Note your reactions—agreement, disagreement, surprise, delight, puzzlement, anger. Are all the parts of the work consistent with each other, or are there inconsistencies or contradictions? Do some ideas or elements get repeated? Do you see a pattern taking shape? What parts do not fit the pattern?
   - If there are particular features of the text, words it uses, or ideas it outlines that you find striking or unusual, underline or circle them.

As an example, here are some of the notes that freshman student Zak Owen made in the margins of a poem by Seamus Heaney:

Digging

SEAMUS HEANEY (1939–), *born in Castledawson, County Derry, Northern Ireland, won the Nobel Prize for Literature in 1995.*

Whoa! Is he angry at someone? I thought the pen was resting. How did it turn into a weapon?

Between my finger and my thumb
The <u>squat</u> pen <u>rests</u>; <u>snug</u> as a <u>gun</u>.

Under my window, a clean <u>rasping</u> sound
When the spade sinks into gravelly ground.
My father, digging. I look down

Not a very dignified position. Is this supposed to be funny?

5

Till his straining rump among the flowerbeds
Bends low, comes up twenty years away
Stooping in rhythm through potato drills
Where he was digging.

What's a potato drill? The dictionary has a "drill" meaning a trench or furrow for planting seeds—that must be it, not an instrument for boring holes or the German cotton or the W. African baboon.

[1]Of course, this advice pertains only if you have "writing rights" over a text. If you need to be actively engaged with something from a library, photocopy it so that you can respond fully without intruding on the experience of later readers.

The coarse boot <u>nestled</u> on the <u>lug</u>, the shaft | *A coarse boot nestling on* 10
Against the inside knee was <u>levered</u> firmly. | *a lug? Weird idea.*
He rooted out tall tops, buried the bright edge deep
To scatter new potatoes that we picked
Loving their cool hardness in our hands.

By God, the old man could handle a spade. | *Admires them both. Like* 15
Just like his old man. | *me watching my dad.*

My grandfather cut more turf in a day | *Didn't take any time for*
Than any other man on Toner's bog. | *himself. (Or to say thank*
Once I carried him milk in a bottle | *you to his grandson?) A*
Corked sloppily with paper. He straightened up | *tough guy.*
To drink it, then fell to right away | 20

<u>Nicking</u> and <u>slicing</u> neatly, heaving sods | *What's good turf? Why are*
Over his shoulder, going down and down | *these men digging turf?*
For the good turf. Digging.

The cold smell of potato mould, the <u>squelch and slap</u> | *Can't he just buy one?* 25
Of soggy peat, the <u>curt cuts</u> of an edge | *What's the problem? Why*
Through living roots awaken in my head. | *so powerless?*
But I've no spade to follow men like them.

Between my finger and my thumb | *Repeats the first words of*
The squat pen rests. | *the poem exactly.* 30
I'll dig with it.   [1966]

Zak's markings, comments, and questions—especially the ones that record his reactions or open up problems and questions—give him an entrance into the poem when he rereads it.

2. **Keep a reading journal:** You can also record your responses/ questions/problems in a separate notebook or computer file. If you choose paper, make it a "double-entry" journal, dividing the pages in half, putting notes about content on one side and your questions and comments on the other. (You can color-code them, if you like.) If you prefer your computer, you can use different fonts or colors to differentiate your descriptive notes from your response and evaluation.

When Zak Owen read Seamus Heaney's poem "Digging," he had a strong reaction to it, in part because he could identify with the narrator's respect for his father's and grandfather's skills and work ethic. In order to capture his reaction, after he read the poem, he wrote this journal entry in a computer file, using two fonts—the first for his descriptive notes, and the second for his evaluation of and responses to the text:

> This man has a lot of respect for his father and grandfather's ability to dig: l. 15: "By God, the old man could handle a spade." He almost makes digging sound like a craft—but that's a funny word for it since digging is really taking something apart, not crafting something, which is putting something together.

> But the respect reminds me of how I used to feel when I watched my father building our patio. He mixed the mortar and then used a trowel to scoop up just the right amount of mortar to join the slabs of stones and then smooth the join. I remember the scrape of the trowel on the stone. But he was building something. I was small and took it all for granted. But he must have been very strong to hoist those stones and fit them together so well. But it is easy to admire his process. He was making something—he designed it and years later, it's still there.

Back to Heaney: Let's see how he can make taking something apart look creative.

3. **Make an idea map:** Use a larger-than-ordinary sheet of paper, or an unlined sheet of paper, or rotate your notebook 90 degrees—anything minor but nonhabitual that can help free your thinking. Write the major ideas *in* the piece with your ideas *about* the piece in no particular order, perhaps color-coding them to keep them distinct. Then draw lines between the ones that are related. For instance, if objects or kinds of objects, or sounds or other sensory data are mentioned more than once, you can connect them. For "Digging," the map might include the words naming tools or the different things that have to be dug for.

4. **Make a list:** Go through the work rereading the notes you wrote in the margins; make a list of them, noting carefully where they came from so that you can retrace your steps when you need to.

5. **Freewrite:** This technique is based on the idea that you know more than you think you know and that if you commit yourself to keeping the flow of words going, you will discover ideas about a text that you did not know you had. The trick is to refuse to lift the pen from the paper (or your fingers from your keyboard). When you run out of ideas, don't stop. Don't worry about grammar and write anything—even "I don't know what to write, I don't know what to write, I don't know what to write"—in order to keep the flow going.

Whatever technique you use, the idea is to join the conversation with and about the text. Doing so will help you prepare to participate in your classes, prepare to write, and prepare for exams. Once you have read actively and critically, you have something to say about complex and ambitious texts—and you'll be on your way to creating your own.

INVENTION STRATEGIES:
STARTING WITH THE ASSIGNMENT

All writing, no matter what kind, requires invention. But very few writers publish their first drafts. Most find that a major part of writing is *re*writing, in response to varying amounts of input from other people. Ultimately, writers have to decide which suggestions to take and how to use them, but many find that their final draft surprises them. As a result of their internal dialogue, as they re-see their own texts and talk with other people, a text often changes radically from first draft to last.

As a student writing for classes, you may get suggestions from friends, family, classmates, and teachers. You are ultimately responsible for what goes on the page, but you will probably find that the creativity of writing comes from revision as well as from the original process of invention. This chapter offers guidance for both stages.

Most of the writing that you will do for this class will be in response to texts of various kinds and will be prompted by assignments. Because an assignment from a teacher will guide your response, you should always start by reading it very carefully. Pay special attention to the verbs signifying what you are to do:

Respond personally: You are being asked to find a kind of human connection with the characters, setting, or events of the text. What in your experience is like—or unlike—the people, places, or events of the text?

Summarize: You are being asked to say what is in a text, but in a form shorter than the text itself. Summarizing implies restating—in your own words—its most important features or points.

Analyze: You are being asked to divide the text into its component parts, identifying its features and the role that each plays in the whole. Does the work seem to fall naturally into sections? What is the function of each?

Interpret: You are being asked to explain the significance of a written text beyond its surface meaning. You might look for patterns created by repetition of words, actions, or images, or look for themes by examining the relationships among characters. How do the various components of the work fit together? (These techniques are examined in Chapters 4–7, as well as in Appendix A.)

Apply: You are being asked to take materials from one area and to use them to understand something in another. For instance, when you examine the relationships among literary characters, a concept from psychology might help you see something new about them. This technique is the focus of Chapters 9 and 10.

Define: You are being asked what something is or what category it belongs to. To fulfill such an assignment, you need to know what's required for membership in that category. If you want to know whether a play is a comedy, for example, first you have to decide what a comedy is, and only then examine the play in question to see if it meets the necessary criteria.

Evaluate: You are being asked to say whether something is good or bad. Answering that question is like defining because it, too, requires criteria. You need to know not only what it takes to make a play a comedy, but also what makes a play a *good* comedy. To evaluate is to decide whether something is a successful example of its genre, achieving its purpose.

Most chapters in this book include checklists that suggest particular approaches to texts. They are invention aids for the most common kinds of assignments in English classes. When responding to other kinds of assignments, make sure you understand the terms they use.

SHAPING AN ARGUMENT IN WRITING

Finding and Developing a Thesis

Most academic writing that responds to written texts has a unifying idea or a main claim called a **thesis.** When you write about texts, you will use your maps, lists, journal entries, and marginal notes to invent your thesis. The shape it takes will depend on your reading of the text and on what the assignment asks you to do.

As you examine the work and your notes on it, stay flexible. Be ready to modify your first idea for a thesis: as you look back and forth between the work you are examining and your essay, you will probably discover new elements that don't fit into your first idea about the work. That doesn't mean you have to jettison your first idea; it may be possible to recast it so that it can include the new elements.

Students are often given the advice, "Narrow your thesis." Sometimes this is exactly what is needed to make a topic manageable. But sometimes narrowing is not what is called for. If, in the light of fuller insights, early formulations of a thesis are too simple, the thesis needs widening, not narrowing.

For instance, Zak Owen wanted to use his journal entry on Seamus Heaney's "Digging" as the basis for an assignment that asked him to analyze and interpret a poem by examining the details of its language. Unsure about how to move from a personal response to a more objective claim about the meaning of the poem, he reviewed his marginal notes and journal entry about the poem and tried a session of freewriting:

OK, it looks to me like he admires his father and grandfather—why? Because they could work so hard, because they could work so well. That could be a thesis, I'll come back to that—admires work. The work is digging and there are different kinds of digging in the poem—the garden now, potatoes in the past and the past is also when they cut peat. Potatoes and peat, what's that about? But how come there's this hint of violence at the beginning of the poem, why does a pen make him think of a gun? The pen is mightier than the sword, but who's ever seen a gun that looks like a pen? James Bond maybe. This feels like a dead end. Nowhere to go, like the poem doesn't go anywhere because its last line is the same as the first. Maybe it's a dead end for him, too, but if I have to keep writing I'll ask who this guy wants to shoot. Maybe there's something there.

Zak is worried about dead ends here but writes past them, partly by writing an internal monologue about writing. Rather than letting his internal censors stop his writing ("this isn't leading anywhere," "this is stupid"), writing about his worry gives his hand something to do while his brain catches up and finds the next step. The freewriting produces a problem: "the narrator admires his father and grandfather" was too simplistic a thesis to carry him forward. When he returned to his marginal notes, Zak saw that the speaker in the poem felt bad about himself and his inability to follow in their footsteps because he has no spade to dig with (l. 28). He wondered if the self-criticism was the source of the undercurrent of violence in the poem.

Zak didn't abandon his provisional thesis about admiration. Instead, he reformulated it: "Seamus Heaney's 'Digging' is about the narrator's complicated feelings about his father, his grandfather, and himself." This more abstract formulation ("complicated feelings" are more general than "admiration") is more inclusive and therefore worked much better as an umbrella for all the things Zak saw in the poem. As Zak worked with the poem, he refined his thesis further, but this version allowed him to work comfortably with the poem while developing his ideas about it to fulfill the assignment.

Drafting

Movies about writers often show them sitting down to write with blank sheets of white paper or empty computer screens. The stereotype has them repeatedly yanking paper out of the typewriter, crumpling it up, and hurling it toward overflowing wastebaskets, or pounding keyboards, or otherwise abusing defenseless computers. Liberal sprinklings of alcohol and off-color language emphasize the sufferings of human and machine.

While no one denies that starting is hard, it needn't conform to Hollywood clichés of writerly pain. Bypassing the pain is the purpose of the invention strategies presented in this text. When you sit down to compose, the blank paper or screen should be surrounded with other texts, including your own notes, to help you decide where to begin. You can come to the desk with lists of ideas, lists of passages in other works that you want to talk about, and, if not a formal outline, at least some sense of the order in which you want to discuss things.

There are two excellent pieces of advice about drafting an essay that any good textbook must pass along:

Important Drafting Tips

1. It is often helpful to start drafting with the introduction.
2. It is often helpful to start drafting anywhere but the introduction.

Tip #1 is vital because if you can get the introduction right, that will guide the rest of your composing and make it easier to structure the essay—especially if the introduction indicates the topics of the essay and the order in which they will be discussed. This is certainly true if the introduction says, "There are four parts to this concept," and the body of the paper unwaveringly discusses all four in order.

But since writing aids thinking, it is important to get started even if your ideas haven't taken shape yet. Then Tip #2 may save you a great deal of anxiety. Just plunge into the part of the paper that you are most ready to write, and then, after you write your way to your main idea, you can revise in the light of it and create an introduction to reflect what you have done. This may take some reorganizing, but you can't revise what's not on the page, so Tip #2 may jumpstart the drafting process.

So take your pick. But in either case, since the structure of the essay may change as you work on it, the introduction is probably going to be the last thing that you revise. The widely quoted writerly question, "How can I tell what I think 'til I see what I say?" is an apt response to the fact that writing is a process of discovery. Once you have written a draft, read it and outline it to see what you've said. You can then revise the organization to improve its logic and revise the introduction to predict what you actually say.

The more invention work you have done before you face the blank page or blank screen, the less painful the actual drafting will be. Drafting, however, is not just a matter of transcription. I have heard students say, "I have all my ideas; I just have to write them down." This notion treats the generation of ideas and the process of composing as if they are entirely separate. New ideas can keep coming as you draft, and you should keep playing with them. The discoveries make composing exciting, even when you are working on writing tasks you did not choose yourself. They become yours as you write and revise your responses.

If we could write an essay the way we decorate a Christmas tree, we could add ornaments as we liked, placing one on a high branch, one below it, one closer to the trunk, one farther away, as our fancy took us, or as the ornaments came out of the boxes in which they were stored. We wouldn't need to create transitions between one branch and another because trees already have structure. But when we make our own structures, we are always in search of words that can make transitions from one part to another. It is often in the making of transitions, the linking, that new ideas can arise.

Using Categories to Organize a Draft

One thing that can help to make the links is finding categories for different kinds of evidence used to support a thesis. Take as an example Zak Owen's thesis about Seamus Heaney's poem "Digging": "Seamus Heaney's 'Digging' is about the narrator's complicated feelings about his father, his grandfather, and himself." Zak was first attracted to the poem partly by the words in it. He started by listing (according to line number) the words that he liked, enjoyed the sound of, or was puzzled by because they are uncommon or are used in interesting ways:

2. Rests, Squat, Snug, Gun
10. Nestled
25. Squelch, Slap
26. Curt, Cuts

When he examined the list, he found that they were all fairly simple words—except for "nestled," all have only one syllable—that were vivid partly because of how they sounded. "Squelch" is even listed in the dictionary as being "imitative," that is, sounding like what it is supposed to name. Some of them come in pairs that make their sound more noticeable because they have the same first letter, like "squelch and slap" (l. 25) and "curt cuts" (26), or because they sound similar, like "snug as a gun" (2). And some of them are used in surprising ways: we do not often think of guns being "snug" or boots being "nestled" on spades. These words usually bring to mind things that are soft and warm, not hard and cold.

Making the list gave Zak one large category of evidence he could use to support his claim: the words of the poem. In trying to decide how to discuss them, Zak considered just going through the poem line by line and pointing these words out as they appeared. This section of the paper would be about words.

But working with the list—rereading it and rereading the poem—gave Zak several smaller groupings that allowed him to gather the words under subheadings: words with vivid sounds and words used in unexpected ways. A structure was beginning to take shape. Zak now had these categories:

Overarching theme: complex feelings
   Words indicating feelings
      Sound effects of words
      Words with warm associations paired with cold objects

The subheadings allowed Zak to group like things together so that his essay could break away from the order of the poem. They also help Zak make transitions. Zak created the list below to reflect this new organization:

Informal outline of part of a paper on the words of "Digging"
[Introduction:] 1. In "Digging," Heaney uses words in two interesting ways.
[Paragraph(s) on] 2. words and phrases with special sound effects
[Transitional sentence at the beginning of new paragraph:] 3. Words in "Digging" are not used only for their sound patterns, but also for **their associations.**
[Paragraph(s) on] 4. words with **warm associations** used to describe cold metal objects

The two subcategories—sound patterns and associations—are marked here by italics and bold, respectively. You can see that the third item in the outline, the transitional sentence, uses both fonts, because the first part of the sentence looks backward to the discussion of sound patterns, and the second part looks forward to the discussion of word associations. The transitional sentence is really a hinge, allowing readers to move from one part of the essay to another.

Supporting a Thesis with Evidence

Since most of the rest of this book is concerned with the development of ideas, this section will confine itself to some general remarks on this process. In order to defend thesis statements about written works, you usually have to provide evidence from the work itself. Even if you are bringing in something from outside the work—something to compare it to or something to provide background for it—you must ordinarily base your claims on a deep acquaintance with the work and how it functions. Even if you come to your claims with a sudden flash of insight, you need to seek out support from the work itself. As you can see from Zak Owen's search for a thesis about Seamus Heaney's "Digging" that took into account not only his own response but all the details of the poem, the process involves going back and forth between generalizations ("This poem is about . . .") and the details of the text ("line 26 says . . . "). If you follow this procedure, by the time you arrive at a plausible thesis, you are also on your way to knowing how to defend it.

There are several ways of presenting textual evidence, including reference, paraphrase, brief quotation, and quotation with analysis. These are all just ways of pointing to a place in the text. You will probably use all of these methods at various times, depending on your purpose and on how much the details of the language matter to your argument at any given time. Below are examples of all four ways of "pointing" to a passage in a text:

Digging

Between my finger and my thumb   1
The squat pen rests; snug as a gun.   2

Neither quotation nor paraphrase is used—this description of the theme and where it appears in the text requires neither.

Reference: Early in the poem we hear a theme that will reappear later—the intimate relationship between part of a man's body and a piece of equipment he is using (ll. 1–2).

No quotation is used, but the precise image is rephrased in the writer's own words.

Paraphrase: The narrator contemplates the comfortable fit between his hand and his pen (ll. 1–2).

The poem's line is trimmed to a single word in order to merge it more smoothly with the writer's sentence.

Brief quotation: The comfortable fit between the narrator's hand and the pen is indicated by the fact that the pen "rests" in his hand (l. 2).

Quotation with analysis: The complexity of the narrator's feelings about his profession surfaces immediately in the first two lines: "Between my finger and my thumb / The squat pen rests; snug as a gun" (ll. 1–2). The first sentence seems to end with the idea of "rest." The pen seems comfortable, at peace. But the fragment that follows is anything but restful. Suddenly the pen becomes, by analogy, a gun. Maybe it is comfortable, but are we? What is cradled in the poet's hand is now a weapon. Who is he going after with it?

*This example shows a very familiar rhythm for textual commentary: **introduction** of the quotation, the **quotation**, and then **analysis** of the quotation.*

It's your job to decide which of these strategies to use at any given point in your paper. If the point you want to make does not require the exact words of the text, you may not need to give a long quotation—a simple reference, paraphrase, or a short quotation might do the job. If you *do* quote a substantial passage, however, make it worth the time it takes your audience to read it by showing them the significance of the details of the quotation.

Introducing and Concluding

Because words and ideas come one at a time in writing, you have to decide on their order. What comes first, what comes last? In very general terms, since endings naturally get a lot of emphasis, you might want to put your strongest ideas and examples last. Of course, you want to start with something vivid enough to engage your readers and end with something strong enough to clinch their opinion that you are insightful and right-thinking. The next section considers the jobs to be done by beginnings and endings.

Introductions

No matter where you start drafting, you eventually have to decide what to include in the introduction of the essay, and the conventions of beginning are, not surprisingly, related to genre. Essays meant for a wide readership often start with a "hook," a provocative statement or an anecdote to attract readers' attention. When you write for academic audiences, it is best not to start too far away from your topic. An essay on psychological approaches to sibling rivalry does not have to begin, "From time immemorial, children have been competing with their brothers and sisters," or something equally broad. It would be more appropriate to get more directly to the topic: "There are currently three important psychological theories about sibling rivalry."

On the one hand, since the end of the introduction is one of the most important parts of a paper, it should probably contain some clear indication of what the paper is going to do. On the other, if you give too much detail, you steal your own thunder and make the body of the paper boringly repetitious.

There are several ways to chart a smooth course between these two equal and opposite dangers. For one, you can give a somewhat general version of the thesis. The audience is thus prepared for the topic and your approach to it but must read on to get the particulars.

A second way to invite your readers in without giving too much away is to refrain from giving the thesis at all. Instead, set up a problem and predict that the paper will provide the solution, or ask a question for which the paper will provide the answer.

In the introduction to his paper on "Digging," Zak steers a middle course. He first refers to what is "well known" about the poem, establishing a degree of common ground with his audience; he next suggests ("But . . .") where he is going in the paper clearly enough to entice his reader to continue but does not give all the details about his thesis:

> Seamus Heaney's poem "Digging" is well known for the narrator's expression of respect for his father and grandfather's work ethic and how it leads to his discovery of his own dedication to writing. But for an in-depth understanding of the poem, we have to notice where there are also some more negative feelings in the poem, too. If we look very closely at the words in the poem, we will better understand his complicated feelings about his relatives and himself.

Zak's statement of his thesis is abstract enough to avoid giving away the paper's strongest points too soon, but it does clearly state an agenda: what you will see if you read this paper is a close examination of the words in the poem.

Conclusions

Just as introductions need to anticipate the paper's content and important ideas but also need to avoid anticipating so much that the audience doesn't really need to read the paper, conclusions need to recapitulate the paper's main insights but cannot repeat so much detail that they are boring.

Working to avoid too much repetition can introduce a different risk: bringing in new material that seems unrelated. Introducing something new in the conclusion can be an advantage, but it must be a carefully calibrated newness that doesn't open up a whole different topic. Instead, the conclusion should come back to the original thesis but do so in a way that captures a new aspect of it or puts it into a slightly larger context. Zak found that he needed no more than a few sentences to pull together the main points of his paper:

> The resolve to write provides a resolution for the negative feelings in the poem. The gun disappears, to be replaced by a declaration of professional intention. The narrator is ready to take his place beside his admired relatives. Writing gives him a better picture of them and a better attitude toward himself.

As I said at the start of this chapter, few people want to "publish" their first drafts, whether that means sending them to the *New York Times* or giving them to a teacher. If you have time to put the draft in a drawer for a while, you might find that you have a fresh view of it when you take it out, but in any case there are several steps required to polish rough drafts, including revising, editing, and proofreading.

REVISING

Much of writing is revising, but what you revise *for* will depend on your assignment, its purpose, and your audience. But there are also some standards that are applicable for many different kinds of writing. Work on the larger issues first:

- **Unity:** All of the parts of a good essay contribute to its main idea or ideas. That unifying theme can be complex so that the essay might cover many topics, but all of them will have a clear relationship to the central focus.
- **Argument:** The claims of a good essay are reasonable and insightful, and they are well supported by enough relevant evidence to be persuasive.
- **Organization:** The parts of a good essay are arranged in a logical order that puts more important ideas in places that receive natural emphasis, such as the ends of sections.[2] The conclusion fulfills goals established at the beginning.

Even if you don't outline before you write a draft, it is often a good idea to outline a paper *after* you draft it so that you can adjust its organization. The outline does not have to be very formal—just list in the margins each new topic as it arrives. Then you can review the list to see whether the essay is unified, whether there is sufficient evidence to support your claims, and whether the topics arrive in a good sequence.

EDITING FOR STYLE

After you have addressed the large issues of unity, argument, and organization, you can turn your attention to style, a subject addressed in more detail in Chapter 6. A good essay is smoothly written in clear, concise, and lively prose:

- It uses vocabulary appropriate to its purpose;
- Its sentences are varied in length and structure and flow well;
- It puts important ideas in places that get natural emphasis in sentences.

[2]For more on the relationship between natural emphasis and purposeful placement of elements, see Joseph Williams, *Style: Ten Lessons in Clarity and Grace* (New York: Longman, 2002), and George Gopen, *The Sense of Structure: Writing from the Reader's Point of View* (New York: Longman, 2004).

PROOFREADING

After you have revised for the bigger issues and edited for style, it's time to fuss over grammar and spelling. If the essay is in electronic form, use programs that check grammar and spelling. As with advice from friends and classmates, of course, you are ultimately responsible for whether to take the programs' suggestions. They are far from perfect and sometimes offer strange (that is, incorrect) suggestions.

Be sure to use the appropriate conventions for quoting and documenting sources. Double-check capitalization, spacing, punctuation, and your references to outside sources.

If you follow the pattern suggested here, revising for argument and organization first, and only then turning to style, grammar, and mechanics, you will use your time efficiently. There is no sense in polishing sentences and paragraphs for correctness and grace if they should really be radically reshaped or even cut. First revise for the big ideas and overall order; then go for the flow.

Checklist for Improving Drafts

_____Does the draft fulfill the assignment? Does it accomplish goals that the major verbs of the assignment call for?

_____What is the thesis? How can it be made clearer?

_____Does the introduction predict what happens in the draft without stealing its own thunder?

_____Does the conclusion recapitulate without being boring?

_____How does the conclusion offer something new without going off on an irrelevant tangent?

_____Does the draft divide its material into appropriate categories and subcategories?

_____Does it put them in a logical order with appropriate transitions between them?

_____Does the draft offer enough relevant evidence to support its thesis? What further evidence could be added? What contradictory evidence does it ignore?

_____Does it use references, paraphrases, and quotations to gather evidence?

_____How could its style be improved?

_____How can its grammar and mechanical errors be corrected?

SAMPLE STUDENT PAPER

Here is the final draft of Zak Owen's essay on Seamus Heaney's "Digging":

Digging for Meaning

Seamus Heaney's poem "Digging" is well known for the narrator's expression of respect for his father and grandfather's work ethic and how it leads to his discovery of his own dedication to writing. But for a deeper understanding of the poem, we have to notice where there are also some more negative feelings in the poem. If we look very closely at the words in the poem, we will better understand his complicated feelings about his relatives and himself.

The complexity of the narrator's feelings about his profession surfaces immediately in the first two lines:

Between my finger and my thumb

The squat pen rests; snug as a gun. (ll. 1—2)

The first sentence seems like it is going to end quietly. The pen seems comfortable, at peace. But what follows is anything but comfortable. First of all, it is a sentence fragment. No grammar, no peace. And second, the very letters of the word "snug" get rearranged to form the word "gun." Maybe the gun is "snug" and cozy, but are we? The thing snuggling in the poet's fingers is now a weapon. Does he want to shoot somebody?

It's hard to know for sure whom the narrator could be angry at, but there are clues in l. 2 and l. 28. In l. 2, he's contemplating the pen in his hand. Maybe he is sitting at a desk with paper in front of him. But he's not writing. The pen is resting. In l. 3, he is listening. The listening brings him to the window to watch his father digging flowers (3—6), the watching makes him remember his father and grandfather digging potatoes and turf, both much more important to the family welfare than flowers (7—27), and makes him admire both men, and the remembering and admiring make him feel inadequate. His father and grandfather make him feel bad about himself because he

isn't living up to their example. Maybe they are his role
models, but he is not picking up the role. He says he does
not have the right equipment ("I've no spade") and so cannot "follow men like them" (28). So perhaps the gun comes
into his mind because he is mad at his relatives for setting a standard so high that it prevents them from being
civil (20—21) or setting a standard so high that he cannot
meet it. Or maybe he is just mad at himself for being
inferior.

But by the time he works through all the memories in
such a way that he is able to state his inferiority so
directly in l. 28, something important has changed. Something has come up that allows him to restate the very first
lines of the poem, but this time, instead of the gun, there
is a solution to the problem of his negative feelings. He
does not state it directly, but it seems that what allows
him to move from hostility to his declaration of his
intention to write is his pleasure in language.

The descriptions of his father and grandfather are full
of play with words—odd words, simple words used in unusual
ways, and words arranged so that their sounds create patterns. The poem is a festival of one-syllable words. Most
of them are plain and familiar. Except for the vivid
"squelch" (25), we might hear any of them in everyday
conversation. Some of them are put to unusual uses. For
instance, it is surprising to hear that "the coarse boot
nestled on the lug" (10). Nestling is an activity that we
might associate with small soft living creatures, not boots
and lugs, but the point is to show us the affinity that
these men have with their tools.

Heaney does not use rhyme in this poem, but just listing
the words shows how similar many of them sound: "thumb" (1),
"snug" (2), "gun" (2), "rump" (6), and "lug" (10) all have
a similar vowel sound. The same is true of "man," "handle,"
and "man" (15—16). In l. 25, "cold" and "mould" are so

close that they actually do rhyme. Then there are a number
of pairs that start with the same letter: "digging . . .
down" (5), "drills . . . digging" (8–9), "buried . . .
bright" (12), "hardness . . . hands" (14), "slicing . . .
sods" (22), "squelch . . . slap . . . soggy" (25–26), and
"curt cuts" (26). The words in l. 25 are actually about
sound, but Heaney is using many of the plain words that
make up his vocabulary in this poem in a way that turns
them into music.

It seems to be the music of the words that allows the
narrator to think that his pen could be equipment as worthy
as the spades of his father and grandfather. Thus, by the
time he has written about the intimacy of boot and lug,
knee and shaft (10–11), the intimacy between hand and pen
stops making the gun a weapon and turns it into another
instrument for digging. And if the activity of digging/
writing can use word music to "awaken in my head" (27) such
clear memories of these worthy forebears, it, too, now
seems worthy.

The resolve to write provides a resolution for the
negative feelings in the poem. The gun disappears, to be
replaced by a declaration of professional intention. The
narrator is ready to take his place beside his admired
relatives. Writing gives him a better picture of them and
a better attitude toward himself.

ACTIVITY 1: *Revising for Organization*

Considering what Zak Owen's paper does to analyze Heaney's poem, there
are other ways he could have written the introduction. Write a different
introductory paragraph for Zak's paper.

ACTIVITY 2: *A Reading Journal Entry*

Reread Sylvia Plath's poem "Cut" or Tobias Wolff's story "Powder" from Chapter 1. Choose one of them and write a journal entry in which you describe the work and your responses to it. If there are words or phrases that strike you as particularly meaningful, say why they are effective. You can separate your more objective from your subjective responses to the work with different colored ink or, as Zak did in his entry on "Digging," with different fonts.

 ACTIVITY 3: *Active Reading*

Review Pam Belluck's article "Nuns Offer Clues to Alzheimer's and Aging" from Chapter 1. Use several of the ideas listed under "Active Reading" in order to summarize and evaluate it for a friend or relative. For instance: annotate it, make a list of its important ideas, and use a sheet of blank paper to map the ideas and events it describes and your reactions to them.

CHAPTER THREE

Kinds of Literature: The Major Genres

GENRE AND FORM

In Chapters 1 and 2, we saw some of the differences between writing for a wide public audience and writing for an academic audience. Writing for these different audiences and with different purposes in mind produces texts with different features. For instance, civic writers usually don't use formal systems for referring to writers whose ideas they want to borrow. If they want to give credit to other writers, they simply mention them. Academic writers, in contrast, have elaborate systems for revealing their sources, from footnotes to works cited lists and parenthetical references tucked into their prose. So in a very straightforward way, civic writing usually looks different from academic writing. When we notice this, we are noticing genre. Each genre or kind of writing has different characteristics.

   You are probably used to making such distinctions in music. You probably recognize the rhythm that usually underlies rap or hip-hop, the themes of country and western music, and the instrumental sounds that mark bebop jazz. You can also probably subdivide the major genres, differentiating punk rock from grunge or metal from heavy metal, and understand the artists who "cross over," or mix the genres, leavening hip-hop with pop, for instance, or enriching pop with the instruments and rhythms of world music.

The same sort of subdividing and mixing goes on with writing. For example, newspaper articles are usually shorter than those in magazines like *The Atlantic* and *The New Yorker*. Letters to the editors of both newspapers and magazines look different from the articles. They begin with a salutation ("To the editor:"); in the first or second paragraph, they usually announce that they are responding to an earlier but recent letter or article in the same publication; and they are usually short. As you discover when you send one to the editor of your favorite publication, if you want your letter to get published, you have to follow the rules. In a "To the Reader" column, Thomas Feyer, the letters editor of the *New York Times*, says he looks as well for "fresh, bright writing that stands out through its own charm" in under 150 words.[1]

Nevertheless, new forms are being invented all the time by ignoring the rules or combining old rules in new ways. There are books by academic writers published by academic presses with—surprisingly—no footnotes, but rather lists of sources for "Further Reading." This hybrid form is meant as a "crossover" book for both academic and nonacademic audiences.

Like language itself, genre is a social phenomenon. The conventions that make a poem a poem or a particular kind of poem are not in the control of individuals. We inherit them as the gifts of our culture. You cannot decide alone that your thirteen-line poem is a sonnet. It may be called a sonnet someday, but only after a slow widening of the definition of the form. And you cannot do it yourself because such definitions are collective agreements. They evolve, but as the result not of individual efforts but of collaboration between readers and writers. If as writers we want our work to be accepted, we have to follow the formal rules of genre.

In Chapters 1 and 2, we separated civic and academic writing from imaginative literature, which can also be divided into genres. The simplest generic categorization separates poetry, fiction, drama, and literary essays. Each one of those gets divided into kinds. In this chapter, we'll spend a little time on the different rules or conventions for each one. But first, a few guidelines:

1. There isn't a single perfect definition of each genre, with perfect examples that follow all the rules. Definitions are slippery, or at least arguable, and they can change.

2. Looking at the features that distinguish the genres from one another, we should remember that there are also features that they share. (These features will be explored in Chapters 4–6 of this book.)

---

[1] Thomas Feyer, "To the Reader," *New York Times*, 14 September 2003, section 4, p. 10.

Poetry

What separates poetry from prose? Some people think it is dense language full of figures of speech such as metaphors and similes. This trait describes some poetry but not all, however, and prose writers can use those figures of speech as freely as poets can.

Some people think the defining characteristic of poetry is meter or rhyme, and during some eras, that was a valid distinction. In the days before printing, when poetry was not read silently but performed, there had to be something audible that would signal a change to a new line. In the early Middle Ages, it was patterns of repeated sounds at the beginning of words—in other words, alliteration. When the repeating sound changed, you were listening to a new line.

Starting in the later Middle Ages, repetition of sounds at the end of words at the end of lines became the signal—in other words, **rhyme.** In combination with patterns of alternating accented and unaccented syllables (called **meter**), rhyme can create patterns recognizable to listening audiences. Even people who were not educated in poetic forms, some of whom were illiterate, could actually hear the shape of the poems. For example, the sounds at the end of the first lines of Chaucer's poem *The Canterbury Tales* rhyme, thus indicating the shift from one line to the next:

From *The "General Prologue" to* The Canterbury Tales

GEOFFREY CHAUCER *(d. 1400) is known as the father of English poetry partly because instead of composing in French (the language of the Normans, who had conquered England in 1066), he was one of the first poets to return to composing in English.*

Whan that Aprill, with his shoures soote°
The droghte of March hath perced to the roote
And bathed every veyne in swich licour,°
Of which vertu engendred is the flour° . . .   [Late fourteenth century]

---

[1]**shoures soote** sweet showers   [3]**swich licour** such liquid   [4]**Of which vertu engendred is the flour** the power of which gives rise to flowers

Chaucer is writing in rhymed couplets with ten syllables per line. He was the first to do so in English, and others imitated him. Other poetic patterns that arose over the centuries defined different subgenres of poetry, like the sonnet, a fourteen-line poem with a specific rhyme pattern. The limerick is another. Chances are, you know a limerick, and you also know how many syllables each line needs and where the rhymes should occur. If you need a reminder, read this one out loud:

There was a young woman named Bright,
Whose speed was much faster than light.
She set out one day
In a relative way,
And returned on the previous night.   [Date unknown]

During the English Renaissance, poets like John Milton experimented with poetry that had meter but no rhyme. It was called **blank verse,** and you could hear the switch from one line to another only if you were very good at keeping track of the number of syllables. Have a friend read aloud the beginning of *Paradise Lost,* Milton's retelling of the fall of Satan and his tempting of Adam and Eve in the Garden of Eden. Can you keep track of when a new line begins just by listening?

From **Paradise Lost**

JOHN MILTON *(1608–74) was part of the Puritan Revolution against the English monarchy from 1640 to its end in 1660, writing many political and religious tracts. Paradise Lost is an epic retelling of the story of Adam and Eve in the Garden of Eden.*

Of Man's First Disobedience, and the Fruit
Of that Forbidden Tree, whose mortal taste
Brought Death into the World, and all our woe . . . .   [1667–74]

Should this kind of poetry be called prose? It flourished because more and more people were reading. When literacy rates went up, poetry didn't have to clang the bell of rhyme for people to know when a new line was beginning. They could see it on the page.

Then in the nineteenth century, some poets, mostly American, dispensed with regular meter, too. Walt Whitman brought the poetic line much closer to natural speech, as you can see at the beginning of his long poem, "Song of Myself."

From *Song of Myself*

WALT WHITMAN *(1819–92), typesetter, journalist, and newspaper editor, tended wounded soldiers during the Civil War. He published the first edition of* Leaves of Grass, *a collection of his poems, in 1855, expanding and revising it for the rest of his life.*

I celebrate myself, and sing myself,
And what I assume you shall assume,
For every atom belonging to me as good belongs to you.

I loaf and invite my soul,
5 I lean and loaf at my ease observing a spear of summer grass.

My tongue, every atom of my blood, form'd from this soil, this air,
Born here of parents born here from parents the same, and their parents the same,
I, now thirty-seven years old in perfect health begin,
Hoping to cease not till death.   [1855–92]

These lines are rhythmic without conforming to the patterns of formal meter. But you wouldn't call it prose if you accept this rather simple definition: *Poetry is that form of writing in which the author, not the printer, determines the right-hand margin.* If you want to claim that language that has meter and rhyme is poetry, you will probably be right, but those criteria will exclude much else that we also call poetry. Nevertheless, what we might want to include in the genre is not infinite. Under special circumstances, a shopping list could be called a "found poem," but not all shopping lists. You might think of Marcel Duchamp's 1917 "Fountain," actually a porcelain urinal mounted as a sculpture.[2] Some of the function of modern art seems to be to challenge our ideas of what art is. The debate about what constitutes poetry continues today when reviewers accuse post-Whitman free verse practitioners of writing prose chopped up into arbitrary lines.[3] It is the job of the poet to convince us that the breaks are not arbitrary.

Here are the first lines of W.H. Auden's "September 1, 1939":

From *September 1, 1939*

W.H. AUDEN *(1907–73) was born in England and educated at Oxford but moved in 1939 to the United States, where he became a citizen. The title of the poem is the date on which the German invasion of Poland initiated World War II.*

I sit in one of the dives
On Fifty-second Street
Uncertain and afraid . . .   [1940]

The poem would change considerably if it began with lines as long as Whitman's:

I sit in one of the dives on Fifty-second Street, uncertain and afraid . . . .

There are small hesitations as the eye makes the turn from line 1 to line 2 and line 2 to line 3. In that delay, the little pause allows us to be surprised by the feelings the speaker reveals in line 3. The surprise creates just enough emphasis for us to register them. They seem a little weightier because they take up a line of their own. We don't rush past them. In the decision about where to break the line lies much of the work's specifically *poetic* power.

---

[2]http://www.beatmuseum.org/duchamp/fountain.html.
[3]E.g., Daniel Anderson, "Sounds and Sweet Airs: *The Norton Anthology* May Be Bigger, But Is It Any Better?" *Harper's Magazine*, September 2002, 84–88.

In addition, it might be assumed that some of the poem's power, and one of the reasons it was so widely read after the destruction of the World Trade Center on September 11, 2001 (see Chapter 1, "Why Read Imaginative Literature?"), is that by starting out with the first person pronoun "I," it creates a human voice. This is one of the characteristics of the subgenre of **lyric poetry,** which often uses the immediacy of that voice. In Chapters 5 through 7, we will talk about some of these resources of language, including point of view, tone of voice, and sound patterns, and discuss what poets can do with them.

Fiction

What we usually mean by fiction is a story that never actually happened. Usually, what we call "fiction" is written in prose, either as novels or short stories. (Of course, poetry and drama can also tell stories—in fact, before the advent of the novel in early modern England, most fictional narratives were in poetry.)

A **narrative** is a storyteller's presentation of a sequence of events that happened to a set of characters.[4] The requirement of a teller means that a list of appointments on a calendar isn't enough. The sequence of events is not usually just a list of things that occur one after another. The news that it rained Monday, was clear on Tuesday, and clouded up on Wednesday is not, at first glance, a story, but rather a set of chronological events. What can make a weather report into a story is the shaping hand of a teller who attributes actions to characters trying to accomplish something and for whom the weather is an obstacle or a cause of **conflict.**

We call the episodes ordered by the creator of a verbal work, whether prose narrative, poetry, or drama, the **plot.** Here is a typical pattern:

1. **Exposition:** Characters and setting, as well as a conflict or problem, are introduced.
2. **Rising action:** The conflict intensifies, building toward a crisis.
3. **Crisis:** The conflict comes to a head. The point of maximum tension, after which subsequent events seem inevitable. The conflict or problem is either resolved or revealed to be unresolvable.
4. **Falling action:** The **denouement** (from the French for "untying") offers a resolution, either smoothing remaining entanglements to establish a new status quo or revealing the full extent of the catastrophe.

---

[4]Robert Scholes and Robert Kellogg, *The Nature of Narrative* (Oxford: Oxford University Press, 1966), 4.

The stages rarely receive equal weight. In most mystery novels, the rising action takes more time than the falling action and denouement. In the modern short story, conflicts are sometimes introduced without much exposition. Sometimes resolutions are hardly even suggested; many stories are left open-ended, with only vague gestures toward the future. According to sociolinguist William Labov, however, the basic pattern holds true not only for "artistic" writing, but also for the simplest of anecdotes.[5] It seems "natural," at least to people brought up in Western cultures.

This storytelling pattern is a tendency, not a straightjacket, and there will be variations as different people use it. There is some leeway, but eventually the deviations from the pattern might be so great that we would say that a given anecdote was not an example of the common pattern at all. Try the activity below to see how common the pattern is in your own storytelling and what tolerances you find in the system.

ACTIVITY 1 (GROUP ACTIVITY): *Telling Anecdotes and Analyzing Structures*

Divide into small groups and take turns telling each other stories of things that have happened to you in the last year. If you have trouble thinking of anecdotes, see whether any of these patterns jog your memory:

- You were supposed to be at a certain place at a certain time but had trouble getting there.
- You wanted to find something that was not easily available.
- You wanted a friend or relative to do something s/he didn't want to do.
- Someone tried to convince you to do something and you had to decide whether or not to do it.

Choose a recorder to report the results of the discussion to the class as a whole. Once each of you has told a story, as a group choose one of them and explore the ways it does or does not conform to the typical structure of stories with exposition, rising action, a crisis, and falling action leading to a denouement. Do the stories that the class chooses confirm or contradict the usual pattern?

---

[5]William Labov, *Language in the Inner City: Black English Vernacular* (Philadelphia: University of Pennsylvania Press, 1972). According to Labov, anecdotes often include an evaluation of some kind, which offers the "lesson learned" from the events related.

John Updike's "A & P" lets us take a look at a published story:

A & P

JOHN UPDIKE *(1932–), while he was an undergraduate, not only edited but wrote and drew for his college humor magazine,* The Harvard Lampoon. *After a stint as a reporter and writer for* The New Yorker *magazine, he began publishing novels and short stories that have earned him awards (including two Pulitzer Prizes) and acclaim as one of the best chroniclers of modern American life.*

In walks these three girls in nothing but bathing suits. I'm in the third checkout slot, with my back to the door, so I don't see them until they're over by the bread. The one that caught my eye first was the one in the plaid green two-piece. She was a chunky kid, with a good tan and a sweet broad soft-looking can with those two crescents of white just under it, where the sun never seems to hit, at the top of the backs of her legs. I stood there with my hand on a box of HiHo crackers trying to remember if I rang it up or not. I ring it up again and the customer starts giving me hell. She's one of these cash-register-watchers, a witch about fifty with rouge on her cheekbones and no eyebrows, and I know it made her day to trip me up. She'd been watching cash registers for fifty years and probably never seen a mistake before.

By the time I got her feathers smoothed and her goodies into a bag—she gives me a little snort in passing, if she'd been born at the right time they would have burned her over in Salem—by the time I get her on her way the girls had circled around the bread and were coming back, without a pushcart, back my way along the counters, in the aisle between the checkouts and the Special bins. They didn't even have shoes on. There was this chunky one, with the two-piece—it was bright green and the seams on the bra were still sharp and her belly was still pretty pale so I guessed she just got it (the suit)—there was this one, with one of those chubby berry-faces, the lips all bunched together under her nose, this one, and a tall one, with black hair that hadn't quite frizzed right, and one of these sunburns right across under the eyes, and a chin that was too long—you know, the kind of girl other girls think is very "striking" and "attractive" but never quite makes it, as they very well know, which is why they like her so much—and then the third one, that wasn't quite so tall. She was the queen. She kind of led them, the other two peeking around and making their shoulders round. She didn't look around, not this queen, she just walked straight on slowly, on these long white prima-donna legs. She came down a little hard on her heels, as if she didn't walk in her bare feet that much, putting down her heels and then letting the weight move along to her toes as if she was testing the floor with every step, putting a little deliberate extra action into it. You never know for sure how girls' minds work (do they really think it's a mind in there or just a little buzz like a bee in a glass jar?) but you got the idea she had talked the other two into coming in here with her, and now she was showing them how to do it, walk slow and hold yourself straight.

She had on a kind of dirty pink—beige maybe, I don't know—bathing suit with a little nubble all over it and, what got me, the straps were down. They were off her shoulders looped loose around the cool tops of her arms, and I guess as a result the suit had slipped on her, so all around the top of the cloth there was this shining rim. If it hadn't been there you wouldn't have known there could have been anything whiter than those shoulders. With the straps pushed off, there was nothing between the top of the suit and the top of her head except just *her,* this clean bare plane of the top of her chest down from the shoulder bones like a dented sheet of metal tilted in the light. I mean, it was more than pretty.

She had sort of oaky hair that the sun and salt had bleached, done up in a bun that was unravelling, and a kind of prim face. Walking into the A & P with your straps down, I suppose it's the only kind of face you *can* have. She held her head so high her neck, coming up out of those white shoulders, looked kind of stretched, but I didn't mind. The longer her neck was, the more of her there was.

She must have felt in the corner of her eye me and over my shoulder Stokesie   5 in the second slot watching, but she didn't tip. Not this queen. She kept her eyes moving across the racks, and stopped, and turned so slow it made my stomach rub the inside of my apron, and buzzed to the other two, who kind of huddled against her for relief, and then they all three of them went up the cat and dog food-breakfast cereal-macaroni-rice-raisins-seasonings-spreads-spaghetti-soft drinks-crackers-and-cookies aisle. From the third slot I look straight up this aisle to the meat counter, and I watched them all the way. The fat one with the tan sort of fumbled with the cookies, but on second thought she put the package back. The sheep pushing their carts down the aisle—the girls were walking against the usual traffic (not that we have one-way signs or anything)—were pretty hilarious. You could see them, when Queenie's white shoulders dawned on them, kind of jerk, or hop, or hiccup, but their eyes snapped back to their own baskets and on they pushed. I bet you could set off dynamite in the A & P and the people would by and large keep reaching and checking oatmeal off their lists and muttering "Let me see, there was a third thing, began with A, asparagus, no, ah, yes, applesauce!" or whatever it is they do mutter. But there was no doubt, this jiggled them. A few house slaves in pin curlers even look around after pushing their carts past to make sure what they had seen was correct.

You know, it's one thing to have a girl in a bathing suit down on the beach, where what with the glare nobody can look at each other much anyway, and another thing in the cool of the A & P, under the fluorescent lights, against all those stacked packages, with her feet paddling along naked over our checkerboard green-and-cream rubber-tile floor.

"Oh, Daddy," Stokesie said beside me. "I feel so faint."

"Darling," I said. "Hold me tight." Stokesie's married, with two babies chalked up on his fuselage already, but as far as I can tell that's the only difference. He's twenty-two, and I was nineteen this April.

"Is it done?" he asks, the responsible married man finding his voice. I forgot to say he thinks he's going to be a manager some sunny day, maybe in 1990 when it's called the Great Alexandrov and Petrooshki Tea Company or something.

10 What he meant was, our town is five miles from a beach, with a big summer colony out on the Point, but we're right in the middle of town, and the women generally put on a shirt or shorts or something before they get out of the car into the street. And anyway these are usually women with six children and varicose veins mapping their legs and nobody, including them, could care less. As I say, we're right in the middle of town, and if you stand at our front doors you can see two banks and the Congregational church and the newspaper store and three real estate offices and about twenty-seven old freeloaders tearing up Central Street because the sewer broke again. It's not as if we're on the Cape; we're north of Boston and there's people in this town haven't seen the ocean for twenty years.

The girls had reached the meat counter and were asking McMahon something. He pointed, they pointed, and they shuffled out of sight behind a pyramid of Diet Delight peaches. All that was left for us to see was old McMahon patting his mouth and looking after them sizing up their joints. Poor kids, I began to feel sorry for them, they couldn't help it.

Now here comes the sad part of the story, at least my family says it's sad, but I don't think it's so sad myself. The store's pretty empty, it being Thursday afternoon, so there was nothing much to do except lean on the register and wait for the girls to show up again. The whole store was like a pinball machine and I didn't know which tunnel they'd come out of. After a while they come around out of the far aisle, around the light bulbs, records at discount of the Caribbean Six or Tony Martin Sings or some such gunk you wonder they waste the wax on, six-packs of candy bars, and plastic toys done up in cellophane that fall apart when a kid looks at them anyway. Around they come, Queenie still leading the way, and holding a little gray jar in her hand. Slots Three through Seven are unmanned and I could see her wondering between Stokes and me, but Stokesie with his usual luck draws an old party in baggy gray pants who stumbles up with four giant cans of pineapple juice (what do these bums *do* with all that pineapple juice? I've often asked myself) so the girls come to me. Queenie puts down the jar and I take it into my fingers icy cold. Kingfish Fancy Herring Snacks in Pure Sour Cream: 49¢. Now her hands are empty, not a ring or a bracelet, bare as God made them, and I wonder where the money's coming from. Still with the prim look she lifts a folded dollar bill out of the hollow at the center of her nubbled pink top. The jar went heavy in my hand. Really, I thought that was so cute.

Then everybody's luck begins to run out. Lengel comes in from haggling with a truck full of cabbages on the lot and is about to scuttle into the door marked MANAGER behind which he hides all day when the girls touch his eye. Lengel's pretty dreary, teaches Sunday school and the rest, but he doesn't miss that much. He comes over and says, "Girls, this isn't the beach."

Queenie blushes, though maybe it's just a brush of sunburn I was noticing for the first time, now that she was so close. "My mother asked me to pick up a jar of herring snacks." Her voice kind of startled me, the way voices do when you see the people first, coming out so flat and dumb yet kind of tony, too, the way it ticked over "pick up" and "snacks." All of a sudden I slid right down her voice into her living room. Her father and the other men were standing around in ice-cream coats and bow ties and the women were in sandals picking up herring snacks on toothpicks off a big glass plate and they were all holding drinks the color of water with olives and sprigs of mint in them. When my parents have somebody over they get lemonade and if it's a real racy affair Schlitz in tall glasses with "They'll Do It Every Time" cartoons stencilled on.

"That's all right," Lengel said. "But this isn't the beach." His repeating this struck me as funny, as if it had just occurred to him, and he had been thinking all these years the A & P was a great big dune and he was the head lifeguard. He didn't like my smiling—as I say he doesn't miss much—but he concentrates on giving the girls that sad Sunday-school-superintendent stare. 15

Queenie's blush was no sunburn now, and the plump one in plaid, that I liked better from the back—a really sweet can—pipes up, "We weren't doing any shopping. We just came in for the one thing."

"That makes no difference," Lengel tells her, and I could see from the way his eyes went that he hadn't noticed she was wearing a two-piece before. "We want you decently dressed when you come in here."

"We *are* decent," Queenie says suddenly, her lower lip pushing, getting sore now that she remembers her place, a place from which the crowd that runs the A & P must look pretty crummy. Fancy Herring Snacks flashed in her very blue eyes.

"Girls, I don't want to argue with you. After this come in here with your shoulders covered. It's our policy." He turns his back. That's policy for you. Policy is what the kingpins want. What the others want is juvenile delinquency.

All this while, the customers had been showing up with their carts but, you know, sheep, seeing a scene, they had all bunched up on Stokesie, who shook open a paper bag as gently as peeling a peach, not wanting to miss a word. I could feel in the silence everybody getting nervous, most of all Lengel, who asks me, "Sammy, have you rung up this purchase?" 20

I thought and said "No" but it wasn't about that I was thinking. I go through the punches, 4, 9, GROC, TOT—it's more complicated than you think and after you do it often enough, it begins to make a little song, that you hear words to, in my case "Hello (*bing*) there, you (*gung*) hap-py *peepul* (*splat*)!"—the *splat* being the drawer flying out. I uncrease the bill, tenderly as you may imagine, it just having come from between the two smoothest scoops of vanilla I had ever known were there, and pass a half and a penny into her narrow pink palm and nestle the herrings in a bag and twist its neck and hand it over, all the time thinking.

The girls, and who'd blame them, are in a hurry to get out, so I say "I quit" to Lengel quick enough for them to hear, hoping they'll stop and watch me, their unsuspected hero. They keep right on going, into the electric eye; the door flies open and they flicker across the lot to their car, Queenie and Plaid and Big Tall Goony-Goony (not that as raw material she was so bad), leaving me with Lengel and a kink in his eyebrow.

"Did you say something, Sammy?"

"I said I quit."

"I thought you did." 25

"You didn't have to embarrass them."

"It was they who were embarrassing us."

I started to say something that came out "Fiddle-de-doo." It's a saying of my grandmother's, and I know she would have been pleased.

"I don't think you know what you're saying," Lengel said.

30 "I know you don't," I said. "But I do." I pull the bow at the back of my apron and start shrugging it off my shoulders. A couple customers that had been heading for my slot begin to knock against each other, like scared pigs in a chute.

Lengel sighs and begins to look very patient and old and gray. He's been a friend of my parents for years. "Sammy, you don't want to do this to your Mom and Dad," he tells me. It's true, I don't. But it seems to me that once you begin a gesture it's fatal not to go through with it. I fold the apron, "Sammy" stitched in red on the pocket, and put it on the counter, and drop the bow tie on top of it. The bow tie is theirs, if you've ever wondered. "You'll feel this for the rest of your life," Lengel says, and I know that's true, too, but remembering how he made that pretty girl blush makes me so scrunchy inside I punch the No Sale tab and the machine whirs "pee-pul" and the drawer splats out. One advantage to this scene taking place in summer, I can follow this up with a clean exit, there's no fumbling around getting your coat and galoshes, I just saunter into the electric eye in my white shirt that my mother ironed the night before, and the door heaves itself open, and outside the sunshine is skating round on the asphalt.

I look around for my girls, but they're gone, of course. There wasn't anybody but some young married screaming with her children about some candy they didn't get by the door of a powder-blue Falcon station wagon. Looking back in the big windows, over the bags of peat moss and aluminum lawn furniture stacked on the pavement, I could see Lengel in my place in the slot, checking the sheep through. His face was dark gray and his back stiff, as if he'd just had an injection of iron, and my stomach kind of fell as I felt how hard the world was going to be to me hereafter. [1962]

 ACTIVITY 2: *Analyzing "A & P" for Narrative Pattern*

- Does "A & P" conform to the common pattern for narrative outlined above? Label the moments in the story that correspond to the stages of a typical narrative. Are there any parts of the story that do not seem to follow the typical pattern?
- Within the basic pattern of narrative, there are different types—coming of age stories, mysteries, the perennial "boy meets girl, boy loses girl," etc. Western literature tends to revolve around a number of familiar plots, repeating them, varying them, making them new. Does "A & P" resemble any of these "types"? How? In what way(s) does it diverge from type?

No matter how a story is structured, it cannot exist without someone to tell it. Like lyric poetry, stories imply the existence of a speaker. The speaker, brought to life by an author's use of language, may be a participant in the story, like Sammy in "A & P," or distanced from it in time and space. Creating that relationship, as well as the speaker's relationship to the audience, is part of the art of narrative, and various ways to do it will concern us in Chapter 4.

No matter how a story is structured or who tells it, stories seem to be a natural part of the way humans relate to the world. As communication researchers have shown, we *live* stories, that is, tend to think of our own and others' lives in terms of narrative patterns that our culture makes available. The girl who is prettier than her classmates and is treated as stupid by teachers has to discover her own intellectual capabilities. The younger sister of the prom queen feels worthless until she is discovered to have a beautiful singing voice. A boy growing up in a poor neighborhood has to discover his own sources of self-esteem in order to avoid the bad choices offered by delinquent friends. A family has it all—status, financial security, a large house, private schools for the children—but none of its members are happy until they abandon it all to sail around the world. These are all familiar patterns.

You can probably envision the movies that could be based on any of these simple stories. The difference between stories that can be told in twenty-page short stories or ninety-minute movies and the stories of our lives is that life stories are not resolved until people die, and even then the resolution may not be satisfying. As Eric Eisenberg says in his article, "Building a Mystery," some people get stuck in stories that keep them from living satisfying lives. Perhaps the drive to tell stories is the drive to give a meaningful shape to a sequence of events in the "laboratory" of fiction as we cannot do in life.[6]

 ACTIVITY 3: *Making a Sequence a Story*

> Make the weather report given above, "it rained Monday, was clear on Tuesday, and clouded up on Wednesday," part of a story rather than just a sequence of unrelated events.

Drama

Not surprisingly, the definition of drama overlaps with the definitions of some of the other genres we have already examined. Like storytelling and the recitation of poetry, the impulse to imitate a sequence of actions before

---

[6]Eric M. Eisenberg, "Building a Mystery: Toward a New Theory of Communication and Identity," *Journal of Communication* 51 (2001): 346–48.

a group of onlookers seems to be very old. For drama as for fiction, the sequence of actions usually has a pattern. In the staged drama that we are used to and the films that present drama through a slightly different medium, the logic of the sequence is often the same as that for short stories, novels, and narrative poems: a character or group of characters has a conflict or problem that gets worse, producing a crisis that either resolves it or demonstrates that it cannot be resolved. A new status quo is thus established.

What drama shares less frequently with fiction is the presence of a teller who narrates the plot. (A few plays, such as Thornton Wilder's *Our Town* and Tennessee Williams's *The Glass Menagerie* have narrators, but they are in the minority.) Instead of being *told*, the stories of most plays and films are *enacted*.

When you read a play, you can see the playwright's instructions to the company producing it, which can be quite sparse or can elaborate on details of how things look (costume, sets, lighting, for instance) and what happens on stage (what the actors are doing while they talk and how they sound). To read it is to produce it in one's head.

To see a play on stage is to see the interpretations of actors, directors, and costume, setting, and lighting designers. Seeing actions played by human actors with human bodies can be quite powerful. That does nothing to detract from the ability of films or the written word to move us. But another element comes in when human actors are present on the stage. A new layer of intimacy and of interpretation is added when a play is "en-acted" by a real actor impersonating a fictional character. Whenever possible, read plays by reading them out loud—ideally, with a group, with different people taking on different parts.

ACTIVITY 4: *Reflecting on (a) Performance*

Many colleges and universities have active drama programs, and many communities have groups, whether amateur or professional, that produce plays for the public. Attend a play, either on or off campus. After the performance, make some notes about how the audience behaved. (When was it noisy, when was it quiet? How did it know when to switch from one to the other?) What cues were there on stage to locate the action in time and space?

You can see from Christopher Graybill's "Go Look" how little it takes to create a "scene" in which dramatic action can happen. Elaborate sets and a cast of thousands are unnecessary for this piece, published in a series called *Ten-Minute Plays*. Yet even with very little attempt to copy reality in any detail, "Go Look" puts us right in the middle of a situation, a relationship, and a pair of psyches.

Go Look

CHRISTOPHER GRAYBILL *is a playwright whose "Eye to Eye" was produced at the Twice as Loud Theatre Company in London in 1996 and at the seventh annual East West Players Network Showcase at the David Henry Hwang Theatre. His play "Deep End" was part of the Baltimore Theatre Festival in 1990. "Go Look" was produced at the Festival of Ten-Minute Plays at the Playwrights Theatre of Milwaukee in 2000.*

Characters

Kath—twenties

Danny—twenties

Time & Place

The present. Two a.m.

A tent in a wilderness area.

DARKNESS. FOREST NOISES. KATH switches on a flashlight.

Kath: What was that?
Danny: Hunh?
Kath: I heard something.
Danny: What did it sound . . .
Kath: Shhh.   5
Danny: OK.
Kath: It's stopped.
Danny: Good.
Kath: Go look.
Danny: What?   10
Kath: Go look outside. Around the tent.
Danny: What for?
Kath: It might be something.
Danny: Kath . . .
Kath: Please.   15
Danny: I'm not dressed.
Kath: Who's going to see you?
Danny: Whatever made the noise.
Kath: It won't care if you have clothes on.
Danny: It? What kind of it?   20
Kath: I don't know.
Danny: You mean like a bear?
Kath: No. Not necessarily.
Danny: You want me to go look for something that's not necessarily a bear. In the middle of the night. In the middle of nowhere. In my underwear.

25 *Kath:* Take the flashlight.

Danny: Why don't you go?

Kath: You're the man.

Danny: Right. I forgot.

Kath: I was kidding.

30 *Danny:* No gun, no knife. But I've got the dick. What am I going to do with that? Piss on him? Fuck him?

Kath: You are gross.

Danny: Thank you.

Kath: I was only kidding anyway—about you being the man.

Danny: Why don't you go?

35 *Kath:* Me?

Danny: Yeah, stuff the flashlight in your jeans. The bear will think you're *really* dangerous.

Kath: You are disgusting. Just forget it.

(Beat.)

Danny: There aren't any bears around here.

Kath: I'm sleeping.

40 *Danny:* There isn't a bear within a hundred miles. Snakes, maybe.

Kath: Get off of me.

Danny: There might be one in your sleeping bag.

Kath: Quit!

Danny: But no bears.

(Beat.)

45 *Kath:* I never said it was a bear.

Danny: So, what? Wild animals?

Kath: No.

Danny: Murderers? Monsters? Your mother?

Kath: Shut up.

50 *Danny:* Come on, Kath. What did you think?

Kath: What I always think in the woods.

Danny: Which is?

Kath: That it will come for me.

Danny: Ooooh. What?

55 *Kath:* I don't know.

Danny: What does it look like?

Kath: I don't know.

Danny: Now we're getting someplace.

Kath: I don't want to talk about him.

60 *Danny:* You said "him." How do you know it's a he?

Kath: I've heard his growl. It sounds deep.

Danny: Like this? I mean, *(Bass.)* like this?

Kath: You're a riot, Danny.

Danny: The growling bogeyman.

65 *Kath:* It's not a bogeyman.

Danny: If you say so.

Kath: It's a real man.

Danny: Oh, a *real* man.

Kath: I mean a person, moron. On the outside. But inside . . .

Danny: Yeah?   70

Kath: Rage.

Danny: Rage?

Kath: No limits.

Danny: Right. And where does this angry guy come from?

Kath: Far from here. Deep in the forest. Where there are no footprints, not even   75
animal tracks. Just thick vines and roots and leaves that shine icy white in
the moonlight.

Danny: He lives there.

Kath: No. That's where he's born. Sometimes at night the leaves and vines shift,
all by themselves, to make a clearing, as if an invisible hand was sweeping
away the underbrush.

Danny: Uh, oh.

Kath: The bare ground forms a mound that puckers at the top.

Danny: Sounds like a pimple.   80

Kath: Danny . . .

Danny: All right. Then what?

Kath: There's a groaning sound that starts way underground. It builds up, louder
and louder.

He bursts out of the ground. Running. On all fours. No hesitation. Tearing
over fields and rocks. Straight toward me. The closer he comes, the faster he
runs. Until he sees where I am.

Then he stops on the side of a hill. He stands there. Looking down at me.
At our tent, lit like a Chinese lantern. I can't see his face. But I know he's
waiting. Teeth bared. Grinning. Growling.

Danny: That's the end?

Kath: I never let myself think further than that.   85

Danny: What would happen?

Kath: If he got me?

Danny: If he got you.

Kath: I would be destroyed.

Danny: You mean killed.   90

Kath: More than that. Everything. Gone.

Danny: Why is he after you?

Kath: I attract him.

Danny: In what way?

Kath: I don't know.   95

Danny: Maybe he knows you won't face him.

Kath: What?

Danny: You'll consent to be destroyed.

Kath: That's awful.

Danny: But true.   100

Kath: No. I don't think so. You never know until the moment.

Danny: Some people do.

Kath: They say they do.

Danny: But not you. The innocent victim. The noble victim.

105 *Kath:* That's a terrible thing to say.

Danny: A worse one to be.

Kath: Why are you being so nasty?

Danny: Because I hate this shit. An angry Man erupts out of the night. He's going to destroy the Woman. It's straight out of a cheap horror movie. I can't stand all this self-righteous . . .

Kath: Danny . . .

110 *Danny:* Poor, helpless you. Big, bad men. I'm sick of taking the blame.

Kath: Shut up a second. I heard it again.

(THEY listen. Silence.)

Kath: Turn off the flashlight. (*HE does so.*)

Danny: That won't matter.

Kath: Why not?

115 *Danny:* He doesn't have eyes.

Kath: How do you know?

Danny: You said so.

Kath: No. I didn't.

Danny: Well, he doesn't. He doesn't need them. He knows where he's going. From the instant he comes out of the ground. Spit out of the earth like something rancid.

120 *Kath:* Are you making fun of . . .

Danny: Running. Speeding over hills, tree stumps, a dry creek bed. Sharp stones cut his feet. Racing, fast as a pulse. Closer. On the horizon. Closer. On the hillside. He pauses.

Kath: All right, Danny.

Danny: Facing but not seeing. No eyes. Or nose. A blank face. A jagged hole of a mouth. Breathing fast. Grinning. Now he's ready. He starts moving.

Kath: Stop. I mean it.

125 *Danny:* Sweeping down the hill. Toward the dark tent. Doesn't need eyes or nose. Not stalking. Drawn. Reeled in. Fast. Almost here. Outside the tent. Growling.

Kath: Quit!

Danny: Through the flap. Past you. And into me. (*HE turns on the flashlight.*)

Kath: OK. The end. Roll the credits.

Danny: I know your Wild Man, Kath. I've met him.

130 *Kath:* The movie's over.

Danny: Whenever we go to the woods. And other times. The line gets stretched very thin. I could cross it. Couldn't you?

Kath: I don't know what you mean.

Danny: I mean I know I could do terrible things. Violent things.

Kath: You're serious.

135 *Danny:* For me, it would be easy. I could pick up a hammer or a flashlight and pound everyone and everything into pulp. Even the people I love most in the

world. Pick it up and do it. And sometimes I want to, I really want to, for no
reason at all. It pulls at me. Don't you ever feel that way?

Kath: I don't know.

Danny: If you did, you'd know it.

Kath: Everybody has bad thoughts, Danny.

Danny: It's not the thoughts. That's not it. It's what's underneath. The
exhilaration. The savage, howling joy of hurting. Or killing. The release.
That's what makes me wonder what I am.

(Beat.)

Kath: I don't know what to say.   140

Danny: Well, you're a fucking saint.

Kath: No. It scares me.

Danny: It must be the testosterone talking. Since I'm the man.

Kath: I'm going to sleep.

(Pause.)

Kath: Danny?   145

Danny: What?

Kath: Last weekend at Mother's. It was a nice day. She told me to push her out
on the back patio.

Danny: So?

Kath: She said something. I don't remember what. Not very nasty, not for her.
Something about my shoes. It was nothing, really. But for an instant I felt
like letting go. Just letting go and watching gravity work. I imagined her
chair rolling down the slope, over the edge, and bouncing down the back
steps. All the way to the garage. And when the police and ambulance
would come, I'd be crying and sobbing and explaining. But inside I'd be
dancing.

Danny: But you didn't do it.   150

Kath: No.

Danny: Too bad. We haven't been dancing for a long time.

(Beat.)

Kath: When you have those thoughts—do you have them toward me, too?

Danny: Yes. Sometimes. I'm sorry, Kath.

Kath: But you don't do anything.   155

Danny: No. Not so far.

Kath: So far, so good.

(Beat. There is a DISTINCT SOUND in the woods.)

Kath: What's that?

Danny: I don't know. *(HE moves to exit.)*

Kath: Wait. *(SHE rises.)* Let's go.   160

(THEY exit together. Curtain.)

The End   [1995]

"Go Look" demonstrates that plots do not require a great deal of physical action. The actors hardly have to move. And yet the conversation can cover quite a lot of territory.

ACTIVITY 5: *Mapping the Plot of "Go Look"*

Map the plot of "Go Look." Then answer the following questions:

1. What are the conflicts in the play?
2. If you were directing the play, what kind of "forest noises" would immediately precede Kath's first speech? Would they be soft sounds like breezes making trees sway and small animals rustling in undergrowth, or would they be loud grunts and knocks? What interpretation of the play would motivate your choice?
3. Describe each character.
4. What do Danny and Kath discover about themselves in the course of the play? What do they discover about each other? Has the couple's relationship changed by the end of the play compared to what it was at the beginning? If so, how?
5. How do the conflicts in the plot affect your reading of the major themes of the play?
6. Write a different ending for the play.

The Essay

An **essay** is a fairly short piece of writing that expresses the views of its author or authors. "Fairly short" is inexact, but it cannot be pinned down to a number of words or pages because the definition of this flexible genre is not very formal. In length, the essay is somewhere between the epigram and the short novel. It can contain exposition, but its chief function is not to convey information. It can contain narrative, but its main goal is not to tell a story. Like lyric poetry, it puts the reader in the presence of a speaker with something to say, but the speakers usually do not speak through fictionalized characters or through a narrator. The authors of essays seem to speak for themselves and are expressing their own opinions and ideas. It can be argued that these "selves" are in fact fictional—but they are fictional only in the way we are all fictional, making up selves out of the raw material provided by our families, our cultures, and the way we have been taught to be in the various worlds we inhabit. Essayists' raw materials are their reactions to whatever they come across in their lives. They use themselves and their experiences as barometers with which to measure the world's weather.

The essay bloomed as a genre with the advent of printing because, unlike poetry, fiction, and drama, it was not a major form of entertainment in the centuries before Gutenberg. The audiences of essays are assumed to be reading. Though early examples exist like the ancient Roman philosopher Marcus Aurelius's *Meditations*, the first writer to use the word *essay* was the sixteenth-century French writer Michel de Montaigne. In the preface to his book, he announces, "So, reader, I am myself the substance of my book."[7] He claims to be "trying out" (*essay* means "trial" or "attempt") his opinions on many subjects that present themselves in the course of everyday life—friendship, education, cruelty, etc.—for the sake of friends and relatives who will outlive him, and he claims that his thoughts are private. But in preserving his thoughts for the future, writing also allows them to spread beyond his personal acquaintances. Many essays—made up of thoughts beautifully written, revealing the nuances of a sensibility worth reading—seem almost to be private thoughts that we are overhearing.

Here is a brief excerpt in which Montaigne's insight is about his mind itself as he notices the way it works. He reports on his attempt to test the theory that if he left his mind to itself, rather than constantly trying to discipline it by setting it to examine "some definite subject which curbs and restrains [it]," it would become more "settled" and "mature." But he found, rather,

> that, on the contrary, like a runaway horse, it is a hundred times more active on its own behalf than ever it was for others. It presents me with so many chimeras and imaginary monsters, one after another, without order or plan, that, in order to contemplate their oddness and absurdity at leisure, I have begun to record them in writing, hoping in time to make my mind ashamed of them. (27–28)

Montaigne might be dismayed to know that he has been less influential in his desire to discipline and disown his whirling thoughts than in his resolve to write them down. The essay flourishes today in the form of meditations, personal essays, and memoirs. Montaigne's modern heirs like Annie Dillard, Joan Didion, and Wendell Berry continue to practice the craft of what we have come to call the belletristic, or literary, essay (see the Anthology for samples from all three writers). Since many modern essays seem not to follow easily classifiable forms and styles but to improvise new forms, many commentators use the rubric "creative nonfiction" to contain the diversity. Such writings take forms that have no rules and can combine modes, for instance, including sections in the format of an

[7]Michel de Montaigne, *Essays*, trans. J.M. Carton (Harmondsworth: Penguin, 1958), 23.

interview, a scientific exposition, or a memoir. They can be experimental and improvisational.[8]

In an essay with observations that range from himself and his family to a more distant time and place, the writer Bernard Cooper develops "The Fine Art of Sighing."

The Fine Art of Sighing

BERNARD COOPER *(1951–), art critic for* Los Angeles Magazine, *has written essays, memoirs, short stories, and a novel. He has taught creative writing and won both the PEN/Hemingway Award and the O. Henry Prize.*

You feel a gradual welling up of pleasure, or boredom, or melancholy. Whatever the emotion, it's more abundant than you ever dreamed. You can no more contain it than your hands can cup a lake. And so you surrender and suck the air. Your esophagus opens, diaphragm expands. Poised at the crest of an exhalation, your body is about to be unburdened, second by second, cell by cell. A kettle hisses. A balloon deflates. Your shoulders fall like two ripe pears, muscles slack at last.

My mother stared out the kitchen window, ashes from her cigarette dribbling into the sink. She'd turned her back on the rest of the house, guarding her own solitude. I'd tiptoe across the linoleum and fix my lunch without making a sound. Sometimes I saw her back expand, then heard her let loose one plummeting note, a sigh so long and weary it might have been her last. Beyond our backyard, above telephone poles and apartment buildings, rose the brown horizon of the city; across it glided an occasional bird, or the blimp that advertised Goodyear tires. She might have been drifting into the distance, or lamenting her separation from it. She might have been wishing she were somewhere else, or wishing she could be happy where she was, a middle-aged housewife dreaming at her sink.

My father's sighs were more melodic. What began as a somber sigh could abruptly change pitch, turn gusty and loose, and suggest by its very transformation that what begins in sorrow might end in relief. He could prolong the rounded vowel of *oy*, or let it ricochet like a echo, as if he were shouting in a tunnel or a cave. Where my mother sighed from ineffable sadness, my father sighed at simple things: the coldness of a drink, the softness of a pillow, or an itch that my mother, following the frantic map of his words, finally found on his back and scratched.

A friend of mine once mentioned that I was given to long and ponderous sighs. Once I became aware of this habit, I heard my father's sighs in my own and knew for a moment his small satisfactions. At other times, I felt my mother's restlessness and wished I could leave my body with my breath, or be happy in the body my breath left behind.

---

[8]See *In Short: A Collection of Brief Creative Nonfiction* (1996) and *In Brief: Short Takes on the Personal* (1990), both edited by Judith Kitchen and Mary Paumier and published by W.W. Norton. Also see the online journal *Brevity: A Journal of Concise Literary Nonfiction*, http://www.creativenonfiction.org/brevity/index.htm.

It's a reflex and a legacy, this soulful species of breathing. Listen closely: My   5
ancestors' lungs are pumping like bellows, men towing boats along the banks of
the Volga, women lugging baskets of rye bread and pike. At the end of each day,
they lift their weary arms in a toast; as thanks for the heat and sting of vodka,
their ahhs condense in the cold Russian air.

At any given moment, there must be thousands of people sighing. A man in
Milwaukee heaves and shivers and blesses the head of his second wife, who's
not too shy to lick his toes. A judge in Munich groans with pleasure after tasting
again the silky bratwurst she ate as a child. Every day, meaningful sighs are
expelled from schoolchildren, driving instructors, forensic experts, certified public
accountants, and dental hygienists, just to name a few. The sighs of widows and
widowers alone must account for a significant portion of the carbon dioxide
released into the atmosphere. Every time a girdle is removed, a foot is submerged
in a tub of warm water, or a restroom is reached on a desolate road . . . you'd think
the sheer velocity of it would create mistrals, siroccos, hurricanes; arrows should be
swarming over satellite maps, weathermen talking a mile a minute, ties flapping
from their necks like flags.

Before I learned that Venetian prisoners were led across it to their execution,
I imagined that the Bridge of Sighs was a feat of invisible engineering, a
structure vaulting above the earth, the girders and trusses, the stay ropes and
cables, the counterweights and safety rails, connecting one human breath to
the next.

Some essays are written for the public on public issues. The writers may
use their own responses to events, making themselves, as Montaigne
claimed, "the substance" of their writing. But their chief aim is to present
material that will contribute to the discussion of public issues. Newspaper
and magazine columnists like George Will, Charles Krauthammer,
Alexander Cockburn, and Barbara Ehrenreich are good examples of this
variety of essayist. We sometimes call them "pundits," from the Hindi term
for someone who knows something. We value their opinions. Most of them
are not scholars, and what we want from them is not just what they know in
the form of information, but what they know because of the way their sensibilities and values filter the world. You know that when you turn to Will and
Krauthammer you will get views from the right of the political spectrum;
Cockburn and Ehrenreich provide views from the left. You might not be able
to figure out Dave Barry's politics, but he will make you laugh. So although
these essayists are not writing personal essays, and they are writing in media
with deadlines that may not allow them to polish their prose styles to perfection, their personalities are part of what they have to offer. As with
Montaigne, their own sensibilities are part of the substance of their writing.

In the months after the destruction of the World Trade Center towers
and part of the Pentagon in September of 2001, many commentators, heads
of arts organizations, and government officials (President George W. Bush
among them) invoked the healing power of art. Here is part of art critic
Christopher Knight's answer to the question of whether art can help a society
heal from the wounds of traumatic events.

From *What Exactly Can Art Heal?*[9]

CHRISTOPHER KNIGHT

Popular in America in the 19th century, when the church had long since ceased to be an important and persuasive cultural patron, the sentiment sprang from a metaphysical void. It's a secular version of venerating the healing power of religious paintings and statues—Matthias Grünewald's famous "Isenheim Altarpiece," say, a monumental machine painted for the chapel of a 16th century monastic hospital in an effort to help patch up those afflicted by a dreaded local disease caused by fungus on rye. It's one heck of a painting, although it didn't cure much gangrene. Still, we cling to the fantasy—even if healing in our post-Freud world is less about physical lesions and more about psychological wounds. Americans' sentimental relationship to art periodically drives us into the suffocating arms of therapeutic culture. The terrorist attacks seem to be doing it again. . . .

Actually, you'd probably do just as well investing in crystals or soliciting by telephone the psychic services of Miss Cleo. But it's instructive that politicians and the political class are the ones who so often champion this old-time conception of art's purpose and value. Extolling "the healing power of art" in the face of massive social trauma handily fudges the failure of politics, and the failure of politics is at the root of things like the '92 riots and the current terrorist nightmare.

[2001]

As regular art critic for the *Los Angeles Times*, Knight must have a regular following, readers who know his style, so they won't be shocked when he calls the beloved Isenheim Altarpiece a "monumental machine," takes a disrespectful tone with flip phrases like "patch up" and "fungus on rye," or calls the healing power of art a "fantasy." Readers who don't know him might be attracted to his wit, even if they disagree with him.

Yet another kind of essay is the **academic essay.** Since its purpose is usually argumentative, it may offer more evidence to support its claims than other kinds of essays, and it will depend for its effect more on the strength and clarity of its argument than on the beauty of its writing style. But it has in common with other kinds of essays the sincerity of its relationship to both subject matter and audience. The writer speaks in his or her own voice, not through a fictional narrator, and wants readers to believe that he or she believes the essay's conclusions—wanting us to believe them, too. The subject matter is not usually personal, and the mind we encounter will not be a mind set free to roam as Montaigne's was in his book. The minds we meet in academic essays address topics within disciplines, the categories into which colleges and universities divide the world of knowledge.

In addition, the disciplines "curb and restrain" inquiry, to use Montaigne's phrase for what he was trying to escape, by providing agreed-upon methods

[9]Christopher Knight, "What Exactly Can Art Heal?" *Los Angeles Times*, 4 November 2001.

of investigating their subjects. So except for rare moments like the one we saw in Chapter 1 when historian J.G.A. Pocock described his pleasure in making a discovery, we will not become as directly intimate with another mind as we will through reading Montaigne. But we will learn how someone with training in a certain subject matter thinks about it. Some academic writers do not use first person pronouns "I," "my," "we," and "our." Nevertheless, they are the sources of their claims and conclusions. When we read them, we are learning about the world from their particular perspectives.

Here is an excerpt from an article in which two psychologists, Wendy Hollway and Tony Jefferson, try to use the concepts of their discipline to understand an adult male psychiatric patient they call "Tommy," whom they interviewed several times.

◎◎◎

From *Narrative, Discourse and the Unconscious: The Case of Tommy*[10]

WENDY HOLLWAY AND TONY JEFFERSON

According to Klein, love and hate are always co-present in our relationships and the challenge is not to overcome the hate, but rather to acknowledge it as belonging in the same place as love. Alford (1989: 165), following Klein, describes a person's integration of love and hate as 'the common task faced by every human being'. This kind of integration enables ambivalence; that is, the capacity to recognise that good and bad exist in the same object. Tommy, as we have seen, is not always good at ambivalence. The capacity for ambivalence through the integration of splits is achieved through reparation; that is, through acknowledging the harm that one might have caused someone, if only in fantasy . . . and attempting to repair it (Klein 1940; Alford 1990). . . .

Our analysis and interpretation of Tommy's narrative aimed at producing a psychosocial account of Tommy. The dominant constructionist paradigm in narrative research meant that it was inadequate for this purpose and so we developed a method of production and analysis of narrative data consistent with the principle of a dynamic unconscious. Pointers to the relation between narrative claims and real experience (or narrated and lived lives) can be found, we believe, in the traces left unconsciously in the text. At the same time, our concern with the discursive positions in which people become invested constantly implicates the social, thus marking the difference between our interest (as social researchers) in the individual case study and that of clinicians working therapeutically with individual lives.   [2000]

---

[10]Wendy Hollway and Tony Jefferson, "Narrative, Discourse and the Unconscious: The Case of Tommy," in *Lines of Narrative: Psychosocial Perspectives*, ed. Molly Andrews, Shelley Day Sclater, Corinne Squire, and Amal Treacher (London: Routledge, 2000), 136–49.

References

Alford, F. (1989) *Melanie Klein and Critical Social Theory*, New Haven: Yale University Press.

———. (1990) 'Reparation and civilization: a Kleinian account of the large group', *Free Associations* 19: 7–30.

Klein, M. (1940) 'Mourning and its relations to manic-depressive states', *International Journal of Psycho-analysis* 21: 125–53.

You might notice that Hollway and Jefferson are bringing together two kinds of material: the theories of psychologists Alford and Klein, who have written before them, and the testimony of their research subject, Tommy. They are applying the theories of Alford and Klein to Tommy's narratives—that is, they are using the theories to try to understand Tommy better. They do not talk about themselves personally, but use first person pronouns "we" and "our" to talk about their ideas and claim them for their own. They give credit to Alford and Klein for the borrowed ideas, referring to their articles through brief references in parentheses in the text, with more complete bibliographic information in the list of references at the end of the article.[11]

At the same time, they take credit for their own contribution, believing that before they put together the work of Alford and Klein, the ideas offered by their field were "inadequate" for understanding the contradictory feelings resulting from Tommy's experience. Using Alford and Klein to understand Tommy is not useful just for Tommy's well-being (Hollway and Jefferson are not therapists, after all, and did not set out to make Tommy feel better). They bring past work to bear on their current project in order to have an impact on their field. In this way, they hope to help not only other researchers, but also therapists and patients.

CONNECTING GENRES

The separate treatment of the different genres in this chapter does not mean that the different worlds of discourse do not communicate. Though genres are separated by the conventions that govern them, they can easily be joined by concern with the same subject matter. They can speak to each other quite well. In fact, literary critics frequently use ideas from arguments in other academic disciplines (the methods and subjects of study in colleges and universities) in order to understand literary works better. This makes sense because imaginative literature portrays human beings feeling and

---

[11]The rules that govern what the parenthetical references and the reference list look like, especially how they are punctuated, are specific to the field of psychology. Since Routledge is a British press and the book was published first in London, it follows British rules rather than American. The particular differences are not important here, only the fact that they exist.

doing all the things that academic scholars and researchers study. Applying the concepts from academic arguments to literature is natural. You might think of the disciplinary idea as a lens that changes our view of something we are looking at or the frame that shapes what we see through a window.

Some of the writings in this chapter offer an opportunity to see interaction between works in different genres. Graybill's play and Hollway and Jefferson's article follow completely different generic conventions, but they might offer each other insights into a common subject matter—the emotional life of human beings. The conversation among works of different genres will be the major concern in Part III of this book.

 ACTIVITY 6: *Connecting Genres*

> Go back to your answers to the questions in Activity 5, particularly those concerning what Danny and Kath discover about themselves and each other. What do their discoveries tell you about the theme of the play? What would Hollway and Jefferson say about the characters' discoveries? Would they think that Danny and Kath are more or less psychologically healthy at the end of the play than they were at the beginning? Do the two characters' paths of discovery differ? If so, how? How might Hollway and Jefferson rewrite the end of the play? How do the generic differences between the article and the play affect your discoveries about their subject matters?

The Elements of Literature

CHAPTER FOUR

Theme, Narrative and Plot, Setting, and Character

In Chapter 1 we explored the different kinds of writing that flow in and around our daily lives; in Chapter 2 we outlined the process of writing in response to texts; in Chapter 3 we discussed the different kinds of imaginative literature. This sequence implies that reading and writing are profoundly linked—as in fact they are. There are two reasons for the connection: First, reading what others write gives us models for writing—it helps us see both *what* can be expressed in writing and *how* it can be expressed. Second, the more deeply we read, the more we have to say. So reading well is an invention strategy for writers.

The rest of this book focuses on reading well in order to write. In this chapter and the next three, we will look at some principal elements of written texts so that you will be able to analyze them in enough detail to make good arguments about them. Many of the examples in the chapters will come from imaginative literature, but where it is useful, I will draw in other kinds of writing, too, since there are many elements that all kinds of writing share.

THEME

Theme is one of the reasons we think that imaginative literature is worth reading—it tells us something valuable about ourselves or our world. While it is true that Shakespeare's Hamlet loved his father, that description is not the theme of the play. If the play had no relevance outside its fictional Denmark and its fictional characters, no one would read it, stage it, or buy tickets to see it. Since it has traveled all around the world and seems always to be in production somewhere, it must mean something beyond its small world, something general enough to apply to other times and places.

A theme is the main or unifying idea in a work. It is different from a topic, a work's general subject matter. For instance, we could say that the topic of *Hamlet* is "vengeance" or "fathers and sons," but theme is better stated as a proposition. It should be a sentence that is general enough to apply to situations other than the single one portrayed in the work, but not so general that it becomes abstract and dull.

Finding the right level of generalization for a statement of theme is not always easy. If we wanted to claim that the theme of *Hamlet* is that young men who hear their dead fathers telling them to murder their uncles become moody and depressed, then we could support the claim by reciting key moments of the plot and noting some moments of Hamlet's emotional volatility. But this statement of theme, like "Hamlet loved his father," is so specific to the situation in the play that it is not very widely applicable to others and hardly explains the appeal of the play. Broadening the statement of theme to "The murder of a father often causes turmoil in his son's life" seems to err the other way, making the theme general enough to become a cliché or a truism that neglects much of the rich complexity of the play.

Most literary works can be seen as presenting more than one theme, especially because readers can view them from more than one angle. Shine a different light on a diamond and it sends back light of a different color. Early in his essay on *Hamlet*, Terence Eagleton piles up examples of the way some characters in the play give each other assignments and some accept assignments to do another's bidding (see his essay from *Shakespeare in Society* reprinted in Chapter 13). On the basis of this evidence, he offers the proposition, "Agency, then, is a central theme in *Hamlet*: society is presented, and is present to each character, as a continuous network of causes, agents, and effects, as a network of men reciprocally using and exploiting one another."

The rest of the essay is a defense of Eagleton's claim through a meticulous examination of some important examples of commands given, accepted, and refused in the play, which builds into a comprehensive analysis of the play as "the tragedy of an authentic man in a false society." But note that when Eagleton introduces his theme, he calls it *"a"* central theme, not *"the"* central theme. There's always room for more interpretation.

There is always room for more interpretation for two principal reasons. First, one can always read more closely, looking at more of the details of a written work (helping you do that is the goal of Chapters 4–8). Second, one can always read with a new point of view, brought in from an academic discipline (the primary method of Chapters 9 and 10) or another work of literature (the method of comparing and contrasting). As we have seen, the themes of literary works can be stated in a number of ways, depending on one's approach. From the point of view of a travel agent, the theme of Tobias Wolff's story "Powder" (see Chapter 1) might be that "people who have obligations in distant towns shouldn't delay their departure from ski resorts when the weather is bad," a pretty trivial version of a theme. It is true enough but reductive because it takes account mostly of setting while ignoring other important elements of the story like the main characters (the narrator and his father), the major conflict (father and son are estranged by the parents' marital difficulties), and how the conflict is resolved.

Other points of view could take more account of the father-son relationship. A family therapist, for instance, might think that the story shows that a good way for estranged fathers and sons to re-establish a bond is to go on trips together. A skiing enthusiast might think that the story shows the particular bonds that skiing trips allow. Although we can and often do draw life lessons from literature's nuanced observations of human behavior, writers do not necessarily aim to give how-to advice. Would the skiing enthusiast insist that Mt. Baker is an especially healing place? Again, as with *Hamlet*, the reader must decide on the appropriate balance of specificity and generalization for a statement of theme.

ACTIVITY 1: *Evaluating Possible Themes for "Powder"*

After reviewing Tobias Wolff's story "Powder" in Chapter 1 (pp. 17–20), examine this list of possible themes for the story. Write a journal entry on which ones you think are both defensible (using details from the story as evidence) and worth defending (that is, they are responsive to the story's main values). Which ones take account of the greatest number of details in the story? What points of view do they reflect?

1. Children emulate their parents.
2. Children rebel against their parents.
3. Marital discord is hard on children.
4. Children want to be seen for who they are.
5. Boys love sports cars.
6. Boys just want to have adventures.
7. Children enjoy respecting their parents and will do their best to find them trustworthy or skillful.
8. Boys love a little danger.
9. Mothers should follow their gut instincts to protect their children from irresponsible fathers.

Since figuring out what authors mean by their works and what the works can mean to us can involve all the subtlety we can bring to bear as readers, looking closely at all the features of a work in order to discover its meaning will be our constant theme in the course of this book. Close reading is necessary because texts do not "speak for themselves." Interpretations need to be supported with evidence. When we try to articulate themes, all the elements of a piece of literature can play a role, so the more deeply we examine it, the more evidence we can marshall in support of our interpretative claims. Even when we use research to put works into contextual frames, we need to start with a close reading.

NARRATIVE AND PLOT

As we saw in Chapter 3, a story is not the simple recitation of a series of events. We cannot report every little thing that happens because it would take too long. When we reproduce the story, we reduce it. And in the process of selecting from the many details, we shape and color the events according to our own attitudes and values.

Conflicts and problems are almost universal elements of Western stories and narratives. We tend not to consider a peaceful continuation of the status quo a story. Conflicts may include clashes or tensions between people or groups who want exclusive possession of the same thing or who have contrasting goals and values. Both can struggle against nature and against their larger society's values and conventions. Problems may include the need for someone to overcome obstacles to complete a journey or achieve a goal. The heightening tension through the rising action of a good stage production of a play results from this pattern. So does our inability to put down a mystery novel; the drive toward the crisis and resolution keeps us turning the pages.

Without too much effort, you can probably name many examples of "great literature" that can be described by problems and conflicts similar to narrative patterns listed in Chapter 3, Activity 1. What is Homer's *Odyssey* but the story of a man who encounters obstacle after obstacle on a journey? Isn't Shakespeare's *Hamlet* an account of a man struggling with a decision about whether to do what someone else wants him to do?

Stories unfold gradually because they are made of language, which parcels out only one word at a time. You might be able to see a whole painting at a glance, but you cannot see the end of a story without either reading it all or skipping ahead to peek. If you read one sentence at a time, you will usually respond to a text by anticipating what will follow. Anticipation causes the tension we find in plots; we speculate about what might happen next and read forward to discover what "really" happens and whether our guesses were right or wrong. Being right can bring satisfaction; being wrong forces us to reevaluate what came before.[1]

[1]For more on this approach to reading, see Wolfgang Iser, *The Act of Reading: A Theory of Aesthetic Response* (Baltimore: The Johns Hopkins University Press, 1978).

In other words, as readers we are not just passive receivers of information. We are busy doing our part to create the narrative, obligingly stepping in to help make connections where they are latent but not obvious. We might fill in some missing stages, assuming that sequential events have a logical connection: "It rained and she did not go to the pond to swim" might lead us to assume that the rain prevented the swim. We might be wrong, of course—perhaps the "she" being spoken of loves swimming in warm gentle rain but on this occasion was too tired or too busy. The tendency to assume that "and" really means "because" is called "post hoc ergo propter hoc" in Latin (*"after* this, *because of* this"). When it is wrongly applied, it is a fallacy. But it is a very natural mistake, and creators of stories depend for tension and surprise on an audience's tendency to see it even where it may not exist.

Another technique that writers use is repetition. It creates emphasis, telling the audience that something is important. But also, because of readers' tendencies to fill in gaps, it also builds expectation, which can be fulfilled or disappointed. Patterns of repetition make readers anticipate the next iteration. You can probably think of many movies and television shows that open with a murder and come to a crisis with the hero or heroine made vulnerable to the same fate at the hands of the same perpetrator. Knowing what happened to the first victim helps us to fear vividly for the protagonist at the end.

Because readers are so sensitive to sequence, we should pay careful attention to the order in which events are narrated, or the **plot,** which may differ from the order in which they are said to have happened. Here are some of the methods writers have for distorting chronology for the sake of a plot:

Flashback: *Inserting* accounts of things that happened in the past
Foreshadowing: *Anticipating* the outcome of an event before it unfolds
Suppressing the full account of an event that happens many times. (We
    may be told about the recurrence but not hear the full description again.)
Starting *in medias res* (Latin for "in the middle of things")

These devices all increase the difference between chronological time and plot time so that a marathon does not take hours to read about.[2] Their usefulness is that they allow writers to shape interpretation: by manipulating the order of events, writers can override chronology in order to control what gets emphasized. Significant events can, for example, be placed at the beginnings and endings of stories, where they will receive more of readers' attention, even if they do not occur first or last chronologically.

We can see how the manipulation of time affects readers' understanding of a story if we look at the beginning and end of John Updike's "A & P" (see Chapter 3, pp. 48–52).

---

[2]Schlomith Rimmon-Kenan uses the terms "story-time" and "discourse-time" in *Narrative Fiction: Contemporary Poetics* (London: Methuen, 1983), 46–56. Also see Gerald Prince, *A Dictionary of Narratology* (Lincoln: University of Nebraska Press, 1987), 58–59, 91.

> In walks these three girls in nothing but bathing suits. I'm in the third check-out slot, with my back to the door, so I don't see them until they're over by the bread. The one that caught my eye first was the one in the plaid green two-piece. She was a chunky kid, with a good tan and a sweet broad soft-looking can with those two crescents of white just under it, where the sun never seems to hit, at the top of the backs of her legs.

When thinking about time in this story, we might quickly notice that the first two sentences are out of chronological order. The narrator, whose name we do not know until several pages later, speaks in the present tense in the first sentence, but he has not yet experienced what he is recounting. Because his back is turned to the door, he does not actually witness the girls' entrance into the store, but we do not know that until the end of the second sentence. A good technique for gauging the impact of this minor disarrangement is to arrange it in a more conventional order:

> I'm in the third check-out slot, with my back to the door. I see three girls wearing nothing but bathing suits over by the bread. The one that caught my eye first was the one in the plaid green two-piece. . . .

This version changes the focus from the girls to the narrator, who can't see them. It therefore takes just a little longer to learn what fascinates Sammy. It is truer to the way things happened, but it is less true to Sammy's reaction to the events. In a sense, Updike's version enacts Sammy's fascination just a little more vividly. He seems to have reconstructed the scene of their entrance in his mind as he remembers their visit to the store.

ACTIVITY 2: *Verb Tense and Chronology in "A & P"*

In Updike's version, the verbs switch from present tense to past. What impact does the change have?

ACTIVITY 3: *More on Chronology in "A & P"*

Here are two sentences from the next-to-last paragraph of "A & P" that also show Updike juggling time:

> Lengel sighs and begins to look very patient and old and gray. He's been a friend of my parents for years. "Sammy, you don't want to do this to your Mom and Dad," he tells me. . . . One advantage to this scene taking place in summer, I can follow this [turning in his apron] up with a clean exit, there's no fumbling around getting your coat and galoshes, I just saunter into the electric eye in my white shirt that my mother ironed the night before, and the door heaves itself open, and outside the sunshine is skating around the asphalt. (Paragraph 31)

Why do you think Updike does not tell the events here in the order in which they occurred?

Writing about Narrative and Plot

In response to the above prompt, freshman Denise Fuentes wrote this journal entry:

Reading the paragraphs of John Updike's "A & P" in the right order, we think that the first thing that happened in this episode that changed the life of the narrator, Sammy, is that three girls in bathing suits walked into the supermarket where he worked. But when we get to the end of the story, we find out some things that happened well before that but which had an effect on the incident. For instance, we find out that Sammy's puritanical boss has been friends with Sammy's parents for a long time. That's probably how Sammy got the job. For another thing, in the more recent past, Sammy's mother ironed the white shirt he wore to work that day (paragraph 31).

These two new pieces of information are related. The boss, Lengel, is trying to remind Sammy of his parents so he will back off from making his romantic grand gesture of quitting his job. Lengel succeeds at least enough to make Sammy think about the fact that his mother ironed his shirt. And it should remind Sammy of the proper way to dress in a supermarket. He should feel superior to the girls because he meets Lengel's standards for propriety and they don't. Both facts are part of how the world tries to get Sammy not to make his gesture.

Since both the friendship and the ironing of the shirt happened before the girls walked into the A & P, we might wonder why Updike doesn't put them first in the narrative. Why didn't he tell the story in chronological order? This version might help answer that question: "Once upon a time in a small New England town, the superintendent of the Sunday school, who managed a grocery store, was friendly with a couple who had a son. When the boy got old enough, the superintendent gave the son a job in the store. The boy's mother ironed the white shirts he wore to work. Then one day. . . ."

I think you can see why Updike mixed things up so they didn't follow chronological order. Chronological order is a bore! The beginning wouldn't grab your interest because it's too much background that we can't understand yet. Updike withholds the excess information and gives it to us on a "need to know" basis. That works better.

Here's a checklist that will help you use our observations on time in imaginative literature:

Checklist on Plot in Imaginative Literature

_____What are the events that occur in the work, as they happen in chronological order?

_____Do the events follow a traditional pattern such as exposition, rising action, crisis, denouement? Or is there at least a conflict, obstacle, problem, or violation of a norm that motivates the rest of the action, with a crisis leading to a resolution?

_____How does the order of presentation in the text differ from the chronological order of the events?

    _____Does the story start *in medias res?*

    _____Are there foreshadowings of future consequences of events?

    _____Are there flashbacks to past events?

    _____Is a repeated event narrated each time it occurs?

    _____Does an event take as long to narrate as it took in the characters' lives?

    _____What comes first in the sequence of events?

    _____What comes last?

_____What difference to a reader's experience and interpretation of the text does the difference between story order and discourse order make?

_____Are there any repeated events that create a pattern? Is the pattern ever varied in a significant way?

 ACTIVITY 4: *Chrono-logic in "Powder" and "The Fine Art of Sighing"*

1. Use the checklist on plot in imaginative literature to make notes on the way Wolff structures time in "Powder" (Chapter 1, pp. 17–20). Refer to the events of the story by paragraph number.

2. Outline Cooper's "The Fine Art of Sighing" (Chapter 3, pp. 62–63) to see whether its sequence makes logical sense. Does the essay have a "plot"?

SETTING

Imaginative literature offers us alternate worlds—not necessarily "alternate" in the sense of science fiction, where the rules of our physical universe may be suspended, but alternate in the sense of different from our own, perhaps in time, place, and customs. In fiction and poetry, either narrators or characters can describe geographical or temporal context. In drama, characters can speak about setting, but most often descriptions by the playwright will appear as stage directions; theater audiences will see only the physical realizations of them offered by directors and set designers. Sometimes the setting provides symbols or circumstances important to the plot. In Charlotte Perkins Gilman's "The Yellow Wallpaper," for instance, the isolated house with its "nursery" with bars on the windows is practically a character in the story. John Donne's poem "The Sun Rising" could take place nowhere but a bedroom. In contrast, Shakespeare's plays have often been updated and transported and have sometimes survived the journey remarkably well. The film of *Hamlet* starring Ethan Hawke, for example, rather successfully turns Denmark into a corporation in modern Manhattan.

One of our jobs as critics is to interpret the relationship between setting and meaning. In general, we judge this relationship according to our own tastes for coherence and subtlety. When the connection between the setting and meaning is very close, critics sometimes complain about implausibility. If every time the main character feels sad, it rains, the connection between mood and weather might be thought too obvious. We might occasionally prefer the ironic contrast between tears and bright sunshine.

Consider the setting of "A & P." The great cornucopia of products available in a supermarket is strictly ordered in organized rows, with products arrayed in categories. In the first sentence, we are told that Sammy is in a "checkout slot," and in the second paragraph, the other parts of the store are listed as "counters," "aisles," and "Special bins": This world has an order so tight that when something doesn't fit because it's "on special," there's a bin for it. The store has a manager (in a labeled bin, of course [paragraph 13]) and it is clearly a managed environment. Updike seems to enjoy recreating this mania for order in his list in paragraph 5: "they all three of them went up the cat and dog food-breakfast cereal-macaroni-rice-raisins-seasoning-spreads-spaghetti-soft drinks-crackers-and-cookies aisle." The items could feed a whole family, with pets, for a whole day, but everything is in a row, in orderly display. It is in this environment that Sammy makes his romantic gesture. Some might say that it is the regimented environment itself that creates the conditions for his gesture, which seems, in contrast, like a rebellion.

 ACTIVITY 5: *Setting in Updike and Wolff*

> Contrast the setting of Updike's "A & P" and the setting of Tobias Wolff's "Powder." How do they differ? What difference do the differences in setting make to the plot of each story and to the actions of the protagonists? How does setting relate to theme?

CHARACTER

In the different worlds that literature creates, we can have experiences different from those provided by our own bodies and narrow physical and social worlds. Through literature, we can "be" (in a limited way, for a limited time) a different sex, a different race or ethnic group, or differently abled, with different opinions and different desires. One of my vivid childhood memories is the night my father suggested that I turn out the light and save the rest of Daphne du Maurier's *The Scapegoat* for another night.[3] I was so much in the grip of this novel about a man deceiving the world by living under an assumed identity that I could only feel sorry for my father because

[3]Dame Daphne du Maurier, *The Scapegoat* (Garden City, NY: Doubleday, 1957).

he didn't know—how could he?—that I was really someone else. All literature, even when it is not specifically about this theme, gives us the brief chance to be someone else.

The characters we encounter through literature are defined by what they think and say, what other characters and the narrator say about them, what they do, and what they look like. This is all the information we have in order to interpret them, to judge them, to inhabit them. In this, our relationships to them are like our relationships to the people in our lives, and they will accordingly be shaped by our personal values. For instance, if you think a good father never takes a young son to night clubs and never lets his son see him disobey a police officer's directive (let alone demand that the son actively participate), then you will think that the man in "Powder" is a bad father. There is good evidence in the story that he is at least an irresponsible blowhard.

But as critics we must ask, is that the judgment offered by the story? Does it account for all the evidence in the story? This short piece of dialogue in "Powder" can contribute to our judgment of the father. The son is challenging him to make good on his earlier claim to know the good points of the narrator's character:

> "Okay then. What are my strong points?"
> "Don't get me started," he said. "It'd take all day."
> "Oh, right. Name one."
> "Easy. You always think ahead."
> True. I always thought ahead. I was a boy who kept his clothes on
> numbered hangers to ensure proper rotation. I bothered my teachers for
> homework assignments far ahead of their due dates so I could make up
> schedules. . . .   (paragraphs 30–34)

Up until this point, the father had seemed to be all talk and no substance. The son's tone in "Oh, right. Name one" seems skeptical; he doesn't believe his father, either. But the father surprises us all by actually producing a description that the son recognizes as correct.

That moment is pivotal. It is a good candidate for being the climax of the story because it allows the son to start enjoying the ride and admiring his father—at least to an extent. He isn't deceived about the man, whom he sees as "rumpled . . . bankrupt of honor," but can now acknowledge that he is kind, a good driver, and observant and caring about his child. The ecstatic description of the drive down the mountain is only possible when the boy accepts his father's regard for him. The story thus offers a new criterion for good fatherhood: love and acceptance of one's children. Using this standard, the manipulative scapegrace of Wolff's story can be seen as flawed but forgivable.

It is not clear whether the father in "Powder" changes or the son just learns something new about him. But at least the change in the son's perspective allows us to see a new side of the father and makes him a more complex character than he was before.

Critics often use the terms "round" and "flat" to describe characters. **Flat characters** tend to be simpler; they are defined by one or two traits, say the same thing repeatedly, or embody an ethnic, gender, or some other stereotype. **Rounded characters,** who are more complex, tend to have a fuller range of thoughts, feelings, or actions, perhaps even in conflict with each other, and might grow, change, or learn something.

When two characters are similar but differ in key areas, they are often said to be **foils** for one another. Comparing them reveals their difference. Tom Sawyer is a foil for Huckleberry Finn in the novels named for them: they are similar enough that Huck is Tom's idol, but their orientation to family and community and their responses to the world ultimately differ in important ways. Tom tends to try to get what he wants by using the rules of society to manipulate people, while Huck tries to bypass the rules by running away.

The relationships among characters might be crucial to interpretation of conflict in a story. If the main character, also called the **protagonist,** seems to have important conflicts with another character, we could call the one who presents the obstacles or difficulties that drive the plot the **antagonist.** The thing (or person or idea) they struggle over will be important to the meaning of the work. What would Robin Hood be without the Sheriff of Nottingham? How would we be able to judge his generosity, love for justice, and loyalty to his king if we didn't watch him opposing the jealous sheriff, who is greedy for power, dictatorial, and treasonous?

Characters are created in other genres besides fiction. Robert Browning's poem "My Last Duchess" (Chapter 5) is spoken by the fairly well-defined speaker, the Duke of Ferrara, whose character we can assess. Lyric poems are often short, but as we will see in the discussion of point of view in Chapter 5, all written language, including poems and nonfiction, implies a speaker whom readers are invited to join and judge.

◎◎◎

Checklist for Writing about Setting and Character

_____What can we tell about the setting for the work? Does it resonate with anything we learn about the characters or what happens to them? What words and details shape our sense of the setting(s)?

_____How do the characters' words and actions define their personalities? How does what others say about them add to the picture?

_____Does anything in the narration or setting or any of the characters' words seem to resonate with meaning that relates to the work as a whole? If so, what are the other places in the work in which this meaning seems relevant?

_____Can you identify protagonist and antagonist among the characters?

_____Do any of the characters function as foils for each other?

_____Do the terms "rounded" and "flat" apply to any of the characters?

ACTIVITY 6: *Character in "A & P"*

> Because Sammy in Updike's "A & P" speaks directly to us, we know how he
> views the world. Along the way he describes everyone who walks through
> the store or stands near it. Interpret Sammy's character through the way he
> characterizes others. Pay close attention to the words and images he uses
> and take account of how his descriptions play off your own values. Use the
> checklist to make sure you are talking about all the relevant aspects of the
> story.
>
> Interpret Sammy's character by looking at Stokesie as his foil.

ACTIVITY 7: *Finding the Themes*

> Taking account of story and narrative, setting, and character, examine the
> details of Tobias Wolff's "Powder" or John Updike's "A & P" to articulate a
> plausible theme for the story. Make a list of details from the story that you
> would use to support your hypothesis about theme.

Point of View and Tone of Voice

POINT OF VIEW

If you find words traced out on the sand of a lonely beach, you imagine the being who put them there. It is part of our human equipment that when faced with language, we look for someone to have created it. The sensation of being talked to is the source of a great deal of the satisfaction of reading. As the critic Walter Slatoff says, when we begin to read, we respond to "the mind of the narrator. Whether we go on reading or not and how attentively or respectfully we do so will depend chiefly on whether we feel the weight of a mind and on how worthy of attention we find it."[1] From language, we infer a mind revealing itself to us. In order to judge it worthy or unworthy, we first inhabit it and try on its ideas. That is, we adopt its **point of view.** This metaphor literally means that we stand where someone is standing, facing in the same direction, in order to see what he or she sees. The angle of vision may be wider than what is physically possible to see from one position and within a piece, the point of view can shift or change. But language implies a speaker with a vantage point.

Every piece of writing included in this book so far, from Pam Belluck's *New York Times* article about the Nun Study in Chapter 1 to Updike's "A & P," implies a point of view. The writer creates a voice whose observations

[1] Walter J. Slatoff, *With Respect to Readers: Dimensions of Literary Response* (Ithaca: Cornell University Press, 1970), 98–99.

we are invited to share. That voice may be close to the actual writer's sensibilities or an entirely fictional character. Sometimes it is hard to tell the difference, but writers create selves for the purpose of addressing a particular audience in a particular situation. We can say that they adopt a **persona,** which means "mask," or refer to them by the terms "speaker," "writer," or "narrator." He or she may speak directly to us, as Sammy does in "A & P" and as the boy does in "Powder," or be unobtrusive, almost hidden by what she presents, as Pam Belluck is. But as Slatoff says, the language implies a mind.

We can see some of the techniques writers use to give readers the sensation of being addressed by another person by examining some of the openings of pieces we have already looked at in this book.

Tobias Wolff, "Powder": Just before Christmas my father took me skiing at Mount Baker.

W. H. Auden, "September 1, 1939": I sit in one of the dives on Fifty-second Street. . . .

Pam Belluck, "Nuns Offer Clues to Alzheimer's and Aging": A spiraling road slopes gently up to Good Counsel Hill, where the convent of the School Sisters of Notre Dame perches peacefully. Within its thick red brick walls are bright paintings of nuns and children. Organ hymns waft from a circular chapel, and nuns attend Mass and murmur rosaries under a white vaulted dome.

But this crucible of faith is also the site of an extraordinary scientific experiment. For 15 years, elderly Catholic nuns here have had their genes analyzed and balance and strength measured. They have been tested on how many words they can remember minutes after reading them on flashcards, how many animals they can name in a minute and whether they can count coins correctly.

Basho: A crow is perched
Upon a leafless withered bough—
The autumn dusk.

David A. Snowdon, Lydia H. Greiner, William R. Markesbery, "Linguistic Ability in Early Life and the Neuropathology of Alzheimer's Disease and Cerebrovascular Disease: Findings from the Nun Study": Findings from the Nun Study indicate that low linguistic ability in early life has a strong association with dementia and premature death in late life. In the present study, we investigated the relationship of linguistic ability in early life to the neuropathology of Alzheimer's disease and cerebrovascular disease.

Bernard Cooper, "The Fine Art of Sighing": You feel a gradual welling up of pleasure, or boredom, or melancholy. Whatever the emotion, it's more abundant than you ever dreamed. You can no more contain it than your hands can cup a lake. And so you surrender and suck the air. Your esophagus opens, diaphragm expands. Poised at the crest of an exhalation, your body is about to be unburdened, second by second, cell by cell.

A kettle hisses. A balloon deflates. Your shoulders fall like two ripe pears, muscles slack at last.

The most obvious way to create a speaker out of language is to use first person pronouns such as Auden's "I," Wolff's "my," and Snowdon and his partners' "we," which all create speakers who invite us to see the world through their eyes. The speakers most closely identified with the authors who wrote the lines are the writers of civic and academic discourse. Since we know that Tobias Wolff is not currently a young boy, we know that he is inventing a teller for the story. Literary critics would call him (and Sammy of Updike's "A & P") a **dramatized narrator,** meaning that he plays a role in the story. He interacts with the other characters and performs some of the actions of the plot. With Auden, it is harder to tell. Since we can't know if this poem is autobiographical, it is safest to refer to the speaker or the narrator of the poem and not give him Auden's name. (You can see, though, that I have given him Auden's gender.)

Of these speakers, who claim to be speaking in their own voices, only one implies that someone is listening. When Cooper addresses his audience as "you," the second person pronoun helps him to name and thereby invite us into a relationship with him, at least for the duration of his essay. In imaginative literature, just as speakers may not coincide with writers, audiences addressed may not be identical to the actual people with books in their hands. There may be a **dramatized listener** within the work. (For an example, see Robert Browning's "My Last Duchess" at the end of this chapter.)

Belluck, because she is a journalist, is the least "present" speaker in this small group of texts. No "I" speaks directly to us and we are not addressed as "you." Nevertheless, there is a speaker. Someone has traveled along "a spiraling road" that "slopes gently up to Good Counsel Hill." Someone can describe the peaceful convent and someone registers the incongruity of scientific work going on in this setting by saying, "But this crucible of faith is also the site of an extraordinary scientific experiment." Someone sees a contrast. Someone says "But." If this were a poem or short story, critics would call Belluck an undramatized narrator here because her part in the action is suppressed.

Basho gives us an objective undramatized narrator who reports from an external point of view and offers no insights into the state of any consciousness. There is a point of view here from which to observe the scene, but there seems to be no one present who could do the observing. But we infer that someone sees, someone reports, and someone makes the connection between the scene and the season.

Literary critics make several other distinctions among kinds of narrators: **omniscient narrators** know everything that happens in a work of imaginative literature, as well as what all the characters are thinking and feeling. A **limited omniscient narrator** knows what *some* characters are thinking and feeling. In addition, as a work develops, some narrators turn out to be **unreliable** because something they say gets contradicted. We usually discover later in the work that they have lied or at least not told the whole truth. They often take advantage of readers' tendency to sympathize with the major characters or the central narrator of a work.

For instance, our great early epic *Beowulf* exploits this habit. Beowulf the Geat sails to Denmark to rescue the Danes from Grendel, the monster who invades from the marshes to kill and eat them at will. After he succeeds, Danes and Geats celebrate with a feast that includes eating, drinking, gift giving, speech making, and story telling. Is it a happy ending? No. Another monster arrives and kills another Dane. Oh, yes. The Danish king now remembers that there were really *two* monsters roaming around out there in the marshes together. But when Beowulf called Grendel a "walker alone," the king didn't correct him or warn him that he would probably have to be heroic twice.[2] Tricky king.

But also tricky narrator. When he originally told us about the first monster, he too implied that Grendel worked solo, calling him a "terrible walker-alone." He just neglected to mention that he sometimes walked together, too, with his terrible mother. We trusted the narrator just as Beowulf trusted the king, so we are just as much seduced and deceived.

Walter Slatoff, whom I quoted above, says that we look, in narrative, for a mind worthy of our attention. But it is hard to judge worthiness during our first reading. Unreliable narrators take advantage of the fact that there is a very strong tendency to sympathize with first-person narrators. We tend to identify with people through whose eyes we are seeing the world and we therefore fill the gaps in our information incorrectly. The guesses that we have to make because we are not fully informed go wrong, and so we find that we have collaborated in our own betrayal.

To summarize what we have learned so far about narrators in imaginative literature: Narrators come in different forms, named for the personal pronouns they use. For example,

1. First person (I, we)
   - Dramatized—play a role in the events narrated, either major or minor
   - Undramatized—not named or described
2. Third person (he, she, they)
   - Omniscient—know what characters feel and think
   - Limited Omniscient—know what some characters feel and think or know some of what characters feel and think
   - Objective—offer no knowledge about characters' feelings and thoughts
3. Reliable
4. Unreliable

[2]E. Talbot Donaldson, trans., *Beowulf: A New Prose Translation* (W.W. Norton, 1966), 4. The Old English is the same word as Beowulf uses later, *āngengea* (l. 165).

All of these narrators, even those who are reliable and objective, because they cannot report all the details of an occurrence or idea, select and shape what they offer their audiences.

And, furthermore:

1. The narrator or persona (the person speaking) is not necessarily identical to the actual author (the person writing).

2. The listener implied by the text is not necessarily identical to the real reader (the person holding the book).

3. Readers tend to trust first-person narrators.

4. Readers will participate in narratives by responding to gaps in the knowledge offered, trying to fill them by inference. They may do it incorrectly, especially if an unreliable narrator is purposely misleading them.

5. Gaps and contradictions in a narrative are sometimes signs that the narrator is not to be trusted.

You can see these principles and terms put to work in the drafts that a student named Derrick White wrote for a paper about "The Shape of the Sword," a short story by Argentinean writer Jorge Luis Borges. We'll start with the assignment Derrick was given, followed by the story.

ACTIVITY 1: *Analyzing "The Shape of the Sword"*

Your Audience: Address readers who have read the story but have very little experience with Borges's work and think it's a little strange, or at least difficult.

Your Purpose: To interpret the story to help your audience understand Borges's manipulations of point of view. Explain his choices and their effects on the story.

Process: Capture your reactions to what Slatoff calls "the mind of the narrator" during your first reading of the story and separate them from your reactions during subsequent readings:

1. Read it once with a pen in your hand to note your responses. If you are puzzled, annoyed, intrigued, amused, etc., note the places and the responses that occurred.

2. Once you know the ending, read the story again with a pen that writes with ink of a different color or a pencil. Note any responses that are different from those of your first reading. Note in particular the ways that Borges keeps first-time readers from finding out who the Englishman really is. What does he withhold? Are there things he does say that could have revealed the secret prematurely?

(Continued)

ACTIVITY 1: *(Continued)*

Once you have read the story several times carefully, use the *Checklist for Writing about Point of View and Tone of Voice* (p. 104). It might be useful to define the narrator or narrators. What kinds of narrators are they? What does the fact that the narrators withhold information from readers tell you about them?

References: Refer to the story (with quotations, paraphrases, and summaries) using paragraph numbers in parentheses.

The Shape of the Sword

JORGE LUIS BORGES *(For biographical notes, see p. 528)*

A spiteful scar crossed his face: an ash-colored and nearly perfect arc that creased his temple at one tip and his cheek at the other. His real name is of no importance; everyone in Tacuarembó called him the "Englishman from La Colorada." Cardoso, the owner of those fields, refused to sell them: I understand that the Englishman resorted to an unexpected argument: he confided to Cardoso the secret of the scar. The Englishman came from the border, from Río Grande del Sur; there are many who say that in Brazil he had been a smuggler. The fields were overgrown with grass, the waterholes brackish; the Englishman, in order to correct those deficiencies, worked fully as hard as his laborers. They say that he was severe to the point of cruelty, but scrupulously just. They say also that he drank: a few times a year he locked himself into an upper room, not to emerge until two or three days later as if from a battle or from vertigo, pale, trembling, confused and as authoritarian as ever. I remember the glacial eyes, the energetic leanness, the gray mustache. He had no dealings with anyone; it is a fact that his Spanish was rudimentary and cluttered with Brazilian. Aside from a business letter or some pamphlet, he received no mail.

The last time I passed through the northern provinces, a sudden overflowing of the Caraguatá stream compelled me to spend the night at La Colorada. Within a few moments, I seemed to sense that my appearance was inopportune; I tried to ingratiate myself with the Englishman; I resorted to the least discerning of passions: patriotism. I claimed as invincible a country with such spirit as England's. My companion agreed, but added with a smile that he was not English. He was Irish, from Dungarvan. Having said this, he stopped short, as if he had revealed a secret.

After dinner we went outside to look at the sky. It had cleared up, but beyond the low hills the southern sky, streaked and gashed by lightning, was conceiving another storm. Into the cleared up dining room the boy who had served dinner brought a bottle of rum. We drank for some time, in silence.

I don't know what time it must have been when I observed that I was drunk; I don't know what inspiration or what exultation or tedium made me mention the scar. The Englishman's face changed its expression; for a few seconds I thought he was going to throw me out of the house. At length he said in his normal voice:

"I'll tell you the history of my scar under one condition: that of not mitigating   5 one bit of the opprobrium, of the infamous circumstances."

I agreed. This is the story that he told me, mixing his English with Spanish, and even with Portuguese:

"Around 1922, in one of the cities of Connaught, I was one of the many who were conspiring for the independence of Ireland. Of my comrades, some are still living, dedicated to peaceful pursuits; others, paradoxically, are fighting on desert and sea under the English flag; another, the most worthy, died in the courtyard of a barracks, at dawn, shot by men filled with sleep; still others (not the most unfortunate) met their destiny in the anonymous and almost secret battles of the civil war. We were Republicans, Catholics; we were, I suspect, Romantics. Ireland was for us not only the utopian future and the intolerable present; it was a bitter and cherished mythology, it was the circular towers and the red marshes, it was the repudiation of Parnell and the enormous epic poems which sang of the robbing of bulls which in another incarnation were heroes and in others fish and mountains . . . One afternoon I will never forget, an affiliate from Munster joined us: one John Vincent Moon.

"He was scarcely twenty years old. He was slender and flaccid at the same time; he gave the uncomfortable impression of being invertebrate. He had studied with fervor and with vanity nearly every page of Lord knows what Communist manual; he made use of dialectical materialism to put an end to any discussion whatever. The reasons one can have for hating another man, or for loving him, are infinite: Moon reduced the history of the universe to a sordid economic conflict. He affirmed that the revolution was predestined to succeed. I told him that for a gentleman only lost causes should be attractive . . . Night had already fallen; we continued our disagreement in the hall, on the stairs, then along the vague streets. The judgments Moon emitted impressed me less than his irrefutable, apodictic note. The new comrade did not discuss: he dictated opinions with scorn and with a certain anger.

"As we were arriving at the outlying houses, a sudden burst of gunfire stunned us. (Either before or afterwards we skirted the blank wall of a factory or barracks.) We moved into an unpaved street; a soldier, huge in the firelight, came out of a burning hut. Crying out, he ordered us to stop. I quickened my pace; my companion did not follow. I turned around: John Vincent Moon was motionless, fascinated, as if eternized by fear. I then ran back and knocked the soldier to the ground with one blow, shook Vincent Moon, insulted him and ordered him to follow. I had to take him by the arm; the passion of fear had rendered him helpless. We fled, into the night pierced by flames. A rifle volley reached out for us, and a bullet nicked Moon's right shoulder; as we were fleeing amid pines, he broke out in weak sobbing.

10   "In that fall of 1923 I had taken shelter in General Berkeley's country house. The general (whom I had never seen) was carrying out some administrative assignment or other in Bengal; the house was less than a century old, but it was decayed and shadowy and flourished in puzzling corridors and in pointless antechambers. The museum and the huge library usurped the first floor: contro-versial and uncongenial books which in some manner are the history of the nineteenth century; scimitars from Nishapur, along whose captured arcs there seemed to persist still the wind and violence of battle. We entered (I seem to recall) through the rear. Moon, trembling, his mouth parched, murmured that the events of the night were interesting; I dressed his wound and brought him a cup of tea; I was able to determine that his 'wound' was superficial. Suddenly he stammered in bewilderment:

"'You know, you ran a terrible risk.'

"I told him not to worry about it. (The habit of the civil war had incited me to act as I did; besides, the capture of a single member could endanger our cause.)

"By the following day Moon had recovered his poise. He accepted a cigarette and subjected me to a severe interrogation on the 'economic resources of our revolutionary party.' His questions were very lucid; I told him (truthfully) that the situation was serious. Deep bursts of rifle fire agitated the south. I told Moon our comrades were waiting for us. My overcoat and my revolver were in my room; when I returned, I found Moon stretched out on the sofa, his eyes closed. He imagined he had a fever; he invoked a painful spasm in his shoulder.

"At that moment I understood that his cowardice was irreparable. I clumsily entreated him to take care of himself and went out. This frightened man morti-fied me, as if I were the coward, not Vincent Moon. Whatever one man does, it is as if all men did it. For that reason it is not unfair that one disobedience in a garden should contaminate all humanity; for that reason it is not unjust that the crucifixion of a single Jew should be sufficient to save it. Perhaps Schopenhauer was right: I am all other men, any man is all men, Shakespeare is in some manner the miserable John Vincent Moon.

15   "Nine days we spent in the general's enormous house. Of the agonies and the successes of the war I shall not speak: I propose to relate the history of the scar that insults me. In my memory, those nine days form only a single day, save for the next to the last, when our men broke into a barracks and we were able to avenge precisely the sixteen comrades who had been machine-gunned in Elphin. I slipped out of the house towards dawn, in the confusion of daybreak. At nightfall I was back. My companion was waiting for me upstairs: his wound did not permit him to descend to the ground floor. I recall him having some vol-ume of strategy in his hand, F. N. Maude or Clausewitz. 'The weapon I prefer is the artillery,' he confessed to me one night. He inquired into our plans; he liked to censure them or revise them. He also was accustomed to denouncing 'our deplorable economic basis'; dogmatic and gloomy, he predicted the disastrous

end. '*C'est une affaire flambée,*'° he murmured. In order to show that he was indifferent to being a physical coward, he magnified his mental arrogance. In this way, for good or for bad, nine days elapsed.

"On the tenth day the city fell definitely to the Black and Tans. Tall, silent horsemen patrolled the roads; ashes and smoke rode on the wind; on the corner I saw a corpse thrown to the ground, an impression less firm in my memory than that of a dummy on which the soldiers endlessly practiced their marks-manship, in the middle of the square . . . I had left when dawn was in the sky; before noon I returned. Moon, in the library, was speaking with someone; the tone of his voice told me he was talking on the telephone. Then I heard my name; then, that I would return at seven; then, the suggestion that they should arrest me as I was crossing the garden. My reasonable friend was reasonably selling me out. I heard him demand guarantees of personal safety.

"Here my story is confused and becomes lost. I know that I pursued the informer along the black, nightmarish halls and along deep stairways of dizzyness. Moon knew the house very well, much better than I. One or two times I lost him. I cornered him before the soldiers stopped me. From one of the general's collections of arms I tore a cutlass: with that half moon I carved into his face forever a half moon of blood. Borges, to you, a stranger, I have made this confession. Your contempt does not grieve me so much."

Here the narrator stopped. I noticed that his hands were shaking.

"And Moon?" I asked him.

"He collected his Judas money and fled to Brazil. That afternoon, in the   20
square, he saw a dummy shot up by some drunken men."

I waited in vain for the rest of the story. Finally I told him to go on.

Then a sob went through his body; and with a weak gentleness he pointed to the whitish curved scar.

"You don't believe me?" he stammered. "Don't you see that I carry written on my face the mark of my infamy? I have told you the story thus so that you would hear me to the end. I denounced the man who protected me: I am Vincent Moon. Now despise me."   [1962]

---

[15]'*C'est une affaire flambée*' It's a combustible (explosive) matter.

SAMPLE STUDENT PAPER IN TWO DRAFTS: "HOW DO YOU SEE IT?" BY DERRICK WHITE

Here are two drafts of the paper Derrick wrote in response to Activity 1. The marginal notes and endnotes for draft 1 are comments by his teacher. In reading the drafts, pay special attention to the changes that Derrick has made on draft 2 in response to his teacher's comments.

First Draft

Derrick White
Prof. J. Ferster
ENG 112
September 12, 2000

Nice title

How Do You See It: A Study of the Use of Perspective and Tone
in Jorge Luis Borge(s') "Shape of the Sword"

"Beauty lies in the eyes of the beholder." This is a
widely known clichés. It is also an excellent way to show
how important one's point of view actually is. While the
aforementioned example refers to practical life and human
relationships, it is also pertinent when addressing literary
works. One author (that) displays exactly how much he grasps

*He's actually
Argentinean.
(1)—See my
numbered
comments at
the end.*

this idea is the <u>Spaniard</u> Jorges Luis Borges.

Borges' work can be perplexing to those with little
experience digesting his material. [It may possibly confound

*Why such
formality?*

one <u>to the degree</u> that he or she may devalue his contribution as a noteworthy author.] However, extensive study of
Borges' use of point of view and tone in his writing will
likely prove his credibility to any detractors.

*Is this your
thesis?*

In the "Shape of the Sword" Borge(s') displays multiple
variations of literary point-of-view techniques. The "Shape
of the Sword" apparently has two different narrators, each
with a separate point of view. The first of these narrators

(2)

appears to be Borges himself. The evidence of this first
person point of view is best observed in the pronouns used
in the passage. For example, in ₱aragraph Øne the narrator   *no caps*
states that "<u>I</u> understand that the Englishman resorted to
an unexpected argument." Furthermore, later in Paragraph
One and Paragraph Two the pronouns primarily used are "I"
and "my"⊙ "Within a few moments, <u>I</u> seemed to sense that

*Yes, but you
don't yet know
his name is
"Borges."*

<u>my</u> appearance was inopportune", states Borges. As a result
of these examples, one would undoubtedly label this first
narrator as first person. This narrator seems to be

(reliable) as he sets the background for the primary portion of
the story. [Although a significant quantity of this narrator's ⁽³⁾
background information relies on secondhand hearsay, it is
clearly visible that his information lacks any claims of
total truth.] For instance, in the first paragraph Borges
states, "His name of no real importance; everyone in
Tacuarembo called him." The phrase "everyone . . . called
him" ⟨ᵢₙₜᵣₒdᵤcₑₛ⟩ ~~shows proof of~~ secondhand information. In the first
paragraph alone there are at least four sentences with the
subject pronoun "they" related to the operative verb "say,"
thus implying hearsay exchange. These ~~aforementioned~~
examples also promote a lack of certainty (on the behalf of) ᵒⁿ ᵗʰᵉ ᵖᵃʳᵗ ᵒᶠ?
the first narrator. This low level of certainty displayed by
the first narrator <u>is arguably an enhancement to his</u>
<u>reliability</u>. If the narrator were to state these claims with
absolute certainty, his reliability as a credible source
would diminish. Given the generality of his statements and
lack of personal description, one might deem the first
narrator to be objective and undramatized. For clarity, one
might <u>examine the ramifications of replacing those statements</u>
<u>containing</u> "they" and "say" with statements of their
relevant subject material as fact. Since the reader obviously
has no way to prove or refute these claims, then false
claims would lead the audience to misinformation.

   The emergence of the second narrator in "Sword" proves
to be a deceptive (one.) Borges uses the reliability of the
first narrator to lull the reader into a false sense of
security. The second narrator is known as the Englishman
who is [retelling his anecdotal recount] of his involvement
in the civil wars of Ireland and Britain in the early
twenties. It is fairly obvious that the second narrator
of the story is ᵗʰᵉ ˡⁱᵏᵉ ᵗʰᵉ ᶠⁱʳˢᵗ ᵒⁿᵉ speaking in first person point-of-view. The
most recognizable feature of first person work is the
presence of defining pronouns. The second narrator
consistently uses the first person pronoun "I". However, the
second narrator also uses the pronouns "we", "me", and "us"

Margin annotations:

How can you tell? What's the basis for this judgment?

redundant— hearsay is 2ndhand

(4) inaccurate quote

the verb form would be livelier than "is" plus the noun form

why such formal vocabulary?

A deceptive emergence? Not clear what that would be. Interesting idea

awkward

(5)

too many
examples for
simple point

which all are used primarily in first person perspective. The first passage of Paragraph Nine states "As <u>we</u> were arriving at the outlying houses, a sudden burst of gunfire stunned <u>us</u>". Paragraph Fifteen's opening sentence further affirms first person perspective. It reads, "Nine days <u>we</u> spent in the general's enormous house. Of the agonies and the successes of the war <u>I</u> shall not speak."

Initially, the second narrator appears to be a reliable source. His account of the conflict is vivid and laden with detail. His level of certainty is very high. In Paragraph Sixteen he states, "On the tenth day the city fell definitely to the Black and Tans. Tall silent horsemen patrolled the roads; ashes and smoke rode on the wind; on the corner I saw a corpse thrown to the ground, an impression less firm in my memory." The opening sentences of this passage support

(6)

a claim of high certainty. However, the phrase, "less firm in my memory", is the reader's initial opportunity to challenge his certainty. It is almost as though Borges is giving us a lead-in to the shocking revelation that the narrator is actually the subject of the Englishman's story. Once the

inconsistent—
double standard

reader realizes what has (occurred) <u>it is then that the second narrator becomes unreliable</u>.

useful?

The fact that "Shape of the Sword" is an imaginative literary work allows room for the presence of an unreliable narrator. However, if this were an academic piece, the reader would need a reliable source. Only in imaginative literature could an author depict a stranger who tells of the betrayal of a patriot by a coward that turns out to be the coward that he speaks of.

Problem of
definition of
"level of
certainty"

Jorge Luis Borges proves his skill at using point-of-view and tone to create an element of surprise. Thus, his writing is very entertaining as well as having worth in literary criticism. However, he also displays to the reader

(7)

the value of possessing the ability to effectively use point-of-view and tone to weave an intricate pattern of literary "genius"; just as he has done for me.

Derrick's instructor wrote these endnotes on his first draft. The numbers are keyed to the numbers in parentheses in the margins of the draft.

1. These two paragraphs are an awfully leisurely start for such a short paper, esp. considering the fact that they don't have much to do with what you actually talk about in the paper. I think you can introduce the paper more efficiently. In fact, it might work well to cut the first two paragraphs completely. The first sentence of the third paragraph is a very good way to begin! You wouldn't want to plunge immediately into the work of this long paragraph, but that sentence could start a small introductory paragraph that presented your thesis.

2. You can label quotations by paragraph number using parenthetical references rather than writing out the word and numbers. See the handbook's explanation of the MLA system of documentation.

3. Oh, I get it now. At the top of p. 2, I ask why you think he's reliable. Then I didn't quite get the logic of the sentence I surrounded with square brackets. But the light dawns: I think you are saying that although he relies on hearsay, he isn't trying to get away with anything because he clearly labels hearsay as hearsay. "This low level of certainty" makes it all clear. I'm wondering if you could make this clearer sooner. For instance, in the second half of the sentence that begins "This narrator seems to be reliable," instead of just saying *when* we get this impression ("as he sets the background"), why not start explaining *why?* Try substituting "because" for "as" and see how the rest of the sentence unfolds.

   I'll also get your point quicker if you revise the sentence that begins "This low level" so I don't have to fight my way through the stiff formality (nouns instead of verbs) of the style.

4. I'd pause over this one a little bit. Is his name really not important? What does your answer to that question do to your estimate of Narrator One's reliability?

5. I don't think you need so many examples to support this fairly simple point. I'd get faster to the deception you introduced at the start of the paragraph, a much meatier matter.

6. Uh oh. I'm not following. How come you give "Borges" all sorts of credit for admitting he doesn't know but when Narrator Two says he's not sure, you decide not to trust him. Seems as though you have a double standard. Then when Number Two finally confesses what is clearly, by the scar on his face, true, you say he's unreliable. Isn't this backwards?

7. Lots of very good material here, Derrick. You're working very well with the text. But I don't think that the payoff is as good as it can be. Things start getting a little thin at the bottom of p. 3. I think you can draw more interesting conclusions from your very interesting observations of what's going on with point of view in this story. And one place to start digging deeper is #4 above. Work some more on "His name of

no real importance." Start by correcting the quote because I think the way you misquote it obscures its real importance.

You could also work more on the corpse thrown to the ground. Doesn't this sound a lot like the dummy shot up by drunks in Brazil? But it would also be worth thinking about how the patriot, who was about to be arrested by English soldiers and was probably killed, knows what Moon saw in Brazil. So this is another place to dig.

Very promising start.

Second Draft

Derrick White

Prof. Ferster

ENG 112

October 15, 2000

How Do You See It? A Story of the Use of Perspective in

Jorge Luis Borges's "Shape of the Sword"

"Beauty lies in the eyes of the beholder." This is a
widely known cliché. It is also an excellent way to show
how important one's point of view actually is. One author
who displays exactly how the use of point of view can
accent literary works is the Argentinean Jorge Luis Borges.
In the "Shape of the Sword" Borges displays multiple
variations of literary point of view techniques.

The "Shape of the Sword" apparently has two different
narrators, each with a separate point of view. The first
appears to be Borges himself, narrating in the first person
with pronouns like "I" and "my" (paragraphs 1 and 2). He
seems to be reliable because he sets the background for the
primary portion of the story and a reader tends to trust
first person guides. In addition, the first narrator adds to
his "pseudo-reliability" by qualifying statements. Although
a significant quantity of this narrator's background
information relied on hearsay, it is clearly visible that
his information lacks claims of total validity. For instance,
Borges states, "His real name is of no importance; everyone
in Tacuarembó called him the 'Englishman . . . .'" The phrase,
"everyone called him" introduces secondhand information. In
the first paragraph alone there are at least four clauses
that start "they say," thus implying hearsay exchange.
These examples also promote a lack of certainty about the
narrator's information. This level of certainty is arguably
an enhancement to the first narrator's reliability. If he
were to state these claims with certainty, his reliability

as a credible source would diminish. We believe him more because he seems to be so careful and honest about how he can't be sure about his information.

However, eventually the reader must come to the conclusion that Borges is not only unreliable, but also that he is sneaky. He is so sneaky that upon my first analysis of "Shape of the Sword," even I thought him to be a reliable narrator. After digesting the material once more, I saw the light. Let's revisit the passage where Borges states, "His real name is of no importance." Although the reader may accept this at first, once the stunning twist is revealed at the conclusion of the story, it is clear that the Englishman's name was more than important. In addition, we can conclude that he blatantly led us to believe that the name of the other character would be an insignificant piece of information in order to produce a surprise ending such as in the movie "The Sixth Sense." Is it justifiable? Maybe it is. Is it reliable? It certainly is not.

The second narrator in "The Shape of the Sword" also proves to be deceptive. Borges uses the reliability of the first narrator to lull the reader into a false sense of security. The second narrator is known as the Englishman. He recalls his involvement in the conflict between Ireland and England in the early twenties. It is fairly obvious from the first person pronouns like "we," "me," "us" that the second narrator, like the first one, is speaking from the first person point of view.

Initially, the second narrator appears to be a reliable source. His account of the conflict is vivid and detailed with a high level of certainty. Ultimately, though, the details get "less firm in my memory," the first sign that something might be wrong. If he is trying to be like the first narrator, maybe he is admitting uncertainty to make us trust him more. He is probably trying to look honest. But he finally turns out to be deceptive because he is not the heroic fighter but the man who betrayed him.

The two narrators turn out to be the same. This demonstrates Borges's skill at creating surprises. His story shows how valuable it is to be able to weave intricate patterns with point of view. In fact, point of view and the reliability of narrators turns out to be what this story is all about.

 ACTIVITY 2: *Analyzing Derrick's Drafts*

Write a response to the changes Derrick has made from the first to the second draft. Say what's different in these categories and whether the changes are beneficial:

• Interpretation of the story
• Support of the interpretation using textual evidence
• Style
• Grammar and mechanics

How well does Derrick manage his own point of view in the essay?

 ACTIVITY 3: *Analyzing Point of View in Another Borges Story*

Use the instructions in Activity 1 as a guide for an essay on another Borges story, "The House of Asterion," which follows. You may note the similarities and differences between the two stories. Whose identity is the chief mystery of this story? When do readers discover the answer? How does Borges confuse us or give us clues about it?

The House of Asterion

JORGE LUIS BORGES *(For biographical notes, see p. 528.)*

> And the queen gave birth to a
> child who was called Asterion.
> Apollodorus: *Bibliotheca*, III, I

I know they accuse me of arrogance, and perhaps of misanthropy, and perhaps of madness. Such accusations (for which I shall extract punishment in due time) are derisory. It is true that I never leave my house, but

1

(Continued)

it is also true that its doors (whose number is infinite)[1] are open day and night to men and to animals as well. Anyone may enter. He will find here no female pomp nor gallant court formality, but he will find quiet and solitude. And he will also find a house like no other on the face of the earth. (There are those who declare there is a similar one in Egypt, but they lie.) Even my detractors admit there is not *one single piece of furniture* in the house. Another ridiculous falsehood has it that I, Asterion, am a prisoner. Shall I repeat that there are no locked doors, shall I add that there are no locks? Besides, one afternoon I did step into the street; if I returned before night, I did so because of the fear that the faces of the common people inspired in me, faces as discolored and flat as the palm of one's hand. The sun had already set, but the helpless crying of a child and the rude supplications of the faithful told me I had been recognized. The people prayed, fled, prostrated themselves; some climbed onto the stylobate of the temple of the Axes, others gathered stones. One of them, I believe, hid himself beneath the sea. Not for nothing was my mother a queen; I cannot be confused with the populace, though my modesty might so desire.

The fact is that I am unique. I am not interested in what one man may transmit to other men; like the philosopher, I think that nothing is communicable by the art of writing. Bothersome and trivial details have no place in my spirit, which is prepared for all that is vast and grand; I have never retained the difference between one letter and another. A certain generous impatience has not permitted that I learn to read. Sometimes I deplore this, for the nights and days are long.

Of course, I am not without distractions. Like the ram about to charge, I run through the stone galleries until I fall dizzy to the floor. I crouch in the shadow of a pool or around a corner and pretend I am being followed. There are roofs from which I let myself fall until I am bloody. At any time I can pretend to be asleep, with my eyes closed and my breathing heavy. (Sometimes I really sleep, sometimes the color of day has changed when I open my eyes.) But of all the games, I prefer the one about the other Asterion. I pretend that he comes to visit me and that I show him my house. With great obeisance I say to him: *Now we shall return to the first intersection* or *Now we shall come out into another courtyard* or *I knew you would like the drain* or *Now you will see a pool that was filled with sand* or *You will soon see how the cellar branches out.* Sometimes I make a mistake and the two of us laugh heartily.

[1] The original says *fourteen*, but there is ample reason to infer that, as used by Asterion, this numeral stands for *infinite*. [Borges's note]

Not only have I imagined these games, I have also meditated on the house. All the parts of the house are repeated many times, any place is another place. There is no one pool, courtyard, drinking trough, manger; the mangers, drinking troughs, courtyards, pools are fourteen (infinite) in number. The house is the same size as the world; or rather, it is the world. However, by dint of exhausting the courtyards with pools and dusty gray stone galleries I have reached the street and seen the temple of the Axes and the sea. I did not understand this until a night vision revealed to me that the seas and temples are also fourteen (infinite) in number. Everything is repeated many times, fourteen times, but two things in the world seem to be only once: above, the intricate sun; below, Asterion. Perhaps I have created the stars and the sun and this enormous house, but I no longer remember.

Every nine years nine men enter the house so that I may deliver them from all evil. I hear their steps or their voices in the depths of the stone galleries and I run joyfully to find them. The ceremony lasts a few minutes. They fall one after another without my having to bloody my hands. They remain where they fell and their bodies help distinguish one gallery from another. I do not know who they are, but I know that one of them prophesied, at the moment of his death, that some day my redeemer would come. Since then my loneliness does not pain me, because I know my redeemer lives and he will finally rise above the dust. If my ear could capture all the sounds of the world, I should hear his steps. I hope he will take me to a place with fewer galleries and fewer doors. What will my redeemer be like?, I ask myself. Will he be a bull or a man? Will he perhaps be a bull with the face of a man? Or will he be like me? 5

The morning sun reverberated from the bronze sword. There was no longer even a vestige of blood.

"Would you believe it, Ariadne?" said Theseus. "The Minotaur scarcely defended himself."   [1962]

TONE IN IMAGINATIVE LITERATURE

Human beings convey their attitudes about themselves, about the people they are speaking to, and about their subject matters with the tones of their voices. There are as many tones as there are attitudes: sincere, enthusiastic, angry, amused, ironic, pleading—the list can include as many adjectives as you have patience to add. Here's a recent poem that takes as its theme the effect of tone on communication.

Tone of Voice

CHARLES HARPER WEBB, *rock singer turned psychotherapist and professor of English at California State University, Long Beach, won the 1997 Morse Poetry Prize and the 1998 Kate Tufts Discovery Award as well as a Whiting Winter's Award for his book* Reading the Water.

It pinks the cheeks of speech, or flushes the forehead.
It's a spring breeze in which words play, a scorching sun
that burns them red, slate clouds that cover them in ice.
Mastering tone, the child outgrows his sticks and stones.
5 "*Okay*," he sneers, twisting the word in Mommie's eye.
El[l]ipses, dashes, all capitals, underlines—
these are tuna nets through which tone's minnows slide.
"I love you" may arrive spiked like a mace,° or snickering.

"State your name" from lawyers' lips can mean "You lie!"
10 Tone leaks the truth despite our best efforts to hide.
It's verbal garlic, mistress on a husband's hands.
Consider dear, when you ask, "Where are my French fries?"
How you may stand in a silk teddy° holding grapes,
a suit of mail holding a lance, a hangman's hood holding
15 a rope. As useless to protest, "I didn't mean that,"
as to tell a corpse, "Stand up. You misinterpreted my car."   [1999]

⁸**mace** a spiked medieval weapon used to attack knights in armor   ¹³**teddy** a woman's one-piece undergarment

Webb captures quite well the way tone functions in conversation and how high the stakes sometimes are. Try Activity 4 to practice imagining the other participants in the conversation.

 ACTIVITY 4: *Analyzing Speaker and Audience in Webb's "Tone of Voice"*

> If Webb's poem is part of an argument that the narrator is having, who is the other participant? What might have been said just before the speaker utters the poem?

Activity 5 is a classic exercise for actors, and it points out the way the voice can interpret words printed on a page.

ACTIVITY 5 (GROUP ACTIVITY): *Analyzing Tone of Voice*

The whole group should choose a short sentence that might occur in ordinary, daily conversation. It might be Webb's "Where are my French fries?" or a simple command or statements like these:

- "Shut the door."
- "Give me the letter."
- "It's raining."

Each class member should spend a moment envisioning several situations in which such a sentence might be uttered. What has happened or what has been said just before your sentence? What is the speakers' relative power? (For instance, is the pair an angry boss and misbehaving employee? A loving couple striving for equality? Older/younger sibling? Parent/child?) Is this the first time the speaker has spoken this line, or has he or she had to repeat it several times?

Go around the room, each person saying the line with the inflection he or she has chosen. See how many different ways to say the line the class can produce. What does the variety of readings reveal about the nature of words on a page?

Charles Harper Webb's poem demonstrates that the ordinary meaning of words does not always indicate speakers' attitudes to their subjects. Print does not easily indicate the tone of voice in which something was said. A possibly apocryphal story is told of a philosopher of language reading a paper at a conference in which he said that although grammatically two negatives make a positive, the reverse is not true: two positives don't make a negative. From the back of the room came the response of another philosopher saying, in a voice dripping with irony, "Yeah, right." Except by saying, "in a voice dripping with irony," I can't put the irony on the page. It is audible only because we've all heard affirmations used this way and we understand the situation. Part of the role of literary critics is to decide what tone words on a page should be spoken with.

Here is a poem that contains a surprise because the meaning of the words seems so different from the attitude of the speaker. This is probably (though there are no clues on the surface level of the language) an example of irony, in which the speaker says one thing but means another.

When the War Is Over

W.S. MERWIN *(1927–) is the author of more than fifteen books of poetry.* The River Sound *was named a* New York Times *Notable Book of the Year. Others of his books have been honored with the Lenore Marshall Poetry Prize, the Pulitzer Prize, the Bollingen Award, the Ruth Lilly Poetry Prize, the Wallace Stevens Award, and numerous fellowships, including the Guggenheim Foundation and the National Endowment for the Arts. He also writes plays, and he lives in Hawaii.*

When the war is over
We will be proud of course the air will be
Good for breathing at last
The water will have been improved the salmon
And the silence of heaven will migrate more perfectly
The dead will think the living are worth it we will know
Who we are
And we will all enlist again.   [1993]

We conjecture that the tone of this poem is ironic despite the lack of surface clues just because we know that war is unlikely to enhance the environment. The words "proud," "good," and "improve" are apt to ring hollow, like the zeugma in ll. 4–5 (see Appendix B). The ordinary meanings of the words seem to be contradicted by the speaker's attitude and the deadpan assertions of ll. 6–8 to mean exactly the opposite of what they seem to claim. What tone of voice would you use to read it aloud?

Checklist for Writing about Point of View and Tone of Voice

_____What is the genre of the text—imaginative literature or academic argument? If argument, is it civic or academic? Something else entirely? To answer this question, it will help to know its purpose and the audience to whom it is addressed. Who are the implied readers?

_____Who is speaking in the text? How "present" is the speaker?

_____What nouns or pronouns are used as subjects of the verbs for speaking or writing? Who is said to be doing the actions described?

_____What are the verbs that name the actions of the piece?

_____How certain are the writers of their claims?

_____If the piece is literary, what kind of narrator does it have? Dramatized? Undramatized? Reliable? Unreliable? Objective? What personal pronouns does the narrator use?

_____If the piece is either literary or nonliterary, characterize its speaker or speakers. How would you describe him or her and his or her attitudes to the subject matter and the audience?

ACTIVITY 6: *Analyzing the Narrator in "My Last Duchess"*

Read the poem "My Last Duchess" by Robert Browning. Use the **Checklist for Writing about Point of View and Tone of Voice** to write an essay in which you analyze the narrator, the duchess, and the various audiences in and of the poem.

Your Audience: Address readers who have read the poem but want to understand it better.

Your Purpose: Attempt to persuade your readers that Browning is a master of point of view and tone of voice. What is the narrator's relationship to the other people in the poem? How is his attitude reflected in his word choice? To whom is he speaking? What is his purpose? Do you think he accomplishes his purpose?

References: Refer to the poem using line numbers (parenthetically).

My Last Duchess³

ROBERT BROWNING *(1812–89) "Home-schooled" by his middle-class London family, Browning wrote plays and some of the best-known poems of the Victorian period, including dramatic monologues like "Fra Lippo Lippi" and "The Bishop Orders his Tomb at Saint Praxed's Church." Many of them reflect his interest in Italy, where he lived for fifteen years with his wife, poet Elizabeth Barrett Browning, with whom he eloped, taking her out of the home of her protective, dictatorial father.*

Ferrara

That's my last Duchess painted on the wall,
Looking as if she were alive. I call
That piece a wonder, now: Frà Pandolf's hands
Worked busily a day, and there she stands.
Will 't please you sit and look at her? I said   5
"Frà Pandolf" by design, for never read
Strangers like you that pictured countenance,
The depth and passion of its earnest glance,
But to myself they turned (since none puts by
The curtain I have drawn for you, but I)   10
And seemed as they would ask me, if they durst,°
How such a glance came there; so, not the first

³The poem is based on the suspicious death of the young wife of Alfonso II d'Este, duke of Ferrara in sixteenth-century Italy.
¹¹**durst** dare

(Continued)

Are you to turn and ask thus. Sir, 'twas not
Her husband's presence only, called that spot
15 Of joy into the Duchess' cheek: perhaps
Frà Pandolf chanced to say, "Her mantle° laps
Over my Lady's wrist too much," or "Paint
Must never hope to reproduce the faint
Half-flush that dies along her throat"; such stuff
20 Was courtesy, she thought, and cause enough
For calling up that spot of joy. She had
A heart . . . how shall I say? . . . too soon made glad,
Too easily impressed; she liked whate'er
She looked on, and her looks went everywhere.
25 Sir, 'twas all one! My favour at her breast,
The dropping of the daylight in the West,
The bough of cherries some officious° fool
Broke in the orchard for her, the white mule
She rode with round the terrace—all and each
30 Would draw from her alike the approving speech,
Or blush, at least. She thanked men,—good; but thanked
Somehow . . . I know not how . . . as if she ranked
My gift of a nine-hundred-years-old name
With anybody's gift. Who'd stoop to blame
35 This sort of trifling? Even had you skill
In speech—(which I have not)—to make your will
Quite clear to such an one, and say, "Just this
Or that in you disgusts me; here you miss,
Or there exceed the mark"—and if she let
40 Herself be lessoned so, nor plainly set
Her wits to yours, forsooth,° and made excuse,
—E'en° then would be some stooping; and I chuse°
Never to stoop. Oh, sir, she smiled, no doubt,
Whene'er I passed her; but who passed without
45 Much the same smile? This grew; I gave commands;
Then all smiles stopped together. There she stands
As if alive. Will 't please you rise? We'll meet
The company below, then. I repeat,
The Count your Master's known munificence°

[16]**mantle** cloak or cape   [27]**officious** too eager to offer something unwanted
[41]**forsooth** in truth   [42]**e'en** even   [42]**chuse** choose   [49]**munificence** generosity
with gifts

Is ample warrant° that no just pretence   50
Of mine for dowry will be disallowed;
Though his fair daughter's self, as I avowed
At starting, is my object. Nay, we'll go
Together down, Sir! Notice Neptune, though,
Taming a sea-horse, thought a rarity,   55
Which Claus of Innsbruck cast in bronze for me.   [1842]

⁵⁰**warrant** guarantee

Word Choice, Figures of Speech, and Word Order

In Chapter 5, we saw that point of view and tone of voice create relationships among writer, reader, and subject—all the elements of the Communications Triangle (see Chapter 1)—and that narrative creates meaning by putting events into a sequence. Writers also create meaning at a "micro" level, by choosing words and putting them into sequences. Understanding the consequences of **diction** (word choice) and **syntax** (word order) can make you not only a stronger reader but a stronger writer, too.

WORD CHOICE

If you've ever reached for a dictionary or thesaurus while writing, or asked a friend for "another way to say" something hard to describe, you have been an active "word chooser." As we will see in the following section, many factors influence our decisions about which words to use for different purposes, and these same factors influence the way we interpret other writers' diction.

Meaning

The first thing we want to know about a word is what it means. Since many words have multiple meanings and multiple uses, finding meaning may not be perfectly straightforward. What a word **denotes,** that is, what it names, can be found in its dictionary definition. A word's **denotation** is what it refers to directly, without emotional coloring. A word's **connotations** convey an attitude towards the thing named.

The first dictionary entry for *head*, for example, defines it as "The uppermost or forwardmost part of the body of a vertebrate, containing the brain and the eyes, ears, nose, mouth, and jaws."[1] When used to point to a part of vertebrate anatomy, *head* is a technical term. When used to designate the foremost member of a committee or department, it connotes responsibility and high status. A person with "a head for business" has a skill or ability. When used to designate a drug addict or the bathroom facilities on a ship, the connotations of *head* are less glamorous.

This example shows that a word can refer to more than one thing and have varied connotations. There are even words that can be used as more than one part of speech. *Head*, for example, can be a verb as well as a noun: You might "head" a commission, a parade, or a soccer ball and might "head" for the library when you need a book. Although so many meanings and uses are available, readers usually do not have trouble figuring out which one is meant in a particular sentence because the context selects out the relevant meanings.

For examples of interpretations of words in texts, you might review Zak Owen's paper on Heaney's poem "Digging" in Chapter 2. Some of his investigations had to do with straightforward questions of designation: Which of the many meanings of "drill" is relevant to the phrase "potato drills"? In the context of potatoes, he could confidently rule out West African baboons.

But in the case of "nestled" in "The coarse boot nestled on the lug" (l. 10), it was precisely the incongruity between the action and its context that was the clue to the poem's meaning. What Zak first labeled a "weird idea" in his marginal notes gave way to a fuller thought in his paper: "Nestling is an activity that we might associate with small soft living creatures, not boots and lugs, but the point is to show us the affinity that these men have with their tools." The affinity with tools helps the speaker overcome the insecurity he feels when he compares himself to his father and grandfather and helps Zak link the narrator's memories with his future ambitions as a writer.

Levels of Diction

You are probably familiar with the idea that we adjust the formality of our speech when we address different audiences. When we say that a deer is "in rut," we are using a formal, technical term. When we complain to our friends that we are "in a rut," we are being conversational and colloquial. Different

[1] *The American Heritage Dictionary*, 3rd ed. (Boston: Houghton Mifflin, 1993), 624. Reprinted with permission.

degrees of formality and informality are called **levels of diction.** Many of us would tell a story to our grandmothers differently from the way we tell it to our friends. (Of course, that depends on how we relate to our grandmothers.) But we would almost certainly tell it in an entirely different way if we had to tell it in court before a judge. "The idiot ran the red light and hit me" might do for a friend, while in court a lawyer might say, "When the defendant ignored the traffic signal, his vehicle collided with my client's."

We typically distinguish among three levels of diction, high, low, and middle, but there are many intermediate registers. For instance:

Formal	"perspire"
Informal	"sweat"
Technical jargon	"diaphoresis," "bodily excretions," or "effluvia"
Slang	"funk juice"
Euphemism	"glow"
Colloquialisms	"sweating blood" (for "working very hard") and "sweating bullets" (for "being very nervous")
Ethnic dialect and regional vocabulary	"schvitz" (Yiddish)
Profanity	There may not be one for "sweat." Feel free to provide your own examples for other bodily functions (or not).

When you are trying to gauge the impact of level of diction on a text, it is sometimes helpful to experiment with a paraphrase. For example, if Lincoln had started the Gettysburg address by saying, "Around eighty seven years ago, a bunch of dissatisfied guys started a country," it probably would not have had the grand ring he wanted for commemorating a cemetery for Union dead.

 ACTIVITY 1: *Paraphrasing Roosevelt*

Think of a way to paraphrase President Franklin Roosevelt's characterization of December 7, 1941, on which the Japanese surprised the U.S. Navy at Pearl Harbor, as a "date that will live in infamy."

 ACTIVITY 2: *Dictionary Definitions*

Pick several of these words and use dictionaries to investigate their various meanings and connotations:

- blow
- rat
- get
- take

(Continued)

ACTIVITY 2: *(Continued)*

How many parts of speech can they represent? How many levels of diction? Besides a collegiate dictionary, you might want to consult an **etymological dictionary** (a dictionary that traces historical changes) and a dictionary of slang.

ACTIVITY 3 (GROUP WORK): *Retelling a Fairy Tale*[2]

As a class, choose a fairy tale most of you know. Divide into small groups. Each group should write a version of the fairy tale using a different level of diction. When you're finished, each group should read the others its version of the tale. Discuss the ways in which the stories have changed from traditional versions.

Word Origins

Words that occupy different levels of diction often entered the English language at different times from different places. English evolved as the islands on which it was spoken received conquerors and immigrants, and as the people who spoke it conquered and emigrated to other places. The language is like a sedimentary rock formation in which layers were laid down over time by the Celtic, Roman, Germanic, Viking, and French peoples who arrived in waves, with additions from places like Australia, East and Southeast Asia, Africa, and the Americas—everywhere that English speakers have roamed.

The Norman Conquest in 1066 brought to England a French ruling class that replaced the old Germanic ruling class. As a result, their language (called "Anglo-Saxon" or "Old English") became the language spoken primarily in everyday life by peasants, while French, spoken by the elite, supplied new words for matters of government, art, education, and religion. Eventually, English became once again the language generally spoken by all classes, but it had been transformed: what we now call "Middle English" kept words stemming from the plain and ordinary vocabulary that had originated in Anglo-Saxon as well as the newer, higher-level vocabulary that had originated in French and Latin. You can hear the two levels of diction in some common English phrases like "last will and testament," which has the one-syllable, plainer Anglo-Saxon "will," as well as the fancier, multi-syllabic, Latinate "testament." This doublet is a witness to the linguistic class divisions of English in the Middle Ages.

This class division and the connotations it carries with it still determine our word choice in some contexts. For example, if a text has a high proportion of technical vocabulary made up of Latinate and formal words, you might guess that it is not meant for a general audience. Conversely, Anglo-Saxon–derived vocabulary can convey earthiness, plainness, or strength. When, for example, Winston Churchill wanted to inspire the suffering

[2]I learned this exercise from my former colleague Tena Helton.

population of Britain during World War II, he admitted that he could offer only "blood, toil, tears, and sweat." Had he offered instead "oxygen-carrying circulating fluid, exertion, saline liquid secreted by the lachrymal glands, and perspiration," his appeal would have been far less vivid.

Since word origins are such an important key to level of diction, think about how you can tell which words come from Anglo-Saxon and which come from French and Latin. Words from romance languages like Latin and French often have more than one syllable and begin with prefixes like "pre-," "post-," "in-," or "ex-," and end with suffixes like "-ment," "-ize," or "-ation." So "prefix," "postpone," "infamous," "exercise," "entertainment," "oxidize," and "oxidation" are easily recognizable as Latinate words.

 ACTIVITY 4: *Latin Origins*

> List other prefixes and suffixes that can be clues to Latin origins and give some examples of words that contain them. Then think of an Anglo-Saxon synonym for each. What are the different connotations of the words in the pairs you find?

The different levels of diction give writers a rich resource for expressing their relationships to their subjects and their audiences. They can show respect, admiration, disapproval, condescension, and many other attitudes. It is rare, however, to find a work in which all words are at the same level of diction. Some of the liveliest writing mixes different kinds of vocabulary. Mixing levels provides special strength to writing when the subject matter is about contrast or tension. You can see that principle at work in #5 of Activity 5 and in the poem in Activity 6 below.

ACTIVITY 5: *Word Choice*

> Here are some passages of poetry and prose with one word removed. At the right, in curved brackets, the missing word appears among other possibilities that the writer could have chosen. Spend a few moments considering the advantages and disadvantages of each choice. Which one would you choose to complete the passage? Be prepared to defend your choice.
>
> **1.** Charmed magic _____ opening on the foam
> {casements, wall openings, windows, apertures}
> Of _____ seas, in faery lands forlorn.   {perilous, dangerous}
> Keats, "Ode to a Nightingale"
>
> **2.** I'll _____ the guts into the neighbor room.
> {carry, convey, lug, bear}
> Shakespeare, *Hamlet*
>
> **3.** Damn it all! All this our South _____ peace.
> {smells, gives off the odor, stinks}
>
> *(Continued)*

ACTIVITY 5: *(Continued)*

> You whoreson dog, Papiols, come! Let's to music!
> I have no life save when the swords clash.
>
> Pound, "Sestina: Altaforte"

4. Much have I traveled in the _____ of gold,
   And many goodly states and kingdoms seen. {regions, realms, counties}

   Keats, "On First Looking into Chapman's Homer"

5. That God of ours, the Great Geometer,
   Does something for us here, where He hath put
   (if you want to put it that way) things in shape,
   Compressing the little lambs in orderly cubes,
   Making the roast a decent cylinder,
   Fairing the tin ellipsoid of a ham,
   Getting the luncheon meat anonymous
   In squares (streamlined, maybe for greater speed).
   Praise Him, he hath conferred aesthetic distance
   Upon our appetites, and on the bloody
   _____ of our birthright, our unseemly need,
   Imposed significant form. {Mess, Disorder, Chaos}

   Nemerov, "Grace to Be Said at the Supermarket"

6. An even more powerful strategy for addressing resistant audiences is a conciliatory strategy, often called *Rogerian argument*, named after psychologist Carl Rogers, who used this strategy to help people _____. {patch up fights, resolve differences, kiss and make up}

   Ramage and Bean, *Writing Arguments*[3]

7. In walks these three girls in nothing but bathing suits. I'm in the third checkout slot, with my back to the door, so I don't see them until they're over by the bread. The one that caught my eye first was the one in the plaid green two-piece. She was a _____, with a good tan and a sweet broad soft-looking can . . .

   {chunky kid, slightly too heavy young female, fat broad}
Updike, "A & P"

8. Under the rule of a series of highly competent emperors . . . the Roman Empire . . . had reached its maximum extent, stretching from the Atlantic Ocean to the Persian Gulf, and from the forests of Germany to the edge of the Sahara, and to contemporaries its demise must have seemed _____. {mind-boggling, inconceivable, unthinkable}

   J.R.S. Phillips, *The Medieval Expansion of Europe*[4]

[3]John Ramage and John Bean, *Writing Arguments: A Rhetoric with Readings*, 4th ed. (Boston: Allyn and Bacon, 1998), 183.

[4]J.R.S. Phillips, *The Medieval Expansion of Europe*, 2nd ed. (Oxford: Oxford University Press, 1998), 3.

ACTIVITY 6: *Word Choice in "I Being Born a Woman and Distressed"*

Edna St. Vincent Millay's poem "I Being Born a Woman and Distressed" will reward the investigation of word choice. Read it several times—at least once out loud—and then, in a journal entry or informal essay, explore answers to these questions:

1. To whom is the narrator speaking? Define her attitude toward him.
2. If there is more than one attitude, how do they differ? How do individual words help her convey them?
3. As you read, mark words that seem unusual or used in unusual ways. Make notes on the way Millay is deploying words of Anglo-Saxon origin as opposed to those of Latin or French origin. What seems to be her purpose? How do her choices contribute to tone?
4. How do tone and level of diction contribute to the meaning of the poem?

I Being Born a Woman and Distressed

EDNA ST. VINCENT MILLAY *(1892–1950), who started publishing poetry when she was in college, was the first woman to win the Pulitzer Prize for Poetry.*

I being born a woman and distressed
By all the needs and notions of my kind,
Am urged by your propinquity° to find
Your person fair and feel a certain zest
To bear your body's weight upon my breast: 5
So subtly is the fume of life designed,
To clarify the pulse and cloud the mind,
And leave me once again undone, possessed.
Think not for this, however, the poor treason
Of my stout blood against my staggering brain,   10
I shall remember you with love, or season
My scorn with pity,—let me make it plain:
I find this frenzy insufficient reason
For conversation when we meet again.   [1927]

³**propinquity** physical nearness

Sometimes, investigation of a word's roots—its **etymology**—will lead to a deeper understanding of how it is being used. There are many places to find information about the history of word meanings, for instance, an etymological dictionary.⁵ The *Oxford English Dictionary* (often affectionately abbreviated *OED*) is a fascinating multivolume resource that is itself the

⁵E.g., *The Oxford Dictionary of English Etymology*, ed. C.T. Onions (Oxford at the Clarendon Press: Oxford University Press, 1966); *Origins: A Short Etymological Dictionary of Modern English*, ed. Eric Partridge (New York: Greenwich House, 1983).

subject of a number of histories. (Many libraries give their patrons access to the online version.)

For an example of how information about etymology can enrich our understanding of a text, go back to the beginning of Sylvia Plath's poem "Cut" in Chapter 1: "What a thrill— /My thumb instead of an onion." Plath's discoveries through her minute examination of the experience of cutting her thumb while cooking might explain why cutting herself is a "thrill." But we will understand even more from the *American Heritage Dictionary*, where the definition includes the word's point of origin in the language called Indo-European that was the ancestor of many now spoken in Europe, the Americas, and South Asia. The asterisk in the entry **terə²** leads us to the Index of Indo-European roots at the back of the dictionary, where we learn that it means "to pass through" [pierce] and produced words like "nostril" (a hole in a nose!). So that to say that piercing the skin is a "thrill" is nothing more than returning to the original sense of the word.

There is a similar reward for investigating the origin of "nestled" in line 10 of Seamus Heaney's "Digging," the subject of Zak Owen's paper in Chapter 2. One reason that Zak felt the incongruity of boots that nestled on lugs is that "nestle" comes from the Anglo-Saxon word *nestlian*, to make a nest. Its meanings therefore include protecting and making comfortable: As an intransitive verb (with no direct object) it means "1. To settle snugly and comfortably. 2. To lie in a sheltered position. 3. To draw or press close, as in affection; snuggle." As a transitive verb, it means "1. To snuggle or press contentedly. 2. To place or settle as if in a nest."[6] The comfort level of that foot on that lug is a key to the poem. One of the words of the definition, *snug*, is even used in the poem (l. 2), helping to connect the narrator's relationship with his preferred instrument and his father's relationship with his.

ACTIVITY 7: *Word Choice in "The Love Song of J. Alfred Prufrock"*

Examine the first few lines of T.S. Eliot's poem "The Love Song of J. Alfred Prufrock" (for biographical notes on Eliot and the complete poem, see Chapter 13):

Let us go then, you and I,
When the evening is spread out against the sky
Like a patient etherized upon a table.

Pick out a few words for investigation of their histories, using either the *OED* or another good dictionary. Which word histories seem to add an extra dimension to the meaning of the lines?

---

[6]*American Heritage Collegiate Dictionary*, 3rd ed. (Boston: Houghton Mifflin, 1993), 916.

Checklist for Writing about Word Choice

_____Do you know the denotative meaning of all the words in the text you are writing about? If not, be sure to look them up.

_____What is the general level of diction in the text? On what evidence do you base this claim? What kinds of words predominate?

_____Do any words, phrases, or larger syntactical units seem to be of a different level? If so, does the variation seem to indicate the writer's inattention or to have a good effect because they are appropriate to the meaning and convey it well?

_____If any words seem particularly resonant and important to meaning, look them up in a dictionary that includes information on etymological histories.

_____Does the work set up a pattern that repeats connotations and etymological meanings that contribute to the meaning of the work as a whole?

FIGURES OF SPEECH

One of the ways that writers can widen the connotations of a word they've chosen is through **figures of speech,** phrases that treat words in unusual, nonliteral ways. The most common figures of speech are described below:

Simile: a comparison. The pairing of two things is signaled by the word *like* or *as.* For instance, in Updike's "A & P" (see Chapter 3), Sammy speculates about what the girls in the store are thinking: "do you think it's a mind in there or just a little buzz like a bee in a glass jar?" (paragraph 2).

Metaphor: a comparison that suppresses the signal, thus treating the two things as if they were identical. When Updike's Sammy sees the women shopping in the supermarket as "sheep pushing their carts down the aisle" (5), he is treating them metaphorically.

Symbol: using one thing to mean something else; often, a material thing stands for something nonmaterial. A snake, for example, might be used as a symbol of sin. For a more complex example, take a look at this poem by William Blake.

The Sick Rose

WILLIAM BLAKE *(For bibliographical notes, see p. 1258.)*

O Rose, thou art sick.
The invisible worm
That flies in the night
In the howling storm

5 Has found out thy bed
Of crimson joy,
And his dark secret love
Does thy life destroy.   [1794]

On a literal level, this is a gardener's lament about the infestation of a flower by a pest. We expect that Blake is writing about something more than a local horticultural nuisance, however. Critics have not settled on what that is. In Western culture, roses are typically symbols of love, and flying worms are dragons.[7] Does the poem refer to the loss of innocence? Loss of virginity? The decline of a culture? Perhaps we still read it because we can't decide.

The lyrics of this song spell out its intentions more clearly.

From *"Love Is a Rose"*

NEIL YOUNG, *the singer/songwriter and guitar player, often sings with the folk/rock group [David] Crosby, [Stephen] Stills, and [Graham] Nash, formed in California in 1968. Their songs include "Suite: Judy Blue Eyes," "Marrakesh Express," and "Woodstock." Young wrote and directed the 2003 film* Greendale, *for which he also composed and performed the music.*

Love is a rose but you'd better not pick it—
Only grows when it's on the vine.
Handful of thorns and you know you've missed it.
Lose your love when you say the word "mine."

Cut roses are often given as tokens of love in our culture, but Young's gloss makes the gesture dangerous. Could Blake's worm be the possessiveness that Young warns against?

ACTIVITY 8 (GROUP ACTIVITY): *Symbols in "The Sick Rose"*

In small groups, brainstorm about how you might investigate the meaning of the symbols in Blake's poem. Where would you look and what would you look for? To think like a historian, start with the dates of Blake's life and this poem. To think like a literary historian, imagine what kinds of sources might have influenced his symbolism. What might Blake have seen that might have provided him with material to borrow from?

---

[7]In the Old English epic *Beowulf*, the word *wyrm*, cognate with the modern *worm*, is used to name the night-flying, fire-breathing dragon or serpent. He does a great deal of damage to the neighborhood, and although he is too big to hide in a rose, dragons like this one must influence Blake's choice of the word for this symbol in his poem.

Allusion: a reference to a historical person, place, or thing, including other works of art. Allusions are one way for a literary work to point to—and thus draw in—the world outside it. In "A & P," when Sammy describes "a pyramid of Diet Delight peaches" (paragraph 11), he is adding to the credibility of the story for all who recognize the brand.

Allusions to other texts put a work into the context of one of its predecessors but (if done well) use the material for new purposes. In a key passage, T.S. Eliot's J. Alfred Prufrock exclaims, "No, I am not Prince Hamlet, nor was meant to be; / Am an attendant lord, one that will do / To swell a progress, start a scene or two" (ll. 111–13). Putting himself into one of Shakespeare's best-known plays is an efficient way for Prufrock to let his audience know how he sees himself—as a minor player in his own life.

In the song "Fishin' 4 Religion," the hip-hop group Arrested Development makes a subtler reference to another song in this couplet: "So on the dock I sit in silence / staring at a sea that's full of violence." If we recognize this allusion to Otis Redding's lines "Sittin' on the dock of the bay, / Watchin' the tide roll away,"[8] we see the peacefulness and stability of his world brought into stark contrast with the violence of Arrested Development's.

"Sampling" in the music world has introduced a new kind of allusion, in which musicians electronically insert a digitally mastered phrase or tune by another composer into their own work. This is different from "covering" another artist's song, which means that someone just sings or plays a song written by another (and presumably pays the appropriate royalties for recording it). Although sampling has at times produced lawsuits for copyright infringement, it is essentially a creative act. If you have a digital "edition" of a song, you can substantially change it by remixing it, changing balances, adding reverberations, and even substituting some of your own words.

ACTIVITY 9: *Allusion in "Tube"*

Here is the opening of a prize-winning slam poem that was written and performed by a group. What do the allusions refer to? What is their purpose in the poem?

From *Tube*

TEAM AUSTIN (*For explanatory notes and the entire poem, see Chapter 18.*)

D: We interrupt your regularly scheduled program to bring you this
P: refreshing
W: gunfire
H: fabulous

(Continued)

[8]"Sittin' on the Dock of the Bay," http://www.otisredding.com/page5.html (accessed 25 June 2001).

> *D:* odor
> *W:* new and improved
> *P:* act of cowardice
> *D:* minty-fresh
> *P:* A must for those who are dieting.
> *W:* You can't find a better set of knives.
> *H:* The death toll continues to rise.
> *D:* Now available on home video
> *P:* free with each box of
> *W:* massive environmental destruction.
> *H:* He scores!
> *D:* He could go all the way!
> *P:* He draws the foul!
> *W:* this game is over.   [1996]

ACTIVITY 10 (GROUP WORK): *Sampling*

> If you listen to a form of music that includes "covers" and "sampling," brain-
> storm with a small group on the relationship between the old material and
> new. What does the inserted material mean in its new context that it didn't
> mean in the old one? What effect does it have on the meaning of the new
> work?

Oxymoron: a phrase that holds together words that seem to be opposites.
The word *oxymoron* means "pointedly foolish" in Greek. In Robert
Herrick's "Delight in Disorder," for example, "wild civility" certainly
qualifies as purposeful foolishness (see p. 126). The contradiction is
emphasized by the words' origins, since *wild* is from Anglo-Saxon and
civility is from Latin.

Personification: the treatment of something nonhuman as if it were human.
Fables like Aesop's, for example, treat animals as if they were people. One
of the usual effects of personification is to invest the thing with special
meaning, more easily evoking empathy in the audience.

Puns: expressions that exploit the multiple meanings of a word or phrase.
Puns, sometimes denigrated as a low form of humor, actually do the
same job of linking and comparing that the other figures of speech do.
The way Nemerov calls upon several meanings of *mess* in "Prayer to Be
Said in the Supermarket" makes a rather profound point about the
human relationship with food (see Chapter 6, Activity 5).

Synecdoche: a reference to something using just a part of it. Synecdoches (the Greek means "to take on a share of") can be found in common usage in phrases like "all hands on deck," "boots on the ground," and "nice wheels."

Often a substitution reveals a writer's or a speaker's attitude toward something. When Hamlet refers to the dead Polonius as the "guts," for instance, he shows his lack of respect for the man. His attitude is revealed by what gets left out.

The Sequence of Images

There are many other figures of speech and ways to classify them. You can find some of them in the Glossary of Terms at the end of this book (Appendix B) and in reference books like *The Princeton Encyclopedia of Poetry and Poetics* and Richard Lanham's *Handlist of Rhetorical Terms.*[9] It is important, however, not merely to identify them, but to see how they function in a text. In a well-constructed text of any kind, whether poetry or prose, imaginative literature or not, different figures of speech often form a pattern or sequence that contributes to its meaning.

Let's look at "The Love Song of J. Alfred Prufrock" (see Chapter 13). After the first simile that describes the evening as "a patient etherised upon a table" (l. 3—see the section on word origins above), the fog is described metaphorically as an animal that falls asleep (l. 22), and the afternoon is personified as being "Asleep . . . tired . . . or it malingers" (l. 77). These lines create a sequence of somnolence that might make us wonder if the atmosphere ever wakes up. At the end of the poem, the narrator imagines that we have "lingered in the chambers of the sea . . . Till human voices wake us, and we drown" (ll. 129–31)—a disastrous climax to the poem. One of the reasons that we can feel its impact is that it reverses the earlier pattern of sleepiness that the poem created, producing not consciousness but death.

Checklist for Writing about Figures of Speech

____What figures of speech does the work include?

____Does the sequence of figures of speech create a pattern that contributes to the meaning of the work? How is the pattern developed and varied?

____How do the figures of speech contribute to the effect of the work?

---

[9]*The Princeton Encyclopedia of Poetry and Poetics*, enlarged edition, ed. Alex Preminger (Princeton: Princeton University Press, 1974); Richard Lanham, *Handlist of Rhetorical Terms: A Guide for Students of English Literature* (Berkeley: University of California Press, 1968).

ACTIVITY 11: *Writing about the Sequence of Images*

John Donne's poem "Batter my Heart" builds a sequence of figures of speech as the narrator prays for a closer relationship with God. Analyze the figures of speech: What do they tell us about the narrator's faith? What difference does the order in which they come make to the impact of the poem?

Holy Sonnet 14, "Batter my heart, three-person'd God"

JOHN DONNE *(For biographical notes, see p. 256.)*

Batter my heart, three-person'd God; for you
As yet but knock, breathe, shine, and seek to mend;
That I may rise, and stand, o'erthrow me and bend
Your force, to break, blow, burn, and make me new.
5 I, like an usurpt town, to another due,
Labour to admit you, but Oh, to no end,
Reason your viceroy in me, me should defend,
But is captiv'd, and proves weak or untrue.
Yet dearly I love you, and would be loved fain,
10 But am betroth'd unto your enemy:
Divorce me, untie, or break that knot again,
Take me to you, imprison me, for I
Except you enthrall me, never shall be free,
Nor ever chaste, except you ravish me.   [1633]

WORD ORDER

Word order is important for the same reasons that narrative order is important: As soon as writers begin a structure (e.g., sentence, paragraph), readers develop expectations about how that structure will continue.[10] Skillful writers are aware of these expectations and take advantage of them for their own purposes, either meeting or disappointing them.

We are not often aware of how, as readers, we are actually writing our anticipatory version of the text, because it normally happens very fast. But paying attention to it will reward us both as readers and as writers.

[10]My thinking about syntax has been shaped by Joseph M. Williams, *Style: Ten Lessons in Clarity and Grace* (New York: Longman, 2002), and Stanley Fish, "Literature in the Reader: Affective Stylistics," *NLH* 2 (1970): 123–62. Reprinted in Stanley Fish, *Self-Consuming Artifact: The Experience of Seventeenth-Century Literature* (Berkeley: University of California Press, 1972), 383–427. Also see George Gopen, *The Sense of Structure: Writing from the Reader's Point of View* (New York: Longman, 2004).

Let's start by looking at two sentences about a horse race.

1. Excalibur broke last from the gate, took the lead by the far turn, then dropped back to fourth coming into the stretch, but rallied to win by a nose.
2. Excalibur won by a nose, though he was fourth coming into the stretch after leading at the far turn despite having broken last from the gate.[11]

Since with a horse race, the important information is usually who won, these accounts chiefly differ in how much they make you wait for the news. The first one makes you wait through the story of the entire race; the second delivers it right at the start. If all you want is to know who won, you don't have to read the second sentence beyond the first clause; you can stop at the comma. Philosopher Nelson Goodman notes the different audiences and purposes of these two sentences: the first a newspaper report that wanted to tell a full story, and the second his own report to a friend who had bet on Excalibur. There's no suspense in the second account because Goodman didn't want to torture his friend.

But there are other decisions that writers make besides where to put the "big news" of the sentence. Grammar has a plot, too, which is driven by readers' understanding of what complete sentences need—chiefly subjects and verbs arranged in independent clauses, structures that can stand alone and make sense. "I am," "you are," and "he is" all qualify as whole sentences because they have subjects and verbs and can stand alone, but there's not much of a grammatical "plot" in these short sentences. Things get more interesting in more complex structures.

Here's another version of Goodman's horse race with the same outcome for those who bet on Excalibur, but a different "plot" in the grammar:

Although Excalibur won by a nose and led at the far turn after having been fourth coming into the stretch, he broke last from the gate.

The news is the same, but the story is different. The story this sentence wants to tell is not about how Excalibur finished the race, but how he *started* it. The start gets emphasis in two ways: it comes last, and it's in the independent clause. This sentence isn't meant for the racing fans at the betting window, but for Excalibur's trainer, pointing out that his bad start created a deficit that he had to make up for on the track.

Here are a number of techniques for creating emphasis:

- **Placement:** The two positions in a sentence that naturally receive emphasis are the beginning and the end. Put the content that deserves emphasis in the places that naturally receive it.
- **Grammar:** Whatever is in the independent clause of a sentence receives emphasis.

[11]Nelson Goodman, "Twisted Tales; or, Story, Study, and Symphony," *Critical Inquiry* 7 (1980); repr. in *On Narrative*, ed. W.J.T. Mitchell (Chicago: University of Chicago Press, 1980, 1981), 99.

- **Delay:** Whatever readers have to wait for receives emphasis. The technique of **embedding** inserts other elements between sentence elements (such as the subject and the verb, or the preposition and its object) to produce delay. Here's an example:

Subject
Excalibur, having broken last from the gate, then having taken the lead by the far turn but

                                                 Verb
dropping back to fourth coming into the stretch, rallied to win by a nose.

- **Weight:** If one part of a sentence is strikingly longer or shorter than others, it may receive extra emphasis.

Meaning is not something we receive homogenized and whole, as we get orange juice from a carton. Finding meaning is more like the process of peeling an orange and then judging its quality section by section. Meaning gets made through the readers' active interpretation as they predict how a sentence will be completed and adjust and revise as their expectations are fulfilled or contradicted.

 ACTIVITY 12: *Rearranging Word Order*

Rearrange the following sentence to put the emphasis on the stretch. (What rhetorical situations might call for such an emphasis?)

Excalibur broke last from the gate, took the lead by the far turn, then dropped back to fourth coming into the stretch, but rallied to win by a nose.

A few more terms for figures of speech that manipulate syntax will help you interpret word order and grammatical structure.

- **Parallelism:** two similar ideas expressed in similar syntactic structures. Parallel structure gives the ideas equal weight: "I came; I saw; I conquered." The parallelism (subject verb; subject verb; subject verb) implies that it didn't take much more than arrival and observation for Julius Caesar to take possession of a territory. The precise balance connotes control and order. (The simplicity of the subject-verb structure also connotes a simple majesty and an air of command. Compare: "I came to Pontus; my army and I looked around; we fought long and hard, through many a battle; thus we conquered the Pontines.")
- **Anaphora:** the repetition of the same word or words at the beginning of successive phrases, clauses, or sentences, commonly in conjunction with parallelism. Julius Caesar's tripartite triumphal declaration above is actually anaphora, as well as parallelism. John F. Kennedy used anaphora in

his inauguration speech: "Ask not what your country can do for you; ask what you can do for your country." If he had said, "Rather than merely planning what demands to make on your government, you ought to be figuring out how you can contribute to your nation's welfare," the lines would probably not be replayed and remembered.

- **Chiasmus:** a syntactical figure of speech that reverses parallelism, for example, in Shakespeare's Sonnet 18: "So long lives this, and this gives life to thee." The pattern—"verb subject, subject verb"—conveys a sense of closure. The repetition of structure reinforces the assertion of shared identity—"oneness"—between the "this" (the sonnet itself) and "thee" (the beloved).

We can see all these techniques at work in all kinds of writing, from the most formal poem to the most humdrum memo. Every sentence structures its "news" in a way that tries to direct readers' attention the way an orchestra conductor does. Look at this sentence from Pam Belluck's *New York Times* piece about the Nun Study (see p. 7):

> Their research has shown **that** folic acid may help stave off Alzheimer's disease; **that** small, barely perceptible strokes may trigger some dementia; and, in an especially striking finding, **that** early language ability may be linked to lower risk of Alzheimer's because nuns who packed more ideas into the sentences of their early autobiographies were less likely to get Alzheimer's disease six decades later.[12]

The research results are packaged in three parallel clauses all beginning with the word *that*. The parallelism makes the three results equivalent to each other. But one of them gets more emphasis than the other two for four reasons: it is last, it is longer than all the others, it is preceded by an interruption, and the interrupting phrase announces its importance. The story this sentence has to tell comes to a satisfying, climactic close with what Belluck seems to consider a very significant announcement.

Checklist for Writing about Grammar and Word Order (Syntax)

_____What are the chief characteristics of the syntax? Is it smooth and clear or is it difficult to read? Does the writer's choice seem appropriate to the subject matter?

_____Are the sentences long or short, simple or complicated in structure?

_____Is sentence length consistent or does it vary? Do the writer's choices about sentence length contribute to the effectiveness of the piece?

_____Does emphasis seem to fall on the appropriate parts of the subject?

_____What techniques does the writer use to give emphasis?

[12]Pam Belluck, "Nuns Offer Clues to Alzheimer's and Aging," *New York Times,* 7 May 2001.

As a way of applying the concepts we've covered here, read the following poem by Robert Herrick, taking special note of its syntax.

Delight in Disorder

ROBERT HERRICK *(1591–1674), who graduated from St. John's College of Cambridge University, became a poet partly by spending time in London in the witty circle of Ben Jonson, which gathered in the Devi's Tavern. After he was ordained an Episcopal priest, he left London with some reservations to become the vicar of a rural parish. The volume of poetry he published in 1648 included religious poems, love poems, and poems about country customs. Known for Royalist sympathies during the ascendancy of the Puritan movement that led to the execution of Charles I in 1649, he was expelled from his parish in 1647 by the government of Oliver Cromwell's Commonwealth. He spent the years of the Commonwealth in London and then, when the monarchy was restored in 1660, returned to his parish for the rest of his life.*

A sweet disorder in the dress
Kindles in clothes a wantonness.
A lawn° about the shoulders thrown
Into a fine distractiön;
5   An erring lace, which here and there
Enthralls the crimson stomacher;°
A cuff neglectful, and thereby
Ribbons to flow confusedly;
A winning wave, deserving note,
10   In the tempestuous petticoat;
A careless shoestring, in whose tie
I see a wild civility;
Do more bewitch me than when art
Is too precise in every part.   [1648]

³**lawn** a finely woven fabric from the French city of Laon   ⁶**stomacher** an item of clothing covering the chest and stomach; often of stiff material sometimes covered with jewels or embroidery

Robert Herrick's poem "Delight in Disorder" is made up of only two sentences, both of which are in the most common order: subject, verb, object. Both sentences convey the same thing: The narrator reveals that he's more attracted to women who are a little sloppy in the way they dress. But the second sentence is harder to read than the first, primarily because of its length. It keeps adding subjects until there's a whole list of items of women's clothing: a lawn (shawl), a bodice piece, lace, a cuff, ribbons, a petticoat, and a shoestring. That means the reader has to wait a long time to get the verb and object of the sentence, which puts emphasis on what is delayed: the declaration that the carelessly worn garments "do more bewitch me."

So talking about word order gets us back to the subject of word choice—there's so much emphasis on "bewitch me" that we're compelled to consider what the word means and how it affects the poem as a whole. Perhaps it indicates that the speaker doesn't take responsibility for his sexual response to slightly disheveled women: He implies that he's helpless because of a magic spell cast over him.

ACTIVITY 13: *Writing about Word Choice and Word Order in Auden*

Following this activity is "Musée des Beaux Arts," a poem in which W.H. Auden responds in the twentieth century to several paintings by sixteenth-century Flemish painter Pieter Brueghel the Elder, "The Massacre of the Innocents" and "Landscape with the Fall of Icarus."[13]

Here are a few suggestions for writing about the poem:

Purpose: Write an essay in which you analyze Auden's use of word choice and word order to convey the message about suffering that he finds in Brueghel's paintings.

Process: Before you draft, read the poem several times with pen in hand. Make notes about the following:

- diction
  - Note words that seem unusual or of a level of diction different from those around them.
  - Note words that seem important carriers of meaning in the poem.
  - Look up words that seem important in a dictionary that gives information on word origin. Take notes on what you find.

- word order
  - Note what grammatical role in the sentences the important actors play. Are they the subjects of independent clauses? Are they fulfilling some other grammatical role?
  - Speculate on how the grammar seems to affect the meaning of the poem. How does the grammatical arrangement mimic or embody the message of the painting?

Audience: Address people who know both the poem and the paintings but want to understand in more detail how they are related to each other.

Documentation: Refer to the poem parenthetically with line numbers.

Musée des Beaux Arts

W.H. Auden *(For biographical notes, see p. 535.)*

About suffering they were never wrong,
The Old Masters: how well they understood
Its human position; how it takes place
While someone else is eating or opening a window or just walking dully along;

[13]The first painting depicts an episode from the life of Jesus in the New Testament and the second an episode from Greek mythology in which, using the wings made by his father Daedalus from wax and feathers, Icarus flies too close to the sun and falls into the sea when the sun melts the wax. See color insert, Figure I-B.

(Continued)

ACTIVITY 13: *(Continued)*

5   How, when the aged are reverently, passionately waiting
For the miraculous birth, there always must be
Children who did not specially want it to happen, skating
On a pond at the edge of the wood:
They never forgot
10   That even the dreadful martyrdom must run its course
Anyhow in a corner, some untidy spot
Where the dogs go on with their doggy life and the torturer's horse
Scratches its innocent behind on a tree.

In Brueghel's Icarus, for instance: how everything turns away
15   Quite leisurely from the disaster; the ploughman may
Have heard the splash, the forsaken cry,
But for him it was not an important failure; the sun shone
As it had to on the white legs disappearing into the green
Water; and the expensive delicate ship that must have seen
20   Something amazing, a boy falling out of the sky,
Had somewhere to get to and sailed calmly on.   [1940]

ACTIVITY 14: *Analyzing Cooper's "The Fine Art of Sighing"*

A. Here is the last sentence of the essay: "Before I learned that Venetian prisoners were led across it to their execution, I imagined that the Bridge of Sighs was a feat of invisible engineering, a structure vaulting above the earth, the girders and trusses, the stay ropes and cables, the counterweights and safety rails connecting one human breath to the next." What is the story told by the grammar and syntax of this sentence?

B. All of the elements of language that we have seen at work in Chapters 5 and 6, including point of view, tone, word choice, figures of speech, and syntax, can be seen at work in nonfiction prose as well as in poetry. Write an essay in which you analyze the way these elements work in Bernard Cooper's essay "The Fine Art of Sighing" (Chapter 3, p. 62).

ACTIVITY 15: *Analyzing Zak Owen's Diction and Syntax in
"Digging for Meaning"*

Review Zak Owen's paper about Seamus Heaney's poem "Digging" (see Chapter 2, pp. 37–39) and in an informal essay use the principles in this chapter to offer Zak some advice on the paper's diction and syntax. What aspects of the diction and syntax work best? Where are they problematic? What suggestions can you make for improvement? As a way to start thinking about this project, you might read the paper out loud.

CHAPTER SEVEN

Sound Patterns, Line Breaks, and Poetic Meter

SOUND PATTERNS: RHYME, ALLITERATION, ASSONANCE, CONSONANCE

Although deliberate sound effects in language are more common in poetry than in nonliterary prose, word music occurs in all kinds of writing—poetry, nonpoetic imaginative literature, and informative and argumentative texts. In poetry, if patterns of sound create structure, you can *see* the patterns on the page. But when you read all kinds of texts out loud, you can *hear* them.

Rhymed words have the same sounds at the ends of the words: house, mouse, louse. **Alliteration** is the repetition of one sound at the beginning of words: house, hesitation, helicopter. **Assonance** and **consonance** repeat vowel or consonant sounds, respectively, but not at the beginning of words.[1] "Mouse" and "lace" share consonant sounds (the spelling does not have to be identical—just the sound). "Mouse" and "lout" share vowel sounds. Assonance marks the list in the last sentence of Bernard Cooper's

---

[1] If both occur together at the end of words, the words rhyme.

essay "The Fine Art of Sighing" (p. 62): "the st<u>ay</u> ropes and c<u>a</u>bles, the counterw<u>ei</u>ghts and s<u>a</u>fety r<u>ai</u>ls."

These devices have historically been used to structure poetry. In Old English alliterative verse, you can tell by listening when a new line has begun because the letter used for alliteration changes, as in the beginning of this riddle about the Old Testament figure, Lot:

Wer sæt æt wīne	mid his wīfum twām
and his twēgen suno	ond his twā dohtor.
[A man sat at wine	with his two wives
and his two sons	and his two daughters.]

Rhyme at the end of lines will do the same thing, telling you when a new line begins, and, if you know the patterns of stanzas, when a new stanza has begun.[2] In modern poetry, and sometimes in other kinds of writing, these devices are usually not structural, but stylistic. They are a way of making language musical and creating emphasis.

Except in political and advertising slogans meant to be catchy, and in some speeches and sermons, civic and argumentative discourse won't rhyme but can use these devices (sparingly) to make prose musical and memorable. Here are two examples of prose, one civic and one academic, that use alliteration for emphasis. In the introductory paragraph of her "Inventing American Reality," Ada Louise Huxtable offers the following: "Some . . . believe the shift mutilates and sells short what it pretends to elevate and embrace."[3] The alliteration (<u>sh</u>ift <u>s</u>ells <u>sh</u>ort; <u>e</u>levate and <u>e</u>mbrace) gives her distinctions weight and earns them attention. Similarly, in an article on what can make an international business team successful, Michael Segalla recommends "vigilant verification"[4]—a vivid vision of a sales success strategy.

You can see how sound patterns can figure into the interpretation of a poem in Zak Owen's paper on Seamus Heaney's "Digging" on p. 37. In fact, Zak considers assonance ("snug," "gun," "rump") and alliteration ("squelch" and "slap") important elements in the meaning of the poem.

As we saw on p. 124, anaphora can give some rhythm to prose; it can do the same for verse. The repetition of phrases at the beginning of lines creates rhythm and structure. For example, Walt Whitman uses anaphora in the following poem (I have put the repeated elements in boldface).

[2]For specific structural patterns, as for different kinds of sonnets, see Appendix B, the Glossary of Literary Terms. Also, see *The Princeton Encyclopedia of Poetry and Poetics*, ed. Alex Preminger, Frank J. Warnke, and O.B. Hardison (Princeton: Princeton University Press, 1974); Paul Fussell Jr., *Poetic Meter and Poetic Form* (New York: Random House, 1965); John Hollander, *Rhyme's Reason: A Guide to English Verse* (New Haven: Yale University Press, 1981).

[3]Ada Louise Huxtable, "Inventing American Reality," *New York Review of Books* (3 July 1992): 191–98.

[4]Michael Segalla, "Factors for the Success or Failure of International Teams: The Special Case of International Research Projects," *Journal of Managerial Psychology*, 13 (1981): 133–36.

From *"Song of Myself," Part 2*

WALT WHITMAN *(For biographical notes, see Chapter 3.)*

Stop this day and night with me and **you shall possess** the origin of all poems,
You shall possess the good of the earth and sun, (there are millions of suns left,)
You shall no longer take things at second or third hand, nor look through the eyes of
    the dead nor feed on the spectres in books,
You shall not look through my eyes either, nor take things from me,
You shall listen to all sides and filter them from your self.   [1881]

"You shall possess," in the first line, is repeated at the start of the next line, and then gets pared down to "You shall," which is repeated in the next three lines. The repetition makes the poem seem almost an incantation, a ritualistic and magical recitation, and so emphasizes the narrator's paradoxical claim: Surrendering yourself to him for the limited period of this poem will make you an independent thinker.

Rhyme creates patterns in poetry, some of which are common enough to have familiar names (for example, **couplets, quatrains,** and **Shakespearean sonnets**). We label the successive rhymes in a poem according to the letters of the alphabet, giving each new rhyming sound a new letter. The sequence of letters, called the **rhyme scheme,** tells us the structure of the verse. The pattern creates an expectation that the poet must follow or purposely violate the rule that the pattern establishes.

One of the most common forms of rhyme in English is the **couplet:** two rhyming lines, often arranged in a sequence (aa bb cc dd ee, etc.). The rhyme scheme of Blake's "The Sick Rose" (p. 117) is abcb defe, with the pattern forming stanzas, or verse "paragraphs." If there were a third stanza, we would expect it to follow the pattern ghih.

Michael Stipe uses both repetition and end rhyme in the following song. (I have put the repeated elements in boldface and the rhymes in italics.)

From *"It's the End of the World as We Know It (And I Feel Fine)"*

MICHAEL STIPE *writes and sings along with Bill Berry, Peter Buck, and Mike Mills as part of the alternative rock group R.E.M. Their albums include "Automatic for the People," "Reveal," "New Adventures in Hi-Fi," and "Document," which includes this song.*

Offer me solutions,
offer me alternatives, and I *decline*.   a

It's the end of the world as we know it.   b
It's the end of the world as we know it.   b
It's the end of the world as we know it and I feel *fine*.   a   [1987]

The strictures and varieties of a number of poetic forms appear in Appendix B.

ACTIVITY 1: *Sound Patterns in John Donne, "The Sun Rising"*

Use the letters of the alphabet to label the rhymes of the poem.

The Sun Rising

JOHN DONNE *(For biographical notes, see p. 256.)*

     Busy old fool, unruly Sun,
     Why dost thou thus,
Through windows, and through curtains, call on us?
Must to thy motions lovers' seasons run?
5   Saucy pedantic wretch, go chide
        Late schoolboys, and sour prentices,
     Go tell court-huntsmen that the king will ride,
     Call country ants to harvest offices,
Love, all alike,° no season knows, nor clime,
10 Nor hours, days, months, which are the rags of time.

     Thy beams, so reverend and strong
     Why shouldst thou think?
I could eclipse and cloud them with a wink,
But that I would not lose her sight so long:
15   If her eyes have not blinded thine,
       Look, and tomorrow late, tell me
     Whether both th'Indias of spice and mine°
     Be where thou leftst them, or lie here with me.
Ask for those kings whom thou saw'st yesterday,
20 And thou shalt hear: "All here in one bed lay."

     She's all states, and all princes I,
     Nothing else is.
Princes do but play us; compared to this,
All honor's mimic, all wealth alchemy.°
25   Thou, sun, art half as happy as we,
      In that the world's contracted thus;

⁹**all alike** unvarying   ¹⁷**both th' Indias of spice and mine** the east Indies (source of spices) and west Indies (source of gold and minerals)   ²⁴**alchemy** counterfeit gold

(Continued)

Thine age asks ease, and since thy duties be
To warm the world, that's done in warming us.
Shine here to us, and thou art everywhere;
This bed thy center is, these walls, thy sphere.° [1633] 30

Underline similar sounds to highlight the assonance, consonance, alliteration, and rhyme. Then write a few paragraphs on the way these sound effects structure the poem and contribute to its impact.

[30]**thy sphere** The image refers to the model of second-century Egyptian cosmologer Ptolemy, in which heavenly bodies revolved in concentric rings around the earth. The Ptolemaic model dominated Western astronomy until Galileo confirmed Copernicus's heliocentric model of what we now call "the solar system." "Everywhere" and "sphere" would have been considered rhymes.

LINE BREAKS IN POETRY

Much poetry in English doesn't rhyme. What makes it poetry, then? The essential characteristic of poetry is not rhyme or alliteration or the other kinds of word music. As we saw in Chapter 3, what distinguishes it from prose is the line break.

When you type on a computer, the setting for page format decides when a new line begins. You hit "return" only for new paragraphs and passages that need special spacing. But if you are writing poetry, you are the one who decides how long a line is and when a new one begins.

This power to determine the length of lines gives poets useful resources for creating experiences for their readers. The first resource is just slowing the reader down.

l(a

E.E. CUMMINGS *(For biographical notes, see p. 538.)*

l(a

le
af
fa

ll

s)
one
l

iness [1958]

This example is so extreme that you can't really read it out loud, but the harvest is rich: the pattern of the mirror-image syllables "af / fa" emerges and we learn that the word "loneliness" contains "one" and the strictly nonsensical but meaningful "one-liness." The single leaf falling becomes a symbol for singlehood and loneliness. Not bad for a four-word poem.

The second resource made available by line breaks is surprise. Punctuation at the end of a line produces a little pause before the next one. If there is no punctuation at the end of a line of poetry, the line is **enjambed,** which means the sentence runs on to the next line and we don't pause at the end of a line when reading it out loud. Even so, there's a little pause as the reader's eye makes the turn to the next line—enough time for expectations to arise about what's coming next. In seventeenth-century poet John Milton's *Paradise Lost,* as Satan watches Adam and Eve and plots their fall, the narrator exclaims,

O Fair Foundation laid wheron° to build
Their ruin!

(4.521–22)

[521]**wheron** on which

"Ruin" is not what usually follows "to build." The line break gives us a split second longer to anticipate the object of the verb as something more positive and thus increases our discomfort when we turn out to be wrong.[5]

Here's an example by Renaissance poet Robert Herrick, whose "Delight in Disorder" we examined in Chapter 6 (p. 126).

Upon a Child

ROBERT HERRICK *(For biographical notes, see p. 126.)*

Here a pretty baby lies
Sung asleep with lullabies:
Pray be silent and not stir
Th'easy earth that covers her.   [1648]

The lullabies of line 2 sing the readers' suspicions to sleep: we assume the "pretty baby" of line 1 is napping. Line 3 ends with the word "stir." Poetic form contributes to our sense of expectations; something will come next to finish the sentence and provide a word that rhymes with "stir" to complete the quatrain. Syntactically, what might we expect? "Stir" could be an intransitive verb and mean "move" or "make a noise," in which case the fourth line could say, "So you will not waken her." It is, then, a rude shock to discover in line 4 that "stir" has an object ("earth") and that the child is dead.

---

[5]My treatment of line break has been shaped by a wonderful article by John Hollander called "'Sense Variously Drawn Out': Some Observations on English Enjambment," in *Literary Theory and Structure: Essays in Honor of William K. Wimsatt,* ed. Frank Brady, John Palmer, and Martin Price (New Haven: Yale University Press, 1973), 201–25. He discusses many striking examples from Milton.

ACTIVITY 2: *Another Version of "Upon a Child"*

Compare the experience of reading Herrick's "Upon a Child" above with the experience of reading this earlier version.

Epitaph Upon a Child That Died

ROBERT HERRICK *(For biographical notes, see p. 126.)*

Here she lies, a pretty bud,
Lately made of flesh and blood:
Who as soon fell fast asleep
As her little eyes did peep.
Give her strewings, but not stir   5
Th'easy earth that covers her.   [1648]

A third resource made available by line break is the expression of various kinds of motion, especially downwardness and turning, since those are the eyes' actions in reading down the page. For example, in John Milton's *Paradise Lost*, the rebellious angels fall from heaven

> . . . with hideous ruin and combustion down
> To bottomless perdition.

> (4.46–47)

The surprise of this line break depends on syntax because the thought is complete; you don't need to go on. But the enjambment leads you on to discover that the angels didn't just fall down; they fell down endlessly. Line 46 has a false bottom that line 47 whisks away to leave the reader with the angels in free fall.[6]

Generally speaking, the more tightly attached the element at the end of one line is to the element that starts the next line, the more pressure there will be to move to the next line. The first line of Herrick's "Upon a Child" exerts little **syntactic pressure**—that is, little urgency to unite the lines—because it is a complete thought. In contrast, e.e. cummings's "a(l" exerts a great deal of pressure because the line break splits a single word into pieces. The stronger that syntactic pressure, the more vulnerable we are to being surprised.

 ACTIVITY 3: *Line Breaks in "Digging"*

Return to Seamus Heaney's poem "Digging" in Chapter 2 (pp. 24–25) and make some notes on how line breaks work in the poem.

---

[6]See John Hollander, "'Sense Variously Drawn Out': Some Observations on English Enjambment."

ACTIVITY 4: *Line Breaks in "Poem"*

Explain how line breaks work in this poem:

Poem

WILLIAM CARLOS WILLIAMS *(For biographical notes, see p. 1092.)*

As the cat
climbed over
the top of

the jamcloset
first the right
forefoot

carefully
then the hind
stepped down

into the pit of
the empty
flowerpot.   [1934]

POETIC METER

The system of describing the rhythmic structures of verse is called
prosody.[7] It codifies and highlights natural elements present in speech.
When we speak, we give different syllables different emphasis or weight.
There are normally three different levels of emphasis given to syllables: **primary,** or heavy stress, **secondary** (relatively less stress), and **unstressed.**
If we use the word *multisyllabic* as an example, we can use accent marks to
show primary stresses on the "u" and the "a," with the "i," "y," and "i" in
the second, third, and fifth syllables unstressed.

múlt ĭ sўl lá bĭc

 ACTIVITY 5: *Marking Stressed and Unstressed Syllables*

Mark the syllables that get relatively more weight in the paragraph above.
For help with the relative stress of multisyllabic words, you can check a
dictionary. Using your annotations, read the paragraph out loud.

Marking the stresses is a way to find the rhythm of language. When rhythm
approaches regular patterns, it is called **meter,** which combines **stressed** and
unstressed (or **accented** and **unaccented**) syllables in verse. Diagramming
metrical patterns by marking stressed and unstressed syllables is called **scanning** a poem, and the system of making such diagrams, **scansion.** To scan

[7]If the word seems too close to "prose," note that it is etymologically related to "ode," a
kind of poem.

verse, we often divide the lines into **feet,** which can be **disyllabic** or **trisyllabic** (two or three syllables long). Here are some common feet:

Disyllabic feet

- iamb: unstressed, stressed: thĕ dánce
- trochee: stressed, unstressed: táblĕ
- spondee: stressed, stressed: "Gét óut!"
- pyrrhic: unstressed, unstressed (almost impossible to demonstrate in isolation)

Trisyllabic feet

- anapest: unstressed, unstressed, stressed (waltz time): ĭntĕrrúpt
- dactyl: stressed, unstressed, unstressed: téndĕrlў, ínfĭltrăte

We name lines of poetry for the kinds of feet and the number of feet they contain, using the Greek prefixes for the number of feet:

- Dimeter: two feet   ˘ / ˘
- Trimeter: three feet   ˘ / ˘ / ˘
- Tetrameter: four feet   ˘ / ˘ / ˘ / ˘
- Pentameter: five feet   ˘ / ˘ / ˘ / ˘ / ˘

The most common line lengths in English poetry are tetrameter and pentameter. The most common kind of verse in English is iambic, because most multisyllabic English words have initial stress, and when you add a definite or indefinite article, iambs result. The same is true when you add an article to a one-syllable word in a stress position:

The fíxture líghts the roóm.
The wórkmen fíxed the streét.
The róck band pláyed a sóng.

The trick with metrical poetry is to follow the pattern of the meter as closely as possible but use language with a rhythm that sounds natural. If readers have to distort the way they usually talk to fit the meter, the verses sound sing-songy and childish. Naturalness might be one way to distinguish between the two versions of Herrick's poem on the dead baby. The slashes indicate the separation of the lines into metric feet:

Hére/ ă prét/ty bá/bў lies
Súng/ ăsleep/ wĭth lúll/ăbiés:
Práy/ bĕ sí/lĕnt ànd/ nŏt stír
Th'eás/ў eárth/ thăt cóv/ĕrs hér.

It reads fairly naturally. Contrast this with the second version:

Hére/ shĕ liés,/ ă prét/tў búd,
Láte/lў máde/ ŏf flésh/ ănd bloód:
Whó/ ăs soón/ fĕll fást/ ăsleép
Ás/ hĕr lít/tle éyes/ dĭd peép.
Gíve/ hĕr stréw/ĭngs, bút/ nŏt stír
Th' eás/ў eárth/ thăt cóv/ĕrs hér.

In this version, the stresses on "Who" in l. 3 and "As" in l. 4 are to my ear a little more strained. Readers probably wouldn't emphasize them if they were in prose. So to surprise, I add more natural meter as a criterion for preferring the shorter version.

 ACTIVITY 6: *Scanning Poetry*

> Use scansion markings to diagram the meter of John Donne's "Sun Rising" (see Activity 1). What is the basic metrical pattern? Where are the metrical variations? Also note where the enjambment pushes you on to the next line.

There are several ways meter gets connected with what a poem says. One way is when the poem is *about* some kind of movement that is associated with a particular pattern. One famous example occurs in Robert Browning's iambic pentameter poem about the Renaissance painter Fra Lippo Lippi, a monk.[8] He watches some girls in the street and notes his reaction to them:

> Scarce had they turned the corner when a titter
> Like the skíp/ping of ráb/bits by moón/light—three slim shapes,
> And a face that looked up . . . zooks, sir, flesh and blood,
> That's all I'm made of . . . .   [1855]

The first line demonstrates the norm in the poem—ten syllables per line in disyllabic feet alternating stressed and unstressed syllables, iambic pentameter. When the girls appear laughing, the meter suddenly shifts into anapests, with thirteen syllables in the line because of this brief trisyllabic moment. How much better anapests can describe the skipping of rabbits—or young girls in a giddy moment—than could iambs! The meter imitates the movement and the spirit of the moment.

As in "Fra Lippo Lippi," in other poems, too, meter often makes its point when there's a variation from the norm: establishment of a pattern, violation of the pattern, and then return to it. After a basically iambic pattern is established, it is very common to find a trochee at the beginning of a line, especially following enjambment. This substitution can give the reader a jolt. Here's the narrator's description of Satan's brooding in Milton's *Paradise Lost*:

> [It] wakes the bitter memory
> Of whát he wás, what ís, and whát must bé
> Wórse: of worse deeds worse sufferings must ensue.
>   (4.24–26)

The meter and syntax of l. 25 seem complete—there are no stresses missing, and the perfectly conventional list of past, present, future seems to have nowhere to go. But the enjambment leads us on, pushes us over into the next

---

[8]I learned about this example from Paul Fussell Jr.'s *Poetic Meter and Poetic Form*.

line where we find an unexpected stress, on an unexpected idea. Satan's fall from heaven might seem bad enough, but apparently greater evil is on the way.

Checklist for Writing about Word Music, Line Breaks in Poetry, and Poetic Meter

_____Does the work use assonance, consonance, alliteration, anaphora, and/or rhyme? Where? Do these features seem arbitrary or do they create emphasis in important places in the work?

_____If the work is poetry, do any of its line breaks contribute to meaning?

_____If the work is metrical poetry, what is the predominant metrical pattern? Where is the pattern varied? How do the variations contribute to the meaning?

 ACTIVITY 7 (GROUP WORK): *Analyzing a Poem*

Following are two poems that use rhythm, meter, syntax, and line break to good effect. Form small groups. Each group should analyze and then report to the class as a whole how one of the poems uses these devices.

When I Heard the Learn'd Astronomer

WALT WHITMAN *(For biographical notes, see p. 44.)*

When I heard the learn'd astronomer,
When the proofs, the figures, were ranged in columns before me,
When I was shown the charts and diagrams, to add, divide, and measure them,
When I sitting heard the astronomer where he lectured with much applause in
  the lecture-room,
How soon unaccountable I became tired and sick,
Till rising and gliding out I wander'd off by myself,
In the mystical moist night-air, and from time to time,
Look'd up in perfect silence at the stars.   [1867]

The Dance

WILLIAM CARLOS WILLIAMS *(For biographical notes, see p. 1092.)*

In Brueghel's great picture,° The Kermess,°
the dancers go round, they go round and
around, the squeal and the blare and the
tweedle of bagpipes, a bugle and fiddles
tipping their bellies (round as the thick-
sided glasses whose wash they impound)°   5

¹See color insert, Figure I-C.   ¹**The Kermess** an outdoor fair in the Low Countries. The word is accented on the first syllable.   ⁶**whose wash they impound** whose fermented liquid they contain

their hips and their bellies off balance
to turn them. Kicking and rolling about
the Fair Grounds, swinging their butts, those
10 shanks must be sound to bear up under such
rollicking measures, prance as they dance
in Brueghel's great picture, The Kermess.   [1944]

WRITING ABOUT SOUND PATTERNS, LINE BREAKS, AND POETIC METER

As you investigate sound patterns, line breaks, and poetic meter in literary works, you will find that they are not all equally important in any given piece. Part of our job as critics is to decide which ones need attention in any particular work. Here is Robert Frost's "Design," followed by an essay assignment and an essay to meet it written by a student named Kenji Takano.

Design

ROBERT FROST *(For biographical notes, see p. 748.)*

I found a dimpled spider, fat and white,
On a white heal-all, holding up a moth
Like a white piece of rigid satin cloth—
Assorted characters of death and blight
5 Mixed ready to begin the morning right,
Like the ingredients of a witches' broth—
A snow-drop spider, a flower like a froth,
And dead wings carried like a paper kite.

What had that flower to do with being white,
10 The wayside blue and innocent heal-all?
What brought the kindred spider to that height,
Then steered the white moth thither in the night?
What but design of darkness to appall?—
If design govern in a thing so small.   [1936]

 ACTIVITY 8: *Writing on Poetry*

> *Purpose:* Write an analysis of a poem using the details of its language (including, where relevant, word choice, figures of speech, word order, sound patterns, line breaks, and meter) to support a claim about its meaning.
>
> *Audience:* Address people who know the poem but want to understand in more detail how it works.
>
> *Documentation:* Use parenthetical references to refer to the poem by line numbers.

Kenji Takano

Prof. Hooker

ENG 207

October 15, 2003

Designing a Poem: The Telling Details in Frost's "Design"

Robert Frost's "Design" turns a morning stroll into an opportunity to ask large questions about why things happen in this world. It involves the reader in these speculations by the way it uses many details of language. We can see how the sonnet works if we look at word choice, figures of speech, word order, sound patterns, line breaks, and poetic meter.

The poem starts out with the narrator's observation of the result of what seems to be a simple event: a spider sitting on a flower has caught a moth. The narrator describes it in appropriately simple language. The syntax is straightforward, with the first two lines providing all the elements of the scene and all the necessary grammatical elements, subject/verb/object. The opening establishes the iambic pattern with one of the most regular lines of the poem. The words are mostly common words that people use in everyday speech. Words like "found," "fat," "white," "holding," and "moth" are originally from Old English, so they seem plain and direct.

Starting in l. 3, the narrator elaborates on the scene by describing it further using figures of speech that add associations that complicate our view. For instance, first he calls the spider a "snow-drop spider" (l. 7). The metaphor, emphasized by the alliteration, starts to make connections among the three elements of the scene. Since a snowdrop *is* a flower (a Eurasian plant of the genus *Galanthus,* commonly white in color), this spider is both *on* a flower and *like* a flower. Is the association a positive one?

We might look at the next image, a simile again empha-sized by alliteration ("a flower like a froth"), to help us answer that question. We encounter froth in a number of circumstances—when we drink beer, when we cook or eat soup or some other food that's boiled or simmered, and when we meet rabid mammals. Like the flower, it tends to be white. Since this simile has both positive and negative connotations, it doesn't answer the question definitively by itself. But it is tempting to add the other nearby similes.

> The scene is
>
> Like the ingredients of a witches' broth—
> A snow-drop spider, a flower like a froth,
> And dead wings carried like a paper kite.
>
> (6—8)

It's hard not to think that the ingredients of l. 7, even though they are pretty innocent by themselves, turn ugly when sandwiched between l. 6 and l. 8.

The cumulative power of the figures of speech decides the answer to our question. The strange rigidity of the satin in l. 3 just adds to the effect. Despite the oddly jolly tone of l. 5 (doesn't it sound like an ad for a breakfast cereal?),[1] the whole scene is rather ominous. Everything matches in color, as if a careful decorator had been at work. But as we find out in the second part of the poem, that is just the problem. Who would decorate in the "characters of death and blight"?

The problem is emphasized by the question that starts l. 9 because the narrator is puzzled about why the heal-all is white since that flower is normally blue. The description of the scene as "Assorted characters of death and blight" may solve the puzzle. Since the word "blight" may be related to the word "bleach," the flower fits into the scene because it has been turned white by disease.[2] Since the word "characters" can refer to marks that are part of writing,

---

[1]The effect is strengthened by the fact that the line starts with one of the few initial spondees in the poem.

[2]C.T. Onions, *The Oxford Dictionary of English Etymology* (Oxford: Oxford University Press, 1966), "Blight," p. 100; Eric Partridge, *A Short Etymological Dictionary of Modern English* (New York: Greenwich House, 1983), "Bleach," #4, p. 49.

the writer of the sonnet is asking whether the "writer" of
the universe uses a destructive alphabet.

The questions of the sonnet's sestet—who arranged this
scene?—leave us with two choices: The first possibility is
that the world is designed and the designer is malevolent,
a force that produces the "design of darkness," which is
emphasized by alliteration (13). If so, the pattern seems
to have a reason for existing: Its purpose is "to appall"
(13). Something wants to shock and horrify whoever sees
this scene. But what is worse, the punning "appall," which
gets emphasis because it is one of the few Latinate words in
the poem, comes from "pallēre," which means "to make pale."[3]
The readers of the poem are, along with the narrator, the
available targets for this whitewashing. No matter what
color we start out, like the blue heal-all, we are made pale
and drawn in to be a part of this scene of destruction. If
we wondered why the spider was called "kindred" in l. 11, we
can now see that it is kin to everything in the scene—not
only the flower and the moth, but also the readers.

Or else there is no force bringing the elements of the
poem together, a possibly even more troubling alternative.
Either we live in a universe guided by a destructive power
that entraps us in its tableaux, or a universe not guided
at all. In a sense the whole poem is a commentary on the
word "design," which can mean either a purposeful pattern
or just an arbitrary pattern produced by chance.

At any rate, these daunting questions are packaged in a
poem that is clearly designed with purpose. The concentrated simplicity of the language is intensified by the unusually small number of rhymes in the poem. Despite repeating
only one word ("white," 1, 9), the rhyme scheme (abba abba
aca acc) uses only three rhyming sounds. That economy makes
the poem a triumph of minimalism, as Frost shows us how
large "a thing so small" can be.

[3]*American Heritage Dictionary* (the same Indo-European root produces *pallid*
and *pallor*).

Now here's a chance for you to try your hand at writing about these elements of literature: Below is Robert Hayden's "Those Winter Sundays," which lends itself to close reading. Use Activity 8 as a guide for an essay about the poem. You may notice that Kenji Takano echoes the writing assignment at the end of his first paragraph, the sentence that announces the agenda of the paper. The paper could then have moved from element to element, taking them in the order of the agenda statement. Proceeding through the poem from top to bottom, as Kenji's paper does, is also an acceptable way to proceed. There is no one right way to organize an essay of this kind.

Those Winter Sundays

ROBERT HAYDEN *(For biographical notes, see p. 906.)*

Sundays, too, my father got up early
and put his clothes on in the blueblack cold,
then with cracked hands that ached
from labor in the weekday weather made
5 banked fires blaze. No one ever thanked him.

I'd wake and hear the cold splintering, breaking.
When the rooms were warm, he'd call,
and slowly I would rise and dress,
fearing the chronic angers of that house.

10 Speaking indifferently to him,
who had driven out the cold
and polished my good shoes as well.
What did I know, what did I know
of love's austere and lonely offices?   [1962]

A CLOSING WORD

Some of the features of language that we examined in Chapters 5 and 6 appear in every kind of text: All writing uses words and puts one after another in a sequence, and all language implies a point of view and a tone of voice. Other features can but do not necessarily appear in every text or every kind of text. Any writer *can* use a simile, but no writer *must* use one. In this chapter, we have looked at some features, such as rhyme, that are important parts of only a few kinds of texts. In this book so far, you have been learning how to recognize these features and notice when they appear in patterns so that you can interpret verbal texts. We started Chapter 4 with a discussion of theme. Now you can see how all the features we have explored contribute to the interpretation of the themes, the central meanings of texts. In the next chapter, we will look more directly at the ways academic writers analyze patterns in order to make arguments.

PART THREE

Argument, Research, and Literature: Conversations among Different Kinds of Writing

Argument

In the earlier chapters of this book, we have seen that literary and nonliterary texts share many features: We can as a rule read expository prose as closely as we read imaginative literature, examining its point of view, word choice, word order, and at times even its symbolism and narrative. In this chapter, we will focus on one feature of nonliterary texts that many literary works do *not* share: argument—not the door-slamming, name-calling kind, but the kind that lays out claims and supports them with reasons and evidence.

Though literature itself is usually not thought of as making arguments (except in the broadest sense of wanting to persuade us of a certain way of viewing the world), we must use argument in order to present our ideas about literature to others. In addition, we will see that understanding other kinds of arguments can sometimes help us better analyze literature. To this end, then, we will examine argument in this chapter—specifically academic argument, which takes place in colleges and universities.

THE ELEMENTS OF ARGUMENT

When everyone agrees, there is no need to argue. Since the observation that every morning the sun appears first in the east is uncontroversial, no one has to make an elaborate argument to defend it. That the earth rotates around the sun, however, is not so easy to observe and was once controversial enough to need support. What is arguable changes in different times and places, but the essential structure of argument does not change. Arguments consist of **claims, reasons, evidence,** and **assumptions.**

Claims

The **claim** in arguments is a statement or proposition that the writer intends to support. All claims want the reader to do or think something, and they all come out of the questions that human beings ask of themselves and their world.

Type of Claim		Questions That Claims Answer	Example
Descriptive claims	Claims of fact	What is true? What things exist? How do they work? What happened?	• School vouchers are violations of the separation of church and state.
	Claims of definition	What are they? What are they made of? What are they part of?	• Microsoft is a monopoly.[1]
	Claims of resemblance; comparison and contrast	What are they like?	• "My love is like a red, red rose."[2]
	Cause and effect	What produces them? What do they produce?	• The military occupation [of Gaza and the West Bank] has made Israel "less secure and less humane."[3]

[1]Joshua Wilner, "Microsoft Declared a Monopoly," *E-Commerce Times*, 5 November 1999, http://www.ecommercetimes.com/perl/story/2479.html (accessed 16 June 2004).

[2]Robert Burns, "A Red, Red Rose."

[3]Ishai Menuchin, "Saying No to Israel's Occupation," *New York Times*, 9 March 2002.

Type of Claim		Questions That Claims Answer	Example
Evaluative claims	Claims of meaning; interpretive claims	What do they signify? How good are they? What is their value?	• *Down from the Mountain* is "an absolutely fabulous album of bluegrass music."[4]
Policy claims		What should we do? What rules should guide our actions?	• "Let's get loud."[5]

In an academic argument, finding claims should be fairly straightforward. Somewhere in the book or essay you should expect to find a clear statement of the main ideas the writer wants to support. Often, as in many essays students write for classes, those ideas will appear at the end of the introduction. Sometimes a journal provides **abstracts,** summaries that appear before the articles; the main claims are likely to appear there as well. The following list provides examples of the different claims different disciplines might make.

Type of Claim	Questions That Claims Answer	Example
Descriptive claims	What exists? (fact)	• Physics: There are three types of neutrinos.[6]
	What happened? (fact)	• History: During the crossing of the Atlantic during the 18th and 19th centuries, mortality was higher among slaves than it was among naval crews and free passengers.[7]
	What are they made of?	• Literary studies: Shakespearean sonnets are 14-line poems with a rhyme scheme of ababcdcdefefgg.
	What are they part of?	• Paleontology: Birds are dinosaurs.[8]

[4]Carrie Attebury, "CD Review: *Down from the Mountain*—Various Artists," *About, Inc.,* http://countrymusic.about.com/library/bldownfromthemountainrev.htm (accessed 16 June 2004).

[5]Jennifer Lopez, "Let's Get Loud," *On the 6,* compact disc, Sony, ASIN: B00000J7RZ, 1999.

[6]Dave Casper, "What's a Neutrino," University of California at Irvine, http://www.ps.uci.edu/~superk/neutrino.html (accessed 16 June 2004).

[7]Raymond L. Cohn, "Maritime Mortality in the Eighteenth and Nineteenth Centuries: A Survey," *International Journal of Maritime History* 1 (1989): 159–91.

[8]University of California, Berkeley, Museum of Paleontology, "DinoBuzz: Current Topics Concerning Dinosaurs, Are Birds Really Dinosaurs?" (revised 22 January 1998), http://www.ucmp.berkeley.edu/diapsids/avians.html (accessed 16 June 2004).

Type of Claim	Questions That Claims Answer	Example
	What are they like? (comparison and contrast)	• Epidemiology: "Low linguistic ability in early life has a strong association with dementia and premature death in late life."[9]
	What produces things? What do things produce? (cause and effect)	• Chemistry: Chlorofluorocarbons damage the ozone layer.[10]
	What do things signify? How do things signify?	• Literary studies: In *Paradise Lost* Milton aims to increase his readers' spiritual capacities by tricking them into making mistakes in interpretation of the verse. They thus learn from Adam's fall by repeating it.[11]
Evaluative claims	How good are things?	• Mechanical engineering: The hydrocarbon mixture R-290/R-600a is a better coolant for small refrigeration units because it is better for the environment than R-12 (Freon) without sacrificing performance.[12]
Policy claims	What should we do? What rules should guide our actions?	• Medicine: Most people diagnosed with multiple sclerosis should quickly begin treatment with one of three available drugs.[13]

ACTIVITY 1: *Identifying Disciplinary Claims*

The list above was not intended to be complete. How would you add to it? For instance:

- What questions might a biologist ask about what something is made of?
- What questions might a sociologist ask about social trends?
- What questions might geologists ask about planet Earth?
- What kinds of claims do researchers in computer science and archaeology make?

[9]David A. Snowdon, Lydia H. Greiner, and William R. Markesbery, "Linguistic Ability in Early Life and the Neuropathology of Alzheimer's Disease and Cerebrovascular Disease: Findings from the Nun Study," *Annals of the New York Academy of Sciences* 903 (2000): 34–38.

[10]M.J. Molina and F.S. Rowland, "Stratospheric Sink for Chlorofluoromethanes: Chlorine Atom Catalyzed Destruction of Ozone," *Nature* 249 (1974): 810.

[11]Stanley Eugene Fish, *Surprised by Sin: The Reader in* Paradise Lost (Berkeley: University of California Press, 1971).

[12]Dongsoo Jung, Chong B. Kim, Byong H. Lim, Hong W. Lee, "Testing of a Hydrocarbon Mixture in Domestic Refrigerators," *ASHRAE Transactions Symposia* 102 (1996): 177–84.

[13]G. Weinstock-Guttman, L.D. Jacobs, "What's New in the Treatment of Multiple Sclerosis?" *Drugs* 59 (2000): 401–10.

ACTIVITY 2: *Identifying the Main Claim*

So that you can do some claim hunting for yourself, here's the first para-graph of an engaging book on language called *Metaphors We Live By*, which was written by linguist George Lakoff and philosopher Mark Johnson. Read the passage carefully. What is the authors' main claim? Where in the para-graph is it located? State it in terms as close as possible to the authors'.

Metaphor is for most people a device of the poetic imagination and the rhetorical flourish—a matter of extraordinary rather than ordinary language. Moreover, metaphor is typically viewed as a characteristic of language alone, a matter of words rather than thought or action. For this reason, most people think they can get along perfectly well without metaphor. We have found, on the contrary, that metaphor is pervasive in everyday life, not just in language but in thought and action. Our ordinary conceptual system, in terms of which we both think and act, is fundamentally metaphorical in nature.

Reasons and Evidence

A claim alone is just an **assertion**—a statement of belief—not an argu-ment. In arguments, claims must be supported with reasons and evidence. Think of a **reason** as a clause that comes after a claim and starts with the word *because*. For instance:

The tomato is a fruit *because* it is the edible, seed-bearing, ripened ovary of a plant.
The tomato is not a fruit *because* the Supreme Court declared it a vegetable in 1893.
The EPA should regulate carbon dioxide emissions *because* they contribute to global warming.
The EPA should not regulate carbon dioxide emissions *because* to do so would hurt the economy.

Reasons have to be backed up with **evidence:** examples, statistics, testi-mony from experts, and, in some cases, personal experience. Biologists can testify about the origin of the edible part of a tomato plant; historians can tell us about why in 1893 the Supreme Court was called upon to define it. Environmentalists can present data about whether or not global warming is occurring, and economists can try to weigh the effects of trying to prevent it. But in all cases, claims worth arguing must be supported.

There are four main requirements for supporting many descriptive claims, which can be easily remembered using the acronym **STAR**.[14] Evidence must be:

- **S**ufficient: There has to be enough of it.
- **T**ypical: Evidence has to be representative, not exceptional.

[14]Richard Fulkerson, *Teaching the Argument in Writing* (Urbana, IL: National Council of Teachers of English, 1996), chapter 6.

- **A**ccurate: Evidence has to be correct.
- **R**elevant: Evidence has to fit the claim.

In the primary research reports of academic discourse, all the things of this world—including both natural objects and what animals and people do and make—are fit subjects of investigation. Evidence in academic arguments, then, consists both of measurement and interpretation of material objects and of observation and interpretation of behavior, whether human or animal. But scholars can't just pile up random pieces of data as evidence to support their claims. The key to drawing conclusions from data involves putting something into a context, that is, placing it next to something else that will reveal something about it.[15] Many academic claims involve this kind of contextualizing. For example, when mechanical engineers Dongsoo Jung, Chong B. Kim, Byong H. Lim, and Hong W. Lee wanted to evaluate an alternative to Freon as a coolant for refrigerators, they had to compare the two substances. Controlled scientific experiments contextualize in exactly this way, by comparing two things or two groups. But claims in disciplines that cannot create control groups in experiments also require comparison, as when paleontologists want to show the relationship between birds and dinosaurs, for example.

ACTIVITY 3: *Supporting a Claim*

> Your friend claims that a significant number of great scientists have also been accomplished in the arts because the two kinds of creativity go together, citing Nobel Prize winners like physicist Richard Feynman, who had one-man shows of his drawings and performed in public on the bongo drum, and other well-known scientists who sculpted, painted, wrote poetry, played instruments, or participated seriously in other arts. You are skeptical about whether the examples he cites can support his claims. What could he do to support them?

Claims, Reasons, and Evidence in Arguments about Literature

Claims about literature come in all varieties and, like claims in most disciplines, they often involve putting something into a context. Sometimes the context comes from the work itself and the claim (a descriptive claim) is that the work is unified (see the entry on "Close Reading and New Criticism" in Appendix A, pp. A-2 and A-3). Or the claim could be that a

---

[15]The word *context* is from the Latin for "to weave together" and is thus related to "textile." Contextualizing thus connects an individual text or object to a larger background. Selecting a different background against which something is displayed can change the way it looks.

particular theme develops in a regular, consistent way throughout the work. In both cases, evidence consists of analysis of passages from different parts of the work to show their similarities and differences. Other claims put a piece of literature into the context of something outside of it (such as other literature that is like it, or something in history or the history of ideas) that can explain what it means, why it was written, or what effect it had on the world.

Here are a few examples of specifically *literary* claims, with discussion of the reasons and evidence necessary to support them:

- **Claims of description** include definition and classification. For instance, to support the claim that "My Last Duchess" is a dramatic monologue, a critic would have to provide a list of characteristics of dramatic monologues and check it against a list of the features of the poem to see if it has all—or enough—of the required characteristics. (The critic and those he or she is trying to persuade have to judge just how many is enough.)

- **Claims of description** can answer the question of how a piece of literature "works." (These claims are based on a metaphor: A poem, of course, has no moving parts, but it is thought of as operating like a machine to produce a given meaning.) In discussing the relationships among various parts of the text (including all the elements discussed in Chapters 4, 5, 6, and 7, such as point of view, narrative, diction, syntax, sequences of images, and so forth), the critic makes it seem dynamic. Showing how it works reveals the text's themes (see Appendix A, New Criticism, pp. A-2 and A-3).

- **Claims of description** can answer the question, "what does it mean?" by showing how the work refers to something outside itself, revealing themes and significance relevant to its audience.

- **Causal claims:** Why did a work get written? What in the author's life or in historical events during his or her lifetime stirred him or her to take up the subject? What previous literary works influenced the work? Did the work cause or influence any actual events?

  An example of a work influencing world events is Harriet Beecher Stowe's *Uncle Tom's Cabin*, which persuaded some people of the justice of the American Civil War through its harsh indictment of slavery. The influences of literary works are rarely quite so easily observed. Catching literature in the act of influencing history is one of the aims of historicism (see Appendix A, pp. A-10 to A-14).

  Causal claims can also focus on the way literary works influence each other, creating a literary history in which scholars reveal, for example, what John Keats learned from Edmund Spenser, what Spenser learned from Geoffrey Chaucer, and what Chaucer learned from his French and Italian sources.

- **Claims of evaluation,** which take the form of **reviews** in both civic and academic argument, are important parts of many interpretive literary arguments. Evaluations pair a work with a set of criteria for what makes something good or bad. Sometimes the context provided for the work being discussed is another work that is similar in some way: perhaps it is of the same genre, by the same author, or from the same time period. Perhaps it is an earlier draft of the same work. In all cases, the standards for judging quality arise from comparison.

There is also some sense of evaluation in many descriptive arguments of interpretation. For example, if a work is said to be an organic whole with a complex meaning to which all its parts contribute, the implication is that it is worthy of close attention.

Assumptions

For an argument to be persuasive, something has to guarantee that a particular reason and a particular claim fit together. This "something" is usually a principle or a rule that will apply in this situation and others. Stephen Toulmin calls such principles **warrants** (a word related to "guarantee" or "warranty," such as that on a consumer product). We can also call them **assumptions** because, although they underpin an argument, they are often unstated.

In earlier chapters, we have seen that readers sometimes need to fill in gaps, and we must do the same with assumptions. Making assumptions explicit gives you tremendous power as both a reader and a writer of argument because it allows you to see whether or not they are really acceptable. Rather than taking them for granted, you can decide whether to grant, or affirm, them.

You can ferret out assumptions by asking the question, "For this reason to support this claim, what else would have to be true?" The answer should take the form of a general rule and therefore should contain a term like *whenever* or *wherever* or *any time*.[16]

Claim: The tomato is a fruit
Reason: because it is the edible, seed-bearing, ripened ovary of a plant.
Assumption: Any edible, seed-bearing, ripened ovary of a plant is a fruit.

As you can see from this example, when the assumption links the claim with the reason very tightly, it can include a term from each of them. But there are other ways to state underlying assumptions:

Claim: The tomato is a vegetable
Reason: because the Supreme Court declared it a vegetable in 1893.
Assumption 1: Whenever the Supreme Court says something is a vegetable, it is a vegetable.
Assumption 2: The Supreme Court has the power to define food.

---

[16]It can be worded with a clause containing *if*: "If you state your assumption as a general rule, it will probably do the job it is meant to do."

The first assumption in this example uses the method of repeating an element from the claim and an element from the reason. The second one states the assumption a little more generally but still makes the link between them. As we will see below, the tomato disagreement need not lead to a war between biologists and the judiciary, but laying it out schematically demonstrates how to discover the assumptions of arguments.

ACTIVITY 4: *Analyzing Claims and Assumptions*

> For each of the paired statements below, answer the following:
> - What kind of claim is this?
> - What are the assumptions that connect the reason with the claim?
>
> **Claim:** The EPA should regulate carbon dioxide emissions
> **Reason:** because they contribute to global warming.
>
> **Claim:** The EPA should not regulate carbon dioxide emissions
> **Reason:** because to do so would hurt the economy.

Assumptions are usually unstated because the audience is expected to know and accept them. They might not be *true*, however, which is why it's important for readers to be aware of them and at times hold them up to the light for examination. In academic argument, the underlying assumptions are often the keys to the methods of the discipline.

Here is an example from psychology. Psychologists Carol Gilligan and Jane Attanucci have distinguished between two basic orientations, one concerned with human relationships (Care orientation) and the other concerned with moral principles (Justice orientation).[17] They interviewed groups of students to see whether there were patterns in men and women's use of the two orientations. For instance, if the research subjects saw a woman stealing money and believed they should report her to the police because stealing is against the law (either religious or secular), they were using the Justice orientation. If they decided not to go to the police because they knew that the woman had recently lost her job and had children to feed, they were using the Care orientation. Gilligan and Attanucci sorted their subjects' descriptions of their dilemmas into the five gradations listed in the table below, then commented on their findings.

---

[17]"Two Moral Orientations: Gender Differences and Similarities," *Merrill-Palmer Quarterly* 34(3), 223–37.

◎◎◎

"Two Moral Orientations: Gender Differences and Similarities"

TABLE 4 *Frequency of Moral Orientation Categories by Gender of Participants*

	Care Only	Care Focus	Care Justice	Justice Focus	Justice Only
Women	5	7	12	6	4
Men	0	1	15	14	16

In Table 4 the distribution of moral orientations for each gender is presented. The statistical test of gender differences is based on a combination of Care Only and Care Focus, as well as a combination of Justice Only and Justice Focus in order to have expected values greater than 5: χ^2 (2, $N = 80$) = 18.33, p < .001. This test demonstrates the relationship between moral orientation and gender in which both men and women present dilemmas in the Care Justice category, but Care Focus is much more likely in the moral dilemma of a woman and Justice Focus more likely in the dilemma of a man. In fact, if women were excluded from a study of moral reasoning, Care Focus could easily be overlooked.

Gilligan and Attanucci are social scientists, but because this research is **quantitative,** that is, it analyzes numerical data in order to draw its conclusions, it shares many terms and methods with the basic and applied sciences. For instance, "N" is the size of the sample, that is, the number of their subjects. "χ^2" is the symbol for the statistical test that is very commonly used to see whether the difference between two groups is greater than a difference that could have been produced randomly. The symbol "p" for "p-value" stands for the probability that the results could have been produced by chance. To call results significant, most researchers demand that p-values be less than .05 (because random coin tossing could have produced the same numbers 5% of the time).[18] In other words, a p-value of .001 is quite good.[19] Nevertheless, since statistical tests are giving a measure of *probability*, not certainty, most scientists state their claims tentatively. Like Gilligan and Attanucci, rather than saying that their results are guaranteed, they are much more likely to say that they are "much more likely."

Now we can lay out the argument Gilligan and Attanucci make:

Claim: "[B]oth men and women present dilemmas in the Care Justice category, but Care Focus is much more likely in the moral dilemma of a woman and Justice Focus more likely in the dilemma of a man"

Reason: because the χ^2 test produced p < .001.

Evidence: Statistics in Table 4.

---

[18]The character "<" means that p is less than .0001. If the open end were on the left, it would mean "greater than."

[19]In general, the smaller the sample size is, the smaller the p-value must be to be persuasive.

Assumption: Any time a statistical test produces a p-value of less than .001, its results probably indicate a significant difference between the groups tested.

This research depends on other assumptions, too—e.g., that 80 subjects are enough and that they were chosen and prompted to speak in ways that do not bias the results. But the assumption about the χ^2 test is instructive because it is fundamental to quantitative research—and the fact that it is so fundamental means that it is hardly ever stated in academic argument. Since academic books and articles are addressed to experts, readers are assumed to understand the nature of statistical tests.

Assumptions in Arguments about Literature[20]

The literary arguments based on close reading that we have been working on in Chapters 4–7 are guided by the principles of formalism, also called New Criticism (see Appendix A, pages A-2 to A-3). Like other disciplines, this kind of interpretation looks for patterns created by the repetition of elements and their variation. We can state some of their common assumptions in the following way:

- If something is repeated, it may be thematically important.
- If a pattern is created by a number of repetitions of an element, a subsequent change to this element may be thematically important. This might be seen, for example, in a shift in meter (say, a nonmetrical passage in a mostly metrical poem) or diction (e.g., a word that is repeated but suddenly appears in a different, disorienting context).
- If every time one element appears, another is also repeated, the connection between them may be thematically important.
- If a work repeats or varies a pattern that is also seen outside of the work, for instance, in the life of the author or in a social or political phenomenon of the author's time, it may be thematically important.
- If a work seems to refer to an external code of significance (e.g., religious or cultural iconography), multiple references or kinds of reference will make the relevance of that code more plausible.
- If a work that appears on the surface to be simple can be shown to have a deeper complexity, or if a work that appears to be disjointed, riven by tensions and contradictions, can be shown to have a deeper unity, it may be evaluated positively.

In addition, the practice of close reading is based on some other deep-seated assumptions, for instance, that a good interpretation discovers unity in a work of literature, but not easily discovered unity. In other words,

---

[20]This list is similar to that of Jeanne Fahnestock and Marie Secor in "The Rhetoric of Literary Criticism," in *Textual Dynamics of the Professions: Historical and Contemporary Studies of Writing in Professional Communities*, ed. by Charles Bazerman and James Paradis (Madison: University of Wisconsin Press, 1991), 76–96.

literary works thought to be worthy of sustained attention are complicated and may be full of tensions and contradictions. New Critics look to see how the tensions and contradictions are resolved. Post-structuralists find them irresoluble. But exploring a work's significant features and the relationships among them is often the first step in finding its meaning.

The student papers included in earlier chapters all show the deep-seated influence of some of these assumptions. In Chapter 2, Zak Owen's awareness of the narrator's contradictory feelings about his forebears in Seamus Heaney's "Digging" helped him shape his thesis statement for the paper. How the narrator resolved them was central to the finished paper. Some of the key evidence Zak offered was the repetition-with-a-difference of the poem's first lines at the end. Zak also piled up examples of word play throughout the poem as evidence that delight in language helped the narrator come to his resolution at the end. In the same way, Derrick White, in discovering similarity between the two seemingly dissimilar narrators of Borges's "Shape of the Sword," finds a pattern. Out of what seems to be diversity, he discovers unity that is a key to the meaning of the work.

Checklist for Finding Assumptions

_____What it would take to guarantee or "warrant" the connection between the claim and the reasons; that is, what makes this a good reason for this claim?

_____Can you state it as a principle or a rule that can be applied to many different situations?

_____Does it include one term from the claim (or a pronoun or more general synonym that refers to a term in the claim) and one term from the reason (or a term that refers to the reason)? (The related term will probably be more general than the one in the claim because now you are stating a principle or rule that can be applied to many different situations.)

_____Does it refer to the belief or action recommended by the claim?

_____Can you state it to include words like *all, any time, whenever,* or *wherever?*[21]

_____Is it likely to be accepted by the audience of this argument?

_____What other broader assumptions underwrite the combination of claims and reasons? That is, what other assumptions are needed to support the main one?

---

[21]These words are not always necessary but it is sometimes helpful to use them. Another formulation of a rule might use the word *if:* E.g., "If a mass of cold air meets a mass of warm air at the correct layer of the atmosphere, it usually rains at the edge of the fronts"; "if you do not take in as many calories as your body burns, you will lose weight."

ACTIVITY 5: *Finding Claims, Evidence, and Assumptions in Literary Argument*

What are some of the claims and assumptions in Kenji Takano's interpretation of Robert Frost's poem "Design" on page 141? What kind of evidence does he use?

ACTIVITY 6: *Identifying Claims, Reasons, and Assumptions*

Lay out the claims, reasons, and assumptions for this abstract from a medical article.

Mortality Associated with Sleep Duration and Insomnia

DANIEL F. KRIPKE, MD; LAWRENCE GARFINKEL, MA; DEBORAH L. WINGARD, PHD; MELVILLE R. KLAUBER, PHD; MATTHEW R. MARLER, PHD[22]

Background Patients often complain about insufficient sleep or chronic insomnia in the belief that they need 8 hours of sleep. Treatment strategies may be guided by what sleep durations predict optimal survival and whether insomnia might signal mortality risks.

Methods In 1982, the Cancer Prevention Study II of the American Cancer Society asked participants about their sleep duration and frequency of insomnia. Cox proportional hazards survival models were computed to determine whether sleep duration or frequency of insomnia was associated with excess mortality up to 1988, controlling simultaneously for demographics, habits, health factors, and use of various medications.

Results Participants were more than 1.1 million men and women from 30 to 102 years of age. The best survival was found among those who slept 7 hours per night. Participants who reported sleeping 8 hours or more experienced significantly increased mortality hazard, as did those who slept 6 hours or less. The increased risk exceeded 15% for those reporting more than 8.5 hours sleep or less than 3.5 or 4.5 hours. In contrast, reports of "insomnia" were not associated with excess mortality hazard. As previously described, prescription sleeping pill use was associated with significantly increased mortality after control for reported sleep durations and insomnia.

Conclusions Patients can be reassured that short sleep and insomnia seem associated with little risk distinct from comorbidities. Slight risks associated with 8 or more hours of sleep and sleeping pill use need further study. Causality is unproven.

[22]Daniel F. Kripke, MD; Lawrence Garfinkel, MA; Deborah L. Wingard, PhD; Melville R. Klauber, PhD; and Matthew R. Marler, PhD, "Mortality Associated with Sleep Duration and Insomnia," *Archives of General Psychiatry* 59 (2002): 131–36.

Qualifiers and Concessions

In our complicated world, most claims are not absolutely true or absolutely false. *Most* fruits are the edible, seed-bearing, ripened ovaries of plants—but not *all* of them are edible. So how you define that item before you on the cutting board depends on how heavily you weigh the different criteria.

Qualifiers can limit the scope of a claim so that it does not seem too extreme. To take account of the complexity of the biological definition, we could say:

> According to most biological criteria, the tomato is a fruit.
>
> or
>
> The tomato is sometimes thought of as a fruit.
>
> or
>
> The tomato is more like a fruit than a vegetable.

To limit claims and reasons having to do with cause and effect, words like *sometimes* or *might* or *can* or *help* are good qualifiers. Many scientists claim that their data "suggest" a conclusion, rather than prove it.

Thinking out the logic of an argument can help us present it to an audience more effectively. Since every point worth arguing has an opposition, arguers have to take the opposition's point of view into account. Understanding claims in the context of the disagreement and understanding the opposition can strengthen them by making arguers look more reasonable. In terms of the Communications Triangle we looked at in Chapter 1 (Figure 1, p. 5), considering the opposition contributes to the *ethos*, or credibility, of the person making the argument. The Supreme Court, after all, did have reasons for classifying tomatoes as vegetables in 1893: Since they are eaten more often with the main meal than as dessert or snacks (another criterion for the definition), it makes some sense to treat them as vegetables for commercial purposes, which is why tomatoes appeared before the Supreme Court in the first place.

To take account of the different kinds of experts who define tomatoes, we could say:

> If we use biological definitions, the tomato is a fruit.
> If we use legal definitions, the tomato is a vegetable.

Or we could concede that our opponents have some right on their side:

> Although the tomato shares many of the characteristics of fruit, it is legally defined as a vegetable.
> Although the tomato is legally defined as a vegetable, many biologists consider it a fruit.

You will be able to find qualifiers and concessions in much academic argument because human research methods rarely produce absolute certainty and controversial subjects are rarely laid permanently to rest.

ACTIVITY 7: *Defining Pluto*

Using principles for interpreting word order and syntax that appear on pp. 122–125, consider the differences among the statements below. How does each one represent the relationship between the two different definitions of Pluto?

1. While long classified as a planet, Pluto is probably a Kuiper Belt object.
2. While probably a Kuiper Belt object, Pluto has long been classified as a planet.
3. Although Pluto is still present on solar system maps as the ninth planet, many astronomers consider it a Kuiper Belt object.
4. Although many astronomers consider it a Kuiper Belt object, Pluto is still present on solar system maps as the ninth planet.
5. "While traditionally classified as a planet, Pluto more likely is a Kuiper Belt object that was pushed into an erratic, Neptune-crossing orbit billions of years ago, according to astronomers."[23]
6. According to astonomers, while Pluto is traditionally classified as a planet, it is more likely a Kuiper Belt object that was pushed into an erratic, Neptune-crossing orbit billions of years ago.

As we have already seen, because of the questions they ask and the methods they use, the disciplines deal in probabilities more than absolutes. This fact makes qualifications an important part of academic argument. Aside from contributing to credibility, qualifying arguments also makes good psychological sense because writers might feel less vulnerable if they are the first to point out the difficulties with their positions.

For example, in his book *Masculinity in the Making*, anthropologist David D. Gilmore wants to claim that in many cultures males must "earn" their masculinity by undergoing tests or trials, whereas females "earn" their femininity differently. In making this claim, Gilmore first has to contend with the argument among anthropologists about whether the differences among cultures are deep or only superficial. He can't settle this argument. But he describes it in order to move past it toward his real subject:

> Whether or not culture is only a thin veneer over a deep structure is a complicated question. . . . But most social scientists would agree that there do exist striking regularities in standard male and female roles across cultural boundaries regardless of other social arrangements (Archer and Lloyd 1985:283–84). The one regularity that concerns me here is the often dramatic ways in which cultures construct an appropriate manhood—the presentation or "imaging" of the male role. In particular, there is a constantly recurring notion that real

[23]Richard Stegner, "Biggest Object in Solar System Found Since Pluto," CNN Science and Space, 7 October 2002, http://www.cnn.com/2002/TECH/space/10/07/ice.object/index.html (accessed 16 June 2004).

manhood is different from simple anatomical maleness, that it is not a natural condition that comes about spontaneously through biological maturation but rather is a precarious or artificial state that boys must win against powerful odds.[24]

In the first sentence, Gilmore deals with the insoluble conflict by acknowledging that it exists and that he isn't going to solve it in this book. Then, in the second sentence, he gives a moderate statement somewhere between the extremes of "they're all the same" and "they're all different." Whatever the truth of the matter, he claims that most social scientists can agree on some "striking regularities." (Note the qualifier "most." There's room for a few who disagree.) Having carved out this middle way, he goes on to state his own thesis.

OTHER FEATURES OF ACADEMIC ARGUMENT

Research Context

All writers must create a context for their own work by choosing the past work that reveals the conflict, the problem, the question, or the gap that their own work addresses. Academic arguments sometimes also look ahead to future work, as well.[25] If you've found a way to shrink cancerous tumors, you undoubtedly think research should go on until your technique is curing as many cancers as possible. As we have seen, scientists usually make this kind of claim in understated ways. Xianming Huang and his team say their work on shrinking tumors in mice by cutting off the blood supply is "an intriguing approach to the eradication of primary solid tumors and vascularized metastases."[26] "Eradication" is a strong promise, but the definition of two particular kinds of tumors limits the claim and "intriguing" is the way the scientists refrain from announcing that they discovered the cure for cancer.

Form

The way academic research reports are arranged depends partly on field and partly on genre. Some differences depend on the style manuals imposed by specific journals. For instance, some journals provide abstracts and some do not. Primary research reports in the sciences and quantitative social sciences

[24]David D. Gilmore, *Masculinity in the Making: Culture Concepts of Masculinity* (New Haven, CT: Yale University Press, 1990), 10–11.

[25]Sometimes cues for future work come out of qualifications and concessions. If you have to acknowledge a problem, you might also want to be the one to solve it, as if you were catching your own rebound.

[26]See for example, Xianming Huang, Grietje Molema, Steven King, Linda Watkins, Thomas S. Edgington, Philip E. Thorpe, "Tumor Infarction in Mice by Antibody-Directed Targeting of Tissue Factor to Tumor Vasculature," *Science* 275 (24 January 1997): 547–50. Their vision of the path for future research is on pp. 549–50.

often have section headings of "Introduction," "Methods," "Results," and "Discussion" (called IMRAD for short). Articles in the humanities and qualitative social sciences tend not to use section headings at all, or, if they do, they are likely to describe the subject matter of the section.

Even without the IMRAD labels, research findings still have to report what got done and what happened. These reports don't, however, usually report all of the false starts, dead ends, crises in confidence, and corrections that produce the final results. Like fictional narrative, they structure the sequence of events to make them rhetorically effective. But the significant methods that produce the results are always present in some way.

In literary arguments that involve close reading, the narrative that makes its way into publication won't begin, "On these dates and at these times I went to the library." When literary critics interpret literature, defining and applying the framework they use for interpretation *is* the "method." Yet, probably no two literary critics apply the same framework to a poem in exactly the same way.

In experimental sciences, however, someone else has to be able to repeat the experiment and get similar results. Outcomes cannot depend on who did it or where it got done. Two physicists claimed some years ago that they had managed to achieve cold fusion, which would have been an enormous energy source without the dangers and dangerous waste products of nuclear fission. Their claim was rejected because no one else could repeat their results.

Style

We already embarked on a study of style in writing in Chapters 4–6 when we talked about tone of voice, diction, and syntax. And we had already begun to explore academic style when comparing Pam Bullock's *New York Times* account of the Nun Study to the scientific research she was reporting (see Activity 5 on p. 13 in Chapter 1). You probably noticed the differences in paragraph length, level of diction, and syntax between the two passages. You may have been surprised to find the scientists using first person pronouns, whereas journalists can't. Academic prose is famously not zippy or graceful because the serious business of advancing knowledge is transacted mostly with sober dignity. But there is some room for personal choices.

Some stylistic distinctions depend on academic discipline. Experimental scientists and social scientists, especially quantitative ones, are known for the use of the passive voice and complex strings of nouns (to get in the spirit, maybe I should say "noun strings").[27] Here's an example by Xianming Huang's team trying to shrink cancer tumors: "The IFN-γ secreted by the tumor cells induces local expression of major histocompatibility complex class II antigens (I-A^d and I-E^d) on the tumor vascular endothelium" (547).[28] Some adjectives sneak in there, but the nouns are denser than in the writing of most humanists.

[27]Alan G. Gross, *The Rhetoric of Science* (Cambridge: Harvard University Press, 1990), 70.

[28]See above for full reference to this article.

There is a logic to this style. For one thing, it condenses narrative and classification. The sentence needn't say, "*First* the tumor cells secreted the substance, *and then* the substance induced the tumor vascular endothelium to express the antigens *which are of* the histocompatibility Class II." The passive verb and the noun strings are much more compact—harder to read, maybe, but efficient. Perhaps the more important advantage is the way they combine to foreground the physical objects and events that science investigates.[29] The world, not the investigator, is the focus.

The right style is part of the equipment for getting your ideas heard in a discipline. And so is knowing where to use it. Rhetorician Kathryn Riley has claimed that passive verbs appear most frequently in the methods and results sections of scientific articles.[30] If a team has done an experiment, it shouldn't make much difference who did what. If it does make a difference, that means replication isn't possible, which is a problem, since replicability is the goal. So it makes sense to say, not "Smith heated it and Jones titrated it," but rather "It was heated and titrated." In fact, Huang et al. do use the first person and Riley's analysis correctly predicts when it appears—in the introduction of their article (paragraphs 2 and 3: "We explored the feasibility . . ."; "We reasoned that . . ."; "To test this concept, we used . . .") and in the last paragraph ("Our experiments illustrate . . .").

Humanists and social scientists have at least as much leeway in deciding whether to use the first person. For them, too, conclusions and the end of introductions are likely places to find it. But they can sometimes be less diffident than scientists in the way they state their claims. Notice the way political scientist Andrew Scott introduces a journal article:

From "Henry George, Henry Adams, and the Dominant American Ideology"[31]

Americans are generally considered, and generally consider themselves, to be nonideological. Our most notable political thinkers died before the industrial age was fairly under way, and systematic political and social doctrines have not flourished in the United States since the early days of the Republic. Acceptance of formal theory, however, is not the only way to be ideological. In this article, I will argue that a matrix of assumptions, precepts, injunctions and cultural values has persisted in America for some time and constitutes a dominant ideology. The content of this ideology has inhibited those associated with the growth of complexity and interdependence.

I will look at certain aspects of the writings of Henry George and Henry Adams and will argue that, despite the fact that these men are familiar figures, important elements in their thought have been persistently overlooked.   [234]

---

[29]Gross, *The Rhetoric of Science* 72–73.

[30]Kathryn Riley, "Passive Voice and Rhetorical Role in Scientific Writing," *Technical Writing and Communication* 21 (1991): 239–57.

[31]Andrew M. Scott, "Henry George, Henry Adams, and the Dominant American Ideology," *South Atlantic Quarterly* 76 (1977): 234–51.

Scott uses the first person at the start of his article, both to lay out his claim ("I will argue that a matrix . . ."; "I . . . will argue that despite . . .") and to lay out his procedure ("I will look at certain aspects . . ."). Now his readers know *what* they will get if they read this article and *how* they will get it. Furthermore, the claim that they hear is not limited by qualifiers. This boldness is something we rarely see in quantitative research—an unapologetically causal claim: "The content of this ideology has inhibited . . ."

No matter what the conventions of a discipline, the rules aren't inflexible, and there are always individual choices to be made. Much depends upon the personality and preferences of writers—and their talents for communicating. According to rhetorician John Swales, the average length of sentences in academic prose is twenty-five words.[32] But an average doesn't tell us much about sentence structure or the rhythm established by the alternation of long and short sentences, which can be hallmarks of individual style.

 ACTIVITY 8: *Analyzing Academic Style*

> Most of the excerpts we have examined in this chapter have been primary research reports. Here's part of the introduction of a book review, a different academic genre. After you read it, compare its style to the style of the other academic passages in this chapter. Make sure your claims are backed up with reasons and evidence.
>
> ### *"Site Reading"*[33]
>
> #### NICHOLAS J. SAUNDERS
>
> Of all the issues in American archaeology, few have been so bitterly contested as that concerning the origins of the continent's human settlers. . . . Until now, there have been two schools of thought: that championing the Clovis people around 11,000 years ago, and another that favoured much earlier dates, anywhere between 13,000 and 30,000 years ago. . . .
>
> Those who advocated a pre-Clovis human presence saw their discoveries undermined by accusations of controversial dating, problematic stratigraphy, wishful thinking and endless debates about whether or not chipped stones and bones were manmade tools or naturally occurring 'eco-facts.'
>
> Into this cockpit of competing egos and academic reputations came Tom D. Dillegay and the Chilean site of Monte Verde in 1997. From the start, Monte Verde was excitingly different. . . .   [145]

---

[32]John Swales, *Genre Analysis: English in Academic and Research Settings* (Cambridge: Cambridge University Press, 1990), 115.

[33]Nicholas J. Saunders, "Site Reading" (rev. of *Monte Verde—A Late Pleistocene Settlement in Chile*, Vol. 2: *The Archaeological Context and Interpretation*), *Nature* 392 (12 March 1998): 145. *Nature* is a British journal, hence the spelling of "favoured."

◎◎◎

Checklist for a Descriptive Analysis of Academic Argument

Determining purpose:

_____What is the genre of the piece you are analyzing? (Is it a primary research report? Review article that synthesizes many sources? Review of a single book? Something else?)

_____To what kind of audience is it addressed? What does it aim to offer its readers?

Analyzing argument:

_____What is the main claim? Are there others? Where are they given?

_____What are the reasons?

_____What kinds of evidence support the reasons?

_____What are the assumptions? Are they stated explicitly?

_____Are any qualifications given?

Analyzing the research context:

_____What is the narrative of previous research that shapes the field in such a way as to make the current work necessary?

_____Does the writer make suggestions for the direction of future research? Where?

_____How are other researchers referred to in the text? By name? Through reference flags only?

_____Are there quotations from previous work? What are they used for?

_____What documentation system is used? Is it the system used most commonly by that discipline?

_____What are the elements of the citations? Title? Date? Place of publication? Page number? Other information? In what order are they given?

Analyzing form:

_____How is the piece structured: Is it divided into sections? What kind of titles do they have?

_____Where do the different parts of the argument appear?

_____Does the arrangement of the piece help make the ideas clear or does it obscure them?

_____What functions do the various parts of the piece perform?

Analyzing style and rhetorical relationships:

_____What is the general level of diction? How can you tell?

_____Are there individual words that deviate from the most dominant level of diction? What is their effect on style? Are they lively variations or do they strike you as inappropriate? Is there a large percentage of technical terms?

_____What is the general sentence length?

_____Are there a variety of sentence lengths? Are they managed effectively for emphasis, for instance through a sequence of long sentences followed by a short dramatic one or short and building to long?

_____Are there a variety of sentence structures? Are they managed so as to put emphasis on the important elements? Is there smooth flow between sentences? Is subordination used to indicate logical relationships?

_____What relationship is established between writer and reader? How present is the writer in the text? Is the first person used? Whom does it include? Do active or passive verbs predominate? Are the different kinds distributed evenly in all parts of the piece or concentrated in specific sections? Does the implied relationship between writer and reader change in different parts of the piece?

_____What is the relationship between writer and subject matter? Is it implied or overt? What, if anything, reveals it?

ACTIVITY 9: *Writing a Comparative Analysis of Two Academic Arguments*[34]

Choose two very different academic disciplines, such as music history and biochemistry or engineering and archaeology. Choosing different *kinds* of fields (historical and experimental, for instance, interpretive vs. quantitative) will help you choose papers that are different. Find a paper that interests you in each field. Photocopy them and turn in the copies with your drafts.

Purpose: Write an essay characterizing them and claiming that the differences between them indicate something about the nature of the writing in the fields they are part of. Use the categories in the Checklist for a Descriptive Analysis of Academic Argument as guides. Remember that every description is a claim of fact that may need to be substantiated by examples from the chosen text.

References: Use the MLA documentation system, consulting Appendix D of this book.

Note: This assignment can be done collaboratively.

[34]This assignment as well as some of the categories of analysis in this chapter (especially research context and form) have been influenced by Chris M. Anson and Dennis L. Wilcox, *A Field Guide to Writing* (New York: Addison-Wesley, 1992).

SAMPLE STUDENT PAPER*

Rami Al-Khalidi

Michael Cheng

Deborah Cooper

Susan O'Quinn

Mr. Porter

English 113

January 26, 2004

A Comparative Analysis of Two Academic Arguments: Carol
Gilligan and Jane Attanucci, "Two Moral Orientations:
Gender Differences and Similarities" and Jennifer Mather
Saul, "Women's 'Different' Voice"

Despite the fact that Carol Gilligan and Jane
Attanucci's "Two Moral Orientations: Gender Differences and
Similarities" and Jennifer Mather Saul's "Women's
'Different' Voice" are about the same thing, they look very
different (Gilligan and Attanucci, 1988; Saul, 2003). You
might think that the reason they look different is that they
disagree, but that's not the case. If we examine them both
in more detail, we will be able to see the real reasons for
their different features. This essay will compare them
by looking at their ways of setting up a relationship to
previous research, their methods of arguing, their format,
and their style in order to show why they differ.

Relationship to Previous Research

Every academic argument has to show how it is rooted
in—but yet goes beyond—previous research. This usually
happens at the beginning because the researchers have to
show on the one hand that they know the literature and
on the other hand that there is still something missing.
Conclusions could be extended or there's a problem that
needs to be solved. For Gilligan and Attanucci, there are
several problems: the one about method is that subjects in
experiments were asked about hypothetical moral situations

*Portions of these sources are posted on the Web site www.mhhe.com/ferster.

and not real ones. They think real ones are better (paragraph 2). Another problem is that "Psychologists studying moral development have equated morality with justice" (8). This is especially true of L. Kohlberg, who was very influential. If women use the care orientation more than the justice orientation (defined in paragraph 6), this equation is inaccurate because it leaves women out. You could almost say that it is unjust. So they designed their study to find out first if people tend to use one orientation more than another and second if men and women are different (17). Their research questions come out of their analysis of what's wrong with previous research.

Saul's research questions come out of her analysis of what's wrong with Gilligan. Although she does not specifically examine the 1988 article written with Attanucci, her overall criticisms of Gilligan's work apply to this article, too, because Gilligan's focus is still pretty much trying to correct Kohlberg. So in order to establish her own relationship to previous research, Saul has to look at what Kohlberg says and what Gilligan says about what Kohlberg says, focusing mostly on Gilligan's book *In a Different Voice* (1982). She repeats pretty extensively the views of each, down to Kohlberg's scale of moral development (10) and even the views of both on the examples of Jake and Amy. Saul praises some of what Gilligan does, saying that she "beautifully" exposes the sexism of past psychology and "rightly" criticizes Kohlberg (9, 12). But she also promises to "take a close and critical look at the consequences of her claims" (9).

Gilligan and Attanucci obviously think that Kohlberg is important because otherwise they would not spend so much time attacking him, but they never praise him the way Saul praises Gilligan. Aside from that, the arguments are very similar in the way they establish their relationships to previous research.

Methods of Arguing

The chief difference between the two arguments is that Gilligan and Attanucci actually did experiments and Saul just read things and thought about them. That means that the psychologists set up groups to compare with each other, the comparisons produced numbers, and the numbers were run through the χ^2 test, a statistical test that separates meaningful results from results that could have been produced by chance. Saul did not do experiments. She compares things, but what she compares is Gilligan with Kohlberg, the researcher who came before her, and Gilligan with the researchers who came after her. She does not have numerical data but she has her own ideas and observations.

There are really two reasons for the differences between the arguments. One is that the disciplines of the writers are different. Gilligan and Attanucci are psychologists who do quantitative research, while Saul is a philosopher who does not work with numbers. Another is that the genres are different. "Two Moral Orientations" is a primary research report, while "Women's 'Different' Voice" is a commentary. The whole chapter can almost be seen as a review article in which the author summarizes and analyzes the trends in a field.

Format

The most obvious difference is that the Gilligan and Attanucci article uses the IMRAD format, giving an introductory literature review section and then labeled sections for "Methods," "Results," and "Discussion." The "Method" section is further broken down into sections with labels according to their topics and the authors give the data in the form of tables. Saul cannot do that because she did not count anything. She divides her argument into subcategories with labels like "Women's Moral Thinking" and "Criticisms of Kohlberg," but they relate to her subject matter, not the scientific method. This difference has to do with the writers' different disciplines and the different genres they write in, primary research report versus commentary and analysis.

Both pieces use the APA system for documenting sources, with parenthetical citations in the text and a list of References at the end. They are different in their parenthetical habits in that when Gilligan and Attanucci mention the name of a previous researcher in their text, they do not repeat the name inside the parentheses (e.g., 24). Saul does. Saul is also different in that she often includes page numbers from the sources that she cites. This modification is an option with the APA system. It is not clear exactly why Saul, a humanist, chooses the social science system in the first place.

Style

Both pieces proceed with pretty conventional academic styles with medium long sentences and middle level diction. Some of Saul's paragraphs are notably longer (e.g., 9). Gilligan and Attanucci, unsurprisingly, use more undefined technical terms and symbols ("binomial distribution," "χ^2 goodness of fit test," "N," 29); this is the language of quantitative research. They are also slightly less expressive of feelings than Saul. While she is willing to say that something is "shocking" (9), they report the fact that "if women were excluded from a story of moral reasoning, Care Focus could easily be overlooked" (30) in a mild, almost deadpan manner. They don't react; they just report. They do not chide Piaget for thinking that since the judgments of girls are "anomalous," it is better to study boys as moral thinkers. They let readers draw their own conclusions about his sexism. In contrast, Saul is willing to say that "claims about male and female nature have a long and often *ugly* history (emphasis ours 58)."

Gilligan and Attanucci use a lot of passive verbs ("The distinction . . . was made," 2) and often use the impersonal constructions of science. They often make their study rather than themselves the subjects of their sentences: "The present exploration . . . has demonstrated" (34), "This finding provides . . . " (36), "The findings presented here suggest . . . " (40). The two stylistic habits come together in a very important sentence, the beginning of the last paragraph of the introduction, which is a kind of statement of their agenda in the article: "In the present study two questions were posed . . . " (17).

Once in a while they refer to themselves in the first person, for instance "we offer" (44), "our findings" (39), and "our research" (44), but not very often. When they do use the first person, it is in the discussion section, where many scientists are willing to step forward and identify with their claims. They do not do it boldly, but they do it.

The other thing that Gilligan and Attanucci have in common with natural scientists is their modesty about their claims. They once say that their exploration "has demon-strated" (34) but that's as definitive as they get. They use the verb "suggest" (40; see also 35, 45), discuss ways that their results could possibly be skewed (43), and use the word "likely" to describe the tendency of females to use the care orientation (30). This vocabulary is very much in keeping with the talk of scientists who use statistical tests to analyze data. What statistical tests reveal is probability. That's probably why they go on to discuss possible directions of future research (39): They know their results are not definitive or final. They are modest here, too: further research "*may* expand" knowledge (emphasis ours 47).

Saul makes a gesture of humility when she says that "it is difficult to discern" differences between men and women and "what consequences follow from these differences" (56), but after that, draws "some points" from the debate, seeming much more confident than Gilligan and Attanucci in her claims. For instance, she says, without hedging, "it is wrong either to praise or to condemn traditionally female traits and activities simply on the grounds that they are *traditionally* female" (emphasis original). She urges caution on feminists who think about moral orientation, but gives advice definitively: "We should always move with great caution . . . " (57). These judgments rest on her analysis of the psychological literature and she states them confidently.

Saul's use of first person pronouns is slightly different from Gilligan and Attanucci's. She uses "me" once (54) and "we" more than they do (55, 57), not to say she has a co-author, but to refer to herself and her readers together (9, 57). However, she is like Gilligan and Attanucci in the way she places her first person pronouns in sections that could be called her discussion.

These two arguments address the same topic and in fact represent a subject on which philosophy and psychology come together. But examination of how they set up their relationships to previous research, their methods of arguing, their formats, and their styles reveals differences that have more to do with their different disciplines and different genres than they do with the convergence of their subject matters.

Works Cited

Gilligan, Carol, and Jane Attanucci. "Two Moral Orientations: Gender Differences and Similarities." Merrill-Palmer Quarterly 34 (1988): 223-37.

Saul, Jennifer Mather. "Women's 'Different' Voice." Feminism: Issues & Arguments. New York: Oxford University Press, 2003. 199—231.

CHAPTER NINE

Exploring Literature through Other Disciplines

Much of Part II is concerned with interpreting literature by reading it closely, without much "background information" about its author's life or the time in which it was written. Then in Chapter 8, when we explored the elements and strategies of academic argument, we saw that making a claim about the meaning of a literary work involved more than merely gathering sufficient amounts of relevant evidence from the work. It involved choices about which elements were significant and how they might form patterns in the work. We saw that literary criticism, like most other disciplines, provides methods that allow researchers to make and support claims about the significance of the patterns, as well as assumptions that link claims and reasons.

These assumptions form the methodology of the discipline and give us a framework with which to approach individual pieces of literature. In literary studies, another source of frameworks that can help interpret literary texts is other academic disciplines. This is not unusual in the academy—there is a great deal of cross-fertilization among different fields of study. Literary critics join enthusiastically in this exchange of ideas and methods, borrowing good ideas wherever they are available. You can see some of the results in Appendix A—critical approaches that employ some of the best ideas of psychologists, historians, sociologists, anthropologists, and political scientists. The purpose of this chapter is to help you invent and apply such interpretive frameworks for yourself.

INTERPRETIVE FRAMEWORKS IN ACADEMIC DISCOURSE

Imagine yourself looking through the lens of a camera. The world you see is different from what you see of the world unframed. The frame selects out just a portion of what is visible and it puts something in the middle and other things around the periphery. If you turn or move the camera up or down, you will create a different picture. Something else will be in the center and it will have a different relationship to what surrounds it.

The painting mentioned in Auden's poem "Musée des Beaux Arts" (p. 127) demonstrates how crucial framing is because the subject for which the painting is named, the fall of Icarus, is in the lower right-hand corner of the frame. Based on what is at the center, the title of the painting might be "A farmer plows his field." To focus the picture on Icarus, the frame would have to be shifted down and to the right. Since Brueghel's point is that one person's catastrophe is not necessarily at the center of someone else's consciousness, his meaning is very precisely a claim *about* framing.

Ideas borrowed from other fields and used as frames can produce whole new kinds of interpretation. For instance, literary critics noticing signs of class struggle between characters and groups in literature produce Marxist interpretation, and those noticing evidence of the workings of the unconscious produce Freudian criticism. But smaller ideas from other fields can be imported, too.

Wilbur's "For C" and Fraley and Shaver's "Airport Separations"

Here are two texts that illustrate the way academic research from another field can contribute to interpretation of a literary work. We will start with a fairly recent poem by Richard Wilbur, who has held the position of Poet Laureate of the United States. The poem addresses "C," the speaker's partner of many years, about what happens when one of them takes a trip alone. Read it several times, at least once aloud, and annotate it to capture your reactions.

For C

RICHARD WILBUR *(For biographical notes, see p. 264.)*

After the clash of elevator gates
And the long sinking, she emerges where,
A slight thing in the morning's crosstown glare,
She looks up toward the window where he waits,

Then in a fleeting taxi joins the rest
Of the huge traffic bound forever west. 6

On such grand scale do lovers say goodbye—
Even this other pair whose high romance
Had only the duration of a dance,
And who, now taking leave with stricken eye,
See each in each a whole new life forgone.
For them, above the darkling clubhouse lawn, 12

Bright Perseids flash and crumble; while for these
Who part now on the dock, weighed down by grief
And baggage, yet with something like relief,
It takes three thousand miles of knitting seas
To cancel out their crossing, and unmake
The amorous rough and tumble of their wake. 18

We are denied, my love, their fine tristesse
And bittersweet regrets, and cannot share
The frequent vistas of their large despair,
Where love and all are swept to nothingness;
Still, there's a certain scope in that long love
Which constant spirits are the keepers of, 24

And which, though taken to be tame and staid,
Is a wild sostenuto of the heart,
A passion joined to courtesy and art
Which has the quality of something made,
Like a good fiddle, like the rose's scent,
Like a rose window or the firmament. [1997] 30

ACTIVITY 1: *Analyzing "For C"*

1. The poem proceeds by means of one major contrast. With what kind of couples is the speaker comparing himself and his partner? What is his hypothesis about why they are different?
2. There are other smaller comparisons that appear in the course of the poem. What are they and what do they contribute to Wilbur's meaning?
3. I heard Wilbur read this poem at a public reading in the late 1990s. I remember that toward the end of the poem, the audience got very quiet and then at the last line made a collective sound as if all had been holding their breath and could now start to breathe again. Can you explain why listeners might have had that reaction to the end of the poem?

Now let's see what work in another discipline can contribute to a reading of the poem. When my student Deborah Baker was working on an interpretation of Wilbur's poem, she wanted to know whether the phenomenon Wilbur describes is idiosyncratic, experienced only by him and C, or shared with other couples in longstanding relationships. After a search of electronic databases that index social science journals, she found a relevant article by a pair of social psychologists at the University of California, Davis. Not everything in the article is relevant to the poem, and the article can't answer Deborah's question completely, but it sheds very interesting light on the two different kinds of "parting" that the poem describes.

Following are some of the relevant passages of the article. Read them several times to make sure you understand them, underlining important passages and writing your reactions in the margins as you read.

From *Airport Separations: A Naturalistic Study of Adult Attachment Dynamics in Separating Couples**

R. CHRIS FRALEY AND PHILLIP R. SHAVER

5 Before describing the airport study in detail, we briefly review the major tenets of attachment theory as it has been applied to children and adults. Specifically, we review some of the factors responsible for the organization of attachment behavior in children and discuss the role these factors may play in organizing responses to airport separations in adults.

The Nature, Function, and Dynamics of Attachment in Childhood

6 Bowlby (1969/1982) observed that infants of many mammalian species require the care and protection of adults in order to survive. As a result, Bowlby proposed that infants are born with various features (e.g., large eyes) and behavioral responses (e.g., cuddling) that attract the attention of potential caregivers. In addition to these relatively simple adaptations, however, infants are theorized to possess a more complex motivational system, the *attachment behavioral system*, for regulating proximity to caregivers. Adopting ideas from control theory and ethology, Bowlby argued that the attachment system has the set goal of maintaining proximity to one or a few individuals. When these individuals, or *attachment figures*, are perceived as available and responsive, the infant feels secure and explores the environment confidently but continues to maintain contact in subtle ways (e.g., with brief glances or intermittent vocalizations). In contrast, when

*R. Chris Fraley and Phillip R. Shaver, "Airport Separations: A Naturalistic Study of Adult Attachment Dynamics in Separating Couples," *Journal of Personality and Social Psychology* 75 (1998): 1198–1212.

an attachment figure's availability is judged to be uncertain, the child experiences anxiety and vigorously attempts to maintain or reestablish contact by engaging in various protest behaviors, such as crying, searching, following, and clinging. According to Bowlby, these *attachment behaviors* are adaptive because they help to reestablish proximity to an absent attachment figure or prevent an attachment figure from leaving.

One of the major objectives of research on attachment in infancy is to identify the factors that contribute to the regulation of attachment behavior. . . . 7

One of the most widely studied variables known to influence the organization of attachment behavior is *attachment style,* a set of knowledge structures or *working models* representing the responsiveness and availability of attachment figures.[2] . . . 9

In summary, research on children indicates that the way attachment behavior is organized in a particular situation depends on several factors, including physical accessibility of the attachment figure, duration of the attachment relationship, and working models of attachment. Theoretically, each of these factors plays a role in determining whether the child judges the attachment figure to be accessible or inaccessible, and, hence, whether the set goal of proximity is exceeded or not. As explained below, if the dynamics of romantic relationships are driven by the same motivational systems present in childhood, then the same factors should contribute to the regulation of attachment behavior in the context of airport separations. 10

Adult Attachment and the Regulation of Behavior

In the late 1980s, Hazan and Shaver published a series of articles in which they argued that attachment dynamics in adult romantic relationships are similar to infant–caregiver attachment dynamics (Hazan & Shaver, 1987; Shaver & Hazan, 1988; Shaver, Hazan, & Bradshaw, 1988). Shaver et al. noted that when a romantic partner is nearby and accessible, adults, like infants, feel secure and are more willing to explore their environments confidently. However, when a person is threatened with harm or a partner's availability or responsiveness is questionable, many adults experience considerable anxiety and, like infants, attempt to regain the attention and proximity of their partners. According to Hazan and Shaver (1987, 1994), these dynamics reflect, in part, the operation of the attachment-behavioral system and function to keep partners in close proximity. . . . 11

As with research on childhood attachment processes, a major goal of adult attachment research is to uncover the factors that shape the organization of attachment behavior in adult relationships. Most of the research to date has focused exclusively on the influence of working models. As discussed above, 13

[2]Technically, the term *attachment style* refers to the observable patterns of behavior exhibited by an individual, not the unobservable variables (such as working models) that shape these patterns. Nonetheless, as is customary in the literature on attachment, we use the terms *attachment style* and *working models* interchangeably throughout the present article to refer to the internal mechanisms theorized to shape attachment behavior.

however, research on infant–caregiver attachment processes indicates that a number of other variables, such as the accessibility of the attachment figure and the length of the relationship, shape the organization of attachment behavior in a given situation. Thus, it is likely that these variables affect adult attachment dynamics as well. Below, we discuss the influence of these factors on the regulation of attachment behavior in the context of airport separations. . . .

15   Paralleling attachment theory and research on children (e.g., Marvin, 1977), the intensity of protest responses should diminish as the length of the relationship increases. As romantic relationships develop and evolve, partners should establish a kind of mutual understanding concerning each other's anxieties and the significance of brief separations. Therefore, brief separations such as those commonly taking place at an airport should elicit less attachment behavior from long-term couples. . . .

18   In summary, adult attachment theory posits that similar motivational systems underlie adult–adult attachment and infant–caregiver attachment (Hazan & Shaver, 1987, 1994; Shaver et al., 1988). Existing research on adult attachment dynamics has focused almost exclusively, however, on working models as regulators of attachment-related behavior despite the fact that attachment theory proposes a number of additional variables (such as the accessibility of the partner and the duration of the relationship) that are also responsible for the organization of attachment behavior. In the present article, we examine the influence of three kinds of variables in shaping attachment behavior: partner accessibility, relationship length, and working models. By doing so, we hope to advance the understanding of attachment dynamics in the domain of romantic relationships.

Overview of the Present Study

19   In the study reported here, we sought to determine how attachment behavior is manifested during romantic separations and how the organization of attachment behavior is influenced by factors known to regulate attachment behavior in infancy (i.e., accessibility of the attachment figure, length of the relationship, and working models). To answer these questions, we conducted a two-phase observational study of couples who were separating from one another in a small metropolitan airport. In Phase 1, we observed and took detailed notes on the behavior and interactions of couple members who were about to separate from each other. On the basis of these observations, we were able to delineate the major behavioral patterns exhibited by separating adults.[4] This information was used to create a standardized coding form for behavioral observation in the second phase of the study. In Phase 2, we observed and coded the behaviors of both couples who were separating and couples who were flying together. Before coding these couples, however, a member of our research team asked each partner to complete a brief questionnaire designed to assess various demographic variables,

---

[4]In the ethological literature, such a record, or partial record, is called an *ethogram*. An *ethogram* is a relatively comprehensive description of the characteristic behavioral patterns of a particular species (Lehner, 1979).

relationship length, and attachment style. This procedure allowed us to examine relations between variables theoretically associated with the regulation of attachment behavior and the natural expression of attachment behavior.

Phase 2: An Examination of Adult Attachment Dynamics

Method

For the second phase of the study, we designed a one-page (double-sided) [28] questionnaire containing questions about (a) demographics, (b) relationship history, (c) feelings about the impending separation, and (d) attachment style.[5] The demographic items inquired about participants' age, sex, and ethnicity. The relationship history items assessed the length of the relationship ("How long have you been involved, dating or married, with this person?") and the kind of relationship (i.e., dating, marital). Three items were designed to measure the level of distress the participant was experiencing with respect to separation ("How upset are you about being away from him or her?" "How angry are you about the separation?" "How sad are you about being away from him or her?"). These items were rated on a 1 (*not at all*) to 3 (*very much so*) scale and were averaged to create a composite self-report index of separation distress ($\alpha = .78$ for men and $\alpha = .77$ for women). To assess attachment style or working models, we asked participants to rate 18 items from Griffin and Bartholomew's (1994a) Relationship Styles Questionnaire (RSQ) on a 1 (*absolutely disagree*) to 7 (*absolutely agree*) scale. The RSQ includes items designed to measure the dimensions of Avoidance (e.g., "I find it difficult to depend on other people") and Anxiety (e.g., "I worry about being alone"). After we collected the data, these items were factor analyzed, using principal-axis factoring with varimax rotation, to yield factor scores on the two dimensions of Avoidance and Anxiety.

Results

Relationship length and attachment behavior. According to our inference [36] from attachment theory, attachment behavior should be less pronounced among couples who have been involved for a longer period of time. Thus, we predicted that the intensity of attachment behavior would vary as a negative function of relationship length. Our preliminary analyses of this association indicated that attachment behavior varied roughly as a negative loglinear function of relationship length. Consequently, in the analyses that follow, relationship length was log-transformed to help meet the assumptions of the linear models employed.

[5] For separating couples, we also assessed the frequency with which similar separations had occurred in the past (rated on a scale with the following metric: 1 = *never*, 2 = *once a year*, 3 = *twice a year*, 4 = *once a month*, 5 = *twice a month*). Sixty-nine percent of the sample endorsed one of the last two options, indicating that most members of this sample were accustomed to brief separations. There was a tendency for couples who were rarely separated to express more attachment behavior than couples who were more accustomed to separations. However, the low number of couples experiencing few separations made it difficult to estimate this association unambiguously. Analyses of the separation-frequency variable are available from R. Chris Fraley on request.

TABLE 1   *A Sampling of Behaviors Exhibited by Separating Couples in Phase 1*

Brief hug
Before boarding, he reads the newspaper and she leans her head on his shoulder
Massages her inner thigh
Kissed several times when she tries to leave
Both hold each other for approximately 5 min
When they separated, neither turned around to take "one last look" at the other
Eye-to-eye contact
Extended hug and stroking (lasts for about 5 min)
She stands on her tip-toes to give him a kiss
Tears in eyes; both members wipe the other's tears away
She goes back to the window and watches the plane leave
Holding hands
Petting other's head
She is still at the window 20 min after the plane leaves
Looks at wristwatch
Crying
At departure, she is the last to board the plane
She gives him money to buy coffee
Extended hand stretch
He leaves before she boards the plane but watches her from a distance without her
    knowledge
Intimate kiss
He waves "good bye" when boarding plane
He kisses her head several times
He leaves quickly
She walks away crying
Long hug; both are crying
Sitting close
She whispers "I love you" to him as she boards
Prolonged hug at the gate
She, in a comforting manner, strokes his face

Note: These descriptions were taken from field notes taken in Phase 1 of the airport study and are
provided to illustrate some of the major behavior patterns observed in separating couples. These
descriptions are listed in no particular order, and, in some cases, more than one of these behaviors is from the same couple.

37   Correlations between attachment behavior and relationship length were
computed separately for separating and nonseparating groups within each
gender. Data from 99 couples (58 separating and 41 flying together) were
available for these analyses. There are two noteworthy features of these
results. . . . First, the expression of attachment behavior tended to decrease as
a function of relationship length, indicating that couples who had been together
longer were less distressed by the impending separation. Second, although
couple members who were flying together exhibited substantially fewer attachment behaviors than couple members who were separating . . . , the expression
of attachment behavior also decreased as a function of relationship length
among nonseparating individuals. This suggests that the negative association
between attachment behavior and relationship length is not dependent on the

threat of separation per se.[10] The findings for the nonseparating couples are compatible with the possibility that additional sources of anxiety and threat (e.g., fear of flying, late departures) were active among nonseparating individuals. Longer term couples may express less proximity-maintenance behavior in such circumstances because they are more certain of each other's willingness to provide comfort if needed, without signals of availability having to be provided in advance. . . .

Summary of findings. In summary, these data indicate that some of the 42 factors shaping the organization of attachment behavior in childhood also contribute to the organization of attachment behavior in the context of adult romantic relationships. In an airport setting, attachment behaviors were most pronounced in couples who were separating. Specifically, separating couples exhibited higher levels of attachment behavior and more behavioral variability than nonseparating couples. We also found that separating individuals who had been involved for a shorter period of time exhibited the strongest levels of attachment behavior. . . .

General Discussion

Relationship Length and the Organization of Attachment Behavior

Although attachment behavior in the airport was heightened during an 50 impending separation, several factors contributed to the degree to which attachment behavior was expressed. Attachment behavior was expressed less strongly for couples who had been involved for a longer time. This finding is consistent with the idea that couples who have been together for a long time view brief separations as fairly inconsequential to the long-term stability of the relationship. A negative association between relationship length and attachment behavior was also observed among nonseparating couples. Although nonseparating individuals exhibited low levels of attachment behavior (their modal score was zero), those who did exhibit such behavior were more likely to have been involved for relatively short periods of time. This may indicate that there were (unmeasured) sources of mild anxiety and threat sufficient to activate attachment concerns and that these concerns were more likely to be expressed among shorter term couples. . . .

[10]As one reviewer noted, the association between relationship length and attachment behavior might have been due to age rather than relationship duration per se. In fact, relationship length and age were correlated .57 in the present sample. In a supplementary set of analyses, we examined the association between relationship length and attachment behavior while holding age constant. The overall result of holding this variable constant was equivalent to subtracting .10 from each of the correlations in Table 3. Relationship length still accounted for approximately 4% to 10% of the variance in Contact Seeking, Contact Maintenance, Caregiving, Sexuality, and self-reported distress for separating and nonseparating men and women. Thus, the negative association between relationship length and attachment behavior is observed even when age is held constant.

Conclusion

63   In summary, this study provides unique and valuable insights into the operation of the attachment system in adulthood. Our observations suggest that attachment behavior serves similar functions in adulthood and childhood. Moreover, many of the factors contributing to the organization of attachment behavior in children (e.g., availability of the attachment figure, duration of the relationship, and working models of attachment) were associated with the organization of attachment behavior in adults in theoretically meaningful ways. These findings help to substantiate and extend the application of attachment theory to adult romantic relationships.

References

Bowlby, J. (1982). *Attachment and loss: Vol. 1. Attachment.* New York: Basic Books. (Original work published 1969)

Griffin, D. W., & Bartholomew, K. (1994a). The metaphysics of measurement: The case of adult attachment. In K. Bartholomew & D. Perlman (Eds.), *Advances in personal relationships: Vol. 5. Attachment processes in adulthood* (pp. 17–52). London: Jessica Kingsley.

Hazan, C., & Shaver, P. R. (1987). Romantic love conceptualized as an attachment process. *Journal of Personality and Social Psychology, 59,* 511–524.

Hazan, C., & Shaver, P. R. (1994). Attachment as an organizational framework for research on close relationships. *Psychological Inquiry, 5,* 1–22.

Lehner, P. N. (1979). *Handbook of ethological methods.* New York: Garland STPM Press.

Marvin, R. S. (1977). An ethological–cognitive model for the attenuation of mother–child attachment behavior. In T. M. Alloway, P. Pliner, & L. Krames (Eds.), *Advances in the study of communication and affect: Vol. 3. Attachment behavior* (pp. 25–60). New York: Plenum.

Shaver, P. R., & Hazan, C. (1988). A biased overview of the study of love. *Journal of Social and Personal Relationships, 5,* 473–501.

Shaver, P. R., Hazan, C., & Bradshaw, D. (1988). Love as attachment: The integration of three behavioral systems. In R. J. Sternberg & M. L. Barnes (Eds.), *The psychology of love* (pp. 68–99). New Haven, CT: Yale University Press.

The juxtaposition of Wilbur's poem and Fraley and Shaver's article shows the fruitful conversation that can take place between the different kinds of texts. Both discuss how couples behave when parting. The distinction between people in short relationships and those in long relationships is crucial in both texts. Both find that the long-standing couples are less demonstrative when separating temporarily at airports: they cling to each other less desperately and express their sorrow less dramatically (Fraley and Shaver paragraphs 36, 37, 50, 63). Fraley and Shaver confirm through the techniques of social science Wilbur's explanation of differences in the different kinds of couples.

Of course, not everything in Fraley and Shaver's study is relevant to the poem, and they can't comment on every aspect of what interests Wilbur about relationships. We don't know enough about Wilbur's speaker and C to know what their "attachment styles" or "working models" are (see Fraley and Shaver's paragraph 9). And Fraley and Shaver don't have any evidence about couples who are in the process of ending their relationships, while Wilbur, because he is imagining the relationships he "reports" on, does. But the texts have useful things to say to each other. Fraley and Shaver can't report the feelings of the less demonstrative couples on the basis of their limited questionnaires—we need poets for that kind of information. Wilbur's speaker, being generously frank about his own experience, adds information that the psychologists could not get.

A MORE EXTENDED TRACING OF PARALLELS: POE'S "CASK OF AMONTILLADO" AND GOFFMAN'S *THE PRESENTATION OF SELF IN EVERYDAY LIFE*

Let's look together at another pair of texts: "The Cask of Amontillado," a short story by Edgar Allan Poe, the nineteenth-century American writer of poetry, essays, and fiction, and an excerpt from *The Presentation of Self in Everyday Life*, a book by sociologist Erving Goffman. As you will see, Goffman's understanding of the way humans interact might answer some questions that the story raises.

Start by reading the story carefully two or more times. As you read the story, make notes about your response to it, either in the book or on separate sheets of paper—or both. Refer to passages in the story by paragraph number so that you can locate them precisely when you return to the story. Notice its formal features: its narrative technique and the point of view from which it is told, its characters, its setting, its structure, its diction, and its syntax. Underline or circle important words and passages. Note turns of events or expressions that please, annoy, or surprise you.

Remember that as a critic, your reactions to a piece of literature are your raw materials. When you go back later to interpret the work, either for a paper or a class discussion, notes about your first responses can help you shape your interpretation.

The Cask of Amontillado°

EDGAR ALLAN POE *(For biographical notes, see p. 319.)*

The thousand injuries of Fortunato I had borne as I best could, but when he
ventured upon insult, I vowed revenge. You, who so well know the nature of
my soul, will not suppose, however, that I gave utterance to a threat. At *length*
I would be avenged; this was a point definitely settled—but the very definitiveness with which it was resolved precluded the idea of risk. I must not only
punish, but punish with impunity. A wrong is unredressed when retribution
overtakes its redresser. It is equally unredressed when the avenger fails to make
himself felt as such to him who has done the wrong.

It must be understood that neither by word nor deed had I given Fortunato
cause to doubt my good will. I continued, as was my wont, to smile in his face,
and he did not perceive that my smile *now* was at the thought of his immolation.

He had a weak point—this Fortunato—although in other regards he was a
man to be respected and even feared. He prided himself on his connoisseurship
in wine. Few Italians have the true virtuoso spirit. For the most part their
enthusiasm is adopted to suit the time and opportunity to practice imposture
upon the British and Austrian *millionaires*. In painting and gemmary Fortunato,
like his countrymen, was a quack, but in the matter of old wines he was sincere.
In this respect I did not differ from him materially;—I was skillful in the Italian
vintages myself, and bought largely whenever I could.

It was about dusk, one evening during the supreme madness of the carnival
season, that I encountered my friend. He accosted me with excessive warmth, for
he had been drinking much. The man wore motley. He had on a tight-fitting
parti-striped dress, and his head was surmounted by the conical cap and bells. I was
so pleased to see him, that I thought I should never have done wringing his hand.

5   I said to him—"My dear Fortunato, you are luckily met. How remarkably
well you are looking to-day! But I have received a pipe° of what passes for
Amontillado, and I have my doubts."

"How?" said he, "Amontillado? A pipe? Impossible! And in the middle of the
carnival?"

"I have my doubts," I replied; "and I was silly enough to pay the full
Amontillado price without consulting you in the matter. You were not to be
found, and I was fearful of losing a bargain."

"Amontillado!"

"I have my doubts."

10   "Amontillado!"

"And I must satisfy them."

"Amontillado!"

"As you are engaged, I am on my way to Luchesi. If any one has a critical
turn, it is he. He will tell me—"

---

^{Title}**Amontillado** pale dry sherry from the region of Montilla in Spain   ⁵**pipe** wine cask

"Luchesi cannot tell Amontillado from Sherry."

"And yet some fools will have it that his taste is a match for your own."   15

"Come, let us go."

"Whither?"

"To your vaults."

"My friend, no; I will not impose upon your good nature. I perceive you have an engagement. Luchesi—"

"I have no engagement; come."   20

"My friend, no. It is not the engagement, but the severe cold with which I perceive you are afflicted. The vaults are insufferably damp. They are encrusted with nitre."

"Let us go, nevertheless. The cold is merely nothing. Amontillado! You have been imposed upon; and as for Luchesi, he cannot distinguish Sherry from Amontillado."

Thus speaking, Fortunato possessed himself of my arm. Putting on a mask of black silk, and drawing a *roquelaure*° closely about my person, I suffered him to hurry me to my palazzo.

There were no attendants at home; they had absconded to make merry in honor of the time. I had told them that I should not return until the morning, and had given them explicit orders not to stir from the house. These orders were sufficient, I well knew, to insure their immediate disappearance, one and all, as soon as my back was turned.

I took from their sconces two flambeaux, and giving one to Fortunato, bowed   25 him through several suites of rooms to the archway that led into the vaults. I passed down a long and winding staircase, requesting him to be cautious as he followed. We came at length to the foot of the descent, and stood together on the damp ground of the catacombs of the Montresors.

The gait of my friend was unsteady, and the bells upon his cap jingled as he strode.

"The pipe," said he.

"It is farther on," said I; "but observe the white web-work which gleams from these cavern walls."

He turned towards me, and looked into my eyes with two filmy orbs that distilled the rheum of intoxication.

"Nitre?" he asked, at length.   30

"Nitre," I replied, "How long have you had that cough?"

"Ugh! ugh! ugh!—ugh! ugh! ugh!—ugh! ugh! ugh!—ugh! ugh! ugh!—ugh! ugh! ugh!"

My poor friend found it impossible to reply for many minutes.

"It is nothing," he said, at last.

"Come," I said, with decision, "we will go back; your health is precious. You   35 are rich, respected, admired, beloved; you are happy, as once I was. You are a man to be missed. For me it is no matter. We will go back; you will be ill, and I cannot be responsible. Besides, there is Luchesi—"

---

[23]*roquelaure* short cloak

"Enough," he said; "the cough is a mere nothing: it will not kill me. I shall not die of a cough."

"True—true," I replied; "and, indeed, I had no intention of alarming you unnecessarily—but you should use all proper caution. A draught of this Medoc will defend us from the damps."

Here I knocked off the neck of a bottle which I drew from a long row of its fellows that lay upon the mould.

"Drink," I said, presenting him the wine.

40   He raised it to his lips with a leer. He paused and nodded to me familiarly, while his bells jingled.

"I drink," he said, "to the buried that repose around us."

"And I to your long life."

He again took my arm, and we proceeded.

"These vaults," he said, "are extensive."

45   "The Montresors," I replied, "were a great and numerous family."

"I forget your arms."

"A huge human foot d'or, in a field azure; the foot crushes a serpent rampant whose fangs are imbedded in the heel."

"And the motto?"

Nemo me impune lacessit.°

50   "Good!" he said.

The wine sparkled in his eyes and the bells jingled. My own fancy grew warm with the Medoc. We had passed through walls of piled bones, with casks and puncheons intermingling, into the inmost recesses of the catacombs. I paused again, and this time I made bold to seize Fortunato by an arm above the elbow.

"The nitre!" I said; "see, it increases. It hangs like moss upon the vaults. We are below the river's bed. The drops of moisture tickle among the bones. Come, we will go back ere it is too late. Your cough—"

"It is nothing," he said; "let us go on. But first, another draught of the Medoc."

I broke and reached him a flagon of De Grâve. He emptied it at a breath. His eyes flashed with a fierce light. He laughed and threw the bottle upwards with a gesticulation I did not understand.

55   I looked at him in surprise. He repeated the movement—a grotesque one.

"You do not comprehend?" he said.

"Not I," I replied.

"Then you are not of the brotherhood."

"How?"

60   "You are not of the masons."°

"Yes, yes," I said, "yes, yes."

"You? Impossible! A mason?"

"A mason," I replied.

"A sign," he said.

---

[49]*Nemo me impune lacessit.* No one attacks me with impunity.   [60]**of the masons** a member of the Freemasons, an international secret fraternity

"It is this," I answered, producing a trowel from beneath the folds of my   65
roquelaure.

"You jest," he exclaimed, recoiling a few paces. "But let us proceed to the
Amontillado."

"Be it so," I said, replacing the tool beneath the cloak, and again offering him
my arm. He leaned upon it heavily. We continued our route in search of the
Amontillado. We passed through a range of low arches, descended, passed on,
and descending again, arrived at a deep crypt, in which the foulness of the air
caused our flambeaux rather to glow than flame.

At the most remote end of the crypt there appeared another less spacious. Its
walls had been lined with human remains piled to the vault overhead, in the fashion of the great catacombs of Paris. Three sides of this interior crypt were still
ornamented in this manner. From the fourth the bones had been thrown down,
and lay promiscuously upon the earth, forming at one point a mound of some
size. Within the wall thus exposed by the displacing of the bones, we perceived a
still interior recess, in depth about four feet, in width three, in height six or seven.
It seemed to have been constructed for no especial use within itself, but formed
merely the interval between two of the colossal supports of the roof of the catacombs, and was backed by one of their circumscribing walls of solid granite.

It was in vain that Fortunato, uplifting his dull torch, endeavored to pry into
the depths of the recess. Its termination the feeble light did not enable us to see.

"Proceed," I said; "herein is the Amontillado. As for Luchesi—"   70

"He is an ignoramus," interrupted my friend, as he stepped unsteadily forward, while I followed immediately at his heels. In an instant he had reached
the extremity of the niche, and finding his progress arrested by the rock, stood
stupidly bewildered. A moment more and I had fettered him to the granite. In its
surface were two iron staples, distant from each other about two feet, horizontally. From one of these depended a short chain, from the other a padlock.
Throwing the links about his waist, it was but the work of a few seconds to
secure it. He was too much astounded to resist. Withdrawing the key I stepped
back from the recess.

"Pass your hand," I said, "over the wall; you cannot help feeling the nitre.
Indeed it is *very* damp. Once more let me *implore* you to return. No? Then I must
positively leave you. But I must first render you all the little attentions in my
power."

"The Amontillado!" ejaculated my friend, not yet recovered from his
astonishment.

"True," I replied; "the Amontillado."

As I said these words I busied myself among the pile of bones of which I have   75
before spoken. Throwing them aside, I soon uncovered a quantity of building-
stone and mortar. With these materials and with the aid of my trowel, I began
vigorously to wall up the entrance of the niche.

I had scarcely laid the first tier of masonry when I discovered that the intoxication of Fortunato had in a great measure worn off. The earliest indication I
had of this was a low moaning cry from the depth of the recess. It was *not* the
cry of a drunken man. There was then a long and obstinate silence. I laid the

second tier, and the third, and the fourth; and then I heard the furious vibrations of the chain. The noise lasted for several minutes, during which, that I might hearken to it with the more satisfaction, I ceased my labors and sat down upon the bones. When at last the clanking subsided, I resumed the trowel, and finished without interruption the fifth, the sixth, and the seventh tier. The wall was now nearly upon a level with my breast. I again paused, and holding the flambeaux over the masonwork, threw a few feeble rays upon the figure within.

A succession of loud and shrill screams, bursting suddenly from the throat of the chained form, seemed to thrust me violently back. For a brief moment I hesitated—I trembled. Unsheathing my rapier, I began to grope with it about the recess; but the thought of an instant reassured me. I placed my hand upon the solid fabric of the catacombs, and felt satisfied. I reapproached the wall. I replied to the yells of him who clamored. I re-echoed—I aided—I surpassed them in volume and in strength. I did this, and the clamorer grew still.

It was now midnight, and my task was drawing to a close. I had completed the eighth, the ninth, and the tenth tier. I had finished a portion of the last and the eleventh; there remained but a single stone to be fitted and plastered in. I struggled with its weight; I placed it partially in its destined position. But now there came from out the niche a low laugh that erected the hairs upon my head. It was succeeded by a sad voice, which I had difficulty in recognizing as that of the noble Fortunato. The voice said—

"Ha! ha! ha!—he! he! he!—a very good joke indeed—an excellent jest. We will have many a rich laugh about it at the palazzo—he! he! he!—over our wine—he! he! he!"

80   "The Amontillado!" I said.

"He! he! he!—he! he! he!—yes, the Amontillado. But is it not getting late? Will not they be awaiting us at the palazzo, the Lady Fortunato and the rest? Let us be gone."

"Yes," I said, "let us be gone."

"For the love of God, Montresor!"

"Yes," I said, "for the love of God!"

85   But to these words I hearkened in vain for a reply. I grew impatient. I called aloud:

"Fortunato!"

No answer. I called again:

"Fortunato!"

No answer still, I thrust a torch through the remaining aperture and let it fall within. There came forth in return only a jingling of the bells. My heart grew sick—on account of the dampness of the catacombs. I hastened to make an end of my labor. I forced the last stone into its position; I plastered it up. Against the new masonry I reerected the old rampart of bones. For the half of a century no mortal has disturbed them. *In pace requiescat!*°   [1846]

---

[89]*In pace requiescat!* May he rest in peace!

ACTIVITY 2 (GROUP ACTIVITY): *Sharing Notes on Texts*

Divide up into small groups; each group should have a recorder. In each group, the members will share the results of their reading and annotating of the story on one of these topics: narrative technique and point of view, character, setting, structure, diction, syntax, theme. When the groups come back to the class as a whole, the recorders will report the results of the group discussions.

ACTIVITY 3: *Writing a Journal Entry on Poe*

Write a journal entry for Poe's "The Cask of Amontillado" in which you reflect on the nature of the narrator and your response to him.

In response to this assignment, a student named Lisa Rodrigues used her annotations of the story to write the journal entry on the following page:

Well, "The Cask of Amontillado" clearly has a dramatized narrator. He's the main actor in the story, so he's not omniscient. He obviously knows everything he does and most of what he feels about it. But he doesn't know what the other characters feel and I think he fools himself sometimes about what he's feeling. For example, when he says he feels sick at the end (89) because of the dampness in the vaults, he's probably trying to cover up the fact that he felt bad about committing murder. He seems to want to come off as a tough guy. So the damp is just an excuse.

The narrator—we learn late in the story that his name is Montresor—starts out seeming to be reliable. After all, he's talking with someone who knows him pretty well—even knows "the nature of my soul"—so why would he lie? But he doesn't really make it clear 'til very late that he's going to murder Fortunato. In fact, I didn't figure it out until about the same time as Fortunato did. If the "you" in the second sentence of paragraph 1 really knows Montresor as well as he's supposed to, maybe he figured it out sooner because he knew Montresor was a dangerous man. But I didn't guess and then I felt cheated because it seemed like Montresor was crazy and why would I want to read a story about a crazy man? We never found out what Fortunato did to Montresor, so we don't know if Montresor's actions are justified and I'm not interested in such extreme behavior. I like to read about people who are more normal. I don't think it's a good story because it isn't realistic. And besides, it gives me the creeps.

Lisa read her journal entry in class, where it sparked some good discussion:

Michael: What do you mean by "normal"?

Lisa: The dictionary says, "sincere," or "natural"—not acting on grudges that don't seem to be based on anything real.

Carlos: I'm not sure "sincere" and "natural" really mean "normal." We don't really know why Montresor hated Fortunato—maybe it was a mistake (Fortunato might not have meant to offend him—maybe he would have apologized if he'd had the chance). Or maybe it was Montresor's character flaw—maybe he was paranoid and needed to think someone was out to insult him. It seems to me that Montresor's kind of an extreme character, but not all that different from "normal" people. I don't think "sincerity" can be a standard for "normal" because everyone is at least a little insincere in everyday life.

Lisa: I don't think so at all—my friends and I are always honest with each other.

Carlos: Montresor may be a bit out of touch with reality—I mean, he does seem obsessed with getting revenge on Fortunato—but I don't think that Montresor and Fortunato are all that different.

Lisa: Well, yes, I did notice some ways they seem to be alike, in paragraph 3, for example, and a lot of other times they "echo" each other in the story. But that doesn't make Montresor normal—or even make him interesting to a sane reader.

There are a number of issues embedded in this discussion. One is the proper function of literature—is it supposed to be realistic, so that we should judge it on the basis of how well it reflects reality? Or should we value it when it provides pictures of and commentary on extreme versions of human behavior? That is, should it help us understand our lives, or should it expand the range of our experience beyond the kind of thing we see every day?

But another important issue lurking behind this discussion is the definition of ordinary human interaction itself. Do people tend to show their true thoughts and feelings, or disguise them? The class couldn't really argue about this issue. They made claims—some, like Lisa, said there was more honesty in the world than hypocrisy, and some said it depended on the people you were with, noting that people were different in different situations.

There were plenty of claims, but not much evidence beyond personal experience, and the class felt that the stories they had read weren't much help because each one dealt with a limited group of characters over a limited span of time. It was hard to generalize from the data available to them. The teacher suggested that several of the social sciences offer a firmer basis for generalizations and in particular suggested that the class read some of the work of sociologist Erving Goffman. His ideas could serve as an interpretive framework for the story because he offers evidence that the way people behave in public is, at least in part, performance. He uses metaphors from the theater to suggest that when people are in public, they aren't "themselves" in any simple way. His insights offer the kind of conceptual scheme that allows us to see Poe's story in a new way.

The students began with the first chapter of his book, *The Presentation of Self in Everyday Life*. Here is part of that chapter. As always, when you read, try to identify the important ideas. Annotate your own copy and make notes on a separate sheet of paper, referring to parts of the text by paragraph number.

◎◎◎

From *The Presentation of Self in Everyday Life*

ERVING GOFFMAN *(1922–82) received his B.A. from the University of Toronto and his Ph.D. in sociology from the University of Chicago, doing the fieldwork for his dissertation on one of the Shetland Islands north of Scotland. His observations of interactions there formed the basis of* The Presentation of Self in Everyday Life, *a book that has had wide influence on the sociological field of symbolic interactionism. He taught at the University of California at Berkeley and the University of Pennsylvania. His other books include* Relations in Public: Micro-Studies of the Public Order, Frame Analysis: Essays on the Organization of Experience, *and* Asylums: Essays on the Social Situation of Mental Patients and Other Inmates. *He received the McIver Prize and was a fellow of the American Academy of Arts and Sciences.*

1   When an individual enters the presence of others, they commonly seek to acquire information about him or to bring into play information about him already possessed. They will be interested in his general socioeconomic status, his conception of self, his attitude toward them, his competence, his trustworthiness, etc. Although some of this information seems to be sought almost as an end in itself, there are usually quite practical reasons for acquiring it. Information about the individual helps to define the situation, enabling others to know in advance what he will expect of them and what they may expect of him. Informed in these ways, the others will know how best to act in order to call forth a desired response from him.

2   For those present, many sources of information become accessible and many carriers (or "sign-vehicles") become available for conveying this information. If unacquainted with the individual, observers can glean clues from his conduct and appearance which allow them to apply their previous experience with individuals roughly similar to the one before them or, more important, to apply untested stereotypes to him. They can also assume from past experience that only individuals of a particular kind are likely to be found in a given social setting. They can rely on what the individual says about himself or on documentary evidence he provides as to who and what he is. If they know, or know of, the individual by virtue of experience prior to the interaction, they can rely on assumptions as to the persistence and generality of psychological traits as a means of predicting his present and future behavior.

However, during the period in which the individual is in the immediate presence of the others, few events may occur which directly provide the others with the conclusive information they will need if they are to direct wisely their own activity. Many crucial facts lie beyond the time and place of interaction or lie concealed within it. For example, the "true" or "real" attitudes, beliefs, and emotions of the individual can be ascertained only indirectly, through his avowals or through what appears to be involuntary expressive behavior. Similarly, if the individual offers the others a product or service, they will often find that during the interaction there will be no time and place immediately available for eating the pudding that the proof can be found in. They will be forced to accept some events as conventional or natural signs of something not directly available to the senses. In Ichheiser's terms,[1] the individual will have to act so that he intentionally or unintentionally *expresses* himself, and the others will in turn have to be *impressed* in some way by him. . . .

Taking communication in both its narrow and broad sense, one finds that when the individual is in the immediate presence of others, his activity will have a promissory character. The others are likely to find that they must accept the individual on faith, offering him a just return while he is present before them in exchange for something whose true value will not be established until after he has left their presence. (Of course, the others also live by inference in their dealings with the physical world, but it is only in the world of social interaction that the objects about which they make inferences will purposely facilitate and hinder this inferential process.) The security that they justifiably feel in making inferences about the individual will vary, of course, depending on such factors as the amount of information they already possess about him, but no amount of such past evidence can entirely obviate the necessity of acting on the basis of inferences. As William I. Thomas suggested:

> It is also highly important for us to realize that we do not as a matter of fact lead our lives, make our decisions, and reach our goals in everyday life either statistically or scientifically. We live by inference. I am, let us say, your guest. You do not know, you cannot determine scientifically, that I will not steal your money or your spoons. But inferentially I will not, and inferentially you have me as a guest.[2]

Let us now turn from the others to the point of view of the individual who presents himself before them. He may wish them to think highly of him, or to think that he thinks highly of them, or to perceive how in fact he feels toward them, or to obtain no clearcut impression; he may wish to ensure sufficient harmony so that the interaction can be sustained, or to defraud, get rid of, confuse, mislead, antagonize, or insult them. Regardless of the particular objective which the individual has in mind and of his motive for having this

[1]Gustav Ichheiser, "Misunderstandings in Human Relations," Supplement to *The American Journal of Sociology*, 55 (September, 1949): 6–7.
[2]Quoted in E. H. Volkart, editor, *Social Behavior and Personality*, Contributions of W. I. Thomas to Theory and Social Research (New York: Social Science Research Council, 1951), p. 5.

objective, it will be in his interests to control the conduct of the others, especially their responsive treatment of him.[3] This control is achieved largely by influencing the definition of the situation which the others come to formulate, and he can influence this definition by expressing himself in such a way as to give them the kind of impression that will lead them to act voluntarily in accordance with his own plan. Thus, when an individual appears in the presence of others, there will usually be some reason for him to mobilize his activity so that it will convey an impression to others which it is in his interests to convey. Since a girl's dormitory mates will glean evidence of her popularity from the calls she receives on the phone, we can suspect that some girls will arrange for calls to be made, and Willard Waller's finding can be anticipated.

> It has been reported by many observers that a girl who is called to the telephone in the dormitories will often allow herself to be called several times, in order to give all the other girls ample opportunity to hear her paged.[4]

Of the two kinds of communication—expressions given and expressions given off—this report will be primarily concerned with the latter, with the more theatrical and contextual kind, the non-verbal, presumably unintentional kind, whether this communication be purposely engineered or not. . . .

9   There is one aspect of the others' response that bears special comment here. Knowing that the individual is likely to present himself in a light that is favorable to him, the others may divide what they witness into two parts: a part that is relatively easy for the individual to manipulate at will, being chiefly his verbal assertions, and a part in regard to which he seems to have little concern or control, being chiefly derived from the expressions he gives off. The others may then use what are considered to be the ungovernable aspects of his expressive behavior as a check upon the validity of what is conveyed by the governable aspects. In this a fundamental asymmetry is demonstrated in the communication process, the individual presumably being aware of only one stream of his communication, the witness of this stream and one other. . . .

10   Now given the fact that others are likely to check up on the more controllable aspects of behavior by means of the less controllable, one can expect that sometimes the individual will try to exploit this very possibility, guiding the impression he makes through behavior felt to be reliably informing.[6] For example, in gaining admission to a tight social circle, the participant observer may not only wear an accepting look while listening to an informant, but may

[3]Here I owe much to an unpublished paper by Tom Burns of the University of Edinburgh. He presents the argument that in all interaction a basic underlying theme is the desire of each participant to guide and control the responses made by the others present. A similar argument has been advanced by Jay Haley in a recent unpublished paper, but in regard to a special kind of control, that having to do with defining the nature of the relationship of those involved in the interaction.

[4]Willard Waller, "The Rating and Dating Complex," *American Sociological Review*, 2:730.

[6]The widely read and rather sound writings of Stephen Potter are concerned in part with signs that can be engineered to give a shrewd observer the apparently incidental cues he needs to discover concealed virtues the gamesman does not in fact possess.

also be careful to wear the same look when observing the informant talking to others; observers of the observer will then not as easily discover where he actually stands. . . .

This kind of control upon the part of the individual reinstates the symmetry 11 of the communication process, and sets the stage for a kind of information game—a potentially infinite cycle of concealment, discovery, false revelation, and rediscovery. It should be added that since the others are likely to be relatively unsuspicious of the presumably unguided aspect of the individual's conduct, he can gain much by controlling it. The others of course may sense that the individual is manipulating the presumably spontaneous aspects of his behavior, and seek in this very act of manipulation some shading of conduct that the individual has not managed to control. This again provides a check upon the individual's behavior, this time his presumably uncalculated behavior, thus reestablishing the asymmetry of the communication process. Here I would like only to add the suggestion that the arts of piercing an individual's effort at calculated unintentionality seem better developed than our capacity to manipulate our own behavior, so that regardless of how many steps have occurred in the information game, the witness is likely to have the advantage over the actor, and the initial asymmetry of the communication process is likely to be retained.

When we allow that the individual projects a definition of the situation when 12 he appears before others, we must also see that the others, however passive their role may seem to be, will themselves effectively project a definition of the situation by virtue of their response to the individual and by virtue of any lines of action they initiate to him. Ordinarily the definitions of the situation projected by the several different participants are sufficiently attuned to one another so that open contradiction will not occur. I do not mean that there will be the kind of consensus that arises when each individual present candidly expresses what he really feels and honestly agrees with the expressed feelings of the others present. This kind of harmony is an optimistic ideal and in any case not necessary for the smooth working of society. Rather, each participant is expected to suppress his immediate heartfelt feelings, conveying a view of the situation which he feels the others will be able to find at least temporarily acceptable. The maintenance of this surface of agreement, this veneer of consensus, is facilitated by each participant concealing his own wants behind statements which assert values to which everyone present feels obliged to give lip service. Further, there is usually a kind of division of definitional labor. Each participant is allowed to establish the tentative official ruling regarding matters which are vital to him but not immediately important to others, e.g., the rationalizations and justifications by which he accounts for his past activity. In exchange for this courtesy he remains silent or noncommittal on matters important to others but not immediately important to him. We have then a kind of interactional *modus vivendi.* Together, the participants contribute to a single over-all definition of the situation which involves not so much a real argument as to what exists but rather a real agreement as to whose claims concerning what issues will be temporarily honored. Real agreement will also exist concerning the desirability of avoiding an open conflict of definitions of the situation.[7] I will refer to this level of agreement as a "working consensus." It is to be understood that the working consensus established in one interaction setting will be quite different in content from the working consensus established in a different type of setting. Thus, between two friends at lunch, a reciprocal show of affection, respect, and concern for the other is maintained. In service occupations, on the other hand, the specialist often maintains an image of disinterested involvement in the problem of the client, while the client responds with a show of respect for the competence and integrity of the specialist. Regardless of such differences in content, however, the general form of these working arrangements is the same. . . .

15   Given the fact that the individual effectively projects a definition of the situation when he enters the presence of others, we can assume that events may occur within the interaction which contradict, discredit, or otherwise throw doubt upon this projection. When these disruptive events occur, the interaction itself may come to a confused and embarrassed halt. Some of the assumptions upon which the responses of the participants had been predicted become untenable, and the participants find themselves lodged in an interaction for which the situation has been wrongly defined and is now no longer defined. At such moments the individual whose presentation has been discredited may feel ashamed while the others present may feel hostile, and all the participants may come to feel ill at ease, nonplussed, out of countenance, embarrassed, experiencing the kind of anomy that is generated when the minute social system of face-to-face interaction breaks down. . . .

17   One cannot judge the importance of definitional disruptions by the frequency with which they occur, for apparently they would occur more frequently were not constant precautions taken. We find that preventive practices are constantly employed to avoid these embarrassments and that corrective practices are constantly employed to compensate for discrediting occurrences that have not been successfully avoided. When the individual employs these strategies and tactics to protect his own projections, we may refer to them as "defensive practices"; when a participant employs them to save the definition of the situation projected by another, we speak of "protective practices" or "tact." Together, defensive and protective practices comprise the techniques employed to safeguard the impression fostered by an individual during his presence before others. It should be added that while we may be ready to see that no fostered impression would survive if defensive practices were not employed, we

[7]An interaction can be purposely set up as a time and place for voicing differences in opinion, but in such cases participants must be careful to agree not to disagree on the proper tone of voice, vocabulary, and degree of seriousness in which all arguments are to be phrased, and upon the mutual respect which disagreeing participants must carefully continue to express toward one another. This debaters' or academic definition of the situation may also be invoked suddenly and judiciously as a way of translating a serious conflict of views into one that can be handled within a framework acceptable to all present.

are less ready perhaps to see that few impressions could survive if those who received the impression did not exert tact in their reception of it.

In addition to the fact that precautions are taken to prevent disruption of projected definitions, we may also note that an intense interest in these disruptions comes to play a significant role in the social life of the group. Practical jokes and social games are played in which embarrassments which are to be taken unseriously are purposely engineered.[12] Fantasies are created in which devastating exposures occur. Anecdotes from the past—real, embroidered, or fictitious—are told and retold, detailing disruptions which occurred, almost occurred, or occurred and were admirably resolved. There seems to be no grouping which does not have a ready supply of these games, reveries, and cautionary tales, to be used as a source of humor, a catharsis for anxieties, and a sanction for inducing individuals to be modest in their claims and reasonable in their projected expectations. . . .   18

To summarize, then, I assume that when an individual appears before others he will have many motives for trying to control the impression they receive of the situation.   19

[12]Erving Goffman, "Communication Conduct in an Island Community" (unpublished Ph.D. dissertation, Department of Sociology, University of Chicago, 1953), pp. 319–27.

ACTIVITY 4: *Theatricality in Everyday Life*

To think your way into Goffman's idea of everyday life as theatrical, try this thought experiment: Imagine that you have a meeting to accomplish a particular purpose with someone you know only slightly. You plan to *ask* the person for information or help on a project, or you intend to *give* the person either of those things; you want to get to know the person a little better (for instance, on a date), or you want to see whether you two can cooperate on something you care about. Make a list of the things you would do to prepare for such a meeting.

Now separate the various preparatory moves you make into two categories: those you are willing to share with your class and those you are not willing to share. Did the exercise help you understand Goffman's point?

As you could see from her journal entry, when Lisa read "The Cask of Amontillado," she thought that she and her friends were categorically different from Montresor. It wasn't just that he was a murderer and they weren't, but that he was hypocritical and they weren't. For this reason, she first read Goffman skeptically, resisting the idea that human beings put on "performances" for each other. After the class had read Goffman and done Activity 4, this discussion ensued:

Michael: When I meet people in my organic chemistry class, I wonder how smart they are and how well they really get the chemistry. That's because I wonder if they'd be good to have in a study group. I also wonder if they might become friends of mine. Or, if they're female, even more than friends.

Dinesh: Yeah, and you're inferring—just what Goffman says. I was thinking about this time I was leaving the dorm—it's locked and somebody wants to come in. He claims to live there but says he's lost his key. If I let him in, I'm inferring that he's a student and he's OK.

Teacher: What do you base your inference on?

Dinesh: Age, I guess. And how he's dressed. If he's got a bookbag, that helps.

Keesha: But here's an example from the other side. I'm an engineering major and when adults who are talking to me find that out, the whole way they treat me changes. Suddenly, they start talking about technical things. It's like they respect me a little bit more.

Lisa: But you're all talking about situations where people don't know each other. I can see Goffman's ideas working between strangers, but not when people are friends. If everybody's acting all the time, what does friendship mean?

Teacher: Do you think we act the same with all the people we're friendly with?

Lisa: I'm not sure.

Gregory: I think I eat differently in my room and in the dining hall, even if I'm by myself in both places. I notice I don't eat with my fingers as much if I think other people might be watching. And that includes my friends. So if my real self likes to eat with his fingers, I'm not being totally "myself" with my friends.

Michael: Yeah, I probably eat a little differently if my women friends are around. Guys don't care if I eat with my fingers.

Lisa: I read in a magazine once that women eat *less* when men are around.

Jennifer: Heterosexual women.

Lisa: Yeah, I guess. Maybe there are degrees of intimacy—you don't always show everyone everything. Maybe you have to be pretty close with someone not to be thinking at all of how you'll come off.

Hearing some of her classmates' stories and recollections and remembering some of her own helped Lisa relate to Goffman's ideas.

Now, review your notes on Goffman's chapter and the results of your speculations in Activity 4, and then think about what Goffman might see in the dialogues between the two main characters of Poe's story. Montresor has elaborately set the stage for his encounter with Fortunato, bringing the "props" he needs—stone and mortar—to the right place in the vault and hiding them under a pile of bones (75) and carrying the trowel in his cloak. He has arranged that no servants be present at his house to witness his journey to the vaults with Fortunato (24).

But these are not the only things important to the setting of the stage. Goffman would also be interested not just in Montresor as stage designer and director but also in Montresor as actor. He would have things to say about what Montresor does to control the way that Fortunato sees him and about why he does it. He could help us understand why, if Montresor really hates Fortunato all that much, he doesn't just shoot him or stab him under the cover of carnival chaos. Why the elaborate preparation? Goffman's understanding of human interaction helps explain what we're seeing in this short story. More generally, it helps us answer the question of whether a twentieth-century sociologist can contribute to the understanding of nineteenth-century fiction.

Think about these questions on your own; then read the following essay that Lisa wrote to answer some of them:

SAMPLE STUDENT PAPER

Lisa Rodrigues

Ms. Washington

English 113

November 1, 2003

     Poe's Old Literary Wine in New Sociological Bottles

     Some people might think a modern-day sociologist might
not have anything relevant to say about how to interpret a
nineteenth-century short story, but he does. Matching up
the major ideas in Erving Goffman's *The Presentation of
Self in Everyday Life* with the interactions in Edgar Allan
Poe's "The Cask of Amontillado" can show just how useful
sociology can be for interpreting fiction.

     One of Goffman's major ideas is that people want to
control each other in a number of ways: They want to
control how others see them (5, 9) and what others do (6).
At first, you might think that wanting to control how others
see them makes it sound like everyone is a phony. There are
clearly some who are, but it's true of others in small and
not necessarily evil ways. Some, as Aretha Franklin says in
her song, just want some "R-E-S-P-E-C-T" and try to arrange
the impression they give so that they get it. Everyone is
involved in some way in the "information game" in which we
try to look good and try to find out whether other people
are as good as they look. There's the same kind of variety
in people's wish to control each other's behavior. Some
people want to be dictators, but some just want you to come
to their parties.

     The reason everyone is part of the information game is
that it's so hard to know someone else's heart. We have to
guess, or as Goffman quotes William I. Thomas as saying,
"We live by inference" (5). In "The Cask of Amontillado,"
Montresor takes advantage of this distance between people
by acting so that Fortunato can infer that Montresor is
still his friend. Montresor tells us frankly about his

hypocrisy: "It must be understood that neither by word nor deed had I given Fortunato cause to doubt my good will" (2). In Goffman's list of impressions people try to give others, Montresor fits the second: A person in front of others "may wish them . . . to think that he thinks highly of them" (6). Montresor wants Fortunato to think he, Montresor, thinks Fortunato is an expert on wine and can help him authenticate the Amontillado he has just bought (7, 9, 11, 13). Of course, Montresor is inferring, too, for instance, when he says, "he did not perceive that my smile *now* was at the thought of his immolation" (2). He's probably right, but he is not an omniscient narrator and doesn't really know what Fortunato knows or what he's thinking.

Another of Goffman's important ideas can help explain why Montresor's verbal maneuvering is so elaborate at the beginning of the story, when he tells Fortunato about the Amontillado, which may not really be there, and pretends to need expert help. Montresor wants Fortunato to be the one to suggest a visit to the catacombs. According to Goffman, the best way to get people to do what you want them to do is "by influencing the definition of the situation . . . in such a way as to give them the kind of impression that will lead them to act voluntarily in accordance" with your wishes (6). The key word is "voluntarily." Montresor accomplishes that by pretending that he is going to ask another wine expert, Luchesi, to judge what's in the cask Montresor says he bought (13). Fortunato is just vain enough and jealous enough to want to be the expert in the case (14), as Montresor guessed he would be (3). When Fortunato hears that Montresor might consult Luchesi, he brings up the idea of going down to the caverns to inspect the cask. Of course Montresor has already prepared for this trip by making sure that his servants wouldn't be home so no one would see them going in (24), but he pretends to be surprised by Fortunato's idea (17) and even unwilling (19). Once they're started on the trip, Montresor keeps trying to turn back, which Fortunato resists (e.g., 35–36, 52–53). But of course Fortunato in the vault is exactly what Montresor has wanted all along. Still, it's much better that Fortunato thinks it's his own idea. Montresor is being a dictator, but he didn't have to kidnap Fortunato because he's doing it by controlling the definition of the situation—inept wine buyer needs help from expert. So even though they're alike in some important ways—especially in their interest in and knowledge of wine—Montresor gets control of Fortunato by pretending to know less. But Fortunato doesn't notice and Montresor has gotten the upper hand by playing dumb.

Another of Goffman's concepts is illustrated by the end of the story. Fortunato has a number of reactions to being chained to the wall: he's bewildered and says, "The Amontillado!" (73); he gives "a low moaning cry" and rattles the chains (76); he screams (77); he laughs and calls what Montresor has done "a very good joke" (79, 81); he cries, *"For the love of God, Montresor!"* (83); and then he falls silent (85, 87, 89). Several of these (i.e., the moans and screams) seem like heartfelt responses to his awful predicament, so they fall outside Goffman's concepts. They're too genuine. The ones Goffman can explain best are the attempt to call this whole episode a joke and the silence. The attempt to call this encounter a joke shows that Fortunato still has enough presence of mind to try to play the information game. He proves Goffman's point that the game is "a potentially infinite cycle of concealment, discovery, false revelation, and rediscovery" (11). It doesn't work, of course; it's too late for Fortunato to win the game. But it's amazing that he can still play at all.

What about the silence? After Fortunato pleads desperately and futilely, *"For the love of God, Montresor!"* Montresor echoes him cruelly: "'Yes,' I said, 'For the love of God!'" (83–84). Montresor wants a response and calls

Fortunato's name several times. When he doesn't get one, he tries to look into the chamber and "My heart grew sick" (89). We can see this as another move in the infinite information game. By calling repeatedly, Montresor tips his hand that he wants something from Fortunato. Probably what he wants is signs of suffering. He seemed to enjoy that earlier when he first began building the wall to shut Fortunato in and Fortunato rattled his chains: "The noise lasted for several minutes, during which, that I might hearken to it with the more satisfaction, I ceased my labors and sat down upon the bones" (76). Maybe Fortunato gets the message that this is the last thing he can do to exercise power over Montresor. It's pathetically little, but it's all he's got left so he uses it. And possibly it works, upsetting Montresor enough that he rushes to complete the wall and leave the area and doesn't tell Fortunato why he has done this to him. According to his definition of revenge at the beginning of the story (1), this makes his revenge incomplete. So maybe this is one very small way that Fortunato wins. Fortunato is dead, but fifty years later Montresor is still telling the story.

So Erving Goffman's ideas do turn out to be useful for interpreting the story because the story is an example of some of the things Goffman is talking about. Of course, most people aren't crazed murderers. But Montresor isn't completely different from ordinary people. He's an extreme example of impression management, but an example just the same. Goffman is helpful for the reader of the story because he uses an inductive method of argument and piles up example after example, from which he draws his generalizations. His examples come from his own research, other sociologists, memoirs, and even a novel, so he seems to think that fiction can help him make his points. The story is one more example and it does just that, but the principles Goffman talks about in his chapter give us a way to understand it.

Works Cited

Goffman, Erving. <u>The Presentation of Self in Everyday Life</u>.
  New York: Doubleday Anchor Books, 1959. 1—16.

Poe, Edgar Allan. "The Cask of Amontillado" (1846). <u>The
  Complete Edgar Allan Poe: Tales</u>. New York: Avenel Books,
  1981.

Lisa's paper demonstrates how conceptual frameworks can guide interpretation. The following exercises ask you to make suggestions that would help her go even further with her analysis.

 ACTIVITY 5: *Applying Poe to Goffman*

Lisa's paper does a good job of applying Goffman's concepts to Poe's story as an interpretive frame. Examine your notes about the match-up of Poe and Goffman. Does Poe have anything to teach sociologists like Goffman? That is, are there any actions or interactions in the story that Goffman does not have a term for but which sociologists ought to be interested in?

You can see from her essay that Lisa's ideas about how people present themselves have grown, thanks to Goffman. But she still thinks some things—like Fortunato's groans and screams—lie outside Goffman's conceptual scheme. She uses Goffman's ideas where they are appropriate, but also points out their limits. This is entirely appropriate. The application of an interpretive framework to material from another field is essentially an exercise in comparison, and as with any two similar but not identical things, there are differences as well as similarities. Responsible writers acknowledge these differences.

The two pairs of texts in this chapter, "For C" and "Airport Separations," and "The Cask of Amontillado" and *The Presentation of Self in Everyday Life,* show different kinds of texts interacting in different ways. But in both cases, the concepts offered by the academic text could deepen our understanding of the literary one. The next chapter will show you how to research frameworks from other disciplines that will help you interpret literary works of your own choosing.

CHAPTER TEN

Using Research to Write about Literature

APPLYING A FRAMEWORK FROM ANOTHER DISCIPLINE TO A LITERARY TEXT

In Chapter 9, you saw students analyzing literary works by using concepts from another discipline. The methods of close reading in literary criticism and research in sociology combined to enrich our understanding of literary works. Using concepts from both disciplines is possible because both are at base about the ways that human beings think, feel, and behave.

This chapter will help you make similar connections for yourself. First, it lays out the kind of assignment that Lisa Rodrigues was responding to with her paper on pp. 202–05 ("Poe's Old Literary Wine in New Sociological Bottles"). Then it helps you work through the stages of producing such an analysis, from reading the assignment to writing a conclusion.

ACTIVITY 1: *The Research Assignment: Applying a Framework from Another Discipline to a Literary Text*

For this assignment, you will

1. choose your own literary work or works from the Anthology (a poem or group of poems, a short story, or a play);
2. through research choose some academic frame(s) through which to view it; and
3. write an analysis in which you interpret the work, calling on the principles and concepts in the academic sources where appropriate.

Your application should be based on careful close reading of the text: Pay careful attention to word choice, syntax, imagery, point of view, and other features subject to formalist analysis (see Appendix A).

Audience: Address an academic audience that knows the literary work but wants to understand it better.

Purpose: To persuade your audience that your argument has merit by supporting your claims with reasons and sufficient, typical, accurate, and relevant evidence.

Format: Your paper, starting with the first draft, should have a works cited list using MLA style.

Reading the Assignment

As we saw in Chapter 2, among the important things to look for in any assignment are the verbs that indicate what you are to *do*. For the writing assignment given in Activity 1, you will be *choosing* a literary work or works, *doing research* to find sources in other disciplines, and then *writing an analysis* that joins the two kinds of texts.

The subsequent parts of the assignment flesh out the communications triangle. For instance, the note on audience tells you what kind of readers to envision as you write. The fact that your readers know the work means that you can leave out plot summary. The fact that your audience is academic explains the note on format: Since readers have to be able to follow the trail of your research, you have to provide references.

The word *persuade* in the note on purpose tells you that you are writing an argument. The possibility of opening someone's mind shows you that you are not expected to *prove* that your interpretation is correct so much as to *make a good case* by supporting it adequately.

Choosing a Literary Work

In choosing a literary work to write about, you have several things to consider. First, is it rich enough to repay all the attention that you will give it in the course of this analysis? The richer the work you start with, the easier it will be to find links to the academic disciplines. A zipper's functioning doesn't depend on its length, but on its teeth: There has to be a full set on each side. Pick a literary work with lots of teeth.

Second, your literary work should interest you because of its subject matter or the way it treats it. It helps to start out liking it, though I have often had the experience of learning to like a work only in the process of trying to understand it. So being puzzled or even annoyed by a work can be the spur to a good paper and a rewarding experience.

Deciding Which Disciplines to Investigate

The crucial link between the literary work and the disciplinary frameworks is theme (see Chapter 4). For this reason, you should spend some time doing a close reading of the work and putting together an argument about its theme that takes account of as many as possible of the features analyzed in Chapters 4 through 7. If your teacher doesn't ask you to write this formally, make notes for yourself.

Once you can make an argument about what the work means, you can decide which academic disciplines address a similar subject and so might have something valuable to offer. It is helpful at this stage and also, as we'll see later, at the writing stage, to see the work as generating a problem or a question that leads you into other disciplines for answers. A few examples follow:

- Several of my students wondered why people would do something that seems as cruel as the ritual in Shirley Jackson's story "The Lottery." Each of them turned up different resources in anthropology and psychology journals to help them answer that question.
- In Edgar Allan Poe's "The Tell-Tale Heart," the narrator is so insistent that he is not mad that my student Erin was prompted to ask whether he was merely a criminal or an *insane* criminal. She explored sources in psychology, sociology, and criminology, finally finding a sociology article entitled "Critical Elements of Criminal Behavior Explanation" that helped her decide whether the narrator's strange behavior could be classified as criminal or just peculiar. She also found a folklore article on the concept of the "evil eye," which helped her understand his motive for the murder.

Thinking of literary works in terms of problems and questions will help you integrate outside research. Useful scholarship is often found in the humanities and social sciences—for instance, in psychology, sociology, history, philosophy, anthropology, communications, and folklore studies. Medicine is also sometimes quite useful, and there are occasionally ways to bring in other natural sciences. Your teacher and reference librarians can help you figure out which disciplines might offer useful approaches.

Doing Research

The Internet

The Internet has changed research by putting huge amounts of information literally at our fingertips. Search engines like Google.com can quickly scan millions of Web pages in order to present you with matches to the precise word or phrase you choose. As you probably already know, these search engines are especially useful for researching topics for civic writing (and for shopping, listening to music, finding news and sports scores, and many other everyday activities). Academic sources are scarcer there, however, and often difficult to distinguish from the mass of other information.

For instance, a student named Tracy Greenwald was interested in writing about David Kaplan's short story, "Doe Season," in which a nine-year-old girl accompanies her father on a deer-hunting trip and discovers not only her society's traditional discomfort with females as hunters, but also her own distaste for it. So that you can better follow Tracy's research, read the story now.

Doe Season°

DAVID MICHAEL KAPLAN *(1946–), who has a B.A. from Yale University and an M.F.A. from the University of Iowa, has published short stories in many magazines and journals, including* The Atlantic, Playboy, Redbook, TriQuarterly, Doubletake, Ohio Review, *and* Crazyhorse. *He teaches at Loyola University of Chicago and has also written about writing in* Revision: A Creative Approach to Writing and Rewriting Fiction. *"Doe Season," which is from Kaplan's first story collection,* Comfort *(1987), was selected for the collection* Best American Short Stories of 1985.

They were always the same woods, she thought sleepily as they drove through the early morning darkness—deep and immense, covered with yesterday's snowfall, which had frozen overnight. They were the same woods that lay behind her house, *and they stretch all the way to here,* she thought, *for miles and miles, longer than I could walk in a day, or a week even, but they are still the same woods.* The thought made her feel good: it was like thinking of God; it was like thinking of the space between here and the moon; it was like thinking of all the foreign countries from her geography book where even now, Andy knew, people were going to bed, while they—she and her father and Charlie Spoon and Mac, Charlie's eleven-year-old son—were driving deeper into the Pennsylvania countryside, to go hunting.

They had risen long before dawn. Her mother, yawning and not trying to hide her sleepiness, cooked them eggs and French toast. Her father smoked a cigarette and flicked ashes into his saucer while Andy listened, wondering *Why doesn't he come?* and *Won't he ever come?* until at last a car pulled into the graveled drive and honked. "That will be Charlie Spoon," her father said; he always said "Charlie Spoon," even though his real name was Spreun, because

---

°Title The government regulates the hunting of certain animals in order to try to control their populations. The "season" is that limited time of year during which it is legal to kill a particular species or subgroup of that species. In "doe season," it is legal to kill female but not male deer.

Charlie was, in a sense, shaped like a spoon, with a large head and a narrow waist and chest.

Andy's mother kissed her and her father and said, "Well, have a good time" and "Be careful." Soon they were outside in the bitter dark loading gear by the back-porch light, their breath steaming. The woods behind the house were then only a black streak against the wash of night.

Andy dozed in the car and woke to find that it was half light. Mac—also sleeping—had slid against her. She pushed him away and looked out the window. Her breath clouded the glass, and she was cold; the car's heater didn't work right. They were riding over gentle hills, the woods on both sides now—the same woods, she knew, because she had been watching the whole way, even while she slept. They had been in her dreams, and she had never lost sight of them.

Charlie Spoon was driving. "I don't understand why she's coming," he said to her father. "How old is she anyway—eight?" 5

"Nine," her father replied. "She's small for her age."

"So—nine. What's the difference? She'll just add to the noise and get tired besides."

"No, she won't," her father said. "She can walk me to death. And she'll bring good luck, you'll see. Animals—I don't know how she does it, but they come right up to her. We go walking in the woods, and we'll spot more raccoons and possums and such than I ever see when I'm alone."

Charlie grunted.

"Besides, she's not a bad little shot, even if she doesn't hunt yet. She shoots 10 the .22 real good."

"Popgun," Charlie said, and snorted. "And target shooting ain't deer hunting."

"Well, she's not gonna be shooting anyway, Charlie," her father said. "Don't worry. She'll be no bother."

"I still don't know why she's coming," Charlie said.

"Because she wants to, and I want her to. Just like you and Mac. No difference."

Charlie turned onto a side road and after a mile or so slowed down. "That's 15 it!" he cried. He stopped, backed up, and entered a narrow dirt road almost hidden by trees. Five hundred yards down, the road ran parallel to a fenced-in field. Charlie parked in a cleared area deeply rutted by frozen tractor tracks. The gate was locked. *In the spring,* Andy thought, *there will be cows here, and a dog that chases them,* but now the field was unmarked and bare.

"This is it," Charlie Spoon declared. "Me and Mac was up here just two weeks ago, scouting it out, and there's deer. Mac saw the tracks."

"That's right," Mac said.

"Well, we'll just see about that," her father said, putting on his gloves. He turned to Andy. "How you doing, honeybun?"

"Just fine," she said.

Andy shivered and stamped as they unloaded: first the rifles, which they 20 unsheathed and checked, sliding the bolts, sighting through scopes, adjusting the slings; then the gear, their food and tents and sleeping bags and stove stored in

four backpacks—three big ones for Charlie Spoon and her father and Mac, and a
day pack for her.

"That's about your size," Mac said, to tease her.

She reddened and said, "Mac, I can carry a pack big as yours any day." He
laughed and pressed his knee against the back of hers, so that her leg buckled.
"Cut it out," she said. She wanted to make an iceball and throw it at him, but
she knew that her father and Charlie were anxious to get going, and she didn't
want to displease them.

Mac slid under the gate, and they handed the packs over to him. Then they slid
under and began walking across the field toward the same woods that ran all the
way back to her home, where even now her mother was probably rising again to
wash their breakfast dishes and make herself a fresh pot of coffee. *She is there, and we
are here:* the thought satisfied Andy. There was no place else she would rather be.

Mac came up beside her. "Over there's Canada," he said, nodding toward the
woods.

25   "Huh!" she said. "Not likely."

"I don't mean *right* over there. I mean farther up north. You think I'm
dumb?"

Dumb as your father, she thought.

"Look at that," Mac said, pointing to a piece of cow dung lying on a spot
scraped bare of snow. "A frozen meadow muffin." He picked it up and sailed it at
her. "Catch!"

"Mac!" she yelled. His laugh was as gawky as he was. She walked faster. He
seemed different today somehow, bundled in his yellow-and-black-checkered
coat, a rifle in hand, his silly floppy hat not quite covering his ears. They all
seemed different as she watched them trudge through the snow—Mac and her
father and Charlie Spoon—bigger, maybe, as if the cold landscape enlarged
rather than diminished them, so that they, the only figures in that landscape,
took on size and meaning just by being there. If they weren't there, everything
would be quieter, and the woods would be the same as before. *But they are here,*
Andy thought, looking behind her at the boot prints in the snow, *and I am too,
and so it's all different.*

30   "We'll go down to the cut where we found those deer tracks," Charlie said as
they entered the woods. "Maybe we'll get lucky and get a late one coming
through."

The woods descended into a gully. The snow was softer and deeper here, so
that often Andy sank to her knees. Charlie and Mac worked the top of the gully
while she and her father walked along the base some thirty yards behind them.
"If they miss the first shot, we'll get the second," her father said, and she nodded
as if she had known this all the time. She listened to the crunch of their boots,
their breathing, and the drumming of a distant woodpecker. And the crackling.
In winter the woods crackled as if everything were straining, ready to snap like
dried chicken bones.

We are hunting, Andy thought. The cold air burned her nostrils.

They stopped to make lunch by a rock outcropping that protected them from
the wind. Her father heated the bean soup her mother had made for them, and

they ate it with bread already stiff from the cold. He and Charlie took a few pulls from a flask of Jim Beam while she scoured the plates with snow and repacked them. Then they all had coffee with sugar and powdered milk, and her father poured her a cup too. "We won't tell your momma," he said, and Mac laughed. Andy held the cup the way her father did, not by the handle but around the rim. The coffee tasted smoky. She felt a little queasy, but she drank it all.

Charlie Spoon picked his teeth with a fingernail. "Now, you might've noticed one thing," he said.

"What's that?" her father asked.   35

"You might've noticed you don't hear no rifles. That's because there ain't no other hunters here. We've got the whole damn woods to ourselves. Now, I ask you—do I know how to find 'em?"

"We haven't seen deer yet, neither."

"Oh, we will," Charlie said, "but not for a while now." He leaned back against the rock. "Deer're sleeping, resting up for the evening feed."

"I seen a deer behind our house once, and it was afternoon," Andy said.

"Yeah, honey, but that was *before* deer season," Charlie said, grinning. "They   40
know something now. They're smart that way."

"That's right," Mac said.

Andy looked at her father—had she said something stupid?

"Well, Charlie," he said, "if they know so much, how come so many get themselves shot?"

"Them's the ones that don't *believe* what they know," Charlie replied. The men laughed. Andy hesitated, and then laughed with them.

They moved on, as much to keep warm as to find a deer. The wind became   45
even stronger. Blowing through the treetops, it sounded like the ocean, and once Andy thought she could smell salt air. But that was impossible; the ocean was *hundreds* of miles away, farther than Canada even. She and her parents had gone last summer to stay for a week at a motel on the New Jersey shore. That was the first time she'd seen the ocean, and it frightened her. It was huge and empty, yet always moving. Everything lay hidden. If you walked in it, you couldn't see how deep it was or what might be below; if you swam, something could pull you under and you'd never be seen again. Its musky, rank smell made her think of things dying. Her mother had floated beyond the breakers, calling to her to come in, but Andy wouldn't go farther than a few feet into the surf. Her mother swam and splashed with animal-like delight while her father, smiling shyly, held his white arms above the waist-deep water as if afraid to get them wet. Once a comber rolled over and sent them both tossing, and when her mother tried to stand up, the surf receding behind, Andy saw that her mother's swimsuit top had come off, so that her breasts swayed free, her nipples like two dark eyes. Embarrassed, Andy looked around: except for two women under a yellow umbrella farther up, the beach was empty. Her mother stood up unsteadily, regained her footing. Taking what seemed the longest time, she calmly refixed her top. Andy lay on the beach towel and closed her eyes. The sound of the surf made her head ache.

And now it was winter; the sky was already dimming, not just with the absence of light but with a mist that clung to the hunters' faces like cobwebs. They made camp early. Andy was chilled. When she stood still, she kept wiggling her toes to make sure they were there. Her father rubbed her arms and held her to him briefly, and that felt better. She unpacked the food while the others put up the tents.

"How about rounding us up some firewood, Mac?" Charlie asked.

"I'll do it," Andy said. Charlie looked at her thoughtfully and then handed her the canvas carrier.

There wasn't much wood on the ground, so it took her a while to get a good load. She was about a hundred yards from camp, near a cluster of high, lichen-covered boulders, when she saw through a crack in the rock a buck and two does walking gingerly, almost daintily, through the alder trees. She tried to hush her breathing as they passed not more than twenty yards away. There was nothing she could do. If she yelled, they'd be gone; by the time she got back to camp, they'd be gone. The buck stopped, nostrils quivering, tail up and alert. He looked directly at her. Still she didn't move, not one muscle. He was a beautiful buck, the color of late-turned maple leaves. Unafraid, he lowered his tail, and he and his does silently merged into the trees. Andy walked back to camp and dropped the firewood.

50   "I saw three deer," she said. "A buck and two does."

"Where?" Charlie Spoon cried, looking behind her as if they might have followed her into camp.

"In the woods yonder. They're gone now."

"Well, hell!" Charlie banged his coffee cup against his knee.

"Didn't I say she could find animals?" her father said, grinning.

55   "Too late to go after them," Charlie muttered. "It'll be dark in a quarter hour. Damn!"

"Damn," Mac echoed.

"They just walk right up to her," her father said.

"Well, leastwise this proves there's deer here." Charlie began snapping long branches into shorter ones. "You know, I think I'll stick with you," he told Andy, "since you're so good at finding deer and all. How'd that be?"

"Okay, I guess," Andy murmured. She hoped he was kidding; no way did she want to hunt with Charlie Spoon. Still, she was pleased he had said it.

60   Her father and Charlie took one tent, she and Mac the other. When they were in their sleeping bags, Mac said in the darkness, "I bet you really didn't see no deer, did you?"

She sighed. "I did, Mac. Why would I lie?"

"How big was the buck?"

"Four point. I counted."

Mac snorted.

65   "You just believe what you want, Mac," she said testily.

"Too bad it ain't buck season," he said. "Well, I got to go pee."

"So pee."

She heard him turn in his bag. "You ever see it?" he asked.

"It? What's 'it'?"

"It. A pecker."

"Sure," she lied.

"Whose? Your father's?"

She was uncomfortable. "No," she said.

"Well, whose then?"

"Oh I don't know! Leave me be, why don't you?"   75

"Didn't see a deer, didn't see a pecker," Mac said teasingly.

She didn't answer right away. Then she said, "My cousin Lewis. I saw his."

"Well, how old's he?"

"One and a half."

"Ha! A baby! A baby's is like a little worm. It ain't a real one at all."   80

If he says he'll show me his, she thought, *I'll kick him. I'll just get out of my bag and kick him.*

"I went hunting with my daddy and Versh and Danny Simmons last year in buck season," Mac said, "and we got ourselves one. And we hog-dressed the thing. You know what that is, don't you?"

"No," she said. She was confused. What was he talking about now?

"That's when you cut him open and take out all his guts, so the meat don't spoil. Makes him lighter to pack out, too."

She tried to imagine what the deer's guts might look like, pulled from the   85
gaping hole. "What do you do with them?" she said. "The guts?"

"Oh, just leave 'em for the bears."

She ran her finger like a knife blade along her belly.

"When we left them on the ground," Mac said, "they smoked. Like they were cooking."

"Huh," she said.

"They cut off the deer's pecker, too, you know."   90

Andy imagined Lewis's pecker and shuddered. "Mac, you're disgusting."

He laughed. "Well, I gotta go pee." She heard him rustle out of his bag. "Broo!" he cried, flapping his arms. "It's cold!"

He makes so much noise, she thought, *just noise and more noise.*

Her father woke them before first light. He warned them to talk softly and said that they were going to the place where Andy had seen the deer, to try to cut them off on their way back from their night feeding. Andy couldn't shake off her sleep. Stuffing her sleeping bag into its sack seemed to take an hour, and tying her boots was the strangest thing she'd ever done. Charlie Spoon made hot chocolate and oatmeal with raisins. Andy closed her eyes and, between beats of her heart, listened to the breathing of the forest. *When I open my eyes, it will be lighter,* she decided. But when she did, it was still just as dark, except for the swaths of their flashlights and the hissing blue flame of the stove. *There has to be just one moment when it all changes from dark to light,* Andy thought. She had missed it yesterday, in the car; today she would watch more closely.

But when she remembered again, it was already first light and they had moved   95
to the rocks by the deer trail and had set up shooting positions—Mac and Charlie Spoon on the up-trail side, she and her father behind them, some six feet

up on a ledge. The day became brighter, the sun piercing the tall pines, raking the hunters, yet providing little warmth. Andy now smelled alder and pine and the slightly rotten odor of rock lichen. She rubbed her hand over the stone and considered that it must be very old, had probably been here before the giant pines, *before anyone was in these woods at all*. A chipmunk sniffed on a nearby branch. She aimed an imaginary rifle and pressed the trigger. The chipmunk froze, then scurried away. Her legs were cramping on the narrow ledge. Her father seemed to doze, one hand in his parka, the other cupped lightly around the rifle. She could smell his scent of old wool and leather. His cheeks were speckled with gray-black whiskers, and he worked his jaws slightly, as if chewing a small piece of gum.

Please let us get a deer, she prayed.

A branch snapped on the other side of the rock face. Her father's hand stiffened on the rifle, startling her—*He hasn't been sleeping at all*, she marveled—and then his jaw relaxed, as did the lines around his eyes, and she heard Charlie Spoon call, "Yo, don't shoot, it's us." He and Mac appeared from around the rock. They stopped beneath the ledge. Charlie solemnly crossed his arms.

"I don't believe we're gonna get any deer here," he said drily.

Andy's father lowered his rifle to Charlie and jumped down from the ledge. Then he reached up for Andy. She dropped into his arms and he set her gently on the ground.

100   Mac sidled up to her. "I knew you didn't see no deer," he said.

"Just because they don't come when you want 'em to don't mean she didn't see them," her father said.

Still, she felt bad. Her telling about the deer had caused them to spend the morning there, cold and expectant, with nothing to show for it.

They tramped through the woods for another two hours, not caring much about noise. Mac found some deer tracks, and they argued about how old they were. They split up for a while and then rejoined at an old logging road that deer might use, and followed it. The road crossed a stream, which had mostly frozen over but in a few spots still caught leaves and twigs in an icy swirl. They forded it by jumping from rock to rock. The road narrowed after that, and the woods thickened.

They stopped for lunch, heating up Charlie's wife's corn chowder. Andy's father cut squares of applesauce cake with his hunting knife and handed them to her and Mac, who ate his almost daintily. Andy could faintly taste knife oil on the cake. She was tired. She stretched her leg; the muscle that had cramped on the rock still ached.

105   "Might as well relax," her father said, as if reading her thoughts. "We won't find deer till suppertime."

Charlie Spoon leaned back against his pack and folded his hands across his stomach. "Well, even if we don't get a deer," he said expansively, "it's still great to be out here, breathe some fresh air, clomp around a bit. Get away from the house and the old lady." He winked at Mac, who looked away.

"That's what the woods are all about, anyway," Charlie said. "It's where the women don't want to go." He bowed his head toward Andy. "With your exception, of course, little lady." He helped himself to another piece of applesauce cake.

"She ain't a woman," Mac said.

"Well, she damn well's gonna be," Charlie said. He grinned at her. "Or will you? You're half a boy anyway. You go by a boy's name. What's your real name? Andrea, ain't it?"

"That's right," she said. She hoped that if she didn't look at him, Charlie 110
would stop.

"Well, which do you like? Andy or Andrea?"

"Don't matter," she mumbled. "Either."

"She's always been Andy to me," her father said.

Charlie Spoon was still grinning. "So what are you gonna be, Andrea? A boy or a girl?"

"I'm a girl," she said. 115

"But you want to go hunting and fishing and everything, huh?"

"She can do whatever she likes," her father said.

"Hell, you might as well have just had a boy and be done with it!" Charlie exclaimed.

"That's funny," her father said, and chuckled. "That's just what her momma tells me."

They were looking at her, and she wanted to get away from them all, even 120
from her father, who chose to joke with them.

"I'm going to walk a bit," she said.

She heard them laughing as she walked down the logging trail. She flapped her arms; she whistled. *I don't care how much noise I make,* she thought. Two grouse flew from the underbrush, startling her. A little farther down, the trail ended in a clearing that enlarged into a frozen meadow; beyond it the woods began again. A few moldering posts were all that was left of a fence that had once enclosed the field. The low afternoon sunlight reflected brightly off the snow, so that Andy's eyes hurt. She squinted hard. A gust of wind blew across the field, stinging her face. And then, as if it had been waiting for her, the doe emerged from the trees opposite and stepped cautiously into the field. Andy watched: it stopped and stood quietly for what seemed a long time and then ambled across. It stopped again about seventy yards away and began to browse in a patch of sugar grass uncovered by the wind. Carefully, slowly, never taking her eyes from the doe, Andy walked backward, trying to step into the boot points she'd already made. When she was far enough back into the woods, she turned and walked faster, her heart racing. *Please let it stay,* she prayed.

"There's doe in the field yonder," she told them.

They got their rifles and hurried down the trail.

"No use," her father said. "We're making too much noise any way you look 125
at it."

"At least we got us the wind in our favor," Charlie Spoon said, breathing heavily. But the doe was still there, grazing.

"Good Lord," Charlie whispered. He looked at her father. "Well, whose shot?"

"Andy spotted it," her father said in a low voice. "Let her shoot it."

"What!" Charlie's eyes widened. 130

Andy couldn't believe what her father had just said. She'd only shot tin cans and targets; she'd never even fired her father's .30-.30, and she'd never killed anything.

"I can't," she whispered.

"That's right, she can't," Charlie Spoon insisted. "She's not old enough and she don't have a license even if she was!"

"Well, who's to tell?" her father said in a low voice. "Nobody's going to know but us." He looked at her. "Do you want to shoot it, punkin?"

135   *Why doesn't it hear us?* she wondered. *Why doesn't it run away?* "I don't know," she said.

"Well, I'm sure as hell gonna shoot it," Charlie said. Her father grasped Charlie's rifle barrel and held it. His voice was steady.

"Andy's a good shot. It's her deer. She found it, not you. You'd still be sitting on your ass back in camp." He turned to her again. "Now—do you want to shoot it, Andy? Yes or no."

He was looking at her; they were all looking at her. Suddenly she was angry at the deer, who refused to hear them, who wouldn't run away even when it could. "I'll shoot it," she said. Charlie turned away in disgust.

She lay on the ground and pressed the rifle stock against her shoulder bone. The snow was cold through her parka; she smelled oil and wax and damp earth. She pulled off one glove with her teeth. "It sights just like the .22," her father said gently. "Cartridge's already chambered." As she had done so many times before, she sighted down the scope; now the doe was in the reticle. She moved the barrel until the cross hairs lined up. Her father was breathing beside her.

140   "Aim where the chest and legs meet, or a little above, punkin," he was saying calmly. "That's the killing shot."

But now, seeing it in the scope, Andy was hesitant. Her finger weakened on the trigger. Still, she nodded at what her father said and sighted again, the cross hairs lining up in exactly the same spot—the doe had hardly moved, its brownish-gray body outlined starkly against the blue-backed snow. *It doesn't know,* Andy thought. *It just doesn't know.* And as she looked, deer and snow and faraway trees flattened within the circular frame to become like a picture on a calendar, not real, and she felt calm, as if she had been dreaming everything— the day, the deer, the hunt itself. And she, finger on trigger, was only a part of that dream.

"Shoot!" Charlie hissed.

Through the scope she saw the deer look up, ears high and straining.

Charlie groaned, and just as he did, and just at the moment when Andy knew—*knew*—the doe would bound away, as if she could feel its haunches tensing and gathering power, she pulled the trigger. Later she would think, *I felt the recoil, I smelled the smoke, but I don't remember pulling the trigger.* Through the scope the deer seemed to shrink into itself, and then slowly knelt, hind legs first, head raised as if to cry out. It trembled, still straining to keep its head high, as if that alone would save it; failing, it collapsed, shuddered, and lay still.

145   "Whoee!" Mac cried.

"One shot! One shot!" her father yelled, clapping her on the back. Charlie Spoon was shaking his head and smiling dumbly.

"I told you she was a great little shot!" her father said. "I told you!" Mac danced and clapped his hands. She was dazed, not quite understanding what had happened. And then they were crossing the field toward the fallen doe, she walking dreamlike, the men laughing and joking, released now from the tension of silence and anticipation. Suddenly Mac pointed and cried out, "Look at that!"

The doe was rising, legs unsteady. They stared at it, unable to comprehend, and in that moment the doe regained its feet and looked at them, as if it too were trying to understand. Her father whistled softly. Charlie Spoon unslung his rifle and raised it to his shoulder, but the doe was already bounding away. His hurried shot missed, and the deer disappeared into the woods.

"Damn, damn, damn," he moaned.

"I don't believe it," her father said. "That deer was dead."   150

"Dead, hell!" Charlie yelled. "It was gutshot, that's all. Stunned and gutshot. Clean shot, my ass!"

What have I done? Andy thought.

Her father slung his rifle over his shoulder. "Well, let's go. It can't get too far."

"Hell, I've seen deer run ten miles gutshot," Charlie said. He waved his arms. "We may never find her!"

As they crossed the field, Mac came up to her and said in a low voice,   155
"Gutshoot a deer, you'll go to hell."

"Shut up, Mac," she said, her voice cracking. It was a terrible thing she had done, she knew. She couldn't bear to think of the doe in pain and frightened. *Please let it die,* she prayed.

But though they searched all the last hour of daylight, so that they had to recross the field and go up the logging trail in a twilight made even deeper by thick, smoky clouds, they didn't find the doe. They lost its trail almost immediately in the dense stands of alderberry and larch.

"I am cold, and I am tired," Charlie Spoon declared. "And if you ask me, that deer's in another county already."

"No one's asking you, Charlie," her father said.

They had a supper of hard salami and ham, bread, and the rest of the   160
applesauce cake. It seemed a bother to heat the coffee, so they had cold chocolate instead. Everyone turned in early.

"We'll find it in the morning, honeybun," her father said, as she went to her tent.

"I don't like to think of it suffering." She was almost in tears.

"It's dead already, punkin. Don't even think about it." He kissed her, his breath sour and his beard rough against her cheek.

Andy was sure she wouldn't get to sleep; the image of the doe falling, falling, then rising again, repeated itself whenever she closed her eyes. Then she heard an owl hoot and realized that it had awakened her, so she must have been asleep after all. She hoped the owl would hush, but instead it hooted louder. She wished her father or Charlie Spoon would wake up and do something about it, but no one moved in the other tent, and suddenly she was afraid that they had all decamped, wanting nothing more to do with her. She whispered, "Mac, Mac," to the sleeping bag where he should be, but no one answered. She tried to find the flashlight she always kept by her side, but couldn't, and she cried in panic, "Mac, are you there?" He mumbled something, and immediately she felt foolish and hoped he wouldn't reply.

165   When she awoke again, everything had changed. The owl was gone, the woods were still, and she sensed light, blue and pale, light where before there had been none. *The moon must have come out,* she thought. And it was warm, too, warmer than it should have been. She got out of her sleeping bag and took off her parka—it was that warm. Mac was asleep, wheezing like an old man. She unzipped the tent and stepped outside.

The woods were more beautiful than she had ever seen them. The moon made everything ice-rimmed glimmer with a crystallized, immanent light, while underneath that ice the branches of trees were as stark as skeletons. She heard a crunching in the snow, the one sound in all that silence, and there, walking down the logging trail into their camp, was the doe. Its body, like everything around her, was silvered with frost and moonlight. It walked past the tent where her father and Charlie Spoon were sleeping and stopped no more than six feet from her. Andy saw that she had shot it, yes, had shot it cleanly, just where she thought she had, the wound a jagged, bloody hole in the doe's chest.

A heart shot, she thought.

The doe stepped closer, so that Andy, if she wished, could have reached out and touched it. It looked at her as if expecting her to do this, and so she did, running her hand, slowly at first, along the rough, matted fur, then down to the edge of the wound, where she stopped. The doe stood still. Hesitantly, Andy felt the edge of the wound. The torn flesh was sticky and warm. The wound parted under her touch. And then, almost without her knowing it, her fingers were within, probing, yet still the doe didn't move. Andy pressed deeper, through flesh and muscle and sinew, until her whole hand and more was inside the wound and she had found the doe's heart, warm and beating. She cupped it gently in her hand. *Alive,* she marveled. *Alive.*

The heart quickened under her touch, becoming warmer and warmer until it was hot enough to burn. In pain, Andy tried to remove her hand, but the wound closed about it and held her fast. Her hand was burning. She cried out in agony, sure they would all hear and come help, but they didn't. And then her hand pulled free, followed by a steaming rush of blood, more blood than she ever could have imagined—it covered her hand and arm, and she saw to her horror that her hand was steaming. She moaned and fell to her knees and plunged her hand into the snow. The doe looked at her gently and then turned and walked back up the trail.

170   In the morning, when she woke, Andy could still smell the blood, but she felt no pain. She looked at her hand. Even though it appeared unscathed, it felt weak and withered. She couldn't move it freely and was afraid the others would notice. *I will hide it in my jacket pocket,* she decided, *so nobody can see.* She ate the oatmeal that her father cooked and stayed apart from them all. No one spoke to her, and that suited her. A light snow began to fall. It was the last day of their hunting trip. She wanted to be home.

Her father dumped the dregs of his coffee. "Well, let's go look for her," he said.

Again they crossed the field. Andy lagged behind. She averted her eyes from the spot where the doe had fallen, already filling up with snow. Mac and Charlie entered the woods first, followed by her father. Andy remained in the field and considered the smear of gray sky, the nearby flock of crows pecking at unyielding stubble. *I will stay here,* she thought, *and not move for a long while.* But now someone—Mac—was yelling. Her father appeared at the woods' edge and waved for her to come. She ran and pushed through a brake of alderberry and larch. The thick underbrush scratched her face. For a moment she felt lost and looked wildly about. Then, where the brush thinned, she saw them standing quietly in the falling snow. They were staring down at the dead doe. A film covered its upturned eye, and its body was lightly dusted with snow.

"I told you she wouldn't get too far," Andy's father said triumphantly. "We must've just missed her yesterday. Too blind to see."

"We're just damn lucky no animal got to her last night," Charlie muttered.

Her father lifted the doe's foreleg. The wound was blood-clotted, brown, and caked like frozen mud. "Clean shot," he said to Charlie. He grinned. "My little girl." 175

Then he pulled out his knife, the blade gray as the morning. Mac whispered to Andy, "Now watch this," while Charlie Spoon lifted the doe from behind by its forelegs so that its head rested between his knees, its underside exposed. Her father's knife sliced thickly from chest to belly to crotch, and Andy was running from them, back to the field and across, scattering the crows who cawed and circled angrily. And now they were all calling to her—Charlie Spoon and Mac and her father—crying *Andy Andy* (but that wasn't her name, she would no longer be called that); yet louder than any of them was the wind blowing through the treetops, like the ocean where her mother floated in green water, also calling *Come in, come in,* while all around her roared the mocking of the terrible, now inevitable, sea.   [1985]

Tracy decided to look for relevant books and articles by doing a simple Google search using the terms *women hunting*. In .26 second, Google found 676,000 Web pages that use those words. Tracy quickly saw, though, that most of the URLs in the early results ended in ".com," meaning that the sites were commercial and not peer reviewed (that is, experts have not checked them to see if the information in them is accurate). As it turns out, the first ten were selling equipment to women who hunt.

In order to gather more academic sources, Tracy hypothesized that the academic discipline most likely to study the subject of women as hunters was anthropology. She therefore refined her search, using these keywords: *anthropology studies women hunting*. The academic sources she turned up included a site offering job-hunting advice to anthropology majors, anthropology term papers for sale(!),[1] a site with pictures of head hunters in Southeast Asia, and a description of an anthropology conference on related topics—the last of

---

[1] These are a dangerous resource, of course, since they are as available to teachers hunting for students' unnamed sources as they are to students hunting for shortcuts.

which she bookmarked, as being possibly useful at a later stage of her research. In other words, there were a few remote possibilities there, but the search was long and arduous. In order to target her search more effectively, Tracy decided to take a look at her school library's electronic resources via its home page. The next section will discuss what she found there.

Library Research: Indexes and Electronic Databases

The best places to search for academic sources are library **catalogues** (indexes to the library's books, journals, newspapers, films, audio and video recordings, and other materials), **periodicals indexes** (indexes to articles in magazines, newspapers, and academic journals), and specialized **bibliographies** (lists of sources on specific topics). When these resources are available electronically—some in the form of CD-ROMs, and some online—they are referred to as **databases.**

Search terms. Once you have formulated your research question, you need to choose the catalogues, bibliographies, and databases most relevant to your project. Databases are usually dedicated to one field or group of related fields and include built-in search engines. You will typically be asked to choose from several kinds of searches:

- Author searches
- Title searches
- Subject searches
- Keyword searches

You can use *author* and *title searches* if you know one of those facts about a source and want to know where to find it. *Subject searches* categorize works according to content. Libraries are organized in this way, with each item assigned a call number that indicates its content (British literature call numbers start with PR, for instance, and American, PS). If you are physically present in a library, you might see the large books of *Library of Congress Subject Headings*. These are useful for determining which subjects have been defined *as* subjects—a subject search on a subject not listed in the Library of Congress indexes is not likely to turn up useful information.

Keyword searches can be most useful when you're not sure of author, title, or subject, because they do not depend on the judgment and conventions of cataloguers—they flag the actual words used in the records about the source. Keywords typically include the subject headings, the main words of the title, and the author's name, which can be entered in any combination in a search. Some databases' keyword searches will search the entire text of the article, as well.

Periodicals indexes and bibliographies. If you've searched your library's catalogue for relevant books and would now like to see what journal articles are available, you need to use a periodicals index or bibliography. Tracy's university library allows patrons to choose from an alphabetical list of online databases or from this broad list of disciplines (Figure 1):

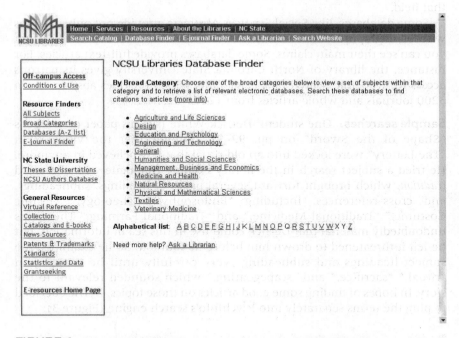

FIGURE 1

Clicking on Humanities and Social Sciences gets you this list of disciplines (Figure 2):

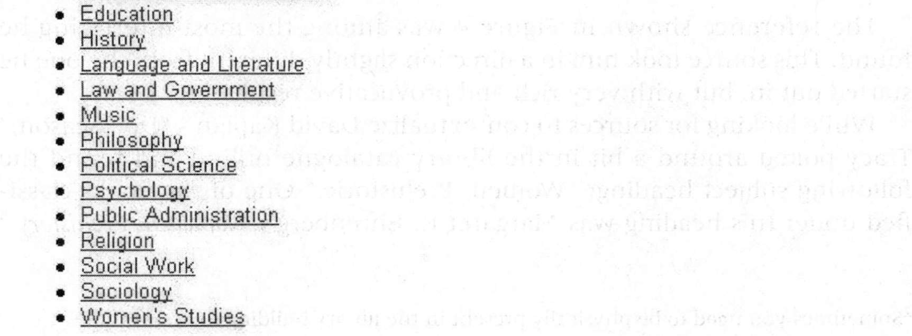

Humanities and Social Sciences

Choose one of the **subjects** below to view a set of more specific resources within that subject.

- African American Studies
- Anthropology and Archaeology
- Art, Architecture and Design
- Communication and Media
- Education
- History
- Language and Literature
- Law and Government
- Music
- Philosophy
- Political Science
- Psychology
- Public Administration
- Religion
- Social Work
- Sociology
- Women's Studies

FIGURE 2

Clicking on any one of these areas produces a list of databases that cover that field.

Some databases, like Social Sciences Abstracts, provide not only citations with bibliographical information, but also the abstracts of articles so that you can see their main claims. Some databases provide full-text articles. For instance, the library of North Carolina State University gives its patrons access to Academic Search Full TEXT Elite, which provides abstracts from 3200 journals and whole articles from 1200.[2]

Sample searches. One student, Derrick White (see his paper on Borges's "Shape of the Sword" on pp. 92–9), thought that the villagers in "The Lottery" were locked into an old ritual that few believed in anymore. He tried a subject search in the library's online catalogue with the word *tradition*, which brought forward several pages of headings, subheadings, and cross-references, including "Philosophy," "Theology," "Ethnic Costume," "Traditional Medicine," and "Traditional Farming." There was undoubtedly material that Derrick could use in this sea of information, but he felt it threatened to drown him before he found it. So he examined the subject headings and subheadings very carefully until he came upon "ritual," "sacrifice," and "scapegoating," which sounded relevant to the story. In hopes of finding some good articles on those topics, Derrick decided to plug the terms separately into PsychInfo's search engine (Figure 3):

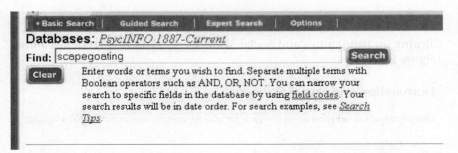

FIGURE 3

The reference shown in Figure 4 was among the most interesting he found. This source took him in a direction slightly different from the one he started out in, but with very rich and provocative results.

While looking for sources to contextualize David Kaplan's "Doe Season," Tracy poked around a bit in the library catalogue online and found the following subject heading: "Women, Prehistoric." One of the books classified under this heading was Margaret R. Ehrenberg's *Women in Prehistory*.[3]

---

[2]Sometimes you need to be physically present in the library building to access these resources successfully or at least at remote computers hardwired to the library's system.

[3]Margaret R. Ehrenberg, *Women in Prehistory* (Norman, OK: University of Oklahoma Press, 1989).

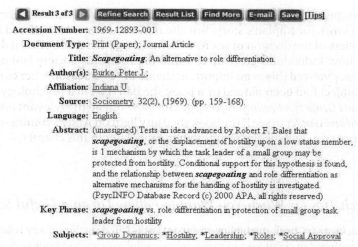

FIGURE 4

When Tracy located the book in her library, it turned out that it only spent a few paragraphs on gender divisions in hunting and other food gathering tasks (pp. 41–44). But one of the articles that Ehrenberg referred to in a footnote sounded promising because according to Ehrenberg, its author, Ernestine Friedl, "explains in more detail than here why present-day foragers divide food collection tasks along gender lines." Tracy first located the full citation for this article in Ehrenberg's bibliography:

Friedl, Ernestine. "Society and Sex Roles." *Human Nature* 1.4 (1978): 68–75.

Then she found the article itself by searching her library's online catalogue for the journal *Human Nature* (Figure 5):

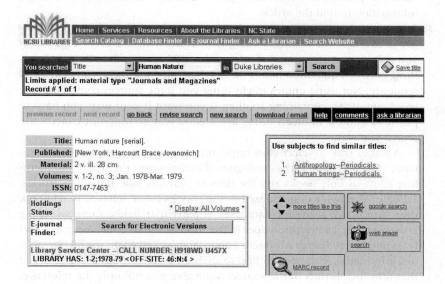

FIGURE 5

When she read Friedl's article, Tracy realized that it would make a very use-ful framework for Kaplan's story. But she noticed that while it offered a per-suasive view of the division of sex roles in hunter-gatherer societies, it did not explain how individuals grew up to fulfill the roles that society laid out for them. Tracy viewed this as an important theme in "Doe Season"; her curiosity on the subject had been piqued by a book she had read in a psychology class, *Women and Gender: A Feminist Psychology.* She now reread the relevant portions of *Women and Gender* to see if the book shed any light on Andy's coming-of-age experience. You will see the results in her paper later in this chapter.

Research Tips for When You Want to Follow Up on a Useful Source

Going backward: Check the bibliography or Works Cited section of any reliable source: they can point you to many other useful articles and books.

Going forward: There is a way to trace research that happens *after* the publica-tion of an article: **citation indexes.** These compilations of references, usually published according to field, list references to a given academic researcher. Using the Social Sciences Citation Index, for example, one stu-dent traced the reception of Stanley Milgram's controversial ideas about obedience, which she wanted to use as a frame for Jackson's "The Lottery." The citation index revealed critiques and refinements of his research.

Going from civic to academic sources: Articles in newspapers and magazines aimed at wide nonacademic audiences can at times be helpful. Though they don't usually have footnotes and lists of references, when they report on academic research, they often give researchers' names and sometimes the academic journal in which an important result was announced, enough information to find the article.

Tailoring searches to your own needs: Many search engines use Boolean lan-guage to shape the results. Joining two words with "AND" in caps brings you only sources that contain both words. "OR" brings either. Putting some-thing between quotation marks means that you want those words in exact sequence. Not using quotes might bring you some sources containing one word and others containing another. If you want it your way, you have to put it in quotes. Boolean filters are a good way to pinpoint exactly the search you want.

Another way to select your target is to choose a more specialized data-base. WorldCat gathers the catalogues of libraries over the world, but there-fore contains only books and the titles of journals, not individual articles. Wildlife Worldwide is specialized in the way its name implies. In addition, there are many academic databases in particular fields, some sweeping rather broadly, as PsychInfo does in the social sciences, some more narrow-ly, as does Bacteriology Abstracts. Some databases give you the bibliograph-ical information you need to find sources on a given topic; some give you that plus the abstract of the source; some give you not only the reference, but when the source is an article, the article itself. Sometimes you can download it to the computer you are working on so that you can produce a printed copy.

Some engines allow you to distinguish between peer-reviewed and non–peer-reviewed journals, ensuring that you can find academic sources.

As you explore some of these powerful tools, don't hesitate to ask your libraries' reference librarians for help. Many of the tools were developed by the discipline in which they were trained, and library science prepares them to navigate the wide seas of available knowledge.

Evaluating sources. Once you find sources, you have to decide whether they're good enough to use for your paper. You have to evaluate them in two ways, first deciding whether they are **reliable,** supplying information that is true, and then deciding whether they're **relevant**—that is, whether they usefully relate to your project and illuminate it.

Evaluating the reliability of sources. Knowledge follows a predictable path, from discovery through evaluation and dissemination:

1. Primary research reports (articles in academic journals and books)
   ↓
2. Review articles and books that synthesize the results of past research
   ↓
3. Specialized encyclopedias and reference books
   ↓
4. Textbooks
   ↓
5. General encyclopedias and reference books like almanacs and atlases

It takes a while for discoveries to be accepted and incorporated into more "general-interest" sources. This means that on the one hand, you can't assume that there is a consensus about everything that you read in the most recent primary sources, and, on the other hand, you wouldn't try to find the latest research news in the *Encyclopaedia Britannica.*

ACTIVITY 2: *Charting Controversies*

Pick one of the once-controversial claims listed below and see if you can chart its course from initial controversial offering to wider acceptance. Does it move from one kind of publication to another? Have questions been raised about it even after it seemed to be secure?

- Stomach ulcers are often caused by the bacterium *Helicobacter pylori*, not emotional stress.
- A diet high in fiber helps to prevent colon cancer.
- A diet high in saturated fat contributes to heart disease.
- Smoking causes cancer.

There are three important criteria for judging reliability:

1. **Credentials**
   - What, specifically, lends this person the authority to make his or her claims?
   - What academic degrees or experience does the author have on the topic?
   - What other works has the author published, and how have they been received?
   - Does the author appear to have any biases that might affect his or her claims?

2. **Context**
   - What press, journal, or other institution thought enough of the author's work to publish it?
   - Was it reviewed by academic experts before publication?

3. **Consistency**
   - Is the work consistent with other credible information you have, both in terms of form and of content?
   - Does it agree with these sources on basic factual matters?
   - Does it follow the conventions of the discipline to which it belongs?
   - Is it grammatical?

Given that almost everything is arguable, a good habit when evaluating both print and Internet sources is to look for **duplication:** Can you find the same information elsewhere? Do experts in the field know about it, confirm it, or at least argue with it as if it deserves reasonable opposition? Finding the reference to Friedl's article in Ehrenberg's book, which was published by a university press, assured Tracy Greenwald that Friedl's ideas are taken seriously by at least several other anthropologists.

Checklist for Evaluating the Reliability of Print and Internet Sources

_____What are the credentials of the writers? What claims to expertise do they have? Relevant graduate degrees? Relevant experience in universities, government, or business? Do they seem to have any ties to an organization or company that would bias their opinions? Have they accounted for the possibility of that kind of influence?

_____Is the information confirmed elsewhere, in other sources?

_____How recent is the source? Has its information been superceded?

As you're no doubt well aware, vast quantities of material are posted on the Internet daily, most of it without peer review or another vetting process—anybody with a modem can post anything. For this reason, here are a few questions specifically for judging Internet materials.

◎◎◎
Checklist for Evaluating Websites[4]

_____Who wrote the page? Are the author's qualifications given? Contact information?

_____When was the page written? Depending on the content, more recent can be better.

_____Has the page been updated recently? (Sometimes this information is given; if it is not, you may be able to tell something about its currency by noting whether its links are functional.)

_____What domain is indicated by its address: .gov, .mil, .edu, .com, .net, .org, or something else? Addresses that end in .gov and .mil are government and military sites; .com and .net are commercial sites; .edu, educational organizations; and .org, nonprofit organizations. (This can give you a rough sense of who might and might not have authorization to post a page on these sites, but will *not* necessarily tell you by itself whether specific information on them is credible.)

_____Are there references for citations? Their presence tends to point to a more academic source, or at least a source that expects a certain amount of scrutiny.

_____Is the page connected to a group, company, or institution that might bias its views? Is it frank about these connections?

_____Can the information on the page be confirmed from other sources, electronic or print?

Use these questions as well as all the tools you have for critical thinking, including the methods for analyzing argument discussed in Chapter 8, as you collect and read the many sources available to you.

Evaluating the relevance of sources. If your searches are even moderately successful, you probably can't carefully read everything that they turn up; you will need to sort through your sources to find the ones that will be most useful for your project. You can make the first cut by looking at titles. One of the topics Tracy Greenwald explored for her paper on "Doe Season" was empathy, because Andy's feelings for the animals that are hunted is an important element in the story. Tracy's search on the Library of Congress Subject Heading "empathy" retrieved a list of twenty-nine books, including books called *Empathy and Counseling: Explorations in Theory and Research* and *Creating Harmonious Relationships: A Practical Guide to the Power of True Empathy*. Tracy guessed that these books were addressed to psychotherapists or other counselors and were not likely to be relevant to her project. One title, though, *Empathy, Fantasy, and Helping*, attracted Tracy's attention. Andy had a dream in the story that Tracy thought was significant; if it could be called a "fantasy," perhaps the book would be relevant to Tracy's paper.

---

[4]For a fuller list, see Jim Kapoun, "Teaching Undergrads WEB Evaluation: A Guide for Library Instruction," http://www.ala.org/acrl/undwebev.html, a site maintained by the American Library Association.

If a title seems promising, check out any other information the record contains: a book's table of contents, an article's abstract, or (if you're lucky) even its complete text. Try to judge from this material whether the piece warrants a closer look, concentrating on the introductions and conclusions, since those places that receive natural emphasis (see Chapter 6) often state the main claims.

Be sure not to eliminate a source just because it seems to disagree with your initial hypothesis. Not only might your early ideas change as you work, but also, sources with opposing views might very usefully outline the topic, define key terms, and present important arguments that you need to understand.

Active Reading

Once you find sources that pass these preliminary tests, read them carefully. Print them out or photocopy them so that you can write on the copies. As Chapter 2 recommends, if you use highlighters to mark important passages, also use pens or pencils to take notes with more content.

At the very least, when I find an idea in an outside source that corresponds to something in the literary work I'm writing on, I note the relevant line, paragraph, or page number of the literary work in the margin and jot something down there about the connection. By the time I am finished with the article, it contains a fragmentary "review" pointing to the passages in the literary work relevant to my interpretation. I often do the same thing for the literary work (but in the opposite direction) so that before I draft, I have a collection of texts that all point to each other in ways that help me remember, as I go back and forth among them, what I thought I could do with them.

Writing the Paper

When you've gathered relevant, reliable sources and read them, you'll have to begin actually writing the paper. We have already covered the details of this process in Chapter 2, but we'll briefly review the process here, using the progress of Tracy Greenwald's paper on "Doe Season" as an example.

Invention: Finding and Developing a Thesis

When you have annotated all your texts carefully, you need to take a step back and get a sense of the larger shape of your project. One method for gathering your thoughts is to use a large sheet of white, unlined paper. Start with your core idea or main claim at the very center of the page and then, in whatever order they come to you, place your subtopics around it and supporting details around *them*, with the line, paragraph, or page numbers that will help you retrace your steps. Take advantage of the absence of lines (if there are lines, ignore them) by writing at angles, in corners, or along the vertical margins: It's better to "create chaos" first. Turn off your internal censors; at this stage, don't discard ideas because they are "stupid" or "far-fetched."

Tracy's first attempt looked like Figure 6:

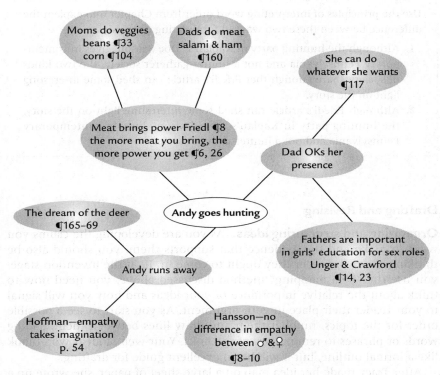

FIGURE 6 *Tracy Greenwald's Idea Map*

All this mapping and shuffling serves the purpose of finding a thesis or claim to defend. Since claims and your defense of them constitute the main structure of a paper, finding them is a crucial step.

Qualifying Claims and Making Concessions

Remember that arguments that apply concepts from other disciplines to literature are like metaphors or similes or any comparison: No matter how close the correspondences, there are always limits to the similarities. You will almost certainly want to make some concessions to the limits of your comparison, at the same time stressing that the limitation does not make the comparison meaningless.

For instance, when Tracy Greenwald wanted to interpret David Kaplan's "Doe Season" using the framework provided by Ernestine Friedl's "Sex and Society," she thought it best to show her readers that she knew the people in the story were not hunter-gatherers. In this case, a simple subordinate clause took care of it: "*Although the hunting party in Kaplan's 'Doe Season' lives in contemporary Pennsylvania and not a hunter-gatherer society*, the two kinds of society share enough that Friedl's article can shed some interesting light on the story."

ACTIVITY 3: *Formulating Concessions*

Use the principles of interpreting word order from Chapter 6 to explain the difference between these two ways of formulating concessions:

1. Although the hunting party in Kaplan's "Doe Season" lives in contemporary Pennsylvania and not a hunter-gatherer society, the two kinds of society share enough that Friedl's article can shed some interesting light on the story.

2. Although Friedl's article can shed some interesting light on the story, the hunting party in Kaplan's "Doe Season" lives in contemporary Pennsylvania and not a hunter-gatherer society.

Drafting and Revising

Organizing and structuring ideas. As you are developing the claims you want to make and the evidence that supports them, you should also be thinking about the order they ought to come in. If, at the invention stage, you use the "idea mapping" method discussed above, you need now to think about the relative importance of your ideas and how you will signal to your reader their place in your argument. As you start to see a possible order for the topics, number them and draw lines between them, adding words or phrases to remind you of the links. Your web of ideas won't look like a formal outline, but it will be an excellent guide for drafting.

After Tracy made her idea map on a large sheet of paper, she wrote up a separate informal outline—a list of topics she wanted to cover in an order that made sense:

Why men want to keep the woods as a male preserve:
    Friedl: Power comes from meat, the scarce good—¶8.
        The more meat women provide, the more power they have—¶23.
Why Andy's father escapes this mindset:
    Unger and Crawford: People want sons to be companions to fathers (¶14), so fathers give girls more leeway than they give boys for cross-gendered behavior—¶23.
    Andy's father's different idea: She can do what she wants to do—¶117.
But at the end of the story, she runs from the woods. Why?
What sends her swinging from one sphere to the other is her empathy for the deer—paragraphs 87,162.
Imagination helps you have empathy—Hoffman p. 54.
Andy has imagination: paragraphs 87, 162, dream 165–69.
No gender difference in empathy (Hansson et al., paragraphs 8–10), but Andy still buys into the separation of male and female spheres: Mom's there; I'm here—¶23.
At the end, she runs toward the sea—¶176.

Some writers take this one step further and do a *formal* outline at this stage; teachers often require a formal outline at some stage in the writing process. The conventional arrangement is a simple but effective way of recording the relationships among the elements of your argument. Here's Tracy's:

I. In our society, men want to keep the woods as a male preserve.
   A. Meat is a scarce resource.
   B. The woods are a source of meat.
   C. Whoever provides meat acquires power (Friedl ¶8, ¶23).

II. Nevertheless, Andy's father takes Andy into the woods.
   A. Andy's father escapes typical mindset about sex roles: Andy can do what she wants to do (¶117).
   B. People want sons to be companions to fathers, so fathers give girls more leeway than they give boys for cross-gendered behavior (Unger and Crawford ¶14, ¶23).

III. At the end of the story, Andy runs from the woods. Why?
   A. What sends her swinging from one sphere to the other is her empathy for the deer (¶87, ¶162).
      1. Her imagination (paragraphs 87, 162, dream 165–69) gives rise to her empathy (Hoffman p. 54).
      2. There is no real gender difference in empathy (Hansson et al. ¶8–10).
   B. Andy still buys into the separation of male and female spheres: She thinks, "mom's there; I'm here" (¶23).

The rough draft. Once she had put her major ideas in order, Tracy felt prepared to draft the body of her paper. Here's what her first draft looked like, with comments from her teacher in the margins:

As soon as Andy and her father meet up with her father's friend Charlie and his eleven-year-old son Mac, Andy is under attack. Charlie wants to keep her out of the woods.

You provide a few examples in the rest of the paragraph (there are more) but you could be more specific in the first sentence—an attack about what?

He says that the woods are "where the women don't want to go" (¶107). The fact that Andy does want to go there makes him accuse her of being unfeminine: "You're half a boy anyway. You go by a boy's name" (109). That night, Mac talks about male genitalia and her lack of it (68—81) and tries to gross her out with talk of gutting a deer (82—91).

Is this the same tactic Charlie uses, or a variation? (Also: watch slang.) This paragraph isn't really fulfilling the function of an intro. Can you provide a better one?

Why are Charlie and Mac so set on keeping her out of the woods? Anthropologist Ernestine Friedl's theory helps to explain their attitude. According to Friedl, in foraging societies, animal protein could be traded with other groups for other important goods (8). In other words, meat was money. "The greater the male monopoly on the distribution of scarce items, the stronger their control of women seems to be" (8). Where women bring in no food and the diet is almost completely animal protein provided by men, like the Eskimos, women are "used, abused, and traded by men" (34). Where women participated in communal hunts for smaller animals, like the Washo Indians of California and Nevada, men and women "were not segregated from each other" and there was "relative equality of the sexes" (26).

Which theory? Be specific.

Why? Explain.

This is a bit choppy—see if you can smooth out transitions. Also, watch syntax.

The families in the story divide the labor of providing food like hunter-gatherers. The wives, who presumably "don't want to go" to hunt in the woods, prepare food at home and send it on the trip. Andy's mother sends bean soup (33) and Mac's mother sends corn chowder (104), two vegetables. The adult men bring "hard salami and ham" (160). And the men alone go to the woods to hunt deer.

But aren't there differences, too? We're talking about the modern era, here.

Beans and corn both have a lot of protein.

But why is Andy's father so different? In their textbook, *Women and Gender*, psychologists Rhoda Unger and

Needs a smoother transition. Different from what?

Mary Crawford talk about how children act out (the usual sex roles.) The chapter called "Becoming Gendered: The Social-ization of Girls and Boys" makes the argument that children have to be taught them. Some of the most powerful factors in teaching children sex roles are the attitudes of par-ents. Studies showed that many people preferred male chil-dren to female. In one study, 78% of women and 90% of men said they would want their child to be a boy (14).

You're getting choppy again here—how does this all fit together?

? Clarify.

Needs more context—were the research and story from the same era?

It turned out that fathers were especially important in how children turned out, and fathers were stricter with boys than with girls in making them act out sex roles (31). Only 40% of fathers of girls saw the girls as "very feminine" but 66% of fathers of boys saw them as "very masculine" (23). We don't know for certain that Andy is an only child, but an important conversation between her father and Charlie seems to show that. Just after Andy's father gives his speech about how Andy should be treated equally, we hear this:

Interesting! Are all these facts related, though? Show how they're connected.

> "Hell, you might as well have just had a boy and be done with it!" Charlie exclaimed.
>
> "That's funny," her father said, and chuckled.
>
> "That's just what her momma tells me."

Good passage to quote. You need a parenthetical reference.

So it is at least plausible that Andy's father, who likes to leave his wife at home and go hunting, treats Andy the way he does so that he can have a child to keep him company on his walks in the woods.

Does he treat her like a boy in every respect?

Then why does Andy go running from the woods at the end of the story thinking that she must act more like a girl? Her father seems to be a big influence on her. When he gives her coffee, promising not to tell "your momma," Andy drinks it all, despite the fact that it makes her feel "a little queasy." Maybe killing the deer is like drinking the coffee: she does it to please her father. Just as drinking the coffee made her feel queasy, shooting the deer but thinking she hadn't killed it instantly gave her a troubled night.

There's a leap here. Can you smooth out the transition between paragraphs?

Good example— flesh this out a bit more. What does the parallel show?

For Andy, the crucial experience of the trip is when she dreams of seeing the deer in the woods. Andy discovers that she can empathize with it, as psychologist Martin Hoffman says. When Mac is tormenting her by describing the hog-dressing of a dead deer, which involves slitting its body open, Andy responds by imagining herself as the deer: "She ran her finger like a knife blade along her belly" (87) "from chest to belly to crotch" (176). Then in her dream, Andy imagines herself touching its heart (168). In the morning, she still seems to feel the heat and smell the doe's blood. At this point, for the first time in the story, she "wanted to be home" (170). It is as if to be daddy's girl, Andy had to be a boy, and for her the limit to her boyishness is going to be killing things.

One problem with this analysis is that Hansson et al. say that psychologists haven't found a difference between empathy in men and women (8–10). They see a relationship between someone's powers of imagining and empathy (1), and Andy clearly has a strong imagination, but the research didn't make a connection to gender.

But Andy seems to think there's something unnatural about the way she acted. As she runs away from the scene where her father cuts up the doe, Andy decides to shed her androgynous nickname (presumably to become "Andrea") (176). The reason is because Andy has accepted the sex role divisions of her society. We can see this as the party drives off to the woods at the beginning of the story. Thinking of her mother washing the dishes at home, she tells herself, "She is there, and we are here" and she is happy to be heading out with her father (23).

Margin annotations:

OK, careful here with Hoffman—his theories on empathy are relevant, but don't imply that he talks about the story.

Unclear

OK, fine—what do you do with this research that doesn't quite "fit"? Putting it so late and in its own paragraph gives it a lot of weight. Do you want to emphasize it so much? Or, if it's going to get so much emphasis, can you do more with it?

Good, but the way she acted when?

So she never really had a chance to be comfortable hunting? I don't understand the connection between her happiness at the start and her change of mind at the end. Can you explain more?

Watch syntax!

You need a conclusion.

Drafting Notes

Verb tense: Notice Tracy talks about the events of the story as if they are just happening: "Andy and her father **meet** . . ."; "Andy **is**. . . ." That decision represents standard practice in literary criticism: The activities taking place in texts are generally written about in the **present tense.**

Pronouns: In the concluding sentence of the second version, Tracy uses "we." Academic writers sometimes use "I" ("I will show . . .") and rarely use "you" (as in "you will be able to see"). Literary critics often use "we" (including themselves and readers).

Integrating references. There are many ways to join texts drawn from other disciplines to literature. Phrases like this can express the relationship:

Smith's concept *can help explain/shed light on/illuminate* the actions of the characters in Jones's play.

The action of the characters in Jones's play *provides an example of/reflects/ demonstrates* Smith's concept.

We can *understand* the action of the character in Jones's play *better* if we can see its relationship to Smith's principle.

In writing your paper, don't imply that Smith actually talks about Jones's play (unless she did, of course). Usually, you will be the one making the connection. So it is incorrect to say that "According to psychologists Unger and Crawford, Andy's father really wanted a boy." Instead, it is more accurate to say, "The conversations among the males in 'Doe Season' seem to corroborate Unger and Crawford's observations about gender preferences in a majority of parents."

Using quotations and citing material. Make sure that you don't just plunk quotations from your sources down in the midst of your own prose. First, introduce them in such a way that you link your thoughts smoothly with theirs. Second, decide whether to use direct quotation, paraphrase, or summary to bring the ideas of others into your text. It often helps to put the contextualizing phrases at the start of sentences, where they will make smooth transitions from your thoughts.

Tracy Greenwald uses this strategy to introduce some of the relevant research she found:

> In their textbook, *Women and Gender*, psychologists Rhoda Unger and Mary Crawford talk about how children act out the usual sex roles.

 ACTIVITY 4: *Integrating References*

What are the different advantages of the following two ways of introducing a text? What kind of context does each one fit into appropriately? Revise the second one to use an active rather than a passive verb.

(Continued)

ACTIVITY 4: *(Continued)*

1. "Rhoda Unger and Mary Crawford synthesize a great deal of research . . . in their 1993 textbook *Women and Gender*."
2. "In Rhoda Unger and Mary Crawford's 1993 textbook *Women and Gender*, a great deal of research done in the late 20th century on how children come to occupy the sex roles that society sets out for them . . . was synthesized."

In citing material, place the parenthetical references to the relevant text at the end of the sentence, if possible. But if one sentence has ideas or quotations from several places, you might need several parentheses, one after each piece of text that requires one. You can see these conventions operating in the first paragraph of Tracy Greenwald's early draft:

> Andy's mother sends bean soup (33) and Mac's mother sends corn chowder (104), two vegetables. The adult men bring "hard salami and ham" (160).

Note that in the first sentence, the parentheses follow references to places in the text, not quotations. It isn't only quotations, but also summaries and paraphrases that require textual references so that you are clearly marking your use of texts and allowing your readers to follow your thinking.

Using parenthetical references (33) to give paragraph numbers is very helpful to readers when paragraphs are numbered in the texts, but unusual enough that Tracy announces that that is what the numbers represent. She doesn't need the label in subsequent parentheses—until she changes to page numbers for a different text.

Many of the sources that Tracy found for her paper also refer to and cite other sources. This will be true of most of the scholarly sources you find and is a great help in pointing you to more useful material. It is important, however, to cite your sources' sources correctly. For instance, Tracy Greenwald found the results of key surveys reported in *Women and Gender* by Unger and Crawford. If she wanted to use the names of the researchers who did the various surveys, she would either have to go find their own reports of their work so that she could refer to them directly, or she would have to make it clear that she has only found them in Unger and Crawford. She can do the latter in the parenthetical references: (Hammer, 1970, qtd. in Unger and Crawford 21). Either way, she must make it possible for anyone who wants to follow up on Hammer's results to find her report.

Introductions.   Using the processes we have discussed for finding imaginative literature to interpret and academic literature to frame it, and letting close reading of all the texts lead her toward comparing them, Tracy dove into her draft without writing a formal introduction. That's fine, but eventually she did have to compose one.

It is sometimes possible to use in the introduction the research question that started you off on your trip through the catalogues and databases in the first place. Posing a question is often a good way to launch an interpretive paper. It engages readers and gives them a reason to stick with the paper. Either you will give the answer to your question and they will want to see how it is supported in the course of the paper, or you will just hint at it and promise the details as the paper proceeds. In either case, they will be motivated to read on.

Tracy Greenwald developed two different versions of an introduction to her paper on David Kaplan's "Doe Season":

Version 1:

At the start of David Kaplan's short story, "Doe Season," the main character, Andy, a nine-year-old girl, seems to be extremely content to be walking through the woods with her father on a hunting trip: "There was no place else she would rather be" (paragraph 23). And yet, by the end of the story, having killed her first deer with a "clean shot" that makes her father proud (175), Andy runs away from the scene, imagining that she is running out of the woods toward the ocean, a realm she associates with her mother. She dreads the ocean, but seems to think it is her only way of escape from the aspects of hunting she turns out to hate. The sea, though "terrible," is now "inevitable" (176). What happens to Andy in the course of the hunt that makes her change her mind?

Version 2 (same as Version 1, with the addition of the following final sentence):

If we read the story closely with some important concepts from psychology and anthropology in mind, we will be able to see that Andy's conflict about hunting is a conflict with her society's traditional separation of the sex roles of men and women.

The first version ends with a question that the paper will presumably answer. The second ends with the explicit intention to answer the question, an agenda statement that predicts how the paper will proceed ("If we read the story closely with some important concepts from psychology and anthropology in mind") and what it will find ("we will be able to see that Andy's conflict about hunting is a conflict with her society's traditional separation of the sex roles of men and women").

Either one of these introductions would do. As it happens, they represent two different stages of Tracy's work on the paper. She understood the question she was asking early on but couldn't add the last sentence of the second version until she was able to lay out her answer.

Conclusions. Having written solid drafts of the introduction and the body for her paper, Tracy needed a conclusion. As we saw in Chapter 2, conclusions have to perform two functions: They summarize or review what went before in the paper, and they remind readers of what the paper has accomplished. The trick is to do something new enough to be interesting but not new enough to seem unrelated. Good tactics are to try to put something in a new context or think about implications for the future or future research.

Tracy had brought the story's heroine to the end of the plot but felt she had not provided a satisfying end for her reader. After all the work she'd done, Tracy was still faced with a question: Why does Andy run away at the end of the story? She felt that the paper ought to try to answer that question.

In addition, Tracy knew that a theme had to have a wider relevance than its particular characters and events (see "Theme" in Chapter 4) but wasn't sure how to generalize the events of the story to draw a conclusion about a theme. These were some possibilities she considered:

1. Girls can't handle the realities of hunting.
2. A nine-year-old girl is too young to witness the dressing of a deer.
3. A nine-year-old girl with a special feeling for animals is too young to witness the hog-dressing of a deer.
4. A nine-year-old girl with a special feeling for her father is too young to witness him hog-dressing a female deer.
5. Even with the encouragement of her father, a nine-year-old girl can't always overcome the pressure to conform to traditional sex roles.
6. Traditional sex roles are natural and innately programmed and thus almost impossible to escape.

Tracy found it hard to juggle these different possibilities. The first one seemed too broad, so she narrowed the category of girls to girls of Andy's age. But was it hunting that was too daunting for nine-year-olds (numbers 2–4), or the whole social apparatus that helps teach children traditional sex roles (5)? Or does the story suggest that traditional sex roles were so persistent because they are programmed biologically, not just learned? Was the story taking a position on the nature/nurture debate (6)?

Tracy presented the puzzle to her teacher, wondering whether she needed another academic source to fit the pieces together. The teacher had two suggestions: Since #4 has a Freudian ring to it, Tracy could do some research to see what Freud had to say about pre-adolescent girls' feelings for their fathers. But whether or not she took that route, she needed to return to the text of the story to see what could be gleaned from the details of the language.

Deciding to return to the text first, Tracy reread the last few paragraphs of the story. The lines that jumped out at her came just after Andy's father examined the doe's wound to see whether it was well (lethally) aimed:

"Clean shot," he said to Charlie. He grinned. "My little girl."

This comment made Tracy think that Andy's father was not quite as "liberated" as she had thought at first, which meant that the choice between "woods" and "ocean," male and female realms, was not as clear as it had at first seemed. Tracy saw how to complete her paper without Freud. Her strategy can be found in the complete text of her paper below.

Titles. Papers need titles that do more than announce the subject matter. A title might come to you at the very beginning of your research, or it might be the last thing you do. In any case, it should announce your topic, reflect your perspective on it, and, ideally, engage a reader's attention. It must be true to the paper, however; a clever title that misrepresents what follows won't help win readers to your argument.

Documenting sources. The mirror image of searching for materials on a topic is documenting the sources you find. When you search, you follow the trails laid down by others in footnotes, bibliographies, and searchable databases. When you document what you have found, labeling them according to their locations, you are laying down a trail that others can follow. This is courteous to your readers and it also establishes a responsible and honest relationship with your sources: You are giving credit where it is due.

As we saw in Chapter 8, different disciplines use different systems for documenting their sources. Your choice of a documentation style will usually be determined by the audience you are addressing: follow your teacher's instructions. (You will find guidelines for using the MLA and APA styles in Appendix D.)

Tracy Greenwald's works cited list gives the bibliographical information for the sources she refers to in her paper. (Note that it isn't a bibliography and therefore doesn't record everything she read while doing research on her topic.)

Checklist for Improving Drafts

Argument:

_____What are the **main claims** of the paper? What are the subsidiary claims? Are the claims clear? Plausible? Are they specific enough to be worthy of a reader's attention? Are they stated in a reasoned or dogmatic way? In what ways are they qualified? Where the paper is applying a model or concept from another field, does it acknowledge that the fit between the model and the text is not perfect? How could the claim be improved?

_____Are the **assumptions** that link the claims and reasons plausible? Do they accord with acceptable assumptions for literary argument? Are they explicitly stated? Should they be?

Organization:

_____What is the **order** in which the paper proposes to discuss its topics? Does it follow that order? Is this the most effective order, or would a different order work better? Does it discuss everything it announces it will discuss?

_____Does each paragraph have a clear **focus?** If there are any paragraphs that stray from their announced topics, note them.

Development:

_____What **evidence** does the paper offer for its claims? Is it sufficient? Underline the strongest pieces of evidence and on the paper itself. What are the weakest? Should these be eliminated or could they be strengthened? How? How could other points be strengthened?

_____Are there places in the story or articles that the writer doesn't discuss but that could help the writer support his/her claims? What are they? Are there places in the story or articles that do not support the claims? Does the writer acknowledge them? Should s/he?

Style:

_____Is the **writing style** pleasing and consistent? Underline sections that are stylistically awkward. Make suggestions on the draft about how they could be revised.

_____Is the writer's **diction** appropriate? Is it lively? Provide suggestions for improving it.

_____How about the writer's **syntax?** Are the important ideas appropriately placed in positions where they get emphasis? What sentences might be revised to improve either emphasis or flow into the next sentence? Make suggestions on the draft.

_____Are **references** meshed smoothly with the writer's prose? Where they do not blend well, make suggestions on the draft.

Grammar:

_____Circle grammatical problems in the draft. Are there recurring problems?

Mechanics:

_____Are the parenthetical citations in the correct form, with correct punctuation?

Tracy Greenwald

Mr. Wallis

English 112

November 21, 2003

Learning to Be a Girl in David Kaplan's "Doe Season"

At the start of David Kaplan's short story, "Doe Season," the main character, a nine-year-old girl named Andy, seems completely content to be walking through the woods with her father on a hunting trip: "There was no place else she would rather be" (paragraph 23). And yet, by the end of the story, having killed her first deer with a "clean shot" that makes her father proud (175), Andy runs away from the scene, imagining that she is running out of the woods toward the ocean, a realm she associates with her mother (45). She dreads the ocean, but seems to think it is her only way of escape from the aspects of hunting she turns out to hate. The sea, though "terrible," is now "inevitable" (176). What happens to Andy in the course of the hunt that makes her change her mind? If we read the story closely with some important concepts from psychology and anthropology in mind, we will see that Andy's conflict about hunting is a conflict with her whole society's traditional separation of the sex roles of men and women.

As soon as Andy and her father meet up with her father's friend Charlie and his eleven-year-old son Mac, Andy finds herself in a battle about whether or not men and women should inhabit separate spheres. In the car on the way to the woods, Charlie begins the list of complaints about Andy's presence: She'll make too much noise and she'll get too tired (7; Mac chimes in at 21). Andy and her father both answer the charges (8, 22). But these complaints are not

*Martin Hoffman's "Empathy, Its Arousal, and Prosocial Functioning," (Chapter 2 of *Empathy and Moral Development: Implications for Caring and Justice*) is in Chapter 16; other sources of Tracy's paper are posted on the Web site at www.mhhe.com/ferster.

really the issue. What really matters are the deeper convictions: In general men and women have different roles and, specifically, women do not hunt. The woods, Charlie says, are "where the women don't want to go" (107). The fact that Andy does want to go there makes her femininity vulnerable to his attack: "You're half a boy anyway. You go by a boy's name" (109). That night, Mac takes over with a different tactic, using her femininity against her: He tries to humiliate her with talk of male genitalia and her lack of it (68—81) and disgust her with talk of gutting a deer, with a brief return to the subject of male genitalia (82—91).

Why are Charlie and Mac so set on defending hunting in the woods as a male-only activity? Anthropologist Ernestine Friedl's theory about the relationship of sex roles to food-providing roles in hunter-gatherer societies helps to explain their attitude. According to Friedl, in foraging societies, animal protein was in such short supply that it can be traded with other groups for other important goods (8). In other words, meat was money. Therefore, whoever brought in more of it had more power in the group. "The greater the male monopoly on the distribution of scarce items, the stronger their control of women seems to be" (8). In most hunter-gatherer societies, only men hunt big game. Where women bring in no food and the diet is almost completely animal protein provided by men, as among the Eskimo, women are "used, abused, and traded by men" (34). Where women participated in communal hunts for smaller animals, as among the Washo Indians of California and Nevada, men and women "were not segregated from each other" and there was "relative equality of the sexes" (26).

Now it is true that the families in Kaplan's stories do not live primarily by hunting. One of the adults in each probably has a job for pay and the trip in the story is a vacation. But while they live in modern Pennsylvania, not a hunter-gatherer society, the families in the story divide the labor of providing food in a way that echoes hunter-gatherer patterns. The two wives, who presumably

"don't want to go" to hunt in the woods, prepare food at
home and send it on the trip. Andy's mother sends bean soup
(33) and Mac's mother sends corn chowder (104), two good
sources of protein, but vegetable, not animal. Both adult
men cook oatmeal (94, 170), but they also bring "hard
salami and ham" (160), provisions not attributed to either
wife. And the males alone, with a condescending nod to Andy
(107) and a conspiratorial wink from Charlie to Mac about
escaping the wife and mother of that family (106), go to
the woods to hunt deer. We don't know if the women work or
who bought the corn and beans, but in a very general way,
the pattern of many subsistence societies applies: The
women provide vegetable protein and the men provide animal
protein. If animal protein still symbolizes the power that
comes from scarcity, it is no wonder that Charlie and Mac
do not want to share the woods with women.

   Understanding Charlie and Mac's attitude in this way
with the help of Ernestine Friedl raises a new question.
If males are likely to guard the privilege gained from
supplying the scarce goods of a society, how does Andy's
father become so egalitarian that he walks with his daughter in the woods, teaches her to shoot, brings her on a
male-dominated hunting trip, and defends her right to "do
whatever she likes" (117)? In their textbook, *Women and
Gender,* psychologists Rhoda Unger and Mary Crawford synthesized a great deal of research done in the late 20th century
(the story was written in 1985) on how children come to
occupy the sex roles that society sets out for them. The
chapter called "Becoming Gendered: The Socialization of
Girls and Boys" makes the argument that children are not
innately programmed to conform to sex roles but have to be
taught. Some of the most powerful factors influencing
children's learning of sex roles (that is, socialization)
are the attitudes and actions of parents. For instance,
many studies showed that even before becoming parents, many
people preferred male children to female. In one study, 78%

of women and 90% of men said that if they could only have one child, they would want it to be a boy (14).

This is important because once a child was born, it turned out that fathers were especially influential in shaping children's sex roles, and fathers imposed traditional roles on little boys more strictly than on very young girls (31). One sign of this is that only 40% of fathers of girls saw the girls as "very feminine" but 66% of fathers of boys saw them as "very masculine" (23). Unger and Crawford do not connect these facts, but it might be true that the father of a girl who had really wanted a boy would give his daughter more leeway to act like a boy than the father of a boy would give his son permission to act like a girl. This is more likely because one of the most common reasons people give for wanting a boy is that the boys could keep their fathers company (31). We don't know for certain that Andy is an only child, but an important conversation between her father and Charlie seems to show that. Just after Andy's father gives his speech about how Andy deserves equal opportunity, we hear this:

> "Hell, you might as well have just had a boy and be done with it!" Charlie exclaimed.
>
> "That's funny," her father said, and chuckled.
>
> "That's just what her momma tells me."(118—19)

So it is at least plausible that Andy's father, who likes to leave his wife at home and go hunting, learns to be more egalitarian on behalf of his daughter so he can have a child to keep him company on his walks in the woods and hunting trips. It seems from the nicknames he calls her that he knows she's a girl ("punkin," 134; "honeybun," 161), but he seems to want her to be as much of a boy as she can be.

Understanding Andy's father in this way, with the help of Unger and Crawford, raises another question: If fathers are so important in sex role training and Andy's father has the idea that girls can do whatever they want and acts on

it, then why does Andy go running from the woods at the end
of the story thinking that she must take on a more traditional female role? It is clear that she loves her father
and tries to please him. When her father gives Andy coffee,
promising not to tell "your momma," Andy drinks it all,
despite the fact that it makes her feel "a little queasy."
Perhaps even more important, she imitates his way of drinking it, holding the cup "the way her father did" (33).

In some ways, killing the deer is just like drinking the
coffee: She isn't comfortable doing it, would not have done
it on her own, but does it to please her father. When he
offers to let her shoot it, despite the fact that she does
not have a license and has never shot anything but "cans
and targets" (131), her first reaction is "I can't" (132).
After much delay and both arguments and pressure from
Charlie, she shoots and hits the deer, who falls but then
gets up and runs away (133—48). Just as drinking the coffee
made her feel queasy, shooting the deer but thinking she
hadn't instantly killed it gave her a troubled night.
Living up to her father's expectations seems to make her
uncomfortable in both cases.

For Andy, the crucial experience of the trip comes
between the shooting of the deer and the discovery of its
dead body the next morning in a grove. What happens during
that time is that Andy finds that she has sympathy with the
doe ("I don't like to think of it suffering," she tells her
father; 162). Then she dreams of encountering it in the
woods, having it look at her, exploring its wound with her
hand, discovering its heart, and then feeling as if her
whole hand and arm are burning up.

Having this experience while she is uncertain about
whether the doe is dead or alive allows Andy to discover
that she identifies with the doe and can empathize with it,
that is, mentally experience the doe's pain. According to
psychologist Martin L. Hoffman, the ability to feel empathy
for someone else is greatly enhanced when people can imagine

how they would feel if they were in the same position and
directly imagine how the other person feels (page 54). Of
course, Hoffman is talking about empathy with other people,
not animals, but we can see Andy's imagination working in
both ways to produce empathy with the deer. One way is when
Mac is tormenting her by describing the hog-dressing of a
dead deer, which involves slitting its body open "from chest
to belly to crotch" (176) to empty out the internal organs.
Andy responds to Mac's description with an action that puts
her in the deer's position: "She ran her finger like a knife
blade along her belly" (87). This is the first kind of
imaginative empathy that Hoffman mentions, putting oneself
in the other's position.

Andy's dream is the second kind of empathy that Hoffman
mentions, empathizing directly with the other. This is what
Andy does when she tells her father that she is bothered by
the idea of its suffering (162) and what she does in her
dream when she imagines herself touching its heart, touching
its life (168). In the morning, she still seems to feel the
heat and smell the doe's blood, as if the doe's suffering
has been transferred to her. She tries to hide her hand,
as if ashamed of what she has done to the deer (170). At
this point, for the first time in the story, she "wanted to
be home" (170). It is as if to be daddy's girl, Andy had
to be a boy, and for her the limit to her boyishness is going
to be killing large animals, especially female ones. She
sympathizes too much with the female deer to be a boy.

One problem with this analysis is that Robert
O. Hansson et al. say that they have not found a difference
between the empathetic capacities of men and women
(paragraphs 8—10). They did see a relationship between
someone's powers of imagining another's experience and a
tendency to empathize (1), and Andy clearly has a strong
imagination, but the research did not find significant gender
differences in either one. Another problem, of course, is
that there are many modern women who hunt. So feeling

empathetic does not mean you have to fulfill a rigid traditional feminine role, and fulfilling a feminine role does
not keep you from hunting.

But those choices seem to be exactly what Andy thinks
she must make. As she runs away from the scene where her
father slices her doe "from chest to belly to crotch" (176),
Andy vows to shed her androgynous nickname (probably to
become "Andrea"; 176). The reason for this vow seems to be
that Andy has accepted the rigid sex role divisions of her
society. Despite her father's openness to her boyish activities, she seems caught in an either/or game in which a child
has to choose the traits of one and only one sex. We can see
her acceptance of the traditional sex role divisions as the
party drives off to the woods at the beginning of the story.
Thinking of her mother washing the dishes at home, she tells
herself, "She is there, and we are here," and she is happy
to be heading out with her father (23). Although the first
paragraph ends with a long sentence culminating in a vision
of the woods that seems to unify all the countries of the
world, still the realms of men and women are far apart. She
associates her father with the woods and her mother with the
kitchen at home and with the sea.

Maybe the research of the psychologists can help here.
Although Hansson et al. did not find a difference between
males' and females' powers to empathize, they did find that
among women, the most empathetic were also the most
androgynous (9—10). Empathetic female subjects had the
"freedom to be comfortable with an 'inappropriate' self
concept and 'inappropriate' role behaviors" (10). But maybe
Andy is just too young to be comfortable opposing such a
strong social norm. Instead, the hunting trip is an
occasion for what Unger and Crawford call the "unlearning"
of the roles usually associated with the other sex (75).

Andy cannot seem to make her way between the too-extreme
choices of woods and ocean, male and female. Despite her
father's accepting attitude, she gives in to the stereotyped

thinking of Charlie and Mac. The stereotypes seem just too strong for a nine-year-old girl. Unger and Crawford are most interested in the way boys unlearn the behavior of girls that they once participated in (67–68), but the story suggests that sometimes girls have to unlearn, too.

Works Cited

Friedl, Ernestine. "Society and Sex Roles." <u>Human Nature</u> 1.4 (1978): 68–75.

Hansson, Robert O., Mary E. Chernovetz, and Warren Jones. "Self Perception: Empathy and Androgyny." <u>Empathy, Fantasy, and Helping</u>. Ed. Ezra Stotland, Kenneth E. Mathews Jr., Stanley E. Sherman, Robert O. Hansson, and Barbara Z. Richardson. Sage Library of Social Research 65. Thousand Oaks, CA: Sage Publications, 1978. 97–102.

Hoffman, Martin L., "Empathy, Its Arousal, and Prosocial Functioning," <u>Empathy and Moral Development: Implications for Caring and Justice</u>. New York: Cambridge University Press, 2000. 29–62 (Chapter 2).

Kaplan, David Michael. "Doe Season." <u>Comfort</u>. New York: Viking, 1987. 1–22.

Unger, Rhoda, and Mary Crawford. "Becoming Gendered: The Socialization of Girls and Boys." <u>Women and Gender: A Feminist Psychology</u>. New York: McGraw-Hill, 1993.

A CLOSING WORD

This chapter brings together the methods presented in all of the previous chapters—moving through the stages of the writing process (Chapter 2), the close reading of literary texts (Chapters 4 through 7), making and analyzing arguments (Chapter 8), and using concepts from the disciplines to interpret literature (Chapter 9). The writing assignment at the start of this chapter makes use of them all. In my classes, assignments calling on these skills have led students to many discoveries that have been deeply rewarding on both the human and intellectual levels. I hope that readers of this book have had equally rich experiences and can take these skills with them as they go forward as both readers and writers.

An Anthology
of Readings

CHAPTER ELEVEN

Body

INTRODUCTION

Having a body is the foundation of our relationships with the world and with ourselves. It is the vehicle for our birth and our death and it is the way we sense where we are and who we are. Because our sense organs pick out particular qualities of the physical world to register, they shape and limit what we notice and respond to. They developed so that they could pick out properties of the particular world we live in, but not every property. They give us limited views. Can we imagine what it would be like to have a beagle's sense of smell, a cat's night vision, a bat's hearing, or a bee's perception of ultraviolet light? Because the senses are not faultless and can be led astray, deceit and mistakes are constant parts of our experience.

The body is obviously a source of pleasure and pain, and perhaps, less obviously, at least one source of thoughts and feelings. The intricacies of the connection between body, mind, and spirit are perennial subjects of fascination. Every religion and school of philosophy explores the implications of human existence in a material realm; cultures and families have assumptions about how to treat the body embedded in their codes of dress, rules for eating, and social mores. For instance, why do some cultures rule out eating foods that others feast on happily? Why do members of some cultures define normal apparel as nothing much, while others wrap themselves from head to toe? Is our capacity for pleasure ennobling or dangerous? Should it be nurtured or governed? And how should we grapple with the fact that the body doesn't survive forever?

To prepare yourself to think about this theme, you might spend a little time noticing what it's like to live in your own body and attempting to become aware of your assumptions about its care and feeding. You can probably see most of the selections in this anthology as having something to say about embodiment and the themes suggested here would be excellent starts for essays on any of them.

If you are choosing among the selections below as possible subjects of an essay, think about how they explore such topics. What are the relationships among the various selections? Do they speak to each other or present strictly separate aspects of the subject? Reading them as closely as possible will help you make hypotheses about their themes that will, in turn, help you determine the areas in which to do research.

POETRY

*Swarthy smoke-blackened smiths**

Swarthy smoke-blackened smiths, smudged with soot,
Drive me to death with the din of their banging.
Men never knew such a noise at night!
Such clattering and clanging, such clamour of scoundrels!
Crabbed and crooked, they cry, 'Coal! Coal!'   5
And blow with their bellows till their brains burst.
'Huff! Puff!' pants one: 'Haff! Paff!' another.
They spit and they sprawl and they spin many yarns.
They grate and grind their teeth, and groan together,
Hot with the heaving of their hard hammers.   10
Aprons they have, of hide of the bull,°
And greaves° as leg-guards against glowing sparks.
Heavy hammers they have, and hit hard with them;
Sturdy strokes they strike on their steel anvils.
Lus, bus! Las, bas! they beat in turn—°   15
Such a doleful din, may the Devil destroy it!
The smith stretches a scrap, strikes a smaller,
Twines the two together, and tinkles a treble note°:
Tik, tak! Hic, hac! Tiket, taket! Tyk, tak!
Bus, lus! Bas, las! Such a life they lead,   20

---

*This is a translation of an anonymous Middle English poem found in a mid-13th century manuscript labeled Arundel 292 in the British Museum. Translation by Brian Stone.

[11]**hide of the bull** leather   [12]**greaves** protectors for the lower leg   [15]**Lus, bus, etc.** nonsense syllables attempting to capture the noise of the smithing process   [18]**tinkles a treble note** strikes a high note with a hammer

These Dobbin-dressers°: Christ doom them to misery!
There's no rest at night for the noise of their water-fizzing.°   [13th c.]

[21]**Dobbin-dressers** ones who dress (prepare, outfit, equip with horseshoes) broken-down or worthless horses   [22]**water-fizzing** the sound made when heated iron is plunged into cold water

1. This translation of a Middle English lyric reveals that industry created noise well before the Industrial Revolution of the nineteenth century. What is the speaker's attitude toward the sounds of the blacksmiths' production process? What is the speaker's attitude toward the smiths themselves? How can you tell?
2. What are the poet's techniques for portraying the sounds of the blacksmiths' industry?
3. How can you put this poem into a historical context?

LUCILLE CLIFTON

LUCILLE CLIFTON *(1936–), née Sayles, graduated from the State University of New York College at Fredonia in 1955. In 1958 she married, worked as a claims clerk in the New York State Division of Employment in Buffalo, and later was employed as a literature assistant in the Office of Education in Washington, D.C. In 1969, her collection of poetry,* Good Times, *was published. From then on she held posts as Writer in Residence at colleges and universities, including Columbia University, George Washington University, and the University of California at Santa Cruz. In 1979, she was named Poet Laureate of Maryland. Her poetry collections include* Next: New Poems *(1987),* Quilting: Poems 1987–1990 *(1991), and* The Terrible Stories *(1996). Prose pieces, memoirs, and many children's books written with the African-American audience in mind have brought her prizes, television appearances, fellowships, and grants. Her prizes include the Shelley Memorial Prize, the Charity Randall Prize, the Shestack Prize, and an Emmy Award. Since 1991, she has been the Distinguished Professor of Humanities at St. Mary's College of Maryland. She has raised six children and lives in Columbia, Maryland.*

Homage to My Hips

these hips are big hips.
they need space to
move around in.
they don't fit into little
5 petty places. these hips
are free hips.
they don't like to be held back.
these hips have never been enslaved,
they go where they want to go

they do what they want to do.   10
these hips are mighty hips.
these hips are magic hips.
i have known them
to put a spell on a man and
spin him like a top!   [1972]   15

   1. Why does the speaker isolate one part of her body? Explain how you can
      detect her attitude toward it.
   2. What kind of psychological or sociological context might illuminate this poem?

EMILY DICKINSON

OLC

EMILY DICKINSON *(1830–86) was born in Amherst, Massachusetts, and attended
Mount Holyoke Female Seminary in South Hadley, but because of homesickness,
returned home after one year. After that, she seldom left her house, except for a trip
to Philadelphia, where she met the Reverend Charles Wadsworth. He visited her in
1860, but decided to live on the West Coast, leaving her desolate. From then on, she
lived in almost total isolation, depending on correspondences and books for company
and contact with the outside world. Her poetry reflects her loneliness, but goes far
beyond that to metaphysical and almost mystical contact with the natural world.
She sent poems in many of her letters, but kept most of them in a drawer at home.
She was not published until after her death. She is now considered, with Walt
Whitman, one of the founders of a uniquely American poetry.*

(A Narrow Fellow in the Grass)

A narrow Fellow in the grass
Occasionally rides—
You may have met Him—did you not
His notice sudden is—

The Grass divides as with a Comb   5
A spotted shaft is seen—
And then it closes at your feet
And opens further on—

He likes a Boggy Acre,
A floor too cool for Corn—   10
Yet when a Boy, and Barefoot,
I more than once at Noon,

Have passed, I thought, a Whip lash
Unbraiding in the Sun
When stooping to secure it   15
It wrinkled, and was gone—

Several of Nature's People
I know, and they know me—

I feel for them a transport
20 Of cordiality—

But never met this Fellow
Attended, or alone
Without a tighter breathing,
And Zero at the Bone—   [1866]

1. How would you describe the form of this poem? What difference does it make?
2. Describe the poem's point of view. What difference does it make that it changes as the poem proceeds?
3. What difference does it make to the poem that Dickinson spent most of her life in Massachusetts?
4. What difference do the poem's poetic devices make to the poem?
5. What is the poem's theme?
6. What sort of conceptual framework might illuminate the poem's meaning?

JOHN DONNE

JOHN DONNE *(1573–1631) was born in London to a Roman Catholic family. Home-schooled, he was quite learned in languages and science, but his education at Oxford and Cambridge universities ended because Catholicism forbade taking the oath that declared the king the head of the church rather than the pope. His career in court as secretary to various high officials was cut short by the discovery of his secret marriage to Anne More, to whom he told the news of their misfortune with the famous message: "John Donne, Anne Donne, Un-done." After much struggle and hesitation, he took orders in the Church of England and signed the oath, eventually becoming Dean of St. Paul's Cathedral. He became famous for his eloquent sermons, one hundred and sixty of which survive. Few of his poems were published during his lifetime, but circulated among friends and other readers; both the secular and religious poems were known for their combination of intellectual wit and passion.*

The Sun Rising

    Busy old fool, unruly sun,
      Why dost thou thus
Through windows and through curtains call on us?
Must to thy motions lovers' seasons run?
5   Saucy pedantic wretch, go chide
      Late schoolboys and sour prentices,
  Go tell court huntsmen that the King will ride,
  Call country ants to harvest offices;
Love, all alike,° no season knows nor clime,

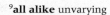

°**all alike** unvarying

Nor hours, days, months, which are the rags of time.   10

    Thy Beams, so reverend and strong
    Why shouldst thou think?
I could eclipse and cloud them with a wink,
But that I would not lose her sight so long;
    If her eyes have not blinded thine,   15
    Look, and tomorrow late, tell me,
  Whether both th' Indias of spice and mine°
Be where thou leftst them, or lie here with me.
Ask for those kings whom thou saw'st yesterday,
And thou shalt hear, All here in one bed lay.   20

    She's all states, and all princes I,
    Nothing else is.
Princes do but play us; compared to this,
All honor's mimic, all wealth alchemy.°
    Thou, sun, art half as happy as we,   25
    In that the world's contracted thus;
  Thine age asks ease, and since thy duties be
To warm the world, that's done in warming us.
Shine here to us, and thou art everywhere;
This bed thy center is, these walls thy sphere.°   [1633] 30

¹⁷**both th' Indias of spice and mine** the east Indies (source of spices) and west Indies
(source of gold and minerals)   ²⁴**alchemy** counterfeit gold   ³⁰The image refers to the
Ptolomaic cosmology, in which heavenly bodies revolved in concentric rings around the
earth. The model of second-century Egyptian Ptolomy dominated Western astronomy
until Galileo confirmed the heliocentric model of Copernicus. "Everywhere" and "sphere"
would have been considered rhymes.

    1. How do rhyme and meter structure this poem?
    2. Who is speaking? To whom? For what purpose?
    3. What is the poem's argument?
    4. To what other poems in this section can this poem be compared?

GALWAY KINNELL

GALWAY KINNELL *(1927–), a native of Providence, Rhode Island, received his
Bachelor of Arts degree from Princeton and his Master of Arts from the University of
Rochester. He served in the navy and has taught writing in many countries, including
France, Australia, and Iran. He has served as Director of the Creative Writing
Program at SUNY Binghamton and New York University. He has been a journalist
and an activist, serving as a field worker for the Congress of Racial Equality in
Louisiana. His poetry began in traditional forms and has changed and become freer
along the way. His books include* Selected Poems *(1982), which won the National
Book Award as well as the Pulitzer Prize,* Imperfect Thirst *(1994),* The Past *(1995),*
The Book of Nightmares *(1971), and translations of French poetry. He is currently
Erich Maria Remarque Professor of Creative Writing at New York University.*

Rapture

I can feel she has got out of bed.
That means it is seven A.M.
I have been lying with eyes shut,
thinking, or possibly dreaming,
5   of how she might look if, at breakfast,
I spoke about the hidden place in her
which, to me, is like a soprano's tremolo,
and right then, over toast and bramble jelly,
if such things are possible, she came.
10 I imagine she would show it while trying to conceal it.
I imagine her hair would fall about her face
and she would become apparently downcast,
as she does at a concert when she is moved.
The hypnopompic° play passes, and I open my eyes
15 and there she is, next to the bed,
bending to a low drawer, picking over
various small smooth black, white,
and pink items of underwear. She bends
so low her back runs parallel to the earth,
20 but there is no sway in it, there is little burden, the day has hardly begun.
The two mounds of muscles for walking, leaping, lovemaking,
lift toward the east—what can I say?
Simile is useless; there is nothing like them on earth.
Her breasts fall full; the nipples
25 are deep pink in the glare shining up through the iron bars
of the gate under the earth where those who could not love
press, wanting to be born again.
I reach out and take her wrist
and she falls back into bed and at once starts unbuttoning my pajamas.
30 Later, when I open my eyes, there she is again,
rummaging in the same low drawer.
The clock shows eight. Hmmm.
With huge, silent effort of great,
mounded muscles the earth has been turning.
35 She takes a piece of silken cloth
from the drawer and stands up. Under the falls
of hair her face has become quiet and downcast,
as if she will be, all day among strangers,
looking down inside herself at our rapture.   [1996]

¹⁴**hypnopompic** The hypnopompic state is the state between sleeping and waking, which for some people includes visual and auditory hallucinations.

1. The obvious subject of this poem is sexual pleasure. How is it treated to create a theme? To what other poems in this section can this poem be compared?
2. The narrator seems to have a position on simile. What is it? How does it affect the meaning of the poem?
3. What conceptual frameworks can enhance our view of this poem?

SHARON OLDS

SHARON OLDS *(1942–) describes herself as having been brought up as a "hellfire Calvinist" in Berkeley, California. She graduated from Stanford and then earned her doctorate in English literature at Columbia University, vowing on graduation day to give up all that she had learned about poetry in order to write in her own voice. She spent seven years in learning how to do that, including an apprenticeship under Muriel Rukeyser, and saw her first book published in 1980,* Satan Says. *In* The Dead and the Living, *she explored themes of bodily experience, winning both the Lamont Poetry Selection and the National Book Critics Circle Award. She then enlarged her interests to include matters of political and social concern, publishing* The Gold Cell *in 1987.* The Wellspring *reflects life experiences, including material concerning her grown children. Olds published* The Unswept Room *in 2002. She is an Associate Professor at New York University and conducts a number of writing workshops across the country. She is one of the founders of NYU's creative writing program for the physically disabled at the Goldwater Hospital in New York City.* The Father, *from which the following poems are taken, appeared in 1992.*

Letter to My Father from 40,000 Feet

Dear Dad, I saw your double today
through the curtain to First Class. Reddish faced,
he had the pitted, swelled, fruit-sucker
skin cheeks lips of the alcoholic, still a
businessman, not fired yet.   5
He sat on the arm of his seat, chatting
across the aisle, I saw your salesman's
gaze, the eyes open and canny,
he had the shorn head, the loosened
tie, the shirt, the belt. I stared   10
through the split in the seats between us, and I wanted—
I wanted to go very close to him,
I did not want to gaze at him or kiss him,
I just wanted to put my long
arms around him, smell the ironed   15
cotton, feel the heat of his chest
against my cheek, the big male body
free of cancer, the fine sifted
lumpless batter of the flesh. Well, that's it, really,

20 just checking in. Isn't it something
    the way I can't get over you, this
    long, deep, unearned desire
    you made when you made me, even after your death
    it beams toward you, even when I'm dead I will be
25 facing you, my non-self
    aiming this ardent non-love
    steadily toward you. I guess I am saying
    I hate you, too, there's a way I want
    to take that first-class toper° and throw him
30 down on the ground, arm-wrestle him
    and win, bang his forearm on the earth
    long after he cries out.   [1992]

²⁹**toper** one who topes, that is, drinks a great deal

1. What kind of language does the narrator use in this poem? What are its most poetic properties?
2. What is the narrator's attitude toward her father?
3. What conceptual frames will enhance our view of this poem?

Waste Sonata

    I think at some point I looked at my father
    and thought *He's full of shit*. How did I
    know fathers talked to their children,
    kissed them? I knew. I saw him and judged him.
5   Whatever he poured into my mother
    she hated, her face rippled like a thin
    wing, sometimes, when she happened to be near him,
    and the liquor he knocked into his body
    felled him, slew the living tree,
10 loops of its grain started to cube,
    petrify, coprofy, he was a
    shit, but I felt he hated being a shit,
    he had never imagined it could happen, this drunken
    sleep was a spell laid on him—
15 by my mother! Well, I left to them
    the passion of who did what to whom, it was a
    baby in their bed they were rolling over on,
    but I could not live with hating him.
    I did not see that I had to. I stood
20 in that living room and saw him drowse
    like the prince, in slobbrous beauty, I began
    to think he was a kind of chalice,

a grail, his love the goal of a quest,
yes! He was the god of love
and I was a shit. I looked down at my forearm—   25
whatever was inside there
was not good, it was white stink,
bad manna.° I looked in the mirror
and as I looked at my face the blemishes
arose, like pigs up out of the ground   30
to the witch's call. It was strange to me
that my body smelled sweet, it was proof I was
demonic, but at least I breathed out,
from the sour dazed scum within,
my father's truth. Well it's fun talking about this,   35
I love the terms of foulness. I have learned
to get pleasure from speaking of pain.
But to die, like this. To grow old and die
a child, lying to herself.
My father was not a shit. He was a man   40
failing at life. He had little shits
travelling through him while he lay there unconscious—
sometimes I don't let myself say
I loved him, anymore, but I feel
I almost love those shits that move through him,   45
shapely, those waste foetuses,
my mother, my sister, my brother, and me
in that purgatory.   [1992]

²⁸**manna** in the Bible, food produced miraculously for the Israelites as they wandered in
the desert after they were freed from slavery in Egypt

1. What are the narrator's insights into her own embodiment?
2. What are the striking features of the language in this poem?
3. What conceptual frameworks can enhance our view of this poem?

LINDA PASTAN

LINDA PASTAN *(1932–) was born in New York City, graduated from Radcliffe
College, and received a master's degree from Brandeis University. She is the
recipient of many awards and honors, including a Pushcart Prize, a Dylan Thomas
Award, the post of Poet Laureate of Maryland, and, in 2003, the Ruth Lilly Poetry
Prize lifetime achievement award for poetry. Her books include* The Last Uncle
(2002), Carnival Evening: New and Selected Poems 1968–1998 *(1998),* An
Early Afterlife *(1995),* Heroes in Disguise *(1991),* The Imperfect Paradise
(1988), PM/AM: New and Selected Poems *(1982),* The Five Stages of Grief
(1978), and A Perfect Circle of Sun *(1971), in which this poem appears.*

Notes from the Delivery Room

Strapped down
victim in an old comic book,
I have been here before,
this place where pain winces
5 off the walls
like too bright light.
Bear down a doctor says,
foreman to sweating laborer,
but this work, this forcing
10 of one life from another
is something that I signed for
at a moment when I would have signed anything.
Babies should grow in fields;
Common as beets or turnips
15 they should be picked and held
root end up, soil spilling
from between their toes—
and how much easier it would be later,
returning them to earth.
20 Bear up . . . bear down . . . the audience
grows restive, and I'm a new magician
Who can't produce the rabbit
from my swollen hat.
She's crowning, someone says,
25 but there is no one royal here,
just me, quite barefoot,
greeting my barefoot child.

[1971]

1. What are the effects of the poet's choices of language in the poem?
2. Compare the poem to Atwood's story "Giving Birth."

MARGE PIERCY

MARGE PIERCY *(1936–) was born into a Detroit family of a Jewish mother and a
non-religious Presbyterian father. The first person in her family to attend college,
she graduated from the University of Michigan. After a short sojourn in France, she
took part-time jobs in Chicago and wrote several novels about working class people
and politics, both of which made her work difficult to publish. In the 1960s, Piercy
became involved in politics in response to the war in Vietnam, especially with the
Students for a Democratic Society. Active in politics by day, she wrote only at night.
Working in that way, she published* Dance the Eagle to Sleep. *Having moved to
Cape Cod, Piercy began* Small Changes *and the Tarot poems. She is now married*

to Ira Wood, a writer with whom she collaborated on a play, and has founded the
Leapfrog Press. She is active in reviving Jewish religion and culture and continues
to write.

Belly Good

A heap of wheat, says the Song of Songs
but I've never seen wheat in a pile.
Apples, potatoes, cabbages, carrots
make lumpy stacks, but you are sleek
as a seal hauled out in the winter sun.   5

I can see you as a great goose egg
or a single juicy and fully ripe peach.
You swell like a natural grassy hill.
You are symmetrical as a Hopewell mound,°
with the eye of the navel wide open,   10

the eye of my apple, the pear's port
window. You're not supposed to exist
at all this decade. You're to be flat
as a kitchen table, so children with
roller skates can speed over you   15

like those sidewalks of my childhood
that each gave a different roar under
my wheels. You're required to show
muscle striations like the ocean
sand at ebb tide, but brick hard.   20

Clothing is not designed for women
of whose warm and flagrant bodies
you are a swelling part. Yet I confess
I meditate with my hands folded on you,
a maternal cushion radiating comfort.   25

Even when I have been at my thinnest,
you have never abandoned me but curled
round as a sleeping cat under my skirt.
When I spread out, so do you. You like
to eat, drink and bang on another belly.   30

In anxiety I clutch you with nervous fingers
as if you were a purse full of calm.
In my grandmother standing in the fierce sun
I see your cauldron that held eleven children
shaped under the tent of her summer dress.   35

°**Hopewell mound** earthworks, including mounds up to 30' high, created by Native
American groups between 200 BCE and 500 BCE in the eastern United States, esp. the
Ohio River Valley

I see you in my mother at thirty
in her flapper gear,° skinny legs
and then you knocking on the tight dress.
We hand you down like a prize feather quilt.
40 You are our female shame and sunburst strength.   [1992]

³⁷**flapper gear** the clothing of a flapper, a young woman of the 1920s, the Jazz Age, an
era characterized by new freedoms for women indicated by shorter hair, shorter skirts, and
the passage of the Twentieth Amendment securing the vote

1. Why does the speaker isolate one part of her body? Explain how you can
   detect her attitude toward it.
2. What kind of psychological or sociological context might illuminate this poem?
3. Compare this poem to Lucille Clifton's "Homage to My Hips."

SAPPHO

SAPPHO *was born on Lesbos and lived and wrote lyric poetry in the early part of
the sixth century BCE in Greece. The facts of her life have been obscured by legend,
but she is considered the most important lyric poet of early Greek times even though
her work exists only in fragments. She is known for love lyrics characterized by
expressions of passion under the perfect control of meter.*

*Pain Penetrates**

Pain penetrates
Me drop
by drop   [sixth c. BCE]

*Translation by Mary Barnard.

1. What is the metaphor that the narrator is using to characterize pain?
2. What disciplines might illuminate this poem?

RICHARD WILBUR

RICHARD WILBUR *(1921–) lives in Cummington, Massachusetts, and Key
West, Florida. He became the Poet Laureate of the United States in 1987 after a
distinguished career as poet, teacher, translator, and lyricist. A graduate of Amherst
College, he saw action in Italy, France, and Germany with the U.S. Army in World
War II and earned his master's degree at Harvard. He has been on the faculties
of Harvard, Wellesley, Wesleyan, and Smith. His books include* The Beautiful
Changes *(1947),* Things of This World *(1957),* Advice to a Prophet *(1961),*
Walking to Sleep *(1969), and* New and Collected Poems *(1989). He has
published two books for children and a collection of prose pieces, has edited the
poetry of Shakespeare and Poe, has done witty translations of the plays of Molière,*

and has written the libretto for Leonard Bernstein's opera Candide. *He has won
the Pulitzer Prize, National Book Award, Bollinger Award, Edna St. Vincent Millay
Memorial Award, Ford Foundation Award, a Guggenheim Fellowship, and a
Prix de Rome Fellowship. He has also won the Aiken Taylor Award for Modern
American Poetry and is a member of the American Institute of Arts and Letters, the
American Academy of Arts and Sciences, and the Academy of American Poets. He
was elected a chevalier of the Ordre des Palms Academiques.*

A Late Aubade

You could be sitting now in a carrel
Turning some liver-spotted page,
Or rising in an elevator-cage
Toward Ladies' Apparel.

You could be planting a raucous bed   5
Of salvia, in rubber gloves,
Or lunching through a screed of someone's loves
With pitying head,

Or making some unhappy setter
Heel, or listening to a bleak   10
Lecture on Schoenberg's serial technique.
Isn't this better?

Think of all the time you are not
Wasting, and would not care to waste,
Such things, thank God, not being to your taste.   15
Think what a lot

Of time, by woman's reckoning,
You've saved, and so may spend on this,
You who had rather lie in bed and kiss
Than anything.   20

It's almost noon, you say? If so,
Time flies, and I need not rehearse
The rosebuds-theme of centuries of verse.°
If you *must* go,

Wait for a while, then slip downstairs   25
And bring us up some chilled white wine,
And some blue cheese, and crackers, and some fine
Ruddy-skinned pears.   [1988]

²³**rosebuds-theme of centuries of verse** the theme of "carpe diem," or "seize the day"
exemplified in Robert Herrick's poem, "To the Virgins, to Make Much of Time." The first
stanza is:

Gather ye rosebuds while ye may,
Old Time is still a-flying:
And [this] same flower that smiles today
Tomorrow will be dying.

1. What is the structure of the poem? The important features of its language?
2. Who is speaking? To whom? What is the narrator's argument in the poem? What argumentative tactics does the narrator use to try to get his way? Compare it to the argument in "To His Coy Mistress" (see Chapter 13). To what other poems in this section can this poem be compared?
3. What disciplines could shed light on this poem?

FRAMEWORKS

Looking at Shakespeare through Medicine

SHAKESPEARE, *Sonnets 65, 72, 73*

HOBART WALLING, *"Life's Brief Candle: A Shakespearean Guide to Death and Dying for Compassionate Physicians"*

OLC

WILLIAM SHAKESPEARE

WILLIAM SHAKESPEARE *(1564–1616) was born at Stratford-on-Avon to a middle-class family. Many of the theories that someone else wrote his plays are motivated by the fact that little is known about his education. He seems to have been educated at the free grammar school in Stratford and to have been, possibly, a schoolmaster there, but there is no record of any time at a university. Some find it hard to explain how a person without university training could have had as much knowledge about the natural world, the arts and sciences, the practical arts, and classical literature as is revealed in the works. But the plays and poems show not only learning, but also a keen ear for language, great wit, and deep insights into the complexities of human character. Shakespeare invented words and developed the genres of Renaissance tragedy and the blank verse line in agile and inventive ways. After marrying Anne Hathaway, and possibly having a pair of twins named Hamnet and Judith, he moved to London, where he became an actor in a very successful acting company and a shareholder in the Globe Theatre. There he wrote, produced, and acted in a stream of plays that are cherished around the world and have been given continuously in every possible medium. When he died in Stratford, he bequeathed his second-best bed to his wife. To the world, he bequeathed poems, including the "Sonnets," "Venus and Adonis," and "The Rape of Lucrece" and a trove of comedies, tragedies, and histories that have influenced writers all over the world.*

Shakespeare, Sonnets 65, 72, 73

A number of Renaissance poets produced sequences of sonnets, including Sir Philip Sidney ("Astrophel and Stella"), Edmund Spenser ("Amoretti"), and Shakespeare, whose 154 sonnets consider themes of love, life, death, and art.

Sonnet 65

Since brass, nor stone, nor earth, nor boundless sea,
But sad mortality o'ersways their power,
How with this rage shall beauty hold a plea,
Whose action is no stronger than a flower?
O! how shall summer's honey breath hold out,   5
Against the wrackful siege of battering days,
When rocks impregnable are not so stout,
Nor gates of steel so strong but Time decays?
O fearful meditation! where, alack,
Shall Time's best jewel from Time's chest lie hid?   10
Or what strong hand can hold his swift foot back?
Or who his spoil of beauty can forbid?
O! none, unless this miracle have might,
That in black ink my love may still shine bright.   [1609]

Sonnet 72

O! lest the world should task you to recite
What merit lived in me, that you should love
After my death,—dear love, forget me quite,
For you in me can nothing worthy prove.
Unless you would devise some virtuous lie,   5
To do more for me than mine own desert,
And hang more praise upon deceased I
Than niggard truth would willingly impart:
O! lest° your true love may seem false in this
That you for love speak well of me untrue,   10
My name be buried where my body is,
And live no more to shame nor me nor you.
For I am shamed by that which I bring forth,
And so should you, to love things nothing worth.   [1609]

⁹**lest** for fear that

Sonnet 73

That time of year thou mayst in me behold
When yellow leaves, or none, or few, do hang
Upon those boughs which shake against the cold,
Bare ruined choirs, where late the sweet birds sang.
In me thou see'st the twilight of such day   5
As after sunset fadeth in the west;
Which by and by black night doth take away,
Death's second self, that seals up all in rest.
In me thou see'st the glowing of such fire,
That on the ashes of his youth doth lie,   10

As the death-bed, whereon it must expire,
Consum'd with that which it was nourish'd by.
This thou perceiv'st, which makes thy love more strong,
To love that well, which thou must leave ere long.   [1609]

To be sure that you understand the poems, first do a close reading of them, noting their structure and meaning. Look up any words you don't understand or think might have deeper meanings that would help illuminate the poems.

1. Who is speaking? What is the point of view?
2. To whom is the speaker speaking?
3. What can you tell about the relationship between the speaker and the person to whom he is speaking? What is the speaker trying to accomplish with the poem?
4. How does the rhyme scheme structure each sonnet?
5. What are the dominant figures of speech in each sonnet? Which sonnet relies less heavily on images than the others? What effect does this have? What other poetic devices play a role?
6. In each sonnet, what effect does the couplet have on the meaning of what comes before?
7. What might Anatole Broyard have said about the images in 73?
8. To what does "that" in l. 14 of Sonnet 73 refer? Who is leaving what?

HOBART W. WALLING

HOBART W. WALLING, PH.D., *is a pharmacologist in the Pharmacological and Physiological Department of the Health Sciences Center of St. Louis University. He has contributed to* Preparation for USMLE Step 1 Basic Sciences Review Book *and other professional publications. In his article* "Life's Brief Candle: A Shakespearean Guide to Death and Dying for Compassionate Physicians," *Dr. Walling examines the plays of Shakespeare to see whether some of his characters manifest the stages that psychiatrist Elizabeth Kübler-Ross predicts for those grappling with imminent death. We can continue the chain of analysis by applying Walling's observations to other works of Shakespeare's—not his plays but his sonnets.*

Life's Brief Candle: A Shakespearean Guide to Death and Dying for Compassionate Physicians*†

Death is a part of the human experience, a necessary consequence of life that we all must face. It is incongruous that death, which remains the ultimate fruition of medicine and, indeed, the only panacea, has been scientifically neglected.

*The lines from William Shakespeare quoted in this article are taken from *The Plays and Sonnets of William Shakespeare*, Volumes 1 and 2. Clarke WG, Wright WA, editors. Great Books of the Western World. Chicago (Ill): Encyclopaedia Britannica, Inc; 1952 [Walling's note]
†Hobart W. Walling, "Life's Brief Candle: A Shakespearean Guide to Death and Dying for Compassionate Physicians," *Western Journal of Medicine* 166 (1997): 280–84.

For example, a search of the medical literature published in 1996 identifies 112 papers that contain the keyword "death," a topic that directly affects everyone. In contrast, a similar search reveals more than 1,000 references pertaining to schizophrenia, a disorder with a population prevalence of about 1%.

Perhaps this relative paucity of information reflects an avoidance of death in the traditional medical model. The care of dying patients receives little attention during medical education, and as a result, "many physicians receive inadequate training in how to manage the dying process, and many enter into such situations with limited confidence."[1(p268)] Perhaps this contributes to the adversarial attitude many physicians have toward death, viewing it as "just one more disease to be conquered, a tenacious but not invincible foe."[2(p226)] Because physicians' emotions and fears "are inextricably bound up with the suffering and death of their patients. . . . [however, e]xtreme stress and unnerving ambiguity sometimes lead to exhaustion, emotional fragmentation, and the erosion of meaning in their lives."[3(p233)]

Because physicians are often in a unique position in the profound moments between life and death, it is important to have an appreciation of the emotional aspects of the dying process and to be comfortable in discussing them. Drawing upon expressions in literature can facilitate this,[4] and the work of William Shakespeare provides ample material.

Elizabeth Kübler-Ross, MD, was a pioneer in speaking with dying patients about their feelings.[5] She described five stages of coping with death: denial, anger, bargaining, depression, and acceptance.[6] Obviously, individual responses can vary greatly, and these stages are not intended to be either sequential or all-inclusive. An analysis of Shakespeare's work provides examples of each of these stages. This suggests that the human experience of death has changed little over the past four centuries and offers further credibility to Kübler-Ross's formulation. Moreover, central to Kübler-Ross's writings is the concept that "the psychological needs of dying patients tend to change, and compassionate care requires that physicians tune into these changes and meet new needs as they arise."[1(p270)]

Denial

In Kübler-Ross's model, disbelief about the prognosis is the first response. Denial is reported to be a common emotion in those facing death from illness; it is also experienced by the bereaved. Initially, "denial can be a useful and necessary defense"[7] that precedes other coping strategies. It "removes the idea of death from our everyday deliberations and conveniently stores it just outside of sight or consciousness."[5(p238)] Denial may be an adaptive mechanism that prepares us to manage death maturely.

Interestingly, the denial of death is not a common theme in Shakespeare. Most characters are well aware of their mortality, and many do not hesitate to face death. Notably, military characters often tend to equate death with honor and hold the latter in higher regard. For example, the title character in *Julius Caesar* declares, "Set honor in one eye and death i' the other, / And I will look on both indifferently" (Act I, scene ii, lines 86–87). This cavalier attitude may reflect a desensitization stemming from having risked death many times. Alternatively, it may be interpreted as a mechanical aphorism reflecting a denial of death's power by one who has avoided serious reflection on it.

A notable antithesis to this mentality is demonstrated by a comic character in *King Henry IV, Part I*. Falstaff is a lackluster soldier who rationalizes his reluctance to fight in the following soliloquy (Act V, scene i, lines 126–139):

Prince: Why, thou owest God a death. [*Exits*]
Falstaff: 'Tis not due yet; I would be loath to pay him before his day. What need
I be so forward with him that calls not on me? Well, 'tis no matter; honor
pricks me on. Yea, but how if honor prick me off when I come on? how
then? Can honor set to a leg? no: Or an arm? no: Or take away the grief of
a wound? no. Honor hath no skill in surgery, then? no. What is honor? A
word. What is in that word honor? air. A trim reckoning! Who hath it? he
that died o' Wednesday. Doth he feel it? no. Doth he hear it? no. 'Tis insensi-
ble, then? Yea, to the dead. But will it not live with the living? no. Why?
detraction will not suffer it. Therefore I'll none of it. Honor is a mere
scutcheon: and so ends my catechism.

In valuing life above recognition, Falstaff's reaction seems to be more human than does Caesar's. In "denying" death, he embraces life. Interestingly, Falstaff goes on to feign his own death in battle and is later knighted for his heroism.

Anger

10 Kübler-Ross cites anger as a second stage of dying. This animosity can be directed toward oneself, God, one's physicians, or whomever one holds responsible. [*sic*] It is understandable for those facing death to be angry with their circumstance. Death may often seem to be an undeserved punishment. The unfairness may engender the attitude that "As flies to wanton boys, are we to the gods, / They kill us for their sport" (*King Lear*, Act IV, scene i, lines 37–38). The following example shows anger mingled with a sense of desperation (*Macbeth*, Act III, scene i, lines 108–114):

2nd Murderer: I am one, my liege,
Whom the vile blows and buffets of the world
Have so incensed that I am reckless what
I do to spite the world.
. . .
1st Murderer: So weary with disasters, tugg'd with fortune,
That I would set my life on any chance,
To mend it, or be rid on't.

This reaction might be similar to that of a chronically ill patient considering further chemotherapy. It conveys a sense of exhausted defeat mingled with both reluctance and hope.

The prospect of death may be especially bitter when faced by a person in the prime of life. Some cultures in the past (and present) have blamed misfortune on astrologic processes. For example, on hearing (counterfeit) news of his bride's death, Romeo vents his contempt for fate, saying, "then I defy you, stars!" (*Romeo and Juliet*, Act V, scene i, line 24). Similarly, Othello blames his woes on an aberrant lunar orbit, saying, "It is the very error of the moon." (*Othello, the Moor of Venice*, Act V, scene ii, line 109). It is important for compassionate physicians to recognize that patients express animosity in response to myriad emotions and to accept angry outbursts with equanimity.

Bargaining

A period of bargaining is described in Kübler-Ross's model. This may be an internally or externally directed negotiation to "be on one's best behavior" and thus in some way alter or improve the future. For example, persons coping with impending death might demonstrate increased compliance with a medical regimen, or alternatively, they might propel themselves toward religion in the hope of divine reward. The need to bargain may be brought about by the fleeting nature of life, as time seems to vanish faster the less of it we have: "I wasted time, and now doth time waste me; / For now hath time made me his numbering clock; / My thoughts are minutes" (*The Tragedy of King Richard II*, Act V, scene v, lines 49–51).

A striking example of bargaining is found in *Othello*. The title character has been treacherously deceived by his servant Iago into believing that his wife, Desdemona, has been adulterous. Othello confronts her and makes known his intention to kill her for the crime he imagines she has committed (Act V, scene ii, lines 36, 78–84):

Desdemona: I hope you will not kill me. . . . O banish me, my lord, but kill me not!
Othello: Down, strumpet!
Desdemona: Kill me to-morrow; let me live tonight!
Othello: Nay, if you strive—
Desdemona: But half an hour!
Othello: Being done, there is no pause.
Desdemona: But while I say one prayer!
Othello: It is too late.

Pathetically, the goals of Desdemona's pleas become more humble as the outlook becomes increasingly dismal. Later, Iago's illusion comes to light, and Othello bargains for his reputation before destroying himself (Act V, scene ii, lines 295, 340–345).

Nought I did in hate, but all in honor.

. . .

I pray you, in your letters,

When you shall these unlucky deeds relate,
Speak of me as I am; nothing extenuate,
Nor set down aught in malice. Then you must speak
Of one that loved not wisely but too well.

Although when presented with "bargaining" patients whose hopes may hinge on their physicians' words, it may be tempting to be placatory, it is essential to incorporate honesty with optimism.

Depression

20   Depression is a fourth stage of coping with dying. This is a complex psychological state that can manifest in countless variations. Depression may be a corollary to feelings of powerlessness, hopelessness, guilt, loss of one's integrity, regret at abandoning unrealized dreams or unresolved conflicts, and fear of the unknown. It may be a cause or a consequence of physical or emotional suffering.

Shakespeare's tragic heroes adroitly plumb the depths of depression with highly evocative imagery and language. Hamlet is perhaps the definitive crestfallen protagonist; his sorrowful soliloquies are inarguably among the most renowned passages in literature. Hamlet's depression ironically stems not from an unwillingness to die, but rather from a reluctance to live (*Hamlet, the Prince of Denmark*, Act I, scene ii, lines 129–134):

O, that this too too solid flesh would melt,
Thaw, and resolve itself into a dew!
Or that the Everlasting had not fix'd
His canon 'gainst self-slaughter! O God, God!
How weary, stale, flat, and unprofitable,
Seem to me all the uses of this world.

The origin of Hamlet's anhedonia is the politically motivated murder of his father and his ensuing hesitation in avenging this death. Hamlet's longing for release is tempered by a respect for biblical law and is emblematic of a defense strategy of intellectualization that is taken to the point of indecision.

Shakespeare's command of diction allows readers to enter into the mental state of his characters. Those coping with their impending death convey a palpable mood of despondency through their figurative language. King Richard II's dark, depressive broodings serve to distance him from readers, as in this excerpt: "And nothing can we call our own but death / And that small model of the barren earth / Which serves as paste and cover to our bones" (*Richard II*, Act III, scene ii, lines 152–153).

Macbeth is one of Shakespeare's most pathetic and detestable characters, as his downfall is self-induced and premeditated. He does not deserve our sympathy as a victim of fate or misunderstanding (as Romeo or Othello might). His ambition leaves a trail stained with the innocent blood of his friends. Before his physical demise (which occurs offstage), Macbeth's soul dies a slow death in self-revulsion and despair. His depression pulsates through his dark words (*Macbeth,* Act V, scene v, lines 19–28):

To-morrow, and to-morrow, and to-morrow,
Creeps in this petty pace from day to day
To the last syllable of recorded time,
And all our yesterdays have lighted fools
The way to dusty death. Out, out, brief candle!
Life's but a walking shadow, a poor player
That struts and frets his hour upon the stage,
And then is heard no more. It is a tale
Told by an idiot, full of sound and fury,
Signifying nothing.

There is the sense that each new day is seen as "heralding increased sickness, pain, or disability, never as the beginning of better times."[8p639] Later, Macbeth's depression translates into a longing for death: "I 'gin to be aweary of the sun, / And wish the estate o' the world were now undone" (Act V, scene v, lines 49–50). In the following passage, he sadly decries his lost innocence, but he merely demonstrates regret for his personal loss rather than remorse for the evil his actions have wrought (*Macbeth,* Act V, scene iii, lines 22–28):

I have lived long enough; my way of life
Is fall'n into the sear, the yellow leaf;
And that which should accompany old age,
As honor, love, obedience, troops of friends,
I must not look to have; but, in their stead,
Curses, not loud but deep, mouth-honor, breath,
Which the poor heart would fain deny, and dare not.

It is important that physicians learn to perceive the signs of depression in their patients, dying or otherwise, and to take the appropriate management steps. By communicating effectively, a physician can "actually reduce patients' suffering by recognizing their personal needs, feelings, and expectations."[5p237]

Acceptance

Acceptance is appropriately Kübler-Ross's final stage in handling death. It is the culmination of intense introspection and interpersonal communication. Ideally, the dying person has resolved all the issues that represented previous conflicts. The most mature acceptance of one's mortality would likely involve placing one's life into perspective, feeling at ease with one's place in the Cosmos, and being ready, albeit reluctant, to die. Though this process is often eased with the help of family and friends, physicians should not exclude themselves from this challenging role.

There are a number of mental approaches dying persons may take to reconcile themselves with death. For some, dying may offer the opportunity for restoration, in the sense that "personal relationships with others and with the world are defined and made explicit."[9p138] Although religious faith provides a source of strength for some, others may take secular comfort in accepting the cyclic nature of life. Theology and the concept of a higher intelligence that cares for and rewards us is central to the psyche of vast millions of people. Indeed, "religion is often invoked as a repository of time-tested wisdom and practical guidance as we deal with our natural fear of finitude."[3(p231)] People facing death may take comfort in the belief that they are participating in God's plan. Indeed, some are confident that life is a mere prelude to what lies beyond. A fatalistic sense of calm is displayed by Hamlet (Act V, scene ii, lines 208–213):

> There's a special providence in the fall of a sparrow. If it be now, 'tis not to come; if it be not to come, it will be now; if it be not now, yet it will come; the readiness is all. Since no man has aught of what he leaves, what is 't to leave betimes? Let be.

This sentiment is echoed by Edgar in *King Lear:* "Men must endure / Their going hence, even as their coming hither: / Ripeness is all" (Act V, scene ii, lines 8–10). The spiritual inclinations of both Hamlet and Edgar reflect the belief in a God who has knowledge of and control over the lives of all creatures. Inherent in this ethos is the idea that good behavior and prayer serve to prepare the soul for judgment. These concepts may make the prospect of death more acceptable.

30   The next two passages also demonstrate a reconciliation with approaching death without directly referring to religion. The first is from *Cymbeline* (Act IV, scene ii, lines 258–263):

> Fear no more the heat o' the sun,
> Nor the furious winter's rages;
> Thou thy worldly task hast done,
> Home art gone, and ta'en thy wages.
> Golden lads and girls all must,
> As chimney-sweepers, come to dust.

The next passage is spoken by Romeo, whose mistaken belief that the sleeping Juliet is dead prompts him to consume a poison (*Romeo and Juliet,* Act V, scene iii, lines 109–115):

> O, here will I set up my everlasting rest
> And shake the yoke of inauspicious stars
> From this world-wearied flesh. Eyes, look your last!
> Arms, take your last embrace! and lips, O you
> The doors of breath, seal with a righteous kiss
> A dateless bargain to engrossing death!

Both passages connote somewhat positive feelings toward death, and the acceptance appears to be a product of the recognition of its inevitability. Each also refers to death as offering a release from the travails of life, specifically from harsh elements and labor in the former and from fate and fatigue in the latter. Romeo's lines also exude a quality of regret, and the motif of being "star-crossed" is reiterated.

Death can also be accepted with ambivalence, as in the following lines: "If thou and nature can so gently part, / The stroke of death is as a lover's pinch, / Which hurts, and is desired" (*Antony and Cleopatra*, Act V, scene ii, lines 297–299).

Dramatic interests often impede Shakespeare's characters from attaining a healthy degree of resolution concerning their death. The following examples demonstrate a rather morbid, less salubrious acceptance of death: "If I must die, / I will encounter darkness as a bride, / And hug it in my arms" (*Measure for Measure*, Act III, scene i, lines 83–85); "but I will be / A bridegroom in my death, and run into 't / As to a lover's bed" (*Antony and Cleopatra*, Act IV, scene xiv, lines 99–101). The next example takes this seemingly pathologic ratification of death to an extreme, employing imagery of putrefaction to instill a sense of horror (*The Life and Death of King John*, Act III, scene iv, lines 25–36):

Death, death; O amiable, lovely death!
Thou odoriferous stench! sound rottenness!
Arise forth from the couch of lasting night,
Thou hate and terror to prosperity,
And I will kiss thy detestable bones
And put my eyeballs in thy vaulty brows,
And ring these fingers with thy household worms
And stop this gap of breath with fulsome dust,
And be a carrion monster like thyself.
Come, grin on me, and I will think thou smilest
And buss thee as thy wife. Misery's love,
O come to me!

Each of the three preceding excerpts compares death to marriage, a seemingly paradoxic metaphor, as marriage is typically equated with joy and procreation. But the comparison is effective in revealing the disturbed emotions of the characters. The acceptance of death is not simply an acquiescence, but a willingness. Indeed, positive anticipation of one's own death may warrant intervention.

A unifying example of Kübler-Ross's model of death is found toward the end of *King Lear*. The following passage may be interpreted as tracing Lear's rapid progression through each stage of dying in response to the death of his daughter, Cordelia. A selfish and short-sighted character throughout most of the play, Lear ironically gains a sense of gallantry and empathy for others only moments before his own death. Psychologically, his grief over his daughter's death may be seen as a subconscious transference or a reciprocal reflection of the response to his own imminent demise. In his process of mourning, he concisely demonstrates denial, bargaining, anger, and depression (but dies before achieving any acceptance) (Act V, scene iii, lines 258–272):

She's gone for ever!
I know when one is dead, and when one lives;
She's dead as earth. Lend me a looking-glass;
If that her breath will mist or stain the stone,
Why, then she lives.
. . . .

This feather stirs; she lives! if it be so,
It is a chance which does redeem all sorrows
That ever I have felt.
. . . .

A plague upon you, murderers, traitors all!
I might have saved her; now she's gone for ever!
Cordelia, Cordelia, stay a little. Ha!
What is't thou say'st?

    Act V, scene iii, lines 305–308:

No, no, no life!
Why should a dog, a horse, a rat, have life,
And thou no breath at all? Thou'lt come no more,
Never, never, never, never, never!

Conclusion

Looking at responses to death in Shakespeare's work can help in grasping life's final voyage. The topic merits contemplation, in that our medical progress has "permitted the prolongation of life without [offering] parallel guidelines for its termination."[10] When confronted by uncomfortable emotional situations, even experienced physicians may react by retreating into the familiar arena of jargon and technology, which does little to promote communication and understanding. Indeed, "when the personal needs of the dying patient are greatest and the need for technical expertise is lessening, the defining attributes of the good physician can be displayed at their finest."[9p141] Perhaps it is most apt to conclude this essay with the words of Kübler-Ross[11]:

> Death is the key to the door of life. It is through accepting the finiteness of our individual existences that we are enabled to find the strength and courage to reject those extrinsic roles and expectations and to devote each day of our lives—however long they may be—to growing as fully as we are able.

Acknowledgment

Ms Carolyn Walling and Gail Furman, PhD, provided helpful suggestions and support.

References

1. Gavrin J, Chapman CR. Clinical management of dying patients. In: Cassel CK, Omenn GS, editors. Caring for patients at the end of life [special issue]. West J Med 1995 Sep; 163:268–277
2. Callahan D. Frustrated mastery: the cultural context of death in America. In: Cassel CK, Omenn GS, editors. Caring for patients at the end of life [special issue]. West J Med 1995 Sep; 163:226–230
3. O'Connell LJ. Religious dimensions of dying and death. In: Cassel CK, Omenn GS, editors. Caring for patients at the end of life [special issue]. West J Med 1995 Sep; 163:231–235

4. Cassel CK, Omenn GS. Dimensions of care of the dying patient. In: Caring for patients at the end of life [special issue]. West J Med 1995 Sep; 163:224–225

5. McCormick TR, Conley BJ. Patients' perspectives on dying and on the care of dying patients. In: Cassel CK, Omenn GS, editors. Caring for patients at the end of life [special issue]. West J Med 1995 Sep; 163:236–243

6. Kübler-Ross E. On death and dying. New York (NY): Macmillan; 1969

7. Dane BO. Anticipatory mourning of middle-aged parents of adult children with AIDS. Families in Society 1991; 72(2):108–115

8. Cassel EJ. The nature of suffering and the goals of medicine. N Engl J Med 1982; 306(11):639–645

9. Mermann AC. Spiritual aspects of death and dying. Yale J Biol Med 1992; 65(2):137–142

10. Boyarsky S, North CS, Boyarsky RE. Thanatology: a new clinical specialty to help confront death. Mo Med 1992; 89(2):95–97

11. Kübler-Ross E. Death: the final stage of growth. Englewood Cliffs (NJ): Prentice-Hall; 1975, p. 164. Cited in Kane RS. The defeat of aging versus the importance of death. J Am Geriatr Soc 1996; 44(3):321–325

[1997]

1. What is Walling's motive for writing the article?
2. What are the article's main ideas?
3. Can you think of other uses for the idea of the stages with which one deals with one's own death?
4. Walling's article is itself an application of psychological concepts to the works of Shakespeare. Do you think that the article can help Walling meet his aim?

The Article and the Poems

1. In applying the concepts of Walling's article to the sonnets, do you find that the poems exhibit any of the stages listed by Walling? Which ones do you see in which lines of which poem?
2. Do the poems exhibit any stages that Walling doesn't list? Do you think psychologists' schema should be amended to incorporate other stages?

FICTION

MARGARET ATWOOD

OLC

MARGARET ATWOOD *(1939–) is a Canadian novelist, poet, short story writer, illustrator, and cartoonist. Her first novel,* Surfacing *(1972), sounded some of the themes of nature and wilderness that recur in her work, as well as individual identity and the sometimes uneasy relationship between Canada and the United States.*

A Handmaid's Tale *is a dystopian fantasy. Her recent novel* The Blind Assassin, *a* tour de force *satire with stories within stories, family dramas, social commentary, and sagas of both world wars, won the prestigious Booker Prize in 2000.*

Giving Birth

But who gives it? And to whom is it given? Certainly it doesn't feel like giving, which implies a flow, a gentle handing over, no coercion. But there is scant gentleness here; it's too strenuous, the belly like a knotted fist, squeezing, the heavy trudge of the heart, every muscle in the body tight and moving, as in a slow-motion shot of a high-jump, the faceless body sailing up, turning, hanging for a moment in the air, and then—back to real time again—the plunge, the rush down, the result. Maybe the phrase was made by someone viewing the result only: in this case, the rows of babies to whom birth has occurred, lying like neat packages in their expertly wrapped blankets, pink or blue, with their labels Scotch Taped to their clear plastic cots, behind the plate-glass window.

No one ever says *giving death*, although they are in some ways the same, events, not things. And *delivering*, that act the doctor is generally believed to perform: who delivers what? Is it the mother who is delivered, like a prisoner being released? Surely not; nor is the child delivered to the mother like a letter through a slot. How can you be both the sender and the receiver at once? Was someone in bondage, is someone made free? Thus language, muttering in its archaic tongues of something, yet one more thing, that needs to be re-named.

It won't be by me, though. These are the only words I have, I'm stuck with them, stuck in them. (That image of the tar sands, old tableau in the Royal Ontario Museum, second floor north, how persistent it is. Will I break free, or will I be sucked down, fossilized, a sabre-toothed tiger or lumbering brontosaurus who ventured out too far? Words ripple at my feet, black, sluggish, lethal. Let me try once more, before the sun gets me, before I starve or drown, while I can. It's only a tableau after all, it's only a metaphor. See, I can speak, I am not trapped, and you on your part can understand. So we will go ahead as if there were no problem about language.)

This story about giving birth is not about me. In order to convince you of that I should tell you what I did this morning, before I sat down at this desk—a door on top of two filing cabinets, radio to the left, calendar to the right, these devices by which I place myself in time. I got up at twenty-to-seven, and, halfway down the stairs, met my daughter, who was ascending, autonomously she thought, actually in the arms of her father. We greeted each other with hugs and smiles; we then played with the alarm clock and the hot water bottle, a ritual we go through only on the days her father has to leave the house early to drive into the city. This ritual exists to give me the illusion that I am sleeping in. When she finally decided it was time for me to get up, she began pulling my hair. I got dressed while she explored the bathroom scales and the mysterious white altar of the toilet. I took her downstairs and we had the usual struggle over her clothes. Already she is wearing miniature jeans, miniature T-shirts. After this she fed herself: orange, banana, muffin, porridge.

We then went out to the sun porch, where we recognized anew, and by their names, the dog, the cats and the birds, blue jays and goldfinches at this time of year, which is winter. She puts her fingers on my lips as I pronounce these words; she hasn't yet learned the secret of making them. I am waiting for her first word: surely it will be miraculous, something that has never yet been said. But if so, perhaps she's already said it and I, in my entrapment, my addiction to the usual, have not heard it.

In her playpen I discovered the first alarming thing of the day. It was a small naked woman, made of that soft plastic from which jiggly spiders and lizards and the other things people hang in their car windows are also made. She was given to my daughter by a friend, a woman who does props for movies, she was supposed to have been a prop but she wasn't used. The baby loved her and would crawl around the floor holding her in her mouth like a dog carrying a bone, with the head sticking out one side and the feet out the other. She seemed chewy and harmless, but the other day I noticed that the baby had managed to make a tear in the body with her new teeth. I put the woman into the cardboard box I use for toy storage.

But this morning she was back in the playpen and the feet were gone. The baby must have eaten them, and I worried about whether or not the plastic would dissolve in her stomach, whether it was toxic. Sooner or later, in the contents of her diaper, which I examine with the usual amount of maternal brooding, I knew I would find two small pink plastic feet. I removed the doll and later, while she was still singing to the dog outside the window, dropped it into the garbage. I am not up to finding tiny female arms, breasts, a head, in my daughter's disposable diapers, partially covered by undigested carrots and the husks of raisins, like the relics of some gruesome and demented murder.

Now she's having her nap and I am writing this story. From what I have said, you can see that my life (despite these occasional surprises, reminders of another world) is calm and orderly, suffused with that warm, reddish light, those well-placed blue highlights and reflecting surfaces (mirrors, plates, oblong window-panes) you think of as belonging to Dutch genre paintings; and like them it is realistic in detail and slightly sentimental. Or at least it has an aura of sentiment. (Already I'm having moments of muted grief over those of my daughter's baby clothes which are too small for her to wear any more. I will be a keeper of hair, I will store things in trunks, I will weep over photos.) But above all it's solid, everything here has solidity. No more of those washes of light, those shifts, nebulous effects of cloud, Turner sunsets, vague fears, the impalpables Jeanie used to concern herself with.

I call this woman Jeanie after the song. I can't remember any more of the song, only the title. The point (for in language there are always these "points," these reflections; this is what makes it so rich and sticky, this is why so many have disappeared beneath its dark and shining surface, why you should never try to see your own reflection in it; you will lean over too far, a strand of your hair will fall in and come out gold, and, thinking it is gold all the way down, you yourself will follow, sliding into those outstretched arms, towards the mouth you think is opening to pronounce your name but instead, just before your ears fill with pure sound, will form a word you have never heard before. . . .)

10   The point, for me, is in the hair. My own hair is not light brown, but Jeanie's was. This is one difference between us. The other point is the dreaming; for Jeanie isn't real in the same way that I am real. But by now, and I mean your time, both of us will have the same degree of reality, we will be equal: wraiths, echoes, reverberations in your own brain. At the moment though Jeanie is to me as I will someday be to you. So she is real enough.

    Jeanie is on her way to the hospital, to give birth, to be delivered. She is not quibbling over these terms. She's sitting in the back seat of the car, with her eyes closed and her coat spread over her like a blanket. She is doing her breathing exercises and timing her contractions with a stopwatch. She has been up since two-thirty in the morning, when she took a bath and ate some lime Jell-O, and it's now almost ten. She has learned to count, during the slow breathing, in numbers (from one to ten while breathing in, from ten to one while breathing out) which she can actually see while she is silently pronouncing them. Each number is a different colour and, if she's concentrating very hard, a different typeface. They range from plain roman to ornamented circus numbers, red with gold filigree and dots. This is a refinement not mentioned in any of the numerous books she's read on the subject. Jeanie is a devotee of handbooks. She has at least two shelves of books that cover everything from building kitchen cabinets to auto repairs to smoking your own hams. She doesn't do many of these things, but she does some of them, and in her suitcase, along with a washcloth, a package of lemon Life Savers, a pair of glasses, a hot water bottle, some talcum powder and a paper bag, is the book that suggested she take along all of these things.

    (By this time you may be thinking that I've invented Jeanie in order to distance myself from these experiences. Nothing could be further from the truth. I am, in fact, trying to bring myself closer to something that time has already made distant. As for Jeanie, my intention is simple: I am bringing her back to life.)

    There are two other people in the car with Jeanie. One is a man, whom I will call A., for convenience. A. is driving. When Jeanie opens her eyes, at the end of every contraction, she can see the back of his slightly balding head and his reassuring shoulders. A. drives well and not too quickly. From time to time he asks her how she is, and she tells him how long the contractions are lasting and how long there is between them. When they stop for gas he buys them each a Styrofoam container of coffee. For months he has helped her with the breathing exercises, pressing on her knee as recommended by the book, and he will be present at the delivery. (Perhaps it's to him that the birth will be given, in the same sense that one gives a performance.) Together they have toured the hospital maternity ward, in company with a small group of other pairs like them: one thin solicitous person, one slow bulbous person. They have been shown the rooms, shared and private, the sitzbaths, the delivery room itself, which gave the impression of being white. The nurse was light-brown, with limber hips and elbows; she laughed a lot as she answered questions.

"First they'll give you an enema. You know what it is? They take a tube of water and put it up your behind. Now, the gentlemen must put on this—and these, over your shoes. And these hats, this one for those with long hair, this for those with short hair."

"What about those with no hair?" says A.

The nurse looks up at his head and laughs. "Oh, you still have some," she says. "If you have a question, do not be afraid to ask."

They have also seen the film made by the hospital, a full-colour film of a woman giving birth to, can it be a baby? "Not all babies will be this large at birth," the Australian nurse who introduces the movie says. Still, the audience, half of which is pregnant, doesn't look very relaxed when the lights go on. ("If you don't like the visuals," a friend of Jeanie's has told her, "you can always close your eyes.") It isn't the blood so much as the brownish-red disinfectant that bothers her. "I've decided to call this whole thing off," she says to A., smiling to show it's a joke. He gives her a hug and says, "Everything's going to be fine."

And she knows it is. Everything will be fine. But there is another woman in the car. She's sitting in the front seat, and she hasn't turned or acknowledged Jeanie in any way. She, like Jeanie, is going to the hospital. She too is pregnant. She is not going to the hospital to give birth, however, because the words, the words, are too alien to her experience, the experience she is about to have, to be used about it at all. She's wearing a cloth coat with checks in maroon and brown, and she has a kerchief tied over her hair. Jeanie has seen her before, but she knows little about her except that she is a woman who did not wish to become pregnant, who did not choose to divide herself like this, who did not choose any of these ordeals, these initiations. It would be no use telling her that everything is going to be fine. The word in English for unwanted intercourse is rape. But there is no word in the language for what is about to happen to this woman.

Jeanie has seen this woman from time to time throughout her pregnancy, always in the same coat, always with the same kerchief. Naturally, being pregnant herself has made her more aware of other pregnant women, and she has watched them, examined them covertly, every time she has seen one. But not every other pregnant woman is this woman. She did not, for instance, attend Jeanie's pre-natal classes at the hospital, where the women were all young, younger than Jeanie.

"How many will be breast-feeding?" asks the Australian nurse with the hefty shoulders.

All hands but one shoot up. A modern group, the new generation, and the one lone bottle-feeder, who might have (who knows?) something wrong with her breasts, is ashamed of herself. The others look politely away from her. What they want most to discuss, it seems, are the differences between one kind of disposable diaper and another. Sometimes they lie on mats and squeeze each other's hands, simulating contractions and counting breaths. It's all very hopeful. The Australian nurse tells them not to get in and out of the bathtub by themselves. At the end of an hour they are each given a glass of apple juice.

There is only one woman in the class who has already given birth. She's there, she says, to make sure they give her a shot this time. They delayed it last time and she went through hell. The others look at her with mild disapproval. *They* are not clamouring for shots, they do not intend to go through hell. Hell comes from the wrong attitude, they feel. The books talk about *discomfort*.

"It's not discomfort, it's pain, baby," the woman says.

The others smile uneasily and the conversation slides back to disposable diapers.

25   Vitaminized, conscientious, well-read Jeanie, who has managed to avoid morning sickness, varicose veins, stretch marks, toxemia and depression, who has had no aberrations of appetite, no blurrings of vision—why is she followed, then, by this other? At first it was only a glimpse now and then, at the infants' clothing section in Simpson's Basement, in the supermarket lineup, on street corners as she herself slid by in A.'s car: the haggard face, the bloated torso, the kerchief holding back the too-sparse hair. In any case, it was Jeanie who saw her, not the other way around. If she knew she was following Jeanie she gave no sign.

As Jeanie has come closer and closer to this day, the unknown day on which she will give birth, as time has thickened around her so that it has become something she must propel herself through, a kind of slush, wet earth underfoot, she has seen this woman more and more often, though always from a distance. Depending on the light, she has appeared by turns as a young girl of perhaps twenty to an older woman of forty or forty-five, but there was never any doubt in Jeanie's mind that it was the same woman. In fact it did not occur to her that the woman was not real in the usual sense (and perhaps she was, originally, on the first or second sighting, as the voice that causes an echo is real), until A. stopped for a red light during this drive to the hospital and the woman, who had been standing on the corner with a brown paper bag in her arms, simply opened the front door of the car and got in. A. didn't react, and Jeanie knows better than to say anything to him. She is aware that the woman is not really there: Jeanie is not crazy. She could even make the woman disappear by opening her eyes wider, by staring, but it is only the shape that would go away, not the feeling. Jeanie isn't exactly afraid of this woman. She is afraid for her.

When they reach the hospital, the woman gets out of the car and is through the door by the time A. has come around to help Jeanie out of the back seat. In the lobby she is nowhere to be seen. Jeanie goes through Admission in the usual way, unshadowed.

There has been an epidemic of babies during the night and the maternity ward is overcrowded. Jeanie waits for her room behind a dividing screen. Nearby someone is screaming, screaming and mumbling between screams in what sounds like a foreign language. Portuguese, Jeanie thinks. She tells herself that for them it is different, you're supposed to scream, you're regarded as queer if you don't scream, it's a required part of giving birth. Nevertheless she knows that the woman screaming is the other woman and she is screaming from pain. Jeanie listens to the other voice, also a woman's, comforting, reassuring: her mother? A nurse?

A. arrives and they sit uneasily, listening to the screams. Finally Jeanie is sent for and she goes for her prep. Prep school, she thinks. She takes off her clothes—when will she see them again?—and puts on the hospital gown. She is examined, labelled around the wrist and given an enema. She tells the nurse she can't take Demerol because she's allergic to it, and the nurse writes this down. Jeanie doesn't know whether this is true or not but she doesn't want Demerol, she has read the books. She intends to put up a struggle over her pubic hair—surely she will lose her strength if it is all shaved off—but it turns out the nurse doesn't have very strong feelings about it. She is told her contractions are not far enough along to be taken seriously, she can even have lunch. She puts on her dressing gown and rejoins A., in the freshly vacated room, eats some tomato soup and a veal cutlet, and decides to take a nap while A. goes out for supplies.

Jeanie wakes up when A. comes back. He has brought a paper, some detective novels for Jeanie and a bottle of Scotch for himself. A. reads the paper and drinks Scotch, and Jeanie reads *Poirot's Early Cases*. There is no connection between Poirot and her labour, which is now intensifying, unless it is the egg-shape of Poirot's head and the vegetable marrows he is known to cultivate with strands of wet wool (placentae? umbilical cords?). She is glad the stories are short; she is walking around the room now, between contractions. Lunch was definitely a mistake. 30

"I think I have back labour," she says to A. They get out the handbook and look up the instructions for this. It's useful that everything has a name. Jeanie kneels on the bed and rests her forehead on her arms while A. rubs her back. A. pours himself another Scotch, in the hospital glass. The nurse, in pink, comes, looks, asks about the timing, and goes away again. Jeanie is beginning to sweat. She can only manage half a page or so of Poirot before she has to clamber back up on the bed again and begin breathing and running through the coloured numbers.

When the nurse comes back, she has a wheelchair. It's time to go down to the labour room, she says. Jeanie feels stupid sitting in the wheelchair. She tells herself about peasant women having babies in the fields, Indian women having them on portages with hardly a second thought. She feels effete. But the hospital wants her to ride, and considering the fact that the nurse is tiny, perhaps it's just as well. What if Jeanie were to collapse, after all? After all her courageous talk. An image of the tiny pink nurse, antlike, trundling large Jeanie through the corridors, rolling her along like a heavy beach ball.

As they go by the check-in desk a woman is wheeled past on a table, covered by a sheet. Her eyes are closed and there's a bottle feeding into her arm through a tube. Something is wrong. Jeanie looks back—she thinks it was the other woman—but the sheeted table is hidden now behind the counter.

In the dim labour room Jeanie takes off her dressing gown and is helped up onto the bed by the nurse. A. brings her suitcase, which is not a suitcase actually but a small flight bag, the significance of this has not been lost on Jeanie, and in fact she now has some of the apprehensive feelings she associates with planes, including the fear of a crash. She takes out her Life Savers, her glasses, her washcloth and the other things she thinks she will need. She removes her contact lenses and places them in their case, reminding A. that they must not be lost. Now she is purblind.

35   There is something else in her bag that she doesn't remove. It's a talisman, given to her several years ago as a souvenir by a travelling friend of hers. It's a rounded oblong of opaque blue glass, with four yellow-and-white eye shapes on it. In Turkey, her friend has told her, they hang them on mules to protect against the Evil Eye. Jeanie knows this talisman probably won't work for her, she is not Turkish and she isn't a mule, but it makes her feel safer to have it in the room with her. She had planned to hold it in her hand during the most difficult part of labour but somehow there is no longer any time for carrying out plans like this.

There is an old woman, a fat old woman dressed all in green, comes into the room and sits beside Jeanie. She says to A., who is sitting on the other side of Jeanie, "That is a good watch. They don't make watches like that any more." She is referring to his gold pocket watch, one of his few extravagances, which is on the night table. Then she places her hand on Jeanie's belly to feel the contraction. "This is good," she says, her accent is Swedish or German. "This, I call a contraction. Before, it was nothing." Jeanie can no longer remember having seen her before. "Good. Good."

"When will I have it?" Jeanie asks, when she can talk, when she is no longer counting.

The old woman laughs. Surely that laugh, those tribal hands, have presided over a thousand beds, a thousand kitchen tables . . . "A long time yet," she says. "Eight, ten hours."

"But I've been *doing* this for twelve hours already," Jeanie says.

40   "Not hard labour," the woman says. "Not good, like this."

Jeanie settles into herself for the long wait. At the moment she can't remember why she wanted to have a baby in the first place. That decision was made by someone else, whose motives are now unclear. She remembers the way women who had babies used to smile at one another, mysteriously, as if there was something they knew that she didn't, the way they would casually exclude her from their frame of reference. What was the knowledge, the mystery, or was having a baby really no more inexplicable than having a car accident or an orgasm? (But these too were indescribable, events of the body, all of them; why should the mind distress itself trying to find a language for them?) She has sworn she will never do that to any woman without children, engage in those passwords and exclusions. She's old enough, she's been put through enough years of it to find it tiresome and cruel.

But—and this is the part of Jeanie that goes with the talisman hidden in her bag, not with the part that longs to build kitchen cabinets and smoke hams—she is, secretly, hoping for a mystery. Something more than this, something else, a vision. After all she is risking her life, though it's not too likely she will die. Still, some women do. Internal bleeding, shock, heart failure, a mistake on the part of someone, a nurse, a doctor. She deserves a vision, she deserves to be allowed to bring something back with her from this dark place into which she is now rapidly descending.

She thinks momentarily about the other woman. Her motives, too, are unclear. Why doesn't she want to have a baby? Has she been raped, does she have ten other children, is she starving? Why hasn't she had an abortion? Jeanie doesn't know, and in fact it no longer matters why. *Uncross your fingers,* Jeanie thinks to her. Her face, distorted with pain and terror, floats briefly behind Jeanie's eyes before it too drifts away.

Jeanie tries to reach down to the baby, as she has many times before, sending waves of love, colour, music, down through her arteries to it, but she finds she can no longer do this. She can no longer feel the baby as a baby, its arms and legs poking, kicking, turning. It has collected itself together, it's a hard sphere, it does not have time right now to listen to her. She's grateful for this because she isn't sure anyway how good the message would be. She no longer has control of the numbers either, she can no longer see them, although she continues mechanically to count. She realizes she has practised for the wrong thing, A. squeezing her knee was nothing, she should have practised for this, whatever it is.

"Slow down," A. says. She's on her side now, he's holding her hand. "Slow it right down."   45

"I can't, I can't do it, I can't do this."

"Yes, you can."

"Will I sound like that?"

"Like what?" A. says. Perhaps he can't hear it: it's the other woman, in the room next door or the room next door to that. She's screaming and crying, screaming and crying. While she cries she is saying, over and over, "It hurts. It hurts."

"No, you won't," he says. So there is someone, after all.   50

A doctor comes in, not her own doctor. They want her to turn over on her back.

"I can't," she says. "I don't like it that way." Sounds have receded, she has trouble hearing them. She turns over and the doctor gropes with her rubber-gloved hand. Something wet and hot flows over her thighs.

"It was just ready to break," the doctor says. "All I had to do was touch it. Four centimetres," she says to A.

"Only *four*?" Jeanie says. She feels cheated; they must be wrong. The doctor says her own doctor will be called in time. Jeanie is outraged at them. They have not understood, but it's too late to say this and she slips back into the dark place, which is not hell, which is more like being inside, trying to get out. *Out,* she says or thinks. Then she is floating, the numbers are gone, if anyone told her to get up, go out of the room, stand on her head, she would do it. From minute to minute she comes up again, grabs for air.

"You're hyperventilating," A. says. "Slow it down." He is rubbing her back   55
now, hard, and she takes his hand and shoves it viciously further down, to the right place, which is not the right place as soon as his hand is there. She remembers a story she read once, about the Nazis tying the legs of Jewish women together during labour. She never really understood before how that could kill you.

A nurse appears with a needle. "I don't want it," Jeanie says.

"Don't be hard on yourself," the nurse says. "You don't have to go through pain like that." What pain? Jeanie thinks. When there is no pain she feels nothing, when there is pain, she feels nothing because there is no *she*. This, finally, is the disappearance of language. *You don't remember afterwards,* she has been told by almost everyone.

Jeanie comes out of a contraction, gropes for control. "Will it hurt the baby?" she says.

"It's a mild analgesic," the doctor says. "We wouldn't allow anything that would hurt the baby." Jeanie doesn't believe this. Nevertheless she is jabbed, and the doctor is right, it is very mild, because it doesn't seem to do a thing for Jeanie, though A. later tells her she has slept briefly between contractions.

60   Suddenly she sits bolt upright. She is wide awake and lucid. "You have to ring that bell right now," she says. "This baby is being born."

A. clearly doesn't believe her. "I can feel it, I can feel the head," she says. A. pushes the button for the call bell. A nurse appears and checks, and now everything is happening too soon, nobody is ready. They set off down the hall, the nurse wheeling Jeanie feels fine. She watches the corridors, the edges of everything shadowy because she doesn't have her glasses on. She hopes A. will remember to bring them. They pass another doctor.

"Need me?" she asks.

"Oh no," the nurse answers breezily. "Natural childbirth."

Jeanie realizes that this woman must have been the anaesthetist. "What?" she says, but it's too late now, they are in the room itself, all those glossy surfaces, tubular strange apparatus like a science-fiction movie, and the nurse is telling her to get onto the delivery table. No one else is in the room.

"You must be crazy," Jeanie says.

65   "Don't push," the nurse says.

"What do you mean?" Jeanie says. This is absurd. Why should she wait, why should the baby wait for them because they're late?

"Breathe through your mouth," the nurse says. "Pant," and Jeanie finally remembers how. When the contraction is over she uses the nurse's arm as a lever and hauls herself across onto the table.

From somewhere her own doctor materializes, in her doctor suit already, looking even more like Mary Poppins than usual, and Jeanie says, "Bet you weren't expecting to see me so soon!" The baby is being born when Jeanie said it would, though just three days ago the doctor said it would be at least another week, and this makes Jeanie feel jubilant and smug. Not that she knew, she'd believed the doctor.

She's being covered with a green tablecloth, they are taking far too long, she feels like pushing the baby out now, before they are ready. A. is there by her head, swathed in robes, hats, masks. He has forgotten her glasses. "Push now," the doctor says. Jeanie grips with her hands, grits her teeth, face, her whole body together, a snarl, a fierce smile, the baby is enormous, a stone, a boulder, her bones unlock, and, once, twice, the third time, she opens like a birdcage turning slowly inside out.

A pause; a wet kitten slithers between her legs. "Why don't you look?" says   70
the doctor, but Jeanie still has her eyes closed. No glasses, she couldn't have seen
a thing anyway. "Why don't you look?" the doctor says again.

Jeanie opens her eyes. She can see the baby, who has been wheeled up beside
her and is fading already from the alarming birth purple. A good baby, she
thinks, meaning it as the old woman did: *a good watch*, well-made, substantial.
The baby isn't crying; she squints in the new light. Birth isn't something that has
been given to her, nor has she taken it. It was just something that has happened
so they could greet each other like this. The nurse is stringing beads for her
name. When the baby is bundled and tucked beside Jeanie, she goes to sleep.

As for the vision, there wasn't one. Jeanie is conscious of no special
knowledge; already she's forgetting what it was like. She's tired and very cold;
she is shaking, and asks for another blanket. A. comes back to the room with
her; her clothes are still there. Everything is quiet, the other woman is no longer
screaming. Something has happened to her, Jeanie knows. Is she dead? Is the
baby dead? Perhaps she is one of those casualties (and how can Jeanie herself
be sure, yet, that she will not be among them) who will go into postpartum
depression and never come out. "You see, there was nothing to be afraid of," A.
says before he leaves, but he was wrong.

The next morning Jeanie wakes up when it's light. She's been warned about
getting out of bed the first time without the help of a nurse, but she decides to
do it anyway (peasant in the field! Indian on the portage!). She's still running
adrenaline, she's also weaker than she thought, but she wants very much to
look out the window. She feels she's been inside too long, she wants to see the
sun come up. Being awake this early always makes her feel a little unreal, a little
insubstantial, as if she's partly transparent, partly dead.

(It was to me, after all, that the birth was given, Jeanie gave it, I am the
result. What would she make of me? Would she be pleased?)

The window is two panes with a venetian blind sandwiched between them; it   75
turns by a knob at the side. Jeanie has never seen a window like this before. She
closes and opens the blind several times. Then she leaves it open and looks out.

All she can see from the window is a building. It's an old stone building,
heavy and Victorian, with a copper roof oxidized to green. It's solid, hard,
darkened by soot, dour, leaden. But as she looks at this building, so old and
seemingly immutable, she sees that it's made of water. Water, and some tenuous
jelly-like substance. Light flows through it from behind (the sun is coming up),
the building is so thin, so fragile, that it quivers in the slight dawn wind. Jeanie
sees that if the building is this way (a touch could destroy it, a ripple of the
earth, why has no one noticed, guarded it against accidents?) then the rest of
the world must be like this too, the entire earth, the rocks, people, trees, everything needs to be protected, cared for, tended. The enormity of this task defeats
her; she will never be up to it, and what will happen then?

Jeanie hears footsteps in the hall outside her door. She thinks it must be
the other woman, in her brown-and-maroon-checked coat, carrying her paper
bag, leaving the hospital now that her job is done. She has seen Jeanie safely
through, she must go now to hunt through the streets of the city for her next

case. But the door opens, it's a nurse, who is just in time to catch Jeanie as she sinks to the floor, holding on to the edge of the air-conditioning unit. The nurse scolds her for getting up too soon.

After that the baby is carried in, solid, substantial, packed together like an apple, Jeanie examines her, she is complete, and in the days that follow Jeanie herself becomes drifted over with new words, her hair slowly darkens, she ceases to be what she was and is replaced, gradually, by someone else.

[1982]

1. What kind of narrator is this? What is the result of the way the narrative is structured?
2. Who is Jeanie and what is her role in the story?
3. What is the relationship between chronology of events and the plot of the story? What difference does the difference make?
4. The narrator says the experience is "indescribable." What does she do to help overcome this obstacle to verbal representation?
5. The narrator says that Jeanie wants "a mystery. Something more than this, something else, a vision." Does she get it?
6. What does the story have to offer people who have never been pregnant and may never give birth?

RALPH ELLISON

RALPH ELLISON *(1914–94), brought up in Oklahoma, attended Tuskegee Institute, studying music and writing, but left because of financial problems. He moved to New York and met Richard Wright, the novelist, who encouraged him to become a writer. His novel* Invisible Man *contains elements of both Wright's and his own lives and describes the loneliness and stresses of modern city life, especially for a black man. It brought him international fame. This version of "Battle Royal" is the first chapter.*

Battle Royal

It goes a long way back, some twenty years. All my life I had been looking for something, and everywhere I turned someone tried to tell me what it was. I accepted their answers too, though they were often in contradiction and even self-contradictory. I was naïve. I was looking for myself and asking everyone except myself questions which I, and only I, could answer. It took me a long time and much painful boomeranging of my expectations to achieve a realization everyone else appears to have been born with: That I am nobody but myself. But first I had to discover that I am an invisible man!

And yet I am no freak of nature, nor of history. I was in the cards, other things having been equal (or unequal) eighty-five years ago. I am not ashamed of my grandparents for having been slaves. I am only ashamed of myself for having at one time been ashamed. About eighty-five years ago they were told that they were free, united with others of our country in everything pertaining to the common good, and, in everything social, separate like the fingers of the hand. And they believed it. They exulted in it. They stayed in their place, worked hard, and brought up my father to do the same. But my grandfather is the one. He was an odd old guy, my grandfather, and I am told I take after him. It was he who caused the trouble. On his deathbed he called my father to him and said, "Son, after I'm gone I want you to keep up the good fight. I never told you, but our life is a war and I have been a traitor all my born days, a spy in the enemy's country ever since I give up my gun back in the Reconstruction. Live with your head in the lion's mouth. I want you to overcome 'em with yeses, undermine 'em with grins, agree 'em to death and destruction, let 'em swoller you till they vomit or bust wide open." They thought the old man had gone out of his mind. He had been the meekest of men. The younger children were rushed from the room, the shades drawn and the flame of the lamp turned so low that it sputtered on the wick like the old man's breathing. "Learn it to the younguns," he whispered fiercely; then he died.

But my folks were more alarmed over his last words than over his dying. It was as though he had not died at all, his words caused so much anxiety. I was warned emphatically to forget what he had said and, indeed, this is the first time it has been mentioned outside the family circle. It had a tremendous effect upon me, however. I could never be sure of what he meant. Grandfather had been a quiet old man who never made any trouble, yet on his deathbed he had called himself a traitor and a spy, and he had spoken of his meekness as a dangerous activity. It became a constant puzzle which lay unanswered in the back of my mind. And whenever things went well for me I remembered my grandfather and felt guilty and uncomfortable. It was as though I was carrying out his advice in spite of myself. And to make it worse, everyone loved me for it. I was praised by the most lily-white men of the town. I was considered an example of desirable conduct—just as my grandfather had been. And what puzzled me was that the old man had defined it as *treachery*. When I was praised for my conduct I felt a guilt that in some way I was doing something that was really against the wishes of the white folks, that if they had understood they would have desired me to act just the opposite, that I should have been sulky and mean, and that that really would have been what they wanted, even though they were fooled and thought they wanted me to act as I did. It made me afraid that some day they would look upon me as a traitor and I would be lost. Still I was more afraid to act any other way because they didn't like that at all. The old man's words were like a curse. On my graduation day I delivered an oration in which I showed that humility was the secret, indeed, the very essence of progress. (Not that I believed this—how could I, remembering my grandfather?—I only believed that it worked.) It was a great success. Everyone praised me and I was invited to give the speech at a gathering of the town's leading white citizens. It was a triumph for our whole community.

It was in the main ballroom of the leading hotel. When I got there I discovered that it was on the occasion of a smoker, and I was told that since I was to be there anyway I might as well take part in the battle royal to be fought by some of my schoolmates as part of the entertainment. The battle royal came first.

All of the town's big shots were there in their tuxedoes, wolfing down the buffet foods, drinking beer and whiskey and smoking black cigars. It was a large

5

room with a high ceiling. Chairs were arranged in neat rows around three sides of a portable boxing ring. The fourth side was clear, revealing a gleaming space of polished floor. I had some misgivings over the battle royal, by the way. Not from a distaste for fighting, but because I didn't care too much for the other fellows who were to take part. They were tough guys who seemed to have no grandfather's curse worrying their minds. No one could mistake their toughness. And besides, I suspected that fighting a battle royal might detract from the dignity of my speech. In those pre-invisible days I visualized myself as a potential Booker T. Washington.° But the other fellows didn't care too much for me either, and there were nine of them. I felt superior to them in my way, and I didn't like the manner in which we were all crowded together into the servants' elevator. Nor did they like my being there. In fact, as the warmly lighted floors flashed past the elevator we had words over the fact that I, by taking part in the fight, had knocked one of their friends out of a night's work.

We were led out of the elevator through a rococo hall into an anteroom and told to get into our fighting togs. Each of us was issued a pair of boxing gloves and ushered out into the big mirrored hall, which we entered looking cautiously about us and whispering, lest we might accidentally be heard above the noise of the room. It was foggy with cigar smoke. And already the whiskey was taking effect. I was shocked to see some of the most important men of the town quite tipsy. They were all there—bankers, lawyers, judges, doctors, fire chiefs, teachers, merchants. Even one of the more fashionable pastors. Something we could not see was going on up front. A clarinet was vibrating sensuously and the men were standing up and moving eagerly forward. We were a small tight group, clustered together, our bare upper bodies touching and shining with anticipatory sweat; while up front the big shots were becoming increasingly excited over something we still could not see. Suddenly I heard the school superintendent, who had told me to come, yell. "Bring up the shines, gentlemen! Bring up the little shines!"

We were rushed up to the front of the ballroom, where it smelled even more strongly of tobacco and whiskey. Then we were pushed into place. I almost wet my pants. A sea of faces, some hostile, some amused, ringed around us, and in the center, facing us, stood a magnificent blonde—stark naked. There was dead silence. I felt a blast of cold air chill me. I tried to back away, but they were behind me and around me. Some of the boys stood with lowered heads, trembling. I felt a wave of irrational guilt and fear. My teeth chattered, my skin turned to goose flesh, my knees knocked. Yet I was strongly attracted and looked in spite of myself. Had the price of looking been blindness, I would have looked. The hair was yellow like that of a circus kewpie doll, the face heavily powdered and rouged, as though to form an abstract mask, the eyes hollow and smeared a cool blue, the color of a baboon's butt. I felt a desire to spit upon her as my eyes brushed slowly over her body. Her breasts were firm and round as the domes of East Indian temples, and I stood so close as to see the fine skin texture and beads

---

[5]**Booker T. Washington** (1856–1915), founder of the Tuskegee Normal and Industrial Institute in the Black Belt of Alabama, advocated teaching practical skills to Blacks. His autobiography, *Up from Slavery*, was published in 1901.

of pearly perspiration glistening like dew around the pink and erected buds of her nipples. I wanted at one and the same time to run from the room, to sink through the floor, or go to her and cover her from my eyes and the eyes of the others with my body; to feel the soft thighs, to caress her and destroy her, to love her and murder her, to hide from her, and yet to stroke where below the small American flag tattooed upon her belly her thighs formed a capital V. I had a notion that of all in the room she saw only me with her impersonal eyes.

And then she began to dance, a slow sensuous movement; the smoke of a hundred cigars clinging to her like the thinnest of veils. She seemed like a fair bird-girl girdled in veils calling to me from the angry surface of some gray and threatening sea. I was transported. Then I became aware of the clarinet playing and the big shots yelling at us. Some threatened us if we looked and others if we did not. On my right I saw one boy faint. And now a man grabbed a silver pitcher from a table and stepped close as he dashed ice water upon him and stood him up and forced two of us to support him as his head hung and moans issued from his thick bluish lips. Another boy began to plead to go home. He was the largest of the group, wearing dark red fighting trunks much too small to conceal the erection which projected from him as though in answer to the insinuating low-registered moans of the clarinet. He tried to hide himself with his boxing gloves.

And all the while the blonde continued dancing, smiling faintly at the big shots who watched her with fascination, and faintly smiling at our fear. I noticed a certain merchant who followed her hungrily, his lips loose and drooling. He was a large man who wore diamond studs in a shirtfront which swelled with the ample paunch underneath, and each time the blonde swayed her undulating hips he ran his hand through the thin hair of his bald head and, with his arms upheld, his posture clumsy like that of an intoxicated panda, wound his belly in a slow and obscene grind. This creature was completely hypnotized. The music had quickened. As the dancer flung herself about with a detached expression on her face, the men began reaching out to touch her. I could see their beefy fingers sink into her soft flesh. Some of the others tried to stop them and she began to move around the floor in graceful circles, as they gave chase, slipping and sliding over the polished floor. It was mad. Chairs went crashing, drinks were spilt, as they ran laughing and howling after her. They caught her just as she reached a door, raised her from the floor, and tossed her as college boys are tossed at a hazing, and above her red, fixed-smiling lips I saw the terror and disgust in her eyes, almost like my own terror and that which I saw in some of the other boys. As I watched, they tossed her twice and her soft breasts seemed to flatten against the air and her legs flung wildly as she spun. Some of the more sober ones helped her to escape. And I started off the floor, heading for the anteroom with the rest of the boys.

Some were still crying and in hysteria. But as we tried to leave we were 10 stopped and ordered to get into the ring. There was nothing to do but what we were told. All ten of us climbed under the ropes and allowed ourselves to be blindfolded with broad bands of white cloth. One of the men seemed to feel a bit sympathetic and tried to cheer us up as we stood with our backs against the ropes. Some of us tried to grin. "See that boy over there?" one of the men said.

"I want you to run across at the bell and give it to him right in the belly. If you don't get him, I'm going to get you. I don't like his looks." Each of us was told the same. The blindfolds were put on. Yet even then I had been going over my speech. In my mind each word was as bright as flame. I felt the cloth pressed into place, and frowned so that it would be loosened when I relaxed.

But now I felt a sudden fit of blind terror. I was unused to darkness. It was as though I had suddenly found myself in a dark room filled with poisonous cotton-mouths. I could hear the bleary voices yelling insistently for the battle royal to begin.

"Get going in there!"

"Let me at that big nigger!"

I strained to pick up the school superintendent's voice, as though to squeeze some security out of that slightly more familiar sound.

15   "Let me at those black sonsabitches!" someone yelled.

"No, Jackson, no!" another voice yelled. "Here, somebody, help me hold Jack."

"I want to get at that ginger-colored nigger. Tear him limb from limb," the first voice yelled.

I stood against the ropes trembling. For in those days I was what they called ginger-colored, and he sounded as though he might crunch me between his teeth like a crisp ginger cookie.

Quite a struggle was going on. Chairs were being kicked about and I could hear voices grunting as with a terrific effort. I wanted to see, to see more desperately than ever before. But the blindfold was as tight as a thick skin-puckering scab and when I raised my gloved hands to push the layers of white aside a voice yelled, "Oh, no you don't, black bastard! Leave that alone!"

20   "Ring the bell before Jackson kills him a coon!" someone boomed in the sudden silence. And I heard the bell clang and the sound of the feet scuffling forward.

A glove smacked against my head. I pivoted, striking out stiffly as someone went past, and felt the jar ripple along the length of my arm to my shoulder. Then it seemed as though all nine of the boys had turned upon me at once. Blows pounded me from all sides while I struck out as best I could. So many blows landed upon me that I wondered if I were not the only blindfolded fighter in the ring, or if the man called Jackson hadn't succeeded in getting me after all.

Blindfolded, I could no longer control my motions. I had no dignity. I stumbled about like a baby or a drunken man. The smoke had become thicker and with each new blow it seemed to sear and further restrict my lungs. My saliva became like hot bitter glue. A glove connected with my head, filling my mouth with warm blood. It was everywhere. I could not tell if the moisture I felt upon my body was sweat or blood. A blow landed hard against the nape of my neck. I felt myself going over, my head hitting the floor. Streaks of blue light filled the black world behind the blindfold. I lay prone, pretending that I was knocked out, but felt myself seized by hands and yanked to my feet. "Get going, black boy! Mix it up!" My arms were like lead, my head smarting from blows. I managed to feel my way to the ropes and held on, trying to catch my breath. A glove landed in my midsection and I went over again, feeling as though the smoke had become a knife jabbed into my guts. Pushed this way and that by the legs milling around me, I finally pulled erect and discovered that I could see the black, sweat-washed forms weaving in the smoky-blue atmosphere like drunken dancers weaving to the rapid drum-like thuds of blows.

Everyone fought hysterically. It was complete anarchy. Everybody fought everybody else. No group fought together for long. Two, three, four, fought one, then turned to fight each other, were themselves attacked. Blows landed below the belt and in the kidney, with the gloves open as well as closed, and with my eye partly opened now there was not so much terror. I moved carefully, avoiding blows, although not too many to attract attention, fighting from group to group. The boys groped about like blind, cautious crabs crouching to protect their mid-sections, their heads pulled in short against their shoulders, their arms stretched nervously before them, with their fists testing the smoke-filled air like the knobbed feelers of hypersensitive snails. In one corner I glimpsed a boy violently punching the air and heard him scream in pain as he smashed his hand against a ring post. For a second I saw him bent over holding his hand, then going down as a blow caught his unprotected head. I played one group against the other, slipping and throwing a punch then stepping out of range while pushing the others into the melee to take the blows blindly aimed at me. The smoke was agonizing and there were no rounds, no bells at three minute intervals to relieve our exhaustion. The room spun round me, a swirl of lights, smoke, sweating bodies surrounded by tense white faces. I bled from both nose and mouth, the blood spattering upon my chest.

The men kept yelling, "Slug him, black boy! Knock his guts out!"

"Uppercut him! Kill him! Kill that big boy!"

25

Taking a fake fall, I saw a boy going down heavily beside me as though we were felled by a single blow, saw a sneaker-clad foot shoot into his groin as the two who had knocked him down stumbled upon him. I rolled out of range, feeling a twinge of nausea.

The harder we fought the more threatening the men became. And yet, I had begun to worry about my speech again. How would it go? Would they recognize my ability? What would they give me?

I was fighting automatically and suddenly I noticed that one after another of the boys was leaving the ring. I was surprised, filled with panic, as though I had been left alone with an unknown danger. Then I understood. The boys had arranged it among themselves. It was the custom for the two men left in the ring to slug it out for the winner's prize. I discovered this too late. When the bell sounded two men in tuxedoes leaped into the ring and removed the blindfold. I found myself facing Tatlock, the biggest of the gang. I felt sick at my stomach. Hardly had the bell stopped ringing in my ears than it clanged again and I saw him moving swiftly toward me. Thinking of nothing else to do I hit him smash on the nose. He kept coming, bringing the rank sharp violence of stale sweat. His face was a black bank of a face, only his eyes alive—with hate of me and aglow with a feverish terror from what had happened to us all. I became anxious. I wanted to deliver my speech and he came at me as though he meant to beat it out of me. I smashed him again and again, taking his blows as they came. Then on a sudden impulse I struck him lightly as we clinched, I whispered, "Fake like I knocked you out, you can have the prize."

"I'll break your behind," he whispered hoarsely.

30   "For *them?*"

"For *me*, sonofabitch!"

They were yelling for us to break it up and Tatlock spun me half around with a blow, and as a joggled camera sweeps in a reeling scene, I saw the howling red faces crouching tense beneath the cloud of blue-gray smoke. For a moment the world wavered, unraveled, flowed, then my head cleared and Tatlock bounced before me. That fluttering shadow before my eyes was his jabbing left hand. Then falling forward, my head against his damp shoulder, I whispered.

"I'll make it five dollars more."

"Go to hell!"

35   But his muscles relaxed a trifle beneath my pressure and I breathed, "Seven!"

"Give it to your ma," he said, ripping me beneath the heart.

And while I still held him I butted him and moved away. I felt myself bombarded with punches. I fought back with hopeless desperation. I wanted to deliver my speech more than anything else in the world, because I felt that only these men could judge truly my ability, and now this stupid clown was ruining my chances. I began fighting carefully now, moving in to punch him and out again with my greater speed. A lucky blow to his chin and I had him going too—until I heard a loud voice yell, "I got my money on the big boy."

Hearing this, I almost dropped my guard. I was confused: Should I try to win against the voice out there? Would not this go against my speech, and was not this a moment for humility, for nonresistance? A blow to my head as I danced about sent my right eye popping like a jack-in-the-box and settled my dilemma. The room went red as I fell. It was a dream fall, my body languid and fastidious as to where to land, until the floor became impatient and smashed up to meet me. A moment later I came to. An hypnotic voice said FIVE emphatically. And I lay there, hazily watching a dark red spot of my own blood shaping itself into a butterfly, glistening and soaking into the soiled gray world of the canvas.

When the voice drawled TEN I was lifted up and dragged to a chair. I sat dazed. My eye pained and swelled with each throb of my pounding heart and I wondered if now I would be allowed to speak. I was wringing wet, my mouth still bleeding. We were grouped along the wall now. The other boys ignored me as they congratulated Tatlock and speculated as to how much they would be paid. One boy whimpered over his smashed hand. Looking up front, I saw attendants in white jackets rolling the portable ring away and placing a small square rug in the vacant space surrounded by chairs. Perhaps, I thought, I will stand on the rug to deliver my speech.

40   Then the M.C. called to us, "Come on up here boys and get your money." We ran forward to where the men laughed and talked in their chairs, waiting. Everyone seemed friendly now.

"There it is on the rug," the man said. I saw the rug covered with coins of all dimensions and a few crumpled bills. But what excited me, scattered here and there, were the gold pieces.

"Boys, it's all yours," the man said. "You get all you grab."

"That's right, Sambo," a blond man said, winking at me confidentially.

I trembled with excitement, forgetting my pain. I would get the gold and the bills, I thought. I would use both hands. I would throw my body against the boys nearest me to block them from the gold.

"Get down around the rug now," the man commanded, "and don't anyone touch it until I give the signal." 45

"This ought to be good," I heard.

As told, we got around the square rug on our knees. Slowly the man raised his freckled hand as we followed it upward with our eyes.

I heard, "These niggers look like they're about to pray!"

Then, "Ready," the man said. "Go!"

I lunged for a yellow coin lying on the blue design of the carpet, touching it and sending a surprised shriek to join those rising around me. I tried frantically to remove my hand but could not let go. A hot, violent force tore through my body, shaking me like a wet rat. The rug was electrified. The hair bristled up on my head as I shook myself free. My muscles jumped, my nerves jangled, writhed. But I saw that this was not stopping the other boys. Laughing in fear and embarrassment, some were holding back and scooping up the coins knocked off by the painful contortions of the others. The men roared above us as we struggled. 50

"Pick it up, goddamnit, pick it up!" someone called like a bass-voiced parrot. "Go on, get it!"

I crawled rapidly around the floor, picking up the coins, trying to avoid the coppers and to get greenbacks and the gold. Ignoring the shock by laughing, as I brushed the coins off quickly, I discovered that I could contain the electricity—a contradiction, but it works. Then the men began to push us onto the rug. Laughing embarrassedly, we struggled out of their hands and kept after the coins. We were all wet and slippery and hard to hold. Suddenly I saw a boy lifted into the air, glistening with sweat like a circus seal, and dropped, his wet back landing flush upon the charged rug, heard him yell and saw him literally dance upon his back, his elbows beating a frenzied tattoo upon the floor, his muscles twitching like the flesh of a horse stung by many flies. When he finally rolled off, his face was gray and no one stopped him when he ran from the floor amid booming laughter.

"Get the money," the M.C. called. "That's good hard American cash!"

And we snatched and grabbed, snatched and grabbed. I was careful not to come too close to the rug now, and when I felt the hot whiskey breath descend upon me like a cloud of foul air I reached out and grabbed the leg of a chair. It was occupied and I held on desperately.

"Leggo, nigger! Leggo!" 55

The huge face wavered down to mine as he tried to push me free. But my body was slippery and he was too drunk. It was Mr. Colcord, who owned a chain of movie houses and "entertainment palaces." Each time he grabbed me I slipped out of his hands. It became a real struggle. I feared the rug more than I did the drunk, so I held on, surprising myself for a moment by trying to topple *him* upon the rug. It was such an enormous idea that I found myself actually carrying it out. I tried not to be obvious, yet when I grabbed his leg, trying to tumble him out of the chair, he raised up roaring with laughter, and, looking at me with soberness dead in the eye, kicked me viciously in the chest. The chair leg flew out of my hand. I felt myself going and rolled. It was as though I had rolled through a bed of hot coals. It seemed a whole century would pass before I would roll free, a century in which I was seared through the deepest levels of my body to the fearful breath within me and the breath seared and heated to the point of explosion. It'll all be over in a flash, I thought as I rolled clear. It'll all be over in a flash.

But not yet, the men on the other side were waiting, red faces swollen as though from apoplexy as they bent forward in their chairs. Seeing their fingers coming toward me I rolled away as a fumbled football rolls off the receiver's fingertips, back into the coals. That time I luckily sent the rug sliding out of place and heard the coins ringing against the floor and the boys scuffling to pick them up and the M.C. calling, "All right, boys, that's all. Go get dressed and get your money."

I was limp as a dish rag. My back felt as though it had been beaten with wires.

When we had dressed the M.C. came in and gave us each five dollars, except Tatlock, who got ten for being the last in the ring. Then he told us to leave. I was not to get a chance to deliver my speech, I thought. I was going out into the dim alley in despair when I was stopped and told to go back. I returned to the ballroom, where the men were pushing back their chairs and gathering in groups to talk.

60   The M.C. knocked on a table for quiet. "Gentlemen," he said, "we almost forgot an important part of the program. A most serious part, gentlemen. This boy was brought here to deliver a speech which he made at his graduation yesterday. . . ."

"Bravo!"

"I'm told that he is the smartest boy we've got out there in Greenwood. I'm told that he knows more big words than a pocket-sized dictionary."

Much applause and laughter.

"So now, gentlemen, I want you to give him your attention."

65   There was still laughter as I faced them, my mouth dry, my eye throbbing. I began slowly, but evidently my throat was tense, because they began shouting, "Louder! Louder!"

"We of the younger generation extol the wisdom of that great leader and educator," I shouted, "who first spoke these flaming words of wisdom: 'A ship lost at sea for many days suddenly sighted a friendly vessel. From the mast of the unfortunate vessel was seen a signal: "Water, water; we die of thirst!" The answer from the friendly vessel came back: "Cast down your bucket where you are." The captain of the distressed vessel, at last heeding the injunction, cast down his bucket, and it came up full of fresh sparkling water from the mouth of the Amazon River.' And like him I say, and in his words. 'To those of my race who depend upon bettering their condition in a foreign land, or who underesti-mate the importance of cultivating friendly relations with the Southern white man, who is his next-door neighbor, I would say: "Cast down your bucket where you are"—cast it down in making friends in every manly way of the people of all races by whom we are surrounded. . . .'"

I spoke automatically and with such fervor that I did not realize that the men were still talking and laughing until my dry mouth, filling up with blood from the cut, almost strangled me. I coughed, wanting to stop and go to one of the tall brass, sand-filled spittoons to relieve myself, but a few of the men, especially the superintendent, were listening and I was afraid. So I gulped it down, blood, saliva and all, and continued. (What powers of endurance I had during those days! What enthusiasm! What a belief in the rightness of things!) I spoke even louder in spite of the pain. But still they talked and still they laughed, as though deaf with cotton in dirty ears. So I spoke with greater emotional emphasis. I closed my ears and swallowed blood until I was nauseated. The speech seemed a hundred times as long as before, but I could not leave out a single word. All had to be said, each memorized nuance considered, rendered. Nor was that all. Whenever I uttered a word of three or more syllables a group of voices would yell for me to repeat it. I used the phrase "social responsibility" and they yelled:

"What's the word you say, boy?"

"Social responsibility," I said.

"What?"   70

"Social . . ."

"Louder."

". . . responsibility."

"More!"

"Respon—"   75

"Repeat!"

"— sibility."

The room filled with the uproar of laughter until, no doubt, distracted by having to gulp down my blood, I made a mistake and yelled a phrase I had often seen denounced in newspaper editorials, heard debated in private.

"Social . . ."

"What?" they yelled.   80

". . . equality—"

The laughter hung smokelike in the sudden stillness. I opened my eyes, puzzled. Sounds of displeasure filled the room. The M.C. rushed forward. They shouted hostile phrases at me. But I did not understand.

A small dry mustached man in the front row blared out, "Say that slowly, son!"

"What sir?"

"What you just said!"   85

"Social responsibility, sir." I said.

"You weren't being smart, were you, boy?" he said, not unkindly.

"No, sir!"

"You sure that about 'equality' was a mistake?"

"Oh, yes, sir," I said. "I was swallowing blood."   90

"Well, you had better speak more slowly so we can understand. We mean to do right by you, but you've got to know your place at all times. All right, now, go on with your speech."

I was afraid. I wanted to leave but I wanted also to speak and I was afraid they'd snatch me down.

"Thank you, sir," I said, beginning where I had left off, and having them ignore me as before.

Yet when I finished there was a thunderous applause. I was surprised to see the superintendent come forth with a package wrapped in white tissue paper, and gesturing for quiet, address the men.

95   "Gentlemen, you see that I did not overpraise this boy. He makes a good speech and some day he'll lead his people in the proper paths. And I don't have to tell you that that is important in these days and times. This is a good, smart boy, and so to encourage him in the right direction, in the name of the Board of Education I wish to present him a prize in the form of this . . ."

He paused, removing the tissue paper and revealing a gleaming calfskin brief case.

". . . in the form of this first-class article from Shad Whitmore's shop."

"Boy," he said, addressing me, "take this prize and keep it well. Consider it a badge of office. Prize it. Keep developing as you are and some day it will be filled with important papers that will help shape the destiny of your people."

I was so moved that I could hardly express my thanks. A rope of bloody saliva forming a shape like an undiscovered continent drooled upon the leather and I wiped it quickly away. I felt an importance that I had never dreamed.

100   "Open it and see what's inside," I was told.

My fingers a-tremble, I complied, smelling the fresh leather and finding an official-looking document inside. It was a scholarship to the state college for Negroes. My eyes filled with tears and I ran awkwardly off the floor.

I was overjoyed; I did not even mind when I discovered that the gold pieces I had scrambled for were brass pocket tokens advertising a certain make of automobile.

When I reached home everyone was excited. Next day the neighbors came to congratulate me. I even felt safe from grandfather, whose deathbed curse usually spoiled my triumphs. I stood beneath his photograph with my brief case in hand and smiled triumphantly into his stolid black peasant's face. It was a face that fascinated me. The eyes seemed to follow everywhere I went.

That night I dreamed I was at a circus with him and that he refused to laugh at the clowns no matter what they did. Then later he told me to open my brief case and read what was inside and I did, finding an official envelope stamped with the state seal; and inside the envelope I found another and another, end-lessly, and I thought I would fall of weariness: "Them's years," he said, "Now open that one." And I did and in it I found an engraved document containing a short message in letters of gold. "Read it," my grandfather said. "Out loud."

105   "To Whom It May Concern," I intoned. "Keep This Nigger-Boy Running."

I awoke with the old man's laughter ringing in my ears.

(It was a dream I was to remember and dream again for many years after. But at the time I had no insight into its meaning. First I had to attend college.)

[1953]

1. In the Prologue of *Invisible Man,* the novel of which "Battle Royal" is the first chapter, the narrator explains the novel's title: "I am invisible . . . simply because people refuse to see me . . . Nor is my invisibility exactly a matter of a bio-chemical accident to my epidermis. That invisibility to which I refer occurs because of a peculiar disposition of the eyes of those with whom I come in contact. A matter of the construction of their *inner* eyes, those eyes with which they look through their physical eyes upon reality."[1]

   How does this definition relate to the narrator's grandfather's dying words? Is the incident in "Battle Royal" an example of not being seen? Who else in the story is incorrectly understood?
2. What kind of narrator is this? What kinds of details does he share about this episode? What difference does that make?
3. Does the part of the speech we hear fulfill the grandfather's commandment? Does it live up to the characterization of the narrator by the M.C.?
4. What disciplines would shed light on this story?

[1]Ralph Ellison, *Invisible Man* (New York: New American Library, 1947), 7.

LOUISE ERDRICH

LOUISE ERDRICH *(1954–) was born of German-American and Chippewa parents in Minnesota and brought up in Wahpeton, North Dakota, where both her parents worked for the Bureau of Indian Affairs running the government school on a reservation. Encouraged to write from an early age, she was admitted to Dartmouth College in 1972, one of the first women to matriculate there, majoring in English and creative writing. She earned her degree in Native American Studies and a master's degree in creative writing from the Johns Hopkins University. When she returned to Dartmouth as a writer-in-residence, she married Michael Dorris, the head of the Native American Studies program. In addition to her own work, she collaborated with her husband on a novel in 1991. After the loss of a child and the death of her husband, she moved back to the West to be near her parents. She is a poet, essayist, and writer of nonfiction books, but is best known for her novels. Her books include* The Blue Jay's Dance: A Birth Year *(1995),* Love Medicine *(1984 and 1993),* The Beet Queen *(1986),* Tracks *(from which "Fleur" is taken, 1988),* The Bingo Palace *(1994), and* Tales of Burning Love *(1996). Her short stories have been published in prestigious magazines and her prose has won her many literary prizes and a Guggenheim Fellowship.*

Fleur

The first time she drowned in the cold and glassy waters of Lake Turcot, Fleur Pillager was only a girl. Two men saw the boat tip, saw her struggle in the waves. They rowed over to the place she went down, and jumped in. When they dragged her over the gunwales, she was cold to the touch and stiff, so they slapped her face, shook her by the heels, worked her arms back and forth, and pounded her back until she coughed up lake water. She shivered all over like a dog, then took a breath. But it wasn't long afterward that those two men disappeared. The first wandered off, and the other, Jean Hat, got himself run over by a cart.

It went to show, my grandma said. It figured to her, all right. By saving Fleur Pillager, those two men had lost themselves.

The next time she fell in the lake, Fleur Pillager was twenty years old and no one touched her. She washed onshore, her skin a dull dead gray, but when George Many Women bent to look closer, he saw her chest move. Then her eyes spun open, sharp black riprock, and she looked at him. "You'll take my place," she hissed. Everybody scattered and left her there, so no one knows how she dragged herself home. Soon after that we noticed Many Women changed, grew afraid, wouldn't leave his house, and would not be forced to go near water. For his caution, he lived until the day that his sons brought him a new tin bathtub. Then the first time he used the tub he slipped, got knocked out, and breathed water while his wife stood in the other room frying breakfast.

Men stayed clear of Fleur Pillager after the second drowning. Even though she was good-looking, nobody dared to court her because it was clear that Misshepeshu, the waterman, the monster, wanted her for himself. He's a devil, that one, love-hungry with desire and maddened for the touch of young girls, the strong and daring especially, the ones like Fleur.

5   Our mothers warn us that we'll think he's handsome, for he appears with green eyes, copper skin, a mouth tender as a child's. But if you fall into his arms, he sprouts horns, fangs, claws, fins. His feet are joined as one and his skin, brass scales, rings to the touch. You're fascinated, cannot move. He casts a shell necklace at your feet, weeps gleaming chips that harden into mica on your breasts. He holds you under. Then he takes the body of a lion or a fat brown worm. He's made of gold. He's made of beach moss. He's a thing of dry foam, a thing of death by drowning, the death a Chippewa cannot survive.

Unless you are Fleur Pillager. We all knew she couldn't swim. After the first time, we thought she'd never go back to Lake Turcot. We thought she'd keep to herself, live quiet, stop killing men off by drowning in the lake. After the first time, we thought she'd keep the good ways. But then, after the second drowning, we knew that we were dealing with something much more serious. She was haywire, out of control. She messed with evil, laughed at the old women's advice, and dressed like a man. She got herself into some half-forgotten medicine, studied ways we shouldn't talk about. Some say she kept the finger of a child in her pocket and a powder of unborn rabbits in a leather thong around her neck. She laid the heart of an owl on her tongue so she could see at night, and went out, hunting, not even in her own body. We know for sure because the next morning, in the snow or dust, we followed the tracks of her bare feet and saw where they changed, where the claws sprang out, the pad broadened and pressed into the dirt. By night we heard her chuffing cough, the bear cough. By day her silence and the wide grin she threw to bring down our guard made us frightened. Some thought that Fleur Pillager should be driven off the reservation, but not a single person who spoke like this had the nerve. And finally, when people were just about to get together and throw her out, she left on her own and didn't come back all summer. That's what this story is about.

During that summer, when she lived a few miles south in Argus, things happened. She almost destroyed that town.

When she got down to Argus in the year of 1920, it was just a small grid of six streets on either side of the railroad depot. There were two elevators, one central, the other a few miles west. Two stores competed for the trade of the three hundred citizens, and three churches quarreled with one another for their souls. There was a frame building for Lutherans, a heavy brick one for Episcopalians, and a long narrow shingled Catholic church. This last had a tall slender steeple, twice as high as any building or tree.

No doubt, across the low, flat wheat, watching from the road as she came near Argus on foot, Fleur saw that steeple rise, a shadow thin as a needle. Maybe in that raw space it drew her the way a lone tree draws lightning. Maybe, in the end, the Catholics are to blame. For if she hadn't seen that sign of pride, that slim prayer, that marker, maybe she would have kept walking.

But Fleur Pillager turned, and the first place she went once she came into town was to the back door of the priest's residence attached to the landmark church. She didn't go there for a handout, although she got that, but to ask for work. She got that too, or the town got her. It's hard to tell which came out worse, her or the men or the town, although the upshot of it all was that Fleur lived. 10

The four men who worked at the butcher's had carved up about a thousand carcasses between them, maybe half of that steers and the other half pigs, sheep, and game animals like deer, elk, and bear. That's not even mentioning the chickens, which were beyond counting. Pete Kozka owned the place, and employed Lily Veddar, Tor Grunewald, and my stepfather, Dutch James, who had brought my mother down from the reservation the year before she disappointed him by dying. Dutch took me out of school to take her place. I kept house half the time and worked the other in the butcher shop, sweeping floors, putting sawdust down, running a hambone across the street to a customer's bean pot or a package of sausage to the corner. I was a good one to have around because until they needed me, I was invisible. I blended into the stained brown walls, a skinny, big-nosed girl with staring eyes. Because I could fade into a corner or squeeze beneath a shelf, I knew everything, what the men said when no one was around, and what they did to Fleur.

Kozka's Meats served farmers for a fifty-mile area, both to slaughter, for it had a stock pen and chute, and to cure the meat by smoking it or spicing it in sausage. The storage locker was a marvel, made of many thicknesses of brick, earth insulation, and Minnesota timber, lined inside with sawdust and vast blocks of ice cut from Lake Turcot, hauled down from home each winter by horse and sledge.

A ramshackle board building, part slaughterhouse, part store, was fixed to the low, thick square of the lockers. That's where Fleur worked. Kozka hired her for her strength. She could lift a haunch or carry a pole of sausages without stumbling, and she soon learned cutting from Pete's wife, a string thin blonde who chain-smoked and handled the razor-sharp knives with nerveless precision, slicing close to her stained fingers. Fleur and Fritzie Kozka worked afternoons, wrapping their cuts in paper, and Fleur hauled the packages to the lockers. The meat was left outside the heavy oak doors that were only opened at 5:00 each afternoon, before the men ate supper.

Sometimes Dutch, Tor, and Lily ate at the lockers, and when they did I stayed too, cleaned floors, restoked the fires in the front smokehouses, while the men sat around the squat cast-iron stove spearing slats of herring onto hardtack bread. They played long games of poker or cribbage on a board made from the planed end of a salt crate. They talked and I listened, although there wasn't much to hear since almost nothing ever happened in Argus. Tor was married, Dutch had lost my mother, and Lily read circulars. They mainly discussed about the auctions to come, equipment, or women.

15   Every so often, Pete Kozka came out front to make a whist, leaving Fritzie to smoke cigarettes and fry raised doughnuts in the back room. He sat and played a few rounds but kept his thoughts to himself. Fritzie did not tolerate him talking behind her back, and the one book he read was the New Testament. If he said something, it concerned weather or a surplus of sheep stomachs, a ham that smoked green or the markets for corn and wheat. He had a good-luck talisman, the opal-white lens of a cow's eye. Playing cards, he rubbed it between his fingers. That soft sound and the slap of cards was about the only conversation.

Fleur finally gave them a subject.

Her cheeks were wide and flat, her hands large, chapped, muscular. Fleur's shoulders were broad as beams, her hips fishlike, slippery, narrow. An old green dress clung to her waist, worn thin where she sat. Her braids were thick like the tails of animals, and swung against her when she moved, deliberately, slowly in her work, held in and half-tamed, but only half. I could tell, but the others never saw. They never looked into her sly brown eyes or noticed her teeth, strong and curved and very white. Her legs were bare, and since she padded around in beadwork moccasins they never saw that her fifth toes were missing. They never knew she'd drowned. They were blinded, they were stupid, they only saw her in the flesh.

And yet it wasn't just that she was a Chippewa, or even that she was a woman, it wasn't that she was good-looking or even that she was alone that made their brains hum. It was how she played cards.

Women didn't usually play with men, so the evening that Fleur drew a chair up to the men's table without being so much as asked, there was a shock of surprise.

20   "What's this," said Lily. He was fat, with a snake's cold pale eyes and precious skin, smooth and lily-white, which is how he got his name. Lily had a dog, a stumpy mean little bull of a thing with a belly drum-tight from eating pork rinds. The dog liked to play cards just like Lily, and straddled his barrel thighs through games of stud, rum poker, vingt-un. The dog snapped at Fleur's arm that first night, but cringed back, its snarl frozen, when she took her place.

"I thought," she said, her voice soft and stroking, "you might deal me in."

There was a space between the heavy bin of spiced flour and the wall where I just fit. I hunkered down there, kept my eyes open, saw her black hair swing over the chair, her feet solid on the wood floor. I couldn't see up on the table where the cards slapped down, so after they were deep in their game I raised myself up in the shadows, and crouched on a sill of wood.

I watched Fleur's hands stack and ruffle, divide the cards, spill them to each player in a blur, rake them up and shuffle again. Tor, short and scrappy, shut one eye and squinted the other at Fleur. Dutch screwed his lips around a wet cigar.

"Gotta see a man," he mumbled, getting up to go out back to the privy. The others broke, put their cards down, and Fleur sat alone in the lamplight that glowed in a sheen across the push of her breasts. I watched her closely, then she paid me a beam of notice for the first time. She turned, looked straight at me, and grinned the white wolf grin a Pillager turns on its victims, except that she wasn't after me.

"Pauline there," she said, "how much money you got?"   25

We'd all been paid for the week that day. Eight cents was in my pocket.

"Stake me," she said, holding out her long fingers. I put the coins in her palm and then I melted back to nothing, part of the walls and tables. It was a long time before I understood that the men would not have seen me no matter what I did, how I moved. I wasn't anything like Fleur. My dress hung loose and my back was already curved, an old woman's. Work had roughened me, reading made my eyes sore, caring for my mother before she died had hardened my face. I was not much to look at, so they never saw me.

When the men came back and sat around the table, they had drawn together. They shot each other small glances, stuck their tongues in their cheeks, burst out laughing at odd moments, to rattle Fleur. But she never minded. They played their vingt-un, staying even as Fleur slowly gained. Those pennies I had given her drew nickels and attracted dimes until there was a small pile in front of her.

Then she hooked them with five-card draw, nothing wild. She dealt, discarded, drew, and then she sighed and her cards gave a little shiver. Tor's eye gleamed, and Dutch straightened in his seat.

"I'll pay to see that hand," said Lily Veddar.   30

Fleur showed, and she had nothing there, nothing at all.

Tor's thin smile cracked open, and he threw his hand in too.

"Well, we know one thing," he said, leaning back in his chair, "the squaw can't bluff."

With that I lowered myself into a mound of swept sawdust and slept. I woke up during the night, but none of them had moved yet, so I couldn't either. Still later, the men must have gone out again, or Fritzie come out to break the game, because I was lifted, soothed, cradled in a woman's arms and rocked so quiet that I kept my eyes shut while Fleur rolled me into a closet of grimy ledgers, oiled paper, balls of string, and thick files that fit beneath me like a mattress.

The game went on after work the next evening. I got my eight cents back five   35
times over, and Fleur kept the rest of the dollar she'd won for a stake. This time they didn't play so late, but they played regular, and then kept going at it night after night. They played poker now, or variations, for one week straight, and

each time Fleur won exactly one dollar, no more and no less, too consistent for luck.

By this time, Lily and the other men were so lit with suspense that they got Pete to join the game with them. They concentrated, the fat dog sitting tense in Lily Veddar's lap, Tor suspicious, Dutch stroking his huge square brow, Pete steady. It wasn't that Fleur won that hooked them in so, because she lost hands too. It was rather that she never had a freak hand or even anything above a straight. She only took on her low cards, which didn't sit right. By chance, Fleur should have gotten a full or flush by now. The irritating thing was she beat with pairs and never bluffed, because she couldn't, and still she ended up each night with exactly one dollar. Lily couldn't believe, first of all, that a woman could be smart enough to play cards, but even if she was, that she would then be stupid enough to cheat for a dollar a night. By day I watched him turn the problem over, his hard white face dull, small fingers probing at his knuckles, until he finally thought he had Fleur figured out as a bit-time player, caution her game. Raising the stakes would throw her.

More than anything now, he wanted Fleur to come away with something but a dollar. Two bits less or ten more, the sum didn't matter, just so he broke her streak.

Night after night she played, won her dollar, and left to stay in a place that just Fritzie and I knew about. Fleur bathed in the slaughtering tub, then slept in the unused brick smokehouse behind the lockers, a windowless place tarred on the inside with scorched fats. When I brushed against her skin I noticed that she smelled of the walls, rich and woody, slightly burnt. Since that night she put me in the closet I was no longer afraid of her, but followed her close, stayed with her, became her moving shadow that the men never noticed, the shadow that could have saved her.

August, the month that bears fruit, closed around the shop, and Pete and Fritzie left for Minnesota to escape the heat. Night by night, running, Fleur had won thirty dollars, and only Pete's presence had kept Lily at bay. But Pete was gone now, and one payday, with the heat so bad no one could move but Fleur, the men sat and played and waited while she finished work. The cards sweat, limp in their fingers, the table was slick with grease, and even the walls were warm to the touch. The air was motionless. Fleur was in the next room boiling heads.

40   Her green dress, drenched, wrapped her like a transparent sheet. A skin of lakeweed. Black snarls of veining clung to her arms. Her braids were loose, half-unraveled, tied behind her neck in a thick loop. She stood in steam, turning skulls through a vat with a wooden paddle. When scraps boiled to the surface, she bent with a round tin sieve and scooped them out. She'd filled two dishpans.

"Ain't that enough now?" called Lily. "We're waiting." The stump of a dog trembled in his lap, alive with rage. It never smelled me or noticed me above Fleur's smoky skin. The air was heavy in my corner, and pressed me down. Fleur sat with them.

"Now what do you say?" Lily asked the dog. It barked. That was the signal for the real game to start.

"Let's up the ante," said Lily, who had been stalking this night all month. He had a roll of money in his pocket. Fleur had five bills in her dress. The men had each saved their full pay.

"Ante a dollar then," said Fleur, and pitched hers in. She lost, but they let her scrape along, cent by cent. And then she won some. She played unevenly, as if chance was all she had. She reeled them in. The game went on. The dog was stiff now, poised on Lily's knees, a ball of vicious muscle with its yellow eyes slit in concentration. It gave advice, seemed to sniff the lay of Fleur's cards, twitched and nudged. Fleur was up, then down, saved by a scratch. Tor dealt seven cards, three down. The pot grew, round by round, until it held all the money. Nobody folded. Then it all rode on one last card and they went silent. Fleur picked hers up and blew a long breath. The heat lowered like a bell. Her card shook, but she stayed in.

Lily smiled and took the dog's head tenderly between his palms.   45

"Say, Fatso," he said, crooning the words, "you reckon that girl's bluffing?"

The dog whined and Lily laughed. "Me too," he said, "let's show." He swept his bills and coins into the pot and then they turned their cards over.

Lily looked once, looked again, then he squeezed the dog up like a fist of dough and slammed it on the table.

Fleur threw her arms out and drew the money over, grinning that same wolf grin that she'd used on me, the grin that had them. She jammed the bills in her dress, scooped the coins up in waxed white paper that she tied with string.

"Let's go another round," said Lily, his voice choked with burrs. But Fleur   50
opened her mouth and yawned, then walked out back to gather slops for the one big hog that was waiting in the stock pen to be killed.

The men sat still as rocks, their hands spread on the oiled wood table. Dutch had chewed his cigar to damp shreds, Tor's eye was dull. Lily's gaze was the only one to follow Fleur. I didn't move. I felt them gathering, saw my stepfather's veins, the ones in his forehead that stood out in anger. The dog had rolled off the table and curled in a knot below the counter, where none of the men could touch it.

Lily rose and stepped out back to the closet of ledgers where Pete kept his private stock. He brought back a bottle, uncorked and tipped it between his fingers. The lump in his throat moved, then he passed it on. They drank, quickly felt the whiskey's fire, and planned with their eyes things they couldn't say out loud.

When they left, I followed. I hid out back in the clutter of broken boards and chicken crates beside the stock pen, where they waited. Fleur could not be seen at first, and then the moon broke and showed her, slipping cautiously along the rough board chute with a bucket in her hand. Her hair fell, wild and coarse, to her waist, and her dress was a floating patch in the dark. She made a pig-calling sound, rang the tin pail lightly against the wood, froze suspiciously. But too late. In the sound of the ring Lily moved, fat and nimble, stepped right behind Fleur and put out his creamy hands. At his first touch, she whirled and doused him with the bucket of sour slops. He pushed her against the big fence and the package of coins split, went clinking and jumping, winked against the wood. Fleur rolled over once and vanished in the yard.

The moon fell behind a curtain of ragged clouds, and Lily followed into the dark muck. But he tripped, pitched over the huge flank of the pig, who lay mired to the snout, heavily snoring. I sprang out of the weeds and climbed the side of the pen, stuck like glue. I saw the sow rise to her neat, knobby knees, gain her balance, and sway, curious, as Lily stumbled forward. Fleur had backed into the angle of rough wood just beyond, and when Lily tried to jostle past, the sow tipped up on her hind legs and struck, quick and hard as a snake. She plunged her head into Lily's thick side and snatched a mouthful of his shirt. She lunged again, caught him lower, so that he grunted in pained surprise. He seemed to ponder, breathing deep. Then he launched his huge body in a swimmer's dive.

55   The sow screamed as his body smacked over hers. She rolled, striking out with her knife-sharp hooves, and Lily gathered himself upon her, took her foot-long face by the ears and scraped her snout and cheeks against the trestles of the pen. He hurled the sow's tight skull against an iron post, but instead of knocking her dead, he merely woke her from her dream.

She reared, shrieked, drew him with her so that they posed standing upright. They bowed jerkily to each other, as if to begin. Then his arms swung and flailed. She sank her black fangs into his shoulder, clasping him, dancing him forward and backward through the pen. Their steps picked up pace, went wild. The two dipped as one, box-stepped, tripped each other. She ran her split foot through his hair. He grabbed her kinked tail. They went down and came up, the same shape and then the same color, until the men couldn't tell one from the other in that light and Fleur was able to launch herself over the gates, swing down, hit gravel.

The men saw, yelled, and chased her at a dead run to the smokehouse. And Lily too, once the sow gave up in disgust and freed him. That is where I should have gone to Fleur, saved her, thrown myself on Dutch. But I went stiff with fear and couldn't unlatch myself from the trestles or move at all. I closed my eyes and put my head in my arms, tried to hide, so there is nothing to describe but what I couldn't block out, Fleur's hoarse breath, so loud it filled me, her cry in the old language, and my name repeated over and over among the words.

The heat was still dense the next morning when I came back to work. Fleur was gone but the men were there, slack-faced, hung over. Lily was paler and softer than ever, as if his flesh had steamed on his bones. They smoked, took pulls off a bottle. It wasn't noon yet. I worked awhile, waiting shop and sharpening steel. But I was sick, I was smothered, I was sweating so hard that my hands slipped on the knives, and I wiped my fingers clean of the greasy touch of the customers' coins. Lily opened his mouth and roared once, not in anger. There was no meaning to the sound. His boxer dog, sprawled limp beside his foot, never lifted its head. Nor did the other men.

They didn't notice when I stepped outside, hoping for a clear breath. And then I forgot them because I knew that we were all balanced, ready to tip, to fly, to be crushed as soon as the weather broke. The sky was so low that I felt the weight of it like a yoke. Clouds hung down, witch teats, a tornado's green-brown cones, and as I watched one flicked out and became a delicate probing

thumb. Even as I picked up my heels and ran back inside, the wind blew
suddenly, cold, and then came rain.

Inside, the men had disappeared already and the whole place was trembling 60
as if a huge hand was pinched at the rafters, shaking it. I ran straight through,
screaming for Dutch or for any of them, and then I stopped at the heavy doors
of the lockers, where they had surely taken shelter. I stood there a moment.
Everything went still. Then I heard a cry building in the wind, faint at first, a
whistle and then a shrill scream that tore through the walls and gathered
around me, spoke plain so I understood that I should move, put my arms out,
and slam down the great iron bar that fit across the hasp and lock.

Outside, the wind was stronger, like a hand held against me. I struggled
forward. The bushes tossed, the awnings flapped off storefronts, the rails of
porches rattled. The odd cloud became a fat snout that nosed along the earth
and sniffled, jabbed, picked at things, sucked them up, blew them apart, rooted
around as if it was following a certain scent, then stopped behind me at the
butcher shop and bored down like a drill.

I went flying, landed somewhere in a ball. When I opened my eyes and
looked, stranger things were happening.

A herd of cattle flew through the air like giant birds, dropping dung, their
mouths opened in stunned bellows. A candle, still lighted, blew past, and tables,
napkins, garden tools, a whole school of drifting eyeglasses, jackets on hangers,
hams, a checkerboard, a lampshade, and at last the sow from behind the lockers,
on the run, her hooves a blur, set free, swooping, diving, screaming as everything
in Argus fell apart and got turned upside down, smashed, and thoroughly wrecked.

Days passed before the town went looking for the men. They were bachelors,
after all, except for Tor, whose wife had suffered a blow to the head that made
her forgetful. Everyone was occupied with digging out, in high relief because
even though the Catholic steeple had been torn off like a peaked cap and sent
across five fields, those huddled in the cellar were unhurt. Walls had fallen,
windows were demolished, but the stores were intact and so were the bankers
and shop owners who had taken refuge in their safes or beneath their cash
registers. It was a fair-minded disaster, no one could be said to have suffered
much more than the next, at least not until Fritzie and Pete came home.

Of all the businesses in Argus, Kozka's Meats had suffered worst. The boards of 65
the front building had been split to kindling, piled in a huge pyramid, and the shop
equipment was blasted far and wide. Pete paced off the distance the iron bathtub
had been flung—a hundred feet. The glass candy case went fifty, and landed without so much as a cracked pane. There were other surprises as well, for the back
rooms where Fritzie and Pete lived were undisturbed. Fritzie said the dust still coated
her china figures, and upon her kitchen table, in the ashtray, perched the last
cigarette she'd put out in haste. She lit it up and finished it, looking through the
window. From there, she could see that the old smokehouse Fleur had slept in was
crushed to a reddish sand and the stockpens were completely torn apart, the rails
stacked helter-skelter. Fritzie asked for Fleur. People shrugged. Then she asked
about the others and, suddenly, the town understood that three men were missing.

There was a rally of help, a gathering of shovels and volunteers. We passed boards from hand to hand, stacked them, uncovered what lay beneath the pile of jagged splinters. The lockers, full of the meat that was Pete and Fritzie's investment, slowly came into sight, still intact. When enough room was made for a man to stand on the roof, there were calls, a general urge to hack through and see what lay below. But Fritzie shouted that she wouldn't allow it because the meat would spoil. And so the work continued, board by board, until at last the heavy oak doors of the freezer were revealed and people pressed to the entry. Everyone wanted to be the first, but since it was my stepfather lost, I was let go in when Pete and Fritzie wedged through into the sudden icy air.

Pete scraped a match on his boot, lit the lamp Fritzie held, and then the three of us stood still in its circle. Light glared off the skinned and hanging carcasses, the crates of wrapped sausages, the bright and cloudy blocks of lake ice, pure as winter. The cold bit into us, pleasant at first, then numbing. We must have stood there a couple of minutes before we saw the men, or more rightly, the humps of fur, the iced and shaggy hides they wore, the bearskins they had taken down and wrapped around themselves. We stepped closer and tilted the lantern beneath the flaps of fur into their faces. The dog was there, perched among them, heavy as a doorstop. The three had hunched around a barrel where the game was still laid out, and a dead lantern and an empty bottle, too. But they had thrown down their last hands and hunkered tight, clutching one another, knuckles raw from beating at the door they had also attacked with hooks. Frost stars gleamed off their eyelashes and the stubble of their beards. Their faces were set in concentration, mouths open as if to speak some careful thought, some agreement they'd come to in each other's arms.

Power travels in the bloodlines, handed out before birth. It comes down through the hands, which in the Pillagers were strong and knotted, big, spidery, and rough, with sensitive fingertips good at dealing cards. It comes through the eyes, too, belligerent, darkest brown, the eyes of those in the bear clan, impolite as they gaze directly at a person.

In my dreams, I look straight back at Fleur, at the men. I am no longer the watcher on the dark sill, the skinny girl.

70 The blood draws us back, as if it runs through a vein of earth. I've come home and, except for talking to my cousins, live a quiet life. Fleur lives quiet too, down on Lake Turcot with her boat. Some say she's married to the waterman, Misshepeshu, or that she's living in shame with white men or windigos, or that she's killed them all. I'm about the only one here who ever goes to visit her. Last winter, I went to help out in her cabin when she bore the child, whose green eyes and skin the color of an old penny made more talk, as no one could decide if the child was mixed blood or what, fathered in a smokehouse, or by a man with brass scales, or by the lake. The girl is bold, smiling in her sleep, as if she knows what people wonder, as if she hears the old men talk, turning the story over. It comes up different every time and has no ending, no beginning. They get the middle wrong too. They only know that they don't know anything.

[1986]

1. Analyze the structure of the story's plot. What insights can be gained from such an analysis?
2. Who is the narrator and what is her point of view on events?
3. What kind of woman is Fleur and what difference does it make to how she is treated?
4. I once got a speeding ticket while listening to this story on tape in my car. Not to excuse such thoughtlessness, can you see the techniques that Erdrich uses to make the language intense?
5. What disciplinary frameworks might enrich our view of the story?

ALICE MUNRO

ALICE MUNRO *(1931–) published "Boys and Girls" in her first collection of short stories,* Dance of the Happy Shades *(1968). Born on a farm in Wingham, Ontario, in central Canada, she may have been drawing on personal experience in her account of farm life in "Boys and Girls." Her other fiction includes story collections* Lives of Girls and Women *(1971),* Who Do You Think You Are? *(1978),* Progress of Love *(1986), and the novel* Moons of Jupiter *(1982). She regularly publishes new stories in the* New Yorker.

Boys and Girls

My father was a fox farmer. That is, he raised silver foxes, in pens; and in the fall and early winter, when their fur was prime, he killed them and skinned them and sold their pelts to the Hudson's Bay Company or the Montreal Fur Traders. These companies supplied us with heroic calendars to hang, one on each side of the kitchen door. Against a background of cold blue sky and black pine forests and treacherous northern rivers, plumed adventurers planted the flags of England or of France; magnificent savages bent their backs to the portage.

For several weeks before Christmas, my father worked after supper in the cellar of our house. The cellar was whitewashed, and lit by a hundred-watt bulb over the worktable. My brother Laird and I sat on the top step and watched. My father removed the pelt inside-out from the body of the fox, which looked surprisingly small, mean and rat-like, deprived of its arrogant weight of fur. The naked, slippery bodies were collected in a sack and buried at the dump. One time the hired man, Henry Bailey, had taken a swipe at me with this sack, saying, "Christmas present!" My mother thought that was not funny. In fact she disliked the whole pelting operation—that was what the killing, skinning, and preparation of the furs was called—and wished it did not have to take place in the house. There was the smell. After the pelt had been stretched inside-out on a long board my father scraped away delicately, removing the little clotted webs of blood vessels, the bubbles of fat; the smell of blood and animal fat, with the strong primitive odor of the fox itself, penetrated all parts of the house. I found it reassuringly seasonal, like the smell of oranges and pine needles.

Henry Bailey suffered from bronchial troubles. He would cough and cough until his narrow face turned scarlet, and his light blue, derisive eyes filled up with tears; then he took the lid off the stove, and, standing well back, shot out a great clot of phlegm—hsss—straight into the heart of the flames. We admired him for this performance and for his ability to make his stomach growl at will, and for his laughter, which was full of high whistlings and gurglings and involved the whole faulty machinery of his chest. It was sometimes hard to tell what he was laughing at, and always possible that it might be us.

After we had been sent to bed we could still smell fox and still hear Henry's laugh, but these things, reminders of the warm, safe, brightly lit downstairs world, seemed lost and diminished, floating on the stale cold air upstairs. We were afraid at night in the winter. We were not afraid of *outside* though this was the time of year when snowdrifts curled around our house like sleeping whales and the wind harassed us all night, coming up from the buried fields, the frozen swamp, with its old bugbear chorus of threats and misery. We were afraid of *inside*, the room where we slept. At this time the upstairs of our house was not finished. A brick chimney went up one wall. In the middle of the floor was a square hole, with a wooden railing around it; that was where the stairs came up. On the other side of the stairwell were the things that nobody had any use for any more—a soldiery roll of linoleum, standing on end, a wicker baby carriage, a fern basket, china jugs and basins with cracks in them, a picture of the Battle of Balaclava, very sad to look at. I had told Laird, as soon as he was old enough to understand such things, that bats and skeletons lived over there; whenever a man escaped from the county jail, twenty miles away, I imagined that he had some-how let himself in the window and was hiding behind the linoleum. But we had rules to keep us safe. When the light was on, we were safe as long as we did not step off the square of worn carpet which defined our bedroom-space; when the light was off no place was safe but the beds themselves. I had to turn out the light kneeling on the end of my bed, and stretching as far as I could to reach the cord.

5   In the dark we lay on our beds, our narrow life rafts, and fixed our eyes on the faint light coming up the stairwell, and sang songs. Laird sang "Jingle Bells," which he would sing any time, whether it was Christmas or not, and I sang "Danny Boy." I loved the sound of my own voice, frail and supplicating, rising in the dark. We could make out the tall frosted shapes of the windows now, gloomy and white. When I came to the part, *When I am dead, as dead I well may be*—a fit of shivering caused not by the cold sheets but by pleasurable emotion almost silenced me. *You'll kneel and say, an Ave there above me*—What was an Ave? Every day I forgot to find out.

Laird went straight from singing to sleep. I could hear his long, satisfied, bub-bly breaths. Now for the time that remained to me, the most perfectly private and perhaps the best time of the whole day, I arranged myself tightly under the covers and went on with one of the stories I was telling myself from night to night. These stories were about myself, when I had grown a little older; they took place in a world that was recognizably mine, yet one that presented opportunities for courage, boldness and self-sacrifice, as mine never did. I rescued people from a bombed building (it discouraged me that the real war had gone on so far away from Jubilee). I shot two rabid wolves who were menacing the schoolyard (the teachers cowered terrified at my back). I rode a fine horse spiritedly down the main street of Jubilee, acknowledging the townspeople's gratitude for some yet-to-be-worked-out piece of heroism (nobody ever rode a horse there, except King Billy in the Orangemen's Day parade). There was always riding and shooting in these stories, though I had only been on a horse twice—bareback because we did not own a saddle—and the second time I had slid right around and dropped under the horse's feet; it had stepped placidly over me. I really was learning to shoot, but I could not hit anything yet, not even tin cans on fence posts.

Alive, the foxes inhabited a world my father made for them. It was surrounded by a high guard fence, like a medieval town, with a gate that was padlocked at night. Along the streets of this town were ranged large, sturdy pens. Each of them had a real door that a man could go through, a wooden ramp along the wire, for the foxes to run up and down on, and a kennel—something like a clothes chest with airholes—where they slept and stayed in winter and had their young. There were feeding and watering dishes attached to the wire in such a way that they could be emptied and cleaned from the outside. The dishes were made of old tin cans, and the ramps and kennels of odds and ends of old lumber. Everything was tidy and ingenious; my father was tirelessly inventive and his favorite book in the world was Robinson Crusoe. He had fitted a tin drum on a wheelbarrow, for bringing water to the pens. This was my job in summer, when the foxes had to have water twice a day. Between nine and ten o'clock in the morning, and again after supper, I filled the drum at the pump and trundled it down through the barnyard to the pens, where I parked it, and filled my watering can and went along the streets. Laird came too, with his little cream and green gardening can, filled too full and knocking against his legs and slopping water on his canvas shoes. I had the real watering can, my father's, though I could only carry it three-quarters full.

The foxes all had names, which were printed on a tin plate and hung beside their doors. They were not named when they were born, but when they survived the first year's pelting and were added to the breeding stock. Those my father had named were called names like Prince, Bob, Wally and Betty. Those I had named were called Star or Turk, or Maureen or Diana. Laird named one Maud after a hired girl we had when he was little, one Harold after a boy at school, and one Mexico, he did not say why.

Naming them did not make pets out of them, or anything like it. Nobody but my father ever went into the pens, and he had twice had blood-poisoning from bites. When I was bringing them their water they prowled up and down on the paths they had made inside their pens, barking seldom—they saved that for night-time, when they might get up a chorus of community frenzy—but always watching me, their eyes burning, clear gold, in their pointed, malevolent faces. They were beautiful for their delicate legs and heavy, aristocratic tails and the bright fur sprinkled on dark down their backs—which gave them their name—but especially for their faces, drawn exquisitely sharp in pure hostility, and their golden eyes.

Besides carrying water I helped my father when he cut the long grass, and the lamb's quarter and flowering money-musk, that grew between the pens. He

10

cut with the scythe and I raked into piles. Then he took a pitchfork and threw fresh-cut grass all over the top of the pens to keep the foxes cooler and shade their coats, which were browned by too much sun. My father did not talk to me unless it was about the job we were doing. In this he was quite different from my mother, who, if she was feeling cheerful, would tell me all sorts of things—the name of a dog she had had when she was a little girl, the names of boys she had gone out with later on when she was grown up, and what certain dresses of hers had looked like—she could not imagine now what had become of them. Whatever thoughts and stories my father had were private, and I was shy of him and would never ask him questions. Nevertheless I worked willingly under his eyes, and with a feeling of pride. One time a feed salesman came down into the pens to talk to him and my father said, "Like to have you meet my new hired man." I turned away and raked furiously, red in the face with pleasure.

"Could of fooled me," said the salesman. "I thought it was only a girl."

After the grass was cut, it seemed suddenly much later in the year. I walked on stubble in the earlier evening, aware of the reddening skies, the entering silences, of fall. When I wheeled the tank out of the gate and put the padlock on, it was almost dark. One night at this time I saw my mother and father standing on the little rise of ground we called the gangway, in front of the barn. My father had just come from the meathouse; he had his stiff bloody apron on, and a pail of cut-up meat in his hand.

It was an odd thing to see my mother down at the barn. She did not often come out of the house unless it was to do something—hang out the wash or dig potatoes in the garden. She looked out of place, with her bare lumpy legs, not touched by the sun, her apron still on and damp across the stomach from the supper dishes. Her hair was tied up in a kerchief, wisps of it falling out. She would tie her hair up like this in the morning, saying she did not have time to do it properly, and it would stay tied up all day. It was true, too; she really did not have time. These days our back porch was piled with baskets of peaches and grapes and pears, bought in town, and onions and tomatoes and cucumbers grown at home, all waiting to be made into jelly and jam and preserves, pickles and chili sauce. In the kitchen there was a fire in the stove all day, jars clinked in boiling water, sometimes a cheesecloth bag was strung on a pole between two chairs straining blue-black grape pulp for jelly. I was given jobs to do and I would sit at the table peeling peaches that had been soaked in the hot water, or cutting up onions, my eyes smarting and streaming. As soon as I was done I ran out of the house, trying to get out of earshot before my mother thought of what she wanted me to do next. I hated the hot dark kitchen in summer, the green blinds and the flypapers, the same old oilcloth table and wavy mirror and bumpy linoleum. My mother was too tired and preoccupied to talk to me, she had no heart to tell about the Normal School Graduation Dance; sweat trickled over her face and she was always counting under her breath, pointing at jars, dumping cups of sugar. It seemed to me that work in the house was endless, dreary and peculiarly depressing; work done out of doors, and in my father's service, was ritualistically important.

I wheeled the tank up to the barn, where it was kept, and I heard my mother saying, "Wait till Laird gets a little bigger, then you'll have a real help."

What my father said I did not hear. I was pleased by the way he stood listening, politely as he would to a salesman or a stranger, but with an air of wanting to get on with his real work. I felt my mother had no business down here and I wanted him to feel the same way. What did she mean about Laird? He was no help to anybody. Where was he now? Swinging himself sick on the swing, going around in circles, or trying to catch caterpillars. He never once stayed with me till I was finished.

"And then I can use her more in the house," I heard my mother say. She had a dead-quiet, regretful way of talking about me that always made me uneasy. "I just get my back turned and she runs off. It's not like I had a girl in the family at all."

I went and sat on a feed bag in the corner of the barn, not wanting to appear when this conversation was going on. My mother, I felt, was not to be trusted. She was kinder than my father and more easily fooled, but you could not depend on her, and the real reasons for the things she said and did were not to be known. She loved me, and she sat up late at night making a dress of the difficult style I wanted, for me to wear when school started, but she was also my enemy. She was always plotting. She was plotting now to get me to stay in the house more, although she knew I hated it (*because* she knew I hated it) and keep me from working for my father. It seemed to me she would do this simply out of perversity, and to try her power. It did not occur to me that she could be lonely, or jealous. No grown-up could be; they were too fortunate. I sat and kicked my heels monotonously against a feed bag, raising dust, and did not come out till she was gone.

At any rate, I did not expect my father to pay any attention to what she said. Who could imagine Laird doing my work—Laird remembering the padlock and cleaning out the watering dishes with a leaf on the end of a stick, or even wheeling the tank without it tumbling over? It showed how little my mother knew about the way things really were.

I have forgotten to say what the foxes were fed. My father's bloody apron reminded me. They were fed horsemeat. At this time most farmers still kept horses, and when a horse got too old to work, or broke a leg or got down and would not get up, as they sometimes did, the owner would call my father, and he and Henry went out to the farm in the truck. Usually they shot and butchered the horse there, paying the farmer from five to twelve dollars. If they had already too much meat on hand, they would bring the horse back alive, and keep it for a few days or weeks in our stable, until the meat was needed. After the war the farmers were buying tractors and gradually getting rid of horses altogether, so it sometimes happened that we got a good healthy horse, that there was just no use for any more. If this happened in the winter we might keep the horse in our stable till spring, for we had plenty of hay and if there was a lot of snow—and the plow did not always get our road cleared—it was convenient to be able to go to town with a horse and cutter.

The winter I was eleven years old we had two horses in the stable. We did not know what names they had had before, so we called them Mack and Flora. Mack was an old black workhorse, sooty and indifferent. Flora was a sorrel mare, a driver. We took them both out in the cutter. Mack was slow and easy to handle. Flora was given to fits of violent alarm, veering at cars and even at other horses, but we loved her speed and high-stepping, her general air of gallantry and abandon. On Saturdays we went down to the stable and as soon as we opened the door on its cosy, animal-smelling darkness Flora threw up her head, rolled her eyes, whinnied despairingly and pulled herself through a crisis of nerves on the spot. It was not safe to go into her stall; she would kick.

This winter also I began to hear a great deal more on the theme my mother had sounded when she had been talking in front of the barn. I no longer felt safe. It seemed that in the minds of the people around me there was a steady under-current of thought, not to be deflected, on this one subject. The word girl had formerly seemed to me innocent and unburdened, like the word *child;* now it appeared that it was no such thing. A girl was not, as I had supposed, simply what I was; it was what I had to become. It was a definition, always touched with emphasis, with reproach and disappointment. Also it was a joke on me. Once Laird and I were fighting, and for the first time ever I had to use all my strength against him; even so, he caught and pinned my arm for a moment, really hurting me. Henry saw this, and laughed, saying, "Oh, that there Laird's gonna show you, one of these days!" Laird was getting a lot bigger. But I was getting bigger too.

My grandmother came to stay with us for a few weeks and I heard other things. "Girls don't slam doors like that." "Girls keep their knees together when they sit down." And worse still, when I asked some questions, "That's none of girls' business." I continued to slam the doors and sit as awkwardly as possible, thinking by such measures I kept myself free.

When spring came, the horses were let out in the barnyard. Mack stood against the barn wall trying to scratch his neck and haunches, but Flora trotted up and down and reared at the fences, clattering her hooves against the rails. Snow drifts dwindled quickly, revealing the hard gray and brown earth, the familiar rise and fall of the ground, plain and bare after the fantastic landscape of winter. There was a great feeling of opening-out, of release. We just wore rubbers now, over our shoes; our feet felt ridiculously light. One Saturday we went to the stable and found all the doors open, letting in the unaccustomed sunlight and fresh air. Henry was there, just idling around looking at his collection of calendars which were tacked up behind the stalls in a part of the stable my mother had probably never seen.

"Come to say goodbye to your old friend Mack?" Henry said. "Here, you give him a taste of oats." He poured some oats in Laird's cupped hands and Laird went to feed Mack. Mack's teeth were in bad shape. He ate very slowly, patiently shifting the oats around in his mouth, trying to find a stump of a molar to grind it on. "Poor old Mac," said Henry mournfully. "When a horse's teeth's gone, he's gone. That's about the way."

25   "Are you going to shoot him today?" I said. Mack and Flora had been in the stable so long I had almost forgotten they were going to be shot.

Henry didn't answer me. Instead he started to sing in a high, trembly, mocking-sorrowful voice. *Oh, there's no more work, for poor Uncle Ned, he's gone where the good darkies go.* Mack's thick, blackish tongue worked diligently at Laird's hand. I went out before the song was ended and sat down on the gangway.

I had never seen them shoot a horse, but I knew where it was done. Last summer Laird and I had come upon a horse's entrails before they were buried. We had thought it was a big black snake, coiled up in the sun. That was around in the field that ran up beside the barn. I thought that if we went inside the barn, and found a wide crack or a knothole to look through, we would be able to see them do it. It was not something I wanted to see; just the same, if a thing really happened, it was better to see, and know.

My father came down from the house, carrying the gun.

"What are you doing here?" he said.

"Nothing."

"Go on up and play around the house."   30

He sent Laird out of the stable. I said to Laird, "Do you want to see them shoot Mack?" and without waiting for an answer led him around to the front door of the barn, opened it carefully, and went in. "Be quiet or they'll hear us," I said. We could hear Henry and my father talking in the stable; then the heavy, shuffling steps of Mack being backed out of his stall.

In the loft it was cold and dark. Thin crisscrossed beams of sunlight fell through the cracks. The hay was low. It was a rolling country, hills and hollows, slipping under our feet. About four feet up was a beam going around the walls. We piled hay up in one corner and I boosted Laird up and hoisted myself. The beam was not very wide; we crept along it with our hands flat on the barn walls. There were plenty of knotholes, and I found one that gave me the view I wanted—a corner of the barnyard, the gate, part of the field. Laird did not have a knothole and began to complain.

I showed him a widened crack between two boards. "Be quiet and wait. If they hear you you'll get us in trouble."

My father came in sight carrying the gun. Henry was leading Mack by the   35
halter. He dropped it and took out his cigarette papers and tobacco; he rolled cigarettes for my father and himself. While this was going on Mack nosed around in the old, dead grass along the fence. Then my father opened the gate and they took Mack through. Henry led Mack away from the path to a patch of ground and they talked together, not loud enough for us to hear. Mack again began searching for a mouthful of fresh grass, which was not to be found. My father walked away in a straight line, and stopped short at a distance which seemed to suit him. Henry was walking away from Mack too, but sideways, still negligently holding on to the halter. My father raised the gun and Mack looked up as if he had noticed something and my father shot him.

Mack did not collapse at once but swayed, lurched sideways and fell, first on his side; then he rolled over on his back and, amazingly, kicked his legs for a few seconds in the air. At this Henry laughed, as if Mack had done a trick for him. Laird, who had drawn a long, groaning breath of surprise when the shot was fired, said out loud, "He's not dead." And it seemed to me it might be true. But his legs stopped, he rolled on his side again, his muscles quivered and sank. The two men walked over and looked at him in a businesslike way; they bent down and examined his forehead where the bullet had gone in, and now I saw his blood on the brown grass.

"Now they just skin him and cut him up," I said. "Let's go." My legs were a little shaky and I jumped gratefully down into the hay. "Now you've seen how they shoot a horse," I said in a congratulatory way, as if I had seen it many times before. "Let's see if any barn cat's had kittens in the hay." Laird jumped. He seemed young and obedient again. Suddenly I remembered how, when he was little, I had brought him into the barn and told him to climb the ladder to the top beam. That was in the spring, too, when the hay was low. I had done it out of a need for excitement, a desire for something to happen so that I could tell about it. He was wearing a little bulky brown and white checked coat, made down from one of mine. He went all the way up just as I told him, and sat down on the top beam with the hay far below him on one side, and the barn floor and some old machinery on the other. Then I ran screaming to my father. "Laird's up on the top beam!" My father came, my mother came, my father went up the ladder talking very quietly and brought Laird down under his arm, at which my mother leaned against the ladder and began to cry. They said to me, "Why weren't you watching him?" but nobody ever knew the truth. Laird did not know enough to tell. But whenever I saw the brown and white checked coat hanging in the closet, or at the bottom of the rag bag, which was where it ended up, I felt a weight in my stomach, the sadness of unexorcised guilt.

I looked at Laird, who did not even remember this, and I did not like the look on this thin, winter-pale face. His expression was not frightened or upset, but remote, concentrating. "Listen," I said, in an unusually bright and friendly voice, "you aren't going to tell, are you?"

"No," he said absently.

"Promise."

"Promise," he said. I grabbed the hand behind his back to make sure he was not crossing his fingers. Even so, he might have a nightmare; it might come out that way. I decided I had better work hard to get all thoughts of what he had seen out of his mind—which, it seemed to me, could not hold very many things at a time. I got some money I had saved and that afternoon we went into Jubilee and saw a show, with Judy Canova, at which we both laughed a great deal. After that I thought it would be all right.

Two weeks later I knew they were going to shoot Flora. I knew from the night before, when I heard my mother ask if the hay was holding out all right, and my father said, "Well, after tomorrow there'll just be the cow, and we should be able to put her out to grass in another week." So I knew it was Flora's turn in the morning.

This time I didn't think of watching it. That was something to see just one time. I had not thought about it very often since, but sometimes when I was busy, working at school, or standing in front of the mirror combing my hair and wondering if I would be pretty when I grew up, the whole scene would flash into my mind: I would see the easy, practiced way my father raised the gun, and hear Henry laughing when Mack kicked his legs in the air. I did not have any great feeling of horror and opposition, such as a city child might have had; I was too used to seeing the death of animals as a necessity by which we lived. Yet I felt a little ashamed, and there was a new wariness, a sense of holding-off, in my attitude to my father and his work.

It was a fine day, and we were going around the yard picking up tree branches that had been torn off in winter storms. This was something we had been told to do, and also we wanted to use them to make a teepee. We heard Flora whinny, and then my father's voice and Henry's shouting, and we ran down to the barnyard to see what was going on.

The stable door was open. Henry had just brought Flora out, and she had broken away from him. She was running free in the barnyard, from one end to the other. We climbed up on the fence. It was exciting to see her running, whinnying, going up on her hind legs, prancing and threatening like a horse in a Western movie, an unbroken ranch horse, though she was just an old driver, an old sorrel mare. My father and Henry ran after her and tried to grab the dangling halter. They tried to work her into a corner, and they had almost succeeded when she made a run between them, wild-eyed, and disappeared around the corner of the barn. We heard the rails clatter down as she got over the fence, and Henry yelled. "She's into the field now!"

That meant she was in the long L-shaped field that ran up by the house. If she got around the center, heading towards the lane, the gate was open; the truck had been driven into the field this morning. My father shouted to me, because I was on the other side of the fence, nearest the lane. "Go shut the gate!"

I could run very fast. I ran across the garden, past the tree where our swing was hung, and jumped across a ditch into the lane. There was the open gate. She had not got out, I could not see her up the road; she must have run to the other end of the field. The gate was heavy, I lifted it out of the gravel and carried it across the roadway. I had it halfway across when she came in sight, galloping straight toward me. There was just time to get the chain on. Laird came scrambling through the ditch to help me.

Instead of shutting the gate, I opened it as wide as I could. I did not make any decision to do this, it was just what I did. Flora never slowed down; she galloped straight past me, and Laird jumped up and down, yelling "Shut it, shut it!" even after it was too late. My father and Henry appeared in the field a moment too late to see what I had done. They only saw Flora heading for the township road. They would think I had not got there in time.

They did not waste any time asking about it. They went back to the barn and got the gun and the knives they used, and put these in the truck; then they turned the truck around and came bouncing up the field toward us. Laird called to them, "Let me go too, let me go too!" and Henry stopped the truck and they took him in. I shut the gate after they were all gone.

I supposed Laird would tell. I wondered what would happen to me. I had never disobeyed my father before, and I could not understand why I had done it. Flora would not really get away. They would catch up with her in the truck. Or if they did not catch her this morning somebody would see her and telephone us this afternoon or tomorrow. There was no wild country here for her to run to, only farms. What was more, my father had paid for her, we needed the meat to feed the foxes, we needed the foxes to make our living. All I had done was make more work for my father who worked hard enough already. And when my father found out about it he was not going to trust me any more; he would know that I was not entirely on his side. I was on Flora's side, and that made me no use to anybody, not even to her. Just the same, I did not regret it; when she came running at me and I held the gate open, that was the only thing I could do.

I went back to the house, and my mother said. "What's all the commotion?" I told her that Flora had kicked down the fence and got away. "Your poor father," she said, "now he'll have to go chasing over the countryside. Well, there isn't any use planning dinner before one." She put up the ironing board. I wanted to tell her, but thought better of it and went upstairs and sat on my bed.

Lately I had been trying to make my part of the room fancy, spreading the bed with old lace curtains, and fixing myself a dressing table with some leftovers of cretonne for a skirt. I planned to put up some kind of barricade between my bed and Laird's, to keep my section separate from his. In the sunlight, the lace curtains were just dusty rags. We did not sing at night any more. One night when I was singing Laird said, "You sound silly," and I went right on but the next night I did not start. There was not so much need to anyway, we were no longer afraid. We knew it was just old furniture over there, old jumble and confusion. We did not keep to the rules. I still stayed awake after Laird was asleep and told myself stories, but even in these stories something different was happening, mysterious alterations took place. A story might start off in the old way, with a spectacular danger, a fire or wild animals, and for a while I might rescue people; then things would change around, and instead, somebody would be rescuing me. It might be a boy from our class at school, or even Mr. Campbell, our teacher, who tickled girls under the arms. And at this point the story concerned itself at great length with what I looked like—how long my hair was, and what kind of dress I had on; by the time I had these details worked out the real excitement of the story was lost.

It was later than one o'clock when the truck came back. The tarpaulin was over the back, which meant there was meat in it. My mother had to heat dinner up all over again. Henry and my father had changed from their bloody overalls into ordinary working overalls in the barn, and they washed their arms and necks and faces at the sink, and splashed water on their hair and combed it. Laird lifted his arm to show off a streak of blood. "We shot old Flora," he said, "and cut her up in fifty pieces."

"Well I don't want to hear about it," my mother said. "And don't come to my table like that."

55   My father made him go and wash the blood off.

We sat down and my father said grace and Henry pasted his chewing-gum on the end of his fork, the way he always did; when he took it off he would have us admire the pattern. We began to pass the bowls of steaming, overcooked vegetables. Laird looked across the table at me and said proudly, distinctly, "Anyway it was her fault Flora got away."

"What?" my father said.

"She could of shut the gate and she didn't. She just open' it up and Flora run out."

"Is that right?" my father said.

Everybody at the table was looking at me. I nodded, swallowing food with 60
great difficulty. To my shame, tears flooded my eyes.

My father made a curt sound of disgust. "What did you do that for?"

I did not answer. I put down my fork and waited to be sent from the table,
still not looking up.

But this did not happen. For some time nobody said anything, then Laird said
matter-of-factly, "She's crying."

"Never mind," my father said. He spoke with resignation, even good humor,
the words which absolved and dismissed me for good. "She's only a girl," he
said.

I didn't protest that, even in my heart. Maybe it was true. [1968] 65

1. One of the important themes of this story is how people learn sex roles. In
    what way are physical bodies implicated in the way the story treats this
    theme? Consider both humans and animals as physical creatures.
2. Compare this story to David Kaplan's "Doe Season" in Chapter 10. How
    does it relate to the academic texts associated with Chapter 10?

EDGAR ALLAN POE

OLC

EDGAR ALLAN POE *(1809–49), orphaned before he was three, was raised by
foster parents and educated well, but his gambling debts at the University of
Virginia angered his guardian, who withdrew support. After an equally abortive
sojourn at West Point, he worked as a magazine editor and literary critic. He wrote
critically successful short stories and poems but was never financially secure. He
struggled with alcohol throughout his life and in 1849, after a brief disappearance,
was found almost unconscious in a Baltimore street. He died three days later at
40 years old.*

The Tell-Tale Heart

True!—nervous—very, very dreadfully nervous I had been and am; but why *will*
you say that I am mad? The disease had sharpened my senses—not destroyed—
not dulled them. Above all was the sense of hearing acute. I heard all things in
the heaven and in the earth.° I heard many things in hell. How, then, am I mad?
Hearken! and observe how healthily—how calmly I can tell you the whole story.

It is impossible to say how first the idea entered my brain; but, once conceived,
it haunted me day and night. Object there was none. Passion there was none.
I loved the old man. He had never wronged me. He had never given me insult.
For his gold I had no desire. I think it was his eye! yes, it was this! One of his
eyes resembled that of a vulture—a pale blue eye, with a film over it. Whenever

---

[1]**all things in the heaven and in the earth** an allusion to the New Testament Philippians
2.10: "That at the name of Jesus every knee should bow, of things in heaven, and things
on earth, and things under the earth."

it fell upon me, my blood ran cold; and so by degrees—very gradually—I made up my mind to take the life of the old man, and thus rid myself of the eye forever.

Now this is the point. You fancy me mad. Madmen know nothing. But you should have seen *me*. You should have seen how wisely I proceeded—with what caution—with what foresight—with what dissimulation I went to work! I was never kinder to the old man than during the whole week before I killed him. And every night, about midnight, I turned the latch of his door and opened it— oh, so gently! And then, when I had made an opening sufficient for my head, I put in a dark lantern,° all closed, closed, so that no light shone out, and then I thrust in my head. Oh, you would have laughed to see how cunningly I thrust it in! I moved it slowly—very, very slowly, so that I might not disturb the old man's sleep. It took me an hour to place my whole head within the opening so far that I could see him as he lay upon his bed. Ha!—would a madman have been so wise as this? And then, when my head was well in the room, I undid the lantern cautiously—oh, so cautiously—cautiously (for the hinges creaked)— I undid it just so much that a single thin ray fell upon the vulture eye. And this I did for seven long nights—every night just at midnight—but I found the eye always closed; and so it was impossible to do the work; for it was not the old man who vexed me, but his Evil Eye.° And every morning, when the day broke, I went boldly into the chamber, and spoke courageously to him, calling him by name in a hearty tone and inquiring how he had passed the night. So you see he would have been a very profound old man, indeed, to suspect that every night, just at twelve, I looked in upon him while he slept.

Upon the eighth night I was more than usually cautious in opening the door. A watch's minute hand moves more quickly than did mine. Never, before that night, had I *felt* the extent of my own powers—of my sagacity. I could scarcely contain my feelings of triumph. To think that there I was, opening the door, little by little, and he not even to dream of my secret deeds or thoughts. I fairly chuckled at the idea; and perhaps he heard me; for he moved on the bed suddenly, as if startled. Now you may think that I drew back—but no. His room was black as pitch with the thick darkness, (for the shutters were close fastened, through fear of robbers,) and so I knew that he could not see the opening of the door, and I kept pushing it on steadily, steadily.

5   I had my head in, and was about to open the lantern, when my thumb slipped upon the tin fastening, and the old man sprang up in the bed, crying out—"Who's there?"

I kept quite still and said nothing. For a whole hour I did not move a muscle, and in the meantime I did not hear him lie down. He was still sitting up in the bed, listening;—just as I have done, night after night, hearkening to the death-watches in the wall.°

Presently I heard a slight groan, and I knew it was the groan of mortal terror. It was not a groan of pain or of grief—oh, no!—it was the low stifled sound that

³**dark lantern** a lantern that has shutters or panels that can close off the light   **Evil Eye** the superstitious belief that someone can harm other people by looking at them   ⁶**death-watches in the wall** beetles of the family of Anobiidae make a clicking sound as they burrow into wood, a sound thought to indicate approaching death

arises from the bottom of the soul when overcharged with awe. I knew the sound well. Many a night, just at midnight, when all the world slept, it has welled up from my own bosom, deepening, with its dreadful echo, the terrors that distracted me. I say I knew it well. I knew what the old man felt, and pitied him, although I chuckled at heart. I knew that he had been lying awake ever since the first slight noise, when he had turned in the bed. His fears had been ever since growing upon him. He had been trying to fancy them causeless, but could not. He had been saying to himself—"It is nothing but the wind in the chimney—it is only a mouse crossing the floor," or "it is merely a cricket which has made a single chirp." Yes, he had been trying to comfort himself with these suppositions: but he had found all in vain. *All in vain;* because Death, in approaching him, had stalked with his black shadow before him, and enveloped the victim. And it was the mournful influence of the unperceived shadow that caused him to feel—although he neither saw nor heard—to *feel* the presence of my head within the room.

When I had waited a long time, very patiently, without hearing him lie down, I resolved to open a little—a very, very little crevice in the lantern. So I opened it— you cannot imagine how stealthily, stealthily—until, at length, a single dim ray, like the thread of the spider, shot from out the crevice and fell upon the vulture eye.

It was open—wide, wide open—and I grew furious as I gazed upon it. I saw it with perfect distinctness—all a dull blue, with a hideous veil over it that chilled the very marrow in my bones; but I could see nothing else of the old man's face or person: for I had directed the rays as if by instinct, precisely upon the damned spot.

And now—have I not told you that what you mistake for madness is but over acuteness of the senses?—now, I say, there came to my ears a low, dull, quick sound, such as a watch makes when enveloped in cotton. I knew *that* sound well, too. It was the beating of the old man's heart. It increased my fury, as the beating of a drum stimulates the soldier into courage. 10

But even yet I refrained and kept still. I scarcely breathed. I held the lantern motionless. I tried how steadily I could maintain the ray upon the eye. Meantime the hellish tattoo of the heart increased. It grew quicker and quicker, and louder and louder every instant. The old man's terror *must* have been extreme! It grew louder, I say, louder every moment!—do you mark me well? I have told you that I am nervous: so I am. And now at the dead hour of the night, amid the dreadful silence of that old house, so strange a noise as this excited me to uncontrollable terror. Yet, for some minutes longer I refrained and stood still. But the beating grew louder, louder! I thought the heart must burst. And now a new anxiety seized me—the sound would be heard by a neighbor! The old man's hour had come! With a loud yell, I threw open the lantern and leaped into the room. He shrieked once—once only. In an instant I dragged him to the floor, and pulled the heavy bed over him. I then smiled gaily, to find the deed so far done. But, for many minutes, the heart beat on with a muffled sound. This, however, did not vex me; it would not be heard through the wall. At length it ceased. The old man was dead. I removed the bed and examined the corpse. Yes, he was stone, stone dead. I placed my hand upon the heart and held it there many minutes. There was no pulsation. He was stone dead. His eye would trouble me no more.

If you still think me mad, you will think so no longer when I describe the wise precautions I took for the concealment of the body. The night waned, and I worked hastily, but in silence. First of all I dismembered the corpse. I cut off the head and the arms and the legs.

I then took up three planks from the flooring of the chamber, and deposited all between the scantlings.° I then replaced the boards so cleverly, so cunningly, that no human eye—not even *his*—could have detected anything wrong. There was nothing to wash out—no stain of any kind—no bloodspot whatever. I had been too wary for that. A tub had caught all—ha! ha!

When I had made an end of these labors, it was four o'clock—still dark as midnight. As the bell sounded the hour, there came a knocking at the street door. I went down to open it with a light heart,—for what had I *now* to fear? There entered three men, who introduced themselves, with perfect suavity, as officers of the police. A shriek had been heard by a neighbor during the night; suspicion of foul play had been aroused; information had been lodged at the police office, and they (the officers) had been deputed to search the premises.

15   I smiled,—for *what* had I to fear? I bade the gentlemen welcome. The shriek, I said, was my own in a dream. The old man, I mentioned, was absent in the country. I took my visiters all over the house. I bade them search—search *well*. I led them, at length, to *his* chamber. I showed them his treasures, secure, undis- turbed. In the enthusiasm of my confidence, I brought chairs into the room and desired them *here* to rest from their fatigues, while I myself, in the wild audacity of my perfect triumph, placed my own seat upon the very spot beneath which reposed the corpse of the victim.

The officers were satisfied. My *manner* had convinced them. I was singularly at ease. They sat, and while I answered cheerily, they chatted of familiar things. But, ere long, I felt myself getting pale and wished them gone. My head ached, and I fancied a ringing in my ears: but still they sat and still they chatted. The ringing became more distinct:—it continued and became more distinct: I talked more freely to get rid of the feeling: but it continued and gained definitiveness—until, at length, I found that the noise was *not* within my ears.

No doubt I now grew *very* pale;—but I talked more fluently, and with a heightened voice. Yet the sound increased—and what could I do? It was *a low, dull, quick sound—much such a sound as a watch makes when enveloped in cotton.* I gasped for breath—and yet the officers heard it not. I talked more quickly—more vehemently; but the noise steadily increased. I arose and argued about trifles, in a high key and with violent gesticulations; but the noise steadily increased. Why *would* they not be gone? I paced the floor to and fro with heavy strides, as if excited to fury by the observations of the men—but the noise steadily increased. Oh God! what *could* I do? I foamed—I raved—I swore! I swung the chair upon which I had been sitting, and grated it upon the boards, but the noise arose over all and con- tinually increased. It grew louder—louder—*louder!* And still the men chatted pleasantly, and smiled. Was it possible they heard not? Almighty God!—no, no! They heard!—they suspected!—they *knew!*—they were making a mockery of my horror!—this I thought, and this I think. But anything was better than this agony! Anything was more tolerable than this derision! I could bear those

---

[13]**scantlings** timbers underpinning floorboards

hypocritical smiles no longer! I felt that I must scream or die!—and now—again!—hark! louder! louder! louder! *louder!*—

"Villains!" I shrieked, "dissemble no more! I admit the deed!—tear up the planks!—here, here!—It is the beating of his hideous heart!" [1843]

1. Characterize the narrative technique of this story.
2. The fourth and fifth sentences allude to the New Testament, Philippians 2:10: "that at the name of Jesus every knee should bow, of things in heaven, and things on earth, and things under the earth." How does the allusion work in the story?
3. What does this story have to say about the body?
4. Compare the story with A. R. Ammons's poem, "Still."

DRAMA

MAX MITCHELL

MAX MITCHELL *is a Canadian actor who also writes plays that have been mounted in New York, Florida, and Los Angeles. He directed the 2002 film* Get Your Stuff. Life Support *first appeared at the West Coast Ensemble in Hollywood, California, directed by Fred Gorelick and starring Forrest Witt. It was included in* The Best American Short Plays of 94/95 *along with plays by Elaine May, Steve Martin, David Mamet, and Thornton Wilder.*

Life Support

Characters:

David

Patrick

AT RISE:

A hospital room. A man lies on a bed with tubes sticking in his arms and a machine connected. He is unconscious, his eyes closed.

Man's Voice: [*O.s.*] I'll bring it back!

[Patrick, *late thirties, enters pushing a wheel chair full of bags. He wears a silk shirt and tie.*]

Patrick: . . . later.

[*He looks at the man in the bed and nods his head. He crosses to the man in the bed and kisses him on the forehead.*]

Patrick: Today's the big day. [*He lifts the blankets to look under.*] Just as I thought. You're not even dressed. Typical. I go to a lot of trouble to organize a party and you don't even care. Typical. Well, I brought some of your friends.

[*He takes an urn out of one of his bags.*] Since his untimely death, Michael's been to London, Palm Springs, Fire Island, and twice to Barney's half price sale. [*To the urn.*] Haven't you, Michael? More than when you were living. Say, hello to David. Hello. Hello. Hello. Here, you sit over here. [*He puts the urn on the bedside table and takes another urn out of another bag.*] And, of course, your friend, Bruce. Hello. Hello. They won't travel in the same bag. You sit over here and try to get along. [*He places Bruce's urn on the bedside table on the opposite side of the bed. He takes some decorations out of the bag.*] I spoke to your doctor. She said nothing's changed. We thought maybe you . . . well. Typical. [*He holds up some streamers and balloons.*] Do you like these colors? Knowing you, I should've hired a decorator but on what I make I'd have to . . . but then, I never met a decorator I'd wanna' . . . Oh, I brought your favorite flowers. [*He takes some fresia out of one of the bags, smells them.*] They smell like heaven. [*He places them in a vase and then goes about tacking up streamers.*] I went to that Course in Miracles and they said death is just another part of life. Well, what have we all been so upset about? Right? Doesn't really matter one way or the other. Dead, alive, just as good. Well, look at Michael and Bruce. They travel, get to the important sales, don't have to work, I suppose it's not a bad . . . death at all. I do all the work. Course, you don't either, but still, you're . . . [*He stops and speaks directly to* David.] I mean they don't even listen, they're above it all . . . but you . . . are you listening, Sweetheart? [*He begins to blow up a couple of balloons. He speaks between puffs.*] No . . . of course not . . . typical . . . we have to be out by one . . . it's like the damn Best Western. Speaking of Best Western, I'm taking the towels . . . I know . . . but with what your insurance pays for the room, the towels should be included . . . and thicker . . . soon be fourth of July . . . would you like to go to the island . . . we're going . . . can't miss an invasion . . . there . . . starting to look festive, huh? . . . oh, your favorite . . . [*He takes a bottle of champagne and four champagne flutes out of a bag and puts them on the table, one by each urn.*] . . . champagne . . . I didn't get the cheap stuff, so shutup . . . they can't hold their booze anymore, but if I don't give them a glass, they act like two-year-olds. You know how it is. Bruce has a stemware fetish. [*He attempts to pop the cork. When it's corked, he pours four shots.*] I didn't know what to wear, so I put on your clothes. The tie I gave you for Christmas. And your silk shirt. I've never done this before. It's not something anybody gets to do . . . much. They say it's an act of love. I don't know how they got to that. Do you? Those course in miracles people . . . they've probably reframed it . . . reconceptualized it . . . so it's like a christening or something . . . What, Michael? Oh, you're right. Toast. Toast. [*He raises his glass. Party time.*] To a wonderful man who used to be . . . [*Pause. He puts his glass down.*] I called your parents. Three times. Last time your father wouldn't come to the phone. I told them to come. I told them this was their last chance. They just don't wanna' hear anything. Anything. I told your father if he didn't come and visit you that I'd move to Alberta and rent the house across the street. And tell everyone I was their son-in-law. They didn't think it was funny. Well, fuck 'em. Right? It's beyond me. If they hadn't given birth to you, I wouldn't believe they were humans. I forgot . . . the

President . . . the President sent a telegram. [*He takes a piece of paper from his pocket.*] "Dear David, on this momentous occasion, the First Lady and I hope that you party hard." That's just the White House. What did I do with Buckingham Palace? It's . . . never mind. [*He raises his glass once more.*] To you. To a sweet beautiful guy who . . . I miss. I can't sleep, you know. Can't decide which side of the bed to stay on. I take them . . . [*Points at urns.*] . . . to bed with me . . . and I wear your . . . I wear your t-shirts to bed . . . [*Breaks down.*] . . . so I can feel close to you . . . so I can sleep. [*He pulls himself up.*] But soon you'll be home and we'll sleep together every night, just like before, and I'll hold you against my cheek the whole night just like before, and we'll be happy. [*He takes a new urn out of the bag. He places it beside the bed. Beat.*] I suppose it might be construed as bad taste to show you your urn before you . . . but I saw this one, I liked it, it was . . . okay, it was on sale . . . and if I didn't buy it this week, I'd have to pay thirty-five dollars more. I know, typical. You like it? It's Limoges. You love Limoges. I hope it fits. I'd hate to have to put the overflow in a drawer or something. [*He examines the machine.*] The doctor told me how it's done, I guess this is the . . . [*He touches one of the buttons. Beat. Seriously. He looks up.*] God? Can't you make a miracle? Just this once? Why him? What did he ever do to anybody? He signalled all his turns and gave money to the homeless and . . . God? Are you sure I'm supposed to do this? God? I can't hear you. Okay. Okay. I know. [*He walks to* David *and speaks into his ear.*] Are you ready? [*Nothing. He takes a party hat from a bag and puts it on* David's *head. He puts a hat on each of Michael and Bruce's urns. He puts one on himself.*] I forgot the hats. Aren't they horrible? Oh, well. We're going for that cheap frivolité. Make it fun. Right? Right. There. Out with a bang. You'll like it on the other side. No muss, no fuss, they say. Right, Guys? You'll all be together. I'll be the one alone. Typical. [*Beat.*] But none of me. It's your party. The music! I'm such a mess. I can't remember anything. [*He takes a cassette tape from his pocket and puts it in a ghetto blaster that sits on the table. He sits on the bed, takes another drink of champagne, finishes it, and drinks from one of the other glasses.*] Excuse me. [*He looks at* David.] I won't say goodbye. I hate goodbyes. You're just changing shape. You'll just be easier to carry. But if there was anything I could do to bring you back to the way you were five years ago . . . when we were happy just to sit on the couch holding hands and watch the news . . . [*He loses control.*] . . . I would. But I'm not that strong. I'm sorry. I'm not that strong. [*Regaining it.*] Let's just get on with it. Okay? Okay. [*He goes to the machine. He reaches for a switch and hesitates.*] No. No. No. [*Beat. He looks at* David.] I don't think I can do this. Can't you just . . . do it yourself? [*Beat.*] Where is an incompetent nurse when you need one? Maybe I shouldn't. Maybe I . . . [*Beat. He sits on the bed and strokes* David's *forehead.*] You're right. There's nothing left but fuss. "Fuss, fuss, fuss. Nothing but fuss," said the King. Nothing but pain and fuss. When your whole existence is pain . . . [*Beat. He thinks. He looks at the machine.*] I can't. I . . . just can't. You understand. You'll just be done when you're done. It's not for me to say. [*Beat. He picks up his drink. He walks to the door. He takes a drink. Thinks. Puts the drink down. He walks over to the machine, takes a deep breath, closes his eyes, shudders, and*

solemnly and deliberately flicks a switch. Nothing happens. The machine is supposed to
shut off but doesn't.] Oh, my God. Shit. I'm sorry. It's . . . [*He starts to laugh.*] Aw
shit. It doesn't work. Typical. [*He laughs. It's ridiculous. He looks around to see if*
anyone is nearby.]Candid Camera? Look, I'll just . . . [*Flying into a rage he kicks*
the machine. Nothing happens again. He kicks it again. Nothing.] Shit! Fuck! [*He*
starts to laugh.] I'm . . . really sorry. I . . . typical. [*Beat. He absent-mindedly*
reaches over and simply pulls the plug out of the wall. The machine dies. David's body
spasms.] What was that? Oh. Right. It's off? It's off. It's off. Okay. Goodbye.
Goodbye. Goodbye. [*Beat. Quiet. He places his hand on* David's *forehead.*] Peace.
No more fuss. [*To Bruce and Michael's urns.*] Right guys? Peace and quiet.
[*He hits the tape player and Edith Piaf's voice rises singing "Milord." He tops off the*
other glasses and raises his glass, sits on the bed, strokes David's forehead, and sings
along.]
Patrick: [*Cont'd.*] [*Quietly.*] "*Allez, venez, Milord, vous assoira Milord . . .*"
[*Etc.*]
[*Slow fade to black.*]   [1994]

1. When Patrick enters, he seems determined to carry out his mission, which
   he has planned for carefully. Yet he claims late in the play that he can't do
   it. Why? What is his conflict? What allows him to go ahead and carry out
   his plan? What is the climactic moment that allows the play to move toward
   resolution?
2. What is the involvement of the medical profession in the end of David's
   life?
3. How does the language of the play contribute to its effect?
4. What difference does it make that the play was published in 1994?
5. What are the issues the play raises? What disciplines can shed light on them?

NONFICTION PROSE

ANATOLE BROYARD

ANATOLE BROYARD *(1920–91) was born into an African-American family*
in Brooklyn, New York. His skin tone was light enough that when he became
estranged from his family, he lived as a white man. He attended Brooklyn College,
later married, and sought a literary career. He did not reveal his race even to his
own children; becoming a prominent writer for the New York Times Book
Review, *he hoped to be accepted as a writer, rather than a "black writer." His first*
book, Sunday Dinner in Brooklyn, *was followed by a memoir inspired by his life*
in the Greenwich Village of the 1940s, Kafka Was the Rage, *which critics called*
lively, stylish, and witty. However, Broyard's writing life was actually centered in
his full-time career as essayist, reviewer, and editor of the New York Times. *Until*
his death in 1991 from cancer, he appears never to have resolved the conflict with
his origins and his identity. Speaking of that conflict in Thirteen Ways of Looking

at a Black Man, *Henry Louis Gates views him as "a living paradox . . . want[ing]*
to be appreciated not for being black but for being a writer, even though his
pretending . . . was stopping him from writing."

Intoxicated by My Illness*

So much of a writer's life consists of assumed suffering, rhetorical suffering, that
I felt something like relief, even elation, when the doctor told me that I had cancer of the prostate. Suddenly there was in the air a rich sense of crisis—real crisis, yet one that also contained echoes of ideas like the crisis of language, the crisis of literature, or of personality. It seemed to me that my existence, whatever I
thought, felt, or did, had taken on a kind of meter, as in poetry or in taxis.

When you learn that your life is threatened, you can turn toward this knowledge
or away from it. I turned toward it. It was not a choice but an automatic shifting of
gears, a tacit agreement between my body and my brain. I thought that time had
tapped me on the shoulder, that I had been given a real deadline at last. It wasn't
that I believed the cancer was going to kill me, even though it had spread beyond
the prostate—it could probably be controlled, either by radiation or hormonal
manipulation. No. What struck me was the startled awareness that one day something, whatever it might be, was going to interrupt my leisurely progress. It sounds
trite, yet I can only say that I realized for the first time that I don't have forever.

Time was no longer innocuous, nothing was casual anymore. I understood
that living itself had a deadline—like the book I had been working on. How
sheepish I would feel if I couldn't finish it. I had promised it to myself and to my
friends. Though I wouldn't say this out loud, I had promised it to the world. All
writers privately think this way.

When my friends heard I had cancer, they found me surprisingly cheerful and
talked about my courage. But it has nothing to do with courage, at least not for me.
As far as I can tell, it's a question of desire. I'm filled with desire—to live, to write,
to do everything. Desire itself is a kind of immortality. While I've always had trouble concentrating, I now feel as concentrated as a diamond or a microchip.

I remember a time in the 1950s when I tried to talk a friend of mine named Jules   5
out of committing suicide. He had already made one attempt, and when I went to
see him he said, "Give me a good reason to go on living." He was thirty years old.

I saw what I had to do. I started to sell life to him, like a real estate agent. Just
look at the world, I said. How can you not be curious about it? The streets, the
houses, the trees, the shops, the people, the movement, and the stillness. Look at
the women, so appealing, each in her own way. Think of all the things you can
do with them, the places you can go together. Think of books, paintings, music.
Think of your friends.

While I was talking I wondered, Am I telling Jules the truth? He didn't think so,
because he put his head in the oven a week later. As for me, I don't know whether
I believed what I said or not, because I just went on behaving like everybody else.

---

*Anatole Broyard, "Intoxicated by My Illness," in *Intoxicated by My Illness and Other Writings*
on Life and Death, compiled and edited by Alexandra Broyard (New York: Clarkson Potter,
1992), 3–7.

But I believe it now. When my wife made me a hamburger the other day I thought it was the most fabulous hamburger in the history of the world.

With this illness one of my recurrent dreams has finally come true. Several times in the past I've dreamed that I had committed a crime—or perhaps I was only accused of a crime, it's not clear. When brought to trial I refused to have a lawyer—I got up instead and made an impassioned speech in my own defense. This speech was so moving that I could feel myself tingling with it. It was inconceivable that the jury would not acquit me—only each time I woke before the verdict. Now cancer is the crime I may or may not have committed, and the eloquence of being alive, the fervor of the survivor, is my best defense.

The way my friends have rallied around me is wonderful. They remind me of a flock of birds rising from a body of water into the sunset. If that image seems a bit extravagant or tinged with satire, it's because I can't help thinking there's something comical about my friends' behavior—all these witty men suddenly saying pious, inspirational things.

10　　They are not intoxicated as I am by my illness, but sobered. Since I refuse to, they've taken on the responsibility of being serious. They appear abashed or chagrined in their sobriety. Stripped of their playfulness these pals of mine seem plainer, homelier—even older. It's as if they had all gone bald overnight.

Yet one of the effects of their fussing over me is that I feel vivid, multicolored, sharply drawn. On the other hand—and this is ungrateful—I remain outside of their solicitude, their love and best wishes. I'm isolated from them by the grandiose conviction that I am the healthy person and they are the sick ones. Like an existential hero, I have been cured by the truth while they still suffer the nausea of the uninitiated.

I've had eight-inch needles thrust into my belly, where I could feel them tickling my metaphysics.° I've worn Pampers. I've been licked by the flames, and my sense of self has been singed. Sartre was right: You have to live each moment as if you're prepared to die.

Now at last I understand the conditional nature of the human condition. Yet, unlike Kierkegaard° and Sartre,° I'm not interested in the irony of my position. Cancer cures you of irony. Perhaps my irony was all in my prostate. A dangerous illness fills you with adrenaline and makes you feel very smart. I can afford now, I said to myself, to draw conclusions. All those grand generalizations toward which I have been building for so many years are finally taking shape. As I look back at how I used to be, it seems to me that an intellectual is a person who thinks that the classical clichés don't apply to him, that he is immune to homely truths. I know better now. I see everything with a summarizing eye. Nature is a terrific editor.

---

¹²**metaphysics** a division of philosophy concerned with the nature of reality
¹³**Kierkegaard** Sören Keirkegaard, Danish philosopher and Christian theologian (*The Sickness unto Death, The Concept of Dread*) known as the founder of existentialism. Accepting that human beings can't know whether the world is organized in a rational way, he saw individuals as free to make—or not make—a "leap of faith" in a meaningful universe.
Sartre Twentieth-century French philosopher Jean-Paul Sartre explored an atheistic version of existentialism in his book *Being and Nothingness* and his plays and novels, including the play *No Exit*.

In the first stages of my illness, I couldn't sleep, urinate, or defecate—the word *ordeal* comes to mind. Then, when my doctor changed all this and everything worked again, what a voluptuous pleasure it was! With a cry of joy I realized how marvelous it is simply to function. My body, which in the last decade or two had become a familiar, no-longer-thrilling old flame, was reborn as a brand-new infatuation. I realize of course that this elation I feel is just a phase, just a rush of consciousness, a splash of perspective, a hot flash of ontological alertness.° But I'll take it, I'll use it. I'll use everything I can while I wait for the next phase. Illness is primarily a drama, and it should be possible to enjoy it as well as to suffer it. I see now why the Romantics were so fond of illness—the sick man sees everything as metaphor. In this phase I'm infatuated with my cancer. It stinks of revelation.

As I look ahead, I feel like a man who has awakened from a long afternoon nap to find the evening stretched out before me. I'm reminded of D'Annunzio, the Italian poet, who said to a duchess he had just met at a party in Paris, "Come, we will have a profound evening." Why not? I see the balance of my life—everything comes in images now—as a beautiful paisley shawl thrown over a grand piano.

Why a paisley shawl, precisely? Why a grand piano? I have no idea. That's the way the situation presents itself to me. I have to take my imagery along with my medicine.   [1992]

[14]**hot flash of ontological awareness** Hot flashes are symptoms of menopause in which a woman experiences a feeling of rising temperature sometimes accompanied by sweating. Ontology is the branch of metaphysics concerned with the nature of being, the nature of what exists in the world.

1. In paragraph 14, Broyard announces that "the sick man sees everything as metaphor." How does the essay confirm that claim? Anayze its figures of speech and puns. What are they and how do they function in the essay?
2. What is the tone of the essay? In a journal entry, Broyard wrote: "There is a sudden pathos. I had seemed to friends and acquaintances to be good for another twenty years. They found a dying Anatole easier to like, more interesting. I have become a ghost who is at the same time more real than they are. I have lost my remorselessness. I find it difficult to be serious, to give up a lifetime of irony."[1] Does this ring true for the way he presents himself in the essay?
3. Lauren Slater has written essays and a memoir about her experience of mental illness. After a very negative review in the *New York Times* by Janet Maslin, Slater wrote an essay in which she said, "No author authors alone. Every text is a joint construction of meaning. Every illness memoir came from the world you and I co-created, and thus we all, together, Janet Maslin included, write and continue to write this long story of sickness[.] For what?"[2] How would you answer her question?

[1]Anatole Broyard, "Journal Notes May–September 1990," *Intoxicated by My Illness and Other Writings on Life and Death*, compiled and edited by Alexandra Broyard (New York: Clarkson Potter/Publishers, 1992), 68.

[2]Lauren Slater, "One Nation, Under the Weather," *Writing Creative Nonfiction*, ed. Carolyn Forché and Philip Gerard (Cincinnati: Story, 2001), 164–69. Quoted on pp. 318–19 of Harriet Malinowitz, "Business, Pleasure, and the Personal Essay," *College English* 65.3 (2003): 305–22.

⊚⊚⊚

CORNEL WEST

CORNEL WEST *(1953–), a Tulsa, Oklahoma, native educated in many locations until his family settled in Sacramento, California, has degrees from Harvard and Princeton. He has held chairs in Afro-American Studies and Philosophy of Religion at Yale and Harvard and is currently at Princeton University. He has been an activitist since his youth, and an intellectual leader all his adult life. His gifts were apparent to his teachers from his earliest years. Since then he has had a great deal of influence on the thinking about race, religion, and social and ethical concerns of our time. He is the author of many articles and books, including* Race Matters, The Cornel West Reader, *and* Keeping Faith: Philosophy and Race in America. *He wrote* The Future of American Progressivism: An Initiative for Political and Economic Reform *with Roberto Mangabeira Unger,* The War Against Parents; What We Can Do for America's Beleaguered Moms and Dads *with Sylvia Ann Hewlett,* Breaking Bread: Insurgent Black Intellectual Life *with bell hooks,* The Future of the Race *with Henry Louis Gates Jr., and* Jews and Blacks: Let the Healing Begin *with Rabbi Michael Lerner. Artemis Records released his rap album* Sketches of My Culture *in 2001.*

*Black Sexuality: The Taboo Subject**

"Here," she said, "in this here place, we flesh; flesh that weeps, laughs; flesh that dances on bare feet in grass. Love it. Love it hard. Yonder they do not love your flesh. They despise it. They don't love your eyes; they'd just as soon pick em out. No more do they love the skin on your back. Yonder they flay it. And O my people they do not love your hands. Those they only use, tie, bind, chop off and leave empty. Love your hands! Love them. Raise them up and kiss them. Touch others with them, pat them together, stroke them on your face 'cause they don't love that either. You got to love it, You! . . . This is flesh I'm talking about here. Flesh that needs to be loved."

TONI MORRISON, *Beloved* (1987)

Americans are obsessed with sex and fearful of black sexuality. The obsession has to do with a search for stimulation and meaning in a fast-paced, market-driven culture; the fear is rooted in visceral feelings about black bodies fueled by sexual myths of black women and men. The dominant myths draw black women and men either as threatening creatures who have the potential for sexual power over whites, or as harmless, desexed underlings of a white culture. There is Jezebel° (the seductive temptress), Sapphire° (the evil, manipulative bitch), or Aunt Jemima° (the sexless, long-suffering nurturer). There is

*Cornel West, "Black Sexuality: The Taboo Subject," in *Race Matters* (Boston: Beacon Press, 1993; reprinted with new epilogue, New York: Vintage Books, 1994), 83–91.
[1]**Jezebel** wife of King Ahab of Israel (1 Kings 16:31) **Sapphire** a rude, aggressive female character in the 1930s through 1950s radio show, "Amos 'n Andy," in which white actors portrayed stereotyped black characters **Aunt Jemima** the image of an older black woman used in advertisements for pancake mix and maple syrup

Bigger Thomas° (the mad and mean predatory craver of white women), Jack Johnson° (the super performer—be it in athletics, entertainment, or sex—who excels others naturally and prefers women of a lighter hue), or Uncle Tom° (the spineless, sexless—or is it impotent?—sidekick of whites). The myths offer distorted, dehumanized creatures whose bodies—color of skin, shape of nose and lips, type of hair, size of hips—are already distinguished from the white norm of beauty and whose feared sexual activities are deemed disgusting, dirty, or funky and considered less acceptable.

Yet the paradox of the sexual politics of race in America is that, behind closed doors, the dirty, disgusting, and funky sex associated with black people is often perceived to be more intriguing and interesting, while in public spaces talk about black sexuality is virtually taboo. Everyone knows it is virtually impossible to talk candidly about race without talking about sex. Yet most social scientists who examine race relations do so with little or no reference to how sexual perceptions influence racial matters. My thesis is that black sexuality is a taboo subject in white and black America and that a candid dialogue about black sexuality between and within these communities is requisite for healthy race relations in America.

The major cultural impact of the 1960s was not to demystify black sexuality but rather to make black bodies more accessible to white bodies *on an equal basis*. The history of such access up to that time was primarily one of brutal white rape and ugly white abuse. The Afro-Americanization of white youth—given the disproportionate black role in popular music and athletics—has put white kids in closer contact with their own bodies and facilitated more humane interaction with black people. Listening to Motown records in the sixties or dancing to hip hop music in the nineties may not lead one to question the sexual myths of black women and men, but when white and black kids buy the same billboard hits and laud the same athletic heroes the result is often a shared cultural space where some humane interaction takes place.

This subterranean cultural current of interracial interaction increased during the 1970s and 1980s even as racial polarization deepened on the political front. We miss much of what goes on in the complex development of race relations in America if we focus solely on the racial card played by the Republican Party and overlook the profound multicultural mix of popular culture that has occurred in the past two decades. In fact, one of the reasons Nixon, Reagan, and Bush had to play a racial card, that is, had to code their language about race, rather than simply call a spade a spade, is due to the changed *cultural* climate of race and sex in America. The classic scene of Senator Strom Thurmond—staunch segregationist and longtime opponent of interracial sex and marriage—strongly defending Judge Clarence Thomas—married to a white woman and an alleged avid

[1]**Bigger Thomas** the main character of Richard Wright's novel *Native Son*   **Jack Johnson** (1878–1946) the world's first African-American heavyweight boxing champion   **Uncle Tom** the eponymous character of Harriet Beecher Stowe's novel about the antebellum South, *Uncle Tom's Cabin*

consumer of white pornography—shows how this change in climate affects even reactionary politicians in America.

5   Needless to say, many white Americans still view black sexuality with disgust. And some continue to view their own sexuality with disgust. Victorian morality and racist perceptions die hard. But more and more white Americans are willing to interact sexually with black Americans *on an equal basis*—even if the myths still persist. I view this as neither cause for celebration nor reason for lament. Any-time two human beings find genuine pleasure, joy, and love, the stars smile and the universe is enriched. Yet as long as that pleasure, joy, and love is still predicated on myths of black sexuality, the more fundamental challenge of humane interaction remains unmet. Instead, what we have is white access to black bodies on an equal basis—but not yet the demythologizing of black sexuality.

This demythologizing of black sexuality is crucial for black America because much of black self-hatred and self-contempt has to do with the refusal of many black Americans to love their own black bodies—especially their black noses, hips, lips, and hair. Just as many white Americans view black sexuality will disgust, so do many black Americans—but for very different reasons and with very different results. White supremacist ideology is based first and foremost on the degradation of black bodies in order to control them. One of the best ways to instill fear in people is to terrorize them. Yet this fear is best sustained by convincing them that their bodies are ugly, their intellect is inherently underdeveloped, their culture is less civilized, and their future warrants less concern than that of other peoples. Two hundred and forty-four years of slavery and nearly a century of institutionalized terrorism in the form of segregation, lynchings, and second-class citizenship in America were aimed at precisely this devaluation of black people. This white supremacist venture was, in the end, a relative failure—thanks to the courage and creativity of millions of black people and hundreds of exceptional white folk like John Brown, Elijah Lovejoy, Myles Horton, Russell Banks, Anne Braden, and others.° Yet this white dehumanizing endeavor has left its toll in the psychic scars and personal wounds now inscribed in the souls of black folk. These scars and wounds are clearly etched on the canvass of black sexuality.

How does one come to accept and affirm a body so despised by one's fellow citizens? What are the ways in which one can rejoice in the intimate moments of black sexuality in a culture that questions the aesthetic beauty of one's body? Can genuine human relationships flourish for black people in a society that assaults black intelligence, black moral character, and black possibility?

These crucial questions were addressed in those black social spaces that affirmed black humanity and warded off white contempt—especially in black families, churches, mosques, schools, fraternities, and sororities. These precious

---

°**John Brown** executed in 1859 for attempting to inspire and lead a slave revolt in Harper's Ferry, Virginia   **Elijah Lovejoy** an early nineteenth-century abolitionist minister and journalist killed defending his press   **Myles Horton** founder of the Highlander Folk School in Monteagle, Tennessee, which became important during the civil rights movement   **Russell Banks** contemporary fiction writer, poet, and essayist   **Anne Braden** mid-twentieth-century civil rights activist in the South

black institutions forged a mighty struggle against the white supremacist bombardment of black people. They empowered black children to learn against the
odds and supported damaged black egos so they could keep fighting; they
preserved black sanity in an absurd society in which racism ruled unabated;
and they provided opportunities for black love to stay alive. But these grand
yet flawed black institutions refused to engage one fundamental issue: *black
sexuality*. Instead, they ran from it like the plague. And they obsessively
condemned those places where black sexuality was flaunted: the streets, the
clubs, and the dance-halls.

Why was this so? Primarily because these black institutions put a premium
on black survival in America. And black survival required accommodation with
and acceptance from white America. Accommodation avoids any sustained association with the subversive and transgressive—be it communism or miscegena-
tion. Did not the courageous yet tragic lives of Paul Robeson and Jack Johnson
bear witness to this truth? And acceptance meant that only "good" negroes
would thrive—especially those who left black sexuality at the door when they
"entered" and "arrived." In short, struggling black institutions made a Faustian
pact with white America: avoid any substantive engagement with black sexuality
and your survival on the margins of American society is, at least, possible.

White fear of black sexuality is a basic ingredient of white racism. And for
whites to admit this deep fear even as they try to instill and sustain fear in blacks
is to acknowledge a weakness—a weakness that goes down to the bone. Social
scientists have long acknowledged that interracial sex and marriage is the most
perceived source of white fear of black people—just as the repeated castrations of
lynched black men cries *[sic]* out for serious psychocultural explanation.

Black sexuality is a taboo subject in America principally because it is a form of
black power over which whites have little control—yet its visible manifestations
evoke the most visceral of white responses, be it one of seductive obsession
or downright disgust. On the one hand, black sexuality among blacks simply
does not include whites, nor does it make them a central point of reference. It
proceeds as if whites do not exist, as if whites are invisible and simply don't
matter. This form of black sexuality puts black agency center stage with no white
presence at all. This can be uncomfortable for white people accustomed to being
the custodians of power.

On the other hand, black sexuality between blacks and whites proceeds
based on underground desires that Americans deny or ignore in public and
over which laws have no effective control. In fact, the dominant sexual myths
of black women and men portray whites as being "out of control"—seduced,
tempted, overcome, overpowered by black bodies. This form of black sexuality
makes white passivity the norm—hardly an acceptable self-image for a white-
run society.

Of course, neither scenario fully accounts for the complex elements that
determine how any particular relationship involving black sexuality *actually*
takes place. Yet they do accent the crucial link between black sexuality and black
power in America. In this way, to make black sexuality a taboo subject is to
silence talk about a particular kind of power black people are perceived to have

10

over whites. On the surface, this "golden" side is one in which black people simply have an upper hand sexually over whites given the dominant myths in our
society.

Yet there is a "brazen" side—a side perceived long ago by black people. If
black sexuality is a form of black power in which black agency and white passivity are interlinked, then are not black people simply acting out the very roles to
which the racist myths of black sexuality confine them? For example, most black
churches shunned the streets, clubs, and dance-halls in part because these black
spaces seemed to confirm the very racist myths of black sexuality to be rejected.
Only by being "respectable" black folk, they reasoned, would white America see
their good works and shed its racist skin. For many black church folk, black
agency and white passivity in sexual affairs was neither desirable nor tolerable.
It simply permitted black people to play the role of the exotic "other"—closer to
nature (removed from intelligence and control) and more prone to be guided by
base pleasures and biological impulses.

15   Is there a way out of this Catch-22 situation in which black sexuality either
liberates black people from white control in order to imprison them in racist
myths or confines blacks to white "respectability" while they make their own
sexuality a taboo subject? There indeed are ways out, but there is no one way
out for all black people. Or, to put it another way, the ways out for black men
differ vastly from those for black women. Yet, neither black men nor black
women can make it out unless both get out since the degradation of both are
[sic] inseparable though not identical.

Black male sexuality differs from black female sexuality because black men
have different self-images and strategies of acquiring power in the patriarchal
structures of white America and black communities. Similarly, black male heterosexuality differs from black male homosexuality owing to the self-perceptions
and means of gaining power in the homophobic institutions of white America
and black communities. The dominant myth of black male sexual prowess
makes black men desirable sexual partners in a culture obsessed with sex. In
addition, the Afro-Americanization of white youth has been more a male than a
female affair given the prominence of male athletes and the cultural weight of
male pop artists. This process results in white youth—male and female—imitating
and emulating black male styles of walking, talking, dressing, and gesticulating
in relation to others. One irony of our present moment is that just as young
black men are murdered, maimed, and imprisoned in record numbers, their
styles have become disproportionately influential in shaping popular culture. For
most young black men, power is acquired by stylizing their bodies over space
and time in such a way that their bodies reflect their uniqueness and provoke
fear in others. To be "bad" is good not simply because it subverts the language of
the dominant white culture but also because it imposes a unique kind of order
for young black men on their own distinctive chaos and solicits an attention that
makes others pull back with some trepidation. This young black male style is a
form of self-identification and resistance in a hostile culture; it also is an instance
of machismo identity ready for violent encounters. Yet in a patriarchal society,
machismo identity is expected and even exalted—as with Rambo and Reagan.

Yet a black machismo style solicits primarily sexual encounters with women and violent encounters with other black men or aggressive police. In this way, the black male search for power often reinforces the myth of black male sexual prowess—a myth that tends to subordinate black and white women as objects of sexual pleasure. This search for power also usually results in a direct confrontation with the order-imposing authorities of the status quo, that is, the police or criminal justice system. The prevailing cultural crisis of many black men is the limited stylistic options of self-image and resistance in a culture obsessed with sex yet fearful of black sexuality.

This situation is even bleaker for most black gay men who reject the major stylistic option of black machismo identity, yet who are marginalized in white America and penalized in black America for doing so. In their efforts to be themselves, they are told they are not really "black men," not machismo-identified. Black gay men are often the brunt of talented black comics like Arsenio Hall and Damon Wayans. Yet behind the laughs lurks a black tragedy of major proportions: the refusal of white and black America to entertain seriously new stylistic options for black men caught in the deadly endeavor of rejecting black machismo identities.

The case of black women is quite different, partly because the dynamics of white and black patriarchy° affect them differently and partly because the degradation of black female heterosexuality in America makes black female lesbian sexuality a less frightful jump to make. This does not mean that black lesbians suffer less than black gays—in fact, they suffer more, principally owing to their lower economic status. But this does mean that the subculture of black lesbians is fluid and the boundaries are less policed precisely because black female sexuality in general is more devalued, hence more marginal in white and black America.

The dominant myth of black female sexual prowess constitutes black women as desirable sexual partners—yet the central role of the ideology of white female beauty attenuates the expected conclusion. Instead of black women being the most sought after "objects of sexual pleasure"—as in the case of black men—white women tend to occupy this "upgraded," that is, degraded, position primarily because white beauty plays a weightier role in sexual desirability for women in racist patriarchal America. The ideal of female beauty in this country puts a premium on lightness and softness mythically associated with white women and downplays the rich stylistic manners associated with black women. This operation is not simply more racist to black women than that at work in relation to black men; it also is more devaluing of women in general than that at work in relation to men in general. This means that black women are subject to more multilayered bombardments of racist assaults than black men in addition to the sexist assaults they receive from black men. Needless to say, most black men—especially professional ones—simply recycle this vulgar operation along

[18]**patriarchy** a system of organizing society so that inheritance passes through the fathers of families rather than mothers and, more generally, men have more authority, power, and legal rights than women

the axis of lighter hues that results in darker black women bearing more of the brunt than their already devalued lighter sisters. The psychic bouts with self-confidence, the existential agony over genuine desirability, and the social burden of bearing and usually nurturing black children under these circumstances breeds a spiritual strength of black women unbeknownst to most black men and nearly all other Americans.

20   As long as black sexuality remains a taboo subject, we cannot acknowledge, examine, or engage these tragic psychocultural facts of American life. Furthermore, our refusal to do so limits our ability to confront the overwhelming realities of the AIDS epidemic in America in general and in black America in particular. Although the dynamics of black male sexuality differ from those of black female sexuality, new stylistic options of self-image and resistance can be forged only when black women and men do so together. This is so not because all black people should be heterosexual or with black partners, but rather because all black people—including black children of so-called "mixed" couples—are affected deeply by the prevailing myths of black sexuality. These myths are part of a wider network of white supremacist lies whose authority and legitimacy must be undermined. In the long run, there is simply no way out for all of us other than living out the truths we proclaim about genuine humane interaction in our psychic and sexual lives. Only by living against the grain can we keep alive the possibility that the visceral feelings about black bodies fed by racist myths and promoted by market-driven quests for stimulation do not forever render us obsessed with sexuality and fearful of each other's humanity.

[1993]

1. West is an academic, a professor of religion and director of the Afro-American Studies program at Princeton University. What is West's *ethos* in this chapter? How does it relate to his style and the audience he intends to address?

2. West begins the chapter by saying, "Americans are obsessed with sex and fearful of black sexuality." At the end of the second paragraph, he says, "My thesis is that black sexuality is a taboo subject in white and black America and that a candid dialogue about black sexuality between and within these communities is requisite for healthy race relations in America." Some might perceive a contradiction between obsession and taboo. How does he try to explain that both can be true at the same time? Is his explanation plausible?

3. How does he support the second part of his thesis? Is his analysis useful over a decade after he wrote the chapter?

CHAPTER TWELVE

Spirit

INTRODUCTION

No matter how much science has learned about the workings of the human body, so far it has not explained consciousness or how consciousness arises from the chemistry and physics of what Hamlet called "this machine." Nevertheless, human beings have a persistent longing to think that there is an aspect of themselves that cannot be explained as merely material. Science might say that the universe was created by the operation of physical processes that were not driven by necessity to produce life. No natural laws required that life or the particular human form of it would be an outcome of their operation. Yet there seems to be a universal desire to understand who we are and why we are. Sometimes speculation about such questions involves the positing of and belief in a supernatural being who created and in one way or another governs the universe; sometimes people do not look to a deity to guarantee the value of the world or impose requirements for how people should behave in it. To look in other ways at the same contrast, we can note that the word *sacred* can apply to something set apart for and dedicated to a deity, but that the word *holy* comes from the Old English word for "whole," as if something is worthy of veneration when it is complete. Either way, humans seem to want to understand our relationship to the universe and the reasons for and meaning of our existence.

Some of the selections here are taken from sacred texts that have been considered foundational for one or more of the major religions of the world. The Hebrew Bible, the New Testament, and the Qur'an are considered to be, for their respective communities, repositories of truths regarding things of the spirit and guides for living. All of the selections engage questions such as what it means to be human, what we owe ourselves, and what we owe each other. You will find these themes in the selections of this unit as well as in others in the anthology. As you read, think about the ways that their writers use the techniques of literature to suggest transcendent themes.

POETRY

ARRESTED DEVELOPMENT

ARRESTED DEVELOPMENT, *as described in* Rolling Stone *magazine, is a group founded by Todd Thomas, a.k.a. Speech, who grew up in Tennessee and moved to Atlanta, Georgia, where he studied music business and management and decided to start a band. Arrested Development became Thomas's family and the springboard for his successful career as a songwriter. The band dissolved in 1996 and Speech has been a solo performer since.*

Fishin' 4 Religion

Grab the hook, grab the line
Grab the bait, grab the box and wait
Tackle and shackle the topic the faculty has chosen
Chosen by many, chosen by plenty, chosen by any
5   man or woman who understand
the topic that's known and
[Go by the dock] flock and clock the topic
as I drop my hook and get a bite
The reason I'm fishin' 4 a new religion
10 is my church makes me fall asleep
They're praising a God that watches you weep
and doesn't want you to do a damn thing about it
When they want change the preacher says "shout it"
Does shouting bring about change? I doubt it
15 All shouting does is make you lose your voice
So on the dock I sit in silence
staring at a sea that's full of violence
Scared to put my line in that water
coz it seems like there's no religion in there
20 Naively so I give it another go
Sitting in church hearing legitimate woes
Pastor tells the lady it'll be alright
Just pray so you can see the pearly gates so white
The lady prays and prays and prays and prays
25 and prays and prays and prays and prays . . . it's everlasting
"There's nothing wrong with praying?" It's what she's asking

She's asking the Lord to let her cope
so one day she can see the golden ropes
What you pray for God will give
to be able to cope in this world we live   30
The word "cope" and the word "change"
is directly opposite, not the same
She should have been praying to change her woes
but pastor said "Pray to cope with those"
The government is happy with most baptist churches   35
coz they don't do a damn thing to try to nurture
brothers and sisters on a revolution
Baptist teaches dying is the only solution
Passiveness causes others to pass us by
I throw my line till I've made my decision   40
until then, I'm still fishin' 4 religion

Fishin' 4 religion (11×)
Fish
[Believe !]
[Everybody in the house tonight . . . C'mon let me hear you say]   45
[Fishin' !]
                                                                  [1992]

1. What is the narrator's attitude toward the religion he finds in church?
2. Like most hip-hop, Arrested Development's song provides a great many
    sound effects in the verse. What are they?
3. What academic disciplines would help shed light on this song?

ASHVAGHOSHA

ASHVAGHOSHA, *first century Indian poet, wrote the first full-length biography of*
the Buddha. It is called Buddhacarita, or The Acts of the Buddha.

From The Legend of the Buddha Shakyamuni

4. The Awakening

In the course of time the women told him° how much they loved the groves
near the city, and how delightful they were. So, feeling like an elephant locked
up inside a house, he set his heart on making a journey outside the palace. The
king heard of the plans of his dearly beloved son, and arranged a pleasure excursion which would be worthy of his own affection and royal dignity, as well as of
his son's youth. But he gave orders that all the common folk with any kind of

---

[1]The protagonist, unnamed in the first paragraph, is Siddartha Gautama, who later became
a buddha. Born in 560 BCE in Nepal in the foothills of the Himalayas, he was the son of
Suddhodana, king of the Sakhyas.

affliction should be kept away from the royal road, because he feared that they might agitate the prince's sensitive mind. Very gently all cripples were driven away, and all those who were crazy, aged, ailing, and the like, and also all wretched beggars. So the royal highway became supremely magnificent.

The citizens jubilantly acclaimed the prince. But the Gods of the Pure Abode, when they saw that everyone was happy as if in Paradise, conjured up the illusion of an *old man,* so as to induce the king's son to leave his home. The prince's charioteer explained to him the meaning of old age. The prince reacted to this news like a bull when a lightning-flash crashes down near him. For his under-standing was purified by the noble intentions he had formed in his past lives and by the good deeds he had accumulated over countless aeons. In consequence his lofty soul was shocked to hear of old age. He sighed deeply, shook his head, fixed his gaze on the old man, surveyed the festive multitude, and, deeply perturbed, said to the charioteer: 'So that is how old age destroys indiscriminately the memory, beauty, and strength of all! And yet with such a sight before it the world goes on quite unperturbed. This being so, my son, turn round the horses, and travel back quickly to our palace! How can I delight to walk about in parks when my heart is full of fear of ageing?' So at the bidding of his master's son the charioteer reversed the chariot. And the prince went back into his palace, which now seemed empty to him, as a result of his anxious reflections.

On a second pleasure excursion the same gods created a *man with a diseased body.* When this fact was explained to him, the son of Shuddhodana was dismayed, trembled like the reflection of the moon on rippling water, and in his compassion he uttered these words in a low voice: 'This then is the calamity of disease, which afflicts people! The world sees it, and yet does not lose its confi-dent ways. Greatly lacking in insight it remains gay under the constant threat of disease. We will not continue this excursion, but go straight back to the palace! Since I have learnt of the danger of illness, my heart is repelled by pleasures and seems to shrink into itself.'

On a third excursion the same gods displayed a *corpse,* which only the prince and his charioteer could see being borne along the road. The charioteer again explained the meaning of this sight to the prince. Courageous though he was, the king's son, on hearing of death, was suddenly filled with dismay. Leaning his shoulder against the top of the chariot rail, he spoke these words in a forceful voice: 'This is the end which has been fixed for all, and yet the world forgets its fears and takes no heed! The hearts of men are surely hardened to fears, for they feel quite at ease even while travelling along the road to the next life. Turn back the chariot! This is no time or place for pleasure excursions. How could an intelligent person pay no heed at a time of disaster, when he knows of his impending destruction?'

5. Withdrawal from the Women

5 From then onwards the prince withdrew from contact with the women in the palace, and in answer to the reproaches of Udayin, the king's counsellor, he explained his new attitude in the following words: 'It is not that I despise the objects of sense, and I know full well that they make up what we call the

"world". But when I consider the impermanence of everything in this world, then I can find no delight in it. Yes, if this triad of old age, illness, and death did not exist, then all this loveliness would surely give me great pleasure. If only this beauty of women were imperishable, then my mind would certainly indulge in the passions, though, of course, they have their faults. But since even women attach no more value to their bodies after old age has drunk them up, to delight in them would clearly be a sign of delusion. If people, doomed to undergo old age, illness, and death, are carefree in their enjoyment with others who are in the same position, they behave like birds and beasts. And when you say that our holy books tell us of gods, sages, and heroes who, though high-minded, were addicted to sensuous passions, then that by itself should give rise to agitation, since they also are now extinct. Successful high-mindedness seems to me incompatible with both extinction and attachment to sensory concerns, and appears to require that one is in full control of oneself. This being so, you will not prevail upon me to devote myself to ignoble sense pleasures, for I am afflicted by ill and it is my lot to become old and to die. How strong and powerful must be your own mind, that in the fleeting pleasures of the senses you find substance! You cling to sense-objects among the most frightful dangers, even while you cannot help seeing all creation on the way to death. By contrast I become frightened and greatly alarmed when I reflect on the dangers of old age, death, and disease. I find neither peace nor contentment, and enjoyment is quite out of the question, for the world looks to me as if ablaze with an all-consuming fire. If a man has once grasped that death is quite inevitable, and if nevertheless greed arises in his heart, then he must surely have an iron will not to weep in this great danger, but to enjoy it.' This discourse indicated that the prince had come to a final decision and had combated the very foundations of sensuous passion. And it was the time of sunset.

6. The Flight

Even amidst the allure of the finest opportunities for sensuous enjoyment the Shakya king's son felt no contentment, and he could not regain a feeling of safety. He was, in fact, like a lion hit in the region of the heart by an arrow smeared with a potent poison. In the hope that a visit to the forest might bring him some peace, he left his palace with the king's consent, accompanied by an escort of ministers' sons, who were chosen for their reliability and their gift for telling entertaining stories. The prince rode out on the good horse Kanthaka, which looked splendid, for the bells of its bit were of fresh gold and its golden trappings beautiful with waving plumes. The beauties of the landscape and his longing for the forest carried him deep into the countryside. There he saw the soil being ploughed, and its surface, broken with the tracks of the furrows, looked like rippling water. The ploughs had torn up the sprouting grass, scattering tufts of grass here and there, and the land was littered with tiny creatures who had been killed and injured, worms, insects, and the like. The sight of all this grieved the prince as deeply as if he had witnessed the slaughter of his own kinsmen. He observed the ploughmen, saw how they suffered from wind, sun, and dust, and how the oxen were worn down by the labour of drawing. And in the supreme nobility of his mind he performed an act of supreme pity. He then alighted from his horse and walked gently and slowly over the ground, overcome with grief. He reflected on the generation and the passing of all living things, and in his distress he said to himself: 'How pitiful all this!'

His mind longed for solitude, he withdrew from the good friends who walked behind him, and went to a solitary spot at the foot of a rose-apple tree. The tree's lovely leaves were in constant motion, and the ground underneath it salubrious and green like beryl. There he sat down, reflected on the origination and passing away of all that lives, and then he worked on his mind in such a way that, with this theme as a basis, it became stable and concentrated. When he had won through to mental stability, he was suddenly freed from all desire for sense-objects and from cares of any kind. He had reached the first stage of trance, which is calm amidst applied and discursive thinking. In his case it had already at this stage a supramundane purity. He had obtained that concentration of mind which is born of detachment, and is accompanied by the highest rapture and joy, and in this state of trance his mind considered the destiny of the world correctly, as it is: 'Pitiful, indeed, that these people who themselves are helpless and doomed to undergo illness, old age, and destruction, should, in the ignorant blindness of their self-intoxication, show so little respect for others who are likewise victims of old age, disease, and death! But now that I have discerned this supreme Dharma, it would be unworthy and unbecoming if I, who am so constituted, should show no respect for others whose constitution is essentially the same as mine.' When he thus gained insight into the fact that the blemishes of disease, old age, and death vitiate the very core of this world, he lost at the same moment all self-intoxication, which normally arises from pride in one's own strength, youth, and vitality. He now was neither glad nor grieved; all doubt, lassitude, and sleepiness disappeared; sensuous excitements could no longer influence him; and hatred and contempt for others were far from his mind.

7. The Apparition of a Mendicant

As this understanding, pure and dustless, grew farther in his noble soul, he saw a man glide towards him, who remained invisible to other men, and who appeared in the guise of a *religious mendicant*. The king's son asked him: 'Tell me who you are', and the answer was: 'O Bull among men, I am a recluse who, terrified by birth and death, ha[s] adopted a homeless life to win salvation. Since all that lives is to extinction doomed, salvation from this world is what I wish, and so I search for that most blessed state in which extinction is unknown. Kinsmen and strangers mean the same to me, and greed and hate for all this world of sense have ceased to be. Wherever I may be, that is my home—the root of a tree, a deserted sanctuary, a hill or wood. Possessions I have none, no expectations either. Intent on the supreme goal I wander about, accepting any alms I may receive.' Before the prince's very eyes he then flew up into the sky. For he was a denizen of the heavens, who had seen other Buddhas in the past, and who had come to him in this form so as to remind him of the task before him.

When that being had risen like a bird into the sky, the best of men was elated and amazed. Then and there he intuitively perceived the Dharma, and made plans to leave his palace for the homeless life. And soon after returning to his palace he decided to escape during the night. The gods knew of his intention, and saw to it that the palace doors were open. He descended from the upper part of the palace, looked with disgust upon the women lying about in all kinds of disorderly positions, and unhesitatingly went to the stables in the outermost courtyard. He roused Chandaka, the groom, and ordered him quickly to bring the horse Kanthaka. 'For I want to depart from here to-day, and win the deathless state!'

8. The Dismissal of Chandaka

They rode off, till they came to a hermitage, where the prince took off his jewels, gave them to Chandaka and dismissed him with this message to his father, king Shuddhodana: 'So that my father's grief may be dispelled, tell him that I have gone to this penance grove for the purpose of putting an end to old age and death, and by no means because I yearn for Paradise, or because I feel no affection for him, or from moody resentment. Since I have left for the homeless life with this end in view, there is no reason why he should grieve for me. Some day in any case all unions must come to an end, however long they may have lasted. It is just because we must reckon with perpetual separation that I am determined to win salvation, for then I shall no more be torn away from my kindred. There is no reason to grieve for me who have left for the homeless life so as to quit all grief. Rather should one grieve over those who greedily cling to those sensuous passions in which all grief is rooted. My father will perhaps say that it was too early for me to leave for the forest. But then there is no such thing as a wrong season for Dharma, our hold on life being so uncertain. This very day therefore I will begin to strive for the highest good— that is my firm resolve! Death confronts me all the time—how do I know how much of life is still at my disposal?'

The charioteer once more tried to dissuade the prince, and received this reply: 'Chandaka, stop this grief over parting from me! All those whom birth estranged from the oneness of Dharma must one day go their separate ways. Even if affection should prevent me from leaving my kinsfolk just now of my own accord, in due course death would tear us apart, and in that we would have no say. Just think of my mother, who bore me in her womb with great longing and with many pains. Fruitless proves her labour now. What am I now to her, what she to me? Birds settle on a tree for a while, and then go their separate ways again. The meeting of all living beings must likewise inevitably end in their parting. Clouds meet and then they fly apart again, and in the same light I see the union of living beings and their parting. This world passes away, and disappoints all hopes of everlasting attachment. It is therefore unwise to have a sense of ownership for people who are united with us as in a dream—for a short while only, and not in fact. The colouring of their leaves is connate to trees, and yet they must let it go; how much more must this apply to the separation of disparate things! This being so, you had better go away now, and cease, my friend, from grieving! But if your love for me still holds you back, go now to the king, and then return to me. And, please, give this message to the people in Kapilavastu who keep their eyes on me: "Cease to feel affection for him, and hear his unshakeable resolve: 'Either he will extinguish old age and death, and then you shall quickly see him again; or he will go to perdition, because his strength has failed him and he could not achieve his purpose'."'

9. The Practice of Austerities

From then onwards the prince led a religious life, and diligently studied the various systems practised among ascetics and yogins. After a time the sage, in search of a lonely retreat, went to live on the bank of the river Nairañjana, the purity of which appealed to that of his own valour. Five mendicants had gone there before him to lead a life of austerity, in scrupulous observance of their religious vows, and proud of their control over the five senses. When the monks saw him there, they waited upon him in their desire for liberation, just as the objects of sense wait upon a lordly man to whom the merits of his past lives have given wealth, and the health to enjoy them. They greeted him reverently, bowed before him, followed his instructions, and placed themselves as pupils under his control, just as the restless senses serve the mind. He, however, embarked on further austerities, and particularly on starvation as the means which seemed most likely to put an end to birth and death. In his desire for quietude he emaciated his body for six years, and carried out a number of strict methods of fasting, very hard for men to endure. At mealtimes he was content with a single jujube fruit, a single sesamum seed, and a single grain of rice—so intent he was on winning the further, the unbounded, shore of Samsara. The bulk of his body was greatly reduced by this self-torture, but by way of compensation his psychic power grew correspondingly more and more. Wasted away though he was, his glory and majesty remained unimpaired, and his sight gladdened the eyes of those who looked upon him. It was as welcome to them as the full moon in autumn to the white lotuses that bloom at night. His fat, flesh, and blood had all gone. Only skin and bone remained. Exhausted though he was, his depth seemed unexhausted like that of the ocean itself.

After a time, however, it became clear to him that this kind of excessive self-torture merely wore out his body without any useful result. Impelled both by his dread of becoming and by his longing for Buddhahood, he reasoned as follows: 'This is not the Dharma° which leads to dispassion, to enlightenment, to emancipation. That method which some time ago I found under the rose-apple tree (see paragraphs 6–7), that was more certain in its results. But those meditations cannot be carried out in this weakened condition; therefore I must take steps to increase again the strength of this body. When that is worn down and exhausted by hunger and thirst, the mind in its turn must feel the strain, that mental organ which must reap the fruit. No, inward calm is needed for success! Inward calm cannot be maintained unless physical strength is constantly and

[13]**Dharma** the teachings of the Buddha

intelligently replenished. Only if the body is reasonably nourished can undue
strain on the mind be avoided. When the mind is free from strain and is serene,
then the faculty of Transic concentration can arise in it. When thought is joined
to Transic concentration, then it can advance through the various stages of
trance. We can then win the dharmas which finally allow us to gain that highest
state, so hard to reach, which is tranquil, ageless, and deathless. And without
proper nourishment this procedure is quite impossible.'

10. Nandabala's Gift

His courage was unbroken, but his boundless intellect led him to the decision
that from now on again he needed proper food. In preparation for his first meal
he went into the Nairañjana river to bathe. Afterwards he slowly and painfully
worked his way up the river bank, and the trees on the slope reverently bent
low their branches to give him a helping hand. At the instigation of the deities,
Nandabala, daughter of the overseer of the cowherds, happened to pass there,
her heart bursting with joy. She looked like the foamy blue waters of the
Yamuna river, with her blue dress, and her arms covered with blazing white
shells. When she saw him, faith further increased her joy, her lotus eyes opened
wide, she prostrated herself before him, and begged him to accept milk-rice from
her. He did, and his meal marked the most fruitful moment of her life. For
himself, however, he gained the strength to win enlightenment. Now that his
body had been nourished, the Sage's bodily frame became fully rounded again.
But the five mendicants left him, because they had formed the opinion that he
had now quite turned away from the holy life—just as in the Samkhya system
the five elements leave the thinking soul once it is liberated. Accompanied only
by his resolution, he proceeded to the root of a sacred fig-tree, where the ground
was carpeted with green grass. For he was definitely determined to win full
enlightenment soon.

The incomparable sound of his footsteps woke Kala, a serpent of high rank,   15
who was as strong as a king elephant. Aware that the great Sage had definitely
determined on enlightenment, he uttered this eulogy: 'Your steps, O Sage,
resound like thunder reverberating in the earth; the light that issues from your
body shines like the sun: No doubt that you to-day will taste the fruit you so
desire! The flocks of blue jays which are whirling round up in the sky show their
respect by keeping their right sides towards you; the air is full of gentle breezes:
It is quite certain that to-day you will become a Buddha.'

The Sage thereupon collected fresh grass from a grass cutter, and, on reaching
the foot of the auspicious great tree, sat down and made a vow to win enlightenment. He then adopted the cross-legged posture, which is the best of all because
so immovable, the limbs being massive like the coils of a sleeping serpent. And
he said to himself: 'I shall not change this my position so long as I have not done
what I set out to do!' Then the denizens of the heavens felt exceedingly joyous,
the herds of beasts, as well as the birds, made no noise at all, and even the trees
ceased to rustle when struck by the wind: for the Lord had seated himself with
his spirit quite resolved.

11. The Defeat of Mara

Because the great Sage, the scion of a line of royal seers, had made his vow to win emancipation, and had seated himself in the effort to carry it out, the whole world rejoiced—but Mara, the inveterate foe of the true Dharma, shook with fright. People address him gladly as the God of Love, the one who shoots with flower-arrows, and yet they dread this Mara as the one who rules events connected with a life of passion, as one who hates the very thought of freedom. He had with him his three sons—Flurry, Gaiety, and Sullen Pride—and his three daughters—Discontent, Delight, and Thirst. These asked him why he was so disconcerted in his mind. And he replied to them with these words: 'Look over there at that sage, clad in the armour of determination, with truth and spiritual virtue as his weapons, the arrows of his intellect drawn ready to shoot! He has sat down with the firm intention of conquering my realm. No wonder that my mind is plunged in deep despondency! If he should succeed in overcoming me, and could proclaim to the world the way to final beatitude, then my realm would be empty to-day, like that of the king of Videha of whom we hear in the Epics that he lost his kingdom because he misconducted himself by carrying off a Brahmin's daughter. But so far he has not yet won the eye of full knowledge. He is still within my sphere of influence. While there is time I therefore will attempt to break his solemn purpose, and throw myself against him like the rush of a swollen river breaking against the embankment!'

But Mara could achieve nothing against the Bodhisattva, and he and his army were defeated, and fled in all directions—their elation gone, their toil rendered fruitless, their rocks, logs, and trees scattered everywhere. They behaved like a hostile army whose commander had been slain in battle. So Mara, defeated, ran away together with his followers. The great seer, free from the dust of passion, victorious over darkness' gloom, had vanquished him. And the moon, like a maiden's gentle smile, lit up the heavens, while a rain of sweet-scented flowers, filled with moisture, fell down on the earth from above.

12. The Enlightenment

Now that he had defeated Mara's violence by his firmness and calm, the Bodhisattva, possessed of great skill in Transic meditation, put himself into trance, intent on discerning both the ultimate reality of things and the final goal of existence. After he had gained complete mastery over all the degrees and kinds of trance:

20   1. In the *first watch* of the night he recollected the successive series of his former births. 'There was I so and so; that was my name; deceased from there I came here'—in this way he remembered thousands of births, as though living them over again. When he had recalled his own births and deaths in all these various lives of his, the Sage, full of pity, turned his compassionate mind towards other living beings, and he thought to himself: 'Again and again they must leave the people they regard as their own, and must go on elsewhere, and that without ever stopping. Surely this world is unprotected and helpless, and like a wheel it turns round and round.' As he continued steadily to recollect the past

thus, he came to the definite conviction that this world of Samsara is as unsubstantial as the pith of a plantain tree.

2. Second to none in valour, he then, in the *second watch* of the night, acquired the supreme heavenly eye, for he himself was the best of all those who have sight. Thereupon with the perfectly pure heavenly eye he looked upon the entire world, which appeared to him as though reflected in a spotless mirror. He saw that the decease and rebirth of beings depend on whether they have done superior or inferior deeds. And his compassionateness grew still further. It became clear to him that no security can be found in this flood of Samsaric existence, and that the threat of death is ever-present. Beset on all sides, creatures can find no resting place. In this way he surveyed the five places of rebirth with his heavenly eye. And he found nothing substantial in the world of becoming, just as no core of heartwood is found in a plantain tree when its layers are peeled off one by one.

3. Then, as the *third watch* of that night drew on, the supreme master of trance turned his meditation to the real and essential nature of this world: 'Alas, living beings wear themselves out in vain! Over and over again they are born, they age, die, pass on to a new life, and are reborn! What is more, greed and dark delusion obscure their sight, and they are blind from birth. Greatly apprehensive, they yet do not know how to get out of this great mass of ill.' He then surveyed the twelve links of conditioned co-production, and saw that, beginning with ignorance, they lead to old age and death, and, beginning with the cessation of ignorance, they lead to the cessation of birth, old age, death, and all kinds of ill.

When the great seer had comprehended that where there is no ignorance whatever, there also the karma-formations are stopped—then he had achieved a correct knowledge of all there is to be known, and he stood out in the world as a Buddha. He passed through the eight stages of Transic insight, and quickly reached their highest point. From the summit of the world downwards he could detect no self anywhere. Like the fire, when its fuel is burnt up, he became tranquil. He had reached perfection, and he thought to himself: 'This is the authentic Way on which in the past so many great seers, who also knew all higher and all lower things, have travelled on to ultimate and real truth. And now I have obtained it!'

4. At that moment, in the *fourth watch* of the night, when dawn broke and all the ghosts that move and those that move not went to rest, the great seer took up the position which knows no more alteration, and the leader of all reached the state of all-knowledge. When, through his Buddhahood, he had cognized this fact, the earth swayed like a woman drunken with wine, the sky shone bright with the Siddhas who appeared in crowds in all the directions, and the mighty drums of thunder resounded through the air. Pleasant breezes blew softly, rain fell from a cloudless sky, flowers and fruits dropped from the trees out of season—in an effort, as it were, to show reverence for him. Mandarava flowers and lotus blossoms, and also water lilies made of gold and beryl, fell from the sky on to the ground near the Shakya sage, so that it looked like a place in the world of the gods. At that moment no one anywhere was angry, ill, or sad;

no one did evil, none was proud; the world became quite quiet, as though it had reached full perfection. Joy spread through the ranks of those gods who longed for salvation; joy also spread among those who lived in the regions below. Everywhere the virtuous were strengthened, the influence of Dharma increased, and the world rose from the dirt of the passions and the darkness of ignorance. Filled with joy and wonder at the Sage's work, the seers of the solar race who had been protectors of men, who had been royal seers, who had been great seers, stood in their mansions in the heavens and showed him their reverence. The great seers among the hosts of invisible beings could be heard widely proclaiming his fame. All living things rejoiced and sensed that things went well. Mara alone felt deep displeasure, as though subjected to a sudden fall.

25   For seven days He dwelt there—his body gave him no trouble, his eyes never closed, and he looked into his own mind. He thought: 'Here I have found freedom', and he knew that the longings of his heart had at last come to fulfilment. Now that he had grasped the principle of causation, and finally convinced himself of the lack of self in all that is, he roused himself again from his deep trance, and in his great compassion he surveyed the world with his Buddha-eye, intent on giving it peace. When, however, he saw on the one side the world lost in low views and confused efforts, thickly covered with the dirt of the passions, and saw on the other side the exceeding subtlety of the Dharma of emancipation, he felt inclined to take no action. But when he weighed up the significance of the pledge to enlighten all beings he had taken in the past, he became again more favourable to the idea of proclaiming the path to Peace. Reflecting in his mind on this question, he also considered that, while some people have a great deal of passion, others have but little. As soon as Indra and Brahma, the two chiefs of those who dwell in the heavens, had grasped the Sugata's intention to proclaim the path to Peace, they shone brightly and came up to him, the weal of the world their concern. He remained there on his seat, free from all evil and successful in his aim. The most excellent Dharma which he had seen was his most excellent companion. His two visitors gently and reverently spoke to him these words, which were meant for the weal of the world: 'Please do not condemn all those that live as unworthy of such treasure! Oh, please engender pity in your heart for beings in this world! So varied is their endowment, and while some have much passion, others have only very little. Now that you, O Sage, have yourself crossed the ocean of the world of becoming, please rescue also the other living beings who have sunk so deep into suffering! As a generous lord shares his wealth, so may also you bestow your own virtues on others! Most of those who know what for them is good in this world and the next, act only for their own advantage. In the world of men and in heaven it is hard to find anyone who is impelled by concern for the weal of the world.' Having made this request to the great seer, the two gods returned to their celestial abode by the way they had come. And the sage pondered over their words. In consequence he was confirmed in his decision to set the world free.

Then came the time for the alms-round, and the World-Guardians of the four quarters presented the seer with begging-bowls. Gautama accepted the four, but for the sake of his Dharma he turned them into one. At that time two merchants of a passing caravan came that way. Instigated by a friendly deity, they joyfully saluted the seer, and, elated in their hearts, gave him alms. They were the first to do so.

After that the sage saw that Arada and Udraka Ramaputra were the two people best equipped to grasp the Dharma. But then he saw that both had gone to live among the gods in heaven. His mind thereupon turned to the five mendicants. In order to proclaim the path to Peace, thereby dispelling the darkness of ignorance, just as the rising sun conquers the darkness of night, Gautama betook himself to the blessed city of Kashi, to which Bhimaratha gave his love, and which is adorned with the Varanasi river and with many splendid forests. Then, before he carried out his wish to go into the region of Kashi, the Sage, whose eyes were like those of a bull, and whose gait like that of an elephant in rut, once more fixed his steady gaze on the root of the Bodhi-tree, after he had turned his entire body like an elephant.

13. The Meeting with the Mendicant

He had fulfilled his task, and now, calm and majestic, went on alone, though it seemed that a large retinue accompanied him. A mendicant, intent on Dharma, saw him on the road, and in wonderment folded his hands and said to him: 'The senses of others are restless like horses, but yours have been tamed. Other beings are passionate, but your passions have ceased. Your form shines like the moon in the night-sky, and you appear to be refreshed by the sweet savour of a wisdom newly tasted. Your features shine with intellectual power, you have become master over your senses, and you have the eyes of a mighty bull. No doubt that you have achieved your aim. Who then is your teacher, who has taught you this supreme felicity?' But he replied: 'No teacher have I. None need I venerate, and none must I despise. Nirvana have I now obtained, and I am not the same as others are. Quite by myself, you see, have I the Dharma won. Completely have I understood what must be understood, though others failed to understand it. That is the reason why I am a Buddha. The hostile forces of defilement I have vanquished. That is the reason why I should be known as one whose self is calmed. And, having calmed myself, I now am on my way to Varanasi, to work the weal of fellow-beings still oppressed by many ills. There shall I beat the deathless Dharma's drum, unmoved by pride, not tempted by renown. Having myself crossed the ocean of suffering, I must help others to cross it. Freed myself, I must set others free. This is the vow which I made in the past when I saw all that lives in distress.' In reply the mendicant whispered to himself, 'Most remarkable, indeed!' and he decided that it would be better not to stay with the Buddha. He accordingly went his way, although repeatedly he looked back at Him with eyes full of wonderment, and not without some degree of longing desire. . . .   [1ˢᵗ c. CE]

1. What initially leads the prince to reconsider his life and what emotion drives him?
2. In Buddhism, the human being is described sometimes as a chariot: The horses are the senses, the ground the world over which we go, the mind

is the reins, and the driver the soul. What are some of the other images used by the writer in this first part of the story?

3. What, in section 6, is the first step in the prince's journey to understanding?

4. What are the lessons and implied criticisms in the sections on austerity (9 and 10)?

5. There are serpents in many cultures' traditions; with what forces does Kala seem to be aligned?

6. Once the Sage, as we must now call him, sits beneath the tree and vows to "do what he has set out to do," he must go through several trials to achieve his aim. In your own words what are they?

7. What images are used to describe Buddhahood?

8. In your own words, describe what the Sage had found.

JOHN DONNE

For biographical notes, see p. 256.

Holy Sonnet 10: Death, Be Not Proud

Death, be not proud, though some have called thee
Mighty and dreadful, for thou art not so;
For those whom thou think'st thou dost overthrow,
Die not, poor Death, nor yet canst thou kill me.
5 From rest and sleep, which but thy pictures be,
Much pleasure; then from thee much more must flow,
And soonest our best men with thee do go,
Rest of their bones, and soul's delivery.
Thou art slave to fate, chance, kings, and desperate men,
10 And dost with poison, war, and sickness dwell;
And poppy° or charms can make us sleep as well
And better than thy stroke; why swell'st thou then?
One short sleep past, we wake eternally,
And death shall be no more; Death, thou shalt die.   [1611]

[11]**poppy** the flower of the opium plant, which can be turned into a drug

1. The "some" in line 1 might include people like Sir Walter Raleigh, who wrote in his *History of the World,*

   O eloquent, just and mighty Death! Whom none could advise, thou hast persuaded; what none hath dared, thou has done; and whom all the world hath flattered, thou only hath cast out of the world and despised: thou hast drawn together all the far stretched greatness, all the pride, cruelty and ambition of man, and covered it over with these two narrow words, Hic jacet [here lies . . .].[1]

In "Holy Sonnet 10," how does Donne argue against this view?

2. Are the arguments effective? What difference does it make that the poem takes several different approaches? How does the final threat at the end of l. 14 affect your opinion of the arguments that precede it?

3. How does the rhyme scheme of this sonnet compare to the Petrarchan and Shakespearean patterns? How does it influence the shape of the poem?

4. How might this poem relate to Holy Sonnet 14 (see p. 122)?

[1]Quoted in John Carey, *John Donne, Life, Mind and Art* (New York: Oxford University Press, 1981), 198.

THOM GUNN

THOM GUNN *(1929–) was brought up in wartime London, completing two years of National Service in the British Army. He received a degree at Cambridge University and his first book of poetry,* Fighting Terms, *was published in 1954. That year, he entered Stanford as a graduate student and then taught at Berkeley, where he is a Senior Lecturer in English. A resident of San Francisco since 1961, he was the recipient of a MacArthur Fellowship. His book,* The Man with Night Sweats, *centers on street people and people with AIDS.*

Memory Unsettled

Your pain still hangs in air,
Sharp motes of it suspended;
The voice of your despair—
That also is not ended:

When near your death a friend   5
Asked you what he could do,
'Remember me,' you said.
We will remember you.

Once when you went to see
Another with a fever   10
In a like hospital bed,
With terrible hothouse cough
And terrible hothouse shiver
That soaked him and then dried him,
And you perceived that he   15
Had to be comforted,

You climbed in there beside him
And hugged him plain in view,
Though you were sick enough,
And had your own fears too.   20

[1994]

1. What does the form of this poem tell you about its meaning?
2. Can you explain the title of the poem? What is the meaning of the sick friend's act?

HEBREW BIBLE
Book of Leviticus
Chapter 19

And HaShem° spoke unto Moses, saying:

Speak unto all the congregation of the children of Israel, and say unto them:
 Ye shall be holy; for I HaShem your G-d° am holy.

Ye shall fear every man his mother, and his father, and ye shall keep My
 sabbaths: I am HaShem your G-d.

Turn ye not unto the idols, nor make to yourselves molten gods: I am
 HaShem your G-d.

5 And when ye offer a sacrifice of peace-offerings unto HaShem, ye shall offer
 it that ye may be accepted.

It shall be eaten the same day ye offer it, and on the morrow; and if aught
 remain until the third day, it shall be burnt with fire.

And if it be eaten at all on the third day, it is a vile thing; it shall not be
 accepted.

But every one that eateth it shall bear his iniquity, because he hath profaned
 the holy thing of HaShem; and that soul shall be cut off from his people.

And when ye reap the harvest of your land, thou shalt not wholly reap the
 corner of thy field, neither shalt thou gather the gleaning of thy harvest.

10 And thou shalt not glean thy vineyard, neither shalt thou gather the fallen
 fruit of thy vineyard; thou shalt leave them for the poor and for the
 stranger: I am HaShem your G-d.

Ye shall not steal; neither shall ye deal falsely, nor lie one to another.

And ye shall not swear by My name falsely, so that thou profane the name of
 thy G-d: I am HaShem.

Thou shalt not oppress thy neighbour, nor rob him; the wages of a hired
 servant shall not abide with thee all night until the morning.

Thou shalt not curse the deaf, nor put a stumbling-block before the blind, but
 thou shalt fear thy G-d: I am HaShem.

15 Ye shall do no unrighteousness in judgment; thou shalt not respect the
 person of the poor, nor favour the person of the mighty; but in
 righteousness shalt thou judge thy neighbour.

Thou shalt not go up and down as a talebearer among thy people; neither
 shalt thou stand idly by the blood of thy neighbour: I am HaShem.

[1]**HaShem** the Lord [2]**HaShem your G-d** the Lord your God (Some devout Jews use the
hyphen to avoid writing down the name of God.)

Thou shalt not hate thy brother in thy heart; thou shalt surely rebuke thy neighbour, and not bear sin because of him.

Thou shalt not take vengeance, nor bear any grudge against the children of thy people, but thou shalt love thy neighbour as thyself: I am HaShem.

Ye shall keep My statutes. Thou shalt not let thy cattle gender with a diverse kind; thou shalt not sow thy field with two kinds of seed; neither shall there come upon thee a garment of two kinds of stuff mingled together.

And whosoever lieth carnally with a woman, that is a bondmaid, designated 20 for a man, and not at all redeemed, nor was freedom given her; there shall be inquisition; they shall not be put to death, because she was not free.

And he shall bring his forfeit unto HaShem, unto the door of the tent of meeting, even a ram for a guilt-offering.

And the priest shall make atonement for him with the ram of the guilt-offering before HaShem for his sin which he hath sinned; and he shall be forgiven for his sin which he hath sinned.

And when ye shall come into the land, and shall have planted all manner of trees for food, then ye shall count the fruit thereof as forbidden; three years shall it be as forbidden unto you; it shall not be eaten.

And in the fourth year all the fruit thereof shall be holy, for giving praise unto HaShem.

But in the fifth year may ye eat of the fruit thereof, that it may yield unto 25 you more richly the increase thereof: I am HaShem your G-d.

Ye shall not eat with the blood; neither shall ye practise divination nor sooth-saying.

Ye shall not round the corners of your heads, neither shalt thou mar the corners of thy beard.

Ye shall not make any cuttings in your flesh for the dead, nor imprint any marks upon you: I am HaShem.

Profane not thy daughter, to make her a harlot, lest the land fall into harlotry, and the land become full of lewdness.

Ye shall keep My sabbaths, and reverence My sanctuary: I am HaShem. 30

Turn ye not unto the ghosts, nor unto familiar spirits; seek them not out, to be defiled by them: I am HaShem your G-d.

Thou shalt rise up before the hoary head, and honour the face of the old man, and thou shalt fear thy G-d: I am HaShem.

And if a stranger sojourn with thee in your land, ye shall not do him wrong.

The stranger that sojourneth with you shall be unto you as the home-born among you, and thou shalt love him as thyself; for ye were strangers in the land of Egypt: I am HaShem your G-d.

Ye shall do no unrighteousness in judgment, in meteyard,° in weight, or in 35 measure.

---

[35]**meteyard** a measure of length

Just balances, just weights, a just ephah,° and a just hin,° shall ye have: I am
   HaShem your G-d, who brought you out of the land of Egypt.
And ye shall observe all My statutes, and all Mine ordinances, and do them: I
   am HaShem.   [7th c. BCE]

³⁶**ephah** a dry measure of grain   **hin** a liquid measure

1. Leviticus gives a second version of the giving of the Ten Commandments
   (the first is in Exodus), with less emphasis on narrative and more on laws,
   of which there are, in this version, many more than ten. It is presented as
   the voice of God[1] speaking to Moses, who is to transmit it to the whole
   community. The formula in verse 2 is repeated in various forms throughout
   the chapter. What is its argument? You might find it useful to compare the
   Jewish Publication Society translation above to these other translations:
   King James: Ye shall be holy: for I the LORD your
   God am holy.[2]
   Kaplan Annotated Pentateuch (Jewish Interpretation): You must be holy, since
   I am God your Lord [and] I am holy.[3]
2. What does the selection of laws in this chapter tell us about what God values?
3. What are the arguments implied by 34 and 36?

[1]The text deforms the word because committing the holy name of the infinite God to a
material substance that will decay is considered sacrilege.
[2]The Bible, King James Version, The Electronic Text Center, University of Virginia,
http://etext.lib.virginia.edu/kjv.browse.html (accessed 27 June 2004).
[3]Navigating the Bible II,
http://bible.ort.org/books/pentd2.asp?ACTION=displaypage&BOOK=3&CHAPTER=
19#P19 (accessed 27 June 2004).

GERARD MANLEY HOPKINS

GERARD MANLEY HOPKINS *(1844–89), the eldest of five children in a High
Anglican family, won a scholarship to Balliol College, Oxford. Attracted to the idea
of becoming a painter in the style of the Pre-Raphaelites, Hopkins was even more
deeply committed to the Catholic religion through his contact with John Henry
Newman, and not only converted, but became a Jesuit priest. At first, he felt that
poetry was not seemly for a priest, but in a few years, once again began to write,
learned Welsh, and began to apply its rhythms to his theories and practice of
"sprung rhythm." Because many of his poetic innovations seemed too radical to be
printed, he published very little in his lifetime.*

[As Kingfishers Catch Fire, Dragonflies Draw Flame]

As kingfishers catch fire, dragonflies draw flame;
   As tumbled over rim in roundy wells
   Stones ring; like each tucked° string tells, each hung bell's

³**tucked** touched

Bow swung finds tongue to fling out broad its name;
Each mortal thing does one thing and the same: 5
    Deals out that being indoors each one dwells;
    Selves—goes itself; *myself* it speaks and spells,
Crying *What I do is me: for that I came.*

I say more: the just man justices;
    Keeps gráce: thát keeps all his goings graces;   10
Acts in God's eye what in God's eye he is—
    Chríst. For Christ plays in ten thousand places,
Lovely in limbs, and lovely in eyes not his
    To the Father through the features of men's faces.   [1918]

1. What is the effect of the similes at the start of the poem? Why are there so many?
2. What is the "more" that the sestet promises?
3. How does the form of the poem relate to traditional sonnets?
4. The poem may be talking about something similar to Maslow's self-actualization (see p. 436). Does his term seem useful for understanding the poem? What in the poem suggests the analogy? What are the limits of Maslow's piece as an interpretive framework for the poem?

THE KING JAMES BIBLE

Luke 10: 25–37

And, behold, a certain lawyer stood up, and tempted him, saying, Master,   25
    what shall I do to inherit eternal life?
He said unto him, What is written in the law? how readest thou?
And he answering said, Thou shalt love the Lord thy God with all thy heart,
    and with all thy soul, and with all thy strength, and with all thy mind;
    and thy neighbour as thyself.
And he said unto him, Thou hast answered right: this do, and thou shalt live.
But he, willing to justify himself, said unto Jesus, And who is my neighbour?
And Jesus answering said, A certain man went down from Jerusalem to   30
    Jericho, and fell among thieves, which stripped him of his raiment, and
    wounded him, and departed, leaving him half dead.
And by chance there came down a certain priest that way: and when he saw
    him, he passed by on the other side.
And likewise a Levite,° when he was at the place, came and looked on him,
    and passed by on the other side.
But a certain Samaritan,° as he journeyed, came where he was: and when he
    saw him, he had compassion on him,

---

[32]**Levite** member of the tribe of Levi, one of the families of Israel   [33]**Samaritan** a Jew
from a tradition different from that of the Levite

And went to him, and bound up his wounds, pouring in oil and wine, and set him on his own beast, and brought him to an inn, and took care of him.

35 And on the morrow when he departed, he took out two pence, and gave them to the host, and said unto him, Take care of him; and whatsoever thou spendest more, when I come again, I will repay thee.

Which now of these three, thinkest thou, was neighbour unto him that fell among the thieves?

And he said, He that shewed mercy on him. Then said Jesus unto him, Go, and do thou likewise. [Late 1ˢᵗ c. CE]

1. This story is commonly classified as a parable, that is to say, a story meant to teach. What is being taught here?
2. There is a great deal of detail given in the story regarding the specific things that the Good Samaritan does to assist the victim of the thieves. Why?
3. What is the relationship between this passage and Leviticus 19.18? What is its relationship to Sura 89 in the Qur'an?

THE GENEROUS QUR'AN

Sura 89
The Dawn

In the Name of God the Compassionate the Caring

By the dawn
By the nights ten
By the odd and the even
By the night as it eases away
5 Is there not in that an oath for the thoughtful mind

Did you not see what your lord did to 'Ad°—
great pillared Íram°
like nothing created in this land before—
and Thamúd° with its carvings in the river bed rock
10 and Pharoah of the tent pegs
who spread oppression through their lands
and compounded their corruption?

Your lord brought down upon them the lash of pain
Your lord is in hiding and waits

---

⁶**Ad** an ancient Arabian civilization, the destruction of which is often mentioned as an example to Thamúd ⁷**Íram** a city with many pillars ⁹**Thamúd** an ancient Arabian civilization mentioned in the writings of Aristo, Ptolemy, and Pliny. It was defeated by the Babylonian king, Sargon II (8th century BCE).

Such is the human being that when his lord tries him with generosity   15
    and bounty he says: my lord has honored me
but when his lord tries him with hunger and lack he says:
    my lord has treated me with disdain

But no. To the orphan you are ungiving
You do not demand food for those who hunger
You feed on inheritances and devour
You love possessions with a love consuming   20

Rather. When the earth is split apart, splitting, splitting
When the lord and the angels approach rank on rank arrayed
When on that day Jahannam° is brought close then the human being will
    remember and what good will it do him that he remembers?
Saying: If only I had made provision for my life
On that day no one else will suffer his pain   25
No one will be held to the covenant he made but he

O soul made peaceful
return to your lord accepted and accepting
Come in among my servants
and in my garden, enter   [Early 7th c. CE]   30

²³**Jahannam** hell

1. This sura seems to address itself particularly to the concerns of the orphan.
   Why?
2. The tone of this sura shifts toward the final lines. Describe this shift and its
   implications for meaning.
3. In this sura, as in many of our readings, the implication could be that
   misfortune eventually falls upon those who lack generosity though they
   prosper. Does this suggest a world-view in which people are ultimately
   responsible for what they suffer?

DYLAN THOMAS

DYLAN THOMAS *(1914–53) was interested in literature and language from an
early age, but was shy and sickly, and dropped out of school at sixteen. His first
book,* Eighteen Poems, *published to great acclaim when he was twenty,
announced his departure from the classical forms and social themes of Eliot and
Auden and his immersion in intense lyricism and idiosyncratic language. His
reading tours in the United States made him immensely popular; his theatrical
delivery, heavy drinking, roaring public displays of temper, and the tremendously
moving way he read his poetry aloud created a persona that made him a legend. He
died after a long drinking bout in New York City in 1953 at the age of 39. His books
include* Twenty-five Poems *(1936),* The World I Breathe *(1939),* The Map of

Love *(1939)*, New Poems *(1942)*, New Poems *(1943)*, Deaths and Entrances *(1946)*, In Country Sleep, and Other Poems *(1952)*, Collected Poems *(1952)*, *and* Poems *(1971). He was the author of essays, short stories, and drama as well as poetry. Some of these volumes include* The Portrait of the Artist as a Young Dog *(1940)*, A Child's Christmas in Wales *(1954)*, Adventures in the Skin Trade, and Other Stories *(1955)*, *and* Under Milk Wood *(1954)*.

A Refusal to Mourn the Death, by Fire, of a Child in London

Never until the mankind making
Bird beast and flower
Fathering and all humbling darkness
Tells with silence the last light breaking
5 And the still hour
Is come of the sea rumbling in harness

And I must enter again the round
Zion of the water bead
And the synagogue of the ear of corn
10 Shall I let pray the shadow of a sound
Or sow my salt seed
In the least valley of sackcloth to mourn

The majesty and burning of the child's death.
I shall not murder
15 The mankind of her going with a grave truth
Nor blaspheme down the stations of the breath
With any further
Elegy of innocence and youth.

Deep with the first dead lies London's daughter,
20 Robed in the long friends,
The grains beyond age, the dark veins of her mother,
Secret by the unmourning water
Of the riding Thames.°
After the first death, there is no other.   [1946]

²³**Thames** the river on the banks of which London was built

1. The first two stanzas, plus the first line of the third stanza, are all one sentence. Read these lines aloud until you feel you have their rhythm and begin to understand their meaning. Then try to write a sentence of your own that conveys their meaning.
2. The first sentence justifies the decision of the poet not to mourn the child's death. Explain his reasoning.
3. In the third stanza, starting with the second line, the poet promises not to "murder" or "blaspheme" the child's death with "grave truth" or an "elegy of innocence and youth." Why does he refuse to do these things, when ordinarily, speeches containing these elements are considered appropriate at funerals and memorial services?

4. Does the poet stand by his promise not to mourn? How does the last stanza of the poem live up to it?
5. Discuss this stanza in terms of the way it relates to the losses suffered in the destruction of the World Trade Center on September 11, 2001. Would this poem, with certain small changes to describe the people who were lost in New York, satisfy the need for a poem to read in mourning those who died there? Do you think it would be comforting for the mourners? How does it compare with other poetic responses to the occasion?

WALT WHITMAN

WALT WHITMAN *(1819–91) was born on Long Island of a mother of Dutch Quaker origin and a father of English descent. His mother was loving and supportive, his father a stern disciplinarian; he was taken from school to learn the printer's trade at the age of twelve. He fell in love with the printed word, reading everything he could, including the Bible, Homer, Dante, Shakespeare, and Sir Walter Scott. He began to teach in a one-room schoolhouse when he was seventeen, and later became a journalist and then editor for a number of newspapers. He worked in Brooklyn and then New Orleans, where he witnessed the evils of slavery. He founded the* Brooklyn Freeman, *a newspaper, upon returning there. During the Civil War he nursed wounded soldiers brought to Washington, D.C., to recover from battle. He then began writing the poetry that was eventually published as* Leaves of Grass, *some four hundred poems rewritten, revised, and added to throughout his life. His body of work established him as the pre-eminent poet of America of the nineteenth century, one who had great influence on poets and writers who followed him.*

A Noiseless Patient Spider

A noiseless patient spider,
I mark'd where on a little promontory it stood isolated,
Mark'd how to explore the vacant vast surrounding,
It launch'd forth filament, filament, filament, out of itself,
Ever unreeling them, ever tirelessly speeding them. 5

And you O my soul where you stand,
Surrounded, detached, in measureless oceans of space,
Ceaselessly musing, venturing, throwing, seeking the spheres to connect them,
Till the bridge you will need be form'd, till the ductile anchor hold,
Till the gossamer° thread you fling catch somewhere, O my soul. [1881] 10

¹⁰**gossamer** as a noun, a film of cobwebs; adj., light, delicate, insubstantial

1. How does Whitman create the parallel between the spider and his soul?
2. What is the limit of the analogy?
3. What is its purpose?

◎◎◎

RICHARD WILBUR

For biographical notes, see p. 264.

Mayflies

In sombre forest, when the sun was low,
I saw from unseen pools a mist of flies
    In their quadrillions° rise
And animate a ragged patch of glow
5 With sudden glittering—as when a crowd
    Of stars appear
Through a brief gap in black and driven cloud,
One arc of their great round-dance showing clear.

It was no muddled swarm I witnessed, for
10 In entrechats° each fluttering insect there
    Rose two steep yards in air,
Then slowly floated down to climb once more,
So that they all composed a manifold
    And figured scene,
15 And seemed the weavers of some cloth of gold,
Or the fine pistons of some bright machine.

Watching those lifelong dancers of a day
As night closed in, I felt myself alone
    In a life too much my own,
20 More mortal in my separateness than they—
Unless, I thought, I had been called to be
    Not fly or star
But one whose task is joyfully to see
How fair the fiats° of the caller are.

[1999]

³**quadrillions** ten to the fifteenth power   ¹⁰**entrechats** a leap during which a ballet dancer crosses his or her legs, beating them together repeatedly   ²⁴**fiats** commands or creative acts; Latin "let there be"

1. The first stanza of this poem is packed with information, including the declaration that it is about seeing. Talk about the way the poet establishes the scene and how he characterizes what it is he sees. Notice that he uses the past tense; how does this affect the relationship between the poet and the reader?

2. This poem is written in three octaves, or octets, an eight-line stanza that was used often by Chaucer, Byron, and other poets. Octaves also make up the larger section of a Petrarchan (Italian) sonnet. Although the rhyme scheme and rhythmic pattern of "Mayflies" differ significantly from the sonnet form, it manifestly draws on a long formal tradition of both narrative

and lyric poetry. Can you justify this choice of a traditional form as it relates to the poem's meaning?

3. Now that you have discovered some of the poem's overarching themes, go back and notice particularly how well the word choices work to become its meanings. Pick out some of the compelling word choices that you consider to be carriers of meaning. Talk about their sounds, their origins, their various meanings, and how these are related to one or more effects and ideas in the poem.

4. How might Louise Antony, author of the essay "The 'Faith' of an Atheist" (p. 504), reflect on the claim made in the poem?

PAUL ZIMMER

PAUL ZIMMER *(1934–), a native of Canton, Ohio, was educated at Kent State University. He has written enough poems to fill more than a dozen poetry collections, including* The Great Bird of Love, *a selection for the National Poetry Series in 1998. Zimmer has directed the presses at the University of Georgia, the University of Iowa, and the University of Pittsburgh and has founded an influential poetry series at each. His latest book is* Crossing to Sunlight: Selected Poems, *a retrospective of his best-known work.*

The Day Zimmer Lost Religion

The first Sunday I missed Mass on purpose
I waited all day for Christ to climb down
Like a wiry flyweight° from the cross and
Club me on my irreverent teeth, to wade into
My blasphemous gut and drop me like a   5
Red hot thurible,° the devil roaring in
Reserved seats until he got the hiccups.

It was a long cold way from the old days
When cassocked° and surpliced° I mumbled Latin
At the old priest and rang his obscure bell.   10
A long way from the dirty wind that blew
The soot like venial sins across the school yard
Where God reigned as a threatening,
One-eyed triangle° high in the fleecy sky.

The first Sunday I missed Mass on purpose   15
I waited all day for Christ to climb down

---

³**flyweight** a boxer who weighs not more than 112 pounds   ⁶**thurible** an incense burner on a chain swung during religious services   ⁹**cassocked** wearing a cassock, an ankle-length garment worn during religious services by clergy and assistants   **surpliced** wearing the loose white garment worn during religious services by clergy and assistants
¹⁴**One-eyed triangle** symbol like the pyramid on the American one dollar bill

Like the playground bully, the cuts and mice
Upon his face agleam, and pound me
Till my irreligious tongue hung out.
20 But of course He never came, knowing that
I was grown up and ready for Him now.   [1976]

1. What do we learn from the title and the first line of the poem? How does the last line fit in?
2. Who is the narrator? What is his relation to the poem's protagonist?
3. How do the figures of speech contribute to the meaning of the poem?

FICTION

OLC

D. H. LAWRENCE

D. H. LAWRENCE (1885–1930) did not fit into the coal-mining town in England where he was born. He received a scholarship to attend the high school, but did not excel academically and dropped out to clerk in a factory. When he met Jessie Chambers, the two became friends and she tutored and encouraged him to begin writing and to finish his education at University College, Nottingham. He eloped with Frieda Weekly, the German wife of a professor at Nottingham. The couple traveled in Europe and married when Frieda's divorce became final. During the First World War, they lived in poverty in England and returned to Italy after the war. Lawrence died in Vence, France, of tuberculosis. Lawrence's stance on sexuality gave him notoriety and caused his works to be censored, especially in the United States. Lady Chatterley's Lover *and* Sons and Lovers *are two of his best-known novels, the former especially because of the court case that focused on whether it should be banned.*

The Rocking-Horse Winner

There was a woman who was beautiful, who started with all the advantages, yet she had no luck. She married for love, and the love turned to dust. She had bonny children, yet she felt they had been thrust upon her, and she could not love them. They looked at her coldly, as if they were finding fault with her. And hurriedly she felt she must cover up some fault in herself. Yet what it was that she must cover up she never knew. Nevertheless, when her children were present, she always felt the centre of her heart go hard. This troubled her, and in her manner she was all the more gentle and anxious for her children, as if she loved them very much. Only she herself knew that at the centre of her heart was a hard little place that could not feel love, no, not for anybody. Everybody else said of her: "She is such a good mother. She adores her children." Only she herself, and her children themselves, knew it was not so. They read it in each other's eyes.

There were a boy and two little girls. They lived in a pleasant house, with a garden, and they had discreet servants, and felt themselves superior to anyone in the neighbourhood.

Although they lived in style, they felt always an anxiety in the house. There was never enough money. The mother had a small income, and the father had a small income, but not nearly enough for the social position which they had to keep up. The father went into town to some office. But though he had good prospects, these prospects never materialised. There was always the grinding sense of the shortage of money, though the style was always kept up.

At last the mother said: "I will see if *I* can't make something." But she did not know where to begin. She racked her brains, and tried this thing and the other, but could not find anything successful. The failure made deep lines come into her face. Her children were growing up, they would have to go to school. There must be more money, there must be more money. The father, who was always very handsome and expensive in his tastes, seemed as if he never *would* be able to do anything worth doing. And the mother, who had a great belief in herself, did not succeed any better, and her tastes were just as expensive.

And so the house came to be haunted by the unspoken phrase: *There must be more money! There must be more money!* The children could hear it all the time, though nobody said it aloud. They heard it at Christmas, when the expensive and splendid toys filled the nursery. Behind the shining modern rocking-horse, behind the smart doll's house, a voice would start whispering: "There *must* be more money! There *must* be more money!" And the children would stop playing, to listen for a moment. They would look into each other's eyes, to see if they had all heard. And each one saw in the eyes of the other two that they too had heard. "There *must* be more money! There *must* be more money!"

It came whispering from the springs of the still-swaying rocking-horse, and even the horse, bending his wooden, champing head, heard it. The big doll, sitting so pink and smirking in her new pram, could hear it quite plainly, and seemed to be smirking all the more self-consciously because of it. The foolish puppy, too, that took the place of the teddy-bear, he was looking so extraordinarily foolish for no other reason but that he heard the secret whisper all over the house: "There *must* be more money!"

Yet nobody ever said it aloud. The whisper was everywhere, and therefore no one spoke it. Just as no one ever says: "We are breathing!" in spite of the fact that breath is coming and going all the time.

"Mother," said the boy Paul one day, "why don't we keep a car of our own? Why do we always use uncle's, or else a taxi?"

"Because we're the poor members of the family," said the mother.

"But why *are* we, mother?"

"Well—I suppose," she said slowly and bitterly, "it's because your father has no luck."

The boy was silent for some time.

"Is luck money, mother?" he said, rather timidly.

"No, Paul. Not quite. It's what causes you to have money."

15   "Oh!" said Paul vaguely. "I thought when Uncle Oscar said *filthy lucker*, it
meant money."

"*Filthy lucre* does mean money," said the mother. "But it's lucre, not luck."

"Oh!" said the boy. "Then what *is* luck, mother?"

"It's what causes you to have money. If you're lucky you have money. That's
why it's better to be born lucky than rich. If you're rich, you may lose your
money. But if you're lucky, you will always get more money."

"Oh! Will you? And is father not lucky?"

20   "Very unlucky, I should say," she said bitterly.

The boy watched her with unsure eyes.

"Why?" he asked.

"I don't know. Nobody ever knows why one person is lucky and another
unlucky."

"Don't they? Nobody at all? Does *nobody* know?"

25   "Perhaps God. But He never tells."

"He ought to, then. And aren't you lucky either, mother?"

"I can't be, if I married an unlucky husband."

"But by yourself, aren't you?"

"I used to think I was, before I married. Now I think I am very unlucky
indeed."

30   "Why?"

"Well—never mind! Perhaps I'm not really," she said.

The child looked at her to see if she meant it. But he saw, by the lines of her
mouth, that she was only trying to hide something from him.

"Well, anyhow," he said stoutly, "I'm a lucky person."

"Why?" said his mother, with a sudden laugh.

35   He stared at her. He didn't even know why he had said it.

"God told me," he asserted, brazening it out.

"I hope He did, dear!" she said, again with a laugh, but rather bitter.

"He did, mother!"

"Excellent!" said the mother, using one of her husband's exclamations.

40   The boy saw she did not believe him; or rather, that she paid no attention to
his assertion. This angered him somewhere, and made him want to compel her
attention.

He went off by himself, vaguely, in a childish way, seeking for the clue to
"luck." Absorbed, taking no heed of other people, he went about with a sort of
stealth, seeking inwardly for luck. He wanted luck, he wanted it, he wanted it.
When the two girls were playing dolls in the nursery, he would sit on his big
rocking-horse, charging madly into space, with a frenzy that made the little girls
peer at him uneasily. Wildly the horse careered, the waving dark hair of the boy
tossed, his eyes had a strange glare in them. The little girls dared not speak
to him.

When he had ridden to the end of his mad little journey, he climbed down
and stood in front of his rocking-horse, staring fixedly into its lowered face. Its
red mouth was slightly open, its big eye was wide and glassy-bright.

"Now!" he would silently command the snorting steed. "Now, take me to
where there is luck! Now take me!"

And he would slash the horse on the neck with the little whip he had asked Uncle Oscar for. He *knew* the horse could take him to where there was luck, if only he forced it. So he would mount again and start on his furious ride, hoping at last to get there. He knew he could get there.

"You'll break your horse, Paul!" said the nurse.   45

"He's always riding like that! I wish he'd leave off!" said his elder sister Joan.

But he only glared down on them in silence. Nurse gave him up. She could make nothing of him. Anyhow, he was growing beyond her.

One day his mother and his Uncle Oscar came in when he was on one of his furious rides. He did not speak to them.

"Hallo, you young jockey! Riding a winner?" said his uncle.

"Aren't you growing too big for a rocking-horse? You're not a very little boy   50
any longer, you know," said his mother.

But Paul only gave a blue glare from his big, rather close-set eyes. He would speak to nobody when he was in full tilt. His mother watched him with an anxious expression on her face.

At last he suddenly stopped forcing his horse into the mechanical gallop and slid down.

"Well, I got there!" he announced fiercely, his blue eyes still flaring, and his sturdy long legs straddling apart.

"Where did you get to?" asked his mother.

"Where I wanted to go," he flared back at her.   55

"That's right, son!" said Uncle Oscar. "Don't you stop till you get there. What's the horse's name?"

"He doesn't have a name," said the boy.

"Gets on without all right?" asked the uncle.

"Well, he has different names. He was called Sansovino last week."

"Sansovino, eh? Won the Ascot. How did you know this name?"   60

"He always talks about horse-races with Bassett," said Joan.

The uncle was delighted to find that his small nephew was posted with all the racing news. Bassett, the young gardener, who had been wounded in the left foot in the war and had got his present job through Oscar Cresswell, whose batman° he had been, was a perfect blade of the "turf." He lived in the racing events, and the small boy lived with him.

Oscar Cresswell got it all from Bassett.

"Master Paul comes and asks me, so I can't do more than tell him, sir," said Bassett, his face terribly serious, as if he were speaking of religious matters.

"And does he ever put anything on a horse he fancies?"   65

"Well—I don't want to give him away—he's a young sport, a fine sport, sir. Would you mind asking him himself? He sort of takes a pleasure in it, and perhaps he'd feel I was giving him away, sir, if you don't mind."

Bassett was serious as a church.

The uncle went back to his nephew and took him off for a ride in the car.

"Say, Paul, old man, do you ever put anything on a horse?" the uncle asked.

°**batman** a soldier assigned to serve a superior officer

70   The boy watched the handsome man closely.

"Why, do you think I oughtn't to?" he parried.

"Not a bit of it! I thought perhaps you might give me a tip for the Lincoln."

The car sped on into the country, going down to Uncle Oscar's place in Hampshire.

"Honour bright?" said the nephew.

75   "Honour bright, son!" said the uncle.

"Well, then, Daffodil."

"Daffodil! I doubt it, sonny. What about Mirza?"

"I only know the winner," said the boy. "That's Daffodil."

"Daffodil, eh?"

80   There was a pause. Daffodil was an obscure horse comparatively.

"Uncle!"

"Yes, son?"

"You won't let it go any further, will you? I promised Bassett."

"Bassett be damned, old man! What's he got to do with it?"

85   "We're partners. We've been partners from the first. Uncle, he lent me my first five shillings, which I lost. I promised him, honour bright, it was only between me and him; only you gave me that ten-shilling note I started winning with, so I thought you were lucky. You won't let it go any further, will you?"

The boy gazed at his uncle from those big, hot, blue eyes, set rather close together. The uncle stirred and laughed uneasily.

"Right you are, son! I'll keep your tip private. Daffodil, eh? How much are you putting on him?"

"All except twenty pounds," said the boy. "I keep that in reserve."

The uncle thought it a good joke.

90   "You keep twenty pounds in reserve, do you, you young romancer? What are you betting, then?"

"I'm betting three hundred," said the boy gravely. "But it's between you and me, Uncle Oscar! Honour bright?"

The uncle burst into a roar of laughter.

"It's between you and me all right, you young Nat Gould,° " he said, laughing. "But where's your three hundred?"

"Bassett keeps it for me. We're partners."

95   "You are, are you! And what is Bassett putting on Daffodil?"

"He won't go quite as high as I do, I expect. Perhaps he'll go a hundred and fifty."

"What, pennies?" laughed the uncle.

"Pounds," said the child, with a surprised look at his uncle. "Bassett keeps a bigger reserve than I do."

Between wonder and amusement Uncle Oscar was silent. He pursued the matter no further, but he determined to take his nephew with him to the Lincoln races.

---

[93]**Nat Gould** author of novels having to do with horse racing

"Now, son," he said, "I'm putting twenty on Mirza, and I'll put five on for you on any horse you fancy. What's your pick?" 100

"Daffodil, uncle."

"No, not the fiver on Daffodil!"

"I should if it was my own fiver," said the child.

"Good! Good! Right you are! A fiver for me and a fiver for you on Daffodil."

The child had never been to a race-meeting before, and his eyes were blue 105
fire. He pursed his mouth tight and watched. A Frenchman just in front had put his money on Lancelot. Wild with excitement, he flayed his arms up and down, yelling *"Lancelot! Lancelot!"* in his French accent.

Daffodil came in first, Lancelot second, Mirza third. The child, flushed and with eyes blazing, was curiously serene. His uncle brought him four five-pound notes, four to one.

"What am I to do with these?" he cried, waving them before the boy's eyes.

"I suppose we'll talk to Bassett," said the boy. "I expect I have fifteen hundred now; and twenty in reserve; and this twenty."

His uncle studied him for some moments.

"Look here, son!" he said. "You're not serious about Bassett and that fifteen 110
hundred, are you?"

"Yes, I am. But it's between you and me, uncle. Honour bright?"

"Honour bright all right, son! But I must talk to Bassett."

"If you'd like to be a partner, uncle, with Bassett and me, we could all be partners. Only, you'd have to promise, honour bright, uncle, not to let it go beyond us three. Bassett and I are lucky, and you must be lucky, because it was your ten shillings I started winning with. . . ."

Uncle Oscar took both Bassett and Paul into Richmond Park for an afternoon, and there they talked.

"It's like this, you see, sir," Bassett said. "Master Paul would get me talking 115
about racing events, spinning yarns, you know, sir. And he was always keen on knowing if I'd made or if I'd lost. It's about a year since, now, that I put five shillings on Blush of Dawn for him: and we lost. Then the luck turned, with that ten shillings he had from you: that we put on Singhalese. And since that time, it's been pretty steady, all things considering. What do you say, Master Paul?"

"We're all right when we're sure," said Paul. "It's when we're not quite sure that we go down."

"Oh, but we're careful then," said Bassett.

"But when are you *sure?*" smiled Uncle Oscar.

"It's Master Paul, sir," said Bassett in a secret, religious voice. "It's as if he had it from heaven. Like Daffodil, now, for the Lincoln. That was as sure as eggs."

"Did you put anything on Daffodil?" asked Oscar Cresswell. 120

"Yes, sir. I made my bit."

"And my nephew?"

Bassett was obstinately silent, looking at Paul.

"I made twelve hundred, didn't I, Bassett? I told uncle I was putting three hundred on Daffodil."

"That's right," said Bassett, nodding. 125

"But where's the money?" asked the uncle.

"I keep it safe locked up, sir. Master Paul he can have it any minute he likes to ask for it."

"What, fifteen hundred pounds?"

"And twenty! And *forty*, that is, with the twenty he made on the course."

130 "It's amazing!" said the uncle.

"If Master Paul offers you to be partners, sir, I would, if I were you: if you'll excuse me," said Bassett.

Oscar Cresswell thought about it.

"I'll see the money," he said.

They drove home again, and, sure enough, Bassett came round to the garden-house with fifteen hundred pounds in notes. The twenty pounds reserve was left with Joe Glee, in the Turf Commission deposit.

135 "You see, it's all right, uncle, when I'm *sure!* Then we go strong, for all we're worth. Don't we, Bassett?"

"We do that, Master Paul."

"And when are you sure?" said the uncle, laughing.

"Oh, well, sometimes I'm *absolutely* sure, like about Daffodil," said the boy; "and sometimes I have an idea; and sometimes I haven't even an idea, have I, Bassett? Then we're careful, because we mostly go down."

"You do, do you! And when you're sure, like about Daffodil, what makes you sure, sonny?"

140 "Oh, well, I don't know," said the boy uneasily. "I'm sure, you know, uncle; that's all."

"It's as if he had it from heaven, sir," Bassett reiterated.

"I should say so!" said the uncle.

But he became a partner. And when the Leger was coming on Paul was "sure" about Lively Spark, which was a quite inconsiderable horse. The boy insisted on putting a thousand on the horse, Bassett was for five hundred, and Oscar Cresswell two hundred. Lively Spark came in first, and the betting had been ten to one against him. Paul had made ten thousand.

"You see," he said, "I was absolutely sure of him."

145 Even Oscar Cresswell had cleared two thousand.

"Look here, son," he said, "this sort of thing makes me nervous."

"It needn't, uncle! Perhaps I shan't be sure again for a long time."

"But what are you going to do with your money?" asked the uncle.

"Of course," said the boy, "I started it for mother. She said she had no luck, because father is unlucky, so I thought if *I* was lucky, it might stop whispering."

150 "What might stop whispering?"

"Our house. I *hate* our house for whispering."

"What does it whisper?"

"Why—why"—the boy fidgeted—"why, I don't know. But it's always short of money, you know, uncle."

"I know it, son, I know it."

155 "You know people send mother writs, don't you, uncle?"

"I'm afraid I do," said the uncle.

"And then the house whispers, like people laughing at you behind your back. It's awful, that is! I thought if I was lucky——"

"You might stop it," added the uncle.

The boy watched him with big blue eyes, that had an uncanny cold fire in them, and he said never a word.

"Well, then!" said the uncle. "What are we doing?"

"I shouldn't like mother to know I was lucky," said the boy.

"Why not, son?"

"She'd stop me."

"I don't think she would."

"Oh!"—and the boy writhed in an odd way—"I *don't* want her to know, uncle."

"All right, son! We'll manage it without her knowing."

They managed it very easily. Paul, at the other's suggestion, handed over five thousand pounds to his uncle, who deposited it with the family lawyer, who was then to inform Paul's mother that a relative had put five thousand pounds into his hands, which sum was to be paid out a thousand pounds at a time, on the mother's birthday, for the next five years.

"So she'll have a birthday present of a thousand pounds for five successive years," said Uncle Oscar. "I hope it won't make it all the harder for her later."

Paul's mother had her birthday in November. The house had been "whispering" worse than ever lately, and, even in spite of his luck, Paul could not bear up against it. He was very anxious to see the effect of the birthday letter, telling his mother about the thousand pounds.

When there were no visitors, Paul now took his meals with his parents, as he was beyond the nursery control. His mother went into town nearly every day. She had discovered that she had an odd knack of sketching furs and dress materials, so she worked secretly in the studio of a friend who was the chief "artist" for the leading drapers. She drew the figures of ladies in furs and ladies in silk and sequins for the newspaper advertisements. This young woman artist earned several thousand pounds a year, but Paul's mother only made several hundreds, and she was again dissatisfied. She so wanted to be first in something, and she did not succeed, even in making sketches for drapery advertisements.

She was down to breakfast on the morning of her birthday. Paul watched her face as she read her letters. He knew the lawyer's letter. As his mother read it, her face hardened and became more expressionless. Then a cold, determined look came on her mouth. She hid the letter under the pile of others, and said not a word about it.

"Didn't you have anything nice in the post for your birthday, mother?" said Paul.

"Quite moderately nice," she said, her voice cold and absent.

She went away to town without saying more.

But in the afternoon Uncle Oscar appeared. He said Paul's mother had had a long interview with the lawyer, asking if the whole five thousand could not be advanced at once, as she was in debt.

"What do you think, uncle?" said the boy.

"I leave it to you, son."

"Oh, let her have it, then! We can get some more with the other," said the boy.

"A bird in the hand is worth two in the bush, laddie!" said Uncle Oscar.

180 "But I'm sure to *know* for the Grand National; or the Lincolnshire; or else the Derby. I'm sure to know for *one* of them," said Paul.

So Uncle Oscar signed the agreement, and Paul's mother touched the whole five thousand. Then something very curious happened. The voices in the house suddenly went mad, like a chorus of frogs on a spring evening. There were certain new furnishings, and Paul had a tutor. He was *really* going to Eton, his father's school, in the following autumn. There were flowers in the winter, and a blossoming of the luxury Paul's mother had been used to. And yet the voices in the house, behind the sprays of mimosa and almondblossom, and from under the piles of iridescent cushions, simply trilled and screamed in a sort of ecstasy: "There *must* be more money! Oh-h-h; there *must* be more money. Oh, now now-w! Now-w-w—there *must* be more money!—more than ever! More than ever!"

It frightened Paul terribly. He studied away at his Latin and Greek with his tutor. But his intense hours were spent with Bassett. The Grand National had gone by: he had not "known," and had lost a hundred pounds. Summer was at hand. He was in agony for the Lincoln. But even for the Lincoln he didn't "know," and he lost fifty pounds. He became wild-eyed and strange, as if something were going to explode in him.

"Let it alone, son! Don't you bother about it!" urged Uncle Oscar. But it was as if the boy couldn't really hear what his uncle was saying.

"I've got to know for the Derby! I've got to know for the Derby!" the child reiterated, his big blue eyes blazing with a sort of madness.

185 His mother noticed how overwrought he was.

"You'd better go to the seaside. Wouldn't you like to go now to the seaside, instead of waiting? I think you'd better," she said, looking down at him anxiously, her heart curiously heavy because of him.

But the child lifted his uncanny blue eyes.

"I couldn't possibly go before the Derby, mother!" he said. "I couldn't possibly!"

"Why not?" she said, her voice becoming heavy when she was opposed. "Why not? You can still go from the seaside to see the Derby with your Uncle Oscar, if that's what you wish. No need for you to wait here. Besides, I think you care too much about these races. It's a bad sign. My family has been a gambling family, and you won't know till you grow up how much damage it has done. But it has done damage. I shall have to send Bassett away, and ask Uncle Oscar not to talk racing to you, unless you promise to be reasonable about it: go away to the seaside and forget it. You're all nerves!"

190 "I'll do what you like, mother, so long as you don't send me away till after the Derby," the boy said.

"Send you away from where? Just from this house?"

"Yes," he said, gazing at her.

"Why, you curious child, what makes you care about this house so much, suddenly? I never knew you loved it."

He gazed at her without speaking. He had a secret within a secret, something he had not divulged, even to Bassett or to his Uncle Oscar.

But his mother, after standing undecided and a little bit sullen for some moments, said:

"Very well, then! Don't go to the seaside till after the Derby, if you don't wish it. But promise me you won't let your nerves go to pieces. Promise you won't think so much about horse-racing and *events*, as you call them!"

"Oh no," said the boy casually. "I won't think much about them, mother. You needn't worry. I wouldn't worry, mother, if I were you."

"If you were me and I were you," said his mother, "I wonder what we *should* do!"

"But you know you needn't worry, mother, don't you?" the boy repeated.

"I should be awfully glad to know it," she said wearily.

"Oh, well, you *can*, you know. I mean, you *ought* to know you needn't worry," he insisted.

"Ought I? Then I'll see about it," she said.

Paul's secret of secrets was his wooden horse, that which had no name. Since he was emancipated from a nurse and nursery-governess, he had had his rocking-horse removed to his own bedroom at the top of the house.

"Surely you're too big for a rocking-horse!" his mother had remonstrated.

"Well, you see, mother, till I can have a *real* horse, I like to have *some* sort of animal about," had been his quaint answer.

"Do you feel he keeps you company?" she laughed.

"Oh yes! He's very good, he always keeps me company, when I'm there," said Paul.

So the horse, rather shabby, stood in an arrested prance in the boy's bedroom.

The Derby was drawing near, and the boy grew more and more tense. He hardly heard what was spoken to him, he was very frail, and his eyes were really uncanny. His mother had sudden strange seizures of uneasiness about him. Sometimes, for half an hour, she would feel a sudden anxiety about him that was almost anguish. She wanted to rush to him at once, and know he was safe.

Two nights before the Derby, she was at a big party in town, when one of her rushes of anxiety about her boy, her first-born, gripped her heart till she could hardly speak. She fought with the feeling, might and main, for she believed in common sense. But it was too strong. She had to leave the dance and go downstairs to telephone to the country. The children's nursery-governess was terribly surprised and startled at being rung up in the night.

"Are the children all right, Miss Wilmot?"

"Oh yes, they are quite all right."

"Master Paul? Is he all right?"

"He went to bed as right as a trivet. Shall I run up and look at him?"

"No," said Paul's mother reluctantly. "No! Don't trouble. It's all right. Don't sit up. We shall be home fairly soon." She did not want her son's privacy intruded upon.

"Very good," said the governess.

It was about one o'clock when Paul's mother and father drove up to their house. All was still. Paul's mother went to her room and slipped off her white fur cloak. She had told her maid not to wait up for her. She heard her husband downstairs, mixing a whisky and soda.

And then, because of the strange anxiety at her heart, she stole upstairs to her son's room. Noiselessly she went along the upper corridor. Was there a faint noise? What was it?

She stood, with arrested muscles, outside his door, listening. There was a strange, heavy, and yet not loud noise. Her heart stood still. It was a soundless noise, yet rushing and powerful. Something huge, in violent, hushed motion. What was it? What in God's name was it? She ought to know. She felt that she knew the noise. She knew what it was.

220 Yet she could not place it. She couldn't say what it was. And on and on it went, like a madness.

Softly, frozen with anxiety and fear, she turned the doorhandle.

The room was dark. Yet in the space near the window, she heard and saw something plunging to and fro. She gazed in fear and amazement.

Then suddenly she switched on the light, and saw her son, in his green pyjamas, madly surging on the rocking-horse. The blaze of light suddenly lit him up, as he urged the wooden horse, and lit her up, as she stood, blonde, in her dress of pale green and crystal, in the doorway.

"Paul!" she cried. "Whatever are you doing?"

225 "It's Malabar!" he screamed in a powerful, strange voice. "It's Malabar!"

His eyes blazed at her for one strange and senseless second, as he ceased urging his wooden horse. Then he fell with a crash to the ground, and she, all her tormented motherhood flooding upon her, rushed to gather him up.

But he was unconscious, and unconscious he remained, with some brain-fever. He talked and tossed, and his mother sat stonily by his side.

"Malabar! It's Malabar! Bassett, Bassett, I *know*! It's Malabar!"

So the child cried, trying to get up and urge the rocking-horse that gave him his inspiration.

230 "What does he mean by Malabar?" asked the heart-frozen mother.

"I don't know," said the father stonily.

"What does he mean by Malabar?" she asked her brother Oscar.

"It's one of the horses running for the Derby," was the answer.

And, in spite of himself, Oscar Cresswell spoke to Bassett, and himself put a thousand on Malabar: at fourteen to one.

235 The third day of the illness was critical: they were waiting for a change. The boy, with his rather long, curly hair, was tossing ceaselessly on the pillow. He neither slept nor regained consciousness, and his eyes were like blue stones. His mother sat, feeling her heart had gone, turned actually into a stone.

In the evening, Oscar Cresswell did not come, but Bassett sent a message, saying could he come up for one moment, just one moment? Paul's mother was very angry at the intrusion, but on second thoughts she agreed. The boy was the same. Perhaps Bassett might bring him to consciousness.

The gardener, a shortish fellow with a little brown moustache and sharp little brown eyes, tiptoed into the room, touched his imaginary cap to Paul's mother, and stole to the bedside, staring with glittering, smallish eyes at the tossing, dying child.

"Master Paul!" he whispered. "Master Paul! Malabar came in first all right, a clean win. I did as you told me. You've made over seventy thousand pounds, you have; you've got over eighty thousand. Malabar came in all right, Master Paul."

"Malabar! Malabar! Did I say Malabar, mother? Did I say Malabar? Do you think I'm lucky, mother! I knew Malabar, didn't I? Over eighty thousand pounds! I call that lucky, don't you mother? Over eighty thousand pounds! I knew, didn't I know I knew? Malabar came in all right. If I ride my horse till I'm sure, then I tell you, Bassett, you can go as high as you like. Did you go for all you were worth, Bassett?"

"I went a thousand on it, Master Paul."

240

"I never told you, mother, that if I can ride my horse, and *get there*, then I'm absolutely sure—oh, absolutely! Mother, did I ever tell you? I *am* lucky!"

"No, you never did," said his mother.

But the boy died in the night.

And even as he lay dead, his mother heard her brother's voice saying to her: "My God, Hester, you're eighty-odd thousand to the good, and a poor devil of a son to the bad. But, poor devil, poor devil, he's best gone out of a life where he rides his rocking-horse to find a winner."

[1926]

1. Characterize the mother in the story. What are her values? What role does she play in Paul's behavior? Would you call the narrator's characterization of the mother fair?
2. Paul most frequently interacts with two older men, not his father. Describe Bassett and Uncle Oscar. Characterize their relationships with Paul.
3. What is the significance of the rocking-horse?
4. What themes are invoked by the story?
5. To what other works in this section can this story be related?

FLANNERY O'CONNOR

OLC

FLANNERY O'CONNOR *(1925–64) was born in Savannah, Georgia, and died in Milledgeville, Georgia, of lupus thirty-nine years later. She graduated from the Georgia State College for Women (now Georgia College) and received the Master of Fine Arts degree from the State University of Iowa. Her awards and honors included a Kenyon Review fellowship in fiction, a National Institute of Arts and Letters grant in literature, and several O. Henry Memorial Awards first prizes. During her working life she wrote two novels, thirty-two short stories, and reviews and commentaries, and is considered one of the major American writers of the twentieth century.*

A Good Man Is Hard to Find

The grandmother didn't want to go to Florida. She wanted to visit some of her connections in east Tennessee and she was seizing at every chance to change Bailey's mind. Bailey was the son she lived with, her only boy. He was sitting on the edge of his chair at the table, bent over the orange sports section of the *Journal*. "Now look here, Bailey," she said, "see here, read this," and she stood with one hand on her thin hip and the other rattling the newspaper at his bald head. "Here this fellow that calls himself The Misfit is aloose from the Federal Pen and headed toward Florida and you read here what it says he did to these people. Just you read it. I wouldn't take my children in any direction with a criminal like that aloose in it. I couldn't answer to my conscience if I did."

Bailey didn't look up from his reading so she wheeled around then and faced the children's mother, a young woman in slacks, whose face was as broad and innocent as a cabbage and was tied around with a green headkerchief that had two points on the top like a rabbit's ears. She was sitting on the sofa, feeding the baby his apricots out of a jar. "The children have been to Florida before," the old lady said. "You all ought to take them somewhere else for a change so they would see different parts of the world and be broad. They never have been to east Tennessee."

The children's mother didn't seem to hear her but the eight-year-old boy, John Wesley, a stocky child with glasses, said, "If you don't want to go to Florida, why dontcha stay at home?" He and the little girl, June Star, were reading the funny papers on the floor.

"She wouldn't stay at home to be queen for a day," June Star said without raising her yellow head.

5   "Yes and what would you do if this fellow, The Misfit, caught you?" the grandmother asked.

"I'd smack his face," John Wesley said.

"She wouldn't stay at home for a million bucks," June Star said. "Afraid she'd miss something. She has to go everywhere we go."

"All right, Miss," the grandmother said. "Just remember that the next time you want me to curl your hair."

June Star said her hair was naturally curly.

10   The next morning the grandmother was the first one in the car, ready to go. She had her big black valise that looked like the head of a hippopotamus in one corner, and underneath it she was hiding a basket with Pitty Sing, the cat, in it. She didn't intend for the cat to be left alone in the house for three days because he would miss her too much and she was afraid he might brush against one of the gas burners and accidentally asphyxiate himself. Her son, Bailey, didn't like to arrive at a motel with a cat.

She sat in the middle of the back seat with John Wesley and June Star on either side of her. Bailey and the children's mother and the baby sat in front and they left Atlanta at eight forty-five with the mileage on the car at 55890. The grandmother wrote this down because she thought it would be interesting to say how many miles they had been when they got back. It took them twenty minutes to reach the outskirts of the city.

The old lady settled herself comfortably, removing her white cotton gloves and putting them up with her purse on the shelf in front of the back window. The children's mother still had on slacks and still had her head tied up in a green kerchief, but the grandmother had on a navy blue straw sailor hat with a bunch of white violets on the brim and a navy blue dress with a small white dot in the print. Her collars and cuffs were white organdy trimmed with lace and at her neckline she had pinned a purple spray of cloth violets containing a sachet. In case of an accident, anyone seeing her dead on the highway would know at once that she was a lady.

She said she thought it was going to be a good day for driving, neither too hot nor too cold, and she cautioned Bailey that the speed limit was fifty-five miles an hour and that the patrolmen hid themselves behind billboards and small clumps of trees and sped out after you before you had a chance to slow down. She pointed out interesting details of the scenery: Stone Mountain; the blue granite that in some places came up to both sides of the highway; the brilliant red clay banks slightly streaked with purple; and the various crops that made rows of green lace-work on the ground. The trees were full of silver-white sunlight and the meanest of them sparkled. The children were reading comic magazines and their mother had gone back to sleep.

"Let's go through Georgia fast so we won't have to look at it much," John Wesley said.

"If I were a little boy," said the grandmother, "I wouldn't talk about my native state that way. Tennessee has the mountains and Georgia has the hills." 15

"Tennessee is just a hillbilly dumping ground," John Wesley said, "and Georgia is a lousy state too."

"You said it," June Star said.

"In my time," said the grandmother, folding her thin veined fingers, "children were more respectful of their native states and their parents and everything else. People did right then. Oh look at the cute little pickaninny!" she said and pointed to a Negro child standing in the door of a shack. "Wouldn't that make a picture, now?" she asked and they all turned and looked at the little Negro out of the back window. He waved.

"He didn't have any britches on," June Star said.

"He probably didn't have any," the grandmother explained. "Little niggers in the country don't have things like we do. If I could paint, I'd paint that picture," she said. 20

The children exchanged comic books.

The grandmother offered to hold the baby and the children's mother passed him over the front seat to her. She set him on her knee and bounced him and told him about the things they were passing. She rolled her eyes and screwed up her mouth and stuck her leathery thin face into his smooth bland one. Occasionally he gave her a faraway smile. They passed a large cotton field with five or six graves fenced in the middle of it, like a small island. "Look at the graveyard!" the grandmother said, pointing it out. "That was the old family burying ground. That belonged to the plantation."

"Where's the plantation?" John Wesley asked.

"Gone With the Wind," said the grandmother. "Ha. Ha."

25   When the children finished all the comic books they had brought, they opened the lunch and ate it. The grandmother ate a peanut butter sandwich and an olive and would not let the children throw the box and the paper napkins out the window. When there was nothing else to do they played a game by choosing a cloud and making the other two guess what shape it suggested. John Wesley took one the shape of a cow and June Star guessed a cow and John Wesley said, no, an automobile, and June Star said he didn't play fair, and they began to slap each other over the grandmother.

The grandmother said she would tell them a story if they would keep quiet. When she told a story, she rolled her eyes and waved her head and was very dramatic. She said once when she was a maiden lady she had been courted by a Mr. Edgar Atkins Teagarden from Jasper, Georgia. She said he was a very good-looking man and a gentleman and that he brought her a watermelon every Saturday afternoon with his initials cut in it, E. A. T. Well, one Saturday, she said, Mr. Teagarden brought the watermelon and there was nobody at home and he left it on the front porch and returned in his buggy to Jasper, but she never got the watermelon, she said, because a nigger boy ate it when he saw the initials, E. A. T.! This story tickled John Wesley's funny bone and he giggled and giggled but June Star didn't think it was any good. She said she wouldn't marry a man that just brought her a watermelon on Saturday. The grandmother said she would have done well to marry Mr. Teagarden because he was a gentleman and had bought Coca-Cola stock when it first came out and that he died only a few years ago, a very wealthy man.

They stopped at The Tower for barbecued sandwiches. The Tower was a part stucco and part wood filling station and dance hall set in a clearing outside of Timothy. A fat man named Red Sammy Butts ran it and there were signs stuck here and there on the building and for miles up and down the highway saying, TRY RED SAMMY'S FAMOUS BARBECUE. NONE LIKE FAMOUS RED SAMMY'S! RED SAM! THE FAT BOY WITH THE HAPPY LAUGH. A VETERAN! RED SAMMY'S YOUR MAN!

Red Sammy was lying on the bare ground outside The Tower with his head under a truck while a gray monkey about a foot high, chained to a small chinaberry tree, chattered nearby. The monkey sprang back into the tree and got on the highest limb as soon as he saw the children jump out of the car and run toward him.

Inside, The Tower was a long dark room with a counter at one end and tables at the other and dancing space in the middle. They all sat down at a board table next to the nickelodeon and Red Sam's wife, a tall burnt-brown woman with hair and eyes lighter than her skin, came and took their order. The children's mother put a dime in the machine and played "The Tennessee Waltz," and the grandmother said that tune always made her want to dance. She asked Bailey if he would like to dance but he only glared at her. He didn't have a naturally sweet disposition like she did and trips made him nervous. The grandmother's brown eyes were very bright. She swayed her head from side to side and pretended she was dancing in her chair. June Star said play something she could tap to so the children's mother put in another dime and played a fast number and June Star stepped out onto the dance floor and did her tap routine.

"Ain't she cute?" Red Sam's wife said, leaning over the counter. "Would you   30
like to come be my little girl?"

"No I certainly wouldn't," June Star said. "I wouldn't live in a broken-down place like this for a million bucks!" and she ran back to the table.

"Ain't she cute?" the woman repeated, stretching her mouth politely.

"Aren't you ashamed?" hissed the grandmother.

Red Sam came in and told his wife to quit lounging on the counter and hurry up with these people's order. His khaki trousers reached just to his hip bones and his stomach hung over them like a sack of meal swaying under his shirt. He came over and sat down at a table nearby and let out a combination sigh and yodel. "You can't win," he said. "You can't win," and he wiped his sweating red face off with a gray handkerchief. "These days you don't know who to trust," he said. "Ain't that the truth?"

"People are certainly not nice like they used to be," said the grandmother.   35

"Two fellers come in here last week," Red Sammy said, "driving a Chrysler. It was a old beat-up car but it was a good one and these boys looked all right to me. Said they worked at the mill and you know I let them fellers charge the gas they bought? Now why did I do that?"

"Because you're a good man!" the grandmother said at once.

"Yes'm, I suppose so," Red Sam said as if he were struck with this answer.

His wife brought the orders, carrying the five plates all at once without a tray, two in each hand and one balanced on her arm. "It isn't a soul in this green world of God's that you can trust," she said. "And I don't count nobody out of that, not nobody," she repeated, looking at Red Sammy.

"Did you read about that criminal, The Misfit, that's escaped?" asked the   40
grandmother.

"I wouldn't be a bit surprised if he didn't attact this place right here," said the woman. "If he hears about it being here, I wouldn't be none surprised to see him. If he hears it's two cent in the cash register, I wouldn't be at all surprised if he . . ."

"That'll do," Red Sam said. "Go bring these people their Co'-Colas," and the woman went off to get the rest of the order.

"A good man is hard to find," Red Sammy said. "Everything is getting terrible. I remember the day you could go off and leave your screen door unlatched. Not no more."

He and the grandmother discussed better times. The old lady said that in her opinion Europe was entirely to blame for the way things were now. She said the way Europe acted you would think we were made of money and Red Sam said it was no use talking about it, she was exactly right. The children ran outside into the white sunlight and looked at the monkey in the lacy chinaberry tree.

He was busy catching fleas on himself and biting each one carefully between his teeth as if it were a delicacy.

45   They drove off again into the hot afternoon. The grandmother took cat naps and woke up every few minutes with her own snoring. Outside of Toombsboro she woke up and recalled an old plantation that she had visited in this neighborhood once when she was a young lady. She said the house had six white columns across the front and that there was an avenue of oaks leading up to it and two little wooden trellis arbors on either side in front where you sat down with your suitor after a stroll in the garden. She recalled exactly which road to turn off to get to it. She knew that Bailey would not be willing to lose any time looking at an old house, but the more she talked about it, the more she wanted to see it once again and find out if the little twin arbors were still standing. "There was a secret panel in this house," she said craftily, not telling the truth but wishing that she were, "and the story went that all the family silver was hidden in it when Sherman came through but it was never found . . ."

"Hey!" John Wesley said. "Let's go see it! We'll find it! We'll poke all the woodwork and find it! Who lives there? Where do you turn off at? Hey Pop, can't we turn off there?"

"We never have seen a house with a secret panel!" June Star shrieked. "Let's go to the house with the secret panel! Hey Pop, can't we go see the house with the secret panel!"

"It's not far from here, I know," the grandmother said. "It wouldn't take over twenty minutes."

Bailey was looking straight ahead. His jaw was as rigid as a horseshoe. "No," he said.

50   The children began to yell and scream that they wanted to see the house with the secret panel. John Wesley kicked the back of the front seat and June Star hung over her mother's shoulder and whined desperately into her ear that they never had any fun even on their vacation, that they could never do what THEY wanted to do. The baby began to scream and John Wesley kicked the back of the seat so hard that his father could feel the blows in his kidney.

"All right!" he shouted and drew the car to a stop at the side of the road. "Will you all shut up? Will you all just shut up for one second? If you don't shut up, we won't go anywhere."

"It would be very educational for them," the grandmother murmured.

"All right," Bailey said, "but get this: this is the only time we're going to stop for anything like this. This is the one and only time."

"The dirt road that you have to turn down is about a mile back," the grandmother directed. "I marked it when we passed."

55   "A dirt road," Bailey groaned.

After they had turned around and were headed toward the dirt road, the grandmother recalled other points about the house, the beautiful glass over the front doorway and the candle-lamp in the hall. John Wesley said that the secret panel was probably in the fireplace.

"You can't go inside this house," Bailey said. "You don't know who lives there."

"While you all talk to the people in front, I'll run around behind and get in a window," John Wesley suggested.

"We'll all stay in the car," his mother said.

They turned onto the dirt road and the car raced roughly along in a swirl of pink dust. The grandmother recalled the times when there were no paved roads and thirty miles was a day's journey. The dirt road was hilly and there were sudden washes in it and sharp curves on dangerous embankments. All at once they would be on a hill, looking down over the blue tops of trees for miles around, then the next minute, they would be in a red depression with the dust-coated trees looking down on them.

"This place had better turn up in a minute," Bailey said, "or I'm going to turn around."

The road looked as if no one had traveled on it in months.

"It's not much farther," the grandmother said and just as she said it, a horrible thought came to her. The thought was so embarrassing that she turned red in the face and her eyes dilated and her feet jumped up, upsetting her valise in the corner. The instant the valise moved, the newspaper top she had over the basket under it rose with a snarl and Pitty Sing, the cat, sprang onto Bailey's shoulder.

The children were thrown to the floor and their mother, clutching the baby, was thrown out the door onto the ground; the old lady was thrown into the front seat. The car turned over once and landed right-side-up in a gulch off the side of the road. Bailey remained in the driver's seat with the cat—gray-striped with a broad white face and an orange nose—clinging to his neck like a caterpillar.

As soon as the children saw they could move their arms and legs, they scrambled out of the car, shouting, "We've had an ACCIDENT!" The grandmother was curled up under the dashboard, hoping she was injured so that Bailey's wrath would not come down on her all at once. The horrible thought she had had before the accident was that the house she had remembered so vividly was not in Georgia but in Tennessee.

Bailey removed the cat from his neck with both hands and flung it out the window against the side of a pine tree. Then he got out of the car and started looking for the children's mother. She was sitting against the side of the red gutted ditch, holding the screaming baby, but she only had a cut down her face and a broken shoulder. "We've had an ACCIDENT!" the children screamed in a frenzy of delight.

"But nobody's killed," June Star said with disappointment as the grandmother limped out of the car, her hat still pinned to her head but the broken front brim standing up at a jaunty angle and the violet spray hanging off the side. They all sat down in the ditch, except the children, to recover from the shock. They were all shaking.

"Maybe a car will come along," said the children's mother hoarsely.

"I believe I have injured an organ," said the grandmother, pressing her side, but no one answered her. Bailey's teeth were clattering. He had on a yellow sport shirt with bright blue parrots designed in it and his face was as yellow as the shirt. The grandmother decided that she would not mention that the house was in Tennessee.

70 The road was about ten feet above and they could see only the tops of the trees on the other side of it. Behind the ditch they were sitting in there were more woods, tall and dark and deep. In a few minutes they saw a car some distance away on top of a hill, coming slowly as if the occupants were watching them. The grandmother stood up and waved both arms dramatically to attract their attention. The car continued to come on slowly, disappeared around a bend and appeared again, moving even slower, on top of the hill they had gone over. It was a big black battered hearse-like automobile. There were three men in it.

It came to a stop just over them and for some minutes, the driver looked down with a steady expressionless gaze to where they were sitting, and didn't speak. Then he turned his head and muttered something to the other two and they got out. One was a fat boy in black trousers and a red sweat shirt with a silver stallion embossed on the front of it. He moved around on the right side of them and stood staring, his mouth partly open in a kind of loose grin. The other had on khaki pants and a blue striped coat and a gray hat pulled down very low, hiding most of his face. He came around slowly on the left side. Neither spoke.

The driver got out of the car and stood by the side of it, looking down at them. He was an older man than the other two. His hair was just beginning to gray and he wore silver-rimmed spectacles that gave him a scholarly look. He had a long creased face and didn't have on any shirt or undershirt. He had on blue jeans that were too tight for him and was holding a black hat and a gun. The two boys also had guns.

"We've had an ACCIDENT!" the children screamed.

The grandmother had the peculiar feeling that the bespectacled man was someone she knew. His face was as familiar to her as if she had known him all her life but she could not recall who he was. He moved away from the car and began to come down the embankment, placing his feet carefully so that he wouldn't slip. He had on tan and white shoes and no socks, and his ankles were red and thin. "Good afternoon," he said. "I see you all had you a little spill."

75 "We turned over twice!" said the grandmother.

"Oncet," he corrected. "We seen it happen. Try their car and see will it run, Hiram," he said quietly to the boy with the gray hat.

"What you got that gun for?" John Wesley asked. "Watcha gonna do with that gun?"

"Lady," the man said to the children's mother, "would you mind calling them children to sit down by you? Children make me nervous. I want all you all to sit down right together there where you're at."

"What are you telling US what to do for?" June Star asked.

80 Behind them the line of woods gaped like a dark open mouth. "Come here," said their mother.

"Look here now," Bailey began suddenly, "we're in a predicament! We're in . . ."

The grandmother shrieked. She scrambled to her feet and stood staring. "You're The Misfit!" she said. "I recognized you at once!"

"Yes'm," the man said, smiling slightly as if he were pleased in spite of himself to be known, "but it would have been better for all of you, lady, if you hadn't of reckernized me."

Bailey turned his head sharply and said something to his mother that shocked even the children. The old lady began to cry and The Misfit reddened.

"Lady," he said, "don't you get upset. Sometimes a man says things he don't mean. I don't reckon he meant to talk to you thataway."

"You wouldn't shoot a lady, would you?" the grandmother said and removed a clean handkerchief from her cuff and began to slap at her eyes with it.

The Misfit pointed the toe of his shoe into the ground and made a little hole and then covered it up again. "I would hate to have to," he said.

"Listen," the grandmother almost screamed, "I know you're a good man. You don't look a bit like you have common blood. I know you must come from nice people!"

"Yes mam," he said, "finest people in the world." When he smiled he showed a row of strong white teeth. "God never made a finer woman than my mother and my daddy's heart was pure gold," he said. The boy with the red sweat shirt had come around behind them and was standing with his gun at his hip. The Misfit squatted down on the ground. "Watch them children, Bobby Lee," he said. "You know they make me nervous." He looked at the six of them huddled together in front of him and he seemed to be embarrassed as if he couldn't think of anything to say. "Ain't a cloud in the sky," he remarked, looking up at it. "Don't see no sun but don't see no cloud neither."

"Yes, it's a beautiful day," said the grandmother. "Listen," she said, "you shouldn't call yourself The Misfit because I know you're a good man at heart. I can just look at you and tell."

"Hush!" Bailey yelled. "Hush! Everybody shut up and let me handle this!" He was squatting in the position of a runner about to sprint forward but he didn't move.

"I pre-chate that, lady," The Misfit said and drew a little circle in the ground with the butt of his gun.

"It'll take a half a hour to fix this here car," Hiram called, looking over the raised hood of it.

"Well, first you and Bobby Lee get him and that little boy to step over yonder with you," The Misfit said, pointing to Bailey and John Wesley. "The boys want to ast you something," he said to Bailey. "Would you mind stepping back in them woods there with them?"

"Listen," Bailey began, "we're in a terrible predicament! Nobody realizes what this is," and his voice cracked. His eyes were as blue and intense as the parrots in his shirt and he remained perfectly still.

The grandmother reached up to adjust her hat brim as if she were going to the woods with him but it came off in her hand. She stood staring at it and

85

90

95

after a second she let it fall on the ground. Hiram pulled Bailey up by the arm as if he were assisting an old man. John Wesley caught hold of his father's hand and Bobby Lee followed. They went off toward the woods and just as they reached the dark edge, Bailey turned and supporting himself against a gray naked pine trunk, he shouted, "I'll be back in a minute, Mamma, wait on me!"

"Come back this instant!" his mother shrilled but they all disappeared into the woods.

"Bailey Boy!" the grandmother called in a tragic voice but she found she was looking at The Misfit squatting on the ground in front of her. "I just know you're a good man," she said desperately. "You're not a bit common!"

"Nome, I ain't a good man," The Misfit said after a second as if he had considered her statement carefully, "but I ain't the worst in the world neither. My daddy said I was a different breed of dog from my brothers and sisters. 'You know,' Daddy said, 'it's some that can live their whole life out without asking about it and it's others has to know why it is, and this boy is one of the latters. He's going to be into everything!'" He put on his black hat and looked up suddenly and then away deep into the woods as if he were embarrassed again. "I'm sorry I don't have on a shirt before you ladies," he said, hunching his shoulders slightly. "We buried our clothes that we had on when we escaped and we're just making do until we can get better. We borrowed these from some folks we met," he explained.

100   "That's perfectly all right," the grandmother said. "Maybe Bailey has an extra shirt in his suitcase."

"I'll look and see terrectly," The Misfit said.

"Where are they taking him?" the children's mother screamed.

"Daddy was a card himself," The Misfit said. "You couldn't put anything over on him. He never got in trouble with the Authorities though. Just had the knack of handling them."

"You could be honest too if you'd only try," said the grandmother. "Think how wonderful it would be to settle down and live a comfortable life and not have to think about somebody chasing you all the time."

105   The Misfit kept scratching in the ground with the butt of his gun as if he were thinking about it. "Yes'm, somebody is always after you," he murmured.

The grandmother noticed how thin his shoulder blades were just behind his hat because she was standing up looking down on him. "Do you ever pray?" she asked.

He shook his head. All she saw was the black hat wiggle between his shoulder blades. "Nome," he said.

There was a pistol shot from the woods, followed closely by another. Then silence. The old lady's head jerked around. She could hear the wind move through the tree tops like a long satisfied insuck of breath. "Bailey Boy!" she called.

"I was a gospel singer for a while," The Misfit said. "I been most everything. Been in the arm service, both land and sea, at home and abroad, been twict married, been an undertaker, been with the railroads, plowed Mother Earth,

been in a tornado, seen a man burnt alive oncet," and he looked up at the
children's mother and the little girl who were sitting close together, their faces
white and their eyes glassy; "I even seen a woman flogged," he said.

"Pray, pray," the grandmother began, "pray, pray . . ." 110

"I never was a bad boy that I remember of," The Misfit said in an almost
dreamy voice, "but somewheres along the line I done something wrong and got
sent to the penitentiary. I was buried alive," and he looked up and held her
attention to him by a steady stare.

"That's when you should have started to pray," she said. "What did you do to
get sent to the penitentiary that first time?"

"Turn to the right, it was a wall," The Misfit said, looking up again at the
cloudless sky. "Turn to the left, it was a wall. Look up it was a ceiling, look down
it was a floor. I forget what I done, lady. I set there and set there, trying to
remember what it was I done and I ain't recalled it to this day. Oncet in a while,
I would think it was coming to me, but it never come."

"Maybe they put you in by mistake," the old lady said vaguely.

"Nome," he said. "It wasn't no mistake. They had the papers on me." 115

"You must have stolen something," she said.

The Misfit sneered slightly. "Nobody had nothing I wanted," he said. "It was a
head-doctor at the penitentiary said what I had done was kill my daddy but I
known that for a lie. My daddy died in nineteen ought nineteen of the epidemic
flu and I never had a thing to do with it. He was buried in the Mount Hopewell
Baptist churchyard and you can go there and see for yourself."

"If you would pray," the old lady said, "Jesus would help you."

"That's right," The Misfit said.

"Well then, why don't you pray?" she asked trembling with delight suddenly. 120

"I don't want no hep," he said. "I'm doing all right by myself."

Bobby Lee and Hiram came ambling back from the woods. Bobby Lee was
dragging a yellow shirt with bright blue parrots in it.

"Thow me that shirt, Bobby Lee," The Misfit said. The shirt came flying at
him and landed on his shoulder and he put it on. The grandmother couldn't
name what the shirt reminded her of. "No, lady," The Misfit said while he was
buttoning it up, "I found out the crime don't matter. You can do one thing or
you can do another, kill a man or take a tire off his car, because sooner or later
you're going to forget what it was you done and just be punished for it."

The children's mother had begun to make heaving noises as if she couldn't
get her breath. "Lady," he asked, "would you and that little girl like to step off
yonder with Bobby Lee and Hiram and join your husband?"

"Yes, thank you," the mother said faintly. Her left arm dangled helplessly and 125
she was holding the baby, who had gone to sleep, in the other. "Hep that lady
up, Hiram," The Misfit said as she struggled to climb out of the ditch, "and
Bobby Lee, you hold onto that little girl's hand."

"I don't want to hold hands with him," June Star said. "He reminds me of a
pig."

The fat boy blushed and laughed and caught her by the arm and pulled her
off into the woods after Hiram and her mother.

Alone with The Misfit, the grandmother found that she had lost her voice. There was not a cloud in the sky nor any sun. There was nothing around her but woods. She wanted to tell him that he must pray. She opened and closed her mouth several times before anything came out. Finally she found herself saying, "Jesus, Jesus," meaning, Jesus will help you, but the way she was saying it, it sounded as if she might be cursing.

"Yes'm," The Misfit said as if he agreed. "Jesus thown everything off balance. It was the same case with Him as with me except He hadn't committed any crime and they could prove I had committed one because they had the papers on me. Of course," he said, "they never shown me my papers. That's why I sign myself now. I said long ago, you get you a signature and sign everything you do and keep a copy of it. Then you'll know what you done and you can hold up the crime to the punishment and see do they match and in the end you'll have something to prove you ain't been treated right. I call myself The Misfit," he said, "because I can't make what all I done wrong fit what all I gone through in punishment."

130   There was a piercing scream from the woods, followed closely by a pistol report. "Does it seem right to you, lady, that one is punished a heap and another ain't punished at all?"

"Jesus!" the old lady cried. "You've got good blood! I know you wouldn't shoot a lady! I know you come from nice people! Pray! Jesus, you ought not to shoot a lady. I'll give you all the money I've got!"

"Lady," The Misfit said, looking beyond her far into the woods, "there never was a body that give the undertaker a tip."

There were two more pistol reports and the grandmother raised her head like a parched old turkey hen crying for water and called, "Bailey Boy, Bailey Boy!" as if her heart would break.

"Jesus was the only One that ever raised the dead," The Misfit continued, "and He shouldn't have done it. He thown everything off balance. If He did what He said, then it's nothing for you to do but thow away everything and follow Him, and if He didn't, then it's nothing for you to do but enjoy the few minutes you got left the best way you can—by killing somebody or burning down his house or doing some other meanness to him. No pleasure but meanness," he said and his voice became almost a snarl.

135   "Maybe He didn't raise the dead," the old lady mumbled, not knowing what she was saying and feeling so dizzy that she sank down in the ditch with her legs twisted under her.

"I wasn't there so I can't say He didn't," The Misfit said. "I wisht I had of been there," he said, hitting the ground with his fist. "It ain't right I wasn't there because if I had of been there I would of known. Listen, lady," he said in a high voice, "if I had of been there I would of known and I wouldn't be like I am now." His voice seemed about to crack and the grandmother's head cleared for an instant. She saw the man's face twisted close to her own as if he were going to cry and she murmured, "Why you're one of my babies. You're one of my own children!" She reached out and touched him on the shoulder. The Misfit sprang back as if a snake had bitten him and shot her three times through the chest. Then he put his gun down on the ground and took off his glasses and began to clean them.

Hiram and Bobby Lee returned from the woods and stood over the ditch, looking down at the grandmother who half sat and half lay in a puddle of blood with her legs crossed under her like a child's and her face smiling up at the cloudless sky.

Without his glasses, The Misfit's eyes were red-rimmed and pale and defenseless-looking. "Take her off and thow her where you thown the others," he said, picking up the cat that was rubbing itself against his leg.

"She was a talker, wasn't she?" Bobby Lee said, sliding down the ditch with a yodel.

"She would of been a good woman," The Misfit said, "if it had been somebody there to shoot her every minute of her life." 140

"Some fun!" Bobby Lee said.

"Shut up, Bobby Lee," The Misfit said. "It's no real pleasure in life."

[1955]

1. What is this story's tone? How does it shift when The Misfit enters the scene?
2. What is the significance of the title of this story?
3. What does The Misfit mean at the end of the story when he says "She would of been a good woman . . . if it had been somebody there to shoot her every minute of her life"?
4. Flannery O'Connor was a devout Roman Catholic, and she once stated that each of her stories was about "the action of grace and its effect upon a character."[1] Can you pinpoint the "action of grace" in this story? Can you determine its effect?
5. O'Connor was often criticized for the degree of violence in her stories. Is the violence in this story gratuitous? Or does it serve a thematic purpose?
6. O'Connor's fiction has troubled some readers in its liberal use of racial epithets. In what way, if at all, does the grandmother's racial insensitivity serve the theme of the story?

[1]Sally Fitzgerald, ed. *The Habit of Being: Letters of Flannery O'Connor* (New York: Farrar Strauss and Giroux, 1979), 373.

FRANK O'CONNOR

FRANK O'CONNOR (1903–66), *short story writer, essayist, literary critic, travel writer, translator, and biographer, was a prolific and popular author. His* Collected Stories *edited by Richard Ellman appeared in 1981; the best-known are "Guests of the Nation," "My Oedipus Complex," and "First Confession."*

Guests of the Nation

1

At dusk the big Englishman, Belcher, would shift his long legs out of the ashes and say "Well, chums, what about it?" and Noble or me would say "All right, chum" (for we had picked up some of their curious expressions), and the little Englishman, Hawkins, would light the lamp and bring out the cards. Sometimes Jeremiah Donovan would come up and supervise the game and get excited over Hawkins's cards, which he always played badly, and shout at him as if he was one of our own, "Ah, you divil, you, why didn't you play the tray?"

But ordinarily Jeremiah was a sober and contented poor devil like the big Englishman, Belcher, and was looked up to only because he was a fair hand at documents, though he was slow enough even with them. He wore a small cloth hat and big gaiters over his long pants, and you seldom saw him with his hands out of his pockets. He reddened when you talked to him, tilting from toe to heel and back, and looking down all the time at his big farmer's feet. Noble and me used to make fun of his broad accent, because we were from the town.

I couldn't at the time see the point of me and Noble guarding Belcher and Hawkins at all, for it was my belief that you could have planted that pair down anywhere from this to Claregalway° and they'd have taken root there like a native weed. I never in my short experience seen two men to take to the country as they did.

They were handed on to us by the Second Battalion when the search for them became too hot, and Noble and myself, being young, took over with a natural feeling of responsibility, but Hawkins made us look like fools when he showed that he knew the country better than we did.

5 "You're the bloke they calls Bonaparte," he says to me. "Mary Brigid O'Connell told me to ask you what you done with the pair of her brother's socks you borrowed."

For it seemed, as they explained it, that the Second used to have little evenings, and some of the girls of the neighborhood turned in, and, seeing they were such decent chaps, our fellows couldn't leave the two Englishmen out of them. Hawkins learned to dance "The Walls of Limerick," "The Siege of Ennis," and "The Waves of Tory"° as well as any of them, though, naturally, we couldn't return the compliment, because our lads at that time did not dance foreign dances on principle.

So whatever privileges Belcher and Hawkins had with the Second they just naturally took with us, and after the first day or two we gave up all pretense of keeping a close eye on them. Not that they could have got far, for they had accents you could cut with a knife and wore khaki tunics and overcoats with civilian pants and boots. But it's my belief that they never had any idea of escaping and were quite content to be where they were.

It was a treat to see how Belcher got off with the old woman of the house where we were staying. She was a great warrant to scold, and cranky even with

---

³**Claregalway** a village in County Galway, Ireland ⁶**"The Walls of Limerick," "The Siege of Ennis," "The Waves of Tory"** Irish folk dances

us, but before ever she had a chance of giving our guests, as I may call them, a lick of her tongue, Belcher had made her his friend for life. She was breaking sticks, and Belcher, who hadn't been more than ten minutes in the house, jumped up from his seat and went over to her.

"Allow me, madam," he says, smiling his queer little smile, "please allow me"; and he takes the bloody hatchet. She was struck too paralytic to speak, and after that, Belcher would be at her heels, carrying a bucket, a basket, or a load of turf, as the case might be. As Noble said, he got into looking before she leapt, and hot water, or any little thing she wanted, Belcher would have it ready for her. For such a huge man (and though I am five foot ten myself I had to look up at him) he had an uncommon shortness—or should I say lack?—of speech. It took us some time to get used to him, walking in and out, like a ghost, without a word. Especially because Hawkins talked enough for a platoon, it was strange to hear big Belcher with his toes in the ashes come out with a solitary "Excuse me, chum," or "That's right, chum." His one and only passion was cards, and I will say for him that he was a good cardplayer. He could have fleeced myself and Noble, but whatever we lost to him Hawkins lost to us, and Hawkins played with the money Belcher gave him.

Hawkins lost to us because he had too much old gab, and we probably lost to Belcher for the same reason. Hawkins and Noble would spit at one another about religion into the early hours of the morning, and Hawkins worried the soul out of Noble, whose brother was a priest, with a string of questions that would puzzle a cardinal. To make it worse, even in treating of holy subjects, Hawkins had a deplorable tongue. I never in all my career met a man who could mix such a variety of cursing and bad language into an argument. He was a terrible man, and a fright to argue. He never did a stroke of work, and when he had no one else to talk to, he got stuck in the old woman.

He met his match in her, for one day when he tried to get her to complain profanely of the drought, she gave him a great come-down by blaming it entirely on Jupiter Pluvius (a deity neither Hawkins nor I had ever heard of, though Noble said that among the pagans it was believed that he had something to do with the rain). Another day he was swearing at the capitalists for starting the German war° when the old lady laid down her iron, puckered up her little crab's mouth, and said: "Mr. Hawkins, you can say what you like about the war, and think you'll deceive me because I'm only a simple poor countrywoman, but I know what started the war. It was the Italian Count that stole the heathen divinity out of the temple in Japan. Believe me, Mr. Hawkins, nothing but sorrow and want can follow the people that disturb the hidden powers."

A queer old girl, all right.

2

We had our tea one evening, and Hawkins lit the lamp and we all sat into cards. Jeremiah Donovan came in too, and sat down and watched us for a while, and it suddenly struck me that he had no great love for the two Englishmen. It

[11]**the German war** World War I, 1914–1918

came as a great surprise to me, because I hadn't noticed anything about him
before.

Late in the evening a really terrible argument blew up between Hawkins and
Noble, about capitalists and priests and love of your country.

"The capitalists," says Hawkins with an angry gulp, "pays the priests to tell
you about the next world so as you won't notice what the bastards are up to in
this."

"Nonsense, man!" says Noble, losing his temper. "Before ever a capitalist was
thought of, people believed in the next world."

5   Hawkins stood up as though he was preaching a sermon.

"Oh, they did, did they?" he says with a sneer. "They believed all the things
you believe, isn't that what you mean? And you believe that God created Adam,
and Adam created Shem, and Shem created Jehoshaphat. You believe all that
silly old fairytale about Eve and Eden and the apple. Well, listen to me, chum. If
you're entitled to hold a silly belief like that, I'm entitled to hold my silly
belief—which is that the first thing your God created was a bleeding capitalist,
with morality and Rolls-Royce complete. Am I right, chum?" he says to Belcher.

"You're right, chum," says Belcher with his amused smile, and got up from
the table to stretch his long legs into the fire and stroke his moustache. So,
seeing that Jeremiah Donovan was going, and that there was no knowing when
the argument about religion would be over, I went out with him. We strolled
down to the village together, and then he stopped and started blushing and
mumbling and saying I ought to be behind, keeping guard on the prisoners.
I didn't like the tone he took with me, and anyway I was bored with life in the
cottage, so I replied by asking him what the hell we wanted guarding them at
all for. I told him I'd talked it over with Noble, and that we'd both rather be out
with a fighting column.

"What use are those fellows to us?" says I.

He looked at me in surprise and said: "I thought you knew we were keeping
them as hostages."

10   "Hostages?" I said.

"The enemy have prisoners belonging to us," he says, "and now they're
talking of shooting them. If they shoot our prisoners, we'll shoot theirs."

"Shoot them?" I said.

"What else did you think we were keeping them for?" he says.

"Wasn't it very unforeseen of you not to warn Noble and myself of that in the
beginning?" I said.

15   "How was it?" says he. "You might have known it."

"We couldn't know it, Jeremiah Donovan," says I. "How could we when they
were on our hands so long?"

"The enemy have our prisoners as long and longer," says he.

"That's not the same thing at all," says I.

"What difference is there?" says he.

20   I couldn't tell him, because I knew he wouldn't understand. If it was only an
old dog that was going to the vet's, you'd try and not get too fond of him, but
Jeremiah Donovan wasn't a man that would ever be in danger of that.

"And when is this thing going to be decided?" says I.

"We might hear tonight," he says. "Or tomorrow or the next day at latest. So if it's only hanging round here that's a trouble to you, you'll be free soon enough."

It wasn't the hanging round that was a trouble to me at all by this time. I had worse things to worry about. When I got back to the cottage the argument was still on. Hawkins was holding forth in his best style, maintaining that there was no next world, and Noble was maintaining that there was; but I could see that Hawkins had had the best of it.

"Do you know what, chum?" he was saying with a saucy smile. "I think you're just as big a bleeding unbeliever as I am. You say you believe in the next world, and you know just as much about the next world as I do, which is sweet damn-all. What's heaven? You don't know. Where's heaven? You don't know. You know sweet damn-all! I ask you again, do they wear wings?"

"Very well, then," says Noble, "they do. Is that enough for you? They do wear wings." 25

"Where do they get them, then? Who makes them? Have they a factory for wings? Have they a sort of store where you hands in your chit and takes your bleeding wings?"

"You're an impossible man to argue with," says Noble. "Now, listen to me—" And they were off again.

It was long after midnight when we locked up and went to bed. As I blew out the candle I told Noble what Jeremiah Donovan was after telling me. Noble took it very quietly. When we'd been in bed about an hour he asked me did I think we ought to tell the Englishmen. I didn't think we should, because it was more than likely that the English wouldn't shoot our men, and even if they did, the brigade officers, who were always up and down with the Second Battalion and knew the Englishmen well, wouldn't be likely to want them plugged. "I think so too," says Noble. "It would be great cruelty to put the wind up them now."

"It was very unforeseen of Jeremiah Donovan anyhow," says I.

It was next morning that we found it so hard to face Belcher and Hawkins. 30 We went about the house all day scarcely saying a word. Belcher didn't seem to notice; he was stretched into the ashes as usual, with his usual look of waiting in quietness for something unforeseen to happen, but Hawkins noticed and put it down to Noble's being beaten in the argument of the night before.

"Why can't you take a discussion in the proper spirit?" he says severely. "You and your Adam and Eve! I'm a Communist, that's what I am. Communist or anarchist, it all comes to much the same thing." And for hours he went round the house, muttering when the fit took him. "Adam and Eve! Adam and Eve! Nothing better to do with their time than picking bleeding apples!"

3

I don't know how we got through that day, but I was very glad when it was over, the tea things were cleared away, and Belcher said in his peaceable way: "Well, chums, what about it?" We sat round the table and Hawkins took out the cards, and just then I heard Jeremiah Donovan's footstep on the path and a dark presentiment crossed my mind. I rose from the table and caught him before he reached the door.

"What do you want?" I asked.

"I want those two soldier friends of yours," he says, getting red.

"Is that the way, Jeremiah Donovan?" I asked.

5 "That's the way. There were four of our lads shot this morning, one of them a boy of sixteen."

"That's bad," I said.

At that moment Noble followed me out, and the three of us walked down the path together, talking in whispers. Feeney, the local intelligence officer, was standing by the gate.

"What are you going to do about it?" I asked Jeremiah Donovan.

"I want you and Noble to get them out; tell them they're being shifted again; that'll be the quietest way."

10 "Leave me out of that," says Noble under his breath.

Jeremiah Donovan looks at him hard.

"All right," he says. "You and Feeney get a few tools from the shed and dig a hole by the far end of the bog. Bonaparte and myself will be after you. Don't let anyone see you with the tools. I wouldn't like it to go beyond ourselves."

We saw Feeney and Noble go round to the shed and went in ourselves. I left Jeremiah Donovan to do the explanations. He told them that he had orders to send them back to the Second Battalion. Hawkins let out a mouthful of curses, and you could see that though Belcher didn't say anything, he was a bit upset too. The old woman was for having them stay in spite of us, and she didn't stop advising them until Jeremiah Donovan lost his temper and turned on her. He had a nasty temper, I noticed. It was pitch-dark in the cottage by this time, but no one thought of lighting the lamp, and in the darkness the two Englishmen fetched their topcoats and said good-bye to the old woman.

"Just as a man makes a home of a bleeding place, some bastard at headquarters thinks you're too cushy and shunts you off," says Hawkins, shaking her hand.

15 "A thousand thanks, madam," says Belcher. "A thousand thanks for everything"—as though he'd made it up.

We went round to the back of the house and down towards the bog. It was only then that Jeremiah Donovan told them. He was shaking with excitement.

"There were four of our fellows shot in Cork° this morning and now you're to be shot as a reprisal."

"What are you talking about?" snaps Hawkins. "It's bad enough being mucked about as we are without having to put up with your funny jokes."

"It isn't a joke," says Donovan. "I'm sorry, Hawkins, but it's true," and begins on the usual rigmarole about duty and how unpleasant it is.

20 I never noticed that people who talk a lot about duty find it much of a trouble to them.

"Oh, cut it out!" says Hawkins.

[17] **Cork** city in southwest Ireland

"Ask Bonaparte," says Donovan, seeing that Hawkins isn't taking him seriously. "Isn't it true, Bonaparte?"

"It is," I say, and Hawkins stops.

"Ah, for Christ's sake, chum."

"I mean it, chum," I say.

"You don't sound as if you meant it."

"If he doesn't mean it, I do," says Donovan, working himself up.

"What have you against me, Jeremiah Donovan?"

"I never said I had anything against you. But why did your people take out four of our prisoners and shoot them in cold blood?"

He took Hawkins by the arm and dragged him on, but it was impossible to make him understand that we were in earnest. I had the Smith and Wesson° in my pocket and I kept fingering it and wondering what I'd do if they put up a fight for it or ran, and wishing to God they'd do one or the other. I knew if they did run for it, that I'd never fire on them. Hawkins wanted to know was Noble in it, and when we said yes, he asked why Noble wanted to plug him. Why did any of us want to plug him? What had he done to us? Weren't we all chums? Didn't we understand him and didn't he understand us? Did we imagine for an instant that he'd shoot us for all the so-and-so officers in the so-and-so British Army?

By this time we'd reached the bog, and I was so sick I couldn't even answer him. We walked along the edge of it in the darkness, and every now and then Hawkins would call a halt and begin all over again, as if he was wound up, about our being chums, and I knew that nothing but the sight of the grave would convince him that we had to do it. And all the time I was hoping that something would happen; that they'd run for it or that Noble would take over the responsibility from me. I had the feeling that it was worse on Noble than on me.

4

At last we saw the lantern in the distance and made towards it. Noble was carrying it, and Feeney was standing somewhere in the darkness behind him, and the picture of them so still and silent in the bogland brought it home to me that we were in earnest, and banished the last bit of hope I had.

Belcher, on recognizing Noble, said: "Hallo, chum," in his quiet way, but Hawkins flew at him at once, and the argument began all over again, only this time Noble had nothing to say for himself and stood with his head down, holding the lantern between his legs.

It was Jeremiah Donovan who did the answering. For the twentieth time, as though it was haunting his mind, Hawkins asked if anybody thought he'd shoot Noble.

"Yes, you would," says Jeremiah Donovan.

"No, I wouldn't, damn you!"

"You would, because you'd know you'd be shot for not doing it."

[30]**Smith and Wesson** revolver made in America

"I wouldn't, not if I was to be shot twenty times over. I wouldn't shoot a pal. And Belcher wouldn't—isn't that right, Belcher?"

"That's right, chum," Belcher said, but more by way of answering the question than of joining in the argument. Belcher sounded as though whatever unforeseen thing he'd always been waiting for had come at last.

"Anyway, who says Noble would be shot if I wasn't? What do you think I'd do if I was in his place, out in the middle of a blasted bog?"

10 "What would you do?" asks Donovan.

"I'd go with him wherever he was going, of course. Share my last bob° with him and stick by him through thick and thin. No one can ever say of me that I let down a pal."

"We had enough of this," says Jeremiah Donovan, cocking his revolver. "Is there any message you want to send?"

"No, there isn't."

"Do you want to say your prayers?"

15 Hawkins came out with a cold-blooded remark that even shocked me and turned on Noble again.

"Listen to me, Noble," he says. "You and me are chums. You can't come over to my side, so I'll come over to your side. That show you I mean what I say? Give me a rifle and I'll go along with you and the other lads."

Nobody answered him. We knew that was no way out.

"Hear what I'm saying?" he says. "I'm through with it. I'm a deserter or anything else you like. I don't believe in your stuff, but it's no worse than mine. That satisfy you?"

Noble raised his head, but Donovan began to speak and he lowered it again without replying.

20 "For the last time, have you any messages to send?" says Donovan in a cold, excited sort of voice.

"Shut up, Donovan! You don't understand me, but these lads do. They're not the sort to make a pal and kill a pal. They're not the tools of any capitalist."

I alone of the crowd saw Donovan raise his Webley° to the back of Hawkin's neck, and as he did so I shut my eyes and tried to pray. Hawkins had begun to say something else when Donovan fired, and as I opened my eyes at the bang, I saw Hawkins stagger at the knees and lie out flat at Noble's feet, slowly and as quiet as a kid falling asleep, with the lantern-light on his lean legs and bright farmer's boots. We all stood very still, watching him settle out in the last agony.

Then Belcher took out a handkerchief and began to tie it about his own eyes (in our excitement we'd forgotten to do the same for Hawkins), and, seeing it wasn't big enough, turned and asked for the loan of mine. I gave it to him and he knotted the two together and pointed with his foot at Hawkins.

"He's not quite dead," he says. "Better give him another."

25 Sure enough, Hawkins's left knee is beginning to rise. I bend down and put my gun to his head; then, recollecting myself, I get up again. Belcher understands what's in my mind.

---

¹¹**bob** British coin worth one shilling, or 12 pence   ²²**Webley** British-made revolver

"Give him his first," he says. "I don't mind. Poor bastard, we don't know what's happening to him now."

I knelt and fired. By this time I didn't seem to know what I was doing. Belcher, who was fumbling a bit awkwardly with the handkerchiefs, came out with a laugh as he heard the shot. It was the first time I heard him laugh and it sent a shudder down my back; it sounded so unnatural.

"Poor bugger!" he said quietly. "And last night he was so curious about it all. It's very queer, chums, I always think. Now he knows as much about it as they'll ever let him know, and last night he was all in the dark."

Donovan helped him to tie the handkerchiefs about his eyes. "Thanks, chum," he said. Donovan asked if there were any messages he wanted sent.

"No, chum," he says. "Not for me. If any of you would like to write to   30
Hawkins's mother, you'll find a letter from her in his pocket. He and his mother were great chums. But my missus left me eight years ago. Went away with another fellow and took the kid with her. I like the feeling of a home, as you may have noticed, but I couldn't start again after that."

It was an extraordinary thing, but in those few minutes Belcher said more than in all the weeks before. It was just as if the sound of the shot had started a flood of talk in him and he could go on the whole night like that, quite happily, talking about himself. We stood round like fools now that he couldn't see us any longer. Donovan looked at Noble, and Noble shook his head. Then Donovan raised his Webley, and at that moment Belcher gives his queer laugh again. He may have thought we were talking about him, or perhaps he noticed the same thing I'd noticed and couldn't understand it.

"Excuse me, chums," he says. "I feel I'm talking the hell of a lot, and so silly about my being so handy about a house and things like that. But this thing came on me suddenly. You'll forgive me, I'm sure."

"You don't want to say a prayer?" asked Donovan.

"No, chum," he says. "I don't think it would help. I'm ready, and you boys want to get it over."

"You understand that we're only doing our duty?" says Donovan.   35

Belcher's head was raised like a blind man's, so that you could only see his chin and the tip of his nose in the lantern-light.

"I never could make out what duty was myself," he said. "I think you're all good lads, if that's what you mean. I'm not complaining."

Noble, just as if he couldn't bear any more of it, raised his fist at Donovan, and in a flash Donovan raised his gun and fired. The big man went over like a sack of meal, and this time there was no need of a second shot.

I don't remember much about the burying, but that it was worse than all this rest because we had to carry them to the grave. It was all mad lonely with nothing but a patch of lantern-light between ourselves and the dark, and birds hooting and screeching all round, disturbed by the guns. Noble went through Hawkins's belongings to find the letter from his mother, and then joined his hands together. He did the same with Belcher. Then, when we'd filled in the grave, we separated from Jeremiah Donovan and Feeney and took our tools back to the shed. All the way we didn't speak a word. The kitchen was dark and cold as we'd left it, and the old woman was sitting over the hearth, saying her beads. We walked past her into the room, and Noble struck a match to light the lamp. She rose quietly and came to the doorway with all her cantankerousness gone.

40   "What did ye do with them?" she asked in a whisper, and Noble started so that the match went out in his hand.

"What's that?" he asked without turning round.

"I heard ye," she said.

"What did you hear?" asked Noble.

"I heard ye. Do ye think I didn't hear ye, putting the spade back in the houseen?"°

45   Noble struck another match and this time the lamp lit for him.

"Was that what ye did to them?" she asked.

Then, by God, in the very doorway, she fell on her knees and began praying, and after looking at her for a minute or two Noble did the same by the fireplace. I pushed my way out past her and left them at it. I stood at the door, watching the stars and listening to the shrieking of the birds dying out over the bogs. It is so strange what you feel at times like that you can't describe it. Noble says he saw everything ten times the size, as though there were nothing in the whole world but that little patch of bog with the two Englishmen stiffening into it, but with me it was as if the patch of bog where the Englishmen were was a million miles away, and even Noble and the old woman, mumbling behind me, and the birds and the bloody stars were all far away, and I was somehow very small and very lost and lonely like a child astray in the snow. And anything that happened to me afterwards, I never felt the same about again.   [1931]

44**houseen** small house

1. What kind of narrator tells this story? What information does he give about himself?
2. Why does Belcher suddenly become talkative towards the end of the story, when he realizes that his death is immanent? How does this shift in characterization affect how the reader experiences him?
3. The story explores the different effects that religious belief and unbelief can have upon different people. Do belief in God and compassion go together in this story? What about unbelief? What is the story's attitude toward duty?
4. Put the story into a historical context.

DOROTHY PARKER

DOROTHY PARKER *(1893–1967), née Dorothy Rothschild, one of the most successful and influential women writers of her era, was born in West End, New Jersey, child of a Scottish mother and Jewish father. Her mother died when Dorothy was four, and her father's unhappy remarriage affected her deeply, as did the death of her brother*

aboard the Titanic *and of her father a year later. She moved to New York City at eigh-
teen, living in a boarding house and working as a piano player for a dancing school.
She began submitting her writing to magazines and a poem of hers was accepted by*
Vanity Fair. *She was soon hired by* Vogue *as a writer, later transferring to* Vanity
Fair, *and became New York's only drama critic. An invitation to move into the
Algonquin Hotel made her the only female founding member of the famous
Algonquin Round Table, a circle of intellectuals that included Robert Benchley,
Robert Sherwood, James Thurber, George Kaufman, and many others. She wrote her
first short story, divorced her husband Edwin Parker, moved permanently into the
Algonquin, and contributed articles to the first issues of the smart new magazine, the*
New Yorker. *Her first play,* Close Harmony, *came out, and then her book of poems,*
Enough Rope. *Her short story "Big Blonde" earned her the O. Henry Award for that
year. She moved to Hollywood, met and married Alan Campbell, and they became
screen-writing partners. In 1936 she helped found the Anti-Nazi League, and the
next year won an Academy Award for her screenplay,* A Star Is Born. *In the '50s she
was called before the House Un-American Activities Committee and asked to name
Communists she knew, remaining silent, even though evidence was entered against
her for her previous involvement with the Sacco–Vanzetti case and her membership
in the Socialist Party. She was inducted into the American Academy of Arts and
Letters in 1959 and was a distinguished Visiting Professor of English at California
State College in Los Angeles. She bequeathed her entire estate to the NAACP.*

The Custard Heart

No living eye, of human being or caged wild beast or dear, domestic animal, had
beheld Mrs. Lanier when she was not being wistful. She was dedicated to
wistfulness, as lesser artists to words and paint and marble. Mrs. Lanier was not
of the lesser; she was of the true. Surely the eternal example of the true artist is
Dickens's actor who blacked himself all over to play Othello. It is safe to assume
that Mrs. Lanier was wistful in her bathroom, and slumbered soft in wistfulness
through the dark and secret night.

If nothing should happen to the portrait of her by Sir James Weir, there she
will stand, wistful for the ages. He has shown her at her full length, all in yellows,
the delicately heaped curls, the slender, arched feet like elegant bananas, the
shining stretch of the evening gown; Mrs. Lanier habitually wore white in the
evening, but white is the devil's own hue to paint, and could a man be expected
to spend his entire six weeks in the States on the execution of a single commission? Wistfulness rests, immortal, in the eyes dark with sad hope, in the pleading
mouth, the droop of the little head on the sweet long neck, bowed as if in submission to the three ropes of Lanier pearls. It is true that, when the portrait was
exhibited, one critic expressed in print his puzzlement as to what a woman who
owned such pearls had to be wistful about; but that was doubtless because he had
sold his saffron-colored soul for a few pennies to the proprietor of a rival gallery.
Certainly, no man could touch Sir James on pearls. Each one is as distinct, as
individual as is each little soldier's face in a Meissonier° battle scene.

[2]**Meissonier** Jean-Louis-Ernest Meissonier, French painter (1815–91)

For a time, with the sitter's obligation to resemble the portrait, Mrs. Lanier wore yellow of evenings. She had gowns of velvet like poured country cream and satin with the lacquer of buttercups and chiffon that spiraled about her like golden smoke. She wore them, and listened in shy surprise to the resulting comparisons to daffodils, and butterflies in the sunshine, and such; but she knew.

"It just isn't me," she sighed at last, and returned to her lily draperies. Picasso had his blue period, and Mrs. Lanier her yellow one. They both knew when to stop.

5   In the afternoons, Mrs. Lanier wore black, thin and fragrant, with the great pearls weeping on her breast. What her attire was by morning, only Gwennie, the maid who brought her breakfast tray, could know; but it must, of course, have been exquisite. Mr. Lanier—certainly there was a Mr. Lanier; he had even been seen—stole past her door on his way out to his office, and the servants glided and murmured, so that Mrs. Lanier might be spared as long as possible from the bright new cruelty of the day. Only when the littler, kinder hours had succeeded noon could she bring herself to come forth and face the recurrent sorrows of living.

There was duty to be done, almost daily, and Mrs. Lanier made herself brave for it. She must go in her town car to select new clothes and to have fitted to her perfection those she had ordered before. Such garments as hers did not just occur; like great poetry, they required labor. But she shrank from leaving the shelter of her house, for everywhere without were the unlovely and the sad, to assail her eyes and her heart. Often she stood shrinking for several minutes by the baroque mirror in her hall before she could manage to hold her head high and brave, and go on.

There is no safety for the tender, no matter how straight their route, how innocent their destination. Sometimes, even in front of Mrs. Lanier's dressmaker's or her furrier's or her lingère's or her milliner's, there would be a file of thin girls and small, shabby men, who held placards in their cold hands and paced up and down and up and down with slow, measured steps. Their faces would be blue and rough from the wind, and blank with the monotony of their treadmill. They looked so little and poor and strained that Mrs. Lanier's hands would fly to her heart in pity. Her eyes would be luminous with sympathy and her sweet lips would part as if on a whisper of cheer, as she passed through the draggled line into the shop.

Often there would be pencil-sellers in her path, a half of a creature set upon a sort of roller-skate thrusting himself along the pavement by his hands, or a blind man shuffling after his wavering cane. Mrs. Lanier must stop and sway, her eyes closed, one hand about her throat to support her lovely, stricken head. Then you could actually see her force herself, could see the effort ripple her body, as she opened her eyes and gave these miserable ones, the blind and the seeing alike, a smile of such tenderness, such sorrowful understanding, that it was like the exquisite sad odor of hyacinths on the air. Sometimes, if the man was not too horrible, she could even reach in her purse for a coin and, holding it as lightly as if she had plucked it from a silvery stem, extend her slim arm and drop it in his cup. If he was young and new at his life, he would offer her pencils for the worth of her money; but Mrs. Lanier wanted no returns. In gentlest delicacy she would slip away, leaving him with mean wares intact, not a worker for his livelihood like a million others, but signal and set apart, rare in the fragrance of charity.

So it was, when Mrs. Lanier went out. Everywhere she saw them, the ragged, the wretched, the desperate, and to each she gave her look that spoke with no words.

"Courage," it said. "And you—oh, wish me courage, too!" 10

Frequently, by the time she returned to her house, Mrs. Lanier would be limp as a freesia. Her maid Gwennie would have to beseech her to lie down, to gain the strength to change her gown for a filmier one and descend to her drawing-room, her eyes darkly mournful, but her exquisite breasts pointed high.

In her drawing-room, there was sanctuary. Here her heart might heal from the blows of the world, and be whole for its own sorrow. It was a room suspended above life, a place of tender fabrics and pale flowers, with never a paper or a book to report the harrowing or describe it. Below the great sheet of its window swung the river, and the stately scows went by laden with strange stuff in rich tapestry colors; there was no necessity to belong to the sort who must explain that it was garbage. An island with a happy name lay opposite, and on it stood a row of prim, tight buildings, naive as a painting by Rousseau. Sometimes there could be seen on the island the brisk figures of nurses and internes, sporting in the lanes. Possibly there were figures considerably less brisk beyond the barred windows of the buildings, but that was not to be wondered about in the presence of Mrs. Lanier. All those who came to her drawing-room came in one cause: to shield her heart from hurt.

Here in her drawing-room, in the lovely blue of the late day, Mrs. Lanier sat upon opalescent taffeta and was wistful. And here to her drawing-room, the young men came and tried to help her bear her life.

There was a pattern to the visits of the young men. They would come in groups of three or four or six, for a while; and then there would be one of them who would stay a little after the rest had gone, who presently would come a little earlier than the others. Then there would be days when Mrs. Lanier would cease to be at home to the other young men, and that one young man would be alone with her in the lovely blue. And then Mrs. Lanier would no longer be at home to that one young man, and Gwennie would have to tell him and tell him, over the telephone, that Mrs. Lanier was out, that Mrs. Lanier was ill, that Mrs. Lanier could not be disturbed. The groups of young men would come again; that one young man would not be with them. But there would be, among them, a new young man, who presently would stay a little later and come a little earlier, who eventually would plead with Gwennie over the telephone.

Gwennie—her widowed mother had named her Gwendola, and then, as if 15 realizing that no other dream would ever come true, had died—was little and compact and unnoticeable. She had been raised on an upstate farm by an uncle and aunt hard as the soil they fought for their lives. After their deaths, she had no relatives anywhere. She came to New York, because she had heard stories of jobs; her arrival was at the time when Mrs. Lanier's cook needed a kitchen-maid. So in her own house, Mrs. Lanier had found her treasure.

Gwennie's hard little farm-girl's fingers could set invisible stitches, could employ a flatiron as if it were a wand, could be as summer breezes in the robing of Mrs. Lanier and the tending of her hair. She was as busy as the day was long; and her days frequently extended from daybreak to daybreak. She was never tired, she had no grievance, she was cheerful without being expressive about it. There was nothing in her presence or the sight of her to touch the heart and thus cause discomfort.

Mrs. Lanier would often say that she didn't know what she would do without her little Gwennie; if her little Gwennie should ever leave her, she said, she just couldn't go on. She looked so lorn and fragile as she said it that one scowled upon Gwennie for the potentialities of death or marriage that the girl carried within her. Yet there was no pressing cause for worry, for Gwennie was strong as a pony and had no beau. She had made no friends at all, and seemed not to observe the omission. Her life was for Mrs. Lanier; like all others who were permitted close, Gwennie sought to do what she could to save Mrs. Lanier from pain.

They could all assist in shutting out reminders of the sadness abroad in the world, but Mrs. Lanier's private sorrow was a more difficult matter. There dwelt a yearning so deep, so secret in her heart that it would often be days before she could speak of it, in the twilight, to a new young man.

"If I only had a little baby," she would sigh, "a little, little baby, I think I could be almost happy." And she would fold her delicate arms, and lightly, slowly rock them, as if they cradled that little, little one of her dear dreams. Then, the denied madonna, she was at her most wistful, and the young man would have lived or died for her, as she bade him.

20 Mrs. Lanier never mentioned why her wish was unfulfilled; the young man would know her to be too sweet to place blame, too proud to tell. But, so close to her in the pale light, he would understand, and his blood would swirl with fury that such clods as Mr. Lanier remained unkilled. He would beseech Mrs. Lanier, first in halting murmurs, then in rushes of hot words, to let him take her away from the hell of her life and try to make her almost happy. It would be after this that Mrs. Lanier would be out to the young man, would be ill, would be incapable of being disturbed.

Gwennie did not enter the drawing-room when there was only one young man there; but when the groups returned she served unobtrusively; drawing a curtain or fetching a fresh glass. All the Lanier servants were unobtrusive, light of step and correctly indistinct of feature. When there must be changes made in the staff, Gwennie and the housekeeper arranged the replacements and did not speak of the matter to Mrs. Lanier, lest she should be stricken by desertions or saddened by tales of woe. Always the new servants resembled the old, alike in that they were unnoticeable. That is, until Kane, the new chauffeur, came.

The old chauffeur had been replaced because he had been the old chauffeur too long. It weighs cruelly heavy on the tender heart when a familiar face grows lined and dry, when familiar shoulders seem daily to droop lower, a familiar nape is hollow between cords. The old chauffeur saw and heard and functioned with no difference; but it was too much for Mrs. Lanier to see what was befalling him. With pain in her voice, she had told Gwennie that she could stand the sight of him no longer. So the old chauffeur had gone, and Kane had come.

Kane was young, and there was nothing depressing about his straight shoulders and his firm, full neck to one sitting behind them in the town car. He stood, a fine triangle in his fitted uniform, holding the door of the car open for Mrs. Lanier and bowed his head as she passed. But when he was not at work, his head was held high and slightly cocked, and there was a little cocked smile on his red mouth.

Often, in the cold weather when Kane waited for her in the car, Mrs. Lanier would humanely bid Gwennie to tell him to come in and wait in the servants' sitting-room. Gwennie brought him coffee and looked at him. Twice she did not hear Mrs. Lanier's enameled electric bell.

Gwennie began to observe her evenings off; before, she had disregarded them and stayed to minister to Mrs. Lanier. There was one night when Mrs. Lanier had floated late to her room, after a theater and a long conversation, done in murmurs, in the drawing-room. And Gwennie had not been waiting, to take off the white gown, and put away the pearls, and brush the bright hair that curled like the petals of forsythia. Gwennie had not yet returned to the house from her holiday. Mrs. Lanier had had to arouse a parlor-maid and obtain unsatisfactory aid from her. 25

Gwennie had wept, next morning, at the pathos of Mrs. Lanier's eyes; but tears were too distressing for Mrs. Lanier to see, and the girl stopped them. Mrs. Lanier delicately patted her arm, and there had been nothing more of the matter, save that Mrs. Lanier's eyes were darker and wider for this new hurt.

Kane became a positive comfort to Mrs. Lanier. After the sorry sights of the streets, it was good to see Kane standing by the car, solid and straight and young, with nothing in the world the trouble with him. Mrs. Lanier came to smile upon him almost gratefully, yet wistfully, too, as if she would seek of him the secret of not being sad.

And then, one day, Kane did not appear at his appointed time. The car, which should have been waiting to convey Mrs. Lanier to her dressmaker's, was still in the garage, and Kane had not appeared there all day. Mrs. Lanier told Gwennie immediately to telephone the place where he roomed and find out what this meant. The girl had cried out at her, cried out that she had called and called and called, and he was not there and no one there knew where he was. The crying out must have been due to Gwennie's loss of head in her distress at this disruption of Mrs. Lanier's day; or perhaps it was the effect on her voice of an appalling cold she seemed to have contracted, for her eyes were heavy and red and her face pale and swollen.

There was no more of Kane. He had had his wages paid him on the day before he disappeared, and that was the last of him. There was never a word and not another sight of him. At first, Mrs. Lanier could scarcely bring herself to believe that such betrayal could exist. Her heart, soft and sweet as a perfectly made crème renversée, quivered in her breast, and in her eyes lay the far light of suffering.

30   "Oh, how could he do this to me?" she asked piteously of Gwennie. "How could he do this to poor me?"

There was no discussion of the defection of Kane; it was too painful a subject. If a caller heedlessly asked whatever had become of that nice-looking chauffeur, Mrs. Lanier would lay her hand over her closed lids and slowly wince. The caller would be suicidal that he had thus unconsciously added to her sorrows, and would strive his consecrated best to comfort her.

Gwennie's cold lasted for an extraordinarily long time. The weeks went by, and still, every morning, her eyes were red and her face white and puffed. Mrs. Lanier often had to look away from her when she brought the breakfast tray.

She tended Mrs. Lanier as carefully as ever; she gave no attention to her holidays, but stayed to do further service. She had always been quiet, and she became all but silent, and that was additionally soothing. She worked without stopping and seemed to thrive, for, save for the effects of the curious cold, she looked round and healthy.

"See," Mrs. Lanier said in tender raillery, as the girl attended the group in the drawing-room, "see how fat my little Gwennie's getting! Isn't that cute?"

35   The weeks went on, and the pattern of the young men shifted again. There came the day when Mrs. Lanier was not at home to a group; when a new young man was to come and be alone with her, for his first time, in the drawing-room. Mrs. Lanier sat before her mirror and lightly touched her throat with perfume, while Gwennie heaped the golden curls.

The exquisite face Mrs. Lanier saw in the mirror drew her closer attention, and she put down the perfume and leaned toward it. She drooped her head a little to the side and watched it closely; she saw the wistful eyes grow yet more wistful, the lips curve to a pleading smile. She folded her arms close to her sweet breast and slowly rocked them, as if they cradled a dream-child. She watched the mirrored arms sway gently, caused them to sway a little slower.

"If I only had a little baby," she sighed. She shook her head. Delicately she cleared her throat, and sighed again on a slightly lower note. "If I only had a little, little baby, I think I could be almost happy."

There was a clatter from behind her, and she turned, amazed. Gwennie had dropped the hair-brush to the floor and stood swaying, with her face in her hands.

"Gwennie!" said Mrs. Lanier. "Gwennie!"

The girl took her hands from her face, and it was as if she stood under a green light.

40   "I'm sorry," she panted. "Sorry. Please excuse me. I'm—oh, I'm going to be sick!"

She ran from the room so violently that the floor shook.

Mrs. Lanier sat looking after Gwennie, her hands at her wounded heart. Slowly she turned back to her mirror, and what she saw there arrested her; the artist knows the masterpiece. Here was the perfection of her career, the sublimation of wistfulness; it was that look of grieved bewilderment that did it. Carefully she kept it upon her face as she rose from the mirror and, with her lovely hands still shielding her heart, went down to the new young man.   [1939]

1. Mrs. Lanier's appearance, actions, and mental processes are described in vivid, minute detail throughout the story. What is the importance of such detail to the story's theme?
2. How does Dorothy Parker alert the reader immediately to the shallowness of Mrs. Lanier's character?
3. What kind of narrator is this and what is the narrator's relationship to the point of view of Mrs. Lanier?
4. In many twentieth-century American short stories, characters are led, through the course of events, to a higher level of self-knowledge. Not in this story, however. To what end does Parker keep her characters static?
5. How does Mrs. Lanier succeed in giving the impression that she has empathy for "the ragged, the wretched, the desperate" while managing to do so little for them?
6. Why does Mrs. Lanier project the illusion that she is being denied the opportunity to bear a child?
7. What is the crisis point of the story? Does it resolve the conflicts of the plot? How does Goffman's concept of theatricality of self-presentation (see p. 194) help us understand it?
8. How do Leviticus 19 in the Hebrew Bible (p. 352), Luke 10:25–37 in the New Testament (p. 355), and Sura 89 in the Qur'an (p. 356) reflect on Mrs. Lanier's actions and self-understanding?

PHILIP ROTH

PHILIP ROTH *(1933–) was born and educated in Newark, New Jersey. He attended Bucknell University and the University of Chicago, where he completed his master's degree and taught English. He also taught creative writing at Iowa and Princeton. His first book,* Goodbye, Columbus, *depicted Jewish life in America after World War II. It gained him the National Book Award but it incensed many in the Jewish community, who felt betrayed. His first full-length novel was* Letting Go, *also centered in the issues of the 1950s, followed by* When She Was Good, *another realistic novel, this time with a woman as narrator.* Portnoy's Complaint, *his depiction of a man speaking to his psychiatrist and revealing everything about his domineering mother and his sexual practices, brought Roth fame and notoriety. His celebrity status was described acutely in* Zuckerman Unbound *and led to more novels with comic and satiric bite. Like others of his books,* Operation Shylock, *which was hailed by critics, explores the relationship of fact and fiction and purports to be a memoir or autobiography or a novel, but where the line is drawn remains in question. Roth was married for a time to Clare Bloom, the British stage and movie actress, and lives in Connecticut in a semireclusive way, devoting himself to writing novels and personal and critical essays. Given numerous medals, awards, and fellowships, he has been elected to the National Institute of Arts and Letters. He won the Pulitzer Prize for* American Pastoral *in 1997 and the PEN/Faulkner Award for Fiction for* The Human Stain *in 2000, which was the basis for the 2003 film of the same name starring Anthony Hopkins, Nicole Kidman, and Gary Sinise.*

The Conversion of the Jews

"You're a real one for opening your mouth in the first place," Itzie said. "What do you open your mouth all the time for?"

"I didn't bring it up, Itz, I didn't," Ozzie said.

"What do you care about Jesus Christ for anyway?"

"I didn't bring up Jesus Christ. He did. I didn't even know what he was talking about. Jesus is historical, he kept saying. Jesus is historical." Ozzie mimicked the monumental voice of Rabbi Binder.

5   "Jesus was a person that lived like you and me," Ozzie continued. "That's what Binder said—"

"Yeah? . . . So what! What do I give two cents whether he lived or not. And what do you gotta open your mouth!" Itzie Lieberman favored closed-mouthedness, especially when it came to Ozzie Freedman's questions. Mrs. Freedman had to see Rabbi Binder twice before about Ozzie's questions and this Wednesday at four-thirty would be the third time. Itzie preferred to keep *his* mother in the kitchen; he settled for behind-the-back subtleties such as gestures, faces, snarls and other less delicate barnyard noises.

"He was a real person, Jesus, but he wasn't like God, and we don't believe he is God." Slowly, Ozzie was explaining Rabbi Binder's position to Itzie, who had been absent from Hebrew School the previous afternoon.

"The Catholics," Itzie said helpfully, "they believe in Jesus Christ, that he's God." Itzie Lieberman used "the Catholics" in its broadest sense—to include the Protestants.

Ozzie received Itzie's remark with a tiny head bob, as though it were a footnote, and went on. "His mother was Mary, and his father probably was Joseph," Ozzie said. "But the New Testament says his real father was God."

10   "His *real* father?"

"Yeah," Ozzie said, "that's the big thing, his father's supposed to be God."

"Bull."

"That's what Rabbi Binder says, that it's impossible—"

"Sure it's impossible. That stuff's all bull. To have a baby you gotta get laid," Itzie theologized. "Mary hadda get laid."

15   "That's what Binder says: 'The only way a woman can have a baby is to have intercourse with a man.'"

"He said *that,* Ozz?" For a moment it appeared that Itzie had put the theological question aside. "He said that, intercourse?" A little curled smile shaped itself in the lower half of Itzie's face like a pink mustache. "What you guys do, Ozz, you laugh or something?"

"I raised my hand."

"Yeah? Whatja say?"

"That's when I asked the question."

20   Itzie's face lit up. "Whatja ask about—intercourse?"

"No, I asked the question about God, how if He could create the heaven and earth in six days, and make all the animals and the fish and the light in six days—the light especially, that's what always gets me, that He could make the light. Making fish and animals, that's pretty good—"

"That's damn good." Itzie's appreciation was honest but unimaginative: it was as though God had just pitched a one-hitter.

"But making light . . . I mean when you think about it, it's really something," Ozzie said. "Anyway, I asked Binder if He could make all that in six days, and He could *pick* the six days he wanted right out of nowhere, why couldn't He let a woman have a baby without having intercourse."

"You said intercourse, Ozz, to Binder?"

"Yeah." 25

"Right in class?"

"Yeah."

Itzie smacked the side of his head.

"I mean, no kidding around," Ozzie said, "that'd really be nothing. After all that other stuff, that'd practically be nothing."

Itzie considered a moment. "What'd Binder say?" 30

"He started all over again explaining how Jesus was historical and how he lived like you and me but he wasn't God. So I said I under*stood* that. What I wanted to know was different."

What Ozzie wanted to know was always different. The first time he had wanted to know how Rabbi Binder could call the Jews "The Chosen People" if the Declaration of Independence claimed all men to be created equal. Rabbi Binder tried to distinguish for him between political equality and spiritual legitimacy, but what Ozzie wanted to know, he insisted vehemently, was different. That was the first time his mother had to come.

Then there was the plane crash. Fifty-eight people had been killed in a plane crash at La Guardia. In studying a casualty list in the newspaper his mother had discovered among the list of those dead eight Jewish names (his grandmother had nine but she counted Miller as a Jewish name); because of the eight she said the plane crash was "a tragedy." During free-discussion time on Wednesday Ozzie had brought to Rabbi Binder's attention this matter of "some of his relations" always picking out the Jewish names. Rabbi Binder had begun to explain cultural unity and some other things when Ozzie stood up at his seat and said that what he wanted to know was different. Rabbi Binder insisted that he sit down and it was then that Ozzie shouted that he wished all fifty-eight were Jews. That was the second time his mother came.

"And he kept explaining about Jesus being historical, and so I kept asking him. No kidding, Itz, he was trying to make me look stupid."

"So what he finally do?" 35

"Finally he starts screaming that I was deliberately simple-minded and a wise guy, and that my mother had to come, and this was the last time. And that I'd never get bar-mitzvahed if he could help it. Then, Itz, then he starts talking in that voice like a statue, real slow and deep, and he says that I better think over what I said about the Lord. He told me to go to his office and think it over." Ozzie leaned his body towards Itzie. "Itz, I thought it over for a solid hour, and now I'm convinced God could do it."

Ozzie had planned to confess his latest transgression to his mother as soon as she came home from work. But it was a Friday night in November and already dark, and when Mrs. Freedman came through the door she tossed off her coat, kissed Ozzie quickly on the face, and went to the kitchen table to light the three yellow candles, two for the Sabbath° and one for Ozzie's father.

When his mother lit the candles she would move her two arms slowly towards her, dragging them through the air, as though persuading people whose minds were half made up. And her eyes would get glassy with tears. Even when his father was alive Ozzie remembered that her eyes had gotten glassy, so it didn't have anything to do with his dying. It had something to do with lighting the candles.

As she touched the flaming match to the unlit wick of a Sabbath candle, the phone rang, and Ozzie, standing only a foot from it, plucked it off the receiver and held it muffled to his chest. When his mother lit candles Ozzie felt there should be no noise; even breathing if you could manage it, should be softened. Ozzie pressed the phone to his breast and watched his mother dragging whatever she was dragging, and he felt his own eyes get glassy. His mother was a round, tired, gray-haired penguin of a woman whose gray skin had begun to feel the tug of gravity and the weight of her own history. Even when she was dressed up she didn't look like a chosen person. But when she lit candles she looked like something better; like a woman who knew momentarily that God could do anything.

40 After a few mysterious minutes she was finished. Ozzie hung up the phone and walked to the kitchen table where she was beginning to lay the two places for the four-course Sabbath meal. He told her that she would have to see Rabbi Binder next Wednesday at four-thirty, and then he told her why. For the first time in their life together she hit Ozzie across the face with her hand.

All through the chopped liver and chicken soup part of the dinner Ozzie cried; he didn't have any appetite for the rest.

On Wednesday, in the largest of the three basement classrooms of the synagogue, Rabbi Marvin Binder, a tall, handsome, broad-shouldered man of thirty with thick strong-fibered black hair, removed his watch from his pocket and saw that it was four o'clock. At the rear of the room Yakov Blotnik, the seventy-one-year-old custodian, slowly polished the large window, mumbling to himself, unaware that it was four o'clock or six o'clock, Monday or Wednesday. To most of the students Yakov Blotnik's mumbling, along with his brown curly beard, scythe nose, and two heel-trailing black cats, made of him an object of wonder, a foreigner, a relic, towards whom they were alternately fearful and disrespectful. To Ozzie the mumbling had always seemed a monotonous, curious prayer; what made it curious was that old Blotnik had been mumbling so steadily for so many years, Ozzie suspected he had memorized the prayers and forgotten all about God.

"It is now free-discussion time," Rabbi Binder said. "Feel free to talk about any Jewish matter at all—religion, family, politics, sports—"

There was silence. It was a gusty, clouded November afternoon and it did not seem as though there ever was or could be a thing called baseball. So nobody this week said a word about that hero from the past, Hank Greenberg—which limited free discussion considerably.

---

[37]**two for the Sabbath** Jews observe the Sabbath from sundown Friday night to sundown Saturday night, starting it by saying prayers to bless two Sabbath candles.

And the soul-battering Ozzie Freedman had just received from Rabbi Binder   45
had imposed its limitation. When it was Ozzie's turn to read aloud from the
Hebrew book the rabbi had asked him petulantly why he didn't read more
rapidly. He was showing no progress. Ozzie said he could read faster but that if
he did he was sure not to understand what he was reading. Nevertheless, at the
rabbi's repeated suggestion Ozzie tried, and showed a great talent, but in the
midst of a long passage he stopped short and said he didn't understand a word
he was reading, and started in again at a drag-footed pace. Then came the
soul-battering.

Consequently when free-discussion time rolled around none of the students
felt too free. The rabbi's invitation was answered only by the mumbling of feeble
old Blotnik.

"Isn't there anything at all you would like to discuss?" Rabbi Binder asked
again, looking at his watch. "No questions or comments?"

There was a small grumble from the third row. The rabbi requested that Ozzie
rise and give the rest of the class the advantage of his thought.

Ozzie rose. "I forget it now," he said, and sat down in his place.

Rabbi Binder advanced a seat towards Ozzie and poised himself on the edge   50
of the desk. It was Itzie's desk and the rabbi's frame only a dagger's-length away
from his face snapped him to sitting attention.

"Stand up again, Oscar," Rabbi Binder said calmly, "and try to assemble your
thoughts."

Ozzie stood up. All his classmates turned in their seats and watched as he
gave an unconvincing scratch to his forehead.

"I can't assemble any," he announced, and plunked himself down.

"Stand up!" Rabbi Binder advanced from Itzie's desk to the one directly in
front of Ozzie; when the rabbinical back was turned Itzie gave it five-fingers off
the tip of his nose, causing a small titter in the room. Rabbi Binder was too
absorbed in squelching Ozzie's nonsense once and for all to bother with titters.
"Stand up, Oscar. What's your question about?"

Ozzie pulled a word out of the air. It was the handiest word. "Religion."   55

"Oh, now you remember?"

"Yes."

"What is it?"

Trapped, Ozzie blurted the first thing that came to him. "Why can't He make
anything He wants to make!"

As Rabbi Binder prepared an answer, a final answer, Itzie, ten feet behind   60
him, raised one finger on his left hand, gestured it meaningfully towards the
rabbi's back, and brought the house down.

Binder twisted quickly to see what had happened and in the midst of the
commotion Ozzie shouted into the rabbi's back what he couldn't have shouted
to his face. It was a loud, toneless sound that had the timbre of something stored
inside for about six days.

"You don't know! You don't know anything about God!"

The rabbi spun back towards Ozzie. "What?"

"You don't know—you don't—"

65 "Apologize, Oscar, apologize!" It was a threat.

"You don't—"

Rabbi Binder's hand flicked out at Ozzie's cheek. Perhaps it had only been meant to clamp the boy's mouth shut, but Ozzie ducked and the palm caught him squarely on the nose.

The blood came in a short, red spurt on to Ozzie's shirt front.

The next moment was all confusion. Ozzie screamed, "You bastard, you bastard!" and broke for the classroom door. Rabbi Binder lurched a step backwards, as though his own blood had started flowing violently in the opposite direction, then gave a clumsy lurch forward and bolted out the door after Ozzie. The class followed after the rabbi's huge blue-suited back, and before old Blotnik could turn from his window, the room was empty and everyone was headed full speed up the three flights leading to the roof.

70 If one should compare the light of day to the life of man: sunrise to birth; sunset—the dropping down over the edge—to death; then as Ozzie Freedman wiggled through the trapdoor of the synagogue roof, his feet kicking backwards bronco-style at Rabbi Binder's outstretched arms—at that moment the day was fifty years old. As a rule fifty or fifty-five reflects accurately the age of late afternoons in November, for it is in that month, during those hours, that one's awareness of light seems no longer a matter of seeing, but of hearing: light begins clicking away. In fact, as Ozzie locked shut the trapdoor in the rabbi's face, the sharp click of the bolt into the lock might momentarily have been mistaken for the sound of the heavier gray that had just throbbed through the sky.

With all his weight Ozzie kneeled on the locked door; any instant he was certain that Rabbi Binder's shoulder would fling it open, splintering the wood into shrapnel and catapulting his body into the sky. But the door did not move and below him he heard only the rumble of feet, first loud then dim, like thunder rolling away.

A question shot through his brain. "Can this be *me?*" For a thirteen-year-old who had just labeled his religious leader a bastard, twice, it was not an improper question. Louder and louder the question came to him—"Is it me? Is it me?"—until he discovered himself no longer kneeling, but racing crazily towards the edge of the roof, his eyes crying, his throat screaming, and his arms flying everywhichway as though not his own.

"Is it me? Is it me Me Me Me Me! It has to be me—but is it!"

It is the question a thief must ask himself the night he jimmies open his first window, and it is said to be the question with which bridegrooms quiz themselves before the altar.

75 In the few wild seconds it took Ozzie's body to propel him to the edge of the roof, his self-examination began to grow fuzzy. Gazing down at the street, he became confused as to the problem beneath the question: was it, is-it-me-who-called-Binder-a-bastard? or, is-it-me-prancing-around-on-the-roof? However, the scene below settled all, for there is an instant in any action when whether it is you or somebody else is academic. The thief crams the money in his pockets and scoots out the window. The bridegroom signs the hotel register for two. And

the boy on the roof finds a streetful of people gaping at him, necks stretched backwards, faces up, as though he were the ceiling of the Hayden Planetarium.° Suddenly you know it's you.

"Oscar! Oscar Freedman!" A voice rose from the center of the crowd, a voice that, could it have been seen, would have looked like the writing on a scroll. "Oscar Freedman, get down from there. Immediately!" Rabbi Binder was point-ing one arm stiffly up at him; and at the end of that arm, one finger aimed men-acingly. It was the attitude of a dictator, but one—the eyes confessed all—whose personal valet had spit neatly in his face.

Ozzie didn't answer. Only for a blink's length did he look towards Rabbi Binder. Instead his eyes began to fit together the world beneath him, to sort out people from places, friends from enemies, participants from spectators. In little jagged starlike clusters his friends stood around Rabbi Binder, who was still pointing. The topmost point on a star compounded not of angels but of five ado-lescent boys was Itzie. What a world it was, with those stars below, Rabbi Binder below . . . Ozzie, who a moment earlier hadn't been able to control his own body, started to feel the meaning of the word control: he felt Peace and he felt Power.

"Oscar Freedman, I'll give you three to come down."

Few dictators give their subjects three to do anything; but, as always, Rabbi Binder only looked dictatorial.

"Are you ready, Oscar?"   80

Ozzie nodded his head yes, although he had no intention in the world—the lower one or the celestial one he'd just entered—of coming down even if Rabbi Binder should give him a million.

"All right then," said Rabbi Binder. He ran a hand through his black Samson hair as though it were the gesture prescribed for uttering the first digit. Then, with his other hand cutting a circle out of the small piece of sky around him, he spoke. "One!"

There was no thunder. On the contrary, at that moment, as though "one" was the cue for which he had been waiting, the world's least thunderous person appeared on the synagogue steps. He did not so much come out the synagogue door as lean out, onto the darkening air. He clutched at the doorknob with one hand and looked up at the roof.

"Oy!"

Yakov Blotnik's old mind hobbled slowly, as if on crutches, and though he   85
couldn't decide precisely what the boy was doing on the roof, he knew it wasn't good—that is, it wasn't-good-for-the-Jews. For Yakov Blotnik life had fractionat-ed itself simply: things were either good-for-the-Jews or no-good-for-the-Jews. He smacked his free hand to his in-sucked cheek, gently. "Oy! Gut!" And then quickly as he was able, he jacked down his head and surveyed the street. There was Rabbi Binder (like a man at an auction with only three dollars in his pocket, he had just delivered a shaky "Two!"); there were the students, and that was all.

---

[75]**Hayden Planetarium** Planetariums are domed buildings where displays projected onto the ceiling depict various aspects of the cosmos. The Hayden Planetarium is part of the Museum of Natural History in New York City.

So far it-wasn't-so-bad-for-the-Jews. But the boy had to come down immediately, before anybody saw. The problem: how to get the boy off the roof?

Anybody who has ever had a cat on the roof knows how to get him down. You call the fire department. Or first you call the operator and you ask her for the fire department. And the next thing there is great jamming of brakes and clanging of bells and shouting of instructions. And then the cat is off the roof. You do the same thing to get a boy off the roof.

That is, you do the same thing if you are Yakov Blotnik and you once had a cat on the roof.

When the engines, all four of them, arrived, Rabbi Binder had four times given Ozzie the count of three. The big hook-and-ladder swung around the corner and one of the firemen leaped from it, plunging headlong towards the yellow fire hydrant in front of the synagogue. With a huge wrench he began to unscrew the top nozzle. Rabbi Binder raced over to him and pulled at his shoulder.

90 "There's no fire . . ."

The fireman mumbled back over his shoulder and, heatedly, continued working at the nozzle.

"But there's no fire, there's no fire . . ." Binder shouted. When the fireman mumbled again, the rabbi grasped his face with both his hands and pointed it up at the roof.

To Ozzie it looked as though Rabbi Binder was trying to tug the fireman's head out of his body, like a cork from a bottle. He had to giggle at the picture they made: it was a family portrait—rabbi in black skullcap, fireman in red fire hat, and the little yellow hydrant squatting beside like a kid brother, bareheaded. From the edge of the roof Ozzie waved at the portrait, a one-handed, flapping, mocking wave; in doing it his right foot slipped from under him. Rabbi Binder covered his eyes with his hands.

Firemen work fast. Before Ozzie had even regained his balance, a big, round, yellowed net was being held on the synagogue lawn. The firemen who held it looked up at Ozzie with stern, feelingless faces.

95 One of the firemen turned his head towards Rabbi Binder. "What, is the kid nuts or something?"

Rabbi Binder unpeeled his hands from his eyes, slowly, painfully, as if they were tape. Then he checked: nothing on the sidewalk, no dents in the net.

"Is he gonna jump, or what?" the fireman shouted.

In a voice not at all like a statue, Rabbi Binder finally answered. "Yes, yes, I think so . . . He's been threatening to . . ."

Threatening to? Why, the reason he was on the roof, Ozzie remembered, was to get away; he hadn't even thought about jumping. He had just run to get away, and the truth was that he hadn't really headed for the roof as much as he'd been chased there.

100 "What's his name, the kid?"

"Freedman," Rabbi Binder answered. "Oscar Freedman."

The fireman looked up at Ozzie. "What is it with you, Oscar? You gonna jump, or what?"

Ozzie did not answer. Frankly, the question had just arisen.

"Look, Oscar, if you're gonna jump, jump—and if you're not gonna jump, don't jump. But don't waste our time, willya?"

Ozzie looked at the fireman and then at Rabbi Binder. He wanted to see   105
Rabbi Binder cover his eyes one more time.

"I'm going to jump."

And then he scampered around the edge of the roof to the corner, where there was no net below, and he flapped his arms at his sides, swishing the air and smacking his palms to his trousers on the downbeat. He began screaming like some kind of engine, "Wheeeee . . . wheeeeee," and leaning way out over the edge with the upper half of his body. The firemen whipped around to cover the ground with the net. Rabbi Binder mumbled a few words to Somebody and covered his eyes. Everything happened quickly, jerkily, as in a silent movie. The crowd, which had arrived with the fire engines, gave out a long, Fourth-of-July fireworks oooh-aahhh. In the excitement no one had paid the crowd much heed, except, of course, Yakov Blotnik, who swung from the doorknob counting heads. "Fier und tsvantsik . . . finf und tsvantsik . . . Oy, Gut!" It wasn't like this with the cat.

Rabbi Binder peeked through his fingers, checked the sidewalk and net. Empty. But there was Ozzie racing to the other corner. The firemen raced with him but were unable to keep up. Whenever Ozzie wanted to he might jump and splatter himself upon the sidewalk, and by the time the firemen scooted to the spot all they could do with their net would be to cover the mess.

"Wheeeee . . . wheeeee . . ."

"Hey, Oscar," the winded fireman yelled, "What the hell is this, a game or   110
something?"

"Wheeeee . . . wheeeee . . . "

"Hey, Oscar—"

But he was off now to the other corner, flapping his wings fiercely. Rabbi Binder couldn't take it any longer—the fire engines from nowhere, the screaming suicidal boy, the net. He fell to his knees, exhausted, and with his hands curled together in front of his chest like a little dome, he pleaded, "Oscar, stop it, Oscar. Don't jump, Oscar. Please come down . . . Please don't jump."

And further back in the crowd a single voice, a single young voice, shouted a lone word to the boy on the roof.   115

"Jump!"

It was Itzie. Ozzie momentarily stopped flapping.

"Go ahead, Ozz—jump!" Itzie broke off his point of the star and courageously, with the inspiration not of a wise-guy but of a disciple, stood alone. "Jump, Ozz, jump!"

Still on his knees, his hands still curled, Rabbi Binder twisted his body back. He looked at Itzie, then, agonizingly, back to Ozzie.

"OSCAR, DON'T JUMP! PLEASE, DON'T JUMP . . . please please . . ."

"Jump!" This time it wasn't Itzie but another point of the star. By the time   120
Mrs. Freedman arrived to keep her four-thirty appointment with Rabbi Binder,

the whole little upside down heaven was shouting and pleading for Ozzie to jump, and Rabbi Binder no longer was pleading with him not to jump, but was crying into the dome of his hands.

Understandably Mrs. Freedman couldn't figure out what her son was doing on the roof. So she asked.

"Ozzie, my Ozzie, what are you doing? My Ozzie, what is it?"

Ozzie stopped wheeeeeing and slowed his arms down to a cruising flap, the kind birds use in soft winds, but he did not answer. He stood against the low, clouded, darkening sky—light clicked down swiftly now, as on a small gear—flapping softly and gazing down at the small bundle of a woman who was his mother.

"What are you doing, Ozzie?" She turned towards the kneeling Rabbi Binder and rushed so close that only a paper-thickness of dusk lay between her stomach and his shoulders.

125 "What is my baby doing?"

Rabbi Binder gaped up at her but he too was mute. All that moved was the dome of his hands; it shook back and forth like a weak pulse.

"Rabbi, get him down! He'll kill himself. Get him down, my only baby . . ."

"I can't," Rabbi Binder said, "I can't . . ." and he turned his handsome head towards the crowd of boys behind him. "It's them. Listen to them."

And for the first time Mrs. Freedman saw the crowd of boys, and she heard what they were yelling.

130 "He's doing it for them. He won't listen to me. It's them." Rabbi Binder spoke like one in a trance.

"For them?"

"Yes."

"Why for them?"

"They want him to . . ."

135 Mrs. Freedman raised her two arms upward as though she were conducting the sky. "For them he's doing it!" And then in a gesture older than pyramids, older than prophets and floods, her arms came slapping down to her sides. "A martyr I have. Look!" She tilted her head to the roof. Ozzie was still flapping softly. "My martyr."

"Oscar, come down, *please*," Rabbi Binder groaned.

In a startlingly even voice Mrs. Freedman called to the boy on the roof. "Ozzie, come down, Ozzie. Don't be a martyr, my baby."

As though it were a litany, Rabbi Binder repeated her words, "Don't be a martyr, my baby. Don't be a martyr."

"Gawhead, Ozz—*be* a Martin!" It was Itzie. "Be a Martin, be a Martin," and all the voices joined in singing for Martindom, whatever *it* was. "Be a Martin, be a Martin . . ."

140 Somehow when you're on a roof the darker it gets the less you can hear. All Ozzie knew was that two groups wanted two new things: his friends were spirited and musical about what they wanted; his mother and the rabbi were even-toned, chanting, about what they didn't want. The rabbi's voice was without tears now and so was his mother's.

The big net stared up at Ozzie like a sightless eye. The big, clouded sky pushed down. From beneath it looked like a gray corrugated board. Suddenly, looking up into that unsympathetic sky, Ozzie realized all the strangeness of what these people, his friends, were asking: they wanted him to jump, to kill himself; they were singing about it now—it made them that happy. And there was an even greater strangeness: Rabbi Binder was on his knees, trembling. If there was a question to be asked now it was not "Is it me?" but rather "Is it us? . . . Is it us?"

Being on the roof, it turned out, was a serious thing. If he jumped would the singing become dancing? Would it? What would jumping stop? Yearningly, Ozzie wished he could rip open the sky, plunge his hands through, and pull out the sun; and on the sun, like a coin, would be stamped JUMP or DON'T JUMP.

Ozzie's knees rocked and sagged a little under him as though they were setting him for a dive. His arms tightened, stiffened, froze, from shoulders to fingernails. He felt as if each part of his body were going to vote as to whether he should kill himself or not—and each part as though it were independent of *him*.

The light took an unexpected click down and the new darkness, like a gag, hushed the friends singing for this and the mother and rabbi chanting for that.

Ozzie stopped counting votes, and in a curiously high voice, like one who wasn't prepared for speech, he spoke.   145

"Mamma?"

"Yes, Oscar."

"Mamma, get down on your knees, like Rabbi Binder."

"Oscar—"

"Get down on your knees," he said, "or I'll jump."   150

Ozzie heard a whimper, then a quick rustling, and when he looked down where his mother had stood he saw the top of a head and beneath that a circle of dress. She was kneeling beside Rabbi Binder.

He spoke again. "Everybody kneel." There was the sound of everybody kneeling.

Ozzie looked around. With one hand he pointed towards the synagogue entrance. "Make *him* kneel."

There was a noise, not of kneeling, but of body-and-cloth stretching. Ozzie could hear Rabbi Binder saying in a gruff whisper, ". . . or he'll *kill* himself," and when next he looked there was Yakov Blotnik off the doorknob and for the first time in his life upon his knees in the Gentile posture of prayer.

As for the firemen—it is not as difficult as one might imagine to hold a net   155
taut while you are kneeling.

Ozzie looked around again; and then he called to Rabbi Binder.

"Rabbi?"

"Yes, Oscar."

"Rabbi Binder, do you believe in God?"

"Yes."   160

"Do you believe God can do Anything?" Ozzie leaned his head out into the darkness. "Anything?"

"Oscar, I think—"

"Tell me you believe God can do Anything."

There was a second's hesitation. Then: "God can do Anything."

165 "Tell me you believe God can make a child without intercourse."

"He can."

"Tell me!"

"God," Rabbi Binder admitted, "can make a child without intercourse."

"Mamma, you tell me."

170 "God can make a child without intercourse," his mother said.

"Make *him* tell me." There was no doubt who *him* was.

In a few moments Ozzie heard an old comical voice say something to the increasing darkness about God.

Next, Ozzie made everybody say it. And then he made them all say they believed in Jesus Christ—first one at a time, then all together.

When the catechizing was through it was the beginning of evening. From the street it sounded as if the boy on the roof might have sighed.

175 "Ozzie?" A woman's voice dared to speak. "You'll come down now?"

There was no answer, but the woman waited, and when a voice finally did speak it was thin and crying, and exhausted as that of an old man who has just finished pulling the bells.

"Mamma, don't you see—you shouldn't hit me. He shouldn't hit me. You shouldn't hit me about God, Mamma. You should never hit anybody about God—"

"Ozzie, please come down now."

"Promise me, promise me you'll never hit anybody about God."

180 He had asked only his mother, but for some reason everyone kneeling in the street promised he would never hit anybody about God.

Once again there was silence.

"I can come down now, Mamma," the boy on the roof finally said. He turned his head both ways as though checking the traffic lights. "Now I can come down . . ."

And he did, right into the center of the yellow net that glowed in the evening's edge like an overgrown halo.   [1955]

1. This story takes place in a closely defined ethnic setting. The conflict that Ozzie faces is a conflict peculiar to Jews within a Christian culture. How is this story relevant to non-Jews? How does Roth manage to universalize the conflict?

2. When Ozzie is on the rooftop, the language of the story becomes noticeably more lyrical. What purpose does this heightening of the language serve?

3. Would you say that Ozzie is a kind of "Christ-figure" in this story? Define a Christ-figure and then decide whether Ozzie meets the criteria.

4. How does the story lead us to judge Rabbi Binder? What kind of person is he and how do we know?

5. The phrase in the title of the story is usually an allusion to the end of the world when impossible things will happen and Jesus Christ will return to earth. What does the story suggest about how the term "conversion" might be understood in a Jewish context? Does it necessarily imply conversion to Christianity?

Looking at Dinesen through Psychology

ISAK DINESEN (KAREN BLIXEN), "Babette's Feast"

ABRAHAM MASLOW, "Self-Actualizing and Beyond," "Various Meanings of Transcendence," from *The Farther Reaches of Human Nature*

ISAK DINESEN

ISAK DINESEN (KAREN BLIXEN) *(1885–1962) Born on her family's estate in Denmark, Blixen was educated in private schools and published her first stories at twenty-two. In love with Hans von Blixen, she married his brother Bror instead, and moved with him to Africa. After treatment in Denmark for syphilis contracted from her husband, she returned to Africa and she and Blixen enlarged their coffee plantations. At thirty-three she met the English hunter Denys Finch Hatton, separated from Bror, and took over the management of the farms. Years of plantation life followed, during which she wrote and spent increasing amounts of time with Finch Hatton. In spite of her efforts to keep the farms profitable, worldwide depression eventually forced her to sell them. After the death of Finch Hatton in a plane crash, Blixen returned to Denmark, where, except for a much-publicized tour of the United States to promote her book of stories,* Winter's Tales, *Blixen lived on in ill health at her family home until her death.*

Babette's Feast

I. Two Ladies of Berlevaag

In Norway there is a fjord—a long narrow arm of the sea between tall mountains—named Berlevaag Fjord. At the foot of the mountains the small town of Berlevaag looks like a child's toy-town of little wooden pieces painted gray, yellow, pink and many other colors.

Sixty-five years ago two elderly ladies lived in one of the yellow houses. Other ladies at that time wore a bustle, and the two sisters might have worn it as gracefully as any of them, for they were tall and willowy. But they had never possessed any article of fashion; they had dressed demurely in gray or black all their lives. They were christened Martine and Philippa, after Martin Luther° and his friend Philip Melanchton.° Their father had been a Dean and a prophet, the founder of a pious ecclesiastic party or sect, which was known and looked up to in all the country of Norway. Its members renounced the pleasures of this world,

[2]**Martin Luther** (1483–1546) the German priest who touched off the Reformation by nailing 95 statements about why the Catholic Church's practice of selling "indulgences" for sin was contrary to the Bible   **Philip Melanchton** (1497–1560), humanist and colleague of Martin Luther

for the earth and all that it held to them was but a kind of illusion, and the true reality was the New Jerusalem toward which they were longing. They swore not at all, but their communication was yea yea and nay nay, and they called one another Brother and Sister.

The Dean had married late in life and by now had long been dead. His disciples were becoming fewer in number every year, whiter or balder and harder of hearing; they were even becoming somewhat querulous and quarrelsome, so that sad little schisms would arise in the congregation. But they still gathered together to read and interpret the Word. They had all known the Dean's daughters as little girls; to them they were even now very small sisters, precious for their dear father's sake. In the yellow house they felt that their Master's spirit was with them; here they were at home and at peace.

These two ladies had a French maid-of-all-work, Babette.

5   It was a strange thing for a couple of Puritan° women in a small Norwegian town; it might even seem to call for an explanation. The people of Berlevaag found the explanation in the sisters' piety and kindness of heart. For the old Dean's daughters spent their time and their small income in works of charity; no sorrowful or distressed creature knocked on their door in vain. And Babette had come to that door twelve years ago as a friendless fugitive, almost mad with grief and fear.

But the true reason for Babette's presence in the two sisters' house was to be found further back in time and deeper down in the domain of human hearts.

II. Martine's Lover

As young girls, Martine and Philippa had been extraordinarily pretty, with the almost supernatural fairness of flowering fruit trees or perpetual snow. They were never to be seen at balls or parties, but people turned when they passed in the streets, and the young men of Berlevaag went to church to watch them walk up the aisle. The younger sister also had a lovely voice, which on Sundays filled the church with sweetness. To the Dean's congregation earthly love, and marriage with it, were trivial matters, in themselves nothing but illusions; still it is possible that more than one of the elderly Brothers had been prizing the maidens far above rubies° and had suggested as much to their father. But the Dean had declared that to him in his calling his daughters were his right and left hand. Who could want to bereave him of them? And the fair girls had been brought up to an ideal of heavenly love; they were all filled with it and did not let themselves be touched by the flames of this world.

All the same they had upset the peace of heart of two gentlemen from the great world outside Berlevaag.

---

[5]**Puritan** 16th and 17th century religious movement that grew up in opposition to Roman Catholicism with emphasis on members reading the Bible for themselves rather than relying on priests and emphasis on human sinfulness, especially the need to have faith in Jesus as savior and to live austere lives to overcome temptation   [1]**far above rubies** an allusion to the Hebrew Bible: Proverbs, 31:10: "Who can find a virtuous woman? for her price is far above rubies."

There was a young officer named Lorens Loewenhielm, who had led a gay life in his garrison town and had run into debt. In the year of 1854, when Martine was eighteen and Philippa seventeen, his angry father sent him on a month's visit to his aunt in her old country house of Fossum near Berlevaag, where he would have time to meditate and to better his ways. One day he rode into town and met Martine in the marketplace. He looked down at the pretty girl, and she looked up at the fine horseman. When she had passed him and disappeared he was not certain whether he was to believe his own eyes.

In the Loewenhielm family there existed a legend to the effect that long ago a gentleman of the name had married a Huldre, a female mountain spirit of Norway, who is so fair that the air round her shines and quivers. Since then, from time to time, members of the family had been second-sighted. Young Lorens till now had not been aware of any particular spiritual gift in his own nature. But at this one moment there rose before his eyes a sudden, mighty vision of a higher and purer life, with no creditors, dunning letters or parental lectures, with no secret, unpleasant pangs of conscience and with a gentle, golden-haired angel to guide and reward him.

Through his pious aunt he got admission to the Dean's house, and saw that   5
Martine was even lovelier without a bonnet. He followed her slim figure with adoring eyes, but he loathed and despised the figure which he himself cut in her nearness. He was amazed and shocked by the fact that he could find nothing at all to say, and no inspiration in the glass of water before him. "Mercy and Truth, dear brethren, have met together," said the Dean. "Righteousness and Bliss have kissed one another." And the young man's thoughts were with the moment when Lorens and Martine should be kissing each other. He repeated his visit time after time, and each time seemed to himself to grow smaller and more insignificant and contemptible.

When in the evening he came back to his aunt's house he kicked his shining riding-boots to the corners of his room; he even laid his head on the table and wept.

On the last day of his stay he made a last attempt to communicate his feelings to Martine. Till now it had been easy for him to tell a pretty girl that he loved her, but the tender words stuck in his throat as he looked into this maiden's face. When he had said good-bye to the party, Martine saw him to the door with a candlestick in her hand. The light shone on her mouth and threw upwards the shadows of her long eyelashes. He was about to leave in dumb despair when on the threshold he suddenly seized her hand and pressed it to his lips.

"I am going away forever!" he cried. "I shall never, never see you again! For I have learned here that Fate is hard, and that in this world there are things which are impossible!"

When he was once more back in his garrison town he thought his adventure over, and found that he did not like to think of it at all. While the other young officers talked of their love affairs, he was silent on his. For seen from the officers' mess, and so to say with its eyes, it was a pitiful business. How had it come to pass that a lieutenant of the hussars had let himself be defeated and frustrated by a set of long-faced sectarians, in the bare-floored rooms of an old Dean's house?

10   Then he became afraid; panic fell upon him. Was it the family madness which made him still carry with him the dream-like picture of a maiden so fair that she made the air round her shine with purity and holiness? He did not want to be a dreamer; he wanted to be like his brother-officers.

    So he pulled himself together, and in the greatest effort of his young life made up his mind to forget what had happened to him in Berlevaag. From now on, he resolved, he would look forward, not back. He would concentrate on his career, and the day was to come when he would cut a brilliant figure in a brilliant world.

    His mother was pleased with the result of his visit to Fossum, and in her letters expressed her gratitude to his aunt. She did not know by what queer, winding roads her son had reached his happy moral standpoint.

    The ambitious young officer soon caught the attention of his superiors and made unusually quick advancement. He was sent to France and to Russia, and on his return he married a lady-in-waiting to Queen Sophia. In these high circles he moved with grace and ease, pleased with his surroundings and with himself. He even in the course of time benefited from words and turns which had stuck in his mind from the Dean's house, for piety was now in fashion at Court.

    In the yellow house of Berlevaag, Philippa sometimes turned the talk to the handsome, silent young man who had so suddenly made his appearance, and so suddenly disappeared again. Her elder sister would then answer her gently, with a still, clear face, and find other things to discuss.

III. Philippa's Lover

A year later a more distinguished person even than Lieutenant Loewenhielm came to Berlevaag.

    The great singer Achille Papin of Paris had sung for a week at the Royal Opera of Stockholm, and had carried away his audience there as everywhere. One evening a lady of the Court, who had been dreaming of a romance with the artist, had described to him the wild, grandiose scenery of Norway. His own romantic nature was stirred by the narration, and he had laid his way back to France round the Norwegian coast. But he felt small in the sublime surroundings; with nobody to talk to he fell into that melancholy in which he saw himself as an old man, at the end of his career, till on a Sunday, when he could think of nothing else to do, he went to church and heard Philippa sing.

    Then in one single moment he knew and understood all. For here were the snowy summits, the wild flowers and the white Nordic nights, translated into his own language of music, and brought him in a young woman's voice. Like Lorens Loewenhielm he had a vision.

    "Almighty God," he thought, "Thy power is without end, and Thy mercy reacheth unto the clouds! And here is a prima donna of the opera who will lay Paris at her feet."

5   Achille Papin at this time was a handsome man of forty, with curly black hair and a red mouth. The idolization of nations had not spoilt him; he was a kind-hearted person and honest toward himself.

He went straight to the yellow house, gave his name—which told the Dean nothing—and explained that he was staying in Berlevaag for his health, and the while would be happy to take on the young lady as a pupil.

He did not mention the Opera of Paris, but described at length how beautifully Miss Philippa would come to sing in church, to the glory of God.

For a moment he forgot himself, for when the Dean asked whether he was a Roman Catholic he answered according to truth, and the old clergyman, who had never seen a live Roman Catholic, grew a little pale. All the same the Dean was pleased to speak French, which reminded him of his young days when he had studied the works of the great French Lutheran writer, Lefèvre d'Etaples. And as nobody could long withstand Achille Papin when he had really set his heart on a matter, in the end the father gave his consent, and remarked to his daughter: "God's paths run across the sea and the snowy mountains, where man's eye sees no track."

So the great French singer and the young Norwegian novice set to work together. Achille's expectation grew into certainty and his certainty into ecstasy. He thought: "I have been wrong in believing that I was growing old. My greatest triumphs are before me! The world will once more believe in miracles when she and I sing together!"

After a while he could not keep his dreams to himself, but told Philippa about 10 them.

She would, he said, rise like a star above any diva of the past or present. The Emperor and Empress, the Princes, great ladies and *bels esprits* of Paris would listen to her, and shed tears. The common people too would worship her, and she would bring consolation and strength to the wronged and oppressed. When she left the Grand Opera upon her master's arm, the crowd would unharness her horses, and themselves draw her to the Café Anglais, where a magnificent supper awaited her.

Philippa did not repeat these prospects to her father or her sister, and this was the first time in her life that she had had a secret from them.

The teacher now gave his pupil the part of Zerlina in Mozart's opera *Don Giovanni* to study. He himself, as often before, sang Don Giovanni's part.

He had never in his life sung as now. In the duet of the second act—which is called the seduction duet—he was swept off his feet by the heavenly music and the heavenly voices. As the last melting note died away he seized Philippa's hands, drew her toward him and kissed her solemnly, as a bridegroom might kiss his bride before the altar. Then he let her go. For the moment was too sublime for any further word or movement; Mozart himself was looking down on the two.

Philippa went home, told her father that she did not want any more singing 15 lessons and asked him to write and tell Monsieur Papin so.

The Dean said: "And God's paths run across the rivers, my child."

When Achille got the Dean's letter he sat immovable for an hour. He thought: "I have been wrong. My day is over. Never again shall I be the divine Papin. And this poor weedy garden of the world has lost its nightingale!"

A little later he thought: "I wonder what is the matter with that hussy? Did I kiss her, by any chance?"

In the end he thought: "I have lost my life for a kiss, and I have no remembrance at all of the kiss! Don Giovanni kissed Zerlina, and Achille Papin pays for it! Such is the fate of the artist!"

20   In the Dean's house Martine felt that the matter was deeper than it looked, and searched her sister's face. For a moment, slightly trembling, she too imagined that the Roman Catholic gentleman might have tried to kiss Philippa. She did not imagine that her sister might have been surprised and frightened by something in her own nature.

Achille Papin took the first boat from Berlevaag.

Of this visitor from the great world the sisters spoke but little; they lacked the words with which to discuss him.

IV. A Letter from Paris

Fifteen years later, on a rainy June night of 1871, the bell-rope of the yellow house was pulled violently three times. The mistresses of the house opened the door to a massive, dark, deadly pale woman with a bundle on her arm, who stared at them, took a step forward and fell down on the doorstep in a dead swoon. When the frightened ladies had restored her to life she sat up, gave them one more glance from her sunken eyes and, all the time without a word, fumbled in her wet clothes and brought out a letter which she handed to them.

The letter was addressed to them all right, but it was written in French. The sisters put their heads together and read it. It ran as follows:

Ladies!

Do you remember me? Ah, when I think of you I have the heart filled with wild lilies-of-the-valley! Will the memory of a Frenchman's devotion bend your hearts to save the life of a Frenchwoman?

5   The bearer of this letter, Madame Babette Hersant, like my beautiful Empress herself, has had to flee from Paris. Civil war° has raged in our streets. French hands have shed French blood. The noble Communards, standing up for the Rights of Man, have been crushed and annihilated. Madame Hersant's husband and son, both eminent ladies' hairdressers, have been shot. She herself was arrested as a Pétroleuse—(which word is used here for women who set fire to houses with petroleum)—and has narrowly escaped the blood-stained hands of General Galliffet. She has lost all she possessed and dares not remain in France.

A nephew of hers is cook to the boat *Anna Colbioernsson,* bound for Christiania—(as I believe, the capital of Norway)—and he has obtained shipping opportunity for his aunt. This is now her last sad resort!

Knowing that I was once a visitor to your magnificent country she comes to me, asks me if there be any good people in Norway and begs me, if it be so, to supply her with a letter to them. The two words of 'good people' immediately bring before my eyes your picture, sacred to my heart. I send her to you. How

---

[5] **Civil war** In 1870–1871, as many as 100,000 Parisian workers demonstrated against Napoleon III and established the Commune, an alternative, anti-capitalist society. The movement ended when the army retook the city, arrested tens of thousands, some to be deported, and killed tens of thousands.

she is to get from Christiania to Berlevaag I know not, having forgotten the map of Norway. But she is a Frenchwoman, and you will find that in her misery she has still got resourcefulness, majesty and true stoicism.

I envy her in her despair: she is to see your faces.

As you receive her mercifully, send a merciful thought back to France.

For fifteen years, Miss Philippa, I have grieved that your voice should never   10
fill the Grand Opera of Paris. When tonight I think of you, no doubt surrounded
by a gay and loving family, and of myself: gray, lonely, forgotten by those who
once applauded and adored me, I feel that you may have chosen the better part
in life. What is fame? What is glory? The grave awaits us all!

And yet, my lost Zerlina, and yet, soprano of the snow! As I write this I feel
that the grave is not the end. In Paradise I shall hear your voice again. There you
will sing, without fears or scruples, as God meant you to sing. There you will be
the great artist that God meant you to be. Ah! how you will enchant the angels.

Babette can cook.

Deign to receive, my ladies, the humble homage of the friend who was once

Achille Papin

At the bottom of the page, as a P.S. were neatly printed the first two bars of
the duet between Don Giovanni and Zerlina, like this:

The two sisters till now had kept only a small servant of fifteen to help them   15
in the house and they felt that they could not possibly afford to take on an
elderly, experienced housekeeper. But Babette told them that she would serve
Monsieur Papin's good people for nothing, and that she would take service with
nobody else. If they sent her away she must die. Babette remained in the house
of the Dean's daughters for twelve years, until the time of this tale.

V. Still Life

Babette had arrived haggard and wild-eyed like a hunted animal, but in her
new, friendly surroundings she soon acquired all the appearance of a
respectable and trusted servant. She had appeared to be a beggar; she turned
out to be a conqueror. Her quiet countenance and her steady, deep glance had
magnetic qualities; under her eyes things moved, noiselessly, into their proper
places.

Her mistresses at first had trembled a little, just as the Dean had once done, at
the idea of receiving a Papist under their roof. But they did not like to worry a
hard-tried fellow-creature with catechization; neither were they quite sure of
their French. They silently agreed that the example of a good Lutheran life
would be the best means of converting their servant. In this way Babette's
presence in the house became, so to say, a moral spur to its inhabitants.

They had distrusted Monsieur Papin's assertion that Babette could cook. In France, they knew, people ate frogs. They showed Babette how to prepare a split cod and an ale-and-bread-soup; during the demonstration the Frenchwoman's face became absolutely expressionless. But within a week Babette cooked a split cod and an ale-and-bread-soup as well as anybody born and bred in Berlevaag.

The idea of French luxury and extravagance next had alarmed and dismayed the Dean's daughters. The first day after Babette had entered their service they took her before them and explained to her that they were poor and that to them luxurious fare was sinful. Their own food must be as plain as possible; it was the soup-pails and baskets for their poor that signified. Babette nodded her head; as a girl, she informed her ladies, she had been cook to an old priest who was a saint. Upon this the sisters resolved to surpass the French priest in asceticism. And they soon found that from the day when Babette took over the housekeeping its cost was miraculously reduced, and the soup-pails and baskets acquired a new, mysterious power to stimulate and strengthen their poor and sick.

5   The world outside the yellow house also came to acknowledge Babette's excellence. The refugee never learned to speak the language of her new country, but in her broken Norwegian she beat down the prices of Berlevaag's flintiest tradesmen. She was held in awe on the quay and in the marketplace.

The old Brothers and Sisters, who had first looked askance at the foreign woman in their midst, felt a happy change in their little sisters' life, rejoiced at it and benefited by it. They found that troubles and cares had been conjured away from their existence, and that now they had money to give away, time for the confidences and complaints of their old friends and peace for meditating on heavenly matters. In the course of time not a few of the brotherhood included Babette's name in their prayers, and thanked God for the speechless stranger, the dark Martha in the house of their two fair Marys. The stone which the builders had almost refused had become the headstone of the corner.

The ladies of the yellow house were the only ones to know that their corner-stone had a mysterious and alarming feature to it, as if it was somehow related to the Black Stone of Mecca, the Kaaba itself.

Hardly ever did Babette refer to her past life. When in early days the sisters had gently condoled her upon her losses, they had been met with that majesty and stoicism of which Monsieur Papin had written. "What will you ladies?" she had answered, shrugging her shoulders. "It is Fate."

But one day she suddenly informed them that she had for many years held a ticket in a French lottery, and that a faithful friend in Paris was still renewing it for her every year. Some time she might win the *grand prix* of ten thousand francs. At that they felt that their cook's old carpetbag was made from a magic carpet; at a given moment she might mount it and be carried off, back to Paris.

10   And it happened when Martine or Philippa spoke to Babette that they would get no answer, and would wonder if she had even heard what they said. They would find her in the kitchen, her elbows on the table and her temples on her hands, lost in the study of a heavy black book which they secretly suspected to be a popish prayer-book. Or she would sit immovable on the three-legged kitchen chair, her strong hands in her lap and her dark eyes wide open, as

enigmatical and fatal as a Pythia upon her tripod.° At such moments they realized that Babette was deep, and that in the soundings of her being there were passions, there were memories and longings of which they knew nothing at all.

A little cold shiver ran through them, and in their hearts they thought: "Perhaps after all she had indeed been a Pétroleuse."

VI. Babette's Good Luck

The fifteenth of December was the Dean's hundredth anniversary.

His daughters had long been looking forward to this day and had wished to celebrate it, as if their dear father were still among his disciples. Therefore it had been to them a sad and incomprehensible thing that in this last year discord and dissension had been raising their heads in his flock. They had endeavored to make peace, but they were aware that they had failed. It was as if the fine and lovable vigor of their father's personality had been evaporating, the way Hoffmann's anodyne will evaporate when left on the shelf in a bottle without a cork. And his departure had left the door ajar to things hitherto unknown to the two sisters, much younger than his spiritual children. From a past half a century back, when the unshepherded sheep had been running astray in the mountains, uninvited dismal guests pressed through the opening on the heels of the worshippers and seemed to darken the little rooms and to let in the cold. The sins of old Brothers and Sisters came, with late piercing repentance like a toothache, and the sins of others against them came back with bitter resentment, like a poisoning of the blood.

There were in the congregation two old women who before their conversion had spread slander upon each other, and thereby to each other ruined a marriage and an inheritance. Today they could not remember happenings of yesterday or a week ago, but they remembered this forty-year-old wrong and kept going through the ancient accounts; they scowled at each other. There was an old Brother who suddenly called to mind how another Brother, forty-five years ago, had cheated him in a deal; he could have wished to dismiss the matter from his mind, but it stuck there like a deep-seated, festering splinter. There was a gray, honest skipper and a furrowed, pious widow, who in their young days, while she was the wife of another man, had been sweethearts. Of late each had begun to grieve, while shifting the burden of guilt from his own shoulders to those of the other and back again, and to worry about the possible terrible consequences, through all eternity, to himself, brought upon him by one who had pretended to hold him dear. They grew pale at the meetings in the yellow house and avoided each other's eyes.

As the birthday drew nearer, Martine and Philippa felt the responsibility growing heavier. Would their ever-faithful father look down to his daughters and call them by name as unjust stewards? Between them they talked matters

---

[10]**a Pythia upon her tripod** In Greek mythology, Pythia were priestesses at Delphi, who, perched on a tripod over a sacred site where fumes issued from a crevice in the earth, could enter into a trance and relay Apollo's cryptic answers to questions posed about the correct course of action.

over and repeated their father's saying: that God's paths were running even across the salt sea, and the snow-clad mountains, where man's eye sees no track.

5   One day of this summer the post brought a letter from France to Madame Babette Hersant. This in itself was a surprising thing, for during these twelve years Babette had received no letter. What, her mistresses wondered, could it contain? They took it into the kitchen to watch her open and read it. Babette opened it, read it, lifted her eyes from it to her ladies' faces and told them that her number in the French lottery had come out. She had won ten thousand francs.

The news made such an impression on the two sisters that for a full minute they could not speak a word. They themselves were used to receiving their modest pension in small instalments; it was difficult to them even to imagine the sum of ten thousand francs in a pile. Then they pressed Babette's hand, their own hands trembling a little. They had never before pressed the hand of a person who the moment before had come into possession of ten thousand francs.

After a while they realized that the happenings concerned themselves as well as Babette. The country of France, they felt, was slowly rising before their servant's horizon, and correspondingly their own existence was sinking beneath their feet. The ten thousand francs which made her rich—how poor did they not make the house she had served! One by one old forgotten cares and worries began to peep out at them from the four corners of the kitchen. The congratulations died on their lips, and the two pious women were ashamed of their own silence.

During the following days they announced the news to their friends with joyous faces, but it did them good to see these friends' faces grow sad as they listened to them. Nobody, it was felt in the Brotherhood, could really blame Babette: birds will return to their nests and human beings to the country of their birth. But did that good and faithful servant realize that in going away from Berlevaag she would be leaving many old and poor people in distress? Their little sisters would have no more time for the sick and sorrowful. Indeed, indeed, lotteries were ungodly affairs.

In due time the money arrived through offices in Christiania and Berlevaag. The two ladies helped Babette to count it, and gave her a box to keep it in. They handled, and became familiar with, the ominous bits of paper.

10   They dared not question Babette upon the date of her departure. Dared they hope that she would remain with them over the fifteenth of December?

The mistresses had never been quite certain how much of their private conversation the cook followed or understood. So they were surprised when on a September evening Babette came into the drawing room, more humble or subdued than they had ever seen her, to ask a favor. She begged them, she said, to let her cook a celebration dinner on the Dean's birthday.

The ladies had not intended to have any dinner at all. A very plain supper with a cup of coffee was the most sumptuous meal to which they had ever asked any guest to sit down. But Babette's dark eyes were as eager and pleading as a dog's; they agreed to let her have her way. At this the cook's face lighted up.

But she had more to say. She wanted, she said, to cook a French dinner, a real French dinner, for this one time. Martine and Philippa looked at each other. They did not like the idea; they felt that they did not know what it might imply. But the very strangeness of the request disarmed them. They had no arguments wherewith to meet the proposition of cooking a real French dinner.

Babette drew a long sigh of happiness, but still she did not move. She had one more prayer to make. She begged that her mistresses would allow her to pay for the French dinner with her own money.

"No, Babette!" the ladies exclaimed. How could she imagine such a thing? Did she believe that they would allow her to spend her precious money on food and drink—or on them? No, Babette, indeed.

Babette took a step forward. There was something formidable in the move, like a wave rising. Had she stepped forth like this, in 1871, to plant a red flag on a barricade? She spoke, in her queer Norwegian, with classical French eloquence. Her voice was like a song.

Ladies! Had she ever, during twelve years, asked you a favor? No! And why not? Ladies, you who say your prayers every day, can you imagine what it means to a human heart to have no prayer to make? What would Babette have had to pray for? Nothing! Tonight she had a prayer to make, from the bottom of her heart. Do you not then feel tonight, my ladies, that it becomes you to grant it her, with such joy as that with which the good God has granted you your own?

The ladies for a while said nothing. Babette was right; it was her first request these twelve years; very likely it would be her last. They thought the matter over. After all, they told themselves, their cook was now better off than they, and a dinner could make no difference to a person who owned ten thousand francs.

Their consent in the end completely changed Babette. They saw that as a young woman she had been beautiful. And they wondered whether in this hour they themselves had not, for the very first time, become to her the "good people" of Achille Papin's letter.

VII. The Turtle

In November Babette went for a journey.

She had preparations to make, she told her mistresses, and would need a leave of a week or ten days. Her nephew, who had once got her to Christiania, was still sailing to that town; she must see him and talk things over with him. Babette was a bad sailor; she had spoken of her one sea-voyage, from France to Norway, as of the most horrible experiences of her life. Now she was strangely collected; the ladies felt that her heart was already in France.

After ten days she came back to Berlevaag.

Had she got things arranged as she wished? the ladies asked. Yes, she answered, she had seen her nephew and given him a list of the goods which he was to bring her from France. To Martine and Philippa this was a dark saying, but they did not care to talk of her departure, so they asked her no more questions.

Babette was somewhat nervous during the next weeks. But one December day she triumphantly announced to her mistresses that the goods had come to

Christiania, had been transshipped there, and on this very day had arrived at Berlevaag. She had, she added, engaged an old man with a wheelbarrow to have them conveyed from the harbor to the house.

But what goods, Babette? the ladies asked. Why, Mesdames, Babette replied, the ingredients for the birthday dinner. Praise be to God, they had all arrived in good condition from Paris.

By this time Babette, like the bottled demon of the fairy tale, had swelled and grown to such dimensions that her mistresses felt small before her. They now saw the French dinner coming upon them, a thing of incalculable nature and range. But they had never in their life broken a promise; they gave themselves into their cook's hands.

All the same when Martine saw a barrow load of bottles wheeled into the kitchen, she stood still. She touched the bottles and lifted up one. "What is there in this bottle, Babette?" she asked in a low voice. "Not wine?" "Wine, Madame!" Babette answered. "No, Madame. It is a Clos Vougeot 1846!" After a moment she added: "From Philippe, in Rue Montorgueil!" Martine had never suspected that wines could have names to them, and was put to silence.

Late in the evening she opened the door to a ring, and was once more faced with the wheelbarrow, this time with a red-haired sailor-boy behind it, as if the old man had by this time been worn out. The youth grinned at her as he lifted a big, undefinable object from the barrow. In the light of the lamp it looked like some greenish-black stone, but when set down on the kitchen floor it suddenly shot out a snake-like head and moved it slightly from side to side. Martine had seen pictures of tortoises, and had even as a child owned a pet tortoise, but this thing was monstrous in size and terrible to behold. She backed out of the kitchen without a word.

10   She dared not tell her sister what she had seen. She passed an almost sleepless night; she thought of her father and felt that on his very birthday she and her sister were lending his house to a witches' sabbath. When at last she fell asleep she had a terrible dream, in which she saw Babette poisoning the old Brothers and Sisters, Philippa and herself.

Early in the morning she got up, put on her gray cloak and went out in the dark street. She walked from house to house, opened her heart to her Brothers and Sisters, and confessed her guilt. She and Philippa, she said, had meant no harm; they had granted their servant a prayer and had not foreseen what might come of it. Now she could not tell what, on her father's birthday, her guests would be given to eat or drink. She did not actually mention the turtle, but it was present in her face and voice.

The old people, as has already been told, had all known Martine and Philippa as little girls; they had seen them cry bitterly over a broken doll. Martine's tears brought tears into their own eyes. They gathered in the afternoon and talked the problem over.

Before they again parted they promised one another that for their little sisters' sake they would, on the great day, be silent upon all matters of food and drink. Nothing that might be set before them, be it even frogs or snails, should wring a word from their lips.

"Even so," said a white-bearded Brother, "the tongue is a little member and boasteth great things. The tongue can no man tame; it is an unruly evil, full of deadly poison. On the day of our master we will cleanse our tongues of all taste and purify them of all delight or disgust of the senses, keeping and preserving them for the higher things of praise and thanksgiving."

So few things ever happened in the quiet existence of the Berlevaag brotherhood 15 that they were at this moment deeply moved and elevated. They shook hands on their vow, and it was to them as if they were doing so before the face of their Master.

VIII. The Hymn

On Sunday morning it began to snow. The white flakes fell fast and thick; the small windowpanes of the yellow house became pasted with snow.

Early in the day a groom from Fossum brought the two sisters a note. Old Mrs. Loewenhielm still resided in her country house. She was now ninety years old and stone-deaf, and she had lost all sense of smell or taste. But she had been one of the Dean's first supporters, and neither her infirmity nor the sledge journey would keep her from doing honor to his memory. Now, she wrote, her nephew, General Lorens Loewenhielm, had unexpectedly come on a visit; he had spoken with deep veneration of the Dean, and she begged permission to bring him with her. It would do him good, for the dear boy seemed to be in somewhat low spirits.

Martine and Philippa at this remembered the young officer and his visits; it relieved their present anxiety to talk of old happy days. They wrote back that General Loewenhielm would be welcome. They also called in Babette to inform her that they would now be twelve for dinner; they added that their latest guest had lived in Paris for several years. Babette seemed pleased with the news, and assured them that there would be food enough.

The hostesses made their little preparations in the sitting room. They dared not set foot in the kitchen, for Babette had mysteriously nosed out a cook's mate from a ship in the harbor—the same boy, Martine realized, who had brought in the turtle—to assist her in the kitchen and to wait at table, and now the dark woman and the red-haired boy, like some witch with her familiar spirit, had taken possession of these regions. The ladies could not tell what fires had been burning or what cauldrons bubbling there from before daybreak.

Table linen and plate had been magically mangled° and polished, glasses and 5 decanters brought, Babette only knew from where. The Dean's house did not possess twelve dining-room chairs, the long horse-hair-covered sofa had been moved from the parlor to the dining room, and the parlor, ever sparsely furnished, now looked strangely bare and big without it.

Martine and Philippa did their best to embellish the domain left to them. Whatever troubles might be in wait for their guests, in any case they should not be cold; all day the sisters fed the towering old stove with birch-knots. They hung a garland of juniper round their father's portrait on the wall, and placed candlesticks on their mother's small working table beneath it; they burned juniper-twigs to make the room smell nice. The while they wondered if in this weather the sledge from Fossum would get through. In the end they put on

---

⁵**mangled** run through a machine for pressing fabric with heated rollers

their old black best frocks and their confirmation gold crosses. They sat down, folded their hands in their laps and committed themselves unto God.

The old Brothers and Sisters arrived in small groups and entered the room slowly and solemnly.

This low room with its bare floor and scanty furniture was dear to the Dean's disciples. Outside its windows lay the great world. Seen from in here the great world in its winter-whiteness was ever prettily bordered in pink, blue and red by the row of hyacinths on the window-sills. And in summer, when the windows were open, the great world had a softly moving frame of white muslin curtains to it.

Tonight the guests were met on the doorstep with warmth and sweet smell, and they were looking into the face of their beloved Master, wreathed with evergreen. Their hearts like their numb fingers thawed.

One very old Brother, after a few moments' silence, in his trembling voice struck up one of the Master's own hymns:

> *"Jerusalem, my happy home*
> *name ever dear to me . . ."*

One by one the other voices fell in, thin quivering women's voices, ancient seafaring Brothers' deep growls, and above them all Philippa's clear soprano, a little worn with age but still angelic. Unwittingly the choir had seized one another's hands. They sang the hymn to the end, but could not bear to cease and joined in another:

> *"Take not thought for food or raiment*
> *careful one, so anxiously . . ."*

The mistresses of the house somewhat reassured by it, the words of the third verse:

> *"Wouldst thou give a stone, a reptile*
> *to thy pleading child for food? . . ."*

went straight to Martine's heart and inspired her with hope.

In the middle of this hymn sledge bells were heard outside; the guests from Fossum had arrived.

Martine and Philippa went to receive them and saw them into the parlor. Mrs. Loewenhielm with age had become quite small, her face colorless like parchment, and very still. By her side General Loewenhielm, tall, broad and ruddy, in his bright uniform, his breast covered with decorations, strutted and shone like an ornamental bird, a golden pheasant or a peacock, in this sedate party of black crows and jackdaws.

IX. General Loewenhielm

General Loewenhielm had been driving from Fossum to Berlevaag in a strange mood. He had not visited this part of the country for thirty years. He had come now to get a rest from his busy life at Court, and he had found no rest. The old house of Fossum was peaceful enough and seemed somehow pathetically small after the Tuileries and the Winter Palace. But it held one disquieting figure: young Lieutenant Loewenhielm walked in its rooms.

General Loewenhielm saw the handsome, slim figure pass close by him. And as he passed, the boy gave the elder man a short glance and a smile, the haughty, arrogant smile which youth gives to age. The General might have smiled back, kindly and a little sadly, as age smiles at youth, if it had not been that he was really in no mood to smile; he was, as his aunt had written, in low spirits.

General Loewenhielm had obtained everything that he had striven for in life and was admired and envied by everyone. Only he himself knew of a queer fact, which jarred with his prosperous existence: that he was not perfectly happy. Something was wrong somewhere, and he carefully felt his mental self all over, as one feels a finger over to determine the place of a deep-seated, invisible thorn.

He was in high favor with royalty, he had done well in his calling, he had friends everywhere. The thorn sat in none of these places.

His wife was a brilliant woman and still good-looking. Perhaps she neglected 5
her own house a little for her visits and parties; she changed her servants every three months and the General's meals at home were served unpunctually. The General, who valued good food highly in life, here felt a slight bitterness against the lady, and secretly blamed her for the indigestion from which he sometimes suffered. Still the thorn was not here either.

Nay, but an absurd thing had lately been happening to General Loewenhielm: he would find himself worrying about his immortal soul. Did he have any reason for doing so? He was a moral person, loyal to his king, his wife and his friends, an example to everybody. But there were moments when it seemed to him that the world was not a moral, but a mystic, concern. He looked into the mirror, examined the row of decorations on his breast and sighed to himself: "Vanity, vanity, all is vanity!"

The strange meeting at Fossum had compelled him to make out the balance-sheet of his life.

Young Lorens Loewenhielm had attracted dreams and fancies as a flower attracts bees and butterflies. He had fought to free himself of them; he had fled and they had followed. He had been scared of the Huldre of the family legend and had declined her invitation to come into the mountain; he had firmly refused the gift of second sight.

The elderly Lorens Loewenhielm found himself wishing that one little dream would come his way, and a gray moth of dusk look him up before nightfall. He found himself longing for the faculty of second sight, as a blind man will long for the normal faculty of vision.

Can the sum of a row of victories in many years and in many countries be 10
a defeat? General Loewenhielm had fulfilled Lieutenant Loewenhielm's wishes and had more than satisfied his ambitions. It might be held that he had gained the whole world. And it had come to this, that the stately, worldly-wise older man now turned toward the naïve young figure to ask him, gravely, even bitterly, in what he had profited? Somewhere something had been lost.

When Mrs. Loewenhielm had told her nephew of the Dean's anniversary and he had made up his mind to go with her to Berlevaag, his decision had not been an ordinary acceptance of a dinner invitation.

He would, he resolved, tonight make up his account with young Lorens Loewenhielm, who had felt himself to be a shy and sorry figure in the house of the Dean, and who in the end had shaken its dust off his riding boots. He would let the youth prove to him, once and for all, that thirty-one years ago he had made the right choice. The low rooms, the haddock and the glass of water on the table before him should all be called in to bear evidence that in their milieu the existence of Lorens Loewenhielm would very soon have become sheer misery.

He let his mind stray far away. In Paris he had once won a *concours hippique*° and had been feted by high French cavalry officers, princes and dukes among them. A dinner had been given in his honor at the finest restaurant of the city. Opposite him at table was a noble lady, a famous beauty whom he had long been courting. In the midst of dinner she had lifted her dark velvet eyes above the rim of her champagne glass and without words had promised to make him happy. In the sledge he now all of a sudden remembered that he had then, for a second, seen Martine's face before him and had rejected it. For a while he listened to the tinkling of the sledge bells, then he smiled a little as he reflected how he would tonight come to dominate the conversation round that same table by which young Lorens Loewenhielm had sat mute.

Large snowflakes fell densely; behind the sledge the tracks were wiped out quickly. General Loewenhielm sat immovable by the side of his aunt, his chin sunk in the high fur collar of his coat.

X. Babette's Dinner

As Babette's red-haired familiar opened the door to the dining room, and the guests slowly crossed the threshold, they let go one another's hands and became silent. But the silence was sweet, for in spirit they still held hands and were still singing.

Babette had set a row of candles down the middle of the table; the small flames shone on the black coats and frocks and on the one scarlet uniform, and were reflected in clear, moist eyes.

General Loewenhielm saw Martine's face in the candlelight as he had seen it when the two parted, thirty years ago. What traces would thirty years of Berlevaag life have left on it? The golden hair was now streaked with silver; the flower-like face had slowly been turned into alabaster. But how serene was the forehead, how quietly trustful the eyes, how pure and sweet the mouth, as if no hasty word had ever passed its lips.

When all were seated, the eldest member of the congregation said grace in the Dean's own words:

"May my food my body maintain,
  may my body my soul sustain,
  may my soul in deed and word
  give thanks for all things to the Lord."

[13]*concours hippique* horse race

At the word of "food" the guests, with their old heads bent over their folded 5
hands, remembered how they had vowed not to utter a word about the subject,
and in their hearts they reinforced the vow: they would not even give it a
thought! They were sitting down to a meal, well, so had people done at the
wedding of Cana. And grace has chosen to manifest itself there, in the very
wine, as fully as anywhere.

Babette's boy filled a small glass before each of the party. They lifted it to their
lips gravely, in confirmation of their resolution.

General Loewenhielm, somewhat suspicious of his wine, took a sip of it,
startled, raised the glass first to his nose and then to his eyes, and sat it down
bewildered. "This is very strange!" he thought. "Amontillado!° And the finest
Amontillado that I have ever tasted." After a moment, in order to test his senses,
he took a small spoonful of his soup, took a second spoonful and laid down his
spoon. "This is exceedingly strange!" he said to himself. "For surely I am eating
turtle-soup—and what turtle-soup!" He was seized by a queer kind of panic and
emptied his glass.

Usually in Berlevaag people did not speak much while they were eating. But
somehow this evening tongues had been loosened. An old Brother told the
story of his first meeting with the Dean. Another went through that sermon
which sixty years ago had brought about his conversion. An aged woman, the
one to whom Martine had first confided her distress, reminded her friends how
in all afflictions any Brother or Sister was ready to share the burden of any
other.

General Loewenhielm, who was to dominate the conversation of the dinner
table, related how the Dean's collection of sermons was a favorite book of the
Queen's. But as a new dish was served he was silenced. "Incredible!" he told
himself. "It is Blinis Demidoff!"° He looked round at his fellow-diners. They
were all quietly eating their Blinis Demidoff, without any sign of either surprise
or approval, as if they had been doing so every day for thirty years.

A Sister on the other side of the table opened on the subject of strange hap- 10
penings which had taken place while the Dean was still amongst his children,
and which one might venture to call miracles. Did they remember, she asked,
the time when he had promised a Christmas sermon in the village the other side
of the fjord? For a fortnight the weather had been so bad that no skipper or
fisherman would risk the crossing. The villagers were giving up hope, but the
Dean told them that if no boat would take him, he would come to them walking
upon the waves. And behold! Three days before Christmas the storm stopped,
hard frost set in, and the fjord froze from shore to shore—and this was a thing
which had not happened within the memory of man!

The boy once more filled the glasses. This time the Brothers and Sisters knew
that what they were given to drink was not wine, for it sparkled. It must be
some kind of lemonade. The lemonade agreed with their exalted state of mind
and seemed to lift them off the ground, into a higher and purer sphere.

---

[7]**Amontillado** sherry, or fortified wine from one region of Spain   [9]**Blinis Demidoff**
Russian dish consisting of a small pancake served with sour cream and caviar

General Loewenhielm again set down his glass, turned to his neighbor on the right and said to him: "But surely this is a Veuve Cliquot° 1860?" His neighbor looked at him kindly, smiled at him and made a remark about the weather.

Babette's boy had his instructions; he filled the glasses of the Brotherhood only once, but he refilled the General's glass as soon as it was emptied. The General emptied it quickly time after time. For how is a man of sense to behave when he cannot trust his senses? It is better to be drunk than mad.

Most often the people in Berlevaag during the course of a good meal would come to feel a little heavy. Tonight it was not so. The *convives*° grew lighter in weight and lighter of heart the more they ate and drank. They no longer needed to remind themselves of their vow. It was, they realized, when man has not only altogether forgotten but has firmly renounced all ideas of food and drink that he eats and drinks in the right spirit.

15   General Loewenhielm stopped eating and sat immovable. Once more he was carried back to that dinner in Paris of which he had thought in the sledge. An incredibly recherché° and palatable dish had been served there; he had asked its name from his fellow diner, Colonel Galliffet, and the Colonel had smilingly told him that it was named "Cailles en Sarcophage."° He had further told him that the dish had been invented by the chef of the very café in which they were dining, a person known all over Paris as the greatest culinary genius of the age, and—most surprisingly—a woman! "And indeed," said Colonel Galliffet, "this woman is now turning a dinner at the Café Anglais into a kind of love affair—into a love affair of the noble and romantic category in which one no longer distinguishes between bodily and spiritual appetite or satiety! I have, before now, fought a duel for the sake of a fair lady. For no woman in all Paris, my young friend, would I more willingly shed my blood!" General Loewenhielm turned to his neighbor on the left and said to him: "But this is Cailles en Sarcophage!" The neighbor, who had been listening to the description of a miracle, looked at him absent-mindedly, then nodded his head and answered: "Yes, Yes, certainly. What else would it be?"

From the Master's miracles the talk round the table had turned to the smaller miracles of kindliness and helpfulness daily performed by his daughters. The old Brother who had first struck up the hymn quoted the Dean's saying: "The only things which we may take with us from our life on earth are those which we have given away!" The guests smiled—what nabobs would not the poor, simple maidens become in the next world!

General Loewenhielm no longer wondered at anything. When a few minutes later he saw grapes, peaches and fresh figs before him, he laughed to his neighbor across the table and remarked: "Beautiful grapes!" His neighbor replied: "'And they came onto the brook of Eshcol, and cut down a branch with one cluster of grapes. And they bare it two upon a staff.'"°

Then the General felt that the time had come to make a speech. He rose and stood up very straight.

---

[12]**Veuve Cliquot** a prestigious brand of champagne   [14]*convives* those enjoying the meal together   [15]**recherché** exotic, rare   **Cailles en Sarcophage** an elaborate preparation of quail in a pastry shell   [17]**And they came . . . two upon a staff** a quotation from Numbers 13:23

Nobody else at the dinner table had stood up to speak. The old people lifted their eyes to the face above them in high, happy expectation. They were used to seeing sailors and vagabonds dead drunk with the crass gin of the country, but they did not recognize in a warrior and courtier the intoxication brought about by the noblest wine of the world.

XI. General Loewenhielm's Speech

"Mercy and truth, my friends, have met together," said the General. "Righteousness and bliss shall kiss one another."

He spoke in a clear voice which had been trained in drill grounds and had echoed sweetly in royal halls, and yet he was speaking in a manner so new to himself and so strangely moving that after his first sentence he had to make a pause. For he was in the habit of forming his speeches with care, conscious of his purpose, but here, in the midst of the Dean's simple congregation, it was as if the whole figure of General Loewenhielm, his breast covered with decorations, were but a mouthpiece for a message which meant to be brought forth.

"Man, my friends," said General Loewenhielm, "is frail and foolish. We have all of us been told that grace is to be found in the universe. But in our human foolishness and short-sightedness we imagine divine grace to be finite. For this reason we tremble . . ." Never till now had the General stated that he trembled; he was genuinely surprised and even shocked at hearing his own voice proclaim the fact. "We tremble before making our choice in life, and after having made it again tremble in fear of having chosen wrong. But the moment comes when our eyes are opened, and we see and realize that grace is infinite. Grace, my friends, demands nothing from us but that we shall await it with confidence and acknowledge it in gratitude. Grace, brothers, makes no conditions and singles out none of us in particular; grace takes us all to its bosom and proclaims general amnesty. See! that which we have chosen is given us, and that which we have refused is, also and at the same time, granted us. Ay, that which we have rejected is poured upon us abundantly. For mercy and truth have met together, and righteousness and bliss have kissed one another!"

The Brothers and Sisters had not altogether understood the General's speech, but his collected and inspired face and the sound of well-known and cherished words had seized and moved all hearts. In this way, after thirty-one years, General Loewenhielm succeeded in dominating the conversation at the Dean's dinner table.

Of what happened later in the evening nothing definite can here be stated. None of the guests later on had any clear remembrance of it. They only knew that the rooms had been filled with a heavenly light, as if a number of small halos had blended into one glorious radiance. Taciturn old people received the gift of tongues; ears that for years had been almost deaf were opened to it. Time itself had merged into eternity. Long after midnight the windows of the house shone like gold, and golden song flowed out into the winter air.

The two old women who had once slandered each other now in their hearts went back a long way, past the evil period in which they had been stuck, to those days of their early girlhood when together they had been preparing for confirmation and hand in hand had filled the roads round Berlevaag with singing. A Brother in the congregation gave another a knock in the ribs, like a rough caress between boys, and cried out: "You cheated me on that timber, you old scoundrel!" The Brother thus addressed almost collapsed in a heavenly burst of laughter, but tears ran from his eyes. "Yes, I did so, beloved Brother," he answered. "I did so." Skipper Halvorsen and Madam Oppegaarden suddenly found themselves close together in a corner and gave one another that long, long kiss, for which the secret uncertain love affair of their youth had never left them time.

The old Dean's flock were humble people. When later in life they thought of this evening it never occurred to any of them that they might have been exalted by their own merit. They realized that the infinite grace of which General Loewenhielm had spoken had been allotted to them, and they did not even wonder at the fact, for it had been but the fulfillment of an ever-present hope. The vain illusions of this earth had dissolved before their eyes like smoke, and they had seen the universe as it really is. They had been given one hour of the millennium.

Old Mrs. Loewenhielm was the first to leave. Her nephew accompanied her, and their hostesses lighted them out. While Philippa was helping the old lady into her many wraps, the General seized Martine's hand and held it for a long time without a word. At last he said:

"I have been with you every day of my life. You know, do you not, that it has been so?"

10   "Yes," said Martine, "I know that it has been so."

"And," he continued, "I shall be with you every day that is left to me. Every evening I shall sit down, if not in the flesh, which means nothing, in spirit, which is all, to dine with you, just like tonight. For tonight I have learned, dear sister, that in this world anything is possible."

"Yes, it is so, dear brother," said Martine. "In this world anything is possible."

Upon this they parted.

When at last the company broke up it had ceased to snow. The town and the mountains lay in white, unearthly splendor and the sky was bright with thousands of stars. In the street the snow was lying so deep that it had become difficult to walk. The guests from the yellow house wavered on their feet, staggered, sat down abruptly or fell forward on their knees and hands and were covered with snow, as if they had indeed had their sins washed white as wool, and in this regained innocent attire were gamboling like little lambs. It was, to each of them, blissful to have become as a small child; it was also a blessed joke to watch old Brothers and Sisters, who had been taking themselves so seriously, in this kind of celestial second childhood. They stumbled and got up, walked on or stood still, bodily as well as spiritually hand in hand, at moments performing the great chain of a beatified *lanciers*.°

15   "Bless you, bless you, bless you," like an echo of the harmony of the spheres° rang on all sides.

Martine and Philippa stood for a long time on the stone steps outside the house. They did not feel the cold. "The stars have come nearer," said Philippa.

---

[14]*lanciers* French square dance for four couples; related to the quadrille   [15]**the harmony of the spheres** Ancient Greek philosophers and mathematicians thought of the universe as consisting of concentric spheres rotating around a center. The motions of the spheres were thought to produce harmonic vibrations.

"They will come every night," said Martine quietly. "Quite possibly it will never snow again."

In this, however, she was mistaken. An hour later it again began to snow, and such a heavy snowfall had never been known in Berlevaag. The next morning people could hardly push open their doors against the tall snowdrifts. The windows of the houses were so thickly covered with snow, it was told for years afterwards, that many good citizens of the town did not realize that daybreak had come, but slept on till late in the afternoon.

XII. The Great Artist

When Martine and Philippa locked the door they remembered Babette. A little wave of tenderness and pity swept through them: Babette alone had had no share in the bliss of the evening.

So they went out into the kitchen, and Martine said to Babette: "It was quite a nice dinner, Babette."

Their hearts suddenly filled with gratitude. They realized that none of their guests had said a single word about the food. Indeed, try as they might, they could not themselves remember any of the dishes which had been served. Martine bethought herself of the turtle. It had not appeared at all, and now seemed very vague and far away; it was quite possible that it had been nothing but a nightmare.

Babette sat on the chopping block, surrounded by more black and greasy pots and pans than her mistresses had ever seen in their life. She was as white and as deadly exhausted as on the night when she first appeared and had fainted on their doorstep.

After a long time she looked straight at them and said: "I was once cook at the Café Anglais."

Martine said again: "They all thought that it was a nice dinner." And when   5
Babette did not answer a word she added: "We will all remember this evening when you have gone back to Paris, Babette."

Babette said: "I am not going back to Paris."

"You are not going back to Paris?" Martine exclaimed.

"No," said Babette. "What will I do in Paris? They have all gone. I have lost them all, Mesdames."

The sisters' thoughts went to Monsieur Hersant and his son, and they said: "Oh, my poor Babette."

"Yes, they have all gone," said Babette. "The Duke of Morny, the Duke of   10
Decazes, Prince Narishkine, General Galliffet, Aurélian Scholl, Paul Daru, the Princesse Pauline! All!"

The strange names and titles of people lost to Babette faintly confused the two ladies, but there was such an infinite perspective of tragedy in her announcement that in their responsive state of mind they felt her losses as their own, and their eyes filled with tears.

At the end of another long silence Babette suddenly smiled slightly at them and said: "And how would I go back to Paris, Mesdames? I have no money."

"No money?" the sisters cried as with one mouth.

"No," said Babette.

15   "But the ten thousand francs?" the sisters asked in a horrified gasp.

"The ten thousand francs have been spent, Mesdames," said Babette.

The sisters sat down. For a full minute they could not speak.

"But ten thousand francs?" Martine slowly whispered.

"What will you, Mesdames," said Babette with great dignity. "A dinner for twelve at the Café Anglais would cost ten thousand francs."

20   The ladies still did not find a word to say. The piece of news was incomprehensible to them, but then many things tonight in one way or another had been beyond comprehension.

Martine remembered a tale told by a friend of her father's who had been a missionary in Africa. He had saved the life of an old chief's favorite wife, and to show his gratitude the chief had treated him to a rich meal. Only long afterwards the missionary learned from his own black servant that what he had partaken of was a small fat grandchild of the chief's, cooked in honor of the great Christian medicine man. She shuddered.

But Philippa's heart was melting in her bosom. It seemed that an unforgettable evening was to be finished off with an unforgettable proof of human loyalty and self-sacrifice.

"Dear Babette," she said softly, "you ought not to have given away all you had for our sake."

Babette gave her mistress a deep glance, a strange glance. Was there not pity, even scorn, at the bottom of it?

25   "For your sake?" she replied. "No. For my own."

She rose from the chopping block and stood up before the two sisters.

"I am a great artist!" she said.

She waited a moment and then repeated: "I am a great artist, Mesdames."

Again for a long time there was deep silence in the kitchen.

30   Then Martine said: "So you will be poor now all your life, Babette?"

"Poor?" said Babette. She smiled as if to herself. "No, I shall never be poor. I told you that I am a great artist. A great artist, Mesdames, is never poor. We have something, Mesdames, of which other people know nothing."

While the elder sister found nothing more to say, in Philippa's heart deep, forgotten chords vibrated. For she had heard, before now, long ago, of the Café Anglais. She had heard, before now, long ago, the names on Babette's tragic list. She rose and took a step toward her servant.

"But all those people whom you have mentioned," she said, "those princes and great people of Paris whom you named, Babette? You yourself fought against them. You were a Communard! The General you named had your husband and son shot! How can you grieve over them?"

Babette's dark eyes met Philippa's.

35   "Yes," she said, "I was a Communard. Thanks be to God, I was a Communard! And those people whom I named, Mesdames, were evil and cruel. They let the people of Paris starve; they oppressed and wronged the poor. Thanks be to God, I stood upon a barricade; I loaded the gun for my menfolk! But all the same, Mesdames, I shall not go back to Paris, now that those people of whom I have spoken are no longer there."

She stood immovable, lost in thought.

"You see, Mesdames," she said, at last, "those people belonged to me, they were mine. They had been brought up and trained, with greater expense than you, my little ladies, could ever imagine or believe, to understand what a great artist I am. I could make them happy. When I did my very best I could make them perfectly happy."

She paused for a moment.

"It was like that with Monsieur Papin too," she said.

"With Monsieur Papin?" Philippa asked.

"Yes, with your Monsieur Papin, my poor lady," said Babette. "He told me so himself: 'It is terrible and unbearable to an artist,' he said, 'to be encouraged to do, to be applauded for doing, his second best.' He said: 'Through all the world there goes one long cry from the heart of the artist: Give me leave to do my utmost!'"

Philippa went up to Babette and put her arms round her. She felt the cook's body like a marble monument against her own, but she herself shook and trembled from head to foot.

For a while she could not speak. Then she whispered:

"Yet this is not the end! I feel, Babette, that this is not the end. In Paradise you will be the great artist that God meant you to be! Ah!" she added, the tears streaming down her cheeks. "Ah, how you will enchant the angels!"

[1958]

1. What can we learn by outlining the plot of the story? What is the purpose of the flashbacks? Is there a turning point that seems to determine the succeeding events? What are the conflicts that drive the plot?
2. Do any of the characters change in the course of the story?

ABRAHAM MASLOW

ABRAHAM MASLOW *(1908–70) was born in Brooklyn, New York, to uneducated Russian Jewish immigrants who pushed him hard for academic success. He studied law at the City College of New York and Cornell University and, against his parents' wishes, married his first cousin. The couple moved to Wisconsin so that he could study psychology at the university, where he worked with Harry Harlow, studying what factors allowed baby rhesus monkeys to become attached to maternal figures (food alone wasn't sufficient to produce well-adjusted monkeys). A return to New York and Columbia University led to research on human sexuality. His teaching appointment at Brooklyn College enabled him to come into contact with many of the European intellectuals who were coming to New York at the time, including Alfred Adler, Erich Fromm, Karen Horney, and several Gestalt and Freudian psychologists. His appointment to the chair of Psychology at Brandeis University led to his introduction to the work of Kurt Goldstein and the beginning of his own theoretical work in self-actualization and humanistic psychology.*

40

Self-Actualizing and Beyond*

In this chapter, I plan to discuss ideas that are in midstream rather than ready for formulation into a final version. I find that with my students and with other people with whom I share these ideas, the notion of self-actualization gets to be almost like a Rorschach inkblot. It frequently tells me more about the person using it than about reality. What I would like to do now is to explore some aspects of the nature of self-actualization, not as a grand abstraction, but in terms of the operational meaning of the self-actualizing process. What does self-actualization mean in moment-to-moment terms? What does it mean on Tuesday at four o'clock?

The Beginnings of Self-Actualization Studies. My investigations on self-actualization were not planned to be research and did not start out as research. They started out as the effort of a young intellectual to try to understand two of his teachers whom he loved, adored, and admired and who were very, very wonderful people. It was a kind of high-IQ devotion. I could not be content simply to adore, but sought to understand why these two people were so different from the run-of-the-mill people in the world. These two people were Ruth Benedict and Max Wertheimer. They were my teachers after I came with a Ph.D. from the West to New York City, and they were most remarkable human beings. My training in psychology equipped me not at all for understanding them. It was as if they were not quite people but something more than people. My own investigation began as a prescientific or nonscientific activity. I made descriptions and notes on Max Wertheimer, and I made notes on Ruth Benedict. When I tried to understand them, think about them, and write about them in my journal and my notes, I realized in one wonderful moment that their two patterns could be generalized. I was talking about a kind of person, not about two non-comparable individuals. There was wonderful excitement in that. I tried to see whether this pattern could be found elsewhere, and I did find it elsewhere, in one person after another.

By ordinary standards of laboratory research, i.e., of rigorous and controlled research, this simply was not research at all. My generalizations grew out of *my* selection of certain kinds of people. Obviously, other judges are needed. So far, one man has selected perhaps two dozen people whom he liked or admired very much and thought were wonderful people and then tried to figure them out and found that he was able to describe a syndrome—the kind of pattern that seemed to fit all of them. These were people only from Western cultures, people selected with all kinds of built-in biases. Unreliable as it is, that was the only operational definition of self-actualizing people as I described them in my first publication on the subject.

After I published the results of my investigations, there appeared perhaps six, eight, or ten other lines of evidence that supported the findings, not by replication, but by approaches from different angles. Carl Rogers' findings (128) and those of his students add up to corroboration for the whole syndrome. Bugental

*Abraham H. Maslow, "Self-Actualizing and Beyond" in *The Farther Reaches of Human Nature* (New York: The Viking Press, 1971), Chapter 3.

(20, pp. 266–275) has offered confirmatory evidence from psychotherapy. Some of the work with LSD (116), some of the studies on the effects of therapy (good therapy, that is) some test results—in fact everything I know adds up to corroborative support, though not replicated support, for that study. I personally feel very confident about its major conclusions. I cannot conceive of any research that would make major changes in the pattern, though I am sure there will be minor changes. I have made some of those myself. But my confidence in my rightness is not a scientific datum. If you question the kind of data I have from my researches with monkeys and dogs, you are bringing my competence into doubt or calling me a liar, and I have a right to object. If you question my findings on self-actualizing people (95, pp. 203–205; 89), you may reasonably do so because you don't know very much about the man who selected the people on whom all the conclusions are based. The conclusions are in the realm of pre-science, but the affirmations are set forth in a form that can be put to test. In that sense, they are scientific.

The people I selected for my investigation were older people, people who had lived much of their lives out and were visibly successful. We do not yet know about the applicability of the findings to young people. We do not know what self-actualization means in other cultures, although studies of self-actualization in China and in India are now in process. We do not know what the findings of these new studies will be, but of one thing I have no doubt: When you select out for careful study very fine and healthy people, strong people, creative people, saintly people, sagacious people—in fact, exactly the kind of people I picked out—then you get a different view of mankind. You are asking how tall can people grow, what can a human being become?

There are other things that I feel very confident about—"my smell tells me," so to speak. Yet I have even fewer objective data on these points than I had on those discussed above. Self-actualization is hard enough to define. How much harder it is to answer the question: Beyond self-actualization, what? Or, if you will: Beyond authenticity, what? Just being honest is, after all, not sufficient in all this. What else can we say of self-actualizing people?

Being-Values. Self-actualizing people are, without one single exception, involved in a cause outside their own skin, in something outside of themselves. They are devoted, working at something, something which is very precious to them—some calling or vocation in the old sense, the priestly sense. They are working at something which fate has called them to somehow and which they work at and which they love, so that the work-joy dichotomy in them disappears. One devotes his life to the law, another to justice, another to beauty or truth. All, in one way or another, devote their lives to the search for what I have called (89) the "being" values ("B" for short), the ultimate values which are intrinsic, which cannot be reduced to anything more ultimate. There are about fourteen of these B-Values, including the truth and beauty and goodness of the ancients and perfection, simplicity, comprehensiveness, and several more. These B-Values are described in Chapter 9, and in the appendix to my book *Religions, Values, and Peak-Experiences* (85). They are the values of being.

Metaneeds and Metapathologies.° The existence of these B-Values adds a whole set of complications to the structure of self-actualization. These B-Values behave like needs. I have called them *metaneeds*. Their deprivation breeds certain kinds of pathologies which have not yet been adequately described but which I call *metapathologies*—the sicknesses of the soul which come, for example, from living among liars all the time and not trusting anyone. Just as we need counselors to help people with the simpler problems of unmet needs, so we may need *metacounselors* to help with the soul-sicknesses that grow from the unfulfilled metaneeds. In certain definable and empirical ways, it is necessary for man to live in beauty rather than ugliness, as it is necessary for him to have food for an aching belly or rest for a weary body. In fact, I would go so far as to claim that these B-Values are the meaning of life for most people, but many people don't even recognize that they have these metaneeds. Part of the counselors' job may be to make them aware of these needs in themselves, just as the classical psychoanalyst made his patients aware of their instinctoid basic needs. Ultimately, perhaps, some professionals shall come to think of themselves as philosophical or religious counselors.

Some of us try to help our conselees move and grow toward self-actualization. These people are often all wrapped up in value problems. Many are youngsters who are, in principle, very wonderful people, though in actuality they often seem to be little more than snotty kids. Nevertheless, I assume (in the face of all behavioral evidence sometimes) that they are, in the classical sense, idealistic. I assume that they are looking for values and that they would love to have something to devote themselves to, to be patriotic about, to worship, adore, love. These youngsters are making choices from moment to moment of going forward or retrogressing, moving away from or moving toward self-actualization. What can counselors, or metacounselors, tell them about becoming more fully themselves?

Behaviors Leading to Self-Actualization

10 What does one do when he self-actualizes? Does he grit his teeth and squeeze? What does self-actualization mean in terms of actual behavior, actual procedure? I shall describe eight ways in which one self-actualizes.

First, self-actualization means experiencing fully, vividly, selflessly, with full concentration and total absorption. It means experiencing without the self-consciousness of the adolescent. At this moment of experiencing, the person is wholly and fully human. This is a self-actualizing moment. This is a moment when the self is actualizing itself. As individuals, we all experience such moments occasionally. As counselors, we can help clients to experience them more often. We can encourage them to become totally absorbed in something and to forget their poses and their defenses and their shyness—to go at it

[8]***Metaneeds, metapathologies*** *meta-* comes from the Greek meaning "beside" or "after." It could mean "after" in terms of time or in a higher state of development, more comprehensive, as in "meta-analysis," techniques for synthesizing the results of previous studies to combine and evaluate them to reach new conclusions.

"whole-hog." From the outside, we can see that this can be a very sweet moment. In those youngsters who are trying to be very tough and cynical and sophisticated, we can see the recovery of some of the guilelessness of childhood; some of the innocence and sweetness of the face can come back as they devote themselves fully to a moment and throw themselves fully into the experiencing of it. The key word for this is "selflessly," and our youngsters suffer from too little selflessness and too much self-consciousness, self-awareness.

Second, let us think of life as a process of choices, one after another. At each point there is a progression choice and a regression choice. There may be a movement toward defense, toward safety, toward being afraid; but over on the other side, there is the growth choice. To make the growth choice instead of the fear choice a dozen times a day is to move a dozen times a day toward self-actualization. *Self-actualization is an ongoing process;* it means making each of the many single choices about whether to lie or be honest, whether to steal or not to steal at a particular point, and it means to make each of these choices as a growth choice. This is movement toward self-actualization.

Third, to talk of self-actualization implies that there is a self to be actualized. A human being is not a *tabula rasa,*° not a lump of clay or Plasticine. He is something which is already there, at least a "cartilaginous" structure of some kind. A human being is, at minimum, his temperament, his biochemical balances, and so on. There is a self, and what I have sometimes referred to as "listening to the impulse voices" means letting the self emerge. Most of us, most of the time (and especially does this apply to children, young people), listen not to ourselves but to Mommy's introjected voice or Daddy's voice or to the voice of the Establishment, of the Elders, of authority, or of tradition.

As a simple first step toward self-actualization, I sometimes suggest to my students that when they are given a glass of wine and asked how they like it, they try a different way of responding. First, I suggest that they *not* look at the label on the bottle. Thus they will not use it to get any cue about whether or not they *should* like it. Next, I recommend that they close their eyes if possible and that they "make a hush." Now they are ready to look within themselves and try to shut out the noise of the world so that they may savor the wine on their tongues and look to the "Supreme Court" inside themselves. Then, and only then, they may come out and say, "I like it" or "I don't like it." A statement so arrived at is different from the usual kind of phoniness that we all indulge in. At a party recently, I caught myself looking at the label on a bottle and assuring my hostess that she had indeed selected a very good Scotch. But then I stopped myself: What was I saying? I know little about Scotches. All I knew was what the advertisements said. I had no idea whether this one was good or not; yet this is the kind of thing we all do. Refusing to do it is part of the ongoing process of actualizing oneself. Does *your* belly hurt? Or does it feel good? Does this taste good on *your* tongue? Do *you* like lettuce?

Fourth, when in doubt, be honest rather than not. I am covered by that phrase "when in doubt," so that we need not argue too much about diplomacy.

15

---

[13]*tabula rasa* Latin for "blank slate"

Frequently, when we are in doubt we are not honest. Clients are not honest much of the time. They are playing games and posing. They do not take easily to the suggestion to be honest. Looking within oneself for many of the answers implies taking responsibility. That is in itself a great step toward actualization. This matter of responsibility has been little studied. It doesn't turn up in our textbooks, for who can investigate responsibility in white rats? Yet it is an almost tangible part of psychotherapy. In psychotherapy, one can see it, can feel it, can know the moment of responsibility. Then there is a clear knowing of what it feels like. This is one of the great steps. Each time one takes responsibility, this is an actualizing of the self.

Fifth, we have talked so far of experiencing without self-awareness, of making the growth choice rather than the fear choice, of listening to the impulse voices, and of being honest and taking responsibility. All these are steps toward self-actualization, and all of them guarantee better life choices. A person who does each of these little things each time the choice point comes will find that they add up to better choices about what is constitutionally right for him. He comes to know what his destiny is, who his wife or husband will be, what his mission in life will be. One cannot choose wisely for a life unless he dares to listen to himself, *his own self,* at each moment in life, and to say calmly, "No, I don't like such and such."

The art world, in my opinion, has been captured by a small group of opinion- and taste-makers about whom I feel suspicious. That is an *ad hominem* judgment, but it seems fair enough for people who set themselves up as able to say, "You like what I like or else you are a fool." We must teach people to listen to their own tastes. Most people don't do it. When standing in a gallery before a puzzling painting, one rarely hears, "That is a puzzling painting." We had a dance program at Brandeis University not too long ago—a weird thing altogether, with electronic music, tapes, and people doing surrealistic° and Dada° things. When the lights went up everybody looked stunned, and nobody knew what to say. In that kind of situation most people will make some smart chatter instead of saying, "I would like to think about this." Making an honest statement involves daring to be different, unpopular, nonconformist. If clients, young or old, cannot be taught about being prepared to be unpopular, counselors might just as well give up right now. To be courageous rather than afraid is another version of the same thing.

Sixth, self-actualization is not only an end state but also the process of actualizing one's potentialities at any time, in any amount. It is, for example, a matter of becoming smarter by studying if one is an intelligent person.

---

[17]**surrealistic** Surrealism was a movement in twentieth-century art and literature that attempted to get beyond the everyday by using fantastic images and surprising juxtapositions of unrelated things.   **Dada** an early twentieth-century artistic and literary movement that rejected conventional aesthetics and taste through nonsense, travesty, and incongruity. Dada was an inspiration for a number of subsequent movements including Surrealism, Constructivism, Pop- and Op-Art, Conceptual Art, and Minimalism, as well as the Yippies and Guerrilla theater movements of the 1960s.

Self-actualization means using one's intelligence. It does not mean doing some far-out thing necessarily, but it may mean going through an arduous and demanding period of preparation in order to realize one's possibilities. Self-actualization can consist of finger exercises at a piano keyboard. Self-actualization means working to do well the thing that one wants to do. To become a second-rate physician is not a good path to self-actualization. One wants to be first-rate or as good as he can be.

Seventh, peak experiences (85, 89) are transient moments of self-actualization. They are moments of ecstasy which cannot be bought, cannot be guaranteed, cannot even be sought. One must be, as C. S. Lewis wrote, "surprised by joy." But one can set up the conditions so that peak experiences are more likely, or one can perversely set up the conditions so that they are less likely. Breaking up an illusion, getting rid of a false notion, learning what one is not good at, learning what one's potentialities are *not*—these are also part of discovering what one is in fact.

Practically everyone does have peak experiences, but not everyone knows it. Some people wave these small mystical experiences aside. Helping people to recognize these little moments of ecstasy (124) when they happen is one of the jobs of the counselor or metacounselor. Yet, how does one's psyche, with nothing external in the world to point at—there is no blackboard there—look into another person's secret psyche and then try to communicate? We have to work out a new way of communication. I have tried one. It is described in another appendix in that same book, *Religions, Values, and Peak-Experiences,* under the title "Rhapsodic Communications." I think that kind of communication may be more of a model for teaching, and counseling, for helping adults to become as fully developed as they can be, than the kind we are used to when we see teachers writing on the board. If I love Beethoven and I hear something in a quartet that you don't, how do I teach you to hear? The noises are there, obviously. But I hear something very, very beautiful, and you look blank. You hear the sounds. How do I get you to hear the beauty? That is more our problem in teaching than making you learn the ABC's or demonstrating arithmetic on the board or pointing to a dissection of a frog. These latter things are external to both people; one has a pointer, and both can look at the same time. This kind of teaching is easy; the other kind is much harder, but it is part of the counselor's job. It is meta-counseling.

Eighth, finding out who one is, what he is, what he likes, what he doesn't like, what is good for him and what bad, where he is going and what his mission is—opening oneself up to himself—means the exposure of psychopathology. It means identifying defenses, and after defenses have been identified, it means finding the courage to give them up. This is painful because defenses are erected against something which is unpleasant. But giving up the defenses is worthwhile. If the psychoanalytic literature has taught us nothing else, it has taught us that repression is not a good way of solving problems.

Desacralizing. Let me talk about one defense mechanism that is not mentioned in the psychology textbooks, though it is a very important defense mechanism to some youngsters of today. It is the defense mechanism of *desacralizing.* These youngsters mistrust the possibility of values and virtues. They feel themselves swindled or thwarted in their lives. Most of them have, in fact, dopey parents whom they don't respect very much, parents who are quite confused themselves about values and who, frequently, are simply terrified of their children and never punish them or stop them from doing things that are wrong. So you have a situation where the youngsters simply despise their elders—often for good and sufficient reason. Such youngsters have learned to make a big generalization: They won't listen to anybody who is grown-up, especially if the grown-up uses the same words which they've heard from the hypocritical mouth. They have heard their fathers talk about being honest or brave or bold, and they have seen their fathers being the opposite of all these things.

The youngsters have learned to reduce the person to the concrete object and to refuse to see what he might be or to refuse to see him in his symbolic values or to refuse to see him or her eternally. Our kids have desacralized sex, for example. Sex is nothing; it is a natural thing, and they have made it so natural that it has lost its poetic qualities in many instances, which means that it has lost practically everything. Self-actualization means giving up this defense mechanism and learning or being taught to resacralize.[1]

Resacralizing. Resacralizing means being willing, once again, to see a person "under the aspect of eternity," as Spinoza says, or to see him in the medieval Christian unitive perception, that is, being able to see the sacred, the eternal, the symbolic. It is to see Woman with a capital "W" and everything which that implies, even when one looks at a particular woman. Another example: One goes to medical school and dissects a brain. Certainly something is lost if the medical student isn't awed but, without the unitive perception, sees the brain only as one concrete thing. Open to resacralization, one sees a brain as a sacred object also, sees its symbolic value, sees it as a figure of speech, sees it in its poetic aspects.

25   Resacralization often means an awful lot of corny talk—"very square," the kids would say. Nevertheless, for the counselor, especially for the counselor of older people, where these philosophical questions about religion and the meaning of life come up, this is a most important way of helping the person to move toward self-actualization. The youngsters may say that it is square, and the logical positivists may say that it is meaningless, but for the person who seeks our help in this process, it is obviously very meaningful and very important, and we had better answer him, or we're not doing what it is our job to do.

Put all these points together, and we see that self-actualization is not a matter of one great moment. It is not true that on Thursday at four o'clock the trumpet blows and one steps into the pantheon° forever and altogether. Self-actualization is a matter of degree, of little accessions accumulated one by one. Too often our

---

[1]I have had to make up these words because the English language is rotten for good people. It has no decent vocabulary for the virtues. Even the nice words get all smeared up—"love," for instance.

[26]**pantheon** a circular temple in ancient Rome dedicated to all the gods, and so, in general, a temple dedicated to all gods

clients are inclined to wait for some kind of inspiration to strike so that they can say, "At 3:23 on this Thursday I became self-actualized!" People selected as self-actualizing subjects, people who fit the criteria, go about it in these little ways: They listen to their own voices; they take responsibility; they are honest; and they work hard. They find out who they are and what they are, not only in terms of their mission in life, but also in terms of the way their feet hurt when they wear such and such a pair of shoes and whether they do or do not like eggplant or stay up all night if they drink too much beer. All this is what the real self means. They find their own biological natures, their congenital natures, which are irreversible or difficult to change.

The Therapeutic Attitude

These are the things people do as they move toward self-actualization. Who, then, is a counselor? How can he help the people who come to him to make this movement in the direction of growth?

Seeking a Model. I have used the words "therapy," "psychotherapy," and "patient." Actually, I hate all these words, and I hate the medical model that they imply because the medical model suggests that the person who comes to the counselor is a sick person, beset by disease and illness, seeking a cure. Actually, of course, we hope that the counselor will be the one who helps to foster the self-actualization of people, rather than the one who helps to cure a disease.

The helping model has to give way, too; it just doesn't fit. It makes us think of the counselor as the person or the professional who knows and reaches down from his privileged position above to the poor jerks below who don't know and have to be helped in some way. Nor is the counselor to be a teacher, in the usual sense, because what teachers have specialized in and gotten to be very good at is "extrinsic learning". . . . The process of growing into the best human being one can be is, instead, "intrinsic learning."

The existential therapists have wrestled with this question of models, and I can recommend Bugental's book, *The Search for Authenticity* (20), for a discussion of the matter. Bugental suggests that we call counseling or therapy "ontogogy," which means trying to help people to grow to their fullest possible height. Perhaps that's a better word than the one I once suggested, a word derived from a German author, "psychogogy," which means the education of the psyche. Whatever the word we use, I think that the concept we will eventually have to come to is one that Alfred Adler suggested a long, long time ago when he spoke of the "older brother." The older brother is the loving person who takes responsibility, just as one does for his young, kid brother. Of course, the older brother knows more; he's lived longer, but he is not qualitatively different, and he is not in another realm of discourse. The wise and loving older brother tries to improve the younger, and he tries to make him better than he is, in the younger's own style. See how different this is from the "teaching-somebody-who-doesn't-know-nothin'" model!

Counseling is not concerned with training or with molding or with teaching in the ordinary sense of telling people what to do and how to do it. It is not concerned with propaganda. It is a Taoistic uncovering and *then* helping. Taoistic

30

means the noninterfering, the "letting be." Taoism is not a laissez-faire philosophy or a philosophy of neglect or of refusal to help or care. As a kind of model of this process we might think of a therapist who, if he is a decent therapist and also a decent human being, would never dream of imposing himself upon his patients or propagandizing in any way or of trying to make a patient into an imitation of himself.

What the good clinical therapist does is to help his particular client to unfold, to break through the defenses against his own self-knowledge, to recover himself, and to get to know himself. Ideally, the therapist's rather abstract frame of reference, the textbooks he has read, the schools that he has gone to, his beliefs about the world—these should never be perceptible to the patient. Respectful of the inner nature, the being, the essence of this "younger brother," he would recognize that the best way for him to lead a good life is to be more fully himself. The people we call "sick" are the people who are not themselves, the people who have built up all sorts of neurotic defenses against being human. Just as it makes no difference to the rosebush whether the gardener is Italian or French or Swedish, so it should make no difference to the younger brother how his helper learned to be a helper. What the helper has to give is certain services that are independent of his being Swedish or Catholic or Mohammedan or Freudian or whatever he is.

These basic concepts include, imply, and are completely in accord with the basic concepts of Freudian and other systems of psychodynamics. It is a Freudian principle that unconscious aspects of the self are repressed and that the finding of the true self requires the uncovering of these unconscious aspects. Implicit is a belief that truth heals much. Learning to break through one's repressions, to know one's self, to hear the impulse voices, to uncover the triumphant nature, to reach knowledge, insight, and the truth—these are the requirements.

Lawrence Kubie (64), in "The Forgotten Man in Education," some time ago made the point that one, ultimate goal of education is to help the person become a human being, as fully human as he can possibly be.

Especially with adults we are not in a position in which we have nothing to work with. We already have a start; we already have capacities, talents, direction, missions, callings. The job is, if we are to take this model seriously, to help them to be more perfectly what they already are, to be more full, more actualizing, more realizing in fact what they are in potentiality.   [1971]

Various Meanings of Transcendence*

1. Transcendence in the sense of loss of self-consciousness, of self-awareness, and of self-observing of the adolescent depersonalization type. It is the same kind of self-forgetfulness which comes from getting absorbed, fascinated, concentrated. In this sense, meditation or concentration on something outside one's own psyche can produce self-forgetfulness and therefore loss of self-consciousness, and in this particular sense of transcendence of the ego or of the conscious self.

*Abraham H. Maslow, "Various Meanings of Transcendence," in *The Farther Reaches of Human Nature* (New York: The Viking Press, 1971), Chapter 21.

2. Transcendence in the metapsychological sense of transcending one's own skin and body and bloodstream, as in identification with the B-Values so that they become intrinsic to the Self itself.

3. Transcendence of time. For example, my experience of being bored in an academic procession and feeling slightly ridiculous in cap and gown, and suddenly slipping over into being a symbol under the aspect of eternity rather than just a bored and irritated individual in the moment and in the specific place. My vision or imagining was that the academic procession stretched way, way out into the future, far, far away, further than I could see, and it had Socrates° at its head, and the implication was, I suppose, that many of the people far ahead had been there and in previous generations, and that I was a successor and a follower of all the great academics and professors and intellectuals. Then the vision was also of the procession stretching out behind me into a dim, hazy infinity where there were people not yet born who would join the academic procession, the procession of scholars, of intellectuals, of scientists and philosophers. And I thrilled at being in such a procession and felt the great dignity of it, of my robes, and even of myself as a person who belonged in this procession. That is, I became a symbol; I stood for something outside my own skin. I was not exactly an individual. I was also a "role" of the eternal teacher. I was the Platonic essence of the teacher.

This kind of transcendence of time is also true in another sense, namely that I can feel friendly, in a very personal and affectionate way, with Spinoza,° Abraham Lincoln,° Jefferson,° William James,° Whitehead,° etc., as if they still lived. Which is to say that in specific ways they *do* still live.

In still another sense, one can transcend time, namely in the sense of working 5 hard for not yet born great-grandchildren or other successors. But this is in the sense in which Allen Wheelis° (157) in his novel, *The Seeker,* had his hero on the point of death thinking that the best thing he could do would be to plant trees for future generations.

4. Transcendence of culture. In a very specific sense, the self-actualizing man, or the transcendent self-actualizing man, is the universal man. He is a member of the human species. He is rooted in a particular culture but he rises above that culture and can be said to be independent of it in various ways and to look down upon it from a height, perhaps like a tree which has its roots in the soil but whose branches are spread out very high above and are unable to look down upon the soil in which the roots are rooted: I have written about the

[3]**Socrates** ancient Greek philosopher (469–399 BCE), known primarily through the works of Plato, particularly as the leader of conversations aimed at discovering the principles that guide human life   [4]**Spinoza** Dutch philosopher Benedict (Baruch) Spinoza (1632–77)   **Abraham Lincoln** (1809–65) sixteenth president of the United States   **[Thomas] Jefferson** (1743–1826) third president of the United States   **William James** philosopher (see headnote p. 1144)   **Alfred North Whitehead** (1861–1947) British mathematician, logician, and philosopher   [5]**Allen Wheelis** (1915–) a psychoanalyst, author of the novel *The Seeker* as well as other books including *On Not Knowing How to Live, How People Change, The Quest for Identity,* and a memoir, *The Listener: A Psychoanalyst Examines His Life*

resistance to enculturation of the self-actualizing person. One can examine one's own culture in which one is rooted in a detached and objective way of a certain kind. This parallels the process in psychotherapy of simultaneously experiencing and of self-observing one's own experience in a kind of critical or editorial or detached and removed way so that one can criticize it, approve or disapprove of it and assume control, and, therefore, the possibility of changing it exists. One's attitude toward one's culture, the parts of it which one has consciously accepted, is quite different from the unthinking and blind, unaware, unconscious total identification with one's culture in a nondiscriminating way.

5. Transcendence of one's past. Two attitudes toward one's past are possible. One attitude may be said to be a transcendent attitude. One can have a B-cognition of one's own past. That is, one's own past can be embraced and accepted into one's present self. This means full acceptance. It means forgiving one's self because of understanding one's self. It means the transcendence of remorse, regret, guilt, shame, embarrassment, and the like.

This is different from viewing the past as something before which one was helpless, something that happened to one, situations in which one was only passive and completely determined by outside determinants. In a certain sense this is like taking responsibility for one's past. It means "having become an agent as well as now being an agent."

6. Transcendence of ego, self, selfishness, ego-centering, etc., when we respond to the demand-character of external tasks, causes, duties, responsibilities to others and to the world of reality. When one is doing one's duty, this also can be seen to be under the aspect of eternity and can represent a transcendence of the ego, of the lower needs of the self. Actually, of course, it is ultimately a form of metamotivation, and identification with what "calls for" doing. This is a sensitivity to extrapsychic requiredness. This in turn means a kind of Taoistic° attitude. The phrase "being in harmony with nature" implies this ability to yield, to be receptive to, or respond to, to live with extrapsychic reality as if one belonged with it, or were in harmony with it.

10   7. Transcendence as mystical experience. Mystic fusion, either with another person or with the whole cosmos or with anything in between. I mean here the mystical experience as classically described by the religious mystics in the various religious literatures.

8. Transcendence of death, pain, sickness, evil, etc., when one is at a level high enough to be reconciled with the necessity of death, pain, etc. From a godlike, or Olympian° point of view, all these are necessary, and can be understood as necessary. If this attitude is achieved, as for instance it can be in the B-cognition, then bitterness, rebelliousness, anger, resentment may all disappear or at least be much lessened.

9. (Overlaps with above.) Transcendence is to accept the natural world, is to let *it* be *itself* in the Taoistic fashion, is the transcendence of the lower needs of the

°**Taoistic** having to do with Taoism, the philosophy and system of religion begun by Lao-tzu in China in the sixth century BCE   [11]**Olympian** In ancient Greek mythology, Mount Olympus was the home of the gods.

self—that is, of one's selfish within-the-skin demands, of one's egocentric judgments upon extrapsychic things as being dangerous or not dangerous, edible or not edible, useful or not useful, etc. This is the ultimate meaning of the phrase "to perceive the world objectively." This is one necessary aspect of B-cognition. B-cognition implies a transcendence of one's ego, lower needs, selfishness, etc.

10. Transcendence of the We-They polarity. Transcendence of the Zero-Sum game° as between persons. This means to ascend up to the level of synergy (interpersonal synergy, synergy of social institutions or of cultures).

11. Transcendence of the basic needs (either by gratifying them so that they disappear normally from consciousness, or by being able to give up the gratifications and to conquer the needs). This is another way of saying "to become primarily metamotivated." It implies identification with the B-Values.

12. Identification-love is a kind of transcendence, e.g., for one's child, or for one's beloved friend. This means "unselfish." This means transcendence of the selfish Self. It implies also a wider circle of identifications, i.e., with more and more and more people approaching the limit of identification with all human beings. This can also be phrased as the more and more inclusive Self. The limit here is identification with the human species. This can also be expressed intrapsychically, phenomenologically, as experiencing one's self to be one of the band of brothers, to belong to the human species.

13. All examples of Angyal-type homonomy,° either high or low (5).

14. Getting off the merry-go-round. Walking through the abattoir° without getting bloody. To be clean even in the midst of filth. To transcend advertising means to be above it, to be unaffected by it, to be untouched. In this sense one can transcend all kinds of bondage, slavery, etc., in the same way that Frankl,° Bettelheim,° *et al.* could transcend even the concentration camp situation. Use the example of *The New York Times* front-page picture in 1933 of an old Jewish man with a beard being paraded before the jeering crowd in Berlin in a garbage truck. It was my impression that he had compassion for the crowd and that he looked upon them with pity and perhaps forgiveness, thinking of them as unfortunate and sick and subhuman. Being independent of other people's evil or ignorance or stupidity or immaturity even when this is directed toward oneself is possible, though very difficult. And yet one *can*, in such a situation, gaze upon the whole situation—including oneself in the midst of the situation—as if one were looking upon it objectively, detachedly from a great and impersonal or suprapersonal height.

15. Transcending the opinions of others, i.e., of reflected appraisals. This means a self-determining Self. It means to be able to be unpopular when this is the right thing to be, to become an autonomous, self-deciding Self; to write

[13]**Zero-Sum game** a game in which whatever one player gains, the other player loses
[16]**Angyal-type homonomy** Psychiatrist Andras Angyal saw human beings as striving for both autonomy (self-determination), and homonomy (relating to and feeling part of a larger whole). [17]**abattoir** slaughterhouse **[Victor] Frankl** (1905–97) psychoanalyst, author of books such as *Man's Search for Meaning*; interned in Auschwitz concentration camp during World War II **[Bruno] Bettleheim** (1903–90) Austrian psychoanalyst who studied with Sigmund Freud and was famous particularly for work with children; interned in Dachau and Buchenwald concentration camps during World War II

one's own lines, to be one's own man, to be not manipulatable or seduceable. These are the resisters (rather than the conformers) in the Asch-type experiment.° Resistance to being rubricized, to be able to be role-free, i.e., to transcend one's role and to be a person rather than being the role. This includes resisting suggestion, propaganda, social pressures, being outvoted, etc.

16. Transcending the Freudian superego and coming up to the level of intrinsic conscience, and intrinsic guilt, deserved and suitable remorse, regret, shame.

17. Transcendence of one's own weakness and dependency, to transcend being a child, to become one's own mother and father to one's self, to become parental and not only filial, to be able to be strong and responsible in addition to being dependent, to transcend one's own weakness, and to rise to being strong. Since we always have both of these within us simultaneously, this is really a matter of degree in large part. But after all, it can be said meaningfully, of some individuals, that they are primarily weak, and that they primarily relate to all other human beings as the weak relate to the strong, and that all mechanisms of adaptation, coping mechanisms, defense mechanisms, are the defenses of weakness against strength. It's the same for dependency and independence. It's the same for irresponsibility and responsibility. It's the same for being the captain of the ship, or the driver of the car on the one hand, and of being merely the passenger on the other hand.

18. Transcending the present situation in the sense of Kurt Goldstein° (39), "to relate to existence also in terms of the possible as well as the actual." This is, to rise above being stimulus-bound and here-now situation-bound, and actuality-bound. Goldstein's reduction to the concrete can be transcended. Perhaps the best phrase here is to rise to the realm of the possible as well as of the actual.

19. Transcendence of dichotomies (polarities, black and white oppositions, either-or, etc.). To rise from dichotomies to superordinate wholes. To transcend atomism in favor of hierarchical-integration. To bind separates together into an integration. The ultimate limit here is the holistic perceiving of the cosmos as a unity. This is the ultimate transcendence, but any step along the way to this ultimate limit is itself a transcendence. Any dichotomy may be used as an example; for instance, selfish versus unselfish, or masculine versus feminine, or parent versus child, teacher versus student, etc. All these can be transcended so that the mutual exclusiveness and oppositeness and Zero-Sum game quality is transcended, in the sense of rising above to a higher viewpoint where one can see that these mutually exclusive differences in opposites can be coordinated into a unity which would be more realistic, more true, more in accord with actual reality.

20. Transcendence of the D-realm in the B-realm. (Of course this overlaps with every other kind of transcendence. As a matter of fact, they each overlap with each other.)

21. Transcendence of one's own will (in favor of the spirit of "not my will be done but Thine"). To yield to one's destiny or fate and to fuse with it, to love it

---

[18]**Asch-type experiment** an experiment aimed at understanding people's decisions about changing their behavior or opinions as a result of real or imagined pressure from others
[21]**Kurt Goldstein** (1878–1965) holistic neurologist from Germany with close ties to the Gestalt psychologists

in the Spinoza sense or in the Taoistic sense. To embrace, lovingly, one's own destiny. This is a rising above one's own personal will, being in charge, taking control, *needing* control, etc.

22. The word transcend also means "surpass" in the sense simply of being able to do more than one thought one could do, or more than one had done in the past, e.g., simply to be able to run faster than one used to, or to be a better dancer or pianist, or a better carpenter, or whatever.

23. Transcendence also means to become divine or godlike, to go beyond the merely human. But one must be careful here not to make anything extrahuman or supernatural out of this kind of statement. I am thinking of using the word "metahuman" or "B-human" in order to stress that this becoming very high or divine or godlike is part of human nature even though it is not often seen in fact. It is still a potentiality of human nature.

To rise above dichotomized nationalism, patriotism, or enthnocentrism, in the sense of "them" against "us," or of we-they, or Ardrey's (6) enmity-amity complex. For example, Piaget's° little Genevan boy who couldn't imagine being both Genevan and Swiss. He could think of being only either Genevan or Swiss. It takes more development in order to able to be more inclusive and superordinate, more integrative. My identification with nationalism, patriotism, or with my culture does not necessarily mitigate against my identification and more inclusive and higher patriotism with the human species or with the United Nations. As a matter of fact, such a superordinate patriotism is, of course, not only more inclusive, but therefore more healthy, more fully-human, than the strict localism which is regarded as antagonistic or as excluding others. That is, I can be a good American, and of course *must* be an American (that's the culture I grew up in, which I can never shake off and I don't want to shake off in favor of being a world citizen). Stress that the world citizen who has no roots, who doesn't belong any place, who is utterly and merely cosmopolitan, is not as good a world citizen as one who grew up in the family, in a place, in a home with a particular language, in a particular culture, and therefore has a sense of belongingness on which to build toward higher need and metaneed levels. To be a full member of the human species does not mean repudiating the lower levels; it means rather including them in the hierarchical integration, e.g., cultural pluralism, enjoying the differences, enjoying different kinds of restaurants with different kinds of food, enjoying travel to other countries, enjoying the ethnological study of other cultures, etc.

24. Transcendence can mean to live in the realm of Being, speaking the language of Being, B-cognizing, plateau-living. It can mean the serene B-cognition as well as the climactic peak-experience kind of B-cognition. After the insight or the great conversion, or the great mystic experience, or the great illumination, or the great full awakening, one can calm down as the novelty disappears, and as one gets used to good things or even great things, live casually in heaven and be on easy terms with the eternal and the infinite. To have got over being surprised and startled and to live calmly and serenely among the Platonic essences, or

[27][Jean] Piaget (1896–1980) Swiss psychologist who specialized in the mental development of children

among the B-Values. The phrase to use here for contrast with the climactic or emotionally poignant great insight and B-cognition would be plateau-cognition. Peak experiences must be transient, and in fact are transient so far as I can make out. And yet an illumination or an insight remains with the person. He can't really become naïve or innocent again or ignorant again in the same way that he was. He cannot "un-see." He can't become blind again. And yet there must be a language to describe getting used to the conversion or the illumination or to living in the Garden of Eden. Such an awakened person normally proceeds in a unitive way or in a B-cognizing way as an everyday kind of thing—certainly, whenever he wishes to. This serene B-cognition or plateau-cognition can come under one's own control. One can turn it off or on as one pleases.

The (transient) attainment of full-humanness or of finality or being an end is an example of transcendence.

25. The attainment of Taoistic (B-level) objectivity in the transcendence of noninvolved, neutral, noncaring, spectator-type objectivity (which itself transcends the purely egocentric and immature lack of objectivity).

26. Transcending—the split between facts and values. Fusion of facts and values in which they become one. . . .

27. A transcendence of negatives (which include evil, pain, death, etc., but also include more than that) is seen in the report from the peak experiences in which the world is accepted as good and one is reconciled to the evils that one perceives. But this is also a transcendence of inhibitions, of blocks, of denials, of refusals.

28. Transcendence of space. This can be in the very simplest sense of getting so absorbed in something that one forgets where one is. But it can also rise to the very highest sense in which one is identified with the whole human species and therefore in which one's brothers on the other side of the earth are part of oneself, so that in a certain sense one is on the other side of the earth as well as being here in space. The same is true for the introjection of the B-Values since they are everywhere, and since they are defining characteristics of the self, and one's self is everywhere too.

29. Overlapping with several of the above is the transcendence of effort and of striving, of wishing and hoping, of any vectorial or intentional characteristics. In the simplest sense this is, of course, the sheer enjoyment of the state of gratification, of hope fulfilled and attained, of being there rather than of striving to get there, of having arrived rather than of traveling toward. This is also in the sense of "being fortuitous" or of Mrs. Garrett's use of the phrase, "high carelessness." It is the Taoistic feeling of letting things happen rather than of making them happen, and of being perfectly happy and accepting of this state of nonstriving, nonwishing, noninterfering, noncontrolling, nonwilling. This is the transcendence of ambition, of efficiencies. This is the state of having rather than of not having. Then of course one lacks nothing. This means it is possible to go over to the state of happiness, of contentment, of being satisfied with what is. Pure appreciation. Pure gratitude. The state and the feeling of good fortune, good luck, the feeling of grace, of gratuitous grace.

Being in an end-state means the transcendence of means in various senses. But this has to be very carefully spelled out.

30. Specially noteworthy for research purposes as well as therapy purposes is to pick out of the special kinds of transcendence, the transcendence of fear into the state of not-fearing or of courage (these are not quite the same thing).

31. Also useful would be Bucke's (18) use of cosmic consciousness. This is a special phenomenological state in which the person somehow perceives the whole cosmos or at least the unity and integration of it and of everything in it, including his Self. He then feels as if he belongs by right in the cosmos. He becomes one of the family rather than an orphan. He comes inside rather than being outside looking in. He feels simultaneously small because of the vastness of the universe, but also an important being because he is there in it by absolute right. He is part of the universe rather than a stranger to it or an intruder in it. The sense of belongingness can be very strongly reported here, as contrasting with the sense of ostracism, isolation, aloneness, of rejection, of not having any roots, of belonging no place in particular. After such a perception, apparently one can feel permanently this sense of belonging, of having a place, of being there by right, etc. (I have used this cosmic consciousness type of B-cognition in the peak experience to contrast with another type, namely, that which comes from narrowing down consciousness and zeroing in in an intense and total absorption and fascination with one person or one thing or one happening which somehow then stands for the whole world, the whole cosmos. I have called this the narrowing-down kind of peak experience and B-cognition.)

32. Perhaps a special and separate statement ought to be made of transcendence in the particular meaning of introjection of and identification with B-Values, with the state of being primarily motivated by them thereafter.

33. One can even transcend individual differences in a very specific sense. The highest attitude toward individual differences is to be aware of them, to accept them, but also to enjoy them and finally to be profoundly grateful for them as a beautiful instance of the ingenuity of the cosmos—the recognition of their value, and wonder at individual differences. This is certainly a higher attitude and I suppose therefore a kind of transcendence. But also, and quite different from this ultimate gratitude for individual differences, is the other attitude of rising above them in the recognition of the essential commonness and mutual belongingness and identification with all kinds of people in ultimate humanness or species-hood, in the sense that everyone is one's brother or sister, then individual differences and even the differences between the sexes have been transcended in a very particular way. That is, at different times one can be very aware of the differences between individuals; but at another time one can wave aside these individual differences as relatively unimportant for the moment by contrast with the universal humanness and *similarities* between human beings.

34. A particular kind of transcendence useful for certain theoretical purposes is the transcendence of human limits, imperfections, shortcomings, and finiteness. This comes either in the acute end experiences of perfection or in the plateau experiences of perfection, in which one can *be* an end, a god, a perfection, an essence, a Being (rather than a Becoming), sacred, divine. This can be phrased as a transcendence of ordinary, everyday humanness in favor of extraordinary humanness or metahumanness or some such phrasing. This can

be an actual phenomenological state; it can be a kind of cognizing; it can also be a conceived limit of philosophy or ideal—for instance, the platonic essences or ideas. In such acute moments, or to some extent in plateau cognition, one becomes perfect, or can see oneself as perfect, e.g., in that moment I can love all and accept all, forgive all, be reconciled even to the evil that hurts me. I can understand and enjoy the way things are. And I can then even feel some subjective equivalent of what has been attributed to the gods only, i.e., omniscience, omnipotence, ubiquity (i.e., in a certain sense one can *become* in such moments a god, a sage, a saint, a mystic). Perhaps the best word in order to stress that this is part of human nature, even though at its best, is the word metahumanness.

35. Transcendence of one's own credo, or system of values, or system of beliefs. This is worth discussing separately because of the special situation in psychology in which the first force, the second force, and the third force have been seen as mutually exclusive by many. Of course this is erroneous. Humanistic psychology is more inclusive rather than exclusive. It is epi-Freudian and epipositivistic science. These two points of view are not so much wrong or incorrect as they are limited and partial. Their essence fits very nicely into a larger and inclusive structure. Of course integrating them into this larger and more inclusive structure certainly changes them in some ways, corrects them, points to certain mistakes, but yet includes their most essential, though partial, characteristics. There can be the enmity-amity complex among intellectuals, in which loyalty to Freud or to Clark Hull, or for that matter to Galileo or Einstein or Darwin, can be a kind of local excluding-others type of patriotism in which one forms a club or fraternity as much to keep other people out as to include some in. This is a special case of inclusiveness or hierarchical integration or holism, but it is useful to make a special point of it for psychologists, as well as for philosophers, scientists, and intellectual areas where there is a tendency to divide into so-called "schools of thought." This is to say that one can take either the dichotomous or the integrative attitude toward a school of thought.

A condensed statement. Transcendence refers to the very highest and most inclusive or holistic levels of human consciousness, behaving and relating, as ends rather than as means, to oneself, to significant others, to human beings in general, to other species, to nature, and to the cosmos. (Holism in the sense of hierarchical integration is assumed; so also is cognitive and value isomorphism.)

Bibliography

ANGYAL, A. *Foundations for a Science of Personality*, Cambridge, Mass.: Commonwealth Fund, 1941.

ARDREY, R. *The Territorial Imperative*. New York: Atheneum Press, 1966.

BUCKE, R. *Cosmic Consciousness*. New York: E. P. Dutton, 1923.

BUGENTAL, J. F. (ed.). *The Search for Authenticity*. New York: Holt, Rinehart and Winston, 1965.

GOLDSTEIN, K. *The Organism*. New York: American Book Co., 1939.

KUBIE, L. The forgotten man in education. *Harvard Alumni Bulletin,* 1953–1954, 56: 349–353.

MASLOW, A. H. *Religions, Values, and Peak-Experiences.* Columbus, Ohio: Ohio State University Press, 1964; Paperback ed., New York: The Viking Press, 1970.

———. *Toward a Psychology of Being.* Princeton, N.J.: Van Nostrand, 1962. (Rev. ed., 1968.)

———. *Motivation and Personality.* New York: Harper & Bros., 1954. (Rev. ed., 1970.)

MOGAR, R. E. Psychedelic (LSD) research: a critical review of methods and results. In J. F. Bugental (ed.), *Challenges of Humanistic Psychology.* New York: McGraw-Hill, 1967.

OTTO, H. The Minerva Experience: an initial report. In J. F. Bugental (ed.), *Challenges of Humanistic Psychology.* New York: McGraw-Hill, 1967.

ROGERS, C. R. *On Becoming a Person.* Boston: Houghton Mifflin, 1961.

WHEELIS, A. *The Seeker.* New York: Random House, 1960.   [1971]

1. Characterize Maslow's voice in these chapters.
2. In 1981, Daniel Yankelovich objected to the influence of Maslow's idea of self-actualization: Although it benefits some individuals, it is "a moral and social absurdity. It gives moral sanction to desires that do not contribute to society's well-being. It contains no principle for synchronizing the requirements of the society with the goals of the individual. It fails to discriminate between socially valuable desires and socially destructive ones, and often works perversely against the real goals of both individuals and society. It provides no principle other than hedonism for interpreting the meaning of the changes and sacrifices we must make to adapt to new economic-political conditions."[1] Is Maslow guilty as charged?
3. Are there any ways you can see the dichotomy between desacralizing and resacralizing in the contemporary world?

[1]Daniel Yankelovich "New Rules in American Life: Searching for Self-Fulfillment in a World Turned Upside Down," *Psychology Today* (April 1981): 35–91, P. 47.

The Story and the Chapters

1. Does Maslow's definition of "self-actualizing" people shed any light on the behavior of the characters of the story? What are the limits of the application?
2. Would Yankelovich call the story "a moral and social absurdity"? Would you?
3. Are any of the various meanings of transcendence that Maslow lists relevant to the story? What about to other works in this section or other sections of the anthology?
4. What other disciplines might shed some light on this story?

DRAMA

WOLE SOYINKA

WOLE SOYINKA *(1934–), born in western Nigeria, was educated there at
University College of Ibadan and then in England at the University of Leeds. He
was a dramaturge at the Royal Court Theatre in London from 1957 to 1959 and
returned to Nigeria to study African drama on a Rockefeller grant and to write a
play celebrating the nation's independence* (A Dance of the Forests). *He has been
teaching and writing in various universities in Ibadan, Lagos, and Ife, where
since 1975 he has been professor of comparative literature. During the civil war
in Nigeria he was arrested, accused of conspiring with the Biafra rebels, and
imprisoned for 22 months. He has published about twenty works of drama, fiction,
and poetry, writing in English. Comedies, satire, mixed media plays with music and
dance, philosophic plays, and opera are all part of his published works. His dramas
include* A Play of Giants *(1984) and* Requiem for a Futurologist *(1985). Two
novels,* The Interpreters *(1996) and* Season of Anomy *(1973), demonstrate the
range and depth of his interests. Books of poetry include* Idanre and Other Poems
(1967), Poems from Prison *(1969),* A Shuttle in the Crypt *(1972), and*
Mandela's Earth and Other Poems *(1988). In 1986, Wole Soyinka was awarded
the Nobel Prize for Literature.*

Death and the King's Horseman

*Dedicated
In Affectionate Greeting
to
My Father, Ayodele
who lately danced, and joined the Ancestors.*

Author's Note

This play is based on events which took place in Oyo, ancient Yoruba city of
Nigeria, in 1946. That year, the lives of Elesin (Olori Elesin), his son, and the
Colonial District Officer intertwined with the disastrous results set out in the
play. The changes I have made are in matters of detail, sequence and of course
characterisation. The action has also been set back two or three years to while
the war was still on, for minor reasons of dramaturgy.

The factual account still exists in the archives of the British Colonial
Administration. It has already inspired a fine play in Yoruba (Oba Wàjà)
by Duro Ladipo. It has also misbegotten a film by some German television
company.

The bane of themes of this genre is that they are no sooner employed
creatively than they acquire the facile tag of "clash of cultures," a prejudicial
label which, quite apart from its frequent misapplication, presupposes a potential

equality *in every given situation* of the alien culture and the indigenous, on the actual soil of the latter. (In the area of misapplication, the overseas prize for illiteracy and mental conditioning undoubtedly goes to the blurb-writer for the American edition of my novel *Season of Anomy* who unblushingly declares that this work portrays the "clash between old values and new ways, between western methods and African traditions"!) It is thanks to this kind of perverse mentality that I find it necessary to caution the would-be producer of this play against a sadly familiar reductionist tendency, and to direct his vision instead to the far more difficult and risky task of eliciting the play's threnodic° essence.

One of the more obvious alternative structures of the play would be to make the District Officer the victim of a cruel dilemma. This is not to my taste and it is not by chance that I have avoided dialogue or situation which would encourage this. No attempt should be made in production to suggest it. The Colonial Factor is an incident, a catalytic incident merely. The confrontation in the play is largely metaphysical, contained in the human vehicle which is Elesin and the universe of the Yoruba mind—the world of the living, the dead and the unborn, and the numinous° passage which links all: transition. *Death and the King's Horseman* can be fully realised only through an evocation of music from the abyss of transition.

—W.S.

Characters

Praise-Singer
Elesin, *Horseman of the King*
Iyaloja, *"Mother" of the market*
Simon Pilkings, *District Officer*
Jane Pilkings, *his wife*
Sergeant Amusa Joseph, *houseboy to the Pilkingses*
Bride
H.R.H. The Prince
The Resident
Aide-de-Camp
Olunde, *eldest son of Elesin*

Drummers, Women, Young Girls, Dancers at the Ball

The play should run without an interval. For rapid scene changes, one adjustable outline set is very appropriate.

Scene 1

(A passage through a market in its closing stages. The stalls are being emptied, mats folded. A few women pass through on their way home, loaded with baskets. On a cloth-stand, bolts of cloth are taken down, display pieces folded and piled on a tray. Elesin Oba enters along a passage before the market, pursued by his drummers and praise-singers. He is a man of enormous vitality, speaks, dances and sings with that infectious enjoyment of life which accompanies all his actions.)

Author's Note**threnodic** A threnody is a song of mourning. **numinous** associated with the supernatural or the spiritually elevated

Praise-Singer:° Elesin o! Elesin Oba! Howu! What tryst is this the cockerel goes to keep with such haste that he must leave his tail behind?

Elesin (slows down a bit, laughing): A tryst where the cockerel needs no adornment.

Praise-Singer: O-oh, you hear that my companions? That's the way the world goes. Because the man approaches a brand new bride he forgets the long faithful mother of his children.

Elesin: When the horse sniffs the stable does he not strain at the bridle? The market is the long-suffering home of my spirit and the women are packing up to go. That Esu-harassed° day slipped into the stewpot while we feasted. We ate it up with the rest of the meat. I have neglected my women.

5 *Praise-Singer:* We know all that. Still it's no reason for shedding your tail on this day of all days. I know the women will cover you in damask and alari° but when the wind blows cold from behind, that's when the fowl knows his true friends.

Elesin: Olohun-iyo!°

Praise-Singer: Are you sure there will be one like me on the other side?

Elesin: Olohun-iyo!

Praise-Singer: Far be it for me to belittle the dwellers of that place but, a man is either born to his art or he isn't. And I don't know for certain that you'll meet my father, so who is going to sing these deeds in accents that will pierce the deafness of the ancient ones. I have prepared my going—just tell me: Olohun-iyo, I need you on this journey and I shall be behind you.

10 *Elesin:* You're like a jealous wife. Stay close to me, but only on this side. My fame, my honour are legacies to the living; stay behind and let the world sip its honey from your lips.

Praise-Singer: Your name will be like the sweet berry a child places under his tongue to sweeten the passage of food. The world will never spit it out.

Elesin: Come then. This market is my roost. When I come among the women I am a chicken with a hundred mothers. I become a monarch whose palace is built with tenderness and beauty.

Praise-Singer: They love to spoil you but beware. The hands of women also weaken the unwary.

Elesin: This night I'll lay my head upon their lap and go to sleep. This night I'll touch feet with their feet in a dance that is no longer of this earth. But the smell of their flesh, their sweat, the smell of indigo on their cloth, this is the last air I wish to breathe as I go to meet my great forebears.

15 *Praise-Singer:* In their time the world was never tilted from its groove, it shall not be in yours.

Elesin: The gods have said No.

---

[1]**Praise-Singer** poet who chronicles the accomplishments of a leader [4]**Esu-harassed** bothered or tormented by a destructive deity [5]**alari** rich woven cloth from the Yoruba area of Nigeria [6]**Olohun-iyo** praise singer

Praise-Singer: In their time the great wars came and went, the little wars came and went; the white slavers came and went, they took away the heart of our race, they bore away the mind and muscle of our race. The city fell and was rebuilt; the city fell and our people trudged through mountain and forest to find a new home but—Elesin Oba do you hear me?

Elesin: I hear your voice Olohun-iyo.

Praise-Singer: Our world was never wrenched from its true course.

Elesin: The gods have said No.   20

Praise-Singer: There is only one home to the life of a river-mussel; there is only one home to the life of a tortoise; there is only one shell to the soul of man; there is only one world to the spirit of our race. If that world leaves its course and smashes on boulders of the great void, whose world will give us shelter?

Elesin: It did not in the time of my forebears, it shall not in mine.

Praise-Singer: The cockerel must not be seen without his feathers.

Elesin: Nor will the Not-I bird be much longer without his nest.

Praise-Singer (stopped in his lyric stride): The Not-I bird, Elesin?   25

Elesin: I said, the Not-I bird.

Praise-Singer: All respect to our elders but, is there really such a bird?

Elesin: What! Could it be that he failed to knock on your door?

Praise-Singer (smiling): Elesin's riddles are not merely the nut in the kernel that breaks human teeth; he also buries the kernel in hot embers and dares a man's fingers to draw it out.

Elesin: I am sure he called on you, Olohun-iyo. Did you hide in the loft and push   30
out the servant to tell him you were out?

(Elesin *executes a brief, half-taunting dance. The* Drummer *moves in and draws a rhythm out of his steps.* Elesin *dances towards the market-place as he chants the story of the Not-I bird, his voice changing dexterously to mimic his characters. He performs like a born raconteur,° infecting his retinue with his humour and energy. More* Women *arrive during his recital, including* Iyaloja.)

Death came calling
Who does not know his rasp of reeds?
A twilight whisper in the leaves before
The great araba° falls? Did you hear it?
Not I! swears the farmer. He snaps
His fingers round his head, abandons
A hard-worn harvest and begins
A rapid dialogue with his legs.

"Not I," shouts the fearless hunter, "but—
It's getting dark, and this night-lamp
Has leaked out all its oil. I think
It's best to go home and resume my hunt
Another day." But now he pauses, suddenly
Lets out a wail: "Oh foolish mouth, calling

³⁰**raconteur** one who tells (recounts) stories   **araba** a large tree of coastal Africa

Down a curse on your own head! Your lamp
Has leaked out all its oil, has it?"
Forwards or backwards now he dare not move.
To search for leaves and make etutu°
On that spot? Or race home to the safety
Of his hearth? Ten market-days have passed
My friends, and still he's rooted there
Rigid as the plinth° of Orayan.°

The mouth of the courtesan barely
Opened wide enough to take a ha'penny robo°
When she wailed: "Not I." All dressed she was
To call upon my friend the Chief Tax Officer.
But now she sends her go-between instead:
"Tell him I'm ill: my period has come suddenly
But not—I hope—my time."

Why is the pupil crying?
His hapless head was made to taste
The knuckles of my friend the Mallam:
"If you were then reciting the Koran
Would you have ears for idle noises
Darkening the trees, you child of ill omen?"
He shuts down school before its time
Runs home and rings himself with amulets.
And take my good kinsman Ifawomi.
His hands were like a carver's, strong
And true. I saw them
Tremble like wet wings of a fowl.
One day he cast his time-smoothed opele°
Across the divination board. And all because
The supplicant looked him in the eye and asked,
"Did you hear that whisper in the leaves?"
"Not I," was his reply; "perhaps I'm growing deaf—
Good-day." And Ifa spoke no more that day
The priest locked fast his doors,
Sealed up his leaking roof—but wait!
This sudden care was not for Fawomi
But for Osanyin,° a courier-bird of Ifa's°
Heart of wisdom. I did not know a kite
Was hovering in the sky

---

³⁰**etutu** rites meant to placate or heal, meant to restore balance when a code or rule has
been breached   **plinth** the base of a pedestal, column, or statue   **Orayan** descendant
of the founder of the Yoruba people   **robo** small delicacy made from melon seeds
opele chain or string of beads used for divination; made of seeds and pods   **Osanyin**
deity of herbal medicine   **Ifa** ancient African philosophy and spiritual practice

And Ifa now a twittering chicken in
The brood of Fawomi the Mother Hen.

Ah, but I must not forget my evening
Courier from the abundant palm, whose groan
Became Not I, as he constipated down
A wayside bush. He wonders if Elegbara°
Has tricked his buttocks to discharge
Against a sacred grove. Hear him
Mutter spells to ward off penalties
For an abomination he did not intend.
If any here
Stumbles on a gourd of wine, fermenting
Near the road, and nearby hears a stream
Of spells issuing from a crouching form.
Brother to a sigidi,° bring home my wine,
Tell my tapper I have ejected
Fear from home and farm. Assure him,
All is well.

Praise-Singer: In your time we do not doubt the peace of farmstead and home,
the peace of road and hearth, we do not doubt the peace of the forest.

Elesin: There was fear in the forest too.
Not-I was lately heard even in the lair
Of beasts. The hyena cackled loud. Not I,
The civet twitched his fiery tail and glared:
Not I. Not-I became the answering-name
Of the restless bird, that little one
Whom Death found nesting in the leaves
When whisper of his coming ran
Before him on the wind. Not-I
Has long abandoned home. This same dawn
I heard him twitter in the gods' abode.
Ah, companions of this living world
What a thing this is, that even those
We call immortal
Should fear to die.

Iyaloja: But you, husband of multitudes?

Elesin: I, when that Not-I bird perched
Upon my roof, bade him seek his nest again.
Safe, without care or fear. I unrolled
My welcome mat for him to see. Not-I
Flew happily away, you'll hear his voice
No more in this lifetime—You all know
What I am.

---

³⁰**Elegbara** a male trickster figure   **sigidi** a carved figure, an aspect of Esu that protects
the inhabitants of a place

35 *Praise-Singer:* That rock which turns its open lodes
　　　Into the path of lightning. A gay
　　　Thoroughbred whose stride disdains
　　　To falter though an adder reared
　　　Suddenly in his path.
Elesin: My rein is loosened.
　　　I am master of my Fate. When the hour comes
　　　Watch me dance along the narrowing path
　　　Glazed by the soles of my great precursors.
　　　My soul is eager. I shall not turn aside.
Women: You will not delay?
Elesin: Where the storm pleases, and when, it directs
　　　The giants of the forest. When friendship summons
　　　Is when the true comrade goes.
Women: Nothing will hold you back?
40 *Elesin:* Nothing. What! Has no one told you yet
　　　I go to keep my friend and master company.
　　　Who says the mouth does not believe in
　　　"No, I have chewed all that before?" I say I have.
　　　The world is not a constant honey-pot.
　　　Where I found little I made do with little.
　　　Where there was plenty I gorged myself.
　　　My master's hands and mine have always
　　　Dipped together and, home or sacred feast,
　　　The bowl was beaten bronze, the meats
　　　So succulent our teeth accused us of neglect.
　　　We shared the choicest of the season's
　　　Harvest of yams. How my friend would read
　　　Desire in my eyes before I knew the cause—
　　　However rare, however precious, it was mine.
Women: The town, the very land was yours.
Elesin: The world was mine. Our joint hands
　　　Raised housepots of trust that withstood
　　　The siege of envy and the termites of time.
　　　But the twilight hour brings bats and rodents—
　　　Shall I yield them cause to foul the rafters?
Praise-Singer: Elesin Oba! Are you not that man who
　　　Looked out of doors that stormy day
　　　The god of luck limped by, drenched
　　　To the very lice that held
　　　His rags together? You took pity upon
　　　His sores and wished him fortune.
　　　Fortune was footloose this dawn, he replied,
　　　Till you trapped him in a heartfelt wish
　　　That now returns to you. Elesin Oba!
　　　I say you are that man who

Chanced upon the calabash° of honour
You thought it was palm wine and
Drained its contents to the final drop.

Elesin: Life has an end. A life that will outlive
Fame and friendship begs another name.
What elder takes his tongue to his plate,
Licks it clean of every crumb? He will encounter
Silence when he calls on children to fulfill
The smallest errand! Life is honour.
It ends when honour ends.

Women: We know you for a man of honour.   45

Elesin: Stop! Enough of that!

Women (puzzled, they whisper among themselves, turning mostly to Iyaloja): What is it?
Did we say something to give offence? Have we slighted him in some way?

Elesin: Enough of that sound I say. Let me hear no more in that vein. I've heard
enough.

Iyaloja: We must have said something wrong. *(Comes forward a little.)* Elesin Oba,
we ask forgiveness before you speak.

Elesin: I am bitterly offended.   50

Iyaloja: Our unworthiness has betrayed us. All we can do is ask your forgiveness.
Correct us like a kind father.

Elesin: This day of all days . . .

Iyaloja: It does not bear thinking. If we offend you now we have mortified the
gods. We offend heaven itself. Father of us all, tell us where we went astray.
(She kneels, the other women follow.)

Elesin: Are you not ashamed? Even a tear-veiled
Eye preserves its function of sight.
Because my mind was raised to horizons
Even the boldest man lowers his gaze
In thinking of, must my body here
Be taken for a vagrant's?

Iyaloja: Horseman of the King, I am more baffled than ever.   55

Praise-Singer: The strictest father unbends his brow when the child is penitent,
Elesin. When time is short, we do not spend it prolonging the riddle. Their
shoulders are bowed with the weight of fear lest they have marred your day
beyond repair. Speak now in plain words and let us pursue the ailment to the
home of remedies.

Elesin: Words are cheap. "We know you for
A man of honour." Well tell me, is this how
A man of honour should be seen?
Are these not the same clothes in which
I came among you a full half-hour ago?

---

[43]**calabash** The large smooth gourds of the calabash tree can be made into containers for
liquid.

(He roars with laughter and the women, relieved, rise and rush into stalls to fetch rich clothes.)

Women: The gods are kind. A fault soon remedied is soon forgiven. Elesin Oba, even as we match our words with deed, let your heart forgive us completely.

Elesin: You who are breath and giver of my being
　　　How shall I dare refuse you forgiveness
　　　Even if the offence was real.

60 *Iyaloja (dancing round him. Sings):*
　　　He forgives us. He forgives us.
　　　What a fearful thing it is when
　　　The voyager sets forth
　　　But a curse remains behind.

Women: For a while we truly feared
　　　Our hands had wrenched the world adrift
　　　In emptiness.

Iyaloja: Richly, richly, robe him richly
　　　The cloth of honour is alari
　　　Sanyan° is the band of friendship
　　　Boa-skin makes slippers of esteem.

Women: For a while we truly feared
　　　Our hands had wrenched the world adrift
　　　In emptiness.

Praise-Singer: He who must, must voyage forth
　　　The world will not roll backwards
　　　It is he who must, with one
　　　Great gesture overtake the world.

65 *Women:* For a while we truly feared
　　　Our hands had wrenched the world adrift
　　　In emptiness.

Praise-Singer: The gourd you bear is not for shirking.
　　　The gourd is not for setting down
　　　At the first crossroad or wayside grove.
　　　Only one river may know its contents.

Women: We shall all meet at the great market
　　　We shall all meet at the great market
　　　He who goes early takes the best bargains
　　　But we shall meet, and resume our banter.

(Elesin stands resplendent in rich clothes, cap, shawl, etc. His sash is of a bright red alari cloth. The Women dance round him. Suddenly, his attention is caught by an object off-stage.)

Elesin: The world I know is good.
Women: We know you'll leave it so.

°62**sanyan** wild raw silk

Elesin: The world I know is the bounty   70
  Of hives after bees have swarmed.
  No goodness teems with such open hands
  Even in the dreams of deities.
Women: And we know you'll leave it so.
Elesin: I was born to keep it so. A hive
  Is never known to wander. An anthill
  Does not desert its roots. We cannot see
  The still great womb of the world—
  No man beholds his mother's womb—
  Yet who denies it's there? Coiled
  To the navel of the world is that
  Endless cord that links us all
  To the great origin. If I lose my way
  The trailing cord will bring me to the roots.
Women: The world is in your hands.

  *(The earlier distraction, a beautiful young girl, comes along the passage through which
  Elesin first made his entry.)*

Elesin: I embrace it. And let me tell you, women—
  I like this farewell that the world designed,
  Unless my eyes deceive me, unless
  We are already parted, the world and I,
  And all that breeds desire is lodged
  Among our tireless ancestors. Tell me friends,
  Am I still earthed in that beloved market
  Of my youth? Or could it be my will
  Has outleapt the conscious act and I have come
  Among the great departed?
Praise-Singer: Elesin Oba why do your eyes roll like a bush-rat who sees his fate   75
  like his father's spirit, mirrored in the eye of a snake? And all those questions!
  You're standing on the same earth you've always stood upon. This voice you
  hear is mine, Olohun-iyo, not that of an acolyte° in heaven.
Elesin: How can that be? In all my life
  As Horseman of the King, the juiciest
  Fruit on every tree was mine. I saw,
  I touched, I wooed, rarely was the answer No.
  The honour of my place, the veneration I
  Received in the eye of man or woman
  Prospered my suit and
  Played havoc with my sleeping hours.
  And they tell me my eyes were a hawk
  In perpetual hunger. Split an iroko° tree
  In two, hide a woman's beauty in its heartwood

°⁷⁵**acolyte** one who assists in religious ceremony   ⁷⁶**iroko** an African hardwood tree

And seal it up again—Elesin, journeying by,
Would make his camp beside that tree
Of all the shades in the forest.
Praise-Singer: Who would deny your reputation, snake-on-the-loose in dark
passages of the market! Bed-bug who wages war on the mat and receives
the thanks of the vanquished! When caught with his bride's own sister he
protested—but I was only prostrating myself to her as becomes a grateful in-
law. Hunter who carries his powder-horn on the hips and fires crouching or
standing! Warrior who never makes that excuse of the whining coward—but
how can I go to battle without my trousers?—trouserless or shirtless it's all
one to him. Oka-rearing-from-a-camouflage-of-leaves, before he strikes the
victim is already prone! Once they told me, Howu, a stallion does not feed on
the grass beneath him: he replied, true, but surely he can roll on it!
Women: Ba-a-a-ba O!
Praise-Singer: Ah, but listen yet. You know there is the leaf-nibbling grub and
there is the cola-chewing beetle; the leaf-nibbling grub lives on the leaf, the
cola-chewing beetle lives in the colanut.° Don't we know what our man feeds
on when we find him cocooned in a woman's wrapper?
80 *Elesin:* Enough, enough, you all have cause
To know me well. But, if you say this earth
Is still the same as gave birth to those songs,
Tell me who was that goddess through whose lips
I saw the ivory pebbles of Oya's river-bed.
Iyaloja, who is she? I saw her enter
Your stall; all your daughters I know well.
No, not even Ogun°-of-the-farm toiling
Dawn till dusk on his tuber patch
Not even Ogun with the finest hoe he ever
Forged at the anvil could have shaped
That rise of buttocks, not though he had
The richest earth between his fingers.
Her wrapper was no disguise
For thighs whose ripples shamed the river's
Coils around the hills of Ilesi. Her eyes
Were new-laid eggs glowing in the dark.
Her skin . . .
Iyaloja: Elesin Oba . . .
Elesin: What! Where do you all say I am?
Iyaloja: Still among the living.
Elesin: And that radiance which so suddenly
Lit up this market I could boast
I knew so well?

---

[79]**colanut** the edible seed of several African trees, which contain caffeine and are chewed
to relieve fatigue and hunger; the origin of "cola" soft drinks (which now use mostly
chemical replacements for the flavor)   [80]**Ogun** Yoruban deity known for strength and
perseverance

Iyaloja: Has one step already in her husband's home. She is betrothed.

Elesin (irritated): Why do you tell me that? 85

> (Iyaloja *falls silent. The* Women *shuffle uneasily.*)

Iyaloja: Not because we dare give you offence Elesin. Today is your day and the whole world is yours. Still, even those who leave town to make a new dwelling elsewhere like to be remembered by what they leave behind.

Elesin: Who does not seek to be remembered?
Memory is Master of Death, the chink
In his armour of conceit. I shall leave
That which makes my going the sheerest
Dream of an afternoon. Should voyagers
Not travel light? Let the considerate traveller
Shed, of his excessive load, all
That may benefit the living.

Women (relieved): Ah Elesin Oba, we knew you for a man of honour.

Elesin: Then honour me. I deserve a bed of honour to lie upon.

Iyaloja: The best is yours. We know you for a man of honour. You are not one 90
who eats and leaves nothing on his plate for children. Did you not say it
yourself? Not one who blights the happiness of others for a moment's
pleasure.

Elesin: Who speaks of pleasure? O women, listen!
Pleasure palls. Our acts should have meaning.
The sap of the plantain° never dries.
You have seen the young shoot swelling
Even as the parent stalks begins to wither.
Women, let my going be likened to
The twilight hour of the plantain.

Women: What does he mean Iyaloja? This language is the language of our elders,
we do not fully grasp it.

Iyaloja: I dare not understand you yet Elesin.

Elesin: All you who stand before the spirit that dares
The opening of the last door of passage,
Dare to rid my going of regrets! My wish
Transcends the blotting out of thought
In one mere moment's tremor of the senses.
Do me credit. And do me honour.
I am girded for the route beyond
Burdens of waste and longing.
Then let me travel light. Let
Seed that will not serve the stomach
On the way remain behind. Let it take root
In the earth of my choice, in this earth
I leave behind.

°¹**plantain** tropical fruit like a banana

95 *Iyaloja (turns to* Women*)*: The voice I hear is already touched by the waiting
   fingers of our departed. I dare not refuse.

Woman: But Iyaloja . . .

Iyaloja: The matter is no longer in our hands.

Woman: But she is betrothed to your own son. Tell him.

Iyaloja: My son's wish is mine. I did the asking for him, the loss can be remedied.
   But who will remedy the blight of closed hands on the day when all should
   be openness and light? Tell him, you say! You wish that I burden him with
   knowledge that will sour his wish and lay regrets on the last moments of his
   mind. You pray to him who is your intercessor to the world—don't set this
   world adrift in your own time; would you rather it was my hand whose
   sacrilege wrenched it loose?

100 *Woman:* Not many men will brave the curse of a dispossessed husband.

Iyaloja: Only the curses of the departed are to be feared. The claims of one whose
   foot is on the threshold of their abode surpasses even the claims of blood. It is
   impiety even to place hindrances in their ways.

Elesin: What do my mothers say? Shall I step
   Burdened into the unknown?

Iyaloja: Not we, but the very earth says No. The sap in the plantain does not dry.
   Let grain that will not feed the voyager at his passage drop here and take root
   as he steps beyond this earth and us. Oh you who fill the home from hearth
   to threshold with the voices of children, you who now bestride the hidden
   gulf and pause to draw the right foot across and into the resting-home of the
   great forebears, it is good that your loins be drained into the earth we know,
   that your last strength be ploughed back into the womb that gave you being.

Praise-Singer: Iyaloja, mother of multitudes in the teeming market of the world,
   how your wisdom transfigures you!

105 *Iyaloja (smiling broadly, completely reconciled)*: Elesin, even at the narrow end of the
   passage I know you will look back and sigh a last regret for the flesh that
   flashed past your spirit in flight. You always had a restless eye. Your choice
   has my blessing. *(To the* Women.*)* Take the good news to our daughter and
   make her ready. *(Some* Women *go off.)*

Elesin: Your eyes were clouded at first.

Iyaloja: Not for long. It is those who stand at the gateway of the great change to
   whose cry we must pay heed. And then, think of this—it makes the mind
   tremble. The fruit of such a union is rare. It will be neither of this world nor
   of the next. Nor of the one behind us. As if the timelessness of the ancestor
   world and the unborn have joined spirits to wring an issue of the elusive
   being of passage . . . Elesin!

Elesin: I am here. What is it?

Iyaloja: Did you hear all I said just now?

110 *Elesin:* Yes.

Iyaloja: The living must eat and drink. When the moment comes, don't turn the
   food to rodents' droppings in their mouth. Don't let them taste the ashes of
   the world when they step out at dawn to breathe the morning dew.

Elesin: This doubt is unworthy of you Iyaloja.

Iyaloja: Eating the awusa nut° is not so difficult as drinking water afterwards.

Elesin: The waters of the bitter stream are honey to a man
Whose tongue has savoured all.

Iyaloja: No one knows when the ants desert their home; they leave the mound   115
intact. The swallow is never seen to peck holes in its nest when it is time to
move with the season. There are always throngs of humanity behind the
leave-taker. The rain should not come through the roof for them, the wind
must not blow through the walls at night.

Elesin: I refuse to take offence.

Iyaloja: You wish to travel light. Well, the earth is yours. But be sure the seed
you leave in it attracts no curse.

Elesin: You really mistake my person Iyaloja.

Iyaloja: I said nothing. Now we must go prepare your bridal chamber. Then these
same hands will lay your shrouds.

Elesin (exasperated): Must you be so blunt? *(Recovers.)* Well, weave your shrouds,   120
but let the fingers of my bride seal my eyelids with earth and wash my body.

Iyaloja: Prepare yourself Elesin.

(She gets up to leave. At that moment the Women *return, leading the* Bride. *Elesin's face
glows with pleasure. He flicks the sleeves of his agbada° with renewed confidence and steps
forward to meet the group. As the girl kneels before* Iyaloja, *lights fade out on the scene.)*

Scene 2

*(The verandah of the District Officer's bungalow. A tango is playing from an old hand-
cranked gramophone and, glimpsed through the wide windows and doors which open
onto the forestage verandah are the shapes of* Simon Pilkings *and his wife,* Jane, *tango-
ing in and out of shadows in the living-room. They are wearing what is immediately
apparent as some form of fancy-dress. The dance goes on for some moments and then the
figure of a "Native Administration" Policeman emerges and climbs up the steps onto the
verandah. He peeps through and observes the dancing couple, reacting with what is obviously a long-standing bewilderment. He stiffens suddenly, his expression changes to one of
disbelief and horror. In his excitement he upsets a flower-pot and attracts the attention of
the couple. They stop dancing.)*

Pilkings: Is there anyone out there?

Jane: I'll turn off the gramophone.

Pilkings (approaching the verandah): I'm sure I heard something fall over. *(The*
Constable *retreats slowly, open-mouthed as* Pilkings *approaches the verandah.)* Oh
it's you Amusa. Why didn't you just knock instead of knocking things over?

Amusa (stammers badly and points a shaky finger at his dress): Mista Pirinkin . . .
Mista Pirinkin . . .

Pilkings: What is the matter with you?

Jane (emerging): Who is it dear? Oh, Amusa . . .   5

---

[113] **awusa nut** a nut that sticks in the throat unless thoroughly chewed   [121] **agbada** a
flowing robe, hand-woven, hand-embroidered, with long, full sleeves

Pilkings: Yes it's Amusa, and acting most strangely.

Amusa (his attention now transferred to Mrs Pilkings*):* Mammadam . . . you too!

Pilkings: What the hell is the matter with you man!

Jane: Your costume darling. Our fancy dress.

10 *Pilkings:* Oh hell, I'd forgotten all about that. *(Lifts the face mask over his head showing his face. His* Wife *follows suit.)*

Jane: I think you've shocked his big pagan heart bless him.

Pilkings: Nonsense, he's a Moslem. Come on Amusa, you don't believe in all that nonsense do you? I thought you were a good Moslem.

Amusa: Mista Pirinkin, I beg you sir, what you think you do with that dress? It belong to dead cult, not for human being.

Pilkings: Oh Amusa, what a let down you are. I swear by you at the club you know—thank God for Amusa, he doesn't believe in any mumbo-jumbo. And now look at you!

15 *Amusa:* Mista Pirinkin, I beg you, take it off. Is not good for man like you to touch that cloth.

Pilkings: Well, I've got it on. And what's more Jane and I have bet on it we're taking first prize at the ball. Now, if you can just pull yourself together and tell me what you wanted to see me about . . .

Amusa: Sir, I cannot talk this matter to you in that dress. I no fit.

Pilkings: What's that rubbish again?

Jane: He is dead earnest too Simon. I think you'll have to handle this delicately.

20 *Pilkings:* Delicately my . . . ! Look here Amusa, I think this little joke has gone far enough hm? Let's have some sense. You seem to forget that you are a police officer in the service of His Majesty's Government. I order you to report your business at once or face disciplinary action.

Amusa: Sir, it is a matter of death. How can man talk against death to person in uniform of death? Is like talking against government to person in uniform of police. Please sir, I go and come back.

Pilkings (roars): Now! *(Amusa switches his gaze to the ceiling suddenly, remains mute.)*

Jane: Oh Amusa, what is there to be scared of in the costume? You saw it confiscated last month from those egungun° men who were creating trouble in town. You helped arrest the cult leaders yourself—if the juju° didn't harm you at the time how could it possibly harm you now? And merely by looking at it?

Amusa (without looking down): Madam, I arrest the ringleaders who make trouble but me I no touch egungun. That egungun itself, I no touch. And I no abuse 'am. I arrest ringleader but I treat egungun with respect.

25 *Pilkings:* It's hopeless. We'll merely end up missing the best part of the ball. When they get this way there is nothing you can do. It's simply hammering against a brick wall. Write your report or whatever it is on that pad Amusa and take yourself out of here. Come on Jane. We only upset his delicate sensibilities by remaining here.

---

[23]**egungun** the masked ancestors of the Yoruba   **juju** magic charm

(Amusa *waits for them to leave, then writes in the notebook, somewhat laboriously. Drumming from the direction of the town wells up.* Amusa *listens, makes a movement as if he wants to recall* Pilkings *but changes his mind. Completes his note and goes. A few moments later* Pilkings *emerges, picks up the pad and reads.*)

Jane!

Jane (from the bedroom): Coming darling. Nearly ready.
Pilkings: Never mind being ready, just listen to this.
Jane: What is it?
Pilkings: Amusa's report. Listen. "I have to report that it come to my information that one prominent chief, namely, the Elesin Oba, is to commit death tonight as a result of native custom. Because this is criminal offence I await further instruction at charge office. Sergeant Amusa."

(Jane *comes out onto the verandah while he is reading.*)

Jane: Did I hear you say commit death? 30
Pilkings: Obviously he means murder.
Jane: You mean a ritual murder?
Pilkings: Must be. You think you've stamped it all out but it's always lurking under the surface somewhere.
Jane: Oh. Does it mean we are not getting to the ball at all?
Pilkings: No-o. I'll have the man arrested. Everyone remotely involved. In any 35 case there may be nothing to it. Just rumours.
Jane: Really? I thought you found Amusa's rumours generally reliable.
Pilkings: That's true enough. But who knows what may have been giving him the scare lately. Look at his conduct tonight.
Jane (laughing): You have to admit he had his own peculiar logic. (*Deepens her voice.*) How can man talk against death to person in uniform of death? (*Laughs.*) Anyway, you can't go into the police station dressed like that.
Pilkings: I'll send Joseph with instructions. Damn it, what a confounded nuisance!
Jane: But don't you think you should talk first to the man, Simon? 40
Pilkings: Do you want to go to the ball or not?
Jane: Darling, why are you getting rattled? I was only trying to be intelligent. It seems hardly fair just to lock up a man—and a chief at that—simply on the er . . . what is the legal word again?—uncorroborated word of a sergeant.
Pilkings: Well, that's easily decided. Joseph!
Joseph (from within): Yes master.
Pilkings: You're quite right of course, I am getting rattled. Probably the effect of 45 those bloody drums. Do you hear how they go on and on?
Jane: I wondered when you'd notice. Do you suppose it has something to do with this affair?
Pilkings: Who knows? They always find an excuse for making a noise . . . (*Thoughtfully.*) Even so . . .
Jane: Yes Simon?
Pilkings: It's different Jane. I don't think I've heard this particular—sound— before. Something unsettling about it.

50   *Jane:* I thought all bush drumming sounded the same.

Pilkings: Don't tease me now Jane. This may be serious.

Jane: I'm sorry. *(Gets up and throws her arms around his neck. Kisses him. The houseboy enters, retreats and knocks.)*

Pilkings (wearily): Oh, come in Joseph! I don't know where you pick up all these elephantine notions of tact. Come over here.

Joseph: Sir?

55   *Pilkings:* Joseph, are you a Christian or not?

Joseph: Yessir.

Pilkings: Does seeing me in this outfit bother you?

Joseph: No sir, it has no power.

Pilkings: Thank God for some sanity at last. Now Joseph, answer me on the honour of a Christian—what is supposed to be going on in town tonight?

60   *Joseph:* Tonight sir? You mean the chief who is going to kill himself?

Pilkings: What?

Jane: What do you mean, kill himself?

Pilkings: You do mean he is going to kill somebody don't you?

Joseph: No master. He will not kill anybody and no one will kill him. He will simply die.

65   *Jane:* But why Joseph?

Joseph: It is native law and custom. The King die last month. Tonight is his burial. But before they can bury him, the Elesin must die so as to accompany him to heaven.

Pilkings: I seem to be fated to clash more often with that man than with any of the other chiefs.

Joseph: He is the King's Chief Horseman.

Pilkings (in a resigned way): I know.

70   *Jane:* Simon, what's the matter?

Pilkings: It would have to be him!

Jane: Who is he?

Pilkings: Don't you remember? He's that chief with whom I had a scrap some three or four years ago. I helped his son get to a medical school in England, remember? He fought tooth and nail to prevent it.

Jane: Oh now I remember. He was that very sensitive young man. What was his name again?

75   *Pilkings:* Olunde. Haven't replied to his last letter come to think of it. The old pagan wanted him to stay and carry on some family tradition or the other. Honestly I couldn't understand the fuss he made. I literally had to help the boy escape from close confinement and load him onto the next boat. A most intelligent boy, really bright.

Jane: I rather thought he was much too sensitive you know. The kind of person you feel should be a poet munching rose petals in Bloomsbury.

Pilkings: Well, he's going to make a first-class doctor. His mind is set on that. And as long as he wants my help he is welcome to it.

Jane (after a pause): Simon.

Pilkings: Yes?

80   *Jane:* This boy, he was the eldest son wasn't he?

Pilkings: I'm not sure. Who could tell with that old ram?

Jane: Do you know, Joseph?

Joseph: Oh yes Madam. He was the eldest son. That's why Elesin cursed master good and proper. The eldest son is not supposed to travel away from the land.

Jane (giggling): Is that true Simon? Did he really curse you good and proper?

Pilkings: By all accounts I should be dead by now.   85

Joseph: Oh no, master is white man. And good Christian. Black man juju can't touch master.

Jane: If he was his eldest, it means that he would be the Elesin to the next king. It's a family thing isn't it Joseph?

Joseph: Yes madam. And if this Elesin had died before the King, his eldest son must take his place.

Jane: That would explain why the old chief was so mad you took the boy away.

Pilkings: Well it makes me all the more happy I did.   90

Jane: I wonder if he knew.

Pilkings: Who? Oh, you mean Olunde?

Jane: Yes. Was that why he was so determined to get away? I wouldn't stay if I knew I was trapped in such a horrible custom.

Pilkings (thoughtfully): No, I don't think he knew. At least he gave no indication. But you couldn't really tell with him. He was rather close you know, quite unlike most of them. Didn't give much away, not even to me.

Jane: Aren't they all rather close, Simon?   95

Pilkings: These natives here? Good gracious. They'll open their mouths and yap with you about their family secrets before you can stop them. Only the other day . . .

Jane: But Simon, do they really give anything away? I mean, anything that really counts. This affair for instance, we didn't know they still practised that custom did we?

Pilkings: Ye-e-es, I suppose you're right there. Sly, devious bastards.

Joseph (stiffly): Can I go now master? I have to clean the kitchen.

Pilkings: What? Oh, you can go. Forgot you were still here.   100

(*Joseph goes.*)

Jane: Simon, you really must watch your language. Bastard isn't just a simple swear-word in these parts, you know.

Pilkings: Look, just when did you become a social anthropologist, that's what I'd like to know.

Jane: I'm not claiming to know anything. I just happen to have overheard quarrels among the servants. That's how I know they consider it a smear.

Pilkings: I thought the extended family system took care of all that. Elastic family, no bastards.

Jane (shrugs): Have it your own way.   105

(*Awkward silence. The drumming increases in volume.* Jane *gets up suddenly, restless.*)

That drumming Simon, do you think it might really be connected with this ritual? It's been going on all evening.

Pilkings: Let's ask our native guide. Joseph! Just a minute Joseph. *(Joseph re-enters.)* What's the drumming about?

Joseph: I don't know master.

Pilkings: What do you mean you don't know? It's only two years since your conversion. Don't tell me all that holy water nonsense also wiped out your tribal memory.

Joseph (visibly shocked): Master!

110 *Jane:* Now you've done it.

Pilkings: What have I done now?

Jane: Never mind. Listen Joseph, just tell me this. Is that drumming connected with dying or anything of that nature?

Joseph: Madam, this is what I am trying to say: I am not sure. It sounds like the death of a great chief and then, it sounds like the wedding of a great chief. It really mix me up.

Pilkings: Oh get back to the kitchen. A fat lot of help you are.

115 *Joseph:* Yes master. *(Goes.)*

Jane: Simon . . .

Pilkings: All right, all right. I'm in no mood for preaching.

Jane: It isn't my preaching you have to worry about, it's the preaching of the missionaries who preceded you here. When they make converts they really convert them. Calling holy water nonsense to our Joseph is really like insult-ing the Virgin Mary before a Roman Catholic. He's going to hand in his notice tomorrow you mark my word.

Pilkings: Now you're being ridiculous.

120 *Jane:* Am I? What are you willing to bet that tomorrow we are going to be without a steward-boy? Did you see his face?

Pilkings: I am more concerned about whether or not we will be one native chief short by tomorrow. Christ! Just listen to those drums. *(He strides up and down, undecided.)*

Jane (getting up): I'll change and make up some supper.

Pilkings: What's that?

Jane: Simon, it's obvious we have to miss this ball.

125 *Pilkings:* Nonsense. It's the first bit of real fun the European club has managed to organise for over a year, I'm damned if I'm going to miss it. And it is a rather special occasion. Doesn't happen every day.

Jane: You know this business has to be stopped Simon. And you are the only man who can do it.

Pilkings: I don't have to stop anything. If they want to throw themselves off the top of a cliff or poison themselves for the sake of some barbaric custom what is that to me? If it were ritual murder or something like that I'd be duty-bound to do something. I can't keep an eye on all the potential suicides in this province. And as for that man—believe me it's good riddance.

Jane (laughs): I know you better than that Simon. You are going to have to do something to stop it—after you've finished blustering.

Pilkings (shouts after her): And suppose after all it's only a wedding? I'd look a proper fool if I interrupted a chief on his honeymoon, wouldn't I? *(Resumes his angry stride, slows down.)* Ah well, who can tell what those chiefs actually do on their honeymoon anyway? *(He takes up the pad and scribbles rapidly on it.)* Joseph! Joseph! Joseph! *(Some moments later* Joseph *puts in a sulky appearance.)* Did you hear me call you? Why the hell didn't you answer?

Joseph: I didn't hear master. 130

Pilkings: You didn't hear me! How come you are here then?

Joseph (stubbornly): I didn't hear master.

Pilkings (controls himself with an effort): We'll talk about it in the morning. I want you to take this note directly to Sergeant Amusa. You'll find him at the charge office. Get on your bicycle and race there with it. I expect you back in twenty minutes exactly. Twenty minutes, is that clear?

Joseph: Yes master. *(Going.)*

Pilkings: Oh er . . . Joseph. 135

Joseph: Yes Master?

Pilkings (between gritted teeth): Er . . . forget what I said just now. The holy water is not nonsense. *I* was talking nonsense.

Joseph: Yes master. *(Goes.)*

Jane (pokes her head round the door): Have you found him?

Pilkings: Found who? 140

Jane: Joseph. Weren't you shouting for him?

Pilkings: Oh yes, he turned up finally.

Jane: You sounded desperate. What was it all about?

Pilkings: Oh nothing. I just wanted to apologise to him. Assure him that the holy water isn't really nonsense.

Jane: Oh? And how did he take it? 145

Pilkings: Who the hell gives a damn! I had a sudden vision of our Very Reverend Macfarlane drafting another letter of complaint to the Resident about my unchristian language towards his parishioners.

Jane: Oh I think he's given up on you by now.

Pilkings: Don't be too sure. And anyway, I wanted to make sure Joseph didn't "lose" my note on the way. He looked sufficiently full of the holy crusade to do some such thing.

Jane: If you've finished exaggerating, come and have something to eat.

Pilkings: No, put it all away. We can still get to the ball. 150

Jane: Simon . . .

Pilkings: Get your costume back on. Nothing to worry about. I've instructed Amusa to arrest the man and lock him up.

Jane: But that station is hardly secure Simon. He'll soon get his friends to help him escape.

Pilkings: A-ah, that's where I have out-thought you. I'm not having him put in the station cell. Amusa will bring him right here and lock him up in my study. And he'll stay with him till we get back. No one will dare come here to incite him to anything.

Jane: How clever of you darling. I'll get ready. 155

Pilkings: Hey.

Jane: Yes darling.

Pilkings: I have a surprise for you. I was going to keep it until we actually got to the ball.

Jane: What is it?

160 *Pilkings:* You know the Prince is on a tour of the colonies don't you? Well, he docked in the capital only this morning but he is already at the Residency. He is going to grace the ball with his presence later tonight.

Jane: Simon! Not really.

Pilkings: Yes he is. He's been invited to give away the prizes and he has agreed. You must admit old Engleton is the best Club Secretary we ever had. Quick off the mark that lad.

Jane: But how thrilling.

Pilkings: The other provincials are going to be damned envious.

165 *Jane:* I wonder what he'll come as.

Pilkings: Oh I don't know. As a coat-of-arms perhaps. Anyway it won't be anything to touch this.

Jane: Well that's lucky. If we are to be presented I won't have to start looking for a pair of gloves. It's all sewn on.

Pilkings (laughing): Quite right. Trust a woman to think of that. Come on, let's get going.

Jane (rushing off): Won't be a second. *(Stops.)* Now I see why you've been so edgy all evening. I thought you weren't handling this affair with your usual brilliance—to begin with that is.

170 *Pilkings (his mood is much improved):* Shut up woman and get your things on.

Jane: All right boss, coming.

(Pilkings suddenly begins to hum the tango to which they were dancing before. Starts to execute a few practice steps. Lights fade.)

Scene 3

(A swelling, agitated hum of women's voices rises immediately in the background. The lights come on and we see the frontage of a converted cloth stall in the market. The floor leading up to the entrance is covered in rich velvets and woven cloth. The Women *come on stage, borne backwards by the determined progress of Sergeant* Amusa *and his two* Constables *who already have their batons out and use them as a pressure against the* Women. *At the edge of the cloth-covered floor however the* Women *take a determined stand and block all further progress of the* Men. *They begin to tease them mercilessly.)*

Amusa: I am tell you women for last time to commot° my road. I am here on official business.

Woman: Official business you white man's eunuch?° Official business is taking place where you want to go and it's a business you wouldn't understand.

Woman (makes a quick tug at the Constable*'s baton):* That doesn't fool anyone you know. It's the one you carry under your government knickers that counts. *(She bends low as if to peep under the baggy shorts. The embarrassed* Constable *quickly puts his knees together. The* Women *roar.)*

¹**commot** come out, get off of   ²**eunuch** a castrated man; an emasculated, ineffectual man

Woman: You mean there is nothing there at all?

Woman: Oh there was something. You know that handbell which the white man 5
uses to summon his servants . . . ?

Amusa (he manages to preserve some dignity throughout): I hope you women know
that interfering with officer in execution of his duty is criminal offence.

Woman: Interfere? He says we're interfering with him. You foolish man we're
telling you there's nothing to interfere with.

Amusa: I am order you now to clear the road.

Woman: What road? The one your father built?

Woman: You are a policeman not so? Then you know what they call trespassing 10
in court. Or—*(Pointing to the cloth-lined steps.)*—do you think that kind of road
is built for every kind of feet.

Woman: Go back and tell the white man who sent you to come himself.

Amusa: If I go I will come back with reinforcement. And we will all return
carrying weapons.

Woman: Oh, now I understand. Before they can put on those knickers the white
man first cuts off their weapons.

Woman: What a cheek! You mean you come here to show power to women and
you don't even have a weapon.

Amusa (shouting above the laughter): For the last time I warn you women to clear 15
the road.

Woman: To where?

Amusa: To that hut. I know he dey dere.

Woman: Who?

Amusa: The chief who call himself Elesin Oba.

Woman: You ignorant man. It is not he who calls himself Elesin Oba, it is his 20
blood that says it. As it called out to his father before him and will to his son
after him. And that is in spite of everything your white man can do.

Woman: Is it not the same ocean that washes this land and the white man's land?
Tell your white man he can hide our son away as long as he likes. When the
time comes for him, the same ocean will bring him back.

Amusa: The government say dat kin' ting must stop.

Woman: Who will stop it? You? Tonight our husband and father will prove
himself greater than the laws of strangers.

Amusa: I tell you nobody go prove anything tonight or anytime. Is ignorant and
criminal to prove dat kin' prove.

Iyaloja (entering from the hut. She is accompanied by a group of young girls who have 25
been attending the Bride*):* What is it Amusa? Why do you come here to disturb
the happiness of others?

Amusa: Madame Iyaloja, I glad you come. You know me, I no like trouble but
duty is duty. I am here to arrest Elesin for criminal intent. Tell these women
to stop obstructing me in the performance of my duty.

Iyaloja: And you? What gives you the right to obstruct our leader of men in the
performance of his duty?

Amusa: What kin' duty be dat one Iyaloja?

Iyaloja: What kin' duty? What kin' duty does a man have to his new bride?

30   *Amusa (bewildered, looks at the women and at the entrance to the hut):* Iyaloja, is it
        wedding you call dis kin' ting?
     Iyaloja: You have wives haven't you? Whatever the white man has done to you
        he hasn't stopped you having wives. And if he has, at least he is married. If
        you don't know what a marriage is, go and ask him to tell you.
     Amusa: This no to wedding.
     Iyaloja: And ask him at the same time what he would have done if anyone had
        come to disturb him on his wedding night.
     Amusa: Iyaloja, I say dis no to wedding.
35   *Iyaloja:* You want to look inside the bridal chamber? You want to see for yourself
        how a man cuts the virgin knot?
     Amusa: Madam . . .
     Woman: Perhaps his wives are still waiting for him to learn.
     Amusa: Iyaloja, make you tell dese women make den no insult me again. If I
        hear dat kin' insult once more . . .
     Girl (pushing her way through): You will do what?
40   *Girl:* He's out of his mind. It's our mothers you're talking to, do you know that?
        Not to any illiterate villager you can bully and terrorise. How dare you
        intrude here anyway?
     Girl: What a cheek, what impertinence!
     Girl: You've treated them too gently. Now let them see what it is to tamper with
        the mothers of this market.
     Girl: Your betters dare not enter the market when the women say no!
     Girl: Haven't you learnt that yet, you jester in khaki and starch?
45   *Iyaloja:* Daughters . . .
     Girl: No no Iyaloja, leave us to deal with him. He no longer knows his mother,
        we'll teach him.

        (With a sudden movement they snatch the batons of the two Constables. *They begin to
        hem him in.)*

     Girl: What next? We have your batons? What next? What are you going to do?

        (With equally swift movements they knock off their hats.)

     Girl: Move if you dare. We have your hats, what will you do about it? Didn't the
        white man teach you to take off your hats before women?
     Iyaloja: It's a wedding night. It's a night of joy for us. Peace . . .
50   *Girl:* Not for him. Who asked him here?
     Girl: Does he dare go to the Residency without an invitation?
     Girl: Not even where the servants eat the left-overs.
     Girls (in turn. In an "English" accent): Well well it's Mister Amusa. Were you invited?
        (Play-acting to one another. The older women encourage them with their titters.)
        —Your invitation card please?
        —Who are you? Have we been introduced?
        —And who did you say you were?
        —Sorry, I didn't quite catch your name.
        —May I take your hat?

—If you insist. May I take yours? *(Exchanging the* Policemen*'s hats.)*
—How very kind of you.
—Not at all. Won't you sit down?
—After you.
—Oh no.
—I insist.
—You're most gracious.
—And how do you find the place?
—The natives are all right.
—Friendly?
—Tractable.
—Not a teeny-weeny bit restless?
—Well, a teeny-weeny bit restless.
—One might even say, difficult?
—Indeed one might be tempted to say, difficult.
—But you do manage to cope?
—Yes indeed I do. I have a rather faithful ox called Amusa.
—He's loyal?
—Absolutely.
—Lay down his life for you what?
—Without a moment's thought.
—Had one like that once. Trust him with my life.
—Mostly of course they are liars.
—Never known a native to tell the truth.
—Does it get rather close around here?
—It's mild for this time of the year.
—But the rains may still come.
—They are late this year aren't they?
—They are keeping African time.
—Ha ha ha ha
—Ha ha ha ha
—The humidity is what gets me.
—It used to be whisky.
—Ha ha ha ha
—Ha ha ha ha
—What's your handicap old chap?
—Is there racing by golly?
—Splendid golf course, you'll like it.
—I'm beginning to like it already.
—And a European club, exclusive.
—You've kept the flag flying.
—We do our best for the old country.
—It's a pleasure to serve.
—Another whisky old chap?
—You are indeed too too kind.
—Not at all sir. Where is that boy? *(With a sudden bellow.)* Sergeant!

Amusa (snaps to attention): Yessir!

(*The* Women *collapse with laughter.*)

55 *Girl:* Take your men out of here.

Amusa (realising the trick, he rages from loss of face): I'm give you warning . . .

Girl: All right then. Off with his knickers! (*They surge slowly forward.*)

Iyaloja: Daughters, please.

Amusa (squaring himself for defence): The first woman wey touch me . . .

60 *Iyaloja:* My children, I beg of you . . .

Girl: Then tell him to leave this market. This is the home of our mothers. We don't want the eater of white left-overs at the feast their hands have prepared.

Iyaloja: You heard them Amusa. You had better go.

Girl: Now!

Amusa (commencing his retreat): We dey go now, but make you no say we no warn you.

65 *Girl:* Now!

Girls: Before we read the riot act—you should know all about that.

Amusa: Make we go. (*They depart, more precipitately.*)

(*The* Women *strike their palms across in the gesture of wonder.*)

Woman: Do they teach you all that at school?

Woman: And to think I nearly kept Apinke away from the place.

70 *Woman:* Did you hear them? Did you see how they mimicked the white man?

Woman: The voices exactly. Hey, there are wonders in this world!

Iyaloja: Well, our elders have said it: Dada may be weak, but he has a younger sibling who is truly fearless.

Woman: The next time the white man shows his face in this market I will set Wuraola on his tail.

(*A* Woman *bursts into song and dance of euphoria—"Tani l'awa o l'ogbeja? Kayi! A l'ogbeja. Omo Kekere l'ogbeja."° The rest of the* Women *join in, some placing the* Girls *on their back like infants, others dancing round them. The dance becomes general, mounting in excitement. Elesin appears, in wrapper only. In his hands a white velvet cloth folded loosely as if it held some delicate object. He cries out.*)

Elesin: Oh you mothers of beautiful brides! (*The dancing stops. They turn and see him, and the object in his hands. Iyaloja approaches and gently takes the cloth from him.*) Take it. It is no mere virgin stain, but the union of life and the seeds of passage. My vital flow, the last from this flesh is intermingled with the promise of future life. All is prepared. Listen! (*A steady drumbeat from the distance.*) Yes. It is nearly time. The King's dog has been killed. The King's favourite horse is about to follow his master. My brother chiefs know their task and perform it well. (*He listens again.*)

73**Tani l'awa o l'ogbeja? Kayi! A l'ogbeja. Omo Kekere l'ogbeja** a well-known drum lyric meaning, "Who says we haven't a defender? Silence! We have our defenders. Little children are our champions."

(The Bride *emerges, stands shyly by the door. He turns to her.)*

Our marriage is not yet wholly fulfilled. When earth and passage wed, the
consummation is complete only when there are grains of earth on the eyelids of
passage. Stay by me till then. My faithful drummers, do me your last service. This
is where I have chosen to do my leave-taking, in this heart of life, this hive which
contains the swarm of the world in its small compass. This is where I have known
love and laughter away from the palace. Even the richest food cloys when eaten
days on end; in the market, nothing ever cloys. Listen. *(They listen to the drums.)*
They have begun to seek out the heart of the King's favourite horse. Soon it will
ride in its bolt of raffia° with the dog at its feet. Together they will ride on the
shoulders of the King's grooms through the pulse centres of the town. They know
it is here I shall await them. I have told them. *(His eyes appear to cloud. He passes his
hand over them as if to clear his sight. He gives a faint smile.)* It promises well; just then
I felt my spirit's eagerness. The kite makes for wide spaces and the wind creeps up
behind its tail; can the kite say less than—thank you, the quicker the better? But
wait a while my spirit. Wait. Wait for the coming of the courier of the King. Do
you know friends, the horse is born to this one destiny, to bear the burden that is
man upon its back. Except for this night, this night alone when the spotless
stallion will ride in triumph on the back of man. In the time of my father I witnessed the strange sight. Perhaps tonight also I shall see it for the last time. If they
arrive before the drums beat for me, I shall tell him to let the Alafin° know I follow swiftly. If they come after the drums have sounded, why then, all is well for I
have gone ahead. Our spirits shall fall in step along the great passage. *(He listens to
the drums. He seems again to be falling into a state of semi-hypnosis; his eyes scan the sky
but it is in a kind of daze. His voice is a little breathless.)* The moon has fed, a glow from
its full stomach fills the sky and air, but I cannot tell where is that gateway
through which I must pass. My faithful friends, let our feet touch together this last
time, lead me into the other market with sounds that cover my skin with down
yet make my limbs strike earth like a thoroughbred. Dear mothers, let me dance
into the passage even as I have lived beneath your roofs. *(He comes down progres-
sively among them. They make way for him, the drummers playing. His dance is one of
solemn, regal motions, each gesture of the body is made with a solemn finality. The* Women
join him, their steps a somewhat more fluid version of his. Beneath the Praise-Singer's
exhortations the Women *dirge "Ale le le, awo mi lo".)*

Praise-Singer: Elesin Alafin, can you hear my voice? 75
Elesin: Faintly, my friend, faintly.
Praise-Singer: Elesin Alafin, can you hear my call?
Elesin: Faintly my king, faintly.
Praise-Singer: Is your memory sound Elesin?
  Shall my voice be a blade of grass and
  Tickle the armpit of the past?
Elesin: My memory needs no prodding but 80
  What do you wish to say to me?

[74]**raffia** cloth made of the fibers of an African palm tree   **Alafin** title for a ruler of Oyo, a
Yoruban state

Praise-Singer: Only what has been spoken. Only what concerns
    The dying wish of the father of all.
Elesin: It is buried like seed-yam in my mind
    This is the season of quick rains, the harvest
    Is this moment due for gathering.
Praise-Singer: If you cannot come, I said, swear
    You'll tell my favourite horse. I shall
    Ride on through the gates alone.
Elesin: Elesin's message will be read
    Only when his loyal heart no longer beats.
85 *Praise-Singer:* If you cannot come Elesin, tell my dog.
    I cannot stay the keeper too long
    At the gate.
Elesin: A dog does not outrun the hand
    That feeds it meat. A horse that throws its rider
    Slows down to a stop. Elesin Alafin
    Trusts no beasts with messages between
    A king and his companion.
Praise-Singer: If you get lost my dog will track
    The hidden path to me.
Elesin: The seven-way crossroads confuses
    Only the stranger. The Horseman of the King
    Was born in the recesses of the house.
Praise-Singer: I know the wickedness of men. If there is
    Weight on the loose end of your sash, such weight
    As no mere man can shift; if your sash is earthed
    By evil minds who mean to part us at the last . . .
90 *Elesin:* My sash is of the deep purple alari;
    It is no tethering-rope. The elephant
    Trails no tethering-rope; that king
    Is not yet crowned who will peg an elephant—
    Not even you my friend and King.
Praise-Singer: And yet this fear will not depart from me
    The darkness of this new abode is deep
    Will your human eyes suffice?
Elesin: In a night which falls before our eyes
    However deep, we do not miss our way.
Praise-Singer: Shall I now not acknowledge I have stood
    Where wonders met their end? The elephant deserves
    Better than that we say "I have caught
    A glimpse of something." If we see the tamer
    Of the forest let us say plainly, we have seen
    An elephant.
Elesin (his voice is drowsy):
    I have freed myself of earth and now
    It's getting dark. Strange voices guide my feet.

Praise-Singer: The river is never so high that the eyes
    Of a fish are covered. The night is not so dark
    That the albino fails to find his way. A child
    Returning homewards craves no leading by the hand.
    Gracefully does the mask regain his grove at the end of the day . . .
    Gracefully. Gracefully does the mask dance
    Homeward at the end of the day, gracefully . . .

    (Elesin's trance appears to be deepening, his steps heavier.)

Iyaloja: It is the death of war that kills the valiant,
    Death of water is how the swimmer goes
    It is the death of markets that kills the trader
    And death of indecision takes the idle away
    The trade of the cutlass blunts its edge
    And the beautiful die the death of beauty.
    It takes an Elesin to die the death of death . . .
    Only Elesin . . . dies the unknowable death of death . . .
    Gracefully, gracefully does the horseman regain
    The stables at the end of day, gracefully . . .

Praise-Singer: How shall I tell what my eyes have seen? The Horseman gallops on
before the courier, how shall I tell what my eyes have seen? He says a dog
may be confused by new scents of beings he never dreamt of, so he must
precede the dog to heaven. He says a horse may stumble on strange boulders
and be lamed, so he races on before the horse to heaven. It is best, he says, to
trust no messenger who may falter at the outer gate; oh how shall I tell what
my ears have heard? But do you hear me still Elesin, do you hear your
faithful one?

(Elesin in his motions appears to feel for a direction of sound, subtly, but he only sinks deeper into his trance-dance.)

Elesin Alafin, I no longer sense your flesh. The drums are changing now but
you have gone far ahead of the world. It is not yet noon in heaven; let those
who claim it is begin their own journey home. So why must you rush like an
impatient bride: why do you race to desert your Olohun-iyo?

(Elesin is now sunk fully deep in his trance, there is no longer sign of any awareness of his surroundings.)

Does the deep voice of gbedu° cover you then, like the passage of royal elephants? Those drums that brook no rivals, have they blocked the passage to
your ears that my voice passes into wind, a mere leaf floating in the night? Is
your flesh lightened Elesin, is that lump of earth I slid between your slippers
to keep you longer slowly sifting from your feet? Are the drums on the other
side now tuning skin to skin with ours in osugbo?° Are there sounds there

---

⁹⁷**gbedu** a tall carved drum beaten at public and religious ceremonies   **osugbo** a grade or
rank of society or the place it meets

I cannot hear, do footsteps surround you which pound the earth like gbedu, roll like thunder round the dome of the world? Is the darkness gathering in your head Elesin? Is there now a streak of light at the end of the passage, a light I dare not look upon? Does it reveal whose voices we often heard, whose touches we often felt, whose wisdoms come suddenly into the mind when the wisest have shaken their heads and murmured: It cannot be done? Elesin Alafin, don't think I do not know why your lips are heavy, why your limbs are drowsy as palm oil in the cold of harmattan.° I would call you back but when the elephant heads for the jungle, the tail is too small a handhold for the hunter that would pull him back. The sun that heads for the sea no longer heeds the prayers of the farmer. When the river begins to taste the salt of the ocean, we no longer know what deity to call on, the river-god or Olokun.° No arrow flies back to the string, the child does not return through the same passage that gave it birth. Elesin Oba, can you hear me at all? Your eyelids are glazed like a courtesan's, is it that you see the dark groom and master of life? And will you see my father? Will you tell him that I stayed with you to the last? Will my voice ring in your ears awhile, will you remember Olohun-iyo even if the music on the other side surpasses his mortal craft? But will they know you over there? Have they eyes to gauge your worth, have they the heart to love you, will they know what thoroughbred prances towards them in caparisons° of honour? If they do not Elesin, if any there cuts your yam with a small knife, or pours you wine in a small calabash, turn back and return to welcoming hands. If the world were not greater than the wishes of Olohun-iyo, I would not let you go . . .

(He appears to break down. Elesin *dances on, completely in a trance. The dirge wells up louder and stronger.* Elesin*'s dance does not lose its elasticity but his gestures become, if possible, even more weighty. Lights fade slowly on the scene.)*

Scene 4

(A Masque. The front side of the stage is part of a wide corridor around the great hall of the Residency extending beyond vision into the rear and wings. It is redolent of the tawdry decadence of a far-flung but key imperial frontier. The Couples *in a variety of fancy-dress are ranged around the walls, gazing in the same direction. The guest-of-honour is about to make an appearance. A portion of the local police brass band with its white* Conductor *is just visible. At last, the entrance of* Royalty. *The band plays "Rule Britannia," badly, beginning long before he is visible. The couples bow and curtsey as he passes by them. Both he and his companions are dressed in seventeenth century European costume. Following behind are the* Resident *and his* Partner *similarly attired. As they gain the end of the hall where the orchestra dais begins the music comes to an end. The* Prince *bows to the guests. The* Band *strikes up a Viennese waltz and the* Prince *formally opens the floor. Several bars later the* Resident *and his companion follow suit. Others*

[97]**harmattan** a season of dry, cold weather   **Olokun** god of oceans   **caparisons** decorative coverings for a horse

follow in appropriate pecking order. The orchestra's waltz rendition is not of the highest musical standard.

Some time later the Prince *dances again into view and is settled into a corner by the* Resident *who then proceeds to select* Couples *as they dance past for introduction, sometimes threading his way through the dancers to tap the lucky* Couple *on the shoulder. Desperate efforts from many to ensure that they are recognised in spite of, perhaps, their costume. The ritual of introductions soon takes in* Pilkings *and his* Wife. *The* Prince *is quite fascinated by their costume and they demonstrate the adaptations they have made to it, pulling down the mask to demonstrate how the egungun normally appears, then showing the various press-button controls they have innovated for the face flaps, the sleeves, etc. They demonstrate the dance steps and the guttural sounds made by the* egungun, *harass other dancers in the hall,* Mrs Pilkings *playing the "restrainer" to* Pilkings' *manic darts. Everyone is highly entertained, the Royal Party especially who lead the applause.*

At this point a liveried Footman *comes in with a note on a salver and is intercepted almost absent-mindedly by the* Resident *who takes the note and reads it. After polite coughs he succeeds in excusing the* Pilkings *from the* Prince *and takes them aside. The* Prince *considerately offers the* Resident's *Wife his hand and dancing is resumed.*

On their way out the Resident *gives an order to his* Aide-de-Camp. *They come into the side corridor where the* Resident *hands the note to* Pilkings.)

Resident: As you see it says "emergency" on the outside. I took the liberty of opening it because His Highness was obviously enjoying the entertainment. I didn't want to interrupt unless really necessary.

Pilkings: Yes, yes of course, Sir.

Resident: Is it really as bad as it says? What's it all about?

Pilkings: Some strange custom they have, sir. It seems because the King is dead some important chief has to commit suicide.

Resident: The King? Isn't it the same one who died nearly a month ago? 5

Pilkings: Yes, sir.

Resident: Haven't they buried him yet?

Pilkings: They take their time about these things, sir. The pre-burial ceremonies last nearly thirty days. It seems tonight is the final night.

Resident: But what has it got to do with the market women? Why are they rioting? We've waived that troublesome tax haven't we?

Pilkings: We don't quite know that they are exactly rioting yet, sir. Sergeant 10 Amusa is sometimes prone to exaggerations.

Resident: He sounds desperate enough. That comes out even in his rather quaint grammar. Where is the man anyway? I asked my aide-de-camp to bring him here.

Pilkings: They are probably looking in the wrong verandah. I'll fetch him myself.

Resident: No no you stay here. Let your wife go and look for them. Do you mind my dear . . . ?

Jane: Certainly not, your Excellency. (*Goes.*)

Resident: You should have kept me informed, Pilkings. You realise how disastrous 15 it would have been if things had erupted while His Highness was here.

Pilkings: I wasn't aware of the whole business until tonight, sir.

Resident: Nose to the ground Pilkings, nose to the ground. If we all let these little things slip past us where would the empire be eh? Tell me that. Where would we all be?

Pilkings (low voice): Sleeping peacefully at home I bet.

Resident: What did you say, Pilkings?

20 *Pilkings:* It won't happen again, sir.

Resident: It mustn't, Pilkings. It mustn't. Where is that damned sergeant? I ought to get back to His Highness as quickly as possible and offer him some plausible explanation for my rather abrupt conduct. Can you think of one, Pilkings?

Pilkings: You could tell him the truth, sir.

Resident: I could? No no no no Pilkings, that would never do. What! Go and tell him there is a riot just two miles away from him? This is supposed to be a secure colony of His Majesty, Pilkings.

Pilkings: Yes, sir.

25 *Resident:* Ah, there they are. No, these are not our native police. Are these the ring-leaders of the riot?

Pilkings: Sir, these are my police officers.

Resident: Oh, I beg your pardon officers. You do look a little . . . I say, isn't there something missing in their uniform? I think they used to have some rather colourful sashes. If I remember rightly I recommended them myself in my young days in the service. A bit of colour always appeals to the natives, yes, I remember putting that in my report. Well well well, where are we? Make your report man.

Pilkings (moves close to Amusa, *between his teeth):* And let's have no more superstitious nonsense from you Amusa or I'll throw you in the guardroom for a month and feed you pork!

Resident: What's that? What has pork to do with it?

30 *Pilkings:* Sir, I was just warning him to be brief. I'm sure you are most anxious to hear his report.

Resident: Yes yes yes of course. Come on man, speak up. Hey, didn't we give them some colourful fez hats with all those wavy things, yes, pink tassels . . .

Pilkings: Sir, I think if he was permitted to make his report we might find that he lost his hat in the riot.

Resident: Ah yes indeed. I'd better tell His Highness that. Lost his hat in the riot, ha ha. He'll probably say well, as long as he didn't lose his head. *(Chuckles to himself.)* Don't forget to send me a report first thing in the morning young Pilkings.

Pilkings: No, sir.

35 *Resident:* And whatever you do, don't let things get out of hand. Keep a cool head and—nose to the ground Pilkings. *(Wanders off in the general direction of the hall.)*

Pilkings: Yes, sir.

Aide-de-Camp: Would you be needing me, sir?

Pilkings: No thanks, Bob. I think His Excellency's need of you is greater than ours.

Aide-de-Camp: We have a detachment of soldiers from the capital, sir. They accompanied His Highness up here.

Pilkings: I doubt if it will come to that but, thanks, I'll bear it in mind. Oh, could you send an orderly with my cloak. 40

Aide-de-Camp: Very good, sir. *(Goes.)*

Pilkings: Now, sergeant.

Amusa: Sir . . . *(Makes an effort, stops dead. Eyes to the ceiling.)*

Pilkings: Oh, not again.

Amusa: I cannot against death to dead cult. This dress get power of dead. 45

Pilkings: All right, let's go. You are relieved of all further duty Amusa. Report to me first thing in the morning.

Jane: Shall I come, Simon?

Pilkings: No, there's no need for that. If I can get back later I will. Otherwise get Bob to bring you home.

Jane: Be careful Simon . . . I mean, be clever.

Pilkings: Sure I will. You two, come with me. *(As he turns to go, the clock in the* 50 *Residency begins to chime.* Pilkings *looks at his watch then turns, horror-stricken, to stare at his* Wife. *The same thought clearly occurs to her. He swallows hard. An* Orderly *brings his cloak.)* It's midnight. I had no idea it was that late.

Jane: But surely . . . they don't count the hours the way we do. The moon, or something . . .

Pilkings: I am . . . not so sure.

(He turns and breaks into a sudden run. The two Constables *follow, also at a run.* Amusa, *who has kept his eyes on the ceiling throughout waits until the last of the footsteps has faded out of hearing. He salutes suddenly but without once looking in the direction of the* Woman.*)*

Amusa: Goodnight, madam.

Jane: Oh. *(She hesitates.)* Amusa . . . *(He goes off without seeming to have heard.)* Poor Simon . . . *(A figure emerges from the shadows, a young black* Man *dressed in a sober western suit. He peeps into the hall, trying to make out the figures of the dancers.)* Who is that?

Olunde (emerges into the light): I didn't mean to startle you madam. I am looking 55 for the District Officer.

Jane: Wait a minute . . . don't I know you? Yes, you are Olunde, the young man who . . .

Olunde: Mrs Pilkings! How fortunate. I came here to look for your husband.

Jane: Olunde! Let's look at you. What a fine young man you've become. Grand but solemn. Good God, when did you return? Simon never said a word. But you do look well Olunde. Really!

Olunde: You are . . . well, you look quite well yourself Mrs Pilkings. From what little I can see of you.

Jane: Oh, this. It's caused quite a stir I assure you, and not all of it very pleasant. 60 You are not shocked I hope?

Olunde: Why should I be? But don't you find it rather hot in there? Your skin must find it difficult to breathe.

Jane: Well, it is a little hot I must confess, but it's all in a good cause.

Olunde: What cause Mrs Pilkings?

Jane: All this. The ball. And His Highness being here in person and all that.

65 *Olunde (mildly):* And that is the good cause for which you desecrate an ancestral mask?

Jane: Oh, so you are shocked after all. How disappointing.

Olunde: No I am not shocked, Mrs Pilkings. You forget that I have now spent four years among your people. I discovered that you have no respect for what you do not understand.

Jane: Oh. So you've returned with a chip on your shoulder. That's a pity Olunde. I am sorry.

(An uncomfortable silence follows.)

I take it then that you did not find your stay in England altogether edifying.

Olunde: I don't say that. I found your people quite admirable in many ways, their conduct and courage in this war for instance.

70 *Jane:* Ah yes, the war. Here of course it is all rather remote. From time to time we have a black-out drill just to remind us that there is a war on. And the rare convoy passes through on its way somewhere or on manoeuvres. Mind you there is the occasional bit of excitement like that ship that was blown up in the harbour.

Olunde: Here? Do you mean through enemy action?

Jane: Oh no, the war hasn't come that close. The captain did it himself. I don't quite understand it really. Simon tried to explain. The ship had to be blown up because it had become dangerous to the other ships, even to the city itself. Hundreds of the coastal population would have died.

Olunde: Maybe it was loaded with ammunition and had caught fire. Or some of those lethal gases they've been experimenting on.

Jane: Something like that. The captain blew himself up with it. Deliberately. Simon said someone had to remain on board to light the fuse.

75 *Olunde:* It must have been a very short fuse.

Jane (shrugs): I don't know much about it. Only that there was no other way to save lives. No time to devise anything else. The captain took the decision and carried it out.

Olunde: Yes . . . I quite believe it. I met men like that in England.

Jane: Oh just look at me! Fancy welcoming you back with such morbid news. Stale too. It was at least six months ago.

Olunde: I don't find it morbid at all. I find it rather inspiring. It is an affirmative commentary on life.

80 *Jane:* What is?

Olunde: That captain's self-sacrifice.

Jane: Nonsense. Life should never be thrown deliberately away.

Olunde: And the innocent people around the harbour?

Jane: Oh, how does one know? The whole thing was probably exaggerated anyway.

85 *Olunde:* That was a risk the captain couldn't take. But please Mrs Pilkings, do you think you could find your husband for me? I have to talk to him.

Jane: Simon? *(As she recollects for the first time the full significance of* Olunde's *presence.)* Simon is . . . there is a little problem in town. He was sent for. But . . . when did you arrive? Does Simon know you're here?

Olunde (suddenly earnest): I need your help Mrs Pilkings. I've always found you somewhat more understanding than your husband. Please find him for me and when you do, you must help me talk to him.

Jane: I'm afraid I don't quite . . . follow you. Have you seen my husband already?

Olunde: I went to your house. Your houseboy told me you were here. *(He smiles.)* He even told me how I would recognise you and Mr Pilkings.

Jane: Then you must know what my husband is trying to do for you.   90

Olunde: For me?

Jane: For you. For your people. And to think he didn't even know you were coming back! But how do you happen to be here? Only this evening we were talking about you. We thought you were still four thousand miles away.

Olunde: I was sent a cable.

Jane: A cable? Who did? Simon? The business of your father didn't begin till tonight.

Olunde: A relation sent it weeks ago, and it said nothing about my father. All it   95
said was, Our King is dead. But I knew I had to return home at once so as to bury my father. I understood that.

Jane: Well, thank God you don't have to go through that agony. Simon is going to stop it.

Olunde: That's why I want to see him. He's wasting his time. And since he has been so helpful to me I don't want him to incur the enmity of our people. Especially over nothing.

Jane (sits down open-mouthed): You . . . you Olunde!

Olunde: Mrs Pilkings, I came home to bury my father. As soon as I heard the news I booked my passage home. In fact we were fortunate. We travelled in the same convoy as your Prince, so we had excellent protection.

Jane: But you don't think your father is also entitled to whatever protection is   100
available to him?

Olunde: How can I make you understand? He *has* protection. No one can undertake what he does tonight without the deepest protection the mind can conceive. What can you offer him in place of his peace of mind, in place of the honour and veneration of his own people? What would you think of your Prince if he refused to accept the risk of losing his life on this voyage? This . . . showing-the-flag tour of colonial possessions.

Jane: I see. So it isn't just medicine you studied in England.

Olunde: Yet another error into which your people fall. You believe that everything which appears to make sense was learnt from you.

Jane: Not so fast Olunde. You have learnt to argue I can tell that, but I never said you made sense. However clearly you try to put it, it is still a barbaric custom. It is even worse—it's feudal! The king dies and a chieftain must be buried with him. How feudalistic can you get!

Olunde (waves his hand towards the background. The Prince *is dancing past again—to a   105
different step—and all the guests are bowing and curtseying as he passes):* And this?

Even in the midst of a devastating war, look at that. What name would you give to that?

Jane: Therapy, British style. The preservation of sanity in the midst of chaos.

Olunde: Others would call it decadence. However, it doesn't really interest me. You white races know how to survive; I've seen proof of that. By all logical and natural laws this war should end with all the white races wiping out one another, wiping out their so-called civilisation for all time and reverting to a state of primitivism the like of which has so far only existed in your imagination when you thought of us. I thought all that at the beginning. Then I slowly realised that your greatest art is the art of survival. But at least have the humility to let others survive in their own way.

Jane: Through ritual suicide?

Olunde: Is that worse than mass suicide? Mrs Pilkings, what do you call what those young men are sent to do by their generals in this war? Of course you have also mastered the art of calling things by names which don't remotely describe them.

110 *Jane:* You talk! You people with your long-winded, roundabout way of making conversation.

Olunde: Mrs Pilkings, whatever we do, we never suggest that a thing is the opposite of what it really is. In your newsreels I heard defeats, thorough, murderous defeats described as strategic victories. No wait, it wasn't just on your newsreels. Don't forget I was attached to hospitals all the time. Hordes of your wounded passed through those wards. I spoke to them. I spent long evenings by their bedsides while they spoke terrible truths of the realities of that war. I know now how history is made.

Jane: But surely, in a war of this nature for the morale of the nation you must expect . . .

Olunde: That a disaster beyond human reckoning be spoken of as a triumph? No. I mean, is there no mourning in the home of the bereaved that such blasphemy is permitted?

Jane (after a moment's pause): Perhaps I can understand you now. The time we picked for you was not really one for seeing us at our best.

115 *Olunde:* Don't think it was just the war. Before that even started I had plenty of time to study your people. I saw nothing, finally, that gave you the right to pass judgement on other peoples and their ways. Nothing at all.

Jane (hesitantly): Was it the . . . colour thing? I know there is some discrimination.

Olunde: Don't make it so simple, Mrs Pilkings. You make it sound as if when I left, I took nothing at all with me.

Jane: Yes . . . and to tell the truth, only this evening, Simon and I agreed that we never really knew what you left with.

Olunde: Neither did I. But I found out over there. I am grateful to your country for that. And I will never give it up.

120 *Jane:* Olunde, please . . . promise me something. Whatever you do, don't throw away what you have started to do. You want to be a doctor. My husband and I believe you will make an excellent one, sympathetic and competent. Don't let anything make you throw away your training.

Olunde (genuinely surprised): Of course not. What a strange idea. I intend to return
  and complete my training. Once the burial of my father is over.
Jane: Oh, please . . . !
Olunde: Listen! Come outside. You can't hear anything against that music.
Jane: What is it?
Olunde: The drums. Can you hear the drums? Listen.   125

  (The drums come over, still distant but more distinct. There is a change of rhythm, it rises to
  a crescendo and then, suddenly, it is cut off. After a silence, a new beat begins, slow and
  resonant.)

  There, it's all over.
Jane: You mean he's . . .
Olunde: Yes, Mrs Pilkings, my father is dead. His will-power has always been
  enormous; I know he is dead.
Jane (screams): How can you be so callous! So unfeeling! You announce your
  father's own death like a surgeon looking down on some strange . . .
  stranger's body! You're just a savage like all the rest.
Aide-de-Camp (rushing out): Mrs Pilkings. Mrs Pilkings. *(She breaks down, sobbing.)*
  Are you all right, Mrs Pilkings?
Olunde: She'll be all right. *(Turns to go.)*   130
Aide-de-Camp: Who are you? And who the hell asked your opinion?
Olunde: You're quite right, nobody. *(Going.)*
Aide-de-Camp: What the hell! Did you hear me ask you who you were?
Olunde: I have business to attend to.
Aide-de-Camp: I'll give you business in a moment you impudent nigger. Answer   135
  my question!
Olunde: I have a funeral to arrange. Excuse me. *(Going.)*
Aide-de-Camp: I said stop! Orderly!
Jane: No, no, don't do that. I'm all right. And for heaven's sake don't act so
  foolishly. He's a family friend.
Aide-de-Camp: Well he'd better learn to answer civil questions when he's asked
  them. These natives put a suit on and they get high opinions of themselves.
Olunde: Can I go now?   140
Jane: No, no, don't go. I must talk to you. I'm sorry about what I said.
Olunde: It's nothing, Mrs Pilkings. And I'm really anxious to go. I couldn't see my
  father before, it's forbidden for me, his heir and successor to set eyes on him
  from the moment of the King's death. But now . . . I would like to touch his
  body while it is still warm.
Jane: You will. I promise I shan't keep you long. Only, I couldn't possibly let you
  go like that. Bob, please excuse us.
Aide-de-Camp: If you're sure . . .
Jane: Of course I'm sure. Something happened to upset me just then, but I'm all   145
  right now. Really.

  (The Aide-de-Camp *goes, somewhat reluctantly.)*

Olunde: I mustn't stay long.

Jane: Please, I promise not to keep you. It's just that . . . oh you saw yourself what happens to one in this place. The Resident's man thought he was being helpful, that's the way we all react. But I can't go in among that crowd just now and if I stay by myself somebody will come looking for me. Please, just say something for a few moments and then you can go. Just so I can recover myself.

Olunde: What do you want me to say?

Jane: Your calm acceptance for instance, can you explain that? It was so unnatural. I don't understand that at all. I feel a need to understand all I can.

150 *Olunde:* But you explained it yourself. My medical training perhaps. I have seen death too often. And the soldiers who returned from the front, they died on our hands all the time.

Jane: No. It has to be more than that. I feel it has to do with the many things we don't really grasp about your people. At least you can explain.

Olunde: All these things are part of it. And anyway, my father has been dead in my mind for nearly a month. Ever since I learnt of the King's death. I've lived with my bereavement so long now that I cannot think of him alive. On that journey on the boat, I kept my mind on my duties as the one who must perform the rites over his body. I went through it all again and again in my mind as he himself had taught me. I didn't want to do anything wrong, something which might jeopardise the welfare of my people.

Jane: But he had disowned you. When you left he swore publicly you were no longer his son.

Olunde: I told you, he was a man of tremendous will. Sometimes that's another way of saying stubborn. But among our people, you don't disown a child just like that. Even if I had died before him I would still be buried like his eldest son. But it's time for me to go.

155 *Jane:* Thank you. I feel calmer. Don't let me keep you from your duties.

Olunde: Goodnight, Mrs Pilkings.

Jane: Welcome home.

(She holds out her hand. As he takes it footsteps are heard approaching the drive. A short while later a woman's sobbing is also heard.)

Pilkings (off): Keep them here till I get back. *(He strides into view, reacts at the sight of Olunde but turns to his Wife.)* Thank goodness you're still here.

Jane: Simon, what happened?

160 *Pilkings:* Later Jane, please. Is Bob still here?

Jane: Yes, I think so. I'm sure he must be.

Pilkings: Try and get him out here as quickly as you can. Tell him it's urgent.

Jane: Of course. Oh Simon, you remember . . .

Pilkings: Yes yes. I can see who it is. Get Bob out here. *(She runs off.)* At first I thought I was seeing a ghost.

165 *Olunde:* Mr Pilkings, I appreciate what you tried to do. I want you to believe that. I can tell you it would have been a terrible calamity if you'd succeeded.

Pilkings (opens his mouth several times, shuts it): You . . . said what?

Olunde: A calamity for us, the entire people.

Pilkings (sighs): I see. Hm.

Olunde: And now I must go. I must see him before he turns cold.

Pilkings: Oh ah . . . em . . . but this is a shock to see you. I mean er thinking all   170
this while you were in England and thanking God for that.

Olunde: I came on the mail boat. We travelled in the Prince's convoy.

Pilkings: Ah yes, a-ah, hm . . . er well . . .

Olunde: Goodnight. I can see you are shocked by the whole business. But you
must know by now there are things you cannot understand—or help.

Pilkings: Yes. Just a minute. There are armed policemen that way and they have
instructions to let no one pass. I suggest you wait a little. I'll er . . . give you
an escort.

Olunde: That's very kind of you. But do you think it could be quickly arranged.   175

Pilkings: Of course. In fact, yes, what I'll do is send Bob over with some men to
the er . . . place. You can go with them. Here he comes now. Excuse me a
minute.

Aide-de-Camp: Anything wrong sir?

Pilkings (takes him to one side): Listen Bob, that cellar in the disused annexe of the
Residency, you know, where the slaves were stored before being taken down
to the coast . . .

Aide-de-Camp: Oh yes, we use it as a storeroom for broken furniture.

Pilkings: But it's still got the bars on it?   180

Aide-de-Camp: Oh yes, they are quite intact.

Pilkings: Get the keys please. I'll explain later. And I want a strong guard over
the Residency tonight.

Aide-de-Camp: We have that already. The detachment from the coast . . .

Pilkings: No, I don't want them at the gates of the Residency. I want you to
deploy them at the bottom of the hill, a long way from the main hall so they
can deal with any situation long before the sound carries to the house.

Aide-de-Camp: Yes of course.   185

Pilkings: I don't want His Highness alarmed.

Aide-de-Camp: You think the riot will spread here?

Pilkings: It's unlikely but I don't want to take a chance. I made them believe I was
going to lock the man up in my house, which was what I had planned to do
in the first place. They are probably assailing it by now. I took a roundabout
route here so I don't think there is any danger at all. At least not before dawn.
Nobody is to leave the premises of course—the native employees I mean.
They'll soon smell something is up and they can't keep their mouths shut.

Aide-de-Camp: I'll give instructions at once.

Pilkings: I'll take the prisoner down myself. Two policemen will stay with him   190
throughout the night. Inside the cell.

Aide-de-Camp: Right sir. *(Salutes and goes off at the double.)*

Pilkings: Jane. Bob is coming back in a moment with a detachment. Until he gets
back please stay with Olunde. *(He makes an extra warning gesture with his eyes.)*

Olunde: Please, Mr Pilkings . . .

Pilkings: I hate to be stuffy old son, but we have a crisis on our hands. It has to
do with your father's affair if you must know. And it happens also at a time

when we have His Highness here. I am responsible for security so you'll simply have to do as I say. I hope that's understood. *(Marches off quickly, in the direction from which he made his first appearance.)*

195 *Olunde:* What's going on? All this can't be just because he failed to stop my father killing himself.

Jane: I honestly don't know. Could it have sparked off a riot?

Olunde: No. If he'd succeeded that would be more likely to start the riot. Perhaps there were other factors involved. Was there a chieftaincy dispute?

Jane: None that I know of.

Elesin (an animal bellow from off): Leave me alone! Is it not enough that you have covered me in shame! White man, take your hand from my body!

(Olunde stands frozen to the spot. Jane *understanding at last, tries to move him.)*

200 *Jane:* Let's go in. It's getting chilly out here.

Pilkings (off): Carry him.

Elesin: Give me back the name you have taken away from me you ghost from the land of the nameless!

Pilkings: Carry him! I can't have a disturbance here. Quickly! Stuff up his mouth.

Jane: Oh God! Let's go in. Please Olunde.

(Olunde does not move.)

205 *Elesin:* Take your albino's hand from me you . . .

(Sounds of a struggle. His voice chokes as he is gagged.)

Olunde (quietly): That was my father's voice.

Jane: Oh you poor orphan, what have you come home to?

(There is a sudden explosion of rage from off-stage and powerful steps come running up the drive.)

Pilkings: You bloody fools, after him!

(Immediately Elesin, *in handcuffs, comes pounding in the direction of* Jane *and* Olunde, *followed some moments afterwards by* Pilkings *and the* Constables. Elesin *confronted by the seeming statue of his son, stops dead.* Olunde *stares above his head into the distance. The* Constables *try to grab him.* Jane *screams at them.)*

Jane: Leave him alone! Simon, tell them to leave him alone.

210 *Pilkings:* All right, stand aside you. *(Shrugs.)* Maybe just as well. It might help to calm him down.

(For several moments they hold the same position. Elesin *moves a step forward, almost as if he's still in doubt.)*

Elesin: Olunde? *(He moves his head, inspecting him from side to side.)* Olunde! *(He collapses slowly at* Olunde's *feet.)* Oh son, don't let the sight of your father turn you blind!

Olunde (he moves for the first time since he heard his voice, brings his head slowly down to look on him): I have no father, eater of left-overs.

(He walks slowly down the way his father had run. Light fades out on Elesin, *sobbing into the ground.)*

Scene 5

(A wide iron-barred gate stretches almost the whole width of the cell in which Elesin *is imprisoned. His wrists are encased in thick iron bracelets, chained together; he stands against the bars, looking out. Seated on the ground to one side on the outside is his recent* Bride, *her eyes bent perpetually to the ground. Figures of the two* Guards *can be seen deeper inside the cell, alert to every movement* Elesin *makes.* Pilkings *now in a police officer's uniform enters noiselessly, observes him a while. Then he coughs ostentatiously and approaches. Leans against the bars near a corner, his back to* Elesin. *He is obviously trying to fall in mood with him. Some moments' silence.)*

Pilkings: You seem fascinated by the moon.

Elesin (after a pause): Yes, ghostly one. Your twin-brother up there engages my thoughts.

Pilkings: It is a beautiful night.

Elesin: Is that so?

Pilkings: The light on the leaves, the peace of the night . . .   5

Elesin: The night is not at peace, District Officer.

Pilkings: No? I would have said it was. You know, quiet . . .

Elesin: And does quiet mean peace for you?

Pilkings: Well, nearly the same thing. Naturally there is a subtle difference . . .

Elesin: The night is not at peace, ghostly one. The world is not at peace. You have   10
shattered the peace of the world for ever. There is no sleep in the world
tonight.

Pilkings: It is still a good bargain if the world should lose one night's sleep as the
price of saving a man's life.

Elesin: You did not save my life, District Officer. You destroyed it.

Pilkings: Now come on . . .

Elesin: And not merely my life but the lives of many. The end of the night's work
is not over. Neither this year nor the next will see it. If I wished you well, I
would pray that you do not stay long enough on our land to see the disaster
you have brought upon us.

Pilkings: Well, I did my duty as I saw it. I have no regrets.   15

Elesin: No. The regrets of life always come later.

(Some moments' pause.)

You are waiting for dawn, white man. I hear you saying to yourself: only so
many hours until dawn and then the danger is over. All I must do is to keep
him alive tonight. You don't quite understand it all but you know that
tonight is when what ought to be must be brought about. I shall ease your
mind even more, ghostly one. It is not an entire night but a moment of the
night, and that moment is past. The moon was my messenger and guide.
When it reached a certain gateway in the sky, it touched that moment for
which my whole life has been spent in blessings. Even I do not know the
gateway. I have stood here and scanned the sky for a glimpse of that door
but, I cannot see it. Human eyes are useless for a search of this nature. But in
the house of osugbo, those who keep watch through the spirit recognised the

moment, they sent word to me through the voice of our sacred drums to prepare myself. I heard them and I shed all thoughts of earth. I began to follow the moon to the abode of the gods . . . servant of the white king, that was when you entered my chosen place of departure on feet of desecration.

Pilkings: I'm sorry, but we all see our duty differently.

Elesin: I no longer blame you. You stole from me my first-born, sent him to your country so you could turn him into something in your own image. Did you plan it all beforehand? There are moments when it seems part of a larger plan. He who must follow my footsteps is taken from me, sent across the ocean. Then, in my turn, I am stopped from fulfilling my destiny. Did you think it all out before, this plan to push our world from its course and sever the cord that links us to the great origin?

Pilkings: You don't really believe that. Anyway, if that was my intention with your son, I appear to have failed.

20 *Elesin:* You did not fail in the main, ghostly one. We know the roof covers the rafters, the cloth covers blemishes; who would have known that the white skin covered our future, preventing us from seeing the death our enemies had prepared for us. The world is set adrift and its inhabitants are lost. Around them, there is nothing but emptiness.

Pilkings: Your son does not take so gloomy a view.

Elesin: Are you dreaming now, white man? Were you not present at my reunion of shame? Did you not see when the world reversed itself and the father fell before his son, asking forgiveness?

Pilkings: That was in the heat of the moment. I spoke to him and . . . if you want to know, he wishes he could cut out his tongue for uttering the words he did.

Elesin: No. What he said must never be unsaid. The contempt of my own son rescued something of my shame at your hands. You have stopped me in my duty but I know now that I did give birth to a son. Once I mistrusted him for seeking the companionship of those my spirit knew as enemies of our race. Now I understand. One should seek to obtain the secrets of his enemies. He will avenge my shame, white one. His spirit will destroy you and yours.

25 *Pilkings:* That kind of talk is hardly called for. If you don't want my consolation . . .

Elesin: No white man, I do not want your consolation.

Pilkings: As you wish. Your son anyway, sends his consolation. He asks your forgiveness. When I asked him not to despise you his reply was: I cannot judge him, and if I cannot judge him, I cannot despise him. He wants to come to you and say goodbye and to receive your blessing.

Elesin: Goodbye? Is he returning to your land?

Pilkings: Don't you think that's the most sensible thing for him to do? I advised him to leave at once, before dawn, and he agrees that is the right course of action.

30 *Elesin:* Yes, it is best. And even if I did not think so, I have lost the father's place of honour. My voice is broken.

Pilkings: Your son honours you. If he didn't he would not ask your blessing.

Elesin: No. Even a thoroughbred is not without pity for the turf he strikes with his hoof. When is he coming?

Pilkings: As soon as the town is a little quieter. I advised it.

Elesin: Yes, white man, I am sure you advised it. You advise all our lives although on the authority of what gods, I do not know.

Pilkings (opens his mouth to reply, then appears to change his mind. Turns to go.   35
    Hesitates and stops again.): Before I leave you, may I ask just one thing of you?

Elesin: I am listening.

Pilkings: I wish to ask you to search the quiet of your heart and tell me—do you not find great contradictions in the wisdom of your own race?

Elesin: Make yourself clear, white one.

Pilkings: I have lived among you long enough to learn a saying or two. One came to my mind tonight when I stepped into the market and saw what was going on. You were surrounded by those who egged you on with song and praises. I thought, are these not the same people who say: the elder grimly approaches heaven and you ask him to bear your greetings yonder; do you really think he makes the journey willingly? After that, I did not hesitate.

(A pause. Elesin sighs. Before he can speak a sound of running feet is heard.)

Jane (off): Simon! Simon!   40

Pilkings: What on earth . . . ! *(Runs off.)*

(Elesin turns to his new Wife, gazes on her for some moments.)

Elesin: My young bride, did you hear the ghostly one? You sit and sob in your silent heart but say nothing to all this. First I blamed the white man, then I blamed my gods for deserting me. Now I feel I want to blame you for the mystery of the sapping of my will. But blame is a strange peace offering for a man to bring a world he has deeply wronged, and to its innocent dwellers. Oh little mother, I have taken countless women in my life but you were more than a desire of the flesh. I needed you as the abyss across which my body must be drawn, I filled it with earth and dropped my seed in it at the moment of preparedness for my crossing. You were the final gift of the living to their emissary to the land of the ancestors, and perhaps your warmth and youth brought new insights of this world to me and turned my feet leaden on this side of the abyss. For I confess to you, daughter, my weakness came not merely from the abomination of the white man who came violently into my fading presence, there was also a weight of longing on my earth-held limbs. I would have shaken it off, already my foot had begun to lift but then, the white ghost entered and all was defiled.

(Approaching voices of Pilkings and his Wife.)

Jane: Oh Simon, you will let her in won't you?

Pilkings: I really wish you'd stop interfering.

(They come into view. Jane is in a dressing-gown. Pilkings is holding a note to which he refers from time to time.)

Jane: Good gracious, I didn't initiate this. I was sleeping quietly, or trying to   45
    anyway, when the servant brought it. It's not my fault if one can't sleep undisturbed even in the Residency.

Pilkings: He'd have done the same thing if we were sleeping at home so don't sidetrack the issue. He knows he can get round you or he wouldn't send you the petition in the first place.

Jane: Be fair Simon. After all he was thinking of your own interests. He is grateful you know, you seem to forget that. He feels he owes you something.

Pilkings: I just wish they'd leave this man alone tonight, that's all.

Jane: Trust him Simon. He's pledged his word it will all go peacefully.

50 *Pilkings:* Yes, and that's the other thing. I don't like being threatened.

Jane: Threatened? *(Takes the note.)* I didn't spot any threat.

Pilkings: It's there. Veiled, but it's there. The only way to prevent serious rioting tomorrow—what a cheek!°

Jane: I don't think he's threatening you Simon.

Pilkings: He's picked up the idiom all right. Wouldn't surprise me if he's been mixing with commies or anarchists over there. The phrasing sounds too good to be true. Damn! If only the Prince hadn't picked this time for his visit.

55 *Jane:* Well, even so Simon, what have you got to lose? You don't want a riot on your hands, not with the Prince here.

Pilkings (going up to Elesin*):* Let's see what he has to say. Chief Elesin, there is yet another person who wants to see you. As she is not a next-of-kin I don't really feel obliged to let her in. But your son sent a note with her, so it's up to you.

Elesin: I know who that must be. So she found out your hiding-place. Well, it was not difficult. My stench of shame is so strong, it requires no hunter's dog to follow it.

Pilkings: If you don't want to see her, just say so and I'll send her packing.

Elesin: Why should I not want to see her? Let her come. I have no more holes in my rag of shame. All is laid bare.

60 *Pilkings:* I'll bring her in. *(Goes off.)*

Jane (hesitates, then goes to Elesin*):* Please, try and understand. Everything my husband did was for the best.

Elesin (he gives her a long strange stare, as if he is trying to understand who she is): You are the wife of the District Officer?

Jane: Yes. My name is Jane.

Elesin: That is my wife sitting down there. You notice how still and silent she sits? My business is with your husband.

(Pilkings returns with Iyaloja.*)*

65 *Pilkings:* Here she is. Now first I want your word of honour that you will try nothing foolish.

Elesin: Honour? White one, did you say you wanted my word of honour?

Pilkings: I know you to be an honourable man. Give me your word of honour you will receive nothing from her.

Elesin: But I am sure you have searched her clothing as you would never dare touch your own mother. And there are these two lizards of yours who roll their eyes even when I scratch.

---

⁵²**what a cheek** British slang: "what nerve"

Pilkings: And I shall be sitting on that tree trunk watching even how you blink. Just the same I want your word that you will not let her pass anything to you.

Elesin: You have my honour already. It is locked up in that desk in which you   70
will put away your report of this night's events. Even the honour of my people you have taken already; it is tied together with those papers of treachery which make you masters in this land.

Pilkings: All right. I am trying to make things easy but if you must bring in politics we'll have to do it the hard way. Madam, I want you to remain along this line and move no nearer to the cell door. Guards! *(They spring to attention.)* If she moves beyond this point, blow your whistle. Come on Jane. *(They go off.)*

Iyaloja: How boldly the lizard struts before the pigeon when it was the eagle itself he promised us he would confront.

Elesin: I don't ask you to take pity on me Iyaloja. You have a message for me or you would not have come. Even if it is the curses of the world, I shall listen.

Iyaloja: You made so bold with the servant of the white king who took your side against death. I must tell your brother chiefs when I return how bravely you waged war against him. Especially with words.

Elesin: I more than deserve your scorn.   75

Iyaloja (with sudden anger): I warned you, if you must leave a seed behind, be sure it is not tainted with the curses of the world. Who are you to open a new life when you dared not open the door to a new existence? I say who are you to make so bold? *(The* Bride *sobs and* Iyaloja *notices her. Her contempt noticeably increases as she turns back to* Elesin.*)* Oh you self-vaunted stem of the plantain, how hollow it all proves. The pith is gone in the parent stem, so how will it prove with the new shoot? How will it go with that earth that bears it? Who are you to bring this abomination on us!

Elesin: My powers deserted me. My charms, my spells, even my voice lacked strength when I made to summon the powers that would lead me over the last measure of earth into the land of the fleshless. You saw it, Iyaloja. You saw me struggle to retrieve my will from the power of the stranger whose shadow fell across the doorway and left me floundering and blundering in a maze I had never before encountered. My senses were numbed when the touch of cold iron came upon my wrists. I could do nothing to save myself.

Iyaloja: You have betrayed us. We fed you sweetmeats such as we hoped awaited you on the other side. But you said No, I must eat the world's left-overs. We said you were the hunter who brought the quarry down; to you belonged the vital portions of the game. No, you said, I am the hunter's dog and I shall eat the entrails of the game and the faeces of the hunter. We said you were the hunter returning home in triumph, a slain buffalo pressing down on his neck; you said wait, I first must turn up this cricket hole with my toes. We said yours was the doorway at which we first spy the tapper° when he comes down from the tree, yours was the blessing of the twilight wine, the purl that brings night spirits out of doors to steal their portion before the light of day.

---

[78]**tapper** a person who collects the milky, sweet liquid from lontar palm trees

We said yours was the body of wine whose burden shakes the tapper like a
sudden gust on his perch. You said, No, I am content to lick the dregs from
each calabash when the drinkers are done. We said, the dew on earth's surface was for you to wash your feet along the slopes of honour. You said No, I
shall step in the vomit of cats and the droppings of mice; I shall fight them for
the left-overs of the world.

Elesin: Enough Iyaloja, enough.

80 *Iyaloja:* We called you leader and oh, how you led us on. What we have no
intention of eating should not be held to the nose.

Elesin: Enough, enough. My shame is heavy enough.

Iyaloja: Wait. I came with a burden.

Elesin: You have more than discharged it.

Iyaloja: I wish I could pity you.

85 *Elesin:* I need neither pity nor the pity of the world. I need understanding. Even
I need to understand. You were present at my defeat. You were part of the
beginnings. You brought about the renewal of my tie to earth, you helped in
the binding of the cord.

Iyaloja: I gave you warning. The river which fills up before our eyes does not
sweep us away in its flood.

Elesin: What were warnings beside the moist contact of living earth between my
fingers? What were warnings beside the renewal of famished embers lodged
eternally in the heart of man. But even that, even if it overwhelmed one
with a thousand-fold temptations to linger a little while, a man could overcome it. It is when the alien hand pollutes the source of will, when a stranger
force of violence shatters the mind's calm resolution, this is when a man is
made to commit the awful treachery of relief, commit in his thought the
unspeakable blasphemy of seeing the hand of the gods in this alien rupture of
his world. I know it was this thought that killed me, sapped my powers and
turned me into an infant in the hands of unnamable strangers. I made to
utter my spells anew but my tongue merely rattled in my mouth. I fingered
hidden charms and the contact was damp; there was no spark left to sever
the life-strings that should stretch from every fingertip. My will was
squelched in the spittle of an alien race, and all because I had committed this
blasphemy of thought—that there might be the hand of the gods in a
stranger's intervention.

Iyaloja: Explain it how you will, I hope it brings you peace of mind. The bush-rat
fled his rightful cause, reached the market and set up a lamentation. "Please
save me!"—are these fitting words to hear from an ancestral mask? "There's a
wild beast at my heels" is not becoming language from a hunter.

Elesin: May the world forgive me.

90 *Iyaloja:* I came with a burden I said. It approaches the gates which are so well
guarded by those jackals whose spittle will from this day be on your food and
drink. But first, tell me, you who were once Elesin Oba, tell me, you who
know so well the cycle of the plantain: is it the parent shoot which withers to
give sap to the younger or, does your wisdom see it running the other way?

Elesin: I don't see your meaning Iyaloja.

Iyaloja: Did I ask you for a meaning? I asked a question. Whose trunk withers to give sap to the other? The parent shoot or the younger?

Elesin: The parent.

Iyaloja: Ah. So you do know that. There are sights in this world which say different Elesin. There are some who choose to reverse the cycle of our being. Oh you emptied bark that the world once saluted for a pith-laden being, shall I tell you what the gods have claimed of you?

(In her agitation she steps beyond the line indicated by Pilkings *and the air is rent by piercing whistles. The two* Guards *also leap forward and place safe-guarding hands on* Elesin. Iyaloja *stops, astonished.* Pilkings *comes racing in, followed by* Jane.)

Pilkings: What is it? Did they try something?   95

Guard: She stepped beyond the line.

Elesin (in a broken voice): Let her alone. She meant no harm.

Iyaloja: Oh Elesin, see what you've become. Once you had no need to open your mouth in explanation because evil-smelling goats, itchy of hand and foot had lost their senses. And it was a brave man indeed who dared lay hands on you because Iyaloja stepped from one side of the earth onto another. Now look at the spectacle of your life. I grieve for you.

Pilkings: I think you'd better leave. I doubt you have done him much good by coming here. I shall make sure you are not allowed to see him again. In any case we are moving him to a different place before dawn, so don't bother to come back.

Iyaloja: We foresaw that. Hence the burden I trudged here to lay beside your   100 gates.

Pilkings: What was that you said?

Iyaloja: Didn't our son explain? Ask that one. He knows what it is. At least we hope the man we once knew as Elesin remembers the lesser oaths he need not break.

Pilkings: Do you know what she is talking about?

Elesin: Go to the gates, ghostly one. Whatever you find there, bring it to me.

Iyaloja: Not yet. It drags behind me on the slow, weary feet of women. Slow as it   105 is Elesin, it has long overtaken you. It rides ahead of your laggard will.

Pilkings: What is she saying now? Christ! Must your people forever speak in riddles?

Elesin: It will come white man, it will come. Tell your men at the gates to let it through.

Pilkings (dubiously): I'll have to see what it is.

Iyaloja: You will. *(Passionately.)* But this is one oath he cannot shirk. White one, you have a king here, a visitor from your land. We know of his presence here. Tell me, were he to die would you leave his spirit roaming restlessly on the surface of earth? Would you bury him here among those you consider less than human? In your land have you no ceremonies of the dead?

Pilkings: Yes. But we don't make our chiefs commit suicide to keep him company.   110

Iyaloja: Child, I have not come to help your understanding. *(Points to* Elesin.*)* This is the man whose weakened understanding holds us in bondage to you. But ask him if you wish. He knows the meaning of a king's passage; he was not born yesterday. He knows the peril to the race when our dead father, who goes as intermediary, waits and waits and knows he is betrayed. He knows when the narrow gate was opened and he knows it will not stay for laggards who drag their feet in dung and vomit, whose lips are reeking of the left-overs of lesser men. He knows he has condemned our King to wander in the void of evil with beings who are enemies of life.

Pilkings: Yes er . . . but look here . . .

Iyaloja: What we ask is little enough. Let him release our King so he can ride on homewards alone. The messenger is on his way on the backs of women. Let him send word through the heart that is folded up within the bolt. It is the least of all his oaths, it is the easiest fulfilled.

(*The* Aide-de-Camp *runs in.*)

Pilkings: Bob?

115 *Aide-de-Camp:* Sir, there's a group of women chanting up the hill.

Pilkings (rounding on Iyaloja*):* If you people want trouble . . .

Jane: Simon, I think that's what Olunde referred to in his letter.

Pilkings: He knows damned well I can't have a crowd here! Damn it, I explained the delicacy of my position to him. I think it's about time I got him out of town. Bob, send a car and two or three soldiers to bring him in. I think the sooner he takes his leave of his father and gets out the better.

Iyaloja: Save your labour white one. If it is the father of your prisoner you want, Olunde, he who until this night we knew as Elesin's son, he comes soon himself to take his leave. He has sent the women ahead, so let them in.

(Pilkings *remains undecided.*)

120 *Aide-de-Camp:* What do we do about the invasion? We can still stop them far from here.

Pilkings: What do they look like?

Aide-de-Camp: They're not many. And they seem quite peaceful.

Pilkings: No men?

Aide-de-Camp: Mm, two or three at the most.

125 *Jane:* Honestly, Simon, I'd trust Olunde. I don't think he'll deceive you about their intentions.

Pilkings: He'd better not. All right then, let them in Bob. Warn them to control themselves. Then hurry Olunde here. Make sure he brings his baggage because I'm not returning him into town.

Aide-de-Camp: Very good, sir. (*Goes.*)

Pilkings (to Iyaloja*):* I hope you understand that if anything goes wrong it will be on your head. My men have orders to shoot at the first sign of trouble.

Iyaloja: To prevent one death you will actually make other deaths? Ah, great is the wisdom of the white race. But have no fear. Your Prince will sleep peacefully. So at long last will ours. We will disturb you no further, servant of the white king. Just let Elesin fulfil his oath and we will retire home and pay homage to our King.

Jane: I believe her Simon, don't you? 130

Pilkings: Maybe.

Elesin: Have no fear ghostly one. I have a message to send my King and then you have nothing more to fear.

Iyaloja: Olunde would have done it. The chiefs asked him to speak the words but he said no, not while you lived.

Elesin: Even from the depths to which my spirit has sunk, I find some joy that this little has been left to me.

(*The* Women *enter, intoning the dirge "Ale le le" and swaying from side to side. On their shoulders is borne a longish object roughly like a cylindrical bolt, covered in cloth. They set it down on the spot where* Iyaloja *had stood earlier, and form a semi-circle round it. The* Praise-Singer *and* Drummer *stand on the inside of the semi-circle but the drum is not used at all. The* Drummer *intones under the* Praise-Singer's *invocations.*)

Pilkings (as they enter): What is that? 135

Iyaloja: The burden you have made white one, but we bring it in peace.

Pilkings: I said *what* is it?

Elesin: White man, you must let me out. I have a duty to perform.

Pilkings: I most certainly will not.

Elesin: There lies the courier of my King. Let me out so I can perform what is 140 demanded of me.

Pilkings: You'll do what you need to do from inside there or not at all. I've gone as far as I intend to with this business.

Elesin: The worshipper who lights a candle in your church to bear a message to his god bows his head and speaks in a whisper to the flame. Have I not seen it ghostly one? His voice does not ring out to the world. Mine are not words for anyone's ears. They are not words even for the bearers of this load. They are words I must speak secretly, even as my father whispered them in my ears and I in the ears of my first-born. I cannot shout them to the wind and the open night-sky.

Jane: Simon . . .

Pilkings: Don't interfere. Please!

Iyaloja: They have slain the favourite horse of the king and slain his dog. They 145 have borne them from pulse to pulse centre of the land receiving prayers for their king. But the rider has chosen to stay behind. Is it too much to ask that he speak his heart to heart of the waiting courier? (Pilkings *turns his back on her.*) So be it. Elesin Oba, you see how even the mere leavings are denied you. (*She gestures to the* Praise-Singer.)

Praise-Singer: Elesin Oba! I call you by that name only this last time. Remember when I said, if you cannot come, tell my horse. (*Pause.*) What? I cannot hear you? I said, if you cannot come, whisper in the ears of my horse. Is your tongue severed from the roots? Elesin? I can hear no response. I said, if there are boulders you cannot climb, mount my horse's back, this spotless black stallion, he'll bring you over them. (*Pauses.*) Elesin Oba, once you had a tongue that darted like a drummer's stick. I said, if you get lost my dog will track a path to me. My memory fails me but I think you replied: My feet have found the path, Alafin.

(The dirge rises and falls.)

I said at the last, if evil hands hold you back, just tell my horse there is weight on the hem of your smock. I dare not wait too long.

(The dirge rises and falls.)

There lies the swiftest ever messenger of a king, so set me free with the errand of your heart. There lie the head and heart of the favourite of the gods, whisper in his ears. Oh my companion, if you had followed when you should, we would not say that the horse preceded its rider. If you had followed when it was time, we would not say the dog has raced beyond and left his master behind. If you had raised your will to cut the thread of life at the summons of the drums, we would not say your mere shadow fell across the gateway and took its owner's place at the banquet. But the hunter, laden with slain buffalo, stayed to root in the cricket's hole with his toes. What now is left? If there is a dearth of bats, the pigeon must serve us for the offering. Speak the words over your shadow which must now serve in your place.

Elesin: I cannot approach. Take off the cloth. I shall speak my message from heart to heart of silence.

Iyaloja (moves forward and removes the covering): Your courier Elesin, cast your eyes on the favoured companion of the King.

(Rolled up in the mat, his head and feet showing at either end, is the body of Olunde.*)*

There lies the honour of your household and of our race. Because he could not bear to let honour fly out of doors, he stopped it with his life. The son has proved the father Elesin, and there is nothing left in your mouth to gnash but infant gums.

Praise-Singer: Elesin, we placed the reins of the world in your hands yet you watched it plunge over the edge of the bitter precipice. You sat with folded arms while evil strangers tilted the world from its course and crashed it beyond the edge of emptiness—you muttered, there is little that one man can do, you left us floundering in a blind future. Your heir has taken the burden on himself. What the end will be, we are not gods to tell. But this young shoot has poured its sap into the parent stalk, and we know this is not the way of life. Our world is tumbling in the void of strangers, Elesin.

(Elesin has stood rock-still, his knuckles taut on the bars, his eyes glued to the body of his son. The stillness seizes and paralyses everyone, including Pilkings *who has turned to look. Suddenly* Elesin *flings one arm round his neck once, and with the loop of the chain, strangles himself in a swift, decisive pull. The* Guards *rush forward to stop him but they are only in time to let his body down.* Pilkings *has leapt to the door at the same time and struggles with the lock. He rushes within, fumbles with the handcuffs and unlocks them, raises the body to a sitting position while he tries to give resuscitation. The* Women *continue their dirge, unmoved by the sudden event.)*

150 *Iyaloja:* Why do you strain yourself? Why do you labour at tasks for which no one, not even the man lying there, would give you thanks? He is gone at last

into the passage but oh, how late it all is. His son will feast on the meat and throw him bones. The passage is clogged with droppings from the King's stallion; he will arrive all stained in dung.

Pilkings (in a tired voice): Was this what you wanted?

Iyaloja: No child, it is what you brought to be, you who play with strangers' lives, who even usurp the vestments of our dead, yet believe that the stain of death will not cling to you. The gods demanded only the old expired plantain but you cut down the sap-laden shoot to feed your pride. There is your board, filled to overflowing. Feast on it. *(She screams at him suddenly, seeing that* Pilkings *is about to close* Elesin*'s staring eyes.)* Let him alone! However sunk he was in debt he is no pauper's carrion abandoned on the road. Since when have strangers donned clothes of indigo° before the bereaved cries out his loss?

(She turns to the Bride *who has remained motionless throughout.)*

Child.

(The girl takes up a little earth, walks calmly into the cell and closes Elesin*'s eyes. She then pours some earth over each eyelid and comes out again.)*

Now forget the dead, forget even the living. Turn your mind only to the unborn.

(She goes off, accompanied by the Bride. *The dirge rises in volume and the* Women *continue their sway. Lights fade to a black-out.)* [1975]

---

¹⁵²**indigo** a dark blue dye often used for mourning clothes

1. The play is based on an actual event in Oyo, a Yoruba city in western Nigeria. Soyinka changed the date by a few years to have the play take place during World War II. What are the consequences of setting it during a major war among Western powers?
2. In his "Author's Note" at the beginning of the published text, Soyinka resists the idea that the play is about "the clash of cultures" because that label "presupposes a potential equality in every given situation of the alien culture and the indigenous, on the actual soil of the latter." Discuss the play's depiction of the relationship between the two cultures in a way that does not assume their equality. Pay careful attention to the different styles in which the characters speak.
3. On what moral basis can one group demand changes in the culture of another? How does the play help us answer that question?
4. Soyinka directs us to "the play's threnodic essence" (paragraph 4). He sees the theme as "largely metaphysical, contained in the human vehicle which is Elesin and the universe of the Yoruba mind—the world of the living, the dead and the unborn, and the numinous passage which links all: transition" (paragraph 5). What is the relationship between the theme of two contrasting cultures and the theme of transition?

5. What is the significance of clothing in the play?
6. What is the effect of our not actually seeing the scene in which Elesin's suicide is prevented? What do we learn about it afterwards? With what consequence for the meaning of the play?
7. What is the significance of the death of Olunde?
8. What is the effect of the visit of the English Prince of Wales?
9. Put the play into the context of Soyinka's life and work.

NONFICTION PROSE

LOUISE M. ANTONY

LOUISE M. ANTONY *(1953–) is a professor of philosophy at Ohio State University. She earned her undergraduate degree at Syracuse University and her Ph.D. at Harvard University. She co-edited the collections* A Mind of One's Own: Feminist Essays on Reason and Objectivity *and* Chomsky and His Critics. *In lively articles such as "Equal Rights for Swamp-Persons," "Sisters, Please, I'd Rather Do It Myself: A Defense of Individualism in Epistemology," and "What Are You Thinking? Character and Content in the Language of Thought," she explores issues having to do with the nature of thought and its relation to human language and the nature-nurture controversies in psychology and feminist theory.*

The "Faith" of an Atheist*

Several years ago, in Raleigh, North Carolina, I attended a debate between the well-known fundamentalist theologian and preacher, William Lane Craig, and my then colleague, a Hobbes° scholar and philosopher of science, Douglas Jesseph.[1] The audience, packed with Christian students bussed in from campuses all over the state, voted to determine the winner. Despite a good showing from the region's infidel-infested philosophy departments, Craig won in a landslide. No surprise; Doug's feelings weren't hurt. But for my daughter, then an eight-year-old evangelical atheist who had been brought up in a home in which a well-wrought counterexample had the power to restore lost television privileges, the verdict was disheartening. "Doug's arguments were better," she pouted, "and they don't even care."

Indeed. Doug's arguments were better, and it was not only the audience who didn't care. Craig himself didn't care. He wasn't trying to persuade the atheists in the audience of anything—instead, his entire presentation was a set piece, a performance designed to reassure the faithful that a Christian could mix it up with a scientifically sophisticated secularist and come out on top. "You don't

[1]You can read a transcript of the debate at http://www.infidels.org/library/modern/doug_jesseph/.

[1][**Thomas] Hobbes** (1588–1679) seventeenth-century British materialist philosopher

*Louise Antony, "The 'Faith' of an Atheist," *Philosophic Exchange*, 32 (2001–2002), 4–17.

have to be embarrassed to be a believer" was the point of the exercise—and whatever Doug said, Craig was going to counter with a reiteration of that message. Craig's favorite tactic was to quote distinguished analytic philosophers to support his pro-God position—sometimes avowedly Christian philosophers, like Alvin Plantinga,° but sometimes—to the great delight of the audience— secularist thinkers whose words Craig would twist to his own purpose.

Now Doug *was* trying to persuade people—or rather, he was trying to make good arguments that would be persuasive to anyone prepared to consider the matter on its merits. He didn't think he had much chance of success, because he didn't think that many people there *were* prepared to consider the matter on its merits. *I* didn't think he had much chance of success either, but for a slightly different reason. I don't want to say that the audience was full of close-minded people. I happen to think that if one has thought very hard for a long time about an issue, and come to some conclusion, then it's unlikely that something one hears in the space of a two hour debate is going to change one's mind. I don't think it necessarily *should* change one's mind.

I am, after all, a philosophy teacher—it's my job to raise puzzling questions about things that students came to my class taking for granted, and I'm good enough at it that I can often raise objections that my students cannot figure out how to answer—at least not in the space of a class period. Indeed, what would I think if a student came up to me after a lecture on skepticism and announced that, on the strength of the considerations raised in class, she had given up a number of her most fundamental beliefs, that she was now genuinely unsure whether she had a body, whether I had a mind, or if the world had been created seven minutes ago, and could I please help? Horrors! The point I generally mean to be making with such lectures is that there's a puzzle to be worked out, a knot to be untied: On the one hand, there are these beliefs that it seems impossible to shed—belief in the external world, in the existence of other minds, in the reality of the past—and on the other hand, there are these apparently good arguments that seem to say that I have no justification for holding on to them. The puzzle doesn't get solved if you just give up and say "OK—you win; I don't know any of those things after all"; it's only a puzzle in the first place because of the fact that giving up these beliefs is not really a practical option. (With this point in mind, let me call attention to Cleanthes's *ad hominem* against the skeptic Philo in Hume's° *Dialogues Concerning Natural Religion*: "Whether your scepticism be as absolute and sincere as you pretend, we shall learn by and by, when the company breaks up: We shall then see, whether you go out at the door or the window."[2]) When we get down to the business of figuring out what we actually

---

[2]David Hume, *Dialogues Concerning Natural Religion* (Indianapolis: Hackett Publishing Company, 1980) Fourth Printing, p. 5.

[2]**Alvin Plantinga** American philosopher who teaches at the University of Notre Dame
[4][David] Hume** (1711–76) eighteenth-century British philosopher known for his secular moral theories. The dialogues are conversations of fictional characters representing differ- ent positions: a religious believer (called Demea), one who defends God on the basis of the argument from design (Cleanthes), and a skeptic (Philo).

think about things, how could a philosophical argument *ever* carry the day against something as banally certain as that I have a body?

5 Now what I think is that for many religious people, belief in God is as basic, as fundamental, and as unassailable as my belief in my own physical reality.[3] I suspect that this was true for many of the audience members the night of that debate. And I imagine that Doug's arguments struck them rather the way I think arguments for skepticism *ought* to strike any sensible person—as puzzles, intellectual exercises, the good of which in this case—though it was certainly not Doug's intention that his arguments would serve this end—would manifest itself, ultimately, in the strengthening of their faith.

OK, but is belief in God really basic in the same way as belief in the external world or belief in other minds? What makes these last two beliefs fundamental is the way in which they are implicated in virtually everything we do and say, on a daily basis. We do, like Hume's Philo, leave rooms by their doors and not by their windows, because we really do believe there are bodies and that, when unsupported by floors or stairs, these bodies fall, and crash to the floor, and that if the crashing body is ours, it will hurt quite a lot. Solipsism—skepticism about other minds—isn't an option, at least for the vast majority of us, because our world is so thoroughly social, and because the only way to negotiate a socially complex world is by treating the people in it as having beliefs, desires, and feelings. Would we ever venture into traffic if we seriously doubted that there were minds controlling those half-ton tin cans rocketing along the streets? Indeed, Philo's response to Cleanthes's challenge was to point out the unliveability of a thorough-going skepticism:

> To whatever length any one may push his speculative principles of scepticism, he must act, I own, and live, and converse, like other men; and for this conduct he is not obliged to give any other reason, than the absolute necessity he lies under of so doing.[4]

Hume is, I believe, pointing to a way of justifying belief that is somewhat different from the kind of evidential or logical justification that we prize so highly in science and philosophy. It is a *pragmatic* justification of belief: it is to say, "believing this is imperative if I am to live the kind of life I want to live, the kind of life that is worth living."[5]

What makes life worth living? I don't pretend to have the definitive list, but see if you don't agree that the following items, at least, ought to be on it:

moral value—a kind of goodness that is different from that which I happen to like or want or feel good about; a kind that is objective in that it belongs to the world, and in the world; a kind that exerts a pull on us to behave in certain ways and not in others.

[3]I thank Amy-Hope Dyson for the suggestion of putting the matter in this light.
[4]Hume, pp. 6–7.
[5]For a discussion of the difference between these two kinds of reasons for believing, see Gilbert Harman, "Pragmatism and Reasons for Belief," in *Reasoning, Meaning, and Mind* (Oxford: Clarendon Press of Oxford University Press, 1999), pp. 93–116.

meaning—something that our lives, and our activities within it, are *for*; a purpose
or significance; something transformative, something to ward off the absurd,
to distinguish the motions and sounds of our bodies from the pointless frenzy
of mindless matter.

love—a depth of feeling for someone, and even for some things, outside
ourselves; the possibility of genuine connection with others, an end to
loneliness.

I'm sure this list is not complete,[6] but it will do for now. Now here's what I
believe theists think: God is the *sine qua non*° of all of these things. It is God who
grounds objective moral value, God who gives meaning and purpose to our
lives, God who is the original and most capacious source of love. This, for theists
is the "absolute necessity" under which they lie: a life worth living requires God.

But I think that theists are inclined to go one step further: it's not just that
God is the ground of morality, meaning, and love—it's that *belief* in God is
necessary for the realization of morality, meaning, and love. They think, in other
words, that there is something additional required for human beings to achieve
a life worth living, namely:

faith—we have need of some kind of sustaining belief that lives worth living are
lives it is *possible* to live. There is a great deal in our experience to threaten
the notion that there is objective moral value in the world, that our
individual existence has worth or value at all, that love can be found.
Something must be there in the background that we can turn to, to reassure
ourselves, even in the face of massive evidence to the contrary, that there is
reason to go on.

Now I agree that *faith*—in the sense I've just laid out—is, as a practical
matter, essential to a life worth living. But in that case, why aren't I a believer?

There are two reasons. The first is that I can't believe something that I don't
believe. Self-deception only takes one so far, and no matter how useful it might
be to me in my everyday life if I could manage it, I simply cannot persuade
myself that there is a God. God seems as fanciful to me as fairies and Santa
Claus. God is a non-starter. But of course, the kind of "persuasion" I seem to be
talking about now lies within the realm of evidence and argument. Didn't I just
explain that there were different ways of justifying belief, and that pragmatic
necessity might, in a certain sense, warrant belief in cases where the belief is
indispensable? Quite so. And that brings me to the second reason: God is not

10

[6]I've left out beauty, that's for sure. But I don't have anything much to say about beauty
vis a vis God. I've also left out truth and knowledge. The issue with these is that I'm not
sure they're real consensus candidates, and in any case, I don't imagine that nearly as
many people think these require God as do the other things on my list, Descartes
notwithstanding. Let me also register the fact that many philosophers reject the conception
of morality presupposed in my characterization of what all of humanity wants. That's as
may be—I'm still betting I've got it right about what we think we need.

[9]*sine qua non* Latin for "without which not," that one thing in any system on which
everything else depends

the *sine qua non*. As it turns out, God has nothing to do with morality, meaning, love or truth. But then what about faith? While it is true that religion has been instrumental in bringing a kind of faith to many human lives, I believe that there is a deeper and more perfect form available to the atheist. Hard to come by, but worth the effort. In the rest of this paper, I'll try to explain why I believe all this.

Let's start with morality. Many, many people believe that without God, there can be no moral value. William Lane Craig says simply: "If God does not exist, then objective moral values do not exist"[7] and he cites the authority of J.L. Mackie° and Friedrich Nietzsche° to back him up. But there's a well-known argument that seems to me to show decisively that this claim is false. The argument comes from Plato's° dialogue *Euthyphro,* which is concerned with the nature of piety. Early on, Socrates asks the morally zealous Euthyphro what piety is. Euthyphro, after some false starts, finally settles on this: piety is that which is pleasing to the gods. Ah, says Socrates, that raises another question: what is the relation between an act's being pious, and its being pleasing to the gods? Specifically: do the gods love the pious acts because they are pious, or are the acts pious because the gods love them? Euthyphro and the average undergraduate find this question pretty confusing, but with some judicious probing, both eventually see what Socrates is getting at.

Translating the question into modern terms, we get this: supposing that there is a God, and that He loves all (morally) good things, is it the case that He loves them because of their (moral) goodness, or is it rather that it is His loving them that makes them good? Is it, in other words, the goodness of various acts, persons, thoughts, and so forth that accounts for God's loving them, or is it the other way around—that in themselves, they are neither good nor bad, but that God's loving them makes them good? Here's an analogy that sometimes works in my classroom, adapted from an example Sally Haslanger developed in a different context: on the supposition that cool people are popular, we might reasonably wonder whether the popularity is due to the coolness, or whether, instead, the coolness is an artifact of the popularity. My own extensive experience as an unpopular, uncool adolescent leads me to think that it's the second—that there are absolutely no constraints on what can turn out to be cool—it depends entirely—even explicitly—on the arbitrary decrees of the popular set. (When *I* first wore clogs in 1967, *I* was a dork. Two months later when Christine Heddleson wore them, they were *in*. Don't get me started.)

15   You see where I'm going with this. If it is the popular people's decrees that make things cool, if it's being loved by the popular that *constitutes* coolness, then

[7]Craig, *op. cit.*

[13]**J.L. Mackie** (1917–81)Australian philosopher   **Friedrich Nietzsche** (1844–1900) German philosopher   **Plato** ancient Greek philosopher (about 427–347 BCE), a student of Athenian philosopher Socrates. Some of his works take the form of dialogues in which a fictionalized Socrates asks an interlocutor (for instance, Euthyphro) probing questions on philosophical issues.

it is, in an important way, *arbitrary* what's cool and what's not. It's to say that the popular have no *reasons* for the decreeing one thing rather than another. For if they had reasons—if there were something about the things they choose in virtue of which those things are cool, then it would be *those other* properties that constituted the coolness, not the mere decree of the popular.

So suppose someone wants to defend this line, to deny that cool is constituted by the consensus of the popular, and affirm that it is constituted instead by some property that cool things have independently of what the popular decide. It might be thought that taking this position involves rejecting the generalization with which we began, viz., that the popular and the cool coincide. For after all, one might reason, if the popular don't simply determine what's cool, if what's cool is independent of them, isn't there the possibility of their making a mistake, of getting it wrong whether something is cool or not? Well, making coolness an independently existing property does give it a kind of independence from the judgments of the popular, but this is consistent with the popular people always being correct in their judgments of coolness: It's perfectly possible that coolness, being, as it were, *cool,* leads naturally to popularity. We can even add to the story the detail that the popular are, as a matter of objective fact, excellent cool-detectors. We can *rely* on the judgments of the popular to guide us in selecting the cool. That is why, in fact, the judgments of the popular so reliably coincide with the facts about what's cool.

There are clear lessons here: as with the popular, so with God. (If there is a God, He is in all things. Including high school.) If, on the one hand, the theist insists that God is literally the *source* of goodness, that it is God's decree that renders anything good or bad, she is saying, in effect, that God's judgments are not really judgments—they are arbitrary stipulations. "Today I shall wear red and ban murder." Why *arbitrary?* Because: as in the case of judgments about the cool, if God's judgments about what is morally permissible and what is not are *not* arbitrary, then they are based on something. And then there must be something present in the thing, antecedent to God's judgment, that determines it to be good or bad. In other words, if the things God is choosing among are not *already* good or bad, prior to His choice, how could He be properly said to *choose* among them?

So to say that God chooses, and does not capriciously stipulate, is to concede that goodness and badness exist prior to, and thus independently of, God's decision. And again, as in the case of cool, this position does not conflict with the claim that what God chooses precisely coincides with what is morally good. It simply requires that we take the position that God is a perfect moral agent; that he is absolutely reliable when it comes to telling the good from the bad.

I think this is a real knock-down argument; I'd love to know if anyone can think of an objection to it. But beyond it's being a knock-down argument, I think it shows something important for religious faith. I think that theists especially should take the second of these two views about God and the good, viz., the view that moral good is inherently good, and that God, being Himself perfectly good, prefers it. To accept instead the view that goodness is constituted by God's preferring it seems to me to be a kind of insult to God. This non-recommended view, by the way, is called "divine command theory," and it has long seemed to me that if divine command theory is true, then God is a petty tyrant, and our attempts at living moral lives are ridiculous. Imagine a parent who arbitrarily chooses foods—not on the basis of their palatability, or their nutritional value, but randomly—and commands her child to eat those and only those foods, and punishes the child if [he or she disobeys]. A parent who did this would rightly be thought abusive. If she derived any amusement or satisfaction from watching her child struggle to eat the foods she happened to select, she would be a monster. But how would such a parent be any different from a God who randomly decrees that his creatures shall do this and shall not do that? The only way to maintain a conception of a truly just and loving God, I contend, is to accept that moral value exists independently of God's will.

20   Consider the story of Abraham and Isaac.° This has always bothered me. Here is Abraham, a man deprived of children until his dotage, then finally granted a single son. He loves the child fiercely. Now what happens? God, with whom Abraham has made a pact, demands that Abraham slaughter this son, as a sacrifice. The traditional interpretation of this demand is that God was testing Abraham's faith. This is, I think, pretty harsh, but it's not the part that really bothers me. What really bothers me is that Abraham is prepared to do it—he's prepared to kill his beloved son—*and that that counts as passing the test.* Huh??? Why is God so pleased? What righteous being wants loyalty like that? Here's the way I would have liked the story to go instead: God says, "Abraham, you must sacrifice your only son to me" and Abraham says, "I don't know who you are, buster, but you sure aren't God—God would never ask me to do anything wrong, much less something as grotesquely, outrageously wrong as this." And *then* God would be pleased.

     The Abraham story raises another problem for the theist who wants to ground morality in God's commands, and that is the *epistemological* problem of knowing *what God's commands are*. It must be conceded all around, I think, that God has not made Himself entirely clear on this point. There is—to put it mildly—some disagreement about what is, and what is not, the will of God. Being a person of the book doesn't help a great deal; for one thing, there is more than one book, and more than one view about how many books there are. Moreover, the book(s) is(are) written in languages that few contemporary theists know anything about. In point of fact, and despite the protestations of some fundamentalists, the understanding of the sacred texts possessed by the majority of those who consider themselves Jews or Christians is one that has been heavily filtered through translation, interpretation, and inference, so that there can be no credible pretence for any but the most erudite scholars that one knows, never mind believes, the literal Word of God. Moreover, the most potent interpretative tool at the religious person's disposal is, I submit, the following dictum: interpret God's commands so that He comes out commanding what is, in fact, good. I see this at work over and over again, whenever religious people of conscience try to come to grips with some new moral challenge to their particular orthodoxy: feminism, gay rights, abortion, premarital sex, euthanasia—the procedure is the same—figure out what's right, attribute that to God.

[20]**Abraham and Isaac** Hebrew Bible, Genesis 12

So here's where I think things stand on the matter of moral value: it is not only not required that there be a God in order for there to be objective moral value; it is (ironically) a more pious approach to theism to assume the existence of an independent moral order. And assuming that the moral order is independent of God's commands, one obtains the additional pay-off that one has at least some hope of determining what it is that God wants.

On to meaning.

What is it that we want when we want our lives to have meaning? To answer this question, I think we need to start small. What are the kinds of examples we might give from everyday life to illustrate what it is to have meaning? One kind of meaning is "sentimental value." I don't consider this to be a trivial kind of meaning. The things in our lives to which we attach sentimental value are things that serve as tangible reminders of people, events, places that are important to us. In helping us remember, they keep us connected with our pasts; they help us, as some academicians say, to construct a narrative of our lives. They can also serve to revive those feelings that enliven us: the flush of excitement at the beginning of a love affair, the tenderness with which we viewed our newborn child. So "sentimental value" is a kind of meaning that matters to self-conscious creatures, creatures who reflect upon and order their experiences.

Another kind of meaning is purpose. We feel that our actions are meaningful when they are directed at some purpose. If we think that some activities are more meaningful than others, it is often because some activities are done for the sake of something. Notably, we tend to ascribe purpose even to some purposeless activities, activities, that is, that are performed for their own sake, and not for the sake of something else: Reflecting on our needs, as animal creatures, for rest, amusement, and pleasure, we invent the dummy concept, "wellbeing," for which we then "need" relaxation, play and sex. So another kind of meaning is the kind that is invested in those things that further some end of ours.

Both these kinds of meaning are what we might call "agent-centered"—they advert to the values or goals of an agent. But there may be another kind of meaning, one that is not agent-centered. The creation of something beautiful, the discovery of something interesting, the achievement of something morally grand—these are all meaningful accomplishments. Their meanings derive from the inherent value of beauty, knowledge, and goodness. Things done "for the sake of" these or some other value are not exactly things done for the sake of something else—it's not like "the Good" has a set of interests which our morally praiseworthy actions help to further. Nor is it that we perform morally good actions as a means to obtaining the Good. A morally good action *is* good. Morally good actions are meaningful because they are good.

Still, one might wonder, would this kind of meaning exist if there were no agents? Is this another kind of agent-centered value after all? I really don't know what to say about beauty, because I'm not sure that aesthetic value does not in some way derive from the discriminative capacities of sentient creatures. Knowledge cannot exist without knowers, so if knowledge is valuable, there must be agents around. Ditto for moral value—the value can be absolute, but there will be no instantiations of it unless there are moral agents.

One more point: the agent-centered values of the second sort—the ones where meaning comes from the fact that one is furthering some purpose—may now appear in a new light. Actions done for a purpose, cannot, if they are to be meaningful, be done for just any old purpose—they must be done for a purpose that bottoms out, either in something that is meaningful to me, the agent, or else in something that is valuable in an agent-independent way. Studying at college is meaningful, perhaps, because doing so will enable one to become a doctor. Being a doctor is a meaningful occupation because it helps people. Helping people is inherently valuable.

Significantly, many of us look for meaning in our occupations; we want the purpose of our work to be something more than merely keeping us alive. Famously, Marx° contended that one of the forms of alienation distinctive of capitalism was the worker's "alienation from his species being." By this Marx meant that work—that which should express the worker's distinctively human capacity to transform matter in accordance with his own intentions—becomes the mere means to keep the worker animal alive: one works to live instead of living to work.

30   So in everyday affairs, we can find the following sources of meaning: our own interests and values, whatever they happen to be, and the things we recognize as valuable in their own right: moral goodness, knowledge, and so forth. That's quite a lot of meaning, when you think of it. Why do we need more? Why do so many people seem to have the feeling that if that's all there is, then there'd be no point in going on? Why aren't these sources of meaning—which are, after all, what most of us rely on most of the time—enough? It may be that there's a fallacy in the air: one might think that, if meaning is attached to activities when they are done for some purpose, then there must be some ultimate purpose for which everything is done, on pain of infinite regress. But we've already seen that there is no threat of regress. As long as there are *some* sources of inherent value, the meaning of activities done for the sake of something can be grounded. There doesn't have to be the same grounded source of meaning for every activity.

But leave that aside. Suppose we could make out the case for some kind of ultimate meaning, the Mother of all meaning, the source of all value that grounds all instrumentally important things. Why think that that could be God?

What are the possibilities here? One is that God, as an agent, has purposes, and that it therefore gives my life meaning to try to fulfill them. But in ordinary life, we do not generally think that the mere fact that someone else has some purpose—getting in shape to run a marathon, for example—has implications for what will be meaningful in our lives. That's not to say that we do not do things for the sake of others. Indeed we do, and "other people" should go on the list of

[29][**Karl**] **Marx** (1818–83) economic and political theorist who described historical changes as the result of the conflict between segments of society or classes with different relationships to the instruments and raw materials to create the goods of a society. In modern capitalist industrial societies, the bourgeoisie (as opposed to the state or government) owns the means of production (e.g., factories) as private property and members of the proletariat (workers) sell their labor to the owners for wages.

sources of inherent meaning. And we do, also, sometimes devote ourselves to an agenda set by someone else, as when we work for someone's campaign. But in those cases, it is not the fact that we are doing something for someone else's purposes that carries the significance—rather it's the value of the objective that makes the work important. And it doesn't matter for this issue whether the value attaching to the goal is inherent, or derivative from interests of one's own. If I decide to dedicate my fortunes to helping the career of the world's leading tiddly winks player, and her career flourishes as a result of my investment, then I'm getting good value for my money—I'm getting meaning. Still—to return to the main point—*my* determination to make tiddly winks an Olympic sport doesn't give *you* any reason to support my efforts. Enthusiasms of this sort are idiosyncratic; my having such an enthusiasm gives no reason for anyone else to have it, too.

So if God's purposes are similarly idiosyncratic, it's difficult to see why one should feel one's life would be more meaningful if one fulfilled God's purposes than if one "merely" fulfilled one's own. But now it will surely be objected that God is different; He's not just any old "other person." In particular, God doesn't have purposes that are capricious or idiosyncratic. We can count on God to have *good* purposes, purposes that involve the creation of beauty and the development of our distinctive capacities. But now we're back in the company of Euthyphro. If the reason that fulfilling God's purposes gives meaning to our lives is that His purposes are inherently excellent, then the fact that they are *God's* purposes plays no essential role—the excellence of the purposes stands alone.

One other reason that people might feel that life would be meaningless without God is that they are troubled by the extreme transiency of our achievements, indeed of our lives. One hundred years from now, who will remember this? Who will remember me? God, that's who. God, being eternal, is always available for recognizing and appreciating. God will always remember our good works, even after our sun has super-nova'ed. But I'm not sure why this thought should be particularly comforting. The assumption underlying it seems to me to be disturbing—the assumption is that it's pointless to care about things that are going to go away. I think quite the reverse is true—loving something, caring about it, despite knowing that it will not always be with you (or that you will no longer be with it) seems to me to represent a particular kind of courage. I can only imagine the bravery of parents to whom are born extremely ill or congenitally afflicted children, who must commit their hearts fully to a person who they know may be with them only a short time. Surely the value of that which is valuable—and what is more valuable than a person?—is not a function of how long the valuable thing survives. While it's there, it's there, and it can ground meaning as well as anything else.

What about love?

For most, if not all, human beings, love is a necessity. This is true in the most straightforward, literal way, as well as in deeper ways. We are a species with a long period of immaturity. It is not until we are four years old or so that we can do even the most minimally necessary things for ourselves, and even then, of course, we would be extremely vulnerable without the protection of an adult. (The more complex our societies become, the longer the period of functional immaturity.) What, except love, would induce adults to devote to—it must be said—largely ungrateful juveniles the immense amount of care and attention necessary to bring these juveniles to the point of even probable self-sufficiency? (Someone's going to bring up evolution at this point—adults don't *really* love their children, they'll say; what we call "love" is simply an adaptive response that functions to ensure the preservation of our gene-carriers. Such claims evince a confusion: even if it's true that natural selection *explains why* we love, it hardly shows *thereby,* that there's no such thing as love.)

Of course, parental love is not the only form of love; there is also romantic love, and the kind of love involved in deep friendships. We also seem to be capable of, and to thrive on, a kind of love of or for abstractions—we at least express love-like feelings for such things as countries and principles. And as we give love, so do we seem to want—need—to receive love. "Unrequited love" is the stock-in-trade of human drama; reciprocity is a part of the ideal, if not always the reality, of love.

But love turns out to be difficult to obtain, and once obtained, fragile. The things we love, are, for the most part, mortal. The prospect of losing a loved one is sometimes so painful that people choose not to love at all (at least if the pop psychology books are to be believed). Alternatively, some people become so desperate for love that they endure humiliation and even physical abuse for the sake of some few crumbs of something that can pass, now and then, for love.

I suggest that one of the reasons that the need for love is so powerful among human beings is that love confirms one's own *value*. If I am loved, then I am love*able*. If I am a source of meaning for someone else, then I am a source of meaning, *simpliciter*.° Being loved by someone else, particularly by someone whom one loves in return, provides a short route to this knowledge, and an argument the force of which can be felt in the gut. If I was right before, if human beings are valuable in themselves, then perhaps this sort of demonstration shouldn't be necessary. But life being as it is, and humans being as we are, the proposition that we are each inherently valuable can be hard to really grasp, absent the testimony provided by the caring gaze of another person.

40 Another thing that can make it difficult to remember that one is inherently valuable is the fact that we are, each of us, flawed. We're ugly, or we're fat, or we have bad skin; we have a tendency to lie our way out of a tight spot, we drink too much, we're lazy; we disappoint our spouses, we don't spend enough time with our kids. In short, we're just not nearly as good as we'd like to be. Every day, it may seem, brings new evidence that we are *not,* in fact, lovable. So in light of our many faults, how much less likely is love?

How wonderful, then, if there were someone *guaranteed* to love us; and how much more wonderful if that someone was guaranteed to exist! To be always there, faithful and unchanging in His love. And how superlatively wonderful if the wonderfulness of this perfect Lover were also guaranteed. To be loved by the

---

[39]*simpliciter* Latin for "simply" or "naturally"

most perfect Being possible—how could one doubt one's lovableness in the face of such affection?

So it's not mysterious why mere mortals might wish for a God. The problem comes in getting from the wish to the belief. After all, it's not immediately evident, if one looks around at the variety of ills that routinely afflict us, that any such universal lover exists. This is a "loving parent," after all, who punishes the dutiful alongside—indeed, sometimes instead of—the perverse. Being the beneficiary of divine love, therefore, does not ensure that anyone will experience *any* of the comforts that normally flow from the human variety. I may have the Cause of Being in my corner, but this does not mean that I won't get sucker-punched in the very next round.

Now I am, in a way, raising the familiar "problem of evil," but for a different purpose than is usual.[8] I am not now raising it in order to question the possibility of a loving and omnipotent God, nor even to suggest that we lack good evidence for the existence of such a God. Rather, I am raising a question about the phenomenology of the experience of "Divine love." From the point of view of our ordinary expectations, if God were a husband, many of us would be battered wives. God loves us all, we're told. But in that case, it must be consistent with God's love that we be abandoned, starved, maimed, gassed by Nazis, bombed by Americans. Knowing that, how does belief in God's love *sustain* anyone?[9] When I pose this sort of question to my religious friends (yes, some of my best friends . . .) they tell me, with or without a condescending smile, that the effect of God's love on their lives is different from the kind of effect I'm looking for. The word they use, again and again, is "transformation." Knowing that God loves them, they say, changes them so that they see the world differently, so that they see other people differently. Sometimes they put this in terms of "grace"—awareness of God's love, they say, is an awareness of the world *as infused with* God's grace.

Often—not always, but often enough—when I listen to these people talk in this way, and when I reflect on their lives, and on their way of being in the world, I begin to see something of what they're talking about. I see people with, first, a real capacity for joy, and second, with a kind of equilibrium, a steadiness in the midst of the turmoil into which life is constantly erupting. I see sensitive and perceptive people—people who do not deny the reality of pain, but are not dominated by their consciousness of it. Above all, I see in these people a caring regard for *other* people—a sustained appreciation of the human that is not predicated on individual achievements or merits, an attitude as close as any human attitude can come to unconditional love.

I believe the Christian term for this is *agape,* and its possibility seems to me to be the single best prudential argument for religion that could ever be made. But

45

---

[8]This is the problem of reconciling the perfect benevolence and omnipotence of God with the existence of suffering.

[9]It's like Joni Mitchell says in her song "The Last Time I Saw Richard": "I am as constant as the Northern Star"/"Constant in the darkness?/Where's that at?/If you want me, I'll be in the bar."

even this argument is not good enough. One of the things I've realized over the years as I've been engaged in peace work together with religious people is that the kind of transformation they ascribe to their apprehension of Divine love is due, really, to their own efforts. Everything that they see in this mortal world that moves them, everything that testifies, in their minds, to God's loving nature, has been there all the time. The "transformation" they experience is self-induced: it amounts to a willful alteration of focus, an enlargement of the capacity for attention. They become people who *choose to see* what there is to value in other people, and to fend off the distractions amply provided by our all-too-human failings.

Why, after all, is it said that God created human beings in "His own image"? It cannot be that human beings had first come to know God's nature, and then saw it reflected in themselves. No theologian would be so impious as to suggest that: if it is not an article of faith that God's nature is unknowable, it is still reckoned to be, in its fullness, beyond human comprehension. Rather (as I believe the standard story goes), we find in *ourselves* qualities, or least potentialities, that we can recognize as having transcendent value, and as being, in this way, divine. When our grasp of these qualities—our subjectivity, our ability to generate meaning by creating ends, our capacity for joy and for pain, our awareness of a world around us, and above all, our ability to apprehend that our fellow human beings also possess these qualities—when our grasp of all this becomes sure and reliable, then we *do* come to see the world in a new way.

The ability to "love" other people in this special and somewhat peculiar sense of "love" gives rise, I think, to an ability to love ourselves. By that I mean: when we become fully alive to the humanity of every person, when we become able to see every person as—in Kantian° terms—an end in [him- or herself], then we become able to see and appreciate ourselves in the same way. (One religious basis for objecting to suicide is that it is the destruction of one of God's children, something no one of us has the right to do. This reasoning seems to me insightful, if not terribly helpful to the despondent person.) What I have in mind is the development of a *habit* of sympathy, a recognition that we all come into this world equipped, to a large extent, with the same basic equipment, and responsible to the same set of basic imperatives. If we can come to see how, for example, rude behavior can be the result of frustration, exhaustion, disappointment, anxiety, ignorance, or even just a poverty of spirit, then we can begin to see acts of rudeness committed against us in something like the light in which we are accustomed to viewing and excusing such acts when we commit them ourselves. And it works the other way, too: if we are harsher on ourselves than on others, a habit of agape can remind us that we are, ourselves, "only human"—no more obliged to be perfect than the next person. "Forgive us our trespasses as we forgive those who trespass against us": an appeal and a resolution at the same time.

The vulnerabilities that I spoke of earlier, may, perhaps, be mitigated to a large extent if this view of persons can be cultivated and maintained. The assurance that one is, at core, a valuable thing, worthy of respect and care, can

°⁴⁷**Kantian** principles derived from the work of German philosopher Immanuel Kant (1724–1804)

be sustaining even if one cannot achieve or preserve all of the more familiar loving relationships one might wish for.

This, then, is the "faith" of an atheist: the sustaining belief that humankind is worth something. It is not a belief based on wishful thinking, but based instead on a clearheaded recognition of both the potentialities and limitations inherent in this human life. And it has this advantage over theistic faith: it is not hostage to the truth of a myth. There is nothing that I need believe that goes beyond evidence that lies plainly about me, that may be threatened by the latest discoveries of science or of history. It is, I claim, the firmest faith of all.   [2002]

1. What is Antony's purpose in the essay? Compare it with her claim about Jesseph's purpose in the debate on the existence of God and Antony's own purpose in her philosophy classes.
2. What are Antony's main claims and how does she support them?
3. How does the analogy between cool/uncool and right/wrong (paragraphs 14–19) work?
4. What has your relationship to popular trends been? Have you started any? Have you joined any? From whom did you take your cues? If you were "the first on your block" to wear or do something, what determined that choice? Do you consider yourself a leader? If no one followed your lead, did you stick with it anyway?
5. How would you define Antony's *ethos*? How does it relate to her style and her target audience? What is the effect of her phrase, "infidel-infested philosophy departments" (paragraph 1)?

KAREN ARMSTRONG

KAREN ARMSTRONG *(1945–), author, teacher, and lecturer, is the author of the* New York Times *bestseller,* A History of God. *Karen Armstrong took vows as a Roman Catholic nun at seventeen and left her order seven years later. Her 2004 memoir about this experience is* The Spiral Staircase: My Climb Out of Darkness. *She earned her degree at Oxford University and taught modern literature and has now become one of the foremost British commentators on religious affairs. She teaches at London's Leo Baeck College for the Study of Judaism and the Training of Rabbis and Teachers. She is also an honorary member of the Association of Muslim Social Sciences. Her books include:* The Gospel According to Women, Holy War, *and* Muhammad: A Biography of the Prophet. *The following excerpt is from Chapter 1 of her book,* Buddha.

From *Renunciation**

One night toward the end of the sixth century B.C.E., a young man called Siddhatta Gotama walked out of his comfortable home in Kapilavatthu in

*Karen Armstrong, "Renunciation," in *Buddha: A Penguin Life* (New York: Viking Book, 1991), 1–19.

the foothills of the Himalayas and took to the road.[1] We are told that he was twenty-nine years old. His father was one of the leading men of Kapilavatthu and had surrounded Gotama with every pleasure he could desire; he had a wife and a son who was only a few days old, but Gotama had felt no pleasure when the child was born. He had called the little boy Rāhula, or "fetter": the baby, he believed, would shackle him to a way of life that had become abhorrent.[2] He had a yearning for an existence that was "wide open" and as "complete and pure as a polished shell," but even though his father's house was elegant and refined, Gotama found it constricting, "crowded" and "dusty." A miasma of petty tasks and pointless duties sullied everything. Increasingly he had found himself longing for a lifestyle that had nothing to do with domesticity, and which the ascetics of India called "homelessness."[3] The thick luxuriant forests that fringed the fertile plain of the Ganges river° had become the haunt of thousands of men and even a few women who had all shunned their families in order to seek what they called "the holy life" (*brahmacariya*), and Gotama had made up his mind to join them.

It was a romantic decision, but it caused great pain to the people he loved. Gotama's parents, he recalled later, wept as they watched their cherished son put on the yellow robe that had become the uniform of the ascetics and shave his head and beard.[4] But we are also told that before he left, Sidhatta stole upstairs, took one last look at his sleeping wife and son, and crept away without saying goodbye.[5] It is almost as though he did not trust himself to hold true to his resolve should his wife beg him to stay. And this was the nub of the problem, since, like many of the forest-monks, he was convinced that it was his attachment to things and people which bound him to an existence that seemed mired in pain and sorrow. Some of the monks used to compare this kind of passion and craving for perishable things to a "dust" which weighed the soul down and prevented it from soaring to the pinnacle of the universe. This may have been what Siddhatta meant when he described his home as "dusty." His father's house was not dirty, but it was filled with people who pulled at his heart and with objects that he treasured. If he wanted to live in holiness, he had to cut these fetters and break free. Right from the start, Siddhatta Gotama took it for granted that family life was incompatible with the highest forms of spirituality. It was a perception shared not only by the other ascetics of India, but also by

[1]The date of Gotama's birth and "Going Forth" are now disputed. Western scholars once imagined that he had been born in about 563 and would, therefore, have left home in about 534, but recent scholarship indicates that Gotama could have left home as late as 450 B.C.E. Heinz Berchant, "The Date of the Buddha Reconsidered," *Indologia Taurinensin*, 10.

[2]Gotama's son was called Rāhula, which has traditionally been understood to mean "fetter." Some modern scholarship has questioned this derivation.

[3]*Majjhima Nikāya*, 36, 100.

[4]Ibid., 26, 36, 85, 100.

[5]*Jātaka*, I:62.

°**Ganges river** major river of the Indian subcontinent

Jesus, who would later tell potential disciples that they must leave their wives and children and abandon their aged relatives if they wanted to follow him.[6]

Gotama would not, therefore, have agreed with our current cult of "family values." Nor would some of his contemporaries or near-contemporaries in other parts of the world, such as Confucius° (551–479) and Socrates° (469–399), who were certainly not family-minded men, but who would, like Gotama himself, become key figures in the spiritual and philosophical development of humanity during this period. Why this rejectionism? The later Buddhist scriptures would evolve elaborate mythological accounts of Gotama's renunciation of domesticity and his "Going Forth" into homelessness, and we shall consider these later in this chapter. But the earlier texts of the Pāli Canon give a starker version of the young man's decision. When he looked at human life, Gotama could see only a grim cycle of suffering, which began with the trauma of birth and proceeded inexorably to "aging, illness, death, sorrow and corruption."[7] He himself was no exception to this universal rule. At present he was young, healthy and handsome, but whenever he reflected on the suffering that lay ahead, all the joy and confidence of youth drained out of him. His luxurious lifestyle seemed meaningless and trivial. He could not afford to feel "revolted" when he saw a decrepit old man or somebody who was disfigured by a loathsome illness. The same fate—or something even worse—would befall him and everybody he loved.[8] His parents, his wife, his baby son and his friends were equally frail and vulnerable. When he clung to them and yearned tenderly toward them, he was investing emotion in what could only bring him pain. His wife would lose her beauty, and little Rāhula could die tomorrow. To seek happiness in mortal, transitory things was not only irrational: the suffering in store for his loved ones as well as for himself cast a dark shadow over the present and took away all his joy in these relationships.

But why did Gotama see the world in such bleak terms? Mortality is a fact of life that is hard to bear. Human beings are the only animals who have to live with the knowledge that they will die one day, and they have always found this vision of extinction difficult to contemplate. But most of us manage to find some solace in the happiness and affection that is also part of the human experience. Some people simply bury their heads in the sand and refuse to think about the sorrow of the world, but this is an unwise course, because, if we are entirely unprepared, the tragedy of life can be devastating. From the very earliest times, men and women devised religions to help them cultivate a sense that our existence has some ultimate meaning and value, despite the dispiriting evidence

[6]Luke 9:57–62; 14:25–27; 18:28–30.
[7]*Majjhima Nikāya*, 26.
[8]*Aṇguttara Nikāya*, 3:38.

[3]**Confucius** Chinese philosopher, whose teachings, collected in the *Analects*, influences much Chinese thought on ethics, society, and government **Socrates** Ancient Greek philosopher whose method of teaching through dialogue used critical reasoning to question commonly held assumptions. We have no writings of his, but through the work of his contemporaries like Aristophanes and Xenophon and his student Plato, he helped to establish the foundations of Western philosophy.

to the contrary. But sometimes the myths and practices of faith seem incredible. People then turn to other methods of transcending the sufferings and frustrations of daily life: to art, music, sex, drugs, sport or philosophy. We are beings who fall very easily into despair, and we have to work very hard to create within ourselves a conviction that life is good, even though all around us we see pain, cruelty, sickness and injustice. When he decided to leave home, Gotama, one might think, appeared to have lost this ability to live with the unpalatable facts of life and to have fallen prey to a profound depression.

5   Yet that was not the case. Gotama had indeed become disenchanted with domestic life in an ordinary Indian household, but he had not lost hope in life itself. Far from it. He was convinced that there was a solution to the puzzle of existence, and that he could find it. Gotama subscribed to what has been called the "perennial philosophy," because it was common to all peoples in all cultures in the premodern world.[9] Earthly life was obviously fragile and overshadowed by death, but it did not constitute the whole of reality. Everything in the mundane world had, it was thought, its more powerful, positive replica in the divine realm. All that we experienced here below was modeled on an archetype in the celestial sphere; the world of the gods was the original pattern of which human realities were only a pale shadow. This perception informed the mythology, ritual and social organizations of most of the cultures of antiquity and continues to influence more traditional societies in our own day. It is a perspective that is difficult for us to appreciate in the modern world, because it cannot be proved empirically and lacks the rational underpinning which we regard as essential to truth. But the myth does express our inchoate sense that life is incomplete and that this cannot be all there is; there *must* be something better, fuller and more satisfying elsewhere. After an intense and eagerly awaited occasion, we often feel that we have missed something that remains just outside our grasp. Gotama shared this conviction, but with an important difference. He did not believe that this "something else" was confined to the divine world of the gods; he was convinced that he could make it a demonstrable reality in this mortal world of suffering, grief and pain.

Thus, he reasoned to himself, if there was "birth, aging, illness, death, sorrow and corruption" in our lives, these sufferings states must have their positive counterparts; there must be another mode of existence, therefore, and it was up to him to find it. "Suppose," he said, "I start to look for the *un*born, the *un*aging, *un*ailing, death*less*, sorrow*less*, *in*corrupt and supreme freedom from this bondage?" He called this wholly satisfactory state Nibbāṇa ("blowing out").[10] Gotama was convinced that it was possible to "extinguish" the passions, attachments and delusions that cause human beings so much pain, rather as we snuff out a flame. To attain Nibbāṇa would be similar to the "cooling" we

[9]Mircea Eliade, *The Myth of the Eternal Return or Cosmos and History* (trans. Willard J. Trask), Princeton, NJ, 1954.
[10]*Majjhima Nikāya*, 26.

experience after we recover from a fever: in Gotama's time, the related adjective *nibbuta* was a term in daily use to describe a convalescent. So Gotama was leaving home to find a cure for the sickness that plagues humanity and which fills men and women with unhappiness. This universal suffering which makes life so frustrating and miserable was not something that we were doomed to bear forever. If our experience of life was currently awry, then, according to the law of archetypes, there must be another form of existence that was *not* contingent, flawed and transient. "There *is* something that has not come to birth in the usual way, which has neither been created and which remains undamaged," Gotama would insist in later life. "If it did not exist, it would be impossible to find a way out."[11]

A modern person may smile at the naïveté of this optimism, and find the myth of eternal archetypes wholly incredible. But Gotama would claim that he *did* find a way out and that Nibbāna did, therefore, exist. Unlike many religious people, however, he did not regard this panacea as supernatural. He did not rely on divine aid from another world, but was convinced that Nibbāna was a state that was entirely natural to human beings and could be experienced by any genuine seeker. Gotama believed that he could find the freedom he sought right in the midst of this imperfect world. Instead of waiting for a message from the gods, he would search within himself for the answer, explore the furthest reaches of his mind, and exploit all his physical resources. He would teach his disciples to do the same, and insisted that nobody must take his teaching on hearsay. They must validate his solutions empirically, in their own experience, and find for themselves that his method really worked. They could expect no help from the gods. Gotama believed that gods existed, but was not much interested in them. Here again, he was a man of his time and culture. The people of India had worshipped gods in the past: Indra, the god of war; Varuna, the guardian of the divine order; Agni, the fire god. But by the sixth century, these deities had begun to recede from the religious consciousness of the most thoughtful people. They were not exactly regarded as worthless, but they had become unsatisfactory as objects of worship. Increasingly, people were aware that the gods could not provide them with real and substantial help. The sacrifices performed in their honor did not in fact alleviate human misery. More and more men and women decided that they must rely entirely on themselves. They believed that the cosmos was ruled by impersonal laws to which even the gods were subject. Gods could not show Gotama the way to Nibbāna; he would have to depend upon his own efforts.

Nibbāna was not, therefore, a place like the Christian Heaven to which a believer would repair after death. Very few people in the ancient world at this point hoped for a blissful immortality. Indeed, by Gotama's day, the people of India felt imprisoned eternally in their present painful mode of existence, as we can see from the doctrine of reincarnation, which had become widely accepted

[11]*Udāna*, 8:3.

by the sixth century. It was thought that a man or a woman would be reborn after death into a new state that would be determined by the quality of their actions (*kamma*) in their present life. Bad *kamma* would mean that you would be reborn as a slave, an animal or a plant; good *kamma* would ensure a better existence next time: you could be reborn as a king or even as a god. But rebirth in one of the heavens was not a happy ending, because divinity was no more permanent than any other state. Eventually, even a god would exhaust the good *kamma* which had divinized him; he would then die and be reborn in a less advantageous position on earth. All beings were, therefore, caught up in an endless cycle of *saṃsāra* ("keeping going"), which propelled them from one life to another. It sounds like a bizarre theory to an outsider, but it was a serious attempt to address the problem of suffering, and can be seen as inherently more satisfactory than attributing human fate to the frequently erratic decisions of a personalized god, who often seems to ensure that the wicked prosper. The law of *kamma* was a wholly impersonal mechanism that applied fairly and without discrimination to everybody. But the prospect of living one life after another filled Gotama, like most other people in northern India, with horror.

This is perhaps difficult to understand. Today many of us feel that our lives are too short and would love the chance to do it all again. But what preoccupied Gotama and his contemporaries was not so much the possibility of rebirth as the horror of redeath. It was bad enough to have to endure the process of becoming senile or chronically sick and undergoing a frightening, painful death *once*, but to be forced to go through all this again and again seemed intolerable and utterly pointless. Most of the religious solutions of the day were designed to help people extricate themselves from *saṃsāra* and achieve a final release. The freedom of Nibbāna was inconceivable because it was so far removed from our everyday experience. We have no terms to describe or even to envisage a mode of life in which there is no frustration, sorrow or pain, and which is not conditioned by factors beyond our control. But Indian sages of Gotama's day were convinced that this liberation was a genuine possibility. Western people often describe Indian thought as negative and nihilistic. Not so. It was breathtakingly optimistic and Gotama shared this hope to the full.

10   When he left his father's house clad in the yellow robes of a mendicant monk who begged for his food, Gotama believed that he was setting out on an exciting adventure. He felt the lure of the "wide open" road, and the shining, perfect state of "homelessness." Everybody spoke of the "holy life" at this time as a noble quest. Kings, merchants and wealthy householders alike honored these *bhikkhus* ("almsmen") and vied with one another for the privilege of feeding them. Some became their regular patrons and disciples. This was no passing craze. The people of India can be as materialistic as anybody else, but they have a long tradition of venerating those who seek the spiritual, and they continue to support them. Still, there was a special urgency in the Ganges region in the late sixth century B.C.E. People did not regard the renunciants as feeble dropouts. There was a spiritual crisis in the region. The sort of disillusion and anomie that Gotama had experienced was widespread, and people were desperately aware that they needed a new religious solution. The monk was thus engaged in a

quest that would benefit his fellows, often at huge cost to himself. Gotama was often described in heroic imagery, suggesting strength, energy and mastery. He was compared to a lion, a tiger and a fierce elephant. As a young man, he was seen as a "handsome nobleman, capable of leading a crack army or a troop of elephants."[12] People regarded the ascetics as pioneers: they were exploring the realms of the spirit to bring succor to suffering men and women. As a result of the prevailing unrest, many yearned for a Buddha, a man who was "enlightened," who had "woken up" to the full potential of humanity and would help others to find peace in a world that had suddenly become alien and desolate.

Why did the people of India feel this dis-ease with life? This malaise was not confined to the subcontinent, but afflicted people in several far-flung regions of the civilized world. An increasing number had come to feel that the spiritual practices of their ancestors no longer worked for them, and an impressive array of prophetic and philosophical geniuses made supreme efforts to find a solution. Some historians call this period (which extended from about 800 to 200 B.C.E.) the "Axial Age" because it proved pivotal to humanity. The ethos forged during this era has continued to nourish men and women to the present day.[13] Gotama would become one of the most important and most typical of the luminaries of the Axial Age, alongside the great Hebrew prophets of the eighth, seventh and sixth centuries; Confucius and Lao Tzu,° who reformed the religious traditions of China in the sixth and fifth centuries; the sixth-century Iranian sage Zoroaster;° and Socrates and Plato° (c. 427–327), who urged the Greeks to question even those truths which appeared to be self-evident. People who participated in this great transformation were convinced that they were on the brink of a new era and that nothing would ever be the same again.

The Axial Age marks the beginning of humanity as we now know it. During this period, men and women became conscious of their existence, their own nature and their limitations in an unprecedented way.[14] Their experience of utter impotence in a cruel world impelled them to seek the highest goals and an absolute reality in the depths of their being. The great sages of the time taught human beings how to cope with the misery of life, transcend their weakness, and live in peace in the midst of this flawed world. The new religious systems that emerged during this period—Taoism and Confucianism in China, Buddhism and Hinduism in India, monotheism in Iran and the Middle East, and Greek rationalism in Europe—all shared fundamental characteristics beneath their

---

[12]*Sutta-Nipāta*, 3:1.

[13]Karl Jaspers, *The Origin and Goal of History,* trans. Michael Bullock, London, 1953.

[14]Ibid., 2–12.

[11]**Lao Tzu** sixth-century BCE Chinese philosopher regarded as the founder of Taoism **Zoroaster** Zarathustra, prophet of Zoroastrianism **Plato** ancient Greek philosopher (about 427 BCE–347 BCE), a student of Athenian philosopher Socrates. Some of his works take the form of dialogues in which a fictionalized Socrates asks an interlocutor probing questions on philosophical issues.

obvious differences. It was only by participating in this massive transformation that the various peoples of the world were able to progress and join the forward march of history.[15] Yet despite its great importance, the Axial Age remains mysterious. We do not know what caused it, nor why it took root only in three core areas: in China; in India and Iran; and in the eastern Mediterranean. Why was it that only the Chinese, Iranians, Indians, Jews and Greeks experienced these new horizons and embarked on this quest for enlightenment and salvation? The Babylonians and the Egyptians had also created great civilizations, but they did not evolve an Axial ideology at this point, and only participated in the new ethos later: in Islam or Christianity, which were restatements of the original Axial impulse. But in the Axial countries, a few men sensed fresh possibilities and broke away from the old traditions. They sought change in the deepest reaches of their beings, looked for greater inwardness in their spiritual lives, and tried to become one with a reality that transcended normal mundane conditions and categories. After this pivotal era, it was felt that only by reaching beyond their limits could human beings become most fully themselves.

Recorded history only begins in about 3000 B.C.E.; until that time we have little documentary evidence of the way human beings lived and organized their societies. But people always tried to imagine what the 20,000 years of prehistory had been like, and to root their own experience in it. All over the world, in every culture, these ancient days were depicted in mythology, which had no historical foundation but which spoke of lost paradises and primal catastrophes.[16] In the Golden Age, it was said, gods had walked the earth with human beings. The story of the Garden of Eden, recounted in the Book of Genesis, the lost paradise of the West, was typical: once upon a time, there had been no rift between humanity and the divine: God strolled in the garden in the cool of the evening. Nor were human beings divided from one another. Adam and Eve lived in harmony, unaware of their sexual difference or of the distinction between good and evil.[17] It is a unity that is impossible for us to imagine in our more fragmented existence, but in almost every culture, the myth of this primal concord showed that human beings continued to yearn for a peace and wholeness that they felt to be the proper state of humanity. They experienced the dawning of self-consciousness as a painful fall from grace. The Hebrew Bible calls this state of wholeness and completeness *shalōm;* Gotama spoke of Nibbāṇa and left his home in order to find it. Human beings, he believed, had lived in this peace and fulfillment before, but they had forgotten the path that led to it.

As we have seen, Gotama felt that his life had become meaningless. A conviction that the world was awry was fundamental to the spirituality that emerged in the Axial countries. Those who took part in this transformation felt restless—just as Gotama did. They were consumed by a sense of helplessness, were obsessed by their mortality and felt a profound terror of and alienation

[15]Ibid., 7, 13.
[16]Ibid., 28–46.
[17]Genesis 2–3.

from the world.[18] They expressed this malaise in different ways. The Greeks saw life as a tragic epic, a drama in which they strove for *katharsis* and release. Plato spoke of man's separation from the divine, and yearned to cast off the impurity of our present state and achieve unity with the Good. The Hebrew prophets of the eighth, seventh and sixth centuries felt a similar alienation from God, and saw their political exile as symbolic of their spiritual condition. The Zoroastrians of Iran saw life as a cosmic battle between Good and Evil, while in China, Confucius lamented the darkness of his age, which had fallen away from the ideals of the ancestors. In India, Gotama and the forest monks were convinced that life was *dukkha:* it was fundamentally "awry," filled with pain, grief and sorrow. The world had become a frightening place. The Buddhist scriptures speak of the "terror, awe and dread" that people experienced when they ventured outside the city and went into the woods.[19] Nature had become obscurely menacing, rather as it had become inimical to Adam and Eve after their lapse. Gotama did not leave home to commune happily with nature in the woods, but experienced a continuous "fear and horror."[20] If a deer approached or if the wind rustled in the leaves, he recalled later, his hair stood on end.

What had happened? Nobody has fully explained the sorrow that fueled Axial Age spirituality. Certainly men and women had experienced anguish before. Indeed, tablets have been found in Egypt and Mesopotamia from centuries before this time that express similar disillusion. But why did the experience of suffering reach such a crescendo in the three core Axial regions? Some historians see the invasions of the nomadic Indo-European horsemen as a common factor in all these areas. These Āryan° tribesmen came out of Central Asia and reached the Mediterranean by the end of the third millennium, were established in India and Iran by about 1200 B.C.E. and were in China by the end of the second millennium. They brought with them a sense of vast horizons and limitless possibilities, and, as a master race, had developed a tragically epic consciousness. They replaced the old stable and more primitive communities, but only after periods of intense conflict and distress, which might account for the Axial Age malaise.[21] But the Jews and their prophets had no contact with these Āryan horsemen, and these invasions occurred over millennia, whereas the chief Axial transformations were remarkably contemporaneous.

Moreover, the type of culture developed by the Āryans in India, for example, bore no relation to the creativity of the Axial Age. By 1000 B.C.E., the Āryan tribesmen had settled down and established agricultural communities in most

15

---

[18]Joseph Campbell, *Oriental Mythology, The Masks of God*, New York, 1962, 211–18.

[19]Vinaya: *Cullavagga*, 6:4; 7:1.

[20]*Majjhima Nikāya*, 4.

[21]Alfred Weber, *Kulturgeschichte als Kultursoziologie*, Leiden, 1935; *Das Tragische und die Geschichte*, Hamburg, 1943 passim.

[15]**Āryan** a speaker of proto-Indo-European, the language that was the source of a family of languages including most of the languages of Europe, the Indian subcontinent, and other parts of Asia

regions of the subcontinent. They dominated India[n] society to such an extent that we now know almost nothing about the indigenous, pre-Āryan civilization of the Indus valley. Despite the dynamism of its origins, however, Āryan India was static and conservative, like most pre-Axial cultures. It divided the people into four distinct classes, similar to the four estates which would develop later in feudal Europe. The *brahmins* were the priestly caste, with responsibility for the cult: they became the most powerful. The warrior *ksatriya* class was devoted to government and defense; the *vaiśya* were farmers and stockbreeders who kept the economy afloat; and the *sudras* were slaves or outcastes who were unable to assimilate into the Āryan system. Originally the four classes were not hereditary; native Indians could become *ksatriyas* or *brahmins* if they possessed the requisite skills. But by Gotama's time, the stratification of society had acquired a sacred significance and become immutable, since it was thought to mirror the archetypal order of the cosmos.[22] There was no possibility of changing this order by moving from one caste to another.

Āryan spirituality was typical of the ancient, pre-Axial religions, which were based on acceptance of the status quo, involved little speculative thought about the meaning of life and saw sacred truth as something that was given and unchangeable; not sought but passively received. The Āryans cultivated the drug soma, which put the *brahmins* into a state of ecstatic trance in which they "heard" (*sruti*) the inspired Sanskrit° texts known as the Vedas.[23] These were not thought to be dictated by the gods but to exist eternally and to reflect the fundamental principles of the cosmos. A universal law, governing the lives of gods and human beings alike, was also a common feature of ancient religion. The Vedas were not written down, since writing was unknown in the subcontinent. It was, therefore, the duty of the *brahmins* to memorize and preserve these eternal truths from one generation to another, passing down this hereditary lore from father to son, since this sacred knowledge put human beings in touch with *brahman*, the underlying principle that made the world holy and enabled it to survive. Over the centuries, Sanskrit, the language of the original Āryan tribesmen, was superseded by local dialects and became incomprehensible to everybody but the *brahmins*—a fact which inevitably enhanced the *brahmins'* power and prestige. They alone knew how to perform the sacrificial ritual prescribed in the Vedas, which was thought to keep the whole world in existence.

It was said that at the beginning of time, a mysterious Creator had performed a primal sacrifice that brought gods, humans and the entire cosmos into

[22]Richard F. Gombrich, *Theravāda Buddhism: A Social History from Ancient Benares to Modern Columbo*, London and New York, 1988, 33–59.

[23]Ibid., 33–34; Hermann Oldenberg, *The Buddha: His Life, His Doctrine, His Order* (trans. William Hoey), London, 1882, 19–21, 44–48; Trevor Ling, *The Buddha: Buddhist Civilization in India and Ceylon*, London, 1973, 66–67.

[17]**Sanskrit** ancient language of India

existence. This primeval sacrifice was the archetype of the animal sacrifices performed by the *brahmins,* which gave them power over life and death. Even the gods depended upon these sacrifices and would suffer if the ritual was not performed correctly. The whole of life therefore centered around these rites. The *brahmins* were clearly crucial to the cult, but the *ksatriyas* and *vaiśyas* also had important roles. Kings and noblemen paid for the sacrifices, and the *vaiśyas* reared the cattle as victims. Fire was of great importance in Vedic religion. It symbolized humanity's control over the forces of nature, and the *brahmins* carefully tended three sacred fires in shrines. Each householder also honored his own domestic hearth with family rites. On the "quarter" (*uposatha*) days of each lunar month, special offerings were made to the sacred fire. On the eve of the *uposatha, brahmins* and ordinary householders alike would fast, abstain from sex and work, and keep night vigil at the hearth. It was a holy time, known as the *upavasatha,* when the gods "dwelt near" the householder and his family beside the fire.[24]

Vedic faith was thus typical of pre-Axial religion. It did not develop or change; it conformed to an archetypal order and did not aspire to anything different. It depended upon external rites, which were magical in effect and intended to control the universe; it was based on arcane, esoteric lore known only to a few.[25] This deeply conservative spirituality sought security in a reality that was timeless and changeless. It was completely different from the new Axial ethos. One need only think of Socrates, who was never content to accept traditional certainties as final, however august they might be. He believed that instead of receiving knowledge from outside, like the *sruti* Vedas, each person must find the truth within his own being. Socrates questioned everything, infecting his interlocutors with his own perplexity, since confusion was the beginning of the philosophical quest. The Hebrew prophets overturned some of the old mythical certainties of ancient Israel: God was no longer automatically on the side of his people, as he had been at the time of the Exodus from Egypt. He would now use the Gentile nations to punish Jews, each of whom had a personal responsibility to act with justice, equity and fidelity. Salvation and survival no longer depended upon external rites; there would be a new law and covenant written in the heart of each of the people. God demanded mercy and compassion rather than sacrifice. Axial faith put the onus on the individual. Wherever they looked, as we have seen, the Axial sages and prophets saw exile, tragedy and *dukkha*. But the truth that they sought enabled them to find peace, despite cruelty, injustice and political defeat. We need only recall the luminous calm of Socrates during his execution by a coercive state. The individual would still suffer and die; there was no attempt to avert fate by the old magical means; but he or she could enjoy a calm in the midst of life's tragedies that gave meaning to existence in such a flawed world.

[24]Sukumar Dutt, *Buddhist Monks and Monasteries of India,* London, 1962, 73.
[25]Jaspers, *Origin and Goal,* 48–49.

20   The new religions sought inner depth rather than magical control. The sages were no longer content with external conformity but were aware of the profound psychic inwardness that precedes action. Crucial was the desire to bring unconscious forces and dimly perceived truths into the light of day. For Socrates, men already knew the truth, but only as an obscure memory within; they had to awaken this knowledge and become fully conscious of it by means of his dialectical method of questioning. Confucius studied the ancient customs of his people, which had hitherto been taken for granted and had remained unexamined. Now the values that they enshrined must be consciously fostered in order to be restored to their original radiance. Confucius wanted to make explicit ideas which had previously been merely intuited, and put elusive, half-understood intimations into clear language. Human beings must study themselves, analyze the reasons for their failures and thus find a beauty and order in the world that was not rendered meaningless by the fact of death. The Axial sages scrutinized the old mythology and reinterpreted it, giving the old truths an essentially ethical dimension. Morality had become central to religion. It was by ethics, not magic, that humanity would wake up to itself and its responsibilities, realize its full potential and find release from the darkness that pressed in on all sides. The sages were conscious of the past, and believed that the world had gone awry because men and women had forgotten the fundamentals of existence. All were convinced that there was an absolute reality that transcended the confusions of this world—God, Nibbāna, the Tao, *brahman*— and sought to integrate it within the conditions of daily life. . . .   [1991]

1. According to Karen Armstrong's writing on the Axial Age, a change in focus redirected human energy to a new kind of effort that had its source within each individual. How does Ashvaghosha's account of the Buddha's teaching (p. 339) reflect this? Can you compare what the Buddha says on this issue with any other philosophy or religion you know?

JORGE LUIS BORGES

JORGE LUIS BORGES *(1899–1986) studied in Europe, traveled a great deal in his youth, and wrote poetry, essays, and arresting short stories that experiment with abstract ideas. In 1955 after the fall of the government of dictator Juan Perón, he was appointed director of the National Library of Argentina and professor of English and American Literature at the University of Buenos Aires, the city of his birth, a post that reflects his love for British and American literature. His books include* Ficciones, The Book of Sand, *and* Labyrinths, *from which this essay is taken.*

Everything and Nothing*

There was no one in him; behind his face (which even through the bad paintings of those times resembles *[sic]* no other) and his words, which were copious, fantastic and stormy, there was only a bit of coldness, a dream dreamt by no one. At first

*Jorge Luis Borges, "Everything and Nothing," in *Labyrinths,* ed. Donald Yates & James E. Irby (New York: New Directions, 1964), 248–49.

he thought that all people were like him, but the astonishment of a friend to whom he had begun to speak of this emptiness showed him his error and made him feel always that an individual should not differ in outward appearance. Once he thought that in books he would find a cure for his ill and thus he learned the small Latin and less Greek a contemporary would speak of; later he considered that what he sought might well be found in an elemental rite of humanity, and let himself be initiated by Anne Hathaway° one long June afternoon. At the age of twenty-odd years he went to London. Instinctively he had already become proficient in the habit of simulating that he was someone, so that others would not discover his condition as no one; in London he found the profession to which he was predestined, that of the actor, who on a stage plays at being another before a gathering of people who play at taking him for that other person. His histrionic tasks brought him a singular satisfaction, perhaps the first he had ever known; but once the last verse had been acclaimed and the last dead man withdrawn from the stage, the hated flavor of unreality returned to him. He ceased to be Ferrex or Tamerlane and became no one again. Thus hounded, he took to imagining other heroes and other tragic fables. And so, while his flesh fulfilled its destiny as flesh in the taverns and brothels of London, the soul that inhabited him was Caesar, who disregards the augur's admonition, and Juliet, who abhors the lark, and Macbeth, who converses on the plain with the witches who are also Fates. No one has ever been so many men as this man, who like the Egyptian Proteus could exhaust all the guises of reality. At times he would leave a confession hidden away in some corner of his work, certain that it would not be deciphered; Richard affirms that in his person he plays the part of many and Iago claims with curious words "I am not what I am." The fundamental identity of existing, dreaming and acting inspired famous passages of his.

For twenty years he persisted in that controlled hallucination, but one morning he was suddenly gripped by the tedium and the terror of being so many kings who die by the sword and so many suffering lovers who converge, diverge and melodiously expire. That very day he arranged to sell his theater. Within a week he had returned to his native village, where he recovered the trees and rivers of his childhood and did not relate them to the others his muse had celebrated, illustrious with mythological allusions and Latin terms. He had to be someone; he was a retired impresario who had made his fortune and concerned himself with loans, lawsuits and petty usury. It was in this character that he dictated the arid will and testament known to us, from which he deliberately excluded all traces of pathos or literature. His friends from London would visit his retreat and for them he would take up again his role as poet.

History adds that before or after dying he found himself in the presence of God and told Him: "I who have been so many men in vain want to be one and myself." The voice of the Lord answered from a whirlwind: "Neither am I anyone; I have dreamt the world as you dreamt your work, my Shakespeare, and among the forms in my dream are you, who like myself are many and no one."

Translated by J. E. I.

[1964]

---

¹**Anne Hathaway** Shakespeare's wife

1. Why does Borges wait for the end of this essay (the editors call it a parable) to name its subject?
2. How does Borges's claim for Shakespeare relate to Maslow's concept of transcendence?
3. What is Borges trying to explain with the analogy in this essay?

JOAN DIDION

JOAN DIDION *(1934–) A fifth-generation Californian, Didion was brought up in central California. As an undergraduate English major at the University of California, Berkeley, she won a* Vogue *essay prize, was hired by the magazine, moved to New York, and eventually became associate editor. Soon after the publication of her first novel,* Run River, *she married the writer John Gregory Dunne and returned with him to her home state, where they lived for twenty-five years. Her essay collections,* Slouching toward Bethlehem *and* The White Album *are among her best work. She has written more novels as well, and two documentary studies,* Salvador *and* Miami.

*On Self-Respect**

Once, in a dry season, I wrote in large letters across two pages of a notebook that innocence ends when one is stripped of the delusion that one likes oneself. Although now, some years later, I marvel that a mind on the outs with itself should have nonetheless made painstaking record of its every tremor, I recall with embarrassing clarity the flavor of those particular ashes. It was a matter of misplaced self-respect.

I had not been elected to Phi Beta Kappa.° This failure could scarcely have been more predictable or less ambiguous (I simply did not have the grades), but I was unnerved by it; I had somehow thought myself a kind of academic Raskolnikov, curiously exempt from the cause-effect relationships which hampered others. Although even the humorless nineteen-year-old that I was must have recognized that the situation lacked real tragic stature, the day that I did not make Phi Beta Kappa nonetheless marked the end of something, and innocence may well be the word for it. I lost the conviction that lights would always turn green for me, the pleasant certainty that those rather passive virtues which had won me approval as a child automatically guaranteed me not only

[2]**Phi Beta Kappa** honor society for college students who earn high grades, the main symbol of which is a gold key inscribed with the three Greek letters of its name

*Joan Didion, "On Self Respect," in *Slouching Toward Bethlehem* (New York: Simon and Schuster, 1968), 142–48.

Phi Beta Kappa keys but happiness, honor, and the love of a good man; lost a certain touching faith in the totem power of good manners, clean hair, and proven competence on the Stanford-Binet scale. To such doubtful amulets had my self-respect been pinned, and I faced myself that day with the nonplused apprehension of someone who has come across a vampire and has no crucifix at hand.

Although to be driven back upon oneself is an uneasy affair at best, rather like trying to cross a border with borrowed credentials, it seems to me now the one condition necessary to the beginnings of real self-respect. Most of our platitudes notwithstanding, self-deception remains the most difficult deception. The tricks that work on others count for nothing in that very well-lit back alley where one keeps assignations with oneself: no winning smiles will do here, no prettily drawn lists of good intentions. One shuffles flashily but in vain through one's marked cards—the kindness done for the wrong reason, the apparent triumph which involved no real effort, the seemingly heroic act into which one had been shamed. The dismal fact is that self-respect has nothing to do with the approval of others—who are, after all, deceived easily enough; has nothing to do with reputation, which, as Rhett Butler told Scarlett O'Hara,° is something people with courage can do without.

To do without self-respect, on the other hand, is to be an unwilling audience of one to an interminable documentary that details one's failings, both real and imagined, with fresh footage spliced in for every screening. *There's the glass you broke in anger, there's the hurt on X's face; watch now, this next scene, the night Y came back from Houston, see how you muff this one.* To live without self-respect is to lie awake some night, beyond the reach of warm milk, phenobarbital, and the sleeping hand on the coverlet, counting up the sins of commission and omission, the trusts betrayed, the promises subtly broken, the gifts irrevocably wasted through sloth or cowardice or carelessness. However long we postpone it, we eventually lie down alone in that notoriously uncomfortable bed, the one we make ourselves. Whether or not we sleep in it depends, of course, on whether or not we respect ourselves.

To protest that some fairly improbable people, some people who *could not possibly respect themselves,* seem to sleep easily enough is to miss the point entirely, 5 as surely as those people miss it who think that self-respect has necessarily to do with not having safety pins in one's underwear. There is a common superstition that "self-respect" is a kind of charm against snakes, something that keeps those who have it locked in some unblighted Eden, out of strange beds, ambivalent conversations, and trouble in general. It does not at all. It has nothing to do with the face of things, but concerns instead a separate peace, a private reconciliation.

---

³**Rhett Butler, Scarlett O'Hara** principal characters in Margaret Mitchell's 1936 novel *Gone with the Wind,* made into a film in 1939 starring Clark Gable and Vivien Leigh in the roles of Butler and O'Hara

Although the careless, suicidal Julian English in *Appointment in Samarra*° and the careless, incurably dishonest Jordan Baker in *The Great Gatsby*° seem equally improbable candidates for self-respect, Jordan Baker had it, Julian English did not. With that genius for accommodation more often seen in women than in men, Jordan took her own measure, made her own peace, avoided threats to that peace: "I hate careless people," she told Nick Carraway. "It takes two to make an accident."

Like Jordan Baker, people with self-respect have the courage of their mistakes. They know the price of things. If they choose to commit adultery, they do not then go running, in an access of bad conscience, to receive absolution from the wronged parties; nor do they complain unduly of the unfairness, the undeserved embarrassment, of being named co-respondent. In brief, people with self-respect exhibit a certain toughness, a kind of moral nerve; they display what was once called *character,* a quality which, although approved in the abstract, sometimes loses ground to other, more instantly negotiable virtues. The measure of its slipping prestige is that one tends to think of it only in connection with homely children and United States senators who have been defeated, preferably in the primary, for reelection. Nonetheless, character—the willingness to accept responsibility for one's own life—is the source from which self-respect springs.

Self-respect is something that our grandparents, whether or not they had it, knew all about. They had instilled in them, young, a certain discipline, the sense that one lives by doing things one does not particularly want to do, by putting fears and doubts to one side, by weighing immediate comforts against the possibility of larger, even intangible, comforts. It seemed to the nineteenth century admirable, but not remarkable, that Chinese Gordon° put on a clean white suit and held Khartoum against the Mahdi; it did not seem unjust that the way to free land in California involved death and difficulty and dirt. In a diary kept during the winter of 1846, an emigrating twelve-year-old named Narcissa Cornwall noted coolly: "Father was busy reading and did not notice that the house was being filled with strange Indians until Mother spoke about it." Even lacking any clue as to what Mother said, one can scarcely fail to be impressed by the entire incident: the father reading, the Indians filing in, the mother choosing the words that would not alarm, the child duly recording the event and noting further that those particular Indians were not, "fortunately for us," hostile. Indians were simply part of the *donnée.*°

---

[5]*Appointment in Samarra* 1934 novel by John O'Hara   *The Great Gatsby* 1925 novel by F. Scott Fitzgerald   [7]**Chinese Gordon** Charles "Chinese" Gordon (1833–85) was a British general who held the city of Khartoum, capital of Sudan, against a siege by the Mahdi, an Islamic leader, for 312 days. British troops who arrived to help lift the siege were too late to save Gordon and his Sudanese supporters.   *donnée* a French word meaning "given"

In one guise or another, Indians always are. Again, it is a question of recognizing that anything worth having has its price. People who respect themselves are willing to accept the risk that the Indians will be hostile, that the venture will go bankrupt, that the liaison may not turn out to be one in which *every day is a holiday because you're married to me.* They are willing to invest something of themselves; they may not play at all, but when they do play, they know the odds.

That kind of self-respect is a discipline, a habit of mind that can never be faked but can be developed, trained, coaxed forth. It was once suggested to me that, as an antidote to crying, I put my head in a paper bag. As it happens, there is a sound physiological reason, something to do with oxygen, for doing exactly that, but the psychological effect alone is incalculable: it is difficult in the extreme to continue fancying oneself Cathy in *Wuthering Heights* with one's head in a Food Fair bag. There is a similar case for all the small disciplines, unimportant in themselves; imagine maintaining any kind of swoon, commiserative or carnal, in a cold shower.

But those small disciplines are valuable only insofar as they represent larger ones. To say that Waterloo was won on the playing fields of Eton is not to say that Napoleon might have been saved by a crash program in cricket; to give formal dinners in the rain forest would be pointless did not the candlelight flickering on the liana call forth deeper, stronger disciplines, values instilled long before. It is a kind of ritual, helping us to remember who and what we are. In order to remember it, one must have known it.

To have that sense of one's intrinsic worth which constitutes self-respect is potentially to have everything: the ability to discriminate, to love and to remain indifferent. To lack it is to be locked within oneself, paradoxically incapable of either love or indifference. If we do not respect ourselves, we are on the one hand forced to despise those who have so few resources as to consort with us, so little perception as to remain blind to our fatal weaknesses. On the other, we are peculiarly in thrall to everyone we see, curiously determined to live out—since our self-image is untenable—their false notions of us. We flatter ourselves by thinking this compulsion to please others an attractive trait: a gist for imaginative empathy, evidence of our willingness to give. *Of course* I will play Francesca to your Paolo, Helen Keller to anyone's Annie Sullivan: no expectation is too misplaced, no role too ludicrous. At the mercy of those we cannot but hold in contempt, we play roles doomed to failure before they are begun, each defeat generating fresh despair at the urgency of divining and meeting the next demand made upon us.

It is the phenomenon sometimes called "alienation from self." In its advanced stages, we no longer answer the telephone, because someone might want something; that we could say *no* without drowning in self-reproach is an idea alien to this game. Every encounter demands too much, tears the nerves, drains the will, and the specter of something as small as an unanswered letter arouses such disproportionate guilt that answering it becomes out of the question. To assign unanswered letters their proper weight, to free us from the expectations of others, to give us back to ourselves—there lies the great, the singular power of self-respect. Without it, one eventually discovers the final turn of the screw: one runs away to find oneself, and finds no one at home.   [1961]

1. What is the paradox at the heart of this essay?
2. Why does the essay start with an incident from the author's distant past?

CHAPTER THIRTEEN

Acting and Authenticity

INTRODUCTION

"Acting" can mean merely doing something, taking an action, but in conjunction with "authenticity" it takes on the meaning of playing a part in a genre where one pretends to be something one isn't. Drama, whether through theater, television, radio, or film, requires turning away from what we call reality for an imitation of it. The pair of words implies that acting, or playing a role, is different from or even the opposite of being sincere, authentic. Challenges to this simple binary opposition come from many quarters. Sociologists like Erving Goffman (see p. 194) use theatrical metaphors to claim that people normally behave as if they are playing parts with objectives they wish to achieve in the way of audience response. Psychologists and therapists who try to help people achieve new habits sometimes encourage people to try out patterns of behavior before the patterns feel natural. The adventitious "false" smile uses different muscles from real ones but sometimes actually make people feel better and lead to real ones. And furthermore, things we think we do spontaneously and perfectly freely may be conditioned and limited by social norms. The works in this section give you a chance to explore the boundaries between the "real," the "actual," or the "sincere" and its (supposedly) less real copy.

POETRY

W.H. AUDEN

W[YSTAN] H[UGH] AUDEN *(1907–73) was born in York, England, and was educated at Christ's Church, Oxford, where his precocity as a poet was recognized immediately, and he formed lifelong friendships with two fellow writers,*

Stephen Spender and Christopher Isherwood. His first collection, Poems, *established his reputation as the leading voice in the revival of classical forms in poetry. His subjects ranged widely over popular culture, current events, literature, art, social and political theories, and science and technology. He wrote satire and parody, traveled widely, took part in the Spanish Civil War, and moved to the United States, where he met Chester Kallman, his long-time companion, and became a citizen. Playwright, librettist, editor, and essayist, he is considered the foremost poet of his generation and still exerts a strong influence on poetry of both England and America.*

The Unknown Citizen

(To JS/07/M/378/
This Marble Monument Is Erected by the State)

He was found by the Bureau of Statistics to be
One against whom there was no official complaint,
And all the reports on his conduct agree
That, in the modern sense of an old-fashioned word, he was a saint,
5 For in everything he did he served the Greater Community.
Except for the War till the day he retired
He worked in a factory and never got fired
But satisfied his employers, Fudge Motors Inc.
Yet he wasn't a scab or odd in his views,
10 For his Union reports that he paid his dues,
(Our report on his Union shows it was sound)
And our Social Psychology workers found
That he was popular with his mates and liked a drink.
The Press are convinced that he bought a paper every day
15 And that his reactions to advertisements were normal in every way.
Policies taken out in his name prove that he was fully insured,
And his Health-card shows he was once in hospital but left it cured.
Both Producers Research and High-Grade Living declare
He was fully sensible to the advantages of the Installment Plan
20 And had everything necessary to the Modern Man,
A phonograph, a radio, a car and a frigidaire.
Our researchers into Public Opinion are content
That he held the proper opinions for the time of year;
When there was peace, he was for peace: when there was war, he went.
25 He was married and added five children to the population,
Which our Eugenist° says was the right number for a parent of his generation.
And our teachers report that he never interfered with their education.
Was he free? Was he happy? The question is absurd:
Had anything been wrong, we should certainly have heard.   [1940]

---

²⁶**Eugenist** Auden probably means "eugenicist," a practitioner of the now largely discredited science of eugenics, attempts to manipulate human reproduction for racial or political purposes.

1. Auden's satiric voice makes itself heard in this poem in some sly ways. Notice the irregular length of line as it contrasts with the rhythm and rhyme scheme. You might want to mark some of the humorous twists that slyly dig at the official attitude toward citizens.
2. This assessment of the life and attitudes of the unknown citizen tells the reader a lot about the unknown citizen's life and about the society in which he lived (and about the narrator's attitude, too). How many of these attributes could apply to what we expect of our fellows in present-day life in the United States?

GWENDOLYN BROOKS

OLC

GWENDOLYN BROOKS *(1917–2000) was born in Topeka, Kansas, the grand-daughter of a runaway slave, and was the child of parents who wanted her to grow up in Chicago, a city with which she was associated all of her life. By the age of four she was rhyming, and she had her first poem published in a children's magazine when she was thirteen. As a student she met the poets Langston Hughes and James Weldon Johnson, who suggested that she read modern poets like Eliot and Cummings. At seventeen, she began submitting her work to an African-American newspaper. By the time she was twenty, she had published many poems, appeared in two anthologies, and made a crucial step in her career when she and her new husband, Henry Blakely III, enrolled in a poetry workshop run by Inez Cunningham Stark. Recognition followed at the Midwestern Writer's conference. She published her first book,* A Street in Bronzeville, *named for her Chicago neighborhood, and was selected as one of* Mademoiselle *magazine's "Ten Young Women of the Year."* Annie Allen *won the Pulitzer Prize, the first ever awarded to an African-American poet. She wrote more than twenty books of poems and was named Poet Laureate of Illinois. In 2000, she completed her last book of poems and died at age 83 of cancer.*

We Real Cool

The Pool Players.
Seven at the Golden Shovel.

We real cool. We
Left School. We

Lurk late. We
Strike straight. We
Sing sin. We   5
Thin gin. We

Jazz June. We
Die soon.   [1960]

1. What are the poetic techniques that give this poem its power?
2. What difference does it make that these young men form a group?
3. What disciplines could help interpret the poem?

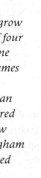

OLC

E.E. CUMMINGS

E[DWARD] E[STLIN] CUMMINGS (1894–1962), born in Cambridge, Massachusetts, began writing poetry as a child. He earned B.A. and M.A. degrees from Harvard and was an ambulance driver during World War I, eventually serving a sentence in a French internment camp for a mistaken suspicion of treason. In 1922 he wrote about this experience in The Enormous Room, *a great critical success. He then began to publish the collections of free verse, lower-case poetry that was full of the typographical games and strange punctuation marks that established him as America's foremost avant-garde poet. At the time of his death, he was the second most widely read poet in the United States after Robert Frost. His work, mostly experimental, even radical at times, was simple and playful enough to appeal to many readers. He resided in Greenwich Village and rural Connecticut, frequently visiting Paris. His books of poetry include* Tulips and Chimneys, &, Viva, No Thanks, 1x1, *and* Complete Poems.

anyone lived in a pretty how town

anyone lived in a pretty how town
(with up so floating many bells down)
spring summer autumn winter
he sang his didn't he danced his did

5   Women and men (both little and small)
cared for anyone not at all
they sowed their isn't they reaped their same
sun moon stars rain

children guessed (but only a few
10   and down they forgot as up they grew
autumn winter spring summer)
that noone loved him more by more

when by now and tree by leaf
she laughed his joy she cried his grief
15   bird by snow and stir by still
anyone's any was all to her

someones married their everyones
laughed their cryings and did their dance
(sleep wake hope and then) they
20   said their nevers they slept their dream

stars rain sun moon
(and only the snow can begin to explain
how children are apt to forget to remember
with up so floating many bells down)

25   one day anyone died i guess
(and noone stooped to kiss his face)

busy folk buried them side by side
little by little and was by was

all by all and deep by deep
and more by more they dream their sleep   30
noone and anyone earth by april
wish by spirit and if by yes.

Women and men (both dong and ding)
summer autumn winter spring
reaped their sowing and went their came   35
sun moon stars rain   [1940]

1. This poem claims to be about someone named or called "anyone." As you
   read it, does it seem to you that it is really about anyone, or are there
   particulars in the life of "anyone" that differentiate this person from others?
   What's the effect of the claim of universality?
2. Characterize the disruptions in language that mark the poem.
3. What effect do the rhythm and rhyme have?
4. What is the impact of the repeated references to the seasonal cycle?
5. Does the poem imply that the townspeople lead less authentic lives than
   anyone and noone?

EMILY DICKINSON

(For biographical notes, see p. 255.)   OLC

(I Like a Look of Agony)

I like a look of Agony,
Because I know it's true—
Men do not sham Convulsion,
Nor simulate, a Throe—

The Eyes glaze once—and that is Death—   5
Impossible to feign
The Beads upon the Forehead
By homely Anguish strung.   [c. 1861]

1. What is the reason the persona gives for the shocking title of the poem? Do
   you agree?
2. Explain the poetic devices in the poem.

(I'm Nobody! Who Are You?)

I'm nobody! Who are you?
Are you—Nobody—too?
Then there's a pair of us!

Don't tell! they'd banish us—you know!

5 How dreary—to be—Somebody!
How public—like a Frog—
To tell your name—the livelong June
To an admiring Bog!

[c. 1861]

1. How do you think Dickinson is defining what it means to be nobody?
   What's the difference between being "nobody" and being "*a* nobody"?
   What's wrong with being somebody?
2. What difference does it make that the speaker is addressing another
   nobody?
3. What are the poetic techniques that give the poem its shape and emphasis?
   How do diction and syntax help to produce its effect?
4. How might the ideas of sociologist Erving Goffman (see *The Presentation of
   Self in Everyday Life,* p. 194) help to interpret this poem?
5. How does this poem relate to the psychology of Buddhism as it is portrayed
   in Ashvaghosha's "The Legend of the Buddha Shakyamuni" (see
   p. 339)?

PAUL LAURENCE DUNBAR

PAUL LAURENCE DUNBAR *(1872–1906), a classmate at the University of Dayton
of aviation pioneer Orville Wright, was born in Cincinnati, Ohio, and became a
prolific writer of short stories, novels, librettos, plays, songs, and essays as well as
the poetry that made his reputation. He wrote classical verse in both standard
English and the dialect of the turn-of-the-century black community. His dialect
poetry conveyed character in the way that Mark Twain's use of dialect conveyed it
in his prose.*

We Wear the Mask

We wear the mask that grins and lies,
It hides our cheeks and shades our eyes—
This debt we pay to human guile;
With torn and bleeding hearts we smile,
5 And mouth with myriad subtleties.

Why should the world be over-wise,
In counting all our tears and sighs?
Nay, let them only see us, while
    We wear the mask.

10 We smile, but, O great Christ, our cries
To thee from tortured souls arise.
We sing, but oh the clay is vile
Beneath our feet, and long the mile;
But let the world dream otherwise,
15   We wear the mask!

[1913]

1. Is this poem demonstrating the principles that Erving Goffman expounds in *The Presentation of Self in Everyday Life* (see p. 194)?
2. Who are the "we" and "them" the poem refers to?
3. What is the purpose of the mask?

T.S. ELIOT

OLC

T[HOMAS] S[TEARNS] ELIOT *(1888–1965) was born in St. Louis, Missouri, but as an adult settled in London and became a British citizen. His first work,* Prufrock and Other Observations, *was published in 1917. The* Wasteland, *which was given some of its density and terseness by the editorial blue pencil of Ezra Pound, appeared in 1922. By 1930 Eliot was the foremost poetic voice in English poetry of his time. He made use of influences from the Metaphysical poets and the French Symbolists and forged radical innovations in technique and subject matter into a new poetry that reflected the disillusionment of the post–World War I generation. Two more books of poetry,* Ash Wednesday *and* Four Quartets, *his books of literary and social criticism, and verse plays such as* Murder in the Cathedral, The Family Reunion, *and* The Cocktail Party *complete his oeuvre. He received the Nobel Prize for Literature in 1948.*

The Love Song of J. Alfred Prufrock

S'io credesse che mia risposta fosse
A persona che mai tornasse al mondo,
Questa fiamma staria senza piu scosse.
Ma perciocche giammai di questo fondo
Non torno vivo alcun, s'i'odo il vero,
Senza tema d'infamia ti rispondo.°

Let us go then, you and I,
When the evening is spread out against the sky
Like a patient etherised upon a table;
Let us go, through certain half-deserted streets,
The muttering retreats   5
Of restless nights in one-night cheap hotels
And sawdust restaurants with oyster-shells:

Epigraph Canto 27 ll. 61–66 of the "Inferno" section of Dante's *Divine Comedy,* a thirteenth-century account of a trip through hell, purgatory, and heaven. When the narrator asks military and political leader Guido da Montefeltro, who is encased in flame, why he is in hell, Guido begins his story with this proviso (as translated by John Ciardi):

"If I believed that my reply were made
to one who could ever climb to the world again,
this flame would shake no more. But since no shade
ever returned—if what I am told is true—
from this blind world into the living light
without fear of dishonor I can answer you."

Streets that follow like a tedious argument
Of insidious intent

10 To lead you to an overwhelming question . . .
Oh, do not ask, "What is it?"
Let us go and make our visit.

In the room the women come and go
Talking of Michelangelo.°

15 The yellow fog that rubs its back upon the window-panes,
The yellow smoke that rubs its muzzle on the window-panes
Licked its tongue into the corners of the evening,
Lingered upon the pools that stand in drains,
Let fall upon its back the soot that falls from chimneys,

20 Slipped by the terrace, made a sudden leap,
And seeing that it was a soft October night,
Curled once about the house, and fell asleep.

And indeed there will be time
For the yellow smoke that slides along the street,

25 Rubbing its back upon the window-panes;
There will be time, there will be time
To prepare a face to meet the faces that you meet;
There will be time to murder and create,
And time for all the works and days of hands

30 That lift and drop a question on your plate;
Time for you and time for me,
And time yet for a hundred indecisions,
And for a hundred visions and revisions,
Before the taking of a toast and tea.

35 In the room the women come and go
Talking of Michelangelo.

And indeed there will be time
To wonder, "Do I dare?" and, "Do I dare?"
Time to turn back and descend the stair,

40 With a bald spot in the middle of my hair—
[They will say: "How his hair is growing thin!"]
My morning coat, my collar mounting firmly to the chin,
My necktie rich and modest, but asserted by a simple pin—
[They will say: "But how his arms and legs are thin!"]

45 Do I dare
Disturb the universe?
In a minute there is time
For decisions and revisions which a minute will reverse.

[14]**Michelangelo** master artist and architect of the Italian Renaissance (1475–1564); sculpted the statue of the young David for Florence and the Pietà for St. Peter's Basilica in Rome; painted the frescoes on the ceiling of the Sistene Chapel in the Vatican in Rome

For I have known them all already, known them all:—
Have known the evenings, mornings, afternoons,   50
I have measured out my life with coffee spoons;
I know the voices dying with a dying fall
Beneath the music from a farther room.
    So how should I presume?

And I have known the eyes already, known them all—   55
The eyes that fix you in a formulated phrase,
And when I am formulated, sprawling on a pin,
When I am pinned and wriggling on the wall,
Then how should I begin
To spit out all the butt-ends of my days and ways?   60
    And how should I presume?

And I have known the arms already, known them all—
Arms that are braceleted and white and bare
[But in the lamplight, downed with light brown hair!]
Is it perfume from a dress   65
That makes me so digress?
Arms that lie along a table, or wrap about a shawl.
    And should I then presume?
    And how should I begin?

        .   .   .   .

Shall I say, I have gone at dusk through narrow streets   70
And watched the smoke that rises from the pipes
Of lonely men in shirt-sleeves, leaning out of windows? . . .

I should have been a pair of ragged claws
Scuttling across the floors of silent seas.

        .   .   .   .

And the afternoon, the evening, sleeps so peacefully!   75
Smoothed by long fingers,
Asleep . . . tired . . . or it malingers,
Stretched on the floor, here beside you and me.
Should I, after tea and cakes and ices,
Have the strength to force the moment to its crisis?   80
But though I have wept and fasted, wept and prayed,
Though I have seen my head [grown slightly bald] brought in upon a platter,
I am no prophet—and here's no great matter;
I have seen the moment of my greatness flicker,
And I have seen the eternal Footman hold my coat, and snicker,   85
And in short, I was afraid.

And would it have been worth it, after all,
After the cups, the marmalade, the tea,
Among the porcelain, among some talk of you and me,
Would it have been worth while,   90

To have bitten off the matter with a smile,
To have squeezed the universe into a ball
To roll it toward some overwhelming question,
To say: "I am Lazarus, come from the dead,
95 Come back to tell you all, I shall tell you all"—
If one, settling a pillow by her head,
    Should say: "That is not what I meant at all.
    That is not it, at all."

And would it have been worth it, after all,
100 Would it have been worth while,
After the sunsets and the dooryards and the sprinkled streets,
After the novels, after the teacups, after the skirts that trail along the floor—
And this, and so much more?—
It is impossible to say just what I mean!
105 But as if a magic lantern threw the nerves in patterns on a screen:
Would it have been worth while
If one, settling a pillow or throwing off a shawl,
And turning toward the window, should say:
    "That is not it at all,
110   That is not what I meant, at all."

. . . . . .

No! I am not Prince Hamlet, nor was meant to be;
Am an attendant lord, one that will do
To swell a progress, start a scene or two,
Advise the prince; no doubt, an easy tool,
115 Deferential, glad to be of use,
Politic, cautious, and meticulous;
Full of high sentence, but a bit obtuse;
At times, indeed, almost ridiculous—
Almost, at times, the Fool.

120 I grow old . . . I grow old . . .
I shall wear the bottoms of my trousers rolled.

Shall I part my hair behind? Do I dare to eat a peach?
I shall wear white flannel trousers, and walk upon the beach.
I have heard the mermaids singing, each to each.
125 I do not think that they will sing to me.

I have seen them riding seaward on the waves
Combing the white hair of the waves blown back
When the wind blows the water white and black.

We have lingered in the chambers of the sea
130 By sea-girls wreathed with seaweed red and brown
Till human voices wake us, and we drown.   [1917]

1. As you accompany the narrator on his travels in his social and psychic worlds ("Let us go, then, you and I"), characterize him. How does he present himself to the audience of the poem?
2. What is the tone of the poem?
3. What is the "crisis" that Prufrock seems to long to produce in l. 80? Why can't he do it? What is he afraid of?
4. Why does Prufrock think he "should have been a pair of ragged claws / Scuttling across the floors of silent seas" (ll. 73–74)?
5. How does literary allusion function in the poem?
6. What would Erving Goffman make of this poem (see p. 194)? Terence Eagleton (see p. 702)?

THOM GUNN

(For biographical notes, see p. 351.)

Night Taxi

for Rod Taylor
wherever he is

Open city
uncluttered as a map.
I drive through empty streets
scoured by the winds
of midnight. My shift   5
is only beginning and I am fresh
and excitable, master of the taxi.
I relish my alert reflexes
where all else
is in hiding. I have   10
by default it seems
conquered me a city.

My first address: I
press the doorbell, I lean back
against the hood, my headlights   15
scalding a garage door, my engine
drumming in the driveway,
the only sound on the block.
There the fare finds me
like a date, jaunty,   20
shoes shined, I am
proud of myself, on my toes,
obliging but not subservient.

I take shortcuts, picking up
25 speed, from time to time
I switch on the dispatcher's
litany of addresses,
China Basin to Twin Peaks,
Harrison Street° to the Ocean.

30 I am thinking tonight
my fares are like affairs
—no, more like tricks to turn:
quick, lively, ending up
with a cash payment.
35 I do not anticipate a holdup.
I can make friendly small talk.
I do not go on about Niggers,
women drivers or the Chinese.
It's all on my terms but
40 I let them think it's on theirs.

Do I pass through the city
or does it pass through me?
I know I have to be loose,
like my light embrace of the wheel,
45 loose but in control
—though hour by hour I tighten
minutely in the routine,
smoking my palate to ash,
till the last hour of all
50 will be drudgery, nothing else.

I zip down Masonic Avenue,
the taxi sings beneath the streetlights
a song to the bare city, it is
my instrument, I woo with it,
55 bridegroom and conqueror.

I jump out to open the door,
fixing the cap on my head
to, you know, firm up my role,
and on my knuckle
60 feel a sprinkle of wet.

Glancing upward I see
high above the lamppost
but touched by its farthest light
a curtain of rain already blowing
65 against black eucalyptus tops.

[1994]

28–29**China Basin, Twin Peaks, Harrison Street** places in San Francisco

1. What are the images the narrator uses to characterize himself? What effect do they have on the poem?
2. How would Erving Goffman (see p. 194) understand the poem?
3. To what other literary works in this section can you compare it?

LINDA HOGAN

LINDA HOGAN *(1947–) is a Chickasaw poet, novelist, essayist, playwright, and activist. Her work reflects her deep interest in the environment and a holistic philosophy that affirms the interconnectedness of all life. Daughter of a Chickasaw father and a non–Native American mother, she was born in Denver, Colorado, but considers Oklahoma, where her father's family lives, to be her true home. She came to poetry through her reading as an adult, commuting to the University of Colorado and earning an M.A. in English and Creative Writing. She has won many awards, including a Yaddo Colony Fellowship, a Guggenheim, and a Pulitzer Prize. She is the author of books of poetry, novels, criticism, and drama. A committed feminist, she is the mother of two adopted daughters of Oglaga Lakota heritage. Her books include* Calling Myself Home *(1978),* Seeing Through the Sun *(1985),* Mean Spirit *(1990),* Book of Medicines *(1993),* The Woman Who Watches Over the World: A Native Memoir *(2001), and* Sightings: The Gray Whales' Mysterious Journey *(2002).*

First Light

In early morning
I forget I'm in this world
with crooked chiefs
who make federal deals.

In the first light   5
I remember who rewards me for living,
not bosses
but singing birds and blue sky.

I know I can bathe and stretch,
make jewelry and love   10
the witch and wise woman
living inside, needing to be silenced
and put at rest for work's long day.

In the first light
I offer cornmeal   15
and tobacco.
I say hello to those who came before me,
and to birds
under the eaves,
and budding plants.   20

I know the old ones are here.
And every morning I remember the song
about how buffalo left through a hole in the sky
and how the grandmothers look out from those holes
25 watching over us
from there and from there.

[1991]

1. Implicit in this poem is a theory of selfhood, with the self divided into
several parts. What are they and what's the relationship between them?
2. To what other works in this section can you compare Hogan's poem?
3. What are the striking features of the language of this poem?

Langston Hughes

OLC

Langston Hughes *(1902–67) was born in Joplin, Missouri, raised by his
grandmother until he was twelve and then by his mother and stepfather. In his
high school years he began writing poetry and spent a year in Mexico and a year at
Columbia University, after which he traveled in Africa and Europe. He finished his
education at Lincoln University in Pennsylvania. He moved to New York, where
he was a major contributor to the Harlem Renaissance of the 1920s. He claimed
Dunbar, Sandburg, and Whitman as primary influences; he listened avidly to jazz
and blues, and their rhythms permeated his work. From the twenties through the
sixties, in novels, short stories, plays, and poetry, he wrote about black life in
America. His house on East 127th Street in Harlem has been designated a
landmark, and the street has been renamed "Langston Hughes Place."*

Theme for English B

The instructor said,

Go home and write
A page tonight.

And let that page come out of you—
5   Then, it will be true.

I wonder if it's that simple?

I am twenty-two, colored, born in Winston-Salem.
I went to school there, then Durham,° then here
To this college on the hill above Harlem.°
10 I am the only colored student in my class.
The steps from the hill lead down to Harlem,
Through a park, then I cross St. Nicholas,
Eighth Avenue, Seventh, and I come to the Y,

7–8**Winston-Salem, Durham** towns in central North Carolina   9**Harlem** a predominantly
black area of Manhattan, New York City

The Harlem Branch Y, where I take the elevator
Up to my room, sit down, and write this page: 15

It's not easy to know what is true for you or me
At twenty-two, my age. But I guess I'm what
I feel and see and hear. Harlem, I hear you:
Hear you, hear me—we two—you, me talk on this page.
(I hear New York, too.) Me—who?   20
Well, I like to eat, sleep, drink, and be in love.
I like to work, read, learn, and understand life.
I like a pipe for a Christmas present,
Or records—Bessie,° bop,° or Bach.°

I guess being colored doesn't make me not like   25
The same things other folks like who are other races.
So will my page be colored that I write?
Being me, it will not be white.
But it will be
A part of you instructor.   30
You are white—
Yet a part of me, as I am part of you.
That's American.

Sometimes perhaps you don't want to be a part of me.
Nor do I often want to be a part of you.   35
But we are, that's true!
As I learn from you,
I guess you learn from me—
Although you're older—and white—
And somewhat more free.   40

This is my page for English B.   [1949]

²⁴**Bessie** Bessie Smith (1895–1937) was a popular jazz and blues singer in the 1920s and
'30s.   **bop** a kind of jazz played in the 1950s and '60s by such musicians as Art Blakey,
John Coltrane, Miles Davis, Art Farmer, Charles Mingus, Sonny Rollins, Max Roach, and
others   **Bach** Johann Sebastian Bach, German composer (1685–1750)

1. What roles does the narrator adopt in this poem?
2. What does the narrator have to teach his teacher?

ANDREW MARVELL

ANDREW MARVELL *(1621–78), English poet, was born at Winestead, son of a
clergyman. He was educated at Trinity College, Cambridge, traveled abroad,
probably as a tutor, and then worked for John Milton during the Commonwealth of
Oliver Cromwell, although he kept his ties to the Royalists. After the monarchy was
restored in 1660, his influence helped Milton avoid a long prison sentence. Always
politically engaged, he represented his hometown of Hull in Parliament for almost*

twenty years. He became well known as a writer of political pamphlets and satirical verse. He is best known today for lyrics such as "The Garden," "Upon Appleton House," "The Definition of Love," and "To His Coy Mistress," most of which were not published until after his death.

To His Coy Mistress

Had we but world enough, and time,
This coyness, Lady, were no crime
We would sit down and think which way
To walk and pass our long love's day.
5 Thou by the Indian Ganges'° side
Shouldst rubies find: I by the tide
Of Humber° would complain. I would
Love you ten years before the Flood,
And you should, if you please, refuse
10 Till the conversion of the Jews.
My vegetable love should grow
Vaster than empires, and more slow;
An hundred years should go to praise
Thine eyes and on thy forehead gaze;
15 Two hundred to adore each breast,
But thirty thousand to the rest;
An age at least to every part,
And the last age should show your heart.
For, Lady, you deserve this state,
20 Nor would I love at lower rate.
    But at my back I always hear
Time's wingèd chariot hurrying near;
And yonder all before us lie
Deserts of vast eternity.
25 Thy beauty shall no more be found,
Nor, in thy marble vault, shall sound
My echoing song: then worms shall try
That long preserved virginity,
And your quaint honour turn to dust,
30 And into ashes all my lust:
The grave's a fine and private place,
But none, I think, do there embrace.
    Now therefore, while the youthful hue
Sits on thy skin like morning dew,
35 And while thy willing soul transpires
At every pore with instant fires,
Now let us sport us while we may,

---

⁵**Ganges** one of the main rivers of India   ⁷**Humber** a river in England

And now, like amorous birds of prey,
Rather at once our time devour
Than languish in his slow-chapt power.   40
Let us roll all our strength and all
Our sweetness up into one ball,
And tear our pleasures with rough strife
Thorough the iron gates of life:
Thus, though we cannot make our sun   45
Stand still, yet we will make him run.   [1641]

1. Analyze the narrator of the poem. What is his tone?
2. What arguments is the narrator making to the "coy mistress" (that is, the reluctant woman) he addresses in the poem?

SYLVIA PLATH

SYLVIA PLATH *(1932–63) was born to German immigrants in Jamaica Plain,*
Massachusetts, and lost her father through illness when she was eight. She was an   OLC
*excellent student and was accepted to Smith College on a scholarship, but she lived
in fear that others would discover that she was not a perfectly happy person. She
won a prize from* Mademoiselle *magazine for her short story, "Sunday at the
Mintons," which gave her the opportunity to be a guest editor at the magazine. She
came home exhausted, and after being rejected for Frank O'Connor's creative writing
course at Harvard, she attempted suicide. She was institutionalized and treated with
insulin therapy and shock treatments at McLean Hospital. These experiences were
material for her novel* The Bell Jar *and for a short story, "Johnny Panic and the
Bible of Dreams." She then attended Cambridge University on a Fulbright scholarship and met Ted Hughes, the poet, in 1956; they were married that same year.
They separated upon her discovery that he was having an affair. The Ariel poems in
1962 followed. She took the couple's two children with her to London and moved
into the former home of poet William Butler Yeats.* The Bell Jar *was published
under the pseudonym Victoria Lucas in January of 1963. In February, she
committed suicide.*

Lady Lazarus

I have done it again.
One year in every ten
I manage it——

A sort of walking miracle, my skin
Bright as a Nazi° lampshade,   5
My right foot

---

⁵**Nazi** the fascist party that controlled Germany from 1933–45. Among the practices often
condemned after they were discovered after World War II, the Nazis reportedly made
lampshades out of the skin of murdered Jews.

A paperweight,
My face a featureless, fine
Jew linen.

10 Peel off the napkin
O my enemy.
Do I terrify?——

The nose, the eye pits, the full set of teeth?
The sour breath
15 Will vanish in a day.

Soon, soon the flesh
The grave cave ate will be
At home on me

And I a smiling woman.
20 I am only thirty.
And like the cat I have nine times to die.

This is Number Three.
What a trash
To annihilate each decade.

25 What a million filaments.
The peanut-crunching crowd
Shoves in to see

Them unwrap me hand and foot——
The big strip tease.
30 Gentleman, ladies,

These are my hands,
My knees.
I may be skin and bone,

Nevertheless, I am the same, identical woman.
35 The first time it happened I was ten.
It was an accident.

The second time I meant
To last it out and not come back at all.
I rocked shut

40 As a seashell.
They had to call and call
And pick the worms off me like sticky pearls.

Dying
Is an art, like everything else.
45 I do it exceptionally well.

I do it so it feels like hell.
I do it so it feels real.
I guess you could say I've a call.

It's easy enough to do it in a cell.
It's easy enough to do it and stay put.   50
It's the theatrical

Comeback in broad day
To the same place, the same face, the same brute
Amused shout:

"A miracle!"   55
That knocks me out.
There is a charge

For the eyeing of my scars, there is a charge
For the hearing of my heart——
It really goes.   60

And there is a charge, a very large charge,
For a word or a touch
Or a bit of blood

Or a piece of my hair or my clothes.
So, so, Herr° Doktor.   65
So, Herr Enemy.

I am your opus,
I am your valuable,
The pure gold baby

That melts to a shriek.   70
I turn and burn.
Do not think I underestimate your great concern.

Ash, ash——
You poke and stir.
Flesh, bone, there is nothing there——   75

A cake of soap,
A wedding ring,
A gold filling.

Herr God, Herr Lucifer,
Beware   80
Beware.

Out of the ash
I rise with my red hair
And I eat men like air.   [1962]

1. Can we see this poem as a response to Emily Dickinson's "I Like a Look of Agony?" How does it relate to T.S. Eliot's "The Love Song of J. Alfred Prufrock"?
2. Explain the title of the poem. What are the other allusions in the poem?
3. What is the tone of the poem?

⁶⁵**Herr** term of address for a man (like "Mr.") in German

FICTION

SANDRA CISNEROS

SANDRA CISNEROS *(1954–) writes about Mexican and Mexican-American women, drawing from her experience as a child born to a Mexican father and Mexican-American mother in Chicago, Illinois. She was educated sporadically in the many schools she attended during the course of many family moves so that she became shy and introverted, a careful and quiet observer of the people and events around her. In the tenth grade she was encouraged to write by one of her teachers and was able to attend Loyola University in Chicago to study English. Her education as a writer was further nurtured at the Iowa Writer's Workshop, where in spite of her fears, she was finally able to view her unique life experience as a gift that she could make use of in her writing.* The House on Mango Street *(1983) was the result of that insight, although the struggle for acceptance and financial security was a long one.* My Wicked, Wicked Ways, *a book of poetry, followed, but did not provide the success and recognition she needed, although she even passed out fliers in supermarkets to publicize it. Sad and broke, she left Texas, where she had been living, and took a teaching job at a branch of California State University. Another money grant helped her write* Women Hollering Creek and Other Stories, *which Random House published. She was the first Chicana author to receive a major publishing contract for a work about Mexican-American women and was critically acclaimed.* Loose Women, *a book of poetry, children's books, and translations followed, so that Cisneros's reputation is now secure. Her battle with the city board of San Antonio over painting her house purple lasted for two years until the house finally faded to a color that the city deemed "historically appropriate."*

Mericans

We're waiting for the awful grandmother who is inside dropping pesos° into *la ofrenda* box° before the altar to La Divina Providencia. Lighting votive candles and genuflecting. Blessing herself and kissing her thumb. Running a crystal rosary between her fingers. Mumbling, mumbling, mumbling.

There are so many prayers and promises and thanks-be-to-God to be given in the name of the husband and the sons and the only daughter who never attend mass. It doesn't matter. Like La Virgen de Guadalupe,° the awful grandmother intercedes on their behalf. For the grandfather who hasn't believed in anything since the first PRI° elections. For my father, El Periquín, so skinny he needs his sleep. For Auntie Light-skin, who only a few hours before was breakfasting on brain and goat tacos after dancing all night in the pink zone.° For Uncle Fat-face,

---

¹**pesos** Mexican currency   *la ofrenda* **box** Spanish for a container for monetary offerings in a church   ²**La Virgen de Guadalupe** the Virgin Mary as she reportedly appeared to a boy in Mexico City in the sixteenth century   **PRI** Institutional Revolutionary Party of Mexico   **pink zone** a Mexican-American district

the blackest of the black sheep—*Always remember your Uncle Fat-face in your prayers.* And Uncle Baby—*You go for me, Mamá—God listens to you.*

The awful grandmother has been gone a long time. She disappeared behind the heavy leather outer curtain and the dusty velvet inner. We must stay near the church entrance. We must not wander over to the balloon and punch-ball vendors. We cannot spend our allowance on fried cookies or Familia Burrón comic books or those clear cone-shaped suckers that make everything look like a rainbow when you look through them. We cannot run off and have our picture taken on the wooden ponies. We must not climb the steps up the hill behind the church and chase each other through the cemetery. We have promised to stay right where the awful grandmother left us until she returns.

There are those walking to church on their knees. Some with fat rags tied around their legs and others with pillows, one to kneel on, and one to flop ahead. There are women with black shawls crossing and uncrossing themselves. There are armies of penitents carrying banners and flowered arches while musicians play tinny trumpets and tinny drums.

La Virgen de Guadalupe is waiting inside behind a plate of thick glass. There's also a gold crucifix bent crooked as a mesquite tree when someone once threw a bomb. La Virgen de Guadalupe on the main altar because she's a big miracle, the crooked crucifix on a side altar because that's a little miracle.

But we're outside in the sun. My big brother Junior hunkered against the wall with his eyes shut. My little brother Keeks running around in circles.

Maybe and most probably my little brother is imagining he's a flying feather dancer, like the ones we saw swinging high up from a pole on the Virgin's birthday. I want to be a flying feather dancer too, but when he circles past me he shouts, "I'm a B-Fifty-two bomber, you're a German," and shoots me with an invisible machine gun. I'd rather play flying feather dancers, but if I tell my brother this, he might not play with me at all.

"*Girl.* We can't play with a *girl.*" *Girl.* It's my brothers' favorite insult now instead of "sissy." "You *girl,*" they yell at each other. "You throw that ball like a *girl.*"

I've already made up my mind to be a German when Keeks swoops past again, this time yelling, "I'm Flash Gordon. You're Ming the Merciless and the Mud People."° I don't mind being Ming the Merciless, but I don't like being the Mud People. Something wants to come out of the corners of my eyes, but I don't let it. Crying is what *girls* do.

I leave Keeks running around in circles—"I'm the Lone Ranger, you're Tonto." I leave Junior squatting on his ankles and go look for the awful grandmother.

Why do churches smell like the inside of an ear? Like incense and the dark and candles in blue glass? And why does holy water smell of tears? The awful grandmother makes me kneel and fold my hands. The ceiling high and everyone's prayers bumping up there like balloons.

If I stare at the eyes of the saints long enough, they move and wink at me, which makes me a sort of saint too. When I get tired of winking saints, I count

⁹**Flash Gordon, Ming the Merciless and the Mud People** the science fiction hero from magazine, television serial, and film, and his enemies

the awful grandmother's mustache hairs while she prays for Uncle Old, sick from the worm,° and Auntie Cuca, suffering from a life of troubles that left half her face crooked and the other half sad.

There must be a long, long list of relatives who haven't gone to church. The awful grandmother knits the names of the dead and the living into one long prayer fringed with the grandchildren born in that barbaric country with its barbarian ways.

I put my weight on one knee, then the other, and when they both grow fat as a mattress of pins, I slap them each awake. *Micaela, you may wait outside with Alfredito and Enrique.* The awful grandmother says it all in Spanish, which I understand when I'm paying attention. "What?" I say, though it's neither proper nor polite. "What?" which the awful grandmother hears as "*¿Güat?*" But she only gives me a look and shoves me toward the door.

15   After all that dust and dark, the light from the plaza makes me squinch my eyes like if I just came out of the movies. My brother Keeks is drawing squiggly lines on the concrete with a wedge of glass and the heel of his shoe. My brother Junior squatting against the entrance, talking to a lady and man.

They're not from here. Ladies don't come to church dressed in pants. And everybody knows men aren't supposed to wear shorts.

"*¿Quieres chicle?*"° the lady asks in a Spanish too big for her mouth.

"*Gracias.*"° The lady gives him a whole handful of gum for free, little cellophane cubes of Chiclets, cinnamon and aqua and the white ones that don't taste like anything but are good for pretend buck teeth.

"*Por favor,*"° says the lady. "*¿Un foto?*"° pointing to her camera.

20   "*Si.*"°

She's so busy taking Junior's picture, she doesn't notice me and Keeks.

"Hey, Michele, Keeks. You guys want gum?"

"But you speak English!"

"Yeah," my brother says, "we're Mericans."

25   We're Mericans, we're Mericans, and inside the awful grandmother prays.

[1991]

---

¹²**sick from the worm** hung over   ¹⁷*¿Quieres chicle?* Would you like a Chiclet [chewing gum]?   ¹⁸*Gracias* Thank you.   ¹⁹*Por favor* Please.   *¿Un foto?* [May I take your] photograph?   ²⁰*Si* Yes.

1. What do we learn from the children's encounter with the tourists?
2. Why does Junior answer the woman in Spanish?

CHARLOTTE PERKINS GILMAN

CHARLOTTE PERKINS GILMAN (1860–1935), *raised by her struggling single mother after her father abandoned the family, was related through her great-grandfather, Lyman Beecher, American Protestant educator, reformer, and*

temperance advocate, to Harriet Beecher Stowe, anti-slavery novelist, to Catherine Esther Beecher, advocate of education for women, and to Henry Ward Beecher, advocate of women's suffrage. It was an activist family. She began to write and lecture on feminism after a bout of depression following the birth of her daughter led to an unhappy stay at the sanatorium of Dr. S. Weir Mitchell for a month of "rest cure," which is the basis for "The Yellow Wallpaper." Gilman's revolutionary book, Women and Economics, *written in 1898, became a bestseller and was translated into seven languages. It criticized and debunked love, marriage, and domesticity as the main goals for women. She lectured widely and wrote extensively, producing nonfiction, novels, nearly 200 short stories, hundreds of poems and plays, thousands of essays, and her autobiography,* The Living of Charlotte Perkins Gilman. *Her magazine* The Forerunner *became an important medium for educating both men and women on the importance to society of equal rights for women. Her second marriage began in 1900. She ended her own life in 1935 when suffering from terminal cancer.*

The Yellow Wallpaper

It is very seldom that mere ordinary people like John and myself secure ancestral halls for the summer.

A colonial mansion, a hereditary estate. I would say a haunted house, and reach the height of romantic felicity—but that would be asking too much of fate!

Still I will proudly declare that there is something queer about it.

Else, why should it be let so cheaply? And why have stood so long untenanted?

John laughs at me, of course, but one expects that in marriage.   5

John is practical in the extreme. He has no patience with faith, an intense horror of superstition, and he scoffs openly at any talk of things not to be felt and seen and put down in figures.

John is a physician, and *perhaps*—(I would not say it to a living soul, of course, but this is dead paper and a great relief to my mind)—*perhaps* that is one reason I do not get well faster.

You see he does not believe I am sick!

And what can one do?

If a physician of high standing, and one's own husband, assures friends and   10
relatives that there is really nothing the matter with one but temporary nervous depression—a slight hysterical tendency—what is one to do?

My brother is also a physician, and also of high standing, and he says the same thing.

So I take phosphates or phosphites—whichever it is, and tonics, and journeys, and air, and exercise, and am absolutely forbidden to "work" until I am well again.

Personally, I disagree with their ideas.

Personally, I believe that congenial work, with excitement and change, would do me good.

15   But what is one to do?

I did write for a while in spite of them: but it *does* exhaust me a good deal—having to be so sly about it, or else meet with heavy opposition.

I sometimes fancy that in my condition if I had less opposition and more society and stimulus—but John says the very worst thing I can do is to think about my condition, and I confess it always makes me feel bad.

So I will let it alone and talk about the house.

The most beautiful place! It is quite alone, standing well back from the road, quite three miles from the village. It makes me think of English places that you read about, for there are hedges and walls and gates that lock, and lots of separate little houses for the gardeners and people.

20   There is a *delicious* garden! I never saw such a garden—large and shady, full of box-bordered paths, and lined with long grapecovered arbors with seats under them.

There were greenhouses, too, but they are all broken now. There was some legal trouble. I believe, something about the heirs and coheirs: anyhow, the place has been empty for years.

That spoils my ghostliness. I am afraid, but I don't care—there is something strange about the house—I can feel it.

I even said so to John one moonlight evening, but he said what I felt was a *draught,* and shut the window.

I get unreasonably angry with John sometimes. I'm sure I never used to be so sensitive. I think it is due to this nervous condition.

25   But John says if I feel so, I shall neglect proper self-control: so I take pains to control myself—before him, at least, and that makes me very tired.

I don't like our room a bit. I wanted one downstairs that opened on the piazza and had roses all over the window, and such pretty old-fashioned chintz hangings! but John would not hear of it.

He said there was only one window and not room for two beds, and no near room for him if he took another.

He is very careful and loving, and hardly lets me stir without special direction.

I have a schedule prescription for each hour in the day: he takes all care from me, and so I feel basely ungrateful not to value it more.

30   He said we came here solely on my account, that I was to have perfect rest and all the air I could get. "Your exercise depends on your strength, my dear," said he, "and your food somewhat on your appetite; but air you can absorb all the time." So we took the nursery at the top of the house.

It is a big, airy room, the whole floor nearly, with windows that look all ways, and air and sunshine galore. It was nursery first and then playroom and gymnasium, I should judge; for the windows are barred for little children, and there are rings and things in the walls.

The paint and paper look as if a boys' school had used it. It is stripped off—the paper—in great patches all around the head of my bed, about as far as I can reach, and in a great place on the other side of the room low down. I never saw a worse paper in my life.

One of those sprawling flamboyant patterns committing every artistic sin.

It is dull enough to confuse the eye in following, pronounced enough to constantly irritate and provoke study, and when you follow the lame uncertain curves for a little distance they suddenly commit suicide—plunge off at outrageous angles, destroy themselves in unheard of contradictions.

The color is repellent, almost revolting: a smouldering unclean yellow, strangely faded by the slow-turning sunlight.

It is a dull yet lurid orange in some places, a sickly sulphur tint in others.

No wonder the children hated it! I should hate it myself if I had to live in this room long.

There comes John, and I must put this away,—he hates to have me write a word.

We have been here two weeks, and I haven't felt like writing before, since that first day.

I am sitting by the window now, up in this atrocious nursery, and there is nothing to hinder my writing as much as I please, save lack of strength.

John is away all day, and even some nights when his cases are serious.

I am glad my case is not serious!

But these nervous troubles are dreadfully depressing.

John does not know how much I really suffer. He knows there is no *reason* to suffer, and that satisfies him.

Of course it is only nervousness. It does weigh on me so not to do my duty in any way!

I meant to be such a help to John, such a real rest and comfort, and here I am a comparative burden already!

Nobody would believe what an effort it is to do what little I am able,—to dress and entertain, and order things.

It is fortunate Mary is so good with the baby. Such a dear baby!

And yet I *cannot* be with him, it makes me so nervous.

I suppose John never was nervous in his life. He laughs at me so about this wallpaper!

At first he meant to repaper the room, but afterwards he said that I was letting it get the better of me, and that nothing was worse for a nervous patient than to give way to such fancies.

He said that after the wallpaper was changed it would be the heavy bedstead, and then the barred windows, and then that gate at the head of the stairs, and so on.

"You know the place is doing you good," he said, "and really, dear, I don't care to renovate the house just for a three months' rental."

"Then do let us go downstairs." I said, "there are such pretty rooms there."

Then he took me in his arms and called me a blessed little goose, and said he would go down to the cellar, if I wished, and have it whitewashed into the bargain.

But he is right enough about the beds and windows and things.

It is an airy and comfortable room as any one need wish, and, of course, I would not be so silly as to make him uncomfortable just for a whim.

I'm really getting quite fond of the big room, all but that horrid paper.

Out of one window I can see the garden, those mysterious deep-shaded arbors, the riotous old-fashioned flowers, and bushes and gnarly trees.

60 Out of another I get a lovely view of the bay and a little private wharf belonging to the estate. There is a beautiful shaded lane that runs down there from the house. I always fancy I see people walking in these numerous paths and arbors, but John has cautioned me not to give way to fancy in the least. He says that with my imaginative power and habit of story-making, a nervous weakness like mine is sure to lead to all manner of excited fancies, and that I ought to use my will and good sense to check the tendency. So I try.

I think sometimes that if I were only well enough to write a little it would relieve the press of ideas and rest me.

But I find I get pretty tired when I try.

It is so discouraging not to have any advice and companionship about my work. When I get really well, John says we will ask Cousin Henry and Julia down for a long visit; but he says he would as soon put fireworks in my pillow-case as to let me have those stimulating people about now.

I wish I could get well faster.

65 But I must not think about that. This paper looks to me as if it *knew* what a vicious influence it had!

There is a recurrent spot where the pattern lolls like a broken neck and two bulbous eyes stare at you upside down.

I get positively angry with the impertinence of it and the everlastingness. Up and down and sideways they crawl, and those absurd, unblinking eyes are everywhere. There is one place where two breadths didn't match, and the eyes go all up and down the line, one a little higher than the other.

I never saw so much expression in an inanimate thing before, and we all know how much expression they have! I used to lie awake as a child and get more entertainment and terror out of blank walls and plain furniture than most children could find in a toystore.

I remember what a kindly wink the knobs of our big, old bureau used to have, and there was one chair that always seemed like a strong friend.

70 I used to feel that if any of the other things looked too fierce I could always hop into that chair and be safe.

The furniture in this room is no worse than inharmonious, however, for we had to bring it all from downstairs. I suppose when this was used as a playroom they had to take the nursery things out, and no wonder! I never saw such ravages as the children have made here.

The wallpaper, as I said before, is torn off in spots, and it sticketh closer than a brother—they must have had perseverance as well as hatred.

Then the floor is scratched and gouged and splintered, the plaster itself is dug out here and there, and this great heavy bed which is all we found in the room, looks as if it had been through the wars.

But I don't mind it a bit—only the paper.

75 There comes John's sister. Such a dear girl as she is, and so careful of me! I must not let her find me writing.

She is a perfect and enthusiastic housekeeper, and hopes for no better profession. I verily believe she thinks it is the writing which made me sick!

But I can write when she is out, and see her a long way off from these windows.

There is one that commands the road, a lovely shaded winding road, and one that just looks off over the country. A lovely country, too, full of great elms and velvet meadows.

This wallpaper has a kind of sub-pattern in a different shade, a particularly irritating one, for you can only see it in certain lights, and not clearly then.

But in the places where it isn't faded and where the sun is just so—I can see ⁸⁰ a strange, provoking, formless sort of figure, that seems to skulk about behind that silly and conspicuous front design.

There's sister on the stairs!

Well, the Fourth of July is over! The people are all gone and I am tired out. John thought it might do me good to see a little company, so we just had mother and Nellie and the children down for a week.

Of course I didn't do a thing. Jennie sees to everything now. But it tired me all the same.

John says if I don't pick up faster he shall send me to Weir Mitchell° in the fall. ⁸⁵

But I don't want to go there at all. I had a friend who was in his hands once, and she says he is just like John and my brother, only more so!

Besides, it is such an undertaking to go so far.

I don't feel as if it was worth while to turn my hand over for anything, and I'm getting dreadfully fretful and querulous.

I cry at nothing, and cry most of the time.

Of course I don't when John is here, or anybody else, but when I am alone.

And I am alone a good deal just now. John is kept in town very often by ⁹⁰ serious cases, and Jennie is good and lets me alone when I want her to.

So I walk a little in the garden or down that lovely lane, sit on the porch under the roses, and lie down up here a good deal.

I'm getting really fond of the room in spite of the wallpaper. Perhaps *because* of the wallpaper.

It dwells in my mind so!

I lie here on this great immovable bed—it is nailed down, I believe—and follow that pattern about by the hour. It is as good as gymnastics, I assure you. I start, we'll say, at the bottom, down in the corner over there where it has not been touched, and I determine for the thousandth time that I *will* follow that pointless pattern to some sort of a conclusion.

I know a little of the principle of design, and I know this thing was not ⁹⁵ arranged on any laws of radiation, or alternation, or repetition, or symmetry, or anything else that I ever heard of.

⁸⁴**Weir Mitchell** a late-nineteenth-century neurologist who developed his rest cure partly to alleviate the symptoms of "nervous women." It was also used for soldiers suffering from shell shock.

It is repeated, of course, by the breadths, but not otherwise.

Looked at in one way each breadth stands alone, the bloated curves and flourishes—a kind of "debased Romanesque° with *delirium tremens*°—go waddling up and down in isolated columns of fatuity.

But, on the other hand, they connect diagonally, and the sprawling outlines run off in great slanting waves of optic horror, like a lot of wallowing seaweeds in full chase.

The whole thing goes horizontally, too, at least it seems so, and I exhaust myself in trying to distinguish the order of its going in that direction.

100   They have used a horizontal breadth for a frieze, and that adds wonderfully to the confusion.

There is one end of the room where it is almost intact, and there, when the crosslights fade and the low sun shines directly upon it, I can almost fancy radiation after all,—the interminable grotesques seem to form around a common center and rush off in headlong plunges of equal distraction.

It makes me tired to follow it. I will take a nap I guess.

I don't know why I should write this.

I don't want to.

105   I don't feel able.

And I know John would think it absurd. But I *must* say what I feel and think in some way—it is such a relief.

But the effort is getting to be greater than the relief!

Half the time now I am awfully lazy, and lie down ever so much.

John says I mustn't lose my strength, and has me take cod liver oil and lots of tonics and things, to say nothing of ale and wine and rare meat.

110   Dear John! He loves me very dearly, and hates to have me sick. I tried to have a real earnest reasonable talk with him the other day, and tell him how I wish he would let me go and make a visit to Cousin Henry and Julia.

But he said I wasn't able to go, nor able to stand it after I got there: and I did not make out a very good case for myself, for I was crying before I had finished.

It is getting to be a great effort for me to think straight. Just this nervous weakness I suppose.

And dear John gathered me up in his arms, and just carried me upstairs and laid me on the bed, and sat by me and read to me till it tired my head.

He said I was his darling and his comfort and all he had, and that I must take care of myself for his sake, and keep well.

115   He says no one but myself can help me out of it, that I must use my will and self-control and not let any silly fancies run away with me.

There's one comfort, the baby is well and happy, and does not have to occupy this nursery with the horrid wallpaper.

If we had not used it, that blessed child would have! What a fortunate escape! Why, I wouldn't have a child of mine, an impressionable little thing, live in such a room for worlds.

[97]**Romanesque** an early medieval architectural style using rounded arches   *delerium tremens* symptoms of withdrawing from an alcohol addiction

I never thought of it before, but it is lucky that John kept me here after all. I can stand it so much easier than a baby, you see.

Of course I never mention it to them any more—I am too wise,—but I keep watch of it all the same.

There are things in that paper that nobody knows but me, or ever will. 120

Behind that outside pattern the dim shapes get clearer every day.

It is always the same shape, only very numerous.

And it is like a woman stooping down and creeping about behind that pattern. I don't like it a bit. I wonder—I begin to think—I wish John would take me away from here!

It is so hard to talk with John about my case, because he is so wise, and because he loves me so.

But I tried last night. 125

It was moonlight. The moon shines in all around just as the sun does.

I hate to see it sometimes, it creeps so slowly, and always comes in by one window or another.

John was asleep and I hated to waken him, so I kept still and watched the moonlight on that undulating wallpaper till I felt creepy.

The faint figure behind seemed to shake the pattern, just as if she wanted to get out.

I got up softly and went to feel and see if the paper *did* move, and when I 130 came back John was awake.

"What is it, little girl?" he said. "Don't go walking about like that—you'll get cold."

I thought it was a good time to talk, so I told him that I really was not gaining here, and that I wished he would take me away.

"Why darling!" said he, "our lease will be up in three weeks, and I can't see how to leave before."

"The repairs are not done at home, and I cannot possibly leave town just now. Of course if you were in any danger, I could and would, but you really are better, dear, whether you can see it or not. I am a doctor, dear, and I know. You are gaining flesh and color, your appetite is better, I feel really much easier about you."

"I don't weigh a bit more," said I, "nor as much: and my appetite may be 135 better in the evening when you are here, but it is worse in the morning when you are away!"

"Bless her little heart!" said he with a big hug, "she shall be as sick as she pleases! But now let's improve the shining hours by going to sleep, and talk about it in the morning!"

"And you won't go away?" I asked gloomily.

"Why, how can I, dear? It is only three weeks more and then we will take a nice little trip of a few days while Jennie is getting the house ready. Really dear you are better!"

"Better in body perhaps—" I began, and stopped short, for he sat up straight and looked at me with such a stern, reproachful look that I could not say another word.

"My darling," said he, "I beg of you, for my sake and for our child's sake, as 140 well as for your own, that you will never for one instant let that idea enter your mind! There is nothing so dangerous, so fascinating, to a temperament like yours. It is a false and foolish fancy. Can you not trust me as a physician when I tell you so?"

So of course I said no more on that score, and we went to sleep before long. He thought I was asleep first, but I wasn't and lay there for hours trying to decide whether that front pattern and the back pattern really did move together or separately.

On a pattern like this, by daylight, there is a lack of sequence, a defiance of law, that is a constant irritant to a normal mind.

The color is hideous enough, and unreliable enough, and infuriating enough, but the pattern is torturing.

You think you have mastered it, but just as you get well underway in following, it turns a back-somersault and there you are. It slaps you in the face, knocks you down, and tramples upon you. It is like a bad dream.

145 The outside pattern is a florid arabesque, reminding one of a fungus. If you can imagine a toadstool in joints, an interminable string of toadstools, budding and sprouting in endless convolutions—why, that is something like it.

That is, sometimes!

There is one marked peculiarity about this paper, a thing nobody seems to notice but myself, and that is that it changes as the light changes.

When the sun shoots in through the east window—I always watch for that first long, straight ray—it changes so quickly that I never can quite believe it.

That is why I watch it always.

150 By moonlight—the moon shines in all night when there is a moon—I wouldn't know it was the same paper.

At night in any kind of light, in twilight, candle light, lamplight, and worst of all by moonlight, it becomes bars! The outside pattern I mean, and the woman behind it is as plain as can be.

I didn't realize for a long time what the thing was that showed behind, that dim sub-pattern, but now I am quite sure it is a woman.

By daylight she is subdued, quiet. I fancy it is the pattern that keeps her so still. It is so puzzling. It keeps me quiet by the hour.

I lie down ever so much now. John says it is good for me, and to sleep all I can.

155 Indeed he started the habit by making me lie down for an hour after each meal.

It is a very bad habit I am convinced, for you see I don't sleep.

And that cultivates deceit, for I don't tell them I'm awake—O no!

The fact is I am getting a little afraid of John.

He seems very queer sometimes, and even Jennie has an inexplicable look.

160 It strikes me occasionally, just as a scientific hypothesis—that perhaps it is the paper!

I have watched John when he did not know I was looking, and come into the room suddenly on the most innocent excuses, and I've caught him several times *looking at the paper!* And Jennie too. I caught Jennie with her hand on it once.

She didn't know I was in the room, and when I asked her in a quiet, a very quiet voice, with the most restrained manner possible, what she was doing with the paper—she turned around as if she had been caught stealing, and looked quite angry—asked me why I should frighten her so!

Then she said that the paper stained everything it touched, that she had found yellow smooches on all my clothes and John's, and she wished we would be more careful!

Did not that sound innocent? But I know she was studying that pattern, and I am determined that nobody shall find it out but myself!

Life is very much more exciting now than it used to be. You see I have   165
something more to expect, to look forward to, to watch. I really do eat better, and am more quiet than I was.

John is so pleased to see me improve! He laughed a little the other day, and said I seemed to be flourishing in spite of my wallpaper.

I turned it off with a laugh. I had no intention of telling him it was *because* of the wallpaper—he would make fun of me. He might even want to take me away.

I don't want to leave now until I have found it out. There is a week more, and I think that will be enough.

I'm feeling ever so much better! I don't sleep much at night, for it is so interesting to watch developments, but I sleep a good deal in the daytime.

In the daytime it is tiresome and perplexing.   170

There are always new shoots on the fungus, and new shades of yellow all over it. I cannot keep count of them, though I have tried conscientiously.

It is the strangest yellow, that wallpaper! It makes me think of all the yellow things I ever saw—not beautiful ones like buttercups, but old foul, bad yellow things.

But there is something else about that paper—the smell! I noticed it the moment we came into the room, but with so much air and sun it was not bad. Now we have had a week of fog and rain, and whether the windows are open or not, the smell is here.

It creeps all over the house.

I find it hovering in the dining-room, skulking in the parlor, hiding in the   175
hall, lying in wait for me on the stairs.

It gets into my hair.

Even when I go to ride, if I turn my head suddenly and surprise it—there is that smell!

Such a peculiar odor, too! I have spent hours in trying to analyze it, to find what it smelled like.

It is not bad—at first, and very gentle, but quite the subtlest, most enduring odor I ever met.

In this damp weather it is awful, I wake up in the night and find it hanging   180
over me.

It used to disturb me at first. I thought seriously of burning the house—to reach the smell.

But now I am used to it. The only thing I can think of that it is like is the *color* of the paper! A yellow smell.

There is a very funny mark on this wall, low down, near the mopboard. A streak that runs round the room. It goes behind every piece of furniture, except the bed, a long, straight, even *smooch*, as if it had been rubbed over and over.

I wonder how it was done and who did it, and what they did it for. Round and round and round—round and round and round—it makes me dizzy!

185   I really have discovered something at last.

Through watching so much at night, when it changes so, I have finally found out.

The front pattern *does* move—and no wonder! The woman behind shakes it!

Sometimes I think there are a great many women behind, and sometimes only one, and she crawls around fast, and her crawling shakes it all over.

Then in the very bright spots she keeps still, and in the very shady spots she just takes hold of the bars and shakes them hard.

190   And she is all the time trying to climb through. But nobody could climb through that pattern—it strangles so: I think that is why it has so many heads.

They get through, and then the pattern strangles them off and turns them upside down, and makes their eyes white!

If those heads were covered or taken off it would not be half so bad.

I think that woman gets out in the daytime!

And I'll tell you why—privately—I've seen her!

195   I can see her out of every one of my windows!

It is the same woman, I know, for she is always creeping, and most women do not creep by daylight.

I see her on that long road under the trees, creeping along, and when a carriage comes she hides under the blackberry vines.

I don't blame her a bit. It must be very humiliating to be caught creeping by daylight!

I always lock the door when I creep by daylight. I can't do it at night, for I know John would suspect something at once.

200   And John is so queer now, that I don't want to irritate him. I wish he would take another room! Besides, I don't want anybody to get that woman out at night but myself.

I often wonder if I could see her out of all the windows at once.

But, turn as fast as I can, I can only see out of one at one time. And though I always see her, she *may* be able to creep faster than I can turn!

I have watched her sometimes away off in the open country, creeping as fast as a cloud shadow in a high wind.

If only that top pattern could be gotten off from the under one! I mean to try it, little by little.

205   I have found out another funny thing, but I shan't tell at this time! It does not do to trust people too much.

There are only two more days to get this paper off, and I believe John is beginning to notice. I don't like the look in his eyes.

And I heard him ask Jennie a lot of professional questions about me. She had a very good report to give.

She said I slept a good deal in the daytime.

John knows I don't sleep very well at night, for all I'm so quiet!

He asked me all sorts of questions, too, and pretended to be very loving and   210
kind.

As if I couldn't see through him!

Still, I don't wonder he acts so, sleeping under this paper for three months.

It only interests me, but I feel sure John and Jennie are secretly affected by it.

Hurrah! This is the last day, but it is enough. John is to stay in town over night, and won't be out until this evening.

Jennie wanted to sleep with me—the sly thing! But I told her I should   215
undoubtedly rest better for a night all alone.

That was clever, for really I wasn't alone a bit! As soon as it was moonlight and that poor thing began to crawl and shake the pattern, I got up and ran to help her.

I pulled and she shook, I shook and she pulled, and before morning we had peeled off yards of that paper.

A strip about as high as my head and half round the room. And then when the sun came and that awful pattern began to laugh at me, I declared I would finish it to-day!

We go away to-morrow, and they are moving all the furniture down again to leave things as they were before.

Jennie looked at the wall in amazement, but I told her merrily that I did it   220
out of pure spite at the vicious thing.

She laughed and said she wouldn't mind doing it herself, but I must not get tired.

How she betrayed herself that time!

But I am here, and no person touches this paper but me—not *alive!*

She tried to get me out of the room—it was too patent! But I said it was so quiet and empty and clean now that I believed I would lie down again and sleep all I could; and not to wake me even for dinner—I would call when I woke.

So now she is gone, and the servants are gone, and the things are gone, and   225
there is nothing left but that great bedstead nailed down, with the canvas mattress we found on it.

We shall sleep downstairs to-night, and take the boat home to-morrow.

I quite enjoy the room, now it is bare again.

How those children did tear about here!

This bedstead is fairly gnawed!

But I must get to work.   230

I have locked the door and thrown the key down into the front path.

I don't want to go out, and I don't want to have anybody come in, till John comes.

I want to astonish him.

I've got a rope up here that even Jennie did not find. If that woman does get
out, and tries to get away, I can tie her!

235 But I forgot I could not reach far without anything to stand on! This bed will
not move!

I tried to lift and push it until I was lame, and then I got so angry I bit off a
little piece at one corner—but it hurt my teeth.

Then I peeled off all the paper I could reach standing on the floor. It sticks
horribly and the pattern just enjoys it! All those strangled heads and bulbous
eyes and waddling fungus growths just shriek with derision!

I am getting angry enough to do something desperate. To jump out of
the window would be admirable exercise, but the bars are too strong even to
try.

Besides I wouldn't do it. Of course not, I know well enough that a step like
that is improper and might be misconstrued.

240 I don't like to *look* out of the windows even—there are so many of those
creeping women, and they creep so fast.

I wonder if they all come out of that wallpaper as I did?

But I am securely fastened now by my well-hidden rope—you don't get *me*
out in the road there!

I suppose I shall have to get back behind the pattern when it comes night,
and that is hard!

It is so pleasant to be out in this great room and creep around as I please!

245 I don't want to go outside. I won't, even if Jennie asks me to.

For outside you have to creep on the ground, and everything is green instead
of yellow.

But here I can creep smoothly on the floor, and my shoulder just fits in that
long smooch around the wall, so I cannot lose my way.

Why there's John at the door!

It is no use, young man, you can't open it!

250 How he does call and pound!

Now he's crying for an axe.

It would be a shame to break down that beautiful door!

"John dear!" said I in the gentlest voice, "the key is down by the front steps,
under a plantain leaf!"

That silenced him for a few moments.

255 Then he said—very quietly indeed, "Open the door, my darling!"

"I can't," said I. "The key is down by the front door under a plantain leaf!"

And then I said it again, several times, very gently and slowly, and said it so
often that he had to go and see, and he got it of course, and came in. He stopped
short by the door.

"What is the matter?" he cried. "For God's sake, what are you doing!"

I kept on creeping just the same, but I looked at him over my shoulder.

260 "I've got out at last," said I, "in spite of you and Jane. And I've pulled off
most of the paper, so you can't put me back!"

Now why should that man have fainted? But he did, and right across my
path by the wall, so that I had to creep over him every time! [1892]

1. Characterize the narrator. What difference does it make that the story is told from her point of view?
2. Compare the method of narration with that of Katherine Anne Porter's "The Jilting of Granny Weatherall" (see p. 1472).
3. Trace the narrator's mental condition through her view of the wallpaper. What is its symbolic value in the story?
4. Given his view of *Hamlet* (see p. 702), how might Terence Eagleton interpret the story?
5. Do some research on the treatment methods invented by Dr. S. Weir Mitchell (paragraph 84) to put the story into its historical context.
6. Put the story into the context of Gilman's life.

LANGSTON HUGHES

(For biographical notes, see p. 548.)

Who's Passing for Who?

One of the great difficulties about being a member of a minority race is that so many kindhearted, well-meaning bores gather around to help you. Usually, to tell the truth, they have nothing to help with, except their company—which is often appallingly dull.

Some members of the Negro race seem very well able to put up with it, though, in these uplifting years. Such was Caleb Johnson, colored social worker, who was always dragging around with him some nondescript white person or two, inviting them to dinner, showing them Harlem,° ending up at the Savoy— much to the displeasure of whatever friends of his might be out that evening for fun, not sociology.

Friends are friends and, unfortunately, overearnest uplifters are uplifters—no matter what color they may be. If it were the white race that was ground down instead of negroes, Caleb Johnson would be one of the first to offer Nordics the sympathy of his utterly inane society, under the impression that somehow he would be doing them a great deal of good.

You see, Caleb, and his white friends, too, were all bores. Or so we, who lived in Harlem's literary bohemia during the "Negro Renaissance," thought. We literary ones in those days considered ourselves too broad-minded to be bothered with questions of color. We liked people of any race who smoked incessantly, drank liberally, wore complexion and morality as loose garments, and made fun of anyone who didn't do likewise. We snubbed and high-hatted any Negro or white luckless enough not to understand Gertrude Stein, Ulysses, Man Ray, the theremin, Jean Toomer, or George Antheil. By the end of the 1920's Caleb was just catching up to Dos Passos. He thought H. G. Wells good.

---

[2]**Harlem** a predominantly black area of Manhattan, New York City

5   We met Caleb one night in Small's. He had three assorted white folks in tow. We would have passed him by with but a nod had he not hailed us enthusiastically, risen, and introduced us with great acclaim to his friends, who turned out to be schoolteachers from Iowa, a woman and two men. They appeared amazed and delighted to meet all at once two Negro writers and a black painter in the flesh. They invited us to have a drink with them. Money being scarce with us, we deigned to sit down at their table.

The white lady said, "I've never met a Negro writer before."

The two men added, "Neither have we."

"Why, we know any number of *white* writers," we three dark bohemians declared with bored nonchalance.

"But Negro writers are much more rare," said the lady.

10   "There are plenty in Harlem," we said.

"But not in Iowa," said one of the men, shaking his mop of red hair.

"There are no good *white* writers in Iowa either, are there?" we asked superciliously.

"Oh yes, Ruth Suckow came from there."

Whereupon we proceeded to light in upon Ruth Suckow as old hat and to anihilate her in favor of Kay Boyle. The way we flung names around seemed to impress both Caleb and his white guests. This, of course, delighted us, though we were too young and too proud to admit it.

15   The drinks came and everything was going well, all of us drinking, and we three showing off in a high-brow manner, when suddenly at the table just behind us a man got up and knocked down a woman. He was a brownskin man. The woman was blonde. As she rose, he knocked her down again. Then the red-haired man from Iowa got up and knocked the colored man down.

He said, "Keep your hands off that white woman."

The man got up and said, "She's not a white woman. She's my wife."

One of the waiters added, "She's not white, sir, she's colored."

Whereupon the man from Iowa looked puzzled, dropped his fists, and said, "I'm sorry."

20   The colored man said, "What are you doing up here in Harlem anyway, interfering with my family affairs?"

The white man said, "I thought she was a white woman."

The woman who had been on the floor rose and said, "Well, I'm not a white woman, I'm colored, and you leave my husband alone."

Then they both lit in on the gentleman from Iowa. It took all of us and several waiters, too, to separate them. When it was over, the manager requested us to kindly pay our bill and get out. He said we were disturbing the peace. So we all left. We went to a fish restaurant down the street. Caleb was terribly apologetic to his white friends. We artists were both mad and amused.

"Why did you say you were sorry," said the colored painter to the visitor from Iowa, "after you'd hit that man—and then found out it wasn't a white woman you were defending, but merely a light colored woman who looked white?"

25   "Well," answered the red-haired Iowan, "I didn't mean to be butting in if they were all the same race."

"Don't you think a woman needs defending from a brute, no matter what race she may be?" asked the painter.

"Yes, but I think it's up to you to defend your own women."

"Oh, so you'd divide up a brawl according to races, no matter who was right?"

"Well, I wouldn't say that."

"You mean you wouldn't defend a colored woman whose husband was knocking her down?" asked the poet.   30

Before the visitor had time to answer, the painter said, "No! you just got mad because you thought a black man was hitting a *white* woman."

"But she *looked* like a white woman," countered the man.

"Maybe she was just passing for colored," I said.

"Like some Negroes pass for white," Caleb interposed.

"Anyhow, I don't like it," said the colored painter, "the way you stopped   35
defending her when you found out she wasn't white."

"No, we don't like it," we all agreed except Caleb.

Caleb said in extenuation, "But Mr. Stubblefield is new to Harlem."

The red-haired white man said, "Yes, it's my first time here."

"Maybe Mr. Stubblefield ought to stay out of Harlem," we observed.

"I agree," Mr. Stubblefield said. "Good night."   40

He got up then and there and left the café. He stalked as he walked. His red head disappeared into the night.

"Oh, that's too bad," said the white couple who remained. "Stubby's temper just got the best of him. But explain to us, are many colored folks really as fair as that woman?"

"Sure, lots of them have more white blood than colored, and pass for white."

"Do they?" said the lady and gentleman from Iowa.

"You never read Nella Larsen?" we asked.   45

"She writes novels," Caleb explained. "She's part white herself."

"Read her," we advised. "Also read the *Autobiography of an Ex-Coloured Man.*"°
Not that we had read it ourselves—because we paid but little attention to the older colored writers—but we knew it was about passing for white.

We all ordered fish and settled down comfortably to shocking our white friends with tales about how many Negroes there were passing for white all over America. We were determined to *épater le bourgeois*° real good via this white couple we had cornered, when the woman leaned over the table in the midst of our dissertations and said, "Listen, gentlemen, you needn't spread the word, but me and my husband aren't white either. We've just been *passing* for white for the last fifteen years."

"What?"

"We're colored, too, just like you," said the husband. "But it's better passing   50
for white because we make more money."

Well, that took the wind out of us. It took the wind out of Caleb, too. He thought all the time he was showing some fine white folks Harlem—and they were as colored as he was!

---

[47]***Autobiography of an Ex-Coloured Man*** a novel published in 1912 by James Weldon Johnson about a black man who passes for white   [48]***épater le bourgeois*** shock or amaze the middle class

Caleb almost never cursed. But this time he said, "I'll be damned!"

Then everybody laughed. And laughed! We almost had hysterics. All at once we dropped our professionally self-conscious "Negro" manners, became natural, ate fish, and talked and kidded freely like colored folks do when there are no white folks around. We really had fun then, joking about that red-haired guy who mistook a fair colored woman for white. After the fish we went to two or three more night spots and drank until five o'clock in the morning.

Finally we put the light-colored people in a taxi heading downtown. They turned to shout a last good-by. The cab was just about to move off when the woman called to the driver to stop.

55   She leaned out the window and said with a grin, "Listen, boys! I hate to confuse you again. But, to tell the truth, my husband and I aren't really colored at all. We're white. We just thought we'd kid you by passing for colored a little while—just as you said Negroes sometimes pass for white."

She laughed as they sped off toward Central Park, waving, "Good-by!"

We didn't say a thing. We just stood there on the corner in Harlem dumbfounded—not knowing now *which* way we'd been fooled. Were they really white—passing for colored? Or colored—passing for white?

Whatever race they were, they had had too much fun at our expense—even if they did pay for the drinks.   [1963]

1. What is the opening tone of the narrator?
2. What are the assumptions revealed by the man from Iowa's gallantry?
3. According to Cornel West, "White fear of black sexuality is a basic ingredient of white racism. . . . Social scientists have long acknowledged that interracial sex and marriage is the most *perceived* source of white fear of black people—just as the repeated castrations of lynched black men cries out for serious psychocultural explanation" (see p. 330). Does that idea resonate with the episode of the man from Iowa's gallantry at the restaurant?
4. What do we learn about human behavior from the contrast between what the narrator calls "professionally self-conscious 'Negro' manners" and their acting more naturally as "colored folk do when there are no white folks around"? How can the ideas of Erving Goffman (see p. 194) help us understand what happens as the racial identity of the couple from Iowa shifts from white to colored and back again?

RICHARD WRIGHT

RICHARD WRIGHT *(1908–60), born near Natchez, Mississippi, to an illiterate sharecropper and a schoolteacher, had a childhood marred by poverty, insecurity, and frequent moves. His family was held together by his mother and aunts. He showed early promise in school and read contemporary novelists voraciously. He found a job working for the post office, but lost it during the Depression. During the*

Depression, he barely eked out a living but continued to write. He joined the Communist party and contributed his stories and poems to its publications. He worked for the Federal Writers' Project researching the history of Illinois and of the Negro in Chicago, moving to New York City in 1937 where he became Harlem editor of the Daily Worker. *Not too long after that, he completed the first draft of his famous novel,* Native Son, *won a Guggenheim Fellowship, and married.* Native Son *was published in 1940 as a Book-of-the-Month Selection, was banned in Birmingham, Alabama, became a best seller, and made Wright internationally famous. He left the Communist Party in 1943, and in 1945 he published* Black Boy, *another very successful book. His subsequent novels failed to sell well; his attempts at being a playwright and even his short stories were not well received. He died in Paris of a heart attack and was cremated there with a copy of* Black Boy.

Big Black Good Man

Through the open window Olaf Jenson could smell the sea and hear the occasional foghorn of a freighter; outside, rain pelted down through an August night, drumming softly upon the pavements of Copenhagen,° inducing drowsiness, bringing dreamy memory, relaxing the tired muscles of his work-wracked body. He sat slumped in a swivel chair with his legs outstretched and his feet propped atop an edge of his desk. An inch of white ash tipped the end of his brown cigar and now and then he inserted the end of the stogie° into his mouth and drew gently upon it, letting wisps of blue smoke eddy from the corners of his wide, thin lips. The watery gray irises behind the thick lenses of his eyeglasses gave him a look of abstraction, of absentmindedness, of an almost genial idiocy. He sighed, reached for his half-empty bottle of beer, and drained it into his glass and downed it with a long slow gulp, then licked his lips. Replacing the cigar, he slapped his right palm against his thigh and said half aloud:

"Well, I'll be sixty tomorrow. I'm not rich, but I'm not poor either. . . . Really, I can't complain. Got good health. Traveled all over the world and had my share of girls when I was young . . . And my Karen's a good wife. I own my home. Got no debts. And I love digging in my garden in the spring . . . Grew the biggest carrots of anybody last year. Ain't saved much money, but what the hell . . . Money ain't everything. Got a good job. Night portering ain't too bad." He shook his head and yawned. "Karen and I could of had some children, though. Would of been good company . . . 'Specially for Karen. And I could of taught 'em languages . . . English, French, German, Danish, Dutch, Swedish, Norwegian, and Spanish . . ." He took the cigar out of his mouth and eyed the white ash critically. "Hell of a lot of good language learning did me . . . Never got anything out of it. But those ten years in New York were fun . . . Maybe I could of got rich if I'd stayed in America . . . Maybe. But I'm satisfied. You can't have everything."

Behind him the office door opened and a young man, a medical student occupying room number nine, entered.

---

[1]**Copenhagen** capital of Denmark   **stogie** inexpensive cigar

"Good evening," the student said.

5 "Good evening," Olaf said, turning.

The student went to the keyboard and took hold of the round, brown knob that anchored his key.

"Rain, rain, rain," the student said.

"That's Denmark for you," Olaf smiled at him.

"This dampness keeps me clogged up like a drainpipe," the student complained.

10 "That's Denmark for you," Olaf repeated with a smile.

"Good night," the student said.

"Good night, son," Olaf sighed, watching the door close.

Well, my tenants are my children, Olaf told himself. Almost all of his children were in their rooms now . . . Only seventy-two and forty-four were missing . . . Seventy-two might've gone to Sweden . . . And forty-four was maybe staying at his girl's place tonight, like he sometimes did . . . He studied the pear-shaped blobs of hard rubber, reddish brown like ripe fruit, that hung from the keyboard, then glanced at his watch. Only room thirty, eighty-one, and one hundred and one were empty . . . And it was almost midnight. In a few moments he could take a nap. Nobody hardly ever came looking for accommodations after midnight, unless a stray freighter came in, bringing thirsty, women-hungry sailors. Olaf chuckled softly. Why in hell was I ever a sailor? The whole time I was at sea I was thinking and dreaming about women. Then why didn't I stay on land where women could be had? Hunh? Sailors are crazy . . .

But he liked sailors. They reminded him of his youth, and there was something so direct, simple, and childlike about them. They always said straight out what they wanted, and what they wanted was almost always women and whisky . . . "Well, there's no harm in that . . . Nothing could be more natural," Olaf sighed, looking thirstily at his empty beer bottle. No; he'd not drink any more tonight; he'd had enough; he'd go to sleep . . .

15 He was bending forward and loosening his shoelaces when he heard the office door crack open. He lifted his eyes, then sucked in his breath. He did not straighten; he just stared up and around at the huge black thing that filled the doorway. His reflexes refused to function; it was not fear; it was just simple astonishment. He was staring at the biggest, strangest, and blackest man he'd ever seen in all his life.

"Good evening," the black giant said in a voice that filled the small office. "Say, you got a room?"

Olaf sat up slowly, not to answer but to look at this brooding black vision; it towered darkly some six and a half feet into the air, almost touching the ceiling, and its skin was so black that it had a bluish tint. And the sheer bulk of the man! . . . His chest bulged like a barrel; his rocklike and humped shoulders hinted of mountain ridges; the stomach ballooned like a threatening stone; and the legs were like telephone poles . . . The big black cloud of a man now lumbered into the office, bending to get its buffalolike head under the door frame, then advanced slowly upon Olaf, like a stormy sky descending.

"You got a room?" the big black man asked again in a resounding voice.

Olaf now noticed that the ebony giant was well dressed, carried a wonderful new suitcase, and wore black shoes that gleamed despite the raindrops that peppered their toes.

"You're American?" Olaf asked him.   20

"Yeah, man; sure," the black giant answered.

"Sailor?"

"Yeah. American Continental Lines."

Olaf had not answered the black man's question. It was not that the hotel did not admit men of color; Olaf took in all comers—blacks, yellows, whites, and browns . . . To Olaf, men were men, and, in his day, he'd worked and eaten and slept and fought with all kinds of men. But this particular black man . . . Well, he didn't seem human. Too big, too black, too loud, too direct, and probably too violent to boot . . . . Olaf's five feet seven inches scarcely reached the black giant's shoulder and his frail body weighed less, perhaps, than one of the man's gigantic legs . . . There was something about the man's intense blackness and ungainly bigness that frightened and insulted Olaf; he felt as though this man had come here expressly to remind him how puny, how tiny, and how weak and how white he was. Olaf knew, while registering his reactions, that he was being irrational and foolish; yet, for the first time in his life, he was emotionally determined to refuse a man a room solely on the basis of the man's size and color . . . Olaf's lips parted as he groped for the right words in which to couch his refusal, but the black giant bent forward and boomed:

"I asked you if you got a room. I got to put up somewhere tonight, man."   25

"Yes, we got a room," Olaf murmured.

And at once he was ashamed and confused. Sheer fear had made him yield. And he seethed against himself for his involuntary weakness. Well, he'd look over his book and pretend that he'd made a mistake; he'd tell this hunk of blackness that there was really no free room in the hotel, and that he was so sorry . . . Then, just as he took out the hotel register to make believe that he was pouring over it, a thick roll of American bank notes, crisp and green, was thrust under his nose.

"Keep this for me, will you?" the black giant commanded. "Cause I'm gonna get drunk tonight and I don't wanna lose it."

Olaf stared at the roll; it was huge, in denominations of fifties and hundreds. Olaf's eyes widened.

"How much is there?" he asked.   30

"Two thousand six hundred," the giant said. "Just put it into an envelope and write 'Jim' on it and lock it in your safe, hunh?"

The black mass of man had spoken in a manner that indicated that it was taking it for granted that Olaf would obey. Olaf was licked. Resentment clogged the pores of his wrinkled white skin. His hands trembled as he picked up the money. No; he couldn't refuse this man . . . The impulse to deny him was strong, but each time he was about to act upon it something thwarted him, made him shy off. He clutched about desperately for an idea. Oh yes, he could say that if he planned to stay for only one night, then he could not have the room, for it was against the policy of the hotel to rent rooms for only one night . . .

"How long are you staying? Just tonight?" Olaf asked.

"Naw. I'll be here for five or six days, I reckon," the giant answered offhandedly.

35 "You take room number thirty," Olaf heard himself saying. "It's forty kroner a day."

"That's all right with me," the giant said.

With slow, stiff movements, Olaf put the money in the safe and then turned and stared helplessly up into the living, breathing blackness looming above him. Suddenly he became conscious of the outstretched palm of the black giant; he was silently demanding the key to the room. His eyes downcast, Olaf surrendered the key, marveling at the black man's tremendous hands . . . He could kill me with one blow, Olaf told himself in fear.

Feeling himself beaten, Olaf reached for the suitcase, but the black hand of the giant whisked it out of his grasp.

"That's too heavy for you, big boy; I'll take it," the giant said.

40 Olaf let him. He thinks I'm nothing . . . He led the way down the corridor, sensing the giant's lumbering presence behind him. Olaf opened the door of number thirty and stood politely to one side, allowing the black giant to enter. At once the room seemed like a doll's house, so dwarfed and filled and tiny it was with a great living blackness . . . Flinging his suitcase upon a chair, the giant turned. The two men looked directly at each other now. Olaf saw that the giant's eyes were tiny and red, buried, it seemed, in muscle and fat. Black cheeks spread, flat and broad, topping the wide and flaring nostrils. The mouth was the biggest that Olaf had ever seen on a human face; the lips were thick, pursed, parted, showing snow-white teeth. The black neck was like a bull's . . . The giant advanced upon Olaf and stood over him.

"I want a bottle of whisky and a woman," he said. "Can you fix me up?"

"Yes," Olaf whispered, wild with anger and insult.

But what was he angry about? He'd had requests like this every night from all sorts of men and he was used to fulfilling them; he was a night porter in a cheap, water-front Copenhagen hotel that catered to sailors and students. Yes, men needed women, but this man, Olaf felt, ought to have a special sort of woman. He felt a deep and strange reluctance to phone any of the women whom he habitually sent to men. Yet he had promised. Could he lie and say that none was available? No. That sounded too fishy. The black giant sat upon the bed, staring straight before him. Olaf moved about quickly, pulling down the window shades, taking the pink coverlet off the bed, nudging the giant with his elbow to make him move as he did so . . . That's the way to treat 'im . . . Show 'im I ain't scared of 'im . . . But he was still seeking for an excuse to refuse. And he could think of nothing. He felt hypnotized, mentally immobilized. He stood hesitantly at the door.

"You send the whisky and the woman quick, pal?" the black giant asked, rousing himself from a brooding stare.

45 "Yes," Olaf grunted, shutting the door.

Goddamn, Olaf sighed. He sat in his office at his desk before the phone. Why did *he* have to come here? . . . I'm not prejudiced . . . No, not at all . . .

But . . . He couldn't think any more. God oughtn't make men as big and black as that . . . But what the hell was he worrying about? He'd send women of all races to men of all colors . . . So why not a woman to the black giant? Oh, only if the man were small, brown, and intelligent-looking . . . Olaf felt trapped.

With a reflex movement of his hand, he picked up the phone and dialed Lena. She was big and strong and always cut him in for fifteen per cent instead of the usual ten per cent. Lena had four small children to feed and clothe. Lena was willing; she was, she said, coming over right now. She didn't give a good goddamn about how big and black the man was . . .

"Why you ask me that?" Lena wanted to know over the phone. "You never asked that before . . . "

"But this one is *big*," Olaf found himself saying.

"He's just a man," Lena told him, her voice singing stridently, laughingly over the wire. "You just leave that to me. You don't have to do anything. *I'll* handle 'im." 50

Lena had a key to the hotel door downstairs, but tonight Olaf stayed awake. He wanted to see her. Why? He didn't know. He stretched out on the sofa in his office, but sleep was far from him. When Lena arrived, he told her again how big and black the man was.

"You told me that over the phone," Lena reminded him.

Olaf said nothing. Lena flounced off on her errand of mercy. Olaf shut the office door, then opened it and left it ajar. But why? He didn't know. He lay upon the sofa and stared at the ceiling. He glanced at his watch; it was almost two o'clock . . . She's staying in there a long time . . . Ah, God, but he could do with a drink . . . Why was he so damned worked up and nervous about a nigger and a white whore? . . . He'd never been so upset in all his life. Before he knew it, he had drifted off to sleep. Then he heard the office door swinging, creakingly open on its rusty hinges. Lena stood in it, grim and businesslike, her face scrubbed free of powder and rouge. Olaf scrambled to his feet, adjusting his eyeglasses, blinking.

"How was it?" he asked her in a confidential whisper.

Lena's eyes blazed. 55

"What the hell's that to you?" she snapped. "There's your cut," she said, flinging him his money, tossing it upon the covers of the sofa. "You're sure nosy tonight. You wanna take over my work?"

Olaf's pasty cheeks burned red.

"You go to hell," he said, slamming the door.

"I'll meet you there!" Lena's shouting voice reached him dimly.

He was being a fool; there was no doubt about it. But, try as he might, he could not shake off a primitive hate for that black mountain of energy, of muscle, of bone; he envied the easy manner in which it moved with such a creeping and powerful motion; he winced at the booming and commanding voice that came to him when the tiny little eyes were not even looking at him; he shivered at the sight of those vast and clawlike hands that seemed always to hint of death . . . 60

Olaf kept his counsel. He never spoke to Karen about the sordid doings at the hotel. Such things were not for women like Karen. He knew instinctively that Karen would have been amazed had he told her that he was worried sick about a nigger and a blonde whore . . . . No; he couldn't talk to anybody about it, not even the hard-bitten old bitch who owned the hotel. She was concerned only about money; she didn't give a damn about how big and how black a client was as long as he paid his room rent.

Next evening, when Olaf arrived for duty, there was no sight or sound of the black giant. A little later after one o'clock in the morning he appeared, left his key, and went out wordlessly. A few moments past two the giant returned, took his key from the board, and paused.

"I want that Lena again tonight. And another bottle of whiskey," he said boomingly.

"I'll call her and see if she's in," Olaf said.

65   "Do that," the black giant said and was gone.

He thinks he's God, Olaf fumed. He picked up the phone and ordered Lena and a bottle of whiskey, and there was a taste of ashes in his mouth. On the third night came the same request: Lena and whiskey. When the black giant appeared on the fifth night, Olaf was about to make a sarcastic remark to the effect that maybe he ought to marry Lena, but he checked it in time . . . . After all, he could kill me with one hand, he told himself.

Olaf was nervous and angry with himself for being nervous. Other black sailors came and asked for girls and Olaf sent them, but with none of the fear and loathing that he sent Lena and a bottle of whiskey to the giant . . . All right, the black giant's stay was almost up. He'd said that he was staying for five or six nights; tomorrow night was the sixth night and that ought to be the end of this nameless terror.

On the sixth night Olaf sat in his swivel chair with his bottle of beer and waited, his teeth on edge, his fingers drumming the desk. But what the hell am I fretting for? . . . The hell with 'im . . . Olaf sat and dozed. Occasionally he'd awaken and listen to the foghorns of freighters sounding as ships came and went in the misty Copenhagen harbor. He was half asleep when he felt a rough hand on his shoulder. He blinked his eyes open. The giant, black and vast and powerful, all but blotted out his vision.

"What I owe you, man?" the giant demanded. "And I want my money."

70   "Sure," Olaf said, relieved, but filled as always with fear of this living wall of black flesh.

With fumbling hands, he made out the bill and received payment, then gave the giant his roll of money, laying it on the desk so as not to let his hands touch the flesh of the black mountain. Well, his ordeal was over. It was past two o'clock in the morning. Olaf even managed a wry smile and muttered a guttural "Thanks" for the generous tip that the giant tossed him.

Then a strange tension entered the office. The office door was shut and Olaf was alone with the black mass of power, yearning for it to leave. But the black mass of power stood still, immobile, looking down at Olaf. And Olaf could not, for the life of him, guess at what was transpiring in that mysterious black mind.

The two of them simply stared at each other for a full two minutes, the giant's tiny little beady eyes blinking slowly as they seemed to measure and search Olaf's face. Olaf's vision dimmed for a second as terror seized him and he could feel a flush of heat overspread his body. Then Olaf sucked in his breath as the devil of blackness commanded:

"Stand up!"

Olaf was paralyzed. Sweat broke on his face. His worst premonitions about this black beast were coming true. This evil blackness was about to attack him, maybe kill him . . . Slowly Olaf shook his head, his terror permitting him to breathe:

"What're you talking about?"

"Stand up, I say!" the black giant bellowed.

As though hypnotized, Olaf tried to rise; then he felt the black paw of the beast helping him roughly to his feet.

They stood an inch apart. Olaf's pasty-white features were glued to the giant's swollen black face. The ebony ensemble of eyes and nose and mouth and cheeks looked down at Olaf, silently; then, with a slow and deliberate movement of his gorillalike arms, he lifted his mammoth hands to Olaf's throat. Olaf had long known and felt that this dreadful moment was coming; he felt trapped in a nightmare. He could not move. He wanted to scream, but could find no words. His lips refused to open; his tongue felt icy and inert. Then he knew that his end had come when the giant's black fingers slowly, softly encircled his throat while a horrible grin of delight broke out on the sooty face . . . Olaf lost control of the reflexes of his body and he felt a hot stickiness flooding his underwear . . . He stared without breathing, gazing into the grinning blackness of the face that was bent over him, feeling the black fingers caressing his throat and waiting to feel the sharp, stinging ache and pain of the bones in his neck being snapped, crushed . . . He knew all along that I hated 'im . . . Yes, and now he's going to kill me for it, Olaf told himself with despair.

The black fingers still circled Olaf's neck, not closing, but gently massaging it, as it were, moving to and fro, while the obscene face grinned into his. Olaf could feel the giant's warm breath blowing on his eyelashes and he felt like a chicken about to have its neck wrung and its body tossed to flip and flap dyingly in the dust of the barnyard . . . Then suddenly the black giant withdrew his fingers from Olaf's neck and stepped back a pace, still grinning. Olaf sighed, trembling, his body seeming to shrink; he waited. Shame sheeted him for the hot wetness that was in his trousers. Oh, God, he's teasing me . . . He's showing me how easily he can kill me . . . He swallowed, waiting, his eyes stones of gray.

The giant's barrel-like chest gave forth a low, rumbling chuckle of delight.

"You laugh?" Olaf asked whimperingly.

"Sure I laugh," the giant shouted.

"Please don't hurt me," Olaf managed to say.

"I wouldn't hurt you, boy," the giant said in a tone of mockery. "So long."

And he was gone. Olaf fell limply into the swivel chair and fought off losing consciousness. Then he wept. He was showing me how easily he could kill

75

80

85

me . . . He made me shake with terror and then laughed and left . . . Slowly, Olaf recovered, stood, then gave vent to a string of curses:

"Goddamn 'im! My gun's right there in the desk drawer; I should of shot 'im. Jesus, I hope the ship he's on sinks . . . I hope he drowns and the sharks eat 'im . . . "

Later, he thought of going to the police, but sheer shame kept him back; and, anyway, the giant was probably on board his ship by now. And he had to get home and clean himself. Oh, Lord, what could he tell Karen? Yes, he would say that his stomach had been upset . . . He'd change clothes and return to work. He phoned the hotel owner that he was ill and wanted an hour off; the old bitch said that she was coming right over and that poor Olaf could have the evening off.

Olaf went home and lied to Karen. Then he lay awake the rest of the night dreaming of revenge. He saw that freighter on which the giant was sailing; he saw it springing a dangerous leak and saw a torrent of sea water flooding, gushing into all the compartments of the ship until it found the bunk in which the black giant slept. Ah, yes, the foamy, surging waters would surprise that sleeping black bastard of a giant and he would drown, gasping and choking like a trapped rat, his tiny eyes bulging until they glittered red, the bitter water of the sea pounding his lungs until they ached and finally burst . . . The ship would sink slowly to the bottom of the cold, black, silent depths of the sea and a shark, a *white* one, would glide aimlessly about the shut portholes until it found an open one and it would slither inside and nose about until it found that swollen, rotting, stinking carcass of the black beast and it would then begin to nibble at the decomposing mass of tarlike flesh, eating the bones clean . . . Olaf always pictured the giant's bones as being jet black and shining.

Once or twice, during these fantasies of cannibalistic revenge, Olaf felt a little guilty about all the many innocent people, women and children, all white and blonde, who would have to go down into watery graves in order that that white shark could devour the evil giant's black flesh . . . But, despite feelings of remorse, the fantasy lived persistently on, and when Olaf found himself alone, it would crowd and cloud his mind to the exclusion of all else, affording him the only revenge he knew. To make me suffer just for the pleasure of it, he fumed. Just to show me how strong he was . . . Olaf learned how to hate, and got pleasure out of it.

90   Summer fled on wings of rain. Autumn flooded Denmark with color. Winter made rain and snow fall on Copenhagen. Finally spring came, bringing violets and roses. Olaf kept to his job. For many months he feared the return of the black giant. But when a year had passed and the giant had not put in an appearance, Olaf allowed his revenge fantasy to peter out, indulging in it only when recalling the shame that the black monster had made him feel.

Then one rainy August night, a year later, Olaf sat drowsing at his desk, his bottle of beer before him, tilting back in his swivel chair, his feet resting atop a corner of his desk, his mind mulling over the more pleasant aspects of his life. The office door cracked open. Olaf glanced boredly up and around. His heart jumped and skipped a beat. The black nightmare of terror and shame that he

had hoped that he had lost forever was again upon him . . . Resplendently
dressed, suitcase in hand, the black looming mountain filled the doorway. Olaf's
thin lips parted and a silent moan, half a curse, escaped them.

"Hi," the black giant boomed from the doorway.

Olaf could not reply. But a sudden resolve swept him: this time he would
even the score. If this black beast came within so much as three feet of him,
he would snatch his gun out of the drawer and shoot him dead, so help him
God . . .

"No rooms tonight," Olaf heard himself announcing in a determined voice.

The black giant grinned; it was the same infernal grimace of delight and tri-   95
umph that he had had when his damnable black fingers had been around his
throat . . .

"Don't want no room tonight," the giant announced.

"Then what are you doing here?" Olaf asked in a loud but tremulous voice.

The giant swept toward Olaf and stood over him; and Olaf could not move,
despite his oath to kill him . . .

"What do you want then?" Olaf demanded once more, ashamed that he
could not lift his voice above a whisper.

The giant still grinned, then tossed what seemed the same suitcase upon   100
Olaf's sofa and bent over it; he zippered it open with a sweep of his clawlike
hand and rummaged in it, drawing forth a flat, gleaming white object done up
in glowing cellophane. Olaf watched with lowered lids, wondering what trick
was now being played on him. Then, before he could defend himself, the giant
had whirled and again long, black, snakelike fingers were encircling Olaf's
throat . . . Olaf stiffened, his right hand clawing blindly for the drawer where the
gun was kept. But the giant was quick.

"Wait," he bellowed, pushing Olaf back from the desk.

The giant turned quickly to the sofa and, still holding his fingers in a wide circle that seemed a noose for Olaf's neck, he inserted the rounded fingers into the
top of the flat, gleaming object. Olaf had the drawer open and his sweaty fingers
were now touching the gun, but something made him freeze. The flat, gleaming
object was a shirt and the black giant's circled fingers were fitting themselves
into its neck . . .

"A perfect fit!" the giant shouted.

Olaf stared, trying to understand. His fingers loosened about the gun. A mixture of a laugh and a curse struggled in him. He watched the giant plunge his
hands into the suitcase and pull out other flat, gleaming shirts.

"One, two, three, four, five, six," the black giant intoned, his voice crisp and   105
businesslike. "Six nylon shirts. And they're all yours. One shirt for each time
Lena came . . . See, Daddy-O?"

The black, cupped hands, filled with billowing nylon whiteness, were
extended under Olaf's nose. Olaf eased his damp fingers from his gun and
pushed the drawer closed, staring at the shirts and then at the black giant's
grinning face.

"Don't you like 'em?" the giant asked.

Olaf began to laugh hysterically, then suddenly he was crying, his eyes so flooded with tears that the pile of dazzling nylon looked like snow in the dead of winter. Was this true? Could he believe it? Maybe this too was a trick? But, no. There were six shirts, all nylon, and the black giant had had Lena six nights.

"What's the matter with you, Daddy-O?" the giant asked. "You blowing your top? Laughing and crying . . . ."

110 Olaf swallowed, dabbed his withered fists at his dimmed eyes; then he realized that he had his glasses on. He took them off and dried his eyes and sat up. He sighed, the tension and shame and fear and haunting dread of his fantasy went from him, and he leaned limply back in his chair . . .

"Try one on," the giant ordered.

Olaf fumbled with the buttons of his shirt, let down his suspenders, and pulled the shirt off. He donned a gleaming nylon one and the giant began buttoning it for him.

"Perfect, Daddy-O," the giant said.

His spectacled face framed in sparkling nylon, Olaf sat with trembling lips. So he'd not been trying to kill me after all.

115 "You want Lena, don't you?" he asked the giant in a soft whisper. "But I don't know where she is. She never came back here after you left—"

"I know where Lena is," the giant told him. "We been writing to each other. I'm going to her house. And, Daddy-O, I'm late." The giant zippered the suitcase shut and stood a moment gazing down at Olaf, his tiny little red eyes blinking slowly. Then Olaf realized that there was a compassion in that stare that he had never seen before.

"And I thought you wanted to kill me," Olaf told him. "I was scared of you . . ."

"Me? Kill you?" the giant blinked. "When?"

"That night when you put your fingers around my throat—"

120 "What?" the giant asked, then roared with laughter. "Daddy-O, you're a funny little man. I wouldn't hurt you. I like you. You a *good* man. You helped me."

Olaf smiled, clutching the pile of nylon shirts in his arms.

"You're a good man too," Olaf murmured. Then loudly, "You're a big black good man."

"Daddy-O, you're crazy," the giant said.

He swept his suitcase from the sofa, spun on his heel, and was at the door in one stride.

125 "Thanks!" Olaf cried after him.

The black giant paused, turned his vast black head, and flashed a grin.

"Daddy-O, drop dead," he said and was gone. [1957]

1. What kind of narrator is this? What is the effect of structuring the narrative in this way?
2. Olaf tries to figure out a way to deny the guest a room at the hotel. Yet he leads him to room 30. Why?

DRAMA

F R A M E W O R K S

Looking at Shakespeare through Literary Criticism

WILLIAM SHAKESPEARE, *Hamlet, Prince of Denmark*

TERENCE EAGLETON, *"Hamlet," from* Shakespeare and Society: Critical Studies in Shakespearean Drama

WILLIAM SHAKESPEARE

(For biographical notes, see p. 266.)

Hamlet, Prince of Denmark

[*Dramatis Personae*

Ghost *of Hamlet, the former King of Denmark*
Claudius, *King of Denmark, the former King's brother*
Gertrude, *Queen of Denmark, widow of the former King and now wife of Claudius*
Hamlet, *Prince of Denmark, son of the late King and of Gertrude*

Polonius, *councillor to the King*
Laertes, *his son*
Ophelia, *his daughter*
Reynaldo, *his servant*

Horatio, *Hamlet's friend and fellow student*

Voltimand,
Cornelius,
Rosencrantz,
Guildenstern,   } *members of the Danish court*
Osric,
A Gentleman,
A Lord,

Bernardo,
Francisco,   } *officers and soldiers on watch*
Marcellus,

Fortinbras, *Prince of Norway*
Captain *in his army*

Three or Four Players, *taking the roles of* Prologue, Player King, Player Queen, *and*
    Lucianus

Two Messengers
First Sailor
Two Clowns, *a gravedigger and his companion*
Priest
First Ambassador *from England*

Lords, Soldiers, Attendants, Guards, other Players, Followers of Laertes, other Sailors,
    another Ambassador or Ambassadors from England

Scene: *Denmark*]

1.1   *Enter Bernardo and Francisco, two sentinels, [meeting].*

Bernardo: Who's there?
Francisco: Nay, answer me. Stand and unfold yourself.
Bernardo: Long live the King!
Francisco: Bernardo?
5 *Bernardo:* He.
Francisco: You come most carefully upon your hour.
Bernardo: 'Tis now struck twelve. Get thee to bed, Francisco.
Francisco: For this relief much thanks. 'Tis bitter cold,
    And I am sick at heart.
10 *Bernardo:* Have you had quiet guard?
Francisco: Not a mouse stirring.
Bernardo: Well, good night.
    If you do meet Horatio and Marcellus,
    The rivals of my watch, bid them make haste.

         Enter Horatio and Marcellus.

15 *Francisco:* I think I hear them.—Stand, ho! Who is there?
Horatio: Friends to this ground.
Marcellus: And liegemen to the Dane.
Francisco: Give you good night.
Marcellus: O, farewell, honest soldier. Who hath relieved you?
20 *Francisco:* Bernardo hath my place. Give you good night.
                  Exit Francisco.
Marcellus: Holla! Bernardo!
Bernardo: Say, what, is Horatio there?
Horatio: A piece of him.
Bernardo: Welcome, Horatio. Welcome, good Marcellus.
25 *Horatio:* What, has this thing appeared again tonight?
Bernardo: I have seen nothing.

1.1. Location: Elsinore castle. A guard platform.
[2]**me** (Francisco emphasizes that *he* is the sentry currently on watch.)   **unfold yourself**
reveal your identity   [14]**rivals** partners   [16]**ground** country, land   [17]**liegemen to the**
Dane men sworn to serve the Danish king   [18]**Give** i.e., may God give

Marcellus: Horatio says 'tis but our fantasy,
    And will not let belief take hold of him
    Touching this dreaded sight twice seen of us.
    Therefore I have entreated him along   30
    With us to watch the minutes of this night,
    That if again this apparition come
    He may approve our eyes and speak to it.
Horatio: Tush, tush, 'twill not appear.
Bernardo: Sit down awhile,
    And let us once again assail your ears,   35
    That are so fortified against our story,
    What we have two nights seen.
Horatio: Well, sit we down,
    And let us hear Bernardo speak of this.
Bernardo: Last night of all,
    When yond same star that's westward from the pole   40
    Had made his course t' illume that part of heaven
    Where now it burns, Marcellus and myself,
    The bell then beating one—

                    Enter Ghost.

Marcellus: Peace, break thee off! Look where it comes again!
Bernardo: In the same figure like the King that's dead.   45
Marcellus: Thou art a scholar. Speak to it, Horatio.
Bernardo: Looks 'a not like the King? Mark it, Horatio.
Horatio: Most like. It harrows me with fear and wonder.
Bernardo: It would be spoke to.
Marcellus: Speak to it, Horatio.
Horatio: What art thou that usurp'st this time of night,   50
    Together with that fair and warlike form
    In which the majesty of buried Denmark
    Did sometime march? By heaven, I charge thee, speak!
Marcellus: It is offended.
Bernardo: See, it stalks away.
Horatio: Stay! Speak, speak! I charge thee, speak!   *Exit Ghost.*   55
Marcellus: 'Tis gone and will not answer.
Bernardo: How now, Horatio? You tremble and look pale.
    Is not this something more than fantasy?
    What think you on 't?

---

[27]**fantasy** imagination   [30]**along** to come along   [31]**watch** keep watch during
[33]**approve** corroborate   [37]**What** with what   [39]**Last . . . all** i.e., this *very* last night
(Emphatic.)   [40]**pole** polestar, north star   [41]**his** its   **illume** illuminate   [46]**scholar**
one learned enough to know how to question a ghost properly   [47]**'a** he   [49]**It . . . to**
(It was commonly believed that a ghost could not speak until spoken to.)   [50]**usurp'st**
wrongfully takes over   [52]**buried Denmark** the buried King of Denmark
[53]**sometime** formerly   [59]**on 't** of it

60 *Horatio:* Before my God, I might not this believe
Without the sensible and true avouch
Of mine own eyes.
Marcellus: Is it not like the King?
Horatio: As thou art to thyself.
Such was the very armor he had on
65 When he the ambitious Norway combated.
So frowned he once when, in an angry parle,
He smote the sledded Polacks on the ice.
'Tis strange.
Marcellus: Thus twice before, and jump at this dead hour,
70 With martial stalk hath he gone by our watch.
Horatio: In what particular thought to work I know not,
But in the gross and scope of mine opinion
This bodes some strange eruption to our state.
Marcellus: Good now, sit down, and tell me, he that knows,
75 Why this same strict and most observant watch
So nightly toils the subject of the land,
And why such daily cast of brazen cannon
And foreign mart for implements of war,
Why such impress of shipwrights, whose sore task
80 Does not divide the Sunday from the week.
What might be toward, that this sweaty haste
Doth make the night joint-laborer with the day?
Who is 't that can inform me?
Horatio: That can I;
At least, the whisper goes so. Our last king,
85 Whose image even but now appeared to us,
Was, as you know, by Fortinbras of Norway,
Thereto pricked on by a most emulate pride,
Dared to the combat; in which our valiant Hamlet—
For so this side of our known world esteemed him—
90 Did slay this Fortinbras; who by a sealed compact
Well ratified by law and heraldry
Did forfeit, with his life, all those his lands
Which he stood seized of, to the conqueror;

[61]**sensible** confirmed by the senses   **avouch** warrant, evidence   [65]**Norway** King of
Norway   [66]**parle** parley   [67]**sledded** traveling on sleds   **Polacks** Poles   [69]**jump**
exactly   [70]**stalk** stride   [71]**to work** i.e., to collect my thoughts and try to understand this
[72]**gross and scope** general drift   [74]**Good now** (An expression denoting entreaty or
expostulation.)   [76]**toils** causes to toil   **subject** subjects   [77]**cast** casting   [78]**mart**
buying and selling   [79]**impress** impressment, conscription   [81]**toward** in preparation
[87]**Thereto . . . pride** (Refers to old Fortinbras, not the Danish King.)   **pricked on** incited
emulate emulous, ambitious   [89]**this . . . world** i.e., all Europe, the Western world
[90]**sealed** certified, confirmed   [93]**seized** possessed

Against the which a moiety competent
Was gagèd by our king, which had returned   95
To the inheritance of Fortinbras
Had he been vanquisher, as, by the same cov'nant
And carriage of the article designed,
His fell to Hamlet. Now, sir, young Fortinbras,
Of unimprovèd mettle hot and full,   100
Hath in the skirts of Norway here and there
Sharked up a list of lawless resolutes
For food and diet to some enterprise
That hath a stomach in 't, which is no other—
As it doth well appear unto our state—   105
But to recover of us, by strong hand
And terms compulsatory, those foresaid lands
So by his father lost. And this, I take it,
Is the main motive of our preparations,
The source of this our watch, and the chief head   110
Of this posthaste and rummage in the land.
Bernardo: I think it be no other but e'en so.
    Well may it sort that this portentous figure
    Comes armèd through our watch so like the King
    That was and is the question of these wars.   115
Horatio: A mote it is to trouble the mind's eye.
    In the most high and palmy state of Rome,
    A little ere the mightiest Julius fell,
    The graves stood tenantless, and the sheeted dead
    Did squeak and gibber in the Roman streets;   120
    As stars with trains of fire and dews of blood,
    Disasters in the sun; and the moist star
    Upon whose influence Neptune's empire stands
    Was sick almost to doomsday with eclipse.
    And even the like precurse of feared events,   125

---

[94] **Against the** in return for   **moiety competent** corresponding portion   [95] **gagèd**
engaged, pledged   **had returned** would have passed   [96] **inheritance** possession
[97] **cov'nant** i.e., the *sealed compact* of line 90   [98] **carriage . . . designed** carrying out of
the article or clause drawn up to cover the point   [100] **unimprovèd mettle** untried,
undisciplined spirits   [101] **skirts** outlying regions, outskirts   [102] **Sharked up** gathered up,
as a shark takes fish   **list** i.e., troop   **resolutes** desperadoes   [103] **For food and diet** i.e.,
they are to serve as *food*, or "means," *to some enterprise;* also they serve in return for
the rations they get   [104] **stomach** (1) a spirit of daring (2) an appetite that is fed by the
lawless resolutes   [110] **head** source   [111] **rummage** bustle, commotion   [113] **sort** suit
[115] **question** focus of contention   [116] **mote** speck of dust   [117] **palmy** flourishing
[119] **sheeted** shrouded   [121] **As** (This abrupt transition suggests that matter is possibly
omitted between lines 120 and 121.)   **trains** trails   [122] **Disasters** unfavorable signs or
aspects   **moist star** i.e., moon, governing tides   [123] **Neptune** god of the sea   **stands**
depends   [124] **sick . . . doomsday** (See Matthew 24:29 and Revelation 6:12.)
[125] **precurse** heralding, foreshadowing

As harbingers preceding still the fates
And prologue to the omen coming on,
Have heaven and earth together demonstrated
Unto our climatures and countrymen.

       Enter Ghost.

130   But soft, behold! Lo, where it comes again!
I'll cross it, though it blast me. (*It spreads his arms.*) Stay, illusion!
If thou hast any sound or use of voice,
Speak to me!
If there be any good thing to be done
135   That may to thee do ease and grace to me,
Speak to me!
If thou art privy to thy country's fate,
Which, happily, foreknowing may avoid,
O, speak!
140   Or if thou hast uphoarded in thy life
Extorted treasure in the womb of earth,
For which, they say, you spirits oft walk in death,
Speak of it! (*The cock crows.*) Stay and speak!—Stop it, Marcellus.
Marcellus: Shall I strike at it with my partisan?
145 *Horatio:* Do, if it will not stand.   [*They strike at it.*]
Bernardo: 'Tis here!
Horatio: 'Tis here!   [*Exit Ghost.*]
Marcellus: 'Tis gone.
We do it wrong, being so majestical,
150   To offer it the show of violence;
For it is as the air invulnerable,
And our vain blows malicious mockery.
Bernardo: It was about to speak when the cock crew.
Horatio: And then it started like a guilty thing
155   Upon a fearful summons. I have heard
The cock, that is the trumpet to the morn,
Doth with his lofty and shrill-sounding throat
Awake the god of day, and at his warning,
Whether in sea or fire, in earth or air,
160   Th' extravagant and erring spirit hies
To his confine; and of the truth herein
This present object made probation.

---

[126]**harbingers** forerunners **still** continually [127]**omen** calamitous event [129]**climatures** regions [130]**soft** i.e., enough, break off [131]**cross** stand in its path, confront
blast wither, strike with a curse s.d.**his** its [137]**privy to** in on the secret of
[138]**happily** haply, perchance [144]**partisan** long-handled spear [156]**trumpet** trumpeter
[160]**extravagant and erring** wandering beyond bounds (The words have similar
meaning.) **hies** hastens [162]**probation** proof

Marcellus: It faded on the crowing of the cock.

   Some say that ever 'gainst that season comes
   Wherein our Savior's birth is celebrated,   165
   This bird of dawning singeth all night long,
   And then, they say, no spirit dare stir abroad;
   The nights are wholesome, then no planets strike,
   No fairy takes, nor witch hath power to charm,
   So hallowed and so gracious is that time.   170

Horatio: So have I heard and do in part believe it.

   But, look, the morn in russet mantle clad
   Walks o'er the dew of yon high eastward hill.
   Break we our watch up, and by my advice
   Let us impart what we have seen tonight   175
   Unto young Hamlet; for upon my life,
   This spirit, dumb to us, will speak to him.
   Do you consent we shall acquaint him with it,
   As needful in our loves, fitting our duty?

Marcellus: Let's do 't, I pray, and I this morning know   180
   Where we shall find him most conveniently.

                                                              Exeunt.

1.2   *Flourish. Enter Claudius, King of Denmark, Gertrude the Queen, [the]*
Council, as Polonius and his son Laertes, Hamlet, cum aliis [including Voltimand and
Cornelius].

King: Though yet of Hamlet our dear brother's death

   The memory be green, and that it us befitted
   To bear our hearts in grief and our whole kingdom
   To be contracted in one brow of woe,
   Yet so far hath discretion fought with nature   5
   That we with wisest sorrow think on him
   Together with remembrance of ourselves.
   Therefore our sometime sister, now our queen,
   Th' imperial jointress to this warlike state,
   Have we, as 'twere with a defeated joy—   10
   With an auspicious and a dropping eye,
   With mirth in funeral and with dirge in marriage,
   In equal scale weighing delight and dole—
   Taken to wife. Nor have we herein barred

164**'gainst** just before   168**strike** destroy by evil influence   169**takes** bewitches
170**gracious** full of grace
1.2. Location: The castle.
s.d.**as** i.e., such as, including   **cum aliis** with others   1**our** my (The royal "we"; also
in the following lines.)   8**sometime** former   9**jointress** woman possessing property
with her husband   11**With . . . eye** with one eye smiling and the other weeping
13**dole** grief

15   Your better wisdoms, which have freely gone
      With this affair along. For all, our thanks.
      Now follows that you know young Fortinbras,
      Holding a weak supposal of our worth,
      Or thinking by our late dear brother's death
20   Our state to be disjoint and out of frame,
      Co-leaguèd with this dream of his advantage,
      He hath not failed to pester us with message
      Importing the surrender of those lands
      Lost by his father, with all bonds of law,
25   To our most valiant brother. So much for him.
      Now for ourself and for this time of meeting.
      Thus much the business is: we have here writ
      To Norway, uncle of young Fortinbras—
      Who, impotent and bed-rid, scarcely hears
30   Of this his nephew's purpose—to suppress
      His further gait herein, in that the levies,
      The lists, and full proportions are all made
      Out of his subject; and we here dispatch
      You, good Cornelius, and you, Voltimand,
35   For bearers of this greeting to old Norway,
      Giving to you no further personal power
      To business with the King more than the scope
      Of these dilated articles allow.   [*He gives a paper.*]
      Farewell, and let your haste commend your duty.
40 *Cornelius, Voltimand:* In that, and all things, will we show our duty.
    King: We doubt it nothing. Heartily farewell.   [*Exeunt Voltimand and Cornelius.*]
      And now, Laertes, what's the news with you?
      You told us of some suit; what is 't, Laertes?
      You cannot speak of reason to the Dane
45   And lose your voice. What wouldst thou beg, Laertes,
      That shall not be my offer, not thy asking?
      The head is not more native to the heart,
      The hand more instrumental to the mouth,
      Than is the throne of Denmark to thy father.

---

[17]**that you know** what you know already, that; or, that you be informed as follows
[18]**weak supposal** low estimate   [21]**Co-leaguèd with** joined to, allied with
dream . . . advantage illusory hope of having the advantage. (His only ally is this hope.)
[23]**Importing** pertaining to   [24]**bonds** contracts   [29]**impotent** helpless   [31]**His** i.e.,
Fortinbras'   **gait** proceeding   [31-33]**in that . . . subject** since the levying of troops
and supplies is drawn entirely from the King of Norway's own subjects   [38]**dilated** set
out at length   [39]**let . . . duty** let your swift obeying of orders, rather than mere words,
express your dutifulness   [41]**nothing** not at all   [44]**the Dane** the Danish king
[45]**lose your voice** waste your speech   [47]**native** closely connected, related
[48]**instrumental** serviceable

What wouldst thou have, Laertes?

Laertes: My dread lord,   50
   Your leave and favor to return to France,
   From whence though willingly I came to Denmark
   To show my duty in your coronation,
   Yet now I must confess, that duty done,
   My thoughts and wishes bend again toward France   55
   And bow them to your gracious leave and pardon.

King: Have you your father's leave? What says Polonius?

Polonius: H'ath, my lord, wrung from me my slow leave
   By laborsome petition, and at last
   Upon his will I sealed my hard consent.   60
   I do beseech you, give him leave to go.

King: Take thy fair hour, Laertes. Time be thine,
   And thy best graces spend it at thy will!
   But now, my cousin Hamlet, and my son—

Hamlet: A little more than kin, and less than kind.   65

King: How is it that the clouds still hang on you?

Hamlet: Not so, my lord. I am too much in the sun.

Queen: Good Hamlet, cast thy nighted color off,
   And let thine eye look like a friend on Denmark.
   Do not forever with thy vailèd lids   70
   Seek for thy noble father in the dust.
   Thou know'st 'tis common, all that lives must die,
   Passing through nature to eternity.

Hamlet: Ay, madam, it is common.

Queen: If it be,
   Why seems it so particular with thee?   75

Hamlet: Seems, madam? Nay, it is. I know not "seems."
   'Tis not alone my inky cloak, good Mother,
   Nor customary suits of solemn black,
   Nor windy suspiration of forced breath,

---

[51]**leave and favor** kind permission   [56]**bow . . . pardon** entreatingly make a deep bow, asking your permission to depart   [58]**H'ath** he has   [60]**sealed** (as if sealing a legal document)   **hard** reluctant   [62]**Take thy fair hour** enjoy your time of youth   [63]**And . . . will** and may your finest qualities guide the way you choose to spend your time   [64]**cousin** any kin not of the immediate family   [65]**A little . . . kind** i.e., closer than an ordinary nephew (since I am stepson), and yet more separated in natural feeling (with pun on *kind* meaning "affectionate" and "natural," "lawful." This line is often read as an aside, but it need not be. The King chooses perhaps not to respond to Hamlet's cryptic and bitter remark.)   [67]**the sun** i.e., the sunshine of the King's royal favor (with pun on *son*)   [68]**nighted color** (1) mourning garments of black (2) dark melancholy   [69]**Denmark** the King of Denmark   [70]**vailèd lids** lowered eyes   [72]**common** of universal occurrence (But Hamlet plays on the sense of "vulgar" in line 74.)   [75]**particular** personal   [78]**customary** (1) socially conventional (2) habitual with me   [79]**suspiration** sighing

80   No, nor the fruitful river in the eye,
    Nor the dejected havior of the visage,
    Together with all forms, moods, shapes of grief,
    That can denote me truly. These indeed seem,
    For they are actions that a man might play.
85   But I have that within which passes show;
    These but the trappings and the suits of woe.
  King: 'Tis sweet and commendable in your nature, Hamlet,
    To give these mourning duties to your father.
    But you must know your father lost a father,
90   That father lost, lost his, and the survivor bound
    In filial obligation for some term
    To do obsequious sorrow. But to persever
    In obstinate condolement is a course
    Of impious stubbornness. 'Tis unmanly grief.
95   It shows a will most incorrect to heaven,
    A heart unfortified, a mind impatient,
    An understanding simple and unschooled.
    For what we know must be and is as common
    As any the most vulgar thing to sense,
100   Why should we in our peevish opposition
    Take it to heart? Fie, 'tis a fault to heaven,
    A fault against the dead, a fault to nature,
    To reason most absurd, whose common theme
    Is death of fathers, and who still hath cried,
105   From the first corpse till he that died today,
    "This must be so." We pray you, throw to earth
    This unprevailing woe and think of us
    As of a father; for let the world take note,
    You are the most immediate to our throne,
110   And with no less nobility of love
    Than that which dearest father bears his son
    Do I impart toward you. For your intent
    In going back to school in Wittenberg,
    It is most retrograde to our desire,
115   And we beseech you bend you to remain
    Here in the cheer and comfort of our eye,
    Our chiefest courtier, cousin, and our son.

---

[80]**fruitful** abundant   [81]**havior** expression   [82]**moods** outward expression of feeling   [92]**obsequious** suited to obsequies or funerals   **persever** persevere   [93]**condolement** sorrowing   [96]**unfortified** i.e., against adversity   [97]**simple** ignorant   [99]**As . . . sense** as the most ordinary experience   [104]**still** always   [105]**the first corpse** (Abel's)   [107]**unprevailing** unavailing, useless   [109]**most immediate** next in succession   [112]**impart toward** i.e., bestow my affection on   **For** as for   [113]**to school** i.e., to your studies   **Wittenberg** famous German university founded in 1502   [114]**retrograde** contrary   [115]**bend you** incline yourself

Queen: Let not thy mother lose her prayers, Hamlet.
   I pray thee, stay with us, go not to Wittenberg.
Hamlet: I shall in all my best obey you, madam.   120
King: Why, 'tis a loving and a fair reply.
   Be as ourself in Denmark. Madam, come.
   This gentle and unforced accord of Hamlet
   Sits smiling to my heart, in grace whereof
   No jocund health that Denmark drinks today   125
   But the great cannon to the clouds shall tell,
   And the King's rouse the heaven shall bruit again,
   Respeaking earthly thunder. Come away.
                    Flourish. Exeunt all but Hamlet.
Hamlet: O, that this too too sullied flesh would melt,
   Thaw, and resolve itself into a dew!   130
   Or that the Everlasting had not fixed
   His canon 'gainst self-slaughter! O God, God,
   How weary, stale, flat, and unprofitable
   Seem to me all the uses of this world!
   Fie on 't, ah fie! 'Tis an unweeded garden   135
   That grows to seed. Things rank and gross in nature
   Possess it merely. That it should come to this!
   But two months dead—nay, not so much, not two.
   So excellent a king, that was to this
   Hyperion to a satyr, so loving to my mother   140
   That he might not beteem the winds of heaven
   Visit her face too roughly. Heaven and earth,
   Must I remember? Why, she would hang on him
   As if increase of appetite had grown
   By what it fed on, and yet within a month—   145
   Let me not think on 't; frailty, thy name is woman!—
   A little month, or ere those shoes were old
   With which she followed my poor father's body,
   Like Niobe, all tears, why she, even she—

---

[120]**in all my best** to the best of my ability   [124]**to** i.e., at   **grace** thanksgiving
[125]**jocund** merry   [127]**rouse** drinking of a draft of liquor   **bruit again** loudly echo
[128]**thunder** i.e., of trumpet and kettledrum, sounded when the King drinks; see 1.4.8–12
[129]**sullied** defiled (The early quartos reads *sallied;* the Folio, *solid.*)   [132]**canon** law
[134]**all the uses** the whole routine   [137]**merely** completely   [139]**to** in comparison to
[140]**Hyperion** Titan sun-god, father of Helios   **satyr** a lecherous creature of classical
mythology, half-human but with a goat's legs, tail, ears, and horns   [141]**beteem** allow
[147]**or ere** even before   [149]**Niobe** Tantalus' daughter, Queen of Thebes, who boasted
that she had more sons and daughters than Leto; for this, Apollo and Artemis, children of
Leto, slew her fourteen children. She was turned by Zeus into a stone that continually
dropped tears.

150 O God, a beast, that wants discourse of reason,
Would have mourned longer—married with my uncle,
My father's brother, but no more like my father
Than I to Hercules. Within a month,
Ere yet the salt of most unrighteous tears
155 Had left the flushing in her gallèd eyes,
She married. O, most wicked speed, to post
With such dexterity to incestuous sheets!
It is not, nor it cannot come to good.
But break, my heart, for I must hold my tongue.

Enter Horatio, Marcellus, and Bernardo.

Horatio: Hail to your lordship!
160 *Hamlet:*   I am glad to see you well.
    Horatio!—or I do forget myself.
Horatio: The same, my lord, and your poor servant ever.
Hamlet: Sir, my good friend; I'll change that name with you.
    And what make you from Wittenberg, Horatio?
165   Marcellus.
Marcellus: My good lord.
Hamlet: I am very glad to see you. [*To Bernardo.*] Good even, sir.—
    But what in faith make you from Wittenberg?
Horatio: A truant disposition, good my lord.
170 *Hamlet:* I would not hear your enemy say so,
    Nor shall you do my ear that violence
    To make it truster of your own report
    Against yourself. I know you are no truant.
    But what is your affair in Elsinore?
175   We'll teach you to drink deep ere you depart.
Horatio: My lord, I came to see your father's funeral.
Hamlet: I prithee, do not mock me, fellow student;
    I think it was to see my mother's wedding.
Horatio: Indeed, my lord, it followed hard upon.
180 *Hamlet:* Thrift, thrift, Horatio! The funeral baked meats
    Did coldly furnish forth the marriage tables.
    Would I had met my dearest foe in heaven
    Or ever I had seen that day, Horatio!
    My father!—Methinks I see my father.

150wants . . . reason lacks the faculty of reason   **155gallèd** irritated, inflamed   **156post**
hasten   **157incestuous** (In Shakespeare's day, the marriage of a man like Claudius to
his deceased brother's wife was considered incestuous.)   **163change that name** i.e., give
and receive reciprocally the name of "friend" (rather than talk of "servant")   **164make
you from** are you doing away from   **179hard** close   **180baked meats** meat pies
181coldly i.e., as cold leftovers   **182dearest** closest (and therefore deadliest)   **183Or ever**
before

Horatio: Where, my lord?

Hamlet: In my mind's eye, Horatio.   185

Horatio: I saw him once. 'A was a goodly king.

Hamlet: 'A was a man. Take him for all in all,
　I shall not look upon his like again.

Horatio: My lord, I think I saw him yesternight.

Hamlet: Saw? Who?   190

Horatio: My lord, the King your father.

Hamlet: The King my father?

Horatio: Season your admiration for a while
　With an attent ear till I may deliver,
　Upon the witness of these gentlemen,   195
　This marvel to you.

Hamlet: For God's love, let me hear!

Horatio: Two nights together had these gentlemen,
　Marcellus and Bernardo, on their watch,
　In the dead waste and middle of the night,
　Been thus encountered. A figure like your father,   200
　Armèd at point exactly, cap-à-pie,
　Appears before them, and with solemn march
　Goes slow and stately by them. Thrice he walked
　By their oppressed and fear-surprisèd eyes
　Within his truncheon's length, whilst they, distilled   205
　Almost to jelly with the act of fear,
　Stand dumb and speak not to him. This to me
　In dreadful secrecy impart they did,
　And I with them the third night kept the watch,
　Where, as they had delivered, both in time,   210
　Form of the thing, each word made true and good,
　The apparition comes. I knew your father;
　These hands are not more like.

Hamlet: But where was this?

Marcellus: My lord, upon the platform where we watch.

Hamlet: Did you not speak to it?

Horatio: My lord, I did,   215
　But answer made it none. Yet once methought
　It lifted up its head and did address
　Itself to motion, like as it would speak;
　But even then the morning cock crew loud,
　And at the sound it shrunk in haste away   220
　And vanished from our sight.

---

[186]**'A** he   [193]**Season your admiration** restrain your astonishment   [194]**attent** attentive
[199]**dead waste** desolate stillness   [201]**at point** correctly in every detail   **cap-à-pie** from
head to foot   [205]**truncheon** officer's staff   **distilled** dissolved   [206]**act** action, operation
[208]**dreadful** full of dread   [217–218]**did . . . speak** began to move as though it were about to
speak   [219]**even then** at that very instant

Hamlet: 'Tis very strange.

Horatio: As I do live, my honored lord, 'tis true,
    And we did think it writ down in our duty
    To let you know of it.

225   *Hamlet:* Indeed, indeed, sirs. But this troubles me.
    Hold you the watch tonight?

All: We do, my lord.

Hamlet: Armed, say you?

All: Armed, my lord.

Hamlet: From top to toe?

230   *All:* My lord, from head to foot.

Hamlet: Then saw you not his face?

Horatio: O, yes, my lord, he wore his beaver up.

Hamlet: What looked he, frowningly?

Horatio: A countenance more in sorrow than in anger.

235   *Hamlet:* Pale or red?

Horatio: Nay, very pale.

Hamlet: And fixed his eyes upon you?

Horatio: Most constantly.

Hamlet: I would I had been there.

240   *Horatio:* It would have much amazed you.

Hamlet: Very like, very like. Stayed it long?

Horatio: While one with moderate haste might tell a hundred.

Marcellus, Bernardo: Longer, longer.

Horatio: Not when I saw 't.

245   *Hamlet:* His beard was grizzled—no?

Horatio: It was, as I have seen it in his life,
    A sable silvered.

Hamlet: I will watch tonight.
    Perchance 'twill walk again.

Horatio: I warrant it will.

Hamlet: If it assume my noble father's person,

250   I'll speak to it though hell itself should gape
    And bid me hold my peace. I pray you all,
    If you have hitherto concealed this sight,
    Let it be tenable in your silence still,
    And whatsoever else shall hap tonight,

255   Give it an understanding but no tongue.
    I will requite your loves. So, fare you well.
    Upon the platform twixt eleven and twelve
    I'll visit you.

All: Our duty to your honor.

---

[232]**beaver** visor on the helmet   [233]**What** how   [242]**tell** count   [245]**grizzled** gray
[247]**sable silvered** black mixed with white   [248]**warrant** assure you   [253]**tenable** held

Hamlet: Your loves, as mine to you. Farewell.

                         Exeunt [all but Hamlet].

My father's spirit in arms! All is not well.   260

I doubt some foul play. Would the night were come!

Till then sit still, my soul. Foul deeds will rise,

Though all the earth o'erwhelm them, to men's eyes.

                              Exit.

1.3   *Enter Laertes and Ophelia, his sister.*

Laertes: My necessaries are embarked. Farewell.

    And, sister, as the winds give benefit

    And convoy is assistant, do not sleep

    But let me hear from you.

Ophelia: Do you doubt that?

Laertes: For Hamlet, and the trifling of his favor,   5

    Hold it a fashion and a toy in blood,

    A violet in the youth of primy nature,

    Forward, not permanent, sweet, not lasting,

    The perfume and suppliance of a minute—

    No more.

Ophelia: No more but so?

Laertes: Think it no more.   10

    For nature crescent does not grow alone

    In thews and bulk, but as this temple waxes

    The inward service of the mind and soul

    Grows wide withal. Perhaps he loves you now,

    And now no soil nor cautel doth besmirch   15

    The virtue of his will; but you must fear,

    His greatness weighed, his will is not his own.

    For he himself is subject to his birth.

    He may not, as unvalued persons do,

    Carve for himself, for on his choice depends   20

    The safety and health of this whole state,

    And therefore must his choice be circumscribed

    Unto the voice and yielding of that body

---

²⁶¹**doubt** suspect

1.3. Location: Polonius' chambers.

³**convoy is assistant** means of conveyance are available   ⁶**toy in blood** passing amorous fancy   ⁷**primy** in its prime, springtime   ⁸**Forward** precocious   ⁹**suppliance** supply, filler   ¹¹**crescent** growing, waxing   ¹²**thews** bodily strength   **temple** i.e., body ¹⁴**Grows wide withal** grows along with it   ¹⁵**soil** blemish   **cautel** deceit   ¹⁶**will** desire ¹⁷**His greatness weighed** if you take into account his high position   ²⁰**Carve** i.e., choose ²³**voice and yielding** assent, approval

Whereof he is the head. Then if he says he loves you,
25 It fits your wisdom so far to believe it
As he in his particular act and place
May give his saying deed, which is no further
Than the main voice of Denmark goes withal.
Then weigh what loss your honor may sustain
30 If with too credent ear you list his songs,
Or lose your heart, or your chaste treasure open
To his unmastered importunity.
Fear it, Ophelia, fear it, my dear sister,
And keep you in the rear of your affection,
35 Out of the shot and danger of desire.
The chariest maid is prodigal enough
If she unmask her beauty to the moon.
Virtue itself scapes not calumnious strokes.
The canker galls the infants of the spring
40 Too oft before their buttons be disclosed,
And in the morn and liquid dew of youth
Contagious blastments are most imminent.
Be wary then; best safety lies in fear.
Youth to itself rebels, though none else near.
45 *Ophelia:* I shall the effect of this good lesson keep
As watchman to my heart. But, good my brother,
Do not, as some ungracious pastors do,
Show me the steep and thorny way to heaven,
Whiles like a puffed and reckless libertine
50 Himself the primrose path of dalliance treads,
And recks not his own rede.

Enter Polonius.

Laertes: O, fear me not.
I stay too long. But here my father comes.
A double blessing is a double grace;
Occasion smiles upon a second leave.
55 *Polonius:* Yet here, Laertes? Aboard, aboard, for shame!
The wind sits in the shoulder of your sail,

---

[26]**in . . . place** in his particular restricted circumstances   [28]**main voice** general assent **withal** along with   [30]**credent** credulous   **list** listen to   [34]**keep . . . affection** don't advance as far as your affection might lead you (A military metaphor.)   [36]**chariest** most scrupulously modest   [37]**If she unmask** if she does no more than show her beauty **moon** (Symbol of chastity.)   [39]**canker galls** cankerworm destroys   [40]**buttons** buds **disclosed** opened   [41]**liquid dew** i.e., time when dew is fresh and bright   [42]**blastments** blights   [44]**Youth . . . rebels** youth is inherently rebellious   [47]**ungracious** ungodly [49]**puffed** bloated, or swollen with pride   [51]**recks** heeds   **rede** counsel   **fear me not** don't worry on my account   [53]**double** (Laertes has already bid his father good-bye.) [54]**Occasion . . . leave** happy is the circumstance that provides a second leave-taking. (The goddess Occasion, or Opportunity, smiles.)

And you are stayed for. There—my blessing with thee!
And these few precepts in thy memory
Look thou character. Give thy thoughts no tongue,
Nor any unproportioned thought his act.   60
Be thou familiar, but by no means vulgar.
Those friends thou hast, and their adoption tried,
Grapple them unto thy soul with hoops of steel,
But do not dull thy palm with entertainment
Of each new-hatched, unfledged courage. Beware   65
Of entrance to a quarrel, but being in,
Bear 't that th' opposèd may beware of thee.
Give every man thy ear, but few thy voice;
Take each man's censure, but reserve thy judgment.
Costly thy habit as thy purse can buy,   70
But not expressed in fancy; rich, not gaudy,
For the apparel oft proclaims the man,
And they in France of the best rank and station
Are of a most select and generous chief in that.
Neither a borrower nor a lender be,   75
For loan oft loses both itself and friend,
And borrowing dulleth edge of husbandry.
This above all: to thine own self be true,
And it must follow, as the night the day,
Thou canst not then be false to any man.   80
Farewell. My blessing season this in thee!

Laertes: Most humbly do I take my leave, my lord.

Polonius: The time invests you. Go, your servants tend.

Laertes: Farewell, Ophelia, and remember well
What I have said to you.   85

Ophelia: 'Tis in my memory locked,
And you yourself shall keep the key of it.

Laertes: Farewell.   *Exit Laertes.*

Polonius: What is 't, Ophelia, he hath said to you?

Ophelia: So please you, something touching the Lord Hamlet.   90

Polonius: Marry, well bethought.
'Tis told me he hath very oft of late

---

[59]**Look** be sure that **character** inscribe [60]**unproportioned** badly calculated, intemperate **his** its [61]**familiar** sociable **vulgar** common [62]**and their adoption tried** and also their suitability for adoption as friends having been tested [64]**dull thy palm** i.e., shake hands so often as to make the gesture meaningless [65]**courage** young man of spirit [67]**Bear 't that** manage it so that [69]**censure** opinion, judgment [70]**habit** clothing [71]**fancy** excessive ornament, decadent fashion [74]**Are . . . that** are of a most refined and well-bred preeminence in choosing what to wear [77]**husbandry** thrift [81]**season** mature [83]**invests** besieges, presses upon **tend** attend, wait [91]**Marry** i.e., by the Virgin Mary (A mild oath.)

Given private time to you, and you yourself
Have of your audience been most free and bounteous.
95   If it be so—as so 'tis put on me,
And that in way of caution—I must tell you
You do not understand yourself so clearly
As it behooves my daughter and your honor.
What is between you? Give me up the truth.
100   *Ophelia:* He hath, my lord, of late made many tenders
Of his affection to me.
Polonius: Affection? Pooh! You speak like a green girl,
Unsifted in such perilous circumstance.
Do you believe his tenders, as you call them?
105   *Ophelia:* I do not know, my lord, what I should think.
Polonius: Marry, I will teach you. Think yourself a baby
That you have ta'en these tenders for true pay
Which are not sterling. Tender yourself more dearly,
Or—not to crack the wind of the poor phrase,
110   Running it thus—you'll tender me a fool.
Ophelia: My lord, he hath importuned me with love
In honorable fashion.
Polonius: Ay, fashion you may call it. Go to, go to.
Ophelia: And hath given countenance to his speech, my lord,
115   With almost all the holy vows of heaven.
Polonius: Ay, springes to catch woodcocks. I do know,
When the blood burns, how prodigal the soul
Lends the tongue vows. These blazes, daughter,
Giving more light than heat, extinct in both
120   Even in their promise as it is a-making,
You must not take for fire. From this time
Be something scanter of your maiden presence.
Set your entreatments at a higher rate
Than a command to parle. For Lord Hamlet,
125   Believe so much in him that he is young,
And with a larger tether may he walk

---

[95]**put on** impressed on, told to   [98]**behooves** befits   [100]**tenders** offers   [103]**Unsifted** i.e., untried   [108]**sterling** legal currency   **Tender** hold, look after, offer   [109]**crack the wind** i.e., run it until it is broken-winded   [110]**tender me a fool** (1) show yourself to me as a fool (2) show me up as a fool (3) present me with a grandchild (*Fool* was a term of endearment for a child.)   [113]**fashion** mere form, pretense   **Go to** (An expression of impatience.)   [114]**countenance** credit, confirmation   [116]**springes** snares   **woodcocks** birds easily caught; here used to connote gullibility   [117]**prodigal** prodigally   [120]**it** i.e., the promise   [122]**something** somewhat   [123]**entreatments** negotiations for surrender (A military term.)   [124]**parle** discuss terms with the enemy (Polonius urges his daughter, in the metaphor of military language, not to meet with Hamlet and consider giving in to him merely because he requests an interview.)   [125]**so . . . him** this much concerning him

Than may be given you. In few, Ophelia,
Do not believe his vows, for they are brokers,
Not of that dye which their investments show,
But mere implorators of unholy suits,   130
Breathing like sanctified and pious bawds,
The better to beguile. This is for all:
I would not, in plain terms, from this time forth
Have you so slander any moment leisure
As to give words or talk with the Lord Hamlet.   135
Look to 't, I charge you. Come your ways.
Ophelia: I shall obey, my lord.   *Exeunt.*

1.4   *Enter Hamlet, Horatio, and Marcellus.*

Hamlet: The air bites shrewdly; it is very cold.
Horatio: It is a nipping and an eager air.
Hamlet: What hour now?
Horatio: I think it lacks of twelve.
Marcellus: No, it is struck.
Horatio: Indeed? I heard it not.
   It then draws near the season   5
   Wherein the spirit held his wont to walk.
            A flourish of trumpets, and two pieces go off [within].
   What does this mean, my lord?
Hamlet: The King doth wake tonight and takes his rouse,
   Keeps wassail, and the swaggering upspring reels;
   And as he drains his drafts of Rhenish down,   10
   The kettledrum and trumpet thus bray out
   The triumph of his pledge.
Horatio: Is it a custom?
Hamlet: Ay, marry, is 't,
   But to my mind, though I am native here
   And to the manner born, it is a custom   15
   More honored in the breach than the observance.

---

¹²⁷**In few** briefly   ¹²⁸**brokers** go-betweens, procurers   ¹²⁹**dye** color or sort
investments clothes (The vows are not what they seem.)   ¹³⁰**mere implorators** out
and out solicitors   ¹³¹**Breathing** speaking   ¹³²**for all** once for all, in sum   ¹³⁴**slander**
abuse, misuse   **moment** moment's   ¹³⁶**Come your ways** come along
1.4. Location: The guard platform.
¹**shrewdly** keenly, sharply   ²**eager** biting   ³**lacks of** is just short of   ⁵**season** time
⁶**held his wont** was accustomed   ˢ·ᵈ·**pieces** i.e., of ordnance, cannon   ⁸**wake** stay
awake and hold revel   **takes his rouse** carouses   ⁹**wassail** carousal   **upspring** wild
German dance   **reels** dances   ¹⁰**Rhenish** Rhine wine   ¹²**The triumph . . . pledge**
i.e., his feat in draining the wine in a single draft   ¹⁵**manner** custom (of drinking)
¹⁶**More . . . observance** better neglected than followed

This heavy-headed revel east and west
Makes us traduced and taxed of other nations.
They clepe us drunkards, and with swinish phrase
20 Soil our addition; and indeed it takes
From our achievements, though performed at height,
The pith and marrow of our attribute.
So, oft it chances in particular men,
That for some vicious mole of nature in them,
25 As in their birth—wherein they are not guilty,
Since nature cannot choose his origin—
By their o'ergrowth of some complexion,
Oft breaking down the pales and forts of reason,
Or by some habit that too much o'erleavens
30 The form of plausive manners, that these men,
Carrying, I say, the stamp of one defect,
Being nature's livery or fortune's star,
His virtues else, be they as pure as grace,
As infinite as man may undergo,
35 Shall in the general censure take corruption
From that particular fault. The dram of evil
Doth all the noble substance often dout
To his own scandal.

        Enter Ghost.

Horatio: Look, my lord, it comes!
Hamlet: Angels and ministers of grace defend us!
40 Be thou a spirit of health or goblin damned,
Bring with thee airs from heaven or blasts from hell,
Be thy intents wicked or charitable,
Thou com'st in such a questionable shape
That I will speak to thee. I'll call thee Hamlet,
45 King, father, royal Dane. O, answer me!

---

[17]**east and west** i.e., everywhere   [18]**taxed of** censured by   [19]**clepe** call   **with swinish phrase** i.e., by calling us swine   [20]**addition** reputation   [21]**at height** outstandingly   [22]**The pith . . . attribute** the essence of the reputation that others attribute to us   [24]**for** on account of   **mole of nature** natural blemish in one's constitution   [26]**his** its   [27]**their o'ergrowth . . . complexion** the excessive growth in individuals of some natural trait   [28]**pales** palings, fences (as of a fortification)   [29]**o'erleavens** induces a change throughout (as yeast works in dough)   [30]**plausive** pleasing   [32]**nature's livery** sign of one's servitude to nature   **fortune's star** the destiny that chance brings   [33]**His virtues else** i.e., the other qualities of *these men* (line 30)   [34]**may undergo** can sustain   [35]**general censure** general opinion that people have of him   [36-38]**The dram . . . scandal** i.e., the small drop of evil blots out or works against the noble substance of the whole and brings it into disrepute. To *dout* is to blot out. (A famous crux.)   [39]**ministers of grace** messengers of God   [40]**Be thou** whether you are   **spirit of health** good angel   [41]**Bring** whether you bring   [42]**Be thy intents** whether your intentions are   [43]**questionable** inviting question

Let me not burst in ignorance, but tell
Why thy canonized bones, hearsèd in death,
Have burst their cerements; why the sepulcher
Wherein we saw thee quietly inurned
Hath oped his ponderous and marble jaws   50
To cast thee up again. What may this mean,
That thou, dead corpse, again in complete steel,
Revisits thus the glimpses of the moon,
Making night hideous, and we fools of nature
So horridly to shake our disposition   55
With thoughts beyond the reaches of our souls?
Say, why is this? Wherefore? What should we do?

             [The Ghost] beckons [Hamlet].

Horatio: It beckons you to go away with it,
   As if it some impartment did desire
   To you alone.

Marcellus: Look with what courteous action   60
   It wafts you to a more removèd ground.
   But do not go with it.

Horatio: No, by no means.

Hamlet: It will not speak. Then I will follow it.

Horatio: Do not, my lord!

Hamlet: Why, what should be the fear?
   I do not set my life at a pin's fee,   65
   And for my soul, what can it do to that,
   Being a thing immortal as itself?
   It waves me forth again. I'll follow it.

Horatio: What if it tempt you toward the flood, my lord,
   Or to the dreadful summit of the cliff   70
   That beetles o'er his base into the sea,
   And there assume some other horrible form
   Which might deprive your sovereignty of reason
   And draw you into madness? Think of it.
   The very place puts toys of desperation,   75
   Without more motive, into every brain
   That looks so many fathoms to the sea
   And hears it roar beneath.

---

[47]**canonized** buried according to the canons of the church   **hearsèd** coffined
[48]**cerements** grave clothes   [49]**inurned** entombed   [52]**complete steel** full armor
[53]**glimpses of the moon** pale and uncertain moonlight   [54]**fools of nature** mere men,
limited to natural knowledge and subject to nature   [55]**So . . . disposition** to distress
our mental composure so violently   [59]**impartment** communication   [65]**fee** value
[69]**flood** sea   [71]**beetles o'er** overhangs threateningly (like bushy eyebrows)   **his** its
[73]**deprive . . . reason** take away the rule of reason over your mind   [75]**toys of
desperation** fancies of desperate acts, i.e., suicide

Hamlet: It wafts me still.—Go on, I'll follow thee.

Marcellus: You shall not go, my lord.   [*They try to stop him.*]

80 *Hamlet:*   Hold off your hands!

Horatio: Be ruled. You shall not go.

Hamlet: My fate cries out,

  And makes each petty artery in this body

  As hardy as the Nemean lion's nerve.

  Still am I called. Unhand me, gentlemen.

85   By heaven, I'll make a ghost of him that lets me!

  I say, away!—Go on, I'll follow thee.

  Exeunt Ghost and Hamlet.

Horatio: He waxes desperate with imagination.

Marcellus: Let's follow. 'Tis not fit thus to obey him.

Horatio: Have after. To what issue will this come?

90 *Marcellus:* Something is rotten in the state of Denmark.

Horatio: Heaven will direct it.

Marcellus: Nay, let's follow him.   *Exeunt.*

1.5   *Enter Ghost and Hamlet.*

Hamlet: Whither wilt thou lead me? Speak. I'll go no further.

Ghost: Mark me.

Hamlet: I will.

Ghost: My hour is almost come,

  When I to sulfurous and tormenting flames

  Must render up myself.

Hamlet: Alas, poor ghost!

5 *Ghost:* Pity me not, but lend thy serious hearing

  To what I shall unfold.

Hamlet: Speak. I am bound to hear.

Ghost: So art thou to revenge, when thou shalt hear.

Hamlet: What?

10 *Ghost:* I am thy father's spirit,

  Doomed for a certain term to walk the night,

  And for the day confined to fast in fires,

  Till the foul crimes done in my days of nature

  Are burnt and purged away. But that I am forbid

---

[81]**My fate cries out** my destiny summons me   [82]**petty** weak   **artery** (through which the vital spirits were thought to have been conveyed)   [83]**Nemean lion** one of the monsters slain by Hercules in his twelve labors   **nerve** sinew   [85]**lets** hinders
[89]**Have after** let's go after him   **issue** outcome   [91]**it** i.e., the outcome
1.5. Location: The battlements of the castle.
[7]**bound** (1) ready (2) obligated by duty and fate (The Ghost, in line 8, answers in the second sense.)   [12]**fast** do penance by fasting   [13]**crimes** sins   **of nature** as a mortal
[14]**But that** were it not that

To tell the secrets of my prison house,   15
I could a tale unfold whose lightest word
Would harrow up thy soul, freeze thy young blood,
Make thy two eyes like stars start from their spheres,
Thy knotted and combinèd locks to part,
And each particular hair to stand on end   20
Like quills upon the fretful porcupine.
But this eternal blazon must not be
To ears of flesh and blood. List, list, O, list!
If thou didst ever thy dear father love—

Hamlet: O God!   25

Ghost: Revenge his foul and most unnatural murder.

Hamlet: Murder?

Ghost: Murder most foul, as in the best it is,
    But this most foul, strange, and unnatural.

Hamlet: Haste me to know 't, that I, with wings as swift   30
    As meditation or the thoughts of love,
    May sweep to my revenge.

Ghost: I find thee apt;
    And duller shouldst thou be than the fat weed
    That roots itself in ease on Lethe wharf,
    Wouldst thou not stir in this. Now, Hamlet, hear.   35
    'Tis given out that, sleeping in my orchard,
    A serpent stung me. So the whole ear of Denmark
    Is by a forgèd process of my death
    Rankly abused. But know, thou noble youth,
    The serpent that did sting thy father's life   40
    Now wears his crown.

Hamlet: O, my prophetic soul! My uncle!

Ghost: Ay, that incestuous, that adulterate beast,
    With witchcraft of his wit, with traitorous gifts—
    O wicked wit and gifts, that have the power   45
    So to seduce!—won to his shameful lust
    The will of my most seeming-virtuous queen.
    O Hamlet, what a falling off was there!
    From me, whose love was of that dignity
    That it went hand in hand even with the vow   50

---

[17]**harrow up** lacerate, tear   [18]**spheres** i.e., eye-sockets, here compared to the orbits or transparent revolving spheres in which, according to Ptolemaic astronomy, the heavenly bodies were fixed   [19]**knotted . . . locks** hair neatly arranged and confined   [22]**eternal blazon** revelation of the secrets of eternity   [28]**in the best** even at best   [33]**shouldst thou be** you would have to be   **fat** torpid, lethargic   [34]**Lethe** the river of forgetfulness in Hades   [36]**orchard** garden   [38]**forgèd process** falsified account   [39]**abused** deceived   [43]**adulterate** adulterous   [44]**gifts** (1) talents (2) presents   [50]**even with the vow** with the very vow

I made to her in marriage, and to decline
Upon a wretch whose natural gifts were poor
To those of mine!
But virtue, as it never will be moved,
55   Though lewdness court it in a shape of heaven,
So lust, though to a radiant angel linked,
Will sate itself in a celestial bed
And prey on garbage.
But soft, methinks I scent the morning air.
60   Brief let me be. Sleeping within my orchard,
My custom always of the afternoon,
Upon my secure hour thy uncle stole,
With juice of cursèd hebona in a vial,
And in the porches of my ears did pour
65   The leprous distillment, whose effect
Holds such an enmity with blood of man
That swift as quicksilver it courses through
The natural gates and alleys of the body,
And with a sudden vigor it doth posset
70   And curd, like eager droppings into milk,
The thin and wholesome blood. So did it mine,
And a most instant tetter barked about,
Most lazar-like, with vile and loathsome crust,
All my smooth body.
75   Thus was I, sleeping, by a brother's hand
Of life, of crown, of queen at once dispatched,
Cut off even in the blossoms of my sin,
Unhouseled, disappointed, unaneled,
No reckoning made, but sent to my account
80   With all my imperfections on my head.
O, horrible! O, horrible, most horrible!
If thou hast nature in thee, bear it not.
Let not the royal bed of Denmark be
A couch for luxury and damnèd incest.
85   But, howsoever thou pursues this act,

---

[53]**To** compared to   [54]**virtue, as it** as virtue   [55]**shape of heaven** heavenly form
[57]**sate . . . bed** cease to find sexual pleasure in a virtuously lawful marriage   [62]**secure**
confident, unsuspicious   [63]**hebona** a poison (The word seems to be a form of *ebony*,
though it is thought perhaps to be related to *henbane*, a poison, or to *ebenus*, "yew.")
[64]**porches of my ears** ears as a porch or entrance of the body   [65]**leprous distillment**
distillation causing leprosylike disfigurement   [69]**posset** coagulate, curdle   [70]**eager** sour,
acid   [72]**tetter** eruption of scabs   **barked** covered with a rough covering, like bark on a
tree   [73]**lazar-like** leperlike   [76]**dispatched** suddenly deprived   [78]**Unhouseled** without
having received the Sacrament   **disappointed** unready (spiritually) for the last journey
unaneled without having received extreme unction   [79]**reckoning** settling of accounts
[82]**nature** i.e., the promptings of a son   [84]**luxury** lechery

Taint not thy mind nor let thy soul contrive
Against thy mother aught. Leave her to heaven
And to those thorns that in her bosom lodge,
To prick and sting her. Fare thee well at once.
The glowworm shows the matin to be near,   90
And 'gins to pale his uneffectual fire.
Adieu, adieu, adieu! Remember me.   [*Exit.*]
Hamlet: O all you host of heaven! O earth! What else?
And shall I couple hell? O, fie! Hold, hold, my heart,
And you, my sinews, grow not instant old,   95
But bear me stiffly up. Remember thee?
Ay, thou poor ghost, whiles memory holds a seat
In this distracted globe. Remember thee?
Yea, from the table of my memory
I'll wipe away all trivial fond records,   100
All saws of books, all forms, all pressures past
That youth and observation copied there,
And thy commandment all alone shall live
Within the book and volume of my brain,
Unmixed with baser matter. Yes, by heaven!   105
O most pernicious woman!
O villain, villain, smiling, damnèd villain!
My tables—meet it is I set it down
That one may smile, and smile, and be a villain.
At least I am sure it may be so in Denmark.   [*Writing.*]   110
So, uncle, there you are. Now to my word:
It is "Adieu, adieu! Remember me."
I have sworn 't.

Enter Horatio and Marcellus.

Horatio: My lord, my lord!
Marcellus: Lord Hamlet!   115
Horatio: Heavens secure him!
Hamlet: So be it.
Marcellus: Hilo, ho, ho, my lord!
Hamlet: Hillo, ho, ho, boy! Come, bird, come.
Marcellus: How is 't, my noble lord?   120

---

[90] **matin** morning   [91] **his** its   [94] **couple** add   **Hold** hold together   [95] **instant** instantly
[98] **globe** (1) head (2) world   [99] **table** tablet, slate   [100] **fond** foolish   [101] **saws** wise sayings
forms shapes or images copied onto the slate; general ideas   **pressures** impressions
stamped   [108] **tables** writing tablets   **meet it is** it is fitting   [111] **there you are** i.e., there,
I've written that down against you   [116] **secure him** keep him safe   [119] **Hillo . . . come**
(A falconer's call to a hawk in air. Hamlet mocks the hallooing as though it were a part of
hawking.)

Horatio: What news, my lord?

Hamlet: O, wonderful!

Horatio: Good my lord, tell it.

Hamlet: No, you will reveal it.

125 *Horatio:* Not I, my lord, by heaven.

Marcellus: Nor I, my lord.

Hamlet: How say you, then, would heart of man once think it?
But you'll be secret?

Horatio, Marcellus: Ay, by heaven, my lord.

Hamlet: There's never a villain dwelling in all Denmark

130 But he's an arrant knave.

Horatio: There needs no ghost, my lord, come from the grave
To tell us this.

Hamlet: Why, right, you are in the right.
And so, without more circumstance at all,
I hold it fit that we shake hands and part,

135 You as your business and desire shall point you—
For every man hath business and desire,
Such as it is—and for my own poor part,
Look you, I'll go pray.

Horatio: These are but wild and whirling words, my lord.

140 *Hamlet:* I am sorry they offend you, heartily;
Yes, faith, heartily.

Horatio: There's no offense, my lord.

Hamlet: Yes, by Saint Patrick, but there is, Horatio,
And much offense too. Touching this vision here,
It is an honest ghost, that let me tell you.

145 For your desire to know what is between us,
O'ermaster 't as you may. And now, good friends,
As you are friends, scholars, and soldiers,
Give me one poor request.

Horatio: What is 't, my lord? We will.

150 *Hamlet:* Never make known what you have seen tonight.

Horatio, Marcellus: My lord, we will not.

Hamlet: Nay, but swear 't.

Horatio: In faith, my lord, not I.

Marcellus: Nor I, my lord, in faith.

127**once** ever   130**arrant** thoroughgoing   133**circumstance** ceremony, elaboration
142**Saint Patrick** (The keeper of Purgatory and patron saint of all blunders and confusion)
143**offense** (Hamlet deliberately changes Horatio's "no offense taken" to "an offense
against all decency.")   144**an honest ghost** i.e., a real ghost and not an evil spirit
153**In faith . . . I** i.e., I swear not to tell what I have seen. (Horatio is not refusing to swear.)

Hamlet: Upon my sword.   [*He holds out his sword.*]   155

Marcellus: We have sworn, my lord, already.

Hamlet: Indeed, upon my sword, indeed.

Ghost (cries under the stage): Swear.

Hamlet: Ha, ha, boy, sayst thou so? Art thou there, truepenny?

    Come on, you hear this fellow in the cellarage.   160

    Consent to swear.

Horatio: Propose the oath, my lord.

Hamlet: Never to speak of this that you have seen,

    Swear by my sword.

Ghost [beneath]: Swear.   [*They swear.*]

Hamlet: Hic et ubique? Then we'll shift our ground.   [*He moves to another spot.*]   165

    Come hither, gentlemen,

    And lay your hands again upon my sword.

    Swear by my sword

    Never to speak of this that you have heard.

Ghost [beneath]: Swear by his sword.   [*They swear*]   170

Hamlet: Well said, old mole. Canst work i' th' earth so fast?

    A worthy pioner!—Once more remove, good friends.   [*He moves again.*]

Horatio: O day and night, but this is wondrous strange!

Hamlet: And therefore as a stranger give it welcome.

    There are more things in heaven and earth, Horatio,   175

    Than are dreamt of in your philosophy.

    But come;

    Here, as before, never, so help you mercy,

    How strange or odd soe'er I bear myself—

    As I perchance hereafter shall think meet   180

    To put an antic disposition on—

    That you, at such times seeing me, never shall,

    With arms encumbered thus, or this headshake,

    Or by pronouncing of some doubtful phrase

    As "Well, we know," or "We could, an if we would,"   185

---

[155]**sword** i.e., the hilt in the form of a cross   [156]**We . . . already** i.e., we swore *in faith*
[159]**truepenny** honest old fellow   [164s.d.]**They swear** (Seemingly they swear here, and
at lines 170 and 190, as they lay their hands on Hamlet's sword. Triple oaths would have
particular force; these three oaths deal with what they have seen, what they have heard,
and what they promise about Hamlet's *antic disposition*.)   [165]**Hic et ubique** here and
everywhere (Latin.)   [172]**pioner** foot soldier assigned to dig tunnels and excavations
[174]**as a stranger** i.e., needing your hospitality   [176]**your philosophy** this subject called
"natural philosophy" or "science" that people talk about   [178]**so help you mercy** as you
hope for God's mercy when you are judged   [181]**antic** fantastic   [183]**encumbered** folded
[185]**an if** if

Or "If we list to speak," or "There be, an if they might,"
Or such ambiguous giving out, to note
That you know aught of me—this do swear,
So grace and mercy at your most need help you.
190 *Ghost [beneath]:* Swear.　　*[They swear.]*
Hamlet: Rest, rest, perturbèd spirit! So, gentlemen,
With all my love I do commend me to you;
And what so poor a man as Hamlet is
May do t' express his love and friending to you,
195 God willing, shall not lack. Let us go in together,
And still your fingers on your lips, I pray.
The time is out of joint. O cursèd spite
That ever I was born to set it right!　*[They wait for him to leave first.]*
Nay, come, let's go together.　*Exeunt.*

2.1　　*Enter old Polonius with his man [Reynaldo].*

Polonius: Give him this money and these notes, Reynaldo.
　　[He gives money and papers.]
Reynaldo: I will, my lord.
Polonius: You shall do marvelous wisely, good Reynaldo,
Before you visit him, to make inquire
Of his behavior.
5 *Reynaldo:*　　　My lord, I did intend it.
Polonius: Marry, well said, very well said. Look you, sir,
Inquire me first what Danskers are in Paris,
And how, and who, what means, and where they keep,
What company, at what expense; and finding
10 By this encompassment and drift of question
That they do know my son, come you more nearer
Than your particular demands will touch it.
Take you, as 'twere, some distant knowledge of him,
As thus, "I know his father and his friends,
15 And in part him." Do you mark this, Reynaldo?

---

[186]**list** wished　**There . . . might** i.e., there are people here (we, in fact) who could tell news if we were at liberty to do so　[187]**giving out** intimation　**note** draw attention to the fact　[188]**aught** i.e., something secret　[192]**do . . . you** entrust myself to you
[194]**friending** friendliness　[195]**lack** be lacking　[196]**still** always　[197]**The time** the state of affairs　**spite** i.e., the spite of Fortune　[199]**let's go together** (Probably they wait for him to leave first, but he refuses this ceremoniousness.)
2.1. Location: Polonius' chambers.
[3]**marvelous** marvelously　[4]**inquire** inquiry　[7]**Danskers** Danes　[8]**what means** what wealth (they have)　**keep** dwell　[10]**encompassment** roundabout talking　**drift** gradual approach or course　[11–12]**come . . . it** you will find out more this way than by asking pointed questions (*particular demands*)　[13]**Take you** assume, pretend

Reynaldo: Ay, very well, my lord.

Polonius: "And in part him, but," you may say, "not well.

But if 't be he I mean, he's very wild,

Addicted so and so," and there put on him

What forgeries you please—marry, none so rank　　　　　20

As may dishonor him, take heed of that,

But, sir, such wanton, wild, and usual slips

As are companions noted and most known

To youth and liberty.

Reynaldo: As gaming, my lord.　　　　　25

Polonius: Ay, or drinking, fencing, swearing,

Quarreling, drabbing—you may go so far.

Reynaldo: My lord, that would dishonor him.

Polonius: Faith, no, as you may season it in the charge.

You must not put another scandal on him　　　　　30

That he is open to incontinency;

That's not my meaning. But breathe his faults so quaintly

That they may seem the taints of liberty,

The flash and outbreak of a fiery mind,

A savageness in unreclaimèd blood,　　　　　35

Of general assault.

Reynaldo: But, my good lord—

Polonius: Wherefore should you do this?

Reynaldo: Ay, my lord, I would know that.

Polonius: Marry, sir, here's my drift,　　　　　40

And I believe it is a fetch of warrant.

You laying these slight sullies on my son,

As 'twere a thing a little soiled wi' the working,

Mark you,

Your party in converse, him you would sound,　　　　　45

Having ever seen in the prenominate crimes

The youth you breathe of guilty, be assured

He closes with you in this consequence:

"Good sir," or so, or "friend," or "gentleman,"

According to the phrase or the addition　　　　　50

Of man and country.

Reynaldo: 　　　　　Very good, my lord.

---

[19]**put on** impute to　[20]**forgeries** invented tales　**rank** gross　[22]**wanton** sportive, unrestrained　[27]**drabbing** whoring　[29]**season** temper, soften　[31]**incontinency** habitual sexual excess　[32]**quaintly** artfully, subtly　[33]**taints of liberty** faults resulting from free living　[35-36]**A savageness . . . assault** a wildness in untamed youth that assails all indiscriminately　[41]**fetch of warrant** legitimate trick　[43]**soiled wi' the working** soiled by handling while it is being made, i.e., by involvement in the ways of the world　[45]**converse** conversation　**sound** i.e., sound out　[46]**Having ever** if he has ever　**prenominate crimes** before-mentioned offenses　[47]**breathe** speak　[48]**closes . . . consequence** takes you into his confidence in some fashion, as follows　[50]**addition** title

Polonius: And then, sir, does 'a this—'a does—what was I about to say? By the
Mass, I was about to say something. Where did I leave?

Reynaldo: At "closes in the consequence."

55 *Polonius:* At "closes in the consequence," ay, marry.
He closes thus: "I know the gentleman,
I saw him yesterday," or "th' other day,"
Or then, or then, with such or such, "and as you say,
There was 'a gaming," "there o'ertook in 's rouse,"

60 "There falling out at tennis," or perchance
"I saw him enter such a house of sale,"
Videlicet a brothel, or so forth. See you now,
Your bait of falsehood takes this carp of truth;
And thus do we of wisdom and of reach,

65 With windlasses and with assays of bias,
By indirections find directions out.
So by my former lecture and advice
Shall you my son. You have me, have you not?

Reynaldo: My lord, I have.

Polonius: God b'wi' ye; fare ye well.

70 *Reynaldo:* Good my lord.

Polonius: Observe his inclination in yourself.

Reynaldo: I shall, my lord.

Polonius: And let him ply his music.

Reynaldo: Well, my lord.

Polonius: Farewell.   *Exit Reynaldo.*

Enter Ophelia.

75   How now, Ophelia, what's the matter?

Ophelia: O my lord, my lord, I have been so affrighted!

Polonius: With what, i' the name of God?

Ophelia: My lord, as I was sewing in my closet,
Lord Hamlet, with his doublet all unbraced,

80 No hat upon his head, his stockings fouled,
Ungartered, and down-gyvèd to his ankle,
Pale as his shirt, his knees knocking each other,
And with a look so piteous in purport
As if he had been loosèd out of hell

85 To speak of horrors—he comes before me.

---

[59]**o'ertook in 's rouse** overcome by drink   [60]**falling out** quarreling   [62]**Videlicet** namely
[63]**carp** a fish   [64]**reach** capacity, ability   [65]**windlasses** i.e., circuitous paths (Literally,
circuits made to head off the game in hunting.)   **assays of bias** attempts through
indirection (like the curving path of the bowling ball, which is biased or weighted to one
side)   [66]**directions** i.e., the way things really are   [68]**have** understand   [69]**b' wi'** be with
[71]**in yourself** in your own person (as well as by asking questions)   [78]**closet** private
chamber   [79]**doublet** close-fitting jacket   **unbraced** unfastened   [81]**down-gyvèd** fallen
to the ankles (like gyves or fetters)   [83]**in purport** in what it expressed

Polonius: Mad for thy love?

Ophelia: My lord, I do not know,
     But truly I do fear it.

Polonius: What said he?

Ophelia: He took me by the wrist and held me hard.
     Then goes he to the length of all his arm,
     And, with his other hand thus o'er his brow   90
     He falls to such perusal of my face
     As 'a would draw it. Long stayed he so.
     At last, a little shaking of mine arm
     And thrice his head thus waving up and down,
     He raised a sigh so piteous and profound   95
     As it did seem to shatter all his bulk
     And end his being. That done, he lets me go,
     And with his head over his shoulder turned
     He seemed to find his way without his eyes,
     For out o' doors he went without their helps,   100
     And to the last bended their light on me.

Polonius: Come, go with me. I will go seek the King.
     This is the very ecstasy of love,
     Whose violent property fordoes itself
     And leads the will to desperate undertakings   105
     As oft as any passion under heaven
     That does afflict our natures. I am sorry.
     What, have you given him any hard words of late?

Ophelia: No, my good lord, but as you did command
     I did repel his letters and denied   110
     His access to me.

Polonius: That hath made him mad.
     I am sorry that with better heed and judgment
     I had not quoted him. I feared he did but trifle
     And meant to wrack thee. But beshrew my jealousy!
     By heaven, it is as proper to our age   115
     To cast beyond ourselves in our opinions
     As it is common for the younger sort
     To lack discretion. Come, go we to the King.
     This must be known, which, being kept close, might move
     More grief to hide than hate to utter love.   120
     Come.   *Exeunt.*

---

⁹²**As** as if (also in line 96)   ⁹⁶**bulk** body   ¹⁰³**ecstasy** madness   ¹⁰⁴**property** nature
fordoes destroys   ¹¹³**quoted** observed   ¹¹⁴**wrack** ruin, seduce   **beshrew my
jealousy** a plague upon my suspicious nature   ¹¹⁵**proper . . . age** characteristic of us
(old) men   ¹¹⁶**cast beyond** overshoot, miscalculate (A metaphor from hunting.)
¹¹⁹**known** made known (to the King)   **close** secret   ¹¹⁹⁻¹²⁰**might . . . love** i.e., might
cause more grief (because of what Hamlet might do) by hiding the knowledge of Hamlet's
strange behavior to Ophelia than unpleasantness by telling it

2.2   *Flourish. Enter King and Queen, Rosencrantz, and Guildenstern [with others].*

King: Welcome, dear Rosencrantz and Guildenstern.
  Moreover that we much did long to see you,
  The need we have to use you did provoke
  Our hasty sending. Something have you heard
5 Of Hamlet's transformation—so call it,
  Sith nor th' exterior nor the inward man
  Resembles that it was. What it should be,
  More than his father's death, that thus hath put him
  So much from th' understanding of himself,
10 I cannot dream of. I entreat you both
  That, being of so young days brought up with him,
  And sith so neighbored to his youth and havior,
  That you vouchsafe your rest here in our court
  Some little time, so by your companies
15 To draw him on to pleasures, and to gather
  So much as from occasion you may glean,
  Whether aught to us unknown afflicts him thus
  That, opened, lies within our remedy.
Queen: Good gentlemen, he hath much talked of you,
20 And sure I am two men there is not living
  To whom he more adheres. If it will please you
  To show us so much gentry and good will
  As to expend your time with us awhile
  For the supply and profit of our hope,
25 Your visitation shall receive such thanks
  As fits a king's remembrance.
Rosencrantz: Both Your Majesties
  Might, by the sovereign power you have of us,
  Put your dread pleasures more into command
  Than to entreaty.
Guildenstern: But we both obey,
30 And here give up ourselves in the full bent
  To lay our service freely at your feet,
  To be commanded.
King: Thanks, Rosencrantz and gentle Guildenstern.

2.2. Location: The castle.
²**Moreover that** besides the fact that   ⁶**Sith nor** since neither   ⁷**that** what
¹¹**of . . . days** from such early youth   ¹²**And sith so neighbored to** and since you are
(or, and since that time you are) intimately acquainted with   **havior** demeanor
¹³**vouchsafe your rest** please to stay   ¹⁶**occasion** opportunity   ¹⁸**opened** being
revealed   ²²**gentry** courtesy   ²⁴**supply . . . hope** aid and furtherance of what we hope
for   ²⁶**As fits . . . remembrance** as would be a fitting gift of a king who rewards true
service   ²⁷**of** over   ²⁸**dread** inspiring awe   ³⁰**in . . . bent** to the utmost degree of our
capacity (An archery metaphor.)

Queen: Thanks, Guildenstern and gentle Rosencrantz.
 And I beseech you instantly to visit   35
 My too much changèd son. Go, some of you,
 And bring these gentlemen where Hamlet is.
Guildenstern: Heavens make our presence and our practices
 Pleasant and helpful to him!
Queen: Ay, amen!

            Exeunt Rosencrantz and Guildenstern [with some attendants].

         Enter Polonius.

Polonius: Th' ambassadors from Norway, my good lord,   40
 Are joyfully returned.
King: Thou still hast been the father of good news.
Polonius: Have I, my lord? I assure my good liege
 I hold my duty, as I hold my soul,
 Both to my God and to my gracious king;   45
 And I do think, or else this brain of mine
 Hunts not the trail of policy so sure
 As it hath used to do, that I have found
 The very cause of Hamlet's lunacy.
King: O, speak of that! That do I long to hear.   50
Polonius: Give first admittance to th' ambassadors.
 My news shall be the fruit to that great feast.
King: Thyself do grace to them and bring them in.   *[Exit Polonius.]*
 He tells me, my dear Gertrude, he hath found
 The head and source of all your son's distemper.   55
Queen: I doubt it is no other but the main,
 His father's death and our o'erhasty marriage.

         Enter Ambassadors [Voltimand and Cornelius, with Polonius].

King: Well, we shall sift him.—Welcome, my good friends!
 Say, Voltimand, what from our brother Norway?
Voltimand: Most fair return of greetings and desires.   60
 Upon our first, he sent out to suppress
 His nephew's levies, which to him appeared
 To be a preparation 'gainst the Polack,
 But, better looked into, he truly found
 It was against Your Highness. Whereat grieved   65

---

³⁸**practices** doings   ⁴²**still** always   ⁴⁴**hold** maintain   **as** as firmly as   ⁴⁷**policy** sagacity
⁵²**fruit** dessert   ⁵³**grace** honor (punning on *grace* said before a *feast*, line 52)   ⁵⁶**doubt**
fear, suspect   **main** chief point, principal concern   ⁵⁸**sift him** question Polonius closely
⁵⁹**brother** fellow king   ⁶⁰**desires** good wishes   ⁶¹**Upon our first** at our first words on
the business

That so his sickness, age, and impotence
Was falsely borne in hand, sends out arrests
On Fortinbras, which he, in brief, obeys,
Receives rebuke from Norway, and in fine
70 Makes vow before his uncle never more
To give th' assay of arms against Your Majesty.
Whereon old Norway, overcome with joy,
Gives him three thousand crowns in annual fee
And his commission to employ those soldiers,
75 So levied as before, against the Polack,
With an entreaty, herein further shown,   [*giving a paper*]
That it might please you to give quiet pass
Through your dominions for this enterprise
On such regards of safety and allowance
As therein are set down.
80 *King:*   It likes us well,
And at our more considered time we'll read,
Answer, and think upon this business.
Meantime we thank you for your well-took labor.
Go to your rest; at night we'll feast together.
Most welcome home!   *Exeunt Ambassadors.*
85 *Polonius:*   This business is well ended.
My liege, and madam, to expostulate
What majesty should be, what duty is,
Why day is day, night night, and time is time,
Were nothing but to waste night, day, and time.
90 Therefore, since brevity is the soul of wit,
And tediousness the limbs and outward flourishes,
I will be brief. Your noble son is mad.
Mad call I it, for, to define true madness,
What is 't but to be nothing else but mad?
But let that go.
95 *Queen:* More matter, with less art.
Polonius: Madam, I swear I use no art at all.
That he's mad, 'tis true; 'tis true 'tis pity,
And pity 'tis 'tis true—a foolish figure,
But farewell it, for I will use no art.
100 Mad let us grant him, then, and now remains

---

[66]**impotence** helplessness   [67]**borne in hand** deluded, taken advantage of   **arrests**
orders to desist   [69]**in fine** in conclusion   [71]**give th' assay** make trial of strength,
challenge   [79]**On . . . allowance** i.e., with such considerations for the safety of Denmark
and permission for Fortinbras   [80]**likes** pleases   [81]**considered** suitable for deliberation
[86]**expostulate** expound, inquire into   [90]**wit** sense or judgment   [98]**figure** figure of
speech

That we find out the cause of this effect,
Or rather say, the cause of this defect,
For this effect defective comes by cause.
Thus it remains, and the remainder thus.
Perpend.   105
I have a daughter—have while she is mine—
Who, in her duty and obedience, mark,
Hath given me this. Now gather and surmise.
[*He reads the letter.*]   "To the celestial and my soul's
idol, the most beautified Ophelia"—   110
That's an ill phrase, a vile phrase; "beautified" is a
vile phrase. But you shall hear. Thus: [*He reads.*]
"In her excellent white bosom, these, etc."
Queen: Came this from Hamlet to her?
Polonius: Good madam, stay awhile, I will be faithful.   [*He reads.*]   115
    "Doubt thou the stars are fire,
        Doubt that the sun doth move,
        Doubt truth to be a liar,
            But never doubt I love.
O dear Ophelia, I am ill at these numbers. I have not   120
art to reckon my groans. But that I love thee best, O
most best, believe it. Adieu.
                Thine evermore, most dear lady, whilst this
                        machine is to him, Hamlet."
This in obedience hath my daughter shown me,   125
And, more above, hath his solicitings,
As they fell out by time, by means, and place,
All given to mine ear.
King: But how hath she
    Received his love?
Polonius: What do you think of me?
King: As of a man faithful and honorable.   130
Polonius: I would fain prove so. But what might you think,
    When I had seen this hot love on the wing—
    As I perceived it, I must tell you that,
    Before my daughter told me—what might you,
    Or my dear Majesty your queen here, think,   135
    If I had played the desk or table book,

[103]**For . . . cause** i.e., for this defective behavior, this madness, has a cause
[105]**Perpend** consider   [108]**gather and surmise** draw your own conclusions
[113]**In . . . bosom** (The letter is poetically addressed to her heart.)   **these** i.e., the letter
[115]**stay** wait   **faithful** i.e., in reading the letter accurately   [118]**Doubt** suspect
[120]**ill . . . numbers** unskilled at writing verses   [121]**reckon** (1) count (2) number
metrically, scan   [124]**machine** i.e., body   [126]**more above** moreover   [127]**fell out**
occurred   **by** according to   [128]**given . . . ear** i.e., told me about   [131]**fain** gladly
[136]**played . . . table book** i.e., remained shut up, concealing the information

Or given my heart a winking, mute and dumb,
Or looked upon this love with idle sight?
What might you think? No, I went round to work,
140 And my young mistress thus I did bespeak:
"Lord Hamlet is a prince out of thy star;
This must not be." And then I prescripts gave her,
That she should lock herself from his resort,
Admit no messengers, receive no tokens.
145 Which done, she took the fruits of my advice;
And he, repellèd—a short tale to make—
Fell into a sadness, then into a fast,
Thence to a watch, thence into a weakness,
Thence to a lightness, and by this declension
150 Into the madness wherein now he raves,
And all we mourn for.
King [to the Queen]:   Do you think 'tis this?
Queen: It may be, very like.
Polonius: Hath there been such a time—I would fain know that—
That I have positively said "'Tis so,"
When it proved otherwise?
155 *King:*   Not that I know.
Polonius: Take this from this, if this be otherwise.
If circumstances lead me, I will find
Where truth is hid, though it were hid indeed
Within the center.
King: How may we try it further?
160 *Polonius:* You know sometimes he walks four hours together
Here in the lobby.
Queen: So he does indeed.
Polonius: At such a time I'll loose my daughter to him.
Be you and I behind an arras then.
Mark the encounter. If he love her not
165 And be not from his reason fall'n thereon,
Let me be no assistant for a state,
But keep a farm and carters.

---

[137]**given . . . winking** closed the eyes of my heart to this   [138]**with idle sight** complacently or incomprehendingly   [139]**round** roundly, plainly   [140]**bespeak** address   [141]**out of thy star** above your sphere, position   [142]**prescripts** orders   [143]**his resort** his visits   [148]**watch** state of sleeplessness   [149]**lightness** lightheadedness   **declension** decline, deterioration (with a pun on the grammatical sense)   [151]**all we** all of us, or, into everything that we   [156]**Take this from this** (The actor probably gestures, indicating that he means his head from his shoulders, or his staff of office or chain from his hands or neck, or something similar.)   [159]**center** middle point of the earth (which is also the center of the Ptolemaic universe)   **try** test, judge   [162]**loose** (as one might release an animal that is being mated)   [163]**arras** hanging, tapestry   [165]**thereon** on that account   [167]**carters** wagon drivers

King: We will try it.

              Enter Hamlet [reading on a book].

Queen: But look where sadly the poor wretch comes reading.

Polonius: Away, I do beseech you both, away.

   I'll board him presently. O, give me leave.   170

               Exeunt King and Queen [with attendants].

   How does my good Lord Hamlet?

Hamlet: Well, God-a-mercy.

Polonius: Do you know me, my lord?

Hamlet: Excellent well. You are a fishmonger.

Polonius: Not I, my lord.   175

Hamlet: Then I would you were so honest a man.

Polonius: Honest, my lord?

Hamlet: Ay, sir. To be honest, as this world goes, is to be one man picked out of ten thousand.

Polonius: That's very true, my lord.   180

Hamlet: For if the sun breed maggots in a dead dog, being a good kissing carrion—Have you a daughter?

Polonius: I have, my lord.

Hamlet: Let her not walk i' the sun. Conception is a blessing, but as your daughter may conceive, friend, look to 't.   185

Polonius [aside]: How say you by that? Still harping on my daughter. Yet he knew me not at first; 'a said I was a fishmonger. 'A is far gone. And truly in my youth I suffered much extremity for love, very near this. I'll speak to him again.—What do you read, my lord?

Hamlet: Words, words, words.   190

Polonius: What is the matter, my lord?

Hamlet: Between who?

Polonius: I mean, the matter that you read, my lord.

Hamlet: Slanders, sir; for the satirical rogue says here that old men have gray beards, that their faces are wrinkled, their eyes purging thick amber and   195
plum-tree gum, and that they have a plentiful lack of wit, together with most weak hams. All which, sir, though I most powerfully and potently believe, yet I hold it not honesty to have it thus set down, for yourself, sir, shall grow old as I am, if like a crab you could go backward.

---

[168]**sadly** seriously   [170]**board** accost   **presently** at once   **give me leave** i.e., excuse me, leave me alone (Said to those he hurries offstage, including the King and Queen.) [172]**God-a-mercy** God have mercy, i.e., thank you   [174]**fishmonger** fish merchant [181–182]**a good kissing carrion** i.e., a good piece of flesh for kissing, or for the sun to kiss [184]**i' the sun** in public (with additional implication of the sunshine of princely favors) **Conception** (1) understanding (2) pregnancy   [187]**'a** he   [191]**matter** substance (But Hamlet plays on the sense of "basis for a dispute.")   [195]**purging** discharging   **amber** i.e., resin, like the resinous *plum-tree gum*   [196]**wit** understanding   [198]**honesty** decency, decorum   **old** as old

200 *Polonius [aside]:* Though this be madness, yet there is method in 't.—Will you
　　 walk out of the air, my lord?

　　 Hamlet: Into my grave.

　　 Polonius: Indeed, that's out of the air. [*Aside.*] How pregnant sometimes his
　　 replies are! A happiness that often madness hits on, which reason and sanity
205 could not so prosperously be delivered of. I will leave him and suddenly con-
　　 trive the means of meeting between him and my daughter.—My honorable
　　 lord, I will most humbly take my leave of you.

　　 Hamlet: You cannot, sir, take from me anything that I will more willingly part
　　 withal—except my life, except my life, except my life.

　　　　　　　　　 Enter Guildenstern and Rosencrantz.

210 *Polonius:* Fare you well, my lord.

　　 Hamlet: These tedious old fools!

　　 Polonius: You go to seek the Lord Hamlet. There he is.

　　 Rosencrantz [to Polonius]: God save you, sir!　　 [*Exit Polonius.*]

　　 Guildenstern: My honored lord!

215 *Rosencrantz:* My most dear lord!

　　 Hamlet: My excellent good friends! How dost thou, Guildenstern? Ah,
　　 Rosencrantz! Good lads, how do you both?

　　 Rosencrantz: As the indifferent children of the earth.

　　 Guildenstern: Happy in that we are not overhappy.

220 　　 On Fortune's cap we are not the very button.

　　 Hamlet: Nor the soles of her shoe?

　　 Rosencrantz: Neither, my lord.

　　 Hamlet: Then you live about her waist, or in the middle of her favors?

　　 Guildenstern: Faith, her privates we.

225 *Hamlet:* In the secret parts of Fortune? O, most true, she is a strumpet. What
　　 news?

　　 Rosencrantz: None, my lord, but the world's grown honest.

　　 Hamlet: Then is doomsday near. But your news is not true. Let me question
　　 more in particular. What have you, my good friends, deserved at the hands of
230 Fortune that she sends you to prison hither?

　　 Guildenstern: Prison, my lord?

　　 Hamlet: Denmark's a prison.

　　 Rosencrantz: Then is the world one.

---

[201]**out of the air** (The open air was considered dangerous for sick people.)　[203]**pregnant** quick-witted, full of meaning　[204]**happiness** felicity of expression　[205]**prosperously** successfully　**suddenly** immediately　[209]**withal** with　[211]**old fools** i.e., old men
like Polonius　[218]**indifferent** ordinary, at neither extreme of fortune or misfortune
[223]**favors** i.e., sexual favors　[224]**her privates we** i.e., (1) we are sexually intimate with
Fortune, the fickle goddess who bestows her favors indiscriminately (2) we are her
private citizens　[225]**strumpet** prostitute (A common epithet for indiscriminate Fortune;
see line 431.)

Hamlet: A goodly one, in which there are many confines, wards, and dungeons, Denmark being one o' the worst. 235

Rosencrantz: We think not so, my lord.

Hamlet: Why then 'tis none to you, for there is nothing either good or bad but thinking makes it so. To me it is a prison.

Rosencrantz: Why then, your ambition makes it one. 'Tis too narrow for your mind. 240

Hamlet: O God, I could be bounded in a nutshell and count myself a king of infinite space, were it not that I have bad dreams.

Guildenstern: Which dreams indeed are ambition, for the very substance of the ambitious is merely the shadow of a dream.

Hamlet: A dream itself is but a shadow. 245

Rosencrantz: Truly, and I hold ambition of so airy and light a quality that it is but a shadow's shadow.

Hamlet: Then are our beggars bodies, and our monarchs and outstretched heroes the beggars' shadows. Shall we to the court? For, by my fay, I cannot reason.

Rosencrantz, Guildenstern: We'll wait upon you. 250

Hamlet: No such matter. I will not sort you with the rest of my servants, for, to speak to you like an honest man, I am most dreadfully attended. But, in the beaten way of friendship, what make you at Elsinore?

Rosencrantz: To visit you, my lord, no other occasion.

Hamlet: Beggar that I am, I am even poor in thanks; but I thank you, and sure, 255 dear friends, my thanks are too dear a halfpenny. Were you not sent for? Is it your own inclining? Is it a free visitation? Come, come, deal justly with me. Come, come. Nay, speak.

Guildenstern: What should we say, my lord?

Hamlet: Anything but to the purpose. You were sent for, and there is a kind of 260 confession in your looks which your modesties have not craft enough to color. I know the good King and Queen have sent for you.

Rosencrantz: To what end, my lord?

Hamlet: That you must teach me. But let me conjure you, by the rights of our fellowship, by the consonancy of our youth, by the obligation of our ever- 265 preserved love, and by what more dear a better proposer could charge you withal, be even and direct with me whether you were sent for or no.

---

[234]**confines** places of confinement   **wards** cells   [243–244]**the very . . . ambitious** that seemingly very substantial thing that the ambitious pursue   [248]**bodies** i.e., solid substances rather than shadows (since beggars are not ambitious)   **outstretched** (1) far-reaching in their ambition (2) elongated as shadows   [249]**fay** faith   [250]**wait upon** accompany, attend (But Hamlet uses the phrase in the sense of providing menial service.)   [251]**sort** class, categorize   [252]**dreadfully attended** waited upon in slovenly fashion   [253]**beaten way** familiar path, tried-and-true course   **make** do   [256]**too dear a halfpenny** (1) too expensive at even a halfpenny, i.e., of little worth (2) too expensive *by* a halfpenny in return for worthless kindness   [257]**free** voluntary   [260]**Anything but to the purpose** anything except a straightforward answer (Said ironically.)   [261]**modesties** sense of shame   [262]**color** disguise   [264]**conjure** adjure, entreat   [265]**the consonancy of our youth** our closeness in our younger days   [266]**better** more skillful   **charge** urge   [267]**even** straight, honest

Rosencrantz [aside to Guildenstern]: What say you?

Hamlet [aside]: Nay, then, I have an eye of you.—If you love me, hold not off.

270 *Guildenstern:* My lord, we were sent for.

Hamlet: I will tell you why; so shall my anticipation prevent your discovery, and your secrecy to the King and Queen molt no feather. I have of late—but wherefore I know not—lost all my mirth, forgone all custom of exercises; and indeed it goes so heavily with my disposition that this goodly frame, the

275 earth, seems to me a sterile promontory; this most excellent canopy, the air, look you, this brave o'erhanging firmament, this majestical roof fretted with golden fire, why, it appeareth nothing to me but a foul and pestilent congregation of vapors. What a piece of work is a man! How noble in reason, how infinite in faculties, in form and moving how express and admirable, in

280 action how like an angel, in apprehension how like a god! The beauty of the world, the paragon of animals! And yet, to me, what is this quintessence of dust? Man delights not me—no, nor woman neither, though by your smiling you seem to say so.

Rosencrantz: My lord, there was no such stuff in my thoughts.

285 *Hamlet:* Why did you laugh, then, when I said man delights not me?

Rosencrantz: To think, my lord, if you delight not in man, what Lenten entertainment the players shall receive from you. We coted them on the way, and hither are they coming to offer you service.

Hamlet: He that plays the king shall be welcome; His Majesty shall have tribute

290 of me. The adventurous knight shall use his foil and target, the lover shall not sigh gratis, the humorous man shall end his part in peace, the clown shall make those laugh whose lungs are tickle o' the sear, and the lady shall say her mind freely, or the blank verse shall halt for 't. What players are they?

Rosencrantz: Even those you were wont to take such delight in, the tragedians of

295 the city.

Hamlet: How chances it they travel? Their residence, both in reputation and profit, was better both ways.

Rosencrantz: I think their inhibition comes by the means of the late innovation.

---

²⁶⁹**of** on **hold not off** don't hold back ²⁷¹**so . . . discovery** in that way my saying it first will spare you from revealing the truth ²⁷²**molt no feather** i.e., not diminish in the least ²⁷⁶**brave** splendid **fretted** adorned (with fretwork, as in a vaulted ceiling) ²⁷⁸**congregation** mass **piece of work** masterpiece ²⁷⁹**express** well-framed, exact, expressive ²⁸⁰**apprehension** power of comprehending ²⁸¹**quintessence** the fifth essence of ancient philosophy, beyond earth, water, air, and fire, supposed to be the substance of the heavenly bodies and to be latent in all things ²⁸⁶⁻²⁸⁷**Lenten entertainment** meager reception (appropriate to Lent) ²⁸⁷**coted** overtook and passed by ²⁸⁹**tribute** (1) applause (2) homage paid in money ²⁹⁰**of** from **foil and target** sword and shield ²⁹¹**gratis** for nothing **humorous man** eccentric character, dominated by one trait or "humor" **in peace** i.e., with full license ²⁹²**tickle o' the sear** easy on the trigger, ready to laugh easily (A *sear* is part of a gunlock.) ²⁹³**halt** limp ²⁹⁴**tragedians** actors ²⁹⁶**residence** remaining in their usual place, i.e., in the city ²⁹⁸**inhibition** formal prohibition (from acting plays in the city) **late** recent **innovation** i.e., the new fashion in satirical plays performed by boy actors in the "private" theaters; or possibly a political uprising; or the strict limitations set on the theaters in London in 1600

Hamlet: Do they hold the same estimation they did when I was in the city? Are
they so followed? 300

Rosencrantz: No, indeed are they not.

Hamlet: How comes it? Do they grow rusty?

Rosencrantz: Nay, their endeavor keeps in the wonted pace. But there is, sir, an
aerie of children, little eyases, that cry out on the top of question and are
most tyrannically clapped for 't. These are now the fashion, and so berattle 305
the common stages—so they call them—that many wearing rapiers are afraid
of goose quills and dare scarce come thither.

Hamlet: What, are they children? Who maintains 'em? How are they escoted?
Will they pursue the quality no longer than they can sing? Will they not say
afterwards, if they should grow themselves to common players—as it is most 310
like, if their means are no better—their writers do them wrong to make them
exclaim against their own succession?

Rosencrantz: Faith, there has been much to-do on both sides, and the nation
holds it no sin to tar them to controversy. There was for a while no money
bid for argument unless the poet and the player went to cuffs in the 315
question.

Hamlet: Is 't possible?

Guildenstern: O, there has been much throwing about of brains.

Hamlet: Do the boys carry it away?

Rosencrantz: Ay, that they do, my lord—Hercules and his load too. 320

Hamlet: It is not very strange; for my uncle is King of Denmark, and those that
would make mouths at him while my father lived give twenty, forty, fifty, a
hundred ducats apiece for his picture in little. 'Sblood, there is something in
this more than natural, if philosophy could find it out.

A flourish [of trumpets within].

[302-320]**How . . . load too** (The passage, omitted from the early quartos, alludes to the
so-called War of the Theaters, 1599–1602, the rivalry between the children's companies
and the adult actors.) [303]**keeps** continues **wonted** usual [304]**aerie** nest
eyases young hawks **cry . . . question** speak shrilly, dominating the controversy
(in decrying the public theaters) [305]**tyrannically** outrageously **berattle** berate,
clamor against [306]**common stages** public theaters **many wearing rapiers**
i.e., many men of fashion, afraid to patronize the common players for fear of being
satirized by the poets writing for the boy actors [307]**goose quills** i.e., pens of satirists
[308]**escoted** maintained [309]**quality** (acting) profession **no longer . . . sing**
i.e., only until their voices change [310]**common** regular, adult [311]**like** likely
if . . . better if they find no better way to support themselves [312]**succession** i.e., future
careers [313]**to-do** ado [314]**tar** set on (as dogs) [314-316]**There . . . question** i.e., for a
while, no money was offered by the acting companies to playwrights for the plot to a play
unless the satirical poets who wrote for the boys and the adult actors came to blows in
the play itself [319]**carry it away** i.e., win the day [320]**Hercules . . . load** (Thought to be
an allusion to the sign of the Globe Theatre, which was Hercules bearing the world on his
shoulders.) [322]**mouths** faces [323]**ducats** gold coins **in little** in miniature **'Sblood**
by God's (Christ's) blood [324]**philosophy** i.e., scientific inquiry

325 *Guildenstern:* There are the players.

Hamlet: Gentlemen, you are welcome to Elsinore. Your hands, come then. Th'
appurtenance of welcome is fashion and ceremony. Let me comply with you
in this garb, lest my extent to the players, which, I tell you, must show fairly
outwards, should more appear like entertainment than yours. You are
330 welcome. But my uncle-father and aunt-mother are deceived.

Guildenstern: In what, my dear lord?

Hamlet: I am but mad north-north-west. When the wind is southerly I know a
hawk from a handsaw.

> *Enter Polonius.*

Polonius: Well be with you, gentlemen!

335 *Hamlet:* Hark you, Guildenstern, and you too; at each ear a hearer. That great
baby you see there is not yet out of his swaddling clouts.

Rosencrantz: Haply he is the second time come to them, for they say an old man
is twice a child.

Hamlet: I will prophesy he comes to tell me of the players. Mark it.—You say
340 right, sir, o' Monday morning, 'twas then indeed.

Polonius: My lord, I have news to tell you.

Hamlet: My lord, I have news to tell you. When Roscius was an actor in Rome—

Polonius: The actors are come hither, my lord.

Hamlet: Buzz, buzz!

345 *Polonius:* Upon my honor—

Hamlet: Then came each actor on his ass.

Polonius: The best actors in the world, either for tragedy, comedy, history,
pastoral, pastoral-comical, historical-pastoral, tragical-historical, tragical-
comical-historical-pastoral, scene individable, or poem unlimited. Seneca
350 cannot be too heavy, nor Plautus too light. For the law of writ and the liberty,
these are the only men.

Hamlet: O Jephthah, judge of Israel, what a treasure hadst thou!

Polonius: What a treasure had he, my lord?

---

[327]**appurtenance** proper accompaniment   **comply** observe the formalities of courtesy   [328]**garb** i.e., manner   **my extent** that which I extend, i.e., my polite behavior   [328-329]**show fairly outwards** show every evidence of cordiality   [329]**entertainment** a (warm) reception   [332]**north-north-west** just off true north, only partly   [333]**hawk, handsaw** i.e., two very different things, though also perhaps meaning a mattock (or *hack*) and a carpenter's cutting tool, respectively; also birds, with a play on *hernshaw*, or heron   [336]**swaddling clouts** cloths in which to wrap a newborn baby   [337]**Haply** perhaps   [342]**Roscius** a famous Roman actor who died in 62 B.C.   [344]**Buzz** (An interjection used to denote stale news.)   [349]**scene individable** a play observing the unity of place; or perhaps one that is unclassifiable, or performed without intermission   **poem unlimited** a play disregarding the unities of time and place; one that is all-inclusive   **Seneca** writer of Latin tragedies   [350]**Plautus** writer of Latin comedy   **law . . . liberty** dramatic composition both according to the rules and disregarding the rules   [351]**these** i.e., the actors   [352]**Jephthah . . . Israel** (Jephthah had to sacrifice his daughter; see Judges 11. Hamlet goes on to quote from a ballad on the theme.)

Hamlet: Why,

>"One fair daughter, and no more,
>The which he lovèd passing well."   355

Polonius [aside]: Still on my daughter.

Hamlet: Am I not i' the right, old Jephthah?

Polonius: If you call me Jephthah, my lord, I have a daughter that I love passing
well.   360

Hamlet: Nay, that follows not.

Polonius: What follows then, my lord?

Hamlet: Why,

>"As by lot, God wot,"

and then, you know,   365

>"It came to pass, as most like it was"—

the first row of the pious chanson will show you more, for look where my
abridgement comes.

>*Enter the Players.*

You are welcome, masters; welcome, all. I am glad to see thee well. Welcome,
good friends. O, old friend! Why, thy face is valanced since I saw thee last. 370
Com'st thou to beard me in Denmark? What, my young lady and mistress!
By 'r Lady, your ladyship is nearer to heaven than when I saw you last, by
the altitude of a chopine. Pray God your voice, like a piece of uncurrent gold,
be not cracked within the ring. Masters, you are all welcome. We'll e'en to 't
like French falconers, fly at anything we see. We'll have a speech straight.   375
Come, give us a taste of your quality. Come, a passionate speech.

First Player: What speech, my good lord?

Hamlet: I heard thee speak me a speech once, but it was never acted, or if it was,
not above once, for the play, I remember, pleased not the million; 'twas caviar
to the general. But it was—as I received it, and others, whose judgments in   380
such matters cried in the top of mine—an excellent play, well digested in the
scenes, set down with as much modesty as cunning. I remember one said
there were no sallets in the lines to make the matter savory, nor no matter in
the phrase that might indict the author of affectation, but called it an honest
method, as wholesome as sweet, and by very much more handsome than   385
fine. One speech in 't I chiefly loved: 'twas Aeneas' tale to Dido, and

---

[356]**passing** surpassingly   [364]**lot** chance   **wot** knows   [366]**like** likely, probable
[367]**row** stanza   **chanson** ballad, song   [367-368]**my abridgment** something that cuts short
my conversation; also, a diversion   [370]**valanced** fringed (with a beard)   [371]**beard**
confront, challenge (with obvious pun)   **young lady** i.e., boy playing women's parts
[372]**By 'r Lady** by Our Lady   [373]**chopine** thick-soled shoe of Italian fashion   **uncurrent**
not passable as lawful coinage   [374]**cracked . . . ring** i.e., changed from adolescent to
male voice, no longer suitable for women's roles (Coins featured rings enclosing the sovereign's head; if the coin was cracked within this ring, it was unfit for currency.)   **e'en
to 't** go at it   [375]**straight** at once   [376]**quality** professional skill   [379-380]**caviar to the
general** caviar to the multitude, i.e., a choice dish too elegant for coarse tastes   [381]**cried
in the top of** i.e., spoke with greater authority than   **digested** arranged, ordered
[382]**modesty** moderation, restraint   **cunning** skill   [383]**sallets** i.e., something savory,
spicy improprieties   [384]**indict** convict   [385]**handsome** well-proportioned   [386]**fine** elaborately ornamented, showy

thereabout of it especially when he speaks of Priam's slaughter. If it live in
your memory, begin at this line: let me see, let me see—

"The rugged Pyrrhus, like th' Hyrcanian beast"—

390 'Tis not so. It begins with Pyrrhus:

"The rugged Pyrrhus, he whose sable arms,
Black as his purpose, did the night resemble
When he lay couchèd in the ominous horse,
Hath now this dread and black complexion smeared

395 With heraldry more dismal. Head to foot
Now is he total gules, horridly tricked
With blood of fathers, mothers, daughters, sons,
Baked and impasted with the parching streets,
That lend a tyrannous and a damnèd light

400 To their lord's murder. Roasted in wrath and fire,
And thus o'ersizèd with coagulate gore,
With eyes like carbuncles, the hellish Pyrrhus
Old grandsire Priam seeks."

So proceed you.

405 *Polonius:* 'Fore God, my lord, well spoken, with good accent and good discretion.

First Player: "Anon he finds him

Striking too short at Greeks. His antique sword,
Rebellious to his arm, lies where it falls,
Repugnant to command. Unequal matched,

410 Pyrrhus at Priam drives, in rage strikes wide,
But with the whiff and wind of his fell sword
Th' unnervèd father falls. Then senseless Ilium,
Seeming to feel this blow, with flaming top
Stoops to his base, and with a hideous crash

415 Takes prisoner Pyrrhus' ear. For, lo! His sword,
Which was declining on the milky head
Of reverend Priam, seemed i' th' air to stick,

[387]**Priam's slaughter** the slaying of the ruler of Troy, when the Greeks finally took the
city   [389]**Pyrrhus** a Greek hero in the Trojan War, also known as Neoptolemus, son of
Achilles—another avenging son   **Hyrcanian beast** i.e., tiger (On the death of Priam,
see Virgil, *Aeneid*, 2.506 ff.; compare the whole speech with Marlowe's *Dido Queen of
Carthage*, 2.1.214 ff. On the *Hyrcanian* tiger, see *Aeneid*, 4.366–367. Hyrcania is on the
Caspian Sea.)   [391]**rugged** shaggy, savage   **sable** black (for reasons of camouflage
during the episode of the Trojan horse)   [393]**couchèd** concealed   **ominous horse**
fateful Trojan horse, by which the Greeks gained access to Troy   [395]**dismal** ill-omened
[396]**total gules** entirely red (A heraldic term.)   **tricked** spotted and smeared (Heraldic.)
[398]**impasted** crusted, like a thick paste   **with . . . streets** by the parching heat of the
streets (because of the fires everywhere)   [399]**tyrannous** cruel   [400]**their lord's** i.e.,
Priam's   [401]**o'ersizèd** covered as with size or glue   [402]**carbuncles** large fiery-red
precious stones thought to emit their own light   [407]**antique** ancient, long-used
[409]**Repugnant** disobedient, resistant   [411]**fell** cruel   [412]**unnervèd** strengthless
senseless Ilium inanimate citadel of Troy   [414]**his** its   [416]**declining** descending
milky white-haired

So as a painted tyrant Pyrrhus stood,
And, like a neutral to his will and matter,
Did nothing. 420
But as we often see against some storm
A silence in the heavens, the rack stand still,
The bold winds speechless, and the orb below
As hush as death, anon the dreadful thunder
Doth rend the region, so, after Pyrrhus' pause, 425
A rousèd vengeance sets him new a-work,
And never did the Cyclops' hammers fall
On Mars's armor forged for proof eterne
With less remorse than Pyrrhus' bleeding sword
Now falls on Priam. 430
Out, out, thou strumpet Fortune! All you gods
In general synod take away her power!
Break all the spokes and fellies from her wheel,
And bowl the round nave down the hill of heaven
As low as to the fiends!" 435

Polonius: This is too long.

Hamlet: It shall to the barber's with your beard.—Prithee, say on. He's for a jig or
a tale of bawdry, or he sleeps. Say on; come to Hecuba.

First Player: "But who, ah woe! had seen the moblèd queen"—

Hamlet: "The moblèd queen?" 440

Polonius: That's good. "Moblèd queen" is good.

First Player: "Run barefoot up and down, threat'ning the flames
With bisson rheum, a clout upon that head
Where late the diadem stood, and, for a robe,
About her lank and all o'erteemèd loins 445
A blanket, in the alarm of fear caught up—
Who this had seen, with tongue in venom steeped,
'Gainst Fortune's state would treason have pronounced.
But if the gods themselves did see her then
When she saw Pyrrhus make malicious sport 450
In mincing with his sword her husband's limbs,
The instant burst of clamor that she made,
Unless things mortal move them not at all,

[418]**painted** i.e., painted in a picture   [419]**like . . . matter** i.e., as though suspended
between his intention and its fulfillment   [421]**against** just before   [422]**rack** mass of clouds
[423]**orb** globe, earth   [425]**region** sky   [427]**Cyclops** giant armor makers in the smithy of
Vulcan   [428]**proof eterne** eternal resistance to assault   [429]**remorse** pity   [432]**synod**
assembly   [433]**fellies** pieces of wood forming the rim of a wheel   [434]**nave** hub   **hill of
heaven** Mount Olympus   [437]**jig** comic song and dance often given at the end of a play
[438]**Hecuba** wife of Priam   [439]**who . . . had** anyone who had (also in line 447)
moblèd muffled   [442]**threat'ning the flames** i.e., weeping hard enough to dampen the
flames   [443]**bisson rheum** blinding tears   **clout** cloth   [444]**late** lately
[445]**all o'erteemèd** utterly worn out with bearing children   [448]**state** rule, managing
pronounced proclaimed

Would have made milch the burning eyes of heaven,
And passion in the gods."

Polonius: Look whe'er he has not turned his color and has tears in 's eyes.
Prithee, no more.

Hamlet: 'Tis well; I'll have thee speak out the rest of this soon.—Good my lord,
will you see the players well bestowed? Do you hear, let them be well used,
for they are the abstract and brief chronicles of the time. After your death
you were better have a bad epitaph than their ill report while you live.

Polonius: My lord, I will use them according to their desert.

Hamlet: God's bodikin, man, much better. Use every man after his desert, and
who shall scape whipping? Use them after your own honor and dignity. The
less they deserve, the more merit is in your bounty. Take them in.

Polonius: Come, sirs.   [*Exit.*]

Hamlet: Follow him, friends. We'll hear a play tomorrow. [*As they start to leave,
Hamlet detains the First Player.*] Dost thou hear me, old friend? Can you play
The Murder of Gonzago?

First Player: Ay, my lord.

Hamlet: We'll ha 't tomorrow night. You could, for a need, study a speech of
some dozen or sixteen lines which I would set down and insert in 't, could
you not?

First Player: Ay, my lord.

Hamlet: Very well. Follow that lord, and look you mock him not. (*Exeunt Players.*)
My good friends, I'll leave you till night. You are welcome to Elsinore.

Rosencrantz: Good my lord!

Exeunt [*Rosencrantz and Guildenstern*].

Hamlet: Ay, so, goodbye to you.—Now I am alone.
O, what a rogue and peasant slave am I!
Is it not monstrous that this player here,
But in a fiction, in a dream of passion,
Could force his soul so to his own conceit
That from her working all his visage wanned,
Tears in his eyes, distraction in his aspect,
A broken voice, and his whole function suiting
With forms to his conceit? And all for nothing!
For Hecuba!
What's Hecuba to him, or he to Hecuba,

---

⁴⁵⁴**milch** milky, moist with tears   **burning eyes of heaven** i.e., heavenly bodies
⁴⁵⁵**passion** overpowering emotion   ⁴⁵⁶**whe'er** whether   ⁴⁵⁹**bestowed** lodged
⁴⁶⁰**abstract** summary account   ⁴⁶³**God's bodikin** by God's (Christ's) little body, *bodykin.*
(Not to be confused with *bodkin,* "dagger.")   **after** according to   ⁴⁷¹**ha 't** have it   **study**
memorize   ⁴⁸¹**But** merely   ⁴⁸²**force . . . conceit** bring his innermost being so entirely
into accord with his conception (of the role)   ⁴⁸³**from her working** as a result of,
or in response to, his soul's activity   **wanned** grew pale   ⁴⁸⁴**aspect** look, glance
⁴⁸⁵–⁴⁸⁶**his whole . . . conceit** all his bodily powers responding with actions to suit his
thought

That he should weep for her? What would he do
Had he the motive and the cue for passion   490
That I have? He would drown the stage with tears
And cleave the general ear with horrid speech,
Make mad the guilty and appall the free,
Confound the ignorant, and amaze indeed
The very faculties of eyes and ears. Yet I,   495
A dull and muddy-mettled rascal, peak
Like John-a-dreams, unpregnant of my cause,
And can say nothing—no, not for a king
Upon whose property and most dear life
A damned defeat was made. Am I a coward?   500
Who calls me villain? Breaks my pate across?
Plucks off my beard and blows it in my face?
Tweaks me by the nose? Gives me the lie i' the throat
As deep as to the lungs? Who does me this?
Ha, 'swounds, I should take it; for it cannot be   505
But I am pigeon-livered and lack gall
To make oppression bitter, or ere this
I should ha' fatted all the region kites
With this slave's offal. Bloody, bawdy villain!
Remorseless, treacherous, lecherous, kindless villain!   510
O, vengeance!
Why, what an ass am I! This is most brave,
That I, the son of a dear father murdered,
Prompted to my revenge by heaven and hell,
Must like a whore unpack my heart with words   515
And fall a-cursing, like a very drab,
A scullion! Fie upon 't, foh! About, my brains!
Hum, I have heard
That guilty creatures sitting at a play
Have by the very cunning of the scene   520
Been struck so to the soul that presently
They have proclaimed their malefactions;

---

[492]**the general ear** everyone's ear   **horrid** horrible   [493]**appall** (Literally, make pale.)
free innocent   [494]**Confound the ignorant** i.e., dumbfound those who know nothing
of the crime that has been committed   **amaze** stun   [496]**muddy-mettled** dull-spirited
peak mope, pine   [497]**John-a-dreams** a sleepy, dreaming idler   **unpregnant of** not
quickened by   [499]**property** i.e., the crown; also character, quality   [500]**damned
defeat** damnable act of destruction   [501]**pate** head   [503]**Gives . . . throat** calls me an
out-and-out liar   [505]**'swounds** by his (Christ's) wounds   [506]**pigeon-livered**
(The pigeon or dove was popularly supposed to be mild because it secreted no gall.)
[507]**bitter** i.e., bitter to me   [508]**region kites** kites (birds of prey) of the air   [509]**offal**
entrails   [510]**Remorseless** pitiless   **kindless** unnatural   [512]**brave** fine, admirable
(Said ironically.)   [516]**drab** whore   [517]**scullion** menial kitchen servant (apt to be
foul-mouthed)   **About** about it, to work   [520]**cunning** art, skill   **scene** dramatic
presentation   [521]**presently** at once

For murder, though it have no tongue, will speak
With most miraculous organ. I'll have these players
525 Play something like the murder of my father
Before mine uncle. I'll observe his looks;
I'll tent him to the quick. If 'a do blench,
I know my course. The spirit that I have seen
May be the devil, and the devil hath power
530 T' assume a pleasing shape; yea, and perhaps,
Out of my weakness and my melancholy,
As he is very potent with such spirits,
Abuses me to damn me. I'll have grounds
More relative than this. The play's the thing
535 Wherein I'll catch the conscience of the King.   *Exit.*

3.1   *Enter King, Queen, Polonius, Ophelia, Rosencrantz, Guildenstern, lords.*

King: And can you by no drift of conference
Get from him why he puts on this confusion,
Grating so harshly all his days of quiet
With turbulent and dangerous lunacy?
5 *Rosencrantz:* He does confess he feels himself distracted,
But from what cause 'a will by no means speak.
Guildenstern: Nor do we find him forward to be sounded,
But with a crafty madness keeps aloof
When we would bring him on to some confession
Of his true state.
10 *Queen:*   Did he receive you well?
Rosencrantz: Most like a gentleman.
Guildenstern: But with much forcing of his disposition.
Rosencrantz: Niggard of question, but of our demands
Most free in his reply.
Queen: Did you assay him
15 To any pastime?
Rosencrantz: Madam, it so fell out that certain players
We o'erraught on the way. Of these we told him,
And there did seem in him a kind of joy
To hear of it. They are here about the court,
20 And, as I think, they have already order
This night to play before him.

527**tent** probe   **the quick** the tender part of a wound, the core   **blench** quail, flinch
532**spirits** humors (of melancholy)   533**Abuses** deludes   534**relative** cogent, pertinent
3.1. Location: The castle.
1**drift of conference** directing of conversation   7**forward** willing   **sounded** questioned
12**disposition** inclination   13**Niggard** stingy   **question** conversation   14**assay** try to
win   17**o'erraught** overtook

Polonius: 'Tis most true,
   And he beseeched me to entreat Your Majesties
   To hear and see the matter.
King: With all my heart, and it doth much content me
   To hear him so inclined.   25
   Good gentlemen, give him a further edge
   And drive his purpose into these delights.
Rosencrantz: We shall, my lord.

              Exeunt Rosencrantz and Guildenstern.
King: Sweet Gertrude, leave us too,
   For we have closely sent for Hamlet hither,
   That he, as 'twere by accident, may here   30
   Affront Ophelia.
   Her father and myself, lawful espials,
   Will so bestow ourselves that seeing, unseen,
   We may of their encounter frankly judge,
   And gather by him, as he is behaved,   35
   If 't be th' affliction of his love or no
   That thus he suffers for.
Queen: I shall obey you.
   And for your part, Ophelia, I do wish
   That your good beauties be the happy cause
   Of Hamlet's wildness. So shall I hope your virtues   40
   Will bring him to his wonted way again,
   To both your honors.
Ophelia: Madam, I wish it may.   [*Exit Queen.*]
Polonius: Ophelia, walk you here.—Gracious, so please you,
   We will bestow ourselves. [*To Ophelia.*] Read on this book,   [*giving her a book*]
That show of such an exercise may color   45
   Your loneliness. We are oft to blame in this—
   'Tis too much proved—that with devotion's visage
   And pious action we do sugar o'er
   The devil himself.
King [aside]: O, 'tis too true!   50
   How smart a lash that speech doth give my conscience!
   The harlot's cheek, beautied with plastering art,
   Is not more ugly to the thing that helps it

---

²⁶**edge** incitement   ²⁹**closely** privately   ³¹**Affront** confront, meet   ³²**espials** spies
⁴¹**wonted** accustomed   ⁴³**Gracious** Your Grace (i.e., the King)   ⁴⁴**bestow** conceal
⁴⁵**exercise** religious exercise (The book she reads is one of devotion.)   **color** give a
plausible appearance to   ⁴⁶**loneliness** being alone   ⁴⁷**too much proved** too often
shown to be true, too often practiced   ⁵³**to** compared to   **the thing** i.e., the cosmetic

Than is my deed to my most painted word.
55 O heavy burden!
Polonius: I hear him coming. Let's withdraw, my lord.

[*The King and Polonius withdraw.*]

Enter Hamlet. [*Ophelia pretends to read a book.*]

Hamlet: To be, or not to be, that is the question:
Whether 'tis nobler in the mind to suffer
The slings and arrows of outrageous fortune,
60 Or to take arms against a sea of troubles
And by opposing end them. To die, to sleep—
No more—and by a sleep to say we end
The heartache and the thousand natural shocks
That flesh is heir to. 'Tis a consummation
65 Devoutly to be wished. To die, to sleep;
To sleep, perchance to dream. Ay, there's the rub,
For in that sleep of death what dreams may come,
When we have shuffled off this mortal coil,
Must give us pause. There's the respect
70 That makes calamity of so long life.
For who would bear the whips and scorns of time,
Th' oppressor's wrong, the proud man's contumely,
The pangs of disprized love, the law's delay,
The insolence of office, and the spurns
75 That patient merit of th' unworthy takes,
When he himself might his quietus make
With a bare bodkin? Who would fardels bear,
To grunt and sweat under a weary life,
But that the dread of something after death,
80 The undiscovered country from whose bourn
No traveler returns, puzzles the will,
And makes us rather bear those ills we have
Than fly to others that we know not of?
Thus conscience does make cowards of us all;
85 And thus the native hue of resolution
Is sicklied o'er with the pale cast of thought,

56s.d.**withdraw** (The King and Polonius may retire behind an arras. The stage
directions specify that they "enter" again near the end of the scene.)   59**slings** missiles
66**rub** (Literally, an obstacle in the game of bowls.)   68**shuffled** sloughed, cast   **coil**
turmoil   69**respect** consideration   70**of . . . life** so long-lived, something we willingly
endure for so long (also suggesting that long life is itself a calamity)   72**contumely**
insolent abuse   73**disprized** unvalued   74**office** officialdom   **spurns** insults   75**of . . .**
takes receives from unworthy persons   76**quietus** acquitance; here, death   77**a bare**
bodkin a mere dagger, unsheathed   **fardels** burdens   80**bourn** frontier, boundary
85**native hue** natural color, complexion   86**cast** tinge, shade of color

And enterprises of great pitch and moment
With this regard their currents turn awry
And lose the name of action.—Soft you now,
The fair Ophelia. Nymph, in thy orisons 90
Be all my sins remembered.

Ophelia: Good my lord,
How does your honor for this many a day?

Hamlet: I humbly thank you; well, well, well.

Ophelia: My lord, I have remembrances of yours,
That I have longèd long to redeliver. 95
I pray you, now receive them. [*She offers tokens.*]

Hamlet: No, not I, I never gave you aught.

Ophelia: My honored lord, you know right well you did,
And with them words of so sweet breath composed
As made the things more rich. Their perfume lost, 100
Take these again, for to the noble mind
Rich gifts wax poor when givers prove unkind.
There, my lord. [*She gives tokens.*]

Hamlet: Ha, ha! Are you honest?

Ophelia: My lord? 105

Hamlet: Are you fair?

Ophelia: What means your lordship?

Hamlet: That if you be honest and fair, your honesty should admit no discourse
to your beauty.

Ophelia: Could beauty, my lord, have better commerce than with honesty? 110

Hamlet: Ay, truly, for the power of beauty will sooner transform honesty from
what it is to a bawd than the force of honesty can translate beauty into his
likeness. This was sometime a paradox, but now the time gives it proof. I did
love you once.

Ophelia: Indeed, my lord, you made me believe so. 115

Hamlet: You should not have believed me, for virtue cannot so inoculate our old
stock but we shall relish of it. I loved you not.

Ophelia: I was the more deceived.

Hamlet: Get thee to a nunnery. Why wouldst thou be a breeder of sinners? I am
myself indifferent honest, but yet I could accuse me of such things that it 120
were better my mother had not borne me: I am very proud, revengeful,

---

[87]**pitch** height (as of a falcon's flight) **moment** importance [88]**regard** respect,
consideration **currents** courses [89]**Soft you** i.e., wait a minute, gently [90]**orisons**
prayers [104]**honest** (1) truthful (2) chaste [106]**fair** (1) beautiful (2) just, honorable
[108]**your honesty** your chastity [108–109]**discourse to** familiar dealings with
[110]**commerce** dealings, intercourse [112]**his** its [113]**sometime** formerly **a paradox**
a view opposite to commonly held opinion **the time** the present age [116]**inoculate**
graft, be engrafted to [117]**but . . . it** that we do not still have about us a taste of the old
stock, i.e., retain our sinfulness [119]**nunnery** convent (with possibly an awareness that
the word was also used derisively to denote a brothel) [120]**indifferent honest** reasonably
virtuous

ambitious, with more offenses at my beck than I have thoughts to put them in, imagination to give them shape, or time to act them in. What should such fellows as I do crawling between earth and heaven? We are arrant knaves all; believe none of us. Go thy ways to a nunnery. Where's your father?

125

Ophelia: At home, my lord.

Hamlet: Let the doors be shut upon him, that he may play the fool nowhere but in 's own house. Farewell.

Ophelia: O, help him, you sweet heavens!

130 *Hamlet:* If thou dost marry, I'll give thee this plague for thy dowry: be thou as chaste as ice, as pure as snow, thou shalt not escape calumny. Get thee to a nunnery, farewell. Or, if thou wilt needs marry, marry a fool, for wise men know well enough what monsters you make of them. To a nunnery, go, and quickly too. Farewell.

135 *Ophelia:* Heavenly powers, restore him!

Hamlet: I have heard of your paintings too, well enough. God hath given you one face, and you make yourselves another. You jig, you amble, and you lisp, you nickname God's creatures, and make your wantonness your ignorance. Go to, I'll no more on 't; it hath made me mad. I say we will have no more

140 marriage. Those that are married already—all but one—shall live. The rest shall keep as they are. To a nunnery, go.   *Exit.*

Ophelia: O, what a noble mind is here o'erthrown!
The courtier's, soldier's, scholar's, eye, tongue, sword,
Th' expectancy and rose of the fair state,

145 The glass of fashion and the mold of form,
Th' observed of all observers, quite, quite down!
And I, of ladies most deject and wretched,
That sucked the honey of his music vows,
Now see that noble and most sovereign reason

150 Like sweet bells jangled out of tune and harsh,
That unmatched form and feature of blown youth
Blasted with ecstasy. O, woe is me,
T' have seen what I have seen, see what I see!

Enter King and Polonius.

King: Love? His affections do not that way tend;

155 Nor what he spake, though it lacked form a little,
Was not like madness. There's something in his soul

---

¹²²**beck** command   ¹³³**monsters** (An illusion to the horns of a cuckold.)   **you** i.e., you women   ¹³⁷**jig** dance   **amble** move coyly   ¹³⁸**you nickname . . . creatures** i.e., you give trendy names to things in place of their God-given names   **make . . . ignorance** i.e., excuse your affectation on the grounds of pretended ignorance   ¹³⁹**on 't** of it
¹⁴⁴**expectancy** hope   **rose** ornament   ¹⁴⁵**The glass . . . form** the mirror of true self-fashioning and the pattern of courtly behavior   ¹⁴⁶**Th' observed . . . observers** i.e., the center of attention and honor in the court   ¹⁴⁸**music** musical, sweetly uttered   ¹⁵¹**blown** blooming   ¹⁵²**Blasted** withered   **ecstasy** madness   ¹⁵⁴**affections** emotions, feelings

O'er which his melancholy sits on brood,
And I do doubt the hatch and the disclose
Will be some danger; which for to prevent,
I have in quick determination
Thus set it down: he shall with speed to England   160
For the demand of our neglected tribute.
Haply the seas and countries different
With variable objects shall expel
This something-settled matter in his heart,
Whereon his brains still beating puts him thus   165
From fashion of himself. What think you on 't?

Polonius: It shall do well. But yet do I believe
The origin and commencement of his grief
Sprung from neglected love.—How now, Ophelia?
You need not tell us what Lord Hamlet said;   170
We heard it all.—My lord, do as you please,
But, if you hold it fit, after the play
Let his queen-mother all alone entreat him
To show his grief. Let her be round with him;   175
And I'll be placed, so please you, in the ear
Of all their conference. If she find him not,
To England send him, or confine him where
Your wisdom best shall think.

King: It shall be so.
Madness in great ones must not unwatched go.   180

                    Exeunt.

3.2   *Enter Hamlet and three of the Players.*

Hamlet: Speak the speech, I pray you, as I pronounced it to you, trippingly on the
tongue. But if you mouth it, as many of our players do, I had as lief the town
crier spoke my lines. Nor do not saw the air too much with your hand, thus,
but use all gently; for in the very torrent, tempest, and, as I may say, whirlwind of your passion, you must acquire and beget a temperance that may give   5
it smoothness. O, it offends me to the soul to hear a robustious periwig-pated
fellow tear a passion to tatters, to very rags, to split the ears of the groundlings,

---

[157]**sits on brood** sits like a bird on a nest, about to *hatch* mischief (line 158)   [158]**doubt**
fear   **disclose** disclosure, hatching   [161]**set it down** resolved   [162]**For . . . of** to
demand   [164]**variable objects** various sights and surroundings to divert him   [165]**This
something . . . heart** the strange matter settled in his heart   [166]**still** continually
[167]**From . . . himself** out of his natural manner   [174]**queen-mother** queen and mother
[175]**round** blunt   [177]**find him not** fails to discover what is troubling him
3.2. Location: The castle.
[2]**our players** players nowadays   **I had as lief** I would just as soon   [6]**robustious** violent,
boisterous   **periwig-pated** wearing a wig   [7]**groundlings** spectators who paid least and
stood in the yard of the theater

who for the most part are capable of nothing but inexplicable dumb shows and noise. I would have such a fellow whipped for o'erdoing Termagant. It

10   out-Herods Herod. Pray you, avoid it.

First Player: I warrant your honor.

Hamlet: Be not too tame neither, but let your own discretion be your tutor. Suit the action to the word, the word to the action, with this special observance, that you o'erstep not the modesty of nature. For anything so o'erdone is from

15   the purpose of playing, whose end, both at the first and now, was and is to hold as 't were the mirror up to nature, to show virtue her feature, scorn her own image, and the very age and body of the time his form and pressure. Now this overdone or come tardy off, though it makes the unskillful laugh, cannot but make the judicious grieve, the censure of the which one must in

20   your allowance o'erweigh a whole theater of others. O, there be players that I have seen play, and heard others praise, and that highly, not to speak it profanely, that, neither having th' accent of Christians nor the gait of Christian, pagan, nor man, have so strutted and bellowed that I have thought some of nature's journeymen had made men and not made them well, they

25   imitated humanity so abominably.

First Player: I hope we have reformed that indifferently with us, sir.

Hamlet: O, reform it altogether. And let those that play your clowns speak no more than is set down for them; for there be of them that will themselves laugh, to set on some quantity of barren spectators to laugh too, though in

30   the meantime some necessary question of the play be then to be considered. That's villainous, and shows a most pitiful ambition in the fool that uses it. Go make you ready.   [*Exeunt Players.*]

Enter Polonius, Guildenstern, and Rosencrantz.

How now, my lord, will the King hear this piece of work?

Polonius: And the Queen too, and that presently.

35   *Hamlet:* Bid the players make haste.   [*Exit Polonius.*]

Will you two help to hasten them?

Rosencrantz: Ay, my lord.   *Exeunt they two.*

Hamlet: What ho, Horatio!

---

[8]**capable of** able to understand   **dumb shows** mimed performances, often used before Shakespeare's time to precede a play or each act   [9]**Termagant** a supposed deity of the Mohammedans, not found in any English medieval play but elsewhere portrayed as violent and blustering   [10]**Herod** Herod of Jewry (A character in *The Slaughter of the Innocents* and other cycle plays. The part was played with great noise and fury.)   [14]**modesty** restraint, moderation   **from** contrary to   [16]**scorn** i.e., something foolish and deserving of scorn   [17]**the very . . . time** i.e., the present state of affairs   **his** its   **pressure** stamp, impressed character   [18]**come tardy off** inadequately done   **the unskillful** those lacking in judgment   [19]**the censure . . . one** the judgment of even one of whom.   [20]**your allowance** your scale of values   [21-22]**not . . . profanely** (Hamlet anticipates his idea in lines 23–25 that some men were not made by God at all.)   [22]**Christians** i.e., ordinary decent folk   [23]**nor man** i.e., nor any human being at all   [24]**journeymen** laborers who are not yet masters in their trade   [25]**abominably** (Shakespeare's usual spelling, *abhominably*, suggests a literal though etymologically incorrect meaning, "removed from human nature.")   [26]**indifferently** tolerably   [28]**of them** some among them   [29]**barren** i.e., of wit   [34]**presently** at once

Enter Horatio.

Horatio: Here, sweet lord, at your service.
Hamlet: Horatio, thou art e'en as just a man   40
    As e'er my conversation coped withal.
Horatio: O, my dear lord—
Hamlet: Nay, do not think I flatter,
    For what advancement may I hope from thee
    That no revenue hast but thy good spirits
    To feed and clothe thee? Why should the poor be flattered?   45
    No, let the candied tongue lick absurd pomp,
    And crook the pregnant hinges of the knee
    Where thrift may follow fawning. Dost thou hear?
    Since my dear soul was mistress of her choice
    And could of men distinguish her election,   50
    Sh' hath sealed thee for herself, for thou hast been
    As one, in suffering all, that suffers nothing,
    A man that Fortune's buffets and rewards
    Hast ta'en with equal thanks; and blest are those
    Whose blood and judgment are so well commeddled   55
    That they are not a pipe for Fortune's finger
    To sound what stop she please. Give me that man
    That is not passion's slave, and I will wear him
    In my heart's core, ay, in my heart of heart,
    As I do thee.—Something too much of this.—   60
    There is a play tonight before the King.
    One scene of it comes near the circumstance
    Which I have told thee of my father's death.
    I prithee, when thou seest that act afoot,
    Even with the very comment of thy soul   65
    Observe my uncle. If his occulted guilt
    Do not itself unkennel in one speech,
    It is a damnèd ghost that we have seen,
    And my imaginations are as foul
    As Vulcan's stithy. Give him heedful note,   70
    For I mine eyes will rivet to his face,
    And after we will both our judgments join
    In censure of his seeming.

---

[41]**my . . . withal** my dealings encountered   [46]**candied** sugared, flattering   [47]**pregnant** compliant   [48]**thrift** profit   [50]**could . . . election** could make distinguishing choices among persons   [51]**sealed thee** (Literally, as one would seal a legal document to mark possession.)   [55]**blood** passion   **commeddled** commingled   [57]**stop** hole in a wind instrument for controlling the sound   [65]**very . . . soul** your most penetrating observation and consideration   [66]**occulted** hidden   [67]**unkennel** (As one would say of a fox driven from its lair.)   [68]**damnèd** in league with Satan   [70]**stithy** smithy, place of stiths (anvils)   [73]**censure of his seeming** judgment of his appearance or behavior

Horatio: Well, my lord.
    If 'a steal aught the whilst this play is playing
75   And scape detecting, I will pay the theft.

        [*Flourish.*] *Enter trumpets and kettledrums, King, Queen, Polonius, Ophelia,*
        [*Rosencrantz, Guildenstern, and other lords, with guards carrying torches*].

Hamlet: They are coming to the play. I must be idle. Get you a place.

        [*The King, Queen, and courtiers sit.*]

King: How fares our cousin Hamlet?

Hamlet: Excellent, i' faith, of the chameleon's dish: I eat the air,
    promise-crammed. You cannot feed capons so.

80 *King:* I have nothing with this answer, Hamlet. These words are not mine.

Hamlet: No, nor mine now. [*To Polonius.*] My lord, you played once i' th'
    university, you say?

Polonius: That did I, my lord, and was accounted a good actor.

Hamlet: What did you enact?

85 *Polonius:* I did enact Julius Caesar. I was killed i' the Capitol; Brutus killed me.

Hamlet: It was a brute part of him to kill so capital a calf there.—Be the players
    ready?

Rosencrantz: Ay, my lord. They stay upon your patience.

Queen: Come hither, my dear Hamlet, sit by me.

90 *Hamlet:* No, good Mother, here's metal more attractive.

Polonius [to the King]: O, ho, do you mark that?

Hamlet: Lady, shall I lie in your lap?   [*Lying down at Ophelia's feet.*]

Ophelia: No, my lord.

Hamlet: I mean, my head upon your lap?

95 *Ophelia:* Ay, my lord.

Hamlet: Do you think I meant country matters?

Ophelia: I think nothing, my lord.

Hamlet: That's a fair thought to lie between maids' legs.

Ophelia: What is, my lord?

100 *Hamlet:* Nothing.

Ophelia: You are merry, my lord.

Hamlet: Who, I?

---

[74]**If 'a steal aught** if he gets away with anything   [76]**idle** (1) unoccupied (2) mad
[77]**cousin** i.e., close relative   [78]**chameleon's dish** (Chameleons were supposed to feed
on air. Hamlet deliberately misinterprets the King's *fares* as "feeds." By his phrase *eat the
air* he also plays on the idea of feeding himself with the promise of succession, of being
the *heir.*)   [79]**capons** roosters castrated and *crammed* with feed to make them succulent
[80]**have . . . with** make nothing of, or gain nothing from   **are not mine** do not respond
to what I asked   [81]**nor mine now** (Once spoken, words are proverbially no longer the
speaker's own—and hence should be uttered warily.)   [86]**brute** (The Latin meaning of
brutus, "stupid," was often used punningly with the name Brutus.)   **part** (1) deed (2) role
calf fool   [88]**stay upon** await   [90]**metal** substance that is *attractive,* i.e., magnetic,
but with suggestion also of *mettle,* "disposition"   [96]**country matters** sexual intercourse
(making a bawdy pun on the first syllable of *country*)   [100]**Nothing** the figure zero or
naught, suggesting the female sexual anatomy (*Thing* not infrequently has a bawdy
connotation of male or female anatomy, and the reference here could be male.)

Ophelia: Ay, my lord.

Hamlet: O God, your only jig maker. What should a man do but be merry? For look you how cheerfully my mother looks, and my father died within 's two hours.   105

Ophelia: Nay, 'tis twice two months, my lord.

Hamlet: So long? Nay then, let the devil wear black, for I'll have a suit of sables. O heavens! Die two months ago, and not forgotten yet? Then there's hope a great man's memory may outlive his life half a year. But, by 'r Lady, 'a must build churches, then, or else shall 'a suffer not thinking on, with the hobby-horse, whose epitaph is "For O, for O, the hobbyhorse is forgot."   110

The trumpets sound. Dumb show follows.

Enter a King and a Queen [very lovingly]; the Queen embracing him, and he her. [She kneels, and makes show of protestation unto him.] He takes her up, and declines his head upon her neck. He lies him down upon a bank of flowers. She, seeing him asleep, leaves him. Anon comes in another man, takes off his crown, kisses it, pours poison in the sleeper's ears, and leaves him. The Queen returns, finds the King dead, makes passionate action. The Poisoner with some three or four come in again, seem to condole with her. The dead body is carried away. The Poisoner woos the Queen with gifts; she seems harsh awhile, but in the end accepts love.

[*Exeunt players.*]

Ophelia: What means this, my lord?

Hamlet: Marry, this' miching mallico; it means mischief.

Ophelia: Belike this show imports the argument of the play.   115

Enter Prologue.

Hamlet: We shall know by this fellow. The players cannot keep counsel; they'll tell all.

Ophelia: Will 'a tell us what this show meant?

Hamlet: Ay, or any show that you will show him. Be not you ashamed to show, he'll not shame to tell you what it means.   120

Ophelia: You are naught, you are naught. I'll mark the play.

---

[104]**only jig maker** very best composer of jigs, i.e., pointless merriment (Hamlet replies sardonically to Ophelia's observation that he is merry by saying, "If you're looking for someone who is really merry, you've come to the right person.")   [105]**within 's** within this (i.e., these)   [108]**suit of sables** garments trimmed with the fur of the sable and hence suited for a wealthy person, not a mourner (but with a pun on *sable*, "black," ironically suggesting mourning once again)   [111]**suffer . . . on** undergo oblivion   [112]**For . . . forgot** (Verse of a song occurring also in *Love's Labor's Lost*, 3.1.27–28. The hobbyhorse was a character made up to resemble a horse and rider, appearing in the morris dance and such May-game sports. This song laments the disappearance of such customs under pressure from the Puritans.)   [114]**this' miching mallico** this is sneaking mischief   [115]**Belike** probably   **argument** plot   [116]**counsel** secret   [119]**Be not you** provided you are not   [121]**naught** indecent (Ophelia is reacting to Hamlet's pointed remarks about not being ashamed to show all.)

Prologue: For us, and for our tragedy,
    Here stooping to your clemency,
    We beg your hearing patiently.   [*Exit.*]
125 *Hamlet:* Is this a prologue, or the posy of a ring?
Ophelia: 'Tis brief, my lord.
Hamlet: As woman's love.

Enter [*two Players as*] King and Queen.

Player King: Full thirty times hath Phoebus' cart gone round
    Neptune's salt wash and Tellus' orbèd ground,
130   And thirty dozen moons with borrowed sheen
    About the world have times twelve thirties been,
    Since love our hearts and Hymen did our hands
    Unite commutual in most sacred bands.
Player Queen: So many journeys may the sun and moon
135   Make us again count o'er ere love be done!
    But, woe is me, you are so sick of late,
    So far from cheer and from your former state,
    That I distrust you. Yet, though I distrust,
    Discomfort you, my lord, it nothing must.
140   For women's fear and love hold quantity;
    In neither aught, or in extremity.
    Now, what my love is, proof hath made you know,
    And as my love is sized, my fear is so.
    Where love is great, the littlest doubts are fear;
145   Where little fears grow great, great love grows there.
Player King: Faith, I must leave thee, love, and shortly too;
    My operant powers their functions leave to do.
    And thou shalt live in this fair world behind,
    Honored, beloved; and haply one as kind
150   For husband shalt thou—
Player Queen: O, confound the rest!
    Such love must needs be treason in my breast.
    In second husband let me be accurst!
    None wed the second but who killed the first.

---

[123]**stooping** bowing   [125]**posy . . . ring** brief motto in verse inscribed in a ring
[128]**Phoebus' cart** the sun-god's chariot, making its yearly cycle   [129]**salt wash** the sea
Tellus goddess of the earth, of the *orbèd ground*   [130]**borrowed** i.e., reflected   [132]**Hymen**
god of matrimony   [133]**commutual** mutually   **bands** bonds   [138]**distrust** am anxious
about   [139]**Discomfort** distress   **nothing** not at all   [140]**hold quantity** keep proportion
with one another   [141]**In . . . extremity** i.e., women fear and love either too little or too
much, but the two, fear and love, are equal in either case   [142]**proof** experience
[143]**sized** in size   [147]**operant powers** vital functions   **leave to do** cease to perform
[148]**behind** after I have gone   [153]**None** i.e., let no woman   **but who** except the one who

Hamlet: Wormwood, wormwood.

Player Queen: The instances that second marriage move 155
 Are base respects of thrift, but none of love.
 A second time I kill my husband dead
 When second husband kisses me in bed.

Player King: I do believe you think what now you speak,
 But what we do determine oft we break. 160
 Purpose is but the slave to memory,
 Of violent birth, but poor validity,
 Which now, like fruit unripe, sticks on the tree,
 But fall unshaken when they mellow be.
 Most necessary 'tis that we forget 165
 To pay ourselves what to ourselves is debt.
 What to ourselves in passion we propose,
 The passion ending, doth the purpose lose.
 The violence of either grief or joy
 Their own enactures with themselves destroy. 170
 Where joy most revels, grief doth most lament;
 Grief joys, joy grieves, on slender accident.
 This world is not for aye, nor 'tis not strange
 That even our loves should with our fortunes change;
 For 'tis a question left us yet to prove, 175
 Whether love lead fortune, or else fortune love.
 The great man down, you mark his favorite flies;
 The poor advanced makes friends of enemies.
 And hitherto doth love on fortune tend;
 For who not needs shall never lack a friend, 180
 And who in want a hollow friend doth try
 Directly seasons him his enemy.
 But, orderly to end where I begun,
 Our wills and fates do so contrary run
 That our devices still are overthrown; 185
 Our thoughts are ours, their ends none of our own.
 So think thou wilt no second husband wed,
 But die thy thoughts when thy first lord is dead.

---

[154]**Wormwood** i.e., how bitter (Literally, a bitter-tasting plant.) [155]**instances** motives **move** motivate [156]**base . . . thrift** ignoble considerations of material prosperity [161]**Purpose . . . memory** our good intentions are subject to forgetfulness [162]**validity** strength, durability [163]**Which** i.e., purpose [165–166]**Most . . . debt** it's inevitable that in time we forget the obligations we have imposed on ourselves [170]**enactures** fulfillments [171–172]**Where . . . accident** the capacity for extreme joy and grief go together, and often one extreme is instantly changed into its opposite on the slightest provocation [173]**aye** ever [177]**down** fallen in fortune [178]**The poor . . . enemies** when one of humble station is promoted, you see his enemies suddenly becoming his friends [179]**hitherto** up to this point in the argument, or, to this extent **tend** attend [180]**who not needs** he who is not in need (of wealth) [181]**who in want** he who, being in need. **try** test (his generosity) [182]**seasons him** ripens him into [184]**Our . . . run** what we want and what we get go so contrarily [185]**devices still** intentions continually [186]**ends** results

Player Queen: Nor earth to me give food, nor heaven light,

190   Sport and repose lock from me day and night,
    To desperation turn my trust and hope,
    An anchor's cheer in prison be my scope!
    Each opposite that blanks the face of joy
    Meet what I would have well and it destroy!

195   Both here and hence pursue me lasting strife
    If, once a widow, ever I be wife!

Hamlet: If she should break it now!

Player King: 'Tis deeply sworn. Sweet, leave me here awhile;
    My spirits grow dull, and fain I would beguile
    The tedious day with sleep.

200 *Player Queen:*   Sleep rock thy brain,
    And never come mischance between us twain!

                [*He sleeps.*] *Exit* [*Player Queen*].

Hamlet: Madam, how like you this play?

Queen: The lady doth protest too much, methinks.

Hamlet: O, but she'll keep her word.

205 *King:* Have you heard the argument? Is there no offense in 't?

Hamlet: No, no, they do but jest, poison in jest. No offense i' the world.

King: What do you call the play?

Hamlet: The Mousetrap. Marry, how? Tropically. This play is the image of a murder
    done in Vienna. Gonzago is the Duke's name, his wife, Baptista. You shall see

210   anon. 'Tis a knavish piece of work, but what of that? Your Majesty, and we
    that have free souls, it touches us not. Let the galled jade wince, our withers
    are unwrung.

                    Enter Lucianus.

    This is one Lucianus, nephew to the King.

Ophelia: You are as good as a chorus, my lord.

215 *Hamlet:* I could interpret between you and your love, if I could see the puppets
    dallying.

---

[189]**Nor** let neither   [190]**Sport . . . night** may day deny me its pastimes and night its
repose   [192]**anchor's cheer** anchorite's or hermit's fare   **my scope** the extent of my
happiness   [193-194]**Each . . . destroy** may every adverse thing that causes the face of joy to
turn pale meet and destroy everything that I desire to see prosper   [193]**blanks** causes to
blanch or grow pale   [195]**hence** in the life hereafter   [199]**spirits** vital spirits   [203]**doth . . .
much** makes too many promises and protestations   [205]**argument** plot   [205-206]**offense . . .
offense** cause for objection . . . actual injury, crime   [206]**jest** make believe   [208]**Tropically**
figuratively (The First Quarto reading, *trapically,* suggests a pun on *trap* in *Mousetrap.*)
[209]**Duke's** i.e., King's (A slip that may be due to Shakespeare's possible source, the alleged
murder of the Duke of Urbino by Luigi Gonzaga in 1538.)   [211]**free** guiltless   **galled jade**
horse whose hide is rubbed by saddle or harness   **withers** the part between the horse's
shoulder blades   [212]**unwrung** not rubbed sore   [214]**chorus** (In many Elizabethan plays,
the forthcoming action was explained by an actor known as the "chorus"; at a puppet
show, the actor who spoke the dialogue was known as an "interpreter," as indicated by the
lines following.)   [215]**interpret** (1) ventriloquize the dialogue, as in puppet show (2) act as
pander   [215-216]**puppets dallying** (With suggestion of sexual play, continued in *keen,* "sexually aroused," *groaning,* "moaning in pregnancy," and *edge,* "sexual desire" or "impetuosity.")

Ophelia: You are keen, my lord, you are keen.

Hamlet: It would cost you a groaning to take off mine edge.

Ophelia: Still better, and worse.

Hamlet: So you mis-take your husbands. Begin, murderer; leave thy damnable   220
faces and begin. Come, the croaking raven doth bellow for revenge.

Lucianus: Thoughts black, hands apt, drugs fit, and time agreeing,

  Confederate season, else no creature seeing,

  Thou mixture rank, of midnight weeds collected,

  With Hecate's ban thrice blasted, thrice infected,   225

  Thy natural magic and dire property

  On wholesome life usurp immediately.

               [*He pours the poison into the sleeper's ear.*]

Hamlet: 'A poisons him i' the garden for his estate. His name's Gonzago. The
story is extant, and written in very choice Italian. You shall see anon how the
murderer gets the love of Gonzago's wife.   [*Claudius rises.*]   230

Ophelia: The King rises.

Hamlet: What, frighted with false fire?

Queen: How fares my lord?

Polonius: Give o'er the play.

King: Give me some light. Away!   235

Polonius: Lights, lights, lights!

              Exeunt all but Hamlet and Horatio.

Hamlet:

  "Why, let the strucken deer go weep,

    The hart ungallèd play.

  For some must watch, while some must sleep;   240

    Thus runs the world away."

  Would not this, sir, and a forest of feathers—if the rest of my fortunes turn
Turk with me—with two Provincial roses on my razed shoes, get me a
fellowship in a cry of players?

Horatio: Half a share.

---

[217]**keen** sharp, bitter   [219]**Still . . . worse** more keen, always *bettering* what other people say
with witty wordplay, but at the same time more offensive   [220]**So** even thus (in marriage)
mis-take take falseheartedly and cheat on (The marriage vows say "for better, for worse.")
[223]**Confederate season** the time and occasion conspiring (to assist the murderer)
else otherwise **seeing** seeing me   [225]**Hecate's ban** the curse of Hecate, the goddess of
witchcraft [226]**dire property** baleful quality [228]**estate** i.e., the kingship **His** i.e., the
King's [232]**false fire** the blank discharge of a gun loaded with powder but no shot
[237-240]**Why . . . away** (Probably from an old ballad, with allusion to the popular belief that
a wounded deer retires to weep and die; compare with *As You Like It*, 2.1.33–66.)
[238]**ungallèd** unafflicted [239]**watch** remain awake [240]**Thus . . . away** thus the world goes
[241]**this** i.e., the play **feathers** (Allusion to the plumes that Elizabethan actors were fond
of wearing.) [241-242]**turn Turk with** turn renegade against, go back on [242]**Provincial
roses** rosettes of ribbon, named for roses grown in a part of France **razed** with
ornamental slashing [243]**fellowship . . . players** partnership in a theatrical company
cry pack (of hounds)

245 *Hamlet:* A whole one, I.
     "For thou dost know, O Damon dear,
       This realm dismantled was
      Of Jove himself, and now reigns here
       A very, very—pajock."
250 *Horatio:* You might have rhymed.
Hamlet: O good Horatio, I'll take the ghost's word for a thousand pound. Didst
  perceive?
Horatio: Very well, my lord.
Hamlet: Upon the talk of the poisoning?
255 *Horatio:* I did very well note him.

    Enter Rosencrantz and Guildenstern.

Hamlet: Aha! Come, some music! Come, the recorders.
    "For if the King like not the comedy,
     Why then, belike, he likes it not, perdy."
    Come, some music.
260 *Guildenstern:* Good my lord, vouchsafe me a word with you.
Hamlet: Sir, a whole history.
Guildenstern: The King, sir—
Hamlet: Ay, sir, what of him?
Guildenstern: Is in his retirement marvelous distempered.
265 *Hamlet:* With drink, sir?
Guildenstern: No, my lord, with choler.
Hamlet: Your wisdom should show itself more richer to signify this to the doctor,
  for for me to put him to his purgation would perhaps plunge him into more
  choler.
270 *Guildenstern:* Good my lord, put your discourse into some frame and start not so
  wildly from my affair.
Hamlet: I am tame, sir. Pronounce.
Guildenstern: The Queen, your mother, in most great affliction of spirit, hath sent
  me to you.
275 *Hamlet:* You are welcome.

---

[246]**Damon** the friend of Pythias, as Horatio is friend of Hamlet; or, a traditional pastoral name   [247-249]**This realm . . . pajock** i.e., Jove, representing divine authority and justice, has abandoned this realm to its own devices, leaving in his stead only a peacock or vain pretender to virtue (though the rhyme-word expected in place of *pajock* or "peacock" suggests that the realm is now ruled over by an "ass").   [247]**dismantled** stripped, divested   [256]**recorders** wind instruments of the flute kind   [258]**perdy** (A corruption of the French *par dieu,* "by God.")   [264]**retirement** withdrawal to his chambers   **distempered** out of humor (But Hamlet deliberately plays on the wider application to any illness of mind or body, as in line 295, especially to drunkenness.)   [266]**choler** anger (But Hamlet takes the word in its more basic humoral sense of "bilious disorder.")   [268]**purgation** (Hamlet hints at something going beyond medical treatment to bloodletting and the extraction of confession.)   [270]**frame** order   **start** shy or jump away (like a horse; the opposite of *tame* in line 272)

Guildenstern: Nay, good my lord, this courtesy is not of the right breed. If it shall please you to make me a wholesome answer, I will do your mother's commandment; if not, your pardon and my return shall be the end of my business.

Hamlet: Sir, I cannot. 280

Rosencrantz: What, my lord?

Hamlet: Make you a wholesome answer; my wit's diseased. But, sir, such answer as I can make, you shall command, or rather, as you say, my mother. Therefore no more, but to the matter. My mother, you say—

Rosencrantz: Then thus she says: your behavior hath struck her into amazement 285 and admiration.

Hamlet: O wonderful son, that can so stonish a mother!
But is there no sequel at the heels of this mother's admiration? Impart.

Rosencrantz: She desires to speak with you in her closet ere you go to bed. 290

Hamlet: We shall obey, were she ten times our mother.
Have you any further trade with us?

Rosencrantz: My lord, you once did love me.

Hamlet: And do still, by these pickers and stealers.

Rosencrantz: Good my lord, what is your cause of distemper? You do surely bar 295 the door upon your own liberty if you deny your griefs to your friend.

Hamlet: Sir, I lack advancement.

Rosencrantz: How can that be, when you have the voice of the King himself for your succession in Denmark?

Hamlet: Ay, sir, but "While the grass grows"—the proverb is something musty. 300

    Enter the Players with recorders.

O, the recorders. Let me see one. [*He takes a recorder.*]
To withdraw with you: why do you go about to recover the wind of me, as if you would drive me into a toil?

Guildenstern: O, my lord, if my duty be too bold, my love is too unmannerly.

Hamlet: I do not well understand that. Will you play upon this pipe? 305

Guildenstern: My lord, I cannot.

Hamlet: I pray you.

Guildenstern: Believe me, I cannot.

Hamlet: I do beseech you.

[276]**breed** (1) kind (2) breeding, manners   [278]**pardon** permission to depart
[286]**admiration** bewilderment   [290]**closet** private chamber   [294]**pickers and stealers**
i.e., hands (So called from the catechism, "to keep my hands from picking and stealing.")
[296]**liberty** i.e., being freed from *distemper,* line 295; but perhaps with a veiled threat as well
deny refuse to share   [300]**While . . . grows** (The rest of the proverb is "the silly
horse starves"; Hamlet may not live long enough to succeed to the kingdom.)
something somewhat   s.d.**Players** actors   [302]**withdraw** speak privately
recover the wind get to the windward side (thus driving the game into the *toil,* or "net")
[303]**toil** snare   [304]**if . . . unmannerly** if I am using an unmannerly boldness, it is my
love that occasions it   [305]**I . . . that** i.e., I don't understand how genuine love can be
unmannerly

310 *Guildenstern:* I know no touch of it, my lord.

Hamlet: It is as easy as lying. Govern these ventages with your fingers and thumb, give it breathe with your mouth, and it will discourse most eloquent music. Look you, these are the stops.

Guildenstern: But these cannot I command to any utterance of harmony. I have

315 not the skill.

Hamlet: Why, look you now, how unworthy a thing you make of me! You would play upon me, you would seem to know my stops, you would pluck out the heart of my mystery, you would sound me from my lowest note to the top of my compass, and there is much music, excellent voice, in this little organ, yet

320 cannot you make it speak. 'Sblood, do you think I am easier to be played on than a pipe? Call me what instrument you will, though you can fret me, you cannot play upon me.

     Enter Polonius.

    God bless you, sir!

Polonius: My lord, the Queen would speak with you, and presently.

325 *Hamlet:* Do you see yonder cloud that's almost in shape of a camel?

Polonius: By the Mass and 'tis, like a camel indeed.

Hamlet: Methinks it is like a weasel.

Polonius: It is backed like a weasel.

Hamlet: Or like a whale.

330 *Polonius:* Very like a whale.

Hamlet: Then I will come to my mother by and by. [*Aside.*] They fool me to the top of my bent.—I will come by and by.

Polonius: I will say so.   [*Exit.*]

Hamlet: "By and by" is easily said. Leave me, friends.   [*Exeunt all but Hamlet.*]

335   'Tis now the very witching time of night,

When churchyards yawn and hell itself breathes out

Contagion to this world. Now could I drink hot blood

And do such bitter business as the day

Would quake to look on. Soft, now to my mother.

340 O heart, lose not thy nature! Let not ever

The soul of Nero enter this firm bosom.

Let me be cruel, not unnatural;

I will speak daggers to her, but use none.

---

[311]**ventages** finger-holes or *stops* (line 313) of the recorder   [318]**sound** (1) fathom (2) produce sound in   [319]**compass** range (of voice)   **organ** musical instrument [321]**fret** irritate (with a quibble on *fret*, meaning the piece of wood, gut, or metal that regulates the fingering on an instrument)   [324]**presently** at once   [331]**by and by** quite soon   **fool me** trifle with me, humor my fooling   [332]**top of my bent** limit of my ability or endurance (Literally, the extent to which a bow may be bent.)   [335]**witching time** time when spells are cast and evil is abroad   [339]**nature** natural feeling   [341]**Nero** murderer of his mother, Agrippina

My tongue and soul in this be hypocrites:
How in my words soever she be shent,   345
To give them seals never my soul consent!   *Exit.*

3.3 *Enter King, Rosencrantz, and Guildenstern.*

King: I like him not, nor stands it safe with us
    To let his madness range. Therefore prepare you.
    I your commission will forthwith dispatch,
    And he to England shall along with you.
    The terms of our estate may not endure   5
    Hazard so near 's as doth hourly grow
    Out of his brows.
Guildenstern: We will ourselves provide.
    Most holy and religious fear it is
    To keep those many many bodies safe
    That live and feed upon Your Majesty.   10
Rosencrantz: The single and peculiar life is bound
    With all the strength and armor of the mind
    To keep itself from noyance, but much more
    That spirit upon whose weal depends and rests
    The lives of many. The cess of majesty   15
    Dies not alone, but like a gulf doth draw
    What's near it with it; or it is a massy wheel
    Fixed on the summit of the highest mount,
    To whose huge spokes ten thousand lesser things
    Are mortised and adjoined, which, when it falls,   20
    Each small annexment, petty consequence,
    Attends the boisterous ruin. Never alone
    Did the King sigh, but with a general groan.
King: Arm you, I pray you, to this speedy voyage,
    For we will fetters put about this fear,   25
    Which now goes too free-footed.
Rosencrantz: We will haste us.
            Exeunt gentlemen [*Rosencrantz and Guildenstern*].

        Enter Polonius.

---

[345]**How . . . soever** however much by my words   **shent** rebuked   [346]**give them seals**
i.e., confirm them with deeds
3.3. Location: The castle.
[1]**him** i.e., his behavior   [3]**dispatch** prepare, cause to be drawn up   [5]**terms of our estate**
circumstances of my royal position   [7]**Out of his brows** i.e., from his brain, in the form of
plots and threats   [8]**religious fear** sacred concern   [11]**single and peculiar** individual and
private   [13]**noyance** harm   [15]**cess** decease, cessation   [16]**gulf** whirlpool   [17]**massy**
massive   [20]**mortised** fastened (as with a fitted joint)   **when it falls** i.e., when it
descends, like the wheel of Fortune, bringing a king down with it   [21]**Each . . .
consequence** i.e., every hanger-on and unimportant person or thing connected with the
King   [22]**Attends** participates in   [24]**Arm** prepare

Polonius: My lord, he's going to his mother's closet.
Behind the arras I'll convey myself
To hear the process. I'll warrant she'll tax him home,
30 And, as you said—and wisely was it said—
'Tis meet that some more audience than a mother,
Since nature makes them partial, should o'erhear
The speech, of vantage. Fare you well, my liege.
I'll call upon you ere you go to bed
And tell you what I know.
35 *King:*   Thanks, dear my lord.

                         Exit [Polonius].

O, my offense is rank! It smells to heaven.
It hath the primal eldest curse upon 't,
A brother's murder. Pray can I not,
Though inclination be as sharp as will;
40 My stronger guilt defeats my strong intent,
And like a man to double business bound
I stand in pause where I shall first begin,
And both neglect. What if this cursèd hand
Were thicker than itself with brother's blood,
45 Is there not rain enough in the sweet heavens
To wash it white as snow? Whereto serves mercy
But to confront the visage of offense?
And what's in prayer but this twofold force,
To be forestallèd ere we come to fall,
50 Or pardoned being down? Then I'll look up.
My fault is past. But O, what form of prayer
Can serve my turn? "Forgive me my foul murder"?
That cannot be, since I am still possessed
Of those effects for which I did the murder:
55 My crown, mine own ambition, and my queen.
May one be pardoned and retain th' offense?
In the corrupted currents of this world
Offense's gilded hand may shove by justice,

---

[28]**arras** screen of tapestry placed around the walls of household apartments (On the Elizabethan stage, the arras was presumably over a door or discovery space in the tiring-house facade.)   [29]**process** proceedings   **tax him home** reprove him severely   [31]**meet** fitting   [33]**of vantage** from an advantageous place, or, in addition   [37]**the primal eldest curse** the curse of Cain, the first murderer; he killed his brother Abel   [39]**Though . . . will** though my desire is as strong as my determination   [41]**bound** (1) destined (2) obliged (The King wants to repent and still enjoy what he has gained.)   [46-47]**Whereto . . . offense?** what function does mercy serve other than to meet sin face to face?   [49]**forestallèd** prevented (from sinning)   [56]**th' offense** the thing for which one offended   [57]**currents** courses   [58]**gilded hand** hand offering gold as a bribe   **shove by** thrust aside

And oft 'tis seen the wicked prize itself
Buys out the law. But 'tis not so above.   60
There is no shuffling, there the action lies
In his true nature, and we ourselves compelled,
Even to the teeth and forehead of our faults,
To give in evidence. What then? What rests?
Try what repentance can. What can it not?   65
Yet what can it, when one cannot repent?
O wretched state, O bosom black as death,
O limèd soul that, struggling to be free,
Art more engaged! Help, angels! Make assay.
Bow, stubborn knees, and heart with strings of steel,   70
Be soft as sinews of the newborn babe!
All may be well.   [*He kneels.*]

    Enter Hamlet.

Hamlet: Now might I do it pat, now 'a is a-praying;
And now I'll do 't. [*He draws his sword.*] And so 'a goes to heaven,
And so am I revenged. That would be scanned: 75
A villain kills my father, and for that,
I, his sole son, do this same villain send
To heaven.
Why, this is hire and salary, not revenge.
'A took my father grossly, full of bread,   80
With all his crimes broad blown, as flush as May;
And how his audit stands who knows save heaven?
But in our circumstance and course of thought
'Tis heavy with him. And am I then revenged,
To take him in the purging of his soul,   85
When he is fit and seasoned for his passage?
No!
Up, sword, and know thou a more horrid hent.   [*He puts up his sword.*]
When he is drunk asleep, or in his rage,
Or in th' incestuous pleasure of his bed,   90
At game, a-swearing, or about some act

[59]**wicked prize** prize won by wickedness [61]**There** i.e., in heaven **shuffling** escape by trickery **the action lies** the accusation is made manifest (A legal metaphor.) [62]**his** its [63]**to the teeth and forehead** face to face, concealing nothing [64]**give in** provide **rests** remains [68]**limèd** caught as with birdlime, a sticky substance used to ensnare birds [69]**engaged** entangled **assay** trial (Said to himself.) [73]**pat** opportunely [75]**would be scanned** needs to be looked into, or, would be interpreted as follows [80]**grossly, full of bread** i.e., enjoying his worldly pleasures rather than fasting (See Ezekiel 16:49.) [81]**crimes broad blown** sins in full bloom **flush** vigorous [82]**audit** account **save** except for [83]**in . . . thought** as we see it from our mortal perspective [86]**seasoned** matured, readied [88]**know . . . hent** await to be grasped by me on a more horrid occasion **hent** act of seizing [89]**drunk . . . rage** dead drunk, or in a fit of sexual passion [91]**game** gambling

That has no relish of salvation in 't—
Then trip him, that his heels may kick at heaven,
And that his soul may be as damned and black

95   As hell, whereto it goes. My mother stays.
This physic but prolongs thy sickly days. *Exit.*
King: My words fly up, my thoughts remain below.
Words without thoughts never to heaven go. *Exit.*

3.4   *Enter [Queen] Gertrude and Polonius.*

Polonius: 'A will come straight. Look you lay home to him.
Tell him his pranks have been too broad to bear with,
And that Your Grace hath screened and stood between
Much heat and him. I'll shroud me even here.

5   Pray you, be round with him.
Hamlet (within): Mother, Mother, Mother!
Queen: I'll warrant you, fear me not.
Withdraw, I hear him coming.   [*Polonius hides behind the arras.*]

              Enter Hamlet.

Hamlet: Now, Mother, what's the matter?
10   *Queen:* Hamlet, thou hast thy father much offended.
Hamlet: Mother, you have my father much offended.
Queen: Come, come, you answer with an idle tongue.
Hamlet: Go, go, you question with a wicked tongue.
Queen: Why, how now, Hamlet?
Hamlet: What's the matter now?
Queen: Have you forgot me?
15   *Hamlet:*   No, by the rood, not so:
You are the Queen, your husband's brother's wife,
And—would it were not so!—you are my mother.
Queen: Nay, then, I'll set those to you that can speak.
Hamlet: Come, come, and sit you down; you shall not budge.
20   You go not till I set you up a glass
Where you may see the inmost part of you.

---

⁹²**relish** trace, savor   ⁹⁵**stays** awaits (me)   ⁹⁶**physic** purging (by prayer), or, Hamlet's
postponement of the killing
3.4. Location: The Queen's private chamber.
¹**lay home** thrust to the heart, reprove him soundly   ²**broad** unrestrained   ⁴**Much heat**
i.e., the King's anger   **shroud** conceal (with ironic fitness to Polonius' imminent death.
The word is only in the First Quarto; the Second Quarto and the Folio read "silence.")
⁵**round** blunt   ¹⁰**thy father** i.e., your stepfather, Claudius   ¹²**idle** foolish   ¹⁵**forgot me**
i.e., forgotten that I am your mother   **rood** cross of Christ   ¹⁸**speak** i.e., to someone so
rude

Queen: What wilt thou do? Thou wilt not murder me?

    Help, ho!

Polonius [behind the arras]: What ho! Help!

Hamlet [drawing]: How now? A rat? Dead for a ducat, dead!   25

              [He thrusts his rapier through the arras.]

Polonius [behind the arras]:

    O, I am slain! *[He falls and dies.]*

Queen: O me, what hast thou done?

Hamlet: Nay, I know not. Is it the King?

Queen: O, what a rash and bloody deed is this!

Hamlet: A bloody deed—almost as bad, good Mother,

    As kill a king, and marry with his brother.   30

Queen: As kill a king!

Hamlet: Ay, lady, it was my word.

            [He parts the arras and discovers Polonius.]

    Thou wretched, rash, intruding fool, farewell!

    I took thee for thy better. Take thy fortune.

    Thou find'st to be too busy is some danger.—

    Leave wringing of your hands. Peace, sit you down,   35

    And let me wring your heart, for so I shall,

    If it be made of penetrable stuff,

    If damnèd custom have not brazed it so

    That it be proof and bulwark against sense.

Queen: What have I done, that thou dar'st wag thy tongue   40

    In noise so rude against me?

Hamlet: Such an act

    That blurs the grace and blush of modesty,

    Calls virtue hypocrite, takes off the rose

    From the fair forehead of an innocent love

    And sets a blister there, makes marriage vows   45

    As false as dicers' oaths. O, such a deed

    As from the body of contraction plucks

    The very soul, and sweet religion makes

    A rhapsody of words. Heaven's face does glow

    O'er this solidity and compound mass   50

    With tristful visage, as against the doom,

    Is thought-sick at the act.

---

[25]**Dead for a ducat** i.e., I bet a ducat he's dead; or, a ducat is his life's fee   [34]**busy** nosey
[38]**damnèd custom** habitual wickedness **brazed** brazened, hardened   [39]**proof** armor
sense feeling   [45]**sets a blister** i.e., brands as a harlot   [47]**contraction** the marriage contract   [48]**sweet religion makes** i.e., makes marriage vows   [49]**rhapsody** senseless string
[49–52]**Heaven's . . . act** heaven's face blushes at this solid world compounded of the various
elements, with sorrowful face as though the day of doom were near, and is sick with horror at the deed (i.e., Gertrude's marriage)

Queen: Ay me, what act,
     That roars so loud and thunders in the index?
Hamlet [showing her two likenesses]:
     Look here upon this picture, and on this,
55   The counterfeit presentment of two brothers.
     See what a grace was seated on this brow:
     Hyperion's curls, the front of Jove himself,
     An eye like Mars to threaten and command,
     A station like the herald Mercury
60   New-lighted on a heaven-kissing hill—
     A combination and a form indeed
     Where every god did seem to set his seal
     To give the world assurance of a man.
     This was your husband. Look you now what follows:
65   Here is your husband, like a mildewed ear,
     Blasting his wholesome brother. Have you eyes?
     Could you on this fair mountain leave to feed
     And batten on this moor? Ha, have you eyes?
     You cannot call it love, for at your age
70   The heyday in the blood is tame, it's humble,
     And waits upon the judgment, and what judgment
     Would step from this to this? Sense, sure, you have,
     Else could you not have motion, but sure that sense
     Is apoplexed, for madness would not err,
75   Nor sense to ecstasy was ne'er so thralled,
     But it reserved some quantity of choice
     To serve in such a difference. What devil was 't
     That thus hath cozened you at hoodman-blind?
     Eyes without feeling, feeling without sight,
80   Ears without hands or eyes, smelling sans all,
     Or but a sickly part of one true sense
     Could not so mope. O shame, where is thy blush?
     Rebellious hell,

---

[53]**index** table of contents, prelude or preface   [55]**counterfeit presentment** portrayed
representation   [57]**Hyperion's** the sun-god's   **front** brow   [58]**Mars** god of war
[59]**station** manner of standing   **Mercury** winged messenger of the gods
[60]**New-lighted** newly alighted   [62]**set his seal** i.e., affix his approval   [65]**ear** i.e., of grain
[66]**Blasting** blighting   [67]**leave** cease   [68]**batten** gorge   **moor** barren or marshy ground
(suggesting also "dark-skinned")   [70]**heyday** state of excitement   **blood** passion
[72]**Sense** perception through the five senses (the functions of the middle or sensible soul)
[74]**apoplexed** paralyzed (Hamlet goes on to explain that, without such a paralysis of will,
mere madness would not so err, nor would the five senses so enthrall themselves to
ecstasy or lunacy; even such deranged states of mind would be able to make the obvious
choice between Hamlet Senior and Claudius.)   **err** so err   [76]**But** but that   [77]**To . . .
difference** to help in making a choice between two such men   [78]**cozened** cheated
hoodman-blind blindman's buff (In this game, says Hamlet, the devil must have pushed
Claudius toward Gertrude while she was blindfolded.)   [80]**sans** without   [82]**mope** be
dazed, act aimlessly

If thou canst mutine in a matron's bones,
To flaming youth let virtue be as wax   85
And melt in her own fire. Proclaim no shame
When the compulsive ardor gives the charge,
Since frost itself as actively doth burn,
And reason panders will.

Queen: O Hamlet, speak no more!   90
Thou turn'st mine eyes into my very soul,
And there I see such black and grainèd spots
As will not leave their tinct.

Hamlet: Nay, but to live
In the rank sweat of an enseamèd bed,
Stewed in corruption, honeying and making love   95
Over the nasty sty!

Queen: O, speak to me no more!
These words like daggers enter in my ears.
No more, sweet Hamlet!

Hamlet: A murderer and a villain,
A slave that is not twentieth part the tithe
Of your precedent lord, a vice of kings,   100
A cutpurse of the empire and the rule,
That from a shelf the precious diadem stole
And put it in his pocket!

Queen: No more!   105

               Enter Ghost [in his nightgown].

Hamlet: A king of shreds and patches—
Save me, and hover o'er me with your wings,
You heavenly guards! What would your gracious figure?

Queen: Alas, he's mad!

Hamlet: Do you not come your tardy son to chide,   110
That, lapsed in time and passion, lets go by
Th' important acting of your dread command?
O, say!

Ghost: Do not forget. This visitation
Is but to whet thy almost blunted purpose.   115
But look, amazement on thy mother sits.
O, step between her and her fighting soul!

---

[84]**mutine** incite mutiny   [85–86]**be as wax . . . fire** melt like a candle or stick of sealing wax held over the candle flame   [86–89]**Proclaim . . . will** call it no shameful business when the compelling ardor of youth delivers the attack, i.e., commits lechery, since the *frost* of advanced age burns with as active a fire of lust and reason perverts itself by fomenting lust rather than restraining it   [92]**grainèd** dyed in grain, indelible   [93]**leave their tinct** surrender their color   [94]**enseamèd** saturated in the grease and filth of passionate lovemaking   [95]**Stewed** soaked, bathed (with a suggestion of "stew," brothel)   [100]**tithe** tenth part   [101]**precedent lord** former husband   **vice** buffoon (A reference to the Vice of the morality plays.)   [106]**shreds and patches** i.e., motley, the traditional costume of the clown or fool   [111]**lapsed** delaying   [112]**important** importunate, urgent   [116]**amazement** distraction

Conceit in weakest bodies strongest works.
Speak to her, Hamlet.

Hamlet: How is it with you, lady?

120 *Queen:* Alas, how is 't with you,
That you do bend your eye on vacancy,
And with th' incorporal air do hold discourse?
Forth at your eyes your spirits wildly peep,
And, as the sleeping soldiers in th' alarm,
125 Your bedded hair, like life in excrements,
Start up and stand on end. O gentle son,
Upon the heat and flame of thy distemper
Sprinkle cool patience. Whereon do you look?

Hamlet: On him, on him! Look you how pale he glares!
130 His form and cause conjoined, preaching to stones,
Would make them capable.—Do not look upon me,
Lest with this piteous action you convert
My stern effects. Then what I have to do
Will want true color—tears perchance for blood.

135 *Queen:* To whom do you speak this?
Hamlet: Do you see nothing there?
Queen: Nothing at all, yet all that is I see.
Hamlet: Nor did you nothing hear?
Queen: No, nothing but ourselves.
140 *Hamlet:* Why, look you there, look how it steals away!
My father, in his habit as he lived!
Look where he goes even now out at the portal!

Exit Ghost.

Queen: This is the very coinage of your brain.
This bodiless creation ecstasy
145 Is very cunning in.

Hamlet: Ecstasy?
My pulse as yours doth temperately keep time,
And makes as healthful music. It is not madness
That I have uttered. Bring me to the test,
150 And I the matter will reword, which madness

---

[118]**Conceit** imagination   [122]**incorporal** immaterial   [124]**as . . . alarm** like soldiers called
out of sleep by an alarum   [125]**bedded** laid flat   **like life in excrements** i.e., as though
hair, an outgrowth of the body, had a life of its own (Hair was thought to be lifeless
because it lacks sensation, and so its standing on end would be unnatural and ominous.)
[127]**distemper** disorder   [130]**His . . . conjoined** his appearance joined to his cause for
speaking   [131]**capable** receptive   [132-133]**convert . . . effects** divert me from my stern
duty   [134]**want . . . blood** lack plausibility so that (with a play on the normal sense of
color) I shall shed colorless tears instead of blood   [141]**habit** clothes   **as** as when
[143]**very** mere   [144-145]**This . . . in** Madness is skillful in creating this kind of hallucination
[150]**reword** repeat word for word

Would gambol from. Mother, for love of grace,
Lay not that flattering unction to your soul
That not your trespass but my madness speaks.
It will but skin and film the ulcerous place,
Whiles rank corruption, mining all within,   155
Infects unseen. Confess yourself to heaven,
Repent what's past, avoid what is to come,
And do not spread the compost on the weeds
To make them ranker. Forgive me this my virtue;
For in the fatness of these pursy times   160
Virtue itself of vice must pardon beg,
Yea, curb and woo for leave to do him good.
Queen: O Hamlet, thou hast cleft my heart in twain.
Hamlet: O, throw away the worser part of it,
And live the purer with the other half.   165
Good night. But go not to my uncle's bed;
Assume a virtue, if you have it not.
That monster, custom, who all sense doth eat,
Of habits devil, is angel yet in this,
That to the use of actions fair and good   170
He likewise gives a frock or livery
That aptly is put on. Refrain tonight,
And that shall lend a kind of easiness
To the next abstinence; the next more easy;
For use almost can change the stamp of nature,   175
And either . . . the devil, or throw him out
With wondrous potency. Once more, good night;
And when you are desirous to be blest,
I'll blessing beg of you. For this same lord,   [*pointing to Polonius*]
I do repent; but heaven hath pleased it so   180
To punish me with this, and this with me,
That I must be their scourge and minister.

---

[151]**gambol** skip away   [152]**unction** ointment   [154]**skin** grow a skin for   [155]**mining** working under the surface   [158]**compost** manure   [159]**this my virtue** my virtuous talk in reproving you   [160]**fatness** grossness   **pursy** flabby, out of shape   [162]**curb** bow, bend the knee   **leave** permission   [168]**who . . . eat** which consumes all proper or natural feeling, all sensibility   [169]**Of habits devil** devil-like in prompting evil habits   [171]**livery** an outer appearance, a customary garb (and hence a predisposition easily assumed in time of stress)   [172]**aptly** readily   [175]**use** habit   **the stamp of nature** our inborn traits   [176]**And either** (A defective line, usually emended by inserting the word *master* after *either*, following the Fourth Quarto and early editors.)   [178–179]**when . . . you** i.e., when you are ready to be penitent and seek God's blessing, I will ask your blessing as a dutiful son should   [182]**their scourge and minister** i.e., agent of heavenly retribution (By *scourge,* Hamlet also suggests that he himself will eventually suffer punishment in the process of fulfilling heaven's will.)

I will bestow him, and will answer well
The death I gave him. So, again, good night.

185 I must be cruel only to be kind.
This bad begins, and worse remains behind.
One word more, good lady.

Queen: What shall I do?

Hamlet: Not this by no means that I bid you do:
Let the bloat king tempt you again to bed,

190 Pinch wanton on your cheek, call you his mouse,
And let him, for a pair of reechy kisses,
Or paddling in your neck with his damned fingers,
Make you to ravel all this matter out
That I essentially am not in madness,

195 But mad in craft. 'Twere good you let him know,
For who that's but a queen, fair, sober, wise,
Would from a paddock, from a bat, a gib,
Such dear concernings hide? Who would do so?
No, in despite of sense and secrecy,

200 Unpeg the basket on the house's top,
Let the birds fly, and like the famous ape,
To try conclusions, in the basket creep
And break your own neck down.

Queen: Be thou assured, if words be made of breath,

205 And breath of life, I have no life to breathe
What thou hast said to me.

Hamlet: I must to England. You know that?

Queen: Alack,
I had forgot. 'Tis so concluded on.

Hamlet: There's letters sealed, and my two schoolfellows,

210 Whom I will trust as I will adders fanged,
They bear the mandate; they must sweep my way
And marshal me to knavery. Let it work.
For 'tis the sport to have the enginer

---

[183] **bestow** stow, dispose of   **answer** account or pay for   [186] **This** i.e., the killing of
Polonius   **behind** to come   [189] **bloat** bloated   [190] **Pinch wanton** i.e., leave his love
pinches on your cheeks, branding you as wanton   [191] **reechy** dirty, filthy   [192] **paddling**
fingering amorously   [193] **ravel . . . out** unravel, disclose   [195] **in craft** by cunning
good (Said sarcastically; also the following eight lines.)   [197] **paddock** toad   **gib** tomcat
[198] **dear concernings** important affairs   [199] **sense and secrecy** secrecy that common
sense requires   [200] **Unpeg the basket** open the cage, i.e., let out the secret
[201] **famous ape** (In a story now lost.)   [202] **try conclusions** test the outcome (in which
the ape apparently enters a cage from which birds have been released and then tries to
fly out of the cage as they have done, falling to its death)   [203] **down** in the fall; utterly
[211-212] **sweep . . . knavery** sweep a path before me and conduct me to some knavery
or treachery prepared for me   [212] **work** proceed   [213] **enginer** maker of military
contrivances

Hoist with his own petard, and 't shall go hard
But I will delve one yard below their mines   215
And blow them at the moon. O, 'tis most sweet
When in one line two crafts directly meet
This man shall set me packing.
I'll lug the guts into the neighbor room.
Mother, good night indeed. This counselor   220
Is now most still, most secret, and most grave,
Who was in life a foolish prating knave.—
Come, sir, to draw toward an end with you.—
Good night, Mother.

Exeunt [separately, Hamlet dragging in Polonius].

4.1   *Enter King and Queen, with Rosencrantz and Guildenstern.*

King: There's matter in these sighs, these profound heaves.
   You must translate; 'tis fit we understand them.
   Where is your son?
Queen: Bestow this place on us a little while.   [*Exeunt Rosencrantz and Guildenstern.*]
   Ah, mine own lord, what have I seen tonight!   5
King: What, Gertrude? How does Hamlet?
Queen: Mad as the sea and wind when both contend
   Which is the mightier. In his lawless fit,
   Behind the arras hearing something stir,
   Whips out his rapier, cries, "A rat, a rat!"   10
   And in this brainish apprehension kills
   The unseen good old man.
King: O heavy deed!
   It had been so with us, had we been there.
   His liberty is full of threats to all—
   To you yourself, to us, to everyone.   15

---

²¹⁴**Hoist with** blown up by   **petard** an explosive used to blow in a door or make a
breach   ²¹⁴⁻²¹⁵**'t shall . . . will** unless luck is against me, I will   ²¹⁵**mines** tunnels used
in warfare to undermine the enemy's emplacements; Hamlet will countermine by going
under their mines   ²¹⁷**in one line** i.e., mines and countermines on a collision course,
or the countermines directly below the mines   **crafts** acts of guile, plots   ²¹⁸**set me
packing** set me to making schemes, and set me to lugging (him), and, also, send me off
in a hurry   ²²³**draw . . . end** finish up (with a pun on *draw,* "pull")
4.1. Location: The castle.
ˢ·ᵈ·**Enter . . . Queen** (Some editors argue that Gertrude never exits in 3.4 and that the
scene is continuous here, as suggested in the Folio, but the Second Quarto marks an
entrance for her and at line 35 Claudius speaks of Gertrude's *closet* as though it were
elsewhere. A short time has elapsed, during which the King has become aware of her
highly wrought emotional state.)   ¹**matter** significance   **heaves** heavy sighs
¹¹**brainish apprehension** headstrong conception   ¹²**heavy** grievous   ¹³**us** i.e., me
(The royal "we"; also in line 15.)

Alas, how shall this bloody deed be answered?
It will be laid to us, whose providence
Should have kept short, restrained, and out of haunt
This mad young man. But so much was our love,
20 We would not understand what was most fit,
But, like the owner of a foul disease,
To keep it from divulging, let it feed
Even on the pith of life. Where is he gone?
Queen: To draw apart the body he hath killed,
25 O'er whom his very madness, like some ore
Among a mineral of metals base,
Shows itself pure: 'a weeps for what is done.
King: O Gertrude, come away!
The sun no sooner shall the mountains touch
30 But we will ship him hence, and this vile deed
We must with all our majesty and skill
Both countenance and excuse.—Ho, Guildenstern!
            Enter Rosencrantz and Guildenstern.
Friends both, go join you with some further aid.
Hamlet in madness hath Polonius slain,
35 And from his mother's closet hath he dragged him.
Go seek him out, speak fair, and bring the body
Into the chapel. I pray you, haste in this.
            [*Exeunt Rosencrantz and Guildenstern.*]
Come, Gertrude, we'll call up our wisest friends
And let them know both what we mean to do
40 And what's untimely done . . . .
Whose whisper o'er the world's diameter,
As level as the cannon to his blank,
Transports his poisoned shot, may miss our name
And hit the woundless air. O, come away!
45 My soul is full of discord and dismay.   *Exeunt.*

4.2   *Enter Hamlet.*

Hamlet: Safely stowed.
Rosencrantz, Guildenstern (within): Hamlet! Lord Hamlet!

---

[16]**answered** explained   [17]**providence** foresight   [18]**short** i.e., on a short tether   **out of haunt** secluded   [22]**divulging** becoming evident   [25]**ore** vein of gold   [26]**mineral** mine   [32]**countenance** put the best face on   [40]**And . . . done** (A defective line; conjectures as to the missing words include *So, haply, slander* [Capell and others]; *For, haply, slander* [Theobald and others]; and *So envious slander* [Jenkins].)   [41]**diameter** extent from side to side   [42]**As level** with as direct aim   **his blank** its target at point-blank range   [44]**woundless** invulnerable
4.2. Location: The castle.

Hamlet: But soft, what noise? Who calls on Hamlet? O, here they come.

       Enter Rosencrantz and Guildenstern.

Rosencrantz: What have you done, my lord, with the dead body?

Hamlet: Compounded it with dust, whereto 'tis kin.   5

Rosencrantz: Tell us where 'tis, that we may take it thence
    And bear it to the chapel.

Hamlet: Do not believe it.

Rosencrantz: Believe what?

Hamlet: That I can keep your counsel and not mine own. Besides, to be   10
    demanded of a sponge, what replication should be made by the son of a king?

Rosencrantz: Take you me for a sponge, my lord?

Hamlet: Ay, sir, that soaks up the King's countenance, his rewards, his authori-
    ties. But such officers do the King best service in the end. He keeps them, like
    an ape, an apple, in the corner of his jaw, first mouthed to be last swallowed.   15
    When he needs what you have gleaned, it is but squeezing you, and, sponge,
    you shall be dry again.

Rosencrantz: I understand you not, my lord.

Hamlet: I am glad of it. A knavish speech sleeps in a foolish ear.

Rosencrantz: My lord, you must tell us where the body is and go with us to the   20
    King.

Hamlet: The body is with the King, but the King is not with the body. The King
    is a thing—

Guildenstern: A thing, my lord?

Hamlet: Of nothing. Bring me to him. Hide fox, and all after!   *Exeunt [running].*   25

4.3   *Enter King, and two or three.*

King: I have sent to seek him, and to find the body.
    How dangerous is it that this man goes loose!
    Yet must not we put the strong law on him.
    He's loved of the distracted multitude,
    Who like not in their judgment, but their eyes,   5

---

[10]**That . . . own** i.e., that I can follow your advice (by telling where the body is) and
still keep my own secret   [11]**demanded of** questioned by   **replication** reply
[13]**countenance** favor   [13–14]**authorities** delegated power, influence   [19]**sleeps in** has no
meaning to   [22]**The . . . body** (Perhaps alludes to the legal commonplace of "the king's
two bodies," which drew a distinction between the sacred office of kingship and the
particular mortal who possessed it at any given time. Hence, although Claudius' body is
necessarily a part of him, true kingship is not contained in it. Similarly, Claudius will have
Polonius' body when it is found, but there is no kingship in this business either.)
[25]**Of nothing** (1) of no account (2) lacking the essence of kingship, as in line 22 and note
[25]**Hide . . . after** (An old signal cry in the game of hide-and-seek, suggesting that Hamlet
now runs away from them.)
4.3. Location: The castle.
[4]**of** by   **distracted** fickle, unstable   [5]**Who . . . eyes** who choose not by judgment but by
appearance

And where 'tis so, th' offender's scourge is weighed,
But never the offense. To bear all smooth and even,
This sudden sending him away must seem
Deliberate pause. Diseases desperate grown
By desperate appliance are relieved,
Or not at all.

Enter Rosencrantz, [Guildenstern,] and all the rest.

How now, what hath befall'n?
Rosencrantz: Where the dead body is bestowed, my lord,
We cannot get from him.
King: But where is he?
Rosencrantz: Without, my lord; guarded, to know your pleasure.
King: Bring him before us.
Rosencrantz: Ho! Bring in the lord.

They enter [with Hamlet].

King: Now, Hamlet, where's Polonius?
Hamlet: At supper.
King: At supper? Where?
Hamlet: Not where he eats, but where 'a is eaten. A certain convocation of politic
worms are e'en at him. Your worm is your only emperor for diet. We fat all
creatures else to fat us, and we fat ourselves for maggots. Your fat king and
your lean beggar is but variable service—two dishes, but to one table. That's
the end.
King: Alas, alas!
Hamlet: A man may fish with the worm that hath eat of a king, and eat of the
fish that hath fed of that worm.
King: What dost thou mean by this?
Hamlet: Nothing but to show you how a king may go a progress through the guts
of a beggar.
King: Where is Polonius?
Hamlet: In heaven. Send thither to see. If your messenger find him not there,
seek him i' th' other place yourself. But if indeed you find him not within
this month, you shall nose him as you go up the stairs into the lobby.
King [to some attendants]: Go seek him there.
Hamlet: 'A will stay till you come. [Exeunt attendants.]
King: Hamlet, this deed, for thine especial safety—
Which we do tender, as we dearly grieve

⁶**scourge** punishment (Literally, blow with a whip.) **weighed** sympathetically
considered ⁷**To . . . even** to manage the business in an unprovocative way ⁹**Deliberate
pause** carefully considered action ¹⁰**appliance** remedies ¹⁹⁻²⁰**politic worms** crafty
worms (suited to a master spy like Polonius) ²⁰**e'en** even now **Your worm** your average worm (Compare *your fat king and your lean beggar* in lines 21–22.) **diet** food, eating
(with a punning reference to the Diet of Worms, a famous *convocation* held in 1521)
²²**variable service** different courses of a single meal ²⁵**eat** eaten (Pronounced *et.*)
²⁸**progress** royal journey of state ³⁷**tender** regard, hold dear **dearly** intensely

For that which thou hast done—must send thee hence
With fiery quickness. Therefore prepare thyself.
The bark is ready, and the wind at help,   40
Th' associates tend, and everything is bent
For England.

Hamlet: For England!

King: Ay, Hamlet.

Hamlet: Good.   45

King: So is it, if thou knew'st our purposes.

Hamlet: I see a cherub that sees them. But come, for England! Farewell, dear
mother.

King: Thy loving father, Hamlet.

Hamlet: My mother. Father and mother is man and wife, man and wife is one   50
flesh, and so, my mother. Come, for England!   *Exit.*

King: Follow him at foot; tempt him with speed aboard.
Delay it not. I'll have him hence tonight.
Away! For everything is sealed and done
That else leans on th' affair. Pray you, make haste.   55
                [*Exeunt all but the King.*]
And, England, if my love thou hold'st at aught—
As my great power thereof may give thee sense,
Since yet thy cicatrice looks raw and red
After the Danish sword, and thy free awe
Pays homage to us—thou mayst not coldly set   60
Our sovereign process, which imports at full,
By letters congruing to that effect,
The present death of Hamlet. Do it, England,
For like the hectic in my blood he rages,
And thou must cure me. Till I know 'tis done,   65
Howe'er my haps, my joys were ne'er begun.   *Exit.*

4.4   *Enter Fortinbras with his army over the stage.*

Fortinbras: Go, Captain, from me greet the Danish king.
Tell him that by his license Fortinbras

---

[40]**bark** sailing vessel   [41]**tend** wait   **bent** in readiness   [47]**cherub** (Cherubim are angels
of knowledge. Hamlet hints that both he and heaven are onto Claudius' tricks.)
[52]**at foot** close behind, at heel   [55]**leans on** bears upon, is related to   [56]**England** i.e.,
King of England   **at aught** at any value   [57]**As . . . sense** for so my great power may
give you a just appreciation of the importance of valuing my love   [58]**cicatrice** scar
[59]**free awe** voluntary show of respect   [60]**coldly set** regard with indifference   [61]**process**
command   **imports at full** conveys specific directions for   [62]**congruing** agreeing
[63]**present** immediate   [64]**hectic** persistent fever   [66]**haps** fortunes
4.4 Location: The coast of Denmark.
[2]**license** permission

Craves the conveyance of a promised march
Over his kingdom. You know the rendezvous.

5   If that His Majesty would aught with us,
We shall express our duty in his eye;
And let him know so.

Captain: I will do 't, my lord.

Fortinbras: Go softly on.   [*Exeunt all but the Captain.*]

         Enter Hamlet, Rosencrantz, [Guildenstern,] etc.

10 *Hamlet:* Good sir, whose powers are these?

Captain: They are of Norway, sir.

Hamlet: How purposed, sir, I pray you?

Captain: Against some part of Poland.

Hamlet: Who commands them, sir?

15 *Captain:* The nephew to old Norway, Fortinbras.

Hamlet: Goes it against the main of Poland, sir,
Or for some frontier?

Captain: Truly to speak, and with no addition,
We go to gain a little patch of ground

20   That hath in it no profit but the name.
To pay five ducats, five, I would not farm it;
Nor will it yield to Norway or the Pole
A ranker rate, should it be sold in fee.

Hamlet: Why, then the Polack never will defend it.

25 *Captain:* Yes, it is already garrisoned.

Hamlet: Two thousand souls and twenty thousand ducats
Will not debate the question of this straw.
This is th' impostume of much wealth and peace,
That inward breaks, and shows no cause without

30   Why the man dies. I humbly thank you, sir.

Captain: God b' wi' you, sir.   [*Exit.*]

Rosencrantz: Will 't please you go, my lord?

Hamlet: I'll be with you straight. Go a little before.   [*Exeunt all except Hamlet.*]
How all occasions do inform against me
And spur my dull revenge! What is a man,

35   If his chief good and market of his time
Be but to sleep and feed? A beast, no more.

---

³**the conveyance of** escort during   ⁶**duty** respect   **eye** presence   ⁹**softly** slowly,
circumspectly   ¹⁰**powers** forces   ¹⁶**main** main part   ¹⁸**addition** exaggeration
²¹**To pay** i.e., for a yearly rental of   **farm it** take a lease of it   ²³**ranker** higher
in fee fee simple, outright   ²⁷**debate . . . straw** settle this trifling matter   ²⁸**impostume**
abscess   ³³**inform against** denounce, betray; take shape against   ³⁵**market of** profit of,
compensation for

Sure he that made us with such large discourse,
Looking before and after, gave us not
That capability and godlike reason
To fust in us unused. Now, whether it be   40
Bestial oblivion, or some craven scruple
Of thinking too precisely on th' event—
A thought which, quartered, hath but one part wisdom
And ever three parts coward—I do not know
Why yet I live to say "This thing's to do,"   45
Sith I have cause, and will, and strength, and means
To do 't. Examples gross as earth exhort me:
Witness this army of such mass and charge,
Led by a delicate and tender prince,
Whose spirit with divine ambition puffed   50
Makes mouths at the invisible event,
Exposing what is mortal and unsure
To all that fortune, death, and danger dare,
Even for an eggshell. Rightly to be great
Is not to stir without great argument,   55
But greatly to find quarrel in a straw
When honor's at the stake. How stand I, then,
That have a father killed, a mother stained,
Excitements of my reason and my blood,
And let all sleep, while to my shame I see   60
The imminent death of twenty thousand men
That for a fantasy and trick of fame
Go to their graves like beds, fight for a plot
Whereon the numbers cannot try the cause,
Which is not tomb enough and continent   65
To hide the slain? O, from this time forth
My thoughts be bloody or be nothing worth!   *Exit.*

---

[37]**discourse** power of reasoning   [38]**Looking before and after** able to review past events and anticipate the future   [40]**fust** grow moldy   [41]**oblivion** forgetfulness   **craven** cowardly   [42]**precisely** scrupulously   **event** outcome   [46]**Sith** since   [47]**gross** obvious   [48]**charge** expense   [49]**delicate and tender** of fine and youthful qualities   [51]**Makes mouths** makes scornful faces   **invisible event** unforeseeable outcome   [53]**dare** could do (to him)   [54–57]**Rightly . . . stake** true greatness does not normally consist of rushing into action over some trivial provocation; however, when one's honor is involved, even a trifling insult requires that one respond greatly (?)   [57]**at the stake** (A metaphor from gambling or bearbaiting.)   [59]**Excitements of** promptings by   [62]**fantasy** fanciful caprice, illusion   **trick** trifle, deceit   [63]**plot** plot of ground   [64]**Whereon . . . cause** on which there is insufficient room for the soldiers needed to engage in a military contest   [65]**continent** receptacle, container

4.5 *Enter Horatio, [Queen] Gertrude, and a Gentleman.*

Queen: I will not speak with her.

Gentleman: She is importunate,
    Indeed distract. Her mood will needs be pitied.

Queen: What would she have?

Gentleman: She speaks much of her father, says she hears
5   There's tricks i' the world, and hems, and beats her heart,
    Spurns enviously at straws, speaks things in doubt
    That carry but half sense. Her speech is nothing,
    Yet the unshapèd use of it doth move
    The hearers to collection; they yawn at it,
10   And botch the words up fit to their own thoughts,
    Which, as her winks and nods and gestures yield them,
    Indeed would make one think there might be thought,
    Though nothing sure, yet much unhappily.

Horatio: 'Twere good she were spoken with, for she may strew
15   Dangerous conjectures in ill-breeding minds.

Queen: Let her come in.   *[Exit Gentleman.]*
    [Aside.] To my sick soul, as sin's true nature is,
    Each toy seems prologue to some great amiss.
    So full of artless jealousy is guilt,
20   It spills itself in fearing to be spilt.

Enter Ophelia [distracted].

Ophelia: Where is the beauteous majesty of Denmark?

Queen: How now, Ophelia?

Ophelia (she sings):
    "How should I your true love know
      From another one?
25   By his cockle hat and staff,
      And his sandal shoon."

Queen: Alas, sweet lady, what imports this song?

Ophelia: Say you? Nay, pray you, mark.
    "He is dead and gone, lady,   *(Song.)*
30   He is dead and gone;

4.5. Location: The castle.
²**distract** distracted   ⁵**tricks** deceptions   **hems** makes "hmm" sounds   **heart** i.e., breast
⁶**Spurns . . . straws** kicks spitefully, takes offense at trifles   **in doubt** obscurely
⁸**unshapèd use** incoherent manner   ⁹**collection** inference, a guess at some sort of
meaning   **yawn** gape, wonder; grasp (The Folio reading, *aim*, is possible.)   ¹⁰**botch**
patch   ¹¹**Which** which words   **yield** deliver, represent   ¹²**thought** intended
¹³**unhappily** unpleasantly near the truth, shrewdly   ¹⁵**ill-breeding** prone to suspect the
worst and to make mischief   ¹⁸**toy** trifle   **amiss** calamity   ¹⁹⁻²⁰**So . . . spilt** Guilt is so
full of suspicion that it unskillfully betrays itself in fearing betrayal.   ²⁰ˢ·ᵈ·**Enter Ophelia**
(In the First Quarto, Ophelia enters, "playing on a lute, and her hair down, singing.")
²⁵**cockle hat** hat with cockleshell stuck in it as a sign that the wearer had been a pilgrim
to the shrine of Saint James of Compostella in Spain   ²⁶**shoon** shoes

At his head a grass-green turf,
>At his heels a stone."
O, ho!

Queen: Nay, but Ophelia—

Ophelia: Pray you, mark.   35

[*Sings.*] "White his shroud as the mountain snow"—

>*Enter King.*

Queen: Alas, look here, my lord.

Ophelia: "Larded with sweet flowers;   (*Song.*)
>Which bewept to the ground did not go
>>With true-love showers."   40

King: How do you, pretty lady?

Ophelia: Well, God 'ild you! They say the owl was a baker's daughter. Lord, we
know what we are, but know not what we may be. God be at your table!

King: Conceit upon her father.

Ophelia: Pray let's have no words of this; but when they ask you what it means,   45
say you this:

>"Tomorrow is Saint Valentine's day,   (*Song.*)
>>All in the morning betime,
>And I a maid at your window,
>>To be your Valentine.   50
>Then up he rose, and donned his clothes,
>>And dupped the chamber door,
>Let in the maid, that out a maid
>>Never departed more."

King: Pretty Ophelia—   55

Ophelia: Indeed, la, without an oath, I'll make an end on 't:

[*Sings.*] "By Gis and by Saint Charity,
>>Alack, and fie for shame!
>Young men will do 't, if they come to 't;
>>By Cock, they are to blame.   60
>Quoth she, 'Before you tumbled me,
>>You promised me to wed.'"

He answers:

>"'So would I ha' done, by yonder sun,
>>An thou hadst not come to my bed.'"   65

King: How long hath she been thus?

Ophelia: I hope all will be well. We must be patient, but I cannot choose but
weep to think they would lay him i' the cold ground. My brother shall know

---

[38]**Larded** decorated   [40]**showers** i.e., tears   [42]**God 'ild** God yield or reward   **owl**
(Refers to a legend about a baker's daughter who was turned into an owl for being
ungenerous when Jesus begged a loaf of bread.)   [44]**Conceit** brooding   [48]**betime** early
[52]**dupped** did up, opened   [57]**Gis** Jesus   [60]**Cock** (A perversion of "God" in oaths; here
also with a quibble on the slang word for penis.)   [65]**An** if

of it. And so I thank you for your good counsel. Come, my coach! Good
70   night, ladies, good night, sweet ladies, good night, good night.   [*Exit.*]
King [to Horatio]: Follow her close. Give her good watch, I pray you.   [*Exit Horatio.*]
O, this is the poison of deep grief; it springs
All from her father's death—and now behold!
O Gertrude, Gertrude,
75   When sorrows come, they come not single spies,
But in battalions. First, her father slain;
Next, your son gone, and he most violent author
Of his own just remove; the people muddied,
Thick and unwholesome in their thoughts and whispers
80   For good Polonius' death—and we have done but greenly,
In hugger-mugger to inter him; poor Ophelia
Divided from herself and her fair judgment,
Without the which we are pictures or mere beasts;
Last, and as much containing as all these,
85   Her brother is in secret come from France,
Feeds on this wonder, keeps himself in clouds,
And wants not buzzers to infect his ear
With pestilent speeches of his father's death,
Wherein necessity, of matter beggared,
90   Will nothing stick our person to arraign
In ear and ear. O my dear Gertrude, this,
Like to a murdering piece, in many places
Gives me superfluous death.   *A noise within.*
Queen: Alack, what noise is this?
95   *King:* Attend!
Where is my Switzers? Let them guard the door.

        Enter a Messenger.

What is the matter?
Messenger: Save yourself, my lord!
The ocean, overpeering of his list,

---

[75]**spies** scouts sent in advance of the main force   [78]**remove** removal   **muddied** stirred
up, confused   [80]**greenly** in an inexperienced way, foolishly   [81]**hugger-mugger** secret
haste   [84]**as much containing** as full of serious matter   [86]**Feeds . . . clouds** feeds his
resentment or shocked grievance, holds himself inscrutable and aloof amid all this rumor
[87]**wants** lacks   **buzzers** gossipers, informers   [89]**necessity** i.e., the need to invent some
plausible explanation   **of matter beggared** unprovided with facts   [90–91]**Will . . . ear**
will not hesitate to accuse my (royal) person in everybody's ears   [92]**murdering piece**
cannon loaded so as to scatter its shot   [93]**Gives . . . death** kills me over and over
[95]**Attend** i.e., guard me   [96]**Switzers** Swiss guards, mercenaries   [98]**overpeering of his
list** overflowing its shore, boundary

Eats not the flats with more impetuous haste
Than young Laertes, in a riotous head,   100
O'erbears your officers. The rabble call him lord,
And, as the world were now but to begin,
Antiquity forgot, custom not known,
The ratifiers and props of every word,
They cry, "Choose we! Laertes shall be king!"   105
Caps, hands, and tongues applaud it to the clouds,
"Laertes shall be king, Laertes king!"
Queen: How cheerfully on the false trail they cry!

A noise within.

O, this is counter, you false Danish dogs!

Enter Laertes with others.

King: The doors are broke.   110
Laertes: Where is this King?—Sirs, stand you all without.
All: No, let's come in.
Laertes: I pray you, give me leave.
All: We will, we will.
Laertes: I thank you. Keep the door. [*Exeunt followers.*] O thou vile king,   115
   Give me my father!
Queen [restraining him]: Calmly, good Laertes.
Laertes: That drop of blood that's calm proclaims me bastard,
   Cries cuckold to my father, brands the harlot
   Even here, between the chaste unsmirchèd brow   120
   Of my true mother.
King: What is the cause, Laertes,
   That thy rebellion looks so giantlike?
   Let him go, Gertrude. Do not fear our person.
   There's such divinity doth hedge a king
   That treason can but peep to what it would,   125
   Acts little of his will. Tell me, Laertes,
   Why thou art thus incensed. Let him go, Gertrude.
   Speak, man.
Laertes: Where is my father?
King: Dead.
Queen: But not by him.

---

[99]**flats** i.e., flatlands near shore   **impetuous** violent (perhaps also with the meaning of *impiteous* [*impitious*, Q2], "pitiless")   [100]**head** insurrection   [102]**as** as if   [104]**The ratifiers . . . word** i.e., *antiquity* (or tradition) and *custom* ought to confirm (*ratify*) and underprop our every word or promise   [106]**Caps** (The caps are thrown in the air.)   [109]**counter** (A hunting term meaning to follow the trail in a direction opposite to that which the game has taken.)   [120]**between** in the middle of   [123]**fear our** fear for my   [124]**hedge** protect, as with a surrounding barrier   [125]**can . . . would** can only peep furtively, as through a barrier, at what it would intend   [126]**Acts . . . will** (but) performs little of what it intends

King: Let him demand his fill.

130 *Laertes:* How came he dead? I'll not be juggled with.
       To hell, allegiance! Vows, to the blackest devil!
       Conscience and grace, to the profoundest pit!
       I dare damnation. To this point I stand,
       That both the worlds I give to negligence,
135   Let come what comes, only I'll be revenged
       Most throughly for my father.

King: Who shall stay you?

Laertes: My will, not all the world's.
       And for my means, I'll husband them so well
       They shall go far with little.

140 *King:*   Good Laertes,
       If you desire to know the certainty
       Of your dear father, is 't writ in your revenge
       That, swoopstake, you will draw both friend and foe,
       Winner and loser?

145 *Laertes:* None but his enemies.

King: Will you know them, then?

Laertes: To his good friends thus wide I'll ope my arms,
       And like the kind life-rendering pelican
       Repast them with my blood.

King: Why, now you speak
150   Like a good child and a true gentleman.
       That I am guiltless of your father's death,
       And am most sensibly in grief for it,
       It shall as level to your judgment 'pear
       As day does to your eye.   *A noise within.*

Laertes: How now, what noise is that?

       Enter Ophelia.

155 *King:*   Let her come in.

Laertes: O heat, dry up my brains! Tears seven times salt
       Burn out the sense and virtue of mine eye!
       By heaven, thy madness shall be paid with weight

130**juggled with** cheated, deceived   133**To . . . stand** I am resolved in this   134**both . . . negligence** i.e., both this world and the next are of no consequence to me
136**throughly** thoroughly   138**My will . . . world's** I'll stop (stay) when my will is accomplished, not for anyone else's.   139**for** as for   143**swoopstake** i.e., indiscriminately (Literally, taking all stakes on the gambling table at once. *Draw* is also a gambling term, meaning "take from.")   148**pelican** (Refers to the belief that the female pelican fed its young with its own blood.)   149**Repast** feed   152**sensibly** feelingly   153**level** plain
157**virtue** faculty, power   158**paid with weight** repaid, avenged equally or more

Till our scale turn the beam. O rose of May!
Dear maid, kind sister, sweet Ophelia!   160
O heavens, is 't possible a young maid's wits
Should be as mortal as an old man's life?
Nature is fine in love, and where 'tis fine
It sends some precious instance of itself
After the thing it loves.   165

Ophelia:
    "They bore him barefaced on the bier,   *(Song.)*
      Hey non nonny, nonny, hey nonny,
    And in his grave rained many a tear—"
Fare you well, my dove!

Laertes: Hadst thou thy wits and didst persuade revenge,   170
  It could not move thus.

Ophelia: You must sing "A-down a-down," and you "call him a-down-a." O, how
the wheel becomes it! It is the false steward that stole his master's daughter.

Laertes: This nothing's more than matter.

Ophelia: There's rosemary, that's for remembrance; pray you, love, remember.   175
And there is pansies; that's for thoughts.

Laertes: A document in madness, thoughts and remembrance fitted.

Ophelia: There's fennel for you, and columbines. There's rue for you, and here's
some for me; we may call it herb of grace o' Sundays. You must wear your
rue with a difference. There's a daisy. I would give you some violets, but they   180
withered all when my father died. They say 'a made a good end—
  [*Sings.*]   "For bonny sweet Robin is all my joy."

Laertes: Thought and affliction, passion, hell itself,
  She turns to favor and to prettiness.

Ophelia:
    "And will 'a not come again?   *(Song.)*   185
    And will 'a not come again?
      No, no, he is dead.
      Go to thy deathbed,
    He never will come again.

[159]**beam** crossbar of a balance   [163]**fine in** refined by [164]**instance** token [165]**After . . .
loves** i.e., into the grave, along with Polonius [170]**persuade** argue cogently for
[172]**You . . . a-down-a** (Ophelia assigns the singing of refrains, like her own "Hey non
nonny," to others present.) [173]**wheel** spinning wheel as accompaniment to the song, or
refrain **false steward** (The story is unknown.) [174]**This . . . matter** this seeming
nonsense is more eloquent than sane utterance [175]**rosemary** (Used as a symbol of
remembrance both at weddings and at funerals.) [176]**pansies** (Emblems of love and
courtship; perhaps from French *pensées,* "thoughts.") [177]**document** instruction, lesson
[178]**fennel** (Emblem of flattery.) **columbines** (Emblems of unchastity or ingratitude.)
rue (Emblem of repentance—a signification that is evident in its popular name, *herb of
grace.*) [180]**with a difference** (A device used in heraldry to distinguish one family from
another on the coat of arms, here suggesting that Ophelia and the others have different
causes of sorrow and repentance; perhaps with a play on rue in the sense of "ruth,"
"pity.") **daisy** (Emblem of dissembling, faithlessness.) **violets** (Emblems of
faithfulness.) [183]**Thought** melancholy **passion** suffering [184]**favor** grace, beauty

190   "His beard was as white as snow,
          All flaxen was his poll.
               He is gone, he is gone,
               And we cast away moan.
          God ha' mercy on his soul!"

195   And of all Christian souls, I pray God. God b' wi' you.

                    [*Exit, followed by Gertrude.*]

Laertes: Do you see this, O God?

King: Laertes, I must commune with your grief,
          Or you deny me right. Go but apart,
          Make choice of whom your wisest friends you will,
200   And they shall hear and judge twixt you and me.
          If by direct or by collateral hand
          They find us touched, we will our kingdom give,
          Our crown, our life, and all that we call ours
          To you in satisfaction; but if not,
205   Be you content to lend your patience to us,
          And we shall jointly labor with your soul
          To give it due content.

Laertes: Let this be so.
          His means of death, his obscure funeral—
          No trophy, sword, nor hatchment o'er his bones,
210   No noble rite, nor formal ostentation—
          Cry to be heard, as 'twere from heaven to earth,
          That I must call 't in question.

King: So you shall,
          And where th' offense is, let the great ax fall.
          I pray you, go with me.   *Exeunt.*

4.6   *Enter Horatio and others.*

Horatio: What are they that would speak with me?

Gentleman: Seafaring men, sir. They say they have letters for you.

Horatio: Let them come in.   [*Exit Gentleman.*]
          I do not know from what part of the world
5   I should be greeted, if not from Lord Hamlet.

---

¹⁹¹**poll** head   ¹⁹⁹**whom** whichever of   ²⁰¹**collateral hand** indirect agency
²⁰²**us touched** me implicated   ²⁰⁹**trophy** memorial   **hatchment** tablet displaying the
armorial bearings of a deceased person   ²¹⁰**ostentation** ceremony   ²¹²**That** so that
call 't in question demand an explanation
4.6 Location: The castle.

Enter Sailors.

First Sailor: God bless you, sir.

Horatio: Let him bless thee too.

First Sailor: 'A shall, sir, an 't please him. There's a letter for you, sir—it came
   from th' ambassador that was bound for England—if your name be Horatio,
   as I am let to know it is.   [*He gives a letter.*]   10

Horatio [reads]: "Horatio, when thou shalt have overlooked this, give these fellows some means to the King; they have letters for him. Ere we were two
   days old at sea, a pirate of very warlike appointment gave us chase. Finding
   ourselves too slow of sail, we put on a compelled valor, and in the grapple I
   boarded them. On the instant they got clear of our ship, so I alone became   15
   their prisoner. They have dealt with me like thieves of mercy, but they knew
   what they did: I am to do a good turn for them. Let the King have the letters
   I have sent, and repair thou to me with as much speed as thou wouldest fly
   death. I have words to speak in thine ear will make thee dumb, yet are they
   much too light for the bore of the matter. These good fellows will bring thee   20
   where I am. Rosencrantz and Guildenstern hold their course for England. Of
   them I have much to tell thee. Farewell.

                                        He that thou knowest thine, Hamlet."

   Come, I will give you way for these your letters,
   And do 't the speedier that you may direct me   25
   To him from whom you brought them.   *Exeunt.*

4.7   *Enter King and Laertes.*

King: Now must your conscience my acquittance seal,
   And you must put me in your heart for friend,
   Sith you have heard, and with a knowing ear,
   That he which hath your noble father slain
   Pursued my life.

Laertes: It well appears. But tell me   5
   Why you proceeded not against these feats
   So crimeful and so capital in nature,
   As by your safety, greatness, wisdom, all things else,
   You mainly were stirred up.

---

[8]**an 't** if it   [9]**th' ambassador** (Evidently Hamlet. The sailor is being circumspect.)
[11]**overlooked** looked over   [12]**means** means of access   [13]**appointment** equipage
[16]**thieves of mercy** merciful thieves   [18]**repair** come   [20]**bore** caliber, i.e., importance
[24]**way** means of access
4.7. Location: The castle.
[1]**my acquittance seal** confirm or acknowledge my innocence   [3]**Sith** since   [6]**feats** acts
[7]**capital** punishable by death   [9]**mainly** greatly

10 *King:* O, for two special reasons,
    Which may to you perhaps seem much unsinewed,
    But yet to me they're strong. The Queen his mother
    Lives almost by his looks, and for myself—
    My virtue or my plague, be it either which—
15 She is so conjunctive to my life and soul
    That, as the star moves not but in his sphere,
    I could not but by her. The other motive
    Why to a public count I might not go
    Is the great love the general gender bear him,
20 Who, dipping all his faults in their affection,
    Work like the spring that turneth wood to stone,
    Convert his gyves to graces, so that my arrows,
    Too slightly timbered for so loud a wind,
    Would have reverted to my bow again
25 But not where I had aimed them.
Laertes: And so have I a noble father lost,
    A sister driven into desperate terms,
    Whose worth, if praises may go back again,
    Stood challenger on mount of all the age
30 For her perfections. But my revenge will come.
King: Break not your sleeps for that. You must not think
    That we are made of stuff so flat and dull
    That we can let our beard be shook with danger
    And think it pastime. You shortly shall hear more.
35 I loved your father, and we love ourself;
    And that, I hope, will teach you to imagine—

                Enter a Messenger with letters.

    How now? What news?
Messenger: Letters, my lord, from Hamlet:
    This to Your Majesty, this to the Queen.   [*He gives letters.*]
King: From Hamlet? Who brought them?

---

¹¹**unsinewed** weak   ¹⁵**conjunctive** closely united (An astronomical metaphor.)
¹⁶**his** its   **sphere** one of the hollow spheres in which, according to Ptolemaic astronomy,
the planets were supposed to move   ¹⁸**count** account, reckoning, indictment
¹⁹**general gender** common people   ²¹**Work** operate, act   **spring** i.e., a spring with such
a concentration of lime that it coats a piece of wood with limestone, in effect gilding and
petrifying it   ²²**gyves** fetters (which, gilded by the people's praise, would look like badges
of honor)   ²³**slightly timbered** light   **loud** (suggesting public outcry on Hamlet's
behalf)   ²⁴**reverted** returned   ²⁷**terms** state, condition   ²⁸**go back** i.e., recall what she
was   ²⁹**on mount** set up on high

Messenger: Sailors, my lord, they say. I saw them not.   40
    They were given me by Claudio. He received them
    Of him that brought them.
King: Laertes, you shall hear them.—
    Leave us.   [*Exit Messenger.*]
    [*He reads.*] "High and mighty, you shall know I am set naked on your
    kingdom. Tomorrow shall I beg leave to see your kingly eyes, when I shall,   45
    first asking your pardon, thereunto recount the occasion of my sudden and
    more strange return.   Hamlet."
    What should this mean? Are all the rest come back?
    Or is it some abuse, and no such thing?
Laertes: Know you the hand?
King: 'Tis Hamlet's character. "Naked!"   50
    And in a postscript here he says "alone."
    Can you devise me?
Laertes: I am lost in it, my lord. But let him come.
    It warms the very sickness in my heart
    That I shall live and tell him to his teeth,   55
    "Thus didst thou."
King: If it be so, Laertes—
    As how should it be so? How otherwise?—
    Will you be ruled by me?
Laertes: Ay, my lord,
    So you will not o'errule me to a peace.
King: To thine own peace. If he be now returned,   60
    As checking at his voyage, and that he means
    No more to undertake it, I will work him
    To an exploit, now ripe in my device,
    Under the which he shall not choose but fall;
    And for his death no wind of blame shall breathe,   65
    But even his mother shall uncharge the practice
    And call it accident.
Laertes: My lord, I will be ruled,
    The rather if you could devise it so
    That I might be the organ.

---

[44]**naked** destitute, unarmed, without following   [46]**pardon** permission   [49]**abuse** deceit
no such thing not what it appears   [50]**character** handwriting   [52]**devise** explain to
[56]**Thus didst thou** i.e., here's for what you did to my father   [57]**As . . . otherwise** how
can this (Hamlet's return) be true? Yet how otherwise than true (since we have the
evidence of his letter)?   [59]**So** provided that   [61]**checking at** i.e., turning aside from (like
a falcon leaving the quarry to fly at a chance bird)   **that** if   [63]**device** devising, invention
[66]**uncharge the practice** acquit the stratagem of being a plot   [69]**organ** agent, instrument

King: It falls right.

70   You have been talked of since your travel much,
        And that in Hamlet's hearing, for a quality
        Wherein they say you shine. Your sum of parts
        Did not together pluck such envy from him
        As did that one, and that, in my regard,
75   Of the unworthiest siege.

Laertes: What part is that, my lord?

King: A very ribbon in the cap of youth,
        Yet needful too, for youth no less becomes
        The light and careless livery that it wears
80   Than settled age his sables and his weeds
        Importing health and graveness. Two months since
        Here was a gentleman of Normandy.
        I have seen myself, and served against, the French,
        And they can well on horseback, but this gallant
85   Had witchcraft in 't; he grew unto his seat,
        And to such wondrous doing brought his horse
        As had he been incorpsed and demi-natured
        With the brave beast. So far he topped my thought
        That I in forgery of shapes and tricks
        Come short of what he did.

90 *Laertes:*   A Norman was 't?

King: A Norman.

Laertes: Upon my life, Lamord.

King: The very same.

Laertes: I know him well. He is the brooch indeed
        And gem of all the nation.

95 *King:* He made confession of you,
        And gave you such a masterly report
        For art and exercise in your defense,
        And for your rapier most especial,
        That he cried out 'twould be a sight indeed
100   If one could match you. Th' escrimers of their nation,
        He swore, had neither motion, guard, nor eye
        If you opposed them. Sir, this report of his
        Did Hamlet so envenom with his envy

---

[72]**Your . . . parts** i.e., all your other virtues   [75]**unworthiest siege** least important
rank   [78]**no less becomes** is no less suited by   [80]**his sables** its rich robes furred with
sable   **weeds** garments   [81]**Importing . . . graveness** signifying a concern for health
and dignified prosperity; also, giving an impression of comfortable prosperity
[84]**can well** are skilled   [87]**As . . . demi-natured** as if he had been of one body and
nearly of one nature (like the centaur)   [88]**topped** surpassed   [89]**forgery** imagining
[93]**brooch** ornament   [95]**confession** testimonial, admission of superiority
[97]**For . . . defense** with respect to your skill and practice with your weapon
[100]**escrimers** fencers

That he could nothing do but wish and beg
Your sudden coming o'er, to play with you.
Now, out of this— 105

Laertes: What out of this, my lord?

King: Laertes, was your father dear to you?
Or are you like the painting of a sorrow,
A face without a heart?

Laertes: Why ask you this? 110

King: Not that I think you did not love your father,
But that I know love is begun by time,
And that I see, in passages of proof,
Time qualifies the spark and fire of it.
There lives within the very flame of love
A kind of wick or snuff that will abate it, 115
And nothing is at a like goodness still,
For goodness, growing to a pleurisy,
Dies in his own too much. That we would do,
We should do when we would; for this "would" changes
And hath abatements and delays as many 120
As there are tongues, are hands, are accidents,
And then this "should" is like a spendthrift sigh,
That hurts by easing. But, to the quick o' th' ulcer:
Hamlet comes back. What would you undertake
To show yourself in deed your father's son 125
More than in words?

Laertes: To cut his throat i' the church.

King: No place, indeed, should murder sanctuarize;
Revenge should have no bounds. But good Laertes,
Will you do this, keep close within your chamber.
Hamlet returned shall know you are come home. 130
We'll put on those shall praise your excellence
And set a double varnish on the fame
The Frenchman gave you, bring you in fine together,

---

[105]**sudden** immediate   **play** fence   [111]**begun by time** i.e., created by the right circumstance and hence subject to change   [112]**passages of proof** actual instances that prove it   [113]**qualifies** weakens, moderates   [115]**snuff** the charred part of a candlewick   [116]**nothing . . . still** nothing remains at a constant level of perfection   [117]**pleurisy** excess, plethora (Literally, a chest inflammation.)   [118]**in . . . much** of its own excess   **That** that which   [120]**abatements** diminutions   [121]**As . . . accidents** as there are tongues to dissuade, hands to prevent, and chance events to intervene   [122]**spendthrift sigh** (An allusion to the belief that sighs draw blood from the heart.)   [123]**hurts by easing** i.e., costs the heart blood and wastes precious opportunity even while it affords emotional relief   **quick o' th' ulcer** i.e., heart of the matter   [127]**sanctuarize** protect from punishment (Alludes to the right of sanctuary with which certain religious places were invested.)   [129]**Will you do this** if you wish to do this   [131]**put on those shall** arrange for some to   [133]**in fine** finally

And wager on your heads. He, being remiss,
135   Most generous, and free from all contriving,
Will not peruse the foils, so that with ease,
Or with a little shuffling, you may choose
A sword unbated, and in a pass of practice
Requite him for your father.

Laertes: I will do 't,
140   And for that purpose I'll anoint my sword.
I bought an unction of a mountebank
So mortal that, but dip a knife in it,
Where it draws blood no cataplasm so rare,
Collected from all simples that have virtue
145   Under the moon, can save the thing from death
That is but scratched withal. I'll touch my point
With this contagion, that if I gall him slightly,
It may be death.

King: Let's further think of this,
Weigh what convenience both of time and means
150   May fit us to our shape. If this should fail,
And that our drift look through our bad performance,
'Twere better not assayed. Therefore this project
Should have a back or second, that might hold
If this did blast in proof. Soft, let me see.
155   We'll make a solemn wager on your cunnings—
I ha 't!
When in your motion you are hot and dry—
As make your bouts more violent to that end—
And that he calls for drink, I'll have prepared him
160   A chalice for the nonce, whereon but sipping,
If he by chance escape your venomed stuck,
Our purpose may hold there. [*A cry within.*] But stay, what noise?

         Enter Queen.

Queen: One woe doth tread upon another's heel,
So fast they follow. Your sister's drowned, Laertes.
165 *Laertes:* Drowned! O, where?
Queen: There is a willow grows askant the brook,
That shows his hoar leaves in the glassy stream;

[134]**remiss** negligently unsuspicious   [135]**generous** noble-minded   [138]**unbated** not
blunted, having no button   **pass of practice** treacherous thrust   [141]**unction** ointment
mountebank quack doctor   [143]**cataplasm** plaster or poultice   [144]**simples** herbs
virtue potency   [145]**Under the moon** i.e., anywhere (with reference perhaps to the
belief that herbs gathered at night had a special power)   [147]**gall** graze, wound   [150]**shape**
part we propose to act   [151]**drift . . . performance** intention should be made visible by
our bungling   [154]**blast in proof** burst in the test (like a cannon)   [155]**cunnings** respective
skills   [158]**As** i.e., and you should   [160]**nonce** occasion   [161]**stuck** thrust (From *stoccado*, a
fencing term.)   [166]**askant** aslant   [167]**hoar leaves** white or gray undersides of the leaves

Therewith fantastic garlands did she make
Of crowflowers, nettles, daisies, and long purples,
That liberal shepherds give a grosser name,   170
But our cold maids do dead men's fingers call them.
There on the pendent boughs her crownet weeds
Clamb'ring to hang, an envious sliver broke,
When down her weedy trophies and herself
Fell in the weeping brook. Her clothes spread wide,   175
And mermaidlike awhile they bore her up,
Which time she chanted snatches of old lauds,
As one incapable of her own distress,
Or like a creature native and endued
Unto that element. But long it could not be   180
Till that her garments, heavy with their drink,
Pulled the poor wretch from her melodious lay
To muddy death.

Laertes: Alas, then she is drowned?

Queen: Drowned, drowned.

Laertes: Too much of water hast thou, poor Ophelia,   185
And therefore I forbid my tears. But yet
It is our trick; nature her custom holds,
Let shame say what it will. [*He weeps.*] When these are gone,
The woman will be out. Adieu, my lord.
I have a speech of fire that fain would blaze,   190
But that this folly douts it.   *Exit.*

King: Let's follow, Gertrude.
How much I had to do to calm his rage!
Now fear I this will give it start again;
Therefore let's follow.   *Exeunt.*

5.1   *Enter two Clowns [with spades and mattocks].*

First Clown: Is she to be buried in Christian burial, when she willfully seeks her
    own salvation?

---

¹⁶⁹**long purples** early purple orchids   ¹⁷⁰**liberal** free-spoken   **a grosser name** (The
testicle-resembling tubers of the orchid, which also in some cases resemble *dead men's fin-*
gers, have earned various slang names like "dogstones" and "cullions.")   ¹⁷¹**cold** chaste
¹⁷²**pendent** overhanging   **crownet** made into a chaplet or coronet   ¹⁷³**envious**
sliver malicious branch   ¹⁷⁴**weedy** i.e., of plants   ¹⁷⁷**lauds** hymns   ¹⁷⁸**incapable of**
lacking capacity to apprehend   ¹⁷⁹**endued** adapted by nature   ¹⁸⁷**It is our trick** i.e.,
weeping is our natural way (when sad)   ^{188–189}**When . . . out** when my tears are all shed,
the woman in me will be expended, satisfied   ¹⁹¹**douts** extinguishes (The Second Quarto
reads "drowns.")
5.1. Location: A churchyard.
^{s.d.}**Clowns** rustics   ²**salvation** (A blunder for "damnation," or perhaps a suggestion that
Ophelia was taking her own shortcut to heaven.)

Second Clown: I tell thee she is; therefore make her grave straight. The crowner hath sat on her, and finds it Christian burial.

5 *First Clown:* How can that be, unless she drowned herself in her own defense?

Second Clown: Why, 'tis found so.

First Clown: It must be *se offendendo*, it cannot be else. For here lies the point: if I drown myself wittingly, it argues an act, and an act hath three branches—it is to act, to do, and to perform. Argal, she drowned herself wittingly.

10 *Second Clown:* Nay, but hear you, goodman delver—

First Clown: Give me leave. Here lies the water; good. Here stands the man; good. If the man go to this water and drown himself, it is, will he, nill he, he goes, mark you that. But if the water come to him and drown him, he drowns not himself. Argal, he that is not guilty of his own death shortens not his

15 own life.

Second Clown: But is this law?

First Clown: Ay, marry, is 't—crowner's quest law.

Second Clown: Will you ha' the truth on 't? If this had not been a gentlewoman, she should have been buried out o' Christian burial.

20 *First Clown:* Why, there thou sayst. And the more pity that great folk should have countenance in this world to drown or hang themselves, more than their even-Christian. Come, my spade. There is no ancient gentlemen but gardeners, ditchers, and grave makers. They hold up Adam's profession.

Second Clown: Was he a gentleman?

25 *First Clown:* 'A was the first that ever bore arms.

Second Clown: Why, he had none.

First Clown: What, art a heathen? How dost thou understand the Scripture? The Scripture says Adam digged. Could he dig without arms? I'll put another question to thee. If thou answerest me not to the purpose, confess thyself—

30 *Second Clown:* Go to.

First Clown: What is he that builds stronger than either the mason, the shipwright, or the carpenter?

Second Clown: The gallows maker, for that frame outlives a thousand tenants.

First Clown: I like thy wit well, in good faith. The gallows does well. But how

35 does it well? It does well to those that do ill. Now thou dost ill to say the

---

[3]**straight** straightway, immediately (But with a pun on *strait*, "narrow.") **crowner** coroner [4]**sat on her** conducted an inquest on her case **finds it** gives his official verdict that her means of death was consistent with [6]**found so** determined so in the coroner's verdict [7]**se offendendo** (A comic mistake for *se defendendo*, a term used in verdicts of justifiable homicide.) [9]**Argal** (Corruption of *ergo*, "therefore.") [10]**goodman** (An honorific title often used with the name of a profession or craft.) [12]**will he, nill he** whether he will or no, willy-nilly [17]**quest** inquest [20]**there thou sayst** i.e., that's right [21]**countenance** privilege [22]**even-Christian** fellow Christians **ancient** going back to ancient times [23]**hold up** maintain [25]**bore arms** (To be entitled to bear a coat of arms would make Adam a gentleman, but as one who bore a spade, our common ancestor was an ordinary delver in the earth.) [28]**arms** i.e., the arms of the body [29]**confess thyself** (The saying continues, "and be hanged.") [33]**frame** (1) gallows (2) structure [34]**does well** (1) is an apt answer (2) does a good turn

gallows is built stronger than the church. Argal, the gallows may do well to thee. To 't again, come.

Second Clown: "Who builds stronger than a mason, a shipwright, or a carpenter?"

First Clown: Ay, tell me that, and unyoke.

Second Clown: Marry, now I can tell.   40

First Clown: To 't.

Second Clown: Mass, I cannot tell.

Enter Hamlet and Horatio [at a distance].

First Clown: Cudgel thy brains no more about it, for your dull ass will not mend his pace with beating; and when you are asked this question next, say "a grave maker." The houses he makes lasts till doomsday. Go get thee in and   45
fetch me a stoup of liquor.   [*Exit Second Clown. First Clown digs.*]

Song.

"In youth, when I did love, did love,
  Methought it was very sweet,
To contract—O—the time for—a—my behove,
  O, methought there—a—was nothing—a—meet."   50

Hamlet: Has this fellow no feeling of his business, 'a sings in grave-making?

Horatio: Custom hath made it in him a property of easiness.

Hamlet: 'Tis e'en so. The hand of little employment hath the daintier sense.

First Clown: Song.

"But age with his stealing steps
  Hath clawed me in his clutch,   55
And hath shipped me into the land,
  As if I had never been such."

[*He throws up a skull.*]

Hamlet: That skull had a tongue in it and could sing once. How the knave jowls it to the ground, as if 'twere Cain's jawbone, that did the first murder! This might be the pate of a politician, which this ass now o'erreaches, one that   60
would circumvent God, might it not?

---

[39]**unyoke** i.e., after this great effort, you may unharness the team of your wits
[42]**Mass** by the Mass   [46]**stoup** two-quart measure   [47]**In . . . love** (This and the two following stanzas, with nonsensical variations, are from a poem attributed to Lord Vaux and printed in *Tottel's Miscellany*, 1557. The *O* and *a* [for "ah"] seemingly are the grunts of the digger.)   [49]**To contract . . . behove** i.e., to shorten the time for my own advantage (Perhaps he means to *prolong* it.)   [50]**meet** suitable, i.e., more suitable   [51]**'a** that he
[52]**property of easiness** something he can do easily and indifferently   [53]**daintier sense** more delicate sense of feeling   [56]**into the land** i.e., toward my grave (?) (But note the lack of rhyme in *steps, land.*)   [58]**jowls** dashes (with a pun on *jowl*, "jawbone")
[60]**politician** schemer, plotter   **o'erreaches** circumvents, gets the better of (with a quibble on the literal sense)

Horatio: It might, my lord.

Hamlet: Or of a courtier, which could say, "Good morrow, sweet lord! How dost thou, sweet lord?" This might be my Lord Such-a-one, that praised my Lord

65 Such-a-one's horse when 'a meant to beg it, might it not?

Horatio: Ay, my lord.

Hamlet: Why, e'en so, and now my Lady Worm's, chapless, and knocked about the mazard with a sexton's spade. Here's fine revolution, an we had the trick to see 't. Did these bones cost no more the breeding but to play at loggets

70 with them? Mine ache to think on 't.

First Clown: *Song.*

"A pickax and a spade, a spade,
    For and a shrouding sheet;
O, a pit of clay for to be made
    For such a guest is meet."

[*He throws up another skull.*]

75 *Hamlet:* There's another. Why may not that be the skull of a lawyer? Where be his quiddities now, his quillities, his cases, his tenures, and his tricks? Why does he suffer this mad knave now to knock him about the sconce with a dirty shovel, and will not tell him of his action of battery? Hum, this fellow might be in 's time a great buyer of land, with his statutes, his recognizances,

80 his fines, his double vouchers, his recoveries. Is this the fine of his fines and the recovery of his recoveries, to have his fine pate full of fine dirt? Will his vouchers vouch him no more of his purchases, and double ones too, than the length and breadth of a pair of indentures? The very conveyances of his lands will scarcely lie in this box, and must th' inheritor himself have no more, ha?

85 *Horatio:* Not a jot more, my lord.

Hamlet: Is not parchment made of sheepskins?

Horatio: Ay, my lord, and of calves' skins too.

---

[67]**chapless** having no lower jaw   [68]**mazard** i.e., head (Literally, a drinking vessel.) **revolution** turn of Fortune's wheel, change   **an** if   [68–69]**trick to see** knack of seeing   [69]**cost . . . but** involve so little expense and care in upbringing that we may   **loggets** a game in which pieces of hard wood shaped like Indian clubs or bowling pins are thrown to lie as near as possible to a stake   [72]**For and** and moreover   [76]**quiddities** subtleties, quibbles (From Latin *quid*, "a thing.")   **quillities** verbal niceties, subtle distinctions (Variation of *quiddities*.)   **tenures** the holding of a piece of property or office, or the conditions or period of such holding   [77]**sconce** head   [78]**action of battery** lawsuit about physical assault   [79]**statutes, recognizances** legal documents guaranteeing a debt by attaching land and property   [80]**fines, recoveries** ways of converting entailed estates into "fee simple" or freehold   **double** signed by two signatories   **vouchers** guarantees of the legality of a title to real estate   [80–81]**fine of his fines . . . fine pate . . . fine dirt** end of his legal maneuvers . . . elegant head . . . minutely sifted dirt   [83]**pair of indentures** legal document drawn up in duplicate on a single sheet and then cut apart on a zigzag line so that each pair was uniquely matched (Hamlet may refer to two rows of teeth or dentures.)   **conveyances** deeds   [84]**box** (1) deed box (2) coffin. ("Skull" has been suggested.)   **inheritor** possessor, owner

Hamlet: They are sheep and calves which seek out assurance in that. I will speak to this fellow.—Whose grave's this, sirrah?

First Clown: Mine, sir. 90

   [*Sings.*] "O, pit of clay for to be made
        For such a guest is meet."

Hamlet: I think it be thine, indeed, for thou liest in 't.

First Clown: You lie out on 't, sir, and therefore 'tis not yours. For my part, I do not lie in 't, yet it is mine. 95

Hamlet: Thou dost lie in 't, to be in 't and say it is thine. 'Tis for the dead, not for the quick; therefore thou liest.

First Clown: 'Tis a quick lie, sir; 'twill away again from me to you.

Hamlet: What man dost thou dig it for?

First Clown: For no man, sir. 100

Hamlet: What woman, then?

First Clown: For none, neither.

Hamlet: Who is to be buried in 't?

First Clown: One that was a woman, sir, but, rest her soul, she's dead.

Hamlet: How absolute the knave is! We must speak by the card, or equivocation 105
will undo us. By the Lord, Horatio, this three years I have took note of it: the age is grown so picked that the toe of the peasant comes so near the heel of the courtier, he galls his kibe.—How long hast thou been grave maker?

First Clown: Of all the days i' the year, I came to 't that day that our last king Hamlet overcame Fortinbras. 110

Hamlet: How long is that since?

First Clown: Cannot you tell that? Every fool can tell that. It was that very day that young Hamlet was born—he that is mad and sent into England.

Hamlet: Ay, marry, why was he sent into England?

First Clown: Why, because 'a was mad. 'A shall recover his wits there, or if 'a do 115
not, 'tis no great matter there.

Hamlet: Why?

First Clown: 'Twill not be seen in him there. There the men are as mad as he.

Hamlet: How came he mad?

First Clown: Very strangely, they say. 120

Hamlet: How strangely?

First Clown: Faith, e'en with losing his wits.

Hamlet: Upon what ground?

First Clown: Why, here in Denmark. I have been sexton here, man and boy, thirty years. 125

Hamlet: How long will a man lie i' th' earth ere he rot?

---

[88] **assurance in that** safety in legal parchments   [89] **sirrah** (A term of address to inferiors.)   [97] **quick** living   [105] **absolute** strict, precise   **by the card** i.e., with precision (Literally, by the mariner's compass-card, on which the points of the compass were marked.) **equivocation** ambiguity in the use of terms   [106] **took** taken   [107] **picked** refined, fastidious   [108] **galls his kibe** chafes the courtier's chilblain   [123] **ground** cause (But, in the next line, the gravedigger takes the word in the sense of "land," "country.")

First Clown: Faith, if 'a be not rotten before 'a die—as we have many pocky
    corpses nowadays, that will scarce hold the laying in—'a will last you some
    eight year or nine year. A tanner will last you nine year.

130 *Hamlet:* Why he more than another?

First Clown: Why, sir, his hide is so tanned with his trade that 'a will keep out
    water a great while, and your water is a sore decayer of your whoreson dead
    body. [*He picks up a skull.*] Here's a skull now hath lien you i' th' earth three-
    and-twenty years.

135 *Hamlet:* Whose was it?

First Clown: A whoreson mad fellow's it was. Whose do you think it was?

Hamlet: Nay, I know not.

First Clown: A pestilence on him for a mad rogue! 'A poured a flagon of Rhenish
    on my head once. This same skull, sir, was, sir, Yorick's skull, the King's jester.

140 *Hamlet:* This?

First Clown: E'en that.

Hamlet: Let me see. [*He takes the skull.*] Alas, poor Yorick! I knew him, Horatio, a
    fellow of infinite jest, of most excellent fancy. He hath bore me on his back a
    thousand times, and now how abhorred in my imagination it is! My gorge

145   rises at it. Here hung those lips that I have kissed I know not how oft. Where
    be your gibes now? Your gambols, your songs, your flashes of merriment that
    were wont to set the table on a roar? Not one now, to mock your own grin-
    ning? Quite chopfallen? Now get you to my lady's chamber and tell her, let
    her paint an inch thick, to this favor she must come. Make her laugh at that.

150   Prithee, Horatio, tell me one thing.

Horatio: What's that, my lord?

Hamlet: Dost thou think Alexander looked o' this fashion i' th' earth?

Horatio: E'en so.

Hamlet: And smelt so? Pah! [*He throws down the skull.*]

155 *Horatio:* E'en so, my lord.

Hamlet: To what base uses we may return, Horatio! Why may not imagination
    trace the noble dust of Alexander till 'a find it stopping a bunghole?

Horatio: 'Twere to consider too curiously to consider so.

Hamlet: No, faith, not a jot, but to follow him thither with modesty enough,

160   and likelihood to lead it. As thus: Alexander died, Alexander was buried,
    Alexander returneth to dust, the dust is earth, of earth we make loam, and
    why of that loam whereto he was converted might they not stop a beer barrel?

---

[127]**pocky** rotten, diseased (Literally, with the pox, or syphilis.)   [128]**hold the laying in**
hold together long enough to be interred   **last you** last (*You* is used colloquially here
and in the following lines.)   [132]**sore** i.e., terrible, great   **whoreson** i.e., vile, scurvy
[133]**lien you** lain (See the note at line 128.)   [138]**Rhenish** Rhine wine   [143]**bore** borne
[144-145]**My gorge rises** i.e., I feel nauseated   [147]**were wont** used   [147-148]**mock your
own grinning** mock at the way your skull seems to be grinning (just as you used to mock
at yourself and those who grinned at you)   [148]**chopfallen** (1) lacking the lower jaw
(2) dejected   [149]**favor** aspect, appearance   [157]**bunghole** hole for filling or emptying a
cask   [158]**curiously** minutely   [159]**modesty** plausible moderation   [161]**loam** mortar
consisting chiefly of moistened clay and straw

Imperious Caesar, dead and turned to clay,
Might stop a hole to keep the wind away.
O, that that earth which kept the world in awe   165
Should patch a wall t' expel the winter's flaw!

> *Enter King, Queen, Laertes, and the corpse [of Ophelia, in procession, with Priest, lords, etc.].*

But soft, but soft awhile! Here comes the King,
The Queen, the courtiers. Who is this they follow?
And with such maimèd rites? This doth betoken
The corpse they follow did with desperate hand   170
Fordo its own life. 'Twas of some estate.
Couch we awhile and mark.

> *[He and Horatio conceal themselves.*
> *Ophelia's body is taken to the grave.]*

Laertes: What ceremony else?
Hamlet [to Horatio]: That is Laertes, a very noble youth. Mark.
Laertes: What ceremony else?   175
Priest: Her obsequies have been as far enlarged
   As we have warranty. Her death was doubtful,
   And but that great command o'ersways the order
   She should in ground unsanctified been lodged
   Till the last trumpet. For charitable prayers,   180
   Shards, flints, and pebbles should be thrown on her.
   Yet here she is allowed her virgin crants,
   Her maiden strewments, and the bringing home
   Of bell and burial.
Laertes: Must there no more be done?
Priest: No more be done.   185
   We should profane the service of the dead
   To sing a requiem and such rest to her
   As to peace-parted souls.
Laertes: Lay her i' th' earth,
   And from her fair and unpolluted flesh
   May violets spring! I tell thee, churlish priest,   190
   A ministering angel shall my sister be
   When thou liest howling.

---

[163]**Imperious** imperial   [166]**flaw** gust of wind   [167]**soft** i.e., wait, be careful
[169]**maimèd** mutilated, incomplete   [171]**Fordo** destroy **estate** rank   [172]**Couch we** let's
hide, lie low   [177]**warranty** i.e., ecclesiastical authority   [178]**great . . . order** orders
from on high overrule the prescribed procedures   [179]**She should . . . lodged** she
should have been buried in unsanctified ground   [180]**For** in place of   [181]**Shards**
broken bits of pottery   [182]**crants** garlands betokening maidenhood   [183]**strewments**
flowers strewn on a coffin   [183–184]**bringing . . . burial** laying the body to rest, to the
sound of the bell   [187]**such rest** i.e., to pray for such rest   [188]**peace-parted souls**
those who have died at peace with God   [190]**violets** (See 4.5.180 and note.)   [192]**howling**
i.e., in hell

Hamlet [to Horatio]: What, the fair Ophelia!

Queen [scattering flowers]: Sweets to the sweet! Farewell.

    I hoped thou shouldst have been my Hamlet's wife.

195   I thought thy bride-bed to have decked, sweet maid,

    And not t' have strewed thy grave.

Laertes: O, treble woe

    Fall ten times treble on that cursèd head

    Whose wicked deed thy most ingenious sense

    Deprived thee of! Hold off the earth awhile,

200   Till I have caught her once more in mine arms.

          [He leaps into the grave and embraces Ophelia.]

    Now pile your dust upon the quick and dead,

    Till of this flat a mountain you have made

    T' o'ertop old Pelion or the skyish head

    Of blue Olympus.

Hamlet [coming forward]: What is he whose grief

205   Bears such an emphasis, whose phrase of sorrow

    Conjures the wandering stars and makes them stand

    Like wonder-wounded hearers? This is I,

    Hamlet the Dane.

Laertes [grappling with him]: The devil take thy soul!

Hamlet: Thou pray'st not well.

210   I prithee, take thy fingers from my throat,

    For though I am not splenitive and rash,

    Yet have I in me something dangerous,

    Which let thy wisdom fear. Hold off thy hand.

King: Pluck them asunder.

215 *Queen:* Hamlet, Hamlet!

All: Gentlemen!

Horatio: Good my lord, be quiet. *[Hamlet and Laertes are parted.]*

Hamlet: Why, I will fight with him upon this theme

    Until my eyelids will no longer wag.

220 *Queen:* O my son, what theme?

---

¹⁹⁸**ingenious sense** a mind that is quick, alert, of fine qualities ^{203–204}**Pelion, Olympus** sacred mountains in the north of Thessaly; see also *Ossa*, below, at line 235 ²⁰⁵**emphasis** i.e., rhetorical and florid emphasis (*Phrase* has a similar rhetorical connotation.) ²⁰⁶**wandering stars** planets ²⁰⁷**wonder-wounded** struck with amazement ²⁰⁸**the Dane** (This title normally signifies the King; see 1.1.17 and note.) ^{s.d.}**grappling with him** The testimony of the First Quarto that *"Hamlet leaps in after Laertes"* and the "Elegy on Burbage" ("Oft have I seen him leap into the grave") seem to indicate one way in which this fight was staged; however, the difficulty of fitting two contenders and Ophelia's body into a confined space (probably the trapdoor) suggests to many editors the alternative, that Laertes jumps out of the grave to attack Hamlet.) ²¹¹**splenitive** quick-tempered ²¹⁹**wag** move (A fluttering eyelid is a conventional sign that life has not yet gone.)

Hamlet: I loved Ophelia. Forty thousand brothers
    Could not with all their quantity of love
    Make up my sum. What wilt thou do for her?
King: O, he is mad, Laertes.
Queen: For love of God, forbear him.   225
Hamlet: 'Swounds, show me what thou'lt do.
    Woo't weep? Woo't fight? Woo't fast? Woo't tear thyself?
    Woo't drink up eisel? Eat a crocodile?
    I'll do 't. Dost come here to whine?
    To outface me with leaping in her grave?   230
    Be buried quick with her, and so will I.
    And if thou prate of mountains, let them throw
    Millions of acres on us, till our ground,
    Singeing his pate against the burning zone,
    Make Ossa like a wart! Nay, an thou'lt mouth,   235
    I'll rant as well as thou.
Queen: This is mere madness,
    And thus awhile the fit will work on him;
    Anon, as patient as the female dove
    When that her golden couplets are disclosed,
    His silence will sit drooping.   240
Hamlet: Hear you, sir.
    What is the reason that you use me thus?
    I loved you ever. But it is no matter.
    Let Hercules himself do what he may,
    The cat will mew, and dog will have his day.
               Exit Hamlet.
King: I pray thee, good Horatio, wait upon him.   245
             [Exit Horatio.]
    [To Laertes.] Strengthen your patience in our last night's speech;
    We'll put the matter to the present push.—
    Good Gertrude, set some watch over your son.—

---

[225]**forbear him** leave him alone   [226]**'Swounds** by His (Christ's) wounds   [227]**Woo't**
wilt thou   [228]**drink up** drink deeply   **eisel** vinegar   **crocodile** (Crocodiles were tough
and dangerous, and were supposed to shed hypocritical tears.)   [231]**quick** alive
[234]**his pate** its head, i.e., top   **burning zone** zone in the celestial sphere containing the
sun's orbit, between the tropics of Cancer and Capricorn   [235]**Ossa** another mountain in
Thessaly. (In their war against the Olympian gods, the giants attempted to heap Ossa on
Pelion to scale Olympus.)   **an** if   **mouth** i.e., rant   [236]**mere** utter   [239]**golden**
couplets two baby pigeons, covered with yellow down   **disclosed** hatched
[243–244]**Let . . . day** i.e., (1) even Hercules couldn't stop Laertes' theatrical rant (2) I, too,
will have my turn; i.e., despite any blustering attempts at interference, every person will
sooner or later do what he or she must do   [246]**in** i.e., by recalling   [247]**present push**
immediate test

This grave shall have a living monument.

250 An hour of quiet shortly shall we see;

Till then, in patience our proceeding be. *Exeunt.*

5.2 *Enter Hamlet and Horatio.*

Hamlet: So much for this, sir; now shall you see the other.

You do remember all the circumstance?

Horatio: Remember it, my lord!

Hamlet: Sir, in my heart there was a kind of fighting

5 That would not let me sleep. Methought I lay

Worse than the mutines in the bilboes. Rashly,

And praised be rashness for it—let us know

Our indiscretion sometimes serves us well

When our deep plots do pall, and that should learn us

10 There's a divinity that shapes our ends,

Rough-hew them how we will—

Horatio: That is most certain.

Hamlet: Up from my cabin,

My sea-gown scarfed about me, in the dark

Groped I to find out them, had my desire,

15 Fingered their packet, and in fine withdrew

To mine own room again, making so bold,

My fears forgetting manners, to unseal

Their grand commission; where I found, Horatio—

Ah, royal knavery!—an exact command,

20 Larded with many several sorts of reasons

Importing Denmark's health and England's too,

With, ho! such bugs and goblins in my life,

That on the supervise, no leisure bated,

No, not to stay the grinding of the ax,

25 My head should be struck off.

Horatio: Is 't possible?

Hamlet [giving a document]: Here's the commission. Read it at more leisure.

But wilt thou hear now how I did proceed?

Horatio: I beseech you.

249living lasting (For Laertes' private understanding, Claudius also hints that Hamlet's death will serve as such a monument.)   **250hour of quiet** time free of conflict
5.2. Location: The castle.
1see the other hear the other news   **6mutines** mutineers   **bilboes** shackles   **Rashly** on impulse (This adverb goes with lines 12 ff.)   **7know** acknowledge   **8indiscretion** lack of foresight and judgment (not an indiscreet act)   **9pall** fail, falter, go stale   **learn** teach   **11Rough-hew** shape roughly   **13sea-gown** seaman's coat   **scarfed** loosely wrapped   **14them** i.e., Rosencrantz and Guildenstern   **15Fingered** pilfered, pinched   **in fine** finally, in conclusion   **20Larded** garnished   **several** different   **21Importing** relating to   **22bugs** bugbears, hobgoblins   **in my life** i.e., to be feared if I were allowed to live   **23supervise** reading   **leisure bated** delay allowed   **24stay** await

Hamlet: Being thus benetted round with villainies—
    Ere I could make a prologue to my brains, 30
    They had begun the play—I sat me down,
    Devised a new commission, wrote it fair.
    I once did hold it, as our statists do,
    A baseness to write fair, and labored much
    How to forget that learning, but, sir, now 35
    It did me yeoman's service. Wilt thou know
    Th' effect of what I wrote?
Horatio: Ay, good my lord.
Hamlet: An earnest conjuration from the King,
    As England was his faithful tributary,
    As love between them like the palm might flourish, 40
    As peace should still her wheaten garland wear
    And stand a comma 'tween their amities,
    And many suchlike "as"es of great charge,
    That on the view and knowing of these contents,
    Without debatement further more or less, 45
    He should those bearers put to sudden death,
    Not shriving time allowed.
Horatio: How was this sealed?
Hamlet: Why, even in that was heaven ordinant.
    I had my father's signet in my purse,
    Which was the model of that Danish seal; 50
    Folded the writ up in the form of th' other,
    Subscribed it, gave 't th' impression, placed it safely,
    The changeling never known. Now, the next day
    Was our sea fight, and what to this was sequent
    Thou knowest already. 55
Horatio: So Guildenstern and Rosencrantz go to 't.
Hamlet: Why, man, they did make love to this employment.
    They are not near my conscience. Their defeat
    Does by their own insinuation grow.
    'Tis dangerous when the baser nature comes 60

[30-31]**Ere . . . play** before I could consciously turn my brain to the matter, it had started working on a plan   [32]**fair** in a clear hand   [33]**statists** statesmen   [34]**baseness** i.e., lower-class trait   [36]**yeoman's** i.e., substantial, faithful, loyal   [37]**effect** purport   [38]**conjuration** entreaty   [40]**palm** (An image of health; see Psalm 92:12.)   [41]**still** always **wheaten garland** (Symbolic of fruitful agriculture, of peace and plenty.)   [42]**comma** (Indicating continuity, link.)   [43]**"as"es** (1) the "whereases" of a formal document (2) asses   **charge** (1) import (2) burden (appropriate to asses)   [47]**shriving time** time for confession and absolution   [48]**ordinant** directing   [49]**signet** small seal   [50]**model** replica   [51]**writ** writing   [52]**Subscribed** signed (with forged signature)   **impression** i.e., with a wax seal   [53]**changeling** i.e., substituted letter (Literally, a fairy child substituted for a human one.)   [54]**was sequent** followed   [58]**defeat** destruction [59]**insinuation** intrusive intervention, sticking their noses in my business   [60]**baser** of lower social station

Between the pass and fell incensèd points
Of mighty opposites.

Horatio: Why, what a king is this!

Hamlet: Does it not, think thee, stand me now upon—

He that hath killed my king and whored my mother,

65   Popped in between th' election and my hopes,

Thrown out his angle for my proper life,

And with such cozenage—is 't not perfect conscience

To quit him with this arm? And is 't not to be damned

To let this canker of our nature come

70   In further evil?

Horatio: It must be shortly known to him from England

What is the issue of the business there.

Hamlet: It will be short. The interim is mine,

And a man's life's no more than to say "one."

75   But I am very sorry, good Horatio,

That to Laertes I forgot myself,

For by the image of my cause I see

The portraiture of his. I'll court his favors.

But, sure, the bravery of his grief did put me

Into a tow'ring passion.

80 *Horatio:*   Peace, who comes here?

Enter a Courtier [Osric].

Osric: Your lordship is right welcome back to Denmark.

Hamlet: I humbly thank you, sir. [*To Horatio.*] Dost know this water fly?

Horatio: No, my good lord.

Hamlet: Thy state is the more gracious, for 'tis a vice to know him. He hath much

85   land, and fertile. Let a beast be lord of beasts, and his crib shall stand at the

King's mess. 'Tis a chuff, but, as I say, spacious in the possession of dirt.

Osric: Sweet lord, if your lordship were at leisure, I should impart a thing to you

from His Majesty.

Hamlet: I will receive it, sir, with all diligence of spirit. Put your bonnet to his

90   right use; 'tis for the head.

Osric: I thank your lordship, it is very hot.

Hamlet: No, believe me, 'tis very cold. The wind is northerly.

Osric: It is indifferent cold, my lord, indeed.

---

[61]**pass** thrust   **fell** fierce   [62]**opposites** antagonists   [63]**stand me now upon** become
incumbent on me now   [65]**election** (The Danish monarch was "elected" by a small
number of high-ranking electors.)   [66]**angle** fishhook   **proper** very   [67]**cozenage**
trickery   [68]**quit** requite; pay back   [69]**canker** ulcer   [69-70]**come In** grow into
[74]**a man's . . . "one"** one's whole life occupies such a short time, only as long as it takes to
count to 1   [79]**bravery** bravado   [85-86]**Let . . . mess** i.e., if a man, no matter how
beastlike, is as rich in livestock and possessions as Osric, he may eat at the King's table
[85]**crib** manger   [86]**chuff** boor, churl (The Second Quarto spelling, *chough*, is a variant
spelling that also suggests the meaning here of "chattering jackdaw.")   [89]**bonnet** any kind
of cap or hat   **his** its   [93]**indifferent** somewhat

Hamlet: But yet methinks it is very sultry and hot for my complexion.

Osric: Exceedingly, my lord. It is very sultry, as 'twere—I cannot tell how. My   95
lord, His Majesty bade me signify to you that 'a has laid a great wager on
your head. Sir, this is the matter—

Hamlet: I beseech you, remember.   [*Hamlet moves him to put on his hat.*]

Osric: Nay, good my lord; for my ease, in good faith. Sir, here is newly come to
court Laertes—believe me, an absolute gentleman, full of most excellent   100
differences, of very soft society and great showing. Indeed, to speak feelingly
of him, he is the card or calendar of gentry, for you shall find in him the
continent of what part a gentleman would see.

Hamlet: Sir, his definement suffers no perdition in you, though I know to divide
him inventorially would dozy th' arithmetic of memory, and yet but yaw   105
neither in respect of his quick sail. But, in the verity of extolment, I take him
to be a soul of great article, and his infusion of such dearth and rareness as, to
make true diction of him, his semblable is his mirror and who else would
trace him his umbrage, nothing more.

Osric: Your lordship speaks most infallibly of him.   110

Hamlet: The concernancy, sir? Why do we wrap the gentleman in our more
rawer breath?

Osric: Sir?

Horatio: Is 't not possible to understand in another tongue? You will do 't, sir,
really.   115

Hamlet: What imports the nomination of this gentleman?

Osric: Of Laertes?

Horatio [to Hamlet]: His purse is empty already; all 's golden words are spent.

Hamlet: Of him, sir.

---

[94]**complexion** temperament   [99]**for my ease**   (A conventional reply declining the
invitation to put his hat back on.)   [100]**absolute** perfect   [101]**differences** special qualities
soft society agreeable manners   **great showing** distinguished appearance   **feelingly**
with just perception   [102]**card** chart, map   **calendar** guide   **gentry** good breeding
[102–103]**the continent . . . see** one who contains in him all the qualities a gentleman would
like to see (A *continent* is that which contains.)   [104]**definement** definition (Hamlet
proceeds to mock Osric by throwing his lofty diction back at him.)   **perdition** loss,
diminution   **you** your description   [104–105]**divide him inventorially** enumerate his
graces   [105]**dozy** dizzy   **yaw** swing unsteadily off course (Said of a ship.)   [106]**neither** for
all that   **in respect of** in comparison with   **in . . . extolment** in true praise (of him)
[107]**of great article** one with many articles in his inventory   **infusion** essence, character
infused into him by nature   **dearth and rareness** rarity   [108]**make true diction** speak
truly   **semblable** only true likeness   [108–109]**who . . . trace** any other person who would
wish to follow   [109]**umbrage** shadow   [111]**concernancy** import, relevance
[112]**rawer breath** unrefined speech that can only come short in praising him   [114]**to
understand . . . tongue** i.e., for you, Osric, to understand when someone else speaks
your language. (Horatio twits Osric for not being able to understand the kind of flowery
speech he himself uses, when Hamlet speaks in such a vein. Alternatively, all this could
be said to Hamlet.)   **You will do 't** i.e., you can if you try, or, you may well have to try
(to speak plainly)   [116]**nomination** naming

120 *Osric:* I know you are not ignorant—

Hamlet: I would you did, sir. Yet in faith if you did, it would not much approve me. Well, sir?

Osric: You are not ignorant of what excellence Laertes is—

Hamlet: I dare not confess that, lest I should compare with him in excellence. But
125 to know a man well were to know himself.

Osric: I mean, sir, for his weapon; but in the imputation laid on him by them, in his meed he's unfellowed.

Hamlet: What's his weapon?

Osric: Rapier and dagger.

130 *Hamlet:* That's two of his weapons—but well.

Osric: The King, sir, hath wagered with him six Barbary horses, against the which he has impawned, as I take it, six French rapiers and poniards, with their assigns, as girdle, hangers, and so. Three of the carriages, in faith, are very dear to fancy, very responsive to the hilts, most delicate carriages, and of very
135 liberal conceit.

Hamlet: What call you the carriages?

Horatio [to Hamlet]: I knew you must be edified by the margent ere you had done.

Osric: The carriages, sir, are the hangers.

140 *Hamlet:* The phrase would be more germane to the matter if we could carry a cannon by our sides; I would it might be hangers till then. But, on: six Barbary horses against six French swords, their assigns, and three liberal-conceited carriages; that's the French bet against the Danish. Why is this impawned, as you call it?

145 *Osric:* The King, sir, hath laid, sir, that in a dozen passes between yourself and him, he shall not exceed you three hits. He hath laid on twelve for nine, and it would come to immediate trial, if your lordship would vouchsafe the answer.

Hamlet: How if I answer no?

150 *Osric:* I mean, my lord, the opposition of your person in trial.

---

[121]**approve** commend   [124–125]**I dare . . . himself** I dare not boast of knowing Laertes' excellence lest I seem to imply a comparable excellence in myself. Certainly, to know another person well, one must know oneself.   [126]**for** i.e., with   **imputation . . . them** reputation given him by others   [127]**meed** merit   **unfellowed** unmatched   [130]**but well** but never mind   [132]**he** i.e., Laertes   **impawned** staked, wagered   **poniards** daggers   [133]**assigns** appurtenances   **hangers** straps on the sword belt (*girdle*), from which the sword hung   **and so** and so on   **carriages** (An affected way of saying *hangers*; literally, gun carriages.)   [134]**dear to fancy** delightful to the fancy   **responsive** corresponding closely, matching or well adjusted   **delicate** (i.e., in workmanship)   [135]**liberal conceit** elaborate design   [137]**margent** margin of a book, place for explanatory notes   [145]**laid** wagered   **passes** bouts (The odds of the betting are hard to explain. Possibly the King bets that Hamlet will win at least five out of twelve, at which point Laertes raises the odds against himself by betting he will win nine.)   [147–148]**vouchsafe the answer** be so good as to accept the challenge (Hamlet deliberately takes the phrase in its literal sense of replying.)

Hamlet: Sir, I will walk here in the hall. If it please His Majesty, it is the breathing
time of day with me. Let the foils be brought, the gentleman willing, and the
King hold his purpose, I will win for him an I can; if not, I will gain nothing
but my shame and the odd hits.

Osric: Shall I deliver you so? 155

Hamlet: To this effect, sir—after what flourish your nature will.

Osric: I commend my duty to your lordship.

Hamlet: Yours, yours. [*Exit Osric.*] 'A does well to commend it himself; there are
no tongues else for 's turn.

Horatio: This lapwing runs away with the shell on his head. 160

Hamlet: 'A did comply with his dug before 'a sucked it. Thus has he—and many
more of the same breed that I know the drossy age dotes on—only got the
tune of the time and, out of an habit of encounter, a kind of yeasty collection,
which carries them through and through the most fanned and winnowed
opinions; and do but blow them to their trial, the bubbles are out. 165

      Enter a Lord.

Lord: My lord, His Majesty commended him to you by young Osric, who brings
back to him that you attend him in the hall. He sends to know if your pleasure hold to play with Laertes, or that you will take longer time.

Hamlet: I am constant to my purposes; they follow the King's pleasure. If his
fitness speaks, mine is ready; now or whensoever, provided I be so able as 170
now.

Lord: The King and Queen and all are coming down.

Hamlet: In happy time.

Lord: The Queen desires you to use some gentle entertainment to Laertes before
you fall to play. 175

Hamlet: She well instructs me.   [*Exit Lord.*]

Horatio: You will lose, my lord.

[151–152]**breathing time** exercise period   [152]**Let** i.e., if   [155]**deliver you** report what you
say   [157]**commend** commit to your favor (A conventional salutation, but Hamlet wryly
uses a more literal meaning, "recommend," "praise," in line 158.)   [159]**for 's turn** for his
purposes, i.e., to do it for him   [160]**lapwing** (A proverbial type of youthful forwardness.
Also, a bird that draws intruders away from its nest and was thought to run about with
its head in the shell when newly hatched; a seeming reference to Osric's hat.)
[161]**comply . . . dug** observe ceremonious formality toward his nurse's or mother's teat
[162]**drossy** laden with scum and impurities, frivolous   [163]**tune** temper, mood, manner of
speech   **an habit of encounter** a demeanor in conversing (with courtiers of his own
kind)   **yeasty** frothy   **collection** i.e., of current phrases   [164–165]**carries . . . opinions**
sustains them right through the scrutiny of persons whose opinions are select and refined
(Literally, like grain separated from its chaff. Osric is both the chaff and the bubbly
froth on the surface of the liquor that is soon blown away.)   [165]**and do** yet do
blow . . . out test them by merely blowing on them, and their bubbles burst   [168]**that** if
[169–170]**If . . . ready** if he declares his readiness, my convenience waits on his   [173]**In happy
time** (A phrase of courtesy indicating that the time is convenient.)   [174]**entertainment**
greeting

Hamlet: I do not think so. Since he went into France, I have been in continual practice; I shall win at the odds. But thou wouldst not think how ill all's here
180   about my heart; but it is no matter.

Horatio: Nay, good my lord—

Hamlet: It is but foolery, but it is such a kind of gaingiving as would perhaps trouble a woman.

Horatio: If your mind dislike anything, obey it. I will forestall their repair hither
185   and say you are not fit.

Hamlet: Not a whit, we defy augury. There is special providence in the fall of a sparrow. If it be now, 'tis not to come; if it be not to come, it will be now; if it be not now; yet it will come. The readiness is all. Since no man of aught he leaves knows, what is 't to leave betimes? Let be.

A table prepared. [Enter] trumpets, drums, and officers with cushions; King, Queen, [Osric,] and all the state; foils, daggers, [and wine borne in;] and Laertes.

190   *King:* Come, Hamlet, come and take this hand from me.

[The King puts Laertes' hand into Hamlet's.]

Hamlet [to Laertes]: Give me your pardon, sir. I have done you wrong,
But pardon 't as you are a gentleman.
This presence knows,
And you must needs have heard, how I am punished
195   With a sore distraction. What I have done
That might your nature, honor, and exception
Roughly awake, I here proclaim was madness.
Was 't Hamlet wronged Laertes? Never Hamlet.
If Hamlet from himself be ta'en away,
200   And when he's not himself does wrong Laertes,
Then Hamlet does it not, Hamlet denies it.
Who does it, then? His madness. If 't be so,
Hamlet is of the faction that is wronged;
His madness is poor Hamlet's enemy.
205   Sir, in this audience
Let my disclaiming from a purposed evil
Free me so far in your most generous thoughts
That I have shot my arrow o'er the house
And hurt my brother.

Laertes: I am satisfied in nature,
210   Whose motive in this case should stir me most
To my revenge. But in my terms of honor

---

¹⁸²**gaingiving** misgiving   ¹⁸⁴**repair** coming   ¹⁸⁸⁻¹⁸⁹**Since . . . Let be** since no one has knowledge of what he is leaving behind, what does an early death matter after all? Enough; don't struggle against it.   ¹⁹³**presence** royal assembly   ¹⁹⁴**punished** afflicted ¹⁹⁶**exception** disapproval   ²⁰³**faction** party   ²⁰⁸**That I have** as if I had   ²⁰⁹**in nature** i.e., as to my personal feelings   ²¹⁰**motive** prompting

I stand aloof, and will no reconcilement
Till by some elder masters of known honor
I have a voice and precedent of peace
To keep my name ungored. But till that time   215
I do receive your offered love like love,
And will not wrong it.

Hamlet: I embrace it freely,
And will this brothers' wager frankly play.—
Give us the foils. Come on.

Laertes: Come, one for me.

Hamlet: I'll be your foil, Laertes. In mine ignorance   220
Your skill shall, like a star i' the darkest night,
Stick fiery off indeed.

Laertes: You mock me, sir.

Hamlet: No, by this hand.

King: Give them the foils, young Osric. Cousin Hamlet,
You know the wager?

Hamlet: Very well, my lord.   225
Your Grace has laid the odds o' the weaker side.

King: I do not fear it; I have seen you both.
But since he is bettered, we have therefore odds.

Laertes: This is too heavy. Let me see another.   [*He exchanges his foil for another.*]

Hamlet: This likes me well. These foils have all a length?   [*They prepare to play.*]   230

Osric: Ay, my good lord.

King: Set me the stoups of wine upon that table.
If Hamlet give the first or second hit,
Or quit in answer of the third exchange,
Let all the battlements their ordnance fire.   235
The King shall drink to Hamlet's better breath,
And in the cup an union shall he throw
Richer than that which four successive kings
In Denmark's crown have worn. Give me the cups,
And let the kettle to the trumpet speak,   240

214**voice** authoritative pronouncement   **of peace** for reconciliation   215**name ungored** reputation unwounded   218**frankly** without ill feeling or the burden of rancor   220**foil** thin metal background which sets a jewel off (with pun on the blunted rapier for fencing) 222**Stick fiery off** stand out brilliantly   226**laid the odds o'** bet on, backed   228**is bettered** has improved; is the odds-on favorite (Laertes' handicap is the "three hits" specified in line 146.)   230**likes me** pleases me   234**Or . . . exchange** i.e., or requites Laertes in the third bout for having won the first two   236**better breath** improved vigor 237**union** pearl (So called, according to Pliny's *Natural History*, 9, because pearls are *unique*, never identical.)   240**kettle** kettledrum

The trumpet to the cannoneer without,
The cannons to the heavens, the heaven to earth,
"Now the King drinks to Hamlet." Come, begin.

Trumpets the while.

And you, the judges, bear a wary eye.

245 *Hamlet:* Come on, sir.
Laertes: Come, my lord.   [*They play. Hamlet scores a hit.*]
Hamlet: One.
Laertes: No.
Hamlet: Judgment.
Osric: A hit, a very palpable hit.

Drum, trumpets, and shot. Flourish. A piece goes off.

250 *Laertes:* Well, again.
King: Stay, give me drink. Hamlet, this pearl is thine.

[*He drinks, and throws a pearl in Hamlet's cup.*]

Here's to thy health. Give him the cup.
Hamlet: I'll play this bout first. Set it by awhile.
Come. [*They play.*] Another hit; what say you?
255 *Laertes:* A touch, a touch, I do confess 't.
King: Our son shall win.
Queen: He's fat and scant of breath.
Here, Hamlet, take my napkin, rub thy brows.
The Queen carouses to thy fortune, Hamlet.
Hamlet: Good madam!
260 *King:* Gertrude, do not drink.
Queen: I will, my lord, I pray you pardon me.   [*She drinks.*]
King [aside]: It is the poisoned cup. It is too late.
Hamlet: I dare not drink yet, madam; by and by.
Queen: Come, let me wipe thy face.
Laertes [to King]: My lord, I'll hit him now.
265 *King:*   I do not think 't.
Laertes [aside]: And yet it is almost against my conscience.
Hamlet: Come, for the third, Laertes. You do but dally.
I pray you, pass with your best violence;
I am afeard you make a wanton of me.
270 *Laertes:* Say you so? Come on.   [*They play.*]
Osric: Nothing neither way.

---

[256]**fat** not physically fit, out of training   [257]**napkin** handkerchief   [258]**carouses** drinks a
toast   [268]**pass** thrust   [269]**make . . . me** i.e., treat me like a spoiled child, trifle with me

Laertes: Have at you now!

> [*Laertes wounds Hamlet; then, in scuffling, they change*
> *rapiers, and Hamlet wounds Laertes.*]

King: Part them! They are incensed.

Hamlet: Nay, come, again.   [*The Queen falls.*]

Osric: Look to the Queen there, ho!

Horatio: They bleed on both sides. How is it, my lord?

Osric: How is 't, Laertes?   275

Laertes: Why, as a woodcock to mine own springe, Osric;

   I am justly killed with mine own treachery.

Hamlet: How does the Queen?

King: She swoons to see them bleed.

Queen: No, no, the drink, the drink—O my dear Hamlet—

   The drink, the drink! I am poisoned.   [*She dies.*]   280

Hamlet: O villainy! Ho, let the door be locked!

   Treachery! Seek it out.   [*Laertes falls. Exit Osric.*]

Laertes: It is here, Hamlet. Hamlet, thou art slain.

   No med'cine in the world can do thee good;

   In thee there is not half an hour's life.   285

   The treacherous instrument is in thy hand,

   Unbated and envenomed. The foul practice

   Hath turned itself on me. Lo, here I lie,

   Never to rise again. Thy mother's poisoned.

   I can no more. The King, the King's to blame.   290

Hamlet: The point envenomed too? Then, venom, to thy work.

> [*He stabs the King.*]

All: Treason! Treason!

King: O, yet defend me, friends! I am but hurt.

Hamlet [forcing the King to drink]:

   Here, thou incestuous, murderous, damnèd Dane,

   Drink off this potion. Is thy union here?   295

   Follow my mother.   [*The King dies.*]

Laertes: He is justly served.

   It is a poison tempered by himself.

272s.d.**in scuffling, they change rapiers** (This stage direction occurs in the Folio.
According to a widespread stage tradition, Hamlet receives a scratch, realizes that Laertes'
sword is unbated, and accordingly forces an exchange.)   276**woodcock** a bird, a type of
stupidity or as a decoy   **springe** trap, snare   287**Unbated** not blunted with a button
practice plot   295**union** pearl (See line 237; with grim puns on the word's other
meanings: marriage, shared death.)   297**tempered** mixed

Exchange forgiveness with me, noble Hamlet.
Mine and my father's death come not upon thee,
300 Nor thine on me!   [*He dies.*]
Hamlet: Heaven make thee free of it! I follow thee.
I am dead, Horatio. Wretched Queen, adieu!
You that look pale and tremble at this chance,
That are but mutes or audience to this act,
305 Had I but time—as this fell sergeant, Death,
Is strict in his arrest—O, I could tell you—
But let it be. Horatio, I am dead;
Thou livest. Report me and my cause aright
To the unsatisfied.
Horatio: Never believe it.
310 I am more an antique Roman than a Dane.
Here's yet some liquor left.
                 [*He attempts to drink from the poisoned cup. Hamlet prevents him.*]
Hamlet: As thou'rt a man,
Give me the cup! Let go! By heaven, I'll ha 't.
O God, Horatio, what a wounded name,
Things standing thus unknown, shall I leave behind me!
315 If thou didst ever hold me in thy heart,
Absent thee from felicity awhile,
And in this harsh world draw thy breath in pain
To tell my story.   *A march afar off* [*and a volley within*]. What warlike noise is this?

Enter Osric.

320 Osric: Young Fortinbras, with conquest come from Poland,
To th' ambassadors of England gives
This warlike volley.
Hamlet: O, I die, Horatio!
The potent poison quite o'ercrows my spirit.
I cannot live to hear the news from England,
325 But I do prophesy th' election lights
On Fortinbras. He has my dying voice.
So tell him, with th' occurrents more and less
Which have solicited—the rest is silence.   [*He dies.*]
Horatio: Now cracks a noble heart. Good night, sweet prince,
330 And flights of angels sing thee to thy rest!   [*March within.*]

303**chance** mischance   304**mutes** silent observers (Literally, actors with nonspeaking parts.)
305**fell** cruel   **sergeant** sheriff's officer   306**strict** (1) severely just (2) unavoidable   **arrest**
(1) taking into custody (2) stopping my speech   310**Roman** (Suicide was an honorable
choice for many Romans as an alternative to a dishonorable life.)   323**o'ercrows** triumphs
over (like the winner in a cockfight)   326**voice** vote   327**occurrents** events, incidents
328**solicited** moved, urged (Hamlet doesn't finish saying what the events have prompted—
presumably, his acts of vengeance, or his reporting of those events to Fortinbras.)

Why does the drum come hither?

> *Enter Fortinbras, with the [English] Ambassadors [with drum, colors, and attendants].*

Fortinbras: Where is this sight?

Horatio: What is it you would see?

If aught of woe or wonder, cease your search.

Fortinbras: This quarry cries on havoc. O proud Death,

What feast is toward in thine eternal cell,   335

That thou so many princes at a shot

So bloodily hast struck?

First Ambassador: The sight is dismal,

And our affairs from England come too late.

The ears are senseless that should give us hearing,

To tell him his commandment is fulfilled,   340

That Rosencrantz and Guildenstern are dead.

Where should we have our thanks?

Horatio: Not from his mouth,

Had it th' ability of life to thank you.

He never gave commandment for their death.

But since, so jump upon this bloody question,   345

You from the Polack wars, and you from England,

Are here arrived, give order that these bodies

High on a stage be placèd to the view,

And let me speak to th' yet unknowing world

How these things came about. So shall you hear   350

Of carnal, bloody, and unnatural acts,

Of accidental judgments, casual slaughters,

Of deaths put on by cunning and forced cause,

And, in this upshot, purposes mistook

Fall'n on th' inventors' heads. All this can I   355

Truly deliver.

Fortinbras: Let us haste to hear it,

And call the noblest to the audience.

For me, with sorrow I embrace my fortune.

I have some rights of memory in this kingdom,

Which now to claim my vantage doth invite me.   360

Horatio: Of that I shall have also cause to speak,

And from his mouth whose voice will draw on more.

---

[334]**quarry** heap of dead   **cries on havoc** proclaims a general slaughter   [335]**feast** i.e., Death feasting on those who have fallen   **toward** in preparation   [340]**his** i.e., Claudius'   [345]**jump** precisely, immediately   **question** dispute, affair   [348]**stage** platform   [352]**judgments** retributions   **casual** occurring by chance   [353]**put on** instigated   **forced cause** contrivance   [359]**of memory** traditional, remembered, unforgotten   [360]**vantage** favorable opportunity   [362]**voice . . . more** vote will influence still others

But let this same be presently performed,
Even while men's minds are wild, lest more mischance
On plots and errors happen.

365 *Fortinbras:*   Let four captains
Bear Hamlet, like a soldier, to the stage,
For he was likely, had he been put on,
To have proved most royal; and for his passage,
The soldiers' music and the rite of war

370 Speak loudly for him.
Take up the bodies. Such a sight as this
Becomes the field, but here shows much amiss.
Go bid the soldiers shoot.

Exeunt [marching, bearing off the dead bodies; a peal of ordnance is shot off].

363**presently** immediately   365**On** on the basis of; on top of   367**put on** i.e., invested in royal office and so put to the test   368**passage** i.e., from life to death   370**Speak** (let them) speak   372**Becomes the field** suits the field of battle

Act 1 Scene 1

1. What do we learn in the first scene about the national concerns of Denmark?
2. What can we tell about the relationship between Bernardo and Francisco from the first two lines of their conversation?

1.2

1. What can we tell about Claudius as king from his first speech in this scene? Can we tell from his words to the court whether he is a good king?
2. What can we learn from the interaction between Claudius and Hamlet? Is Claudius's argument that Hamlet should mourn less a good one?

1.3

1. Characterize the relationships among Laertes, Ophelia, and Polonius.

1.5

1. What is Hamlet's reaction to the ghost?
2. Since the high platform of a castle would have no basement, the idea in l. 160 that the ghost is in the "cellarage" is mysterious. What is its import in this scene?

2.1

1. How do the two halves of this scene fit together?

2.2

1. How does the conversation between Rosencrantz and Guildenstern and Claudius and Gertrude relate to 2.1?
2. What do we learn about Polonius when he reports to the king and queen about Hamlet's behavior to Ophelia? What do we learn about Hamlet?

3. What is the effect of the arrival of the players at this point in the scene? The speech that Hamlet asks the player to recite, although it pertains to the Trojan War, contains a number of parallels with the situation in Denmark. What do we learn from the part of it that Hamlet focuses on?

4. When talking to Polonius, Hamlet refers to Jephthah, a judge of ancient Israel. How does the allusion work in the scene?

3.1

1. Hamlet's speech beginning "To be, or not to be" is one of the most famous speeches in the play (and perhaps all plays). What difference does it make if Hamlet knows that Ophelia is within earshot and that Claudius and Polonius are also listening in?

2. What are the themes sounded in the conversation between Hamlet and Ophelia? If Hamlet knows that Claudius and Polonius are watching, how does that change our view of the scene?

3. Claudius does not seem to buy Polonius's theory that Hamlet is mad with frustrated love for Ophelia (154). What might his purpose be for l. 180?

3.2

1. What do we learn from Hamlet's advice to the players?

2. Why does Hamlet change the subject midway through his speech to Horatio (l. 60)?

3. Hamlet calls this play within the play *The Mousetrap*. Notice that Hamlet has the actors dramatize the perfidy of Gertrude and Claudius twice—once in the dumb show, and once in a spoken dramatic scene of great directness. You might be interested in looking for as many examples in the play of doubling, puns, and sets of opposites as you can find, since doubleness, duplicity, and two-facedness are all related to the matters on his mind.

4. Hamlet has engineered the "play within the play" in order to test Claudius's reaction to an image of his murder of Hamlet Sr. as it is recounted by the ghost. He is satisfied that Claudius is "frighted with false fire" (232) and rises "Upon the talk of the poisoning" (254). What do we learn from his commentary on the action of the play within the play?

5. What do we learn from Hamlet's interrogation of Rosencrantz and Guildenstern?

6. The scene ends with a short soliloquy in which Hamlet restates the theme of Hecate and witchcraft and hell. Why do you think Shakespeare puts these images and allusions into Hamlet's speech? What does Hamlet fear? What does he vow? What is the effect of Hamlet's being "as good as a chorus" (214) during the play?

3.3

1. What is the dramatic irony in ll. 39–99?

2. How does Hamlet's decision not to kill Claudius here influence your estimation of his character?

3.4

1. Hamlet's unwitting murder of Polonius has now made him the murderer he has tried to avoid becoming. What does he predict will be the effect of this action on him?

2. Hamlet goes to his mother's private room because she asks him to come, but in so doing, he sets out to accomplish something in the interview. What are his goals in speaking to her as he does? Explain. Think about the themes of authenticity he plays on as he shows her and comments on the two (doubles again) portraits.

3. First Ophelia and then Gertrude eagerly seize on the idea that Hamlet is mad. How do you explain that fact? Are you beginning to believe it yourself, or are you still convinced that he is playing at madness?

4. Think about the demands to act a certain way that he now makes on her. Contrast them with what she asked of him in Act I. Notice a little later on her "O, Hamlet, thou hast cleft my heart in *twain*." Do you think that she is responding to him as a madman here, or as her beloved and sensitive son?

5. Why does the ghost re-appear in this scene?

6. What does Hamlet tell his mother about what will be happening to him? What does he plan to do about it?

7. The last part of the speech begins with the lines, "This man shall set me packing." Hamlet obviously refers to Polonius. Why does he put it this way? He says good night to his mother and she leaves. He follows, doing what he says he will do, namely: "I'll lug the guts into the neighbor room." He has just killed the father of Ophelia (who might have become his father-in-law) and the chief counselor of his uncle-father and chief enemy, Claudius. Why doesn't he seem to be upset about it?

4.1

1. Gertrude calls Hamlet "Mad as the sea and wind when both contend / Which is the mightier," and she describes him as weeping for "what's done." We haven't been witness to any such behavior, and there doesn't seem to have been time for any such thing to occur. If these things have not been part of Hamlet's behavior, why does she lie?

4.2

1. What other scenes in the play does this scene relate to?

4.3

1. In this scene, the mocking answers Hamlet gives to Rosencrantz and Guildenstern are part of his "madness," but they are also deliberately ironic and sarcastic, and yet they verge on the philosophic. When this bitter mode of discourse continues, how does Claudius react to some of the jibes, such as "Nothing but to show you how a king may go a progress through the guts of a beggar" (28–29)?

4.4

1. The army of Fortinbras on its passage through Denmark is now the focus of Hamlet's attention. In "How all occasions do inform against me" (33ff.), he

expresses his dissatisfaction with his own inaction. Notice that once more he compares himself to another young man. List the others to whom he compares himself and describe how he feels he looks in comparison.

4.5

1. Ophelia's speech reveals that one of the causes of her madness is her father's death. Do you see any others? Explain.
2. What are Claudius's concerns with regard to Ophelia's condition?
3. What does Laertes demand and how does Claudius deal with him?

4.6 & 4.7

1. Scene 4.6 tells us what has happened to Hamlet through a letter to Horatio. What does it say and what does Hamlet want?
2. In the second letter from Hamlet (4.7), addressed this time to Claudius, Hamlet declares himself to be returning "naked and alone" to Denmark. What does Claudius plan for Laertes in response? What is Laertes's response to the plan? How do you feel about him when you hear his plan?
3. By the end of the scene, Laertes has even more reason to feel justified in becoming both avenger and executioner. Is his sister's death entirely Hamlet's fault?

5.1

1. The graveyard scene, probably the most famous in all of dramatic literature, opens with clowns. Can you explain this choice?
2. The whole scene is replete with puns, ironies, sarcasms, and serious thoughts about the physical and metaphysical aspects of death. What kinds of thoughts about death does the discovery of Yorick's skull arouse in Hamlet?
3. Hamlet has just arrived in Denmark and at first does not know whose funeral procession this is. When he sees Laertes jump into the grave, what effect does it have on him? Do you think he is acting when he does this, or is he expressing authentic feelings about Ophelia?

5.2

1. At the beginning of the scene, Hamlet relates his sea adventure to Horatio. Notice the entirely different tone of the scene and of Hamlet's discourse. Do you see any signs that he is approaching the resolution and reconciliation that befits a tragic hero?
2. Does Hamlet feel remorse at the fate of Rosencrantz and Guildenstern? Should he?
3. Osric is a character Shakespeare introduces at the last minute. Why do you think he made this happen?
4. How does Hamlet feel about the forthcoming duel with Laertes? Notice that he makes peace with Laertes before they begin, asking for forgiveness because he was "not himself," then chooses a foil. How much care does Hamlet take in selecting it?
5. At the end, Hamlet and Laertes are poisoned in the duel and the queen is poisoned by the drink Claudius has prepared for Hamlet; Laertes blames the

king and Hamlet finally kills Claudius with the poisoned foil. Do you see a certain poetic justice and symbolic meaning in these deaths?

6. Why does Hamlet use his last strength to prevent Horatio from following him in the Roman fashion?

7. Fortinbras comes in to restore order to the poisoned kingdom. What is his tribute to Hamlet? Is he right?

8. The play ends with the rhyming couplet, "Take up the bodies. Such a sight as this / Becomes the field, but here shows much amiss." Then he issues one more direction: "Go bid the soldiers shoot." The last thing we see is the body borne aloft by soldiers. How would you stage and light this scene in order to make it a fitting ending for a tragedy?

Comparison

The play has often been compared to Sophocles' *Oedipus Rex* (see Chapter 16, p. 1158). Is the comparison useful?

TERENCE EAGLETON

TERENCE (TERRY) EAGLETON *(1953–), born in Salford, England, of third-generation, poor Irish immigrants, suffered the indignities of poverty, asthma, and the sadistic practices of his schoolmates. As an undergraduate at Trinity College of Cambridge University, he was influenced by the Marxist critic Raymond Williams and, after taking a "starred first" at graduation, was offered a research fellowship at Jesus College, Cambridge. After some years as a Don at Oxford, he moved to the University of Manchester. Marxism supplanted his early forays into active leftist Catholicism when he found the church immovable. He married Rosemary Galpin, a registered nurse, during his first year at Cambridge, had two children, and divorced after ten years of marriage. He married the American academic Willa Murphy in 1997 and became a father again. He has written extensively on literary theory but also has taken new approaches to major figures like Hardy, Dickens, and the Brontës, always basing his social and political analysis on close readings of the texts. He has also written on the language and culture of Ireland. Not wanting to confine himself strictly to academic writing, he has also published a novel, several plays, and a memoir. "Hamlet" is the second chapter of Eagleton's 1967 book,* Shakespeare and Society: Critical Studies in Shakespearean Drama.

*Hamlet**

The plot of *Hamlet* turns on the fact that in Act I Scene 5 Hamlet is given a task to fulfil by his father's ghost—a task which he leaves undone until the very end of the play. But this is only one of a number of assignments which people lay on other people throughout the play. Claudius appoints Cornelius and Voltemand as ambassadors to the King of Norway, and Rosencrantz and Guildenstern to discover the truth about Hamlet; Polonius instructs Reynaldo to spy on Laertes,

*Terry Eagleton, *Shakespeare and Society: Critical Studies in Shakespearean Drama* (London: Chatto & Windus, 1967), Chapter 2.

uses Ophelia as bait to trap Hamlet, and is Claudius's self-appointed agent; Hamlet orders Polonius to look after the actors, and uses the actors as bait to catch Claudius; Gertrude uses Rosencrantz, Guildenstern and Polonius to bear messages to Hamlet, and Claudius uses Osric for the same purpose; Claudius uses Laertes to kill Hamlet, and Hamlet uses the English authorities to get rid of Rosencrantz and Guildenstern; Horatio is told by the dying Hamlet to give the succession of Denmark to Fortinbras, and the play ends with Fortinbras's order for ceremonial shots to be fired. Messages and reports are constantly being given by or about one person to another via a third: Hamlet's friends tell him about the Ghost; Ophelia tells Polonius about Hamlet, and Polonius tells the King; Hamlet describes his sea-voyage to Horatio; the Queen describes Ophelia's death to Laertes. The process almost parodies itself in Act IV Scene 6, where a message passes from Hamlet to sailors to an attendant to Horatio to Claudius, and Claudius's command before the duel images the movement:

> . . . Give me the cups;
> And let the kettle to the trumpet speak,
> The trumpet to the cannoneer without,
> The cannons to the heavens, the heaven to earth,
> 'Now the King drinks to Hamlet'.   (V, 2)

Agency, then, is a central theme in *Hamlet*: society is presented, and is present to each character, as a continuous network of causes, agents, and effects, a network of men reciprocally using and exploiting one another. The reciprocity is important: men both use others and are used, and as a result they have two senses of themselves, as source and as agent (or object). Polonius is a professional go-between, almost at times a pandar, but we see him also as a father, severe to Ophelia, paternalistic to Laertes. Ophelia is used as a pawn by Claudius and her father, but when she confronts Hamlet she forgets her role of agent and becomes herself. Laertes is a source when advising Ophelia but exploited as an agent by Claudius; Horatio executes Hamlet's wishes but remains solid in his integrity, his self-possession. Marcellus and Bernardo reduce themselves to dutiful agents in reporting the news of the Ghost to Hamlet, but we have seen them already, in the first scene of the play, as full, independent human beings; even the players, who hardly move or speak outside their role as actors, gain some independent humanity from Hamlet's personal dealing with them.

Rosencrantz, Guildenstern and Osric, on the other hand, have no existence at all outside their role as agents. They are defined totally by the way society uses them, and they accept and enact this definition, seeing themselves as society sees them. This is especially evident in the case of Rosencrantz and Guildenstern, who consciously consign whatever integrity they might have into Claudius's possession, as a free act:

> But we both obey,
> And here give up ourselves, in the full bent,
> To lay our service freely at your feet,
> To be commanded.   (II, 2)

Both men voluntarily surrender themselves to be controlled, and by actively consenting to being Claudius's puppets they authenticate their appointed roles, make them personally real; from this point on we see them only in this function. Osric does not even personally authenticate his role as agent: he is incapable even of this degree of individual choice. He is whatever men care to make him, an obedient reflection of other men's views:

> *Osric:* I thank your lordship; it is very hot.
> *Hamlet:* No, believe me, 'tis very cold; the wind is northerly.
> *Osric:* It is indifferent cold, my lord, indeed.
> *Hamlet:* But yet methinks it is very sultry and hot for my complexion.
> *Osric:* Exceedingly, my lord . . .   (V, 2)

Osric serves to hold the mirror up to nature, but the image is not intended to shape the reality it reflects, as Hamlet says an actor should do, as the mirror of his own scorn shows Gertrude her vices. The agent in *Hamlet* is not like the mediator in *Troilus and Cressida:* in *Troilus,* the mediator helps to create a new reality, actively shaping experience; in *Hamlet* the agent's task is to transmit what is entrusted to him intact to the receiver, cancelling his own identity in the process. This is what the clown in the graveyard scene refuses to do when questioned by Hamlet; he refuses to pass on information intact, colouring it constantly with his own personality:

> *Hamlet:* How came he mad?
> *Clown:* Very strangely, they say.
> *Hamlet:* How strangely?
> *Clown:* Faith, e'en with losing his wits.
> *Hamlet:* Upon what ground?
> *Clown:* Why, here in Denmark. I have been sexton here, man and boy, thirty
>   years.   (V, 1)

The clown is all the time more concerned with exercising his wit than with giving Hamlet a straight answer; he can't keep himself out of the conversation, and turns the dialogue as soon as he can to himself. The scene immediately precedes Hamlet's encounter with Osric, and is meant to contrast with it: the clown asserts himself as an autonomous human being, causing Hamlet some dry amusement at his refusal to be servile; Osric has no humanity apart from his servility.

Throughout the play, the self as source and the self as agent (what A. P. Rossiter calls 'mind-sense' and 'self-sense')* are at odds: some men, like Claudius, appear almost totally autonomous, fulfilling themselves by using others as agents, manipulating them into action; other men, like Osric, are objects, tools to be used. But generally the tension between self as subject and self as object is an interior one, between how a man sees himself, and his conception of how others see him or how he is actually used by others. Laertes has to be reduced carefully by Claudius from passionate self-affirmation to a pliable object capable of being turned against Hamlet; Ophelia lives at the point of tension between seeing herself as the obedient daughter of Polonius, subject to his will, and asserting her authentic self in her love for Hamlet: with her, the

---

*'Angel with Horns', Longmans, Chapter 9.

tension is finally destructive. Polonius consciously turns himself into an object, by becoming a self-appointed spy: he uses himself. Polonius's family provides a minor, reflecting image of the larger social network which includes it: Polonius is a source for Ophelia and Laertes, giving them both advice; Laertes is a source for Ophelia, advising her against receiving Hamlet's advances, but is suddenly objectified himself as Ophelia becomes herself a source, warning Laertes to obey his own advice.

The opposition is brought out in a peculiar way by a continual verbal play between 'eyes' or 'voice', and 'ears'. In the first scene, Marcellus wishes that Horatio will 'approve (their) eyes', confirm his experience, by seeing the Ghost which so far only he and Bernardo have seen: they tell him to sit down so that they may once more assail his ears. When Horatio finally sees the Ghost, he stresses the significance of his actual, personal seeing, as grounds for belief:

> *Before my God, I might not this believe*
> *Without the sensible and true avouch*
> *Of mine own eyes.* (I, 1)

and this contrasts with his mere half-belief in what he *hears*, when the story of the cock which sings all night at Christmas is told him:

> So have I heard, and do in part believe it.

'Eyes' or 'voice', and 'ears', are used throughout the play as the symbols, respectively, for the self as subject and the self as object. It is what men see with their own eyes that is most genuinely personal: to look or speak is to act as subject. To hear is to become, even if only temporarily, an object, the passive recipient of another's subjective experience, and being reduced to this status of object can be dangerous: Laertes warns Ophelia not to receive Hamlet's overtures with 'too credent ear', and Ophelia in return reminds him to follow his own advice—to keep an adjustment between his subjective self and his public actions. Polonius's advice a few minutes later is the opposite: he warns Laertes to 'Give every man thine ear, but few thy voice', to make a conscious dislocation between his authentic, subjective self and the self which is present to others in the world.

The fact of the Ghost *speaking* to Hamlet also assumes importance, and the word is given emphasis; it is dumb to Marcellus and Bernardo, present to them only as an object; but it engages in dialogue with Hamlet, disclosing itself as a subject with a will. It makes him an object, calling on him to hear, and then lays a duty on him, making him an agent. The danger involved in being made into an object is revealed in the Ghost's account of his murder: the poison which killed him was poured in at the ear. A similar play between subject and object occurs in Act I Scene 2, where Gertrude appears to Hamlet to 'let (his) eye look like a friend on Denmark', and a few minutes later Claudius echoes her remark:

> . . . For your intent
> In going back to school in Wittenberg,
> It is most retrograde to our desire;
> And we beseech you bend you to remain
> Here, in the cheer and comfort of our eye . . .

Denmark is to be in Hamlet's eye, which means he is to possess and control it as something which can be used or enjoyed. But Hamlet, in turn, is to be in Claudius's eye: controlled, defined by Claudius, assigned his proper place at court, reduced perhaps to an object. Men can put themselves at the mercy of others, surrendering themselves up as Rosencrantz and Guildenstern do, in a kind of suicide, and later in the same scene Hamlet warns Horatio against doing this, when Horatio accuses himself of a truant disposition:

> I would not hear your enemy say so;
> Nor shall you do my ear that violence,
> To make it truster of your own report
> Against yourself.

A man's act can be taken from him and used against him: by saying too much, by unpacking his heart publicly, a man can hand himself into the control of a listener, who then becomes a subject, manipulating him as an object; Hamlet has just warned himself before Horatio's entrance to hold his tongue. Words can't be reclaimed: like all actions, they detach themselves from the performer, who can then disown responsibility for them but also lose control over their consequences:

> *King:* I have nothing with this answer, Hamlet; these words are not mine.
> *Hamlet:* No, nor mine now.   (III, 2)

Ophelia is warned by her father not to speak to Hamlet: a denial of speech, in this society, is a denial of self-giving, presenting oneself to the other merely as an object. Love, in these terms, is an engagement of two selves which does not demand the reduction of either to the status of objects,* and it is this which breaks down when Ophelia closes herself off from Hamlet, makes herself opaque to him. Ophelia tells Polonius of Hamlet's behaviour, and this information, 'given to (his) ear', he gives in turn to the ear of Claudius. Claudius hides himself to spy on Hamlet's encounter with Ophelia: he and Polonius

> Will so bestow ourselves that, *seeing unseen,*
> We may of their encounter frankly judge . . .   (III, 1)

'Seeing unseen' is the ideal situation for a man: he can be purely himself without being objectified by the look of another, as Hamlet feels himself seen and exploited when he becomes aware of Polonius in hiding. Claudius, generally in total control of others, a source and not an agent, rarely puts himself in a position where he can be reduced to an object; he is objectified in this way only twice in the play, once when he betrays himself during the play-scene under the scrutiny of Hamlet and Horatio ('Even with the very comment of thy

---

*Real love, in the play, involves that knowledge of the centre of another which in this society is generally resisted because it is seen as an attempt to possess and objectify: Hamlet wears Horatio 'in his heart's core', Gertrude is 'conjunctive' to Claudius's 'heart and soul'. In contrast, Polonius's resolve to discover the truth about Hamlet 'though it were hid, indeed, within the centre' is an attempt to control him.

soul,/Observe my uncle'), and finally when he is stabbed by Hamlet at the end of the play.

The conflict of self as subject and self as object comes out strongly in Hamlet's confrontation of his mother in Act III Scene 4. They begin as two subjects, each powerfully self-asserting and confident. The quick, thrusting give-and-take of their opening duel confirms this:

> *Queen:* Hamlet, thou hast thy father much offended.
> *Hamlet:* Mother, you have my father much offended.
> *Queen:* Come, come, you answer with an idle tongue.
> *Hamlet:* Go, go, you question with a wicked tongue.

The Conflict is equally balanced, the two selves directly clashing: the reference in both cases is to 'tongues', to the self as subject and source. Gertrude then tries to gain control by a threat—'Nay then, I'll set those to you that can speak'— intended to reduce Hamlet to an object, chastised by the voices of others. Hamlet sweeps this aside with a direct command:

> Come, come, and sit you down; you shall not budge.
> You go not till I set you up a glass
> Where you may see the inmost part of you.

He forces her, in physical posture, into a passive position, and rather than objectify her himself will be the glass in which she will see herself as she is. Gertrude's control breaks: she is reduced to fright and calls for Polonius. But now Hamlet is completely in control, as his cool response to Polonius's death indicates*: he shows his mother the portraits of her two husbands, noting the 'eye like Mars' of his father and describing Claudius as 'a mildew'd ear'. He cannot believe that Gertrude could have eyes and choose Claudius:

> Eyes without feeling, feeling without sight,
> Ears without hands or eyes, smelling sans all,
> Or but a sickly part of one true sense
> Could not so mope.

Even someone without a subjective, choosing self could hardly have been so blind. Gertrude is finally reduced to repentance:

> O Hamlet, speak no more!
> Thou turn'st my eyes into my very soul;
> And there I see such black and grained spots
> As will not leave their tinct.

Hamlet's words enter her ears like daggers, forcing her to objectify her sins. But the situation changes when the Ghost appears: now it is Hamlet who is

---

*Hamlet's reaction to Polonius's body, like his reaction to Yorick's skull, is to wonder at the distinction between the living, subjective self, and the dumb, objective corpse:
> . . . Indeed, this counsellor
> Is now most still, most secret, and most grave,
> Who was in life a foolish prating knave.   [Eagleton's note]

objectified, both by the Ghost and by Gertrude. The Ghost objectifies both Hamlet and Gertrude, noting Gertrude's amazement and rebuking Hamlet for his delay; he tells Hamlet to reassure his mother, using him as an agent. Hamlet turns back to Gertrude, concerned for her, to find that she is concerned for him, objectifying him as mad. Each thinks the other is seeing wrongly: Gertrude thinks Hamlet is having hallucinations, Hamlet can't understand why she can't see what to him is evidently there. The two selves clash again as subjects, asserting their own versions of seeing against each other. Finally Hamlet regains control: Gertrude submits to his advice and asks what she should do. But Hamlet's aim is a reconciliation, not merely a chance to reduce her to submission:

> Forgive me this my virtue;
> For in the fatness of these pursy times
> Virtue itself of vice must pardon beg,
> Yea, curb and woo for leave to do him good.

Hamlet wants to give Gertrude moral advice without reducing her to an object within his control: he wants, simultaneously, to have a real relationship with her. The only way he can achieve these conflicting ends, to see her both as subject and object, is to give her advice while asking her pardon for it: in this way he makes himself the object of her pardon as he makes her the object of his moralising.

Hamlet ends by laying on the Queen an injunction not to reveal to Claudius what he has said, and she assures him that she will be silent:

> Be thou assur'd, if words be made of breath
> And breath of life, I have no life to breathe
> What thou hast said to me.

Speech is deeply connected with personal life, with self-giving; Gertrude is not merely saying that she will repress what Hamlet has told her, but that her silence will be part of her deepest life, part of her truth-to-self: she makes Hamlet's restriction part of her authentic life as, in a different way, Rosencrantz and Guildenstern personally authenticate Claudius's commands. Hamlet's last words to her are a reminder that he has to leave for England: it is he, now, who is to be used by others. But he intends to manipulate those who will try to control him:

> . . . Let it work;
> For 'tis the sport to have the engineer
> Hoist with his own petar; and't shall go hard
> But I will delve one yard below their mines
> And blow them at the moon.

Those who expect to use him as an object will find him an active subject, objectifying his manipulators:

> . . . O 'tis most sweet
> When in one line two crafts directly meet.

He expects a head-on collision of two subjective wills, each out to control the other, which was how his interview with his mother began.

More instances of the opposition of subject and object occur in the court's consternation at the death of Polonius. The corpse, Hamlet says, is at supper, 'not where he eats, but where he is eaten'. Eating provides a good image of the opposition: it has been used already in Hamlet's reference to Gertrude's lust as an increase of appetite growing from what it feeds on (I, 2). To feed is to use another creature as object to strengthen oneself as subject, and the process can be circular: 'we fat all creatures else to fat us, and we fat ourselves for maggots . . . a man may fish with the worm that hath eat of a king, and eat of the fish that hath fed of that worm.' All creatures simultaneously eat and are eaten, in endless reciprocity.

Laertes returns to Denmark, his ear 'infected' by 'buzzers'; he bursts in with an unruly crowd at his heels, over whom his control is shaky:

> *Laertes:* Where is this king?—Sirs, stand you all without.
> *All:* No, let's come in.
> *Laertes:* I pray you give me leave.
> *All:* We will, we will.   (IV, 5)

This is not just to show the crowd's fickleness: it reveals again the tension of subject and object. Laertes can gain a personal wish which is denied to him when he appeals as subject to the crowd, by making himself instead the object of their permission. Claudius, similarly, lets Laertes rage on, and then begins to direct the rage to his own ends, slowly, until Laertes is ready to be commanded:

> My lord, I will be rul'd
> The rather, if you could devise it so
> That I might be the organ.   (IV, 7)

Laertes positively demands to become the King's agent, his tool, because he sees this as a role within which he can enact his own subjective resolution to kill Hamlet. But from Claudius's viewpoint, Laertes as subject and as object are quite different: as Claudius's tool he will be killing Hamlet for reasons entirely distinct from his personal grievances.

When Laertes and Hamlet finally meet for the duel, Hamlet tries to diminish the hostility by offering to reduce himself to an object:

> I'll be your foil, Laertes; in mine ignorance
> Your skill shall, like a star i' th' darkest night,
> Stick fiery off indeed.   (V, 2)

In duelling, two selves come physically into conflict, and the aim, for Laertes anyway, is to reduce Hamlet to the purest objectivity possible to man, a corpse. The reciprocity of the conflict is imaged in the changing of rapiers: Laertes stabs Hamlet with the poisoned blade, and is then stabbed with the same weapon. But Hamlet, even when dying, is a source rather than an agent: he kills Claudius, instructs Horatio to stay alive to tell his story, and gives his 'dying voice' to Fortinbras—he reaches out beyond his death as an active voice, transmitted in both Horatio and Fortinbras. The ambassador from England comes too late with the news of the deaths of Rosencrantz and Guildenstern: the man who arranged their deaths has himself been killed, and 'the ears are senseless' to receive the information.

* * *

We can see the society of *Hamlet* as a continuous network of reciprocal human definitions, as we saw the society of *Troilus and Cressida*. As with *Troilus*, this inter-definition is felt both as limiting and circular: men's realities are reflected to them by the particular nexus of their society, and this can differ radically from the way they see themselves, from their authentic selves. In this condition, a man can either consent to finding his real self only in the margin of society, in nonofficial activities and relationships; he can sell himself over, alternatively, to the public definition, become as he is valued; or he can continue to assert his authentic life and risk destruction. In *Hamlet* we find all three experiments tried, and they are all inadequate.

The *Hamlet* society resembles the Greek camp in its enclosedness, its sense of the public eye, but it is a much more claustrophobic society, one riddled with spying and secrecy, with attempts to hunt down and possess the truth of others. In this context, self-repression is vital, just for survival: the fear and hesitancy of the first scenes, the sense of concealed rottenness and the doubt about the Ghost's identity, [are] part of the whole atmosphere of a society where men are forced to close themselves off from each other, falsifying their identities. To expose oneself is to risk manipulation, as Polonius warns Ophelia: she must learn that being in society, part of the complex network of cause and effect, involves self-concealment. As a result, the tension between authentic desire and public role can become crippling: it can only be eased by inauthentic choosing, by consenting to be an object, like Rosencrantz and Guildenstern. By actively choosing this self, they can mould themselves to the required role, really become what they are expected to be. Polonius, too, actively accepts and authenticates his role as Claudius's tool, although he allows himself some autonomy in the margin, in the privacy of his family.

15   These are the terms, then, in which survival in Denmark is possible, and they are the terms available to Hamlet as well as to everyone else. Hamlet has a particular function in society—that of prince—and the specific function, given to him by his father, of killing Claudius. But Hamlet, like Troilus, conceives of himself as pure fluidity: like Achilles, his whole character is geared to resisting any externally imposed definition. The first time we see him he is concerned to point out that he is something more than he appears, that there is a discontinuity between his real self, and the objective self present to the world: forms, moods and shapes cannot denote him truly, for

> . . . I have that within which passes show—
> These but the trappings and the suits of woe.   (I, 2)

This, in the whole context of the play, is more than a rejection of the specifically distorting appearances of mourning: it is also a rejection of any attempt to be fully identified. It is not just that black garments can falsify the self: any posture at all, any particular commitment, is in itself falsifying because it seems to deny the possibility of other postures. Like Troilus, Hamlet's self can be defined only in terms of process: the disowning of 'appearances' is, more deeply, the disowning of any particular action as an adequate image of self. This is the real motivation behind the twisting, evasive conversation, the cryptic comments and disowning of imputed attitudes. Hamlet deliberately confuses others about his real self, creating several different versions which refuse to mesh into a single image.

Hamlet, like Claudius, is a source rather than an agent, and it is this which Claudius recognises as dangerous: he is a difficult man to manipulate. The court find Hamlet impenetrable: they are disturbed both by his silence, his cryptic, uncommunicative presence at their proceedings, and by the evasive, fast-talking self he reveals when he breaks out of this shell. Hamlet uses both methods to keep the court at bay, to resist any imposed definition from outside: he refuses objectification both by shifting his ground so quickly that it is impossible to pin him down (as in his banter with Polonius, and his interchange with Ophelia in the play-scene), and by keeping silent, by withholding his real self and thus staying untrapped:

> You would play upon me; you would seem to know my stops; you would pluck out the heart of my mystery. . . . 'Sblood, do you think I am easier to be play'd on than a pipe? Call me what instrument you will, though you can fret me, yet you cannot play upon me.   (III, 2)

Hamlet's fine, fluid mind is amusedly indignant that Rosencrantz and Guildenstern should have so low an opinion of him as to think that he could actually be fully known to them as a man: he breaks free of any definition the court can provide, as he breaks out of the restraining arms of his friends to follow the Ghost. Those who can be fully known, whose real selves are fully embodied in their objective functions and roles, are inauthentic men like Osric, assembled by society; on these terms, the real man is the one who can keep something of himself in reserve, who can retain some integrity. This means a willingness to be inactive, to avoid full involvement with the world. To be fully involved is to be fully known, completely available to others and therefore vulnerable, exposed to exploitation. A real man, for Hamlet, is one who can only be described in terms of himself:

> . . . I take him to be a soul of great article, and his infusion of such dearth and rareness as, to make true diction of him, his semblable is his mirror, and who else would trace him, his umbrage, nothing more.   (V, 2)

Horatio's reply in Act I Scene 1 to Marcellus's question 'Is it not like the King?', referring to the Ghost, is 'As thou art to thyself': the ultimate criterion of similarity is a man's own absolute likeness to himself. Comparison with others, for Hamlet, is part of that whole process of public judgements which forms the basis of the Greek sense of identity in *Troilus*, and which Cressida and Pandarus come to reject for an essentialist, individualist view of men as beings-in-themselves, unique. Hamlet's deliberately meaningless communication to his eager friends after the Ghost has left him—

> There's never a villain dwelling in all Denmark
> But he's an arrant knave.   (I, 5)

—is an echo of this feeling that men can be defined only in relation to themselves. But this process, like the inter-definition of a whole society, is closed and circular: as in *Troilus*, both ways of living are inadequate. Polonius comes close to the same sense of things-in-themselves when he announces to the King and Queen that true madness is to be nothing else but mad: to describe it further would be as pointless as trying to explain why day is day and night night. Things are as they are, independent of human valuations: Hamlet's melancholy leads him to see the sky as a pestilent congregation of vapours and man as a quintessence of dust, but he recognises this for what it is, a personal feeling, a personal interpretation:

> I am but mad north-north-west; when the wind is southerly I know a hawk from
> a handsaw.   (II, 2)

The self can be defined only with reference to itself, because it is always deeper and more complex than any of its manifestations in action in the public world. For this reason, the common process of judgement and evaluation of the individual which was the mainspring of the Greek view of society in *Troilus* is rejected: the authentic individual is always ultimately behind and beyond his actions as they are present to others, and their judgement can therefore only ever be partial. Hamlet's contempt for the common judgement comes out in his contempt for the 'general', the theatre audiences whose judgement must always be ignored in favour of the opinions of a few, select men. We see, in this kind of attitude, how close his rejection of social definition is to a generally aristocratic stance, a feeling that full involvement in a social role is crudely limiting, that the true man will always keep some distance between himself and his actions. A full definition of an authentic man is as impossible as a definition of a ghost; indeed the wonder and questioning of Marcellus and Bernardo when confronted with the Ghost reflects the attitude of the court to Hamlet himself. The Ghost is present to Marcellus and Bernardo only as an object, dumb and mysterious; but it has, also, all the fluid evasiveness of pure subjectivity, in a quite physical sense: it appears suddenly, without warning, and seems to dissolve into the air:

> We do it wrong, being so majestical,
> To offer it the show of violence;
> For it is, as the air, invulnerable,
> And our vain blows malicious mockery.   (I, 2)

Marcellus's words, stretched a little, could almost be taken as applying to Hamlet: this is essentially the way the court sees Hamlet, as a figure invulnerable in his elusiveness, and it is Horatio's ability to take the buffets and rewards of Fortune with equal thanks that Hamlet most admires in him. Hamlet 'eats the air', as he remarks to Claudius (III, 2), a comment which echoes Marcellus's remark about the Ghost. When Hamlet encounters the Ghost, he compares it to himself:

> I do not set my life at a pin's fee;
> And for my soul, what can it do to that,
> Being a thing immortal as itself?   (I, 4)

Hamlet sets his physical existence in society at nothing; but his real self, his soul, is as immortal as the Ghost itself.

The play begins by creating a sense of fluidity, hesitation, doubt: the quick, confused questioning of the sentries, the anxious mutual establishment of identity, leads on to the doubt about the Ghost and the uncommitted scepticism of Horatio. Doubt is expressed in terms of a number of open possibilities:

> If thou hast any sound or use of voice,
> Speak to me.
> If there be any good thing to be done,
> That may to thee do ease and grace to me,
> Speak to me.
> If thou art privy to thy country's fate,
> Which happily foreknowing may avoid,
> O speak! . . .   (I, 1)

and Hamlet's later questioning of the Ghost echoes this:

> Be thou a spirit of health or goblin damn'd,
> Bring with thee airs from heaven or blasts from hell.
> Be thy intents wicked or charitable,
> Thou com'st in such a questionable shape
> That I will speak to thee.*   (I, 4)

It is speaking, mutual engagement in dialogue, which establishes meaning and identity: this is why both Horatio and Hamlet emphasise the importance of speaking so much. Until speech is established and the self disclosed, the other exists only in terms of a number of possibilities, or as an object, impenetrable to enquiry. Hamlet's encounter with Gertrude in Act III Scene 4 is seen by him as this kind of direct and ultimate grappling with another, a final establishment of the truth: it is deliberately a high-point, a set piece, a confrontation in which Hamlet is determined to break through to the truth of his mother, to wring her heart 'if it be made of penetrable stuff'.

The Ghost's evasiveness, then, is of two kinds, like Hamlet's: it has a fluidity which evades localisation (' 'Tis here! . . . 'Tis here! . . . 'Tis gone!'), a ubiquitousness (it is *'Hic et ubique'*, in Hamlet's words, everywhere at once, following Hamlet's shifts of ground); it is also, at first, a dumb object, resisting enquiry.

---

*The same sense of a number of possibilities, a fluidity, is there in Polonius's announcement of the actors' programme: 'tragedy, comedy, history, pastoral, pastoral-comical, historical-pastoral . . . (II, 2). The actors, like Hamlet, have identities which are completely flexible, capable of any posture.   [Eagleton's note]

These two conditions are imaged respectively in its two different states of being: during the night it wanders, during the day it is confined in the prison-house of purgatory. Its self-disclosure to Hamlet has to be made quickly, before it is forced to return to confinement; when it confronts Marcellus, Bernardo and Horatio, it is caught at the point of tension between self-disclosure in speech and the pressures which draw it back into prison and silence. The tension is essentially the one we have seen in other characters, between the self as subject and as object, between free self-giving and self-concealment. The Ghost as subject is 'extravagant and erring', but in this condition it can speak and be known for what it is; imprisoned in purgatory it is dumb. It fades on the point of action, of speech: it fails, at first, to realise itself in free disclosure, and even when it talks to Hamlet it is continually aware of the pressures of purgatory at work, drawing it back.

20   The Ghost's appearance reduces Marcellus and Bernardo to a fluidity like its own, making them incapable of action:

> . . . thrice he walk'd
> By their oppress'd and fear-surprised eyes,
> Within his truncheon's length; whilst they, distill'd
> Almost to jelly with the act of fear,
> Stand dumb and speak not to him.   (I, 2)

The jelly to which Marcellus and Bernardo are reduced is like the dew into which Hamlet wishes his too-solid flesh would dissolve: it is a state of pure subjectivity which is incapable of objectifying itself in action. This is the condition in which Hamlet lives throughout the play, resisting the objectification of action and a fixed social role. He is a source, not an agent or an object: when Polonius brings him the news of the actors' arrival his reply is 'Buzz, buzz'—stale news. He is not the kind of man to be given news by Polonius: he knows it already. Polonius is not even allowed the minute degree of power over Hamlet which telling him something he did not know before would involve. In their encounter in Act II Scene 2, Hamlet refuses to be Polonius's agent even in the most basic sense of giving straight answers to questions seeking information: like the clown, he twists the questions and throws back ambiguous answers, reducing the questioner to confusion, exploiting him. Laertes's view of Hamlet, expounded to Ophelia, is thus powerfully ironic:

> . . . Perhaps he loves you now,
> And now no soil nor cautel doth besmirch
> The virtue of his will; but you must fear,
> His greatness weigh'd, his will is not his own;
> For he himself is subject to his birth:
> He may not, as unvalued persons do,
> Carve for himself; for on his choice depends
> The sanity and health of this whole state;
> And therefore must his choice be circumscrib'd
> Unto the voice and yielding of that body
> Whereof he is the head.   (I, 3)

To Laertes, Hamlet must be taken as a man only within the public role which officially identifies him: he must confine his authentic life within this public definition, making himself what society makes him. His choices and actions must be socially responsible, answerable to the whole society whose values he should focus and shape. But Hamlet does, in fact, carve for himself all the time: by evading the formal definitions society lays on him, by cutting through expected behaviour and approaching Ophelia with a directly personal appeal after the shock of the Ghost's announcement, he is acting counter to the patterns prescribed for him: his 'authentic' and 'social' selves, his own sense of himself and the way others see him, are at odds.

Society denies Hamlet authenticity: it asks him to surrender up his own desires, his love for Ophelia and his reluctance to be limited by a fixed role, and take on an official function. Life on these terms, on the terms of Osric and Rosencrantz and Guildenstern, is clearly unacceptable for Hamlet: he is intent on not being a puppet. But Hamlet's insistence on not being a puppet leads, finally, to a delight in resisting any kind of definition: it becomes, in fact, socially irresponsible, a merely negative response. This is the really tragic tension in the play, the central dilemma. The significant actions which are available to Hamlet as formal modes of self-definition, the actions of killing Claudius and behaving as prince, are not the actions in which he can find himself authentically; therefore he is unable to act. But the real tragedy of a man who is unable to find self-definition within formal social patterns, who can preserve his sense of identity only in opposition to these patterns, is that this identity then becomes unreal, negative. A self which can know itself only in constant opposition to its context finally destroys itself. This is the savage irony of the authentic man in a false society, the irony, to some degree, of Achilles in *Troilus;* the man who can find himself only outside his society's terms will disintegrate because of his very lack of that offered social verification of his existence which he is rejecting as false. Society may indeed be seen as false, its offered definitions as distorting, but it is still the only available way for a man to confirm himself as real, to objectify and know himself in public action. A man who does not objectify himself in action becomes unreal, as Achilles, according to Ulysses, is unreal; he loses, too, that spontaneity and truth-to-self which is the very ground of his opposition to the society.

This is Hamlet's situation. Hamlet must refuse to act in the public ways open to him because they seem to him false definitions of himself; but his refusal to act means that he begins to lose hold on his identity, to lose spontaneous life. He turns from the public roles and actions to the personal relationship with Ophelia, looking there for a kind of definition, to find that this too has been absorbed into the public pattern: Ophelia has made an inauthentic choice, like Rosencrantz and Guildenstern, she has wavered between Polonius and Hamlet and chosen the former. Hamlet, now, cannot even find the authentic self-expression he is looking for in the margins of society: he is stirred into spontaneous life only momentarily, with Horatio or the actors. He can now preserve his integrity only by evading the offered definitions, and this involves a state of constant fluidity: to be himself he must keep himself free from the limiting

demands of society, he must keep one jump ahead all the time. But the effort
of doing this, paradoxically, is destructive of the very integrity he hopes to
preserve; he, like the court, becomes involved in secretive and calculating
politics, only in his case the politics, ironically, is a way of staying free from the
machinations of the others. In a false society, there are a number of ways of
preserving integrity, but they are all self-defeating. A man, to avoid the exploitation of others, may make himself opaque, refuse self-disclosure in action, as
Hamlet does; but to refuse action is to stagnate, to lose spontaneity. He may, on
the other hand, try to play the society's game of manipulation, and by playing it
better than they do hoist them with their own petard; again, this involves a
surrender of integrity, a sharing in the shifty tactics of others. Hamlet does this,
and becomes like Claudius:

> *Hamlet:* 'Tis dangerous when the baser nature comes
> Between the pass and fell incensed points
> Of mighty opposites.
>
> *Horatio:* Why, what a king is this!   (V, 2)

Hamlet is completely trapped: he can find authenticity neither within nor
outside society, since both to step outside the official nexus of the court, and to
commit himself to it, involves loss of integrity, disintegration.

Hamlet's society is characterised by Claudius's first speech to the court in Act I
Scene 2. It is, above all, a society which weighs and measures, balancing consequences according to a fixed and rational scale of values: Claudius has weighed
delight and dole in equal scale, considered additional factors like the opinions of
the court, and made a decision: his efficient mind, moving easily from topic to
topic, is offended by the disproportion of Hamlet's obstinate persistence in grief.
For Claudius, feeling and action must be adjusted, according to reason; Hamlet,
like Troilus, emphasises the human response, the human energy:

> *Polonius:* My lord, I will use them according to their desert.
>
> *Hamlet:* God's bodykins, man, much better. Use every man after his desert, and
> who shall scape whipping? Use them after your own honour and dignity: the less
> they deserve, the more merit is in your bounty.   (II, 2)

Hamlet rejects the ethic of rational weighing, as Troilus does, in favour of a
free, spontaneous self-giving which disturbs rational calculations. This is a
viewpoint which the society cannot tolerate: it is bounty, free self-giving, which
Laertes and Polonius criticise in Ophelia: she must be chary of herself, not
prodigal, set her entreatments at a 'higher rate'. To act spontaneously, disproportionately, is to be vulnerable, to overstep the safe limits of social role and
expose one's true self freely, without balanced calculation. This can be socially
disruptive: for society to function, men must suit the action to the word and
the word to the action, as Hamlet reminds the player; like clowns and ambassadors, men must not speak more than is set down for them. The contrast is
between spontaneous self-expression and reflective restraint, between the pure,

fluid freedom of the subjective self, and the defined, known limits of the self as object.

The society of *Hamlet* lacks spontaneous life: men have to stifle themselves in the interests of the State. But this, at least, means that action can be socially responsible, in a way that spontaneous action often is not. It is Guildenstern, the hollow man, who seals Hamlet's death-warrant with his reminder that kingship is a massy wheel, to whose spokes ten thousand lesser things are adjoined: the symbol of social responsibility is one of unity, coherence. Hamlet is described in terms of diffusion: his sighs seem to Ophelia to 'shatter all his bulk', the Ghost warns him that his 'knotted and combined locks' will part, 'and each particular hair stand on end', when he hears his story. The tragedy of the authentic man in a false society is that he is driven into a position where his authenticity becomes negative, a cynical withdrawal from all commitment, from responsibility. For Hamlet, as for Achilles, society becomes merely stuff for personal self-expression, old men to be parodied. Like Troilus, Hamlet is a man who sees himself in terms of process, and who therefore resists social function; subjectivity refuses to be objectified and becomes self-consuming. It is the deadlock of *Troilus* again, the incompatibility of authentic and responsible action, of action-for-self and action-for-others. To be true to oneself, to preserve integrity, may well involve falseness to others, in spite of what Polonius says.   [1967]

1. In the introduction to *Shakespeare and Society,* from which this essay is taken, Eagleton says that the book is an attempt to deepen our understanding of the relationship between the individual and society. He says, "In this book I try to show the tension in some of Shakespeare's plays between the self as it seems to a man in its personal depth, and as it seems in action, to others, as part of and responsible to a whole society" (11). But "what must be avoided, in maintaining this essential tension, is the habit of seeing society as inevitably external, a repressive mechanism which by definition threatens individual authenticity." We must understand that "individual experience is no more merely private than society is merely public" (10–11). Does the chapter on Hamlet meet these goals? If so, how?
2. How do Eagleton's concepts of how selves operate in society relate to those of Erving Goffman (see p. 194)?

The Play and The Chapter

1. Unlike other disciplinary material paired with literary works in other sections of this book, Eagleton talks directly about the play. He provides terms such as agency and the contrast between being a source and a subject, and then applies them to the play. Do you think that in the process of doing so, he has done justice to the play? Has he distorted it in any way? Has he helped us understand it? Are there important passages or aspects of the play that he neglects?

NONFICTION PROSE

JAMES BALDWIN

JAMES BALDWIN *(1924–87) was the vital literary voice of civil rights activism in the 1950s and '60s. Born in Harlem, he relates the circumstances of his youth including his calling as a preacher at the age of fourteen in the partly autobiographical* Go Tell It on the Mountain *(1953).* Notes of a Native Son *(1955),* Nobody Knows My Name *(1961), and* The Fire Next Time *(1963) were influential in teaching a white audience about black experience. He made his home in the south of France, but returned often to his native country to lecture and teach. Later works written for the stage attempted to come to terms with the racial and gay sexual tensions among New York intellectuals and offered powerful depictions of racism. These dramas,* Blues for Mister Charlie, Going to Meet the Man, *and* Tell Me How Long the Train's Been Gone, *were all written and produced in the 1960s.*

The Discovery of What It Means To Be an American*

"It is a complex fate to be an American," Henry James observed, and the principal discovery an American writer makes in Europe is just how complex this fate is. America's history, her aspirations, her peculiar triumphs, her even more peculiar defeats, and her position in the world—yesterday and today—are all so profoundly and stubbornly unique that the very word "America" remains a new, almost completely undefined and extremely controversial proper noun. No one in the world seems to know exactly what it describes, not even we motley millions who call ourselves Americans.

I left America because I doubted my ability to survive the fury of the color problem here. (Sometimes I still do.) I wanted to prevent myself from becoming *merely* a Negro; or, even, merely a Negro writer. I wanted to find out in what way the *specialness* of my experience could be made to connect me with other people instead of dividing me from them. (I was as isolated from Negroes as I was from whites, which is what happens when a Negro begins, at bottom, to believe what white people say about him.)

In my necessity to find the terms on which my experience could be related to that of others, Negroes and whites, writers and non-writers, I proved, to my astonishment, to be as American as any Texas G.I. And I found my experience was shared by every American writer I knew in Paris. Like me, they had been divorced from their origins, and it turned out to make very little difference that the origins of white Americans were European and mine were African—they were no more at home in Europe than I was.

*Baldwin, James, "The Discovery of What It Means To Be an American," *Collected Essays* (New York: Library Classics of the United States, 1998), 137–42.

The fact that I was the son of a slave and they were the sons of free men meant less, by the time we confronted each other on European soil, than the fact that we were both searching for our separate identities. When we had found these, we seemed to be saying, why, then, we would no longer need to cling to the shame and bitterness which had divided us so long.

It became terribly clear in Europe, as it never had been here, that we knew more   5
about each other than any European ever could. And it also became clear that, no matter where our fathers had been born, or what they had endured, the fact of Europe had formed us both was part of our identity and part of our inheritance.

I had been in Paris a couple of years before any of this became clear to me. When it did, I, like many a writer before me upon the discovery that his props have all been knocked out from under him, suffered a species of breakdown and was carried off to the mountains of Switzerland. There, in that absolutely alabaster landscape, armed with two Bessie Smith° records and a typewriter, I began to try to re-create the life that I had first known as a child and from which I had spent so many years in flight.

It was Bessie Smith, through her tone and her cadence, who helped me to dig back to the way I myself must have spoken when I was a pickaninny,° and to remember the things I had heard and seen and felt. I had buried them very deep. I had never listened to Bessie Smith in America (in the same way that, for years, I would not touch watermelon°), but in Europe she helped to reconcile me to being a "nigger."

I do not think that I could have made this reconciliation here. Once I was able to accept my role—as distinguished, I must say, from my "place"—in the extraordinary drama which is America, I was released from the illusion that I hated America.

The story of what can happen to an American Negro writer in Europe simply illustrates, in some relief, what can happen to any American writer there. It is not meant, of course, to imply that it happens to them all, for Europe can be very crippling, too; and, anyway, a writer, when he has made his first break-through, has simply won a crucial skirmish in a dangerous, unending and unpredictable battle. Still, the breakthrough is important, and the point is that an American writer, in order to achieve it, very often has to leave this country.

The American writer, in Europe, is released, first of all, from the necessity of   10
apologizing for himself. It is not until he *is* released from the habit of flexing his muscles and proving that he is just a "regular guy" that he realizes how crippling this habit has been. It is not necessary for him, there, to pretend to be something he is not, for the artist does not encounter in Europe the same suspicion he encounters here. Whatever the Europeans may actually think of artists, they have killed enough of them off by now to know that they are as real—and as persistent—as rain, snow, taxes or businessmen.

---

⁶**Bessie Smith** (1895–1937) a popular jazz and blues singer in the 1920s and '30s
⁷**pickaninny** African-American child, often derogatory   **watermelon** racially stereotyped depictions of African-Americans often included slices of watermelon

Of course, the reason for Europe's comparative clarity concerning the different functions of men in society is that European society has always been divided into classes in a way that American society never has been. A European writer considers himself to be part of an old and honorable tradition—of intellectual activity, of letters—and his choice of a vocation does not cause him any uneasy wonder as to whether or not it will cost him all his friends. But this tradition does not exist in America.

On the contrary, we have a very deep-seated distrust of real intellectual effort (probably because we suspect that it will destroy, as I hope it does, that myth of America to which we cling so desperately). An American writer fights his way to one of the lowest rungs on the American social ladder by means of pure bull-headedness and an indescribable series of odd jobs. He probably *has* been a "regular fellow" for much of his adult life, and it is not easy for him to step out of that lukewarm bath.

We must, however, consider a rather serious paradox: though American society is more mobile than Europe's, it is easier to cut across social and occupational lines there than it is here. This has something to do, I think, with the problem of status in American life. Where everyone has status, it is also perfectly possible, after all, that no one has. It seems inevitable, in any case, that a man may become uneasy as to just what his status is.

But Europeans have lived with the idea of status for a long time. A man can be as proud of being a good waiter as of being a good actor, and, in neither case, feel threatened. And this means that the actor and the waiter can have a freer and more genuinely friendly relationship in Europe than they are likely to have here. The waiter does not feel, with obscure resentment, that the actor has "made it," and the actor is not tormented by the fear that he may find himself, tomorrow, once again a waiter.

15   This lack of what may roughly be called social paranoia causes the American writer in Europe to feel—almost certainly for the first time in his life—that he can reach out to everyone, that he is accessible to everyone and open to everything. This is an extraordinary feeling. He feels, so to speak, his own weight, his own value.

It is as though he suddenly came out of a dark tunnel and found himself beneath the open sky. And, in fact, in Paris, I began to see the sky for what seemed to be the first time. It was borne in on me—and it did not make me feel melancholy—that this sky had been there before I was born and would be there when I was dead. And it was up to me, therefore, to make of my brief opportunity the most that could be made.

I was born in New York, but have lived only in pockets of it. In Paris, I lived in all parts of the city—on the Right Bank and the Left, among the bourgeoisie and among *les misérables,* and knew all kinds of people, from pimps and prostitutes in Pigalle to Egyptian bankers in Neuilly. This may sound extremely unprincipled or even obscurely immoral: I found it healthy. I love to talk to people, all kinds of people, and almost everyone, as I hope we still know, loves a man who loves to listen.

This perpetual dealing with people very different from myself caused a shattering in me of preconceptions I scarcely knew I held. The writer is meeting in Europe people who are not American, whose sense of reality is entirely different from his own. They may love or hate or admire or fear or envy this country—they see it, in any case, from another point of view, and this forces the writer to reconsider many things he had always taken for granted. This reassessment, which can be very painful, is also very valuable.

This freedom, like all freedom, has its dangers and its responsibilities. One day it begins to be borne in on the writer, and with great force, that he is living in Europe as an American. If he were living there as a European, he would be living on a different and far less attractive continent.

This crucial day may be the day on which an Algerian taxi-driver tells him how it feels to be an Algerian in Paris. It may be the day on which he passes a café terrace and catches a glimpse of the tense, intelligent and troubled face of Albert Camus.° Or it may be the day on which someone asks him to explain Little Rock° and he begins to feel that it would be simpler—and, corny as the words may sound, more honorable—to *go* to Little Rock than sit in Europe, on an American passport, trying to explain it.

This is a personal day, a terrible day, the day to which his entire sojourn has been tending. It is the day he realizes that there are no untroubled countries in this fearfully troubled world; that if he has been preparing himself for anything in Europe, he has been preparing himself—for America. In short, the freedom that the American writer finds in Europe brings him, full circle, back to himself, with the responsibility for his development where it always was: in his own hands.

Even the most incorrigible maverick has to be born somewhere. He may leave the group that produced him—he may be forced to—but nothing will efface his origins, the marks of which he carries with him everywhere. I think it is important to know this and even find it a matter for rejoicing, as the strongest people do, regardless of their station. On this acceptance, literally, the life of a writer depends.

The charge has often been made against American writers that they do not describe society, and have no interest in it. They only describe individuals in opposition to it, or isolated from it. Of course, what the American writer is describing is his own situation. But what is *Anna Karenina* describing if not the tragic fate of the isolated individual, at odds with her time and place?

The real difference is that Tolstoy° was describing an old and dense society in which everything seemed—to the people in it, though not to Tolstoy—to be

[20]**Albert Camus** existentialist Algerian writer (1913–60), author of novels including *The Plague* and *The Stranger* and plays including *Caligula* and *Cross Purpose*. In 1957, he won the Nobel Prize for Literature.   **Little Rock** capital of Arkansas, where in 1957, attempts to desegregate the high school led to race riots (see notes for Gwendolyn Brooks's "*The Chicago Defender* Sends a Man to Little Rock" in Chapter 15)   [24]**Tolstoy** Count Leo Tolstoy: (1828–1910) Russian writer whose works include the novels *Anna Karenina* and *War and Peace*

fixed forever. And the book is a masterpiece because Tolstoy was able to fathom, and make us see, the hidden laws which really governed this society and made Anna's doom inevitable.

25   American writers do not have a fixed society to describe. The only society they know is one in which nothing is fixed and in which the individual must fight for his identity. This is a rich confusion, indeed, and it creates for the American writer unprecedented opportunities.

That the tensions of American life, as well as the possibilities, are tremendous is certainly not even a question. But these are dealt with in contemporary literature mainly compulsively; that is, the book is more likely to be a symptom of our tension than an examination of it. The time has come, God knows, for us to examine ourselves, but we can only do this if we are willing to free ourselves of the myth of America and try to find out what is really happening here.

Every society is really governed by hidden laws, by unspoken but profound assumptions on the part of the people, and ours is no exception. It is up to the American writer to find out what these laws and assumptions are. In a society much given to smashing taboos without thereby managing to be liberated from them, it will be no easy matter.

It is no wonder, in the meantime, that the American writer keeps running off to Europe. He needs sustenance for his journey and the best models he can find. Europe has what we do not have yet, a sense of the mysterious and inexorable limits of life, a sense, in a word, of tragedy. And we have what they sorely need: a new sense of life's possibilities.

In this endeavor to wed the vision of the Old World with that of the New, it is the writer, not the statesman, who is our strongest arm. Though we do not wholly believe it yet, the interior life is a real life, and the intangible dreams of people have a tangible effect on the world.   [1959]

1. Since this is a personal essay, we can equate the narrator with the writer, James Baldwin. What kind of *ethos* does he create in the essay?
2. How does the essay define what Baldwin calls "the color problem"?
3. Why does moving to Europe solve the color problem for him? What does this tell us about the nature of the self? Has Baldwin arrived at an authentic self?
4. How does the fact that he is a writer figure into his experience in Europe?

RICHARD FORD

RICHARD FORD (1944–), *the fiction writer, was born in Jackson, Mississippi, and holds degrees from Michigan State University (B.A.) and the University of California (M.F.A.). He won a PEN/Faulkner citation for* The Sportswriter *and that same award plus a Pulitzer Prize for its sequel,* Independence Day. *It was the first time those two awards were given for a single work. When he was growing up in Jackson, Ford lived across the street from Eudora Welty (see p. 989) and at her death became her literary executor.*

In the Face*

I've hit a lot of people in the face in my life. Too many, I'm certain. Where I grew up, in Mississippi and Arkansas, in the fifties, to be willing to hit another person in the face with your fist meant something. It meant you were—well, brave. It meant you were experienced, too. It also meant you were brash, winningly impulsive, considerate of but not intimidated by consequence, admittedly but not too admittedly theatrical, and probably dangerous. As a frank, willed act, hitting in the face was a move toward adulthood, the place we were all headed—a step in the right direction.

I have likewise been hit in the face by others, also quite a few times. Usually just before or just after the former experience. Being hit in the face *goes with* doing the hitting yourself; and, while much less to be wished for, it was also important. It signaled some of those same approved character values (along with rugged resilience), and one had to be willing to endure it.

I can't with accuracy say where this hitting impulse came from, although it wasn't, I'm sure, mere peer pressure. My grandfather was a boxer, and to be "quick with your fists" was always a good trait in his view. He referred to hitting someone as "biffing." "I biffed him," he would say, then nod and sometimes even smile, which meant it was good, or at least admirably mischievous. Once, in Memphis in 1956, at a college football game in Crump Stadium, he "biffed" a man right in front of me—some drunk he got tired of and who, as we were heading up the steep concrete steps toward an exit, had kicked his heel not once but twice. The biff he delivered that day was a short, heavy boxer's punch from the shoulder. Technically a hook. There was only one blow, but the other guy, a man in a felt hat (it was autumn), took it on the chin and went over backward and right down the concrete steps into the midst of some other people. He was biffed. We just kept going.

There were other times my grandfather did that, too: once, right in the lobby of the hotel he ran—putting a man down on the carpet with two rather clubbing blows that seemed to me to originate in his legs. I don't remember what the man had done. Another time was at a hunting camp. A man we were riding with in a pickup truck somehow allowed a deer rifle to discharge *inside* the cab with us and blow a hole through the door—a very, very loud noise. The man was our host and was, naturally enough, drunk. But it scared us all nearly to death, and my grandfather, whose boxing name was Kid Richard, managed to biff this man by reaching over me and connecting right across the truck seat. It was ten o'clock at night. We were parked in a soybean field, hoping to see some deer. I never thought about it much afterward except to think that what he, my grandfather, did was unarguably the best response.

Later, when I was sixteen and my father had suddenly died, my grandfather escorted me to the YMCA—this was in Little Rock—and there, along with the boys training for the Golden Gloves, he worked out the solid mechanics of hitting for me: the need for bodily compactness, the proper tight fist, the confident step forward, the focus of the eyes, the virtue of the three-punch

*Ford, Richard. "In the Face," *The Best American Essays 1997*, ed. Ian Frazier and Robert Atwan (Boston: Houghton Mifflin, 1997), 51–55.

combination. And he taught me to "cut" a punch—the snapping, inward quarter-rotation of the fist, enacted at the precise moment of impact, and believed by him to magnify an otherwise hard jolt into a form of detonation. Following this, I tried out all I'd learned on the Golden Gloves boys, although with not very positive effects to myself. They were, after all, stringy, small-eyed, stingy-mouthed boys from rural Arkansas, with more to lose than I had—which is to say, they were tougher than I was. Still, in years to come, I tried to practice all I'd learned, always made the inward cut, took the step forward, always looked where I was hitting. These, I considered, were the crucial aspects of the science. Insider's knowledge. A part of who I was.

I of course remember the first occasion when I was hit in my own face— hit, that is, by someone who meant to hurt me, break my cheek or my nose (which happened), knock my teeth out, ruin my vision, cut me, deliver me to unconsciousness: kill me, at least figuratively. Ronnie Post was my opponent's name. It was 1959. We were fifteen and had experienced a disagreement over some trivial school business. (We later seemed to like each other.) But he and his friend, a smirky boy named Johnny Petit, found me after class one day and set on me with a torrent of blows. Others were present, too, and I did some wild, inex- pert swinging myself—nothing like what I would later learn. None of it lasted very long or did terrible damage. There was no spectacle. No one "boxed." But I got hit a lot, and I remember the feeling of the very first punch, which I saw coming yet could not avoid. The sensation was like a sound more than a shock you'd feel—two big cymbals being clanged right behind my head, followed almost immediately by cold traveling from my neck down into my toes. It didn't particularly hurt or knock me down. (It's not so easy to knock a person down.) And it didn't scare me. I may even have bragged about it later. But when I think about it now, after thirty-seven years, I can hear that cymbals sound and I go light-headed and cold again, as if the air all around me had suddenly gotten rarer.

Over the years since then, there have been other occasions for this sort of blunt but pointed response to the world's contingent signals—all occasions I think now to be regrettable. I once hit my best friend at the time flush in the cheek in between downs in a football game where we were playing shirts and skins. We were never friends after that. I once hit a fraternity brother a cheap shot in the nose, because he'd humiliated me in public, plus I simply didn't like him. At a dinner after a friend's funeral (of all places) I punched one of the other mourners, who, due to his excessive style of mourning, was making life and grief worse for everybody, and "needed" it, or so I felt. And many, many years ago, on a Saturday afternoon in the middle of May, on a public street in Jackson, Mississippi, I bent over and kissed another boy's bare butt for the express pur- pose of keeping him from hitting me. (There is very little to learn from all this, I'm afraid, other than where glory does not reside.)

I can hardly speak for the larger culture, but it's been true all my life that when I've been faced with what seemed to me to be an absolutely unfair, undeserved, and insoluble dilemma, I have thought about hitting it or its human emissary in the face. I've felt this about authors of unfair book reviews. I've felt it about other story writers whom I considered perfidious and due for some suffering. I've felt it about my wife on a couple of occasions. I once took a reckless swing at my own father, a punch that missed but brought on very bad consequences for me. I even felt it about my neighbor across the street, who, in the heat of an argument over nothing less than a barking dog, hit me in the face very hard, provoking me (or so I judged it) to hit him until he was down on the sidewalk and helpless. I was forty-eight years old when that happened—an adult in every way.

Today, by vow, I don't do that kind of thing anymore, and pray no one does it to me. But hitting in the face is still an act the possibility of which I *retain* as an idea—one of those unerasable personal facts we carry around in deep memory and inventory almost every day, and that represent the seemingly realest, least unequivocal realities we can claim access to. These facts are entries in our bottom line, which for each of us is always composed of plenty we're not happy about. Oddly enough, I don't think about hitting much when I attend an actual boxing match, where plenty of hitting happens. Boxing *seems* to be about so much more than hitting—about not getting hit, about certain attempts at grace, even about compassion or pathos or dignity. Though hitting in the face may be *all* boxing's about—that and money—and its devotees have simply fashioned suave mechanisms of language to defend against its painful redundancy. This is conceivably why A. J. Liebling wrote less about boxing than about boxers, and why he called it a science, not an art: because hitting in the face is finally not particularly interesting, inasmuch as it lacks even the smallest grain of optimism.

Part of my bottom line is that to myself I'm a man—fairly, unfairly, uninter- estingly, stupidly—who could be willing to hit you in the face. And there are still moments when I think this or that—some enmity, some affront, some inequity or malfeasance—will conclude in blows. Possibly I am all unwholesome violence inside, and what I need is therapy or to start life over again on a better tack. Or possibly there's just a meanness in the world and, as Auden wrote, "we are not any of us very nice." But that thought—hitting—thrilling and awful at the same time, is still one crude but important calibration for what's serious to me, and a guide, albeit extreme, to how I *could* confront the serious if I had to. In this way, I suppose it is a part of my inner dramaturgy, and relatable, as interior dramas and many perversions are, to a sense of justice. And in the end it seems simply better and more generally informative that I know at least this much about myself—and learn caution from it, forbearance, empathy—rather than know nothing about it at all.   [1997]

1. What is the theory of self implicit in this essay?
2. How might Eagleton's essay on *Hamlet* (see p. 702) help us interpret this essay?

LUCY GREALY

LUCY GREALY (1964–2002) *developed a bony growth on her jaw at the age of nine, which was found after a number of misdiagnoses to be Ewing's sarcoma, a rare and often fatal form of cancer. Half her jaw was removed in an effort to save*

her, after which she embarked on radiation, chemotherapy, and a decade of plastic
surgery to restore her face. Her book about the ordeal, Autobiography of a Face,
was one of the most celebrated of 1994. She committed suicide at age thirty-nine.

Mirrorings*

There was a long period of time, almost a year, during which I never looked in a
mirror. It wasn't easy, for I'd never suspected just how omnipresent are our own
images. I began by merely avoiding mirrors, but by the end of the year I found
myself with an acute knowledge of the reflected image, its numerous tricks and
wiles, how it can spring up at any moment: a glass tabletop, a well-polished door
handle, a darkened window, a pair of sunglasses, a restaurant's otherwise
magnificent brass-plated coffee machine sitting innocently by the cash register.

At the time, I had just moved, alone, to Scotland and was surviving on the dole,
as Britain's social security benefits are called. I didn't know anyone and had no
idea how I was going to live, yet I went anyway because by happenstance I'd met a
plastic surgeon there who said he could help me. I had been living in London,
working temp jobs. While in London, I'd received more nasty comments about
my face than I had in the previous three years, living in Iowa, New York, and
Germany. These comments, all from men and all odiously sexual, hurt and disoriented me. I also had journeyed to Scotland because after more than a dozen operations in the States my insurance had run out, along with my hope that further
operations could make any *real* difference. Here, however, was a surgeon who had
some new techniques, and here, amazingly enough, was a government willing to
foot the bill: I didn't feel I could pass up yet another chance to "fix" my face, which
I confusedly thought concurrent with "fixing" my self, my soul, my life.

Twenty years ago, when I was nine and living in America, I came home
from school one day with a toothache. Several weeks and misdiagnoses later,
surgeons removed most of the right side of my jaw in an attempt to prevent the
cancer they found there from spreading. No one properly explained the operation to me, and I awoke in a cocoon of pain that prevented me from moving or
speaking. Tubes ran in and out of my body, and because I was temporarily
unable to speak after the surgery and could not ask questions, I made up my
own explanations for the tubes' existence. I remember the mysterious manner
the adults displayed toward me. They asked me to do things: lie still for x-rays,
not cry for needles, and so on, tasks that, although not easy, never seemed equal
to the praise I received in return. Reinforced to me again and again was how I
was "a brave girl" for not crying, "a good girl" for not complaining, and soon I
began defining myself this way, equating strength with silence.

Then the chemotherapy began. In the seventies chemo was even cruder than
it is now, the basic premise being to poison patients right up to the very brink
of their own death. Until this point I almost never cried and almost always
received praise in return. Thus I got what I considered the better part of the deal.
But now it was like a practical joke that had gotten out of hand. Chemotherapy

*Grealy, Lucy, "Mirrorings," in *Autobiography of a Face* (Boston: Houghton Mifflin, 1994).

was a nightmare and I wanted it to stop; I didn't want to be brave anymore. Yet I had grown so used to defining myself as "brave"—i.e., *silent*—that the thought of losing this sense of myself was even more terrifying. I was certain that if I broke down I would be despicable in the eyes of both my parents and the doctors.

The task of taking me into the city for the chemo injections fell mostly on my mother, though sometimes my father made the trip. Overwhelmed by the sight of the vomiting and weeping, my father developed the routine of "going to get the car," meaning that he left the doctor's office before the injection was administered, on the premise that then he could have the car ready and waiting when it was all over. Ashamed of my suffering, I felt relief when he was finally out of the room. When my mother took me, she stayed in the room, yet this only made the distance between us even more tangible. She explained that it was wrong to cry *before* the needle went in; afterward was one thing, but before, that was mere fear, and hadn't I demonstrated my bravery earlier? Every Friday for two and a half years I climbed up onto that big doctor's table and told myself not to cry, and every week I failed. The two large syringes were filled with chemicals so caustic to the vein that each had to be administered very slowly. The whole process took about four minutes; I had to remain utterly still. Dry retching began in the first fifteen seconds, then the throb behind my eyes gave everything a yellow-green aura, and the bone-deep pain of alternating extreme hot and cold flashes made me tremble, yet still I had to sit motionless and not move my arm. No one spoke to me—not the doctor, who was a paradigm of the cold-fish physician; not the nurse, who told my mother I reacted much more violently than many of "the other children"; and not my mother, who, surely overwhelmed by the sight of her child's suffering, thought the best thing to do was remind me to be brave, to try not to cry. All the while I hated myself for having wept before the needle went in, convinced that the nurse and my mother were right, that I was "overdoing it," that the throwing up was psychosomatic, that my mother was angry with me for not being good or brave enough.

Yet each week, two or three days after the injection, there came the first flicker of feeling better, the always forgotten and gratefully rediscovered understanding that to simply be well in my body was the greatest thing I could ask for. I thought other people felt this appreciation and physical joy all the time, and I felt cheated because I was able to feel it only once a week.

Because I'd lost my hair, I wore a hat constantly, but this fooled no one, least of all myself. During this time, my mother worked in a nursing home in a Hasidic community. Hasidic law dictates that married women cover their hair, and most commonly this is done with a wig. My mother's friends were now all too willing to donate their discarded wigs, and soon the house seemed filled with them. I never wore one, for they frightened me even when my mother insisted I looked better in one of the few that actually fit. Yet we didn't know how to say no to the women who kept graciously offering their wigs. The cats enjoyed sleeping on them and the dogs playing with them, and we grew used to having to pick a wig up off a chair we wanted to sit in. It never struck us as odd until one day a visitor commented wryly as he cleared a chair for himself, and suddenly a great wave of shame overcame me. I had nightmares about wigs and flushed if I even heard the word, and one night I put myself out of my misery by getting up after everyone was asleep and gathering all the wigs except for one the dogs were fond of and that they had chewed up anyway. I hid all the rest in an old chest.

When you are only ten, which is when the chemotherapy began, two and a half years seem like your whole life, yet it did finally end, for the cancer was gone. I remember the last day of treatment clearly because it was the only day on which I succeeded in not crying, and because later, in private, I cried harder than I had in years; I thought now I would no longer be "special," that without the arena of chemotherapy in which to prove myself no one would ever love me, that I would fade unnoticed into the background. But this idea about *not being different* didn't last very long. Before, I foolishly believed that people stared at me because I was bald. After my hair eventually grew in, it didn't take long before I understood that I looked different for another reason. My face. People stared at me in stores, and other children made fun of me to the point that I came to expect such reactions constantly, wherever I went. School became a battleground.

Halloween, that night of frights, became my favorite holiday because I could put on a mask and walk among the blessed for a few brief, sweet hours. Such freedom I felt, walking down the street, my face hidden! Through the imperfect oval holes I could peer out at other faces, masked or painted or not, and see on those faces nothing but the normal faces of childhood looking back at me, faces I mistakenly thought were the faces everyone else but me saw all the time, faces that were simply curious and ready for fun, not the faces I usually braced myself for, the cruel, lonely, vicious ones I spent every day other than Halloween waiting to see around each corner. As I breathed in the condensed, plastic-scented air under the mask, I somehow thought that I was breathing in normality, that this joy and weightlessness were what the world was composed of, and that it was only my face that kept me from it, my face that was my own mask that kept me from knowing the joy I was sure everyone but me lived with intimately. How could the other children not know it? Not know that to be free of the fear of taunts and the burden of knowing no one would ever love you was all that anyone could ever ask for? I was a pauper walking for a short while in the clothes of the prince, and when the day ended I gave up my disguise with dismay.

10 I was living in an extreme situation, and because I did not particularly care for the world I was in, I lived in others, and because the world I did live in was dangerous now, I incorporated this danger into my secret life. I imagined myself to be an Indian. Walking down the streets, I stepped through the forest, my body ready for any opportunity to fight or flee one of the big cats that I knew stalked me. Vietnam and Cambodia, in the news then as scenes of catastrophic horror, were other places I walked through daily. I made my way down the school hall, knowing a land mine or a sniper might give themselves away at any moment with the subtle metal click I'd read about. Compared with a land mine, a mere insult about my face seemed a frivolous thing.

In those years, not yet a teenager, I secretly read—knowing it was somehow inappropriate—works by Primo Levi and Elie Wiesel, and every book by a survivor I could find by myself without asking the librarian. Auschwitz, Birkenau: I felt the blows of the capos and somehow knew that because at any moment we might be called upon to live for a week on one loaf of bread and some water called soup, the peanut-butter sandwich I found on my plate was nothing less than a miracle, an utter and sheer miracle capable of making me literally weep with joy.

I decided to become a "deep" person. I wasn't exactly sure what this would entail, but I believed that if I could just find the right philosophy, think the right thoughts, my suffering would end. To try to understand the world I was in, I undertook to find out what was "real," and I quickly began seeing reality as existing in the lowest common denominator, that suffering was the one and only dependable thing. But rather than spend all of my time despairing, though certainly I did plenty of that, I developed a form of defensive egomania: I felt I was the only one walking about in the world who understood what was really important. I looked upon people complaining about the most mundane things—nothing on TV, traffic jams, the price of new clothes—and felt joy because I knew how unimportant those things really were and felt unenlightened superiority because other people didn't. Because in my fantasy life I had learned to be thankful for each cold, blanketless night that I survived on the cramped wooden bunks, my pain and despair were a stroll through the country in comparison. I was often miserable, but I knew that to feel warm instead of cold was its own kind of joy, that to eat was a reenactment of the grace of some god whom I could only dimly define, and that to simply be alive was a rare, ephemeral gift.

As I became a teenager, my isolation began. My nonidentical twin sister started going out with boys, and I started—my most tragic mistake of all—to listen to and believe the taunts thrown at me daily by the very boys she and the other girls were interested in. I was a dog, a monster, the ugliest girl they had ever seen. Of all the remarks, the most damaging wasn't even directed at me but was really an insult to "Jerry," a boy I never saw because every day between fourth and fifth periods, when I was cornered by a particular group of kids, I was too ashamed to lift my eyes off the floor. "Hey, look, it's Jerry's girlfriend!" they shrieked when they saw me, and I felt such shame, knowing that this was the deepest insult to Jerry that they could imagine.

When pressed to it, one makes compensations. I came to love winter, when I could wrap up the disfigured lower half of my face in a scarf: I could speak to people and they would have no idea to whom and to what they were really speaking. I developed the bad habits of letting my long hair hang in my face and of always covering my chin and mouth with my hand, hoping it might be mistaken as a thoughtful, accidental gesture. I also became interested in horses and got a job at a rundown local stable. Having those horses to go to each day after school saved my life; I spent all of my time either with them or thinking about them. Completely and utterly repressed by the time I was sixteen, I was convinced that I would never want a boyfriend, not ever, and wasn't it convenient for me, even a blessing, that none would ever want me. I told myself I was free to concentrate on the "true reality" of life, whatever that was. My sister and her friends put on blue eye shadow, blow-dried their hair, and spent interminable hours in the local mall, and I looked down on them for this, knew they were misleading themselves and being overly occupied with the "mere surface" of living. I'd had thoughts like this when I was younger, ten or twelve, but now my philosophy was haunted by desires so frightening I was unable even to admit they existed.

15   Throughout all of this, I was undergoing reconstructive surgery in an attempt to rebuild my jaw. It started when I was fifteen, two years after chemo ended. I had known for years I would have operations to fix my face, and at night I fantasized about how good my life would finally be then. One day I got a clue that maybe it wouldn't be so easy. An older plastic surgeon explained the process of "pedestals" to me, and told me it would take *ten years* to fix my face. Ten years? Why even bother, I thought; I'll be ancient by then. I went to a medical library and looked up the "pedestals" he talked about. There were gruesome pictures of people with grotesque tubes of their own skin growing out of their bodies, tubes of skin that were harvested like some kind of crop and then rearranged, with results that did not look at all normal or acceptable to my eye. But then I met a younger surgeon, who was working on a new way of grafting that did not involve pedestals, and I became more hopeful and once again began to await the fixing of my face, the day when I would be whole, content, loved.

Long-term plastic surgery is not like in the movies. There is no one single operation that will change everything, and there is certainly no slow unwrapping of the gauze in order to view the final, remarkable result. There is always swelling, sometimes to a grotesque degree, there are often bruises, and always there are scars. After each operation, too frightened to simply go look in the mirror, I developed an oblique method, with several stages. First, I tried to catch my reflection in an overhead lamp: the roundness of the metal distorted my image just enough to obscure details and give no true sense of size or proportion. Then I slowly worked my way up to looking at the reflection in someone's eyeglasses, and from there I went to walking as briskly as possible by a mirror, glancing only quickly. I repeated this as many times as it would take me, passing the mirror slightly more slowly each time until finally I was able to stand still and confront myself.

The theory behind most reconstructive surgery is to take large chunks of muscle, skin, and bone and slap them into the roughly appropriate place, then slowly begin to carve this mess into some sort of shape. It involves long, major operations, countless lesser ones, a lot of pain, and many, many years. And also, it does not always work. With my young surgeon in New York, who with each passing year was becoming not so young, I had two or three soft-tissue grafts, two skin grafts, a bone graft, and some dozen other operations to "revise" my face, yet when I left graduate school at the age of twenty-five I was still more or less in the same position I had started in: a deep hole in the right side of my face and a rapidly shrinking left side and chin, a result of the radiation I'd had as a child and the stress placed upon the bone by the other operations. I was caught in a cycle of having a big operation, one that would force me to look monstrous from the swelling for many months, then having the subsequent revision operations that improved my looks tremendously, and then slowly, over the period of a few months or a year, watching the graft reabsorb back into my body, slowly shrinking down and leaving me with nothing but the scarred donor site the graft had originally come from.

It wasn't until I was in college that I finally allowed that maybe, just maybe, it might be nice to have a boyfriend. I went to a small, liberal, predominantly female school and suddenly, after years of alienation in high school, discovered that there were other people I could enjoy talking to who thought me intelligent and talented. I was, however, still operating on the assumption that no one, not ever, would be physically attracted to me, and in a curious way this shaped my personality. I became forthright and honest in the way that only the truly self-confident are, who do not expect to be rejected, and in the way of those like me, who do not even dare to ask acceptance from others and therefore expect no rejection. I had come to know myself as a person, but I would be in graduate school before I was literally, physically able to use my name and the word "woman" in the same sentence.

Now my friends repeated for me endlessly that most of it was in my mind, that, granted, I did not look like everyone else, but that didn't mean I looked bad. I am sure now that they were right some of the time. But with the constant surgery I was in a perpetual state of transfiguration. I rarely looked the same for more than six months at a time. So ashamed of my face, I was unable even to admit that this constant change affected me; I let everyone who wanted to know that it was only what was inside that mattered, that I had "grown used to" the surgery, that none of it bothered me at all. Just as I had done in childhood, I pretended nothing was wrong, and this was constantly mistaken by others for bravery. I spent a great deal of time looking in the mirror in private, positioning my head to show off my eyes and nose, which were not only normal but quite pretty, as my friends told me often. But I could not bring myself to see them for more than a moment: I looked in the mirror and saw not the normal upper half of my face but only the disfigured lower half.

People still teased me. Not daily, as when I was younger, but in ways that caused me more pain than ever before. Children stared at me, and I learned to cross the street to avoid them; this bothered me, but not as much as the insults I got from men. Their taunts came at me not because I was disfigured but because I was a disfigured *woman*. They came from boys, sometimes men, and almost always from a group of them. I had long, blond hair, and I also had a thin figure. Sometimes, from a distance, men would see a thin blonde and whistle, something I dreaded more than anything else because I knew that as they got closer, their tune, so to speak, would inevitably change; they would stare openly or, worse, turn away quickly in shame or repulsion. I decided to cut my hair to avoid any misconception that anyone, however briefly, might have about my being attractive. Only two or three times have I ever been teased by a single person, and I can think of only one time when I was ever teased by a woman.

Had I been a man, would I have had to walk down the street while a group of young women followed and denigrated my sexual worth?

Not surprisingly, then, I viewed sex as my salvation. I was sure that if only I could get someone to sleep with me, it would mean I wasn't ugly, that I was attractive, even lovable. This line of reasoning led me into the beds of several manipulative men who liked themselves even less than they liked me, and I in turn left each short-term affair hating myself, obscenely sure that if only I had been prettier it would have worked—he would have loved me and it would have been like those other love affairs that I was certain "normal" women had all the time. Gradually, I became unable to say "I'm depressed" but could say only "I'm ugly," because the two had become inextricably linked in my mind. Into that universal lie, that sad equation of "if only . . . ." that we are all prey to, I was sure that if only I had a normal face, then I would be happy.

The new surgeon in Scotland, Oliver Fenton, recommended that I undergo a procedure involving something called a tissue expander, followed by a bone graft. A tissue expander is a small balloon placed under the skin and then slowly blown up over the course of several months, the object being to stretch out the skin and create room and cover for the new bone. It's a bizarre, nightmarish thing to do to your face, yet I was hopeful about the end results and I was also able to spend the three months that the expansion took in the hospital. I've always felt safe in hospitals: they're the one place I feel free from the need to explain the way I look. For this reason the first tissue expander was bearable— just—and the bone graft that followed it was a success; it did not melt away like the previous ones.

The surgical stress this put upon what remained of my original jaw instigated the deterioration of that bone, however, and it became unhappily apparent that I was going to need the same operation I'd just had on the right side done to the left. I remember my surgeon telling me this at an outpatient clinic. I planned to be traveling down to London that same night on an overnight train, and I barely made it to the station on time, such a fumbling state of despair was I in.

I could not imagine going through it *again*, and just as I had done all my life, I searched and searched through my intellect for a way to make it okay, make it bearable, for a way to *do* it. I lay awake all night on that train, feeling the tracks slip beneath me with an odd eroticism, when I remembered an afternoon from my three months in the hospital. Boredom was a big problem those long after-noons, the days marked by meals and television programs. Waiting for the after-noon tea to come, wondering desperately how I could make time pass, it had suddenly occurred to me that I didn't have to make time pass, that it would do it of its own accord, that I simply had to relax and take no action. Lying on the train, remembering that, I realized I had no obligation to improve my situation, that I didn't have to explain or understand it, that I could just simply let it happen. By the time the train pulled into King's Cross station, I felt able to bear it yet again, not entirely sure what other choice I had.

25   But there was an element I didn't yet know about. When I returned to Scotland to set up a date to have the tissue expander inserted, I was told quite

casually that I'd be in the hospital only three or four days. Wasn't I going to spend the whole expansion time in the hospital? I asked in a whisper. What's the point of that? came the answer. You can just come in every day to the outpatient ward to have it expanded. Horrified by this, I was speechless. I would have to live and move about in the outside world with a giant balloon inside the tissue of my face? I can't remember what I did for the next few days before I went into the hospital, but I vaguely recall that these days involved a great deal of drinking alone in bars and at home.

I had the operation and went home at the end of the week. The only things that gave me any comfort during the months I lived with my tissue expander were my writing and Franz Kafka. I started a novel and completely absorbed myself in it, writing for hours each day. The only way I could walk down the street, could stand the stares I received, was to think to myself, "I'll bet none of them are writing a novel." It was that strange, old, familiar form of egomania, directly related to my dismissive, conceited thoughts of adolescence. As for Kafka, who had always been one of my favorite writers, he helped me in that I felt permission to feel alienated, and to have that alienation be okay, bearable, noble even. In the same way that imagining I lived in Cambodia helped me as a child, I walked the streets of my dark little Scottish city by the sea and knew without doubt that I was living in a story Kafka would have been proud to write.

The one good thing about a tissue expander is that you look so bad with it in that no matter what you look like once it's finally removed, your face has to look better. I had my bone graft and my fifth soft-tissue graft and, yes, even I had to admit I looked better. But I didn't look like me. Something was wrong: was *this* the face I had waited through eighteen years and almost thirty operations for? I somehow just couldn't make what I saw in the mirror correspond to the person I thought I was. It wasn't only that I continued to feel ugly; I simply could not conceive of the image as belonging to me. My own image was the image of a stranger, and rather than try to understand this, I simply stopped looking in the mirror. I perfected the technique of brushing my teeth without a mirror, grew my hair in such a way that it would require only a quick, simple brush, and wore clothes that were simply and easily put on, no complex layers or lines that might require even the most minor of visual adjustments.

On one level I understood that the image of my face was merely that, an image, a surface that was not directly related to any true, deep definition of the self. But I also knew that it is only through appearances that we experience and make decisions about the everyday world, and I was not always able to gather the strength to prefer the deeper world to the shallower one. I looked for ways to find a bridge that would allow me access to both, rather than riding out the constant swings between peace and anguish. The only direction I had to go in to achieve this was to strive for a state of awareness and self-honesty that sometimes, to this day, occasionally rewards me. I have found, I believe, that our whole lives are dominated, though it is not always so clearly translatable, by the question "How do I look?" Take all the many nouns in our lives—car, house, job, family, love, friends—and substitute the personal pronoun "I." It is not that we are all so self-obsessed; it is that all things eventually relate back to ourselves, and it is our own sense of how we appear to the world by which we chart our lives, how we navigate our personalities, which would otherwise be adrift in the ocean of *other* people's obsessions.

One evening toward the end of my year-long separation from the mirror, I was sitting in a café talking to someone—an attractive man, as it happened—and we were having a lovely, engaging conversation. For some reason I suddenly wondered what I looked like to him. What was he *actually* seeing when he saw me? So many times I've asked this of myself, and always the answer is this: a warm, smart woman, yes, but an unattractive one. I sat there in the café and asked myself this old question, and startlingly, for the first time in my life, I had no answer readily prepared. I had not looked in a mirror for so long that I quite simply had no clue as to what I looked like. I studied the man as he spoke; my entire life I had seen my ugliness reflected back to me. But now, as reluctant as I was to admit it, the only indication in my companion's behavior was positive.

30   And then, that evening in that café, I experienced a moment of the freedom I'd been practicing for behind my Halloween mask all those years ago. But whereas as a child I expected my liberation to come as a result of gaining something, a new face, it came to me now as the result of shedding something, of shedding my image. I once thought that truth was eternal, that when you understood something it was with you forever. I know now that this isn't so, that most truths are inherently unretainable, that we have to work hard all our lives to remember the most basic things. Society is no help; it tells us again and again that we can most be ourselves by looking like someone else, leaving our own faces behind to turn into ghosts that will inevitably resent and haunt us. It is no mistake that in movies and literature the dead sometimes know they are dead only after they can no longer see themselves in the mirror; and as I sat there feeling the warmth of the cup against my palm, this small observation seemed like a great revelation to me. I wanted to tell the man I was with about it, but he was involved in his own topic and I did not want to interrupt him, so instead I looked with curiosity toward the window behind him, its night-darkened glass reflecting the whole café, to see if I could, now, recognize myself.   [1993]

1. As you read through the essay, jot down the coping strategies Grealy acquired throughout her long ordeal.
2. What is your reaction to the description of the multiple operations Grealy undergoes during doctors' attempt to rebuild her jaw?
3. Notice that in addition to the period of avoidance of her own reflection described at the beginning of the essay, as a college girl, Grealy spent a lot of time looking in the mirror. She says that she did not see the prettiness her friends told her about, but only the disfigurement; nevertheless she lets us know that she was blond and had a good figure. Then she tells us the shocking truth: "Their taunts came at me not because I was disfigured but because I was a disfigured *woman*." What explains the difference between the way men reacted to her and the way women did?

4. "Something was wrong: was *this* the face I had waited . . . for?" At this point, Grealy tells us that her "own image was the image of a stranger," so she "simply stopped looking in the mirror." Then follows the experience of seeing herself reflected in the eyes of the man she is with in the café. Her experience of "shedding her image" is crucial to the understanding of the essay and what it is trying to tell us. Talk about what you think will happen this time when she is finally able to "see if I could, now, recognize myself."

5. What are the mistakes Grealy thinks she makes? What are the advantages her ordeal gives her?

6. Why is Grealy so averse to seeing her image when she admits that she looks better after use of the tissue exapander?

7. What insights does Grealy offer to people who are not disfigured?

8. How can Eagleton's essay on *Hamlet* (see p. 702) help us understand Grealy's essay?

9. Characterize Grealy as a narrator.

GERMAINE GREER

GERMAINE GREER *(1949–) wrote* The Female Eunuch, *from which "The Stereotype" is taken, in 1970 while she was a lecturer in English and Comparative Literary Studies at Warwick. On its publication in 1971, it became an important text in the "Second Wave" of the feminist movement (the "First Wave" was the movement for women's suffrage in the early twentieth century). Greer's other publications include studies of women writers and painters, of Shakespeare, and books such as* Daddy, We Hardly Know You *(1999) and* The Change: Women, Aging and the Menopause *(1991). She runs her own press and has published the work of other women writers. Her 1999 book,* The Whole Woman, *addresses the state of the feminist movement.*

The Stereotype*

In that mysterious dimension where the body meets the soul the stereotype is born and has her being. She is more body than soul, more soul than mind. To her belongs all that is beautiful, even the very word beauty itself. All that exists, exists to beautify her.

Taught from infancy that beauty is woman's sceptre, the mind shapes itself to the body, and roaming round its gilt cage, only seeks to adorn its prison.

Mary Wollstonecraft,°
A Vindication of the Rights of Woman, *1792, p. 90*

---

*Greer, Germaine, "The Stereotype," in *The Female Eunuch* (New York: McGraw-Hill, 1971).

[1]**Mary Wollstonecraft** (1759–97), nineteenth-century writer and social critic, began her career of social commentary with a pamphlet that responded to the French Revolution by supporting the right of the English to remove a bad king from the throne, as the French had done. The *Vindication of the Rights of Woman* supported education and the vote for women and argued that if women were financially dependent on men, marriage was legal prostitution, controversial ideas in the late eighteenth century.

The sun shines only to burnish her skin and gild her hair; the wind blows only to whip up the color in her cheeks; the sea strives to bathe her; flowers die gladly so that her skin may luxuriate in their essence. She is the crown of creation, the masterpiece. The depths of the sea are ransacked for pearl and coral to deck her; the bowels of the earth are laid open that she might wear gold, sapphires, diamonds and rubies. Baby seals are battered with staves, unborn lambs ripped from their mothers' wombs, millions of moles, muskrats, squirrels, minks, ermines, foxes, beavers, chinchillas, ocelots, lynxes, and other small and lovely creatures die untimely deaths that she might have furs. Egrets, ostriches and peacocks, butterflies and beetles yield her their plumage. Men risk their lives hunting leopards for her coats, and crocodiles for her handbags and shoes. Millions of silkworms offer her their yellow labors; even the seamstresses roll seams and whip lace by hand, so that she might be clad in the best that money can buy.

The men of our civilization have stripped themselves of the fineries of the earth so that they might work more freely to plunder the universe for treasures to deck my lady in. New raw materials, new processes, new machines are all brought into her service. My lady must therefore be the chief spender as well as the chief symbol of spending ability and monetary success. While her mate toils in his factory, she totters about the smartest streets and plushiest hotels with his fortune upon her back and bosom, fingers and wrists, continuing that essential expenditure in his house which is her frame and her setting, enjoying that silken idleness which is the necessary condition of maintaining her mate's prestige and her qualification to demonstrate it.[1] Once upon a time only the aristocratic lady could lay claim to the title of crown of creation: only her hands were white enough, her feet tiny enough, her waist narrow enough, her hair long and golden enough; but every well-to-do burgher's wife set herself up to ape my lady and to follow fashion, until my lady was forced to set herself out like a gilded doll overlaid with monstrous rubies and pearls like pigeons' eggs. Nowadays the Queen of England still considers it part of her royal female role to sport as much of the family jewelery as she can manage at any one time on all public occasions, although the male monarchs have escaped such showcase duty, which devolves exclusively upon their wives.

At the same time as woman was becoming the showcase for wealth and caste, while men were slipping into relative anonymity and "handsome is as handsome does," she was emerging as the central emblem of western art. For the Greeks the male and female body had beauty of a human, not necessarily a sexual, kind; indeed they may have marginally favored the young male form as the most powerful and perfectly proportioned. Likewise the Romans showed no bias towards the depiction of femininity in their predominantly monumental art. In the Renaissance the female form began to predominate, not only as the mother in the predominant emblem of *madonna col bambino,* but as an aesthetic study in herself. At first naked female forms took their chances in crowd scenes or diptychs of Adam and Eve, but gradually Venus claims ascendancy, Mary Magdalene ceases to be wizened and emaciated, and becomes nubile and ecstatic, portraits of anonymous young women, chosen only for their prettiness, begin to appear, are

[1]Thorstein Veblen (*op. cit.*), *passim.*

gradually disrobed, and renamed Flora or Primavera. Painters begin to paint their own wives and mistresses and royal consorts as voluptuous beauties, divesting them of their clothes if desirable, but not of their jewelry. Susanna keeps her bracelets on in the bath, and Hélène Fourment keeps ahold of her fur as well!

What happened to women in painting happened to her in poetry as well. Her beauty was celebrated in terms of the riches which clustered around her: her hair was gold wires, her brow ivory, her lips ruby, her teeth gates of pearl, her breasts alabaster veined with lapis lazuli, her eyes as black as jet.[2] The fragility of her loveliness was emphasized by the inevitable comparisons with the rose, and she was urged to employ her beauty in love-making before it withered on the stem.[3] She was for consumption; other sorts of imagery spoke of her in terms of cherries and cream, lips as sweet as honey and skin white as milk, breasts like cream uncrudded, hard as apples.[4] Some celebrations yearned over her finery as well, her lawn more transparent than morning mist, her lace as delicate as gossamer, the baubles that she toyed with and the favors that she gave.[5] Even now

[2]E.g.,

> I thought my mistress' hairs were gold,
> And in her locks my heart I fold;
> Her amber tresses were the sight
> That wrapped me in vain delight;
>
> Her ivory front, her pretty chin,
> Were stales that drew me on to sin;
> Her starry looks, her crystal eyes
> Brighter than the sun's arise.
>   (Robert Greene, *Francesco's Fortunes*)

[3]E.g.,

> When I admire the rose,
> That Nature makes repose
> In you the best of many,
> And see how curious art
> Hath decked every part,
> I think with doubtful view
> Whether you be the rose or the rose be you.
>   (Thomas Lodge, *William Longbeard*)

[4]E.g.,

> Her cheeks like apples which the sun hath rudded,
> Her lips like cherries charming men to bite,
> Her breasts like to a bowl of cream uncrudded . . .
>   (Edmund Spenser, *Epithalamion*)

[5]E.g.,

> The outside of her garments were of lawn,
> The lining purple silk, with gilt stars drawn,
> Her wide sleeves green and bordered with many a grove . . .
> Buskins of shells all silvered used she
> Branched with blushing coral to the knee,
> Where sparrows perched, of hollow pearl and gold,
> Such as the world would wonder to behold;
> Those with sweet water oft her handmaid fills,
> Which as she went would chirrup through the bills.

It is only proper to point out that in this passage Marlowe is setting Hero up as a foil to the natural beauty of Leander, beloved of the gods, who is presented quite naked. Hero as a stereotype might be considered one of the themes of the poem.

we find the thriller hero describing his classy dames' elegant suits, cheeky hats, well-chosen accessories and footwear; the imagery no longer dwells on jewels and flowers but the consumer emphasis is the same. The mousy secretary blossoms into the feminine stereotype when she reddens her lips, lets down her hair, and puts on something frilly.

5   Nowadays women are not expected, unless they are Paola di Liegi or Jackie Onassis, and then only on gala occasions, to appear with a king's ransom deployed upon their bodies, but they are required to look expensive, fashionable, well-groomed, and not to be seen in the same dress twice. If the duty of the few may have become less onerous, it has also become the duty of the many. The stereotype marshals an army of servants. She is supplied with cosmetics, underwear, foundation garments, stockings, wigs, postiches and hairdressing as well as her outer garments, her jewels and furs. The effect is to be built up layer by layer, and it is expensive. Splendor has given way to fit, line and cut. The spirit of competition must be kept up, as more and more women struggle towards the top drawer, so that the fashion industry can rely upon an expanding market. Poorer women fake it, ape it, pick up on the fashions a season too late, use crude effects, mistaking the line, the sheen, the gloss of the high-class article for a garish simulacrum. The business is so complex that it must be handled by an expert. The paragons of the stereotype must be dressed, coifed and painted by the experts and the style-setters, although they may be encouraged to give heart to the housewives studying their lives in pulp magazines by claiming a lifelong fidelity to their own hair and soap and water. The boast is more usually discouraging than otherwise, unfortunately.

As long as she is young and personable, every woman may cherish the dream that she may leap up the social ladder and dim the sheen of luxury by sheer natural loveliness; the few examples of such a feat are kept before the eye of the public. Fired with hope, optimism and ambition, young women study the latest forms of the stereotype, set out in *Vogue, Nova, Queen* and other glossies, where the mannequins stare from among the advertisements for fabulous real estate, furs and jewels. Nowadays the uniformity of the year's fashions is severely affected by the emergence of the pert female designers who direct their appeal to the working girl, emphasizing variety, comfort, and simple, striking effects. There is no longer a single face of the year: even Twiggy has had to withdraw into marketing and rationed personal appearances, while the Shrimp works mostly in New York. Nevertheless the stereotype is still supreme. She has simply allowed herself a little more variation.

The stereotype is the Eternal Feminine. She is the Sexual Object sought by all men, and by all women. She is of neither sex, for she has herself no sex at all. Her value is solely attested by the demand she excites in others. All she must contribute is her existence. She need achieve nothing, for she is the reward of achievement. She need never give positive evidence of her moral character because virtue is assumed from her loveliness, and her passivity. If any man who has no right to her be found with her she will not be punished, for she is morally neuter. The matter is solely one of male rivalry. Innocently she may drive men to madness and war. The more trouble she can cause, the more her stocks go up, for possession of her means more the more demand she excites. Nobody wants a girl whose beauty is imperceptible to all but him; and so men welcome the stereotype because it directs their taste into the most commonly recognized areas of value, although they may protest because some aspects of it do not tally with their fetishes. There is scope in the stereotype's variety for most fetishes. The leg man may follow miniskirts, the tit man can encourage see-through blouses and plunging necklines, although the man who likes fat women may

> *The myth of the strong black woman is the other side of the coin of the myth of the beautiful dumb blonde. The white man turned the white woman into a weak-minded, weak-bodied, delicate freak, a sex pot, and placed her on a pedestal; he turned the black woman into a strong self-reliant Amazon and deposited her in his kitchen. . . . The white man turned himself into the Omnipotent Administrator and established himself in the Front Office.*
>
> Eldridge Cleaver,°
> "The Allegory of the Black Eunuchs,"
> Soul on Ice, 1968, p. 162

feel constrained to enjoy them in secret. There are stringent limits to the variations on the stereotype, for nothing must interfere with her function as sex object. She may wear leather, as long as she cannot actually handle a motorbike: she may wear rubber, but it ought not to indicate that she is an expert diver or waterskier. If she wears athletic clothes the purpose is to underline her unathleticism. She may sit astride a horse, looking soft and curvy, but she must not crouch over its neck with her rump in the air.

> *She was created to be the toy of man, his rattle, and it must jingle in his ears whenever, dismissing reason, he chooses to be amused.*
>
> Mary Wollstonecraft,
> A Vindication of the Rights of Woman, 1792, p. 66

Because she is the emblem of spending ability and the chief spender, she is also the most effective seller of this world's goods. Every survey ever held has shown that the image of an attractive woman is the most effective advertising gimmick. She may sit astride the mudguard of a new car, or step into it ablaze with jewels; she may lie at a man's feet stroking his new socks; she may hold the petrol pump in a challenging pose, or dance through woodland glades in slow motion in all the glory of a new shampoo; whatever she does her image sells. The gynolatry of our civilization is written large upon its face, upon hoardings, cinema screens, television, newspapers, magazines, tins, packets, cartons, bottles, all consecrated to the reigning deity, the female fetish. Her dominion must not be thought to entail the rule of women, for she is not a woman. Her glossy lips and mat complexion, her unfocused eyes and flawless fingers, her extraordinary hair all floating and shining, curling and gleaming, reveal the inhuman triumph of cosmetics, lighting, focusing and printing, cropping and composition. She

[7]**Eldridge Cleaver** (1935–98) a Black Panther activist in the 1960s. He wrote *Soul on Ice,* his collection of essays about racism, while in prison.

sleeps unruffled, her lips red and juicy and closed, her eyes as crisp and black as if new painted, and her false lashes immaculately curled. Even when she washes her face with a new and creamier toilet soap her expression is as tranquil and vacant and her paint as flawless as ever. If ever she should appear tousled and troubled, her features are miraculously smoothed to their proper veneer by a new washing powder or a bouillon cube. For she is a doll: weeping, pouting or smiling, running or reclining, she is a doll. She is an idol, formed of the concatenation of lines and masses, signifying the lineaments of satisfied impotence.

Her essential quality is castratedness. She absolutely must be young, her body hairless, her flesh buoyant, and *she must not have a sexual organ.* No musculature must distort the smoothness of the lines of her body, although she may be painfully slender or warmly cuddly. Her expression must betray no hint of humor, curiosity or intelligence, although it may signify hauteur to an extent that is actually absurd, or smoldering lust, very feebly signified by drooping eyes and a sullen mouth (for the stereotype's lust equals irrational submission), or, most commonly, vivacity and idiot happiness. Seeing that the world despoils itself for this creature's benefit, she must be happy; the entire structure would topple if she were not. So the image of woman appears plastered on every surface imaginable, smiling interminably. An apple pie evokes a glance of tender beatitude, a washing machine causes hilarity, a cheap box of chocolates brings forth meltingly joyous gratitude, a Coke is the cause of a rictus of unutterable brilliance, even a new stick-on bandage is saluted by a smirk of satisfaction. A real woman licks her lips and opens her mouth and flashes her teeth when photographers appear: *she* must arrive at the premiere of her husband's film in a paroxysm of delight, or his success might be murmured about. The occupational

---

Discretion is the better part of Valerie
though all of her is nice
lips as warm as strawberries
eyes as cold as ice
the very best of everything
only will suffice
not for her potatoes
and puddings made of rice

Roger McGough,° Discretion

---

hazard of being a Playboy Bunny is the aching facial muscles brought on by the obligatory smiles.

10   So what is the beef? Maybe I couldn't make it. Maybe I don't have a pretty smile, good teeth, nice tits, long legs, a cheeky arse, a sexy voice. Maybe I don't know how to handle men and increase my market value, so that the rewards due to the feminine will accrue to me. Then again, maybe I'm sick of the masquerade. I'm sick of pretending eternal youth. I'm sick of belying my own

---

[9]**Roger McGough** (1937–) the English writer of over fifty books and films, among them the script for the Beatles' film *Yellow Submarine.*

intelligence, my own will, my own sex. I'm sick of peering at the world through false eyelashes, so everything I see is mixed with a shadow of bought hairs; I'm sick of weighting my head with a dead mane, unable to move my neck freely, terrified of rain, of wind, of dancing too vigorously in case I sweat into my lacquered curls. I'm sick of the Powder Room. I'm sick of pretending that some fatuous male's self-important pronouncements are the objects of my undivided attention, I'm sick of going to films and plays when someone else wants to, and sick of having no opinions of my own about either. I'm sick of being a transvestite. I refuse to be a female impersonator. I am a woman, not a castrate.

April Ashley was born male. All the information supplied by genes, chromosomes, internal and external sexual organs added up to the same thing. April was a man. But he longed to be a woman. He longed for the stereotype, not to embrace, but to be. He wanted soft fabrics, jewels, furs, makeup, the love and

> To what end is the laying out of the embroidered Hair, embared Breasts; vermilion Cheeks, alluring looks, Fashion gates, and artfull Countenances, effeminate intangling and insnaring Gestures, their Curls and Purls of proclaiming Petulancies, boulstered and laid out with such example and authority in these our days, as with Allowance and beseeming Conveniency?
>
> Doth the world wax barren through decrease of Generations, and become, like the Earth, less fruitful heretofore? Doth the Blood lose his Heat or do the Sunbeams become waterish and less fervent, than formerly they have been, that men should be thus inflamed and persuaded on to lust?
>
> Alex. Niccholes,° A Discourse of Marriage and Wiving,
> 1615, pp. 143–52

protection of men. So he was impotent. He couldn't fancy women at all, although he did not particularly welcome homosexual addresses. He did not think of himself as a pervert, or even as a transvestite, but as a woman cruelly transmogrified into manhood. He tried to die, became a female impersonator, but eventually found a doctor in Casablanca who came up with a more acceptable alternative. He was to be castrated, and his penis used as the lining of a surgically constructed cleft, which would be a vagina. He would be infertile, but that has never affected the attribution of femininity. April returned to England, resplendent. Massive hormone treatment had eradicated his beard, and formed tiny breasts: he had grown his hair and bought feminine clothes during the time he had worked as an impersonator. He became a model, and began to illustrate the feminine stereotype as he was perfectly qualified to do, for he was elegant, voluptuous, beautifully groomed, and in love with his own image. On an ill-fated day he married the heir to a peerage, the Hon. Arthur Corbett, acting out the highest achievement of the feminine dream, and went to live with him in a villa in Marbella. The marriage was never consummated. April's incompetence as a woman is what we must expect from a castrate, but it is not

[11]**Alexander Niccholes** seventeenth century English writer of a manual teaching men "[h]ow to choose a good wife rather than a bad one."

so very different after all from the impotence of feminine women, who submit to sex without desire, with only the infantile pleasure of cuddling and affection, which is their favorite reward. As long as the feminine stereotype remains the definition of the female sex, April Ashley is a woman, regardless of the legal decision ensuing from her divorce.[6] She is as much a casualty of the polarity of the sexes as we all are. Disgraced, unsexed April Ashley is our sister and our symbol.

[6]*Corbett* v. *Corbett* (otherwise Ashley) before Mr. Justice Ormerod (Law Report, February 2, 1970, Probate, Divorce and Admiralty Division). *News of the World,* February 8, 1970, *Sunday Mirror,* February 3, 8, 15, 1970.

1. This is a chapter of Greer's 1971 book, *The Female Eunuch.* It has been published separately a number of times. What is its structure?
2. As the narrator asks at the beginning of paragraph 10, "what is the beef?" What's wrong with the stereotype?
3. What is the effect of the embedded quotation by Alexander Niccholes?
4. Put the chapter into its historical context.

CHAPTER FOURTEEN

Gender, Sex, and Love

INTRODUCTION

That heterosexuals should desire sex is required for the continuation of the species. But why they should desire it during pregnancy, when it is not necessary for reproduction, or why women should desire it after they are no longer fertile, or why homosexuals should desire it is not as immediately obvious. Nor is it clear why human beings create highly elaborate codes and ideologies of love that surround sexual behavior. Why don't we just do it, rather than writing poems, plays, songs, and stories about it and talking about it for hours with our friends?

Perhaps our highly developed love talk is just what happened to sex when the human cortex increased in size enough to influence the animal functions like eating, sleeping, and exercising that are controlled by older parts of the brain. But as they learn to describe the way neglected babies fail to grow and the way people without friends and family become sick more often, scientists are beginning to be able to explain the function, if not the purpose, of love.

But even as we are learning about the biological value of love, some of its varieties are also subjects of fascinated exploration, not only how it affects adult pairings, but also its other forms such as filial, parental, patriotic, and universal. Scholars also study how it interacts with gender—the way we define masculine and feminine roles, as opposed to biological sex. This inquiry is especially important since the way society defines and enforces sex roles often entails the unequal distribution of power.

You will be able to see the way literary and nonliterary writers depict these themes in this section and will be able to see their relationship to works in Body, Spirit, and other sections, as well.

POETRY

MATTHEW ARNOLD

MATTHEW ARNOLD (1822–88) *grew up in Surrey, England, where his father was the head of the elite Rugby School. Arnold, having graduated from Oxford, where he won the Newdigate Prize for poetry, also became involved in education and worked for most of his adult life as an inspector of schools. He also wrote poetry, served as a professor of poetry at Oxford, and wrote literary and social criticism, arguing for literature as a source of moral values for society.*

Dover Beach

The sea is calm tonight.
The tide is full, the moon lies fair
Upon the straits;—on the French coast the light
Gleams and is gone; the cliffs of England stand,
5 Glimmering and vast, out in the tranquil bay.
Come to the window, sweet is the night-air!
Only, from the long line of spray
Where the sea meets the moon-blanched° land,
Listen! you hear the grating roar
10 Of pebbles which the waves draw back, and fling,
At their return, up the high strand,°
Begin, and cease, and then again begin,
With tremulous cadence slow, and bring
The eternal note of sadness in.
15 Sophocles° long ago
Heard it on the Aegean,° and it brought
Into his mind the turbid ebb and flow
Of human misery; we
Find also in the sound a thought,
20 Hearing it by this distant northern sea.

The Sea of Faith
Was once, too, at the full, and round earth's shore
Lay like the folds of a bright girdle furled.
But now I only hear
25 Its melancholy, long, withdrawing roar,
Retreating, to the breath
Of the night-wind, down the vast edges drear

---

[8]**moon-blanched** made pale or white by moonlight   [11]**strand** shore, beach
[15]**Sophocles** Greek playwright (496–406 BCE) who wrote plays such as *Antigone* and *Oedipus Rex*   [16]**Aegean** an area of the Mediterranean Sea east of Greece

And naked shingles° of the world.
Ah, love, let us be true
To one another! for the world, which seems   30
To lie before us like a land of dreams,
So various, so beautiful, so new,
Hath really neither joy, nor love, nor light,
Nor certitude, nor peace, nor help for pain;
And we are here as on a darkling° plain   35
Swept with confused alarms of struggle and flight,
Where ignorant armies clash by night.   [1867]

²⁸**shingles** pebble beaches   ³⁵**darkling** dark

1. How would you describe the form of this poem? How does the form reveal
   or affect the content?
2. What is the effect of Arnold's invocation of Sophocles?
3. Why the contrast between the calm beginning and the turbulent ending
   ("And we are here as on a darkling plain / Swept with confused alarms of
   struggle and flight / Where ignorant armies clash by night.")?
4. Why is this a love poem? What does this poem say about Arnold's understanding of love?

Elizabeth Bishop

Elizabeth Bishop *(1911–79) grew up in Canada and Massachusetts, graduating
from Vassar College in 1934, where she and her friends founded a literary magazine. She traveled extensively in Europe, lived in Key West, Florida, New York, and
Brazil, and taught at Harvard for seven years. Meanwhile, she won almost every
prestigious poetry prize in the country, including the Houghton Mifflin Poetry
Award, the Pulitzer Prize, the National Book Award, and the National Book Critics
Circle Award. She wrote for the* New Yorker, *translated Brazilian works, and
received honorary degrees from many colleges and universities. From 1949–1950,
she was consultant in poetry to the Library of Congress. Her books include* North &
South, Questions of Travel, The Complete Poems, Geography III, The
Complete Poems, 1927–1979, *and* The Collected Prose, *these last two books
published posthumously in 1983 and 1984.*

One Art

The art of losing isn't hard to master;
so many things seem filled with the intent
to be lost that their loss is no disaster.

Lose something every day. Accept the fluster
of lost door keys, the hour badly spent.   5
The art of losing isn't hard to master.

Then practice losing farther, losing faster:
places, and names, and where it was you meant
to travel. None of these will bring disaster.

10 I lost my mother's watch. And look! my last, or
next-to-last, of three loved houses went.
The art of losing isn't hard to master.

I lost two cities, lovely ones. And, vaster,
some realms I owned, two rivers, a continent.
15 I miss them, but it wasn't a disaster.

—Even losing you (the joking voice, a gesture
I love) I shan't have lied. It's evident
the art of losing's not too hard to master
though it may look like (*Write* it!) like disaster.   [1976]

1. Why the singularity of "one" art? Aren't there other arts, poetry for
   instance?
2. Describe the rhyme scheme and how it informs the content of the poem.
3. What does the content of the poem reveal about the poet's outlook on love?
4. How do parentheses function as part of this poem?
5. What is the tone of the poem?

JOHN DONNE

(For biographical notes, see p. 256.)

Song

Go, and catch a falling star,
   Get with child° a mandrake root,°
Tell me, where all past years are,
   Or who cleft the devil's foot,
5 Teach me to hear mermaids singing
Or to keep off envy's stinging,
      And find
      What wind
Serves to advance an honest mind.

10 If thou beest born to strange sights,
   Things invisible to see,
Ride ten thousand days and nights,

²**get with child** impregnate   **mandrake root** the root of a Mediterranean herb
sometimes used to promote conception. Because of its forked shape, it was thought to
resemble the form of a person.

Till age snow white hairs on thee;
Thou, when thou return'st, wilt tell me
All strange wonders that befell thee, 15
    And swear,
    No where
Lives a woman true, and fair.

If thou find'st one, let me know:
    Such a pilgrimage were sweet. 20
Yet do not, I would not go,
    Though at next door we might meet:
Though she were true when you met her,
And last till you write your letter,
    Yet she 25
    Will be
False, ere I come, to two, or three.

                                           [1633]

1. Relate the speaker's attitude towards love to Bishop's perception in "One Art."
2. Why is this a "Song"? What is the effect of his magical challenges?
3. What is the connection between love and faithfulness? Are they mutually exclusive?
4. What is the effect of poetic form and the deployment of language in stanza three?

A Valediction: Forbidding Mourning

As virtuous men pass mildly away,
    And whisper to their souls to go,
Whilst some of their sad friends do say,
    "The breath goes now," and some say, "No,"

So let us melt, and make no noise, 5
    No tear-floods, nor sigh-tempests move;
'Twere profanation of our joys
    To tell the laity° our love.

Moving of the earth° brings harms and fears,
    Men reckon what it did and meant; 10
But trepidation of the spheres,°
    Though greater far, is innocent.

Dull sublunary° lovers' love
    (Whose soul is sense) cannot admit
Absence, because it doth remove 15
    Those things which elemented° it.

---

[8]**laity** the secular public, as opposed to the clergy of a particular religion
[9]**Moving of the earth** earthquake   [11]**trepidation of the spheres** motions or the orbits of the heavenly bodies and realms of the universe thought to be structured as concentric rings   [13]**sublunary** below the moon, that is, earthly   [16]**elemented** composed

But we, by a love so much refined
    That our selves know not what it is,
Inter-assured of the mind,
20   Care less, eyes, lips, and hands to miss.

Our two souls therefore, which are one,
    Though I must go, endure not yet
A breach, but an expansion,
    Like gold to airy thinness beat.°

25 If they be two, they are two so
    As stiff twin compasses° are two:
Thy soul, the fixed foot, makes no show
    To move, but doth, if the other do;

And though it in the center sit,
30   Yet when the other far doth roam,
It leans, and hearkens after it,
    And grows erect, as that comes home.

Such wilt thou be to me, who must,
    Like the other foot, obliquely run;
35 Thy firmness makes my circle just,
    And makes me end where I begun.

                                                            [1633]

[24]**gold to airy thinness beat** gold beaten to gold leaf decreases in thickness   [26]**twin compasses** the device with two prongs connected by a hinge for drawing circles around a fixed center point

1. Describe the form of the poem.
2. How does Donne make use of scientific or technical imagery, and how does this affect the poem?
3. What does the poet's advice reveal about his attitudes towards the differences between men and women?

ROBERT FROST

OLC

ROBERT FROST (*1874–1963*) *was born in San Francisco, moving as a child to New England. He attended Dartmouth College and Harvard without taking a degree, working as a teacher, cobbler, and editor of the local newspaper in Lawrence, Massachusetts. His marriage to Elinor White in 1895 lasted until her death in 1938. In 1912, after their New England farm failed, they moved to England, where Frost came under the influence of poets Edward Thomas, Rupert Brooke, and Robert Graves. His friendship with Ezra Pound led to the publication of* A Boy's Will *and* North of Boston. *These two books won him recognition for his poetry, making him the most celebrated poet in America. His fame and honors*

grew with each book, four of which garnered Pulitzer prizes. West-Running
Brook *(1928) and* A Further Range *(1936) are among these. His much-admired
simplicity is the vehicle for layers of ambiguity and irony. Frost taught at a number
of colleges and universities and delivered the Inaugural Poem for President John F.
Kennedy in 1961.*

Home Burial

He saw her from the bottom of the stairs
Before she saw him. She was starting down,
Looking back over her shoulder at some fear.
She took a doubtful step and then undid it
To raise herself and look again. He spoke 5
Advancing toward her: "What is it you see
From up there always—for I want to know."
She turned and sank upon her skirts at that,
And her face changed from terrified to dull.
He said to gain time: "What is it you see," 10
Mounting until she cowered under him.
"I will find out now—you must tell me, dear."
She, in her place, refused him any help
With the least stiffening of her neck and silence.
She let him look, sure that he wouldn't see, 15
Blind creature; and a while he didn't see.
But at last he murmured, "Oh," and again, "Oh."

"What is it—what?" she said.

                              "Just that I see."

"You don't," she challenged. "Tell me what it is." 20

"The wonder is I didn't see at once.
I never noticed it from here before.
I must be wonted to it—that's the reason.
The little graveyard where my people are!
So small the window frames the whole of it. 25
Not so much larger than a bedroom, is it?
There are three stones of slate and one of marble,
Broad-shouldered little slabs there in the sunlight
On the sidehill. We haven't to mind *those*.
But I understand: it is not the stones, 30
But the child's mound—"

"Don't, don't, don't, don't," she cried.

She withdrew shrinking from beneath his arm
That rested on the banister, and slid downstairs;
And turned on him with such a daunting look, 35
He said twice over before he knew himself:
"Can't a man speak of his own child he's lost?"

"Not you! Oh, where's my hat? Oh, I don't need it!
I must get out of here. I must get air.
40 I don't know rightly whether any man can."

"Amy! Don't go to someone else this time.
Listen to me. I won't come down the stairs."
He sat and fixed his chin between his fists.
"There's something I should like to ask you, dear."

45 "You don't know how to ask it."

"Help me, then."
Her fingers moved the latch for all reply.

"My words are nearly always an offence.
I don't know how to speak of anything
50 So as to please you. But I might be taught
I should suppose. I can't say I see how.
A man must partly give up being a man
With women-folk. We could have some arrangement
By which I'd bind myself to keep hands off
55 Anything special you're a-mind to name.
Though I don't like such things 'twixt those that love.
Two that don't love can't live together without them.
But two that do can't live together with them."
She moved the latch a little. "Don't—don't go.
60 Don't carry it to someone else this time.
Tell me about it if it's something human.
Let me into your grief. I'm not so much
Unlike other folks as your standing there
Apart would make me out. Give me my chance.
65 I do think, though, you overdo it a little.
What was it brought you up to think it the thing
To take your mother-loss of a first child
So inconsolably—in the face of love.
You'd think his memory might be satisfied—"

70 "There you go sneering now!"

"I'm not, I'm not!
You make me angry. I'll come down to you.
God, what a woman! And it's come to this,
A man can't speak of his own child that's dead."

75 "You can't because you don't know how.
If you had any feelings, you that dug
With your own hand—how could you?—his little grave;
I saw you from that very window there,
Making the gravel leap and leap in air,
80 Leap up, like that, like that, and land so lightly
And roll back down the mound beside the hole.

I thought, Who is that man? I didn't know you.
And I crept down the stairs and up the stairs
To look again, and still your spade kept lifting.
Then you came in. I heard your rumbling voice   85
Out in the kitchen, and I don't know why,
But I went near to see with my own eyes.
You could sit there with the stains on your shoes
Of the fresh earth from your own baby's grave
And talk about your everyday concerns.   90
You had stood the spade up against the wall
Outside there in the entry, for I saw it."

"I shall laugh the worst laugh I ever laughed.
I'm cursed. God, if I don't believe I'm cursed."

"I can repeat the very words you were saying.   95
'Three foggy mornings and one rainy day
Will rot the best birch fence a man can build.'
Think of it, talk like that at such a time!
What had how long it takes a birch to rot
To do with what was in the darkened parlour.   100
You *couldn't* care! The nearest friends can go
With anyone to death, comes so far short
They might as well not try to go at all.
No, from the time when one is sick to death,
One is alone, and he dies more alone.   105
Friends make pretence of following to the grave,
But before one is in it, their minds are turned
And making the best of their way back to life
And living people, and things they understand.
But the world's evil. I won't have grief so   110
If I can change it. Oh, I won't, I won't!"

"There, you have said it all and you feel better.
You won't go now. You're crying. Close the door.
The heart's gone out of it: why keep it up.
Amy! There's someone coming down the road!"   115

"*You*—oh, you think the talk is all. I must go—
Somewhere out of this house. How can I make you—"

"If—you—do!" She was opening the door wider.
Where do you mean to go? First tell me that.
I'll follow and bring you back by force. I *will!*—"   [1914] 120

1. What is the nature of the argument the two characters are having?
2. Why does the male character cry out, "I'm cursed"?
3. What's the significance of the title "Home Burial"? What else does it relate
   to besides the child's grave?

THOM GUNN

(For biographical notes, see p. 351.)

Waitress

At one they hurry in to eat.
Loosed from the office job they sit
But somehow emptied out by it
And eager to fill up with meat.
5   *Salisbury Steak with Garden Peas.*

The boss who orders them about
Lunches elsewhere and they are free
To take a turn at ordering me.
I watch them hot and heavy shout:
10 *Waitress I want the Special please.*

My little breasts, my face, my hips,
My legs they study while they feed
Are not found on the list they read
While wiping gravy off their lips.
15 *Here Honey gimme one more scoop.*

I dream that while they belch and munch
And talk of Pussy, Ass, and Tits,
And sweat into their double knits,
I serve them up their Special Lunch:
20 *Bone Hash, Grease Pie, and Leather Soup.*

1. What difference does it make that the waitress is female and her customers
   are male? What connection does the language of the poem make between
   the men's work and their treatment of the waitress?
2. Is the waitress's "dream meal" for her male customers appropriate? Why or
   why not?
3. To what other works in this Anthology can you compare this poem?

HỒ XUÂN HƯƠNG

HỒ XUÂN HƯƠNG *(1775 or 1780–1820?), whose name means "spring essence,"
was the second wife of the governor of Yên Quảng province of Vietnam. In a time
when few women wrote poetry, she produced a group of poems remarkable in many
ways: they include frank observations about the declining status of women and the
indignities of being a second wife or concubine; and they both decry the corruption
of the Buddhist hierarchy and celebrate some of its precepts. They use the demanding
four- and eight-line verse form, the lu-shih, which is comparable in its intricacy to
the sonnet; they exploit the tonal nature of the Vietnamese language (the same word*

spoken at different pitches has different meanings) to produce racy double entendres; instead of using the symbol system based on Chinese characters used by literate elites, they use Nôm, a writing system representing Vietnamese speech.

On Sharing a Husband*

Screw the fate that makes you share a man.
One cuddles under cotton blankets; the other's cold.

Every now and then, well, maybe or maybe not.
Once or twice a month, oh, it's like nothing.

You try to stick to it like a fly on rice   5
but the rice is rotten. You slave like the maid,

but without pay. If I had known how it would go
I think I would have lived alone.   [18th or early 19th c]

*Translated by John Balaban.

1. What is "every now and then, well, maybe or maybe not"?
2. What is the effect of reading a poem in translation?
3. Compare the bitterness of this poem to the frustration of "Amy" in "Home Burial."
4. Compare the resignation of the poet to Mrs. Mallard in "The Story of an Hour."

JAMES W. JOHNSON

JAMES WELDON JOHNSON *(1871–1938), lawyer, professor, civil rights activist, ambassador (to three different South American countries), and founder of the first black newspaper in the United States, wrote in many genres, including songs (200 for Broadway and the words of the black anthem, "Lift Every Voice and Sing") and fiction (including the novel* Autobiography of an Ex-Colored Man, *about a black person passing for white). When he taught literature at Fisk University, he wrote his own autobiography,* Along This Way. *When he was killed in a car accident in New Hampshire, over 2,000 people attended his funeral in Harlem.*

The Glory of the Day Was in Her Face

The glory of the day was in her face,
The beauty of the night was in her eyes.
And over all her loveliness, the grace
Of morning blushing in the early skies.

And in her voice, the calling of the dove;   5
Like music of a sweet, melodious part.
And in her smile, the breaking light of love;
And all the gentle virtues in her heart.

And now the glorious day, the beauteous night,
The birds that signal to their mates at dawn,   10

To my dull ears, to my tear-blinded sight
Are one with all the dead, since she is gone.   [1935]

1. How has Johnson characterized "her"?
2. Compare this sonnet to Shakespeare's "My mistress' eyes . . .". (Sonnet 130; see p. 758.)

MICHAEL LASSELL

MICHAEL LASSELL *(1947–) holds degrees from Colgate, California Institute of the Arts, and Yale, and lives in New York City, where he is the features editor of* Metropolitan Home *magazine. His books of poetry, fiction, and nonfiction include* A Flame for the Touch That Matters *(1998) and* Decade Dance *(1990), which won a Lambda Literary Award. He is also the editor of five books, including an anthology of lesbian and gay poetry.*

How to Watch Your Brother Die

For Carl Morse

When the call comes, be calm.
Say to your wife, "My brother is dying. I have to fly
to California."
Try not to be shocked that he already looks like
5   a cadaver.
Say to the young man sitting by your brother's side,
"I'm his brother."
Try not to be shocked when the young man says,
"I'm his lover. Thanks for coming."
10 Listen to the doctor with a steel face on.
Sign the necessary forms.
Tell the doctor you will take care of everything.
Wonder why doctors are so remote.

Watch the lover's eyes as they stare into
15 your brother's eyes as they stare into
space.
Wonder what they see there.

Remember the time he was jealous and
opened your eyebrow with a sharp stick.
20 Forgive him out loud
even if he can't
understand you.
Realize the scar will be
all that's left of him.

25 Over coffee in the hospital cafeteria
say to the lover, "You're an extremely good-looking

young man."
Hear him say,
"I never thought I was good enough looking to
deserve your brother."

Watch the tears well up in his eyes. Say,
"I'm sorry, I don't know what it means to be
the lover of another man."
Hear him say,
"It's just like a wife, only the commitment is
deeper because the odds against you are so much
greater."
Say nothing, but
take his hand like a brother's.

Drive to Mexico for unproved drugs that might
help him live longer.
Explain what they are to the border guard.
Fill with rage when he informs you,
"You can't bring those across."

Begin to grow loud.
Feel the lover's hand on your arm
restraining you. See in the guard's eye
how much a man can hate another man.
Say to the lover, "How can you stand it?"
Hear him say, "You get used to it."
Think of one of your children getting used to
another man's hatred.

Call your wife on the telephone. Tell her,
"He hasn't much time.
I'll be home soon." Before you hang up, say,
"How could anyone's commitment be deeper than
a husband and wife?" Hear her say,
"Please. I don't want to know all the details."

When he slips into an irrevocable coma,
hold his lover in your arms while he sobs,
no longer strong. Wonder how much longer
you will be able to be strong.
Feel how it feels to hold a man in your arms
whose arms are used to holding men.
Offer God anything to bring your brother back.
Know you have nothing God could possibly want.
Curse God, but do not
abandon Him.

Stare at the face of the funeral director
when he tells you he will not
embalm the body for fear of
contamination. Let him see in your eyes

how much a man can hate another man.

Stand beside a casket covered in flowers,
75 white flowers. Say,
"Thank you for coming," to each of several
hundred men
who file past in tears, some of them
holding hands. Know that your brother's life
80 was not what you imagined. Overhear two
mourners say, "I wonder who'll be next?" and
"I don't care anymore,
as long as it isn't you."

Arrange to take an early flight home,
85 his lover will drive you to the airport.
When your flight is announced say,
awkwardly, "If I can do anything, please
let me know." Do not flinch when he says,
"Forgive yourself for not wanting to know him
90 after he told you. He did."
Stop and let it soak in. Say,
"He forgave me, or he knew himself?"
"Both," the lover will say, not knowing what else
to do. Hold him like a brother while he
95 kisses you on the cheek. Think that
you haven't been kissed by a man since
your father died. Think,
"This is no moment not to be strong."

Fly first class and drink Scotch. Stroke
100 your split eyebrow with a finger and
think of your brother alive. Smile
at the memory and think
how your children will feel in your arms,
warm and friendly and without challenge.   [1990]

1. Characterize the poet's attitude towards his brother's homosexuality.
2. Why is this poem a "how to" list? Compare the sentiments in this poem
   to those in Robert Frost's "Home Burial" (see p. 749). Is there anything
   distinctly male about the poetry?
3. How does this poem reflect the saga of AIDS in America?

ADRIENNE RICH

ADRIENNE RICH *(1929–) began writing poetry as a child under her father's
tutelage. Her first book of poems,* A Change of World, *was published before she
graduated from Radcliffe College and was selected by W. H. Auden to receive the*

Yale Younger Poets Prize. Subsequent books of poetry and prose came out of her experiences as a wife and mother, a political activist protesting the Vietnam War, and a lesbian feminist. Her 1973 book of poems Diving into the Wreck *won the National Book Award. She has also been awarded the Bollingen Prize, the Ruth Lilly Poetry Prize, the Lenore Marshall Poetry Prize, the Wallace Stevens Award, and a MacArthur Fellowship.*

Planetarium

Thinking of Caroline Herschel (1750–1848)
astronomer, sister of William;° and others.

A woman in the shape of a monster
a monster in the shape of a woman
the skies are full of them

a woman   'in the snow
among the Clocks and instruments   5
or measuring the ground with poles'
in her 98 years to discover
8 comets

she whom the moon ruled
like us   10
levitating into the night sky
riding the polished lenses

Galaxies of women, there
doing penance for impetuousness
ribs chilled   15
in those spaces   of the mind

An eye,

       'virile, precise and absolutely certain'
       from the mad webs of Uranusborg°

                    encountering the NOVA°   20

every impulse of light exploding
from the core
as life flies out of us

       Tycho whispering at last
       'Let me not seem to have lived in vain'°   25

What we see, we see
and seeing is changing

Epigraph**William [Herschel]** (1738–1822), astronomer, discoverer of Uranus
[19]**Uranusborg** a version of Uranienborg, sky castle, the name Danish astronomer Tycho Brahe (1546–1601) gave to his observatory   [20]**NOVA** Brahe discovered a "New Star" in the constellation of Cassiopeia.   [25]Brahe's last words

the light that shrivels a mountain
and leaves a man alive

30 Heartbeat of the pulsar
heart sweating through my body

The radio impulse
pouring in from Taurus°

    I am bombarded yet   I stand

35 I have been standing all my life in the
direct path of a battery of signals
the most accurately transmitted most
untranslatable language in the universe
I am a galactic cloud so deep   so invo-

40 luted that a light wave° could take 15
years to travel through me   And has
taken   I am an instrument in the shape
of a woman trying to translate pulsations
into images   for the relief of the body

45 and the reconstruction of the mind.

                                              [1968]

³³**Taurus** constellation   ⁴⁰**light wave** Distances in space are measured according to the
number of years they can be crossed by something traveling at the speed of light (light
years).

1. What is the relationship between the woman and the galaxy?
2. What does the poet mean when she says "I am a galactic cloud . . ."?
3. How does this poem reflect a conception of femininity?

WILLIAM SHAKESPEARE

OLC

(For biographical notes, see p. 266.)

Sonnet 130

My mistress' eyes are nothing like the sun;
Coral is far more red than her lips' red;
If snow be white, why then her breasts are dun;
If hairs be wires, black wires grow on her head.

5 I have seen roses damasked red and white,
But no such roses see I in her cheeks;
And in some perfumes is there more delight
Than in the breath that from my mistress reeks.
I love to hear her speak, yet well I know

10 That music hath a far more pleasing sound;

I grant I never saw a goddess go:°
My mistress, when she walks, treads on the ground.
    And yet, by heaven, I think my love as rare
    As any she, belied with false compare.

                                                 [1609]

¹¹**go** walk, move from place to place

1. Describe the form of this sonnet.
2. Why is this sonnet an unorthodox love poem?
3. What does this poem tell us about ideal beauty in Shakespeare's time?

ALAN SHAPIRO

ALAN SHAPIRO *(1952–) has won major awards for his teaching (at the University of North Carolina at Chapel Hill), memoirs (*Vigil*, about his sister's death, won the Discovery Award from the New England Booksellers' Association), and poetry (for instance, the O.B. Hardison Jr. Poetry Prize at the Folger Shakespeare Library).* Mixed Company *won the Los Angeles Book Award for poetry in 1996. Shapiro also writes literary criticism, for which there aren't so many prizes.*

Lover

To love thou blam'st me not, for love thou saist
Leads up to Heav'n, is both the way and guide;
Bear with me then, if lawful what I ask;
Love not the heav'nly Spirits, and how thir Love
Express they, by looks onely, or do they mix
Irradiance, virtual or immediate touch?
         —Adam to Raphael, Book VIII, *Paradise Lost*°

Since we can greet and be greeted only
    through the separate
and not entirely intelligible

languages of "membrane, joynt or limb,"
    and therefore
must with every greeting yearn

more urgently for the angelic
    congress°
we are barred from forever—

                                                 5

^{Epigraph}These are ll. 612–17 of Book III of John Milton's *Paradise Lost*, a passage in which Adam is asking the Archangel Raphael whether angels love, and if so, how they experience it. The angel's answer is that love is a requirement for happiness and since angels are happy, that means they love. Since they do not have physical bodies, their love is unencumbered by "membrane, joynt or limb" (*Paradise Lost* 3.625; "Lover," l. 4). "Easier than air, if spirits embrace, / Total they mix, Union of Pure with Pure / Desiring . . ." (ll. 626–28). ⁸**congress** meeting, sexual intercourse. Etymologically, a coming together, from the Latin.

¹⁰ spirits intermixing "easier
than air with air";°
since it is only distance here

that joins us in the misaligned
or unequal
¹⁵ effort we exert to overcome it,

and all distance, even the smallest,
even when we seem
to touch, to understand each other,

is a desert, what can we finally do
²⁰ but love the desert,
love the shimmering air

of one another that recedes
as we approach it,
love most of all the approach,

²⁵ the heat, the thirst that can make
of our ever
meeting here together,

in any way at all,
a virtual,
³⁰ if not miraculous, water.

[1996]

^{10–11}**"easier / than air with air"** *Paradise Lost* 3.626

1. How does the passage from *Paradise Lost* inform your reading of the poem?
2. Compare Shapiro's ideas about spiritual and physical love to Donne's in "A Valediction: Forbidding Mourning." See p. 747.
3. What evidence can you provide from this poem and other readings to support Shapiro's assertion that "we can greet and be greeted only / through the separate / and not entirely intelligible / languages"?
4. What is the solution he offers to the problem of the distance between people?

CATHY SONG

CATHY SONG *(1955–) was born in Honolulu, Hawai'i, where she worked with poet-critic John Unterecker when she attended the University of Hawaii. She received a B.A. from Wellesley College and an M.F.A. from Boston University. She married Dr. Douglas Davenport and has two children. She returned to Hawai'i in 1987, where she is a member of the Bamboo Ridge study group and teaches in the Poets in the Schools program. She has received the 1982 Yale Series of Younger Poets Award, the Shelley Memorial Award from the Poetry Society of America, the Hawai'i Award for Literature, and a National Endowment for the Arts Fellowship.*

Books by Cathy Song include Picture Bride *(1983),* Frameless Windows, Squares of Light *(1988),* School Figures *(1994), and* The Land of Bliss *(2001).*

The Hand That Feeds

I lift my blouse
and pop a breast into his mouth.
Clever with a grin,
a ring of eight pearly teeth
like beads on a rattle,   5
he is careful not to bite
the hand that feeds.
He closes his eyes,
anxious to settle down
and begin the slow swim   10
back to the primordial waters,
sluggish,
dark without stars.
He begins to suck and
suck, all night   15
if he could,
his tongue in the mouth
working its patient tasting.
This is his first pleasure.

Pinned under the platypus   20
weight of his body,
I am trapped
until the sucking stops
and I can pry my nipple,
its little piece of meat,   25
out of his slack mouth.
Once he's asleep his teeth clamp
shut like the bars of a cage.
Until then I am stuck,
beached among the living.   30
I can only listen
to their movements upstairs,
the clatter of dishes,
the ringing of the telephone,
a chair scraping across the hardwood floor.   35
The living take down messages for me.

He grunts and chuckles
in his dream of returning
upstream, one hand pinching
whichever nipple is free.   40
His fingers twist and turn

the little knob of nipple
as if it were a radio dial.
And with an ear pressed flat against
45 the knocking of my heartbeat,
as close as we'll ever be,
he listens for the right frequency,
adjusting sleep
to the rhythm of the absolute.   [1992]

1. Contrast the first stanza with the second. What's the significance of the change in tone?
2. What does the difference in tone revealed in the previous question suggest about the breast-feeding woman in the poem? What does the poem in its entirety suggest about breast-feeding in general? Which specific lines can you use as evidence?
3. Compare the complicated nature of a mother's love to the complicated nature of a sexual relationship.

FICTION

RAYMOND CARVER

RAYMOND CARVER *(1938–88), born to a working-class family, lived most of his life in the Pacific Northwest, where he wrote both fiction and poetry that have been translated into twenty languages, as well as essays and* Doestoevsky, A Screenplay. *Among his awards were a Guggenheim Fellowship, grants from the National Endowment for the Arts, the Harold Strauss Living award,* Poetry *magazine's Levinson Prize, a Brandeis Citation for fiction, and election to the American Academy and Institute of Arts and Letters. He married early and had two children by his first wife. He was troubled throughout his adult life by alcoholism, for which he was hospitalized in serious condition four times. Shortly after his divorce, he gave up alcohol and was sober for the last ten years of his life. He died of cancer at the age of fifty. His published fiction includes* Put Yourself in My Shoes, Furious Seasons and Other Stories, Where I'm Calling From, *and* Elephant and Other Stories. *His books of poetry include* Near Klamath, Winter Insomnia, Ultramarine, *and* A New Path to the Waterfall. *The following story is from the collection of the same name.*

What We Talk About When We Talk About Love

My friend Mel McGinnis was talking. Mel McGinnis is a cardiologist, and sometimes that gives him the right.

The four of us were sitting around his kitchen table drinking gin. Sunlight filled the kitchen from the big window behind the sink. There were Mel and me and his second wife, Teresa—Terri, we called her—and my wife, Laura. We lived in Albuquerque then. But we were all from somewhere else.

There was an ice bucket on the table. The gin and the tonic water kept going around, and we somehow got on the subject of love. Mel thought real love was nothing less than spiritual love. He said he'd spent five years in a seminary before quitting to go to medical school. He said he still looked back on those years in the seminary as the most important years in his life.

Terri said the man she lived with before she lived with Mel loved her so much he tried to kill her. Then Terri said, "He beat me up one night. He dragged me around the living room by my ankles. He kept saying, 'I love you, I love you, you bitch.' He went on dragging me around the living room. My head kept knocking on things." Terri looked around the table. "What do you do with love like that?"

She was a bone-thin woman with a pretty face, dark eyes, and brown hair   5
that hung down her back. She liked necklaces made of turquoise, and long pendant earrings.

"My God, don't be silly. That's not love, and you know it," Mel said. "I don't know what you'd call it, but I sure know you wouldn't call it love."

"Say what you want to, but I know it was," Terri said. "It may sound crazy to you, but it's true just the same. People are different, Mel. Sure, sometimes he may have acted crazy. Okay. But he loved me. In his own way maybe, but he loved me. There was love there, Mel. Don't say there wasn't."

Mel let out his breath. He held his glass and turned to Laura and me. "The man threatened to kill me," Mel said. He finished his drink and reached for the gin bottle. "Terri's a romantic. Terri's of the kick-me-so-I'll-know-you-love-me school. Terri, hon, don't look that way." Mel reached across the table and touched Terri's cheek with his fingers. He grinned at her.

"Now he wants to make up," Terri said.

"Make up what?" Mel said. "What is there to make up? I know what I know.   10
That's all."

"How'd we get started on this subject, anyway?" Terri said. She raised her glass and drank from it. "Mel always has love on his mind," she said. "Don't you, honey?" She smiled, and I thought that was the last of it.

"I just wouldn't call Ed's behavior love. That's all I'm saying, honey," Mel said. "What about you guys?" Mel said to Laura and me. "Does that sound like love to you?"

"I'm the wrong person to ask," I said. "I didn't even know the man. I've only heard his name mentioned in passing. I wouldn't know. You'd have to know the particulars. But I think what you're saying is that love is an absolute."

Mel said, "The kind of love I'm talking about is. The kind of love I'm talking about, you don't try to kill people."

Laura said, "I don't know anything about Ed, or anything about the situation.   15
But who can judge anyone else's situation?"

I touched the back of Laura's hand. She gave me a quick smile. I picked up Laura's hand. It was warm, the nails polished, perfectly manicured. I encircled the broad wrist with my fingers, and I held her.

"When I left, he drank rat poison," Terri said. She clasped her arms with her hands. "They took him to the hospital in Santa Fe. That's where we lived then, about ten miles out. They saved his life. But his gums went crazy from it. I mean they pulled away from his teeth. After that, his teeth stood out like fangs. My God," Terri said. She waited a minute, then let go of her arms and picked up her glass.

"What people won't do!" Laura said.

"He's out of the action now," Mel said. "He's dead."

20 Mel handed me the saucer of limes. I took a section, squeezed it over my drink, and stirred the ice cubes with my finger.

"It gets worse," Terri said. "He shot himself in the mouth. But he bungled that too. Poor Ed," she said. Terri shook her head.

"Poor Ed nothing," Mel said. "He was dangerous."

Mel was forty-five years old. He was tall and rangy with curly soft hair. His face and arms were brown from the tennis he played. When he was sober, his gestures, all his movements, were precise, very careful.

"He did love me though, Mel. Grant me that," Terri said. "That's all I'm asking. He didn't love me the way you love me. I'm not saying that. But he loved me. You can grant me that, can't you?"

25 "What do you mean, he bungled it?" I said.

Laura leaned forward with her glass. She put her elbows on the table and held her glass in both hands. She glanced from Mel to Terri and waited with a look of bewilderment on her open face, as if amazed that such things happened to people you were friendly with.

"How'd he bungle it when he killed himself?" I said.

"I'll tell you what happened," Mel said. "He took this twenty-two pistol he'd bought to threaten Terri and me with. Oh, I'm serious, the man was always threatening. You should have seen the way we lived in those days. Like fugitives. I even bought a gun myself. Can you believe it? A guy like me? But I did. I bought one for self-defense and carried it in the glove compartment. Sometimes I'd have to leave the apartment in the middle of the night. To go to the hospital, you know? Terri and I weren't married then, and my first wife had the house and kids, the dog, everything, and Terri and I were living in this apartment here. Sometimes, as I say, I'd get a call in the middle of the night and have to go in to the hospital at two or three in the morning. It'd be dark out there in the parking lot, and I'd break into a sweat before I could even get to my car. I never knew if he was going to come up out of the shrubbery or from behind a car and start shooting. I mean, the man was crazy. He was capable of wiring a bomb, anything. He used to call my service at all hours and say he needed to talk to the doctor, and when I'd return the call, he'd say, 'Son of a bitch, your days are numbered.' Little things like that. It was scary, I'm telling you."

"I still feel sorry for him," Terri said.

30 "It sounds like a nightmare," Laura said. "But what exactly happened after he shot himself?"

Laura is a legal secretary. We'd met in a professional capacity. Before we knew it, it was a courtship. She's thirty-five, three years younger than I am. In addition to being in love, we like each other and enjoy one another's company. She's easy to be with.

"What happened?" Laura said.

Mel said, "He shot himself in the mouth in his room. Someone heard the shot and told the manager. They came in with a passkey, saw what had happened, and called an ambulance. I happened to be there when they brought him in, alive but past recall. The man lived for three days. His head swelled up to twice the size of a normal head. I'd never seen anything like it, and I hope I never do again. Terri wanted to go in and sit with him when she found out about it. We had a fight over it. I didn't think she should see him like that. I didn't think she should see him, and I still don't."

"Who won the fight?" Laura said.

"I was in the room with him when he died," Terri said. "He never came up out of it. But I sat with him. He didn't have anyone else." 35

"He was dangerous," Mel said. "If you call that love, you can have it."

"It was love," Terri said. "Sure, it's abnormal in most people's eyes. But he was willing to die for it. He did die for it."

"I sure as hell wouldn't call it love," Mel said. "I mean, no one knows what he did it for. I've seen a lot of suicides, and I couldn't say anyone ever knew what they did it for."

Mel put his hands behind his neck and tilted his chair back. "I'm not interested in that kind of love," he said. "If that's love, you can have it."

Terri said, "We were afraid. Mel even made a will out and wrote to his brother in California who used to be a Green Beret. Mel told him who to look for if something happened to him." 40

Terri drank from her glass. She said, "But Mel's right—we lived like fugitives. We were afraid. Mel was, weren't you, honey? I even called the police at one point, but they were no help. They said they couldn't do anything until Ed actually did something. Isn't that a laugh?" Terri said.

She poured the last of the gin into her glass and waggled the bottle. Mel got up from the table and went to the cupboard. He took down another bottle.

"Well, Nick and I know what love is," Laura said. "For us, I mean," Laura said. She bumped my knee with her knee. "You're supposed to say something now," Laura said, and turned her smile on me.

For an answer, I took Laura's hand and raised it to my lips. I made a big production out of kissing her hand. Everyone was amused.

"We're lucky," I said. 45

"You guys," Terri said. "Stop that now. You're making me sick. You're still on the honeymoon, for God's sake. You're still gaga, for crying out loud. Just wait. How long have you been together now? How long has it been? A year? Longer than a year?"

"Going on a year and a half," Laura said, flushed and smiling.

"Oh, now," Terri said. "Wait awhile."

She held her drink and gazed at Laura.

"I'm only kidding," Terri said. 50

Mel opened the gin and went around the table with the bottle.

"Here, you guys," he said. "Let's have a toast. I want to propose a toast. A toast to love. To true love," Mel said.

We touched glasses.

"To love," we said.

55   Outside in the backyard, one of the dogs began to bark. The leaves of the aspen that leaned past the window ticked against the glass. The afternoon sun was like a presence in this room, the spacious light of ease and generosity. We could have been anywhere, somewhere enchanted. We raised our glasses again and grinned at each other like children who had agreed on something forbidden.

"I'll tell you what real love is," Mel said. "I mean, I'll give you a good example. And then you can draw your own conclusions." He poured more gin into his glass. He added an ice cube and a sliver of lime. We waited and sipped our drinks. Laura and I touched knees again. I put a hand on her warm thigh and left it there.

"What do any of us really know about love?" Mel said. "It seems to me we're just beginners at love. We say we love each other and we do, I don't doubt it. I love Terri and Terri loves me, and you guys love each other too. You know the kind of love I'm talking about now. Physical love, that impulse that drives you to someone special, as well as love of the other person's being, his or her essence, as it were. Carnal love and, well, call it sentimental love, the day-to-day caring about the other person. But sometimes I have a hard time accounting for the fact that I must have loved my first wife too. But I did, I know I did. So I suppose I am like Terri in that regard. Terri and Ed." He thought about it and then he went on. "There was a time when I thought I loved my first wife more than life itself. But now I hate her guts. I do. How do you explain that? What happened to that love? What happened to it, is what I'd like to know. I wish someone could tell me. Then there's Ed. Okay, we're back to Ed. He loves Terri so much he tries to kill her and he winds up killing himself." Mel stopped talking and swallowed from his glass. "You guys have been together eighteen months and you love each other. It shows all over you. You glow with it. But you both loved other people before you met each other. You've both been married before, just like us. And you probably loved other people before that too, even. Terri and I have been together five years, been married for four. And the terrible thing, the terrible thing is, but the good thing too, the saving grace, you might say, is that if something happened to one of us—excuse me for saying this—but if something happened to one of us tomorrow, I think the other one, the other person, would grieve for a while, you know, but then the surviving party would go out and love again, have someone else soon enough. All this, all of this love we're talking about, it would just be a memory. Maybe not even a memory. Am I wrong? Am I way off base? Because I want you to set me straight if you think I'm wrong. I want to know. I mean, I don't know anything, and I'm the first one to admit it."

"Mel, for God's sake," Terri said. She reached out and took hold of his wrist. "Are you getting drunk? Honey? Are you drunk?"

"Honey, I'm just talking," Mel said. "All right? I don't have to be drunk to say what I think. I mean, we're all just talking, right?" Mel said. He fixed his eyes on her.

60   "Sweetie, I'm not criticizing," Terri said.

She picked up her glass.

"I'm not on call today," Mel said. "Let me remind you of that. I am not on call," he said.

"Mel, we love you," Laura said.

Mel looked at Laura. He looked at her as if he could not place her, as if she was not the woman she was.

"Love you too, Laura," Mel said. "And you, Nick, love you too. You know something?" Mel said. "You guys are our pals," Mel said.   65

He picked up his glass.

Mel said, "I was going to tell you about something. I mean, I was going to prove a point. You see, this happened a few months ago, but it's still going on right now, and it ought to make us feel ashamed when we talk like we know what we're talking about when we talk about love."

"Come on now," Terri said. "Don't talk like you're drunk if you're not drunk."

"Just shut up for once in your life," Mel said very quietly. "Will you do me a favor and do that for a minute? So as I was saying, there's this old couple who had this car wreck out on the interstate. A kid hit them and they were all torn to shit and nobody was giving them much chance to pull through."

Terri looked at us and then back at Mel. She seemed anxious, or maybe that's   70 too strong a word.

Mel was handing the bottle around the table.

"I was on call that night," Mel said. "It was May or maybe it was June. Terri and I had just sat down to dinner when the hospital called. There'd been this thing out on the interstate. Drunk kid, teenager, plowed his dad's pickup into this camper with this old couple in it. They were up in their mid-seventies, that couple. The kid—eighteen, nineteen, something—he was DOA. Taken the steering wheel through his sternum. The old couple, they were alive, you understand. I mean, just barely. But they had everything. Multiple fractures, internal injuries, hemor-rhaging, contusions, lacerations, the works, and they each of them had them-selves concussions. They were in a bad way, believe me. And, of course, their age was two strikes against them. I'd say she was worse off than he was. Ruptured spleen along with everything else. Both kneecaps broken. But they'd been wear-ing their seatbelts and, God knows, that's what saved them for the time being."

"Folks, this is an advertisement for the National Safety Council," Terri said. "This is your spokesman, Dr. Melvin R. McGinnis, talking." Terri laughed. "Mel," she said, "sometimes you're just too much. But I love you, hon," she said.

"Honey, I love you," Mel said.

He leaned across the table. Terri met him halfway. They kissed.   75

"Terri's right," Mel said as he settled himself again. "Get those seatbelts on. But seriously, they were in some shape, those oldsters. By the time I got down there, the kid was dead, as I said. He was off in a corner, laid out on a gurney. I took one look at the old couple and told the ER nurse to get me a neurologist and an orthopedic man and a couple of surgeons down there right away."

He drank from his glass. "I'll try to keep this short," he said. "So we took the two of them up to the OR and worked like fuck on them most of the night. They had these incredible reserves, those two. You see that once in a while. So we did everything that could be done, and toward morning we're giving them a fifty-fifty chance, maybe less than that for her. So here they are, still alive the next morning. So, okay, we move them into the ICU, which is where they both kept plugging away at it for two weeks, hitting it better and better on all the scopes. So we transfer them out to their own room."

Mel stopped talking. "Here," he said, "let's drink this cheapo gin the hell up. Then we're going to dinner, right? Terri and I know a new place. That's where we'll go, to this new place we know about. But we're not going until we finish up this cut-rate, lousy gin."

Terri said, "We haven't actually eaten there yet. But it looks good. From the outside, you know."

80   "I like food," Mel said. "If I had it to do all over again, I'd be a chef, you know? Right, Terri?" Mel said.

He laughed. He fingered the ice in his glass.

"Terri knows," he said. "Terri can tell you. But let me say this. If I could come back again in a different life, a different time and all, you know what? I'd like to come back as a knight. You were pretty safe wearing all that armor. It was all right being a knight until gunpowder and muskets and pistols came along."

"Mel would like to ride a horse and carry a lance," Terri said.

"Carry a woman's scarf with you everywhere," Laura said.

85   "Or just a woman," Mel said.

"Shame on you," Laura said.

Terri said, "Suppose you came back as a serf. The serfs didn't have it so good in those days," Terri said.

"The serfs never had it good," Mel said. "But I guess even the knights were vessels to someone. Isn't that the way it worked? But then everyone is always a vessel to someone. Isn't that right? Terri? But what I liked about knights, besides their ladies, was that they had that suit of armor, you know, and they couldn't get hurt very easy. No cars in those days, you know? No drunk teenagers to tear into your ass."

"Vassals," Terri said.

90   "What?" Mel said.

"Vassals," Terri said. "They were called vassals, not vessels."

"Vassals, vessels," Mel said, "what the fuck's the difference? You knew what I meant anyway. All right," Mel said. "So I'm not educated. I learned my stuff. I'm a heart surgeon, sure, but I'm just a mechanic. I go in and fuck around and I fix things. Shit," Mel said.

"Modesty doesn't become you," Terri said.

"He's just a humble sawbones," I said. "But sometimes they suffocated in all that armor, Mel. They'd even have heart attacks if it got too hot and they were too tired and worn out. I read somewhere that they'd fall off their horses and not be able to get up because they were too tired to stand with all that armor on them. They got trampled by their own horses sometimes."

95   "That's terrible," Mel said. "That's a terrible thing, Nicky. I guess they'd just lay there and wait until somebody came along and made a shish kebab out of them."

"Some other vessel," Terri said.

"That's right," Mel said. "Some vassal would come along and spear the bastard in the name of love. Or whatever the fuck it was they fought over in those days."

"Same things we fight over these days," Terri said.

Laura said, "Nothing's changed."

The color was still high in Laura's cheeks. Her eyes were bright. She brought her glass to her lips.   100

Mel poured himself another drink. He looked at the label closely as if studying a long row of numbers. Then he slowly put the bottle down on the table and slowly reached for the tonic water.

"What about the old couple?" Laura said. "You didn't finish that story you started."

Laura was having a hard time lighting her cigarette. Her matches kept going out.

The sunshine inside the room was different now, changing, getting thinner. But the leaves outside the window were still shimmering, and I stared at the pattern they made on the panes and on the Formica counter. They weren't the same patterns, of course.

"What about the old couple?" I said.   105

"Older but wiser," Terri said.

Mel stared at her.

Terri said, "Go on with your story, hon. I was only kidding. Then what happened?"

"Terri, sometimes," Mel said.

"Please, Mel," Terri said. "Don't always be so serious, sweetie. Can't you take   110
a joke?"

"Where's the joke?" Mel said.

He held his glass and gazed steadily at his wife.

"What happened?" Laura said.

Mel fastened his eyes on Laura. He said, "Laura, if I didn't have Terri and if I didn't love her so much, and if Nick wasn't my best friend, I'd fall in love with you. I'd carry you off, honey," he said.

"Tell your story," Terri said. "Then we'll go to that new place, okay?"   115

"Okay," Mel said. "Where was I?" he said. He stared at the table and then he began again.

"I dropped in to see each of them every day, sometimes twice a day if I was up doing other calls anyway. Casts and bandages, head to foot, the both of them. You know, you've seen it in the movies. That's just the way they looked, just like in the movies. Little eye-holes and nose-holes and mouth-holes. And she had to have her legs slung up on top of it. Well, the husband was very depressed for the longest while. Even after he found out that his wife was going to pull through, he was still very depressed. Not about the accident, though. I mean, the accident was one thing, but it wasn't everything. I'd get up to his mouth-hole, you know, and he'd say no, it wasn't the accident exactly but it was because he couldn't see her through his eye-holes. He said that was what was making him feel so bad. Can you imagine? I'm telling you, the man's heart was breaking because he couldn't turn his goddamn head and *see* his goddamn wife."

Mel looked around the table and shook his head at what he was going to say.

"I mean, it was killing the old fart just because he couldn't *look* at the fucking woman."

120   We all looked at Mel.

"Do you see what I'm saying?" he said.

Maybe we were a little drunk by then. I know it was hard keeping things in focus. The light was draining out of the room, going back through the window where it had come from. Yet nobody made a move to get up from the table to turn on the overhead light.

"Listen," Mel said. "Let's finish this fucking gin. There's about enough here for one shooter all around. Then let's go eat. Let's go to the new place."

"He's depressed," Terri said. "Mel, why don't you take a pill?"

125   Mel shook his head. "I've taken everything there is."

"We all need a pill now and then," I said.

"Some people are born needing them," Terri said.

She was using her finger to rub at something on the table. Then she stopped rubbing.

"I think I want to call my kids," Mel said. "Is that all right with everybody? I'll call my kids," he said.

130   Terri said, "What if Marjorie answers the phone? You guys, you've heard us on the subject of Marjorie? Honey, you know you don't want to talk to Marjorie. It'll make you feel even worse."

"I don't want to talk to Marjorie," Mel said. "But I want to talk to my kids."

"There isn't a day goes by that Mel doesn't say he wishes she'd get married again. Or else die," Terri said. "For one thing," Terri said, "she's bankrupting us. Mel says it's just to spite him that she won't get married again. She has a boyfriend who lives with her and the kids, so Mel is supporting the boyfriend too."

"She's allergic to bees," Mel said. "If I'm not praying she'll get married again, I'm praying she'll get herself stung to death by a swarm of fucking bees."

"Shame on you," Laura said.

135   "Bzzzzzzz," Mel said, turning his fingers into bees and buzzing them at Terri's throat. Then he let his hands drop all the way to his sides.

"She's vicious," Mel said. "Sometimes I think I'll go up there dressed like a beekeeper. You know, that hat that's like a helmet with the plate that comes down over your face, the big gloves, and the padded coat? I'll knock on the door and let loose a hive of bees in the house. But first I'd make sure the kids were out, of course."

He crossed one leg over the other. It seemed to take him a lot of time to do it. Then he put both feet on the floor and leaned forward, elbows on the table, his chin cupped in his hands.

"Maybe I won't call the kids, after all. Maybe it isn't such a hot idea. Maybe we'll just go eat. How does that sound?"

"Sounds fine to me," I said. "Eat or not eat. Or keep drinking. I could head right on out into the sunset."

"What does that mean, honey?" Laura said. 140

"It just means what I said," I said. "It means I could just keep going. That's all it means."

"I could eat something myself," Laura said. "I don't think I've ever been so hungry in my life. Is there something to nibble on?"

"I'll put out some cheese and crackers," Terri said.

But Terri just sat there. She did not get up to get anything.

Mel turned his glass over. He spilled it out on the table. 145

"Gin's gone," Mel said.

Terri said, "Now what?"

I could hear my heart beating. I could hear everyone's heart. I could hear the human noise we sat there making, not one of us moving, not even when the room went dark. [1981]

1. What types of love do the characters discuss in this story?
2. Alcohol plays an important role in this story. What do the characters drink and how much? What effect does the alcohol have on them? How does Carver connect their consumption of alcohol to the passing of time?
3. Does the article by R. Chris Fraley and Phillip R. Shaver, "Airport Separations: A Naturalistic Study of Adult Attachment Dynamics in Separating Couples" (see Chapter 9, p. 178) shed any light on the physical behavior of the couples?
4. How does the narrator of James Weldon Johnson's "The Glory of the Day Was in Her Face" relate to the various couples in this story?
5. This story contains two examples of love expressed in a very extreme way: Ed and Terri and the older couple who were injured. What do these two couples have in common, or more specifically, what are the similarities and differences between their "love"? What is Mel's reaction to these couples and the details of their relationships?

KATE CHOPIN

OLC

KATE (O'FLAHERTY) CHOPIN *(1850–1904), from a prosperous family in St. Louis, lived for over a decade in New Orleans with her husband, the French-Creole corn merchant Oscar Chopin. After he died of malaria, she returned with her six children to St. Louis and began to write fiction, eventually producing numerous short stories and six novels. The Awakening was received with great disapproval because of its main character's adultery and was removed from libraries, its author publicly denounced. However, it was this novel that after her death gained her lasting fame. Many of the short stories, including "The Story of an Hour," were similarly controversial.*

The Story of an Hour

Knowing that Mrs. Mallard was afflicted with a heart trouble, great care was taken to break to her as gently as possible the news of her husband's death.

It was her sister Josephine who told her, in broken sentences; veiled hints that revealed in half concealing. Her husband's friend Richards was there, too, near her. It was he who had been in the newspaper office when intelligence of the railroad disaster was received, with Brently Mallard's name leading the list of "killed." He had only taken the time to assure himself of its truth by a second telegram, and had hastened to forestall any less careful, less tender friend in bearing the sad message.

She did not hear the story as many women have heard the same, with a paralyzed inability to accept its significance. She wept at once, with sudden, wild abandonment, in her sister's arms. When the storm of grief had spent itself she went away to her room alone. She would have no one follow her.

There stood, facing the open window, a comfortable, roomy armchair. Into this she sank, pressed down by a physical exhaustion that haunted her body and seemed to reach into her soul.

5 She could see in the open square before her house the tops of trees that were all aquiver with the new spring life. The delicious breath of rain was in the air. In the street below a peddler was crying his wares. The notes of a distant song which some one was singing reached her faintly, and countless sparrows were twittering in the eaves.

There were patches of blue sky showing here and there through the clouds that had met and piled one above the other in the west facing her window.

She sat with her head thrown back upon the cushion of the chair, quite motionless, except when a sob came up into her throat and shook her, as a child who has cried itself to sleep continues to sob in its dreams.

She was young, with a fair, calm face, whose lines bespoke repression and even a certain strength. But now there was a dull stare in her eyes, whose gaze was fixed away off yonder on one of those patches of blue sky. It was not a glance of reflection, but rather indicated a suspension of intelligent thought.

There was something coming to her and she was waiting for it, fearfully. What was it? She did not know; it was too subtle and elusive to name. But she felt it, creeping out of the sky, reaching toward her through the sounds, the scents, the color that filled the air.

10 Now her bosom rose and fell tumultuously. She was beginning to recognize this thing that was approaching to possess her, and she was striving to beat it back with her will—as powerless as her two white slender hands would have been.

When she abandoned herself a little whispered word escaped her slightly parted lips. She said it over and over under her breath: "Free, free, free!" The vacant stare and the look of terror that had followed it went from her eyes. They stayed keen and bright. Her pulses beat fast, and the coursing blood warmed and relaxed every inch of her body.

She did not stop to ask if it were or were not a monstrous joy that held her. A clear and exalted perception enabled her to dismiss the suggestion as trivial.

She knew that she would weep again when she saw the kind, tender hands folded in death; the face that had never looked save with love upon her, fixed and gray and dead. But she saw beyond that bitter moment a long procession of years to come that would belong to her absolutely. And she opened and spread her arms out to them in welcome.

There would be no one to live for during those coming years; she would live for herself. There would be no powerful will bending hers in that blind persistence with which men and women believe they have a right to impose a private will upon a fellow-creature. A kind intention or a cruel intention made the act seem no less a crime as she looked upon it in that brief moment of illumination.

And yet she had loved him—sometimes. Often she had not. What did it matter! What could love, the unsolved mystery, count for in face of this possession of self-assertion which she suddenly recognized as the strongest impulse of her being! 15

"Free! Body and soul free!" she kept whispering.

Josephine was kneeling before the closed door with her lips to the keyhole, imploring for admission. "Louise, open the door! I beg, open the door—you will make yourself ill. What are you doing, Louise? For heaven's sake open the door."

"Go away. I am not making myself ill." No; she was drinking in a very elixir of life through that open window.

Her fancy was running riot along those days ahead of her. Spring days, and summer days, and all sorts of days that would be her own. She breathed a quick prayer that life might be long. It was only yesterday she had thought with a shudder that life might be long.

She arose at length and opened the door to her sister's importunities. There was a feverish triumph in her eyes, and she carried herself unwittingly like a goddess of Victory. She clasped her sister's waist, and together they descended the stairs. Richards stood waiting for them at the bottom. 20

Some one was opening the front door with a latchkey. It was Brently Mallard who entered, a little travel-stained, composedly carrying his grip-sack and umbrella. He had been far from the scene of accident, and did not even know there had been one. He stood amazed at Josephine's piercing cry; at Richards' quick motion to screen him from the view of his wife.

But Richards was too late.

When the doctors came they said she had died of heart disease—of joy that kills. [1894]

1. Why is Louise Mallard introduced as Mrs. Mallard? What is the significance of her last name?
2. How does Louise Mallard react to the news of her husband's death? What is the significance of the scene she views from her bedroom window?
3. When she's alone in her room, what does she think about her marriage? How does she envision the future without Brently Mallard?
4. "The Story of an Hour" begins and ends with references to problems with Louise Mallard's heart. What is the nature of her "heart trouble"? How is this related to the "joy that kills"?
5. What does this story suggest about marriage? Would the story have the same effect if the gender roles were reversed?

SUSAN GLASPELL

SUSAN GLASPELL (1882–1948) graduated from Drake University and became a journalist on the staff of the Des Moines Daily News, *leaving that job when her stories for magazines enabled her to become a full-time writer. She met the stage director George Cook in 1915 and the two founded the Provincetown Players on Cape Cod, Massachusetts. Glaspell wrote ten plays for this company, which included Eugene O'Neill and Edna St. Vincent Millay as well as actors, directors, and writers of note. Her plays included* Women's Honor, Bernice, The Inheritors, *and* The Verge. *In 1922, Glaspell and Cook married and moved to New York City, where she wrote mostly fiction. In 1939 she won the Pulitzer Prize for* Alison's House, *a play based on the life of Emily Dickinson. She retired to Cape Cod, where she continued writing until her death.*

A Jury of Her Peers

When Martha Hale opened the storm-door and got a cut of the north wind, she ran back for her big woolen scarf. As she hurriedly wound that round her head her eye made a scandalized sweep of her kitchen. It was no ordinary thing that called her away—it was probably further from ordinary than anything that had ever happened in Dickson County. But what her eye took in was that her kitchen was in no shape for leaving: her bread all ready for mixing, half the flour sifted and half unsifted.

She hated to see things half done; but she had been at that when the team from town stopped to get Mr. Hale, and then the sheriff came running in to say his wife wished Mrs. Hale would come too—adding, with a grin, that he guessed she was getting scary and wanted another woman along. So she had dropped everything right where it was.

"Martha!" now came her husband's impatient voice. "Don't keep folks waiting out here in the cold."

She again opened the storm-door, and this time joined the three men and the one woman waiting for her in the big two-seated buggy.

5   After she had the robes tucked around her she took another look at the woman who sat beside her on the back seat. She had met Mrs. Peters the year before at the county fair, and the thing she remembered about her was that she didn't seem like a sheriff's wife. She was small and thin and didn't have a strong voice. Mrs. Gorman, sheriff's wife before Gorman went out and Peters came in, had a voice that somehow seemed to be backing up the law with every word. But if Mrs. Peters didn't look like a sheriff's wife, Peters made it up in looking like a sheriff. He was to a dot the kind of man who could get himself elected sheriff—a heavy man with a big voice, who was particularly genial with the law-abiding, as if to make it plain that he knew the difference between criminals and non-criminals. And right there it came into Mrs. Hale's mind, with a stab, that this man who was so pleasant and lively with all of them was going to the Wrights' now as a sheriff.

"The country's not very pleasant this time of year," Mrs. Peters at last ventured, as if she felt they ought to be talking as well as the men.

Mrs. Hale scarcely finished her reply, for they had gone up a little hill and could see the Wright place now, and seeing it did not make her feel like talking. It looked very lonesome this cold March morning. It had always been a lonesome-looking place. It was down in a hollow, and the poplar trees around it were lonesome-looking trees. The men were looking at it and talking about what had happened. The county attorney was bending to one side of the buggy, and kept looking steadily at the place as they drew up to it.

"I'm glad you came with me," Mrs. Peters said nervously, as the two women were about to follow the men in through the kitchen door.

Even after she had her foot on the door-step, her hand on the knob, Martha Hale had a moment of feeling she could not cross that threshold. And the reason it seemed she couldn't cross it now was simply because she hadn't crossed it before. Time and time again it had been in her mind, "I ought to go over and see Minnie Foster"—she still thought of her as Minnie Foster, though for twenty years she had been Mrs. Wright. And then there was always something to do and Minnie Foster would go from her mind. But *now* she could come.

The men went over to the stove. The women stood close together by the door. Young Henderson, the county attorney, turned around and said, "Come up to the fire, ladies." 10

Mrs. Peters took a step forward, then stopped. "I'm not—cold," she said.

And so the two women stood by the door, at first not even so much as looking around the kitchen.

The men talked for a minute about what a good thing it was the sheriff had sent his deputy out that morning to make a fire for them, and then Sheriff Peters stepped back from the stove, unbuttoned his outer coat, and leaned his hands on the kitchen table in a way that seemed to mark the beginning of official business. "Now, Mr. Hale," he said in a sort of semi-official voice, "before we move things about, you tell Mr. Henderson just what it was you saw when you came here yesterday morning."

The county attorney was looking around the kitchen.

"By the way," he said, "has anything been moved?" He turned to the sheriff. "Are things just as you left them yesterday?" 15

Peters looked from cupboard to sink; from that to a small worn rocker a little to one side of the kitchen table.

"It's just the same."

"Somebody should have been left here yesterday," said the county attorney.

"Oh—yesterday," returned the sheriff, with a little gesture as of yesterday having been more than he could bear to think of. "When I had to send Frank to Morris Center for that man who went crazy—let me tell you, I had my hands full *yesterday*. I knew you could get back from Omaha by today, George, and as long as I went over everything here myself—"

"Well, Mr. Hale," said the county attorney, in a way of letting what was past and gone go, "tell just what happened when you came here yesterday morning." 20

Mrs. Hale, still leaning against the door, had that sinking feeling of the mother whose child is about to speak a piece. Lewis often wandered along and got things mixed up in a story. She hoped he would tell this straight and plain, and not say unnecessary things that would just make things harder for

Minnie Foster. He didn't begin at once, and she noticed that he looked queer—
as if standing in that kitchen and having to tell what he had seen there yesterday morning made him almost sick.

"Yes, Mr. Hale?" the county attorney reminded.

"Harry and I had started to town with a load of potatoes," Mrs. Hale's
husband began.

Harry was Mrs. Hale's oldest boy. He wasn't with them now, for the very
good reason that those potatoes never got to town yesterday and he was taking
them this morning, so he hadn't been home when the sheriff stopped to say he
wanted Mr. Hale to come over to the Wright place and tell the county attorney
his story there, where he could point it all out. With all Mrs. Hale's other emotions came the fear now that maybe Harry wasn't dressed warm enough—they
hadn't any of them realized how that north wind did bite.

25   "We come along this road," Hale was going on, with a motion of his hand to
the road over which they had just come, "and as we got in sight of the house I
says to Harry, 'I'm goin' to see if I can't get John Wright to take a telephone.'
You see," he explained to Henderson, "unless I can get somebody to go in with
me they won't come out this branch road except for a price I can't pay. I'd spoke
to Wright about it once before; but he put me off, saying folks talked too much
anyway, and all he asked was peace and quiet—guess you know about how
much he talked himself. But I thought maybe if I went to the house and talked
about it before his wife, and said all the women-folks liked the telephones, and
that in this lonesome stretch of road it would be a good thing—well, I said to
Harry that that was what I was going to say—though I said at the same time that
I didn't know as what his wife wanted made much difference to John—"

Now there he was!—saying things he didn't need to say. Mrs. Hale tried to
catch her husband's eye, but fortunately the county attorney interrupted with:

"Let's talk about that a little later, Mr. Hale. I do want to talk about that, but
I'm anxious now to get along to just what happened when you got here."

When he began this time, it was very deliberately and carefully:

"I didn't see or hear anything. I knocked at the door. And still it was all quiet
inside. I knew they must be up—it was past eight o'clock. So I knocked again,
louder, and I thought I heard somebody say, 'Come in.' I wasn't sure—I'm not
sure yet. But I opened the door—this door," jerking a hand toward the door by
which the two women stood, "and there, in that rocker"—pointing to it—"sat
Mrs. Wright."

30   Everyone in the kitchen looked at the rocker. It came into Mrs. Hale's mind
that that rocker didn't look in the least like Minnie Foster—the Minnie Foster of
twenty years before. It was a dingy red, with wooden rungs up the back, and the
middle rung was gone, and the chair sagged to one side.

"How did she—look?" the county attorney was inquiring.

"Well," said Hale, "she looked—queer."

"How do you mean—queer?"

As he asked it he took out a note-book and pencil. Mrs. Hale did not like the
sight of that pencil. She kept her eye fixed on her husband, as if to keep him from
saying unnecessary things that would go into that note-book and make trouble.

Hale did speak guardedly, as if the pencil had affected him too.

"Well, as if she didn't know what she was going to do next. And kind of—done up."

"How did she seem to feel about your coming?"

"Why, I don't think she minded—one way or other. She didn't pay much attention. I said, 'Ho' do, Mrs. Wright? It's cold, ain't it?' And she said. 'Is it?'—and went on pleatin' at her apron.

"Well, I was surprised. She didn't ask me to come up to the stove, or to sit down, but just set there, not even lookin' at me. And so I said: 'I want to see John.'

"And then she—laughed. I guess you would call it a laugh.

"I thought of Harry and the team outside, so I said, a little sharp, 'Can I see John?' 'No,' says she—kind of dull like. 'Ain't he home?' says I. Then she looked at me. 'Yes,' says she, 'he's home.' 'Then why can't I see him?' I asked her, out of patience with her now. ''Cause he's dead' says she, just as quiet and dull—and fell to pleatin' her apron. 'Dead?' says I, like you do when you can't take in what you've heard.

"She just nodded her head, not getting a bit excited, but rockin' back and forth.

"'Why—where is he?' says I, not knowing *what* to say.

"She just pointed upstairs—like this"—pointing to the room above.

"I got up, with the idea of going up there myself. By this time I—didn't know what to do. I walked from there to here; then I says: 'Why, what did he die of?'

"'He died of a rope around his neck,' says she; and just went on pleatin' at her apron."

Hale stopped speaking, and stood staring at the rocker, as if he were still seeing the woman who had sat there the morning before. Nobody spoke; it was as if every one were seeing the woman who had sat there the morning before.

"And what did you do then?" the county attorney at last broke the silence.

"I went out and called Harry. I thought I might—need help. I got Harry in, and we went upstairs." His voice fell almost to a whisper. "There he was—lying over the—"

"I think I'd rather have you go into that upstairs," the county attorney inter- rupted, "where you can point it all out. Just go on now with the rest of the story."

"Well, my first thought was to get that rope off. It looked—"

He stopped, his face twitching.

"But Harry, he went up to him, and he said, 'No, he's dead all right, and we'd better not touch anything.' So we went downstairs.

"She was still sitting that same way. 'Has anybody been notified?' I asked. 'No,' says she, unconcerned.

"'Who did this, Mrs. Wright?' said Harry. He said it business-like, and she stopped pleatin' at her apron. 'I don't know,' she says. 'You don't *know*?' says Harry. 'Weren't you sleepin' in the bed with him?' 'Yes,' says she, 'but I was on the inside.' 'Somebody slipped a rope round his neck and strangled him, and you didn't wake up?' says Harry. 'I didn't wake up,' she said after him.

"We may have looked as if we didn't see how that could be, for after a minute she said, 'I sleep sound.'

"Harry was going to ask her more questions, but I said maybe that weren't our business; maybe we ought to let her tell her story first to the coroner or the sheriff. So Harry went fast as he could over to High Road—the Rivers' place, where there's a telephone."

"And what did she do when she knew you had gone for the coroner?" The attorney got his pencil in his hand all ready for writing.

"She moved from that chair to this one over here"—Hale pointed to a small chair in the corner—"and just sat there with her hands held together and lookin' down. I got a feeling that I ought to make some conversation, so I said I had come in to see if John wanted to put in a telephone; and at that she started to laugh, and then she stopped and looked at me—scared."

60   At the sound of a moving pencil the man who was telling the story looked up.

"I dunno—maybe it wasn't scared," he hastened: "I wouldn't like to say it was. Soon Harry got back, and then Dr. Lloyd came, and you, Mr. Peters, and so I guess that's all I know that you don't."

He said that last with relief, and moved a little, as if relaxing. Everyone moved a little. The county attorney walked toward the stair door.

"I guess we'll go upstairs first—then out to the barn and around there."

He paused and looked around the kitchen.

65   "You're convinced there was nothing important here?" he asked the sheriff. "Nothing that would—point to any motive?"

The sheriff too looked all around, as if to re-convince himself.

"Nothing here but kitchen things," he said, with a little laugh for the insignificance of kitchen things.

The county attorney was looking at the cupboard—a peculiar, ungainly structure, half closet and half cupboard, the upper part of it being built in the wall, and the lower part just the old-fashioned kitchen cupboard. As if its queerness attracted him, he got a chair and opened the upper part and looked in. After a moment he drew his hand away sticky.

"Here's a nice mess," he said resentfully.

70   The two women had drawn nearer, and now the sheriff's wife spoke.

"Oh—her fruit," she said, looking to Mrs. Hale for sympathetic understanding. She turned back to the county attorney and explained: "She worried about that when it turned so cold last night. She said the fire would go out and her jars might burst."

Mrs. Peters' husband broke into a laugh.

"Well, can you beat the women! Held for murder, and worrying about her preserves!"

The young attorney set his lips.

75   "I guess before we're through with her she may have something more serious than preserves to worry about."

"Oh, well," said Mrs. Hale's husband, with good-natured superiority, "women are used to worrying over trifles."

The two women moved a little closer together. Neither of them spoke. The county attorney seemed suddenly to remember his manners—and think of his future.

"And yet," said he, with the gallantry of a young politician, "for all their worries, what would we do without the ladies?"

The women did not speak, did not unbend. He went to the sink and began washing his hands. He turned to wipe them on the roller towel—whirled it for a cleaner place.

"Dirty towels! Not much of a housekeeper, would you say, ladies?"   80

He kicked his foot against some dirty pans under the sink.

"There's a great deal of work to be done on a farm," said Mrs. Hale stiffly.

"To be sure. And yet"—with a little bow to her—"I know there are some Dickson County farm-houses that do not have such roller towels." He gave it a pull to expose its full length again.

"Those towels get dirty awful quick. Men's hands aren't always as clean as they might be."

"Ah, loyal to your sex, I see," he laughed. He stopped and gave her a keen   85
look, "But you and Mrs. Wright were neighbors. I suppose you were friends, too."

Martha Hale shook her head.

"I've seen little enough of her of late years. I've not been in this house—it's more than a year."

"And why was that? You didn't like her?"

"I liked her well enough," she replied with spirit. "Farmers' wives have their hands full, Mr. Henderson. And then—" She looked around the kitchen.

"Yes?" he encouraged.   90

"It never seemed a very cheerful place," said she, more to herself than to him.

"No," he agreed; "I don't think anyone would call it cheerful. I shouldn't say she had the home-making instinct."

"Well, I don't know as Wright had, either," she muttered.

"You mean they didn't get on very well?" he was quick to ask.

"No; I don't mean anything," she answered, with decision. As she turned a   95
little away from him, she added: "But I don't think a place would be any the cheerfuler for John Wright's bein' in it."

"I'd like to talk to you about that a little later, Mrs. Hale," he said. "I'm anxious to get the lay of things upstairs now."

He moved toward the stair door, followed by the two men.

"I suppose anything Mrs. Peters does'll be all right?" the sheriff inquired. "She was to take in some clothes for her, you know—and a few little things. We left in such a hurry yesterday."

The county attorney looked at the two women whom they were leaving alone there among the kitchen things.

"Yes—Mrs. Peters," he said, his glance resting on the woman who was not   100
Mrs. Peters, the big farmer woman who stood behind the sheriff's wife. "Of course Mrs. Peters is one of us," he said, in a manner of entrusting responsibility.

"And keep your eye out, Mrs. Peters, for anything that might be of use. No telling; you women might come upon a clue to the motive—and that's the thing we need."

Mr. Hale rubbed his face after the fashion of a showman getting ready for a pleasantry.

"But would the women know a clue if they did come upon it?" he said; and, having delivered himself of this, he followed the others through the stair door.

The women stood motionless and silent, listening to the footsteps, first upon the stairs, then in the room above them.

Then, as if releasing herself from something strange, Mrs. Hale began to arrange the dirty pans under the sink, which the county attorney's disdainful push of the foot had deranged.

105   "I'd hate to have men comin' into my kitchen," she said testily—"snoopin' round and criticizin'."

"Of course it's no more than their duty," said the sheriff's wife, in her manner of timid acquiescence.

"Duty's all right," replied Mrs. Hale bluffly; "but I guess that deputy sheriff that come out to make the fire might have got a little of this on." She gave the roller towel a pull. "Wish I'd thought of that sooner! Seems mean to talk about her for not having things slicked up, when she had to come away in such a hurry."

She looked around the kitchen. Certainly it was not "slicked up." Her eye was held by a bucket of sugar on a low shelf. The cover was off the wooden bucket, and beside it was a paper bag—half full.

Mrs. Hale moved toward it.

110   "She was putting this in there," she said to herself—slowly.

She thought of the flour in her kitchen at home—half sifted, half not sifted. She had been interrupted, and had left things half done. What had interrupted Minnie Foster? Why had that work been left half done? She made a move as if to finish it,—unfinished things always bothered her,—and then she glanced around and saw that Mrs. Peters was watching her—and she didn't want Mrs. Peters to get that feeling she had got of work begun and then—for some reason—not finished.

"It's a shame about her fruit," she said, and walked toward the cupboard that the county attorney had opened, and got on the chair, murmuring: "I wonder if it's all gone."

It was a sorry enough looking sight, but "Here's one that's all right," she said at last. She held it toward the light. "This is cherries, too." She looked again. "I declare I believe that's the only one."

With a sigh, she got down from the chair, went to the sink, and wiped off the bottle.

115   "She'll feel awful bad, after all her hard work in the hot weather. I remember the afternoon I put up my cherries last summer.

She set the bottle on the table, and, with another sigh, started to sit down in the rocker. But she did not sit down. Something kept her from sitting down in that chair. She straightened—stepped back, and, half turned away, stood looking at it, seeing the woman who had sat there "pleatin' at her apron."

The thin voice of the sheriff's wife broke in upon her: "I must be getting those things from the front-room closet." She opened the door into the other room, started in, stepped back. "You coming with me, Mrs. Hale?" she asked nervously. "You—you could help me get them."

They were soon back—the stark coldness of that shut-up room was not a thing to linger in.

"My!" said Mrs. Peters, dropping the things on the table and hurrying to the stove.

Mrs. Hale stood examining the clothes the woman who was being detained in town had said she wanted. 120

"Wright was close!°" she exclaimed, holding up a shabby black skirt that bore the marks of much making over. "I think maybe that's why she kept so much to herself. I s'pose she felt she couldn't do her part; and then, you don't enjoy things when you feel shabby. She used to wear pretty clothes and be lively—when she was Minnie Foster, one of the town girls, singing in the choir. But that—oh, that was twenty years ago."

With a carefulness in which there was something tender, she folded the shabby clothes and piled them at one corner of the table. She looked up at Mrs. Peters, and there was something in the other woman's look that irritated her.

"She don't care," she said to herself. "Much difference it makes to her whether Minnie Foster had pretty clothes when she was a girl."

Then she looked again, and she wasn't so sure; in fact, she hadn't at any time been perfectly sure about Mrs. Peters. She had that shrinking manner, and yet her eyes looked as if they could see a long way into things.

"This all you was to take in?" asked Mrs. Hale. 125

"No," said the sheriff's wife; "she said she wanted an apron. Funny thing to want," she ventured in her nervous little way, "for there's not much to get you dirty in jail, goodness knows. But I suppose just to make her feel more natural. If you're used to wearing an apron—. She said they were in the bottom drawer of this cupboard. Yes—here they are. And then her little shawl that always hung on the stair door."

She took the small gray shawl from behind the door leading upstairs, and stood a minute looking at it.

Suddenly Mrs. Hale took a quick step toward the other woman.

"Mrs. Peters!"

"Yes, Mrs. Hale?" 130

"Do you think she—did it?"

A frightened look blurred the other thing in Mrs. Peters' eyes.

"Oh, I don't know," she said, in a voice that seemed to shrink away from the subject.

"Well, I don't think she did," affirmed Mrs. Hale stoutly. "Asking for an apron, and her little shawl. Worryin' about her fruit."

"Mr. Peters says—." Footsteps were heard in the room above; she stopped, looked up, then went on in a lowered voice: "Mr. Peters says—it looks bad for 135

---

[121]**close** ungenerous, tight with money

her. Mr. Henderson is awful sarcastic in a speech, and he's going to make fun of her saying she didn't—wake up."

For a moment Mrs. Hale had no answer. Then, "Well, I guess John Wright didn't wake up—when they was slippin' that rope under his neck," she muttered.

"No, it's *strange*," breathed Mrs. Peters. "They think it was such a—funny way to kill a man."

She began to laugh; at the sound of the laugh, abruptly stopped.

"That's just what Mr. Hale said," said Mrs. Hale, in a resolutely natural voice. "There was a gun in the house. He says that's what he can't understand."

140   "Mr. Henderson said, coming out, that what was needed for the case was a motive. Something to show anger—or sudden feeling."

"Well, I don't see any signs of anger around here," said Mrs. Hale, "I don't—"

She stopped. It was as if her mind tripped on something. Her eye was caught by a dish-towel in the middle of the kitchen table. Slowly she moved toward the table. One half of it was wiped clean, the other half messy. Her eyes made a slow, almost unwilling turn to the bucket of sugar and the half empty bag beside it. Things begun—and not finished.

After a moment she stepped back, and said, in that manner of releasing herself:

"Wonder how they're finding things upstairs? I hope she had it a little more red up° up there. You know,"—she paused, and feeling gathered,—"it seems kind of *sneaking*: locking her up in town and coming out here to get her own house to turn against her!"

145   "But, Mrs. Hale," said the sheriff's wife, "the law is the law."

"I s'pose 'tis," answered Mrs. Hale shortly.

She turned to the stove, saying something about that fire not being much to brag of. She worked with it a minute, and when she straightened up she said aggressively:

"The law is the law—and a bad stove is a bad stove. How'd you like to cook on this?"—pointing with the poker to the broken lining. She opened the oven door and started to express her opinion of the oven; but she was swept into her own thoughts, thinking of what it would mean, year after year, to have that stove to wrestle with. The thought of Minnie Foster trying to bake in that oven—and the thought of her never going over to see Minnie Foster—.

She was startled by hearing Mrs. Peters say: "A person gets discouraged—and loses heart."

150   The sheriff's wife had looked from the stove to the sink—to the pail of water which had been carried in from outside. The two women stood there silent, above them the footsteps of the men who were looking for evidence against the woman who had worked in that kitchen. That look of seeing into things, of seeing through a thing to something else, was in the eyes of the sheriff's wife now. When Mrs. Hale next spoke to her, it was gently:

"Better loosen up your things, Mrs. Peters. We'll not feel them when we go out."

---

^{144}**red up** neat, orderly

Mrs. Peters went to the back of the room to hang up the fur tippet she was wearing. A moment later she exclaimed, "Why, she was piecing a quilt," and held up a large sewing basket piled high with quilt pieces.

Mrs. Hale spread some of the blocks on the table.

"It's log-cabin pattern," she said, putting several of them together, "Pretty, isn't it?"

They were so engaged with the quilt that they did not hear the footsteps on the stairs. Just as the stair door opened Mrs. Hale was saying: 155

"Do you suppose she was going to quilt it or just knot it?"

The sheriff threw up his hands.

"They wonder whether she was going to quilt it or just knot it!"

There was a laugh for the ways of women, a warming of hands over the stove, and then the county attorney said briskly:

"Well, let's go right out to the barn and get that cleared up."   160

"I don't see as there's anything so strange," Mrs. Hale said resentfully, after the outside door had closed on the three men—"our taking up our time with little things while we're waiting for them to get the evidence. I don't see as it's anything to laugh about."

"Of course they've got awful important things on their minds," said the sheriff's wife apologetically.

They returned to an inspection of the block for the quilt. Mrs. Hale was looking at the fine, even sewing, and preoccupied with thoughts of the woman who had done that sewing, when she heard the sheriff's wife say, in a queer tone:

"Why, look at this one."

She turned to take the block held out to her.   165

"The sewing," said Mrs. Peters, in a troubled way, "All the rest of them have been so nice and even—but—this one. Why, it looks as if she didn't know what she was about!"

Their eyes met—something flashed to life, passed between them; then, as if with an effort, they seemed to pull away from each other. A moment Mrs. Hale sat there, her hands folded over that sewing which was so unlike all the rest of the sewing. Then she had pulled a knot and drawn the threads.

"Oh, what are you doing, Mrs. Hale?" asked the sheriff's wife, startled.

"Just pulling out a stitch or two that's not sewed very good," said Mrs. Hale mildly.

"I don't think we ought to touch things," Mrs. Peters said, a little helplessly.   170

"I'll just finish up this end," answered Mrs. Hale, still in that mild, matter-of-fact fashion.

She threaded a needle and started to replace bad sewing with good. For a little while she sewed in silence. Then, in that thin, timid voice, she heard:

"Mrs. Hale!"

"Yes, Mrs. Peters?"

"What do you suppose she was so—nervous about?"   175

"Oh, *I* don't know," said Mrs. Hale, as if dismissing a thing not important enough to spend much time on. "I don't know as she was—nervous. I sew awful queer sometimes when I'm just tired."

She cut a thread, and out of the corner of her eye looked up at Mrs. Peters. The small, lean face of the sheriff's wife seemed to have tightened up. Her eyes had that look of peering into something. But next moment she moved, and said in her thin, indecisive way:

"Well, I must get those clothes wrapped. They may be through sooner than we think. I wonder where I could find a piece of paper—and string."

"In that cupboard, maybe," suggested Mrs. Hale, after a glance around.

180   One piece of the crazy sewing remained unripped. Mrs. Peter's back turned, Martha Hale now scrutinized that piece, compared it with the dainty, accurate sewing of the other blocks. The difference was startling. Holding this block made her feel queer, as if the distracted thoughts of the woman who had perhaps turned to it to try and quiet herself were communicating themselves to her.

Mrs. Peters' voice roused her.

"Here's a bird-cage," she said. "Did she have a bird, Mrs. Hale?"

"Why, I don't know whether she did or not." She turned to look at the cage Mrs. Peters was holding up. "I've not been here in so long." She sighed. "There was a man round last year selling canaries cheap—but I don't know as she took one. Maybe she did. She used to sing real pretty herself."

Mrs. Peters looked around the kitchen.

185   "Seems kind of funny to think of a bird here." She half laughed—an attempt to put up a barrier. "But she must have had one—or why would she have a cage? I wonder what happened to it."

"I suppose maybe the cat got it," suggested Mrs. Hale, resuming her sewing.

"No; she didn't have a cat. She's got that feeling some people have about cats—being afraid of them. When they brought her to our house yesterday, my cat got in the room, and she was real upset and asked me to take it out."

"My sister Bessie was like that," laughed Mrs. Hale.

The sheriff's wife did not reply. The silence made Mrs. Hale turn round. Mrs. Peters was examining the bird-cage.

190   "Look at this door," she said slowly. "It's broke. One hinge has been pulled apart."

Mrs. Hale came nearer.

"Looks as if someone must have been—rough with it."

Again their eyes met—startled, questioning, apprehensive. For a moment neither spoke nor stirred. Then Mrs. Hale, turning away, said brusquely:

"If they're going to find any evidence, I wish they'd be about it. I don't like this place."

195   "But I'm awful glad you came with me, Mrs. Hale." Mrs. Peters put the bird-cage on the table and sat down. "It would be lonesome for me—sitting here alone."

"Yes, it would, wouldn't it?" agreed Mrs. Hale, a certain determined natural-ness in her voice. She had picked up the sewing, but now it dropped in her lap, and she murmured in a different voice: "But I tell you what I *do* wish, Mrs. Peters. I wish I had come over sometimes when she was here. I wish—I had."

"But of course you were awful busy, Mrs. Hale. Your house—and your children."

"I could've come," retorted Mrs. Hale shortly. "I stayed away because it weren't cheerful—and that's why I ought to have come. I"—she looked around—"I've never liked this place. Maybe because it's down in a hollow and you don't see the road. I don't know what it is, but it's a lonesome place, and always was. I wish I had come over to see Minnie Foster sometimes. I can see now—" She did not put it into words.

"Well, you mustn't reproach yourself," counseled Mrs. Peters. "Somehow, we just don't see how it is with other folks till—something comes up."

"Not having children makes less work," mused Mrs. Hale, after a silence, "but it makes a quiet house—and Wright out to work all day—and no company when he did come in. Did you know John Wright, Mrs. Peters?" 200

"Not to know him. I've seen him in town. They say he was a good man."

"Yes—good," conceded John Wright's neighbor grimly. "He didn't drink, and kept his word as well as most, I guess, and paid his debts. But he was a hard man, Mrs. Peters. Just to pass the time of day with him—." She stopped, shivered a little. "Like a raw wind that gets to the bone." Her eye fell upon the cage on the table before her, and she added, almost bitterly: "I should think she would've wanted a bird!"

Suddenly she leaned forward, looking intently at the cage. "But what do you s'pose went wrong with it?"

"I don't know," returned Mrs. Peters; "unless it got sick and died."

But after she said it she reached over and swung the broken door. Both 205 women watched it as if somehow held by it.

"You didn't know—her?" Mrs. Hale asked, a gentler note in her voice.

"Not till they brought her yesterday," said the sheriff's wife.

"She—come to think of it, she was kind of like a bird herself. Real sweet and pretty, but kind of timid and—fluttery. How—she—did—change."

That held her for a long time. Finally, as if struck with a happy thought and relieved to get back to everyday things, she exclaimed:

"Tell you what, Mrs. Peters, why don't you take the quilt in with you? It 210 might take up her mind."

"Why, I think that's a real nice idea, Mrs. Hale," agreed the sheriff's wife, as if she too were glad to come into the atmosphere of a simple kindness. "There couldn't possibly be any objection to that, could there? Now, just what will I take? I wonder if her patches are in here—and her things?"

They turned to the sewing basket.

"Here's some red," said Mrs. Hale, bringing out a roll of cloth. Underneath that was a box. "Here, maybe her scissors are in here—and her things." She held it up. "What a pretty box! I'll warrant that was something she had a long time ago—when she was a girl."

She held it in her hand a moment; then, with a little sigh, opened it.

Instantly her hand went to her nose. 215

"Why—!"

Mrs. Peters drew nearer—then turned away.

"There's something wrapped up in this piece of silk," faltered Mrs. Hale.

"This isn't her scissors," said Mrs. Peters, in a shrinking voice.

220   Her hand not steady, Mrs. Hale raised the piece of silk. "Oh, Mrs. Peters!" she cried. "It's—"

Mrs. Peters bent closer.

"It's the bird," she whispered.

"But, Mrs. Peters!" cried Mrs. Hale. "*Look* at it! Its *neck*—look at its neck! It's all—other side *to*."

She held the box away from her.

225   The sheriff's wife again bent closer.

"Somebody wrung its neck," said she, in a voice that was slow and deep.

And then again the eyes of the two women met—this time clung together in a look of dawning comprehension, of growing horror. Mrs. Peters looked from the dead bird to the broken door of the cage. Again their eyes met. And just then there was a sound at the outside door.

Mrs. Hale slipped the box under the quilt pieces in the basket, and sank into the chair before it. Mrs. Peters stood holding to the table. The county attorney and the sheriff came in from outside.

"Well, ladies," said the county attorney, as one turning from serious things to little pleasantries, "have you decided whether she was going to quilt it or knot it?"

230   "We think," began the sheriff's wife in a flurried voice, "that she was going to—knot it."

He was too preoccupied to notice the change that came in her voice on that last.

"Well, that's very interesting, I'm sure," he said tolerantly. He caught sight of the bird-cage. "Has the bird flown?"

"We think the cat got it," said Mrs. Hale in a voice curiously even.

He was walking up and down, as if thinking something out.

235   "Is there a cat?" he asked absently.

Mrs. Hale shot a look up at the sheriff's wife.

"Well, not *now*," said Mrs. Peters. "They're superstitious, you know; they leave."

She sank into her chair.

The county attorney did not heed her. "No sign at all of anyone having come in from the outside," he said to Peters, in the manner of continuing an interrupted conversation. "Their own rope. Now let's go upstairs again and go over it, piece by piece. It would have to have been someone who knew just the—"

240   The stair door closed behind them and their voices were lost.

The two women sat motionless, not looking at each other, but as if peering into something and at the same time holding back. When they spoke now it was as if they were afraid of what they were saying, but as if they could not help saying it.

"She liked the bird," said Martha Hale, low and slowly. "She was going to bury it in that pretty box."

"When I was a girl," said Mrs. Peters, under her breath, "my kitten—there was a boy took a hatchet, and before my eyes—before I could get there—" She covered her face an instant. "If they hadn't held me back I would have"—she

caught herself, looked upstairs where footsteps were heard, and finished weakly—
"hurt him."

Then they sat without speaking or moving.

"I wonder how it would seem," Mrs. Hale at last began, as if feeling her way   245
over strange ground—"never to have had any children around?" Her eyes made
a slow sweep of the kitchen, as if seeing what that kitchen had meant through
all the years. "No, Wright wouldn't like the bird," she said after that—"a thing
that sang. She used to sing. He killed that too." Her voice tightened.

Mrs. Peters moved uneasily.

"Of course we don't know who killed the bird."

"I knew John Wright," was Mrs. Hale's answer.

"It was an awful thing was done in this house that night, Mrs. Hale," said the
sheriff's wife. "Killing a man while he slept—slipping a thing round his neck that
choked the life out of him."

Mrs. Hale's hand went out to the bird cage.   250

"His neck. Choked the life out of him."

"We don't *know* who killed him," whispered Mrs. Peters wildly. "We don't *know*."

Mrs. Hale had not moved. "If there had been years and years of—nothing,
then a bird to sing to you, it would be awful—still—after the bird was still."

It was as if something within her not herself had spoken, and it found in Mrs.
Peters something she did not know as herself.

"I know what stillness is," she said, in a queer, monotonous voice. "When we   255
homesteaded in Dakota, and my first baby died—after he was two years old—
and me with no other then—"

Mrs. Hale stirred.

"How soon do you suppose they'll be through looking for the evidence?"

"I know what stillness is," repeated Mrs. Peters, in just that same way. Then
she too pulled back. "The law has got to punish crime, Mrs. Hale," she said in
her tight little way.

"I wish you'd seen Minnie Foster," was the answer, "when she wore a white
dress with blue ribbons, and stood up there in the choir and sang."

The picture of that girl, the fact that she had lived neighbor to that girl for   260
twenty years, and had let her die for lack of life, was suddenly more than she
could bear.

"Oh, I *wish* I'd come over here once in a while!" she cried. "That was a crime!
Who's going to punish that?"

"We mustn't take on," said Mrs. Peters, with a frightened look toward the stairs.

"I might 'a' *known* she needed help! I tell you, it's *queer*, Mrs. Peters. We live
close together, and we live far apart. We all go through the same things—it's all
just a different kind of the same thing! If it weren't—why do you and I *understand*? Why do we *know*—what we know this minute?"

She dashed her hand across her eyes. Then, seeing the jar of fruit on the table
she reached for it and choked out:

"If I was you I wouldn't *tell* her her fruit was gone! Tell her it *ain't*. Tell her it's   265
all right—all of it. Here—take this in to prove it to her! She—she may never
know whether it was broke or not."

She turned away.

Mrs. Peters reached out for the bottle of fruit as if she were glad to take it—as if touching a familiar thing, having something to do, could keep her from something else. She got up, looked about for something to wrap the fruit in, took a petticoat from the pile of clothes she had brought from the front room, and nervously started winding that round the bottle.

"My!" she began, in a high, false voice, "it's a good thing the men couldn't hear us! Getting all stirred up over a little thing like a—dead canary." She hurried over that. "As if that could have anything to do with—with—My, wouldn't they *laugh*?"

Footsteps were heard on the stairs.

270 "Maybe they would," muttered Mrs. Hale—"maybe they wouldn't."

"No, Peters," said the county attorney incisively; "it's all perfectly clear, except the reason for doing it. But you know juries when it comes to women. If there was some definite thing—something to show. Something to make a story about. A thing that would connect up with this clumsy way of doing it."

In a covert way Mrs. Hale looked at Mrs. Peters. Mrs. Peters was looking at her. Quickly they looked away from each other. The outer door opened and Mr. Hale came in.

"I've got the team° round now," he said. "Pretty cold out there."

"I'm going to stay here awhile by myself," the county attorney suddenly announced. "You can send Frank out for me, can't you?" he asked the sheriff. "I want to go over everything. I'm not satisfied we can't do better."

275 Again, for one brief moment, the two women's eyes found one another.

The sheriff came up to the table.

"Did you want to see what Mrs. Peters was going to take in?"

The county attorney picked up the apron. He laughed.

"Oh, I guess they're not very dangerous things the ladies have picked out."

280 Mrs. Hale's hand was on the sewing basket in which the box was concealed. She felt that she ought to take her hand off the basket. She did not seem able to. He picked up one of the quilt blocks which she had piled on to cover the box. Her eyes felt like fire. She had a feeling that if he took up the basket she would snatch it from him.

But he did not take it up. With another little laugh, he turned away, saying:

"No; Mrs. Peters doesn't need supervising. For that matter, a sheriff's wife is married to the law. Ever think of it that way, Mrs. Peters?"

Mrs. Peters was standing beside the table. Mrs. Hale shot a look up at her; but she could not see her face. Mrs. Peters had turned away. When she spoke, her voice was muffled.

"Not—just that way," she said.

285 "Married to the law!" chuckled Mrs. Peters' husband. He moved toward the door into the front room, and said to the county attorney:

"I just want you to come in here a minute, George. We ought to take a look at these windows."

"Oh—windows," said the county attorney scoffingly.

°273**team** team of horses

"We'll be right out, Mr. Hale," said the sheriff to the farmer, who was still waiting by the door.

Hale went to look after the horses. The sheriff followed the county attorney into the other room. Again—for one final moment—the two women were alone in that kitchen.

Martha Hale sprang up, her hands tight together, looking at that other woman, with whom it rested. At first she could not see her eyes, for the sheriff's wife had not turned back since she turned away at that suggestion of being married to the law. But now Mrs. Hale made her turn back. Her eyes made her turn back. Slowly, unwillingly, Mrs. Peters turned her head until her eyes met the eyes of the other woman. There was a moment when they held each other in a steady, burning look in which there was no evasion or flinching. Then Martha Hale's eyes pointed the way to the basket in which was hidden the thing that would make certain the conviction of the other woman—that woman who was not there and yet who had been there with them all through that hour.

For a moment Mrs. Peters did not move. And then she did it. With a rush forward, she threw back the quilt pieces, got the box, tried to put it in her handbag. It was too big. Desperately she opened it, started to take the bird out. But there she broke—she could not touch the bird. She stood there helpless, foolish.

There was the sound of a knob turning in the inner door. Martha Hale snatched the box from the sheriff's wife, and got it in the pocket of her big coat just as the sheriff and the county attorney came back into the kitchen.

"Well, Henry," said the county attorney facetiously, "at least we found out that she was not going to quilt it. She was going to—what is it you call it, ladies?"

Mrs. Hale's hand was against the pocket of her coat.

"We call it—knot it, Mr. Henderson."   [1917]   295

1. What are the conflicts in this story and how do they develop? How are they resolved? What is the crisis point in the plot?
2. Glaspell wrote this story first as a play, a year later as a short story. For the story version, she had to decide how to handle point of view. How does she do it and what are the consequences of her choices?

JAMES JOYCE

OLC

JAMES JOYCE (1882–1941) *was the eldest of twelve children in a family whose fortunes gradually fell because of the father's alcoholism. Nevertheless, Joyce received a strong education at a Jesuit boarding school and University College, Dublin. By the end of his school years, he had rejected Catholicism and pledged himself to literature. At the age of twenty he left Ireland, which remained the resonant setting of most of his writing, including the autobiographically inspired* Portrait of the Artist as a Young Man, Ulysses *(which was for a time banned in the United States), and the story collection* Dubliners, *from which "Araby" is taken.*

Araby

North Richmond Street, being blind,° was a quiet street except at the hour when the Christian Brothers' School set the boys free. An uninhabited house of two stories stood at the blind end, detached from its neighbors in a square ground. The other houses of the street, conscious of decent lives within them, gazed at one another with brown imperturbable faces.

The former tenant of our house, a priest, had died in the back drawing-room. Air, musty from having been long enclosed, hung in all the rooms, and the waste room behind the kitchen was littered with old useless papers. Among these I found a few paper-covered books, the pages of which were curled and damp: *The Abbot,*° by Walter Scott, *The Devout Communicant*° and *The Memoirs of Vidocq.*° I liked the last best because its leaves were yellow. The wild garden behind the house contained a central apple-tree and a few straggling bushes under one of which I found the late tenant's rusty bicycle-pump. He had been a very charitable priest; in his will he had left all his money to institutions and the furniture of his house to his sister.

When the short days of winter came dusk fell before we had well eaten our dinners. When we met in the street the houses had grown sombre. The space of sky above us was the colour of ever-changing violet and towards it the lamps of the street lifted their feeble lanterns. The cold air stung us and we played till our bodies glowed. Our shouts echoed in the silent street. The career of our play brought us through the dark muddy lanes behind the houses where we ran the gauntlet of the rough tribes from the cottages, to the back doors of the dark dripping gardens where odours arose from the ashpits, to the dark odorous stables where a coachman smoothed and combed the horse or shook music from the buckled harness. When we returned to the street light from the kitchen windows had filled the areas. If my uncle was seen turning the corner we hid in the shadow until we had seen him safely housed. Or if Mangan's sister came out on the doorstep to call her brother in to his tea we watched her from our shadow peer up and down the street. We waited to see whether she would remain or go in and, if she remained, we left our shadow and walked up to Mangan's steps resignedly. She was waiting for us, her figure defined by the light from the half-opened door. Her brother always teased her before he obeyed and I stood by the railings looking at her. Her dress swung as she moved her body and the soft rope of her hair tossed from side to side.

Every morning I lay on the floor in the front parlour watching her door. The blind was pulled down to within an inch of the sash so that I could not be seen. When she came out on the doorstep my heart leaped. I ran to the hall, seized my books and followed her. I kept her brown figure always in my eye and, when we came near the point at which our ways diverged, I quickened my pace and passed

---

[1]**blind** a dead end, a street with no outlet   [2]***The Abbot*** a nineteenth-century Romantic novel by Sir Walter Scott about Catholics in Scotland   ***The Devout Communicant*** a religious manual for Roman Catholics   ***The Memoirs of Vidocq*** the memoirs of Eugène François Vidocq (1775–1857), a French detective, published in four volumes between 1828–29

her. This happened morning after morning. I had never spoken to her, except for a few casual words, and yet her name was like a summons to all my foolish blood.

Her image accompanied me even in places the most hostile to romance. On Saturday evenings when my aunt went marketing I had to go to carry some of the parcels. We walked through the flaring streets, jostled by drunken men and bargaining women, amid the curses of labourers, the shrill litanies of shop-boys who stood on guard by the barrels of pigs' cheeks, the nasal chanting of street-singers, who sang a *come-all-you* about O'Donovan Rossa, or a ballad about the troubles in our native land. These noises converged in a single sensation of life for me: I imagined that I bore my chalice safely through a throng of foes. Her name sprang to my lips at moments in strange prayers and praises which I myself did not understand. My eyes were often full of tears (I could not tell why) and at times a flood from my heart seemed to pour itself out into my bosom. I thought little of the future. I did not know whether I would ever speak to her or not or, if I spoke to her, how I could tell her of my confused adoration. But my body was like a harp and her words and gestures were like fingers running upon the wires.

One evening I went into the back drawing-room in which the priest had died. It was a dark rainy evening and there was no sound in the house. Through one of the broken panes I heard the rain impinge upon the earth, the fine incessant needles of water playing in the sodden beds. Some distant lamp or lighted window gleamed below me. I was thankful that I could see so little. All my senses seemed to desire to veil themselves and, feeling that I was about to slip from them, I pressed the palms of my hands together until they trembled, murmuring: "*O love! O love!*" many times.

At last she spoke to me. When she addressed the first words to me I was so confused that I did not know what to answer. She asked me was I going to Araby. I forget whether I answered yes or no. It would be a splendid bazaar, she said; she would love to go.

"And why can't you?" I asked.

While she spoke she turned a silver bracelet round and round her wrist. She could not go, she said, because there would be a retreat that week in her convent.° Her brother and two other boys were fighting for their caps and I was alone at the railings. She held one of the spikes, bowing her head towards me. The light from the lamp opposite our door caught the white curve of her neck, lit up her hair that rested there and, falling, lit up the hand upon the railing. It fell over one side of her dress and caught the white border of a petticoat, just visible as she stood at ease.

"It's well for you," she said.

"If I go," I said, "I will bring you something."

What innumerable follies laid waste my waking and sleeping thoughts after that evening! I wished to annihilate the tedious intervening days. I chafed against the work of school. At night in my bedroom and by day in the classroom her image came between me and the page I strove to read. The syllables of the

---

⁹**convent** Catholic school for girls

word *Araby*° were called to me through the silence in which my soul luxuriated and cast an Eastern enchantment over me. I asked for leave to go to the bazaar on Saturday night. My aunt was surprised and hoped it was not some Freemason affair. I answered few questions in class. I watched my master's face pass from amiability to sternness; he hoped I was not beginning to idle. I could not call my wandering thoughts together. I had hardly any patience with the serious work of life which, now that it stood between me and my desire, seemed to me child's play, ugly monotonous child's play.

On Saturday morning I reminded my uncle that I wished to go to the bazaar in the evening. He was fussing at the hall-stand, looking for the hat-brush, and answered me curtly:

"Yes, boy, I know."

15   As he was in the hall I could not go into the front parlour and lie at the window. I left the house in bad humour and walked slowly towards the school. The air was pitilessly raw and already my heart misgave me.

When I came home to dinner my uncle had not yet been home. Still it was early. I sat staring at the clock for some time and, when its ticking began to irritate me, I left the room. I mounted the staircase and gained the upper part of the house. The high cold empty gloomy rooms liberated me and I went from room to room singing. From the front window I saw my companions playing below in the street. Their cries reached me weakened and indistinct and, leaning my forehead against the cool glass, I looked over at the dark house where she lived. I may have stood there for an hour, seeing nothing but the brown-clad figure cast by my imagination, touched discreetly by the lamplight at the curved neck, at the hand upon the railings and at the border below the dress.

When I came downstairs again I found Mrs. Mercer sitting at the fire. She was an old garrulous woman, a pawnbroker's widow, who collected used stamps for some pious purpose. I had to endure the gossip of the tea-table. The meal was prolonged beyond an hour and still my uncle did not come. Mrs Mercer stood up to go: she was sorry she couldn't wait any longer, but it was after eight o'clock and she did not like to be out late, as the night air was bad for her. When she had gone I began to walk up and down the room, clenching my fists. My aunt said:

"I'm afraid you may put off your bazaar for this night of Our Lord."

At nine o'clock I heard my uncle's latchkey in the halldoor. I heard him talking to himself and heard the hallstand rocking when it had received the weight of his overcoat. I could interpret these signs. When he was midway through his dinner I asked him to give me the money to go to the bazaar. He had forgotten.

20   "The people are in bed and after their first sleep now," he said.

I did not smile. My aunt said to him energetically:

"Can't you give him the money and let him go? You've kept him late enough as it is."

My uncle said he was very sorry he had forgotten. He said he believed in the old saying: "All work and no play makes Jack a dull boy." He asked me where I was going and, when I had told him a second time he asked me did I know

---

¹²**Araby** old-fashioned way to refer to the Middle East

The Arab's Farewell to His Steed. When I left the kitchen he was about to recite the opening lines of the piece to my aunt.

I held a florin° tightly in my hand as I strode down Buckingham Street towards the station. The sight of the streets thronged with buyers and glaring with gas recalled to me the purpose of my journey. I took my seat in a third-class carriage of a deserted train. After an intolerable delay the train moved out of the station slowly. It crept onward among ruinous houses and over the twinkling river. At Westland Row Station a crowd of people pressed to the carriage doors; but the porters moved them back, saying that it was a special train for the bazaar. I remained alone in the bare carriage. In a few minutes the train drew up beside an improvised wooden platform. I passed out on to the road and saw by the lighted dial of a clock that it was ten minutes to ten. In front of me was a large building which displayed the magical name.

I could not find any sixpenny entrance and, fearing that the bazaar would be   25
closed, I passed in quickly through a turnstile, handing a shilling to a weary-looking man. I found myself in a big hall girdled at half its height by a gallery. Nearly all the stalls were closed and the greater part of the hall was in darkness. I recognized a silence like that which pervades a church after a service. I walked into the center of the bazaar timidly. A few people were gathered about the stalls which were still open. Before a curtain, over which the words *Café Chantant* were written in coloured lamps, two men were counting money on a salver. I listened to the fall of the coins.

Remembering with difficulty why I had come I went over to one of the stalls and examined porcelain vases and flowered tea-sets. At the door of the stall a young lady was talking and laughing with two young gentlemen. I remarked their English accents and listened vaguely to their conversation.

"O, I never said such a thing!"

"O, but you did!"

"O, but I didn't!"

"Didn't she say that?"   30

"Yes. I heard her."

"O, there's a . . . fib!"

Observing me the young lady came over and asked me did I wish to buy anything. The tone of her voice was not encouraging; she seemed to have spoken to me out of a sense of duty. I looked humbly at the great jars that stood like eastern guards at either side of the dark entrance to the stall and murmured:

"No, thank you."

The young lady changed the position of one of the vases and went back to   35
the two young men. They began to talk of the same subject. Once or twice the young lady glanced at me over her shoulder.

I lingered before her stall, though I knew my stay was useless, to make my interest in her wares seem the more real. Then I turned away slowly and walked down the middle of the bazaar. I allowed the two pennies to fall against the sixpence in my pocket. I heard a voice call from one end of the gallery that the light was out. The upper part of the hall was now completely dark.

---

²⁴**florin** British coin worth two shillings, or 24 pence

Gazing up into the darkness I saw myself as a creature driven and derided by vanity; and my eyes burned with anguish and anger.   [1914]

1. How would you characterize the relationship between the narrator and Mangan's sister?
2. Why does he want to buy her something at the bazaar? What is the symbolic significance of this gift? In what ways is this emblematic of courtly love?
3. After spending so much time worrying about going to the bazaar so that he can buy a gift for Mangan's sister, the narrator ends up buying nothing. Why?
4. Compare this story with John Updike's "A & P" (see Chapter 3, p. 48).

◯ F R A M E W O R K S ◯

Looking at Mason through Psychology

BOBBIE ANN MASON, *"Shiloh"*

MARK KARPEL, *"Individuation: From Fusion to Dialogue"*

◎◎◎

BOBBIE ANN MASON

BOBBIE ANN MASON (1940–), *born on a farm in Mayfield, Kentucky, graduated from the University of Kentucky in 1962. She moved to New York in order to work in publishing and to write for magazines. In 1966 she received a master's degree from SUNY–Binghamton and in 1972 her doctorate at the University of Connecticut. Her fiction, literary criticism, and short stories have been published in* The New Yorker, Redbook, *and other magazines and her first book of fiction,* Shiloh and Other Stories, *was awarded the Ernest Hemingway Award in 1983. She has been the recipient of several fellowships and has written* In Country *and* Spence + Lila, *both in 1988. She currently lives in rural Pennsylvania.*

Shiloh

Leroy Moffitt's wife, Norma Jean, is working on her pectorals. She lifts three-pound dumbbells to warm up, then progresses to a twenty-pound barbell. Standing with her legs apart, she reminds Leroy of Wonder Woman.

"I'd give anything if I could just get these muscles to where they're real hard," says Norma Jean. "Feel this arm. It's not as hard as the other one."

"That's 'cause you're right-handed," says Leroy, dodging as she swings the barbell in an arc.

"Do you think so?"

"Sure."

Leroy is a truckdriver. He injured his leg in a highway accident four months ago, and his physical therapy, which involves weights and a pulley, prompted Norma Jean to try building herself up. Now she is attending a body-building class. Leroy has been collecting temporary disability since his tractor-trailer jack-knifed in Missouri, badly twisting his left leg in its socket. He has a steel pin in his hip. He will probably not be able to drive his rig again. It sits in the backyard, like a gigantic bird that has flown home to roost. Leroy has been home in Kentucky for three months, and his leg is almost healed, but the accident frightened him and he does not want to drive any more long hauls. He is not sure what to do next. In the meantime, he makes things from craft kits. He started by building a miniature log cabin from notched Popsicle sticks. He varnished it and placed it on the TV set, where it remains. It reminds him of a rustic Nativity scene. Then he tried string art (sailing ships on black velvet), a macramé owl kit, a snap-together B-17 Flying Fortress, and a lamp made out of a model truck, with a light fixture screwed in the top of the cab. At first the kits were diversions, something to kill time, but now he is thinking about building a full-scale log house from a kit. It would be considerably cheaper than building a regular house, and besides, Leroy has grown to appreciate how things are put together. He has begun to realize that in all the years he was on the road he never took time to examine anything. He was always flying past scenery.

"They won't let you build a log cabin in any of the new subdivisions," Norma Jean tells him.

"They will if I tell them it's for you," he says, teasing her. Ever since they were married, he has promised Norma Jean he would build her a new home one day. They have always rented, and the house they live in is small and nondescript. It does not even feel like a home, Leroy realizes now.

Norma Jean works at the Rexall drugstore, and she has acquired an amazing amount of information about cosmetics. When she explains to Leroy the three stages of complexion care, involving creams, toners, and moisturizers, he thinks happily of other petroleum products—axle grease, diesel fuel. This is a connection between him and Norma Jean. Since he has been home, he has felt unusually tender about his wife and guilty over his long absences. But he can't tell what she feels about him. Norma Jean has never complained about his traveling; she has never made hurt remarks, like calling his truck a "widow-maker." He is reasonably certain she has been faithful to him, but he wishes she would celebrate his permanent homecoming more happily. Norma Jean is often startled to find Leroy at home, and he thinks she seems a little disappointed about it. Perhaps he reminds her too much of the early days of their marriage, before he went on the road. They had a child who died as an infant, years ago. They never speak about their memories of Randy, which have almost faded, but now that Leroy is home all the time, they sometimes feel awkward around each other, and Leroy wonders if one of them should mention the child. He has the feeling that they are waking up out of a dream together—that they must create a new marriage, start afresh. They are lucky they are still married. Leroy has read that for most people losing a child destroys the marriage—or else he heard this on *Donahue*.° He can't always remember where he learns things anymore.

10   At Christmas, Leroy bought an electric organ for Norma Jean. She used to play the piano when she was in high school. "It don't leave you," she told him once. "It's like riding a bicycle."

The new instrument had so many keys and buttons that she was bewildered by it at first. She touched the keys tentatively, pushed some buttons, then pecked out "Chopsticks." It came out in an amplified fox-trot rhythm, with marimba sounds.

"It's an orchestra!" she cried.

The organ had a pecan-look finish and eighteen preset chords, with optional flute, violin, trumpet, clarinet, and banjo accompaniments. Norma Jean mastered the organ almost immediately. At first she played Christmas songs. Then she bought *The Sixties Songbook* and learned every tune in it, adding variations to each with the rows of brightly colored buttons.

"I didn't like these old songs back then," she said. "But I have this crazy feeling I missed something."

15   "You didn't miss a thing," said Leroy.

Leroy likes to lie on the couch and smoke a joint and listen to Norma Jean play "Can't Take My Eyes Off You" and "I'll Be Back." He is back again. After fifteen years on the road, he is finally settling down with the woman he loves. She is still pretty. Her skin is flawless. Her frosted curls resemble pencil trimmings.

Now that Leroy has come home to stay, he notices how much the town has changed. Subdivisions are spreading across western Kentucky like an oil slick. The sign at the edge of town says "Pop: 11,500"—only seven hundred more than it said twenty years before. Leroy can't figure out who is living in all the new houses. The farmers who used to gather around the courthouse square on Saturday afternoons to play checkers and spit tobacco juice have gone. It has been years since Leroy has thought about the farmers, and they have disappeared without his noticing.

Leroy meets a kid named Stevie Hamilton in the parking lot at the new shopping center. While they pretend to be strangers meeting over a stalled car, Stevie tosses an ounce of marijuana under the front seat of Leroy's car. Stevie is wearing orange jogging shoes and a T-shirt that says CHATTAHOOCHEE SUPER-RAT. His father is a prominent doctor who lives in one of the expensive subdivisions in a new white-columned brick house that looks like a funeral parlor. In the phone book under his name there is a separate number, with the listing "Teenagers."

"Where do you get this stuff?" asks Leroy. "From your pappy?"

20   "That's for me to know and you to find out," Stevie says. He is slit-eyed and skinny.

"What else you got?"

°**Donahue** Phil Donahue had a syndicated television talk show from 1969 to 1996.

"What you interested in?"

"Nothing special. Just wondered."

Leroy used to take speed on the road. Now he has to go slowly. He needs to be mellow. He leans back against the car and says, "I'm aiming to build me a log house, soon as I get time. My wife, though, I don't think she likes the idea."

"Well, let me know when you want me again," Stevie says. He has a cigarette   25
in his cupped palm, as though sheltering it from the wind. He takes a long drag, then stomps it on the asphalt and slouches away.

Stevie's father was two years ahead of Leroy in high school. Leroy is thirty-four. He married Norma Jean when they were both eighteen, and their child Randy was born a few months later, but he died at the age of four months and three days. He would be about Stevie's age now. Norma Jean and Leroy were at the drive-in, watching a double feature (*Dr. Strangelove*° and *Lover Come Back*°), and the baby was sleeping in the back seat. When the first movie ended, the baby was dead. It was the sudden infant death syndrome. Leroy remembers handing Randy to a nurse at the emergency room, as though he were offering her a large doll as a present. A dead baby feels like a sack of flour. "It just happens sometimes," said the doctor, in what Leroy always recalls as a nonchalant tone. Leroy can hardly remember the child anymore, but he still sees vividly a scene from *Dr. Strangelove* in which the President of the United States was talking in a folksy voice on the hot line to the Soviet premier about the bomber accidentally headed toward Russia. He was in the War Room, and the world map was lit up. Leroy remembers Norma Jean standing catatonically beside him in the hospital and himself thinking: Who is this strange girl? He had forgotten who she was. Now scientists are saying that crib death is caused by a virus. Nobody knows anything, Leroy thinks. The answers are always changing.

When Leroy gets home from the shopping center, Norma Jean's mother, Mabel Beasley, is there. Until this year, Leroy has not realized how much time she spends with Norma Jean. When she visits, she inspects the closets and then the plants, informing Norma Jean when a plant is droopy or yellow. Mabel calls the plants "flowers," although there are never any blooms. She always notices if Norma Jean's laundry is piling up. Mabel is a short, overweight woman whose tight, brown-dyed curls look more like a wig than the actual wig she sometimes wears. Today she has brought Norma Jean an off-white dust ruffle she made for the bed; Mabel works in a custom-upholstery shop.

"This is the tenth one I made this year," Mabel says. "I got started and couldn't stop."

"It's real pretty," says Norma Jean.

"Now we can hide things under the bed," says Leroy, who gets along with his   30
mother-in-law primarily by joking with her. Mabel has never really forgiven him for disgracing her by getting Norma Jean pregnant. When the baby died, she said that fate was mocking her.

---

[26]**Dr. Strangelove** the 1964 film, *Dr. Strangelove, Or: How I Learned to Stop Worrying and Love the Bomb*, starring Peter Sellers and directed by Stanley Kubrick   **Lover Come Back** the 1962 film with Rock Hudson and Doris Day

"What's that thing?" Mabel says to Leroy in a loud voice, pointing to a tangle of yarn on a piece of canvas.

Leroy holds it up for Mabel to see. "It's my needlepoint," he explains. "This is a *Star Trek* pillow cover."

"That's what a woman would do," says Mabel. "Great day in the morning!"

"All the big football players on TV do it," he says.

35 "Why, Leroy, you're always trying to fool me. I don't believe you for one minute. You don't know what to do with yourself—that's the whole trouble. Sewing!"

"I'm aiming to build us a log house," says Leroy. "Soon as my plans come."

"Like *heck* you are," says Norma Jean. She takes Leroy's needlepoint and shoves it into a drawer. "You have to find a job first. Nobody can afford to build now anyway."

Mabel straightens her girdle and says, "I still think before you get tied down y'all ought to take a little run to Shiloh."

"One of these days, Mama," Norma Jean says impatiently.

40 Mabel is talking about Shiloh, Tennessee. For the past few years, she has been urging Leroy and Norma Jean to visit the Civil War battleground there. Mabel went there on her honeymoon—the only real trip she ever took. Her husband died of a perforated ulcer when Norma Jean was ten, but Mabel, who was accepted into the United Daughters of the Confederacy in 1975, is still preoccupied with going back to Shiloh.

"I've been to kingdom come and back in that truck out yonder," Leroy says to Mabel, "but we never yet set foot in that battleground. Ain't that something? How did I miss it?"

"It's not even that far," Mabel says.

After Mabel leaves, Norma Jean reads to Leroy from a list she has made. "Things you could do," she announces. "You could get a job as a guard at Union Carbide, where they'd let you set on a stool. You could get on at the lumberyard. You could do a little carpenter work, if you want to build so bad. You could—"

"I can't do something where I'd have to stand up all day."

45 "You ought to try standing up all day behind a cosmetics counter. It's amazing that I have strong feet, coming from two parents that never had strong feet at all." At the moment Norma Jean is holding on to the kitchen counter, raising her knees one at a time as she talks. She is wearing two-pound ankle weights.

"Don't worry," says Leroy. "I'll do something."

"You could truck calves to slaughter for somebody. You wouldn't have to drive any big old truck for that."

"I'm going to build you this house," says Leroy. "I want to make you a real home."

"I don't want to live in any log cabin."

50 "It's not a cabin. It's a house."

"I don't care. It looks like a cabin."

"You and me together could lift those logs. It's just like lifting weights."

Norma Jean doesn't answer. Under her breath, she is counting. Now she is marching through the kitchen. She is doing goose steps.

Before his accident, when Leroy came home he used to stay in the house with Norma Jean, watching TV in bed and playing cards. She would cook fried chicken, picnic ham, chocolate pie—all his favorites. Now he is home alone much of the time. In the mornings, Norma Jean disappears, leaving a cooling place in the bed. She eats a cereal called Body Buddies, and she leaves the bowl on the table, with the soggy tan balls floating in a milk puddle. He sees things about Norma Jean that he never realized before. When she chops onions, she stares off into a corner, as if she can't bear to look. She puts on her house slippers almost precisely at nine o'clock every evening and nudges her jogging shoes under the couch. She saves bread heels for the birds. Leroy watches the birds at the feeder. He notices the peculiar way goldfinches fly past the window. They close their wings, then fall, then spread their wings to catch and lift themselves. He wonders if they close their eyes when they fall. Norma Jean closes her eyes when they are in bed. She wants the lights turned out. Even then, he is sure she closes her eyes.

He goes for long drives around town. He tends to drive a car rather carelessly.   55
Power steering and an automatic shift make a car feel so small and inconsequential that his body is hardly involved in the driving process. His injured leg stretches out comfortably. Once or twice he has almost hit something, but even the prospect of an accident seems minor in a car. He cruises the new subdivisions, feeling like a criminal rehearsing for a robbery. Norma Jean is probably right about a log house being inappropriate here in the new subdivisions. All the houses look grand and complicated. They depress him.

One day when Leroy comes home from a drive he finds Norma Jean in tears. She is in the kitchen making a potato and mushroom-soup casserole, with grated-cheese topping. She is crying because her mother caught her smoking.

"I didn't hear her coming. I was standing here puffing away pretty as you please," Norma Jean says, wiping her eyes.

"I knew it would happen sooner or later," says Leroy, putting his arm around her.

"She don't know the meaning of the word 'knock,'" says Norma Jean. "It's a wonder she hadn't caught me years ago."

"Think of it this way," Leroy says. "What if she caught me with a joint?"   60

"You better not let her!" Norma Jean shrieks. "I'm warning you, Leroy Moffitt!"

"I'm just kidding. Here, play me a tune. That'll help you relax."

Norma Jean puts the casserole in the oven and sets the timer. Then she plays a ragtime tune, with horns and banjo, as Leroy lights up a joint and lies on the couch, laughing to himself about Mabel's catching him at it. He thinks of Stevie Hamilton—a doctor's son pushing grass. Everything is funny. The whole town seems crazy and small. He is reminded of Virgil Mathis, a boastful policeman Leroy used to shoot pool with. Virgil recently led a drug bust in a back room at a bowling alley, where he seized ten thousand dollars' worth of marijuana. The newspaper had a picture of him holding up the bags of grass and grinning widely. Right now, Leroy can imagine Virgil breaking down the door and arresting him with a lungful of smoke. Virgil would probably have been alerted to the scene because of all the racket Norma Jean is making. Now she sounds like a hard-rock band. Norma Jean is terrific. When she switches to a Latin-rhythm version of "Sunshine Superman," Leroy hums along. Norma Jean's foot goes up and down, up and down.

"Well, what do you think?" Leroy says, when Norma Jean pauses to search through her music.

65   "What do I think about what?"

His mind has gone blank. Then he says, "I'll sell my rig and build us a house." That wasn't what he wanted to say. He wanted to know what she thought— what she *really* thought—about them.

"Don't start in on that again," says Norma Jean. She begins playing "Who'll Be the Next in Line?"

Leroy used to tell hitchhikers his whole life story—about his travels, his hometown, the baby. He would end with a question: "Well, what do you think?" It was just a rhetorical question. In time, he had the feeling that he'd been telling the same story over and over to the same hitchhikers. He quit talking to hitchhikers when he realized how his voice sounded—whining and self-pitying, like some teenage-tragedy song. Now Leroy has the sudden impulse to tell Norma Jean about himself, as if he had just met her. They have known each other so long they have forgotten a lot about each other. They could become reacquainted. But when the oven timer goes off and she runs to the kitchen, he forgets why he wants to do this.

The next day, Mabel drops by. It is Saturday and Norma Jean is cleaning. Leroy is studying the plans of his log house, which have finally come in the mail. He has them spread out on the table—big sheets of stiff blue paper, with diagrams and numbers printed in white. While Norma Jean runs the vacuum, Mabel drinks coffee. She sets her coffee cup on a blueprint.

70   "I'm just waiting for time to pass," she says to Leroy drumming her fingers on the table.

As soon as Norma Jean switches off the vacuum, Mabel says in a loud voice, "Did you hear about the datsun dog that killed the baby?"

Norma Jean says, "The word is 'dachshund.'"

"They put the dog on trial. It chewed the baby's legs off. The mother was in the next room all the time." She raises her voice. "They thought it was neglect."

Norma Jean is holding her ears. Leroy manages to open the refrigerator and get some Diet Pepsi to offer Mabel. Mabel still has some coffee and she waves away the Pepsi.

75   "Datsuns are like that," Mabel says. "They're jealous dogs. They'll tear a place to pieces if you don't keep an eye on them."

"You better watch out what you're saying, Mabel," says Leroy.

"Well, facts is facts."

Leroy looks out the window at his rig. It is like a huge piece of furniture gathering dust in the backyard. Pretty soon it will be an antique. He hears the vacuum cleaner. Norma Jean seems to be cleaning the living room rug again.

Later, she says to Leroy, "She just said that about the baby because she caught me smoking. She's trying to pay me back."

"What are you talking about?" Leroy says, nervously shuffling blueprints.   80

"You know good and well," Norma Jean says. She is sitting in a kitchen chair with her feet up and her arms wrapped around her knees. She looks small and helpless. She says, "The very idea, her bringing up a subject like that! Saying it was neglect."

"She didn't mean that," Leroy says.

"She might not have thought she meant it. She always says things like that. You don't know how she goes on."

"But she didn't really mean it. She was just talking."

Leroy opens a king-sized bottle of beer and pours it into two glasses, dividing it   85 carefully. He hands a glass to Norma Jean and she takes it from him mechanically. For a long time, they sit by the kitchen window watching the birds at the feeder.

Something is happening. Norma Jean is going to night school. She has graduated from her six-week body-building course and now she is taking an adult-education course in composition at Paducah Community College. She spends her evenings outlining paragraphs.

"First you have a topic sentence," she explains to Leroy. "Then you divide it up. Your secondary topic has to be connected to your primary topic."

To Leroy, this sounds intimidating. "I never was any good in English," he says.

"It makes a lot of sense."

"What are you doing this for, anyhow?"   90

She shrugs. "It's something to do." She stands up and lifts her dumbbells a few times.

"Driving a rig, nobody cared about my English."

"I'm not criticizing your English."

Norma Jean used to say, "If I lose ten minutes' sleep, I just drag all day." Now she stays up late, writing compositions. She got a B on her first paper—a how-to theme, on soup-based casseroles. Recently Norma Jean has been cooking unusual foods—tacos, lasagna, Bombay chicken. She doesn't play the organ anymore, though her second paper was called "Why Music Is Important to Me." She sits at the kitchen table, concentrating on her outlines, while Leroy plays with his log house plans, practicing with a set of Lincoln Logs. The thought of getting a truckload of notched, numbered logs scares him, and he wants to be prepared. As he and Norma Jean work together at the kitchen table, Leroy has the hopeful thought that they are sharing something, but he knows he is a fool to think this. Norma Jean is miles away. He knows he is going to lose her. Like Mabel, he is just waiting for time to pass.

One day, Mabel is there before Norma Jean gets home from work, and Leroy   95 finds himself confiding in her. Mabel, he realizes, must know Norma Jean better than he does.

"I don't know what's got into that girl," Mabel says. "She used to go to bed with the chickens. Now you say she's up all hours. Plus her a-smoking. I like to died."

"I want to make her this beautiful home," Leroy says, indicating the Lincoln Logs. "I don't think she even wants it. Maybe she was happier with me gone."

"She don't know what to make of you, coming home like this."

"Is that it?"

100   Mabel takes the roof off his Lincoln Log cabin. "You couldn't get *me* in a log cabin," she says. "I was raised in one. It's no picnic, let me tell you."

"They're different now," says Leroy.

"I tell you what," Mabel says, smiling oddly at Leroy.

"What?"

"Take her on down to Shiloh. Y'all need to get out together, stir a little. Her brain's all balled up over them books."

105   Leroy can see traces of Norma Jean's features in her mother's face. Mabel's worn face has the texture of crinkled cotton, but suddenly she looks pretty. It occurs to Leroy that Mabel has been hinting all along that she wants them to take her with them to Shiloh.

"Let's all go to Shiloh," he says. "You and me and her. Come Sunday."

Mabel throws up her hands in protest. "Oh, no, not me. Young folks want to be by theirselves."

When Norma Jean comes in with groceries, Leroy says excitedly, "Your mama here's been dying to go to Shiloh for thirty-five years. It's about time we went, don't you think?"

"I'm not going to butt in on anybody's second honeymoon," Mabel says.

110   "Who's going on a honeymoon, for Christ's sake?" Norma Jean says loudly.

"I never raised no daughter of mine to talk that-a-way," Mabel says.

"You ain't seen nothing yet," says Norma Jean. She starts putting away boxes and cans, slamming cabinet doors.

"There's a log cabin at Shiloh," Mabel says. "It was there during the battle. There's bullet holes in it."

"When are you going to *shut up* about Shiloh, Mama?" asks Norma Jean.

115   "I always thought Shiloh was the prettiest place, so full of history," Mabel goes on. "I just hoped y'all could see it once before I die, so you could tell me about it." Later, she whispers to Leroy, "You do what I said. A little change is what she needs."

"Your name means 'the king,'" Norma Jean says to Leroy that evening. He is trying to get her to go to Shiloh, and she is reading a book about another century.

"Well, I reckon I ought to be right proud."

"I guess so."

"Am I still king around here?"

120   Norma Jean flexes her biceps and feels them for hardness. "I'm not fooling around with anybody, if that's what you mean," she says.

"Would you tell me if you were?"

"I don't know."

"What does *your* name mean?"

"It was Marilyn Monroe's real name."

"No kidding!" 125

"Norma comes from the Normans. They were invaders," she says. She closes her book and looks hard at Leroy. "I'll go to Shiloh with you if you'll stop staring at me."

On Sunday, Norma Jean packs a picnic and they go to Shiloh. To Leroy's relief, Mabel says she does not want to come with them. Norma Jean drives, and Leroy, sitting beside her, feels like some boring hitchhiker she has picked up. He tries some conversation, but she answers him in monosyllables. At Shiloh, she drives aimlessly through the park, past bluffs and trails and steep ravines. Shiloh is an immense place, and Leroy cannot see it as a battleground. It is not what he expected. He thought it would look like a golf course. Monuments are every-where, showing through the thick clusters of trees. Norma Jean passes the log cabin Mabel mentioned. It is surrounded by tourists looking for bullet holes.

"That's not the kind of log house I've got in mind," says Leroy apologetically.

"I know *that.*"

"This is a pretty place. Your mama was right." 130

"It's O.K.," says Norma Jean. "Well, we've seen it. I hope she's satisfied."

They burst out laughing together.

At the park museum, a movie on Shiloh is shown every half hour, but they decide that they don't want to see it. They buy a souvenir Confederate flag for Mabel, and then they find a picnic spot near the cemetery. Norma Jean has brought a picnic cooler, with pimiento sandwiches, soft drinks, and Yodels. Leroy eats a sandwich and then smokes a joint, hiding it behind the picnic cooler. Norma Jean has quit smoking altogether. She is picking cake crumbs from the cellophane wrapper, like a fussy bird.

Leroy says, "So the boys in gray ended up in Corinth. The Union soldiers zapped 'em finally. April 7, 1862."

They both know that he doesn't know any history. He is just talking about 135 some of the historical plaques they have read. He feels awkward, like a boy on a date with an older girl. They are still just making conversation.

"Corinth is where Mama eloped to," says Norma Jean.

They sit in silence and stare at the cemetery for the Union dead and, beyond, at a tall cluster of trees. Campers are parked nearby, bumper to bumper, and small children in bright clothing are cavorting and squealing. Norma Jean wads up the cake wrapper and squeezes it tightly in her hand. Without looking at Leroy, she says, "I want to leave you."

Leroy takes a bottle of Coke out of the cooler and flips off the cap. He holds the bottle poised near his mouth but cannot remember to take a drink. Finally he says, "No, you don't."

"Yes, I do."

"I won't let you." 140

"You can't stop me."

"Don't do me that way."

Leroy knows Norma Jean will have her own way. "Didn't I promise to be home from now on?" he says.

"In some ways, a woman prefers a man who wanders," says Norma Jean. "That sounds crazy, I know."

145 "You're not crazy."

Leroy remembers to drink from his Coke. Then he says, "Yes, you *are* crazy. You and me could start all over again. Right back at the beginning."

"We *have* started all over again," says Norma Jean. "And this is how it turned out."

"What did I do wrong?"

"Nothing."

150 "Is this one of those women's lib things?" Leroy asks.

"Don't be funny."

The cemetery, a green slope dotted with white markers, looks like a subdivision site. Leroy is trying to comprehend that his marriage is breaking up, but for some reason he is wondering about white slabs in a graveyard.

"Everything was fine till Mama caught me smoking," says Norma Jean, standing up. "That set something off."

"What are you talking about?"

155 "She won't leave me alone—*you* won't leave me alone." Norma Jean seems to be crying, but she is looking away from him. "I feel eighteen again. I can't face that all over again." She starts walking away. "No, it *wasn't* fine. I don't know what I'm saying. Forget it."

Leroy takes a lungful of smoke and closes his eyes as Norma Jean's words sink in. He tries to focus on the fact that thirty-five hundred soldiers died on the grounds around him. He can only think of that war as a board game with plastic soldiers. Leroy almost smiles, as he compares the Confederates' daring attack on the Union camps and Virgil Mathis's raid on the bowling alley. General Grant, drunk and furious, shoved the Southerners back to Corinth, where Mabel and Jet Beasley were married years later, when Mabel was still thin and good-looking. The next day, Mabel and Jet visited the battleground, and then Norma Jean was born, and then she married Leroy and they had a baby, which they lost, and now Leroy and Norma Jean are here at the same battleground. Leroy knows he is leaving out a lot. He is leaving out the insides of history. History was always just names and dates to him. It occurs to him that building a house out of logs is similarly empty—too simple. And the real inner workings of a marriage, like most of history, have escaped him. Now he sees that building a log house is the dumbest idea he could have had. It was clumsy of him to think Norma Jean would want a log house. It was a crazy idea. He'll have to think of something else, quickly. He will wad the blueprints into tight balls and fling them into the lake. Then he'll get moving again. He opens his eyes. Norma Jean has moved away and is walking through the cemetery, following a serpentine brick path.

Leroy gets up to follow his wife, but his good leg is asleep and his bad leg still hurts him. Norma Jean is far away, walking rapidly toward the bluff by the river, and he tries to hobble toward her. Some children run past him, screaming noisily. Norma Jean has reached the bluff, and she is looking out over the Tennessee River. Now she turns toward Leroy and waves her arms. Is she beckoning to him? She seems to be doing an exercise for her chest muscles. The sky is unusually pale—the color of the dust ruffle Mabel made for their bed.   [1982]

1. What is the point of view in the story and how is it established? What kind of narrator tells the story? What are the results of these choices?
2. Compare and contrast what we know of Norma Jean and Leroy as characters.
3. What role does Mabel play in the story?
4. What is the crisis in the plot? How is it resolved?

MARK KARPEL

MARK KARPEL, M.S., *a therapist at the Psychological Services Center of the University of Massachusetts, has edited* Family Resources: The Hidden Partner in Family Therapy *(New York: The Guilford Press, 1986) and written* Evaluating Couples: A Handbook for Practitioners *(W.W. Norton & Co., Inc., 1994). In the article excerpted here, he offers a way of understanding and categorizing couples according to how comfortable the partners are with their own and the other's separate identity.*

Individuation: From Fusion to Dialogue*

Growing interest in concepts of fusion and individuation within a number of different theoretical systems of psychotherapy suggests an emerging shift in perspective in the conceptualization of psychopathology and psychotherapy. This shift may represent a first step in the integration of individual and relational dynamic theories. A theoretical framework for the exploration of processes of fusion and individuation is presented, with suggested applications for the study of problems experienced by adult couples. The process of individuation from fusion to dialogue is outlined in the description of four modes of relationship. In this context, the paper suggests ways in which a variety of problematic relational patterns seen in couples may be viewed as reflecting the partners' struggles to move from fusion to dialogue.

In recent years, the literature of psychotherapy has paid increasing attention to what have been called "symbiotic," "merged," or "fused" relationships and to the related process of "differentiation," "individuation," or "self-delineation." These concepts have been developing along similar lines in areas as nominally disparate as psychoanalytic and family-systems theory until quite recently the concept of individuation seems to have emerged as a field of inquiry in its own right. This convergence of interest suggests the first outlines of a developing paradigm-shift in the conceptualization of psychopathology and psychotherapy.

*Mark Karpel, "Individuation: From Fusion to Dialogue," *Family Process* 15 (1976): 65–82.

Its significance lies in its potential for integrating phenomenological and transactional concepts and for achieving a synthesis of psychoanalytic and family-systems orientations.

At first glance, the phenomenon of fusion seems to be an exotic form of relational psychopathology, with a kind of quaint status accorded to *folie-à-deux°* in textbooks of abnormal psychology. The study of this phenomenon, however, has led a number of different theorists to redefine it in ways that have significant implications for our understanding of all forms of psychopathology and psychotherapy, of human personality and relatedness. Psychoanalytic thinkers, such as Searles (16, 17), Fairbairn (7), Guntrip (9), Jacobson (10), and Mahler (11), and family therapists, such as Bowen (3), Minuchin (12, 13), Satir (15), and Boszormenyi-Nagy (2) have all addressed themselves to issues of fusion and individuation in a variety of relational contexts, including the mother-infant dyad, the nuclear family, the adult couple, and the patient-therapist dyad. This paper will concentrate on points of convergence and areas of conceptual complementarity between these various theoretical systems in order to sketch the outlines of this still nascent perspective more clearly. In addition, its relevance for the study of problems experienced by adult couples will be explored. The theoretical framework to be presented draws heavily on the work of several theorists, particularly that of Searles (16, 17) on the felt experience and underlying dynamics of fusion, Bowen (3) on the transactional structure of fusion and individuation, Fairbairn (7) on the stages of development of object-relations, and Boszormenyi-Nagy (2) on the dialectical process of self-delineation and the structure of dialogic relationships. Other influences include Perls' (14) perspective on individuation and Buber's (4, 5, 6) work on dialogic relationships.

The term "individuation" refers to the process by which a person becomes increasingly differentiated from a past or present relational context. This process encompasses a multitude of intrapsychic and interpersonal changes that share a common direction. In different relational contexts, the specific changes may vary greatly. They may involve an infant's gradual realization that the source of his gratifications is an object, a body, which is separate from his own and which becomes for him "mother"; an adolescent's determination to violate an unwritten family rule that mother chooses all the children's clothing; a husband's struggle to see himself as capable of surviving without the painful relationship that exists between his wife and himself; a mother's recognition that her child is, in fact, *not* as anxious, dependent, shy or whatever, as she has felt herself to be. Individuation involves the subtle but crucial phenomenological shifts by which a person comes to see him/herself as separate and distinct within the relational context in which s/he has been embedded. It is the increasing definition of an "I" within a "We." The term "fusion" is used to describe the person's state of embeddedness in, of undifferentiation within, the relational context. The essence of this perspective is the perception of the process of individuation from fusion as a universal developmental and existential struggle and as a fundamental organizing principle of human growth. From this standpoint, a wide variety

---

[3]*folie-à-deux* a madness shared by two people

of individual and relational problems may be seen as deriving from this struggle. More precisely, specific symptoms may be seen as reflecting either *consequences* of, *defenses* against, or *ambivalence* over the persistence of the state of fusion, whether internally in the person's experience, externally in a relationship structured to maintain it, or both, in later life.

The Theoretical Context

To understand the problems of fusion and individuation, we must consider them within a matrix of two different dimensions. One dimension concerns the nature of self in relation, the dilemma of "I" and "We," which Bakan (1) has referred to as "the duality of human existence," and which Buber (5) speaks of as man's ability either to "set others at a distance" or to "enter into relation with others." We can, in different ways and at different moments in our lives, choose either to set ourselves apart, as an "I" separate from others, or to enter into relationship with another or others, to become part of a "We." The second dimension is that of maturation. The immature stage of human development is characterized by minimal individuation and an inability to form relationships based on differentiation. In this stage, the urge to give over responsibility for oneself is relatively undiluted, even if present only at an unconscious level as in the minimally differentiated but unrelated schizoid° position. The mature stage is characterized by the willingness and ability to accept responsibility for oneself and by relationships based on differentiation and not identification. Fairbairn (7) has described these stages with his distinction between "infantile dependence" and "mature dependence." Perls (14) has emphasized the change from "environmental-" to "self-support." These sets of concepts are partial and complementary, in that Perls conveys the sense of increasing *individual responsibility* but neglects the movement from immature to *mature relation* which Fairbairn supplies.

At the simplest level, we might postulate four possible modes of being and relating based on the interaction of these two dimensions. Diagramatically, this is represented below in Figure 1. This matrix suggests two important and related types of omissions in the work of some theorists in this area. The first involves an emphasis on the dimension of distance and relation while ignoring that of

	IMMATURE	MATURE
RELATION	fusion	dialogue
DISTANCE	unrelatedess	individuation

FIGURE 1

°**schizoid** relating to or resulting from the mental illness of schizophrenia

maturity. Bakan's (1) distinction between agency and communion is an example of one such theory. Here one senses an emphasis on the potential pathology of agency or distance. In Bowen's (3) alternation of fusion and individuation, we see another, in this case with an emphasis on the potential pathology of fusion or relation. Tom Fogarty (8), a family therapist, has used the metaphor of two magnets to describe a couple's attempts to find an optimal distance between them. He suggests the couple should feel close enough to feel the emotional tug without fusing. The metaphor is helpful in suggesting a midground between fusion and lack of relation but again misleads by ignoring the maturational processes that make this midground possible. A second and more important type of omission can be seen in the tendency of some theorists to view individuation as an end in itself and to ignore the question of the nature of mature, non-fused relationships. In terms of the matrix presented here, there has been a tendency to ignore the nature of "dialogue," a term used to describe a mature relationship between individuated partners.

There remains an element to be added in order to complete a theoretical framework within which issues of fusion, individuation, and dialogue can be explored. This is the inclusion of a transitional stage between the immature and mature stages described above. If the immature stage represents *relatively* undiluted regressive desires for fusion and the mature stage represents *relatively* undiluted progressive desires for individuation, the transitional stage is that in which the struggle, the conflict and ambivalence, between the two is most intense. For this reason, as we will see later, the transitional stage is the least stable of the three. In other words, in spite of (or, more accurately, precisely because of) the fact that it is developmentally more mature, the transitional stage is *less* stable than the immature stage.

The combination of the two poles of distance and relation with the three stages of development yields six possible positions as illustrated in Figure 2.

The three stages of development can also be differentiated by the ways in which individuals within a stage integrate the duality of distance and relation, the poles of "I" and "We." In the immature stage, there is an attempt to rigidly eliminate one pole or the other. Theoretically, unrelatedness (which corresponds to the schizoid position) excludes the possibility of any "We" relation, just as the mode of pure fusion permits no intrusion of the "I." During the transitional stage, the experience of both "I" and "We" become available to the person, but

	IMMATURE	TRANSITIONAL	MATURE
RELATION	pure fusion	ambivalent fusion	dialogue
DISTANCE	unrelatedness	ambivalent isolation	individuation

FIGURE 2

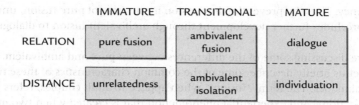

FIGURE 3

they co-exist as conflicting alternatives. The only options available are either loss of self to the "We" or unrelatedness as an "I." The person may feel either suffocated in the "We" or isolated as a lonely and unrelated "I." The lack of integration may be seen in a variety of uneasy compromises between the two, which we will describe later. In the mature stage, individuation and dialogue— the mature poles of "I" and "We"—are integrated in such a way that they nourish one another and are, in fact, meaningless without one another. The more strongly individuated the couple, the more capable they are of forming a differentiated "We," a dialogic relationship that furthers their continuing self-delineation. These differences between stages in the integration of "I" and "We" suggest four theoretical *modes of relationship*—(a) unrelatedness, (b) pure fusion, (c) ambivalent fusion, and (d) dialogue—as represented diagramatically in Figure 3.[1] This ordering of the four modes is not meant to suggest that unrelatedness precedes pure fusion, as will be clarified below. We begin, however, with the mode of unrelatedness in order to simplify presentation.

Modes of Relationship

The relational mode of *unrelatedness* corresponds to the schizoid position. It is "relational" only in that the position taken vis-à-vis relationship is one of rejection and denial. Unrelatedness is characterized by the elimination of the "We" from the person's life. Obviously, there must exist to some extent a set of internal relational others for any self-concept to exist, but close external relationships are largely avoided. Unrelatedness represents an interruption of the original state of pure fusion that exists between mother and infant. The reasons for this interruption are far too complex to pursue in this paper. Searles (16) has suggested that the infant is expelled from symbiotic attachment in response to the mother's anxiety. Fairbairn (7) relates the schizoid position to the infant's conviction that his/her love is destructive to the other. Regardless of terminology, what remains significant is the perception of unrelatedness as a detour (and dead-end in terms of the development of object-relationships) from the natural process of individuation from pure fusion. Just as pure fusion represents the acceptance of the state of total infantile dependency that characterizes early development, unrelatedness represents an attempt to reject or deny this state of

[1]The third and fourth relational modes take their names from the relational pole of their particular stage.

dependency. Thus, by preventing immersion in the state of pure fusion, unrelatedness precludes further development through ambivalent fusion to dialogue.

Before discussing some of the differences between pure and ambivalent fusion, let us briefly describe some of the common characteristics of these two relational modes. The term, "fusion," when applied to adult couples, refers to the transactional and experiential phenomenon that is created when two minimally individuated persons form a close, emotional relationship. The defining characteristic of the relationship is the high degree of identification that exists between partners. Searles (16, p. 39) has said that partners equate "relatedness with a process of engulfment, in which [one] personality is in the process of devouring or being devoured by the personality of the other . . . " Fairbairn (7, pp. 314–315) has described this as "both a mutual swallowing and a mutual merging, and the [person] is never quite sure at any given moment whether he feels most as if he is being swallowed or doing the swallowing." Partners experience the relationship with the feeling of absolute, needy dependence that characterizes a young infant. Their inordinate dependence on one another drives them to be almost exclusively relationship-oriented. Energy goes into seeking love or approval or into attacking the other for not providing it. Little or no energy is devoted to the task of developing self-support.

Searles (16) has made clear the degree to which the relationship must be characterized, due to the identification between partners, by a confusion of intrapsychic and interpersonal processes. Partners possess to an unusual degree "a galaxy of repressed concepts" (p. 225) of themselves, which they project onto the other, who is then responded to, not as a real other person, but as "the personification of the unacceptable, projected part-aspects of the patient's self, or, . . . as a personification of his own repressed self-images" (pp. 721–722). Boszormenyi-Nagy (2) has pointed out how great a part is played in these relationships by partners' "vicarious participation" in the life of the other, suggesting, for example, that crucial determinants of one partner's acting-out be sought in the other's unconscious desires for such behavior.

Because partners see the other as essential for their very survival and because the boundary between self and other is so indistinct, object-loss, that is, the loss of the other, is tantamount to ego-loss and is, in fact, experienced in just this way. Because the only mode of relatedness possible at this level is identification and because security is seen as lying in this fusion of identities, any indications of difference, growth, or change are perceived as threatening, not only to the relationship but, as suggested above, to the person's very survival. Partners experience a terror of difference and separation, and they seek to create a stable transactional structure that eliminates these distressing intrusions into their one-ness. Growth, change, the development of other relationships—any indications of separateness—are perceived in the other, and in oneself, as disloyalty and betrayal and generate guilt, blame, and anxiety.

One of the hallmarks of fusion is the blurring of boundaries of individual responsibility. Partners share a fantasy of absolute responsibility for the other—for the other's happiness and pain, faults and failures, life decisions, his or her very survival. In this way, endless cycles of guilt and blame may be created. Each must remain the same as the other and a fraction of him/her self, even if this is, as it must be, crippling, and each expects no less than this from the other. Each may bully, threaten, seduce, or cajole the other into taking responsibility for his/her partner in a futile attempt to deny and evade the burden of separateness and ultimate responsibility for oneself.

In order to erase individual differences and to eliminate movements toward growth, the partners must develop a rigid, highly predictable transactional system. Bowen (3) sees this as an automatic, unconscious chain-reaction pattern. Partners eventually come to feel like helpless objects within this predictable transactional system but participate in an unconscious collusion to maintain it, since they feel unable to tolerate its modification or dissolution. They each respect an unspoken agreement to respond to the other in predictable ways in return for the other's unspoken but demonstrated willingness to do the same. 15

Like unrelatedness, *pure fusion* represents the immature stage. It corresponds to Bowen's "comfortable fusion," Searles' "pre-ambivalent symbiosis," and Nagy's "merger." It is characterized by both individuals' and the relational system's complete acceptance of infantile dependence. The relationship is almost exclusively based on identification, and there is virtually no conflict (within or between partners) between progressive and regressive tendencies, since the latter dominate so strongly. In other words, both partners are fixated at so immature a level that there is none of the conflict or struggle of the transitional stage, and the relational system is structured to support the maintenance of these infantile features.

The most salient aspects of pure fusion for our discussion are its gratifications. These include, in Searles' (16) words, "the deep contentment," "the felt communion that needs no words," (p. 339), which, as he points out, can characterize the loving relationship between a nursing mother and her child. Fusion offers the presence of a "soulmate" to assuage the partners' loneliness and insecurity, the comforting hope that one can slide out from under the burden of one's own life by handing that responsibility over to another and by escaping into a dreamy idyllic haven from life. It promises that no foreign and threatening intrusion of another person's real otherness or growth will shatter the predictable security of the relationship. There is no need to face the fears, the losses, the uncertainty of growing up. It is noteworthy that many descriptions of fused relationships tend toward metaphors of biological re-union.

Pure fusion may be only a theoretical possibility in adult couples. Searles (17) has recently written: " . . . I have come to regard it as impossible to find any clearly defined, long-sustained instance of pre-ambivalent symbiosis" (p. 248). It seems unlikely that a relationship could be at such an immature level that there would be no anxiety or struggle over individuation. In any case, a consideration of the theoretical significance of pure fusion contributes to a greater comprehension of the more prevalent mode of ambivalent fusion.

The third relational mode, *ambivalent fusion,* characterizes the transitional stage. It is comparable to Bowen's "uncomfortable fusion," and Searles' "ambivalent symbiosis." It is seen as much more prevalent than the relational mode of pure fusion and subsumes a wide variety of relational and "individual" problems.

The essence of the transitional period is the conflict between progressive tendencies toward differentiation and regressive tendencies toward identification, between the responsibility and self-support that characterize individuation and the blame, guilt, and manipulation for environmental-support that characterize fusion. It is often experienced as being caught between the fear of being swallowed in a fusion that threatens ego-loss and the fear of being totally alone, unrelated, with a responsibility for one's existence that feels too great to bear. In Fairbairn's (7) words: "the behavior of the individual is characterized both by desperate endeavors . . . to separate himself from the object and desperate endeavors to achieve re-union with the object—desperate attempts to 'escape from prison' and desperate attempts to 'return home'" (p. 43).

For these reasons, partners in an ambivalently fused relationship experience not only the gratifications but the anxieties of fusion. They have differentiated sufficiently to feel threatened by the loss of self that accompanies fusion. However, they have no haven outside of the fused state, since they are not sufficiently individuated to feel comfortable as separate persons. Outside the fusion, they are always lonely, never just alone. In addition, each will be repeatedly faced with his/her partner's attempts to avoid fusion and with all the anxiety over loss of self through loss of the other that this creates. Because of these conflicting tendencies and the anxieties they entail, the ambivalently fused relational mode is the least stable psychologically. The relationship cannot settle into either a regressive but secure infantile form or a structurally sound, dialogic form. Even if its transactional patterns are quite predictable and inflexible, the relationship provides a minimum of psychological security and stability to the partners. The awareness that a decrease in relational stability may actually reflect greater individuation may help couples in treatment and the therapists who guide them to understand and tolerate the often noted phenomenon of periods of intensified conflict and upheaval that may accompany or follow real progress.

20 As already stated, the relational forms this conflict can take may vary greatly. Some of the more common patterns are described below as an illustration of how different relational problems can be understood in the light of the theoretical framework presented here. Each of these relational patterns represents the joint translation of both partners' internal psychological experience into a predictable transactional structure. For this reason, we will focus on how each particular pattern represents a struggle between the regressive tendency toward fusion and the progressive tendency toward individuation.

(a) *One Partner Distancing*. The couple maintain contact without fusion by establishing a pattern in which one partner keeps up a facade of distance (which both consciously accept as real), while the other pursues. It is as though one partner were collusively chosen to embody the desire for individuation (expressed here at a less mature level as mere distance). The fact that this is not simply a case of one really wanting less closeness and the other wanting more, that both act to perpetuate this pattern that is painful for both, becomes apparent in their unwillingness to change the pattern and by the fact that if, at rare moments, they are shaken out of it, their roles will most likely reverse. This then begins to resemble and may actually develop into (b).

(b) *Alternating Distancing.* The pattern of distancing is the same as in (a) except that a larger cycle is created in which both partners take turns. The roles of distancer and pursuer are traded back and forth. This pattern demonstrates one way in which fused couples may experience frequent role switches because of the degree of identification and projection involved in the relationship. The end result of the couple's simultaneous steps toward and away from one another is that roughly the same degree and quality of distance is maintained throughout, despite both partners' movements. Here it is as though the couple move in a synchronized but alternating fashion to act out the basic conflict transactionally. At one point in the cycle, one embodies "We" and the other "I"; at the next shift, the roles are reversed, and so on.

(c) Another coordinated pattern is one in which both partners shuttle between poles together, creating *cycles of fusion and unrelatedness* in the relationship as a whole. Partners move toward one another until a degree of fusion is reached that is threatening to both, leading to a rush by both away from each other until anxiety over unrelatedness leads to another approach to fusion. Here again both partners embody movement between the poles of "I" and "We" but now in such a way that the relationship itself is characterized by one pole or the other at any given moment.

(d) *Continual Conflict.* The couple maintains a constant level of antagonism that represents a sort of uneasy compromise between fusion and unrelatedness. Boszormenyi-Nagy (2) has pointed out how this pattern of "chronic bickering," by steering a course between the poles of fused "We" and unrelated "I," may represent an "optimal definition of the members' ego boundaries" (p. 69), since it provides (conflictual) contact without a merger of identities. One frequent form this pattern takes is for the couple to "triangle" around some issue or object that serves as the focus of the conflict, such as a child, an extramarital sexual affair, alcohol, drugs, career, etc. It is as if they collude to place a protective buffer between themselves.

(e) *Impairment of One Partner.* In this relational pattern, the transactional 25
expression of the partners' needs for fusion and individuation is less clear because these needs are cloaked by a relational facade of one mature, responsible, self-confident partner (A) and one helpless, dependent partner (B). Both collude at an unconscious level to create this facade while they accept it as accurate consciously. In a sense, they make an unconscious tradeoff. At the price of losing his/her own strength and self-support, B, the "weaker" partner, gets to give over much of his/her individual responsibility to A. However, B resents this loss of independence and may blame A for what they have together colluded to give over to A. Meanwhile, A has to take on additional responsibility for B but gets to project all his/her own weakness and dependence onto B. In other words, A is permitted to view his/her self as much stronger than it really is. However, he/she may always resent B for the burden they have together colluded to dump on A. The relationship provides a complementary self-delineation for both partners that is demanded by their regressive needs to remain immature but is frustrating to their progressive desires to mature and individuate.

These five relational patterns represent one attempt to organize the diversity of problems presented to the therapist, with an eye on the underlying conflicts of ambivalent fusion. They are not seen as pure or static types. Couples may be in continual conflict over one partner's distancing. They may alternate distancing within a context of one partner's impairment. Relationships may move from one relational pattern to another. The point of such an organization is not to propose these as fixed types but to demonstrate how a wide variety of relational problems can be understood as resulting from the partners' struggles between regressive tendencies toward fusion and progressive attempts at individuation. For what differentiates ambivalent from pure fusion is the introduction of the "I," at first isolated, insecure, and unrelated, but with a potential to become stronger and more centered both alone and in relation.

Hopefully, these patterns also begin to suggest a way of looking at people in which the interpenetration and complementarity of individual and relational dynamic theories is more visible. In Boszormenyi-Nagy's (2) terms, the experience of Self depends on the availability of a matching Not-Self. A person forms the "figure" of him/herself against the "ground" of another. External transactions and internal experience are related facets of one unitary process—both partners' simultaneous self-delineation in relationship. We can no more speak of the person without the system than we can of the system without the person.

Boszormenyi-Nagy's (2) discussion of the relational positions of "being-the-subject" and "being-the-object" illuminates an important aspect of ambivalent fusion and provides a set of concepts that will later help describe the transactional structure of dialogue. In relationships we would characterize as ambivalently fused, there does exist some boundary between partners; there is some awareness of a separate "I." In Boszormenyi-Nagy's terms, there is a subject-object polarity. There is also, for all the reasons described so far, an inflexible process by which partners are assigned fixed and extremely limited roles vis-à-vis one another. Boszormenyi-Nagy believes that, to varying degrees, partners may be accurately described as being in one of two possible positions. The person who succeeds in forcing the other into an object-role assignment that is satisfying, on some level, to his/her own self-image but from which the other is unable to escape, is "being-the-subject." That is, s/he has the power of definition in the relationship. The other is trapped in the role of "being-the-object." Particular object role assignments may vary greatly. "You are—the 'sick' one, the 'strong' one, the 'nurturant' one, the 'selfish' one, the 'good' one, the 'quiet' one," etc. The pain of "being-the-object" lies not in the "negative" status of the role imposed but in the inescapable imposition of the role, whether "positive" or "negative." In some relationships, partners may be essentially fixed in one position or the other; in others, they may take up different positions in different areas ("I force you to be the 'sick' one sexually, but I am forced to be the 'sick' one parentally"); in still others, partners may take turns forcing one another into the same narrow object-role assignments.

The intensity of fusion between partners increases as the insulation of the relational system from outside influences is increased. And, in a sense, the dynamics of fusion move the relationship naturally toward greater insulation. The degree of fusion within the couple is directly related to the partners' subjective distance from outside relationships due to their inability to form non-fused relationships. In this way, a vicious cycle is created that moves toward a stagnant endpoint of complete investment within the fused dyad with no meaningful relationships outside the dyad.

The fourth relational mode, *dialogue*, represents the mature stage of human development, in which the poles of "I" and "We" are integrated in such a way that they nourish and foster one another. Individuation (the differentiated "I") and dialogue (the differentiated "We") are complementary parts of the overall process of both partners' simultaneous self-delineation in relationship. The more highly individuated the partners, the better prepared they are for a dialogic relationship. In Buber's (4) words: ". . . in order to be able to go out to the other you must have the starting place, you must have been, you must be, with yourself" (p. 21). Elsewhere (6), he asserts:

> Every real relation in the world rests on individuation. This is its joy—for only in this way is mutual knowledge of different beings won—and its limitations—for in this way perfect knowledge and being known are foregone. (p. 99)

At the same time, dialogue represents the mode of relationship that maximally fosters continuing individuation for both partners. Unlike fusion where difference is avoided, in dialogue it is sought and affirmed. Partners aim toward an ideal of responding to the other as a whole and truly *other* person and not merely as a part of their own experience. Their *ability* and their *decision* to respond to the other in this way provides an optimal context for the increasing individuation of each. Where difference and change are felt as threatening and responded to as betrayal, individuation is crippled. Where they are accepted and valued, individuation is enhanced. The cycle is completed in that each partner's increased individuation makes him/her more capable of accepting the otherness of the other. Partners in a dialogic relationship are more willing to accept individual responsibility for their own lives. They try to accept and respond to unpredictability, to see themselves and to act, over and over, as separate, self-directed individuals.

Several theorists have discussed the process through which a person's or a couple's individuation is facilitated. Searles (16) points out that in psychotherapy, once the patient and therapist have formed a "therapeutic symbiosis," the patient's individuation often begins, in a sense, in the intrapsychic experience of the therapist.

> . . . the therapist comes to sense, time after time, newly emerging tendrils of differentiation in the patient, before the latter himself is conscious of them. In responding to these with spontaneity as they show themselves, . . . the therapist helps the patient to become aware that they are a part of him. (p. 314)

Bowen (3) has identified the process of a couple's joint individuation out of fusion as a coordinated sequence marked by a series of "controlled emotional crises." The "differentiating one" makes a move toward individuation; the other tries to lure, manipulate, threaten or bully him/her back into the predictable pattern of fusion. When s/he can withstand this pressure, can resist the impulse to respond in the old predictable way, the chain-reaction is interrupted. The other can no longer maintain his/her own fused stance and is forced, if the relationship is to be maintained, to re-align him/herself at a more highly individuated level. When one partner refuses to respond solely as the "sick" one or the "nurturant" one, the other must give up his/her own limited role as the "healthy" one or the "one who is fed."

The rigid, predictable patterns displayed in fused relationships reflect transactionally the partners' experiential avoidance of difference. Partners hope to derive security from the exclusion of everything new and different, which contributes to the sense of constriction and stagnation in the relationship. In dialogue, difference, otherness, unpredictability, and change are accepted. Even a dialogic relationship will inevitably develop predictable or patterned interchanges that contribute to the security and continuity, the sense of being "at home," in the relationship. However, patterns will be more flexible, more responsive to spontaneity and change because they are not compelled to constantly serve the function of eliminating difference and change.

Security in the relational mode of dialogue derives not from rigid predictability but from what Boszormenyi-Nagy (2) has referred to as the "structural requisite" of trust. He recognizes that a necessary prerequisite for a successful dialogic relationship is each partner's sensitivity to the other's needs. He goes further, however, to insist that what must follow this is a willingness on the part of each partner to offer him/herself temporarily as an object for the self-delineation of the other.

> What is referred to here . . . amounts primarily to helping the Other to be delineated as a subject opposite to oneself as an object of the Other's needs. Since offering oneself as an object to the Other amounts to "giving," the act of mutually trusting the Other is an important structural requisite of the dialogue. The trust, i.e., the anticipated reciprocation on the part of the Other, removes the emotional flavor of being used or taken advantage of. The atmosphere of trust changes the *economy* of "giving emotionally." (pp. 56–57)

Boszormenyi-Nagy uses the concept of trust in a way that illustrates the interpenetration of intrapsychic experience and interpersonal transactions. Trust is the experiential expectation that the other will cooperate in transactions that facilitate the partner's own self-delineation. It is based on past transactions and "predicts" future ones. Both partners' willingness to serve as object for the other in the expectation that the other will do the same is, for Boszormenyi-Nagy, the core of dialogue. The form this mutual trusting takes, transactionally and experientially, is that of a constant *alteration* of subject and object roles between partners.

> As the "dialogue of needs" becomes established, it becomes one of the greatest sources of relational security and trust. Its accomplishment permits the posing of real demands, i.e., of transiently non-reciprocal kinds of object-role assignments, in the knowledge that the Other will subsequently feel free to demand the same in return . . . . . The structure of dialogue is not based on a constant complementation of needs. Instead, it is a contract for the free exchange of both partners' non-complementary need assertions, based on their reliance on the over-all mutuality of each other's object availability. (p. 77)

These factors—the transactional structure and psychological experience of trust, the complementarity of the poles of (the now differentiated) "I" and "We," and the optimal satisfaction of self-delineational needs—contribute to the psychological and relational stability of the relational mode of dialogue. This does not imply a guarantee of longevity for these relationships. Quite the contrary, dialogue is based on the acceptance by both partners that there are no "guarantees," for the assumption of a relational guarantee is, in fact, the unrealistic promise never to grow or change that characterizes fusion. It does suggest that dialogic relationships are relatively free of the inherent anxiety and ambivalence, as well as the various forms of discord and symptomatology they can take, that characterize ambivalent fusion. Dialogue describes a relational structure that is highly conducive to both partners' continuing growth. The possibility that they will grow in ways that might lead them to end the relationship always exists. However, a variety of forces combine to produce a dynamic counterweight to this potential for growing apart. These forces include the partners' feelings that their relational needs are, to their satisfaction, optimally met in the particular relationship, their needs for relational continuity and stability over time, and their sense of commitment to one another.

What we have already said concerning other relational modes and the different relational patterns seen in couples applies equally well to the relational mode of dialogue. It is neither pure nor static. The mature stage of human development is *largely characterized* by increasing individuation and by the formation of close, differentiated relationships. Mature relationships will be *largely characterized* by those features we have described as dialogic. But features that characterize less mature forms of relationship will always be present to varying degrees at varying moments. In Searles' (17) words:

> . . . individuation is not a once-and-for-all, irreversible process. . . . A healthy adult . . . lives a daily and yearly life which involves, in its most essential ingredients, experiences—whether measured in moments or phases of his life—of symbiotic relatedness and re-individuation. (p. 250)

Summary

Psychotherapists who are guided in their work by psychoanalytic and family-systems perspectives have been troubled by the seemingly unbridgeable gap between theories of individual dynamics, on the one hand, and relational dynamics, on the other. They have sought a common language that would permit a cross-fertilization of phenomenological and transactional concepts. Recently, a number of different theoretical systems have begun, independently of one another, to focus on the phenomenon of fused relationships and the related concept of individuation or differentiation. This convergence of interest may represent the first stages of an emerging paradigm-shift in the conceptualization of psychopathology and psychotherapy, one that seems to qualify as a significant first step toward such a common language. This paper represents one attempt to weave some of the strands of these different theoretical systems into a coherent whole in order to give greater definition to the outlines of this perspective. The reader should bear in mind that significant areas of disagreement among theoretical systems have been avoided and consideration of many crucial theoretical questions, such as the application of these concepts to family systems with more than two members, has been omitted. Although well advanced in some respects, the theoretical perspective described here is, in terms of its own differentiation from its "parent" systems as a distinct theory of human personality and relatedness, still in the infant stage.

References

1. BAKAN, D., *The Duality of Human Existence: An Essay on Psychology and Religion,* Chicago, Rand McNally and Company, 1966.

2. BOSZORMENYI-NAGY, I., "A Theory of Relationships: Experience and Transaction" in I. Boszormenyi-Nagy, and J. L. Framo, (Eds.), *Intensive Family Therapy,* New York, Harper and Row, 1965.

3. BOWEN, M., "Family Therapy and Family Group Therapy" in H. I. Kaplan, and B. J. Sadock, (Eds.), *Comprehensive Group Psychotherapy,* Baltimore, Williams and Wilkins, 1971.

4. BUBER, M., *Between Man and Man,* New York, Macmillan Company, 1965.

5. BUBER, M., "Distance and Relation," *Psychiatry,* 20: 97–104, 1955.

6. BUBER, M., *I and Thou,* New York, Charles Scribner's Sons, 1958.

7. FAIRBAIRN, W. R. D., *Psychoanalytic Studies of the Personality,* London, Tavistock Publications, 1952.

8. FOGARTY, T., "The Systems Theory Point of View," Paper presented at second annual family therapy conference, "Differentiation and Integration in the family" of the Family Studies Unit, North Shore University Hospital Manhasset, New York, January 24–26, 1974.

9. GUNTRIP, H. J., *Personality Structure and Human Interaction,* New York, International Universities Press, Inc., 1961.

10. JACOBSON, E. *The Self and the Object World,* New York, International Universities Press, Inc., 1964.

11. MAHLER, M. S., "Thoughts about Development and Individuation" in *The Psychoanalytic Study of the Child,* Volume XVIII, New York, International Universities Press, Inc., 1963.

12. MINUCHIN, S., *Families and Family Therapy,* Cambridge, Harvard University Press, 1974.

13. MINUCHIN, S., and Montalvo, B., *et al., Families of the Slums,* New York, Basic Books, 1967.

14. PERLS, F. *Gestalt Therapy Verbatim,* Moab, Utah, Real People Press, 1969.

15. SATIR, V. *Conjoint Family Therapy,* Palo Alto, Science and Behavior Books, Inc., 1967.

16. SEARLES, H. F., *Collected Papers on Schizophrenia and Related Subjects,* New York, International Universities Press, Inc., 1965.

17. SEARLES, H. F., "Concerning Therapeutic Symbiosis," *The Annual of Psychoanalysis,* 1: 247–262, 1973.
[1976]

1. How does Karpel make his claim for the usefulness of the article?
2. For what other literary works in this section might Karpel provide a useful interpretive frame?

The Story and the Article

1. What is the nature of Leroy and Norma Jean's relationship? How would Mark Karpel categorize it? What part of the relationship is Karpel's schema unable to account for?
2. Sociologist Nancy Chodorow thinks it likely "that from their children's earliest childhood, mothers and women tend to identify more with daughters and to help them differentiate less, and that processes of separation and individuation are made more difficult for girls. On the other hand, a mother tends to identify less with her son, and to push him toward differentiation and the taking on of a male role unsuitable to his age, and undesirable at any age in his relationship to her."[1] How does this theory help explain some of the elements in the story?
3. What role does the Civil War battlefield in Shiloh play in the story? How does it bring together some of the elements offered by the analyses of Karpel and Chodorow?

[1]Nancy Chodorow, "Family Structure and the Feminine Personality," in *Women, Culture, and Society,* edited by Michelle Zimbalist Rosaldo and Louise Lamphere, 43–66 (Stanford: Stanford University Press, 1974), p. 48.

DRAMA

AUGUST WILSON

AUGUST WILSON *(1945–), child of a biracial family, voraciously read the works of black authors in the public library of the poor community in Pittsburgh where he grew up. His first play was staged in 1981, but he was catapulted to fame by the success of* Ma Rainey's Black Bottom, *which was produced at Yale and later staged in New York in 1984. Wilson's work with Lloyd Richards, dean of the Yale School of Drama, established him as the pre-eminent African-American playwright.* Joe Turner's Come and Gone *opened on Broadway to great acclaim and was voted Best New Play of the Year by the New York Drama Critics' Circle.* The Piano Lesson *was also honored by the Drama Critics' Circle and garnered his second Pulitzer Prize for Drama. He is the recipient of other awards as well, continuing to distill the experiences of his childhood and youth and his understanding of the American scene. He has set himself the task of writing a ten-play cycle that chronicles each decade of the black experience in the 20th century and focuses on what Wilson sees as the most important issue for blacks in each of these periods. His second play,* Fences, *about an embittered Negro League baseball player, won him his first Pulitzer Prize.*

Fences

for Lloyd Richards,
who adds to whatever he touches

> When the sins of our fathers visit us
> We do not have to play host.
> We can banish them with forgiveness
> As God, in His Largeness and Laws.

—*August Wilson*

List of Characters

Troy Maxson
Jim Bono, *Troy's friend*
Rose, *Troy's wife*
Lyons, *Troy's oldest son by previous marriage*
Gabriel, *Troy's brother*
Cory, *Troy and Rose's son*
Raynell, *Troy's daughter*

Setting: *The setting is the yard which fronts the only entrance to the Maxson household, an ancient two-story brick house set back off a small alley in a big-city neighborhood. The entrance to the house is gained by two or three steps leading to a wooden porch badly in need of paint.*

A relatively recent addition to the house and running its full width, the porch lacks congruence. It is a sturdy porch with a flat roof. One or two chairs of dubious value sit at one end where the kitchen window opens onto the porch. An old-fashioned icebox stands silent guard at the opposite end.

The yard is a small dirt yard, partially fenced, except for the last scene, with a wooden saw horse, a pile of lumber, and other fence-building equipment set off to the side. Opposite is a tree from which hangs a ball made of rags. A baseball bat leans against the tree. Two oil drums serve as garbage receptacles and sit near the house at right to complete the setting.

The Play: *Near the turn of the century, the destitute of Europe sprang on the city with tenacious claws and an honest and solid dream. The city devoured them. They swelled its belly until it burst into a thousand furnaces and sewing machines, a thousand butcher shops and bakers' ovens, a thousand churches and hospitals and funeral parlors and money-lenders. The city grew. It nourished itself and offered each man a partnership limited only by his talent, his guile, and his willingness and capacity for hard work. For the immigrants of Europe, a dream dared and won true.*

The descendants of African slaves were offered no such welcome or participation. They came from places called the Carolinas and the Virginias, Georgia, Alabama, Mississippi, and Tennessee. They came strong, eager, searching. The city rejected them and they fled and settled along the riverbanks and under bridges in shallow, ramshackle houses made of sticks and tarpaper. They collected rags and wood. They sold the use of their muscles and their bodies. They cleaned houses and washed clothes, they shined shoes, and in quiet desperation and vengeful pride, they stole, and lived in pursuit of their own dream. That they could breathe free, finally, and stand to meet life with the force of dignity and whatever eloquence the heart could call upon.

By 1957, the hard-won victories of the European immigrants had solidified the industrial might of America. War had been confronted and won with new energies that used loyalty and patriotism as its fuel. Life was rich, full, and flourishing. The Milwaukee Braves won the World Series, and the hot winds of change that would make the sixties a turbulent, racing, dangerous, and provocative decade had not yet begun to blow full.

Act 1
Scene 1

It is 1957. Troy *and* Bono *enter the yard, engaged in conversation.* Troy *is fifty-three years old, a large man with thick, heavy hands; it is this largeness that he strives to fill out and make an accommodation with. Together with his blackness, his largeness informs his sensibilities and the choices he has made in his life.*

Of the two men, Bono *is obviously the follower. His commitment to their friendship of thirty-odd years is rooted in his admiration of* Troy's *honesty, capacity for hard work, and his strength, which* Bono *seeks to emulate.*

It is Friday night, payday, and the one night of the week the two men engage in a ritual of talk and drink. Troy *is usually the most talkative and at times he can be crude and almost vulgar, though he is capable of rising to profound heights of expression. The men carry lunch buckets and wear or carry burlap aprons and are dressed in clothes suitable to their jobs as garbage collectors.*

Bono: Troy, you ought to stop that lying!

Troy: I ain't lying! The nigger had a watermelon this big. *[He indicates with his hands.]* Talking about . . . "What watermelon, Mr. Rand?" I liked to fell out! "What watermelon, Mr. Rand?". . . And it sitting there big as life.

Bono: What did Mr. Rand say?

Troy: Ain't said nothing. Figure if the nigger too dumb to know he carrying a watermelon, he wasn't gonna get much sense out of him. Trying to hide that great big old watermelon under his coat. Afraid to let the white man see him carry it home.

Bono: I'm like you . . . I ain't got no time for them kind of people.   5

Troy: Now what he look like getting mad cause he see the man from the union talking to Mr. Rand?

Bono: He come to me talking about . . . "Maxson gonna get us fired." I told him to get away from me with that. He walked away from me calling you a troublemaker. What Mr. Rand say?

Troy: Ain't said nothing. He told me to go down the Commissioner's office next Friday. They called me down there to see them.

Bono: Well, as long as you got your complaint filed, they can't fire you. That's what one of them white fellows tell me.

Troy: I ain't worried about them firing me. They gonna fire me cause I asked a   10
question? That's all I did. I went to Mr. Rand and asked him, "Why? Why you got the white mens driving and the colored lifting?" Told him, "what's

the matter, don't I count? You think only white fellows got sense enough to drive a truck. That ain't no paper job! Hell, anybody can drive a truck. How come you got all whites driving and the colored lifting?" He told me "take it to the union." Well, hell, that's what I done! Now they wanna come up with this pack of lies.

Bono: I told Brownie if the man come and ask him any questions . . . just tell the truth! It ain't nothing but something they done trumped up on you cause you filed a complaint on them.

Troy: Brownie don't understand nothing. All I want them to do is change the job description. Give everybody a chance to drive the truck. Brownie can't see that. He ain't got that much sense.

Bono: How you figure he be making out with that gal be up at Taylor's all the time . . . that Alberta gal?

Troy: Same as you and me. Getting just as much as we is. Which is to say nothing.

15   *Bono:* It is, huh? I figure you doing a little better than me . . . and I ain't saying what I'm doing.

Troy: Aw, nigger, look here . . . I know you. If you had got anywhere near that gal, twenty minutes later you be looking to tell somebody. And the first one you gonna tell . . . that you gonna want to brag to . . . is me.

Bono: I ain't saying that. I see where you be eyeing her.

Troy: I eye all the women. I don't miss nothing. Don't never let nobody tell you Troy Maxson don't eye the women.

Bono: You been doing more than eyeing her. You done bought her a drink or two.

20   *Troy:* Hell yeah, I bought her a drink! What that mean? I bought you one, too. What that mean cause I buy her a drink? I'm just being polite.

Bono: It's all right to buy her one drink. That's what you call being polite. But when you wanna be buying two or three . . . that's what you call eyeing her.

Troy: Look here, as long as you known me . . . you ever known me to chase after women?

Bono: Hell yeah! Long as I done known you. You forgetting I knew you when.

Troy: Naw, I'm talking about since I been married to Rose?

25   *Bono:* Oh, not since you been married to Rose. Now, that's the truth, there. I can say that.

Troy: All right then! Case closed.

Bono: I see you be walking up around Alberta's house. You supposed to be at Taylors' and you be walking up around there.

Troy: What you watching where I'm walking for? I ain't watching after you.

Bono: I seen you walking around there more than once.

30   *Troy:* Hell, you liable to see me walking anywhere! That don't mean nothing cause you see me walking around there.

Bono: Where she come from anyway? She just kinda showed up one day.

Troy: Tallahassee. You can look at her and tell she one of them Florida gals. They got some big healthy women down there. Grow them right up out the ground. Got a little bit of Indian in her. Most of them niggers down in Florida got some Indian in them.

Bono: I don't know about that Indian part. But she damn sure big and healthy. Woman wear some big stockings. Got them great big old legs and hips as wide as the Mississippi River.

Troy: Legs don't mean nothing. You don't do nothing but push them out of the way. But them hips cushion the ride!

Bono: Troy, you ain't got no sense.   35

Troy: It's the truth! Like you riding on Goodyears!

> Rose *enters from the house. She is ten years younger than* Troy, *her devotion to him stems from her recognition of the possibilities of her life without him: a succession of abusive men and their babies, a life of partying and running the streets, the Church, or aloneness with its attendant pain and frustration. She recognizes* Troy's *spirit as a fine and illuminating one and she either ignores or forgives his faults, only some of which she recognizes. Though she doesn't drink, her presence is an integral part of the Friday night rituals. She alternates between the porch and the kitchen, where supper preparations are under way.*

Rose: What you all out here getting into?

Troy: What you worried about what we getting into for? This is men talk, woman.

Rose: What I care what you all talking about? Bono, you gonna stay for supper?

Bono: No, I thank you, Rose. But Lucille say she cooking up a pot of pigfeet.   40

Troy: Pigfeet! Hell, I'm going home with you! Might even stay the night if you got some pigfeet. You got something in there to top them pigfeet, Rose?

Rose: I'm cooking up some chicken. I got some chicken and collard greens.

Troy: Well, go on back in the house and let me and Bono finish what we was talking about. This is men talk. I got some talk for you later. You know what kind of talk I mean. You go on and powder it up.

Rose: Troy Maxson, don't you start that now!

Troy [puts his arm around her]: Aw, woman . . . come here. Look here, Bono . . .   45
when I met this woman . . . I got out that place, say, "Hitch up my pony, saddle up my mare . . . there's a woman out there for me somewhere. I looked here. Looked there. Saw Rose and latched on to her." I latched on to her and told her—I'm gonna tell you the truth—I told her, "Baby, I don't wanna marry, I just wanna be your man." Rose told me . . . tell him what you told me, Rose.

Rose: I told him if he wasn't the marrying kind, then move out the way so the marrying kind could find me.

Troy: That's what she told me. "Nigger, you in my way. You blocking the view! Move out the way so I can find me a husband." I thought it over two or three days. Come back—

Rose: Ain't no two or three days nothing. You was back the same night.

Troy: Come back, told her . . . "Okay, baby . . . but I'm gonna buy me a banty rooster and put him out there in the backyard . . . and when he see a stranger come, he'll flap his wings and crow . . ." Look here, Bono, I could watch the front door by myself . . . it was that back door I was worried about.

Rose: Troy, you ought not talk like that. Troy ain't doing nothing but telling a lie.   50

Troy: Only thing is . . . when we first got married . . . forget the rooster . . . we ain't had no yard!

Bono: I hear you tell it. Me and Lucille was staying down there on Logan Street. Had two rooms with the outhouse in the back. I ain't mind the outhouse none. But when that goddamn wind blow through there in the winter . . . that's what I'm talking about! To this day I wonder why in the hell I ever stayed down there for six long years. But see, I didn't know I could do no better. I thought only white folks had inside toilets and things.

Rose: There's a lot of people don't know they can do no better than they doing now. That's just something you got to learn. A lot of folks still shop at Bella's.

Troy: Ain't nothing wrong with shopping at Bella's. She got fresh food.

55 *Rose:* I ain't said nothing about if she got fresh food. I'm talking about what she charge. She charge ten cents more than the A&P.

Troy: The A&P ain't never done nothing for me: I spends my money where I'm treated right. I go down to Bella, say, "I need a loaf of bread, I'll pay you Friday." She give it to me. What sense that make when I got money to go and spend it somewhere else and ignore the person who done right by me? That ain't in the Bible.

Rose: We ain't talking about what's in the Bible. What sense it make to shop there when she overcharge?

Troy: You shop where you want to. I'll do my shopping where the people been good to me.

Rose: Well, I don't think it's right for her to overcharge. That's all I was saying.

60 *Bono:* Look here . . . I got to get on. Lucille going be raising all kind of hell.

Troy: Where you going, nigger? We ain't finished this pint. Come here, finish this pint.

Bono: Well, hell, I am . . . if you ever turn the bottle loose.

Troy [hands him the bottle]: The only thing I say about the A&P is I'm glad Cory got that job down there. Help him take care of his school clothes and things. Gabe done moved out and things getting tight around here. He got that job. . . . He can start to look out for himself.

Rose: Cory done went and got recruited by a college football team.

65 *Troy:* I told that boy about that football stuff. The white man ain't gonna let him get nowhere with that football. I told him when he first come to me with it. Now you come telling me he done went and got more tied up in it. He ought to go and get recruited in how to fix cars or something where he can make a living.

Rose: He ain't talking about making no living playing football. It's just something the boys in school do. They gonna send a recruiter by to talk to you. He'll tell you he ain't talking about making no living playing football. It's a honor to be recruited.

Troy: It ain't gonna get him nowhere. Bono'll tell you that.

Bono: If he be like you in the sports . . . he's gonna be all right. Ain't but two men ever played baseball as good as you. That's Babe Ruth° and Josh Gibson.° Them's the only two men ever hit more home runs than you.

---

[68]**Babe Ruth** (1895–1948), major league baseball player who hit 60 home runs in one season and 708 in his years with the New York Yankees and Boston Red Sox
Josh Gibson (1911–47), known as "the Babe Ruth of the Negro Leagues," hit 84 home runs in one season and, according to his Baseball Hall of Fame plaque, "almost 800" over the course of his career

Troy: What it ever get me? Ain't got a pot to piss in or a window to throw it out of.

Rose: Times have changed since you was playing baseball, Troy. That was before   70
the war. Times have changed a lot since then.

Troy: How in hell they done changed?

Rose: They got lots of colored boys playing ball now. Baseball and football.

Bono: You right about that, Rose. Times have changed, Troy. You just come along
too early.

Troy: There ought not never have been no time called too early! Now you take
that fellow . . . what's that fellow they had playing right field for the Yankees
back then? You know who I'm talking about, Bono. Used to play right field
for the Yankees.

Rose: Selkirk?°   75

Troy: Selkirk! That's it! Man batting .269, understand? .269. What kind of sense
that make? I was hitting .432 with thirty-seven home runs! Man batting .269
and playing right field for the Yankees! I saw Josh Gibson's daughter yesterday.
She walking around with raggedy shoes on her feet. Now I bet you Selkirk's
daughter ain't walking around with raggedy shoes on the feet! I bet you that!

Rose: They got a lot of colored baseball players now. Jackie Robinson° was the
first. Folks had to wait for Jackie Robinson.

Troy: I done seen a hundred niggers play baseball better than Jackie Robinson.
Hell, I know some teams Jackie Robinson couldn't even make! What you
talking about Jackie Robinson. Jackie Robinson wasn't nobody. I'm talking
about if you could play ball then they ought to have let you play. Don't care
what color you were. Come telling me I come along too early. If you could
play . . . then they ought to have let you play.

Troy takes a long drink from the bottle.

Rose: You gonna drink yourself to death. You don't need to be drinking like that.

Troy: Death ain't nothing. I done seen him. Done wrassled with him. You can't   80
tell me nothing about death. Death ain't nothing but a fastball on the outside
corner. And you know what I'll do to that! Lookee here, Bono . . . am I lying?
You get one of them fastballs, about waist high, over the outside corner of the
plate where you can get the meat of the bat on it . . . and good god! You can
kiss it goodbye. Now, am I lying?

Bono: Naw, you telling the truth there. I seen you do it.

Troy: If I'm lying . . . that 450 feet worth of lying! *[Pause.]* That's all death is to
me. A fastball on the outside corner.

Rose: I don't know why you want to get on talking about death.

Troy: Ain't nothing wrong with talking about death. That's part of life. Everybody gonna die. You gonna die, I'm gonna die. Bono's gonna die. Hell, we all
gonna die.

---

[75]**Selkirk** (1908–87) George Selkirk played for the New York Yankees from 1934–42.

[77]**Jackie Robinson** (1919–72) the first African-American major league baseball player,
playing for the Brooklyn Dodgers from 1947–56. He won the National League's Most
Valuable Player award in 1949.

85 *Rose:* But you ain't got to talk about it. I don't like to talk about it.

Troy: You the one brought it up. Me and Bono was talking about baseball . . . you tell me I'm gonna drink myself to death. Ain't that right, Bono? You know I don't drink this but one night out of the week. That's Friday night. I'm gonna drink just enough to where I can handle it. Then I cuts it loose. I leave it alone. So don't you worry about me drinking myself to death. 'Cause I ain't worried about Death. I done seen him. I done wrestled with him.

Look here, Bono . . . I looked up one day and Death was marching straight at me. Like Soldiers on Parade! The Army of Death was marching straight at me. The middle of July, 1941. It got real cold just like it be winter. It seem like Death himself reached out and touched me on the shoulder. He touch me just like I touch you. I got cold as ice and Death standing there grinning at me.

Rose: Troy, why don't you hush that talk.

Troy: I say . . . what you want, Mr. Death? You be wanting me? You done brought your army to be getting me? I looked him dead in the eye. I wasn't fearing nothing. I was ready to tangle. Just like I'm ready to tangle now. The Bible say be ever vigilant. That's why I don't get but so drunk. I got to keep watch.

Rose: Troy was right down there in Mercy Hospital. You remember he had pneumonia? Laying there with a fever talking plumb out of his head.

90 *Troy:* Death standing there staring at me . . . carrying that sickle in his hand. Finally he say, "You want bound over for another year?" See, just like that . . . "You want bound over for another year?" I told him, "Bound over hell! Let's settle this now!"

It seem like he kinda fell back when I said that, and all the cold went out of me. I reached down and grabbed that sickle and threw it just as far as I could throw it . . . and me and him commenced to wrestling.

We wrestled for three days and three nights. I can't say where I found the strength from. Everytime it seemed like he was gonna get the best of me, I'd reach way down deep inside myself and find the strength to do him one better.

Rose: Everytime Troy tell that story he find different ways to tell it. Different things to make up about it.

Troy: I ain't making up nothing. I'm telling you the facts of what happened. I wrestled with Death for three days and three nights and I'm standing here to tell you about it. *[Pause.]* All right. At the end of the third night we done weakened each other to where we can't hardly move. Death stood up, throwed on his robe . . . had him a white robe with a hood on it. He throwed on that robe and went off to look for his sickle. Say, "I'll be back." Just like that. "I'll be back." I told him, say, "Yeah, but . . . you gonna have to find me!" I wasn't no fool. I wasn't going looking for him. Death ain't nothing to play with. And I know he's gonna get me. I know I got to join his army . . . his camp followers. But as long as I keep my strength and see him coming . . . as long as I keep up my vigilance . . . he's gonna have to fight to get me. I ain't going easy.

Bono: Well, look here, since you got to keep up your vigilance . . . let me have the bottle.

Troy: Aw hell, I shouldn't have told you that part. I should have left out that part.

Rose: Troy be talking that stuff and half the time don't even know what he be   95
talking about.

Troy: Bono know me better than that.

Bono: That's right. I know you. I know you got some Uncle Remus° in your
blood. You got more stories that the devil got sinners.

Troy: Aw hell, I done seen him too! Done talked with the devil.

Rose: Troy, don't nobody wanna be hearing all that stuff.

Lyons *enters the yard from the street. Thirty-four years old,* Troy's *son by a previous
marriage, he sports a neatly trimmed goatee, sport coat, white shirt, tieless and
buttoned at the collar. Though he fancies himself a musician, he is more caught up in
the rituals and "idea" of being a musician than in the actual practice of the music. He
has come to borrow money from* Troy, *and while he knows he will be successful, he is
uncertain as to what extent his lifestyle will be held up to scrutiny and ridicule.*

Lyons: Hey, Pop.   100

Troy: What you come "Hey, Popping" me for?

Lyons: How you doing, Rose? *[He kisses her.]* Mr. Bono. How you doing?

Bono: Hey, Lyons . . . how you been?

Troy: He must have been doing all right. I ain't seen him around here last week.

Rose: Troy, leave your boy alone. He come by to see you and you wanna start all   105
that nonsense.

Troy: I ain't bothering Lyons. *[Offers him the bottle.]* Here . . . get you a drink. We
got an understanding. I know why he come by to see me and he know I
know.

Lyons: Come on, Pop . . . I just stopped by to say hi . . . see how you was doing.

Troy: You ain't stopped by yesterday.

Rose: You gonna stay for supper, Lyons? I got some chicken cooking in the oven.

Lyons: No, Rose . . . thanks. I was just in the neighborhood and thought I'd stop   110
by for a minute.

Troy: You was in the neighborhood all right, nigger. You telling the truth there.
You was in the neighborhood cause it's my payday.

Lyons: Well, hell, since you mentioned it . . . let me have ten dollars.

Troy: I'll be damned! I'll die and go to hell and play blackjack with the devil
before I give you ten dollars.

Bono: That's what I wanna know about . . . that devil you done seen.

Lyons: What . . . Pop done seen the devil? You too much, Pops.   115

Troy: Yeah, I done seen him. Talked to him too!

Rose: You ain't seen no devil. I done told you that man ain't had nothing to do
with the devil. Anything you can't understand, you want to call it the devil.

Troy: Look here, Bono . . . I went down to see Hertzberger about some furniture.
Got three rooms for two-ninety-eight. That what it say on the radio. "Three
rooms . . . two-ninety-eight." Even made up a little song about it. Go down
there . . . man tell me I can't get no credit. I'm working every day and can't

---

°⁹⁷**Uncle Remus** the narrator of a collection of traditional tales by Joel Chandler Harris

get no credit. What to do? I got an empty house with some raggedy furniture in it. Cory ain't got no bed. He's sleeping on a pile of rags on the floor. Working every day and can't get no credit. Come back here—Rose'll tell you—madder than hell. Sit down . . . try to figure what I'm gonna do. Come a knock on the door. Ain't been living here but three days. Who know I'm here? Open the door . . . devil standing there bigger than life. White fellow . . . white fellow . . . got on good clothes and everything. Standing there with a clipboard in his hand. I ain't had to say nothing. First words come out of his mouth was . . . "I understand you need some furniture and can't get no credit." I liked to fell over. He say, "I'll give you all the credit you want, but you got to pay the interest on it." I told him, "Give me three rooms worth and charge whatever you want." Next day a truck pulled up here and two men unloaded them three rooms. Man what drove the truck give me a book. Say send ten dollars, first of every month to the address in the book and every thing will be all right. Say if I miss a payment the devil was coming back and it'll be hell to pay. That was fifteen years ago. To this day . . . the first of the month I send my ten dollars, Rose'll tell you.

Rose: Troy lying.

120 *Troy:* I ain't never seen that man since. Now you tell me who else that could have been but the devil? I ain't sold my soul or nothing like that, you understand. Naw, I wouldn't have truck with the devil about nothing like that. I got my furniture and pays my ten dollars the first of the month just like clockwork.

Bono: How long you say you been paying this ten dollars a month?

Troy: Fifteen years!

Bono: Hell, ain't you finished paying for it yet? How much the man done charged you?

Troy: Ah hell, I done paid for it. I done paid for it ten times over! The fact is I'm scared to stop paying it.

125 *Rose:* Troy lying. We got that furniture from Mr. Glickman. He ain't paying no ten dollars a month to nobody.

Troy: Aw hell, woman. Bono know I ain't that big a fool.

Lyons: I was just getting ready to say . . . I know where there's a bridge for sale.

Troy: Look here, I'll tell you this . . . it don't matter to me if he was the devil. It don't matter if the devil give credit. Somebody has got to give it.

Rose: It ought to matter. You going around talking about having truck with the devil . . . God's the one you gonna have to answer to. He's the one gonna be at the Judgment.

130 *Lyons:* Yeah, well, look here, Pop . . . Let me have that ten dollars. I'll give it back to you. Bonnie got a job working at the hospital.

Troy: What I tell you, Bono? The only time I see this nigger is when he wants something. That's the only time I see him.

Lyons: Come on, Pop, Mr. Bono don't want to hear all that. Let me have the ten dollars. I told you Bonnie working.

Troy: What that mean to me? "Bonnie working." I don't care if she working. Go ask her for the ten dollars if she working. Talking about "Bonnie working." Why ain't you working?

Lyons: Aw, Pop, you know I can't find no decent job. Where am I gonna get a job at? You know I can't get no job.

Troy: I told you I know some people down there. I can get you on the rubbish if   135
you want to work. I told you that the last time you came by here asking me for something.

Lyons: Naw, Pop . . . thanks. That ain't for me. I don't wanna be carrying nobody's rubbish. I don't wanna be punching nobody's time clock.

Troy: What's the matter, you too good to carry people's rubbish? Where you think that ten dollars you talking about come from? I'm just supposed to haul people's rubbish and give my money to you cause you too lazy to work. You too lazy to work and wanna know why you ain't got what I got.

Rose: What hospital Bonnie working at? Mercy?

Lyons: She's down at Passavant working in the laundry.

Troy: I ain't got nothing as it is. I give you that ten dollars and I got to eat beans   140
the rest of the week. Naw . . . you ain't getting no ten dollars here.

Lyons: You ain't got to be eating no beans. I don't know why you wanna say that.

Troy: I ain't got no extra money. Gabe done moved over to Miss Pearl's paying her the rent and things done got tight around here. I can't afford to be giving you every payday.

Lyons: I ain't asked you to give me nothing. I asked you to loan me ten dollars. I know you got ten dollars.

Troy: Yeah, I got it. You know why I got it? Cause I don't throw my money away out there in the streets. You living the fast life . . . wanna be a musician . . . running around in them clubs and things . . . then, you learn to take care of yourself. You ain't gonna find me going and asking nobody for nothing. I done spent too many years without.

Lyons: You and me is two different people, Pop.   145

Troy: I done learned my mistake and learned to do what's right by it. You still trying to get something for nothing. Life don't owe you nothing. You owe it to yourself. Ask Bono. He'll tell you I'm right.

Lyons: You got your way of dealing with the world . . . I got mine. The only thing that matters to me is the music.

Troy: Yeah, I can see that! It don't matter how you gonna eat . . . where your next dollar is coming from. You telling the truth there.

Lyons: I know I got to eat. But I got to live too. I need something that gonna help me to get out of the bed in the morning. Make me feel like I belong in the world. I don't bother nobody. I just stay with the music cause that's the only way I can find to live in the world. Otherwise there ain't no telling what I might do. Now I don't come criticizing you and how you live. I just come by to ask you for ten dollars. I don't wanna hear all that about how I live.

Troy: Boy, your mamma did a hell of a job raising you.   150

Lyons: You can't change me, Pop. I'm thirty-four years old. If you wanted to change me, you should have been there when I was growing up. I come by to see you . . . ask for ten dollars and you want to talk about how I was raised. You don't know nothing about how I was raised.

Rose: Let the boy have ten dollars, Troy.

Troy [to Lyons*]:* What the hell you looking at me for? I ain't got no ten dollars. You know what I do with my money. *[To* Rose.*]* Give him ten dollars if you want him to have it.

Rose: I will. Just as soon as you turn it loose.

155   *Troy [handing* Rose *the money]:* There it is. Seventy-six dollars and forty-two cents. You see this, Bono? Now, I ain't gonna get but six of that back.

Rose: You ought to stop telling that lie. Here, Lyons. *[She hands him the money.]*

Lyons: Thanks, Rose. Look . . . I got to run . . . I'll see you later.

Troy: Wait a minute. You gonna say, "thanks, Rose" and ain't gonna look to see where she got that ten dollars from? See how they do me, Bono?

Lyons: I know she got it from you, Pop. Thanks. I'll give it back to you.

160   *Troy:* There he go telling another lie. Time I see that ten dollars . . . he'll be owing me thirty more.

Lyons: See you, Mr. Bono.

Bono: Take care, Lyons!

Lyons: Thanks, Pop. I'll see you again.

   Lyons *exits the yard.*

Troy: I don't know why he don't go and get him a decent job and take care of that woman he got.

165   *Bono:* He'll be all right, Troy. The boy is still young.

Troy: The *boy* is thirty-four years old.

Rose: Let's not get off into all that.

Bono: Look here . . . I got to be going. I got to be getting on. Lucille gonna be waiting.

Troy [puts his arm around Rose*]:* See this woman, Bono? I love this woman. I love this woman so much it hurts. I love her so much . . . I done run out of ways of loving her. So I got to go back to basics. Don't you come by my house Monday morning talking about time to go to work . . . 'cause I'm still gonna be stroking!

170   *Rose:* Troy! Stop it now!

Bono: I ain't paying him no mind, Rose. That ain't nothing but gin-talk. Go on, Troy. I'll see you Monday.

Troy: Don't you come by my house, nigger! I done told you what I'm gonna be doing.

   The lights go down to black.

Scene 2

The lights come up on Rose *hanging up clothes. She hums and sings softly to herself. It is the following morning.*

Rose [sings]: Jesus, be a fence all around me every day

   Jesus, I want you to protect me as I travel on my way.

   Jesus, be a fence all around me every day.

   Troy *enters from the house.*

   Jesus, I want you to protect me

As I travel on my way.

[To Troy.*]* 'Morning. You ready for breakfast? I can fix it soon as I finish hanging up these clothes?

Troy: I got the coffee on. That'll be all right. I'll just drink some of that this morning.

Rose: That 651 hit yesterday. That's the second time this month. Miss Pearl hit for a dollar . . . seem like those that need the least always get lucky. Poor folks can't get nothing.

Troy: Them numbers don't know nobody. I don't know why you fool with them. You and Lyons both.

Rose: It's something to do.   5

Troy: You ain't doing nothing but throwing your money away.

Rose: Troy, you know I don't play foolishly. I just play a nickel here and a nickel there.

Troy: That's two nickels you done thrown away.

Rose: Now I hit sometimes . . . that makes up for it. It always comes in handy when I do hit. I don't hear you complaining then.

Troy: I ain't complaining now. I just say it's foolish. Trying to guess out of six   10
hundred ways which way the number gonna come. If I had all the money niggers, these Negroes, throw away on numbers for one week—just one week—I'd be a rich man.

Rose: Well, you wishing and calling it foolish ain't gonna stop folks from playing numbers. That's one thing for sure. Besides . . . some good things come from playing numbers. Look where Pope done bought him that restaurant off of numbers.

Troy: I can't stand niggers like that. Man ain't had two dimes to rub together. He walking around with his shoes all run over bumming money for cigarettes. All right. Got lucky there and hit the numbers . . .

Rose: Troy, I know all about it.

Troy: Had good sense, I'll say that for him. He ain't throwed his money away. I seen niggers hit the numbers and go through two thousand dollars in four days. Man bought him that restaurant down there . . . fixed it up real nice . . . and then didn't want nobody to come in it! A Negro go in there and can't get no kind of service. I seen a white fellow come in there and order a bowl of stew. Pope picked all the meat out of the pot for him. Man ain't had nothing but a bowl of meat! Negro come behind him and ain't got nothing but the potatoes and carrots. Talking about what numbers do for people, you picked a wrong example. Ain't done nothing but make a worser fool out of him than he was before.

Rose: Troy, you ought to stop worrying about what happened at work yesterday.   15

Troy: I ain't worried. Just told me to be down there at the Commissioner's office on Friday. Everybody think they gonna fire me. I ain't worried about them firing me. You ain't got to worry about that. *[Pause.]* Where's Cory? Cory in the house? *[Calls.]* Cory?

Rose: He gone out.

Troy: Out, huh? He gone out 'cause he know I want him to help me with this fence. I know how he is. That boy scared of work.

Gabriel *enters. He comes halfway down the alley and, hearing* Troy's *voice, stops.*

Troy *[continues]:* He ain't done a lick of work in his life.

20   *Rose:* He had to go to football practice. Coach wanted them to get in a little extra practice before the season start.

Troy: I got his practice . . . running out of here before he get his chores done.

Rose: Troy, what is wrong with you this morning? Don't nothing set right with you. Go on back in there and go to bed . . . get up on the other side.

Troy: Why something got to be wrong with me? I ain't said nothing wrong with me.

Rose: You got something to say about everything. First it's the numbers . . . then it's the way the man runs his restaurant . . . then you done got on Cory. What's it gonna be next? Take a look up there and see if the weather suits you . . . or is it gonna be how you gonna put up the fence with the clothes hanging in the yard.

25   *Troy:* You hit the nail on the head then.

Rose: I know you like I know the back of my hand. Go on in there and get you some coffee . . . see if that straighten you up. 'Cause you ain't right this morning.

    Troy *starts into the house and sees* Gabriel. Gabriel *starts singing.* Troy's *brother, he is seven years younger than* Troy. *Injured in World War II, he has a metal plate in his head. He carries an old trumpet tied around his waist and believes with every fiber of his being that he is the Archangel Gabriel. He carries a chipped basket with an assortment of discarded fruits and vegetables he has picked up in the strip district and which he attempts to sell.*

Gabriel *[singing]:* Yes, ma'am I got plums

     You ask me how I sell them

     Oh ten cents apiece

     Three for a quarter

     Come and buy now

     'Cause I'm here today

     And tomorrow I'll be gone

     Gabriel *enters.*

     Hey, Rose!

Rose: How you doing Gabe?

Gabriel: There's Troy . . . Hey, Troy!

30   *Troy:* Hey, Gabe.

    Exit into kitchen.

Rose [to Gabriel*]:* What you got there?

Gabriel: You know what I got, Rose. I got fruits and vegetables.

Rose [looking in basket]: Where's all these plums you talking about?

Gabriel: I ain't got no plums today, Rose. I was just singing that. Have some tomorrow. Put me in a big order for plums. Have enough plums tomorrow for St. Peter and everybody.

    Troy *reenters from kitchen, crosses to steps.*

    [To Rose.*]* Troy's mad at me.

35   *Troy:* I ain't mad at you. What I got to be mad at you about? You ain't done nothing to me.

Gabriel: I just moved over to Miss Pearl's to keep out from in your way. I ain't mean no harm by it.

Troy: Who said anything about that? I ain't said anything about that.

Gabriel: You ain't mad at me, is you?

Troy: Naw . . . I ain't mad at you, Gabe. If I was mad at you I'd tell you about it.

Gabriel: Got me two rooms. In the basement. Got my own door too. Wanna see   40
my key? *[He holds up a key.]* That's my own key! My two rooms!

Troy: Well, that's good, Gabe. You got your own key . . . that's good.

Rose: You hungry, Gabe? I was just fixing to cook Troy his breakfast.

Gabriel: I'll take some biscuits. You got some biscuits? Did you know when I was
in heaven . . . every morning me and St. Peter would sit down by the gate
and eat some big fat biscuits? Oh, yeah! We had us a good time. We'd sit
there and eat us them biscuits and then St. Peter would go off to sleep and
tell me to wake him up when it's time to open the gates for the judgment.

Rose: Well, come on . . . I'll make up a batch of biscuits.

Rose *exits into the house.*

Gabriel: Troy . . . St. Peter got your name in the book. I seen it. It say . . . Troy   45
Maxson. I say . . . I know him! He got the same name like what I got. That's
my brother!

Troy: How many times you gonna tell me that, Gabe?

Gabriel: Ain't got my name in the book. Don't have to have my name. I done
died and went to heaven. He got your name though. One morning St. Peter
was looking at his book . . . marking it up for the judgment . . . and he let me
see your name. Got it in there under M. Got Rose's name . . . I ain't seen it
like I seen yours . . . but I know it's in there. He got a great big book. Got
everybody's name what was ever been born. That's what he told me. But I
seen your name. Seen it with my own eyes.

Troy: Go on in the house there. Rose going to fix you something to eat.

Gabriel: Oh, I ain't hungry. I done had breakfast with Aunt Jemimah. She come
by and cooked me up a whole mess of flapjacks. Remember how we used to
eat them flapjacks?

Troy: Go on in the house and get you something to eat now.   50

Gabriel: I got to sell my plums. I done sold some tomatoes. Got me two quarters.
Wanna see? *[He shows* Troy *his quarters.]* I'm gonna save them and buy me a
new horn so St. Peter can hear me when it's time to open the gates. *[Gabriel
stops suddenly. Listens.]* Hear that? That's the hellhounds. I got to chase them
out of here. Go on get out of here! Get out!

Gabriel *exits singing.*

Better get ready for the judgment

Better get ready for the judgment

My Lord is coming down

Rose *enters from the house.*

Troy: He's gone off somewhere.

Gabriel [offstage]: Better get ready for the judgment

Better get ready for the judgment morning

Better get ready for the judgment

My God is coming down

Rose: He ain't eating right. Miss Pearl say she can't get him to eat nothing.

55 *Troy:* What you want me to do about it, Rose? I done did everything I can for the man. I can't make him get well. Man got half his head blown away . . . what you expect?

Rose: Seem like something ought to be done to help him.

Troy: Man don't bother nobody. He just mixed up from that metal plate he got in his head. Ain't no sense for him to go back into the hospital.

Rose: Least he be eating right. They can help him take care of himself.

Troy: Don't nobody wanna be locked up, Rose. What you wanna lock him up for? Man go over there and fight the war . . . messin' around with them Japs, get half his head blow off . . . and they give him a lousy three thousand dollars. And I had to swoop down on that.

60 *Rose:* Is you fixing to go into that again?

Troy: That's the only way I got a roof over my head . . . cause of that metal plate.

Rose: Ain't no sense you blaming yourself for nothing. Gabe wasn't in no condition to manage that money. You done what was right by him. Can't nobody say you ain't done what was right by him. Look how long you took care of him . . . till he wanted to have his own place and moved over there with Miss Pearl.

Troy: That ain't what I'm saying, woman! I'm just stating the facts. If my brother didn't have that metal plate in his head . . . I wouldn't have a pot to piss in or a window to throw it out of. And I'm fifty-three years old. Now see if you can understand that!

Troy gets up from the porch and starts to exit the yard.

Rose: Where you going off to? You been running out of here every Saturday for weeks. I thought you was gonna work on this fence?

65 *Troy:* I'm gonna walk down to Taylors'. Listen to the ball game. I'll be back in a bit. I'll work on it when I get back.

He exits the yard. The lights go to black.

Scene 3

The lights come up on the yard. It is four hours later. Rose *is taking down the clothes from the line.* Cory *enters carrying his football equipment.*

Rose: Your daddy like to had a fit with you running out of here this morning without doing your chores.

Cory: I told you I had to go to practice.

Rose: He say you were supposed to help him with this fence.

Cory: He been saying that the last four or five Saturdays, and then he don't never do nothing, but go down to Taylors'. Did you tell him about the recruiter?

5 *Rose:* Yeah, I told him.

Cory: What he say?

Rose: He ain't said nothing too much. You get in there and get started on your chores before he gets back. Go on and scrub down them steps before he gets back here hollering and carrying on.

Cory: I'm hungry. What you got to eat, Mama?

Rose: Go on and get started on your chores. I got some meat loaf in there. Go on and make you a sandwich . . . and don't leave no mess in there.

Cory *exits into the house.* Rose *continues to take down the clothes.*

Troy *enters the yard and sneaks up and grabs her from behind.*

Troy! Go on, now. You liked to scared me to death. What was the score of the game? Lucille had me on the phone and I couldn't keep up with it.

Troy: What I care about the game? Come here, woman. *[He tries to kiss her.]*   10

Rose: I thought you went down Taylors' to listen to the game. Go on, Troy! You supposed to be putting up this fence.

Troy [attempting to kiss her again]: I'll put it up when I finish with what is at hand.

Rose: Go on, Troy. I ain't studying you.

Troy [chasing after her]: I'm studying you . . . fixing to do my homework!

Rose: Troy, you better leave me alone.   15

Troy: Where's Cory? That boy brought his butt home yet?

Rose: He's in the house doing his chores.

Troy [calling]: Cory! Get your butt out here, boy!

Rose *exits into the house with the laundry.* Troy *goes over to the pile of wood, picks up a board, and starts sawing.* Cory *enters from the house.*

Troy: You just now coming in here from leaving this morning?

Cory: Yeah, I had to go to football practice.   20

Troy: Yeah, what?

Cory: Yessir.

Troy: I ain't but two seconds off you noway. The garbage sitting in there overflowing . . . you ain't done none of your chores . . . and you come in here talking about "Yeah."

Cory: I was just getting ready to do my chores now, Pop . . .

Troy: Your first chore is to help me with this fence on Saturday. Everything else   25
come after that. Now get that saw and cut them boards.

Cory *takes the saw and begins cutting the boards.* Troy *continues working. There is a long pause.*

Cory: Hey, Pop . . . why don't you buy a TV?

Troy: What I want with a TV? What I want one of them for?

Cory: Everybody got one. Earl, Ba Bra . . . Jesse!

Troy: I ain't asked you who had one. I say what I want with one?

Cory: So you can watch it. They got lots of things on TV. Baseball games and   30
everything. We could watch the World Series.

Troy: Yeah . . . and how much this TV cost?

Cory: I don't know. They got them on sale for around two hundred dollars.

Troy: Two hundred dollars, huh?

Cory: That ain't that much, Pop.

Troy: Naw, it's just two hundred dollars. See that roof you got over your head at   35
night? Let me tell you something about that roof. It's been over ten years
since that roof was last tarred. See now . . . the snow come this winter and sit
up there on that roof like it is . . . and it's gonna seep inside. It's just gonna be
a little bit . . . ain't gonna hardly notice it. Then the next thing you know, it's
gonna be leaking all over the house. Then the wood rot from all that water

and you gonna need a whole new roof. Now, how much you think it cost to get that roof tarred?

Cory: I don't know.

Troy: Two hundred and sixty-four dollars . . . cash money. While you thinking about a TV, I got to be thinking about the roof . . . and whatever else go wrong here. Now if you had two hundred dollars, what would you do . . . fix the roof or buy a TV?

Cory: I'd buy a TV. Then when the roof started to leak . . . when it needed fixing . . . I'd fix it.

Troy: Where you gonna get the money from? You done spent it for a TV. You gonna sit up and watch the water run all over your brand new TV.

40 *Cory:* Aw, Pop. You got money. I know you do.

Troy: Where I got it at, huh?

Cory: You got it in the bank.

Troy: You wanna see my bankbook? You wanna see that seventy-three dollars and twenty-two cents I got sitting up in there?

Cory: You ain't got to pay for it all at one time. You can put a down payment on it and carry it on home with you.

45 *Troy:* Not me. I ain't gonna owe nobody nothing if I can help it. Miss a payment and they come and snatch it right out of your house. Then what you got? Now, soon as I get two hundred dollars clear, then I'll buy a TV. Right now, as soon as I get two hundred and sixty-four dollars, I'm gonna have this roof tarred.

Cory: Aw . . . Pop!

Troy: You go on and get you two hundred dollars and buy one if ya want it. I got better things to do with my money.

Cory: I can't get no two hundred dollars. I ain't never seen two hundred dollars.

Troy: I'll tell you what . . . you get you a hundred dollars and I'll put the other hundred with it.

50 *Cory:* All right, I'm gonna show you.

Troy: You gonna show me how you can cut them boards right now.

 Cory *begins to cut the boards. There is a long pause.*

Cory: The Pirates won today. That makes five in a row.

Troy: I ain't thinking about the Pirates. Got an all-white team. Got that boy . . . that Puerto Rican boy . . . Clemente. Don't even half-play him. That boy could be something if they give him a chance. Play him one day and sit him on the bench the next.

Cory: He gets a lot of chances to play.

55 *Troy:* I'm talking about playing regular. Playing every day so you can get your timing. That's what I'm talking about.

Cory: They got some white guys on the team that don't play every day. You can't play everybody at the same time.

Troy: If they got a white fellow sitting on the bench . . . you can bet your last dollar he can't play! The colored guy got to be twice as good before he get on the team. That's why I don't want you to get all tied up in them sports. Man on the team and what it get him? They got colored on the team and don't use them. Same as not having them. All them teams the same.

Cory: The Braves got Hank Aaron and Wes Covington. Hank Aaron hit two home runs today. That makes forty-three.

Troy: Hank Aaron ain't nobody. That what you supposed to do. That's how you supposed to play the game. Ain't nothing to it. It's just a matter of timing . . . getting the right follow-through. Hell, I can hit forty-three home runs right now!

Cory: Not off no major-league pitching, you couldn't.   60

Troy: We had better pitching in the Negro leagues. I hit seven home runs off of Satchel Paige.° You can't get no better than that!

Cory: Sandy Koufax. He's leading the league in strikeouts.

Troy: I ain't thinking of no Sandy Koufax.

Cory: You got Warren Spahn and Lew Burdette. I bet you couldn't hit no home runs off of Warren Spahn.

Troy: I'm through with it now. You go on and cut them boards. *[Pause.]* Your   65
mama tell me you done got recruited by a college football team? Is that right?

Cory: Yeah. Coach Zellman say the recruiter gonna be coming by to talk to you. Get you to sign the permission papers.

Troy: I thought you supposed to be working down there at the A&P. Ain't you suppose to be working down there after school?

Cory: Mr. Stawicki say he gonna hold my job for me until after the football season. Say starting next week I can work weekends.

Troy: I thought we had an understanding about this football stuff? You suppose to keep up with your chores and hold that job down at the A&P. Ain't been around here all day on a Saturday. Ain't none of your chores done . . . and now you telling me you done quit your job.

Cory: I'm going to be working weekends.   70

Troy: You damn right you are! And ain't no need for nobody coming around here to talk to me about signing nothing.

Cory: Hey, Pop . . . you can't do that. He's coming all the way from North Carolina.

Troy: I don't care where he coming from. The white man ain't gonna let you get nowhere with that football noway. You go on and get your book-learning so you can work yourself up in that A&P or learn how to fix cars or build houses or something, get you a trade. That way you have something can't nobody take away from you. You go on and learn how to put your hands to some good use. Besides hauling people's garbage.

Cory: I get good grades, Pop. That's why the recruiter wants to talk with you. You got to keep up your grades to get recruited. This way I'll be going to college. I'll get a chance . . .

Troy: First you gonna get your butt down there to the A&P and get your job back.   75

Cory: Mr. Stawicki done already hired somebody else 'cause I told him I was playing football.

---

[61] **Satchel Paige** (1906–82), one of the best pitchers for the Negro Leagues; when he pitched in the Major Leagues, starting with the Cleveland Indians in 1948, he was the oldest rookie in its history. He was inducted into the Baseball Hall of Fame in 1971.

Troy: You a bigger fool than I thought . . . to let somebody take away your job so you can play some football. Where you gonna get your money to take out your girlfriend and whatnot? What kind of foolishness is that to let somebody take away your job?

Cory: I'm still gonna be working weekends.

Troy: Naw . . . naw. You getting your butt out of here and finding you another job.

80 *Cory:* Come on, Pop! I got to practice. I can't work after school and play football too. The team needs me. That's what Coach Zellman say . . .

Troy: I don't care what nobody else say. I'm the boss . . . you understand? I'm the boss around here. I do the only saying what counts.

Cory: Come on, Pop!

Troy: I asked you . . . did you understand?

Cory: Yeah . . .

85 *Troy:* What?!

Cory: Yessir.

Troy: You go on down there to that A&P and see if you can get your job back. If you can't do both . . . then you quit the football team. You've got to take the crookeds with the straights.

Cory: Yessir. *[Pause.]* Can I ask you a question?

Troy: What the hell you wanna ask me? Mr. Stawicki the one you got the questions for.

90 *Cory:* How come you ain't never liked me?

Troy: Liked you? Who the hell say I got to like you? What law is there say I got to like you? Wanna stand up in my face and ask a damn foolass question like that. Talking about liking somebody. Come here, boy, when I talk to you.

Cory *comes over to where* Troy *is working. He stands slouched over and* Troy *shoves him on his shoulder.*

Straighten up, goddammit! I asked you a question . . . what law is there say I got to like you?

Cory: None.

Troy: Well, all right then! Don't you eat every day? *[Pause.]* Answer me when I talk to you! Don't you eat every day?

Cory: Yeah.

95 *Troy:* Nigger, as long as you in my house, you put that sir on the end of it when you talk to me.

Cory: Yes . . . sir.

Troy: You eat every day.

Cory: Yessir!

Troy: Got a roof over your head.

100 *Cory:* Yessir!

Troy: Got clothes on your back.

Cory: Yessir.

Troy: Why you think that is?

Cory: Cause of you.

105 *Troy:* Ah, hell I know it's cause of me . . . but why do you think that is?

Cory [hesitant]: Cause you like me.

Troy: Like you? I go out of here every morning . . . bust my butt . . . putting up with them crackers every day . . . cause I like you? You are the biggest fool I ever saw. *[Pause.]* It's my job. It's my responsibility! You understand that? A man got to take care of his family. You live in my house . . . sleep you behind on my bedclothes . . . fill you belly up with my food . . . cause you my son. You my flesh and blood. Not cause I like you! Cause it's my duty to take care of you. I owe a responsibility to you! Let's get this straight right here . . . before it go along any further . . . I ain't got to like you. Mr. Rand don't give me my money come payday cause he likes me. He gives me cause he owe me. I done give you everything I had to give you. I gave you your life! Me and your mama worked that out between us. And liking your black ass wasn't part of the bargain. Don't you try and go through life worrying about if somebody like you or not. You best be making sure they doing right by you. You understand what I'm saying boy?

Cory: Yessir.

Troy: Then get the hell out of my face, and get on down to that A&P.

Rose *has been standing behind the screen door for much of the scene. She enters as* Cory *exits.*

Rose: Why don't you let the boy go ahead and play football, Troy? Ain't no harm   110
in that. He's just trying to be like you with the sports.

Troy: I don't want him to be like me! I want him to move as far away from my life as he can get. You the only decent thing that ever happened to me. I wish him that. But I don't wish him a thing else from my life. I decided seventeen years ago that boy wasn't getting involved in no sports. Not after what they did to me in the sports.

Rose: Troy, why don't you admit you was too old to play in the major leagues? For once . . . why don't you admit that?

Troy: What do you mean too old? Don't come telling me I was too old. I just wasn't the right color. Hell, I'm fifty-three years old and can do better than Selkirk's .269 right now!

Rose: How's was you gonna play ball when you were over forty? Sometimes I can't get no sense out of you.

Troy: I got good sense, woman. I got sense enough not to let my boy get hurt   115
over playing no sports. You been mothering that boy too much. Worried about if people like him.

Rose: Everything that boy do . . . he do for you. He wants you to say "Good job, son." That's all.

Troy: Rose, I ain't got time for that. He's alive. He's healthy. He's got to make his own way. I made mine. Ain't nobody gonna hold his hand when he get out there in that world.

Rose: Times have changed from when you was young, Troy. People change. The world's changing around you and you can't even see it.

Troy [slow, methodical]: Woman . . . I do the best I can do. I come in here every Friday. I carry a sack of potatoes and a bucket of lard. You all line up at the door with your hands out. I give you the lint from my pockets. I give you my sweat and my blood. I ain't got no tears. I done spent them. We go upstairs in that room at night . . . and I fall down on you and try to blast a hole into for-ever. I get up Monday morning . . . find my lunch on the table. I go out. Make my way. Find my strength to carry me through to the next Friday. *[Pause.]* That's all I got, Rose. That's all I got to give. I can't give nothing else.

Troy *exits into the house. The lights go down to black.*

Scene 4

It is Friday. Two weeks later. Cory *starts out of the house with his football equipment. The phone rings.*

Cory *[calling]:* I got it! *[He answers the phone and stands in the screen door talking.]* Hello? Hey, Jesse. Naw . . . I was just getting ready to leave now.

Rose *[calling]:* Cory!

Cory: I told you, man, them spikes is all tore up. You can use them if you want, but they ain't no good. Earl got some spikes.

Rose *[calling]:* Cory!

5 Cory *[calling to* Rose*]:* Mam? I'm talking to Jesse. *[Into phone.]* When she say that? *[Pause.]* Aw, you lying, man. I'm gonna tell her you said that.

Rose *[calling]:* Cory, don't you go nowhere!

Cory: I got to go to the game, Ma! *[Into the phone.]* Yeah, hey, look, I'll talk to you later. Yeah, I'll meet you over Earl's house. Later. Bye, Ma.

Cory *exits the house and starts out the yard.*

Rose: Cory, where you going off to? You got that stuff all pulled out and thrown all over your room.

Cory *[in the yard]:* I was looking for my spikes. Jesse wanted to borrow my spikes.

10 Rose: Get up there and get that cleaned up before your daddy get back in here.

Cory: I got to go to the game! I'll clean it up *when I get back.*

Cory *exits.*

Rose: That's all he need to do is see that room all messed up.

Rose *exits into the house.* Troy *and* Bono *enter the yard.* Troy *is dressed in clothes other than his work clothes.*

Bono: He told him the same thing he told you. Take it to the union.

Troy: Brownie ain't got that much sense. Man wasn't thinking about nothing. He wait until I confront them on it . . . then he wanna come crying seniority. *[Calls.]* Hey, Rose!

15 Bono: I wish I could have seen Mr. Rand's face when he told you.

Troy: He couldn't get it out of his mouth! Liked to bit his tongue! When they called me down there to the Commissioner's office . . . he thought they was gonna fire me. Like everybody else.

Bono: I didn't think they was gonna fire you. I thought they was gonna put you on the warning paper.

Troy: Hey, Rose! *[To* Bono.*]* Yeah, Mr. Rand like to bit his tongue.

Troy *breaks the seal on the bottle, takes a drink, and hands it to* Bono.

Bono: I see you run right down to Taylors' and told that Alberta gal.

20 Troy *[calling]:* Hey Rose! *[To* Bono.*]* I told everybody. Hey, Rose! I went down there to cash my check.

Rose [entering from the house]: Hush all that hollering, man! I know you out here. What they say down there at the Commissioner's office?

Troy: You supposed to come when I call you, woman. Bono'll tell you that. [*To* Bono.] Don't Lucille come when you call her?

Rose: Man, hush your mouth. I ain't no dog . . . talk about "come when you call me."

Troy [puts his arm around Rose]: You hear this, Bono? I had me an old dog used to get uppity like that. You say, "C'mere, Blue!" . . . and he just lay there and look at you. End up getting a stick and chasing him away trying to make him come.

Rose: I ain't studying you and your dog. I remember you used to sing that old song.   25

Troy [he sings]: Hear it ring! Hear it ring! I had a dog his name was Blue.

Rose: Don't nobody wanna hear you sing that old song.

Troy [sings]: You know Blue was mighty true.

Rose: Used to have Cory running around here singing that song.

Bono: Hell, I remember that song myself.   30

Troy [sings]: You know Blue was a good old dog.
  Blue treed a possum in a hollow log.
  That was my daddy's song. My daddy made up that song.

Rose: I don't care who made it up. Don't nobody wanna hear you sing it.

Troy [makes a song like calling a dog]: Come here, woman.

Rose: You come in here carrying on, I reckon they ain't fired you. What they say down there at the Commissioner's office?

Troy: Look here, Rose . . . Mr. Rand called me into his office today when I got   35
  back from talking to them people down there . . . it come from up top . . . he called me in and told me they was making me a driver.

Rose: Troy, you kidding!

Troy: No I ain't. Ask Bono.

Rose: Well, that's great, Troy. Now you don't have to hassle them people no more.
  Lyons *enters from the street.*

Troy: Aw hell, I wasn't looking to see you today. I thought you was in jail. Got it all over the front page of the *Courier* about them raiding Sefus's place . . . where you be hanging out with all them thugs.

Lyons: Hey, Pop . . . that ain't got nothing to do with me. I don't go down there   40
  gambling. I go down there to sit in with the band. I ain't got nothing to do with the gambling part. They got some good music down there.

Troy: They got some rogues . . . is what they got.

Lyons: How you been, Mr. Bono? Hi, Rose.

Bono: I see where you playing down at the Crawford Grill tonight.

Rose: How come you ain't brought Bonnie like I told you? You should have brought Bonnie with you, she ain't been over in a month of Sundays.

Lyons: I was just in the neighborhood . . . thought I'd stop by.   45

Troy: Here he come . . .

Bono: Your daddy got a promotion on the rubbish. He's gonna be the first colored driver. Ain't got to do nothing but sit up there and read the paper like them white fellows.

Lyons: Hey, Pop . . . if you knew how to read you'd be all right.

Bono: Naw . . . naw . . . you mean if the nigger knew how to drive he'd be all right. Been fighting with them people about driving and ain't even got a license. Mr. Rand know you ain't got no driver's license?

50 *Troy:* Driving ain't nothing. All you do is point the truck where you want it to go. Driving ain't nothing.

Bono: Do Mr. Rand know you ain't got no driver's license? That's what I'm talking about. I ain't asked if driving was easy. I asked if Mr. Rand know you ain't got no driver's license.

Troy: He ain't got to know. The man ain't got to know my business. Time he find out, I have two or three driver's licenses.

Lyons [going into his pocket]: Say, look here, Pop . . .

Troy: I knew it was coming. Didn't I tell you, Bono? I know what kind of "Look here, Pop" that was. The nigger fixing to ask me for some money. It's Friday night. It's my payday. All them rogues down there on the avenue . . . the ones that ain't in jail . . . and Lyons is hopping in his shoes to get down there with them.

55 *Lyons:* See, Pop . . . if you give somebody else a chance to talk sometimes, you'd see that I was fixing to pay you back your ten dollars like I told you. Here . . . I told you I'd pay you when Bonnie got paid.

Troy: Naw . . . you go ahead and keep that ten dollars. Put it in the bank. The next time you feel like you wanna come by here and ask me for something . . . you go on down there and get that.

Lyons: Here's your ten dollars, Pop. I told you I don't want you to give me nothing. I just wanted to borrow ten dollars.

Troy: Naw . . . you go on and keep that for the next time you want to ask me.

Lyons: Come on, Pop . . . here go your ten dollars.

60 *Rose:* Why don't you go on and let the boy pay you back, Troy?

Lyons: Here you go, Rose. If you don't take it I'm gonna have to hear about it for the next six months. *[He hands her the money.]*

Rose: You can hand yours over here too, Troy.

Troy: You see this, Bono. You see how they do me.

Bono: Yeah, Lucille do me the same way.

    Gabriel *is heard singing off stage. He enters.*

65 *Gabriel:* Better get ready for the Judgment! Better get ready for . . . Hey! . . . Hey! . . . There's Troy's boy!

Lyons: How are you doing, Uncle Gabe?

Gabriel: Lyons . . . The King of the Jungle! Rose . . . hey, Rose. Got a flower for you. *[He takes a rose from his pocket.]* Picked it myself. That's the same rose like you is!

Rose: That's right nice of you, Gabe.

Lyons: What you been doing, Uncle Gabe?

70 *Gabriel:* Oh, I been chasing hellhounds and waiting on the time to tell St. Peter to open the gates.

Lyons: You been chasing hellhounds, huh? Well . . . you doing the right thing, Uncle Gabe. Somebody got to chase them.

Gabriel: Oh, yeah . . . . I know it. The devil's strong. The devil ain't no pushover. Hellhounds snipping at everybody's heels. But I got my trumpet waiting on the judgment time.

Lyons: Waiting on the Battle of Armageddon, huh?

Gabriel: Ain't gonna be too much of a battle when God get to waving that Judgment sword. But the people's gonna have a hell of a time trying to get into heaven if them gates ain't open.

Lyons [putting his arm around Gabriel*]:* You hear this, Pop. Uncle Gabe, you all right!   75

Gabriel [laughing with Lyons*]:* Lyons! King of the Jungle.

Rose: You gonna stay for supper, Gabe? Want me to fix you a plate?

Gabriel: I'll take a sandwich, Rose. Don't want no plate. Just wanna eat with my hands. I'll take a sandwich.

Rose: How about you, Lyons? You staying? Got some short ribs cooking.

Lyons: Naw, I won't eat nothing till after we finished playing. *[Pause.]* You ought   80
to come down and listen to me play, Pop.

Troy: I don't like that Chinese music. All that noise.

Rose. Go on in the house and wash up, Gabe . . . I'll fix you a sandwich.

Gabriel [to Lyons, *as he exits]:* Troy's mad at me.

Lyons: What you mad at Uncle Gabe for, Pop?

Rose: He thinks Troy's mad at him cause he moved over to Miss Pearl's.   85

Troy: I ain't mad at the man. He can live where he want to live at.

Lyons: What he move over there for? Miss Pearl don't like nobody.

Rose: She don't mind him none. She treats him real nice. She just don't allow all that singing.

Troy: She don't mind that rent he be paying . . . that's what she don't mind.

Rose: Troy, I ain't going through that with you no more. He's over there cause he   90
want to have his own place. He can come and go as he please.

Troy: Hell, he could come and go as he please here. I wasn't stopping him. I ain't put no rules on him.

Rose: It ain't the same thing, Troy. And you know it.

Gabriel *comes to the door.*

Now, that's the last I wanna hear about that. I don't wanna hear nothing else about Gabe and Miss Pearl. And next week . . .

Gabriel: I'm ready for my sandwich, Rose.

Rose: And next week . . . when that recruiter come from that school . . . I want you to sign that paper and go on and let Cory play football. Then that'll be the last I have to hear about that.

Troy [to Rose *as she exits into the house]:* I ain't thinking about Cory nothing.   95

Lyons: What . . . Cory got recruited? What school he going to?

Troy: That boy walking around here smelling his piss . . . thinking he's grown. Thinking he's gonna do what he want, irrespective of what I say. Look here, Bono . . . I left the Commissioner's office and went down to the A&P . . . that boy ain't working down there. He lying to me. Telling me he got his job back . . . telling me he working weekends . . . telling me he working after school . . . Mr. Stawicki tell me he ain't working down there at all!

Lyons: Cory just growing up. He's just busting at the seams trying to fill out your shoes.

Troy: I don't care what he's doing. When he get to the point where he wanna disobey me . . . then it's time for him to move on. Bono'll tell you that. I bet he ain't never disobeyed his daddy without paying the consequences.

100 *Bono:* I ain't never had a chance. My daddy came on through . . . but I ain't never knew him to see him . . . or what he had on his mind or where he went. Just moving on through. Searching out the New Land. That's what the old folks used to call it. See a fellow moving around from place to place . . . woman to woman . . . called it searching out the New Land. I can't say if he ever found it. I come along, didn't want no kids. Didn't know if I was gonna be in one place long enough to fix on them right as their daddy. I figured I was going searching too. As it turned out I been hooked up with Lucille near about as long as your daddy been with Rose. Going on sixteen years.

Troy: Sometimes I wish I hadn't known my daddy. He ain't cared nothing about no kids. A kid to him wasn't nothing. All he wanted was for you to learn how to walk so he could start you to working. When it come time for eating . . . he ate first. If there was anything left over, that's what you got. Man would sit down and eat two chickens and give you the wing.

Lyons: You ought to stop that, Pop. Everybody feed their kids. No matter how hard times is . . . everybody care about their kids. Make sure they have something to eat.

Troy: The only thing my daddy cared about was getting them bales of cotton in to Mr. Lubin. That's the only thing that mattered to him. Sometimes I used to wonder why he was living. Wonder why the devil hadn't come and got him. "Get them bales of cotton in to Mr. Lubin" and find out he owe him money . . .

Lyons: He should have just went on and left when he saw he couldn't get nowhere. That's what I would have done.

105 *Troy:* How he gonna leave with eleven kids? And where he gonna go? He ain't knew how to do nothing but farm. No, he was trapped and I think he knew it. But I'll say this for him . . . he felt a responsibility toward us. Maybe he ain't treated us the way I felt he should have . . . but without that responsibility he could have walked off and left us . . . made his own way.

Bono: A lot of them did. Back in those days what you talking about . . . they walk out their front door and just take on down one road or another and keep on walking.

Lyons: There you go! That's what I'm talking about.

Bono: Just keep on walking till you come to something else. Ain't you never heard of nobody having the walking blues? Well, that's what you call it when you just take off like that.

Troy: My daddy ain't had them walking blues! What you talking about? He stayed right there with his family. But he was just as evil as he could be. My mama couldn't stand him. Couldn't stand that evilness. She run off when I was about eight. She sneaked off one night after he had gone to sleep. Told me she was coming back for me. I ain't never seen her no more. All his women run off and left him. He wasn't good for nobody.

When my turn come to head out, I was fourteen and got to sniffing around Joe Canewell's daughter. Had us an old mule we called Greyboy. My daddy sent me out to do some plowing and I tied up Greyboy and went to fooling around with Joe Canewell's daughter. We done found us a nice little spot, got real cozy with each other. She about thirteen and we done figured we was grown anyway . . . so we down there enjoying ourselves . . . ain't thinking about nothing. We didn't know Greyboy had got loose and wandered back to the house and my daddy was looking for me. We down there by the creek enjoying ourselves when my daddy come up on us. Surprised us. He had them leather straps off the mule and commenced to whupping me like there was no tomorrow. I jumped up, mad and embarrassed. I was scared of my daddy. When he commenced to whupping on me . . . quite naturally I run to get out of the way. *[Pause.]* Now I thought he was mad cause I ain't done my work. But I see where he was chasing me off so he could have the gal for himself. When I see what the matter of it was, I lost all fear of my daddy. Right there is where I become a man . . . at fourteen years of age. *[Pause.]* Now it was my turn to run him off. I picked up them same reins that he had used on me. I picked up them reins and commenced to whupping on him. The gal jumped up and run off . . . and when my daddy turned to face me, I could see why the devil had never come to get him . . . cause he was the devil himself. I don't know what happened. When I woke up, I was laying right there by the creek, and Blue . . . this old dog we had . . . was licking my face. I thought I was blind. I couldn't see nothing. Both my eyes were swollen shut. I laid there and cried. I didn't know what I was gonna do. The only thing I knew was the time had come for me to leave my daddy's house. And right there the world suddenly got big. And it was a long time before I could cut it down to where I could handle it.

Part of that cutting down was when I got to the place where I could feel him kicking in my blood and knew that the only thing that separated us was the matter of a few years.

Gabriel *enters from the house with a sandwich.*

Lyons: What you got there, Uncle Gabe?

Gabriel: Got me a ham sandwich. Rose gave me a ham sandwich.

Troy: I don't know what happened to him. I done lost touch with everybody except Gabriel. But I hope he's dead. I hope he found some peace.

Lyons: That's a heavy story, Pop. I didn't know you left home when you was fourteen.

Troy: And didn't know nothing. The only part of the world I knew was the forty-two acres of Mr. Lubin's land. That's all I knew about life.

Lyons: Fourteen's kinda young to be out on your own. *[Phone rings.]* I don't even think I was ready to be out on my own at fourteen. I don't know what I would have done.

Troy: I got up from the creek and walked on down to Mobile. I was through with farming. Figured I could do better in the city. So I walked the two hundred miles to Mobile.

Lyons: Wait a minute . . . you ain't walked no two hundred miles, Pop. Ain't nobody gonna walk no two hundred miles. You talking about some walking there.

Bono: That's the only way you got anywhere back in them days.

Lyons: Shhh. Damn if I wouldn't have hitched a ride with somebody!

120 *Troy:* Who you gonna hitch it with? They ain't had no cars and things like they got now. We talking about 1918.

Rose [entering]: What you all out here getting into?

Troy [to Rose]: I'm telling Lyons how good he got it. He don't know nothing about this I'm talking.

Rose: Lyons, that was Bonnie on the phone. She say you supposed to pick her up.

Lyons: Yeah, okay, Rose.

125 *Troy:* I walked on down to Mobile and hitched up with some of them fellows that was heading this way. Got up here and found out . . . not only couldn't you get a job . . . you couldn't find no place to live. I thought I was in freedom. Shhh. Colored folks living down there on the riverbanks in whatever kind of shelter they could find for themselves. Right down there under the Brady Street Bridge. Living in shacks made of sticks and tarpaper. Messed around there and went from bad to worse. Started stealing. First it was food. Then I figured, hell, if I steal money I can buy me some food. Buy me some shoes too! One thing led to another. Met your mama. I was young and anxious to be a man. Met your mama and had you. What I do that for? Now I got to worry about feeding you and her. Got to steal three times as much. Went out one day looking for somebody to rob . . . that's what I was, a robber. I'll tell you the truth. I'm ashamed of it today. But it's the truth. Went to rob this fellow . . . pulled out my knife . . . and he pulled out a gun. Shot me in the chest. I felt just like somebody had taken a hot branding iron and laid it on me. When he shot me I jumped at him with my knife. They told me I killed him and they put me in the penitentiary and locked me up for fifteen years. That's where I met Bono. That's where I learned how to play baseball. Got out that place and your mama had taken you and went on to make life without me. Fifteen years was a long time for her to wait. But that fifteen years cured me of that robbing stuff. Rose'll tell you. She asked me when I met her if I had gotten all that foolishness out of my system. And I told her, "Baby, it's you and baseball all what count with me." You hear me, Bono? I meant it too. She say, "Which one comes first?" I told her, "Baby, ain't no doubt it's baseball . . . but you stick and get old with me and we'll both outlive this baseball." Am I right, Rose? And it's true.

Rose: Man, hush your mouth. You ain't said no such thing. Talking about, "Baby you know you'll always be number one with me." That's what you was talking.

Troy: You hear that, Bono. That's why I love her.

Bono: Rose'll keep you straight. You get off the track, she'll straighten you up.

Rose: Lyons, you better get on up and get Bonnie. She waiting on you.

130 *Lyons [gets up to go]:* Hey, Pop, why don't you come on down to the Grill and hear me play?

Troy: I ain't going down there. I'm too old to be sitting around in them clubs.

Bono: You got to be good to play down at the Grill.

Lyons: Come on, Pop . . .

Troy: I got to get up in the morning.

Lyons: You ain't got to stay long.   135

Troy: Naw, I'm gonna get my supper and go on to bed.

Lyons: Well, I got to go. I'll see you again.

Troy: Don't you come around my house on my payday.

Rose: Pick up the phone and let somebody know you coming. And bring Bonnie
   with you. You know I'm always glad to see her.

Lyons: Yeah, I'll do that, Rose. You take care now. See you, Pop. See you,   140
   Mr. Bono. See you, Uncle Gabe.

Gabriel: Lyons! King of the Jungle!

   Lyons *exits.*

Troy: Is supper ready, woman? Me and you got some business to take care of. I'm
   gonna tear it up too.

Rose: Troy, I done told you now!

Troy [puts his arm around Bono]: Aw hell, woman . . . this is Bono. Bono like family. I done known this nigger since . . . how long I done know you?

Bono: It's been a long time.   145

Troy: I done know this nigger since Skippy was a pup. Me and him done been
   through some times.

Bono: You sure right about that.

Troy: Hell, I done know him longer than I known you. And we still standing
   shoulder to shoulder. Hey, look here, Bono . . . a man can't ask for no more
   than that. *[Drinks to him.]* I love you, nigger.

Bono: Hell, I love you too . . . I got to get home see my woman. You got yours in
   hand. I got to get mine.

   Bono starts to exit as Cory *enters the yard, dressed in his football uniform. He gives*
   Troy *a hard, uncompromising look.*

Cory: What you do that for, Pop?   150

   He throws his helmet down in the direction of Troy.

Rose: What's the matter? Cory . . . what's the matter?

Cory: Papa done went up to the school and told Coach Zellman I can't play football no more. Wouldn't even let me play the game. Told him to tell the
   recruiter not to come.

Rose: Troy . . .

Troy: What you Troying me for. Yeah, I did it. And the boy know why I did it.

Cory: Why you wanna do that to me? That was the one chance I had.   155

Rose: Ain't nothing wrong with Cory playing football, Troy.

Troy: The boy lied to me. I told the nigger if he wanna play football . . . to keep
   up his chores and hold down that job at the A&P. That was the conditions.
   Stopped down there to see Mr. Stawicki . . .

Cory: I can't work after school during the football season, Pop! I tried to tell you
   that Mr. Stawicki's holding my job for me. You don't never want to listen to
   nobody. And then you wanna go and do this to me!

Troy: I ain't done nothing to you. You done it to yourself.

160 *Cory:* Just cause you didn't have a chance! You just scared I'm gonna be better than you, that's all.

Troy: Come here.

Rose: Troy . . .

Cory *reluctantly crosses over to* Troy.

Troy: All right! See. You done made a mistake.

Cory: I didn't even do nothing!

165 *Troy:* I'm gonna tell you what your mistake was. See . . . you swung at the ball and didn't hit it. That's strike one. See, you in the batter's box now. You swung and you missed. That's strike one. Don't you strike out!

Lights fade to black.

Act 2
Scene 1

The following morning. Cory *is at the tree hitting the ball with the bat. He tries to mimic* Troy, *but his swing is awkward, less sure.* Rose *enters from the house.*

Rose: Cory, I want you to help me with this cupboard.

Cory: I ain't quitting the team. I don't care what Poppa say.

Rose: I'll talk to him when he gets back. He had to go see about your Uncle Gabe. The police done arrested him. Say he was disturbing the peace. He'll be back directly. Come on in here and help me clean out the top of this cupboard.

Cory *exits into the house.* Rose *sees* Troy *and* Bono *coming down the alley.*

Troy . . . what they say down there?

Troy: Ain't said nothing. I give them fifty dollars and they let him go. I'll talk to you about it. Where's Cory?

5 *Rose:* He's in there helping me clean out these cupboards.

Troy: Tell him to get his butt out here.

Troy *and* Bono *go over to the pile of wood.* Bono *picks up the saw and begins sawing.*

Troy *[to Bono]:* All they want is the money. That makes six or seven times I done went down there and got him. See me coming they stick out their hands.

Bono: Yeah. I know what you mean. That's all they care about . . . that money. They don't care about what's right. *[Pause.]* Nigger, why you got to go and get some hard wood? You ain't doing nothing but building a little old fence. Get you some soft pine wood. That's all you need.

Troy: I know what I'm doing. This is outside wood. You put pine wood inside the house. Pine wood is inside wood. This here is outside wood. Now you tell me where the fence is gonna be?

10 *Bono:* You don't need this wood. You can put it up with pine wood and it'll stand as long as you gonna be here looking at it.

Troy: How you know how long I'm gonna be here, nigger? Hell, I might just live forever. Live longer than old man Horsely.

Bono: That's what Magee used to say.

Troy: Magee's damn fool. Now you tell me who you ever heard of gonna pull their own teeth with a pair of rusty pliers.

Bono: The old folks . . . my granddaddy used to pull his teeth with pliers. They ain't had no dentists for the colored folks back then.

Troy: Get clean pliers! You understand? Clean pliers! Sterilize them! Besides we   15
ain't living back then. All Magee had to do was walk over to Doc Goldblum's.

Bono: I see where you and that Tallahassee gal . . . that Alberta . . . I see where you all done got tight.

Troy: What you mean "got tight"?

Bono: I see where you be laughing and joking with her all the time.

Troy: I laughs and jokes with all of them, Bono. You know me.

Bono: That ain't the kind of laughing and joking I'm talking about.   20
Cory *enters from the house.*

Cory: How you doing, Mr. Bono?

Troy: Cory? Get that saw from Bono and cut some wood. He talking about the wood's too hard to cut. Stand back there, Jim, and let that young boy show you how it's done.

Bono: He's sure welcome to it.
Cory *takes the saw and begins to cut the wood.*
Whew-e-e! Look at that. Big old strong boy. Look like Joe Louis. Hell, must be getting old the way I'm watching that boy whip through that wood.

Cory: I don't see why Mama want a fence around the yard noways.

Troy: Damn if I know either. What the hell she keeping out with it? She ain't got   25
nothing nobody want.

Bono: Some people build fences to keep people out . . . and other people build fences to keep people in. Rose wants to hold on to you all. She loves you.

Troy: Hell, nigger, I don't need nobody to tell me my wife loves me. Cory . . . go on in the house and see if you can find that other saw.

Cory: Where's it at?

Troy: I said find it! Look for it till you find it!
Cory *exits into the house.*
What's that supposed to mean? Wanna keep us in?

Bono: Troy . . . I done known you seem like damn near my whole life. You and   30
Rose both. I done know both of you all for a long time. I remember when you met Rose. When you was hitting them baseball out the park. A lot of them old gals was after you then. You had the pick of the litter. When you picked Rose, I was happy for you. That was the first time I knew you had any sense. I said . . . My man Troy knows what he's doing . . . I'm gonna follow this nigger . . . he might take me somewhere. I been following you too. I done learned a whole heap of things about life watching you. I done learned how to tell where the shit lies. How to tell it from the alfalfa. You done learned me a lot of things. You showed me how to not make the same mistakes . . . to take life as it comes along and keep putting one foot in front of the other. *[Pause.]* Rose a good woman, Troy.

Troy: Hell, nigger, I know she a good woman. I been married to her for eighteen years. What you got on your mind, Bono?

Bono: I just say she a good woman. Just like I say anything. I ain't got to have nothing on your mind.

Troy: You just gonna say she a good woman and leave it hanging out there like that? Why you telling me she a good woman?

Bono: She loves you, Troy. Rose loves you.

35 *Troy:* You saying I don't measure up. That's what you trying to say. I don't measure up cause I'm seeing this other gal. I know what you trying to say.

Bono: I know what Rose means to you, Troy. I'm just trying to say I don't want to see you mess up.

Troy: Yeah, I appreciate that, Bono. If you was messing around on Lucille I'd be telling you the same thing.

Bono: Well, that's all I got to say. I just say that because I love you both.

Troy: Hell, you know me . . . I wasn't out there looking for nothing. You can't find a better woman than Rose. I know that. But seems like this woman just stuck onto me where I can't shake her loose. I done wrestled with it, tried to throw her off me . . . but she just stuck on tighter. Now she's stuck on for good.

40 *Bono:* You's in control . . . that's what you tell me all the time. You responsible for what you do.

Troy: I ain't ducking the responsibility of it. As long as it sets right in my heart . . . then I'm okay. Cause that's all I listen to. It'll tell me right from wrong every time. And I ain't talking about doing Rose no bad turn. I love Rose. She done carried me a long ways and I love and respect her for that.

Bono: I know you do. That's why I don't want to see you hurt her. But what you gonna do when she find out? What you got then? If you try and juggle both of them . . . sooner or later you gonna drop one of them. That's common sense.

Troy: Yeah, I hear what you saying, Bono. I been trying to figure a way to work it out.

Bono: Work it out right, Troy. I don't want to be getting all up between you and Rose's business . . . but work it so it come out right.

45 *Troy:* Ah hell, I get all up between you and Lucille's business. When you gonna get that woman that refrigerator she been wanting? Don't tell me you ain't got no money now. I know who your banker is. Mellon don't need that money bad as Lucille want that refrigerator. I'll tell you that.

Bono: Tell you what I'll do . . . when you finish building this fence for Rose . . . I'll buy Lucille that refrigerator.

Troy: You done stuck your foot in your mouth now!

Troy *grabs up a board and begins to saw.* Bono *starts to walk out the yard.*

Hey, nigger . . . where you going?

Bono: I'm going home. I know you don't expect me to help you now. I'm protecting my money. I wanna see you put that fence up by yourself. That's what I want to see. You'll be here another six months without me.

Troy: Nigger, you ain't right.

50 *Bono:* When it comes to my money . . . I'm right as fireworks on the Fourth of July.

Troy: All right, we gonna see now. You better get out your bankbook.

Bono *exits, and* Troy *continues to work.* Rose *enters from the house.*

Rose: What they say down there? What's happening with Gabe?

Troy: I went down there and got him out. Cost me fifty dollars. Say he was disturbing the peace. Judge set up a hearing for him in three weeks. Say to show cause why he shouldn't be recommitted.

Rose: What was he doing that cause them to arrest him?

Troy: Some kids was teasing him and he run them off home. Say he was howling 55 and carrying on. Some folks seen him and called the police. That's all it was.

Rose: Well, what's you say? What'd you tell the judge?

Troy: Told him I'd look after him. It didn't make no sense to recommit the man. He stuck out his big greasy palm and told me to give him fifty dollars and take him on home.

Rose: Where's he at now? Where'd he go off to?

Troy: He's gone about his business. He don't need nobody to hold his hand.

Rose: Well, I don't know. Seem like that would be the best place for him if they 60 did put him into the hospital. I know what you're gonna say. But that's what I think would be best.

Troy: The man done had his life ruined fighting for what? And they wanna take and lock him up. Let him be free. He don't bother nobody.

Rose: Well, everybody got their own way of looking at it I guess. Come on and get your lunch. I got a bowl of lima beans and some cornbread in the oven. Come and get something to eat. Ain't no sense you fretting over Gabe.

Rose *turns to go into the house.*

Troy: Rose . . . got something to tell you.

Rose: Well, come on . . . wait till I get this food on the table.

Troy: Rose! 65

She *stops and turns around.*

I don't know how to say this. *[Pause.]* I can't explain it none. It just sort of grows on you till it gets out of hand. It starts out like a little bush . . . and the next thing you know it's a whole forest.

Rose: Troy . . . what is you talking about?

Troy: I'm talking, woman, let me talk. I'm trying to find a way to tell you . . . I'm gonna be a daddy. I'm gonna be somebody's daddy.

Rose: Troy . . . you're not telling me this? You're gonna be . . . what?

Troy: Rose . . . now . . . see . . .

Rose: You telling me you gonna be somebody's daddy? You telling your *wife* this? 70

Gabriel *enters from the street. He carries a rose in his hand.*

Gabriel: Hey, Troy! Hey, Rose!

Rose: I have to wait eighteen years to hear something like this.

Gabriel: Hey, Rose . . . I got a flower for you. *[He hands it to her.]* That's a rose. Same rose like you is.

Rose: Thanks, Gabe.

Gabriel: Troy, you ain't mad at me is you? Them bad mens come and put me 75 away. You ain't mad at me is you?

Troy: Naw, Gabe, I ain't mad at you.

Rose: Eighteen years and you wanna come with this.

Gabriel [takes a quarter out of his pocket]: See what I got? Got a brand new quarter.

Troy: Rose . . . it's just . . .

80   *Rose:* Ain't nothing you can say, Troy. Ain't no way of explaining that.

Gabriel: Fellow that give me this quarter had a whole mess of them. I'm gonna keep this quarter till it stop shining.

Rose: Gabe, go on in the house there. I got some watermelon in the Frigidaire. Go on and get you a piece.

Gabriel: Say, Rose . . . you know I was chasing hellhounds and them bad mens come and get me and take me away. Troy helped me. He come down there and told them they better let me go before he beat them up. Yeah, he did!

Rose: You go on and get you a piece of watermelon, Gabe. Them bad mens is gone now.

85   *Gabriel:* Okay, Rose . . . gonna get me some watermelon. The kind with the stripes on it.

    Gabriel *exits into the house.*

Rose: Why, Troy? Why? After all these years to come dragging this in to me now. It don't make no sense at your age. I could have expected this ten or fifteen years ago, but not now.

Troy: Age ain't got nothing to do with it, Rose.

Rose: I done tried to be everything a wife should be. Everything a wife could be. Been married eighteen years and I got to live to see the day you tell me you been seeing another woman and done fathered a child by her. And you know I ain't never wanted no half nothing in my family. My whole family is half. Everybody got different fathers and mothers . . . my two sisters and my brother. Can't hardly tell who's who. Can't never sit down and talk about Papa and Mama. It's your papa and your mama and my papa and my mama . . .

Troy: Rose . . . stop it now.

90   *Rose:* I ain't never wanted that for none of my children. And now you wanna drag your behind in here and tell me something like this.

Troy: You ought to know. It's time for you to know.

Rose: Well, I don't want to know, goddamn it!

Troy: I can't just make it go away. It's done now. I can't wish the circumstance of the thing away.

Rose: And you don't want to either. Maybe you want to wish me and my boy away. Maybe that's what you want? Well, you can't wish us away. I've got eighteen years of my life invested in you. You ought to have stayed upstairs in my bed where you belong.

95   *Troy:* Rose . . . now listen to me . . . we can get a handle on this thing. We can talk this out . . . come to an understanding.

Rose: All of a sudden it's "we." Where was "we" at when you was down there rolling around with some godforsaken woman? "We" should have come to an understanding before you started making a damn fool of yourself. You're a day late and a dollar short when it comes to an understanding with me.

Troy: It's just . . . She gives me a different idea . . . a different understanding about myself. I can step out of this house and get away from the pressures and problems . . . be a different man. I ain't got to wonder how I'm gonna

pay the bills or get the roof fixed. I can just be a part of myself that I ain't
never been.

Rose: What I want to know . . . is do you plan to continue seeing her. That's all
you can say to me.

Troy: I can sit up in her house and laugh. Do you understand what I'm saying. I
can laugh out loud . . . and it feels good. It reaches all the way down to the
bottom of my shoes. *[Pause.]* Rose, I can't give that up.

Rose: Maybe you ought to go on and stay down there with her . . . if she's a   100
better woman than me.

Troy: It ain't about nobody being a better woman or nothing. Rose, you ain't the
blame. A man couldn't ask for no woman to be a better wife than you've
been. I'm responsible for it. I done locked myself into a pattern trying to take
care of you all that I forgot about myself.

Rose: What the hell was I there for? That was my job, not somebody else's.

Troy: Rose, I done tried all my life to live decent . . . to live a clean . . . hard . . .
useful life. I tried to be a good husband to you. In every way I knew how.
Maybe I come into the world backwards, I don't know. But . . . you born
with two strikes on you before you come to the plate. You got to guard it
closely . . . always looking for the curve ball on the inside corner. You can't
afford to let none get past you. You can't afford a call strike. If you going
down . . . you going down swinging. Everything lined up against you. What
you gonna do. I fooled them, Rose. I bunted. When I found you and Cory
and a halfway decent job . . . I was safe. Couldn't nothing touch me. I wasn't
gonna strike out no more. I wasn't going back to the penitentiary. I wasn't
gonna lay in the streets with a bottle of wine. I was safe. I had me a family.
A job. I wasn't gonna get that last strike. I was on first looking for one of
them boys to knock me in. To get me home.

Rose: You should have stayed in my bed, Troy.

Troy: Then when I saw that gal . . . she firmed up my backbone. And I got to   105
thinking that if I tried . . . I just might be able to steal second. Do you understand after eighteen years I wanted to steal second.

Rose: You should have held me tight. You should have grabbed me and held on.

Troy: I stood on first base for eighteen years and I thought . . . well, goddamn it . . .
go on for it!

Rose: We're not talking about baseball! We're talking about you going off to lay
in bed with another woman . . . and then bring it home to me. That's what
we're talking about. We ain't talking about no baseball.

Troy: Rose, you're not listening to me. I'm trying the best I can to explain it to
you. It's not easy for me to admit that I been standing in the same place for
eighteen years.

Rose: I been standing with you! I been right here with you, Troy. I got a life too. I   110
gave eighteen years of my life to stand in the same spot with you. Don't you
think I ever wanted other things? Don't you think I had dreams and hopes?
What about my life? What about me. Don't you think it ever crossed my
mind to want to know other men? That I wanted to lay up somewhere and
forget about my responsibilities? That I wanted someone to make me laugh

so I could feel good? You not the only one who's got wants and needs. But I held on to you, Troy. I took all my feelings, my wants and needs, my dreams . . . and I buried them inside you. I planted a seed and watched and prayed over it. I planted myself inside you and waited to bloom. And it didn't take me no eighteen years to find out the soil was hard and rocky and it wasn't never gonna bloom.

But I held on to you, Troy. I held you tighter. You was my husband. I owed you everything I had. Every part of me I could find to give you. And upstairs in that room . . . with the darkness falling in on me . . . I gave everything I had to try and erase the doubt that you wasn't the finest man in the world. And wherever you was going . . . I wanted to be there with you. Cause you was my husband. Cause that's the only way I was gonna survive as your wife. You always talking about what you give . . . and what you don't have to give. But you take too. You take . . . and don't even know nobody's giving!

Rose *turns to exit into the house;* Troy *grabs her arm.*

Troy: You say I take and don't give!

Rose: Troy! You're hurting me!

Troy: You say I take and don't give!

Rose: Troy . . . you're hurting my arm! Let go!

115 Troy: I done give you everything I got. Don't you tell that lie on me.

Rose: Troy!

Troy: Don't you tell that lie on me!

Cory *enters from the house.*

Cory: Mama!

Rose: Troy. You're hurting me.

120 Troy: Don't you tell me about no taking and giving.

Cory *comes up behind* Troy *and grabs him.* Troy, *surprised, is thrown off balance just as* Cory *throws a glancing blow that catches him on the chest and knocks him down.* Troy *is stunned, as is* Cory.

Rose: Troy. Troy. No!

Troy *gets to his feet and starts at* Cory.

Troy . . . no. Please! Troy!

Rose *pulls on* Troy *to hold him back.* Troy *stops himself.*

Troy [to Cory]: All right. That's strike two. You stay away from around me, boy. Don't you strike out. You living with a full count. Don't you strike out.

Troy *exits out the yard as the lights go down.*

Scene 2

It is six months later, early afternoon. Troy *enters from the house and starts to exit the yard.* Rose *enters from the house.*

Rose: Troy, I want to talk to you.

Troy: All of a sudden, after all this time, you want to talk to me, huh? You ain't wanted to talk to me for months. You ain't wanted to talk to me last night. You ain't wanted no part of me then. What you wanna talk to me about now?

Rose: Tomorrow's Friday.

Troy: I know what day tomorrow is. You think I don't know tomorrow's Friday? My whole life I ain't done nothing but look to see Friday coming and you got to tell me it's Friday.

Rose: I want to know if you're coming home.

Troy: I always come home, Rose. You know that. There ain't never been a night I ain't come home.

Rose: That ain't what I mean . . . and you know it. I want to know if you're coming straight home after work.

Troy: I figure I'd cash my check . . . hang out at Taylors' with the boys . . . maybe play a game of checkers . . .

Rose: Troy, I can't live like this. I won't live like this. You livin' on borrowed time with me. It's been going on six months now you ain't been coming home.

Troy: I be here every night. Every night of the year. That's 365 days.

Rose: I want you to come home tomorrow after work.

Troy: Rose . . . I don't mess up my pay. You know that now. I take my pay and I give it to you. I don't have no money but what you give me back. I just want to have a little time to myself . . . a little time to enjoy life.

Rose: What about me? When's my time to enjoy life?

Troy: I don't know what to tell you, Rose. I'm doing the best I can.

Rose: You ain't been home from work but time enough to change your clothes and run out . . . and you wanna call that the best you can do?

Troy: I'm going over to the hospital to see Alberta. She went into the hospital this afternoon. Look like she might have the baby early. I won't be gone long.

Rose: Well, you ought to know. They went over to Miss Pearl's and got Gabe today. She said you told them to go ahead and lock him up.

Troy: I ain't said no such thing. Whoever told you that is telling a lie. Pearl ain't doing nothing but telling a big fat lie.

Rose: She ain't had to tell me. I read it on the papers.

Troy: I ain't told them nothing of the kind.

Rose: I saw it right there on the papers.

Troy: What it say, huh?

Rose: It said you told them to take him.

Troy: Then they screwed that up, just the way they screw up everything. I ain't worried about what they got on the paper.

Rose: Say the government send part of his check to the hospital and the other part to you.

Troy: I ain't got nothing to do with that if that's the way it works. I ain't made up the rules about how it work.

Rose: You did Gabe just like you did Cory. You wouldn't sign the paper for Cory . . . but you signed for Gabe. You signed that paper.

The telephone is heard ringing inside the house.

Troy: I told you I ain't signed nothing, woman! The only thing I signed was the release form. Hell, I can't read, I don't know what they had on that paper! I ain't signed nothing about sending Gabe away.

Rose: I said send him to the hospital . . . you said let him be free . . . now you done went down there and signed him to the hospital for half his money. You went back on yourself, Troy. You gonna have to answer for that.

30   *Troy:* See now . . . you been over there talking to Miss Pearl. She done got mad cause she ain't getting Gabe's rent money. That's all it is. She's liable to say anything.

Rose: Troy, I seen where you signed the paper.

Troy: You ain't seen nothing I signed. What she doing got papers on my brother anyway? Miss Pearl telling a big fat lie. And I'm gonna tell her about it too! You ain't seen nothing I signed. Say . . . you ain't seen nothing I signed.

Rose exits into the house to answer the telephone. Presently she returns.

Rose: Troy . . . that was the hospital. Alberta had the baby.

Troy: What she have? What is it?

35   *Rose:* It's a girl.

Troy: I better get on down to the hospital to see her.

Rose: Troy . . .

Troy: Rose . . . I got to go see her now. That's only right . . . what's the matter . . . the baby's all right, ain't it?

Rose: Alberta died having the baby.

40   *Troy:* Died . . . you say she's dead? Alberta's dead?

Rose: They said they done all they could. They couldn't do nothing for her.

Troy: The baby? How's the baby?

Rose: They say it's healthy. I wonder who's gonna bury her.

Troy: She had family, Rose. She wasn't living in the world by herself.

45   *Rose:* I know she wasn't living in the world by herself.

Troy: Next thing you gonna want to know if she had any insurance.

Rose: Troy, you ain't got to talk like that.

Troy: That's the first thing that jumped out your mouth. "Who's gonna bury her?" Like I'm fixing to take on that task for myself.

Rose: I am your wife. Don't push me away.

50   *Troy:* I ain't pushing nobody away. Just give me some space. That's all. Just give me some room to breathe.

Rose exits into the house. Troy *walks about the yard.*

Troy [with a quiet rage that threatens to consume him]: All right . . . Mr. Death. See now . . . I'm gonna tell you what I'm gonna do. I'm gonna take and build me a fence around this yard. See? I'm gonna build me a fence around what belongs to me. And then I want you to stay on the other side. See? You stay over there until you're ready for me. Then you come on. Bring your army. Bring your sickle. Bring your wrestling clothes. I ain't gonna fall down on my vigilance this time. You ain't gonna sneak up on me no more. When you ready for me . . . when the top of your list say Troy Maxson . . . that's when you come around here. You come up and knock on the front door. Ain't nobody else got nothing to do with this. This is between you and me. Man to man. You stay on the other side of that fence until you ready for me. Then you come up and knock on the front door. Anytime you want. I'll be ready for you.

The lights go down to black.

Scene 3

The lights come up on the porch. It is late evening three days later. Rose *sits listening to the ball game waiting for* Troy. *The final out of the game is made and* Rose *switches off the radio.* Troy *enters the yard carrying an infant wrapped in blankets. He stands back from the house and calls.*

Rose *enters and stands on the porch. There is a long, awkward silence, the weight of which grows heavier with each passing second.*

Troy: Rose . . . I'm standing here with my daughter in my arms. She ain't but a wee bittie little old thing. She don't know nothing about grownups' business. She innocent . . . and she ain't got no mama.

Rose: What you telling me for, Troy?

She turns and exits into the house.

Troy: Well . . . I guess we'll just sit out here on the porch.

He sits down on the porch. There is an awkward indelicateness about the way he handles the baby. His largeness engulfs and seems to swallow it. He speaks loud enough for Rose *to hear.*

A man's got to do what's right for him. I ain't sorry for nothing I done. It felt right in my heart. *[To the baby.]* What you smiling at? Your daddy's a big man. Got these great big old hands. But sometimes he's scared. And right now your daddy's scared cause we sitting out here and ain't got no home. Oh, I been homeless before. I ain't had no little baby with me. But I been homeless. You just be out on the road by your lonesome and you see one of them trains coming and you just kinda go like this . . .

He sings as a lullaby.

   Please, Mr. Engineer let a man ride the line
   Please, Mr. Engineer let a man ride the line
   I ain't got no ticket please let me ride the blinds.

Rose *enters from the house.* Troy, *hearing her steps behind him, stands and faces her.*
She's my daughter, Rose. My own flesh and blood. I can't deny her no more than I can deny them boys. *[Pause.]* You and them boys is my family. You and them and this child is all I got in the world. So I guess what I'm saying is . . . I'd appreciate it if you'd help me take care of her.

Rose: Okay, Troy . . . you're right. I'll take care of your baby for you . . . cause . . . like you say . . . she's innocent . . . and you can't visit the sins of the father upon the child. A motherless child has got a hard time. *[She takes the baby from him.]* From right now . . . this child got a mother. But you a womanless man.
Rose *turns and exits into the house with the baby. Lights go down to black.*

Scene 4

It is two months later. Lyons *enters the street. He knocks on the door and calls.*

Lyons: Hey, Rose! *[Pause.]* Rose!

Rose *[from inside the house]:* Stop that yelling. You gonna wake up Raynell. I just got her to sleep.

Lyons: I just stopped by to pay Papa this twenty dollars I owe him. Where's Papa at?

Rose: He should be here in a minute. I'm getting ready to go down to the church. Sit down and wait on him.

5   *Lyons:* I got to go pick up Bonnie over her mother's house.

Rose: Well, sit it down there on the table. He'll get it.

Lyons [enters the house and sets money on the table]: Tell Papa I said thanks. I'll see you again.

Rose: All right, Lyons. We'll see you.

Lyons *starts to exit as* Cory *enters.*

Cory: Hey, Lyons.

10   *Lyons:* What's happening, Cory? Say man, I'm sorry I missed your graduation. You know I had a gig and couldn't get away. Otherwise, I would have been there, man. So what you doing?

Cory: I'm trying to find a job.

Lyons: Yeah I know how that go, man. It's rough out here. Jobs are scarce.

Cory: Yeah, I know.

Lyons: Look here, I got to run. Talk to Papa . . . he know some people. He'll be able to help get you a job. Talk to him . . . see what he say.

15   *Cory:* Yeah . . . all right, Lyons.

Lyons: You take care. I'll talk to you soon. We'll find some time to talk.

Lyons *exits the yard.* Cory *wanders over to the tree, picks up the bat, and assumes a batting stance. He studies an imaginary pitcher and swings. Dissatisfied with the result, he tries again.* Troy *enters. They eye each other for a beat.* Cory *puts the bat down and exits the yard.* Troy *starts into the house as* Rose *exits with* Raynell. *She is carrying a cake.*

Troy: I'm coming in and everybody's going out.

Rose: I'm taking this cake down to the church for the bake sale. Lyons was by to see you. He stopped by to pay you your twenty dollars. It's laying in there on the table.

Troy [going into his pocket]: Well . . . here go this money.

20   *Rose:* Put it in there on the table, Troy. I'll get it.

Troy: What time you coming back?

Rose: Ain't no use in you studying me. It don't matter what time I come back.

Troy: I just asked you a question, woman. What's the matter . . . can't I ask you a question?

Rose: Troy, I don't want to go into it. Your dinner's in there on the stove. All you got to do is heat it up. And don't you be eating the rest of them cakes in there. I'm coming back for them. We having a bake sale at the church tomorrow.

Rose *exits the yard.* Troy *sits down on the steps, takes a pint bottle from his pocket, opens it, and drinks. He begins to sing.*

25   *Troy:* Hear it ring! Hear it ring!

Had an old dog his name was Blue
You know Blue was mighty true
You know Blue as a good old dog
Blue trees a possum in a hollow log
You know from that he was a good old dog.

Bono *enters the yard*.

Bono: Hey, Troy.

Troy: Hey, what's happening, Bono?

Bono: I just thought I'd stop by to see you.

Troy: What you stop by and see me for? You ain't stopped by in a month of Sundays. Hell, I must owe you money or something.

Bono: Since you got your promotion I can't keep up with you. Used to see you every day. Now I don't even know what route you working.   30

Troy: They keep switching me around. Got me out in Greentree now . . . hauling white folks' garbage.

Bono: Greentree, huh? You lucky, at least you ain't got to be lifting them barrels. Damn if they ain't getting heavier. I'm gonna put in my two years and call it quits.

Troy: I'm thinking about retiring myself.

Bono: You got it easy. You can drive for another five years.

Troy: It ain't the same, Bono. It ain't like working the back of the truck. Ain't got   35
nobody to talk to . . . feel like you working by yourself. Naw, I'm thinking about retiring. How's Lucille?

Bono: She all right. Her arthritis get to acting up on her sometime. Saw Rose on my way in. She going down to the church, huh?

Troy: Yeah, she took up going down there. All them preachers looking for somebody to fatten their pockets. *[Pause.]* Got some gin here.

Bono: Naw, thanks. I just stopped by to say hello.

Troy: Hell, nigger . . . you can take a drink. I ain't never known you to say no to a drink. You ain't got to work tomorrow.

Bono: I just stopped by. I'm fixing to go over to Skinner's. We got us a domino   40
game going over his house every Friday.

Troy: Nigger, you can't play no dominoes. I used to whup you four games out of five.

Bono: Well, that learned me. I'm getting better.

Troy: Yeah? Well, that's all right.

Bono: Look here . . . I got to be getting on. Stop by sometime, huh?

Troy: Yeah, I'll do that, Bono. Lucille told Rose you bought her a new   45
refrigerator.

Bono: Yeah, Rose told Lucille you had finally built your fence . . . so I figured we'd call it even.

Troy: I knew you would.

Bono: Yeah . . . okay. I'll be talking to you.

Troy: Yeah, take care, Bono. Good to see you. I'm gonna stop over.

Bono: Yeah. Okay, Troy.   50

Bono *exits*. Troy *drinks from the bottle*.

Troy: Old Blue died and I dig his grave
    Let him down with a golden chain
    Every night when I hear old Blue bark
    I know Blue treed a possum in Noah's Ark.
    Hear it ring! Hear it ring!

Cory *enters the yard. They eye each other for a beat.* Troy *is sitting in the middle of the steps.* Cory *walks over.*

Cory: I got to get by.

Troy: Say what? What's you say?

Cory: You in my way. I got to get by.

55   *Troy:* You got to get by where? This is my house. Bought and paid for. In full. Took me fifteen years. And if you wanna go in my house and I'm sitting on the steps . . . you say excuse me. Like your mama taught you.

Cory: Come on, Pop . . . I got to get by.

Cory *starts to maneuver his way past* Troy. Troy *grabs his leg and shoves him back.*

Troy: You just gonna walk over top of me?

Cory: I live here too!

Troy [advancing toward him]: You just gonna walk over top of me in my own house?

60   *Cory:* I ain't scared of you.

Troy: I ain't asked if you was scared of me. I asked you if you was fixing to walk over top of me in my own house? That's the question. You ain't gonna say excuse me? You just gonna walk over top of me?

Cory: If you wanna put it like that.

Troy: How else am I gonna put it?

Cory: I was walking by you to go into the house cause you sitting on the steps drunk, singing to yourself. You can put it like that.

65   *Troy:* Without saying excuse me???

Cory *doesn't respond.*

I asked you a question. Without saying excuse me???

Cory: I ain't got to say excuse me to you. You don't count around here no more.

Troy: Oh, I see . . . I don't count around here no more. You ain't got to say excuse me to your daddy. All of a sudden you done got so grown that your daddy don't count around here no more . . . . Around here in his own house and yard that he done paid for with the sweat of his brow. You done got so grown to where you gonna take over. You gonna take over my house. Is that right? You gonna wear my pants. You gonna go in there and stretch out on my bed. You ain't got to say excuse me cause I don't count around here no more. Is that right?

Cory: That's right. You always talking this dumb stuff. Now, why don't you just get out my way?

Troy: I guess you got someplace to sleep and something to put in your belly. You got that, huh? You got that? That's what you need. You got that, huh?

70   *Cory:* You don't know what I got. You ain't got to worry about what I got.

Troy: You right! You one hundred percent right! I done spent the last seventeen years worrying about what you got. Now it's your turn, see? I'll tell you what to do. You grown . . . we done established that. You a man. Now, let's see you act like one. Turn your behind around and walk out this yard. And when you get out there in the alley . . . you can forget about this house. See? Cause this is my house. You go on and be a man and get your own house. You can forget about this. Cause this is mine. You go on and get yours cause I'm through with doing for you.

Cory: You talking about what you did for me . . . what'd you ever give me?

Troy: Them feet and bones! That pumping heart, nigger! I give you more than anybody else is ever gonna give you.

Cory: You ain't never gave me nothing! You ain't never done nothing but hold me back. Afraid I was gonna be better than you. All you ever did was try and make me scared of you. I used to tremble every time you called my name. Every time I heard your footsteps in the house. Wondering all the time . . . what's Papa gonna say if I do this? . . . What's he gonna say if I do that? . . . What's Papa gonna say if I turn on the radio? And Mama, too . . . she tries . . . but she's scared of you.

Troy: You leave your mama out of this. She ain't got nothing to do with this. 75

Cory: I don't know how she stand you . . . after what you did to her.

Troy: I told you to leave your mama out of this!

    He advances toward Cory.

Cory: What you gonna do . . . give me a whupping? You can't whup me no more. You're too old. You just an old man.

Troy [shoves him on his shoulder]: Nigger! That's what you are. You just another nigger on the street to me!

Cory: You crazy! You know that? 80

Troy: Go on now! You got the devil in you. Get on away from me!

Cory: You just a crazy old man . . . talking about I got the devil in me.

Troy: Yeah, I'm crazy! If you don't get on the other side of that yard . . . I'm gonna show you how crazy I am! Go on . . . get the hell out of my yard.

Cory: It ain't your yard. You took Uncle Gabe's money he got from the army to buy this house and then you put him out.

Troy [advances on Cory*]:* Get your black ass out of my yard! 85

    Troy's *advance backs* Cory *up against the tree.* Cory *grabs up the bat.*

Cory: I ain't going nowhere! Come on . . . put me out! I ain't scared of you.

Troy: That's my bat!

Cory: Come on!

Troy: Put my bat down!

Cory: Come on, put me out. 90

    Cory *swings at* Troy, *who backs across the yard.*

    What's the matter? You so bad . . . put me out!

    Troy *advances toward* Cory.

Cory [backing up]: Come on! Come on!

Troy: You're gonna have to use it! You wanna draw that bat back on me . . . you're gonna have to use it.

Cory: Come on! . . . Come on!

    Cory *swings the bat at* Troy *a second time. He misses.* Troy *continues to advance toward him.*

Troy: You're gonna have to kill me! You wanna draw that bat back on me. You're gonna have to kill me.

    Cory, *backed up against the tree, can go no farther.* Troy *taunts him. He sticks out his head and offers him a target.*

    Come on! Come on!

Cory *is unable to swing the bat.* Troy *grabs it.*

95 *Troy:* Then I'll show you.

Cory *and* Troy *struggle over the bat. The struggle is fierce and fully engaged.* Troy *ultimately is the stronger and takes the bat from* Cory *and stands over him ready to swing. He stops himself.*

Go on and get away from around my house.

Cory, *stung by his defeat, picks himself up, walks slowly out of the yard and up the alley.*

Cory: Tell Mama I'll be back for my things.

Troy: They'll be on the other side of that fence.

Cory *exits.*

Troy: I can't taste nothing. Helluljah! I can't taste nothing no more. *[*Troy *assumes a batting posture and begins to taunt Death, the fastball on the outside corner.]* Come on! It's between you and me now! Come on! Anytime you want! Come on! I be ready for you . . . but I ain't gonna be easy.

The lights go down on the scene.

Scene 5

The time is 1965. The lights come up in the yard. It is the morning of Troy's *funeral. A funeral plaque with a light hangs beside the door. There is a small garden plot off to the side. There is noise and activity in the house as* Rose, Lyons, *and* Bono *have gathered. The door opens and* Raynell, *seven years old, enters dressed in a flannel nightgown. She crosses to the garden and pokes around with a stick.* Rose *calls from the house.*

Rose: Raynell!

Raynell: Mam?

Rose: What you doing out there?

Raynell: Nothing.

Rose *comes to the door.*

5 *Rose:* Girl, get in here and get dressed. What you doing?

Raynell: Seeing if my garden growed.

Rose: I told you it ain't gonna grow overnight. You got to wait.

Raynell: It don't look like it never gonna grow. Dag!

Rose: I told you a watched pot never boils. Get in here and get dressed.

10 *Raynell:* This ain't even no pot, Mama.

Rose: You just have to give it a chance. It'll grow. Now you come on and do what I told you. We got to be getting ready. This ain't no morning to be playing around. You hear me?

Raynell: Yes, mam.

Rose *exits into the house.* Raynell *continues to poke at her garden with a stick.* Cory *enters. He is dressed in a Marine corporal's uniform, and carries a duffelbag. His posture is that of a military man, and his speech has a clipped sternness.*

Cory [to Raynell*]:* Hi. *[Pause.]* I bet your name is Raynell.

Raynell: Uh huh.

15 *Cory:* Is your mama home?

Raynell *runs up on the porch and calls through the screen door.*

Raynell: Mama . . . there's some man out here. Mama?

Rose *comes to the door.*

Rose: Cory? Lord have mercy! Look here, you all!

Rose *and* Cory *embrace in a tearful reunion as* Bono *and* Lyons *enter from the house dressed in funeral clothes.*

Bono: Aw, looka here . . .

Rose: Done got all grown up!

Cory: Don't cry, Mama. What you crying about?   20

Rose: I'm just so glad you made it.

Cory: Hey Lyons. How you doing, Mr. Bono.

Lyons *goes to embrace* Cory.

Lyons: Look at you, man. Look at you. Don't he look good, Rose. Got them
Corporal stripes.

Rose: What took you so long?

Cory: You know how the Marines are, Mama. They got to get all their paperwork   25
straight before they let you do anything.

Rose: Well, I'm sure glad you made it. They let Lyons come. Your Uncle Gabe's
still in the hospital. They don't know if they gonna let him out or not. I just
talked to them a little while ago.

Lyons: A Corporal in the United States Marines.

Bono: Your daddy knew you had it in you. He used to tell me all the time.

Lyons: Don't he look good, Mr. Bono?

Bono: Yeah, he remind me of Troy when I first met him. *[Pause.]* Say, Rose,   30
Lucille's down at the church with the choir. I'm gonna go down and get the
pallbearers lined up. I'll be back to get you all.

Rose: Thanks, Jim.

Cory: See you, Mr. Bono.

Lyons [with his arm around Raynell*]:* Cory . . . look at Raynell. Ain't she precious?
She gonna break a whole lot of hearts.

Rose: Raynell, come and say hello to your brother. This is your brother, Cory. You
remember Cory.

Raynell: No, Mam.   35

Cory: She don't remember me, Mama.

Rose: Well, we talk about you. She heard us talk about you. *[To* Raynell.*]* This is
your brother, Cory. Come on and say hello.

Raynell: Hi.

Cory: Hi. So you're Raynell. Mama told me a lot about you.

Rose: You all come on into the house and let me fix you some breakfast. Keep up   40
your strength.

Cory: I ain't hungry, Mama.

Lyons: You can fix me something, Rose. I'll be in there in a minute.

Rose: Cory, you sure you don't want nothing? I know they ain't feeding you
right.

Cory: No, Mama . . . thanks. I don't feel like eating. I'll get something later.

Rose: Raynell . . . get on upstairs and get that dress on like I told you.   45

Rose *and* Raynell *exit into the house.*

Lyons: So . . . I hear you thinking about getting married.

Cory: Yeah, I done found the right one, Lyons. It's about time.

Lyons: Me and Bonnie been split up about four years now. About the time Papa retired. I guess she just got tired of all them changes I was putting her through. *[Pause.]* I always knew you was gonna make something out yourself. Your head was always in the right direction. So . . . you gonna stay in . . . make it a career . . . put in your twenty years?

Cory: I don't know. I got six already, I think that's enough.

50 *Lyons:* Stick with Uncle Sam and retire early. Ain't nothing out here. I guess Rose told you what happened with me. They got me down the workhouse. I thought I was being slick cashing other people's checks.

Cory: How much time you doing?

Lyons: They give me three years. I got that beat now. I ain't got but nine more months. It ain't so bad. You learn to deal with it like anything else. You got to take the crookeds with the straights. That's what Papa used to say. He used to say that when he struck out. I seen him strike out three times in a row . . . and the next time up he hit the ball over the grandstand. Right out there in Homestead Field. He wasn't satisfied hitting in the seats . . . he want to hit it over everything! After the game he had two hundred people standing around waiting to shake his hand. You got to take the crookeds with the straights. Yeah, Papa was something else.

Cory: You still playing?

Lyons: Cory . . . you know I'm gonna do that. There's some fellows down there we got us a band . . . we gonna try and stay together when we get out . . . but yeah, I'm still playing. It still helps me to get out of bed in the morning. As long as it do that I'm gonna be right there playing and trying to make some sense out of it.

55 *Rose [calling]:* Lyons, I got these eggs in the pan.

Lyons: Let me go on and get these eggs, man. Get ready to go bury Papa. *[Pause.]* How you doing? You doing all right?

Cory *nods.* Lyons *touches him on the shoulder and they share a moment of silent grief.* Lyons *exits into the house.* Cory *wanders about the yard.* Raynell *enters.*

Raynell: Hi.

Cory: Hi.

Raynell: Did you used to sleep in my room?

60 *Cory:* Yeah . . . that used to be my room.

Raynell: That's what Papa call it. "Cory's room." It got your football in the closet.

Rose *comes to the door.*

Rose: Raynell, get in there and get them good shoes on.

Raynell: Mama, can't I wear these? Them other one hurt my feet.

Rose: Well, they just gonna have to hurt your feet for a while. You ain't said they hurt your feet when you went down to the store and got them.

65 *Raynell:* They didn't hurt then. My feet done got bigger.

Rose: Don't you give me no backtalk now. You get in there and get them shoes on.

Raynell *exits into the house.*

Ain't too much changed. He still got that piece of rag tied to that tree. He was out here swinging that bat. I was just ready to go back in the house. He swung that bat and then he just fell over. Seem like he swung it and stood there with this grin on his face . . . and then he just fell over. They carried him on down to the hospital, but I knew there wasn't no need . . . why don't you come on in the house?

Cory: Mama . . . I got something to tell you. I don't know how to tell you this . . . but I've got to tell you . . . I'm not going to Papa's funeral.

Rose: Boy, hush your mouth. That's your daddy you talking about. I don't want hear that kind of talk this morning. I done raised you to come to this? You standing there all healthy and grown talking about you ain't going to your daddy's funeral?

Cory: Mama . . . listen . . .

Rose: I don't want to hear it, Cory. You just get that thought out of your head.　70

Cory: I can't drag Papa with me everywhere I go. I've got to say no to him. One time in my life I've got to say no.

Rose: Don't nobody have to listen to nothing like that. I know you and your daddy ain't seen eye to eye, but I ain't got to listen to that kind of talk this morning. Whatever was between you and your daddy . . . the time has come to put it aside. Just take it and set it over there on the shelf and forget about it. Disrespecting your daddy ain't gonna make you a man, Cory. You got to find a way to come to that on your own. Not going to your daddy's funeral ain't gonna make you a man.

Cory: The whole time I was growing up . . . living in his house . . . Papa was like a shadow that followed you everywhere. It weighed on you and sunk into your flesh. It would wrap around you and lay there until you couldn't tell which one was you anymore. That shadow digging in your flesh. Trying to crawl in. Trying to live through you. Everywhere I looked, Troy Maxson was staring back at me . . . hiding under the bed . . . in the closet. I'm just saying I've got to find a way to get rid of that shadow, Mama.

Rose: You just like him. You got him in you good.

Cory: Don't tell me that, Mama.　75

Rose: You Troy Maxson all over again.

Cory: I don't want to be Troy Maxson. I want to be me.

Rose: You can't be nobody but who you are, Cory. That shadow wasn't nothing but you growing into yourself. You either got to grow into it or cut it down to fit you. But that's all you got to make life with. That's all you got to measure yourself against that world out there. Your daddy wanted you to be everything he wasn't . . . and at the same time he tried to make you into everything he was. I don't know if he was right or wrong . . . but I do know he meant to do more good than he meant to do harm. He wasn't always right. Sometimes when he touched he bruised. And sometimes when he took me in his arms he cut.

When I first met your daddy I thought . . . Here is a man I can lay down with and make a baby. That's the first thing I thought when I seen him. I was thirty years old and had done seen my share of men. But when he walked up to me and said, "I can dance a waltz that'll make you dizzy," I thought, Rose Lee, here is a man that you can open yourself up to and be filled to bursting. Here is a man that can fill all them empty spaces you been tipping around the edges of. One of them empty spaces was being somebody's mother.

I married your daddy and settled down to cooking his supper and keeping clean sheets on the bed. When your daddy walked through the house he was so big he filled it up. That was my first mistake. Not to make him leave some room for me. For my part in the matter. But at that time I wanted that. I wanted a house that I could sing in. And that's what your daddy gave me. I didn't know to keep up his strength I had to give up little pieces of mine. I did that. I took on his life as mine and mixed up the pieces so that you couldn't hardly tell which was which anymore. It was my choice. It was my life and I didn't have to live it like that. But that's what life offered me in the way of being a woman and I took it. I grabbed hold of it with both hands.

By the time Raynell came into the house, me and your daddy had done lost touch with one another. I didn't want to make my blessing off of nobody's misfortune . . . but I took on to Raynell like she was all them babies I had wanted and never had.

The phone rings.

Like I'd been blessed to relive a part of my life. And if the Lord see fit to keep up my strength . . . I'm gonna do her just like your daddy did you . . . I'm gonna give her the best of what's in me.

Raynell [entering, still with her old shoes]: Mama . . . Reverend Tollivier on the phone.

Rose *exits into the house.*

80 *Raynell:* Hi.

Cory: Hi.

Raynell: You in the Army or the Marines?

Cory: Marines.

Raynell: Papa said it was the Army. Did you know Blue?

85 *Cory:* Blue? Who's Blue?

Raynell: Papa's dog what he sing about all the time.

Cory [singing]: Hear it ring! Hear it ring!

    I had a dog his name was Blue

    You know Blue was mighty true

    You know Blue was a good old dog

    Blue treed a possum in a hollow log

    You know from that he was a good old dog.

    Hear it ring! Hear it ring!

Raynell *joins in singing.*

Cory and Raynell: Blue treed a possum out on a limb

    Blue looked at me and I looked at him

    Grabbed that possum and put him in a sack

    Blue stayed there till I came back

    Old Blue's feets was big and round

    Never allowed a possum to touch the ground.

    Old Blue died and I dug his grave

    I dug his grave with a silver spade

    Let him down with a golden chain

    And every night I call his name

    Go on Blue, you good dog you

    Go on Blue, you good dog you.

Raynell: Blue laid down and died like a man 90
    Blue laid down and died . . .
Both: Blue laid down and died like a man
    Now he's treeing possums in the Promised Land
    I'm gonna tell you this to let you know
    Blue's gone where the good dogs go
    When I hear old Blue bark
    When I hear old Blue bark
    Blue treed a possum in Noah's Ark
    Blue treed a possum in Noah's Ark.
    Rose *comes to the screen door.*
Rose: Cory, we gonna be ready to go in a minute.
Cory [to Raynell*]:* You go on in the house and change them shoes like Mama told
    you so we can go to Papa's funeral.
Raynell: Okay, I'll be back.
    Raynell *exits into the house.* Cory *gets up and crosses over to the tree.* Rose *stands in*
    the screen door watching him. Gabriel *enters from the alley.*
Gabriel [calling]: Hey, Rose! 95
Rose: Gabe?
Gabriel: I'm here, Rose. Hey Rose, I'm here!
    Rose *enters from the house.*
Rose: Lord . . . Look here, Lyons!
Lyons: See, I told you, Rose . . . I told you they'd let him come.
Cory: How you doing, Uncle Gabe? 100
Lyons: How you doing, Uncle Gabe?
Gabriel: Hey, Rose. It's time. It's time to tell St. Peter to open the gates. Troy, you
    ready? You ready, Troy. I'm gonna tell St. Peter to open the gates. You get
    ready now.
    Gabriel, *with great fanfare, braces himself to blow. The trumpet is without a*
    mouthpiece. He puts the end of it into his mouth and blows with great force, like a
    man who has been waiting some twenty-odd years for this single moment. No
    sound comes out of the trumpet. He braces himself and blows again with the same
    result. A third time he blows. There is a weight of impossible description that falls
    away and leaves him bare and exposed to a frightful realization. It is a trauma that a
    sane and normal mind would be unable to withstand. He begins to dance. A slow,
    strange dance, eerie and life-giving. A dance of atavistic signature and ritual. Lyons
    attempts to embrace him. Gabriel *pushes* Lyons *away. He begins to howl in what is*
    an attempt at song, or perhaps a song turning back into itself in an attempt at
    speech. He finishes his dance and the gates of heaven stand open as wide as God's
    closet.
    That's the way that go!

                (BLACKOUT) [1987]

1. What is the significance of the play's setting in time? How does it reflect on
    Rose's claim in Act 1 Scene 1 that times have changed in ways that Troy
    hasn't acknowledged?

2. What is the effect of Troy's understanding of the relationship between blacks and whites in America on his relationship with his son Cory?

3. What is Cory's understanding of why his father doesn't want him to play football?

4. What do fences mean in the context of this play?

5. Troy claims to love his wife Rose. Why, then, does he have an adulterous affair?

6. What is Rose's understanding of sex roles in marriage? How does it affect her response to Troy's affair?

7. At the end of the play, Cory is struggling with the question of whether to go to Troy's funeral. Rose tries to mediate between Cory and his now-dead father, saying, "Not going to your daddy's funeral ain't going to make you a man." How does what literary critic Carla McDonough calls the "complex matrix of gender and racial identity"[1] make it difficult for Cory to grow into his own manhood?

8. In Act 1.1 do the arguments of Troy and Rose accord with the predictions that would be made by Gilligan and Attanucci in their article "Two Moral Orientations" (see Chapter 8, p. 156 and the Sample Student Paper, p. 168)?

9. Compare the family situation in "Fences" to that in Robert Hayden's poem, "Those Winter Sundays" (see Chapter 7, p. 144).

10. What role does Gabriel play?

[1]Carla J. McDonough. *Staging masculinity: male identity in contemporary American drama.* Jefferson, N.C: McFarland & Co., 1997, p. 150.

NONFICTION PROSE

SUSAN MOLLER OKIN WITH RESPONDENTS

SUSAN MOLLER OKIN *(1946–2004), a native of New Zealand and graduate of the University of Auckland, studied at Oxford, earning the M. Phil. in Politics, and at Harvard, where she was awarded a Ph.D. in Government. She began her teaching career at Vassar College, going on to teach at Brandeis University and then at Stanford, where she was Marta Sutton Weeks Professor of Ethics in Society and Professor of Political Science. She is the author of* Women in Western Political Thought *(Princeton, 1979) and* Justice, Gender, and the Family *(Basic Books, 1989). A whole range of topics makes up her list of published articles, including nuclear deterrence, gender, and economic development. She is considered by her peers to be among the foremost feminist scholars.* Is Multiculturalism Bad for Women? *(Princeton, 1999), a compilation of Okin's essay and responses from fifteen scholars in diverse fields, has garnered international attention and spurred considerable public debate.*

Thanks to Elizabeth Beaumont for research assistance and to Beaumont and Joshua Cohen for helpful comments on an earlier draft.   [Okin's note]

Is Multiculturalism Bad for Women?*

Until the past few decades, minority groups—immigrants as well as indigenous peoples—were typically expected to assimilate into majority cultures. This assimilationist expectation is now often considered oppressive, and many Western countries are seeking to devise new policies that are more responsive to persistent cultural differences. The appropriate policies vary with context: countries such as England, with established churches or state-supported religious education, find it difficult to resist demands to extend state support to minority religious schools; countries such as France, with traditions of strictly secular public education, struggle over whether the clothing required by minority religions may be worn in the public schools. But one issue recurs across all contexts, though it has gone virtually unnoticed in current debate: what should be done when the claims of minority cultures or religions clash with the norm of gender equality that is at least formally endorsed by liberal states (however much they continue to violate it in their practices)?

In the late 1980s, for example, a sharp public controversy erupted in France about whether Magrébin girls could attend school wearing the traditional Muslim head scarves regarded as proper attire for postpubescent young women. Staunch defenders of secular education lined up with some feminists and far-right nationalists against the practice; much of the Old Left supported the multiculturalist demands for flexibility and respect for diversity, accusing opponents of racism or cultural imperialism. At the very same time, however, the public was virtually silent about a problem of vastly greater importance to many French Arab and African immigrant women: polygamy.

During the 1980s, the French government quietly permitted immigrant men to bring multiple wives into the country, to the point where an estimated 200,000 families in Paris are now polygamous.° Any suspicion that official concern over head scarves was motivated by an impulse toward gender equality is belied by the easy adoption of a permissive policy on polygamy, despite the burdens this practice imposes on women and the warnings disseminated by women from the relevant cultures.[1] On this issue, no politically effective opposition galvanized. But once reporters finally got around to interviewing the wives, they discovered what the government could have learned years earlier: that the women affected by polygamy regarded it as an inescapable and barely tolerable institution in their African countries of origin, and an unbearable imposition in the French context. Overcrowded apartments and the lack of private space for each wife led to immense hostility, resentment, even violence both among the wives and against each other's children.

In part because of the strain on the welfare system caused by families with twenty to thirty members, the French government has recently decided to

---

*Susan Moller Okin, with Respondents, *Is Multiculturalism Bad for Women?* Ed. Joshua Cohen, Matthew Howard, and Martha Nussbaum (Princeton: Princeton University Press, 1999).

[1] *International Herald Tribune,* 2 February 1996, News section.

° **polygamous** having more than one mate at the same time, technically referring to either sex. The more specific term is "polygyny," having more than one wife at the same time.

recognize only one wife and to consider all the other marriages annulled. But what will happen to all the other wives and children? Having ignored women's views on polygamy for so long, the government now seems to be abdicating its responsibility for the vulnerability that its rash policy has inflicted on women and children.

5   The French accommodation of polygamy illustrates a deep and growing tension between feminism and multiculturalist concern for protecting cultural diversity. I think we—especially those of us who consider ourselves politically progressive and opposed to all forms of oppression—have been too quick to assume that feminism and multiculturalism are both good things which are easily reconciled. I shall argue instead that there is considerable likelihood of tension between them—more precisely, between feminism and a multiculturalist commitment to group rights for minority cultures.

A few words to explain the terms and focus of my argument. By *feminism*, I mean the belief that women should not be disadvantaged by their sex, that they should be recognized as having human dignity equal to that of men, and that they should have the opportunity to live as fulfilling and as freely chosen lives as men can. *Multiculturalism* is harder to pin down, but the particular aspect that concerns me here is the claim, made in the context of basically liberal democracies, that minority cultures or ways of life are not sufficiently protected by the practice of ensuring the individual rights of their members, and as a consequence these should also be protected through special *group* rights or privileges. In the French case, for example, the right to contract polygamous marriages clearly constituted a group right not available to the rest of the population. In other cases, groups have claimed rights to govern themselves, to have guaranteed political representation, or to be exempt from certain generally applicable laws.

Demands for such group rights are growing—from indigenous native populations, minority ethnic or religious groups, and formerly colonized peoples (at least when the latter immigrate to the former colonial state). These groups, it is argued, have their own "societal cultures" which—as Will Kymlicka, the foremost contemporary defender of cultural group rights, says—provide "members with meaningful ways of life across the full range of human activities, including social, educational, religious, recreational, and economic life, encompassing both public and private spheres."[2] Because societal cultures play so pervasive and fundamental a role in the lives of their members, and because such cultures are threatened with extinction, minority cultures should be protected by special rights. That, in essence, is the case for group rights.

Some proponents of group rights argue that even cultures that "flout the rights of [their individual members] in a liberal society"[3] should be accorded group rights or privileges if their minority status endangers the culture's continued existence. Others do not claim that all minority cultural groups should have special rights, but rather that such groups—even illiberal ones that violate their individual members'

[2]Will Kymlicka, *Multicultural Citizenship: A Liberal Theory of Minority Rights* (Oxford: Oxford University Press, 1995), pp. 89, 76. See also Kymlicka, *Liberalism, Community, and Culture* (Oxford: The Clarendon Press, 1989). It should be noted that Kymlicka himself does not argue for extensive or permanent group rights for those who have voluntarily immigrated.

[3]Avishai Margalit and Moshe Halbertal, "Liberalism and the Right to Culture," *Social Research* 61, 3 (Fall 1994): 491.

rights, requiring them to conform to group beliefs or norms—have the right to be "left alone" in a liberal society.[4] Both claims seem clearly inconsistent with the basic liberal value of individual freedom, which entails that group rights should not trump the individual rights of its members; thus I will not address the additional problems they present for feminists here.[5] But some defenders of multiculturalism confine their defense of group rights largely to groups that are internally liberal.[6] Even with these restrictions, feminists—everyone, that is, who endorses the moral equality of men and women—should remain skeptical. So I will argue.

Gender and Culture

Most cultures are suffused with practices and ideologies concerning gender. Suppose, then, that a culture endorses and facilitates the control of men over women in various ways (even if informally, in the private sphere of domestic life). Suppose, too, that there are fairly clear disparities in power between the sexes, such that the more powerful, male members are those who are generally in a position to determine and articulate the group's beliefs, practices, and interests. Under such conditions, group rights are potentially, and in many cases actually, antifeminist. They substantially limit the capacities of women and girls of that culture to live with human dignity equal to that of men and boys, and to live as freely chosen lives as they can.

Advocates of group rights for minorities within liberal states have not adequately addressed this simple critique of group rights, for at least two reasons. First, they tend to treat cultural groups as monoliths—to pay more attention to differences between and among groups than to differences within them. Specifically, they accord little or no recognition to the fact that minority cultural groups, like the societies in which they exist (though to a greater or lesser extent), are themselves *gendered*, with substantial differences in power and advantage between men and women. Second, advocates of group rights pay little or no attention to the private sphere. Some of the most persuasive liberal defenses of group rights urge that individuals need "a culture of their own," and that only within such a culture can people develop a sense of self-esteem or self-respect, as well as the capacity to decide what kind of life is good for them. But such arguments typically neglect both the different roles that cultural groups impose on their members and the context in which persons' senses of themselves and their capacities are first formed *and* in which culture is first transmitted—the realm of domestic or family life.

When we correct for these deficiencies by paying attention to internal differences and to the private arena, two particularly important connections between culture and gender come into sharp relief, both of which underscore the force of this simple critique of group rights. First, the sphere of personal, sexual, and

[4]For example, Chandran Kukathas, "Are There Any Cultural Rights?," *Political Theory* 20, 1 (1992): 105–39.

[5]Okin, "Feminism and Multiculturalism: Some Tensions," *Ethics* 108, 4 (July 1998): 661–84.

[6]For example, Kymlicka, *Liberalism, Community, and Culture* and *Multicultural Citizenship* (esp. chap. 8). Kymlicka does not apply his requirement that groups be internally liberal to those he terms "national minorities," but I will not address that aspect of his theory here.

reproductive life functions as a central focus of most cultures, a dominant theme in cultural practices and rules. Religious or cultural groups often are particularly concerned with "personal law"—the laws of marriage, divorce, child custody, division and control of family property, and inheritance.[7] As a rule, then, the defense of "cultural practices" is likely to have much greater impact on the lives of women and girls than on those of men and boys, since far more of women's time and energy goes into preserving and maintaining the personal, familial, and reproductive side of life. Obviously, culture is not only about domestic arrangements, but they do provide a major focus of most contemporary cultures. Home is, after all, where much of culture is practiced, preserved, and transmitted to the young. On the other hand, the distribution of responsibilities and power at home has a major impact on who can participate in and influence the more public parts of the cultural life, where rules and regulations about both public and private life are made. The more a culture requires or expects of women in the domestic sphere, the less opportunity they have of achieving equality with men in either sphere.

The second important connection between culture and gender is that most cultures have as one of their principal aims the control of women by men.[8] Consider, for example, the founding myths of Greek and Roman antiquity, and of Judaism, Christianity, and Islam: they are rife with attempts to justify the control and subordination of women. These myths consist of a combination of denials of women's role in reproduction; appropriations by men of the power to reproduce themselves; characterizations of women as overly emotional, untrustworthy, evil, or sexually dangerous; and refusals to acknowledge mothers' rights over the disposition of their children.[9] Think of Athena, sprung from the head of Zeus, and of Romulus and Remus, reared without a human mother. Or Adam, made by a male God, who then (at least according to one of the two biblical versions of the story) created Eve out of part of Adam. Consider Eve, whose weakness led Adam astray. Think of all those endless "begats" in Genesis, where women's primary role in reproduction is completely ignored, or of the textual justifications for polygamy, once practiced in Judaism, still practiced in many parts of the Islamic world and (though illegally) by Mormons in some parts of the United States. Consider, too, the story of Abraham, a pivotal turning point in the development

---

[7] See, for example, Kirti Singh, "Obstacles to Womens' Rights in India," in *Human Rights of Women: National and International Perspectives*, ed. Rebecca J. Cook (Philadelphia: University of Pennsylvania Press, 1994), pp. 375–96, esp. pp. 378–89.

[8] I cannot discuss here the roots of this male preoccupation, except to say (following feminist theorists Dorothy Dinnerstein, Nancy Chodorow, Jessica Benjamin, and, before them, Jesuit anthropologist Walter Ong) that it seems to have a lot to do with female primary parenting. It is also clearly related to the uncertainty of paternity, which technology has now counteracted. If these issues are at the root of it, then the cultural preoccupation with controlling women is not an inevitable fact of human life but a contingent factor that feminists have a considerable interest in changing.

[9] See, for example, Arvind Sharma, ed., *Women in World Religions* (Albany: SUNY Press, 1987); John Stratton Hawley, ed., *Fundamentalism and Gender* (Oxford: Oxford University Press, 1994).

of monotheism.[10] God commands Abraham to sacrifice "his" beloved son. Abraham prepares to do exactly what God asks of him, without even telling, much less asking, Isaac's mother, Sarah. Abraham's absolute obedience to God makes him the central, fundamental model of faith for all three religions.

Although the powerful drive to control women—and to blame and punish them for men's difficulty in controlling their own sexual impulses—has been softened considerably in the more progressive, reformed versions of Judaism, Christianity, and Islam, it remains strong in their more orthodox or fundamentalist versions. Moreover, it is by no means confined to Western or monotheistic cultures. Many of the world's traditions and cultures, including those practiced within formerly conquered or colonized nation-states—which certainly encompasses most of the peoples of Africa, the Middle East, Latin America, and Asia—are quite distinctly patriarchal. They too have elaborate patterns of socialization, rituals, matrimonial customs, and other cultural practices (including systems of property ownership and control of resources) aimed at bringing women's sexuality and reproductive capabilities under men's control. Many such practices make it virtually impossible for women to choose to live independently of men, to be celibate or lesbian, or to decide not to have children.

Those who practice some of the most controversial of such customs—clitoridectomy,° polygamy, the marriage of children or marriages that are otherwise coerced—sometimes explicitly defend them as necessary for controlling women and openly acknowledge that the customs persist at men's insistence. In an interview with *New York Times* reporter Celia Dugger, practitioners of clitoridectomy in Côte d'Ivoire and Togo explained that the practice "helps insure a girl's virginity before marriage and fidelity afterward by reducing sex to a marital obligation." As a female exciser said, "[a] woman's role in life is to care for her children, keep house and cook. If she has not been cut, [she] might think about her own sexual pleasure."[11] In Egypt, where a law banning female genital cutting was recently overturned by a court, supporters of the practice say it "curbs a girl's sexual appetite and makes her more marriageable."[12] Moreover, in such societies, many women have no economically viable alternative to marriage.

In polygamous cultures, too, men readily acknowledge that the practice accords with their self-interest and is a means of controlling women. As a French immigrant from Mali said in a recent interview: "When my wife is sick and I don't have another, who will care for me? . . . [O]ne wife on her own is trouble. When there are several, they are forced to be polite and well behaved. If they misbehave, you threaten that you'll take another wife." Women apparently see polygamy very differently. French African immigrant women deny that they

15

---

[10]See Carol Delaney, *Abraham on Trial: The Social Legacy of Biblical Myth* (Princeton: Princeton University Press, 1998). Note that in the Qur'anic version, it is not Isaac but Ishmael whom Abraham prepares to sacrifice.

[11]*New York Times*, 5 October 1996, A4. The role that older women in such cultures play in perpetuating these practices is important but complex and cannot be addressed here.

[12]*New York Times*, 26 June 1997, A9.

[14]**cliteridectomy** a form of female genital mutilation in which all or part of the clitoris is removed

like polygamy and say that not only are they given "no choice" in the matter, but their female forebears in Africa did not like it either.[13] As for child or otherwise coerced marriage: this practice is clearly a way not only of controlling who the girls or young women marry but also of ensuring that they are virgins at the time of marriage and, often, of enhancing the husband's power by creating a significant age difference between husbands and wives.

Consider, too, the practice—common in much of Latin America, rural Southeast Asia and parts of West Africa—of pressuring or even requiring a rape victim to marry the rapist. In many such cultures—including fourteen countries in Central and South America—rapists are legally exonerated if they marry or (in some cases) simply offer to marry their victims. Clearly, rape is not seen in these cultures primarily as a violent assault on the girl or woman herself but rather as a serious injury to her family and its honor. By marrying his victim, the rapist can help restore the family's honor and relieve it of a daughter who, as "damaged goods," has become unmarriageable. In Peru, this barbaric law was amended for the worse in 1991: the codefendants in a gang rape now are all exonerated if just one of them offers to marry the victim (feminists are fighting to get the law repealed). As a Peruvian taxi driver explained: "Marriage is the right and proper thing to do after a rape. A raped woman is a used item. No one wants her. At least with this law the woman will get a husband."[14] It is difficult to imagine a worse fate for a woman than being pressured into marrying the man who has raped her. But worse fates do exist in some cultures—notably in Pakistan and parts of the Arab Middle East, where women who bring rape charges quite frequently are charged themselves with the serious Muslim offense of *zina*, or sex outside of marriage. Law allows for the whipping or imprisonment of such women, and culture condones the killing or pressuring into suicide of a raped woman by relatives intent on restoring the family's honor.[15]

Thus many culturally based customs aim to control women and render them, especially sexually and reproductively, servile to men's desires and interests. Sometimes, moreover, "culture" or "traditions" are so closely linked with the control of women that they are virtually equated. In a recent news report about a small community of Orthodox Jews living in the mountains of Yemen, the elderly leader of this small polygamous sect is quoted as saying: "We are Orthodox Jews, very keen on our traditions. If we go to Israel, we will lose hold over our daughters, our wives and our sisters." One of his sons added, "We are like Muslims, we do not allow our women to uncover their faces."[16] Thus the servitude of women is presented as virtually synonymous with "our traditions." (Ironically, from a feminist point of view, the story was entitled "Yemen's Small Jewish Community Thrives on Mixed Traditions." Only blindness to sexual

---

[13]*International Herald Tribune,* 2 February 1996, News section.

[14]*New York Times,* 12 March 1997, A8.

[15]This practice is discussed in Henry S. Richardson, *Practical Reasoning about Final Ends* (Cambridge: Cambridge University Press, 1994), esp. pp. 240–43, 262–63, 282–84.

[16]*Agence France Presse,* 18 May 1997, International News section.

servitude can explain the title; it is inconceivable that the article would have carried such a title if it were about a community that practiced any kind of slavery but sexual slavery.)

While virtually all of the world's cultures have distinctly patriarchal pasts, some—mostly, though by no means exclusively, Western liberal cultures—have departed far further from them than others. Western cultures, of course, still practice many forms of sex discrimination. They place far more importance on beauty, thinness, and youth in females and on intellectual accomplishment, skill, and strength in males. They expect women to perform for no economic reward far more than half of the unpaid work related to home and family, whether or not they also work for wages; partly as a consequence of this and partly because of workplace discrimination, women are far more likely than men to become poor. Girls and women are also subjected by men to a great deal of (illegal) violence, including sexual violence. But women in more liberal cultures are, at the same time, legally guaranteed many of the same freedoms and opportunities as men. In addition, most families in such cultures, with the exception of some religious fundamentalists, do not communicate to their daughters that they are of less value than boys, that their lives are to be confined to domesticity and service to men and children, and that their sexuality is of value only in marriage, in the service of men, and for reproductive ends. This situation, as we have seen, is quite different from that of women in many of the world's other cultures, including many of those from which immigrants to Europe and North America come.

Group Rights?

Most cultures are patriarchal, then, and many (though not all) of the cultural minorities that claim group rights are more patriarchal than the surrounding cultures. So it is no surprise that the cultural importance of maintaining control over women shouts out to us in the examples given in the literature on cultural diversity and group rights within liberal states. Yet, though it shouts out, it is seldom explicitly addressed.[17]

A paper by Sebastian Poulter about the legal rights and culture-based claims of various immigrant groups and Gypsies in contemporary Britain mentions the roles and status of women as "one very clear example" of the "clash of cultures."[18] In it, Poulter discusses claims put forward by members of such groups for special legal treatment on account of their cultural differences. A few are non–gender-related claims; for example, a Muslim schoolteacher's being allowed to be absent part of Friday afternoons in order to pray, and Gypsy children's being subject to less stringent schooling requirements than others on account of their itinerant lifestyle. But the vast majority of the examples concern

20

---

[17]See, however, Bhikhu Parekh's "Minority Practices and Principles of Toleration," *International Migration Review* (April 1996): 251–84, in which he directly addresses and critiques a number of cultural practices that devalue the status of women.

[18]Sebastian Poulter, "Ethnic Minority Customs, English Law, and Human Rights," *International and Comparative Law Quarterly* 36, 3 (1987): 589–615.

gender inequalities: child marriages, forced marriages, divorce systems biased against women, polygamy, and clitoridectomy. Almost all of the legal cases discussed by Poulter stemmed from women's or girls' claims that their individual rights were being truncated or violated by the practices of their own cultural groups. In a recent article by political philosopher Amy Gutmann, fully half her examples have to do with gender issues—polygamy, abortion, sexual harassment, clitoridectomy, and purdah.[19] This is quite typical in the literature on subnational multicultural issues. Moreover, the same linkage between culture and gender occurs in practice in the international arena, where women's human rights are often rejected by the leaders of countries or groups of countries as incompatible with their various cultures.[20]

Similarly, the overwhelming majority of "cultural defenses" that are increasingly being invoked in U.S. criminal cases involving members of cultural minorities are connected with gender—in particular with male control over women and children.[21] Occasionally, cultural defenses are cited in explanation of expectable violence among men or the ritual sacrifice of animals. Much more common, however, is the argument that, in the defendant's cultural group, women are not human beings of equal worth but rather subordinates whose primary (if not only) function is to serve men sexually and domestically. Indeed, the four types of cases in which cultural defenses have been used most successfully are: (1) kidnap and rape by Hmong men who claim that their actions are part of their cultural practice of *zij poj niam*, or "marriage by capture"; (2) wife-murder by immigrants from Asian and Middle Eastern countries whose wives have either committed adultery or treated their husbands in a servile way; (3) murder of children by Japanese or Chinese mothers who have also tried but failed to kill themselves, and who claim that because of their cultural backgrounds the shame of their husbands' infidelity drove them to the culturally condoned practice of mother-child suicide; and (4) in France—though not yet in the United States, in part because the practice was criminalized only in 1996—clitoridectomy. In a number of such cases, expert testimony about the accused's or defendant's cultural background has resulted in dropped or reduced charges, culturally based assessments of *mens rea*, or significantly reduced sentences. In a well-known recent case in the United States, an immigrant from rural Iraq married his two daughters, aged 13 and 14, to two of his friends, aged 28 and 34. Subsequently, when the older daughter ran away with her 20-year-old boyfriend, the father

[19]Amy Gutmann, "The Challenge of Multiculturalism in Political Ethics," *Philosophy and Public Affairs* 22, 3 (Summer 1993): 171–204.

[20]Mahnaz Afkhami, ed., *Faith and Freedom: Women's Human Rights in the Muslim World* (Syracuse: Syracuse University Press, 1995); Valentine M. Moghadam, ed., *Identity Politics and Women: Cultural Reassertions and Feminisms in International Perspective* (Boulder, CO: Westview Press, 1994); Susan Moller Okin, "Culture, Religion, and Female Identity Formation" (unpublished manuscript, 1997).

[21]For one of the best and most recent accounts of this, and for legal citations for the cases mentioned below, see Doriane Lambelet Coleman, "Individualizing Justice through Multiculturalism: The Liberals' Dilemma," *Columbia Law Review* 96, 5 (1996): 1093–1167.

sought the help of the police in finding her. When they located her, they charged the father with child abuse and the two husbands and boyfriend with statutory rape. The Iraqis' defense is based in part on their cultural marriage practices.[22]

As the four examples show, the defendants are not always male, nor the victims always female. Both a Chinese immigrant man in New York who battered his wife to death for committing adultery and a Japanese immigrant woman in California who drowned her children and tried to drown herself because her husband's adultery had shamed the family relied on cultural defenses to win reduced charges (from first-degree murder to second-degree murder or involuntary manslaughter). It might seem, then, that the cultural defense was biased toward the male in the first case and the female in the second. But though defendants of different sexes were cited, in both cases, the cultural message is similarly gender-biased: women (and children, in the second case) are ancillary to men and should bear the blame and the shame for any departure from monogamy. Whoever is guilty of the infidelity, the wife suffers: in the first case, by being brutally killed on account of her husband's rage at her shameful infidelity; in the second, by being so shamed and branded such a failure by his infidelity that she is driven to kill herself and her children. Again, the idea that girls and women are first and foremost sexual servants of men—that their virginity before marriage and fidelity within it are their preeminent virtues—emerges in many of the statements made in defense of cultural practices.

Western majority cultures, largely at the urging of feminists, have recently made substantial efforts to preclude or limit excuses for brutalizing women. Well within living memory, American men were routinely held less accountable for killing their wives if they explained their conduct as a crime of passion, driven as they were by jealousy and rage over the wife's infidelity. Also not long ago, female rape victims who did not have completely celibate pasts or who did not struggle—even when to do so meant endangering themselves—were routinely blamed for the attack. Things have now changed to some extent, and doubts about the turn toward cultural defenses undoubtedly are prompted in part by a concern to preserve recent advances. Another concern is that such defenses can distort perceptions of minority cultures by drawing excessive attention to negative aspects of them. But perhaps the primary concern is that, by failing to protect women and sometimes children of minority cultures from male and sometimes maternal violence, cultural defenses violate women's and children's rights to equal protection of the laws.[23] When a woman from a more patriarchal culture comes to the United States (or some other Western, basically liberal, state), why should she be less protected from male violence than other women are? Many women from minority cultures have protested the double standard that is being applied on behalf of their aggressors.[24]

---

[22]*New York Times*, 2 December 1996, A6.

[23]See Coleman, "Individualizing Justice through Multiculturalism."

[24]See, for example, Nilda Rimonte, "A Question of Culture: Cultural Approval of Violence against Women in the Asian-Pacific Community and the Cultural Defense," *Stanford Law Review* 43 (1991): 1311–26.

Liberal Defense

Despite all this evidence of cultural practices that control and subordinate women, none of the prominent defenders of multicultural group rights has adequately or even directly addressed the troubling connections between gender and culture or the conflicts that arise so commonly between feminism and multiculturalism. Will Kymlicka's discussion is, in this respect, representative.

25   Kymlicka's arguments for group rights are based on the rights of individuals and confine such privileges and protection to cultural groups that are internally liberal. Following John Rawls, Kymlicka emphasizes the fundamental importance of self-respect in a person's life. He argues that membership in a "rich and secure cultural structure,"[25] with its own language and history, is essential both for the development of self-respect and for giving persons a context in which they can develop the capacity to make choices about how to lead their lives. Cultural minorities need special rights, then, because their cultures may otherwise be threatened with extinction, and cultural extinction would be likely to undermine the self-respect and freedom of group members. Special rights, in short, put minorities on an equal footing with the majority.

The value of freedom plays an important role in Kymlicka's argument. As a result, except in rare circumstances of cultural vulnerability, a group that claims special rights must govern itself by recognizably liberal principles, neither infringing on the basic liberties of its own members by placing internal restrictions on them nor discriminating among them on grounds of sex, race, or sexual preference.[26] This requirement is of great importance to a consistently liberal justification of group rights, because a "closed" or discriminatory culture cannot provide the context for individual development that liberalism requires, and because otherwise collective rights might result in subcultures of oppression within and facilitated by liberal societies. As Kymlicka says, "To inhibit people from questioning their inherited social roles can condemn them to unsatisfying, even oppressive lives."[27]

As Kymlicka acknowledges, this requirement of internal liberalism rules out the justification of group rights for the "many fundamentalists of all political and religious stripes who think that the best community is one in which all but their preferred religious, sexual, or aesthetic practices are outlawed." For the promotion and support of *these* cultures undermines "the very reason we had for being concerned with cultural membership—that it allows for meaningful individual choice."[28] But the examples I cited earlier suggest that far fewer minority cultures than Kymlicka seems to think will be able to claim group rights under his liberal justification. Though they may not impose their beliefs or practices on others, and though they may appear to respect the basic civil and political liberties

[25]Kymlicka, *Liberalism, Community, and Culture*, p. 165.

[26]Ibid., pp. 168–72, 195–98.

[27]Kymlicka, *Multicultural Citizenship*, p. 92.

[28]Kymlicka, *Liberalism, Community, and Culture*, pp. 171–72.

of women and girls, many cultures do not, especially in the private sphere, treat them with anything like the same concern and respect with which men and boys are treated, or allow them to enjoy the same freedoms. Discrimination against and control of the freedom of females are practiced, to a greater or lesser extent, by virtually all cultures, past and present, but especially by religious ones and those that look to the past—to ancient texts or revered traditions— for guidelines or rules about how to live in the contemporary world. Sometimes more patriarchal minority cultures exist in the midst of less patriarchal majority cultures; sometimes the reverse is true. In either case, the degree to which each culture is patriarchal and its willingness to become less so should be crucial factors in judgment about the justifications of group rights—once women's equality is taken seriously.

Clearly, Kymlicka regards cultures that discriminate overtly and formally against women—by denying them education or the right to vote or hold office— as not deserving special rights.[29] But sex discrimination is often far less overt. In many cultures, strict control of women is enforced in the private sphere by the authority of either actual or symbolic fathers, often acting through, or with the complicity of, the older women of the culture. In many cultures in which women's basic civil rights and liberties are formally assured, discrimination practiced against women and girls within the household not only severely constrains their choices but also seriously threatens their well-being and even their lives.[30] And such sex discrimination—whether severe or more mild—often has very powerful *cultural* roots.

Although Kymlicka rightly objects, then, to the granting of group rights to minority cultures that practice overt sex discrimination, his arguments for multiculturalism fail to register what he acknowledges elsewhere: that the subordination of women is often informal and private, and that virtually no culture in the world today, minority or majority, could pass his "no sex discrimination" test if it were applied in the private sphere.[31] Those who defend group rights on liberal grounds need to address these very private, culturally reinforced kinds of discrimination. For surely self-respect and self-esteem require more than simple membership in a viable culture. Surely it is *not* enough for one to be able to "question one's inherited social roles" and to have the capacity to make choices about the life one wants to lead, that one's culture be protected. At least as important to the development of self-respect and self-esteem is *our place within our culture*. And at least as pertinent to our capacity to question our social roles is *whether our culture instills in us and forces on us particular social roles*. To the extent that a girl's culture is patriarchal, in both these respects her healthy development is endangered.

[29]Kymlicka, *Multicultural Citizenship*, pp. 153, 165.

[30]See, for example, Amartya Sen, "More Than One Hundred Million Women Are Missing," *New York Review of Books*, 20 December 1990.

[31]Will Kymlicka, *Contemporary Political Philosophy: An Introduction* (Oxford: The Clarendon Press, 1990), pp. 239–62.

Part of the Solution?

30   It is by no means clear, then, from a feminist point of view, that minority group rights are "part of the solution." They may well exacerbate the problem. In the case of a more patriarchal minority culture in the context of a less patriarchal majority culture, no argument can be made on the basis of self-respect or freedom that the female members of the culture have a clear interest in its preservation. Indeed, they *might* be much better off if the culture into which they were born were either to become extinct (so that its members would become integrated into the less sexist surrounding culture) or, preferably, to be encouraged to alter itself so as to reinforce the equality of women—at least to the degree to which this value is upheld in the majority culture. Other considerations would, of course, need to be taken into account, such as whether the minority group speaks a language that requires protection, and whether the group suffers from prejudices such as racial discrimination. But it would take significant factors weighing in the other direction to counterbalance evidence that a culture severely constrains women's choices or otherwise undermines their well-being.

What some of the examples discussed above illustrate is how culturally endorsed practices that are oppressive to women can often remain hidden in the private or domestic sphere. In the Iraqi child marriage case mentioned above, if the father himself had not called in agents of the state, his daughters' plight might well not have become public. And when Congress in 1996 passed a law criminalizing clitoridectomy, a number of U.S. doctors objected to the law on the basis that it concerned a private matter which, as one said, "should be decided by a physician, the family, and the child."[32] It can take more or less extraordinary circumstances for such abuses of girls or women to become public or for the state to be able to intervene protectively.

Thus it is clear that many instances of private-sphere discrimination against women on cultural grounds are never likely to emerge in public, where courts can enforce the women's rights and political theorists can label such practices as illiberal and therefore unjustified violations of women's physical or mental integrity. Establishing group rights to enable some minority cultures to preserve themselves may not be in the best interests of the girls and women of those cultures, even if it benefits the men.

Those who make liberal arguments for the rights of groups, then, must take special care to look at inequalities within those groups. It is especially important to consider inequalities between the sexes, since they are likely to be less public, and thus less easily discernible. Moreover, policies designed to respond to the needs and claims of cultural minority groups must take seriously the urgency of adequately representing less powerful members of such groups. Because attention to the rights of minority cultural groups, if it is to be consistent with the fundamentals of liberalism, must ultimately be aimed at furthering the well-being of the members of these groups, there can be no justification for assuming

[32]*New York Times,* 12 October 1996, A6. Similar views were expressed on National Public Radio.

that the groups' self-proclaimed leaders—invariably composed mainly of their older and their male members—represent the interests of all of the groups' members. Unless women—and, more specifically, young women (since older women often are co-opted into reinforcing gender inequality)—are fully represented in negotiations about group rights, their interests may be harmed rather than promoted by the granting of such rights.   [1999]

Is Multiculturalism Bad for Women?

Part 2: Responses

WILL KYMLICKA

WILL KYMLICKA, *the eminent Canadian political scientist, is on the faculty of Queen's University, where he is professor of philosophy and a recurrent visiting professor in the Nationalism Studies program at the Central European University in Budapest. His works have been translated into twenty-one languages, and include five books published by the Oxford University Press:* Liberalism, Community, and Culture *(1989),* Contemporary Political Philosophy *(1990),* Multicultural Citizenship *(1995), which was awarded the Macpherson Prize by the Canadian Political Science Association and the Bunche Award by the American Political Science Association,* Finding our Way: Rethinking Ethnocultural Relations in Canada *(1998), and* Politics in the Vernacular: Nationalism, Multiculturalism, Citizenship *(2002). He has also edited and co-edited several collections of works on politics and political philosophy.*

Liberal Complacencies

I agree with the basic claim of Okin's paper—that a liberal[1] egalitarian (and feminist) approach to multiculturalism must look carefully at intragroup inequalities, and specifically at gender inequalities, when examining the legitimacy of minority group rights. Justice within ethnocultural groups is as important as justice between ethnocultural groups. Group rights are permissible if they help promote justice between ethnocultural groups, but are impermissible if they create or exacerbate gender inequalities within the group.

In my recent work, I have tried to emphasize this point by distinguishing between two kinds of "group rights." Sometimes an ethnocultural group claims rights against its own members—in particular, the right to restrict individual choice in the name of cultural "tradition" or cultural "integrity." I call such group rights "internal restrictions," since their aim is to restrict the ability of individuals within the group (particularly women) to question, revise, or abandon traditional cultural roles and practices. A liberal theory of minority group

---

[1]The word "liberal" is here used in relation to its original meaning of "free" to refer to modern states that are designed to promote and protect freedom, not to the policies of particular political parties.

rights, I have argued, cannot accept such internal restrictions, since they violate the autonomy of individuals and create injustice within the group.

However, liberals can accept a second sort of group rights—namely, rights that a minority group claims against the larger society in order to reduce its vulnerability to the economic or political power of the larger society. Such rights, which I call "external protections," can take the form of language rights, guaranteed political representation, funding of ethnic media, land claims, compensation for historical injustice, or the regional devolution of power. All of these can help to promote justice between ethnocultural groups, by ensuring that members of the minority have the same effective capacity to promote their interests as the majority.

Okin argues, in effect, that my account of "internal restrictions" is too narrow. I defined internal restrictions as those claims by a group which involve limiting the civil and political liberties of individual members, but Okin insists that the ability of women to question and revise their traditional gender roles can be drastically curtailed even when their civil rights are formally protected in the public sphere.

5 I accept this point. In fact, I had not intended "individual freedoms" to be interpreted in a purely formal or legalistic way, and I would consider the domestic oppressions that Okin discusses to be paradigmatic examples of the sorts of "internal restrictions" which liberals must oppose.

So I accept Okin's claim that we need a more subtle account of internal restrictions which helps us identify limitations on the freedom of women within ethnocultural groups. But it still seems to me that the basic distinction is sound—i.e., liberals can accept external protections which promote justice between groups, but must reject internal restrictions which reduce freedom within groups. Okin is suggesting a constructive elaboration of this distinction, but I see no reason to reject the underlying principle.

Yet Okin seems to think that feminists should therefore be deeply skeptical about the very category of minority group rights. More generally, she suggests that feminists should view multiculturalism not as a likely ally in a broader struggle for a more inclusive justice, but as a likely threat to whatever gains feminists have made over the last few decades.

I think this way of opposing feminism and multiculturalism is regrettable. After all, both are making the same point about the inadequacy of the traditional liberal conception of individual rights. In her own work, Okin has argued that women's equality cannot be achieved solely through women's being given the same set of formal individual rights which men possess. We must also pay attention to the structure of societal institutions (e.g., the workplace, family, etc.), and to the sorts of images and expectations people are exposed to in schools and the media, since these are typically gendered in an unfair way, using the male as the "norm."

Similarly, multiculturalists argue that we cannot achieve justice between ethnocultural groups simply by guaranteeing to ethnocultural minorities the same set of formal individual rights which the majority possesses. We must also examine the structure of institutions (e.g., the language, calendar, and uniforms that they use), and the content of schooling and media, since all of these take the majority culture as the "norm."

Moreover, both feminists and multiculturalists provide the same explanation 10 for why traditional liberal theories are not satisfactory. Historically, liberal theorists were explicitly prejudiced against women and ethnic or racial minorities. Today, however, the problem is one of invisibility. In her work, Okin has shown how liberal theorists implicitly or explicitly operate with the assumption that the citizen is a man, and never ask what sorts of institutions or principles women would choose (e.g., if they were behind Rawls's "veil of ignorance"). In my work, I show that liberal theorists have operated with the assumption that citizens share the same language and national culture, and never ask what sorts of institutions would be chosen by ethnocultural minorities. In both cases, the distinctive needs and interests of women and ethnocultural minorities are simply never addressed in the theory. And in both cases, the result is that liberalism has been blind to grave injustices which limit the freedom and harm the self-respect of women and ethnocultural minorities.

Finally, both feminism and multiculturalism look to similar remedies. Okin says that she is concerned about the view that the members of a minority "are not sufficiently protected by the practice of ensuring the individual rights of their members," and minority group members are demanding "a group right not available to the rest of the population." But many feminists have made precisely the same argument about gender equality—i.e., that true equality will require rights for women that are not available to men, such as affirmative action, women-only classrooms, gender-specific prohibitions on pornography, gender-specific health programs, and the like. Others have made similar arguments about the need for group-specific rights and benefits for the disabled, or for gays and lesbians. All of these movements are challenging the traditional liberal assumption that equality requires identical treatment.

So I see multiculturalism and feminism as allies engaged in related struggles for a more inclusive conception of justice. Indeed, my own thoughts on ethnocultural justice have been deeply influenced by Okin's work on gender justice, since I think there are many comparable historical patterns and contemporary lessons.

Okin worries that the currently fashionable attention to multiculturalism is obscuring the older struggle for gender inequality. This is true of some multiculturalists, just as it is true that some feminists have been blind to issues of cultural difference. But it would be a mistake—in both theory and practice—to think that struggling against gender inequality within ethnocultural groups requires denying or downplaying the extent of injustice between groups. These are both grave injustices, and liberalism's historic inability to recognize them is rooted in similar theoretical mistakes. The same attitudes and habits of mind that enabled liberals to ignore the just claims of women have also enabled them to ignore the just claims of ethnocultural minorities. We have a common interest in fighting these liberal complacencies.

KATHA POLLITT

KATHA POLLITT *(1949–) received her B.A. from Harvard and her M.F.A. from Columbia. Her book of poems,* Antarctic Traveler, *won the National Book Critics Circle Award. She writes a regular column for the weekly magazine* The Nation, *and has published several collections of her essays, including* Reasonable Creatures: Essays on Women and Feminism *(1994) and* Subject to Debate: Sense and Dissents on Women, Politics, and Culture *(2001).*

Whose Culture?

Susan Okin writes that multiculturalism and feminism are in "tension," and sometimes even in opposition to each other. She argues that defenders of "cultural" or "group rights" for minority cultures have failed to notice that there are considerable differences of power within those cultures, and that those differences are gendered, with men having power over women. She also claims that group-rights advocates fail to pay enough attention to the private, domestic sphere, in which these oppressive and gendered cultural traditions tend to be most freely exercised.

Coming in late to this debate, I have to say I've had a hard time understanding how anyone could find these arguments controversial. Feminism and multiculturalism may find themselves allied in academic politics, where white women and minority women and men face common enemies (Great Books, dead white men, old boy networks, job discrimination, and so forth). But as political visions in the larger world they are very far apart. In its demand for equality for women, feminism sets itself in opposition to virtually every culture on earth. You could say that multiculturalism demands respect for all cultural traditions, while feminism interrogates and challenges all cultural traditions. Feminists might disagree about strategic issues: what needs changing first, or how to ensure one isn't just making things worse, or how to win over enough people. Feminists might even disagree about what true equality is in a given instance. But fundamentally, the ethical claims of feminism run counter to the cultural relativism of "group rights" multiculturalism.

Okin notes that the flashpoints for cultural rights tend to be around issues of gender, a.k.a. "the family," and she cites a number of prominent legal cases in which immigrants have put forward cultural defenses against charges of wife murder, child murder, the forced marriage of underage daughters to strangers, clitoridectomy, and so forth. (She might have included the role that multicultural arguments play in cases involving the harsh disciplining of children, homophobia, and sex education.) Although she herself sets aside, as clearly unmeritorious, the notion of "group rights" for immigrants, who have, after all, made a decision to come here, these cases raise interesting questions: What is a culture, and how do you know? A Chinese immigrant murders his supposedly unfaithful wife and says this is the way they do things back home. Many were outraged, and rightly so, that this multicultural equivalent of the Twinkie Defense was successful as a legal strategy. Not so many paused to wonder whether the defense argument was based on fact. Is it really legal in modern China for husbands to murder their wives if they think their wives are having affairs? China has undergone a great deal of social change in the twentieth century—change that includes dramatic, if uneven, gains in rights for women. Maybe in China lots of husbands kill their wives; maybe, as in the United States, such men are motivated by tacit cultural values (men who can't control their wives are impotent wimps, crimes of passion aren't so bad, etc.), but this is a different story from the one told by the defendant's lawyer, which portrayed him as the naive product of a rigid, static society who somehow found himself living in New York City and who could not be expected to adapt.

True or (in my view) false, you'll note that this is not an argument that just any immigrant can make. A Russian, an Italian, could not justify beating his wife to death by referring to the customs of dear old Moscow or Calabria, although Russian women are killed by their male partners at astronomical rates and parts of Italy are very old-fashioned indeed about these matters. That is partly because of multiculturalism's connections to Third Worldism, and the appeals Third Worldism makes to white liberal guilt, and partly because Americans understand that Russia and Italy are dynamic societies in which change is constant and interests clash. The cultural rights argument works best for cultures that most Americans know comparatively little about: cultures that in our ignorance we can imagine as stable, timeless, ancient, lacking in internal conflict, premodern. But where on the globe today is such a society? Even the supposedly ancient traditions defended by group-rights advocates sometimes turn out to be of rather recent vintage. Clitoridectomy, it's worth remembering, was falling into desuetude in Kenya when nationalists revived it as part of their rejection of British colonialism. Israeli family law, which is extremely unfair to women—divorce is unilateral for men only, for example, as under Islamic law—is the result of a political deal between the religious and secular Zionists who founded the state.

That cultural-rights movements have centered on gender is a telling fact about them. It's related to the way in which nationalism tends to identify the nation with the bodies of its women: they are the ones urged into "traditional" dress, conceptualized as the producers of babies for the fatherland and keepers of the hearth for the men at the front, punished for sleeping with outsiders, raped by the nation's enemies, and so forth. But it's also partly due to the fact that gender and family are retrograde areas of most majority cultures, too: these are accommodations majority cultures have often been willing to make. How far would an Algerian immigrant get, I wonder, if he refused to pay the interest on his Visa bill on the grounds that Islam forbids interest on borrowed money? Or a Russian who argued that the cradle-to-grave social security provided by the former Soviet Union was part of his cultural tradition and should be extended to him in Brooklyn as well? Everyone understands that money is much too important to be handed out in this whimsical fashion. Women and children are another story.

An older friend of mine was in Paris while the dispute over Muslim schoolgirls' head scarves was going on. A gentle, tolerant, worldly-wise leftist, she sided with the girls against the government: why shouldn't they be able to dress as they

5

wished, to follow their culture? Then she came across a television debate in which a Muslim girl said she wanted the ban to stay because without it, her family would force her to wear a scarf. That changed my friend's view of the matter: the left, and feminist, position, she now thought, was to support this girl and the ones like her in their struggle to be independent modern women—not the parents, the neighbors, the community and religious "leaders." I think my friend was right.

SUSAN MOLLER OKIN

From *Reply*

10   . . . Janet Halley, Katha Pollitt, Raz, and Tamir° all want to extend the argument I make about women to other less powerful subgroups and individuals within cultures, and I appreciate and applaud their ideas. I have by no means exhausted the subject of oppression within groups that is often justified in the name of cultural preservation or religious toleration. Children, gays and lesbians, persons of minority races, disabled persons, and dissenters are all liable to varying kinds and degrees of mistreatment within many societies, including our own, and we should work to eliminate this mistreatment, in part by paying attention to those aspects of the culture that reinforce them. For example, the general level of violence that is portrayed in films and other media in the United States undoubtedly affects the level of violence—often targeted toward vulnerable persons—that actually occurs, although violence is not formally reinforced, taught as a necessary part of, or justified by, our culture.[1] (Violence against gays may be a partial exception to the last point, since homosexuality is explicitly named a sin or vice by many religious groups.). . .

Toward a Feminist, More Egalitarian Multiculturalism

27   Finally, I agree with Will Kymlicka's important observation that multiculturalism and feminism are, in some ways, related struggles. Both seek the recognition of difference in the context of norms that are universal in theory, but not in practice. Still, an essential difference remains. The few special rights that women claim qua women do not give more powerful women the right to control less powerful women. In contrast, cultural group rights do often (in not-so-obvious ways) reinforce existing hierarchies. As Kymlicka indicates, he and I share this concern, though he tends to prioritize cultural group rights and I, as is by now obvious, prioritize women's equality. What we need to strive toward is a form of multiculturalism that gives the issues of gender and other intragroup inequalities

---

[1] For a recent argument to this effect, see James Hamilton, *Channeling Violence* (Princeton: Princeton University Press, 1998).

[10] **Janet Halley, Katha Pollitt, [Joseph] Raz, and [Yael] Tamir** respondents to Okin's essay in the book

their due—that is to say, a multiculturalism that effectively treats all persons as each other's moral equals.

1. This cluster of texts is from the book, *Is Multiculturalism Bad for Women?*, which gathers political theorist Okin's essay for the *Boston Review*, fifteen responses to it, and Okin's reply. The article and subsequent book are responses to some of the legal cases that have come out of the mixing into modern America of many varieties of ethnic cultures. What do people bring with them when they look to settle here? And what do indigenous cultures seek to preserve? The cases Okin lists arose because immigrants did things in America that are not generally accepted in American law. Their defenses sometimes claimed, in the words of one commentator, "My Culture Made Me Do It."[1] The debate in the book addresses the occasional conflicts between, on the one hand, the rights of individuals, and, on the other hand, between the rights of individuals and the rights of groups. What is Okin's worry about accepting a legal defense on the basis of culture?

2. In an earlier book, Okin claimed that since the family is the place most people learn their ideas of justice, if we want to promote equality between men and women, we should make sure our family structures follow that principle. This means equal sharing of childcare, household maintenance, and financial support.[2] How does this view relate to her critique of the theory of group rights?

3. Once she has summarized Kymlicka's position, which, she concedes, does take account of discrimination against women, what does Okin object to about it? What is the logical consequence of her objection?

4. Characterize Kymlicka's response to Okin and its consequences.

5. Looking carefully at the dialogue between Okin and Kymlicka, explain whether the two merely reiterate their positions or whether the exchange has produced a new synthesis.

6. What does Pollitt contribute to the debate?

7. Does this discussion between Okin and Kymlicka say anything relevant to Soyinka's "Death and the King's Horseman" (see Chapter 12, p. 454)?

[1]Bonnie Honig, "My Culture Made Me Do It," in *Is Multiculturalism Bad for Women?*, Ed. Joshua Cohen, Matthew Howard, and Martha Nussbaum, 35–40 (Princeton: Princeton University Press, 1999).

[2]Susan Moller Okin, *Justice, Gender, and the Family* (New York: Basic Books, 1989). See esp. Chapter 8.

CHAPTER FIFTEEN

Race and Ethnicity

INTRODUCTION

Religious and spiritual visionaries love humankind as one community. Some widen their scope to include all beings or the whole planet. Yet another powerful impulse categorizes, sometimes separating "people like me" from "people not like me." Even while aspiring to love widely, we seem to need ties to subsets of people or creatures. But the criteria for sorting change according to our needs and aims. We often sort by family status (Mothers Against Drunk Driving), professional activities (National Council of Teachers of English), political preferences (Republicans), relationships (Parents and Friends of Lesbians and Gays), and hobbies (Chess League of America). We all have so many different affiliations that it wouldn't be too much of a stretch to imagine one person who could belong to all of these groups.

Two of the most persistent ways of sorting people in contemporary America are race and ethnicity, despite the uncertainty about how to define these categories and how they relate to each other. Racial differences look physical, but many scientists reject race as a biological distinction, saying that there is as much diversity among members of one race as there is between supposedly different races. For instance, some Asian Indians, who are Caucasians, have more skin pigmentation than some African-Americans, so what does melanin mean? Yet since the mapping of the human genome, we are better able to track genetic differences among groups. How many mutations does it take to make a race? Some think that geographical origin is a more meaningful distinction than race, with people dividing into five groups according to the continents their ancestors came from. Some traits can be located more particularly. Swedes are the group least liable to be lactose intolerant as adults, but no one would point to a Swedish "race." Jews have more Tay-Sachs disease than other groups, but not all Jews, mainly those with Eastern European ancestry. African-Americans have, as a group, more sickle cell anemia than other groups, but not all people of African descent carry genes for the disease, and not all sufferers have ancestry in sub-Saharan Africa, where the disease originated.

How we sort members of our species has important results because it can influence the way we structure medical trials of new drugs or the way we ask people to identify themselves on a census. But however scientists debate these issues, whatever the results for policies, society must come to terms with the dynamics between groups that have, on the one hand, different cultures and customs, and on the other, different amounts of power and influence in society. The selections in this unit all deal with the consequences of those differences.

POETRY

GWENDOLYN BROOKS

OLC

(For biographical notes, see p. 537.)

The Chicago Defender *Sends a Man to Little Rock*°
Fall, 1957°

In Little Rock the people bear
Babes, and comb and part their hair
And watch the want ads, put repair
To roof and latch. While wheat toast burns
A woman waters multiferns.   5

Time upholds or overturns
The many, tight, and small concerns.

In Little Rock the people sing
Sunday hymns like anything,
Through Sunday pomp and polishing.   10

And after testament and tunes,
Some soften Sunday afternoons
With lemon tea and Lorna Doones.°

Title*The Chicago Defender* is a weekly African-American newspaper.   Date**1957** As a result of the unanimous Supreme Court decision in the 1954 case of *Brown* v. *Board of Education,* nine African-American students attempted to enter the high school in Little Rock, Arkansas, in 1957. Their arrival set off riots protesting desegregation. The conflict eventually led to a confrontation between Arkansas Governor Orval Faubus and President Dwight D. Eisenhower and to more legal battles.   13**Lorna Doones** commercially available cookies

I forecast
15   And I believe
Come Christmas Little Rock will cleave
To Christmas tree and trifle, weave,
From laugh and tinsel, texture fast.

In Little Rock is baseball; Barcarolle.°
20   That hotness in July . . . the uniformed figures raw and implacable
And not intellectual,
Batting the hotness or clawing the suffering dust.
The Open Air Concert, on the special twilight green. . . .
When Beethoven is brutal or whispers to lady-like air.
25   Blanket-sitters are solemn, as Johann troubles to lean

To tell them what to mean. . . .
There is love, too, in Little Rock. Soft women softly
Opening themselves in kindness,
Or, pitying one's blindness,
30   Awaiting one's pleasure
In azure
Glory with anguished rose at the root. . . .
To wash away old semi-discomfitures.
They re-teach purple and unsullen blue.
35   The wispy soils go. And uncertain
Half-havings have they clarified to sures.

In Little Rock they know
Not answering the telephone is a way of rejecting life,
That it is our business to be bothered, is our business
40   To cherish bores or boredom, be polite
To lies and love and many-faceted fuzziness.
I scratch my head, massage the hate-I-had.
I blink across my prim and pencilled pad.
The saga I was sent for is not down.
45   Because there is a puzzle in this town.
The biggest News I do not dare
Telegraph to the Editor's chair:
"They are like people everywhere."

The angry Editor would reply
50   In hundred harryings of Why.

And true, they are hurling spittle, rock,
Garbage and fruit in Little Rock.
And I saw coiling storm a-writhe
On bright madonnas. And a scythe
55   Of men harassing brownish girls.

---

¹⁹**Barcarolle** the song of a gondolier on the canals of Venice or a musical composition
using alternating strong and weak beats to imitate the rhythm of rowing

(The bows and barrettes in the curls
And braids declined away from joy.)
I saw a bleeding brownish boy. . . .
The lariat lynch-wish I deplored.
The loveliest lynchee was our Lord.   [1960]   60

1. Who is the narrator of the poem?
2. What is the puzzle of Little Rock?
3. How does Brooks indicate the difference between the view of the citizens of
   Little Rock as ordinary, church-going, family-oriented people and the view
   of the rioters at the end of the poem?

JOSHUA COBEN

JOSHUA COBEN *(1965–) was born and educated in St. Louis, Missouri,
graduating from Washington University in 1990. He received his M.Ed. from
Boston University. He did a junior year abroad at the Université de Caen, France,
and after Boston University spent a year in France on a Fulbright teaching
assistantship. He then taught for nine years in a "total immersion" public
elementary school that conducts most of its classes in French. After taking a leave of
absence to act as a full-time father, homemaker, and writer, he returned to teaching.
His poems have appeared in* College English, Pleides, RE:AL, Plainsongs, *and
other publications.*

Ishmael°

We share a face:
sunbit river mud
beset with scrub, lit
and soiled from within
like an oil lamp.   5
I glimpse myself
in your market stare,
glaze my teeth
in the fruit you eat
and in your kefiya   10
bind my hair.
Rumor would have us
same-grain brothers

Title According to the account in Genesis 16–21, Ishmael was the son of Abraham and his
servant Hagar, exiled after the long-awaited birth of Isaac, son of Abraham and his wife
Sarah. Ishmael is considered to be the founder of the Arab peoples, as Isaac is a patriarch
of the Jews.

in a lineage of sand
15 and Dead Sea salt.
History is the sod
we are made of,
layers seething
at the pores
20 the way embers sweat
blood through ash.

We are a body bent
on its own suicidal
defense: skin that salves
25 and suffocates, combustible
bones that prod,
uphold, afflict.

Go to our father.
Tell him you've
30 come home. Tell him
you never left.   [1997]

1. Who is the narrator of this poem? What is his discovery? How is our
   understanding of the poem enriched by the story from the Hebrew Bible of
   Ishmael and Isaac, the sons of Abraham?
2. What are the poetic techniques through which the poem makes its
   impact?

COUNTEE CULLEN

COUNTEE CULLEN *(1903–46) was raised in a Methodist parsonage in New York
City, attended De Witt Clinton High School, and began writing poetry at fourteen. In
1922 he matriculated at New York University. His first published poems appeared
in magazines, first in* The Crisis *and* Opportunity, *and then in* Harper's,
Century Magazine, *and* Poetry. *His poem,* "Ballad of the Brown Girl," *won him
awards, and his first volume of verse,* Color, *was published the year of his
graduation. He subsequently received a Master of Arts degree from Harvard
University. His second book of poetry,* Copper Sun *(1927), was controversial for its
lack of attention to race, even though it had been the focus of his first book. He had
gone beyond it, feeling, since he had been raised in a primarily white milieu, that
his background did not provide him with further material for his writing. He relied
on traditional forms and subject matter in the Romantic tradition for his work and
resisted both the style and content of the literature of the Harlem Renaissance and
the Modernists of his time. His books also include* The Black Christ and Other
Poems *(1929),* The Medea and Some Other Poems *(1935), two books of
children's stories, and a play,* St. Louis Woman *(1946), co-written with Arna
Bontemps.*

Incident

(For Eric Walrond)

Once riding in old Baltimore,
Heart-filled, head-filled with glee,
I saw a Baltimorean
Keep looking straight at me.

Now I was eight and very small,   5
And he was no whit bigger,
And so I smiled, but he poked out
His tongue, and called me, "Nigger."

I saw the whole of Baltimore
From May until December: 10
Of all the things that happened there
That's all that I remember.   [1925]

1. What is the relationship between the poem and its title?
2. During his lifetime, Cullen was sometimes criticized for using poetic forms
   out of fashion in the era of the Harlem Renaissance. Why do you think he
   used a formal verse structure in this poem?
3. How does l. 6 add to the effect of the poem?

NIKKI GIOVANNI

NIKKI GIOVANNI *(1943–) was born in Tennessee and raised in Ohio. She graduated from Fisk University, where she joined the Writer's Workshop and edited the
literary magazine. She entered graduate school at the University of Pennsylvania.
In her first two collections,* Black Feeling, Black Talk *and* Black Judgement, *she
reflects on African-American identity. Her recent books are* Blues for All the
Changes: New Poems *and* Selected Poems of Nikki Giovanni. *Her honors
include the NAACP Image Award for Literature, the Langston Hughes Award for
Distinguished Contributions to Art and Letters, and Woman of the Year for*
Essence, Mademoiselle, *and* Ladies Home Journal. *She is a professor of
English and Black Studies at Virginia Tech.*

Ego Tripping

(there may be a reason why)

I was born in the congo
I walked to the fertile crescent and built
   the sphinx
I designed a pyramid so tough that a star
   that only glows every one hundred years falls   5
   into the center giving divine perfect light
I am bad

I sat on the throne
    drinking nectar with allah
10 I got hot and sent an ice age to europe
    to cool my thirst
My oldest daughter is nefertiti
    the tears from my birth pains
    created the nile
15 I am a beautiful woman

I gazed on the forest and burned
    out the sahara desert
    with a packet of goat's meat
    and a change of clothes
20 I crossed it in two hours
I am a gazelle so swift
    so swift you can't catch me

    For a birthday present when he was three
I gave my son hannibal° an elephant
25   He gave me rome for mother's day
My strength flows ever on

My son noah° built new/ark and
I stood proudly at the helm
    as we sailed on a soft summer day
30 I turned myself into myself and was
    jesus
    men intone my loving name
    All praises All praises
I am the one who would save

35 I sowed diamonds in my back yard
My bowels deliver uranium
    the filings from my fingernails are
    semi-precious jewels
    On a trip north
40 I caught a cold and blew
My nose giving oil to the arab world
I am so hip even my errors are correct
I sailed west to reach east and had to round off
    the earth as I went
45   The hair from my head thinned
    and gold was laid across three continents

[24]**Hannibal** important Carthaginian general in the Punic Wars between ancient Rome and Carthage, 3rd century BCE   [27]**Noah** according to Genesis 6–10, a righteous man who, on God's instructions, built an ark to save himself, his family, and two of each of the earth's animals from the flood of forty days and nights in which God destroyed the rest of the world

I am so perfect so divine so ethereal so surreal
I cannot be comprehended
   except by my permission

I mean . . . I . . . can fly   50
   like a bird in the sky . . .   [1973]

1. Point out some of the poetic techniques that contribute to the effect of the poem.
2. Imagery associated with the Renaissance Italian poet Petrarch typically exaggerates the power of love and its effects on the lover. Look at the Petrarchan imagery in the second stanza of John Donne's "Canonization." How does Giovanni's imagery compare?

      Alas, alas, who's injur'd by my love?   10
        What merchant's ships have my sighs drown'd?
        Who says my tears have overflow'd his ground?
        When did my colds a forward spring remove?
          When did the heats which my veins fill
          Add one more to the plaguy bill?   15
      Soldiers find wars, and lawyers find out still
        Litigious men, which quarrels move,
        Though she and I do love.
3. Put the poem into the context of Giovanni's life and of its time (1973).

SUHEIR HAMMAD

SUHEIR HAMMAD *(1977–) is a Palestinian by birth and now an American poet and political activist. She is the author of a book of poems,* Born Palestinian, Born Black, *and a memoir,* Drops of This Story, *and is the recipient of the Audre Lourde Writing Award from Hunter College, as well as other awards. She makes frequent appearances as a reader at New York reading venues, has performed on the radio and in person with various bands, has produced a documentary film, and is writing a film entitled* From Beirut to Brooklyn, *based on her memoir. She is a spokesperson on issues of domestic violence, sexual abuse, racism, and homophobia, edits the literary journal* Butter Phoenix, *and writes a literary column for* Stress *magazine. Starting in 2002 she had a leading role in "Russell Simmons Def Poetry Jam on Broadway."*

Exotic

don't wanna be your exotic
        some delicate   fragile   colorful bird
     imprisoned   caged
     in a land foreign to the stretch of her wings

5   don't wanna be your exotic
                women everywhere are just like me
                some taller   darker   nicer than me
                but like me but just the same
                women everywhere carry my nose on their faces
10   my name on their spirits

    don't wanna
                don't seduce yourself with
                my otherness   my hair
                wasn't put on top my head to entice
15   you into some mysterious black vodou
                the beat of my lashes against each other
                ain't some dark desert beat
                it's just a blink
                get over it

20   don't wanna be your exotic
                your lovin of my beauty ain't more than
                funky fornication°   plain pink perversion
                in fact   nasty necrophilia°
                cause my beauty is dead to you
25   i am dead to you

    not your
                harem girl   geisha° doll   banana picker
                pom pom girl°   pum pum shorts   coffee maker
                town whore   belly dancer   private dancer°
30   la malinche°   venus hottentot°   laundry girl°
                your immaculate vessel emasculating princess

    don't wanna be
        your erotic
    not your exotic
                                                                    [1996]

---

²²**fornication** sexual intercourse between people who are not married to each other
²³**necrophilia** sexual fascination with dead bodies   ²⁷**geisha** a Japanese woman trained
to sing, dance, and converse politely in order to entertain at professional meetings of men
²⁸**pom pom girl** young woman dressed as a cheerleader posed in pornographic pictures
²⁹**private dancer** euphemism for prostitute   ³⁰**la malinche** an Aztec woman who
interpreted for Cortes as he led his army across Mexico; regarded as a traitor by some for
facilitating the relationship between the conqueror and the indigenous leader Montezuma;
sometimes characterized as a slave or prostitute   **venus hottentot** Sara Baartman was
an indigenous South African woman brought to England in the early nineteenth century.
She became a symbol of black female sexuality. In one widely circulated picture, she is
posed with exposed buttocks while several people peer at her; one comments, "Oh! God
Damn what roast beef!" Her remains were returned to South Africa in 2002.   **laundry
girl** nineteenth- and early twentieth-century term for a woman who worked in laundries
run by Catholic convents as a result of public shame like prostitution or bearing children
out of wedlock

1. How is the form of this poem created and what effect does it have?
2. Who is the implied audience, that audience to which the poem seems to be addressed? What is the speaker's attitude toward that audience?
3. What reasons does the narrator give for her attitude?
4. What is the effect of stanza 3?
5. What is the effect of the diction of the poem?
6. How does l. 31 work in the poem?

LANGSTON HUGHES

(For biographical notes, see p. 548.)

Harlem

What happens to a dream deferred?

> Does it dry up
> like a raisin in the sun?
> Or fester like a sore—
> And then run?
> Does it stink like rotten meat?
> Or crust and sugar over—
> like a syrupy sweet?

> Maybe it just sags
> like a heavy load.

> *Or does it explode?*   [1951]

5

10

Same in Blues

I said to my baby,
Baby, take it slow.
I can't, she said, I can't!
I got to go!

> There's a certain
> amount of traveling
> in a dream deferred.

5

Lulu said to Leonard,
I want a diamond ring.
Leonard said to Lulu,
You won't get a goddamn thing!

10

> A certain
> amount of nothing
> in a dream deferred.

Daddy, daddy, daddy,
All I want is you.

15

You can have me, baby—
but my lovin' days is through.

A certain
20 amount of impotence
in a dream deferred.

Three parties
On my party line—
But that third party,
25 Lord, ain't mine!

There's liable
to be confusion
in a dream deferred.

From river to river
30 Uptown and down,
There's liable to be confusion
when a dream gets kicked around.

You talk like
they don't kick
35 dreams around
Downtown.

I expect they do—
But I'm talking about
Harlem to you!
40 Harlem to you!
Harlem to you!
Harlem to you!

[1951]

1. How would you describe and account for the differing impacts of these two poems?
2. What is the dream and why is it deferred?

CLAUDE MCKAY

CLAUDE MCKAY *(1889–1948) was the grandson of slaves and the son of freeborn Jamaicans. He was taught at home by his elder brother and went to school to become a wheelwright and cabinetmaker but during his lifetime worked as a farmer, restaurant owner, police officer, porter, janitor, newspaper editor, and butler. He spent time in Morocco, England, Russia, and the United States, where he eventually became a citizen, living in New York and Chicago. Encouraged by an English friend, he wrote verses in Jamaican dialect. Among his books of poetry are* Songs of Jamaica *(1912) and* Constab Ballads *(1912). He also wrote novels, nonfiction, and an autobiography.*

The White City

I will not toy with it nor bend an inch.
Deep in the secret chambers of my heart
I muse my life-long hate, and without flinch
I bear it nobly as I live my part.
My being would be a skeleton, a shell,   5
If this dark Passion that fills my every mood,
And makes my heaven in the white world's hell,
Did not forever feed me vital blood.
I see the mighty city through a mist—
The strident trains that speed the goaded mass,   10
The poles and spires and towers vapor-kissed,
The fortressed port through which the great ships pass,
The tides, the wharves, the dens I contemplate,
Are sweet like wanton loves because I hate.

[1922]

1. The city in question is possibly New York. Describe conditions for African-Americans in New York in 1922 in a way that makes sense of the poem.
2. What is the dark Passion of l. 6? In what sense does it make the speaker more than a "skeleton" or "shell"?
3. Explicate the diction of ll. 11 and 12.
4. How does the poem's form figure into its meaning?
5. Look at Wordsworth's "Upon Westminster Bridge" (see p. 1272). How does Wordsworth's response to London compare with McKay's to New York?

PAT MORA

PAT MORA *(1942–), a leading figure in contemporary Hispanic poetry, graduated from Texas Western College and received her master's degree from the University of Texas in 1967. She has taught at the University of New Mexico, was a museum director, and worked with youth. Her recent books include* My Own True Name: New and Selected Poems for Young Adults, 1984–1999, Aunt Carmen's Book of Practical Saints, *and* Agua Santa: Holy Water. *She is the recipient of the Kellogg National Leadership Fellowship, fellowships in poetry from the National Endowment for the Arts, four Southwest Book awards, and the Premio Aztlan Literature Award. She has written many children's books and now lives in Santa Fe, New Mexico, and Cincinnati, Ohio.*

Immigrants

wrap their babies in the American flag,
feed them mashed hot dogs and apple pie,
name them Bill and Daisy,
buy them blonde dolls that blink

5   blue eyes or a football and tiny cleats
     before the baby can even walk,
     speak to them in thick English,
          hallo, babee, hallo.
     whisper in Spanish or Polish
10   when the babies sleep, whisper
     in a dark parent bed, that dark
     parent fear, "Will they like
     our boy, our girl, our fine american
     boy, our fine american girl?"   [1986]

1. What do the actions of the parents indicate about their wishes for their
    children?
2. What is the significance of ll. 9–10?

SHARON OLDS

(For biographical notes, see p. 259.)

On the Subway

     The boy and I face each other.
     His feet are huge, in black sneakers
     laced with white in a complex pattern like a
     set of intentional scars. We are stuck on
5   opposite sides of the car, a couple of
     molecules stuck in a rod of light
     rapidly moving through darkness. He has the
     casual cold look of a mugger,
     alert under hooded lids. He is wearing
10   red, like the inside of the body
     exposed. I am wearing dark fur, the
     whole skin of an animal taken and
     used. I look at his raw face,
     he looks at my fur coat, and I don't
15   know if I am in his power—
     he could take my coat so easily, my
     briefcase, my life—
     or if he is in my power, the way I am
     living off his life, eating the steak
20   he does not eat, as if I am taking
     the food from his mouth. And he is black
     and I am white, and without meaning or
     trying to I must profit from his darkness,
     the way he absorbs the murderous beams of the

nation's heart, as black cotton
absorbs the heat of the sun and holds it. There is
no way to know how easy this
white skin makes my life, this
life he could take so easily and
break across his knee like a stick the way his   30
own back is being broken, the
rod of his soul that at birth was dark and
fluid and rich as the heart of a seedling
ready to thrust up into any available light.   [1992]

25

1. What are the racial dynamics the narrator perceives between herself and
   the young man?
2. Is it possible that the narrator is wrong about her relationship with the
   young man? What conclusions can we draw about the narrator from her
   meditation about the man?

JIM SAGEL

JIM SAGEL *(1947–98) grew up in Northern New Mexico speaking a mix of
Spanish and English, but because he often writes in Spanish, he decided early to
compete for the prestigious El Premio Casa de las Americas, a prize awarded in
Cuba. Inspired to continue writing by winning the coveted prize, he wrote* Citra vez
en la movida, *which gained him another important prize, this one from Venezuela
for the best book of poetry in Spanish that year. He teaches in Taos, working with
teachers and students to support and develop the Spanish language as it grows and
changes in the United States. He sees the Hispanic culture in the Southwest as the
key to integrating new immigrants and as a bridge to Latin America.*

Baca° Grande

Una vaca se topó con un ratón y le dice:
"Tú—¿tan chiquito y con bigote?" Y le responde el ratón:
"Y tú tan grandota—¿y sin brassiere?"°

It was nearly a miracle
James Baca remembered anyone at all
from the old hometown gang
having been two years at Yale
   no less   5
and halfway through law school
at the University of California at Irvine

Title**Baca** a phonetic version of the Spanish word for "cow"   Epigraph A cow met a rat and
said, "You—so small and with a moustache?" The rat replied, "And you—so big and
without a bra?"

They hardly recognized him either
in his three-piece grey business suit
10 and surfer-swirl haircut
with just the menacing hint
of a tightly trimmed Zapata° moustache
        for cultural balance
and relevance

15 He had come to deliver the keynote address
to the graduating class of 80
at his old alma mater
and show off his well-trained lips
which laboriously parted
20   each Kennedyish "R"°
and drilled the first person pronoun
through the microphone
like an oil bit
with the slick, elegantly honed phrases
25 that slid so smoothly
off his meticulously bleached
        tongue
He talked Big Bucks
with astronautish fervor and if he
30   the former bootstrapless James A. Baca
could dazzle the ass
off the universe
then even you
        yes you
35 Joey Martinez toying with your yellow
        tassle
and staring dumbly into space
could emulate Mr. Baca someday
        possibly
40 well
there was of course
such a thing
as being an outrageously successful
gas station attendant too
45   let us never forget
it doesn't really matter what you do

---

¹²**Zapata** Emiliano Zapata (1879–1919), leader in the Mexican Revolution of 1910, the uprising of the lower classes against the government of General Díaz. Assassinated in 1919, he was a popular folk hero.   ²⁰**Kennedyish "R"** Thirty-fifth president of the United States (1961–63), John F. Kennedy spoke in a dialect that sometimes put the sound of the letter "r" at the end of a word ending in "a."

so long as you excel
    James said
never believing a word
of it
for he had already risen
    as high as they go

Wasn't nobody else
from this deprived environment
who'd ever jumped
    straight out of college
into the Governor's office
and maybe one day
he'd sit in that big chair
    himself   60
and when he did
he'd forget this damned town
and all the petty little people
in it
once and for all   65

That much he promised himself   [1982]

1. Characterize the narrator of this poem. What tone does he take about James
   Baca?
2. What is the import of the "bleached tongue" in ll. 26–27?
3. Compare the attitude in this poem about assimilation to that in Mora's
   "Immigrants."
4. What part would Baca play in "Los Vendidos"?

WILLIAM JAY SMITH

WILLIAM JAY SMITH *(1918–), an "army brat," was educated at Washington
University in St. Louis, Missouri, and served in the U.S. Navy from 1941 to 1945.
He then attended Columbia University and the Universities of Oxford and Florence,
served in the Vermont House of Representatives, and, from 1968 to 1970, was
consultant in poetry to the Library of Congress. His children's poetry, translations,
and studies of well-known literary hoaxes and lampoons emphasize his interest in
humor and wit in poetry. His narrative poetry and experiments with free verse can
be found in* Poems, Celebration at Dark, Tin Can and Other Poems, *and*
Collected Poems.

Old Cherokee Woman's Song

They have taken my land,
they have taken my home;
they have driven me here

to the edges of the water.
5   Cold is the ground
and cold the red water.
At night the men come
to circle the campground;
they carry tall reeds,
10   each topped with a feather,
a bright eagle feather
to draw our eyes upward
and bring us all hope
for the bitter long journey.
15   But for me the reed's broken
and the sky it has fallen
where black storm clouds gather.
Cold is the ground
and cold the red water.
20   My blood it will mix
with the flowing red water:
they have taken my land,
they have taken my home;
I go now to die
25   beyond the red water.

[2000]

1. Put the old woman's experience into its historical context.
2. Does the narrator's response to the men who bring the tall reeds resonate
    with anything about the Cherokee's historical experience?
3. According to Smith, "I like to think that the still center from which I believe
    my poetry springs has much in common with the reverential attitude of the
    Native American towards the elements, the sensory and spiritual connection
    between earth and sky. . . . The visual element in my work may owe some-
    thing to my Choctaw heritage" (http://www.state.lib.la.us/). Can you see
    these elements in the poem?

MITSUYE YAMADA

MITSUYE YAMADA (1923–), *poet, educator, and founder of Multicultural Women
Writers of Orange County, California, was born in Japan. Her father was a poet
and interpreter for the U.S. Immigration Service who was arrested for spying right
after the attack on Pearl Harbor. She and her mother and brother were sent to a
relocation camp in Idaho but were allowed to leave because they renounced loyalty
to the emperor. Yamada moved to Cincinnati, went to college there, and continued
at New York University and the University of Chicago. She taught ethnic and
children's literature and creative writing and is currently a professor of English at*

Cypress College in Seattle, Washington. Her works include Camp Notes and Other Poems, *a biographical documentary on Public Television that recounts the family's immigrant story. Her latest volume,* Desert Run: Poems and Stories, *returns to the experience of the internment camp and deals with problems of retaining her cultural heritage as well as feminist and other issues.*

To the Lady

The one in San Francisco who asked:
Why did the Japanese Americans let
the government put them in
those camps without protest?
Come to think of it I   5
   should've run off to Canada
   should've hijacked a plane to Algeria
   should've pulled myself up from my
   bra straps
   and kicked'm in the groin   10
   should've bombed a bank
   should've tried self-immolation
   should've holed myself up in a
   woodframe house
   and let you watch me   15
   burn up on the six o'clock news
   should've run howling down the street
   naked and assaulted you at breakfast
   by AP wirephoto
   should've screamed bloody murder   20
   like Kitty Genovese°
Then
YOU would've
   come to my aid in shining armor
   laid yourself across the railroad track
   marched on Washington°   25
   tatooed a Star of David on your arm

[21]**Kitty Genovese** murdered in Kew Gardens, New York, as she was walking home. Thirty-eight people reportedly heard her cries but did not try to help her ward off her attacker.   [26]**marched on Washington** a reference to the tradition of organizing mass gatherings on the Mall in Washington, D.C., to protest or support government policies. One of the largest and most famous was the August 28, 1963, March on Washington organized by such groups as the National Association for the Advancement of Colored People, Congress of Racial Equality (CORE), Southern Christian Leadership Conference, Urban League, Student Non-Violent Coordinating Committee, and the Negro American Labor Committee. The March was an important moment in the Civil Rights movement. Over 250,000 marchers heard Dr. Martin Luther King, who delivered his "I Have a Dream" speech, and other speakers.

written six million° enraged
letters to Congress

30 But we didn't draw the line
anywhere
law and order Executive Order 9066°
social order moral order internal order

You let'm
35 I let'm
All are punished.   [1976]

[28]**six million** a reference to Jews killed by the Nazis during World War II, many of whom
had had identifying numbers tattooed on their forearms   [32]**Executive Order 9066**
President Franklin Delano Roosevelt's Executive Order 9066 authorized the relocation of
over 100,000 Japanese and Japanese Americans on the West Coast to internment camps
after the Japanese bombed Pearl Harbor on December 7, 1941.

1. What is the effect of the poem's double list structure: "I should've . . . Then
   YOU would've . . ."?
2. How do the allusions to protests and actions in other situations add to the
   impact of the poem?

⟳ F R A M E W O R K S ⟳

Looking at Hayden through History and Psychology

ROBERT HAYDEN, *Middle Passage*

From Argument of **JOHN QUINCY ADAMS,** before the Supreme Court of the United
States, in the case of the United States, Appellants, *vs.* Cinque, and others,
Africans Captured in the Schooner *Amistad,* by Lieut. Gedney, Delivered on the
24th of February and 1st of March, 1841

DANIEL BROWN, From *Stress and Emotion: Implications for Illness Development and
Wellness*

RAYMOND L. COHN, From *Maritime Mortality in the Eighteenth and Nineteenth
Centuries: A Survey*

JAMES A. RAWLEY, *The Middle Passage*

⟳⟳⟳

ROBERT HAYDEN

ROBERT HAYDEN *(1913–80) was raised in a poor area of Detroit by friends of
his parents, who divorced when he was young. He took the name of his parents'
friends and didn't find out his parents' name until he was an adult. He earned a*

*B.A. at Detroit City College (now Wayne State University) and an M.A. at the
University of Michigan, where he studied with W.H. Auden. He taught at Fisk
University and at the University of Michigan, publishing a number of books of
poetry, including* Ballad of Remembrance, *which won the grand prize at the
First World Festival of Negro Arts in Dakar, Senegal, in 1966 and* Words in the
Mourning Time *(1970),* Night-Blooming Cereus *(1972),* Angle of Ascent
(1975), and American Journal *(1978 and 1982). In 1979 he was the first
African-American appointed as the Consultant in Poetry to the Library of Congress
(a post that later became Poet Laureate).*

Middle Passage°

1

Jesús, Estrella, Esperanza, Mercy:°

    Sails flashing to the wind like weapons,
    sharks following the moans the fever and the dying;
    horror the corposant° and compass rose.°

Middle Passage: 5
        voyage through death
                to life upon these shores.

    "10 April 1800—
    Blacks rebellious. Crew uneasy. Our linguist says
    their moaning is a prayer for death,   10
    ours and their own. Some try to starve themselves.
    Lost three this morning leaped with crazy laughter
    to the waiting sharks, sang as they went under."

Desire, Adventure, Tartar, Ann:°

    Standing to° America, bringing home   15
    black gold, black ivory, black seed.

        Deep in the festering hold thy father lies,
        of his bones New England pews are made,
        those are altar lights that were his eyes.

Jesus   Saviour   Pilot   Me   20
Over   Life's   Tempestuous   Sea°

Title**Middle Passage** The transatlantic transport of slaves to the Americas was referred to as the middle part of a triangular trading route. Having delivered slaves from Africa, captains would use the money from the sale of slaves to buy sugar, tobacco, and rum to be sold in England and Europe. With the money from the sale of the commodities, they would return to Africa. 1,14ship names 4**corposant** holy body of Jesus crucified, a Portuguese and obsolete Spanish word (from Latin) for St. Elmo's fire, visible electrical discharges traveling between high points such as ship masts during thunderstorms **compass rose** the card at the bottom of a compass against which the needle swings indicating the direction of travel 15**Standing to** sailing toward 20–21**Jesus . . . Sea** a Christian hymn composed by Edward Hopper (1816–88) and John E. Gould (1822–75)

We pray that Thou wilt grant, O Lord,
safe passage to our vessels bringing
heathen souls unto Thy chastening.

25 Jesus Saviour

     "8 bells. I cannot sleep, for I am sick
     with fear, but writing eases fear a little
     since still my eyes can see these words take shape
     upon the page & so I write, as one
30   would turn to exorcism. 4 days scudding,°
     but now the sea is calm again. Misfortune
     follows in our wake like sharks (our grinning
     tutelary gods°). Which one of us
     has killed an albatross?° A plague among
35   our blacks—Ophthalmia:° blindness—& we
     have jettisoned the blind to no avail.
     It spreads, the terrifying sickness spreads.
     Its claws have scratched sight from the Capt.'s eyes
     & there is blindness in the fo'c'sle°
40   & we must sail 3 weeks before we come
     to port."

         What port awaits us, Davy Jones°
         or home? I've heard of slavers drifting, drifting,
         playthings of wind and storm and chance, their crews
45   *gone blind, the jungle hatred*
         crawling up on deck.

Thou Who Walked on Galilee

     "Deponent° further sayeth *The Bella J*
     left the Guinea Coast
50   with cargo of five hundred blacks and odd
     for the barracoons° of Florida:

     "That there was hardly room 'tween-decks for half
     the sweltering cattle stowed spoon-fashion there;
     that some went mad of thirst and tore their flesh
55   and sucked the blood:

     "That Crew and Captain lusted with the comeliest
     of the savage girls kept naked in the cabins;
     that there was one they called The Guinea Rose
     and they cast lots and fought to lie with her:

---

³⁰**scudding** running before a gale   ³³**tutelary gods** deities taking the function of
guardians   ³³⁻³⁴**Which . . . albatross?** In sea lore, it is bad luck to kill an albatross.
³⁵**Ophthalmia** contagious inflammation of the eye   ³⁹**fo'c'sle** phonetic spelling of
forecastle; the forward part of a ship where the crew is lodged   ⁴²**Davy Jones** the
bottom of the sea personified   ⁴⁸**Deponent** a person who gives evidence in a legal case
⁵¹**barracoons** enclosures or barracks for confining slaves or convicts

"That when the Bo's'n° piped all hands,° the flames　　　　60
spreading from starboard already were beyond
control, the negroes howling and their chains
entangled with the flames:

"That the burning blacks could not be reached,
that the Crew abandoned ship,　　　　65
leaving their shrieking negresses behind,
that the Captain perished drunken with the wenches:

"Further Deponent sayeth not."

Pilot Oh Pilot Me

2

Aye, lad, and I have seen those factories,　　　　70
Gambia,° Rio Pongo,° Calabar;°
have watched the artful mongos° baiting traps
of war wherein the victor and the vanquished

Were caught as prizes for our barracoons.
Have seen the nigger kings whose vanity　　　　75
and greed turned wild black hides of Fellatah,°
Mandingo,° Ibo,° Kru° to gold for us.

And there was one—King Anthracite° we named him—
fetish face beneath French parasols
of brass and orange velvet, impudent mouth　　　　80
whose cups were carven skulls of enemies:

He'd honor us with drum and feast and conjo°
and palm-oil glistening wenches deft in love,
and for tin crowns that shone with paste,
red calico and German-silver trinkets　　　　85

Would have the drums talk war and send
his warriors to burn the sleeping villages
and kill the sick and old and lead the young
in coffles° to our factories.

Twenty years a trader, twenty years,　　　　90
for there was wealth aplenty to be harvested
from those black fields, and I'd be trading still
but for the fevers melting down my bones.

3

Shuttles in the rocking loom of history,
the dark ships move, the dark ships move,　　　　95

⁶⁰**Bo's'n** phonetic spelling of boatswain, officer on a ship having charge of hull maintenance
piped all hands used a musical pipe to summon all sailors　　⁷¹**Gambia** a country in West
Africa　　**Rio Pongo** river in West Africa　　**Calabar** Nigerian port city　　⁷²**mongos** slave-
traders　　⁷⁶**Fellatah** a Muslim people　　⁷⁷**Mandingo** a West African people　　**Ibo** a people
of southwestern Nigeria　　**Kru** Liberian tribesmen　　⁷⁸**Anthracite** a hard coal of high
luster　　⁸²**conjo** magic　　⁸⁹**coffles** a line of slaves or animals fastened together

their bright ironical names
like jests of kindness on a murderer's mouth;
plough through thrashing glister toward
fata morgana's° lucent melting shore,
100   weave toward New World littorals° that are
mirage and myth and actual shore.

Voyage through death,

                 voyage whose chartings are unlove.

A charnel stench, effluvium of living death
105   spreads outward from the hold,
where the living and the dead, the horribly dying,
lie interlocked, lie foul with blood and excrement.

Deep in the festering hold thy father lies,
the corpse of mercy rots with him,
110   *rats eat love's rotten gelid eyes.*

But, oh, the living look at you
with human eyes whose suffering accuses you,
whose hatred reaches through the swill of dark
to strike you like a leper's claw.

115   *You cannot stare that hatred down*
or chain the fear that stalks the watches
and breathes on you its fetid scorching breath;
cannot kill the deep immortal human wish,
the timeless will.

120   "But for the storm that flung up barriers
of wind and wave, *The Amistad*,° señores,
would have reached the port of Principe° in two,
three days at most; but for the storm we should
have been prepared for what befell.
125   Swift as the puma's leap it came. There was
that interval of moonless calm filled only
with the water's and the rigging's usual sounds,
then sudden movement, blows and snarling cries
and they had fallen on us with machete
130   and marlinspike.° It was as though the very
air, the night itself were striking us.
Exhausted by the rigors of the storm,

---

⁹⁹**fata morgana** mirage (literally, Morgan le Fay: half-sister of the mythical King Arthur,
she had magical powers)   ¹⁰⁰**littorals** coastal regions   ¹²¹***The Amistad*** a Spanish slave
ship seized by the slaves. When it reached American waters, it was captured by the
American Navy. The owners of the ship brought suit to have the ship and the Africans
found aboard it returned to them as their property. The case went to the Supreme Court
in 1841.   ¹²²**Principe** an island off the coast of western Africa in the Gulf of Guinea
¹³⁰**marlinspike** pointed tool used to separate the strands of rope or wire

we were no match for them. Our men went down
before the murderous Africans. Our loyal
Celestino ran from below with gun   135
and lantern and I saw, before the cane-
knife's wounding flash, Cinquez,°
that surly brute who calls himself a prince,
directing, urging on the ghastly work.
He hacked the poor mulatto down, and then   140
he turned on me. The decks were slippery
when daylight finally came. It sickens me
to think of what I saw, of how these apes
threw overboard the butchered bodies of
our men, true Christians all, like so much jetsam.   145
Enough, enough. The rest is quickly told:
Cinquez was forced to spare the two of us
you see to steer the ship to Africa,
and we like phantoms doomed to rove the sea
voyaged east by day and west by night,   150
deceiving them, hoping for rescue,
prisoners on our own vessel, till
at length we drifted to the shores of this
your land, America, where we were freed
from our unspeakable misery. Now we   155
demand, good sirs, the extradition of
Cinquez and his accomplices to La
Havana. And it distresses us to know
there are so many here who seem inclined
to justify the mutiny of these blacks.   160
We find it paradoxical indeed
that you whose wealth, whose tree of liberty
are rooted in the labor of your slaves
should suffer the august John Quincy Adams°
to speak with so much passion of the right   165
of chattel slaves to kill their lawful masters
and with his Roman rhetoric weave a hero's
garland for Cinquez. I tell you that
we are determined to return to Cuba
with our slaves and there see justice done. Cinquez—   170
or let us say 'the Prince'—Cinquez shall die."

---

[137]**Cinquez** an African rice farmer (his African name was Sengbeh Pieh) who became the leader of the slaves. After the trial, he returned to Africa, living in Sierra Leone until he died in 1879.   [164]**John Quincy Adams** Former U.S. president John Quincy Adams was part of the legal team that successfully argued before the Supreme Court that the "self-emancipated" slaves were now free.

The deep immortal human wish,
the timeless will:

> Cinquez its deathless primaveral image,
175   life that transfigures many lives.

Voyage through death
          to life upon these shores.   [1962]

1. The poem consists of a number of voices speaking from different points of view with no clear transitions between them. Characterize the different speakers and their subjects. What are the effects of constructing the poem through these points of view? Are there any elements that provide unity for the collection of speakers?

2. What are the effects of the references to Christianity in the poem?

3. "Middle Passage" contains several allusions to Ariel's song to Ferdinand in *The Tempest* when Ferdinand thinks his father has been drowned. In the play, the song is an image of transformation:

> Four fathom five thy father lies.
> Of his bones are coral made.
> Those were pearls that were his eyes.
> Nothing of him that doth fade
> But doth suffer a sea change
> Into something rich and strange.
> Sea nymphs hourly ring his knell.   (1.2.398–404)

What are the effects of the transformation of the song in Hayden's poem?

4. What is the effect of putting the story of the *Amistad* mutiny in the last section of the poem?

John Quincy Adams

John Quincy Adams (1767–1848), *son of Abigail Adams and John Adams, second president of the United States, himself became the sixth. Having witnessed the Revolution as a boy, he accompanied his father on diplomatic missions to Europe, acquiring skill in languages and diplomacy along the way and finishing his education at Harvard. As Secretary of State, he helped to define America's northern border with Canada, to secure from Spain all the territory east of the Mississippi, and to acquire Florida. He also shaped the Monroe Doctrine, which declared U.S. opposition to European influence in the Americas. After his term as president, he was elected to the House of Representatives, where he served for the rest of his life despite those who thought it too lowly a position for an ex-president. As a congressman, he opposed the spread of slavery to new states and territories. During this time, the Spanish ship* Amistad, *which had been taken over by the Africans it was bringing to America to sell as slaves, was taken in the waters off Long Island. When President Van Buren's government sought to return the ship and its "cargo" to its Spanish owners, Adams defended the freedom of the Africans in a case tried before the Supreme Court. What follows is an excerpt from his argument in the case.*

From *Argument of John Quincy Adams, before the Supreme Court of the United States, in the case of the United States, Appellants, vs. Cinque, and others, Africans Captured in the Schooner Amistad, by Lieut. Gedney, Delivered on the 24ᵗʰ of February and 1ˢᵗ of March, 1841**

The charge I make against the present Executive administration is that in all their proceedings relating to these unfortunate men, instead of that *Justice*, which they were bound not less than this honorable Court itself to observe, they have substituted *Sympathy!*—sympathy with one of the parties in this conflict of justice, and *Antipathy* to the other. Sympathy with the white, antipathy to the black—and in proof of this charge I adduce the admission and avowal of the Secretary of State himself. In the letter of Mr. Forsyth° to the Spanish Minister d'Argaiz, of 13th of December, 1839, [Document H. R. N. S. 185,] defending the course of the administration against the reproaches utterly groundless, but not the less bitter of the Spanish Envoy, he says:

"The undersigned cannot conclude this communication without calling the attention of the Chevalier d'Argaiz to *the fact*, that with the single exception of the vexatious detention to which Messrs. Montes and Ruiz° have been subjected in consequence of the civil suit instituted against them, *all the proceedings in the matter, on the part both the Executive and Judicial branches of the government have had their foundation in the* ASSUMPTION *that these persons* ALONE *were the parties aggrieved; and that their claims to the surrender of the property was founded in fact and in justice.*" [pp. 29, 30.]

At the date of this letter, this statement of Mr. Forsyth was strictly true. All the proceedings of the government, Executive and Judicial, in this case had been founded on the *assumption* that the two Spanish slave-dealers were the *only* parties aggrieved—that all the right was on their side, and all the wrong on the side of their surviving self-emancipated victims. I ask your honors, was this JUSTICE? No. It was not so considered by Mr. Forsyth himself. It was *sympathy*, and he so calls it, for in the preceding page of the same letter referring to the proceedings of this Government from the very first intervention of Lieut. Gedney, he says:

"Messrs. Ruiz and Montes were first found near the coast of the United States, deprived of their property and of their freedom, suffering from *lawless violence* in their persons, and in imminent and constant danger of being deprived of their lives also. They were found in this distressing and perilous situation by

---

*Argument of John Quincy Adams Before the Supreme Court of the United States in the Case of the United States, Appellants, vs. Cinque, and others, Africans, Captured in the Schooner *Amistad*, by Lieut. Gedney, Delivered in the 24ᵗʰ of February and 1ˢᵗ of March, 1841 (New York: Negro Universities Press, 1969). Originally published in 1841, S.W. Benedict. Paragraph numbers in this selection do not reflect editorial deletions.

¹**Mr. Forsyth** John Forsyth was the Secretary of State during the Van Buren administration. He owned slaves in his home state of Georgia and had been minister to Spain from 1819 to 1823.   ²**Messrs. [Pedro] Montes and [José] Ruiz** the Spanish owners of the *Amistad*.

officers of the United States, who, moved towards them *by sympathetic feeling which subsequently became as it were national,* immediately rescued them from personal danger, restored them to freedom, secured *their oppressors* that they might abide the consequences of the acts of violence *perpetrated* upon them, and placed under the safeguard of the laws all the property which they claimed as their own, to remain in safety until the competent authority could examine their title to it, and pronounce upon the question of ownership agreeably to the provisions of the 9th article of the treaty of 1795."

5   This sympathy with Spanish slave-traders is declared by the Secretary to have been first felt by Lieutenant Gedney.° I hope this is not correctly represented. It is imputed to him and declared to have become in a manner national. The national sympathy with the slave-traders of the baracoons° is officially declared to have been the prime motive of action of the government: And this fact is given as an answer to all the claims, demands and reproaches of the Spanish minister! I cannot urge the same objection to this that was brought against the assertion in the libel—that it said the thing which is not—too unfortunately it was so, as he said. The sympathy of the Executive government, and as it were of the nation, in favor of the slave-traders, and against these poor, unfortunate, helpless, tongueless, defenceless Africans, was the cause and foundation and motive of all these proceedings, and has brought this case up for trial before your honors.

I do not wish to blame the first sympathies of Lieut. Gedney, nor the first action of the District and Circuit Courts. The seizure of the vessel, with the arrest and examination of the Africans, was intended for inquiry, and to lead to an investigation of the rights of all parties. This investigation has ultimated in the decision of the District Court, confirmed by the Circuit Court, which it is now the demand of the Executive should be reversed by this Court. The District Court has exercised its jurisdiction over the parties in interest, and has found that the right was with the other party, that the decisions of JUSTICE were not in accordance with the impulses of sympathy, and that consequently the sympathy was wrong before. And consequently it now appears that everything which has flowed from this mistaken or misapplied sympathy, was wrong from the beginning.

For I inquire by what *right,* all this sympathy, from Lieut. Gedney to the Secretary of State, and from the Secretary of State, *as it were,* to the nation, was extended to the two Spaniards from Cuba exclusively, and utterly denied to the fifty-two victims of *their* lawless violence? By what *right* was it denied to the men who had restored themselves to freedom, and secured their oppressors to abide the consequences of the acts of violence perpetrated by them, and why was it extended to the perpetrators of those acts of violence themselves? When the Amistad first came within the territorial jurisdiction of the United States, acts of violence had passed between the two parties, the Spaniards and Africans on board of her, but on which side these acts were *lawless,* on which side were the

---

[5]**Lieutenant Gedney** the officer of the U.S.S. *Washington,* the ship that seized the *Amistad* in the waters off Long Island   **baracoons** enclosures or barracks for confining slaves or convicts

oppressors, was a question of right and wrong, for the settlement of which, if the government and people of the United States interfered at all, they were bound in duty to extend their sympathy to them all; and if they intervened at all *between* them, the duty incumbent upon this intervention was not of favor, but of impartiality—not of sympathy, but of JUSTICE, dispensing to every individual *his own right.*

Thus the Secretary of State himself declares that the motive for all the proceedings of the government of the United States, until that time, had been governed by sympathetic feeling towards one of the parties, and by the *assumption* that all the right was on one side and all the wrong on the other. It was the motive of Lieut. Gedney: the same influence had prevailed even in the judicial proceedings until then: the very language of the Secretary of State in this letter breathes the same spirit as animating the executive administration, and has continued to govern all its proceedings on this subject to the present day. It is but too true that the same spirit of sympathy and antipathy has nearly pervaded the whole nation, and it is against them that I am in duty bound to call upon this Court to restrain itself in the sacred name of JUSTICE.

One of the Judges who presided in some of the preceding trials, is said to have called this an anomalous case. It is indeed anomalous, and I know of no law, but one which I am not at liberty to argue before this Court, no law, statute or constitution, no code, no treaty, applicable to the proceedings of the Executive or the Judiciary, except that law, (pointing to the copy of the Declaration of Independence, hanging against one of the pillars of the court room,) that law, two copies of which are ever before the eyes of your Honors. I know of no other law that reaches the case of my clients, but the law of Nature and of Nature's God on which our fathers placed our own national existence. The circumstances are so peculiar, that no code or treaty has provided for such a case. That law, in its application to my clients, I trust will be the law on which the case will be decided by this Court.

In the sequel to the diplomatic correspondence between the Secretary of State and the Spanish minister Argaiz, relating to the case of the Amistad, recently communicated by the President of the United States to the Senate, [Doc. 179. 12 Feb. 1841,] the minister refers with great apparent satisfaction to certain resolutions of the Senate, adopted at the instance of Mr. Calhoun,° on the 15th of April, 1840, as follows:

1. "*Resolved*—That a ship or vessel on the high seas, in time of peace, engaged in a lawful voyage, is according to the laws of nations under the exclusive jurisdiction of the state to which her flag belongs as much as if constituting a part of its own domain."

[10]**Mr. Calhoun** John Caldwell Calhoun (1782–1850), currently serving as senator from South Carolina (at other times congressman, secretary of war, vice president, secretary of state, and again senator). He had played a role in the administration of Adams when he was president, but was on the ticket as vice president in Andrew Jackson's successful campaign, depriving Adams of a second term. Although he did not live to see the Civil War, he was a major player in the conflict between the North and South, taking an active part in the intellectual and political support of slavery.

2. *"Resolved*—That if such ship or vessel should be forced, by stress of weather, or other unavoidable cause into the port, and under the jurisdiction of a friendly power, she and her cargo, and persons on board, with their property, and all the rights belonging to their personal relations, as established by the laws of the state to which they belong, would be placed under the protection which the laws of nations extend to the unfortunate under such circumstances."

Without entering into any discussion as to the correctness of these principles, let us admit them to be true to their fullest extent, and what is their application to the case of the Amistad? If the first of the resolutions declares a sound principle of national law, neither Lieut. Gedney, nor Lieut. Meade, nor any officer of the brig Washington had the shadow of a right even to set foot on board of the Amistad. According to the second resolution, the Africans in possession of the vessel were entitled to all the kindness and good offices due from a humane and Christian nation to the unfortunate; and if the Spaniards were entitled to the same, it was by the territorial right and jurisdiction of the State of New York and of the Union, only to the extent of liberating their persons from imprisonment. Chevalier d'Argaiz, therefore, totally misapprehends the application of the principles asserted in these resolutions of the Senate, as indeed Mr. Forsyth appears by his answer to this letter of the Chevalier to be fully aware. From the decisiveness with which on this solitary occasion he meets the pretensions of the Spanish Envoy, a fair inference may be drawn that the Secretary himself perceived that the Senatorial resolutions, instead of favoring the cause of Montes and Ruiz, have a bearing point blank against them.

The Africans were in possession, and had the presumptive right of ownership; they were in peace with the United States; the Courts have decided, and truly, that they were not pirates; they were on a voyage to their native homes—their *dulces Argos;* they had acquired the right and so far as their knowledge extended they had the power of prosecuting the voyage; the ship was theirs, and being in immediate communication with the shore, was in the territory of the State of New York; or, if not, at least half the number were actually on the soil of New York, and entitled to all the provisions of the law of nations, and the protection and comfort which the laws of that State secure to every human being within its limits.

15   In this situation Lieut. Gedney, without any charge or authority from his government, without warrant of law, by force of fire arms, seizes and disarms them, then being in the peace of that Commonwealth and of the United States, drives them on board the vessel, seizes the vessel and transfers it against the will of its possessors to another State. I ask in the name of justice, by what law was this done? Even admitting that it had been a case of actual piracy, which your courts have properly found it was not, there are questions arising here of the deepest interest to the liberties of the people of this Union, and especially of the State of New York. Have the officers of the U.S. Navy a right to seize men by force, on the territory of New York, to fire at them, to overpower them, to disarm them, to put them on board of a vessel and carry them by force and against their will to another State, without warrant or form of law? I am not arraigning Lieut. Gedney, but I ask this Court, in the name of justice, to settle it in their minds, by what law it was done, and how far the principle it embraces is to be carried.

The whole of my argument to show that the appeal should be dismissed, is founded on an averment that the proceedings on the part of the United States are all wrongful from the beginning. The first act, of seizing the vessel, and these men, by an officer of the navy, was a wrong. The forcible arrest of these men, or a part of them, on the soil of New York, was a wrong. After the vessel was brought into the jurisdiction of the District Court of Connecticut, the men were first seized and imprisoned under a criminal process for murder and piracy on the high seas. Then they were libelled by Lieut. Gedney, as property, and salvage claimed on them, and under that process were taken into the custody of the marshal as property. Then they were claimed by Ruiz and Montes and again taken into custody by the court. The District Attorney of Connecticut wrote to the Secretary of State, September 5th, giving him an account of the matter, stating that "the blacks are indicted for the murder of the captain and mate," and "are now in jail at New Haven;" that "the next term of our Circuit Court sits on the 17th instant, at which time I suppose,"—that is in italics in the printed document—"I *suppose* it will be my duty to bring them to trial, unless they are in some other way disposed of." This is the first intimation of the District Attorney; it is easy to understand in what "other way" he wished them disposed of. And he closes by saying—"should you have any instructions to give on the subject, I should like to receive them as soon as may be."

On the 9th of September, he writes again that he has examined the law, which has brought him fully to the conclusion that the Courts of the United States cannot take cognizance of any offence these people may have committed, as it was done on board a vessel belonging to a foreign state. And then he says,

"I would respectfully inquire, sir, whether there are no treaty stipulations with the Government of Spain that would authorize our Government to deliver them up to the Spanish authorities; and if so, whether it could be done before our court sits?" . . .

M. Calderon de la Barca then refers to several treaty stipulations in support of his demand, and particularly the 8th, 9th, and 10th articles of the treaty of 1795, continued in force by the treaty of 1819.

"ART. 8. In case the subjects and inhabitants of either party, with their ship- 20
ping, whether public and of war, or private and of merchants, be forced, through stress of weather, pursuit of pirates or enemies, or any other urgent necessity, for seeking of shelter and harbor, to retreat and enter into any of the rivers, bays, roads, or ports, belonging to the other party, they shall be received and treated with all humanity, and enjoy all favor, protection, and help; and they shall be permitted to refresh and provide themselves, at reasonable rates, with victuals and all things needful for the subsistence of their persons, or reparation of their ships, and prosecution of their voyage; and they shall noways be hindered from returning out of the said ports or roads, but may remove and depart when and whither they please, without any let or hindrance."

This is a provision for vessels with their owners, driven into port by distress. Who was the Spanish owner here with his ship? There was none. I say the Africans were here *with their ship*. If you say the original owner is referred to, in whose name the ship's register was given, he was dead, he was not on board, and could not claim the benefit of this article. The vessel either belonged to the Africans, in whose possession it was found, and who certainly had what is everywhere the first evidence of property, or there was no person to whom this article could apply, and it was not *casus fœderis.*° The truth is, this article was not intended to apply to such a case as this, but to the common case, in regard to which it has doubtless been carried into execution hundreds of times, in meeting the common disasters of maritime life.

The Africans, who certainly had the *prima facie* title to the property, did not bring the vessel into our waters themselves, but were brought here against their will, by the two Spaniards, by stratagem and deception. Now, if this court should consider, as the courts below have done, that the original voyage from Lomboko, in Africa, was continued by the Spaniards in the Amistad, and that pursuing that voyage was a violation of the laws of the United States, then the Spaniards are responsible for that offence. The deed begun in Africa was not consummated according to its original intention, until the negroes were landed at their port of final destination in Porto Principe. The clandestine landing in Havana, the unlawful sale in the barracoons, the shipment on board the Amistad, were all parts of the original transaction. And it was in pursuit of that original unlawful intent that the Spaniards brought the vessel by stratagem into a port of the United States. Does the treaty apply to such voyages? Suppose the owner had been on board, and his voyage lawful, what does the treaty secure to him? Why, that he might repair his ship, and purchase refreshments, and continue his voyage. Ruiz and Montes could not continue the voyage. But, suppose the article applicable, and what were the United States to do? They must place those on board the ship in the situation they were in when taken, that is, the Africans in possession, with the two Spaniards as their prisoners, or their slaves, as the case might be; the negroes as masters of the ship, to continue *their* voyage, which on their part was certainly lawful.

If any part of the article was applicable to the case it was in favor of the Africans. They were in distress, and were brought into our waters by their enemies, by those who sought, and who are still seeking, to reduce them from freedom to slavery, as a reward for having spared their lives in the fight. If the good offices of the government are to be rendered to the proprietors of shipping in distress, they are due to the Africans only, and the United States are now bound to restore the ship to the Africans, and replace the Spaniards on board as prisoners. But the article is not applicable at all. It is not a *casus fœderis.* The parties to the treaty never could have had any such case in view. The transaction on board of the vessel after leaving Havana entirely changed the circumstances of the parties, and conferred rights on my most unfortunate clients, which cannot but be regarded by this honorable court.

Next we have article 9:

25   "ART. 9. All ships and merchandise, of what nature soever, which shall be rescued out of the hands of any pirates or robbers on the high seas, shall be brought into some port of either state, and shall be delivered to the custody of

----

[21]*casus fœderis* a set of circumstances meant to be covered by a treaty

the officers of that port, in order to be taken care of, and restored entire to the true proprietor, as soon as due and sufficient proof shall be made concerning the property thereof."

Was this ship rescued out of the hands of pirates and robbers? Is this Court competent to declare it? The Courts below have decided that they have no authority to try, criminally, what happened on board the vessel. They have then no right to regard those who forcibly took possession of the vessel as pirates and robbers. If the sympathies of Lieutenant Gedney, which the Secretary of State says had become national, had been felt for all the parties, in due proportion to their sufferings and their deserts, who were the pirates and robbers? Were they the Africans? When they were brought from Lomboko, in the Tecora, against the laws of Spain, against the laws of the United States, and against the law of nations, so far as the United States, and Spain, and Great Britain, are concerned, who were the robbers and pirates? And when the same voyage, in fact, was continued in the Amistad, and the Africans were in a perishing condition in the hands of Ruiz, dropping dead from day to day under his treatment, were *they* the pirates and robbers? This honorable Court will observe from the record that there were fifty-four Africans who left the Havana. Ruiz says in his libel that nine had died before they reached our shores. The marshal's return shows that they were dying day after day from the effects of their sufferings. One died before the Court sat at New London. Three more died before the return was made to the Court at Hartford—only seventeen days—and three more between that and November. Sixteen fell victims before November, and from that time not one has died. Think only of the relief and benefit of being restored to the absolute wants of human nature. Although placed in a condition which, if applied to forty citizens of the United States, we should call cruel, shut up eighteen months in a prison, and enjoying only the tenderness which our laws provide for the worst of criminals, so great is the improvement of their condition from what it was in the hands of Ruiz, that they have perfectly recovered their health, and not one has died; when, before that time, they were perishing from hour to hour.

At the great day of accounts, may it please the Court, who is to be responsible for those sixteen souls that died? Ruiz claims those sixteen as his property, as merchandise. How many of them, at his last hour, will pass before him and say, "Let me sit heavy on thy soul to-morrow!"

Who, then, are the tyrants and oppressors against whom our laws are invoked? Who are the innocent sufferers, for whom we are called upon to protect this ship against enemies and robbers? Certainly not Ruiz and Montes.

But, independently of this consideration, the article cannot apply to slaves. It says ships and merchandise. Is that language applicable to human beings? Will this Court so affirm? It says they shall be restored entire. Is it a treaty between cannibal nations, that a stipulation is needed for the restoration of merchandise entire, to prevent parties from cutting off the legs and arms of human beings before they are delivered up? The very word entire in the stipulation is of itself a sufficient exclusion of human beings from the scope of the article. But if it was intended to embrace human beings, the article would have included a provision for their subsistence until they are restored, and an indemnification for their maintenance to the officers who are charged with the execution of the stipulation. And there is perhaps needed a provision with regard to the institutions of the free states, to prevent a difficulty in keeping human beings in the custom house, without having them liable to the operation of the local law, the habeas corpus, and the rights of freedom.

30   But with regard to article 9, I will speak of my own knowledge, for it happened that on the renewal of the treaty in 1819, the whole of the negotiations with the then minister of Spain passed through my hands, and I am certain that neither of us ever entertained an idea that this word *merchandise* was to apply to human beings. . . .

The argument with much hesitation concludes that the African slave trade is *not* contrary to the Law of Nations—but it begins with admitting, also with hesitation, that it *is* contrary to the law of nature. He says—"That it *is* contrary to the law of nature will *scarcely* be denied. That every man has a natural right to the fruits of his own labor, is *generally* admitted; and that no other person can rightfully deprive him of those fruits, and appropriate them against his will *seems* to be the necessary result of this admission.

"*Seems*, Madam—Nay it *is*—I know not *seems*."

Surely never was this exclamation more suitable than on this occasion; but the cautious and wary manner of stating the moral principle, proclaimed in the Declaration of Independence, as *self-evident truth*, is because the argument is obliged to encounter it with matter of fact. To the *moral principle* the Chief Justice opposes *general usage*—fact against right. "From the earliest times war has existed, and war confers rights in which all have acquiesced. Among the most enlightened nations of antiquity, one of these was, that the victor might enslave the vanquished—

"Slavery, then, has its origin in force; but as the world has agreed that it is a legitimate result of force, the state of things which is thus produced by general consent *cannot be pronounced unlawful.*

35   "Throughout Christendom, this *harsh* rule has been exploded, and war is no longer considered as giving a right to enslave captives. But this triumph of humanity has not been universal. The parties to the modern law of nations do not propagate their principles by force; and Africa has not yet adopted them. Throughout the whole extent of that immense continent, so far as we know its history, it is still the law of nations that prisoners are slaves. *Can those who have themselves renounced this law, be permitted to participate in its effects, by purchasing the beings who are its victims?*

"Whatever might be the answer of a *moralist* to this question, a jurist must search for its legal solution in those principles of action which are sanctioned by the usages, the national acts, and the general assent, of that portion of the world of which he considers himself a part, and to whose law the appeal is made. If we resort to this standard as the test of international law, the question as has already been observed, is decided in favor of the legality of the trade. Both Europe and America embarked in it; and for nearly two centuries, it was carried on without opposition and without censure."

With all possible reverence for the memory of Chief Justice Marshall, and with all *due* respect for his argument in this case, I must here be permitted to say, that here begins its fallacy. He admits that throughout all Christendom, the victors in war have no right to enslave the vanquished. As between Christian nations therefore, slavery as a legitimate consequence of war is totally abolished. So totally abolished that slaves captured in war, cannot be held by the captors, as slaves; but must be emancipated, or exchanged as prisoners of war.

But Africa, says the Chief Justice, still enslaves her captives in war, and for nearly two centuries, Europe and America purchased African slaves without "opposition and without censure." This may prove that the African slave-trade was *heretofore*, not contrary to the international law of Europe and of Christendom. But how was it, when the Antelope was in judgment before Christian Admiralty Courts in 1820–21, and '25? How is it now?

For nearly forty years it has been prohibited by the laws of the United States, as a crime of enormous magnitude—and when the Antelope was tried by their judicial Courts, it was proclaimed piracy, punishable with death—

It was piracy by the laws of Great Britain.   40

By the 10th Article of the Treaty of Ghent, concluded on the 24th of December, 1814, between Great Britain and the United States, the traffic in slaves had been declared irreconcilable with the principles of humanity and justice, and both parties did thereby stipulate and contract to use their best endeavors to promote *its entire abolition.* . . .

And such is the history of the case of the Antelope in the judicial tribunals of the United States. That vessel, commanded by a citizen of the United States, was taken in the very act of smuggling 258 Africans into the United States for sale as slaves, and by the plain, unquestionable letter of the 4th section of an act of Congress of 20th April, 1818, was forfeited; while, by an act in addition to the acts prohibiting the slave-trade, of 3d March, 1819, every African thus imported in the Antelope was made free,—subject only to safe keeping, support, and removal beyond the limits of the United States, by direction of their President.

After seven years of litigation in the Courts of the United States, and, of course, of captivity to nearly all of these Africans who survived the operation; after decrees of the District Court, reversed by the Circuit Court, and three successive annual reversals by the Supreme Court of the decrees of the Circuit Court; what was the *result* of this *most troublesome charge?*

The vessel was restored to certain Spanish slave-traders in the island of Cuba. Of the Africans, about fifty had perished by the benignity of their treatment in this land of liberty, during its suspended animation as to them; sixteen, drawn *by lot* from the whole number, (by the merciful dispensation of the Circuit Court, under the arbitrary enlargement of the tender mercies of the District Judge, which had limited the number to *seven*,)—sixteen had drawn the prize of *liberty*, to which the whole number were entitled by the letter of the law; and, of the remainder, THIRTY-NINE, upon evidence inadmissible upon the most trifling question of property in any court of justice, were, under *the very peculiar circumstances of the case*, surrendered! delivered up to the Spanish vice-consul—AS SLAVES! To the rest was at last extended the benefit of the laws which had foreordained their emancipation. They were delivered over to safe keeping, support, and transportation, as freemen, beyond the limits of the United States, by the Chief Magistrate of the Union.

45   And now, by what possible process of reasoning can any decision of the Supreme Court of the United States in the case of the Antelope, be adduced as authorizing the President of the United States to seize and deliver up to the order of the Spanish minister the captives of the Amistad? Even the judge of the District Court in Georgia, who would have enslaved all the unfortunates of the Antelope but seven, distinctly admitted, that, if they had been bought in Africa *after* the prohibition of the trade by Spain, he would have liberated them all.

In delivering the opinion of the Supreme Court, on their first decree in the case of the Antelope, Chief Justice Marshall, after reviewing the decisions in the British Courts of Admiralty, says, "The principle common to these cases is, that the legality of the capture of a vessel engaged in the slave-trade depends on the law of the country to which the vessel belongs. If that law gives its sanction to the trade, restitution will be decreed: if that law prohibits it, the vessel and cargo will be condemned as good prize."

It was by the application of *this* principle, to the fact, that, at the time when the Antelope was taken by the Arraganta, the slave-trade, in which the Antelope was engaged, had not yet been made unlawful by Spain, that the Supreme Court affirmed so much of the decree of the Circuit Court as directed restitution to the Spanish claimant of the Africans found on board the Antelope when captured by the Arraganta.

But by the same *identical principle*, applied to the case of the Amistad, if, when captured by Lieutenant Gedney, she and her cargo had been in possession of the Spaniards, and the Africans in the condition of slaves, the vessel would have been condemned, and the slaves liberated, by the laws of the United States; because she was engaged in the slave-trade in violation of the laws of Spain. She was in possession of the Africans, self-emancipated, and not in the condition of slaves. *That*, surely, could not legalize the trade in which she had been engaged. By the principle asserted in the opinion of the Supreme Court, declared by Chief Justice Marshall, it would have saved the vessel, at once, from condemnation and from restitution, and would have relieved the Court from the necessity of restoring to the Africans their freedom. Thus the opinion of the Supreme Court, as declared by the Chief Justice, in the case of the Antelope, was a fact, an authority in point, against the surrender of the Amistad, and in favor of the liberation of the Africans taken in her, even if they had been, when taken, in the condition of slaves. How monstrous, then, is the claim upon the Courts of the United States to re-inslave them, as thralls to the Spaniards, Ruiz and Montes! or to transport them beyond the seas, at the demand of the Minister of Spain!

I said, when I began this plea, that my final reliance for success in this case was on this Court as a court of JUSTICE; and in the confidence this fact inspired, that, in the administration of justice, in a case of no less importance than the liberty and the life of a large number of persons, this Court would not decide but on a due consideration of all the rights, both natural and social, of *every one* of these individuals. I have endeavored to show that they are entitled to their liberty from this Court. I have avoided, purposely avoided, and this Court will do justice to the motive for which I have avoided, a recurrence to those first principles of liberty which might well have been invoked in the argument of this cause. I have shown that Ruiz and Montes, the only parties in interest here, for whose sole benefit this suit is carried on by the Government, were acting at the time in a way that is forbidden by the laws of Great Britain, of Spain, and of the United States, and that the mere signature of the Governor General of Cuba ought not to prevail over the ample evidence in the case that these negroes were free and had a right to assert their liberty. I have shown that the papers in question are absolutely null and insufficient as passports for persons, and still more invalid to convey or prove a title to property.

The review of the case of the Antelope, and my argument in behalf of the   50
captives of the Amistad, is closed.   [1841]

1. Sympathy is often thought of as a positive trait. What does Adams think is wrong with it here? Why does he quote the Secretary of State's letter? What is the tone of his response?
2. Why does Adams agree with a judge in the previous trial that the case of the *Amistad* is anomalous?
3. How does Adams answer the claims that Calhoun's Senate Resolution of April 14, 1840, and the treaty with Spain demand the return of the *Amistad* to Spain?
4. The situation of the *Amistad* was often compared to the case of another slave ship, the *Antelope,* which was eventually returned to the country of origin, also Spain. How does Adams use that case to support his own claim that the *Amistad* and its "merchandise" should not be returned to Spain?
5. When the Supreme Court ruled that the *Antelope* should be returned to Spain, one of the reasons given (Adams attributes it to Chief Justice Marshall) was that although Christian countries had agreed that victors in war should not enslave their captives, the practice still survived in Africa, so that it was legally acceptable to support Spain's claim to own the Africans on board the *Antelope,* who had been sold to the ship's owners by other Africans. How do the points of view in "Is Multiculturalism Bad for Women?" (see p. 869) reflect on this reasoning?
6. From your experience of legal trials, actual or fictional, can you detect anything in Adams's behavior in these passages that might have been unusual lawyerly behavior?

DANIEL BROWN

DANIEL BROWN *received his B.S. in Microbiology from the University of Massachusetts and his Ph.D. in Religion and Psychological Studies from the University of Chicago. He is Assistant Clinical Professor in Psychology, Harvard*

Medical School, teaches at the Simmons School of Social Work, and directs the Center for Integrative Psychotherapy. Among the books he has written are Hypnotherapy and Hypnoanalysis *(with E. Fromm),* Hypnosis and Behavioral Medicine, Creative Mastery in Hypnosis and Hypnoanalysis, *and (with A.W. Scheflin and D.C. Hammond) the award-winning* Memory, Trauma Treatment and the Law. *A sign of his continuing interest in the subject of the paper excerpted here is his presenting a workshop in 2003 for the Southern California Society of Clinical Hypnosis on the immune system and the mind.*

From Stress and Emotion: Implications for Illness Development and Wellness*

This chapter is about the relationship between affect and physical health. With the growing interest in body/mind therapies in medicine and behavioral medicine, this volume would be incomplete without some attempt to address health issues. Specifically, this chapter addresses the questions What is the relationship between affective development, illness development, and health maintenance? How does affective development contribute to physical wellness? and what constitutes optimal mental health or well-being?

Definition of Stress

The contribution of affect to illness development is less understood, but many studies have clearly demonstrated the relationship between stress and illness development. To clarify how the concept of stress is defined in research, first, stress is usually associated with an externally perceived situation. Whereas Freud defined an affect, specifically anxiety, as a "response to an internal danger" (Freud, 1926), stress usually refers to an external event or situation, for example, life change, daily hassles, environmental pollution, and social isolation. Second, stress refers more to the perception of stress than to the stressful situation per se. Not all people react to the same situation in the same way; what is stressful for one may not be stressful for another. What is and is not perceived as stressful depends largely too on the range and adequacy of coping resources available to the individual (Roskies and Lazarus, 1980) and on the extent to which the person perceives his or her control over the situation (Marlatt and Gordon, 1985). Third, stress is primarily a biological construct, not an affect construct. Selye's (1956) pioneering work on the "general adaptation [or stress] syndrome" defines stress in terms of gross biological effects, meaning in terms of observable tissue change, for example, an enlarged adrenal cortex or a shrunken

*Daniel Brown, "Stress and Emotion: Implications for Illness Development and Wellness," in Steven L. Ablon, Daniel Brown, Edward J. Khantzian, and John E. Mack, *Human Feelings: Explorations in Affect Development and Meaning* (Hillsdale, NJ: The Analytic Press, 1993): 281–301.

thalamus. The generally accepted understanding of the stress effects has been primarily either disregulation of the autonomic nervous system° (Cannon, 1923; Gellhorn, 1967) or disregulation of specific organ systems (Schwartz, 1977, 1979; Weiner, 1975). Thus, the relationship between stress, or affect for that matter, and illness development pertains primarily to biological consequences, not to subjective experience.

Stress and Illness Development

The earliest work on stress and illness development focused on life change stress (Holmes and Rahe, 1967). Significant changes in the established routines of daily life such as loss, marriage, birth, change in work status, change in residence, and financial change were associated with the increased probability of subsequent illness. Current research on stress has shifted the emphasis to an understanding of daily hassles such as misplacing or losing things, having too many phone calls to return, getting stuck in traffic, and having to fill out forms (Kanner et al., 1981). These minor stressors accumulate and contribute to physiological disregulation and the development of physical symptoms. Other researchers have focused on the environment as a source of stress. Extreme temperature change (especially exposure to cold); barometric and weather changes; and exposure to toxic substances, radiation, and certain toxic foodstuffs also are associated with illness. In the social environment, extremes of isolation and chronic loneliness on one hand and overcrowding and lack of solitude on the other can contribute to the development of illness. The well-known Alameda County study clearly demonstrates that those who lack social support are at high risk and those with healthy social support systems are more resistant to illness development (Berkman and Syme, 1979).

Mechanisms of Illness Development

Two mechanisms by which stress can affect human physiology and contribute to illness development are disregulation of the nervous autonomic system, which in turn is associated with a variety of psychophysiological conditions, such as headache, hypertension, and asthma, and disregulation of the immune system, which in turn is associated with the development of a variety of immune-related conditions, such as infections, cancer, allergy, and autoimmune disease.

Autonomic Disregulation and Psychophysiological Disorders

Chronic stress results in repeated reactivation of the autonomic nervous system   5
and, ultimately, in a condition of sustained sympathetic activation without

---

[2]**the autonomic nervous system** governs involuntary actions like the beating of the heart and peristalsis

intervening periods of rest. Chronic sympathetic° activation without habituation contributes to a variety of harmful physiological changes in which the neurons in the autonomic nervous system may become sensitized and thereby stress reactive with little external provocation. Thus, high levels of sympathetic activation may occur readily and frequently, even in the absence of clear-cut external stressors. In this sense, sympathetic activation becomes conditioned as part of a chronic stress-response cycle. Furthermore, such readiness to activation is associated with a cascade of biochemical substances, namely catecholamines and corticosteroids, which are released into the tissues of the body.

The autonomic nervous system mediates the activity of the vasomotor system, the striate musculature, and other physiological systems. Chronic disregulation of the autonomic nervous system can lead to long-term disregulation of vasomotor and striate muscle activation, which in turn can contribute to the development of a variety of psychophysiological conditions. Autonomic hyperactivity is associated with bronchospasm in certain individuals with stress-reactive asthma (Magonet, 1960; Mathe and Knapp, 1971). Disregulation of normal cardiovascular response patterns is critical to the development of essential hypertension (Brown and Fromm, 1987; Fahrion, 1980). Autonomic hyperactivity (Bruyn, 1980; Sargent, Walters, and Green, 1973) with associated vasomotor disregulation (Dalessio, 1980; Graham and Wolff, 1938; Marshall, 1978) and chronic disregulation of striate muscle activation (Bakal and Kaganov, 1977; Budzynski, et al., 1973; Philips, 1977) contribute to a psychobiological predisposition to headache (Bakal, 1982).

Immune Disregulation

The immune system functions to protect the body from invasion by external agents like bacteria and viruses and to preserve the molecular integrity of the body over and against aberrant cell formations like tumors and cancer. This "complex recognition system" (Besedovsky and Sorkin, 1981, p. 546) is composed of several categories of cells, a complex differentiation of labor between the cell types, and multiple regulatory processes: the humoral, or B-cell, system, which manufactures and secretes a variety of immunoglobulins or circulating antibodies that protect the body from infectious agents or antigens such as bacteria and viruses; the cell-mediated, or T-cell, system, which acts by "molecular touch" (Locke and Colligan, 1986, p. 58) on indigenous cells mistakenly transformed either by genetic mutation or by viral infection (Burnet, 1971); highly mobile natural killer (NK) cells, constituting the first line of defense, which search and destroy bacteria, viruses, and indigenous tumor and virus-infected cells when they first appear in the body and prior to involvement with B and T lymphocytes° (Herberman and Holden, 1979); and a system of larger cells, the monocyte-macrophage system, which engulf bacteria, virus-infected

---

[5]**sympathetic** The sympathetic nervous system is part of the autonomic nervous system.
[7]**B and T lymphocytes** white blood cells that are made in the bone marrow and circulate in the blood. They recognize and destroy harmful substances that enter the body. NK (natural killer) lymphocytes are specifically targeted to cancerous cells and cells infected with viruses.

tumor cells, and other antigens. The complex interactions between all of these systems function in the service of "immunological surveillance" to protect the organism from invasion by bacteria and viruses and from spontaneous muta- tions during reproduction of the body's own cells (Burnet, 1971).

The entire operation of the immune system is dependent on a complex biochemical signaling system consisting largely of neuropeptides (Pert, 1986; Toy, 1983). Biochemical messengers signal the general activation of the immune system in response to an antigen and also signal the specific activation and coor- dination of the B, T, and NK lymphocytes. Catecholamines (Crary et al., 1983), corticosteroids (Dennis and Mond, 1986), and certain opioid peptides (Shavit et al., 1984; Brown and Epps, 1985; Nair, Cilik, and Schwartz, 1986)—part of the stress response system—have the effect of suppressing immune functioning.

Stress is capable of affecting disregulation of the immune system. Research on animals has firmly established that a wide variety of acute and chronic stressors result in immunosuppression° and illness development (Monjan, 1981; Monjan and Collector, 1977; Riley, Fitzmaurice, and Spackman, 1981). In humans, a number of studies have documented the relationship between stress, coping ability, immune functioning, and illness development (Dohrenwald and Dohrenwald, 1974; Holmes and Rahe, 1967; Levy, 1982; Locke et al., 1984). Other studies have suggested that bereavement (Bartrup et al., 1977; Linn, Linn, and Jensen, 1982; Stoddard and Henry, 1985), depression (Schleifer et al., 1980), and trauma (burns, accidental injuries, and surgery) (Goodwin, Bromberg, and Staszak, 1981; Munster, 1976) can affect immune functioning, yet these studies have been received with some skepticism because of method- ological limitations (Stein, Miller, and Trestman, 1991).

Perhaps the most elegant research on the links between stress, immune functioning, and illness development has recently come from the laboratories of Kiecolt-Glaser and McClelland. Kiecolt-Glaser and associates studied the immune functioning of medical students throughout an academic year. Repeated measures of immune functioning such as NK activity, percentage of T cells, and helper-suppressor ratio were consistently lower around the time of academic examinations and higher during periods free from exams. When the population of medical students was further investigated along the dimensions of life change stress and social isolation, it became clear that immunosuppression around exams was greatest for the lonelier students and students who experi- enced life change stress (Kiecolt-Glaser, Garner, et al., 1984; Kiecolt-Glaser, Ricker, et al., 1984; Kiecolt-Glaser et al., 1986). In order to demonstrate the three-way association between stress, immunosuppression, and illness development, Kiecolt-Glaser examined the relationship between medical exam stress, loneliness, immune functioning, and illness incidence, such as incidence of upper respiratory infection and response to the Epstein-Barr virus and other herpesviruses in vitro (Glaser et al., 1985).

10

⁹**immunosuppression** In immunosuppression the immune system, which protects the body from harmful substances, functions at less than its full capacity.

In other studies, Kiecolt-Glaser and associates investigated the relationship between stress, immunosuppression, and tumor/cancer vulnerability. Tumor development results from genetic mutation, or alteration of the genetic material of the cell. Normal cells are equipped with an enzyme system that repairs faulty replicated DNA. Psychiatric inpatients were subdivided into high-stress and low-stress groups. The high-distress groups had significantly poorer ability to repair the DNA of lymphocytes exposed to irradiation. Because the ability to repair DNA and the efficiency of NK activity are both necessary to control carcinogenesis and immunosurveillance of tumor cells, respectively, the researchers' findings suggest the possible mechanisms by which tumor or cancer cells may develop and proliferate in the stressed individual (Kiecolt-Glaser, Glaser, et al., 1985; Kiecolt-Glaser, Stephens, et al., 1985).

McClelland and associates have shed light on the enduring personality factors associated with immune functioning (McClelland et al., 1980; McClelland and Jemmott, 1980). Most of their work has centered on the notion of the inhibited power motive. Exam stress in students was associated with increases in catecholamine levels and decreases in immunoglobulin (IgA) activity as expected, but only in the subgroup of students who manifested an inhibited power motive (Jemmott et al., 1983; McClelland, Ross, and Patel, 1985). Another study clarified the link between immune functioning and illness development. High stress in people with high inhibited power motive but not in others was associated with decreased IgA and a greater incidence of upper respiratory infections (McClelland, Alexander, and Marks, 1982).

Various diseases associated with the immune system occur when the regulation of the complex functions of the immune system is disturbed. One or another of the branches of the immune system may become dysfunctional (Solomon, Amkraut, and Kasper, 1974). According to Melnechuk (1986, personal communication), infections and cancer occur when immune functioning is hypoactive and therefore fails to recognize and destroy antigens. Allergies and autoimmune diseases occur when immune functioning is hyperactive. B-cell activity is not held in check by the suppressor T cells, and seemingly neutral targets are mistakenly recognized as antigens—external neutral stimuli (in the case of allergies), and internal normal cell populations (in the case of autoimmune disease). Figure 1 summarizes the various types of immune disregulation.

Antigen	Hyperactive Immune Functioning	Hypoactive Immune Functioning
endogenous	autoimmunity	cancer
exogenous	allergy	infection

FIGURE 1 *Classification of Diseases Associated with Disregulation of Immune Functioning. (Adapted with permission from Theodore Melnechuk, 1986, personal communication.)*

Affect and Illness Development

The contribution of affect to illness development is becoming increasingly clear. In the case of asthma, for example, emotional stress can precipitate asthmatic episodes. Discussion of unpleasant memories and situations can increase bronchospasm and wheezing (Faulkner, 1941; Stevenson and Ripley, 1952). Dekker and Groen (1956) selected stressful emotional stimuli from the personal history of each of their patients and introduced those stimuli to induce attacks. When certain emotions become associated with asthmatic episodes, distinguishing cause from effect can be difficult. Does the emotion cause the episode, or is the emotion a consequence of the episode? On one hand, more often than not, anxiety, depression, frustration, and anger are the results of having an asthma attack, rather than its cause (Purcell and Weiss, 1970). On the other hand, emotions constitute a powerful class of triggers, at least for some people in whom the experience of certain emotions—fear, anger, excitement—may directly activate the autonomic nervous system, which, in turn, may trigger the bronchospasm (Purcell and Weiss, 1970). Moreover, the expressions accompanying certain emotions are associated with radical changes in air flow, for example, holding one's breath, crying, laughing, and gasping. These emotional expressions can trigger asthma attacks by means of mechanical irritation (Gold, Kessler, and Yu, 1972).

With respect to other psychophysiological disorders, the inhibition of emotional expression has been associated with symptom development. Suppression of emotion, notably anger, can trigger headaches in a subgroup of headache-prone individuals (Fromm-Reichmann, 1937; Harrison, 1975). Vascular headaches have been defined in terms of regional vasomotor disfunction (Dalessio, 1980). Anger, and especially the intentional inhibition of the expression of anger, is associated with pervasive cardiovascular changes. Anger suppression, therefore, can precipitate a headache in an individual whose vasomotor system has become sensitized. . . .

References

Bakal, D. A. (1982), *The Psychobiology of Chronic Headache*. New York: Springer.
———— & Kaganov, J. A. (1977), Muscle contraction and migraine headache: Psychophysiologic comparison. *Headache,* 17:208–215.
Bartrop, R. W., Luckhurst, E. & Lazarus, L. (1977), Depressed lymphocyte function after bereavement. *Lancet,* 1:834–946.
Berkman, L. F. & Syme, S. L. (1979), Social networks, host resistance and morality. *Amer. J. Epidem.,* 109:186–204.
Besedovsky, H. O. & Sorkin, E. (1981), Immunologic-neuroendocrine circuits: Physiological approaches. In: *Psychoneuroimmunology,* ed. R. Adler. New York: Academic Press, pp. 545–574.
Brown, D. & Fromm, E. (1987), *Hypnosis and Behavioral Medicine*. Hillsdale, NJ: Lawrence Erlbaum Associates.
Brown, S. L. & Epps, D. E. (1985), Suppression of T lymphocyte chemotactic factor production by both the opioid peptides B-endorphin and met-emkaphalin. *J. Immun.,* 134:3384–3390.

Bruyn, G. W. (1980), The biochemistry of migraine. *Headache,* 20:235–256.

Budzynski, T. H., Stoyva, J. M., Adler, C. S. & Mullaney, D. J. (1973), EMG biofeedback and tension headache: A controlled outcome study. *Psychosom. Med.,* 35:484–496.

Burnet, F. M. (1971), Immunological surveillance in neoplasia. *Transplant Rev.,* 7:3–25.

Cannon, W. B. (1923), *Traumatic Shock.* New York: Appleton.

Crary, B., Hauser, S. L., Borysenko, M., Kutz, I., Hoban, C., Ault, K. A., Weiner, H. L. & Benson, H. (1983), Epinephrine-induced changes in the distribution of lymphocyte subsets in peripheral blood of humans. *J. Immun.,* 131:1178–1181.

Dalessio, D. J. (1980), *Wolff's Headache and Other Pain.* New York: Oxford University Press.

Dekker, E. & Groen, J. (1956), Reproducible psychogenic attacks of asthma. *J. Psychosom. Res.,* 1:58–67.

Dennis, G. J. & Mond, J. J. (1986), Corticosteroid-induced suppression of murine B cell immune response antigens. *J. Immun.,* 136:1600–1604.

Dohrenwend, B. S. & Dohrenwend, B. P., eds. (1974), *Stressful Life Events: Their Nature and Effects.* New York: Wiley.

Fahrion, S. L. (1980), Etiology and intervention in essential hypnotension: A biobehavioral approach. Unpublished manuscript, The Menninger Foundation.

Faulkner, W. B. (1941), Influence of suggestion of the size of the bronchial lumen. *Northwest Med.,* 40:367–368.

Freud, S. (1926), Inhibitions, symptoms and anxiety. *Standard Edition,* 20. London: Hogarth Press, pp. 87–172.

Fromm-Reichman, F. (1937), Contribution to the psychogenesis of migraine. *Psychoanal. Rev.,* 24:26–33.

Gellhorn, E. (1967), *Principles of Autonomic-Somatic Integrations: Physiological Basis and Psychological and Clinical Implications.* Minneapolis, MN: University of Minnesota Press.

Glaser, R., Thorn, B. E., Tarr, K. L., Kiecolt-Glaser, J. K. & D'Ambrosio, S. M. (1985), Effects of stress on methyltransferase synthesis: An important DNA repair enzyme. *Health Psychol.,* 4:403–412.

Gold, W. M., Kessler, G. F. & Yu, D. Y. C. (1972), Role of vagus nerve in experimental asthma in allergic dogs. *J. Applied Physiol.,* 33:719–725.

Goodwin, J. S., Bromberg, S. & Staszak, C. (1981), Effect of physical stress on sensitivity of lymphocytes to inhibition by prostaglandin E2. *J. Immun.,* 127:518–522.

Graham, J. R. & Wolff, H. G. (1938), Mechanism of migraine headache and action of ergotamine tartrate. *Arch. Neurolog. Psychiat.,* 39:737–763.

Harrison, R. H. (1975), Psychological testing in headache. *Headache,* 14:177–185.

Herberman, R. B. & Holden, H. T. (1979), Natural killer cells and antitumor effector cells. *J. Natl. Cancer Inst.,* 62:441–445.

Race and Ethnicity **931**

Holmes, T. H. & Rahe, R. H. (1967), The social readjustment rating scale. *J. Psychosom. Res.*, 11:213–218.

Jemmott, J. B., Borysenko, J. Z., Borysenko, M., McClelland, D. C., Chapman, R., Meyer, D. & Benson, H. (1983), Academic stress, power motivation, and decrease in salivary immunoglobulin A secretion rate. *Lancet*, 1:1400–1402.

Kanner, A. D., Coyne, J. C., Schaefer, C. & Lazarus, R. S. (1981), Comparison of two models of stress measurement: Daily hassles and uplifts versus major life events. *J. Nervous and Mental Disord.*, 125:181–201.

Kielcolt-Glaser, J. K., Garner, W., Speicher, C., Penn, G. M., Holliday, J. & Glaser, R. (1984), Psychosocial modifiers of immunocompetence in medical students. *Psychosom. Med.*, 46:7–17.

———— ———— Strain, E. C., Stout, J. C., Tarr, K. L., Holliday, J. E. & Speicher, C. E. (1986), Modulation of cellular immunity in medical students. *J. Behav. Med.*, 9:5–21.

———— Ricker, D., George, J., Messick, G., Speicher, C. E., Garner, W. & Glaser, R. (1984), Urinary cortisol levels, cellular immunocompetency and loneliness in psychiatric inpatients. *Psychosom. Med.*, 46:15–23.

———— Stephens, R. E., Lipetz, P. D., Speicher, C. E. & Glaser, R. (1985), Distress and DNA repair in human lymphocytes. *J. Behav. Med.*, 8:311–320.

Levy, S. M. (1982), Biobehavioral interventions in behavioral medicine: An overview. *Cancer*, 50:1928–1935.

Linn, B. S., Linn, M. W. & Jensen, J. (1982), Degree of depression and immune responsiveness. *Psychosom. Med.*, (Abstract), 44:128.

Locke, S. & Colligan, D. (1986), *The Healer Within: The New Medicine of Mind and Body*. New York: Dutton.

———— Kraus, L., Leserman, J., Hurst, M. W., Heisel, J. S. & Williams, M. (1984), Life change stress, psychiatric symptoms and natural killer cell activity. *Psychosom. Med.*, 46:441–453.

Magonet, A. P. (1960), Hypnosis in asthma. *Internat. J. Clin. Exper. Hypno.*, 8:121–127.

Marlatt, G. A. & Gordon, J. R. (1985), *Relapse prevention: Maintenance Strategies in the Treatment of Addictive Behaviors*. New York: Guilford.

Marshall, J. (1978), Cerebral blood flow in migraine without headache. *Research & Clinical Studies in Headache*, 6:1–5.

Mathe, A. A. & Knapp, P. H. (1971), Emotional and adrenal reactions to stress in bronchial asthma. *Psychosom. Med.*, 33:323–340.

McClelland, D. C., Alexander, C. & Marks, E. (1982), The need for power, stress, immune function, and illness among male prisoners. *J. Abnor. Psychol.*, 91:61–70.

———— & Jemmott, J. B. (1980), Power motivation, stress and physical illness. *J. Human Stress*, 6:6–15.

———— Floor, W., Davidson, R. J., & Saron, C. (1980), Stressed power motivation, sympathetic activation, immune function & illness. *J. Human Stress*, 6:11–19.

———— Ross, G. & Patel, V. (1985), The effect of an academic examination of salivary norepinephrine and immunoglobulin levels. *J. Human Stress*, 11:52–59.

Monjan, A. A. (1981), Stress and immunologic competence: Studies in animals. In: *Psychoneuroimmunology,* ed. R. Ader. New York: Academic Press, pp. 185–228.

——— & Collector, M. I. (1977), Stress-induced modulation of the immune response. *Science,* 196:307–308.

Munster, A. M. (1976), Post-traumatic immunosuppression is due to activation of suppressor T cells. *Lancet,* 1329–1330.

Nair, M. P. N., Cilik, J. M. & Schwartz, S. A. (1986). Histamine-induced suppressor factor inhibition of NK cells: reversal with Interferon and Interleukin 2. *J. Immunol.,* 136:2456–2462.

Pert, C. B. (1986), The wisdom of the receptors: Neuropeptides, the emotions, and bodymind. *Advances,* 3:8–16.

Philips, C. (1977), A psychological analysis of tension headache. In: *Contributions to Medical Psychology,* ed. S. Rachman. New York: Pergamon, pp. 91–113.

Purcell, K. & Weiss, J. H. (1970), Asthma. In: *Symptoms of Psychopathology,* ed. C. G. Costello. New York: Wiley, pp. 597–623.

Riley, V. M., Fitzmaurice, M. A. & Spackman, D. H. (1981), Psychoneuroimmunologic factors in neoplasis: Studies in animals. In: *Psychoneuroimmunology,* ed. R. Ader. New York: Academic Press, pp. 31–102.

Roskies, E. & Lazarus, R. S. (1980), Coping theory and the teaching of coping skills. In: *Behavioral Medicine: Changing Health Lifestyles,* eds. P. O. Davidson & S. M. Davidson. New York: Brunner/Mazel, pp. 38–69.

Sargent, J. D., Walters, E. D. & Green, E. F. (1973), Psychosomatic self-regulation of migraine headaches. *Seminars in Psychiat.,* 5:415–428.

Schleifer, S. J., Keller, S. E., McKegney, F. P. & Stein, M. (1980), Bereavement and lymphocyte function. Presented at the annual meeting of the American Psychiatric Association. San Francisco, CA.

Schwartz, G. E. (1977), Biofeedback and the self-management of disregulation disorders. In: *Behavioral Self-Management: Strategies, Techniques and Outcomes,* ed. R. B. Stuart. New York: Brunner/Mazel, pp. 49–70.

——— (1979), Disregulation and systems theory: A biobehavioral framework for biofeedback and behavioral medicine. In: *Biofeedback and Behavioral Medicine.* New York: Aldine, pp. 27–56.

Selye, H. (1956), *The Stress of Life.* New York: McGraw-Hill.

Shavit, Y., Lewis, J. W., Terman, G. W., Gale, R. P. & Liebeskind, J. C. (1984), Opioid peptides mediate the suppressive effect of stress on natural killer cell cytotoxicity. *Science,* 233:188–190.

Solomon, G. F. (1985), The emerging field of psychoneuroimmunology. *Advances,* 2:6–19.

——— Amkraut, A. A. & Kasper, P. (1974), Immunity, emotions and stress. *Annals Clin. Res.,* 6:313–322.

Stein, M., Miller, A. H. & Trestmen, R. L. (1991), Depression, the immune system, and health and illness. *Arch. Gen. Psychiat.,* 48:171–177.

Stevenson, I. & Ripley, H. S. (1952), Variations in respiration symptoms during changes in emotion. *Psychosom. Med.,* 14:476–490.

Stoddard, F. J. & Henry, J. P. (1985), Affectional bonding and the impact of bereavement. *Advances,* 2:19–28.

Toy, J. L. (1983), The interferons. *Clin. & Exper. Immunol.*, 54:1–13.
Weiner, H. (1975), Are "psychosomatic" diseases, diseases of regulation?
   Psychosom. Med., 37:289–291.   [1993]

1. The essay from which this passage is taken is a chapter in the book *Human Feelings: Explorations in Affect Development and Meaning.*[1] The chapter makes connections between stress and specific health problems like heart disease and cancer, and it ends with exploration of the question of what psychotherapists and educators can do to help people with psychological development that will contribute to their physical health. What is the purpose of these first sections of the chapter?
2. How do these sections proceed? What kind of evidence do they use?

[1]Steven L. Ablon, Daniel Brown, Edward J. Khantzian, and John E. Mack, *Human Feelings: Explorations in Affect Development and Meaning* (Hillsdale, NJ: The Analytic Press, 1993) 281–301.

RAYMOND L. COHN

RAYMOND L. COHN *earned his Ph.D. at the University of Oregon, where he has been a member of the faculty ever since in the field of Economic History and International Migration. His research is focused on the study of patterns of immigration in the United States in the nineteenth century. His latest research investigates the determinants of mortality on various types of ship.*

From *Maritime Mortality in the Eighteenth and Nineteenth Centuries: A Survey**

. . . The data show that the crew aboard the French slave ships died at rates substantially below those for the slaves they carried. An almost identical crew mortality rate probably occurred on the Dutch trade. The figures for Britain imply a somewhat higher mortality rate, but it should be noted that the short time periods covered by the British figures may make them unrepresentative. While the slave ship's crew died at rates below those for slaves, the crew aboard the slavers may have suffered at higher rates than crews on other trades. This finding makes sense as other crews would not spend time along the African coast, where crew mortality was so high. As no voyage length information is available for the other trades, however, this finding must remain uncertain.

   In summary, what have economists and historians discovered concerning the size of mortality among various groups at different periods of time? Four points deserve emphasis. First, the highest mortality rates were suffered by slaves. Except for a few cases that have not been well studied (such as the Chinese in the early 1860s) or that consist of a small sample (such as convicts shipped to

30

*Raymond L. Cohn, "Maritime Mortality in the Eighteenth and Nineteenth Centuries: A Survey," *International Journal of Maritime History* 1.1 (1989): 159–91.

the American colonies in the early part of the eighteenth century), mortality rates for *every* other shipboard group were lower. More importantly, the difference in mortality was substantial. While slaves died at a monthly rate greater than fifty per thousand, it was unusual for mortality rates among the other groups to exceed twenty per thousand; in fact, the average was frequently much lower. It is difficult to rank the non-slave groups in terms of mortality, though the available data imply that Chinese and some Indians and non-slave Africans died at relatively high rates. The second point is that substantial evidence exists that shipboard mortality rates fell over time among most non-slave groups, but not among the slaves. The data on immigration provide some evidence that rates were lower in the nineteenth than in the eighteenth century. Stronger evidence for this secular decline is shown in the convict voyages. Additionally, some of the lowest mortality rates were found among the voyages of contract labourers, especially for the better studied cases of the Indians and the Pacific Islanders. The information for the contract labour voyages are also for the later time period—after 1850. Examining all the non-slave voyages together implies a secular decline in mortality. While mortality rates fell among the non-slave groups, it should be emphasized that, even after 1850, rates on the ships were still higher than for non-migrants. This point is the third one that deserves emphasis. Transporting people on sailing ships increased the rate at which they died. Society suffered lost output from the inactivity of the migrants during the voyage, but also sacrificed the future output of those who died. The high costs of migration, of which the mortality suffered was an important component, point out how great the benefits of migration must have been to the non-slave migrants that voluntarily undertook such a hazardous journey. . . .

The last point that must be emphasized is that much more could be done to improve our knowledge of the size and trend of mortality rates. It can be suggested that we should extend our data base, particularly for immigrants and contract labour voyages, and that the systematic analysis of such new bodies of data could modify some of our findings.

Explaining Maritime Mortality Rates

This section will discuss the various theories that have been presented to explain why mortality was higher among slaves, why it declined over time among non-slave groups, and why it was higher among all migrant compared to non-sailing groups. The first information needed to answer this question is knowledge of the causes of death on the voyages. The major cause of death among all sailing groups was disease. Some individuals died from other factors, such as accidents, shipwrecks, suicide, and violence; in total, these other factors generally accounted for only a small percentage of total deaths.[37] At a first approximation,

[37]For slaves, see Steckel and Jensen, "New Evidence." For the crew on slave ships, see Stein, "Mortality." For immigrants, see F. Kapp, *Immigration and the Commissioners of Emigration* (New York, 1969, reprint of 1870 edition). For contract labour movements to Fiji and Australia, see Shlomowitz, "Pacific Labour Trade."

therefore, the three major findings of the last section can be answered. First, slaves must have been particularly susceptible to diseases during their migration and this situation must have continued over time. Second, for the non-slave groups, something must have reduced the incidence of disease on the ships over time. Third, the voyage must have caused sailing groups to become more susceptible to disease compared to their non-sailing counterparts, a statement that is particularly striking given that, at least for voluntary immigrants, we would expect the individuals who sailed to be healthier than the general population.

The major diseases that led to death differed among sailing groups, at least partly because of the different climatic zones of the voyages. For slaves, virtually every researcher mentions dysentery, smallpox, and scurvy as major causes of death. Yellow fever, measles, yaws, pneumonia, tuberculosis, ophthalmia, and influenza have also been mentioned, though the importance placed on these diseases varies substantially. For example, among these other factors, Curtin blames pneumonia, tuberculosis, and influenza; Klein and Engerman blame yellow fever and measles; and Steckel and Jensen blame fevers.[38] Similarly, other groups died from a wide variety of diseases. The crews on slave ships were most susceptible to malaria, yellow fever, and gastrointestinal diseases (such as dysentery), though the importance ascribed to each varies among researchers.[39] For European immigrants to North America, typhus and cholera were the primary killers.[40] For convicts, typhus and dysentery were the major diseases.[41] On Indian voyages to Fiji, cholera and meningitis were important, and on Pacific Islander voyages to Fiji and Queensland, dysentery was important.[42]

Though the diseases that were important differed, a common characteristic among them was that they were acute infectious diseases, not chronic ones. This factor led to a common characteristic of mortality found in virtually every data set. The majority of deaths usually occurred on a small number of ships, which then had mortality rates substantially above the average, while most ships suffered mortality at rates below the average. The probability of dying on the voyage depended largely on the particular voyage examined. If an individual was lucky enough to be on a voyage where there was no outbreak of an infectious

35

[38]Causes of slave deaths are given in the following sources: Philip D. Curtin, *The Atlantic Slave Trade: A Census* (Madison, Wis., 1969), 283; Joseph C. Miller, "Mortality in the Atlantic Slave Trade: Statistical Evidence on Causality," *Journal of Interdisciplinary History,* XI, No. 3 (Winter 1981), 412; Herbert S. Klein and Stanley L. Engerman, "A Note on Mortality in the French Slave Trade in the Eighteenth Century," in Gemery and Hogendorn (eds.), *The Uncommon Market,* 271; Johannes Postma, "Mortality in the Dutch Slave Trade, 1675–1795," ibid., 252; and Steckel and Jensen, "New Evidence," 60–63.

[39]Curtin, *Atlantic Slave Trade,* 283, mentions yellow fever and malaria. Steckel and Jensen, "New Evidence," 61–63, also mention gastrointestinal diseases.

[40]Kapp, *Immigration*; Oliver MacDonagh, *A Pattern of Government Growth, 1800–1860* (London, 1961); United States, Senate, "Report of the Select Committee on the Sickness and Mortality on Board Emigrant Ships," 33rd Congress, 1st Session, Senate Reports (#386), 1854; and Cecil Woodham-Smith, *The Great Hunger–Ireland: 1845–1849* (New York, 1962).

[41]McDonald and Shlomowitz, "Mortality on Convict Voyages," 3.

[42]Shlomowitz, "Pacific Labour Trade."

disease, the chances of survival were much better than the average mortality rate for the entire group would lead us to believe. On the other hand, an outbreak of infectious disease on the voyage substantially raised the probability of death. For example, in the 1077 immigrant ships in Cohn's sample, the average percent loss per ship was 1.36%. Some 621 (fifty-eight percent) of the ships suffered losses of one percent or less, another 279 (twenty-eight percent) suffered losses between one and two percent, while forty-four (four percent) of the ships suffered losses of over five percent of the passengers embarked. While the probability of sailing on a ship that suffered such a high rate of loss was small (about one in twenty-five), the consequences of doing so were severe; an individual on such a ship was, at a minimum, four times as likely to die. All sailing groups faced this same situation and, for some, the differential was larger. For slaves, there may have been as much as a twelve times difference in mortality rates among different voyages.[43]

While there is general agreement that acute infectious diseases were the major cause of deaths, there is much less agreement concerning the factors that led to epidemics occurring on ocean voyages. Three general hypotheses have been advanced. The first two emphasize the situation faced by the migrant before boarding the ship while the third emphasizes the situation faced by the migrant on the ship. Of course, there may have been some interactive effects among the factors. The pre-boarding situation could have increased mortality in two similar, but distinct, ways. In the process of moving from where he/she lived, the migrant could have moved into or through a different disease environment, one which contained diseases for which the migrant had no immunities. The migrant would then be exposed to these new diseases. As many infectious diseases have an incubation period, migrants could have boarded the ships between being exposed to the disease and its actual outbreak. Even subjecting the migrant to a pre-boarding medical check (an unusual event) would not prevent these diseases from being carried on board. This hypothesis will be called the Epidemiology Hypothesis. Before the migrant could board the ship, he/she frequently encountered a wait for a ship. The waiting was often done in an unsanitary, frequently crowded environment, factors which could have led to exposure of migrants to infectious diseases. For the same reasons just discussed, it is possible that the diseases would not actually show up until the migrant was on the ship. This hypothesis will be called the Waiting Hypothesis. Once on the ship, the migrant faced crowded and unsanitary conditions, may have had inadequate or contaminated food, usually had little access to (admittedly questionable) medical care, and sometimes faced unexpectedly long voyages, all factors which could have increased the susceptibility of the migrant to catching an infectious disease. This hypothesis will be called the Onboard Hypothesis.

Note that each hypothesis leads to an emphasis on different steps that needed to be taken in order to lower mortality. The hypothesis least favorable to migrants is the Epidemiology Hypothesis. It implies that very little could have

---

[43]Cohn, "Mortality." For slaves, see the estimates given in Eltis. *Economic Growth*, Appendix D.

been done to lower mortality until medical knowledge advanced sufficiently so that potential migrants could be inoculated against the infectious diseases. The only possible factor would have been pre-boarding checks to have prevented obviously sick migrants from boarding the ships. Given incubation periods, it is doubtful how successful these checks would have been. Also, while pre-boarding checks may have lowered shipboard mortality, they may not have affected the degree of mortality suffered by the migrant over their entire trip. If the Waiting Hypothesis is correct, then mortality could have been lowered by providing healthier environments where migrants could have waited for their ships. The difference here compared to the Epidemiology Hypothesis is that something concrete could have been done *at the time* that would have led to lower mortality. The Onboard Hypothesis is similar to the Waiting Hypothesis in its implications. If ships had been less crowded and cleaner, and if better quality food and medical care had been available, all possible at the time, mortality would have been lower. While the Epidemiology and Waiting Hypotheses are similar in blaming pre-boarding conditions for the large shipboard mortality, the Waiting and the Onboard Hypotheses are similar in that each implies that steps could have been taken at the time that would have lowered mortality.[44]

The three hypotheses have been used to explain the findings of the last section concerning mortality. Consider first the high mortality on the slave trade compared to the other sailing groups. The factors behind all three hypotheses could have increased mortality. Slaves were usually captured in the interior of Africa and had to be transported to the coast in order to be shipped. While on the coast, the slaves were kept in enclosures to prevent escape. The Epidemiology Hypothesis stresses that during the journey to the coast and while on the coast, the slaves would encounter diseases for which they had no immunity.[45] As other sailing groups either did not change disease environments or did not move through as severe a change in disease environments, their mortality was lower.

Acceptance of the Epidemiology Hypothesis as the major cause of the higher slave mortality requires that slaves moved through different disease environments within Africa. As slaves were generally captured inland and moved to the coast, it is certainly possible that the disease environment changed. Two pieces of evidence are usually used to support this claim. The first is an article by Curtin which shows that individuals who lived in a disease environment different than the one in which they were born suffered higher mortality than individuals who lived in the same disease environment in which they were born. In this article, Curtin showed that African troops serving in a part of Africa different from the one in which they were born suffered an increase in mortality, the implication being that Africa was made up of a series of separate disease environments. While

[44]Analyses of maritime mortality at the time emphasized either the Waiting or Onboard Hypothesis, a not surprising finding given the lack of medical knowledge.

[45]The clearest expressions of this view are found in Miller, "Mortality," and Eltis, *Economic Growth*, Appendix D. With respect to Miller, also see Raymond L. Cohn and Richard A. Jensen, "Comment and Controversy: Mortality in the Atlantic Slave Trade," *Journal of Interdisciplinary History*, XII, No. 2 (Autumn 1982), 317–329.

it is true that mortality was higher than typical for the African troops, the differential found was only about fifty percent, much too small by itself to fully explain the higher slave mortality on the ships.[46] The second piece of evidence advanced in support of the Epidemiology Hypothesis is that maritime mortality rates differed substantially by the African port of embarkation, the implication being that disease environments differed substantially by port.[47] While many studies have found a difference by port, not all have. In particular, a study by Galenson finds that the difference by port for his data set is due strictly to differences in ship size and voyage duration, that is, when these other factors are controlled, the difference by port disappears.[48] The studies that have found differences by port have either used a model not as complete as that used by Galenson or have not used mortality *rates* as an explanatory variable.[49] On the other hand, Galenson's sample was comprised of only thirty-five ships; the other studies have used significantly larger samples. Thus, to what extent mortality differed by port of embarkation is uncertain. It would be useful for someone to re-examine the evidence connecting mortality and port of origin in order to clarify the relationship.

40   Eltis, a proponent of the Epidemiology Hypothesis, has claimed that "if the death rates for the best months had held for the rest of the year, Africans on most slave-trade routes would have died at rates much closer to those experienced by contemporary European migrants in the North Atlantic."[50] While it is obviously true that slave mortality would have been closer to that of other groups if the high mortality months are deleted, it is incorrect to imply that the rates for the best months are at all comparable to those of other groups, especially when it is realized that Eltis' data are for the nineteenth century. For ships sailing from the Bight of Benin, the mortality rate for the lowest month was fourteen per thousand, a rate one and one-half times higher than that for European migrants.[51] This rate is comparable to Curtin's fifty percent figure, but it is for only one route. For the other five routes examined by Eltis, the monthly

[46]Philip D. Curtin, "Epidemiology and the Slave Trade," *Political Science Quarterly,* LXXXIII, No. 2 (June 1968), 190–216. Of course, slaves were moving through a new disease environment for the first time, while the troops were stationed in an area with a different disease environment. Also, see Philip D. Curtin, "African Health at Home and Abroad," *Social Science History,* X, No. 4 (Winter 1986), 369–398.

[47]See Eltis, *Economic Growth,* App. D; Curtin, *The Atlantic Slave Trade,* 279–280; Klein, *The Middle Passage,* 56, 85, 162, 199; E. van de Boogaart and P.C. Emmer, "The Dutch Participation in the Atlantic Slave Trade, 1596–1650," in Gemery and Hogendorn (eds.), *The Uncommon Market,* 353–376; Postma, "Mortality," 250.

[48]Galenson, *Traders, Planters, and Slaves,* 46–48.

[49]For an example of the former, see David Eltis, "Mortality in the Nineteenth Century Slave Trade" (unpublished manuscript). For an example of the latter, see Klein, *The Middle Passage,* 56, 85, 162, 199. Steckel and Jensen, "New Evidence," do find differences by port but their sample has an overall slave mortality rate of 9.6 per thousand, an extremely low figure. . . . Their rate is low because their sample includes a lower incidence of ships from higher mortality ports. Whether the relationships they found would still hold if their overall mortality rate was a more typical thirty or sixty per thousand is not known.

[50]Eltis, *Economic Growth,* 266.

[51]*Ibid.,* 267.

rates in the best months were twenty-five, forty-six, forty-seven, fifty-seven, and eighty-three, rates *much* above those suffered by European migrants. Additionally, Eltis shows that mortality was statistically higher only in certain months. Instead of simply using the lowest month, one could calculate a weighted (by number of ships) average of mortality for the set of months with the lowest mortality that are not statistically different from each other. Calculating such a rate for the Bight of Benin yields a weighted average of 33.7, a mortality figure over three times as large as that for European migrants. For all other routes Eltis considered, the weighted average would give a mortality rate substantially greater than the single month rates given above. Thus, while some evidence exists that implies mortality differed by port for slaves, the strength of the evidence is unclear and, at best, can likely explain only part of the reason that slaves died at rates higher than those for other sailing groups.

The Waiting Hypothesis would explain high slave mortality by pointing out that slaves were frequently held along the coast in a very unhealthy environment. Slaves were ill-fed and ill-housed and exposed to diseases carried by other slaves and their captors. These factors could have led to high rates of mortality once the slaves were on the ships. All in all, this Hypothesis has been least developed for the slave trade.[52]

The Onboard Hypothesis specifies that conditions onboard the ships caused the high mortality suffered by slaves. This hypothesis implies that the crowded and unsanitary conditions found on slave ships in combination with unhealthy and contaminated food and/or unexpectedly long voyages led to higher mortality.[53] Researchers have tried to test the Onboard Hypothesis primarily by looking for a relationship between crowding and mortality rates. While there is some discussion of the proper way to measure crowding, almost *none* of the major data sets for the slave trade (or for any other migrant group) find any significant correlation between crowding and mortality.[54] There are three studies that do find a positive relationship between the variables. First, Steckel and Jensen find a relationship during the loading phase of the slave trade, but not during the Middle Passage.[55] They acquire their data from slavers' log books kept on the

[52]It is very difficult to distinguish between deaths caused simply by being in a different disease environment and those caused strictly by the waiting conditions faced. Steckel and Jensen, "New Evidence," provide an analysis of slave deaths and how they differed during the loading phase compared to the actual voyage. As this article was going to press, the author became aware of Joseph C. Miller, *Way of Death: Merchant Capitalism and the Angolan Slave Trade, 1730–1830* (Madison, Wis., 1988), 379–442, which emphasizes poor nutrition of slaves beginning with their capture as an important cause of mortality on the ships.

[53]For example, see Raymond L. Cohn and Richard A. Jensen, "The Determinants of Slave Mortality Rates in the Middle Passage," *Explorations in Economic History,* XIX, No. 3 (July 1982), 269–282.

[54]For problems with the measurement of crowding, see Klein, *The Middle Passage,* 195–196. Studies that find no significant correlation between crowding and slave mortality are Klein, *The Middle Passage,* 195–196; Herbert S. Klein and Stanley L. Engerman, "Slave Mortality on British Ships," in Roger Anstey and P. E. H. Hair (eds.), *Liverpool, the African Slave Trade, and Abolition* (Bristol, 1976), 113–125; Postma, "Mortality," 249–250; Galenson, *Traders, Planters and Slaves,* 42. Cohn, "Mortality," finds similar results for European immigration to New York.

[55]Steckel and Jensen, "New Evidence."

British trade during the 1790s. As noted before, however, it is unclear how representative their sample is since it has a monthly mortality rate of [only] 9.6 per thousand. . . .[56] Second, Eltis finds a positive relationship between crowding and mortality during the nineteenth century, but argues that it holds only for one decade and that traders increased crowding in response to higher mortality rather than the other way around.[57] Third, McDonald and Shlomowitz found a positive relationship between mortality and crowding in their study of immigration to Australia.[58] Thus, the relationship between crowding and mortality is very uncertain *within* any trade. It does not seem, however, that this approach is the only way of relating crowding and mortality. Critics of the slave trade argued (at least in part) that slave ship mortality was higher because the slave ships were more crowded *compared to voyages of other groups.* Slaves were crowded on the ships at rates around two per ton, while European immigrants to the U.S. were crowded at rates under 0.4 per ton. Every other group for which crowding estimates are available give rates substantially less than those for slaves.[59] Variations in crowding within each group may not have affected mortality (except for extreme variations such as those analyzed by Steckel and Jensen for slaves), but variations among groups could have had a substantial effect. No one has put all the crowding figures together for the different trades, however, so that this possibility could be better tested.[60] Nor has anyone found a way to determine the extent to which inadequate or contaminated food affected mortality.

One way that researchers have tried to distinguish among the three hypotheses is by examining when slaves died during the voyage. If most deaths occurred near the start of the voyage, then, assuming an incubation period, slaves were likely exposed to the disease before boarding. On the other hand, if deaths occurred near the end of the voyage, then slaves were likely exposed to the disease during the course of the voyage. The statistical evidence on this point is contradictory. Miller has claimed that, except for extraordinarily long voyages, mortality rates were higher near the beginning of the voyage.[61] Miller's empirical techniques have been questioned, however, by Cohn and Jensen who found

[56]See the discussion in footnote 49.

[57]Eltis, "Mortality in the Nineteenth Century," 6.

[58]McDonald and Shlomowitz, "Mortality on Immigrant Voyages."

[59]For estimates of crowding of slaves, see Klein, *The Middle Passage,* 87, 194–196. For crowding of European immigrants to the U.S., see Cohn, "Mortality." Similar levels are found in McDonald and Shlomowitz, "Mortality on Immigrant Ships" for immigrants to Australia, and in McDonald and Shlomowitz, "Mortality on Convict Ships" for convicts.

[60]One would almost certainly obtain a positive relationship between mortality and crowding if the suggested test was run. Interpreting the results is another matter. Few slave (immigrant) ships sailed in which there was as much (little) space per passenger as on immigrant (slave) ships. One thus has a positive relationship but little overlap within the data among the different groups. The point is not that this type of test would prove that crowding was an important determinant of mortality, rather it is to illustrate that, when viewed in a broader comparative context, crowding *could* have been important.

[61]Miller, "Mortality."

no evidence of declining mortality rates using the same data.[62] In another article, Cohn and Jensen, using sophisticated statistical techniques, have found a positive relationship between voyage length and mortality rates for unexpectedly long voyages, while both Galenson and Eltis have failed to find a relationship.[63] Recently, Steckel and Jensen have claimed that most slave deaths occurred near the middle of the voyage.[64] No consensus currently exists on when slaves died during the voyage; whether additional data exist that can adequately answer this question is unclear.

One other recent study has some bearing on which hypothesis most accurately explains the high mortality rate suffered by slaves. Shlomowitz has recently analyzed some additional data concerning the shipment of liberated slaves from St. Helena, Rio de Janeiro, and Sierra Leone to the West Indies.[65] He found that mortality rates on these voyages fell precipitously after 1850. . . . Shlomowitz explains that the decline was due to administrative reforms that led to improvements in the screening of passengers before boarding. This result lends some support to the Waiting Hypothesis because it implies that better screening of slaves before boarding could have similarly lowered the mortality rate on slave ships. It is possible, however, that the reforms only reduced *shipboard* mortality. If epidemiological factors were indeed the primary reason for the death of slaves, it could be argued that more of the slaves died in the depot before or after the ship sailed rather than on the ships. In other words, the reforms could have just changed the distribution of slave deaths by location.

In the final analysis, it may be impossible to determine which of the three hypotheses best explains the high slave mortality. Slaves moved between different disease environments, waited for ships in very miserable conditions, and sailed on very crowded and unsanitary ships. None of the other sailing groups encountered such a drastic change in disease environments or waited in such miserable conditions or sailed under such bad conditions. In fact, maritime historians may be taking the wrong approach by arguing about which of the hypotheses is correct. It is possible that no one hypothesis *by itself* explains the high slave mortality. All the factors discussed may very well have contributed to the high maritime mortality suffered by slaves. Good theoretical reasons exist to believe that each factor should have independently raised mortality. The fact that slaves faced the worst conditions on all counts may explain their high rate of death. . . .   [1989]

45

[62]Cohn and Jensen, "Comment and Controversy."

[63]Cohn and Jensen, "Determinants of Slave Mortality Rates;" Eltis, "Mortality;" Galenson, *Traders, Planters, and Slaves*, 40–42.

[64]Steckel and Jensen, "New Evidence." Steckel's and Jensen's sample is to be preferred to that of Miller and others. Steckel's and Jensen's data were for deaths on particular ships, whereas the others use deaths and voyage lengths across ships. On the other hand, as noted in footnote 49, it is unclear how representative is Steckel's and Jensen's sample.

[65]Shlomowitz, "Mortality and Voyages of Liberated Africans."

1. What is Cohn's purpose in this selection?

JAMES A. RAWLEY

JAMES A. RAWLEY *(1916–), born in Terre Haute, Indiana, has had a distinguished career in the field of history as an author and educator. He is a graduate of
the University of Michigan, where he received both a bachelor's and master's
degree, and of Columbia University, where he received his doctorate. He taught at
Columbia, at Sweet Briar College, and then at the University of Nebraska-Lincoln,
where he is currently the Carl Adolph Happold Professor of History (Emeritus). He
is a Fellow of the Royal Historical Society, the Society of American Historians, and
the National Endowment for the Humanities. He was a board member and president of the board of directors of the Nebraska State Historical Society, and served
on the board of the Nebraska Council for the Humanities Foundation. His works
include numerous articles, letters, and papers on such topics as the Civil War,
United States politics and government from 1845 to 1861, and race relations.*

The Middle Passage*

Few stereotypes about the Atlantic slave trade are more familiar than popular
impressions of the Middle Passage—the crossing from Africa to America. Huge
ships—crammed to the gunwales with Africans, packed together like spoons,
chained to one another, daily exposed to white brutality, meager provisions, and
hygienical neglect—in long, slow voyages suffered abnormally high mortality
rates for their hapless passengers.

A diagram of the Liverpool slave vessel, the *Brookes,* has for nearly two centuries nourished this stereotype. A nauseous sketch depicted a large ship of three
hundred and twenty tons, whose narrow and shallow decks were packed with
slaves "like books on a shelf." The diagram was printed in 1788 when Parliament was deliberating upon a law which in effect would have restricted the
Brookes to a cargo of no more than 454 slaves. It was calculated that if every man
slave was allowed six feet by one foot, four inches, platform space, every woman
five feet ten by one foot four, every boy five feet by one foot two, and every girl
four feet six by one foot, the *Brookes* could hold 451 slaves. A witness who had
been on the *Brookes'*s voyage of 1783 testified that "they bought upwards of 600
slaves, and lost about seventy in the voyage."[1]

The sketch and the calculation were the work of the London abolition committee, based upon dimensions that the government investigator, Captain Perry,
had brought back from Liverpool. The print, Thomas Clarkson declared, "seemed
to make an instantaneous impression of horror upon all who saw it." Abolitionists circulated the print in Great Britain and abroad. Clarkson carried a copy to
Paris where the revolutionary Mirabeau had a small model built for display in

*James A. Rawley, *The Transatlantic Slave Trade: A History* (New York: W.W. Norton, 1981),
Chapter XII, "The Middle Passage," 283–306.
[1]PP, *A&P*, 1790, XXX (699), 37.

his dining room. In Philadelphia some 3,700 copies were distributed. Since then nearly all popular accounts of the slave trade, as well as a good many scholarly studies, reproduce this print.[2]

Ships of three hundred and twenty tons were not uncommon in the trade in the 1780s, though they were not the standard. Certainly for the long years before the middle of the eighteenth century most slave ships were much smaller, as we have seen. Nor were most slave ships specially built to transport human cargoes. In this chapter we shall try to thread our way through the controversial topic of the Middle Passage.

Witnesses before the parliamentary investigators at the end of the eighteenth   5 century offered often contradictory points of view, drawing on their own experience in the trade. This welter of views serves to point to the complexity of the subject. It also serves to point to the partisan atmosphere in which abolitionists and defenders of the trade were giving testimony to shape legislation. Wilberforce scored the testimony of the Liverpool slave trader, Robert Norris, who "had painted the accommodations on board a slaveship in the most glowing colours." He then proceeded to depict the misery of the slaves, fettered to one another, cramped for space, amidst stench, without sufficient water or food, forced to eat, forced to exercise, singing not songs of joy but of lamentation for the loss of their homeland, subject to brutality and severe mortality.[3]

For analysis of the problems posed by the Middle Passage we shall look at rates of mortality for Europeans and for whites in Africa, for crew members, tropical medicine in the slave era, government regulation of the trade, causes of mortality, care of slaves in transit, brutality, "tight packing," disaster at sea, preembarkation mortality, and postembarkation mortality.

Comparison of Middle Passage mortality for slaves with white mortality rates is based on the fact that Africans and Europeans were accustomed to different disease environments. But it seems impossible to compare the "normal" death rate in West Africa with that of western Europe. Close in comparability are British military forces (though in the period 1817 to 1836) who had a death rate in the American tropics ranging from 85 to 138 per thousand, and in West Africa ranging from 483 to 668 per thousand.

Sir William Young in 1801 comparing the mortality of white and Negro troops in the West Indies, recognizing variations in islands and stations, found that annual mortality rates were 11 per cent and 5 per cent respectively, viz., the white rate was more than double the Negro. During the American Revolutionary War years of 1776 to 1780, white troops from Britain and Germany sent to the West Indies and North America incurred mortality losses averaging 11 per cent for the West Indies and at least 8 per cent for North America.[4] These comparisons suffer not only from the question of differing immunities to disease environments, but also differing factors such as space in ships, diet, and medical

[2]Clarkson, *History*, II, 111. Donnan, *Documents*, II, 592–593. Klein, *Middle Passage*.
[3]Clarkson, *History*, II, 48–52. *Parliamentary History*, XXVIII, 41–67, has Wilberforce's great oration.
[4]Klein, *Middle Passage*, 68–71. Young, *West-India Common-Place Book*, 221.

care. Certain it is that when epidemics struck, Europeans and Africans could be felled in large numbers, and shipwrecks at sea were no respecters of race.

A close look at the mortality of white persons in Africa confirms the saying that Africa was the "white man's grave." Employees of the Royal African Company for the years 1684 to 1732 suffered an appalling loss which doubtless would have discouraged recruits had they known the grim story. A recent study starkly concluded that three out of five Europeans stationed in Africa died during the first year. The first and second months, notably the second, were the most devastating, accounting for 23.5 per cent of newcomers, and risk ran high for the first eight months. Moreover, the scholar K. G. Davies saw no certainty that more than 10 per cent returned to England. Of 1,080 persons sent out to Africa by the Company of Merchants Trading to Africa from 1751 to 1788, 653 died; 333 of these perished during the first year, with a somewhat higher mortality for military than for civil employees.[5]

10   The Gold Coast was the healthiest part of Africa that Davies studied. His finding was confirmed by an analysis of the Europeans employed by the Dutch West India Company on the Gold Coast from 1719 to 1760. This analysis concluded that the mortality rate was just under 20 per cent per year.[6] The variant conclusion is a reminder that it is risky to generalize about mortality rates, either for "the white man's grave," or for the Middle Passage.

The mortality of crews on slave ships is perhaps the best standard of comparison with slave mortality on the Middle Passage. It is an imperfect standard, owing among other things to the facts that white crewmen came from a different disease environment than did Africans, they had three passages (to Africa, the Middle Passage, and the return home), and they were not subjected to the same treatment that was inflicted upon black slaves. Moreover, studies do not normally separate crew mortality on the Middle Passage from mortality on the other two legs of the voyage. Further complicating matters is the fact that numerous sailors left ship in America.

Lord Rodney, victor over the French in the West Indies in two wars, in giving testimony on the slave trade in 1790, expressed his belief that the British West-India trade was "a considerable nursery for seamen, and without the African trade the West Indies . . . could not be supported."[7] Defenders of the slave trade adopted this view and made the phrase "nursery for seamen" familiar. Lore and fact should have disabused contemporaries of this belief. The toll of seamen's lives taken by the Guinea trade had been put into popular verse:

> Beware and take care
> Of the Bight of Benin;
> For one that comes out,
> There are forty go in.

[5]K. G. Davies, "The Living and the Dead: White Mortality in West Africa, 1684–1732," in Engerman and Genovese, eds., *Race and Slavery*, 83–98.

[6]H. M. Feinberg, "New Data on European Mortality in West Africa: The Dutch on the Gold Coast, 1719–1760," *JAfH*, XV (1974), 357–371.

[7]PP, *A&P*, 1790, XXX (699), 471.

Writing in 1682 of slaving in Old Calabar, the Frenchman John Barbot, after observing that "the trade goes on there very slowly," remarked, "The air in this river is very malignant, and occasions a great mortality among our sailors, that make any long stay." Besides the problem of malignancy in the air and the long stay in the river, he noted the problem of the strong ocean current that carried ships toward Cameroon River, "which gives a great fatigue to sailors that come out of Old Calabar, to turn up a ship for three weeks or a month in the gulph to gain Prince's island," or other port to take on water and provisions before making the long crossing. The shift of slaving activity in the latter part of the eighteenth century to the eastern coast of Lower Guinea doubtless had deleterious effects upon the mortality of seamen.[8]

Shocking facts about slave-crew mortality had been uncovered by Thomas Clarkson in his visits to Bristol and Liverpool and published in a Board of Trade Report in 1789. Alive to Englishmen's pride in their seamen, he copied muster rolls of Bristol ships, becoming "able to prove," as he said, "that more persons would be found dead in three slave-vessels from Bristol, in a given time, than in all the other vessels put together, numerous as they were, belonging to the same port." His inquiry at Liverpool entered another debit to England's maritime strength—returning survivors of slave voyages, men "rendered incapable, by disease, of continuing their occupation at sea."

He presented Parliament with his statistics, offering a comparative view of crew mortality in the Bristol slave trade as against trade to the West Indies, Petersburg, Newfoundland, Greenland, and East India. Death was three times more common among seamen in the first as in all the other trades. Nearly one in four of the Bristol seamen perished, nearly one in five of the Liverpool seamen. Instead of the slave trade being the nursery for seamen, it was "the grave of the British marine."[9] Clarkson's figures made a deep impact upon both contemporaries and later writers about the trade. Little notice has been given to the fact that he failed to recognize that the death rate for sailors in the nonslave trade to Africa was as great as for those in the slave trade, nor that most of the voyages he chose for comparison were shorter than the triangular voyage.

The death toll for Nantes seamen in the Guinea trade was as grim as for English seamen. Mortality for these sailors, who, be it remembered, had longer voyages, was also higher than for the slaves; for both classes the losses declined in the eighteenth century. As suggested in British parliamentary testimony, the African coast was more perilous for sailors than the Middle Passage. A study of Nantes slave trade mortality by Herbert S. Klein, superseding earlier studies by French scholars, disclosed a mortality loss for crew of 18.3 per cent and for slaves of 14.9 per cent. High incidence of slave mortality was often attended by high incidence of crew mortality. Although the voyage in 1768–69 of the *Marie-Gabrielle* cost the lives not of thirty-one of thirty-nine crewmen, as has been asserted, but thirty of fifty-four, it had a ghastly toll.[10]

15

[8]Donnan, *Documents*, I, 300.

[9]Clarkson, *History*, I, 326, 394–395; II, 59–61, 69.

[10]Klein, *Middle Passage*, 194, 197–198. Mettas, "Pour une histoire," 38, corrects Curtin, *Atlantic Slave Trade*, 282 and Gaston-Martin on the figures for the *Marie-Gabrielle*.

Sailors well into the nineteenth century in ordinary service as well as in the slave trade were dealt with harshly. There are numerous accounts of cruelty and occasional death from brutal masters. But as the English captain William Littleton testified in 1789 about slave ship captains, "Some are more severe than others." He had never known any instance of notorious cruelty in the captains of slave ships. "It is their interest to take care of the seamen, the success of the voyage depending on it."[11] The British Parliament in 1789, responding to complaints, laid down minimal requirements for sleeping and victualing sailors in the slave trade.

The foregoing figures for white mortality in Europe, in America, in Africa, and on slave ships become meaningful only when compared against figures for black mortality on the Middle Passage. Thomas Clarkson put the mortality of Negroes, under the most favorable circumstances, at 45 per cent, and in many instances above 80 per cent. Traditional estimates of such mortality have ranged from 8 to above 30 per cent. These estimates have often been gross, not taking into account factors of differing origins and destinations, carrying nations, and time. Writers have not agreed whether the trend was up or down in the nineteenth century, some presuming that in an era of illegal trade the trend must be upward, soaring as high as 50 per cent.

Recent scholarship has gone far to rationalize these previous estimates. The trade conducted by the Portuguese and Brazilians was the largest single trade, as we have seen, and examination of its mortality patterns is illuminating. To begin, the careful scholar Joseph C. Miller, who has investigated the trade from 1760 to 1830, has emphasized that causes of slave mortality were to be found not in the Atlantic passage as much as in Africa. There were, he found, significant variations in each African port. Conditions in Africa, he concluded, were more meaningful than those at sea. These conditions most importantly included factors of drought, famine, and epidemics, and formed the background for death on the Atlantic crossing. Added to these was the factor of demand for slaves; in times of heavy demand mortality rose, apparently resulting from the dispatch of weak persons to meet demand. Similarly, delays in loading affected mortality. A ready supply of healthy slaves who were swiftly loaded could reduce the death rate.

20   Mortality losses examined by African ports at different periods reveal sharp differences for ports and for periods of time. Thus for ships sailing to Rio from 1795 to 1811 the Luanda departures had a loss of 10.4 per cent and the Benguela departures only 7.8 per cent; but from 1811 to 1830 the overall loss dropped; they were for Luanda 8.4 per cent, for Benguela 5.8 per cent, and for Ambriz/Cabinda only 4.1 per cent. Examining arrivals in Rio from 1795 to 1811 by broad African regions or origin, it was ascertained that slaves from West Africa suffered a 6.3 per cent mortality, from Southwest Africa 8.9 per cent, and from distant East Africa a disastrous 23.4 per cent. The season of arrival at Rio was also related to mortality; slaves arriving in the winter months had a mortality loss nearly double that of summer arrivals. In the last years of legal trade to Rio, 1825–1830, mortality losses by African region stood at low

[11]PP, *A&P*, 1789, XXIV (633), 106.

percentages: for the Congo 3.3, for Angola 6.25, and for East Africa 12.1 per cent. If mortality losses dropped in the eighteenth and first third of the nineteenth centuries, what of the death rate during the period of illegal trading? The evidence is fragmentary but points to a higher death rate for slaves during the years of illicit trade than before 1830. Slaves exported from Congo North and Angola from 1830 to 1843 appear to have been subjected to a mortality of near- ly 17 per cent. This last finding is in keeping with the claims of contemporary abolitionists that the illegal trade was more deadly than the lawful one.[12]

Comparative studies of mortality by national carrier now exist, revealing some variations in mortality percentage losses, but in all indicating a mortality loss for the eighteenth century below 18 per cent and tending to decline during the century. For the Danish trade, random samples between 1698 and 1733 dis- closed losses ranging from 10 to 25 per cent, and a more systematic study of thirty-five slavers sailing between 1777 and 1788 showed an average loss of 14.9 per cent.[13] In the Dutch experience the mortality loss was just below 17 per cent, with the average slightly lower for the Dutch West India ships, which drew slaves from shore installations rather than from ship trade.[14]

In the French trade there are unusually full data for Nantes, the major slave port. For the eighteenth century they show an overall mortality loss of 13.1 per cent. African place of embarkation played a significant role in mortality, with a high loss of 15.6 per cent for slaves exported from the Gold Coast, with its adverse westerly winds and a low loss of 11.1 per cent for departures from Angola. The overall loss in the early part of the century was somewhat greater than in the latter part of the century.[15]

It was in Great Britain that abolitionists painted death in the Middle Passage in the most vivid colors. The investigation by the Committee of the Privy Council reported a death loss of 23.5 per cent for the years 1680–88. T. F. Buxton, sampling losses for the year 1792, computed a loss of 17 per cent; and Wilberforce in 1789 told Parliament the loss was not less than 12.5 per cent. A painstaking study by a modern scholar, Roger Anstey, showed a loss varying from 8.5 per cent to 9.6 per cent from 1761 to 1791, and thereafter to 1807 a declining loss dropping to 2.7 per cent in 1795 and averaging 4 per cent during the last decade of the lawful trade. Anstey halved Buxton's estimate for 1792 to 8.4 per cent. African coastal region was an important factor in variation of the death toll, the region from the Senegal to the Volta rivers having a loss of 4.1 per cent, from the Volta to Gabon 13.1 per cent, and from Loango to Angola 2.8 per cent. Placing British experience against that of the rest of Europe in the

---

[12]Curtin, *Atlantic Slave Trade*, 275–276. Miller, "Legal Portuguese Slaving from Angola," 135–176. In a paper that he kindly let me read in manuscript, Professor Miller has pointed out that scholars have confused percentage losses with mortality rates. The latter are pro- duced by dividing percentage losses by time. I have sought to describe percentage losses. Klein, *Middle Passage*, 56, 63n. Eltis, "Export of Slaves from Africa, 1821–1843," 426.

[13]Klein, *Middle Passage*, 66, 161.

[14]Johannes Postma, "Mortality in the Dutch Slave Trade, 1675–1795," in Gemery and Hogendorn, eds., *Uncommon Market*.

[15]Klein, *Middle Passage*, 199.

half-century after 1760, Anstey concluded the British loss was below the rest, which he estimated overall at 10 per cent.[16]

A specialized study of 301 British ships in the Jamaica trade for the years 1782 to 1808 found a death loss of 5.6 per cent. The scholar excluded ships that had no report of mortality, and pointed to the lateness of the period in a century of declining mortality rates. Like other scholars he demonstrated that place of origin in Africa was related to mortality, the Bight of Biafra exacting the heaviest toll.[17]

25   North Americans in the slave trade have left a sparse and unsatisfactory record. A study of only thirty-seven voyages, beginning in 1734, that excluded three catastrophic voyages which together lost 58 per cent of their cargo, put the American mortality loss at about 10 per cent. An analysis of less than one hundred Rhode Island voyages made from 1752–1807 resulted in a percentage loss of 12 per cent. As under other flags the loss fell with the advance of the century. The rate and the trend were consistent with the record of continental European traders. In the American case it should be noted that two factors probably served to raise the rate: Americans tended to ply the ship instead of the shore trade and they slaved in heavy proportions on the Lower Guinea Coast.[18]

What were the causes of mortality in the Middle Passage? Popular understanding attributed the high incidence of death to a variety of causes: disease, poor hygiene, medical neglect, inadequate food and water, white brutality, slave mutinies, and overcrowding.

First let us consider the trauma of the Middle Passage—the morbid condition produced upon Africans who were taken from their familiar surroundings, sold to white strangers, imprisoned, manacled, confined on a ship that would sail into the alien sea for an unknown destination and unknown purposes. These hapless slaves penned few accounts, but there exists one written by an Ibo, Olaudah Equiano, captured as a child and taken to the sea coast where he was placed on a slave ship. "I was now persuaded that I had gotten into a world of bad spirits and that they [the crew] were going to kill me." When he looked around and saw a large copperpot boiling, "and a multitude of black people of every description chained together, every one of their countenances expressing dejection and sorroe, I no longer doubted my fate: and quite overpowered with horror and anguish, I fell motionless on the deck and fainted." He learned from other blacks that he was not to be eaten, but, "Soon after this the blacks who brought me on board went off, and left me abandoned to despair."[19]

The psychological impact of the Middle Passage upon the involuntary passengers was noted by contemporaries. The surgeon on the *Elizabeth*, Isaac Wilson,

[16]Anstey, *Atlantic Slave Trade*, 31, 415.

[17]Klein, *Middle Passage*, 160.

[18]Tommy Todd Hamm, "The American Slave Trade with Africa, 1620–1807," unpublished Ph.D. dissertation, Indiana University, 1975, 206–210. Jay Alan Coughtry, "The Notorious Triangle: Rhode Island and the African Slave Trade, 1700–1807," unpublished Ph.D. dissertation, University of Wisconsin, 1978, 388–389.

[19]Paul Edwards, ed., *Equiano's Travels* (2 vols., London, 1969), I, 70–72, 16–26.

observed that when the slaves were brought on board, "a gloomy pensiveness seemed to overcast their countenances and continued in a great many." The mortality of this voyage was 155 slaves of 602 on board, and Wilson was persuaded that two-thirds of the deaths resulted from melancholy. He could cure none who had the melancholy, but some of the slaves who did not have the melancholy "took medicines with very good effect." Melancholy, he ventured the opinion, was the remote cause of dysentery. Dr. Alexander Falconbridge, despairing that he could never cure a slave from a bad case of dysentery, went on to remark that he had known a few slaves to recover, "who seemed not to reflect on their situation." There seems to be little doubt that mortality was fostered by the traumatic impact of the Middle Passage.[20]

Without doubt disease was a relentless killer of slaves on shipboard. Dysentery, "fever," measles, smallpox, and scurvy were formidable causes of death. Dysentery, often called by contemporaries "the flux," was perhaps the most common disease. Outbreaks occurred when ships had been at sea for some time and when slaves had been confined below for several days. Medicine was of little avail, but one form of treatment comprised of isolating the patient, withholding food for two days, and then feeding him meat, onions, vinegar or lime juice and sometimes both.[21]

Tropical medicine was more helpful for dealing with smallpox, malaria, and scurvy. A primitive inoculation for smallpox was occasionally practiced in the first half of the century, and precautions sometimes taken. A South Sea Company agent in 1738 reported the spread of smallpox in Jamaica. He had the vessel *Clara* "smoakt with brimstone and tar before the Negroes were put on board. And the vessell ordred to the Keys to prevent the smallpox breaking out. . . ." A slave-ship doctor noted that it was necessary to keep patients at a distance from the ship's company. "I have heard," he said, "of Guineamen towing them in a longboat." Not until the end of the century did Dr. Edward Jenner discover a safe way to inoculate against smallpox. By the opening of the nineteenth century some slaves were being inoculated before being transported.[22]

Scurvy early in the eighteenth century was a scourge of seamen, those in the navy as well as in the slave trade. The Dutch ship *Beeksteyn*, transporting 753 slaves from Elmina to Surinam in 1731, running short of food and water, experienced an epidemic, and at least 150 slaves succumbed to scurvy.[23] In the naval war of the 1740s Great Britain lost more men to scurvy than to the Spanish and French fleets. In his circumnavigation of the globe, 1740–1744, Lord Anson had 75 per cent of the crews of five ships die of scurvy. A Scottish doctor, James Lind, who served as naval surgeon in the war, published the results of his observations and experiments in a work entitled *A Treatise on the Scurvy* (1754),

[20]PP, *A&P*, 1790, XXX (699), 562–581, 591.
[21]Hamm, "American Slave Trade," 224. David Richardson, unpublished manuscript on the English slave trade, ch. 5, 14.
[22]Donnan, *Documents*, II, 461–462. T. Trotter, *The Health of Seamen*, C. Lloyd, ed. (London, 1965), 310.
[23]Postma, "Mortality in the Dutch Slave Trade."

dedicated to Lord Anson. Trying a variety of remedies on twelve patients sick with scurvy, Dr. Lind discovered, "the most sudden and visible good effects were perceived from the use of oranges and lemons. . . ." His book, affirming the use of oranges, lemons, and limes as antiscorbutics, was translated into French and won wide attention in Europe. Lind in 1761 proved that the steam from salt water was fresh, and he soon was urging that ships supply themselves with fresh water by distillation. Dr. Thomas Trotter, who briefly served as a slave ship-surgeon, in 1786 published his *Observations on Scurvy*. Numerous slave ships from the middle of the eighteenth century benefited from progress in tropical medicine; it is worth noting that not until 1795 did the British Admiralty order that the navy be supplied with lemon juice. The term "limey" to describe a British sailor comes from the practice of taking lime juice as antiscorbutic. The use of Peruvian bark from the cinchona tree to treat malaria had been introduced into Europe in the mid-seventeenth century. Captain Hills in giving testimony to Parliament in 1789 stated that he made the sailors he sent on shore in Africa take "the bark."[24]

The medical lore available to ameliorate conditions on the Middle Passage by 1788 was presented to the British Committee of the Privy Council by Archibald Dalzel. He urged regulation of the trade by creating a government body with authority to inspect ships in order to see that they carried not only an abundance of provisions and water, but also antiscorbutics to combat scurvy and other medicines, and a still to convert salt water into fresh water. Parliament did not enact these suggestions, but it did by Dolben's Act in 1788 provide that every ship have a certified surgeon who would keep and file a journal of mortality on the voyage.

The word "fever" was often recorded as a cause of death. To modern medicine, fever is a vague description, but in the eighteenth century fevers were sometimes systematically classified as intermittent, continued, putrid, ardent, and inflammatory. The author of a manual for the use of young sea doctors in the slave trade warned against improper diagnosis of fevers. Writing in 1729 Dr. T. Aubrey cautioned:

> Abundance of these poor Creatures are lost on Board Ships to the great prejudice of the Owners and Scandal of the Surgeon, merely thro' the Surgeon's Ignorance, because he knows not what they are afflicted with, but supposing it to be a Fever, bleeds and purges, or vomits them, and so casts them into an incurable *Diarrhoea*, and in a few Days they become a Feast for some hungry Shark."[25]

[24]"James Lind," *DNB*, XI, 1150–1151. H. H. Scott, *A History of Tropical Medicine* (2 vols., London, 1939), II, 933–934. R. B. Sheridan, "The Guinea Surgeons on the Middle Passage," unpublished paper delivered at the Pacific Coast Branch of the American Historical Association meeting, LaJolla, Calif., 1976. I have greatly benefited from Professor Sheridan's paper.

[25]Christopher Lloyd and J. L. S. Coulter, *Medicine and the Navy, 1200–1900* (4 vols., Edinburgh, 1957–63), III, 293–358. Philip Curtin, *The Image of Africa* (Madison, Wis., 1964), 72–81. Quotation in Sheridan, "Guinea Surgeons," 14.

The inflammation of eye called ophthalmia, contagious and a cause of blindness, afflicted Africans in great numbers. Familiar with the illness, Africans treated it in a number of ways; one was with the juice of a pear-shaped fruit variously known as pan-a-pánnee or tontáy. The French slaver *Le Rodeur* in 1819 set out with 160 slaves from Bonny for Guadeloupe. After the slaves had been confined to the lower hold for several days following a revolt, ophthalmia broke out among them. The ship's surgeon advised the captain the disease was beyond his management. All of the slaves and all of the crew, except one seaman, were at one time blind; and at this time the French ship spoke a Spanish ship on which everyone was blind. Most persons on *Le Rodeur* recovered entirely or partially. Thirty-nine slaves who remained sightless were thrown into the sea, the captain expecting to recover his losses from the underwriters.[26]

The yaws, a chronic, contagious Negro disease characterized by raspberrylike swellings, contributed heavily to mortality on the Middle Passage. Sometimes acquired in childhood, the disease was hard to cure, as the pimples and ulcers persisted. Dr. T. Aubrey declared that the "yaws flux" was "the mortal Disease that cuts off three parts in four of the Negroes, that are commonly lost on Board ships." 35

Intestinal worms were another common source of illness among slaves. Infestation often began in childhood, and in addition many slaves seem to have acquired worms on their trek to the coast. Dr. Thomas Winterbottom, who had been physician to the colony of Sierra Leone, said that slaves provided by the Foolas were invariably infested with worms. "This probably arises," he explained, "from the very scanty and wretched diet which they are fed in the *path*, as they term the journey, and which, from the distance they are brought inland, often lasts for many weeks, at the same time that their strength is further reduced by the heavy loads they are obliged to carry."[27]

Knowledge of hygiene was also meager in the slave trade era. Many ships' masters understood the importance of cleanliness. Captain John Newton in 1750 recorded in his journal the death of a slave woman, "taken with a lethargic disorder." Under his instructions sailors, "Scraped the rooms, then smoked the ship with tar, tobacco and brimstone for 2 hours, afterwards washed with vinegar." Newton's practice was common in the latter part of the century. Slave decks were routinely scrubbed with a combination of lime juice and vinegar, following which they were dried by burning tar, tobacco, and brimstone.[28]

The importance of fresh air to hygiene was recognized. In good weather slaves spent the day on open deck. Captain William Littleton testified in 1789 that it was a general rule to keep the slaves on deck as much as possible, "with prudence," he added. He thought that all slave ships were equipped with air

---

[26]French Clandestine Slave Trade Collection, Henry E. Huntington Library, HM43994. George F. Dow, *Slave Ships and Sailing* (Salem, Mass., 1927; reprinted New York 1970), xxvii–xxxv, from "an old book of voyages."

[27]Sheridan, "Guinea Surgeons," 16–17.

[28]John Newton, *Journal of a Slave Trader* (London, 1962 reprint of 1788 work).

ports and gratings; sometimes the slaves, when below, complained of too much air and begged to have tarpaulins placed over the openings.[29]

Another slave-ship captain, William Sherwood, was asked whether the construction and "conveniences" of a ship were not more important than confining the number of slaves to a certain tonnage. In response he said, "I think the construction is more material than the tonnage; in a long narrow ship the air circulates more freely: a short quarter deck, no top-gallant forecastle, no gangway, and a very low waist, are Circumstances of greater advantage than a mere extension of tonnage."[30]

40 Slave ships were equipped with a medical manual, such as Dr. T. Aubrey's *The Sea-Surgeon, or the Guinea Man's Vade Mecum*, which was published as early as 1729. The Dutch West India Companies and subsequent free-trade companies gave detailed instructions about medical, hygienic, and dietary care of slaves. The company in 1733 dismissed a doctor who had been guilty of ignorant and negligent treatment of slaves on the ship *Beschutter*.[31]

The presence of doctors on slave ships demonstrates concern about the health of the cargo. In the seventeenth century the Royal African Company gave attention to health and hygiene. Its ships employed surgeons, who were paid so much per head for slaves landed in America in good health, a practice known as paying head money.[32] The Dutch appear commonly to have had surgeons aboard, and in the French trade the presence of a surgeon was required; on large vessels two or more were often in attendance.[33] North American slavers seem rarely to have carried doctors. In the absence of surgeons, slave-ship captains were expected to diagnose and treat illness.[34] Surgeons in the era of the slave trade secured their training as apprentices, sometimes going on to hospitals and to universities.

The quality of the Guinea surgeons ranged widely; some of them seem to have been highly capable and conscientious, but many seem to have been "generally driven to engage in so disagreeable an employ by the confined state of their finances," like Archibald Dalzel. One captain complained that his surgeon "has turned out a Drunken Rascal and Mutinous with all." A report from Bance Island in 1721 related, "19 slaves dead since their being put on board. Mr. Trashall the Doctor Negligent."[35]

[29]PP, *A&P*, 1789, XXIV (633), 215–216.

[30]Ibid., 1790, XXIX (698), 495.

[31]Postma, "Dutch Participation," 211.

[32]Davies, *Royal African Company*, 292.

[33]Stein, *French Slave Trade*, 68. Léon Vignols, "La Compagne Négrière de *la Perle* (1755–1757)," *Revue Historique*, CLXIII (1930), 70–71.

[34]Darold D. Wax, "A Philadelphia Surgeon on a Slaving Voyage to Africa, 1749–1751," *Pennsylvania Magazine of History and Biography*, XCII (1968), 465–493. Coughtry, "Notorious Triangle," 389.

[35]Alexander Falconbridge, *An Account of the Slave Trade on the Coast of Africa* (London, 1788; reprinted New York, 1973), 28. William Roper to James Rogers, PRO C107/5. Donnan, *Documents*, II, 285.

The British law of 1788, by which Parliament first regulated the slave trade, required every slave ship to employ at least one certified surgeon, without whom the ship would not be cleared for Africa. The surgeon was ordered to keep a journal recording the number of slaves, the deaths of slaves and crew, and the causes of death. Upon certification that not more than three slaves in the hundred had died from the time of the ship's arrival in Africa to the time of arrival in the West Indies, the surgeon would be paid twenty-five pounds and the captain fifty pounds. This law, which likewise limited the number of slaves per ton, had a sequel, though delayed, in reduced mortality.

The duties of a slaver's surgeon began before departure for Africa. Dr. Aubrey cautioned young surgeons taking up the Guinea practice that they should make certain the ship stocked not only a sufficient supply of medicine, but also of food, tobacco, and pipes.[36]

It was on the African coast that in the eyes of slave merchants surgeons began 45 to justify their cost. Slave merchants wanted healthy slaves, who could command a good price in America. Dr. Arnold declared that "the slaves are examined to see if they are physically fit, have healthy eyes, good teeth, stand over four feet high, and if men, are not ruptured; if females, have not 'fallen breasts.'"[37] The stay on the African coast, often stretching over months, occasioned care of those slaves who had been acquired, for beginning surgeons the coping with baffling problems, and necessitated preparation for the Middle Passage. The diet of Africans and the adequacy of water supplies were special cares.

On the Middle Passage the ship's surgeon had both routine duties and extraordinary ones. The French slaver *Aurore,* Captain Herpin, in 1718 received these instructions: "We order Sieur Herpin, all his officers and the surgeon, to take great care of the health of the negroes, to prevent lewdness between the negresses and the negroes and the crew, to have them all properly cared for and to have the space between decks cleaned and scraped every day in order that no corruption at all may be generated there."[38]

It was the duty of the surgeon to make a daily examination of the slaves, going below the first thing in the morning before the slaves were brought on deck. Because the slaves were crowded below, Dr. Isaac Wilson, with great sensitivity, usually removed his shoes before going down, and then walked cautiously lest he tread on the slaves. Sick slaves were separated from the others by being placed in the hospital, which often was nothing more than a reserved place, with no accommodations and with bare planks. Body sores commonly resulted from hospitalization, but if plasters and bandages were applied the slaves frequently removed them. Men were taken out of their irons [shackles]. Surgeons attended the patients with medicines brought from the home port and prescribed a diet; wine and sago (a kind of starch) were commonly given to the sick. On the ships he was in, Falconbridge said that the surgeon and his mate

[36]Sheridan, "Guinea Surgeons," 6–7.
[37]PP, *A&P,* 1789 (646a).
[38]Quotation in Dart, "First Cargo of Slaves for Louisiana," 164.

were responsible for the cleanliness of women slaves, and the first mate for the men.[39]

The outbreak of an epidemic on shipboard placed an extraordinary strain upon the surgeon, increasing the number of visits to hospital and hold, and keeping him busy administering medicines and supervising hygiene. When measles broke out on the *Wolf,* Dr. William Chancellor recorded, "There is scarce a day now passes without my being in the utmost anxiety. . . ." Guinea surgeons often suffered from a sense of helplessness in the face of epidemics.[40]

Slave-ship surgeon's duties sometimes extended to preparing the slaves for market. Preparations were designed to heal as well as hide diseases. Black skins were made to glow with oil, wounds closed, and scars concealed with ointments. Mercury and other drugs employed in these artifices could later cause a disease to erupt with even greater virulence. Slaves who were obviously sick or maimed were often sold separately, sometimes as speculations against the chance they might improve in health. Ecroide Claxton, surgeon on the brig *Young Hero,* advised the seller's agent in the West Indies that fourteen slaves were going to die. The agent responded that it would be best to dispose of them immediately, except for those who afforded hopes of recovery; these he would buy for himself.[41]

50   The Guinea surgeons have mainly been ignored by historians, except to draw on them for horror tales of the Middle Passage. Employed by slave shipowners out of economic rather than humanitarian motives, the surgeons by their presence in fact demonstrate a concern to abate sickness and mortality on the Passage. Often of questionable ability, the surgeons conducted a practice that had unusual difficulties. They worked in a milieu that was largely controlled by shipowners and merchants, who dictated the numbers to be carried in a ship as well as the quantities of provisions and medicines. They were practicing unfamiliar aspects of medicine, still a quasi-science, which called for a knowledge of nautical medicine, tropical medicine, and of the mingling of disease environments. A small monthly salary, head money for slaves, generally one male and one female out of the cargo—more valuable if well than ill—were allowed surgeons "in consideration for their care and trouble in the management of Slaves on board the ship."[42]

The feeding of slaves early in the trade became routinized. It was customary to give two meals a day, placing ten slaves about small tubs containing their victuals. Each slave was provided with a wooden spoon. A staple on English ships was horse beans, brought from England and stored in dry vats until they were boiled in lard until they formed a pulp. Slaves were said to have a good stomach for beans, and besides, as James Barbot remarked, "it is a proper fattening food

[39]PP, *A&P*, 1790, XXX (699), 561–581, esp. 562, 574 (Wilson); 581–632, esp. 632 (Falconbridge).

[40]Wax, "A Philadelphia Surgeon," 487. PP, *A&P*, 1790, XXX (699), 630.

[41]MacPherson, *Annals*, IV, 146. PP, *A&P*, 1789, XXVI (646a), part III. PP, *A&P*, 1791, XXIV (748), 39.

[42]Wax, "A Philadelphia Surgeon," 492. PP, *A&P*, 1790, XXIV (698), 29–30.

for captives." Rice, available both in Europe and Africa, was a second staple; it was sometimes boiled with yams, available in Africa. Meat, whether beef or pork, was rarely offered. Slaves from the Bight were accustomed to yams; those from the Windward and Gold coasts were accustomed to rice. Palm oil, flour, water, and pepper mixed together produced *slabber-sauce*. Corn [wheat] vegetables, lemons, and limes from time to time appeared in this regimen. Vessels often made a landfall before reaching their ultimate destination, as at Prince's Island in the eastern Atlantic, or at the outer rim of the Caribbean, to take on provisions. North American slavers commonly fed their slaves rice and corn, both of which were available in America and Africa, and black-eyed peas. The rice was boiled in an iron pot and corn was fried into cakes. Water was the usual beverage, sometimes flavored with molasses by the Americans. Wine and spirits were administered as medicines, and the smoking of tobacco in pipes was often encouraged.[43]

Men slaves, but not women or children, were placed in shackles as soon as they were put aboard ship. They were bound together in pairs, left leg to right leg, left wrist to right wrist. Some masters removed the shackles once out to sea, others only during the day, and some not until the destination had been attained. Shipboard security varied with the origins of slaves. Captain James Fraser said he seldom confined Angola slaves, "being very peaceable," took off the handcuffs of Windward and Gold Coast slaves as soon as the ship was out of sight of land, and soon after that the leg irons, but Bonny slaves, whom he thought vicious, were kept under stricter confinement.[44]

Violently removed from their customary way of life, cramped in narrow, floating quarters, dominated by white-skinned men, despondent and often in trauma, Africans were exposed to acts of brutality, incited to revolt on shipboard, and driven to taking their own lives. On the Middle Passage there was little check to sadism and lust. Perhaps the most infamous atrocity in the annals of the slave trade was committed by Luke Collingwood, captain of the *Zong*. In 1781 he loaded his ship at Saint Thomas on the African coast with a cargo of four hundred slaves and proceeded toward Jamaica, 6 September. By 29 November he had lost seven white people, over sixty slaves, and had many more who were sick. Discovering that he had left only two hundred gallons of fresh water, he ascertained that, if the slaves died a natural death, it would be the loss of the shipowners, but if the slaves were thrown alive into the sea, it would be the loss of the insurers. He designated sick and weak slaves, and on that day fifty-four were thrown into the sea. On 1 December forty-two more were thrown overboard; on that day a heavy rain enabled the ship to collect in casks enough water for eleven days' full allowance. Even so, twenty-six more slaves, their hands bound, were thrown into the sea, and ten more, about to be bound for disposal, jumped into the sea.

---

[43]Donnan, *Documents*, I, 462–463. Falconbridge, *An Account of the Slave Trade*, 21–23. Hamm, "American Slave Trade," 214–215.

[44]PP, *A&P*, 1790, XXIV (698), 3–60, esp. 38, 26, 24. Newton, *Journal*, 25.

The underwriters refused to pay insurance, and the owners, the Gregsons and others of Liverpool, brought suit, asking thirty pounds for each slave lost in this manner, which was described as "the perils of the seas." The Court of King's Bench gave a verdict in favor of the shipowners. The affair was taken up by abolitionists, serving their cause. "The horrible murder," Granville Sharp declared, "must surely demonstrate an absolute necessity for the Nation to put an entire stop to Slavedealing." In time the *Zong* atrocity led to the enactment of two laws restricting recovery through insurance for slave losses at sea.[45]

55   Shipwrecks were common in the era of the slave trade, and took their toll on the Middle Passage. The first ship sent out by the French Asiento Company to Buenos Aires, carrying 325 slaves, was lost "par une tempête terrible." Captivity could compound the tragedy of shipwreck. The Dutch ship *Leusden* in 1737 lost 700 of 716 slaves—one of the most calamitous voyages in the trade's history.[46]

Slave rebellions added to the hazards and mortality of the Middle Passage. The authors of a popular history of the slave trade have counted fifty-five rebellions recorded in detail, passing references to more than a hundred more, and a number about as great of ships "cut-off" by Africans all in the period from 1699 to 1845. The historian of the Rhode Island slave trade, Jay Coughtry, counted only seventeen slave revolts in that trade from 1730 to 1807, or approximately one every four and a half years; one in every fifty-five voyages. This compares with estimates of the French trade of one every one and a half years or one in every fifteen voyages, and of the British trade of one every two years.[47]

For a large number of slaves suicide was preferable to slavery. Many slaveship accounts record death through refusal to eat or by violence. A considerable record of slave insurrections and resistance to the slave trade shows that the tradition of African acquiescence and docility is in error. "A Cormantee," an observer warned in 1764, "will never brook servitude; though young, but will either destroy himself, or murder his master." Slaves sought opportunities to escape, refused to eat, formed conspiracies, rose in revolt, took their own lives, and killed and wounded their captors. It was with good reason that male slaves were kept in irons. Some slaves were thought by contemporaries to be more rebellious than others. John Barbot wrote in 1682 that "Fida and Ardra slaves are of all the others, the most apt to revolt aboard ships."[48]

---

[45] A standard account is Prince Hoare, *Memoirs of Granville Sharpe* (London, 1828), app. viii, pp. xvii–xviii. The case was taken to the Court of King's Bench in a hearing for a new trial; Henry Roscoe, *Reports of Cases Argued and Determined in the Court of King's Bench* (1782–1785), III, 232–235. A diligent search by the present writer, with much help from staff members of the Public Record Office, failed to find a record of a second trial. G. Sharp to W. Dilwyn, 18 May 1783, Sharp MSS., British and Foreign Bible Society, London.

[46] Bonnaisseux, *Les Grandes Compagnies de Commerce*, 390–391. Johannes Postma, "Mortality in the Dutch Slave Trade, 1675–1795," in Gemery and Hogendorn, eds., *The Uncommon Market.* "Dutch Participation," 236–237.

[47] Mannix and Cowley, *Black Cargoes*, 111. Coughtry, "Notorious Triangle," 398–399.

[48] Darold D. Wax, "Negro Resistance to the Early American Slave Trade," *JNH*, LI (1966), 1–15. *Gentleman's Magazine*, XXXIV, 1764, 487. Donnan, *Documents*, I, 207 for the *James;* 295 for Barbot.

Few notions of the Middle Passage are more fixed than that overcrowding or "tight packing," was a major cause of mortality. Abolitionists exploited the notion; the diagram of the *Brookes* exhibited it; and Clarkson extolled the horrors of cramped quarters. Slaves were said to be packed like spoons, or like books on a shelf. Slave-ship captains acknowledged that on occasion slaves might not have sufficient space for all to lie on their backs.

Numerous captains and other contemporaries asserted that overcrowding was lethal. Two Barbados factors in 1664 reported a "great mortality" "through so many sick and decaying negroes being thronghed together." In listing the cause of "the great mortality, which so often happens in slave ships," James Barbot placed first, "taking in too many." This contemporary opinion has been reaffirmed by a modern scholar, who has asserted "That overcrowding was a factor affecting mortality. . . ."[49]

Yet not all contemporaries shared this belief. Captain Knox, who had also been a ship's surgeon, said he never supposed a slave died from overcrowding. And Dr. George Pinckard, comparing slave ships with troop transports from his vantage point on Barbados in 1795–1796, declared that "The slaves are much more crowded than the soldiers, yet far more healthy."[50] It is the conclusion of some present-day scholars that "tight packing" was not a major cause of mortality on the Middle Passage.   60

Scholars, especially Herbert S. Klein, have made statistical analyses of the relationship between mortality and "tight packing" for aspects of the Portuguese, French, British, and Dutch slave trades. A study of the mortality of slaves arriving in Rio from 1795 to 1811, based upon numbers of slaves per ship leaving Africa, concluded that "there is no significant correlation between the number of slaves carried and the rate of mortality." Findings on the French trade, based upon slaves per ton ratio, also indicate "that the extent of crowding on ships of a given size did not appear to affect mortality." A third inquiry into mortality on British ships from 1791 to 1797 found that mortality rates could not be explained by ships' tonnage or the number of slaves carried per ton. Investigation of cargo density in the Dutch slave trade failed to discover any relationship between crowding and mortality. Comparison of the largest and smallest cargoes resulted in the finding that "more than half . . . showed a higher rate of death among the less crowded cargoes." The findings should be considered as suggestive rather than definitive, because in the Brazilian study tonnage data were not available and in the other studies the varying time lengths of voyages were not taken into account.[51]

If "tight packing" is a less meaningful explanation than once believed, what were the causes of slave mortality on the Middle Passage, emphasized by

---

[49]*CSP, Col*, 1661–1668, 94. Donnan, *Documents*, I, 460. Anstey, *Atlantic Slave Trade*, 30.

[50]PP, *A&P*, 1789, XXIV (633), 83. George Pinckard, *Notes on the West Indies* (3 vols., London, 1806; reprinted New York, 1970), II. 9.

[51]Klein, *Middle Passage*, 66, 194–195. Klein and Engerman, "Slave Mortality on British Ships," 118. Postma, "Mortality in the Dutch Slave Trade," 12–13. I am indebted to Joseph C. Miller for the point about caution in receiving these findings.

modern scholarship? First of all, the length of the voyage had much to do with the death rate. Scholars have shown a positive correlation between time at sea and mortality—the longer the time the higher the loss. Thus, ships from East Africa had a higher loss than those from West Africa. The incidence of mortality rose if a passage was slow and protracted, in the case of East Africa ships longer than 70 days, and in the case of West African ships in the Portuguese trade longer than 50. Moreover, a ship that ran short of provisions and water on a passage longer than contemplated was liable to a heavy mortality loss. A study of the eighteenth-century French trade disclosed that ships with a passage of 40 days incurred a loss of only 8.3 per cent as against ships with a passage of over 141 days which incurred a loss of 21.3 per cent.[52]

Similarly, studies of the Dutch and nineteenth-century trades stress time at sea as an important factor. Dutch slavers in the free-trade era, plying the passage from Angola to the Caribbean, suffered a mortality rate of 10.65, while those plying the much longer passage from the Guinea Coast suffered a rate of 17.4 per cent. The investigator concluded, "The duration of the middle passage provides the most systematic explanation of mortality patterns." In the nineteenth century, fragmentary data for the slave trade to Brazil from 1817 to 1843 disclose that ships making the voyage in twenty to twenty-nine days incurred a mortality loss of 5.1 per cent, while those making the voyage in sixty-one or more days incurred a loss of 25.9 per cent.[53]

If time at sea was an important contributor to mortality, so too was African region, separate from distance to America. Here, as we have earlier seen, historians stress conditions in Africa rather than on the voyage. These conditions include the health of the slaves before embarkation, the length of the trip from the interior, the pressures on African merchants of supply and demand, and length of detention at port or on shipboard before sailing. Some African areas produced a higher mortality rate than others; and twentieth-century scholarship has confirmed the eighteenth-century belief that the Bight of Biafra and the Bight of Benin were particularly deadly.[54]

65 Slave mortality on the Middle Passage declined in the eighteenth century. The reasons for this remain in part speculative, but we may cite the growing experience of slave traders, changes in shipping, gains in medicine and hygiene, and profit considerations. The growing experience of slave traders facilitated the African transaction and mitigated the evils of the passage. From the middle of the century the trade centered in the hands of large-scale merchants gathering this experience among regular traders. Familiarity with the complexities of the voyage as well as with the African market on the part of these bodies of specialized merchants could only result in reducing the human losses of the Middle Passage.

[52]Klein, *Middle Passage*, 86–90, 198–200. Mettas, "Honfleur et la Traite des Noirs," 20.
[53]Postma, "Mortality in the Dutch Slave Trade," 250. Curtin, *Atlantic Slave Trade*, 282.
[54]Klein and Engerman, "Slave Mortality on British Ships," 117–118.

Two changes in shipping were significant. One was the development of vessels designed for the slave trade. Of middle-range tonnage, built to specifications, they enhanced commerce in slaves. The other change was the resort to copper sheathing, which increased the speed of ships and reduced travel time. Knowledge of nautical medicine, with a growing body of knowledge of tropical medicine and a concern about hygiene and diet, combined to abate the perils of the passage.

Beyond all this there lay strong economic incentives to minimize mortality at sea. Slaves were a perishable cargo whose death meant a debit. The costs of slaves in Africa were rising in the century, it would appear in more rapid proportion than prices in America; shipping costs were also on the rise. These economic factors, taken together, gave slaving interests a strong inducement to maintain the lives and indeed the health of slaves.

The poet Heinrich Heine saw a large profit after a 50 per cent mortality. He did not envision the much larger profit through preventing high mortality. In his memorable poem, "The Slave Ship," he has the supercargo say:

> Six hundred niggers I bought dirt-cheap
> Where the Senegal river is flowing;
> Their flesh is firm, and their sinews tough
> As the finest iron going.

> I got them by barter, and gave in exchange
> Glass beads, steel goods, and some brandy;
> I shall make at least eight hundred per cent,
> With but half of them living and handy.

Slave merchants and ship masters alike were keenly aware of the pecuniary importance of a high survival rate on the Middle Passage. Examples abound of mercantile instructions to masters to care for their human cargo. The Vernons of Newport, Rhode Island, enjoined Captain Godfrey to let the slaves "have a sufficiency of good Diet," adding, "as you are Sensible your voyage depends upon their Health." Masters, mates, and surgeons each had a financial stake in landing the cargo alive and in good condition; commissions, privilege slaves, and head money for the surgeon were realistic incentives to care for the slaves. Captain Knox of the British trade summed it up in 1789, "The captains, mates, and surgeon's profits, all but a trifle, depend on preserving the slaves' health."[55]

Governments for the most part gave little legislative attention to the regulation of conditions of the Middle Passage. An exception was Portugal, which as early as 1684 enacted a measure regulating the slave-carrying capacity of a ship. It provided that officials measure a ship by its deck areas rather than volume, and fix the capacity by a factor, which customarily was five slaves for each

[55]Vernons to Captain Godfrey, 8 Nov. 1755, Vernon MSS., New York Historical Society. PP, *A&P*, 1789, XXIV (633), 106.

measured two tons, though space with portholes could carry seven slaves per ton. It also decreed the quantity of provisions a slaver must carry: enough for a voyage of thirty-five days to Pernambuco, for forty days to Bahia, and for fifty days to Rio. These voyage times were about average for the seventeenth and eighteenth centuries; and therefore the law did not contemplate above-average crossings. Antedating the British Regulatory Act of 1788 by more than a century, the Portuguese law disproves the assertion of a British historian that no other European nation than Britain "imposed official restrictions."[56]

The British law of 1788 was brought forward in Parliament by Sir William Dolben, who was a correspondent of the London committee on the slave trade. The law, as we have already noted, required employment of a trained surgeon and imposed certain obligations upon him. It also offered premiums to surgeons and captains if the mortality rate of a Middle Passage was no more than 3 per cent. Beyond that it looked to the question of crowding; Dolben at first proposing to apportion five slaves to every ton in ships under 150 tons tons burden. During the ensuing debate witnesses from Liverpool opposed regulation, and the prime minister, Pitt, dispatched Captain Perry to Liverpool to examine slave vessels then in port, resulting in the famous diagram of the *Brookes.* The law as finally passed restricted the carriage to five slaves for every 3 tons up to 201 tons and one slave for each additional ton. The law outlawed insurance on any cargo of slaves, with exceptions such as perils of the sea and fire. When renewed the next year it contained provisions, it may be remembered, that looked to the welfare of crew members. When extended in 1799 the regulation shifted its basis from tonnage ratio to space measurements between decks, further reducing ship capacity. The effect, one scholar has concluded, was to reduce the slaves' per-ton-ratio from 2.6 per ton in the prereform period to one slave per ton in the final decade of the British trade.[57]

Scholars' analyses of losses on the Middle Passage do not normally reckon slave losses before departure from Africa. Preembarkation mortality significantly augmented the totality of deaths in the transit from Africa to America. The journal of the ship *Arthur,* sailing for the Royal African Company in 1677–1678, contained the melancholy record, "died of our negroes befor such tyme as wee could gett over the Barr 12 men 6 woman and 1 Boy: have severall others sick"; thirty-six more perished before the ship left Africa. An early nineteenth-century American account of mortality in the Bight trade underscored the high

[56]Joseph C. Miller, "Sources and Knowledge of the Slave Trade in the Southern Atlantic," unpublished paper kindly supplied me by Professor Miller, 37–38, 43n., 70. Anstey, *Atlantic Slave Trade,* 31.

[57]Namier and Brooke, *History of Parliament,* II, 329. *Parliamentary History,* XXVII, 54. Clarkson, *History,* 1, 514, 517, 520. The text of the Act is in Donnan, *Documents,* II, 582–589. Klein, *Middle Passage,* 145. James W. LoGerfo, "Sir William Dolben and 'The Cause of Humanity': The Passage of the Slave Trade Regulation Act of 1788," *Eighteenth Century Studies,* VI (1972), 431–451.

preembarkation toll. "The greater part of this mortality often happens during the time the ships stay in Affrica [*sic*]," it noted.[58]

A systematic study of preembarkation mortality in the Dutch trade found an estimated 3 to 5 per cent loss during the years of the West India Company. These slaves often endured a long waiting period for ships in the forts and castles of the company. The major castle at Elmina had a dungeon with a planned capacity for three hundred slaves into which four hundred were frequently crammed. With the reduction of the storage period in the free-trade era, the estimated mortality rate in Africa in the Dutch experience fell to 1.5 per cent to 2.5.[59]

Postcrossing mortality before sale heightened the tragic loss of life in the passage from Africa to America. Here there was often a waiting period before disembarkation and perhaps another before sale. Wilberforce in 1789 gave the specific loss in the West Indies at 4.5 per cent. Spanish policy required a health inspection before slaves could be landed. If there were delays, deaths among the slaves "often mounted so rapidly that importers faced financial ruin." After landing, there was at Cartagena a minimum two-week waiting period before customs clearance could be secured. During this interval slaves were confined in pens or barracoons, where in the early seventeenth century the mortality was not less than 10 per cent of the cargo. The policy of refreshment in the West Indies before reexportation to Cartagena together with improved conditions in the late eighteenth century effected a fall in the barracoon death rate to about 1 per cent. A committee of the Jamaica assembly reported that from 1655 to 1787, 31,181 slaves had died in the harbor of 676,276 reported at the customshouse as arrived. Slave-ship captains in giving evidence about mortality often omitted deaths in the harbor, which at Jamaica amounted to about 4.1 per cent.[60] In the assessment of the morality incurred by Africans in their forced migration from one continent to another the preembarkation and postembarkation deaths before they were sold into American slavery should be noted.

In this chapter on the Middle Passage we have seen that ships were on average smaller than those in the stereotype, and often not filled, that the death rates for the most nearly comparable white groups were often higher than for blacks, that the question of disease environments complicates comparisons, and that there were factors which help account for death other than greed, brutality, neglect, and disease.

Modern scholarship, acknowledging that the Middle Passage was repugnant and on occasion horrifying, and affirming that the mortality rate declined in the eighteenth century, analyzes the theme with discrimination as well as compassion. It stresses conditions in Africa, including drought, famine, epidemics, and

75

---

[58]Donnan, *Documents*, I, 230 (for the *Arthur*). Undated manuscript, "On the African slave carrying trade," Boston Public Library, accession no. 1450.

[59]Postma, "Mortality in the Dutch Slave Trade," 242–243.

[60]*Parliamentary History*, XXVIII, 65. David L. Chandler, "Health Conditions in the Slave Trade of Colonial New Granada," in R. B. Toplin, ed., *Slavery and Race Relations in Latin America* (Westport, Conn., 1974), 51–88. MacPherson, *Annals*, IV, 146n. PP, *A&P*, 1789 (646a), part III.

waiting time before embarkation, that bear upon the health of slaves during the
Middle Passage. It notes variations in mortality with reference to African place of
origins; thus slaves from the Bights suffered higher rates than those from Sierra
Leone. It takes account of length of time on shipboard; long confinement of
slaves on shipboard led to high death tolls. It scrutinizes the state of knowledge
in the field of tropical medicine, seeing its limitations but also its advances. It
runs up statistics of sizes of ships and human cargoes and discounts the factor
of "tight packing." Not abating moral condemnation of the traffic, it strives to
understand the economics of the slave trade as significant in explaining death in
transit. The sway of the forces of supply and demand is observed. And finally,
modern scholarship sees the countervailing influence of human greed, how
economic incentives to deliver a cargo alive and well served to reduce the
severity of the Middle Passage.   [1981]

1. This chapter from Rawley's book is concerned, like Cohn's article, with mortality during the Middle Passage. What are the causes he offers for death on
the journey? How does his explanation compare to Cohn's?

The Poem and the Nonfiction Sources

1. Adams reports that Lieutenant Gedney, who found the *Amistad* floating in
U.S. waters, was moved to feel sympathy for the two Spanish slave traders
Ruiz and Montes and the U.S. government was sympathetic enough with
them to join the suit. What is Adams's view of these reactions? How does
the issue of sympathy resonate with the poem?
2. According to Adams, one of the arguments supporting the slave trade even
after "all Christendom" accepted that "victors in war have no right to
enslave the vanquished" (paragraph 37) was that Africans themselves
claimed prisoners of war as slaves. Therefore, Europeans who bought slaves
from Africans were not creating slaves, merely trading in humans who had
been made slaves by their own culture. Adams rejects this justification. How
does this idea appear in the poem?
3. How does Adams use American ideals to argue that the slaves ought to be
freed?
4. Cohn and Rawley consider some of the conditions that might have caused
the high levels of slave mortality on the Middle Passage. How might the
point of view in Brown's chapter help them explain why, even though they
were exposed to the same diseases for the same amount of time at sea, more
slaves than white crew members died on the trip?
5. What other ideas in the articles help to contextualize the poem?
6. In Part 3 of the poem, the Spanish slave trader objects to the "Roman
rhetoric" with which John Quincy Adams wove "a hero's / garland for
Cinquez" (167–68). "Roman rhetoric" might include the use of subordinate
clauses to create complicated syntax. In the passages you have here, does
Adams use these structures and other devices of elevated, formal language
to make his case?

FICTION

CHINUA ACHEBE

CHINUA ACHEBE *(1930–) was born of a Christian family in Ogidi, Nigeria, and attended Government College in Unuahia and University College in Ibadan. He received a B.A. from London University in 1953 and studied broadcasting at the BBC. Married in 1961, he has four children. He was one of the founders of the new literature in Nigeria and is considered to be one the finest writers in English anywhere. He works from the African oral tradition, often basing his stories on the ancestor myths that he says serve a human purpose. He writes of the rhythms of community life as he finds them in his native country and shows how they are changed by the pressures of colonialization and modernization.*

Dead Men's Path

Michael Obi's hopes were fulfilled much earlier than he had expected. He was appointed headmaster of Ndume Central School in January 1949. It had always been an unprogressive school, so the Mission authorities decided to send a young and energetic man to run it. Obi accepted this responsibility with enthusiasm. He had many wonderful ideas and this was an opportunity to put them into practice. He had had sound secondary school education which designated him a "pivotal teacher" in the official records and set him apart from the other headmasters in the mission field. He was outspoken in his condemnation of the narrow views of these older and often less-educated ones.

"We shall make a good job of it, shan't we?" he asked his young wife when they first heard the joyful news of his promotion.

"We shall do our best," she replied. "We shall have such beautiful gardens and everything will be just *modern* and delightful . . ." In their two years of married life she had become completely infected by his passion for "modern methods" and his denigration of "these old and superannuated people in the teaching field who would be better employed as traders in the Onitsha market." She began to see herself already as the admired wife of the young headmaster, the queen of the school.

The wives of the other teachers would envy her position. She would set the fashion in everything . . . Then, suddenly, it occurred to her that there might not be other wives. Wavering between hope and fear, she asked her husband, looking anxiously at him.

"All our colleagues are young and unmarried," he said with enthusiasm which for once she did not share. "Which is a good thing," he continued.

"Why?"

"Why? They will give all their time and energy to the school."

Nancy was downcast. For a few minutes she became sceptical about the new school; but it was only for a few minutes. Her little personal misfortune could not blind her to her husband's happy prospects. She looked at him as he sat

5

folded up in a chair. He was stoop-shouldered and looked frail. But he sometimes surprised people with sudden bursts of physical energy. In his present posture, however, all his bodily strength seemed to have retired behind his deep-set eyes, giving them an extraordinary power of penetration. He was only twenty-six, but looked thirty or more. On the whole, he was not unhandsome.

"A penny for your thoughts, Mike," said Nancy after a while, imitating the woman's magazine she read.

10   "I was thinking what a grand opportunity we've got at last to show these people how a school should be run."

Ndume School was backward in every sense of the word. Mr. Obi put his whole life into the work, and his wife hers too. He had two aims. A high standard of teaching was insisted upon, and the school compound was to be turned into a place of beauty. Nancy's dream-gardens came to life with the coming of the rains, and blossomed. Beautiful hibiscus and allamanda hedges in brilliant red and yellow marked out the carefully tended school compound from the rank neighbourhood bushes.

One evening as Obi was admiring his work he was scandalized to see an old woman from the village hobble right across the compound, through a marigold flower-bed and the hedges. On going up there he found faint signs of an almost disused path from the village across the school compound to the bush on the other side.

"It amazes me," said Obi to one of his teachers who had been three years in the school, "that you people allowed the villagers to make use of this footpath. It is simply incredible." He shook his head.

"The path," said the teacher apologetically, "appears to be very important to them. Although it is hardly used, it connects the village shrine with their place of burial."

15   "And what has that got to do with the school?" asked the headmaster.

"Well, I don't know," replied the other with a shrug of the shoulders. "But I remember there was a big row some time ago when we attempted to close it."

"That was some time ago. But it will not be used now," said Obi as he walked away. "What will the Government Education Officer think of this when he comes to inspect the school next week? The villagers might, for all I know, decide to use the schoolroom for a pagan ritual during the inspection."

Heavy sticks were planted closely across the path at the two places where it entered and left the school premises. These were further strengthened with barbed wire.

Three days later the village priest of *Ani* called on the headmaster. He was an old man and walked with a slight stoop. He carried a stout walking-stick which he usually tapped on the floor, by way of emphasis, each time he made a new point in his argument.

20   "I have heard," he said after the usual exchange of cordialities, "that our ancestral footpath has recently been closed . . ."

"Yes," replied Mr. Obi. "We cannot allow people to make a highway of our school compound."

"Look here, my son," said the priest bringing down his walking-stick, "this path was here before you were born and before your father was born. The whole life of this village depends on it. Our dead relatives depart by it and our ancestors visit us by it. But most important it is the path of children coming in to be born . . .

"The whole purpose of our school," he said finally, "is to eradicate just such beliefs as that. Dead men do not require footpaths. The whole idea is just fantastic. Our duty is to teach your children to laugh at such ideas."

"What you say may be true," replied the priest, "but we follow the practices of our fathers. If you re-open the path we shall have nothing to quarrel about. What I always say is: let the hawk perch and let the eagle perch." He rose to go.

"I am sorry," said the young headmaster. "But the school compound cannot be a thoroughfare. It is against our regulations. I would suggest your constructing another path, skirting our premises. We can even get our boys to help in building it. I don't suppose the ancestors will find the little detour too burdensome."

"I have no more words to say," said the old priest, already outside.

Two days later a young woman in the village died in childbed. A diviner was immediately consulted and he prescribed heavy sacrifices to propitiate ancestors insulted by the fence.

Obi woke up next morning among the ruins of his work. The beautiful hedges were torn up not just near the path but right round the school, the flowers trampled to death and one of the school buildings pulled down . . . That day, the white Supervisor came to inspect the school and wrote a nasty report on the state of the premises but more seriously about the "tribal-war situation developing between the school and the village, arising in part from the misguided zeal of the new headmaster." [1973]

1. What kind of narrator is telling the story? What effect does that have on the story?
2. Are there any signs early in the story that things will not turn out as well as Mr. and Mrs. Obi hope?
3. Why didn't Obi's suggestion for a compromise work? Can you think of suggestions that would have created a more successful resolution?
4. How would the priest's proverb have been different if he had said, "let the hawk and the eagle perch"?
5. What difference does it make that the story takes place in 1949? What is the significance of the school's being run by "Mission authorities"?
6. Is the Supervisor right that Obi's "zeal" is "misguided"?
7. What is the significance of the similarity between the description of Michael Obi as "stoop-shouldered" and of the priest as walking "with a slight stoop"?

⊚⊚⊚

Chitra B. Divakaruni

Chitra Banerjee Divakaruni (1957–) lived in her birthplace, Calcutta, India, until the age of nineteen when she came to Wright State University in Dayton, Ohio, to continue her education in the field of English. She received her Ph.D. from the University of California, Berkeley, holding many odd jobs along the way. She is the author of Sister of My Heart, The Mistress of Spices, *and* Vine of Desire, *a book of short stories,* The Unknown Errors of Our Lives, *and several books of poems. Her work has been included in over thirty anthologies, including* Best American Short Stories *and the Pushcart Prize anthology. Her first book of stories,* Arranged Marriage, *was the winner of several prestigious awards for fiction. She now lives in San Francisco with her husband and two children.*

Mrs. Dutta Writes a Letter

When the alarm goes off at 5:00 A.M., buzzing like a trapped wasp, Mrs. Dutta has been lying awake for quite a while. She still has difficulty sleeping on the Perma Rest mattress that Sagar and Shyamoli, her son and daughter-in-law, have bought specially for her, though she has had it now for two months. It is too American-soft, unlike the reassuringly solid copra° ticking she used at home. *But this is home now,* she reminds herself. She reaches hurriedly to turn off the alarm, but in the dark her fingers get confused among the knobs, and the electric clock falls with a thud to the floor. Its angry metallic call vibrates through the walls of her room, and she is sure it will wake everyone. She yanks frantically at the wire until she feels it give, and in the abrupt silence that follows she hears herself breathing, a sound harsh and uneven and full of guilt.

Mrs. Dutta knows, of course, that this ruckus is her own fault. She should just not set the alarm. She does not need to get up early here in California, in her son's house. But the habit, taught her by her mother-in-law when she was a bride of seventeen, *A good wife wakes before the rest of the household,* is one she finds impossible to break. How hard it was then to pull her unwilling body away from the sleep-warm clasp of her husband, Sagar's father, whom she had just learned to love; to stumble to the kitchen that smelled of stale garam masala and light the coal stove so that she could make morning tea for them all—her parents-in-law, her husband, his two younger brothers, and the widowed aunt who lived with them.

After dinner, when the family sits in front of the TV, she tries to tell her grandchildren about those days. "I was never good at starting that stove—the smoke stung my eyes, making me cough and cough. Breakfast was never ready on time, and my mother-in-law—oh, how she scolded me, until I was in tears. Every night I'd pray to Goddess Durga, please let me sleep late, just one morning!"

"Mmmm," Pradeep says, bent over a model plane.

---

¹**copra** a product made from dried coconut

"Oooh, how awful," Mrinalini says, wrinkling her nose politely before she turns back to a show filled with jokes that Mrs. Dutta does not understand.

"That's why you should sleep in now, Mother," Shyamoli says, smiling at her from the recliner where she sits looking through *The Wall Street Journal*. With her legs crossed so elegantly under the shimmery blue skirt she has changed into after work, and her unusually fair skin, she could pass for an American, thinks Mrs. Dutta, whose own skin is as brown as roasted cumin. The thought fills her with an uneasy pride.

From the floor where he leans against Shyamoli's knee, Sagar adds, "We want you to be comfortable, Ma. To rest. That's why we brought you to America."

In spite of his thinning hair and the gold-rimmed glasses that he has recently taken to wearing, Sagar's face seems to Mrs. Dutta still that of the boy she used to send off to primary school with his metal tiffin box. She remembers how he crawled into her bed on stormy monsoon nights, how when he was ill, no one else could make him drink his barley water. Her heart lightens in sudden gladness because she is really here, with him and his children in America. "Oh, Sagar," she says, smiling, "now you're talking like this! But did you give me a moment's rest while you were growing up?" And she launches into a description of childhood pranks that has him shaking his head indulgently while disembodied TV laughter echoes through the room.

But later he comes into her bedroom and says, a little shamefaced, "Mother, please don't get up so early in the morning. All that noise in the bathroom—it wakes us up, and Molli has such a long day at work . . ."

And she, turning a little so that he won't see her foolish eyes filling with tears, as though she were a teenage bride again and not a woman well over sixty, nods her head, *yes, yes.*

Waiting for the sounds of the stirring household to release her from the embrace of her Perma Rest mattress, Mrs. Dutta repeats the 108 holy names of God. *Om Keshavaya Namah, Om Narayanaya Namah, Om Madhavaya Namah.*° But underneath she is thinking of the bleached-blue aerogram from Mrs. Basu that has been waiting unanswered on her bedside table all week, filled with news from home. Someone robbed the Sandhya jewelry store. The bandits had guns, but luckily no one was hurt. Mr. Joshi's daughter, that sweet-faced child, has run away with her singing teacher. Who would've thought it? Mrs. Barucha's daughter-in-law had one more baby girl. Yes, their fourth. You'd think they'd know better than to keep trying for a boy. Last Tuesday was Bangla Bandh, another labor strike, everything closed down, not even the buses running. But you can't really blame them, can you? After all, factory workers have to eat too. Mrs. Basu's tenants, whom she'd been trying to evict forever, finally moved out. Good riddance, but you should see the state of the flat.

At the very bottom Mrs. Basu wrote, *Are you happy in America?*

[11]***Om Keshavaya Namah, Om Narayanaya Namah, Om Madhavaya Namah*** from the chant honoring the 108 names for Shiva, the Hindu god of destruction and regeneration

Mrs. Dutta knows that Mrs. Basu, who has been her closest friend since they both moved to Ghoshpara Lane as young brides, cannot be fobbed off with descriptions of Fisherman's Wharf and the Golden Gate Bridge, or even with anecdotes involving grandchildren. And so she has been putting off her reply, while in her heart family loyalty battles with insidious feelings of—but she turns from them quickly and will not name them even to herself.

Now Sagar is knocking on the children's doors—a curious custom this, children being allowed to close their doors against their parents. With relief Mrs. Dutta gathers up her bathroom things. She has plenty of time. Their mother will have to rap again before Pradeep and Mrinalini open their doors and stumble out. Still, Mrs. Dutta is not one to waste the precious morning. She splashes cold water on her face and neck (she does not believe in pampering herself), scrapes the night's gumminess from her tongue with her metal tongue cleaner, and brushes vigorously, though the minty toothpaste does not leave her mouth feeling as clean as does the bittersweet neem stick° she's been using all her life. She combs the knots out of her hair. Even at her age it is thicker and silkier than her daughter-in-law's permed curls. *Such vanity,* she scolds her reflection, *and you a grandmother and a widow besides.* Still, as she deftly fashions her hair into a neat coil, she remembers how her husband would always compare it to monsoon clouds.

15   She hears a sudden commotion outside.

"Pat! Minnie! What d'you mean you still haven't washed up? I'm late to work every morning nowadays because of you kids."

"But, Mom, *she's* in there. She's been there forever . . ." Mrinalini says.

Pause. Then, "So go to the downstairs bathroom."

"But all our stuff is here," Pradeep says, and Mrinalini adds, "It's not fair. Why can't *she* go downstairs?"

20   A longer pause. Mrs. Dutta hopes that Shyamoli will not be too harsh with the girl. But a child who refers to elders in that disrespectful way ought to be punished. How many times did she slap Sagar for something far less, though he was her only one, the jewel of her eye, come to her after she had been married for seven years and everyone had given up hope? Whenever she lifted her hand to him, her heart was pierced through and through. Such is a mother's duty.

But Shyamoli only says, in a tired voice, "That's enough! Go put on your clothes, hurry!"

The grumblings recede. Footsteps clatter down the stairs. Inside the bathroom Mrs. Dutta bends over the sink, fists tight in the folds of her sari. Hard with the pounding in her head to think what she feels most—anger at the children for their rudeness, or at Shyamoli for letting them go unrebuked. Or is it shame she feels (but why?), this burning, acid and indigestible, that coats her throat in molten metal?

It is 9:00 A.M., and the house, after the flurry of departures, of frantic "I can't find my socks" and "Mom, he took my lunch money" and "I swear I'll leave you

---

[14]**neem stick** made from the bark of a tropical tree used in Ayurvedic medicine, an ancient Indian art of healing

kids behind if you're not in the car in exactly one minute," has settled into its quiet daytime rhythms.

Busy in the kitchen, Mrs. Dutta has recovered her spirits. Holding on to grudges is too exhausting, and besides, the kitchen—sunlight spilling across its countertops while the refrigerator hums reassuringly in the background—is her favorite place.

Mrs. Dutta hums too as she fries potatoes for alu dum. Her voice is rusty and   25 slightly off-key. In India she would never have ventured to sing, but with everyone gone the house is too quiet, all that silence pressing down on her like the heel of a giant hand, and the TV voices, with their strange foreign accents, are no help at all. As the potatoes turn golden-brown, she permits herself a moment of nostalgia for her Calcutta kitchen—the new gas stove she bought with the birthday money Sagar sent, the scoured-shiny brass pots stacked by the meat safe, the window with the lotus-pattern grille through which she could look down on white-uniformed children playing cricket after school. The mouth-watering smell of ginger and chili paste, ground fresh by Reba, the maid, and, in the evening, strong black Assam tea brewing in the kettle when Mrs. Basu came by to visit. In her mind she writes to Mrs. Basu: *Oh, Roma, I miss it all so much. Sometimes I feel that someone has reached in and torn out a handful of my chest.*

But only fools indulge in nostalgia, so Mrs. Dutta shakes her head clear of images and straightens up the kitchen. She pours the half-drunk glasses of milk down the sink, though Shyamoli has told her to save them in the refrigerator. But surely Shyamoli, a girl from a good Hindu family, doesn't expect her to put contaminated *jutha*° things with the rest of the food. She washes the breakfast dishes by hand instead of letting them wait inside the dishwasher till night, breeding germs. With practiced fingers she throws an assortment of spices into the blender: coriander, cumin, cloves, black pepper, a few red chilies for vigor. No stale bottled curry powder for her. *At least the family's eating well since I arrived*, she writes in her mind. *Proper Indian food, puffed-up chapatis,° fish curry in mustard sauce, and real pulao° with raisins and cashews and ghee°—the way you taught me, Roma—instead of Rice-a-roni.* She would like to add, *They love it*, but thinking of Shyamoli, she hesitates.

At first Shyamoli was happy enough to have someone take over the cooking. "It's wonderful to come home to a hot dinner," she'd say. Or "Mother, what crispy papads,° and your fish curry is out of this world." But recently she has taken to picking at her food, and once or twice from the kitchen Mrs. Dutta has caught wisps of words, intensely whispered: "cholesterol," "all putting on weight," "she's spoiling you." And though Shyamoli always says no when the children ask if they can have burritos from the freezer instead, Mrs. Dutta suspects that she would really like to say yes.

---

[26]*jutha* leftovers of food offered to a deity, who takes the food's essence
chapatis Indian breads   *pulao* an Indian rice dish   *ghee* clarified butter, that is, butter with milk solids and water removed; an important ingredient in Indian cuisine
[27]*papads* light Indian cracker made of lentils

The children. A heaviness pulls at Mrs. Dutta's entire body when she thinks of them. Like so much in this country, they have turned out to be—yes, she might as well admit it—a disappointment.

For this she blames, in part, the Olan Mills portrait. Perhaps it was foolish of her to set so much store by a photograph, especially one taken years ago. But it was such a charming scene—Mrinalini in a ruffled white dress with her arm around her brother, Pradeep chubby and dimpled in a suit and bow tie, a glorious autumn forest blazing red and yellow behind them. (Later Mrs. Dutta was saddened to learn that the forest was merely a backdrop in a studio in California, where real trees did not turn such colors.)

30   The picture had arrived, silver-framed and wrapped in a plastic sheet filled with bubbles, with a note from Shyamoli explaining that it was a Mother's Day gift. (A strange concept, a day set aside to honor mothers. Did the sahibs not honor their mothers the rest of the year, then?) For a week Mrs. Dutta could not decide where it should be hung. If she put it in the drawing room, visitors would be able to admire her grandchildren, but if she put it on the bedroom wall, she would be able to see the photo last thing before she fell asleep. She finally opted for the bedroom, and later, when she was too ill with pneumonia to leave her bed for a month, she was glad of it.

Mrs. Dutta was accustomed to living on her own. She had done it for three years after Sagar's father died, politely but stubbornly declining the offers of various relatives, well-meaning and otherwise, to come and stay with her. In this she surprised herself as well as others, who thought of her as a shy, sheltered woman, one who would surely fall apart without her husband to handle things for her. But she managed quite well. She missed Sagar's father, of course, especially in the evenings, when it had been his habit to read to her the more amusing parts of the newspaper while she rolled out chapatis. But once the grief receded, she found she enjoyed being mistress of her own life, as she confided to Mrs. Basu. She liked being able, for the first time ever, to lie in bed all evening and read a new novel of Shankar's straight through if she wanted, or to send out for hot eggplant pakoras on a rainy day without feeling guilty that she wasn't serving up a balanced meal.

When the pneumonia hit, everything changed.

Mrs. Dutta had been ill before, but those illnesses had been different. Even in bed she'd been at the center of the household, with Reba coming to find out what should be cooked, Sagar's father bringing her shirts with missing buttons, her mother-in-law, now old and tamed, complaining that the cook didn't brew her tea strong enough, and Sagar running in crying because he'd had a fight with the neighbor boy. But now she had no one to ask her, querulously, *Just how long do you plan to remain sick?* No one waited in impatient exasperation for her to take on her duties again. No one's life was inconvenienced the least bit by her illness.

Therefore she had no reason to get well.

35   When this thought occurred to Mrs. Dutta, she was so frightened that her body grew numb. The walls of the room spun into blackness; the bed on which she lay, a vast four-poster she had shared with Sagar's father since their wedding, rocked like a dinghy caught in a storm; and a great hollow roaring reverberated

inside her head. For a moment, unable to move or see, she thought, *I'm dead.* Then her vision, desperate and blurry, caught on the portrait. *My grandchildren.* With some difficulty she focused on the bright, oblivious sheen of their faces, the eyes so like Sagar's that for a moment heartsickness twisted inside her like a living thing. She drew a shudder of breath into her aching lungs, and the roaring seemed to recede. When the afternoon post brought another letter from Sagar— *Mother, you really should come and live with us. We worry about you all alone in India, especially when you're sick like this*—she wrote back the same day, with fingers that still shook a little, *You're right: my place is with you, with my grandchildren.*

But now that she is here on the other side of the world, she is wrenched by doubt. She knows the grandchildren love her—how can it be otherwise among family? And she loves them, she reminds herself, even though they have put away, somewhere in the back of a closet, the vellum-bound *Ramayana for Young Readers* that she carried all the way from India in her hand luggage. Even though their bodies twitch with impatience when she tries to tell them stories of her girlhood. Even though they offer the most transparent excuses when she asks them to sit with her while she chants the evening prayers. *They're flesh of my flesh, blood of my blood,* she reminds herself. But sometimes when she listens, from the other room, to them speaking on the phone, their American voices rising in excitement as they discuss a glittering, alien world of Power Rangers, Metallica, and Spirit Week at school, she almost cannot believe what she hears.

Stepping into the back yard with a bucket of newly washed clothes, Mrs. Dutta views the sky with some anxiety. The butter-gold sunlight is gone, black-bellied clouds have taken over the horizon, and the air feels still and heavy on her face, as before a Bengal storm. What if her clothes don't dry by the time the others return home?

Washing clothes has been a problem for Mrs. Dutta ever since she arrived in California.

"We can't, Mother," Shyamoli said with a sigh when Mrs. Dutta asked Sagar to put up a clothesline for her in the back yard. (Shyamoli sighed often nowadays. Perhaps it was an American habit? Mrs. Dutta did not remember that the Indian Shyamoli, the docile bride she'd mothered for a month before putting her on a Pan Am flight to join her husband, pursed her lips in quite this way to let out a breath at once patient and exasperated.) "It's just not *done*, not in a nice neighborhood like this one. And being the only Indian family on the street, we have to be extra careful. People here sometimes—" She broke off with a shake of her head. "Why don't you just keep your dirty clothes in the hamper I've put in your room, and I'll wash them on Sunday along with everyone else's."

Afraid of causing another sigh, Mrs. Dutta agreed reluctantly. She knew she should not store unclean clothes in the same room where she kept the pictures of her gods. That would bring bad luck. And the odor. Lying in bed at night she could smell it distinctly, even though Shyamoli claimed that the hamper was air-tight. The sour, starchy old-woman smell embarrassed her. 40

She was more embarrassed when, on Sunday afternoons, Shyamoli brought the laundry into the family room to fold. Mrs. Dutta would bend intently over her knitting, face tingling with shame, as her daughter-in-law nonchalantly shook out the wisps of lace, magenta and sea-green and black, that were her panties, placing them next to a stack of Sagar's briefs. And when, right in front of everyone, Shyamoli pulled out Mrs. Dutta's crumpled, baggy bras from the heap, she wished the ground would open up and swallow her, like the Sita of mythology.

Then one day Shyamoli set the clothes basket down in front of Sagar.

"Can you do them today, Sagar?" (Mrs. Dutta, who had never, through the forty-two years of her marriage, addressed Sagar's father by name, tried not to wince.) "I've *got* to get that sales report into the computer by tonight."

Before Sagar could respond, Mrs. Dutta was out of her chair, knitting needles dropping to the floor.

45   "No, no, no, clothes and all is no work for the man of the house. I'll do it." The thought of her son's hands searching through the basket and lifting up his wife's—and her own—underclothes filled her with horror.

"Mother!" Shyamoli said. "This is why Indian men are so useless around the house. Here in America we don't believe in men's work and women's work. Don't I work outside all day, just like Sagar? How'll I manage if he doesn't help me at home?"

"I'll help you instead," Mrs. Dutta ventured.

"You don't understand, do you, Mother?" Shyamoli said with a shaky smile. Then she went into the study.

Mrs. Dutta sat down in her chair and tried to understand. But after a while she gave up and whispered to Sagar that she wanted him to teach her how to run the washer and dryer.

50   "Why, Mother? Molli's quite happy to . . ."

"I've got to learn it . . ." Her voice was low and desperate as she rummaged through the tangled heap for her clothes.

Her son began to object and then shrugged. "Oh, very well. If it makes you happy."

But later, when she faced the machines alone, their cryptic symbols and rows of gleaming knobs terrified her. What if she pressed the wrong button and flooded the entire floor with soapsuds? What if she couldn't turn the machines off and they kept going, whirring maniacally, until they exploded? (This had happened on a TV show just the other day. Everyone else had laughed at the woman who jumped up and down, screaming hysterically, but Mrs. Dutta sat stiff-spined, gripping the armrests of her chair.) So she has taken to washing her clothes in the bathtub when she is alone. She never did such a chore before, but she remembers how the village washerwomen of her childhood would beat their saris clean against river rocks. And a curious satisfaction fills her as her clothes hit the porcelain with the same solid wet *thunk*.

My small victory, my secret.

55   This is why everything must be dried and put safely away before Shyamoli returns. Ignorance, as Mrs. Dutta knows well from years of managing a household, is a great promoter of harmony. So she keeps an eye on the menacing advance of the clouds as she hangs up her blouses and underwear, as she drapes

her sari° along the redwood fence that separates her son's property from the neighbor's, first wiping the fence clean with a dish towel she has secretly taken from the bottom drawer in the kitchen. But she isn't worried. Hasn't she managed every time, even after that freak hailstorm last month, when she had to use the iron from the laundry closet to press everything dry? The memory pleases her. In her mind she writes to Mrs. Basu: *I'm fitting in so well here, you'd never guess I came only two months back. I've found new ways of doing things, of solving problems creatively. You would be most proud if you saw me.*

When Mrs. Dutta decided to give up her home of forty-five years, her relatives showed far less surprise than she had expected. "Oh, we all knew you'd end up in America sooner or later," they said. She had been foolish to stay on alone so long after Sagar's father, may he find eternal peace, passed away. Good thing that boy of hers had come to his senses and called her to join him. Everyone knows a wife's place is with her husband, and a widow's is with her son.

Mrs. Dutta had nodded in meek agreement, ashamed to let anyone know that the night before she had awakened weeping.

"Well, now that you're going, what'll happen to all your things?" they asked.

Mrs. Dutta, still troubled over those traitorous tears, had offered up her household effects in propitiation. "Here, Didi, you take this cutwork bedspread. Mashima, for a long time I have meant for you to have these Corning Ware dishes; I know how much you admire them. And Boudi, this tape recorder that Sagar sent a year back is for you. Yes, yes, I'm quite sure. I can always tell Sagar to buy me another one when I get there."

Mrs. Basu, coming in just as a cousin made off triumphantly with a bone-china tea set, had protested. "Prameela, have you gone crazy? That tea set used to belong to your mother-in-law."

60

"But what'll I do with it in America? Shyamoli has her own set—"

A look that Mrs. Dutta couldn't read flitted across Mrs. Basu's face. "But do you want to drink from it for the rest of your life?"

"What do you mean?"

Mrs. Basu hesitated. Then she said, "What if you don't like it there?"

"How can I not like it, Roma?" Mrs. Dutta's voice was strident, even to her own ears. With an effort she controlled it and continued. "I'll miss my friends, I know—and you most of all. And the things we do together—evening tea, our walk around Rabindra Sarobar Lake, Thursday night Bhagavad Gita class. But Sagar—they're my only family. And blood is blood, after all."

65

"I wonder," Mrs. Basu said drily, and Mrs. Dutta recalled that though both of Mrs. Basu's children lived just a day's journey away, they came to see her only on occasions when common decency dictated their presence. Perhaps they were tightfisted in money matters, too. Perhaps that was why Mrs. Basu had started renting out her downstairs a few years earlier, even though, as anyone in Calcutta knew, tenants were more trouble than they were worth. Such filial

---

⁵⁵**sari** a garment worn by southern Indian women consisting of several yards of cloth that is wrapped around the body to form a skirt and then draped to cover one shoulder or the head

neglect must be hard to take, though Mrs. Basu, loyal to her children as indeed a mother should be, never complained. In a way, Mrs. Dutta had been better off, with Sagar too far away for her to put his love to the test.

"At least don't give up the house," Mrs. Basu was saying. "You won't be able to find another place in case . . ."

"In case what?" Mrs. Dutta asked, her words like stone chips. She was surprised to find that she was angrier with Mrs. Basu than she'd ever been. Or was she afraid? *My son isn't like yours,* she'd been on the verge of spitting out. She took a deep breath and made herself smile, made herself remember that she might never see her friend again.

"Ah, Roma," she said, putting her arm around Mrs. Basu. "You think I'm such an old witch that my Sagar and my Shyamoli will be unable to live with me?"

70   Mrs. Dutta hums a popular Tagore° song as she pulls her sari from the fence. It's been a good day, as good as it can be in a country where you might stare out the window for hours and not see one living soul. No vegetable vendors with enormous wicker baskets balanced on their heads, no knife sharpeners with their distinctive call—*scissors-knives-choppers, scissors-knives-choppers*—to bring the children running. No peasant women with colorful tattoos on their arms to sell you cookware in exchange for your old silk saris. Why, even the animals that frequented Ghoshpara Lane had personality—stray dogs that knew to line up outside the kitchen door just when the leftovers were likely to be thrown out; the goat that maneuvered its head through the garden grille hoping to get at her dahlias; cows that planted themselves majestically in the center of the road, ignoring honking drivers. And right across the street was Mrs. Basu's two-story house, which Mrs. Dutta knew as well as her own. How many times had she walked up the stairs to that airy room, painted sea-green and filled with plants, where her friend would be waiting for her?

What took you so long today, Prameela? Your tea is cold already.

Wait till you hear what happened, Roma. Then you won't scold me for being late—

Stop it, you silly woman, Mrs. Dutta tells herself severely. *Every single one of your relatives would give an arm and a leg to be in your place, you know that. After lunch you're going to write a nice letter to Roma telling her exactly how delighted you are to be here.*

From where Mrs. Dutta stands, gathering up petticoats and blouses, she can look into the next yard. Not that there's much to see—just tidy grass and a few pale-blue flowers whose name she doesn't know. Two wooden chairs sit under a tree, but Mrs. Dutta has never seen anyone using them. *What's the point of having such a big yard if you're not even going to sit in it?* she thinks. Calcutta pushes itself into her mind again, with its narrow, blackened flats where families of six and eight and ten squeeze themselves into two tiny rooms, and her heart fills with a sense of loss she knows to be illogical.

[70]**Tagore** Rabindranath Tagore (1861–1941), Nobel laureate for literature (1913), poet, and the composer of independent India's national anthem

When she first arrived in Sagar's home, Mrs. Dutta wanted to go over and   75
meet her next-door neighbors, maybe take them some of her special sweet raso-
gollahs, as she'd often done with Mrs. Basu. But Shyamoli said she shouldn't.
Such things were not the custom in California, she explained earnestly. You
didn't just drop in on people without calling ahead. Here everyone was busy;
they didn't sit around chatting, drinking endless cups of sugar-tea. Why, they
might even say something unpleasant to her.

"For what?" Mrs. Dutta had asked disbelievingly, and Shyamoli had said,
"Because Americans don't like neighbors to"—here she used an English phrase—
"invade their privacy." Mrs. Dutta, who didn't fully understand the word "privacy,"
because there was no such term in Bengali, had gazed at her daughter-in-law in
some bewilderment. But she understood enough not to ask again. In the following months, though, she often looked over the fence, hoping to make contact.
People were people, whether in India or in America, and everyone appreciated a
friendly face. When Shyamoli was as old as Mrs. Dutta, she would know that too.

Today, just as she is about to turn away, out of the corner of her eye Mrs.
Dutta notices a movement. At one of the windows a woman is standing, her
hair a sleek gold like that of the TV heroines whose exploits baffle Mrs. Dutta
when she tunes in to an afternoon serial. She is smoking a cigarette, and a curl
of gray rises lazily, elegantly, from her fingers. Mrs. Dutta is so happy to see
another human being in the middle of her solitary day that she forgets how
much she disapproves of smoking, especially in women. She lifts her hand in the
gesture she has seen her grandchildren use to wave an eager hello.

The woman stares back at Mrs. Dutta. Her lips are a perfect painted red, and
when she raises her cigarette to her mouth, its tip glows like an animal's eye.
She does not wave back or smile. Perhaps she is not well? Mrs. Dutta feels sorry
for her, alone in her illness in a silent house with only cigarettes for solace, and
she wishes the etiquette of America did not prevent her from walking over with
a word of cheer and a bowl of her fresh-cooked alu dum.°

Mrs. Dutta rarely gets a chance to be alone with her son. In the morning
he is in too much of a hurry even to drink the fragrant cardamom tea that she
(remembering how as a child he would always beg for a sip from her cup) offers
to make him. He doesn't return until dinnertime, and afterward he must help
the children with their homework, read the paper, hear the details of Shyamoli's
day, watch his favorite TV crime show in order to unwind, and take out the
garbage. In between, for he is a solicitous son, he converses with Mrs. Dutta. In
response to his questions she assures him that her arthritis is much better now;
no, no, she's not growing bored being at home all the time; she has everything
she needs—Shyamoli has been so kind. But perhaps he could pick up a few
aerograms on his way back tomorrow? She obediently recites for him an edited
list of her day's activities, and smiles when he praises her cooking. But when he
says, "Oh, well, time to turn in, another working day tomorrow," she feels a
vague pain, like hunger, in the region of her heart.

---

⁷⁸**alu dum** potato curry

80   So it is with the delighted air of a child who has been offered an unexpected
gift that she leaves her half-written letter to greet Sagar at the door today, a good
hour before Shyamoli is due back. The children are busy in the family room
doing homework and watching cartoons (mostly the latter, Mrs. Dutta suspects).
But for once she doesn't mind, because they race in to give their father hurried
hugs and then race back again. And she has him, her son, all to herself in a
kitchen filled with the familiar, pungent odors of tamarind° sauce and chopped
coriander leaves.

"Khoka," she says, calling him by a childhood name she hasn't used in years,
"I could fry you two-three hot-hot luchis, if you like." As she waits for his reply,
she can feel, in the hollow of her throat, the rapid thud of her heart. And when
he says yes, that would be very nice, she shuts her eyes tight and takes a deep
breath, and it is as though merciful time has given her back her youth, that
sweet, aching urgency of being needed again.

Mrs. Dutta is telling Sagar a story.

"When you were a child, how scared you were of injections! One time, when
the government doctor came to give us compulsory typhoid shots, you locked
yourself in the bathroom and refused to come out. Do you remember what your
father finally did? He went into the garden and caught a lizard and threw it in
the bathroom window, because you were even more scared of lizards than of
shots. And in exactly one second you ran out screaming—right into the waiting
doctor's arms."

Sagar laughs so hard that he almost upsets his tea (made with real sugar,
because Mrs. Dutta knows it is better for her son than that chemical powder
Shyamoli likes to use). There are tears in his eyes, and Mrs. Dutta, who had not
dared to hope that he would find her story so amusing, feels gratified. When he
takes off his glasses to wipe them, his face is oddly young, not like a father's at
all, or even a husband's, and she has to suppress an impulse to put out her hand
and rub away the indentations that the glasses have left on his nose.

85   "I'd totally forgotten," Sagar says. "How can you keep track of those old, old
things?"

Because it is the lot of mothers to remember what no one else cares to, Mrs. Dutta
thinks. *To tell those stories over and over, until they are lodged, perforce, in family lore.
We are the keepers of the heart's dusty corners.*

But as she starts to say this, the front door creaks open, and she hears the
faint click of Shyamoli's high heels. Mrs. Dutta rises, collecting the dirty dishes.

"Call me fifteen minutes before you're ready to eat, so that I can fry fresh
luchis for everyone," she tells Sagar.

"You don't have to leave, Mother," he says.

90   Mrs. Dutta smiles her pleasure but doesn't stop. She knows that Shyamoli
likes to be alone with her husband at this time, and today, in her happiness, she
does not grudge her this.

---

[80]**tamarind** the sharp and sweet pulp that surrounds the seeds of the tropical tamarind
tree, used in south and southeast Asian cooking

"You think I've nothing to do, only sit and gossip with you?" she mock-scolds. "I want you to know I have a very important letter to finish."

Somewhere behind her she hears a thud—a briefcase falling over. This surprises her. Shyamoli is always careful with it, because it was a gift from Sagar when she was finally made a manager in her company.

"Hi!" Sagar calls, and when there's no answer, "Hey, Molli, you okay?"

Shyamoli comes into the room slowly, her hair disheveled as though she has been running her fingers through it. Hot color blotches her cheeks.

"What's the matter, Molli?" Sagar walks over to give her a kiss. "Bad day at   95
work?" Mrs. Dutta, embarrassed as always by this display of marital affection, turns toward the window, but not before she sees Shyamoli move her face away.

"Leave me alone." Her voice is low, shaking. "Just leave me alone."

"But what is it?" Sagar says with concern.

"I don't want to talk about it right now." Shyamoli lowers herself into a kitchen chair and puts her face in her hands. Sagar stands in the middle of the room, looking helpless. He raises his hand and lets it fall, as though he wants to comfort his wife but is afraid of what she might do.

A protective anger for her son surges inside Mrs. Dutta, but she moves away silently. In her mind-letter she writes, *Women need to be strong, not react to every little thing like this. You and I, Roma, we had far worse to cry about, but we shed our tears invisibly. We were good wives and daughters-in-law, good mothers. Dutiful, uncomplaining. Never putting ourselves first.*

A sudden memory comes to her, one she hasn't thought of in years—a day   100
when she scorched a special kheer dessert. Her mother-in-law had shouted at her, "Didn't your mother teach you anything, you useless girl?" As punishment she refused to let Mrs. Dutta go with Mrs. Basu to the cinema, even though *Sahib, Bibi aur Ghulam,* which all Calcutta was crazy about, was playing, and their tickets were bought already. Mrs. Dutta had wept the entire afternoon, but before Sagar's father came home, she washed her face carefully with cold water and applied *kajal°* to her eyes so that he wouldn't know.

But everything is getting mixed up, and her own young, trying-not-to-cry face blurs into another—why, it's Shyamoli's—and a thought hits her so sharply in the chest that she has to hold on to her bedroom wall to keep from falling. *And what good did it do? The more we bent, the more people pushed us, until one day we'd forgotten that we could stand up straight. Maybe Shyamoli's the one with the right idea after all . . .*

Mrs. Dutta lowers herself heavily onto her bed, trying to erase such an insidious idea from her mind. Oh, this new country, where all the rules are upside down, it's confusing her. The space inside her skull feels stirred up, like a pond in which too many water buffaloes have been wading. Maybe things will settle down if she can focus on the letter to Roma.

Then she remembers that she has left the half-written aerogram on the kitchen table. She knows she should wait until after dinner, after her son and his wife have sorted things out. But a restlessness—or is it defiance?—has taken

---

°*kajal* Indian cream used as eyeliner

hold of her. She is sorry that Shyamoli is upset, but why should she have to waste her evening because of that? She'll go get her letter—it's no crime, is it? She'll march right in and pick it up, and even if Shyamoli stops in mid-sentence with another one of those sighs, she'll refuse to feel apologetic. Besides, by now they're probably in the family room, watching TV.

Really, Roma, she writes in her head, as she feels her way along the unlighted corridor, *the amount of TV they watch here is quite scandalous. The children, too, sitting for hours in front of that box like they've been turned into painted dolls, and then talking back when I tell them to turn it off.* Of course she will never put such blasphemy into a real letter. Still, it makes her feel better to be able to say it, if only to herself.

In the family room the TV is on, but for once no one is paying it any attention. Shyamoli and Sagar sit on the sofa, conversing. From where she stands in the corridor, Mrs. Dutta cannot see them, but their shadows—enormous against the wall where the table lamp has cast them—seem to flicker and leap at her.

105   She is about to slip unseen into the kitchen when Shyamoli's rising voice arrests her. In its raw, shaking unhappiness it is so unlike her daughter-in-law's assured tones that Mrs. Dutta is no more able to move away from it than if she had heard the call of the *nishi,* the lost souls of the dead, the subject of so many of the tales on which she grew up.

"It's easy for you to say 'Calm down.' I'd like to see how calm *you'd* be if she came up to you and said, 'Kindly tell the old lady not to hang her clothes over the fence into my yard.' She said it twice, like I didn't understand English, like I was a savage. All these years I've been so careful not to give these Americans a chance to say something like this, and now—"

"Shhh, Shyamoli, I *said* I'd talk to Mother about it."

"You always say that, but you never *do* anything. You're too busy being the perfect son, tiptoeing around her feelings. But how about mine? Aren't I a person too?"

"Hush, Molli, the children . . ."

110   "Let them hear. I don't care anymore. Besides, they're not stupid. They already know what a hard time I've been having with her. You're the only one who refuses to see it."

In the passage Mrs. Dutta shrinks against the wall. She wants to move away, to hear nothing else, but her feet are formed of cement, impossible to lift, and Shyamoli's words pour into her ears like fire.

"I've explained over and over, and she still does what I've asked her not to— throwing away perfectly good food, leaving dishes to drip all over the counter- tops. Ordering my children to stop doing things I've given them permission to do. She's taken over the entire kitchen, cooking whatever she likes. You come in the door and the smell of grease is everywhere, in all our clothes even. I feel like this isn't my house anymore."

"Be patient, Molli. She's an old woman, after all."

"I know. That's why I tried so hard. I know having her here is important to you. But I can't do it any longer. I just can't. Some days I feel like taking the kids and leaving." Shyamoli's voice disappears into a sob.

A shadow stumbles across the wall to her, and then another. Behind the   115
weatherman's nasal tones, announcing a week of sunny days, Mrs. Dutta can
hear a high, frightened weeping. The children, she thinks. This must be the first
time they've seen their mother cry.

"Don't talk like that, sweetheart." Sagar leans forward, his voice, too,
anguished. All the shadows on the wall shiver and merge into a single dark
silhouette.

Mrs. Dutta stares at that silhouette, the solidarity of it. Sagar and Shyamoli's
murmurs are lost beneath the noise in her head, a dry humming—like thirsty
birds, she thinks wonderingly. After a while she discovers that she has reached
her room. In darkness she lowers herself onto her bed very gently, as though her
body were made of the thinnest glass. Or perhaps ice—she is so cold. She sits for
a long time with her eyes closed, while inside her head thoughts whirl faster and
faster until they disappear in a gray dust storm.

When Pradeep finally comes to call her for dinner, Mrs. Dutta follows him to
the kitchen, where she fries luchis for everyone, the perfect circles of dough puffing
up crisp and golden as always. Sagar and Shyamoli have reached a truce of some
kind: she gives him a small smile, and he puts out a casual hand to massage the
back of her neck. Mrs. Dutta shows no embarrassment at this. She eats her dinner.
She answers questions put to her. She laughs when someone makes a joke. If her
face is stiff, as though she had been given a shot of Novocain, no one notices.
When the table is cleared, she excuses herself, saying she has to finish her letter.

Now Mrs. Dutta sits on her bed, reading over what she wrote in the innocent
afternoon.

Dear Roma,   120

*Although I miss you, I know you will be pleased to hear how happy I am in America.
There is much here that needs getting used to, but we are no strangers to adjusting, we old
women. After all, haven't we been doing it all our lives?*

*Today I'm cooking one of Sagar's favorite dishes, alu dum. It gives me such pleasure to
see my family gathered around the table, eating my food. The children are still a little shy of
me, but I am hopeful that we'll soon be friends. And Shyamoli, so confident and successful—
you should see her when she's all dressed for work. I can't believe she's the same timid bride
I sent off to America just a few years ago. But Sagar, most of all, is the joy of my old age. . . .*

With the edge of her sari Mrs. Dutta carefully wipes a tear that has fallen on
the aerogram. She blows on the damp spot until it is completely dry, so the pen
will not leave a telltale smudge. Even though Roma would not tell a soul, she
cannot risk it. She can already hear them, the avid relatives in India who've
been waiting for something just like this to happen. *That Dutta-ginni, so set in her
ways, we knew she'd never get along with her daughter-in-law.* Or, worse, *Did you hear
about poor Prameela? How her family treated her? Yes, even her son, can you imagine?*

This much surely she owes to Sagar.

And what does she owe herself, Mrs. Dutta, falling through black night with   125
all the certainties she trusted in collapsed upon themselves like imploded stars,
and only an image inside her eyelids for company? A silhouette—man, wife,

children, joined on a wall—showing her how alone she is in this land of young people. And how unnecessary.

She is not sure how long she sits under the glare of the overhead light, how long her hands clench themselves in her lap. When she opens them, nail marks line the soft flesh of her palms, red hieroglyphs—her body's language, telling her what to do.

Dear Roma, Mrs. Dutta writes,

I cannot answer your question about whether I am happy, for I am no longer sure I know what happiness is. All I know is that it isn't what I thought it to be. It isn't about being needed. It isn't about being with family either. It has something to do with love, I still think that, but in a different way than I believed earlier, a way I don't have the words to explain. Perhaps we can figure it out together, two old women drinking cha° in your down-stairs flat (for I do hope you will rent it to me on my return) while around us gossip falls—but lightly, like summer rain, for that is all we will allow it to be. If I'm lucky—and perhaps, in spite of all that has happened, I am—the happiness will be in the figuring out.

Pausing to read over what she has written, Mrs. Dutta is surprised to discover this: now that she no longer cares whether tears blotch her letter, she feels no need to weep.   [1998]

[128]*cha* spiced Indian tea

1. What are the conflicts between Mrs. Dutta and her son's family and what are their sources?
2. The story has a complicated time line. What are the various periods it depicts? How does story time relate to narrative time? Narrative time to chronological time? How do the multiple time lines contribute to the crisis of the story and the resolution of the conflicts?
3. How does the letter mentioned in the title function in the story?
4. How does Mrs. Dutta's definition of happiness change through her experience in America?

WILLIAM FAULKNER

WILLIAM FAULKNER *(1897–1962), one of the great American novelists of the twentieth century and winner of the 1949 Nobel Prize, was born into an old Southern family. His first book was a collection of poems. He attended the University of Mississippi and lived in Paris briefly, returning home to buy and occupy a pre–Civil War mansion in Oxford, Mississippi, where he lived, a virtual recluse, for the rest of his life. Most of his novels are set in the rural South and explore the conditions and particularities of Southern life, which can be viewed as a microcosm of the greater world outside. His stream of consciousness technique and brilliant rhetorical style are put to the service of his compassionate understanding of the anguish of a divided and troubled society still recovering from the Civil War.*

Wash

Sutpen stood above the pallet bed on which the mother and child lay. Between the shrunken planking of the wall the early sunlight fell in long pencil strokes, breaking upon his straddled legs and upon the riding whip in his hand, and lay across the still shape of the mother, who lay looking up at him from still, inscrutable, sullen eyes, the child at her side wrapped in a piece of dingy though clean cloth. Behind them an old Negro woman squatted beside the rough hearth where a meager fire smoldered.

"Well, Milly," Sutpen said, "too bad you're not a mare. Then I could give you a decent stall in the stable."

Still the girl on the pallet did not move. She merely continued to look up at him without expression, with a young, sullen, inscrutable face still pale from recent travail. Sutpen moved, bringing into the splintered pencils of sunlight the face of a man of sixty. He said quietly to the squatting Negress, "Griselda foaled this morning."

"Horse or mare?" the Negress said.

"A horse. A damned fine colt. . . . What's this?" He indicated the pallet with   5
the hand which held the whip.

"That un's a mare, I reckon."

"Hah," Sutpen said. "A damned fine colt. Going to be the spit and image of old Rob Roy when I rode him North in '61. Do you remember?"

"Yes, Marster."

"Hah." He glanced back towards the pallet. None could have said if the girl still watched him or not. Again his whip hand indicated the pallet. "Do whatever they need with whatever we've got to do it with." He went out, passing out the crazy doorway and stepping down into the rank weeds (there yet leaned rusting against the corner of the porch the scythe which Wash had borrowed from him three months ago to cut them with) where his horse waited, where Wash stood holding the reins.

When Colonel Sutpen rode away to fight the Yankees, Wash did not go. "I'm   10
looking after the Kernal's place and niggers," he would tell all who asked him and some who had not asked—a gaunt, malaria-ridden man with pale, questioning eyes, who looked about thirty-five, though it was known that he had not only a daughter but an eight-year-old granddaughter as well. This was a lie, as most of them—the few remaining men between eighteen and fifty—to whom he told it, knew, though there were some who believed that he himself really believed it, though even these believed that he had better sense than to put it to the test with Mrs. Sutpen or the Sutpen slaves. Knew better or was just too lazy and shiftless to try it, they said, knowing that his sole connection with the Sutpen plantation lay in the fact that for years now Colonel Sutpen had allowed him to squat in a crazy shack on a slough in the river bottom on the Sutpen place, which Sutpen had built for a fishing lodge in his bachelor days and which had since fallen into dilapidation from disuse, so that now it looked like an aged or sick wild beast crawled terrifically there to drink in the act of dying.

The Sutpen slaves themselves heard of his statement. They laughed. It was not the first time they had laughed at him, calling him white trash behind his back. They began to ask him themselves, in groups, meeting him in the faint road which led up from the slough and the old fish camp, "Why ain't you at de war, white man?"

Pausing, he would look about the ring of black faces and white eyes and teeth behind which derision lurked. "Because I got a daughter and family to keep," he said. "Get out of my road, niggers."

"Niggers?" they repeated; "niggers?" laughing now. "Who him, calling us niggers?"

"Yes," he said. "I ain't got no niggers to look after my folks if I was gone."

15   "Nor nothing else but dat shack down yon dat Cunnel wouldn't *let* none of us live in."

Now he cursed them; sometimes he rushed at them, snatching up a stick from the ground while they scattered before him, yet seeming to surround him still with that black laughing, derisive, evasive, inescapable, leaving him panting and impotent and raging. Once it happened in the very back yard of the big house itself. This was after bitter news had come down from the Tennessee mountains and from Vicksburg, and Sherman had passed through the plantation, and most of the Negroes had followed him. Almost everything else had gone with the Federal troops, and Mrs. Sutpen had sent word to Wash that he could have the scuppernongs ripening in the arbor in the back yard. This time it was a house servant, one of the few Negroes who remained; this time the Negress had to retreat up the kitchen steps, where she turned. "Stop right dar, white man. Stop right whar you is. You ain't never crossed dese steps whilst Cunnel here, and you ain't ghy' do hit now."

This was true. But there was this of a kind of pride: he had never tried to enter the big house, even though he believed that if he had, Sutpen would have received him, permitted him. "But I ain't going to give no black nigger the chance to tell me I can't go nowhere," he said to himself. "I ain't even going to give Kernel the chance to have to cuss a nigger on my account." This, though he and Sutpen had spent more than one afternoon together on those rare Sundays when there would be no company in the house. Perhaps his mind knew that it was because Sutpen had nothing else to do, being a man who could not bear his own company. Yet the fact remained that the two of them would spend whole afternoons in the scuppernong arbor, Sutpen in the hammock and Wash squatting against a post, a pail of cistern water between them, taking drink for drink from the same demijohn. Meanwhile on weekdays he would see the fine figure of the man—they were the same age almost to the day, though neither of them (perhaps because Wash had a grandchild while Sutpen's son was a youth in school) ever thought of himself as being so—on the fine figure of the black stallion, galloping about the plantation. For that moment his heart would be quiet and proud. It would seem to him that that world in which Negroes, whom the Bible told him had been created and cursed by God to be brute and vassal to all men of white skin, were better found and housed and even clothed than he and his; that world in which he sensed always about him mocking echoes of black laughter was but a dream and an illusion, and that the actual world was this one across which his own lonely apotheosis seemed to gallop on the black thoroughbred, thinking how the Book said also that all men were created in the image of God and hence all men made the same image in God's eyes at least; so that he could say, as though speaking of himself, "A fine proud man. If God Himself was to come down and ride the natural earth, that's what He would aim to look like."

Sutpen returned in 1865, on the black stallion. He seemed to have aged ten years. His son had been killed in action the same winter in which his wife had died. He returned with his citation for gallantry from the hand of General Lee to a ruined plantation, where for a year now his daughter had subsisted partially on the meager bounty of the man to whom fifteen years ago he had granted permission to live in that tumbledown fishing camp whose very existence he had at the time forgotten. Wash was there to meet him, unchanged: still gaunt, still ageless, with his pale, questioning gaze, his air diffident, a little servile, a little familiar, "Well, Kernel," Wash said, "they kilt us but they ain't whupped us yit, air they?"

That was the tenor of their conversation for the next five years. It was inferior whisky which they drank now together from a stoneware jug, and it was not in the scuppernong arbor. It was in the rear of the little store which Sutpen managed to set up on the highroad: a frame shelved room where, with Wash for clerk and porter, he dispensed kerosene and staple foodstuffs and stale gaudy candy and cheap beads and ribbons to Negroes or poor whites of Wash's own kind, who came afoot or on gaunt mules to haggle tediously for dimes and quarters with a man who at one time could gallop (the black stallion was still alive; the stable in which his jealous get lived was in better repair than the house where the master himself lived) for ten miles across his own fertile land and who had led troops gallantly in battle; until Sutpen in fury would empty the store, close and lock the doors from the inside. Then he and Wash would repair to the rear and the jug. But the talk would not be quiet now, as when Sutpen lay in the hammock, delivering an arrogant monologue while Wash squatted guffawing against his post. They both say now, though Sutpen had the single chair while Wash used whatever box or keg was handy, and even this for just a little while, because soon Sutpen would reach that stage of impotent and furious undefeat in which he would rise, swaying and plunging, and declare again that he would take his pistol and the black stallion and ride single-handed into Washington and kill Lincoln, dead now, and Sherman, now a private citizen. "Kill them!" he would shout. "Shoot them down like the dogs they are—"

"Sho, Kernel; sho, Kernel," Wash would say, catching Sutpen as he fell. Then he would commandeer the first passing wagon or, lacking that, he would walk the mile to the nearest neighbor and borrow one and return and carry Sutpen home. He entered the house now. He had been doing so for a long time, taking Sutpen home in whatever borrowed wagon might be, talking him into locomotion with cajoling murmurs as though he were a horse, a stallion himself. The daughter would meet them and hold open the door without a word. He would carry his burden through the once white formal entrance, surmounted by a fanlight imported piece by piece from Europe and with a board now nailed over a missing pane, across a velvet carpet from which all nap was now gone, and up a formal stairs, now but a fading ghost of bare boards between two strips of fading paint, and into the bedroom. It would be dusk by now, and he would let his burden sprawl onto the bed and undress it and then he would sit quietly in a chair beside. After a time the daughter would come to the door. "We're all right now," he would tell her. "Don't you worry none, Miss Judith."

Then it would become dark, and after a while he would lie down on the floor beside the bed, though not to sleep, because after a time—sometimes before midnight—the man on the bed would stir and groan and then speak. "Wash?"

"Hyer I am, Kernel. You go back to sleep. We ain't whupped yit, air we? Me and you kin do hit."

Even then he had already seen the ribbon about his granddaughter's waist. She was now fifteen, already mature, after the early way of her kind. He knew where the ribbon came from; he had been seeing it and its kind daily for three years, even if she had lied about where she got it, which she did not, at once bold, sullen, and fearful. "Sho now," he said, "Ef Kernel wants to give hit to you, I hope you minded to thank him."

His heart was quiet, even when he saw the dress, watching her secret, defiant, frightened face when she told him that Miss Judith, the daughter, had helped her to make it. But he was quite grave when he approached Sutpen after they closed the store that afternoon, following the other to the rear.

25   "Get the jug," Sutpen directed.

"Wait," Wash said. "Not yit for a minute."

Neither did Sutpen deny the dress. "What about it?" he said.

But Wash met his arrogant stare; he spoke quietly. "I've knowed you for going on twenty years. I ain't never yit denied to do what you told me to do. And I'm a man nigh sixty. And she ain't nothing but a fifteen-year-old gal."

"Meaning that I'd harm a girl? I, a man as old as you are?"

30   "If you was ara other man, I'd say you was as old as me. And old or no old, I wouldn't let her keep that dress nor nothing else that come from your hand. But you are different."

"How different?" But Wash merely looked at him with his pale, questioning, sober eyes. "So that's why you are afraid of me?"

Now Wash's gaze no longer questioned. It was tranquil, serene. "I ain't afraid. Because you air brave. It ain't that you were a brave man at one minute or day of your life and got a paper to show hit from General Lee. But you air brave, the same as you air alive and breathing. That's where hit's different. Hit don't need no ticket from nobody to tell me that. And I know that whatever you handle or tech, whether hit's a regiment of men or a ignorant gal or just a hound dog, that you will make hit right."

Now it was Sutpen who looked away, turning suddenly, brusquely. "Get the jug," he said sharply.

"Sho, Kernel," Wash said.

35   So on that Sunday dawn two years later, having watched the Negro midwife, which he had walked three miles to fetch, enter the crazy door beyond which his granddaughter lay wailing, his heart was still quiet though concerned. He

knew what they had been saying—the Negroes in cabins about the land, the white men who loafed all day long about the store, watching quietly the three of them; Sutpen, himself, his granddaughter with her air of brazen and shrinking defiance as her condition became daily more and more obvious, like three actors that came and went upon a stage. "I know what they say to one another," he thought. "I can almost hyear them: *Wash Jones has fixed old Sutpen at last. Hit taken him twenty years, but he has done hit at last.*"

It would be dawn after a while, though not yet. From the house, where the lamp shone dim beyond the warped doorframe, his granddaughter's voice came steadily as though run by a clock, while thinking went slowly and terrifically, fumbling, involved somehow with a sound of galloping hooves, until there broke suddenly free in mid-gallop the fine proud figure of the man on the fine proud stallion, galloping; and then that at which thinking fumbled, broke free too and quite clear, not in justification nor even explanation, but as the apotheosis, lonely, explicable, beyond all fouling by human touch: "He is bigger than all them Yankees that kilt his son and his wife and taken his niggers and ruined his land, bigger than this hyer durn country that he fit for and that has denied him into keeping a little country store; bigger than the denial which hit helt to his lips like the bitter cup in the Book. And how could I have lived this nigh to him for twenty years without being teched and changed by him? Maybe I ain't as big as him and maybe I ain't done none of the galloping. But at least I done been drug along. Me and him kin do hit, if so be he will show me what he aims for me to do."

Then it was dawn. Suddenly he could see the house, and the old Negress in the door looking at him. Then he realized that his granddaughter's voice had ceased. "It's a girl," the Negress said. "You can go tell him if you want to." She reentered the house.

"A girl," he repeated; "a girl"; in astonishment, hearing the galloping hooves, seeing the proud galloping figure emerge again. He seemed to watch it pass, galloping through avatars which marked the accumulation of years, time, to the climax where it galloped beneath a brandished saber and a shot-torn flag rushing down a sky in color like thunderous sulphur, thinking for the first time in his life that perhaps Sutpen was an old man like himself. "Gittin a gal," he thought in that astonishment; then he thought with the pleased surprise of a child: "Yes, sir. Be dawg if I ain't lived to be a great-grandpaw after all."

He entered the house. He moved clumsily, on tiptoe as if he no longer lived there, as if the infant which had just drawn breath and cried in light had dispossessed him, but it of his own blood too though it might. But even above the pallet he could see little save the blur of his granddaughter's exhausted face. Then the Negress squatting at the hearth spoke, "You better gawn tell him if you going to. Hit's daylight now."

But that was not necessary. He had no more than turned the corner of the porch where the scythe leaned which he had borrowed three months ago to clear away the weeds through which he walked, when Sutpen himself rode up on the old stallion. He did not wonder how Sutpen had got the word. He took it for granted that this was what had brought the other out at this hour on Sunday

40

morning, and he stood while the other dismounted, and he took the reins from Sutpen's hand, an expression on his gaunt face almost imbecile with a kind of weary triumph, saying, "Hit's a gal, Kernel. I be dawg if you ain't as old as I am—" until Sutpen passed him and entered the house. He stood there with the reins in his hand and heard Sutpen cross the floor to the pallet. He heard what Sutpen said, and something seemed to stop dead in him before going on.

The sun was now up, the swift sun of Mississippi latitudes, and it seemed to him that he stood beneath a strange sky, in a strange scene, familiar only as things are familiar in dreams, like the dreams of falling to one who has never climbed. "I kain't have heard what I thought I heard," he thought quietly. "I know I kain't." Yet the voice, the familiar voice which had said the words was still speaking, talking now to the old Negress about a colt foaled that morning. "That's why he was up so early," he thought. "That was hit. Hit ain't me and mine. Hit ain't even hisn that got him outten bed."

Sutpen emerged. He descended into the weeds, moving with the heavy deliberation which would have been haste when he was younger. He had not yet looked full at Wash. He said, "Dicey will stay and tend to her. You better—" Then he seemed to see Wash facing him and paused. "What?" he said.

"You said—" To his own ears Wash's voice sounded flat and ducklike, like a deaf man's. "You said if she was a mare, you could give her a good stall in the stable."

"Well?" Sutpen said. His eyes widened and narrowed, almost like a man's fists flexing and shutting, as Wash began to advance towards him, stooping a little. Very astonishment kept Sutpen still for the moment, watching that man whom in twenty years he had no more known to make any motion save at command than he had the horse which he rode. Again his eyes narrowed and widened; without moving he seemed to rear suddenly upright. "Stand back," he said suddenly and sharply. "Don't you touch me."

45 "I'm going to tech you, Kernel," Wash said in that flat, quiet, almost soft voice, advancing.

Sutpen raised the hand which held the riding whip; the old Negress peered around the crazy door with her black gargoyle face of a worn gnome. "Stand back, Wash," Sutpen said. Then he struck. The old Negress leaped down into the weeds with the agility of a goat and fled. Sutpen slashed Wash again across the face with the whip, striking him to his knees. When Wash rose and advanced once more he held in his hands the scythe which he had borrowed from Sutpen three months ago and which Sutpen would never need again.

When he reentered the house his granddaughter stirred on the pallet bed and called his name fretfully. "What was that?" she said.

"What was what, honey?"

"That ere racket out there."

50 "'Twarn't nothing," he said gently. He knelt and touched her hot forehead clumsily. "Do you want ara thing?"

"I want a sup of water," she said querulously. "I been laying here wanting a sup of water a long time, but don't nobody care enough to pay me no mind."

"Sho now," he said soothingly. He rose stiffly and fetched the dipper of water and raised her head to drink and laid her back and watched her turn to the child

with an absolutely stonelike face. But a moment later he saw that she was crying quietly. "Now, now," he said. "I wouldn't do that. Old Dicey says hit's a right
fine gal. Hit's all right now. Hit's all over now. Hit ain't no need to cry now."

But she continued to cry quietly, almost sullenly, and he rose again and stood
uncomfortably above the pallet for a time, thinking as he had thought when his
own wife lay so and then his daughter in turn: "Women. Hit's a mystry to me.
They seem to want em, and yit when they git em they cry about hit. Hit's a
mystry to me. To ara man." Then he moved away and drew a chair up to the
window and sat down.

Through all that long, bright, sunny forenoon he sat at the window, waiting.
Now and then he rose and tiptoed to the pallet. But his granddaughter slept
now, her face sullen and calm and weary, the child in the crook of her arm.
Then he returned to the chair and sat again, waiting, wondering why it took
them so long, until he remembered that it was Sunday. He was sitting there at
mid-afternoon when a half-grown white boy came around the corner of the
house upon the body and gave a choked cry and looked up and glared for a
mesmerized instant at Wash in the window before he turned and fled. Then
Wash rose and tiptoed again to the pallet.

The granddaughter was awake now, wakened perhaps by the boy's cry with-   55
out hearing it. "Milly," he said, "air you hungry?" She didn't answer, turning her
face away. He built up the fire on the hearth and cooked the food which he had
brought home the day before: fatback it was, and cold corn pone; he poured
water into the stale coffee pot and heated it. But she would not eat when he carried the plate to her, so he ate himself, quietly, alone, and left the dishes as they
were and returned to the window.

Now he seemed to sense, feel, the men who would be gathering with horses
and guns and dogs—the curious, and the vengeful: men of Sutpen's own kind,
who had made the company about Sutpen's table in the time when Wash himself had yet to approach nearer to the house than the scuppernong arbor—men
who had also shown the lesser ones how to fight in battle, who maybe also had
signed papers from the generals saying that they were among the first of the
brave; who had also galloped in the old days arrogant and proud on the fine
horses across the fine plantations—symbols also of admiration and hope;
instruments too of despair and grief.

That was whom they would expect him to run from. It seemed to him that he
had no more to run from than he had to run to. If he ran, he would merely be
fleeing one set of bragging and evil shadows for another just like them, since
they were all of a kind throughout all the earth which he knew, and he was old,
too old to flee far even if he were to flee. He could never escape them, no matter
how much or how far he ran: a man going on sixty could not run that far. Not
far enough to escape beyond the boundaries of earth where such men lived, set
the order and the rule of living. It seemed to him that he now saw for the first
time, after five years, how it was that Yankees or any other living armies had
managed to whip them: the gallant, the proud, the brave; the acknowledged and
chosen best among them all to carry courage and honor and pride. Maybe if he
had gone to the war with them he would have discovered them sooner. But if he

had discovered them sooner, what would he have done with his life since? How could he have borne to remember for five years what his life had been before?

Now it was getting toward sunset. The child had been crying; when he went to the pallet he saw his granddaughter nursing it, her face still bemused, sullen, inscrutable. "Air you hungry yit?" he said.

"I don't want nothing."

60   "You ought to eat."

This time she did not answer at all, looking down at the child. He returned to his chair and found that the sun had set. "Hit kain't be much longer," he thought. He could feel them quite near now, the curious and the vengeful. He could even seem to hear what they were saying about him, the undercurrent of believing beyond the immediate fury: *Old Wash Jones he come a tumble at last. He thought he had Sutpen, but Sutpen fooled him. He thought he had Kernel where he would have to marry the gal or pay up. And Kernel refused.* "But I never expected that, Kernel!" he cried aloud, catching himself at the sound of his own voice, glancing quickly back to find his granddaughter watching him.

"Who you talking to now?" she said.

"Hit ain't nothing. I was just thinking and talked out before I knowed hit."

Her face was becoming indistinct again, again a sullen blur in the twilight. "I reckon so. I reckon you'll have to holler louder than that before he'll hear you, up yonder at that house. And I reckon you'll need to do more than holler before you get him down here too."

65   "Sho now," he said. "Don't you worry none." But already thinking was going smoothly on: "You know I never. You know how I ain't never expected or asked nothing from ara living man but what I expected from you. And I never asked that. I didn't think hit would need. I said, *I don't need to. What need has a fellow like Wash Jones to question or doubt the man that General Lee himself says in a handwrote ticket that he was brave?* Brave," he thought. "Better if nara one of them had never rid back home in '65"; thinking *Better if his kind and mine too had never drawn the breath of life on this earth. Better than all who remain of us be blasted from the face of earth than that another Wash Jones should see his whole life shredded from him and shrivel away like a dried shuck thrown onto the fire.*

He ceased, became still. He heard the horses, suddenly and plainly; presently he saw the lantern and the movement of men, the glint of gun barrels, in its moving light. Yet he did not stir. It was quite dark now, and he listened to the voices and the sounds of underbrush as they surrounded the house. The lantern itself came on; its light fell upon the quiet body in the weeds and stopped, the horses tall and shadowy. A man descended and stooped in the lantern light, above the body. He held a pistol; he rose and faced the house. "Jones," he said.

"I'm here," Wash said quietly from the window. "That you, Major?"

"Come out."

"Sho," he said quietly. "I just want to see to my granddaughter."

70   "We'll see to her. Come on out."

"Sho, Major. Just a minute."

"Show a light. Light your lamp."

"Sho. In just a minute." They could hear his voice retreat into the house, though they could not see him as he went swiftly to the crack in the chimney where he kept the butcher knife: the one thing in his slovenly life and house in which he took pride, since it was razor sharp. He approached the pallet, his granddaughter's voice:

"Who is it? Light the lamp, grandpaw."

"Hit won't need no light, honey. Hit won't take but a minute," he said, kneeling, fumbling toward her voice, whispering now. "Where air you?"   75

"Right here," she said fretfully. "Where would I be? What is . . ." His hand touched her face. "What is . . . Grandpaw! Grand. . . ."

"Jones!" the sheriff said. "Come out of there!"

"In just a minute, Major," he said. Now he rose and moved swiftly. He knew where in the dark the can of kerosene was, just as he knew that it was full, since it was not two days ago that he had filled it at the store and held it there until he got a ride home with it, since the five gallons were heavy. There were still coals on the hearth; besides, the crazy building itself was like tinder: the coals, the hearth, the walls exploding in a single blue glare. Against it the waiting men saw him in a wild instant springing toward them with the lifted scythe before the horses reared and whirled. They checked the horses and turned them back toward the glare, yet still in wild relief against it the gaunt figure ran toward them with the lifted scythe.

"Jones!" the sheriff shouted; "stop! Stop, or I'll shoot. Jones! *Jones!*" Yet still the gaunt, furious figure came on against the glare and roar of the flames. With the scythe lifted, it bore down upon them, upon the wild glaring eyes of the horses and the swinging glints of gun barrels, without any cry, any sound.

[1934]

1. The story differentiates among several categories of living creatures, including "the fine figure of a man," Colonel Sutpen; "the fine figure of a black stallion," Colonel Sutpen's horse; poor whites like Wash; and "Negroes" who were slaves before the war and free after. How do different people in the story rank them differently according to their relative status, and how do the rankings change in the course of the plot?
2. How does dialect figure into the relative status of the various groups of people in the story?
3. What is the relationship between the narrative time and chronological time of this story? What is the crisis point of the plot?
4. How does Faulkner's style contribute to the effect of the story?

EUDORA WELTY

EUDORA WELTY *(1909–2001) was born in Jackson, Mississippi, where she spent most of her life. She received her degree from the University of Washington and did a year of postgraduate work at Columbia University. Upon her return home, she worked for the local radio station and then took a job as a publicist with President Franklin Roosevelt's Works Progress Administration. She traveled all over Mississippi to promote efforts to bring economic progress to the area. Selections from her many photographs of rural life in Depression-era Mississippi were exhibited in*

New York and have been published as books, including One Time, One Place: Mississippi in the Depression: A Snapshot Album *(1978) and* Photographs *(1989). In 1936, she published her first important short story and, from then on, her writing career saw the publication of many novels and short stories, which have been collected in anthologies edited by Richard Ford and Michael Kreyling. She published right through her seventies, working especially on* One Writer's Beginnings, *an autobiography. There she talked about the relationship between her writing and photography: "Life doesn't hold still," she said. "Photography taught me that to be able to capture transience, by being ready to click the shutter at the crucial moment, was the greatest need I had" (84).*

A Worn Path

It was December—a bright frozen day in the early morning. Far out in the country there was an old Negro woman with her head tied in a red rag, coming along a path through the pinewoods. Her name was Phoenix Jackson. She was very old and small and she walked slowly in the dark pine shadows, moving a little from side to side in her steps, with the balanced heaviness and lightness of a pendulum in a grandfather clock. She carried a thin, small cane made from an umbrella, and with this she kept tapping the frozen earth in front of her. This made a grave and persistent noise in the still air, that seemed meditative like the chirping of a solitary little bird.

She wore a dark striped dress reaching down to her shoe tops, and an equally long apron of bleached sugar sacks, with a full pocket: all neat and tidy, but every time she took a step she might have fallen over her shoelaces, which dragged from her unlaced shoes. She looked straight ahead. Her eyes were blue with age. Her skin had a pattern all its own of numberless branching wrinkles and as though a whole little tree stood in the middle of her forehead, but a golden color ran underneath, and the two knobs of her cheeks were illumined by a yellow burning under the dark. Under the red rag her hair came down on her neck in the frailest of ringlets, still black, and with an odor like copper.

Now and then there was a quivering in the thicket. Old Phoenix said, "Out of my way, all you foxes, owls, beetles, jack rabbits, coons and wild animals! . . . Keep out from under these feet, little bob-whites. . . . Keep the big wild hogs out of my path. Don't let none of those come running my direction. I got a long way." Under her small black-freckled hand her cane, limber as a buggy whip, would switch at the brush as if to rouse up any hiding things.

On she went. The woods were deep and still. The sun made the pine needles almost too bright to look at, up where the wind rocked. The cones dropped as light as feathers. Down in the hollow was the mourning dove—it was not too late for him.

5   The path ran up a hill. "Seem like there is chains about my feet, time I get this far," she said, in the voice of argument old people keep to use with themselves. "Something always take a hold of me on this hill—pleads I should stay."

After she got to the top she turned and gave a full, severe look behind her where she had come. "Up through pines," she said at length. "Now down through oaks."

Her eyes opened their widest, and she started down gently. But before she got to the bottom of the hill a bush caught her dress.

Her fingers were busy and intent, but her skirts were full and long, so that before she could pull them free in one place they were caught in another. It was not possible to allow the dress to tear. "I in the thorny bush," she said. "Thorns, you doing your appointed work. Never want to let folks pass, no sir. Old eyes thought you was a pretty little *green* bush."

Finally, trembling all over, she stood free, and after a moment dared to stoop for her cane.

"Sun so high!" she cried, leaning back and looking, while the thick tears went over her eyes. "The time getting all gone here."   10

At the foot of this hill was a place where a log was laid across the creek.

"Now comes the trial," said Phoenix.

Putting her right foot out, she mounted the log and shut her eyes. Lifting her skirt, leveling her cane fiercely before her, like a festival figure in some parade, she began to march across. Then she opened her eyes and she was safe on the other side.

"I wasn't as old as I thought," she said.

But she sat down to rest. She spread her skirts on the bank around her and   15
folded her hands over her knees. Up above her was a tree in a pearly cloud of mistletoe. She did not dare to close her eyes, and when a little boy brought her a plate with a slice of marble-cake on it she spoke to him. "That would be acceptable," she said. But when she went to take it there was just her own hand in the air.

So she left that tree, and had to go through a barbed-wire fence. There she had to creep and crawl, spreading her knees and stretching her fingers like a baby trying to climb the steps. But she talked loudly to herself: she could not let her dress be torn now, so late in the day, and she could not pay for having her arm or her leg sawed off if she got caught fast where she was.

At last she was safe through the fence and risen up out in the clearing. Big dead trees, like black men with one arm, were standing in the purple stalks of the withered cotton field. There sat a buzzard.

"Who you watching?"

In the furrow she made her way along.

"Glad this not the season for bulls," she said, looking sideways, "and the good   20
Lord made his snakes to curl up and sleep in the winter. A pleasure I don't see no two-headed snake coming around that tree, where it come once. It took a while to get by him, back in the summer."

She passed through the old cotton and went into a field of dead corn. It whispered and shook and was taller than her head. "Through the maze now," she said, for there was no path.

Then there was something tall, black, and skinny there, moving before her.

At first she took it for a man. It could have been a man dancing in the field. But she stood still and listened, and it did not make a sound. It was as silent as a ghost.

"Ghost," she said sharply, "who be you the ghost of? For I have heard of nary death close by."

25   But there was no answer—only the ragged dancing in the wind.

She shut her eyes, reached out her hand, and touched a sleeve. She found a coat and inside that an emptiness, cold as ice.

"You scarecrow," she said. Her face lighted. "I ought to be shut up for good," she said with laughter. "My senses is gone. I too old. I the oldest people I ever know. Dance, old scarecrow," she said, "while I dancing with you."

She kicked her foot over the furrow, and with mouth drawn down, shook her head once or twice in a little strutting way. Some husks blew down and whirled in streamers about her skirts.

Then she went on, parting her way from side to side with the cane, through the whispering field. At last she came to the end, to a wagon track where the silver grass blew between the red ruts. The quail were walking around like pullets, seeming all dainty and unseen.

30   "Walk pretty," she said. "This is the easy place. This the easy going."

She followed the track, swaying through the quiet bare fields, through the little strings of trees silver in their dead leaves, past cabins silver from weather, with the doors and windows boarded shut, all like old women under a spell sitting there. "I walking in their sleep," she said, nodding her head vigorously.

In a ravine she went where a spring was silently flowing through a hollow log. Old Phoenix bent and drank. "Sweet-gum makes the water sweet," she said, and drank more. "Nobody know who made this well, for it was here when I was born."

The track crossed a swampy part where the moss hung as white as lace from every limb. "Sleep on, alligators, and blow your bubbles." Then the track went into the road.

Deep, deep the road went down between the high green-colored banks. Overhead the live-oaks met, and it was as dark as a cave.

35   A black dog with a lolling tongue came up out of the weeds by the ditch. She was meditating, and not ready, and when he came at her she only hit him a little with her cane. Over she went in the ditch, like a little puff of milkweed.

Down there, her senses drifted away. A dream visited her, and she reached her hand up, but nothing reached down and gave her a pull. So she lay there and presently went to talking. "Old woman," she said to herself, "that black dog come up out of the weeds to stall you off, and now there he sitting on his fine tail, smiling at you."

A white man finally came along and found her—a hunter, a young man, with his dog on a chain.

"Well, Granny!" he laughed. "What are you doing there?"

"Lying on my back like a June-bug waiting to be turned over, mister," she said, reaching up her hand.

40   He lifted her up, gave her a swing in the air, and set her down. "Anything broken, Granny?"

"No sir, them old dead weeds is springy enough," said Phoenix, when she had got her breath. "I thank you for your trouble."

"Where do you live, Granny?" he asked, while the two dogs were growling at each other.

"Away back yonder, sir, behind the ridge. You can't even see it from here."

"On your way home?"

"No sir, I going to town."   45

"Why, that's too far! That's as far as I walk when I come out myself, and I get something for my trouble." He patted the stuffed bag he carried, and there hung down a little closed claw. It was one of the bob-whites, with its beak hooked bitterly to show it was dead. "Now you go on home, Granny!"

"I bound to go to town, mister," said Phoenix. "The time come around."

He gave another laugh, filling the whole landscape. "I know you old colored people! Wouldn't miss going to town to see Santa Claus!"

But something held old Phoenix very still. The deep lines in her face went into a fierce and different radiation. Without warning, she had seen with her own eyes a flashing nickel fall out of the man's pocket onto the ground.

"How old are you, Granny?" he was saying.   50

"There is no telling, mister," she said, "no telling."

Then she gave a little cry and clapped her hands and said, "Git on away from here, dog! Look! Look at that dog!" She laughed as if in admiration. "He ain't scared of nobody. He a big black dog." She whispered, "Sic him!"

"Watch me get rid of that cur," said the man. "Sic him, Pete! Sic him!"

Phoenix heard the dogs fighting, and heard the man running and throwing sticks. She even heard a gunshot. But she was slowly bending forward by that time, further and further forward, the lid stretched down over her eyes, as if she were doing this in her sleep. Her chin was lowered almost to her knees. The yellow palm of her hand came out from the fold of her apron. Her fingers slid down and along the ground under the piece of money with the grace and care they would have in lifting an egg from under a setting hen. Then she slowly straightened up, she stood erect, and the nickel was in her apron pocket. A bird flew by. Her lips moved. "God watching me the whole time. I come to stealing."

The man came back, and his own dog panted about them. "Well, I scared him   55 off that time," he said, and then he laughed and lifted his gun and pointed it at Phoenix.

She stood straight and faced him.

"Doesn't the gun scare you?" he said, still pointing it.

"No, sir, I seen plenty go off closer by, in my day, and for less than what I done," she said, holding utterly still.

He smiled, and shouldered the gun. "Well, Granny," he said, "you must be a hundred years old, and scared of nothing. I'd give you a dime if I had any money with me. But you take my advice and stay home, and nothing will happen to you."

"I bound to go on my way, mister," said Phoenix. She inclined her head in   60 the red rag. Then they went in different directions, but she could hear the gun shooting again and again over the hill.

She walked on. The shadows hung from the oak trees to the road like curtains. Then she smelled wood-smoke, and smelled the river, and she saw a steeple and the cabins on their steep steps. Dozens of little black children whirled around her. There ahead was Natchez shining. Bells were ringing. She walked on.

In the paved city it was Christmas time. There were red and green electric lights strung and crisscrossed everywhere, and all turned on in the daytime. Old Phoenix would have been lost if she had not distrusted her eyesight and depended on her feet to know where to take her.

She paused quietly on the sidewalk where people were passing by. A lady came along in the crowd, carrying an armful of red-, green- and silver-wrapped presents; she gave off perfume like the red roses in hot summer, and Phoenix stopped her.

"Please, missy, will you lace up my shoe?" She held up her foot.

65   "What do you want, Grandma?"

"See my shoe," said Phoenix. "Do all right for out in the country, but would't look right to go in a big building."

"Stand still then, Grandma," said the lady. She put her packages down on the sidewalk beside her and laced and tied both shoes tightly.

"Can't lace 'em with a cane," said Phoenix. "Thank you, missy. I doesn't mind asking a nice lady to tie up my shoe, when I gets out on the street."

Moving slowly and from side to side, she went into the big building, and into a tower of steps, where she walked up and around and around until her feet knew to stop.

70   She entered a door, and there she saw nailed up on the wall the document that had been stamped with the gold seal and framed in the gold frame, which matched the dream that was hung up in her head.

"Here I be," she said. There was a fixed and ceremonial stiffness over her body.

"A charity case, I suppose," said an attendant who sat at the desk before her.

But Phoenix only looked above her head. There was sweat on her face, the wrinkles in her face shone like a bright net.

"Speak up, Grandma," the woman said. "What's your name? We must have your history, you know. Have you been here before? What seems to be the trouble with you?"

75   Old Phoenix only gave a twitch to her face as if a fly were bothering her.

"Are you deaf?" cried the attendant.

But then the nurse came in.

"Oh, that's just old Aunt Phoenix," she said. "She doesn't come for herself— she has a little grandson. She makes these trips just as regular as clockwork. She lives away back off the Old Natchez Trace." She bent down. "Well, Aunt Phoenix, why don't you just take a seat? We won't keep you standing after your long trip." She pointed.

The old woman sat down, bolt upright in the chair.

80   "Now, how is the boy?" asked the nurse.

Old Phoenix did not speak.

"I said, how is the boy?"

But Phoenix only waited and stared straight ahead, her face very solemn and withdrawn into rigidity.

"Is his throat any better?" asked the nurse. "Aunt Phoenix, don't you hear me? Is your grandson's throat any better since the last time you came for the medicine?"

With her hands on her knees, the old woman waited, silent, erect and motionless, just as if she were in armor.   85

"You mustn't take up our time this way, Aunt Phoenix," the nurse said. "Tell us quickly about your grandson, and get it over. He isn't dead, is he?"

At last there came a flicker and then a flame of comprehension across her face, and she spoke.

"My grandson. It was my memory had left me. There I sat and forgot why I made my long trip."

"Forgot?" The nurse frowned. "After you came so far?"

Then Phoenix was like an old woman begging a dignified forgiveness for waking   90
up frightened in the night. "I never did go to school, I was too old at the Surrender,"°
she said in a soft voice. "I'm an old woman without an education. It was my memory fail me. My little grandson, he is just the same, and I forgot it in the coming."

"Throat never heals, does it?" said the nurse, speaking in a loud, sure voice to old Phoenix. By now she had a card with something written on it, a little list. "Yes. Swallowed lye. When was it?—January—two-three years ago—"

Phoenix spoke unasked now. "No, missy, he not dead, he just the same. Every little while his throat begin to close up again, and he not able to swallow. He not get his breath. He not able to help himself. So the time come around, and I go on another trip for the soothing medicine."

"All right. The doctor said as long as you came to get it, you could have it," said the nurse. "But it's an obstinate case."

"My little grandson, he sit up there in the house all wrapped up, waiting by himself," Phoenix went on. "We is the only two left in the world. He suffer and it don't seem to put him back at all. He got a sweet look. He going to last. He wear a little patch quilt and peep out holding his mouth open like a little bird. I remembers so plain now. I not going to forget him again, no, the whole enduring time. I could tell him from all the others in creation."

"All right." The nurse was trying to hush her now. She brought her a bottle of   95
medicine. "Charity," she said, making a check mark in a book.

Old Phoenix held the bottle close to her eyes, and then carefully put it into her pocket.

"I thank you," she said.

"It's Christmas time, Grandma," said the attendant. "Could I give you a few pennies out of my purse?"

"Five pennies is a nickel," said Phoenix stiffly.

"Here's a nickel," said the attendant.   100

Phoenix rose carefully and held out her hand. She received the nickel and then fished the other nickel out of her pocket and laid it beside the new one. She stared at her palm closely, with her head on one side.

Then she gave a tap with her cane on the floor.

"This is what come to me to do," she said. "I going to the store and buy my child a little windmill they sells, made out of paper. He going to find it hard to

---

°**Surrender** Confederate General Robert E. Lee's surrender to Union General Ulysses S. Grant ended the Civil War on April 9, 1865.

believe there such a thing in the world. I'll march myself back where he waiting, holding it straight up in this hand."

She lifted her free hand, gave a little nod, turned around, and walked out of the doctor's office. Then her slow step began on the stairs, going down.

[1940]

1. What character traits of Phoenix do we learn about as the story progresses?
2. What do we learn from her encounter with the hunter?
3. What can we learn from how the staff members at the clinic treat her?
4. What disciplines might offer concepts and data that would help explain the story?

DRAMA

ATHOL FUGARD

ATHOL FUGARD (1932–), *born of white English and Afrikaner parents, was brought up in Port Elizabeth, South Africa, with English as his mother tongue. He dropped out of the University of Cape Town just before exams to hitchhike through Africa and sail the world as a deckhand. His interest in acting led to a career in writing plays, almost always plays about his own country, especially about apartheid and post-apartheid politics and problems. His work with a group of actors who were influenced by Strasburg's Method Acting led to his first play,* No Good Friday, *and his first international success,* Blood Knot, *a play about the psychology of racism that led to his being exiled by the pro-apartheid South African government. Fugard's work has been performed in Africa, the United States, and elsewhere. In 2003, a revival of* "Master Harold" . . . and the Boys *was staged on Broadway with Christopher Denham as Hally, Michael Boatman as Willie, and Danny Glover as Sam.*

"Master Harold" . . . and the Boys

Characters

Willy
Sam
Hally

(*Scene: The St. George's Park Tea Room on a wet and windy Port Elizabeth afternoon.*)

(*Tables and chairs have been cleared and are stacked on one side except for one which stands apart with a single chair. On this table a knife, fork, spoon and side plate in anticipation of a simple meal, together with a pile of comic books.*)

(*Other elements: a serving counter with a few stale cakes under glass and a not very impressive display of sweets, cigarettes and cool drinks, etc.; a few cardboard advertising handouts—Cadbury's Chocolate, Coca-Cola—and a blackboard on which an untrained hand has chalked up the prices of Tea, Coffee, Scones, Milkshakes—all flavors—and Cool Drinks; a few sad ferns in pots; a telephone; an old-style jukebox.)*

(There is an entrance on one side and an exit into a kitchen on the other.)

(Leaning on the solitary table, his head cupped in one hand as he pages through one of the comic books, is Sam. A black man in his mid-forties. He wears the white coat of a waiter. Behind him on his knees, mopping down the floor with a bucket of water and a rag, is Willie. Also black and about the same age as Sam. He has his sleeves and trousers rolled up.)

(The year: 1950.)

Willie *(singing as he works)*: "She was scandalizin' my name, she took my money, she called me honey but she was scandalizin' my name. Called it love but was playin' a game. . . ."

(He gets up and moves the bucket. Stands thinking for a moment, then, raising his arms to hold an imaginary partner, he launches into an intricate ballroom dance step. Although a mildly comic figure, he reveals a reasonable degree of accomplishment.)

Hey, Sam.

(Sam, absorbed in the comic book, does not respond.)

Hey, Boet° Sam!

(Sam looks up.)

I'm getting it. The quickstep. Look now and tell me. *(He repeats the step.)* Well?

Sam *(encouragingly)*: Show me again.

Willie: Okay, count for me.

Sam: Ready?

Willie: Ready.

Sam: Five, six, seven, eight. . . . *(Willie starts to dance.)* A-n-d one two three four . . . and one two three four. . . . *(Ad libbing as Willie dances.)* Your shoulders, Willie . . . your shoulders! Don't look down! Look happy, Willie! Relax, Willie!   5

Willie *(desperate but still dancing)*: I am relax.

Sam: No, you're not.

Willie *(he falters)*: Ag no man, Sam! Mustn't talk. You make me make mistakes.

Sam: But you're stiff.   10

Willie: Yesterday I'm not straight . . . today I'm too stiff!

Sam: Well, you are. You asked me and I'm telling you.

Willie: Where?

Sam: Everywhere. Try to glide through it.

Willie: Glide?   15

Sam: Ja, make it smooth. And give it more style. It must look like you're enjoying yourself.

Willie *(emphatically)*: I wasn't.

Sam: Exactly.

Willie: How can I enjoy myself? Not straight, too stiff and now it's also glide, give it more style, make it smooth. . . . Haai! Is hard to remember all those things, Boet Sam.

---

[1]**Boet** brother

20 *Sam:* That's your trouble. You're trying too hard.

Willie: I try hard because it *is* hard.

Sam: But don't let me see it. The secret is to make it look easy. Ballroom must look happy, Willie, not like hard work. It must. . . . Ja! . . . it must look like romance.

Willie: Now another one! What's romance?

Sam: Love story with happy ending. A handsome man in tails, and in his arms, smiling at him, a beautiful lady in evening dress!

25 *Willie:* Fred Astaire, Ginger Rogers.°

Sam: You got it. Tapdance or ballroom, it's the same. Romance. In two weeks' time when the judges look at you and Hilda, they must see a man and a woman who are dancing their way to a happy ending. What I saw was you holding her like you were frightened she was going to run away.

Willie: Ja! Because that is what she wants to do! I got no romance left for Hilda anymore, Boet Sam.

Sam: Then pretend. When you put your arms around Hilda, imagine she is Ginger Rogers.

Willie: With no teeth? You try.

30 *Sam:* Well, just remember, there's only two weeks left.

Willie: I know, I know! (*To the jukebox.*) I do it better with music. You got sixpence for Sarah Vaughan°?

Sam: That's a slow foxtrot. You're practicing the quickstep.

Willie: I'll practice slow foxtrot.

Sam (*shaking his head*): It's your turn to put money in the jukebox.

35 *Willie:* I only got bus fare to go home. (*He returns disconsolately to his work.*) Love story and happy ending! She's doing it all right, Boet Sam, but is not me she's giving happy endings. Fuckin' whore! Three nights now she doesn't come practice. I wind up gramophone, I get record ready and I sit and wait. What happens? Nothing. Ten o'clock I start dancing with my pillow. You try and practice romance by yourself, Boet Sam. Struesgod, she doesn't come tonight I take back my dress and ballroom shoes and I find me new partner. Size twenty-six. Shoes size seven. And now she's also making trouble for me with the baby again. Reports me to Child Wellfed, that I'm not giving her money. She lies! Every week I am giving her money for milk. And how do I know is my baby? Only his hair looks like me. She's fucking around all the time I turn my back. Hilda Samuels is a bitch! (*Pause.*) Hey, Sam!

Sam: Ja.

Willie: You listening?

Sam: Ja.

Willie: So what you say?

40 *Sam:* About Hilda?

Willie: Ja.

Sam: When did you last give her a hiding?

Willie (*reluctantly*): Sunday night.

Sam: And today is Thursday.

[25]**Fred Astaire, Ginger Rogers** actors whose collaborative movies often included singing and dancing, both tap and ballroom   [31]**Sarah Vaughan** jazz singer

Willie (he knows what's coming): Okay.   45

Sam: Hiding on Sunday night, then Monday, Tuesday, and Wednesday she doesn't
  come to practice . . . and you are asking me why?

Willie: I said okay, Boet Sam!

Sam: You hit her too much. One day she's going to leave you for good.

Willie: So? She makes me the hell-in too much.

Sam (emphasizing his point): *Too* much and *too* hard. You had the same trouble   50
  with Eunice.

Willie: Because she also make the hell-in, Boet Sam. She never got the steps
  right. Even the waltz.

Sam: Beating her up every time she makes a mistake in the waltz? (*Shaking his
  head.*) No, Willie! That takes the pleasure out of ballroom dancing.

Willie: Hilda is not too bad with the waltz, Boet Sam. Is the quickstep where the
  trouble starts.

Sam (teasing him gently): How's your pillow with the quickstep?

Willie (ignoring the tease): Good! And why? Because it got no legs. That's her trou-   55
  ble. She can't move them quick enough, Boet Sam. I start the record and before
  halfway Count Basie° is already winning. Only time we catch up with him is
  when gramophone runs down. (*Sam laughs.*) Haaikona, Boet Sam, is not funny.

Sam (snapping his fingers): I got it! Give her a handicap.

Willie: What's that?

Sam: Give her a ten-second start and then let Count Basie go. Then I put my
  money on her. Hot favorite in the Ballroom Stakes: Hilda Samuels ridden by
  Willie Malopo.

Willie (turning away): I'm not talking to you no more.

Sam (relenting): Sorry, Willie. . . .   60

Willie: It's finish between us.

Sam: Okay, okay . . . I'll stop.

Willie: You can also fuck off.

Sam: Willie, listen! I want to help you!

Willie: No more jokes?   65

Sam: I promise.

Willie: Okay. Help me.

Sam (his turn to hold an imaginary partner): Look and learn. Feet together. Back
  straight. Body relaxed. Right hand placed gently in the small of her back and
  wait for the music. Don't start worrying about making mistakes or the judges
  or the other competitors. It's just you, Hilda and the music, and you're going
  to have a good time. What Count Basie do you play?

Willie: "You the cream in my coffee, you the salt in my stew."

Sam: Right. Give it to me in strict tempo.   70

Willie: Ready?

Sam: Ready.

Willie: A-n-d . . . (*Singing.*) "You the cream in my coffee. You the salt in my stew.
  You will always be my necessity. I'd be lost without you. . . ." (*etc.*)

---

[55]**Count Basie** jazz pianist, composer, and leader of a jazz band

(Sam launches into the quickstep. He is obviously a much more accomplished dancer than Willie. Hally enters. A seventeen-year-old white boy. Wet raincoat and school case. He stops and watches Sam. The demonstration comes to an end with a flourish. Applause from Hally and Willie.)

Hally: Bravo! No question about it. First place goes to Mr. Sam Semela.

75   *Willie (in total agreement):* You was gliding with style, Boet Sam.

Hally (cheerfully): How's it, chaps?

Sam: Okay, Hally.

Willie (springing to attention like a soldier and saluting): At your service, Master Harold!

Hally: Not long to the big event, hey!

80   *Sam:* Two weeks.

Hally: You nervous?

Sam: No.

Hally: Think you stand a chance?

Sam: Let's just say I'm ready to go out there and dance.

85   *Hally:* It looked like it. What about you, Willie?

(*Willie groans.*)

What's the matter?

Sam: He's got leg trouble.

Hally (innocently): Oh, sorry to hear that, Willie.

Willie: Boet Sam! You promised. (*Willie returns to his work.*)

(Hally deposits his school case and takes off his raincoat. His clothes are a little neglected and untidy: black blazer with school badge, gray flannel trousers in need of an ironing, khaki shirt and tie, black shoes. Sam has fetched a towel for Hally to dry his hair.)

Hally: God, what a lousy bloody day. It's coming down cats and dogs out there. Bad for business, chaps. . . . (*Conspiratorial whisper.*) . . . but it also means we're in for a nice quiet afternoon.

90   *Sam:* You can speak loud. Your Mom's not here.

Hally: Out shopping?

Sam: No. The hospital.

Hally: But it's Thursday. There's no visiting on Thursday afternoons. Is my Dad okay?

Sam: Sounds like it. In fact, I think he's going home.

95   *Hally (stopped short by Sam's remark):* What do you mean?

Sam: The hospital phoned.

Hally: To say what?

Sam: I don't know. I just heard your Mom talking.

Hally: So what makes you say he's going home?

100   *Sam:* It sounded as if they were telling her to come and fetch him.

(*Hally thinks about what Sam has said a few seconds.*)

Hally: When did she leave?

Sam: About an hour ago. She said she would phone you. Want to eat?

(*Hally doesn't respond.*)

Hally, want your lunch?

Hally: I suppose so. (*His mood has changed.*) What's on the menu? . . . as if I don't know.

Sam: Soup, followed by meat pie and gravy.

Hally: Today's? 105

Sam: No.

Hally: And the soup?

Sam: Nourishing pea soup.

Hally: Just the soup. (*The pile of comic books on the table.*) And these?

Sam: For your Dad. Mr. Kempston brought them. 110

Hally: You haven't been reading them, have you?

Sam: Just looking.

Hally (*examining the comics*): Jungle Jim . . . Batman and Robin . . . Tarzan . . . God, what rubbish! Mental pollution. Take them away.

  (*Sam exits waltzing into the kitchen. Hally turns to Willie.*)

Hally: Did you hear my Mom talking on the telephone, Willie?

Willie: No, Master Hally. I was at the back. 115

Hally: And she didn't say anything to you before she left?

Willie: She said I must clean the floors.

Hally: I mean about my Dad.

Willie: She didn't say nothing to me about him, Master Hally.

Hally (*with conviction*): No! It can't be. They said he needed at least another three 120 weeks of treatment. Sam's definitely made a mistake.

  (*Rummages through his school case, finds a book and settles down at the table to read.*)

  So, Willie!

Willie: Yes, Master Hally! Schooling okay today?

Hally: Yes, okay. . . . (*He thinks about it.*) . . . No, not really. Ag, what's the difference? I don't care. And Sam says you've got problems.

Willie: Big problems.

Hally: Which leg is sore?

  (*Willie groans.*)

  Both legs.

Willie: There is nothing wrong with my legs. Sam is just making jokes. 125

Hally: So then you *will* be in the competition.

Willie: Only if I can find a partner.

Hally: But what about Hilda?

Sam (*returning with a bowl of soup*): She's the one who's got trouble with her legs.

Hally: What sort of trouble, Willie? 130

Sam: From the way he describes it, I think the lady has gone a bit lame.

Hally: Good God! Have you taken her to see a doctor?

Sam: I think a vet would be better.

Hally: What do you mean?

Sam: What do you call it again when a racehorse goes very fast? 135

Hally: Gallop?

Sam: That's it!

Willie: Boet Sam!

Hally: "A gallop down the homestretch to the winning post." But what's that got
    to do with Hilda?

140 *Sam:* Count Basie always gets there first.

    (*Willie lets fly with his slop rag. It misses Sam and hits Hally.*)

Hally (*furious*): For Christ's sake, Willie! What the hell do you think you're doing?
Willie: Sorry, Master Hally, but it's him. . . .
Hally: Act your bloody age! (*Hurls the rag back at Willie.*) Cut out the nonsense
    now and get on with your work. And you too, Sam. Stop fooling around.

    (*Sam moves away*)

    No. Hang on. I haven't finished! Tell me exactly what my Mom said.
Sam: I have. "When Hally comes, tell him I've gone to the hospital and I'll phone
    him."

145 *Hally:* She didn't say anything about taking my Dad home?
Sam: No. It's just that when she was talking on the phone. . . .
Hally (*interrupting him*): No, Sam. They can't be discharging him. She would have
    said so if they were. In any case, we saw him last night and he wasn't in good
    shape at all. Staff nurse even said there was talk about taking more X-rays.
    And now suddenly today he's better? If anything, it sounds more like a bad
    turn to me . . . which I sincerely hope it isn't. Hang on . . . how long ago did
    you say she left?
Sam: Just before two . . . (*his wrist watch*) . . . hour and a half.
Hally: I know how to settle it. (*Behind the counter to the telephone. Talking as he
    dials.*) Let's give her ten minutes to get to the hospital, ten minutes to load
    him up, another ten, at the most, to get home, and another ten to get him
    inside. Forty minutes. They should have been home for at least half an hour
    already. (*Pause—he waits with the receiver to his ear.*) No reply, chaps. And you
    know why? Because she's at his bedside in hospital helping him pull through
    a bad turn. You definitely heard wrong.

150 *Sam:* Okay.

    (*As far as Hally is concerned, the matter is settled. He returns to his table, sits down,
    and divides his attention between the book and his soup. Sam is at his school case and
    picks up a textbook.*)

    Modern Graded Mathematics for Standards Nine and Ten. (*Opens it at random and
    laughs at something he sees.*) Who is this supposed to be?

Hally: Old fart-face Prentice.
Sam: Teacher?
Hally: Thinks he is. And believe me, that is not a bad likeness.
Sam: Has he seen it?

155 *Hally:* Yes.
Sam: What did he say?
Hally: Tried to be clever, as usual. Said I was no Leonardo da Vinci and that bad
    art had to be punished. So, six of the best, and his are bloody good.
Sam: On your bum?
Hally: Where else? The days when I got them on my hands are gone forever, Sam.

Sam: With your trousers down! 160

Hally: No. He's not quite that barbaric.

Sam: That's the way they do it in jail.

Hally (flicker of morbid interest): Really?

Sam: Ja. When the magistrate sentences you to "strokes with a light cane."

Hally: Go on. 165

Sam: They make you lie down on a bench. One policeman pulls down your trousers and holds your ankles, another one pulls your shirt over your head and holds your arms. . . .

Hally: Thank you! That's enough.

Sam: . . . and the one that gives you the strokes talks to you gently and for a long time between each one. (*He laughs.*)

Hally: I've heard enough, Sam! Jesus! It's a bloody awful world when you come to think of it. People can be real bastards.

Sam: That's the way it is, Hally. 170

Hally: It doesn't *have* to be that way. There is something called progress, you know. We don't exactly burn people at the stake anymore.

Sam: Like Joan of Arc.

Hally: Correct. If she was captured today, she'd be given a fair trial.

Sam: And then the death sentence.

Hally (a world-weary sigh): I know, I know! I oscillate between hope and despair 175 for this world as well, Sam. But things will change, you wait and see. One day somebody is going to get up and give history a kick up the backside and get it going again.

Sam: Like who?

Hally (after thought): They're called social reformers. Every age, Sam, has got its social reformer. My history book is full of them.

Sam: So where's ours?

Hally: Good question. And I hate to say it, but the answer is: I don't know. Maybe he hasn't even been born yet. Or is still only a babe in arms at his mother's breast. God, what a thought.

Sam: So we just go on waiting. 180

Hally: Ja, looks like it. (*Back to his soup and the book.*)

Sam (reading from the textbook): "Introduction: In some mathematical problems only the magnitude. . . ." (*He mispronounces the word "magnitude."*)

Hally (correcting him without looking up): Magnitude.

Sam: What's it mean?

Hally: How big it is. The size of the thing. 185

Sam (reading): ". . . magnitude of the quantities is of importance. In other problems we need to know whether these quantities are negative or positive. For example, whether there is a debit or credit bank balance . . ."

Hally: Whether you're broke or not.

Sam: ". . . whether the temperature is above or below Zero. . . ."

Hally: Naught degrees. Cheerful state of affairs! No cash and you're freezing to death. Mathematics won't get you out of that one.

Sam: "All these quantities are called . . ." (*spelling the word*) . . . s-c-a-l. . . . 190

Hally: Scalars.

Sam: Scalars! (*Shaking his head with a laugh.*) You understand all that?

Hally (*turning a page*)*:* No. And I don't intend to try.

Sam: So what happens when the exams come?

195 *Hally:* Failing a maths exam isn't the end of the world, Sam. How many times have I told you that examination results don't measure intelligence?

Sam: I would say about as many times as you've failed one of them.

Hally (*mirthlessly*)*:* Ha, ha, ha.

Sam (*simultaneously*)*:* Ha, ha, ha.

Hally: Just remember Winston Churchill° didn't do particularly well at school.

200 *Sam:* You've also told me that one many times.

Hally: Well, it just so happens to be the truth.

Sam (*enjoying the word*)*:* Magnitude! Magnitude! Show me how to use it.

Hally (*after thought*)*:* An intrepid social reformer will not be daunted by the magnitude of the task he has undertaken.

Sam (*impressed*)*:* Couple of jaw-breakers in there!

205 *Hally:* I gave you three for the price of one. Intrepid, daunted, and magnitude. I did that once in an exam. Put five of the words I had to explain in one sentence. It was half a page long.

Sam: Well, I'll put my money on you in the English exam.

Hally: Piece of cake. Eighty percent without even trying.

Sam (*another textbook from Hally's case*)*:* And history?

Hally: So-so. I'll scrape through. In the fifties if I'm lucky.

210 *Sam:* You didn't do too badly last year.

Hally: Because we had World War One. That at least has some action. You try to find that in the South African Parliamentary system.

Sam (*reading from the history textbook*)*:* "Napoleon and the principle of equality." Hey! This sounds interesting. "After concluding peace with Britain in 1802, Napoleon used a brief period of calm to in-sti-tute . . ."

Hally: Introduce.

Sam: ". . . many reforms. Napoleon regarded all people as equal before the law and wanted them to have equal opportunities for advancement. All ves-ti-ges of the feu-dal sys-tem with its oppression of the poor were abol-ished." Vestiges, feudal system, and abolished. I'm all right on oppression.

215 *Hally:* I'm thinking. He swept away . . . abolished . . . the last remains . . . vestiges . . . of the bad old days . . . feudal system.

Sam: Ha! There's the social reformer we're waiting for. He sounds like a man of some magnitude.

Hally: I'm not so sure about that. It's a damn good title for a book, though. A man of magnitude!

Sam: He sounds pretty big to me, Hally.

Hally: Don't confuse historical significance with greatness. But maybe I'm being a bit prejudiced. Have a look in there and you'll see he's two chapters long.

---

[199] **Winston Churchill** prime minister who led Great Britain through World War II

And hell! . . . has he only got dates, Sam, all of which you've got to remember! This campaign and that campaign, and then, because of all the fighting, the next thing is we get Peace Treaties all over the place. And what's the end of the story? Battle of Waterloo, which he loses. Wasn't worth it. No, I don't know about him as a man of magnitude.

Sam: Then who would you say was?   220

Hally: To answer that, we need a definition of greatness, and I suppose that would be somebody who . . . somebody who benefited all mankind.

Sam: Right. But like who?

Hally (he speaks with total conviction): Charles Darwin. Remember him? That big book from the library. *The Origin of the Species.*

Sam: Him?

Hally: Yes. For his Theory of Evolution.   225

Sam: You didn't finish it.

Hally: I ran out of time. I didn't finish it because my two weeks was up. But I'm going to take it out again after I've digested what I read. It's safe. I've hidden it away in the Theology section. Nobody ever goes in there. And anyway who are you to talk? You hardly even looked at it.

Sam: I tried. I looked at the chapters in the beginning and I saw one called "The Struggle for an Existence." Ah ha, I thought. At last! But what did I get? Something called the mistletoe which needs the apple tree and there's too many seeds and all are going to die except one . . . ! No, Hally.

Hally (intellectually outraged): What do you mean, No! The poor man had to start somewhere. For God's sake, Sam, he revolutionized science. Now we know.

Sam: What?   230

Hally: Where we come from and what it all means.

Sam: And that's a benefit to mankind? Anyway, I still don't believe it.

Hally: God, you're impossible. I showed it to you in black and white.

Sam: Doesn't mean I got to believe it.

Hally: It's the likes of you that kept the Inquisition in business. It's called bigotry.   235
Anyway, that's my man of magnitude. Charles Darwin! Who's yours?

Sam (without hesitation): Abraham Lincoln.

Hally: I might have guessed as much. Don't get sentimental, Sam. You've never been a slave, you know. And anyway we freed your ancestors here in South Africa long before the Americans. But if you want to thank somebody on their behalf, do it to Mr. William Wilberforce.° Come on. Try again. I want a real genius.

(Now enjoying himself, and so is Sam. Hally goes behind the counter and helps himself to a chocolate.)

Sam: William Shakespeare.

Hally (no enthusiasm): Oh. So you're also one of them, are you? You're basing that opinion on only one play, you know. You've only read my

---

[237]**William Wilberforce** the British reformer who led the successful fights to abolish first the slave trade (1798) and then slavery (1833) in Britain

Julius Caesar and even I don't understand half of what they're talking about. They should do what they did with the old Bible: bring the language up to date.

240   *Sam:* That's all you've got. It's also the only one *you've* read.

Hally: I know, I admit it. That's why I suggest we reserve our judgment until we've checked up on a few others. I've got a feeling, though, that by the end of this year one is going to be enough for me, and I can give you the names of twenty-nine other chaps in the Standard Nine class of the Port Elizabeth Technical College who feel the same. But if you want him, you can have him. My turn now. (*Pacing.*) This is a damned good exercise, you know! It started off looking like a simple question and here it's got us really probing into the intellectual heritage of our civilization.

Sam: So who is it going to be?

Hally: My next man . . . and he gets the title on two scores: social reform and literary genius . . . is Leo Nikolaevich Tolstoy.

Sam: That Russian.

245   *Hally:* Correct. Remember the picture of him I showed you?

Sam: With the long beard.

Hally (Trying to look like Tolstoy): And those burning, visionary eyes. My God, the face of a social prophet if ever I saw one! And remember my words when I showed it to you? Here's a *man*, Sam!

Sam: Those were words, Hally.

Hally: Not many intellectuals are prepared to shovel manure with the peasants and then go home and write a "little book" called *War and Peace*. Incidentally, Sam, he was somebody else who, to quote, ". . . did not distinguish himself scholastically."

250   *Sam:* Meaning?

Hally: He was also no good at school.

Sam: Like you and Winston Churchill.

Hally (mirthlessly): Ha, ha, ha.

Sam (simultaneously): Ha, ha, ha.

255   *Hally:* Don't get clever, Sam. That man freed his serfs of his own free will.

Sam: No argument. He was a somebody, all right. I accept him.

Hally: I'm sure Count Tolstoy will be very pleased to hear that. Your turn. Shoot. (*Another chocolate from behind the counter.*) I'm waiting, Sam.

Sam: I've got him.

Hally: Good. Submit your candidate for examination.

260   *Sam:* Jesus.

Hally (stopped dead in his tracks): Who?

Sam: Jesus Christ.

Hally: Oh, come on, Sam!

Sam: The Messiah.

265   *Hally:* Ja, but still . . . No, Sam. Don't let's get started on religion. We'll just spend the whole afternoon arguing again. Suppose I turn around and say Mohammed?

Sam: All right.

Hally: All right. You can't have them both on the same list!

Sam: Why not? You like Mohammed, I like Jesus.

Hally: I *don't* like Mohammed. I never have. I was merely being hypothetical. As far as I'm concerned, the Koran is as bad as the Bible. No. Religion is out! I'm not going to waste my time again arguing with you about the existence of God. You know perfectly well I'm an atheist . . . and I've got homework to do.

Sam: Okay, I take him back.   270

Hally: You've got time for one more name.

Sam (after thought): I've got one I know we'll agree on. A simple straightforward great Man of Magnitude . . . and no arguments. And *he* really *did* benefit all mankind.

Hally: I wonder. After your last contribution I'm beginning to doubt whether anything in the way of an intellectual agreement is possible between the two of us. Who is he?

Sam: Guess.

Hally: Socrates? Alexandre Dumas? Karl Marx? Dostoevsky? Nietzsche?   275

(*Sam shakes his head after each name.*)

Give me a clue.

Sam: The letter *P* is important. . . .

Hally: Plato!

Sam: . . . and his name begins with an *F*.

Hally: I've got it. Freud and Psychology.

Sam: No. I didn't understand him.   280

Hally: That makes two of us.

Sam: Think of moldy apricot jam.

Hally (after a delighted laugh): Penicillin and Sir Alexander Fleming! And the title of the book: *The Microbe Hunters.* (*Delighted.*) Splendid, Sam! Splendid. For once we are in total agreement. The major breakthrough in medical science in the Twentieth Century. If it wasn't for him, we might have lost the Second World War. It's deeply gratifying, Sam, to know that I haven't been wasting my time in talking to you. (*Strutting around proudly.*) Tolstoy may have educated his peasants, but I've educated you.

Sam: Standard Four to Standard Nine.

Hally: Have we been at it as long as that?   285

Sam: Yep. And my first lesson was geography.

Hally (intrigued): Really? I don't remember.

Sam: My room there at the back of the old Jubilee Boarding House. I had just started working for your Mom. Little boy in short trousers walks in one afternoon and asks me seriously: "Sam, do you want to see South Africa?" Hey man! Sure I wanted to see South Africa!

Hally: Was that me?

Sam: . . . So the next thing I'm looking at a map you had just done for   290
homework. It was your first one and you were very proud of yourself.

Hally: Go on.

Sam: Then came my first lesson. "Repeat after me, Sam: Gold in the Transvaal, mealies° in the Free State, sugar in Natal, and grapes in the Cape." I still know it!

Hally: Well, I'll be buggered. So that's how it all started.

Sam: And your next map was one with all the rivers and the mountains they came from. The Orange, the Vaal, the Limpopo, the Zambezi. . . .

295 *Hally:* You've got a phenomenal memory!

Sam: You should be grateful. That is why you started passing your exams. You tried to be better than me.

(*They laugh together. Willie is attracted by the laughter and joins them.*)

Hally: The old Jubilee Boarding House. Sixteen rooms with board and lodging, rent in advance and one week's notice. I haven't thought about it for donkey's years . . . and I don't think that's an accident. God, was I glad when we sold it and moved out. Those years are not remembered as the happiest ones of an unhappy childhood.

Willie (*knocking on the table and trying to imitate a woman's voice*): "Hally, are you there?"

Hally: Who's that supposed to be?

300 *Willie:* "What you doing in there, Hally? Come out at once!"

Hally (*to Sam*): What's he talking about?

Sam: Don't you remember?

Willie: "Sam, Willie . . . is he in there with you boys?"

Sam: Hiding away in our room when your mother was looking for you.

305 *Hally* (*another good laugh*): Of course! I used to crawl and hide under your bed! But finish the story, Willie. Then what used to happen? You chaps would give the game away by telling her I was in there with you. So much for friendship.

Sam: We couldn't lie to her. She knew.

Hally: Which meant I got another rowing for hanging around the "servants' quarters." I think I spent more time in there with you chaps than anywhere else in that dump. And do you blame me? Nothing but bloody misery wherever you went. Somebody was always complaining about the food, or my mother was having a fight with Micky Nash because she'd caught her with a petty officer in her room. Maud Meiring was another one. Remember those two? They were prostitutes, you know. Soldiers and sailors from the troopships. Bottom fell out of the business when the war ended. God, the flotsam and jetsam that life washed up on our shores! No joking, if it wasn't for your room, I would have been the first certified ten-year-old in medical history. Ja, the memories are coming back now. Walking home from school and thinking: "What can I do this afternoon?" Try out a few ideas, but sooner or later I'd end up in there with you fellows. I bet you I could still find my way to your room with my eyes closed. (*He does exactly that.*) Down the corridor . . . telephone on the right, which my Mom keeps locked because somebody is using it on the sly and not paying . . . past the kitchen and unappetizing cooking smells. . . around the corner into the backyard, hold my breath again because there are more smells coming when I pass your lavatory,

---

²⁹²**mealies** corn

then into that little passageway, first door on the right and into your room.
How's that?

Sam: Good. But, as usual, you forgot to knock.

Hally: Like that time I barged in and caught you and Cynthia . . . at it. Remember?
God, was I embarrassed! I didn't know what was going on at first.

Sam: Ja, that taught you a lesson.   310

Hally: And about a lot more than knocking on doors, I'll have you know, and I
don't mean geography either. Hell, Sam, couldn't you have waited until it
was dark?

Sam: No.

Hally: Was it that urgent?

Sam: Yes, and if you don't believe me, wait until your time comes.

Hally: No, thank you. I am not interested in girls. (*Back to his memories. . . . Using a*   315
few chairs he re-creates the room as he lists the items.) A gray little room with a
cold cement floor. Your bed against that wall . . . and I now know why the
mattress sags so much! . . . Willie's bed . . . it's propped up on bricks because
one leg is broken . . . that wobbly little table with the washbasin and jug of
water . . . Yes! . . . stuck to the wall above it are some pin-up pictures from
magazines. Joe Louis. . . .

Willie: Brown Bomber. World Title. (*Boxing pose.*) Three rounds and knockout.

Hally: Against who?

Sam: Max Schmeling.

Hally: Correct. I can also remember Fred Astaire and Ginger Rogers, and Rita
Hayworth in a bathing costume which always made me hot and bothered
when I looked at it. Under Willie's bed is an old suitcase with all his clothes in
a mess, which is why I never hide there. Your things are neat and tidy in a
trunk next to your bed, and on it there is a picture of you and Cynthia in
your ballroom clothes, your first silver cup for third place in a competition
and an old radio which doesn't work anymore. Have I left out anything?

Sam: No.   320

Hally: Right, so much for the stage directions. Now the characters. (*Sam and
Willie move to their appropriate positions in the bedroom.*) Willie is in bed, under
his blankets with his clothes on, complaining nonstop about something, but
we can't make out a word of what he's saying because he's got his head
under the blankets as well. You're on your bed trimming your toenails with a
knife—not a very edifying sight—and as for me. . . . What am I doing?

Sam: You're sitting on the floor giving Willie a lecture about being a good loser
while you get the checkerboard and pieces ready for a game. Then you go to
Willie's bed, pull off the blankets and make him play with you first because
you know you're going to win, and that gives you the second game with me.

Hally: And you certainly were a bad loser, Willie!

Willie: Haai!

Hally: Wasn't he, Sam? And so slow! A game with you almost took the whole   325
afternoon. Thank God I gave up trying to teach you how to play chess.

Willie: You and Sam cheated.

Hally: I never saw Sam cheat, and mine were mostly the mistakes of youth.

Willie: Then how is it you two was always winning?

Hally: Have you ever considered the possibility, Willie, that it was because we were better than you?

330 *Willie:* Every time better?

Hally: Not every time. There were occasions when we deliberately let you win a game so that you would stop sulking and go on playing with us. Sam used to wink at me when you weren't looking to show me it was time to let you win.

Willie: So then you two didn't play fair.

Hally: It was for your benefit, Mr. Malopo, which is more than being fair. It was an act of self-sacrifice. (*To Sam.*) But you know what my best memory is, don't you?

Sam: No.

335 *Hally:* Come on, guess. If your memory is so good, you must remember it as well.

Sam: We got up to a lot of tricks in there, Hally.

Hally: This one was special, Sam.

Sam: I'm listening.

Hally: It started off looking like another of those useless nothing-to-do after-noons. I'd already been down to Main Street looking for adventure, but nothing had happened. I didn't feel like climbing trees in the Donkin Park or pretending I was a private eye and following a stranger . . . so as usual: See what's cooking in Sam's room. This time it was you on the floor. You had two thin pieces of wood and you were smoothing them down with a knife. It didn't look particularly interesting, but when I asked you what you were doing, you just said, "Wait and see, Hally. Wait . . . and see" . . . in that secret sort of way of yours, so I knew there was a surprise coming. You teased me, you bugger, by being deliberately slow and not answering my questions!

(*Sam laughs.*)

And whistling while you worked away! God, it was infuriating! I could have brained you! It was only when you tied them together in a cross and put that down on the brown paper that I realized what you were doing. "Sam is making a kite?" And when I asked you and you said "Yes". . . ! (*Shaking his head with disbelief.*) The sheer audacity of it took my breath away. I mean, seriously, what the hell does a black man know about flying a kite? I'll be honest with you, Sam, I had no hopes for it. If you think I was excited and happy, you got another guess coming. In fact, I was shit-scared that we were going to make fools of ourselves. When we left the boarding house to go up onto the hill, I was praying quietly that there wouldn't be any other kids around to laugh at us.

340 *Sam* (*enjoying the memory as much as Hally*): Ja, I could see that.

Hally: I made it obvious, did I?

Sam: Ja. You refused to carry it.

Hally: Do you blame me? Can you remember what the poor thing looked like? Tomato-box wood and brown paper! Flour and water for glue! Two of my mother's old stockings for a tail, and then all those bits and pieces of string you made me tie together so that we could fly it! Hell, no, that was now only asking for a miracle to happen.

Sam: Then the big argument when I told you to hold the string and run with it
   when I let go.

Hally: I was prepared to run, all right, but straight back to the boarding house.   345

Sam (knowing what's coming): So what happened?

Hally: Come on, Sam, you remember as well as I do.

Sam: I want to hear it from you.

   (Hally pauses. He wants to be as accurate as possible.)

Hally: You went a little distance from me down the hill, you held it up ready to
   let it go. . . . "This is it," I thought. "Like everything else in my life, here
   comes another fiasco." Then you shouted, "Go, Hally!" and I started to run.
   (Another pause.) I don't know how to describe it, Sam. Ja! The miracle happened! I was running, waiting for it to crash to the ground, but instead suddenly there was something alive behind me at the end of the string, tugging
   at it as if it wanted to be free. I looked back . . . *(Shakes his head.)* . . . I still
   can't believe my eyes. It was flying! Looping around and trying to climb even
   higher into the sky. You shouted to me to let it have more string. I did, until
   there was none left and I was just holding that piece of wood we had tied it
   to. You came up and joined me. You were laughing.

Sam: So were you. And shouting, "It works, Sam! We've done it!"   350

Hally: And we had! I was so proud of us! It was the most splendid thing I had
   ever seen. I wished there were hundreds of kids around to watch us. The part
   that scared me, though, was when you showed me how to make it dive
   down to the ground and then just when it was on the point of crashing,
   swoop up again!

Sam: You didn't want to try yourself.

Hally: Of course not! I would have been suicidal if anything had happened to it.
   Watching you do it made me nervous enough. I was quite happy just to see it
   up there with its tail fluttering behind it. You left me after that, didn't you?
   You explained how to get it down, we tied it to the bench so that I could sit
   and watch it, and you went away. I wanted you to stay, you know. I was a little scared of having to look after it by myself.

Sam (quietly): I had work to do, Hally.

Hally: It was sort of sad bringing it down, Sam. And it looked sad again when it   355
   was lying there on the ground. Like something that had lost its soul. Just
   tomato-box wood, brown paper and two of my mother's old stockings! But,
   hell, I'll never forget that first moment when I saw it up there. I had a stiff
   neck the next day from looking up so much.

   (Sam laughs. Hally turns to him with a question he never thought of asking before.)

   Why did you make that kite, Sam?

Sam (evenly): I can't remember.

Hally: Truly?

Sam: Too long ago, Hally.

Hally: Ja, I suppose it was. It's time for another one, you know.

Sam: Why do you say that?   360

Hally: Because it feels like that. Would't be a good day to fly it, though.

Sam: No. You can't fly kites on rainy days.

Hally (He studies Sam. Their memories have made him conscious of the man's presence in his life.): How old are you, Sam?

Sam: Two score and five.

365 *Hally:* Strange, isn't it?

Sam: What?

Hally: Me and you.

Sam: What's strange about it?

Hally: Little white boy in short trousers and a black man old enough to be his father flying a kite. It's not every day you see that.

370 *Sam:* But why strange? Because the one is white and the other black?

Hally: I don't know. Would have been just as strange, I suppose, if it had been me and my Dad . . . cripple man and a little boy! Nope! There's no chance of me flying a kite without it being strange. (*Simple statement of fact—no self-pity.*) There's a nice little short story there. "The Kite-Flyers." But we'd have to find a twist in the ending.

Sam: Twist?

Hally: Yes. Something unexpected. The way it ended with us was too straightforward . . . me on the bench and you going back to work. There's no drama in that.

Willie: And me?

375 *Hally:* You?

Willie: Yes me.

Hally: You want to get into the story as well, do you? I got it! Change the title: "Afternoons in Sam's Room" . . . expand it and tell all the stories. It's on its way to being a novel. Our days in the old Jubilee. Sad in a way that they're over. I almost wish we were still in that little room.

Sam: We're still together.

Hally: That's true. It's just that life felt the right size in there . . . not too big and not too small. Wasn't so hard to work up a bit of courage. It's got so bloody complicated since then.

(*The telephone rings. Sam answers it.*)

380 *Sam:* St. George's Park Tea Room . . . Hello, Madam . . . Yes, Madam, he's here. . . . Hally, it's your mother.

Hally: Where is she phoning from?

Sam: Sounds like the hospital. It's a public telephone.

Hally (relieved): You see! I told you. (*The telephone.*) Hello, Mom . . . Yes . . . Yes no fine. Everything's under control here. How's things with poor old Dad? . . . Has he had a bad turn? . . . What? . . . Oh, God! . . . Yes, Sam told me, but I was sure he'd made a mistake. But what's this all about, Mom? He didn't look at all good last night. How can he get better so quickly? . . . Then very obviously you must say no. Be firm with him. You're the boss. . . . You know what it's going to be like if he comes home. . . . well then, don't blame me when I fail my exams at the end of the year. . . . Yes! How am I expected to be fresh for school when I spend half the night massaging his gammy leg? . . . So am I! . . . So tell him a white lie. Say Dr. Colley wants more X-rays of his stump.

Or bribe him. We'll sneak in double tots of brandy in future. . . . What? . . . Order him to get back into bed at once! If he's going to behave like a child, treat him like one. . . . All right, Mom! I was just trying to . . . I'm sorry. . . . I said I'm sorry. . . . Quick, give me your number. I'll phone you back. (*He hangs up and waits a few seconds.*) Here we go again! (*He dials.*) I'm sorry, Mom. . . . Okay. . . . But now listen to me carefully. All it needs is for you to put your foot down. Don't take no for an answer. . . . Did you hear me? And whatever you do, don't discuss it with him. . . . Because I'm frightened you'll give in to him. . . . Yes, Sam gave me lunch. . . . I ate all of it! . . . No, Mom not a soul. It's still raining here. . . . Right, I'll tell them. I'll just do some homework and then lock up. . . . But remember now, Mom. Don't listen to anything he says. And phone me back and let me know what happens. . . . Okay. Bye, Mom. (*He hangs up. The men are staring at him.*) My Mom says that when you're finished with the floors you must do the windows. (*Pause.*) Don't misunderstand me, chaps. All I want is for him to get better. And if he was, I'd be the first person to say: "Bring him home." But he's not, and we can't give him the medical care and attention he needs at home. That's what hospitals are there for. (*Brusquely.*) So don't just stand there! Get on with it!

(*Sam clears Hally's table.*)

You heard right. My Dad wants to go home.

Sam: Is he better?

Hally (sharply): No! How the hell can he be better when last night he was groan-   385
ing with pain? This is not an age of miracles!

Sam: Then he should stay in hospital.

Hally (seething with irritation and frustration): Tell me something I don't know, Sam.
What the hell do you think I was saying to my Mom? All I can say is fuck-it-all.

Sam: I'm sure he'll listen to your Mom.

Hally: You don't know what she's up against. He's already packed his shaving kit
and pajamas and is sitting on his bed with his crutches, dressed and ready to
go. I know him when he gets in that mood. If she tries to reason with him,
we've had it. She's no match for him when it comes to a battle of words. He'll
tie her up in knots. (*Trying to hide his true feelings.*)

Sam: I suppose it gets lonely for him in there.   390

Hally: With all the patients and nurses around? Regular visits from the Salvation
Army? Balls! It's ten times worse for him at home. I'm at school and my
mother is here in the business all day.

Sam: He's at least got you at night.

Hally (before he can stop himself): And we've got him! Please! I don't want to talk
about it anymore. (*Unpacks his school case, slamming down books on the table.*)
Life is just a plain bloody mess, that's all. And people are fools.

Sam: Come on, Hally.

Hally: Yes, they are! They bloody well deserve what they get.   395

Sam: Then don't complain.

Hally: Don't try to be clever, Sam. It doesn't suit you. Anybody who thinks
there's nothing wrong with this world needs to have his head examined. Just

when things are going along all right, without fail someone or something will come along and spoil everything. Somebody should write that down as a fundamental law of the Universe. The principle of perpetual disappointment. If there is a God who created this world, he should scrap it and try again.

Sam: All right, Hally, all right. What you got for homework?

Hally: Bullshit, as usual. (*Opens an exercise book and reads.*) "Write five hundred words describing an annual event of cultural or historical significance."

400   *Sam:* That should be easy enough for you.

Hally: And also plain bloody boring. You know what he wants, don't you? One of their useless old ceremonies. The commemoration of the landing of the 1820 Settlers, or if it's going to be culture, Carols by Candlelight every Christmas.

Sam: It's an impressive sight. Make a good description, Hally. All those candles glowing in the dark and the people singing hymns.

Hally: And it's called religious hysteria. (*Intense irritation.*) Please, Sam! Just leave me alone and let me get on with it. I'm not in the mood for games this afternoon. And remember my Mom's orders . . . you're to help Willie with the windows. Come on now, I don't want any more nonsense in here.

Sam: Okay, Hally, okay.

(*Hally settles down to his homework; determined preparations . . . pen, ruler, exercise book, dictionary, another cake. . . all of which will lead to nothing.*)

(*Sam waltzes over to Willie and starts to replace tables and chairs. He practices a ballroom step while doing so. Willie watches. When Sam is finished, Willie tries.*)

Good! But just a little bit quicker on the turn and only move in to her after she's crossed over. What about this one?

(*Another step. When Sam is finished, Willie again has a go.*)

Much better. See what happens when you just relax and enjoy yourself? Remember that in two weeks' time and you'll be all right.

405   *Willie:* But I haven't got partner, Boet Sam.

Sam: Maybe Hilda will turn up tonight.

Willie: No, Boet Sam. (*Reluctantly.*) I gave her a good hiding.

Sam: You mean a bad one.

Willie: Good bad one.

410   *Sam:* Then you mustn't complain either. Now you pay the price for losing your temper.

Willie: I also pay two pounds ten shilling entrance fee.

Sam: They'll refund you if you withdraw now.

Willie (*appalled*): You mean, don't dance?

Sam: Yes.

415   *Willie:* No! I wait too long and I practice too hard. If I find me a new partner, you think I can be ready in two weeks? I ask Madam for my leave now and we practice every day.

Sam: Quickstep nonstop for two weeks. World record, Willie, but you'll be mad at the end.

Willie: No jokes, Boet Sam.

Sam: I'm not joking.

Willie: So then what?

Sam: Find Hilda. Say you're sorry and promise you won't beat her again.   420

Willie: No.

Sam: Then withdraw. Try again next year.

Willie: No.

Sam: Then I give up.

Willie: Haaikona, Boet Sam, you can't.   425

Sam: What do you mean, I can't? I'm telling you: I give up.

Willie (adamant): No! (*Accusingly.*) It was you who start me ballroom dancing.

Sam: So?

Willie: Before that I use to be happy. And is you and Miriam who bring me to
    Hilda and say here's partner for you.

Sam: What are you saying, Willie?   430

Willie: You!

Sam: But me what? To blame?

Willie: Yes.

Sam: Willie . . .? (*Bursts into laughter.*)

Willie: And now all you do is make jokes at me. You wait. When Miriam leaves   435
    you is my turn to laugh. Ha! Ha! Ha!

Sam (he can't take Willie seriously any longer): She can leave me tonight! I know
    what to do. (*Bowing before an imaginary partner.*) May I have the pleasure?
    (*He dances and sings.*)

"Just a fellow with his pillow . . .
Dancin' like a willow . . .
In an autumn breeze. . . ."

Willie: There you go again!

(*Sam goes on dancing and singing.*)

Boet Sam!

Sam: There's the answer to your problem! Judges' announcement in two weeks'
    time: "Ladies and gentlemen, the winner in the open section . . . Mr. Willie
    Malopo and his pillow!"

(*This is too much for a now really angry Willie. He goes for Sam, but the latter is too
quick for him and puts Hally's table between the two of them.*)

Hally (exploding): For Christ's sake, you two!

Willie (still trying to get at Sam): I donner you, Sam! Struesgod!   440

Sam (still laughing): Sorry, Willie . . . Sorry. . . .

Hally: Sam! Willie! (*Grabs his ruler and gives Willie a vicious whack on the bum.*) How
    the hell am I supposed to concentrate with the two of you behaving like
    bloody children!

Willie: Hit him too!

Hally: Shut up, Willie.

Willie: He started jokes again.   445

Hally: Get back to your work. You too, Sam. (*His ruler.*) Do you want another
    one, Willie?

(Sam and Willie return to their work. Hally uses the opportunity to escape from his unsuccessful attempt at homework. He struts around like a little despot, ruler in hand, giving vent to his anger and frustration.)

Suppose a customer had walked in then? Or the Park Superintendent. And seen the two of you behaving like a pair of hooligans. That would have been the end of my mother's license, you know. And your jobs? Well, this is the end of it. From now on there will be no more of your ballroom nonsense in here. This is a business establishment, not a bloody New Brighton dancing school. I've been far too lenient with the two of you. *(Behind the counter for a green cool drink and a dollop of ice cream. He keeps up his tirade as he prepares it.)* But what really makes me bitter is that I allow you chaps a little freedom in here when business is bad and what do you do with it? The foxtrot! Specially you, Sam. There's more to life than trotting around a dance floor and I thought at least you knew it.

Sam: It's a harmless pleasure, Hally. It doesn't hurt anybody.

Hally: It's also a rather simple one, you know.

Sam: You reckon so? Have you ever tried?

450 *Hally:* Of course not.

Sam: Why don't you? Now.

Hally: What do you mean? Me dance?

Sam: Yes. I'll show you a simple step—the waltz—then you try it.

Hally: What will that prove?

455 *Sam:* That it might not be as easy as you think.

Hally: I didn't say it was easy. I said it was simple—like in simple-minded, meaning mentally retarded. You can't exactly say it challenges the intellect.

Sam: It does other things.

Hally: Such as?

Sam: Make people happy.

460 *Hally (the glass in his hand):* So do American cream sodas with ice cream. For God's sake, Sam, you're not asking me to take ballroom dancing serious, are you?

Sam: Yes.

Hally (sigh of defeat): Oh, well, so much for trying to give you a decent education. I've obviously achieved nothing.

Sam: You still haven't told me what's wrong with admiring something that's beautiful and then trying to do it yourself.

Hally: Nothing. But we happen to be talking about a foxtrot, not a thing of beauty.

465 *Sam:* But that is just what I'm saying. If you were to see two champions doing, two masters of the art . . . !

Hally: Oh, God, I give up. So now it's also art!

Sam: Ja.

Hally: There's a limit, Sam. Don't confuse art and entertainment.

Sam: So then what is art?

470 *Hally:* You want a definition?

Sam: Ja.

Hally (he realizes he has got to be careful. He gives the matter a lot of thought before answering): Philosophers have been trying to do that for centuries. What is Art? What is Life? But basically I suppose it's . . . the giving of meaning to matter.

Sam: Nothing to do with beautiful?

Hally: It goes beyond that. It's the giving of form to the formless.

Sam: Ja, well, maybe it's not art, then. But I still say it's beautiful. 475

Hally: I'm sure the word you mean to use is entertaining.

Sam (adamant): No. Beautiful. And if you want proof come along to the Centenary Hall in New Brighton in two weeks' time.

(*The mention of the Centenary Hall draws Willie over to them.*)

Hally: What for? I've seen the two of you prancing around in here often enough.

Sam (he laughs): This isn't the real thing, Hally. We're just playing around in here.

Hally: So? I can use my imagination. 480

Sam: And what do you get?

Hally: A lot of people dancing around and having a so-called good time.

Sam: That all?

Hally: Well, basically it is that, surely.

Sam: No, it isn't. Your imagination hasn't helped you at all. There's a lot more to 485 it than that. We're getting ready for the championships, Hally, not just another dance. There's going to be a lot of people, all right, and they're going to have a good time, but they'll only be spectators, sitting around and watching. It's just the competitors out there on the dance floor. Party decorations and fancy lights all around the walls! The ladies in beautiful evening dresses!

Hally: My mother's got one of those, Sam, and, quite frankly, it's an embarrassment every time she wears it.

Sam (undeterred): Your imagination left out the excitement.

(*Hally scoffs.*)

Oh, yes. The finalists are not going to be out there just to have a good time. One of those couples will be the 1950 Eastern Province Champions. And your imagination left out the music.

Willie: Mr. Elijah Gladman Guzana and his Orchestral Jazzonions.

Sam: The sound of the big band, Hally. Trombone, trumpet, tenor and alto sax. And then, finally, your imagination also left out the climax of the evening when the dancing is finished, the judges have stopped whispering among themselves and the Master of Ceremonies collects their scorecards and goes up onto the stage to announce the winners.

Hally: All right. So you make it sound like a bit of a do. It's an occasion. 490 Satisfied?

Sam (victory): So you admit that!

Hally: Emotionally yes, intellectually no.

Sam: Well, I don't know what you mean by that, all I'm telling you is that it is going to be *the* event of the year in New Brighton. It's been sold out for two weeks already. There's only standing room left. We've got competitors coming from Kingwilliamstown, East London, Port Alfred.

(*Hally starts pacing thoughtfully.*)

Hally: Tell me a bit more.

Sam: I thought you weren't interested . . . intellectually. 495

Hally (mysteriously): I've got my reasons.

Sam: What do you want to know?

Hally: It takes place every year?

Sam: Yes. But only every third year in New Brighton. It's East London's turn to have the championships next year.

500 *Hally:* Which, I suppose, makes it an even more significant event.

Sam: Ah ha! We're getting somewhere. Our "occasion" is now a "significant event."

Hally: I wonder.

Sam: What?

Hally: I wonder if I would get away with it.

505 *Sam:* But what?

Hally (to the table and his exercise book): "Write five hundred words describing an annual event of cultural or historical significance." Would I be stretching poetic license a little too far if I called your ballroom championships a cultural event?

Sam: You mean . . . ?

Hally: You think we could get five hundred words out of it, Sam?

Sam: Victor Sylvester has written a whole book on ballroom dancing.

510 *Willie:* You going to write about it, Master Hally?

Hally: Yes, gentlemen, that is precisely what I am considering doing. Old Doc Bromely—he's my English teacher—is going to argue with me, of course. He doesn't like natives. But I'll point out to him that in strict anthropological terms the culture of a primitive black society includes its dancing and singing. To put my thesis in a nutshell: The war-dance has been replaced by the waltz. But it still amounts to the same thing: the release of primitive emotions through movement. Shall we give it a go?

Sam: I'm ready.

Willie: Me also.

Hally: Ha! This will teach the old bugger a lesson. (*Decision taken.*) Right. Let's get ourselves organized. (*This means another cake on the table. He sits.*) I think you've given me enough general atmosphere, Sam, but to build the tension and suspense I need facts. (*Pencil poised.*)

515 *Willie:* Give him facts, Boet Sam.

Hally: What you called the climax . . . how many finalists?

Sam: Six couples.

Hally (making notes): Go on. Give me the picture.

Sam: Spectators seated right around the hall. (*Willie becomes a spectator.*)

520 *Hally:* . . . and it's a full house.

Sam: At one end, on the stage, Gladman and his Orchestral Jazzonions. At the other end is a long table with the three judges. The six finalists go onto the dance floor and take up their positions. When they are ready and the spectators have settled down, the Master of Ceremonies goes to the microphone. To start with, he makes some jokes to get people laughing. . . .

Hally: Good touch. (*As he writes.*) ". . . creating a relaxed atmosphere which will change to one of tension and drama as the climax is approached."

Sam (onto a chair to act out the M.C.): "Ladies and gentlemen, we come now to the great moment you have all been waiting for this evening. . . . The finals of the 1950 Eastern Province Open Ballroom Dancing Championships. But first

let me introduce the finalists! Mr. and Mrs. Welcome Tchabalala from
Kingwilliamstown . . ."

Willie (he applauds after every name): Is when the people clap their hands and
whistle and make a lot of noise, Master Hally.

Sam: "Mr. Mulligan Njikelane and Miss Nomhle Nkonyeni of Grahamstown;   525
Mr. and Mrs. Norman Nchinga from Port Alfred; Mr. Fats Bokolane and
Miss Dina Plaatjies from East London; Mr. Sipho Dugu and Mrs. Mable Magada
from Peddie; and from New Brighton our very own Mr. Willie Malopo and
Miss Hilda Samuels."

(*Willie can't believe his ears. He abandons his role as spectator and scrambles into
position as a finalist.*)

Willie: Relaxed and ready to romance!

Sam: The applause dies down. When everybody is silent, Gladman lifts up his
sax, nods at the Orchestral Jazzonions. . . .

Willie: Play the jukebox please, Boet Sam!

Sam: I also only got bus fare, Willie.

Hally: Hold it, everybody. (*Heads for the cash register behind the counter.*) How much   530
is in the till, Sam?

Sam: Three shillings. Hally . . . Your Mom counted it before she left.

(*Hally hesitates.*)

Hally: Sorry, Willie. You know how she carried on the last time I did it. We'll just
have to pool our combined imaginations and hope for the best. (*Returns to the
table.*) Back to work. How are the points scored, Sam?

Sam: Maximum of ten points each for individual style, deportment, rhythm, and
general appearance.

Willie: Must I start?

Hally: Hold it for a second, Willie. And penalties?   535

Sam: For what?

Hally: For doing something wrong. Say you stumble or bump into somebody . . .
do they take off any points?

Sam (aghast): Hally . . . !

Hally: When you're dancing. If you and your partner collide into another couple.

(*Hally can get no further. Sam has collapsed with laughter. He explains to Willie.*)

Sam: If me and Miriam bump into you and Hilda. . . .   540

(*Willie joins him in another good laugh.*)

Hally, Hally . . . !

Hally (perplexed): Why? What did I say?

Sam: There's no collisions out there, Hally. Nobody trips or stumbles or bumps
into anybody else. That's what that moment is all about. To be one of those
finalists on that dance floor is like . . . like being in a dream about a world in
which accidents don't happen.

Hally (genuinely moved by Sam's image): Jesus, Sam! That's beautiful!

Willie (can endure waiting no longer): I'm starting!

(*Willie dances while Sam talks.*)

545 *Sam:* Of course it is. That's what I've been trying to say to you all afternoon. And it's beautiful because that is what we want life to be like. But instead, like you said, Hally, we're bumping into each other all the time. Look at the three of us this afternoon: I've bumped into Willie, the two of us have bumped into you, you've bumped into your mother, she bumping into your Dad. . . . None of us knows the steps and there's no music playing. And it doesn't stop with us. The whole world is doing it all the time. Open a newspaper and what do you read? America has bumped into Russia, England is bumping into India, rich man bumps into poor man. Those are big collisions, Hally. They make for a lot of bruises. People get hurt in all that bumping, and we're sick and tired of it now. It's been going on for too long. Are we never going to get it right? . . . Learn to dance life like champions instead of always being just a bunch of beginners at it?

Hally (deep and sincere admiration of the man): You've got a vision, Sam!

Sam: Not just me. What I'm saying to you is that everybody's got it. That's why there's only standing room left for the Centenary Hall in two weeks' time. For as long as the music lasts, we are going to see six couples get it right, the way we want life to be.

Hally: But is that the best we can do, Sam . . . watch six finalists dreaming about the way it should be?

Sam: I don't know. But it starts with that. Without the dream we won't know what we're going for. And anyway I reckon there are a few people who have got past just dreaming about it and are trying for something real. Remember that thing we read once in the paper about the Mahatma Gandhi?° Going without food to stop those riots in India?

550 *Hally:* You're right. He certainly was trying to teach people to get the steps right.

Sam: And the Pope.

Hally: Yes, he's another one. Our old General Smuts° as well, you know. He's also out there dancing. You know, Sam, when you come to think of it, that's what the United Nations boils down to . . . a dancing school for politicians!

Sam: And let's hope they learn.

Hally (a little surge of hope): You're right. We mustn't despair. Maybe there's some hope for mankind after all. Keep it up, Willie. (*Back to his table with determination.*) This is a lot bigger than I thought. So what have we got? Yes, our title: "A World Without Collisions."

555 *Sam:* That sounds good! "A World Without Collisions."

Hally: Subtitle: "Global Politics on the Dance Floor." No. A bit too heavy, hey? What about "Ballroom Dancing as a Political Vision"?

(*The telephone rings. Sam answers it.*)

Sam: St. George's Park Tea Room . . . Yes, Madam . . . Hally, it's your Mom.

549**Mahatma Gandhi** the leader who helped the Indian people use the philosophy of nonviolent direct action to drive the British out of India, making way for the establishment of the independent Indian state in 1947   552**General Smuts** South African leader who fought the British in the Boer War and helped to found both the Union of South Africa in 1910 and the United Nations in 1945

Hally (back to reality): Oh, God, yes! I'd forgotten all about that. Shit! Remember
my words, Sam! Just when you're enjoying yourself, someone or something
will come along and wreck everything.

Sam: You haven't heard what she's got to say yet.

Hally: Public telephone?   560

Sam: No.

Hally: Does she sound happy or unhappy?

Sam: I couldn't tell. (*Pause.*) She's waiting, Hally.

Hally (to the telephone): Hello, Mom . . . No, everything is okay here. Just doing
my homework. . . . What's your news? . . . You've what? . . . (*Pause. He takes
the receiver away from his ear for a few seconds. In the course of Hally's telephone conversation, Sam and Willie discreetly position the stacked tables and chairs. Hally places
the receiver back to his ear.*) Yes, I'm still here. Oh, well, I give up now. Why did
you do it, Mom? . . . Well, I just hope you know what you've let us in for. . . .
(*Loudly.*) I said I hope you know what you've let us in for! It's the end of the
peace and quiet we've been having. (*Softly.*) Where is he? (*Normal voice.*) He
can't hear us from in there. But for God's sake, Mom, what happened? I told
you to be firm with him. . . . Then you and the nurses should have held him
down, taken his crutches away. . . . I know only too well he's my father! . . .
I'm not being disrespectful, but I'm sick and tired of emptying stinking chamber pots full of phlegm and piss. . . . Yes, I do! When you're not there, he asks
me to do it. . . . If you really want to know the truth, that's why I've got no
appetite for my food. . . . Yes! There's a lot of things you don't know about.
For your information, I still haven't got that science textbook I need. And you
know why? He borrowed the money you gave me for it. . . . Because I didn't
want to start another fight between you two. . . . He says that every time. . . .
All right, Mom! (*Viciously.*) Then just remember to start hiding your bag away
again, because he'll be at your purse before long for money for booze. And
when he's well enough to come down here, you better keep an eye on the till
as well, because that is also going to develop a leak. . . . Then don't complain
to me when he starts his old tricks. . . . Yes, you do. I get it from you on one
side and from him on the other, and it makes life hell for me. I'm not going to
be the peacemaker anymore. I'm warning you now: when the two of you
start fighting again, I'm leaving home. . . . Mom, if you start crying, I'm going
to put down the receiver. . . . Okay. . . . (*Lowering his voice to a vicious whisper.*)
Okay, Mom, I heard you. (*Desperate.*) No. . . . Because I don't want to. I'll see
him when I get home! Mom! . . . (*Pause. When he speaks again, his tone changes
completely. It is not simply pretense. We sense a genuine emotional conflict.*) Welcome
home, chum! . . . What's that? . . . Don't be silly, Dad. You being home is just
about the best news in the world. . . . I bet you are. Bloody depressing there
with everybody going on about their ailments, hey! . . . How you feeling? . . .
Good. . . . Here as well, pal. Coming down cats and dogs. . . . That's right. Just
the day for a kip° and a toss in your old Uncle Ned. . . . Everything's just
hunky-dory on my side, Dad. . . . Well, to start with, there's a nice pile of

---

°⁵⁶⁴**kip** nap

comics for you on the counter. . . . Yes, old Kemple brought them in. *Batman and Robin, Submariner* . . . just your cup of tea. . . . I will. . . . Yes, we'll spin a few yarns tonight. . . . Okay, chum, see you in a little while. . . . No, I promise. I'll come straight home. . . . (*Pause—his mother comes back on the phone.*) Mom? Okay. I'll lock up now. . . . What? . . . Oh, the brandy . . . Yes, I'll remember! . . . I'll put it in my suitcase now, for God's sake. I know well enough what will happen if he doesn't get it. . . . (*Places a bottle of brandy on the counter.*) I was kind to him, Mom. I didn't say anything nasty! . . . All right. Bye. (*End of telephone conversation. A desolate Hally doesn't move. A strained silence.*)

565   *Sam* (*quietly*): That sounded like a bad bump, Hally.

Hally (*Having a hard time controlling his emotions. He speaks carefully.*): Mind your own business, Sam.

Sam: Sorry. I wasn't trying to interfere. Shall we carry on? Hally? (*He indicates the exercise book. No response from Hally.*)

Willie (*also trying*): Tell him about when they give out the cups, Boet Sam.

Sam: Ja! That's another big moment. The presentation of the cups after the winners have been announced. You've got to put that in.

(*Still no response from Hally.*)

570   *Willie:* A big silver one, Master Hally, called floating trophy for the champions.

Sam: We always invite some big-shot personality to hand them over. Guest of honor this year is going to be His Holiness Bishop Jabulani of the All African Free Zionist Church.

(*Hally gets up abruptly, goes to his table, and tears up the page he was writing on.*)

Hally: So much for a bloody world without collisions.

Sam: Too bad. It was on its way to being a good composition.

Hally: Let's stop bullshitting ourselves, Sam.

575   *Sam:* Have we been doing that?

Hally: Yes! That's what all our talk about a decent world has been . . . just so much bullshit.

Sam: We did say it was still only a dream.

Hally: And a bloody useless one at that. Life's a fuckup and it's never going to change.

Sam: Ja, maybe that's true.

580   *Hally:* There's no maybe about it. It's a blunt and brutal fact. All we've done this afternoon is waste our time.

Sam: Not if we'd got your homework done.

Hally: I don't give a shit about my homework, so, for Christ's sake, just shut up about it. (*Slamming books viciously into his school case.*) Hurry up now and finish your work. I want to lock up and get out of here. (*Pause.*) And then go where? Home-sweet-fucking-home. Jesus, I hate that word.

(*Hally goes to the counter to put the brandy bottle and comics in his school case. After a moment's hesitation, he smashes the bottle of brandy. He abandons all further attempts to hide his feelings. Sam and Willie work away as unobtrusively as possible.*)

Do you want to know what is really wrong with your lovely little dream,
Sam? It's not just that we are all bad dancers. That does happen to be perfectly
true, but there's more to it than just that. You left out the cripples.

Sam: Hally!

Hally (now totally reckless): Ja! Can't leave them out, Sam. That's why we
always end up on our backsides on the dance floor. They're also out there
dancing . . . like a bunch of broken spiders trying to do the quickstep!
(*An ugly attempt at laughter.*) When you come to think of it, it's a bloody
comical sight. I mean, it's bad enough on two legs . . . but one and a pair of
crutches! Hell, no, Sam. That's guaranteed to turn that dance floor into a
shambles. Why you shaking your head? Picture it, man. For once this
afternoon let's use our imaginations sensibly.

Sam: Be careful, Hally.   585

Hally: Of what? The truth? I seem to be the only one around here who is prepared to face it. We've had the pretty dream, it's time now to wake up and
have a good long look at the way things really are. Nobody knows the steps,
there's no music, the cripples are also out there tripping up everybody and
trying to get into the act, and it's all called the All-Comers-How-to-Make-a-
Fuckup-of-Life Championships. (*Another ugly laugh.*) Hang on, Sam! The best
bit is still coming. Do you know what the winner's trophy is? A beautiful big
chamber pot with roses on the side, and it's full to the brim with piss. And
guess who I think is going to be this year's winner.

Sam (almost shouting): Stop now!

Hally (suddenly appalled by how far he has gone): Why?

Sam: Hally? It's your father you're talking about.

Hally: So?   590

Sam: Do you know what you've been saying?

(*Hally can't answer. He is rigid with shame. Sam speaks to him sternly.*)

No, Hally, you mustn't do it. Take back those words and ask for forgiveness!
It's a terrible sin for a son to mock his father with jokes like that. You'll be
punished if you carry on. Your father is your father, even if he is a . . . cripple
man.

Willie: Yes, Master Hally. Is true what Sam say.

Sam: I understand how you are feeling, Hally, but even so. . . .

Hally: No, you don't!

Sam: I think I do.   595

Hally: And I'm telling you you don't. Nobody does. (*Speaking carefully as his shame
turns to rage at Sam.*) It's your turn to be careful, Sam. Very careful! You're
treading on dangerous ground. Leave me and my father alone.

Sam: I'm not the one who's been saying things about him.

Hally: What goes on between me and my Dad is none of your business!

Sam: Then don't tell me about it. If that's all you've got to say about him, I don't
want to hear.

(*For a moment Hally is at loss for a response.*)

Hally: Just get on with your bloody work and shut up.   600

Sam: Swearing at me won't help you.

Hally: Yes, it does! Mind your own fucking business and shut up!

Sam: Okay. If that's the way you want it, I'll stop trying.

(*He turns away. This infuriates Hally even more.*)

Hally: Good. Because what you've been trying to do is meddle in something you know nothing about. All that concerns you in here, Sam, is to try and do what you get paid for—keep the place clean and serve the customers. In plain words, just get on with your job. My mother is right. She's always warning me about allowing you to get too familiar. Well, this time you've gone too far. It's going to stop right now.

(*No response from Sam.*)

You're only a servant in here, and don't forget it.

(*Still no response. Hally is trying hard to get one.*)

And as far as my father is concerned, all you need to remember is that he is your boss.

605 *Sam (needed at last):* No, he isn't. I get paid by your mother.

Hally: Don't argue with me, Sam!

Sam: Then don't say he's my boss.

Hally: He's a white man and that's good enough for you.

Sam: I'll try to forget you said that.

610 *Hally:* Don't! Because you won't be doing me a favor if you do. I'm telling you to remember it.

(*A pause. Sam pulls himself together and makes one last effort.*)

Sam: Hally, Hally . . . ! Come on now. Let's stop before it's too late. You're right. We *are* on dangerous ground. If we're not careful, somebody is going to get hurt.

Hally: It won't be me.

Sam: Don't be so sure.

Hally: I don't know what you're talking about, Sam.

615 *Sam:* Yes, you do.

Hally (furious): Jesus, I wish you would stop trying to tell me what I do and what I don't know.

(*Sam gives up. He turns to Willie.*)

Sam: Let's finish up.

Hally: Don't turn your back on me! I haven't finished talking.

(*He grabs Sam by the arm and tries to make him turn around. Sam reacts with a flash of anger.*)

Sam: Don't do that, Hally! (*Facing the boy.*) All right, I'm listening. Well? What do you want to say to me?

620 *Hally (pause as Hally looks for something to say):* To begin with, why don't you also start calling me Master Harold, like Willie.

Sam: Do you mean that?

Hally: Why the hell do you think I said it?

Sam: And if I don't?

Hally: You might just lose your job.

Sam (quietly and very carefully): If you make me say it once, I'll never call you anything else again.   625

Hally: So? (*The boy confronts the man.*) Is that meant to be a threat?

Sam: Just telling you what will happen if you make me do that. You must decide what it means to you.

Hally: Well, I have. It's good news. Because that is exactly what Master Harold wants from now on. Think of it as a little lesson in respect, Sam, that's long overdue, and I hope you remember it as well as you do your geography. I can tell you now that somebody who will be glad to hear I've finally given it to you will be my Dad. Yes! He agrees with my Mom. He's always going on about it as well. "You must teach the boys to show you more respect, my son."

Sam: So now you can stop complaining about going home. Everybody is going to be happy tonight.

Hally: That's perfectly correct. You see, you mustn't get the wrong idea about me   630
and my Dad, Sam. We also have our good times together. Some bloody good laughs. He's got a marvelous sense of humor. Want to know what our favorite joke is? He gives out a big groan, you see, and says: "It's not fair, is it, Hally?" Then I have to ask: "What, chum?" And then he says: "A nigger's arse". . . and we both have a good laugh.

(*The men stare at him with disbelief.*)

What's the matter, Willie? Don't you catch the joke? You always were a bit slow on the uptake. It's what is called a pun. You see, fair means both light in color and to be just and decent. (*He turns to Sam.*) I thought *you* would catch it, Sam.

Sam: Oh ja, I catch it all right.

Hally: But it doesn't appeal to your sense of humor.

Sam: Do you really laugh?

Hally: Of course.

Sam: To please him? Make him feel good?   635

Hally: No, for heavens sake! I laugh because I think it's a bloody good joke.

Sam: You're really trying hard to be ugly, aren't you? And why drag poor old Willie into it? He's done nothing to you except show you the respect you want so badly. That's also not being fair, you know . . . and I mean just or decent.

Willie: It's all right, Sam. Leave it now.

Sam: It's me you're after. You should just have said "Sam's arse" . . . because that's the one you're trying to kick. Anyway, how do you know it's not fair? You've never seen it. Do you want to? (*He drops his trousers and underpants and presents his backside for Hally's inspection.*) Have a good look. A real Basuto arse . . . which is about as nigger as they can come. Satisfied? (*Trousers up.*) Now you can make your Dad even happier when you go home tonight. Tell him I showed you my arse and he is quite right. It's not fair. And if it will give him an even better laugh next time, I'll also let *him* have a look. Come, Willie, let's finish up and go.

(*Sam and Willie start to tidy up the tea room. Hally doesn't move. He waits for a moment when Sam passes him.*)

640 *Hally (quietly):* Sam . . .

> *(Sam stops and looks expectantly at the boy. Hally spits in his face. A long and heartfelt groan from Willie. For a few seconds Sam doesn't move.)*

Sam (taking out a handkerchief and wiping his face): It's all right, Willie.

> *(To Hally.)*

Ja, well, you've done it . . . Master Harold. Yes, I'll start calling you that from now on. It won't be difficult anymore. You've hurt yourself, Master Harold. I saw it coming. I warned you, but you wouldn't listen. You've just hurt yourself *bad*. And you're a coward, Master Harold. The face you should be spitting in is your father's . . . but you used mine, because you think you're safe inside your fair skin . . . and this time I don't mean just or decent. *(Pause, then moving violently toward Hally.)* Should I hit him, Willie?

Willie (stopping Sam): No, Boet Sam.

Sam (violently): Why not?

Willie: It won't help, Boet Sam.

645 *Sam:* I don't want to help! I want to hurt him.

Willie: You also hurt yourself.

Sam: And if he had done it to you, Willie?

Willie: Me? Spit at me like I was a dog? *(A thought that had not occurred to him before. He looks at Hally.)* Ja. Then I want to hit him. I want to hit him hard!

> *(A dangerous few seconds as the men stand staring at the boy. Willie turns away, shaking his head.)*

But maybe all I do is go cry at the back. He's little boy, Boet Sam. Little *white* boy. Long trousers now, but he's still little boy.

Sam (his violence ebbing away into defeat as quickly as it flooded): You're right. So go on, then: groan again, Willie. You do it better than me. *(To Hally.)* You don't know all of what you've just done . . . Master Harold. It's not just that you've made me feel dirtier than I've ever been in my life . . . I mean, how do I wash off yours and your father's filth? . . . I've also failed. A long time ago I promised myself I was going to try and do something, but you've just shown me . . . Master Harold . . . that I've failed. *(Pause.)* I've also got a memory of a little white boy when he was still wearing short trousers and a black man, but they're not flying a kite. It was the old Jubilee days, after dinner one night. I was in my room. You came in and just stood against the wall, looking down at the ground, and only after I'd asked you what you wanted, what was wrong, I don't know how many times, did you speak and even then so softly I almost didn't hear you. "Sam, please help me to go and fetch my Dad." Remember? He was dead drunk on the floor of the Central Hotel Bar. They'd phoned for your Mom, but you were the only one at home. And do you remember how we did it? You went in first by yourself to ask permission for me to go into the bar. Then I loaded him onto my back like a baby and carried him back to the boarding house with you following behind carrying his crutches. *(Shaking his head as he remembers.)* A crowded Main Street with all the people watching a little white boy following his drunk father on a nigger's back! I felt for that little boy . . . Master Harold. I felt for him. After that we still had to clean him up, remember? He'd messed in his trousers, so we had to clean him up and get him into bed.

Hally (great pain): I love him, Sam.   650

Sam: I know you do. That's why I tried to stop you from saying these things about him. It would have been so simple if you could have just despised him for being a weak man. But he's your father. You love him and you're ashamed of him. You're ashamed of so much! . . . And now that's going to include yourself. That was the promise I made to myself: to try and stop that happening. (*Pause.*) After we got him to bed you came back with me to my room and sat in a corner and carried on just looking down at the ground. And for days after that! You hadn't done anything wrong, but you went around as if you owed the world an apology for being alive. I didn't like seeing that! That's not the way a boy grows up to be a man! . . . But the one person who should have been teaching you what that means was the cause of your shame. If you really want to know, that's why I made you that kite. I wanted you to look up, be proud of something, of yourself . . . (*bitter smile at the memory*) . . . and you certainly were that when I left you with it up there on the hill. Oh, ja . . . something else! . . . If you ever do write it as a short story, there *was* a twist in our ending. I couldn't sit down there and stay with you. It was a "Whites Only" bench. You were too young, too excited to notice then. But not anymore. If you're not careful . . . Master Harold . . . you're going to be sitting up there by yourself for a long time to come, and there won't be a kite in the sky. (*Sam has got nothing more to say. He exits into the kitchen, taking off his waiter's jacket.*)

Willie: Is bad. Is all bad in here now.

Hally (books into his school case, raincoat on): Willie . . . (*It is difficult to speak.*) Will you lock up for me and look after the keys?

Willie: Okay.

   (*Sam returns. Hally goes behind the counter and collects the few coins in the cash register. As he starts to leave . . . .*)

Sam: Don't forget the comic books.   655

   (*Hally returns to the counter and puts them in his case. He starts to leave again.*)

Sam (to the retreating back of the boy): Stop . . . Hally. . . .

   (*Hally stops, but doesn't turn to face him.*)

   Hally . . . I've got no right to tell you what being a man means if I don't behave like one myself, and I'm not doing so well at that this afternoon. Should we try again, Hally?

Hally: Try what?

Sam: Fly another kite, I suppose. It worked once, and this time I need it as much as you do.

Hally: It's still raining, Sam. You can't fly kites on rainy days, remember.

Sam: So what do we do? Hope for better weather tomorrow?   660

Hally (helpless gesture): I don't know. I don't know anything anymore.

Sam: You sure of that, Hally? Because it would be pretty hopeless if that was true. It would mean nothing has been learnt in here this afternoon, and there was a hell of a lot of teaching going on . . . one way or the other. But anyway, I don't believe you. I reckon there's one thing you know. You don't *have* to sit up there by yourself. You know what that bench means now, and you can leave it any time you choose. All you've got to do is stand up and walk away from it.

(Hally leaves. Willie goes up quietly to Sam.)

Willie: Is okay, Boet Sam. You see. Is . . . *(he can't find any better words)* . . . is going to be okay tomorrow. *(Changing his tone.)* Hey, Boet Sam! *(He is trying hard.)* You right. I think about it and you right. Tonight I find Hilda and say sorry. And make promise I won't beat her no more. You hear me, Boet Sam?

Sam: I hear you, Willie.

665 *Willie:* And when we practice I relax and romance with her from beginning to end. Nonstop! You watch! Two weeks' time: "First prize for promising new-comers: Mr. Willie Malopo and Miss Hilda Samuels." *(Sudden impulse.)* To hell with it! I walk home. *(He goes to the jukebox, puts in a coin and selects a record. The machine comes to life in the gray twilight, blushing its way through a spectrum of soft, romantic colors.)* How did you say it, Boet Sam? Let's dream. *(Willie sways with the music and gestures for Sam to dance.)*

(Sarah Vaughan sings.)

"Little man you're crying,
I know why you're blue,
Someone took your kiddy car away;
Better go to sleep now,
Little man you've had a busy day." *(etc., etc.)* You lead. I follow.

(The men dance together.)

"Johnny won your marbles,
Tell you what we'll do;
Dad will get you new ones right away;
Better go to sleep now,
Little man you've had a busy day." [1982]

1. A good deal of the play is concerned with characters who never appear, Hally's parents. What do we know about them? Sketch their characters. What is their effect on Hally?

2. This is a one-act play that takes place in real time on one rainy afternoon. There are no stage directions reading "Later that evening" or "Three months later." Rather, the plot takes up the exact time that the play takes to perform. Yet, since much of it is taken up with the characters' memories of the past, it covers a number of years. How does this affect our understanding of the play's meaning?

3. The play takes place in South Africa in 1950, the era of an apartheid system that enforced the separation of the races and discriminated against the indigenous black majority in favor of the whites who had colonized the country. How do the dynamics of race play out in the personal relationships among the characters?

4. What is the role of Hally's schoolwork in the play?

5. What do the changes in the characters' relationships tell us about the nature of selves?

6. What is the usefulness of this play since the dismantling of apartheid in South Africa?

LUIS VALDEZ

LUIS VALDEZ (1940–), rightly called the father of Chicano theater, has nurtured this movement since 1963, when he staged his first play at San Jose State College. He founded El Teatro Campesino, *a touring farmworkers' theater group and produced one-act and longer plays for it and other theaters.* La Carpe de los Rasquachis, El Fin del Mundo, Zoot Suit, *and* Tibercoa Vasques, *and the movie* La Bamba *are some of his works. He writes from the standpoint of his background as one of ten children of migrant farm workers who was able to enter the state university on scholarship, publish plays, join Cesar Chavez's efforts to educate and unionize migrant workers, and eventually mold a theater for that group. The troupe toured widely and won the "Obie" in 1968, staging one-act plays, Mexican theatricals, musical* corridas, *dramatized ballads, religious pageants, and other dramatic forms. Valdez turned to movies, becoming an actor-director after the success of* Zoot Suit. *This play, the first by a Mexican American to run on Broadway, ran for two years in California and New York. These triumphs, and his greatest success, the film* La Bamba, *the story of Richie Valens, the rock and roll singer, made Valdez a mentor who opened the way for Latinos to make careers in film and the theater.*

Los Vendidos

Characters

Honest Sancho
Secretary
Farm Worker
Johnny
Revolucionario
Mexican-American

Scene: Honest Sancho's *Used Mexican Lot and Mexican Curio Shop. Three models are on display in* Honest Sancho's *shop: to the right, there is a* Revolucionario, *complete with sombrero,* carrilleras,° *and carabina 30-30. At center, on the floor, there is the* Farm Worker, *under a broad straw sombrero. At stage left is the* Pachuco,° filero° *in hand.*

(Honest Sancho *is moving among his models, dusting them off and preparing for another day of business.)*

Sancho: Bueno, bueno, mis monos, vamos a ver a quien vendemos ahora, ¿no? *(To audience.)* ¡Quihubo!° I'm Honest Sancho and this is my shop. Antes fui contratista pero ahora logré tener mi negocito.° All I need now is a customer. *(A bell rings offstage.)* Ay, a customer!

Scene*carrilleras* literally chin straps, but may refer to cartridge belts **Pachuco** Chicano slang for 1940s zoot suiter *filero* blade [1]**Bueno, bueno, . . . Quihubo** "Good, good, my cute ones, let's see who we can sell now, O.K.?" **Antes fui . . . negocito** "I used to be a contractor, but now I've succeeded in having my little business."

Secretary (Entering): Good morning, I'm Miss Jiménez from—

Sancho: ¡Ah, una chicana! Welcome, welcome Señorita Jiménez.

Secretary (Anglo pronunciation): JIM-enez.

5 *Sancho:* ¿Qué?

Secretary: My name is Miss JIM-enez. Don't you speak English? What's wrong with you?

Sancho: Oh, nothing, Señorita JIM-enez. I'm here to help you.

Secretary: That's better. As I was starting to say, I'm a secretary from Governor Reagan's office, and we're looking for a Mexican type for the administration.

Sancho: Well, you come to the right place, lady. This is Honest Sancho's Used Mexican lot, and we got all types here. Any particular type you want?

10 *Secretary:* Yes, we were looking for somebody suave—

Sancho: Suave.

Secretary: Debonair.

Sancho: De buen aire.

Secretary: Dark.

15 *Sancho:* Prieto.

Secretary: But of course not too dark.

Sancho: No muy prieto.

Secretary: Perhaps, beige.

Sancho: Beige, just the tone. Así como cafecito con leche,° ¿no?

20 *Secretary:* One more thing. He must be hard-working.

Sancho: That could only be one model. Step right over here to the center of the shop, lady. *(They cross to the* Farm Worker.*)* This is our standard farm worker model. As you can see, in the words of our beloved Senator George Murphy, he is "built close to the ground." Also take special notice of his four-ply Goodyear huaraches,° made from the rain tire. This wide-brimmed sombrero is an extra added feature—keeps off the sun, rain, and dust.

Secretary: Yes, it does look durable.

Sancho: And our farm worker model is friendly. Muy amable.° Watch. *(Snaps his fingers.)*

Farm Worker (Lifts up head): Buenos días, señorita. *(His head drops.)*

25 *Secretary:* My, he's friendly.

Sancho: Didn't I tell you? Loves his patrones! But his most attractive feature is that he's hard-working. Let me show you. *(Snaps fingers.* Farm Worker *stands.)*

Farm Worker: ¡El jale!° *(He begins to work.)*

Sancho: As you can see, he is cutting grapes.

Secretary: Oh, I wouldn't know.

30 *Sancho:* He also picks cotton. *(Snap.* Farm Worker *begins to pick cotton.)*

Secretary: Versatile isn't he?

Sancho: He also picks melons. *(Snap.* Farm Worker *picks melons.)* That's his slow speed for late in the season. Here's his fast speed. *(Snap.* Farm Worker *picks faster.)*

Secretary: ¡Chihuahua! . . . I mean, goodness, he sure is a hard worker.

---

[19]**Así como . . . leche** like coffee with milk.   [21]**huaraches** sandals with tire-rubber soles   [23]**Muy amable** very friendly   [27]**¡El jale!** the job

Sancho (Pulls the Farm Worker *to his feet):* And that isn't the half of it. Do you see these little holes on his arms that appear to be pores? During those hot sluggish days in the field, when the vines or the branches get so entangled, it's almost impossible to move; these holes emit a certain grease that allow our model to slip and slide right through the crop with no trouble at all.

Secretary: Wonderful. But is he economical?   35

Sancho: Economical? Señorita, you are looking at the Volkswagen of Mexicans. Pennies a day is all it takes. One plate of beans and tortillas will keep him going all day. That, and chile. Plenty of chile. Chile jalapenos, chile verde, chile colorado. But, of course, if you do give him chile *(Snap.* Farm Worker *turns left face. Snap.* Farm Worker *bends over.)* then you have to change his oil filter once a week.

Secretary: What about storage?

Sancho: No problem. You know these new farm labor camps our Honorable Governor Reagan has built out by Parlier or Raisin City? They were designed with our model in mind. Five, six, seven, even ten in one of those shacks will give you no trouble at all. You can also put him in old barns, old cars, river banks. You can even leave him out in the field overnight with no worry!

Secretary: Remarkable.

Sancho: And here's an added feature: Every year at the end of the season, this   40
model goes back to Mexico and doesn't return, automatically, until next Spring.

Secretary: How about that. But tell me: does he speak English?

Sancho: Another outstanding feature is that last year this model was programmed to go out on STRIKE! *(Snap.)*

Farm Worker: ¡HUELGA! ¡HUELGA! Hermanos, sálganse de esos files.° *(Snap. He stops.)*

Secretary: No! Oh no, we can't strike in the State Capitol.

Sancho: Well, he also scabs.° *(Snap.)*   45

Farm Worker: Me vendo barato, ¿y qué?° *(Snap.)*

Secretary: That's much better, but you didn't answer my question. Does he speak English?

Sancho: Bueno . . . no pero° he has other—

Secretary: No.

Sancho: Other features.   50

Secretary: NO! He just won't do!

Sancho: Okay, okay pues.° We have other models.

Secretary: I hope so. What we need is something a little more sophisticated.

Sancho: Sophisti—¿qué?

Secretary: An urban model.   55

Sancho: Ah, from the city! Step right back. Over here in this corner of the shop is exactly what you're looking for. Introducing our new 1969 JOHNNY PACHUCO model! This is our fast-back model. Streamlined. Built for speed,

---

⁴³¡HUELGA! ¡HUELGA! . . . esos files "Strike! Strike! Brothers, leave those rows."
⁴⁵scabs works while other employees are on strike   ⁴⁶Me vendo . . . qué? "I come cheap, so what?"   ⁴⁸Bueno . . . no pero "Well, no, but . . ."   ⁵²okay pues okay, then.

low-riding, city life. Take a look at some of these features. Mag shoes, dual exhausts, green chartreuse paint-job, dark-tint windshield, a little poof on top. Let me just turn him on. *(Snap. Johnny walks to stage center with a pachuco bounce.)*

Secretary: What was that?

Sancho: That, señorita, was the Chicano shuffle.

Secretary: Okay, what does he do?

60   *Sancho:* Anything and everything necessary for city life. For instance, survival: He knife fights. *(Snap. Johnny pulls out switch blade and swings at Secretary.)*

(Secretary screams.)

Sancho: He dances. *(Snap.)*

Johnny (Singing): "Angel Baby, my Angel Baby . . ."*(Snap.)*

Sancho: And here's a feature no city model can be without. He gets arrested, but not without resisting, of course. *(Snap.)*

Johnny: ¡En la madre, la placa!° I didn't do it! I didn't do it! *(Johnny turns and stands up against an imaginary wall, legs spread out, arms behind his back.)*

65   *Secretary:* Oh no, we can't have arrests! We must maintain law and order.

Sancho: But he's bilingual!

Secretary: Bilingual?

Sancho: Simón que yes.° He speaks English! Johnny, give us some English. *(Snap.)*

Johnny (Comes downstage.): Fuck-you!

70   *Secretary (Gasps):* Oh! I've never been so insulted in my whole life!

Sancho: Well, he learned it in your school.

Secretary: I don't care where he learned it.

Sancho: But he's economical!

Secretary: Economical?

75   *Sancho:* Nickels and dimes. You can keep Johnny running on hamburgers, Taco Bell tacos, Lucky Lager beer, Thunderbird wine, yesca—

Secretary: Yesca?

Sancho: Mota.

Secretary: Mota?

Sancho: Leños . . .° Marijuana. *(Snap; Johnny inhales on an imaginary joint.)*

80   *Secretary:* That's against the law!

Johnny (Big smile, holding his breath): Yeah.

Sancho: He also sniffs glue. *(Snap. Johnny inhales glue, big smile.)*

Johnny: Tha's too much man, ése.°

Secretary: No, Mr. Sancho, I don't think this—

85   *Sancho:* Wait a minute, he has other qualities I know you'll love. For example, an inferiority complex. *(Snap.)*

Johnny (To Sancho): You think you're better than me, huh ése? *(Swings switch blade.)*

Sancho: He can also be beaten and he bruises, cut him and he bleeds; kick him and he—*(He beats, bruises and kicks Pachuco.)* would you like to try it?

---

[64]**En la . . . placa** "Wow, the police!"   [68]**Simón . . . yes** yeah, sure.   [79]**Leños** "joints" of marijuana   [83]**ése** man, buddy

Secretary: Oh, I couldn't.

Sancho: Be my guest. He's a great scapegoat.

Secretary: No, really.   90

Sancho: Please.

Secretary: Well, all right. Just once. *(She kicks* Pachuco.*)* Oh, he's so soft.

Sancho: Wasn't that good? Try again.

Secretary (Kicks Pachuco*):* Oh, he's so wonderful! *(She kicks him again.)*

Sancho: Okay, that's enough, lady. You ruin the merchandise. Yes, our Johnny   95
Pachuco model can give you many hours of pleasure. Why, the L.A.P.D. just
bought twenty of these to train their rookie cops on. And talk about maintenance. Señorita, you are looking at an entirely self-supporting machine.
You're never going to find our Johnny Pachuco model on the relief rolls. No,
sir, this model knows how to liberate.

Secretary: Liberate?

Sancho: He steals. *(Snap.* Johnny *rushes the* Secretary *and steals her purse.)*

Johnny: ¡Dame esa bolsa, vieja!° *(He grabs the purse and runs. Snap by* Sancho. *He stops.)*

*(*Secretary *runs after* Johnny *and grabs purse away from him, kicking him as she goes.)*

Secretary: No, no, no! We can't have any *more* thieves in the State Administration. Put him back.

Sancho: Okay, we still got other models. Come on, Johnny, we'll sell you to some   100
old lady. *(*Sancho *takes* Johnny *back to his place.)*

Secretary: Mr. Sancho, I don't think you quite understand what we need. What
we need is something that will attract the women voters. Something more
traditional, more romantic.

Sancho: Ah, a lover. *(He smiles meaningfully.)* Step right over here, señorita. Introducing our standard Revolucionario and/or Early California Bandit type. As
you can see he is well-built, sturdy, durable. This is the International Har-
vester of Mexicans.

Secretary: What does he do?

Sancho: You name it, he does it. He rides horses, stays in the mountains, crosses
deserts, plains, rivers, leads revolutions, follows revolutions, kills, can be
killed, serves as a martyr, hero, movie star—did I say movie star? Did you
ever see *Viva Zapata? Viva Villa? Villa Rides? Pancho Villa Returns? Pancho Villa
Goes Back? Pancho Villa Meets Abbot and Costello—*

Secretary: I've never seen any of those.   105

Sancho: Well, he was in all of them. Listen to this. *(Snap.)*

Revolucionario (Scream): ¡VIVA VILLAAAAA!

Secretary: That's awfully loud.

Sancho: He has a volume control. *(He adjusts volume. Snap.)*

Revolucionario (Mousey voice): ¡Viva Villa!   110

Secretary: That's better.

Sancho: And even if you didn't see him in the movies, perhaps you saw him on
TV. He makes commercials. *(Snap.)*

Revolucionario: Is there a Frito Bandito in your house?

Secretary: Oh yes, I've seen that one!

---

[98]**Dame esa. . . . vieja** "Gimme that bag, old lady!"

115 *Sancho:* Another feature about this one is that he is economical. He runs on raw
horsemeat and tequila!

Secretary: Isn't that rather savage?

Sancho: Al contrario,° it makes him a lover. *(Snap.)*

Revolucionario (To Secretary*):* ¡Ay, mamasota, cochota, ven pa'ca!° *(He grabs*
Secretary *and folds her back—Latin-lover style.)*

Sancho: (Snap. Revolucionario *goes back upright.)* Now wasn't that nice?

120 *Secretary:* Well, it was rather nice.

Sancho: And finally, there is one outstanding feature about this model I KNOW
the ladies are going to love: He's a GENUINE antique! He was made in
Mexico in 1910!

Secretary: Made in Mexico?

Sancho: That's right. Once in Tijuana, twice in Guadalajara, three times in
Cuernavaca.

Secretary: Mr. Sancho, I thought he was an American product.

125 *Sancho:* No, but—

Secretary: No, I'm sorry. We can't buy anything but American-made products. He
just won't do.

Sancho: But he's an antique!

Secretary: I don't care. You still don't understand what we need. It's true we need
Mexican models such as these, but it's more important that he be *American.*

Sancho: American?

130 *Secretary:* That's right, and judging from what you've shown me, I don't think
you have what we want. Well, my lunch hour's almost over; I better—

Sancho: Wait a minute! Mexican but American?

Secretary: That's correct.

Sancho: Mexican but . . . *(A sudden flash.)* AMERICAN! Yeah, I think we've got
exactly what you want. He just came in today! Give me a minute. *(He exits. Talks
from backstage.)* Here he is in the shop. Let me just get some papers off. There.
Introducing our new 1970 Mexican-American! Ta-ra-ra-ra-ra-ra-RA-RAAA!

(Sancho brings out the Mexican-American *model, a clean-shaven middle-class type
in business suit, with glasses.)*

Secretary (Impressed): Where have you been hiding this one?

135 *Sancho:* He just came in this morning. Ain't he a beauty? Feast your eyes on
him! Sturdy US STEEL frame, streamlined, modern. As a matter of fact, he is
built exactly like our Anglo models except that he comes in a variety of
darker shades: naugahyde, leather, or leatherette.

Secretary: Naugahyde.

Sancho: Well, we'll just write that down. Yes, señorita, this model represents the
apex of American engineering! He is bilingual, college educated, ambitious! Say
the word "acculturate" and he accelerates. He is intelligent, well-mannered,
clean—did I say clean? *(Snap.* Mexican-American *raises his arm.)* Smell.

Secretary (Smells): Old Sobaco, my favorite.

---

[117]**Al contrario** on the contrary   [118]**Ay, mamasota . . . pa'ca** "Hey, big mama,
[unknown], come here!"

Sancho (Snap. Mexican-American *turns toward* Sancho.): Eric! *(To* Secretary.) We call him Eric Garcia. *(To Eric)* I want you to meet Miss JIM-enez, Eric.

Mexican-American: Miss JIM-enez, I am delighted to make your acquaintance. 140
(*He kisses her hand.)*

Secretary: Oh, my, how charming!

Sancho: Did you feel the suction? He has seven especially engineered suction cups right behind his lips. He's a charmer all right!

Secretary: How about boards? Does he function on boards?

Sancho: You name them, he is on them. Parole boards, draftboards, school boards, taco quality control boards, surfboards, two-by-fours.

Secretary: Does he function in politics? 145

Sancho: Señorita, you are looking at a political MACHINE. Have you ever heard of the OEO, EOC, COD, WAR ON POVERTY? That's our model! Not only that, he makes political speeches.

Secretary: May I hear one?

Sancho: With pleasure. *(Snap.)* Eric, give us a speech.

Mexican-American: Mr. Congressman, Mr. Chairman, members of the board, honored guests, ladies and gentlemen. *(Sancho and* Secretary *applaud.)* Please, please, I come before you as a Mexican-American to tell you about the problems of the Mexican. The problems of the Mexican stem from one thing and one thing alone: He's stupid. He's uneducated. He needs to stay in school. He needs to be ambitious, forward-looking, harder-working. He needs to think American, American, American, AMERICAN, AMERICAN, AMERICAN, GOD BLESS AMERICA! GOD BLESS AMERICA!! *(He goes out of control.)*

(Sancho snaps frantically and the Mexican-American *finally slumps forward, bending at the waist.)*

Secretary: Oh my, he's patriotic too! 150

Sancho: Sí, señorita, he loves his country. Let me just make a little adjustment here. *(Stands* Mexican-American *up.)*

Secretary: What about upkeep? Is he economical?

Sancho: Well, no, I won't lie to you. The Mexican-American costs a little bit more, but you get what you pay for. He's worth every extra cent. You can keep him running on dry martinis, Langendorf bread.

Secretary: Apple pie?

Sancho: Only Mom's. Of course, he's also programmed to eat Mexican food on 155 ceremonial functions, but I must warn you: an overdose of beans will plug up his exhaust.

Secretary: Fine! There's just one more question: HOW MUCH DO YOU WANT FOR HIM?

Sancho: Well, I tell you what I'm gonna do. Today and today only, because you've been so sweet, I'm gonna let you steal this model from me! I'm gonna let you drive him off the lot for the simple price of—let's see taxes and license included—$15,000.

Secretary: Fifteen thousand DOLLARS? For a MEXICAN!

Sancho: Mexican? What are you talking, lady? This is a Mexican-AMERICAN! We had to melt down two pachucos,° a farm worker and three gabachos° to make this model! You want quality, but you gotta pay for it! This is no cheap run-about. He's got class!

160 *Secretary:* Okay, I'll take him.

Sancho: You will?

Secretary: Here's your money.

Sancho: You mind if I count it?

Secretary: Go right ahead.

165 *Sancho:* Well, you'll get your pink slip in the mail. Oh, do you want me to wrap him up for you? We have a box in the back.

Secretary: No, thank you. The Governor is having a luncheon this afternoon, and we need a brown face in the crowd. How do I drive him?

Sancho: Just snap your fingers. He'll do anything you want.

(Secretary *snaps*, Mexican-American *steps forward.*)

Mexican-American: RAZA QUERIDA, ¡VAMOS LEVANTANDO ARMAS PARA LIBERARNOS DE ESTOS DESGRACIADOS GABACHOS QUE NOS EXPLOTAN! VAMOS.°

Secretary: What did he say?

170 *Sancho:* Something about lifting arms, killing white people, etc.

Secretary: But he's not supposed to say that!

Sancho: Look, lady, don't blame me for bugs from the factory. He's your Mexican American: you bought him, now drive him off the lot!

Secretary: But he's broken!

Sancho: Try snapping another finger.

(Secretary *snaps.* Mexican-American *comes to life again.*)

175 *Mexican-American:* ¡ESTA GRAN HUMANIDAD HA DICHO BASTA! Y SE HA PUESTO EN MARCHA! ¡BASTA! ¡BASTA! ¡VIVA LA RAZA! ¡VIVA LA CAUSA! ¡VIVA LA HUELGA! ¡VIVAN LOS BROWN BERETS! ¡VIVAN LOS ESTUDIANTES! ¡CHICANO POWER!°

(The Mexican-American *turns toward the* Secretary, *who gasps and backs up. He keeps turning toward the* Pachuco, Farm Worker, *and* Revolucionario, *snapping his fingers and turning each of them on, one by one.*)

Pachuco (Snap. To Secretary*):* I'm going to get you, baby! ¡Viva La Raza!

Farm Worker (Snap. To Secretary*):* ¡Viva la huelga! ¡Viva la Huelga! ¡VIVA LA HUELGA!

Revolucionario (Snap. To Secretary*):* ¡Viva la revolución! ¡VIVA LA REVOLUCIÓN!

Revolucionario (Snap. To Secretary*):* ¡Viva la revolución! ¡VIVA LA REVOLUCIÓN!

---

[159]**pachucos** Mexican-American teenagers who dress in flamboyant clothes; they have become a symbol of resistance against the homogenizing effects of assimilation
gabachos gringos, foreigners   [168]**RAZA QUERIDA, . . . VAMOS** "Beloved Raza, let's pick up arms to liberate ourselves from those damned whites that exploit us! Let's go."
[175]**ESTA GRAN . . . CHICANO POWER** "This great mass of humanity has said enough: And it begins to march! Enough! Enough! Long live La Raza! Long live the Cause! Long live the strike! Long live the Brown Berets! Long live the students! Chicano Power!"

(The three models join together and advance toward the Secretary *who backs up and runs out of the shop screaming.* Sancho *is at the other end of the shop holding his money in his hand. All freeze. After a few seconds of silence, the* Pachuco *moves and stretches, shaking his arms and loosening up. The* Farm Worker *and* Revolucionario *do the same.* Sancho *stays where he is, frozen to his spot.)*

Johnny: Man, that was a long one, ése. *(Others agree with him.)* 180

Farm Worker: How did we do?

Johnny: Perty good, look all that lana,° man! *(He goes over to* Sancho *and removes the money from his hand.* Sancho *stays where he is.)*

Revolucionario: En la madre, look at all the money.

Johnny: We keep this up, we're going to be rich.

Farm Worker: They think we're machines. 185

Revolucionario: Burros.

Johnny: Puppets.

Mexican-American: The only thing I don't like is—how come I always got to play the goddamn Mexican-American?

Johnny: That's what you get for finishing high school.

Farm Worker: How about our wages, ése? 190

Johnny: Here it comes right now. $3,000 for you, $3,000 for you, $3,000 for you, and $3,000 for me. The rest we put back into the business.

Mexican-American: Too much, man. Heh, where you vatos° going tonight?

Farm Worker: I'm going over to Concha's. There's a party.

Johnny: Wait a minute, vatos. What about our salesman? I think he needs an oil job.

Revolucionario: Leave him to me. 195

(The Pachuco, Farm Worker, *and* Mexican-American *exit, talking loudly about their plans for the night. The* Revolucionario *goes over to* Sancho, *removes his derby hat and cigar, lifts him up and throws him over his shoulder.* Sancho *hangs loose, lifeless.)*

Revolucionario *(To audience):* He's the best model we got! ¡Ajua!° *(Exit.)*

[1967]

¹⁸²**lana** money   ¹⁹²**vatos** guys, dudes   ¹⁹⁶**Ajua** Mexican war cry made famous during the Mexican-American War

1. When and where does this play take place and what difference does it make?
2. What is the significance of the secretary's name and how she pronounces it?
3. What is the import of the end of the play?
4. Compare this play to Sagel's poem "Baca Grande" (p. 901).

NONFICTION PROSE

GORDON ALLPORT

GORDON ALLPORT *(1897–1967) received his Ph.D. in social psychology from Harvard, where he spent most of his teaching career. His work includes the development of theories about prejudice, as well as the development of personality tests. He used the term "propriate functioning" to define the way human behavior* *expresses the self. Besides* The Nature of Prejudice *(1954), excerpted here, his significant works include* Pattern and Growth in Personality *(1965),* The Person in Psychology *(1968), and, appropriately enough for a psychologist with his research interests, autobiographical essays (1967, 1968).*

The Nature of Prejudice*

From **Chapter 1**

Definition

The word *prejudice*, derived from the Latin noun *praejudicium*, has, like most words, undergone a change of meaning since classical times. There are three stages in the transformation.[1]

1. To the ancients, *praejudicium* meant a *precedent*—a judgment based on previous decisions and experiences.
2. Later, the term, in English, acquired the meaning of a judgment formed before due examination and consideration of the facts—a premature or hasty judgment.
3. Finally the term acquired also its present emotional flavor of favorableness or unfavorableness that accompanies such a prior and unsupported judgment.

Perhaps the briefest of all definitions of prejudice is: *thinking ill of others without sufficient warrant.*[2] This crisp phrasing contains the two essential ingredients of all definitions—reference to unfounded judgment and to a feeling-tone. It is, however, too brief for complete clarity.

In the first place, it refers only to *negative* prejudice. People may be prejudiced in favor of others; they may think *well* of them without sufficient warrant. The wording offered by the New English Dictionary recognizes positive as well as negative prejudice:

> *A feeling, favorable or unfavorable, toward a person or thing, prior to, or not based on, actual experience.*

While it is important to bear in mind that biases may be *pro* as well as *con*, it is none the less true that *ethnic* prejudice is mostly negative. A group of students was asked to describe their attitudes toward ethnic groups. No suggestion was made that might lead them toward negative reports. Even so, they reported eight times as many antagonistic attitudes as favorable attitudes. In this volume,

---

*Gordon Allport, *The Nature of Prejudice* (Garden City, NJ: Doubleday, 1958). [6–9, 14–16, 20–27, 43–46]. The paragraph and footnote numbers in this section do not reflect editorial deletions.

[1] Cf. *A New English Dictionary.* (Sir James A. H. Murray, Ed.) Oxford: Clarendon Press, 1909, Vol. VII, Pt. II, 1275.

[2] This definition is derived from the Thomistic moralists who regard prejudice as "rash judgment." The author is indebted to the Rev. J. H. Fichter, S. J., for calling this treatment to his attention. The definition is more fully discussed by the Rev. John LaFarge, S. J., in *The Race Question and the Negro*, New York: Longmans, Green, 1945, 174 ff.

accordingly, we shall be concerned chiefly with prejudice *against*, not with prejudice *in favor of*, ethnic groups.

The phrase "thinking ill of others" is obviously an elliptical expression that must be understood to include feelings of scorn or dislike, of fear and aversion, as well as various forms of antipathetic conduct: such as talking against people, discriminating against them, or attacking them with violence.

Similarly, we need to expand the phrase "without sufficient warrant." A judg-   5
ment is unwarranted whenever it lacks basis in fact. A wit defined prejudice as "being down on something you're not up on."

It is not easy to say how much fact is required in order to justify a judgment. A prejudiced person will almost certainly claim that he has sufficient warrant for his views. He will tell of bitter experiences he has had with refugees, Catholics, or Orientals. But, in most cases, it is evident that his facts are scanty and strained. He resorts to a selective sorting of his own few memories, mixes them up with hearsay, and overgeneralizes. No one can possibly know *all* refugees, Catholics, or Orientals. Hence any negative judgment of these groups *as a whole* is, strictly speaking, an instance of thinking ill without sufficient warrant.

Sometimes, the ill-thinker has no first-hand experience on which to base his judgment. A few years ago most Americans thought exceedingly ill of Turks— but very few had ever seen a Turk nor did they know any person who had seen one. Their warrant lay exclusively in what they had heard of the Armenian massacres and of the legendary crusades. On such evidence they presumed to condemn all members of a nation.

Ordinarily, prejudice manifests itself in dealing with individual members of rejected groups. But in avoiding a Negro neighbor, or in answering "Mr. Greenberg's" application for a room, we frame our action to accord with our categorical generalization of the group as a whole. We pay little or no attention to individual differences, and overlook the important fact that Negro X, our neighbor, is not Negro Y, whom we dislike for good and sufficient reason; that Mr. Greenberg, who may be a fine gentleman, is not Mr. Bloom, whom we have good reason to dislike.

So common is this process that we might define prejudice as:

> an avertive or hostile attitude toward a person who belongs to a group, simply because he belongs to that group, and is therefore presumed to have the objectionable qualities ascribed to the group.

This definition stresses the fact that while ethnic prejudice in daily life is ordinarily a matter of dealing with individual people it also entails an unwarranted idea concerning a group as a whole.

Returning to the question of "sufficient warrant," we must grant that few if   10
any human judgments are based on absolute certainty. We can be reasonably, but not absolutely, sure that the sun will rise tomorrow, and that death and taxes will finally overtake us. The sufficient warrant for any judgment is always a matter of probabilities. Ordinarily our judgments of natural happenings are based on firmer and higher probabilities than our judgments of people. Only rarely do our categorical judgments of nations or ethnic groups have a foundation in high probability.

Take the hostile view of Nazi leaders held by most Americans during World War II. Was it prejudiced? The answer is No, because there was abundant available evidence regarding the evil policies and practices accepted as the official code of the party. True, there may have been good individuals in the party who at heart rejected the abominable program; but the probability was so high that the Nazi group constituted an actual menace to world peace and to humane values that a realistic and justified conflict resulted. The high probability of danger removes an antagonism from the domain of prejudice into that of realistic social conflict.

In the case of gangsters, our antagonism is not a matter of prejudice, for the evidence of their antisocial conduct is conclusive. But soon the line becomes hard to draw. How about an ex-convict? It is notoriously difficult for an ex-convict to obtain a steady job where he can be self-supporting and self-respecting. Employers naturally are suspicious if they know the man's past record. But often they are more suspicious than the facts warrant. If they looked further they might find evidence that the man who stands before them is genuinely reformed, or even that he was unjustly accused in the first place. To shut the door merely because a man has a criminal record has *some* probability in its favor, for many prisoners are never reformed; but there is also an element of unwarranted prejudgment involved. We have here a true borderline instance.

We can never hope to draw a hard and fast line between "sufficient" and "insufficient" warrant. For this reason we cannot always be sure whether we are dealing with a case of prejudice or nonprejudice. Yet no one will deny that often we form judgments on the basis of scant, even nonexistent, probabilities.

Overcategorization is perhaps the commonest trick of the human mind. Given a thimbleful of facts we rush to make generalizations as large as a tub. One young boy developed the idea that all Norwegians were giants because he was impressed by the gigantic stature of Ymir in the saga, and for years was fearful lest he meet a living Norwegian. A certain man happened to know three Englishmen personally and proceeded to declare that the whole English race had the common attributes that he observed in these three.

15   There is a natural basis for this tendency. Life is so short, and the demands upon us for practical adjustments so great, that we cannot let our ignorance detain us in our daily transactions. We have to decide whether objects are good or bad by classes. We cannot weigh each object in the world by itself. Rough and ready rubrics, however coarse and broad, have to suffice.

Not every overblown generalization is a prejudice. Some are simply *misconceptions*, wherein we organize wrong information. One child had the idea that all people living in Minneapolis were "monopolists." And from his father he had learned that monopolists were evil folk. When in later years he discovered the confusion, his dislike of dwellers in Minneapolis vanished.

Here we have the test to help us distinguish between ordinary errors of prejudgment and prejudice. If a person is capable of rectifying his erroneous judgments in the light of new evidence he is not prejudiced. *Prejudgments become prejudices only if they are not reversible when exposed to new knowledge.* A prejudice, unlike a simple misconception, is actively resistant to all evidence that would unseat it. We tend to grow emotional when a prejudice is threatened with contradiction. Thus the difference between ordinary prejudgments and prejudice is that one can discuss and rectify a prejudgment without emotional resistance.

Taking these various considerations into account, we may now attempt a final definition of negative ethnic prejudice—one that will serve us throughout this book. Each phrase in the definition represents a considerable condensation of the points we have been discussing:

> Ethnic prejudice is an antipathy based upon a faulty and inflexible generalization. It may be felt or expressed. It may be directed toward a group as a whole, or toward an individual because he is a member of that group.

The net effect of prejudice, thus defined, is to place the object of prejudice at some disadvantage not merited by his own misconduct. . . .

Acting Out Prejudice

What people actually do in relation to groups they dislike is not always directly related to what they think or feel about them. Two employers, for example, may dislike Jews to an equal degree. One may keep his feelings to himself and may hire Jews on the same basis as any workers—perhaps because he wants to gain goodwill for his factory or store in the Jewish community. The other may translate his dislike into his employment policy, and refuse to hire Jews. Both men are prejudiced, but only one of them practices *discrimination*. As a rule discrimination has more immediate and serious social consequences than has prejudice.

It is true that any negative attitude tends somehow, somewhere, to express itself in action. Few people keep their antipathies entirely to themselves. The more intense the attitude, the more likely it is to result in vigorously hostile action.

We may venture to distinguish certain degrees of negative action from the least energetic to the most.

1. *Antilocution*. Most people who have prejudices talk about them. With like-minded friends, occasionally with strangers, they may express their antagonism freely. But many people never go beyond this mild degree of antipathetic action.

2. *Avoidance*. If the prejudice is more intense, it leads the individual to avoid members of the disliked group, even perhaps at the cost of considerable inconvenience. In this case, the bearer of prejudice does not directly inflict harm upon the group he dislikes. He takes the burden of accommodation and withdrawal entirely upon himself.

3. *Discrimination*. Here the prejudiced person makes detrimental distinctions of an active sort. He undertakes to exclude all members of the group in question from certain types of employment, from residential housing, political rights, educational or recreational opportunities, churches, hospitals, or from some other social privileges. Segregation is

an institutionalized form of discrimination, enforced legally or by common custom.[3]

4. *Physical attack.* Under conditions of heightened emotion prejudice may lead to acts of violence or semiviolence. An unwanted Negro family may be forcibly ejected from a neighborhood, or so severely threatened that it leaves in fear. Gravestones in Jewish cemeteries may be desecrated. The Northside's Italian gang may lie in wait for the Southside's Irish gang.

5. *Extermination.* Lynchings, pogroms, massacres, and the Hitlerian program of genocide mark the ultimate degree of violent expression of prejudice.

This five-point scale is not mathematically constructed, but it serves to call attention to the enormous range of activities that may issue from prejudiced attitudes and beliefs. While many people would never move from antilocution to avoidance; or from avoidance to active discrimination, or higher on the scale, still it is true that activity on one level makes transition to a more intense level easier. It was Hitler's antilocution that led Germans to avoid their Jewish neighbors and erstwhile friends. This preparation made it easier to enact the Nürnberg laws of discrimination which, in turn, made the subsequent burning of synagogues and street attacks upon Jews seem natural. The final step in the macabre progression was the ovens at Auschwitz.

5   From the point of view of social consequences much "polite prejudice" is harmless enough—being confined to idle chatter. But unfortunately, the fateful progression is, in this century, growing in frequency. The resulting disruption in the human family is menacing. And as the peoples of the earth grow ever more interdependent, they can tolerate less well the mounting friction.

From Chapter 2

The Process of Categorization

The human mind must think with the aid of categories (the term is equivalent here to *generalizations*). Once formed, categories are the basis for normal prejudgment. We cannot possibly avoid this process. Orderly living depends upon it.

We may say that the process of categorization has five important characteristics.

(1) **It forms large classes and clusters for guiding our daily adjustments.** We spend most of our waking life calling upon preformed categories for this purpose. When the sky darkens and the barometer falls we prejudge that rain will fall. We adjust to this cluster of happenings by taking along an umbrella. When an angry looking dog charges down the street, we categorize

---

[3]Aware of the world-wide problem of discrimination, the Commission on Human Rights of the United Nations has prepared a thorough analysis of *The main types and causes of discrimination.* United Nations Publications, 1949, XIV, 3.

him as a "mad dog" and avoid him. When we go to a physician with an ailment we expect him to behave in a certain way toward us. On these, and countless other occasions, we "type" a single event, place it within a familiar rubric, and act accordingly. Sometimes we are mistaken: the event does not fit the category. It does not rain; the dog is not mad; the physician behaves unprofessionally. Yet our behavior was rational. It was based on high probability. Though we used the wrong category, we did the best we could.

What all this means is that our experience in life tends to form itself into clusters (concepts, categories), and while we may call on the right cluster at the wrong time, or the wrong cluster at the right time, still the process in question dominates our entire mental life. A million events befall us every day. We cannot handle so many events. If we think of them at all, we type them.

Open-mindedness is considered to be a virtue. But, strictly speaking, it cannot occur. A new experience *must* be redacted into old categories. We cannot handle each event freshly in its own right. If we did so, of what use would past experience be? Bertrand Russell, the philosopher, has summed up the matter in a phrase, "a mind perpetually open will be a mind perpetually vacant." 5

(2) **Categorization assimilates as much as it can to the cluster.** There is a curious inertia in our thinking. We like to solve problems easily. We can do so best if we can fit them rapidly into a satisfactory category and use this category as a means of prejudging the solution. The story is told of the pharmacist's mate in the Navy who had only two categories into which he fitted every ailment that came to his attention on sick call: if you can *see* it put iodine on it; if you *can't*, give the patient a dose of salts. Life was simple for this pharmacist's mate; he ran his whole professional life with the aid of only two categories.

The point may be stated in this way: the mind tends to categorize environmental events in the "grossest" manner compatible with the need for action. If the pharmacist's mate in our story were called to task for his overcrude practice of medicine, he might then mend his ways and learn to employ more discriminated categories. But so long as we can "get away" with coarse overgeneralizations we tend to do so. (Why? Well, it takes less effort, and effort, except in the area of our most intense interests, is disagreeable.)

The bearing of this tendency on our problem is clear. It costs the Anglo employer less effort to guide his daily behavior by the generalization "Mexicans are lazy," than to individualize his workmen and learn the real reasons for their conduct. If I can lump thirteen million of my fellow citizens under a simple formula, "Negroes are stupid, dirty, and inferior," I simplify my life enormously. I simply avoid them one and all. What could be easier?

(3) **The category enables us quickly to identify a related object.** Every event has certain marks that serve as a cue to bring the category of prejudgment into action. When we see a red-breasted bird, we say to ourselves "robin." When we see a crazily swaying automobile, we think, "drunken driver," and act accordingly. A person with dark brown skin will activate whatever concept of Negro is dominant in our mind. If the dominant category is one composed of negative attitudes and beliefs we will automatically avoid him, or adopt whichever habit of rejection (Chapter 1) is most available to us.

10   Thus categories have a close and immediate tie with what we see, how we
judge, and what we do. In fact, their whole purpose seems to be to facilitate
perception and conduct—in other words, to make our adjustment to life
speedy, smooth, and consistent. This principle holds even though we often
make mistakes in fitting events to categories and thus get ourselves into
trouble.

(4) **The category saturates all that it contains with the same ideational and emotional flavor.** Some categories are almost purely intellectual. Such
categories we call concepts. *Tree* is a concept made up of our experience with
hundreds of kinds of trees and with thousands of individual trees, and yet it has
essentially one ideational meaning. But many of our concepts (even *tree*) have in
addition to a "meaning" also a characteristic "feeling." We not only know what
tree is but we *like* trees. And so it is with ethnic categories. Not only do we know
what Chinese, Mexican, Londoner mean, but we may have a feeling tone of
favor or disfavor accompanying the concept.

(5) **Categories may be more or less rational.** We have said that generally
a category starts to grow up from a "kernel of truth." A rational category does
so, and enlarges and solidifies itself through the increment of relevant experience. Scientific laws are examples of rational categories. They are backed up by
experience. Every event to which they pertain turns out in a certain way. Even
if the laws are not 100 percent perfect, we consider them rational if they have a
high probability of predicting a happening.

Some of our ethnic categories are quite rational. It is probable a Negro will have
dark skin (though this is not always true). It is probable that a Frenchman will
speak French better than German (though here, too, are exceptions). But is it true
that the Negro will be superstitious, or that the Frenchman will be morally lax?
Here the probability is much less, perhaps even zero in significance if we compare
the French with people in other nations. Yet our minds seem to make no distinction in category formation: irrational categories are formed as easily as rational.

To make a rational prejudgment of members of a group requires considerable
knowledge of the characteristics of the group. It is unlikely that anyone has
sound evidence that Scots are more penurious than Norwegians, or that Orientals are more wily than Caucasians, yet these beliefs grow as readily as do more
rational beliefs.

> In a certain Guatemalan community there is fierce hatred of the Jews. No resident
> has ever seen a Jew. How did the Jew-is-to-be-hated category grow up? In the
> first place, the community was strongly Catholic. Teachers had told the residents
> that the Jews were Christ-killers. It also so happened that in the local culture was
> an old pagan myth about a devil who killed a god. Thus two powerfully emotional
> ideas converged and created a hostile prejudgment of Jews.

15   We have said that irrational categories are formed as easily as rational categories. Probably they are formed *more* easily, for intense emotional feelings have
a property of acting like sponges. Ideas, engulfed by an overpowering emotion,
are more likely to conform to the emotion than to objective evidence.

An irrational category is one formed without adequate evidence. It may be that
the person is simply *ignorant* of the evidence, in which case a misconception is

formed, as defined in Chapter 1. Many concepts depend on hearsay, on second-hand accounts, and for this reason category-misinformation is often inevitable. A child in school is required to form some general conception of, say, the Tibetan people. He can take into consideration only what his teacher and textbook tell him. The resultant picture may be erroneous, but the child has done the best he can.

Much deeper and more baffling is the type of irrational prejudgment that *disregards* the evidence. There is the story of an Oxford student who once remarked, "I despise all Americans, but have never met one I didn't like." In this case the categorization went against even his first-hand experience. Holding to a prejudgment when we know better is one of the strangest features of prejudice. Theologians tell us that in prejudgments based on ignorance there is no question of sin; but that in prejudgments held in deliberate disregard of evidence, sin is involved.

When Categories Conflict with Evidence

For our purposes it is important to understand what happens when categories conflict with evidence. It is a striking fact that in most instances categories are stubborn and resist change. After all, we have fashioned our generalizations as we have because they have worked fairly well. Why change them to accommodate every new bit of evidence? If we are accustomed to one make of automobile and are satisfied, why admit the merits of another make? To do so would only disturb our satisfactory set of habits.

We selectively admit new evidence to a category if it confirms us in our previous belief. A Scotsman who is penurious delights us because he vindicates our prejudgment. It is pleasant to say, "I told you so." But if we find evidence that is contradictory to our preconception, we are likely to grow resistant.

There is a common mental device that permits people to hold to prejudg-   20
ments even in the face of much contradictory evidence. It is the device of admitting exceptions. "There are nice Negroes but . . ." or "Some of my best friends are Jews but. . . ." This is a disarming device. By excluding a few favored cases, the negative rubric is kept intact for all other cases. In short, contrary evidence is not admitted and allowed to modify the generalization; rather it is perfunctorily acknowledged but excluded.

Let us call this the "re-fencing" device. When a fact cannot fit into a mental field, the exception is acknowledged, but the field is hastily fenced in again and not allowed to remain dangerously open.

A curious instance of re-fencing takes place in many discussions concerning the Negro. When a person with a strong anti-Negro bias is confronted with evidence favorable to the Negro he frequently pops up with the well-known matrimonial question: "Would you want your sister to marry a Negro?" This re-fencing is adroit. As soon as the interlocutor says, "No," or hesitates in his reply, the biased person can say in effect, "See, there just *is* something different and impossible about the Negro," or, "I was right all along—for the Negro has an objectionable essence in his nature."

There are two conditions under which a person will not strive to re-fence his mental field in such a way as to maintain the generalization. The first of these is the somewhat rare condition of *habitual open-mindedness*. There are people who seem to go through life with relatively little of the rubricizing tendency. They are suspicious of all labels, of categories, of sweeping statements. They habitually insist on knowing the evidence for each and every broad generalization. Realizing the complexity and variety in human nature, they are especially chary of ethnic generalizations. If they hold to any at all it is in a highly tentative way, and every contrary experience is allowed to modify the pre-existing ethnic concept.

The other occasion that makes for modification of concepts is plain *self-interest*. A person may learn from bitter failure that his categories are erroneous and must be revised. For example, he may not have known the right classification for edible mushrooms and thus find himself poisoned by toadstools. He will not make the same mistake again: his category will be corrected. Or he may think that Italians are primitive, ignorant, and loud until he falls in love with an Italian girl of a cultured family. Then he finds it greatly to his self-interest to modify his previous generalization and act thereafter on the more correct assumption that there are many, many kinds of Italians.

25 Usually, however, there are good reasons for maintaining the grounds of prejudgment intact. It takes less effort to do so. What is more, we find our prejudgments approved and supported by our friends and associates. It would not be polite for a suburbanite to disagree with his neighbors about admitting Jews to the local country club. It is comforting to find that our categories are similar to those of our neighbors, upon whose goodwill our own sense of status depends. How pointless for me to be perpetually reconsidering all my convictions, especially those that form the groundwork of my life, so long as that groundwork is satisfactory to me and to my neighbors. . . .

Personal Values and Prejudice

It is obvious, then, that the very act of affirming our way of life often leads us to the brink of prejudice. The philosopher Spinoza has defined what he calls "love-prejudice." It consists, he says, "in feeling about anyone through love more than is right." The lover overgeneralizes the virtues of his beloved. Her every act is seen as perfect. The partisan of a church, a club, a nation may also feel about these objects "through love more than is right."

Now there is a good reason to believe that this love-prejudice is far more basic to human life than is its opposite, hate-prejudice (which Spinoza says "consists in feeling about anyone through hate less than is right"). One must first overestimate the things one loves before one can underestimate their contraries. Fences are built primarily for the protection of what we cherish.

Positive attachments are essential to life. The young child could not exist without his dependent relationship on a nurturant person. He must love and identify himself with someone or something before he can learn what to hate. Young children must have family and friendship circles before they can define the "out-groups" which are a menace to them.[1]

---

[1] See G. W. Allport, A psychological approach to love and hate. Chapter 5 in P. A. Sorokin (Ed.), *Explorations in Altruistic Love and Behavior*. Boston: Beacon Press, 1950. Also, M. F. ASHLEY-MONTAGU, *On Being Human*. New York: Henry Schumann, 1950.

Why is it that we hear so little about love-prejudice—the tendency to over-generalize our categories of attachment and affection? One reason is that prejudices of this sort create no social problem. If I am grossly partisan toward my own children, no one will object—unless at the same time it leads me, as it sometimes does, to manifest antagonism toward the neighbor's children. When a person is defending a categorical value of his own, he may do so at the expense of other people's interests or safety. If so, then we note his hate-prejudice, not realizing that it springs from a reciprocal love-prejudice underneath.

Take an example from anti-American prejudice. It has been a long-standing condition among many cultivated Europeans. As long ago as 1854 one of them described the United States with contempt as "a grand bedlam, a rendezvous of European scamps and vagabonds."[2] The abuse was so common that in 1869 James Russell Lowell was moved to chide the European critics in an essay entitled "On a certain condescension in foreigners." But the same type of criticism is still current.

What lies at its root? In the first place, we can be sure that before there was criticism there was self-love—a patriotism, a pride of ancestry and culture, representing the positive values by which the European critics live. Coming to this country they sense a vague threat to their own position. By disparaging America they can feel more secure. It is not that initially they hate America, but that they initially love themselves and their way of life. The formula holds equally well for Americans traveling abroad.

A student in Massachusetts, an avowed apostle of tolerance—so he thought— wrote, "The Negro question will never be solved until those dumb white Southerners get something through their ivory skulls." The student's positive values were idealistic. But ironically enough, his militant "tolerance" brought about a prejudiced condemnation of a portion of the population which he perceived as a threat to his tolerance-value.

Somewhat similar is the case of the lady who said, "Of course I have no prejudice. I had a dear old colored mammy for a nurse. Having grown up in the South and having lived here all my life I understand the problem. The Negroes are much happier if they are just allowed to stay in their place. Northern troublemakers just don't understand the Negro." This lady in her little speech was (psychologically speaking) defending her own privileges, her position, and her cosy way of life. It was not so much that she disliked Negroes or northerners, but she loved the status quo.

It is convenient to believe, if one can, that all of one category is good, all of the other evil. A popular workman in a factory was offered a job in the office by the management of the company. A union official said to him, "Don't take a management job or you'll become a bastard like all the rest of them." Only two classes existed in this official's mind: the workmen and the "bastards."

These instances argue that negative prejudice is a reflex of one's own system of values. We prize our own mode of existence and correspondingly underprize (or actively attack) what seems to us to threaten it. The thought has been expressed by Sigmund Freud: "In the undisguised antipathies and aversion

[2]Merle Curti. The reputation of America overseas (1776–1860). *American Quarterly*, 1949, 1. 58–82.

which people feel towards strangers with whom they have to do, we recognize the expression of self-love, of narcissism."

The process is especially clear in time of war. When an enemy threatens all or nearly all of our positive values we stiffen our resistance and exaggerate the merits of our cause. We feel—and this is an instance of overgeneralization—that we are wholly right. (If we did not believe this we could not marshall all our energies for our defense.) And if we are wholly right then the enemy must be wholly wrong. Since he is wholly wrong, we should not hesitate to exterminate him. But even in this wartime example it is clear that our basic love-prejudice is primary and that the hate-prejudice is a derivative phenomenon.

35   While there may be such things as "just wars," in the sense that threats to one's values are genuine and must be resisted, yet war always entails some degree of prejudice. The very existence of a severe threat causes one to perceive the enemy country as wholly evil, and every citizen therein as a menace. Balance and discrimination become impossible.[3]

Summary

This chapter has argued that man has a propensity to prejudice. This propensity lies in his normal and natural tendency to form generalizations, concepts, categories, whose content represents an oversimplification of his world of experience. His rational categories keep close to first-hand experience, but he is able to form irrational categories just as readily. In these even a kernel of truth may be lacking, for they can be composed wholly of hearsay evidence, emotional projections, and fantasy.

One type of categorization that predisposes us especially to make unwarranted judgments is our personal values. These values, the basis of all human existence, lead easily to love-prejudices. Hate-prejudices are secondary developments, but they may, and often do, arise as a reflex of positive values.

In order to understand better the nature of love-prejudice, which at bottom is responsible for hate-prejudice, we turn our attention next to the formation of in-group loyalties.

From **Chapter 3**

Can Humanity Constitute an In-group?

One's family ordinarily constitutes the smallest and the firmest of one's in-groups. It is probably for this reason that we usually think of in-groups growing weaker and weaker the larger their circle of inclusion. Figure 2 expresses the common feeling that the potency of the membership becomes less as the distance from personal contact grows larger. Only a few sample memberships are included in the diagram in order not to complicate the point at issue.

Such an image implies that a world-loyalty is the most difficult to achieve. In part the implication is correct. There seems to be special difficulty in fashioning

[3]Important relations between war and prejudice are discussed in H. Cantril (Ed.), *Tensions That Cause Wars*. Urbana: Univ. of Illinois Press, 1950.

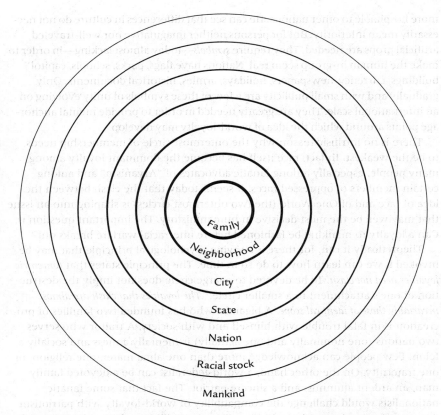

FIGURE 2 *Hypothetical Lessening of In-group Potency as Membership Becomes More Inclusive.*

an in-group out of an entity as embracing as mankind. Even the ardent believer in One World has trouble. Suppose a diplomat is dealing at a conference table with representatives of other countries whose language, manners, and ideology differ from his own. Even if this diplomat believes ardently in One World, still he cannot escape a sense of strangeness in his encounters. His own model of propriety and rightness is his own culture. Other languages and customs inevitably seem outlandish and, if not inferior, at least slightly absurd and unnecessary.

Suppose the delegate is so broadminded that he can see many defects in his own nation, and suppose he sincerely wants to build an ideal society, where the good features of many cultures are blended. Even such an extreme idealism is likely to wring from him only minor concessions. With utmost sincerity he finds himself fighting for his own language, religion, ideology, law, forms of etiquette. After all, his nation's way of life is *his* way of life—and he cannot lightly abrogate the ground of his whole existence.

Such almost reflex preference for the familiar grips us all. To be sure, a well-traveled person, or one who is endowed with cosmopolitan tastes, is relatively

more hospitable to other nations. He can see that differences in culture do not necessarily mean inferiority. But for persons neither imaginative nor well-traveled
artificial props are needed. They require *symbols*—today almost lacking—in order to
make the human in-group seem real. Nations have flags, parks, schools, capitol
buildings, currency, newspapers, holidays, armies, historical documents. Only
gradually and with small publicity are a few of these symbols of unity evolving on
an international scale. They are greatly needed in order to provide mental anchor-
age points around which the idea of world-loyalty may develop.

5   There is no intrinsic reason why the outermost circle of membership needs
to be the weakest. In fact, race itself has become the dominant loyalty among
many people, especially among fanatic advocates of "Aryanism" and among
certain members of oppressed races. It seems today that the clash between the
idea of race and of One World (the two outermost circles) is shaping into an issue
that may well be the most decisive in human history. The important question is,
Can a loyalty to mankind be fashioned before interracial warfare breaks out?

Theoretically it can, for there is a saving psychological principle that may be
invoked if we can learn how to do so in time. The principle states that *concentric
loyalties need not clash*. To be devoted to a large circle does not imply the destruction of one's attachment to a smaller circle.[1] *The loyalties that clash are almost
invariably those of identical scope.* A bigamist who has founded two families of procreation is in fatal trouble with himself and with society. A traitor who serves
two nations (one nominally and one actually) is mentally a mess and socially a
felon. Few people can acknowledge more than one alma mater, one religion, or
one fraternity. On the other hand, a world-federalist can be a devoted family
man, an ardent alumnus, and a sincere patriot. The fact that some fanatic
nationalists would challenge the compatibility of world-loyalty with patriotism
does not change the psychological law. Wendell Willkie and Franklin Roosevelt
were no less patriots because they envisioned a United Nations in One World.

Concentric loyalties take time to develop, and often, of course, they fail completely to do so. In an interesting study of Swiss children Piaget and Weil discovered the resistance of young children to the idea that one loyalty can be included within another. The following record of a seven-year-old is typical of that age:

> Have you heard of Switzerland? *Yes*. What is it? *A canton*. And what is
> Geneva? *A town*. Where is Geneva? *In Switzerland*. (But the child draws
> two circles side by side.) Are you Swiss? *No, I'm Genevese*.

[1]This spatial metaphor has its limitations. The reader may ask, What really is the innermost
circle of loyalty? It is by no means always the family, as Fig. 2 implies. May not the core be the
primordial self-love we discussed in Chapter 2? If we regard self as the central circle, then the
broadening loyalties are, psychologically speaking, simply extensions of the self. But as the self
widens, it may also *re-center* itself, so that what is at first an outer circle may become psychologically the focus. Thus a religious person, for example, may believe that man is made in God's
image: therefore his own love of God and man may, for him, lie in the innermost circle. Both
loyalties and prejudices are features of personality organization, and in the last analysis each
organization is unique. While this criticism is entirely valid, still for our present purposes Fig. 2
can stand as an approximate representation of the fact that for many people the larger the
social system the less easily do they encompass it in their span of understanding and affection.

At a later stage (eight to ten) children grasp the idea that Geneva is enclosed spatially in Switzerland and draw their relationship as one circle enclosing the other. But the idea of concentric loyalty is still elusive.

What is your nationality? *I'm Swiss.* How is that? *Because I live in Switzerland.* You're Genevese too? *No, I can't be.* Why not? *I'm Swiss now and can't be Genevese as well.*

By the age of ten or eleven the child can straighten the matter out.

What is your nationality? *I'm Swiss.* How is that? *Because my parents are Swiss.* Are you Genevese as well? *Naturally, because Geneva is in Switzerland.*

Likewise by the age of ten or eleven the child has an emotional evaluation of his national circle.

I like Switzerland because it's a free country.
I like Switzerland because it's the Red Cross country.
In Switzerland our neutrality makes us charitable.

It is evident that these emotional valuations are learned from teachers and parents, and are adopted ready-made. The mode of teaching ordinarily stops the process of enlargement at this point. Beyond the borders of the native land there is only the domain of "foreigners"—not of fellow men. Michel, aged nine and one-half, answered the interviewer as follows:

Have you ever heard of such people as foreigners? *Yes, the French, the Americans, the Russians, the English.* Quite right. Are there differences between all these people? *Oh yes, they don't speak the same language.* And what else? Try to tell me as much as possible. *The French are not very serious, they don't worry about anything, and it's dirty there.* And what do you think of the Americans? *They're ever so rich and clever. They've discovered the atom bomb.* And what do you think of the Russians? *They're bad, they're always wanting to make war.* Now look, how did you come to know all you've told me? *I don't know . . . I've heard it . . . that's what people say.*

Most children never enlarge their sense of belonging beyond the ties of family, city, nation. The reason seems to be that those with whom the child lives, and whose judgment he mirrors, do not do so. Piaget and Weil write, "Everything suggests that, on discovering the values accepted in his immediate circle, the child feels bound to accept the circle's opinions of all other national groups."[2]

While the national orbit is the largest circle of loyalty that most children learn, there is no necessity for the process to stop there. In some children of twelve and thirteen years of age these investigators found a high sense of "reciprocity," i.e., a willingness to admit that all peoples have equal value and merit, although each prefers its own mode of life. When such a sense of reciprocity is firmly established, the way is prepared for the integrated

[2]J. Piaget and Anne-Marie Weil. The development in children of the idea of the homeland and of relations with other countries. *International Social Science Bulletin*, 1951, 3, 570.

conception of larger and larger units of mankind, to all of which the young person can be loyal without losing his earlier attachments. Until he learns this attitude of reciprocity, he is unlikely to accept other countries as lying within the orbit of his loyalty.

In summary, in-group memberships are vitally important to individual survival. These memberships constitute a web of habits. When we encounter an outsider who follows different customs we unconsciously say, "He breaks my habits." Habit-breaking is unpleasant. We prefer the familiar. We cannot help but feel a bit on guard when other people seem to threaten or even question our habits. Attitudes partial to the in-group, or to the reference group, do not necessarily require that attitudes toward other groups be antagonistic—even though hostility often helps to intensify the in-group cohesion. Narrow circles can, without conflict, be supplemented by larger circles of loyalty. This happy condition is not often achieved, but it remains from the psychological point of view a hopeful possibility.   [1959]

1. Why does Allport think that open-mindedness "cannot occur"?
2. What are the uses of categorical generalizations according to Allport? Why are they hard to change?
3. Try to notice how you use categories to classify the objects that are part of your daily life. Is Allport right about how the categories function for you? When has your evaluation of a category changed? What did it take?
4. Where can you see the workings of the kind of categorization Allport describes in the literary works in this chapter?
5. What about works in other chapters?

TONI MORRISON

TONI MORRISON *(1931–) (Chloe Anthony Wofford) grew up in Lorain, Ohio, in a black working-class family. She studied at Howard and Cornell Universities, pursuing an academic career at Texas Southern, Howard, Yale, and since 1989, Princeton. She has also worked as an editor, lecturer and critic, specializing in African-American literature. Her novels include* The Bluest Eye, Sula, Song of Solomon, Tar Baby, Beloved, *and* Jazz; *she has also written a play and a book of essays. She is the winner of many awards, including the Pulitzer Prize in 1988, and the Nobel Prize for Literature. "Romancing the Shadow" is a chapter of her book,* Playing in the Dark: Whiteness and the Literary Imagination.

From *Romancing the Shadow**

. . . I want to suggest that these concerns—autonomy, authority, newness and difference, absolute power—not only become the major themes and presumptions

*Toni Morrison, "Romancing the Shadow," *Playing in the Dark: Whiteness and the Literary Imagination* (Cambridge: Harvard University Press, 1992; New York: Vintage, 1993 [paperback]). [44–59] The paragraph numbers in this section do not reflect editorial deletions.

of American literature, but that each one is made possible by, shaped by, activated by a complex awareness and employment of a constituted Africanism. It was this Africanism, deployed as rawness and savagery, that provided the staging ground and arena for the elaboration of the quintessential American identity.

Autonomy is freedom and translates into the much championed and revered "individualism"; newness translates into "innocence"; distinctiveness becomes difference and the erection of strategies for maintaining it; authority and absolute power become a romantic, conquering "heroism," virility, and the problematics of wielding absolute power over the lives of others. All the rest are made possible by this last, it would seem—absolute power called forth and played against and within a natural and mental landscape conceived of as a "raw, half-savage world."

Why is it seen as raw and savage? Because it is peopled by a nonwhite indigenous population? Perhaps. But certainly because there is ready to hand a bound and unfree, rebellious but serviceable, black population against which Dunbar and all white men are enabled to measure these privileging and privileged differences.

Eventually individualism fuses with the prototype of Americans as solitary, alienated, and malcontent. What, one wants to ask, are Americans alienated from? What are Americans always so insistently innocent of? Different from? As for absolute power, over whom is this power held, from whom withheld, to whom distributed?

Answers to these questions lie in the potent and ego-reinforcing presence of   5
an Africanist population. This population is convenient in every way, not the least of which is self-definition. This new white male can now persuade himself that savagery is "out there." The lashes ordered (500 applied five times is 2500) are not one's own savagery; repeated and dangerous breaks for freedom are "puzzling" confirmations of black irrationality; the combination of Dean Swift's beatitudes and a life of regularized violence is civilized; and if the sensibilities are dulled enough, the rawness remains external.

These contradictions slash their way through the pages of American literature. How could it be otherwise? As Dominick LaCapra reminds us, "Classic novels are not only worked over . . . by common contextual forces (such as ideologies) but also rework and at least partially work through those forces in critical and at times potentially transformative fashion."*

As for the culture, the imaginative and historical terrain upon which early American writers journeyed is in large measure shaped by the presence of the racial other. Statements to the contrary, insisting on the meaninglessness of race to the American identity, are themselves full of meaning. The world does not become raceless or will not become unracialized by assertion. The act of enforcing racelessness in literary discourse is itself a racial act. Pouring rhetorical acid on the fingers of a black hand may indeed destroy the prints, but not the hand. Besides, what happens in that violent, self-serving act of erasure to the hands, the fingers, the fingerprints of the one who does the pouring? Do they remain acid-free? The literature itself suggests otherwise.

*Dominick LaCapra, *History, Politics and the Novel* (Ithaca: Cornell University Press, 1987), p. 4.

Explicit or implicit, the Africanist presence informs in compelling and inescapable ways the texture of American literature. It is a dark and abiding presence, there for the literary imagination as both a visible and an invisible mediating force. Even, and especially, when American texts are not "about" Africanist presences or characters or narrative or idiom, the shadow hovers in implication, in sign, in line of demarcation. It is no accident and no mistake that immigrant populations (and much immigrant literature) understood their "Americanness" as an opposition to the resident black population. Race, in fact, now functions as a metaphor so necessary to the construction of Americanness that it rivals the old pseudo-scientific and class-informed racisms whose dynamics we are more used to deciphering.

As a metaphor for transacting the whole process of Americanization, while burying its particular racial ingredients, this Africanist presence may be something the United States cannot do without. Deep within the word "American" is its association with race. To identify someone as a South African is to say very little; we need the adjective "white" or "black" or "colored" to make our meaning clear. In this country it is quite the reverse. American means white, and Africanist people struggle to make the term applicable to themselves with ethnicity and hyphen after hyphen after hyphen. Americans did not have a profligate, predatory nobility from which to wrest an identity of national virtue while continuing to covet aristocratic license and luxury. The American nation negotiated both its disdain and its envy in the same way Dunbar did: through a self-reflexive contemplation of fabricated, mythological Africanism. For the settlers and for American writers generally, this Africanist other became the means of thinking about body, mind, chaos, kindness, and love; provided the occasion for exercises in the absence of restraint, the presence of restraint, the contemplation of freedom and of aggression; permitted opportunities for the exploration of ethics and morality, for meeting the obligations of the social contract, for bearing the cross of religion and following out the ramifications of power.

10   Reading and charting the emergence of an Africanist persona in the development of a national literature is both a fascinating project and an urgent one, if the history and criticism of our literature is to become accurate. Emerson's plea for intellectual independence was like the offer of an empty plate that writers could fill with nourishment from an indigenous menu. The language no doubt had to be English, but the content of that language, its subject, was to be deliberately, insistently un-English and anti-European, insofar as it rhetorically repudiated an adoration of the Old World and defined the past as corrupt and indefensible. In the scholarship on the formation of an American character and the production of a national literature, a number of items have been catalogued. A major item to be added to the list must be an Africanist presence—decidedly not American, decidedly other.

The need to establish difference stemmed not only from the Old World but from a difference in the New. What was distinctive in the New was, first of all, its claim to freedom and, second, the presence of the unfree within the heart of the democratic experiment—the critical absence of democracy, its echo, shadow, and silent force in the political and intellectual activity of some not-Americans.

The distinguishing features of the not-Americans were their slave status, their social status—and their color.

It is conceivable that the first would have self-destructed in a variety of ways had it not been for the last. These slaves, unlike many others in the world's history, were visible to a fault. And they had inherited, among other things, a long history on the meaning of color. It was not simply that this slave population had a distinctive color; it was that this color "meant" something. That meaning had been named and deployed by scholars from at least the moment, in the eighteenth century, when other and sometimes the same scholars started to investigate both the natural history and the inalienable rights of man—that is to say, human freedom.

One supposes that if Africans all had three eyes or one ear, the significance of that difference from the smaller but conquering European invaders would also have been found to have meaning. In any case, the subjective nature of ascribing value and meaning to color cannot be questioned this late in the twentieth century. The point for this discussion is the alliance between visually rendered ideas and linguistic utterances. And this leads into the social and political nature of received knowledge as it is revealed in American literature.

Knowledge, however mundane and utilitarian, plays about in linguistic images and forms cultural practice. Responding to culture—clarifying, explicating, valorizing, translating, transforming, criticizing—is what artists everywhere do, especially writers involved in the founding of a new nation. Whatever their personal and formally political responses to the inherent contradiction of a free republic deeply committed to slavery, nineteenth-century writers were mindful of the presence of black people. More important, they addressed, in more or less passionate ways, their views on that difficult presence.

The alertness to a slave population did not confine itself to the personal   15
encounters that writers may have had. Slave narratives were a nineteenth-century publication boom. The press, the political campaigns, and the policy of various parties and elected officials were rife with the discourse of slavery and freedom. It would have been an *isolato* indeed who was unaware of the most explosive issue in the nation. How could one speak of profit, economy, labor, progress, suffragism, Christianity, the frontier, the formation of new states, the acquisition of new lands, education, transportation (freight and passengers), neighborhoods, the military—of almost anything a country concerns itself with—without having as a referent, at the heart of the discourse, at the heart of definition, the presence of Africans and their descendants?

It was not possible. And it did not happen. What did happen frequently was an effort to talk about these matters with a vocabulary designed to disguise the subject. It did not always succeed, and in the work of many writers disguise was never intended. But the consequence was a master narrative that spoke *for* Africans and their descendants, or *of* them. The legislator's narrative could not coexist with a response from the Africanist persona. Whatever popularity the slave narratives had—and they influenced abolitionists and converted antiabolitionists—the slave's own narrative, while freeing the narrator in many ways, did not destroy the master narrative. The master narrative could make any number of adjustments to keep itself intact.

Silence from and about the subject was the order of the day. Some of the silences were broken, and some were maintained by authors who lived with and within the policing narrative. What I am interested in are the strategies for maintaining the silence and the strategies for breaking it. How did the founding writers of young America engage, imagine, employ, and create an Africanist presence and persona? In what ways do these strategies explicate a vital part of American literature? How does excavating these pathways lead to fresh and more profound analyses of what they contain and how they contain it?

*   *   *

Let me propose some topics that need critical investigation.

First, the Africanist character as surrogate and enabler. In what ways does the imaginative encounter with Africanism enable white writers to think about themselves? What are the dynamics of Africanism's self-reflexive properties? Note, for instance, the way Africanism is used to conduct a dialogue concerning American space in *The Narrative of Arthur Gordon Pym*. Through the use of Africanism, Poe meditates on place as a means of containing the fear of border-lessness and trespass, but also as a means of releasing and exploring the desire for a limitless empty frontier. Consider the ways that Africanism in other American writers (Mark Twain, Melville, Hawthorne) serves as a vehicle for regulating love and the imagination as defenses against the psychic costs of guilt and despair. Africanism is the vehicle by which the American self knows itself as not enslaved, but free; not repulsive, but desirable; not helpless, but licensed and powerful; not history-less, but historical; not damned, but innocent; not a blind accident of evolution, but a progressive fulfillment of destiny.

20   A second topic in need of critical attention is the way an Africanist idiom is used to establish difference or, in a later period, to signal modernity. We need to explicate the ways in which specific themes, fears, forms of consciousness, and class relationships are embedded in the use of Africanist idiom: how the dialogue of black characters is construed as an alien, estranging dialect made deliberately unintelligible by spellings contrived to disfamiliarize it; how Africanist language practices are employed to evoke the tension between speech and speechlessness; how it is used to establish a cognitive world split between speech and text, to reinforce class distinctions and otherness as well as to assert privilege and power; how it serves as a marker and vehicle for illegal sexuality, fear of madness, expulsion, self-loathing. Finally, we should look at how a black idiom and the sensibilities it has come to imply are appropriated for the associative value they lend to modernism—to being hip, sophisticated, ultra-urbane.

Third, we need studies of the technical ways in which an Africanist character is used to limn out and enforce the invention and implications of whiteness. We need studies that analyze the strategic use of black characters to define the goals and enhance the qualities of white characters. Such studies will reveal the process of establishing others in order to know them, to display knowledge of the other so as to ease and to order external and internal chaos. Such studies will reveal the process by which it is made possible to explore and penetrate one's own body in the guise of the sexuality, vulnerability, and anarchy of the other—and to control projections of anarchy with the disciplinary apparatus of punishment and largess.

Fourth, we need to analyze the manipulation of the Africanist narrative (that is, the story of a black person, the experience of being bound and/or rejected) as a means of meditation—both safe and risky—on one's own humanity. Such analyses will reveal how the representation and appropriation of that narrative provides opportunities to contemplate limitation, suffering, rebellion, and to speculate on fate and destiny. They will analyze how that narrative is used for discourse on ethics, social and universal codes of behavior, and assertions about and definitions of civilization and reason. Criticism of this type will show how that narrative is used in the construction of a history and a context for whites by positing history-lessness and context-lessness for blacks.

These topics surface endlessly when one begins to look carefully, without restraining, protective agenda beforehand. They seem to me to render the nation's literature a much more complex and rewarding body of knowledge.

Two examples may clarify: one a major American novel that is both a source and a critique of romance as a genre; the other the fulfillment of the promise I made earlier to return to those mute white images of Poe's.

*   *   *

If we supplement our reading of *Huckleberry Finn*, expand it—release it from   25
its clutch of sentimental nostrums about lighting out to the territory, river gods, and the fundamental innocence of Americanness—to incorporate its contestatory, combative critique of antebellum America, it seems to be another, fuller novel. It becomes a more beautifully complicated work that sheds much light on some of the problems it has accumulated through traditional readings too shy to linger over the implications of the Africanist presence at its center. We understand that, at a certain level, the critique of class and race is there, although disguised or enhanced by humor and naiveté. Because of the combination of humor, adventure, and the viewpoint of the naif, Mark Twain's readers are free to dismiss the critique, the contestatory qualities, of the novel and focus on its celebration of savvy innocence, at the same time voicing polite embarrassment over the symptomatic racial attitude it enforces. Early criticism (that is, the reappraisals in the 1950s that led to the reification of *Huckleberry Finn* as a great novel) missed or dismissed the social quarrel in that work because it appears to assimilate the ideological assumptions of its society and culture; because it is narrated in the voice and controlled by the gaze of a child-without-status—someone outside, marginal, and already "othered" by the middle-class society he loathes and seems never to envy; and because the novel masks itself in the comic, parodic, and exaggerated tall-tale format.

On this young but street-smart innocent, Huck, who is virginally uncorrupted by bourgeois yearnings, fury, and helplessness, Mark Twain inscribes a critique of slavery and the pretensions of the would-be middle class, a resistance to the loss of Eden and the difficulty of becoming a social individual. The agency, however, for Huck's struggle is the nigger Jim, and it is absolutely necessary (for reasons I tried to illuminate earlier) that the term *nigger* be inextricable from

Huck's deliberations about who and what he himself is—or, more precisely, is not. The major controversies about the greatness or near greatness of *Huckleberry Finn* as an American (or even "world") novel exist as controversies because they forgo a close examination of the interdependence of slavery and freedom, of Huck's growth and Jim's serviceability within it, and even of Mark Twain's inability to continue, to explore the journey into free territory.

The critical controversy has focused on the collapse of the so-called fatal ending of the novel. It has been suggested that the ending is brilliant finesse that returns Tom Sawyer to the center stage where he should be. Or it is a brilliant play on the dangers and limitations of romance. Or it is a sad and confused ending to the book of an author who, after a long blocked period, lost narrative direction; who changed the serious adult focus back to a child's story out of disgust. Or the ending is a valuable learning experience for Jim and Huck for which we and they should be grateful. What is not stressed is that there is no way, given the confines of the novel, for Huck to mature into a moral human being *in America* without Jim. To let Jim go free, to let him enter the mouth of the Ohio River and pass into free territory, would be to abandon the whole premise of the book. Neither Huck nor Mark Twain can tolerate, in imaginative terms, Jim freed. That would blast the predilection from its mooring.

Thus the fatal ending becomes the elaborate deferment of a necessary and necessarily unfree Africanist character's escape, because freedom has no meaning to Huck or to the text without the specter of enslavement, the anodyne to individualism; the yardstick of absolute power over the life of another; the signed, marked, informing, and mutating presence of a black slave.

The novel addresses at every point in its structural edifice, and lingers over in every fissure, the slave's body and personality: the way it speaks, what passion legal or illicit it is prey to, what pain it can endure, what limits, if any, there are to its suffering, what possibilities there are for forgiveness, compassion, love. Two things strike us in this novel: the apparently limitless store of love and compassion the black man has for his white friend and white masters; and his assumption that the whites are indeed what they say they are, superior and adult. This representation of Jim as the visible other can be read as the yearning of whites for forgiveness and love, but the yearning is made possible only when it is understood that Jim has recognized his inferiority (not as slave, but as black) and despises it. Jim permits his persecutors to torment him, humiliate him, and responds to the torment and humiliation with boundless love. The humiliation that Huck and Tom subject Jim to is baroque, endless, foolish, mind-softening— and it comes *after* we have experienced Jim as an adult, a caring father and a sensitive man. If Jim had been a white ex-convict befriended by Huck, the ending could not have been imagined or written: because it would not have been possible for two children to play so painfully with the life of a white man (regardless of his class, education, or fugitiveness) once he had been revealed to us as a moral adult. Jim's slave status makes play and deferment possible—but it also dramatizes, in style and mode of narration, the connection between slavery and the achievement (in actual and imaginary terms) of freedom. Jim seems unassertive, loving, irrational, passionate, dependent, inarticulate (except for the "talks" he and Huck have, long sweet talks we are not privy to—but what did you talk about, Huck?). It is not what Jim seems that warrants inquiry, but what Mark Twain, Huck, and especially Tom need from him that should solicit our attention. In that sense the book may indeed be "great" because in its structure, in the hell it puts its readers through at the end, the frontal debate it forces, it simulates and describes the parasitical nature of white freedom.

*   *   *

Forty years earlier, in the works of Poe, one sees how the concept of the American 30 self was similarly bound to Africanism, and was similarly covert about its dependency. We can look to "The Gold-Bug" and "How to Write a Blackwood Article" (as well as *Pym*) for samples of the desperate need of this writer with pretensions to the planter class for the literary techniques of "othering" so common to American literature: estranging language, metaphoric condensation, fetishizing strategies, the economy of stereotype, allegorical foreclosure; strategies employed to secure his characters' (and his readers') identity. But there are unmanageable slips. The black slave Jupiter is said to whip his master in "The Gold-Bug"; the black servant Pompey stands mute and judgmental at the antics of his mistress in "A Blackwood Article." And Pym engages in cannibalism *before* he meets the black savages; when he escapes from them and witnesses the death of a black man, he drifts toward the silence of an impenetrable, inarticulate whiteness.

We are reminded of other images at the end of literary journeys into the forbidden space of blackness. Does Faulkner's *Absalom! Absalom!*, after its protracted search for the telling African blood, leave us with just such an image of snow and the eradication of race? Not quite. Shreve sees himself as the inheritor of the blood of African kings; the snow apparently is the wasteland of unmeaning, unfathomable whiteness. Harry's destiny and death dream in Hemingway's Africa is focused on the mountain top "great, high, and unbelievably white in the sun" in "The Snows of Kilimanjaro." *To Have and Have Not* closes with an image of a white boat. William Styron begins and ends Nat Turner's journey with a white, floating marble structure, windowless, doorless, incoherent. In *Henderson the Rain King* Saul Bellow ends the hero's journey to and from his fantastic Africa on the ice, the white frozen wastes. With an Africanist child in his arms, the soul of the Black King in his baggage, Henderson dances, he shouts, over the frozen whiteness, a new white man in a new found land: "leaping, pounding, and tingling over the pure white lining of the gray Arctic silence."

If we follow through on the self-reflexive nature of these encounters with Africanism, it falls clear: images of blackness can be evil *and* protective, rebellious *and* forgiving, fearful *and* desirable—all of the self-contradictory features of the self. Whiteness, alone, is mute, meaningless, unfathomable, pointless, frozen, veiled, curtained, dreaded, senseless, implacable. Or so our writers seem to say.   [1992]

1. In the first chapter of *Playing in the Dark*, Morrison says, "What Africanism became for, and how it functioned in, the literary imagination is of paramount interest because it may be possible to discover, through a close look at literary 'blackness,' the nature—even the cause—of literary 'whiteness.' What is it for? What parts do the invention and development

of whiteness play in the construction of what is loosely described as 'American'?" Does the second chapter, "Romancing the Shadow," contribute to her project? If so, how does it further Morrison's attempt to answer the questions she poses?

2. As a novelist, Morrison has won the Pulitzer Prize for fiction and, in 1993, the Nobel Prize for literature. Characterize her nonfiction writing in this chapter.

3. To what works in this book can Morrison's analysis be applied?

BRENT STAPLES

BRENT STAPLES *(1951–) grew up in poverty, the eldest of nine children in Chester, Pennsylvania. His own brother, a drug dealer, was murdered by one of his "clients." Staples was awarded scholarships to the University of Pennsylvania and to the University of Chicago. His best-selling memoir,* Parallel Time: Growing Up in Black and White, *won awards, but his main occupation has been as a reporter and essayist for newspapers and journals. He writes on education, politics, and culture for the* New York Times *Editorial Board and before that worked as a reporter for the* Chicago Sun Times. *He holds an M.A. and Ph.D. in Psychology from the University of Chicago.*

Black Men and Public Space*

My first victim was a woman—white, well-dressed, probably in her late twenties. I came upon her late one evening on a deserted street in Hyde Park, a relatively affluent neighborhood in an otherwise mean, impoverished section of Chicago. As I swung onto the avenue behind her, there seemed to be a discreet, uninflammatory distance between us. Not so. She cast back a worried glance. To her, the youngish black man—a broad six feet two inches with a beard and billowing hair, both hands shoved into the pockets of a bulky military jacket—seemed menacingly close. After a few more quick glimpses, she picked up her pace and was soon running in earnest. Within seconds, she disappeared into a cross street.

That was more than a decade ago. I was twenty-two years old, a graduate student newly arrived at the University of Chicago. It was in the echo of that terrified woman's footfalls that I first began to know the unwieldy inheritance I'd come into—the ability to alter public space in ugly ways. It was clear that she thought herself the quarry of a mugger, a rapist, or worse. Suffering a bout of insomnia, however, I was stalking sleep, not defenseless wayfarers. As a softy who is scarcely able to take a knife to a raw chicken—let alone hold one to a person's throat—I was surprised, embarrassed, and dismayed all at once. Her flight made me feel like an accomplice in tyranny. It also made it clear that I was indistinguishable from the muggers who occasionally seeped into the area from the surrounding ghetto. That first encounter, and those that followed, signified that a vast, unnerving gulf lay between nighttime pedestrians—particularly

*Brent Staples, "Black Men in Public Spaces," *Harper's* (December, 1986).

women—and me. And I soon gathered that being perceived as dangerous is a hazard in itself. I only needed to turn a corner into a dicey situation, or crowd some frightened, armed person in a foyer somewhere, or make an errant move after being pulled over by a policeman. Where fear and weapons meet—and they often do in urban America—there is always the possibility of death.

In that first year, my first away from my hometown, I was to become thoroughly familiar with the language of fear. At dark, shadowy intersections, I could cross in front of a car stopped at a traffic light and elicit the *thunk*, thunk, thunk, thunk of the driver—black, white, male, or female—hammering down the door locks. On less traveled streets after dark, I grew accustomed to but never comfortable with people crossing to the other side of the street rather than pass me. Then there were the standard unpleasantries with policemen, doormen, bouncers, cabdrivers, and others whose business it is to screen out troublesome individuals *before* there is any nastiness.

I moved to New York nearly two years ago and I have remained an avid night walker. In central Manhattan, the near-constant crowd cover minimizes tense one-on-one street encounters. Elsewhere—in SoHo, for example, where sidewalks are narrow and tightly spaced buildings shut out the sky—things can get very taut indeed.

After dark, on the warrenlike streets of Brooklyn where I live, I often see   5 women who fear the worst from me. They seem to have set their faces on neutral, and with their purse straps strung across their chests bandolier-style, they forge ahead as though bracing themselves against being tackled. I understand, of course, that the danger they perceive is not a hallucination. Women are particularly vulnerable to street violence, and young black males are drastically overrepresented among the perpetrators of that violence. Yet these truths are no solace against the kind of alienation that comes of being ever the suspect, a fearsome entity with whom pedestrians avoid making eye contact.

It is not altogether clear to me how I reached the ripe old age of twenty-two without being conscious of the lethality nighttime pedestrians attributed to me. Perhaps it was because in Chester, Pennsylvania, the small, angry industrial town where I came of age in the 1960s, I was scarcely noticeable against a backdrop of gang warfare, street knifings, and murders. I grew up one of the good boys, had perhaps a half-dozen fistfights. In retrospect, my shyness of combat has clear sources.

As a boy, I saw countless tough guys locked away; I have since buried several, too. They were babies, really—a teenage cousin, a brother of twenty-two, a childhood friend in his mid-twenties—all gone down in episodes of bravado played out in the streets. I came to doubt the virtues of intimidation early on. I chose, perhaps unconsciously, to remain a shadow—timid, but a survivor.

The fearsomeness mistakenly attributed to me in public places often has a perilous flavor. The most frightening of these confusions occurred in the late 1970s and early 1980s, when I worked as a journalist in Chicago. One day, rushing into the office of a magazine I was writing for with a deadline story in hand, I was mistaken for a burglar. The office manager called security and, with an ad hoc posse, pursued me through the labyrinthine halls, nearly to my editor's door. I had no way of proving who I was. I could only move briskly toward the company of someone who knew me.

Another time I was on assignment for a local paper and killing time before an interview. I entered a jewelry store on the city's affluent Near North Side. The proprietor excused herself and returned with an enormous red Doberman pinscher straining at the end of a leash. She stood, the dog extended toward me, silent to my questions, her eyes bulging nearly out of her head. I took a cursory look around, nodded, and bade her good night.

10   Relatively speaking, however, I never fared as badly as another black male journalist. He went to nearby Waukegan, Illinois, a couple of summers ago to work on a story about a murderer who was born there. Mistaking the reporter for the killer, police officers hauled him from his car at gunpoint and but for his press credentials would probably have tried to book him. Such episodes are not uncommon. Black men trade tales like this all the time.

Over the years, I learned to smother the rage I felt at so often being taken for a criminal. Not to do so would surely have led to madness. I now take precautions to make myself less threatening. I move about with care, particularly late in the evening. I give a wide berth to nervous people on subway platforms during the wee hours, particularly when I have exchanged business clothes for jeans. If I happen to be entering a building behind some people who appear skittish, I may walk by, letting them clear the lobby before I return, so as not to seem to be following them. I have been calm and extremely congenial on those rare occasions when I've been pulled over by the police.

And on late-evening constitutionals I employ what has proved to be an excellent tension-reducing measure: I whistle melodies from Beethoven and Vivaldi and the more popular classical composers. Even steely New Yorkers hunching toward nighttime destinations seem to relax, and occasionally they even join in the tune. Virtually everybody seems to sense that a mugger wouldn't be warbling bright, sunny selections from Vivaldi's *Four Seasons*. It is my equivalent of the cowbell that hikers wear when they know they are in bear country.

[1986]

1. Can Allport help to explain why Staples has the effect that he does on strangers on the street? Is their reaction justified in any way? Does Staples think so?
2. Can Allport explain why what Staples calls his "tension-reducing measure" might work?
3. Since the essay is about the impression Staples gives of being threatening, it is important to analyze his *ethos* in the essay. What kind of relationship does he establish with the reader? How does he do it?

VETTA L. SANDERS THOMPSON

VETTA L. SANDERS THOMPSON, *Ph.D., teaches at the University of St. Louis as a member of the core clinical psychology faculty. Her primary research interests are directed to multicultural issues in mental health and racial identification in African Americans. Her primary clinical interests are in the areas of children and families.*

Perceived Experiences of Racism as Stressful Life Events*

ABSTRACT: *The impact of racism on African American personality, behavior, and health has been debated in the psychological literature. There has been little research however, on racism as a stressful life event. The goal of this study was to learn whether perceived racism produces symptoms of subjective distress noted in relationship to other stressful life events. In addition, this study sought to find whether racial identification mediated the psychological impact of perceived experiences of racism. Two hundred African American adults were surveyed. Participants completed a 30 item racial identification measure, a questionnaire that requested information on the experience of racism, and the Impact of Events scale. The results showed that one third of the participants reported a perceived experience of racism within six months of the interview. Mean scores for intrusion symptoms were higher as the seriousness of the reported event increased. While participants reported avoidance symptoms, there were no differences based on the seriousness of the racial incident. Racial identification did not mediate the impact of the experience of racism.*

The issue of the relevance of race, its impact and management, has an extensive recent history in counseling and psychotherapy discussions (Goldberg & Hodes, 1992; Myers & King, 1983; Kupers, 1981; Block, 1980; Griffith, 1977). These issues are difficult to resolve without a discussion of the impact of race and race relations. Traditionally, the impact of racism has been discussed from a sociological perspective and the group impact has received the most attention. A part of the impact, however, involves the individual response and reaction to racism. Yet, a complete consideration of the psychological impact of or reaction to racism has not taken place. The number of hate crimes has increased on college campuses (Youngstrom, 1991) and throughout society (Dovidio, 1993). Events suggest that counselors and therapists must recognize the psychological impact of the experience or perception of racism (Goldberg & Hodes, 1992).

Goldberg & Hodes (1992) noted that many ethnic minorities experience racism. They also note that much of the research conducted fails to provide descriptions of the specific impact of the experience on ethnic minorities. Grier and Cobbs (1968) noted that exposure to racism resulted in suspiciousness, distrust, and anger among African Americans. They viewed these as adaptive responses to racism. The research on the impact of racism has recently focused on the physiological response to a racist event and its health implications. This has occurred although major reviews have suggested that only 12% of the variance in health outcome can be explained by traumatic life events (Anderson, 1991).

Sutherland & Harrell (1986) reported that fearful and racially noxious image scenes resulted in increased heart rate activity. Armstead, Lawler, Gordon, Cross, & Gibbons (1989) noted that exposure to racist stimuli resulted in significant blood pressure increases among African American students. Krieger (1990) reported an association between self reported hypertension and the acceptance of unfair treatment based on race. Anderson (1989), using the experience of racism

*Vetta L. Sanders Thompson, "Perceived Experiences of Racism as Stressful Life Events," *Community Mental Health Journal* 32.3 (June 1996): 223–33.

as a stressor, demonstrated the physiological (increased cardiovascular reactivity) and psychological (anger) reactivity of African Americans to the theme of racism. While these studies focus on the impact of racism on African Americans, it is reasonable to assume that other ethnic group numbers would be similarly affected. In addition, these studies are limited in scope and ignore the need for empirical validation of possible psychological reactions and responses to racism.

Stressful life events have been characterized as those situations that are tension producing and could adversely affect an individual's mental health (Rabkin & Struening, 1976). Lazarus (1984) suggests that stress is a term used to describe an event made up of antecedent, mediating, and response components. Antecedent factors are called stressors, as they are events that elicit a response to stress. The impact of stress is mediated by variables such as self-esteem, racial identity, appraisals and self-efficacy (Anderson, 1991). The response component may involve expressions of distress. Distress is considered a subjective state that occurs when the individual is unable to cope effectively with the stressor.

5   Studies of the psychological response to stressful life events have suggested that intrusion and avoidance symptoms are common (Horowitz, Wilner & Alvarez, 1979). Reports of the subjective impact of stressful life events have included descriptions of troubling dreams, repetitious behavior, and intrusive thoughts and images, characterized as intrusion symptoms. Emotional numbness, denial of the impact and meaning of the event, and blunted sensation are indications of avoidance symptoms (Horowitz, et al., 1979; Horowitz, 1976; Lazarus, 1966). Intrusion and avoidance symptoms are two of the three DSM-IV symptom clusters necessary for a diagnosis of post-traumatic stress disorder (American Psychiatric Association, 1994). The presence of these symptoms, in individuals who report experiences of perceived racism, is therefore diagnostically significant.

Burke (1984), Goldberg & Hodes (1992), and Bullock & Houston (1987) described the responses of individuals of African descent who reported experiences of racism. The reactions appeared consistent with intrusion and avoidance symptoms. Responses included difficulty concentrating, frustration, hypervigilence, denial, withdrawal and avoidance behavior.

Although it has been proposed that the experience of racism is a life stressor (Rabkin & Struening, 1976; Carter, 1982; Kessler & Neighbors, 1986; Miller, 1992), there has been disagreement among professionals regarding the response to victims of racial discrimination (Goldberg & Hodes, 1992; Myers & King, 1983; Thomas & Sillen, 1972). This, besides discomfort with issues of race and ethnicity, has sometimes led therapists to avoid these issues and take a "color-blind" approach (Thomas & Sillen, 1972). Despite Griffith's (1977) suggestion that we discuss race and racial issues in initial therapy sessions with clients, there is a reluctance to do so. Therapists often feel the need for a specific rationale related to potential treatment issues or goals. One method of establishing a rationale for this discussion is to examine whether exposure to racism produces intrusion and avoidance symptoms commonly associated with other stressful life events and post-traumatic stress disorder.

This study was designed to learn whether intrusion and avoidance symptoms occur as individuals respond to perceived experiences of racism. Knowledge of the possible presence or absence of intrusion and avoidance symptoms has treatment implications for counselors and therapists helping clients to cope with these experiences.

While some researchers have explored the impact of racism, little attention has been paid to factors that might mediate the impact of experiencing discrimination. Racial identification may be such a mediating variable. Racial identification refers to the positive and negative attitudes African Americans hold toward the group. Positive racial identification has been noted to have several beneficial outcomes. It purportedly results in a stronger sense of purpose, greater security in self, and an easier acceptance of frustration (Allen & Stukes, 1982). If the outcome of positive racial identity is greater tolerance of frustration and a stronger sense of self, it is plausible that racial identification mediates the impact of racism (Anderson, 1991).

Studies have suggested that strong ethnic identification results in a more active strategy for coping with discrimination (Chavira & Phinney, 1991). Research also suggests that ethnic identity does not mediate the impact of negative messages about the group received from others (Phinney, Chavira & Tate, 1993). This is consistent with Cross's (1985) suggestion that racial identity is a socio-cultural propensity and not a psychological variable. This also suggests that racial identification would not mediate the impact of racism. Thompson Sanders (1991, 1992) suggests that no conclusive results are possible unless racial identification is understood as a multidimensional concept. Resolution of this issue has implications for how therapists work with clients when race related issues are of concern.

In summary, this study attempted to learn whether racism produces the psychological responses noted in relationship to other stressful life events, specifically intrusion and avoidance symptoms. In addition, racial identification was explored as a variable that might mediate the impact of the experience of racism on the individual. Specific hypotheses tested were:

1. Intrusion and avoidance symptoms are noted when there is a perceived experience of racism and the level of distress varies with the type of racism experienced.
2. Psychological, cultural and physical racial identifications mediate the subjective distress reported following a perceived experience of racism, i.e., as psychological, cultural and physical racial identifications increase reported intrusion and avoidance symptoms decrease.
3. Socio-political racial identification has no impact on reported subjective distress.

Method

Subjects

Three hundred and eighteen African Americans were asked to participate in the study. One hundred and eighteen potential participants refused, citing reasons including lack of time, lack of interest, and difficulty understanding what was required. This resulted in a refusal rate of 37 percent. The final sample consisted of 200 participants, including 114 females and 82 males. All participants were eighteen years of age or older and resided in the St. Louis Metropolitan area. The mean age of participants was 33.5 years, with a mean age of 33.5 years for males and 34.0 years for females. The median income for the sample was $22,500. Ten percent of the sample had failed to complete high school, 20.4 percent had completed high school, 37.2 percent had some college, 14.3 percent were college graduates, and 17.7 percent reported graduate education.

Instruments

Dependent Variables: Avoidance and Intrusion Symptoms. The Impact of Events scale is a measure of subjective distress in response to a specific, serious life event (Horowitz, et al., 1979). The scale yields scores for two subscales found to coincide with two major response sets noted in relationship to stressful life events—intrusion and avoidance. Participants were required to describe the event that served as referent in detail. This was done to increase the accuracy of responses related to the event.

Intrusion is characterized by "unbidden thoughts and images, troubled dreams, strong pangs or waves of feelings and repetitive behavior" (Horowitz, et. al., 1979, p. 210). The intrusion scale is composed of seven items. The scale included items such as "I had dreams about it," "Any reminders brought back feelings about it" and "I had strong feelings about it." The scale obtained an internal consistency score, using Cronbach's alpha, of .78. Test-retest reliability was .89. Avoidance was characterized by "ideational constriction, denial of the meanings and consequences of the event, blunted sensation, behavioral inhibition and awareness of emotional numbness" (Horowitz, et al., 1979, p. 210). The avoidance scale is composed of eight items. The scale included items such as "I avoided reminders of it," "I tried not to think of it" and "I tried not to talk about it." The scale obtained an internal consistency score of .82 and test-retest reliability was .79.

15   Participants reported whether each item on the scale had been experienced within the past 10, 30, and 90 days. The most recent racial experience, within six months, served as the referent. Responses to symptoms were reported as not experienced at all, rarely experienced, sometimes experienced, or often experienced.

Racial Identification. The Multi-dimensional Racial Identification Scale was used in this study (Myers & Thompson, in press; Thompson Sanders, 1991). Items were rated on a 5-point Likert scale, with responses ranging from strongly agree to strongly disagree.

Psychological identity items examined the individual's sense of concern for and commitment to the racial group. The 13 items on this subscale included questions concerning the individual's sense of group membership, responsibility, and group pride. The alpha coefficient for this scale was .87 and test-retest reliability at three weeks was .93. Socio-political identity items examined the individual's attitude toward social and economic issues. These five items included questions on attitudes concerned with economic and political opportunity and advancement for African Americans. The internal consistency coefficient was .62 and test-retest reliability at three weeks was .89. Six items on the physical identity subscale examined individual acceptance of physical features associated with African Americans. The internal consistency coefficient was .73 and test-retest reliability at three weeks was .89. There were three items on the cultural subscale that referred to an awareness, knowledge, and acceptance of the cultural and social traditions of African Americans. The internal consistency coefficient was .85 and test-retest reliability at three weeks was .92.

Racism. Participants reported whether they had ever experienced racism and whether they had experienced racism in the last six months. Racism was described as an unfavorable, unfair, or insulting event or action that occurred due to their skin color or group membership. Three examples of racism were provided if, and only if, a participant requested it. The examples were: loss of job due to race, refusal of housing due to race, or derogatory names that were racial in nature. Participants were asked to provide a written description of the most recent racial incident within six months. Incidents coded as racism involved events such as a participant reporting being called a "nigger." The participant said that the slur was used in front of co-workers, yet no action was taken against the employee who made the statement. Another incident involved a family living in a predominantly White neighborhood. They reported police and fire department harassment, although attorneys and City Hall officials reportedly told them that they were not violating city ordinances.

Three raters were trained by the primary investigator to categorize racial incidents. Descriptions were categorized as minor, moderate, and major. Minor incidents were those involving name calling, gestures, obscene or offensive language that was racially motivated or had racial overtones. Moderate incidents involved unfavorable work assignments, grades, evaluations, or treatment believed to be racially motivated. Major events involved personal loss of a job, wages, housing, etc. due to race. Inter-rater reliability was 89.6 percent for 62 participant descriptions.

Procedure

The data were collected between June of 1992 and May of 1993. The 1980 census tract data (U.S. Department of Commerce, 1980) were used to select neighborhoods to be surveyed. Census tracts containing 400 or more African Americans were randomly selected for survey. Five African American research assistants surveyed participants residing within assigned census tract areas.

Surveys were administered individually by research assistants. Solicitation was door to door within an assigned census tract. Participants completed the questionnaire in their home in a single session. The study was described as a project concerned with individual experiences of race relations. A research assistant was available to answer and explain questions. They read items and/or provided writing assistance as requested by participants. There was no remuneration for participation.

Results

The data showed that 33.8 percent of the participants reported an experience of racism within six months of the interview (N = 66). Chi square analyses indicated that there were no significant differences in reporting by sex, education or income. Of those participants reporting experiences of racism, 33.33 percent reported minor experiences; 43.94 percent, moderate experiences; 16.67 percent, severe; and 6.06 percent could not be classified. The mean intrusion score for participants reporting experiences with racism was X = 14.68 (N = 63) at 10 days, X = 14.12 (N = 59) at 30 days and X = 12.04 (N = 57) at 90 days. The mean avoidance score was X = 13.34 (N = 65) at 10 days, X = 16.75 (N = 59) at 30 days and X = 15.23 (N = 57) at 90 days. The mean intrusion and avoidance scores by level of racism experienced are reported in Table 1.

To learn which variables significantly predicted intrusion and avoidance scores in response to the experience of racism, a hierarchical multiple regression analysis was conducted for each scale. Variables of interest entered into each of the multiple regression equations were: sex, level of racism experienced, psychological racial identification, cultural racial identification, physical racial identification, and socio-political racial identification.

The multiple regression equations for intrusion scores at 10 days ($F(6,42)$ = 2.47, $p < .03$; $R^2 = .29$), 30 days ($F(6,42) = 2.75$, $p < .02$; $R^2 = .31$) and 90 days ($F(6,42) = 18$, $p < .001$; $R^2 = .41$) were significant. The multiple regression equations for avoidance scores were not significant at 10 days ($F(6,42) = .86$, $p < .54$; $R^2 = .13$), 30 days ($F(6,42) = .69$, $p < .68$; $R^2 = .10$) and 90 days ($F(6,42) = 1.08$, $p < .39$; $R^2 = .15$). Significance tests for each variable entered into the equation indicated that sex and racial identification were not significantly associated with intrusion or avoidance scores. Significance tests indicated that the level of racism was associated with intrusion scores at 10 days ($t(1,42) = 2.75$, $p < .009$), 30 days ($t(1,42) = 3.54$, $p < .001$) and 90 days ($t(1,42) = 4.09$, $p < .0002$). There was no association between level of racism and avoidance scores. There was a trend for level of racism experienced to affect

TABLE 1 *Mean Intrusion and Avoidance Scores by Level of Racism*

		Level of Racism*				
	Minor		Moderate		Severe	
Intrusion						
10 Days	N = 22	X = 10.57	N = 29	X = 17.63	N = 11	X = 22.33
30 Days†	N = 22	X = 9.68	N = 28	X = 15.28	N = 9	X = 16.56
90 Days‡	N = 22	X = 7.56	N = 27	X = 12.19	N = 9	X = 18.33
Avoidance						
10 Days	N = 22	X = 12.21	N = 29	X = 15.21	N = 11	X = 12.33
30 Days†	N = 22	X = 12.67	N = 28	X = 16.79	N = 9	X = 18.67
90 Days‡	N = 22	X = 10.64	N = 27	X = 16.30	N = 9	X = 19.00

*Four participants provided insufficient information to allow categorization of the level of racism.
†One participant incident was too recent to respond at 30 days.
‡Two participant incidents were too recent to respond at 90 days.

avoidance scores at 90 days (t(1,42) = 2.92, $p < .07$). Hierarchical regression equations were completed to learn whether income or education affected the reported experience of racism. No significant relationship was found.

Scheffe's test for multiple comparisons of means was conducted to detect which differences in mean intrusion scores by level of racism were significant. In cases of minor and moderate, and minor and severe racial experiences, mean intrusion scores were significantly different. The differences between mean intrusion scores for moderate and severe racial experiences were not significant. The differences between mean intrusion scores by level of racism was significant at 10 days (F(42) = 3.20, $p < .05$), 30 days (F(42) = 3.21, $p < .05$) and 90 days (F(42)= 3.23, $p < .05$).

Discussion

The purpose of this study was to learn whether the perception of racism produces measurable psychological distress. One third of the participants in this study reported an experience with racism within the six months before the interview. Mean scores for avoidance and intrusion symptoms suggested that individuals reporting experiences with racism experienced subjective distress. Episodes of intrusive thinking and periods of avoidance were noted. The presence of retrospectively reported intrusion symptoms decreased over time, while retrospectively reported avoidance symptoms increased over time. Avoidance behavior was reported at a clinically significant level at 30 and 90 days. Regression analyses suggested that the type of racial experience was related to the level of intrusion symptoms reported.

While the level of intrusion symptoms was associated with the level of racism reported, only the differences between the mean intrusion scores for minor and moderate and minor and severe levels of racism were significant. There was no difference between mean intrusion scores for moderate and severe levels of racism. The mean avoidance scores did not vary significantly by level of racism experienced. There was a trend toward this effect.

There was no support for the hypothesis that racial identification mediated the impact of the experience of racism. This is consistent with research on the mediating effect of ethnic identification (Phinney, Chavira & Tate, 1993). It is possible that an alternate measure [of] racial identification might have yielded different results. For example, a measure of the stage of racial identification might have provided a psychologically oriented variable that had mediating effects. An alternate hypothesis is that racial identification does not mediate the distress experienced in response to racism because it is a socio-cultural propensity (Cross, 1985). If this view is correct, racial identification might more appropriately be thought to have an influence on attributions made following experiences of racism. It might also influence coping methods when discrimination has occurred. This possibility should be explored in future research.

These results suggest that the experience of racism, like other stressful life events, produces measurable reports of subjective distress. The presence of intrusion and avoidance symptoms suggests a reaction similar to post-traumatic stress disorder. The diagnosis of this disorder also requires arousal symptoms that were not assessed in this study. The perceived experience of racism should be explored further to decide its relationship to a diagnosis of post-traumatic stress disorder.

30   While this study focused on the experiences of African Americans, there is no reason to believe that the psychological impact of racism/discrimination is different for members of other ethnic or racial groups. Future research should consider the impact of racism/discrimination on members of various racial/ethnic groups.

It is important to note that these results were obtained using a non-clinical community solicited sample. However, caution is warranted in the interpretation of the data. The data are retrospective, creating a possible bias in response. Respondents have been found poor historians in the accurate recall of life events. Future studies should focus on individuals who are seeking therapy and/or legal remedy due to the perception of a racially discriminatory experience.

Although it has been proposed that racism is a life stressor (Rabkin & Struening, 1976; Miller, 1992), there has been disagreement among professionals, as well as the larger society, as to the prevalence and impact of racism (Myers & King, 1983; Thomas & Sillen, 1972). The data presented in this study suggest that individuals who perceive the experience of racism experience measurable psychological distress. The results of this study have important implications for the management of racial issues in therapy and counseling. While many studies have focused on the experience of anger, this study suggests that this is not the only concern. One participant wrote a special note to the researcher that emphasized the emotional experience of racism. The experience was described as one of hurt and pain.

As the number of hate crimes increases on college campuses (Youngstrom, 1991) and throughout society (Dovidio, 1993), these data suggest that counselors and therapist[s] must recognize the psychological impact of these events. Mental health professionals must be trained to intervene appropriately with clients who report distress. "Only an awareness of racism and a readiness to hear about its effects will allow therapists to discuss the issue adequately with clients" (Goldberg & Hodes, 1992, p. 63).

References

Allen, W. & Stukes, S. (1982). Black family lifestyles and the mental health of black Americans. In F. Munoz & R. Endo (Eds.), *Perspectives on minority group mental health*, (pp. 43–52). Washington, D.C.: University Press of America, Inc.

American Psychiatric Association (1994). *Diagnostic & Statistical Manual of Mental Disorders, Fourth Edition*. Washington, D.C.: American Psychiatric Association.

Anderson, L.P. (1991). Acculturative stress: A theory of relevance to Black Americans. *Clinical Psychology Review*, 11, 685–702.

Anderson, N.B. (1989). Racial differences in stress-induced cardiovascular reactivity and hypertension: Current status and substantive issues. *Psychological Bulletin*, 105, 89–105.

Armstead, C., Lawler, K., Gordon, G., Cross, J., & Gibbons, J. (1989). Relationship of racial stressors to blood pressure responses and anger expression in black college students. *Health Psychology*, 8, 541–556.

Block, C. (1980). Black Americans and the cross cultural counseling experience. In A.J. Marsella & P.B. Pederson (Eds.). *Cross-cultural counseling and psychotherapy*. New York: Pergamon.

Bullock, S.C. & Houston, E. (1987). Perceptions of racism by Black medical students attending White medical schools. *Journal of the National Medical Association*, 79, 601–608.

Burke, A.W. (1984). Racism and psychological disturbances among West Indians in Britain. *International Journal of Social Psychiatry*, 30, 50–68.

Carter, J.H. (1982). Alcoholism in Black Vietnam veterans: Symptoms of post-traumatic stress disorder. *Journal of the National Medical Association*, 74, 655–660.

Chavira, V. & Phinney, J. (1991). Adolescents' ethnic identity, self-esteem & strategies for dealing with ethnicity and minority status. *Hispanic Journal of Behavioral Sciences*, 13, 226–227.

Cross, W.E. (1985). Black identity: Rediscovering the distinction between personal identity and reference group orientation. In M.B. Spencer, G. Brookins & W.R. Allen (Eds.), *Beginnings: The Social and affective development of black children*, (pp. 155–171). N.J.: Lawrence Erlbaum.

Dovidio, J. (1993). The subtlety of racism. *Training and Development*, 47, 51–57.

Goldberg, D. & Hodes, M. (1992). The poison of racism and the self-poisoning of adolescents. *Journal of Family Therapy*, 14, 51–67.

Grier, W.H. & Cobbs, P.M. (1968). *Black Rage*. New York: Basic Books.

Griffith, M.S. (1977). The influence of race on the psychotherapeutic relationship. *Psychiatry*, 40, 27–40.

Horowitz, M.J. (1976). *Stress Response Syndromes*. New York: Aronson.

Horowitz, M.J., Wilner, N., & Alvarez, W. (1979). Impact of Event Scale: A measure of subjective stress. *Psychosomatic Medicine*, 41, 209–218.

Kessler, R.C. & Neighbors, H.W. (1986). A new perspective on the relationships among race, social class and psychological distress. *Journal of Health and Social Behavior*, 27, 107–115.

Krieger, N. (1990). Racial and gender discrimination: Risk factors for high blood pressure? *Social Science Medicine*, 30, 1273–1281.

Kupers, T. (1981). *Public Therapy: The practice of psychotherapy in the public mental health clinic*. New York: Macmillan.

Lazarus, R.S. (1966). *Psychological Stress and the Coping Process*. New York: McGraw-Hill.

Lazarus, R.S. (1984). Puzzles in the study of daily hassles. *Journal of Behavioral Medicine*, 7, 375–384.

Miller, F.S. (1992). Network structure support: Its relationship to the psychosocial development of black females. In A.K. Burlew, W.C. Banks, H.P. McAdoo, & D.A. ya Azibo (Eds.), *African American Psychology: Theory research, and practice*, (pp. 105–123). Newbury Park: Sage.

Myers, H.F. & King, L.M. (1983). Mental health issues in the development of the black American child. In G. Powell (Ed.), *The psychosocial development of minority group children*, (pp. 275–306). New York: Brunner/Mazel.

Myers, M. & Thompson Sanders, V.L. (in press). An evaluation of two culture specific instruments. *Western Journal of Black Studies.*

Phinney, J., Chavira, V. & Tate, J.(1993). The effect of ethnic threat on ethnic self-concept and own group ratings. *The Journal of Social Psychology*, 133(4), 469–478.

Rabkin, J.G. & Struening, E.L. (1976). Life events, stress, and illness. *Science*, 194, 1013–1020.

Sutherland, M.E. & Harrell, J.P. (1986–87). Individual differences in physiological responses to fearful, racially noxious, and neutral imagery. *Imagination, Cognition, and Personality*, 6, 133–149.

Thompson Sanders, V.L. (1991). A multidimensional approach to the assessment of African American racial identification. *The Western Journal of Black Studies*, 15, 154–158.

Thompson Sanders, V.L. (1992). A multifaceted approach to the conceptualization of African American identification. *Journal of Black Studies*, 23, 75–85.

Thomas, A. & Sillen, S. (1972). *Racism and Psychiatry*. NJ: The Citadel Press.

Uhlenhuth, E.H., Haberman, S.J., Balter, M.D., & Lipman, R.S. (1977). Remembering life events. In J.S. Strauss, H.M. Babigan, & M. Roff (Ed.), *The origins and course of psychopathology* (pp. 117–134). New York: Plenum Press.

Youngstrom, N. (1991). Campus life polluted for many by hate acts. *American Psychological Association Monitor*, 22(#11), 38.   [1996]

1. What hypotheses did Thompson set out to test?
2. How did she test them?
3. What were her conclusions? Lay out the claims, reasons, and assumptions of her research report.
4. What other conclusions was Thompson able to draw from her data?
5. Make a list of the important features of this research report.
6. What was Thompson's motive for doing the study? What is her *ethos* as a narrator of the report?
7. On what other selections in this book can Thompson's article shed light?

CHAPTER SIXTEEN

Ethical Questions

INTRODUCTION

Since life seems constantly to be presenting us with choices of how to feel, think, and act, one of literature's consistent concerns is moral behavior. Literature doesn't often present principles of morality in systematic ways, as moral philosophers do. Rather its strength is the representation of people making choices. Many of the choices have moral implications and raise questions about right and wrong ways to behave. What do we owe to other people and ourselves? How do we define good and bad behavior, virtue and vice, and what are the sources of our definitions? How is our sense of justice related to the laws of a particular society? Since narrative thrives on conflict, it sometimes puts characters in situations calling forth conflicting desires and conflicting duties, asking how they should make their decisions.

Questions like these have already been raised in the selections in other chapters. Most obviously, the texts of the three major monotheisms in Chapter 12, "Spirit," set out human beings' obligations to themselves, each other, and their creator. "The Legend of the Buddha Shakyamuni" does the same in narrative form without reference to a creator. In selections in this chapter, as well as others in the book, you will be able to see how literature can function almost as a laboratory in which characters make and justify moral decisions, allowing you to watch how they choose and the consequences of their choices.

POETRY

JULIA ALVAREZ

JULIA ALVAREZ *(1950–) was born in New York City but raised in the Dominican Republic until her family returned to the United States when she was ten because of her father's political opposition to the dictatorship of Trujillo. The roots of the opposition movement form the basis for her novel* In the Time of Butterflies, *which was made into a film with Salma Hayek, Marc Anthony, and Edward James Olmos. Alvarez's other books include* Homecoming, How the Garcia Girls Lost Their Accents, The Other Side: El Otro Lado, *and* AYO. *She writes essays, stories, and poems for the* New Yorker, USA Weekend, *and other journals.*

On Not Shoplifting Louise Bogan's The Blue Estuaries

Connecticut College, Fall 1968

Your book surprised me on the bookstore shelf—
swans gliding on a blueblack lake;
no blurbs by the big boys on back;
no sassy, big-haired picture
5   to complicate the achievement;
no mentors musing
over how they had discovered
you had it in you
before you even knew
10 you had it in you.
The swans posed on a placid lake,
your name blurred underwater
sinking to the bottom.
I had begun to haunt
15 the poetry shelf at the college store—
thin books crowded in by texts,
reference tomes and a spread
of magazines for persistent teens
on how to get their boys,
20 Chaucer-Milton-Shakespeare-Yeats.
Your name was not familiar,
I took down the book and read.

Page after page, your poems
were stirring my own poems—
25 words rose, breaking the surface,
shattering an old silence.
I leaned closer to the print
until I could almost feel
the blue waters drawn
30 into the tip of my pen.
I bore down on the page,
the lake flowed out again,
the swans, the darkening sky.
For a moment I lost my doubts,
35 my girl's voice, my coming late
into this foreign alphabet.
I read and wrote as I read.

I wanted to own this moment.
My breath came quickly, thinking it over—
I had no money, no one was looking.   40
The swans posed on the cover,
their question-mark necks arced
over the dark waters.
I was asking them what to do . . .
The words they swam over answered.   45
I held the book closed before me
as if it were something else,
a mirror reflecting back
someone I was becoming.
The swans dipped their alphabet necks   50
in the blueblack ink of the lake.
I touched their blank, downy sides, musing,
and I put the book back.   [1995]

1. Why doesn't the speaker steal the book?
2. Characterize the diction of the poem and other qualities of its language.
3. What is the impact of the image in ll. 11–13?

JOHN BALABAN

JOHN BALABAN *(1943–) gave up his student deferment during the Vietnam War,
registering as a conscientious objector and insisting on doing his alternative service
in Vietnam, where he was wounded while working with the Committee of Responsibility to Save War-Injured Children. He returned with a grant because he had been
captivated by Vietnamese poetry. He learned Vietnamese, collected Vietnamese folk
poetry by wandering the countryside with a tape recorder and asking people to
recite (actually sing) the poems they knew, and studied the higher style poetry of
early nineteenth-century court poet Hồ Xuân Hu'o'ng. His translations of her
poetry have been published as* Spring Essence *(see p. 752). He is working with
linguists to digitize and preserve Nôm, the rarified language in which she wrote.
He has written a memoir about his experiences,* Remembering Heaven's Face:
A Story of Rescue in Wartime Vietnam. *With Nguyen Qui Duc, he has edited*
Vietnam: A Traveler's Literary Companion. *Balaban's own book of poetry,*
Locusts at the Edge of Summer *(1997), was nominated for the 1997 National
Book Award and won the William Carlos Williams Award of the Poetry Society of
America. His other books include* After Our War, Blue Mountain, *and* Words
for My Daughter, *which was selected for the 1992 National Poetry Series. He is
Poet-in-Residence and Professor of English at North Carolina State University.*

For the Missing in Action

Hazed with heat and harvest dust
the air swam with flying husks
as men whacked rice sheaves into bins

and all across the sun-struck fields
5   red flags hung from bamboo poles.
Beyond the last treeline on the horizon
beyond the coconut palms and eucalyptus
out in the moon-zone puckered by bombs
the dead earth where no one ventures,
10 the boys found it, foolish boys
riding buffaloes in craterlands
where at night bombs thump and ghosts howl.
A green patch on the raw earth.
And now they've led the farmers here,
15 the kerchiefed women in baggy pants,
the men with sickles and flails, chidren
herding ducks with switches—all
staring from a crater berm; silent:
In that dead place the weeds had formed a man
20 where someone died and fertilized the earth, with flesh
and blood, with tears, with longing for loved ones.
No scrap remained; not even a buckle
survived the monsoons, just a green creature,
a viny man, supine, with posies for eyes,
25 butterflies for buttons, a lily for a tongue.
Now when huddled asleep together
the farmers hear a rustly footfall
as the leaf-man rises and stumbles to them.   [1997]

1. Who are "the Missing in Action" referred to in the poem's title? What context does this phrase immediately create for the poem? What evidence in the poem confirms your answer?
2. This poem weds images of destruction with images of creation. Identify examples of each kind of image and analyze how their union produces the poem's theme.
3. What does the poem argue about the relationship between human beings and the larger world of which they are a part?
4. To what other works in this section can you connect this poem?
5. What disciplines would provide greater context for understanding this poem?

The Guard at the Binh Thuy Bridge

How still he stands as mists begin to move,
as curling, morning billows creep across
his cooplike, concrete sentry perched mid-bridge
over mid-muddy river. Stares at bush green banks
5 which bristle rifles, mortars, men—perhaps.
No convoys shake the timbers. No sound

but water slapping boat sides, bank sides, pilings.
He's slung his carbine barrel down to keep
the boring dry, and two banana-clips instead of one
are taped to make, now, forty rounds instead   10
of twenty. Droplets bead from stock to sight;
they bulb, then strike his boot. He scrapes his heel,
and sees no box bombs floating toward his bridge.
Anchored in red morning mist a narrow junk
rocks its weight. A woman kneels on deck   15
staring at lapping water. Wets her face.
Idly the thick Rach Binh Thuy slides by.
He aims. At her. Then drops his aim. Idly.   [1997]

1. The speaker tells us that the guard stands watch in "his cooplike, concrete
   sentry perched mid-bridge / over mid-muddy river" (ll. 3–4). What does this
   description tell us about the guard's literal and metaphorical position in the
   social context in which he finds himself?
2. What is a "junk"? What does the woman who "kneels on [its] deck"
   (l. 15) represent—for the guard, for the speaker, and for readers of the
   poem?
3. Comment on the significance of the repetition of the word *idly* in the last
   two lines.
4. What disciplines would provide greater context for understanding this
   poem?

☺☺☺

EMILY DICKINSON

(For biographical notes, see p. 255.)

OLC

The Soul selects her own Society

The Soul selects her own Society—
Then—shuts the Door—
To her divine Majority—
Present no more—

Unmoved—she notes the Chariots—pausing—   5
At her low Gate—
Unmoved—an Emperor be kneeling
Upon her Mat—

I've known her—from an ample nation—
Choose One—   10
Then—close the Valves of her attention—
Like Stone—   [1862]

1. Characterize the "soul" described in this poem.
2. What is the effect of the isolationism depicted here? Can individuals successfully close themselves off from the larger world?
3. To what other works in this section can you connect this poem?

ROBERT FROST

OLC

(For biographical notes, see p. 748.)

The Death of the Hired Man

Mary sat musing on the lamp-flame at the table
Waiting for Warren. When she heard his step,
She ran on tip-toe down the darkened passage
To meet him in the doorway with the news
5   And put him on his guard. 'Silas is back.'
She pushed him outward with her through the door
And shut it after her. 'Be kind,' she said.
She took the market things from Warren's arms
And set them on the porch, then drew him down
10   To sit beside her on the wooden steps.

'When was I ever anything but kind to him?
But I'll not have the fellow back,' he said.
'I told him so last haying, didn't I?
"If he left then," I said, "that ended it."
15   What good is he? Who else will harbour him
At his age for the little he can do?
What help he is there's no depending on.
Off he goes always when I need him most.
"He thinks he ought to earn a little pay,
20   Enough at least to buy tobacco with,
So he won't have to beg and be beholden."
"All right," I say, "I can't afford to pay
Any fixed wages, though I wish I could."
"Someone else can." "Then someone else will have to."
25   I shouldn't mind his bettering himself
If that was what it was. You can be certain,
When he begins like that, there's someone at him
Trying to coax him off with pocket-money,—
In haying time, when any help is scarce.
30   In winter he comes back to us. I'm done.'

'Sh! not so loud: he'll hear you,' Mary said.

'I want him to: he'll have to soon or late.'

'He's worn out. He's asleep beside the stove.
When I came up from Rowe's I found him here,
Huddled against the barn-door fast asleep,   35
A miserable sight, and frightening, too—
You needn't smile—I didn't recognise him—
I wasn't looking for him—and he's changed.
Wait till you see.'

        'Where did you say he'd been?'

'He didn't say. I dragged him to the house,   40
And gave him tea and tried to make him smoke.
I tried to make him talk about his travels.
Nothing would do: he just kept nodding off.'

'What did he say? Did he say anything?'

'But little.'   45

        'Anything? Mary, confess
He said he'd come to ditch the meadow for me.'

'Warren!'

        'But did he? I just want to know.'

'Of course he did. What would you have him say?
Surely you wouldn't grudge the poor old man
Some humble way to save his self-respect.   50
He added, if you really care to know,
He meant to clear the upper pasture, too.
That sounds like something you have heard before?
Warren, I wish you could have heard the way
He jumbled everything. I stopped to look   55
Two or three times—he made me feel so queer—
To see if he was talking in his sleep.
He ran on Harold Wilson—you remember—
The boy you had in haying four years since.
He's finished school, and teaching in his college.   60
Silas declares you'll have to get him back.
He says they two will make a team for work:
Between them they will lay this farm as smooth!
The way he mixed that in with other things.
He thinks young Wilson a likely lad, though daft   65
On education—you know how they fought
All through July under the blazing sun,
Silas up on the cart to build the load,
Harold along beside to pitch it on.'

'Yes, I took care to keep well out of earshot.'   70

'Well, those days trouble Silas like a dream.
You wouldn't think they would. How some things linger!

Harold's young college boy's assurance piqued him.
After so many years he still keeps finding
75 Good arguments he sees he might have used.
I sympathise. I know just how it feels
To think of the right thing to say too late.
Harold's associated in his mind with Latin.
He asked me what I thought of Harold's saying
80 He studied Latin like the violin
Because he liked it—that an argument!
He said he couldn't make the boy believe
He could find water with a hazel prong—
Which showed how much good school had ever done him.
85 He wanted to go over that. But most of all
He thinks if he could have another chance
To teach him how to build a load of hay—'

'I know, that's Silas' one accomplishment.
He bundles every forkful in its place,
90 And tags and numbers it for future reference,
So he can find and easily dislodge it
In the unloading. Silas does that well.
He takes it out in bunches like big birds' nests.
You never see him standing on the hay
95 He's trying to lift, straining to lift himself.'

'He thinks if he could teach him that, he'd be
Some good perhaps to someone in the world.
He hates to see a boy the fool of books.
Poor Silas, so concerned for other folk,
100 And nothing to look backward to with pride,
And nothing to look forward to with hope,
So now and never any different.'

Part of a moon was falling down the west,
Dragging the whole sky with it to the hills.
105 Its light poured softly in her lap. She saw it
And spread her apron to it. She put out her hand
Among the harp-like morning-glory strings,
Taut with the dew from garden bed to eaves,
As if she played unheard some tenderness
110 That wrought on him beside her in the night.
'Warren,' she said, 'he has come home to die:
You needn't be afraid he'll leave you this time.'

'Home,' he mocked gently.

                              'Yes, what else but home?
It all depends on what you mean by home.
115 Of course he's nothing to us, any more

Than was the hound that came a stranger to us
Out of the woods, worn out upon the trail.'

'Home is the place where, when you have to go there,
They have to take you in.'

                  'I should have called it
Something you somehow haven't to deserve.'   120

Warren leaned out and took a step or two,
Picked up a little stick, and brought it back
And broke it in his hand and tossed it by.
'Silas has better claim on us you think
Than on his brother? Thirteen little miles   125
As the road winds would bring him to his door.
Silas has walked that far no doubt to-day.
Why didn't he go there? His brother's rich,
A somebody—director in the bank.'

'He never told us that.'   130

                 'We know it though.'

'I think his brother ought to help, of course.
I'll see to that if there is need. He ought of right
To take him in, and might be willing to—
He may be better than appearances.
But have some pity on Silas. Do you think   135
If he had any pride in claiming kin
Or anything he looked for from his brother,
He'd keep so still about him all this time?'

'I wonder what's between them.'

                  'I can tell you.
Silas is what he is—we wouldn't mind him—   140
But just the kind that kinsfolk can't abide.
He never did a thing so very bad.
He don't know why he isn't quite as good
As anybody. Worthless though he is,
He won't be made ashamed to please his brother.'   145

'I can't think Si ever hurt anyone.'

'No, but he hurt my heart the way he lay
And rolled his old head on that sharp-edged chair-back
He wouldn't let me put him on the lounge.
You must go in and see what you can do.   150
I made the bed up for him there to-night.
You'll be surprised at him—how much he's broken.
His working days are done; I'm sure of it.'

'I'd not be in a hurry to say that.'

155 'I haven't been. Go, look, see for yourself.
But, Warren, please remember how it is:
He's come to help you ditch the meadow.
He has a plan. You mustn't laugh at him.
He may not speak of it, and then he may.
160 I'll sit and see if that small sailing cloud
Will hit or miss the moon.'

        It hit the moon.
Then there were three there, making a dim row,
The moon, the little silver cloud, and she.

Warren returned—too soon, it seemed to her,
165 Slipped to her side, caught up her hand and waited.

'Warren?' she questioned.

       'Dead,' was all he answered.   [1915]

1. Identify each of the following characters and their relationship to one
   another: Warren, Mary, Silas, Harold Wilson.
2. This poem presents a debate between husband and wife about their duty to
   a laborer on their farm. Outline the two sides to this debate. Which character presents the stronger case? Why?
3. How does Gilligan and Attanucci's article, "Two Moral Orientations" (see
   p. 156 in Chapter 8) help illuminate the nature of the two opposing
   positions adopted by the husband and wife in this poem?
4. According to Jennifer Saul, men's and women's responses in studies like
   Gilligan and Attanucci can be further analyzed to show that both genders
   tend to use the care orientation in situations having to do with their homes
   and justice orientations in situations having to do with work. Such analysis
   reduces the separation between men's and women's moral orientation (see
   www.mhhe.com/ferster).[1] How might this observation affect our interpretation of the poem?
5. Compare this poem to the other poems by Frost in this section.

OLC   [1]Jennifer Saul, *Feminism: Issues & Arguments* (Oxford: Oxford University Press, 2003). For
more information, see www.mhhe.com/ferster.

Love and a Question

A stranger came to the door at eve,
  And he spoke the bridegroom fair.
He bore a green-white stick in his hand,
  And, for all burden, care.
5 He asked with the eyes more than the lips
  For a shelter for the night,
And he turned and looked at the road afar
  Without a window light.

The bridegroom came forth into the porch
10   With, 'Let us look at the sky,

And question what of the night to be,
  Stranger, you and I.'
The woodbine leaves littered the yard,
  The woodbine berries were blue,
Autumn, yes, winter was in the wind;   15
  'Stranger, I wish I knew.'

Within, the bride in the dusk alone
  Bent over the open fire,
Her face rose-red with the glowing coal
  And the thought of the heart's desire.   20
The bridegroom looked at the weary road,
  Yet saw but her within,
And wished her heart in a case of gold
  And pinned with a silver pin.

The bridegroom thought it little to give   25
  A dole of bread, a purse,
A heartfelt prayer for the poor of God,
  Or for the rich a curse;
But whether or not a man was asked
  To mar the love of two   30
By harboring woe in the bridal house,
  The bridegroom wished he knew.   [1915]

1. What is the question referred to in the title of this poem? Is it answered?
2. How do the time of day, season, and weather relate to the theme of this poem?
3. What conceptual frameworks can enhance our understanding of this poem?

Two Tramps in Mud Time

Out of the mud two strangers came
And caught me splitting wood in the yard.
And one of them put me off my aim
By hailing cheerily "Hit them hard!"
I knew pretty well why he dropped behind   5
And let the other go on a way.
I knew pretty well what he had in mind:
He wanted to take my job for pay.

Good blocks of oak it was I split,
As large around as the chopping block;   10
And every piece I squarely hit
Fell splinterless as a cloven rock.
The blows that a life of self-control
Spares to strike for the common good,
That day, giving a loose to my soul,   15
I spent on the unimportant wood.

The sun was warm but the wind was chill.
You know how it is with an April day
When the sun is out and the wind is still,
20 You're one month on in the middle of May.
But if you so much as dare to speak,
A cloud comes over the sunlit arch,
A wind comes off a frozen peak,
And you're two months back in the middle of March.

25 A bluebird comes tenderly up to alight
And turns to the wind to unruffle a plume
His song so pitched as not to excite
A single flower as yet to bloom.
It is snowing a flake: and he half knew
30 Winter was only playing possum.
Except in color he isn't blue,
But he wouldn't advise a thing to blossom.

The water for which we may have to look
In summertime with a witching wand,
35 In every wheelrut's now a brook,
In every print of a hoof a pond.
Be glad of water, but don't forget
The lurking frost in the earth beneath
That will steal forth after the sun is set
40 And show on the water its crystal teeth.

The time when most I loved my task
These two must make me love it more
By coming with what they came to ask.
You'd think I never had felt before
45 The weight of an ax-head poised aloft,
The grip on earth of outspread feet,
The life of muscles rocking soft
And smooth and moist in vernal heat.

Out of the woods two hulking tramps
50 (From sleeping God knows where last night,
But not long since in the lumber camps).
They thought all chopping was theirs of right.
Men of the woods and lumberjacks,
They judged me by their appropriate tool.
55 Except as a fellow handled an ax,
They had no way of knowing a fool.

Nothing on either side was said.
They knew they had but to stay their stay
And all their logic would fill my head:
60 As that I had no right to play
With what was another man's work for gain.

My right might be love but theirs was need.
And where the two exist in twain
Theirs was the better right—agreed.   [1934]

1. Throughout this poem the speaker contemplates an unspoken argument set
   forth by the two tramps who approach him while he is chopping wood.
   What is this argument, and what are the ethical assumptions on which it is
   based?
2. How does the relationship between human labor and the natural environment illuminate the theme of this poem?
3. Compare this poem to Robert Frost's "Death of the Hired Man" or "Love
   and a Question."

MIROSLAV HOLUB

MIROSLAV HOLUB *(1923–98) was both a poet and a scientist. He was an
internationally acclaimed immunologist with both a Ph.D. from the Czechoslovak
Academy of Sciences and an M.D. His political participation in the attempt to
reform the Communist government of Czechoslovakia in the 1960s caused him to
lose his job at the Microbiological Institute and his publications were banned until
the fall of the government. However, his literary as well as his scientific work had
been translated into many languages and became well-known abroad. The
translations of his poetry into English are so successful that in some circles he is
considered to be a British poet.*

*The Fly**

She sat on a willow-trunk
watching
part of the battle of Crécy,°
the shouts,
the gasps,   5
the groans,
the tramping and the tumbling.

During the fourteenth charge
of the French cavalry
she mated   10
with a brown-eyed male fly
from Vadincourt.

She rubbed her legs together
as she sat on a disembowelled horse

---

*From the Czech (translated by George Theiner)
³**the battle of Crécy** The Battle of Crécy (Saturday, August 26, 1346) was the first battle
of the Hundred Years' War between England and France.

15 meditating
on the immortality of flies.

With relief she alighted
on the blue tongue
of the Duke of Clervaux.

20 When silence settled
and only the whisper of decay
softly circled the bodies

and only
a few arms and legs
25 still twitched jerkily under the trees,

she began to lay her eggs
on the single eye
of Johann Uhr,
the Royal Armourer.

30 And thus it was
that she was eaten by a swift
fleeing
from the fires of Estrées.   [1987]

1. What argument does this poem make about human warfare? How does the
   focus on a fly's experience of a battle contribute to that argument?
2. What is the "swift" (l. 31) referred to in the final stanza? How does the fly's
   fate parallel that of the soldiers?
3. Locate information about the battle of Crécy, which occurred in the fourteenth century. Explain what that sort of contextual information does or
   does not contribute to an understanding of this poem.
4. Compare this poem to John Balaban's "For the Missing in Action."

YUSEF KOMUNYAKAA

YUSEF KOMUNYAKAA *(1947–) was born in Bogalusa, Louisiana, and grew up in
a rural Southern community and in New Orleans, the center of jazz and blues.
The richness of this background is the source of much of his work. Military service
also provided him with formative experiences, including a tour of duty in Vietnam,
where he was a correspondent for* The Southern Cross, *a military newspaper. He
left the army and went to college at the University of Colorado, where he received a
B.A. in 1975, and then an M.A. from Colorado State University, where he studied
with poet Bill Tremblay in the graduate writing program. He earned an M.F.A.
from the University of California at Irvine in 1980. He published two books himself,*
Dedications Other Darkhorses *(1977) and* Lost in the Bonewheel Factory
(1979). His third collection, Copacetic *(1984), his first commercially published book,
returns to childhood memories and jazz themes as they illuminate racial issues. His
1994 collection,* Neon Vernacular, *won a Pulitzer Prize and the Kingsley Tufts
Poetry Award. He is currently a professor in the Council of Humanities and Creative*

Writing Program of Princeton University and a Chancellor of the Academy of American Poets.

Facing It

My black face fades,
hiding inside the black granite.
I said I wouldn't,
dammit: No tears.
I'm stone. I'm flesh.   5
My clouded reflection eyes me
like a bird of prey, the profile of night
slanted against morning. I turn
this way—the stone lets me go.
I turn that way—I'm inside   10
the Vietnam Veterans Memorial°
again, depending on the light
to make a difference.
I go down the 58,022 names,
half-expecting to find   15
my own in letters like smoke.
I touch the name Andrew Johnson;
I see the booby trap's white flash.
Names shimmer on a woman's blouse
but when she walks away   20
the names stay on the wall.
Brushstrokes flash, a red bird's
wings cutting across my stare.
The sky. A plane in the sky.
A white vet's image floats   25
closer to me, then his pale eyes
look through mine. I'm a window.
He's lost his right arm
inside the stone. In the black mirror
a woman's trying to erase names: 30
No, she's brushing a boy's hair.

[1988]

11**Vietnam Veterans Memorial** the memorial on the mall in Washington, D.C., commemorating Americans who died in the Vietnam War. It consists of walls of reflective, polished black granite on which the names of the dead are inscribed.

1. How does the stone memorial described in this poem become a living memory for the speaker?
2. How do the speaker's observations of other visitors to the Vietnam Veterans Memorial reveal multiple experiences of this war (and of war in general)?
3. What kind of psychological or sociological contexts might illuminate this poem?
4. To what other works in this section can you connect this poem?

⊙⊙⊙

WILFRED OWEN

WILFRED OWEN *(1893–1918), poet of the first World War, was educated at the Birkenhead Institute and the University of London, but left there for reasons of health and lived and taught in Bordeaux, France, where he prepared his first book of poems, which was never published. In 1915 he enlisted in the British Army and was commissioned in the Manchester Regiment. After training in England, he left for the front, maturing quickly under fire in trench warfare, and writing poems reflecting the cruelty of war. He was caught in an explosion and evacuated to a hospital in Edinburgh for treatment of what was then termed shell shock. There he met the poet Siegfried Sassoon, who agreed with his antiwar views, and encouraged him and introduced him to his friend Robert Graves. Sassoon influenced him greatly, revolutionizing Owen's conception of poetry. He returned to the front, was awarded the Military Cross for bravery at Amiens, and was killed attempting to lead his men across the Sambre canal at Ors. The news of his death reached his parents on November 11ᵗʰ, Armistice (now Veterans') Day. Sassoon undertook the publication of Owen's war poems, which included "Dulce et Decorum Est" and "Anthem for Doomed Youth."*

Dulce et Decorum Est

Bent double, like old beggars under sacks,
Knock-kneed, coughing like hags, we cursed through sludge,
Till on the haunting flares we turned our backs
And towards our distant rest began to trudge.
5   Men marched asleep. Many had lost their boots
But limped on, blood-shod. All went lame; all blind;
Drunk with fatigue; deaf even to the hoots
Of tired, outstripped Five-Nines° that dropped behind.

Gas! Gas! Quick, boys!—An ecstasy of fumbling,
10   Fitting the clumsy helmets just in time;
But someone still was yelling out and stumbling
And flound'ring like a man in fire or lime . . .
Dim, through the misty panes and thick green light,
As under a green sea, I saw him drowning.
15   In all my dreams, before my helpless sight,
He plunges at me, guttering, choking, drowning.

If in some smothering dreams you too could pace
Behind the wagon that we flung him in,
And watch the white eyes writhing in his face,
20   His hanging face, like a devil's sick of sin;
If you could hear, at every jolt, the blood
Come gargling from the froth-corrupted lungs,
Obscene as cancer, bitter as the cud

⁸**Five-Nines** shells that release poison gas on impact

Of vile, incurable sores on innocent tongues,—
My friend, you would not tell with such high zest   25
To children ardent for some desperate glory,
The old Lie: Dulce et decorum est
Pro patria mori.°   [1920]

27–28**Dulce et decorum est / Pro patria mori** Sweet and fitting it is to die for one's
country. From Horace, *Odes* 3.2.

1. Analyze how this poem juxtaposes the glorification of war with the reality
   of war.
2. The "friend" referred to in line 25 is Jessie Pope, a woman who wrote
   poems celebrating the nobility of death in battle. Does Owen's direct address
   to Pope in this poem support or contradict Gilligan and Attanucci's claim
   about gender differences in responses to ethical dilemmas? (See p. 156.)
3. To what other works in this section can you connect this poem?
4. How does this poem use rhythm, word choice, rhyme, and sound patterns
   to make its meaning?
5. Compare Owen's use of syntax to place the proper emphasis on death to
   Auden's in "Musée des Beaux Arts" (p. 127).

WILLIAM EDGAR STAFFORD

WILLIAM EDGAR STAFFORD *(1914–93) grew up in Kansas, hunting with his
father and moving from town to town during the Depression. The young Stafford
helped by doing odd jobs. He worked his way toward a bachelor's and then a
master's degree from the University of Kansas. His education was interrupted by
World War II when, as a registered pacifist, he worked in camps and projects for
conscientious objectors. During this time, he met and married his wife, Dorothy, in
California. The couple settled in Portland, Oregon, where Stafford taught at Lewis
and Clark College until his retirement, except for his time at the University of Iowa
in pursuit of the Ph.D. in creative writing. He served as Poetry Consultant for the
Library of Congress in 1970. He did not publish poetry until his mid-forties, but for
the rest of his life produced and published hundreds of poems. His collection*
Traveling through the Dark *won the National Book Award for Poetry in 1963.*

Traveling through the Dark

Traveling through the dark I found a deer
dead on the edge of the Wilson River road.
It is usually best to roll them into the canyon:
that road is narrow; to swerve might make more dead.

By glow of the tail-light I stumbled back of the car   5
and stood by the heap, a doe, a recent killing;
she had stiffened already, almost cold.
I dragged her off; she was large in the belly.

My fingers touching her side brought me the reason—
10 her side was warm; her fawn lay there waiting,
alive, still, never to be born.
Beside that mountain road I hesitated.

The car aimed ahead its lowered parking lights;
under the hood purred the steady engine.
15 I stood in the glare of the warm exhaust turning red;
around our group I could hear the wilderness listen.

I thought hard for us all—my only swerving—
then pushed her over the edge into the river.   [1962]

1. What does the narrator mean by "swerve" in the first stanza and by "swerving" in the final one? Explain the significance of the different connotations you identify.
2. .Compare and contrast the descriptions of the deer's body and those of the automobile. Analyze the effect of these juxtaposed images.
3. Why does the speaker hesitate to dispose of the deer's body? What ethical issues does this situation raise? What factors need to be weighted? Is the speaker's resolution of this dilemma satisfying? Why or why not?
4. Explain the effects of the phrases in l. 11.
5. What conceptual frameworks can enhance our view of this poem?

ALFRED, LORD TENNYSON

ALFRED, LORD TENNYSON *(1809–92) Tennyson's father was the poor relation in a wealthy family, a contrast that made the young Tennyson feel particularly impoverished and inclined to worry about money all his life. He was also disturbed about mental disease in the family, but escaped his troubled home at Trinity College, Cambridge. There he joined The Apostles, a group devoted to the discussion of philosophy, the source of lifelong friendships. When one of the group, his good friend Arthur Hallam, died prematurely, Tennyson wrote* In Memoriam, *one of his most important poems, to commemorate the death. His first book of poems was not well received, a matter of such pain to the poet that he did not publish anything for nine years. Unlucky investments worsened his situation, but the success of his late collection of poems made him a popular poet and secured him a government pension. His appointment as Poet Laureate in 1850 finally established him as the most popular poet of the Victorian era.*

Ulysses°

It little profits that an idle king,
By this still hearth, among these barren crags,
Matched with an aged wife, I mete and dole
Unequal laws unto a savage race,

^Title^**Ulysses** Ulysses was the ancient Greek hero of Homer's *Odyssey,* which recounts his ten-year adventure-filled trip home from the Trojan War.

That hoard, and sleep, and feed, and know not me. 5

    I cannot rest from travel; I will drink
Life to the lees. All times I have enjoyed
Greatly, have suffered greatly, both with those
That loved me, and alone; on shore, and when
Through scudding drifts the rainy Hyades 10
Vexed the dim sea. I am become a name;
For always roaming with a hungry heart
Much have I seen and known—cities of men
And manners, climates, councils, governments,
Myself not least, but honored of them all— 15
And drunk delight of battle with my peers,
Far on the ringing plains of windy Troy.
I am a part of all that I have met;
Yet all experience is an arch wherethrough
Gleams that untraveled world whose margin fades 20
Forever and forever when I move.
How dull it is to pause, to make an end,
To rust unburnished, not to shine in use!
As though to breathe were life! Life piled on life
Were all too little, and of one to me 25
Little remains; but every hour is saved
From that eternal silence, something more,
A bringer of new things; and vile it were
For some three suns to store and hoard myself,
And this gray spirit yearning in desire 30
To follow knowledge like a sinking star,
Beyond the utmost bound of human thought.

    This is my son, mine own Telemachus,
To whom I leave the scepter and the isle—
Well-loved of me, discerning to fulfill 35
This labor, by slow prudence to make mild
A rugged people, and through soft degrees
Subdue them to the useful and the good.
Most blameless is he, centered in the sphere
Of common duties, decent not to fail 40
In offices of tenderness, and pay
Meet adoration to my household gods,
When I am gone. He works his work, I mine.

    There lies the port; the vessel puffs her sail;
There gloom the dark, broad seas. My mariners, 45
Souls that have toiled, and wrought, and thought with me—
That ever with a frolic welcome took
The thunder and the sunshine, and opposed
Free hearts, free foreheads—you and I are old,
Old age hath yet his honor and his toil. 50

Death closes all; but something ere the end,
Some work of noble note, may yet be done,
Not unbecoming men that strove with Gods.
The lights begin to twinkle from the rocks
55 The long day wanes; the slow moon climbs; the deep
Moans round with many voices. Come, my friends,
'Tis not too late to seek a newer world.
Push off, and sitting well in order smite
The sounding furrows; for my purpose holds
60 To sail beyond the sunset, and the baths
Of all the western stars, until I die.
It may be that the gulfs will wash us down;
It may be we shall touch the Happy Isles,
And see the great Achilles, whom we knew.
65 Though much is taken, much abides; and though
We are not now that strength which in old days
Moved earth and heaven, that which we are, we are—
One equal temper of heroic hearts,
Made weak by time and fate, but strong in will
70 To strive, to seek, to find, and not to yield.   [1833]

1. What is the speaker's attitude toward his past, present, and future?
    How does his personal vision relate to the larger project of human existence?
2. What disciplines can shed light on the theme of this poem?
3. Compare this poem to Yusef Komunyakaa's "Facing It."

WILLIAM CARLOS WILLIAMS

WILLIAM CARLOS WILLIAMS *(1883–1963) had two main interests throughout his adult life: practicing medicine, which he did in his hometown of Rutherford New Jersey, and writing poetry. As one of the principal poets of the Imagist school, he was devoted to using ordinary language that presents clear pictures of concrete images. He also experimented with new techniques of meter and line arrangement in order to forge a less European and more American poetic style. His epic poem* Paterson, *which he worked on from the 1930s through the early 1960s, was among the works that influenced later poets such as Allen Ginsberg and the Beats.*

The Yachts

contend in a sea which the land partly encloses
shielding them from the too-heavy blows
of an ungoverned ocean which when it chooses

tortures the biggest hulls, the best man knows
5 to pit against its beatings, and sinks them pitilessly.
Mothlike in mists, scintillant in the minute

brilliance of cloudless days, with broad bellying sails
they glide to the wind tossing green water
from their sharp prows while over them the crew crawls

ant-like, solicitously grooming them, releasing,
making fast as they turn, lean far over and having
caught the wind again, side by side, head for the mark.   10

In a well guarded arena of open water surrounded by
lesser and greater craft which, sycophant, lumbering
and flittering follow them, they appear youthful, rare   15

as the light of a happy eye, live with the grace
of all that in the mind is fleckless, free and
naturally to be desired. Now the sea which holds them
is moody, lapping their glossy sides, as if feeling
for some slightest flaw but fails completely.   20
Today no race. Then the wind comes again. The yachts

move, jockeying for a start, the signal is set and they
are off. Now the waves strike at them but they are too
well made, they slip through, though they take in canvas.°

Arms with hands grasping seek to clutch at the prows.   25
Bodies thrown recklessly in the way are cut aside.
It is a sea of faces about them in agony, in despair

until the horror of the race dawns staggering the mind,
the whole sea become an entanglement of watery bodies
lost to the world bearing what they cannot hold. Broken,   30
beaten, desolate, reaching from the dead to be taken up
they cry out, failing, failing! their cries rising
in waves still as the skillful yachts pass over.   [1935]

²⁴**take in canvas** reduce the area of sail exposed to the wind

1. Who is speaking? What kind of narrator is this?
2. What kinds of competition does the poem set up?
3. What is the effect of the figures of speech in the poem?
4. To what other selections in this chapter can this poem be compared?

FICTION

TONI CADE BAMBARA

TONI CADE BAMBARA *(1939–95) began life in New York City and was educated
there as well as in Italy and Paris. As a young woman she worked as an investigator for the New York Department of Social Welfare before finding her career as a
teacher and writer. Bambara was a civil rights activist involved in African-
American life and issues, especially issues pertaining to women's rights. She is the
author of several volumes of short stories, including* Gorilla, My Love *(1972) and*

The Sea Birds Are Still Alive: Collected Stories *(1977), and two novels,* The Salt Eaters *(1980) and* If Blessing Comes *(1987). She edited* The Black Woman: An Anthology *(1970), a groundbreaking collection of African women's literature. In 1996* Deep Sightings and Rescue Missions: Fiction, Essays, and Conversations *was published.*

The Lesson

Back in the days when everyone was old and stupid or young and foolish and me and Sugar were the only ones just right, this lady moved on our block with nappy hair and proper speech and no makeup. And quite naturally we laughed at her, laughed the way we did at the junk man who went about his business like he was some big-time president and his sorry-ass horse his secretary. And we kinda hated her too, hated the way we did the winos who cluttered up our parks and pissed on our handball walls and stank up our hallways and stairs so you couldn't halfway play hide-and-seek without a goddamn gas mask. Miss Moore was her name. The only woman on the block with no first name. And she was black as hell, cept for her feet, which were fish-white and spooky. And she was always planning these boring-ass things for us to do, us being my cousin, mostly, who lived on the block cause we all moved North the same time and to the same apartment then spread out gradual to breathe. And our parents would yank our heads into some kinda shape and crisp up our clothes so we'd be presentable for travel with Miss Moore, who always looked like she was going to church, though she never did. Which is just one of the things the grownups talked about when they talked behind her back like a dog. But when she came calling with some sachet she'd sewed up or some gingerbread she'd made or some book, why then they'd all be too embarrassed to turn her down and we'd get handed over all spruced up. She'd been to college and said it was only right that she should take responsibility for the young ones' education, and she not even related by marriage or blood. So they'd go for it. Specially Aunt Gretchen. She was the main gofer in the family. You got some ole dumb shit foolishness you want somebody to go for, you send for Aunt Gretchen. She been screwed into the go-along for so long, it's a blood-deep natural thing with her. Which is how she got saddled with me and Sugar and Junior in the first place while our mothers were in a la-de-da apartment up the block having a good ole time.

So this one day Miss Moore rounds us all up at the mailbox and it's puredee hot and she's knockin herself out about arithmetic. And school suppose to let up in summer I heard, but she don't never let up. And the starch in my pinafore scratching the shit outta me and I'm really hating this nappy-head bitch and her goddamn college degree. I'd much rather go to the pool or to the show where it's cool. So me and Sugar leaning on the mailbox being surly, which is a Miss Moore word. And Flyboy checking out what everybody brought for lunch. And Fat Butt already wasting his peanut-butter-and-jelly sandwich like the pig he is. And Junebug punchin on Q.T.'s arm for potato chips. And Rosie Giraffe shifting from one hip to the other waiting for somebody to step on her foot or ask her if she from Georgia so she can kick ass, preferably Mercedes'. And Miss Moore asking us do we know what money is, like we a bunch of retards. I mean real money, she say, like it's only poker chips or monopoly papers we lay on the grocer. So right away I'm tired of this and say so. And would much rather snatch Sugar and go to the Sunset and terrorize the West Indian kids and take their hair ribbons and their money too. And Miss Moore files that remark away for next week's lesson on brotherhood, I can tell. And finally I say we oughta get to the subway cause it's cooler and besides we might meet some cute boys. Sugar done swiped her mama's lipstick, so we ready.

So we heading down the street and she's boring up silly about what things cost and what our parents make and how much goes for rent and how money ain't divided up right in this country. And then she gets to the part about we all poor and live in the slums, which I don't feature. And I'm ready to speak on that, but she steps out in the street and hails two cabs just like that. Then she hustles half the crew in with her and hands me a five-dollar bill and tells me to calculate 10 percent tip for the driver. And we're off. Me and Sugar and Junebug and Flyboy hangin out the window and hollering to everybody, putting lipstick on each other cause Flyboy a faggot anyway, and making farts with our sweaty armpits. But I'm mostly trying to figure how to spend this money. But they all fascinated with the meter ticking and Junebug starts laying bets as to how much it'll read when Flyboy can't hold his breath no more. Then Sugar lays bets as to how much it'll be when we get there. So I'm stuck. Don't nobody want to go for my plan, which is to jump out at the next light and run off to the first bar-b-que we can find. Then the driver tells us to get the hell out cause we there already. And the meter reads eighty-five cents. And I'm stalling to figure out the tip and Sugar say give him a dime. And I decide he don't need it bad as I do, so later for him. But then he tries to take off with Junebug's foot still in the door so we talk about his mama something ferocious. Then we check out that we on Fifth Avenue and everybody dressed up in stockings. One lady in a fur coat, hot as it is. White folks crazy.

"This is the place," Miss Moore say, presenting it to us in the voice she uses at the museum. "Let's look in the windows before we go in."

"Can we steal?" Sugar asks very serious like she's getting the ground rules squared away before she plays. "I beg your pardon," say Miss Moore, and we fall out. So she leads us around the windows of the toy store and me and Sugar screamin, "This is mine, that's mine, I gotta have that, that was made for me, I was born for that," till Big Butt drowns us out.

"Hey, I'm goin to buy that there."

"That there? You don't even know what it is, stupid."

"I do so," he say punchin on Rosie Giraffe. "It's a microscope."

"Whatcha gonna do with a microscope, fool?"

"Look at things."

"Like what, Ronald?" ask Miss Moore. And Big Butt ain't got the first notion. So here go Miss Moore gabbing about the thousands of bacteria in a drop of water and the somethinorother in a speck of blood and the million and one living things in the air around us is invisible to the naked eye. And what she say that for? Junebug go to town on that "naked" and we rolling. Then Miss Moore ask what it cost. So we all jam into the window smudgin it up and the price tag say $300. So then she ask how long'd take for Big Butt and Junebug to save up their allowances. "Too long," I say. "Yeh," adds Sugar, "outgrown it by that time." And Miss Moore say no, you never outgrow learning instruments. "Why, even medical students and interns and," blah, blah, blah. And we ready to choke Big Butt for bringing it up in the first damn place.

"This here costs four hundred eighty dollars," say Rosie Giraffe. So we pile up all over her to see what she pointin out. My eyes tell me it's a chunk of glass cracked with something heavy, and different-color inks dripped into the splits, then the whole thing put into a oven or something. But for $480 it don't make sense.

"That's a paperweight made of semi-precious stones fused together under tremendous pressure," she explains slowly, with her hands doing the mining and all the factory work.

"So what's a paperweight?" asks Rosie Giraffe.

15 "To weigh paper with, dumbbell," say Flyboy, the wise man from the East.

"Not exactly," say Miss Moore, which is what she say when you warm or way off too. "It's to weigh paper down so it won't scatter and make your desk untidy." So right away me and Sugar curtsy to each other and then to Mercedes who is more the tidy type.

"We don't keep paper on top of the desk in my class," say Junebug, figuring Miss Moore crazy or lyin one.

"At home, then," she say. "Don't you have a calendar and a pencil case and a blotter and a letter-opener on your desk at home where you do your home-work?" And she know damn well what our homes look like cause she nosys around in them every chance she gets.

"I don't even have a desk," say Junebug. "Do we?"

20 "No. And I don't get no homework neither," says Big Butt.

"And I don't even have a home," say Flyboy like he do at school to keep the white folks off his back and sorry for him. Send this poor kid to camp posters, is his specialty.

"I do," says Mercedes. "I have a box of stationery on my desk and a picture of my cat. My godmother bought the stationery and the desk. There's a big rose on each sheet and the envelopes smell like roses."

"Who wants to know about your smelly-ass stationery," say Rosie Giraffe fore I can get my two cents in.

"It's important to have a work area all your own so that . . ."

25 "Will you look at this sailboat, please," say Flyboy, cuttin her off and pointin to the thing like it was his. So once again we tumble all over each other to gaze at this magnificent thing in the toy store which is just big enough to maybe sail two kittens across the pond if you strap them to the posts tight. We all start recit-ing the price tag like we in assembly. "Handcrafted sailboat of fiberglass at one thousand one hundred ninety-five dollars."

"Unbelievable," I hear myself say and am really stunned. I read it again for myself just in case the group recitation put me in a trance. Same thing. For some reason this pisses me off. We look at Miss Moore and she lookin at us, waiting for I dunno what.

"Who'd pay all that when you can buy a sailboat set for a quarter at Pop's, a tube of glue for a dime, and a ball of string for eight cents? It must have a motor and a whole lot else besides," I say, "My sailboat cost me about fifty cents."

"But will it take water?" say Mercedes with her smart ass.

"Took mine to Alley Pond Park once," say Flyboy. "String broke. Lost it. Pity."

"Sailed mine in Central Park and it keeled over and sank. Had to ask my father for another dollar."   30

"And you got the strap," laugh Big Butt. "The jerk didn't even have a string on it. My old man wailed on his behind."

Little Q.T. was staring hard at the sailboat and you could see he wanted it bad. But he too little and somebody'd just take it from him. So what the hell. "This boat for kids, Miss Moore?"

"Parents silly to buy something like that just to get all broke up," say Rosie Giraffe.

"That much money it should last forever," I figure.

"My father'd buy it for me if I wanted it."   35

"Your father, my ass," say Rosie Giraffe getting a chance to finally push Mercedes.

"Must be rich people shop here," say Q.T.

"You are a very bright boy," say Flyboy. "What was your first clue?" And he rap him on the head with the back of his knuckles, since Q.T. the only one he could get away with. Though Q.T. liable to come up behind you years later and get his licks in when you half expect it.

"What I want to know is," I says to Miss Moore though I never talk to her, I wouldn't give the bitch that satisfaction, "is how much a real boat costs? I figure a thousand'd get you a yacht any day."

"Why don't you check that out," she says, "and report back to the group?"   40
Which really pains my ass. If you gonna mess up a perfectly good swim day least you could do is have some answers. "Let's go in," she say like she got something up her sleeve. Only she don't lead the way. So me and Sugar turn the corner to where the entrance is, but when we get there I kinda hang back. Not that I'm scared, what's there to be afraid of, just a toy store. But I feel funny, shame. But what I got to be shamed about? Got as much right to go in as anybody. But somehow I can't seem to get hold of the door, so I step away from Sugar to lead. But she hangs back too. And I look at her and she looks at me and this is ridiculous. I mean, damn, I have never ever been shy about doing nothing or going nowhere. But then Mercedes steps up and then Rosie Giraffe and Big Butt crowd in behind and shove, and next thing we all stuffed into the doorway with only Mercedes squeezing past us, smoothing out her jumper and walking right down the aisle. Then the rest of us tumble in like a glued-together jigsaw done all wrong. And people lookin at us. And it's like the time me and Sugar crashed into the Catholic church on a dare. But once we got in there and everything so hushed and holy and the candles and the bowin and the handkerchiefs on all the drooping heads, I just couldn't go through with the plan. Which was for me to run up to the altar and do a tap dance while Sugar played the nose flute and

messed around in the holy water. And Sugar kept givin me the elbow. Then later teased me so bad I tied her up in the shower and turned it on and locked her in. And she'd be there till this day if Aunt Gretchen hadn't finally figured I was lyin about the boarder takin a shower.

Same thing in the store. We all walkin on tiptoe and hardly touchin the games and puzzles and things. And I watched Miss Moore who is steady watchin us like she waitin for a sign. Like Mama Drewery watches the sky and sniffs the air and takes note of just how much slant is in the bird formation. Then me and Sugar bump smack into each other, so busy gazing at the toys, 'specially the sailboat. But we don't laugh and go into our fat-lady bump-stomach routine. We just stare at that price tag. Then Sugar run a finger over the whole boat. And I'm jealous and want to hit her. Maybe not her, but I sure want to punch somebody in the mouth.

"Watcha bring us here for, Miss Moore?"

"You sound angry, Sylvia. Are you mad about something?" Givin me one of them grins like she tellin a grown-up joke that never turns out to be funny. And she's lookin very closely at me like maybe she plannin to do my portrait from memory. I'm mad, but I won't give her that satisfaction. So I slouch around the store bein very bored and say, "Let's go."

Me and Sugar at the back of the train watchin the tracks whizzin by large then small then getting gobbled up in the dark. I'm thinkin about this tricky toy I saw in the store. A clown that somersaults on a bar then does chin-ups just cause you yank lightly at his leg. Cost $35. I could see me askin my mother for a $35 birthday clown. "You wanna who that costs what?" she'd say, cocking her head to the side to get a better view of the hole in my head. Thirty-five dollars could buy new bunk beds for Junior and Gretchen's boy. Thirty-five dollars and the whole household could go visit Granddaddy Nelson in the country. Thirty-five dollars would pay for the rent and the piano bill too. Who are these people that spend that much for performing clowns and $1000 for toy sailboats? What kinda work they do and how they live and how come we ain't in on it? Where we are is who we are, Miss Moore always pointin out. But it don't necessarily have to be that way, she always adds then waits for somebody to say that poor people have to wake up and demand their share of the pie and don't none of us know what kind of pie she talking about in the first damn place. But she ain't so smart cause I still got her four dollars from the taxi and she sure ain't gettin it. Messin up my day with this shit. Sugar nudges me in my pocket and winks.

45   Miss Moore lines us up in front of the mailbox where we started from, seem like years ago, and I got a headache for thinkin so hard. And we lean all over each other so we can hold up under the draggy-ass lecture she always finishes us off with at the end before we thank her for borin us to tears. But she just looks at us like she readin tea leaves. Finally she say, "Well, what did you think of F.A.O. Schwarz?"

Rosie Giraffe mumbles, "White folks crazy."

"I'd like to go there again when I get my birthday money," says Mercedes, and we shove her out the pack so she has to lean on the mailbox by herself.

"I'd like a shower. Tiring day," say Flyboy.

Then Sugar surprises me by sayin, "You know, Miss Moore, I don't think all of us here put together eat in a year what that sailboat costs." And Miss Moore lights up like somebody goosed her. "And?" she say, urging Sugar on. Only I'm standin on her foot so she don't continue.

"Imagine for a minute what kind of society it is in which some people can   50 spend on a toy what it would cost to feed a family of six or seven. What do you think?"

"I think," say Sugar pushing me off her feet like she never done before, cause I whip her ass in a minute, "that this is not much of a democracy if you ask me. Equal chance to pursue happiness means an equal crack at the dough, don't it?" Miss Moore is besides herself and I am disgusted with Sugar's treachery. So I stand on her foot one more time to see if she'll shove me. She shuts up, and Miss Moore looks at me, sorrowfully I'm thinkin. And somethin weird is goin on, I can feel it in my chest.

"Anybody else learn anything today?" lookin dead at me. I walk away and Sugar has to run to catch up and don't even seem to notice when I shrug her arm off my shoulder.

"Well, we got four dollars anyway," she says.

"Uh hunh."

"We could go to Hascombs and get half a chocolate layer and then go to the   55 Sunset and still have plenty money for potato chips and ice cream sodas."

"Uh hunh."

"Race you to Hascombs," she say.

We start down the block and she gets ahead which is O.K. by me cause I'm going to the West End and then over to the Drive to think this day through. She can run if she want to and even run faster. But ain't nobody gonna beat me at nuthin.   [1972]

1. What kind of narrator is telling the story? Characterize her tone. What role does her diction play in your determination of tone?
2. What are the children's attitudes to the adults in the story?
3. To what does the title refer? Is the title ironic? Why or why not?
4. Why does the narrator abandon Sugar at the end of the trip to the toy store?
5. What are the story's main themes?
6. What ethical questions does this story raise?

SHIRLEY JACKSON

SHIRLEY JACKSON *(1919–65) came from a comfortable and happy family in California. She showed a precocious interest in writing and excelled at sports during her early years. Her years of study at the college level at the University of Rochester and Syracuse University were also devoted to her writing, where her lifelong habits of discipline in the refining of her craft were forged. She married Stanley Edgar Hyman, with whom she started a literary magazine at Syracuse and found herself* *famous for her story, "The Lottery," which was published in 1948. While her four children were growing up, her output was prodigious; it included, among others, four novels, forty-four short stories, and children's books. Her novel,* The Haunting of Hill House, *became a successful movie. Another novel,* We Have Always Lived in the Castle, *was a best seller. Subject to bouts of anxiety and depression, Jackson also had physical troubles, including asthma, which led to her premature death.*

The Lottery

The morning of June 27th was clear and sunny, with the fresh warmth of a full-summer day; the flowers were blossoming profusely and the grass was richly green. The people of the village began to gather in the square, between the post office and the bank, around ten o'clock; in some towns there were so many people that the lottery took two days and had to be started on June 26th, but in this village, where there were only about three hundred people, the whole lottery took less than two hours, so it could begin at ten o'clock in the morning and still be through in time to allow the villagers to get home for noon dinner.

The children assembled first, of course. School was recently over for the summer, and the feeling of liberty sat uneasily on most of them; they tended to gather together quietly for a while before they broke into boisterous play, and their talk was still of the classroom and the teacher, of books and reprimands. Bobby Martin had already stuffed his pockets full of stones, and the other boys soon followed his example, selecting the smoothest and roundest stones; Bobby and Harry Jones and Dickie Delacroix—the villagers pronounced this name "Dellacroy"—eventually made a great pile of stones in one corner of the square and guarded it against the raids of the other boys. The girls stood aside, talking among themselves, looking over their shoulders at the boys, and the very small children rolled in the dust or clung to the hands of their older brothers or sisters.

Soon the men began to gather, surveying their own children, speaking of planting and rain, tractors and taxes. They stood together, away from the pile of stones in the corner, and their jokes were quiet and they smiled rather than laughed. The women, wearing faded house dresses and sweaters, came shortly after their menfolk. They greeted one another and exchanged bits of gossip as they went to join their husbands. Soon the women, standing by their husbands, began to call to their children, and the children came reluctantly, having to be called four or five times. Bobby Martin ducked under his mother's grasping hand and ran, laughing, back to the pile of stones. His father spoke up sharply, and Bobby came quickly and took his place between his father and his oldest brother.

The lottery was conducted—as were the square dances, the teen-age club, the Halloween program—by Mr. Summers, who had time and energy to devote to civic activities. He was a round-faced, jovial man and he ran the coal business, and people were sorry for him, because he had no children and his wife was a scold. When he arrived in the square, carrying the black wooden box, there was a murmur of conversation among the villagers, and he waved and called, "Little late today, folks." The postmaster, Mr. Graves, followed him, carrying a three-legged stool, and the stool was put in the center of the square and Mr. Summers set the black box down on it. The villagers kept their distance, leaving a space between themselves and the stool, and when Mr. Summers said, "Some of you fellows want to give me a hand?" there was a hesitation before two men, Mr. Martin and his oldest son, Baxter, came forward to hold the box steady on the stool while Mr. Summers stirred up the papers inside it.

The original paraphernalia for the lottery had been lost long ago, and the black box now resting on the stool had been put into use even before Old Man Warner, the oldest man in town, was born. Mr. Summers spoke frequently to the villagers about making a new box, but no one liked to upset even as much tradition as was represented by the black box. There was a story that the present box had been made with some pieces of the box that had preceded it, the one that had been constructed when the first people settled down to make a village here. Every year, after the lottery, Mr. Summers began talking again about a new box, but every year the subject was allowed to fade off without anything's being done. The black box grew shabbier each year; by now it was no longer completely black but splintered badly along one side to show the original wood color, and in some places faded or stained.

Mr. Martin and his oldest son, Baxter, held the black box securely on the stool until Mr. Summers had stirred the papers thoroughly with his hand. Because so much of the ritual had been forgotten or discarded, Mr. Summers had been successful in having slips of paper substituted for the chips of wood that had been used for generations. Chips of wood, Mr. Summers had argued, had been all very well when the village was tiny, but now that the population was more than three hundred and likely to keep on growing, it was necessary to use something that would fit more easily into the black box. The night before the lottery, Mr. Summers and Mr. Graves made up the slips of paper and put them in the box, and it was then taken to the safe of Mr. Summers's coal company and locked up until Mr. Summers was ready to take it to the square next morning. The rest of the year, the box was put away, sometimes one place, sometimes another; it had spent one year in Mr. Graves's barn and another year underfoot in the post office, and sometimes it was set on a shelf in the Martin grocery and left there.

There was a great deal of fussing to be done before Mr. Summers declared the lottery open. There were the lists to make up—of heads of families, heads of households in each family, members of each household in each family. There was the proper swearing-in of Mr. Summers by the postmaster, as the official of the lottery; at one time, some people remembered, there had been a recital of some sort, performed by the official of the lottery, a perfunctory, tuneless chant that had been rattled off duly each year; some people believed that the official of the lottery used to stand just so when he said or sang it, others believed that he was supposed to walk among the people, but years and years ago this part of the ritual had been allowed to lapse. There had been, also, a ritual salute, which the official of the lottery had had to use in addressing each person who came up to draw from the box, but this also had changed with time, until now it was felt necessary only for the official to speak to each person approaching. Mr. Summers was very good at all this; in his clean white shirt and blue jeans, with one hand resting carelessly on the black box, he seemed very proper and important as he talked interminably to Mr. Graves and the Martins.

Just as Mr. Summers finally left off talking and turned to the assembled villagers, Mrs. Hutchinson came hurriedly along the path to the square, her sweater thrown over her shoulders, and slid into place in the back of the crowd. "Clean forgot what day it was," she said to Mrs. Delacroix, who stood next to her, and they both laughed softly. "Thought my old man was out back stacking wood," Mrs. Hutchinson went on, "and then I looked out the window and the kids was gone, and then I remembered it was the twenty-seventh and came a-running." She dried her hands on her apron, and Mrs. Delacroix said, "You're in time, though. They're still talking away up there."

Mrs. Hutchinson craned her neck to see through the crowd and found her husband and children standing near the front. She tapped Mrs. Delacroix on the arm as a farewell and began to make her way through the crowd. The people separated good-humoredly to let her through; two or three people said, in voices just loud enough to be heard across the crowd, "Here comes your Missus, Hutchinson," and "Bill, she made it after all." Mrs. Hutchinson reached her husband, and Mr. Summers, who had been waiting, said cheerfully, "Thought we were going to have to get on without you, Tessie." Mrs. Hutchinson said, grinning, "Wouldn't have me leave m'dishes in the sink, now, would you, Joe?," and soft laughter ran through the crowd as the people stirred back into position after Mrs. Hutchinson's arrival.

10   "Well, now," Mr. Summers said soberly, "guess we better get started, get this over with, so's we can go back to work. Anybody ain't here?"

"Dunbar," several people said. "Dunbar, Dunbar."

Mr. Summers consulted his list. "Clyde Dunbar," he said. "That's right. He's broke his leg, hasn't he? Who's drawing for him?"

"Me, I guess," a woman said, and Mr. Summers turned to look at her. "Wife draws for her husband," Mr. Summers said. "Don't you have a grown boy to do it for you, Janey?" Although Mr. Summers and everyone else in the village knew the answer perfectly well, it was the business of the official of the lottery to ask such questions formally. Mr. Summers waited with an expression of polite interest while Mrs. Dunbar answered.

"Horace's not but sixteen yet," Mrs. Dunbar said regretfully. "Guess I gotta fill in for the old man this year."

15   "Right," Mr. Summers said. He made a note on the list he was holding. Then he asked, "Watson boy drawing this year?"

A tall boy in the crowd raised his hand. "Here," he said. "I'm drawing for m'mother and me." He blinked his eyes nervously and ducked his head as several voices in the crowd said things like "Good fellow, Jack," and "Glad to see your mother's got a man to do it."

"Well," Mr. Summers said, "guess that's everyone. Old Man Warner make it?"

"Here," a voice said, and Mr. Summers nodded.

A sudden hush fell on the crowd as Mr. Summers cleared his throat and looked at the list. "All ready?" he called. "Now, I'll read the names—heads of families first—and the men come up and take a paper out of the box. Keep the paper folded in your hand without looking at it until everyone has had a turn. Everything clear?"

The people had done it so many times that they only half listened to the directions; most of them were quiet, wetting their lips, not looking around. Then Mr. Summers raised one hand high and said, "Adams." A man disengaged himself from the crowd and came forward. "Hi, Steve," Mr. Summers said, and Mr. Adams said, "Hi, Joe." They grinned at one another humorlessly and nervously. Then Mr. Adams reached into the black box and took out a folded paper. He held it firmly by one corner as he turned and went hastily back to his place in the crowd, where he stood a little apart from his family, not looking down at his hand.

"Allen," Mr. Summers said. "Anderson. . . . Bentham."

"Seems like there's no time at all between lotteries any more," Mrs. Delacroix said to Mrs. Graves in the back row. "Seems like we got through with the last one only last week."

"Time sure goes fast," Mrs. Graves said.

"Clark. . . . Delacroix."

"There goes my old man," Mrs. Delacroix said. She held her breath while her husband went forward.

"Dunbar," Mr. Summers said, and Mrs. Dunbar went steadily to the box while one of the women said, "Go on, Janey," and another said, "There she goes."

"We're next," Mrs. Graves said. She watched while Mr. Graves came around from the side of the box, greeted Mr. Summers gravely, and selected a slip of paper from the box. By now, all through the crowd there were men holding the small folded papers in their large hands, turning them over and over nervously. Mrs. Dunbar and her two sons stood together, Mrs. Dunbar holding the slip of paper.

"Harburt. . . . Hutchinson."

"Get up there, Bill," Mrs. Hutchinson said, and the people near her laughed.

"Jones."

"They do say," Mr. Adams said to Old Man Warner, who stood next to him, "that over in the north village they're talking of giving up the lottery."

Old Man Warner snorted. "Pack of crazy fools," he said. "Listening to the young folks, nothing's good enough for *them*. Next thing you know, they'll be wanting to go back to living in caves, nobody work any more, live *that* way for a while. Used to be a saying about 'Lottery in June, corn be heavy soon.' First thing you know, we'd all be eating stewed chickweed and acorns. There's *always* been a lottery," he added petulantly. "Bad enough to see young Joe Summers up there joking with everybody."

"Some places have already quit lotteries," Mrs. Adams said.

"Nothing but trouble in *that*," Old Man Warner said stoutly. "Pack of young fools."

"Martin." And Bobby Martin watched his father go forward. "Overdyke. . . . Percy."

"I wish they'd hurry," Mrs. Dunbar said to her older son. "I wish they'd hurry."

"They're almost through," her son said.

"You get ready to run tell Dad," Mrs. Dunbar said.

Mr. Summers called his own name and then stepped forward precisely and selected a slip from the box. Then he called, "Warner."

40   "Seventy-seventh year I been in the lottery," Old Man Warner said as he went through the crowd. "Seventy-seventh time."

"Watson." The tall boy came awkwardly through the crowd. Someone said, "Don't be nervous, Jack," and Mr. Summers said, "Take your time, son."

"Zanini."

After that, there was a long pause, a breathless pause, until Mr. Summers, holding his slip of paper in the air, said, "All right, fellows." For a minute, no one moved, and then all the slips of paper were opened. Suddenly, all the women began to speak at once, saying, "Who is it?," "Who's got it?," "Is it the Dunbars?," "Is it the Watsons?" Then the voices began to say, "It's Hutchinson. It's Bill," "Bill Hutchinson's got it."

"Go tell your father," Mrs. Dunbar said to her older son.

45   People began to look around to see the Hutchinsons. Bill Hutchinson was standing quiet, staring down at the paper in his hand. Suddenly, Tessie Hutchinson shouted to Mr. Summers, "You didn't give him time enough to take any paper he wanted. I saw you. It wasn't fair!"

"Be a good sport, Tessie," Mrs. Delacroix called, and Mrs. Graves said, "All of us took the same chance."

"Shut up, Tessie," Bill Hutchinson said.

"Well, everyone," Mr. Summers said, "that was done pretty fast, and now we've got to be hurrying a little more to get done in time." He consulted his next list. "Bill," he said, "you draw for the Hutchinson family. You got any other households in the Hutchinsons?"

"There's Don and Eva," Mrs. Hutchinson yelled. "Make *them* take their chance!"

50   "Daughters draw with their husbands' families, Tessie," Mr. Summers said gently. "You know that as well as anyone else."

"It wasn't *fair,*" Tessie said.

"I guess not, Joe," Bill Hutchinson said regretfully. "My daughter draws with her husband's family, that's only fair. And I've got no other family except the kids."

"Then, as far as drawing for families is concerned, it's you," Mr. Summers said in explanation, "and as far as drawing for households is concerned, that's you, too. Right?"

"Right," Bill Hutchinson said.

55   "How many kids, Bill?" Mr. Summers asked formally.

"Three," Bill Hutchinson said. "There's Bill, Jr., and Nancy, and little Dave. And Tessie and me."

"All right, then," Mr. Summers said. "Harry, you got their tickets back?"

Mr. Graves nodded and held up the slips of paper. "Put them in the box, then," Mr. Summers directed. "Take Bill's and put it in."

"I think we ought to start over," Mrs. Hutchinson said, as quietly as she could. "I tell you it wasn't *fair.* You didn't give him time enough to choose. *Every*body saw that."

Mr. Graves had selected the five slips and put them in the box, and he
dropped all the papers but those onto the ground, where the breeze caught them
and lifted them off.

"Listen, everybody," Mrs. Hutchinson was saying to the people around her.

"Ready, Bill?" Mr. Summers asked, and Bill Hutchinson, with one quick
glance around at his wife and children, nodded.

"Remember," Mr. Summers said, "take the slips and keep them folded until
each person has taken one. Harry, you help little Dave." Mr. Graves took the
hand of the little boy, who came willingly with him up to the box. "Take a paper
out of the box, Davy," Mr. Summers said. Davy put his hand into the box and
laughed. "Take just *one* paper," Mr. Summers said. "Harry, you hold it for him."
Mr. Graves took the child's hand and removed the folded paper from the tight
fist and held it while little Dave stood next to him and looked at him
wonderingly.

"Nancy next," Mr. Summers said. Nancy was twelve, and her school friends
breathed heavily as she went forward, switching her skirt, and took a slip
daintily from the box. "Bill, Jr.," Mr. Summers said, and Billy, his face red and
his feet overlarge, nearly knocked the box over as he got a paper out. "Tessie,"
Mr. Summers said. She hesitated for a minute, looking around defiantly, and
then set her lips and went up to the box. She snatched a paper out and held it
behind her.

"Bill," Mr. Summers said, and Bill Hutchinson reached into the box and felt
around, bringing his hand out at last with the slip of paper in it.

The crowd was quiet. A girl whispered, "I hope it's not Nancy," and the sound
of the whisper reached the edges of the crowd.

"It's not the way it used to be," Old Man Warner said clearly. "People ain't the
way they used to be."

"All right," Mr. Summers said. "Open the papers. Harry, you open little
Dave's."

Mr. Graves opened the slip of paper and there was a general sigh through the
crowd as he held it up and everyone could see that it was blank. Nancy and Bill,
Jr., opened theirs at the same time, and both beamed and laughed, turning
around to the crowd and holding their slips of paper above their heads.

"Tessie," Mr. Summers said. There was a pause, and then Mr. Summers
looked at Bill Hutchinson, and Bill unfolded his paper and showed it. It was
blank.

"It's Tessie," Mr. Summers said, and his voice was hushed. "Show us her
paper, Bill."

Bill Hutchinson went over to his wife and forced the slip of paper out of her
hand. It had a black spot on it, the black spot Mr. Summers had made the night
before with the heavy pencil in the coal-company office. Bill Hutchinson held it
up, and there was a stir in the crowd.

"All right, folks," Mr. Summers said. "Let's finish quickly."

Although the villagers had forgotten the ritual and lost the original black box,
they still remembered to use stones. The pile of stones the boys had made earlier
was ready; there were stones on the ground with the blowing scraps of paper
that had come out of the box. Mrs. Delacroix selected a stone so large she had to

60

65

70

pick it up with both hands and turned to Mrs. Dunbar. "Come on," she said. "Hurry up."

75   Mrs. Dunbar had small stones in both hands, and she said, gasping for breath, "I can't run at all. You'll have to go ahead and I'll catch up with you."

The children had stones already, and someone gave little Davy Hutchinson a few pebbles.

Tessie Hutchinson was in the center of a cleared space by now, and she held her hands out desperately as the villagers moved in on her. "It isn't fair," she said. A stone hit her on the side of the head.

Old Man Warner was saying, "Come on, come on, everyone." Steve Adams was in the front of the crowd of villagers, with Mrs. Graves beside him.

"It isn't fair, it isn't right," Mrs. Hutchinson screamed, and then they were upon her.   [1948]

1. Explain the lottery to which the title of this story refers.
2. Early in the story, Mrs. Hutchinson accepts the lottery as an equitable social institution. What assumptions underlie her acceptance of the lottery? How do her assumptions—and her acceptance of the lottery—change when she is later selected as the sacrifice?
3. What psychological, sociological, or philosophical contexts illuminate various issues in this story?
4. To what other works can you connect this short story?

SIR THOMAS MALORY

SIR THOMAS MALORY (?–1471?) seems to have been an English knight of Warwickshire who fought in France during the Hundred Years' War. We don't know the full details of his life and work, but possibly while in prison for various crimes, civic and political, he compiled, translated, and synthesized various English and French versions of the story of King Arthur and his knights of the Round Table. First published by William Caxton in 1485 as one of the first printed English books, Le Morte d'Arthur still engages readers with its stories of knights who take an idealistic oath and their successes and failures in trying to live up to it. This fragment gives the flavor of the loyalties and conflicts it can engender.

Le Morte d'Arthur

Book XVI

Chapter X

HOW SIR BORS LEFT TO RESCUE HIS BROTHER, AND RESCUED THE DAMOSEL; AND HOW IT
    WAS TOLD HIM THAT LIONEL WAS DEAD

Then dressed he him unto the knight the which had the gentlewoman, and then he cried: Sir knight, let your hand off that maiden, or ye be but dead. And then he set down the maiden, and was armed at all pieces save he lacked his spear. Then he dressed his shield, and drew out his sword, and Bors smote him so hard

that it went through his shield and habergeon° on the left shoulder. And
through great strength he beat him down to the earth, and at the pulling out of
Bors' spear there he swooned. Then came Bors to the maid and said: How
seemeth it you? of this knight ye be delivered at this time. Now sir, said she, I
pray you lead me there as this knight had me. So shall I do gladly: and took the
horse of the wounded knight, and set the gentlewoman upon him, and so
brought her as she desired. Sir knight, said she, ye have better sped than ye
weened,° for an° I had lost my maidenhead, five hundred men should have died
for it. What knight was he that had you in the forest? By my faith, said she, he is
my cousin. So wot I never with what engyn the fiend enchafed him,° for yesterday he took me from my father privily; for I nor none of my father's men mistrusted him not, and if he had had my maidenhead he should have died for the
sin, and his body shamed and dishonoured for ever. Thus as she stood talking
with him there came twelve knights seeking after her, and anon° she told them
all how Bors had delivered her; then they made great joy, and besought him to
come to her father, a great lord, and he should be right welcome. Truly, said
Bors, that may not be at this time, for I have a great adventure to do in this
country. So he commended them unto God and departed. Then Sir Bors rode
after Lionel, his brother, by the trace of their horses, thus he rode seeking a great
while. Then he overtook a man clothed in a religious clothing, and rode on a
strong black horse blacker than a bear, and said: Sir knight, what seek you? Sir,
said he, I seek my brother that I saw within a while beaten with two knights.
Ah, Bors, discomfort you not, nor fall into no wanhope,° for I shall tell you tid-
ings such as they be, for truly he is dead. Then showed he him a new slain body
lying in a bush, and it seemed him well that it was the body of Lionel; and then
he made such a sorrow that he fell to the earth all in a swoon, and lay a great
while there. And when he came to himself he said: Fair brother, sith° the company of you and me is departed shall I never have joy in my heart, and now He
which I have taken unto my master, He be my help. And when he had said thus
he took his body lightly in his arms, and put it upon the arson° of his saddle.
And then he said to the man: Canst thou tell me unto some chapel where that I
may bury this body? Come on, said he, here is one fast by;° and so long they
rode till they saw a fair tower, and afore it there seemed an old feeble chapel.
And then they alit both, and put him into a tomb of marble.

Chapter XI

HOW SIR BORS TOLD HIS DREAM TO A PRIEST, WHICH HE HAD DREAMED, AND OF THE
    COUNSEL THAT THE PRIEST GAVE TO HIM

Now leave we him here, said the good man, and go we to our harbour till
to-morrow; we will come here again to do him service. Sir, said Bors, be ye a
priest? Yea forsooth, said he. Then I pray you tell me a dream that befell to me°

---

⁵habergeon jacket of chain mail, shorter than a hauberk   **¹²weened** supposed   **an** if
¹⁴So wot I never with what engyn the fiend enchafed him I don't know by what
device the devil made him hot   **¹⁸anon** soon   **²⁷wanhope** despair   **³¹sith** since
³⁴arson the arch in the front of the saddle   **³⁶fast by** close by
³befell to me happened to me

the last night. Say on, said he. Then he began so much to tell him of the great
5 bird in the forest, and after told him of his birds, one white, another black, and of
the rotten tree, and of the white flowers. Sir, I shall tell you a part now, and the
other dele° to-morrow. The white fowl betokeneth° a gentlewoman, fair and rich,
which loved thee paramours,° and hath loved thee long; and if thou warne° her
love she shall go die anon, if thou have no pity on her. That signifieth the great
10 bird, the which shall make thee to warne her. Now for no fear that thou hast,
nor for no dread that thou hast of God, thou shalt not warne her, but thou
wouldst not do it for to be holden chaste,° for to conquer the loos° of the vain
glory° of the world; for that shall befall thee now an thou warne her, that
Launcelot, the good knight, thy cousin, shall die. And therefore men shall now
15 say that thou art a manslayer, both of thy brother, Sir Lionel, and of thy cousin,
Sir Launcelot du Lake, the which thou mightest have saved and rescued easily,
but thou weenedst to rescue a maid which pertaineth nothing to thee. Now look
thou whether it had been greater harm of thy brother's death, or else to have suffered her to have lost her maidenhood. Then asked he him: Hast thou heard the
20 tokens of thy dream the which I have told to you? Yea forsooth, said Sir Bors, all
your exposition and declaring of my dream I have well understood and heard.
Then said the man in this black clothing: Then is it in thy default if Sir Launcelot,
thy cousin, die. Sir, said Bors, that were me loth,° for wit ye well° there is nothing
in the world but I had lever do it than to see my lord, Sir Launcelot du Lake, to
25 die in my default. Choose ye now the one or the other, said the good man. And
then he led Sir Bors into an high tower, and there he found knights and ladies:
those ladies said he was welcome, and so they unarmed him. And when he was
in his doublet° men brought him a mantle furred with ermine, and put it about
him; and then they made him such cheer that he had forgotten all his sorrow and
30 anguish, and only set his heart in these delights and dainties, and took no
thought more for his brother, Sir Lionel, neither of Sir Launcelot du Lake, his
cousin. And anon came out of a chamber to him the fairest lady that ever he saw,
and more richer bysene° than ever he saw Queen Guenever or any other estate.
Lo, said they, Sir Bors, here is the lady unto whom we owe all our service, and
35 I trow° she be the richest lady and the fairest of all the world, and the which
loveth you best above all other knights, for she will have no knight but you. And
when he understood that language he was abashed.° Not for then she saluted
him, and he her; and then they sat down together and spake° of many things, in
so much that she besought him to be her love, for she had loved him above all
40 earthly men, and she should make him richer than ever was man of his age.
When Bors understood her words he was right evil at ease,° which in no manner
would not break chastity, so wist not he° how to answer her.

---

⁷**dele** part   **betokeneth** signifies   ⁸**paramours** as a lover   **warne** refuse to accept
¹²**for to be holden chaste** to be thought virtuous   **loos** fame, praise; reputation; love
¹²⁻¹³**vain glory** unwarranted pride in accomplishments   ²³**that were me loth** that
would be hateful to me   **for wit ye well** for know you well   ²⁸**doublet** a close-fitting
garment worn by men   ³³**more richer bysene** more richly furnished, equipped
³⁵**I trow** I trust   ³⁷**abashed** astonished   ³⁸**spake** spoke   ⁴¹**right evil at ease** very ill
at ease   ⁴²**so wist not he** as he knew not

Chapter XII

HOW A DEVIL IN WOMAN'S LIKENESS WOULD HAVE TEMPTED SIR BORS, AND HOW BY
  GOD'S GRACE HE ESCAPED

Alas, said she, Bors, shall ye not do my will? Madam, said Bors, there is no lady
in the world whose will I will fulfill as of this thing, for my brother lieth dead
which was slain right late. Ah Bors, said she, I have loved you long for the great
beauty I have seen in you, and the great hardiness that I have heard of you, that
needs ye must lie by me this night, and therefore I pray you grant it me. Truly,   5
said he, I shall not do it in no manner wise.° Then she made him such sorrow as
though she would have died. Well Bors, said she, unto this have ye brought me,
nigh to mine end. And therewith she took him by the hand, and bad him behold
her.° And ye shall see how I shall die for your love. Ah, said then he, that shall I
never see. Then she departed and went up into an high battlement, and led with   10
her twelve gentlewomen; and when they were above, one of the gentlewomen
cried, and said: Ah, Sir Bors, gentle knight have mercy on us all, and suffer my
lady to have her will, and if ye do not we must suffer death with our lady, for to
fall down off this high tower, and if ye suffer us thus to die for so little a thing all
ladies and gentlewomen will say of you dishonour. Then looked he upward,   15
they seemed all ladies of great estate, and richly and well bisene.° Then had he
of them great pity; not for that he was uncounselled in himself that lever° he
had they all had lost their souls than he his, and with that they fell adown all at
once unto the earth. And when he saw that, he was all abashed, and had
thereof great marvel. With that he blessed his body and his visage. And anon he   20
heard a great noise and a great cry, as though all the fiends of hell had been
about him; and therewith he saw neither tower nor lady, nor gentlewoman, nor
no chapel where he brought his brother to. Then held he up both his hands to
the heaven, and said: Fair Father God, I am grievously escaped; and then he
took his arms and his horse and rode on his way. Then he heard a clock smite°   25
on his right hand; and thither he came to an Abbey on his right hand, closed
with high walls, and there was let in. Then they supposed that he was one of the
quest of the Sangreal,° so they led him into a chamber and unarmed him. Sirs,
said Sir Bors, if there be any holy man in this house I pray you let me speak
with him. Then one of them led him unto the Abbot, which was in a Chapel.   30
And then Sir Bors saluted him, and he him again. Sir, said Bors, I am a knight
errant;° and told him all the adventure which he had seen. Sir Knight, said the
Abbot, I wot not what ye be, for I weened never that a knight of your age might
have been so strong in the grace of our Lord Jesu Christ. Not for then ye shall go
unto your rest, for I will not counsel you this day, it is too late, and to-morrow   35
I shall counsel you as I can.

---

[6]**in no manner wise** in no way   [8-9]**bad him behold her** told him to look at her
[16]**well bisene** well furnished, equipped   [17]**lever** rather   [25]**smite** strike   [28]**Sangreal** the
chalice or cup in which the blood of Jesus was said to have been collected at the crucifixion. Having been lost, it was the object of a knightly quest. Legends of the grail are part of
the medieval stories of the Arthurian Round Table.   [31-32]**knight errant** armed fighters
who were willing to travel to do their chivalric duty: "errant" means "wandering"

Chapter XIII

OF THE HOLY COMMUNICATION OF AN ABBOT TO SIR BORS, AND HOW THE ABBOT
  COUNSELLED HIM

And that night was Sir Bors served richly; and on the morn early he heard mass, and the Abbot came to him, and bad him good morrow, and Bors to him again. And then he told him he was a fellow of the quest of the Sangreal, and how he had charge of the holy man to eat bread and water. Then said the Abbot: Our
5 Lord Jesu Christ showed him unto you in the likeness of a soul that suffered great anguish for us, syne He was put upon the cross, and bled His heart blood for mankind: there was the token and the likeness of the Sangreal that appeared afore you, for the blood that the great fowl bled revived the chickens from death to life. And by the bare tree is betokened the world which is naked and without
10 fruit but if it come of Our Lord. Also the lady for whom ye fought for, and King Aniause which was lord there tofore, betokeneth Jesu Christ which is the King of the world. And that ye fought with the champion for the lady, this it betokeneth: for when ye took the battle for the lady, by her shall ye understand the new law of Jesu Christ and Holy Church; and by the other lady ye shall under
15 stand the old law and the fiend, which all day warreth against Holy Church, therefore ye did your battle with right. For ye be Jesu Christ's knights, therefore ye ought to be defenders of Holy Church. And by the black bird might ye understand Holy Church, which sayeth I am black, but he is fair. And by the white bird might men understand the fiend, and I shall tell you how the swan is white
20 without forth, and black within: it is hypocrisy which is without yellow or pale, and seemeth without forth the servants of Jesu Christ, but they be within so horrible of filth and sin, and beguile the world evil. Also when the fiend appeared to thee in likeness of a man of religion, and blamed thee that thou left thy brother for a lady, so led thee where thou seemed thy brother was slain, but
25 he is yet on live; and all was for to put thee in error, and bring thee unto wanhope and lechery, for he knew thou were tender hearted, and all was for thou shouldst not find the blessed adventure of the Sangreal. And the third fowl betokeneth the strong battle against the fair ladies which were all devils. Also the dry tree and the white lily: the dry tree betokeneth thy brother Lionel, which is dry
30 without virtue, and therefore many men ought to call him the rotten tree, and the wormeaten tree, for he is a murderer and doth contrary to the order of knighthood. And the two white flowers signify two maidens, the one is a knight which was wounded the other day, and the other is the gentlewoman which ye rescued; and why the other flower drew nigh the other, that was the knight
35 which would have defouled her and himself both. And Sir Bors, ye had been a great fool and in great peril for to have seen those two flowers perish for to succour the rotten tree, for and they had sinned together they had been damned; and for that° ye rescued them both, men might call you a very knight and servant of Jesu Christ.

---

[38]**for that** because

Chapter XIV

HOW SIR BORS MET WITH HIS BROTHER SIR LIONEL, AND HOW SIR LIONEL WOULD HAVE
SLAIN SIR BORS

Then went Sir Bors from thence and commended the abbot unto God. And then
he rode all that day, and harboured with an old lady. And on the morn he rode
to a castle in a valley, and there he met with a yeoman going a great pace toward
a forest. Say me, said Sir Bors, canst thou tell me of any adventure? Sir, said he,
here shall be under this castle a great and a marvellous tournament. Of what   5
folks shall it be? said Sir Bors. The Earl of Plains shall be in the one party, and
the lady's nephew of Hervin on the other party. Then Bors thought to be there if
he might meet with his brother Sir Lionel, or any other of his fellowship, which
were in the quest of the Sangreal. And then he turned to an hermitage that was
in the entry of the forest. And when he was come thither he found there Sir   10
Lionel, his brother, which sat all armed at the entry of the chapel door for to
abide there harbour till on the morn that the tournament shall be. And when Sir
Bors saw him he had great joy of him, that it were marvel to tell of his joy. And
then he alit off his horse, and said: Fair sweet brother, when came ye hither?
Anon as Lionel saw him he said: Ah Bors, ye may not make none avaunt,° but   15
as for you I might have been slain; when ye saw two knights leading me away
beating me, ye left me for to succour a gentlewoman, and suffered me in peril of
death; for never erst ne did no° brother to another so great an untruth. And for
that misdeed now I ensure you but death, for well have ye deserved it; therefore
keep thee from henceforward, and that shall ye find as soon as I am armed.   20
When Sir Bors understood his brother's wrath he kneeled down to the earth and
cried him mercy, holding up both his hands, and prayed him to forgive him his
evil will. Nay, said Lionel, that shall never be an° I may have the higher hand,
that I make mine avow to God, thou shalt have death for it, for it were pity ye
lived any longer. Right so he went in and took his harness, and mounted upon   25
his horse, and came tofore him and said: Bors, keep thee from me, for I shall do
to thee as I would to a felon or a traitor, for ye be the untruest knight that ever
came out of so worthy an house as was King Bors' de Ganis which was our
father, therefore start upon thy horse, and so shall ye be most at your advantage.
And but if° ye will I will run upon you there as ye stand upon foot, and so the   30
shame shall be mine and the harm yours, but of that shame ne reck I nought.°
When Sir Bors saw that he must fight with his brother or else to die, he nist°
what to do; then his heart counselled him not thereto, inasmuch as Lionel was
born or he,° wherefore he ought to bear him reverence; yet kneeled he down
afore Lionel's horse's feet, and said: Fair sweet brother, have mercy upon me and   35
slay me not, and have in remembrance the great love which ought to be
between us twain. What Sir Bors said to Lionel he recked not,° for the fiend had

---

[15]**ye may not make none avaunt** you can't boast   [18]**never erst ne did no** never
before did any   [23]**an** if   [30]**and but if** and unless   [31]**ne reck I nought** I care nothing,
I do not care   [32]**he nist** he did not know   [34]**or he** before he [was]   [37]**he recked not** he
cared not

brought him in such a will that he should slay him. Then when Lionel saw he
would none other, and that he would not have risen to give him battle, he
40 rushed over him so that he smote° Bors with his horse, feet upward to the
earth, and hurt him so sore that he swooned of distress,° the which he felt in
himself to have died without confession. So when Lionel saw this, he alit off his
horse to have smitten off his head. And so he took him by the helm,° and would
have rent° it from his head. Then came the hermit running unto him, which was
45 a good man and of great age, and well had heard all the words that were between
them, and so fell down upon Sir Bors.

Chapter XV

HOW SIR COLGREVANCE FOUGHT AGAINST SIR LIONEL FOR TO SAVE SIR BORS, AND HOW
    THE HERMIT WAS SLAIN

Then he said to Lionel: Ah gentle knight, have mercy upon me and on thy
brother, for if thou slay him thou shalt be dead of sin, and that were sorrowful,
for he is one of the worthiest knights of the world, and of the best conditions.°
So God help me, said Lionel, sir priest, but if ye flee from him I shall slay you,
5 and he shall never the sooner be quit. Certes, said the good man, I have lever ye
slay me than him, for my death shall not be great harm, not half so much as of
his. Well, said Lionel, I am agreed; and set his hand to his sword and smote him
so hard that his head yede° backward. Not for that he restrained him of his evil
will, but took his brother by the helm, and unlaced it to have stricken° off his
10 head, and had slain° him without fail. But so it happed, Colgrevance, a fellow of
the Round Table, came at that time thither as Our Lord's will was. And when he
saw the good man slain he marvelled much what it might be. And then he
beheld Lionel would have slain his brother, and knew Sir Bors which he loved
right well. Then start he down and took Lionel by the shoulders, and drew him
15 strongly aback from Bors, and said: Lionel, will ye slay your brother, the
worthiest knight of the world one?° and that should no good man suffer. Why,
said Lionel, will ye let me?° therefore if ye intermit you in this° I shall slay you,
and him after. Why, said Colgrevance, is this sooth that ye will slay him? Slay
him will I, said he, whoso say° the contrary, for he hath done so much against
20 me that he hath well deserved it. And so ran upon him, and would have smitten
him through the head, and Sir Colgrevance ran betwixt them, and said: An ye be
so hardy to do so more,° we two shall meddle together.° When Lionel understood his words he took his shield afore him, and asked him what that he was.
And he told him, Colgrevance, one of his fellows. Then Lionel defied him, and
25 gave him a great stroke through the helm. Then he drew his sword, for he was a

---

⁴⁰**smote** struck   ⁴¹**so sore he swooned of distress** so badly that he fainted with the
injury   ⁴³**helm** helmet   ⁴⁴**rent** torn   ³**conditions** rank, family, social position   ⁸**yede**
went   ⁹**stricken** struck   ¹⁰**had slain** would have slain   ¹⁶**worthiest knight of the
world one** one of the worthiest knights of the world   ¹⁷**will ye let me?** will you
prevent me?   **if ye intermit you in this** if you mix yourself up in this   ¹⁹**whoso say**
whoever says   ²¹⁻²²**An ye be so hardy to do so more** if you be so foolhardy as to [fight]
any more   ²²**meddle together** fight

passing good knight, and defended him right manfully. So long dured the battle
that Bors rose up all anguishly, and beheld Colgrevance, the good knight, fought
with his brother for his quarrel; then was he full sorry and heavy, and thought if
Colgrevance slay him that was his brother he should never have joy; and if his
brother slew Colgrevance the shame should ever be mine. Then would he have   30
risen to have departed them, but he had not so much might to stand on foot; so
he abode him so long till Colgrevance had the worse, for Lionel was of great
chivalry and right hardy, for he had pierced the hauberk° and the helm, that he
abode but death, for he had lost much of his blood that it was marvel that he
might stand upright. Then beheld he Sir Bors which sat dressing him upward   35
and said: Ah, Bors, why come ye not to cast me out of peril of death, wherein I
have put me to succour you which were right now nigh the death? Certes,° said
Lionel, that shall not avail you, for none of you shall bear others warrant, but
that ye shall die both of my hand. When Bors heard that, he did so much, he
rose and put on his helm. Then perceived he first the hermit priest which was   40
slain, then made he a marvellous° sorrow upon him.

Chapter XVI

HOW SIR LIONEL SLEW SIR COLGREVANCE, AND HOW AFTER HE WOULD HAVE SLAIN
    SIR BORS

Then often Colgrevance cried upon Sir Bors: Why will ye let me die here for
your sake? if it please you that I die for you the death, it will please me the
better for to save a worthy man. With that word Sir Lionel smote off the helm
from his head. Then Colgrevance saw that he might not escape; then he said:
Fair sweet Jesu, that I have misdone have mercy upon my soul, for such sorrow   5
that my heart suffereth for goodness, and for alms deed that I would have done
here, be to me alygement of penance° unto my soul's health. At these words
Lionel smote him so sore that he bare him to the earth. So he had slain Colgrevance he ran upon his brother as a fiendly man, and gave him such a stroke that
he made him stoop. And he that was full of humility prayed him for God's love   10
to leave this battle: For an it befel, fair brother, that I slew you or ye me, we
should be dead of that sin. Never God me help but if I have on you mercy, an I
may have the better hand. Then drew Bors his sword, all weeping, and said: Fair
brother, God knoweth mine intent. Ah, fair brother, ye have done full evil this
day to slay such an holy priest the which never trespassed. Also ye have slain a   15
gentle knight, and one of our fellows. And well wot° ye that I am not afeared of
you greatly, but I dread the wrath of God, and this is an unkindly° war, therefore God show miracle upon us both. Now God have mercy upon me though
I defend my life against my brother; with that Bors lift up his hand and would
have smitten his brother.   20

---

³³**hauberk** a chain mail tunic that is part of a knight's armor   ³⁷**Certes** Surely
⁴¹**marvellous** great   ⁷**alygement of penance** relief gained from penance   ¹⁶**wot** know
¹⁷**unkindly** unkind, unnatural because it involves "kind," that is, family

Chapter XVII

HOW THERE CAME A VOICE WHICH CHARGED SIR BORS TO TOUCH HIM NOT, AND OF A
CLOUD THAT CAME BETWEEN THEM

And then he heard a voice that said: Flee Bors, and touch him not, or else thou
shall slay him. Right so alit a cloud betwixt them in likeness of a fire and a
marvellous flame, that both their two shields burnt. Then were they sore° afraid,
that they fell both to the earth, and lay there a great while in a swoon. And when
5 they came to themself, Bors saw that his brother had no harm; then he held up
both his hands, for he dread God had taken vengeance upon him. With that he
heard a voice say: Bors, go hence, and bear thy brother no longer fellowship, but
take thy way anon right to the sea, for Sir Percivale abideth thee there. Then he
said to his brother: Fair sweet brother, forgive me for God's love all that I have
10 trespassed unto you. Then he answered: God forgive it thee and I do gladly.
So Sir Bors departed from him and rode the next way to the sea.   [c. 1470]

³**sore** very

1. Who are Sir Bors and Sir Lionel? What is the cause of the conflict between
   them?
2. What dream does Sir Bors have and what temptations does he face? From
   whom does he seek and receive advice about how to deal with these
   dilemmas?
3. What assumptions (or values or beliefs) govern the way Sir Bors resolves
   the dilemmas he confronts?
4. Locate information about King Arthur, his knights, and the code of chivalry
   that united them and provided them a common worldview. How does that
   information illuminate the events in this excerpt?
5. To what other works in this section can you connect this excerpt?

KATHERINE MANSFIELD

KATHERINE MANSFIELD *(1888–1923) was born in New Zealand. Her first love
was the violoncello, but she published her first text when she was nine years old.
The collections of her short stories,* In a German Pension, Bliss, *and* The
Garden-Party, *established her as a major writer. After an unhappy first marriage,
she married the critic John Middleton Murry. She died of tuberculosis at the age of
thirty-five. Her stories, often characterized as delicate, luminous, and evocative, are
simple in form, showing people in moments of decision.*

The Garden-Party

And after all the weather was ideal. They could not have had a more perfect day
for a garden-party if they had ordered it. Windless, warm, the sky without a
cloud. Only the blue was veiled with a haze of light gold, as it is sometimes in
early summer. The gardener had been up since dawn, mowing the lawns and

sweeping them, until the grass and the dark flat rosettes where the daisy plants had been seemed to shine. As for the roses, you could not help feeling they understood that roses are the only flowers that impress people at garden-parties; the only flowers that everybody is certain of knowing. Hundreds, yes, literally hundreds, had come out in a single night; the green bushes bowed down as though they had been visited by archangels.

Breakfast was not yet over before the men came to put up the marquee.

"Where do you want the marquee put, mother?"

"My dear child, it's no use asking me. I'm determined to leave everything to you children this year. Forget I am your mother. Treat me as an honoured guest."

But Meg could not possibly go and supervise the men. She had washed her hair before breakfast, and she sat drinking her coffee in a green turban, with a dark wet curl stamped on each cheek. Jose, the butterfly, always came down in a silk petticoat and a kimono jacket.

"You'll have to go, Laura; you're the artistic one."

Away Laura flew, still holding her piece of bread-and-butter. It's so delicious to have an excuse for eating out of doors, and besides, she loved having to arrange things; she always felt she could do it so much better than anybody else.

Four men in their shirt-sleeves stood grouped together on the garden path. They carried staves covered with rolls of canvas, and they had big tool-bags slung on their backs. They looked impressive. Laura wished now that she had not got the bread-and-butter, but there was nowhere to put it, and she couldn't possibly throw it away. She blushed and tried to look severe and even a little bit short-sighted as she came up to them.

"Good morning," she said, copying her mother's voice. But that sounded so fearfully affected that she was ashamed, and stammered like a little girl, "Oh—er—have you come—is it about the marquee?"

"That's right, miss," said the tallest of the men, a lanky, freckled fellow, and he shifted his tool-bag, knocked back his straw hat and smiled down at her. "That's about it."

His smile was so easy, so friendly that Laura recovered. What nice eyes he had, small, but such dark blue! And now she looked at the others, they were smiling too. "Cheer up, we won't bite," their smile seemed to say. How very nice workmen were! And what a beautiful morning! She mustn't mention the morning; she must be businesslike. The marquee.

"Well, what about the lily-lawn? Would that do?"

And she pointed to the lily-lawn with the hand that didn't hold the bread-and-butter. They turned, they stared in the direction. A little fat chap thrust out his under-lip, and the tall fellow frowned.

"I don't fancy it," said he. "Not conspicuous enough. You see, with a thing like a marquee," and he turned to Laura in his easy way, "you want to put it somewhere where it'll give you a bang slap in the eye, if you follow me."

Laura's upbringing made her wonder for a moment whether it was quite respectful of a workman to talk to her of bangs slap in the eye. But she did quite follow him.

"A corner of the tennis-court," she suggested. "But the band's going to be in one corner."

"H'm, going to have a band, are you?" said another of the workmen. He was pale. He had a haggard look as his dark eyes scanned the tennis-court. What was he thinking?

"Only a very small band," said Laura gently. Perhaps he wouldn't mind so much if the band was quite small. But the tall fellow interrupted.

"Look here, miss, that's the place. Against those trees. Over there. That'll do fine."

20 Against the karakas. Then the karaka-trees would be hidden. And they were so lovely, with their broad, gleaming leaves, and their clusters of yellow fruit. They were like trees you imagined growing on a desert island, proud, solitary, lifting their leaves and fruits to the sun in a kind of silent splendour. Must they be hidden by a marquee?

They must. Already the men had shouldered their staves and were making for the place. Only the tall fellow was left. He bent down, pinched a sprig of lavender, put his thumb and forefinger to his nose and snuffed up the smell. When Laura saw that gesture she forgot all about the karakas in her wonder at him caring for things like that—caring for the smell of lavender. How many men that she knew would have done such a thing? Oh, how extraordinarily nice workmen were, she thought. Why couldn't she have workmen for friends rather than the silly boys she danced with and who came to Sunday night supper? She would get on much better with men like these.

It's all the fault, she decided, as the tall fellow drew something on the back of an envelope, something that was to be looped up or left to hang, of these absurd class distinctions. Well, for her part, she didn't feel them. Not a bit, not an atom. . . . And now there came the chock-chock of wooden hammers. Some one whistled, some one sang out, "Are you right there, matey?" "Matey!" The friendliness of it, the—the—Just to prove how happy she was, just to show the tall fellow how at home she felt, and how she despised stupid conventions, Laura took a big bite of her bread-and-butter as she stared at the little drawing. She felt just like a work-girl.

"Laura, Laura, where are you? Telephone, Laura!" a voice cried from the house.

"Coming!" Away she skimmed, over the lawn, up the path, up the steps, across the veranda, and into the porch. In the hall her father and Laurie were brushing their hats ready to go to the office.

25 "I say, Laura," said Laurie very fast, "you might just give a squiz at my coat before this afternoon. See if it wants pressing."

"I will," said she. Suddenly she couldn't stop herself. She ran at Laurie and gave him a small, quick squeeze. "Oh, I do love parties, don't you?" gasped Laura.

"Ra-ther," said Laurie's warm, boyish voice, and he squeezed his sister too, and gave her a gentle push. "Dash off to the telephone, old girl."

The telephone. "Yes, yes; oh yes. Kitty? Good morning, dear. Come to lunch? Do, dear. Delighted of course. It will only be a very scratch meal—just the sandwich crusts and broken meringue-shells and what's left over. Yes, isn't it a perfect morning? Your white? Oh, I certainly should. One moment—hold the line. Mother's calling." And Laura sat back. "What, mother? Can't hear."

Mrs. Sheridan's voice floated down the stairs. "Tell her to wear that sweet hat she had on last Sunday."

"Mother says you're to wear that *sweet* hat you had on last Sunday. Good. One o'clock. Bye-bye." 30

Laura put back the receiver, flung her arms over her head, took a deep breath, stretched and let them fall. "Huh," she sighed, and the moment after the sigh she sat up quickly. She was still, listening. All the doors in the house seemed to be open. The house was alive with soft, quick steps and running voices. The green baize door that led to the kitchen regions swung open and shut with a muffled thud. And now there came a long, chuckling absurd sound. It was the heavy piano being moved on its stiff castors. But the air! If you stopped to notice, was the air always like this? Little faint winds were playing chase, in at the tops of the windows, out at the doors. And there were two tiny spots of sun, one on the inkpot, one on a silver photograph frame, playing too. Darling little spots. Especially the one on the inkpot lid. It was quite warm. A warm little silver star. She could have kissed it.

The front door bell pealed, and there sounded the rustle of Sadie's print skirt on the stairs. A man's voice murmured; Sadie answered, careless, "I'm sure I don't know. Wait. I'll ask Mrs. Sheridan."

"What is it, Sadie?" Laura came into the hall.

"It's the florist, Miss Laura."

It was, indeed. There, just inside the door, stood a wide, shallow tray full of pots of pink lilies. No other kind. Nothing but lilies—canna lilies, big pink flowers, wide open, radiant, almost frighteningly alive on bright crimson stems. 35

"O-oh Sadie!" said Laura, and the sound was like a little moan. She crouched down as if to warm herself at that blaze of lilies; she felt they were in her fingers, on her lips, growing in her breast.

"It's some mistake," she said faintly. "Nobody ever ordered so many. Sadie, go and find mother."

But at that moment Mrs. Sheridan joined them.

"It's quite right," she said calmly. "Yes, I ordered them. Aren't they lovely?" She pressed Laura's arm. "I was passing the shop yesterday, and I saw them in the window. And I suddenly thought for once in my life I shall have enough canna lilies. The garden-party will be a good excuse."

"But I thought you said you didn't mean to interfere," said Laura. Sadie had gone. The florist's man was still outside at his van. She put her arm round her mother's neck and gently, very gently, she bit her mother's ear. 40

"My darling child, you wouldn't like a logical mother, would you? Don't do that. Here's the man."

He carried more lilies still, another whole tray.

"Bank them up, just inside the door, on both sides of the porch, please," said Mrs. Sheridan. "Don't you agree, Laura?"

"Oh, I *do* mother."

45   In the drawing-room Meg, Jose and good little Hans had at last succeeded in moving the piano.

"Now, if we put this chesterfield against the wall and move everything out of the room except the chairs, don't you think?"

"Quite."

"Hans, move these tables into the smoking-room, and bring a sweeper to take these marks off the carpet and—one moment, Hans—" Jose loved giving orders to the servants, and they loved obeying her. She always made them feel they were taking part in some drama. "Tell mother and Miss Laura to come here at once."

"Very good, Miss Jose."

50   She turned to Meg. "I want to hear what the piano sounds like, just in case I'm asked to sing this afternoon. Let's try over 'This Life is Weary.'"

Pom! Ta-ta-ta *Tee*-ta! The piano burst out so passionately that Jose's face changed. She clasped her hands. She looked mournfully and enigmatically at her mother and Laura as they came in.

> This Life is *Wee*-ary,
> A Tear—a Sigh.
> A Love that *Chan*-ges,
> This Life is *Wee*-ary,
> A Tear—a Sigh.
> A Love that *Chan*-ges,
> And then . . . *Good*-bye!

But at the word "Good-bye," and although the piano sounded more desperate than ever, her face broke into a brilliant, dreadfully unsympathetic smile.

"Aren't I in good voice, mummy?" she beamed.

> This Life is *Wee*-ary,
> Hope comes to Die.
> A Dream—a *Wa*-kening.

But now Sadie interrupted them. "What is it, Sadie?"

55   "If you please, m'm, cook says have you got the flags for the sandwiches?"

"The flags for the sandwiches, Sadie?" echoed Mrs. Sheridan dreamily. And the children knew by her face that she hadn't got them. "Let me see." And she said to Sadie firmly, "Tell cook I'll let her have them in ten minutes."

Sadie went.

"Now, Laura," said her mother quickly. "Come with me into the smoking-room. I've got the names somewhere on the back of an envelope. You'll have to write them out for me. Meg, go upstairs this minute and take that wet thing off your head. Jose, run and finish dressing this instant. Do you hear me, children, or shall I have to tell your father when he comes home to-night? And—and, Jose, pacify cook if you do go into the kitchen, will you? I'm terrified of her this morning."

The envelope was found at last behind the dining-room clock, though how it had got there Mrs. Sheridan could not imagine.

60   "One of you children must have stolen it out of my bag, because I remember vividly—cream cheese and lemon-curd. Have you done that?"

"Yes."

"Egg and—" Mrs. Sheridan held the envelope away from her. "It looks like mice. It can't be mice, can it?"

"Olive, pet," said Laura, looking over her shoulder.

"Yes, of course, olive. What a horrible combination it sounds. Egg and olive."

They were finished at last, and Laura took them off to the kitchen. She found Jose there pacifying the cook, who did not look at all terrifying.

"I have never seen such exquisite sandwiches," said Jose's rapturous voice. "How many kinds did you say there were, cook? Fifteen?"

"Fifteen, Miss Jose."

"Well, cook, I congratulate you."

Cook swept up crusts with the long sandwich knife, and smiled broadly.

"Godber's has come," announced Sadie, issuing out of the pantry. She had seen the man pass the window.

That meant the cream puffs had come. Godber's were famous for their cream puffs. Nobody ever thought of making them at home.

"Bring them in and put them on the table, my girl," ordered cook.

Sadie brought them in and went back to the door. Of course Laura and Jose were far too grown-up to really care about such things. All the same, they couldn't help agreeing that the puffs looked very attractive. Very. Cook began arranging them, shaking off the extra icing sugar.

"Don't they carry one back to all one's parties?" said Laura.

"I suppose they do," said practical Jose, who never liked to be carried back. "They look beautifully light and feathery, I must say."

"Have one each, my dears," said cook in her comfortable voice. "Yer ma won't know."

Oh, impossible. Fancy cream puffs so soon after breakfast. The very idea made one shudder. All the same, two minutes later Jose and Laura were licking their fingers with that absorbed inward look that only comes from whipped cream.

"Let's go into the garden, out by the back way," suggested Laura. "I want to see how the men are getting on with the marquee. They're such awfully nice men."

But the back door was blocked by cook, Sadie, Godber's man and Hans. Something had happened.

"Tuk-tuk-tuk," clucked cook like an agitated hen. Sadie had her hand clapped to her cheek as though she had toothache. Hans's face was screwed up in the effort to understand. Only Godber's man seemed to be enjoying himself; it was his story.

"What's the matter? What's happened?"

"There's been a horrible accident," said Cook. "A man killed."

"A man killed! Where? How? When?"

But Godber's man wasn't going to have his story snatched from under his very nose.

"Know those little cottages just below here, miss?" Know them? Of course, she knew them. "Well, there's a young chap living there, name of Scott, a carter.

His horse shied at a traction-engine, corner of Hawke Street this morning, and he was thrown out on the back of his head. Killed."

"Dead!" Laura stared at Godber's man.

"Dead when they picked him up," said Godber's man with relish. "They were taking the body home as I come up here." And he said to the cook, "He's left a wife and five little ones."

"Jose, come here." Laura caught hold of her sister's sleeve and dragged her through the kitchen to the other side of the green baize door. There she paused and leaned against it. "Jose!" she said, horrified, "however are we going to stop everything?"

90   "Stop everything, Laura!" cried Jose in astonishment. "What do you mean?"

"Stop the garden-party, of course." Why did Jose pretend?

But Jose was still more amazed. "Stop the garden-party? My dear Laura, don't be so absurd. Of course we can't do anything of the kind. Nobody expects us to. Don't be so extravagant."

"But we can't possibly have a garden-party with a man dead just outside the front gate."

That really was extravagant, for the little cottages were in a lane to them-selves at the very bottom of a steep rise that led up to the house. A broad road ran between. True, they were far too near. They were the greatest possible eye-sore, and they had no right to be in that neighbourhood at all. They were little mean dwellings painted a chocolate brown. In the garden patches there was nothing but cabbage stalks, sick hens and tomato cans. The very smoke coming out of their chimneys was poverty-stricken. Little rags and shreds of smoke, so unlike the great silvery plumes that uncurled from the Sheridans' chimneys. Washerwomen lived in the lane and sweeps and a cobbler, and a man whose house-front was studded all over with minute bird-cages. Children swarmed. When the Sheridans were little they were forbidden to set foot there because of the revolting language and of what they might catch. But since they were grown up, Laura and Laurie on their prowls sometimes walked through. It was disgusting and sordid. They came out with a shudder. But still one must go everywhere; one must see everything. So through they went.

95   "And just think of what the band would sound like to that poor woman," said Laura.

"Oh, Laura!" Jose began to be seriously annoyed. "If you're going to stop a band playing every time some one has an accident, you'll lead a very strenuous life. I'm every bit as sorry about it as you. I feel just as sympathetic." Her eyes hardened. She looked at her sister just as she used to when they were little and fighting together. "You won't bring a drunken workman back to life by being sentimental," she said softly.

"Drunk! Who said he was drunk?" Laura turned furiously on Jose. She said, just as they had used to say on those occasions, "I'm going straight up to tell mother."

"Do, dear," cooed Jose.

"Mother, can I come in your room?" Laura turned the big glass door-knob.

"Of course, child. Why, what's the matter? What's given you such a colour?" 100
And Mrs. Sheridan turned round from her dressing-table. She was trying on a
new hat.

"Mother, a man's been killed," began Laura.

"Not in the garden?" interrupted her mother.

"No, no!"

"Oh, what a fright you gave me!" Mrs. Sheridan sighed with relief, and took
off the big hat and held it on her knees.

"But listen, mother," said Laura. Breathless, half-choking, she told the 105
dreadful story. "Of course, we can't have our party, can we?" she pleaded. "The
band and everybody arriving. They'd hear us, mother; they're nearly neighbors!"

To Laura's astonishment her mother behaved just like Jose, it was harder to
bear because she seemed amused. She refused to take Laura seriously.

"But, my dear child, use your common sense. It's only by accident we've
heard of it. If some one had died there normally—and I can't understand how
they keep alive in those poky little holes—we should still be having our party,
shouldn't we?"

Laura had to say "yes" to that, but she felt it was all wrong. She sat down on
her mother's sofa and pinched the cushion frill.

"Mother, isn't it really terribly heartless of us?" she asked.

"Darling!" Mrs. Sheridan got up and came over to her, carrying the hat. Before 110
Laura could stop her she had popped it on. "My child!" said her mother, "the hat
is yours. It's made for you. It's much too young for me. I have never seen you
look such a picture. Look at yourself!" And she held up her hand-mirror.

"But, mother," Laura began again. She couldn't look at herself; she turned
aside.

This time Mrs. Sheridan lost patience just as Jose had done.

"You are being very absurd, Laura," she said coldly. "People like that don't
expect sacrifices from us. And it's not very sympathetic to spoil everybody's
enjoyment as you're doing now."

"I don't understand," said Laura, and she walked quickly out of the room into
her own bedroom. There, quite by chance, the first thing she saw was this
charming girl in the mirror, in her black hat trimmed with gold daisies, and a
long black velvet ribbon. Never had she imagined she could look like that. Is
mother right? she thought. And now she hoped her mother was right. Am I
being extravagant? Perhaps it was extravagant. Just for a moment she had
another glimpse of that poor woman and those little children, and the body
being carried into the house. But it all seemed blurred, unreal, like a picture in
the newspaper. I'll remember it again after the party's over, she decided. And
somehow that seemed quite the best plan. . . .

Lunch was over by half-past one. By half-past two they were all ready for the 115
fray. The green-coated band had arrived and was established in a corner of the
tennis-court.

"My dear!" trilled Kitty Maitland, "aren't they too like frogs for words? You
ought to have arranged them round the pond with the conductor in the middle
on a leaf."

Laurie arrived and hailed them on his way to dress. At the sight of him Laura remembered the accident again. She wanted to tell him. If Laurie agreed with the others, then it was bound to be all right. And she followed him into the hall.

"Laurie!"

"Hallo!" He was half-way upstairs, but when he turned round and saw Laura he suddenly puffed out his cheeks and goggled his eyes at her. "My word, Laura; You do look stunning," said Laurie. "What an absolutely topping hat!"

120   Laura said faintly, "Is it?" and smiled up at Laurie, and didn't tell him after all.

Soon after that people began coming in streams. The band struck up; the hired waiters ran from the house to the marquee. Wherever you looked there were couples strolling, bending to the flowers, greeting, moving on over the lawn. They were like bright birds that had alighted in the Sheridan's garden for this one afternoon, on their way to—where? Ah, what happiness it is to be with people who all are happy, to press hands, press cheeks, smile into eyes.

"Darling Laura, how well you look!"

"What a becoming hat, child!"

"Laura, you look quite Spanish. I've never seen you look so striking."

125   And Laura, glowing, answered softly, "Have you had tea? Won't you have an ice? The passion-fruit ices really are rather special." She ran to her father and begged him. "Daddy darling, can't the band have something to drink?"

And the perfect afternoon slowly ripened, slowly faded, slowly its petals closed.

"Never a more delightful garden-party . . ." "The greatest success . . ." "Quite the most . . ."

Laura helped her mother with the good-byes. They stood side by side in the porch till it was all over.

"All over, all over, thank heaven," said Mrs. Sheridan. "Round up the others, Laura. Let's go and have some fresh coffee. I'm exhausted. Yes, it's been very successful. But oh, these parties, these parties! Why will you children insist on giving parties!" And they all of them sat down in the deserted marquee.

130   "Have a sandwich, daddy dear. I wrote the flag."

"Thanks," Mr. Sheridan took a bite and the sandwich was gone. He took another. "I suppose you didn't hear of a beastly accident that happened to-day?" he said.

"My dear," said Mrs. Sheridan, holding up her hand, "we did. It nearly ruined the party. Laura insisted we should put it off."

"Oh, mother!" Laura didn't want to be teased about it.

"It was a horrible affair all the same," said Mr. Sheridan. "The chap was married too. Lived just below in the lane, and leaves a wife and half a dozen kiddies, so they say."

135   An awkward little silence fell. Mrs. Sheridan fidgeted with her cup. Really, it was very tactless of father. . . .

Suddenly she looked up. There on the table were all those sandwiches, cakes, puffs, all uneaten, all going to be wasted. She had one of her brilliant ideas.

"I know," she said. "Let's make up a basket. Let's send that poor creature some of this perfectly good food. At any rate, it will be the greatest treat for the children. Don't you agree? And she's sure to have neighbours calling in and so on. What a point to have it all ready prepared. Laura!" She jumped up. "Get me the big basket out of the stairs cupboard."

"But, mother, do you really think it's a good idea?" said Laura.

Again, how curious, she seemed to be different from them all. To take scraps from their party. Would the poor woman really like that?

"Of course! What's the matter with you to-day? An hour or two ago you were insisting on us being sympathetic, and now—" 140

Oh, well! Laura ran for the basket. It was filled, it was heaped by her mother.

"Take it yourself, darling," said she. "Run down just as you are. No, wait, take the arum lilies too. People of that class are so impressed by arum lilies."

"The stems will ruin her lace frock," said practical Jose.

So they would. Just in time. "Only the basket, then. And, Laura!"—her mother followed her out of the marquee—"don't on any account—"

"What, mother?" 145

No, better not put such ideas into the child's head! "Nothing! Run along."

It was just growing dusky as Laura shut their garden gates. A big dog ran by like a shadow. The road gleamed white, and down below in the hollow the little cottages were in deep shade. How quiet it seemed after the afternoon. Here she was going down the hill to somewhere where a man lay dead, and she couldn't realize it. Why couldn't she? She stopped a minute. And it seemed to her that kisses, voices, tinkling spoons, laughter, the smell of crushed grass were somehow inside her. She had no room for anything else. How strange! She looked up at the pale sky, and all she thought was, "Yes, it was the most successful party."

Now the broad road was crossed. The lane began, smoky and dark. Women in shawls and men's tweed caps hurried by. Men hung over the palings; the children played in the doorways. A low hum came from the mean little cottages. In some of them there was a flicker of light, and a shadow, crab-like, moved across the window. Laura bent her head and hurried on. She wished now she had put on a coat. How her frock shone! And the big hat with the velvet streamer—if only it was another hat! Were the people looking at her? They must be. It was a mistake to have come; she knew all along it was a mistake. Should she go back even now?

No, too late. This was the house. It must be. A dark knot of people stood outside. Beside the gate an old, old woman with a crutch sat in a chair, watching. She had her feet on a newspaper. The voices stopped as Laura drew near. The group parted. It was as though she was expected, as though they had known she was coming here.

Laura was terribly nervous. Tossing the velvet ribbon over her shoulder, she said to a woman standing by, "Is this Mrs. Scott's house?" and the woman, smiling queerly, said, "It is, my lass." 150

Oh, to be away from this! She actually said, "Help me, God," as she walked up the tiny path and knocked. To be away from those staring eyes, or to be covered up in anything, one of those women's shawls even. I'll just leave the basket and go, she decided. I shan't even wait for it to be emptied.

Then the door opened. A little woman in black showed in the gloom.

Laura said, "Are you Mrs. Scott?" But to her horror the woman answered, "Walk in please, miss," and she was shut in the passage.

"No," said Laura, "I don't want to come in. I only want to leave this basket. Mother sent—"

155 The little woman in the gloomy passage seemed not to have heard her. "Step this way, please, miss," she said in an oily voice, and Laura followed her.

She found herself in a wretched little low kitchen, lighted by a smoky lamp. There was a woman sitting before the fire.

"Em," said the little creature who had let her in. "Em! It's a young lady." She turned to Laura. She said meaningly, "I'm 'er sister, Miss. You'll excuse 'er, won't you?"

"Oh, but of course!" said Laura. "Please, please don't disturb her. I—I only want to leave—"

But at that moment the woman at the fire turned round. Her face, puffed up, red, with swollen eyes and swollen lips, looked terrible. She seemed as though she couldn't understand why Laura was there. What did it mean? Why was this stranger standing in the kitchen with a basket? What was it all about? And the poor face puckered up again.

160 "All right, my dear," said the other. "I'll thenk the young lady."

And again she began, "You'll excuse her, miss, I'm sure," and her face, swollen too, tried an oily smile.

Laura only wanted to get out, to get away. She was back in the passage. The door opened. She walked straight through into the bedroom, where the dead man was lying.

"You'd like a look at 'im, wouldn't you?" said Em's sister, and she brushed past Laura over to the bed. "Don't be afraid, my lass,—" and now her voice sounded fond and sly, and fondly she drew down the sheet—"'e looks a picture. There's nothing to show. Come along, my dear."

There lay a young man, fast asleep—sleeping so soundly, so deeply, that he was far, far away from them both. Oh, so remote, so peaceful. He was dreaming Never wake him up again. His head was sunk in the pillow, his eyes were closed; they were blind under the closed eyelids. He was given up to his dream. What did garden-parties and baskets and lace frocks matter to him? He was far from all those things. He was wonderful, beautiful. While they were laughing and while the band was playing, this marvel had come to the lane. Happy . . . happy. . . . All is well, said that sleeping face. This is just as it should be. I am content.

165 But all the same you had to cry, and she couldn't go out of the room without saying something to him. Laura gave a loud childish sob.

"Forgive my hat," she said.

And this time she didn't wait for Em's sister. She found her way out of the door, down the path, past all those dark people. At the corner of the lane she met Laurie.

He stepped out of the shadow. "Is that you, Laura?"

"Yes."

170 "Mother was getting anxious. Was it all right?"

"Yes, quite. Oh, Laurie!" She took his arm, she pressed up against him.

"I say, you're not crying, are you?" asked her brother.

Laura shook her head. She was.

Laurie put his arm round her shoulder. "Don't cry," he said in his warm, loving voice. "Was it awful?"

"No," sobbed Laura. "It was simply marvellous. But, Laurie—" She stopped,   175
she looked at her brother. "Isn't life," she stammered, "isn't life—" But what life was she couldn't explain. No matter. He quite understood.

"*Isn't* it, darling?" said Laurie.

[1922]

1. What is the relationship of Mr. Scott (the dead man) and his family to the Sheridans, the family having the garden party?
2. Despite Scott's death, the Sheridans hold their garden party as planned. What assumptions underlie and help justify their rationale for doing so?
3. Compare and contrast the two social events depicted in this story. What significance do you observe in their juxtaposition?
4. What conceptual frameworks can enhance our view of this story?
5. Compare this short story to Robert Frost's "The Death of the Hired Man" (p. 1078), to John Balaban's "For the Missing in Action" (p. 1075), or to Ursula LeGuin's "The Ones Who Walk Away from Omelas" (p. 1139).

TIM O'BRIEN

TIM O'BRIEN *(1946–) opposed the war in Vietnam but was drafted after he graduated from Macalester College in 1968, serving from 1969–1970 in the 3rd Platoon, A Co., 5th Battalion 46th infantry and leaving with a Combat Infantry Badge. After the war he spent some time as a graduate student and then as a newspaper reporter, which led him to start writing about his war experience in memoirs like* If I Die in a Combat Zone, Box Me Up and Send Me Home *and fiction like* The Things They Carried, *of which this is the title story.*

The Things They Carried

First Lieutenant Jimmy Cross carried letters from a girl named Martha, a junior at Mount Sebastian College in New Jersey. They were not love letters, but Lieutenant Cross was hoping, so he kept them folded in plastic at the bottom of his rucksack. In the late afternoon, after a day's march, he would dig his foxhole, wash his hands under a canteen, unwrap the letters, hold them with the tips of his fingers, and spend the last hour of light pretending. He would imagine romantic camping trips into the White Mountains in New Hampshire. He would sometimes taste the envelope flaps, knowing her tongue had been there. More than anything, he wanted Martha to love him as he loved her, but the letters were mostly chatty, elusive on the matter of love. She was a virgin, he was almost sure. She was an English major at Mount Sebastian, and she wrote beautifully about her professors and roommates and midterm exams, about her respect for Chaucer and her great affection for Virginia Woolf. She often quoted lines of poetry; she never mentioned the war, except to say, Jimmy, take care of yourself. The letters weighed ten ounces. They were signed "Love, Martha," but Lieutenant Cross understood that "Love" was only a way of signing and did not mean what he sometimes pretended it meant. At dusk, he would carefully return the letters to his rucksack. Slowly, a bit distracted, he would get up and move among his men, checking the perimeter, then at full dark he would return to his hole and watch the night and wonder if Martha was a virgin.

The things they carried were largely determined by necessity. Among the necessities or near necessities were P-38 can openers, pocket knives, heat tabs, wrist watches, dog tags, mosquito repellant, chewing gum, candy, cigarettes, salt tablets, packets of Kool-Aid, lighters, matches, sewing kits, Military Payment Certificates, C rations, and two or three canteens of water. Together, these items weighed between fifteen and twenty pounds, depending upon a man's habits or rate of metabolism. Henry Dobbins, who was a big man, carried extra rations; he was especially fond of canned peaches in heavy syrup over pound cake. Dave Jensen, who practiced field hygiene, carried a toothbrush, dental floss, and several hotel-size bars of soap he'd stolen on R&R° in Sydney, Australia. Ted Lavender, who was scared, carried tranquilizers until he was shot in the head outside the village of Than Khe in mid-April. By necessity, and because it was SOP,° they all carried steel helmets that weighed five pounds including the liner and camouflage cover. They carried the standard fatigue jackets and trousers. Very few carried underwear. On their feet they carried jungle boots—2.1 pounds—and Dave Jensen carried three pairs of socks and a can of Dr. Scholl's foot powder as a precaution against trench foot. Until he was shot, Ted Lavender carried six or seven ounces of premium dope, which for him was a necessity. Mitchell Sanders, the RTO,° carried condoms. Norman Bowker carried a diary. Rat Kiley carried comic books. Kiowa, a devout Baptist, carried an illustrated New Testament that had been presented to him by his father, who taught Sunday school in Oklahoma City, Oklahoma. As a hedge against bad times, however, Kiowa also carried his grandmother's distrust of the white man, his grandfather's old hunting hatchet. Necessity dictated. Because the land was mined and booby-trapped, it was SOP for each man to carry a steel-centered, nylon-covered flak jacket,° which weighed 6.7 pounds, but which on hot days seemed much heavier. Because you could die so quickly, each man carried at least one large compress bandage, usually in the helmet band for easy access. Because the nights were cold, and because the monsoons were wet, each carried a green plastic poncho that could be used as a raincoat or ground sheet or makeshift tent. With its quilted liner, the poncho weighed almost two pounds, but it was worth every ounce. In April, for instance, when Ted Lavender was shot, they used his poncho to wrap him up, then to carry him across the paddy, then to lift him into the chopper that took him away.

---

[2]**R&R** Rest and Recreation   **SOP** Standard Operating Procedure   **RTO** Radio Telephone Operator   **flak jacket** garment made out of heavy fabric with embedded metal plates to protect against shells from weapons

They were called legs or grunts.

To carry something was to "hump" it, as when Lieutenant Jimmy Cross humped his love for Martha up the hills and through the swamps. In its intransitive form, "to hump" meant "to walk," or "to march," but it implied burdens far beyond the intransitive.

Almost everyone humped photographs. In his wallet, Lieutenant Cross   5 carried two photographs of Martha. The first was a Kodachrome snapshot signed "Love," though he knew better. She stood against a brick wall. Her eyes were gray and neutral, her lips slightly open as she stared straight-on at the camera. At night, sometimes, Lieutenant Cross wondered who had taken the picture, because he knew she had boyfriends, because he loved her so much, and because he could see the shadow of the picture taker spreading out against the brick wall. The second photograph had been clipped from the 1968 Mount Sebastian yearbook. It was an action shot—women's volleyball—and Martha was bent horizontal to the floor, reaching, the palms of her hands in sharp focus, the tongue taut, the expression frank and competitive. There was no visible sweat. She wore white gym shorts. Her legs, he thought, were almost certainly the legs of a virgin, dry and without hair, the left knee cocked and carrying her entire weight, which was just over one hundred pounds. Lieutenant Cross remembered touching that left knee. A dark theater, he remembered, and the movie was *Bonnie and Clyde,* and Martha wore a tweed skirt, and during the final scene, when he touched her knee, she turned and looked at him in a sad, sober way that made him pull his hand back, but he would always remember the feel of the tweed skirt and the knee beneath it and the sound of the gunfire that killed Bonnie and Clyde, how embarrassing it was, how slow and oppressive. He remembered kissing her good night at the dorm door. Right then, he thought, he should've done something brave. He should've carried her up the stairs to her room and tied her to the bed and touched that left knee all night long. He should've risked it. Whenever he looked at the photographs, he thought of new things he should've done.

What they carried was partly a function of rank, partly of field specialty.

As a first lieutenant and platoon leader, Jimmy Cross carried a compass, maps, code books, binoculars, and a .45-caliber pistol that weighed 2.9 pounds fully loaded. He carried a strobe light and the responsibility for the lives of his men.

As an RTO, Mitchell Sanders carried the PRC-25 radio, a killer, twenty-six pounds with its battery.

As a medic, Rat Kiley carried a canvas satchel filled with morphine and plasma and malaria tablets and surgical tape and comic books and all the things a medic must carry, including M&M's for especially bad wounds, for a total weight of nearly twenty pounds.

As a big man, therefore a machine gunner, Henry Dobbins carried the M-60,   10 which weighed twenty-three pounds unloaded, but which was almost always loaded. In addition, Dobbins carried between ten and fifteen pounds of ammunition draped in belts across his chest and shoulders.

As PFCs° or Spec 4s,° most of them were common grunts and carried the standard M-16 gas-operated assault rifle. The weapon weighed 7.5 pounds unloaded, 8.2 pounds with its full twenty-round magazine. Depending on numerous factors, such as topography and psychology, the riflemen carried anywhere from twelve to twenty magazines, usually in cloth bandoliers, adding on another 8.4 pounds at minimum, fourteen pounds at maximum. When it was available, they also carried M-16 maintenance gear—rods and steel brushes and swabs and tubes of LSA oil—all of which weighed about a pound. Among the grunts, some carried the M-79 grenade launcher, 5.9 pounds unloaded, a reasonably light weapon except for the ammunition, which was heavy. A single round weighed ten ounces. The typical load was twenty-five rounds. But Ted Lavender, who was scared, carried thirty-four rounds when he was shot and killed outside Than Khe, and he went down under an exceptional burden, more than twenty pounds of ammunition, plus the flak jacket and helmet and rations and water and toilet paper and tranquilizers and all the rest, plus the unweighed fear. He was dead weight. There was no twitching or flopping. Kiowa, who saw it happen, said it was like watching a rock fall, or a big sandbag or something— just boom, then down—not like the movies where the dead guy rolls around and does fancy spins and goes ass over teakettle—not like that, Kiowa said, the poor bastard just flatfuck fell. Boom. Down. Nothing else. It was a bright morning in mid-April. Lieutenant Cross felt the pain. He blamed himself. They stripped off Lavender's canteens and ammo, all the heavy things, and Rat Kiley said the obvious, the guy's dead, and Mitchell Sanders used his radio to report one U.S. KIA° and to request a chopper. Then they wrapped Lavender in his poncho. They carried him out to a dry paddy,° established security, and sat smoking the dead man's dope until the chopper came. Lieutenant Cross kept to himself. He pictured Martha's smooth young face, thinking he loved her more than anything, more than his men, and now Ted Lavender was dead because he loved her so much and could not stop thinking about her. When the dust-off arrived, they carried Lavender aboard. Afterward they burned Than Khe. They marched until dusk, then dug their holes, and that night Kiowa kept explaining how you had to be there, how fast it was, how the poor guy just dropped like so much concrete. Boom-down, he said. Like cement.

In addition to the three standard weapons—the M-60, M-16, and M-79—they carried whatever presented itself, or whatever seemed appropriate as a means of killing or staying alive. They carried catch-as-catch-can. At various times, in various situations, they carried M-14s and CAR-15s and Swedish Ks and grease guns and captured AK-47s and Chi-Coms and RPGs and Simonov carbines and black-market Uzis and .38-caliber Smith & Wesson handguns and 66 mm LAWs and shotguns and silencers and blackjacks and bayonets and C-4 plastic explosives. Lee Strunk carried a slingshot; a weapon of last resort, he called it. Mitchell Sanders carried brass knuckles. Kiowa carried his grandfather's feathered hatchet.

[11]**PFC** Private First Class   **Spec 4** Specialist 4   **KIA** Killed In Action   **paddy** rice field, alternately flooded and drained for the different phases of the growing cycle

Every third or fourth man carried a Claymore antipersonnel mine—3.5 pounds with its firing device. They all carried fragmentation grenades—fourteen ounces each. They all carried at least one M-18 colored smoke grenade—twenty-four ounces. Some carried CS or tear-gas grenades. Some carried white-phosphorus grenades. They carried all they could bear, and then some, including a silent awe for the terrible power of the things they carried.

In the first week of April, before Lavender died, Lieutenant Jimmy Cross received a good-luck charm from Martha. It was a simple pebble, an ounce at most. Smooth to the touch, it was a milky-white color with flecks of orange and violet, oval-shaped, like a miniature egg. In the accompanying letter, Martha wrote that she had found the pebble on the Jersey shoreline, precisely where the land touched water at high tide, where things came together but also separated. It was this separate-but-together quality, she wrote, that had inspired her to pick up the pebble and to carry it in her breast pocket for several days, where it seemed weightless, and then to send it through the mail, by air, as a token of her truest feelings for him. Lieutenant Cross found this romantic. But he wondered what her truest feelings were, exactly, and what she meant by separate-but-together. He wondered how the tides and waves had come into play on that afternoon along the Jersey shoreline when Martha saw the pebble and bent down to rescue it from geology. He imagined bare feet. Martha was a poet, with the poet's sensibilities, and her feet would be brown and bare, the toenails unpainted, the eyes chilly and somber like the ocean in March, and though it was painful, he wondered who had been with her that afternoon. He imagined a pair of shadows moving along the strip of sand where things came together but also separated. It was phantom jealousy, he knew, but he couldn't help himself. He loved her so much. On the march, through the hot days of early April, he carried the pebble in his mouth, turning it with his tongue, tasting sea salts and moisture. His mind wandered. He had difficulty keeping his attention on the war. On occasion he would yell at his men to spread out the column, to keep their eyes open, but then he would slip away into daydreams, just pretending, walking barefoot along the Jersey shore, with Martha, carrying nothing. He would feel himself rising. Sun and waves and gentle winds, all love and lightness.

What they carried varied by mission.

When a mission took them to the mountains, they carried mosquito netting,　15
machetes, canvas tarps, and extra bug juice.

If a mission seemed especially hazardous, or if it involved a place they knew to be bad, they carried everything they could. In certain heavily mined AOs,° where the land was dense with Toe Poppers° and Bouncing Betties,° they took turns humping a twenty-eight-pound mine detector. With its headphones and big sensing plate, the equipment was a stress on the lower back and shoulders, awkward to handle, often useless because of the shrapnel in the earth, but they carried it anyway, partly for safety, partly for the illusion of safety.

---

[16] **AOs** Areas of Operation　**Toe Poppers** land mines　**Bouncing Betties** a weapon that leaps into the air, sending out shrapnel in a 360-degree spray

On ambush, or other night missions, they carried peculiar little odds and ends. Kiowa always took along his New Testament and a pair of moccasins for silence. Dave Jensen carried night-sight vitamins high in carotin. Lee Strunk carried his slingshot; ammo, he claimed, would never be a problem. Rat Kiley carried brandy and M&M's. Until he was shot, Ted Lavender carried the starlight scope, which weighed 6.3 pounds with its aluminum carrying case. Henry Dobbins carried his girlfriend's pantyhose wrapped around his neck as a comforter. They all carried ghosts. When dark came, they would move out single file across the meadows and paddies to their ambush coordinates, where they would quietly set up the Claymores and lie down and spend the night waiting.

Other missions were more complicated and required special equipment. In mid-April, it was their mission to search out and destroy the elaborate tunnel complexes in the Than Khe area south of Chu Lai. To blow the tunnels, they carried one-pound blocks of pentrite high explosives, four blocks to a man, sixty-eight pounds in all. They carried wiring, detonators, and battery-powered clackers. Dave Jensen carried earplugs. Most often, before blowing the tunnels, they were ordered by higher command to search them, which was considered bad news, but by and large they just shrugged and carried out orders. Because he was a big man, Henry Dobbins was excused from tunnel duty. The others would draw numbers. Before Lavender died there were seventeen men in the platoon, and whoever drew the number seventeen would strip off his gear and crawl in head first with a flashlight and Lieutenant Cross's .45-caliber pistol. The rest of them would fan out as security. They would sit down or kneel, not facing the hole, listening to the ground beneath them, imagining cobwebs and ghosts, whatever was down there—the tunnel walls squeezing in—how the flashlight seemed impossibly heavy in the hand and how it was tunnel vision in the very strictest sense, compression in all ways, even time, and how you had to wiggle in—ass and elbows—a swallowed-up feeling—and how you found yourself worrying about odd things—will your flashlight go dead? Do rats carry rabies? If you screamed, how far would the sound carry? Would your buddies hear it? Would they have the courage to drag you out? In some respects, though not many, the waiting was worse than the tunnel itself. Imagination was a killer.

On April 16, when Lee Strunk drew the number seventeen, he laughed and muttered something and went down quickly. The morning was hot and very still. Not good, Kiowa said. He looked at the tunnel opening, then out across a dry paddy toward the village of Than Khe. Nothing moved. No clouds or birds or people. As they waited, the men smoked and drank Kool-Aid, not taking much, feeling sympathy for Lee Strunk but also feeling the luck of the draw. You win some, you lose some, said Mitchell Sanders, and sometimes you settle for a rain check. It was a tired line and no one laughed.

20   Henry Dobbins ate a tropical chocolate bar. Ted Lavender popped a tranquilizer and went off to pee.

After five minutes, Lieutenant Jimmy Cross moved to the tunnel, leaned down, and examined the darkness. Trouble, he thought—a cave-in maybe. And then suddenly, without willing it, he was thinking about Martha. The stresses and fractures, the quick collapse, the two of them buried alive under all that weight. Dense, crushing love. Kneeling, watching the hole, he tried to concentrate on Lee Strunk and the war, all the dangers, but his love was too much for him, he felt paralyzed, he wanted to sleep inside her lungs and breathe her blood and be smothered. He wanted her to be a virgin and not a virgin, all at once. He wanted to know her. Intimate secrets—why poetry? Why so sad? Why the grayness in her eyes? Why so alone? Not lonely, just alone—riding her bike across campus or sitting off by herself in the cafeteria. Even dancing, she danced alone—and it was the aloneness that filled him with love. He remembered telling her that one evening. How she nodded and looked away. And how, later, when he kissed her, she received the kiss without returning it, her eyes wide open, not afraid, not a virgin's eyes, just flat and uninvolved.

Lieutenant Cross gazed at the tunnel. But he was not there. He was buried with Martha under the white sand at the Jersey shore. They were pressed together, and the pebble in his mouth was her tongue. He was smiling. Vaguely, he was aware of how quiet the day was, the sullen paddies, yet he could not bring himself to worry about matters of security. He was beyond that. He was just a kid at war, in love. He was twenty-two years old. He couldn't help it.

A few moments later Lee Strunk crawled out of the tunnel. He came up grinning, filthy but alive. Lieutenant Cross nodded and closed his eyes while the others clapped Strunk on the back and made jokes about rising from the dead.

Worms, Rat Kiley said. Right out of the grave. Fuckin' zombie.

The men laughed. They all felt great relief.   25

Spook City, said Mitchell Sanders.

Lee Strunk made a funny ghost sound, a kind of moaning, yet very happy, and right then, when Strunk made that high happy moaning sound, when he went *Ahhooooo*, right then Ted Lavender was shot in the head on his way back from peeing. He lay with his mouth open. The teeth were broken. There was a swollen black bruise under his left eye. The cheekbone was gone. Oh shit, Rat Kiley said, the guy's dead. The guy's dead, he kept saying, which seemed profound—the guy's dead. I mean really.

The things they carried were determined to some extent by superstition. Lieutenant Cross carried his good-luck pebble. Dave Jensen carried a rabbit's foot. Norman Bowker, otherwise a very gentle person, carried a thumb that had been presented to him as a gift by Mitchell Sanders. The thumb was dark brown, rubbery to the touch, and weighed four ounces at most. It had been cut from a VC° corpse, a boy of fifteen or sixteen. They'd found him at the bottom of an irrigation ditch, badly burned, flies in his mouth and eyes. The boy wore black shorts and sandals. At the time of his death he had been carrying a pouch of rice, a rifle, and three magazines of ammunition.

You want my opinion, Mitchell Sanders said, there's a definite moral here.

---

[28]**VC** Viet Cong: South Vietnamese government's term for the military forces of the National Front for the Liberation of Vietnam

30 He put his hand on the dead boy's wrist. He was quiet for a time, as if counting a pulse, then he patted the stomach, almost affectionately, and used Kiowa's hunting hatchet to remove the thumb.

Henry Dobbins asked what the moral was.

Moral?

You know. *Moral.*

Sanders wrapped the thumb in toilet paper and handed it across to Norman Bowker. There was no blood. Smiling, he kicked the boy's head, watched the flies scatter, and said, It's like with that old TV show—Paladin. Have gun, will travel.

35 Henry Dobbins thought about it.

Yeah, well, he finally said. I don't see no moral.

There it *is*, man.

Fuck off.

They carried USO° stationery and pencils and pens. They carried Sterno, safety pins, trip flares, signal flares, spools of wire, razor blades, chewing tobacco, liberated joss sticks and statuettes of the smiling Buddha, candles, grease pencils, *The Stars and Stripes,*° fingernail clippers, Psy Ops° leaflets, bush hats, bolos, and much more. Twice a week, when the resupply choppers came in, they carried hot chow in green Mermite cans and large canvas bags filled with iced beer and soda pop. They carried plastic water containers, each with a two-gallon capacity. Mitchell Sanders carried a set of starched tiger fatigues for special occasions. Henry Dobbins carried Black Flag insecticide. Dave Jensen carried empty sandbags that could be filled at night for added protection. Lee Strunk carried tanning lotion. Some things they carried in common. Taking turns, they carried the big PRC-77 scrambler radio, which weighed thirty pounds with its battery. They shared the weight of memory. They took up what others could no longer bear. Often, they carried each other, the wounded or weak. They carried infections. They carried chess sets, basketballs, Vietnamese-English dictionaries, insignia of rank, Bronze Stars and Purple Hearts, plastic cards imprinted with the Code of Conduct. They carried diseases, among them malaria and dysentery. They carried lice and ringworm and leeches and paddy algae and various rots and molds. They carried the land itself—Vietnam, the place, the soil—a powdery orange-red dust that covered their boots and fatigues and faces. They carried the sky. The whole atmosphere, they carried it, the humidity, the monsoons, the stink of fungus and decay, all of it, they carried gravity. They moved like mules. By daylight they took sniper fire, at night they were mortared, but it was not battle, it was just the endless march, village to village, without purpose, nothing won or lost. They marched for the sake of the march. They plodded along slowly, dumbly, leaning forward against the heat, unthinking, all blood and bone, simple grunts, soldiering with their legs, toiling up the hills and down

[39]**USO** United Service Organizations for uniformed military personnel   *Stars and Stripes* newspaper for military personnel   **Psy Ops** Psychological Operations

into the paddies and across the rivers and up again and down, just humping, one step and then the next and then another, but no volition, no will, because it was automatic, it was anatomy, and the war was entirely a matter of posture and carriage, the hump was everything, a kind of inertia, a kind of emptiness, a dullness of desire and intellect and conscience and hope and human sensibility. Their principles were in their feet. Their calculations were biological. They had no sense of strategy or mission. They searched the villages without knowing what to look for, not caring, kicking over jars of rice, frisking children and old men, blowing tunnels, sometimes setting fires and sometimes not, then forming up and moving on to the next village, then other villages, where it would always be the same. They carried their own lives. The pressures were enormous. In the heat of early afternoon, they would remove their helmets and flak jackets, walking bare, which was dangerous but which helped ease the strain. They would often discard things along the route of march. Purely for comfort, they would throw away rations, blow their Claymores and grenades, no matter, because by nightfall the resupply choppers would arrive with more of the same, then a day or two later still more, fresh watermelons and crates of ammunition and sunglasses and woolen sweaters—the resources were stunning—sparklers for the Fourth of July, colored eggs for Easter. It was the great American war chest—the fruits of science, the smokestacks, the canneries, the arsenals at Hartford, the Minnesota forests, the machine shops, the vast fields of corn and wheat—they carried like freight trains; they carried it on their backs and shoulders—and for all the ambiguities of Vietnam, all the mysteries and unknowns, there was at least the single abiding certainty that they would never be at a loss for things to carry.

After the chopper took Lavender away, Lieutenant Jimmy Cross led his men   40
into the village of Than Khe. They burned everything. They shot chickens and dogs, they trashed the village well, they called in artillery and watched the wreckage, then they marched for several hours through the hot afternoon, and then at dusk, while Kiowa explained how Lavender died, Lieutenant Cross found himself trembling.

He tried not to cry. With his entrenching tool, which weighed five pounds, he began digging a hole in the earth.

He felt shame. He hated himself. He had loved Martha more than his men, and as a consequence Lavender was now dead, and this was something he would have to carry like a stone in his stomach for the rest of the war.

All he could do was dig. He used his entrenching tool like an ax, slashing, feeling both love and hate, and then later, when it was full dark, he sat at the bottom of his foxhole and wept. It went on for a long while. In part, he was grieving for Ted Lavender, but mostly it was for Martha, and for himself, because she belonged to another world, which was not quite real, and because she was a junior at Mount Sebastian College in New Jersey, a poet and a virgin and uninvolved, and because he realized she did not love him and never would.

Like cement, Kiowa whispered in the dark. I swear to God—boomdown. Not a word.

45   I've heard this, said Norman Bowker.

A pisser, you know? Still zipping himself up. Zapped while zipping.

All right, fine. That's enough.

Yeah, but you had to see it, the guy just—

I *heard,* man. Cement. So why not shut the fuck *up?*

50   Kiowa shook his head sadly and glanced over at the hole where Lieutenant Jimmy Cross sat watching the night. The air was thick and wet. A warm, dense fog had settled over the paddies and there was the stillness that precedes rain.

After a time Kiowa sighed.

One thing for sure, he said. The Lieutenant's in some deep hurt. I mean that crying jag—the way he was carrying on—it wasn't fake or anything, it was real heavy-duty hurt. The man cares.

Sure, Norman Bowker said.

Say what you want, the man does care.

55   We all got problems.

Not Lavender.

No, I guess not, Bowker said. Do me a favor, though.

Shut up?

That's a smart Indian. Shut up.

60   Shrugging, Kiowa pulled off his boots. He wanted to say more, just to lighten up his sleep, but instead he opened his New Testament and arranged it beneath his head a as a pillow. The fog made things seem hollow and unattached. He tried not to think about Ted Lavender, but then he was thinking how fast it was, no drama, down and dead, and how it was hard to feel anything except surprise. It seemed un-Christian. He wished he could find some great sadness, or even anger, but the emotion wasn't there and he couldn't make it happen. Mostly he felt pleased to be alive. He liked the smell of the New Testament under his cheek, the leather and ink and paper and glue, whatever the chemicals were. He liked hearing the sounds of night. Even his fatigue, it felt fine, the stiff muscles and the prickly awareness of his own body, a floating feeling. He enjoyed not being dead. Lying there, Kiowa admired Lieutenant Jimmy Cross's capacity for grief. He wanted to share the man's pain, he wanted to care as Jimmy Cross cared. And yet when he closed his eyes, all he could think was Boomdown, and all he could feel was the pleasure of having his boots off and the fog curling in around him and the damp soil and the Bible smells and the plush comfort of night.

After a moment Norman Bowker sat up in the dark.

What the hell, he said. You want to talk, *talk.* Tell it to me.

Forget it.

No, man, go on. One thing I hate, it's a silent Indian.

65   For the most part they carried themselves with poise, a kind of dignity. Now and then, however, there were times of panic, when they squealed or wanted to squeal but couldn't, when they twitched and made moaning sounds and covered

their heads and said Dear Jesus and flopped around on the earth and fired their weapons blindly and cringed and sobbed and begged for the noise to stop and went wild and made stupid promises to themselves and to God and to their mothers and fathers, hoping not to die. In different ways, it happened to all of them. Afterward, when the firing ended, they would blink and peek up. They would touch their bodies, feeling shame, then quickly hiding it. They would force themselves to stand. As if in slow motion, frame by frame, the world would take on the old logic—absolute silence, then the wind, then sunlight, then voices. It was the burden of being alive. Awkwardly, the men would reassemble themselves, first in private, then in groups, becoming soldiers again. They would repair the leaks in their eyes. They would check for casualties, call in dust-offs, light cigarettes, try to smile, clear their throats and spit and begin cleaning their weapons. After a time someone would shake his head and say, No lie, I almost shit my pants, and someone else would laugh, which meant it was bad, yes, but the guy had obviously not shit his pants, it wasn't that bad, and in any case nobody would ever do such a thing and then go ahead and talk about it. They would squint into the dense, oppressive sunlight. For a few moments, perhaps, they would fall silent, lighting a joint and tracking its passage from man to man, inhaling, holding in the humiliation. Scary stuff, one of them might say. But then someone else would grin or flick his eyebrows and say, Roger-dodger, almost cut me a new asshole, *almost.*

There were numerous such poses. Some carried themselves with a sort of wistful resignation, others with pride or stiff soldierly discipline or good humor or macho zeal. They were afraid of dying but they were even more afraid to show it.

They found jokes to tell.

They used a hard vocabulary to contain the terrible softness. *Greased,* they'd say. *Offed, lit up, zapped while zipping.* It wasn't cruelty, just stage presence. They were actors and the war came at them in 3-D. When someone died, it wasn't quite dying, because in a curious way it seemed scripted, and because they had their lines mostly memorized, irony mixed with tragedy, and because they called it by other names, as if to encyst and destroy the reality of death itself. They kicked corpses. They cut off thumbs. They talked grunt lingo. They told stories about Ted Lavender's supply of tranquilizers, how the poor guy didn't feel a thing, how incredibly tranquil he was.

There's a moral here, said Mitchell Sanders.

They were waiting for Lavender's chopper, smoking the dead man's dope.   70

The moral's pretty obvious, Sanders said, and winked. Stay away from drugs. No joke, they'll ruin your day every time.

Cute, said Henry Dobbins.

Mind-blower, get it? Talk about wiggy—nothing left, just blood and brains.

They made themselves laugh.

There it is, they'd say, over and over, as if the repetition itself were an act of   75
poise, a balance between crazy and almost crazy, knowing without going. There it is, which meant be cool, let it ride, because oh yeah, man, you can't change what can't be changed, there it is, there it absolutely and positively and fucking well *is.*

They were tough.

They carried all the emotional baggage of men who might die. Grief, terror, love, longing—these were intangibles, but the intangibles had their own mass and specific gravity, they had tangible weight. They carried shameful memories. They carried the common secret of cowardice barely restrained, the instinct to run or freeze or hide, and in many respects this was the heaviest burden of all, for it could never be put down, it required perfect balance and perfect posture. They carried their reputations. They carried the soldier's greatest fear, which was the fear of blushing. Men killed, and died, because they were embarrassed not to. It was what had brought them to the war in the first place, nothing positive, no dreams of glory or honor, just to avoid the blush of dishonor. They died so as not to die of embarrassment. They crawled into tunnels and walked point and advanced under fire. Each morning, despite the unknowns, they made their legs move. They endured. They kept humping. They did not submit to the obvious alternative, which was simply to close the eyes and fall. So easy, really. Go limp and tumble to the ground and let the muscles unwind and not speak and not budge until your buddies picked you up and lifted you into the chopper that would roar and dip its nose and carry you off to the world. A mere matter of falling, yet no one ever fell. It was not courage, exactly; the object was not valor. Rather, they were too frightened to be cowards.

By and large they carried these things inside, maintaining the masks of composure. They sneered at sick call. They spoke bitterly about guys who had found release by shooting off their own toes or fingers. Pussies, they'd say. Candyasses. It was fierce, mocking talk, with only a trace of envy or awe, but even so, the image played itself out behind their eyes.

They imagined the muzzle against flesh. They imagined the quick, sweet pain, then the evacuation to Japan, then a hospital with warm beds and cute geisha nurses.

80   They dreamed of freedom birds.

At night, on guard, staring into the dark, they were carried away by jumbo jets. They felt the rush of takeoff. *Gone!* they yelled. And then velocity, wings and engines, a smiling stewardess—but it was more than a plane, it was a real bird, a big sleek silver bird with feathers and talons and high screeching. They were flying. The weights fell off, there was nothing to bear. They laughed and held on tight, feeling the cold slap of wind and altitude, soaring, thinking *It's over, I'm gone!*—they were naked, they were light and free—it was all lightness, bright and fast and buoyant, light as light, a helium buzz in the brain, a giddy bubbling in the lungs as they were taken up over the clouds and the war, beyond duty, beyond gravity and mortification and global entanglements— *Sin loi!*° they yelled, *I'm sorry, motherfuckers, but I'm out of it, I'm goofed, I'm on a space cruise, I'm gone!*—and it was a restful, disencumbered sensation, just riding the light waves, sailing that big silver freedom bird over the mountains and oceans, over America, over the farms and great sleeping cities and cemeteries and highways and the golden arches of McDonald's. It was flight, a kind of

[81]*Sin loi* Vietnamese for "I am sorry"

fleeing, a kind of falling, falling higher and higher, spinning off the edge of the earth and beyond the sun and through the vast, silent vacuum where there were no burdens and where everything weighed exactly nothing. *Gone!* they screamed, *I'm sorry but I'm gone!* And so at night, not quite dreaming, they gave themselves over to lightness, they were carried, they were purely borne.

On the morning after Ted Lavender died, First Lieutenant Jimmy Cross crouched at the bottom of his foxhole and burned Martha's letters. Then he burned the two photographs. There was a steady rain falling, which made it difficult, but he used heat tabs and Sterno to build a small fire, screening it with his body, holding the photographs over the tight blue flame with the tips of his fingers.

He realized it was only a gesture. Stupid, he thought. Sentimental, too, but mostly just stupid.

Lavender was dead. You couldn't burn the blame.

Besides, the letters were in his head. And even now, without photographs, Lieutenant Cross could see Martha playing volleyball in her white gym shorts and yellow T-shirt. He could see her moving in the rain.   85

When the fire died out, Lieutenant Cross pulled his poncho over his shoulders and ate breakfast from a can.

There was no great mystery, he decided.

In those burned letters Martha had never mentioned the war, except to say, Jimmy, take care of yourself. She wasn't involved. She signed the letters "Love," but it wasn't love, and all the fine lines and technicalities did not matter.

The morning came up wet and blurry. Everything seemed part of everything else, the fog and Martha and the deepening rain.

It was a war, after all.   90

Half smiling, Lieutenant Jimmy Cross took out his maps. He shook his head hard, as if to clear it, then bent forward and began planning the day's march. In ten minutes, or maybe twenty, he would rouse the men and they would pack up and head west, where the maps showed the country to be green and inviting. They would do what they had always done. The rain might add some weight, but otherwise it would be one more day layered upon all the other days.

He was realistic about it. There was that new hardness in his stomach.

No more fantasies, he told himself.

Henceforth, when he thought about Martha, it would be only to think that she belonged elsewhere. He would shut down the daydreams. This was not Mount Sebastian, it was another world, where there were no pretty poems or midterm exams, a place where men died because of carelessness and gross stupidity. Kiowa was right. Boomdown, and you were dead, never partly dead.

Briefly, in the rain, Lieutenant Cross saw Martha's gray eyes gazing back at him.   95

He understood.

It was very sad, he thought. The things men carried inside. The things men did or felt they had to do.

He almost nodded at her, but didn't.

Instead he went back to his maps. He was now determined to perform his duties firmly and without negligence. It wouldn't help Lavender, he knew that, but from this point on he would comport himself as a soldier. He would dispose of his good-luck pebble. Swallow it, maybe, or use Lee Strunk's slingshot, or just drop it along the trail. On the march he would impose strict field discipline. He would be careful to send out flank security, to prevent straggling or bunching up, to keep his troops moving at the proper pace and at the proper interval. He would insist on clean weapons. He would confiscate the remainder of Lavender's dope. Later in the day, perhaps, he would call the men together and speak to them plainly. He would accept the blame for what had happened to Ted Lavender. He would be a man about it. He would look them in the eyes, keeping his chin level, and he would issue the new SOPs in a calm, impersonal tone of voice, an officer's voice, leaving no room for argument or discussion. Commencing immediately, he'd tell them, they would no longer abandon equipment along the route of march. They would police up their acts. They would get their shit together, and keep it together, and maintain it neatly and in good working order.

100   He would not tolerate laxity. He would show strength, distancing himself.

Among the men there would be grumbling, of course, and maybe worse, because their days would seem longer and their loads heavier, but Lieutenant Cross reminded himself that his obligation was not to be loved but to lead. He would dispense with love; it was not now a factor. And if anyone quarreled or complained, he would simply tighten his lips and arrange his shoulders in the correct command posture. He might give a curt little nod. Or he might not. He might just shrug and say Carry on, then they would saddle up and form into a column and move out toward the villages of Than Khe.   [1990]

1. Classify the various "things" the soldiers in this story "carry."
2. In addition to the physical burdens the soldiers carry on their persons and in their packs, what emotional ones do they also take into battle with them?
3. How does Lieutenant Cross convince himself that he is to blame for Ted Lavender's death? How does he deal with the guilt engendered by his acceptance of blame? Does this acceptance of blame lighten or increase the emotional load he carries?
4. What other disciplines might provide insight into this story?
5. To what other works in this section can you connect this story?

○ F R A M E W O R K S ○

Looking at LeGuin through Philosophy

URSULA LEGUIN, *The Ones Who Walk Away from Omelas*

WILLIAM JAMES, From *The Moral Philosopher and the Moral Life*

JOHN STUART MILL, From *What Utilitarianism Is*

URSULA LEGUIN

URSULA K. LEGUIN *(1929–), science fiction writer, was born in Berkeley,*
California. Her family life was full of lively conversations and interesting visitors,
who frequently discussed foreign cultures with her father. She has said that this laid
the foundation for her interest in inventing imaginary cultures. The Dispossessed
(1974) and The Left Hand of Darkness *(1969), two of LeGuin's best-known*
science fiction novels, exhibit her interest in exploring contemporary problems by
restating them in terms of other worlds. She continues to expand her idea of the
futuristic novel, including maps and poetry in her book Always Coming Home
and publishing it in conjunction with tapes of music that composer Todd Barton
based on the sequences of amino acids in human DNA (Genome Music).

The Ones Who Walk Away from Omelas
(Variations on a Theme by William James)

With a clamor of bells that set the swallows soaring, the Festival of Summer
came to the city Omelas, bright-towered by the sea. The rigging of the boats in
harbor sparkled with flags. In the streets between houses with red roofs and
painted walls, between old moss-grown gardens and under avenues of trees,
past great parks and public buildings, processions moved. Some were decorous:
old people in long stiff robes of mauve and grey, grave master workmen, quiet,
merry women carrying their babies, and chatting as they walked. In other streets
the music beat faster, a shimmering of gong and tambourine, and the people
went dancing, the procession was a dance. Children dodged in and out, their
high calls rising like the swallows' crossing flights over the music and the
singing. All the processions wound towards the north side of the city, where on
the great water-meadow called the Green Fields boys and girls, naked in the
bright air, with mud-stained feet and ankles and long, lithe arms, exercised their
restive horses before the race. The horses wore no gear at all but a halter without bit. Their manes were braided with streamers of silver, gold, and green. They
flared their nostrils and pranced and boasted to one another; they were vastly
excited, the horse being the only animal who has adopted our ceremonies as his
own. Far off to the north and west the mountains stood up half encircling
Omelas on her bay. The air of morning was so clear that the snow still crowning
the Eighteen Peaks burned with white-gold fire across the miles of sunlit air,
under the dark blue of the sky. There was just enough wind to make the
banners that marked the racecourse snap and flutter now and then. In the
silence of the broad green meadows one could hear the music winding through
the city streets, farther and nearer and ever approaching, a cheerful faint sweetness of the air that from time to time trembled and gathered together and broke
out into the great joyous clanging of the bells.

Joyous! How is one to tell about joy? How describe the citizens of Omelas?
They were not simple folk, you see, though they were happy. But we do not
say the words of cheer much any more. All smiles have become archaic. Given

a description such as this one tends to make certain assumptions. Given a description such as this one tends to look next for the King, mounted on a splendid stallion and surrounded by his noble knights, or perhaps in a golden litter borne by great-muscled slaves. But there was no king. They did not use swords, or keep slaves. They were not barbarians. I do not know the rules and laws of their society, but I suspect that they were singularly few. As they did without monarchy and slavery, so they also get on without the stock exchange, the advertisement, the secret police, and the bomb. Yet I repeat that these were not simple folk, not dulcet shepherds, noble savages, bland utopians. They were not less complex than us. The trouble is that we have a bad habit, encouraged by pedants and sophisticates, of considering happiness as something rather stupid. Only pain is intellectual, only evil interesting. This is the treason of the artist: a refusal to admit the banality of evil and the terrible boredom of pain. If you can't lick 'em join 'em. If it hurts, repeat it. But to praise despair is to condemn delight, to embrace violence is to lose hold of everything else. We have almost lost hold; we can no longer describe a happy man, nor make any celebration of joy. How can I tell you about the people of Omelas? They were not naive and happy children—though their children were, in fact, happy. They were mature, intelligent, passionate adults whose lives were not wretched. O miracle! but I wish I could describe it better. I wish I could convince you. Omelas sounds in my words like a city in a fairy tale, long ago and far away, once upon a time. Perhaps it would be best if you imagined it as your own fancy bids, assuming it will rise to the occasion, for certainly I cannot suit you all. For instance, how about technology? I think that there would be no cars or helicopters in and above the streets; this follows from the fact that the people of Omelas are happy people. Happiness is based on a just discrimination of what is necessary, what is neither necessary nor destructive, and what is destructive. In the middle category, however—that of the unnecessary but undestructive, that of comfort, luxury, exuberance, etc.—they could perfectly well have central heating, subway trains, washing machines, and all kinds of marvelous devices not yet invented here, floating light-sources, fuelless power, a cure for the common cold. Or they could have none of that: it doesn't matter. As you like it. I incline to think that people from towns up and down the coast have been coming in to Omelas during the last days before the Festival on very fast little trains and double-decked trams, and that the train station of Omelas is actually the hand-somest building in town, though plainer than the magnificent Farmers' Market. But even granted trains, I fear that Omelas so far strikes some of you as goody-goody. Smiles, bells, parades, horses, bleh. If so, please add an orgy. If an orgy would help, don't hesitate. Let us not, however, have temples from which issue beautiful nude priests and priestesses already half in ecstasy and ready to copu-late with any man or woman, lover or stranger, who desires union with the deep godhead of the blood, although that was my first idea. But really it would be better not to have any temples in Omelas—at least, not manned temples. Religion yes, clergy no. Surely the beautiful nudes can just wander about, offer-ing themselves like divine souffles to the hunger of the needy and the rapture of the flesh. Let them join the processions. Let tambourines be struck above the copulations, and the glory of desire be proclaimed upon the gongs, and (a not unimportant point) let the offspring of these delightful rituals be beloved and looked after by all. One thing I know there is none of in Omelas is guilt. But what else should there be? I thought at first there were no drugs, but that is puritanical. For those who like it, the faint insistent sweetness of *drooz* may perfume the ways of the city, *drooz* which first brings a great lightness and brilliance to the mind and limbs, and then after some hours a dreamy languor, and wonderful visions at last of the very arcana and inmost secrets of the Universe, as well as exciting the pleasure of sex beyond all belief; and it is not habit-forming. For more modest tastes I think there ought to be beer. What else, what else belongs in the joyous city? The sense of victory, surely, the celebration of courage. But as we did without clergy, let us do without soldiers. The joy built upon successful slaughter is not the right kind of joy; it will not do; it is fearful and it is trivial. A boundless and generous contentment, a magnanimous triumph felt not against some outer enemy but in communion with the finest and fairest in the souls of all men everywhere and the splendor of the world's summer: this is what swells the hearts of the people of Omelas, and the victory they celebrate is that of life. I really don't think many of them need to take *drooz*.

Most of the processions have reached the Green Fields by now. A marvelous smell of cooking goes forth from the red and blue tents of the provisioners. The faces of small children are amiably sticky; in the benign grey beard of a man a couple of crumbs of rich pastry are entangled. The youths and girls have mounted their horses and are beginning to group around the starting line of the course. An old woman, small, fat and laughing, is passing out flowers from a basket, and tall young men wear her flowers in their shining hair. A child of nine or ten sits at the edge of the crowd alone, playing on a wooden flute. People pause to listen, and they smile, but they do not speak to him, for he never ceases playing and never sees them, his dark eyes wholly rapt in the sweet, thin magic of the tune.

He finishes, and slowly lowers his hands holding the wooden flute.   5

As if that little private silence were the signal, all at once a trumpet sounds from the pavilion near the starting line: imperious, melancholy, piercing. The horses rear on their slender legs, and some of them neigh in answer. Soberfaced, the young riders stroke the horses' necks and soothe them, whispering, "Quiet, quiet, there my beauty, my hope. . . ." They begin to form in rank along the starting line. The crowds along the racecourse are like a field of grass and flowers in the wind. The Festival of Summer has begun.

Do you believe? Do you accept the festival, the city, the joy? No? Then let me describe one more thing.

In a basement under one of the beautiful public buildings of Omelas, or perhaps in the cellar of one of its spacious private homes, there is a room. It has one locked door, and no window. A little light seeps in dustily between cracks in the boards, secondhand from a cobwebbed window somewhere across the cellar. In one corner of the little room a couple of mops, with stiff, clotted, foul-smelling heads, stand near a rusty bucket. The floor is dirt, a little damp to the touch, as cellar dirt usually is. The room is about three paces long and two wide: a mere broom closet or disused tool room. In the room a child is sitting. It could be a boy or a girl. It looks about six, but actually is nearly ten. It is feeble-minded. Perhaps it was born defective, or perhaps it has become imbecile through fear, malnutrition, and neglect. It picks its nose and occasionally fumbles vaguely with its toes or genitals, as it sits hunched in the corner farthest from the bucket and the two mops. It is afraid of the mops. It finds them horrible. It shuts its eyes, but it knows the mops are still standing there; and the door is locked; and nobody will come. The door is always locked; and nobody ever comes, except that sometimes—the child has no understanding of time or interval—sometimes the door rattles terribly and opens, and a person, or several people, are there. One of them may come in and kick the child to make it stand up. The others never come close, but peer in at it with frightened, disgusted eyes. The food bowl and the water jug are hastily filled, the door is locked, the eyes disappear. The people at the door never say anything, but the child, who has not always lived in the tool room, and can remember sunlight and its mother's voice, sometimes speaks. "I will be good," it says. "Please let me out. I will be good!" They never answer. The child used to scream for help at night, and cry a good deal, but now it only makes a kind of whining, "eh-haa, eh-haa," and it speaks less and less often. It is so thin there are no calves to its legs; its belly protrudes; it lives on a half-bowl of corn meal and grease a day. It is naked. Its buttocks and thighs a mass of festered sores, as it sits in its own excrement continually.

They all know it is there, all the people of Omelas. Some of them have come to see it, others are content merely to know it is there. They all know that it has to be there. Some of them understand why, and some do not, but they all understand that their happiness, the beauty of their city, the tenderness of their friendships, the health of their children, the wisdom of their scholars, the skill of their makers, even the abundance of their harvest and the kindly weathers of their skies, depends wholly on this child's abominable misery.

10   This is usually explained to children when they are between eight and twelve, whenever they seem capable of understanding; and most of those who come to see the child are young people, though often enough an adult comes, or comes back, to see the child. No matter how well the matter has been explained to them, these young spectators are always shocked and sickened at the sight. They feel disgust, which they had thought themselves superior to. They feel anger, outrage, impotence, despite all the explanations. They would like to do something for the child. But there is nothing they can do. If the child were brought up into the sunlight out of that vile place, if it were cleaned and fed and comforted, that would be a good thing, indeed; but if it were done, in that day and hour all the prosperity and beauty and delight of Omelas would wither and be destroyed. Those are the terms. To exchange all the goodness and grace of every life in Omelas for that single, small improvement: to throw away the happiness of thousands for the chance of the happiness of one: that would be to let guilt within the walls indeed.

The terms are strict and absolute; there may not even be a kind word spoken to the child.

Often the young people go home in tears, or in a tearless rage, when they have seen the child and faced this terrible paradox. They may brood over it for weeks or years. But as time goes on they begin to realize that even if the child could be released, it would not get much good of its freedom: a little vague pleasure of warmth and food, no doubt, but little more. It is too degraded and imbecile to know any real joy. It has been afraid too long even to be free of fear. Its habits are too uncouth for it to respond to humane treatment. Indeed, after so long it would probably be wretched without walls about it to protect it, and darkness for its eyes, and its own excrement to sit in. Their tears at the bitter injustice dry when they begin to perceive the terrible justice of reality, and to accept it. Yet it is their tears and anger, the trying of their generosity and the acceptance of their helplessness, which are perhaps the true source of the splendor of their lives. Theirs is no vapid, irresponsible happiness. They know that they, like the child, are not free. They know compassion. It is the existence of the child, and their knowledge of its existence, that makes possible the nobility of their architecture, and poignancy of their music, the profundity of their science. It is because of the child that they are so gentle with children. They know that if the wretched one were not there snivelling in the dark, the other one, the flute-player, could make no joyful music as the young riders line up in their beauty for the race in the sunlight of the first morning of summer.

Now do you believe in them? Are they not more credible? But there is one more thing to tell, and this is quite incredible.

At times one of the adolescent girls or boys who go to see the child does not go home to weep or rage, does not, in fact, go home at all. Sometimes also a man or woman much older falls silent for a day or two, and then leaves home. These people go out into the street, and walk down the street alone. They keep walking, and walk straight out of the city of Omelas, through the beautiful gates. They keep walking across the farmlands of Omelas. Each one goes alone, youth or girl, man or woman. Night falls; the traveler must pass down village streets, between the houses with yellow-lit windows, and on out into the darkness of the fields. Each alone, they go west or north, towards the mountains. They go on. They leave Omelas, they walk ahead into the darkness, and they do not come back. The place they go towards is a place even less imaginable to most of us than the city of happiness. I cannot describe it at all. It is possible that it does not exist. But they seem to know where they are going, the ones who walk away from Omelas.

1. Although there are no space breaks in this story, it nevertheless can be divided into sections. How would you divide it? How would the sections relate to each other?
2. What kind of narrator is this? How does the narrator function in the story?
3. What moral dilemma is depicted in the story? What is the narrator's attitude toward it? Do you think LeGuin's attitude is the same as the narrator's? What is yours?
4. How might "the ones who walk away from Omelas" support their decision to leave their beloved city? How might those who remain justify their decision? In developing your answer, consider Gilligan and Attanucci's theory of Care and Justice orientations (see p. 156).
5. What is the significance of the narrator's difficulty imagining any place other than Omelas?

6. Compare this story to Shirley Jackson's "The Lottery" (p. 1100) or to
   William Stafford's "Traveling through the Dark" (p. 1089) in this chapter or
   to Sharon Olds's "On the Subway" on p. 900.
7. How does Martin L. Hoffman's concept of the "diffusion of responsibility"
   help us to interpret the story?

WILLIAM JAMES

*WILLIAM JAMES (1842–1910) was born into a wealthy and much-traveled New
York family, so that by the time he was an adolescent, he had lived in the major
cities of Europe, as well as New York and Boston. As he traveled, his education
included foreign schools, different languages and cultures, and the rich intellectual
life of his own family. Visitors to his family included the leaders and great minds of
the time (including John Stuart Mill), and the children were expected to contribute
to the intellectual discussions. William, the eldest, engaged in countless scientific
experiments, forays into art as a career, and then chemistry and physiology at
Harvard. He finally chose medicine, but interrupted his training when a disastrous
specimen-hunting expedition to the Amazon with anti-Darwinian naturalist Louis
Agassiz left him with back pain and weak eyes as a result of a bout of smallpox.
He finished his medical degree but continued to be plagued by depression, anxiety,
and sometimes suicidal thoughts. When he reached a stage he considered a
profound emotional and spiritual crisis, he went to Europe and sought the key to
his breakdown in the study of psychology. An essay on free will helped him climb
out of his depression ("My first act of free will," he said, "shall be to believe in free
will."). He returned to America but without a clear direction in life until he was
offered a position teaching physiology at Harvard. He married and had five children
and enjoyed both marriage and fatherhood. He remained at Harvard for the rest of
his life, working in a variety of fields that reveal the range of his intellectual curiosity. He began to teach psychology as it related to physiology, developing a small laboratory for the course. His studies in science influenced his ideas and teaching and
led to the publication of* The Principles of Psychology *in 1894, which strongly
influenced the development of the field in America. His study of the mind broadened
into philosophical concerns, and he was also interested in religion and education.
A legendary teacher, he had a profound impact on all the disciplines he studied.*

From The Moral Philosopher and The Moral Life[1]*

The main purpose of this paper is to show that there is no such thing possible as
an ethical philosophy dogmatically made up in advance. We all help to determine the content of ethical philosophy so far as we contribute to the race's

[1]An Address to the Yale Philosophical Club, published in the *International Journal of Ethics*,
April, 1891.
*William James, "The Moral Philosopher and the Moral Life," *The Writings of William James:
A Comprehensive Edition*, ed. John J. McDermott (New York: Random House, 1967).

moral life. In other words, there can be no final truth in ethics any more than in physics, until the last man has had his experience and said his say. In the one case as in the other, however, the hypotheses which we now make while waiting, and the acts to which they prompt us, are among the indispensable conditions which determine what that 'say' shall be.

First of all, what is the position of him who seeks an ethical philosophy? To begin with, he must be distinguished from all those who are satisfied to be ethical sceptics. He *will* not be a sceptic; therefore so far from ethical scepticism being one possible fruit of ethical philosophizing, it can only be regarded as that residual alternative to all philosophy which from the outset menaces every would-be philosopher who may give up the quest discouraged, and renounce his original aim. That aim is to find an account of the moral relations that obtain among things, which will weave them into the unity of a stable system, and make of the world what one may call a genuine universe from the ethical point of view. So far as the world resists reduction to the form of unity, so far as ethical propositions seem unstable, so far does the philosopher fail of his ideal. The sub-ject-matter of his study is the ideals he finds existing in the world; the purpose which guides him is this ideal of his own, of getting them into a certain form. This ideal is thus a factor in ethical philosophy whose legitimate presence must never be overlooked; it is a positive contribution which the philosopher himself neces-sarily makes to the problem. But it is his only positive contribution. At the outset of his inquiry he ought to have no other ideals. Were he interested peculiarly in the triumph of any one kind of good, he would *pro tanto* cease to be a judicial investigator, and become an advocate for some limited element of the case.

There are three questions in ethics which must be kept apart. Let them be called respectively the *psychological* question, the *metaphysical* question, and the *casuistic* question. The psychological question asks after the historical *origin* of our moral ideas and judgments; the metaphysical question asks what the very *meaning* of the words 'good,' 'ill,' and 'obligation' are; the casuistic question asks what is the *measure* of the various goods and ills which men recognize, so that the philosopher may settle the true order of human obligations.

I

The psychological question is for most disputants the only question. When your ordinary doctor of divinity has proved to his own satisfaction that an altogether unique faculty called 'conscience' must be postulated to tell us what is right and what is wrong, or when your popular-science enthusiast has proclaimed that 'apriorism' is an exploded superstition, and that our moral judgments have gradually resulted from the teaching of the environment, each of these persons thinks that ethics is settled and nothing more is to be said. The familiar pair of names, Intuitionist and Evolutionist, so commonly used now to connote all possi-ble differences in ethical opinion, really refer to the psychological question alone. The discussion of this question hinges so much upon particular details that it is impossible to enter upon it at all within the limits of this paper. I will therefore only express dogmatically my own belief, which is this,—that the Benthams, the Mills, and the Bains have done a lasting service in taking so many of our human ideals and showing how they must have arisen from the association with acts of simple bodily pleasures and reliefs from pain. Association with many remote pleasures will unquestionably make a thing significant of goodness in our minds; and the more vaguely the goodness is conceived of, the more mysterious will its source appear to be. But it is surely impossible to explain all our sentiments and preferences in this simple way. The more minutely psychology studies human nature, the more clearly it finds there traces of secondary affections, relating the impressions of the environment with one another and with our impulses in quite different ways from those mere associations of coexistence and succession which are practically all that pure empiricism can admit. Take the love of drunkenness; take bashfulness, the terror of high places, the tendency to seasickness, to faint at the sight of blood, the susceptibility to musical sounds; take the emotion of the comical, the passion for poetry, for mathematics, or for metaphysics,—no one of these things can be wholly explained by either association or utility. They go *with* other things that can be so explained, no doubt; and some of them are prophetic of future utilities, since there is nothing in us for which some use may not be found. But their origin is in incidental complications to our cerebral structure, a structure whose original features arose with no reference to the perception of such discords and harmonies as these.

5   Well, a vast number of our moral perceptions also are certainly of this secondary and brain-born kind. They deal with directly felt fitnesses between things, and often fly in the teeth of all the prepossessions of habit and presumptions of utility. The moment you get beyond the coarser and more commonplace moral maxims, the Decalogues and Poor Richard's Almanacs, you fall into schemes and positions which to the eye of common-sense are fantastic and overstrained. The sense for abstract justice which some persons have is as excentric a variation, from the natural-history point of view, as is the passion for music or for the higher philosophical consistencies which consumes the soul of others. The feeling of the inward dignity of certain spiritual attitudes, as peace, serenity, simplicity, veracity; and of the essential vulgarity of others, as querulousness, anxiety, egoistic fussiness, etc.,—are quite inexplicable except by an innate preference of the more ideal attitude for its own pure sake. The nobler thing *tastes* better, and that is all that we can say. 'Experience' of consequences may truly teach us what things are *wicked,* but what have consequences to do with what is *mean* and *vulgar?* If a man has shot his wife's paramour, by reason of what subtle repugnancy in things is it that we are so disgusted when we hear that the wife and the husband have made it up and are living comfortably together again? Or if the hypothesis were offered us of a world in which Messrs. Fourier's and Bellamy's and Morris's utopias should all be outdone, and millions kept permanently happy on the one simple condition that a certain lost soul on the far-off edge of things should lead a life of lonely torture, what except a specifical and independent sort of emotion can it be which would make us immediately feel, even though an impulse arose within us to clutch at the

happiness so offered, how hideous a thing would be its enjoyment when deliberately accepted as the fruit of such a bargain? To what, once more, but subtle brain-born feelings of discord can be due all these recent protests against the entire race-tradition of retributive justice?—I refer to Tolstoï with his ideas of non-resistance, to Mr. Bellamy with his substitution of oblivion for repentance (in his novel of Dr. Heidenhain's Process), to M. Guyau with his radical condemnation of the punitive ideal. All these subtleties of the moral sensibility go as much beyond what can be ciphered out from the 'laws of association' as the delicacies of sentiment possible between a pair of young lovers go beyond such precepts of the 'etiquette to be observed during engagement' as are printed in manuals of social form.

No! Purely inward forces are certainly at work here. All the higher, more penetrating ideals are revolutionary. They present themselves far less in the guise of effects of past experience than in that of probable causes of future experience, factors to which the environment and the lessons it has so far taught us must learn to bend.

This is all I can say of the psychological question now. In the last chapter of a recent work[2] I have sought to prove in a general way the existence, in our thought, of relations which do not merely repeat the couplings of experience. Our ideals have certainly many sources. They are not all explicable as signifying corporeal pleasures to be gained, and pains to be escaped. And for having so constantly perceived this psychological fact, we must applaud the intuitionist school. . . . [1891]

[2]*The Principles of Psychology,* New York, H. Holt & Co., 1890.

JOHN STUART MILL

JOHN STUART MILL *(1806–73) was the son of James Mill, the British philosopher, who educated him at home. Under his father's tutelage, he started learning Greek at age three and became something of an intellectual child prodigy, reading classical writers in their original languages and studying logic, science, and mathematics— mastering many of the subjects of university curricula by his early adolescence. As an adult, he became one of the leaders of utilitarian thought and developed the theories begun by his father, leavening them with humanitarian and socialistic ideas. He was a staunch believer in empiricism as the source of all knowledge. His* On Liberty *(1859) is one of the most famous documents on political economy. He was the originator of many political and social reforms and influenced the events of his own time as well as the ideas of economists and philosophers who followed after him. Among his works are* System of Logic *(1843),* Utilitarianism *(1863), and* Auguste Comte and Positivism *(1865). In his autobiography (1873), he recounts the period of depression in which he realized that his remarkable education had led to the neglect of the emotional side of life and how the poetry of Wordsworth had helped him resolve his personal crisis.*

From Chapter Two: *"What Utilitarianism Is"**

A passing remark is all that needs be given to the ignorant blunder of supposing that those who stand up for utility as the test of right and wrong, use the term in that restricted and merely colloquial sense in which utility is opposed to pleasure. An apology is due to the philosophical opponents of utilitarianism, for even the momentary appearance of confounding them with any one capable of so absurd a misconception; which is the more extraordinary, inasmuch as the contrary accusation, of referring everything to pleasure, and that too in its grossest form, is another of the common charges against utilitarianism: and, as has been pointedly remarked by an able writer, the same sort of persons, and often the very same persons, denounce the theory "as impracticably dry when the word utility precedes the word pleasure, and as too practically voluptuous when the word pleasure precedes the word utility." Those who know anything about the matter are aware that every writer, from Epicurus to Bentham, who maintained the theory of utility, meant by it, not something to be contradistinguished from pleasure, but pleasure itself, together with exemption from pain; and instead of opposing the useful to the agreeable or the ornamental, have always declared that the useful means these, among other things. Yet the common herd, including the herd of writers, not only in newspapers and periodicals, but in books of weight and pretension, are perpetually falling into this shallow mistake. Having caught up the word utilitarian, while knowing nothing whatever about it but its sound, they habitually express by it the rejection, or the neglect, of pleasure in some of its forms; of beauty, of ornament, or of amusement. Nor is the term thus ignorantly misapplied solely in disparagement, but occasionally in compliment; as though it implied superiority to frivolity and the mere pleasures of the moment. And this perverted use is the only one in which the word is popularly known, and the one from which the new generation are acquiring their sole notion of its meaning. Those who introduced the word, but who had for many years discontinued it as a distinctive appellation, may well feel themselves called upon to resume it, if by doing so they can hope to contribute anything towards rescuing it from this utter degradation.[1]

The creed which accepts as the foundation of morals, Utility, or the Greatest Happiness Principle, holds that actions are right in proportion as they tend to promote happiness, wrong as they tend to produce the reverse of happiness. By

---

*John Stuart Mill, "What Utilitarianism Is," *Utilitarianism* (London: Parker, Son, and Bourn, 1863). The copy of Chapter Two excerpted here was prepared by Gary Varner for use in classes at Texas A&M University, http://www.phil.tamu.edu/~gary/intro/paper. mill.html (accessed 9 July 2004).

[1]The author of this essay has reason for believing himself to be the first person who brought the word utilitarian into use. He did not invent it, but adopted it from a passing expression in Mr. Galt's *Annals of the Parish*. After using it as a designation for several years, he and others abandoned it from a growing dislike to anything resembling a badge or watchword of sectarian distinction. But as a name for one single opinion, not a set of opinions—to denote the recognition of utility as a standard, not any particular way of applying it—the term supplies a want in the language, and offers, in many cases, a convenient mode of avoiding tiresome circumlocution.

happiness is intended pleasure, and the absence of pain; by unhappiness, pain, and the privation of pleasure. To give a clear view of the moral standard set up by the theory, much more requires to be said; in particular, what things it includes in the ideas of pain and pleasure; and to what extent this is left an open question. But these supplementary explanations do not affect the theory of life on which this theory of morality is grounded—namely, that pleasure, and freedom from pain, are the only things desirable as ends; and that all desirable things (which are as numerous in the utilitarian as in any other scheme) are desirable either for the pleasure inherent in themselves, or as means to the promotion of pleasure and the prevention of pain.

Now, such a theory of life excites in many minds, and among them in some of the most estimable in feeling and purpose, inveterate dislike. To suppose that life has (as they express it) no higher end than pleasure—no better and nobler object of desire and pursuit—they designate as utterly mean and groveling; as a doctrine worthy only of swine, to whom the followers of Epicurus were, at a very early period, contemptuously likened; and modern holders of the doctrine are occasionally made the subject of equally polite comparisons by its German, French, and English assailants.

When thus attacked, the Epicureans have always answered, that it is not they, but their accusers, who represent human nature in a degrading light; since the accusation supposes human beings to be capable of no pleasures except those of which swine are capable. If this supposition were true, the charge could not be gainsaid, but would then be no longer an imputation; for if the sources of pleasure were precisely the same to human beings and to swine, the rule of life which is good enough for the one would be good enough for the other. The comparison of the Epicurean life to that of beasts is felt as degrading, precisely because a beast's pleasures do not satisfy a human being's conceptions of happiness. Human beings have faculties more elevated than the animal appetites, and when once made conscious of them, do not regard anything as happiness which does not include their gratification. I do not, indeed, consider the Epicureans to have been by any means faultless in drawing out their scheme of consequences from the utilitarian principle. To do this in any sufficient manner, many Stoic, as well as Christian elements require to be included. But there is no known Epicurean theory of life which does not assign to the pleasures of the intellect, of the feelings and imagination, and of the moral sentiments, a much higher value as pleasures than to those of mere sensation. It must be admitted, however, that utilitarian writers in general have placed the superiority of mental over bodily pleasures chiefly in the greater permanency, safety, uncostliness, etc., of the former—that is, in their circumstantial advantages rather than in their intrinsic nature. And on all these points utilitarians have fully proved their case; but they might have taken the other, and, as it may be called, higher ground, with entire consistency. It is quite compatible with the principle of utility to recognize the fact, that some kinds of pleasure are more desirable and more valuable than others. It would be absurd that while, in estimating all other things, quality is considered as well as quantity, the estimation of pleasures should be supposed to depend on quantity alone.

If I am asked, what I mean by difference of quality in pleasures, or what makes one pleasure more valuable than another, merely as a pleasure, except its

5

being greater in amount, there is but one possible answer. Of two pleasures, if there be one to which all or almost all who have experience of both give a decided preference, irrespective of any feeling of moral obligation to prefer it, that is the more desirable pleasure. If one of the two is, by those who are competently acquainted with both, placed so far above the other that they prefer it, even though knowing it to be attended with a greater amount of discontent, and would not resign it for any quantity of the other pleasure which their nature is capable of, we are justified in ascribing to the preferred enjoyment a superiority in quality, so far outweighing quantity as to render it, in comparison, of small account.

Now it is an unquestionable fact that those who are equally acquainted with, and equally capable of appreciating and enjoying, both, do give a most marked preference to the manner of existence which employs their higher faculties. Few human creatures would consent to be changed into any of the lower animals, for a promise of the fullest allowance of a beast's pleasures; no intelligent human being would consent to be a fool, no instructed person would be an ignoramus, no person of feeling and conscience would be selfish and base, even though they should be persuaded that the fool, the dunce, or the rascal is better satisfied with his lot than they are with theirs. They would not resign what they possess more than he for the most complete satisfaction of all the desires which they have in common with him. If they ever fancy they would, it is only in cases of unhappiness so extreme, that to escape from it they would exchange their lot for almost any other, however undesirable in their own eyes. A being of higher faculties requires more to make him happy, is capable probably of more acute suffering, and certainly accessible to it at more points, than one of an inferior type; but in spite of these liabilities, he can never really wish to sink into what he feels to be a lower grade of existence. We may give what explanation we please of this unwillingness; we may attribute it to pride, a name which is given indiscriminately to some of the most and to some of the least estimable feelings of which mankind are capable: we may refer it to the love of liberty and personal independence, an appeal to which was with the Stoics one of the most effective means for the inculcation of it; to the love of power, or to the love of excitement, both of which do really enter into and contribute to it: but its most appropriate appellation is a sense of dignity, which all human beings possess in one form or other, and in some, though by no means in exact, proportion to their higher faculties, and which is so essential a part of the happiness of those in whom it is strong, that nothing which conflicts with it could be, otherwise than momentarily, an object of desire to them.

Whoever supposes that this preference takes place at a sacrifice of happiness—that the superior being, in anything like equal circumstances, is not happier than the inferior—confounds the two very different ideas, of happiness, and content. It is indisputable that the being whose capacities of enjoyment are low, has the greatest chance of having them fully satisfied; and a highly endowed being will always feel that any happiness which he can look for, as the world is constituted, is imperfect. But he can learn to bear its imperfections, if they are at all bearable; and they will not make him envy the being who is indeed unconscious of the imperfections, but only because he feels not at all the good which those imperfections qualify. It is better to be a human being dissatisfied than a pig satisfied; better to be Socrates dissatisfied than a fool satisfied. And if the fool, or the pig, are of a different opinion, it is because they only know their own side of the question. The other party to the comparison knows both sides.

It may be objected, that many who are capable of the higher pleasures, occasionally, under the influence of temptation, postpone them to the lower. But this is quite compatible with a full appreciation of the intrinsic superiority of the higher. Men often, from infirmity of character, make their election for the nearer good, though they know it to be the less valuable; and this no less when the choice is between two bodily pleasures, than when it is between bodily and mental. They pursue sensual indulgences to the injury of health, though perfectly aware that health is the greater good.

It may be further objected, that many who begin with youthful enthusiasm for everything noble, as they advance in years sink into indolence and selfishness. But I do not believe that those who undergo this very common change, voluntarily choose the lower description of pleasures in preference to the higher. I believe that before they devote themselves exclusively to the one, they have already become incapable of the other. Capacity for the nobler feelings is in most natures a very tender plant, easily killed, not only by hostile influences, but by mere want of sustenance; and in the majority of young persons it speedily dies away if the occupations to which their position in life has devoted them, and the society into which it has thrown them, are not favorable to keeping that higher capacity in exercise. Men lose their high aspirations as they lose their intellectual tastes, because they have not time or opportunity for indulging them; and they addict themselves to inferior pleasures, not because they deliberately prefer them, but because they are either the only ones to which they have access, or the only ones which they are any longer capable of enjoying. It may be questioned whether any one who has remained equally susceptible to both classes of pleasures, ever knowingly and calmly preferred the lower; though many, in all ages, have broken down in an ineffectual attempt to combine both.

From this verdict of the only competent judges, I apprehend there can be no   10
appeal. On a question which is the best worth having of two pleasures, or which of two modes of existence is the most grateful to the feelings, apart from its moral attributes and from its consequences, the judgment of those who are qualified by knowledge of both, or, if they differ, that of the majority among them, must be admitted as final. And there needs be the less hesitation to accept this judgment respecting the quality of pleasures, since there is no other tribunal to be referred to even on the question of quantity. What means are there of determining which is the acutest of two pains, or the intensest of two pleasurable sensations, except the general suffrage of those who are familiar with both? Neither pains nor pleasures are homogeneous, and pain is always heterogeneous with pleasure. What is there to decide whether a particular pleasure is worth purchasing at the cost of a particular pain, except the feelings and judgment of the experienced? When, therefore, those feelings and judgment declare the

pleasures derived from the higher faculties to be preferable in kind, apart from the question of intensity, to those of which the animal nature, disjoined from the higher faculties, is susceptible, they are entitled on this subject to the same regard.

I have dwelt on this point, as being a necessary part of a perfectly just conception of Utility or Happiness, considered as the directive rule of human conduct. But it is by no means an indispensable condition to the acceptance of the utilitarian standard; for that standard is not the agent's own greatest happiness, but the greatest amount of happiness altogether; and if it may possibly be doubted whether a noble character is always the happier for its nobleness, there can be no doubt that it makes other people happier, and that the world in general is immensely a gainer by it. Utilitarianism, therefore, could only attain its end by the general cultivation of nobleness of character, even if each individual were only benefitted by the nobleness of others, and his own, so far as happiness is concerned, were a sheer deduction from the benefit. But the bare enunciation of such an absurdity as this last, renders refutation superfluous.

According to the Greatest Happiness Principle, as above explained, the ultimate end, with reference to and for the sake of which all other things are desirable (whether we are considering our own good or that of other people), is an existence exempt as far as possible from pain, and as rich as possible in enjoyments, both in point of quantity and quality; the test of quality, and the rule for measuring it against quantity, being the preference felt by those who in their opportunities of experience, to which must be added their habits of self-consciousness and self-observation, are best furnished with the means of comparison. This, being, according to the utilitarian opinion, the end of human action, is necessarily also the standard of morality; which may accordingly be defined, the rules and precepts for human conduct, by the observance of which an existence such as has been described might be, to the greatest extent possible, secured to all mankind; and not to them only, but, so far as the nature of things admits, to the whole sentient creation.

Against this doctrine, however, arises another class of objectors, who say that happiness, in any form, cannot be the rational purpose of human life and action; because, in the first place, it is unattainable: and they contemptuously ask, what right hast thou to be happy? a question which Mr. Carlyle clenches by the addition, What right, a short time ago, hadst thou even to be? Next, they say, that men can do without happiness; that all noble human beings have felt this, and could not have become noble but by learning the lesson of Entsagen, or renunciation; which lesson, thoroughly learnt and submitted to, they affirm to be the beginning and necessary condition of all virtue.

The first of these objections would go to the root of the matter were it well founded; for if no happiness is to be had at all by human beings, the attainment of it cannot be the end of morality, or of any rational conduct. Though, even in that case, something might still be said for the utilitarian theory; since utility includes not solely the pursuit of happiness, but the prevention or mitigation of unhappiness; and if the former aim be chimerical, there will be all the greater scope and more imperative need for the latter, so long at least as mankind think fit to live, and do not take refuge in the simultaneous act of suicide recommended under certain conditions by Novalis. When, however, it is thus positively asserted to be impossible that human life should be happy, the assertion, if not something like a verbal quibble, is at least an exaggeration. If by happiness be meant a continuity of highly pleasurable excitement, it is evident enough that this is impossible. A state of exalted pleasure lasts only moments, or in some cases, and with some intermissions, hours or days, and is the occasional brilliant flash of enjoyment, not its permanent and steady flame. Of this the philosophers who have taught that happiness is the end of life were as fully aware as those who taunt them. The happiness which they meant was not a life of rapture; but moments of such, in an existence made up of few and transitory pains, many and various pleasures, with a decided predominance of the active over the passive, and having as the foundation of the whole, not to expect more from life than it is capable of bestowing. A life thus composed, to those who have been fortunate enough to obtain it, has always appeared worthy of the name of happiness. And such an existence is even now the lot of many, during some considerable portion of their lives. The present wretched education, and wretched social arrangements, are the only real hindrance to its being attainable by almost all.

The objectors perhaps may doubt whether human beings, if taught to consider happiness as the end of life, would be satisfied with such a moderate share of it. But great numbers of mankind have been satisfied with much less. The main constituents of a satisfied life appear to be two, either of which by itself is often found sufficient for the purpose: tranquillity, and excitement. With much tranquillity, many find that they can be content with very little pleasure: with much excitement, many can reconcile themselves to a considerable quantity of pain. There is assuredly no inherent impossibility in enabling even the mass of mankind to unite both; since the two are so far from being incompatible that they are in natural alliance, the prolongation of either being a preparation for, and exciting a wish for, the other. It is only those in whom indolence amounts to a vice, that do not desire excitement after an interval of repose: it is only those in whom the need of excitement is a disease, that feel the tranquillity which follows excitement dull and insipid, instead of pleasurable in direct proportion to the excitement which preceded it. When people who are tolerably fortunate in their outward lot do not find in life sufficient enjoyment to make it valuable to them, the cause generally is, caring for nobody but themselves. To those who have neither public nor private affections, the excitements of life are much curtailed, and in any case dwindle in value as the time approaches when all selfish interests must be terminated by death: while those who leave after them objects of personal affection, and especially those who have also cultivated a fellow-feeling with the collective interests of mankind, retain as lively an interest in life on the eve of death as in the vigour of youth and health. Next to selfishness, the principal cause which makes life unsatisfactory is want of mental cultivation. A cultivated mind—I do not mean that of a philosopher, but any mind to which the fountains of knowledge have been opened, and which has been taught, in any tolerable degree, to exercise its faculties—finds sources of

15

inexhaustible interest in all that surrounds it; in the objects of nature, the achievements of art, the imaginations of poetry, the incidents of history, the ways of mankind, past and present, and their prospects in the future. It is possible, indeed, to become indifferent to all this, and that too without having exhausted a thousandth part of it; but only when one has had from the beginning no moral or human interest in these things, and has sought in them only the gratification of curiosity.

Now there is absolutely no reason in the nature of things why an amount of mental culture sufficient to give an intelligent interest in these objects of contemplation, should not be the inheritance of every one born in a civilized country. As little is there an inherent necessity that any human being should be a selfish egotist, devoid of every feeling or care but those which center in his own miserable individuality. Something far superior to this is sufficiently common even now, to give ample earnest of what the human species may be made. Genuine private affections and a sincere interest in the public good, are possible, though in unequal degrees, to every rightly brought-up human being. In a world in which there is so much to interest, so much to enjoy, and so much also to correct and improve, every one who has this moderate amount of moral and intellectual requisites is capable of an existence which may be called enviable; and unless such a person, through bad laws, or subjection to the will of others, is denied the liberty to use the sources of happiness within his reach, he will not fail to find this enviable existence, if he escape the positive evils of life, the great sources of physical and mental suffering—such as indigence, disease, and the unkindness, worthlessness, or premature loss of objects of affection. The main stress of the problem lies, therefore, in the contest with these calamities, from which it is a rare good fortune entirely to escape; which, as things now are, cannot be obviated, and often cannot be in any material degree mitigated. Yet no one whose opinion deserves a moment's consideration can doubt that most of the great positive evils of the world are in themselves removable, and will, if human affairs continue to improve, be in the end reduced within narrow limits. Poverty, in any sense implying suffering, may be completely extinguished by the wisdom of society, combined with the good sense and providence of individuals. Even that most intractable of enemies, disease, may be indefinitely reduced in dimensions by good physical and moral education, and proper control of noxious influences; while the progress of science holds out a promise for the future of still more direct conquests over this detestable foe. And every advance in that direction relieves us from some, not only of the chances which cut short our own lives, but, what concerns us still more, which deprive us of those in whom our happiness is wrapped up. As for vicissitudes of fortune, and other disappointments connected with worldly circumstances, these are principally the effect either of gross imprudence, of ill-regulated desires, or of bad or imperfect social institutions.

All the grand sources, in short, of human suffering are in a great degree, many of them almost entirely, conquerable by human care and effort; and though their removal is grievously slow—though a long succession of generations will perish in the breach before the conquest is completed, and this world becomes all that, if will and knowledge were not wanting, it might easily be made—yet every mind sufficiently intelligent and generous to bear a part, however small and inconspicuous, in the endeavor, will draw a noble enjoyment from the contest itself, which he would not for any bribe in the form of selfish indulgence consent to be without.

And this leads to the true estimation of what is said by the objectors concerning the possibility, and the obligation, of learning to do without happiness. Unquestionably it is possible to do without happiness; it is done involuntarily by nineteen-twentieths of mankind, even in those parts of our present world which are least deep in barbarism; and it often has to be done voluntarily by the hero or the martyr, for the sake of something which he prizes more than his individual happiness. But this something, what is it, unless the happiness of others or some of the requisites of happiness? It is noble to be capable of resigning entirely one's own portion of happiness, or chances of it: but, after all, this self-sacrifice must be for some end; it is not its own end; and if we are told that its end is not happiness, but virtue, which is better than happiness, I ask, would the sacrifice be made if the hero or martyr did not believe that it would earn for others immunity from similar sacrifices? Would it be made if he thought that his renunciation of happiness for himself would produce no fruit for any of his fellow creatures, but to make their lot like his, and place them also in the condition of persons who have renounced happiness? All honor to those who can abnegate for themselves the personal enjoyment of life, when by such renunciation they contribute worthily to increase the amount of happiness in the world; but he who does it, or professes to do it, for any other purpose, is no more deserving of admiration than the ascetic mounted on his pillar. He may be an inspiriting proof of what men can do, but assuredly not an example of what they should.

Though it is only in a very imperfect state of the world's arrangements that any one can best serve the happiness of others by the absolute sacrifice of his own, yet so long as the world is in that imperfect state, I fully acknowledge that the readiness to make such a sacrifice is the highest virtue which can be found in man. I will add, that in this condition the world, paradoxical as the assertion may be, the conscious ability to do without happiness gives the best prospect of realizing, such happiness as is attainable. For nothing except that consciousness can raise a person above the chances of life, by making him feel that, let fate and fortune do their worst, they have not power to subdue him: which, once felt, frees him from excess of anxiety concerning the evils of life, and enables him, like many a Stoic in the worst times of the Roman Empire, to cultivate in tranquillity the sources of satisfaction accessible to him, without concerning himself about the uncertainty of their duration, any more than about their inevitable end.

Meanwhile, let utilitarians never cease to claim the morality of self-devotion as a possession which belongs by as good a right to them, as either to the Stoic or to the Transcendentalist. The utilitarian morality does recognise in human beings the power of sacrificing their own greatest good for the good of others. It only refuses to admit that the sacrifice is itself a good. A sacrifice which does not increase, or tend to increase, the sum total of happiness, it considers as wasted. The only self-renunciation which it applauds, is devotion to the happiness, or to

20

some of the means of happiness, of others; either of mankind collectively, or of individuals within the limits imposed by the collective interests of mankind.

I must again repeat, what the assailants of utilitarianism seldom have the justice to acknowledge, that the happiness which forms the utilitarian standard of what is right in conduct, is not the agent's own happiness, but that of all concerned. As between his own happiness and that of others, utilitarianism requires him to be as strictly impartial as a disinterested and benevolent spectator. In the golden rule of Jesus of Nazareth, we read the complete spirit of the ethics of utility. To do as you would be done by, and to love your neighbor as yourself, constitute the ideal perfection of utilitarian morality. As the means of making the nearest approach to this ideal, utility would enjoin, first, that laws and social arrangements should place the happiness, or (as speaking practically it may be called) the interest, of every individual, as nearly as possible in harmony with the interest of the whole; and secondly, that education and opinion, which have so vast a power over human character, should so use that power as to establish in the mind of every individual an indissoluble association between his own happiness and the good of the whole; especially between his own happiness and the practice of such modes of conduct, negative and positive, as regard for the universal happiness prescribes; so that not only he may be unable to conceive the possibility of happiness to himself, consistently with conduct opposed to the general good, but also that a direct impulse to promote the general good may be in every individual one of the habitual motives of action, and the sentiments connected therewith may fill a large and prominent place in every human being's sentient existence. If the impugners of the utilitarian morality represented it to their own minds in this its true character, I know not what recommendation possessed by any other morality they could possibly affirm to be wanting to it; what more beautiful or more exalted developments of human nature any other ethical system can be supposed to foster, or what springs of action, not accessible to the utilitarian, such systems rely on for giving effect to their mandates. . . .

27   Again, Utility is often summarily stigmatized as an immoral doctrine by giving it the name of Expediency, and taking advantage of the popular use of that term to contrast it with Principle. But the Expedient, in the sense in which it is opposed to the Right, generally means that which is expedient for the particular interest of the agent himself; as when a minister sacrifices the interests of his country to keep himself in place. When it means anything better than this, it means that which is expedient for some immediate object, some temporary purpose, but which violates a rule whose observance is expedient in a much higher degree. The Expedient, in this sense, instead of being the same thing with the useful, is a branch of the hurtful. Thus, it would often be expedient, for the purpose of getting over some momentary embarrassment, or attaining some object immediately useful to ourselves or others, to tell a lie. But inasmuch as the cultivation in ourselves of a sensitive feeling on the subject of veracity, is one of the most useful, and the enfeeblement of that feeling one of the most hurtful, things to which our conduct can be instrumental; and inasmuch as any, even unintentional, deviation from truth, does that much towards weakening the trustworthiness of human assertion, which is not only the principal support of

all present social well-being, but the insufficiency of which does more than any one thing that can be named to keep back civilization, virtue, everything on which human happiness on the largest scale depends; we feel that the violation, for a present advantage, of a rule of such transcendent expediency, is not expedient, and that he who, for the sake of a convenience to himself or to some other individual, does what depends on him to deprive mankind of the good, and inflict upon them the evil, involved in the greater or less reliance which they can place in each other's word, acts the part of one of their worst enemies. Yet that even this rule, sacred as it is, admits of possible exceptions, is acknowledged by all moralists; the chief of which is when the withholding of some fact (as of information from a malefactor, or of bad news from a person dangerously ill) would save an individual (especially an individual other than oneself) from great and unmerited evil, and when the withholding can only be effected by denial. But in order that the exception may not extend itself beyond the need, and may have the least possible effect in weakening reliance on veracity, it ought to be recognized, and, if possible, its limits defined; and if the principle of utility is good for anything, it must be good for weighing these conflicting utilities against one another, and marking out the region within which one or the other preponderates. . . .   [1863]

1. Utilitarianism is sometimes summarized as meaning "the greatest good for the greatest number." Is that a fair summary of Mill's chapter?
2. What are the chances that, given the dictates of utilitarianism, a good society could be made up of people who, assuming they had enough resources, spent all of their time indulging in physical pleasures? Would Mill call that society "good"? Would Abraham Maslow (see p. 436)?
3. What problems do you see with Mill's version of utilitarianism?
4. In paragraph 21, Mill invokes the golden rule ("Love your neighbor as yourself"). What problem does he intend to solve with this moral injunction?
5. What is the problem with utilitarianism that James points out in his essay?
6. When James says, "Our ideals have certainly many sources. They are not all explicable as signifying corporeal pleasures to be gained, and pains to be escaped" (paragraph 7), he sounds like he is critiquing utilitarianism. Does that critique damage utilitarianism?
7. Is there any way to solve the problem James sees in utilitarianism?
8. Although James does not use the term "scapegoat" in his essay, he does explore this idea here. Summarize James's discussion of the concept of the scapegoat. How does this concept enter into James's consideration of "the moral life"?

The Philosophers and the Story

1. LeGuin calls her story "Variations on a Theme by William James" and in her book *The Lathe of Heaven* (New York: Perennial Classics, 2003) quotes the passage from "The Moral Philosopher and the Moral Life," paragraph 5 on unacceptable utopias. How does the story reflect James's concerns?

2. In what ways does Mill offer help in understanding the story?

3. Are there any circumstances in which Mill would accept the state of affairs in Omelas?

4. How does LeGuin's science-fictional "thought experiment" about this moral issue relate to real-world distribution of happiness and human notions of morality?

5. In mythic terms, the "certain lost soul on the far-off edge of things" living "a life of lonely torture" (James, paragraph 5) is called a "scapegoat," a figure who absorbs and carries away the sins of a community. Drawing on stories, books, or movies with which you are familiar, try to identify the figure of the scapegoat in other works.

DRAMA

OLC

SOPHOCLES

SOPHOCLES *(?496 BCE–?406 BCE) was the most famous dramatist of ancient Greece. Born in Colonus, near Athens, Sophocles began writing at an early age. He determined to become the best tragedian of all and succeeded well enough to have earned the fame that has kept his works alive. He changed Greek theater to include a third actor, painted scenery, and the enlargement of the chorus from twelve to fifteen. His plays are still presented all over the world and include not only* Oedipus Rex *but* Oedipus at Colonus, Antigone, Ajax, Electra, The Trachiniae, *and* Philoctetes.

Oedipus Rex

An English Version by Dudley Fitts and Robert Fitzgerald

List of Characters

Oedipus
A Priest
Creon
Teiresias
Iocastê
Messenger
Shepherd of Laïos
Second Messenger
Chorus of Theban Elders

Scene: *Before the palace of* Oedipus, *King of Thebes. A central door and two lateral doors open onto a platform which runs the length of the facade. On the platform, right and left, are altars; and three steps lead down into the "orchestra," or chorus-ground. At the beginning of the action these steps are crowded by* Suppliants *who have brought branches and chaplets of olive leaves and who lie in various attitudes of despair.* Oedipus *enters.*

Prologue

Oedipus: My children, generations of the living
    In the line of Kadmos,° nursed at his ancient hearth;
    Why have you strewn yourselves before these altars
    In supplication, with your boughs and garlands?
    The breath of incense rises from the city   5
    With a sound of prayer and lamentation.
                             Children,
    I would not have you speak through messengers,
    And therefore I have come myself to hear you—
    I, Oedipus, who bear the famous name.
    [To a Priest.*]* You, there, since you are eldest in the company,   10
    Speak for them all, tell me what preys upon you,
    Whether you come in dread, or crave some blessing:
    Tell me, and never doubt that I will help you
    In every way I can; I should be heartless
    Were I not moved to find you suppliant here.   15
Priest: Great Oedipus, O powerful King of Thebes!
    You see how all the ages of our people
    Cling to your altar steps: here are boys
    Who can barely stand alone, and here are priests
    By weight of age, as I am a priest of God,   20
    And young men chosen from those yet unmarried;
    As for the others, all that multitude,
    They wait with olive chaplets in the squares,
    At the two shrines of Pallas,° and where Apollo°
    Speaks in the glowing embers.
                      Your own eyes   25
    Must tell you: Thebes is in her extremity
    And cannot lift her head from the surge of death.
    A rust consumes the buds and fruits of the earth;
    The herds are sick; children die unborn,
    And labor is vain. The god of plague and pyre   30
    Raids like detestable lightning through the city,
    And all the house of Kadmos is laid waste,
    All emptied, and all darkened: Death alone
    Battens upon the misery of Thebes.
    You are not one of the immortal gods, we know;   35
    Yet we have come to you to make our prayer
    As to the man of all men best in adversity
    And wisest in the ways of God. You saved us

---

[2]**Kadmos** mythical founder of Thebes   [24]**Pallas** Athena, goddess of wisdom, protectress
of Athens   **Apollo** god of light and healing

From the Sphinx,° that flinty singer, and the tribute
40 We paid to her so long; yet you were never
Better informed than we, nor could we teach you:
It was some god breathed in you to set us free.

Therefore, O mighty King, we turn to you:
Find us our safety, find us a remedy,
45 Whether by counsel of the gods or the men.
A king of wisdom tested in the past
Can act in a time of troubles, and act well.
Noblest of men, restore
Life to your city! Think how all men call you
50 Liberator for your triumph long ago;
Ah, when your years of kingship are remembered,
Let them not say *We rose, but later fell*—
Keep the State from going down in the storm!
Once, years ago, with happy augury,
55 You brought us fortune; be the same again!
No man questions your power to rule the land:
But rule over men, not over a dead city!
Ships are only hulls, citadels are nothing,
When no life moves in the empty passageways.

60 *Oedipus:* Poor children! You may be sure I know
All that you longed for in your coming here.
I know that you are deathly sick; and yet,
Sick as you are, not one is as sick as I.
Each of you suffers in himself alone
65 His anguish, not another's; but my spirit
Groans for the city, for myself, for you.

I was not sleeping, you are not waking me.
No, I have been in tears for a long while
And in my restless thought walked many ways.
70 In all my search, I found one helpful course,
And that I have taken: I have sent Creon,
Son of Menoikeus, brother of the Queen,
To Delphi, Apollo's place of revelation,
To learn there, if he can,
75 What act or pledge of mine may save the city.
I have counted the days, and now, this very day,
I am troubled, for he has overstayed his time.

---

[39]**Sphinx** a monster (body of a lion, wings of a bird, face of a woman) who asked the riddle, "What goes on four legs in the morning, two at noon, and three in the evening?" and who killed those who could not answer. When Oedipus responded correctly that man crawls on all fours in infancy, walks upright in maturity, and uses a staff in old age, the Sphinx destroyed herself.

What is he doing? He has been gone too long.
Yet whenever he comes back, I should do ill
To scant whatever hint the god may give. 80

Priest: It is a timely promise. At this instant
They tell me Creon is here.

Oedipus: O Lord Apollo!
May his news be fair as his face is radiant!

Priest: It could not be otherwise: he is crowned with bay,
The chaplet is thick with berries.

Oedipus: We shall soon know; 85
He is near enough to hear us now.

Enter Creon.

O Prince:
Brother: son of Menoikeus:
What answer do you bring us from the god?

Creon: It is favorable. I can tell you, great afflictions
Will turn out well, if they are taken well. 90

Oedipus: What was the oracle? These vague words
Leave me still hanging between hope and fear.

Creon: Is it your pleasure to hear me with all these
Gathered around us? I am prepared to speak,
But should we not go in?

Oedipus: Let them all hear it. 95
It is for them I suffer, more than myself.

Creon: Then I will tell you what I heard at Delphi.

In plain words
The god commands us to expel from the land of Thebes
An old defilement that it seems we shelter. 100
It is a deathly thing, beyond expiation.
We must not let it feed upon us longer.

Oedipus: What defilement? How shall we rid ourselves of it?

Creon: By exile or death, blood for blood. It was
Murder that brought the plague-wind on the city. 105

Oedipus: Murder of whom? Surely the god has named him?

Creon: My lord: long ago Laïos was our king,
Before you came to govern us.

Oedipus: I know;
I learned of him from others; I never saw him.

Creon: He was murdered; and Apollo commands us now 110
To take revenge upon whoever killed him.

Oedipus: Upon whom? Where are they? Where shall we find a clue
To solve that crime, after so many years?

Creon: Here in this land, he said.

If we make enquiry,
We may touch things that otherwise escape us. 115

Oedipus: Tell me: Was Laïos murdered in his house,
  Or in the fields, or in some foreign country?
Creon: He said he planned to make a pilgrimage.
  He did not come home again.
Oedipus: And was there no one,
120 No witness, no companion, to tell what happened?
Creon: They were all killed but one, and he got away
  So frightened that he could remember one thing only.
Oedipus: What was that one thing? One may be the key
  To everything, if we resolve to use it.
125 *Creon:* He said that a band of highwaymen attacked them,
  Outnumbered them, and overwhelmed the King.
Oedipus: Strange, that a highwayman should be so daring—
  Unless some faction here bribed him to do it.
Creon: We thought of that. But after Laïos' death
130 New troubles arose and we had no avenger.
Oedipus: What troubles could prevent your hunting down the killers?
Creon: The riddling Sphinx's song
  Made us deaf to all mysteries but her own
Oedipus: Then once more I must bring what is dark to light.
135 It is most fitting that Apollo shows,
  As you do, this compunction for the dead.
  You shall see how I stand by you, as I should,
  To avenge the city and the city's god,
  And not as though it were for some distant friend,
140 But for my own sake, to be rid of evil.
  Whoever killed King Laïos might—who knows?—
  Decide at any moment to kill me as well.
  By avenging the murdered king I protect myself.
  Come, then, my children: leave the altar steps,
  Lift up your olive boughs!
145   One of you go
  And summon the people of Kadmos to gather here.
  I will do all that I can; you may tell them that.

                              [Exit a Page.*]*

  So, with the help of God,
  We shall be saved—or else indeed we are lost.
150 *Priest:* Let us rise, children. It was for this we came,
  And now the King has promised it himself.
  Phoibos° has sent us an oracle; may he descend
  Himself to save us and drive out the plague.
  Exeunt Oedipus *and* Creon *into the palace by the central door. The* Priest *and the*
  Suppliants *disperse right and left. After a short pause the* Chorus *enters the*
  orchestra.

152**Phoibos** Phoebus Apollo, the sun god

Párodos

Chorus: What is God singing in his profound   *Strophe 1*
    Delphi of gold and shadow?
    What oracle for Thebes, the sunwhipped city?
    Fear unjoints me, the roots of my heart tremble.
    Now I remember, O Healer, your power, and wonder;   5
    Will you send doom like a sudden cloud, or weave it
    Like nightfall of the past?
    Speak, speak to us, issue of holy sound:
    Dearest to our expectancy: be tender!

    Let me pray to Athenê, the immortal daughter of Zeus,   *Antistrophe 1*   10
    And to Artemis her sister
    Who keeps her famous throne in the market ring,
    And to Apollo, bowman at the far butts of heaven—

    O gods, descend! Like three streams leap against
    The fires of our grief, the fires of darkness;   15
    Be swift to bring us rest!

    As in the old time from the brilliant house
    Of air you stepped to save us, come again!

    Now our afflictions have no end,   *Strophe 2*
    Now all our stricken host lies down   20
    And no man fights off death with his mind;

    The noble plowland bears no grain,
    And groaning mothers cannot bear—
    See, how our lives like birds take wing,
    Like sparks that fly when a fire soars,   25
    To the shore of the god of evening.

    The plague burns on, it is pitiless   *Antistrophe 2*
    Though pallid children laden with death
    Lie unwept in the stony ways,
    And old gray women by every path   30
    Flock to the strand about the altars

    There to strike their breasts and cry
    Worship of Phoibos in wailing prayers:
    Be kind, God's golden child!

    There are no swords in this attack by fire,   *Strophe 3*   35
    No shields, but we are ringed with cries.
    Send the besieger plunging from our homes
    Into the vast sea-room of the Atlantic
    Or into the waves that foam eastward of Thrace—
    For the day ravages what the night spares—   40

    Destroy our enemy, lord of the thunder!
    Let him be riven by lightning from heaven!

Phoibos Apollo, stretch the sun's bowstring,   *Antistrophe 3*
That golden cord, until it sing for us,
Flashing arrows in heaven!

45   Artemis, Huntress,
Race with flaring lights upon our mountains!
O scarlet god, O golden-banded brow,
O Theban Bacchos° in a storm of Maenads,°
Enter Oedipus, *center.*
Whirl upon Death, that all the Undying hate!

50   Come with blinding cressets, come in joy!

Scene I

Oedipus: Is this your prayer? It may be answered. Come,
Listen to me, act as the crisis demands,
And you shall have relief from all these evils.

Until now I was a stranger to this tale,
5   As I had been a stranger to the crime.
Could I track down the murderer without a clue?
But now, friends,

As one who became a citizen after the murder,
I make this proclamation to all Thebans:
10   If any man knows by whose hand Laïos, son of Labdakos,
Met his death, I direct that man to tell me everything,
No matter what he fears for having so long withheld it.
Let it stand as promised that no further trouble
Will come to him, but he may leave the land in safety.

15   Moreover: If anyone knows the murderer to be foreign,
Let him not keep silent: he shall have his reward from me.
However, if he does conceal it, if any man
Fearing for his friend or for himself disobeys this edict,
Hear what I propose to do:

20   I solemnly forbid the people of this country,
Where power and throne are mine, ever to receive that man
Or speak to him, no matter who he is, or let him
Join in sacrifice, lustration, or in prayer.
I decree that he be driven from every house,

25   Being, as he is, corruption itself to us: the Delphic
Voice of Zeus has pronounced this revelation.
Thus I associate myself with the oracle
And take the side of the murdered king.

48**Bacchos** Dionysos, god of wine, thus scarlet-faced   **Maenads** Dionysos's female
attendants

As for the criminal, I pray to God—
Whether it be a lurking thief, or one of a number—
I pray that that man's life be consumed in evil and wretchedness.
And as for me, this curse applies no less
If it should turn out that the culprit is my guest here,
Sharing my hearth.

            You have heard the penalty.
I lay it on you now to attend to this
For my sake, for Apollo's, for the sick
Sterile city that heaven has abandoned.
Suppose the oracle had given you no command:
Should this defilement go uncleansed for ever?
You should have found the murderer: your king,
A noble king, had been destroyed!

            Now I,
Having the power that he held before me,
Having his bed, begetting children there
Upon his wife, as he would have, had he lived—
Their son would have been my children's brother,
If Laïos had had luck in fatherhood!
(But surely ill luck rushed upon his reign)—
I say I take the son's part, just as though
I were his son, to press the fight for him
And see it won! I'll find the hand that brought
Death to Labdakos' and Polydoros' child,
Heir of Kadmos' and Agenor's line.
And as for those who fail me,
May the gods deny them the fruit of the earth,
Fruit of the womb, and may they rot utterly!
Let them be wretched as we are wretched, and worse!

For you, for loyal Thebans, and for all
Who find my actions right, I pray the favor
Of justice, and of all the immortal gods.
Choragos:° Since I am under oath, my lord, I swear
    I did not do the murder, I cannot name
    The murderer. Might not the oracle
    That has ordained the search tell where to find him?
Oedipus: An honest question. But no man in the world
    Can make the gods do more than the gods will.
Choragos: There is one last expedient—
Oedipus: Tell me what it is.
    Though it seem slight, you must not hold it back.

30

35

40

45

50

55

60

65

---

⁶⁰**Choragos** leader of the Chorus

Choragos: A lord clairvoyant to the lord Apollo,
    As we all know, is the skilled Teiresias.
70   One might learn much about this from him, Oedipus.
Oedipus: I am not wasting time:
    Creon spoke of this, and I have sent for him—
    Twice, in fact; it is strange that he is not here.
Choragos: The other matter—that old report—seems useless.
75 *Oedipus:* Tell me. I am interested in all reports.
Choragos: The King was said to have been killed by highwaymen.
Oedipus: I know. But we have no witnesses to that.
Choragos: If the killer can feel a particle of dread,
    Your curse will bring him out of hiding!
Oedipus: No.
80   The man who dared that act will fear no curse.
    Enter the blind seer Teiresias *led by a* Page.
Choragos: But there is one man who may detect the criminal.
    This is Teiresias, this is the holy prophet
    In whom, alone of all men, truth was born.
Oedipus: Teiresias: seer: student of mysteries,
85   Of all that's taught and all that no man tells,
    Secrets of Heaven and secrets of the earth:
    Blind though you are, you know the city lies
    Sick with plague; and from this plague, my lord,
    We find that you alone can guard or save us.

90   Possibly you did not hear the messengers?
    Apollo, when we sent to him,
    Sent us back word that this great pestilence
    Would lift, but only if we established clearly
    The identity of those who murdered Laïos.
    They must be killed or exiled.
95   Can you use
    Birdflight or any art of divination
    To purify yourself, and Thebes, and me
    From this contagion? We are in your hands.
    There is no fairer duty
100   Than that of helping others in distress.
Teiresias: How dreadful knowledge of the truth can be
    When there's no help in truth! I knew this well,
    But did not act on it: else I should not have come.
Oedipus: What is troubling you? Why are your eyes so cold?
105 *Teiresias:* Let me go home. Bear your own fate, and I'll
    Bear mine. It is better so: trust what I say.
Oedipus: What you say is ungracious and unhelpful
    To your native country. Do not refuse to speak.

Teiresias: When it comes to speech, your own is neither temperate
    Nor opportune. I wish to be more prudent.   110
Oedipus: In God's name, we all beg you—
Teiresias: You are all ignorant.
    No; I will never tell you what I know.
    Now it is my misery; then, it would be yours.
Oedipus: What! You do know something, and will not tell us?
    You would betray us all and wreck the State?   115
Teiresias: I do not intend to torture myself, or you.
    Why persist in asking? You will not persuade me.
Oedipus: What a wicked man you are! You'd try a stone's
    Patience! Out with it! Have you no feeling at all?
Teiresias: You call me unfeeling. If you could only see   120
    The nature of your feelings . . .
Oedipus: Why,
    Who would not feel as I do? Who could endure
    Your arrogance toward the city?
Teiresias: What does it matter!
    Whether I speak or not, it is bound to come.
Oedipus: Then, if "it" is bound to come, you are bound to tell me.   125
Teiresias: No, I will not go on. Rage as you please.
Oedipus: Rage? Why not!
                    And I'll tell you what I think:
    You planned it, you had it done, you all but
    Killed him with your own hands: if you had eyes,
    I'd say the crime was yours, and yours alone.   130
Teiresias: So? I charge you, then,
    Abide by the proclamation you have made.
    From this day forth
    Never speak again to these men or to me;
    You yourself are the pollution of this country.   135
Oedipus: You dare say that! Can you possibly think you have
    Some way of going free, after such insolence?
Teiresias: I have gone free. It is the truth sustains me.
Oedipus: Who taught you shamelessness? It was not your craft.
Teiresias: You did. You made me speak. I did not want to.   140
Oedipus: Speak what? Let me hear it again more clearly.
Teiresias: Was it not clear before? Are you tempting me?
Oedipus: I did not understand it. Say it again.
Teiresias: I say that you are the murderer whom you seek.
Oedipus: Now twice you have spat out infamy. You'll pay for it!   145
Teiresias: Would you care for more? Do you wish to be really angry?
Oedipus: Say what you will. Whatever you say is worthless.
Teiresias: I say you live in hideous shame with those
    Most dear to you. You cannot see the evil.

150   *Oedipus:* It seems you can go on mouthing like this for ever.

    Teiresias: I can, if there is power in truth.

    Oedipus: There is:

        But not for you, not for you,

        You sightless, witless, senseless, mad old man!

    Teiresias: You are the madman. There is no one here

155   Who will not curse you soon, as you curse me.

    Oedipus: You child of endless night! You cannot hurt me

        Or any other man who sees the sun.

    Teiresias: True: it is not from me your fate will come.

        That lies within Apollo's competence,

        As it is his concern.

160   *Oedipus:*   Tell me:

        Are you speaking for Creon, or for yourself?

    Teiresias: Creon is no threat. You weave your own doom.

    Oedipus: Wealth, power, craft of statesmanship!

        Kingly position, everywhere admired!

165   What savage envy is stored up against these,

        If Creon, whom I trusted, Creon my friend,

        For this great office which the city once

        Put in my hands unsought—if for this power

        Creon desires in secret to destroy me!

170   He has brought this decrepit fortune-teller, this

        Collector of dirty pennies, this prophet fraud—

        Why, he is no more clairvoyant than I am!

                               Tell us:

        Has your mystic mummery ever approached the truth?

        When that hellcat the Sphinx was performing here,

175   What help were you to these people?

        Her magic was not for the first man who came along:

        It demanded a real exorcist. Your birds—

        What good were they? or the gods, for the matter of that?

        But I came by,

180   Oedipus, the simple man, who knows nothing—

        I thought it out for myself, no birds helped me!

        And this is the man you think you can destroy,

        That you may be close to Creon when he's king!

        Well, you and your friend Creon, it seems to me,

185   Will suffer most. If you were not an old man,

        You would have paid already for your plot.

    Choragos. We cannot see that his words or yours

        Have spoken except in anger, Oedipus,

        And of anger we have no need. How can God's will

190   Be accomplished best? That is what most concerns us.

Teiresias: You are a king. But where argument's concerned
    I am your man, as much a king as you.
    I am not your servant, but Apollo's.
    I have no need of Creon to speak for me.

    Listen to me. You mock my blindness, do you?   195
    But I say that you, with both your eyes, are blind:
    You cannot see the wretchedness of your life,
    Not in whose house you live, no, nor with whom.
    Who are your father and mother? Can you tell me?
    You do not even know the blind wrongs   200
    That you have done them, on earth and in the world below.
    But the double lash of your parents' curse will whip you
    Out of this land some day, with only night
    Upon your precious eyes.
    Your cries then—where will they not be heard?   205
    What fastness of Kithairon° will not echo them?
    And that bridal-descant of yours—you'll know it then,
    The song they sang when you came here to Thebes
    And found your misguided berthing.
    All this, and more, that you cannot guess at now,   210
    Will bring you to yourself among your children.
    Be angry, then. Curse Creon. Curse my words.
    I tell you, no man that walks upon the earth
    Shall be rooted out more horribly than you.
Oedipus: Am I to bear this from him?—Damnation   215
    Take you! Out of this place! Out of my sight!
Teiresias: I would not have come at all if you had not asked me.
Oedipus: Could I have told that you'd talk nonsense, that
    You'd come here to make a fool of yourself, and of me?
Teiresias: A fool? Your parents thought me sane enough.   220
Oedipus: My parents again!—Wait: who were my parents?
Teiresias: This day will give you a father, and break your heart.
Oedipus: Your infantile riddles! Your damned abracadabra!
Teiresias: You were a great man once at solving riddles.
Oedipus: Mock me with that if you like; you will find it true.   225
Teiresias: It was true enough. It brought about your ruin.
Oedipus: But if it saved this town.
Teiresias [to the Page*]:*   Boy, give me your hand.
Oedipus: Yes, boy; lead him away.
                     —While you are here
    We can do nothing. Go; leave us in peace.
Teiresias: I will go when I have said what I have to say.   230
    How can you hurt me? And I tell you again:

[206]**fastness of Kithairon** stronghold in a mountain near Thebes

The man you have been looking for all this time,
The damned man, the murderer of Laïos,
That man is in Thebes. To your mind he is foreignborn,
235   But it will soon be shown that he is a Theban,
A revelation that will fail to please
        A blind man
Who has his eyes now; a penniless man, who is rich now;
And he will go tapping the strange earth with his staff;
To the children with whom he lives now he will be
240   Brother and father—the very same; to her
Who bore him, son and husband—the very same
Who came to his father's bed, wet with his father's blood.

Enough. Go think that over.
If later you find error in what I have said,
245   You may say that I have no skill in prophecy.

Exit Teiresias, *led by his* Page. Oedipus *goes into the palace.*

         Ode I

Chorus: The Delphic stone of prophecies   *Strophe 1*
    Remembers ancient regicide
    And a still bloody hand.
    That killer's hour of flight has come.
5   He must be stronger than riderless
    Coursers of untiring wind,
    For the son of Zeus° armed with his father's thunder
    Leaps in lightning after him;
    And the Furies° follow him, the sad Furies.

10 Holy Parnossos' peak of snow   *Antistrophe 1*
    Flashes and blinds that secret man,
    That all shall hunt him down:
    Though he may roam the forest shade
    Like a bull gone wild from pasture
15 To rage through glooms of stone.
    Doom comes down on him; flight will not avail him;
    For the world's heart calls him desolate,
    And the immortal Furies follow, for ever follow.

    But now a wilder thing is heard   *Strophe 2*
20 From the old man skilled at hearing Fate in the wingbeat of a bird.
    Bewildered as a blown bird, my soul hovers and cannot find
    Foothold in this debate, or any reason or rest of mind.
    But no man ever brought—none can bring
    Proof of strife between Thebes' royal house,

---

[7]**son of Zeus** Apollo   [9]**Furies** avenging deities

Labdakos' line,° and the son of Polybos;° 25
And never until now has any man brought word
Of Laïos' dark death staining Oedipus the King.

Divine Zeus and Apollo hold *Antistrophe 2*
Perfect intelligence alone of all tales ever told;
And well though this diviner works, he works in his own night; 30
No man can judge that rough unknown or trust in second sight,
For wisdom changes hands among the wise.
Shall I believe my great lord criminal
At a raging word that a blind old man let fall?
I saw him, when the carrion woman faced him of old, 35
Prove his heroic mind! These evil words are lies.

Scene II

Creon: Men of Thebes:
I am told that heavy accusations
Have been brought against me by King Oedipus.
I am not the kind of man to bear this tamely.

If in these present difficulties 5
He holds me accountable for any harm to him
Through anything I have said or done—why, then,
I do not value life in this dishonor.
It is not as though this rumor touched upon
Some private indiscretion. The matter is grave. 10
The fact is that I am being called disloyal
To the State, to my fellow citizens, to my friends.
Choragos: He may have spoken in anger, not from his mind.
Creon: But did you hear him say I was the one
Who seduced the old prophet into lying? 15
Choragos: The thing was said; I do not know how seriously.
Creon: But you were watching him! Were his eyes steady?
Did he look like a man in his right mind?
Choragos: I do not know.
I cannot judge the behavior of great men.
But here is the King himself.
Enter Oedipus.

Oedipus: So you dared come back. 20
Why? How brazen of you to come to my house,
You murderer!
Do you think I do not know
That you plotted to kill me, plotted to steal my throne?
Tell me, in God's name: am I coward, a fool,

---

²⁵**Labdakos' line** family of Laïos   **son of Polybos** Oedipus (so the Chorus believes)

25   That you should dream you could accomplish this?
        A fool who could not see your slippery game?
        A coward, not to fight back when I saw it?
        You are the fool, Creon, are you not? hoping
        Without support or friends to get a throne?
30   Thrones may be won or bought: you could do neither.
    Creon: Now listen to me. You have talked; let me talk, too.
        You cannot judge unless you know the facts.
    Oedipus: You speak well: there is one fact; but I find it hard
        To learn from the deadliest enemy I have.
35 *Creon:* That above all I must dispute with you.
    Oedipus: That above all I will not hear you deny.
    Creon: If you think there is anything good in being stubborn
        Against all reason, then I say you are wrong.
    Oedipus: If you think a man can sin against his own kind
40   And not be punished for it, I say you are mad.
    Creon: I agree. But tell me: what have I done to you?
    Oedipus: You advised me to send for that wizard, did you not?
    Creon: I did. I should do it again.
    Oedipus: Very well. Now tell me:
        How long has it been since Laïos—
    Creon: What of Laïos?
45 *Oedipus:* Since he vanished in that onset by the road?
    Creon: It was long ago, a long time.
    Oedipus: And this prophet,
        Was he practicing here then?
    Creon: He was; and with honor, as now.
    Oedipus: Did he speak of me at that time?
    Creon: He never did;
        At least, not when I was present.
    Oedipus: But . . . the enquiry?
        I suppose you held one?
50 *Creon:*   We did, but we learned nothing.
    Oedipus: Why did the prophet not speak against me then?
    Creon: I do not know; and I am the kind of man
        Who holds his tongue when he has no facts to go on.
    Oedipus: There's one fact that you know, and you could tell it.
55 *Creon:* What fact is that? If I know it, you shall have it.
    Oedipus: If he were not involved with you, he could not say
        That it was I who murdered Laïos.
    Creon: If he says that, you are the one that knows it!—
        But now it is my turn to question you.
60 *Oedipus:* Put your questions. I am no murderer.
    Creon: First, then: You married my sister?
    Oedipus: I married your sister.
    Creon: And you rule the kingdom equally with her?

Oedipus: Everything that she wants she has from me.

Creon: And I am the third, equal to both of you?

Oedipus: That is why I call you a bad friend.   65

Creon: No. Reason it out, as I have done.

Think of this first. Would any sane man prefer
Power, with all a king's anxieties,
To that same power and the grace of sleep?
Certainly not I.   70
I have never longed for the king's power—only his rights.
Would any wise man differ from me in this?
As matters stand, I have my way in everything
With your consent, and no responsibilities.
If I were king, I should be a slave to policy.   75
How could I desire a scepter more
Than what is now mine—untroubled influence?
No, I have not gone mad; I need no honors,
Except those with the perquisites I have now.
I am welcome everywhere; every man salutes me,   80
And those who want your favor seek my ear,
Since I know how to manage what they ask.
Should I exchange this ease for that anxiety?
Besides, no sober mind is treasonable.
I hate anarchy   85
And never would deal with any man who likes it.

Test what I have said. Go to the priestess
At Delphi, ask if I quoted her correctly.
And as for this other thing: if I am found
Guilty of treason with Teiresias,   90
Then sentence me to death! You have my word
It is a sentence I should cast my vote for—
But not without evidence!
                         You do wrong
When you take good men for bad, bad men for good.
A true friend thrown aside—why, life itself   95
Is not more precious!
                     In time you will know this well:
For time, and time alone, will show the just man,
Though scoundrels are discovered in a day.

Choragos: This is well said, and a prudent man would ponder it.
Judgments too quickly formed are dangerous.   100

Oedipus: But is he not quick in his duplicity?
And shall I not be quick to parry him?
Would you have me stand still, hold my peace, and let
This man win everything, through my inaction?

Creon: And you want—what is it, then? To banish me?   105

Oedipus: No, not exile. It is your death I want,
    So that all the world may see what treason means.
Creon: You will persist, then? You will not believe me?
Oedipus: How can I believe you?
Creon: Then you are a fool.
Oedipus: To save myself?
110 *Creon:*   In justice, think of me.
Oedipus: You are evil incarnate.
Creon: But suppose that you are wrong?
Oedipus: Still I must rule.
Creon: But not if you rule badly.
Oedipus: O city, city!
Creon: It is my city, too!
Choragos: Now, my lords, be still. I see the Queen,
115   Iocastê, coming from her palace chambers;
    And it is time she came, for the sake of you both.
    This dreadful quarrel can be resolved through her.
    Enter Iocastê.
Iocastê: Poor foolish men, what wicked din is this?
    With Thebes sick to death, is it not shameful
120   That you should rake some private quarrel up?
    [To Oedipus.*]* Come into the house.
                   —And you, Creon, go now:
    Let us have no more of this tumult over nothing.
Creon: Nothing? No, sister: what your husband plans for me
    Is one of two great evils: exile or death.
Oedipus: He is right.
125   Why, woman, I have caught him squarely
    Plotting against my life.
Creon: No! Let me die
    Accurst if ever I have wished you harm!
Iocastê: Ah, believe it, Oedipus!
    In the name of the gods, respect this oath of his
130   For my sake, for the sake of these people here!

Choragos: Open your mind to her, my lord. Be ruled   *Strophe 1*
    by her, I beg you!
Oedipus: What would you have me do?
Choragos: Respect Creon's word. He has never spoken like a fool,
    And now he has sworn an oath.
Oedipus: You know what you ask?
Choragos: I do.
Oedipus: Speak on, then.
135 *Choragos:* A friend so sworn should not be baited so,
    In blind malice, and without final proof.
Oedipus: You are aware, I hope, that what you say
    Means death for me, or exile at the least.

Choragos: No, I swear by Helios,° first in Heaven!   *Strophe 2*
   May I die friendless and accurst,   140
   The worst of deaths, if ever I meant that!
      It is the withering fields
         That hurt my sick heart:
      Must we bear all these ills,
         And now your bad blood as well?   145
Oedipus: Then let him go. And let me die, if I must,
   Or be driven by him in shame from the land of Thebes.
   It is your unhappiness, and not his talk,
   That touches me.
                    As for him—
   Wherever he is, I will hate him as long as I live.   150
Creon: Ugly in yielding, as you were ugly in rage!
   Natures like yours chiefly torment themselves.
Oedipus: Can you not go? Can you not leave me?
Creon: I can.
   You do not know me; but the city knows me,
   And in its eyes I am just, if not in yours.   155

                                                 [Exit Creon.]

Choragos: Lady Iocastê, did you not ask the King   *Antistrophe 1*
   to go to his chambers?
Iocastê: First tell me what has happened.
Choragos: There was suspicion without evidence; yet it rankled
   As even false charges will.
Iocastê: On both sides?
Choragos: On both.
Iocastê: But what was said?
Choragos: Oh let it rest, let it be done with!   160
   Have we not suffered enough?
Oedipus: You see to what your decency has brought you:
   You have made difficulties where my heart saw none.

Choragos: Oedipus, it is not once only I have told you—   *Antistrophe 2*
   You must know I should count myself unwise   165
   To the point of madness, should I now forsake you—
      You, under whose hand,
         In the storm of another time,
      Our dear land sailed out free,
         But now stand fast at the helm!   170
Iocastê: In God's name, Oedipus, inform your wife as well:
   Why are you so set in this hard anger?
Oedipus: I will tell you, for none of these men deserves
   My confidence as you do. It is Creon's work,
   His treachery, his plotting against me.   175
Iocastê: Go on, if you can make this clear to me.

---

[139]**Helios** sun god

Oedipus: He charges me with the murder of Laïos.

Iocastê: Has he some knowledge? Or does he speak from hearsay?

Oedipus: He would not commit himself to such a charge,

180   But he has brought in that damnable soothsayer
    To tell his story.

Iocastê: Set your mind at rest.
    If it is a question of soothsayers, I tell you
    That you will find no man whose craft gives knowledge
    Of the unknowable.

                 Here is my proof.

185   An oracle was reported to Laïos once
    (I will not say from Phoibos himself, but from
    His appointed ministers, at any rate)
    That his doom would be death at the hands of his own son—
    His son, born of his flesh and of mine!

190   Now, you remember the story: Laïos was killed
    By marauding strangers where three highways meet;
    But his child had not been three days in this world
    Before the King had pierced the baby's ankles
    And left him to die on a lonely mountainside.

195   Thus, Apollo never caused that child
    To kill his father, and it was not Laïos' fate
    To die at the hands of his son, as he had feared.
    This is what prophets and prophecies are worth!
    Have no dread of them.

              It is God himself

200   Who can show us what he wills, in his own way.

Oedipus: How strange a shadowy memory crossed my mind,
    Just now while you were speaking; it chilled my heart.

Iocastê: What do you mean? What memory do you speak of?

Oedipus: If I understand you, Laïos was killed
    At a place where three roads meet.

205 *Iocastê:*   So it was said;
    We have no later story.

Oedipus: Where did it happen?

Iocastê: Phokis, it is called: at a place where the Theban Way
    Divides into the roads towards Delphi and Daulia.

Oedipus: When?

Iocastê: We had the news not long before you came

210   And proved the right to your succession here.

Oedipus: Ah, what net has God been weaving for me?

Iocastê: Oedipus! Why does this trouble you?

Oedipus: Do not ask me yet.
    First, tell me how Laïos looked, and tell me
    How old he was.

Iocastê: He was tall, his hair just touched
    With white; his form was not unlike your own.   215
Oedipus: I think that I myself may be accurst
    By my own ignorant edict.
Iocastê: You speak strangely.
    It makes me tremble to look at you, my King.
Oedipus: I am not sure that the blind man cannot see.
    But I should know better if you were to tell me—   220
Iocastê: Anything—though I dread to hear you ask it.
Oedipus: Was the King lightly escorted, or did he ride
    With a large company, as a ruler should?
Iocastê: There were five men with him in all: one was a herald;
    And a single chariot, which he was driving.   225
Oedipus: Alas, that makes it plain enough!

                 But who—
    Who told you how it happened?
Iocastê: A household servant,
    The only one to escape.
Oedipus: And is he still
    A servant of ours?
Iocastê: No; for when he came back at last
    And found you enthroned in the place of the dead king,   230
    He came to me, touched my hand with his, and begged
    That I would send him away to the frontier district
    Where only the shepherds go—
    As far away from the city as I could send him.
    I granted his prayer; for although the man was a slave,   235
    He had earned more than this favor at my hands.
Oedipus: Can he be called back quickly?
Iocastê: Easily.
    But why?
Oedipus: I have taken too much upon myself
    Without enquiry; therefore I wish to consult him.
Iocastê: Then he shall come.

                But am I not one also   240
    To whom you might confide these fears of yours!
Oedipus: That is your right; it will not be denied you,
    Now least of all; for I have reached a pitch
    Of wild foreboding. Is there anyone
    To whom I should sooner speak?   245
    Polybos of Corinth is my father.
    My mother is a Dorian: Meropê.
    I grew up chief among the men of Corinth
    Until a strange thing happened—
    Not worth my passion, it may be, but strange.   250

At a feast, a drunken man maundering in his cups
Cries out that I am not my father's son!

I contained myself that night, though I felt anger
And a sinking heart. The next day I visited
255 My father and mother, and questioned them. They stormed,
Calling it all the slanderous rant of a fool;
And this relieved me. Yet the suspicion
Remained always aching in my mind;
I knew there was talk; I could not rest;
260 And finally, saying nothing to my parents,
I went to the shrine at Delphi.
The god dismissed my question without reply;
He spoke of other things.
                              Some were clear,
Full of wretchedness, dreadful, unbearable:
265 As, that I should lie with my own mother, breed
Children from whom all men would turn their eyes;
And that I should be my father's murderer.

I heard all this, and fled. And from that day
Corinth to me was only in the stars
270 Descending in that quarter of the sky,
As I wandered farther and farther on my way
To a land where I should never see the evil
Sung by the oracle. And I came to this country
Where, so you say, King Laïos was killed.
275 I will tell you all that happened there, my lady.

There were three highways
Coming together at a place I passed;
And there a herald came towards me, and a chariot
Drawn by horses, with a man such as you describe
280 Seated in it. The groom leading the horses
Forced me off the road at his lord's command;
But as this charioteer lurched over toward me
I struck him in my rage. The old man saw me
And brought his double goad down upon my head
As I came abreast.
                          He was paid back, and more!
285 Swinging my club in this right hand I knocked him
Out of his car, and he rolled on the ground.
                          I killed him.
I killed them all.
Now if that stranger and Laïos were—kin,
290 Where is a man more miserable than I?

More hated by the gods? Citizen and alien alike
Must never shelter me or speak to me—
I must be shunned by all.
                              And I myself
Pronounced this malediction upon myself!

Think of it: I have touched you with these hands,   295
These hands that killed your husband. What defilement!

Am I all evil, then? It must be so,
Since I must flee from Thebes, yet never again
See my own countrymen, my own country,
For fear of joining my mother in marriage   300
And killing Polybos, my father.
                              Ah,
If I was created so, born to this fate,
Who could deny the savagery of God?

O holy majesty of heavenly powers!
May I never see that day! Never!   305
Rather let me vanish from the race of men
Than know the abomination destined me!
Choragos: We too, my lord, have felt dismay at this.
But there is hope: you have yet to hear the shepherd.
Oedipus: Indeed, I fear no other hope is left me.   310
Iocastê: What do you hope from him when he comes?
Oedipus: This much:
If his account of the murder tallies with yours,
Then I am cleared.
Iocastê: What was it that I said
Of such importance?
Oedipus: Why, "marauders," you said,
Killed the King, according to this man's story.   315
If he maintains that still, if there were several,
Clearly the guilt is not mine: I was alone.
But if he says one man, singlehanded, did it,
Then the evidence all points to me.
Iocastê: You may be sure that he said there were several;   320
And can he call back that story now? He cannot.
The whole city heard it as plainly as I.
But suppose he alters some detail of it:
He cannot ever show that Laïos' death
Fulfilled the oracle: for Apollo said   325
My child was doomed to kill him; and my child—
Poor baby!—it was my child that died first.

No. From now on, where oracles are concerned,
I would not waste a second thought on any.

Oedipus: You may be right.

330   But come: let someone go
For the shepherd at once. This matter must be settled.

Iocastê: I will send for him.
          I would not wish to cross you in anything,
And surely not in this.—Let us go in.   *[Exeunt into the palace.]*

Ode II

Chorus: Let me be reverent in the ways of right,   *Strophe 1*
          Lowly the paths I journey on;
          Let all my words and actions keep
          The laws of the pure universe
5   From highest Heaven handed down.
          For Heaven is their bright nurse,
          Those generations of the realms of light;
          Ah, never of mortal kind were they begot,
          Nor are they slaves of memory, lost in sleep:
10   Their Father is greater than Time, and ages not.

          The tyrant is a child of Pride   *Antistrophe 1*
          Who drinks from his great sickening cup
          Recklessness and vanity,
          Until from his high crest headlong
15   He plummets to the dust of hope.
          That strong man is not strong.
          But let no fair ambition be denied;
          May God protect the wrestler for the State
          In government, in comely policy,
20   Who will fear God, and on His ordinance wait.

          Haughtiness and the high hand of disdain   *Strophe 2*
          Tempt and outrage God's holy law;
          And any mortal who dares hold
          No immortal Power in awe
25   Will be caught up in a net of pain:
          The price for which his levity is sold.
          Let each man take due earnings, then,
          And keep his hands from holy things,
          And from blasphemy stand apart—
30   Else the crackling blast of heaven
          Blows on his head, and on his desperate heart;
          Though fools will honor impious men,
          In their cities no tragic poet sings.

          Shall we lose faith in Delphi's obscurities,   *Antistrophe 2*
35   We who have heard the world's core
          Discredited, and the sacred wood
          Of Zeus at Elis praised no more?
          The deeds and the strange prophecies

Must make a pattern yet to be understood.
Zeus, if indeed you are lord of all,   40
Throned in light over night and day,
Mirror this in your endless mind:
Our masters call the oracle
Words on the wind, and the Delphic vision blind!
Their hearts no longer know Apollo,   45
And reverence for the gods has died away.

                        Scene III

Enter Iocastê.

Iocastê: Princes of Thebes, it has occurred to me
    To visit the altars of the gods, bearing
    These branches as a suppliant, and this incense.
    Our King is not himself: his noble soul
    Is overwrought with fantasies of dread,   5
    Else he would consider
    The new prophecies in the light of the old.
    He will listen to any voice that speaks disaster,
    And my advice goes for nothing.
She approaches the altar, right.
                              To you, then, Apollo,
    Lycean lord, since you are nearest, I turn in prayer.   10
    Receive these offerings, and grant us deliverance
    From defilement. Our hearts are heavy with fear
    When we see our leader distracted, as helpless sailors
    Are terrified by the confusion of their helmsman.
Enter Messenger.

Messenger: Friends, no doubt you can direct me: 15
    Where shall I find the house of Oedipus,
    Or, better still, where is the King himself?
Choragos: It is this very place, stranger; he is inside.
    This is his wife and mother of his children.
Messenger: I wish her happiness in a happy house,   20
    Blest in all the fulfillment of her marriage.
Iocastê: I wish as much for you: your courtesy
    Deserves a like good fortune. But now, tell me:
    Why have you come? What have you to say to us?
Messenger: Good news, my lady, for your house and your husband.   25
Iocastê: What news? Who sent you here?
Messenger: I am from Corinth.
    The news I bring ought to mean joy for you,
    Though it may be you will find some grief in it.
Iocastê: What is it? How can it touch us in both ways?
Messenger: The people of Corinth, they say,   30
    Intend to call Oedipus to be their king.
Iocastê: But old Polybos—is he not reigning still?

Messenger: No. Death holds him in his sepulchre.

Iocastê: What are you saying? Polybos is dead?

35 *Messenger:* If I am not telling the truth, may I die myself.

Iocastê [to a Maidservant*]:* Go in, go quickly; tell this to your master.

    O riddlers of God's will, where are you now!

    This was the man whom Oedipus, long ago,

    Feared so, fled so, in dread of destroying him—

40   But it was another fate by which he died.

    Enter Oedipus, *center.*

Oedipus: Dearest Iocastê, why have you sent for me?

Iocastê: Listen to what this man says, and then tell me

    What has become of the solemn prophecies.

Oedipus: Who is this man? What is his news for me?

45 *Iocastê:* He has come from Corinth to announce your father's death!

Oedipus: Is it true, stranger? Tell me in your own words.

Messenger: I cannot say it more clearly: the King is dead.

Oedipus: Was it by treason? Or by an attack of illness?

Messenger: A little thing brings old men to their rest.

Oedipus: It was sickness, then?

50 *Messenger:*   Yes, and his many years.

Oedipus: Ah!

    Why should a man respect the Pythian hearth,° or

    Give heed to the birds that jangle above his head?

    They prophesied that I should kill Polybos,

55   Kill my own father; but he is dead and buried,

    And I am here—I never touched him, never,

    Unless he died in grief for my departure,

    And thus, in a sense, through me. No, Polybos

    Has packed the oracles off with him underground.

    They are empty words.

60 *Iocastê:*   Had I not told you so?

Oedipus: You had; it was my faint heart that betrayed me.

Iocastê: From now on never think of those things again.

Oedipus: And yet—must I not fear my mother's bed?

Iocastê: Why should anyone in this world be afraid,

65   Since Fate rules us and nothing can be foreseen?

    A man should live only for the present day.

    Have no more fear of sleeping with your mother.

    How many men, in dreams, have lain with their mothers!

    No reasonable man is troubled by such things.

---

⁵²**Pythian hearth** Delphi (also called Pytho because a great snake had lived there), where
Apollo spoke through a priestess

Oedipus: That is true; only—   70
    If only my mother were not still alive!
    But she is alive. I cannot help my dread.
Iocastê: Yet this news of your father's death is wonderful.
Oedipus: Wonderful. But I fear the living woman.
Messenger: Tell me, who is this woman that you fear?   75
Oedipus: It is Meropê, man; the wife of King Polybos.
Messenger: Meropê? Why should you be afraid of her?
Oedipus: An oracle of the gods, a dreadful saying.
Messenger: Can you tell me about it or are you sworn to silence?
Oedipus: I can tell you, and I will.   80
    Apollo said through his prophet that I was the man
    Who should marry his own mother, shed his father's blood
    With his own hands. And so, for all these years
    I have kept clear of Corinth, and no harm has come—
    Though it would have been sweet to see my parents again.   85
Messenger: And is this the fear that drove you out of Corinth?
Oedipus: Would you have me kill my father?
Messenger: As for that
    You must be reassured by the news I gave you.
Oedipus: If you could reassure me, I would reward you.
Messenger: I had that in mind, I will confess: I thought   90
    I could count on you when you returned to Corinth.
Oedipus: No: I will never go near my parents again.
Messenger: Ah, son, you still do not know what you are doing—
Oedipus: What do you mean? In the name of God tell me!
Messenger: —If these are your reasons for not going home—   95
Oedipus: I tell you, I fear the oracle may come true.
Messenger: And guilt may come upon you through your parents?
Oedipus: That is the dread that is always in my heart.
Messenger: Can you not see that all your fears are groundless?
Oedipus: How can you say that? They are my parents, surely?   100
Messenger: Polybos was not your father.
Oedipus: Not my father?
Messenger: No more your father than the man speaking to you.
Oedipus: But you are nothing to me!
Messenger: Neither was he.
Oedipus: Then why did he call me son?
Messenger: I will tell you:
    Long ago he had you from my hands, as a gift.   105
Oedipus: Then how could he love me so, if I was not his?
Messenger: He had no children, and his heart turned to you.
Oedipus: What of you? Did you buy me? Did you find me by chance?
Messenger: I came upon you in the crooked pass of Kithairon.
Oedipus: And what were you doing there?
Messenger: Tending my flocks.   110

Oedipus: A wandering shepherd?

Messenger: But your savior, son, that day.

Oedipus: From what did you save me?

Messenger: Your ankles should tell you that.

Oedipus: Ah, stranger, why do you speak of that childhood pain?

Messenger: I cut the bonds that tied your ankles together.

115 *Oedipus:* I have had the mark as long as I can remember.

Messenger: That was why you were given the name you bear.°

Oedipus: God! Was it my father or my mother who did it?
     Tell me!

Messenger: I do not know. The man who gave you to me

120 Can tell you better than I.

Oedipus: It was not you that found me, but another?

Messenger: It was another shepherd gave you to me.

Oedipus: Who was he? Can you tell me who he was?

Messenger: I think he was said to be one of Laïos' people.

125 *Oedipus:* You mean the Laïos who was king here years ago?

Messenger: Yes; King Laïos; and the man was one of his herdsmen.

Oedipus: Is he still alive? Can I see him?

Messenger: These men here
     Know best about such things.

Oedipus: Does anyone here
     Know this shepherd that he is talking about?

130 Have you seen him in the fields, or in the town?
     If you have, tell me. It is time things were made plain.

Choragos: I think the man he means is that same shepherd
     You have already asked to see. Iocastê perhaps
     Could tell you something.

Oedipus: Do you know anything

135 About him, Lady? Is he the man we have summoned?
     Is that the man this shepherd means?

Iocastê: Why think of him?
     Forget this herdsman. Forget it all.
     This talk is a waste of time.

Oedipus: How can you say that,
     When the clues to my true birth are in my hands?

140 *Iocastê:* For God's love, let us have no more questioning!
     Is your life nothing to you?
     My own is pain enough for me to bear.

Oedipus: You need not worry. Suppose my mother a slave,
     And born of slaves: no baseness can touch you.

145 *Iocastê:* Listen to me, I beg you: do not do this thing!

Oedipus: I will not listen; the truth must be made known.

Iocastê: Everything that I say is for your own good!

---

[116]**name you bear** *Oedipus* means "swollen-foot"

Oedipus: My own good
   Snaps my patience, then: I want none of it.
Iocastê: You are fatally wrong! May you never learn who you are!
Oedipus: Go, one of you, and bring the shepherd here.   150
   Let us leave this woman to brag of her royal name.
Iocastê: Ah, miserable!
   That is the only word I have for you now.
   That is the only word I can ever have.

Exit into the palace.

Choragos: Why has she left us, Oedipus? Why has she gone   155
   In such a passion of sorrow? I fear this silence:
   Something dreadful may come of it.
Oedipus: Let it come!
   However base my birth, I must know about it.
   The Queen, like a woman, is perhaps ashamed
   To think of my low origin. But I   160
   Am a child of luck; I cannot be dishonored.
   Luck is my mother; the passing months, my brothers,
   Have seen me rich and poor. If this is so,
   How could I wish that I were someone else?
   How could I not be glad to know my birth?   165

Ode III

Chorus: If ever the coming time were known   *Strophe*
   To my heart's pondering,
   Kithairon, now by Heaven I see the torches
   At the festival of the next full moon,
   And see the dance, and hear the choir sing   5
   A grace to your gentle shade:
   Mountain where Oedipus was found,
   O mountain guard of a noble race!
   May the god who heals us lend his aid,
   And let that glory come to pass   10
   For our king's cradling-ground.

   Of the nymphs that flower beyond the years,   *Antistrophe*
   Who bore you, royal child,
   To Pan of the hills or the timberline Apollo,
   Cold in delight where the upland clears,   15
   Or Hermês for whom Kyllenê's° heights are piled?
   Or flushed as evening cloud,
   Great Dionysos, roamer of mountains,
   He—was it he who found you there,

[16]**Hermês . . . Kyllenê's** Hermês, messenger of the gods, was said to have been born on
Mt. Kyllenê

20   And caught you up in his own proud
        Arms from the sweet god-ravisher°
        Who laughed by the Muses' fountains?

                        Scene IV

Oedipus: Sirs: though I do not know the man,
        I think I see him coming, this shepherd we want:
        He is old, like our friend here, and the men
        Bringing him seem to be servants of my house.
5   But you can tell, if you have ever seen him.
        Enter Shepherd *escorted by servants.*
Choragos: I know him, he was Laïos' man. You can trust him.
Oedipus: Tell me first, you from Corinth: is this the shepherd
        We were discussing?
Messenger: This is the very man.
Oedipus [to Shepherd*]:* Come here. No, look at me. You must answer
10   Everything I ask.—You belonged to Laïos?
Shepherd: Yes: born his slave, brought up in his house.
Oedipus: Tell me: what kind of work did you do for him?
Shepherd: I was a shepherd of his, most of my life.
Oedipus: Where mainly did you go for pasturage?
15 *Shepherd:* Sometimes Kithairon, sometimes the hills near-by.
Oedipus: Do you remember ever seeing this man out there?
Shepherd: What would he be doing there? This man?
Oedipus: This man standing here. Have you ever seen him before?
Shepherd: No. At least, not to my recollection.
20 *Messenger:* And that is not strange, my lord. But I'll refresh
        His memory: he must remember when we two
        Spent three whole seasons together, March to September,
        On Kithairon or thereabouts. He had two flocks;
        I had one. Each autumn I'd drive mine home
25   And he would go back with his to Laïos' sheepfold.—
        Is this not true, just as I have described it?
Shepherd: True, yes; but it was all so long ago.
Messenger: Well, then: do you remember, back in those days
        That you gave me a baby boy to bring up as my own?
30 *Shepherd:* What if I did? What are you trying to say?
Messenger: King Oedipus was once that little child.
Shepherd: Damn you, hold your tongue!
Oedipus: No more of that!
        It is your tongue needs watching, not this man's.
Shepherd: My King, my Master, what is it I have done wrong?
35 *Oedipus:* You have not answered his question about the boy.

²¹**the sweet god-ravisher** the presumed mother, the nymph whom the god found
irresistible

Shepherd: He does not know . . . He is only making trouble . . .
Oedipus: Come, speak plainly, or it will go hard with you.
Shepherd: In God's name, do not torture an old man!
Oedipus: Come here, one of you; bind his arms behind him.
Shepherd: Unhappy king! What more do you wish to learn?   40
Oedipus: Did you give this man the child he speaks of?
Shepherd: I did.
   And I would to God I had died that very day.
Oedipus: You will die now unless you speak the truth.
Shepherd: Yet if I speak the truth, I am worse than dead.
Oedipus: Very well; since you insist upon delaying—   45
Shepherd: No! I have told you already that I gave him the boy.
Oedipus: Where did you get him? From your house? From somewhere else?
   From somewhere else?
Shepherd: Not from mine, no. A man gave him to me.
Oedipus: Is that man here? Do you know whose slave he was?
Shepherd: For God's love, my King, do not ask me any more!   50
Oedipus: You are a dead man if I have to ask you again.
Shepherd: Then . . . Then the child was from the palace of Laïos.
Oedipus: A slave child? or a child of his own line?
Shepherd: Ah, I am on the brink of dreadful speech!
Oedipus: And I of dreadful hearing. Yet I must hear.   55
Shepherd: If you must be told, then . . .
                          They said it was Laïos' child,
   But it is your wife who can tell you about that.
Oedipus: My wife!—Did she give it to you?
Shepherd: My lord, she did.
Oedipus: Do you know why?
Shepherd: I was told to get rid of it.
Oedipus: An unspeakable mother!
Shepherd: There had been prophecies . . .   60
Oedipus: Tell me.
Shepherd: It was said that the boy would kill his own father.
Oedipus: Then why did you give him over to this old man?
Shepherd: I pitied the baby, my King,
   And I thought that this man would take him far away
   To his own country.
               He saved him—but for what a fate!   65
   For if you are what this man says you are,
   No man living is more wretched than Oedipus.
Oedipus: Ah God!
        It was true!
         All the prophecies!
                —Now,
   O Light, may I look on you for the last time!   70
   I, Oedipus,

Oedipus, damned in his birth, in his marriage damned,
Damned in the blood he shed with his own hand!
He rushes into the palace.

Ode IV

Chorus: Alas for the seed of men.   *Strophe 1*

What measure shall I give these generations
That breathe on the void and are void
And exist and do not exist?

5   Who bears more weight of joy
Than mass of sunlight shifting in images,
Or who shall make his thought stay on
That down time drifts away?

Your splendor is all fallen.

10   O naked brow of wrath and tears,
O change of Oedipus!
I who saw your days call no man blest—
Your great days like ghosts gone.

That mind was a strong bow.   *Antistrophe 1*
15   Deep, how deep you drew it then, hard archer,
At a dim fearful range,
And brought dear glory down!

You overcame the stranger—
The virgin with her hooking lion claws—
20   And though death sang, stood like a tower
To make pale Thebes take heart.

Fortress against our sorrow!

Divine king, giver of laws,
Majestic Oedipus!
25   No prince in Thebes had ever such renown,
No prince won such grace of power.

And now of all men ever known   *Strophe 2*
Most pitiful is this man's story:
His fortunes are most changed, his state
30   Fallen to a low slave's
Ground under bitter fate.
O Oedipus, most royal one!
The great door that expelled you to the light
Gave it night—ah, gave night to your glory:
35   As to the father, to the fathering son.

All understood too late.

How could that queen whom Laïos won,
The garden that he harrowed at his height,
Be silent when that act was done?

But all eyes fail before time's eye,   *Antistrophe 2*   40
All actions come to justice there.
Though never willed, though far down the deep past,
Your bed, your dread sirings,
Are brought to book at last.
Child by Laïos doomed to die,   45
Then doomed to lose that fortunate little death,
Would God you never took breath in this air
That with my wailing lips I take to cry:

For I weep the world's outcast.

I was blind, and now I can tell why: 50
Asleep, for you had given ease of breath
To Thebes, while the false years went by.

                    Exodos

Enter, from the palace, Second Messenger.
Second Messenger: Elders of Thebes, most honored in this land,
      What horrors are yours to see and hear, what weight
      Of sorrow to be endured, if, true to your birth,
      You venerate the line of Labdakos!
      I think neither Istros nor Phasis, those great rivers,   5
      Could purify this place of the corruption
      It shelters now, or soon must bring to light—
      Evil not done unconsciously, but willed.

      The greatest griefs are those we cause ourselves.
Choragos: Surely, friend, we have grief enough already;   10
      What new sorrow do you mean?
Second Messenger: The Queen is dead.
Choragos: Iocastê? Dead? But at whose hand?
Second Messenger: Her own.
      The full horror of what happened you cannot know,
      For you did not see it; but I, who did, will tell you
      As clearly as I can how she met her death.   15

      When she had left us,
      In passionate silence, passing through the court,
      She ran to her apartment in the house,
      Her hair clutched by the fingers of both hands.
      She closed the doors behind her; then, by that bed   20
      Where long ago the fatal son was conceived—
      That son who should bring about his father's death—

We heard her call upon Laïos, dead so many years,
And heard her wail for the double fruit of her marriage,
A husband by her husband, children by her child.

Exactly how she died I do not know:
For Oedipus burst in moaning and would not let us
Keep vigil to the end: it was by him
As he stormed about the room that our eyes were caught.
From one to another of us he went, begging a sword,
Cursing the wife who was not his wife, the mother
Whose womb had carried his own children and himself.
I do not know: it was none of us aided him,
But surely one of the gods was in control!
For with a dreadful cry
He hurled his weight, as though wrenched out of himself,
At the twin doors: the bolts gave, and he rushed in.
And there we saw her hanging, her body swaying
From the cruel cord she had noosed about her neck.
A great sob broke from him heartbreaking to hear,
As he loosed the rope and lowered her to the ground.

I would blot out from my mind what happened next!
For the King ripped from her gown the golden brooches
That were her ornament, and raised them, and plunged them down
Straight into his own eyeballs, crying, "No more,
No more shall you look on the misery about me,
The horrors of my own doing! Too long you have known
The faces of those whom I should never have seen,
Too long been blind to those for whom I was searching!
From this hour, go in darkness!" And as he spoke,
He struck at his eyes—not once, but many times;
And the blood spattered his beard,
Bursting from his ruined sockets like red hail.

So from the unhappiness of two this evil has sprung,
A curse on the man and woman alike. The old
Happiness of the house of Labdakos
Was happiness enough: where is it today?
It is all wailing and ruin, disgrace, death—all
The misery of mankind that has a name—
And it is wholly and for ever theirs.
Choragos: Is he in agony still? Is there no rest for him?
Second Messenger: He is calling for someone to lead him to the gates
So that all the children of Kadmos may look upon
His father's murderer, his mother's—no,
I cannot say it!
                    And then he will leave Thebes,

25

30

35

40

45

50

55

60

65

Self-exiled, in order that the curse
Which he himself pronounced may depart from the house.
He is weak, and there is none to lead him,
So terrible is his suffering.
                                    But you will see:
Look, the doors are opening; in a moment   70
You will see a thing that would crush a heart of stone.
The central door is opened; Oedipus, blinded, *is led in.*
Choragos: Dreadful indeed for men to see.
    Never have my own eyes
    Looked on a sight so full of fear.

Oedipus!   75
What madness came upon you, what daemon°
Leaped on your life with heavier
Punishment than a mortal man can bear?
No: I cannot even
Look at you, poor ruined one.   80
And I would speak, question, ponder,
If I were able. No.
You make me shudder.
Oedipus: God. God.
    Is there a sorrow greater?   85
    Where shall I find harbor in this world?
    My voice is hurled far on a dark wind.
    What has God done to me?
Choragos: Too terrible to think of, or to see.

Oedipus: O cloud of night,   *Strophe 1*   90
    Never to be turned away: night coming on,
    I cannot tell how: night like a shroud!
    My fair winds brought me here.
                                    Oh God. Again
    The pain of the spikes where I had sight,
    The flooding pain   95
    Of memory, never to be gouged out.
Choragos: This is not strange.
    You suffer it all twice over, remorse in pain,
    Pain in remorse.

Oedipus: Ah dear friend   *Antistrophe 1*   100
    Are you faithful even yet, you alone?
    Are you still standing near me, will you stay here,
    Patient, to care for the blind?
                                    The blind man!
    Yet even blind I know who it is attends me,

---

⁷⁶**daemon** a spirit, not necessarily evil

105   By the voice's tone—
        Though my new darkness hide the comforter.
    Choragos: Oh fearful act!
        What god was it drove you to rake black
        Night across your eyes?

110   *Oedipus:* Apollo. Apollo. Dear   *Strophe 2*
        Children, the god was Apollo.
        He brought my sick, sick fate upon me.
        But the blinding hand was my own!
        How could I bear to see
115   When all my sight was horror everywhere?
    Choragos: Everywhere; that is true.
    Oedipus: And now what is left?
        Images? Love? A greeting even,
        Sweet to the senses? Is there anything?
120   Ah, no, friends: lead me away.
        Lead me away from Thebes.
                      Lead the great wreck
    And hell of Oedipus, whom the gods hate.
    Choragos: Your fate is clear, you are not blind to that.
        Would God you had never found it out!

125   *Oedipus:* Death take the man who unbound   *Antistrophe 2*
        My feet on that hillside
        And delivered me from death to life! What life?
        If only I had died,
        This weight of monstrous doom
130   Could not have dragged me and my darlings down.
    Choragos: I would have wished the same.
    Oedipus: Oh never to have come here
        With my father's blood upon me! Never
        To have been the man they call his mother's husband!
135   Oh accurst! O child of evil,
        To have entered that wretched bed—
                      the selfsame one!
    More primal than sin itself, this fell to me.
    Choragos: I do not know how I can answer you.
        You were better dead than alive and blind.
140   *Oedipus:* Do not counsel me any more. This punishment
        That I have laid upon myself is just.
        If I had eyes,
        I do not know how I could bear the sight
        Of my father, when I came to the house of Death,
145   Or my mother: for I have sinned against them both
        So vilely that I could not make my peace
        By strangling my own life.
                Or do you think my children,

Born as they were born, would be sweet to my eyes?
Ah never, never! Nor this town with its high walls,
Nor the holy images of the gods.
     For I,   150
Thrice miserable—Oedipus, noblest of all the line
Of Kadmos, have condemned myself to enjoy
These things no more, by my own malediction
Expelling that man whom the gods declared
To be a defilement in the house of Laïos.   155
After exposing the rankness of my own guilt,
How could I look men frankly in the eyes?
No, I swear it,
If I could have stifled my hearing at its source,
I would have done it and made all this body   160
A tight cell of misery, blank to light and sound:
So I should have been safe in a dark agony
Beyond all recollection.
     Ah Kithairon!
Why did you shelter me? When I was cast upon you,
Why did I not die? Then I should never   165
Have shown the world my execrable birth.

Ah Polybos! Corinth, city that I believed
The ancient seat of my ancestors: how fair
I seemed, your child! And all the while this evil
Was cancerous within me!
     For I am sick   170
In my daily life, sick in my origin.

O three roads, dark ravine, woodland and way
Where three roads met: you, drinking my father's blood,
My own blood, spilled by my own hand: can you remember
The unspeakable things I did there, and the things   175
I went on from there to do?
     O marriage, marriage!
The act that engendered me, and again the act
Performed by the son in the same bed—
       Ah, the net
Of incest, mingling fathers, brothers, sons,
With brides, wives, mothers: the last evil   180
That can be known by men: no tongue can say
How evil!
   No. For the love of God, conceal me
Somewhere far from Thebes; or kill me; or hurl me
Into the sea, away from men's eyes for ever.
Come, lead me. You need not fear to touch me.   185
Of all men, I alone can bear this guilt.
Enter Creon.

Choragos: We are not the ones to decide; but Creon here
   May fitly judge of what you ask. He only
   Is left to protect the city in your place.
190 *Oedipus:* Alas, how can I speak to him? What right have I
   To beg his courtesy whom I have deeply wronged?
Creon: I have not come to mock you, Oedipus,
   Or to reproach you, either.
      [To Attendants.]   —You, standing there:
   If you have lost all respect for man's dignity,
195   At least respect the flame of Lord Helios:
   Do not allow this pollution to show itself
   Openly here, an affront to the earth
   And Heaven's rain and the light of day. No, take him
   Into the house as quickly as you can.
200   For it is proper
   That only the close kindred see his grief.
Oedipus: I pray you in God's name, since your courtesy
   Ignores my dark expectation, visiting
   With mercy this man of all men most execrable:
205   Give me what I ask—for your good, not for mine.
Creon: And what is it that you would have me do?
Oedipus: Drive me out of this country as quickly as may be
   To a place where no human voice can ever greet me.
Creon: I should have done that before now—only,
210   God's will had not been wholly revealed to me.
Oedipus: But his command is plain: the parricide
   Must be destroyed. I am that evil man.
Creon: That is the sense of it, yes; but as things are,
   We had best discover clearly what is to be done.
215 *Oedipus:* You would learn more about a man like me?
Creon: You are ready now to listen to the god.
Oedipus: I will listen. But it is to you
   That I must turn for help. I beg you, hear me.

   The woman in there—
220   Give her whatever funeral you think proper:
   She is your sister.
         —But let me go, Creon!
   Let me purge my father's Thebes of the pollution
   Of my living here, and go out to the wild hills,
   To Kithairon, that has won such fame with me,
225   The tomb my mother and father appointed for me,
   And let me die there, as they willed I should.
   And yet I know
   Death will not ever come to me through sickness
   Or in any natural way: I have been preserved
230   For some unthinkable fate. But let that be.

As for my sons, you need not care for them.
They are men, they will find some way to live.
But my poor daughters, who have shared my table,
Who never before have been parted from their father—
Take care of them, Creon; do this for me.   235
And will you let me touch them with my hands
A last time, and let us weep together?
Be kind, my lord,
Great prince, be kind!
                    Could I but touch them,
They would be mine again, as when I had my eyes.   240
Enter Antigonê *and* Ismenê, *attended.*
Ah, God!
Is it my dearest children I hear weeping?
Has Creon pitied me and sent my daughters?
Creon: Yes, Oedipus: I knew that they were dear to you
In the old days, and know you must love them still.   245
Oedipus: May God bless you for this—and be a friendlier
Guardian to you than he has been to me!

Children, where are you?
Come quickly to my hands: they are your brother's—
Hands that have brought your father's once clear eyes   250
To this way of seeing—
                    Ah dearest ones,
I had neither sight nor knowledge then, your father
By the woman who was the source of his life!
And I weep for you—having no strength to see you—,
I weep for you when I think of the bitterness   255
That men will visit upon you all your lives.
What homes, what festivals can you attend
Without being forced to depart again in tears?
And when you come to marriageable age,
Where is the man, my daughters, who would dare   260
Risk the bane that lies on all my children?
Is there any evil wanting? Your father killed
His father; sowed the womb of her who bore him;
Engendered you at the fount of his own existence!
That is what they will say of you.
                    Then, whom   265
Can you ever marry? There are no bridegrooms for you,
And your lives must wither away in sterile dreaming.
O Creon, son of Menoikeus!
You are the only father my daughters have,
Since we, their parents, are both of us gone forever.   270
They are your own blood: you will not let them
Fall into beggary and loneliness;

You will keep them from the miseries that are mine!
Take pity on them; see, they are only children,
275 Friendless except for you. Promise me this,
Great Prince, and give me your hand in token of it.
Creon clasps his right hand.
Children:
I could say much, if you could understand me,
But as it is, I have only this prayer for you:
280 Live where you can, be as happy as you can—
Happier, please God, than God has made your father!
Creon: Enough. You have wept enough. Now go within.
Oedipus: I must; but it is hard.
Creon: Time eases all things.
Oedipus: But you must promise—
Creon: Say what you desire.
Oedipus: Send me from Thebes!
285 *Creon:*   God grant that I may!
Oedipus: But since God hates me . . .
Creon: No, he will grant your wish.
Oedipus: You promise?
Creon: I cannot speak beyond my knowledge.
Oedipus: Then lead me in.
Creon.   Come now, and leave your children.
Oedipus: No! Do not take them from me!
Creon: Think no longer
290 That you are in command here, but rather think
How, when you were, you served your own destruction.
Exeunt into the house all but the Chorus; *the* Choragos *chants directly
to the audience.*

Choragos: Men of Thebes: look upon Oedipus.
This is the king who solved the famous riddle
And towered up, most powerful of men.
295 No mortal eyes but looked on him with envy,

Yet in the end ruin swept over him.
Let every man in mankind's frailty
Consider his last day; and let none
Presume on his good fortune until he find
Life, at his death, a memory without pain.

[c. 430 BCE]

1. What troubles the citizens of Thebes at the beginning of the play? What is
Oedipus' role in the community, and how does he plan to solve the city's
problem?
2. Who are Creon and Teiresias? Of what does Oedipus accuse them? How
does Creon defend himself against Oedipus' accusations?

3. The play is about the search for the answer to a mystery and even has elements of courtroom drama. Chart the way tension builds in the course of the plot. What is the crisis point? When do the different characters know the truth?
4. How does Oedipus react to the fateful revelations about his heritage and its effect on his present situation? How does he justify the action he takes?
5. What role does the Chorus play in the drama?
6. What disciplines might provide insight into the events of this play?
7. To what other works in this section can you connect this play?

NONFICTION PROSE

BARBARA EHRENREICH

BARBARA EHRENREICH *(1941–), a social activist and feminist, writes on health care, class, families, and sex.* The American Health Empire: Power, Profits and Politics *(1970),* For Her Own Good: One Hundred Fifty Years of the Experts' Advice to Women *(1978), and* The Hearts of Men: American Dreams and the Flight from Commitment *(1983) are some of her controversial books. A biologist with a Ph.D. from Rockefeller University, she became involved in political activism during the Vitenam War and has written professionally ever since. Her first novel was* Kipper's Game *(1993). She has written for* The Nation, The Progressive, The Atlantic Monthly, The New York Times, *and dozens of other publications.* "Nickel-and-Dimed" *surveys some of the conclusions of her book of the same name for* Harper's *Magazine.*

*Nickel-and-Dimed: On (not) getting by in America**

At the beginning of June 1998 I leave behind everything that normally soothes the ego and sustains the body—home, career, companion, reputation, ATM card—for a plunge into the low-wage workforce. There, I become another, occupationally much diminished "Barbara Ehrenreich"—depicted on job-application forms as a divorced homemaker whose sole work experience consists of housekeeping in a few private homes. I am terrified, at the beginning, of being unmasked for what I am: a middle-class journalist setting out to explore the world that welfare mothers are entering, at the rate of approximately 50,000 a month, as welfare reform kicks in. Happily, though, my fears turn out to be entirely unwarranted: during a month of poverty and toil, my name goes unnoticed and for the most part unuttered. In this parallel universe where my father never got out of the mines and I never got through college, I am "baby," "honey," "blondie," and, most commonly, "girl."

---

*Barbara Ehrenreich, "Nickel-and-Dimed: On (not) getting by in America," *Harper's Magazine,* January 1999 (37–52).

My first task is to find a place to live. I figure that if I can earn $7 an hour—which, from the want ads, seems doable—I can afford to spend $500 on rent, or maybe, with severe economies, $600. In the Key West area, where I live, this pretty much confines me to flophouses and trailer homes—like the one, a pleasing fifteen-minute drive from town, that has no air-conditioning, no screens, no fans, no television, and, by way of diversion, only the challenge of evading the landlord's Doberman pinscher. The big problem with this place, though, is the rent, which at $675 a month is well beyond my reach. All right, Key West is expensive. But so is New York City, or the Bay Area, or Jackson Hole, or Telluride, or Boston, or any other place where tourists and the wealthy compete for living space with the people who clean their toilets and fry their hash browns.[1] Still, it is a shock to realize that "trailer trash" has become, for me, a demographic category to aspire to.

So I decide to make the common trade-off between affordability and convenience, and go for a $500-a-month efficiency thirty miles up a two-lane highway from the employment opportunities of Key West, meaning forty-five minutes if there's no road construction and I don't get caught behind some sun-dazed Canadian tourists. I hate the drive, along a roadside studded with white crosses commemorating the more effective head-on collisions, but it's a sweet little place—a cabin, more or less, set in the swampy back yard of the converted mobile home where my landlord, an affable TV repairman, lives with his bartender girlfriend. Anthropologically speaking, a bustling trailer park would be preferable, but here I have a gleaming white floor and a firm mattress, and the few resident bugs are easily vanquished.

Besides, I am not doing this for the anthropology. My aim is nothing so mistily subjective as to "experience poverty" or find out how it "really feels" to be a long-term low-wage worker. I've had enough unchosen encounters with poverty and the world of low-wage work to know it's not a place you want to visit for touristic purposes; it just smells too much like fear. And with all my real-life assets—bank account, IRA, health insurance, multiroom home—waiting indulgently in the background, I am, of course, thoroughly insulated from the terrors that afflict the genuinely poor.

5   No, this is a purely objective, scientific sort of mission. The humanitarian rationale for welfare reform—as opposed to the more punitive and stingy impulses that may actually have motivated it—is that work will lift poor women out of poverty while simultaneously inflating their self-esteem and hence their future value in the labor market. Thus, whatever the hassles involved in finding child care, transportation, etc., the transition from welfare to work will end happily, in greater prosperity for all. Now there are many problems with this comforting prediction, such as the fact that the economy will inevitably undergo a downturn, eliminating many jobs. Even without a downturn, the influx of a million former welfare recipients into the

[1]According to the Department of Housing and Urban Development, the "fair-market rent" for an efficiency is $551 here in Monroe County, Florida. A comparable rent in the five boroughs of New York City is $704; in San Francisco, $713; and in the heart of Silicon Valley, $808. The fair-market rent for an area is defined as the amount that would be needed to pay rent plus utilities for "privately owned, decent, safe, and sanitary rental housing of a modest (non-luxury) nature with suitable amenities."

low-wage labor market could depress wages by as much as 11.9 percent, according to the Economic Policy Institute (EPI) in Washington, D.C.

But is it really possible to make a living on the kinds of jobs currently available to unskilled people? Mathematically, the answer is no, as can be shown by taking $6 to $7 an hour, perhaps subtracting a dollar or two an hour for child care, multiplying by 160 hours a month, and comparing the result to the prevailing rents. According to the National Coalition for the Homeless, for example, in 1998 it took, on average nationwide, an hourly wage of $8.89 to afford a one-bedroom apartment, and the Preamble Center for Public Policy estimates that the odds against a typical welfare recipient's landing a job at such a "living wage" are about 97 to 1. If these numbers are right, low-wage work is not a solution to poverty and possibly not even to homelessness.

It may seem excessive to put this proposition to an experimental test. As certain family members keep unhelpfully reminding me, the viability of low-wage work could be tested, after a fashion, without ever leaving my study. I could just pay myself $7 an hour for eight hours a day, charge myself for room and board, and total up the numbers after a month. Why leave the people and work that I love? But I am an experimental scientist by training. In that business, you don't just sit at a desk and theorize; you plunge into the everyday chaos of nature, where surprises lurk in the most mundane measurements. Maybe, when I got into it, I would discover some hidden economies in the world of the low-wage worker. After all, if 30 percent of the workforce toils for less than $8 an hour, according to the EPI, they may have found some tricks as yet unknown to me. Maybe—who knows?—I would even be able to detect in myself the bracing psychological effects of getting out of the house, as promised by the welfare wonks at places like the Heritage Foundation. Or, on the other hand, maybe there would be unexpected costs—physical, mental, or financial— to throw off all my calculations. Ideally, I should do this with two small children in tow, that being the welfare average, but mine are grown and no one is willing to lend me theirs for a month-long vacation in penury. So this is not the perfect experiment, just a test of the best possible case: an unencumbered woman, smart and even strong, attempting to live more or less off the land.

On the morning of my first full day of job searching, I take a red pen to the want ads, which are auspiciously numerous. Everyone in Key West's booming "hospitality industry" seems to be looking for someone like me—trainable, flexible, and with suitably humble expectations as to pay. I know I possess certain traits that might be advantageous—I'm white and, I like to think, well-spoken and poised—but I decide on two rules: One, I cannot use any skills derived from my education or usual work—not that there are a lot of want ads for satirical essayists anyway. Two, I have to take the best-paid job that is offered me and of course do my best to hold it; no Marxist rants or sneaking off to read novels in the ladies' room. In addition, I rule out various occupations for one reason or another: Hotel front-desk clerk, for example, which to my surprise is regarded as unskilled and pays around $7 an hour, gets eliminated because it involves standing in one spot for eight hours a day. Waitressing is similarly something I'd like to avoid, because I remember it leaving me bone tired when I was eighteen, and I'm decades of varicosities and back pain beyond that now. Telemarketing, one of the first refuges of the suddenly indigent, can be dismissed on grounds of personality. This leaves certain supermarket jobs, such as deli clerk, or housekeeping in Key West's thousands of hotel and guest rooms. Housekeeping is especially appealing, for reasons both atavistic and practical: it's what my mother did before I came along, and it can't be too different from what I've been doing part-time, in my own home, all my life.

So I put on what I take to be a respectful-looking outfit of ironed Bermuda shorts and scooped-neck T-shirt and set out for a tour of the local hotels and supermarkets. Best Western, Econo Lodge, and HoJo's all let me fill out application forms, and these are, to my relief, interested in little more than whether I am a legal resident of the United States and have committed any felonies. My next stop is Winn-Dixie, the supermarket, which turns out to have a particularly onerous application process, featuring a fifteen-minute "interview" by computer since, apparently, no human on the premises is deemed capable of representing the corporate point of view. I am conducted to a large room decorated with posters illustrating how to look "professional" (it helps to be white and, if female, permed) and warning of the slick promises that union organizers might try to tempt me with. The interview is multiple choice: Do I have anything, such as child-care problems, that might make it hard for me to get to work on time? Do I think safety on the job is the responsibility of management? Then, popping up cunningly out of the blue: How many dollars' worth of stolen goods have I purchased in the last year? Would I turn in a fellow employee if I caught him stealing? Finally, "Are you an honest person?"

10   Apparently, I ace the interview, because I am told that all I have to do is show up in some doctor's office tomorrow for a urine test. This seems to be a fairly general rule: if you want to stack Cheerio boxes or vacuum hotel rooms in chemically fascist America, you have to be willing to squat down and pee in front of some health worker (who has no doubt had to do the same thing herself). The wages Winn-Dixie is offering—$6 and a couple of dimes to start with—are not enough, I decide, to compensate for this indignity.[2]

I lunch at Wendy's, where $4.99 gets you unlimited refills at the Mexican part of the Superbar, a comforting surfeit of refried beans and "cheese sauce." A teenage employee, seeing me studying the want ads, kindly offers me an application form, which I fill out, though here, too, the pay is just $6 and change an hour. Then it's off for a round of the locally owned inns and guesthouses. At "The Palms," let's call it, a bouncy manager actually takes me around to see

[2]According to the *Monthly Labor Review* (November 1996), 28 percent of work sites surveyed in the service industry conduct drug tests (corporate workplaces have much higher rates), and the incidence of testing has risen markedly since the Eighties. The rate of testing is highest in the South (56 percent of work sites polled), with the Midwest in second place (50 percent). The drug most likely to be detected—marijuana, which can be detected in urine for weeks—is also the most innocuous, while heroin and cocaine are generally undetectable three days after use. Prospective employees sometimes try to cheat the tests by consuming excessive amounts of liquids and taking diuretics and even masking substances available through the Internet.

the rooms and meet the existing housekeepers, who, I note with satisfaction, look pretty much like me—faded ex-hippie types in shorts with long hair pulled back in braids. Mostly, though, no one speaks to me or even looks at me except to proffer an application form. At my last stop, a palatial B&B, I wait twenty minutes to meet "Max," only to be told that there are no jobs now but there should be one soon, since "nobody lasts more than a couple weeks." (Because none of the people I talked to knew I was a reporter, I have changed their names to protect their privacy and, in some cases perhaps, their jobs.)

Three days go by like this, and, to my chagrin, no one out of the approximately twenty places I've applied calls me for an interview. I had been vain enough to worry about coming across as too educated for the jobs I sought, but no one even seems interested in finding out how overqualified I am. Only later will I realize that the want ads are not a reliable measure of the actual jobs available at any particular time. They are, as I should have guessed from Max's comment, the employers' insurance policy against the relentless turnover of the low-wage workforce. Most of the big hotels run ads almost continually, just to build a supply of applicants to replace the current workers as they drift away or are fired, so finding a job is just a matter of being at the right place at the right time and flexible enough to take whatever is being offered that day. This finally happens to me at a [sic] one of the big discount hotel chains, where I go, as usual, for housekeeping and am sent, instead, to try out as a waitress at the attached "family restaurant," a dismal spot with a counter and about thirty tables that looks out on a parking garage and features such tempting fare as "Pollish [sic] sausage and BBQ sauce" on 95-degree days. Phillip, the dapper young West Indian who introduces himself as the manager, interviews me with about as much enthusiasm as if he were a clerk processing me for Medicare, the principal questions being what shifts can I work and when can I start. I mutter something about being woefully out of practice as a waitress, but he's already on to the uniform: I'm to show up tomorrow wearing black slacks and black shoes; he'll provide the rust-colored polo shirt with HEARTHSIDE embroidered on it, though I might want to wear my own shirt to get to work, ha ha. At the word "tomorrow," something between fear and indignation rises in my chest. I want to say, "Thank you for your time, sir, but this is just an experiment, you know, not my actual life."

So begins my career at the Hearthside, I shall call it, one small profit center within a global discount hotel chain, where for two weeks I work from 2:00 till 10:00 P.M. for $2.43 an hour plus tips.[3] In some futile bid for gentility, the management has barred employees from using the front door, so my first day I enter through the kitchen, where a red-faced man with shoulder-length blond hair is throwing frozen steaks against the wall and yelling, "Fuck this shit!" "That's just

---

[3]According to the Fair Labor Standards Act, employers are not required to pay "tipped employees," such as restaurant servers, more than $2.13 an hour in direct wages. However, if the sum of tips plus $2.13 an hour falls below the minimum wage, or $5.15 an hour, the employer is required to make up the difference. This fact was not mentioned by managers or otherwise publicized at either of the restaurants where I worked.

Jack," explains Gail, the wiry middle-aged waitress who is assigned to train me. "He's on the rag again"—a condition occasioned, in this instance, by the fact that the cook on the morning shift had forgotten to thaw out the steaks. For the next eight hours, I run after the agile Gail, absorbing bits of instruction along with fragments of personal tragedy. All food must be trayed, and the reason she's so tired today is that she woke up in a cold sweat thinking of her boyfriend, who killed himself recently in an upstate prison. No refills on lemonade. And the reason he was in prison is that a few DUIs caught up with him, that's all, could have happened to anyone. Carry the creamers to the table in a monkey bowl, never in your hand. And after he was gone she spent several months living in her truck, peeing in a plastic pee bottle and reading by candlelight at night, but you can't live in a truck in the summer, since you need to have the windows down, which means anything can get in, from mosquitoes on up.

At least Gail puts to rest any fears I had of appearing overqualified. From the first day on, I find that of all the things I have left behind, such as home and identity, what I miss the most is competence. Not that I have ever felt utterly competent in the writing business, in which one day's success augurs nothing at all for the next. But in my writing life, I at least have some notion of procedure: do the research, make the outline, rough out a draft, etc. As a server, though, I am beset by requests like bees: more iced tea here, ketchup over there, a to-go box for table fourteen, and where are the high chairs, anyway? Of the twenty-seven tables, up to six are usually mine at any time, though on slow afternoons or if Gail is off, I sometimes have the whole place to myself. There is the touch-screen computer-ordering system to master, which is, I suppose, meant to mini-mize server-cook contact, but in practice requires constant verbal fine-tuning: "That's gravy on the mashed, okay? None on the meatloaf," and so forth—while the cook scowls as if I were inventing these refinements just to torment him. Plus, something I had forgotten in the years since I was eighteen: about a third of a server's job is "side work" that's invisible to customers—sweeping, scrub-bing, slicing, refilling, and restocking. If it isn't all done, every little bit of it, you're going to face the 6:00 P.M. dinner rush defenseless and probably go down in flames. I screw up dozens of times at the beginning, sustained in my shame entirely by Gail's support—"It's okay, baby, everyone does that sometime"— because, to my total surprise and despite the scientific detachment I am doing my best to maintain, I care.

15   The whole thing would be a lot easier if I could just skate through it as Lily Tomlin in one of her waitress skits, but I was raised by the absurd Booker T. Washingtonian precept that says: If you're going to do something, do it well. In fact, "well" isn't good enough by half. Do it better than anyone has ever done it before. Or so said my father, who must have known what he was talking about because he managed to pull himself, and us with him, up from the mile-deep copper mines of Butte to the leafy suburbs of the Northeast, ascending from boilermakers to martinis before booze beat out ambition. As in most endeavors I have encountered in my life, doing it "better than anyone" is not a reasonable goal. Still, when I wake up at 4:00 A.M. in my own cold sweat, I am not thinking about the writing deadlines I'm neglecting; I'm thinking about the table whose

order I screwed up so that one of the boys didn't get his kiddie meal until the rest of the family had moved on to their Key Lime pies. That's the other power-ful motivation I hadn't expected—the customers, or "patients," as I can't help thinking of them on account of the mysterious vulnerability that seems to have left them temporarily unable to feed themselves. After a few days at the Hearth-side, I feel the service ethic kick in like a shot of oxytocin, the nurturance hormone. The plurality of my customers are hard-working locals—truck drivers, construction workers, even housekeepers from the attached hotel—and I want them to have the closest to a "fine dining" experience that the grubby circum-stances will allow. No "you guys" for me; everyone over twelve is "sir" or "ma'am." I ply them with iced tea and coffee refills; I return, mid-meal, to inquire how everything is; I doll up their salads with chopped raw mushrooms, summer squash slices, or whatever bits of produce I can find that have survived their sojourn in the cold-storage room mold-free.

There is Benny, for example, a short, tight-muscled sewer repairman, who cannot even think of eating until he has absorbed a half hour of air-conditioning and ice water. We chat about hyperthermia and electrolytes until he is ready to order some finicky combination like soup of the day, garden salad, and a side of grits. There are the German tourists who are so touched by my pidgin "Willkom-men" and "Ist alles gut?" that they actually tip. (Europeans, spoiled by their trade-union-ridden, high-wage welfare states, generally do not know that they are supposed to tip. Some restaurants, the Hearthside included, allow servers to "grat" their foreign customers, or add a tip to the bill. Since this amount is added before the customers have a chance to tip or not tip, the practice amounts to an automatic penalty for imperfect English.) There are the two dirt-smudged les-bians, just off their construction shift, who are impressed enough by my suave handling of the fly in the piña colada that they take the time to praise me to Stu, the assistant manager. There's Sam, the kindly retired cop, who has to plug up his tracheotomy hole with one finger in order to force the cigarette smoke into his lungs.

Sometimes I play with the fantasy that I am a princess who, in penance for some tiny transgression, has undertaken to feed each of her subjects by hand. But the non-princesses working with me are just as indulgent, even when this means flouting management rules—concerning, for example, the number of croutons that can go on a salad (six). "Put on all you want," Gail whispers, "as long as Stu isn't looking." She dips into her own tip money to buy biscuits and gravy for an out-of-work mechanic who's used up all his money on dental surgery, inspiring me to pick up the tab for his milk and pie. Maybe the same high levels of agape can be found throughout the "hospitality industry." I remember the poster deco-rating one of the apartments I looked at, which said "If you seek happiness for yourself you will never find it. Only when you seek happiness for others will it come to you," or words to that effect—an odd sentiment, it seemed to me at the time, to find in the dank one-room basement apartment of a bellhop at the Best Western. At the Hearthside, we utilize whatever bits of autonomy we have to ply our customers with the illicit calories that signal our love. It is our job as servers to assemble the salads and desserts, pouring the dressings and squirting the whipped cream. We also control the number of butter patties our customers get and the amount of sour cream on their baked potatoes. So if you wonder why Americans are so obese, consider the fact that waitresses both express their humanity and earn their tips through the covert distribution of fats.

Ten days into it, this is beginning to look like a livable lifestyle. I like Gail, who is "looking at fifty" but moves so fast she can alight in one place and then another without apparently being anywhere between them. I clown around with Lionel, the teenage Haitian busboy, and catch a few fragments of conversation with Joan, the svelte fortyish hostess and militant feminist who is the only one of us who dares to tell Jack to shut the fuck up. I even warm up to Jack when, on a slow night and to make up for a particularly unwarranted attack on my abilities, or so I imagine, he tells me about his glory days as a young man at "coronary school"—or do you say "culinary"?—in Brooklyn, where he dated a knock-out Puerto Rican chick and learned everything there is to know about food. I finish up at 10:00 or 10:30, depending on how much side work I've been able to get done during the shift, and cruise home to the tapes I snatched up at random when I left my real home—Marianne Faithfull, Tracy Chapman, Enigma, King Sunny Ade, the Violent Femmes—just drained enough for the music to set my cranium resonating but hardly dead. Midnight snack is Wheat Thins and Monterey Jack, accompanied by cheap white wine on ice and whatever AMC has to offer. To bed by 1:30 or 2:00, up at 9:00 or 10:00, read for an hour while my uniform whirls around in the landlord's washing machine, and then it's another eight hours spent following Mao's central instruction, as laid out in the Little Red Book, which was: Serve the people.

I could drift along like this, in some dreamy proletarian idyll, except for two things. One is management. If I have kept this subject on the margins thus far it is because I still flinch to think that I spent all those weeks under the surveillance of men (and later women) whose job it was to monitor my behavior for signs of sloth, theft, drug abuse, or worse. Not that managers and especially "assistant managers" in low-wage settings like this are exactly the class enemy. In the restaurant business, they are mostly former cooks or servers, still capable of pinch-hitting in the kitchen or on the floor, just as in hotels they are likely to be former clerks, and paid a salary of only about $400 a week. But everyone knows they have crossed over to the other side, which is, crudely put, corporate as opposed to human. Cooks want to prepare tasty meals; servers want to serve them graciously; but managers are there for only one reason—to make sure that money is made for some theoretical entity that exists far away in Chicago or New York, if a corporation can be said to have a physical existence at all. Reflecting on her career, Gail tells me ruefully that she had sworn, years ago, never to work for a corporation again. "They don't cut you no slack. You give and you give, and they take."

20   Managers can sit—for hours at a time if they want—but it's their job to see that no one else ever does, even when there's nothing to do, and this is why, for servers, slow times can be as exhausting as rushes. You start dragging out each little chore, because if the manager on duty catches you in an idle moment, he will give you something far nastier to do. So I wipe, I clean, I consolidate

ketchup bottles and recheck the cheesecake supply, even tour the tables to make sure the customer evaluation forms are all standing perkily in their places—wondering all the time how many calories I burn in these strictly theatrical exercises. When, on a particularly dead afternoon, Stu finds me glancing at a *USA Today* a customer has left behind, he assigns me to vacuum the entire floor with the broken vacuum cleaner that has a handle only two feet long, and the only way to do that without incurring orthopedic damage is to proceed from spot to spot on your knees.

On my first Friday at the Hearthside there is a "mandatory meeting for all restaurant employees," which I attend, eager for insight into our overall marketing strategy and the niche (your basic Ohio cuisine with a tropical twist?) we aim to inhabit. But there is no "we" at this meeting. Phillip, our top manager except for an occasional "consultant" sent out by corporate headquarters, opens it with a sneer: "The break room—it's disgusting. Butts in the ashtrays, newspapers lying around, crumbs." This windowless little room, which also houses the time clock for the entire hotel, is where we stash our bags and civilian clothes and take our half-hour meal breaks. But a break room is not a right, he tells us. It can be taken away. We should also know that the lockers in the break room and whatever is in them can be searched at any time. Then comes gossip; there has been gossip; gossip (which seems to mean employees talking among themselves) must stop. Off-duty employees are henceforth barred from eating at the restaurant, because "other servers gather around them and gossip." When Phillip has exhausted his agenda of rebukes, Joan complains about the condition of the ladies' room and I throw in my two bits about the vacuum cleaner. But I don't see any backup coming from my fellow servers, each of whom has subsided into her own personal funk; Gail, my role model, stares sorrowfully at a point six inches from her nose. The meeting ends when Andy, one of the cooks, gets up, muttering about breaking up his day off for this almighty bullshit.

Just four days later we are suddenly summoned into the kitchen at 3:30 P.M., even though there are live tables on the floor. We all—about ten of us—stand around Phillip, who announces grimly that there has been a report of some "drug activity" on the night shift and that, as a result, we are now to be a "drug-free" workplace, meaning that all new hires will be tested, as will possibly current employees on a random basis. I am glad that this part of the kitchen is so dark, because I find myself blushing as hard as if I had been caught toking up in the ladies' room myself: I haven't been treated this way—lined up in the corridor, threatened with locker searches, peppered with carelessly aimed accusations—since junior high school. Back on the floor, Joan cracks, "Next they'll be telling us we can't have sex on the job." When I ask Stu what happened to inspire the crackdown, he just mutters about "management decisions" and takes the opportunity to upbraid Gail and me for being too generous with the rolls. From now on there's to be only one per customer, and it goes out with the dinner, not with the salad. He's also been riding the cooks, prompting Andy to come out of the kitchen and observe—with the serenity of a man whose customary implement is a butcher knife—that "Stu has a death wish today."

Later in the evening, the gossip crystallizes around the theory that Stu is himself the drug culprit, that he uses the restaurant phone to order up marijuana and sends one of the late servers out to fetch it for him. The server was caught, and she may have ratted Stu out or at least said enough to cast some suspicion on him, thus accounting for his pissy behavior. Who knows? Lionel, the busboy, entertains us for the rest of the shift by standing just behind Stu's back and sucking deliriously on an imaginary joint.

The other problem, in addition to the less-than-nurturing management style, is that this job shows no sign of being financially viable. You might imagine, from a comfortable distance, that people who live, year in and year out, on $6 to $10 an hour have discovered some survival stratagems unknown to the middle class. But no. It's not hard to get my co-workers to talk about their living situations, because housing, in almost every case, is the principal source of disruption in their lives, the first thing they fill you in on when they arrive for their shifts. After a week, I have compiled the following survey:

- Gail is sharing a room in a well-known downtown flophouse for which she and a roommate pay about $250 a week. Her roommate, a male friend, has begun hitting on her, driving her nuts, but the rent would be impossible alone.
- Claude, the Haitian cook, is desperate to get out of the two-room apartment he shares with his girlfriend and two other, unrelated, people. As far as I can determine, the other Haitian men (most of whom only speak Creole) live in similarly crowded situations.
- Annette, a twenty-year-old server who is six months pregnant and has been abandoned by her boyfriend, lives with her mother, a postal clerk.
- Marianne and her boyfriend are paying $170 a week for a one-person trailer.
- Jack, who is, at $10 an hour, the wealthiest of us, lives in the trailer he owns, paying only the $400-a-month lot fee.
- The other white cook, Andy, lives on his dry-docked boat, which, as far as I can tell from his loving descriptions, can't be more than twenty feet long. He offers to take me out on it, once it's repaired, but the offer comes with inquiries as to my marital status, so I do not follow up on it.
- Tina and her husband are paying $60 a night for a double room in a Days Inn. This is because they have no car and the Days Inn is within walking distance of the Hearthside. When Marianne, one of the breakfast servers, is tossed out of her trailer for subletting (which is against the trailer-park rules), she leaves her boyfriend and moves in with Tina and her husband.
- Joan, who had fooled me with her numerous and tasteful outfits (hostesses wear their own clothes), lives in a van she parks behind a shopping center at night and showers in Tina's motel room. The clothes are from thrift shops.[4]

---

[4] I could find no statistics on the number of employed people living in cars or vans, but according to the National Coalition for the Homeless's 1997 report "Myths and Facts About Homelessness," nearly one in five homeless people (in twenty-nine cities across the nation) is employed in a full- or part-time job.

It strikes me, in my middle-class solipsism, that there is gross improvidence in   25
some of these arrangements. When Gail and I are wrapping silverware in
napkins—the only task for which we are permitted to sit—she tells me she is
thinking of escaping from her roommate by moving into the Days Inn herself.
I am astounded: How can she even think of paying between $40 and $60 a day?
But if I was afraid of sounding like a social worker, I come out just sounding like
a fool. She squints at me in disbelief, "And where am I supposed to get a
month's rent and a month's deposit for an apartment?" I'd been feeling pretty
smug about my $500 efficiency, but of course it was made possible only by the
$1,300 I had allotted myself for start-up costs when I began my low-wage life:
$1,000 for the first month's rent and deposit, $100 for initial groceries and cash
in my pocket, $200 stuffed away for emergencies. In poverty, as in certain
propositions in physics, starting conditions are everything.

There are no secret economies that nourish the poor; on the contrary, there are
a host of special costs. If you can't put up the two months' rent you need to secure
an apartment, you end up paying through the nose for a room by the week. If you
have only a room, with a hot plate at best, you can't save by cooking up huge
lentil stews that can be frozen for the week ahead. You eat fast food, or the hot
dogs and styrofoam cups of soup that can be microwaved in a convenience store.
If you have no money for health insurance—and the Hearthside's niggardly plan
kicks in only after three months—you go without routine care or prescription
drugs and end up paying the price. Gail, for example, was fine until she ran out of
money for estrogen pills. She is supposed to be on the company plan by now, but
they claim to have lost her application form and need to begin the paperwork all
over again. So she spends $9 per migraine pill to control the headaches she
wouldn't have, she insists, if her estrogen supplements were covered. Similarly,
Marianne's boyfriend lost his job as a roofer because he missed so much time after
getting a cut on his foot for which he couldn't afford the prescribed antibiotic.

My own situation, when I sit down to assess it after two weeks of work,
would not be much better if this were my actual life. The seductive thing about
waitressing is that you don't have to wait for payday to feel a few bills in your
pocket, and my tips usually cover meals and gas, plus something left over to
stuff into the kitchen drawer I use as a bank. But as the tourist business slows in
the summer heat, I sometimes leave work with only $20 in tips (the gross is
higher, but servers share about 15 percent of their tips with the busboys and
bartenders). With wages included, this amounts to about the minimum wage of
$5.15 an hour. Although the sum in the drawer is piling up, at the present rate
of accumulation it will be more than a hundred dollars short of my rent when
the end of the month comes around. Nor can I see any expenses to cut. True, I
haven't gone the lentil-stew route yet, but that's because I don't have a large
cooking pot, pot holders, or a ladle to stir with (which cost about $30 at Kmart,
less at thrift stores), not to mention onions, carrots, and the indispensable bay
leaf. I do make my lunch almost every day—usually some slow-burning, high-
protein combo like frozen chicken patties with melted cheese on top and canned
pinto beans on the side. Dinner is at the Hearthside, which offers its employees a
choice of BLT, fish sandwich, or hamburger for only $2. The burger lasts longest,

especially if it's heaped with gut-puckering jalapeños, but by midnight my stomach is growling again.

So unless I want to start using my car as a residence, I have to find a second, or alternative, job. I call all the hotels where I filled out housekeeping applications weeks ago—the Hyatt, Holiday Inn, Econo Lodge, HoJo's, Best Western, plus a half dozen or so locally run guesthouses. Nothing. Then I start making the rounds again, wasting whole mornings waiting for some assistant manager to show up, even dipping into places so creepy that the front-desk clerk greets you from behind bulletproof glass and sells pints of liquor over the counter. But either someone has exposed my real-life housekeeping habits—which are, shall we say, mellow—or I am at the wrong end of some infallible ethnic equation: most, but by no means all, of the working housekeepers I see on my job searches are African Americans, Spanish-speaking, or immigrants from the Central European post-Communist world, whereas servers are almost invariably white and monolingually English-speaking. When I finally get a positive response, I have been identified once again as server material. Jerry's, which is part of a well-known national family restaurant chain and physically attached here to another budget hotel chain, is ready to use me at once. The prospect is both exciting and terrifying, because, with about the same number of tables and counter seats, Jerry's attracts three or four times the volume of customers as the gloomy old Hearthside.

Picture a fat person's hell, and I don't mean a place with no food. Instead there is everything you might eat if eating had no bodily consequences—cheese fries, chicken-fried steaks, fudge-laden desserts—only here every bite must be paid for, one way or another, in human discomfort. The kitchen is a cavern, a stomach leading to the lower intestine that is the garbage and dishwashing area, from which issue bizarre smells combining the edible and the offal: creamy carrion, pizza barf, and that unique and enigmatic Jerry's scent—citrus fart. The floor is slick with spills, forcing us to walk through the kitchen with tiny steps, like Susan McDougal° in leg irons. Sinks everywhere are clogged with scraps of lettuce, decomposing lemon wedges, waterlogged toast crusts. Put your hand down on any counter and you risk being stuck to it by the film of ancient syrup spills, and this is unfortunate, because hands are utensils here, used for scooping up lettuce onto salad plates, lifting out pie slices, and even moving hash browns from one plate to another. The regulation poster in the single unisex restroom admonishes us to wash our hands thoroughly and even offers instructions for doing so, but there is always some vital substance missing—soap, paper towels, toilet paper—and I never find all three at once. You learn to stuff your pockets with napkins before going in there, and too bad about the customers, who must eat, though they don't realize this, almost literally out of our hands.

30   The break room typifies the whole situation: there is none, because there are no breaks at Jerry's. For six to eight hours in a row, you never sit except to pee. Actually, there are three folding chairs at a table immediately adjacent to

[29]**Susan McDougal** served 18 months in prison in the late 1990s for refusing to answer questions about President and Mrs. Clinton before the Whitewater grand jury.

the bathroom, but hardly anyone ever sits here, in the very rectum of the gastro-architectural system. Rather, the function of the peritoilet area is to house the ashtrays in which servers and dishwashers leave their cigarettes burning at all times, like votive candles, so that they don't have to waste time lighting up again when they dash back for a puff. Almost everyone smokes as if his or her pulmonary well-being depended on it—the multinational mélange of cooks, the Czech dish-washers, the servers, who are all American natives—creating an atmosphere in which oxygen is only an occasional pollutant. My first morning at Jerry's, when the hypoglycemic shakes set in, I complain to one of my fellow servers that I don't understand how she can go so long without food. "Well, I don't understand how you can go so long without a cigarette," she responds in a tone of reproach—because work is what you do for others; smoking is what you do for yourself. I don't know why the antismoking crusaders have never grasped the element of defiant self-nurturance that makes the habit so endearing to its victims—as if, in the American workplace, the only thing people have to call their own is the tumors they are nourishing and the spare moments they devote to feeding them.

Now, the Industrial Revolution is not an easy transition, especially when you have to zip through it in just a couple of days. I have gone from craft work straight into the factory, from the air-conditioned morgue of the Hearthside directly into the flames. Customers arrive in human waves, sometimes disgorged fifty at a time from their tour buses, peckish and whiny. Instead of two "girls" on the floor at once, there can be as many as six of us running around in our bril-liant pink-and-orange Hawaiian shirts. Conversations, either with customers or fellow employees, seldom last more than twenty seconds at a time. On my first day, in fact, I am hurt by my sister servers' coldness. My mentor for the day is an emotionally uninflected twenty-three-year-old, and the others, who gossip a little among themselves about the real reason someone is out sick today and the size of the bail bond someone else has had to pay, ignore me completely. On my second day, I find out why. "Well, it's good to see you again," one of them says in greeting. "Hardly anyone comes back after the first day." I feel powerfully vindicated—a survivor—but it would take a long time, probably months, before I could hope to be accepted into this sorority.

I start out with the beautiful, heroic idea of handling the two jobs at once, and for two days I almost do it: the breakfast/lunch shift at Jerry's, which goes till 2:00, arriving at the Hearthside at 2:10, and attempting to hold out until 10:00. In the ten minutes between jobs, I pick up a spicy chicken sandwich at the Wendy's drive-through window, gobble it down in the car, and change from khaki slacks to black, from Hawaiian to rust polo. There is a problem, though. When during the 3:00 to 4:00 P.M. dead time I finally sit down to wrap silver, my flesh seems to bond to the seat. I try to refuel with a purloined cup of soup, as I've seen Gail and Joan do dozens of times, but a manager catches me and hisses "No eating!" though there's not a customer around to be offended by the sight of food making contact with a server's lips. So I tell Gail I'm going to quit, and she hugs me and says she might just follow me to Jerry's herself.

But the chances of this are minuscule. She has left the flophouse and her annoying roommate and is back to living in her beat-up old truck. But guess what? she reports to me excitedly later that evening: Phillip has given her permission to park overnight in the hotel parking lot, as long as she keeps out of sight, and the parking lot should be totally safe, since it's patrolled by a hotel security guard! With the Hearthside offering benefits like that, how could anyone think of leaving?

Gail would have triumphed at Jerry's, I'm sure, but for me it's a crash course in exhaustion management. Years ago, the kindly fry cook who trained me to waitress at a Los Angeles truck stop used to say: Never make an unnecessary trip; if you don't have to walk fast, walk slow; if you don't have to walk, stand. But at Jerry's the effort of distinguishing necessary from unnecessary and urgent from whenever would itself be too much of an energy drain. The only thing to do is to treat each shift as a one-time-only emergency: you've got fifty starving people out there, lying scattered on the battlefield, so get out there and feed them! Forget that you will have to do this again tomorrow, forget that you will have to be alert enough to dodge the drunks on the drive home tonight—just burn, burn, burn! Ideally, at some point you enter what servers call "a rhythm" and psychologists term a "flow state," in which signals pass from the sense organs directly to the muscles, bypassing the cerebral cortex, and a Zen-like emptiness sets in. A male server from the Hearthside's morning shift tells me about the time he "pulled a triple"—three shifts in a row, all the way around the clock—and then got off and had a drink and met this girl, and maybe he shouldn't tell me this, but they had sex right then and there, and it was like, beautiful.

35   But there's another capacity of the neuromuscular system, which is pain. I start tossing back drugstore-brand ibuprofen pills as if they were vitamin C, four before each shift, because an old mouse-related repetitive-stress injury in my upper back has come back to full-spasm strength, thanks to the tray carrying. In my ordinary life, this level of disability might justify a day of ice packs and stretching. Here I comfort myself with the Aleve commercial in which the cute blue-collar guy asks: If you quit after working four hours, what would your boss say? And the not-so-cute blue-collar guy, who's lugging a metal beam on his back, answers: He'd fire me, that's what. But fortunately, the commercial tells us, we workers can exert the same kind of authority over our painkillers that our bosses exert over us. If Tylenol doesn't want to work for more than four hours, you just fire its ass and switch to Aleve.

True, I take occasional breaks from this life, going home now and then to catch up on e-mail and for conjugal visits (though I am careful to "pay" for anything I eat there), seeing *The Truman Show* with friends and letting them buy my ticket. And I still have those what-am-I-doing-here moments at work, when I get so homesick for the printed word that I obsessively reread the six-page menu. But as the days go by, my old life is beginning to look exceedingly strange. The e-mails and phone messages addressed to my former self come from a distant race of people with exotic concerns and far too much time on their hands. The neighborly market I used to cruise for produce now looks forbiddingly like a Manhattan yuppie emporium. And when I sit down one morning in my real home to pay bills from my past life, I am dazzled at the two- and three-figure sums owed to outfits like Club BodyTech and Amazon.com.

Management at Jerry's is generally calmer and more "professional" than at the Hearthside, with two exceptions. One is Joy, a plump, blowsy woman in her early thirties, who once kindly devoted several minutes to instructing me in the correct one-handed method of carrying trays but whose moods change disconcertingly from shift to shift and even within one. Then there's B.J., a.k.a. B.J.-the-bitch, whose contribution is to stand by the kitchen counter and yell, "Nita, your order's up, move it!" or, "Barbara, didn't you see you've got another table out there? Come on, girl!" Among other things, she is hated for having replaced the whipped-cream squirt cans with big plastic whipped-cream-filled baggies that have to be squeezed with both hands—because, reportedly, she saw or thought she saw employees trying to inhale the propellant gas from the squirt cans, in the hope that it might be nitrous oxide. On my third night, she pulls me aside abruptly and brings her face so close that it looks as if she's planning to butt me with her forehead. But instead of saying, "You're fired," she says, "You're doing fine." The only trouble is I'm spending time chatting with customers: "That's how they're getting you." Furthermore I am letting them "run me," which means harassment by sequential demands: you bring the ketchup and they decide they want extra Thousand Island; you bring that and they announce they now need a side of fries; and so on into distraction. Finally she tells me not to take her wrong. She tries to say things in a nice way, but you get into a mode, you know, because everything has to move so fast.[5]

I mumble thanks for the advice, feeling like I've just been stripped naked by the crazed enforcer of some ancient sumptuary law: No chatting for you, girl. No fancy service ethic allowed for the serfs. Chatting with customers is for the beautiful young college-educated servers in the downtown carpaccio joints, the kids who can make $70 to $100 a night. What had I been thinking? My job is to move orders from tables to kitchen and then trays from kitchen to tables. Customers are, in fact, the major obstacle to the smooth transformation of information into food and food into money—they are, in short, the enemy. And the painful thing is that I'm beginning to see it this way myself. There are the traditional asshole types—frat boys who down multiple Buds and then make a fuss because the steaks are so emaciated and the fries so sparse—as well as the variously impaired—due to age, diabetes, or literacy issues—who require patient nutritional counseling. The worst, for some reason, are the Visible Christians— like the ten-person table, all jolly and sanctified after Sunday-night service, who run me mercilessly and then leave me $1 on a $92 bill. Or the guy with the crucifixion T-shirt (SOMEONE TO LOOK UP TO) who complains that his baked potato is too hard and his iced tea too icy (I cheerfully fix both) and leaves no tip. As a general rule, people wearing crosses or WWJD? (What Would Jesus Do?) buttons look at us disapprovingly no matter what we do, as if they were confusing waitressing with Mary Magdalene's original profession.

---

[5]In *Workers in a Lean World: Unions in the International Economy* (Verso, 1997), Kim Moody cites studies finding an increase in stress-related workplace injuries and illness between the mid-1980s and the early 1990s. He argues that rising stress levels reflect a new system of "management by stress," in which workers in a variety of industries are being squeezed to extract maximum productivity, to the detriment of their health.

I make friends, over time, with the other "girls" who work my shift: Nita, the tattooed twenty-something who taunts us by going around saying brightly, "Have we started making money yet?" Ellen, whose teenage son cooks on the graveyard shift and who once managed a restaurant in Massachusetts but won't try out for management here because she prefers being a "common worker" and not "ordering people around." Easy-going fiftyish Lucy, with the raucous laugh, who limps toward the end of the shift because of something that has gone wrong with her leg, the exact nature of which cannot be determined without health insurance. We talk about the usual girl things—men, children, and the sinister allure of Jerry's chocolate peanut-butter cream pie—though no one, I notice, ever brings up anything potentially expensive, like shopping or movies. As at the Hearthside, the only recreation ever referred to is partying, which requires little more than some beer, a joint, and a few close friends. Still, no one here is homeless, or cops to it anyway, thanks usually to a working husband or boyfriend. All in all, we form a reliable mutual-support group: If one of us is feeling sick or overwhelmed, another one will "bev" a table or even carry trays for her. If one of us is off sneaking a cigarette or a pee,[6] the others will do their best to conceal her absence from the enforcers of corporate rationality.

40   But my saving human connection—my oxytocin receptor, as it were—is George, the nineteen-year-old, fresh-off-the-boat Czech dishwasher. We get to talking when he asks me, tortuously, how much cigarettes cost at Jerry's. I do my best to explain that they cost over a dollar more here than at a regular store and suggest that he just take one from the half-filled packs that are always lying around on the break table. But that would be unthinkable. Except for the one tiny earring signaling his allegiance to some vaguely alternative point of view, George is a perfect straight arrow—crew-cut, hardworking, and hungry for eye contact. "Czech Republic," I ask, "or Slovakia?" and he seems delighted that I know the difference. "Václav Havel," I try. "Velvet Revolution, Frank Zappa?" "Yes, yes, 1989," he says, and I realize we are talking about history.

My project is to teach George English. "How are you today, George?" I say at the start of each shift. "I am good, and how are you today, Barbara?" I learn that he is not paid by Jerry's but by the "agent" who shipped him over—$5 an hour, with the agent getting the dollar or so difference between that and what Jerry's

[6]Until April 1998, there was no federally mandated right to bathroom breaks. According to Marc Linder and Ingrid Nygaard, authors of *Void Where Prohibited: Rest Breaks and the Right to Urinate on Company Time* (Cornell University Press, 1997), "The right to rest and void at work is not high on the list of social or political causes supported by professional or executive employees, who enjoy personal workplace liberties that millions of factory workers can only daydream about. . . . While we were dismayed to discover that workers lacked an acknowledged legal right to void at work, [the workers] were amazed by outsiders' naive belief that their employers would permit them to perform this basic bodily function when necessary. . . . A factory worker, not allowed a break for six-hour stretches, voided into pads worn inside her uniform; and a kindergarten teacher in a school without aides had to take all twenty children with her to the bathroom and line them up outside the stall door when she voided."

pays dishwashers. I learn also that he shares an apartment with a crowd of other Czech "dishers," as he calls them, and that he cannot sleep until one of them goes off for his shift, leaving a vacant bed. We are having one of our ESL sessions late one afternoon when B.J. catches us at it and orders "Joseph" to take up the rubber mats on the floor near the dishwashing sinks and mop underneath. "I thought your name was George," I say loud enough for B.J. to hear as she strides off back to the counter. Is she embarrassed? Maybe a little, because she greets me back at the counter with "George, Joseph—there are so many of them!" I say nothing, neither nodding nor smiling, and for this I am punished later when I think I am ready to go and she announces that I need to roll fifty more sets of silverware and isn't it time I mixed up a fresh four-gallon batch of blue-cheese dressing? May you grow old in this place, B.J., is the curse I beam out at her when I am finally permitted to leave. May the syrup spills glue your feet to the floor.

I make the decision to move closer to Key West. First, because of the drive. Second and third, also because of the drive: gas is eating up $4 to $5 a day, and although Jerry's is as high-volume as you can get, the tips average only 10 percent, and not just for a newbie like me. Between the base pay of $2.15 an hour and the obligation to share tips with the busboys and dishwashers, we're averaging only about $7.50 an hour. Then there is the $30 I had to spend on the regulation tan slacks worn by Jerry's servers—a setback it could take weeks to absorb. (I had combed the town's two downscale department stores hoping for something cheaper but decided in the end that these marked-down Dockers, originally $49, were more likely to survive a daily washing.) Of my fellow servers, everyone who lacks a working husband or boyfriend seems to have a second job: Nita does something at a computer eight hours a day; another welds. Without the forty-five-minute commute, I can picture myself working two jobs and having the time to shower between them.

So I take the $500 deposit I have coming from my landlord, the $400 I have earned toward the next month's rent, plus the $200 reserved for emergencies, and use the $1,100 to pay the rent and deposit on trailer number 46 in the Overseas Trailer Park, a mile from the cluster of budget hotels that constitute Key West's version of an industrial park. Number 46 is about eight feet in width and shaped like a barbell inside, with a narrow region—because of the sink and the stove—separating the bedroom from what might optimistically be called the "living" area, with its two-person table and half-sized couch. The bathroom is so small my knees rub against the shower stall when I sit on the toilet, and you can't just leap out of the bed, you have to climb down to the foot of it in order to find a patch of floor space to stand on. Outside, I am within a few yards of a liquor store, a bar that advertises "free beer tomorrow," a convenience store, and a Burger King—but no supermarket or, alas, laundromat. By reputation, the Overseas park is a nest of crime and crack, and I am hoping at least for some vibrant, multicultural street life. But desolation rules night and day, except for a thin stream of pedestrian traffic heading for their jobs at the Sheraton or 7-Eleven. There are not exactly people here but what amounts to canned labor, being preserved from the heat between shifts.

In line with my reduced living conditions, a new form of ugliness arises at Jerry's. First we are confronted—via an announcement on the computers through which we input orders—with the new rule that the hotel bar is henceforth off-limits to restaurant employees. The culprit, I learn through the grapevine, is the ultra-efficient gal who trained me—another trailer-home dweller and a mother of three. Something had set her off one morning, so she slipped out for a nip and returned to the floor impaired. This mostly hurts Ellen, whose habit it is to free her hair from its rubber band and drop by the bar for a couple of Zins before heading home at the end of the shift, but all of us feel the chill. Then the next day, when I go for straws, for the first time I find the dry-storage room locked. Ted, the portly assistant manager who opens it for me, explains that he caught one of the dishwashers attempting to steal something, and, unfortunately, the miscreant will be with us until a replacement can be found—hence the locked door. I neglect to ask what he had been trying to steal, but Ted tells me who he is—the kid with the buzz cut and the earring. You know, he's back there right now.

45   I wish I could say I rushed back and confronted George to get his side of the story. I wish I could say I stood up to Ted and insisted that George be given a translator and allowed to defend himself, or announced that I'd find a lawyer who'd handle the case pro bono. The mystery to me is that there's not much worth stealing in the dry-storage room, at least not in any fenceable quantity: "Is Gyorgi here, and am having 200—maybe 250—ketchup packets. What do you say?" My guess is that he had taken—if he had taken anything at all—some Saltines or a can of cherry-pie mix, and that the motive for taking it was hunger.

So why didn't I intervene? Certainly not because I was held back by the kind of moral paralysis that can pass as journalistic objectivity. On the contrary, something new—something loathsome and servile—had infected me, along with the kitchen odors that I could still sniff on my bra when I finally undressed at night. In real life I am moderately brave, but plenty of brave people shed their courage in concentration camps, and maybe something similar goes on in the infinitely more congenial milieu of the low-wage American workplace. Maybe, in a month or two more at Jerry's, I might have regained my crusading spirit. Then again, in a month or two I might have turned into a different person altogether—say, the kind of person who would have turned George in.

But this is not something I am slated to find out. When my month-long plunge into poverty is almost over, I finally land my dream job—housekeeping. I do this by walking into the personnel office of the only place I figure I might have some credibility, the hotel attached to Jerry's, and confiding urgently that I have to have a second job if I am to pay my rent and, no, it couldn't be front-desk clerk. "All right," the personnel lady fairly spits, "So it's housekeeping," and she marches me back to meet Maria, the housekeeping manager, a tiny, frenetic Hispanic woman who greets me as "babe" and hands me a pamphlet emphasizing the need for a positive attitude. The hours are nine in the morning till whenever, the pay is $6.10 an hour, and there's one week of vacation a year. I don't have to ask about health insurance once I meet Carlotta, the middle-aged African-American woman who will be training me. Carla, as she tells me to call her, is missing all of her top front teeth.

On that first day of housekeeping and last day of my entire project—although I don't yet know it's the last—Carla is in a foul mood. We have been given nineteen rooms to clean, most of them "checkouts," as opposed to "stay-overs," that require the whole enchilada of bed-stripping, vacuuming, and bathroom-scrubbing. When one of the rooms that had been listed as a stay-over turns out to be a checkout, Carla calls Maria to complain, but of course to no avail. "So make up the motherfucker," Carla orders me, and I do the beds while she sloshes around the bathroom. For four hours without a break I strip and remake beds, taking about four and a half minutes per queen-sized bed, which I could get down to three if there were any reason to. We try to avoid vacuuming by picking up the larger specks by hand, but often there is nothing to do but drag the monstrous vacuum cleaner—it weighs about thirty pounds—off our cart and try to wrestle it around the floor. Sometimes Carla hands me the squirt bottle of "BAM" (an acronym for something that begins, ominously, with "butyric"; the rest has been worn off the label) and lets me do the bathrooms. No service ethic challenges me here to new heights of performance. I just concentrate on removing the pubic hairs from the bathtubs, or at least the dark ones that I can see.

I had looked forward to the breaking-and-entering aspect of cleaning the stay-overs, the chance to examine the secret, physical existence of strangers. But the contents of the rooms are always banal and surprisingly neat—zipped up shaving kits, shoes lined up against the wall (there are no closets), flyers for snorkeling trips, maybe an empty wine bottle or two. It is the TV that keeps us going, from *Jerry* to *Sally* to *Hawaii Five-O* and then on to the soaps. If there's something especially arresting, like "Won't Take No for an Answer" on *Jerry,* we sit down on the edge of a bed and giggle for a moment as if this were a pajama party instead of a terminally dead-end job. The soaps are the best, and Carla turns the volume up full blast so that she won't miss anything from the bathroom or while the vacuum is on. In room 503, Marcia confronts Jeff about Lauren. In 505, Lauren taunts poor cuckolded Marcia. In 511, Helen offers Amanda $10,000 to stop seeing Eric, prompting Carla to emerge from the bathroom to study Amanda's troubled face. "You take it, girl," she advises. "I would for sure."

The tourists' rooms that we clean and, beyond them, the far more expensively 50 appointed interiors in the soaps, begin after a while to merge. We have entered a better world—a world of comfort where every day is a day off, waiting to be filled up with sexual intrigue. We, however, are only gate-crashers in this fantasy, forced to pay for our presence with backaches and perpetual thirst. The mirrors, and there are far too many of them in hotel rooms, contain the kind of person you would normally find pushing a shopping cart down a city street—bedraggled, dressed in a damp hotel polo shirt two sizes too large, and with sweat dribbling down her chin like drool. I am enormously relieved when Carla announces a half-hour meal break, but my appetite fades when I see that the bag of hot-dog rolls she has been carrying around on our cart is not trash salvaged from a check-out but what she has brought for her lunch.

When I request permission to leave at about 3:30, another housekeeper warns me that no one has so far succeeded in combining housekeeping at the hotel with serving at Jerry's: "Some kid did it once for five days, and you're no kid." With that helpful information in mind, I rush back to number 46, down four Advils (the name brand this time), shower, stooping to fit into the stall, and attempt to compose myself for the oncoming shift. So much for what Marx termed the "reproduction of labor power," meaning the things a worker has to do just so she'll be ready to work again. The only unforeseen obstacle to the smooth transition from job to job is that my tan Jerry's slacks, which had looked reasonably clean by 40-watt bulb last night when I handwashed my Hawaiian shirt, prove by daylight to be mottled with ketchup and ranch-dressing stains. I spend most of my hour-long break between jobs attempting to remove the edible portions with a sponge and then drying the slacks over the hood of my car in the sun.

I can do this two-job thing, is my theory, if I can drink enough caffeine and avoid getting distracted by George's ever more obvious suffering.[7] The first few days after being caught he seemed not to understand the trouble he was in, and our chirpy little conversations had continued. But the last couple of shifts he's been listless and unshaven, and tonight he looks like the ghost we all know him to be, with dark half-moons hanging from his eyes. At one point, when I am briefly immobilized by the task of filling little paper cups with sour cream for baked potatoes, he comes over and looks as if he'd like to explore the limits of our shared vocabulary, but I am called to the floor for a table. I resolve to give him all my tips that night and to hell with the experiment in low-wage money management. At eight, Ellen and I grab a snack together standing at the mephitic end of the kitchen counter, but I can only manage two or three mozzarella sticks and lunch had been a mere handful of McNuggets. I am not tired at all, I assure myself, though it may be that there is simply no more "I" left to do the tiredness monitoring. What I would see, if I were more alert to the situation, is that the forces of destruction are already massing against me. There is only one cook on duty, a young man named Jesus ("Hay-Sue," that is) and he is new to the job. And there is Joy, who shows up to take over in the middle of the shift, wearing high heels and a long, clingy white dress and fuming as if she'd just been stood up in some cocktail bar.

Then it comes, the perfect storm. Four of my tables fill up at once. Four tables is nothing for me now, but only so long as they are obligingly staggered. As I bev

---

[7]In 1996, the number of persons holding two or more jobs averaged 7.8 million, or 6.2 percent of the workforce. It was about the same rate for men and for women (6.1 versus 6.2), though the kinds of jobs differ by gender. About two thirds of multiple jobholders work one job full-time and the other part-time. Only a heroic minority—4 percent of men and 2 percent of women—work two full-time jobs simultaneously. (From John F. Stinson Jr., "New Data on Multiple Jobholding Available from the CPS," in the *Monthly Labor Review*, March 1997.)

table 27, tables 25, 28, and 24 are watching enviously. As I bev 25, 24 glowers because their bevs haven't even been ordered. Twenty-eight is four yuppyish types, meaning everything on the side and agonizing instructions as to the chicken Caesars. Twenty-five is a middle-aged black couple, who complain, with some justice, that the iced tea isn't fresh and the tabletop is sticky. But table 24 is the meteorological event of the century: ten British tourists who seem to have made the decision to absorb the American experience entirely by mouth. Here everyone has at least two drinks—iced tea and milk shake, Michelob and water (with lemon slice, please)—and a huge promiscuous orgy of breakfast specials, mozz sticks, chicken strips, quesadillas, burgers with cheese and with-out, sides of hash browns with cheddar, with onions, with gravy, seasoned fries, plain fries, banana splits. Poor Jesus! Poor me! Because when I arrive with their first tray of food—after three prior trips just to refill bevs—Princess Di refuses to eat her chicken strips with her pancake-and-sausage special, since, as she now reveals, the strips were meant to be an appetizer. Maybe the others would have accepted their meals, but Di, who is deep into her third Michelob, insists that everything else go back while they work on their "starters." Meanwhile, the yuppies are waving me down for more decaf and the black couple looks ready to summon the NAACP.

Much of what happened next is lost in the fog of war. Jesus starts going under. The little printer on the counter in front of him is spewing out orders faster than he can rip them off, much less produce the meals. Even the invincible Ellen is ashen from stress. I bring table 24 their reheated main courses, which they immediately reject as either too cold or fossilized by the microwave. When I return to the kitchen with their trays (three trays in three trips), Joy confronts me with arms akimbo: "What is this?" She means the food—the plates of rejected pancakes, hash browns in assorted flavors, toasts, burgers, sausages, eggs. "Uh, scrambled with cheddar," I try, "and that's . . ." "NO," she screams in my face. "Is it a traditional, a super-scramble, an eye-opener?" I pretend to study my check for a clue, but entropy has been up to its tricks, not only on the plates but in my head, and I have to admit that the original order is beyond reconstruction. "You don't know an eye-opener from a traditional?" she demands in outrage. All I know, in fact, is that my legs have lost interest in the current venture and have announced their intention to fold. I am saved by a yuppie (mercifully not one of mine) who chooses this moment to charge into the kitchen to bellow that his food is twenty-five minutes late. Joy screams at him to get the hell out of her kitchen, please, and then turns on Jesus in a fury, hurling an empty tray across the room for emphasis.

I leave. I don't walk out, I just leave. I don't finish my side work or pick up my credit-card tips, if any, at the cash register or, of course, ask Joy's permission to go. And the surprising thing is that you *can* walk out without permission, that the door opens, that the thick tropical night air parts to let me pass, that my car is still parked where I left it. There is no vindication in this exit, no fuck-you surge of relief, just an overwhelming, dank sense of failure pressing down on me and the entire parking lot. I had gone into this venture in the spirit of science, to test a mathematical proposition, but somewhere along the line, in the tunnel vision imposed by long shifts and relentless concentration, it became a test of myself, and clearly I have failed. Not only had I flamed out as a housekeeper/server, I had even forgotten to give George my tips, and, for reasons perhaps best known to hardworking, generous people like Gail and Ellen, this hurts. I don't cry, but I am in a position to realize, for the first time in many years, that the tear ducts are still there, and still capable of doing their job.

When I moved out of the trailer park, I gave the key to number 46 to Gail and arranged for my deposit to be transferred to her. She told me that Joan is still living in her van and that Stu had been fired from the Hearthside. I never found out what happened to George.

In one month, I had earned approximately $1,040 and spent $517 on food, gas, toiletries, laundry, phone, and utilities. If I had remained in my $500 efficiency, I would have been able to pay the rent and have $22 left over (which is $78 less than the cash I had in my pocket at the start of the month). During this time I bought no clothing except for the required slacks and no prescription drugs or medical care (I did finally buy some vitamin B to compensate for the lack of vegetables in my diet). Perhaps I could have saved a little on food if I had gotten to a supermarket more often, instead of convenience stores, but it should be noted that I lost almost four pounds in four weeks, on a diet weighted heavily toward burgers and fries.

How former welfare recipients and single mothers will (and do) survive in the low-wage workforce, I cannot imagine. Maybe they will figure out how to condense their lives—including child-raising, laundry, romance, and meals—into the couple of hours between full-time jobs. Maybe they will take up residence in their vehicles, if they have one. All I know is that I couldn't hold two jobs and I couldn't make enough money to live on with one. And I had advantages unthinkable to many of the long-term poor—health, stamina, a working car, and no children to care for and support. Certainly nothing in my experience contradicts the conclusion of Kathryn Edin and Laura Lein, in their recent book *Making Ends Meet: How Single Mothers Survive Welfare and Low-Wage Work*, that low-wage work actually involves more hardship and deprivation than life at the mercy of the welfare state. In the coming months and years, economic conditions for the working poor are bound to worsen, even without the almost inevitable recession. As mentioned earlier, the influx of former welfare recipients into the low-skilled workforce will have a depressing effect on both wages and the number of jobs available. A general economic downturn will only enhance these effects, and the working poor will of course be facing it without the slight, but nonetheless often saving, protection of welfare as a backup.

The thinking behind welfare reform was that even the humblest jobs are morally uplifting and psychologically buoying. In reality they are likely to be fraught with insult and stress. But I did discover one redeeming feature of the most abject low-wage work—the camaraderie of people who are, in almost all cases, far too smart and funny and caring for the work they do and the wages they're paid. The hope, of course, is that someday these people will come to know what they're worth, and take appropriate action. [1999]

1. What is the significance of the date of Ehrenreich's essay?
2. How would you characterize Ehrenreich's *ethos?* What features of her style contribute to it? What do you think she has in mind when she says that her personality would disqualify her for work in telemarketing (paragraph 8)?
3. What is Ehrenreich's main claim and how does she support it? Where does it appear in the essay? What does her month-long experiment contribute to her argument?
4. Does the essay raise ethical questions?

MARTIN L. HOFFMAN

MARTIN L. HOFFMAN *(1924–), who earned his Ph.D. in social psychology at the University of Michigan, is a professor of psychology at New York University. Interested generally in the relationship between thinking and emotions, he focuses on the role of empathy in the development of character, along with accompanying emotions like "sympathy, guilt, empathetic anger, and feelings of injustice." In other research, he studies the interaction between empathetic emotions and abstract moral principles like "justice."* Empathy and Moral Development: Implications for Caring and Justice *has been translated into Chinese, Japanese, Serbian, and Spanish.*

*Empathy, Its Arousal, and Prosocial Functioning**

People are innocent bystanders when they witness someone in pain, danger, or any other form of distress. The distress can involve physical pain or discomfort due to injury or disease, emotional pain over the loss or expected loss of a loved one, fear of being attacked, anxiety over failure or financial impoverishment, and the like. The moral issue in these situations is whether the bystander is motivated to help and if he is, the extent to which the motivation is self-serving or based on true concern for the victim. The bystander model is the prototypic moral encounter for empathic distress and related empathic affects. It is also the context for my theory of empathy development. In this chapter I give my definition of empathy, provide evidence that it functions as a prosocial motive, and then describe the mechanism by which it is aroused. In chapters 3 and 4, I present the theory of empathy development and discuss four empathy-based feelings that also function as prosocial motives: sympathetic distress, empathy-based anger, empathy-based feeling of injustice, and guilt over inaction. In subsequent chapters I deal with other types of moral encounters.

Definition of Empathy

Empathy has been defined by psychologists in two ways: (a) empathy is the cognitive awareness of another person's internal states, that is, his thoughts, feelings, perceptions, and intentions (see Ickes, 1997, for recent research); (b) empathy is the vicarious affective response to another person. This book

*Martin L. Hoffman, "Empathy, Its Arousal, and Prosocial Functioning," *Empathy and Moral Development: Implications for Caring and Justice* (New York: Cambridge University Press, 2000), 29–62 [Chapter 2].

deals with the second type: affective empathy. Affective empathy seems like a simple concept—one feels what the other feels—and many writers define it in simple outcome terms: One empathizes to the extent that one's feeling matches the other's feeling. The more I study empathy, however, the more complex it becomes. Consequently, I have found it far more useful to define empathy not in terms of outcome (affect match) but in terms of the processes underlying the relationship between the observer's and the model's feeling. The key requirement of an empathic response according to my definition is **the involvement of psychological processes that make a person have feelings that are more congruent with another's situation than with his own situation.** The empathy-arousing processes often produce the same feeling in observer and victim but not necessarily, as when one feels empathic anger on seeing someone attacked even when the victim feels sad or disappointed rather than angry.

This is not to deny the importance of accurate cognitive assessment of another's feelings, what Ickes (1997) calls empathic accuracy. Indeed, a certain amount of empathic accuracy is built into my theory, although, unlike Ickes, I see empathic accuracy as including awareness of the model's relevant past and probable future—the model's life condition—an awareness that contributes importantly to an observer's empathic affect. For this and other reasons, dropping the requirement of an affect match between observer and model affords empathy far more scope and has other advantages, as we shall see.

My focus is **empathic distress** because prosocial moral action usually involves helping someone in discomfort, pain, danger, or some other type of distress.

Empathic Distress as a Prosocial Motive

5 Before reviewing the evidence that empathic distress is a prosocial motive, it is necessary to state what kind of evidence is needed. First, empathic distress must correlate positively with people's helping behavior. Second, empathic distress must not only correlate with but must also precede and contribute to the helping behavior. And third, like other motives, empathic distress should diminish in intensity and one should feel better when one helps, but it should continue at a high level when one does not help. The evidence, which I now present, is supportive on all three counts.

   a. *Empathic distress is associated with helping.* There are countless studies showing that when people witness others in distress, they typically respond empathically or with an overt helpful act, whichever is being investigated, and when data are available on both responses, subjects typically show them both. This research was reviewed by Hoffman (1981) and Eisenberg and Miller (1987). To update these reviews, fill in the gaps, and give you a feeling for the research, here are examples. Berndt (1979) found that a group of empathic sixth graders who discussed a sad incident in another person's life donated more time to making pictures for hospitalized children than did empathic children who discussed a sad event in their own lives. Davis (1983) found that college students who obtained high empathy scores on a paper-and-pencil measure donated more money to the Jerry Lewis Muscular Dystrophy Telethon than did their less empathic classmates. Empathic college students were more likely to volunteer and put in more hours of work at shelters for homeless families (Penner, Fritzsche, Craiger, & Freifeld, 1995). In a study by Otten, Penner, and Altabe (1991), psychotherapists who scored high on empathy measures were more likely to help college students with a work assignment (writing an article on psychotherapy) than psychotherapists who scored low.

In an experimental study, college students watched a confederate of the investigator working on an unpleasant task (Carlo, Eisenberg, Troyer, Switzer & Speer, 1991). The confederate became distressed and asked the subject to take his place. One group of subjects was given the alternative of sitting and watching the confederate suffer or taking his place, and another group had the option of leaving the experiment and going home. Three-quarters of the first group chose to take the confederate's place rather than continue to experience empathic distress. Remarkably, over half the subjects in the second group chose to take the confederate's place rather than go home, and those who did this were the more empathic members of the group.

Finally, it has been found that observers are quicker to help when the victim shows more pain (Geer & Jarmecky, 1973; Weiss, Boyer, Lombardo, & Stitch, 1973) and when their own empathic distress is high rather than low (Gaertner & Dovidio, 1977). The details of these three studies can be found in Hoffman (1978).

b. *Empathic distress precedes helping.* The above research shows the required association between empathic arousal and helping behavior. There is also evidence from 1970s' experimental research reviewed by Hoffman (1978) that empathic arousal precedes and motivates helping. The last and most interesting of these experiments was done by Gaertner and Dovidio (1977). In that study, female undergraduate students witnessed (through earphones) a situation in which another student (a confederate of the experimenter) stopped working on an experimental task in order to straighten out a stack of chairs that she thought was about to topple over on her. A moment later the confederate screamed that the chairs were falling on her, and then was silent. The main findings were that the observers' heart rate began to accelerate an average of 20 seconds before they rose from their chair to help the victim; and the greater an observer's heart-rate acceleration the more quickly she rose from her chair. In other words, the intensity of the observer's physiological (empathic) arousal was systematically related to the speed of her *subsequent* helping action.

c. *Observers feel better after helping.* The most direct evidence that empathic distress diminishes in intensity after an observer helps someone can be found in Darley and Latane's (1968) study in which subjects heard sounds indicating that someone was having an epileptic seizure. The subjects who did not respond overtly continued to be aroused and upset, as indicated by their trembling hands and sweaty palms; the subjects who tried to help showed fewer signs of continued upset. A similar finding was obtained in Murphy's (1937) classic nursery school study: When children helped others their empathic distress appeared to diminish; when they did not help their distress was prolonged. These findings suggest that empathic distress acts like other motives: When it is expressed behaviorally its intensity subsides. In the case of empathic distress, there may be an additional factor: The victim's expression of relief may produce a feeling of empathic relief in the helper—a vicarious reward that is unavailable to observers who do not help.

These findings could be interpreted as showing that people learn from experience that helping others makes them feel good, so when they feel empathic distress they anticipate feeling good and help for that reason—not to alleviate the victim's distress. The counterargument is that the consequences of an action say nothing about the motivation behind it; because helping makes one feel good does not mean that one helps in order to feel good. Furthermore, there is no evidence that people help in order to feel good, and there is evidence to the contrary (Batson & Weeks, 1996; Batson & Shaw, 1991). These investigators reasoned that if observers helped only for self-reward, then it wouldn't matter to them whether or not the victim's distress was alleviated; the sheer act of helping would make them feel better. What they found was that empathic helpers continued to feel empathic distress when, despite their efforts and through no fault of their own, the victim's distress was not alleviated. This implies that empathic helpers do have their eye on the ultimate consequences of their action for the victim and it does matter to them whether their actions reduce the victim's distress. It seems reasonable to conclude that although empathy-based helping makes people feel good by reducing empathic distress and providing empathic relief, the main objective of empathy-based helping is to alleviate the victim's distress. Empathic distress is, in short, a prosocial motive.

The discussion so far might suggest that humans are saintly empathic-distress-leads-to-helping machines. Not so: Empathic distress does not always lead to helping. Why doesn't it? There are several reasons. First, as we know from the classic work of Latane and Darley (1970), the presence of other bystanders may interfere with a person's helping by activating the assumptions of "pluralistic ignorance" (no one else is reacting; it must not be an emergency after all) and "diffusion of responsibility" (I'm sure someone else has already called the police).

Second, when bystanders are alone their motive to help may be checked by powerful egoistic motives revolving around fear, energy expenditure, financial cost, loss of time, opportunities missed, and the like. The bystanders may have learned from experience that helping makes one feel good, but the prospect of feeling good may be overridden by helping's potential cost. As a dramatic case in point, consider this quote from a study comparing Germans who rescued and those who did not rescue Jews from the Nazis during the Holocaust:

> My parents were loving and kind. I learned from them to be helpful and considerate. There was a Jewish family living in our apartment building, but I hardly noticed when they left. Later, when I was working in the hospital as a doctor, a Jewish man was brought to the emergency room by his wife. I knew that he would die unless he was treated immediately. But we were not allowed to treat Jews; they could only be treated at the Jewish hospital. I could do nothing.
> (Oliner & Oliner, 1988, p. 187)

These are the words of a *non*-rescuer, described by Oliner and Oliner as "a kind and compassionate woman predisposed by sentiment and the ethics of her profession to help a dangerously ill man who nonetheless did not do so" (p. 187). As we shall see, those Germans who took risks and rescued Jews were kind and compassionate, but this quote shows that when the costs are high, kindness and compassion may not be enough.

Third, in view of the costs that helping may entail, we might expect people not only to refrain from helping but also to be leery of feeling empathy in the first place for fear of what it may lead them to do: It may lead them to incur the cost of helping, including the cost of experiencing the unpleasantness of empathic distress. People might, therefore, when possible try to forestall feeling for victims in order to escape the motivational consequences of that feeling. A motive to avoid empathy has been demonstrated experimentally by Shaw, Batson, and Todd (1994), who predicted the activation of such a motive when, before being exposed to a person in need, observers are warned that they will be asked to help the person and the helping will be costly. To test this prediction, college students were given the choice of hearing one of two appeals for help made by a homeless man who had lost his job and was very ill: an empathy-inducing appeal in which the man presents his needs emotionally and asks the listener to imagine how he feels and what he is going through, and an appeal in which he presents his needs calmly and objectively. As predicted, the subjects who expected to be given a high-cost opportunity to help (spend several hours meeting and giving him support) were less likely to choose the empathy-inducing appeal than subjects who expected the cost of helping to be low (an hour writing and addressing letters on his behalf).

This analysis of the observer's motives points up the complexity of the bystander model. It is not simply that observers feel empathic distress and the desire to help. Egoistic motives are also evoked that compete with empathic distress, may preclude helping, and when bystanders know the costs in advance, may even lead to efforts to avoid empathizing. **The bystander model, in short, involves conflict between the motive to help and egoistic motives that can be powerful.** This makes it all the more remarkable that empathic distress is an effective prosocial motive. The reason may be its self-reinforcing property: Helpers feel good afterward. If so, it raises the question, Is empathy-based helping prosocial? I say yes (Hoffman, 1981), because it is instigated by another's distress, not one's own, its primary aim is to help another, and one feels good only if the victim is helped.

A final note on empathy's contribution to prosocial behavior. My focus has been on helping others in distress but it is worth noting that empathy has also been found to reduce aggression (Feshbach & Feshbach, 1969; Gibbs, 1987). The aggression-reducing feature of empathy is highlighted in my discussion of the transgressor model . . . and my review of moral education methods used to reduce aggression in delinquent adolescents. . . . A more subtle, less well-known finding bears on empathy's relation to the ability to manipulate people. According to Christie and Geis (1970), who conducted extensive research on the "Machiavellian" personality in the 1960s, effective manipulators are not, as some might think, effective empathizers who use empathy to read other people's motives and then use their knowledge of others' motives to take advantage of them. Indeed, they are *weak* empathizers and poor at reading people's motives. Their "advantage" is precisely that they are not empathic, and their resulting insensitivity to others permits them to "bull their way through in pursuit of their own goals." Similarly, in the novel *Blade Runner* (Dick, 1968), "androids" were deemed a menace and outlawed by society because they could be equipped with an intelligence greater than that of many human beings but were totally incapable of empathy.[1] They were viewed as epitomizing manipulators (and killers) because, lacking empathic distress or grief at another's defeat, nothing short of destroying them could stop them from having their way.

Of course, being incapable of empathy does not doom one to manipulating or killing others. O'Neil (1999) describes patients with an empathic disorder called Asperger's (a type of autism) who "realize, and regret, a gap they can cross only with extreme difficulty" (p. F1). They try to break down behavior that most people master without thinking into discrete fragments that can be memorized; they then practice taking the other's point of view. "Things like, 'Do I have to look him in the eye?' 'Yes, but just a little bit to let him know you're listening'" (p. F4). See also Sacks (1995). This contrasts with most humans whose natural empathic sensitivity keeps them from being detached enough to take full advantage of others.

In other words, empathy not only contributes to helping but it also interferes with aggression and the ability to manipulate others. We now turn to the mechanisms that underlie the arousal of empathic distress.

Arousal of Empathic Distress

There are five empathy-arousing modes, as I originally proposed twenty years ago (Hoffman, 1978) and update here. Three are primitive, automatic, and, most important, involuntary. I describe them first.

Mimicry

20 Mimicry was described a century ago by Lipps (1906), although it was intuitively understood 150 years earlier by Adam Smith (1759/1976) who observed:

> When we see a stroke aimed, and just ready to fall upon the leg or arm of another person, we naturally shrink and draw back our own arm. . . . The mob, when they are gazing at a dancer on the slack rope, naturally writhe and twist and balance their own bodies as they see him do. (pp. 4, 10)

Lipps (1906) defined empathy as an innate, involuntary, isomorphic response to another person's expression of emotion. A close reading of his work shows that he saw the process as involving two distinct steps that operate in rapid sequence (Hoffman, 1978). The observer first automatically imitates and synchronizes changes in his facial expression, voice, and posture with the slightest changes in another person's facial, vocal, or postural expressions of feeling—which Lipps

[1] I thank Krin Gabbard for suggesting I read this book.

called "objective motor mimicry." The resulting changes in the observer's facial, vocal, and postural musculature then trigger afferent feedback which produces feelings in the observer that match the feelings of the victim. To avoid confusion, I refer to the two steps as "imitation" and "feedback" and the entire process as mimicry.

Mimicry has long been neglected by psychologists, probably because it seems like an instinctual explanation. It warrants our attention, however, because intuitively it appears to be the very essence of empathy—one observes another's expression of feeling, automatically imitates his expression, and then the brain takes over and makes one feel what the other feels. Though important, demonstrating mimicry empirically is difficult, and it therefore requires more attention than the other empathy-arousing modes. I note first that despite the neglect of mimicry, recent years have seen a lot of research on imitation and on feedback, though little on the combined process.

1. *Imitation*. Bavelas, Black, Lemery, and Mullett (1987) surveyed the research documenting the existence of imitation or mimicry. They found that people imitate another's expressions of pain, laughter, smiling, affection, embarrassment, discomfort, disgust, stuttering, reaching with effort, and the like, in a broad range of situations. Developmental researchers have found that infants shortly after birth will try to imitate another's facial gestures: They stick out their tongues, purse their lips, and open their mouths (Meltzoff, 1988; Reissland, 1988). By 10 weeks of age they imitate at least the rudimentary features of their mothers' facial expressions of happiness and anger (Haviland & Lelwica, 1987). And 9-month-olds will mirror their mothers' posed expressions of joy and sadness (Termine & Izard, 1988).

Not only do infants imitate their mothers' facial expressions of emotion but mothers imitate their infants' facial expressions as well, often without being aware of what they are doing (O'Toole & Dubin, 1968). Indeed, adults appear to have a natural tendency to mirror the facial expression of children, and of other adults, without awareness.

Most of the research has employed electromyographic procedures (EMG). These procedures can measure movements of the facial skin and connective tissues (folds, lines, wrinkles; brow and mouth movement) caused by emotion-produced contraction of the facial muscles—movements that are so subtle (weak or transient) that they produce no observable facial expression. Dimberg (1990) measured the facial EMG activity of Swedish college students as they looked at photographs of people displaying happy and angry facial expressions. He found that subjects observing happy facial expressions showed increased muscular activity over the "zygomaticus major" (cheek) muscle region. When they observed angry facial expressions, they showed increased muscular activity over the "corrugator supercilia" (brow) muscle region.

In an empathy-EMG study (Mathews, 1991; Mathews, Hoffman, & Cohen, 1991), college students' faces were secretly videotaped as they viewed a 2-minute film of a young women recounting a happy event (a dinner party with her fiancé and his parents) and a sad event (being told that her parents had decided to get divorced). In the happy segment, her facial expression, voice, and gestures

25

conveyed a feeling of extreme joy. In the sad segment, her facial expression, voice, and gestures conveyed deep sadness. The facial EMG activity of the subjects obtained from the videotapes of their faces showed increased activity over their cheek muscles and decreased activity over their brow muscles when they watched the happy account; the reverse pattern was obtained when they watched the sad account. In a later analysis of the data, trained judges who were "blind" as to which segment the subjects observed rated the subjects' faces as happier when viewing the happier segment and sadder when viewing the sad segment. Similar results were obtained by Hatfield, Cacioppo, and Rapson (1992), whose judges rated college students' facial expressions as happy or sad when observing a 3-minute filmed interview of a man recounting a happy or a sad event in his life (a surprise birthday party or his grandfather's funeral which he attended at age 6).

Although most of the research employs facial expression, people have been found to engage in increased lip activity and frequency of eye-blink responses when observing others who stutter or blink their eyes (Berger & Hadley, 1975; Bernal & Berger, 1976). More important is people's tendency to imitate aspects of another person's speech patterns: speed, pitch, rhythm, pausing, duration of utterance (Buder, 1991). Since speech patterns are associated with feelings—happy feelings with a fast tempo, large variations in pitch, and small variations in amplitude (Scherer, 1982)—vocal mimicry becomes a real possibility. The importance of vocal mimicry is that it can occur early in life, possibly in newborns as we shall see, and, unlike facial expression, one's speech pattern is extremely difficult to control, which makes deception less likely.

The evidence is clear, then, that people tend automatically to imitate the emotional expressions of people around them—their facial expression, vocal expression, and probably their posture. The next question is: What about feedback? Does the imitation-based activation of a person's facial and vocal expression lead to afferent feedback that in turn affects his or her subjective emotional experience from one moment to the next?

2. Feedback. Charles Darwin (1877) was the first to state the feedback hypothesis ("He who gives way to violent gestures will increase rage; he who does not control the signs of fear will experience fear in a greater degree," p. 365). William James (1893) went further, postulating that feedback was the key to all emotional experience. The way people know how they feel is by sensing it from their muscular as well as their glandular and visceral responses. The well-known quote is "We feel sorry because we cry, angry because we strike, and afraid because we tremble." James advanced this view a century ago, but it has only recently been put to the test.

In the first serious study of feedback, Laird (1974) told adult subjects that he was interested in studying the action of facial muscles. Laird's experimental room contained apparatus designed to convince the subjects that complicated multichannel recordings of facial muscle activity were about to be made. Silver cup electrodes were attached to their faces between their eyebrows, at the corners of their mouths, and at the corners of their jaws. The experimenter then arranged the subjects' faces into emotional expressions (smiles or angry frowns) without their realizing it, by asking them to contract various muscles. To produce angry frowns he touched the subject lightly between the eyebrows with an electrode and said, "Pull your brows down and together . . . good, now hold it like that"); he then asked the subject to contract the muscles at the corners of his jaw ("clench your teeth"). To produce happy faces the subjects were asked to contract the muscles near the corners of their mouths ("draw the corners of your mouth back and up"). Laird found that the subjects in the frown condition felt angrier and those in the smile condition felt happier than their peers. Furthermore, cartoons viewed when the subjects were "smiling" were rated by them as being funnier than cartoons they viewed when "frowning." And, in a later study, subjects in the "smile" condition were better at recalling happy events in their lives than sad events, whereas subjects in the "frown" condition were better at recalling sad events (Laird, Wagener, Halal, & Szedga, 1982). These comments by a subject in the first study show how the process may have worked:

> When my jaw was clenched and my brows down, I tried not to be angry but it just fit the position. I'm not in an angry mood but I found my thoughts wandering to things that made me angry, which is sort of silly, I guess. I knew I was in an experiment and knew I had no reason to feel that way, but I just lost control. (p. 480)

Other equally ingenious techniques have been used to produce smiles without subjects' awareness. In one experiment, smiles were produced by requiring subjects to fill out rating forms with a pen held in their front teeth, which eases the facial muscles into a smile. These subjects found humorous cartoons funnier than did students who held the pen in their lips, forcing their faces into a frown position (Strack, Martin, & Stepper, 1988). In another experiment, the investigators wanted subjects to furrow their brows without asking them explicitly to move facial muscles. This was achieved by taping two golf tees to the subjects' forehead (inside corner of each eye) and instructing them to move the tees together, a task which gave their faces a sad look. It also made them feel sad: Looking at photographs of starving children and other sad scenes made them feel sadder than control subjects did who looked at the same scenes without tees on their foreheads. At least a dozen other studies have produced similar results: Subjects feel the specific emotions consistent with the facial expressions they adopt and have trouble experiencing emotions incompatible with these poses. Still other methods have been used, for example, asking subjects to exaggerate or try to hide any emotional reactions they might have. These studies as well as those mentioned above and others have been reviewed and the evidence is clear that people's emotional experience tends to be influenced by the facial expressions they adopt (Adelman & Zajonc, 1989; Hatfield, Cacioppo, & Rapson, 1992).

Despite the evidence it remains unclear to me whether the subjects actually felt angry or happy because the changes in their stage-managed facial expression activated afferent neural pathways that produced the particular emotion. The alternative is that they perceived the changes in facial-expression kinesthetically and associated the changes with angry or happy experiences ("When I'm angry,

30

my jaws are clenched and my brows are down"). If the latter explanation is correct, the research cannot be said to support afferent feedback, but a weaker self-perception-and-cognitive-inference version of feedback. This issue is important because if afferent feedback exists and operates in early childhood, then mimicry becomes a particularly important mechanism because it enables infants to empathize with another's feeling even before having had their own direct experience with the same feeling; it might even explain the newborn's reactive cry. . . . But if the only feedback is through self-perception and cognitive inference, which requires previous experience with the particular feeling, then empathy in early childhood can only occur through conditioning and direct association. Laird (1984) claims that people engage in both types of feedback: "Some people are happy because they smile, angry because they scowl, and sad because they pout; others define their emotional experience in terms of situational expectations." Laird also presents evidence for this claim (Laird, 1984; Laird, et al., 1994). This dual-process explanation implies, of course, that afferent feedback exists though it is not used by everyone.

An argument can be made in favor of the strong version of the afferent feedback hypothesis. It begins with psychology's long-held assumption that connections between facial expression and emotion are culturally determined. This assumption was laid to rest by the landmark study of Ekman, Sorenson, and Friesen (1969) in which preliterate New Guinea tribespeople identified a number of emotional facial expressions in the same way that subjects in Japan, Brazil, and the United States did. This finding began a new line of research, and evidence has since accumulated suggesting that there are certain innate emotions, each with its corresponding facial expressions. These innate emotions and expressions provide the foundation for differences in subjective feeling and expression of emotion that are then elaborated by culture and socialization (Ekman, Friesen, O'Sullivan, & Chan, 1987).

More important for our purposes, the evidence suggests that the connections between certain emotions and facial expressions are universal and based on neural integration. This supports the afferent feedback hypothesis. The existence of afferent feedback does not rule out self-perception-and-cognitive-inference feedback and, indeed, may explain it. That is, it may be true that we feel angry because past experience tells us that anger "fits the position" of our stage-managed facial expression, but anger may fit the position in the first place because of afferent feedback. This may also explain in part why feedback based on self-perception and cognitive inference can be as quick-acting, effortless, and involuntary as it appears to be. And, finally, Laird's finding that some people use afferent feedback and others use cognitive inference may be explained by socialization that makes some people more sensitive to situational cues and others more sensitive to internal sensations.

No one to my knowledge has actually demonstrated afferent feedback resulting from imitation. To do this may require investigating imitation-produced changes in facial expression in a realistic setting and assessing the effect of these changes on the subjects' feelings. This seems like a difficult task but Bush, Barr, McHugo, and Lanzetta (1989) may have accomplished it. They asked college students to watch comic routines under different conditions and judge how funny they were. A group that was instructed to "relax and enjoy" the routines, and viewed the routines interspersed with shots focused on the studio audience's laughing faces, imitated the audience's laughing faces and found the routines funnier than a group given the same instructions without seeing the audience. This suggests that the subjects' audience-imitating smiles resulted in afferent feedback that made them feel happier and judge the routines funnier. A more parsimonious interpretation is that feedback was unnecessary: The audience's laughing faces made the subjects both smile and think the routines were funnier. Barr et al. anticipated this, however, and included a group that saw the audience's laughing faces but were instructed to inhibit all bodily and facial movements during the experiment. This group did not find the routines funny. In other words, two groups saw the audience's laughing faces but only the group that imitated the audience found the routines funnier—presumably because of afferent feedback.

A possible problem still remains, it seems to me: Only the imitation group behaved spontaneously. The no-imitation group did not, and to follow the instructions and keep from laughing they might have turned away from the audience or tried to think about non-funny things. If so, then it is possible that had they focused on the audience they would have found the routines funnier despite not imitating the audience's laughing faces, which would rule out an afferent feedback explanation. This is sheer speculation: It seems more reasonable that the authors did it right; the group focused on the audience (in keeping with their instructions) and they did not find the routines funnier because of the lack of afferent feedback.

It seems reasonable to conclude that the weight of the evidence for the universality of emotions plus the evidence for imitation and feedback favors the imitation–feedback sequence and the mimicry process as described by Lipps. This means that mimicry is probably a hard-wired neurologically based empathy-arousing mechanism whose two steps, imitation and feedback, are directed by commands from the central nervous system. This is important for two reasons. First, as noted, a hard-wired mimicry provides a quick-acting mechanism enabling infants to empathize and feel what another feels without previously experiencing that emotion. I say quick-acting, following Davis's (1985) colorful argument that mimicry is too complex and fast-acting to be done consciously. Davis points out that whereas even the lightning-fast Muhammad Ali took 190 milliseconds to spot a light and an additional 40 milliseconds to throw a punch in response, videotapes of college students in conversation show that each student's speech and body motions were synchronized to the other's in 20 milliseconds or less. A second reason for the importance of mimicry's being hard-wired is that besides being involuntary and fast, mimicry is the only empathy-arousing mechanism that assures a match between the observer's feeling and expression of feeling and the victim's feeling and expression of feeling, at least in face-to-face encounters.

This match in emotional expression looms large in the research done by Bavelas et al. (1987) and Bavelas, Black, Chovil, Lemery, and Mullett (1988), which supports their contention that mimicry is a communicative act, conveying a rapid and precise nonverbal message to another person. Specifically, they argue that people are communicating solidarity and involvement ("I am with you" or "I am like you") when they mimic. "By immediately displaying a reaction appropriate to the other's situation (e.g., a wince for the other's pain), the observer conveys precisely and eloquently both awareness of and involvement with the other's situation" (1988, p. 278). If Bavelas et al. are right, then mimicry may not just be another mechanism of empathic arousal that predisposes people to help others, but it may also be a direct means of giving support and comfort to others. That is, mimicry-based empathy may not only be a prosocial motive but also a prosocial act.

Classical Conditioning

Classical conditioning is an important empathy-arousing mechanism in childhood especially in the early, preverbal years. It appears that young children (or anyone for that matter) can acquire empathic feelings of distress as conditioned responses whenever they observe someone in distress at the same time that they are having their own independent experience of distress. Thus Lanzetta and Orr (1986) found that presenting adults with a fear-producing danger signal (shock electrodes) along with an another adult's fearful facial expression, results in fearful faces becoming conditioned stimuli that evoke fear in the subjects even when the shock electrodes are removed from view. Using a similar procedure, happy faces and neutral tones can become conditioned fear-producing stimuli, though not as effectively as fearful faces. At the other extreme, and of greater interest to us, two decades of research have shown, contrary to previous belief, that conditioning is possible in newborns: The sucking response of 1-day-olds, for example, can be conditioned to stroking their forehead (Blass, Ganchrow, & Steiner, 1984).

This pairing of one's actual distress with expressive cues of distress in others may be inevitable in mother–infant interactions, as when the mother's feelings are transferred to the infant in the course of physical handling. For example, when a mother feels anxiety or tension, her body may stiffen and the stiffening may transmit her distress to the infant she is holding. The infant is now distressed; and the stiffening of the mother's body was the direct cause—the unconditioned stimulus. The mother's accompanying facial and verbal expressions then become conditioned stimuli, which can subsequently evoke distress in the child even in the absence of physical contact. This mechanism may explain Sullivan's (1940) definition of empathy as a form of "nonverbal contagion and communion" between mother and infant; and Escalona's finding (1945), in a woman's reformatory where mothers cared for their own infants, that the infants were most upset when their mothers were waiting to appear before a parole board. Furthermore, through generalization of the conditioned stimulus, facial and verbal signs of distress from *anyone*, not only the mother, can make the infant feel distressed.

40 This type of direct physical conditioning is not confined to negative affect. When a mother holds the baby closely, securely, affectionately, and has a smile

on her face, the baby feels good and the mother's smile is associated with that feeling. Later, the mother's smile alone may function as a conditioned stimulus that makes the baby feel good. And, again through stimulus generalization, other people's smiles can make the baby feel good. This process is relevant here because it may contribute to the empathic relief discussed earlier when the person one has helped smiles in gratitude or relief.

Afferent feedback, an essential component of mimicry, may also play a role in conditioning, and it may contribute to a certain degree of match between the observer's and the victim's feeling. That is, changes in the observer's facial expression accompanying empathic distress aroused by conditioning may trigger afferent feedback and produce feelings in the observer that match the victim's feelings, because: (a) all humans have certain distress experiences in common (loss, injury, deprivation), (b) they are structurally similar to each other and therefore likely to process distress-relevant information similarly, and (c) they are therefore likely to respond to similar stressful events with similar feelings (Ekman et al., 1987).

Indeed, conditioning might be thought of, like mimicry, as a two-step process: conditioning of facial expression followed by afferent feedback. There is a big difference of course: Mimicry assures a match between victim's and observer's feeling because it is the only process whose first step (imitation) is a direct response to the victim's facial expression; whereas conditioning can be a response to the victim's situation.

Direct Association

A variant of the conditioning paradigm, described some time ago by Humphrey (1922), is the direct association of cues in the victim's situation that remind observers of similar experiences in their own past and evoke feelings in them that fit the victim's situation. We have a distressing experience; later on we observe someone in a similar situation; and his facial expression, voice, posture, or any other cue in the situation that reminds us of our past experience may evoke a feeling of distress in us. A frequently cited example is the boy who sees another child cut himself and cry. The sight of the blood, the sound of the cry, or any other cue from the victim or the situation that reminds the boy of his own past experiences of pain may evoke an empathic distress response. Another example is children's past experiences of separation from the mother—short daily separation, prolonged separation, or their worrying about the mother's dying—which may facilitate their empathizing with another person whose mother is hospitalized or dies.

Direct association differs from conditioning because it does not require previous experiences in which distress in oneself is actually paired with cues of distress in others. The only requirement is that the observer has had past feelings of pain or discomfort, which can now be evoked by cues of distress from victims or situational cues that are similar to those painful experiences. Direct association thus has more scope than conditioning and provides the basis for a variety of distress experiences in others with which children may empathize. Furthermore, what I said about the possible role of afferent feedback in conditioning may also be true of direct association: Changes in an observer's facial expression resulting from direct association may, through afferent feedback, contribute to a certain degree of match between the observer's and the victim's feeling. Here is a vivid example of direct association described by a college student:

> Getting off the bus I saw a man slip and fall and hit his head on the stairs. I was shocked. An incident flashed through my mind when I slipped on the sidewalk and cracked my skull. I don't know what came over me. I didn't think of anything but to rush to help and somehow get him to feel okay. I remember yelling at the people to call 911. I must have spent over two hours making sure everything was okay. I know myself, and I know I wouldn't have felt okay just to get him up and leave it to someone else to take care of him.

45   To summarize, mimicry, conditioning, and direct association are important mechanisms of empathic arousal for several reasons: (a) they are automatic, quick-acting, and involuntary; (b) they enable infants and preverbal children, as well as adults, to empathize with others in distress; (c) they produce early pairings of children's empathic distress with other people's actual distress, which contributes to children's expectation of distress whenever they are exposed to another's distress; (d) they are self-reinforcing to some extent because the helping behavior they foster may produce empathic relief; (e) they contribute an involuntary dimension to children's future empathy experiences.

The question may be raised whether conditioning and direct association are empathy-arousing processes when triggered by the situation rather than by the victim's feeling. I consider them empathy-arousing processes as long as the observer attends to the victim and the feelings evoked in the observer fit the victim's situation rather than the observer's. In any case, the problem does not exist in face-to-face encounters, where mimicry defines the observer's distress as clearly empathic, and conditioning and association may contribute to the intensity of that distress. The empathy aroused in observers by the combination of mimicry, conditioning, and association is, to be sure, a passive, involuntary response, based on the pull of surface cues and requiring the shallowest level of cognitive processing. It is a potentially powerful empathy-arousing package, nonetheless, precisely because it shows that humans are built in such a way that they can involuntarily and forcefully experience another's emotion—that is, a person's distress is often contingent not on his own but on someone else's painful experience.

It is a limited empathy-arousing package, however, because of the minimal involvement of language and cognition. This limitation makes it necessary for the victim to be present and enables observers to empathize only with simple emotions. The three mechanisms that make up the package also make little or no contribution to mature empathy's metacognitive dimension—the awareness that one's feeling of distress is a response to another's distressing situation. These deficiencies are overcome by language and cognitive development, which are central to the two remaining modes of empathy arousal, mediated association and role-taking, to which we now turn.

Mediated Association

In the fourth empathic arousal mode, verbal mediation, the victim's emotionally distressed state is communicated through language. To highlight the processes involved in mediated association, consider what happens when language provides the only cue about another's affective state, for example, when the other person is not present but we receive a letter describing what happened to him or how he feels. Language might produce an empathic response because of the physical properties of words which have become conditioned stimuli (the sound of the word *cancer* may arouse fear in children who do not know its meaning but associate the sound with adult expressions of fear and anxiety). This is not what is special about language, however.

What is special about language is not the physical properties of words but their semantic meaning. Verbal messages from victims must be semantically processed and decoded. When this happens, language is the mediator or link between the model's feeling and the observer's experience. The message may express the model's feeling (I'm worried), the model's situation (my child was just taken to the hospital), or both. Empathic affect may then be aroused in observers who decode the victim's message and relate it to their own experience. Alternatively, the decoded message enables the observer to conjure up visual (facial expression, posture) or auditory images of the victim (cries, moans) and the observer then responds empathically to these images through direct association or mimicry.

Verbally mediated empathic arousal is interesting for several reasons. First, the time it takes to process a message semantically and relate it to one's experience, though undoubtedly greater than the time required by conditioning, association, and mimicry, varies enormously. Semantic processing can be drawn out but it can also be amazingly fast: It takes less than a second to categorize words in a list (which word is a fruit?) and 2 to 3 seconds to judge whether a word is a synonym of another word (Gitomer, Pellegrino, & Bisanz, 1983; Rogers, Kuiper, & Kirker, 1977). Second, semantic processing undoubtedly requires more mental effort than conditioning, association, and mimicry.

Third, because one is not responding directly to the victim or his situation, semantic processing puts psychological distance between observers and victims due to the decoding and encoding processes that intervene. That is, the victim encodes his feelings into words (sad, afraid). But words are general categories that can only approximate the victim's feelings at the time, and words are the total input available to the observer. In decoding the message the observer must reverse the sequence, going from the general category of feeling represented by the word to his own specific feeling and the associated past events in which he had that feeling. As a result, the observer's feelings have much in common with the victim's feelings, owing to the normative, shared meaning of the victim's words, but there is always some slippage due to encoding and decoding "errors" (and memory lapses for associated past events). These errors can be reduced when victims are expert at putting feelings into words and when observers know the victim well, know how he feels in different situations and can perhaps imagine his facial expression and behavior in the immediate situation. In general, we would expect verbal mediation to reduce the intensity of observer's empathic response below what it would be when victims are present—although there are exceptions to this, which will be discussed in the next chapter.

In most bystander situations the victim *is* present and verbal communication of his distress is accompanied by visual or auditory cues. These cues may have triggered the observer's empathic response in the first place, through conditioning, association, or mimicry because these are faster-acting than semantically processing the verbal message. Semantic processing, I would hypothesize, is more likely to follow and fine-tune the observer's empathic response, although it may at times initiate the empathic process, as when the verbal message precedes the victim's arrival on the scene. Whatever the sequence, the victim's expressive cues, which are likely to be picked up through conditioning, association, and mimicry, may keep the empathic process "alive" because these cues are salient, vivid, and can therefore hold the observer's attention—in contrast to verbal messages, which are distancing and to some extent dampen empathic affect because of the encoding and decoding involved in processing them.

The victim's expressive cues may also keep observers from being misled when victims' words belie their feelings, because of the human tendency to "leak" feelings through involuntary changes in facial expression, posture, and tone of voice. These involuntary changes in expression can be picked up and communicated to the observer by conditioning, association, and mimicry. This points up a second communication function of empathic affect (see Bavelas et al., 1988, above for the first), which is to *inform* its motivational component (Hoffman, 1981). Thus empathic affect is generated both by primitive and verbally mediated mechanisms. The information from these two sources of empathic affect is usually congruent, but when it is not congruent the discrepancy can provide corrective feedback that helps observers to make a more accurate assessment of the victim's state and thus to have a more veridical empathic response.

Verbally mediated empathic distress is illustrated in a study by Batson, Sympson, and Hindman (1996). Adolescent subjects read stories in which someone of the same sex described an upsetting life experience. One story described the acute embarrassment and shame, the enduring cruel remarks and teasing, and the hating to see oneself in the mirror that resulted from having a bad case of acne. The other story described feeling betrayed and rejected, trying to regroup and move on, and experiencing self-doubt and lingering love after being rejected by a long-term dating partner. The subjects reported feeling considerable empathic distress after reading the stories. The female subjects reported even greater empathic distress if they recalled having a similar experience themselves, which suggests verbally mediated association. Verbal mediation probably also enabled all the subjects to imagine themselves in the victim's place, an empathy-arousing mechanism to which we turn in a moment, after this quite different example of cognitively, though not verbally, mediated empathic distress which was described to me by a student.

> When dealing with someone with a terminal illness I was always taught to never discuss that illness with them, just to talk about everyday topics. About five years ago my grandma lapsed into a coma, and for a year she "lived" this way. I would

often speak to her on the phone, identifying myself and talking to her about my life. It was very difficult and painful for me because there would never be a response and I could never question her. I would speak with her in the hope that she would respond some way. She never did.

In this case there were no expressive cues from the victim except silence which would have meant nothing if not for the observer's knowledge and understanding of the victim's plight.

Role-Taking

The fifth mode of empathic arousal requires an advanced level of cognitive processing: putting oneself in the other's place and imagining how he or she feels. The idea that putting oneself in the other's place can make one feel something of what the other feels is not new. Two-and-a-half centuries ago the British philosopher David Hume suggested that because people are constituted similarly and have similar life experiences, when one imagines oneself in another's place one converts the other's situation into mental images that then evoke the same feeling in oneself (Hume, 1751/1957). Adam Smith, a contemporary, agreed with Hume about empathy's importance, and Smith's speculations about the nature of the empathic process foreshadowed some of today's formulations. He realized, for example, that empathy could be a response to direct expressive cues of another's feeling: "Grief and joy strongly expressed in the look and gestures of anyone at once affect the spectator with some degree of a like painful or agreeable emotion" (Smith, 1759/1965, p. 260). He also viewed empathy as universal and involuntary: "Even the greatest ruffian, the most hardened violator of the laws of society is not without it" (p. 257). Though involuntary, empathy is enhanced by cognitive processes.

> By the imagination we place ourselves in the other's situation, we conceive ourselves enduring all the same torments, we enter, as it were, into his body, and become in some measure the same person with him, and thence form some idea of his sensations, and even feel something which, though weaker in degree, is not altogether unlike them. (p. 261)

Despite these early beginnings, role-taking as a mechanism of empathic arousal was not investigated empirically until the mid-1960s. The most pertinent research was done by Stotland (1969). In one study, subjects were instructed to imagine how they would feel and what sensations they would have in their hands if they were exposed to the same painful heat treatment that was being applied to someone they were observing through a one-way mirror. These subjects showed more empathic distress, as measured by palmar sweat and verbal report, than subjects who were instructed to attend closely to the victim's physical movements. They also showed more empathic distress than subjects who were instructed to imagine how the victim felt while undergoing the heat treatment. The first finding indicates that imagining oneself in the victim's place is more empathy-arousing than focusing on his expressive movements. The second finding suggests that imagining oneself in the other's place is more empathy-arousing than focusing one's attention directly on the victim's feeling.

Stotland also found that the subjects who were instructed to imagine themselves in the victim's place did not show an increase in palmar sweat until about 30 seconds after the experimenter announced that the painful heat treatment had begun, which was longer than the time it took for subjects who were simply asked to observe the victim. The delay in empathic responsiveness could have been due to the cognitive demands of role-taking (plus the mental effort involved in following the instructions).

Stotland's research suggested to me that there may be two types of role-taking that have somewhat different effects: One is the usual conception of role-taking in which one imagines oneself in the other's place. In the second type, one focuses directly on the other's feeling. I conducted dozens of interviews asking people to describe instances in which they responded empathically to victims who were present, victims who communicated their distress in writing, and victims whose distress was communicated to them by a third person. The interviews served two purposes: They confirmed the two types of role-taking as well as a third, combined type, and they suggested the cognitive–affective interaction processes that may underlie the types, as follows.

1. *Self-focused role-taking.* When people observe someone in distress they may imagine how they would feel in the same situation. If they can do this vividly enough, they may experience some of the same affect experienced by the victim. And if they are reminded of similar events in their own past, or if they remember worrying about such events happening, then their empathic response to the victim may be enhanced through association with the emotionally charged memory of those actual or worried-about events.

2. *Other-focused role-taking.* On learning of another's misfortune, people may focus directly on the victim and imagine how he feels; and doing this may result in their feeling something of the victim's feeling. This empathic response may be enhanced by bringing in any personal information they have about the victim (his character, life-condition, behavior in similar situations), and any normative knowledge they may have of how most people feel in that situation. It may be enhanced further if they attend to the victim's facial expression, voice tone, or posture, because these nonverbal cues of distress may enlist the more primitive empathy-arousing mechanisms (conditioning, association, mimicry). This can be done even in the victim's absence, as when observers who are closely related to the victim imagine how he looks, "hear" his cries, and respond empathically as if he were present.

60   Based on my interviews, I suggested that Stotland's finding that self-focused role-taking produced more intense empathic distress than other-focused role-taking could be explained as follows:

> Imagining oneself in the other's place reflects processes generated from within the observer . . . in which connections are made between the stimuli impinging on the other person and similar stimulus events in the observer's own past. That is, imagining oneself in the other's place produces an empathic response because it has the power to evoke associations with real events in one's own past in which one actually experienced the affect in question. (Hoffman, 1978, p. 180)

Such internally generated responses are less likely when one focuses on the victim.

The hypothesis that self-focused role-taking produces more intense empathic affect than other-focused role-taking has recently been confirmed in an experimental study by Batson, Early, and Salvarani (1997). Undergraduate subjects listened to a (bogus) radio interview of a young woman in serious need: Her parents and a sister had recently been killed in an automobile crash. She explained that she was desperately trying to take care of her surviving younger brother and sister while she finished her last year of college. If she did not finish, she would not be able to earn enough money to support them and would have to put them up for adoption. One group of subjects was instructed to remain objective while listening, another to imagine how the young woman "feels about what has happened to her and how it has affected her life," and another to imagine how "you yourself would feel if you were experiencing what has happened to her and how this experience would affect your life." The main finding was that both role-taking conditions produced more empathic distress than the objective condition, but the self-focused condition produced more than the other-focused condition. That is, the subjects who imagined how they would feel in the victim's situation experienced more intense empathic distress than those who imagined how the victim felt.[2] The reason, I suggest, is that imagining how oneself would feel activates one's own personal need system.

Self-focused role-taking may have its limitations, however. When people take the victim's place and bring in emotionally charged personal memories, the memories may at times take control of their response and turn their attention away from the victim toward themselves. That is, an observer feels empathic/ sympathetic distress ("I feel so much of your pain. It hurts me so much to see this happen to you"), but when he starts ruminating about a similar perhaps more traumatic experience in his own past (self-focused role-taking), he begins to feel a more personal distress; the empathic pain remains, but the image of the victim recedes into the background. In other words, the observer is overwhelmed by the empathic connection with the victim, and the empathic connection is then severed, ironically, because the empathic affect resonates so effectively with the observer's own needs; and his focus, which was initially on the victim, shifts toward himself. Ruminating about his painful past, he becomes lost in egoistic concerns and the image of the victim that initiated the role-taking process slips out of focus and fades away, aborting or temporarily aborting the empathic process.

I call this loss of empathic connection "egoistic drift" (Hoffman, 1978). Egoistic drift points up empathy's fragility: It highlights the fact that **although humans can empathize with the other they are not the other.** My hypothesis is

---

[2]The actual finding was that both the self- and other-focused conditions produced more empathic/sympathetic distress than the objective condition, but the self-focused condition produced in addition a high degree of relatively "pure" empathic distress (called "personal distress" by Batson et al., 1997). The terms *empathic/sympathetic distress* and *pure empathic distress* will make more sense after reading the next chapter, in which they are discussed at length.

that self-focused role-taking arouses more intense empathic distress because it makes a direct connection between the victim's affective state and the observer's own need system. But this very connection makes it vulnerable to egoistic drift. The result is that self-focused role-taking produces a more intense, but sometimes less stable empathic response than other-focused role-taking. Regardless of the explanation, the observer's affective response, though initially triggered by the victim's affective state, would no longer, in my judgment, qualify as empathy unless the observer returned to his initial focus on the victim.

The following experience, reported by an undergraduate, illustrates both the power of self-focused role-taking to evoke empathic affect and its vulnerability to egoistic drift.

> The movie *Steel Magnolias* is a poignant film focused on the life of a woman, Shelby, struggling with diabetes. Shelby marries Jackson and they have a son. One evening Jackson returns from work to find Shelby unconscious on the floor with the phone in her hand. Their 3-year-old son is crying beside his mother. Shelby goes to the hospital where she dies. Shelby's mother, M'Lynn, is comforted by her closest friends. At the burial of her only daughter, M'Lynn becomes hysterical. She cries not only about the tragic loss of her daughter but also about the grandson who will never know his mother. She wants to know why God took her Shelby; a mother is not supposed to outlive her child.
>
> I was able to keep my composure until that last scene. As M'Lynn became hysterical—her voice, her words, her facial expression—visions of my grandmother emerged. I began to remember witnessing the same actions . . . performed by my grandmother. I became hysterical. My focus was no longer on Shelby and M'Lynn but rather on my grandmother. I remember how I felt after my aunt died leaving behind her two children. I felt the pain and depression all over again. My friends who were watching the movie with me assumed I was crying because of the movie but in actuality the tears were because of my own life.

65 Another student contributed this incident, which shows that one need not have had an experience like the victim's but only to be worried about having one.

> A friend who is pregnant was just told the baby, her fourth, had Down's Syndrome. I felt really sorry for her. I have been thinking about having children lately. I have none and spend a lot of time worrying about what my life would be like if I had a child with a serious deformity. I imagine all the things that might happen to the child, and to me. When my friend told me that, I immediately started thinking about what it would be like if I were just told that the child I was carrying had Down's Syndrome. When this occurred I became so engrossed in my own thoughts about what it would feel like, that I forgot all about my friend and her condition. I was completely consumed by the fear of what might happen to my future rather than what was happening to my friend in the present.

3. Combination. Observers can shift back and forth between "other-focused" and "self-focused" role-taking or experience them as co-occurring parallel processes. My discussion suggests that the combination may be the most powerful because it combines the emotional intensity of self-focused role-taking with the more sustained attention to the victim of other-focused role-taking. Indeed, fully mature role-taking might be defined as imagining oneself in the other's place and integrating the resulting empathic affect with one's personal information about the other and one's general knowledge of how people feel in his or her situation. It could go either way: other-focused role-taking in the service of self-focused role-taking, or self-focused role-taking in the service of other-focused role-taking.

A final word about role-taking. Although spontaneous role-taking has been found in adults and in children as young as 9 years old (Wilson & Cantor, 1985), role-taking is more cognitively demanding than the other empathy-arousing mechanisms and might therefore be expected to have a greater voluntary component. It would seem possible, for example, to avoid role-taking by thinking distracting thoughts. This might be difficult, however, in situations that demand paying attention to the victim or when distress cues from the victim are salient, owing to the pull of primitive empathy-arousing mechanisms (conditioning, association, mimicry). This could explain why a group of Stotland's (1969) subjects who were instructed to attend to the victim but avoid putting themselves in his place showed as much palmar sweat as subjects who were simply instructed to attend to the victim; try as they might, these subjects could not avoid empathizing. It may also explain why most everyone regardless of age finds it difficult to avoid empathizing with victims in the movies. That is, they find it difficult to avoid "suspending disbelief," even though they know it is all "pretend." Role-taking, in other words, may not be as voluntary a process as it first appears to be.

A final developmental hypothesis: other-focused role-taking is more cognitively demanding (one considers another's inner states) and is thus acquired later.

Importance of Many Modes

The importance of many modes of empathic arousal is that they enable observers to respond empathically to whatever distress cues are available. If the only cues are the victim's facial expression, voice, or posture, they can be picked up through mimicry. If the only cues are situational, empathic distress can be aroused through conditioning or direct association. If the victim expresses distress verbally or in writing, or someone else describes his plight, observers can be empathically aroused through verbal mediation or role-taking.

The three primitive modes—mimicry, association, and conditioning—operating together provide a powerful package that may underlie empathic arousal in children's early preverbal years. Mimicry may be particularly important in infancy because it produces a match between observers' and victims' feelings even when observers have not had a similar experience. The three primitive modes also contribute to empathy development beyond infancy by giving young children repeated experiences of feeling distressed as a co-occurring feature of another person's distress, as well as the pleasant experience of empathic relief when they help. Finally, because the three primitive modes are automatic and encompass all the available distress cues, they may account for the involuntary dimension of empathy in adults, which may, among other things, reduce the tendency toward "egoistic drift."

Ordinarily victims are present and all the arousal mechanisms are operating. When that happens there may be a certain division of labor among them. Some arousal mechanisms are more likely to intensify empathic affect or keep one's attention focused on the victim (mimicry). On the other hand, others are more likely to contribute to "egoistic drift" (especially self-focused role-taking). Some mechanisms may start the empathic process but fade away, while others take over for them. Mimicry, for example, may start the empathy-arousing process but then fade away due to facial muscle fatigue; the victim's face is still cognitively represented, however, and the representation of the face may sustain other empathy-arousing mechanisms and keep them operating. Apart from a division of labor, the modes may interact reciprocally: Empathic affect from primitive modes may trigger role-taking, which may then intensify and give broader meaning to empathic affect from the primitive modes. Which mechanism initiates the process, the primitive or the more cognitive, may be a function of personal style and the context.

The various modes should ordinarily produce the same empathic affect (with exceptions discussed in chapters 3 and 4); and the functional redundancy should assure an empathic response in most observers. Indeed, although one's empathic distress may usually be less intense than the victim's actual distress, the combined effects of the arousal modes may sometimes make one's empathic distress more intensely painful than the victim's actual distress. This may explain a phenomenon that fascinated Darwin (1862/1965, p. 216): "It is not a little remarkable that sympathy with the distresses of others should excite more tears more freely than our own distresses; and this is certainly the case." My hypothesis is that what happens is the observer's imagination runs rampant as he or she contemplates being in the victim's place (self-focused role-taking), whereas the victim has had time to accept and come to terms with his or her condition. As a result, the observer's empathic distress can be more intense than the victim's actual distress—and presumably more intense than the *observer's* actual distress would be in the victim's situation. More about this later (chapter 8).

The existence of multiple arousal modes bears on my definition of empathy as not requiring (though often including) a close match between observer's and victim's affect. On the one hand, the many modes virtually assure a certain degree of match between the feelings of observers and victims, even across cultures, for three reasons: First, mimicry, because it is automatic and neurally based, assures a close match in feeling when there is face-to-face contact between observer and victim. Second, even conditioning and association assure some degree of match because all humans are structurally similar and process information similarly; they are therefore likely to respond to similar events with similar feelings. On the other hand, as we shall see, there are occasions in which empathy does not require a match and, indeed, may require a certain *mismatch*, as when the victim's life condition belies his feelings in the immediate situation. These are occasions in which verbal mediation and role-taking are likely to be paramount.

To summarize, empathic distress is a multidetermined, hence reliable human response. The three preverbal modes are crucial in childhood especially in face-to-face situations, but they continue to operate past childhood and provide an important involuntary dimension to empathy throughout life. They not only enable a person to respond to whatever cues are available, but they also *compel* him or her to do that—instantly, automatically, and outside of conscious awareness. An example can be found in empathic avoidance: If a person tries to avoid empathy by refraining from eye contact or not listening to a description of a victim's life condition, he may still be vulnerable to empathic distress through conditioning or association. The two cognitively advanced modes—verbal mediation and role-taking—can be drawn out and subjected to voluntary control, but if one is paying attention to the victim, they too can be fast-acting, involuntary, and triggered immediately on witnessing the victim's situation. What these two cognitively advanced modes contribute is that they add scope to one's empathic capability and enable one to empathize with others who are not present. All of this fits well with the evidence presented earlier for empathy's effectiveness as a prosocial moral motive and with the argument that empathy became a basic part of human nature through natural selection (Hoffman, 1981). It is also in keeping with the finding that empathy has a hereditary component: Identical twins are more similar to each other on empathy measures than are fraternal twins of the same age (Zahn-Waxler, Robinson, Emde, & Plomin, 1992).

Before concluding this chapter, I would like to raise a fundamental question about empathy: why do the various empathy-arousing mechanisms work, that is, why do they elicit feelings in observers that approximate the feelings of those being observed? My answer, implied in the foregoing discussion of mechanisms, is first and foremost that because of the structural similarities in people's physiological and cognitive response systems, similar events evoke similar feelings—similar but not identical for the reasons already given. However, the degree of structural similarity, hence the tendency to empathize with one another, should be greater between people in the same culture who live under similar conditions, and especially between those who interact frequently, than between people from different cultures or who rarely interact. This is obviously true of the cognitive system but it is also true of the physiological system, as evidenced by Levenson and Ruef (1997) who found an increased "physiological synchrony" in humans who spend a lot of time together, for example, an increased covariation of heart-rate changes between patients and their therapists, and between mothers and their infants.

75

References

Adelman, P. K., & Zajonc, R. (1989). Facial efference and the experience of emotion. *Annual Review of Psychology, 40,* 249–280.

Batson, C. D., Early, S., & Salvarani, G. (1997). Perspective taking: Imagining how another feels versus imagining how you would feel. *Personality and Social Psychology Bulletin, 23,* 751–758.

Batson, C. D., & Shaw, L. L. (1991). Evidence for altruism: Toward a pluralism of prosocial motives. *Psychological Inquiry, 2,* 107–122.

Batson, C. D., Sympson, S. C., & Hindman, J. L. (1996). "I've been there, too": Effect on empathy of prior experience with a need. *Personality and Social Psychology Bulletin, 22,* 474–482.

Batson, C. D., & Weeks, J. L. (1996). Mood effects of unsuccessful helping: Another test of the empathy-altruism hypothesis. *Personality and Social Psychology Bulletin, 22,* 148–157.

Bavelas, J. B., Black, A., Chovil, N., Lemery, C. R., & Mullett, J. (1988). Form and function in motor mimicry: Topographical evidence that the primary function is communication. *Human Communication Research,* 14, 275–299.

Bavelas, J. B., Black, A., Lemery, C. R., & Mullett, J. (1987). Motor mimicry as primitive empathy. In N. Eisenberg & J. Strayer (Eds.), *Empathy and its development* (pp. 317–338). New York: Cambridge University Press.

Berger, S. M., & Hadley, S. W. (1975). Some effects of a model's performance on observer electromyographic activity. *American Journal of Psychology, 88,* 263–276.

Bernal, G., & Berger, S. M. (1976). Vicarious eyelid conditioning. *Journal of Personality and Social Psychology, 34,* 62–68.

Berndt, T. (1979). Effect of induced sadness about self or other on helping behavior in high and low empathy children. *Developmental Psychology, 15,* 329–330.

Blass, E. M., Ganchrow, J. R., & Steiner, J. E. (1984). Classical conditioning in newborn humans 2–48 hours of age. *Infant Behavior and Development, 7,* 223–235.

Buder, E. (1991). Vocal synchrony in conversations: Spatial analysis of fundamental voice frequency. Unpublished doctoral dissertation, University of Wisconsin-Madison.

Bush, L. K., Barr, C. L., McHugo, G. J., & Lanzetta, J. T. (1989). The effects of facial control and facial mimicry on subjective reactions to comedy routines. *Motivation and emotion,* 31–53.

Carlo, G., Eisenberg, N., Troyer, D., Switzer, G., & Speer, A. L. (1991). The altruistic personality: In what contexts is it apparent? *Journal of Personality and Social Psychology, 61,* 450–458.

Christie, R., & Geis, F. L. (1970). *Studies in Machiavellianism.* NY: Academic Press.

Darley, J. M., & Latane, B. (1968). Bystander intervention in emergencies: Diffusion of responsibility. *Journal of Personality and Social Psychology, 8,* 377–383.

Darwin, C. (1862/1965). *The expression of the emotions in man and animals.* Chicago: University of Chicago Press.

Darwin, C. (1877). A biological sketch of an infant. *Mind: Quarterly Review of Psychology and Philosophy,* 11, 286–294.

Davis, M. R. (1983). Measuring individual differences in empathy: Evidence for a multi-dimensional approach. *Journal of Personality and Social Psychology, 44,* 113–126.

Davis, M. R. (1985). Perceptual and affective reverberation components. In A. B. Goldstein and G. Y. Michaels (Eds.), *Empathy: Development, training, and consequences* (pp. 62–108). Hillsdale, NJ: Erlbaum.

Dick, P. K. (1968). *Blade runner.* New York: Ballantine Books.

Dimberg, U. (1990). Facial electromyography and emotional reactions. *Psychophysiology, 27,* 481–494.

Eisenberg, N., & Miller, P. (1987). Relation of empathy to prosocial behavior. *Psychological Bulletin,* 101, 91–119.

Ekman, P., Friesen, W., O'Sullivan, M., & Chan, A. (1987). Universals and cultural differences in the judgments of facial expressions of emotion. *Journal of Personality and Social Psychology,* 53, 712–717.

Ekman, P., Sorenson, E., & Friesen, W. (1969). Pan-cultural elements in facial displays of emotion. *Science,* 164, 86–88.

Escalona, S. K. (1945). Feeding disturbances in very young children. *American Journal of Orthopsychiatry,* 15, 76–80.

Feshbach, N. D., & Feshbach, S. (1969). The relationship between empathy and aggression in two age groups. *Developmental Psychology,* 1, 102–107.

Gaertner, S. L., & Dovidio, J. F. (1977). The subtlety of White racism, arousal, and helping behavior. *Journal of Personality and Social Psychology,* 35, 691–707.

Geer, J. H., & Jarmecky, L. (1973). The effect of being responsible for reducing another's pain on subjects' pain and arousal. *Journal of Personality and Social Psychology,* 26, 323–337.

Gibbs, J. C. (1987). Social processes in delinquency: The need to facilitate empathy as well as sociomoral reasoning. In W. M. Kurtines & J. C. Gewirtz (Eds.), *Moral development through social interaction* (pp. 301–321). New York: Wiley.

Gitomer, A., Pellegrino, H., & Bisanz, J. (1983). Developmental changes and invariance in semantic processing. *Journal of Experimental Child Psychology,* 35, 56–80.

Hatfield, E., Cacioppo, J. T., & Rapson, R. L. (1992). Emotional contagion. In M. S. Clark (Ed.), *Review of personality and social psychology: Vol. 14, Emotional and social behavior* (pp. 151–177). Newbury Park, CA: Sage.

Haviland, J. M., & Lelwica, M. (1987). The induced affect response: 10-week-old infants' responses to three emotion expressions. *Developmental Psychology,* 23, 97–104.

Hoffman, M. L. (1978). Empathy, its development and prosocial implications. In C. B. Keasey (Ed.), *Nebraska Symposium on Motivation,* 25, 169–218.

Hoffman, M. L. (1981). Is altruism part of human nature? *Journal of Personality and Social Psychology,* 40, 121–137.

Hume, D. (1751/1957). *An inquiry concerning the principle of morals.* New York: Liberal Arts Press.

Humphrey, G. (1922). The conditioned reflex and the elementary social reaction. *Journal of Abnormal and Social Psychology,* 17, 113–119.

Ickes, W. (1997). *Empathic accuracy.* New York: Guilford.

James, W. (1893). *Psychology.* New York: Holt.

Laird, J. D. (1974). Self-attribution of emotion. The effects of expressive behavior on the quality of emotional experience. *Journal of Personality and Social Psychology,* 29, 475–486.

Laird, J. D. (1984). The real role of facial response in the experience of emotion. *Journal of Personality and Social Psychology,* 47, 909–917.

Laird, J. D., Alibozak, T., Davainis, D., Deignan, K., Fontanella, K., Hong, J., & Pacheco, C. (1994). Individual differences in the effects of spontaneous mimicry on emotional contagion. *Motivation and Emotion*, 18, 231–247.

Laird, J. D., Wagener, J. J., Halal, M., & Szedga, M. (1982). Remembering what you feel: Effects of emotion and memory. *Journal of Personality and Social Psychology*, 42, 646–675.

Lanzetta, J. T., & Orr, S. P. (1986). Excitatory strength of expressive faces: Effects of happy and fear expressions and context on the extinction of a conditioned fear response. *Journal of Personality and Social Psychology*, 50, 190–194.

Latane, B., & Darley, J. M. (1970). *The unresponsive bystander: Why doesn't he help?* New York: Prentice-Hall.

Levenson, R. W., & Ruef, A. M. (1997). Physiological aspects of emotional knowledge and rapport. In W. Ickes (Ed.), *Empathic accuracy* (pp. 44–72). New York: Guilford.

Lipps, T. (1906). Das wissen von fremden Ichen. *PsycholUntersuch*, 1, 694–722.

Mathews, J. D. (1991). Empathy: A facial electromyographic study. Unpublished doctoral dissertation, New York University.

Mathews, J. D., Hoffman, M. L., & Cohen, B. H. (1991). Self-reports and experimental set predict facial responses to empathy-evoking stimuli. American Psychological Science meetings, Washington, DC, June 13.

Meltzoff, A. N. (1988). Infant imitation after a 1-week delay. *Developmental Psychology*, 24, 470–476.

Murphy, L. B. (1937). *Social behavior and child personality.* New York: Columbia University Press.

Oliner, S. P., & Oliner, P. M. (1988). *The altruistic personality.* New York: The Free Press.

O'Neil, J. (1999, April 6). A syndrome with a mix of skills and deficits. *New York Times*, pp. F1, F4.

O'Toole, R. & Dubin, R. (1968). Baby feeding and body sway: An experiment in George Herbert Mead's "taking the role of the other." *Journal of Social and Personality Psychology*, 10, 59–65.

Otten, C. A., Penner, L. A., & Altabe, M. N. (1991). An examination of therapists' and college students' willingness to help a psychologically distressed person. *Journal of Social and Clinical Psychology*, 10, 102–120.

Penner, L. A., Fritzsche, B. A., Craiger, J. P., & Freifeld, T. (1995). Measuring the prosocial personality. In J. N. Butcher & C. D. Spielberger (Eds.), *Advances in Personality Assessment* (Vol. 10). Hillsdale, NJ: Erlbaum.

Reissland, N. (1988). Neonatal imitation in the first hour of life: Observations in rural Nepal. *Developmental Psychology*, 24, 464–469.

Rogers, T. B., Kuiper, N. A., & Kirker, W. S. (1977). Self-reference and the encoding of personal information. *Journal of Personality and Social Psychology*, 35, 677–688.

Sacks, O. W. (1995). *An anthropologist on Mars.* New York: Knopf.

Scherer, K. (1982). Methods of research on verbal communication: Paradigms and parameters. In K. R. Scherer and P. Ekman (Eds.), *Handbook of methods in nonverbal behavior research* (pp. 136–198). New York: Cambridge University Press.

Shaw, L. L., Batson, C. D., & Todd, R. M. (1994). Empathy avoidance: Forestalling feeling for another in order to escape the motivational consequences. *Journal of Personality and Social Psychology, 67,* 879–887.

Smith, A. (1759/1976). *The theory of moral sentiments.* Oxford, England: Clarendon Press.

Stotland, E. (1969). Exploratory investigations of empathy. In L. Berkowitz (Ed.), *Advances in experimental social psychology* (Vol. 4, pp. 271–314). New York: Academic Press.

Strack, F., Martin, L. L., & Stepper, S. (1988). Inhibiting and facilitating conditions of the human smile: A nonobtrusive test of the facial feedback hypothesis. *Journal of Personal and Social Psychology, 54,* 768–776.

Sullivan, H. S. (1940). *Conceptions of modern psychiatry.* London: Havistock Press.

Termine, N. T., & Izard, C. E. (1988). Infants' responses to their mothers' expressions of joy and sadness. *Developmental Psychology, 24,* 223–229.

Weiss, R. F., Boyer, J. L., Lombardo, J. P., & Stitch, M. H. (1973). Altruistic drive and altruistic reinforcement. *Journal of Personality and Social Psychology, 25,* 390–400.

Wilson, B. J., & Cantor, J. (1985). *Journal of Experimental Child Psychology, 39,* 284–299.

Zahn-Waxler, C., Radke-Yarrow, M., Wagner, E., & Chapman, M. (1992). Development of concern for others. *Developmental Psychology, 28,* 126–136.

[2000]

1. Summarize the main components of Hoffman's theory of "empathic distress." How does this concept connect to morality?
2. What is the "bystander model"? Explain the concepts of "pluralistic ignorance" and "diffusion of responsibility" and how they relate to the "bystander model."
3. For what other works in this section would Hoffman's theory of "empathic distress" or the concept of the "bystander model" provide insightful context?

MICHEL DE MONTAIGNE

MICHEL DE MONTAIGNE *(1533–92) came into the world at the chateau of Montaigne in Perigord, France, the family seat established by his great-grandfather, a fish and wine merchant. His father, who married a woman of Jewish origin, was mayor of Bordeaux for two years. Montaigne himself was a child prodigy who was sent to the College of Guyenne at the age of six to be educated. He lived there for seven years, continuing studies in Latin begun at home with his tutor, adding logic, dialectics, and law, and became a member of the court. He married, had five daughters, only one of whom survived him, and at the age of thirty-seven, sold his position of counsellor and retired to his chateau. For the next seven years he worked on his* Essays, *first published in two volumes. During a lengthy journey through France and Italy to Rome, he was appointed mayor of Bordeaux, finally ending his tenure in absentia when the plague broke out. He continued to revise and add to his* Essays *until his death. Although he lived without the benefit of clergy for most of* *his life, he clasped hands during the elevation when a priest at his bedside was giving him the last rites, and the Church considered him to have achieved "a supreme act of faith."*

That our actions should be judged by our intentions*

Death, it is said, releases us from all our obligations. But I know some who have taken this saying in a special sense. King Henry the Seventh of England made an agreement with Don Philip, son of the Emperor Maximilian—or, to give him a higher title, father of the Emperor Charles V—that the said Philip should deliver into his hands his enemy the Duke of Suffolk of the White Rose, who had fled for refuge to the Netherlands, but this on condition that Henry should make no attempt on the life of the said Duke. But when the English king came to die, he commanded his son in his last will to put Suffolk to death immediately after his decease.

More recently in the tragedy of Count Horn and Count Egmont, which the Duke of Alva staged for us at Brussels, a certain incident occurred, among many others worthy of note. Count Egmont, upon whose pledge and assurance Count Horn had surrendered to the Duke, earnestly entreated that he might be the first to die, so that by his death he might be released from his obligation to Count Horn.

Death did not, in my opinion, excuse the English king from his promise, and I think that Egmont would have been excused from his even if he had not died. We cannot be held responsible beyond our strength and means, since the resulting events are quite outside our control and, in fact, we have power over nothing except our will; which is the basis upon which all rules concerning man's duty must of necessity be founded. Count Egmont, therefore, since he considered his whole mind and will to be pledged to his promise, though the power to keep it was not in his hands, would indubitably have been absolved from it even if he had outlived Count Horn. But the English king, having deliberately gone back on his word, cannot be excused merely because he postponed the performance of his treachery till after his death, any more than can the King of Egypt's mason in Herodotus, who kept the secret of his master's treasure faithfully so long as he lived, but revealed it to his children at his death.

I have known several men in my own time whose consciences have pricked them for retaining other men's property, and who have attempted in their wills to set things right after their decease. But it will not help them to fix a term in so urgent a matter; no attempt to redeem an injury at so small a cost and sacrifice to themselves will be of any avail. They owe something of what is really their own. And the more distressing and inconvenient the payment, the more just and meritorious is the restitution. Penitence must be felt as a weight.

5   It is even worse when a man who has concealed some spiteful feelings against a neighbour for the whole of his life gives vent to them in his last will.

*Michel de Montaigne, "That our actions should be judged by our intentions," *Essays*, trans. J.M. Cohen (Harmondsworth, Middlesex, England: Penguin Books, 1958, 1983), Book One, Chapter 7.

He is showing little regard for his own reputation in thus rousing the injured man's anger against his memory, and still less for his conscience in this failure to stifle his malice even in the presence of death, and in extending its life beyond his own. It is an unjust judge who postpones his judgements until the case is outside his jurisdiction.

I shall see to it, if I can, that my death makes no statement that my life has not made already.   [1575]

1. What is Montaigne's main claim?
2. What assumptions does Montaigne make?
3. Evaluate the effectiveness of the examples Montaigne provides to illustrate his argument.
4. How would Montaigne judge the actions of the citizens who walk away from (or remain in) Omelas, of Oedipus, and of the Sheridans?

MARK TWAIN

MARK TWAIN (pseudonym of Samuel Langhorne Clemens; 1835–1910), the fore-most American humorist, became a pilot on the Mississippi River after a boyhood spent in Hannibal, Missouri. He became a journalist and first won notice with his story, "The Celebrated Jumping Frog of Calaveras County." Innocents Abroad, *based on a trip to the Holy Land, was a popular success. He married in 1870 and had homes in New York and Connecticut, where he wrote his masterly depictions of boyhood,* The Adventures of Tom Sawyer *(1876) and* The Adventures of Huckleberry Finn *(1884). Other travel books, including* Life on the Mississippi, *and two novels,* The Prince and the Pauper *and* A Connecticut Yankee in King Arthur's Court, *were successful, but unfortunate investments plunged him into debt and he was forced to travel around the world giving lectures. The loss of his two daughters and his wife turned him into a bitter pessimist, but he continued to foster the public image of a courtly gentleman taking his daily strolls dressed in white, ready to smile and sign autographs for his many admirers.*

The Lowest Animal[1]*

In August, 1572, similar things were occurring in Paris and elsewhere in France. In this case it was Christian against Christian. The Roman Catholics, by previous concert, sprang a surprise upon the unprepared and unsuspecting Protestants, and butchered them by thousands—both sexes and all ages. This was the memorable St. Bartholomew's Day. At Rome the Pope and the Church gave public thanks to God when the happy news came.

During several centuries hundreds of heretics were burned at the stake every year because their religious opinions were not satisfactory to the Roman Church.

---

[1]This was to have been prefaced by newspaper clippings which, apparently, dealt with religious persecutions in Crete. The clippings have been lost. They probably referred to the Cretan revolt of 1897. [B. DV.] [Twain's note]

*Mark Twain, "The Lowest Animal," *Letters from the Earth* (New York: Harper & Row, 1962).

In all ages the savages of all lands have made the slaughtering of their neighboring brothers and the enslaving of their women and children the common business of their lives.

Hypocrisy, envy, malice, cruelty, vengefulness, seduction, rape, robbery, swindling, arson, bigamy, adultery, and the oppression and humiliation of the poor and the helpless in all ways have been and still are more or less common among both the civilized and uncivilized peoples of the earth.

5 For many centuries "the common brotherhood of man" has been urged—on Sundays—and "patriotism" on Sundays and weekdays both. Yet patriotism *contemplates the opposite of a common brotherhood.*

Woman's equality with man has never been conceded by any people, ancient or modern, civilized or savage.

I have been studying the traits and dispositions of the "lower animals" (so-called), and contrasting them with the traits and dispositions of man. I find the result humiliating to me. For it obliges me to renounce my allegiance to the Darwinian theory of the Ascent of Man from the Lower Animals; since it now seems plain to me that that theory ought to be vacated in favor of a new and truer one, this new and truer one to be named the *De*scent of Man from the Higher Animals.

In proceeding toward this unpleasant conclusion I have not guessed or speculated or conjectured, but have used what is commonly called the scientific method. That is to say, I have subjected every postulate that presented itself to the crucial test of actual experiment, and have adopted it or rejected it according to the result. Thus I verified and established each step of my course in its turn before advancing to the next. These experiments were made in the London Zoological Gardens, and covered many months of painstaking and fatiguing work.

Before particularizing any of the experiments, I wish to state one or two things which seem to more properly belong in this place than further along. This in the interest of clearness. The massed experiments established to my satisfaction certain generalizations, to wit:

10 1. That the human race is of one distinct species. It exhibits slight variations—in color, stature, mental caliber, and so on—due to climate, environment, and so forth; but it is a species by itself, and not to be confounded with any other.

2. That the quadrupeds are a distinct family, also. This family exhibits variations—in color, size, food preferences and so on; but it is a family by itself.

3. That the other families—the birds, the fishes, the insects, the reptiles, etc.—are more or less distinct, also. They are in the procession. They are links in the chain which stretches down from the higher animals to man at the bottom.

Some of my experiments were quite curious. In the course of my reading I had come across a case where, many years ago, some hunters on our Great Plains organized a buffalo hunt for the entertainment of an English earl—that, and to provide some fresh meat for his larder. They had charming sport. They killed seventy-two of those great animals; and ate part of one of them and left the seventy-one to rot. In order to determine the difference between an anaconda and an earl—if any—I caused seven young calves to be turned into the anaconda's cage. The grateful reptile immediately crushed one of them and swallowed it, then lay back satisfied. It showed no further interest in the calves, and no disposition to harm them. I tried this experiment with other anacondas; always with the same result. The fact stood proven that the difference between an earl and an anaconda is that the earl is cruel and the anaconda isn't; and that the earl wantonly destroys what he has no use for, but the anaconda doesn't. This seemed to suggest that the anaconda was not descended from the earl. It also seemed to suggest that the earl was descended from the anaconda, and had lost a good deal in the transition.

I was aware that many men who have accumulated more millions of money than they can ever use have shown a rabid hunger for more, and have not scrupled to cheat the ignorant and the helpless out of their poor servings in order to partially appease that appetite. I furnished a hundred different kinds of wild and tame animals the opportunity to accumulate vast stores of food, but none of them would do it. The squirrels and bees and certain birds made accumulations, but stopped when they had gathered a winter's supply, and could not be persuaded to add to it either honestly or by chicane. In order to bolster up a tottering reputation the ant pretended to store up supplies, but I was not deceived. I know the ant. These experiments convinced me that there is this difference between man and the higher animals: he is avaricious and miserly, they are not.

In the course of my experiments I convinced myself that among the animals man is the only one that harbors insults and injuries, broods over them, waits till a chance offers, then takes revenge. The passion of revenge is unknown to the higher animals.   15

Roosters keep harems, but it is by consent of their concubines; therefore no wrong is done. Men keep harems, but it is by brute force, privileged by atrocious laws which the other sex were allowed no hand in making. In this matter man occupies a far lower place than the rooster.

Cats are loose in their morals, but not consciously so. Man, in his descent from the cat, has brought the cat's looseness with him but has left the unconsciousness behind—the saving grace which excuses the cat. The cat is innocent, man is not.

Indecency, vulgarity, obscenity—these are strictly confined to man; he invented them. Among the higher animals there is no trace of them. They hide nothing; they are not ashamed. Man, with his soiled mind, covers himself. He will not even enter a drawing room with his breast and back naked, so alive are he and his mates to indecent suggestion. Man is "The Animal that Laughs." But so does the monkey, as Mr. Darwin pointed out; and so does the Australian bird that is called the laughing jackass. No—Man is the Animal that Blushes. He is the only one that does it—or has occasion to.

At the head of this article we see how "three monks were burnt to death" a few days ago, and a prior "put to death with atrocious cruelty." Do we inquire into the details? No; or we should find out that the prior was subjected to unprintable mutilations. Man—when he is a North American Indian—gouges out his prisoner's eyes; when he is King John, with a nephew to render untroublesome, he uses a red-hot iron; when he is a religious zealot dealing with heretics in the Middle Ages, he skins his captive alive and scatters salt on his back; in the first Richard's time he shuts up a multitude of Jew families in a tower and sets fire to it; in Columbus's time he captures a family of Spanish Jews and—but *that* is not printable; in our day in England a man is fined ten shillings for beating his mother nearly to death with a chair, and another man is fined forty shillings for having four pheasant eggs in his possession without being able to satisfactorily explain how he got them. Of all the animals, man is the only one that is cruel. He is the only one that inflicts pain for the pleasure of doing it. It is a trait that is not known to the higher animals. The cat plays with the frightened mouse; but she has this excuse, that she does not know that the mouse is suffering. The cat is moderate—unhumanly moderate: she only scares the mouse, she does not hurt it; she doesn't dig out its eyes, or tear off its skin, or drive splinters under its nails—man-fashion; when she is done playing with it she makes a sudden meal of it and puts it out of its trouble. Man is the Cruel Animal. He is alone in that distinction.

20   The higher animals engage in individual fights, but never in organized masses. Man is the only animal that deals in that atrocity of atrocities, War. He is the only one that gathers his brethren about him and goes forth in cold blood and with calm pulse to exterminate his kind. He is the only animal that for sordid wages will march out, as the Hessians did in our Revolution, and as the boyish Prince Napoleon did in the Zulu war, and help to slaughter strangers of his own species who have done him no harm and with whom he has no quarrel.

Man is the only animal that robs his helpless fellow of his country—takes possession of it and drives him out of it or destroys him. Man has done this in all the ages. There is not an acre of ground on the globe that is in possession of its rightful owner, or that has not been taken away from owner after owner, cycle after cycle, by force and bloodshed.

Man is the only Slave. And he is the only animal who enslaves. He has always been a slave in one form or another, and has always held other slaves in bondage under him in one way or another. In our day he is always some man's slave for wages, and does that man's work; and this slave has other slaves under him for minor wages, and they do *his* work. The higher animals are the only ones who exclusively do their own work and provide their own living.

Man is the only Patriot. He sets himself apart in his own country, under his own flag, and sneers at the other nations, and keeps multitudinous uniformed assassins on hand at heavy expense to grab slices of other people's countries, and keep *them* from grabbing slices of *his*. And in the intervals between campaigns he washes the blood off his hands and works for "the universal brotherhood of man"—with his mouth.

Man is the Religious Animal. He is the only Religious Animal. He is the only animal that has the True Religion—several of them. He is the only animal that loves his neighbor as himself, and cuts his throat if his theology isn't straight. He has made a graveyard of the globe in trying his honest best to smooth his brother's path to happiness and heaven. He was at it in the time of the Caesars, he was at it in Mahomet's time, he was at it in the time of the Inquisition, he was at it in France a couple of centuries, he was at it in England in Mary's day, he has been at it ever since he first saw the light, he is at it today in Crete—as per the telegrams quoted above—he will be at it somewhere else tomorrow. The higher animals have no religion. And we are told that they are going to be left out, in the Hereafter. I wonder why? It seems questionable taste.

Man is the Reasoning Animal. Such is the claim. I think it is open to dispute. Indeed, my experiments have proven to me that he is the Unreasoning Animal. Note his history, as sketched above. It seems plain to me that whatever he is he is *not* a reasoning animal. His record is the fantastic record of a maniac. I consider that the strongest count against his intelligence is the fact that with that record back of him he blandly sets himself up as the head animal of the lot: whereas by his own standards he is the bottom one.

In truth, man is incurably foolish. Simple things which the other animals easily learn, he is incapable of learning. Among my experiments was this. In an hour I taught a cat and a dog to be friends. I put them in a cage. In another hour I taught them to be friends with a rabbit. In the course of two days I was able to add a fox, a goose, a squirrel and some doves. Finally a monkey. They lived together in peace; even affectionately.

Next, in another cage I confined an Irish Catholic from Tipperary, and as soon as he seemed tame I added a Scotch Presbyterian from Aberdeen. Next a Turk from Constantinople; a Greek Christian from Crete; an Armenian; a Methodist from the wilds of Arkansas; a Buddhist from China; a Brahman from Benares. Finally, a Salvation Army Colonel from Wapping. Then I stayed away two whole days. When I came back to note results, the cage of Higher Animals was all right, but in the other there was but a chaos of gory odds and ends of turbans and fezzes and plaids and bones and flesh—not a specimen left alive. These Reasoning Animals had disagreed on a theological detail and carried the matter to a Higher Court.

One is obliged to concede that in true loftiness of character, Man cannot claim to approach even the meanest of the Higher Animals. It is plain that he is constitutionally incapable of approaching that altitude; that he is constitutionally afflicted with a Defect which must make such approach forever impossible, for it is manifest that this defect is permanent in him, indestructible, ineradicable.

I find this Defect to be *the Moral Sense.* He is the only animal that has it. It is the secret of his degradation. It is the quality *which enables him to do wrong.* It has no other office. It is incapable of performing any other function. It could never have been intended to perform any other. Without it, man could do no wrong. He would rise at once to the level of the Higher Animals.

Since the Moral Sense has but the one office, the one capacity—to enable man to do wrong—it is plainly without value to him. It is as valueless to him as is disease. In fact, it manifestly *is* a disease. *Rabies* is bad, but it is not so bad as this disease. Rabies enables a man to do a thing which he could not do when in a healthy state: kill his neighbor with a poisonous bite. No one is the better man for having rabies. The Moral Sense enables a man to do wrong. It enables him to do wrong in a thousand ways. Rabies is an innocent disease, compared to the Moral Sense. No one, then, can be the better man for having the Moral Sense.

What, now, do we find the Primal Curse to have been? Plainly what it was in the beginning: the infliction upon man of the Moral Sense; the ability to distinguish good from evil; and with it, necessarily, the ability to *do* evil; for there can be no evil act without the presence of consciousness of it in the doer of it.

And so I find that we have descended and degenerated, from some far ancestor—some microscopic atom wandering at its pleasure between the mighty horizons of a drop of water perchance—insect by insect, animal by animal, reptile by reptile, down the long highway of smirchless innocence, till we have reached the bottom stage of development—namable as the Human Being. Below us—nothing. Nothing but the Frenchman.

There is only one possible stage below the Moral Sense; that is the Immoral Sense. The Frenchman has it. Man is but little lower than the angels. This definitely locates him. He is between the angels and the French.

Man seems to be a rickety poor sort of a thing, any way you take him; a kind of British Museum of infirmities and inferiorities. He is always undergoing repairs. A machine that was as unreliable as he is would have no market. On top of his specialty—the Moral Sense—are piled a multitude of minor infirmities; such a multitude, indeed, that one may broadly call them countless. The higher animals get their teeth without pain or inconvenience. Man gets his through months and months of cruel torture; and at a time of life when he is but ill able to bear it. As soon as he has got them they must all be pulled out again, for they were of no value in the first place, not worth the loss of a night's rest. The second set will answer for a while, by being reinforced occasionally with rubber or plugged up with gold; but he will never get a set which can really be depended on till a dentist makes him one. This set will be called "false" teeth—as if he had ever worn any other kind.

In a wild state—a natural state—the Higher Animals have a few diseases; diseases of little consequence; the main one is old age. But man starts in as a child and lives on diseases till the end, as a regular diet. He has mumps, measles, whooping cough, croup, tonsilitis, diphtheria, scarlet fever, almost as a matter of course. Afterward, as he goes along, his life continues to be threatened at every turn: by colds, coughs, asthma, bronchitis, itch, cholera, cancer, consumption, yellow fever, bilious fever, typhus fevers, hay fever, ague, chilblains, piles, inflammation of the entrails, indigestion, toothache, earache, deafness, dumbness, blindness, influenza, chicken pox, cowpox, smallpox, liver complaint, constipation, bloody flux, warts, pimples, boils, carbuncles, abscesses, bunions, corns, tumors, fistulas, pneumonia, softening of the brain, melancholia and fifteen other kinds of insanity; dysentery, jaundice, diseases of the heart, the bones, the skin, the scalp, the spleen, the kidneys, the nerves, the brain, the blood; scrofula, paralysis, leprosy, neuralgia, palsy, fits, headache, thirteen kinds of rheumatism, forty-six of gout, and a formidable supply of gross and unprintable disorders of one sort and another. Also—but why continue the list? The mere names of the agents appointed to keep this shackly machine out of repair would hide him from sight if printed on his body in the smallest type known to the founder's art. He is but a basket of pestilent corruption provided for the support and entertainment of swarming armies of bacilli—armies commissioned to rot him and destroy him, and each army equipped with a special detail of the work. The process of waylaying him, persecuting him, rotting him, killing him, begins with his first breath, and there is no mercy, no pity, no truce till he draws his last one.

Look at the workmanship of him, in certain of its particulars. What are his tonsils for? They perform no useful function; they have no value. They have no business there. They are but a trap. They have but the one office, the one industry: to provide tonsilitis and quinsy and such things for the possessor of them. And what is the vermiform appendix for? It has no value; it cannot perform any useful service. It is but an ambuscaded enemy whose sole interest in life is to lie in wait for stray grapeseeds and employ them to breed strangulated hernia. And what are the male's mammals for? For business, they are out of the question; as an ornament, they are a mistake. What is his beard for? It performs no useful function; it is a nuisance and a discomfort; all nations hate it; all nations persecute it with the razor. And because it is a nuisance and a discomfort, Nature never allows the supply of it to fall short, in any man's case, between puberty and the grave. You never see a man bald-headed on his chin. But his hair! It is a graceful ornament, it is a comfort, it is the best of all protections against certain perilous ailments, man prizes it above emeralds and rubies. And because of these things Nature puts it on, half the time, so that it won't stay. Man's sight, smell, hearing, sense of locality—how inferior they are. The condor sees a corpse at five miles; man has no telescope that can do it. The bloodhound follows a scent that is two days old. The robin hears the earthworm burrowing his course under the ground. The cat, deported in a closed basket, finds its way home again through twenty miles of country which it has never seen.

Certain functions lodged in the other sex perform in a lamentably inferior way as compared with the performance of the same functions in the Higher Animals. In the human being, menstruation, gestation and parturition are terms which stand for horrors. In the Higher Animals these things are hardly even inconveniences.

For style, look at the Bengal tiger—that ideal of grace, beauty, physical perfection, majesty. And then look at Man—that poor thing. He is the Animal of the Wig, the Trepanned Skull, the Ear Trumpet, the Glass Eye, the Pasteboard Nose, the Porcelain Teeth, the Silver Windpipe, the Wooden Leg—a creature that is mended and patched all over, from top to bottom. If he can't get renewals of his bric-a-brac in the next world, what will he look like?

He has just one stupendous superiority. In his intellect he is supreme. The Higher Animals cannot touch him there. It is curious, it is noteworthy, that no heaven has ever been offered him wherein his one sole superiority was provided with a chance to enjoy itself. Even when he himself has imagined a heaven, he has never made provision in it for intellectual joys. It is a striking omission. It seems a tacit confession that heavens are provided for the Higher Animals alone. This is matter for thought; and for serious thought. And it is full of a grim suggestion: that we are not as important, perhaps, as we had all along supposed we were.

[1909]

1. As Bernard DeVoto (*Letters from the Earth,* New York: Harper & Row, 1962, p. 222) points out in a footnote to his edition of Twain's "The Lowest Animal," this essay was intended to follow newspaper articles about the 1897 revolt in Crete. Locate information about this historical event. How does such information provide greater context for the argument Twain sets forth in this essay?

2. What is Twain's claim? Where does he state it?

3. What is the scientific method Twain refers to in paragraph 8? Why does he invoke the scientific method here? How serious is Twain about his use of the scientific method to gather data for his argument? How can you tell?

4. What does Twain argue is humanity's greatest "Defect"? Why? How might you question his argument on this issue?

5. Early in the essay, Twain states that "patriotism *contemplates the opposite of a common brotherhood.*" What does he mean by this assertion? What historical or contemporary events could you use to support this statement? To refute it?

CHAPTER SEVENTEEN

Nature

INTRODUCTION

As human beings, we would be nothing without the natural world, nothing without the physical laws and flora and fauna of our earth. The natural world is a marvelous gift and preserving it can sometimes be a daunting responsibility for modern humanity. Nature is more than something that we merely observe or admire, or something from which we collect merely scientific data. Nature informs and shapes humanity. We are bound to the natural world; moreover, we have arisen from the natural world and are a part of and akin to it. As human beings, we are both stronger and weaker than nature; we are nature's benefactors and beneficiaries as we are the earth's protectors and destroyers.

The selections in this cluster explore issues about the relationship between nature and humankind. There will be opportunities for you to think about the power we have over the natural world, what we seek from it, and what unique challenges and questions we face as its keepers.

POETRY

A.R. AMMONS

A[RCHIE] R[ANDOLPH] AMMONS *(1926–2001) was born in North Carolina and started writing poetry when he was serving aboard a Navy destroyer escort in the South Pacific in World War II. When he came home, he attended Wake Forest University and then worked as a real estate salesman, an editor, and an executive in his father's glass company. He taught at Cornell University in Ithaca, New York, from 1964 to 1998. He published thirty books of poetry. His writing earned such prizes as the National Book Award, the National Book Critics Circle Award for Poetry, and the Bollingen Prize, and he won fellowships from the Guggenheim and MacArthur Foundations and the American Academy of Arts and Letters. Some of his books are* Glare *(1997),* Brink Road *(1996),* The North Carolina Poems *(1994),* Garbage *(1993),* The Really Short Poems *(1991), and* Sumerian Vistas *(1987). There are five volumes of selected poems as well as many earlier books and a volume of prose selections edited by Zofia Burr called* Set in Motion: Essays, Interviews, and Dialogues *(1996).*

Still

I said I will find what is lowly
  and put the roots of my identity
  down there:
each day I'll wake up
5 and find the lowly nearby,
  a handy focus and reminder,
a ready measure of my significance,
the voice by which I would be heard,
the wills, the kinds of selfishness
10 I could
freely adopt as my own:

but though I have looked everywhere,
  I can find nothing
  to give myself to:
15 everything is

magnificent with existence, is in
surfeit of glory:
nothing is diminished,
nothing has been diminished for me:
20 I said what is more lowly than the grass:
  ah, underneath,
  a ground-crust of dry-burnt moss:
  I looked at it closely
and said this can be my habitat: but
25 nestling in I
found
  below the brown exterior
  green mechanisms beyond intellect
awaiting resurrection in rain: so I got up
30 and ran saying there is nothing lowly in the universe:
I found a beggar:
he had stumps for legs: nobody was paying
him any attention: everybody went on by:
  I nestled in and found his life:
35 there, love shook his body like a devastation:

I said
>   though I have looked everywhere
>   I can find nothing lowly
>   in the universe:

I whirled through transfigurations up and down,   40
transfigurations of size and shape and place:
>   at one sudden point came still,
>   stood in wonder:
moss, beggar, weed, tick, pine, self, magnificent
>   with being!   [1986] 45

1. What is the narrator's stated goal in this poem? What cultural resonance
   does it have? Does he achieve it?
2. When the narrator takes his search to the grass (l. 20), lying down to
   examine it, he recalls nineteenth-century American poet Walt Whitman,
   whose major book is called *Leaves of Grass*. Here are a few passages from his
   poem, "Song of Myself." How do they reflect on Ammons's "Still"?

   > I loafe and invite my Soul;
   > I lean and loafe at my ease, observing a spear of summer grass.
   >   (Section 1, ll. 4–5.)

   > A child said, What is the grass? fetching it to me with full hands;
   > How could I answer the child? I do not know what it is, any more than he.

   > I guess it must be the flag of my disposition, out of hopeful green stuff woven.

   > Or I guess it is the handkerchief of the Lord,
   > A scented gift and remembrancer, designedly dropt,
   > Bearing the owner's name someway in the corners, that we may see and
   >   remark, and say Whose?

   > Or I guess the grass is itself a child, the produced babe of the vegetation.

   > Or I guess it is a uniform hieroglyphic;
   > And it means, Sprouting alike in broad zones and narrow zones,
   > Growing among black folks as among white;
   > Kanuck, Tuckahoe, Congressman, Cuff, I give them the same, I receive
   >   them the same.

   > And now it seems to me the beautiful uncut hair of graves.
   >   (Section 6, ll. 1–12.)

   > I believe a leaf of grass is no less than the journey-work of the stars,
   > And the pismire is equally perfect, and a grain of sand, and the egg of the wren,
   > And the tree-toad is a chef-d'oeuvre for the highest,
   > And the running blackberry would adorn the parlors of heaven,
   > And the narrowest hinge in my hand puts to scorn all machinery,
   > And the cow crunching with depress'd head surpasses any statue,
   > And a mouse is miracle enough to stagger sextillions of infidels.
   >   (Section 31, ll. 1–7.)

3. What is the significance of the title to the overall meaning of the poem?

◎◎◎

WILLIAM BLAKE

WILLIAM BLAKE *(1757–1827) was born in London to a prosperous shopkeeper and was educated at home by his mother until he was sent to drawing school. From an early age he was subject to visions of angels and various historical figures. At fourteen he was apprenticed to an engraver and then went to the Royal Academy School, producing watercolors and engraved illustrations for magazines. After his marriage, he taught his wife to be his assistant and opened a print shop, which subsequently failed. A poet from the age of twelve, Blake published his* Poetical Sketches, Songs of Innocence, *and* Songs of Experience, *attracting the attention of many members of the artistic and literary world in England and France at the end of the century. He began to publish his political and social criticism, which was radical, visionary, and prophetic. He hated the Industrial Revolution and espoused radical causes. By 1800 he knew many of the literati and members of the art world and became the protégé of the wealthy William Hayley. He continued to produce his poems, aphorisms, and engravings into his seventies and died debt-free, leaving behind him many admirers, including Wordsworth, who declared him to be mad but a genius. Although he was barely understood in his lifetime, his influence on poetry and art has been felt by the Pre-Raphaelites, W. B. Yeats, the neo-Romantics, the Underground movement of the 60s, and beyond.*

The Tyger

Tyger Tyger. burning bright,
In the forests of the night;
What immortal hand or eye
Could frame thy fearful symmetry?

5 In what distant deeps or skies
Burnt the fire of thine eyes?
On what wings dare he aspire?
What the hand, dare seize the fire?

And what shoulder, & what art,
10 Could twist the sinews of thy heart?
And when thy heart began to beat.
What dread hand? & what dread feet?

What the hammer? what the chain,
In what furnace was thy brain?
15 What the anvil? what dread grasp
Dare its deadly terrors clasp?

When the stars threw down their spears
And watered heaven with their tears:
Did he smile His work to see?
20 Did he who made the lamb make thee?

Tyger Tyger burning bright,
In the forests of the night:
What immortal hand or eye,
Dare frame thy fearful symmetry?   [1794]

1. What lesson does the narrator take from his appreciation of the tiger?
2. What is "fearful" about symmetry?
3. This poem is from Blake's collection, *Songs of Innocence and of Experience*,
   where it is paired with this poem about a lamb, spoken in the voice of a child:

   > Little Lamb, who made thee
   > Dost thou know who made thee
   > Gave thee life & bid thee feed.
   > By the stream & o'er the mead;
   > Gave thee clothing of delight,
   > Softest clothing woolly bright;
   > Gave thee such a tender voice,
   > Making all the vales rejoice:
   > > Little Lamb who made thee
   > > Dost thou know who made thee
   >
   > > Little Lamb I'll tell thee,
   > > Little Lamb I'll tell thee;
   > He is called by thy name,
   > For he calls himself a Lamb:
   > He is meek & he is mild,
   > He became a little child
   > I a child & thou a lamb,
   > We are called by His name,
   > > Little Lamb God bless thee,
   > > Little Lamb God bless thee.

   How do the two poems relate to each other?
4. Compare the attitude toward natural creatures in this poem to that in
   Galway Kinnell's "St. Francis and the Sow" (p. 1264), Sylvia Plath's "Black
   Rook in Rainy Weather" (p. 1270), and Richard Wilbur's "Mayflies" (p. 360).

RICHARD EBERHART

RICHARD EBERHART *(1904–) was educated at Dartmouth College, the University
of Cambridge, and Harvard University. His first book of poems was* A Bravery of
Earth. *He became tutor to the son of King Prajadhipok of Siam (now Thailand) and
then taught at several American universities, particularly Dartmouth. He was consultant in poetry at the Library of Congress and in 1962 was co-winner with John
Hall Wheelock of the Bollingen Prize in Poetry.* Collected Poems, 1930–1976 *was
published in 1976.* Of Poetry and Poets *is one of his books of criticism.*

On Shooting Particles Beyond the World

"White Sands, N. M., Dec. 18 (UP). 'We first throw a little something into the skies,'
Zwicky said. 'Then a little more, then a shipload of instruments—then ourselves.'"

On this day man's disgust is known
Incipient before but now full blown
With minor wars of major consequence,
Duly building empirical delusions.

5 Now this little creature in a rage
Like new-born infant screaming compleat angler°
Objects to the whole globe itself
And with a vicious lunge he throws

Metal particles beyond the orbit of mankind.
10 Beethoven shaking his fist at death,
A giant dignity in human terms,
Is nothing to this imbecile metal fury.

The world is too much for him. The green
Of earth is not enough, love's deities.
15 Peaceful intercourse, happiness of nations,
The wild animal dazzled on the desert.

If the maniac would only realize
The comforts of his padded cell
He would have penetrated the
20 Impenetrability of the spiritual.

It is not intelligent to go too far.
How he frets that he can't go too!
But his particles would maim a star,
His free-floating bombards rock the moon.

25 Good Boy! We pat the baby to eructate,
We pat him then for eructation.°
Good Boy Man! Your innards are put out,
From now all space will be your vomitorium.

The atom bomb accepted this world,
30 Its hatred of man blew death in his face.
But not content, he'll send slugs beyond,
His particles of intellect will spit on the sun.

Not God he'll catch, in the mystery of space.
He flaunts his own out-cast state
35 As he throws his imperfections outward bound
And his shout that gives a hissing sound.

[1960]

⁶**compleat angler** an allusion to Izaak Walton's book on fly fishing, *The Compleat Angler*
²⁶**eructation** belch, burp

1. This poem was written before the launch of the Soviet satellite Sputnik on October 4, 1957, yet the comment from Zwicky seems to have allowed Eberhart to foresee some of the ramifications of space exploration. What is his attitude towards it? What is the tone of the poem? How does the poem's imagery contribute to the tone and theme?

2. What is the alternate course of action the narrator would prefer mankind to take?

3. Line 6 alludes to seventeenth-century writer Izaak Walton's book *The Compleat Angler*. Find out enough about the book to make a hypothesis about how the allusion works in the poem.

4. Here is Shakespeare's Sonnet 29:

> When in disgrace with Fortune and men's eyes,
>   I all alone beweep my outcast state,
>   And trouble deaf heaven with my bootless cries,
>   And look upon my self and curse my fate,
>   Wishing me like to one more rich in hope,
>   Featured like him, like him with friends possessed,
>   Desiring this man's art, and that man's scope,
>   With what I most enjoy contented least,
>   Yet in these thoughts my self almost despising,
>   Haply I think on thee, and then my state,
>   (Like to the lark at break of day arising
>   From sullen earth) sings hymns at heaven's gate,
>   For thy sweet love remembered such wealth brings,
>   That then I scorn to change my state with kings.

Do you think Eberhart's phrase, "his own out-cast state" (l. 34) contains an allusion to the sonnet? If so, what does it accomplish in the poem? To what else does this line allude?

JAMES WELDON JOHNSON

(For biographical notes, see p. 753.)

Deep in the Quiet Wood

Are you bowed down in heart?
Do you but hear the clashing discords and the din of life?
Then come away, come to the peaceful wood,
Here bathe your soul in silence. Listen! Now,
From out the palpitating solitude   5
Do you not catch, yet faint, elusive strains?
They are above, around, within you, everywhere.
Silently listen! Clear, and still more clear, they come.
They bubble up in rippling notes, and swell in singing tones,

10 Not let your soul run the whole gamut of the wondrous scale
Until responsive to the tonic chord,
It touches the diapason° of God's grand cathedral organ,
Filling earth for you heavenly peace
And holy harmonies.   [1935]

¹²**diapason** an outpouring of harmonious sound

1. What is the narrator's purpose in this poem? What is his main claim?
2. How do the images work to support his claim?
3. What is meant by "palpitating solitude" (l. 5)? How does this image work in the poem?
4. What does Johnson gain by his choices for the form of the poem? How do they contribute to its meaning?

GALWAY KINNELL

(For biographical notes, see p. 257.)

The Bear

1.
In late winter
I sometimes glimpse bits of steam
coming up from
some fault in the old snow
5   and bend close and see it is lung-colored
and put it down my nose
and know
the chilly, enduring odor of bear.

2.
I take a wolf's rib and whittle
10 it sharp at both ends
and coil it up
and freeze it in blubber and place it out
on the fairway of the bears.

And when it has vanished
15 I move out on the bear tracks,
roaming in circles
until I come to the first, tentative, dark
splash on the earth.

And I set out
20 running, following the splashes
of blood wandering over the world,
at the cut, gashed resting places
I stop and rest,

at the crawl-marks
where he lay out on his belly   25
to overpass some stretch of bauchy° ice
I lie out
dragging myself forward with bear-knives in my fists.

3.

On the third day I begin to starve,
at nightfall I bend down as I knew I would   30
at a turd sopped in blood,
and hesitate, and pick it up,
and thrust it in my mouth, and gnash it down,
and rise
and go on running.   35

4.

On the seventh day,
living by now on bear blood alone,
I can see his upturned carcass far out ahead, a scraggled,
steamy hulk,
the heavy fur riffling in the wind.   40

I come up to him
and stare at the narrow-spaced, petty eyes,
the dismayed
face laid back on the shoulder, the nostrils
flared, catching   45
perhaps the first taint of me as he
died.

I hack
a ravine in his thigh, and eat and drink,
and tear him down his whole length   50
and open him and climb in
and close him up after me, against the wind,
and sleep.

5.

And dream
of lumbering flatfooted   55
over the tundra,
stabbed twice from within,
splattering a trail behind me,
splattering it out no matter which way I lurch,
no matter which parabola of bear-transcendence,   60
which dance of solitude I attempt,
which gravity-clutched leap,
which trudge, which groan.

---

²⁶**bauchy** In the *Oxford English Dictionary, bauch* means "weak, poor, pithless, without substance or stamina; indifferent, sorry, shaky."

6.

Until one day I totter and fall—
65 fall on this
stomach that has tried so hard to keep up,
to digest the blood as it leaked in,
to break up
and digest the bone itself: and now the breeze
70 blows over me, blows off
the hideous belches of ill-digested bear blood
and rotted stomach
and the ordinary, wretched odor of bear,

blows across
75 my sore, lolled tongue a song
or screech, until I think I must rise up
and dance. And I lie still.

7.

I awaken I think. Marshlights
reappear, geese
80 come trailing again up the flyway.
In her ravine under old snow the dam-bear
lies, licking
lumps of smeared fur
and drizzly eyes into shapes
85 with her tongue. And one
hairy-soled trudge stuck out before me,
the next groaned out,
the next,
the next,
90 the rest of my days I spend
wandering: wondering
what, anyway,
was that sticky infusion, that rank flow of blood, that poetry, by which I lived?

[1967]

1. This is a narrative poem. What are the themes suggested by the story it tells?
   What kind of narrator tells it? What difference does the narrator make?
2. What is the meaning of the last line of the poem?
3. How does the poem's word choice affect its meaning?

St. Francis and the Sow°

The bud
stands for all things,
even those things that don't flower,

Title**St. Francis** probably the medieval Italian founder of the order of Franciscan monks
based on obedience, poverty, and chastity, St. Francis of Assisi, who died in 1226. He was
known for his sympathy with animals.

for everything flowers, from within, of self-blessing;
though sometimes it is necessary   5
to reteach a thing its loveliness,
to put a hand on its brow
of the flower
and retell it in words and in touch
it is lovely   10
until it flowers again from within, of self-blessing;
as St. Francis
put his hand on the creased forehead
of the sow, and told her in words and in touch
blessings of earth on the sow, and the sow   15
began remembering all down her thick length,
from the earthen snout all the way
through the fodder and slops to the spiritual curl of the tail,
from the hard spininess spiked out from the spine
down through the great broken heart   20
to the sheer blue milken dreaminess spurting and shuddering
from the fourteen teats into the fourteen mouths sucking
    and blowing beneath them:
the long, perfect loveliness of sow.   [1980]

1. Is this a religious poem?
2. Characterize the language of this poem.

PHILIP LARKIN

PHILIP LARKIN *(1922–85) led the quiet life of a librarian but wrote tough,*
unsparing memorable poems and became the preeminent poet of his generation. He
and his cohort members of "The Movement," a group of writers who rejected the
neo-Romanticism of Yeats and Dylan Thomas, concentrated, like their mentor
Thomas Hardy, on intense personal emotion without sentimentality or self-pity.
His searing and often mocking wit only set off the dark vision and obsession with
mortality and solitude prevalent in his work. Deeply antisocial and a great lover of
American jazz, he died in Hull, England, in 1985.

Going, Going

I thought it would last my time—
The sense that, beyond the town,
There would always be fields and farms,
Where the village louts could climb
Such trees as were not cut down;   5
I knew there'd be false alarms

In the papers about old streets
And split level shopping, but some
Have always been left so far;
10 And when the old part retreats
As the bleak high-risers come
We can always escape in the car.

Things are tougher than we are, just
As earth will always respond
15 However we mess it about;
Chuck filth in the sea, if you must:
The tides will be clean beyond.
—But what do I feel now? Doubt?

Or age, simply? The crowd
20 Is young in the M1° cafe;
Their kids are screaming for more—
More houses, more parking allowed,
More caravan sites, more pay.
On the Business Page, a score
25 Of spectacled grins approve
Some takeover bid that entails
Five per cent profit (and ten
Per cent more in the estuaries): move
Your works to the unspoilt dales
30 (Grey area grants)! And when

You try to get near the sea
In summer . . .
        It seems, just now,
To be happening so very fast;
35 Despite all the land left free
For the first time I feel somehow
That it isn't going to last,

That before I snuff it, the whole
Boiling will be bricked in
40 Except for the tourist parts—
First slum of Europe: a role
It won't be hard to win,
With a cast of crooks and tarts.

And that will be England gone,
45 The shadows, the meadows, the lanes,
The guildhalls, the carved choirs.
There'll be books; it will linger on
In galleries; but all that remains
For us will be concrete and tyres.

²⁰**M1** highway in England

Most things are never meant. 50
This won't be, most likely; but greeds
And garbage are too thick-strewn
To be swept up now, or invent
Excuses that make them all needs.
I just think it will happen, soon. [1972] 55

1. What is the narrator's worry in the poem? What is the "it" of l. 1? Why has he lost the confidence he refers to in l. 1?
2. Who's to blame?
3. What do the word choice and form contribute to the poem?
4. What is the tone of the poem?

MARY OLIVER

MARY OLIVER *(1935–), born in Cleveland, Ohio, attended Ohio State University and Vassar College. She worked for a time as secretary to Edna St. Vincent Millay's sister and published her own volume of poems in 1963. Her childhood experiences became the basis for more poems in* The River Styx, Ohio, and Other Poems. *More poetry collections followed, along with the Pulitzer Prize, the National Book Award, and other honors. Oliver has also written essays on other poets.*

Rice

It grew in the black mud.
It grew under the tiger's orange paws.
Its stems thinner than candles, and as straight.
Its leaves like feathers of egrets, but green.
The grains cresting, wanting to burst. 5
Oh, blood of the tiger.

I don't want you just to sit down at the table.
I don't want you just to eat, and be content.
I want you to walk out into the fields
where the water is shining, and the rice has risen. 10
I want you to stand there, far from the white tablecloth.
I want you to fill your hands with mud, like a blessing. [1992]

1. What is the purpose of the images in the first stanza?
2. How is the first stanza related to the second?

SIMON ORTIZ

SIMON ORTIZ *(1941–), born and educated in New Mexico, went to college to become a chemist but found he was more interested in writing. He quit college to gain life experience, joining the Army and falling prey to alcoholism. His time in VA hospitals fighting* *that disease was central to his writing. He attended the Iowa Writers' School, receiving a Master of Fine Arts degree, and has since taught creative writing and Native American literature at three universities. His work is infused with Indian history, mythology, and philosophy and is rooted in the oral tradition of the Native American storytellers.*

Earth and Rain, The Plants & Sun

Once near San Ysidro°
on the way to Colorado,
I stopped and looked.

The sound of a meadowlark
5   through smell of fresh cut alfalfa.

Raho would say,
"Look, Dad." A hawk

sweeping
      its wings
10 clear through
     the blue
of whole and pure
     the wind
       the sky.

15 It is writhing
overhead.
Hear. The Bringer.
     The Thunderer.

Sunlight falls
20 through cloud curtains,
a straight bright shaft.

It falls,
    it falls
  down
25   to earth,
a green plant.

Today the Katzina° come.
The dancing prayers.
Many times, the Katzina.
30 The dancing prayers.
It shall not end,
son, it will not end,
this love.

Again and again,
35 the earth is new again.

¹**San Ysidro** town in southern California   ²⁷**Katzina** in Hopi and Zuni culture, spirits
sometimes represented by dolls

They come, listen, listen.
Hold on to your mother's hand.
They come.

O great joy, they come.
The plants with bells.
The stones with voices.
Listen, son, hold my hand.   [1992]

1. Who is speaking and for what purpose?
2. What is the narrator's message about nature and how does the poem convey it?

Vision Shadows

Wind visions are honest.
Eagle clearly soars
into the craggy peaks
of the mind.
The mind is full   5
of Sunprayer
and Childlaughter.

Mountain dreams
about Pine brother and friends,
the mystic realm of boulders   10
which shelter
Rabbit, Squirrel, and Wren.
They believe in the power.
They also believe
in quick Eagle death.   15

Eagle loops
into the wind power.
He can see a million miles
and more because of it.

All believe things   20
of origin and solitude.
        But what has happened
(I hear strange news from Wyoming
of thallium sulphate. Ranchers
bearing arms in helicopters.)   25
        to these visions?
I hear foreign tremors.
Breath comes thin and shredded.
I hear the scabs of strange deaths
falling off.   30

Snake hurries through the grass.
Coyote is befuddled by his own tricks.
And Bear whimpers pain into the wind.

Poisonous fumes cross our sacred paths.
35 The wind is still.
O Blue Sky, O Mountain, O Spirit, O
what has stopped?

Eagle tumbles dumbly into shadow
that swallows him with dull thud.
40 The sage can't breathe.
Jackrabbit is lonely and alone
with Eagle gone.

It is painful, aiiee, without visions
to soothe dry whimpers
45 or repair the flight of Eagle, our own brother.   [1992]

> 1. What is the relationship between shadows and vision in this poem?
> 2. Does the poem suggest how to "de-shadow" or how to reconcile the conflict
>   between industry and nature?

SYLVIA PLATH

OLC

(For biographical notes, see p. 551.)

Black Rook° in Rainy Weather

On the stiff twig up there
Hunches a wet black rook
Arranging and rearranging its feathers in the rain.
I do not expect miracle
5 Or an accident

To set the sight on fire
In my eye, nor seek
Any more in the desultory weather some design,
But let spotted leaves fall as they fall,
10 Without ceremony, or portent.

Although, I admit, I desire,
Occasionally, some backtalk
From the mute sky, I can't honestly complain:
A certain minor light may still
15 Leap incandescent

Out of kitchen table or chair
As if a celestial burning took
Possession of the most obtuse objects now and then—

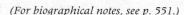

Title**Black Rook** a bird about the size and color of a crow

Thus hallowing an interval
Otherwise inconsequent   20

By bestowing largesse, honour,
One might say love. At any rate, I now walk
Wary (for it could happen
Even in this dull, ruinous landscape); sceptical,
Yet politic; ignorant   25

Of whatever angel may choose to flare
Suddenly at my elbow. I only know that a rook
Ordering its black feathers can so shine
As to seize my senses, haul
My eyelids up, and grant   30

A brief respite from fear
Of total neutrality. With luck,
Trekking stubborn through this season
Of fatigue, I shall
Patch together a content   35

Of sorts. Miracles occur,
If you care to call those spasmodic
Tricks of radiance miracles. The wait's begun again,
The long wait for the angel,
For that rare, random descent.   [1967]   40

1. Characterize the narrator of this poem.
2. How is the meaning of the poem created through its language?

WILLIAM WORDSWORTH

OLC

WILLIAM WORDSWORTH *(1770–1850), one of the great English poets and author
of close to 900 poems, was born in the heart of the English Lake District, the beloved
landscape that gave rise to many of his works. After the early death of his mother,
Wordsworth felt that his boarding school was his true home. He became an orphan
at thirteen when his father died, leaving him and his four siblings almost destitute
because of a large sum of money owed to his lawyer father by the Earl of Lonsdale,
money which was never repaid. Nevertheless, he attended Cambridge, where he
had little interest or success in his studies, but went on a walking tour in France,
where he became a passionate supporter of the French Revolution, educated himself
in aesthetics, and fell in love with Annette Vallon, who bore him a daughter. His
return to England was marked by unhappiness; he became a committed radical and
published nothing. In 1795, a close friend died, leaving him money that enabled
him to devote his life to writing poetry. Wordsworth's friendship with poet Samuel
Taylor Coleridge, the other turning point in his life, combined with his new
financial independence, led him to establish his home with his sister Dorothy near
Coleridge's own home, where the camaraderie of "three persons with one soul" led*

to the publication of Lyrical Ballads. *He married a childhood friend and had five children. His establishment as one of the great poets of the realm led to prizes and the post of Poet Laureate. At his death in 1850, Matthew Arnold announced that "the last poetic voice is dumb." Later that year,* The Prelude *was published under a title suggested by Mary Wordsworth.*

Upon Westminster Bridge°

Earth has not anything to show more fair:
   Dull would he be of soul who could pass by
   A sight so touching in its majesty:
This City now doth like a garment wear
5 The beauty of the morning; silent, bare,
   Ships, towers, domes, theatres, and temples lie
   Open unto the fields, and to the sky;
All bright and glittering in the smokeless air.
Never did sun more beautifully steep
10 In his first splendour valley, rock, or hill;
Ne'er saw I, never felt, a calm so deep!
   The river glideth at his own sweet will:
Dear God! the very houses seem asleep;
   And all that mighty heart is lying still!   [1807]

Title**Westminster Bridge** a bridge over the Thames River in London

1. If you know that Wordsworth is usually thought of as a poet of nature, you might expect that the first line of this sonnet is launching an appreciation of some natural phenomenon. How does Wordsworth arrange the poem to create a surprise for readers with those expectations?
2. What is it that makes Wordsworth admire the city? What is the importance of the word *smokeless* in l. 8?
3. Are there any cities that inspire this kind of admiration in you? In others?

The World Is Too Much with Us

The world is too much with us; late and soon,
Getting and spending, we lay waste our powers:
Little we see in Nature that is ours;
We have given our hearts away, a sordid boon!°
5 This Sea that bares her bosom to the moon;
The winds that will be howling at all hours,
And are up-gathered now like sleeping flowers;

⁴**boon** something given in response to a request

For this, for everything, we are out of tune;
It moves us not.—Great God! I'd rather be
A Pagan suckled in a creed outworn;   10
So might I, standing on this pleasant lea,
Have glimpses that would make me less forlorn;
Have sight of Proteus rising from the sea;
Or hear old Triton blow his wreathèd horn.   [1807]

1. What is the narrator's main complaint in this poem? What is the effect of
   the way he expresses it? What does he mean by "Nature"? What does he
   expect of it?
2. What alternative does the poem offer?
3. What is traditional about the poetic form of this poem and what is not?

FICTION

KATE CHOPIN

OLC

(For biographical notes, see p. 771.)

The Storm

I

The leaves were so still that even Bibi thought it was going to rain. Bobinôt, who
was accustomed to converse on terms of perfect equality with his little son,
called the child's attention to certain sombre clouds that were rolling with
sinister intention from the west, accompanied by a sullen, threatening roar.
They were at Friedheimer's store and decided to remain there till the storm had
passed. They sat within the door on two empty kegs. Bibi was four years old and
looked very wise.

"Mama'll be 'fraid, yes," he suggested with blinking eyes.

"She'll shut the house. Maybe she got Sylvie helpin' her this evenin',"
Bobinôt responded reassuringly.

"No; she ent got Sylvie. Sylvie was helpin' her yistiday," piped Bibi.

Bobinôt arose and going across to the counter purchased a can of shrimps, of   5
which Calixta was very fond. Then he returned to his perch on the keg and sat
stolidly holding the can of shrimps while the storm burst. It shook the wooden
store and seemed to be ripping great furrows in the distant field. Bibi laid his
little hand on his father's knee and was not afraid.

II

Calixta, at home, felt no uneasiness for their safety. She sat at a side window
sewing furiously on a sewing machine. She was greatly occupied and did not

notice the approaching storm. But she felt very warm and often stopped to mop her face on which the perspiration gathered in beads. She unfastened her white sacque at the throat. It began to grow dark, and suddenly realizing the situation she got up hurriedly and went about closing windows and doors.

Out on the small front gallery° she had hung Bobinôt's Sunday clothes to air and she hastened out to gather them before the rain fell. As she stepped outside, Alcée Laballière rode in at the gate. She had not seen him very often since her marriage, and never alone. She stood there with Bobinôt's coat in her hands, and the big rain drops began to fall. Alcée rode his horse under the shelter of a side projection where the chickens had huddled and there were plows and a harrow piled up in the corner.

"May I come and wait on your gallery till the storm is over, Calixta?" he asked.

"Come 'long in, M'sieur Alcée."

His voice and her own startled her as if from a trance, and she seized Bobinôt's vest. Alcée, mounting to the porch, grabbed the trousers and snatched Bibi's braided jacket that was about to be carried away by a sudden gust of wind. He expressed an intention to remain outside, but it was soon apparent that he might as well have been out in the open: the water beat in upon the boards in driving sheets, and he went inside, closing the door after him. It was even necessary to put something beneath the door to keep the water out.

"My! what a rain! It's good two years sence it rain' like that," exclaimed Calixta as she rolled up a piece of bagging and Alcée helped her to thrust it beneath the crack.

She was a little fuller of figure than five years before when she married; but she had lost nothing of her vivacity. Her blue eyes still retained their melting quality; and her yellow hair, dishevelled by the wind and rain, kinked more stubbornly than ever about her ears and temples.

The rain beat upon the low, shingled roof with a force and clatter that threatened to break an entrance and deluge them there. They were in the dining room—the sitting room—the general utility room. Adjoining was her bed room, with Bibi's couch along side her own. The door stood open, and the room with its white, monumental bed, its closed shutters, looked dim and mysterious.

Alcée flung himself into a rocker and Calixta nervously began to gather up from the floor the lengths of a cotton sheet which she had been sewing.

"If this keeps up, *Dieu sait*° if the levees goin' to stan' it!" she exclaimed.

"What have you got to do with the levees?"

"I got enough to do! An' there's Bobinôt with Bibi out in that storm—if he only didn' left Friedheimer's!"

"Let us hope, Calixta, that Bobinôt's got sense enough to come in out of a cyclone."

She went and stood at the window with a greatly disturbed look on her face. She wiped the frame that was clouded with moisture. It was stiflingly hot. Alcée got up and joined her at the window, looking over her shoulder. The rain was

---

°**front gallery** covered porch   °**Dieu sait** God knows (French)

coming down in sheets obscuring the view of far-off cabins and enveloping the distant wood in a gray mist. The playing of the lightning was incessant. A bolt struck a tall chinaberry tree at the edge of the field. It filled all visible space with a blinding glare and the crash seemed to invade the very boards they stood upon.

Calixta put her hands to her eyes, and with a cry, staggered backward. Alcée's arm encircled her, and for an instant he drew her close and spasmodically to him. 20

"*Bonté!*"° she cried, releasing herself from his encircling arm and retreating from the window, "the house'll go next! If I only knew w'ere Bibi was!" She would not compose herself; she would not be seated. Alcée clasped her shoulders and looked into her face. The contact of her warm, palpitating body when he had unthinkingly drawn her into his arms, had aroused all the old-time infatuation and desire for her flesh.

"Calixta," he said, "don't be frightened. Nothing can happen. The house is too low to be struck, with so many tall trees standing about. There! aren't you going to be quiet? say, aren't you?" He pushed her hair back from her face that was warm and steaming. Her lips were as red and moist as pomegranate seed. Her white neck and a glimpse of her full, firm bosom disturbed him powerfully. As she glanced up at him the fear in her liquid blue eyes had given place to a drowsy gleam that unconsciously betrayed a sensuous desire. He looked down into her eyes and there was nothing for him to do but to gather her lips in a kiss. It reminded him of Assumption.°

"Do you remember—in Assumption Calixta?" he asked in a low voice broken by passion. Oh! she remembered; for in Assumption he had kissed her and kissed and kissed her; until his senses would well nigh fail, and to save her he would resort to a desperate flight. If she was not an immaculate dove in those days, she was still inviolate; a passionate creature whose very defenselessness had made her defense, against which his honor forbade him to prevail. Now— well, now—her lips seemed in a manner free to be tasted, as well as her round, white throat and her whiter breasts.

They did not heed the crashing torrents, and the roar of the elements made her laugh as she lay in his arms. She was a revelation in that dim, mysterious chamber; as white as the couch she lay upon. Her firm, elastic flesh that was knowing for the first time its birthright, was like a creamy lily that the sun invites to contribute its breath and perfume to the undying life of the world.

The generous abundance of her passion, without guile or trickery, was like a white flame which penetrated and found response in depths of his own sensuous nature that had never yet been reached. 25

When he touched her breasts they gave themselves up in quivering ecstasy, inviting his lips. Her mouth was a fountain of delight. And when he possessed her, they seemed to swoon together at the very borderland of life's mystery.

He stayed cushioned upon her, breathless, dazed, enervated, with his heart beating like a hammer upon her. With one hand she clasped his head, her lips

---

²¹*Bonté* Heavens!   ²²**Assumption** a parish (county) in Louisiana

lightly touching his forehead. The other hand stroked with a soothing rhythm his muscular shoulders.

The growl of the thunder was distant and passing away. The rain beat softly upon the shingles, inviting them to drowsiness and sleep. But they dared not yield.

The rain was over; and the sun was turning the glistening green world into a place of gems. Calixta, on the gallery, watched Alcée ride away. He turned and smiled at her with a beaming face; and she lifted her pretty chin in the air and laughed aloud.

III

30 Bobinôt and Bibi, trudging home, stopped without at the cistern to make themselves presentable.

"My! Bibi, w'at will yo' mama say! You ought to be ashame'. You oughtn' put on those good pants. Look at 'em! An' that mud on yo' collar! How you got that mud on yo' collar, Bibi? I never saw such a boy!" Bibi was the picture of pathetic resignation. Bobinôt was the embodiment of serious solicitude as he strove to remove from his own person and his son's the signs of their tramp over heavy roads and through wet fields. He scraped the mud off Bibi's bare legs and feet with a stick and carefully removed all traces from his heavy brogans. Then, prepared for the worst—the meeting with an over-scrupulous housewife, they entered cautiously at the back door.

Calixta was preparing supper. She had set the table and was dripping coffee at the hearth. She sprang up as they came in.

"Oh, Bobinôt! You back! My! but I was uneasy. W'ere you been during the rain? An' Bibi? he ain't wet? he ain't hurt?" She had clasped Bibi and was kissing him effusively. Bobinôt's explanations and apologies which he had been composing all along the way, died on his lips as Calixta felt him to see if he were dry, and seemed to express nothing but satisfaction at their safe return.

"I brought you some shrimps, Calixta," offered Bobinôt, hauling the can from his ample side pocket and laying it on the table.

35 "Shrimps! Oh, Bobinôt! you too good fo' anything!" and she gave him a smacking kiss on the cheek that resounded. *"J'vous reponds,*° we'll have a feas' to night! umph-umph!"

Bobinôt and Bibi began to relax and enjoy themselves, and when the three seated themselves at table they laughed much and so loud that anyone might have heard them as far away as Laballière's.

IV

Alcée Laballière wrote to his wife, Clarisse, that night. It was a loving letter, full of tender solicitude. He told her not to hurry back, but if she and the babies liked it at Biloxi, to stay a month longer. He was getting on nicely; and though he

---

[35] *J'vous reponds* I tell you

missed them, he was willing to bear the separation a while longer—realizing that their health and pleasure were the first things to be considered.

V

As for Clarisse, she was charmed upon receiving her husband's letter. She and the babies were doing well. The society was agreeable; many of her old friends and acquaintances were at the bay. And the first free breath since her marriage seemed to restore the pleasant liberty of her maiden days. Devoted as she was to her husband, their intimate conjugal life was something which she was more than willing to forego for a while.

So the storm passed and everyone was happy.   [1898]

1. This story creates a close parallel between Calixta's behavior and the weather. Is this an effective device?
2. Characterize the story's point of view.
3. Chopin's novel *The Awakening*, in which the heroine has an adulterous affair and commits suicide when it ends, had so scandalized readers when it was published in 1899 that publishers were reluctant to publish her subsequent stories. "The Storm" was not published during her lifetime. Do you find the story scandalous? If so, why? Compare its view of marriage to that in "The Story of an Hour" (see p. 772).

ERNEST HEMINGWAY

ERNEST HEMINGWAY *(1899–1961) was born in Oak Park, Illinois, and began his professional writing life as a young newspaper reporter. At the start of World War I, he volunteered in an ambulance unit of the Italian Army and was wounded and decorated. Having returned to America as a reporter, he was soon sent back to Europe to report on the Greek Revolution and later the Spanish Civil War and World War II.*

In 1922, he had settled in Paris, where he wrote The Sun Also Rises, A Farewell to Arms, *and* For Whom the Bell Tolls, *all successful novels reflecting his experiences as reporter, ambulance driver, and avid outdoorsman, and his interest in people working against the difficulties of modern life. He also published* The Old Man and the Sea *and several volumes of short stories, many written in the spare, understated style that was his trademark. He was awarded the Nobel Prize in Literature in 1954. In 1961, he took his own life, as his father had done.*

The Short Happy Life of Francis Macomber

It was now lunch time and they were all sitting under the double green fly of the dining tent pretending that nothing had happened.

"Will you have lime juice or lemon squash?" Macomber asked.

"I'll have a gimlet," Robert Wilson told him.

"I'll have a gimlet too. I need something," Macomber's wife said.

5   "I suppose it's the thing to do," Macomber agreed. "Tell him to make three gimlets."

The mess boy had started them already, lifting the bottles out of the canvas cooling bags that sweated wet in the wind that blew through the trees that shaded the tents.

"What had I ought to give them?" Macomber asked.

"A quid would be plenty," Wilson told him. "You don't want to spoil them."

"Will the headman distribute it?"

10   "Absolutely."

Francis Macomber had, half an hour before, been carried to his tent from the edge of the camp in triumph on the arms and shoulders of the cook, the personal boys, the skinner and the porters. The gun-bearers had taken no part in the demonstration. When the native boys put him down at the door of his tent, he had shaken all their hands, received their congratulations, and then gone into the tent and sat on the bed until his wife came in. She did not speak to him when she came in and he left the tent at once to wash his face and hands in the portable wash basin outside and go over to the dining tent to sit in a comfortable canvas chair in the breeze and the shade.

"You've got your lion," Robert Wilson said to him, "and a damned fine one too."

Mrs. Macomber looked at Wilson quickly. She was an extremely handsome and well-kept woman of the beauty and social position which had, five years before, commanded five thousand dollars as the price of endorsing, with photographs, a beauty product which she had never used. She had been married to Francis Macomber for eleven years.

"He is a good lion, isn't he?" Macomber said. His wife looked at him now. She looked at both these men as though she had never seen them before.

15   One, Wilson, the white hunter, she knew she had never truly seen before. He was about middle height with sandy hair, a stubby mustache, a very red face and extremely cold blue eyes with faint white wrinkles at the corners that grooved merrily when he smiled. He smiled at her now and she looked away from his face at the way his shoulders sloped in the loose tunic he wore with the four big cartridges held in loops where the left breast pocket should have been, at his big brown hands, his old slacks, his very dirty boots and back to his red face again. She noticed where the baked red of his face stopped in a white line that marked the circle left by his Stetson hat that hung now from one of the pegs of the tent pole.

"Well, here's to the lion," Robert Wilson said. He smiled at her again and, not smiling, she looked curiously at her husband.

Francis Macomber was very tall, very well built if you did not mind that length of bone, dark, his hair cropped like an oarsman, rather thin-lipped, and was considered handsome. He was dressed in the same sort of safari clothes that Wilson wore except that his were new, he was thirty-five years old, kept himself very fit, was good at court games, had a number of big-game fishing records, and had just shown himself, very publicly, to be a coward.

"Here's to the lion," he said. "I can't ever thank you for what you did."

Margaret, his wife, looked away from him and back to Wilson.

20

"Let's not talk about the lion," she said.

Wilson looked over at her without smiling and now she smiled at him.

"It's been a very strange day," she said. "Hadn't you ought to put your hat on even under the canvas at noon? You told me that, you know."

"Might put it on," said Wilson.

"You know you have a very red face, Mr. Wilson," she told him and smiled again.

"Drink," said Wilson.

25

"I don't think so," she said. "Francis drinks a great deal, but his face is never red."

"It's red today," Macomber tried a joke.

"No," said Margaret. "It's mine that's red today. But Mr. Wilson's is always red."

"Must be racial," said Wilson. "I say, you wouldn't like to drop my beauty as a topic, would you?"

"I've just started on it."

30

"Let's chuck it," said Wilson.

"Conversation is going to be so difficult," Margaret said.

"Don't be silly, Margot," her husband said.

"No difficulty," Wilson said. "Got a damn fine lion."

Margot looked at them both and they both saw that she was going to cry. Wilson had seen it coming for a long time and he dreaded it. Macomber was past dreading it.

35

"I wish it hadn't happened. Oh, I wish it hadn't happened," she said and started for her tent. She made no noise of crying but they could see that her shoulders were shaking under the rose-colored, sun-proofed shirt she wore.

"Women upset," said Wilson to the tall man. "Amounts to nothing. Strain on the nerves and one thing'n another."

"No," said Macomber. "I suppose that I rate that for the rest of my life now."

"Nonsense. Let's have a spot of the giant killer," said Wilson. "Forget the whole thing. Nothing to it anyway."

"We might try," said Macomber. "I won't forget what you did for me though."

40

"Nothing," said Wilson. "All nonsense."

So they sat there in the shade where the camp was pitched under some wide-topped acacia trees with a boulder-strewn cliff behind them, and a stretch of grass that ran to the bank of a boulder-filled stream in front with forest beyond it, and drank their just-cool lime drinks and avoided one another's eyes while the boys set the table for lunch. Wilson could tell that the boys all knew about it now and when he saw Macomber's personal boy looking curiously at his master while he was putting dishes on the table he snapped at him in Swahili. The boy turned away with his face blank.

"What were you telling him?" Macomber asked.

"Nothing. Told him to look alive or I'd see he got about fifteen of the best."

"What's that? Lashes?"

45

"It's quite illegal," Wilson said. "You're supposed to fine them."

"Do you still have them whipped?"

"Oh, yes. They could raise a row if they chose to complain. But they don't. They prefer it to the fines."

"How strange!" said Macomber.

50 "Not strange, really," Wilson said. "Which would you rather do? Take a good birching or lose your pay?"

Then he felt embarrassed at asking it and before Macomber could answer he went on, "We all take a beating every day, you know, one way or another."

This was no better. "Good God," he thought. "I am a diplomat, aren't I?"

"Yes, we take a beating," said Macomber, still not looking at him. "I'm awfully sorry about that lion business. It doesn't have to go any further, does it? I mean no one will hear about it, will they?"

"You mean will I tell it at the Mathaiga Club?" Wilson looked at him now coldly. He had not expected this. So he's a bloody four-letter man as well as a bloody coward, he thought. I rather liked him too until today. But how is one to know about an American?

55 "No," said Wilson. "I'm a professional hunter. We never talk about our clients. You can be quite easy on that. It's supposed to be bad form to ask us not to talk though."

He had decided now that to break would be much easier. He would eat, then, by himself and could read a book with his meals. They would eat by themselves. He would see them through the safari on a very formal basis—what was it the French called it? Distinguished consideration—and it would be a damn sight easier than having to go through this emotional trash. He'd insult him and make a good clean break. Then he could read a book with his meals and he'd still be drinking their whisky. That was the phrase for it when a safari went bad. You ran into another white hunter and you asked, "How is everything going?" and he answered, "Oh, I'm still drinking their whisky," and you knew everything had gone to pot.

"I'm sorry," Macomber said and looked at him with his American face that would stay adolescent until it became middle-aged, and Wilson noted his crew-cropped hair, fine eyes only faintly shifty, good nose, thin lips and handsome jaw. "I'm sorry I didn't realize that. There are lots of things I don't know."

So what could he do, Wilson thought. He was all ready to break it off quickly and neatly and here the beggar was apologizing after he had just insulted him. He made one more attempt. "Don't worry about me talking," he said. "I have a living to make. You know in Africa no woman ever misses her lion and no white man ever bolts."

"I bolted like a rabbit," Macomber said.

60 Now what in hell were you going to do about a man who talked like that, Wilson wondered.

Wilson looked at Macomber with his flat, blue, machine-gunner's eyes and the other smiled back at him. He had a pleasant smile if you did not notice how his eyes showed when he was hurt.

"Maybe I can fix it up on buffalo," he said. "We're after them next, aren't we?"

"In the morning if you like," Wilson told him. Perhaps he had been wrong. This was certainly the way to take it. You most certainly could not tell a damned thing about an American. He was all for Macomber again. If you could forget the morning. But, of course, you couldn't. The morning had been about as bad as they come.

"Here comes the Memsahib," he said. She was walking over from her tent looking refreshed and cheerful and quite lovely. She had a very perfect oval face, so perfect that you expected her to be stupid. But she wasn't stupid, Wilson thought, no, not stupid.

"How is the beautiful red-faced Mr. Wilson? Are you feeling better, Francis, my pearl?" 65

"Oh, much," said Macomber.

"I've dropped the whole thing," she said, sitting down at the table. "What importance is there to whether Francis is any good at killing lions? That's not his trade. That's Mr. Wilson's trade. Mr. Wilson is really very impressive killing anything. You do kill anything, don't you?"

"Oh, anything," said Wilson. "Simply anything." They are, he thought, the hardest in the world; the hardest, the cruelest, the most predatory and the most attractive and their men have softened or gone to pieces nervously as they have hardened. Or is it that they pick men they can handle? They can't know that much at the age they marry, he thought. He was grateful that he had gone through his education on American women before now because this was a very attractive one.

"We're going after buff in the morning," he told her.

"I'm coming," she said. 70

"No, you're not."

"Oh, yes, I am. Mayn't I, Francis?"

"Why not stay in camp?"

"Not for anything," she said. "I wouldn't miss something like today for anything."

When she left, Wilson was thinking, when she went off to cry, she seemed a 75 hell of a fine woman. She seemed to understand, to realize, to be hurt for him and for herself and to know how things really stood. She is away for twenty minutes and now she is back, simply enamelled in that American female cruelty. They are the damnedest women. Really the damnedest.

"We'll put on another show for you tomorrow," Francis Macomber said.

"You're not coming," Wilson said.

"You're very mistaken," she told him. "And I want so to see you perform again. You were lovely this morning. That is if blowing things' heads off is lovely."

"Here's the lunch," said Wilson. "You're very merry, aren't you?"

"Why not? I didn't come out here to be dull." 80

"Well, it hasn't been dull," Wilson said. He could see the boulders in the river and the high bank beyond with the trees and he remembered the morning.

"Oh, no," she said. "It's been charming. And tomorrow. You don't know how I look forward to tomorrow."

"That's eland he's offering you," Wilson said.

"They're the big cowy things that jump like hares, aren't they?"

85   "I suppose that describes them," Wilson said.

   "It's very good meat," Macomber said.

   "Did you shoot it, Francis?" she asked.

   "Yes."

   "They're not dangerous, are they?"

90   "Only if they fall on you," Wilson told her.

   "I'm so glad."

   "Why not let up on the bitchery just a little, Margot," Macomber said, cutting the eland steak and putting some mashed potato, gravy and carrot on the down-turned fork that tined through the piece of meat.

   "I suppose I could," she said, "since you put it so prettily."

   "Tonight we'll have champagne for the lion," Wilson said. "It's a bit too hot at noon."

95   "Oh, the lion," Margot said. "I'd forgotten the lion!"

   So, Robert Wilson thought to himself, she *is* giving him a ride, isn't she? Or do you suppose that's her idea of putting up a good show? How should a woman act when she discovers her husband is a bloody coward? She's damn cruel but they're all cruel. They govern, of course, and to govern one has to be cruel sometimes. Still, I've seen enough of their damn terrorism.

   "Have some more eland," he said to her politely.

   That afternoon, late, Wilson and Macomber went out in the motor car with the native driver and the two gun-bearers. Mrs. Macomber stayed in the camp. It was too hot to go out, she said, and she was going with them in the early morning. As they drove off Wilson saw her standing under the big tree, looking pretty rather than beautiful in her faintly rosy khaki, her dark hair drawn back off her forehead and gathered in a knot low on her neck, her face as fresh, he thought, as though she were in England. She waved to them as the car went off through the swale of high grass and curved around through the trees into the small hills of orchard bush.

   In the orchard bush they found a herd of impala, and leaving the car they stalked one old ram with long, wide-spread horns and Macomber killed it with a very creditable shot that knocked the buck down at a good two hundred yards and sent the herd off bounding wildly and leaping over one another's backs in long, leg-drawn-up leaps as unbelievable and as floating as those one makes sometimes in dreams.

100   "That was a good shot," Wilson said. "They're a small target."

   "Is it a worth-while head?" Macomber asked.

   "It's excellent," Wilson told him. "You shoot like that and you'll have no trouble."

   "Do you think we'll find buffalo tomorrow?"

   "There's a good chance of it. They feed out early in the morning and with luck we may catch them in the open."

105   "I'd like to clear away that lion business," Macomber said. "It's not very pleasant to have your wife see you do something like that."

   I should think it would be even more unpleasant to do it, Wilson thought, wife or no wife, or to talk about it having done it. But he said, "I wouldn't think about that any more. Any one could be upset by his first lion. That's all over."

But that night after dinner and a whisky and soda by the fire before going to bed, as Francis Macomber lay on his cot with the mosquito bar over him and listened to the night noises it was not all over. It was neither all over nor was it beginning. It was there exactly as it happened with some parts of it indelibly emphasized and he was miserably ashamed at it. But more than shame he felt cold, hollow fear in him. The fear was still there like a cold slimy hollow in all the emptiness where once his confidence had been and it made him feel sick. It was still there with him now.

It had started the night before when he had wakened and heard the lion roaring somewhere up along the river. It was a deep sound and at the end there were sort of coughing grunts that made him seem just outside the tent, and when Francis Macomber woke in the night to hear it he was afraid. He could hear his wife breathing quietly, asleep. There was no one to tell he was afraid, nor to be afraid with him, and, lying alone, he did not know the Somali proverb that says a brave man is always frightened three times by a lion; when he first sees his track, when he first hears him roar and when he first confronts him. Then while they were eating breakfast by lantern light out in the dining tent, before the sun was up, the lion roared again and Francis thought he was just at the edge of camp.

"Sounds like an old-timer," Robert Wilson said, looking up from his kippers and coffee. "Listen to him cough."

"Is he very close?"

"A mile or so up the stream." 110

"Will we see him?"

"We'll have a look."

"Does his roaring carry that far? It sounds as though he were right in camp."

"Carries a hell of a long way," said Robert Wilson. "It's strange the way it car- 115
ries. Hope he's a shootable cat. The boys said there was a very big one about here."

"If I get a shot, where should I hit him," Macomber asked, "to stop him?"

"In the shoulders," Wilson said. "In the neck if you can make it. Shoot for bone. Break him down."

"I hope I can place it properly," Macomber said.

"You shoot very well," Wilson told him. "Take your time. Make sure of him. The first one in is the one that counts."

"What range will it be?" 120

"Can't tell. Lion has something to say about that. Don't shoot unless it's close enough so you can make sure."

"At under a hundred yards?" Macomber asked.

Wilson looked at him quickly.

"Hundred's about right. Might have to take him a bit under. Shouldn't chance a shot at much over that. A hundred's a decent range. You can hit him wherever you want at that. Here comes the Memsahib."

"Good morning," she said. "Are we going after that lion?" 125

"As soon as you deal with your breakfast," Wilson said. "How are you feeling?"

"Marvellous," she said. "I'm very excited."

"I'll just go and see that everything is ready," Wilson went off. As he left the lion roared again.

"Noisy beggar," Wilson said. "We'll put a stop to that."

130   "What's the matter, Francis?" his wife asked him.

"Nothing," Macomber said.

"Yes, there is," she said. "What are you upset about?"

"Nothing," he said.

"Tell me," she looked at him. "Don't you feel well?"

135   "It's that damned roaring," he said. "It's been going on all night, you know."

"Why didn't you wake me," she said. "I'd love to have heard it."

"I've got to kill the damned thing," Macomber said, miserably.

"Well, that's what you're out here for, isn't it?"

"Yes. But I'm nervous. Hearing the thing roar gets on my nerves."

140   "Well then, as Wilson said, kill him and stop his roaring."

"Yes, darling," said Francis Macomber. "It sounds easy, doesn't it?"

"You're not afraid, are you?"

"Of course not. But I'm nervous from hearing him roar all night."

"You'll kill him marvellously," she said. "I know you will. I'm awfully anxious to see it."

145   "Finish your breakfast and we'll be starting."

"It's not light yet," she said. "This is a ridiculous hour."

Just then the lion roared in a deep-chested moaning, suddenly guttural, ascending vibration that seemed to shake the air and ended in a sigh and a heavy, deep-chested grunt.

"He sounds almost here," Macomber's wife said.

"My God," said Macomber. "I hate that damned noise."

150   "It's very impressive."

"Impressive. It's frightful."

Robert Wilson came up then carrying his short, ugly, shockingly big-bored .505 Gibbs and grinning.

"Come on," he said. "Your gun-bearer has your Springfield and the big gun. Everything's in the car. Have you solids?"

"Yes."

155   "I'm ready," Mrs. Macomber said.

"Must make him stop that racket," Wilson said. "You get in front. The Memsahib can sit back here with me."

They climbed into the motor car and, in the gray first daylight, moved off up the river through the trees. Macomber opened the breech of his rifle and saw he had metal-cased bullets, shut the bolt and put the rifle on safety. He saw his hand was trembling. He felt in his pocket for more cartridges and moved his fingers over the cartridges in the loops of his tunic front. He turned back to where Wilson sat in the rear seat of the doorless, box-bodied motor car beside his wife, them both grinning with excitement, and Wilson leaned forward and whispered,

"See the birds dropping. Means the old boy has left his kill."

On the far bank of the stream Macomber could see, above the trees, vultures circling and plummeting down.

160   "Chances are he'll come to drink along here," Wilson whispered. "Before he goes to lay up. Keep an eye out."

They were driving slowly along the high bank of the stream which here cut deeply to its boulder-filled bed, and they wound in and out through big trees as they drove. Macomber was watching the opposite bank when he felt Wilson take hold of his arm. The car stopped.

"There he is," he heard the whisper. "Ahead and to the right. Get out and take him. He's a marvellous lion."

Macomber saw the lion now. He was standing almost broadside, his great head up and turned toward them. The early morning breeze that blew toward them was just stirring his dark mane, and the lion looked huge, silhouetted on the rise of bank in the gray morning light, his shoulders heavy, his barrel of a body bulking smoothly.

"How far is he?" asked Macomber, raising his rifle.

"About seventy-five. Get out and take him." 165

"Why not shoot from where I am?"

"You don't shoot them from cars," he heard Wilson saying in his ear. "Get out. He's not going to stay there all day."

Macomber stepped out of the curved opening at the side of the front seat, onto the step and down onto the ground. The lion still stood looking majestically and coolly toward this object that his eyes only showed in silhouette, bulking like some super-rhino. There was no man smell carried toward him and he watched the object, moving his great head a little from side to side. Then watching the object, not afraid, but hesitating before going down the bank to drink with such a thing opposite him, he saw a man figure detach itself from it and he turned his heavy head and swung away toward the cover of the trees as he heard a cracking crash and felt the slam of a .30–06 220-grain solid bullet that bit his flank and ripped in sudden hot scalding nausea through his stomach. He trotted, heavy, big-footed, swinging wounded full-bellied, through the trees toward the tall grass and cover, and the crash came again to go past him ripping the air apart. Then it crashed again and he felt the blow as it hit his lower ribs and ripped on through, blood sudden hot and frothy in his mouth, and he galloped toward the high grass where he could crouch and not be seen and make them bring the crashing thing close enough so he could make a rush and get the man that held it.

Macomber had not thought how the lion felt as he got out of the car. He only knew his hands were shaking and as he walked away from the car it was almost impossible for him to make his legs move. They were stiff in the thighs, but he could feel the muscles fluttering. He raised the rifle, sighted on the junction of the lion's head and shoulders and pulled the trigger. Nothing happened though he pulled until he thought his finger would break. Then he knew he had the safety on and as he lowered the rifle to move the safety over he moved another frozen pace forward, and the lion seeing his silhouette now clear of the silhouette of the car, turned and started off at a trot, and, as Macomber fired, he heard a whunk that meant that the bullet was home; but the lion kept on going. Macomber shot again and every one saw the bullet throw a spout of dirt beyond the trotting lion. He shot again, remembering to lower his aim, and they all heard the bullet hit, and the lion went into a gallop and was in the tall grass before he had the bolt pushed forward.

170   Macomber stood there feeling sick at his stomach, his hands that held the Springfield still cocked, shaking, and his wife and Robert Wilson were standing by him. Beside him too were the two gun-bearers chattering in Wakamba.

    "I hit him," Macomber said. "I hit him twice."

    "You gut-shot him and you hit him somewhere forward," Wilson said without enthusiasm. The gun-bearers looked very grave. They were silent now.

    "You may have killed him," Wilson went on. "We'll have to wait a while before we go in to find out."

    "What do you mean?"

175   "Let him get sick before we follow him up."

    "Oh," said Macomber.

    "He's a hell of a fine lion," Wilson said cheerfully. "He's gotten into a bad place though."

    "Why is it bad?"

    "Can't see him until you're on him."

180   "Oh," said Macomber.

    "Come on," said Wilson. "The Memsahib can stay here in the car. We'll go to have a look at the blood spoor."

    "Stay here, Margot," Macomber said to his wife. His mouth was very dry and it was hard for him to talk.

    "Why?" she asked.

    "Wilson says to."

185   "We're going to have a look," Wilson said. "You stay here. You can see even better from here."

    "All right."

    Wilson spoke in Swahili to the driver. He nodded and said, "Yes, Bwana."

    Then they went down the steep bank and across the stream, climbing over and around the boulders and up the other bank, pulling up by some projecting roots, and along it until they found where the lion had been trotting when Macomber first shot. There was dark blood on the short grass that the gun-bearers pointed out with grass stems, and that ran away behind the river bank trees.

190   "What do we do?" asked Macomber.

    "Not much choice," said Wilson. "We can't bring the car over. Bank's too steep. We'll let him stiffen up a bit and then you and I'll go in and have a look for him."

    "Can't we set the grass on fire?" Macomber asked.

    "Too green."

    "Can't we send beaters?"

    Wilson looked at him appraisingly. "Of course we can," he said. "But it's just a touch murderous. You see we know the lion's wounded. You can drive an unwounded lion—he'll move on ahead of a noise—but a wounded lion's going to charge. You can't see him until you're right on him. He'll make himself perfectly flat in cover you wouldn't think would hide a hare. You can't very well send boys in there to that sort of a show. Somebody bound to get mauled."

195   "What about the gun-bearers?"

"Oh, they'll go with us. It's their *shauri*.° You see, they signed on for it. They don't look too happy though, do they?"

"I don't want to go in there," said Macomber. It was out before he knew he'd said it.

"Neither do I," said Wilson very cheerily. "Really no choice though." Then, as an afterthought, he glanced at Macomber and saw suddenly how he was trembling and the pitiful look on his face.

"You don't have to go in, of course," he said. "That's what I'm hired for, you know. That's why I'm so expensive."

"You mean you'd go in by yourself? Why not leave him there?" 200

Robert Wilson, whose entire occupation had been with the lion and the problem he presented, and who had not been thinking about Macomber except to note that he was rather windy, suddenly felt as though he had opened the wrong door in a hotel and seen something shameful.

"What do you mean?"

"Why not just leave him?"

"You mean pretend to ourselves he hasn't been hit?"

"No. Just drop it." 205

"It isn't done."

"Why not?"

"For one thing, he's certain to be suffering. For another, some one else might run onto him."

"I see."

"But you don't have to have anything to do with it." 210

"I'd like to," Macomber said. "I'm just scared, you know."

"I'll go ahead when we go in," Wilson said, "with Kongoni tracking. You keep behind me and a little to one side. Chances are we'll hear him growl. If we see him we'll both shoot. Don't worry about anything. I'll keep you backed up. As a matter of fact, you know, perhaps you'd better not go. It might be much better. Why don't you go over and join the Memsahib while I just get it over with?"

"No, I want to go."

"All right," said Wilson. "But don't go in if you don't want to. This is my *shauri* now, you know."

"I want to go," said Macomber. 215

They sat under a tree and smoked.

"Want to go back and speak to the Memsahib while we're waiting?" Wilson asked.

"No."

"I'll just step back and tell her to be patient."

"Good," said Macomber. He sat there, sweating under his arms, his mouth 220 dry, his stomach hollow feeling, wanting to find courage to tell Wilson to go on and finish off the lion without him. He could not know that Wilson was furious because he had not noticed the state he was in earlier and sent him back to his

---

[196]**shauri** duty

wife. While he sat there Wilson came up. "I have your big gun," he said. "Take it. We've given him time, I think. Come on."

Macomber took the big gun and Wilson said:

"Keep behind me and about five yards to the right and do exactly as I tell you." Then he spoke in Swahili to the two gun-bearers who looked the picture of gloom.

"Let's go," he said.

"Could I have a drink of water?" Macomber asked. Wilson spoke to the older gun-bearer, who wore a canteen on his belt, and the man unbuckled it, unscrewed the top and handed it to Macomber, who took it noticing how heavy it seemed and how hairy and shoddy the felt covering was in his hand. He raised it to drink and looked ahead at the high grass with the flat-topped trees behind it. A breeze was blowing toward them and the grass rippled gently in the wind. He looked at the gun-bearer and he could see the gun-bearer was suffering too with fear.

225   Thirty-five yards into the grass the big lion lay flattened out along the ground. His ears were back and his only movement was a slight twitching up and down of his long, black-tufted tail. He had turned at bay as soon as he had reached this cover and he was sick with the wound through his full belly, and weakening with the wound through his lungs that brought a thin foamy red to his mouth each time he breathed. His flanks were wet and hot and flies were on the little openings the solid bullets had made in his tawny hide, and his big yellow eyes, narrowed with hate, looked straight ahead, only blinking when the pain came as he breathed, and his claws dug in the soft baked earth. All of him, pain, sickness, hatred and all of his remaining strength, was tightening into an absolute concentration for a rush. He could hear the men talking and he waited, gathering all of himself into this preparation for a charge as soon as the men would come into the grass. As he heard their voices his tail stiffened to twitch up and down, and, as they came into the edge of the grass, he made a coughing grunt and charged.

Kongoni, the old gun-bearer, in the lead watching the blood spoor, Wilson watching the grass for any movement, his big gun ready, the second gun-bearer looking ahead and listening, Macomber close to Wilson, his rifle cocked, they had just moved into the grass when Macomber heard the blood-choked coughing grunt, and saw the swishing rush in the grass. The next thing he knew he was running; running wildly, in panic in the open, running toward the stream.

He heard the *ca-ra-wong!* of Wilson's big rifle, and again in a second crashing *carawong!* and turning saw the lion, horrible-looking now, with half his head seeming to be gone, crawling toward Wilson in the edge of the tall grass while the red-faced man worked the bolt on the short ugly rifle and aimed carefully as another blasting *carawong!* came from the muzzle, and the crawling, heavy, yellow bulk of the lion stiffened and the huge, mutilated head slid forward and Macomber, standing by himself in the clearing where he had run, holding a loaded rifle, while two black men and a white man looked back at him in contempt, knew the lion was dead. He came toward

Wilson, his tallness all seeming a naked reproach, and Wilson looked at him and said:

"Want to take pictures?"

"No," he said.

That was all any one had said until they reached the motor car. Then Wilson   230
had said:

"Hell of a fine lion. Boys will skin him out. We might as well stay here in the shade."

Macomber's wife had not looked at him nor he at her and he had sat by her in the back seat with Wilson sitting in the front seat. Once he had reached over and taken his wife's hand without looking at her and she had removed her hand from his. Looking across the stream to where the gun-bearers were skinning out the lion he could see that she had been able to see the whole thing. While they sat there his wife had reached forward and put her hand on Wilson's shoulder. He turned and she had leaned forward over the low seat and kissed him on the mouth.

"Oh, I say," said Wilson, going redder than his natural baked color.

"Mr. Robert Wilson," she said. "The beautiful red-faced Mr. Robert Wilson."

Then she sat down beside Macomber again and looked away across the   235
stream to where the lion lay, with uplifted, white-muscled, tendon-marked naked forearms, and white bloating belly, as the black men fleshed away the skin. Finally the gun-bearers brought the skin over, wet and heavy, and climbed in behind with it, rolling it up before they got in, and the motor car started. No one had said anything more until they were back in camp.

That was the story of the lion. Macomber did not know how the lion had felt before he started his rush, nor during it when the unbelievable smash of the .505 with a muzzle velocity of two tons had hit him in the mouth, nor what kept him coming after that, when the second ripping crash had smashed his hind quarters and he had come crawling on toward the crashing, blasting thing that had destroyed him. Wilson knew something about it and only expressed it by saying, "Damned fine lion," but Macomber did not know how Wilson felt about things either. He did not know how his wife felt except that she was through with him.

His wife had been through with him before but it never lasted. He was very wealthy, and would be much wealthier, and he knew she would not leave him ever now. That was one of the few things that he really knew. He knew about that, about motor cycles—that was earliest—about motor cars, about duck-shooting, about fishing, trout, salmon and big-sea, about sex in books, many books, too many books, about all court games, about dogs, not much about horses, about hanging on to his money, about most of the other things his world dealt in, and about his wife not leaving him. His wife had been a great beauty and she was still a great beauty in Africa, but she was not a great enough beauty any more at home to be able to leave him and better herself and she knew it and he knew it. She had missed the chance to leave him and he knew it. If he had been better with women she would probably have started to worry about him getting another new, beautiful wife; but she knew too much about him to worry about him either. Also, he had always had a great tolerance which seemed the nicest thing about him if it were not the most sinister.

All in all they were known as a comparatively happily married couple, one of those whose disruption is often rumored but never occurs, and as the society columnist put it, they were adding more than a spice of *adventure* to their much envied and ever-enduring *Romance* by a *Safari* in what was known as *Darkest Africa* until the Martin Johnsons lighted it on so many silver screens where they were pursuing *Old Simba* the lion, the buffalo, *Tembo* the elephant and as well collecting specimens for the Museum of Natural History. This same columnist had reported them *on the verge* at least three times in the past and they had been. But they always made it up. They had a sound basis of union. Margot was too beautiful for Macomber to divorce her and Macomber had too much money for Margot ever to leave him.

It was now about three o'clock in the morning and Francis Macomber, who had been asleep a little while after he had stopped thinking about the lion, wakened and then slept again, woke suddenly, frightened in a dream of the bloody-headed lion standing over him, and listening while his heart pounded, he realized that his wife was not in the other cot in the tent. He lay awake with that knowledge for two hours.

240   At the end of that time his wife came into the tent, lifted her mosquito bar and crawled cozily into bed.

"Where have you been?" Macomber asked in the darkness.

"Hello," she said. "Are you awake?"

"Where have you been?"

"I just went out to get a breath of air."

245   "You did, like hell."

"What do you want me to say, darling?"

"Where have you been?"

"Out to get a breath of air."

"That's a new name for it. You *are* a bitch."

250   "Well, you're a coward."

"All right," he said. "What of it?"

"Nothing as far as I'm concerned. But please let's not talk, darling, because I'm very sleepy."

"You think that I'll take anything."

"I know you will, sweet."

255   "Well, I won't."

"Please, darling, let's not talk. I'm so very sleepy."

"There wasn't going to be any of that. You promised there wouldn't be."

"Well, there is now," she said sweetly.

"You said if we made this trip that there would be none of that. You promised."

260   "Yes, darling. That's the way I meant it to be. But the trip was spoiled yesterday. We don't have to talk about it, do we?"

"You don't wait long when you have an advantage, do you?"

"Please let's not talk. I'm so sleepy, darling."

"I'm going to talk."

"Don't mind me then, because I'm going to sleep." And she did.

At breakfast they were all three at the table before daylight and Francis 265
Macomber found that, of all the many men that he had hated, he hated Robert
Wilson the most.

"Sleep well?" Wilson asked in his throaty voice, filling a pipe.

"Did you?"

"Topping," the white hunter told him.

You bastard, thought Macomber, you insolent bastard.

So she woke him when she came in, Wilson thought, looking at them both 270
with his flat, cold eyes. Well, why doesn't he keep his wife where she belongs?
What does he think I am, a bloody plaster saint? Let him keep her where she
belongs. It's his own fault.

"Do you think we'll find buffalo?" Margot asked, pushing away a dish of
apricots.

"Chance of it," Wilson said and smiled at her. "Why don't you stay in camp?"

"Not for anything," she told him.

"Why not order her to stay in camp?" Wilson said to Macomber.

"You order her," said Macomber coldly. 275

"Let's not have any ordering, nor," turning to Macomber, "any silliness,
Francis," Margot said quite pleasantly.

"Are you ready to start?" Macomber asked.

"Any time," Wilson told him. "Do you want the Memsahib to go?"

"Does it make any difference whether I do or not?"

The hell with it, thought Robert Wilson. The utter complete hell with it. So 280
this is what it's going to be like. Well, this is what it's going to be like, then.

"Makes no difference," he said.

"You're sure you wouldn't like to stay in camp with her yourself and let me
go out and hunt the buffalo?" Macomber asked.

"Can't do that," said Wilson. "Wouldn't talk rot if I were you."

"I'm not talking rot. I'm disgusted."

"Bad word, disgusted." 285

"Francis, will you please try to speak sensibly?" his wife said.

"I speak too damned sensibly," Macomber said. "Did you ever eat such filthy
food?"

"Something wrong with the food?" asked Wilson quietly.

"No more than with everything else."

"I'd pull yourself together, laddybuck," Wilson said very quietly. "There's a 290
boy waits at table that understands a little English."

"The hell with him."

Wilson stood up and puffing on his pipe strolled away, speaking a few words
in Swahili to one of the gun-bearers who was standing waiting for him. Macomber
and his wife sat on at the table. He was staring at his coffee cup.

"If you make a scene I'll leave you, darling," Margot said quietly.

"No, you won't."

"You can try it and see." 295

"You won't leave me."

"No," she said. "I won't leave you and you'll behave yourself."

"Behave myself? That's a way to talk. Behave myself."

"Yes. Behave yourself."

300   "Why don't *you* try behaving?"

"I've tried it so long. So very long."

"I hate that red-faced swine," Macomber said. "I loathe the sight of him."

"He's really *very* nice."

"Oh, *shut up*," Macomber almost shouted. Just then the car came up and stopped in front of the dining tent and the driver and the two gun-bearers got out. Wilson walked over and looked at the husband and wife sitting there at the table.

305   "Going shooting?" he asked.

"Yes," said Macomber, standing up. "Yes."

"Better bring a woolly. It will be cool in the car," Wilson said.

"I'll get my leather jacket," Margot said.

"The boy has it," Wilson told her. He climbed into the front with the driver and Francis Macomber and his wife sat, not speaking, in the back seat.

310   Hope the silly beggar doesn't take a notion to blow the back of my head off, Wilson thought to himself. Women *are* a nuisance on safari.

The car was grinding down to cross the river at a pebbly ford in the gray daylight and then climbed, angling up the steep bank, where Wilson had ordered a way shovelled out the day before so they could reach the parklike wooded rolling country on the far side.

It was a good morning, Wilson thought. There was a heavy dew and as the wheels went through the grass and low bushes he could smell the odor of the crushed fronds. It was an odor like verbena and he liked this early morning smell of the dew, the crushed bracken and the look of the tree trunks showing black through the early morning mist, as the car made its way through the untracked, parklike country. He had put the two in the back seat out of his mind now and was thinking about buffalo. The buffalo that he was after stayed in the daytime in a thick swamp where it was impossible to get a shot, but in the night they fed out into an open stretch of country and if he could come between them and their swamp with the car, Macomber would have a good chance at them in the open. He did not want to hunt buff with Macomber in thick cover. He did not want to hunt buff or anything else with Macomber at all, but he was a professional hunter and he had hunted with some rare ones in his time. If they got buff today there would only be rhino to come and the poor man would have gone through his dangerous game and things might pick up. He'd have nothing more to do with the woman and Macomber would get over that too. He must have gone through plenty of that before by the look of things. Poor beggar. He must have a way of getting over it. Well, it was the poor sod's own bloody fault.

He, Robert Wilson, carried a double size cot on safari to accommodate any windfalls he might receive. He had hunted for a certain clientele, the international, fast, sporting set, where the women did not feel they were getting their money's worth unless they had shared that cot with the white hunter. He despised them when he was away from them although he liked some of them well enough at the time, but he made his living by them; and their standards were his standards as long as they were hiring him.

They were his standards in all except the shooting. He had his own standards about the killing and they could live up to them or get some one else to hunt them. He knew, too, that they all respected him for this. This Macomber was an odd one though. Damned if he wasn't. Now the wife. Well, the wife. Yes, the wife. Hm, the wife. Well he'd dropped all that. He looked around at them. Macomber sat grim and furious. Margot smiled at him. She looked younger today, more innocent and fresher and not so professionally beautiful. What's in her heart God knows, Wilson thought. She hadn't talked much last night. At that it was a pleasure to see her.

The motor car climbed up a slight rise and went on through the trees and 315 then out into a grassy prairie-like opening and kept in the shelter of the trees along the edge, the driver going slowly and Wilson looking carefully out across the prairie and all along its far side. He stopped the car and studied the opening with his field glasses. Then he motioned to the driver to go on and the car moved slowly along, the driver avoiding wart-hog holes and driving around the mud castles ants had built. Then, looking across the opening, Wilson suddenly turned and said,

"By God, there they are!"

And looking where he pointed, while the car jumped forward and Wilson spoke in rapid Swahili to the driver, Macomber saw three huge, black animals looking almost cylindrical in their long heaviness, like big black tank cars, moving at a gallop across the far edge of the open prairie. They moved at a stiff-necked, stiff bodied gallop and he could see the upswept wide black horns on their heads as they galloped heads out; the heads not moving.

"They're three old bulls," Wilson said. "We'll cut them off before they get to the swamp."

The car was going a wild forty-five miles an hour across the open and as Macomber watched, the buffalo got bigger and bigger until he could see the gray, hairless, scabby look of one huge bull and how his neck was a part of his shoulders and the shiny black of his horns as he galloped a little behind the others that were strung out in that steady plunging gait; and then, the car swaying as though it had just jumped a road, they drew up close and he could see the plunging hugeness of the bull, and the dust in his sparsely haired hide, the wide boss of horn and his outstretched, wide-nostrilled muzzle, and he was raising his rifle when Wilson shouted, "Not from the car, you fool!" and he had no fear, only hatred of Wilson, while the brakes clamped on and the car skidded, plowing sideways to an almost stop and Wilson was out on one side and he on the other, stumbling as his feet hit the still speeding-by of the earth, and then he was shooting at the bull as he moved away, hearing the bullets whunk into him, emptying his rifle at him as he moved steadily away, finally remembering to get his shots forward into the shoulder, and as he fumbled to re-load, he saw the bull was down. Down on his knees, his big head tossing, and seeing the other two still galloping he shot at the leader and hit him. He shot again and missed and he heard the *carawonging* roar as Wilson shot and saw the leading bull slide forward onto his nose.

"Get that other," Wilson said. "Now you're shooting!" 320

But the other bull was moving steadily at the same gallop and he missed, throwing a spout of dirt, and Wilson missed and the dust rose in a cloud and Wilson shouted, "Come on. He's too far!" and grabbed his arm and they were in the car again, Macomber and Wilson hanging on the sides and rocketing swayingly over the uneven ground, drawing up on the steady, plunging, heavy-necked, straight-moving gallop of the bull.

They were behind him and Macomber was filling his rifle, dropping shells onto the ground, jamming it, clearing the jam, then they were almost up with the bull when Wilson yelled "Stop," and the car skidded so that it almost swung over and Macomber fell forward onto his feet, slammed his bolt forward and fired as far forward as he could aim into the galloping, rounded black back, aimed and shot again, then again, then again, and the bullets, all of them hitting, had no effect on the buffalo that he could see. Then Wilson shot, the roar deafening him, and he could see the bull stagger. Macomber shot again, aiming carefully, and down he came, onto his knees.

"All right," Wilson said. "Nice work. That's the three."

Macomber felt a drunken elation.

325   "How many times did you shoot?" he asked.

"Just three," Wilson said. "You killed the first bull. The biggest one. I helped you finish the other two. Afraid they might have got into cover. You had them killed. I was just mopping up a little. You shot damn well."

"Let's go to the car," said Macomber. "I want a drink."

"Got to finish off that buff first," Wilson told him. The buffalo was on his knees and he jerked his head furiously and bellowed in pig-eyed, roaring rage as they came toward him.

"Watch he doesn't get up," Wilson said. Then, "Get a little broadside and take him in the neck just behind the ear."

330   Macomber aimed carefully at the center of the huge, jerking, rage-driven neck and shot. At the shot the head dropped forward.

"That does it," said Wilson. "Got the spine. They're a hell of a looking thing, aren't they?"

"Let's get the drink," said Macomber. In his life he had never felt so good.

In the car Macomber's wife sat very white faced. "You were marvellous, darling," she said to Macomber. "What a ride."

"Was it rough?" Wilson asked.

335   "It was frightful. I've never been more frightened in my life."

"Let's all have a drink," Macomber said.

"By all means," said Wilson. "Give it to the Memsahib." She drank the neat whisky from the flask and shuddered a little when she swallowed. She handed the flask to Macomber who handed it to Wilson.

"It was frightfully exciting," she said. "It's given me a dreadful headache. I didn't know you were allowed to shoot them from cars though."

"No one shot from cars," said Wilson coldly.

340   "I mean chase them from cars."

"Wouldn't ordinarily," Wilson said. "Seemed sporting enough to me though while we were doing it. Taking more chance driving that way across the plain full of holes and one thing and another than hunting on foot. Buffalo could have charged us each time we shot if he liked. Gave him every chance. Wouldn't mention it to any one though. It's illegal if that's what you mean."

"It seemed very unfair to me," Margot said, "chasing those big helpless things in a motor car."

"Did it?" said Wilson.

"What would happen if they heard about it in Nairobi?"

"I'd lose my licence for one thing. Other unpleasantnesses," Wilson said, taking a drink from the flask. "I'd be out of business." 345

"Really?"

"Yes, really."

"Well," said Macomber, and he smiled for the first time all day. "Now she has something on you."

"You have such a pretty way of putting things, Francis," Margot Macomber said. Wilson looked at them both. If a four-letter man marries a five-letter woman, he was thinking, what number of letters would their children be? What he said was, "We lost a gun-bearer. Did you notice it?"

"My God, no," Macomber said. 350

"Here he comes," Wilson said. "He's all right. He must have fallen off when we left the first bull."

Approaching them was the middle-aged gun-bearer, limping along in his knitted cap, khaki tunic, shorts and rubber sandals, gloomy-faced and disgusted looking. As he came up he called out to Wilson in Swahili and they all saw the change in the white hunter's face.

"What does he say?" asked Margot.

"He says the first bull got up and went into the bush," Wilson said with no expression in his voice.

"Oh," said Macomber blankly. 355

"Then it's going to be just like the lion," said Margot, full of anticipation.

"It's not going to be a damned bit like the lion," Wilson told her. "Did you want another drink, Macomber?"

"Thanks, yes," Macomber said. He expected the feeling he had had about the lion to come back but it did not. For the first time in his life he really felt wholly without fear. Instead of fear he had a feeling of definite elation.

"We'll go and have a look at the second bull," Wilson said. "I'll tell the driver to put the car in the shade."

"What are you going to do?" asked Margaret Macomber. 360

"Take a look at the buff," Wilson said.

"I'll come."

"Come along."

The three of them walked over to where the second buffalo bulked blackly in the open, head forward on the grass, the massive horns swung wide.

"He's a very good head," Wilson said. "That's close to a fifty-inch spread." 365

Macomber was looking at him with delight.

"He's hateful looking," said Margot. "Can't we go into the shade?"

"Of course," Wilson said. "Look," he said to Macomber, and pointed. "See that patch of bush?"

"Yes."

370 "That's where the first bull went in. The gun-bearer said when he fell off the bull was down. He was watching us helling along and the other two buff galloping. When he looked up there was the bull up and looking at him. Gun-bearer ran like hell and the bull went off slowly into that bush."

"Can we go in after him now?" asked Macomber eagerly.

Wilson looked at him appraisingly. Damned if this isn't a strange one, he thought. Yesterday he's scared sick and today he's a ruddy fire eater.

"No, we'll give him a while."

"Let's please go into the shade," Margot said. Her face was white and she looked ill.

375 They made their way to the car where it stood under a single, wide-spreading tree and all climbed in.

"Chances are he's dead in there," Wilson remarked. "After a little we'll have a look."

Macomber felt a wild unreasonable happiness that he had never known before.

"By God, that was a chase," he said. "I've never felt any such feeling. Wasn't it marvellous, Margot?"

"I hated it."

380 "Why?"

"I hated it," she said bitterly. "I loathed it."

"You know I don't think I'd ever be afraid of anything again," Macomber said to Wilson. "Something happened in me after we first saw the buff and started after him. Like a dam bursting. It was pure excitement."

"Cleans out your liver," said Wilson. "Damn funny things happen to people."

Macomber's face was shining. "You know something did happen to me," he said. "I feel absolutely different."

385 His wife said nothing and eyed him strangely. She was sitting far back in the seat and Macomber was sitting forward talking to Wilson who turned sideways talking over the back of the front seat.

"You know, I'd like to try another lion," Macomber said. "I'm really not afraid of them now. After all, what can they do to you?"

"That's it," said Wilson. "Worst one can do is kill you. How does it go? Shakespeare. Damned good. See if I can remember. Oh, damned good. Used to quote it to myself at one time. Let's see. 'By my troth, I care not; a man can die but once; we owe God a death and let it go which way it will he that dies this year is quit for the next.' Damned fine, eh?"

He was very embarrassed, having brought out this thing he had lived by, but he had seen men come of age before and it always moved him. It was not a matter of their twenty-first birthday.

It had taken a strange chance of hunting, a sudden precipitation into action without opportunity for worrying beforehand, to bring this about with Macomber, but regardless of how it had happened it had most certainly happened. Look at the beggar now, Wilson thought. It's that some of them stay little boys so long, Wilson thought. Sometimes all their lives. Their figures stay boyish when they're fifty. The great American boy-men. Damned strange people. But he liked this Macomber now. Damned strange fellow. Probably meant the end of cuckoldry too. Well, that would be a damned good thing. Damned good thing. Beggar had probably been afraid all his life. Don't know what started it. But over now. Hadn't had time to be afraid with the buff. That and being angry too. Motor car too. Motor cars made it familiar. Be a damn fire eater now. He'd seen it in the war work the same way. More of a change than any loss of virginity. Fear gone like an operation. Something else grew in its place. Main thing a man had. Made him into a man. Women knew it too. No bloody fear.

From the far corner of the seat Margaret Macomber looked at the two of   390
them. There was no change in Wilson. She saw Wilson as she had seen him the day before when she had first realized what his great talent was. But she saw the change in Francis Macomber now.

"Do you have that feeling of happiness about what's going to happen?" Macomber asked, still exploring his new wealth.

"You're not supposed to mention it," Wilson said, looking in the other's face. "Much more fashionable to say you're scared. Mind you, you'll be scared too, plenty of times."

"But you *have* a feeling of happiness about action to come?"

"Yes," said Wilson. "There's that. Doesn't do to talk too much about all this. Talk the whole thing away. No pleasure in anything if you mouth it up too much."

"You're both talking rot," said Margot. "Just because you've chased some   395
helpless animals in a motor car you talk like heroes."

"Sorry," said Wilson. "I have been gassing too much." She's worried about it already, he thought.

"If you don't know what we're talking about why not keep out of it?" Macomber asked his wife.

"You've gotten awfully brave, awfully suddenly," his wife said contemptuously, but her contempt was not secure. She was very afraid of something.

Macomber laughed, a very natural hearty laugh. "You know I *have*," he said. "I really have."

"Isn't it sort of late?" Margot said bitterly. Because she had done the best she   400
could for many years back and the way they were together now was no one person's fault.

"Not for me," said Macomber.

Margot said nothing but sat back in the corner of the seat.

"Do you think we've given him time enough?" Macomber asked Wilson cheerfully.

"We might have a look," Wilson said. "Have you any solids left?"

"The gun-bearer has some."   405

Wilson called in Swahili and the older gun-bearer, who was skinning out one of the heads, straightened up, pulled a box of solids out of his pocket and brought them over to Macomber, who filled his magazine and put the remaining shells in his pocket.

"You might as well shoot the Springfield," Wilson said. "You're used to it. We'll leave the Mannlicher in the car with the Memsahib. Your gun-bearer can

carry your heavy gun. I've this damned cannon. Now let me tell you about them."
He had saved this until the last because he did not want to worry Macomber.
"When a buff comes he comes with his head high and thrust straight out. The
boss of the horns covers any sort of a brain shot. The only shot is straight into
the nose. The only other shot is into his chest or, if you're to one side, into the
neck or the shoulders. After they've been hit once they take a hell of a lot of
killing. Don't try anything fancy. Take the easiest shot there is. They've finished
skinning out that head now. Should we get started?"

He called to the gun-bearers, who came up wiping their hands, and the older
one got into the back.

"I'll only take Kongoni," Wilson said. "The other can watch to keep the birds
away."

410   As the car moved slowly across the open space toward the island of brushy
trees that ran in a tongue of foliage along a dry water course that cut the open
swale, Macomber felt his heart pounding and his mouth was dry again, but it
was excitement, not fear.

"Here's where he went in," Wilson said. Then to the gun-bearer in Swahili,
"Take the blood spoor."

The car was parallel to the patch of bush. Macomber, Wilson and the
gun-bearer got down. Macomber, looking back, saw his wife, with the rifle by
her side, looking at him. He waved to her and she did not wave back.

The brush was very thick ahead and the ground was dry. The middle-aged
gun-bearer was sweating heavily and Wilson had his hat down over his eyes and
his red neck showed just ahead of Macomber. Suddenly the gun-bearer said
something in Swahili to Wilson and ran forward.

"He's dead in there," Wilson said. "Good work," and he turned to grip
Macomber's hand and as they shook hands, grinning at each other, the gun-bearer
shouted wildly and they saw him coming out of the bush sideways, fast as a crab,
and the bull coming, nose out, mouth tight closed, blood dripping, massive head
straight out, coming in a charge, his little pig eyes bloodshot as he looked at
them. Wilson, who was ahead was kneeling shooting, and Macomber, as he fired,
unhearing his shot in the roaring of Wilson's gun, saw fragments like slate burst
from the huge boss of the horns, and the head jerked, he shot again at the wide
nostrils and saw the horns jolt again and fragments fly, and he did not see Wilson
now and, aiming carefully, shot again with the buffalo's huge bulk almost on him
and his rifle almost level with the on-coming head, nose out, and he could see
the little wicked eyes and the head started to lower and he felt a sudden white-
hot, blinding flash explode inside his head and that was all he ever felt.

415   Wilson had ducked to one side to get in a shoulder shot. Macomber had stood
solid and shot for the nose, shooting a touch high each time and hitting the
heavy horns, splintering and chipping them like hitting a slate roof, and Mrs.
Macomber, in the car, had shot at the buffalo with the 6.5 Mannlicher as it
seemed about to gore Macomber and had hit her husband about two inches up
and a little to one side of the base of his skull.

Francis Macomber lay now, face down, not two yards from where the buffalo
lay on his side and his wife knelt over him with Wilson beside her.

"I wouldn't turn him over," Wilson said.

The woman was crying hysterically.

"I'd get back in the car," Wilson said. "Where's the rifle?"

She shook her head, her face contorted. The gun-bearer picked up the rifle. 420

"Leave it as it is," said Wilson. Then, "Go get Abdulla so that he may witness the manner of the accident."

He knelt down, took a handkerchief from his pocket, and spread it over Francis Macomber's crew-cropped head where it lay. The blood sank into the dry, loose earth.

Wilson stood up and saw the buffalo on his side, his legs out, his thinly-haired belly crawling with ticks. "Hell of a good bull," his brain registered automatically. "A good fifty inches, or better. Better." He called to the driver and told him to spread a blanket over the body and stay by it. Then he walked over to the motor car where the woman sat crying in the corner.

"That was a pretty thing to do," he said in a toneless voice. "He *would* have left you too."

"Stop it," she said. 425

"Of course it's an accident," he said. "I know that."

"Stop it," she said.

"Don't worry," he said. "There will be a certain amount of unpleasantness but I will have some photographs taken that will be very useful at the inquest. There's the testimony of the gun-bearers and the driver too. You're perfectly all right."

"Stop it," she said.

"There's a hell of a lot to be done," he said. "And I'll have to send a truck off 430 to the lake to wireless for a plane to take the three of us into Nairobi. Why didn't you poison him? That's what they do in England."

"Stop it. Stop it. Stop it," the woman cried.

Wilson looked at her with his flat blue eyes.

"I'm through now," he said. "I was a little angry. I'd begun to like your husband."

"Oh, please stop it," she said. "Please, please stop it."

"That's better," Wilson said. "Please is much better. Now I'll stop." 435

[1936]

1. Before World War II, the African safari developed as a form of recreation in which wealthy Westerners hired men familiar with the terrain and habits of animals to guide them on hunting trips. Denis Finch-Hatton, lover of Karen von Blixen, who wrote "Babette's Feast" (see p. 413), might have been one of the models for Robert Wilson, who guided the Macombers. The genre of trips has since been increased by the photographic version in which the shooting is done with cameras. But what relationship to nature can you discern from the practice described in the story?

2. What ethical questions does the story raise?

3. What does the story have to say about gender?

4. What is the relationship between plot and chronology in this story? Why structure the story in this way?

5. How does Hemingway structure point of view in the story? With what effect?

LESLIE MARMON SILKO

LESLIE MARMON SILKO (1948–) *writes about her origins as Laguna, Pueblo, Mexican, and white. She was born and raised in New Mexico on the Laguna Pueblo Reservation and grew up listening to the folk tales and legends of her tribe, which became the material for her first collection of poems,* Laguna Woman. *Her acclaimed novel,* Ceremony, *was published in 1977 and was followed in 1981 by* Storyteller, *a collection of poetry, family history, myths, stories, and photographs and in 1991 by* Almanac of Death. *She lives and works in Tucson, Arizona.*

The Man to Send Rain Clouds

One

They found him under a big cottonwood tree. His Levi jacket and pants were faded light-blue so that he had been easy to find. The big cottonwood tree stood apart from a small grove of winterbare cottonwoods which grew in the wide, sandy arroyo.° He had been dead for a day or more, and the sheep had wandered and scattered up and down the arroyo. Leon and his brother-in-law, Ken, gathered the sheep and left them in the pen at the sheep camp before they returned to the cottonwood tree. Leon waited under the tree while Ken drove the truck through the deep sand to the edge of the arroyo. He squinted up at the sun and unzipped his jacket—it sure was hot for this time of year. But high and northwest the blue mountains were still deep in snow. Ken came sliding down the low, crumbling bank about fifty yards down, and he was bringing the red blanket.

Before they wrapped the old man, Leon took a piece of string out of his pocket and tied a small gray feather in the old man's long white hair. Ken gave him the paint. Across the brown wrinkled forehead he drew a streak of white and along the high cheekbones he drew a strip of blue paint. He paused and watched Ken throw pinches of corn meal and pollen into the wind that fluttered the small gray feather. Then Leon painted with yellow under the old man's broad nose, and finally, when he had painted green across the chin, he smiled.

"Send us rain clouds, Grandfather." They laid the bundle in the back of the pickup and covered it with a heavy tarp before they started back to the pueblo.

They turned off the highway onto the sandy pueblo road. Not long after they passed the store and post office they saw Father Paul's car coming toward them. When he recognized their faces he slowed his car and waved for them to stop. The young priest rolled down the car window.

5   "Did you find old Teofilo?" he asked loudly.

Leon stopped the truck. "Good morning, Father. We were just out to the sheep camp. Everything is O.K. now."

---

¹**arroyo** a gully or channel carved by water in an arid region

"Thank God for that. Teofilo is a very old man. You really shouldn't allow him to stay at the sheep camp alone."

"No, he won't do that any more now."

"Well, I'm glad you understand. I hope I'll be seeing you at Mass this week— we missed you last Sunday. See if you can get old Teofilo to come with you." The priest smiled and waved at them as they drove away.

Two

Louise and Teresa were waiting. The table was set for lunch, and the coffee was   10
boiling on the black iron stove. Leon looked at Louise and then at Teresa.

"We found him under a cottonwood tree in the big arroyo near sheep camp. I guess he sat down to rest in the shade and never got up again." Leon walked toward the old man's head. The red plaid shawl had been shaken and spread carefully over the bed, and a new brown flannel shirt and pair of stiff new Levis were arranged neatly beside the pillow. Louise held the screen door open while Leon and Ken carried in the red blanket. He looked small and shriveled, and after they dressed him in the new shirt and pants he seemed more shrunken.

It was noontime now because the church bells rang the Angelus.° They ate the beans with hot bread, and nobody said anything until after Teresa poured the coffee.

Ken stood up and put on his jacket. "I'll see about the gravediggers. Only the top layer of soil is frozen. I think it can be ready before dark."

Leon nodded his head and finished his coffee. After Ken had been gone for a while, the neighbors and clanspeople came quietly to embrace Teofilo's family and to leave food on the table because the grave-diggers would come to eat when they were finished.

Three

The sky in the west was full of pale-yellow light. Louise stood outside with her   15
hands in the pockets of Leon's green army jacket that was too big for her. The funeral was over, and the old men had taken their candles and medicine bags and were gone. She waited until the body was laid into the pickup before she said anything to Leon. She touched his arm, and he noticed that her hands were still dusty from the corn meal that she had sprinkled around the old man. When she spoke, Leon could not hear her.

"What did you say? I didn't hear you."

"I said that I had been thinking about something."

"About what?"

"About the priest sprinkling holy water° for Grandpa. So he won't be thirsty."

Leon stared at the new moccasins that Teofilo had made for the ceremonial   20
dances in the summer. They were nearly hidden by the red blanket. It was getting

---

¹²**Angelus** in Catholicism, a bell announcing time for a prayer commemorating the Incarnation of Jesus as messiah   ¹⁹**holy water** in Catholicism, water blessed by a priest and used to purify

colder, and the wind pushed gray dust down the narrow pueblo road. The sun
was approaching the long mesa where it disappeared during the winter. Louise
stood there shivering and watching his face. Then he zipped up his jacket and
opened the truck door. "I'll see if he's there."

Ken stopped the pickup at the church, and Leon got out; and then Ken drove
down the hill to the graveyard where people were waiting. Leon knocked at the
old carved door with its symbols of the Lamb. While he waited he looked up at
the twin bells from the king of Spain with the last sunlight pouring around them
in their tower.

The priest opened the door and smiled when he saw who it was. "Come in!
What brings you here this evening?"

The priest walked toward the kitchen, and Leon stood with his cap in his
hand, playing with the earflaps and examining the living room—the brown sofa,
the green armchair, and the brass lamp that hung down from the ceiling by links
of chain. The priest dragged a chair out of the kitchen and offered it to Leon.

"No thank you, Father. I only came to ask you if you would bring your holy
water to the graveyard."

25   The priest turned away from Leon and looked out the window at the patio
full of shadows and the dining-room windows of the nuns' cloister across the
patio. The curtains were heavy, and the light from within faintly penetrated; it
was impossible to see the nuns inside eating supper. "Why didn't you tell me he
was dead? I could have brought the Last Rites° anyway."

Leon smiled. "It wasn't necessary, Father."

The priest stared down at his scuffed brown loafers and the worn hem of his
cassock. "For a Christian burial it was necessary."

His voice was distant, and Leon thought that his blue eyes looked tired.

"It's O.K., Father, we just want him to have plenty of water."

30   The priest sank down in the green chair and picked up a glossy missionary magazine. He turned the colored pages full of lepers and pagans without looking at them.

"You know I can't do that, Leon. There should have been the Last Rites and a
funeral Mass at the very least."

Leon put on his green cap and pulled the flaps down over his ears. "It's getting late, Father. I've got to go."

When Leon opened the door Father Paul stood up and said, "Wait." He left
the room and came back wearing a long brown overcoat. He followed Leon
out the door and across the dim churchyard to the adobe steps in front of the
church. They both stooped to fit through the low adobe entrance. And when
they started down the hill to the graveyard only half of the sun was visible
above the mesa.

The priest approached the grave slowly, wondering how they had managed to
dig into the frozen ground, and then he remembered that this was New Mexico,
and saw the pile of cold loose sand beside the hole. The people stood close to

---

²⁵**Last Rites** the Catholic sacrament in which the body of a sick or dying person is anointed
with holy oil and prayers said for the person's physical and spiritual health through
forgiveness of sins

each other with little clouds of steam puffing from their faces. The priest looked at them and saw a pile of jackets, gloves, and scarves in the yellow, dry tumble-weeds that grew in the graveyard. He looked at the red blanket, not sure that Teofilo was so small, wondering if it wasn't some perverse Indian trick—something they did in March to ensure a good harvest—wondering if maybe old Teofilo was actually at sheep camp corraling the sheep for the night. But there he was, facing into a cold dry wind and squinting at the last sunlight, ready to bury a red wool blanket while the faces of the parishioners were in shadow with the last warmth of the sun on their backs.

His fingers were stiff, and it took them a long time to twist the lid off the holy water. Drops of water fell on the red blanket and soaked into dark icy spots. He sprinkled the grave and the water disappeared almost before it touched the dim, cold sand; it reminded him of something—he tried to remember what it was, because he thought if he could remember he might understand this. He sprin-kled more water; he shook the container until it was empty, and the water fell through the light from sundown like August rain that fell while the sun was still shining, almost evaporating before it touched the wilted squash flowers. ₃₅

The wind pulled at the priest's brown Franciscan robe and swirled away the corn meal and pollen that had been sprinkled on the blanket. They lowered the bundle into the ground, and they didn't bother to untie the stiff pieces of new rope that were tied around the ends of the blanket. The sun was gone, and over on the highway the eastbound lane was full of headlights. The priest walked away slowly. Leon watched him climb the hill, and when he had disappeared within the tall, thick walls, Leon turned to look up at the high blue mountains in the deep snow that reflected a faint red light from the west. He felt good because it was finished, and he was happy about the sprinkling of the holy water, now the old man could send them big thunderclouds for sure.   [1969]

1. What are the major themes of this story? How do you know?
2. What are the major characteristics of the different cultures represented in the story?
3. From whose point of view is the story narrated? What is the effect of this choice?

Nguyen Huy Thiep

Nguyen Huy Thiep *(1950–) was born in Hanoi and raised in a small farming community during the French and American military campaigns in Vietnam. After graduating from the National Vietnamese Teacher's College during the American bombing in 1970, he began teaching history in a rural province, writing and painting in his spare time. Influenced by many European writers and yet deeply involved with life in Vietnam, he began to publish his writing in 1987. The 1987 collection from which this story is taken got a great deal of attention, including some government attempts at censorship.*

Salt of the Jungle

A month after the new year is the best time to be in the jungle. The vegetation is bursting with fresh buds, and its leaves are deep green and moist. Nature is both daunting and delicate, and this is due, in large measure, to the showers of spring rain.

At around this time, your feet sink into carpets of rotting leaves, you inhale pure air, and, sometimes, your body shudders with pleasure, because a drop of water has fallen from a leaf and struck your bare shoulder. Miraculously, the vexations of your daily life can be completely forgotten, because a small squirrel has sprung onto a branch. And, as it happened, it was at just such a time that Mr. Dieu went hunting.

The idea to go hunting had come to him when his son, who was studying in a foreign country, sent him a gift of a double-barreled shotgun. The gun was as light as a toy, and so sleek that he could not have dreamt such a beautiful thing existed. Mr. Dieu was sixty, and, at that age, both a new shotgun and a spring day for the hunt really made life worth living.

To dress for the occasion, he put on a warm quilted coat and trousers, a fur hat, and laced up a pair of high boots. To be well prepared, he also took a ration of sticky rice rolled into a ball the size of his fist. He moved up along the bed of a dry stream toward its source, a mile from which was the fabled kingdom of limestone caves.

5   Mr. Dieu turned onto a beaten track that wound through the jungle. As he moved along, he was aware that the trees on either side were full of bluebirds. Yet, he did not shoot. With a gun like his, it would have been a waste of ammunition, especially when he had already had his fill of bluebirds. They were tasty enough, but had a fishy flavor. In any case, he had no need to shoot birds with a loft full of pigeons at home.

At a turn in the track, Mr. Dieu was startled by a rustling in a bush. A clump of motley vines flew up in front of his face, and, as he caught his breath, a pair of jungle fowls shot out in front of the bush with their heads down, clucking. Mr. Dieu raised his shotgun and aimed. However, the fowls did not present a good target. *I'll miss,* he thought. He considered the situation, and sat down motionless for a very long time, waiting for the jungle to become quiet again. The fowls would think there was nobody there: it would be better that way—for them and for him.

The mountain range was full of towering peaks. Mr. Dieu looked at them as he contemplated his strength. To bag a monkey or a mountain goat would certainly be something. But he knew that mountain goats were difficult game. It was only by some stroke of luck that he would get a good shot at one, and he did not think that luck would come.

As he weighed carefully the pros and cons, Mr. Dieu decided to move along the foot of the limestone mountain range and hunt monkeys in the Dau Da Forest. He would be surer of finding food and wasting less energy. Mount Hoa Qua and Thuy Liem Cave were along the valley and, like the forest, they were legendary monkey haunts. Mr. Dieu also knew that he did not have difficulty shooting monkeys.

He stopped on a piece of rising ground, amid trees covered with climbing vines. This species of tree was unknown to him, with its silver leaves and golden flowers like earrings that hung down to the earth. Mr. Dieu sat quietly and observed, for he wanted to see if there were any monkeys there. These animals are as crafty as human beings; when they gather food they always put out sentries, and monkey sentries are very acute. If you don't see them, there is no hope for the hunt, no hope of hitting the leader of the troop. Of course, the leader was only a monkey. But it was not just any monkey. It would be the one that fate had singled out for him. So he had to wait, had to be cunning if he wanted to shoot his monkey.

Mr. Dieu sat quietly and relaxed for half an hour. The spring weather was warm and silky. It had been a long time since he had had the opportunity to sit as peacefully as this. And as he sat without a care in the world, the tranquillity of the jungle flowed through his being.

Suddenly, a swishing sound came rushing from out of the Dau Da Forest. It was the sound of a large animal moving through the trees. Mr. Dieu knew it was the leader of a monkey troop. He also knew that this monkey was formidable. It would appear with the brutal self-confidence of a king. Mr. Dieu smiled and watched carefully.

The sound continued for a while; then, suddenly, the beast appeared. It rapidly propelled itself through the jungle as though it never rested. Mr. Dieu admired its nimbleness. However, it disappeared in a flash, leaving him with a sharp stab of disappointment that this king-like creature would not be his. The elation he had felt since leaving home that morning was beginning to subside.

As soon as the leader disappeared, a gaggle of about twenty monkeys swung into view, criss-crossing Mr. Dieu's field of vision from very many angles. Some of them appeared on perches high up in the trees, others swung through the branches, and still others sprang to the ground. Within this medley of movement, Mr. Dieu noticed three monkeys that stayed together: a male, a female, and their young baby. He knew immediately that this male monkey was his prey.

Mr. Dieu felt hot. He took off his hat and quilted coat and placed them under a bush. He also placed his ball of sticky rice there. Gradually, he moved into a depression in the ground. He observed carefully, and noticed that the female monkey was standing guard. That was convenient, for with a becoming sense of vanity, she had distracted herself with the task of picking off her body lice.

Mr. Dieu made his calculations, then crept along, keeping windward of the female monkey. He had to get within twenty meters of the troop before he would be able to shoot. He crawled rapidly and skillfully. Once he had located his prey, he was sure he would kill it. That monkey was his. He was so certain of this, he felt that if he stumbled or made a careless move it would not make any difference.

Yet, even though he thought like this, Mr. Dieu still stalked the monkey troop carefully. He knew that nature was full of surprises, that one could never be too cautious.

He rested the shotgun in the fork of a tree, while the family trio had no inkling that disaster was near. The father was perched in a tree plucking fruit and throwing it down to the mother and child. Before he threw it, he always selected the best fruit and ate it himself. *How contemptible,* thought Mr. Dieu as he squeezed the trigger. The shotgun blast stunned the monkey troop for several seconds: the male monkey had fallen heavily to the ground with its arms outstretched.

The confusion into which the shotgun blast had thrown the monkey troop caused Mr. Dieu to tremble. He had done something cruel. His arms and legs went limp, with the kind of sensation that overcomes someone who has just overexerted himself with heavy work, and the troop disappeared into the jungle before he knew it. The female monkey and the baby also ran off after the others, but, after moving some distance, the female suddenly turned around and returned. Her mate, whose shoulder had been shattered by the shotgun pellets, was trying to raise himself but kept falling back to the ground.

The female monkey advanced carefully to where her mate had fallen and looked around, suspicious of the silence. The male monkey let out a pitiful scream, before he became silent again and listened, with a frantic expression on his face.

20   *Oh, get away from there!* Mr. Dieu groaned softly. But the female monkey looked as though she was prepared to sacrifice herself. She went to her mate and lifted him up in her arms. Mr. Dieu angrily raised his shotgun. Her readiness to sacrifice herself made him hate her like some bourgeois madame who paraded her noble nature. He knew all about the deceptions in which such theatrical performances were rooted; she could not deceive an old hunter like him.

As Mr. Dieu prepared to squeeze the trigger, the female monkey turned around and looked at him with terror in her eyes. She dropped the male monkey with a thud and fled. Mr. Dieu breathed a sigh of relief, then laughed quietly. He rose to his feet and left his hiding place.

I've made a mistake! Mr. Dieu cursed under his breath. For when he moved from his hiding place, the female monkey immediately turned around. *She knows I'm human,* he sighed, *the game is up.* Exactly so: the female monkey now kept him in the corner of her eye as she rushed headlong back to her mate. She deftly put her arms around him and hugged him to her chest. The two rolled around in a ball on the ground. She was acting like a crazy old woman. She was going to sacrifice herself recklessly, because of some noble instinct that nature prized. This stirred deep feelings of guilt in Mr. Dieu's heart. He had revealed himself as an assassin, while the female monkey, who faced death, still bared her teeth in a smile. Whatever he did now, he could only suffer, he could never rest, and he could even die two years before his time if he shot the female monkey at this moment. And all of this was because he had come out of his hiding place two minutes too soon.

As if to torment him, the monkeys took each other by the hand and ran off. *You pathetic old figure, Dieu,* he thought sadly. *With a pair of arthritic legs like yours, how are you going to run as fast as a monkey driven by loyalty and devotion?* The female monkey waved her bow legs, grinned, and made obscene gestures. Mr. Dieu angrily hurled his shotgun down in front of him. He wanted to frighten the female monkey into releasing her mate.

At the moment the shotgun hit the ground, the baby monkey suddenly appeared from a rocky mound. It grabbed the sling of the shotgun and dragged it off along the ground. The three monkeys scurried off on all fours, shrieking. Mr. Dieu was struck dumb for a second, then burst out laughing: his predicament was so ridiculous.

He picked up a handful of dirt and stones and threw it at the monkeys, as he 25 took off howling in pursuit. The monkeys, who were terrified by these developments, split up, with the two adults veering off in the direction of the mountains and the baby running toward the cliff. *Losing the shotgun will be disastrous,* thought Mr. Dieu, and he continued to chase the baby monkey. He charged forward and narrowed the distance between them to the extent that only a jagged rock prevented him from reaching his gun.

By chasing the baby monkey, Mr. Dieu had taken a course of action that had extraordinary consequences. These began when the small monkey just rolled over the edge of the precipice, holding the shotgun sling tightly. Evidently, it was too inexperienced to react in any other way.

Mr. Dieu was pale and soaked with sweat. He stood looking down over the cliff with his body shaking. From far below came the echo of a piercing scream, the likes of which he had never heard before. He drew back in fear, as a mist swirled up from the abyss and enveloped the vegetation around him. Very quickly the entire landscape was obscured by eerie vapors. He ran back to the mountain. It was perhaps the first time since childhood that Mr. Dieu had run as though he were being chased by a ghost.

Mr. Dieu was exhausted when he reached the foot of the mountain. He sat down on the ground, looking back in the direction of the precipice, which the mist had now obscured. He remembered suddenly that this was the most feared place in the valley: the place that hunters called Death Hollow. Here, with alarming regularity, somebody perished in the mist each year.

Ghosts? thought Mr. Dieu. *Forsaken spirits usually take the form of white monkeys, don't they?* It had been a white monkey that seized the gun. Moreover, this had been such an extraordinary action that Mr. Dieu began to wonder if what he had been chasing was really a monkey.

Am I dreaming? he wondered, looking around. *Is all of this happening?* He stood 30 up and looked at the mountain wall on the other side of Death Hollow. He was stunned, for now, without a trace of mist, the dome of the sky was clear and vast, and the entire landscape was visible in every detail.

An agitated cry came from somewhere above him. Mr. Dieu looked up and there he saw the wounded monkey lying across a rock ledge. The female monkey was nowhere to be seen, and so, very happy in the certainty that he would now catch his monkey, Mr. Dieu searched for a way to climb up on the rock ledge.

Finding a way up the side of the steep, slippery mountain was both difficult and dangerous. Mr. Dieu gauged his strength. *Whatever way, I'm going to get that monkey,* he murmured to himself, as he calmly used the crevices in the rock face to work his way up.

After about ten minutes, Mr. Dieu felt hot. He chose a spot where he could stand, then took off his boots and outer garments and placed them in the fork of a mulberry tree. He climbed onward quickly with no doubts about his ability to reach the ledge.

The slab of rock on which the wounded monkey lay was smooth and seemed somewhat unstable. Beneath it, there was a crevice as wide as Mr. Dieu's hand, which would allow him to pull himself up. He shuddered, frightened by the feeling that the slab might move and roll down the mountain at any moment. Nature was cruel and might want to test his courage further.

Mr. Dieu finally pulled himself up on the rock ledge with his elbows, and there he saw an extremely beautiful monkey with fine golden hair. It lay prone with its hands raking across the surface of the rock, as if it were trying to pull itself along. Its shoulder was stained red with blood.

Mr. Dieu put his hand on the monkey and felt its feverish body heat. *Easier than putting a hand on a sparrow,* he thought. Next, he slipped his hand under the monkey's chest and lifted it to estimate its weight. However, he withdrew his hand quickly when the chest emitted a low, but very disconcerting *hum,* which made him feel that his intervention had aroused Death's fury. The monkey stirred Mr. Dieu's pity when it trembled and rolled its sluggish eyes toward him. The shotgun pellets had smashed the monkey's shoulder blade and come out through four centimeters of bone. Each time the bones rubbed together, the monkey writhed in pain.

"I can't leave you like that," said Mr. Dieu. He picked up some Lao grass, crumpled it in his hand, and put it in the monkey's mouth. The monkey chewed the grass carefully, while Mr. Dieu applied a handful of leaves to its wound to stem the bleeding. The monkey curled its body into a ball and again turned its moist eyes toward Mr. Dieu. The old man looked away.

The monkey then buried its head in Mr. Dieu's arms, and a stammering sound came out of its mouth. The monkey was like a helpless child imploring him for help. Mr. Dieu felt very miserable. "It is better for me if you resist," he murmured, looking down at the suffering brow of the shriveled monkey. "I am old, and you know the sympathy of old people is easily aroused. What can I use to bandage you, poor monkey?"

Mr. Dieu considered the situation. He had no choice but to take off his shorts and use them to bandage the monkey's wound. When he did this, the bleeding stopped and the monkey no longer groaned.

Naked now, Mr. Dieu picked the monkey up and kept adjusting its weight in his arms as he found his way back down the mountain. Then, suddenly, as though impelled by some force, the mountainside began to slide away with a tremendous roar from about halfway up.

An avalanche!

Mr. Dieu jumped in terror and clung tightly to a rock. A section of the path he had taken to come up the mountain now flashed down past him, leaving only the surface of the rock shorn smooth. Mr. Dieu could no longer see the mulberry tree where he had left his boots and outer garments. To descend that way was now impossible. He would have to circle around behind the mountain. Even though it was farther this way, it was the only safe alternative.

Mr. Dieu groped his way down the mountain for more than two hours before he reached the bottom. He had never had as difficult and as exhausting an ordeal as that. His body was covered in scratches. The monkey hovered between life and death, as he dragged it along the ground. For Mr. Dieu, it was agonizing to have to drag the monkey like that, but he no longer had the strength to carry it in his arms.

When Mr. Dieu reached the clump of bushes and vines he had hidden behind that morning, he stopped to pick up his hat and coat and the ball of sticky rice he had left there. But, to his astonishment, he found that a termites' nest as tall as rice stubble had risen in that spot. The nest was a sticky mound of fresh red earth plastered together with termites' wings. Unfortunately, his things had been mixed up in the nest and turned to mash. Mr. Dieu sighed, turned around in frustration, and lifted the monkey up in his arms. *How humiliating it will be to return home naked,* he scowled angrily. *I'll become a laughing stock.*

He set off, thinking about what he was going to do, and walked around in a circle   45
until he found the track again. *How did this happen?* He burst out laughing. *Who has ever shot a monkey like this? A sparrow-and-a-half of meat on it. Golden hair like dye. You shoot an animal like this even though you've got no clothes? Serves you right, you old fool!*

There was a faint sound of something moving behind him. He gave a start, turned around, and recognized the female monkey, who immediately disappeared behind a bush. It turned out that she had followed Mr. Dieu from the mountain without his realizing it. *How bizarre,* he thought. After moving on for some distance, Mr. Dieu turned around again and, to his exasperation, saw that she was still following him. He put the male monkey down on the ground, gathered some stones, and chased the female monkey away. She gave a high-pitched scream and disappeared. When Mr. Dieu looked around a little later, she still tagged along behind him.

The trio continued to plod on through the jungle. The female monkey was incredibly persistent, and made Mr. Dieu feel that it was all so terribly unfair, that he was being pursued by misfortune.

By now, the male monkey had also recognized the call of his mate. He wriggled around. This wriggling made Mr. Dieu feel extremely wretched, and it so exhausted him that he didn't have the strength to carry the monkey any farther. To make matters worse, the monkey's hands clawed at Mr. Dieu's chest and made it bleed. Mr. Dieu could no longer bear the situation, and, in a fury, he threw the monkey down on the ground.

While the monkey lay sprawled out on a piece of wet grass, Mr. Dieu sat down and looked at it. Not far away, the female monkey bobbed out from behind the foot of a tree to see what was happening. As Mr. Dieu now looked at both of the monkeys, he felt a burning sensation on the bridge of his nose. Profoundly sad, he was overcome by the realization that, in life, responsibility weighs heavily on every living thing.

All right, I'll set you free, declared Mr. Dieu. He sat peacefully for a moment,   50
then stood up without warning, and spat a wad of saliva on the ground near his feet. After hesitating for some time, he finally hurried off. The female monkey shot straight out of her hiding place as though she had been waiting for exactly this moment, and ran quickly to her mate.

Mr. Dieu turned onto another track because he wanted to avoid people. This track was choked with bramble bushes that made the going difficult, but they were covered by masses of *tu huyen* flowers. Mr. Dieu stopped in amazement. *Tu huyen* flowers bloom only once in thirty years, and people that come across them are said to meet with good luck. The flowers are white. They are as small as the head of a toothpick and have a salty taste. People call them "salt of the jungle." When the jungle is braided together with these flowers, it is a sign that the country is blessed with peace and abundant harvests.

When he came out of the valley, Mr. Dieu went down into the fields. The spring rain was gentle but very good for the rice seeds. Naked and lonely, he went on his way. A little later, his shadow faded into the curtain of rain.

In only a few days it would be the beginning of summer. The weather would gradually get warmer. . . .   [1987]

1. What kind of narrator is this and what difference does it make to the story?
2. What is the function of the following passage? How does it reflect on the story's definition of point of view? "The species of tree was unknown to him, with its silver leaves and golden flowers like earrings that hung down to the earth. Mr. Dieu sat quietly and observed, for he wanted to see if there were any monkeys there" (paragraph 9). How does it influence our reading of paragraph 10?
3. Why does Mr. Dieu choose the head of the monkey band as prey?
4. What happens to Mr. Dieu's attitude toward the hunt? How does it happen?
5. What is the climax of the plot?
6. Is Mr. Dieu better or worse off for his adventure in the jungle?
7. Discuss the symbolic significance of the title and any significance to the name "Dieu."
8. To what other works in the book can you compare this story?

DRAMA

FRAMEWORKS

Looking at Frayn through Science

MICHAEL FRAYN, *Copenhagen*

IRVING M. KLOTZ, *Procrustean Distortions of Science*

HARRY LUSTIG AND KIRSTEN SHEPHERD-BARR, From *Science as Theatre*

MICHAEL FRAYN

MICHAEL FRAYN *(1933–), London-born and bred, began his writing career as a newspaper columnist and reporter. He published several collections of his columns and several novels. His plays include* Donkey's Years, Make and Break, *and the farce* Noises Off, *which was made into a film with Carol Burnett, Michael Caine, Christopher Reeve, and John Ritter. The New York production of* Copenhagen *won the Tony Award for Best Play in 2000, and the play was filmed for PBS television with Daniel Craig, Stephen Rea, and Francesca Annis.*

Copenhagen was first performed at the Cottesloe Theatre, Royal National Theatre, London on May 21, 1998, with the following cast:

Margrethe°	Sara Kestelman
Bohr°	David Burke
Heisenberg°	Matthew Marsh

Directed by Michael Blakemore
Designed by Peter J. Davison
Lighting by Mark Henderson
Sound by Simon Baker

Author's note

I should like to record my gratitude to Professor Balázs L. Gyorffy, Professor of Physics at Bristol University, for his kindness in reading the text of the play and making a number of corrections and suggestions.

Michael Frayn, 1998

Copenhagen

Act One

Margrethe: But why?
Bohr: You're still thinking about it?
Margrethe: Why did he come to Copenhagen?
Bohr: Does it matter, my love, now we're all three of us dead and gone?
Margrethe: Some questions remain long after their owners have died. Lingering   5
  like ghosts. Looking for the answers they never found in life.
Bohr: Some questions have no answers to find.
Margrethe: Why did he come? What was he trying to tell you?
Bohr: He did explain later.
Margrethe: He explained over and over again. Each time he explained it became
  more obscure.
Bohr: It was probably very simple, when you come right down to it: he wanted   10
  to have a talk.
Margrethe: A talk? To the enemy? In the middle of a war?
Bohr: Margrethe, my love, we were scarcely the enemy.
Margrethe: It was 1941!

Margrethe [Nørlund Bohr] married Bohr in 1913   **[Niels] Bohr** (1885–1962) the Danish physicist who won the Nobel Prize in 1922 for his work on the implications of quantum theory for the structure of atoms. In Denmark he directed the Theoretical Physics Institute of the University of Copenhagen. Because he was half Jewish, he was in danger from the Nazis, who occupied Denmark during World War II. Having escaped the Nazis in 1943, he went to the lab at Los Alamos, New Mexico, to join America's effort to make an atomic bomb. After the war, he worked on the political problems resulting from the invention of nuclear weapons. He also wrote about the ways that knowledge of physics influence other areas of human life (e.g., *Atomic Physics and Human Knowledge*). **[Werner] Heisenberg** (1901–1976) German physicist who received the Nobel Prize for Physics in 1932. He worked with Bohr in Copenhagen from September 1924 until May 1925 and from May 1926 until 1927.

Bohr: Heisenberg was one of our oldest friends.

15 *Margrethe:* Heisenberg was German. We were Danes. We were under German occupation.

Bohr: It put us in a difficult position, certainly.

Margrethe: I've never seen you as angry with anyone as you were with Heisenberg that night.

Bohr: Not to disagree, but I believe I remained remarkably calm.

Margrethe: I know when you're angry.

20 *Bohr:* It was as difficult for him as it was for us.

Margrethe: So why did he do it? Now no one can be hurt, now no one can be betrayed.

Bohr: I doubt if he ever really knew himself.

Margrethe: And he wasn't a friend. Not after that visit. That was the end of the famous friendship between Niels Bohr and Werner Heisenberg.

Heisenberg: Now we're all dead and gone, yes, and there are only two things the world remembers about me. One is the uncertainty principle,° and the other is my mysterious visit to Niels Bohr in Copenhagen in 1941. Everyone understands uncertainty. Or thinks he does. No one understands my trip to Copenhagen. Time and time again I've explained it. To Bohr himself, and Margrethe. To interrogators and intelligence officers, to journalists and historians. The more I've explained, the deeper the uncertainty has become. Well, I shall be happy to make one more attempt. Now we're all dead and gone. Now no one can be hurt, now no one can be betrayed.

25 *Margrethe:* I never entirely liked him, you know. Perhaps I can say that to you now.

Bohr: Yes, you did. When he was first here in the twenties? Of course you did. On the beach at Tisvilde with us and the boys? He was one of the family.

Margrethe: Something alien about him, even then.

Bohr: So quick and eager.

Margrethe: Too quick. Too eager.

30 *Bohr:* Those bright watchful eyes.

Margrethe: Too bright. Too watchful.

Bohr: Well, he was a very great physicist. I never changed my mind about that.

Margrethe: They were all good, all the people who came to Copenhagen to work with you. You had most of the great pioneers in atomic theory here at one time or another.

Bohr: And the more I look back on it, the more I think Heisenberg was the greatest of them all.

35 *Heisenberg:* So what was Bohr? He was the first of us all, the father of us all. Modern atomic physics began when Bohr realised that quantum theory° applied to matter as well as to energy. 1913. Everything we did was based on that great insight of his.

Bohr: When you think that he first came here as my assistant in 1924 . . .

[24]**uncertainty principle** "The more precisely the position is determined, the less precisely the momentum is known in this instant, and vice versa" (Heisenberg, 1927).
[35]**quantum theory** the idea that radiant energy is divided into finite portions or quantities

Heisenberg: I'd only just finished my doctorate, and Bohr was the most famous atomic physicist in the world.

Bohr: . . . and in just over a year he'd invented quantum mechanics.

Margrethe: It came out of his work with you.

Bohr: Within three he'd got uncertainty.   40

Margrethe: And you'd done complementarity.°

Bohr: We argued them both out together.

Heisenberg: We did most of our best work together.

Bohr: Heisenberg usually led the way.

Heisenberg: Bohr made sense of it all.   45

Bohr: We operated like a business.

Heisenberg: Chairman and managing director.

Margrethe: Father and son.

Heisenberg: A family business.

Margrethe: Even though we had sons of our own.   50

Bohr: And we went on working together long after he ceased to be my assistant.

Heisenberg: Long after I'd left Copenhagen in 1927 and gone back to Germany. Long after I had a chair and a family of my own.

Margrethe: Then the Nazis came to power. . . .

Bohr: And it got more and more difficult. When the war broke out—impossible. Until that day in 1941.

Margrethe: When it finished forever.   55

Bohr: Yes, why did he do it?

Heisenberg: September, 1941. For years I had it down in my memory as October.

Margrethe: September. The end of September.

Bohr: A curious sort of diary memory is.

Heisenberg: You open the pages, and all the neat headings and tidy jottings dissolve   60
around you.

Bohr: You step through the pages into the months and days themselves.

Margrethe: The past becomes the present inside your head.

Heisenberg: September, 1941, Copenhagen. . . . And at once—here I am, getting off the night train from Berlin with my colleague Carl von Weizsäcker.° Two plain civilian suits and raincoats among all the field-grey Wehrmacht uniforms arriving with us, all the naval gold braid, all the well-tailored black of the SS. In my bag I have the text of the lecture I'm giving. In my head is another communication that has to be delivered. The lecture is on astrophysics. The text inside my head is a more difficult one.

Bohr: We obviously can't go to the lecture.

Margrethe: Not if he's giving it at the German Cultural Institute—it's a Nazi   65
propaganda organisation.

---

[41]**complementarity** the idea that one can't separate the behavior of an atomic object from the instruments that measure it. Therefore the information obtained from different experimental conditions can't be added up into one comprehensive understanding, but must be regarded as complementing each other. Light, for example, sometimes behaves like a wave and sometimes like a particle. It can't be seen as both at the same time, but the two descriptions together are better than either one alone.   [63]**Carl von Weizsäcker** German physicist and nuclear scientist

Bohr: He must know what we feel about that.

Heisenberg: Weizsäcker has been my John the Baptist, and written to warn Bohr of my arrival.

Margrethe: He wants to see you?

Bohr: I assume that's why he's come.

70 *Heisenberg:* But how can the actual meeting with Bohr be arranged?

Margrethe: He must have something remarkably important to say.

Heisenberg: It has to seem natural. It has to be private.

Margrethe: You're not really thinking of inviting him to the house?

Bohr: That's obviously what he's hoping.

75 *Margrethe:* Niels! They've occupied our country!

Bohr: He is not they.

Margrethe: He's one of them.

Heisenberg: First of all there's an official visit to Bohr's workplace, the Institute for Theoretical Physics, with an awkward lunch in the old familiar canteen. No chance to talk to Bohr, of course. Is he even present? There's Rozental° . . . Petersen, I think . . . Christian Møller,° almost certainly. . . . It's like being in a dream. You can never quite focus the precise details of the scene around you. At the head of the table—is that Bohr? I turn to look, and it's Bohr, it's Rozental, it's Møller, it's whoever I appoint to be there. . . . A difficult occasion, though—I remember that clearly enough.

Bohr: It was a disaster. He made a very bad impression. Occupation of Denmark unfortunate. Occupation of Poland, however, perfectly acceptable. Germany now certain to win the war.

80 *Heisenberg:* Our tanks are almost at Moscow. What can stop us? Well, one thing, perhaps. One thing.

Bohr: He knows he's being watched, of course. One must remember that. He has to be careful about what he says.

Margrethe: Or he won't be allowed to travel abroad again.

Bohr: My love, the Gestapo° planted microphones in his house. He told Goudsmit° when he was in America. The SS brought him in for interrogation in the basement at the Prinz-Albrecht-Strasse.

Margrethe: And then they let him go again.

85 *Heisenberg:* I wonder if they suspect for one moment how painful it was to get permission for this trip. The humiliating appeals to the Party, the demeaning efforts to have strings pulled by our friends in the Foreign Office.

Margrethe: How did he seem? Is he greatly changed?

Bohr: A little older.

Margrethe: I still think of him as a boy.

Bohr: He's nearly forty. A middle-aged professor, fast catching up with the rest of us.

90 *Margrethe:* You still want to invite him here?

[78]**[Stefan] Rozental** (1903–94) Polish physicist   **Christian Møller** physicist who worked with Bohr in Copenhagen before the war   [83]**Gestapo** German secret police   **[Samuel Abraham] Goudsmit** (1902–78) Dutch physicist who in 1927 emigrated to the United States, where he spent the rest of his career

Bohr: Let's add up the arguments on either side in a reasonably scientific way. Firstly, Heisenberg is a friend. . . .

Margrethe: Firstly, Heisenberg is a German.

Bohr: A White Jew. That's what the Nazis called him. He taught relativity, and they said it was Jewish physics. He couldn't mention Einstein° by name, but he stuck with relativity, in spite of the most terrible attacks.

Margrethe: All the real Jews have lost their jobs. He's still teaching.

Bohr: He's still teaching relativity.   95

Margrethe: Still a professor at Leipzig.

Bohr: At Leipzig, yes. Not at Munich. They kept him out of the chair at Munich.

Margrethe: He could have been at Columbia.

Bohr: Or Chicago. He had offers from both.

Margrethe: He wouldn't leave Germany.   100

Bohr: He wants to be there to rebuild German science when Hitler goes. He told Goudsmit.

Margrethe: And if he's being watched it will all be reported upon. Who he sees. What he says to them. What they say to him.

Heisenberg: I carry my surveillance around like an infectious disease. But then I happen to know that Bohr is also under surveillance.

Margrethe: And you know you're being watched yourself.

Bohr: By the Gestapo?   105

Heisenberg: Does he realise?

Bohr: I've nothing to hide.

Margrethe: By our fellow-Danes. It would be a terrible betrayal of all their trust in you if they thought you were collaborating.

Bohr: Inviting an old friend to dinner is hardly collaborating.

Margrethe: It might appear to be collaborating.   110

Bohr: Yes. He's put us in a difficult position.

Margrethe: I shall never forgive him.

Bohr: He must have good reason. He must have very good reason.

Heisenberg: This is going to be a deeply awkward occasion.

Margrethe: You won't talk about politics?   115

Bohr: We'll stick to physics. I assume it's physics he wants to talk to me about.

Margrethe: I think you must also assume that you and I aren't the only people who hear what's said in this house. If you want to speak privately you'd better go out in the open air.

Bohr: I shan't want to speak privately.

Margrethe: You could go for another of your walks together.

Heisenberg: Shall I be able to suggest a walk?   120

Bohr: I don't think we shall be going for any walks. Whatever he has to say he can say where everyone can hear it.

Margrethe: Some new idea he wants to try out on you, perhaps.

---

[93] **Albert Einstein** (1879–1955) German physicist who worked on the electromagnetic radiation of light, special theory of relativity, general relativity, and the equivalence of mass and energy. He won the Nobel Prize in 1921 for his 1905 work on the photoelectric effect. Visiting the United States when the Nazis came to power in 1933, he never returned to Germany.

Bohr: What can it be, though? Where are we off to next?

Margrethe: So now of course your curiosity's aroused, in spite of everything.

125 *Heisenberg:* So now here I am, walking out through the autumn twilight to the Bohrs' house at Ny-Carlsberg. Followed, presumably, by my invisible shadow. What am I feeling? Fear, certainly—the touch of fear that one always feels for a teacher, for an employer, for a parent. Much worse fear about what I have to say. About how to express it. How to broach it in the first place. Worse fear still about what happens if I fail.

Margrethe: It's not something to do with the war?

Bohr: Heisenberg is a theoretical physicist. I don't think anyone has yet discovered a way you can use theoretical physics to kill people.

Margrethe: It couldn't be something about fission?°

Bohr: Fission? Why would he want to talk to me about fission?

130 *Margrethe:* Because you're working on it.

Bohr: Heisenberg isn't.

Margrethe: Isn't he? Everybody else in the world seems to be. And you're the acknowledged authority.

Bohr: He hasn't published on fission.

Margrethe: It was Heisenberg who did all the original work on the physics of the nucleus. And he consulted you then, he consulted you at every step.

135 *Bohr:* That was back in 1932. Fission's only been around for the last three years.

Margrethe: But if the Germans were developing some kind of weapon based on nuclear fission . . .

Bohr: My love, no one is going to develop a weapon based on nuclear fission.

Margrethe: But if the Germans were trying to, Heisenberg would be involved.

Bohr: There's no shortage of good German physicists.

140 *Margrethe:* There's no shortage of good German physicists in America or Britain.

Bohr: The Jews have gone, obviously.

Heisenberg: Einstein, Wolfgang Pauli,° Max Born° . . . Otto Frisch,° Lise Meitner.° . . . We led the world in theoretical physics! Once.

Margrethe: So who is there still working in Germany?

Bohr: Sommerfeld,° of course. Von Laue.°

145 *Margrethe:* Old men.

Bohr: Wirtz.° Harteck.°

---

[128]**fission** When bombarded by neutrons, the nuclei of atoms split, producing two elements of different mass and giving off large amounts of energy. For instance, uranium can be split into neptunium and plutonium. [142]**Wolfgang Pauli** (1900–58) won the Nobel Prize for Physics in 1945, having spent the years of World War II in the United States   **Max Born** (1882–1970) German physicist who emigrated in 1933 at the rise of the Nazi Party; Nobel Laureate in Physics, 1954   **Otto Frisch** one of the first scientists to realize that a relatively small amount of the fissionable uranium 235 isotope could produce a nuclear explosion   **Lise Meitner** (1878–1968) Austrian physicist; emigrated to Sweden when the Nazis took over Austria; frequent collaborator with Otto Hahn; identified and gave the theoretical explanation of nuclear fission   [144]**[Arnold] Sommerfeld** (1868–1951) German physicist   **[Max] Von Laue** (1879–1960) won the Nobel Prize for Physics in 1914 [146]**[Karl] Wirtz** during World War II, part of the German team of nuclear scientists **[Paul] Harteck** (1926–) German physicist

Margrethe: Heisenberg is head and shoulders above all of them.

Bohr: Otto Hahn°—he's still there. He discovered fission, after all.

Margrethe: Hahn's a chemist. I thought that what Hahn discovered . . .

Bohr: . . . was that Enrico Fermi° had discovered it in Rome four years earlier.   150
Yes—he just didn't realise it was fission. It didn't occur to anyone that the
uranium atom might have split, and turned into an atom of barium and an
atom of krypton. Not until Hahn and Strassmann° did the analysis, and
detected the barium.

Margrethe: Fermi's in Chicago.

Bohr: His wife's Jewish.

Margrethe: So Heisenberg would be in charge of the work?

Bohr: Margrethe, there is no work! John Wheeler° and I did it all in 1939. One
of the implications of our paper is that there's no way in the foreseeable
future in which fission can be used to produce any kind of weapon.

Margrethe: Then why is everyone still working on it?   155

Bohr: Because there's an element of magic in it. You fire a neutron at the
nucleus of a uranium atom and it splits into two other elements. It's what the
alchemists were trying to do—to turn one element into another.

Margrethe: So why is he coming?

Bohr: Now your curiosity's aroused.

Margrethe: My forebodings.

Heisenberg: I crunch over the familiar gravel to the Bohrs' front door, and tug   160
at the familiar bell-pull. Fear, yes. And another sensation, that's become
painfully familiar over the past year. A mixture of self-importance and sheer
helplessness absurdity—that of all the 2,000 million people in this world, I'm the
one who's been charged with this impossible responsibility. . . . The heavy
door swings open.

Bohr: My dear Heisenberg!

Heisenberg: My dear Bohr!

Bohr: Come in, come in . . .

Margrethe: And of course as soon as they catch sight of each other all their caution
disappears. The old flames leap up from the ashes. If we can just negotiate
all the treacherous little opening civilities . . .

Heisenberg: I'm so touched you felt able to ask me.   165

Bohr: We must try to go on behaving like human beings.

Heisenberg: I realise how awkward it is.

Bohr: We scarcely had a chance to do more than shake hands at lunch the
other day.

[148]**Otto Hahn** (1879–1968) a chemist who won the Nobel Prize in 1944
[150]**Enrico Fermi** (1901–54) Italian physicist who won the Nobel Prize in Physics in 1938,
after which he emigrated to America to escape Mussolini's fascist regime. He helped to
create the first controlled nuclear chain reaction and became one of the leaders of the
Manhattan Project for the development of nuclear energy and the atomic bomb.
[Fritz] Strassmann (1902–80) German physicist   [154]**John Wheeler** (1911–) American
physicist who worked with Bohr on fission before World War II

Heisenberg: And Margrethe I haven't seen . . .

170 *Bohr:* Since you were here four years ago.

Margrethe: Niels is right. You look older.

Heisenberg: I had been hoping to see you both in 1938, at the congress in Warsaw . . .

Bohr: I believe you had some personal trouble.

Heisenberg: A little business in Berlin.

175 *Margrethe:* In the Prinz-Albrecht-Strasse?

Heisenberg: A slight misunderstanding.

Bohr: We heard, yes. I'm so sorry.

Heisenberg: These things happen. The question is now resolved. Happily resolved. Entirely resolved. . . . We should all have met in Zürich . . .

Bohr: In September 1939.

180 *Heisenberg:* And of course, sadly . . .

Bohr: Sadly for us as well.

Margrethe: A lot more sadly still for many people.

Heisenberg: Yes. Indeed.

Bohr: Well, there it is.

185 *Heisenberg:* What can I say?

Margrethe: What can any of us say, in the present circumstances?

Heisenberg: No. And your sons?

Margrethe: Are well, thank you. Elisabeth? The children?

Heisenberg: Very well. They send their love, of course.

190 *Margrethe:* They so much wanted to see each other, in spite of everything! But now the moment has come they're so busy avoiding each other's eye that they can scarcely see each other at all.

Heisenberg: I wonder if you realise how much it means to me to be back here in Copenhagen. In this house. I have become rather isolated in these last few years.

Bohr: I can imagine.

Margrethe: Me he scarcely notices. I watch him discreetly from behind my expression of polite interest as he struggles on.

Heisenberg: Have things here been difficult?

195 *Bohr:* Difficult?

Margrethe: Of course. He has to ask. He has to get it out of the way.

Bohr: Difficult. . . . What can I say? We've not so far been treated to the gross abuses that have occurred elsewhere. The race laws have not been enforced.

Margrethe: Yet.

Bohr: A few months ago they started deporting Communists and other anti-German elements.

200 *Heisenberg:* But you personally . . . ?

Bohr: Have been left strictly alone.

Heisenberg: I've been anxious about you.

Bohr: Kind of you. No call for sleepless nights in Leipzig so far, though.

Margrethe: Another silence. He's done his duty. Now he can begin to steer the conversation round to pleasanter subjects.

Heisenberg: Are you still sailing? 205
Bohr: Sailing?
Margrethe: Not a good start.
Bohr: No, no sailing.
Heisenberg: The Sound is . . . ?
Bohr: Mined. 210
Heisenberg: Of course.
Margrethe: I assume he won't ask if Niels has been skiing.
Heisenberg: You've managed to get some skiing?
Bohr: Skiing? In Denmark?
Heisenberg: In Norway. You used to go to Norway. 215
Bohr: I did, yes.
Heisenberg: But since Norway is also . . . well . . .
Bohr: Also occupied? Yes, that might make it easier. In fact I suppose we could
    now holiday almost anywhere in Europe.
Heisenberg: I'm sorry. I hadn't thought of it quite in those terms.
Bohr: Perhaps I'm being a little oversensitive. 220
Heisenberg: Of course not. I should have thought.
Margrethe: He must almost be starting to wish he was back in the Prinz-Albrecht-
    Strasse.
Heisenberg: I don't suppose you feel you could ever come to Germany . . .
Margrethe: The boy's an idiot.
Bohr: My dear Heisenberg, it would be an easy mistake to make, to think that 225
    the citizens of a small nation, of a small nation overrun, wantonly and cruelly
    overrun, by its more powerful neighbour, don't have exactly the same feelings
    of national pride as their conquerors, exactly the same love of their country.
Margrethe: Niels, we agreed.
Bohr: To talk about physics, yes.
Margrethe: Not about politics.
Bohr: I'm sorry.
Heisenberg: No, no—I was simply going to say that I still have my old ski-hut at 230
    Bayrischzell. So if by any chance . . . at any time . . . for any reason . . .
Bohr: Most kind of you.
Heisenberg: Frau Schumacher in the bakery—you remember her?
Bohr: I remember Frau Schumacher.
Heisenberg: She still has the key.
Bohr: Perhaps Margrethe would be kind enough to sew a yellow star on my 235
    ski-jacket.
Heisenberg: Yes. Yes. Stupid of me.
Margrethe: Silence again. Those first brief sparks have disappeared, and the ashes
    have become very cold indeed. So now of course I'm starting to feel almost
    sorry for him. Sitting here all on his own in the midst of people who hate him,
    all on his own against the two of us. He looks younger again, like the boy who
    first came here in 1924. Younger than Christian would have been now. Shy
    and arrogant and anxious to be loved. Homesick and pleased to be away from
    home at last. And, yes, it's sad, because Niels loved him, he was a father to him.

Heisenberg: So . . . what are you working on?

Margrethe: And all he can do is press forward.

240 *Bohr:* Fission, mostly.

Heisenberg: I saw a couple of papers in the *Physical Review*. The velocity-range relations of fission fragments . . . ?

Bohr: And something about the interactions of nuclei with deuterons. And you?

Heisenberg: Various things.

Margrethe: Fission?

245 *Heisenberg:* I sometimes feel very envious of your cyclotron.°

Margrethe: Why? Are you working on fission yourself?

Heisenberg: There are over thirty in the United States. Whereas in the whole of Germany . . . Well. . . . You still get to your country place, at any rate?

Bohr: We still go to Tisvilde, yes.

Margrethe: In the whole of Germany, you were going to say . . .

250 *Bohr:* . . . there is not one single cyclotron.

Heisenberg: So beautiful at this time of year. Tisvilde.

Bohr: You haven't come to borrow the cyclotron, have you? That's not why you've come to Copenhagen?

Heisenberg: That's not why I've come to Copenhagen.

Bohr: I'm sorry. We mustn't jump to conclusions.

255 *Heisenberg:* No, we must none of us jump to conclusions of any sort.

Margrethe: We must wait patiently to be told.

Heisenberg: It's not always easy to explain things to the world at large.

Bohr: I realise that we must always be conscious of the wider audience our words may have. But the lack of cyclotrons in Germany is surely not a military secret.

Heisenberg: I've no idea what's a secret and what isn't.

260 *Bohr:* No secret, either, about why there aren't any. You can't say it but I can. It's because the Nazis have systematically undermined theoretical physics. Why? Because so many people working in the field were Jews. And why were so many of them Jews? Because theoretical physics, the sort of physics done by Einstein, by Schrödinger° and Pauli, by Born and Sommerfeld, by you and me, was always regarded in Germany as inferior to experimental physics, and the theoretical chairs and lectureships were the only ones that Jews could get.

Margrethe: Physics, yes? Physics.

Bohr: This is physics.

Margrethe: It's also politics.

Heisenberg: The two are sometimes painfully difficult to keep apart.

265 *Bohr:* So, you saw those two papers. I haven't seen anything by you recently.

Heisenberg: No.

Bohr: Not like you. Too much teaching?

Heisenberg: I'm not teaching. Not at the moment.

Bohr: My dear Heisenberg—they haven't pushed you out of your chair at Leipzig? That's not what you've come to tell us?

---

[245]**cyclotron** particle accelerator   [260]**[Erwin] Schrödinger** Austrian physicist who won the Nobel Prize in 1933; escaped to Ireland when the Nazis invaded Austria

Heisenberg: No, I'm still at Leipzig. For part of each week.   270
Bohr: And for the rest of the week?
Heisenberg: Elsewhere. The problem is more work, not less.
Bohr: I see. Do I?
Heisenberg: Are you in touch with any of our friends in England? Born?
   Chadwick?
Bohr: Heisenberg, we're under German occupation. Germany's at war with   275
   Britain.
Heisenberg: I thought you might still have contacts of some sort. Or people in
   America? We're not at war with America.
Margrethe: Yet.
Heisenberg: You've heard nothing from Pauli, in Princeton? Goudsmit? Fermi?
Bohr: What do you want to know?
Heisenberg: I was simply curious . . . I was thinking about Robert Oppenheimer°   280
   the other day. I had a great set-to with him in Chicago in 1939.
Bohr: About mesons.°
Heisenberg: Is he still working on mesons?
Bohr: I'm quite out of touch.
Margrethe: The only foreign visitor we've had was from Germany. Your friend
   Weizsäcker was here in March.
Heisenberg: *My* friend? *Your* friend, too. I hope. You know he's come back to   285
   Copenhagen with me? He's very much hoping to see you again.
Margrethe: When he came here in March he brought the head of the German
   Cultural Institute with him.
Heisenberg: I'm sorry about that. He did it with the best of intentions. He may not
   have explained to you that the Institute is run by the Cultural Division of the
   Foreign Office. We have good friends in the foreign service. Particularly at the
   Embassy here.
Bohr: Of course. I knew his father when he was Ambassador in Copenhagen in
   the twenties.
Heisenberg: It hasn't changed so much since then, you know, the German foreign
   service.
Bohr: It's a department of the Nazi government.   290
Heisenberg: Germany is more complex than it may perhaps appear from the
   outside. The different organs of state have quite different traditions. Some
   departments remain stubbornly idiosyncratic, in spite of all attempts at
   reform. Particularly the foreign service. You know how attached diplomats
   are to outmoded conventions. Our people in the Embassy here are quite old-
   fashioned in the way they use their influence. They would certainly be trying
   to see that distinguished local citizens were able to work undisturbed.
Bohr: Are you telling me that I'm being protected by your friends in the Embassy?

---

[280]**[J.] Robert Oppenheimer** (1904–67) American physicist, an early opponent of
fascism who became head of the bomb program at Los Alamos   [281]**mesons** atomic
particles

Heisenberg: What I'm saying, in case Weizsäcker failed to make it clear, is that you would find congenial company there. I know people would be very honoured if you felt able to accept an occasional invitation.

Bohr: To cocktail parties at the German Embassy? To coffee and cakes with the Nazi plenipotentiary?

295 *Heisenberg:* To lectures, perhaps. To discussion groups. Social contacts of any sort could be helpful.

Bohr: I'm sure they could.

Heisenberg: Essential, perhaps, in certain circumstances.

Bohr: In what circumstances?

Heisenberg: I think we both know.

300 *Bohr:* Because I'm half-Jewish?

Heisenberg: We all at one time or another may need the help of our friends.

Bohr: Is this why you've come to Copenhagen? To invite me to watch the deportation of my fellow-Danes from a grandstand seat in the windows of the German Embassy?

Heisenberg: Bohr, please! Please! What else can I do? How else can I help? It's an impossibly difficult situation for you, I understand that. It's also an impossibly difficult one for me.

Bohr: Yes. I'm sorry. I'm sure you also have the best of intentions.

305 *Heisenberg:* Forget what I said. Unless . . .

Bohr: Unless I need to remember it.

Heisenberg: In any case it's not why I've come.

Margrethe: Perhaps you should simply say what it is you want to say.

Heisenberg: What you and I often used to do in the old days was to take an evening stroll.

310 *Bohr:* Often. Yes. In the old days.

Heisenberg: You don't feel like a stroll this evening, for old times' sake?

Bohr: A little chilly tonight, perhaps, for strolling.

Heisenberg: This is so difficult. You remember where we first met?

Bohr: Of course. At Göttingen in 1922.

315 *Heisenberg:* At a lecture festival held in your honour.

Bohr: It was a high honour. I was very conscious of it.

Heisenberg: You were being honoured for two reasons. Firstly because you were a great physicist . . .

Bohr: Yes, yes.

Heisenberg: . . . and secondly because you were one of the very few people in Europe who were prepared to have dealings with Germany. The war had been over for four years, and we were still lepers. You held out your hand to us. You've always inspired love, you know that. Wherever you've been, wherever you've worked. Here in Denmark. In England, in America. But in Germany we worshipped you. Because you held out your hand to us.

320 *Bohr:* Germany's changed.

Heisenberg: Yes. Then we were down. And you could be generous.

Margrethe: And now you're up.

Heisenberg: And generosity's harder. But you held out your hand to us then, and we took it.

Bohr: Yes. . . . No! Not you. As a matter of fact. You bit it.

Heisenberg: Bit it? 325

Bohr: Bit my hand! You did! I held it out, in my most statesmanlike and reconciliatory way, and you gave it a very nasty nip.

Heisenberg: I did?

Bohr: The first time I ever set eyes on you. At one of those lectures I was giving in Göttingen.

Heisenberg: What are you talking about?

Bohr: You stood up and laid into me. 330

Heisenberg: Oh . . . I offered a few comments.

Bohr: Beautiful summer's day. The scent of roses drifting in from the gardens. Rows of eminent physicists and mathematicians, all nodding approval of my benevolence and wisdom. Suddenly, up jumps a cheeky young pup and tells me that my mathematics are wrong.

Heisenberg: They were wrong.

Bohr: How old were you?

Heisenberg: Twenty. 335

Bohr: Two years younger than the century.

Heisenberg: Not quite.

Bohr: December 5th, yes?

Heisenberg: 1.93 years younger than the century.

Bohr: To be precise. 340

Heisenberg: No—to two places of decimals. To be *precise*, 1.928 . . . 7 . . . 6 . . . 7 . . . 1 . . .

Bohr: I can always keep track of you, all the same. And the century.

Margrethe: And Niels has suddenly decided to love him again, in spite of every-thing. Why? What happened? Was it the recollection of that summer's day in Göttingen? Or everything? Or nothing at all? Whatever it was, by the time we've sat down to dinner the cold ashes have started into flame once again.

Bohr: You were always so combative! It was the same when we played table-tennis at Tisvilde. You looked as if you were trying to kill me.

Heisenberg: I wanted to win. Of course I wanted to win. *You* wanted to win. 345

Bohr: I wanted an agreeable game of table-tennis.

Heisenberg: You couldn't see the expression on your face.

Bohr: I could see the expression on yours.

Heisenberg: What about those games of poker in the ski-hut at Bayrischzell, then? You once cleaned us all out! You remember that? With a non-existent straight! We're all mathematicians—we're all counting the cards—we're 90 per cent certain he hasn't got anything. But on he goes, raising us, raising us. This insane confidence. Until our faith in mathematical probability begins to waver, and one by one we all throw in.

Bohr: I thought I *had* a straight! I misread the cards! I bluffed myself! 350

Margrethe: Poor Niels.

Heisenberg: Poor Niels? He won! He bankrupted us! You were insanely competitive! He got us all playing poker once with imaginary cards!

Bohr: You played chess with Weizsäcker on an imaginary board!

Margrethe: Who won?

355 *Bohr:* Need you ask? At Bayrischzell we'd ski down from the hut to get provisions, and he'd make even that into some kind of race! You remember? When we were there with Weizsäcker and someone? You got out a stop-watch.

Heisenberg: It took poor Weizsäcker eighteen minutes.

Bohr: You were down there in ten, of course.

Heisenberg: Eight.

Bohr: I don't recall how long I took.

360 *Heisenberg:* Forty-five minutes.

Bohr: Thank you.

Margrethe: Some rather swift skiing going on here, I think.

Heisenberg: Your skiing was like your science. What were you waiting for? Me and Weizsäcker to come back and suggest some slight change of emphasis?

Bohr: Probably.

365 *Heisenberg:* You were doing seventeen drafts of each slalom?

Margrethe: And without me there to type them out.

Bohr: At least I knew where I was. At the speed you were going you were up against the uncertainty relationship. If you knew where you were when you were down you didn't know how fast you'd got there. If you knew how fast you'd been going you didn't know you were down.

Heisenberg: I certainly didn't stop to think about it.

Bohr: Not to criticise, but that's what might be criticised with some of your science.

370 *Heisenberg:* I usually got there, all the same.

Bohr: You never cared what got destroyed on the way, though. As long as the mathematics worked out you were satisfied.

Heisenberg: If something works it works.

Bohr: But the question is always, What does the mathematics mean, in plain language? What are the philosophical implications?

Heisenberg: I always knew you'd be picking your way step by step down the slope behind me, digging all the capsized meanings and implications out of the snow.

375 *Margrethe:* The faster you ski the sooner you're across the cracks and crevasses.

Heisenberg: The faster you ski the better you think.

Bohr: Not to disagree, but that is most . . . most interesting.

Heisenberg: By which you mean it's nonsense. But it's not nonsense. Decisions make themselves when you're coming downhill at seventy kilometres an hour. Suddenly there's the edge of nothingness in front of you. Swerve left? Swerve right? Or think about it and die? In your head you swerve both ways . . .

Margrethe: Like that particle.

380 *Heisenberg:* What particle?

Margrethe: The one that you said goes through two different slits at the same time.

Heisenberg: Oh, in our old thought-experiment. Yes. Yes!

Margrethe: Or Schrödinger's wretched cat.°

Heisenberg: That's alive and dead at the same time.

Margrethe: Poor beast. 385

Bohr: My love, it was an imaginary cat.

Margrethe: I know.

Bohr: Locked away with an imaginary phial of cyanide.

Margrethe: I know, I know.

Heisenberg: So the particle's here, the particle's there . . . 390

Bohr: The cat's alive, the cat's dead . . .

Margrethe: You've swerved left, you've swerved right . . .

Heisenberg: Until the experiment is over, this is the point, until the sealed chamber is opened, the abyss detoured; and it turns out that the particle has met itself again, the cat's dead . . .

Margrethe: And you're alive.

Bohr: Not so fast, Heisenberg . . . 395

Heisenberg: The swerve itself was the decision.

Bohr: Not so fast, not so fast!

Heisenberg: Isn't that how you shot Hendrik Casimir° dead?

Bohr: Hendrik Casimir?

Heisenberg: When he was working here at the Institute. 400

Bohr: I never shot Hendrik Casimir.

Heisenberg: You told me you did.

Bohr: It was George Gamow.° I shot George Gamow. *You* don't know—it was long after your time.

---

[383]**Schrödinger's cat** A "thought experiment" in which the physicist Erwin Schrödinger tried to show that the atom behaves differently from ordinary reality (E. Schrödinger, *Naturwissenschaften* 23, 807, 1935). Here is the way the website at the National Institute of Standards and Technology explains the contradiction:

"Suppose one places a cat (a macroscopic object) inside a closed box with a vial of cyanide and a radioactive atom initially prepared in the metastable state (a microscopic object). The radioactive atom has a probability of ½ of decaying in one hour. If it decays, then the cyanide is released and the cat dies; if it does not decay, then the cyanide is not released and the cat remains unharmed.

"The paradox arises because the atom, being a microscopic object, must be described by quantum mechanics. After one hour, and before it is observed, the atom is in an equal superposition of being decayed and undecayed. However, if quantum mechanics is a universal and complete theory, it must describe the whole system. And, since the state of the cat is correlated with the state of the atom, the cat must also be in a superposition of being dead and alive. This clearly contradicts our everyday experience of cats!

"This sort of apparent contradiction arises whenever the state of macroscopic objects is correlated with that of microscopic objects. It comes about because in our experience of our macroscopic surroundings, objects are either in one state or another, but never in a superposition of several states at the same time." (http://www.boulder.nist.gov/timefreq/ion/qucomp/cat.htm). [398]**Hendrik Casimir** Dutch physicist [403]**George Gamow** (1904–68) A Russian physicist who spent 1928–29 and 1930–31 as a Fellow of the Theoretical Physics Institute of the University of Copenhagen. In 1934 he emigrated to America, where he spent the rest of his career.

Heisenberg: Bohr, you shot Hendrik Casimir.

405 *Bohr:* Gamow, Gamow. Because he insisted that it was always quicker to act than to react. To make a decision to do something rather than respond to someone else's doing it.

Heisenberg: And for that you shot him?

Bohr: It was him! He went out and bought a pair of pistols! He puts one in his pocket, I put one in mine, and we get on with the day's work. Hours go by, and we're arguing ferociously about—I can't remember—our problems with the nitrogen nucleus, I expect—when suddenly Gamow reaches into his pocket . . .

Heisenberg: Cap-pistols.

Bohr: Cap-pistols, yes. Of course.

410 *Heisenberg:* Margrethe was looking a little worried.

Margrethe: No—a little surprised. At the turn of events.

Bohr: Now you remember how quick he was.

Heisenberg: Casimir?

Bohr: Gamow.

415 *Heisenberg:* Not as quick as me.

Bohr: Of course not. But compared with me.

Heisenberg: A fast neutron. However, or so you're going to tell me . . .

Bohr: However, yes, before his gun is even out of his pocket . . .

Heisenberg: You've drafted your reply.

420 *Margrethe:* I've typed it out.

Heisenberg: You've checked it with Klein.

Margrethe: I've retyped it.

Heisenberg: You've submitted it to Pauli in Hamburg.

Margrethe: I've retyped it again.

425 *Bohr:* Before his gun is even out of his pocket, mine is in my hand.

Heisenberg: And poor Casimir has been blasted out of existence.

Bohr: Except that it was Gamow.

Heisenberg: It was Casimir! He told me!

Bohr: Yes, well, one of the two.

430 *Heisenberg:* Both of them simultaneously alive and dead in our memories.

Bohr: Like a pair of Schrödinger cats. Where were we?

Heisenberg: Skiing. Or music. That's another thing that decides everything for you. I play the piano and the way seems to open in front of me—all I have to do is follow. That's how I had my one success with women. At a musical evening at the Bückings in Leipzig—we've assembled a piano trio. 1937, just when all my troubles with the . . . when my troubles are coming to a head. We're playing the Beethoven G major. We finish the scherzo, and I look up from the piano to see if the others are ready to start the final presto. And in that instant I catch a glimpse of a young woman sitting at the side of the room. Just the briefest glimpse, but of course at once I've carried her off to Bayrischzell, we're engaged, we're married, etc.—the usual hopeless romantic fantasies. Then off we go into the presto, and it's terrifyingly fast—so fast there's no time to be afraid. And suddenly everything in the world seems easy. We reach the end and I just carry on skiing. Get myself introduced to the young woman—see her home—and, yes, a week later I've carried her off to Bayrischzell—another week and we're engaged—three months and we're married. All on the sheer momentum of that presto!

Bohr: You were saying you felt isolated. But you do have a companion, after all.

Heisenberg: Music?

Bohr: Elisabeth!   435

Heisenberg: Oh. Yes. Though, what with the children, and so on . . . I've always envied the way you and Margrethe manage to talk about everything. Your work. Your problems. Me, no doubt.

Bohr: I was formed by nature to be a mathematically curious entity: not one but half of two.

Heisenberg: Mathematics becomes very odd when you apply it to people. One plus one can add up to so many different sums . . .

Margrethe: Silence. What's he thinking about now? His life? Or ours?

Bohr: So many things we think about at the same time. Our lives and our   440
physics.

Margrethe: All the things that come into our heads out of nowhere.

Bohr: Our private consolations. Our private agonies.

Heisenberg: Silence. And of course they're thinking about their children again.

Margrethe: The same bright things. The same dark things. Back and back they come.

Heisenberg: Their four children living, and their two children dead.   445

Margrethe: Harald. Lying alone in that ward.

Bohr: She's thinking about Christian and Harald.

Heisenberg: The two lost boys. Harald . . .

Bohr: All those years alone in that terrible ward.

Heisenberg: And Christian. The firstborn. The eldest son.   450

Bohr: And once again I see those same few moments that I see every day.

Heisenberg: Those short moments on the boat, when the tiller slams over in the heavy sea, and Christian is falling.

Bohr: If I hadn't let him take the helm . . .

Heisenberg: Those long moments in the water.

Bohr: Those endless moments in the water.   455

Heisenberg: When he's struggling towards the lifebuoy.

Bohr: So near to touching it.

Margrethe: I'm at Tisvilde. I look up from my work. There's Niels in the doorway, silently watching me. He turns his head away, and I know at once what's happened.

Bohr: So near, so near! So slight a thing!

Heisenberg: Again and again the tiller slams over. Again and again . . .   460

Margrethe: Niels turns his head away . . .

Bohr: Christian reaches for the lifebuoy . . .

Heisenberg: But about some things even they never speak.

Bohr: About some things even we only think.

Margrethe: Because there's nothing to be said.   465

Bohr: Well . . . perhaps we *should* be warm enough. You suggested a stroll.

Heisenberg: In fact the weather is remarkably warm.

Bohr: We shan't be long.

Heisenberg: A week at most.

470 *Bohr:* What—our great hike through Zealand?

Heisenberg: We went to Elsinore. I often think about what you said there.

Bohr: You don't mind, my love? Half-an-hour?

Heisenberg: An hour, perhaps. No, the whole appearance of Elsinore, you said, was changed by our knowing that Hamlet had lived there. Every dark corner there reminds us of the darkness inside the human soul . . .

Margrethe: So, they're walking again. He's done it. And if they're walking they're talking. Talking in a rather different way, no doubt—I've typed out so much in my time about how differently particles behave when they're unobserved . . . I knew Niels would never hold out if they could just get through the first few minutes. If only out of curiosity. . . . Now they're started an hour will mean two, of course, perhaps three. . . . The first thing they ever did was to go for a walk together. At Göttingen, after that lecture. Niels immediately went to look for the presumptuous young man who'd queried his mathematics, and swept him off for a tramp in the country. Walk—talk—make his acquaintance. And when Heisenberg arrived here to work for him, off they go again, on their great tour of Zealand. A lot of this century's physics they did in the open air. Strolling around the forest paths at Tisvilde. Going down to the beach with the children. Heisenberg holding Christian's hand. They talked on the boat a lot. Was Christian ever on the boat with them? No, he was too young for sailing then. . . . Yes, and every evening in Copenhagen, after dinner, they'd walk round Faelled Park behind the Institute, or out along Langelinie into the harbour. Walk, and talk. Long, long before walls had ears . . . But this time, in 1941, their walk takes a different course. Ten minutes after they set out . . . they're back! I've scarcely had the table cleared when there's Niels in the doorway. I see at once how upset he is—he can't look me in the eye.

475 *Bohr:* Heisenberg wants to say goodbye. He's leaving.

Margrethe: He won't look at me, either.

Heisenberg: Thank you. A delightful evening. Almost like old times. So kind of you.

Margrethe: You'll have some coffee? A glass of something?

Heisenberg: I have to get back and prepare for my lecture.

480 *Margrethe:* But you'll come and see us again before you leave?

Bohr: He has a great deal to do.

Margrethe: It's like the worst moments of 1927 all over again, when Niels came back from Norway and first read Heisenberg's uncertainty paper. Something they both seemed to have forgotten about earlier in the evening, though I hadn't. Perhaps they've both suddenly remembered that time. Only from the look on their faces something even worse has happened.

Heisenberg: Forgive me if I've done or said anything that . . .

Bohr: Yes, yes.

Heisenberg: It meant a great deal to me, being here with you both again. More   485
  perhaps than you realise.
Margrethe: It was a pleasure for us. Our love to Elisabeth.
Bohr: Of course.
Margrethe: And the children.
Heisenberg: Perhaps, when this war is over. . . . If we're all spared. . . . Goodbye.
Margrethe: Politics?   490
Bohr: Physics. He's not right, though. How can he be right? John Wheeler and
  I . . .
Margrethe: A breath of air as we talk, why not?
Bohr: A breath of air?
Margrethe: A turn around the garden. Healthier than staying indoors, perhaps.
Bohr: Oh. Yes.   495
Margrethe: For everyone concerned.
Bohr: Yes. Thank you. . . . How can he possibly be right? Wheeler and I went
  through the whole thing in 1939.
Margrethe: What did he say?
Bohr: Nothing. I don't know. I was too angry to take it in.
Margrethe: Something about fission?   500
Bohr: What happens in fission? You fire a neutron° at a uranium nucleus, it
  splits, and it releases energy.
Margrethe: A huge amount of energy. Yes?
Bohr: About enough to move a speck of dust. But it also releases two or three
  more neutrons. Each of which has the chance of splitting another nucleus.
Margrethe: So then those two or three split nuclei each release energy in their
  turn?
Bohr: And two or three more neutrons.   505
Heisenberg: You start a trickle of snow sliding as you ski. The trickle becomes a
  snowball . . .
Bohr: An ever-widening chain of split nuclei forks through the uranium, doubling and quadrupling in millionths of a second from one generation to the
  next. First two splits, let's say for simplicity. Then two squared, two cubed,
  two to the fourth, two to the fifth, two to the sixth . . .
Heisenberg: The thunder of the gathering avalanche echoes from all the surrounding mountains . . .
Bohr: Until eventually, after, let's say, eighty generations, 2^{80} specks of dust have
  been moved. 2^{80} is a number with 24 noughts. Enough specks of dust to constitute a city, and all who live in it.
Heisenberg: But there is a catch.   510
Bohr: There is a catch, thank God. Natural uranium consists of two different
  isotopes,° U-238 and U-235. Less than one per cent of it is U-235, and this
  tiny fraction is the only part of it that's fissionable by fast neutrons.

---

[501]**neutron** an uncharged atomic particle present in the nuclei of all elements except
hydrogen   [511]**isotopes** species of atoms with the same atomic number and position on
the periodic table of elements but differing mass

Heisenberg: This was Bohr's great insight. Another of his amazing intuitions. It came to him when he was at Princeton in 1939, walking across the campus with Wheeler. A characteristic Bohr moment—I wish I'd been there to enjoy it. Five minutes deep silence as they walked then: 'Now hear this—I have understood everything.'

Bohr: In fact it's a double catch. 238 is not only impossible to fission by fast neutrons—it also absorbs them. So, very soon after the chain reaction starts, there aren't enough fast neutrons left to fission the 235.

Heisenberg: And the chain stops.

515 *Bohr:* Now, you can fission the 235 with slow neutrons as well. But then the chain reaction occurs more slowly than the uranium blows itself apart.

Heisenberg: So again the chain stops.

Bohr: What all this means is that an explosive chain reaction will never occur in natural uranium. To make an explosion you will have to separate out pure 235. And to make the chain long enough for a large explosion . . .

Heisenberg: Eighty generations, let's say . . .

Bohr: . . . you would need many tons of it. And it's extremely difficult to separate.

520 *Heisenberg:* Tantalisingly difficult.

Bohr: Mercifully difficult. The best estimates, when I was in America in 1939, were that to produce even one gram of U-235 would take 26,000 years. By which time, surely, this war will be over. So he's wrong, you see, he's wrong! Or could *I* be wrong? Could I have miscalculated? Let me see. . . . What are the absorption rates for fast neutrons in 238? What's the mean free path of slow neutrons in 235 . . . ?

Margrethe: But what exactly had Heisenberg said? That's what everyone wanted to know, then and forever after.

Bohr: It's what the British wanted to know, as soon as Chadwick managed to get in touch with me. What exactly did Heisenberg say?

Heisenberg: And what exactly did Bohr reply? That was of course the first thing my colleagues asked me when I got back to Germany.

525 *Margrethe:* What did Heisenberg tell Niels—what did Niels reply? The person who wanted to know most of all was Heisenberg himself.

Bohr: You mean when he came back to Copenhagen after the war, in 1947?

Margrethe: Escorted this time not by unseen agents of the Gestapo, but by a very conspicuous minder from British intelligence.

Bohr: I think he wanted various things.

Margrethe: Two things. Food-parcels . . .

530 *Bohr:* For his family in Germany. They were on the verge of starvation.

Margrethe: And for you to agree what you'd said to each other in 1941.

Bohr: The conversation went wrong almost as fast as it did before.

Margrethe: You couldn't even agree where you'd walked that night.

Heisenberg: Where we walked? Faelled Park, of course. Where we went so often in the old days.

535 *Margrethe:* But Faelled Park is behind the Institute, four kilometres away from where we live!

Heisenberg: I can see the drift of autumn leaves under the street-lamps next to the bandstand.

Bohr: Yes, because you remember it as October!

Margrethe: And it was September.

Bohr: No fallen leaves!

Margrethe: And it was 1941. No street-lamps! 540

Bohr: I thought we hadn't got any further than my study. What I can see is the drift of papers under the reading-lamp on my desk.

Heisenberg: We must have been outside! What I was going to say was treasonable. If I'd been overheard I'd have been executed.

Margrethe: So what was this mysterious thing you said?

Heisenberg: There's no mystery about it. There never was any mystery. I remember it absolutely clearly, because my life was at stake, and I chose my words very carefully. I simply asked you if as a physicist one had the moral right to work on the practical exploitation of atomic energy. Yes?

Bohr: I don't recall. 545

Heisenberg: You don't recall, no, because you immediately became alarmed. You stopped dead in your tracks.

Bohr: I was horrified.

Heisenberg: Horrified. Good, you remember that. You stood there gazing at me, horrified.

Bohr: Because the implication was obvious. That you *were* working on it.

Heisenberg: And you jumped to the conclusion that I was trying to provide Hitler 550 with nuclear weapons.

Bohr: And you were!

Heisenberg: No! A reactor!° That's what we were trying to build! A machine to produce power! To generate electricity, to drive ships!

Bohr: You didn't say anything about a reactor.

Heisenberg: I didn't say anything about anything! Not in so many words. I couldn't! I'd no idea how much could be overheard. How much you'd repeat to others.

Bohr: But then I asked you if you actually thought that uranium fission could be 555 used for the construction of weapons.

Heisenberg: Ah! It's coming back!

Bohr: And I clearly remember what you replied.

Heisenberg: I said I now knew that it could be.

Bohr: This is what really horrified me.

Heisenberg: Because you'd always been confident that weapons would need 235, 560 and that we could never separate enough of it.

Bohr: A reactor—yes, maybe, because there it's not going to blow itself apart. You can keep the chain reaction going with slow neutrons in natural uranium.

Heisenberg: What we'd realised, though, was that if we could once get the reactor going . . .

Bohr: The 238 in the natural uranium would absorb the fast neutrons . . .

---

[552]**reactor** nuclear power plant for the generation of electricity

Heisenberg: Exactly as you predicted in 1939—everything we were doing was based on that fundamental insight of yours. The 238 would absorb the fast neutrons. And would be transformed by them into a new element altogether.

565 *Bohr:* Neptunium. Which would decay in its turn into another new element . . .

Heisenberg: At least as fissile as the 235 that we couldn't separate . . .

Margrethe: Plutonium.

Heisenberg: Plutonium.

Bohr: I should have worked it out for myself.

570 *Heisenberg:* If we could build a reactor we could build bombs. That's what had brought me to Copenhagen. But none of this could I say. And at this point you stopped listening. The bomb had already gone off inside your head. I realised we were heading back towards the house. Our walk was over. Our one chance to talk had gone forever.

Bohr: Because I'd grasped the central point already. That one way or another you saw the possibility of supplying Hitler with nuclear weapons.

Heisenberg: You grasped at least four different central points, all of them wrong. You told Rozental that I'd tried to pick your brains about fission. You told Weisskopf that I'd asked you what you knew about the Allied nuclear programme. Chadwick thought I was hoping to persuade you that there was no German programme. But then you seem to have told some people that I'd tried to recruit you to work on it!

Bohr: Very well. Let's start all over again from the beginning. No Gestapo in the shadows this time. No British intelligence officer. No one watching us at all.

Margrethe: Only me.

575 *Bohr:* Only Margrethe. We're going to make the whole thing clear to Margrethe. You know how strongly I believe that we don't do science for ourselves, that we do it so we can explain to others . . .

Heisenberg: In plain language.

Bohr: In plain language. Not your view, I know—you'd be happy to describe what you were up to purely in differential equations if you could—but for Margrethe's sake . . .

Heisenberg: Plain language.

Bohr: Plain language. All right, so here we are, walking along the street once more. And this time I'm absolutely calm, I'm listening intently. What is it you want to say?

580 *Heisenberg:* It's not just what *I* want to say! The whole German nuclear team in Berlin! Not Diebner,° of course, not the Nazis—but Weizsäcker, Hahn, Wirtz, Jensen,° Houtermanns°—they all wanted me to come and discuss it with you. We all see you as a kind of spiritual father.

580[Kurt] Diebner German army physicist and ordnance expert; in 1939, became head of Germany's uranium project to study the possibility of nuclear weapons

[J. Hans D.] Jensen (1907–73) German physicist who won the Nobel Prize in 1963

[Friedrich Georg] Houtermanns [Houtermans] (1903–66) Dutch-Austrian-German physicist

Margrethe: The Pope. That's what you used to call Niels behind his back. And now you want him to give you absolution.

Heisenberg: Absolution? No!

Margrethe: According to your colleague Jensen.

Heisenberg: Absolution is the last thing I want!

Margrethe: You told one historian that Jensen had expressed it perfectly.　　　　585

Heisenberg: Did I? Absolution. . . . Is that what I've come for? It's like trying to remember who was at that lunch you gave me at the Institute. Around the table sit all the different explanations for everything I did. I turn to look . . . Petersen, Rozental, and . . . yes . . . now the word absolution is taking its place among them all . . .

Margrethe: Though I thought absolution was granted for sins past and repented, not for sins intended and yet to be committed.

Heisenberg: Exactly! That's why I was so shocked!

Bohr: *You* were shocked?

Heisenberg: Because you *did* give me absolution! That's exactly what you did! As　　590
we were hurrying back to the house. You muttered something about everyone in wartime being obliged to do his best for his own country. Yes?

Bohr: Heaven knows what I said. But now here I am, profoundly calm and conscious, weighing my words. You don't want absolution. I understand. You want me to tell you *not* to do it? All right. I put my hand on your arm. I look you in the eye in my most papal way. Go back to Germany, Heisenberg. Gather your colleagues together in the laboratory. The whole team—Weizsäcker, Hahn, Wirtz, Jensen, Houtermanns, all the assistants and technicians. Get up on a table and tell them: 'Niels Bohr says that in his considered judgment supplying a homicidal maniac with an improved instrument of mass murder is . . .' What shall I say? '. . . an interesting idea.' No, not even an interesting idea. '. . . a really rather seriously uninteresting idea.' What happens? You all fling down your Geiger counters?

Heisenberg: Obviously not.

Bohr: Because they'll arrest you.

Heisenberg: Whether they arrest us or not it won't make any difference. In fact it will make things worse. I'm running my programme for the Kaiser Wilhelm Institute. But there's a rival one at Army Ordnance, run by Kurt Diebner, and he's a party member. If I go they'll simply get Diebner to take over my programme as well. He should be running it anyway. Wirtz and the rest of them only smuggled me in to keep Diebner and the Nazis out of it. My one hope is to remain in control.

Bohr: So you don't want me to say yes and you don't want me to say no.　　595

Heisenberg: What I want is for you to listen carefully to what I'm going on to say next, instead of running off down the street like a madman.

Bohr: Very well. Here I am, walking very slowly and popishly. And I listen most carefully as you tell me . . . .

Heisenberg: That nuclear weapons will require an enormous technical effort.

Bohr: True.

600 *Heisenberg:* That they will suck up huge resources.

Bohr: Huge resources. Certainly.

Heisenberg: That sooner or later governments will have to turn to scientists and ask whether it's worth committing those resources—whether there's any hope of producing the weapons in time for them to be used.

Bohr: Of course, but . . .

Heisenberg: Wait. So they will have to come to you and me. We are the ones who will have to advise them whether to go ahead or not. In the end the decision will be in our hands, whether we like it or not.

605 *Bohr:* And that's what you want to tell me?

Heisenberg: That's what I want to tell you.

Bohr: That's why you have come all this way, with so much difficulty? That's why you have thrown away nearly twenty years of friendship? Simply to tell me that?

Heisenberg: Simply to tell you that.

Bohr: But, Heisenberg, this is more mysterious than ever! What are you telling it me *for?* What am I supposed to do about it? The government of occupied Denmark isn't going to come to me and ask me whether we should produce nuclear weapons!

610 *Heisenberg:* No, but sooner or later, if I manage to remain in control of our programme, the German government is going to come to *me!* They will ask *me* whether to continue or not! *I* will have to decide what to tell them!

Bohr: Then you have an easy way out of your difficulties. You tell them the simple truth that you've just told me. You tell them how difficult it will be. And perhaps they'll be discouraged. Perhaps they'll lose interest.

Heisenberg: But, Bohr, where will that lead? What will be the consequences if we manage to fail?

Bohr: What can I possibly tell you that you can't tell yourself?

Heisenberg: There was a report in a Stockholm paper that the Americans are working on an atomic bomb.

615 *Bohr:* Ah. Now it comes, now it comes. Now I understand everything. You think I have contacts with the Americans?

Heisenberg: You may. It's just conceivable. If anyone in Occupied Europe does it will be you.

Bohr: So you *do* want to know about the Allied nuclear programme.

Heisenberg: I simply want to know if there is one. Some hint. Some clue. I've just betrayed my country and risked my life to warn you of the German programme . . .

Bohr: And now I'm to return the compliment?

620 *Heisenberg:* Bohr, I have to know! I'm the one who has to decide! If the Allies are building a bomb, what am I choosing for my country? You said it would be easy to imagine that one might have less love for one's country if it's small and defenceless. Yes, and it would be another easy mistake to make, to think that one loved one's country less because it happened to be in the wrong. Germany is where I was born. Germany is where I became what I am. Germany is all the faces of my childhood, all the hands that picked me up when I fell, all the voices that encouraged me and set me on my way, all the

hearts that speak to my heart. Germany is my widowed mother and my impossible brother. Germany is my wife. Germany is our children. I have to know what I'm deciding for them! Is it another defeat? Another nightmare like the nightmare I grew up with? Bohr, my childhood in Munich came to an end in anarchy and civil war. Are more children going to starve, as we did? Are they going to have to spend winter nights as I did when I was a schoolboy, crawling on my hands and knees through the enemy lines, creeping out into the country under cover of darkness in the snow to find food for my family? Are they going to sit up all night, as I did at the age of seventeen, guarding some terrified prisoner, talking to him and talking to him through the small hours, because he's going to be executed in the morning?

Bohr: But, my dear Heisenberg, there's nothing I can tell you. I've no idea whether there's an Allied nuclear programme.

Heisenberg: It's just getting under way even as you and I are talking. And maybe I'm choosing something worse even than defeat. Because the bomb they're building is to be used on us. On the evening of Hiroshima° Oppenheimer said it was his one regret. That they hadn't produced the bomb in time to use on Germany.

Bohr: He tormented himself afterwards.

Heisenberg: Afterwards, yes. At least we tormented ourselves a little beforehand. Did a single one of them stop to think, even for one brief moment, about what they were doing? Did Oppenheimer? Did Fermi, or Teller,° or Szilard?° Did Einstein, when he wrote to Roosevelt in 1939 and urged him to finance research on the bomb? Did you, when you escaped from Copenhagen two years later, and went to Los Alamos?

Bohr: My dear, good Heisenberg, we weren't supplying the bomb to Hitler!   625

Heisenberg: You weren't dropping it on Hitler, either. You were dropping it on anyone who was in reach. On old men and women in the street, on mothers and their children. And if you'd produced it in time they would have been my fellow-countrymen. My wife. My children. That was the intention. Yes?

Bohr: That was the intention.

Heisenberg: You never had the slightest conception of what happens when bombs are dropped on cities. Even conventional bombs. None of you ever experienced it. Not a single one of you. I walked back from the centre of Berlin to the suburbs one night, after one of the big raids. No transport moving, of course. The whole city on fire. Even the puddles in the streets are burning. They're puddles of molten phosphorus. It gets on your shoes like some kind of incandescent dog-muck—I have to keep scraping it off—as if the streets have been fouled by the hounds of hell. It would have made you laugh—my shoes keep bursting into flame. All around me, I suppose, there are people trapped, people in various stages of burning to death. And all I can think is, How will I ever get hold of another pair of shoes in times like these?

---

[622]**Hiroshima** Japanese city, the target of the first atomic bomb, August 6, 1945
[624]**[Edward] Teller** (1908–2003) Hungarian physicist, student of Heisenberg's; emigrated to Denmark in 1934, where he worked with Bohr, then to America in 1935; worked on the atomic bomb at Los Alamos; after World War II, promoted the idea of a hydrogen bomb   **[Leo] Szilard** physicist born in Hungary; emigrated to America, where he worked on the atomic bomb; helped Einstein draft the letter to Roosevelt in 1939

Bohr: You know why Allied scientists worked on the bomb.

630 *Heisenberg:* Of course. Fear.

Bohr: The same fear that was consuming you. Because they were afraid that *you* were working on it.

Heisenberg: But, Bohr, you could have told them!

Bohr: Told them what?

Heisenberg: What I told you in 1941! That the choice is in our hands! In mine—in Oppenheimer's! That if I can tell them the simple truth when they ask me, the simple discouraging truth, so can he!

635 *Bohr:* This is what you want from me? Not to tell you what the Americans are doing but to stop them?

Heisenberg: To tell them that we can stop it together.

Bohr: I had no contact with the Americans!

Heisenberg: You did with the British.

Bohr: Only later.

640 *Heisenberg:* The Gestapo intercepted the message you sent them about our meeting.

Margrethe: And passed it to you?

Heisenberg: Why not? They'd begun to trust me. This is what gave me the possibility of remaining in control of events.

Bohr: Not to criticise, Heisenberg, but if this is your plan in coming to Copenhagen, it's . . . what can I say? It's most interesting.

Heisenberg: It's not a plan. It's a hope. Not even a hope. A microscopically fine thread of possibility. A wild improbability. Worth trying, though, Bohr! Worth trying, surely! But already you're too angry to understand what I'm saying.

645 *Margrethe:* No—why he's angry is because he *is* beginning to understand! The Germans drive out most of their best physicists because they're Jews. America and Britain give them sanctuary. Now it turns out that this might offer the Allies a hope of salvation. And at once you come howling to Niels begging him to persuade them to give it up.

Bohr: Margrethe, my love, perhaps we should try to express ourselves a little more temperately.

Margrethe: But the gall of it! The sheer, breathtaking gall of it!

Bohr: Bold skiing, I have to say.

Heisenberg: But, Bohr, we're not skiing now! We're not playing table-tennis! We're not juggling with cap-pistols and non-existent cards! I refused to believe it, when I first heard the news of Hiroshima. I thought that it was just one of the strange dreams we were living in at the time. They'd got stranger and stranger, God knows, as Germany fell into ruins in those last months of the war. But by then we were living in the strangest of them all. The ruins had suddenly vanished—just the way things do in dreams—and all at once we're in a stately home in the middle of the English countryside. We've been rounded up by the British—the whole team, everyone who worked on atomic research—and we've been spirited away. To Farm Hall,° in

---

649**Farm Hall** country house in Huntingdonshire, England, where German physicists were interned and spied upon after World War II

Huntingdonshire, in the water-meadows of the River Ouse. Our families in Germany are starving, and there are we sitting down each evening to an excellent formal dinner with our charming host, the British officer in charge of us. It's like a pre-war house-party—one of those house-parties in a play, that's cut off from any contact with the outside world, where you know the guests have all been invited for some secret sinister purpose. No one knows we're there—no one in England, no one in Germany, not even our families. But the war's over. What's happening? Perhaps, as in a play, we're going to be quietly murdered, one by one. In the meanwhile it's all delightfully civilised. I entertain the party with Beethoven piano sonatas. Major Rittner, our hospitable gaoler, reads Dickens to us, to improve our English. . . . Did these things really happen to me . . . ? We wait for the point of it all to be revealed to us. Then one evening it is. And it's even more grotesque than the one we were fearing. It's on the radio: you have actually done the deed that we were tormenting ourselves about. That's why we're there, dining with our gracious host, listening to our Dickens. We've been kept locked up to stop us discussing the subject with anyone until it's too late. When Major Rittner tells us I simply refuse to believe it until I hear it with my own ears on the nine o'clock news. We'd no idea how far ahead you'd got. I can't describe the effect it has on us. You play happily with your toy cap-pistol. Then someone else picks it up and pulls the trigger . . . and all at once there's blood every-where and people screaming, because it wasn't a toy at all. . . . We sit up half the night, talking about it, trying to take it in. We're all literally in shock.

Margrethe: Because it had been done? Or because it wasn't you who'd done it?   650

Heisenberg: Both. Both. Otto Hahn wants to kill himself, because it was he who discovered fission, and he can see the blood on his hands. Gerlach, our old Nazi co-ordinator, also wants to die, because his hands are so shamefully clean. You've done it, though. You've built the bomb.

Bohr: Yes.

Heisenberg: And you've used it on a living target.

Bohr: On a living target.

Margrethe: You're not suggesting that Niels did anything wrong in working at   655
Los Alamos?

Heisenberg: Of course not. Bohr has never done anything wrong.

Margrethe: The decision had been taken long before Niels arrived. The bomb would have been built whether Niels had gone or not.

Bohr: In any case, my part was very small.

Heisenberg: Oppenheimer described you as the team's father-confessor.

Bohr: It seems to be my role in life.   660

Heisenberg: He said you made a great contribution.

Bohr: Spiritual, possibly. Not practical.

Heisenberg: Fermi says it was you who worked out how to trigger the Nagasaki° bomb.

Bohr: I put forward an idea.

---

⁶⁶³**Nagasaki** the second Japanese city bombed at the end of World War II, August 9, 1945

665 *Margrethe:* You're not implying that there's anything that *Niels* needs to explain or defend?

Heisenberg: No one has ever expected him to explain or defend anything. He's a profoundly good man.

Bohr: It's not a question of goodness. I was spared the decision.

Heisenberg: Yes, and I was not. So explaining and defending myself was how I spent the last thirty years of my life. When I went to America in 1949 a lot of physicists wouldn't even shake my hand. Hands that had actually built the bomb wouldn't touch mine.

Margrethe: And let me tell you, if you think you're making it any clearer to me now, you're not.

670 *Bohr:* Margrethe, I understand his feelings . . .

Margrethe: I don't. I'm as angry as you were before! It's so easy to make you feel conscience-stricken. Why should he transfer his burden to you? Because what does he do after his great consultation with you? He goes back to Berlin and tells the Nazis that he can produce atomic bombs!

Heisenberg: But what I stress is the difficulty of separating 235.

Margrethe: You tell them about plutonium.

Heisenberg: I tell some of the minor officials. I have to keep people's hopes alive!

675 *Margrethe:* Otherwise they'll send for the other one.

Heisenberg: Diebner. Very possibly.

Margrethe: There's always a Diebner at hand ready to take over our crimes.

Heisenberg: Diebner might manage to get a little further than me.

Bohr: Diebner?

680 *Heisenberg:* Might. Just possibly might.

Bohr: He hasn't a quarter of your ability!

Heisenberg: Not a tenth of it. But he has ten times the eagerness to do it. It might be a very different story if it's Diebner who puts the case at our meeting with Albert Speer,° instead of me.

Margrethe: The famous meeting with Speer.

Heisenberg: But this is when it counts. This is the real moment of decision. It's June 1942. Nine months after my trip to Copenhagen. All research cancelled by Hitler unless it produces immediate results—and Speer is the sole arbiter of what will qualify. Now, we've just got the first sign that our reactor's going to work. Our first increase in neutrons. Not much—thirteen per cent—but it's a start.

685 *Bohr:* June 1942? You're slightly ahead of Fermi in Chicago.

Heisenberg: Only we don't know that. But the RAF have begun terror-bombing. They've obliterated half of Lübeck, and the whole centre of Rostock and Cologne. We're desperate for new weapons to strike back with. If ever there's a moment to make our case, this is it.

Margrethe: You don't ask him for the funding to continue?

Heisenberg: To continue with the reactor? Of course I do. But I ask for so little that he doesn't take the programme seriously.

---

[682] **Albert Speer** (1905–81) chief architect of the Nazi regime during World War II

Margrethe: Do you tell him the reactor will produce plutonium?

Heisenberg: I don't tell him the reactor will produce plutonium. Not Speer, no. I   690
don't tell him the reactor will produce plutonium.

Bohr: A striking omission, I have to admit.

Heisenberg: And what happens? It works! He gives us barely enough money to
keep the reactor programme ticking over. And that is the end of the German
atomic bomb. That is the end of it.

Margrethe: You go on with the reactor, though.

Heisenberg: We go on with the reactor. Of course. Because now there's no risk of
getting it running in time to produce enough plutonium for a bomb. No, we
go on with the reactor all right. We work like madmen on the reactor. We
have to drag it all the way across Germany, from east to west, from Berlin to
Swabia, to get it away from the bombing, to keep it out of the hands of the
Russians. Diebner tries to hijack it on the way. We get it away from him, and
we set it up in a little village in the Swabian Jura.

Bohr: This is Haigerloch?   695

Heisenberg: There's a natural shelter there—the village inn has a wine-cellar cut
into the base of a cliff. We dig a hole in the floor for the reactor, and I keep
that programme going, I keep it under my control, until the bitter end.

Bohr: But, Heisenberg, with respect now, with the greatest respect, you couldn't
even keep the reactor under your control. That reactor was going to kill you.

Heisenberg: It wasn't put to the test. It never went critical.

Bohr: Thank God. Hambro and Perrin examined it after the Allied troops took
over. They said it had no cadmium control rods.° There was nothing to absorb
any excess of neutrons, to slow the reaction down when it overheated.

Heisenberg: No rods, no.   700

Bohr: You believed the reaction would be self-limiting.

Heisenberg: That's what I originally believed.

Bohr: Heisenberg, the reaction would not have been self-limiting.

Heisenberg: By 1945 I understood that.

Bohr: So if you ever had got it to go critical, it would have melted down, and   705
vanished into the centre of the earth!

Heisenberg: Not at all. We had a lump of cadmium to hand.

Bohr: A *lump* of cadmium? What were you proposing to to do with a *lump* of
cadmium?

Heisenberg: Throw it into the water.

Bohr: What water?

Heisenberg: The heavy water. The moderator that the uranium was immersed in.   710

Bohr: My dear good Heisenberg, not to criticise, but you'd all gone mad!

Heisenberg: We were almost there! We had this fantastic neutron growth! We had
670 per cent growth!

Bohr: You'd lost all contact with reality down in that hole!

Heisenberg: Another week. Another fortnight. That's all we needed!

---

[699]**cadmium control rods** Inserted into a nuclear pile, cadmium absorbs enough
neutrons to stop a chain reaction.

715   *Bohr:* It was only the arrival of the Allies that saved you!

Heisenberg: We'd almost reached the critical mass! A tiny bit bigger and the chain would sustain itself indefinitely. All we need is a little more uranium. I set off with Weizsäcker to try and get our hands on Diebner's. Another hair-raising journey all the way back across Germany. Constant air raids—no trains—we try bicycles—we never make it! We end up stuck in a little inn somewhere in the middle of nowhere, listening to the thump of bombs falling all round us. And on the radio someone playing the Beethoven G minor cello sonata . . .

Bohr: And everything was still under your control?

Heisenberg: Under my control—yes! That's the point! Under my control!

Bohr: Nothing was under anyone's control by that time!

720   *Heisenberg:* Yes, because at last we were free of all constraints! The nearer the end came the faster we could work!

Bohr: You were no longer running that programme, Heisenberg. The programme was running you.

Heisenberg: Two more weeks, two more blocks of uranium, and it would have been German physics that achieved the world's first self-sustaining chain reaction.

Bohr: Except that Fermi had already done it in Chicago, two years earlier.

Heisenberg: We didn't know that.

725   *Bohr:* You didn't know anything down in that cave. You were as blind as moles in a hole. Perrin said that there wasn't even anything to protect you all from the radiation.

Heisenberg: We didn't have time to think about it.

Bohr: So if it *had* gone critical . . .

Margrethe: You'd all have died of radiation sickness.

Bohr: My dear Heisenberg! My dear boy!

730   *Heisenberg:* Yes, but by then the reactor would have been running.

Bohr: I should have been there to look after you.

Heisenberg: That's all we could think of at the time. To get the reactor running, to get the reactor running.

Bohr: You always needed me there to slow you down a little. Your own walking lump of cadmium.

Heisenberg: If I had died then, what should I have missed? Thirty years of attempting to explain. Thirty years of reproach and hostility. Even you turned your back on me.

735   *Margrethe:* You came to Copenhagen again. You came to Tisvilde.

Heisenberg: It was never the same.

Bohr: No. It was never the same.

Heisenberg: I sometimes think that those final few weeks at Haigerloch were the last happy time in my life. In a strange way it was very peaceful. Suddenly we were out of all the politics of Berlin. Out of the bombing. The war was coming to an end. There was nothing to think about except the reactor. And we didn't go mad, in fact. We didn't work all the time. There was a monastery on top of the rock above our cave. I used to retire to the organ-loft in the church, and play Bach fugues.

Margrethe: Look at him. He's lost. He's like a lost child. He's been out in the woods all day, running here, running there. He's shown off, he's been brave, he's been cowardly. He's done wrong, he's done right. And now the evening's come, and all he wants is to go home, and he's lost.

Heisenberg: Silence. 740

Bohr: Silence.

Margrethe: Silence.

Heisenberg: And once again the tiller slams over, and Christian is falling.

Bohr: Once again he's struggling towards the lifebuoy.

Margrethe: Once again I look up from my work, and there's Niels in the doorway, 745 silently watching me . . .

Bohr: So, Heisenberg, why did you come to Copenhagen in 1941? It was right that you told us about all the fears you had. But you didn't really think I'd tell you whether the Americans were working on a bomb.

Heisenberg: No.

Bohr: You didn't seriously hope that I'd stop them.

Heisenberg: No.

Bohr: You were going back to work on that reactor whatever I said. 750

Heisenberg: Yes.

Bohr: So, Heisenberg, why did you come?

Heisenberg: Why did I come?

Bohr: Tell us once again. Another draft of the paper. And this time we shall get it right. This time we shall understand.

Margrethe: Maybe you'll even understand yourself. 755

Bohr: After all, the workings of the atom were difficult to explain. We made many attempts. Each time we tried they became more obscure. We got there in the end, however. So—another draft, another draft.

Heisenberg: Why did I come? And once again I go through that evening in 1941. I crunch over the familiar gravel, and tug at the familiar bell-pull. What's in my head? Fear, certainly, and the absurd and horrible importance of someone bearing bad news. But . . . yes . . . something else as well. Here it comes again. I can almost see its face. Something good. Something bright and eager and hopeful.

Bohr: I open the door . . .

Heisenberg: And there he is. I see his eyes light up at the sight of me.

Bohr: He's smiling his wary schoolboy smile. 760

Heisenberg: And I feel a moment of such consolation.

Bohr: A flash of such pure gladness.

Heisenberg: As if I'd come home after a long journey.

Bohr: As if a long-lost child had appeared on the doorstep.

Heisenberg: Suddenly I'm free of all the dark tangled currents in the water. 765

Bohr: Christian is alive, Harald still unborn.

Heisenberg: The world is at peace again.

Margrethe: Look at them. Father and son still. Just for a moment. Even now we're all dead.

Bohr: For a moment, yes, it's the twenties again.

770   *Heisenberg:* And we shall speak to each other and understand each other in the way we did before.

    Margrethe: And from those two heads the future will emerge. Which cities will be destroyed, and which survive. Who will die, and who will live. Which world will go down to obliteration, and which will triumph.

    Bohr: My dear Heisenberg!

    Heisenberg: My dear Bohr!

    Bohr: Come in, come in . . .

Act Two

    Heisenberg: It was the very beginning of spring. The first time I came to Copenhagen, in 1924. March: raw, blustery northern weather. But every now and then the sun would come out and leave that first marvellous warmth of the year on your skin. That first breath of returning life.

    Bohr: You were twenty-two. So I must have been . . . Thirty-eight.

    Bohr: Almost the same age as you were when you came in 1941.

    Heisenberg: So what do we do?

5   *Bohr:* Put on our boots and rucksacks . . .

    Heisenberg: Take the tram to the end of the line . . .

    Bohr: And start walking!

    Heisenberg: Northwards to Elsinore.

    Bohr: If you walk you talk.

10   *Heisenberg:* Then westwards to Tisvilde.

    Bohr: And back by way of Hillerød.

    Heisenberg: Walking, talking, for a hundred miles.

    Bohr: After which we talked more or less non-stop for the next three years.

    Heisenberg: We'd split a bottle of wine over dinner in your flat at the Institute.

15   *Bohr:* Then I'd come up to your room . . .

    Heisenberg: That terrible little room in the servants' quarters in the attic.

    Bohr: And we'd talk on into the small hours.

    Heisenberg: How, though?

    Bohr: How?

20   *Heisenberg:* How did we talk? In Danish?

    Bohr: In German, surely.

    Heisenberg: I lectured in Danish. I had to give my first colloquium when I'd only been here for ten weeks.

    Bohr: I remember it. Your Danish was already excellent.

    Heisenberg: No. You did a terrible thing to me. Half-an-hour before it started you said casually, Oh, I think we'll speak English today.

25   *Bohr:* But when you explained . . . ?

    Heisenberg: Explain to the Pope? I didn't dare. That excellent Danish you heard was my first attempt at English.

    Bohr: My dear Heisenberg! On our own together, though? My love, do you recall?

    Margrethe: What language you spoke when I wasn't there? You think I had microphones hidden?

    Bohr: No, no—but patience, my love, patience!

30   *Margrethe:* Patience?

Bohr: You sounded a little sharp.

Margrethe: Not at all.

Bohr: We have to follow the threads right back to the beginning of the maze.

Margrethe: I'm watching every step.

Bohr: You didn't mind? I hope.   35

Margrethe: Mind?

Bohr: Being left at home?

Margrethe: While you went off on your hike? Of course not. Why should I have minded? You had to get out of the house. Two new sons arriving on top of each other would be rather a lot for any man to put up with.

Bohr: Two new sons?

Margrethe: Heisenberg.   40

Bohr: Yes, yes.

Margrethe: And our own son.

Bohr: Aage?

Margrethe: Ernest!

Bohr: 1924—of course—Ernest.   45

Margrethe: Number five. Yes?

Bohr: Yes, yes, yes. And if it was March, you're right—he couldn't have been much more than . . .

Margrethe: One week.

Bohr: One week? One week, yes. And you really didn't mind?

Margrethe: Not at all. I was pleased you had an excuse to get away. And you   50
always went off hiking with your new assistants. You went off with
Kramers,° when he arrived in 1916.

Bohr: Yes, when I suppose Christian was still only . . .

Margrethe: One week.

Bohr: Yes. . . . Yes. . . . I almost killed Kramers, you know.

Heisenberg: Not with a cap-pistol?

Bohr: With a mine. On our walk.   55

Heisenberg: Oh, the mine. Yes, you told me, on ours. Never mind Kramers—you
almost killed yourself!

Bohr: A mine washed up in the shallows . . .

Heisenberg: And of course at once they compete to throw stones at it. What were
you thinking of?

Bohr: I've no idea.

Heisenberg: A touch of Elsinore there, perhaps.   60

Bohr: Elsinore?

Heisenberg: The darkness inside the human soul.

Bohr: You did something just as idiotic.

Heisenberg: I did?

Bohr: With Dirac° in Japan. You climbed a pagoda.   65

---

[50]**[Hendrik Anthony] Kramers** (1894–1952) Dutch physicist; Bohr's student and then
assistant between 1916 and 1926   [65]**[Paul Adrien Maurice] Dirac** (1902–84) English
physicist (shared the Nobel Prize with Erwin Schrödinger in 1933) who went to Japan
with Heisenberg in 1929

Heisenberg: Oh, the pagoda.

Bohr: Then balanced on the pinnacle. According to Dirac. On one foot. In a high wind. I'm glad I wasn't there.

Heisenberg: Elsinore, I confess.

Bohr: Elsinore, certainly.

70 *Heisenberg:* I was jealous of Kramers, you know.

Bohr: His Eminence. Isn't that what you called him?

Heisenberg: Because that's what he was. Your leading cardinal. Your favourite son. Till I arrived on the scene.

Margrethe: He was a wonderful cellist.

Bohr: He was a wonderful everything.

75 *Heisenberg:* Far too wonderful.

Margrethe: I liked him.

Heisenberg: I was terrified of him. When I first started at the Institute. I was terrified of all of them. All the boy wonders you had here—they were all so brilliant and accomplished. But Kramers was the heir apparent. All the rest of us had to work in the general study hall. Kramers had the private office next to yours, like the electron on the inmost orbit around the nucleus. And he didn't think much of my physics. He insisted you could explain everything about the atom by classical mechanics.

Bohr: Well, he was wrong.

Margrethe: And very soon the private office was vacant.

80 *Bohr:* And there was another electron on the inmost orbit.

Heisenberg: Yes, and for three years we lived inside the atom.

Bohr: With other electrons on the outer orbits around us all over Europe.

Heisenberg: Max Born and Pascual Jordan° in Göttingen.

Bohr: Yes, but Schrödinger in Zürich, Fermi in Rome.

85 *Heisenberg:* Chadwick° and Dirac in England.

Bohr: Joliot° and de Broglie° in Paris.

Heisenberg: Gamow and Landau° in Russia.

Bohr: Everyone in and out of each other's departments.

Heisenberg: Papers and drafts of papers on every international mail-train.

90 *Bohr:* You remember when Goudsmit and Uhlenbeck° did spin?

Heisenberg: There's this one last variable in the quantum state of the atom that no one can make sense of. The last hurdle . . .

Bohr: And these two crazy Dutchmen go back to a ridiculous idea that electrons can spin in different ways.

[83]**Pascual Jordan** (1902–80) German physicist   [85]**[James] Chadwick** (1891–1974) English physicist who won the Nobel Prize in 1935   [86]**Frédéric Joliot** (1900–58) French chemist who won the Nobel Prize in 1935   [86]**[Prince Louis-Victor Pierre Raymond] de Broglie** (1892–1987) French physicist who won the Nobel Prize in 1929 [87]**[Lev Davidovic] Landau** (1908–68) Russian physicist who won the Nobel Prize in 1962   [90]**[George Eugene] Uhlenbeck** (1900–88) Dutch physicist who spent much of his career at the University of Michigan and then Rockefeller University. He wrote a paper with Samuel Goudsmit in 1925 claiming that electrons spin.

Heisenberg: And of course the first thing that everyone wants to know is, What line is Copenhagen going to take?

Bohr: I'm on my way to Leiden, as it happens.

Heisenberg: And it turns into a papal progress! The train stops on the way at Hamburg . . . 95

Bohr: Pauli and Stern° are waiting on the platform to ask me what I think about spin.

Heisenberg: You tell them it's wrong.

Bohr: No, I tell them it's very . . .

Heisenberg: Interesting.

Bohr: I think that is precisely the word I choose. 100

Heisenberg: Then the train pulls into Leiden.

Bohr: And I'm met at the barrier by Einstein and Ehrenfest.° And I change my mind because Einstein—Einstein, you see?—I'm the Pope—he's God—because Einstein has made a relativistic analysis, and it resolves all my doubts.

Heisenberg: Meanwhile I'm standing in for Max Born at Göttingen, so you make a detour there on your way home.

Bohr: And you and Jordan meet me at the station.

Heisenberg: Same question: what do you think of spin? 105

Bohr: And when the train stops at Berlin there's Pauli on the platform.

Heisenberg: Wolfgang Pauli, who never gets out of bed if he can possibly avoid it . . .

Bohr: And who's already met me once at Hamburg on the journey out . . .

Heisenberg: He's travelled all the way from Hamburg to Berlin purely in order to see you for the second time round . . .

Bohr: And find out how my ideas on spin have developed en route. 110

Heisenberg: Oh, those years! Those amazing years! Those three short years!

Bohr: From 1924 to 1927.

Heisenberg: From when I arrived in Copenhagen to become your assistant . . .

Bohr: To when you departed, to take up your chair at Leipzig.

Heisenberg: Three years of raw, bracing northern springtime. 115

Bohr: At the end of which we had quantum mechanics, we had uncertainty . . .

Heisenberg: We had complementarity . . .

Bohr: We had the whole Copenhagen Interpretation.°

Heisenberg: Europe in all its glory again. A new Enlightenment, with Germany back in her rightful place at the heart of it. And who led the way for everyone else?

[96][Otto] Stern (1888–1969) German physicist who emigrated to America in 1933. He won the Nobel Prize in 1943. [102][Paul] Ehrenfest (1880–1933) Austrian physicist. In 1925, Ehrenfest entertained Bohr and Einstein at his house in Leiden, the Netherlands, hoping they could resolve their disagreement about quantum theory. They could not. [118]Copenhagen Interpretation a synthesis of several aspects of quantum theory, particularly Bohr's idea of complementarity and Heisenberg's uncertainty principle, claiming that an electron must be understood as both a particle and a wave

120 *Margrethe:* You and Niels.

Heisenberg: Well, we did.

Bohr: We did.

Margrethe: And that's what you were trying to get back to in 1941?

Heisenberg: To something we did in those three years. . . . Something we said, something we thought. . . . I keep almost seeing it out of the corner of my eye as we talk! Something about the way we worked. Something about the way we did all those things . . .

125 *Bohr:* Together.

Heisenberg: Together. Yes, together.

Margrethe: No.

Bohr: No? What do you mean, no?

Margrethe: Not together. You didn't do any of those things together.

130 *Bohr:* Yes, we did. Of course we did.

Margrethe: No, you didn't. Every single one of them you did when you were apart. *You* first worked out quantum mechanics on Heligoland. You said you couldn't think in Copenhagen.

Heisenberg: No, well, it was summer by then. I had my hay fever.

Margrethe: But on Heligoland, on your own, on a rocky bare island in the middle of the North Sea . . .

Heisenberg: My head began to clear, and I had this very sharp picture of what atomic physics ought to be like. I suddenly realised that we had to limit it to the measurements we could actually make, to what we could actually observe. We can't see the electrons inside the atom . . .

135 *Margrethe:* Any more than Niels can see the thoughts in your head, or you the thoughts in Niels's.

Heisenberg: All we can see are the effects that the electrons produce, on the light that they reflect . . .

Bohr: But the difficulties you were trying to resolve were the ones we'd explored together, over dinner in the flat, on the beach at Tisvilde.

Heisenberg: Of course. But I remember the evening when the mathematics first began to chime with the principle.

Margrethe: On Heligoland.

140 *Heisenberg:* On Heligoland.

Margrethe: On your own.

Heisenberg: It was terribly laborious—I didn't understand matrix calculus then . . . I get so excited I keep making mistakes. But by three in the morning I've got it. I seem to be looking through the surface of atomic phenomena into a strangely beautiful interior world. A world of pure mathematical structures. I'm too excited to sleep. I go down to the southern end of the island. There's a rock jutting out into the sea that I've been longing to climb. I get up it in the half-light before the dawn, and lie on top, gazing out to sea.

Margrethe: On your own.

Heisenberg: On my own. And yes—I was happy.

145 *Margrethe:* Happier than you were back here with us all in Copenhagen the following winter.

Heisenberg: What, with all the Schrödinger nonsense?

Bohr: Nonsense? Come, come. Schrödinger's wave formulation?

Margrethe: Yes, suddenly everyone's turned their backs on your wonderful new matrix mechanics.

Heisenberg: No one can understand it.

Margrethe: And they *can* understand Schrödinger's wave mechanics. 150

Heisenberg: Because they'd learnt it in school! We're going backwards to classical physics! And when I'm a little cautious about accepting it . . .

Bohr: A little cautious? Not to criticise, but . . .

Margrethe: . . . You described it as repulsive!

Heisenberg: I said the physical implications were repulsive. Schrödinger said my mathematics were repulsive.

Bohr: I seem to recall you used the word . . . well, I won't repeat it in mixed 155 company.

Heisenberg: In private. But by that time people had gone crazy.

Margrethe: They thought you were simply jealous.

Heisenberg: Someone even suggested some bizarre kind of intellectual snobbery. You got extremely excited.

Bohr: On your behalf.

Heisenberg: You invited Schrödinger here . . . 160

Bohr: To have a calm debate about our differences.

Heisenberg: And you fell on him like a madman. You meet him at the station—of course—and you pitch into him before he's even got his bags off the train. Then you go on at him from first thing in the morning until last thing at night.

Bohr: I go on? *He* goes on!

Heisenberg: Because you won't make the least concession!

Bohr: Nor will he! 165

Heisenberg: You made him ill! He had to retire to bed to get away from you!

Bohr: He had a slight feverish cold.

Heisenberg: Margrethe had to nurse him!

Margrethe: I dosed him with tea and cake to keep his strength up.

Heisenberg: Yes, while you pursued him even into the sickroom! Sat on his bed 170 and hammered away at him!

Bohr: Perfectly politely.

Heisenberg: You were the Pope and the Holy Office and the Inquisition all rolled into one! And then, and then, after Schrödinger had fled back to Zürich—and this I will never forget, Bohr, this I will never let you forget—you started to take his side! You turned on me!

Bohr: Because *you'd* gone mad by this time! You'd become fanatical! You were refusing to allow wave theory any place in quantum mechanics at all!

Heisenberg: You'd completely turned your coat!

Bohr: I said wave mechanics and matrix mechanics were simply alternative tools. 175

Heisenberg: Something you're always accusing me of. 'If it works it works.' Never mind what it means.

Bohr: Of course I mind what it means.

Heisenberg: What it means in language.

Bohr: In plain language, yes.

180   *Heisenberg:* What something means is what it means in mathematics.

Bohr: You think that so long as the mathematics works out, the sense doesn't matter.

Heisenberg: Mathematics *is* sense! That's what sense is!

Bohr: But in the end, in the end, remember, we have to be able to explain it all to Margrethe!

Margrethe: Explain it to me? You couldn't even explain it to each other! You went on arguing into the small hours every night! You both got so angry!

185   *Bohr:* We also both got completely exhausted.

Margrethe: It was the cloud chamber that finished you.

Bohr: Yes, because if you detach an electron from an atom, and send it through a cloud chamber, you can see the track it leaves.

Heisenberg: And it's a scandal. There shouldn't be a track!

Margrethe: According to your quantum mechanics.

190   *Heisenberg:* There *isn't* a track! No orbits! No tracks or trajectories! Only external effects!

Margrethe: Only there the track is. I've seen it myself, as clear as the wake left by a passing ship.

Bohr: It was a fascinating paradox.

Heisenberg: You actually loved the paradoxes, that's your problem. You revelled in the contradictions.

Bohr: Yes, and you've never been able to understand the suggestiveness of paradox and contradiction. That's *your* problem. You live and breathe paradox and contradiction, but you can no more see the beauty of them than the fish can see the beauty of the water.

195   *Heisenberg:* I sometimes felt as if I was trapped in a kind of windowless hell. You don't realise how aggressive you are. Prowling up and down the room as if you're going to eat someone—and I can guess who it's going to be.

Bohr: That's the way we did the physics, though.

Margrethe: No. No! In the end you did it on your own again! Even you! You went off skiing in Norway.

Bohr: I had to get away from it all!

Margrethe: And you worked out complementarity in Norway, on your own.

200   *Heisenberg:* The speed he skis at he had to do *something* to keep the blood going round. It was either physics or frostbite.

Bohr: Yes, and you stayed behind in Copenhagen . . .

Heisenberg: And started to think at last.

Margrethe: You're a lot better off apart, you two.

Heisenberg: Having him out of town was as liberating as getting away from my hay fever on Heligoland.

205   *Margrethe:* I shouldn't let you sit anywhere near each other, if I were the teacher.

Heisenberg: And that's when I did uncertainty. Walking round Faelled Park on my own one horrible raw February night. It's very late, and as soon as I've turned off into the park I'm completely alone in the darkness. I start to think about what you'd see, if you could train a telescope on me from the mountains of Norway. You'd see me by the street-lamps on the Blegdamsvej, then nothing as I vanished into the darkness, then another glimpse of me as I passed the lamp-post in front of the bandstand. And that's what we see in the cloud chamber. Not a continuous track but a series of glimpses—a series of collisions between the passing electron and various molecules of water vapour. . . . Or think of you, on your great papal progress to Leiden in 1925. What did Margrethe see of that, at home here in Copenhagen? A picture postcard from Hamburg, perhaps. Then one from Leiden. One from Göttingen. One from Berlin. Because what we see in the cloud chamber are not even the collisions themselves, but the water-droplets that condense around them, as big as cities around a traveller—no, vastly bigger still, relatively—complete countries—Germany . . . Holland . . . Germany again. There is no track, there are no precise addresses; only a vague list of countries visited. I don't know why we hadn't thought of it before, except that we were too busy arguing to think at all.

Bohr: You seem to have given up on all forms of discussion. By the time I get back from Norway I find you've done a draft of your uncertainty paper and you've already sent it for publication!

Margrethe: And an even worse battle begins.

Bohr: My dear good Heisenberg, it's not open behaviour to rush a first draft into print before we've discussed it together! It's not the way we work!

Heisenberg: No, the way we work is that you hound me from first thing in the morning till last thing at night! The way we work is that you drive me mad! 210

Bohr: Yes, because the paper contains a fundamental error.

Margrethe: And here we go again.

Heisenberg: No, but I show him the strangest truth about the universe that any of us has stumbled on since relativity—that you can never know everything about the whereabouts of a particle, or anything else, even Bohr now, as he prowls up and down the room in that maddening way of his, because we can't observe it without introducing some new element into the situation, a molecule of water vapour for it to hit, or a piece of light—things which have an energy of their own, and which therefore have an effect on what they hit. A small one, admittedly, in the case of Bohr . . .

Bohr: Yes, if you know where I am with the kind of accuracy we're talking about when we're dealing with particles, you can still measure my velocity to within—what . . . ?

Heisenberg: Something like a billionth of a billionth of a kilometre per second. 215 The theoretical point remains, though, that you have no absolutely determinate situation in the world, which among other things lays waste to the idea of causality, the whole foundation of science—because if you don't know how things are today you certainly can't know how they're going to be tomorrow. I shatter the objective universe around you—and all you can say is that there's an error in the formulation!

Bohr: There is!

Margrethe: Tea, anyone? Cake?

Heisenberg: Listen, in my paper what we're trying to locate is not a free electron° off on its travels through a cloud chamber, but an electron when it's at home, moving around inside an atom . . .

Bohr: And the uncertainty arises not, as you claim, through its indeterminate recoil when it's hit by an incoming photon° . . . .

220   *Heisenberg:* Plain language, plain language!

Bohr: This *is* plain language.

Heisenberg: Listen . . . .

Bohr: The language of classical mechanics.

Heisenberg: Listen! Copenhagen is an atom. Margrethe is its nucleus. About right, the scale? Ten thousand to one?

225   *Bohr:* Yes, yes.

Heisenberg: Now, Bohr's an electron. He's wandering about the city somewhere in the darkness, no one knows where. He's here, he's there, he's everywhere and nowhere. Up in Faelled Park, down at Carlsberg. Passing City Hall, out by the harbour. I'm a photon. A quantum of light. I'm despatched into the darkness to find Bohr. And I succeed, because I manage to collide with him. . . . But what's happened? Look—he's been slowed down, he's been deflected! He's no longer doing exactly what he was so maddeningly doing when I walked into him!

Bohr: But, Heisenberg, Heisenberg! You also have been deflected! If people can see what's happened to you, to their piece of light, then they can work out what must have happened to me! The trouble is knowing what's happened to you! Because to understand how people see you we have to treat you not just as a particle, but as a wave. I have to use not only your particle mechanics, I have to use the Schrödinger wave function.

Heisenberg: I know—I put it in a postscript to my paper.

Bohr: Everyone remembers the paper—no one remembers the postscript. But the question is fundamental. Particles are things, complete in themselves. Waves are disturbances in something else.

230   *Heisenberg:* I know. Complementarity. It's in the postscript.

Bohr: They're either one thing or the other. They can't be both. We have to choose one way of seeing them or the other. But as soon as we do we can't know everything about them.

Heisenberg: And off he goes into orbit again. Incidentally exemplifying another application of complementarity. Exactly where you go as you ramble around is of course completely determined by your genes and the various physical forces acting on you. But it's also completely determined by your own entirely inscrutable whims from one moment to the next. So we can't completely understand your behaviour without seeing it both ways at once, and that's impossible. Which means that your extraordinary peregrinations are not fully objective aspects of the universe. They exist only partially, through the efforts of me or Margrethe, as our minds shift endlessly back and forth between the two approaches.

---

[218]**electron** a negatively charged elementary particle   [219]**photon** an elementary particle, a quantum of electromagnetic radiation

Bohr: You've never absolutely and totally accepted complementarity, have you?

Heisenberg: Yes! Absolutely and totally! I defended it at the Como Conference in 1927! I have adhered to it ever afterwards with religious fervour! You convinced me. I humbly accepted your criticisms.

Bohr: Not before you'd said some deeply wounding things. 235

Heisenberg: Good God, at one point you literally reduced me to tears!

Bohr: Forgive me, but I diagnosed them as tears of frustration and rage.

Heisenberg: I was having a tantrum?

Bohr: I have brought up children of my own.

Heisenberg: And what about Margrethe? Was *she* having a tantrum? Klein told 240 me you reduced *her* to tears after I'd gone, making her type out your endless redraftings of the complementarity paper.

Bohr: I don't recall that.

Margrethe: I do.

Heisenberg: We had to drag Pauli out of bed in Hamburg once again to come to Copenhagen and negotiate peace.

Bohr: He succeeded. We ended up with a treaty. Uncertainty and complementarity became the two central tenets of the Copenhagen Interpretation of Quantum Mechanics.

Heisenberg: A political compromise, of course, like most treaties. 245

Bohr: You see? Somewhere inside you there are still secret reservations.

Heisenberg: Not at all—it works. That's what matters. It works, it works, it works!

Bohr: It works, yes. But it's more important than that. Because you see what we did in those three years, Heisenberg? Not to exaggerate, but we turned the world inside out! Yes, listen, now it comes, now it comes. . . . We put man back at the centre of the universe. Throughout history we keep finding ourselves displaced. We keep exiling ourselves to the periphery of things. First we turn ourselves into a mere adjunct of God's unknowable purposes, tiny figures kneeling in the great cathedral of creation. And no sooner have we recovered ourselves in the Renaissance, no sooner has man become, as Protagoras° proclaimed him, the measure of all things, than we're pushed aside again by the products of our own reasoning! We're dwarfed again as physicists build the great new cathedrals for us to wonder at—the laws of classical mechanics that predate us from the beginning of eternity, that will survive us to eternity's end, that exist whether we exist or not. Until we come to the beginning of the twentieth century, and we're suddenly forced to rise from our knees again.

Heisenberg: It starts with Einstein.

Bohr: It starts with Einstein. He shows that measurement—measurement, on 250 which the whole possibility of science depends—measurement is not an impersonal event that occurs with impartial universality. It's a human act, carried out from a specific point of view in time and space, from the one particular viewpoint of a possible observer. Then, here in Copenhagen in those three years in the mid-twenties we discover that there is no precisely

---

[248]**Protagoras** ancient Greek philosopher (c. 490–c. 420 BCE), one of whose best-known claims is that "man is the measure of all things"

determinable objective universe. That the universe exists only as a series of approximations. Only within the limits determined by our relationship with it. Only through the understanding lodged inside the human head.

Margrethe: So this man you've put at the centre of the universe—is it you, or is it Heisenberg?

Bohr: Now, now, my love.

Margrethe: Yes, but it makes a difference.

Bohr: Either of us. Both of us. Yourself. All of us.

255 *Margrethe:* If it's Heisenberg at the centre of the universe, then the one bit of the universe that he can't see is Heisenberg.

Heisenberg: So . . .

Margrethe: So it's no good asking him why he came to Copenhagen in 1941. He doesn't know!

Heisenberg: I thought for a moment just then I caught a glimpse of it.

Margrethe: Then you turned to look.

260 *Heisenberg:* And away it went.

Margrethe: Complementarity again. Yes?

Bohr: Yes, yes.

Margrethe: I've typed it out often enough. If you're doing something you have to concentrate on you can't also be thinking about doing it, and if you're thinking about doing it then you can't actually be doing it. Yes?

Heisenberg: Swerve left, swerve right, or think about it and die.

265 *Bohr:* But *after* you've done it . . .

Margrethe: You look back and make a guess, just like the rest of us. Only a worse guess, because you didn't see yourself doing it, and we did. Forgive me, but you don't even know why you did uncertainty in the first place.

Bohr: Whereas if *you're* the one at the centre of the universe . . .

Margrethe: Then I can tell you that it was because you wanted to drop a bomb on Schrödinger.

Heisenberg: I wanted to show he was wrong, certainly.

270 *Margrethe:* And Schrödinger was winning the war. When the Leipzig chair first became vacant that autumn he was short-listed for it and you weren't. You needed a wonderful new weapon.

Bohr: Not to criticise, Margrethe, but you have a tendency to make everything personal.

Margrethe: Because everything *is* personal! You've just read us all a lecture about it! You know how much Heisenberg wanted a chair. You know the pressure he was under from his family. I'm sorry, but you want to make everything seem heroically abstract and logical. And when you tell the story, yes, it all falls into place, it all has a beginning and a middle and an end. But I was there, and when I remember what it was like I'm there still, and I look around me and what I see isn't a story! It's confusion and rage and jealousy and tears and no one knowing what things mean or which way they're going to go.

Heisenberg: All the same, it works, it works.

Margrethe: Yes, it works wonderfully. Within three months of publishing your uncertainty paper you're offered Leipzig.

Heisenberg: I didn't mean that. 275
Margrethe: Not to mention somewhere else and somewhere else.
Heisenberg: Halle and Munich and Zürich.
Bohr: And various American universities.
Heisenberg: But I didn't mean that.
Margrethe: And when you take up your chair at Leipzig you're how old? 280
Heisenberg: Twenty-six.
Bohr: The youngest full professor in Germany.
Heisenberg: I mean the Copenhagen Interpretation. The Copenhagen Interpretation works. However we got there, by whatever combination of high principles and low calculation, of most painfully hard thought and most painfully childish tears, it works. It goes on working.
Margrethe: Yes, and why did you both accept the Interpretation in the end? Was it really because you wanted to re-establish humanism?
Bohr: Of course not. It was because it was the only way to explain what the 285 experimenters had observed.
Margrethe: Or was it because now you were becoming a professor you wanted a solidly established doctrine to teach? Because you wanted to have your new ideas publicly endorsed by the head of the church in Copenhagen? And perhaps Niels agreed to endorse them in return for your accepting *his* doctrines. For recognising him as head of the church. And if you want to know why you came to Copenhagen in 1941 I'll tell you that as well. You're right— there's no great mystery about it. You came to show yourself off to us.
Bohr: Margrethe!
Margrethe: No! When he first came in 1924 he was a humble assistant lecturer from a humiliated nation, grateful to have a job. Now here you are, back in triumph—the leading scientist in a nation that's conquered most of Europe. You've come to show us how well you've done in life.
Bohr: This is so unlike you!
Margrethe: I'm sorry, but isn't that really why he's here? Because he's burning to 290 let us know that he's in charge of some vital piece of secret research. And that even so he's preserved a lofty moral independence. Preserved it so famously that he's being watched by the Gestapo. Preserved it so successfully that he's now also got a wonderfully important moral dilemma to face.
Bohr: Yes, well, now you're simply working yourself up.
Margrethe: A chain reaction.° You tell one painful truth and it leads to two more. And as you frankly admit, you're going to go back and continue doing precisely what you were doing before, whatever Niels tells you.
Heisenberg: Yes.
Margrethe: Because you wouldn't dream of giving up such a wonderful opportunity for research.
Heisenberg: Not if I can possibly help it. 295

---

²⁹²**chain reaction** a self-sustaining chemical or nuclear reaction in which the products of one stage cause the next

Margrethe: Also you want to demonstrate to the Nazis how useful theoretical physics can be. You want to save the honour of German science. You want to be there to reestablish it in all its glory as soon as the war's over.

Heisenberg: All the same, I don't tell Speer that the reactor . . .

Margrethe: . . . will produce plutonium, no, because you're afraid of what will happen if the Nazis commit huge resources, and you fail to deliver the bombs. Please don't try to tell us that you're a hero of the resistance.

Heisenberg: I've never claimed to be a hero.

300 *Margrethe:* Your talent is for skiing too fast for anyone to see where you are. For always being in more than one position at a time, like one of your particles.

Heisenberg: I can only say that it worked. Unlike most of the gestures made by heroes of the resistance. It worked! I know what you think. You think I should have joined the plot against Hitler, and got myself hanged like the others.

Bohr: Of course not.

Heisenberg: You don't say it, because there are some things that can't be said. But you think it.

Bohr: No.

305 *Heisenberg:* What would it have achieved? What would it have achieved if you'd dived in after Christian, and drowned as well? But that's another thing that can't be said.

Bohr: Only thought.

Heisenberg: Yes. I'm sorry.

Bohr: And rethought. Every day.

Heisenberg: You had to be held back, I know.

310 *Margrethe:* Whereas you held yourself back.

Heisenberg: Better to stay on the boat, though, and fetch it about. Better to remain alive, and throw the lifebuoy. Surely!

Bohr: Perhaps. Perhaps not.

Heisenberg: Better. Better.

Margrethe: Really it is ridiculous. You reasoned your way, both of you, with such astonishing delicacy and precision into the tiny world of the atom. Now it turns out that everything depends upon these really rather large objects on our shoulders. And what's going on in there is . . .

315 *Heisenberg:* Elsinore.

Margrethe: Elsinore, yes.

Heisenberg: And you may be right. I *was* afraid of what would happen. I *was* conscious of being on the winning side . . . So many explanations for everything I did! So many of them sitting round the lunch-table! Somewhere at the head of the table, I think, is the real reason I came to Copenhagen. Again I turn to look. . . . And for a moment I almost see its face. Then next time I look the chair at the head of the table is completely empty. There's no reason at all. I didn't tell Speer simply because I didn't think of it. I came to Copenhagen simply because I did think of it. A million things we might do or might not do every day. A million decisions that make themselves. Why didn't you kill me?

Bohr: Why didn't I . . .?

Heisenberg: Kill me. Murder me. That evening in 1941. Here we are, walking back towards the house, and you've just leapt to the conclusion that I'm going to arm Hitler with nuclear weapons. You'll surely take any reasonable steps to prevent it happening.

Bohr: By murdering you? 320

Heisenberg: We're in the middle of a war. I'm an enemy. There's nothing odd or immoral about killing enemies.

Bohr: I should fetch out my cap-pistol?

Heisenberg: You won't need your cap-pistol. You won't even need a mine. You can do it without any loud bangs, without any blood, without any spectacle of suffering. As cleanly as a bomb-aimer pressing his release three thousand metres above the earth. You simply wait till I've gone. Then you sit quietly down in your favourite armchair here and repeat aloud to Margrethe, in front of our unseen audience, what I've just told you. I shall be dead almost as soon as poor Casimir. A lot sooner than Gamow.

Bohr: My dear Heisenberg, the suggestion is of course . . .

Heisenberg: Most interesting. So interesting that it never even occurred to you. 325 Complementarity, once again. I'm your enemy; I'm also your friend. I'm a danger to mankind; I'm also your guest. I'm a particle; I'm also a wave. We have one set of obligations to the world in general, and we have other sets, never to be reconciled, to our fellow-countrymen, to our neighbours, to our friends, to our family, to our children. We have to go through not two slits at the same time but twenty-two. All we can do is to look afterwards, and see what happened.

Margrethe: I'll tell you another reason why you did uncertainty: you have a natural affinity for it.

Heisenberg: Well, I must cut a gratifyingly chastened figure when I return in 1947. Crawling on my hands and knees again. My nation back in ruins.

Margrethe: Not really. You're demonstrating that once more you personally have come out on top.

Heisenberg: Begging for food parcels?

Margrethe: Established in Göttingen under British protection, in charge of post-war 330 German science.

Heisenberg: That first year in Göttingen I slept on straw.

Margrethe: Elisabeth said you had a most charming house thereafter.

Heisenberg: I was given it by the British.

Margrethe: Your new foster-parents. Who'd confiscated it from someone else.

Bohr: Enough, my love, enough. 335

Margrethe: No, I've kept my thoughts to myself for all these years. But it's maddening to have this clever son forever dancing about in front of our eyes, forever demanding our approval, forever struggling to shock us, forever begging to be told what the limits to his freedom are, if only so that he can go out and transgress them! I'm sorry, but really. . . . On your hands and knees? It's my dear, good, kind husband who's on his hands and knees! Literally. Crawling down to the beach in the darkness in 1943, fleeing like a thief in the night from his own homeland to escape being murdered. The protection of the German Embassy that you boasted about didn't last for long. We were incorporated into the Reich.

Heisenberg: I warned you in 1941. You wouldn't listen. At least Bohr got across to Sweden.

Margrethe: And even as the fishing-boat was taking him across the Sound two freighters were arriving in the harbour to ship the entire Jewish population of Denmark eastwards. That great darkness inside the human soul was flooding out to engulf us all.

Heisenberg: I did try to warn you.

340   *Margrethe:* Yes, and where are you? Shut away in a cave like a savage, trying to conjure an evil spirit out of a hole in the ground. That's what it came down to in the end, all that shining springtime in the 1920s, that's what it produced— a more efficient machine for killing people.

Bohr: It breaks my heart every time I think of it.

Heisenberg: It broke all our hearts.

Margrethe: And this wonderful machine may yet kill every man, woman, and child in the world. And if we really are the centre of the universe, if we really are all that's keeping it in being, what will be left?

Bohr: Darkness. Total and final darkness.

345   *Margrethe:* Even the questions that haunt us will at last be extinguished. Even the ghosts will die.

Heisenberg: I can only say that I didn't do it. I didn't build the bomb.

Margrethe: No, and why didn't you? I'll tell you that, too. It's the simplest reason of all. Because you couldn't. You didn't understand the physics.

Heisenberg: That's what Goudsmit said.

Margrethe: And Goudsmit knew. He was one of your magic circle. He and Uhlenbeck were the ones who did spin.

350   *Heisenberg:* All the same, he had no idea of what I did or didn't understand about a bomb.

Margrethe: He tracked you down across Europe for Allied Intelligence. He interrogated you after you were captured.

Heisenberg: He blamed me, of course. His parents died in Auschwitz. He thought I should have done something to save them. I don't know what. So many hands stretching up from the darkness for a lifeline, and no lifeline that could ever reach them . . .

Margrethe: He said you didn't understand the crucial difference between a reactor and a bomb.

Heisenberg: I understood very clearly. I simply didn't tell the others.

355   *Margrethe:* Ah.

Heisenberg: I understood, though.

Margrethe: But secretly.

Heisenberg: You can check if you don't believe me.

Margrethe: There's evidence, for once?

360   *Heisenberg:* It was all most carefully recorded.

Margrethe: Witnesses, even?

Heisenberg: Unimpeachable witnesses.

Margrethe: Who wrote it down?

Heisenberg: Who recorded it and transcribed it.

Margrethe: Even though you didn't tell anyone? 365

Heisenberg: I told one person. I told Otto Hahn. That terrible night at Farm Hall, after we'd heard the news. Somewhere in the small hours, after everyone had finally gone to bed, and we were alone together. I gave him a reasonably good account of how the bomb had worked.

Margrethe: After the event.

Heisenberg: After the event. Yes. When it didn't matter any more. All the things Goudsmit said I didn't understand. Fast neutrons in 235. The plutonium option. A reflective shell to reduce neutron escape. Even the method of triggering it.

Bohr: The critical mass.° That was the most important thing. The amount of material you needed to establish the chain-reaction. Did you tell him the critical mass?

Heisenberg: I gave him a figure, yes. You can look it up! Because that was the 370 other secret of the house-party. Diebner asked me when we first arrived if I thought there were hidden microphones. I laughed. I told him the British were far too old-fashioned to know about Gestapo methods. I underestimated them. They had microphones everywhere—they were recording everything. Look it up! Everything we said. Everything we went through that terrible night. Everything I told Hahn alone in the small hours.

Bohr: But the critical mass. You gave him a figure. What was the figure you gave him?

Heisenberg: I forget.

Bohr: Heisenberg . . .

Heisenberg: It's all on the record. You can see for yourself.

Bohr: The figure for the Hiroshima bomb . . . 375

Heisenberg: Was fifty kilograms.

Bohr: So that was the figure you gave Hahn? Fifty kilograms?

Heisenberg: I said about a ton.

Bohr: About a ton? A thousand kilograms? Heisenberg, I believe I am at last beginning to understand something.

Heisenberg: The one thing I was wrong about. 380

Bohr: You were twenty times over.

Heisenberg: The one thing.

Bohr: But, Heisenberg, your mathematics, your mathematics! How could they have been so far out?

Heisenberg: They weren't. As soon as I calculated the diffusion I got it just about right.

Bohr: As soon as you calculated it? 385

Heisenberg: I gave everyone a seminar on it a week later. It's in the record! Look it up!

---

³⁶⁹**critical mass** the amount of material needed to sustain a chain reaction

Bohr: You mean . . . you hadn't calculated it before? You hadn't done the
diffusion equation?

Heisenberg: There was no need to.

Bohr: No need to?

390 *Heisenberg:* The calculation had already been done.

Bohr: Done by whom?

Heisenberg: By Perrin° and Flügge° in 1939.

Bohr: By Perrin and Flügge? But, my dear Heisenberg, that was for natural
uranium. Wheeler and I showed that it was only the 235 that fissioned.

Heisenberg: Your great paper. The basis of everything we did.

395 *Bohr:* So you needed to calculate the figure for pure 235.

Heisenberg: Obviously.

Bohr: And you didn't?

Heisenberg: I didn't.

Bohr: And that's why you were so confident you couldn't do it until you had the
plutonium. Because you spent the entire war believing that it would take not
a few kilograms of 235, but a ton or more. And to make a ton of 235 in any
plausible time . . .

400 *Heisenberg:* Would have needed something like two hundred million separator
units. It was plainly unimaginable.

Bohr: If you'd realised you had to produce only a few kilograms . . .

Heisenberg: Even to make a single kilogram would need something like two
hundred thousand units.

Bohr: But two hundred million is one thing; two hundred thousand is another.
You might just possibly have imagined setting up two hundred thousand.

Heisenberg: Just possibly.

405 *Bohr:* The Americans did imagine it.

Heisenberg: Because Otto Frisch and Rudolf Peierls° actually did the calculation.
They solved the diffusion equation.

Bohr: Frisch was my old assistant.

Heisenberg: Peierls was my old pupil.

Bohr: As Austrian and a German.

410 *Heisenberg:* So they should have been making their calculation for us, at the
Kaiser Wilhelm Institute in Berlin. But instead they made it at the University
of Birmingham, in England.

Margrethe: Because they were Jews.

Heisenberg: There's something almost mathematically elegant about that.

Bohr: They also started with Perrin and Flügge.

Heisenberg: They also thought it would take tons. They also thought it was
unimaginable.

392[**Jean Baptiste] Perrin** (1870–1942) French physicist who won the Nobel Prize for
physics in 1926; emigrated to America in 1940 when France was occupied by Nazi Germany
[**Siegfried] Flügge** German physicist at the Kaiser Wilhelm Institute in Berlin who had
concluded before World War II that uranium fission might be used to make a bomb
406[**Sir Rudolf Ernst] Peierls** (1907–95) British physicist who, in 1940 with Otto
Frisch, calculated the critical mass of Uranium-235 needed to sustain a chain reaction

Bohr: Until one day . . .   415
Heisenberg: They did the calculation.
Bohr: They discovered just how fast the chain reaction would go.
Heisenberg: And therefore how little material you'd need.
Bohr: They said slightly over half a kilogram.
Heisenberg: About the size of a tennis ball.   420
Bohr: They were wrong, of course.
Heisenberg: They were ten times under.
Bohr: Which made it seem ten times more imaginable than it actually was.
Heisenberg: Whereas I left it seeming twenty times less imaginable.
Bohr: So all your agonising in Copenhagen about plutonium was beside the   425
    point. You could have done it without ever building the reactor. You could
    have done it with 235 all the time.
Heisenberg: Almost certainly not.
Bohr: Just possibly, though.
Heisenberg: Just possibly.
Bohr: And *that* question you'd settled long before you arrived in Copenhagen.
    Simply by failing to try the diffusion equation.
Heisenberg: Such a tiny failure.   430
Bohr: But the consequences went branching out over the years, doubling and
    redoubling.
Heisenberg: Until they were large enough to save a city. Which city? Any of the
    cities that we never dropped our bomb on.
Bohr: London, presumably, if you'd had it in time. If the Americans had already
    entered the war, and the Allies had begun to liberate Europe, then . . .
Heisenberg: Who knows? Paris as well. Amsterdam. Perhaps Copenhagen.
Bohr: So, Heisenberg, tell us this one simple thing: why didn't you do the   435
    calculation?
Heisenberg: The question is why Frisch and Peierls *did* do it. It was a stupid waste
    of time. However much 235 it turned out to be, it was obviously going to be
    more than anyone could imagine producing.
Bohr: Except that it wasn't!
Heisenberg: Except that it wasn't.
Bohr: So why . . . ?
Heisenberg: I don't know! I don't know why I didn't do it! Because I never   440
    thought of it! Because it didn't occur to me! Because I assumed it wasn't
    worth doing!
Bohr: Assumed? Assumed? You never assumed things! That's how you got
    uncertainty, because you rejected our assumptions! You calculated, Heisenberg!
    You calculated everything! The first thing you did with a problem was the
    mathematics!
Heisenberg: You should have been there to slow me down.
Bohr: Yes, you wouldn't have got away with it if I'd been standing over you.
Heisenberg: Though in fact you made exactly the same assumption! You thought
    there was no danger for exactly the same reason as I did! Why didn't *you*
    calculate it?

445 *Bohr:* Why didn't *I* calculate it?

Heisenberg: Tell us why *you* didn't calculate it and we'll know why *I* didn't!

Bohr: It's obvious why *I* didn't!

Heisenberg: Go on.

Margrethe: Because he wasn't trying to build a bomb!

450 *Heisenberg:* Yes. Thank you. Because he wasn't trying to build a bomb. I imagine
it was the same with me. Because *I* wasn't trying to build a bomb. Thank you.

Bohr: So, you bluffed yourself, the way I did at poker with the straight I never
had. But in that case . . .

Heisenberg: Why did I come to Copenhagen? Yes, why did I come . . . ?

Bohr: One more draft, yes? One final draft!

Heisenberg: And once again I crunch over the familiar gravel to the Bohrs' front
door, and tug at the familiar bell-pull. Why have I come? I know perfectly
well. Know so well that I've no need to ask myself. Until once again the
heavy front door opens.

455 *Bohr:* He stands on the doorstep blinking in the sudden flood of light from the
house. Until this instant his thoughts have been everywhere and nowhere,
like unobserved particles, through all the slits in the diffraction grating simultaneously. Now they have to be observed and specified.

Heisenberg: And at once the clear purposes inside my head lose all definite shape.
The light falls on them and they scatter.

Bohr: My dear Heisenberg!

Heisenberg: My dear Bohr!

Bohr: Come in, come in . . .

460 *Heisenberg:* How difficult it is to see even what's in front of one's eyes. All we
possess is the present, and the present endlessly dissolves into the past. Bohr
has gone even as I turn to see Margrethe.

Margrethe: Niels is right. You look older.

Bohr: I believe you had some personal trouble.

Heisenberg: Margrethe slips into history even as I turn back to Bohr. And yet how
much more difficult still it is to catch the slightest glimpse of what's behind
one's eyes. Here I am at the centre of the universe, and yet all I can see are
two smiles that don't belong to me.

Margrethe: How is Elisabeth? How are the children?

465 *Heisenberg:* Very well. They send their love, of course . . . I can feel a third smile
in the room, very close to me. Could it be the one I suddenly see for a moment
in the mirror there? And is the awkward stranger wearing it in any way
connected with this presence that I can feel in the room? This all-enveloping,
unobserved presence?

Margrethe: I watch the two smiles in the room, one awkward and ingratiating,
the other rapidly fading from incautious warmth to bare politeness. There's
also a third smile in the room, I know, unchangingly courteous, I hope, and
unchangingly guarded.

Heisenberg: You've managed to get some skiing?

Bohr: I glance at Margrethe, and for a moment I see what she can see and I
can't—myself, and the smile vanishing from my face as poor Heisenberg
blunders on.

Heisenberg: I look at the two of them looking at me, and for a moment I see the third person in the room as clearly as I see them. Their importunate guest, stumbling from one crass and unwelcome thoughtfulness to the next.

Bohr: I look at him looking at me, anxiously, pleadingly, urging me back to the old days, and I see what he sees. And yes—now it comes, now it comes—there's someone missing from the room. He sees me. He sees Margrethe. He doesn't see himself. 470

Heisenberg: Two thousand million people in the world, and the one who has to decide their fate is the only one who's always hidden from me.

Bohr: You suggested a stroll.

Heisenberg: You remember Elsinore? The darkness inside the human soul . . . ?

Bohr: And out we go. Out under the autumn trees. Through the blacked-out streets.

Heisenberg: Now there's no one in the world except Bohr and the invisible other. Who is he, this all-enveloping presence in the darkness? 475

Margrethe: The flying particle wanders the darkness, no one knows where. It's here, it's there, it's everywhere and nowhere.

Bohr: With careful casualness he begins to ask the question he's prepared.

Heisenberg: Does one as a physicist have the moral right to work on the practical exploitation of atomic energy?

Margrethe: The great collision.

Bohr: I stop. He stops . . . 480

Margrethe: This is how they work.

Heisenberg: He gazes at me, horrified.

Margrethe: Now at last he knows where he is and what he's doing.

Heisenberg: He turns away.

Margrethe: And even as the moment of collision begins it's over. 485

Bohr: Already we're hurrying back towards the house.

Margrethe: Already they're both flying away from each other into the darkness again.

Heisenberg: Our conversation's over.

Bohr: Our great partnership.

Heisenberg: All our friendship. 490

Margrethe: And everything about him becomes as uncertain as it was before.

Bohr: Unless . . . yes . . . a thought-experiment. . . . Let's suppose for a moment that I don't go flying off into the night. Let's see what happens if instead I remember the paternal role I'm supposed to play. If I stop, and control my anger, and turn to him. And ask him why.

Heisenberg: Why?

Bohr: Why are you confident that it's going to be so reassuringly difficult to build a bomb with 235? Is it because you've done the calculation?

Heisenberg: The calculation? 495

Bohr: Of the diffusion in 235. No. It's because you haven't calculated it. You haven't considered calculating it. You hadn't consciously realised there was a calculation to be made.

Heisenberg: And of course now I *have* realised. In fact it wouldn't be all that difficult. Let's see. . . . The scattering cross-section's about 6×10^{-24}, so the mean free path would be . . . Hold on . . .

Bohr: And suddenly a very different and very terrible new world begins to take shape . . .

Margrethe: That was the last and greatest demand that Heisenberg made on his friendship with you. To be understood when he couldn't understand himself. And that was the last and greatest act of friendship for Heisenberg that you performed in return. To leave him misunderstood.

500 *Heisenberg:* Yes. Perhaps I should thank you.

Bohr: Perhaps you should.

Margrethe: Anyway, it was the end of the story.

Bohr: Though perhaps there was also something I should thank *you* for. That summer night in 1943, when I escaped across the Sound in the fishing-boat, and the freighters arrived from Germany . . .

Margrethe: What's that to do with Heisenberg?

505 *Bohr:* When the ships arrived on the Wednesday there were eight thousand Jews in Denmark to be arrested and crammed into their holds. On the Friday evening, at the start of the Sabbath, when the SS began their round-up, there was scarcely a Jew to be found.

Margrethe: They'd all been hidden in churches and hospitals, in people's homes and country cottages.

Bohr: But how was that possible? —Because we'd been tipped off by someone in the German Embassy.

Heisenberg: Georg Duckwitz,° their shipping specialist.

Bohr: Your man?

510 *Heisenberg:* One of them.

Bohr: He was a remarkable informant. He told us the day before the freighters arrived—the very day that Hitler issued the order. He gave us the exact time that the SS would move.

Margrethe: It was the Resistance who got them out of their hiding-places and smuggled them across the Sound.

Bohr: For a handful of us in one fishing smack to get past the German patrol-boats was remarkable enough. For a whole armada to get past, with the best part of eight thousand people on board, was like the Red Sea parting.

Margrethe: I thought there *were* no German patrol-boats that night?

515 *Bohr:* No—the whole squadron had suddenly been reported unseaworthy.

Heisenberg: How they got away with it I can't imagine.

Bohr: Duckwitz again?

Heisenberg: He also went to Stockholm and asked the Swedish Government to accept everyone.

Bohr: So perhaps I should thank you.

520 *Heisenberg:* For what?

Bohr: My life. All our lives.

Heisenberg: Nothing to do with me by that time. I regret to say.

---

[508]**Georg Duckwitz** The German official who warned Danish Jews that they were about to be deported by the Nazis, allowing most of them (including Bohr) to escape to Sweden. After the war, he was made ambassador to Denmark.

Bohr: But after I'd gone you came back to Copenhagen.

Heisenberg: To make sure that our people didn't take over the Institute in your absence.

Bohr: I've never thanked you for that, either. 525

Heisenberg: You know they offered me your cyclotron?

Bohr: You could have separated a little 235 with it.

Heisenberg: Meanwhile you were going on from Sweden to Los Alamos.

Bohr: To play my small but helpful part in the deaths of a hundred thousand people.

Margrethe: Niels, you did nothing wrong! 530

Bohr: Didn't I?

Heisenberg: Of course not. You were a good man, from first to last, and no one could ever say otherwise. Whereas I . . .

Bohr: Whereas you, my dear Heisenberg, never managed to contribute to the death of one single solitary person in all your life.

Margrethe: Well, yes.

Heisenberg: Did I? 535

Margrethe: One. Or so you told us. The poor fellow you guarded overnight, when you were a boy in Munich, while he was waiting to be shot in the morning.

Bohr: All right then, one. One single soul on his conscience, to set against all the others.

Margrethe: But that one single soul was emperor of the universe, no less than each of us. Until the morning came.

Heisenberg: No, when the morning came I persuaded them to let him go.

Bohr: Heisenberg, I have to say—if people are to be measured strictly in terms of 540 observable quantities . . .

Heisenberg: Then we should need a strange new quantum ethics. There'd be a place in heaven for me. And another one for the SS man I met on my way home from Haigerloch. That was the end of my war. The Allied troops were closing in; there was nothing more we could do. Elisabeth and the children had taken refuge in a village in Bavaria, so I went to see them before I was captured. I had to go by bicycle—there were no trains or road transport by that time—and I had to travel by night and sleep under a hedge by day, because all through the daylight hours the skies were full of Allied planes, scouring the roads for anything that moved. A man on a bicycle would have been the biggest target left in Germany. Three days and three nights I travelled. Out of Württemberg, down through the Swabian Jura and the first foothills of the Alps. Across my ruined homeland. Was this what I'd chosen for it? This endless rubble? This perpetual smoke in the sky? These hungry faces? Was this my doing? And all the desperate people on the roads. The most desperate of all were the SS. Bands of fanatics with nothing left to lose, roaming around shooting deserters out of hand, hanging them from roadside trees. The second night, and suddenly there it is—the terrible familiar black tunic emerging from the twilight in front of me. On his lips as I stop—the one terrible familiar word. 'Deserter,' he says. He sounds as exhausted as I am. I give him the travel order I've written for myself. But there's hardly enough light in the sky to read by, and he's too weary to bother. He begins to open his holster instead. He's going to shoot me because it's simply less labour. And suddenly I'm thinking very quickly and clearly—it's like skiing, or that night on Heligoland, or the one in Faelled Park. What comes into my mind this time is the pack of American cigarettes I've got in my pocket. And already it's in my hand—I'm holding it out to him. The most desperate solution to a problem yet. I wait while he stands there looking at it, trying to make it out, trying to think, his left hand holding my useless piece of paper, his right on the fastening of the holster. There are two simple words in large print on the pack: Lucky Strike. He closes the holster, and takes the cigarettes instead. . . . It had worked, it had worked! Like all the other solutions to all the other problems. For twenty cigarettes he let me live. And on I went. Three days and three nights. Past the weeping children, the lost and hungry children, drafted to fight, then abandoned by their commanders. Past the starving slave-labourers walking home to France, to Poland, to Estonia. Through Gammertingen and Biberach and Memmingen. Mindelheim, Kaufbeuren, and Schöngau. Across my beloved homeland. My ruined and dishonoured and beloved homeland.

Bohr: My dear Heisenberg! My dear friend!

Margrethe: Silence. The silence we always in the end return to.

Heisenberg: And of course I know what they're thinking about.

545 *Margrethe:* All those lost children on the road.

Bohr: Heisenberg wandering the world like a lost child himself.

Margrethe: Our own lost children.

Heisenberg: And over goes the tiller once again.

Bohr: So near, so near! So slight a thing!

550 *Margrethe:* He stands in the doorway, watching me, then he turns his head away . . .

Heisenberg: And once again away he goes, into the dark waters.

Bohr: Before we can lay our hands on anything, our life's over.

Heisenberg: Before we can glimpse who or what we are, we're gone and laid to dust.

Bohr: Settled among all the dust we raised.

555 *Margrethe:* And sooner or later there will come a time when all our children are laid to dust, and all our children's children.

Bohr: When no more decisions, great or small, are ever made again. When there's no more uncertainty, because there's no more knowledge.

Margrethe: And when all our eyes are closed, when even the ghosts have gone, what will be left of our beloved world? Our ruined and dishonoured and beloved world?

Heisenberg: But in the meanwhile, in this most precious meanwhile, there it is. The trees in Faelled Park. Gammertingen and Biberach and Mindelheim. Our children and our children's children. Preserved, just possibly, by that one short moment in Copenhagen. By some event that will never quite be located or defined. By that final core of uncertainty at the heart of things.   [1998]

1. The play seems to start over several times, repeating its opening scene in almost exactly the same words. Why?

2. In reality, Margrethe was probably not present for all of the encounter between the two men. What is her role in the play?
3. Note Heisenberg's different answers to Margrethe's question about why he came to Copenhagen. Why so many? How do they fit together?
4. The play talks literally about a number of events and objects that are later used as metaphors. List some of them and analyze how they are used in the play.
5. What is the importance of the paradox at the end of the play?

IRVING M. KLOTZ

IRVING M. KLOTZ *(1916–), Ph.D., is Morrison Professor Emeritus in the Departments of Chemistry and of Biochemistry, Molecular Biology, and Cell Biology at Northwestern University. He is the author of books on thermodynamics and biochemical energetics as well as many research papers on ligand-receptor interactions and the structure and function of proteins.*

*Procrustean Distortions of Science**

In classical Greek legends, the robber giant Procrustes, after enticing travelers to his dwelling near Eleusis, would fit each guest snugly into a narrow iron bed of rigid dimensions by stretching or cutting off one's limbs. Thus the term "Bed of Procrustes" has become a proverbial metaphor for tendencies to fit novel concepts and perceptions into the stiff framework of one's preconceptions. During the past century, the most frequent scientific victims of such Procrustean distortions have been the "Theory of Relativity" and the "Uncertainty Principle" which have diffused into much of literature and drama. In recent years, such deceptive casuistry has often also entered narratives of the German atomic bomb project of the Nazi era. It behooves us to examine some of these rhetorical and dramatic exercises to distinguish myth from documented history.

Theory of Relativity

"Relativism" or "the dynamic character of reality" has a long history, far predating Einstein's° unrelated scientific concept of relativity. Anyone with a classical education should recall that the Greeks had concluded at least as long ago as Leucippus of Thrace (fifth century B.C.) that $\Pi\alpha\nu\tau\alpha\ \rho\epsilon\acute{\iota}$, all is change. According to an article in the *New York Times Book Review* of a few years ago, Darwinian ideas (nineteenth century A.D.) "always imply flux," "movement and change."[1] After

---

*Irving M. Klotz, "Procrustean Distortions of Science," *Academic Questions* 14.3 (Summer 2001): 9–21.

[1] G. Levine, "Darwin and the Evolution of Fiction," *New York Times Book Review,* 5 October 1986, 1, 60.

[2] **[Albert] Einstein** (1879–1955) German physicist who worked on the electromagnetic radiation of light, special theory of relativity, general relativity, and the equivalence of mass and energy. He won the Nobel Prize in 1921 for his 1905 work on the photoelectric effect. Visiting the United States when the Nazis came to power in 1933, he never returned to Germany.

the astrophysicist Eddington's dramatic public presentation of the observations from his 1919 solar eclipse expedition, Einstein's name entered the general public's awareness through newspapers and magazines, and a new era opened in which a wide range of critics and commentators viewed "relativity" (and "relativism") as having newly arisen from Einstein's discovery.

Thus, in the 1920s, the critic T. J. Craven announced that Einstein's theory of relativity liberated the artist from the static and led to the adoption of a "new system of coordinates." Even more glowing rhetoric can be found in a review by an art historian[2] near the end of the twentieth century:

> By deleting objects from his work and using only the elements of form, color, line and texture to express content, Kandinsky was among the first to diverge from the path that western art had traveled for the previous 500 years. . . . Kandinsky received theoretical enforcement for his ideas from . . . modern science. . . . In 1905, Albert Einstein published his theory of relativity. Modern science was painting its own picture of the world, one that was as different from its classical predecessor as were Kandinsky's paintings from those of the Renaissance artists. The new science . . . introduced new concepts . . . , the dynamic rather than static character of reality, the overlapping of time and space, the much talked about fourth dimension (time), and the view of nature as an organic space-time continuum, an eternal present without beginning, middle or end . . . a new *dynamic, uncertain and relativistic* world view.

A host of similar misinformed essays on the theory of relativity can be found throughout the arts, humanities, and social sciences.[3]

5   *Relativity theory/invariance theory.* In actual fact, the relativity of space and time is anchored in the *absoluteness* of the two foundation principles of Einstein's theory. The name "relativity theory" was spawned in 1906 (essentially casually) by Max Planck° in a review of the electrodynamics of moving bodies in which he compared three different theories, and coined abbreviated names to label them.[4]

---

[2]J. Scoville, *Journal of the American Medical Association*, Volume 256 (1986), 1679.

[3]See, for instance, A. F. Freedman and C. C. Donley, *Einstein as Myth and Muse* (Cambridge: Cambridge University Press, 1985); Bruno Latour, "A Relativistic Account of Einstein's Relativity," *Social Studies of Science*, Volume 18 (1988), 3; Alan Sokal, "Transformative Hermeneutics of Quantum Gravity," *Social Text*, Volume 46 (1996), 217. Sokal's article is a hoax, a brilliant parody of postmodernist distortions of science [See the concurrent paper, "A Physicist Experiments with Cultural Studies," by Alan Sokal in *Lingua Franca*, May/June 1996, 62]; see also, Alan Sokal and Jean Bricmont, *Fashionable Nonsense: Postmodern Intellectuals' Abuse of Science* (New York: Picador, 1998), also published in Great Britain as *Intellectual Impostures* (Profile Books, 1998), and in France as *Impostures Intellectuelles* (Editions Odile Jacob, 1997).

[4]See A. I. Miller, *Albert Einstein's Special Theory of Relativity* (Reading, MA: Addison-Wesley Press, 1986) (contains an English translation of Einstein's 1905 paper); P. W. Bridgman, *A Sophisticate's Primer of Relativity*, (Middletown, CT: Wesleyan University Press, 1962, second edition 1983); and Irving M. Klotz, "One Culture/Two Cultures: Captives of Our Metaphors," *Speculations in Science and Technology*, Volume 13, Number 2 (1990), 129.

[5]**Max Planck** (1858–1947) German physicist who won the Nobel Prize for Physics in 1918

Einstein himself, at least in his early days, preferred the name "invariance theory," which emphasizes the foundation of his new theory on (1) the invariance of the velocity of light and on (2) the invariance of the laws of physics:[5]

> (1) Light is always propagated in empty space with a definite velocity c regardless of the reference frame considered;
>
> (2) The laws governing changes in physical systems are independent of the reference frames in which they are measured so long as their relative motion is uniform.

Even in 1909, Einstein referred to the "*so-called* relativity theory." Other distinguished physicists also much preferred "invariance theory." As late as 1948, the theoretical physicist Arnold Sommerfeld wrote, "the name of relativity theory was an unfortunate choice; the relativity of space and time is not the essential thing, which is the independence of laws of nature from the viewpoint of the observer."[6]

Nevertheless, "relativity" has been very fertile as a *metaphor* to rationalize innumerable twentieth-century revolutionary ideas in the arts and humanities. Inspired images may arise from misunderstanding and myth. These can be found in the writings of such famous poets and authors as Archibald MacLeish, William Carlos Williams, E. E. Cummings, Lawrence Durrell, Vladimir Nabokov, Virginia Woolf, William Faulkner, and James Joyce.[7]

There have also been many humanists who have been hostile to or unenthusiastic about Einstein's relativity. Moral absolutists, such as Ezra Pound and T. S. Eliot, two of the most influential writers of the twentieth century, objected to the "socialisation" of relativity, to slogans such as "everything is relative." (Perhaps coincidentally, Pound and Eliot also displayed strong Judeophobic sentiments.) They demanded absolute standards for morality and feared the loss of traditional standards. They failed to recognize that they could have adapted alternative metaphors from the absolutist, invariance principles of Einstein's theory to fit their preconceptions if they wished to appeal to his authority. Likewise, religious absolutists, such as Cardinal O'Connell° (in the 1920s), would not have been frightened that relativity "produce[d] universal doubt about God and His Creation" if they had known that it is founded on principles of absolute invariance.[8] Pseudo-knowledge often generates pseudo-problems.

It is not widely appreciated that the two invariance principles by themselves would not have led to the relativities of distance and time. A crucial addition is the experimental observation that the velocity of light (in empty space) is finite, not infinite as Galileo and Newton had every reason to believe in their time. Some may think that the enormous velocity of 299,792,458 meters (186,000 miles)

10

---

[5]See Bridgman, *A Sophisticate's Primer of Relativity,* 143.

[6]See Miller, *Special Theory of Relativity,* 181.

[7]Klotz, "One Culture/Two Cultures," 129.

[8]Ibid., 135.

[9]**Cardinal [William Henry] O'Connell** (d. 1944) Archbishop of Boston

per second is not significantly different from infinite. And in common experience such individuals are right: the difference is trivial. If light traveled at infinite velocity, it would traverse a distance of one meter in zero time, 0.000000000 . . . . . second. At its actual velocity, light traverses one meter in 0.000000003 second. It is that tiny difference that led Einstein to realize that the concept of simultaneity or absolute time is untenable and that distance and time intervals depend on the reference frame in which they are measured. Thus arose the derivative conclusion labeled Einstein's Theory of Special Relativity.

As we shall see, an analogous feature underlies the uncertainty principle.

Indeterminacy/Uncertainty Principle

As with "relativity," another word that has captured the public's imagination, "uncertainty," is one with a long history in discourse and thought about events and experiences at the human scale. In the 1920s, this word was appended to a very subtle and abstract scientific concept, in a domain very far removed from common experience. Thereby, during the past century, the appellation "uncertainty principle"° provided a conduit for a flood of rhetoric from ecclesiastics, literary critics, dramatists, art critics, journalists, etc., trying to erect a scientific foundation for their preconceptions.

The essence of the quantum mechanical concept. The uncertainty principle of Heisenberg° arises from his revolutionary formulation of quantum mechanics in the middle 1920s. It is pertinent to note that he insisted, and argued with Einstein for fifty years,[9] that his (Heisenberg's) analysis was a logical descendant of Einstein's operational approach to fundamental concepts, such as time and space.[10] There are also other parallelisms between the theory of relativity and the uncertainty principle.

As was true with regard to Einstein who used "invariententheorie" to describe the concepts of his (1905) first paper, so with Heisenberg. For the first statement of his principle[11] he selected the term *"unbestimmt"* (indeterminate), not *"unsicher"* (uncertain). *Unbestimmt* has a very different connotation than does *unsicher*. In the exposition of his principle, Heisenberg established the impossibility of specifying simultaneously the exact position and the precise velocity (momentum) of an elementary particle, such as an electron. If one of these two conjugate variables is known definitively, the other is *"unbestimmt."*

[9]Gerald Holton, "Werner Heisenberg and Albert Einstein," *Physics Today,* Volume 53, Number 7 (2000), 38.

[10]P. W. Bridgman, *The Logic of Modern Physics* (New York: Macmillan, 1927).

[11]Werner Heisenberg, "On the Conceptual Content of Quantum Theoretical Kinematics and Mechanics," *Zeitschrift für Physik,* Volume 43 (1927), 172; and N. R. Hanson, *Patterns of Discovery: An Inquiry into the Conceptual Foundations of Science* (London: Cambridge University Press, 1958), 136.

[12]**uncertainty principle** "The more precisely the position is determined, the less precisely the momentum is known in this instant, and vice versa" (Heisenberg, 1927).

[13]**[Werner] Heisenberg** (1901–76), German physicist who received the Nobel Prize for Physics in 1932. His visit to his former mentor and friend Niels Bohr in Copenhagen during World War II when Denmark was occupied by the Nazis is the subject of Michael Frayn's play *Copenhagen* (see p. 1311).

In practice, each variable will have some indeterminacy or uncertainty, $\Delta\chi$ for the position and $\Delta\rho$ for the momentum, and the two are coupled in the Heisenberg equation

$$\Delta\chi \; \Delta\rho = h$$

where h is Planck's constant.

The constant h is a manifestation of the ultimate corpuscular or grainy character of matter (elementary particles) or radiation (photons) as one penetrates to smaller and smaller dimensions. The Planck constant is a very, very small number: 6.626×10^{-34} (joule sec) (that is, a decimal point followed by 33 zeros and then the digits 6626). If matter and radiation were not grainy and the Planck constant was truly equal to zero, the uncertainly principle would not exist.

Reification of Concepts. The electron of the uncertainty principle is an extremely small elementary particle, with a mass ("weight") of 0.000000000000000000000 0000009 gram and a size of about 0.00000001 cm. How can one visualize such an infinitesimally small entity?

As human beings, we approach such a totally unfamiliar situation by projection from common experience at our macroscopic scale. Thus we create a mental image for an electron as a tiny spherical particle of subatomic dimensions, one that would look like an ultra-ultra-miniature billiard ball. But physics of the twentieth century has found that an electron is also wave-like in nature. An entity that is simultaneously a corpuscle (i.e. a particle) and a wave cannot be visualized at the macroscopic scale of human experience; the two different natures are incompatible, contradictory. At our scale of observation, one can always assign to a particle an exact position in space and a precise velocity. Thus we project a corresponding picture on to an elementary particle such as an electron. But an electron is also a wave, which is inherently spread out in space, not localized to a defined point. In common experience, an entity cannot be simultaneously a particle and a wave. Thus the projection of classical concepts from the macroscopic to the ultra-ultra-microscopic needs careful, critical examination.

Actually the hazards of transporting a concept from large scale phenomena to the submicroscopic realm were recognized long before Heisenberg's analysis. Consider, for example, the notion of temperature.

The origin of this idealization was undoubtedly physiological, based on the sensations of heat and cold. Such an approach necessarily is very crude but sufficed for most cultures. In time human beings observed that the heat effects experienced physiologically also produced changes in the measurable properties of matter. Originally, the most obvious of such measurable changes was in the volume of a liquid or gas. From such observations it became possible to define temperature operationally and quantitatively, and, ultimately, to sever its dependence upon physiological sensations.

Early versions of a thermometer were constructed with alcohol or mercury as the liquid. If the thermometer is small and is inserted into a large body, A, which we recognize by our crude physiological sensors as unchanging in temperature, the small thermometer soon reaches a steady volume (or height) reading. We now say the thermometer is in equilibrium with its surroundings. Furthermore, if we insert the thermometer into a second large body, B, and find that the volume reading at equilibrium is the same as that seen with A, we observe that when A and B are brought into contact with each other, there is no change in the condition of either. We then say A and B are at the same temperature. Proceeding further, we even set up a temperature scale, for example, by inserting the thermometer first in ice-water and then in a water-steam system at a specified pressure, to fix the spread of readings on the scale, and thereby to assign a number to a specific temperature. With widespread use of a thermometer, we begin to reify "temperature" so that it becomes an attribute inherent in everything.

For the non-scientific public such a reified concept of temperature is in accord with common experiences. One is confronted with no paradoxes. Most people would be surprised to learn that a mercury thermometer may give a reading different from that of an alcohol thermometer. (Which one is "right"?) It is unlikely that a non-scientist would cover the bulb of one thermometer with lustrous silver paint and of another (as identical in construction as possible) with dull black paint; but if he or she then compared the readings of the temperature of outside air on a beautiful sunny day, the numbers would be different. (Which one is "right"?) There are various ways of measuring the temperature in a very turbulent fluid and the answers obtained may be different (Which one is "right"?), but this is not a problem that a non-specialist worries about.

At some stage one might also become curious about the temperature of an isolated fundamental particle, an electron, an atom, a molecule. Even a little reflection reveals that projection of the macroscopic concept of temperature to the submicroscopic realm is fraught with ambiguities. How could one use a thermometer to gauge the temperature of a single electron? Likewise, if one turns to the opposite extreme, from the familiar and nearby macroscopic to the cosmoscopic region, one might become curious to ascertain the temperature of empty space between the stars. How should that be done?

Critical analyses of these situations soon make it evident that the same word, temperature, is used for very different types of measurements. Nevertheless, in common experiences, we are unaware of these ambiguities, or we simply lose sight of them. We feel "intuitively" that there is a particular, independent thermal intensity inherent in everything and that the technical devices used to measure it are wholly peripheral, irrelevant. So we hypostatize temperature, make it into a separate but intangible entity or quality that pervades the universe. It comes as a shock to most individuals to learn that there is actually *no meaning* to "temperature" of a single molecule, or atom, or electron.

Likewise we hypostatize our macroscopic concepts of position and velocity and assume we can project our pictures from the macroscopic to the submicroscopic domain. But if isolated electrons, or atoms, do not have temperature, color, or odor, why need they have "traditional dimensions, positions and dynamical properties"?[12]

---

[12]Hanson, *Patterns of Discovery*, 122.

Quantum mechanics has supplied alternative perspectives for delineating the   25
behavior of fundamental particles.[13] "The result is radical unpicturability," the
abandonment of reified classical concepts.[14]

Fluidity in the meaning of words. The reverse projection, from an electron of mass
10^{-28} grams to a human being of mass 70,000 grams, is even more deceptive. In
the subatomic region, "uncertainty principle" has a clear, mathematically defined
meaning, whereas in the macroscopic domain "uncertainty" carries a large
rhetorical baggage that it has accumulated over the ages. In rhetorical space,
words have a fluidity that allows them to be fitted into containers of widely
varying shapes. "Uncertainty" means different things in different contexts. To
illustrate this fluidity, let us scrutinize several other words used in common
parlance that also appear in scientific discourse: wrong, imaginary, irrational.

If someone says the Earth is flat, he or she is wrong. An individual who claims
the Earth is a sphere is also wrong (the Earth is a spheroid) but not as wrong as
the first person. If someone announces that the value of π is 10, he is wrong. So
is the individual who states that π is 3.141596 (the actual seventh significant
digit is 3), but not as wrong as the first person. One who claims that a candle
burning in air releases phlogiston into the air is wrong. An individual who states
that when a candle burns in air the increase in weight of matter released into the
air is *exactly* equal to the sum of the loss in weight of the candle and of the oxygen
in the air is wrong, but in a very different sense. We have to recognize that
"wrong" (and "right") are ambiguous, fuzzy concepts.[15] They are not transcen-
dental qualities or attributes that diffuse into a verbal or written statement.

"Imagination" and "imaginary" are also words that appear frequently in
critical writings in the humanities.[16] It also happens that the "imaginary number," $\sqrt{-1}$ is a basic concept in mathematics. So it too is occasionally transposed
into various areas of critical analysis outside of the natural sciences and mathematics. A particularly stunning illustration of a gross distortion, taken from the
writings of J. Lacan,° is the following:

Thus by calculating that signification according to the algebraic method used here,
namely:

$$\frac{S(\text{signifier})}{s(\text{signified})} = s(\text{the statement})$$

with $S = (1)$, produces:

$$s = \sqrt{-1}$$

---

[13]Ibid., 126. See also, R. Penrose, *The Emperor's New Mind* (New York: Oxford University
Press, 1989), 249; and F. Wilczek and B. Devine, *Longing for the Harmonies* (New York:
W. W. Norton Co., 1987), 130.

[14]Hanson, *Patterns of Discovery,* 123.

[15]Isaac Asimov, *Skeptical Inquirer,* Volume 14 (1989), 35.

[16]See, for example, F. Amrine, Editor, *Literature and Science as Modes of Expression*—Boston
Studies in the Philosophy of Science, Vol. 115, Kluwer Academic Publishers, Dordrecht/
Boston/London (1989); and G. Levine, Editor, *Realism and Representation*—A Conference
Sponsored by the Center for Critical Analysis of Contemporary Culture, Rutgers
University, Rutgers, NJ (1989).

[28]**J[acques] Lacan** late twentieth-century French psychoanalytic theorist

From this Lacan concludes that . . . [the erectile organ] is equivalent to the $\sqrt{-1}$ of the signification produced above.[17]

One wonders whether Lacan would have used this allusion to the "imaginary" number in regard to the erectile organ if he had realized that the appellation "imaginary" became widespread only by chance, and in any event is a misleading name for $\sqrt{-1}$. Mathematicians of previous centuries have called the number $\sqrt{-1}$ sophistic, fictitious, subtle, impossible, uninterpretable.[18] Descartes invented the name "imaginary," and his choice has survived.

In any event, $\sqrt{-1}$ is no more imaginary than is $\sqrt{2}$ or -5 or for that matter $+5$.[19] Few of us today are aware that early mathematicians considered even negative numbers, e.g. -1, as meaningless, a construct to be avoided. As John Wallis,° a contemporary of Newton observed, a negative number, taken literally, implies a quantity less than zero, i.e. less than nothing, clearly a ridiculous idea. Until his time, negative numbers that appeared in the extraction of roots of equations were called absurd, false, fictitious, meaningless.[20] It was Wallis who originally suggested a geometrical interpretation: on a straight line with a point selected to represent zero, distances to the left of zero represent negative numbers, complementing positive numbers measured by distances to the right of zero. To Wallis, a negative number is just as real as a positive one "but to be interpreted in a contrary sense."[21] C. F. Gauss° (among others) many years after Wallis, extended the latter's geometric interpretation to $\sqrt{-1}$ by identifying it with a rotation of the line of positive numbers by 90° (instead of the 180° for -1), thereby creating the complex plane, with complex numbers. To emphasize the interrelationships between $+1$, -1 and $\sqrt{-1}$, Gauss proposed the names direct, inverse, and lateral unity. Unfortunately, Descartes' rather arbitrary term "imaginary" maintained its hold.

It is of interest to note in passing that "irrational" numbers are not bereft of reason. In recent years "surreal" numbers have also been introduced into mathematics. These two mathematical concepts have no relation to the same adjectives in rhetorical creations.

Retrojection of the uncertainty principle to the human domain. With this background, we may return to "uncertainty." In recent years, a popular exercise among some writers and dramatists has been to retroject Heisenberg's uncertainty principle back on to its discoverer. For example, in the highly successful play *Copenhagen*[22]

---

[17]Sokal and Bricmont, *Fashionable Nonsense*, (n. 3), 18.

[18]T. Danzig, *Number, The Language of Science,* fourth edition (Garden City, NY: Doubleday and Co., 1954, first edition published by Macmillan in 1930), 184, and P. J. Nahin, *The Story of $\sqrt{-1}$* (Princeton, NJ: Princeton University Press, 1998), 6.

[19]Danzig, op. cit., *Number, the Language of Science,* 191; and Nahin, *The Story of $\sqrt{-1}$,* 104.

[20]Nahin, *The Story of $\sqrt{-1}$,* 6.

[21]Ibid., 42.

[22]M. Frayn, *Copenhagen* (London: Methuen, 1998).

30 John Wallis (1616–1703) English mathematician   **[Johann Carl Friedrich] Gauss** (1777–1855) German mathematician

the playwright, Michael Frayn, adopts the stratagem of assuming that the only available information relevant to the meeting between Heisenberg and Bohr in Copenhagen in September 1941 is the slanted account of the event provided by Heisenberg years afterward.[23] With this premise, he then subtly slides from the "uncertainty principle" to "uncertainty" in human events. On this basis, he improvises a variety of conjectures and speculations about Heisenberg's thoughts, intentions, and motivations during the Nazi period and thereby generates a fog that conceals what actually occurred during that time.[24] Similar uncertainty scenarios have been conjured up by others;[25] Frayn builds on that of Powers.[26]

However, the uncertainty of the quantum theoretical world of the electron introduces no uncertainty in the macroscopic domain of human experience. Ambiguities in reconstructions of past events arise from several other sources.

One is the unreliability of recollections. As an insightful military leader once remarked, "as the years since the war continue to pass, the more vivid become my memories—of things that never really happened." In a more serious vein, the great contemporary poet Czeslaw Milosz expressed the same theme in the following words: "The past is *inaccurate*. Whoever lives long enough knows how much of what he had seen with his own eyes becomes overgrown with rumor, legend, a magnifying or belittling hearsay. [It makes one ache to exclaim] 'it was not like that at all!'"

In addition, many writers and dramatists employ as their mode of exploration a procedure that has been described by the expression *si potest esse, est:* if something can be imagined to have happened, then it did indeed occur.[27] For example, this is the format of Frayn's *Copenhagen*. In a laudatory review, Powers (neglecting to mention that the play he is reviewing is based on his own book) praises Frayn for *"not trying to establish what really happened* [during the Heisenberg-Bohr meeting in September, 1941]; *it is what might, could or should have happened."*[28] Such an approach artificially inflates the uncertainty and intensifies the drama, which captivates the audience, but leaves us with a picture that is fictional not documented history.

[23]R. Jungk, *Brighter Than a Thousand Suns* (New York: Harcourt, Brace, Jovanovich, 1958). Thirty years later, Jungk retracted the views expressed in this book—see A. Pais, *Niels Bohr's Times* (New York: Oxford University Press, 1991), 484.

[24]D. C. Cassidy, *Uncertainty: The Life and Science of Werner Heisenberg* (New York: Freeman, 1992); P. L. Rose, *Heisenberg and the Nazi Atomic Bomb Project* (Berkeley: University of California Press, 1998); J. Logan, "The Critical Mass," *American Scientist,* Volume 84 (1996), 263; P. L. Rose, "Frayn's 'Copenhagen' Plays Well at History's Expense," *Chronicle of Higher Education,* Volume 46, Number 35 (2000), B4; J. Logan, "A Strange New Quantum Ethics," *American Scientist,* Volume 88 (2000), 356; and D. C. Cassidy, "A Historical Perspective on 'Copenhagen,'" *Physics Today,* Volume 53, Number 7 (2000), 28.

[25]Jungk, op. cit., *Brighter Than a Thousand Suns.* Also, M. Walker, *Nazi Science: Myth, Truth and the German Atomic Bomb* (New York: Plenum Press, 1995).

[26]T. Powers, *The Secret History of the German Atomic Bomb,* (New York: Knopf, 1993).

[27]Irving M. Klotz, "Bending Perception," *Nature,* Volume 379 (1996), 411.

[28]T. Powers, "The Unanswered Question," *New York Review of Books,* Volume 47, Number 9 (2000), 4.

Further inflation of uncertainty is promoted by dramatists and writers who ignore or distort records and documentation that contradict their thesis. This is also repeatedly evident in *Copenhagen*. For example, in one scene we are told that in June 1942, Heisenberg's uranium project in Germany was ahead of Fermi's in the United States. Actually, six months later (December, 1942) Fermi's group had successfully constructed the first self-sustaining nuclear reactor, but even three years later, Heisenberg's reactor was still not operational. Furthermore, the German uranium project, in general, was even further behind the American in essentially all other respects. In 1940, Nier, and in 1941, Lawrence, by independent methods, separated samples of fissionable U^{235} from natural forms; and in (March) 1941, Seaborg produced samples of fissionable plutonium, Pu^{239}, from cyclotron bombardment of uranium. In contrast, even at the end of the war, the Germans had not isolated a single atom of U^{235} or of Pu^{239}.

Repeatedly we are told, by Frayn in *Copenhagen* and by such historians as Walker and Powers,[29] that the Germans "knew" about element 94, Pu^{239}, for it is mentioned in their secret wartime documents. But there is even more convincing evidence that most American graduate students in nuclear physics or nuclear chemistry (not engaged in classified work at that time) "knew" about plutonium, for a contemporary textbook, written in 1940–41 and printed in 1942, states that "it was proved by McMillan and Abelson that the resulting [element] 93^{239} decays to 94^{239} [plutonium]."[30] But how do these "knews" compare with the discussion in Louis Turner's paper, submitted in May 1940 to *Physical Review* (held secret and printed in 1946) containing a detailed analysis of how to convert "all of the U^{238} into Pu^{239}"? Clearly the word "knew" has widely disparate meanings that need elaboration before one starts making claims.

Revelations from the Farm Hall Transcripts

Awareness of plutonium, element 94. What little the Germans surmised about element 94, Pu^{239}, in 1940, they did not carry forward to any significant extent. That assessment is unequivocally documented in the Farm Hall transcripts,° surreptitiously recorded conversations (declassified in 1992) of the German atomic scientists during their internment in England from May to December, 1945.[31] These transcripts contain a long wandering discussion, typified by the following excerpts:

> *Hahn:*° The fission of ionium was experimentally proved in the Radium Institute at Vienna. . . . Thorium undergoes fission. . . . Ionium is also fissile.

[38]**Farm Hall transcripts** the transcriptions of conversations secretly recorded at Farm Hall, the country house in Huntingdonshire, England, where German physicists were interned and spied upon after World War II   **[Otto] Hahn** (1879–1968) a chemist who won the Nobel Prize in 1944

[29]M. Walker, op. cit., *Nazi Science: Myth, Truth and the German Atomic Bomb;* Powers, op. cit., *The Secret History of the German Atomic Bomb.*

[30]T. Pollard and W. L. Davidson, *Applied Nuclear Physics* (New York: John Wiley, 1942), 198.

[31]*Epsilon, 1 May to 30 December 1945*, Public Record Office, London, 1992. See also *Operation Epsilon: The Farm Hall Transcripts*, Institute of Physics, Bristol, 1993.

Gerlach: Can one make a bomb with it? Can you make a bomb out of 2 kg ionium?

Hahn: I don't know.

Bagge:° This they call "Pluto." This might be 93.

Heisenberg: I still do not understand what they have done. . . . How they obtained this element [94] is still a mystery.

. . . If they have made it with a machine [that is, a nuclear pile], then there is the fantastically difficult problem that they have had to carry out chemical processes with this terrifically radioactive material. . . . I do not believe that the Americans could have done it. . . . I believe it almost more likely that they have done something quite original such as getting out protactinium in quantity from colossal quantities of material. . . . Perhaps the facts are that they thereby discovered "Pluto." Pluto is a code name. Protactinium also starts with a "P". . . . Perhaps the others have used protactinium; this is almost easier to imagine than all other methods. . . . If one has pure protactinium in considerable quantity, then the whole thing would blow up. . . . You can of course have luck if you make element 94 . . . perhaps just as many [neutrons] come out in the case of protactinium. . . . Let us assume that they have done it with protactinium, which to me at the moment appears to be the most likely. . . . They would have had to work with 140,000 tons of materials. "Pluto" may be a code name.

Moral posturings. More distressing are the distortions, under the guise of uncertainty, of the motivations of the German atomic bomb scientists. A theme that has been repeatedly resurrected and inflated is that the Germans, and particularly Heisenberg, conspired to deny Hitler access to a bomb. This view first received wide dissemination from R. Jungk's 1956 book, *Brighter Than a Thousand Suns* where it is stated as follows:

It seems paradoxical that the German nuclear physicists, living under a saber-rattling dictatorship, obeyed the voice of conscience and attempted to prevent the construction of atom bombs, while their professional colleagues in the democracies, who had no coercion to fear, with very few exceptions, concentrated their whole energies on production of the new weapons.[32]

Some thirty years later, M. Walker opined that

German scientists conspired to deny Hitler a bomb.[33]

Shortly afterward the journalist T. Powers in his self-styled "shadow history" of the German fission project wrote:

It was not dumb luck that saved us from the nightmare [of Hitler with an atom bomb] but the fact that a handful of German scientists—Heisenberg foremost

40

[32]R. Jungk, op. cit. (n. 23), *Brighter Than a Thousand Suns.*

[33]M. Walker, "Heisenberg, Goudsmit, and the German Atomic Bomb," *Physics Today,* Volume 44, Number 5 (1991), 94; see also *Physics Today,* Volume 43, Number 1 (1990), 52.

[38][Eric] **Bagge** a physicist in Leipzig interned at Farm Hall with other German nuclear scientists after World War II

among them—found a way to guarantee that the German bomb died *in utero* . . . Heisenberg did not simply withhold himself, stand aside, let the project die. He killed it.[34]

This same theme is prominent in Frayn's *Copenhagen*, his "work of fiction featur[ing] historical characters and historical events" [Frayn's words]. In this moving drama the following words issue from Heisenberg's mouth:

I understood very clearly [the principle of the atomic bomb]. I simply didn't tell the others.[35]

In fact Heisenberg had disclosed the construction of an atomic bomb repeatedly to Nazi government officials.[36] For example, in the Farm Hall Transcripts, Heisenberg reveals that in the spring of 1942, "we convinced [the Nazi official Rust] that we had absolutely definite proof that it could be done."[37] *Copenhagen* then converts the Jungk-Walker-Powers assertions into a moral formulation:

Does one as a physicist have the moral right to work on the practical exploitation of atomic energy?

(This self-justifying sophistry equates working on an atomic bomb for use by Hitler, after he had subjugated and terrorized essentially all of Europe, with the frantic efforts of terrified refugees and potential new victims to create a weapon that would stop him). However, the moral scruples retroactively formulated by the German atomic scientists after the defeat of Germany are not apparent in their conversations at Farm Hall:

Heisenberg: I can understand someone saying we ought to team up with Russia. . . . We can do it in good conscience. . . . The Russians will make very good offers to some of the physicists. . . . [If] the Russians say "you will get an institute with a yearly budget of half a million [1945 money]," then I would consider if I shouldn't go to the Russians.

Heisenberg: If the Americans have not got so far as we did—that's what it looks like—then we are in luck. There is a possibility of making money. One must do that [nuclear work for the Allies] cleverly. As far as the masses are concerned it will look as though we unfortunately have to continue our scientific work under the wicked Anglo-Saxon control. . . . We will have to appear to accept this control with fury and gnashing of teeth.

Harteck: [If] we had been in Russia and had the necessary material and had to start from nothing, we would undertake to make a machine work in nine months.[38]

---

[34]Powers, op. cit., *The Secret History of the German Atomic Bomb*, 479.

[35]M. Frayn, *Copenhagen*, 82.

[36]J. Logan, op. cit. "The Critical Mass"; P. L. Rose, "Frayn's 'Copenhagen' Plays Well at History's Expense"; J. Logan, "A Strange New Quantum Ethics," 356.

[37]*Operation Epsilon: The Farm Hall Transcripts* (n. 31), 56.

[38]Ibid., 102, 128, 157, 175.

With regard to the sabotaging of the atomic bomb project by the German physi- 45
cists, the following interchanges in the Farm Hall transcripts are enlightening:

> *Weizsacker:* I believe the reason we didn't do it [construct an atomic bomb] was
> because *all the physicists* didn't want to do it on principle.
>
> *Hahn:* I don't believe that.
>
> *Weizsacker:* In our case even the outstanding scientists said it couldn't be done.
>
> *Bagge:* That's not true . . . everyone was asked [Sept. 1941] . . . everyone said it
> must be done at once. [Bothe said] gentlemen it must be done at once . . .
> [Geiger] said if there is the slightest chance it is possible, it must be done. It is
> absurd for Weizsacker to say he did not want the [bomb] to succeed. That may
> be so in his case, but not for all of us.[39]

These quotations clearly contradict writings propagating the myth of cryptic
sabotage by the German atomic bomb scientists. Paraphrasing John Keats, one
may observe that in our time also there are writers who are "content with half
knowledge."[40]

Epilogue

People become infatuated with felicitous expressions. Catchy phrases from
science are used to provide a mantle of scientific authenticity for all kinds of
preconceived beliefs or novel tenets in art, drama, and literature. The terms
theory of relativity, uncertainty principle, chaos, entropy pervade much of
modern literature and art. However, a metaphor is not a syllogism. The eminent
jurist Learned Hand° once said,

> Much of metaphor merely impedes discourse . . . it is ordinarily a symptom of
> confused thinking.[41]

The pertinence of this trenchant insight is repeatedly evident in writings
attempting to infuse Procrustean distortions of scientific concepts into the
humanities.   [2001]

[39]Ibid., 66, 67, 157.
[40]Holton, op. cit. (n. 9), "Werner Heisenberg and Albert Einstein," 38.
[41]See J. T. Noonan, Jr., "The Metaphors of Morals," *Bulletin of the American Academy of Arts and Sciences,* Volume 42, Number 2 (1988), 30.

[47]**Learned Hand** (1872–1961) American federal district court judge, later a judge on the Second Circuit Court of Appeals

1. Characterize Klotz's persona and style as the writer of this essay.
2. What position would Klotz take on C. P. Snow's wish to bridge the gap
   between "the two cultures," which Lustig and Shepherd-Barr define as
   "science on one side and the arts and humanities on the other" (see their
   "Science as Theater" on p. 1378). How does he justify his position?

◎◎◎

Harry Lustig
Kirsten Shepherd-Barr

Harry Lustig *(1925–) is a theoretical nuclear physicist, now professor of physics emeritus and provost emeritus at the City College of the City University of New York. He is also Treasurer Emeritus of the American Physical Society and Adjunct Professor of Physics and Astronomy at the University of New Mexico.*

Kirsten Shepherd-Barr *(1966–) holds a Bachelor of Arts degree from Yale University and a Doctor of Philosophy degree from Oxford University. Her special interests lie in the fields of modern drama, theater history, and theater and science. Her first book,* Ibsen and Early Modernist Theatre, 1890–1900, *was published in 1997. Many articles on theater in America, Scandinavia, and Canada followed. She is particularly interested in cross-cultural, interdisciplinary approaches to drama. Dr. Shepherd-Barr is an Associate Professor at North Carolina State University.*

*Science as Theater**

Two thousand million people in the world, and the one who has to decide their fate is the only one who's always hidden from me. . . .

On a bare stage, actor Hank Stratton, playing the role of Werner Heisenberg in Michael Frayn's acclaimed play *Copenhagen,* muses on the impossibility of self-knowledge. The fictional Heisenberg is agonizing over his role in the Nazi effort to build an atomic bomb and finds himself unsure of his own motivations.

For four years on the London stage, two years on Broadway, and in cities across Europe and America, *Copenhagen* has defied the conventional wisdom that science and art cannot co-exist. Despite or perhaps because of its heady mix of quantum physics and moral dilemmas, it has been popular with critics and audiences alike; it won the Tony Award for Best New Play in 2000 and was filmed for presentation this fall to U.S. public-television audiences. As *New York Times* critic Ben Brantley put it, "Who would have ever thought that three dead, long-winded people talking about atomic physics would be such electrifying companions?"

Yet the success of *Copenhagen* has not been an isolated phenomenon. In recent years, science has become a surprisingly popular subject for playwrights. According to our best count, more than 20 plays on a scientific theme have opened in a professional production over the last five years, although none has yet matched *Copenhagen*'s popular success. At the very least, science is in vogue on stage as it has never been before. The best of these plays go far beyond using science as an ornament or a plot device. They seriously embrace scientific ideas and grapple with their implications. In an era when traditional dramatic subjects such as dysfunctional families have become tired, playwrights have found the lives and discoveries of real scientists to be full of dramatic possibilities and thought-provoking metaphors.

In his famous 1959 essay on "the two cultures," C. P. Snow lamented the widening gulf between science on one side and the arts and humanities on the other, and

*Harry Lustig and Kirsten Shepherd-Barr, "Science as Theater," *American Scientist* 90 (November–December 2002): 550–55.

expressed his hope for a "third culture" of art that would "be on speaking terms with the scientific one." A number of recent science plays show how effective this conversation can be, and suggest that the "third culture" that Snow envisioned may actually be arriving in the intersection between science and the theater.

Anxiety and Distrust

"Science plays" have a long history and a distinguished provenance, starting with Christopher Marlowe's *Dr. Faustus*, published in 1604. Although it does not deal with specific scientific concepts, the play features a scientist who strikes a bargain with the Devil and meets a horrible demise as a result of his lust for knowledge.

Marlowe's distrust of the motives of scientists set the tone for many future plays in the genre. Other playwrights expressed this distrust in more comedic form. Ben Jonson's *The Alchemist* (1610) lampooned both the practitioners of this ancient pseudo-science, unmasked by Jonson as jargon-babbling rogues, and their willing dupes. When Jonson's sly alchemist, Subtle, quizzes his accomplice, Face, Jonson has great fun with the terminology of Renaissance science:

Subtle: Name the vexations, and the martyrisations
    Of metals, in the work.
Face: Sir, putrefaction,
    Solution, ablution, sublimation,
    Cohobation, calcinations, ceration and
    Fixation.
Subtle: This is heathen Greek, to you, now?
    And when comes vivification?
Face: After mortification.

Later, George Bernard Shaw's *The Doctor's Dilemma* (1906) made fun of a passel of medical charlatans with such famous lines as "Stimulate the phagocytes!" But the play also shows that Shaw has genuinely investigated the biochemistry that the doctors discuss.

Bertolt Brecht's *Galileo,* with its portrayal of actual scientists in historical situations, marked a turning point in the history of scientific plays. In a version of the play published in 1939 (but not translated, and therefore not widely known), Brecht took a very positive view of his protagonist; but in later revisions, which were strongly influenced by Hiroshima° and Nagasaki,° he portrayed Galileo as an antihero. The revised play, published in 1947, is the Brecht *Galileo* most widely used and read around the world.

Several other playwrights also saw the bomb in Faustian terms. Friedrich Dürrenmatt, in *The Physicists* (1962), warned of the apocalyptic results of modern physics put into the wrong hands. The play uses the Möbius strip as a central image and is one of the first modern plays to integrate science formally as well as thematically. Another remarkable science play that warns of the dangerous potential of physics, while actually discussing scientific ideas, is Hallie Flanagan Davis's $E = mc^{2}$° (1948). This play is part allegory and part documentary, as it

[8]**Hiroshima** Japanese city, the target of the first atomic bomb, August 6, 1945
Nagasaki the second Japanese city bombed at the end of World War II, August 9, 1945
[9]$E = mc^2$ Albert Einstein's formula expressing the relationship between matter and energy

features a character called Atom and a Professor who explains the physics that the audience needs to know. Much of the play's dialogue is taken directly from transcripts of hearings of the Atomic Energy Commission and contemporary news sources. Davis leaves the fate of the Earth in the audience's hands, pleading with us to choose the right path in our use of atomic energy.

Memory and Duality

10   Even as they retain some elements of skepticism toward science, contemporary science plays explore a broader range of attitudes and, as in $E = mc^2$, have frequently drawn their themes from science itself. No play illustrates this better than the masterpiece of the genre, *Copenhagen*.

Michael Frayn's play, familiar by now to many *American Scientist* readers, re-enacts the 1941 visit of Werner Heisenberg to his mentor and friend Niels Bohr, in Nazi-occupied Denmark. The third "long-winded" character is Bohr's wife Margrethe, who in this play (although probably not in reality) was present for the first part of the conversation. The action takes place outside chronological time, as the three deceased characters struggle, with the hindsight of 60 years of history, to make sense of what happened that afternoon.

From 1939 until Germany's defeat in 1945, Heisenberg was in charge of the most important part of the country's uranium project. As a result of the visit to Copenhagen, the friendship between the two men cooled abruptly. Something had happened, but neither ever explained definitively what it was. Frayn explores the mystery with three alternative scenarios, or "drafts" as the characters call them, each with different outcomes. No concrete answers are provided in the text. Even the characters' own memories of the events prove unreliable.

The questions begin with the very opening lines from Margrethe to her husband: "Why did he [Heisenberg] come to Copenhagen? . . . What was he trying to tell you?" They continue: Did Heisenberg say to Bohr what he had intended? If not, why not? What was Bohr's reaction? What was Heisenberg's? And inevitably, why did the Germans not achieve an atomic bomb, and why, under Heisenberg, did they not even try—or did they? Did Heisenberg deliberately slow down the bomb effort for moral reasons? Was it Heisenberg's or his fellow German scientists' incompetence? Had he made an incorrect calculation, or no calculation at all, of the critical mass required for an explosive chain reaction?

In the script, Frayn dives right into the physics, going far beyond what most theatergoers can be expected to know. The level of sophistication makes the characters believable, and it also conveys crucial plot points. First, the characters explain why they both thought, in 1939, that an atomic bomb could never be produced:

> *Bohr:* What all this means is that an explosive reaction will never occur in natural uranium. To make an explosion you will have to separate pure [uranium-]235. And to make the chain long enough for a large explosion . . .
>
> *Heisenberg:* Eighty generations, let's say . . .
>
> *Bohr:* . . . you would need many tons of it. And it's extremely difficult to separate.
>
> *Heisenberg:* Tantalisingly difficult.

Bohr: Mercifully difficult. The best estimates, when I was in America in 1939, were that to produce even one gram of U-235 would take 26,000 years. By which time, surely, this war will be over.

Later we find out what they had missed:

Heisenberg: Because you'd always been confident that weapons would need 235 and that we could never separate enough of it. [. . .]
Heisenberg: What we'd realised, though, was that if we could once get the reactor going . . .
Bohr: The 238 in the natural uranium would absorb the fast neutrons . . .
Heisenberg: [. . .] And would be transformed by them into a new element altogether.
Bohr: Neptunium. Which would decay in its turn into another new element . . .
Heisenberg: At least as fissile as the 235 that we couldn't separate . . .
Margrethe: Plutonium.
Heisenberg: Plutonium.
Heisenberg: [. . .] If we could build a reactor we could build bombs. That's what had brought me to Copenhagen.

Scientifically, the first passage is not completely accurate, but it is basically correct about what Bohr and Heisenberg had thought at one time. The second passage is scientifically correct, and moreover it is thematically crucial. Heisenberg says he wanted to ask if it was morally right to go on working on the reactor project in light of this apocalyptic discovery; Bohr thinks Heisenberg came to ask for his blessing—or, even worse, for his help. 15

Copenhagen is built out of such dual, and dueling, interpretations. The title itself does double duty, as the location of the action but also as the name of the famous "Copenhagen interpretation" of quantum mechanics developed by Bohr and Heisenberg in the mid-1920s. In this interpretation, the state of a quantum particle is not determined until the act of observation puts it into a definite state. Even then, complementary attributes such as a particle's position and momentum obey an uncertainty relation: The more precisely the observer (who may be a machine) measures one, the less precisely can the other be measured. Quantum-mechanical objects and light behave, to use classical language, sometimes as waves and sometimes as particles. The principle of complementarity states that these two attributes can never be demonstrated in the same experiment or observation.

The uncertainty principle and complementarity are grist for the playwright's mill. The characters cannot agree on anything that happened—not even when and where the conversation took place. The staging of the play reinforces the scientific ideas. In the Broadway and London productions, the stage was round and bare, and the actors' motions around it called to mind the electrons, protons and neutrons moving in an atom. Some of the audience sat in a tribunal at the back of the stage, watching and "judging" the action in stark marble stalls. They were in turn watched by the rest of the audience—the observers observed.

Many philosophers of science have questioned the application of the Copenhagen interpretation to the macroscopic world of human beings, finding it impermissibly reductive. In spite of the fact that this extrapolation is the very premise of the play, in one of his two copious "postscripts" Frayn has said he doesn't take it literally. "The concept of uncertainty is one of those scientific notions that has become common coinage, and generalized to the point of losing much of its original meaning," he writes. Clearly his intent is not to debase the coinage any more. Instead, he uses uncertainty as a metaphor (always part of the artist's license) for the inherent unfathomability of memory, "a systematic limitation which cannot even in theory be circumvented."

Copenhagen has, in its own way, created an observer effect, leading to a reexamination of the historical record that it scrutinizes. In February, a decade ahead of their stated schedule, the Bohr family unsealed, for publication, some letters to Heisenberg that Bohr drafted in the 1950s but never sent. They cast serious doubt on one of the suggestions in the play: that Heisenberg might have been reluctant to work on the bomb for moral reasons. But the new revelations do little to settle the uncertainties in the play and nothing to alter Frayn's essential points about uncertainty. In fact, some lines of Bohr's letters, such as his repeated statement "I am greatly amazed to see how much your memory has deceived you," read as if they could have been written by Frayn.

The Slip of the Screwdriver

20   On May 21, 1946, Louis Slotin, a Canadian physicist at Los Alamos,° repeated a "criticality test" that he had done many times before. He slipped the pieces of a plutonium bomb closer together and farther apart, "flirting" (as Dennis Overbye has written in the *New York Times*) "with the moment when the assembly would be tight enough to achieve critical mass." He had chosen an extraordinarily dangerous partner to flirt with. Richard Feynman once called such experiments "tickling the dragon's tail."

Ordinarily, wooden spacers separated the two halves of the bomb and prevented a chain reaction from getting started. But for the test, Slotin had removed the spacers and was using the blade of a screwdriver to keep the shells apart. The screwdriver slipped, and the assembly clicked together. A blue glow enveloped the room. Slotin pulled the bomb apart instantly, but there was no way to undo the lethal dose of radiation he had received. Seven other men who were in the chamber with him received smaller doses and survived, because they had been shielded by Slotin's body, but he died after nine days of increasing agony at the Los Alamos hospital.

Playwright Paul Mullin has turned this terrible accident into what could be one of the most provocative science plays since *Copenhagen,* called *Louis Slotin Sonata.* (Like several other recent science-based dramas, this play received funding from the Alfred P. Sloan Foundation through a program that encourages playwrights and artists to take on scientific and technological themes.) Where *Copenhagen* is spare and cerebral, *Louis Slotin Sonata* is flamboyant and emotional. In the play, Slotin suffers hallucinations during his final days, giving Mullin a chance to bring on some unlikely characters. J. Robert Oppenheimer is there,

---

[20]**Los Alamos** the laboratories in New Mexico where scientists created the atomic bombs that were dropped on Japan at the end of World War II

repeating his line from the *Bhagavad-Gita:* "I am become death, shatterer of worlds." Einstein shows up—you guessed it—playing dice, and God himself puts in an appearance, dressed in a pinstripe suit and fedora and bearing an uncanny resemblance, as Overbye points out, to Harry S. Truman. Obviously the playwright is giving the audience some strong hints about human beings playing God.

In one of the hallucinations, Josef Mengele, the sadistic Nazi death camp doctor, arrives in Hiroshima to watch the scientists achieve in milliseconds "what took us years to do in stinking, filth-filled camps." To critic Bruce Weber, writing in *The New York Times,* the scene seemed too contrived: "It feels motivated by theatricality rather than drama, especially when Mengele leads the show's weirdest sequence, a parody of a vaudeville chorus line, with scientists singing doggerel about thermodynamics. Like a lot of elements in the play, the scene is ornamental and distracting, presented by the playwright not because he should but because he can."

Louis Slotin Sonata succeeded in provoking a symposium at Los Alamos after a special reading of the play. (The postperformance symposium seems to be turning into a new science/art form; *Copenhagen* has also given rise to several of them.) Many of the Manhattan Project veterans complained bitterly about the antiscientific bias of the play. But the play's excesses do not hide the fact that Mullin has done his homework; as he told Overbye, he plowed through a three-inch-thick file at Los Alamos on the Slotin case. "I vowed to tell it like it was," he said. "Anything less would be grave digging." It seems to us that the playwright has every right to question whether the atomic scientists were heroes or irresponsible "cowboys," playing around with the dragon when there were safer ways to test the bomb assembly. He is also entitled to the conclusion that the bomb should not have been dropped on Hiroshima and Nagasaki, although one might have wished for a more balanced presentation of the argument.

Still, the "two cultures" dichotomy dies hard. Curt Dempster, the artistic director of the Ensemble Studio Theatre, told Overbye after the symposium: "They were running into us, the illusionists. We were running into the reality." *Copenhagen* has decisively undermined the old argument. Illusion and reality do not have to run into each other, if both are treated with respect.

Evolution and Betrayal

In recent years most "science plays" have been physics plays, perhaps because the bomb brought the consequences of modern physics so forcefully to the public's attention, raising powerful ethical and historical issues that science itself could not solve. But biology has taken its own turn on the stage. One example is Timberlake Wertenbaker's play *After Darwin,* dramatizing another explosive scientific topic: the theory of natural selection.

After Darwin borrows a metatheatrical technique from Tom Stoppard's mathematics play *Arcadia,* with scenes alternating between two historical periods. The present-day characters are actors, Tom and Ian, putting on a play about Charles Darwin (played by Tom) and Robert FitzRoy (Ian), the captain of the *Beagle.* The scenes alternate between this historical costume drama and the present, in which Tom and Ian talk with the Bulgarian director, Millie, and the African-American playwright, Lawrence.

As the play progresses, the tension builds in each time frame. Darwin and FitzRoy become estranged, as the very religious captain feels increasingly threatened by the implications of Darwin's discoveries. FitzRoy even threatens his former friend with a pistol. Ian feels threatened, too, when Tom confides to him that he has been hired to appear in a movie and will have to quit the play in order to do so. That would close down the production. In order to save his job, Ian betrays Tom by secretly emailing the film director and telling him (falsely) that Tom is HIV-positive.

Where does evolution by natural selection come in? Wertenbaker relies on the somewhat shopworn parallel between biological Darwinism and social Darwinism, which seems to be defined here as people being incredibly selfish in order to survive. Tom defends his defection to the film project by citing adaptation and survival, and Ian justifies his betrayal in the same terms: "I don't want another two years without work. I want to survive, I want Millie to survive, I want this to survive." Just as FitzRoy wants his faith to remain intact, Ian wants the play to go on; but both of them know in their hearts that Darwin/Tom's decisions are irrevocable. They object to the way that Darwin and Tom "play God," but they fail to see their own interventions in the same hubristic light.

30   The play's subplots strengthen the scientific metaphors. The stories of Millie and Lawrence, who are both transplants of a sort, provide different "takes" on adaptation and the losses and compromises it entails. A second subplot involves Ian's "babysitting" a Tamagotchi toy for his niece. The toy is constantly beeping and interrupting him to demand virtual nourishment, which he must provide speedily lest the creature die. The attention he gives to the virtual pet while betraying his flesh-and-blood colleague sends a bleak message about technology as a dehumanizing force.

After Darwin, which was produced at the Hampstead Theater in London, received mixed reviews. On the one hand, the London-based critic Benedict Nightingale noted that Wertenbaker "bangs away at her theme a bit relentlessly." But on the other hand, Nightingale wrote, "the dramatic brew is rich and mentally nourishing, embracing as it does questions of God and godlessness, determinism and free will, biology and ethics." It remains to be seen whether *After Darwin* presages a lasting subgenre of "biology plays," but it is the first serious attempt to integrate evolutionary theory with the theater both thematically and formally. (As an aside, we would like to note one very worthy successor, Tom McGrath's *Safe Delivery*, a play about gene therapy inspired by the research of the writer's daughter. This play was sponsored by the Wellcome Trust, which has mounted in England a program comparable to the Sloan Foundation's support of U.S. plays about science.)

We hope that the three plays we have chosen to discuss—out of the many that we could have chosen—give some flavor of the variety of treatments of scientific themes in contemporary plays. The infusion of scientific ideas has invigorated a theatrical scene that, as recently as 15 years ago, was criticized by the prominent theater critic and scholar Martin Esslin for the banality of its subject matter and its refusal to treat topics "outside the narrow range of family squabbles." Clearly, science works as theater. And theater can work at conveying the ideas of science. In an article he prepared for the symposium "The Copenhagen Interpretation: Science and History on Stage," physicist John Marburger wrote, "Many stories can be told of [science's] struggles and their consequences, but I doubt that many will rise to the standard set by Frayn's *Copenhagen.* I will end by thanking Michael Frayn for bringing the core issues of this beautiful aspect of science to such a large audience." We hope that other playwrights will take up the challenge.

Bibliography

Bernstein, J. 2001. *Hitler's Uranium Club, the Secret Recordings of Farm Hall.* New York: Copernicus Books.

Bethe, H. A. 2000. The German uranium project. *Physics Today* 53:34–36.

Bohr, N. 1957–1962. Unsent drafts of letters to Heisenberg and memoranda about the 1941 meeting. Released by the Niels Bohr Archive, February 6, 2002. *Naturens Verden* 84(8–9); http://www.nbi.dk/NBA/papers/docs/cover.html

Brantley, B. 2000. "Copenhagen": A fiery power in the behavior of particles and humans. *The New York Times,* April 12:E-1.

Carpenter, C. A. 1999. *Dramatists and the Bomb: American and British Playwrights Confront the Nuclear Age, 1945–1964.* Westport, Conn.: Greenwood Press.

Cassidy, D. In press. New light on *Copenhagen* and the German nuclear project. *Physics in Perspective.*

Frayn, M. 2000. *Copenhagen.* New York: Anchor Books.

Frayn, M. 2002. Post-postscript. http://web.gc.cuny.edu/ashp/nml/artsci/frayn.htm

Haynes, R. D. 1994. *From Faust to Strangelove: Representations of the Scientist in Western Literature.* Baltimore: Johns Hopkins University Press.

Jonson, B. 1987. *The Alchemist* (ed. Peter Bement). London, New York: Methuen.

Logan, J. 2000. "A strange new quantum ethics." *American Scientist* 88:356–359.

Marburger, J. H., III. 2002. On the Copenhagen interpretation of quantum mechanics. http://web.gc.cuny.edu/ashp/nml/artsci/marburger.htm

Overbye, D. 2001. Theatrical elegy recalls a victim of nuclear age. *The New York Times* (April 3):F-4.

Pais, A., and M. Frayn. 2000. What happened in Copenhagen? A physicist's view and the playwright's response. *Hudson Review* 53:2.

Powers, T. 2000. The unanswered question. *New York Review of Books,* May 25.

Rhodes, R. 1995. *The Making of the Atomic Bomb.* New York: Touchstone Books.

Rose, P. L. 2000. Frayn's "Copenhagen" plays well at history's expense. *The Chronicle of Higher Education* (May 5):B4–6.

Ruddick, N. 2001. The search for a quantum ethics: Michael Frayn's "Copenhagen" and other recent British science plays. *Journal of the Fantastic in the Arts* 11:415–29.

Shepherd-Barr, Kirsten. In press. "Copenhagen" and beyond: The "rich and mentally nourishing" interplay between science and theatre. *Gramma.*

Snow, C. P. 1993. *The Two Cultures.* Cambridge, U.K.: Cambridge University Press.

Weber, B. 2001. "Louis Slotin Sonata": A scientist's tragic hubris attains critical mass onstage. *The New York Times* (April 10):E-1.

Wertenbaker, T. 1998. *After Darwin.* London: Faber.   [2002]

1. What is the authors' attitude to what Klotz calls art's "Procrustean distortions" of science?

2. Characterize the argument between Lustig and Shepherd-Barr on the one side and Klotz on the other.

3. According to Heisenberg, "quantum theory provides us with a striking illustration of the fact that we can fully understand a connection though we can only speak of it in images and parables."[1] How does this observation help us in the argument over the use of scientific metaphors in art and in science itself?

4. Review the excerpt from Lakoff and Johnson's *Metaphors We Live By*[2] in Chapter 8 (p. 151). How would the authors weigh in on the debate about metaphor? What difference does it make that so much of modern physics seems to have been debated on long walks?

[1]"Quotations by Werner Heisenberg," School of Mathematics and Statistics, University of St Andrews, Scotland, http://www-history.mcs.st-andrews.ac.uk/Quotations/Heisenberg.html (accessed July 10, 2004).

[2]George Lakoff and Mark Johnson, *Metaphors We Live By* (Chicago: University of Chicago Press, 1980).

The Play and the Essays

1. In his Postscript to the play, Frayn indicates that he knows that the principle of uncertainty, which prevents the simultaneous measurement of the position and the momentum of a subatomic particle, does not apply "directly to our observations of thought and intention." For Klotz, this neither prevents nor excuses the distortions that result from the use of scientific terms metaphorically. Can the play help us decide between Klotz's prohibition against scientific metaphor and Lustig and Shepherd-Barr's insistence on artists' license to use metaphor?

2. Another of Klotz's critiques of the play is that it supports the view, offered by Jungk, Walker, and Powers, that German physicists led by Heisenberg "conspired to deny Hitler access to a bomb." While it is true that after Germany's surrender, in their search for German weapons, the Allies discovered no signs of a German program to make nuclear weapons, the reasons for that absence were unclear. Klotz accuses the play of "propagating the myth of cryptic sabotage by the German atomic bomb scientists." Do you agree? Why or why not?

NONFICTION PROSE

WENDELL BERRY

WENDELL BERRY *(1934–) was born and reared in Kentucky and was educated there, receiving the B.A. and M.A. from the University of Kentucky, teaching on its faculty, and living and writing on his Kentucky farm. He has also taught at a number* *of other universities and began his writing career as a teaching fellow at Stanford University, where he wrote his first novel* Nathan Coulter. *Farming and community life in rural America is the central theme of his novels, essays, and poems, a subject in which he is well-versed, not only through his own experiences, but through the experiences of his family, rooted in Kentucky soil since the 1800s. His father was a pioneer in organic farm principles with Robert Rodale, and Berry himself has written for* The New Farm, *a magazine devoted to the principles of organic farming, principles that Berry follows on his own farm. In writing his numerous essays and articles, he envisions a world in which responsibility for preserving the earth takes precedence over profit and is intent on teaching others the practical ways in which this goal can be met worldwide.*

Life Is a Miracle*

I have been working this morning in front of a window where I have been at work on many mornings for thirty-seven years. Though I have been busy, today as always I have been aware of what has been happening beyond the window. The ground is whitened by patches of melting snow. The river swollen with the runoff, is swift and muddy. I saw four wood ducks riding the current, apparently for fun. A great blue heron was fishing, standing in water up to his belly feathers. Through binoculars I saw him stoop forward, catch, and swallow a fish. At the feeder on the window sill, goldfinches, titmice, chickadees, nuthatches, and cardinals have been busy at a heap of free (to them) sunflower seeds. A flock of crows has found something newsworthy in the cornfield across the river. The woodpeckers are at work, and so are the squirrels. Sometimes from this outlook I have seen wonders: deer swimming across, wild turkeys feeding, a pair of newly fledged owls, otters at play, a coyote taking a stroll, a hummingbird feeding her young, a peregrine falcon eating a snake. When the trees are not in leaf, I can see the wooded slopes on both sides of the valley. I have known this place all my life. I long to protect it and the creatures who belong to it. During the thirty-seven years I have been at work here, I have been thinking a good part of the time about how to protect it. This is a small place, a slender strip of woodland between the river and the road. I know that in two hours a bulldozer could make it unrecognizable to me, and perfectly recognizable to every "developer."

The one thing that I know above all is that even to hope to protect it, I have got to break out of all the categories and confront it as it is; I must be present in its presence. I know at least some of the categories and value them and have found them useful. But here I am in my life, and I know I am not here as a representative white male American human, nor are the birds and animals and plants here as representatives of their sex or species. We all have our ways, forms, and habits. We all are what we are partly because we are here and not in another place. Some of us are mobile; some of us (such as the trees) have to be content merely to be flexible. All of us who are mobile are required by

*Wendell Berry, "Life Is a Miracle," Orion: People and Nature 19.2 (Spring 2000): 29–39.

happenstance and circumstance and accident to make choices that are not instinctive, and that force us out of categories into our lives here and now. Even the trees are under this particularizing influence of place and time. Each one, responding to happenstance and circumstance and accident, has assumed a shape not quite like that of any other tree of its kind. The trees stand rooted in their mysteriously determined places, no place quite like any other, in strange finality. The birds and animals have their nests in holes and burrows and crotches, each one's place a little unlike any other in the world—and so is the nest my mate and I have made.

In all of the thirty-seven years I have worked here, I have been trying to learn a language particular enough to speak of this place as it is and of my being here as I am. My success, as I well know, has been poor enough, and yet I am glad of the effort, for it has helped me to make, and to remember always, the distinction between reduction and the thing reduced. I know the usefulness of reductive language. To know that I am "a white male American human," that a red bird with black wings is "a scarlet tanager," that a tree with white bark is "a sycamore," that this is "a riparian plant community"—all that is helpful to a necessary kind of thought. But when I try to make my language more particular, I see that the life of this place is always emerging beyond expectation or prediction or typicality, that it is unique, given to the world minute by minute, only once, never to be repeated. And then is when I see that this life is a miracle, absolutely worth having, absolutely worth saving.

We are alive within mystery, by miracle. "Life," wrote Erwin Chargaff in *Heraclitean Fire*, "is the continual intervention of the inexplicable." We have more than we can know. We know more than we can say. The constructions of language (which is to say the constructions of thought) are formed *within* experience, not the other way around. Finally, we live beyond words, as also we live beyond computation and beyond theory. There is no reason whatever to assume that the languages of science are less limited than other languages. Perhaps we should wish that after the processes of reduction, scientists would return to the world of our creatureliness and affection, our joy and grief, that precedes and (so far) survives all of our processes.

5   Science speaks properly a language of abstraction and abstract categories when it is properly trying to sort out and put in order the things it knows. But it often assumes improperly that it has said—or known—enough when it has spoken of "the cell" or "the organism," "the genome" or "the ecosystem" and given the correct scientific classification and name. Carried too far, this is a language of false specification and pretentious exactitude, never escaping either abstraction or the cold-heartedness of abstraction.

The giveaway is that even scientists do not speak of their loved ones in categorical terms as "a woman," "a man," "a child," or "a case." Affection requires us to break out of the abstractions, the categories, and confront the creature itself in its life in its place. The importance of this for the cause of conservation can hardly be overstated. For things cannot survive as categories but only as individual creatures living uniquely where they live.

We know enough of our own history by now to be aware that people *exploit* what they have merely concluded to be of value, but they *defend* what they love. To defend what we love we need a particularizing language, for we love what we particularly know. The abstract, "objective," impersonal, dispassionate language of science can, in fact, help us to know certain things, and to know some things with certainty. It can help us, for instance, to know the value of species and of species diversity. But it cannot replace, and it cannot become, the language of familiarity, reverence, and affection by which things of value ultimately are protected.

The abstractions of science are too readily assimilable to the abstractions of industry and commerce, which see everything as interchangeable with or replaceable by something else. There is a kind of egalitarianism which holds that any two things equal in price are equal in value, and that nothing is better than anything that may profitably or fashionably replace it. Forest = field = parking lot; if the price of alteration is right, then there is no point in quibbling over differences. One place is as good as another, one use is as good as another, one life is as good as another—if the price is right. Thus political sentimentality metamorphoses into commercial indifference or aggression. This is the industrial doctrine of the interchangeability of parts, and we apply it to places, to creatures, and to our fellow humans as if it were the law of the world, using all the while a sort of middling language, imitated from the sciences, that cannot speak of heaven or earth but only of concepts. This is a rhetoric of nowhere, which forbids a passionate interest in, let alone a love of, anything in particular.

Directly opposed to this reduction or abstraction of things is the idea of the preciousness of individual lives and places. This does not come from science but from our cultural and religious traditions. It is not derived, and it is not derivable, from any notion of egalitarianism. If all are equal, none can be precious. (And perhaps it is necessary to stop here to say that this ancient delight in the individuality of creatures is not the same thing as what we now mean by "individualism." It is the opposite. Individualism, in present practice, refers to the supposed "right" of an individual to act alone, in disregard of other individuals.)

We now have the phenomenon of "mitigation banking" by which a developer may purchase the "right" to spoil one place by preserving another. Science can measure and balance acreages in this way just as cold-heartedly as commerce; developers involved in such trading undoubtedly have the assistance of ecologists. Nothing insists that one place is not interchangeable with another except affection. If the people who live in such places and love them cannot protect them, nobody can.   10

It is not quite imaginable that people will exert themselves greatly to defend creatures and places that they have dispassionately studied. It is altogether imaginable that they will greatly exert themselves to defend creatures and places that they have involved in their lives and invested their lives in—and of course I know that many scientists make this sort of commitment.

Religion, as empiricists must finally grant, deals with a reality beyond the reach of empiricism. This larger reality does not manifest itself in the manner of laboratory results or in the manner of a newspaper front page. Christ does not come down from the cross and confound his tormentors, as good a movie as that would make. God does not speak loudly from Heaven in the most popular modern languages for all to hear. (If He did, we would have no need for science, or religion either.) It is nevertheless true that people believe in the existence of this larger reality, and accept religious truth as knowledge, because of their *experience*. The walls of the rational, empirical world are famously porous.

What come through are dreams, imaginings, inspirations, visions, revelations. There is no use in stooping over these with a magnifying lens. Beyond any earthly reason we experience beauty in excess of use, justice in excess of anger, mercy in excess of justice, love in excess of deserving or fulfillment. We have known evil beyond imagining and seemingly beyond intention. We have known compassion and forgiveness beyond measure.

Religion, it seems to me, has dealt with this reality clumsily enough, and that is why the history of a religion and its organizations is so frequently a blight on its teachings. But religion at least attempts to deal with religious experience on its own terms; it does not try to explain it by terms that are fundamentally alien to it. And it is explicitly against reductionism. The Bible says that between all creatures and God there is an absolute intimacy. All flesh lives by the spirit and breath of God (Job 34:14–15). We "live, and move, and have our being" in God (Acts 17:28). In the Gospels it is a principle of faith that God's love for the world includes every creature individually, not just races or species. God knows of the fall of every sparrow; He has numbered "the very hairs of your head" (Matthew 10:29–30). William Blake° was being perfectly scriptural when he said that "everything that lives is holy." Julian of Norwich° also was following scriptures when she said that God "wants us to know that not only does he care of great and noble things but equally for little and small, lowly and simple things as well." Stephanie Mills° is witness to the survival of this tradition when she writes: "*A Sand County Almanac*° is suffused with affection for distinct beings."

15   No attentive reader of the Bible can fail to see the writers' alertness to the individuality of things. The characters of humans are sharply observed and are appreciated for their unique abilities. And surely nobody, having read of him once, can forget the warhorse in Job 39:25, who "saith among the trumpets, Ha, ha." I don't know where you could find characterizations more deft and astute than those in the story of the resurrection in John 20:1–17. And again and again the biblical writers write of their pleasure and wonder in the "manifold" works of God, all keenly observed.

People who blame the Bible for the modern destruction of nature have failed to see its delight in the variety and individuality of creatures and its insistence upon

[14]**William Blake** (1757–1827) artist, printmaker, and visionary poet   **Julian of Norwich** (1342–c.1416) English nun and mystic who lived as an anchoress in a small room built into the wall of the church of St. Julian in Norwich, England. She had a number of visions about God's love that she wrote down in two books of revelations and her *Showings*.   **Stephanie Mills** the author of *In Praise of Nature* (Island Press) *A Sand County Almanac* a book by environmentalist Aldo Leopold (Oxford University Press, 1949)

their holiness. But that delight—in, say, the final chapters of Job or the 104th psalm—is far more useful to the cause of conservation than the undifferentiating abstractions of science. Empiricists fail to see how the language of religion (and I mean such language as I have quoted, not pulpit clichés) can speak of a nonempirical reality and convey knowledge, and how it can instruct those who use it in good faith. Reverence gives standing to creatures, and to our perception of them, just as the law gives standing to a citizen. Certain things appear only in certain lights. "The gods' presence in the world," Herakleitos° said, "goes unnoticed by men who do not believe in the gods." To define knowledge as merely empirical is to limit one's ability to know; it enfeebles one's ability to feel and think.

We have come face to face with a paradox that we had better notice. People of faith have always believed in the unity of truth in God, whose works are endlessly and countlessly various. There is a world of difference between this humanly unknowable unity of truth and a theoretical unity of knowledge, which supposes that mere humans can know, in some definitive or final way, the truth. And the results are wonderfully different: Acceptance of the mystery of unitary truth in God leads to glorification of the multiplicity of His works, whereas the goal of a cognitive unity produced by science leads to abstraction and reduction, the opposite of which is not synthesis. The principle that is opposite to reduction—and, when necessary, its sufficient answer—is God's love for all things, for *each* thing for its own sake and not for its category.

There is no reason, as I hope and believe, that science and religion might not live together in amity and peace, so long as they both acknowledge their real differences and each remains within its own competence. Religion, that is, should not attempt to dispute what science has actually proved; and science should not claim to know what it does not know; it should not confuse theory and knowledge; and it should disavow any claim on what is empirically unknowable.

One cannot, in honesty, propose to reconcile Heaven and Earth by denying the existence of Heaven. The danger of this sort of reconciliation, as twentieth-century politics has shown, is that whatever proposes to invalidate or abolish religion is in fact attempting to put itself in religion's place. Science-as-religion is clearly a potent threat to freedom. Beyond that, it endangers real science. Science can function as religion only by making two unscientific claims: that it will *eventually* know everything, and that it will *eventually* solve all human problems.

It is not easily dismissable that virtually from the beginning of the progress of [20] science-technology-and-industry that we call the Industrial Revolution, while some have been confidently predicting that science, going ahead as it has gone, would solve all problems and answer all questions, others have been in mourning. Among these mourners have been people of the highest intelligence and education, who were speaking, not from nostalgia or reaction or superstitious dread, but from knowledge, hard thought, and the promptings of culture.

What were they afraid of? What did they mourn? Without exception, I think, what they feared was the violation of life by an oversimplifying, feelingless utilitarianism; they feared the destruction of creatures, places, communities,

---

[16]**Herakleitos** pre-Socratic Greek philosopher who flourished around 500 BCE

cultures, and human souls; they feared the loss of the old prescriptive definition of humankind, according to which we are neither gods nor beasts, though partaking of the nature of both. What they mourned was the progressive death of the earth.

Wes Jackson° of the Land Institute said once, thinking of the nuclear power and genetic engineering industries, "We ought to stay out of the nuclei." I remember that because I felt that he was voicing, not scientific intelligence, but a wise instinct: an intuition, common enough among human beings, that some things are and ought to be forbidden to us, off-limits, foreign, *properly* strange. I remember it furthermore because my own instinctive wish was to "stay out of the nuclei," and, as I well knew, this wish amounted exactly to nothing. One can hardly find a better example of modern science as a public predicament. For modern scientists work with everybody's proxy, whether or not that proxy has been given. A good many people, presumably, would have chosen to "stay out of the nuclei," but that was a choice they did not have. When a few scientists decided to go in, they decided for everybody. This "freedom of scientific inquiry" was immediately transformed into the freedom of corporate and/or governmental exploitation. And so the freedom of the originators and exploiters has become, in effect, the abduction and imprisonment of all the rest of us. Adam was the first, but not the last, to choose for the whole human race.

The disciplines are different from one another, each distinct in itself, and rightly so. Science and art are neither fundamental nor immutable. They are not life or the world. They are tools. The arts and the sciences are our kit of cultural tools. Science cannot replace art or religion for the same reason that you cannot loosen a nut with a saw or cut a board in two with a wrench. The first question about the disciplines is not how they originated but how and for what they are to be used.

The only reason, really, that we need this kit of tools is to build and maintain our dwelling here on earth. (Those who wish to live or do business in other worlds should be free to depart, but not to return.) Our dwelling here is the proper work of culture. If the tools can be used collaboratively, then maybe we can find what are the appropriate standards for our work and can then build a good and lasting dwelling—which actually would be a diversity of dwellings suited to the diversity of homelands. If the tools cannot be so used, then they will be used to destroy such dwellings as we have accomplished so far, and our homelands as well.

To begin to think of the possibility of collaboration among the disciplines, we must realize that the "two cultures" exist as such because both of them belong to the one culture of division and dislocation, opposition and competition, which is to say the culture of colonialism and industrialism. This culture has steadily increased the dependence of individuals, regions, and nations upon larger and larger collective economies. At the same time it has thrown individuals, regions, and nations into a competitiveness with one another that is limitlessly destructive

[22]**Wes Jackson** founded the Land Institute to promote sustainable agriculture

and demeaning. This state of universal competition understands the world as an anti-pattern in which each thing is opposed to every other thing, and it destroys the self-sufficiency of all places—households, farms, communities, regions, nations—even as it destroys the self-sufficiency of the world.

The collective economy is run for the benefit of a decreasing number of increasingly wealthy corporations. These corporations understand their "global economy" as a producer of money, not of goods. The goods of the world such as topsoil or forests must decline so that the money may increase. To facilitate this process, the corporations patronize the disciplines, chiefly the sciences, but some of the money, as "philanthropy," trickles down upon the arts. The brokers of this patronage are the universities, which are the organizers of the disciplines in our times. Since the universities are always a-building and always in need of money, they accept the economy's fundamental principles of the opposition of money to goods. Having thus accepted as real the world as an anti-pattern of competing opposites, it is merely inevitable that they should organize learning, not as a conversation of collaborating disciplines, but as an anti-system of opposed and competing divisions. They have departmented our one great responsibility to live ably and generously into a nest of irresponsibilities.

Wallace Stegner° knew, both from his personal experience and from his long study of his region, that the two cultures of the American West are not those of the sciences and the arts, but rather those of the two human kinds that he called "boomers" and "stickers," the boomers being "those who pillage and run," and the stickers "those who settle, and love the life they have made and the place they have made it in." This applies to our country as a whole, and maybe to all of Western civilization in modern times. Unquestionably the dominant theme of modern history has been that of the boomer. It is no surprise that the predominant arts and sciences of the modern era have been boomer arts and boomer sciences.

The collaboration of boomer science with the boomer mentality of the industrial corporations has imposed upon us a state of virtually total economy in which it is the destiny of every creature (humans not excepted) to have a price and to be sold. In a total economy, all materials, creatures, and ideas become commodities, interchangeable and disposable. Only such an economy could seek to impose upon the world's abounding geographic and creaturely diversity the tyranny of technological and genetic monoculture. Only in such an economy could "life forms" be patented, or the renewability of nature and culture be destroyed. Monsanto's aptly named "terminator gene"—which, implanted in seed sold by Monsanto, would cause the next generation of seed to be sterile—is as grave an indicator of totalitarian purpose as a concentration camp.

Suppose, then, that we should change the standards, as in fact some scientists and some artists already are attempting to do. Suppose that the ultimate standard of our work were to be, not professionalism and profitability, but the health and

---

²⁶**Wallace Stegner** A writer of both fiction and nonfiction, Stegner founded the creative writing program of Stanford University where he taught, among other well-known writers, Wendell Berry.

durability of human and natural communities. Suppose we learned to ask of any proposed innovation the question so far only the Amish have been wise enough to ask: What will this do to our community? Suppose we attempted the authentic multiculturalism of adapting our ways of life to the nature of the places where we live. Suppose, in short, that we should take seriously the proposition that our arts and sciences have the power to help us adapt and survive. What then?

Well, we certainly would have a healthier, prettier, more diverse and interesting world, a world less toxic and explosive, than we have now.

30   And how might this come about? Again, I have to say that I don't know. I don't like or trust large, official programs of improvement, and I don't want to appear to be inviting any such thing. But perhaps there is no harm in making suggestions, if I acknowledge that the suggestions are only mine, and if I make sure that my suggestions apply primarily to the thinking, work, and conduct of individuals. Here is my list:

1. Rather than the present economic hierarchy of the professions, which results in the denigration and undercompensation of essential jobs of work, particularly in the economies of land use, we should think and work toward an appropriate subordination of all the disciplines to the health of creatures, places, and communities. A science, for example, that served settlement rather than the exploitation of "frontiers" would be subordinate to reverence, fidelity, neighborliness, and stewardship, to affection and delight. It would aim to keep our creatureliness intact.

2. We should banish from our speech and writing any use of the word "machine" as an explanation or definition of anything that is not a machine. Our understanding of creatures and our use of them are not improved by calling them machines.

3. We should abandon the idea that this world and our human life in it can be brought by science to some sort of mechanical perfection or predictability. We are creatures whose intelligence and knowledge are not invariably equal to our circumstances. The radii of knowledge have only pushed back—and enlarged—the circumference of mystery. We live in a world famous for its ability both to surprise us and to deceive us. We are prone to err, ignorantly or foolishly or intentionally or maliciously. One of the oddest things about us is the interdependency of our virtues and our faults. Our moral code depends on our shortcomings as much as our knowledge. It is only where we confess our ignorance that we can see our need for "the law and the prophets." It is only because we err and are ignorant that we make promises, which we keep, not because we are smart, but because we are faithful.

4. We should give up the frontier and its boomer "ethics" of greed, cunning, and violence, and so near too late, accept settlement as our goal. Wes Jackson says that our schools now have only one major, upward mobility, and that we need to offer a major in homecoming. I agree, and would only add that a part of the sense of "homecoming" must be home*making,* for we now must begin sometimes with remnants, sometimes with ruins.

5. We need to require from our teachers, researchers, and leaders—and   35
attempt for ourselves—a responsible accounting of technological progress.
What have we gained by computers, for example, *after* we have subtracted the
ecological costs of making them, using them, and throwing them away, the
value of lost time and work when "the computers are down," and the enormous economic cost of the Y2K correction?

6. We ought conscientiously to reduce our tolerance for ugliness. Why, if
we are in fact "progressing," should so much expense and effort have resulted
in so much ugliness? We ought to begin to ask ourselves what are the limits—of scale, speed, and probably expense as well—beyond which human
work is bound to be ugly.

7. We should recognize the insufficiency, to our life here among living
creatures, of the abstract categories of reductionist thought. Resist classification! Without some use of abstraction, thought is incoherent or unintelligible,
perhaps unthinkable. But abstraction alone is merely dead. And here we
return again to the crucial issue of language.

In our public dialogue (such as it is) we are now using many valuable words
that are losing their power of reference, and have as a consequence become
abstract, merely gestures. I have in mind words such as "patriotism," "freedom,"
"equality," and "rights," or "nature," "human," "wild," and "sustainable." We
could make a longish list of words such as these, which we often use without
thought or feeling, just to show which side we suppose we want to be on. This
situation calls for language that is not sloganish and rhetorical but rather is
capable of reference, specification, precision, and refinement—a language never
far from experience and example. In the great poets, the heavenly and the
earthly are not abstract, but are *present*; the language of those poets is whole and
precise. The middling, politically correct language of the professions is incapable
either of reverence or familiarity; it is headless and footless, loveless, a language
of nowhere.

I believe that this need for a whole, vital, particularizing language applies just
as strongly to the sciences as to the arts and humanities. For the human necessity
is not just to know, but also to cherish and protect the things that are known,
and to know the things that can be known only by cherishing. If we are to protect the world's multitude of places and creatures, then we must know them, not
just conceptually but imaginatively as well. They must be pictured in the mind
and in memory; they must be known with affection, "by heart," so that in seeing
or remembering them the heart may be said to "sing," to make a music peculiar
to its recognition of each particular place or creature that it knows well.

One of the most significant costs of the economic destruction of farm popula-   40
tions is the loss of local memory, local history, and local names. Field names, for
instance, even such colorless names as "the front field" and "the back field," are
vital signs of a culture. If the arts and the sciences ever waken from their rapture
of academic specialization, they will make themselves at home in places they
have helped to spoil, and set about reconstructing histories and remembering
names.

8. We should value familiarity above innovation. Boomer scientists and artists want to discover (so to speak) a place where they have not been. Sticker scientists and artists want to know where they are.

There is nothing intrinsically wrong with an interest in discovery and innovation. It only becomes wrong when it is thought to be the norm of culture and of intellectual life. As such it is in the first place misleading. As I have already suggested, the effort of familiarity is always leading to discovery and the new, just as do the quests of explorers and "original researchers." The difference is that innovation for its own sake, and especially now when it so directly serves the market, is disruptive of human settlement, whereas the revelations of familiarity elaborate the local cultural pattern and tend toward settlement, which they also prevent from becoming static. There is no reason that familiarity cannot be a goal just as worthy, demanding, and exciting as innovation—or, as I would argue, much more so. It would certainly give worthwhile employment to more people. And in fact its boundaries are much larger. Innovation is limited always by human ingenuity and human means; familiarity is limited only by the limits of life. The real infinitude of experience is in familiarity.

My own experience has shown me that it is possible to live in and attentively study the same small place decade after decade, and find that it ceaselessly evades and exceeds comprehension. There is nothing that it can be reduced to because "it" is always, and not predictably, changing. It is never the same two days running, and the better one pays attention the more aware one becomes of these differences. Living and working in the place day by day, one is continuously revising one's knowledge of it, continuously being surprised by it and in error about it. And even if the place stayed the same, one would be getting older and growing in memory and experience, and would need for that reason alone to work from revision to revision. One knows one's place, that is to say, only within limits, and the limits are in one's mind, not in the place. This is a description of life in time in the world.

[2000]

1. How is Berry using the word *miracle* in this essay? Compare his use of it to Sylvia Plath's in her poem "Black Rook in Rainy Weather." Compare his attitude to that of some of the other writers in this section.
2. How does Berry's sense of the miraculousness of life relate to his distinction between the individual, on the one hand, and egalitarianism and individualism, on the other? How does that distinction shape his environmentalism?
3. What is your response to Berry's distinctions among the arts, the sciences, and religion? Why does Berry think religion is necessary? Do you agree?
4. What is Berry's proposal in the essay?
5. With what literary works in the section do Berry's ideas resonate?
6. Study a piece of landscape (a view from a window, a place where you wait for a bus, etc.) for a week and describe it in detail. Comment on what you see and whether or not you think the place is "ugly," how it makes you feel, what part it plays in nature, in the life of the community, whether or not it seems functional and appropriate to you. Take a guess as to how you think

it might have looked fifty years ago and how the differences would change your responses to the place.

7. Describe a place you love from memory and think of it in terms of Berry's essay. What is your reaction to his essay, and to his manifestos, in terms of that place? What are you prepared to assume about the place as a result of reading the essay? What do you think you would be prepared to do in order to preserve it?

8. Make a list of proposals for a "new school," in which children would be educated in order to grow up in the world Berry describes in paragraph 28. Describe the physical plant, the goals, and the program of this school in as much detail as you need to show that such a school could foster a generation of adults who would be likely to live by the eight principles Berry outlines at the end of the essay. Relate each detail to each of his proposals.

HOWARD FRUMKIN

HOWARD FRUMKIN *(1955–), M.D., Dr.PH., FACP, FACOEM, who has degrees from Brown University, Harvard University, and the University of Pennsylvania, is director of the Pediatric Environmental Health Specialty Unit at the Rollins School of Public Health in Atlanta, Georgia. His interests range from occupational and environmental epidemiology to environmental policy and the effects of global warming. He is working on a number of projects having to do with the effects of pollution on both children and migrant workers.*

Beyond Toxicity:
Human Health and the Natural Environment*

Abstract: Research and teaching in environmental health have centered on the hazardous effects of various environmental exposures, such as toxic chemicals, radiation, and biological and physical agents. However, some kinds of environmental exposures may have positive health effects. According to E.O. Wilson's "biophilia" hypothesis, humans are innately attracted to other living organisms. Later authors have expanded this concept to suggest that humans have an innate bond with nature more generally. This implies that certain kinds of contact with the natural world may benefit health. Evidence supporting this hypothesis is presented from four aspects of the natural world: animals, plants, landscapes, and wilderness. Finally, the implications of this hypothesis for a broader agenda for environmental health, encompassing not only toxic outcomes but also salutary ones, are discussed. This agenda implies research on a range of potentially healthful environmental exposures, collaboration among professionals in a range of disciplines from public health to landscape architecture to city planning, and interventions based on research outcomes.

*Howard Frumkin, "Beyond Toxicity: Human Health and the Natural Environment," American Journal of Preventive Medicine 20.3 (2001): 234–40.

Medical Subject Headings (MeSH): animals, ecology, environmental health, nature, plants, trees (Am J Prev Med 2001;20(3):234–240) © 2001 American Journal of Preventive Medicine

Advances in the field of environmental health have taught us much about human health hazards. We know that air pollution can cause respiratory disease,[1] that heavy metals can cause neurotoxicity,[2] and that global climate change is likely to fuel some infectious diseases.[3] Clearly, environmental exposures can threaten health.

But the natural environment, broadly conceived, can also enhance health. A well-recognized example is the many pharmaceuticals that derive from plants and animals—a compelling argument for preserving biodiversity.[4–6] But another example is even more intuitive, both to clinicians and to laypeople. Contact with the natural world may be directly beneficial to health. If so, then the field of environmental health needs to extend beyond toxicity to consider possible health benefits. This article reviews the evidence for health benefits of the natural environment, and suggests some of the research and interventions that such a broader paradigm of environmental health might imply.

Links Between Health and Environment

Fifty years ago the World Health Organization° defined health as "a state of complete physical, mental, and social well-being and not merely the absence of disease or infirmity." Does contact with the natural environment contribute to our "complete physical, mental, and social well-being"?

Many people appreciate a walk in the park, or the sound of a bird's song, or the sight of ocean waves lapping at the seashore. Even if these were only aesthetic preferences, they would be of interest, since they are so common as to seem nearly universal. As one environmental psychologist has written,[7] "Nature matters to people. Big trees and small trees, glistening water, chirping birds, budding bushes, colorful flowers—these are important ingredients in a good life." But perhaps these are more than aesthetic preferences. Perhaps we as a species find tranquility in certain natural environments—a soothing, restorative, and even a healing sense. If so, contact with nature might be an important component of well-being.

5   From an evolutionary perspective, a deep-seated connection with the natural world would be no surprise. Primate evolution began at least 65 million years ago, and the first hominids appeared as much as 5 million years ago. *Homo habilis* probably appeared 2 or 3 million years ago, and our immediate predecessor, *Homo erectus*, appeared about 1.5 million years ago. Human history as we now know it began during the neolithic period just 10,000 or 15,000 years ago, when the last great ice age ended, and global climate and ecology came to resemble those we know. Our *Homo sapiens* ancestors began to form settlements, cultivate crops, domesticate animals, dig mines, and even make art. If the last 2 million years of our species' history were scaled to a single human lifetime of

[3]**World Health Organization** an agency of the United Nations specializing in health

70 years, then the first humans would not have begun settling into villages until 8 months after the 69th birthday. Some people—aboriginal groups in Australia, South America, the Pacific Islands, and elsewhere—would remain hunter-gatherers until a day or two before the 70th birthday. We have broken with long-established patterns of living rather late in our life as a species.

For the great majority of human existence, human biology has been embedded in the natural environment. Those who could smell the water, find the plants, follow the animals, and recognize the safe havens, must have enjoyed survival advantages. According to biologist E.O. Wilson,[8] "It would . . . be quite extraordinary to find that all learning rules related to that world have been erased in a few thousand years, even in the tiny minority of peoples who have existed for more than one or two generations in wholly urban environments." Wilson[9] hypothesized the existence of biophilia, "the innately emotional affiliation of human beings to other living organisms." Building on this theory, others have postulated an affinity for nature that goes beyond living things, to include streams, ocean waves, and wind.[10]

The human relationship with nature, and the idea that this might be a component of good health, have a long history in philosophy, art, and popular culture, from ancient Greece to the New England transcendentalists (e.g., Nash,[11] McLuhan,[12] Mazel,[13] and Murphy[14]). A century ago, the early American conservationist John Muir[15] observed, "Thousands of tired, nerve-shaken, over-civilized people are beginning to find out that going to the mountains is going home; that wilderness is a necessity; and that mountain parks and reservations are useful not only as fountains of timber and irrigating rivers, but as fountains of life." Is there any evidence to support this view, and to suggest that contact with nature can function to enhance health? Evidence is available from four aspects of the natural world—animals, plants, landscapes, and wilderness experience.

Domains of Nature Contact

Animals

Animals have always played a prominent part in human life.[16] Today, more people go to zoos each year than to all professional sporting events.[8] A total of 56% of U.S. households own pets.[17] Animals comprise more than 90% of the characters used in language acquisition and counting in children's preschool books.[18] Numerous studies establish that household animals are considered family members; we talk to them as if they were human, we carry their photographs, we share our bedrooms with them.[19] An estimated 50% of adults and 70% of adolescents confide in their animals.[17]

A wide body of evidence links animals with human health. In a study in a Melbourne cardiovascular disease risk clinic,[20] nearly 6000 patients were divided into those who owned pets and those who did not. Among men, the pet owners had statistically significantly lower systolic blood pressure, cholesterol, and triglycerides than the non–pet owners. Among women, a similar trend was observed. These findings did not appear to be due to differences in exercise levels (say, from dog walking), diet, social class, or other confounders. In a 1995 study,[21] 369 survivors of myocardial infarction were followed for 1 year. Of these, 112 owned pets and 257 did not. The dog owners had a 1-year survival six times higher than that of the non–dog owners, and this benefit was not due to physiological differences. (Cat owners showed no such advantage.)

10   Investigators in Cambridge, England[22] followed 71 adults who had just acquired pets, and compared them with 26 petless controls, over a 10-month period. Within a month of acquiring the pet, the pet owners showed a statistically significant decrease in minor health problems. In the dog owners (but not the cat owners) this improvement was sustained for the entire 10 months of observation. In another study, this one in the United States,[23] 938 Medicare enrollees were divided into pet owners and non–pet owners. The pet owners, especially the dog owners, had fewer physician visits than non–pet owners. Moreover, stressful life events were associated with more doctor visits among the non–pet owners, but not among the pet owners, suggesting that owning a pet helped mediate stress.

The role of animals in helping people handle stress has been tested specifically. In one study,[24] patients about to undergo oral surgery were randomly assigned to one of five conditions: a half-hour looking at an aquarium, with or without hypnosis; a half-hour looking at a picture of a waterfall, with or without hypnosis; and a half-hour of sitting quietly. The patients' comfort and relaxation during surgery were graded independently by the oral surgeon, the investigator, and the patients themselves. The most relaxed patients were those who looked at the aquarium, irrespective of whether they had been hypnotized. The patients who looked at the waterfall picture were almost as relaxed, but only if they had been hypnotized first. Otherwise, they had low relaxation scores, as low as those of the control patients. In another study,[25] 45 women were exposed to a stressful stimulus alone, in the presence of a human friend, and in the presence of their dog. Their autonomic nervous system responses to stress, such as heart rate, were measured. The stress response was marked when subjects were alone, and even more marked when a friend was present. But having a dog present significantly reduced the stress response. Animal facilitated therapy in the treatment of psychiatric conditions is now well established.[26]

Evidence such as this supports the conclusion of animal researchers Alan Beck and N. Marshall Meyers[17]: "Preserving the bond between people and their animals, like encouraging good nutrition and exercise, appears to be in the best interests of those concerned with public health."

Plants

People feel good around plants. In the 1989 National Gardening Survey of more than 2000 randomly selected households,[27] 50.1% of respondents agreed with the statement, "The flowers and plants at theme parks, historic sites, golf courses, and restaurants are important to my enjoyment of visiting there," and 40.0% agreed with the statement, "Being around plants makes me feel calmer and more relaxed." Among residents of retirement communities,[28] 99% indicate that "living within pleasant landscaped grounds" is either essential or important, and 95% indicate that windows facing green, landscaped grounds are either essential or important. Office employees report that plants make them feel calmer and more relaxed, and that an office with plants is a more desirable place to work.[29] In urban settings, gardens and gardening have been linked to social benefits ranging from improved property values to greater conviviality (e.g., Patel[30]). Psychologist Michael Perlman[31] has written of the psychological power of trees, as evidenced by mythology, dreams, and self-reported emotional responses.

Indeed, the concept that plants have a role in mental health is well established. Horticultural therapy evolved as a form of mental health treatment, based on the therapeutic effects of gardening.[32] It is also used today in community-based programs, geriatrics programs, prisons, developmental disabilities programs, and special education.[33] In prisons, although rigorous evidence is not available, observers have noted that gardening has a "strangely soothing effect," making "pacifists of potential battlers,"[34] and seeming to decrease the numbers of assaults among prisoners.[35]

Could contact with plants also contribute to healing from physical ailments?[36] 15 There is a memorable passage in Oliver Sacks' 1984 account[37] of his recovery from a serious leg injury. After more than 2 weeks in a small hospital room with no outside view, and a third week on a dreary surgical ward, he was finally taken out to the hospital garden:

> This was a great joy—to be out in the air—for I had not been outside in almost a month. A pure and intense joy, a blessing, to feel the sun on my face and the wind in my hair, to hear birds, to see, touch, and fondle the living plants. Some essential connection and communion with nature was re-established after the horrible isolation and alienation I had known. Some part of me came alive, when I was taken to the garden, which had been starved, and died, perhaps without my knowing it.

Sacks[37] credited his garden contact with an important role in his recovery, and mused that perhaps more hospitals should have gardens, or even be set in the countryside or near woods.

Swee-Lian Yi[38] was aged 29 when she suffered a severe stroke, and was hospitalized in New York's Rusk Institute for rehabilitation. Like Sacks, she found her first visit to the hospital greenhouse a turning point. "It was when I walked through that building, perfectly quiet, filled with green and growing plants and the sweet smell of healthy soil that my anxiety began to ebb away. In its place came a tranquility I had not experienced since the day of my stroke."[38] In fact, hospitals have traditionally had gardens as an adjunct to recuperation and healing, and despite the depredations of managed care, notable examples survive in many parts of the country.[39] Perhaps this time-honored practice reflects an ancient recognition that proximity to plants, like proximity to animals, may in some circumstances enhance health.

Landscapes

Natural landscapes may have a similar effect. Returning to an evolutionary perspective, human history probably began on the African savanna, a region of open grasslands punctuated by scattered copses of trees and denser woods near rivers and lakes. If this sounds like the choicest real estate in most cities and towns, that may not be a coincidence. As E.O. Wilson[9] points out, "certain key features of the ancient physical habitat match the choices made by modern human beings when they have a say in the matter"—a pattern that repeats in parks, cemeteries, golf courses, and lawns. "It seems that whenever people are given a free choice, they move to open tree-studded land on prominences overlooking water."

Could evolution have selected for certain landscape preferences? Perhaps. According to Wilson,[10] "A crucial step in the lives of most organisms, including humans, is selection of a habitat. If a creature gets into the right place, everything else is likely to be easier. Habitat selection depends on the recognition of objects, sounds, and odors to which the organism responds as if it understood their significance for future behavior and success." For example, many birds use patterns of tree density and vertical arrangement of branches as primary settling cues; presumably these cues are correlated with such crucial information as food availability, concealment from predators, and other benefits. For early humans, a place with an open view would have offered better opportunities to identify food and shelter and to avoid predators, than a spatially restricted setting. But not too open a view: Clumps of trees would offer hiding places in a pinch, and, like streams and lakes, might also signal the presence of prey for the hunter.[40] Going further, perhaps the ability to identify relaxing, restorative settings, and the capacity to recover from fatigue and stress, could also have been adaptive.[40,41] If you can run away from a saber-toothed tiger, your survival is enhanced. But if, having run away, you can get to a peaceful place, relax, and gather your strength, that may further enhance your survival. Perhaps individuals who chose such settings gained a survival advantage.[40]

There is considerable evidence that people's aesthetic preferences conform to this scenario. When offered a variety of landscapes, people react most positively to savanna-like settings, with moderate to high depth or openness, relatively smooth or uniform-length grassy vegetation or ground surfaces, scattered trees or small groupings of trees, and water.[42,43] Notably, these findings emerge cross-culturally, in studies of North Americans, Europeans, Asians, and Africans (e.g., Hull and Revell,[44] Purcell et al.,[45] and Korpela and Hartig[46]).

20   This effect may extend beyond aesthetics, to restoration or stress recovery. Research on recreational activities has shown that savanna-like settings are associated with self-reported feelings of "peacefulness," "tranquility," or "relaxation."[40] Viewing such settings leads to decreased fear and anger, and enhanced positive affect on the Zuckerman Inventory of Personal Reactions.[47] Moreover, viewing nature scenes is associated with enhanced mental alertness, attention, and cognitive performance, as measured by tasks such as proofreading and by formal psychological testing.[48–50]

The same results emerge from studies that directly consider conventional health endpoints. In 1981, Ernest Moore, a University of Michigan architect, took advantage of a natural experiment at the State Prison of Southern Michigan, a massive depression-era structure.[51] Half the prisoners occupied cells along the outside wall, with a window view of rolling farmland and trees, while the other half occupied cells that faced the prison courtyard. Assignment to one or the other kind of cell was random. The prisoners in the inside cells had a 24% higher frequency of sick-call visits, compared to those in exterior cells. Moore could not identify any design feature to explain this difference, and concluded that the outside view "may provide some stress reduction." Like prisoners, employees with views of nature at work report fewer headaches (as well as less job pressure and greater job satisfaction) than those without such a view.[52]

Similar observations have come from health care settings. A short 1984 paper in *Science*[53] bore the provocative title, "View through a window may influence recovery from surgery." Like the Michigan prison study, this study also took advantage of an inadvertent architectural experiment. On the surgical floors of a 200-bed suburban Pennsylvania hospital, some rooms faced a stand of deciduous trees, while others faced a brown brick wall. Postoperative patients were assigned essentially randomly to one or the other kind of room. The records of all cholecystectomy patients over a 10-year interval, restricted to the summer months when the trees were in foliage, were reviewed. Endpoints were the length of hospitalization, the need for pain and anxiety medications, the occurrence of minor medical complications, and nurses' notes. Patients with tree views had statistically significantly shorter hospitalizations (7.96 days compared to 8.70 days), less need for pain medications, and fewer negative comments in the nurses' notes, compared to patients with brick-wall views.

Other evidence is available from therapeutic settings. In a study of dental patients,[54] researchers placed a large mural of an open natural scene on the wall of a dental waiting room during some days, and removed it on others. On the days when the mural was visible, dental patients had lower blood pressure and less self-reported anxiety than on the days when it was taken down. In a study of psychiatric in-patients,[40] patients were exposed to two kinds of wall art: nature scenes such as landscapes, or abstract or symbolic art. Interviews suggested more positive responses to the nature scenes. Moreover, in 15 years of records on patient attacks on the wall art, every attack was on abstract art, none on a nature scene. (No information was provided on how many of the psychiatric patients were artists or art critics.) Viewing landscapes and related nature scenes, whether genuine or in pictures, seems to have a salutary effect.

Wilderness Experience

Wilderness experiences—entering the landscape rather than viewing it—may also be therapeutic. David Cumes[55,56] has described "wilderness rapture," including self-awareness; feelings of awe, wonder, and humility; a sense of comfort in and connection to nature; increased appreciation of others; and a feeling of renewal and vigor. These outcomes are often cited in favorable accounts of so-called wilderness therapy for psychiatric patients[57–60]; emotionally disturbed children and adolescents[61–63]; bereaved people[64,65]; rape and incest survivors[66]; and patients with cancer,[67] end-stage renal disease,[68] post-traumatic distress syndrome (PTSD),[69] addiction disorders,[70,71] and other ailments.[72]

Most documented examples relate to mental health endpoints. A group of emotionally disturbed boys aged 5.5 to 11.5 years attending an outdoor day camp was compared to a group of similar boys not attending the camp.[73] The campers' self-ratings and teachers' ratings of their emotional adjustment were significantly better than those of the controls, although neither parents' ratings nor scores on formal psychological testing showed an improvement. A group of adolescents being treated for depression, substance abuse, or adjustment reactions improved on measures of cooperation and trust following a wilderness experience, while controls did not.[58] Psychiatric in-patients showed improvements in coping ability and locus of control following a wilderness adventure program.[59] In-patients at the Oregon State Mental Hospital showed improved function and greater probability of discharge following wilderness adventure programs.[57] In a convenience sample of more than 700 people who had participated in 2- to 4-week wilderness excursions, 90% described "an increased sense of aliveness, well-being, and energy," and 90% reported that the experience had helped them break an addiction (defined broadly, from nicotine to chocolate).[74]

While this literature is more extensive than the literature on plants and animals,[75] several limitations make it difficult to interpret.[76,77] Much of the published research comes from proponents with a personal or commercial interest in wilderness experiences, such as companies that market adventures. Much of the research refers to structured trips or summer camp programs rather than to the more general phenomenon of contact with wilderness. To the extent that such research seems to show benefits, this may be due to the vacation quality of the experience, to the psychological value of setting and achieving difficult goals, and/or to the group bonding that occurs on some such trips, rather than (or in addition to) a direct effect of wilderness contact. Few studies have been randomized, and selection bias can rarely be excluded. Blinding of subjects has been impossible, and blinding of investigators has not been attempted.

Despite these limitations, many published accounts do suggest some benefit from wilderness experiences. Mental health has been more studied than somatic conditions, and short-term benefit has been demonstrated more than long-term benefit.

There is evidence, then, that contact with the natural world—with animals, plants, landscapes, and wilderness—may offer health benefits. Perhaps this reflects ancient learning habits, preferences, and tastes, which may be echoes of our origins as creatures of the wild. Satisfying these preferences—taking seriously our affiliation with the natural world—may be an effective way to enhance health, not to mention cheaper and freer of side effects than medications. If so, then medicine and the other health professions will need to articulate a broad vision of environmental health, one that stretches from urban planning to landscape architecture, from interior design to forestry, from botany to veterinary medicine.

The Greening of Environmental Health

A paradigm of environmental health that includes health as well as illness, has implications in at least three arenas: research, collaboration, and intervention.

Research

Clinical and epidemiologic research in environmental health addresses many variants of the same question: Is there an association between exposure and outcome? We need a research agenda directed not only at exposures we suspect to be unhealthy, but also at those we suspect to be healthy, and at outcomes that reflect not only impaired health, but also enhanced health. If people have regular contact with flowers or trees, do they report greater well-being, better sleep, fewer headaches, reduced joint pain? Do inner city children who attend a rural summer camp have better health during the next semester of school than their friends who spent the summer in the city? Do patients with cancer or AIDS survive longer, or have fewer infections, or less pain, or higher T-cell counts, if they have pets? Do gardens in hospitals speed postoperative recovery? Can psychotherapy that utilizes contact with nature—known as ecopsychology[78]—have an empirical basis? If any of these therapeutic approaches shows promise, which patients will benefit and what kinds of contact with nature have the greatest efficacy and cost effectiveness?

Research questions like these pose challenges of defining and operationalizing unfamiliar variables. Landscape architects, horticulturists, and environmental psychologists work with the exposure variables, but physicians and clinical investigators do not. Similarly, the outcome variables that reflect health instead of disease are less familiar, and need to be developed and validated. These challenges offer broad opportunities for methods development and hypothesis testing.

Collaboration

Environmental health specialists, from researchers to clinicians, have long recognized the need to collaborate with other professionals. We work with mechanical engineers to build exposure chambers, with chemists to measure exposures, and with software engineers to apply geographic information systems to health data. If we turn our attention to aspects of the environment that may enhance health, we need to open collaborations with a broad range of professionals, such as landscape architects to help identify the salient features of outdoor "exposures," interior designers to do the same in micro-environments, veterinarians and ethologists to help us understand more about human relationships with animals, and urban and regional planners to help link environmental health principles with large-scale environmental design.

Intervention

Finally, as we learn more about the health benefits of particular environments, we need to act on these findings. On the clinical level, this may have implications for patient care. Perhaps we will advise patients to take a few days in the country, to spend time gardening, or to adopt a pet, if clinical evidence offers support for such measures. Perhaps we will build hospitals in scenic locations, or plant gardens in rehabilitation centers. Perhaps the employers and managed care organizations that pay for health care will come to fund such interventions, especially if they prove to rival pharmaceuticals in cost and efficacy.

On the public health level, environmental health has a long history of providing data, and advocating action based on these data to achieve control of environmental hazards, such as more protective air pollution regulations, lower automobile emissions, safer pesticide practices, and cleaner rivers and streams. In the same way, we need to act on emerging evidence of environmental health benefits. Environmental health could be a factor in zoning decisions, transportation planning, and regional development strategies. Environmental health could appear in the curricula of schools of architecture and civil engineering. We take for granted that health experts play a prominent role in the Food and Drug Administration and the Environmental Protection Agency, but how about the National Park Service or the local zoo? As we learn more about the health benefits of contact with the natural world, we need to apply this knowledge in ways that directly enhance the health of the public.

This article was adapted from an Emory University Great Teachers Lecture delivered on 15 October 1998, and from a talk given at the Institute of Medicine Roundtable on Environmental Health Sciences, Research, and Medicine, on 20 June 2000. Partial support came from NIEHS Environmental/Occupational Medicine Academic Award ES00257. Thanks to Beryl Cowan, Bill Harlan, Howard Hu, Dick Jackson, and Melissa Walker for valuable comments.

References

1. American Thoracic Society, Committee of the Environmental and Occupational Health Assembly. Health effects of air pollution. Am J Resp Critical Care Med 1996;153:3–50, 477–98.
2. Feldman RG. Occupational and environmental neurotoxicology. Philadelphia: Lippincott-Raven, 1999.
3. McMichael AJ, Haines A, Slooff R, Kovats S, eds. Climate change and human health. Geneva: World Health Organization, 1996.
4. Wilson EO. The diversity of life. Cambridge: Harvard University Press, 1992.
5. Grifo F, Rosenthal J. Biodiversity and human health. Washington, DC: Island Press, 1996.
6. Cassis G. Biodiversity loss: a human health issue. Med J Australia 1998;169:568–9.
7. Kaplan R. The role of nature in the urban context. In: Altham I, Wohlwill J, eds. Behavior and the natural environment. New York: Plenum, 1983: 127–61.
8. Wilson EO. Biophilia and the conservation ethic. In: Kellert SR, Wilson EO, eds. The biophilia hypothesis. Washington, DC: Island Press, 1993:31–41.
9. Wilson EO. Biophilia: the human bond with other species. Cambridge: Harvard University Press, 1984.
10. Heerwagen JH, Orians GH. Humans, habitats, and aesthetics. In: Kellert SR, Wilson EO, eds. The biophilia hypothesis. Washington, DC: Island Press, 1993:138–72.

11. Nash R. Wilderness and the American mind. 3rd edition. New Haven, CT: Yale University Press, 1982.
12. McLuhan TC. The way of the earth: encounters with nature in ancient and contemporary thought. New York: Simon & Schuster, 1994.
13. Mazel D. American literary environmentalism. Athens, GA: University of Georgia Press, 2000.
14. Murphy PD, Gifford T, Yamazato K. Literature of nature: an international sourcebook. Chicago: Fitzroy Dearborn Publishers, 1998.
15. Fox S. John Muir and his legacy. Boston: Little, Brown, 1981.
16. Clutton-Brock J. Domesticated animals from early times. Austin, TX: University of Texas Press, 1981.
17. Beck AM, Meyers NM. Health enhancement and companion animal ownership. Ann Rev Public Health 1996;17:247–57.
18. Kellert SR. The biological basis for human values of nature. In: Kellert SR, Wilson EO, eds. The biophilia hypothesis. Washington, DC: Island Press, 1993:42–72.
19. Beck A, Katcher A. Between pets and people: the importance of animal companionship. New York: Perigree Books, 1983.
20. Anderson W, Reid C, Jennings G. Pet ownership and risk factors for cardiovascular disease. Med J Australia 1992;157:298–301.
21. Friedmann E, Thomas SA. Pet ownership, social support, and one-year survival after acute myocardial infarction in the cardiac arrhythmia suppression trial (CAST). Am J Cardiol 1995;76:1213–17.
22. Serpell J. Beneficial effects of pet ownership on some aspects of human health and behaviour. J Royal Soc Med 1991;84:717–20.
23. Siegel J. Stressful life events and use of physician services among the elderly: the moderating role of pet ownership. J Personality Social Psychol 1990;58:1081–6.
24. Katcher A, Segal H, Beck A. Comparison of contemplation and hypnosis for the reduction of anxiety and discomfort during dental surgery. Am J Clinical Hypnosis 1984;27:14–21.
25. Allen DT. Effects of dogs on human health. J Am Veterinary Med Assoc 1997;210:1136–9.
26. Draper RJ, Gerber GJ, Layng EM. Defining the role of pet animals in psychotherapy. Psych J Univ Ottawa 1990;15(3):169–72.
27. Butterfield B, Relf D. National survey of attitudes toward plants and gardening. In: Relf D, ed. The role of horticulture in human well-being and social development: a national symposium, 19–21 April 1990, Arlington, Virginia. Portland, OR: Timber Press, 1992:211–2.
28. Browne A. The role of nature for the promotion of well-being in the elderly. In: Relf D, ed. The role of horticulture in human well-being and social development: a national symposium, 19–21 April 1990, Arlington, Virginia. Portland, OR: Timber Press, 1992:75–79.
29. Randall K, Shoemaker CA, Relf D, Geller ES. Effects of plantscapes in an office environment on worker satisfaction. In: Relf D, ed. The role of horticulture in human well-being and social development: a national

symposium, 19–21 April 1990, Arlington, Virginia. Portland, OR: Timber Press, 1992:106–9.

30. Patel IC. Socio-economic impact of community gardening in an urban setting. In: Relf D, ed. The role of horticulture in human well-being and social development: a national symposium, 19–21 April 1990, Arlington, Virginia. Portland, OR: Timber Press, 1992:84–7.

31. Perlman M. The power of trees: the reforesting of the soul. Dallas, TX: Spring Publications, 1994.

32. Lewis CA. Green nature/human nature: the meaning of plants in our lives. Urbana, IL: University of Illinois Press, 1996.

33. Mattson RH. Prescribing health benefits through horticultural activities. In: Relf D, ed. The role of horticulture in human well-being and social development: a national symposium, 19–21 April 1990, Arlington, Virginia. Portland, OR: Timber Press, 1992:161–8.

34. Neese R. Prisoner's escape. Flower Grower 1959:46:39–40.

35. Lewis CA. Effects of plants and gardening in creating interpersonal and community well-being. In: Relf D, ed. The role of horticulture in human well-being and social development: a national symposium, 19–21 April 1990, Arlington, Virginia. Portland, OR: Timber Press, 1992:55–65.

36. Lewis CA. Gardening as healing process. In: Francis M, Hester RT, eds. The meaning of gardens. Cambridge: MIT Press, 1990:244–51.

37. Sacks O. A leg to stand on. New York: HarperCollins, 1984.

38. Yi S-L. A life renewed. National Gardening 1985;8:19–21.

39. Gerlach-Spriggs N, Kaufman RE, Warner SB. Restorative gardens: the healing landscape. New Haven, CT: Yale University Press, 1998.

40. Ulrich RS. Biophilia, biophobia, and natural landscapes. In: Kellert SR, Wilson EO, eds. The biophilia hypothesis. Washington, DC: Island Press, 1993:73–137.

41. Kaplan R, Kaplan S. The experience of nature: a psychological perspective. Cambridge: Cambridge University Press, 1989.

42. Schroeder HW, Green TL. Public preferences for tree density in municipal parks. J Arboriculture 1985;11:272–7.

43. Colan NB. Outward bound: An annotated bibliography (1976–1985). Greenwich, CT. Outward Bound USA, 1986.

44. Hull RB, Revell GRB. Cross-cultural comparison on landscape scenic beauty evaluations: a case study in Bali. J Environmental Psychology 1989;9:177–91.

45. Purcell AT, Lamb RJ, Peron EM, Falchero S. Preference or preferences for landscape? J Environ Psychol 1994;14:195–209.

46. Korpela K, Hartig T. Restorative qualities of favorite places. J Environmental Psychol 1996;16:221–33.

47. Honeyman MK. Vegetation and stress: a comparison study of varying amounts of vegetation in countryside and urban scenes. In: Relf D, ed. The role of horticulture in human well-being and social development: a national symposium, 19–21 April 1990, Arlington, Virginia. Portland, OR: Timber Press, 1992:143–5.

48. Hartig T, Mang M, Evans G. Restorative effects of natural environmental experiences. Environment Behav 1991;23:3–26.
49. Cimprich B. Development of an intervention to restore attention win cancer patients. Cancer Nurs 1993;16:83–92.
50. Tennessen CM, Cimprich B. Views to nature: effects on attention. J Environ Psychol 1995;15:77–85.
51. Moore EO. A prison environment's effect on health care service demands. J Environ Systems 1981–2;11:17–34.
52. Kaplan R. The psychological benefits of nearby nature. In: Relf D, ed. The role of horticulture in human well-being and social development: a national symposium, 19–21 April 1990, Arlington, Virginia. Portland, OR: Timber Press, 1992:125–33.
53. Ulrich RS. View through a window may influence recovery from surgery. Science 1984;224:420–1.
54. Heerwagen JH. The psychological aspects of windows and window design. In: Anthony KH, Choi J, Orland B, eds. Proceedings of the 21st Annual Conference of the Environmental Design Research Association, EDRA 21/1990. Oklahoma City: EDRA, 1990:269–80.
55. Cumes D. Nature as medicine: the healing power of the wilderness. Alternative Therapies 1998;4:79–86.
56. Cumes D. Inner passages outer journeys: wilderness, healing, and the discovery of self. Minneapolis: Llewellyn Publications, 1998.
57. Jerstad L, Stelzer J. Adventure experiences as treatment for residential mental patients. Therapeutic Recreation J 1973;7:8–11.
58. Witman JP. The efficacy of adventure programming in the development of cooperation and trust with adolescents in treatment. Therapeutic Recreation J 1987;21:22–9.
59. Plakun EM, Tucker GJ, Harris PQ. Outward bound: an adjunctive psychiatric therapy. J Psychiatr Treat Eval 1981;3:33–7.
60. Berman DS, Anton MT. A wilderness therapy program as an alternative to adolescent psychiatric hospitalization. Residential Treatment Children Youth 1988;5:41–53.
61. Hobbs TR, Shelton GC. Therapeutic camping for emotionally disturbed adolescents. Hosp Community Psych 1972;23:298–301.
62. Marx JD. An outdoor adventure counseling program for adolescents. Social Work 1988;33:517–20.
63. Davis-Berman J, Berman DS. The wilderness therapy program: an empirical study of its effects with adolescents in an outpatient setting. J Contemporary Psychotherapy 1989;19:271–81.
64. Moyer JA. Bannock bereavement retreat: a camping experience for surviving children. Am J Hospice Care 1988;5:26–30.
65. Birnbaum A. Haven hugs & bugs. Am J Hospice Palliative Care 1991;8:23–9.
66. Levine D. Breaking through barriers: wilderness therapy for sexual assault survivors. Women Therapy 1994;15(3/4):175–84.
67. Pearson J. A wilderness program for adolescents with cancer. J Assoc Pediatric Oncol Nurses 1989;6:24–5.

68. Warady BA. Therapeutic camping for children with end-stage renal disease. Pediatric Nephrol 1994;8:387–90.

69. Hyer L, Boyd S, Scurfield R, Smith D, Burke J. Effects of outward bound experience as an adjunct to inpatient PTSD treatment of war veterans. J Clinical Psychol 1996;52:263–78.

70. Bennett LW, Cardone S, Jarczyk J. Effects of a therapeutic camping program on addiction recovery: The Algonquin Relapse Prevention Program. J Substance Abuse Treatment 1998;15:469–74.

71. Kennedy BP, Minami M. The Beech Hill Hospital/Outward Bound Adolescent Chemical Dependency Treatment Program. J Substance Abuse Treat 1993;10:395–406.

72. Easley AT, Passineau JF, Driver BL, comps. The use of wilderness for personal growth, therapy, and education. Fort Collins, CO: U.S. Department of Agriculture, Forest Service, Rocky Mountain Forest and Range Experiment Station, 1990.

73. Shniderman CM. Impact of therapeutic camping. Social Work 1974;19:354–7.

74. Greenway R. The wilderness effect and ecopsychology. In: Roszak T, Gomes ME, Kanner AD, eds. Ecopsychology: restoring the Earth, healing the mind. San Francisco: Sierra Club Books, 1995:122–35.

75. Kaplan R. The role of nature in the urban context. In: Altham I, Wohlwill J, eds. Behavior and the natural environment. New York: Plenum, 1983:127–61.

76. McNeil EB. The background of therapeutic camping. J Social Issues 1957;13:3–14.

77. Byers ES. Wilderness camping as a therapy for emotionally disturbed children: a critical review. Exceptional Children 1979;45:628–35.

78. Roszak T, Gomes ME, Kanner AD, eds. Ecopsychology: restoring the Earth, healing the mind. San Francisco: Sierra Club Books, 1995.   [2001]

1. Characterize Frumkin as a scientific writer in this article.
2. What is the genre of this essay? What are its important generic features?
3. How might Wendell Berry respond to this article and its companions by Wilson and Stilgoe?
4. What kind of framework do the Frumkin, Wilson, and Stilgoe essays provide for literary works in this section?

JOHN R. STILGOE

JOHN R. STILGOE *(1949–) is the Robert and Lois Orchard Professor in the History of Landscape at Harvard University, where he conducts research on subjects related to landscape and urban design. He is the winner of the 2001 American Institute of Architects medal and author of many articles and books, including* Outside Lies Magic: Regaining History and Awareness in Everyday places, Alongshore, Borderland: Origins of American Suburbs, Shallow Water Dictionary, *and* Common Landscape of America, 1580 to 1845.

*Gone Barefoot Lately?**

Gone barefoot lately? Changing human interaction with natural and built environments began arresting environmental studies scholars in the late 1970s. Geographer Yi-Fu Tuan published two seminal books, *Topophilia: A Study of Environmental Perception, Attitudes, and Values*[1] and *Landscapes of Fear*[2] focused on human attitudes toward wilderness, landscape, and, to a lesser extent, interior structures and spaces ranging from subway stations to office-building lobbies. E. O. Wilson's subsequent biophilia hypothesis[3,4] prompted many researchers to re-evaluate their understanding that plants and small-scale, engineered ecosystems such as parks somehow please people only on the cultural levels Tuan articulated. At the same time, however, environmental studies scholars acknowledged the fact that many Americans spend more and more time inside buildings and vehicles, and that studying people who live mostly in natural environments and traditional open-country landscapes (e.g., dairy farming and ranching ones) means studying ever-shrinking cohorts. Between the appearance of Stanley Milgram's "The Experience of Living in Cities"[5] and Robert E. Lane's *The Loss of Happiness in Market Democracies*,[6] the thrust of environmental studies research has involved the built environment and focused especially on people (many of them unwell) who spend most of their time in artificial (and now virtual) space.

Howard Frumkin[7] does a great service to many disciplines beyond medicine by emphasizing the extent to which humans may have evolved in response to natural systems and the ways such systems promote health. Walking barefoot involves not only tactile knowing of surfaces—say, which stones are cooler than others and so indicate water beneath—but continuously rediscovering how well the unshod foot climbs rocks and trees, moves over grass, and gropes about under water, let alone feels the vibration of underground machinery. But many Americans, especially children, now rarely go barefoot even on beaches, and instead insulate themselves increasingly from the floors of their own homes and from the biosphere Frumkin explicates.

Much of the biosphere is now something at which to look. Contact other than visual, say olfactory or tactile, proves so surprisingly rare that some designers seriously champion erecting plastic trees along highway corridors. Designers essentially accept widespread human insulation from the biosphere and indeed increase it by creating buildings in which temperature never changes, all light is artificial, and smells and sounds are eliminated or inserted.

Insulation originates in fear and marketing. Dissecting U.S. fears perplexes environmental studies scholars trying to make sense of traditional minor threats such as poison ivy contact and novel ones such as Lyme disease and mosquito-borne West Nile infection. Ignorance, often astounding ignorance, keeps some people away from all shrubbery and vines that might be poison ivy. A deepening inability to define degrees of risk complicates outdoor behavior. Many Americans wear beach shoes to reduce the risk of stepping on used hypodermic needles or dead jellyfish; others fear snake bite and so rarely stray off paved trails; still others will not risk getting lost in suburban woods, but few can estimate

*John R. Stilgoe, "Gone Barefoot Lately?" *American Journal of Preventive Medicine* 20.3 (2001): 243–44.

the likelihood of what they fear actually happening. Whatever the origins of incompetence and timidity, designers now accept both, and shape parks, office complexes, vacation resorts, and college campuses as nonthreatening, nonchallenging, essentially visual constructs.

5   Mass-market advertising and media, especially the electronic media desperate to keep viewers indoors and tuned in to phosphorescent bluish light, not only exaggerate many environmental dangers but subsist on advertising for beach shoes, air conditioners, and other goods that insulate people from all sorts of outdoor environmental stimuli. Over 4 decades, television may well have converted many Americans into indoor people fundamentally incompetent outside.

Yet scholars know that many other Americans deliberately choose continual and rich immersion in natural stimuli. Something other than the enduring legacy of the suburban movement orders the behavior of an unknown number of individuals. Eschewing urban amenities, especially high-paying urban jobs, for exurban and rural ones is more difficult to study than fears, because land ownership records remain among the last decentralized databases in the nation and because marketing researchers cannot examine Americans who avoid advertising-based media and malls. But marketing researchers, real estate agents, land developers, and environmental studies scholars now glimpse two emerging patterns.

Some well-to-do Americans will not buy houses downwind from air-polluting industries any more than they will locate within a mile or two of high-tension electric lines. Residence location results in part from careful decisions (often based on Internet-derived mapping information) involving distance from known or suspected environmental minuses. But location also results from fierce determination to live in or adjacent to environmental pluses ranging from high-altitude aspen forests to salt marshes and beaches thought to produce high-quality living, a vague phrase that connotes improved physical and mental health and sustained physical and mental well-being, the latter difficult for many Americans to describe.

On some levels brutally simple issues involving full-range biosphere contact—many runners live in rural places because they loathe breathing urban air while dodging automobiles—grow sophisticated and maddeningly complex when extended to emotional and psychological health. Scattered, again largely anecdotal evidence—collected mostly by deep-background marketing firms sniffing out a new cohort of well-to-do, happy, essentially satisfied Americans somehow immune to advertising—suggests that people remain in or move to wilderness or rural environments both to escape the stresses of high-paced urban and suburban living and to immerse themselves in "soothing" or "healthful" biospheres. Even when collated by ZIP code, U.S. Census data fail to track the vectors of people deserting metropolitan areas or, perhaps more importantly, intending to do so. The rural, sparsely populated, poverty-stricken, but spectacularly beautiful and ordinarily cloudless Colorado county of San Luis has 33,000 nonresident landowners, many of whom value its clean air, bright sunlight, and wind-whispering quiet. In a way that mystifies everyone from land use planners to real estate salesmen, a great many Americans intend moving to rural areas in the future, often for the vaguest of reasons, but in quest of something Frumkin identifies so acutely.

A handful of scholars now suspect that some sort of sensory defensiveness annoys, perhaps even afflicts, many Americans who half-consciously find themselves trapped in high-stress built environments. Too much artificial environment stimulation perhaps exhausts or otherwise debilitates. At least some Americans cannot endure the vibration on the top floors of very tall office buildings that sway slightly in the wind. Others cannot relax with video screens flickering at the edge of their peripheral vision, or read beneath fluorescent lights, or enjoy studying or working indoors when heating and ventilation systems irritate their hearing. Crowding stresses some, something frequently overlooked by educators advocating smaller classes held in standard-size classrooms: a feeling of spaciousness more than increased teacher contact may improve learning. As Theodore R. Sizer and Nancy Faust Sizer explain in *The Students are Watching: Schools and the Moral Contract*,[8] the typical U.S. public high school is the most crowded indoor environment Americans ever confront outside of prison. In an era when architects design windowless schools and so many white-collar workers spend hours in cubicles that frustrate long-distance vision, Frumkin explains the stunning popularity of home offices, the use of remote phones just outside back doors, and the enduring pleasure of sunbathing.

Frumkin decisively advances an argument involving more than cultural spatial preferences and the contemporary significance of the biophilia hypothesis. He signals the beginning of what may well prove to be an astonishingly fruitful collaboration among the medical, design, and environmental studies communities on behalf of a public desperately seeking sustained well-being.   10

References

1. Tuan Y-F. Topophilia: a study of environmental perception, attitudes, and values. Englewood Cliffs, NJ: Prentice-Hall, 1974.
2. Tuan Y-F. Landscapes of fear. New York: Pantheon Books, 1979.
3. Wilson EO. Biophilia and the conservation ethic. In: Kellert Sr, Wilson EO, eds. The biophilia hypothesis. Washington, DC: Island Press, 1993:31–41.
4. Wilson EO. Biophilia: the human bond with other species. Cambridge: Harvard University Press, 1989.
5. Milgram S. The experience of living in cities. Science 1970;167(924): 1461–8.
6. Lane RE. The loss of happiness in market democracies. New Haven, CT: Yale University Press, 2000.
7. Frumkin H. Beyond toxicity: human health and the natural environment. Am J Prev Med 2001;20(3):234–40.
8. Sizer TR, Sizer NF. The students are watching: schools and the moral contract. Boston: Beacon Press, 1999.   [2001]

1. What kinds of responses have you had to artificial and natural environments? Have you ever worked or slept in rooms with no windows? How much time do you spend outdoors?

EDWARD O. WILSON

EDWARD O. WILSON *(1929–) was born in Birmingham, Alabama. He got his Ph.D. in biology at Harvard, where he has been professor for over forty years. As discoverer of many new species, he has been called "the father of biodiversity." His interest in his subject of specialization, ants, originated in large part from a childhood accident that destroyed the sight of his right eye. The resulting decision was to concentrate on insects he could pick up and bring close enough to see. But his focus is not narrow. He has written twenty books, including the controversial* Sociobiology: The New Synthesis, *in which he suggests analogies between animal and human societies that are explicable by genes. A new edition has been released for the book's twenty-fifth anniversary. The even more ambitious* Consilience: The Unity of Knowledge *suggests that the sciences and humanities, in fact, all human endeavors, are based on the same inherent principles. He has won two Pulitzer prizes and many awards and honors from many countries in fields such as education, entomology, and biology.*

Nature Matters*

Howard Frumkin's[1] synthesis in this issue of the *American Journal of Preventive Medicine* belongs in that special class of emergent revolutions whose rationale is in plain sight but whose importance has been missed until pointed out—such as the clear rings that form around fungi growing in bacterial culture plates. Time and again medical research has advanced on the recognition that human beings are a biological species and, in particular, a catarrhine primate closely similar to other catarrhines, such as chimpanzees and rhesus macaques. However refined, however elevated by intelligence and culture, we can learn and benefit a great deal from an understanding of our origins.

Dr. Frumkin reminds us that other animal species are adapted to the environments in which they evolved, in other words fitted by natural selection both physiologically and behaviorally. Instinctive habitat selection is universal, and its analysis has become an important industry within the growing discipline of behavioral ecology. Even tiny species of insects, rotifers, and other invertebrates, whose brains are invisible to the naked eye, follow impressive algorithms of orientation to reach the habitats they need to survive. It should come as no great surprise to find that *Homo sapiens* at least still feels an innate preference for the natural environment that cradled us. Frumkin points to a mass of evidence that such is indeed the case. He argues persuasively for closer attention in preventive medicine of the role of the habitat-seeking instinct by encouraging the union of environmental psychology with medical research.

*Edward O. Wilson, "Nature Matters," *American Journal of Preventive Medicine* 20.3 (2001): 241–42.

[1]Frumkin H. Beyond toxicity: human health and the natural environment. Am J Prev Med 2000;20(3):234–40.

Several disciplines, prominently including biological anthropology, sociobiology, cognitive psychology, and neuroscience, are yielding evidence that other innate algorithms affect the development of human behavior. These algorithms can be blocked or reversed only at the peril of mental health. An example is the negative imprinting that forms the basis of incest avoidance, as follows: When either of two persons lives in close domestic proximity during the first 30 months' life of either one, both are unable to form close sexual bonding later in their lives. The phenomenon, known as the Westermarck effect in honor of the Finnish anthropologist who discovered it a century ago, is evidently widespread if not universal in human beings. Equally impressive, it is shared by all other primate species whose sexual behavioral development has been closely studied.

The nature of the automatic incest-avoidance process, as well as its evolutionary origins, now seems well established by solid research. Similarly, the adaptive advantage it gives to those who react to it correctly is clear: less inbreeding, fewer homozygous defective genes, and more healthy children. The Westermarck effect is an example of an epigenetic rule, defined as an inherited regularity of development. Dr. Frumkin has listed not one, but several major categories of healthy mental response to the natural environment. Will deeper research, guided by evolutionary reasoning and targeting specific phenomena, turn up new epigenetic rules that contribute to our biophilia? I believe that to be likely.

Civilization has, in my opinion, entered the Century of Biology in basic research, and the Century of the Environment in applied science. In the decades ahead, science and technology will turn increasingly inward in order to improve the health and happiness of the human race, as well as the health of the planet on which our species was born and on which we remain entirely dependent. We are also methodologically in the Age of Synthesis, in which research will turn more and more from nearly pure reductionism to the reassembly into wholes of the complex systems whose parts and basic processes have been discovered by reductionism. Synthesis of high quality in environment and health requires inventive new efforts in the collaboration between environmental scientists and biomedical researchers on the one hand, and between environmental and medical policymakers on the other. 5

The engagement of the new forms of preventive medicine envisioned in Frumkin's essay will be welcomed by environmentalists for much the same reason that the intervention of physicians in peacemaking and the care of refugees has been rewarded by two Nobel Peace Prizes, thus far. One of the principal goals of environmental thinkers today is the formulation of a sound conservation ethic grounded in the deep psychological and spiritual needs of human beings. Dr. Frumkin has shown, among his other enlightenments in this essay, why it is wiser, for example, to save the last of the rich old-growth forests in the permanent service of preventive medicine than to cut them down for the short-term purchase of more pharmaceuticals. [2001]

1. What is the relationship between Frumkin's article and Wilson's?
2. What parts of Frumkin's survey does Wilson seem most interested in?

CHAPTER EIGHTEEN

Sight and Insight

INTRODUCTION

This section asks several questions. First, what does it mean to see the world, that is, to process sensory data from the eyes in order to make one's way through the physical world? Then, how do people who cannot literally see understand it? In addition, why do human beings seem to crave representations of the world, versions of it that imitate one or more of its features in visual, oral, or tactile media? Since no art can "capture" life, what is it for? The writers of the works in this section provide various answers.

POETRY

ELIZABETH BISHOP

(For biographical notes, see p. 745.)

Filling Station

Oh, but it is dirty!
—this little filling station,
oil-soaked, oil-permeated
to a disturbing, over-all
5   black translucency.
Be careful with that match!

Father wears a dirty,
oil-soaked monkey suit
that cuts him under the arms,
10 and several quick and saucy

and greasy sons assist him
(it's a family filling station),
all quite thoroughly dirty.

Do they live in the station?
It has a cement porch   15
behind the pumps, and on it
a set of crushed and grease-
impregnated wickerwork;
on the wicker sofa
a dirty dog, quite comfy.   20

Some comic books provide
the only note of color—
of certain color. They lie
upon a big dim doily
draping a taboret   25
(part of the set), beside
a big hirsute begonia.

Why the extraneous plant?
Why the taboret?
Why, oh why, the doily?   30
(Embroidered in daisy stitch
with marguerites, I think,
and heavy with gray crochet.)

Somebody embroidered the doily.
Somebody waters the plant,   35
or oils it, maybe. Somebody
arranges the rows of cans
so that they softly say:
ESSO—SO—SO—SO°
to high-strung automobiles.   40
Somebody loves us all.   [1965]

³⁹**ESSO** one of the petroleum products companies that now make up the Exxon Mobil
Corporation

1. This poem is full of repeated words: *dirty* (four times), *oil-soaked* (twice),
   somebody (three times), *filling station* (twice), *quite* (twice), and *grease-
   impregnated, greasy; wicker, wickerwork*. What impressions relating to the
   meaning of the poem are conveyed by these repeated words and phrases?
2. Discuss contrasts between the masculine and feminine elements and how
   they meet in the poem.
3. The narrator asks four questions during the course of the poem: "Do they
   live in the station?" "Why the extraneous plant?" "Why the taboret?" and
   "Why, oh why, the doily?" The last eight lines are devoted to the answer. If
   you were reading the poem aloud, how would you read the last line? Would

you take a tone of sarcasm, of disgust, of naïve wonder, or of convinced affirmation? Point to elements of the poem that support your reading.

4. Does the narrator's attitude toward the station change during the course of the poem? What is the tone of l. 30?

JOHN KEATS

JOHN KEATS *(1795–1821) Orphaned at an early age by the tuberculosis that haunted his family, Keats was under the care of a guardian who apprenticed him to an apothecary-surgeon, but he never practiced his profession, deciding to become a poet instead. He joined a circle of literary men, among them Leigh Hunt, Percy Shelley, and William Wordsworth. Soon after, he published his first volume,* Poems by John Keats. *In response to Shelley's advice that he produce a larger volume of work, he wrote "Endymion," a long allegorical romance, which was not well received. While nursing his ill brother, Keats wrote "The Fall of Hyperion," a blank-verse epic. In 1820, he published* Lamia, Isabella, The Eve of St. Agnes, and Other Poems. *The three title poems are among his best work. The book contained as well "Ode on a Grecian Urn," "Ode on Melancholy," and "Ode to a Nightingale," all of them among the finest poems in the English language. His anguished love letters to Fanny Brawne have also been published. Keats died at twenty-five of tuberculosis in Rome and is buried there.*

Ode on a Grecian Urn

I

Thou still unravish'd bride of quietness,
   Thou foster-child of silence and slow time,
Sylvan historian, who canst thus express
   A flowery tale more sweetly than our rhyme:
5 What leaf-fring'd legend haunts about thy shape
    Of deities or mortals, or of both,
      In Tempe or the dales of Arcady?°
   What men or gods are these? What maidens loth?
What mad pursuit? What struggle to escape?
10   What pipes and timbrels?° What wild ecstasy?

II

Heard melodies are sweet, but those unheard
   Are sweeter; therefore, ye soft pipes, play on;
Not to the sensual ear, but, more endear'd,
   Pipe to the spirit ditties of no tone:

---

[7] **Arcady** a region of ancient Greece often chosen as the background for pastoral poetry
[10] **timbrels** small hand drums or tambourines

Fair youth, beneath the trees, thou canst not leave   15
   Thy song, nor ever can those trees be bare;
     Bold Lover, never, never canst thou kiss,
Though winning near the goal—yet, do not grieve;
     She cannot fade, though thou hast not thy bliss,
   For ever wilt thou love, and she be fair!   20

III

Ah, happy, happy boughs! that cannot shed
   Your leaves, nor ever bid the Spring adieu;
And, happy melodist, unwearied,
   For ever piping songs for ever new;
More happy love! more happy, happy love!   25
   For ever warm and still to be enjoy'd,
     For ever panting, and for ever young;
All breathing human passion far above,
     That leaves a heart high-sorrowful and cloy'd,
     A burning forehead, and a parching tongue.   30

IV

Who are these coming to the sacrifice?
   To what green altar, O mysterious priest,
Lead'st thou that heifer lowing at the skies,
   And all her silken flanks with garlands drest?
What little town by river or sea shore,   35
   Or mountain-built with peaceful citadel,
     Is emptied of this folk, this pious morn?
And, little town, thy streets for evermore
     Will silent be; and not a soul to tell
     Why thou art desolate, can e'er return.   40

V

O Attic° shape! Fair attitude! with brede
   Of marble men and maidens overwrought,
With forest branches and the trodden weed;
   Thou, silent form, dost tease us out of thought
As doth eternity: Cold Pastoral!°   45
     When old age shall this generation waste,
     Thou shalt remain, in midst of other woe
Than ours, a friend to man, to whom thou say'st,
   "Beauty is truth, truth beauty,"—that is all
   Ye know on earth, and all ye need to know.   [1820]   50

---

[41]**Attic** from an area of Greece of which Athens is the capital; of a style characterized by simplicity, purity, refinement   [45]**Pastoral** having to do with rural life, usually characterized as uncorrupt, simple, and serene

1. The particular artifacts that Keats had in mind when he was writing this poem are not precisely known but probably included several different ones. You can see some objects associated with the poem by visiting the British Museum on the Internet at http://www.thebritishmuseum.ac.uk/. If you click on "Compass" and do a search for "Greek marble urn," you will be able to view "Young cow and Herdsman from the south frieze of the Parthenon" and the Townley vase, a marble urn with sculptural reliefs (see color insert, Figure I-O). What are the scenes depicted on the urn? Try to imagine carefully what Keats describes.

2. Analyze the way the rhyme and meter create the structure of the poem. What are the significant metrical variations? How do syntax and line breaks interact with the poem's structure?

3. Analyze the poem's diction and syntax.

4. Who is talking in the various parts of the poem? To whom?

5. Why is the narrator so fascinated with the scene on the urn? What does he like about the scene? What are the costs of the scene's positive aspects? Does the poem successfully reconcile the positive and negative aspects of the scene? Can you formulate a statement of theme for the poem?

6. What disciplines are likely to shed light on the poem's theme?

X. J. KENNEDY

X. J. KENNEDY (1929–) was named Joseph Charles Kennedy at his birth in Dover, New Jersey. By the time he was twelve he was the publisher of his own science fiction magazine, Terrifying Test-Tube Tales. *A bachelor's degree from Seton Hall University and a master's from Columbia followed. He then served four years in the U.S. Navy, publishing the newspaper for his destroyer at sea. He studied further at the Sorbonne and the University of Michigan and then taught English at the University of North Carolina and Tufts University, where he began teaching in 1963. His first poetry collection,* Nude Descending a Staircase *(1961), won the Lamont Award for that year. Since 1979 Kennedy has been a freelance writer. He prefers metrical forms and rhyme in his poetry. He is the author of several books of poetry for children and several textbooks.*

Nude Descending a Staircase

Toe upon toe, a snowing flesh,
A gold of lemon, root and rind,
She sifts in sunlight down the stairs
With nothing on. Nor on her mind.

5 We spy beneath the banister
A constant thresh of thigh on thigh—
Her lips imprint the swinging air
That parts to let her parts go by.

One-woman waterfall, she wears
Her slow descent like a long cape   10
And pausing, on the final stair
Collects her motions into shape.   [1961]

1. Kennedy's poem is obviously a response to Marcel Duchamp's painting by
    the same name, a painting that, among other things, captures the sense of
    motion involved in descending a staircase (color insert, Figure I-E). That is,
    instead of a static presentation of a woman *at a certain point on the stairs,* the
    painting tries to capture the sequence of her descent. Considering
    Kennedy's diction, syntax, and rhyme scheme, how does he convey the
    sense of motion that he sees in the painting?

YUSEF KOMUNYAKAA

(For biographical notes, see p. 1086.)

Hanoi Hannah°

Ray Charles! His voice
calls from waist-high grass,
& we duck behind gray sandbags.
"Hello, Soul Brothers. Yeah,
Georgia's also on my mind."   5
Flares bloom over the trees.
"Here's Hannah again.
Let's see if we can't
light her goddamn fuse
this time." Artillery   10
shells carve a white arc
against dusk. Her voice rises
from a hedgerow on our left.
"It's Saturday night in the States.
Guess what your woman's doing tonight.   15
I think I'll let Tina Turner
tell you, you homesick GIs."
Howitzers buck like a herd
of horses behind concertina.
"You know you're dead men,   20
don't you? You're dead
as King today in Memphis."

Title **Hanoi Hannah** (her real name was Thu Houng) a DJ on a Radio Hanoi radio show
broadcast in English to American soldiers during the Vietnam War. "Tokyo Rose" made
similar broadcasts in the Pacific theater during World War II.

Boys, you're surrounded by
General Tran Do's division."
25 Her knife-edge song cuts
deep as a sniper's bullet.
"Soul Brothers, what you dying for?"
We lay down a white-klieg
trail of tracers. Phantom jets
30 fan out over the trees.
Artillery fire zeros in.
Her voice grows flesh
& we can see her falling
into words, a bleeding flower
35 no one knows the true name for.
"You're lousy shots, GIs."
Her laughter floats up
as though the airways are
buried under our feet.

[1988]

1. Judging from the poem, what are Hanoi Hannah's aims and how does she try to accomplish them?
2. Is she successful?
3. How do the images help to convey the meaning of the poem?
4. Do some Web research at sites such as http://www.psywarrior.com/hannah. html to look for some details about such radio broadcasts that might shed some light on the poem.

LI-YOUNG LEE

LI-YOUNG LEE *(1957–) was born in Jakarta, Indonesia, of Chinese parents. He fled Indonesia with his family because of President Sukarno's persecution and jailing of his father. The family traveled for five years throughout the Far East before arriving in America. His book* Rose *won the New York University's 1986 Delmore Schwartz Memorial Poetry Award, and* The City in Which I Love You *was the 1990 Lamont Poetry Selection of the Academy of American Poets. Lee currently lives in Chicago with his wife Donna and their two children.*

Persimmons

In sixth grade Mrs. Walker
slapped the back of my head
and made me stand in the corner
for not knowing the difference
5 between persimmon and precision.
How to choose

persimmons. This is precision.
Ripe ones are soft and brown-spotted.
Sniff the bottoms. The sweet one
will be fragrant. How to eat:
put the knife away, lay down the newspaper.
Peel the skin tenderly, not to tear the meat.
Chew on the skin, suck it,
and swallow. Now, eat
the meat of the fruit,
so sweet
all of it, to the heart.

Donna undresses, her stomach is white.
In the yard, dewy and shivering
with crickets, we lie naked,
face-up, face-down,
I teach her Chinese. Crickets: chiu chiu. Dew: I've forgotten.
Naked: I've forgotten.
Ni, wo: you me.
I part her legs,
remember to tell her
she is beautiful as the moon.

Other words
that got me into trouble were
fight and fright, wren and yarn.
Fight was what I did when I was frightened,
fright was what I felt when I was fighting.
Wrens are small, plain birds,
yarn is what one knits with.
Wrens are soft as yarn.
My mother made birds out of yarn.
I loved to watch her tie the stuff;
a bird, a rabbit, a wee man.

Mrs. Walker brought a persimmon to class
and cut it up
so everyone could taste
a Chinese apple. Knowing
it wasn't ripe or sweet, I didn't eat
but watched the other faces.

My mother said every persimmon has a sun
inside, something golden, glowing,
warm as my face.

Once, in the cellar, I found two wrapped in newspaper
forgotten and not yet ripe.
I took them and set them both on my bedroom windowsill,

10

15

20

25

30

35

40

45

50

where each morning a cardinal
sang. The sun, the sun.

Finally understanding
he was going blind,
55   my father would stay up all one night
waiting for a song, a ghost.
I gave him the persimmons, swelled, heavy as sadness,
and sweet as love.

This year, in the muddy lighting
60   of my parents' cellar, I rummage, looking
for something I lost.
My father sits on the tired, wooden stairs,
black cane between his knees,
hand over hand, gripping the handle.

65   He's so happy that I've come home.
I ask how his eyes are, a stupid question.
All gone, he answers.

Under some blankets, I find three scrolls.
I sit beside him and untie
70   three paintings by my father:
Hibiscus leaf and a white flower.
Two cats preening.
Two persimmons, so full they want to drop from the cloth.

He raises both hands to touch the cloth,
75   asks, Which is this?
This is persimmons, Father.

Oh, the feel of the wolftail on the silk,
the strength, the tense
precision in the wrist.
80   I painted them hundreds of times
eyes closed. These I painted blind.
Some things never leave a person:
scent of the hair of one you love,
the texture of persimmons,
85   in your palm, the ripe weight.   [1986]

1. The episode of being struck by the teacher and then being isolated, punished, for "not knowing the difference . . ." is a shocking way to begin
   the poem. How does the episode resonate throughout the rest of the
   poem?
2. In the climactic encounter with his father, the narrator answers his father's
   question with the simple sentence, "This is persimmons, Father." How does
   this sentence fit in with the rest of the poem? Is it true?
3. Who speaks the last stanza? How does it relate to the rest of the poem?

⊙⊙⊙

DENISE LEVERTOV

DENISE LEVERTOV *(1923–98), daughter of a Welsh Christian mother and a Russian-Jewish father, is the author of twenty-three volumes of poetry, essays, and translations. Although she was born in England, she came to the United States in 1948 and is considered to be a leading American poet of the late twentieth century. She was the friend and disciple of William Carlos Williams and was associated with the Black Mountain poets, Robert Creeley, Charles Olson, and Robert Duncan. Levertov's spirituality probably originated with her father, who became a Christian minister in the Church of England, although he never formally converted. Levertov herself later converted to Catholicism. She was a committed feminist active in the antiwar movement of the 60s and 70s and in the later antinuclear movement.*

The Reminder

Composed by nature, time, human art,
an earthly paradise. A haze that is not smog
gentles the light. Mountains delicately frosted,
timbered autumnal hillsides copper and bronze.
Black-green of pine, gray-green of olive.   5
Nothing is missing. Ferries' long wakes pattern the water,
send to the still shores a minor music of waves.
Dark perpendiculars
of cypress, grouped or single, cross immemorial
horizontals of terraced slopes, the outstretched wings,   10
creamy yellow, of villas more elegant
in slight disrepair than anything spick and span
could ever be. And all perceived
not through our own crude gaze alone but by the accretion
of others' vision—language, paint, memory transmitted.   15
Here, just now, the malady
we know the earth endures seems in remission—
or *we* are, from that knowledge that gnaws at us.
But only seems. Down by the lake the sign:
"Swim at your own risk. The lake is polluted."   20
Not badly, someone says, blithely irrelevant.
We can avoid looking that way,
if we choose. That's at our own risk.
Deep underneath remission's fragile peace,
the misshaped cells remain.   [1992]   25

1. Explicate the figures of speech in the poem.
2. What is the effect of the repetition of the idea of risk in ll. 20 and 23?
3. What does the poem tell us about the observation of nature? What role does her insight into seeing play in the poem?
4. What is the narrator's *ethos?*

DAVID RAY

DAVID RAY (1932–) and his wife Judy founded both New Letters Magazine *and the NPR radio program, "New Letters on the Air." He lives in Tucson, conducts workshops and gives readings around the country from his books of poetry, which include* The Tramp's Cup, The Touched Life, Sam's Book, Kangaroo Paws, Wool Highways, The Maharani's New Wall, *and* Demons in the Diner. *He has published a book of stories and a memoir,* The Endless Search, *about his difficult childhood in Oklahoma during the depression.* One Thousand Years: Poems about the Holocaust *was published in 2004. He has twice won the William Carlos Williams Award from the Poetry Society of America and twice been nominated for the Pulitzer Prize. He has received the Allen Ginsberg and the Emily Dickinson Awards and the Richard J. Snyder Memorial Award. He received the 2001 Nuclear Age Peace Foundation Poetry Award and has earned the admiration of other authors, including Studs Terkel, who has written, "David Ray's poetry had always been radiant even though personal tragedy has suffused it."*

A Midnight Diner by Edward Hopper

Your own greyhounds bark at your side.
It is you, dressed like a Siennese,
Galloping, ripping the gown as the fabled
White-skinned woman runs, seeking freedom.
5 Tiny points of birches rise from hills,
Spin like serrulate corkscrews toward the sky;
In other rooms it is your happiness
Flower petals fall for, your brocade
You rediscover, feel bloom upon your shoulder.

10 And freedom's what the gallery's for.
You roam in large rooms and choose your beauty.
Yet, Madman, it's your own life you turn back to:
In one postcard purchase you wipe out
Centuries of light and smiles, golden skin
15 And openness, forest babes and calves.
You forsake the sparkler breast
That makes the galaxies, you betray
The women who dance upon the water.

All for some bizarre hometown necessity!
20 Some ache still found within you!
Now it will go with you, this scene
By Edward Hopper and nothing else.
It will become your own tableau of sadness
Composed of blue and grey already there.
25 Over or not, this suffering will not say Hosanna.
Now a music will not come out of it.

Grey hat, blue suit, you are in a midnight
Diner painted by Edward Hopper.

Here is a man trapped at midnight underneath the El.
He has sought the smoothest counter in the world   30
And found it here in the almost empty street,
Away from everything he has ever said.
Now he has the silence they've insisted on.
Not a squirrel, not an autumn birch,
Not a hound at his side, moves to help him now.   35
His grief is what he'll try to hold in check.
His thumb has found and held his coffee cup.   [1970]

1. What is the question this poem is attempting to answer?
2. Do you think the poem answers it successfully? Is it useful to consider the poem alongside the painting that gives it its name? The narrator describes it in ll. 21–37. What can the comparison with the painting (see color insert, Figure I-I) contribute to our understanding of the poem?
3. According to the poem, what is the function of art?
4. Who is the Madman of l. 12?

ALAN SHAPIRO

(For biographical notes, see p. 759.)

Astronomy Lesson

The two boys lean out on the railing
of the front porch, looking up.
Behind them they can hear their mother
in one room watching "Name That Tune,"°
their father in another watching   5
a Walter Cronkite° Special, the TVs
turned up high and higher till they
each can't hear the other's show.
The older boy is saying that no matter
how many stars you counted there were   10
always more stars beyond them
and beyond the stars black space
going on forever in all directions,
so that even if you flew up
millions and millions of years   15
you'd be no closer to the end

⁴**"Name That Tune"** a popular television quiz show in the 1950s in which contestants competed to be the first to give the names of songs or musical compositions played by a band   ⁶**Walter Cronkite** one of the founders of the CBS Evening News, for which he was the anchorman from 1962 until his retirement in 1981

of it than they were now
here on the porch on Tuesday night
in the middle of summer.
20 The younger boy can think somehow
only of his mother's closet,
how he likes to crawl in back
behind the heavy drapery
of shirts, nightgowns and dresses,
25 into the sheer black where
no matter how close he holds
his hand up to his face
there's no hand ever, no
face to hold it to.

30 A woman from another street
is calling to her stray cat or dog,
clapping and whistling it in,
and farther away deep in the city
sirens now and again
35 veer in and out of hearing.

The boys edge closer, shoulder
to shoulder now, sad Ptolemies,
the older looking up, the younger
as he thinks back straight ahead
40 into the black leaves of the maple
where the street lights flicker
like another watery skein of stars.
"Name That Tune" and Walter Cronkite
struggle like rough water
45 to rise above each other.
And the woman now comes walking
in a nightgown down the middle
of the street, clapping and
whistling, while the older boy
50 goes on about what light years
are, and solar winds, black holes,
and how the sun is cooling
and what will happen to
them all when it is cold.   [1987]

1. Explain the allusion in the phrase "sad Ptolemies." What connection does it
   have to the two boys' activities?
2. What images are repeated in the poem? How do they affect our understanding of the poem and the boys' concerns?
3. Map the spatial organization of images in the poem. How does this organization enhance the poem's meaning?

Wife: The Mirror

The softest part of his anatomy
was the bristling hint of hair on the shaved head.
The t-shirt tight as spandex on the pecs,
the shoulders, the rippling stomach, seemed to sharpen
the definition of what it covered up.   5
With a god's composure, or an animal's,
leaning against the lamp post, he was gazing,
nakedly gazing at all the passing women
(even the ones that other men were with),
gazing and smiling a stainless certitude   10
that they would think it was their privilege
he'd notice them at all.
                    I thought of those
sometimes protracted times when you and I
have been invisible to one another,
distracted, or at odds, and how at such   15
times often after showering I'll watch myself
and feel, though wishing this were firmer, that
were bigger, not entirely displeased,
imagining another woman sees
the way mist on the mirror makes a kind   20
of nimbus all around me as it clears.

I thought of other times as well, times when
you come to me in need of comfort only,
only desiring to be held, and I mistake it,
and either push on in a blind assurance   25
that what I want is really all you need,
or sulk away, to lick the wounded ego.

Suddenly I could see him through your eyes.
I realized the fugitive dislike
you would have showed in face or voice—   30
had you been there with me—would not have been
for that man only, but for the very thing
he purified of hesitation, doubt.
It would have been dislike for that male gaze,
that ever vigilant aim, that too precise,   35
impersonal and solitary heat.   [1996]

---

1. How much looking and seeing is going on in this poem? What is its
   thematic significance?
2. The phrase "that male gaze" (l. 34) comes from film theory, where it
   refers to films in which the camera seems to take the point of view of a

heterosexual male, looking at and judging women as objects of desire.[1] How appropriate is it as the narrator uses it here?

3. What is the structural principle of the poem?

4. What is the relationship between the narrator and the man leaning against the lamp post?

[1]Laura Mulvey, "Afterthoughts on 'Visual Pleasure and Narrative Cinema' Inspired by *Duel in the Sun*," *Feminism and Film Theory*, ed. Constance Penley (New York: Routledge, 1988).

WOLE SOYINKA

(For biographical notes, see p. 454.)

Telephone Conversation

The price seemed reasonable, location
Indifferent. The landlady swore she lived
Off premises. Nothing remained
But self-confession. "Madam," I warned
5 "I hate a wasted journey—I am—African."
Silence. Silenced transmission of
Pressurized good-breeding. Voice, when it came,
Lip-stick coated, long gold-rolled
Cigarette-holder pipped. Caught I was, foully.
10 "HOW DARK?" . . . I had not misheard . . .
    "ARE YOU LIGHT
OR VERY DARK?" Button B. Button A. Stench
Of rancid breath of public-hide-and-speak.
Red booth. Red pillar-box. Red double-tiered
15 Omnibus squelching tar. It *was* real! Shamed
By ill-mannered silence, surrender
Pushed dumbfoundment to beg simplification.
Considerate she was, varying the emphasis—
"ARE YOU DARK? OR VERY LIGHT?" Revelation came.
20 "You mean—like plain or milk chocolate?"
Her assent was clinical, crushing in its light,
Impersonality. Rapidly, wave-length adjusted,
I chose, "West African sepia"—and as an afterthought,
"Down in my passport." Silence for spectroscopic
25 Flight of fancy, till truthfulness clanged her accent
Hard on the mouthpiece. "WHAT'S THAT?" conceding
"DON'T KNOW WHAT THAT IS." "Like brunette."
"THAT'S DARK, ISN'T IT?" "Not altogether.
"Facially, I am brunette, but madam, you should see
30 The rest of me. Palm of my hand, soles of my feet
Are a peroxide blond. Friction, caused—

Foolishly madam—by sitting down, has turned
My bottom raven black—One moment madam!"—sensing
Her receiver rearing on the thunder clap
About my ears—"Madam," I pleaded, "Wouldn't you rather   35
See for yourself?"   [1962]

1. Considering the date of the poem, speculate about when and where
   Soyinka might have had the kind of experience recounted in the poem.
2. The 1960s were a time at which portrayals of telephone conversations became
   cultural artifacts. In their careers as stand-up comedians, actors Bob Newhart
   and Lily Tomlin and actors and directors Mike Nichols and Elaine May used
   the telephone to create comic versions of the genre. Newhart, an accountant
   in his life before show business, often took the role of the reasonable person
   talking to someone being outrageous on the other end of the line. Audiences
   would have to infer the exact dimensions of the unseen speaker's outrageous-
   ness only from Newhart's patient and reasonable responses. In one of their
   comedy routines, Nichols plays a man who has lost his dime in a pay phone,
   and he tries to convince May, who plays the operator, to return his dime. In
   the course of the conversation, she gets more officious and formulaic as he
   gets more desperate. Lily Tomlin's telephone operator Ernestine gave rigid
   answers to an unheard customer who seemed to be getting more and more
   upset with her unresponsiveness. Cold and business-like, she pretended to
   provide service but didn't. The audience's task with both Newhart and Tomlin
   was to judge both the audible speaker and the unheard interlocutor to decide
   who was really reasonable, who was more credible. In the days when the
   telephone company was a monopoly, audiences could usually see around
   Ernestine's false friendliness. By the end of the sketch, her customer would get
   hysterical enough (we guessed) to drive her to abandon the company façade
   to hiss, "We don't care. We don't have to; we're the phone company!"
   Compare Soyinka's poem to this genre of comedy.
3. What is the tone of "pleaded" in l. 35?
4. What are some of the poetic techniques that give the poem its power?
5. The subject of this poem needs no explanation for anyone who has been alive
   recently in any of the "civilized" nations of the world. If the poem burns itself
   into your memory, causes indignation, then gives you the sense of satisfaction that comes when someone has thought of the right answer to an insult at
   the right time, it has fulfilled one of the functions of art. Try turning your
   own experience, or the experience of a family member or friend, into a poem.

WALLACE STEVENS

WALLACE STEVENS (1879–1955), who attended Harvard and earned a degree
from New York Law School, worked for the Hartford Accident and Indemnity Co. in
Connecticut for most of his adult life. In 1914, Harriet Monroe, editor of Poetry,
published four of his poems in the magazine, thereby launching him on a parallel

career as a poet. His first book, Harmonium, *showed his exotic, whimsical, impressionist style. He continued his career in insurance, rising to a vice-presidency of the company, writing his poems on his way to and from work. He is considered one of the major American poets of the century, although he did not receive much recognition until the publication of his* Collected Poems *a year before his death.* The Idea of Order, The Man with the Blue Guitar, Notes towards a Supreme Fiction, *and a collection of essays on poetry,* The Necessary Angel, *comprise the bulk of his work.*

Anecdote of the Jar

I placed a jar in Tennessee,
And round it was, upon a hill.
It made the slovenly wilderness
Surround that hill.

5 The wilderness rose up to it,
And sprawled around, no longer wild.
The jar was round upon the ground
And tall and of a port in air.

It took dominion everywhere.
10 The jar was gray and bare.
It did not give of bird or bush,
Like nothing else in Tennessee.   [1923]

1. What does the jar symbolize? What are its important characteristics?
2. What other works in this section can help us to interpret this poem?

The Man with the Blue Guitar

I

The man bent over his guitar,
A shearsman of sorts. The day was green.

They said, "You have a blue guitar,
You do not play things as they are."

5 The man replied, "Things as they are
Are changed upon the blue guitar."

And they said then, "But play, you must,
A tune beyond us, yet ourselves,

A tune upon the blue guitar
10 Of things exactly as they are."

II

I cannot bring a world quite round,
Although I patch it as I can.

I sing a hero's head, large eye
And bearded bronze, but not a man,

Although I patch him as I can   15
And reach through him almost to man.

If to serenade almost to man
Is to miss, by that, things as they are,

Say that it is the serenade
Of a man that plays a blue guitar.   20

III

Ah, but to play man number one,
To drive the dagger in his heart,

To lay his brain upon the board
And pick the acrid colors out,

To nail his thought across the door,   25
Its wings spread wide to rain and snow,

To strike his living hi and ho,
To tick it, tock it, turn it true,

To bang it from a savage blue,
Jangling the metal of the strings . . .   30

IV

So that's life, then: things as they are?
It picks its way on the blue guitar.

A million people on one string?
And all their manner in the thing,

And all their manner, right or wrong,   35
And all their manner, weak and strong?

The feelings crazily, craftily call,
Life a buzzing of flies in autumn air,

And that's life, then: things as they are,
This buzzing of the blue guitar.   [1936]   40

1. The poem seems to refer to Pablo Picasso's "The Old Guitarist," a 1903 painting from Picasso's "Blue Period," when, saddened by the suicide of a friend, he used a mostly blue palette for a number of paintings of somber, isolated people, among them the bowed guitarist hunched over his instrument (see color insert, Figure I-N). How would you characterize the poem as a response to the painting? What does the blue guitar symbolize?

2. Who are the speakers in this poem? Characterize their interaction. Does it matter that there are no quotation marks after the first stanza?

3. Do ll. 37–40 resolve the conflict depicted in the rest of the poem? What is their tone?

⊙⊙⊙

TEAM AUSTIN

TEAM AUSTIN *has represented Austin, Texas, at the National Poetry Slam (NPS) competition every year since 1995, reaching at least the semi-finals in every annual tournament. Poetry Slams are poetry competitions in which poets perform original work which is judged by members of the audience. Having evolved over the course of a decade into an international grassroots network, slams take place at the local level in dozens of cities, with winning individual poets forming teams that in turn compete at NPS, representing their local poetic scene.*

In 1996, Mike Henry, rock musician, co-owner of the club where the local slam took place, and experienced slammer, coached a team consisting of Hilary Thomas, Wammo, Danny Solis, and Phil West as they prepared for and competed in the National Poetry Slam. Team Austin reached the NPS finals that year, with Wammo advancing to the individual finals. The event, held in Portland, Oregon, was featured in Paul Devlin's award-winning documentary Slam Nation *(http://www.slamnation.com). "Everyone on the team went away and collected images from the media, wrote images and soundbites in the familiar voices we see and hear on TV,"* Henry explains. *"We wove the text and the characters into the four-voice poem."* More information on poetry slams can be found at *http://www.poetryslam.com.*

Tube

D: (with rest of group entering at intervals)
We interrupt your regularly scheduled program to bring you this
P: refreshing
W: gunfire
H: fabulous
5   *D:* odor
W: new and improved
P: act of cowardice
D: minty-fresh
P: A must for those who are dieting.
10   *W:* You can't find a better set of knives.
H: The death toll continues to rise.
D: Now available on home video
P: free with each box of
W: massive environmental destruction.
15   *H:* He scores!
D: He could go all the way!
P: He draws the foul!
W: This game is over.

P: Rounding out the top five movies for the week were "Mighty Ducks XII" and "Weekend at Bernie's
20   *PH:* three"
H: helpings just aren't enough, try family-sized

HD: death count

D: in Rwanda continues to rise as over a hundred children a day perish from starvation and malnutrition-related

DW: diseases

W: and suffering from the Lord Almighty Jehovah who shall rain down a great   25
fire upon all those who would transgress against his precious flock.

ALL: No Americans were killed in the disaster.

P: Moving on to national news,

H: got milk?

W: You're soaking in it.

D: Sylvia, I'm not your uncle, I'm your father.   30

H: But that means my mother is

P: your psychic friend.

W: It tightens your abs while it rids you of

WD: affirmative action.

PWH: No comment *(repeat until Wammo's line)*   35

D: Why DON'T you have a comment, motherfucker?

W: No money down.

P: No credit, no problem.

H: No product on the market works better to insure

HP: eight hours   40

P: of hair raising thrills

PD: watch it and you die a thousand deaths in this

PDW: terror-drenched

WP: blood curdling horror film

H: at eleven   45

D: with our brand new sky cam bringing you the latest

W: miracle

WH: of

WHD: modern

ALL: technology.   50

P: Now here's Sandra with sports.

H: In football news today, a bunch of steroid-laden machoids pranced around in stupid-looking costumes trying to prove what big men they are in a grandiose display of latent homosexual male contact-oriented grunting.

W: Beef. It's what's for dinner.

D: And for more football news, let's go to Steve

WP: at the courthouse   55

H: where we've had reporters working all day.

WH: (whistle Andy Griffith theme over Phil's line)

P: According to police spokesmen, the internal investigation concluded the shooting was accidental. The 17-year old black male suspect is still in serious but stable condition

D: but your guests will not have to worry about that unpleasantness. All they'll see is the nice centerpiece you put together for your small but elegant dinner party.

W: And tonight's winning Lotto numbers are pi,   60

P: doh,

W: null,

P: doh,

W: infinity,

65 *P:* woo-hoo

W: and 666

P: doh,

H: the real thing.

P: The jury returned a verdict of

70 *WD:* A BRAND NEW CAR!

PH: Good and good for you.

D: Now here's Dick with the weather.

W: Stay in your homes.

P: And order pay-per-view for the Poetry Wrestling Sudden-Death Cage Match of the Century!

75 *W:* He lost his belt to Robert "Iron John" Bly in SuperSlamaBama III and he's not about to forget it.

D: Robert Bly°—all those crybabies in the men's movement, all that runnin' around in the woods, paintin' your face, playin' your drums, cryin' about your dead daddy, and especially all that bad poetry you wrote in the '60's ain't gonna save you! You're going down, baby, down!

H: If we get close and he smells, forget it.

P: Hey we're hangin' at the MTV Beach House ready to

D: wreak havoc

80 *W:* and let the angel with the flaming sword cut loose the bonds of sin. Let's check the current contribution totals for this evening, shall we?

PDH: No Americans were killed in the disaster.

W: Hallelujah!

P: The new breakthrough AIDS treatment will cost each patient anywhere from 40 to 60 thousand dollars per year.

W: And we will be saved

85 *D:* More fighting today in the West Bank.

W: by the power of Jesus,

H: This brought to you by . . .

W: our almighty lord who looks down upon us and says . . .

P: We'll get back to warm and sunny weather by Friday.

90 *H:* just in time for the weekend.

W: And in tomorrow's news

D: based on an analysis of current global

DH: trends

[76]**Robert Bly** (1926–) a poet, translator, and editor who has published over 50 books of poetry, including *Iron John: A Book about Men* (1990), an important text for the men's movement in the late 20th century as it tried to understand the roles of men in society and common characterizations of them. Iron John is a "wild man" figure from *Grimm's Fairy Tales* who acts as a mentor for younger men.

H: looking toward the
HP: future   95
P: a team of experts
PD: have predicted
D: our civilization will soon be

ALL: STATIC.   [1996]

1. What difference does it make that this poem is performed by a group?
    Would this poem be more or less effective if recited by a single speaker?
2. What is the poem's attitude toward American culture?

WILLIAM CARLOS WILLIAMS

(For biographical notes, see p. 1092.)

Landscape with the Fall of Icarus°

According to Brueghel
when Icarus fell
it was spring

a farmer was ploughing
his field   5
the whole pageantry

of the year was
awake tingling
near

the edge of the sea   10
concerned
with itself

sweating in the sun
that melted
the wings' wax   15

unsignificantly
off the coast
there was

a splash quite unnoticed
this was   20
Icarus drowning   [1962]

Title A painting by Pieter Brueghel the Elder, c. 1525–69. In classical Greek mythology
Daedalus designed the labyrinth for King Minos of Crete to confine the monstrous half-
bull/half-human offspring of Queen Pasiphae and a bull. When Daedalus himself was
imprisoned in the labyrinth, he made wings out of wax and feathers with which he and
his son Icarus escaped the maze and the island. Icarus flew too high, and when the sun
melted the wax in his wings, he fell to his death in the sea.

1. Pieter Brueghel the Elder's *Landscape with the Fall of Icarus* (see color insert, Figure I-B) is also the focus of W.H. Auden's poem "Musée des Beaux Arts" (see p. 127). Compare and contrast the ways that Williams and Auden treat the painting. Are they responding to it emotionally? Intellectually? Trying to give a version of it in words? What is the significance of the syntax, line breaks, and punctuation? What is the significance of the poems' titles?
2. How does Williams's stanza 5 function in the poem?

FICTION

RAYMOND CARVER

(For biographical notes, see p. 762.)

Cathedral

This blind man, an old friend of my wife's, he was on his way to spend the night. His wife had died. So he was visiting the dead wife's relatives in Connecticut. He called my wife from his in-laws'. Arrangements were made. He would come by train, a five-hour trip, and my wife would meet him at the station. She hadn't seen him since she worked for him one summer in Seattle ten years ago. But she and the blind man had kept in touch. They made tapes and mailed them back and forth. I wasn't enthusiastic about his visit. He was no one I knew. And his being blind bothered me. My idea of blindness came from the movies. In the movies, the blind moved slowly and never laughed. Sometimes they were led by seeing-eye dogs. A blind man in my house was not something I looked forward to.

That summer in Seattle she had needed a job. She didn't have any money. The man she was going to marry at the end of the summer was in officers' training school. He didn't have any money, either. But she was in love with the guy, and he was in love with her, etc. She'd seen something in the paper: HELP WANTED— *Reading to Blind Man*, and a telephone number. She phoned and went over, was hired on the spot. She'd worked with this blind man all summer. She read stuff to him, case studies, reports, that sort of thing. She helped him organize his little office in the county social-service department. They'd become good friends, my wife and the blind man. How do I know these things? She told me. And she told me something else. On her last day in the office, the blind man asked if he could touch her face. She agreed to this. She told me he touched his fingers to every part of her face, her nose—even her neck! She never forgot it. She even tried to write a poem about it. She was always trying to write a poem. She wrote a poem or two every year, usually after something really important had happened to her.

When we first started going out together, she showed me the poem. In the poem, she recalled his fingers and the way they had moved around over her face. In the poem, she talked about what she had felt at the time, about what went through her mind when the blind man touched her nose and lips. I can remember I didn't think much of the poem. Of course, I didn't tell her that.

Maybe I just don't understand poetry. I admit it's not the first thing I reach for when I pick up something to read.

Anyway, this man who'd first enjoyed her favors, the officer-to-be, he'd been her childhood sweetheart. So okay. I'm saying that at the end of the summer she let the blind man run his hands over her face, said goodbye to him, married her childhood etc., who was now a commissioned officer, and she moved away from Seattle. But they'd kept in touch, she and the blind man. She made the first contact after a year or so. She called him up one night from an Air Force base in Alabama. She wanted to talk. They talked. He asked her to send him a tape and tell him about her life. She did this. She sent the tape. On the tape, she told the blind man about her husband and about their life together in the military. She told the blind man she loved her husband but she didn't like it where they lived and she didn't like it that he was a part of the military-industrial thing. She told the blind man she'd written a poem and he was in it. She told him that she was writing a poem about what it was like to be an Air Force officer's wife. The poem wasn't finished yet. She was still writing it. The blind man made a tape. He sent her the tape. She made a tape. This went on for years. My wife's officer was posted to one base and then another. She sent tapes from Moody AFB, McGuire, McConnell, and finally Travis, near Sacramento, where one night she got to feeling lonely and cut off from people she kept losing in that moving-around life. She got to feeling she couldn't go it another step. She went in and swallowed all the pills and capsules in the medicine chest and washed them down with a bottle of gin. Then she got into a hot bath and passed out.

But instead of dying, she got sick. She threw up. Her officer—why should he have a name? he was the childhood sweetheart, and what more does he want?—came home from somewhere, found her, and called the ambulance. In time, she put it all on a tape and sent the tape to the blind man. Over the years, she put all kinds of stuff on tapes and sent the tapes off lickety-split. Next to writing a poem every year, I think it was her chief means of recreation. On one tape, she told the blind man she'd decided to live away from her officer for a time. On another tape, she told him about her divorce. She and I began going out, and of course she told her blind man about it. She told him everything, or so it seemed to me. Once she asked me if I'd like to hear the latest tape from the blind man. This was a year ago. I was on the tape, she said. So I said okay, I'd listen to it. I got us drinks and we settled down in the living room. We made ready to listen. First she inserted the tape into the player and adjusted a couple of dials. Then she pushed a lever. The tape squeaked and someone began to talk in this loud voice. She lowered the volume. After a few minutes of harmless chitchat, I heard my own name in the mouth of this stranger, this blind man I didn't even know! And then this: "From all you've said about him, I can only conclude——" But we were interrupted, a knock at the door, something, and we didn't ever get back to the tape. Maybe it was just as well. I'd heard all I wanted to.

Now this same blind man was coming to sleep in my house.

"Maybe I could take him bowling," I said to my wife. She was at the draining board doing scalloped potatoes. She put down the knife she was using and turned around.

5

"If you love me," she said, "you can do this for me. If you don't love me, okay. But if you had a friend, any friend, and the friend came to visit, I'd make him feel comfortable." She wiped her hands with the dish towel.

"I don't have any blind friends," I said.

10 "You don't have *any* friends," she said. "Period. Besides," she said, "goddamn it, his wife's just died! Don't you understand that? The man's lost his wife!"

I didn't answer. She'd told me a little about the blind man's wife. Her name was Beulah. Beulah! That's a name for a colored woman.

"Was his wife a Negro?" I asked.

"Are you crazy?" my wife said. "Have you just flipped or something?" She picked up a potato. I saw it hit the floor, then roll under the stove. "What's wrong with you?" she said. "Are you drunk?"

"I'm just asking," I said.

15 Right then my wife filled me in with more detail than I cared to know. I made a drink and sat at the kitchen table to listen. Pieces of the story began to fall into place.

Beulah had gone to work for the blind man the summer after my wife had stopped working for him. Pretty soon Beulah and the blind man had themselves a church wedding. It was a little wedding—who'd want to go to such a wedding in the first place?—just the two of them, plus the minister and the minister's wife. But it was a church wedding just the same. It was what Beulah had wanted, he'd said. But even then Beulah must have been carrying the cancer in her glands. After they had been inseparable for eight years—my wife's word, *inseparable*—Beulah's health went into a rapid decline. She died in a Seattle hospital room, the blind man sitting beside the bed and holding on to her hand. They'd married, lived and worked together, slept together—had sex, sure—and then the blind man had to bury her. All this without his having ever seen what the goddamned woman looked like. It was beyond my understanding. Hearing this, I felt sorry for the blind man for a little bit. And then I found myself thinking what a pitiful life this woman must have led. Imagine a woman who could never see herself as she was seen in the eyes of her loved one. A woman who could go on day after day and never receive the smallest compliment from her beloved. A woman whose husband could never read the expression on her face, be it misery or something better. Someone who could wear makeup or not—what difference to him? She could, if she wanted, wear green eye-shadow around one eye, a straight pin in her nostril, yellow slacks and purple shoes, no matter. And then to slip off into death, the blind man's hand on her hand, his blind eyes streaming tears—I'm imagining now—her last thought maybe this: that he never even knew what she looked like, and she on an express to the grave. Robert was left with a small insurance policy and half of a twenty-peso Mexican coin. The other half of the coin went into the box with her. Pathetic.

So when the time rolled around, my wife went to the depot to pick him up. With nothing to do but wait—sure, I blamed him for that—I was having a drink and watching the TV when I heard the car pull into the drive. I got up from the sofa with my drink and went to the window to have a look.

I saw my wife laughing as she parked the car. I saw her get out of the car and shut the door. She was still wearing a smile. Just amazing. She went around to the other side of the car to where the blind man was already starting to get out. This blind man, feature this, he was wearing a full beard! A beard on a blind man! Too much, I say. The blind man reached into the back seat and dragged out a suitcase. My wife took his arm, shut the car door, and, talking all the way, moved him down the drive and then up the steps to the front porch. I turned off the TV. I finished my drink, rinsed the glass, dried my hands. Then I went to the door.

My wife said, "I want you to meet Robert. Robert, this is my husband. I've told you all about him." She was beaming. She had this blind man by his coat sleeve.

The blind man let go of his suitcase and up came his hand.   20

I took it. He squeezed hard, held my hand, and then he let it go.

"I feel like we've already met," he boomed.

"Likewise," I said. I didn't know what else to say. Then I said, "Welcome. I've heard a lot about you." We began to move then, a little group, from the porch into the living room, my wife guiding him by the arm. The blind man was carrying his suitcase in his other hand. My wife said things like, "To your left here, Robert. That's right. Now watch it, there's a chair. That's it. Sit down right here. This is the sofa. We just bought this sofa two weeks ago."

I started to say something about the old sofa. I'd liked that old sofa. But I didn't say anything. Then I wanted to say something else, small-talk, about the scenic ride along the Hudson. How going *to* New York, you should sit on the right-hand side of the train, and coming *from* New York, the left-hand side.

"Did you have a good train ride?" I said. "Which side of the train did you sit   25
on, by the way?"

"What a question, which side!" my wife said. "What's it matter which side?" she said.

"I just asked," I said.

"Right side," the blind man said. "I hadn't been on a train in nearly forty years. Not since I was a kid. With my folks. That's been a long time. I'd nearly forgotten the sensation. I have winter in my beard now," he said. "So I've been told, anyway. Do I look distinguished, my dear?" the blind man said to my wife.

"You look distinguished, Robert," she said. "Robert," she said. "Robert, it's just so good to see you."

My wife finally took her eyes off the blind man and looked at me. I had the   30
feeling she didn't like what she saw. I shrugged.

I've never met, or personally known, anyone who was blind. This blind man was late forties, a heavy-set, balding man with stooped shoulders, as if he carried a great weight there. He wore brown slacks, brown shoes, a light-brown shirt, a tie, a sports coat. Spiffy. He also had this full beard. But he didn't use a cane and he didn't wear dark glasses. I'd always thought dark glasses were a must for the blind. Fact was, I wished he had a pair. At first glance, his eyes looked like anyone else's eyes. But if you looked close, there was something different about them. Too much white in the iris, for one thing, and the pupils seemed to move around in the sockets without his knowing it or being able to stop it. Creepy. As I stared at his face, I saw the left pupil turn in toward his nose while the other made an effort to keep in one place. But it was only an effort, for that eye was on the roam without his knowing it or wanting it to be.

I said, "Let me get you a drink. What's your pleasure? We have a little of everything. It's one of our pastimes."

"Bub, I'm a Scotch man myself," he said fast enough in this big voice.

"Right," I said. Bub! "Sure you are. I knew it."

35   He let his fingers touch his suitcase, which was sitting alongside the sofa. He was taking his bearings. I didn't blame him for that.

"I'll move that up to your room," my wife said.

"No, that's fine," the blind man said loudly. "It can go up when I go up."

"A little water with the Scotch?" I said.

"Very little," he said.

40   "I knew it," I said.

He said, "Just a tad. The Irish actor, Barry Fitzgerald? I'm like that fellow. When I drink water, Fitzgerald said, I drink water. When I drink whiskey, I drink whiskey." My wife laughed. The blind man brought his hand up under his beard. He lifted his beard slowly and let it drop.

I did the drinks, three big glasses of Scotch with a splash of water in each. Then we made ourselves comfortable and talked about Robert's travels. First the long flight from the West Coast to Connecticut, we covered that. Then from Connecticut up here by train. We had another drink concerning that leg of the trip.

I remembered having read somewhere that the blind didn't smoke because, as speculation had it, they couldn't see the smoke they exhaled. I thought I knew that much and that much only about blind people. But this blind man smoked his cigarette down to the nubbin and then lit another one. This blind man filled his ashtray and my wife emptied it.

When we sat down at the table for dinner, we had another drink. My wife heaped Robert's plate with cube steak, scalloped potatoes, green beans. I buttered him up two slices of bread. I said, "Here's bread and butter for you." I swallowed some of my drink. "Now let us pray," I said, and the blind man lowered his head. My wife looked at me, her mouth agape. "Pray the phone won't ring and the food doesn't get cold," I said.

45   We dug in. We ate everything there was to eat on the table. We ate like there was no tomorrow. We didn't talk. We ate. We scarfed. We grazed that table. We were into serious eating. The blind man had right away located his foods, he knew just where everything was on his plate. I watched with admiration as he used his knife and fork on the meat. He'd cut two pieces of meat, fork the meat into his mouth, and then go all out for the scalloped potatoes, the beans next, and then he'd tear off a hunk of buttered bread and eat that. He'd follow this up with a big drink of milk. It didn't seem to bother him to use his fingers once in a while, either.

We finished everything, including half a strawberry pie. For a few moments, we sat as if stunned. Sweat beaded on our faces. Finally, we got up from the table and left the dirty plates. We didn't look back. We took ourselves into the living room and sank into our places again. Robert and my wife sat on the sofa. I took the big chair. We had us two or three more drinks while they talked about the major things that had come to pass for them in the past ten years. For the most part, I just listened. Now and then I joined in. I didn't want him to think I'd left the room, and I didn't want her to think I was feeling left out. They talked of things that had happened to them—to them!—these past ten years. I waited in vain to hear my name on my wife's sweet lips: "And then my dear husband came into my life"—something like that. But I heard nothing of the sort. More talk of Robert. Robert had done a little of everything, it seemed, a regular blind jack-of-all-trades. But most recently he and his wife had had an Amway distributorship, from which, I gathered, they'd earned their living, such as it was. The blind man was also a ham radio operator. He talked in his loud voice about conversations he'd had with fellow operators in Guam, in the Philippines, in Alaska, and even in Tahiti. He said he'd have a lot of friends there if he ever wanted to go visit those places. From time to time, he'd turn his blind face toward me, put his hand under his beard, ask me something. How long had I been in my present position? (Three years.) Did I like my work? (I didn't.) Was I going to stay with it? (What were the options?) Finally, when I thought he was beginning to run down, I got up and turned on the TV.

My wife looked at me with irritation. She was heading toward a boil. Then she looked at the blind man and said, "Robert, do you have a TV?"

The blind man said, "My dear, I have two TVs. I have a color set and a black-and-white thing, an old relic. It's funny, but if I turn the TV on, and I'm always turning it on, I turn on the color set. It's funny, don't you think?"

I didn't know what to say to that. I had absolutely nothing to say to that. No opinion. So I watched the news program and tried to listen to what the announcer was saying.

"This is a color TV," the blind man said. "Don't ask me how, but I can tell." 50

"We traded up a while ago," I said.

The blind man had another taste of his drink. He lifted his beard, sniffed it, and let it fall. He leaned forward on the sofa. He positioned his ashtray on the coffee table, then put the lighter to his cigarette. He leaned back on the sofa and crossed his legs at the ankles.

My wife covered her mouth, and then she yawned. She stretched. She said, "I think I'll go upstairs and put on my robe. I think I'll change into something else. Robert, you make yourself comfortable," she said.

"I'm comfortable," the blind man said.

"I want you to feel comfortable in this house," she said. 55

"I am comfortable," the blind man said.

After she'd left the room, he and I listened to the weather report and then to the sports roundup. By that time, she'd been gone so long I didn't know if she was going to come back. I thought she might have gone to bed. I wished she'd come back downstairs. I didn't want to be left alone with a blind man. I asked him if he wanted another drink, and he said sure. Then I asked if he wanted to smoke some dope with me. I said I'd just rolled a number. I hadn't, but I planned to do so in about two shakes.

"I'll try some with you," he said.

"Damn right," I said. "That's the stuff."

60 I got our drinks and sat down on the sofa with him. Then I rolled us two fat numbers. I lit one and passed it. I brought it to his fingers. He took it and inhaled.

"Hold it as long as you can," I said. I could tell he didn't know the first thing.

My wife came back downstairs wearing her pink robe and her pink slippers.

"What do I smell?" she said.

"We thought we'd have us some cannabis," I said.

65 My wife gave me a savage look. Then she looked at the blind man and said, "Robert, I didn't know you smoked."

He said, "I do now, my dear. There's a first time for everything. But I don't feel anything yet."

"This stuff is pretty mellow," I said. "This stuff is mild. It's dope you can reason with," I said. "It doesn't mess you up."

"Not much it doesn't, bub," he said, and laughed.

My wife sat on the sofa between the blind man and me. I passed her the number. She took it and toked and then passed it back to me. "Which way is this going?" she said. Then she said, "I shouldn't be smoking this. I can hardly keep my eyes open as it is. That dinner did me in. I shouldn't have eaten so much."

70 "It was the strawberry pie," the blind man said. "That's what did it," he said, and he laughed his big laugh. Then he shook his head.

"There's more strawberry pie," I said.

"Do you want some more, Robert?" my wife said.

"Maybe in a little while," he said.

We gave our attention to the TV. My wife yawned again. She said, "Your bed is made up when you feel like going to bed, Robert. I know you must have had a long day. When you're ready to go to bed, say so." She pulled his arm. "Robert?"

75 He came to and said, "I've had a real nice time. This beats tapes, doesn't it?"

I said, "Coming at you," and I put the number between his fingers. He inhaled, held the smoke, and then let it go. It was like he'd been doing it since he was nine years old.

"Thanks, bub," he said. "But I think this is all for me. I think I'm beginning to feel it," he said. He held the burning roach out for my wife.

"Same here," she said. "Ditto. Me, too." She took the roach and passed it to me. "I may just sit here for a while between you two guys with my eyes closed. But don't let me bother you, okay? Either one of you. If it bothers you, say so. Otherwise, I may just sit here with my eyes closed until you're ready to go to bed," she said. "Your bed's made up, Robert, when you're ready. It's right next to our room at the top of the stairs. We'll show you up when you're ready. You wake me up now, you guys, if I fall asleep." She said that and then she closed her eyes and went to sleep.

The news program ended. I got up and changed the channel. I sat back down on the sofa. I wished my wife hadn't pooped out. Her head lay across the back of the sofa, her mouth open. She'd turned so that her robe had slipped away from her legs, exposing a juicy thigh. I reached to draw her robe back over her, and it

was then that I glanced at the blind man. What the hell! I flipped the robe open
again.

"You say when you want some strawberry pie," I said.   80

"I will," he said.

I said, "Are you tired? Do you want me to take you up to your bed? Are you
ready to hit the hay?"

"Not yet," he said. "No, I'll stay up with you, bub. If that's all right. I'll stay
up until you're ready to turn in. We haven't had a chance to talk. Know what I
mean? I feel like me and her monopolized the evening." He lifted his beard and
he let it fall. He picked up his cigarettes and his lighter.

"That's all right," I said. Then I said, "I'm glad for the company."

And I guess I was. Every night I smoked dope and stayed up as long as I could   85
before I fell asleep. My wife and I hardly ever went to bed at the same time.
When I did go to sleep, I had these dreams. Sometimes I'd wake up from one of
them, my heart going crazy.

Something about the church and the Middle Ages was on the TV. Not your
run-of-the-mill TV fare. I wanted to watch something else. I turned to the other
channels. But there was nothing on them, either. So I turned back to the first
channel and apologized.

"Bub, it's all right," the blind man said. "It's fine with me. Whatever you
want to watch is okay. I'm always learning something. Learning never ends. It
won't hurt me to learn something tonight. I got ears," he said.

We didn't say anything for a time. He was leaning forward with his head
turned at me, his right ear aimed in the direction of the set. Very disconcerting.
Now and then his eyelids drooped and then they snapped open again. Now and
then he put his fingers into his beard and tugged, like he was thinking about
something he was hearing on the television.

On the screen, a group of men wearing cowls was being set upon and tormented by men dressed in skeleton costumes and men dressed as devils. The men
dressed as devils wore devil masks, horns, and long tails. This pageant was part of
a procession. The Englishman who was narrating the thing said it took place in
Spain once a year. I tried to explain to the blind man what was happening.

"Skeletons," he said. "I know about skeletons," he said, and he nodded.   90

The TV showed this one cathedral. Then there was a long, slow look at
another one. Finally, the picture switched to the famous one in Paris,° with its
flying buttresses and its spires reaching up to the clouds. The camera pulled
away to show the whole of the cathedral rising above the skyline.

There were times when the Englishman who was telling the thing would
shut up, would simply let the camera move around over the cathedrals. Or else
the camera would tour the countryside, men in fields walking behind oxen. I
waited as long as I could. Then I felt I had to say something. I said, "They're

---

⁹¹**the famous one in Paris** probably Notre Dame de Paris, built in the Gothic style
between 1163 and the early 14th century

showing the outside of this cathedral now. Gargoyles. Little statues carved to look like monsters. Now I guess they're in Italy. Yeah, they're in Italy. There's paintings on the walls of this one church."

"Are those fresco paintings, bub?" he asked, and he sipped from his drink.

I reached for my glass. But it was empty. I tried to remember what I could remember. "You're asking me are those frescoes?" I said. "That's a good question. I don't know."

95   The camera moved to a cathedral outside Lisbon. The differences in the Portuguese cathedral compared with the French and Italian were not that great. But they were there. Mostly the interior stuff. Then something occurred to me, and I said, "Something has occurred to me. Do you have any idea what a cathedral is? What they look like, that is? Do you follow me? If somebody says cathedral to you, do you have any notion what they're talking about? Do you know the difference between that and a Baptist church, say?"

He let the smoke dribble from his mouth. "I know they took hundreds of workers fifty or a hundred years to build," he said. "I just heard the man say that, of course. I know generations of the same families worked on a cathedral. I heard him say that, too. The men who began their life's work on them, they never lived to see the completion of their work. In that wise, bub, they're no different from the rest of us, right?" He laughed. Then his eyelids drooped again. His head nodded. He seemed to be snoozing. Maybe he was imagining himself in Portugal. The TV was showing another cathedral now. This one was in Germany. The Englishman's voice droned on. "Cathedrals," the blind man said. He sat up and rolled his head back and forth. "If you want the truth, bub, that's about all I know. What I just said. What I heard him say. But maybe you could describe one to me? I wish you'd do it. I'd like that. If you want to know, I really don't have a good idea."

I stared hard at the shot of the cathedral on the TV. How could I even begin to describe it? But say my life depended on it. Say my life was being threatened by an insane guy who said I had to do it or else.

I stared some more at the cathedral before the picture flipped off into the countryside. There was no use. I turned to the blind man and said, "To begin with, they're very tall." I was looking around the room for clues. "They reach way up. Up and up. Toward the sky. They're so big, some of them, they have to have these supports. To help hold them up, so to speak. These supports are called buttresses. They remind me of viaducts, for some reason. But maybe you don't know viaducts, either? Sometimes the cathedrals have devils and such carved into the front. Sometimes lords and ladies. Don't ask me why this is," I said.

He was nodding. The whole upper part of his body seemed to be moving back and forth.

100   "I'm not doing so good, am I?" I said.

He stopped nodding and leaned forward on the edge of the sofa. As he listened to me, he was running his fingers through his beard. I wasn't getting through to him, I could see that. But he waited for me to go on just the same. He nodded, like he was trying to encourage me. I tried to think what else to say. "They're really big," I said. "They're massive. They're built of stone. Marble, too, sometimes. In those olden days, when they built cathedrals, men wanted to be close to God. In those olden days, God was an important part of everyone's life. You could tell this from their cathedral-building. I'm sorry," I said, "but it looks like that's the best I can do for you. I'm just no good at it."

"That's all right, bub," the blind man said. "Hey, listen. I hope you don't mind my asking you. Can I ask you something? Let me ask you a simple question, yes or no. I'm just curious and there's no offense. You're my host. But let me ask if you are in any way religious? You don't mind my asking?"

I shook my head. He couldn't see that, though. A wink is the same as a nod to a blind man. "I guess I don't believe in it. In anything. Sometimes it's hard. You know what I'm saying?"

"Sure, I do," he said.

"Right," I said. 105

The Englishman was still holding forth. My wife sighed in her sleep. She drew a long breath and went on with her sleeping.

"You'll have to forgive me," I said. "But I can't tell you what a cathedral looks like. It just isn't in me to do it. I can't do any more than I've done."

The blind man sat very still, his head down, as he listened to me.

I said, "The truth is, cathedrals don't mean anything special to me. Nothing. Cathedrals. They're something to look at on late-night TV. That's all they are."

It was then that the blind man cleared his throat. He brought something up. 110 He took a handkerchief from his back pocket. The he said, "I get it, bub. It's okay. It happens. Don't worry about it," he said. "Hey, listen to me. Will you do me a favor? I got an idea. Why don't you find us some heavy paper? And a pen. We'll do something. We'll draw one together. Get us a pen and some heavy paper. Go on, bub, get the stuff," he said.

So I went upstairs. My legs felt like they didn't have any strength in them. They felt like they did after I'd done some running. In my wife's room, I looked around. I found some ballpoints in a little basket on her table. And then I tried to think where to look for the kind of paper he was talking about.

Downstairs, in the kitchen, I found a shopping bag with onion skins in the bottom of the bag. I emptied the bag and shook it. I brought it into the living room and sat down with it near his legs. I moved some things, smoothed the wrinkles from the bag, spread it out on the coffee table.

The blind man got down from the sofa and sat next to me on the carpet.

He ran his fingers over the paper. He went up and down the sides of the paper. The edges, even the edges. He fingered the corners.

"All right," he said. "All right, let's do her." 115

He found my hand, the hand with the pen. He closed his hand over my hand. "Go ahead, bub, draw," he said. "Draw. You'll see. I'll follow along with you. It'll be okay. Just begin now like I'm telling you. You'll see. Draw," the blind man said.

So I began. First I drew a box that looked like a house. It could have been the house I lived in. Then I put a roof on it. At either end of the roof, I drew spires. Crazy.

"Swell," he said. "Terrific. You're doing fine," he said. "Never thought anything like this could happen in your lifetime, did you, bub? Well, it's a strange life, we all know that. Go on now. Keep it up."

I put in windows with arches. I drew flying buttresses. I hung great doors. I couldn't stop. The TV station went off the air. I put down the pen and closed and opened my fingers. The blind man felt around over the paper. He moved the tips of his fingers over the paper, all over what I had drawn, and he nodded.

120 "Doing fine," the blind man said.

I took up the pen again, and he found my hand. I kept at it. I'm no artist. But I kept drawing just the same.

My wife opened up her eyes and gazed at us. She sat up on the sofa, her robe hanging open. She said, "What are you doing? Tell me, I want to know."

I didn't answer her.

The blind man said, "We're drawing a cathedral. Me and him are working on it. Press hard," he said to me. "That's right. That's good," he said. "Sure. You got it, bub. I can tell. You didn't think you could. But you can, can't you? You're cooking with gas now. You know what I'm saying? We're going to really have us something here in a minute. How's the old arm?" he said. "Put some people in there now. What's a cathedral without people?"

125 My wife said, "What's going on? Robert, what are you doing? What's going on?"

"It's all right," he said to her. "Close your eyes now," the blind man said to me. I did it. I closed them just like he said.

"Are they closed?" he said. "Don't fudge."

"They're closed," I said.

130 "Keep them that way," he said. He said, "Don't stop now. Draw."

So we kept on with it. His fingers rode my fingers as my hand went over the paper. It was like nothing else in my life up to now.

Then he said, "I think that's it. I think you got it," he said. "Take a look. What do you think?"

But I had my eyes closed. I thought I'd keep them that way for a little longer. I thought it was something I ought to do.

"Well?" he said. "Are you looking?"

135 My eyes were still closed. I was in my house. I knew that. But I didn't feel like I was inside anything.

"It's really something," I said.   [1985]

1. Describe the narrator in this story. What kind of narrator is he? What can you deduce about him? How does that affect your view of the story?
2. What is the effect of all the consumption that goes on in the story (alcohol, food, marijuana, television)?
3. Thinking of Robert's deceased wife, the narrator asks us to "Imagine a woman who could never see herself as she was seen in the eyes of her loved one." What does this tell us about the narrator's understandings of identity and about the relationships between men and women?
4. Why is the narrator willing to draw the cathedral with Robert? What is the result of the collaboration?
5. What is it that the narrator is able to "see" once he closes his eyes?

6. Considering Helen Keller's essay, "Three Days to See" (p. 1576), how well does the narrator understand what it is like to be blind? Do any other works in this section help you understand this story?

Don DeLillo

Don DeLillo *(1936–) A major American novelist, playwright, essayist, and short story writer, Don DeLillo paints landscapes of the contemporary American psyche in the form of conspirators, loners, and obsessives. DeLillo cites European film, jazz, and Abstract Impressionism as his major influences for such works as* Ratner's Star *(1976),* Players *(1977),* Running Dog *(1978), and* Amazons *(written under the pseudonym Cleo Birdwell). His breakthrough novel,* White Noise *(1985), came as a result of the shock of returning to the United States after a five-year sojourn in Greece.* Underworld, *which many consider his masterpiece, follows the progress of a famous baseball as it passes from character to character from the Cold War to the advent of the World Wide Web, highlighting the themes of celebrity, conspiracy, and consumerism. DeLillo lives with his wife Barbara in New York and has been the recipient of numerous honors.*

Videotape

It shows a man driving a car. It is the simplest sort of family video. You see a man at the wheel of a medium Dodge.

It is just a kid aiming her camera through the rear window of the family car at the windshield of the car behind her.

You know about families and their video cameras. You know how kids get involved, how the camera shows them that every subject is potentially charged, a million things they never see with the unaided eye. They investigate the meaning of inert objects and dumb pets and they poke at family privacy. They learn to see things twice.

It is the kid's own privacy that is being protected here. She is twelve years old and her name is being withheld even though she is neither the victim nor the perpetrator of the crime but only the means of recording it.

It shows a man in a sport shirt at the wheel of his car. There is nothing else to   5
see. The car approaches briefly, then falls back.

You know how children with cameras learn to work the exposed moments that define the family cluster. They break every trust, spy out the undefended space, catching mom coming out of the bathroom in her cumbrous robe and turbaned towel, looking bloodless and plucked. It is not a joke. They will shoot you sitting on the pot if they can manage a suitable vantage.

The tape has the jostled sort of noneventness that marks the family product. Of course the man in this case is not a member of the family but a stranger in a car, a random figure, someone who has happened along in the slow lane.

It shows a man in his forties wearing a pale shirt open at the throat, the image washed by reflections and sunglint, with many jostled moments.

It is not just another video homicide. It is a homicide recorded by a child who thought she was doing something simple and maybe halfway clever, shooting some tape of a man in a car.

He sees the girl and waves briefly, wagging a hand without taking it off the wheel—an underplayed reaction that makes you like him.

It is unrelenting footage that rolls on and on. It has an aimless determination, a persistence that lives outside the subject matter. You are looking into the mind of home video. It is innocent, it is aimless, it is determined, it is real.

He is bald up the middle of his head, a nice guy in his forties whose whole life seems open to the hand-held camera.

But there is also an element of suspense. You keep on looking not because you know something is going to happen—of course you do know something is going to happen and you do look for that reason but you might also keep on looking if you came across this footage for the first time without knowing the outcome. There is a crude power operating here. You keep on looking because things combine to hold you fast—a sense of the random, the amateurish, the accidental, the impending. You don't think of the tape as boring or interesting. It is crude, it is blunt, it is relentless. It is the jostled part of your mind, the film that runs through your hotel brain under all the thoughts you know you're thinking.

The world is lurking in the camera, already framed, waiting for the boy or girl who will come along and take up the device, learn the instrument, shooting old granddad at breakfast, all stroked out so his nostrils gape, the cereal spoon baby-gripped in his pale fist.

It shows a man alone in a medium Dodge. It seems to go on forever.

There's something about the nature of the tape, the grain of the image, the sputtering black-and-white tones, the starkness—you think this is more real, truer-to-life than anything around you. The things around you have a rehearsed and layered and cosmetic look. The tape is superreal, or maybe underreal is the way you want to put it. It is what lies at the scraped bottom of all the layers you have added. And this is another reason why you keep on looking. The tape has a searing realness.

It shows him giving an abbreviated wave, stiff-palmed, like a signal flag at a siding.

You know how families make up games. This is just another game in which the child invents the rules as she goes along. She likes the idea of videotaping a man in his car. She has probably never done it before and she sees no reason to vary the format or terminate early or pan to another car. This is her game and she is learning it and playing it at the same time. She feels halfway clever and inventive and maybe slightly intrusive as well, a little bit of brazenness that spices any game.

And you keep on looking. You look because this is the nature of the footage, to make a channeled path through time, to give things a shape and a destiny.

Of course if she had panned to another car, the right car at the precise time, she would have caught the gunman as he fired.

The chance quality of the encounter. The victim, the killer, and the child with a camera. Random energies that approach a common point. There's something here that speaks to you directly, saying terrible things about forces beyond your control, lines of intersection that cut through history and logic and every reasonable layer of human expectation.

She wandered into it. The girl got lost and wandered clear-eyed into horror. This is a children's story about straying too far from home. But it isn't the family car that serves as the instrument of the child's curiosity, her inclination to explore. It is the camera that puts her in the tale.

You know about holidays and family celebrations and how somebody shows up with a camcorder and the relatives stand around and barely react because they're numbingly accustomed to the process of being taped and decked and shown on the VCR with the coffee and cake.

He is hit soon after. If you've seen the tape many times you know from the hand wave exactly when he will be hit. It is something, naturally, that you wait for. You say to your wife, if you're at home and she is there, Now here is where he gets it. You say, Janet, hurry up, this is where it happens.

Now here is where he gets it. You see him jolted, sort of wire-shocked—then   25
he seizes up and falls toward the door or maybe leans or slides into the door is the proper way to put it. It is awful and unremarkable at the same time. The car stays in the slow lane. It approaches briefly, then falls back.

You don't usually call your wife over to the TV set. She has her programs, you have yours. But there's a certain urgency here. You want her to see how it looks. The tape has been running forever and now the thing is finally going to happen and you want her to be here when he's shot.

Here it comes all right. He is shot, head-shot, and the camera reacts, the child reacts—there is a jolting movement but she keeps on taping, there is a sympathetic response, a nerve response, her heart is beating faster but she keeps the camera trained on the subject as he slides into the door and even as you see him die you're thinking of the girl. At some level the girl has to be present here, watching what you're watching, unprepared—the girl is seeing this cold and you have to marvel at the fact that she keeps the tape rolling.

It shows something awful and unaccompanied. You want your wife to see it because it is real this time, not fancy movie violence—the realness beneath the layers of cosmetic perception. Hurry up, Janet, here it comes. He dies so fast. There is no accompaniment of any kind. It is very stripped. You want to tell her it is realer than real but then she will ask what that means.

The way the camera reacts to the gunshot—a startle reaction that brings pity and terror into the frame, the girl's own shock, the girl's identification with the victim.

You don't see the blood, which is probably trickling behind his ear and down   30
the back of his neck. The way his head is twisted away from the door, the twist of the head gives you only a partial profile and it's the wrong side, it's not the side where he was hit.

And maybe you're being a little aggressive here, practically forcing your wife to watch. Why? What are you telling her? Are you making a little statement? Like I'm going to ruin your day out of ordinary spite. Or a big statement? Like this is the risk of existing. Either way you're rubbing her face in this tape and you don't know why.

It shows the car drifting toward the guardrail and then there's a jostling sense of two other lanes and part of another car, a split-second blur, and the tape ends here, either because the girl stopped shooting or because some central authority, the police or the district attorney or the TV station, decided there was nothing else you had to see.

This is either the tenth or eleventh homicide committed by the Texas Highway Killer. The number is uncertain because the police believe that one of the shootings may have been a copycat crime.

And there is something about videotape, isn't there, and this particular kind of serial crime? This is a crime designed for random taping and immediate playing. You sit there and wonder if this kind of crime became more possible when the means of taping an event and playing it immediately, without a neutral interval, a balancing space and time, became widely available. Taping-and-playing intensifies and compresses the event. It dangles a need to do it again. You sit there thinking that the serial murderer has found its medium, or vice versa—an act of shadow technology, of compressed time and repeated images, stark and glary and unremarkable.

35   It shows very little in the end. It is a famous murder because it is on tape and because the murderer has done it many times and because the crime was recorded by a child. So the child is involved, the Video Kid as she is sometimes called because they have to call her something. The tape is famous and so is she. She is famous in the modern manner of people whose names are strategically withheld. They are famous without names or faces, spirits living apart from their bodies, the victims and witnesses, the underage criminals, out there somewhere at the edges of perception.

Seeing someone at the moment he dies, dying unexpectedly. This is reason alone to stay fixed to the screen. It is instructional, watching a man shot dead as he drives along on a sunny day. It demonstrates an elemental truth, that every breath you take has two possible endings. And that's another thing. There's a joke locked away here, a note of cruel slapstick that you are willing to appreciate even if it makes you feel a little guilty. Maybe the victim's a chump, a sort of silent-movie dope, classically unlucky. He had it coming, in a sense, for letting himself be caught on camera. Because once the tape starts rolling it can only end one way. This is what the context requires.

You don't want Janet to give you any crap about it's on all the time, they show it a thousand times a day. They show it because it exists, because they have to show it, because this is why they're out there, to provide our entertainment.

The more you watch the tape, the deader and colder and more relentless it becomes. The tape sucks the air right out of your chest but you watch it every time.   [1994]

1. Characterize the narrator of the story. What difference does his point of view make to the story?
2. Characterize the style of the story. What is its effect on the story?

3. The narrator says both that the moment of the man's death is fascinating because it carries the existential truth that every breath could be one's last (paragraph 36) and that television stations exist "to provide our entertainment." Is one of these claims more important than the other?

4. The narrator implies that serial murders are made for and in some sense by videotape: "Taping-and-playing intensifies and compresses the event. It dangles a need to do it again" (34). Does the story confirm or deny this insight? What events do you know of that have been captured by cameras and played repeatedly on television? What was the impact of the repetition? How does videotape affect our ability to understand or perceive things in the "real" world?

KIMBERLY ELKINS

KIMBERLY ELKINS *was a graduate student at Florida State University when her short story, "What Is Visible," was published in the March 2003 issue of* Atlantic Monthly *and chosen for inclusion in* Best New American Voices 2004. *She was a semifinalist in the William Faulkner Creative Writing Competition in 2003 for "Reliquary."*

What Is Visible

I was so fortunate as to hear of the child [Laura Bridgman], and immediately hastened to Hanover to see her . . . The parents were easily induced to consent to her coming to Boston, and [soon] they brought her to the Institution.

—Dr. Samuel Gridley Howe,
quoted in *American Notes*,
Charles Dickens, 1842

Miss Wight says that Julia will be here any minute, and that I must dress to see her. Julia has returned from New York today—a month early, the cook told Miss Wight, *and without Doctor*. I wish that I could have a cameo of Doctor's head to wear as a brooch on the lace collar of my black day dress, above my silver cross. No, no, to wear on all my collars, on all my dresses, every day. And then at night, alone in my bed in my room, I would push the pin of the brooch right through the skin in the hollow of my neck so that his dear face would stay with me the whole night long and I could run my fingers over his raised likeness and never sleep. Miss Wight, my companion, who lives with me here at the Institution, says they almost never make cameos of men, but I don't understand why not. Everyone says that Doctor is the handsomest man in Boston—who would not want him as an ornament? I would carve the cameo myself if I could procure the ivory and a good small knife, and then I might not suffer as unbearably when he's away—six months this time!

I know his features as well as my own: the strong, wide brow and bushy eyebrows; the long prow of his nose between the deep-set eyes; the bristly fur of moustache half covering his upper lip, and the plump lower lip that I have traced with my finger a thousand times, but never met with mine. And his beard, Doctor's beard—I would spend an hour curling each hair with my blade, all the way up to the prominent ridges of his cheekbones. Maybe I could get a large block of ivory with the money I've saved from my sewing and crochet work that people buy on Exhibition Days (oh, look: handkerchiefs embroidered by Laura Bridgman, the deaf, mute, blind girl—we *must* buy a whole set!) and carve a life-size cameo of Doctor's head, large enough to sleep beside me on my pillow. It would be cold to the touch, but it would be something.

Before I work the thick masses of curls for his hair, I might please him with my learning of phrenology—his decade-old passion—by rendering expertly each bump on his skull. Ah, there it is: the well-developed veneration bump right at the top, between firmness and benevolence, evidencing the faculties of his divine creative spirit and his quest for the sublime. I round the twin bumps of ideality at his temples, which display the disposition toward perfection, toward beauty and refinement in all things, and then notch the bulge of individuality between his eyebrows that sets them so far apart and him so far apart from lesser men. And the affection bump on the upper back of his head, so prodigious that the famous phrenologist Dr. Combe cautioned him at forty that he must find an appropriate object on which to bestow its vast benefits—dare I carve that affection with my little knife?

If I had been twenty, as I am now, I think Doctor might have chosen me instead of Julia. Dr. Gallaudet and Mr. Clerc, at the Hartford Asylum for the Deaf, both married their students, and they were just silly deaf girls—nothing like me, the star pupil of Dr. Samuel Gridley Howe, my own dear Doctor, of the world-famous Perkins Institution for the Blind, taught to read with Doctor's miraculous raised-letter books and to write with the finger alphabet (Doctor and I do not believe in Sign). I have been visited by thousands, written about by Mr. Charles Darwin, and given an entire chapter in Mr. Dickens's *American Notes*. Mr. Dickens says that I am the second wonder of North America; apparently, only the roar of Niagara Falls is more impressive than what I have achieved in silence. But I was only thirteen when Doctor's affection bump forced him to choose an object, and look who he chose: Julia Ward, in possession of all five senses and then some, and the author of "The Battle Hymn of the Republic," which, I understand from Miss Wight and others, might be a fitting accompaniment for their married life! And anyone who has eyes to see confirms that Julia has not lost the weight from her last child, and that the fabled blonde locks are now tricked out with gray. Gossip flies into my hands as easily as it does the ears of others, and lands buzzing on my palms like flies.

5   Miss Wight shakes my arm. "Hurry," she spells into my palm. "Julia is waiting for you."

I would like to make her wait, but I am eager for news of Doctor. I tap my way exactly thirty-eight lady's steps down the corridor, take a sharp right, and walk twelve more through the foyer to the public room. My movements are very precise. I enter the room slowly, my head held so high that my bun almost slides down the back of my head, and I am about to take the twenty-eight steps from the door to my visiting chair when the air directly in front of me is suddenly and violently disturbed. Julia has rushed me; she hugs me against her bosom. Though she has three children of her own, I think she fancies herself some sort of mother to me. Does she not realize how I have blossomed and flourished so long and so far without my own mother, with only Doctor to meet my needs (and Miss Wight a little, I suppose)? I pull away from Julia quickly, holding her hand in mine but at a full arm's length. Thank God she no longer stays here at Perkins often, now that she is off waging campaigns with the suffragists and the abolitionists. I gather my skirts and settle into my chair by the hearth, angling it to catch the last of the November afternoon's warmth on my back.

"How was your journey?" I spell into her hand, but before she can switch hands with me, I push on. "How is Doctor? When does he arrive?"

Julia writes a few words about her trip into my hand with her stubby fingers, not half the length of mine. The fingers feel thicker than on her last visit, and her palms, curiously, always sport slight calluses; even Miss Wight, a lady of much lower station, has no calluses. Julia spells as slowly as my uneducated visitors from the country, and I think she should stick to writing songs, because she'd need twenty years to write a book at this slug's pace.

And then finally, in answer to my question: "Doctor Howe will be arriving a week from tomorrow."

"Only a week, not a month?" I quiz her palm, thrilled that I might touch him   10
so soon, but anxious that I have so little time to prepare.

Yes, a week tomorrow, she assures me, and now she is scratching on about her work. I am Doctor's project, and so she must have projects of her own: repressed women, and slaves. I feel a simultaneous affinity and disgust for both.

"Laura, you should speak out on these important humanist topics on Exhibition Days; you have a grand platform from which to share your views. You can write on your chalkboard for the crowds who come to see you, and influence people from all over the world."

"On Exhibition Days," I scribble as fast as I can, knowing she can't keep up and will understand only half of it, "Doctor likes for me to demonstrate my knowledge of geography and—SAUSAGE—reading comprehension—FINGERS— and to show my penmanship, needlework, and ability to recognize people by their hands."

"But, L," she spells now, using only an "L" for "Laura," either because she is lazy or because she mistakenly believes that I must hold her in affection (I allow only Doctor and Miss Wight to use that diminutive), "surely you care that women and Negroes should be free."

"I AM NOT FREE," I write, pushing down so hard that my nails press into her   15
palm. "I am not free to even BE a woman like you."

"Of course you are a woman." Julia's fingers press equally hard, and slide on the valleys of my palm, which has begun to sweat. This almost never happens; I use a dusting of powder to keep my hands fresh and dry, and take pride in my coolness to the touch. No, it is Julia's hands that are wet, and polluting mine! I pull my hands away and wipe them slowly and deliberately on the folds of my skirt.

"You are all black to me," I write. "Everything is dark to me, and everyone is the same. I think it is the same for God." I wish I were brave enough to rip off the fillet that covers my eyes, to force Julia to see what I cannot.

Julia is excited, the tips of her fingers nearly dripping. "You could write that next week for the visitors," she spells. "Exactly that."

"Ask your husband," I telegraph back, and her hand waits and then falls away. I wonder about the bumps on her head, whether Doctor finds them pleasing in their causality. I reach up suddenly, toward where I think the top of her head is, but my fingers instead catch her on the ear, and I hold it for a few seconds, bending the soft, pliable rim up and down, marveling that through this sweet little maze she is able to hear: to let in the whole world and, most of all, the multitude of Doctor's sounds, his laughs and sighs. I know how to laugh too; I laugh a lot. It is apparently the one thing I learned as a baby to do well, before scarlet fever robbed me of four of my senses. And Doctor says my laughter is a beautiful sound, like angels' beating wings. But as I hold Julia's ear, I make one of my other sounds, the ugly ones I am not supposed to make, which Mr. Dickens wrote are "painful to hear." It comes up from the back of my throat, the same sound I have felt from Pozzo, the Institution's dog, thrumming in the cords of his neck. I push my index finger hard into Julia's ear. I push it in again and again, and her hands are on my shoulders and then on my elbow, and so are Miss Wight's, and I could do it harder still, but I take my finger out of her ear and allow them to shove me back into my chair. I feel the vibration in the floor as Julia's chair is moved away from me, out of reach. I slow my breathing and extend both my arms into the air in front of me, my palms facing up in supplication.

20   I know I have been bad, and that Miss Wight has gone to get the gloves, but I am sure Julia is still in the room, waiting. Yes, she takes my hands in hers, trembling, and I let her hold them before I tap on her knuckles to let me spell. I have slapped my teachers many times but never, ever, Doctor or Julia. I have slapped even poor, dear Miss Wight twice this year, and I have grown accustomed, probably too accustomed, to asking for forgiveness both from the persons I have hurt and from God. My friends always forgive me, and so, I am certain, does God— but He absolves me only on the occasions when I am truly sorry. This is not yet one of those occasions.

"I am sorry if I hurt you," I write. "I pray I did not hurt your ear."

"A little," she spells back, "but I am fine. I didn't mean to upset you." Julia is taking this extremely well; I suppose that suffragists and abolitionists also get their dander up from time to time.

"I only wanted to feel for the bumps on your head," I tell her, and she pauses before she answers.

"I do not much believe in the science of phrenology, as my husband does," she writes.

25   I am shocked; to my knowledge, no one has disagreed with Doctor on this, though I myself have had some doubts.

"If we are born with these bumps that govern our character, then how are we to grow and change?" She fills my hand and waits.

I take a long time to gather my thoughts, unsure whether I want to share them with Julia. "I think maybe"—I pause and qualify myself further, this time careful to form each letter slowly and precisely, so that she will understand me fully—"maybe it is possible that phrenology interferes with the idea of free will."

"Yes, yes," Julia writes emphatically, in letters so large that she traces the stem of the first "Y" on my wrist.

"Did Doctor give you the phrenological examination before you were married?" I ask.

"Before we were even pledged," she writes back. Her fingertips bounce lightly   30
up and down on my palm, and I know she is laughing. "Doctor Combe said that my self-esteem was far too elevated. That was the bump of destructiveness you were going for just above my ear, but don't worry, it was not destroyed."

I laugh too, but then Miss Wight tugs on my arm, and all I have time to spell is "Don't tell Doctor," without even a "please," before Miss Wight is pulling the gloves onto my hands. Of course I have to be punished for what I did to Julia, but still she kisses me long on the cheek, and I grab at her skirt as she's walking away. Just a touch, even if only of her scratchy serge, before the glove isolates that hand.

"Tonight and all tomorrow," Miss Wight taps through the thick cotton of the glove. Everyone knows, even the little blind girls when they sidle up and reach for my hands, that I am not allowed conversation when I am wearing the gloves. Though my punishment is deserved, it is worse than the solitary confinement with which they punish criminals: Not only am I cut off from all human contact, I lose all but the roughest impressions of the world itself. Touch is my one intact sense, and it is thickened and furred almost to nullity by the gloves—which on other young ladies would mean they're going out for a stroll. No one can comprehend the multitude of pleasures I receive from my fingertips, the hours I can spend stroking Pozzo's wiry, tangled fur, careening my fingers down the long whip of his tail, rubbing the softness of his firm belly. And the ladies' clothes!: their silks and satins, even the roughness of the out-of-towners' cotton broadcloths, the deep crush of velvet collars, the short, nappy rub of felt hats. And I am never more stirred than when I find the sharp quill of a plume on a hat, and can run my fingers up and down the feather.

Miss Wight taps me on the shoulder, and I know I'm being sent to bed early as further punishment. She takes my arm in hers and walks me down the hallway to my room, but she writes nothing to me tonight, not a word, and I know it's useless to ask her to spell out Doctor's last letter again into my palm. Of course, I have largely memorized all his letters anyway ("L—Yet another phrenologists' conference today—I ought to have my head examined!" "The Parisians feed their dogs at the table." But most of all, "Dear L, I miss you so").

I'm left alone to change into my nightgown; it is the rule that I cannot remove the gloves, even for bed. For my worst punishment, four years ago, I had to wear the gloves in bed every night for a month, because someone—I am still not sure whether it was Miss Wight or, to my greatest horror, maybe Julia, who was staying here because the Institution was short of help for a few weeks—caught me in the act of self-exploration. That wasn't the first time, and it certainly won't be the last, no matter how many times they glove me. I was on my stomach (Tessy, one of the blind girls, let me in on that trick), because of course I can't hear anyone coming, and if I am mightily preoccupied—both hands down, as they were that night—then I won't feel even the slight vibrations from footsteps on the wooden floor. A sudden smack on my upper arm, and I pushed down my nightgown and turned over, my hands up, waiting for the intruder to write upon them. Instead a fist came down on my forehead and NO was rapped across my brow by hard knuckles. I pulled the blankets up under my chin, and a minute later a cold, dripping washcloth was flung at my face. Every night for the next month the gloves were left on top of my nightgown and taken away again the next morning, after I'd changed into my day dress. I made sure that the gloves were spotless and unspoiled each morning, but restraint did not come easily.

35   Though Doctor delayed my religious education until I was sixteen, because he was often away in Europe and did not want me tainted by the doctrines of Calvinism (he is an ardent Unitarian and does not go in much for the actual words of the Holy Bible), I begged him to raise the Bible for me, and after months of labor by the Institution's publishers for the blind, I was given the Bible entire except for Revelation, which he has still refused to let me read. I have devoured that great book (I am a very fast reader), and have never found anything that I believe speaks against my explorations of my body. The spilling of seed is written against, but I don't see how that applies to me. And even if it does (Tessy is the only one who has ever explained the relations between men and women to me, and her effusive ramblings may have left me ill informed, so I could be wrong on this point), I still contend that the unique condition which my Maker has forced upon me for His own unintelligible reasons might also grant me an exception—a special pardon, if you will—when it comes to touching. The sensitive, peaking nipples of my breasts, and that whole silken netherworld, are God's gifts to me. My universe is manifest only through touching, and I refuse to be a stranger to it.

So if Doctor can't ever see his way clear of Julia and the trouble she causes him, then he must at least find me a suitable young man, soft-skinned and well spelled, from among his vast acquaintance. Miss Wight has been promised to the Unitarian minister who has been visiting me; she will leave me soon for this man with deeply ridged fingernails. I am fair to pleasing, I think: dark-haired and pale, my features regular, my nose a little long. "Petite," I have had spelled into my palm many times by visitors, and Mama says I am like a little bird. Who might not love a little bird, I am hopeful, even if it is locked in a dark and silent cage?

But I must remember to eat, to eat more. I vow to chew and swallow all three meals every day to fatten myself for Doctor. My bones poke through my skin, and I think that the soft, plump pillows of Miss Wight's hands are nicer to touch than my birdy bones. Eating is hard, though, when I taste almost nothing;

Art

This section contains a portfolio of artworks chosen as an inspiration for writing. Some of these works of art have been written about by well-known poets; some lend themselves well to comparisons with written works printed elsewhere in this book; all make for interesting "reading" in their own right. Explore the connections listed with the pictures and find some of your own.

Guidelines for Writing about Art

1. Focus on a work of art that presents an interesting connection to a work or several works of literature, or that appeals to you for the thoughts, associations, memories, or feelings it evokes. Make some notes about your responses. Draft a poem, story, analytical essay, or a personal essay in response to one of the artworks.

2. If you intend to write a story or a poem, imagine someone inhabiting the space described by the artwork—that is, imagine the artwork as the setting for characters and action. It might be helpful to think about the influence of setting on character and action in some of the literary works in this book. For instance, the effect of a bedroom on the narrator of Gilman's story "The Yellow Wallpaper" (p. 557) might lead to some thoughts about the painting of Van Gogh's *Bedroom at Arles* (color insert, Figure I-P).

3. You can address the artwork directly—making, for example, an in-depth analysis of it, a description of it, a comparison of literary and artistic treatments of the same subject, or a comparison of two works that resonate with each other—or more obliquely, concentrating more on your response than on the art itself. If you choose to perform a detailed analysis, try to "read" the art as you would read a verbal work. In Chapter 6, we examined how writers use syntax to orchestrate emphasis. How do visual artists indicate what is important? Think about such elements as perspective; tone (ordinarily conveyed by color, contrast, and choice and placement of subjects); "story"; structure and pattern; and mode (realistic? impressionistic? abstract? something else?). How do the elements work together to make meaning? You may, if you like, research the life or career of the artist, artistic techniques used, genesis of the work of art, symbols or stories depicted, or anything else relevant to the work.

4. As always, after you write a first draft, revise carefully. Does your own meaning come through clearly? What elements of your writing (such as point of view, tone of voice, structure, word choice, and word order) might be more effective with revision?

FIGURE I-A *George Bellows (American 1882–1925),* Stag at Sharkey's. *Oil on canvas, 36¼ × 48¼ in. (92.1 × 122.6 cm). 1909. Cleveland Museum of Art, Cleveland, Ohio.*

*Possible connections include Ralph Ellison, "Battle Royal," p. 288 and Richard Ford, "In the Face," p. 723.

FIGURE I-B *Pieter Brueghel, the Elder (Flemish 1525?–69),* Landscape with the Fall of Icarus. *Oil on canvas, 29 × 44 in. (73.5 × 112 cm). 1558. Royal Museum of Fine Arts, Brussels, Belgium.*

See W.H. Auden, "Musée des Beaux Arts," p. 127.

See William Carlos Williams, "Landscape with the Fall of Icarus," p. 1437.

FIGURE I-C *Pieter Brueghel, the Elder (Flemish 1525?–69)*, The Kermess. *Oil on canvas, approximately 45 × 64.5 in. Kunsthistorisches Museum, Vienna, Austria.*
See William Carlos Williams, "The Dance," p. 139.

FIGURE I-D *Pieter Brueghel, the Elder (Flemish 1525?–69)*, The Wedding Dance in the Open Air. *Oil on canvas, 47 × 62 in. 1566. Detroit Institute of Art, Detroit, Michigan.*
See William Carlos Williams, "The Dance," p. 139.

FIGURE I-E *Marcel Duchamp (French 1887–1968)*, Nude Descending a Staircase, No. 2. *Oil on canvas, 58 × 35 in. 1912. Philadelphia Museum of Art, Philadelphia, Pennsylvania.*
See X.J. Kennedy, "Nude Descending a Staircase," p. 1420.

FIGURE I-F *Marko Duricic (Yugoslavian 1956–),* Homage to Cézanne. *Oil on canvas, $76\frac{7}{8} \times 38\frac{1}{8}$ in. 1981. Ackland Art Museum, University of North Carolina at Chapel Hill.*
*Possible connections include Brian Friel, Molly Sweeney, *p. 1487; R.L. Gregory and Jean G. Wallace, "Recovery from Early Blindness: A Case Study," p. 1520; Oliver Sacks, "To See and Not See," p. 1530; Annie Dillard, "Seeing," p. 1559; and Helen Keller, "Three Days to See," p. 1576.*

FIGURE I-G *Willem Claesz Heda (Dutch c. 1594–1680),* Banquet Piece with Mince Pie. *Oil on canvas, 42 × 43¾ in. (106.7 × 111.1 cm).* 1635. *National Gallery of Art, Washington, D.C. Patron's Permanent Fund, 1991.87.1.*
*Possible connections include Isak Dinesen, "Babette's Feast," p. 413.

FIGURE I-H *Winslow Homer (American 1836–1910)*, Hurricane, Bahamas.
Watercolor, $14\frac{1}{2} \times 21$ in. (36.8 $\times$ 53.3 cm). 1874. Metropolitan Museum, New York.
**Possible connections include Kate Chopin, "The Storm," p. 1273 and Marcel
Duchamp,* Nude Descending a Staircase, No. 2 *(color insert, Figure I-E).*

FIGURE I-I *Edward Hopper (American 1882–1967),* Nighthawks. *Oil on canvas, 84.1 × 152.4 cm. 1942. Art Institute of Chicago, Chicago, Illinois.*
*See David Ray, "A Midnight Diner by Edward Hopper," p. 1426.

FIGURE I-J *Frida Kahlo (Mexican 1907–54),* The Two Fridas. *Oil on canvas, 68 × 68 in. (173 × 173 cm). 1939. Museo de Arte Moderno, Mexico City, Mexico. *Possible connections include Chinua Achebe, "Dead Men's Path," p. 963; Sandra Cisneros, "Mericans," p. 554; Chitra B. Divakaruni, "Mrs. Dutta Writes a Letter," p. 966; Pat Mora, "Immigrants," p. 899; and Jim Sagel, "Baca Grande," p. 901.*

FIGURE I-K *Jean-François Millet (French 1814–75),* The Gleaners. *Oil on canvas, approximately 33 × 44 in. (110 × 83 cm). 1857. Louvre, Paris, France.*
*Possible connections include Anonymous, "Swarthy smoke-blackened smiths," p. 253 and Seamus Heaney, "Digging," p. 24.

FIGURE I-L *Claude Monet (French 1840–1926),* Rouen Cathedral West Portal. *Oil on canvas, $42\frac{1}{8} \times 28\frac{3}{4}$ in. (107 × 73 cm). 1894. Musée d'Orsay, Paris, France.*
*Possible connections include Raymond Carver, "Cathedral," p. 1438; color insert, Figure I-F, Marko Duricic, Homage to Cézanne; *Brian Friel,* Molly Sweeney, *p. 1487; R.L. Gregory and Jean G. Wallace, "Recovery from Early Blindness: A Case Study," p. 1520; Oliver Sacks, "To See and Not See," p. 1530; Annie Dillard, "Seeing," p. 1559; and Helen Keller, "Three Days to See," p. 1576.*

FIGURE I-M *Claude Monet (French 1840–1926)* Water Lilies. *Oil on canvas.*
73 × 92 cm. 1903. Musée Marmo, Paris, France.
Possible connections include Basho, "Haiku," p. 14; Marko Duricic, Homage to
Cézanne, color insert, Figure I-F; Brian Friel, Molly Sweeney, *p. 1487; R.L. Gregory*
and Jean G. Wallace, "Recovery from Early Blindness: A Case Study," p. 1520; Oliver
Sacks, "To See and Not See," p. 1530; Annie Dillard, "Seeing," p. 1559; Helen Keller,
"Three Days to See," 1576; and James Wright, "Lying in a Hammock at William
Duffy's Farm in Pine Island, Minnesota," p. 16.

FIGURE I-N *Pablo Picasso (Spanish 1881–1973),* The Old Guitarist. *Oil on canvas, 122.9 × 82.6 cm. 1903–4. The Art Institute of Chicago, Chicago, Illinois.*
*See Wallace Stevens, "Man with the Blue Guitar," p. 1432.

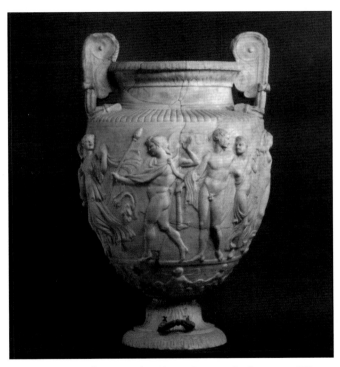

FIGURE I-O The Townley Vase, *Roman, 2nd century AD.*
Found at a villa at Monte Cagnolo, near Rome. The British
Museum, London, England.
*See John Keats, "Ode on a Grecian Urn," p. 1418.

FIGURE 1-P *Vincent Van Gogh (Dutch 1853–90)*, Bedroom at Arles.
Oil on canvas, $22\frac{1}{2} \times 29\frac{1}{3}$ in. (57 × 74 cm). 1889. Musée d'Orsay, Paris, France.
*Possible connections include Charlotte Perkins Gilman, "The Yellow Wallpaper,"
p. 557.

the fever that took my eyes and ears took even the senses of taste and smell. I
move my jaws and grind my teeth and pass my tongue over the lumps of whatever it is that slides from my fork or spoon, but the exercise seems meaningless.
I would much rather dip my fingers into the warm pond of the soup and plumb
its depths for legumes, rend the slick skin from the chicken and peel away the
sheaves of muscle until I reach the hardness of the bone, tear the bread into a
hundred tiny pieces and roll them into buttered balls to juggle over my plate,
squish through the pliant mounds of the potatoes, ravage the soft pulp of the
baked aubergines, and burrow both fists into the pie I will never know the
sweetness of. Soak the whole feast in milk. For me the only delights of food are
in its destruction, and it so disappoints me that I can no longer indulge my play
now—not at my age, not in my position as the world's most famous woman,
second only to Queen Victoria (second only to *Julia!*), and certainly not with
Doctor coming next week.

Yes, yes, he will see me fatter, and I will fatten my affection bump, too. I tried
once before to elevate its standing by beating on it several nights with the ends
of my knitting needles, but that increased it hardly at all. Now I have a whole
week, and this time I will not shy from employing the best tools at my disposal:
the heels of my Sunday dress boots! I slide from my bed and crawl along the
floor to my closet, and there it is: a boot for my affection. After all, Doctor
arranged for Julia to undergo a thorough phrenological examination by the
famed Dr. Combe before they were pledged, so I will make certain that even to
Doctor's less trained eye the enormity of my capacity for love will be impossible
to miss. He hasn't seen me for almost six months, so I think he will perceive my
faculties as not greatly changed but only rendered more pronounced.

I take one boot back to bed with me and pull up the blankets, leaving just the
top of my head uncovered. I hit myself hard on the spot I have studied in the
raised charts he has given me. Harder, harder; and it hurts, yes, it hurts, but my
labors will be worthwhile. Although I do not believe that my character, especially my ability to love faithfully and well, is sealed within the physiognomy of my
skull, Doctor does, and so I rally my cause—Love! Love!—with each shuddering
vibration through my temples and down my jaw. I move the heel of the boot
closer to the front of my head and strike at the positions of benevolence and
veneration, because I know that these are the qualities that impress Doctor most
and that, he reports, are his own largest visible faculties.

Today, today, Doctor arrives today, and I am ready! I have eaten all my meals   40
this week, even asking for seconds on several occasions, much to the surprise
and delight of Miss Wight and the cook. I feel very cheerful and plump, no little
bird but a downy hen. I have been careful, ever so careful, to wear my cotton
bonnet with the string ties all week, so that no one might observe the heightening of my bumps. I have used the excuse of helping to clean and scrub the
premises for Doctor's arrival—I always wear my bonnet when I clean, so that no
strands of my long hair will escape from my bun and be dirtied. Miss Wight has
been pleased, because I am a very good cleaner and she likes to see me clean.
I cannot see the dirt, of course, but if you sit me down in an area and give me

some good rags and a bucket of soapy water, I will scrub and scrub until you tell me the floor is spotless. This quality will also prove me a good wife. The only thing I dislike is wearing the heavy cleaning gloves, but they are necessary to protect the softness of my hands, which Doctor will soon be touching, again and again.

I run the duster over the top of my armoire and let the feathers stroke the heads of my Laura dolls, all sixteen of them. Twelve-inch likenesses of me—with their eyes poked out and little green grosgrain ribbons tied over the eye-holes—were sold across the country and even in England in the days when Doctor's educational exhibitions drew standing-room crowds. As I tickle the tiny molded toes of my Lauras, it occurs to me that if I am to have a *real* life—the *realest* life—then I must no longer allow myself to be quickened by these constant reminders of my fame; and besides, I am too old to play with dolls, to hold mock teas for my sixteen other selves. The little girls who cuddled me are all grown up, and most of them probably have their own babies to play with now, as I intend to. Carefully I take the dolls down from the armoire and place them in a heap on the bed beside me. One at a time, I rock each Laura to sleep, humming a tuneless lullaby I'm sure would make a real baby cry, and before I push the dolls into the dark beneath my bed, I untie the ribbon from the sightless eyes of each porcelain head. I braid the ribbons into a thick, soft plait and then fold it beneath my pillow, because green will bring me luck.

Green is the color I remember with the most pleasure: the green of the grass outside our house, in New Hampshire. Blue still spills from that square of sky visible over the bed where I lay ill for almost a year. Mama says my eyes were bright blue before they shrank behind my lids forever. Red I have a strong and disagreeable sense of, from when they bled me with leeches. And black I know the longest and best, because it is my constant companion. These are the only colors I can recall or imagine with any clarity. Yearning alone glimmers in my darkness, and the shades of my deepest desires cannot be described, just as I am certain that the color that is God is not known to any man.

I pat the hands of my clock's glassless face—Doctor will soon be here. The bonnet comes off, and I check the bumps. They are raised and sore, the veneration one especially; I hope they are not red. I've awakened every morning with a headache from the boot's work, but the pain is nothing compared with gaining my share of life's affections. I arrange my hair in a bun low on the back of my head, so that the bumps will show to their best advantage. I have even plucked a few hairs from the tops of each of them, so that they might be seen more clearly. I change into my best Sunday dress, my only silk one (a rose-pink *robe á l'anglaise* that Miss Wight says gives me color), and lace up the dress boots that have nearly knocked me senseless. I slip the green fillet over my eyes and go to meet Doctor, as nervous as I have ever been.

I know that Doctor is not here yet; I can always tell when he is in a room— the air warms and condenses almost imperceptibly, and its weight tilts me gently in his direction, as if I were borne aloft on the high end of a seesaw but losing balance, sliding slowly toward him on the ground. I sit in my chair by the hearth, pinching at my cheeks to redden them, and wave away Miss Wight's attempts at conversation. I am almost faint with worry when suddenly the air shimmies with heat and I feel the floorboards tense and then shift heavily— Doctor at last! But he doesn't come near me for a good ten minutes, probably talking with Miss Wight, and I force myself to wait patiently for him, like a lady. I used to run whimpering to him like a puppy whenever he came in, but I have learned to wait, no matter how painful it is. Finally the chair beside me is swung around, and his hand takes mine.

"L," he writes, "you're looking very well." 45

I am shaking—he must notice—but I write the next line of our customary greeting: "Thank you, Doctor. And you?" This is our little joke, our routine, and now he lifts my hand to his face so that I can feel for myself how well he is looking.

"Oh, yes," I write, as I limn the familiar perfections of his profile, "you look very well." I round the tip of his nose just as he snorts out a laugh, and my fingers catch his delight. "How was your trip?"

He fills my hand with his travels even as he mouths them, allowing my fingers to float in front of his lips so that I can feel the different forces and velocities of the puffs of air as he exhales the names of places I will never touch: New York, London, and—in a warm fluff of breath—Paris. "Paris," he says again (he knows the exquisite pleasure that the rushing air of any "P" gives me), and in my excitement I rub my fingers against his lips. They are soft but slightly dry—chapped, maybe, from riding in the wind. I am pulling open his lower lip with two fingers when he grasps my wrist firmly and pushes my hand down into my lap. I am too bold today; I have never tried to open Doctor's mouth before. I can tell from the movement of his arm holding mine that he is leaning back and away from me.

"L," he writes, "what has happened to your head?"

"Nothing," I reply. "It is fine, as always." 50

"It looks like a woodpecker got loose on it. Maybe you have banged it on the bed frame."

That is what he sees—an *accident*? I cannot write a thing. My hand is limp under his heavy one, and I don't even let my fingers stray across the beloved hairs on his knuckles.

"Dear L," he writes, as if composing a letter to me, as if we were still corresponding from a long distance apart, though I am trembling right here in his hands, "I have made a special trip back here just to speak with you."

And not to see your beloved wife? I want to write.

"After I returned from Europe, I took a train from New York to New Hampshire 55 to see your family." His fingers stiffen, as if writing is difficult for him, and I worry that he might have contracted the rheumatism. Mama has it, and she can scarcely bend her fingers to converse with me.

"Mama and Papa are well?" I ask.

"Of course," he spells. "They miss you very much, and we all think . . ." His fingers stop, only the heat of them hovering above my palm, and then he etches the words into my soul, firmly and furiously. "We all think it best if you go back to New Hampshire to live with them now."

What happened? Did Julia tell him that I questioned phrenology, or that I hurt her ear? Did Miss Wight tell him? My fingers panic; they scrabble all over his palm, paw at his arm; I am squeezing his hands, reaching for his face. Doctor pulls away until I stop moving and sit perfectly still, my hands shaking but folded in my lap. After an eternity he reaches for my hand again and spells into it very slowly.

"Your education is finished here, L. We have nothing else to teach you."

60   I write as deliberately as he does, though usually we are so quick with each other that no one else could possibly keep up. "Do you not see that I am ready, Doctor, that I am fit for finer things?"

"Do you mean a convent?" he writes, and I realize that he does not see me at all. I shake my head violently "no" and wipe at the wetness soaking through my fillet.

He pats my hand. "Good. I think you have too much temper for a convent."

His fingers strike again in the hollow of my palm, but I am thinking about my favorite Bible passage, Mark 7:32–34. "And they bring unto him one that was deaf, and had an impediment in his speech; and they beseech him to put his hand upon him. And he took him aside from the multitude, and put his fingers into his ears, and he spit and touched his tongue; And looking up to heaven, he sighed, and saith unto him, Eph-phatha, that is, Be opened."

Every night before I go to sleep, I put my fingers in my ears; I spit and touch my tongue; and, looking up to heaven, I sigh and I write the ancient word upon my hand, I spell it across my forehead, I open my thighs and write the letters down that slope, against that place, the only place, that is as dark and silent as the cave inside my head.

65   I pull my hands away from Doctor and stand up. "Eph-phatha," I write across the width of his forehead, between the temples of his ideality, and I laugh because I have finally spelled a word he does not know. I run to the door—it is far fewer steps than twenty-eight when I am running—and down the corridor to my room.

I want to write this all out, but I am denied the pleasure—or pain—of ever being able to read my own words. Doctor will be able to read them, others will be able to read them, but I will not. So I write this out into the air, in a grand and looping cursive, and what is invisible to man will be visible to God.

[2003]

1. Do some research to discover how much of what Elkins writes about in the story is based on fact.
2. Why might a writer want to write a fictional story about a historical character?
3. What part does phrenology play in the story?
4. What role does Julia Ward Howe play in the story?

NATHANIEL HAWTHORNE

OLC

NATHANIEL HAWTHORNE *(1804–64) graduated from Bowdoin College in 1825 and lived reclusively for a number of years in order to write, emerging from his solitude to take his place as a writer. All told, he wrote four novels, including* The Scarlet Letter *and* The House of the Seven Gables, *and over one hundred short stories and sketches. He married Sophia America Peabody in 1842, and in 1853 President Franklin Pierce, a college classmate, appointed him to the consulship of Liverpool, England, a post that he held until 1857. Great-great grandson of one of the judges at the witch trials in Salem, Massachusetts, town of his birth, he explored in his writing the Puritan conscience and the sense of sin and redemption in the American experience.*

Young Goodman Brown

Young Goodman Brown came forth, at sunset, into the street of Salem village,° but put his head back, after crossing the threshold, to exchange a parting kiss with his young wife. And Faith, as the wife was aptly named, thrust her own pretty head into the street, letting the wind play with the pink ribbons of her cap, while she called to Goodman Brown.

'Dearest heart,' whispered she, softly and rather sadly, when her lips were close to his ear, 'pr'y thee, put off your journey until sunrise, and sleep in your own bed to-night. A lone woman is troubled with such dreams and such thoughts, that she's afeard of herself, sometimes. Pray, tarry with me this night, dear husband, of all nights in the year!'

'My love and my Faith,' replied young Goodman Brown, 'of all nights in the year, this one night must I tarry away from thee. My journey, as thou callest it, forth and back again, must needs be done 'twixt now and sunrise. What, my sweet, pretty wife, dost thou doubt me already, and we but three months married!'

'Then, God bless you!' said Faith, with the pink ribbons, 'and may you find all well, when you come back.'

'Amen!' cried Goodman Brown. 'Say thy prayers, dear Faith, and go to bed at dusk, and no harm will come to thee.' 5

So they parted; and the young man pursued his way, until, being about to turn the corner by the meeting-house, he looked back, and saw the head of Faith still peeping after him, with a melancholy air, in spite of her pink ribbons.

'Poor little Faith!' thought he, for his heart smote him. 'What a wretch am I, to leave her on such an errand! She talks of dreams, too. Methought, as she spoke,

---

[1]**Salem village** The time of the story is not stated explicitly, but the use of "Goodman" and "Goody" as titles of address as well as fear of the appearance and actions of the devil on earth suggest that the story is set in Salem, Massachusetts, around the time of the trials for witchcraft in 1692 that resulted in the deaths of twenty people and the imprisonment of hundreds. Hawthorne, who was born in Salem, had an ancestor who served as a judge in some of the witch trials.

there was trouble in her face, as if a dream had warned her what work is to be done to-night. But, no, no! 'twould kill her to think it. Well; she's a blessed angel on earth; and after this one night, I'll cling to her skirts and follow her to Heaven.'

With this excellent resolve for the future, Goodman Brown felt himself justified in making more haste on his present evil purpose. He had taken a dreary road, darkened by all the gloomiest trees of the forest, which barely stood aside to let the narrow path creep through, and closed immediately behind. It was all as lonely as could be; and there is this peculiarity in such a solitude, that the traveller knows not who may be concealed by the innumerable trunks and the thick boughs overhead; so that, with lonely footsteps, he may yet be passing through an unseen multitude.

'There may be a devilish Indian behind every tree,' said Goodman Brown, to himself; and he glanced fearfully behind him, as he added, 'What if the devil himself should be at my very elbow!'

10 His head being turned back, he passed a crook of the road, and looking forward again, beheld the figure of a man, in grave and decent attire, seated at the foot of an old tree. He arose, at Goodman Brown's approach, and walked onward, side by side with him.

'You are late, Goodman Brown,' said he. 'The clock of the Old South was striking as I came through Boston; and that is full fifteen minutes agone.'

'Faith kept me back awhile,' replied the young man, with a tremor in his voice, caused by the sudden appearance of his companion, though not wholly unexpected.

It was now deep dusk in the forest, and deepest in that part of it where these two were journeying. As nearly as could be discerned, the second traveller was about fifty years old, apparently in the same rank of life as Goodman Brown, and bearing a considerable resemblance to him, though perhaps more in expression than features. Still, they might have been taken for father and son. And yet, though the elder person was as simply clad as the younger, and as simple in manner too, he had an indescribable air of one who knew the world, and would not have felt abashed at the governor's dinner-table, or in King William's court, were it possible that his affairs should call him thither. But the only thing about him, that could be fixed upon as remarkable, was his staff, which bore the likeness of a great black snake, so curiously wrought, that it might almost be seen to twist and wriggle itself, like a living serpent. This, of course, must have been an ocular deception, assisted by the uncertain light.

'Come, Goodman Brown!' cried his fellow-traveller, 'this is a dull pace for the beginning of a journey. Take my staff, if you are so soon weary.'

15 'Friend,' said the other, exchanging his slow pace for a full stop, 'having kept covenant by meeting thee here, it is my purpose now to return whence I came. I have scruples, touching the matter thou wot'st of.'

'Sayest thou so?' replied he of the serpent, smiling apart. 'Let us walk on, nevertheless, reasoning as we go, and if I convince thee not, thou shalt turn back. We are but a little way in the forest, yet.'

'Too far, too far!' exclaimed the goodman, unconsciously resuming his walk. 'My father never went into the woods on such an errand, nor his father before him. We have been a race of honest men and good Christians, since the days of the martyrs. And shall I be the first of the name of Brown, that ever took this path, and kept—'

'Such company, thou wouldst say,' observed the elder person, interpreting his pause. 'Well said, Goodman Brown! I have been as well acquainted with your family as with ever a one among the Puritans; and that's no trifle to say. I helped your grandfather, the constable, when he lashed the Quaker woman so smartly through the streets of Salem. And it was I that brought your father a pitch-pine knot, kindled at my own hearth, to set fire to an Indian village, in King Philip's war. They were my good friends, both; and many a pleasant walk have we had along this path, and returned merrily after midnight. I would fain be friends with you, for their sake.'

'If it be as thou sayest,' replied Goodman Brown, 'I marvel they never spoke of these matters. Or, verily, I marvel not, seeing that the least rumor of the sort would have driven them from New-England. We are a people of prayer, and good works, to boot, and abide no such wickedness.'

'Wickedness or not,' said the traveller with the twisted staff, 'I have a very general acquaintance here in New-England. The deacons of many a church have drunk the communion wine with me; the selectmen, of divers towns, make me their chairman; and a majority of the Great and General Court are firm support-ers of my interest. The governor and I, too—but these are state-secrets.'   20

'Can this be so!' cried Goodman Brown, with a stare of amazement at his undisturbed companion. 'Howbeit, I have nothing to do with the governor and council; they have their own ways, and are no rule for a simple husbandman, like me. But, were I to go on with thee, how should I meet the eye of that good old man, our minister, at Salem village? Oh, his voice would make me tremble, both Sabbath-day and lecture-day!'

Thus far, the elder traveller had listened with due gravity, but now burst into a fit of irrepressible mirth, shaking himself so violently, that his snake-like staff actually seemed to wriggle in sympathy.

'Ha! ha! ha!' shouted he, again and again; then composing himself, 'Well, go on, Goodman Brown, go on; but pr'y thee, don't kill me with laughing!'

'Well, then, to end the matter at once,' said Goodman Brown, considerably nettled, 'there is my wife, Faith. It would break her dear little heart; and I'd rather break my own!'

'Nay, if that be the case,' answered the other, 'e'en go thy ways, Goodman   25
Brown. I would not, for twenty old women like the one hobbling before us, that Faith should come to any harm.'

As he spoke, he pointed his staff at a female figure on the path, in whom Goodman Brown recognized a very pious and exemplary dame, who had taught him his catechism, in youth, and was still his moral and spiritual adviser, jointly with the minister and Deacon Gookin.

'A marvel, truly, that Goody Cloyse should be so far in the wilderness, at night-fall!' said he. 'But, with your leave, friend, I shall take a cut through the woods, until we have left this Christian woman behind. Being a stranger to you, she might ask whom I was consorting with, and whither I was going.'

'Be it so,' said his fellow-traveller. 'Betake you to the woods, and let me keep the path.'

Accordingly, the young man turned aside, but took care to watch his companion, who advanced softly along the road, until he had come within a staff's length of the old dame. She, meanwhile, was making the best of her way, with singular speed for so aged a woman, and mumbling some indistinct words, a prayer, doubtless, as she went. The traveller put forth his staff, and touched her withered neck with what seemed the serpent's tail.

30   'The devil!' screamed the pious old lady.

'Then Goody Cloyse knows her old friend?' observed the traveller, confronting her, and leaning on his writhing stick.

'Ah, forsooth, and is it your worship, indeed?' cried the good dame. 'Yea, truly is it, and in the very image of my old gossip, Goodman Brown, the grandfather of the silly fellow that now is. But—would your worship believe it?—my broomstick hath strangely disappeared, stolen, as I suspect, by that unhanged witch, Goody Cory, and that, too, when I was all anointed with the juice of smallage and cinque-foil and wolf's-bane—'

'Mingled with fine wheat and the fat of a new-born babe,' said the shape of old Goodman Brown.

'Ah, your worship knows the receipt,' cried the old lady, cackling aloud. 'So, as I was saying, being all ready for the meeting, and no horse to ride on, I made up my mind to foot it; for they tell me, there is a nice young man to be taken into communion to-night. But now your good worship will lend me your arm, and we shall be there in a twinkling.'

35   'That can hardly be,' answered her friend. 'I may not spare you my arm, Goody Cloyse, but here is my staff, if you will.'

So saying, he threw it down at her feet, where, perhaps, it assumed life, being one of the rods which its owner had formerly lent to the Egyptian Magi. Of this fact, however, Goodman Brown could not take cognizance. He had cast up his eyes in astonishment, and looking down again, beheld neither Goody Cloyse nor the serpentine staff, but his fellow-traveller alone, who waited for him as calmly as if nothing had happened.

'That old woman taught me my catechism!' said the young man; and there was a world of meaning in this simple comment.

They continued to walk onward, while the elder traveller exhorted his companion to make good speed and persevere in the path, discoursing so aptly, that his arguments seemed rather to spring up in the bosom of his auditor, than to be suggested by himself. As they went, he plucked a branch of maple, to serve for a walking-stick, and began to strip it of the twigs and little boughs, which were wet with evening dew. The moment his fingers touched them, they became strangely withered and dried up, as with a week's sunshine. Thus the pair proceeded, at a good free pace, until suddenly, in a gloomy hollow of the road, Goodman Brown sat himself down on the stump of a tree, and refused to go any farther.

'Friend,' said he, stubbornly, 'my mind is made up. Not another step will I budge on this errand. What if a wretched old woman do choose to go to the devil, when I thought she was going to Heaven! Is that any reason why I should quit my dear Faith, and go after her?'

'You will think better of this, by-and-by,' said his acquaintance, composedly. 'Sit here and rest yourself awhile; and when you feel like moving again, there is my staff to help you along.' 40

Without more words, he threw his companion the maple stick, and was as speedily out of sight, as if he had vanished into the deepening gloom. The young man sat a few moments, by the road-side, applauding himself greatly, and thinking with how clear a conscience he should meet the minister, in his morning-walk, nor shrink from the eye of good old Deacon Gookin. And what calm sleep would be his, that very night, which was to have been spent so wickedly, but purely and sweetly now, in the arms of Faith! Amidst these pleasant and praise-worthy meditations, Goodman Brown heard the tramp of horses along the road, and deemed it advisable to conceal himself within the verge of the forest, con-scious of the guilty purpose that had brought him thither, though now so happily turned from it.

On came the hoof-tramps and the voices of the riders, two grave old voices, conversing soberly as they drew near. These mingled sounds appeared to pass along the road, within a few yards of the young man's hiding-place; but owing, doubtless, to the depth of the gloom, at that particular spot, neither the trav-ellers nor their steeds were visible. Though their figures brushed the small boughs by the way-side, it could not be seen that they intercepted, even for a moment, the faint gleam from the strip of bright sky, athwart which they must have passed. Goodman Brown alternately crouched and stood on tip-toe, pulling aside the branches, and thrusting forth his head as far as he durst, without dis-cerning so much as a shadow. It vexed him the more, because he could have sworn, were such a thing possible, that he recognized the voices of the minister and Deacon Gookin, jogging along quietly, as they were wont to do, when bound to some ordination or ecclesiastical council. While yet within hearing, one of the riders stopped to pluck a switch.

'Of the two, reverend Sir,' said the voice like the deacon's, 'I had rather miss an ordination-dinner than to-night's meeting. They tell me that some of our community are to be here from Falmouth and beyond, and others from Connecticut and Rhode-Island; besides several of the Indian powows, who, after their fashion, know almost as much deviltry as the best of us. Moreover, there is a goodly young woman to be taken into communion.'

'Mighty well, Deacon Gookin!' replied the solemn old tones of the minister. 'Spur up, or we shall be late. Nothing can be done, you know, until I get on the ground.'

The hoofs clattered again, and the voices, talking so strangely in the empty air, 45 passed on through the forest, where no church had ever been gathered, nor solitary Christian prayed. Whither, then, could these holy men be journeying, so deep into the heathen wilderness? Young Goodman Brown caught hold of a tree, for support, being ready to sink down on the ground, faint and overburthened with the heavy sickness of his heart. He looked up to the sky, doubting whether there really was a Heaven above him. Yet, there was the blue arch, and the stars brightening in it.

'With Heaven above, and Faith below, I will yet stand firm against the devil!' cried Goodman Brown.

While he still gazed upward, into the deep arch of the firmament, and had lifted his hands to pray, a cloud, though no wind was stirring, hurried across the zenith, and hid the brightening stars. The blue sky was still visible, except directly overhead, where this black mass of cloud was sweeping swiftly northward. Aloft in the air, as if from the depths of the cloud, came a confused and doubtful sound of voices. Once, the listener fancied that he could distinguish the accents of town's-people of his own, men and women, both pious and ungodly, many of whom he had met at the communion-table, and had seen others rioting at the tavern. The next moment, so indistinct were the sounds, he doubted whether he had heard aught but the murmur of the old forest, whispering without a wind. Then came a stronger swell of those familiar tones, heard daily in the sunshine, at Salem village, but never, until now, from a cloud of night. There was one voice, of a young woman, uttering lamentations, yet with an uncertain sorrow, and entreating for some favor, which, perhaps, it would grieve her to obtain. And all the unseen multitude, both saints and sinners, seemed to encourage her onward.

'Faith!' shouted Goodman Brown, in a voice of agony and desperation; and the echoes of the forest mocked him, crying—'Faith! Faith!' as if bewildered wretches were seeking her, all through the wilderness.

The cry of grief, rage, and terror, was yet piercing the night, when the unhappy husband held his breath for a response. There was a scream, drowned immediately in a louder murmur of voices, fading into far-off laughter, as the dark cloud swept away, leaving the clear and silent sky above Goodman Brown. But something fluttered lightly down through the air, and caught on the branch of a tree. The young man seized it, and beheld a pink ribbon.

50 'My Faith is gone!' cried he, after one stupefied moment. 'There is no good on earth; and sin is but a name. Come, devil! for to thee is this world given.'

And maddened with despair, so that he laughed loud and long, did Goodman Brown grasp his staff and set forth again, at such a rate, that he seemed to fly along the forest-path, rather than to walk or run. The road grew wilder and drearier, and more faintly traced, and vanished at length, leaving him in the heart of the dark wilderness, still rushing onward, with the instinct that guides mortal man to evil. The whole forest was peopled with frightful sounds; the creaking of the trees, the howling of wild beasts, and the yell of Indians; while, sometimes, the wind tolled like a distant church-bell, and sometimes gave a broad roar around the traveller, as if all Nature were laughing him to scorn. But he was himself the chief horror of the scene, and shrank not from its other horrors.

'Ha! ha! ha!' roared Goodman Brown, when the wind laughed at him. 'Let us hear which will laugh loudest! Think not to frighten me with your deviltry! Come witch, come wizard, come Indian powow, come devil himself! and here comes Goodman Brown. You may as well fear him as he fear you!'

In truth, all through the haunted forest, there could be nothing more frightful than the figure of Goodman Brown. On he flew, among the black pines, brandishing his staff with frenzied gestures, now giving vent to an inspiration of horrid blasphemy, and now shouting forth such laughter, as set all the echoes of the forest laughing like demons around him. The fiend in his own shape is less hideous, than when he rages in the breast of man. Thus sped the demoniac on his course, until, quivering among the trees, he saw a red light before him, as when the felled trunks and branches of a clearing have been set on fire, and throw up their lurid blaze against the sky, at the hour of midnight. He paused, in a lull of the tempest that had driven him onward, and heard the swell of what seemed a hymn, rolling solemnly from a distance, with the weight of many voices. He knew the tune; it was a familiar one in the choir of the village meeting-house. The verse died heavily away, and was lengthened by a chorus, not of human voices, but of all the sounds of the benighted wilderness, pealing in awful harmony together. Goodman Brown cried out; and his cry was lost to his own ear, by its unison with the cry of the desert.

In the interval of silence, he stole forward, until the light glared full upon his eyes. At one extremity of an open space, hemmed in by the dark wall of the forest, arose a rock, bearing some rude, natural resemblance either to an altar or a pulpit, and surrounded by four blazing pines, their tops aflame, their stems untouched, like candles at an evening meeting. The mass of foliage, that had overgrown the summit of the rock, was all on fire, blazing high into the night, and fitfully illuminating the whole field. Each pendent twig and leafy festoon was in a blaze. As the red light arose and fell, a numerous congregation alternately shone forth, then disappeared in shadow, and again grew, as it were, out of the darkness, peopling the heart of the solitary woods at once.

'A grave and dark-clad company!' quoth Goodman Brown.   55

In truth, they were such. Among them, quivering to-and-fro, between gloom and splendor, appeared faces that would be seen, next day, at the council-board of the province, and others which, Sabbath after Sabbath, looked devoutly heavenward, and benignantly over the crowded pews, from the holiest pulpits in the land. Some affirm, that the lady of the governor was there. At least, there were high dames well known to her, and wives of honored husbands, and widows, a great multitude, and ancient maidens, all of excellent repute, and fair young girls, who trembled, lest their mothers should espy them. Either the sudden gleams of light, flashing over the obscure field, bedazzled Goodman Brown, or he recognized a score of the church-members of Salem village, famous for their especial sanctity. Good old Deacon Gookin had arrived, and waited at the skirts of that venerable saint, his revered pastor. But, irreverently consorting with these grave, reputable, and pious people, these elders of the church, these chaste dames and dewy virgins, there were men of dissolute lives and women of spotted fame, wretches given over to all mean and filthy vice, and suspected even of horrid crimes. It was strange to see, that the good shrank not from the wicked, nor were the sinners abashed by the saints. Scattered, also, among their pale-faced enemies, were the Indian priests, or powows, who had often scared their native forest with more hideous incantations than any known to English witchcraft.

'But, where is Faith?' thought Goodman Brown; and, as hope came into his heart, he trembled.

Another verse of the hymn arose, a slow and mournful strain, such as the pious love, but joined to words which expressed all that our nature can conceive of sin, and darkly hinted at far more. Unfathomable to mere mortals is the lore of fiends. Verse after verse was sung, and still the chorus of the desert swelled between, like the deepest tone of a mighty organ. And, with the final peal of that dreadful anthem, there came a sound, as if the roaring wind, the rushing streams, the howling beasts, and every other voice of the unconverted wilderness, were mingling and according with the voice of guilty man, in homage to the prince of all. The four blazing pines threw up a loftier flame, and obscurely discovered shapes and visages of horror on the smoke-wreaths, above the impious assembly. At the same moment, the fire on the rock shot redly forth, and formed a glowing arch above its base, where now appeared a figure. With reverence be it spoken, the figure bore no slight similitude, both in garb and manner, to some grave divine of the New-England churches.

'Bring forth the converts!' cried a voice, that echoed through the field and rolled into the forest.

60   At the word, Goodman Brown stept forth from the shadow of the trees, and approached the congregation, with whom he felt a loathful brotherhood, by the sympathy of all that was wicked in his heart. He could have well nigh sworn, that the shape of his own dead father beckoned him to advance, looking downward from a smoke-wreath, while a woman, with dim features of despair, threw out her hand to warn him back. Was it his mother? But he had no power to retreat one step, nor to resist, even in thought, when the minister and good old Deacon Gookin seized his arms, and led him to the blazing rock. Thither came also the slender form of a veiled female, led between Goody Cloyse, that pious teacher of the catechism, and Martha Carrier, who had received the devil's promise to be queen of hell. A rampant hag was she! And there stood the proselytes, beneath the canopy of fire.

'Welcome, my children,' said the dark figure, 'to the communion of your race! Ye have found, thus young, your nature and your destiny. My children, look behind you!'

They turned; and flashing forth, as it were, in a sheet of flame, the fiend-worshippers were seen; the smile of welcome gleamed darkly on every visage.

'There,' resumed the sable form, 'are all whom ye have reverenced from youth. Ye deemed them holier than yourselves, and shrank from your own sin, contrasting it with their lives of righteousness, and prayerful aspirations heavenward. Yet, here are they all, in my worshipping assembly! This night it shall be granted you to know their secret deeds; how hoary-bearded elders of the church have whispered wanton words to the young maids of their households; how many a woman, eager for widow's weeds, has given her husband a drink at bedtime, and let him sleep his last sleep in her bosom; how beardless youths have made haste to inherit their fathers' wealth; and how fair damsels—blush not, sweet ones!—have dug little graves in the garden, and bidden me, the sole guest, to an infant's funeral. By the sympathy of your human hearts for sin, ye shall scent out all the places—whether in church, bed-chamber, street, field, or forest—where crime has been committed, and shall exult to behold the whole earth one stain of guilt, one mighty blood-spot. Far more than this! It shall be yours to penetrate, in every bosom, the deep mystery of sin, the fountain of all wicked arts, and which inexhaustibly supplies more evil impulses than human power—than my power, at its utmost!—can make manifest in deeds. And now, my children, look upon each other.'

They did so; and, by the blaze of the hell-kindled torches, the wretched man beheld his Faith, and the wife her husband, trembling before that unhallowed altar.

'Lo! there ye stand, my children,' said the figure, in a deep and solemn tone, almost sad, with its despairing awfulness, as if his once angelic nature could yet mourn for our miserable race. 'Depending upon one another's hearts, ye had still hoped, that virtue were not all a dream. Now are ye undeceived! Evil is the nature of mankind. Evil must be your only happiness. Welcome, again, my children, to the communion of your race!' 65

'Welcome!' repeated the fiend-worshippers, in one cry of despair and triumph.

And there they stood, the only pair, as it seemed, who were yet hesitating on the verge of wickedness, in this dark world. A basin was hollowed, naturally, in the rock. Did it contain water, reddened by the lurid light? or was it blood? or, perchance, a liquid flame? Herein did the Shape of Evil dip his hand, and prepare to lay the mark of baptism upon their foreheads, that they might be partakers of the mystery of sin, more conscious of the secret guilt of others, both in deed and thought, than they could now be of their own. The husband cast one look at his pale wife, and Faith at him. What polluted wretches would the next glance shew them to each other, shuddering alike at what they disclosed and what they saw!

'Faith! Faith!' cried the husband. 'Look up to Heaven, and resist the Wicked One!'

Whether Faith obeyed, he knew not. Hardly had he spoken, when he found himself amid calm night and solitude, listening to a roar of the wind, which died heavily away through the forest. He staggered against the rock and felt it chill and damp, while a hanging twig, that had been all on fire, besprinkled his cheek with the coldest dew.

The next morning, young Goodman Brown came slowly into the street of Salem village, staring around him like a bewildered man. The good old minister was taking a walk along the grave-yard, to get an appetite for breakfast and meditate his sermon, and bestowed a blessing, as he passed, on Goodman Brown. He shrank from the venerable saint, as if to avoid an anathema. Old Deacon Gookin was at domestic worship, and the holy words of his prayer were heard through the open window. 'What God doth the wizard pray to?' quoth Goodman Brown. Goody Cloyse, that excellent old Christian, stood in the early sunshine, at her own lattice, catechising a little girl, who had brought her a pint of morning's milk. Goodman Brown snatched away the child, as from the grasp of the fiend himself. Turning the corner by the meeting-house, he spied the head of Faith, with the pink ribbons, gazing anxiously forth, and bursting into such joy at sight of him, that she skipt along the street, and almost kissed her 70 husband before the whole village. But, Goodman Brown looked sternly and sadly into her face, and passed on without a greeting.

Had Goodman Brown fallen asleep in the forest, and only dreamed a wild dream of a witch-meeting?

Be it so, if you will. But, alas! it was a dream of evil omen for young Goodman Brown. A stern, a sad, a darkly meditative, a distrustful, if not a desperate man, did he become, from the night of that fearful dream. On the Sabbath-day, when the congregation were singing a holy psalm, he could not listen, because an anthem of sin rushed loudly upon his ear, and drowned all the blessed strain. When the minister spoke from the pulpit, with power and fervid eloquence, and, with his hand on the open Bible, of the sacred truths of our religion, and of saint-like lives and triumphant deaths, and of future bliss or misery unutterable, then did Goodman Brown turn pale, dreading, lest the roof should thunder down upon the gray blasphemer and his hearers. Often, awakening suddenly at midnight, he shrank from the bosom of Faith, and at morning or eventide, when the family knelt down at prayer, he scowled, and muttered to himself, and gazed sternly at his wife, and turned away. And when he had lived long, and was borne to his grave, a hoary corpse, followed by Faith, an aged woman, and children and grand-children, a goodly procession, besides neighbors, not a few, they carved no hopeful verse upon his tomb-stone; for his dying hour was gloom.   [1835]

1. Consult the glossary in Appendix B and decide whether the story is an allegory.
2. What does Goodman Brown see in the forest? On the basis of what Brown sees, what does Hawthorne want us to believe about human nature? How does the narrator affect your answer to that question?
3. Characterize the relationship between Young Goodman Brown and his wife Faith.
4. Why does Hawthorne set the story in Salem in the days of the witch trials?
5. What role do Indians play in the story?
6. As lightning flashes reveal respected Salem townspeople at the witch's Sabbath in the woods, Brown cries out, "But where is Faith?" What answer do you think he is hoping for?
7. What is Hawthorne trying to tell us about the Puritan religion and the Puritan imagination? Put the story into the context of Hawthorne's own life.

KATHERINE ANNE PORTER

KATHERINE ANNE PORTER *(1890–1980) was born to a Texas family of four children. Upon the death of her mother when she was two, Katherine, then Callie, and her siblings were cared for by their grandmother. Her death left them all adrift and in financial straits, and Katherine's formal education was over. She continued it on her own by reading and studying for the rest of her life. She and her sisters eked out a meager existence giving lessons in music, physical culture, and dramatic reading,* *and at sixteen she entered on the first of several marriages. After getting a poem published in a trade journal, Porter decided to set out on her own and left for Chicago, intending to divorce her husband and work as a journalist. She soon discovered that she had tuberculosis and had to be in a sanitorium for awhile before she could start work, but after a nearly fatal bout with influenza in the great national epidemic, she became the drama and music critic for the* Rocky Mountain News. *By 1919 she was in Greenwich Village to pursue a writing career, and had published several stories in a children's magazine. Lured to Mexico by friends, she settled there and wrote in English for local newspapers and magazines. Three of her stories were based on these experiences. A move to Connecticut with a number of very gifted writers inspired her and helped her get published. A trip to Bermuda inspired "Flowering Judas," one of her best stories, and another stay in Mexico was followed by a Guggenheim fellowship. She used that money to finance a trip to Europe that formed the basis for her novel* Ship of Fools, *and she formed friendships among the American literati that lasted a lifetime. Upon her return to the United States, she settled in Pennsylvania and completed two of the "short novels" that appeared in* Pale Horse, Pale Rider *in 1939. She separated from her then husband and later married again for a short time, going to Yaddo, the writer's colony, to recuperate. Several moves to New York State, Washington, D.C., and Hollywood, and to many universities for teaching fellowships followed. She gave readings and lectures on radio and television, and the filming of* Ship of Fools *made her financially independent at last. The* Collected Stories *won the National Book Award and a Pulitzer Prize. Her health deteriorated gradually, but she continued to publish almost to the end of her long life.*

The Jilting of Granny Weatherall

She flicked her wrist neatly out of Doctor Harry's pudgy careful fingers and pulled the sheet up to her chin. The brat ought to be in knee breeches. Doctoring around the country with spectacles on his nose! "Get along now, take your schoolbooks and go. There's nothing wrong with me."

Doctor Harry spread a warm paw like a cushion on her forehead where the forked green vein danced and made her eyelids twitch. "Now, now, be a good girl, and we'll have you up in no time."

"That's no way to speak to a woman nearly eighty years old just because she's down. I'd have you respect your elders, young man."

"Well, Missy, excuse me." Doctor Harry patted her cheek. "But I've got to warn you, haven't I? You're a marvel, but you must be careful or you're going to be good and sorry."

"Don't tell me what I'm going to be. I'm on my feet now, morally speaking. It's Cornelia. I had to go to bed to get rid of her."   5

Her bones felt loose, and floated around in her skin, and Doctor Harry floated like a balloon around the foot of the bed. He floated and pulled down his waistcoat and swung his glasses on a cord. "Well, stay where you are, it certainly can't hurt you."

"Get along and doctor your sick," said Granny Weatherall. "Leave a well woman alone. I'll call for you when I want you. . . . Where were you forty years ago when I pulled through milk-leg and double pneumonia? You weren't even born. Don't let Cornelia lead you on," she shouted, because Doctor Harry appeared to float up to the ceiling and out. "I pay my own bills, and I don't throw my money away on nonsense!"

She meant to wave good-by, but it was too much trouble. Her eyes closed of themselves, it was like a dark curtain drawn around the bed. The pillow rose and floated under her, pleasant as a hammock in a light wind. She listened to the leaves rustling outside the window. No, somebody was swishing newspapers: no, Cornelia and Doctor Harry were whispering together. She leaped broad awake, thinking they whispered in her ear.

"She was never like this, *never* like this!" "Well, what can we expect?" "Yes, eighty years old. . . ."

10   Well, and what if she was? She still had ears. It was like Cornelia to whisper around doors. She always kept things secret in such a public way. She was always being tactful and kind. Cornelia was dutiful; that was the trouble with her. Dutiful and good: "So good and dutiful," said Granny, "that I'd like to spank her." She saw herself spanking Cornelia and making a fine job of it.

"What'd you say, Mother?"

Granny felt her face tying up in hard knots.

"Can't a body think, I'd like to know?"

"I thought you might want something."

15   "I do. I want a lot of things. First off, go away and don't whisper."

She lay and drowsed, hoping in her sleep that the children would keep out and let her rest a minute. It had been a long day. Not that she was tired. It was always pleasant to snatch a minute now and then. There was always so much to be done, let me see: tomorrow.

Tomorrow was far away and there was nothing to trouble about. Things were finished somehow when the time came; thank God there was always a little margin over for peace: then a person could spread out the plan of life and tuck in the edges orderly. It was good to have everything clean and folded away, with the hair brushes and tonic bottles sitting straight on the white embroidered linen: the day started without fuss and the pantry shelves laid out with rows of jelly glasses and brown jugs and white stone-china jars with blue whirligigs and words painted on them: coffee, tea, sugar, ginger, cinnamon, allspice: and the bronze clock with the lion on top nicely dusted off. The dust that lion could collect in twenty-four hours! The box in the attic with all those letters tied up, well she'd have to go through that tomorrow. All those letters—George's letters and John's letters and her letters to them both—lying around for the children to find afterwards made her uneasy. Yes, that would be tomorrow's business. No use to let them know how silly she had been once.

While she was rummaging around she found death in her mind and it felt clammy and unfamiliar. She had spent so much time preparing for death there was no need for bringing it up again. Let it take care of itself now. When she was sixty she had felt very old, finished, and went around making farewell trips to see her children and grandchildren, with a secret in her mind: This is the very last of your mother, children! Then she made her will and came down with a long fever. That was all just a notion like a lot of other things, but it was lucky too, for she had once for all got over the idea of dying for a long time. Now she couldn't be worried. She hoped she had better sense now. Her father had lived to be one hundred and two years old and had drunk a noggin of strong hot toddy on his last birthday. He told the reporters it was his daily habit, and he owed his long life to that. He had made quite a scandal and was very pleased about it. She believed she'd just plague Cornelia a little.

"Cornelia! Cornelia!" No footsteps, but a sudden hand on her cheek. "Bless you, where have you been?"

"Here, mother."

"Well, Cornelia, I want a noggin of hot toddy."

"Are you cold, darling?"

"I'm chilly, Cornelia. Lying in bed stops the circulation. I must have told you that a thousand times."

Well, she could just hear Cornelia telling her husband that Mother was getting childish and they'd have to humor her. The thing that most annoyed her was that Cornelia thought she was deaf, dumb, and blind. Little hasty glances and tiny gestures tossed around her and over her head saying, "Don't cross her, let her have her way, she's eighty years old," and she sitting there as if she lived in a thin glass cage. Sometimes Granny almost made up her mind to pack up and move back to her own house where nobody could remind her every minute that she was old. Wait, wait, Cornelia, till your own children whisper behind your back!

In her day she had kept a better house and had got more work done. She wasn't too old yet for Lydia to be driving eighty miles for advice when one of the children jumped the track, and Jimmy still dropped in and talked things over: "Now, Mammy, you've a good business head, I want to know what you think of this? . . ." Old Cornelia couldn't change the furniture around without asking. Little things, little things! They had been so sweet when they were little. Granny wished the old days were back again with the children young and everything to be done over. It had been a hard pull, but not too much for her. When she thought of all the food she had cooked, and all the clothes she had cut and sewed, and all the gardens she had made—well, the children showed it. There they were, made out of her, and they couldn't get away from that. Sometimes she wanted to see John again and point to them and say, Well, I didn't do so badly, did I? But that would have to wait. That was for tomorrow. She used to think of him as a man, but now all the children were older than their father, and he would be a child beside her if she saw him now. It seemed strange and there was something wrong in the idea. Why, he couldn't possibly recognize her. She had fenced in a hundred acres once, digging the post holes herself and clamping the wires with just a negro boy to help. That changed a woman. John would be looking for a young woman with the peaked Spanish comb in her hair and the painted fan. Digging post holes changed a woman. Riding country roads in the winter when women had their babies was another thing: sitting up nights with sick horses and sick negroes and sick children and hardly ever losing one. John, I hardly ever lost one of them! John would see that in a minute, that would be something he could understand, she wouldn't have to explain anything!

It made her feel like rolling up her sleeves and putting the whole place to rights again. No matter if Cornelia was determined to be everywhere at once, there were a great many things left undone on this place. She would start tomorrow and do them. It was good to be strong enough for everything, even if all you made melted and changed and slipped under your hands, so that by the time you finished you almost forgot what you were working for. What was it I set out to do? she asked herself intently, but she could not remember. A fog rose over the valley, she saw it marching across the creek swallowing the trees and moving up the hill like an army of ghosts. Soon it would be at the near edge of the orchard, and then it was time to go in and light the lamps. Come in, children, don't stay out in the night air.

Lighting the lamps had been beautiful. The children huddled up to her and breathed like little calves waiting at the bars in the twilight. Their eyes followed the match and watched the flame rise and settle in a blue curve, then they moved away from her. The lamp was lit, they didn't have to be scared and hang on to mother any more. Never, never, never more. God, for all my life I thank Thee. Without Thee, my God, I could never have done it. Hail, Mary, full of grace.

I want you to pick all the fruit this year and see that nothing is wasted. There's always someone who can use it. Don't let good things rot for want of using. You waste life when you waste good food. Don't let things get lost. It's bitter to lose things. Now, don't let me get to thinking, not when I am tired and taking a little nap before supper. . . .

The pillow rose about her shoulders and pressed against her heart and the memory was being squeezed out of it: oh, push down the pillow, somebody: it would smother her if she tried to hold it. Such a fresh breeze blowing and such a green day with no threats in it. But he had not come, just the same. What does a woman do when she has put on the white veil and set out the white cake for a man and he doesn't come? She tried to remember. No, I swear he never harmed me but in that. He never harmed me but in that . . . and what if he did? There was the day, the day, but a whirl of dark smoke rose and covered it, crept up and over into the bright field where everything was planted so carefully in orderly rows. That was hell, she knew hell when she saw it. For sixty years she had prayed against remembering him and against losing her soul in the deep pit of hell, and now the two things were mingled in one and the thought of him was a smoky cloud from hell that moved and crept in her head when she had just got rid of Doctor Harry and was trying to rest a minute. Wounded vanity, Ellen, said a sharp voice in the top of her mind. Don't let your wounded vanity get the upper hand of you. Plenty of girls get jilted. You were jilted, weren't you? Then stand up to it. Her eyelids wavered and let in streamers of blue-gray light like tissue paper over her eyes. She must get up and pull the shades down or she'd never sleep. She was in bed again and the shades were not down. How could that happen? Better turn over, hide from the light, sleeping in the light gave you nightmares. "Mother, how do you feel now?" and a stinging wetness on her forehead. But I don't like having my face washed in cold water!

30 Hapsy? George? Lydia? Jimmy? No, Cornelia, and her features were swollen and full of little puddles. "They're coming, darling, they'll all be here soon." Go wash your face, child, you look funny.

Instead of obeying, Cornelia knelt down and put her head on the pillow. She seemed to be talking but there was no sound. "Well, are you tongue-tied? Whose birthday is it? Are you going to give a party?"

Cornelia's mouth moved urgently in strange shapes. "Don't do that, you bother me, daughter."

"Oh, no, Mother, oh, no. . . ."

Nonsense. It was strange about children. They disputed your every word. "No what, Cornelia?"

"Here's Doctor Harry."   35

"I won't see that boy again. He just left five minutes ago."

"That was this morning, Mother. It's night now. Here's the nurse."

"This is Doctor Harry, Mrs. Weatherall. I never saw you look so young and happy!"

"Ah, I'll never be young again—but I'd be happy if they'd let me lie in peace and get rested."

She thought she spoke up loudly, but no one answered. A warm weight on   40
her forehead, a warm bracelet on her wrist, and a breeze went on whispering, trying to tell her something. A shuffle of leaves in the everlasting hand of God. He blew on them and they danced and rattled. "Mother, don't mind, we're going to give you a little hypodermic." "Look here, daughter, how do ants get in this bed? I saw sugar ants yesterday." Did you send for Hapsy too?

It was Hapsy she really wanted. She had to go a long way back through a great many rooms to find Hapsy standing with a baby on her arm. She seemed to herself to be Hapsy also, and the baby on Hapsy's arm was Hapsy and himself and herself, all at once, and there was no surprise in the meeting. Then Hapsy melted from within and turned flimsy as gray gauze and the baby was a gauzy shadow, and Hapsy came up close and said, "I thought you'd never come," and looked at her very searchingly and said, "You haven't changed a bit!" They leaned forward to kiss, when Cornelia began whispering from a long way off, "Oh, is there anything you want to tell me? Is there anything I can do for you?"

Yes, she had changed her mind after sixty years and she would like to see George. I want you to find George. Find him and be sure to tell him I forgot him. I want him to know I had my husband just the same and my children and my house like any other woman. A good house too and a good husband that I loved and fine children out of him. Better than I hoped for even. Tell him I was given back everything he took away and more. Oh, no, oh, God, no, there was something else besides the house and the man and the children. Oh, surely they were not all? What was it? Something not given back. . . . Her breath crowded down under her ribs and grew into a monstrous frightening shape with cutting edges; it bored up into her head, and the agony was unbelievable: Yes, John, get the doctor now, no more talk, my time has come.

When this one was born it should be the last. The last. It should have been born first, for it was the one she had truly wanted. Everything came in good time. Nothing left out, left over. She was strong, in three days she would be as well as ever. Better. A woman needed milk in her to have her full health.

"Mother, do you hear me?"

"I've been telling you—"   45

"Mother, Father Connolly's here."

"I went to Holy Communion only last week. Tell him I'm not so sinful as all that."

"Father just wants to speak to you."

He could speak as much as he pleased. It was like him to drop in and inquire about her soul as if it were a teething baby, and then stay on for a cup of tea and a round of cards and gossip. He always had a funny story of some sort, usually about an Irishman who made his little mistakes and confessed them, and the point lay in some absurd thing he would blurt out in the confessional showing his struggles between native piety and original sin. Granny felt easy about her soul. Cornelia, where are your manners? Give Father Connolly a chair. She had her secret comfortable understanding with a few favorite saints who cleared a straight road to God for her. All as surely signed and sealed as the papers for the new Forty Acres. Forever . . . heirs and assigns forever. Since the day the wedding cake was not cut, but thrown out and wasted. The whole bottom dropped out of the world, and there she was blind and sweating with nothing under her feet and the walls falling away. His hand had caught her under the breast, she had not fallen, there was the freshly polished floor with the green rug on it, just as before. He had cursed like a sailor's parrot and said, "I'll kill him for you." Don't lay a hand on him, for my sake leave something to God. "Now, Ellen, you must believe what I tell you. . . ."

50   So there was nothing, nothing to worry about any more, except sometimes in the night one of the children screamed in a nightmare, and they both hustled out shaking and hunting for the matches and calling, "There, wait a minute, here we are!" John, get the doctor now, Hapsy's time has come. But there was Hapsy standing by the bed in a white cap. "Cornelia, tell Hapsy to take off her cap. I can't see her plain."

Her eyes opened very wide and the room stood out like a picture she had seen somewhere. Dark colors with the shadows rising towards the ceiling in long angles. The tall black dresser gleamed with nothing on it but John's picture, enlarged from a little one, with John's eyes very black when they should have been blue. You never saw him, so how do you know how he looked? But the man insisted the copy was perfect, it was very rich and handsome. For a picture, yes, but it's not my husband. The table by the bed had a linen cover and a candle and a crucifix. The light was blue from Cornelia's silk lampshades. No sort of light at all, just frippery. You had to live forty years with kerosene lamps to appreciate honest electricity. She felt very strong and she saw Doctor Harry with a rosy nimbus around him.

"You look like a saint, Doctor Harry, and I vow that's as near as you'll ever come to it."

"She's saying something."

"I heard you, Cornelia. What's all this carrying-on?"

55   "Father Connolly's saying—"

Cornelia's voice staggered and bumped like a cart in a bad road. It rounded corners and turned back again and arrived nowhere. Granny stepped up in the cart very lightly and reached for the reins, but a man sat beside her and she knew him by his hands, driving the cart. She did not look in his face, for she knew without seeing, but looked instead down the road where the trees leaned over and bowed to each other and a thousand birds were singing a Mass. She felt like singing too, but she put her hand in the bosom of her dress and pulled out a rosary, and Father Connolly murmured Latin in a very solemn voice and tickled her feet. My God, will you stop that nonsense? I'm a married woman. What if he did run away and leave me to face the priest by myself? I found another a whole world better. I wouldn't have exchanged my husband for anybody except St. Michael himself, and you may tell him that for me with a thank you in the bargain.

Light flashed on her closed eyelids, and a deep roaring shook her. Cornelia, is that lightning? I hear thunder. There's going to be a storm. Close all the windows. Call the children in. . . . "Mother, here we are, all of us." "Is that you, Hapsy?" "Oh, no, I'm Lydia. We drove as fast as we could." Their faces drifted above her, drifted away. The rosary fell out of her hands and Lydia put it back. Jimmy tried to help, their hands fumbled together, and Granny closed two fingers around Jimmy's thumb. Beads wouldn't do, it must be something alive. She was so amazed her thoughts ran round and round. So, my dear Lord, this is my death and I wasn't even thinking about it. My children have come to see me die. But I can't, it's not time. Oh, I always hated surprises. I wanted to give Cornelia the amethyst set—Cornelia, you're to have the amethyst set, but Hapsy's to wear it when she wants, and, Doctor Harry, do shut up. Nobody sent for you. Oh, my dear Lord, do wait a minute. I meant to do something about the Forty Acres, Jimmy doesn't need it and Lydia will later on, with that worthless husband of hers. I meant to finish the altar cloth and send six bottles of wine to Sister Borgia for her dyspepsia. I want to send six bottles of wine to Sister Borgia, Father Connolly, now don't let me forget.

Cornelia's voice made short turns and tilted over and crashed. "Oh, Mother, oh, Mother, oh, Mother. . . ."

"I'm not going, Cornelia. I'm taken by surprise. I can't go."

You'll see Hapsy again. What about her? "I thought you'd never come." Granny made a long journey outward, looking for Hapsy. What if I don't find her? What then? Her heart sank down and down, there was no bottom to death, she couldn't come to the end of it. The blue light from Cornelia's lampshade drew into a tiny point in the center of her brain, it flickered and winked like an eye, quietly it fluttered and dwindled. Granny lay curled down within herself, amazed and watchful, staring at the point of light that was herself; her body was now only a deeper mass of shadow in an endless darkness and this darkness would curl around the light and swallow it up. God, give a sign! 60

For the second time there was no sign. Again no bridegroom and the priest in the house. She could not remember any other sorrow because this grief wiped them all away. Oh, no, there's nothing more cruel than this—I'll never forgive it. She stretched herself with a deep breath and blew out the light.   [1929]

1. How does Porter establish the point of view in this story? What difference does point of view make to your experience of the story?

2. What is Granny Weatherall's attitude towards death? How does religion function in the story?
3. The story seems to allude to the parable of the ten virgins and the bridegroom (Matthew 25:1–13). How does the parable work in the story?
4. Compare this story to Elkins's "What Is Visible" (p. 1453).

ALICE WALKER

ALICE WALKER (1944–) *was the eighth and youngest child of poor sharecroppers in Georgia, descendants of a slave woman who was forced to walk from Virginia to Georgia with a baby on each arm. On the paternal side, Walker is descended from Cherokee Indians. She attended Spelman College and then received a scholarship to Sarah Lawrence College, but by that time she was immersed in working for the civil rights movement and had to be persuaded to attend. Her college years provided mentors—Muriel Rukeyser, poet, and Jane Cooper, fiction writer. By the time she was twenty-one, Walker had published a short story, "To Hell with Dying," that was praised by Langston Hughes. By the 70s she was teaching at Wellesley College, where she started one of the first women's studies courses in the nation and brought the work of Zora Neale Hurston to light. Walker's writing fame grew with two volumes of short stories and her second novel,* Meridian. The Color Purple *received both critical praise and condemnation from the white and black communities for its harsh realism, won a Pulitzer Prize and the National Book Award, and was made into a movie by Steven Spielberg. More novels, short stories, and literary and social criticism followed, including* The Way Forward Is with a Broken Heart.

Everyday Use

For your grandmama

I will wait for her in the yard that Maggie and I made so clean and wavy yesterday afternoon. A yard like this is more comfortable than most people know. It is not just a yard. It is like an extended living room. When the hard clay is swept clean as a floor and the fine sand around the edges lined with tiny, irregular grooves, anyone can come and sit and look up into the elm tree and wait for the breezes that never come inside the house.

Maggie will be nervous until after her sister goes: she will stand hopelessly in corners homely and ashamed of the burn scars down her arms and legs, eyeing her sister with a mixture of envy and awe. She thinks her sister had held life always in the palm of one hand, that "no" is a word the world never learned to say to her.

You've no doubt seen those TV shows where the child who has "made it" is confronted, as a surprise, by her own mother and father, tottering in weakly from backstage. (A pleasant surprise, of course: What would they do if parent and child came on the show only to curse out and insult each other?) On TV mother and child embrace and smile into each other's faces. Sometimes the mother and father weep, the child wraps them in her arms and leans across the table to tell how she would not have made it without their help. I have seen these programs.

Sometimes I dream a dream in which Dee and I are suddenly brought together on a TV program of this sort. Out of a dark and soft-seated limousine I am ushered into a bright room filled with many people. There I meet a smiling, gray, sporty man like Johnny Carson who shakes my hand and tells me what a fine girl I have. Then we are on the stage and Dee is embracing me with tears in her eyes. She pins on my dress a large orchid, even though she has told me once that she thinks orchids are tacky flowers.

In real life I am a large, big-boned woman with rough, man-working hands.   5
In the winter I wear flannel nightgowns to bed and overalls during the day. I can kill and clean a hog as mercilessly as a man. My fat keeps me hot in zero weather. I can work outside all day, breaking ice to get water for washing. I can eat pork liver cooked over the open fire minutes after it comes steaming from the hog. One winter I knocked a bull calf straight in the brain between the eyes with a sledge hammer and had the meat hung up to chill before nightfall. But of course all this does not show on television. I am the way my daughter would want me to be: a hundred pounds lighter, my skin like an uncooked barley pan-cake. My hair glistens in the hot bright lights. Johnny Carson has much to do to keep up with my quick and witty tongue.

But that is a mistake. I know even before I wake up. Who ever knew a Johnson with a quick tongue? Who can even imagine me looking a strange white man in the eye? It seems to me I have talked to them always with one foot raised in flight, with my head turned in whichever way is farthest from them. Dee, though. She would always look anyone in the eye. Hesitation was no part of her nature.

"How do I look, Mama?" Maggie says, showing just enough of her thin body enveloped in pink skirt and red blouse for me to know she's there, almost hid-den by the door.

"Come out into the yard," I say.

Have you ever seen a lame animal, perhaps a dog run over by some careless person rich enough to own a car, sidle up to someone who is ignorant enough to be kind to him? That is the way my Maggie walks. She has been like this, chin on chest, eyes on ground, feet in shuffle, ever since the fire that burned the other house to the ground.

Dee is lighter than Maggie, with nicer hair and a fuller figure. She's a woman 10
now, though sometimes I forget. How long ago was it that the other house burned? Ten, twelve years? Sometimes I can still hear the flames and feel Maggie's arms sticking to me, her hair smoking and her dress falling off her in little black papery flakes. Her eyes seemed stretched open, blazed open by the flames reflected in them. And Dee. I see her standing off under the sweet gum tree she used to dig gum out of; a look of concentration on her face as she watched the last dingy gray board of the house fall in toward the red-hot brick

chimney. Why don't you do a dance around the ashes? I'd wanted to ask her. She had hated the house that much.

I used to think she hated Maggie, too. But that was before we raised the money, the church and me, to send her to Augusta to school. She used to read to us without pity; forcing words, lies, other folks' habits, whole lives upon us two, sitting trapped and ignorant underneath her voice. She washed us in a river of make-believe, burned us with a lot of knowledge we didn't necessarily need to know. Pressed us to her with the serious way she read, to shove us away at just the moment, like dimwits, we seemed about to understand.

Dee wanted nice things. A yellow organdy dress to wear to her graduation from high school; black pumps to match a green suit she'd made from an old suit somebody gave me. She was determined to stare down any disaster in her efforts. Her eyelids would not flicker for minutes at a time. Often I fought off the temptation to shake her. At sixteen she had a style of her own: and knew what style was.

I never had an education myself. After second grade the school was closed down. Don't ask me why: in 1927 colored asked fewer questions than they do now. Sometimes Maggie reads to me. She stumbles along goodnaturedly but can't see well. She knows she is not bright. Like good looks and money, quickness passed her by. She will marry John Thomas (who has mossy teeth in an earnest face) and then I'll be free to sit here and I guess just sing church songs to myself. Although I never was a good singer. Never could carry a tune. I was always better at a man's job. I used to love to milk till I was hoofed in the side in '49. Cows are soothing and slow and don't bother you, unless you try to milk them the wrong way.

I have deliberately turned my back on the house. It is three rooms, just like the one that burned, except the roof is tin; they don't make shingle roofs any more. There are no real windows, just some holes cut in the sides, like the portholes in a ship, but not round and not square, with rawhide holding the shutters up on the outside. This house is in a pasture, too, like the other one. No doubt when Dee sees it she will want to tear it down. She wrote me once that no matter where we "choose" to live, she will manage to come see us. But she will never bring her friends. Maggie and I thought about this and Maggie asked me, "Mama, when did Dee ever *have* any friends?"

15   She had a few. Furtive boys in pink shirts hanging about on washday after school. Nervous girls who never laughed. Impressed with her they worshiped the well-turned phrase, the cute shape, the scalding humor that erupted like bubbles in lye. She read to them.

When she was courting Jimmy T she didn't have much time to pay to us, but turned all her faultfinding power on him. He *flew* to marry a cheap gal from a family of ignorant flashy people. She hardly had time to recompose herself.

When she comes I will meet—but there they are!

Maggie attempts to make a dash for the house, in her shuffling way, but I stay her with my hand. "Come back here," I say. And she stops and tries to dig a well in the sand with her toe.

It is hard to see them clearly through the strong sun. But even the first glimpse of leg out of the car tells me it is Dee. Her feet were always neat-looking, as if God himself had shaped them with a certain style. From the other side of the car comes a short, stocky man. Hair is all over his head a foot long and hanging from his chin like a kinky mule tail. I hear Maggie suck in her breath. "Uhnnnh," is what it sounds like. Like when you see the wriggling end of a snake just in front of your foot on the road. "Uhnnnh."

Dee next. A dress down to the ground, in this hot weather. A dress so loud   20
it hurts my eyes. There are yellows and oranges enough to throw back the light of the sun. I feel my whole face warming from the heat waves it throws out. Earrings, too, gold and hanging down to her shoulders. Bracelets dangling and making noises when she moves her arm up to shake the folds of the dress out of her armpits. The dress is loose and flows, and as she walks closer, I like it. I hear Maggie go "Uhnnnh" again. It is her sister's hair. It stands straight up like the wool on a sheep. It is black as night and around the edges are two long pigtails that rope about like small lizards disappearing behind her ears.

"Wa-su-zo-Tean-o!" she says, coming on in that gliding way the dress makes her move. The short stocky fellow with the hair to his navel is all grinning and he follows up with "Asalamalakim, my mother and sister!" He moves to hug Maggie but she falls back, right up against the back of my chair. I feel her trembling there and when I look up I see the perspiration falling off her chin.

"Don't get up," says Dee. Since I am stout it takes something of a push. You can see me trying to move a second or two before I make it. She turns, showing white heels through her sandals, and goes back to the car. Out she peeks next with a Polaroid. She stoops down quickly and lines up picture after picture of me sitting there in front of the house with Maggie cowering behind me. She never takes a shot without making sure the house is included. When a cow comes nibbling around the edge of the yard she snaps it and me and Maggie *and* the house. Then she puts the Polaroid in the back seat of the car, and comes up and kisses me on the forehead.

Meanwhile Asalamalakim is going through the motions with Maggie's hand. Maggie's hand is as limp as a fish, and probably as cold, despite the sweat, and she keeps trying to pull it back. It looks like Asalamalakim wants to shake hands but wants to do it fancy. Or maybe he don't know how people shake hands. Anyhow, he soon gives up on Maggie.

"Well," I say. "Dee."

"No, Mama," she says. "Not 'Dee,' Wangero Leewanika Kemanjo!"   25

"What happened to 'Dee'?" I wanted to know.

"She's dead," Wangero said. "I couldn't bear it any longer being named after the people who oppress me."

"You know as well as me you was named after your aunt Dicie," I said. Dicie is my sister. She named Dee. We called her "Big Dee" after Dee was born.

"But who was *she* named after?" asked Wangero.

"I guess after Grandma Dee," I said.   30

"And who was she named after?" asked Wangero.

"Her mother," I said, and saw Wangero was getting tired. "That's about as far back as I can trace it," I said. Though, in fact, I probably could have carried it back beyond the Civil War through the branches.

"Well," said Asalamalakim, "there you are."

"Uhnnnh," I heard Maggie say.

35 "There I was not," I said, "before 'Dicie' cropped up in our family, so why should I try to trace it that far back?"

He just stood there grinning, looking down on me like somebody inspecting a Model A car. Every once in a while he and Wangero sent eye signals over my head.

"How do you pronounce this name?" I asked.

"You don't have to call me by it if you don't want to," said Wangero.

"Why shouldn't I?" I asked. "If that's what you want us to call you, we'll call you."

40 "I know it might sound awkward at first," said Wangero.

"I'll get used to it," I said. "Ream it out again."

Well, soon we got the name out of the way. Asalamalakim had a name twice as long and three times as hard. After I tripped over it two or three times he told me to just call him Hakim-a-barber. I wanted to ask him was he a barber, but I didn't really think he was, so I didn't ask.

"You must belong to those beef-cattle peoples down the road," I said. They said "Asalamalakim" when they met you, too, but they didn't shake hands. Always too busy: feeding the cattle, fixing the fences, putting up saltlick shelters, throwing down hay. When the white folks poisoned some of the herd the men stayed up all night with rifles in their hands. I walked a mile and a half just to see the sight.

Hakim-a-barber said, "I accept some of their doctrines, but farming and raising cattle is not my style." (They didn't tell me, and I didn't ask, whether Wangero [Dee] had really gone and married him.)

45 We sat down to eat and right away he said he didn't eat collards and pork was unclean. Wangero, though, went on through the chitlins and corn bread, the greens and everything else. She talked a blue streak over the sweet potatoes. Everything delighted her. Even the fact that we still used the benches her daddy made for the table when we couldn't afford to buy chairs.

"Oh, Mama!" she cried. Then turned to Hakim-a-barber. "I never knew how lovely these benches are. You can feel the rump prints," she said, running her hands underneath her and along the bench. Then she gave a sigh and her hand closed over Grandma Dee's butter dish. "That's it!" she said. "I knew there was something I wanted to ask you if I could have." She jumped up from the table and went over in the corner where the churn stood, the milk in it clabber by now. She looked at the churn and looked at it.

"This churn top is what I need," she said. "Didn't Uncle Buddy whittle it out of a tree you all used to have?"

"Yes," I said.

"Uh huh," she said happily. "And I want the dasher, too."

50 "Uncle Buddy whittle that, too?" asked the barber.

Dee (Wangero) looked up at me.

"Aunt Dee's first husband whittled the dash," said Maggie so low you almost couldn't hear her. "His name was Henry, but they called him Stash."

"Maggie's brain is like an elephant's," Wangero said, laughing. "I can use the churn top as a centerpiece for the alcove table," she said, sliding a plate over the churn, "and I'll think of something artistic to do with the dasher."

When she finished wrapping the dasher the handle stuck out. I took it for a moment in my hands. You didn't even have to look close to see where hands pushing the dasher up and down to make butter had left a kind of sink in the wood. In fact, there were a lot of small sinks; you could see where thumbs and fingers had sunk into the wood. It was beautiful light yellow wood, from a tree that grew in the yard where Big Dee and Stash had lived.

After dinner Dee (Wangero) went to the trunk at the foot of my bed and   55
started rifling through it. Maggie hung back in the kitchen over the dishpan. Out came Wangero with two quilts. They had been pieced by Grandma Dee and then Big Dee and me had hung them on the quilt frames on the front porch and quilted them. One was in the Lone Star pattern. The other was Walk Around the Mountain. In both of them were scraps of dresses Grandma Dee had worn fifty and more years ago. Bits and pieces of Grandpa Jarrell's paisley shirts. And one teeny faded blue piece, about the piece of a penny matchbox, that was from Great Grandpa Ezra's uniform that he wore in the Civil War.

"Mama," Wangero said sweet as a bird. "Can I have these old quilts?"

I heard something fall in the kitchen, and a minute later the kitchen door slammed.

"Why don't you take one or two of the others?" I asked. "These old things was just done by me and Big Dee from some tops your grandma pieced before she died."

"No," said Wangero. "I don't want those. They are stitched around the borders by machine."

"That's make them last better," I said.   60

"That's not the point," said Wangero. "These are all pieces of dresses Grandma used to wear. She did all this stitching by hand. Imagine!" She held the quilts securely in her arms, stroking them.

"Some of the pieces, like those lavender ones, come from old clothes her mother handed down to her," I said, moving up to touch the quilts. Dee (Wangero) moved back just enough so that I couldn't reach the quilts. They already belonged to her.

"Imagine!" she breathed again, clutching them closely to her bosom.

"The truth is," I said, "I promised to give them quilts to Maggie, for when she marries John Thomas."

She gasped like a bee had stung her.   65

"Maggie can't appreciate these quilts!" she said. "She'd probably be backward enough to put them to everyday use."

"I reckon she would," I said. "God knows I been saving 'em for long enough with nobody using 'em. I hope she will!" I didn't want to bring up how I had offered Dee (Wangero) a quilt when she went away to college. Then she had told me they were old-fashioned, out of style.

"But they're *priceless!*" she was saying now, furiously; for she has a temper. "Maggie would put them on the bed and in five years they'd be in rags. Less than that!"

"She can always make some more," I said. "Maggie knows how to quilt."

70 Dee (Wangero) looked at me with hatred. "You just will not understand. The point is these quilts, *these* quilts!"

"Well," I said, stumped. "What would *you* do with them?"

"Hang them," she said. As if that was the only thing you *could* do with quilts.

Maggie by now was standing in the door. I could almost hear the sound her feet made as they scraped over each other.

"She can have them, Mama," she said, like somebody used to never winning anything, or having anything reserved for her. "I can 'member Grandma Dee without the quilts."

75 I looked at her hard. She had filled her bottom lip with checkerberry snuff and it gave her face a kind of dopey, hangdog look. It was Grandma Dee and Big Dee who taught her how to quilt herself. She stood there with her scarred hands hidden in the folds of her skirt. She looked at her sister with something like fear but she wasn't mad at her. This was Maggie's portion. This was the way she knew God to work.

When I looked at her like that something hit me in the top of my head and ran down to the soles of my feet. Just like when I'm in church and the spirit of God touches me and I get happy and shout. I did something I never had done before: hugged Maggie to me, then dragged her on into the room, snatched the quilts out of Miss Wangero's hands and dumped them into Maggie's lap. Maggie just sat there on my bed with her mouth open.

"Take one or two of the others," I said to Dee.

But she turned without a word and went out to Hakim-a-barber.

"You just don't understand," she said, as Maggie and I came out to the car.

80 "What don't I understand?" I wanted to know.

"Your heritage," she said. And then she turned to Maggie, kissed her, and said, "You ought to try to make something of yourself, too, Maggie. It's really a new day for us. But from the way you and Mama still live you'd never know it."

She put on some sunglasses that hid everything above the tip of her nose and her chin.

Maggie smiled; maybe at the sunglasses. But a real smile, not scared. After we watched the car dust settle I asked Maggie to bring me a dip of snuff. And then the two of us sat there just enjoying, until it was time to go in the house and go to bed. [1973]

1. How is this story about seeing?
2. What would Lucy Grealy have to say about the story (see p. 725)?
3. What role does television play in the story?
4. What disciplines would shed light on the story?
5. Do you think that "art" and "useful things" ought to be in separate categories?
6. This story is often compared to that of the Prodigal Son in Luke 15:11–32. Do you think that the comparison is fruitful?

DRAMA

Looking at Friel through Science

BRIAN FRIEL, *Molly Sweeney*

R. L. GREGORY AND JEAN G. WALLACE, "Recovery from Early Blindness: A Case Study"

OLIVER SACKS, From "To See and Not See"

BRIAN FRIEL

BRIAN FRIEL *(1929–) was educated in Belfast and taught school in Londonderry for ten years. When the* New Yorker *began to publish his stories regularly, he became a full time writer of stories and radio and stage plays. His first dramatic success,* Philadelphia, Here I Come! *was produced at the Dublin Theatre Festival and then in New York City and London to critical and popular acclaim. After that he had plays on the boards almost every year for the next ten years.* Dancing at Lughnasa *won the Tony Award and was made into a film with Meryl Streep.*

Molly Sweeney

Act One

When the lights go up, we discover the three characters—Molly Sweeney, Mr Rice, Frank Sweeney—on stage. All three stay on stage for the entire play.

I suggest that each character inhabits his/her own special acting area—Mr Rice stage left, Molly Sweeney centre stage, Frank Sweeney stage right (left and right from the point of view of the audience).

Molly Sweeney and Frank are in their late thirties/early forties. Mr Rice is older.

Most people with impaired vision look and behave like fully sighted people. The only evidence of their disability is usually a certain vacancy in the eyes or the way the head is held. Molly should indicate her disability in some such subtle way. No canes, no groping, no dark glasses, etc.

Molly: By the time I was five years of age, my father had taught me the names of dozens of flowers and herbs and shrubs and trees. He was a judge and his work took him all over the county. And every evening, when he got home, after he'd had a few quick drinks, he'd pick me up in his arms and carry me out to the walled garden.

'Tell me now,' he'd ask. 'Where precisely are we?'

'We're in your garden.'

'Oh, you're such a clever little missy!' And he'd pretend to smack me.

'Exactly what part of my garden?'

'We're beside the stream.'

'Stream? Do you hear a stream? I don't. Try again.'

'We're under the lime tree.'

'I smell no lime tree. Sorry. Try again.'

'We're beside the sundial.'

'You're guessing. But you're right. And at the bottom of the pedestal there is a circle of petunias. There are about twenty of them all huddled together in one bed. They are—what?—seven inches tall. Some of them are blue-and-white, and some of them are pink, and a few have big, red, cheeky faces. Touch them.'

And he would bend over, holding me almost upside down, and I would have to count them and smell them and feel their velvet leaves and their sticky stems. Then he'd test me.

'Now, Molly. Tell me what you saw.'

'Petunias.'

'How many petunias did you see?'

'Twenty.'

'Colour?'

'Blue-and-white and pink and red.'

'Good. And what shape is their bed?'

'It's a circle.'

'Splendid. Passed with flying colours. You *are* a clever lady.'

And to have got it right for him and to hear the delight in his voice gave me such pleasure.

Then we'd move on to his herb bed and to his rose bed and to his ageratum and his irises and his azaleas and his sedum. And when we'd come to his nemophila, he always said the same thing.

'Nemophila are sometimes called Baby Blue Eyes. I know you can't see them but they have beautiful blue eyes. Just like you. You're my nemophila.'

And then we'd move on to the shrubs and the trees and we'd perform the same ritual of naming and counting and touching and smelling. Then, when our tour was ended, he'd kiss my right cheek and then my left cheek with that old-world formality with which he did everything; and I loved that because his whiskey breath made my head giddy for a second.

'Excellent!' he'd say. 'Excellent testimony! We'll adjourn until tomorrow.'

Then if Mother were away in hospital with her nerves, he and I would make our own meal. But if she were at home she'd appear at the front door—always in her headscarf and wellingtons—and she'd shout, 'Molly! Daddy! Dinner!' I never heard her call him anything but Daddy and the word always seemed to have a mocking edge. And he'd say to me, 'Even scholars must eat. Let us join your mother.'

And sometimes, just before we'd go into that huge, echoing house, sometimes he'd hug me to him and press his mouth against my ear and whisper with fierce urgency, 'I promise you, my darling, you aren't missing a lot; not a lot at all. Trust me.'

Of course I trusted him; completely. But late at night, listening to Mother and himself fighting their weary war downstairs and then hearing him grope his way unsteadily to bed, I'd wonder what he meant. And it was only when I was about the same age as he was then, it was only then that I thought—I thought perhaps I was beginning to understand what he meant. But that was many, many years later. And by then Mother and he were long dead and the old echoing house was gone. And I had been married to Frank for over two years. And by then, too, I had had the operation on the first eye.

Mr Rice:* The day he brought her to my house—the first time I saw them together—my immediate thought was: What an unlikely couple!

I had met him once before about a week earlier; by himself. He had called to ask would I see her, just to give an opinion, if only to confirm that nothing could be done for her. I suggested he phone the hospital and make an appointment in the usual way. But of course he didn't. And within two hours he was back at my door again with an enormous folder of material that had to do with her case and that he had compiled over the years and he'd be happy to go through it with me there and then because not only were the documents and reports and photographs interesting in themselves but they would be essential reading for someone like myself who was going to take her case on.

Yes, an ebullient fellow; full of energy and enquiry and the indiscriminate enthusiasms of the self-taught. And convinced, as they usually are, that his own life story was of compelling interest. He had worked for some charitable organization in Nigeria. Kept goats on an island off the Mayo coast and made cheese. Sold storage batteries for those windmill things that produce electricity. Endured three winters in Norway to ensure the well-being of whales. That sort of thing. Worthy pursuits, no doubt. And he was an agreeable fellow; oh, yes; perfectly agreeable. Frank. That was his name. She was Molly. Reminded me instantly of my wife, Maria. Perhaps the way she held her head. A superficial resemblance. Anyhow. Molly and Frank Sweeney.

I liked her. I liked her calm and her independence; the confident way she shook my hand and found a seat for herself with her white cane. And when she spoke of her disability, there was no self-pity, no hint of resignation. Yes, I liked her.

Her life, she insisted, was uneventful compared with his. An only child. Father a judge. Mother in and out of institutions all her days with nervous trouble. Brought up by various housekeepers. For some reason she had never been sent to a blind school. Said she didn't know why; perhaps because her father thought he could handle the situation best at home.

She had been blind since she was ten months old. She wasn't totally sightless: she could distinguish between light and dark; she could see the direction from which light came; she could detect the shadow of Frank's hand moving

---

***Mr Rice** In Great Britain, doctors are addressed as "Mr." rather than "Dr."

in front of her face. But for all practical purposes she had no useful sight. Other ophthalmologists she had been to over the years had all agreed that surgery would not help. She had a full life and never felt at all deprived. She was now forty-one, married just over two years, and working as a massage therapist in a local health club. Frank and she had met there and had married within a month. They were fortunate they had her earnings to live on because he was out of work at the moment.

She offered this information matter-of-factly. And as she talked, he kept interrupting. 'She knows when I pass my hand in front of her face. So there is some vision, isn't there? So there is hope, isn't there, isn't there?' Perhaps, I said. 'And if there is a chance, any chance, that she might be able to see, we must take it, mustn't we? How can we not take it? She has nothing to lose, has she? What has she to lose? Nothing! Nothing!'

And she would wait without a trace of impatience until he had finished and then she would go on. Yes, I liked her at once.

His 'essential' folder. Across it he had written, typically, *Researched and Compiled by Frank C. Sweeney*. The 'C' stood for Constantine, I discovered. And it did have some interest, the folder. Photographs of her cycling by herself across a deserted beach. Results of tests she had undergone years ago. A certificate for coming first in her physiotherapy exams. Pictures of them on their honeymoon in Stratford-on-Avon—his idea of self-improvement, no doubt. Letters from two specialists she had been to in her late teens. An article he had cut out of a magazine about miraculous ophthalmological techniques once practised in Tibet—or was it Mongolia? Diplomas she had won in provincial swimming championships. And remarkably—in his own furious handwriting—remarkably, extracts from essays by various philosophers on the relationship between vision and knowledge, between seeing and understanding. A strange fellow, indeed.

And when I talked to them on that first occasion I saw them together in my house, I knew that she was there at Frank's insistence, to please him, and not with any expectation that I could help. And as I watched her sitting there, erect in her seat and staring straight ahead, two thoughts flitted across my mind. That her blindness was his latest cause and that it would absorb him just as long as his passion lasted. And then, I wondered, what then? But perhaps that was too stern a judgement.

And the second and much less worthy thought I had was this. No, not a thought; a phantom desire, a fantasy in my head; absurd, bizarre, because I knew only the barest outlines of her case, hadn't even examined her yet; the thought, the bizarre thought that perhaps, perhaps—up here in Donegal—not in Paris or Dallas or Vienna or Milan—but perhaps up here in remote Ballybeg was I about to be given—what is the vulgar parlance?—the chance of a lifetime, the one-in-a-thousand opportunity that can rescue a career—no, no, transform a career—dare I say it, restore a reputation? And if that opportunity were being offered to me and if after all these years I could pull myself together and measure up to it, and if, oh my God, if by some miracle pull it off perhaps . . . (*He laughs in self-mockery.*)

Yes, I'm afraid so. People who live alone frequently enjoy an opulent fantasy life.

Frank: One of the most fascinating discoveries I made when I was in the cheese business—well, perhaps not fascinating, but interesting, definitely interesting—one of the more interesting discoveries I made—this was long before I met Molly—for three and a half years I had a small goat farm on the island of Inis Beag off the Mayo coast—no, no, not a farm for small goats—a farm for ordinary goats—well, extraordinary goats as a matter of fact because I imported two piebald Iranian goats—and I can't tell you how complicated and expensive that whole process was; and the reason I wanted them, the reason I wanted Iranians, was that in all the research I had done and according to all the experts they were reputed to give the highest milk yield—untrue as it turned out—and because their pelts were in great demand as wall coverings in California—equally untrue, I'm afraid; and although they bred very successfully—eventually I had a herd of fourteen—they couldn't endure the Mayo winters with the result that I had to keep them indoors and feed them for six months of the year—in Mayo the winter lasts for six months for God's sake—at least it did on Inis Beag. And of course that threw my whole financial planning into disarray. As you can imagine. And yes, as a matter of interest, they are small animals, Iranian goats. And, as I say, from Iran which, as you know, is an ancient civilization in South West . . . Asia . . .

But I was telling you about—what? The interesting discovery! Yes! Well, perhaps not an interesting discovery in any general sense but certainly of great interest to anybody who hopes to make cheese from the milk of imported Iranian goats, not that there are thousands of those people up and down the country! Anyhow—anyhow—what I discovered was this. I had those goats for three and half years, and even after all that time their metabolism, their internal clock, stayed Iranian; never adjusted to Irish time. Their system never made the transition. They lived in a kind of perpetual jet-lag.

So what, you may ask. So for three and a half years I had to get up to feed them at three in the morning my time because that was 7.00 a.m. their time, their breakfast time! And worse—worse—they couldn't be kept awake and consequently couldn't be milked after eight in the evening because that was midnight their time—and they were lying there, dead out, snoring! Bizarre! Some imprint in the genes remained indelible and immutable. I read a brilliant article once by a professor in an American magazine and he called this imprint an engram, from the Greek word meaning something that is etched, inscribed, on something. He said it accounts for the mind's strange ability to recognize instantly somebody we haven't seen for maybe thirty years. Then he appears. The sight of him connects with the imprint, the engram. And bingo—instant recognition!

Interesting word—engram. The only other time I heard it used was by Mr Rice, Molly's ophthalmologist. In that swanky accent of his—'engram'. And he was born in the village of Kilmeedy in County Limerick for God's sake! I really never did warm to that man. No wonder his wife cleared off with another man. No, no, no, I don't mean that; I really don't mean that; that's a rotten thing to say; sorry; I shouldn't have said that. But I was talking about the word engram and how he pronounced it. That was before any of the operations, and he was explaining to Molly that if by some wonderful, miraculous good fortune her sight were restored, even partially restored, she would still have to learn to see and that would be an enormous and very difficult undertaking.

The way he explained it was this. She knew dozens of flowers; not to see; not by sight. She knew them only if she could touch them and smell them because those tactile engrams were implanted in her brain since she was a child. But if she weren't allowed to touch, to smell, she wouldn't know one flower from another; she wouldn't know a flower from a football. How could she?

And interestingly, interestingly this very same problem was debated three hundred years ago by two philosophers, William Molyneux and his friend, John Locke. I came across this discussion in a Do-It-Yourself magazine of all places! Fascinating stuff, philosophy—absolutely fascinating. Anyhow—anyhow. If you are blind, said Molyneux—he was an Irishman by the way and in fact his wife was blind—if you are blind you can learn to distinguish between a cube and a sphere just by touching them, by feeling them. Right? Right. Now, supposing your vision is suddenly restored, will you be able—by sight alone, without touching, without feeling—will you be able to tell which object is the cube and which the sphere? Sorry, friend, said Locke—incidentally he went to Westminster School where he was flogged regularly—sorry, friend, you will not be able to tell which is which.

Then who comes along to join in the debate but another philosopher, George Berkeley, with his essay entitled *An Essay Towards a New Theory of Vision*. Another Irishman incidentally; Bishop Berkeley. And actually when I say along came the Bishop, his 'Essay' didn't appear until seventeen years after the discussion I told you about between Locke and Molyneux. Anyhow—anyhow. When the problem was put to the Lord Bishop, he came to the same conclusion as his friends. But he went even further. He said that there was no necessary connection *at all* between the tactile world—the world of touch—and the world of sight; and that any connection between the two could be established only by living, only by experience, only by learning the connection.

Which, indeed, is really what Rice said to Molly three hundred years later. That most of us are born with all five senses; and with all the information they give us, we build up a sight world from the day we are born—a world of objects and ideas and meanings. We aren't given that world, he said. We make it ourselves—through our experience, by our memory, by making categories, by interconnections. Now Molly had only ten months of sight and what she had seen in that time was probably forgotten. So, if her sight were restored, everything would have to be learned anew: she would have to *learn* to see. She would have to build up a whole repertory of visual engrams and then, then she would have to establish connections between these new imprints and the tactile engrams she already possessed. Put it another way: she would have to create a whole new world of her own.

How in God's name did I get into all that? The goats! Engrams! Three o'clock every bloody morning! I'll tell you something: three and a half years on that damned island and I lost four stone weight. And not an ounce of cheese—ever!

Not that it mattered, I suppose. I didn't go to Inis Beag to make my fortune. God knows why I went. God knows why I've spent my life at dozens of mad schemes. Crazy . . . Billy Hughes—Billy's an old pal of mine—Billy says I'm haunted for God's sake, always looking for . . . whatever . . .

Anyhow—anyhow. To go back for a second to our friend who knew what a cube was by touching it but couldn't identify it by sight alone. Rice talked a lot to Molly about all that stuff. He said neurologists had a word for people in that condition—seeing but not knowing, not recognizing, what it is they see. A word first used in this context by Freud, apparently. He said that people in that condition are called agnosic. Yes. Agnosic. Strange; because I always thought that word had to do with believing or not believing.

Molly: I didn't like Mr Rice when I first met him. But I got to like him. I suppose because I trusted him. Frank never warmed to him. He was put off by his manner and the way he spoke. But I thought that for all his assurance there was something . . . unassured about him.

He was said to have been one of the most brilliant ophthalmologists ever in the country. Worked in the top eye hospitals all over the world—America, Japan, Germany. Married a Swiss girl. They had two daughters. Then she left him—according to the gossip; went off with a colleague of his from New York. The daughters lived with her parents in Geneva. For years after that there are gaps in his story. Nobody seems to know what became of him. They say that he had a breakdown; that he worked as a labourer in Bolivia; that he ran a pub in Glasgow. Anyhow he turned up here in Ballybeg and got a job in the hospital and took a rented bungalow at the outskirts of the town. He looked after himself in a sort of way. Walked a bit. Did a lot of fly-fishing during the season—Frank said he was beautiful to watch. People thought him a bit prickly, a bit uppity, but that was probably because he didn't mix much. I'm sure a brilliant man like that never thought he'd end up in a Regional Hospital in the north-west of Donegal. When I wondered what he looked like I imagined a face with an expression of some bewilderment.

Maybe I liked him because of all the doctors who examined me over the years he was the only one who never quizzed me about what it felt like to be blind—I suppose because he knew everything about it. The others kept asking me what the idea of colour meant to me, or the idea of space, or the notion of distance. You live in a world of touch, a tactile world, they'd say. You depend almost entirely on tactile perceptions, on knowing things by feeling their shape. Tell us: How do you think your world compares with the world the rest of us know, the world you would share with us if you had visual perception as well?

He never asked me questions like that. He did ask me once did the idea, the possibility, of seeing excite me or frighten me. It certainly excited Frank, I said. But why should it be frightening? A stupid question, I know, he said. Very stupid.

Why indeed should it be frightening? And how could I answer all those other questions? I know only my own world. I didn't think of it as a deprived world. Disadvantaged in some ways; of course it was. But at that stage I never thought of it as deprived. And Mr Rice knew that.

And how could I have told those other doctors how much pleasure my world offered me? From my work, from the radio, from walking, from music, from cycling. But especially from swimming. Oh I can't tell you the joy I got from swimming. I used to think—and I know this sounds silly—but I really did believe I got more pleasure, more delight, from swimming than sighted people can ever get. Just offering yourself to the experience—every pore open and eager for that world of pure sensation, of sensation alone—sensation that could not have been enhanced by sight—experience that existed only by touch and feel; and moving swiftly and rhythmically through that enfolding world; and the sense of such assurance, such liberation, such concordance with it . . . Oh I can't tell you the joy swimming gave me. I used to think that the other people in the pool with me, the sighted people, that in some way their pleasure was actually diminished because they could see, because seeing in some way qualified the sensation; and that if they only knew how full, how total my pleasure was, I used to tell myself that they must, they really must envy me.

Silly I suppose. Of course it was. I tried to explain how I felt to Mr Rice.

'I know what you mean,' he said.

And I think he did know.

Yes, maybe he was a bit pompous. And he could be sarcastic at times. And Frank said he didn't look at all bewildered; ever. But although I never saw my father's face, I imagine it never revealed any bewilderment either.

Mr Rice: In the present state of medicine nothing can be done for people who are born blind, the clinically blind. Their retinas are totally insensitive to light and so are non-functional. There are no recorded cases of recovery from clinical blindness.

Molly Sweeney wasn't born blind. She was functionally blind and lived in a blind world for forty years. But she wasn't clinically blind: her retinas weren't totally insensitive to light. For God's sake how often did the husband, Mr Autodidact, tell me that she was aware of the shadow of his hand in front of her face?

So in theory, perhaps—purely theoretically—her case wasn't exactly hopeless. But I did make a point of giving her and her husband the only statistic available to us; and a dispiriting statistic it is. The number of cases known to us—of people who became blind shortly after birth and had their sight restored many years later—the number of cases over the past ten centuries is not more than twenty. Twenty people in a thousand years.

I know she believed me. I wasn't at all sure Frank Constantine did.

Anyhow, as a result of that first cursory examination in my home I decided to bring her into the clinic for tests.

Frank: Well of course the moment Rice said in that uppity voice of his, 'In   5
theory—in theory—in theory—perhaps in theory—perhaps—perhaps'—
the first time Molly met him—after a few general questions, a very quick
examination—ten o'clock in the morning in his house—I'll never forget it—
the front room in the rented bungalow—no fire—the remains of last night's
supper on a tray in the fireplace—teapot, crusts, cracked mug—well of
course, goddamit, of course the head exploded! Just ex-ploded!

Molly was going to see! I knew it! For all his perhapses! Absolutely no
doubt about it! A new world—a new life! A new life for both of us!

*Miracle of Molly Sweeney. Gift of sight restored to middle-aged woman. 'I've been
given a new world,' says Mrs Sweeney.*

Unemployed husband cries openly.

And why not?

Oh my God . . .

Sight . . .

I saw an Austrian psychiatrist on the television one night. Brilliant man.
Brilliant lecture. He said that when the mind is confronted by a situation
of overwhelming intensity—a moment of terror or ecstasy or tragedy—to
protect itself from overload, from overcharge, it switches off and focuses on
some trivial detail associated with the experience.

And he was right. I know he was. Because that morning in that front
room in the chilly bungalow—immediately after that moment of certainty,
that explosion in the head—my mind went numb; fused; and all I could think
of was that there was smell of fresh whiskey off Rice's breath. And at ten
o'clock in the morning that seemed the most astonishing thing in the world
and I could barely stop myself from saying to Molly, 'Do you not smell the
whiskey off his breath? The man's reeking of whiskey!'

Ridiculous . . .

Mr Rice: Tests revealed that she had thick cataracts on both eyes. But that wasn't
the main problem. She also had retinitis pigmentosa; as the name suggests, a
discoloration of the retina. She seemed to have no useful retinal function. It
wasn't at all surprising that other doctors had been put off.

There were scars of old disease, too. But what was encouraging—to put it
at its very best—was that there was no current, no active disease process. So
that if I were to decide to operate and if the operation were even partially
successful, her vision, however impaired, ought to be stable for the rest of
her life.

So in theory perhaps . . .

Frank: On the morning of Tuesday, October 7, he operated on the right eye to
remove a cataract and implant a new lens.

I was told not to visit her until the following day because the eye would be
bandaged for twenty-four hours and she had to have as much rest and quiet
as possible. Naturally, of course . . .

And a wonderful thing happened that night when I was at home by myself. I got a call from London; from a friend I knew in Nigeria in the old days. Chap called Winterman, Dick Winterman. Inviting me to set up and supervise a food convoy to Ethiopia. Was I interested?

Of course I was interested. The first job I'd been offered in months. But not now. How could I go now for God's sake? Molly was on the verge of a new life. I had to be with her now. Anyhow, as I told Dick, those rambling days were over.

All the same it was nice to be remembered. And to be remembered on that night—I thought that was a good omen.

Mr Rice: I'm ashamed to say that within a week I crossed the frontier into the fantasy life again. The moment I decided I was going to operate on Molly I had an impulse—a dizzying, exuberant, overmastering, intoxicating instinct to phone Roger Bloomstein in New York and Hans Girder in Berlin and Hiroko Matoba in Kyoto—even old Murnahan in Dublin—and tell them what I was about to do. Yes, yes, especially old Murnahan in Dublin; and say to him, 'Paddy Rice here, Professor. Of course you remember him! You called him a rogue star once—oh, yes, that caused a titter. Well, he works in a rundown hospital in Donegal now. And I suspect, I think, I believe for no good reason at all that Paddy Rice is on the trembling verge, Professor. He has a patient who has been blind for forty years. And do you know what? He is going to give her vision—the twenty-first recorded case in over a thousand years! And for the first time in her life—how does Saint Mark put it in the gospel?—for the first time in her life she will 'see men walking as if like trees'.

Delirium . . . hubris . . . the rogue star's token insurrection . . . a final, ridiculous flourish. For God's sake, a routine cataract operation?

Of course I made no calls. Instead I wrote to my daughters, Aisling and Helga in Geneva, and enclosed what money I could afford. Then to Maria, my ex-wife, in New York; yet another open-heart letter, full of candour and dreary honesty. I told her I was busy and in good spirits and involved in a new case that was unusual in some respects.

Then I made supper; had a few drinks; fell asleep in the armchair. I woke again at 4.00 a.m., my usual hour, and sat there waiting for a new day, and said to myself over and over again: Why the agitation over this case? You remove cataracts every day of the week, don't you? And isn't the self-taught husband right? (*angrily*) What has she to lose for Christ's sake? Nothing! Nothing at all!

Molly: What a party we had the night before the operation! Three o'clock in the morning before we got the house cleared. Oh, God! And I had to be in the hospital for ten—fasting. Frank wanted to get a taxi but I said we should walk to get all that alcohol out of the system.

And it wasn't that we had organized anything that night. A few neighbours just dropped in to wish me luck; and then a few more; and then Frank said, 'Come on! This is beginning to feel like a wake!' and away he went to the off-licence and came back with a load of stuff.

Who was there? Tony and Betty from this side; with Molly, their baby; they called her after me; she was just a toddler then. And the Quinns from that side; Jack and Mary. Jack wasn't drinking for some reason and Mary certainly was; so that was a delicate situation. And old Mr O'Neill from across the street; first time outside his house since his wife, Louise, died three months before; and Frank just took him by the arm and said he would fall into a decline if he didn't pull himself together. Anyhow, after two or three beers, what does Mr O'Neill do? Up on top of the table and begins reciting 'A bunch of the boys were whooping it up in the Malamute saloon'—or whatever the right name is! Yes! Little timid Mr O'Neill, the mourning widower! And he acted it out so seriously. And of course we all began to snigger. And the more we sniggered, the more melodramatic he became. So that by the time he got to 'The woman that kissed him and pinched his poke was the lady that's known as Lou'—he always called Louise, his dead wife, Lou'—well of course by that time we were falling about. Oh, he was furious. Sulked in the corner for ages. God!

Who else? Billy Hughes was there; an old bachelor friend of Frank. Years ago Frank and he borrowed money from the bank and bought forty beehives; but I gather that didn't work out. And Dorothy and Joyce; they're physio-therapists in the hospital. And Tom McLaughlin, another of Frank's bachelor friends. He's a great fiddler, Tom. And that was it. And of course Rita, Rita Cairns, my oldest, my closest friend. She managed the health club I was working in. Rita probably knows me better than anybody.

There was a lot of joking that there were thirteen of us if you counted the baby. And Billy Hughes, who was already well tanked by the time he arrived, he suggested that maybe Jack—from that side—maybe Jack would do the decent and volunteer to leave since he was in a bad mood and wasn't drink-ing anyway. And Mary, Jack's wife, she said that was the brightest idea all evening. So that was an even trickier situation.

And at some point in the night—it must have been about two—I'm afraid I had a brainwave. Here we are, all friends together, having a great time; so shouldn't I phone Mr Rice and ask him to join us? Wasn't he a friend, too? And I made for the phone and dialled the number. But Frank, thank God, Frank pulled the phone out of my hand before he answered. Imagine the embarrassment that would have been!

Anyway we chatted and we played tapes and we sang and we drank. And Tony and Betty from this side, Molly's parents, they sang 'Anything You Can Do I Can Do Better' and there was so much tension between them you knew they weren't performing at all. And Dorothy and Joyce did their usual Laurel and Hardy imitation. And Billy Hughes, the bee-man, told some of his jokes that only Frank and he found funny. And as usual Rita, Rita Cairns, sang 'Oft in the Stilly Night', her party piece. That was my father's song, too. She has a sweet voice, really a child's voice, and she sings it beautifully. And as usual, when she had finished, so she tells me, she nodded her head and smiled and cried all at the same time. That's what she—'The Shooting of Dan McGrew'! That's the title of Mr O'Neill's poem! Poor old Mr O'Neill. Somebody told me recently that he's in a hospice now.

And shortly after midnight—long before I had the brainwave to phone Mr Rice—Tom McLaughlin, Tom the fiddler, played 'The Lament for Limerick'! He played it softly, delicately. And suddenly, suddenly I felt

utterly desolate. Maybe it was Rita singing, 'Oft in the Stilly Night' earlier.
Or maybe it was because all that night nobody once mentioned the next day
or how they thought the operation might go; and because nothing was said,
maybe that made the occasion a bit unreal, a bit frantic. Or maybe it was
because I was afraid that if things turned out as Frank and Mr Rice hoped,
I was afraid that I would never again know these people as I knew them
now, with my own special knowledge of each of them, the distinctive sense
each of them exuded for me; and knowing them differently, experiencing
them differently, I wondered—I wondered would I ever be as close to them
as I was now.

And then with sudden anger I thought: Why am I going for this operation?
None of this is my choosing. Then why is this happening to me? I am being
used. Of course I trust Frank. Of course I trust Mr Rice. But how can they
know what they are taking away from me? How do they know what they are
offering me? They don't. They can't. And have I anything to gain? Anything?
Anything?

And then I knew, suddenly I knew why I was so desolate. It was the dread
of exile, of being sent away. It was the desolation of homesickness.

And then a strange thing happened. As soon as Tom played the last note
of 'The Lament for Limerick', I found myself on my feet in the middle of the
sitting-room and calling, 'A hornpipe, Tom! A mad, fast hornpipe!' And the
moment he began to play, I shouted—screamed, 'Now watch me! Just you
watch me!' And in a rage of anger and defiance I danced a wild and furious
dance round and round that room; then out to the hall; then round the
kitchen; then back to the room again and round it a third time. Mad and wild
and frenzied. But so adroit, so efficient. No timidity, no hesitations, no falter-
ings. Not a glass overturned, not a shoulder brushed. Weaving between all
those people, darting between chairs and stools and cushions and bottles and
glasses with complete assurance, with absolute confidence. Until Frank said
something to Tom and stopped him playing.

God knows how I didn't kill myself or injure somebody. Or indeed how
long it lasted. But it must have been terrifying to watch because, when I
stopped, the room was hushed.

Frank whispered something to me. I don't know what he said—I was suddenly lost and anxious and frightened. I remember calling, 'Rita? Where are
you, Rita?'

'Here at the window,' she said. And I stumbled, groped my way to her and
sat beside her. 'Come on, sweetie,' she said. 'We'll have none of that. You're
not allowed to cry. I'm the only one that's allowed to give a performance and
then cry.'

10   *Mr Rice:* The night before I operated on Molly Sweeney I thought about that high
summer in my thirty-second year. Cairo. Another lecture; another conference;
another posh hotel. As usual we all met up: Roger Bloomstein from New York,
Hans Girder from Berlin, Hiroko Matoba from Kyoto, myself. The meteors. The
young turks. The four horsemen. Oslo last month. Helsinki next week. Paris the
week after. That luminous, resplendent life. Those glowing, soaring careers.

Maria left the children with parents in Geneva and flew down to join us. Still wan and translucent after the birth of Helga. And so beautiful; my God, so beautiful. We had a dinner party for her the night she arrived. Roger was master-of-ceremonies. Toasted her with his usual elegance. Said she was our Venus—no, our Galatea. She smiled her secret smile and said each of us was her Icarus.

Insatiable years. Work. Airports. Dinners. Laughter. Operating theatres. Conferences. Gossip. Publications. The professional jealousies and the necessary vigilance. The relentless, devouring excitement. But above all, above all the hunger to accomplish, the greed for achievement.

Shards of those memories came back to me on the night before I operated on Molly Sweeney on Tuesday, October 7. I had had a few drinks. I had had a lot of drinks. The fire was dead. I was drifting in and out of sleep.

Then the phone rang; an anxious sound at two in the morning. By the time I had pulled myself together and got to it, it had stopped. Wrong number probably.

I had another drink and sat beside the dead fire and relived for the hundredth time that other phone-call. The small hours of the morning, too. In Cairo. That high summer of my thirty-second year.

It was Roger Bloomstein. Brilliant Roger. Treacherous Icarus. To tell me that Maria and he were at the airport and about to step on a plane for New York. They were deeply in love. They would be in touch in a few days. He was very sorry to have to tell me this. He hoped that in time I would see the situation from their point of view and come to understand it. And he hung up.

The mind was instantly paralysed. All I could think was: He's confusing seeing with understanding. Come on, Bloomstein. What's the matter with you? Seeing isn't understanding.

You know that! Don't talk rubbish, man!

And then . . . and then . . . oh, Jesus, Maria . . .

Frank: Just as I was about to step into bed that night—that same Tuesday night that Dick Winterman phoned—the night of the operation—I was on the point of stepping into bed when suddenly, suddenly I remembered: Ethiopia is Abyssinia! Abyssinia is Ethiopia! They're the same place! Ethiopia is the new name for the old Abyssinia! For God's sake only last year the *National Geographic* magazine had a brilliant article on it with all these stunning photographs. For God's sake I could write a book about Ethiopia! Absolutely *the* most interesting country in the world! Let me give you one fascinating fact about the name, the name Abyssinia. The name Abyssinia is derived from the word 'habesh'; and the word 'habesh' means mixed—on account of the varied nature of its peoples. But interestingly, interestingly the people themselves always called themselves Ethiopians, never Abyssinians, because they considered the word Abyssinia and Abyssinians as derogatory—they didn't want to be thought of as mixed! So now the place is officially what the people themselves always called it—Ethiopia. Fascinating!

But of course I had to say no to Dick. As I said. Those rambling days were over. Molly was about to inherit a new world; and I had a sense—stupid, I know—I had a sense that maybe I was, too.

Pity to miss Abyssinia all the same—the one place in the whole world I've always dreamed of visiting; a phantom desire, a fantasy in the head. Pity to miss that.

You shouldn't have dangled it in front of me, Dick Winterman. Bloody, bloody heartbreaking.

Molly: I remember so well the first day Frank came to the health club. That was the first time I'd met him. I was on a coffee-break. A Friday afternoon.

I had known of him for years of course. Rita Cairns and his friend Billy Hughes used to go out occasionally and I'd hear his name mentioned. She never said anything bad about him; but when his name came up, you got the feeling he was a bit . . . different.

Anyhow that Friday he came into the club and Rita introduced us and we chatted. And for the whole ten minutes of my coffee-break he gave me a talk about a feasibility study he was doing on the blueback salmon, known in Oregon as sockeye and in Alaska as redfish, and of his plan to introduce it to Irish salmon farmers because it has the lowest wastage rate in all canning factories where it is used.

When he left I said to Rita that I'd never met a more enthusiastic man in my life. And Rita said in her laconic way, 'Sweetie, who wants their enthusiasm focussed on bluebacks for God's sake?'

Anyhow, ten minutes after he left, the phone rang. Could we meet that evening? Saturday? Sunday? What about a walk, a meal, a concert? Just a chat?

I asked him to call me the following Friday.

I thought a lot about him that week. I suppose he was the first man I really knew—apart from my father. And I liked his energy. I liked his enthusiasm. I liked his passion. Maybe what I really liked about him was that he was everything my father wasn't.

Frank: I spent a week in the library—the week after I first met her—one full week immersing myself in books and encyclopaedias and magazines and articles—anything, everything I could find about eyes and vision and eye-diseases and blindness.

Fascinating. I can't tell you—fascinating. I look out of my bedroom window and at a single glance I see the front garden and the road beyond and cars and buses and the tennis-courts on the far side and people playing on them and the hills beyond that. Everything—all those details and dozens more—all seen in one immediate, comprehensive perception. But Molly's world isn't perceived instantly, comprehensively. She composes a world from a sequence of impressions; one after the other, in time. For example, she knows that this is a carving knife because first she can feel the handle; then she can feel this long blade; then this sharp edge. In sequence. In time. What is this object? These are ears. This is a furry body. Those are paws. That is a long tail. Ah, a cat! In sequence. Sequentially.

Right? Right. Now a personal question. You are going to ask this blind lady out for an evening. What would be the ideal entertainment for somebody like her? A meal? A concert? A walk? Maybe a swim? Billy Hughes says she's a wonderful swimmer. (*He shakes his head slowly.*)

The week in the library pays off. Know the answer instantly. Dancing. Take her dancing. With her disability the perfect, the absolutely perfect relaxation. Forget about space, distance, who's close, who's far, who's approaching. Forget about time. This is not a sequence of events. This is one continuous, delightful event. Nothing leads to nothing else. There is only now. There is nothing subsequent. I am your eyes, your ears, your location, your sense of space. Trust me.

Dancing. Obvious.

Straight into a phone-box and asked her would she come with me to the Hikers Club dance the following Saturday. It'll be small, I said; more like a party. What do you say?

Silence.

We'll ask Billy and Rita and we'll make it a foursome and we'll have our own table and our own fun.

Not a word.

Please, Molly.

In my heart of hearts I really didn't think she'd say yes. For God's sake why should she? Middle-aged. No skill. No job. No prospect of a job. Two rooms above Kelly's cake-shop. And not exactly Rudolf Valentino. And when she did speak, when she said very politely, 'Thank you, Frank. I'd love to go,' do you know what I said? 'All right then.' Bloody brilliant.

But I vowed to myself in that phone-box, I made a vow there and then that at the dance on Saturday night I wouldn't open the big mouth—big?— enormous for Christ's sake!—I wouldn't open it once all night, all week.

Talking of Valentino, in point of fact Valentino was no Adonis himself. Average height; average looks; mediocre talent. And if he hadn't died so young—in 1926—he was only 31—and in those mysterious circumstances that were never fully explained—he would never have become the cult figure the studios worked so hard to . . .

Anyhow . . .

Molly: As usual Rita was wonderful. She washed my hair, my bloody useless hair—I can do nothing with it—she washed it in this special shampoo she concocted herself. Then she pulled it all away back from my face and piled it up, just here, and held it in place with her mother's silver ornamental comb. And she gave me her black shoes and her new woollen dress she'd just bought for her brother's wedding.

'There's still something not right,' she said. 'You still remind me of my Aunt Madge. Here—try these.' And she whipped off her earrings and put them on me. 'Now we have it,' she said. 'Bloody lethal. Francis Constantine, you're a dead duck!'

Frank: She had the time of her life. Knew she would. We danced every dance. 15 Sang every song at the top of our voices. Ate an enormous supper. Even won a spot prize: a tin of shortbread and a bottle of Albanian wine. The samba, actually. I wasn't bad at the samba once.

Dancing. I knew. I explained the whole thing to her. She had to agree. For God's sake she didn't have to say a word—she just glowed.

Molly: It was almost at the end of the night—we were doing an old-time waltz—and suddenly he said to me, 'You are such a beautiful woman, Molly.'

Nobody had ever said anything like that to me before. I was afraid I might cry. And before I could say a word, he plunged on: 'Of course I know that the very idea of appearance, of how things look, can't have much meaning for you. I do understand that. And maybe at heart you're a real philosophical sceptic because you question not only the idea of appearance but probably the existence of external reality itself. Do you, Molly?'

Honest to God . . . the second last dance at the Hikers Club . . . a leisurely, old-time waltz . . .

And I knew that night that he would ask me to marry him. Because he liked me—I knew he did. And because of my blindness—oh, yes, that fascinated him. He couldn't resist the different, the strange. I think he believed that some elusive off-beat truth resided in the quirky, the off-beat. I suppose that's what made him such a restless man. Rita of course said it was inevitable he would propose to me. 'All part of the same pattern, sweetie: bees—whales—Iranian goats—Molly Sweeney.'

Maybe she was right.

And I knew, too, after that night in the Hikers Club, that if he did ask me to marry him, for no very good reason at all I would probably say yes.

Mr Rice: The morning of the operation I stood at the window of my office and watched them walk up the hospital drive. It was a blustery morning, threatening rain.

She didn't have her cane and she didn't hold his arm. But she moved briskly with her usual confidence; her head high; her face alert and eager. In her right hand she carried a grey, overnight bag.

He was on her left. Now in the open air a smaller presence in a shabby raincoat and cap; his hands clasped behind his back; his eyes on the ground; his head bowed slightly against the wind so that he looked . . . passive. Not a trace of the assurance, the ebullience, that relentless energy.

And I thought: Are they really such an unlikely couple? And I wondered what hopes moved in them as they came towards me. Were they modest? Reasonable? Outrageous? Of course, of course they were outrageous.

And suddenly and passionately and with utter selflessness I wanted nothing more in the world than that *their* inordinate hopes would be fulfilled, that I could give them their miracle. And I whispered to Hans Girder and to Matoba and to Murnaghan and to Bloomstein—yes, to Bloomstein, too!—to gather round me this morning and steady my unsteady hand and endow me with all their exquisite skills.

Because as I watched them approach the hospital that blustery morning, one head alert, one head bowed, I was suddenly full of anxiety for both of them. Because I was afraid—even though she was in the hands of the best team in the whole world to deliver her miracle, because she was in the hands of the best team in the whole world—I was fearful, I suddenly knew that that courageous woman had everything, everything to lose.

Act Two

Molly: The morning the bandages were to be removed a staff nurse spent half-an-hour preparing me for Mr Rice. It wasn't really her job, she told me; but this was my big day and I had to look my best and she was happy to do it.

So she sponged my face and hands. She made me clean my teeth again. She wondered did I use lipstick—maybe just for today? She did the best she could with my hair, God help her. She looked at my fingernails and suggested that a touch of clear varnish would be nice. She straightened the bow at the front of my nightdress and adjusted the collar of my dressing-gown. She put a dab of her own very special perfume on each of my wrists—she got it from a cousin in Paris. Then she stood back and surveyed me and said,

'Now. That's better. You'll find that from now on—if everything goes well of course—you'll find that you'll become very aware of your appearance. They all do for some reason. Don't be nervous. You look just lovely. He'll be here any minute now.'

I asked her where the bathroom was.

'At the end of the corridor. Last door on the right. I'll bring you.'

'No,' I said. 'I'll find it.'

I didn't need to go to the bathroom. I just wanted to take perhaps a last walk; in my own world; by myself.

I don't know what I expected when the bandages would be removed. I think maybe I didn't allow myself any expectations. I knew that in his heart Frank believed that somehow, miraculously, I would be given the perfect vision that sighted people have, even though Mr Rice had told us again and again that my eyes weren't capable of that vision. And I knew what Mr Rice hoped for: that I would have partial sight. 'That would be a total success for me' is what he said. But I'm sure he meant it would be great for all of us.

As for myself, if I had any hope, I suppose it was that neither Frank nor Mr Rice would be too disappointed because it had all become so important for them.

No, that's not accurate either. Yes, I did want to see. For God's sake of course I wanted to see. But that wasn't an expectation, not even a mad hope. If there was a phantom desire, a fantasy in my head, it was this. That perhaps by some means I might be afforded a brief excursion to this land of vision; not to live there—just to visit. And during my stay to devour it again and again with greedy, ravenous eyes. To gorge on all those luminous sights and wonderful spectacles until I knew every detail intimately and utterly—every ocean, every leaf, every field, every star, every tiny flower. And then, oh yes, then to return home to my own world with all that rare understanding within me for ever.

No, that wasn't even a phantom desire. Just a stupid fantasy. And it came into my head again when that poor nurse was trying to prettify me for Mr Rice. And I thought to myself: It's like being back at school—I'm getting dressed up for the annual excursion.

When Mr Rice did arrive, even before he touched me, I knew by his quick, shallow breathing that he was far more nervous than I was. And then as he took off the bandages his hands trembled and fumbled.

'There we are,' he said. 'All off. How does that feel?'

'Fine,' I said. Even though I felt nothing. Were all the bandages off?

'Now, Molly. In your own time. Tell me what you see.'

Nothing. Nothing at all. Then out of the void a blur; a haze; a body of mist; a confusion of light, colour, movement. It had no meaning.

'Well?' he said. 'Anything? Anything at all?'

I thought: Don't panic; a voice comes from a face; that blur is his face; look at him.

'Well? Anything?'

Something moving; large; white. The nurse? And lines, black lines, vertical lines. The bed? The door?

'Anything, Molly?' A bright light that hurt. The window maybe?

'I'm holding my hand before your eyes, Molly. Can you see it?'

A reddish blob in front of my face; rotating; liquefying; pulsating. Keep calm. Concentrate.

'Can you see my hand, Molly?'

'I think so . . . I'm not sure . . .'

'Now I'm moving my hand slowly.'

'Yes . . . yes . . .'

'Do you see my hand moving?'

'Yes . . .'

'What way is it moving?'

'Yes . . . I do see it . . . up and down . . . up and down . . . Yes! I see it! I do! Yes! Moving up and down! Yes-yes-yes!'

'Splendid!' he said. 'Absolutely splendid! You are a clever lady!'

And there was such delight in his voice. And my head was suddenly giddy. And I thought for a moment—for a moment I thought I was going to faint.

Frank: There was some mix-up about what time the bandages were to be removed. At least I was confused. For some reason I got it into my head that they were to be taken off at eight in the morning, October 8, the day after the operation. A Wednesday, I remember, because I was doing a crash-course in speed-reading and I had to switch from the morning to the afternoon class for that day.

So; eight o'clock sharp; there I was sitting in the hospital, all dickied up— the good suit, the shoes polished, the clean shirt, the new tie, and with my bunch of flowers, waiting to be summoned to Molly's ward.

The call finally did come—at a quarter to twelve. Ward 10. Room 17. And of course by then I knew the operation was a disaster.

Knocked. Went in. Rice was there. And a staff nurse, a tiny little woman. And an Indian man—the anaesthetist, I think. The moment I entered he rushed out without saying a word.

And Molly. Sitting very straight in a white chair beside her bed. Her hair pulled away back from her face and piled up just here. Wearing a lime-green dressing-gown that Rita Cairns had lent her and the blue slippers I got her for her last birthday.

There was a small bruise mark below her right eye.

I thought: How young she looks, and so beautiful, so very beautiful.

'There she is,' said Rice. 'How does she look?'

'She looks well.'

'Well? She looks wonderful! And why not? Everything went brilliantly! A complete success! A dream!'

He was so excited, there was no trace of the posh accent. And he bounced up and down on the balls of his feet. And he took my hand and shook it as if he were congratulating me. And the tiny staff nurse laughed and said 'Brilliant! Brilliant!' and in her excitement knocked the chart off the end of the bed and then laughed even more.

'Speak to her!' said Rice. 'Say something!'

'How are you?' I said to Molly.

'How do I look?'

'You look great.'

'Do you like my black eye?'

'I didn't notice it,' I said.

'I'm feeling great,' she said. 'Really. But what about you?'

'What do you mean?'

'Did you manage all right on your own last night?'

I suppose at that moment and in those circumstances it did sound a bit funny.

Anyhow Rice laughed out loud and of course the staff nurse; and then Molly and I had to laugh, too. In relief, I suppose, really . . .

Then Rice said to me,

'Aren't you going to give the lady her flowers?'

'Sorry,' I said. 'I got Rita to choose them. She said they're your favourite.'

Could she see them? I didn't know what to do. Should I take her hand and put the flowers into it?

I held them in front of her. She reached out confidently and took them from me.

'They're lovely,' she said. 'Thank you. Lovely.'

And she held them at arm's length, directly in front of her face, and turned them round. Suddenly Rice said,

'What colour are they, Molly?'

She didn't hesitate at all.

'They're blue,' she said. 'Aren't they blue?'

'They certainly are! And the paper?' Rice asked. 'What colour is the wrapping paper?'

'Is it . . . yellow?'

'Yes! So you know some colours! Excellent! Really excellent!'

And the staff nurse clapped with delight.

'Now—a really hard question, and I'm not sure I know the answer to it myself. What sort of flowers are they?'

She brought them right up to her face. She turned them upside down. She held them at arm's length again. She stared at them—peered at them really—for what seemed an age. I knew how anxious she was by the way her mouth was working.

'Well, Molly? Do you know what they are?'

We waited. Another long silence. Then suddenly she closed her eyes shut tight. She brought the flowers right up against her face and inhaled in quick gulps and at the same time, with her free hand, swiftly, deftly felt the stems and the leaves and the blossoms. Then with her eyes still shut tight she called out desperately, defiantly,

'They're cornflowers! That's what they are! Cornflowers! Blue cornflowers! Centaurea!'

Then for maybe half-a-minute she cried. Sobbed really.

The staff nurse looked uneasily at Rice. He held up his hand.

'Cornflowers, indeed. Splendid,' he said very softly. 'Excellent. It has been a heady day. But we're really on our way now, aren't we?'

I went back to the hospital again that night after my class. She was in buoyant form. I never saw her so animated.

'I can see, Frank!' she kept saying. 'Do you hear me?—I can see!' Mr Rice was a genius! Wasn't it all wonderful? The nurses were angels! Wasn't I thrilled? She loved my red tie—it was red, wasn't it? And everybody was so kind. Dorothy and Joyce brought those chocolates during their lunch-break. And old Mr O'Neill sent that Get Well card—there—look—on the window-sill. And didn't the flowers look beautiful in that pink vase? She would have the operation on the left eye just as soon as Mr Rice would agree. And then, Frank, and then and then and then and then—oh, God, what then!

I was so happy, so happy for her. Couldn't have been happier for God's sake.

But just as on that first morning in Rice's bungalow when the only thing my mind could focus on was the smell of fresh whiskey off his breath, now all I could think of was some—some—some absurd scrap of information a Norwegian fisherman told me about the eyes of whales.

Whales for God's sake!

Stupid information. Useless, off-beat information. Stupid, useless, quirky mind . . .

Molly was still in full flight when a nurse came in and said that visiting time was long over and that Mrs Sweeney needed all her strength to face tomorrow.

'How do I look?'

'Great,' I said.

'Really, Frank?'

'Honestly. Wonderful.'

'Black eye and all?'

'You wouldn't notice it,' I said.

She caught my hand.

'Do you think . . . ?'

'Do I think what?'

'Do you think I look pretty, Frank?'

'You look beautiful,' I said. 'Just beautiful.'

'Thank you.'

I kissed her on the forehead and, as I said good night to her, she gazed intently at my face as if she were trying to read it. Her eyes were bright; unnaturally bright; burnished. And her expression was open and joyous. But as I said good night I had a feeling she wasn't as joyous as she looked.

Mr Rice: When I look back over my working life I suppose I must have done thousands of operations. Sorry—performed. Bloomstein always corrected me on that: 'Come on, you bloody bogman! We're not mechanics. We're artists. We perform.' (*He shrugs his shoulders in dismissal.*)

And of those thousands I wonder how many I'll remember.

I'll remember Dubai. An Arab gentleman whose left eye had been almost pecked out by one of his peregrines and who sent his private jet to New York for Hans Girder and myself. The eye was saved, really because Girder was a magician. And we spent a week in a palace of marble and gold and played poker with the crew of the jet and lost every penny of the ransom we had just earned.

And I'll remember a city called Frankfort in Kentucky; and an elderly lady called Busty Butterfly who had been blinded in a gas explosion. Hiroko Matoba and I 'performed' that operation. A tricky one, but he and I always worked well together. And Busty Butterfly was so grateful that she wanted me to have her best racehorse and little Hiroko to marry her.

And I'll remember Ballybeg. Of course I'll remember Ballybeg. And the courageous Molly Sweeney. And I'll remember it not because of the operation—the operation wasn't all that complex; nor because the circumstances were special; nor indeed because a woman who had been blind for over forty years got her sight back. Yes, yes, yes, I'll remember it for all those reasons. Of course I will. But the core, the very heart, of the memory will be something different, something altogether different.

Perhaps I should explain that after that high summer of my thirty-second year—that episode in Cairo—the dinner party for Maria—Bloomstein's phone-call—all that tawdry drama—my life no longer . . . cohered. I withdrew from medicine, from friendships, from all the consolations of work and the familiar; and for seven years and seven months—sounds like a fairy tale I used to read to Aisling—I subsided into a terrible darkness . . .

But I was talking of Molly's operation and my memory of that. And the core of that memory is this. That for seventy-five minutes in the theatre on that blustery October morning, the darkness miraculously lifted, and I performed—I watched myself do it—I performed so assuredly and with such skill, so elegantly, so efficiently, so economically—yes, yes, yes, of course it sounds vain—vanity has nothing to do with it—but suddenly, miraculously, all the gifts, all the gifts were mine again, abundantly mine, joyously mine; and on that blustery October morning I had such a feeling of mastery and—how can I put it?—such a sense of playfulness for God's sake that I knew I was restored. No, no, no, not fully restored. Never fully restored. But a sense that a practical restoration, perhaps a restoration to something truer—that was possible. Yes, maybe that was possible . . .

Yes, I'll remember Ballybeg. And when I left that dreary little place, that's the memory I took away with me. The place where I restored her sight to Molly Sweeney. Where the terrible darkness lifted. Where the shaft of light glanced off me again.

Molly: Mr Rice said he couldn't have been more pleased with my progress. He called me his Miracle Molly. I liked him a lot more as the weeks passed.

And as usual Rita was wonderful. She let me off work early every Monday, Wednesday and Friday. And I'd dress up in this new coat I'd bought—a mad splurge to keep the spirits up—brilliant scarlet with a matching beret—Rita said I could be seen from miles away, like a distress signal—anyhow in all my new style I'd walk to the hospital on those three afternoons—without my cane!—and sometimes that was scary, I can tell you. And Mr Rice would examine me and say, 'Splendid, Molly! Splendid!' And then he'd pass me on to a psychotherapist, Mrs Wallace, a beautiful looking young woman according to Frank, and I'd do all sorts of tests with her. And then she'd pass me on to George, her husband, for more tests—he was a behavioural psychologist, if you don't mind, a real genius apparently—the pair of them were writing a book on me. And then I'd go back to Mr Rice again and he'd say 'Splendid!' again. And then I'd walk home—still no cane!—and have Frank's tea waiting for him when he'd get back from the library.

I can't tell you how kind Frank was to me, how patient he was. As soon as tea was over, he'd sit at the top of the table and he'd put me at the bottom and he'd begin my lesson.

He'd put something in front of me—maybe a bowl of fruit—and he'd say, 'What have I got in my hand?'

'A piece of fruit.'

'What sort of fruit?'

'An orange, Frank. I know the colour, don't I?'

'Very clever. Now, what's this?'

'It's a pear.'

'You're guessing.'

'Let me touch it.'

'Not allowed. You already have your tactical engrams. We've got to build up a repertory of visual engrams to connect with them.'

And I'd say, 'For God's sake stop showing off your posh new words, Frank. It's a banana.'

'Sorry. Try again.'

'It's a peach. Right?'

'Splendid!' he'd say in Mr Rice's accent. 'It certainly is a peach. Now, what's this?'

And he'd move on to knives and forks, or shoes and slippers, or all the bits and pieces on the mantelpiece for maybe another hour or more. Every night. Seven nights a week.

Oh, yes, Frank couldn't have been kinder to me.

Rita, too. Even kinder. Even more patient.

And all my customers at the health club, the ones who had massages regularly, they sent me a huge bouquet of pink-and-white tulips. And the club I used to swim with, they sent me a beautiful gardening book. God knows what they thought—that I'd now be able to pick it up and read it? But everyone was great, just great.

Oh, yes, I lived in a very exciting world for those first weeks after the operation. Not at all like that silly world I wanted to visit and devour—none of that nonsense.

No, the world that I now saw—half-saw, peered at really—it was a world of wonder and surprise and delight. Oh, yes; wonderful, surprising, delightful. And joy—such joy, small unexpected joys that came in such profusion and passed so quickly that there was never enough time to savour them.

But it was a very foreign world, too. And disquieting; even alarming. Every shape an apparition, a spectre that appeared suddenly from nowhere and challenged you. And all that movement—nothing ever still—everything in motion all the time; and every movement unexpected, somehow threatening. Even the sudden sparrows in the garden, they seemed aggressive, dangerous.

So that after a time the mind could absorb no more sensation. Just one more colour—light—movement—ghostly shape—and suddenly the head imploded and the hands shook and the heart melted with panic. And the only escape—the only way to live—was to sit absolutely still; and shut the eyes tight; and immerse yourself in darkness; and wait. Then when the hands were still and the heart quiet, slowly open the eyes again. And emerge. And try to find the courage to face it all once more.

I tried to explain to Frank once how—I suppose how *terrifying* it all was. But naturally, naturally he was far more concerned with teaching me practical things. And one day when I mentioned to Mr Rice that I didn't think I'd find things as unnerving as I did, he said in a very icy voice,

'And what sort of world did you expect, Mrs Sweeney?'

Yes, it was a strange time. An exciting time, too—oh, yes, exciting. But so strange. And during those weeks after the operation I found myself thinking more and more about my mother and father, but especially about my mother and what it must have been like for her living in that huge, echoing house.

Mr Rice: I operated on the second eye, the left eye, six weeks after the first operation. I had hoped it might have been a healthier eye. But when the cataract was removed, we found a retina much the same as in the right: traces of pigmentosa, scarred macula, areas atrophied. However, with both eyes functioning to some degree, her visual field was larger and she fixated better. She could now see from a medical point of view. From a psychological point of view she was still blind. In other words she now had to learn to see.

Frank: As we got closer to the end of that year, it was quite clear that Molly was changing—had changed. And one of the most fascinating insights into the

5

state of her mind at that time was given to me by Jean Wallace, the psychotherapist; very interesting woman; brilliant actually; married to George, a behavioural psychologist, a second-rater if you ask me; and what a bore— what a bore! Do you know what that man did? Lectured me one day for over an hour on cheese-making if you don't mind! Anyhow—anyhow—the two of them—the Wallaces—they were doing this book on Molly; a sort of documentation of her 'case-history' from early sight to life-long blindness to sight restored to . . . whatever. And the way Jean explained Molly's condition to me was this.

All of us live on a swing, she said. And the swing normally moves smoothly and evenly across a narrow range of the usual emotions. Then we have a crisis in our life; so that instead of moving evenly from, say, feeling sort of happy to feeling sort of miserable, we now swing from elation to despair, from unimaginable delight to utter wretchedness.

The word she used was 'delivered' to show how passive we are in this terrifying game: We are delivered into one emotional state—snatched away from it—delivered into the opposite emotional state. And we can't help ourselves. We can't escape. Until eventually we can endure no more abuse— become incapable of experiencing anything, feeling anything at all.

That's how Jean Wallace explained Molly's behaviour to me. Very interesting woman. Brilliant actually. And beautiful, too. Oh, yes, all the gifts. And what she said helped me to understand Molly's extraordinary behaviour— difficult behaviour—yes, goddamit, very difficult behaviour over those weeks leading up to Christmas.

For example—for example. One day, out of the blue, a Friday evening in December, five o'clock, I'm about to go to the Hikers Club, and she says, 'I feel like a swim, Frank. Let's go for a swim now.'

At this stage I'm beginning to recognize the symptoms: the defiant smile, the excessive enthusiasm, some reckless, dangerous proposal. 'Fine. Fine,' I say. Even though it's pitch dark and raining. So we'll go to the swimming-pool? Oh, no. She wants to swim in the sea. And not only swim in the sea on a wet Friday night in December, but she wants to go out to the rocks at the far end of Tramore and she wants to climb up on top of Napoleon Rock as we call it locally—it's the highest rock there, a cliff really—and I'm to tell her if the tide is in or out and how close are the small rocks in the sea below and how deep the water is because she's going to dive—to dive for God's sake— the eighty feet from the top of Napoleon down into the Atlantic ocean.

'And why not, Frank? Why not for God's sake?'

Oh, yes, an enormous change. Something extraordinary about all that.

Then there was the night I watched her through the bedroom door. She was sitting at her dressing-table, in front of the mirror, trying her hair in different ways. When she would have it in a certain way, she'd lean close to the mirror and peer into it and turn her head from side to side. But you knew she couldn't read her reflection, could scarcely even see it. Then she would try the hair in a different style and she'd lean into the mirror again until her face was almost touching it and again she'd turn first to one side and then the other. And you knew that all she saw was a blur.

Then after about half-a-dozen attempts she stood up and came to the door—it was then I could see she was crying—and she switched off the light. Then she went back to the dressing-table and sat down again; in the dark; for maybe an hour; sat there and gazed listlessly at the black mirror.

Yes, she did dive into the Atlantic from the top of Napoleon Rock; first time in her life. Difficult times. Oh, I can't tell you. Difficult times for all of us.

Mr Rice: The dangerous period for Molly came—as it does for all patients—when the first delight and excitement at having vision have died away. The old world with its routines, all the consolations of work and the familiar, is gone for ever. A sighted world—a partially sighted world, for that is the best it will ever be—is available. But to compose it, to put it together, demands effort and concentration and patience that are almost superhuman.

So the question she had to ask herself was: How much do I want this world? And am I prepared to make that enormous effort to get it?

Frank: Then there was a new development—as if she hadn't enough troubles already. A frightening new development. She began getting spells of dizziness when everything seemed in a thick fog, all external reality became just a haze. This would hit her for no reason at all—at work, or walking home, or in the house; and it would last for an hour, maybe several hours.

Rice had no explanation for it. But you could see he was concerned.

'It's called "gnosis",' he said.

'How do you spell that?'

'G-n-o-s-i-s.'

'And what is it?'

'It's a condition of impaired vision, Mr Sweeney.'

He really was a right little bastard at times.

Anyhow, I looked it up in the library, and interestingly, interestingly I could find no reference at all to a medical condition called 'gnosis'. But according to the dictionary the word meant a mystical knowledge, a knowledge of spiritual things! And my first thought was: Good old Molly! Molly's full of mystical knowledge! God forgive me; I really didn't mean to be so cheap.

I meant to tell Rice about *that* meaning of the word the next time I met him—just to bring him down a peg. But it slipped my mind. I suppose because the condition disappeared as suddenly as it appeared. And anyway she had so many troubles at that stage that my skirmishes with Rice didn't matter any more.

Molly: Tests—tests—tests—tests—tests! Between Mr Rice and Jean Wallace and George Wallace and indeed Frank himself I must have spent months and months being analysed and answering questions and identifying drawings and making sketches. And, God, those damned tests with photographs and lights and objects—those endless tricks and illusions and distortions—the Zöllner illusion, the Ames distorting room, the Staircase illusion, the Müller-Lyer illusion.* And they never told you if you had passed or failed so you always assumed you failed. Such peace—such peace when they were all finished.

*_____

***Zöllner illusion, the Ames distorting room, the Staircase illusion, the Müller-Lyer illusion** See Gregory and Wallace, "Recovery from Early Blindness," Figure 2a, Test 8, Figure 3b, Figure 4 (pp. 1524, 1525, 1527).

I stopped at the florist one evening to get something for Tony and Betty from this side—what was this side; Molly's father and mother. For their wedding anniversary. And I spotted this little pot of flowers, like large buttercups, about six inches tall, with blue petals and what seemed to me a whitish centre. I thought I recognized them but I wasn't quite sure. And I wouldn't allow myself to touch them.

'I'll take these,' I said to the man.

'Pretty, aren't they?' he said. 'Just in from Holland this morning. And do you know what?—I can't remember what they're called. Do you know?'

'They're nemophila.'

'Are they?'

'Yes,' I said. 'Feel the leaves. They should be dry and feathery.'

'You're right,' he said. 'That's what they are. They have another name, haven't they?'

'Baby Blue Eyes,' I said.

'That's it! I'd forgotten that. Getting too old for this job.'

Yes, that gave me some pleasure. One silly little victory. And when I took them home and held them up to my face and looked closely at them, they weren't nearly as pretty as buttercups. Weren't pretty at all. Couldn't give that as a present next door.

10 *Frank:* It was the clever Jean Wallace who spotted the distress signals first. She said to me: 'We should be seeing a renaissance of personality at this point. Because if that doesn't take place—and it's not—then you can expect a withdrawal.'

And she was right. That's what's happened. Molly just . . . withdrew.

Then in the middle of February she lost her job in the health club. And now Rita was no longer a friend. And that was so unfair—Rita kept making allowances for her long after any other boss would have got rid of her; turning in late; leaving early; maybe not even making an appearance for two or three days. Just sitting alone in her bedroom with her eyes shut, maybe listening to the radio, maybe just sitting there in silence.

I made a last effort on the first of March. I took her new scarlet coat out of the wardrobe and I said, 'Come on, girl! Enough of this. We're going for a long walk on Tramore beach. Then we'll have a drink in Moriarity's. Then we'll have dinner in that new Chinese place. Right? Right!' And I left the coat at the foot of her bed.

And that's where it lay for weeks. And weeks. In fact she never wore it out again.

And at that point I had come to the end of my tether. There seemed to be nothing more I could do.

Mr Rice: In those last few months a new condition appeared. She began showing symptoms of a condition known as blindsight. This is a physiological condition, not psychological. On those occasions she claimed she could see nothing, absolutely nothing at all. And indeed she was telling the truth. But even as she said this, she behaved as if she could see—reach for her purse, avoid a chair that was in her way, lift a book and hand it to you. She *was* indeed receiving visual signals and she *was* indeed responding to them. But because

of a malfunction in part of the cerebral cortex none of this perception
reached her consciousness. She was totally unconscious of seeing anything
at all.

In other words she *had* vision—but a vision that was utterly useless to her.

Blindsight . . . curious word . . .

I remember in Cleveland once, Bloomstein and Maria and I were in a
restaurant and when Maria left the table Bloomstein said to me,

'Beautiful lady. You *do* know that?'

'I know,' I said.

'Do you really?'

I said of course I did.

'That's not how you behave,' he said. 'You behave like a man with blindsight.'

Frank: We were in the pub this night, Billy Hughes and myself, just sitting and
chatting about—yes! I remember what we were talking about! An idea Billy
had of recycling old tea-leaves and turning them into a substitute for tobacco.
We should have followed that up.

Anyhow—anyhow, this man comes up to me in the bar, says he's a journalist from a Dublin paper, asks would I be interested in giving him the full
story about Molly.

He seemed a decent man. I talked to him for maybe an hour at most. Of
course it was stupid. And I really didn't do it for the bloody money.

Jack from next door spotted the piece and brought it in. *Miracle Cure False
Dawn. Molly sulks in darkness. Husband drowns sorrow in pub.*

Of course she heard about it—God knows how. And now I was as bad as
all the others: I had let her down, too.

Molly: During all those years when my mother was in the hospital with her
nerves my father brought me to visit her only three times. Maybe that was
her choice. Or his. I never knew.

But I have a vivid memory of each of those three visits.

One of the voice of a youngish woman. My father and mother are in her
ward, surrounded by a screen, fighting as usual, and I'm standing outside in
the huge echoey corridor. And I can hear a young woman sobbing at the far
end of the corridor. More lamenting than sobbing. And even though a lot of
people are passing along that corridor I remember wondering why nobody
paid any attention to her. And for some reason the sound of that lamentation
stayed with me.

And I remember another patient, an old man, leaning over me and
enveloping me in the smell of snuff. He slipped a coin into my hand and said,
'Go out and buy us a fancy new car, son, and the two of us will drive away to
beautiful Fethard-on-Sea.' And he laughed. He had given me a shilling.

And the third memory is of my mother sitting on the side of her bed,
shouting at my father, screaming at him, 'She should be at a blind school!
You know she should! But you know the real reason you won't send her?
Not because you haven't the money. Because you want to punish me.'

I didn't tell Mr Rice that story when he first asked me about my childhood. Out of loyalty to Father, maybe. Maybe out of loyalty to Mother, too.

Anyhow those memories came into my head the other day. I can't have been more than six or seven at the time.

Mr Rice: In those last few months it was hard to recognize the woman who had first come to my house. The confident way she shook my hand. Her calm and her independence. The way she held her head.

How self-sufficient she had been then—her home, her job, her friends, her swimming; so naturally, so easily experiencing her world with her hands alone.

And we had once asked so glibly: What has she to lose?

15 *Molly:* In those last few months I was seeing less and less. I was living in the hospital then, Mother's old hospital. And what was strange was that there were times when I didn't know if the things I did see were real or was I imagining them. I seemed to be living on a borderline between fantasy and reality.

Yes, that was a strange state. Anxious at first; oh, very anxious. Because it meant that I couldn't trust any more what sight I still had. It was no longer trustworthy.

But as time went on that anxiety receded; seemed to be a silly anxiety. Not that I began trusting my eyes again. Just that trying to discriminate, to distinguish between what might be real and what might be imagined, being guided by what Father used to call 'excellent testimony'—that didn't seem to matter all that much, seemed to matter less and less. And for some reason the less it mattered, the more I thought I could see.

Mr Rice: In those last few months—she was living in the psychiatric hospital at that point—I knew I had lost contact with her. She had moved away from us all. She wasn't in her old blind world—she was exiled from that. And the sighted world, which she had never found hospitable, wasn't available to her any more.

My sense was that she was trying to compose another life that was neither sighted nor unsighted, somewhere she hoped was beyond disappointment; somewhere, she hoped, without expectation.

Frank: The last time I saw Rice was on the following Easter Sunday; April 7; six months to the day after the first operation. Fishing on a lake called Lough Anna away up in the hills. Billy Hughes spotted him first.

'Isn't that your friend, Mr Rice? Wave to him, man!'

And what were Billy and I doing up there in the wilds? Embarrassing. But I'll explain.

Ballybeg got its water supply from Lough Anna and in the summer, when the lake was low, from two small adjoining lakes. So to make the supply more efficient it was decided that at the end of April the two small lakes would be emptied into Lough Anna and it would become the sole reservoir for the town. That would raise the water-level of Anna by fifteen feet and of course ruin the trout fishing there—not that that worried them. So in fact that Easter Sunday would have been Rice's last time to fish there. But he probably knew that because Anna was his favourite lake; he was up there every chance he got; and he had told me once that he had thought of putting a boat on it. Anyhow—anyhow.

Billy Hughes and his crazy scheme. He had heard that there was a pair of badgers in a sett at the edge of the lake. When Anna was flooded in three weeks' time, they would be drowned. They would have to be moved. Would I help him?

Move two badgers! Wonderful! So why did I go with him? Partly to humour the eejit.* But really, I suppose, really because that would be our last day together, that Easter Sunday.

And that's how we spent it—digging two bloody badgers out of their sett. Dug for two-and-a-half hours. Then flung old fishing nets over them to immobilize them. Then lifted them into two wheelbarrows. Then hauled those wheelbarrows along a sheep track up the side of the mountain—and each of those brutes weighed at least thirty pounds—so that we were hauling half-a-hundred-weight of bloody badger-meat up an almost vertical moun-tainside. And then—listen to this—the greatest lunacy of all—then tried to force them into an old, abandoned sett half-way up the mountain! Brilliant Billy Hughes!

Because of course the moment we cut them out of the nets and tried to push them down the new hole, well naturally they went wild; bit Billy's ankle and damn near fractured my arm; and then went careering down the hillside in a mad panic, trailing bits of net behind them. And because they can't see too well in daylight or maybe because they're half-blind anyway, stumbling into bushes and banging into rocks and bumping into each other and sliding and rolling and tumbling all over the place. And where did they head for? Of course—of course—straight back to the old sett at the edge of the water—the one we'd destroyed with all our digging!

Well, what could you do but laugh? Hands blistered, bleeding ankle, sore arm, filthy clothes. Flung ourselves on the heather and laughed until our sides hurt. And then Billy turned to me and said very formally, 'Happy Easter, Frank' and it seemed the funniest thing in the world and off we went again. What an eejit that man was!

Rice joined us when we were putting the wheelbarrows into the back of Billy's van.

'I was watching you from the far side,' he said. 'What in God's name were you doing?'

Billy told him.

'Good heavens!' he said, posh as ever. 'A splendid idea. Always a man for the noble pursuit, Frank.'

The bastard couldn't resist it, I knew. But for some reason he didn't anger me that day; didn't even annoy me. Maybe because his fishing outfit was a couple of sizes too big for him and in those baggy trousers he looked a bit like a circus clown. Maybe because at that moment, after that fiasco with the bad-gers, standing on that shore that would be gone in a few weeks' time, none of the three of us—Billy, Rice, myself—none of the three of us seemed such big shots at that moment. Or maybe he didn't annoy me that Easter Sunday

*__eejit__ idiot

afternoon because I knew I'd probably never see him again. I was heading off to Ethiopia in the morning.

We left the van outside Billy's flat and he walked me part of the way home.

When we got to the courthouse I said he'd come far enough: we'd part here. I hoped he'd get work. I hoped he'd meet some decent woman who'd marry him and beat some sense into him. And I'd be back home soon, very soon, the moment I'd sorted out the economy of Ethiopia . . . The usual stuff.

Then we hugged quickly and he walked away and I looked after him and watched his straight back and the quirky way he threw out his left leg as he walked and I thought, my God, I thought how much I'm going to miss that bloody man.

And when he disappeared round the corner of the courthouse, I thought, too—I thought, too—Abyssinia for Christ's sake—or whatever it's called— Ethiopia—Abyssinia—whatever it's called—who cares what it's called—who gives a damn—who in his right mind wants to go there for Christ's sake? Not you. You certainly don't. Then why don't you stay where you are for Christ's sake? What are you looking for?

Oh, Jesus . . .

Mr Rice: Roger Bloomstein was killed in an air-crash on the evening of the Fourth of July. He was flying his plane from New York to Cape Cod where Maria and he had rented a house for the summer. An eyewitness said the engine stopped suddenly, and for a couple of seconds the plane seemed to sit suspended in the sky, golden and glittering in the setting sun, and then plummeted into the sea just south of Martha's Vineyard.

The body was never recovered.

I went to New York for the memorial service the following month. Hiroko Matoba couldn't come: he had had a massive heart attack the previous week. So of the four horsemen, the brilliant meteors, there were only the two of us: Hans, now the internationally famous Herr Girder, silver-haired, sleek, smiling; and myself, seedy, I knew, after a bad flight and too much whiskey.

Girder asked about Molly. He had read an article George Wallace had written about 'Mrs M' in the *Journal of Psychology*. The enquiry sounded casual but the smiling eyes couldn't conceal the vigilance. So the vigilance was still necessary despite the success, maybe more necessary because of the success.

'Lucky Paddy Rice,' he said. 'The chance of a lifetime. Fell on your feet again.'

'Not as lucky as you, Hans.'

'But it didn't end happily for the lady?'

''Fraid not,' I said.

'Too bad. No happy endings. So she is totally sightless now?'

'Totally.'

'And mentally?'

'Good days—bad days,' I said.

'But she won't survive?'

'Who's to say?' I said.

'No, no. They don't survive. That's the pattern. But they'll insist on having the operation, won't they? And who's to dissuade them?'

'Let me get you a drink,' I said and I walked away.

I watched Maria during the service. Her beauty had always been chameleon. She had an instinctive beauty for every occasion. And today with her drained face and her dazed eyes and that fragile body, today she was utterly vulnerable, and at the same time, within her devastation, wholly intact and untouchable. I had never seen her more beautiful.

When the service was over she came to me and thanked me for coming. We talked about Aisling and Helga. They were having a great time with her parents in Geneva; they loved it there and her parents spoiled them; they weren't good at answering letters but they liked getting mine even though they were a bit scrappy. They were happy girls, she said.

Neither of us spoke Roger's name.

Then she took my hand and kissed it and held it briefly against her cheek. It was a loving gesture. But for all its tenderness, because of its tenderness, I knew she was saying a final goodbye to me.

As soon as I got back to Ballybeg I resigned from the hospital and set about gathering whatever belongings I had. The bungalow was rented, never more than a lodging. So the moving out was simple—some clothes, a few books, the fishing rods. Pity to leave the lakes at that time of year. But the lake I enjoyed most—a lake I had grown to love—it had been destroyed by flooding. So it was all no great upheaval.

I called on Molly the night before I left. The nurse said she was very frail. But she could last for ever or she could slip away tonight. 'It's up to herself,' she said. 'But a lovely woman. No trouble at all. If they were all as nice and quiet . . .'

She was sleeping and I didn't waken her. Propped up against the pillows; her mouth open; her breathing shallow; a scarlet coat draped around her shoulders; the wayward hair that had given her so much trouble now contained in a net.

And looking down at her I remembered—was it all less than a year ago?— I had a quick memory of the first time I saw her in my house, and the phantom desire, the insane fantasy that crossed my mind that day: Was this the chance of a lifetime that might pull my life together, rescue a career, restore a reputation? Dear God, that opulent fantasy life . . .

And looking down at her—the face relaxed, that wayward hair contained in a net—I thought how I had failed her. Of course I had failed her. But at least, at least for a short time she did see men 'walking as if like trees'. And I think, perhaps, yes I think she understood more than any of us what she did see.

Molly: When I first went to Mr Rice I remember him asking me was I able to distinguish between light and dark and what direction light came from. And I remember thinking: Oh my God, he's asking you profound questions about good and evil and about the source of knowledge and about big mystical issues! Careful! Don't make a fool of yourself! And of course all the poor man wanted to know was how much vision I had. And I could answer him easily now: I can't distinguish between light and dark, nor the direction from which light comes, and I certainly wouldn't see the shadow of Frank's hand in front of my face. Yes, that's all long gone. Even the world of touch has shrunk. No, not that it has shrunk; just that I seem to need much less of it now. And after all that anxiety and drudgery we went through with engrams and the need to establish connections between visual and tactile engrams and synchronizing sensations of touch and sight and composing a whole new world. But I suppose all that had to be attempted.

I like this hospital. The staff are friendly. And I have loads of visitors. Tony and Betty and baby Molly from this side—well, what used to be this side. They light an odd fire in the house, too, to keep it aired for Frank. And Mary from that side. She hasn't told me yet but I'm afraid Jack has cleared off. And Billy Hughes; out of loyalty to Frank; every Sunday in life, God help me; God help *him*. And Rita. Of course, Rita. We never talk about the row we had. That's all in the past. I love her visits: she has all the gossip from the club. Next time she's here I must ask her to sing 'Oft in the Stilly Night' for me. And no crying at the end!

And old Mr O'Neill! Yes! Dan McGrew himself! And Louise—Lou—his wife! Last Wednesday she appeared in a crazy green cloche hat and deep purple gloves up to here (*elbow*) and eyeshadow half-way down her cheek and a shocking black woollen dress that scarcely covered her bum! Honestly! He was looking just wonderful; not a day over forty. And he stood in the middle of the ward and did the whole thing for me—'A bunch of the boys were whooping it up in the Malamute saloon'. And Lou gazing at him in admiration and glancing at us as if to say, 'Isn't he just the greatest thing ever?' And he was—he was! Oh, that gave my heart a great lift.

And yesterday I got a letter, twenty-seven pages long. Frank—who else? It took the nurse an hour to read it to me. Ethiopia is paradise. The people are heroes. The climate is hell. The relief workers are completely dedicated. Never in his life has he felt so committed, so passionate, so fulfilled. And they have a special bee out there, the African bee, that produces twice as much honey as our bees and is immune to all known bee diseases and even though it has an aggressive nature he is convinced it would do particularly well in Ireland. Maybe in Leitrim. And in his very limited spare time he has taken up philosophy. It is fascinating stuff. There is a man called Aristotle that he thinks highly of. I should read him, he says. And he sent a money order for two pounds and he'll write again soon.

Mother comes in occasionally; in her pale blue headscarf and muddy wellingtons. Nobody pays much attention to her. She just wanders through the wards. She spent so much time here herself, I suppose she has an affection for the place. She doesn't talk much—she never did. But when she sits uneasily on the edge of my bed, as if she were waiting to be summoned, her face always frozen in that nervous half-smile, I think I know her better than I ever knew her and I begin to love her all over again.

Mr Rice came to see me one night before he went away.

I was propped up in bed, drifting in and out of sleep, and he stood swaying at the side of the bed for maybe five minutes, just gazing at me. I kept my eyes closed. Then he took both my hands in his and said, 'I'm sorry, Molly Sweeney. I'm so sorry.'

And off he went.

I suppose it was mean of me to pretend I was asleep. But the smell of whiskey was suffocating; and the night nurse told me that on his way out the front door he almost fell down the stone steps.

And sometimes Father drops in on his way from court. And we do imaginary tours of the walled garden and compete with each other in the number of flowers and shrubs each of us can identify. I asked him once why he had never sent me to a school for the blind. And as soon as I asked him I knew I sounded as if I was angry about it, as if I wanted to catch him out. But he wasn't at all disturbed. The answer was simple, he said. Mother wasn't well; and when she wasn't in hospital she needed my company at home. But even though I couldn't see the expression on his face, his voice was lying. The truth of the matter was he was always mean with money; he wouldn't pay the blind school fees.

And once—just once—I thought maybe I heard the youngish woman sobbing quietly at the far end of the corridor, more lamenting than sobbing. But I wasn't sure. And when I asked the nurse, she said I must have imagined it; there was nobody like that on our floor. And of course my little old snuff man must be dead years ago—the man who wanted us to drive to beautiful Fethard-on-Sea. He gave me a shilling, I remember; a lot of money in those days.

I think I see nothing at all now. But I'm not absolutely sure of that. Anyhow my borderline country is where I live now. I'm at home there. Well . . . at ease there. It certainly doesn't worry me any more that what I think I see may be fantasy or indeed what I take to be imagined may very well be real—what's Frank's term?—external reality. Real—imagined—fact—fiction—fantasy—reality—there it seems to be. And it seems to be all right.

And why should I question any of it any more?   [1994]

1. Briefly summarize what you know about each of the three characters by the end of the first act. What is the stake each has in the proposed eye operation?
2. Characterize the construction of this play. What are its advantages and disadvantages? Did you become involved—feel any suspense, or have any stake in a possible outcome?
3. If you were the director of a small community theater reading this play among others for possible production, would you consider presenting it? What factors would go into your decision?
4. If you were a film director, would you want to make a movie of this play? What difficulties would it present? How would you solve them? Discuss location, period style, casting, lighting, color effects, and the material in the play that would justify each decision.

5. Summarize the effect of the operation on each of the three characters. What did each have to lose? Do you think the two men were justified in encouraging Molly to have the operation and making it so hard for her to refuse to do it?

6. Why do you think we hear the story of Frank and Billy's attempt to rescue the two badgers from Lough Anna?

R. L. GREGORY AND JEAN G. WALLACE

RICHARD LANGTON GREGORY, *D.Sc., F.R.S., CBE (1923–), is Professor of Neuropsychology and Director of the Brain and Perception Laboratory at the University of Bristol in England and author of* The Oxford Companion to the Mind. *Besides his research and teaching, he has appeared often on radio and television in Great Britain to discuss scientific matters and he set up the Bristol Exploratory, "the UK's first hands-on science center." In 1992, he was elected a Fellow of the Royal Society of London and awarded the Royal Society's Faraday Medal. He has sometimes written with Jean G. Wallace, B.Com. Edin., formerly a Research Associate at the Cambridge Psychological Laboratory.*

   "The recovery from early blindness: a case study," a chapter from Gregory's book, Concepts and Mechanisms of Perception, *tells the story of Gregory's work with S.B., a man functionally blind since his first year whose sight was restored through cornea transplants when he was fifty years old. What seemed initially like good results soon darkened as S.B. had difficulty adjusting, became depressed, and then died prematurely at fifty-six. Gregory says, "His story is in some ways tragic. He suffered one of the greatest handicaps, and yet he lived with energy and enthusiasm. When his handicap was apparently swept away, as by a miracle, he lost his peace and his self-respect. We may feel disappointment at a private dream come true: S.B. found disappointment with what he took to be reality."*

   In 2003, another man's experience with sight recovered after decades of blindness has been happier. Richard Gregory writes about it in Nature Neuro-science 6.9, 9 (September 2003). *In his early years, Michael May had more complete sight than S.B. did in his, and seems to have more emotional and intellectual resources for dealing with the task of learning to see. He also probably had the benefit of the writings about S.B. and other cases of recovered sight.*

From *Recovery from Early Blindness: A Case Study**

This is the case history of a man born in 1906 who lost effective sight in both eyes at about ten months of age, and after fifty years as a blind person received corneal grafts to restore his sight. Such cases are rare, and few have been investigated in any detail, or have available pre-operative records giving their early history. Since cases of recovery from congenital or early blindness have been

* R[ichard] L[angton] Gregory & Jean G. Wallace, "Recovery from Early Blindness: A Case Study," *Experimental Psychology Society Monograph* No. 2 1963 (Cambridge: Cambridge University Press, 1963). Reprinted in *Concepts and Mechanisms of Perception*, ed. R. L. Gregory (New York: Charles Scribner's Sons, 1974). Paragraph numbers in this selection do not reflect editorial deletions.

discussed by philosophers for over three hundred years, and have more recently attracted the interest of experimental psychologists, we feel justified in presenting in full everything which might be regarded as relevant to the case. . . .

First Visual Experiences after Operation

S.B.'s first visual experience, when the bandages were removed, was of the surgeon's face. He described the experience as follows:—

He heard a voice coming from in front of him and to one side: he turned to the source of the sound, and saw a 'blur'. He realized that this must be a face. Upon careful questioning, he seemed to think that he would not have known that this was a face if he had not previously heard the voice and known that voices came from faces.

At the time we first saw him, he did not find faces 'easy' objects. He did not look at a speaker's face, and made nothing of facial expressions. On the other hand, he very rapidly (apparently within a couple of days) distinguished between passing lorries and cars, and would get up at six each morning to look at them some way off. He 'collected' different types of lorry, and took much pleasure recognizing vans, articulated lorries, and so on. His particular interest in cars and lorries may have been in part that they made familiar sounds, which helped in identification; that they could only be driven by sighted people, and so held out particular promise to him. He had spent many hours trying to visualize the shape of cars while washing them, particularly his brother-in-law's car, which he frequently washed down.

He told us that he did not suffer particularly from giddiness when he first opened his eyes.

As in previous cases (Latta, 1904), he experienced marked scale distortion   5
when looking down from a high window. In the famous Cheselden case, objects were at first reported to be touching the eye;[1] this was not true for S.B. but he found that when looking down from a high window (about 30–40 feet above the ground) he thought he could safely lower himself down by his hands. When later he saw the same window from outside, he realized that this would be impossible.

On the whole, his early estimates of the size of objects seem to have been quite accurate providing they were objects already familiar to him by touch. Thus buses seemed to him to be too high but the right length. This may well have been because he was used to walking their length, but not feeling their height; adding the separate tactile sensations of the height of each step and adding enough above the stair-case would be a comparatively difficult and unfamiliar task. In drawings of buses, to be given later, he emphasized the features familiar to touch but ignored the bonnet, which would not easily have been explored by touch, by a blind boy.

He may well have made many mistakes of identification of objects which we did not hear about, but from the beginning he was proud of his ability to name

[1]Although this is often quoted at its face value, it is worth remembering that normally a strong light, particularly if painful, is not regarded so much as 'out there' as in the eye itself. The same is true for intense (and unusual?) stimuli in any sense modality. E.g. a very loud sound is a sensation *in the ear.*

objects correctly, and took no pleasure in allowing others to find out that he made mistakes.

It was very soon obvious (as we had to some extent anticipated) that merely to ask questions about what he saw would not give us much information about his visual capacity. In fact the only example of a curious and interesting mistake was described to us by the Matron, who said that about three days after the operation he saw the moon for the first time. At first he thought it a reflection in the window, but when he realized, or was told, it was the moon, he expressed surprise at its crescent shape, expecting a 'quarter moon' to look like a quarter piece of cake! It is noteworthy that this is the only clear instance of an expression of surprise, or of a clear error of this sort. That it should occur with an object he could not have touched is perhaps significant. It also shows—when it is remembered that the full moon only subtends 0.5°—that his visual acuity must have been reasonably good at that time, a few days after the first operation.

It is also worth noting that reflections fascinated him and continued to do so for at least a year after the operation.

Perceptual Tests

10   One of the difficulties about trying to discover the perceptual world of the blind is that they use the normal words of the sighted, even though they cannot always have the meanings we attach to them. Thus a blind man will say, 'I saw in the paper to-day . . .' when he read it by touch in Braille. When S.B. named an object correctly (say a chair or a vase of flowers) we could not discover what special features he used to decide what object it was. It was obvious that facial expressions meant nothing to him, and that he could not recognize people by their faces, though he could immediately do so by their voices, but we could learn little more.

We tried to get some insight into his previous world by getting him to say what surprised him when vision returned. The attempt failed almost completely, as he seldom admitted to any surprises.

We would have liked to obtain accurate measures of such things beloved by the experimental psychologist as the visual constancies, but this was not practicable, for he tired easily, and we were anxious not to upset either him or the hospital staff. We decided to get him to look at various well-known visual illusions, about which a great deal is known for normal observers, even though explanations for many of them are lacking. The lack of explanation of these illusions did not worry us greatly, for with more knowledge, which is bound to come with further research in perception, they will surely be explained, and then any findings should be relatable to general perceptual issues.[1] It seemed to

---

[1]Since undertaking this investigation, we have made an intensive investigation of the geometrical illusions, and have come to the conclusion that they arise from discrepancy between estimated distance and degree of constancy evoked by such perceptual features as perspective lines. The illusion figures presented here seem to produce distortion of visual space by evoking constancy which is inappropriate to the flat plane (visible as a textured surface) on which the figures lie. On this view, we might say that the anomalous results obtained for S.B. show that these figures did not serve to evoke constancy scaling for him, and thus the illusions were absent.

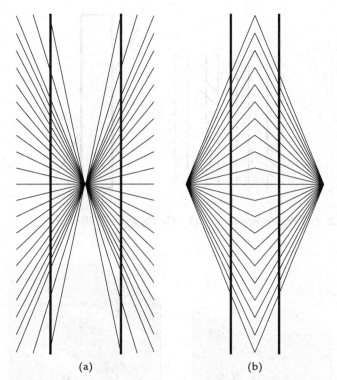

FIGURE 1 *The Hering illusion.* (a) *First form.* (b) *Second form (Wundt).*

us that this would be the best way of getting some reasonably objective information as to his perceptual capacities and peculiarities.

The first three tests to be described here were given on the morning of 26 January, 1959, and the remainder on the same afternoon, when the first three were repeated.

Test 1. The Hering illusion. This is shown in Fig. 1*a* , where it will be seen that although the heavy vertical lines are in fact straight and parallel, they appear to diverge in the middle. This figure was presented to S.B. printed in heavy black lines on a white card of size $10\frac{1}{2}'' \times 4''$. He held it close to his eye, and studied it very carefully in silence.

Result First he said the lines were straight. He then became doubtful, and thought that they might be further apart at the top and middle. When shown the figures again, in the afternoon, he first said: 'One goes out in the middle' and ended by saying that both were straight. We may conclude that the illusion was, if present, considerably less marked than in normal observers. Fig. 1*b* gave a similar result.

Test 2. The Zöllner illusion. Normally, the verticals look non-parallel and may fluctuate in their positions (Fig. 2*a*).

Result He reported the verticals, after careful study, as all parallel, and after questioning about variation he said it was 'all calm.'

15

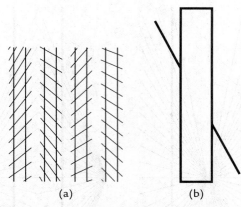

FIGURE 2 (a) *The Zöllner illusion.* (b) *The Poggendorff illusion.*

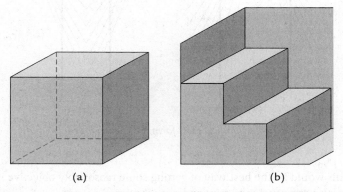

FIGURE 3 *Ambiguous depth illusions.* (a) *Necker cube* (b) *Staircase illusion.*

Test 3. The Poggendorff illusion. Normally, the right-hand section of the slanting line appears to lie below the continuation of the left-hand section (Fig. 2*b*).

Result S.B. reported it as: 'all one line'.

20 *Test 4. Ambiguous depth illusions (reversing figures).* (a) *The Necker cube.* This also is a very well-known illusion: it was shown as presented in Fig. 3*a*. It was displayed on a card 10 cm. × 15 cm. the figure being 5.2 cm. × 8.0 cm. Normally, this figure is seen to reverse at intervals, the side representing the front being ambiguous.

Result This gave a most unusual, possibly unique, result. The figure was evidently *not seen in depth* and it *did not reverse*.

We took the greatest possible care to ensure that he understood what we meant by 'depth' and 'reversal', after he asked us 'What is depth?' We did this by showing him (after first obtaining negative answers to our question as to whether it reversed or was seen in depth) a child's wooden brick we had brought along, and pointed out that it receded from him, by pointing out the

FIGURE 4 *Müller-Lyer illusion.*

depth with a finger, and getting him to touch it while looking at it. When he looked again at the picture cube he said that he could not see depth, and that 'it looks quite different [from the brick].' He tried, rather unsuccessfully, to draw a cube, but unfortunately this drawing is lost.

(*b*) *The staircase illusion.* This is similar to the Necker cube in that it also is a figure reversible in depth. It was presented on a card (Fig. 3*b*).

Result The result was the same; evidently no depth, and no ambiguity was observed.

Test 5. The Müller-Lyer illusion. This famous illusion is shown in Fig. 4. When the shafts of the arrows are in fact of equal length, the arrow with diverging fins is seen as longer than that having converging fins. This was presented to S.B. as two arrows end to end, and was so arranged that it could be varied, and continuously adjusted by the observer, who holds the device in his hand. The length of the fixed arrow was 74 cm., and the movable arrow is normally observed to be *shorter* than this. S.B. adjusted the arrow for apparent equality of length four times, each time with great care.

Result His estimate of length on the four successive readings were as follows:

1. 10.0
2. 16.5
3. 17.0
4. 16.0

These figures meaning the *under-estimation of length* from the standard of 74 cm. His average illusion is thus 14.12 cm, in the normal direction. This may be compared with the mean obtained on ten normal observers on the same apparatus of 20 cm. The extent of the illusion as measured for S.B. is unusually small, though some 'normal' observers can be found with a similar degree of illusion.

Test 6. Perspective size changes. Figure 5 shows four men, all actually the same size, but normally appearing of increasing size as the apparent distance, due to perspective, increases.

Result S.B. reported: 'They don't look far away, it's just as though the men were standing underneath (? the buildings). The first man looks smaller, but the last three look the same.' It should be made clear that these comments were in answer to a request for a description of the relative sizes of the men, and we had to state that the objects depicted *were* men. As will be seen later he was hardly able to identify drawings of such objects as men.

Test 7. Figure and ground. One of the classical problems in the study of perception is how 'figure' is distinguished from 'ground' and whether the distinction is

FIGURE 5 *Perspective size illusion.*

FIGURE 6 *Figure and ground effect.*

innate or learned. Normally objects stand out against a hardly perceived background, for example the objects in a room against the walls, even when highly decorated, but this can be perceptually ambiguous, as when at dusk the sky is sometimes seen as 'object', with the black roofline as unimportant 'background'. Similarly, looking at a map, the land or the sea can be seen as 'object' or 'background'.

The only example given to S.B. was Fig. 6.

TEST 8 *The Ames Room: The child seems to dwarf the adult because, although the room appears to be conventionally proportioned, with 90-degree angles at the corners, it is actually trapezoidal. The adult is twice as far from the camera as the child and so appears smaller.*

Result S.B. made little of it; after some time he said, of the black curved part: 'Is it the case of a fan—a turbine fan?' He meant by this, as questioning elicited, part of the boiler equipment on which he worked. This is particularly interesting, for he had not at that time seen this equipment; he was however certain that he knew what it would look like, from his experience with touch plus his recent visual experience. He gave no response indicating figure-ground fluctuation, and could make nothing of the white part, even when the 'face' was pointed out in detail.

Test 8. The Ames distorting room. The Ames distorting rooms are of importance for studies on 'visual framework'. They emphasize that many judgements of size, shape or distance which may seem to be absolute are relative in the sense that they depend on other features in the visual field.   30

The rooms are non-rectangular, but are so made that they give, from a chosen viewing position, a retinal image corresponding to a rectangular room. Clearly they *must* appear rectangular from the chosen position, since no information is available to indicate otherwise, but they become interesting when objects are introduced into the rooms, for objects in fact at different distances may appear to be the same distance from the observer. When this is so, objects of the same size and the same *apparent* distance will give different sized retinal images. To the normal observer the objects will appear of different sizes even when this is quite contrary to all their past experience. For example, a child can be made to look larger than an adult. It would seem that, at least in a Western culture, where most rooms are rectangular, the walls serve as a reference frame for deciding the ever-present perceptual question: is it a large object far away or a small near object giving this size of retinal image?

We should expect S.B. to see an Ames room as rectangular—or at any rate he should not find its shape surprising—but it was an open question what he would see when identical objects were placed in such a room, at actually different distances though at apparently the same distance.

To test S.B.'s reactions to this special situation, we used a small model Ames room, into which he looked, using one eye.

Result He reported the room to be rectangular (in fact the rear wall receded from him to the right), and this result in no way surprised us since the resulting retinal image would be the same as for a truly rectangular room, or box. We then held a half-penny in each of the two windows in the back wall, one window being in fact further from the observer than the other, this distance not being apparent. S.B. reported that the right hand coin looked smaller than the left. When the right hand coin was replaced by a penny piece, and this compared with a half-penny in the left window, he reported that they were of the same size. This response is quite normal for observers using the particular model Ames room we used for this test. We were, rightly or wrongly, considerably surprised by the result. . . .

Visit to the Science Museum, South Kensington

S.B. had a long-standing interest in tools and machinery; we were thus particularly interested to discover whether the sight of these things would serve to stimulate him, and dispel the lethargy into which he had fallen. . . .

35   The most interesting episode was his reaction to the fine Maudeslay screw cutting lathe which is housed in a special glass case. This is a large and fairly simple example. We chose this object because a lathe would be a tool that he must often have wished to use.

We led him to the glass case, which was closed, and asked him to tell us what was in it. He was quite unable to say anything about it, except that he thought the nearest part was a handle. (He pointed to the handle of the transverse feed.) He complained that he could not see the cutting edge, or the metal being worked, or anything else about it, and appeared rather agitated. We then asked a museum attendant (as previously arranged) for the case to be opened, and S.B. was allowed to touch the lathe. The result was startling; he ran his hands deftly over the machine, touching first the transverse feed handle and confidently naming it as 'a handle', and then on to the saddle, the bed and the head-stock. He ran his hands eagerly over the lathe, with his eyes tight shut. Then he stood back a little and opened his eyes, and said: 'Now that I've felt it I can see'. He then named many of the parts correctly and explained how they would work, though he could not understand the chain of four gears driving the lead screw. . . .

It is of course true that in nearly (though not quite) all these cases of recovery of vision after long-standing blindness the development of perceptual skill is very slow, even when considerable sight was present before operation. But this, we suggest, is due not to the fact that visual learning, whether in the child or the adult, is *inevitably* slow but to lack of practice in making appropriate use of the available input. It would seem that the difficulty is not so much in learning *per se* as in *changing perceptual habits and strategies from touching to seeing.* . . .

The findings that S.B.'s visual space was not disturbed by the geometrical-optical illusions, and that apparent depth was not evoked by perspective drawings, show that his spatial organization was far from normal. Since investigating the case, we have devoted considerable thought to the origin of these illusions and have arrived at the tentative view that they depend upon inappropriate scaling by the mechanism which produces size-constancy. If this should prove correct, it may be surmised that the figures failed to evoke constancy size-scaling in our patient, either through lack of early learning or maturational defect. It would seem of some importance, therefore, to devote attention to the study of these illusions in children with special reference to the development of size constancy.

Perhaps the most important outcome of our study is the evidence it provides for *transfer from early touch experience to vision many years later.* The fact that our patient was able, certainly with a minimum of training—and perhaps with none at all—to recognize by vision upper case letters which he had learned by touch, and that he was *unable* to recognize by vision lower case letters which he had *not* learned by touch, provides strong evidence for cross-modal transfer. It will be borne in mind, too, that it took him many months to learn to recognize by vision letters which he had *not* previously learned by touch. One may point out that the 'control' provided by the lower-case letters is vital to the argument, since we can never wholly rule out the possibility of some residual vision (undoubtedly present in this case). The fact that S.B. could recognize the figures in the Ishihara Plates (perhaps the most surprising observation we made) gives evidence of transfer and, incidentally, renders it most unlikely that the *modus operandi* of transfer lies in identity of motor patterns (i.e. patterns of eye-movement corresponding with patterns of active touch). As has been said, gross observation of eye-movements, which consisted in large and apparently uncontrolled jerks resembling exaggerated saccades, made it impossible to believe that the patient could follow outlines of relatively small figures, such as the Ishihara digits, by controlled movements of the eyes. . . .   [1963]

1. What is your experience of the various optical illusions?
2. Ordinary life can present situations in which our senses are misled. Have there been situations in which your senses have been fooled?

OLIVER SACKS

OLIVER SACKS *(1933–) was born in London, England, and moved to California in 1965. In between, he was educated at St. Paul's School, The Queen's College, Oxford, and the Middlesex hospital. He came to the United States for further training and, after doing research in neurochemistry and neuropathology, returned to clinical work. His work then centered on migraine and on behavioral development and disorders in children, neurological disorders in the elderly, phantom pain, tics, and the care of postencephalitic patients. He described dramatic events pertaining to the care of sleeping-sickness patients in* Awakenings *in 1973, a book that became a film starring Robin Williams and was also the basis of a play by Harold Pinter.*

Sacks is the author of The Man Who Mistook His Wife for a Hat, *published in 1985 and dramatized by Peter Brook. Sacks characterizes himself as a "loner," fond of botany and swimming.*

Virgil's story was fictionalized for the 1999 film, At First Sight, *starring Val Kilmer, Mira Sorvino, and Kelly McGillis.*

From *To See and Not See**

Early in October of 1991, I got a phone call from a retired minister in the Midwest, who told me about his daughter's fiancé, a fifty-year-old man named Virgil, who had been virtually blind since early childhood. He had thick cataracts and was also said to have retinitis pigmentosa, a hereditary condition that slowly but implacably eats away at the retinas. But his fiancée, Amy, who required regular eye checks herself because of diabetes, had recently taken him to see her own ophthalmologist, Dr. Scott Hamlin, and he had given them new hope. Dr. Hamlin, listening carefully to the history, was not so sure that Virgil did have retinitis pigmentosa. It was difficult to be certain at this stage, because the retinas could no longer be seen beneath the thick cataracts, but Virgil could still see light and dark, the direction from which light came, and the shadow of a hand moving in front of his eyes, so obviously there was not a total destruction of the retina. And cataract extraction was a relatively simple procedure, done under local anesthesia, with very little surgical risk. There was nothing to lose—and there might be much to gain. Amy and Virgil would be getting married soon— wouldn't it be fantastic if he could see? If, after a near-lifetime of blindness, his first vision could be his bride, the wedding, the minister, the church! Dr. Hamlin had agreed to operate, and the cataract on Virgil's right eye had been removed a fortnight earlier, Amy's father informed me. And, miraculously, the operation had worked. Amy, who began keeping a journal the day after the operation— the day the bandages were removed—wrote in her initial entry: "Virgil can SEE! . . . Entire office in tears, first time Virgil has sight for forty years. . . . Virgil's family so excited, crying, can't believe it! . . . Miracle of sight restored incredible!" But the following day she remarked problems: "Trying to adjust to being sighted, tough to go from blindness to sighted. Has to think faster, not able to trust vision yet. . . . Like baby just learning to see, everything new, exciting, scary, unsure of what seeing means."

A neurologist's life is not systematic, like a scientist's, but it provides him with novel and unexpected situations, which can become windows, peepholes, into the intricacy of nature—an intricacy that one might not anticipate from the ordinary course of life. "Nature is nowhere accustomed more openly to display her secret mysteries," wrote William Harvey, in the seventeenth century, "than in cases where she shows traces of her workings apart from the beaten path." Certainly this phone call—about the restoration of vision in adulthood to a patient blind from early childhood—hinted of such a case. "In fact," writes the

*Oliver Sacks, "To See and Not See," in *An Anthropologist on Mars: Seven Paradoxical Tales* (New York: Alfred A. Knopf, 1995) 108–52.

ophthalmologist Alberto Valvo, in *Sight Restoration after Long-Term Blindness,* "the number of cases of this kind over the last ten centuries known to us is not more than twenty."

What would vision be like in such a patient? Would it be "normal" from the moment vision was restored? This is what one might think at first. This is the commonsensical notion—that the eyes will be opened, the scales will fall from them, and (in the words of the New Testament) the blind man will "receive" sight.[1]

But could it be that simple? Was not *experience* necessary to see? Did one not have to learn to see? I was not well acquainted with the literature on the subject, though I had read with fascination the great case history published in the *Quarterly Journal of Psychology* in 1963 by the psychologist Richard Gregory (with Jean G. Wallace), and I knew that such cases, hypothetical or real, had riveted the attention of philosophers and psychologists for hundreds of years. The seventeenth-century philosopher William Molyneux, whose wife was blind, posed the following question to his friend John Locke: "Suppose a man born blind, and now adult, and taught by his touch to distinguish between a cube and a sphere [be] made to see: [could he now] by his sight, before he touched them . . . distinguish and tell which was the globe and which the cube?" Locke considers this in his 1690 *Essay Concerning Human Understanding* and decides that the answer is no. In 1709, examining the problem in more detail, and the whole relation between sight and touch, in *A New Theory of Vision,* George Berkeley concluded that there was no necessary connection between a tactile world and a sight world—that a connection between them could be established only on the basis of experience.

Barely twenty years elapsed before these considerations were put to the test— 5 when, in 1728, William Cheselden, an English surgeon, removed the cataracts from the eyes of a thirteen-year-old boy born blind. Despite his high intelligence and youth, the boy encountered profound difficulties with the simplest visual perceptions. He had no idea of distance. He had no idea of space or size. And he was bizarrely confused by drawings and paintings, by the *idea* of a two-dimensional representation of reality. As Berkeley had anticipated, he was able to make sense of what he saw only gradually and insofar as he was able to connect visual experiences with tactile ones. It had been similar with many other patients in the two hundred and fifty years since Cheselden's operation: nearly all had experienced the most profound, Lockean confusion and bewilderment.[2]

And yet, I was informed, as soon as the bandages were removed from Virgil's eye, he saw his doctor and his fiancée, and laughed. Doubtless he saw

[1]There is a hint of something stranger, more complex, in Mark's description of the miracle at Bethsaida, for here, at first, the blind man saw "men as trees, walking," and only subsequently was his eyesight fully restored (Mark 8:22–26).

[2]The removal (or, as was first done, the dislocation or "couching" of the cataracted lens) leaves an eye strongly farsighted and in need of an artificial lens; and the thick lenses used in the eighteenth and nineteenth centuries, and indeed until quite recently, markedly reduced peripheral vision. Thus all patients operated upon for cataract before the present era of contact and implanted lenses had significant optical difficulties to contend with. But it was only those blind from birth or early childhood who had the special Lockean difficulty of not being able to make sense of what they saw.

something—but what did he see? What did "seeing" for this previously not-seeing man mean? What sort of world had he been launched into?

Virgil was born on a small farm in Kentucky soon after the outbreak of the Second World War. He seemed normal enough as a baby, but (his mother thought) had poor eyesight even as a toddler, sometimes bumped into things, seemed not to see them. At the age of three, he became gravely ill with a triple illness—a meningitis or meningoencephalitis (inflammation of the brain and its membranes), polio, and cat-scratch fever. During this acute illness, he had convulsions, became virtually blind, paralyzed in the legs, partly paralyzed in his breathing, and, after ten days, fell into a coma. He remained in a coma for two weeks. When he emerged from it, he seemed, according to his mother, "a different person"; he showed a curious indolence, nonchalance, passivity, seemed nothing at all like the spunky, mischievous boy he had been.

The strength in his legs came back over the next year, and his chest grew stronger, though never entirely normal. His vision also recovered significantly—but his retinas were now gravely damaged. Whether the retinal damage was caused wholly by his acute illness or perhaps partly by a congenital retinal degeneration was never clear.

In Virgil's sixth year, cataracts began to develop in both eyes, and it was evident that he was again becoming functionally blind. That same year, he was sent to a school for the blind, and there he eventually learned to read Braille and to become adept with the use of a cane. But he was not a star pupil; he was not as adventurous or aggressively independent as some blind people are. There was a striking passivity all through his time at school—as, indeed, there had been since his illness.

10   Yet Virgil graduated from the school and, when he was twenty, decided to leave Kentucky, to seek training, work, and a life of his own in a city in Oklahoma. He trained as a massage therapist and soon found employment at a YMCA. He was obviously good at his job, and highly esteemed, and the Y was happy to keep him on its permanent staff and to provide a small house for him across the road, where he lived with a friend, also employed at the Y. Virgil had many clients—it is fascinating to hear the tactile detail with which he can describe them—and seemed to take a real pleasure and pride in his job. Thus, in his modest way, Virgil made a life: had a steady job and an identity, was self-supporting, had friends, read Braille papers and books (though less, with the years, as Talking Books came in). He had a passion for sports, especially baseball, and loved to listen to games on the radio. He had an encyclopedic knowledge of baseball games, players, scores, statistics. On a couple of occasions, he became involved with girlfriends and would cross the city on public transport to meet them. He maintained a close tie with home, and particularly with his mother—he would get hampers of food regularly from the farm and send hampers of laundry back and forth. Life was limited, but stable in its way.

Then, in 1991, he met Amy—or, rather, they met again, for they had known each other well twenty or more years before. Amy's background was different from Virgil's: she came from a cultivated middle-class family, had gone to college in New Hampshire, and had a degree in botany. She had worked at another Y in town, as a swimming coach, and had met Virgil at a cat show in 1968. They dated a bit—she was in her early twenties, he was a few years older—but then Amy decided to go back to graduate school in Arkansas, where she met her first husband, and she and Virgil fell out of contact. She ran her own plant nursery for a while, specializing in orchids, but had to give this up when she developed severe asthma. She and her first husband divorced after a few years, and she returned to Oklahoma. In 1988, out of the blue, Virgil called her, and, after three years of long phone calls between them, they finally met again, in 1991. "All of a sudden it was like twenty years were never there," Amy said.

Meeting again, at this point in their lives, both felt a certain desire for companionship. With Amy, perhaps, this took a more active form. She saw Virgil stuck (as she perceived it) in a vegetative, dull life: going over to the Y, doing his massages; going back home, where, increasingly, he listened to ball games on the radio; going out and meeting people less and less each year. Restoring his sight, she must have felt, would, like marriage, stir him from his indolent bachelor existence and provide them both with a new life.

Virgil was passive here as in so much else. He had been sent to half a dozen specialists over the years, and they had been unanimous in declining to operate, feeling that in all probability he had no useful retinal function; and Virgil seemed to accept this with equanimity. But Amy disagreed. With Virgil being blind already, she said, there was nothing to lose, and there was a real possibility, remote but almost too exciting to contemplate, that he might actually get reasonable sight back and, after nearly forty-five years, see again. And so Amy pushed for the surgery. Virgil's mother, fearing disturbance, was strongly against it. ("He is fine as he is," she said.) Virgil himself showed no preference in the matter; he seemed happy to go along with whatever they decided.

Finally, in mid-September, the day of surgery came. Virgil's right eye had its cataract removed, and a new lens implant was inserted; then the eye was bandaged, as is customary, for twenty-four hours of recovery. The following day, the bandage was removed, and Virgil's eye was finally exposed, without cover, to the world. The moment of truth had finally come.

Or had it? The truth of the matter (as I pieced it together later), if less "miraculous" than Amy's journal suggested, was infinitely stranger. The dramatic moment stayed vacant, grew longer, sagged. No cry ("I can see!") burst from Virgil's lips. He seemed to be staring blankly, bewildered, without focusing, at the surgeon, who stood before him, still holding the bandages. Only when the surgeon spoke—saying "Well?"—did a look of recognition cross Virgil's face. 15

Virgil told me later that in this first moment he had no idea what he was seeing. There was light, there was movement, there was color, all mixed up, all meaningless, a blur. Then out of the blur came a voice that said, "Well?" Then, and only then, he said, did he finally realize that this chaos of light and shadow was a face—and, indeed, the face of his surgeon.

His experience was virtually identical to that of Gregory's patient S.B., who was accidentally blinded in infancy, and received a corneal transplant in his fifties:

> When the bandages were removed . . . he heard a voice coming from in front of him and to one side: he turned to the source of the sound, and saw a "blur." He

realized that this must be a face. . . . He seemed to think that he would not have known that this was a face if he had not previously heard the voice and known that voices came from faces.

The rest of us, born sighted, can scarcely imagine such confusion. For we, born with a full complement of senses, and correlating these, one with the other, create a sight world from the start, a world of visual objects and concepts and meanings. When we open our eyes each morning, it is upon a world we have spent a lifetime *learning* to see. We are not given the world: we make our world through incessant experience, categorization, memory, reconnection. But when Virgil opened his eye, after being blind for forty-five years—having had little more than an infant's visual experience, and this long forgotten—there were no visual memories to support a perception; there was no world of experience and meaning awaiting him. He saw, but what he saw had no coherence. His retina and optic nerve were active, transmitting impulses, but his brain could make no sense of them; he was, as neurologists say, agnosic.

Everyone, Virgil included, expected something much simpler. A man opens his eyes, light enters and falls on the retina: he sees. It is as simple as that, we imagine. And the surgeon's own experience, like that of most ophthalmologists, had been with the removal of cataracts from patients who had almost always lost their sight late in life—and such patients do indeed, if the surgery is successful, have a virtually immediate recovery of normal vision, for they have in no sense lost their ability to see. And so, though there had been a careful surgical discussion of the operation and of possible postsurgical complications, there was little discussion or preparation for the neurological and psychological difficulties that Virgil might encounter.

20   With the cataract out, Virgil was able to see colors and movements, to see (but not identify) large objects and shapes, and, astonishingly, to *read* some letters on the third line of the standard Snellen eye chart—the line corresponding to a visual acuity of about 20/100 or a little better. But though his best vision was a respectable 20/80, he lacked a coherent visual field, because his central vision was poor, and it was almost impossible for the eye to fixate on targets; it kept losing them, making random searching movements, finding them, then losing them again. It was evident that the central, or macular, part of the retina, which is specialized for high acuity and fixation, was scarcely functioning, and that it was only the surrounding *para*macular area that was making possible such vision as he had. The retina itself presented a moth-eaten or piebald appearance, with areas of increased and decreased pigmentation—islets of intact or relatively intact retina alternating with areas of atrophy. The macula was degenerated and pale, and the blood vessels of the entire retina appeared narrowed.

Examination, I was told, suggested the scars or residues of old disease but no current or active disease process; and, this being so, Virgil's vision, such as it was, could be stable for the rest of his life. It could be hoped, moreover (since the worse eye had been operated on first), that the left eye, which was to be operated upon in a few weeks' time, might have considerably more functional retina than the right.

I had not been able to go to Oklahoma straightaway—my impulse was to take the next plane after that initial phone call—but had kept myself informed of Virgil's progress over the ensuing weeks by speaking with Amy, with Virgil's mother, and, of course, with Virgil himself. I also spoke at length with Dr. Hamlin and with Richard Gregory, in England, to discuss what sort of test materials I should bring, for I myself had never seen such a case, nor did I know anyone (apart from Gregory) who had. I gathered together some materials—solid objects, pictures, cartoons, illusions, videotapes, and special perceptual tests designed by a physiologist colleague, Ralph Siegel; I phoned an ophthalmologist friend, Robert Wasserman (we had previously worked together on the case of the colorblind painter), and we started to plan a visit. It was important, we felt, not just to test Virgil but to see how he managed in real life, inside his house, outside, in natural settings and social situations; crucial, too, that we see him as a person, bringing his own life history—his particular dispositions and needs and expectations—to this critical passage; that we meet his fiancée, who had so urged the operation, and with whom his life was now so intimately mingled; that we look not merely at his eyes and perceptual powers but at the whole tenor and pattern of his life.

Virgil and Amy—now newlyweds—greeted us at the exit barrier in the airport. Virgil was of medium height, but exceedingly fat; he moved slowly and tended to cough and puff with the slightest exertion. He was not, it was evident, an entirely well man. His eyes roved to and fro, in searching movements, and when Amy introduced Bob and me he did not seem to see us straightaway—he looked toward us but not quite at us. I had the impression, momentary but strong, that he did not really look at our faces, though he smiled and laughed and listened minutely.

I was reminded of what Gregory had observed of his patient S.B.—that "he did not look at a speaker's face, and made nothing of facial expressions." Virgil's behavior was certainly not that of a sighted man, but it was not that of a blind man, either. It was, rather, the behavior of one *mentally* blind, or agnosic—able to see but not to decipher what he was seeing. He reminded me of an agnosic patient of mine, Dr. P. (the man who mistook his wife for a hat), who, instead of looking at me, taking me in, in the normal way, made sudden strange fixations—on my nose, on my right ear, down to my chin, up to my right eye—not seeing, not "getting," my face as a whole.

We walked out through the crowded airport, Amy holding Virgil's arm, guiding him, and out to the lot where they had parked their car. Virgil was fond of cars, and one of his first pleasures after surgery (as with S.B.) had been to watch them through the window of his house, to enjoy their motions, and spot their colors and shapes—their colors, especially. He was sometimes bewildered by shapes. "What cars do you see?" I asked him as we walked through the lot. He pointed to all the cars we passed. "That's a blue one, that's red—wow, that's a big one!" Some of the shapes he found very surprising. "Look at that one!" he exclaimed once. "I have to look down!" And, bending, he felt it—it was a slinky, streamlined V-12 Jaguar—and confirmed its low profile. But it was only the colors and general profiles he was getting; he would have walked past their own

25

car had Amy not been with him. And Bob and I were struck by the fact that Virgil would look, would attend visually, only if one asked him to or pointed something out—not spontaneously. His sight might be largely restored, but using his eyes, looking, it was clear, was far from natural to him; he still had many of the habits, the behaviors, of a blind man.[3]

The drive from the airport to their house was a long one; it took us through the heart of town, and it gave us an opportunity to talk to Virgil and Amy and to observe Virgil's reactions to his new vision. He clearly enjoyed movement, watching the ever-changing spectacle through the car windows and the movement of other cars on the road. He spotted a speeder coming up very fast behind us and identified cars, buses (he especially loved the bright-yellow school buses), eighteen-wheelers, and, once, on a side road, a slow, noisy tractor. He seemed very sensitive to, and intrigued by, large neon signs and advertisements and liked picking out their letters as we passed. He had difficulty reading entire words, though he often guessed them correctly from one or two letters or from the style of the signs. Other signs he saw but could not read. He was able to see and identify the changing colors of the traffic lights as we got into town.

He and Amy told us of other things he had seen since his operation and of some of the unexpected confusions that could occur. He had seen the moon; it was larger than he expected.[4] On one occasion, he was puzzled by seeing "a fat airplane" in the sky—"stuck, not moving." It turned out to be a blimp. Occasionally, he had seen birds; they made him jump, sometimes, if they came too close. (Of course, they did *not* come that close, Amy explained. Virgil simply had no idea of distance.)

Much of their time recently had been spent shopping—there had been the wedding to prepare for, and Amy wanted to show Virgil off, tell his story to the clerks and shopkeepers they knew, let them see a transformed Virgil for

[3]One does not see, or sense, or perceive, in isolation—perception is always linked to behavior and movement, to reaching out and exploring the world. It is insufficient to see; one must look as well. Though we have spoken, with Virgil, of a perceptual incapacity, or agnosia, there was, equally, a lack of capacity or impulse to *look*, to *act* seeing—a lack of visual *behavior*. Von Senden mentions the case of two children whose eyes had been bandaged from an early age, and who, when the bandages were removed at the age of five, showed no reaction to this, showed no looking, and seemed blind. One has the sense that these children, who had built up their worlds with other senses and behaviors, did not know how to *use* their eyes.

Looking—as an orientation, as a behavior—may even vanish in those who become blind late in life, despite the fact that they have been "lookers" all their lives. Many startling examples of this are given by John Hull in his autobiographical book, *Touching the Rock*. Hull had lived as a sighted man until his midforties, but within five years of becoming totally blind, he had lost the very idea of "facing" people, of "looking" at his interlocutors.

[4]Gregory's patient, too, was startled by the moon: he had expected a quarter moon would be wedge-shaped, like a piece of cake, and was astonished and amused to find it a crescent instead.

themselves.[5] It was fun; the local television station had aired a story about Virgil's operation, and people would recognize him and come up to shake his hand. But supermarkets and other stores were also dense visual spectacles of objects of all kinds, often in bright packaging, and provided good "exercise" for Virgil's new sight. Among the first objects he had recognized, just the day after his bandages came off, were rolls of toilet paper on display. He had picked up a package and given it to Amy to prove he could see. Three days after surgery, they had gone to an IGA, and Virgil had seen shelves, fruit, cans, people, aisles, carts—so much that he got scared. "Everything ran together," he said. He needed to get out of the store and close his eyes for a bit.

He enjoyed uncluttered views, he said, of green hills and grass—especially after the overfull, overrich visual spectacles of shops—though it was difficult for him, Amy indicated, to connect the visual shapes of hills with the tangible hills he had walked up, and he had no idea of size or perspective.[6] But the first month of seeing had been predominantly positive: "Every day seems like a great adventure, seeing more for the first time each day," Amy had written, summarizing it, in her journal.

When we arrived at the house, Virgil, caneless, walked by himself up the path to the front door, pulled out his key, grasped the doorknob, unlocked the door, and opened it. This was impressive—he could never have done it at first, he said, and it was something he had been practicing since the day after surgery. It was his showpiece. But he said that in general he found walking "scary" and

30

---

[5]Robert Scott, a sociologist and anthropologist at the Institute for Advanced Behavioral Study at Stanford, has been especially concerned with societal reactions to the blind, and the social contempt and stigmatization so often accorded them. He has also lectured on "miracle cures," the extravagance of emotion that may attend the restoration of sight. It was Dr. Scott who, some years ago, sent me a copy of Valvo's book.

[6]Sensation itself has no "markers" for size and distance; these have to be learned on the basis of experience. Thus it has been reported that if people who have lived their entire lives in dense rain forest, with a far point no more than a few feet away, are brought into a wide, empty landscape, they may reach out and try to touch the mountaintops with their hands; they have no concept of how far the mountains are.

Helmholtz (in *Thought in Medicine*, an autobiographical memoir) relates how, as a child of two, when walking in a park, he saw what he took to be a little tower with a rail at the top and tiny mannikins or dolls walking around behind the rail. When he asked his mother if she could reach him down one to play with, she exclaimed that the tower was a kilometer away, and two hundred meters high, and these little figures were not mannikins but *people* on the top. As soon as she said this, Helmholtz writes, he suddenly realized the scale of everything, and never again made such a perceptual mistake—though the visual perception of space as a subject never ceased to exercise him. (See Cahan, 1993.)

Poe, in "The Gold Bug," relates an opposite story: how what appeared to be a vast, many-jointed creature on a distant hill turned out to be a tiny bug on the window.

A personal experience, the first time I used marijuana, comes to mind here: gazing at my hand, seen against a blank wall. It seemed to rush away from me, while maintaining the same apparent size, until it appeared like a vast hand, a cosmic hand, across parsecs of space. Probably this illusion was made possible by, among other things, the absence of markers or context to indicate actual size and distance, and perhaps some disturbance of body image and central processing of vision.

"confusing" without touch, without his cane, with his uncertain, unstable judgment of space and distance. Sometimes surfaces or objects would seem to loom, to be on top of him, when they were still quite a distance away; sometimes he would get confused by his own shadow (the whole concept of shadows, of objects blocking light, was puzzling to him) and would come to a stop, or trip, or try to step over it. Steps, in particular, posed a special hazard, because all he could see was a confusion, a flat surface, of parallel and crisscrossing lines; he could not see them (although he knew them) as solid objects going up or coming down in three-dimensional space. Now, five weeks after surgery, he often felt more disabled than he had felt when he was blind, and he had lost the confidence, the ease of moving, that he had possessed then. But he hoped all this would sort itself out with time.

I was not so sure; every patient described in the literature had faced great difficulties after surgery in the apprehension of space and distance—for months, even years. This was the case even in Valvo's highly intelligent patient H.S., who had been normally sighted until, at fifteen, his eyes were scarred by a chemical explosion. He had become totally blind until a corneal transplant was done twenty-two years later. But following this, he encountered grave difficulties of every kind, which he recorded, minutely, on tape:

> During these first weeks [after surgery] I had no appreciation of depth or distance; street lights were luminous stains stuck to the window panes, and the corridors of the hospital were black holes. When I crossed the road the traffic terrified me, even when I was accompanied. I am very insecure while walking; indeed I am more afraid now than before the operation.

We gathered in the kitchen at the back of the house, which had a large white deal table. Bob and I laid out all our test objects—color charts, letter charts, pictures, illusions—on it and set up a video camera to record the testing. As we settled down, Virgil's cat and dog bounded in to greet and check us—and Virgil, we noted, had some difficulty telling which was which. This comic and embarrassing problem had persisted since he returned home from surgery: both animals, as it happened, were black and white, and he kept confusing them—to their annoyance—until he could touch them, too. Sometimes, Amy said, she would see him examining the cat carefully, looking at its head, its ears, its paws, its tail, and touching each part gently as he did so. I observed this myself the next day— Virgil feeling and looking at Tibbles with extraordinary intentness, correlating the cat. He would keep doing this, Amy remarked ("You'd think once was enough"), but the new ideas, the visual recognitions, kept slipping from his mind.

Cheselden described a strikingly similar scene with his young patient in the 1720s:

> One particular only, though it might appear trifling, I will relate: Having often forgot which was the cat, and which the dog, he was ashamed to ask; but catching the cat, which he knew by feeling, he was observed to look at her steadfastly, and then, setting her down, said, So, puss, I shall know you another time. . . . Upon being told what things were . . . he would carefully observe that he might know

them again; and (as he said) at first learned to know, and again forgot, a thousand things in a day.

Virgil's first formal recognitions when the bandages were taken off had been of letters on the ophthalmologist's eye chart, and we decided to test him, first, on letter recognition. He could not see ordinary newsprint clearly—his acuity was still only about 20/80—but he readily perceived letters that were more than a third of an inch high. Here he did rather well, for the most part, and recognized all the commoner letters (at least, capital letters) easily—as he had been able to do from the moment the bandages were removed. How was it that he had so much difficulty recognizing faces, or the cat, and so much difficulty with shapes generally, and with size and distance, and yet so little difficulty, relatively, recognizing letters? When I asked Virgil about this, he told me that he had learned the alphabet by touch at school, where they had used letter blocks, or cutout letters, for teaching the blind. I was struck by this and reminded of Gregory's patient S.B.: "much to our surprise, he could even tell the time by means of a large clock on the wall. We were so surprised at this that we did not at first believe that he could have been in any sense blind before the operation." But in his blind days S.B. had used a large hunter watch with no glass, telling the time by touching the hands, and he had apparently made an instant "cross-modal" transfer, to use Gregory's term, from touch to vision. Virgil too, it seemed, must have been making just such a transfer.

But while Virgil could recognize individual letters easily, he could not string   35
them together—could not read or even see words. I found this puzzling, for he said that they used not only Braille but English in raised or inscribed letters at school—and that he had learned to read fairly fluently. Indeed, he could still easily read the inscriptions on war memorials and tombstones by touch. But his eyes seemed to fix on particular letters and to be incapable of the easy movement, the scanning, that is needed to read. This was also the case with the literate H.S.:

> My first attempts at reading were painful. I could make out single letters, but it was impossible for me to make out whole words; I managed to do so only after weeks of exhausting attempts. In fact, it was impossible for me to remember all the letters together, after having read them one by one. Nor was it possible for me, during the first weeks, to count my own five fingers: I had the feeling that they were all there, but . . . it was not possible for me to pass from one to the other while counting.

Further problems became apparent as we spent the day with Virgil. He would pick up details incessantly—an angle, an edge, a color, a movement—but would not be able to synthesize them, to form a complex perception at a glance. This was one reason the cat, visually, was so puzzling: he would see a paw, the nose, the tail, an ear, but could not see all of them together, see the cat as a whole.

Amy had commented in her journal on how even the most "obvious" connections—visually and logically obvious—had to be learned. Thus, she told us, a few days after the operation "he said that trees didn't look like anything on earth," but in her entry for October 21, a month after the operation, she noted, "Virgil finally put a tree together—he now knows that the trunk and leaves go together to form a complete unit." And on another occasion: "Skyscrapers strange, cannot understand how they stay up without collapsing."

Many—or perhaps all—patients in Virgil's situation had had similar difficulties. One such patient (described by Eduard Raehlmann, in 1891), though she had had a little vision preoperatively and had frequently handled dogs, "had no idea of how the head, legs, and ears were connected to the animal." Valvo quotes his patient T.G.:

> Before the operation I had a completely different idea of space, and I knew that an object could occupy only one tactile point. I knew . . . also that if there were an obstacle or a step at the end of the porch, this obstacle occurred after a certain period of time, to which I was accustomed. After the operation, for many months, I could no longer coordinate visual sensations with my speed of walking. . . . I had to coordinate both vision and the time necessary to cover the distance. That I found very difficult. If any walking were too slow or too fast, I stumbled.

Valvo comments, "The real difficulty here is that simultaneous perception of objects is an unaccustomed way to those used to sequential perception through touch." We, with a full complement of senses, live in space and time; the blind live in a world of time alone. For the blind build their worlds from sequences of impressions (tactile, auditory, olfactory) and are not capable, as sighted people are, of a simultaneous visual perception, the making of an instantaneous visual scene. Indeed, if one can no longer see in space, then the *idea* of space becomes incomprehensible—even for highly intelligent people blinded relatively late in life (this is the central thesis of von Senden's great monograph). And it is power-fully conveyed by John Hull in his remarkable autobiography, *Touching the Rock*, when he speaks of himself, of the blind, as "living in time" almost exclusively. With the blind, he writes,

> this sense of being in a place is less pronounced. . . . Space is reduced to one's own body, and the position of the body is known not by what objects have been passed but by how long it has been in motion. Position is thus measured by time. . . . For the blind, people are not there unless they speak. . . . People are in motion, they are temporal, they come and they go. They come out of nothing; they disappear.

Although Virgil could recognize letters and numbers, and could write them, too, he mixed up some rather similar ones ("A" and "H," for example) and on occasion, wrote some backward. (Hull describes how, after only five years of blindness in his forties, his own visual memories had become so uncertain that he was not sure which way around a "3" went and had to trace it in the air with his fingers. Thus the numeral was retained as a tactile-motor concept, but no longer as a visual concept.) Still, Virgil's performance was an impressive one for a man who had not seen for forty-five years. But the world does not consist of letters and numbers. How would he do with objects and pictures? How would he do with the real world?

His first impressions when the bandages were removed were especially of color, and it seemed to be color, which has no analogue in the world of touch, that excited and delighted him—this was very clear from the way he spoke and from Amy's journal. (The recognition of colors and movement seems to be innate.) It was colors to which Virgil continually alluded, the chromatic unexpectedness of new sights. He had had Greek salad and spaghetti the night before, he told us, and the spaghetti startled him: "White round strings, like fishing line," he said. "I thought it'd be brown."

Seeing light and shape and movements, seeing colors above all, had been completely unexpected and had had a physical and emotional impact almost shocking, explosive. ("I felt the violence of these sensations," wrote Valvo's patient H.S., "like a blow on the head. The violence of the emotion . . . was akin to the very strong emotion I felt on seeing my wife for the first time, and when out in a car, I saw the huge monuments of Rome.")

We found that Virgil easily distinguished a great array of colors and matched them without difficulty. But, confusingly, or confusedly, he sometimes gave colors the wrong names: yellow, for example, he called pink, but he knew that it was the same color as a banana. We wondered at first whether he could have a color agnosia or color anomia—defects of color association and color naming that are due to damage in specific areas of the brain. But his difficulties, it seemed to us, came simply from lack of learning (or from forgetting)—from the fact that early and long blindness had sometimes prevented his associating colors with their names or had caused him to forget some of the associations he had made. Such associations and the neural connections that underlay them, feeble in the first place, had become disestablished in his brain, not through any damage or disease, but simply from disuse.

Although Virgil believed that he had visual memories, including color memories, from the remote past—on our drive from the airport he had spoken of growing up on the farm in Kentucky ("I see the creek running down the middle," "birds on the fences," "the big old white house")—I could not decide whether these were genuine memories, visual images in his mind, or mere verbal descriptions without images (like Helen Keller's).

How was he with shapes? Here matters were more complicated, because in the weeks since his surgery Virgil had been practicing shapes, correlating their look and their feel. No such practice had been required with colors. He had at first been unable to recognize any shapes visually—even shapes as simple as a square or a circle, which he recognized instantly by touch. To him, a touch square in no sense corresponded to a sight square. This was his answer to the Molyneux question. For this reason, Amy had bought, among other things, a child's wooden formboard, with large, simple blocks—square, triangle, circle, and rectangle—to be fitted into corresponding holes, and had got Virgil to practice with it every day. Virgil found the task impossible at first, but quite easy

40

now, after practicing for a month. He still tended to feel the holes and shapes before matching them, but when we forbade this he fitted them together quite fluently by sight alone.

45   Solid objects, it was evident, presented much more difficulty, because their appearance was so variable; and much of the past five weeks had been devoted to the exploration of objects, their unexpected vicissitudes of appearance as they were seen from near or far, or half-concealed, or from different places and angles.

On the day he returned home after the bandages were removed, his house and its contents were unintelligible to him, and he had to be led up the garden path, led through the house, led into each room, and introduced to each chair. Within a week, with Amy's help, he had established a canonical line—a particular line up the path, through the sitting room to the kitchen, with further lines, as necessary, to the bathroom and the bedroom. It was only from this line, at first, that he could recognize anything—though this took a great deal of interpretation and inference; thus he learned, for example, that "a whiteness to the right," to be seen as he came obliquely through the front door, was in fact the dining table in the next room, although at this point neither "table" nor "dining room" was a clear visual concept. If he deviated from the line, he would be totally disoriented. Then, carefully, with Amy's help, he started to use the line as a home base, making short sallies and excursions to either side of it, so that he could see the room, feel its walls and contents from different angles, and build up a sense of space, of solidity, of perspective.

As Virgil explored the rooms of his house, investigating, so to speak, the visual construction of the world, I was reminded of an infant moving his hand to and fro before his eyes, waggling his head, turning it this way and that, in his primal construction of the world. Most of us have no sense of the immensity of this construction, for we perform it seamlessly, unconsciously, thousands of times every day, at a glance. But this is not so for a baby, it was not so for Virgil, and it is not so for, say, an artist who wants to experience his elemental perceptions afresh and anew. Cézanne once wrote, "The same subject seen from a different angle gives a subject for study of the highest interest and so varied that I think I could be occupied for months without changing my place, simply bending more to the right or left."

We achieve perceptual constancy—the correlation of all the different appearances, the transforms of objects—very early, in the first months of life. It constitutes a huge learning task, but is achieved so smoothly, so unconsciously, that its enormous complexity is scarcely realized (though it is an achievement that even the largest supercomputers cannot begin to match). But for Virgil, with half a century of forgetting whatever visual engrams he had constructed, the learning, or relearning, of these transforms required hours of conscious and systematic exploration each day. This first month, then, saw a systematic exploration, by sight and touch, of all the smaller things in the house: fruit, vegetables, bottles, cans, cutlery, flowers, the knickknacks on the mantelpiece— turning them round and round, holding them close to him, then at arm's length, trying to synthesize their varying appearances into a sense of unitary objecthood.[7]

Despite all the vexations that trying to see could entail, Virgil had stuck with this gamely, and he had learned steadily. He had little difficulty now recognizing the fruit, the bottles, the cans in the kitchen, the different flowers in the living room, and other common objects in the house.

Unfamiliar objects were much more difficult. When I took a blood-pressure cuff from my medical bag, he was completely flummoxed and could make nothing of it, but he recognized it immediately when I allowed him to touch it. Moving objects presented a special problem, for their appearance changed constantly. Even his dog, he told me, looked so different at different times that he wondered if it was the same dog.[8] He was utterly lost when it came to the rapid changes in others' physiognomies. Such difficulties are almost universal among the early blinded restored to sight. Gregory's patient S.B. could not recognize individual faces, or their expressions, a year after his eyes had been operated on, despite perfectly normal elementary vision.

What about pictures? Here I had been given conflicting reports about Virgil. He was said to love television, to follow everything on it—and, indeed, a huge new TV stood in the living room, an emblem of Virgil's new life as a seeing person. But when we tried him first on still pictures, pictures in magazines, he had no success at all. He could not see people, could not see objects—did not comprehend the idea of representation. Gregory's patient S.B. had similar problems. When shown a picture of the Cambridge Backs, showing the river and King's Bridge, Gregory tells us,

> He made nothing of this. He did not realize that the scene was of a river, and did not recognize water or bridge. . . . So far as we could tell, S.B. had no idea which

[7]There were similar problems with Gregory's subject, S.B., who never ceased to be "struck by how objects changed their shape when he walked round them. . . . He would look at a lamppost, walk round it, and stand studying it from a different aspect, and wonder why it looked different and yet the same." All newly sighted subjects, indeed, have radical difficulties with appearances, finding themselves suddenly plunged into a world that, for them, may be a chaos of continually shifting, unstable, evanescent appearances. They may find themselves completely lost, at sea, in this flux of appearances, which for them is not yet securely anchored to a world of objects, a world of space. The newly sighted, who have previously depended on senses other than vision, are baffled by the very concept of "appearance," which, being optical, has no analogue in the other senses. We who have been born into the world of appearances (and their occasional illusions, mirages, deceptions) have learned to master it, to feel secure and at home in it, but this is exceedingly difficult for the newly sighted. The philosopher F. H. Bradley wrote a famous book called *Appearance and Reality* (1893)—but for the newly sighted, at first, these have no connection.

[8]When Virgil said this I was reminded of a description in Borges's story "Funes the Memorious," where Funes's difficulty with general concepts leads him into a similar situation:

> It was not only difficult for him to understand that the generic term *dog* embraced so many unlike specimens of different sizes and forms; he was disturbed by the fact that a dog at three-fourteen (seen in profile) should have the same name as the dog at three-fifteen (seen from the front).

objects lay in front of or behind others in any of the color pictures..... We formed the impression that he saw little more than patches of color.

It was similar, again, with Cheselden's young patient:

> We thought he soon knew what pictures represented . . . but we found afterwards we were mistaken; for about two months after he was couched, he discovered at once they represented solid bodies, when to that time he considered them only as party-coloured planes, or surfaces diversified with variety of paint; but even then he was no less surprised, expecting the pictures would feel like the things they represented, . . . and asked which was the lying sense, feeling or seeing?

Nor were things any better with moving pictures on a TV screen. Mindful of Virgil's passion for listening to baseball games, we found a channel with a game in progress. It seemed at first as if he were following it visually, because he could describe who was batting, what was going on. But as soon as we turned off the sound he was lost. It became evident that he himself perceived little beyond streaks of light and colors and motions, and that all the rest (what he *seemed* to see) was interpretation, performed swiftly, and perhaps unconsciously, in consonance with the sound. How it would be with a real game we were far from sure—it seemed possible to us that he might see and enjoy a good deal; it was in the two-dimensional representation of reality, pictorial or televisual, that he was still completely at sea.

Virgil had now had two hours of testing and was beginning to get tired—both visually and cognitively tired, as he had tended to do since the operation—and when he got tired he could see less and less, and had more and more difficulty making sense of what he could see.[9]

Indeed, we were getting restless ourselves and wanted to get out after a morning of testing. We asked him, as a final task before going for a drive, if he felt up to some drawing. We suggested first that he draw a hammer. (A hammer

---

[9]Due to his exhaustion at this point, we could not test him on the visual illusions we had brought along. This was unfortunate, because "seeing" or "not seeing" visual illusions provides an objective and replicable way of examining the visual-constructive capacities of the brain. No one has explored this approach more deeply than Gregory, and his detailed account of S.B.'s responses to visual illusions is therefore of great interest. One such illusion consists of parallel lines that, to normal eyes, seem to diverge because of the effect of diverging lines superimposed on them; no such "gestalt" effect occurred with S.B., who saw the lines as perfectly parallel—a similar lack of "influence" was seen with other illusions. Particularly interesting was S.B.'s response to reversing figures, such as cubes and staircases drawn in perspective, which are normally seen in depth and reverse their apparent configuration at intervals; the figures did not reverse for S.B. and were not seen in depth. There was, similarly, no figure-ground fluctuation with ambiguous figures. He did not, apparently, "see" distance/size changes in illusions, nor did he experience the so-called waterfall effect, the familiar aftereffect of perceived movement. In all these cases, the illusion is "seen" (even though the mind may know the perception to be illusory) by all normally sighted adults. Many of these illusory effects can also be demonstrated in young children, and some in monkeys, and even in Edelman's artificial "creature," DARWIN IV. That S.B. failed to "see" them illustrates how rudimentary his brain's powers of visual construction were, in consequence of the virtual absence of early visual experience.

was the first object S.B. drew.) Virgil agreed and, rather shakily, began to draw. He tended to guide the pencil's movement with his free hand. ("He only does that because he's tired now," said Amy.) Then he drew a car (very high and old-fashioned); a plane (with the tail missing: it would have been hard put to fly); and a house (flat and crude, like a three-year-old's drawing).

When we finally got out, it was a brilliant October morning, and Virgil was blinded for a minute, until he put on a pair of dark-green sunglasses. Even ordinary daylight, he said, seemed far too bright for him, too glary; he felt that he saw best in quite subdued light. We asked him where he would like to go, and after thinking for a little he said, "The zoo." He had never been to a zoo, he said, and he was curious to know how the different animals looked. He had loved animals ever since his childhood days on the farm.

Very striking, as soon as we got to the zoo, was Virgil's sensitivity to motion. He was startled, first, by an odd strutting movement; it made him smile—he had never seen anything like it. "What is it?" he asked.

"An emu."

He was not quite sure what an emu was, so we asked him to describe it to us. He had difficulty and could say only that it was about the same size as Amy— she and the emu were standing side by side at that point—but that its movements were quite different from hers. He wanted to touch it, to feel it all over. If he did that, he thought, he would then see it better. But touching, sadly, was not allowed.

His eye was caught next by a leaping motion nearby, and he immediately realized—or, rather, surmised—that it must be a kangaroo. His eye followed its motions closely, but he could not describe it, he said, unless he could feel it. We were wondering by now exactly what he could see—and what, indeed, he meant by "seeing."

In general, it seemed to us, if Virgil could identify an animal it would be either by its motion or by virtue of a single feature—thus, he might identify a kangaroo because it leapt, a giraffe by its height, or a zebra by its stripes—but he could not form any overall impression of the animal. It was also necessary that the animal be sharply defined against a background; he could not identify the elephants, despite their trunks, because they were at a considerable distance and stood against a slate-colored background.

Finally, we went to the great-ape enclosure; Virgil was curious to see the gorilla. He could not see it at all when it was half-hidden among some trees, and when it finally came into the open he thought that, though it moved differently, it looked just like a large man. Fortunately, there was a life-size bronze statue of a gorilla in the enclosure, and we told Virgil, who had been longing to touch all the animals, that he could, if nothing else, at least examine the statue. Exploring it swiftly and minutely with his hands, he had an air of assurance that he had never shown when examining anything by sight. It came to me—perhaps it came to all of us at this moment—how skillful and self-sufficient he had been as a blind man, how naturally and easily he had experienced his world with his hands, and how much we were now, so to speak, pushing him against the grain: demanding that he renounce all that came easily to him, that he sense the world in a way incredibly difficult for him, and alien.[10]

His face seemed to light up with comprehension as he felt the statue. "It's not like a man at all," he murmured. The statue examined, he opened his eyes, and turned around to the real gorilla standing before him in the enclosure. And now, in a way that would have been impossible before, he described the ape's posture, the way the knuckles touched the ground, the little bandy legs, the great canines, the huge ridge on the head, pointing to each feature as he did so. Gregory writes of a wonderful episode with his patient S.B., who had a long-standing interest in tools and machinery. Gregory took him to the Science Museum in London to see its grand collection:

> The most interesting episode was his reaction to the fine Maudeslay screw cutting lathe which is housed in a special glass case. . . . We led him to the glass case, which was closed, and asked him to tell us what was in it. He was quite unable to say anything about it, except that he thought the nearest part was a handle. . . . We then asked a museum attendant (as previously arranged) for the case to be opened, and S.B. was allowed to touch the lathe. The result was startling. . . . He ran his hands eagerly over the lathe, with his eyes tight shut. Then he stood back a little and opened his eyes and said: "Now that I've felt it I can see."

So it was with Virgil and the gorilla. This spectacular example of how touching could make seeing possible explained something else that had puzzled me. Since the operation, Virgil had begun to buy toy soldiers, toy cars, toy animals, miniatures of famous buildings—an entire Lilliputian world—and to spend hours with them. It was not mere childishness or playfulness that had driven him to such pastimes. Through touching these at the same time he looked at them, he could forge a crucial correlation; he could prepare himself to see the real world by learning first to see this toy world. The disparity of scale did not matter, any more than it mattered to S.B., who was instantly able to tell the time on a large wall clock because he could correlate it with what he knew by touch from his pocket watch. . . .

68   Brain systems in all animals may respond to overwhelming stimulation, or stimulation past a critical point, with a sudden shutdown.[11] Such reactions have

---

[10]Earlier, Virgil had picked up the distant sound of lions roaring in their enclosure; he pricked up his ears and turned instantly in their direction. "Listen!" he said. "It's the lions—they're feeding the lions." The rest of us had completely missed the sound and, even when Virgil drew our attention to it, found it faint and were unsure which direction it came from. We were struck by the quality of Virgil's hearing, his auditory attention and acuteness and orientation, how extremely skilled as a listener he was. Such an acuteness and a heightening of auditory sensitivity occur in many blind people, but above all in those born blind or blinded early in life; it seems to go with the constant focusing of attention and affect and cognitive powers in these spheres, and, with this, a hyperdevelopment of auditory-cognitive systems in the brain.

[11]Pavlov, speaking of such responses in dogs, called this "transmarginal inhibition consequent upon supramaximal stimulation," and regarded these shutdowns as protective in nature.

nothing to do with the individual or his motives. They are purely local and physiological and can occur even in isolated slices of cerebral cortex: they are a biological defense against neural overload.

Still, perceptual-cognitive processes, while physiological, are also personal—it is not a world that one perceives or constructs but *one's own* world—and they lead to, are linked to, a perceptual self, with a will, an orientation, and a style of its own. This perceptual self may itself collapse with the collapse of perceptual systems, altering the orientation and the very identity of the individual. If this occurs, an individual not only becomes blind but ceases to behave as a visual being, offers no report of any change in inner state, is completely oblivious of his own visuality or lack of it. Such a condition, of total psychic blindness (known as Anton's syndrome), may occur if there is massive damage, as from a stroke, to the visual parts of the brain. But it also seemed to occur, on occasion, with Virgil. At such times, indeed, he might talk of "seeing" while in fact appearing blind and showing no visual behavior whatever. One had to wonder whether the whole basis of visual perception and identity in Virgil was as yet so feeble that under conditions of overload or exhaustion he might go in and out of not merely physical blindness but a total Anton-like psychic blindness.

A quite different sort of visual shutdown—a withdrawal—seemed to be associated with situations of great emotional stress or conflict. And for Virgil this period was indeed as stressful a time as he had ever known: he had just had surgery, he had just been married; the even tenor of his blind, bachelor life had been shattered; he was under a tremendous pressure of expectation; and seeing itself was confusing, exhausting. These pressures had increased as his wedding day approached, especially with the convergence of his own family in town; his family had not only opposed the surgery in the first place but now insisted that he was in fact still blind. All this was documented by Amy in her journal:

70

> October 9: Went to church to decorate for wedding. Virgil's vision quite blurry. Not able to distinguish much. It is as though sight has taken a nosedive. Virgil acting "blind" again. . . . Having me lead him around.
>
> October 11: Virgil's family arrives today. His sight seems to have gone on vacation. . . . It is as though he has gone back to being blind! Family arrived. Couldn't believe he could see. Every time he said he could see something they would say, "Ah, you're just guessing." They treated him as though he was totally blind—leading him around, giving him anything he wanted. . . . I am very nervous, and Virgil's sight has disappeared. . . . Want to be sure we are doing the right thing.
>
> October 12: Wedding day. Virgil very calm . . . vision little clearer, but still blurry. . . . Could see me coming down aisle, but was very blurry. . . . Wedding beautiful. Party at Mom's. Virgil surrounded by family. They still cannot accept his sight, he could not see much. Said goodbye to his family tonight. Sight began clearing up right after they left.

In these episodes Virgil was treated by his family as a blind man, his seeing identity denied or undermined, and he responded, compliantly, by acting, or even becoming, blind—a massive withdrawal or regression of part of his ego to a crushing, annihilating denial of identity. Such a regression would have to be seen as motivated, albeit unconsciously—an inhibition on a "functional" basis. Thus there seemed to be two distinct forms of "blind behavior" or "acting blind"—one a collapse of visual processing and visual identity on an organic basis (a "bottom-up" or neuropsychological disturbance, in neurological parlance), the other a collapse or inhibition of visual identity on a functional basis (a "top-down" or psychoneurotic disturbance), though no less real for him. Given the extreme organic weakness of his vision—the instability of his visual systems *and* visual identity at this point—it was very difficult, at times, to know what was going on, to distinguish between the "physiological" and "psychological." His vision was so marginal, so close to the border, that either neural overload or identity conflict might push him over it.[12]

Marius von Senden, reviewing every published case over a three-hundred-year period in his classic book *Space and Sight* (1932), concluded that every newly sighted adult sooner or later comes to a "motivation crisis"—and that not every patient gets through it. He tells of one patient who felt so threatened by sight (which would have meant his leaving the Asylum for the Blind, and his fiancée there) that he threatened to tear his eyes out; he cites case after case of patients who "behave blind" or "refuse to see" after an operation, and of others who, fearful of what sight may entail, refuse operation (one such account, entitled "L'Aveugle qui refuse de voir," was published as early as 1771). Both Gregory and Valvo dilate on the emotional dangers of forcing a new sense on a blind man—how, after an initial exhilaration, a devastating (and even lethal) depression can ensue.

Precisely such a depression descended on Gregory's patient: S.B.'s period in the hospital was full of excitement and perceptual progress. But the promise was not fulfilled. Six months after the operation, Gregory reports,

> we formed a strong impression that his sight was to him almost entirely disappointing. It enabled him to do a little more . . . but it became clear that the opportunities it afforded him were less than he had imagined. . . . He still to a great extent lived the life of a blind man, sometimes not bothering to put on the light at night. . . . He did not get on well with his neighbours [now], who regarded him as "odd," and his workmates [previously so admiring] played tricks on him and teased him for being unable to read.

---

[12]When a specific organic weakness exists, emotional stress can easily press toward a physical form; thus, asthmatics get asthma under stress, parkinsonians become more parkinsonian, and someone like Virgil, with borderline vision, may get pushed over the border and become (temporarily) blind. It was, therefore, exceedingly difficult at times to distinguish between what was physiological vulnerability in him, and what was "motivated behavior."

His depression deepened, he became ill, and, two years after his operation, S.B. died. He had been perfectly healthy, he had once enjoyed life; he was only fifty-four.

Valvo provides us with six exemplary tales, and a profound discussion, of the feelings and behavior of early blinded people when they are confronted with the "gift" of sight and with the necessity of renouncing one world, one identity, for another.[13]

A major conflict in Virgil, as in all newly sighted people, was the uneasy relation of touch and sight—not knowing whether to feel or look. This was obvious in Virgil from the day of the operation and was very evident the day we saw him, when he could hardly keep his hands off the formboard, longed to touch all the animals, and gave up spearing his food. His vocabulary, his whole sensibility, his picture of the world, were couched in tactile—or, at least, nonvisual—terms. He was, or had been until his operation, a touch person through and through.

It has been well established that in congenitally deaf people (especially if they are native signers) some of the auditory parts of the brain are reallocated for visual use. It has also been well established that in blind people who read Braille the reading finger has an exceptionally large representation in the tactile parts of the cerebral cortex. And one would suspect that the tactile (and auditory) parts of the cortex are enlarged in the blind and may even extend into what is normally the visual cortex. What remains of the visual cortex, without visual stimulation, may be largely undeveloped. It seems likely that such a differentiation of cerebral development would follow the early loss of a sense and the compensatory enhancement of other senses.

If this was the case in Virgil, what might happen if visual function was suddenly made possible, demanded? One might certainly expect *some* visual learning, some development of new pathways in the visual parts of the brain. There had never been any documentation of the kindling of activity in the visual cortex of an adult, and we hoped to take special PET scans of Virgil's visual cortex to show this as he learned to see. But what would this learning, this activation, be like? Would it be like a baby first learning to see? (This was Amy's first thought.) But the newly sighted are not on the same starting line, neurologically

[13]In his ironically titled *Letter on the Blind: For the Use of Those Who Can See* (1749), the youthful Diderot maintains a position of epistemological and cultural relativism—that the blind may, in their own way, construct a complete and sufficient world, have a complete "blind identity" and no sense of disability or inadequacy, and that the "problem" of their blindness and the desire to cure this, therefore, is ours, not theirs.

He also feels that intelligence and cultivation may make a fundamental difference to what the blind may understand; may give them, at least, a formal understanding of much that they cannot directly perceive. He is especially drawn to this conclusion by pondering the case of Nicholas Saunderson, the celebrated blind mathematician and Newtonian, who died in 1740. That Saunderson, who never saw light, could conceive it so well, could be (of all things!) a lecturer in optics, could construct, in his own way, a sublime picture of the universe, excites Diderot immensely.

speaking, as babies, whose cerebral cortex is equipotential—equally ready to adapt to any form of perception. The cortex of an early blinded adult such as Virgil has already become highly adapted to organizing perceptions in time and not in space.[14]

An infant merely learns. This is a huge, never-ending task, but it is not one charged with irresoluble conflict. A newly sighted adult, by contrast, has to make a radical switch from a sequential to a visual-spatial mode, and such a switch flies in the face of the experience of an entire lifetime. Gregory emphasizes this, pointing out how conflict and crisis are inevitable if "the perceptual habits and strategies of a lifetime" are to be changed. Such conflicts are built into the nature of the nervous system itself, for the early blinded adult who has spent a lifetime adapting and specializing his brain must now ask his brain to reverse all this. (Moreover, the brain of an adult no longer has the plasticity of a child's brain—that is why learning new languages or new skills becomes more difficult with age. But in the case of a man previously blind, learning to see is not like learning another language; it is, as Diderot puts it, like learning language for the first time.)

80   In the newly sighted, learning to see demands a radical change in neurological functioning and, with it, a radical change in psychological functioning, in self, in identity. The change may be experienced in literally life-and-death terms. Valvo quotes a patient of his as saying, "One must die as a sighted person to be born again as a blind person," and the opposite is equally true: one must die as a blind person to be born again as a seeing person. It is the interim, the limbo—"between two worlds, one dead / The other powerless to be born"—that is so terrible. Though blindness may at first be a terrible privation and loss, it may become less so with the passage of time, for a deep adaptation, or reorientation, occurs, by which one reconstitutes, reappropriates, the world in nonvisual terms. It then becomes a *different* condition, a different form of being, one with its own sensibilities and coherence and

[14]The Canadian psychologist Donald Hebb was deeply interested in the development of seeing and presented much experimental evidence against its being, in higher animals and man, "innate," as had often been supposed. He was fascinated, understandably, by the rare "experiment" (if such a term be allowed) of restoring sight in adult life to the congenitally blind and ponders at length in *The Organization of Behaviour* on the cases collected by von Senden (Hebb himself had no personal experience of such a case). These provided rich confirmation for his thesis that seeing requires experience and learning; indeed he thought that it required, in man, fifteen years of learning to reach its full development.

But one caveat must be made (it is also made by Gregory) with regard to Hebb's comparison of the newly sighted adult to a baby. It may be that the newly sighted adult must indeed go through some of the learning and developmental stages of infancy; yet an adult, neurologically and psychologically, is nothing like a baby—an adult is already committed to a lifetime of perceptual experiences—and such cases cannot, therefore (as Hebb supposes), tell us what a baby's world is like, serve as a window into the otherwise inaccessible development of their perception.

feeling. John Hull calls this "deep blindness" and sees it as "one of the orders of human being."[15]

On October 31, the cataract in Virgil's left eye was removed, revealing a retina, an acuity, similar to the right. This was a great disappointment, for there had been hope that it might be a far better eye—enough to make a crucial difference to his vision. His vision did improve slightly: he fixated better, and the searching eye movements were fewer, and he had a larger visual field.

With both eyes working, Virgil now went back to work, but found, increasingly, that there was another side to seeing, that much of it was confusing, and some downright shocking. He had worked happily at the Y for thirty years, he said, and thought he *knew* all the bodies of his clients. Now he found himself startled by seeing bodies, and skins, that he had previously known only by touch; he was amazed at the range of skin colors he saw and slightly disgusted by blemishes and "stains" in skins that to his hands had seemed perfectly smooth.[16] Virgil found it a relief, when giving massages, to shut his eyes.

He continued to improve, visually, over the ensuing weeks, especially when he was free to set his own pace. He did his utmost to live the life of a sighted man, but he also became more conflicted at this time. He expressed fears, occasionally, that he would have to throw away his cane and walk outside, cross the streets, by vision alone; and, on one occasion, a fear that he might be "expected" to drive and take up an entirely new "sighted" job. This, then, was a time of great striving and real success—but success achieved, one felt, at a psychological cost, at a cost of deepening strain and splitting in himself.

There was one outing, a week before Christmas, when he and Amy went to the ballet. Virgil enjoyed *The Nutcracker:* he had always loved the music, and now, for the first time, he saw something as well. "I could see people jumping around the stage. Couldn't see what they were wearing, though," he said. He thought he would enjoy seeing a live baseball game and looked forward to the start of the season in the spring.

---

[15]If blindness has a positivity of its own, is one of the orders of human being, this is equally (or more) so for deafness, where there is not only a heightening of visual (and, in general, spatial) abilities, but a whole community of deaf people, with their own visuo-gestural language (Sign) and culture. Problems somewhat similar to Virgil's may be encountered by congenitally deaf, or very early deafened, subjects given cochlear implants. Sound, for them, at first has no associations, no meaning—so they find themselves, at least initially, in a world of auditory chaos, or agnosia. But in addition to these cognitive problems there are identity problems, too; in a sense, they must die as deaf people to be born as hearing ones. This, potentially, is much more serious and has ramifying social and cultural implications; for deafness may be not just a personal identity, but a shared linguistic, communal, and cultural one. These very complex issues are discussed by Harlan Lane in *The Mask of Benevolence: Disabling the Deaf Community*.

[16]Gregory observes of S.B., "He also found some things he loved ugly (including his wife and himself!), and he was frequently upset by the blemishes and imperfections of the visible world."

85   Christmas was a particularly festive and important time—the first Christmas after his wedding, his first Christmas as a sighted man—and he returned, with Amy, to the family farm in Kentucky. He saw his mother for the first time in more than forty years—he had scarcely been able to see her, to see anything much, at the time of the wedding—and thought she looked "real pretty." He saw again the old farmhouse, the fences, the creek in the pasture, which he had also not seen since he was a child; he had never ceased to cherish them in his mind. Some of his seeing had been a great disappointment, but seeing home and family was not—it was a pure joy.

No less important was the change in the family's attitude toward him. "He seemed more alert," his sister said. "He would walk, move around the house, without touching the walls—he would just get up and go." She felt that there had been "a big difference" since he was first operated on, and his mother and the rest of the family felt the same.

I phoned them the day before Christmas and spoke to his mother, his sister, and others. They asked me to join them, and I wish I could have done so, for it seemed to be a joyful and affirmative time for them all. The family's initial opposition to Virgil's seeing (and perhaps to Amy, too, for having pushed it) and their disbelief that he *could* actually see had been something that he internalized, something that could literally annihilate his seeing. Now that the family was "converted," a major psychological block, one hoped, might dissolve. Christmas was the climax, but also the resolution, of an extraordinary year.

What would happen, I wondered, in the coming year? What might he hope for, at best? How much of a visual world, a visual life, might still await him? We were, frankly, quite unsure at this point. Grim and frightening though the histories of so many patients were, some, at least, overcame the worst of their difficulties and emerged into a relatively unconflicted new sight.

Valvo, normally cautious in expression, lets himself go a little in describing some of his patients' happier outcomes:

> Once our patients acquire visual patterns, and can work with them autonomously, they seem to experience great joy in visual learning . . . a renaissance of personality. . . . They start thinking about wholly new areas of experience.

90   "A renaissance of personality"—this was just what Amy wanted for Virgil. It was difficult for us to imagine such a renaissance in him, for he seemed so phlegmatic, so set in his ways. And yet, despite a range of problems—retinal, cortical, psychological, possibly medical—he had done remarkably well in a way, had shown a steady increase in his power to apprehend a visual world. With his predominantly positive motivation, and the obvious enjoyment and advantage he could get from seeing, there seemed no reason why he should not progress further. He could never hope to have perfect vision, but he might certainly hope for a life radically enlarged by seeing.

The catastrophe, when it came, was very sudden. On February 8, I had a phone call from Amy: Virgil had collapsed, had been taken, grey and stuporous, to the hospital. He had a lobar pneumonia, a massive consolidation of one lung, and was in the intensive-care unit, on oxygen and intravenous antibiotics.

The first antibiotics used did not work: he grew worse; he grew critical; and for some days he hovered between life and death. Then, after three weeks, the infection was finally mastered, and the lung started to reexpand. But Virgil himself remained gravely ill, for, though the pneumonia itself was clearing, it had tipped him into respiratory failure—a near-paralysis of the respiratory center in the brain, which made it unable to respond properly to levels of oxygen and carbon dioxide in the blood. The oxygen levels in his blood started to fall—fell to less than half of normal. And the level of carbon dioxide started to rise—rose to nearly three times normal. He needed oxygen constantly, but only a little could be given, lest his failing respiratory center be further depressed. With his brain deprived of oxygen and poisoned by carbon dioxide, Virgil's consciousness fluctuated and faded, and on bad days (when the oxygen in his blood was lowest and the carbon dioxide highest) he could see nothing: he was totally blind.

Much contributed to this continuing respiratory crisis: Virgil's lungs themselves were thickened and fibrotic; there was advanced bronchitis and emphysema; there was no movement of the diaphragm on one side, a consequence of his childhood polio; and, on top of all this, he was enormously obese—obese enough to cause a Pickwick syndrome (named after the somnolent fat boy, Joe, in *The Pickwick Papers*). In Pickwick syndrome, there is a grave depression of breathing, and failure to oxygenate the blood fully, associated with a depression of the respiratory center in the brain.

Virgil had probably been getting ill for some years; he had gradually been increasing in weight since 1985. But between his wedding and Christmas he had put on a further forty pounds—had shot up, in a few weeks, to two hundred and eighty pounds—partly from fluid retention caused by heart failure, and partly from nonstop eating, a habit of his under stress.

He now had to spend three weeks in the hospital, his blood oxygen still plummeting to dangerously low levels, despite his being given oxygen—and each time the level grew really low he became lethargic and totally blind. Amy would know the moment she opened his door what sort of day he was having— where the blood oxygen was—depending on whether he used his eyes, looked around, or fumbled and touched, "acted blind." (We wondered, in retrospect, whether the strange fluctuations his vision had shown from almost the day of surgery might also have been caused, at least in part, by fluctuations in his blood oxygen, with consequent retinal or cerebral anoxia. Virgil had probably had a mild Pickwick syndrome for years, and could have been close to respiratory failure and anoxia even before his acute illness.)

There was another, intermediate state, which Amy found very puzzling; at such times, he would *say* that he saw nothing whatever, but would reach for objects, avoid obstacles, and *behave* as if seeing. Amy could make nothing of this singular state, in which he manifestly responded to objects, could locate them, was seeing, and yet denied any consciousness of seeing. This condition—called implicit sight, unconscious sight, or blindsight—occurs if the visual parts of the

95

cerebral cortex are knocked out (as they may be by a lack of oxygen, for instance), but the visual centers in the subcortex remain intact. Visual signals are perceived and are responded to appropriately, but nothing of this perception reaches consciousness at all.

At last, Virgil was able to leave the hospital and return home, but to return a respiratory cripple. He was tethered to an oxygen cylinder and could not even stir from his chair without it. It seemed unlikely at this stage that he would ever recover sufficiently to go out and work again, and the Y now felt that it had to terminate his job. A few months later, he was forced to leave the house where he had lived as an employee of the Y for more than twenty years. This was the situation that summer: Virgil had lost not only his health but his job and his house as well.

By October, however, he was feeling better and was able to go without oxygen for an hour or two at a time. It had not been wholly clear to me, from speaking to Virgil and Amy, what had finally happened to his vision after all these months. Amy said that it had "almost gone" but that now she felt it was coming back as he got better. When I phoned the visual-rehabilitation center where Virgil had been evaluated, I was given a different story. Virgil, I was told, seemed to have lost all the sight restored the previous year, with only a few bits remaining. Kathy, his therapist, thought he saw colors but little else—and some-times colors without objects: thus he might see a haze or halo of pink around a Pepto-Bismol bottle without clearly seeing the bottle itself.[17] This color percep-tion, she said, was the only seeing that was constant; for the rest he appeared almost blind, missed objects, groped, seemed visually lost. He was showing his old, blind random movements of the eyes. And yet sometimes, spontaneously, out of the blue, he would get sudden, startling moments of vision, in which he would see objects, quite small ones. But these percepts would then vanish as suddenly as they came, and he was usually unable to retrieve them. For all practical purposes, she said, Virgil was now blind.

I was shocked and puzzled when Kathy told me this. These were phenomena radically different from anything he had shown before: What was happening now with his eyes and his brain? From a distance, I could not sort out what was happening, especially since Amy, for her part, maintained that Virgil's vision was now improving. Indeed, she got furious when she heard anyone say that Virgil was blind, and she maintained that the visual-rehab center was actually "teaching him to be blind." So in February of 1993, a year after the onset of his devastating illness, we brought Virgil and Amy to New York to see us again and to get some specialized physiological tests of retinal and brain function.

100   As soon as I met Virgil at the arrival gate at LaGuardia Airport, I could see for myself that everything had gone quite terribly wrong. He was now almost fifty

[17]Semir Zeki has observed in some cases of cerebral anoxia that the color-constructing areas of the visual cortex may be relatively spared, so that the patient may see color *and nothing else*—no form, no boundaries, no sense of objects whatsoever.

pounds heavier than when I had met him in Oklahoma. He was carrying a cylinder of oxygen strung over one shoulder. He groped; his eyes wandered; he looked totally blind. Amy guided him, her hand under his elbow, everywhere they went. And yet sometimes as we drove over the Fifty-ninth Street Bridge into the city, he would pick up something—a light on the bridge—not guessing but seeing it quite accurately. But he could never hold it or retrieve it, and so remained visually lost.

When we came to test him in my office—first using large colored targets, then large movements and flashlights—he missed everything. He seemed totally blind—*blinder than he had been before his operations*, because then, at least, even through his cataracts he could consistently detect light, its direction, and the shadow of a hand moving before him. Now he could detect nothing whatever, no longer seemed to have any light-sensitive receptors: it was as if his retinas had gone. Yet not totally gone—that was the odd thing. For once in a while he would see something accurately: once, he saw, described, grasped, a banana; on two occasions, he was able to follow a randomly moving light bar with his hands on a computer screen; and sometimes he would reach for objects, or "guess" them correctly, even though he said he saw "nothing" at such times—the blind-sight that had first been observed in the hospital.

We were dismayed at his near-uniform failure, and he was sinking into a demoralized, defeated state—it was time to stop testing and take a break for lunch. As we passed him a bowl of fruit, and he felt the fruit with swift, sensitive, skillful fingers, his face lighted up, and he regained his animation. He gave us, as he handled the fruit, remarkable tactile descriptions, speaking of the waxy, slick quality of the plum skin, the soft fuzz of peaches and smoothness of nectarines ("like a baby's cheeks"), and the rough, dimpled skin of oranges. He weighed the fruits in his hand, spoke of their weight and consistency, their pips and stones; and then, lifting them to his nose, their different smells. His tactile (and olfactory) appreciation seemed far finer than our own. We included an exceedingly clever wax pear among the real fruit; with its realistic shape and coloring, it had deceived sighted people completely. Virgil was not taken in for a moment: he burst out laughing as soon as he touched it. "It's a candle," he said immediately, somewhat puzzled. "Shaped like a bell or a pear." While he may indeed have been, in von Senden's words, "an exile from spatial reality," he was deeply at home in the world of touch, in time.

But if his sense of touch was perfectly preserved, there were, it was evident, just sparks from his retinas—rare, momentary sparks, from retinas that now seemed to be 99 percent dead. Bob Wasserman, too, who had not seen Virgil since our visit to Oklahoma, was appalled at the degradation of vision and wanted to reexamine the retinas. When he did so, they looked exactly as before—piebald, with areas of increased and decreased pigmentation. There was no evidence of any new disease. Yet the functioning of even the preserved areas of retina had fallen to almost zero. Electroretinograms, designed to record the retina's electrical activity when stimulated by light, were completely flat, and visual evoked potentials, designed to show activity in the visual parts of the brain, were absent, too—there was no longer anything, electrically, going on in either the retinas or the brain that could be recorded. (There may have been rare, momentary sparks of activity, but if so, we failed to catch these in our recordings.) This inactivity could not be attributed to the original disease, retinitis, which had long been inactive. Something else had emerged in the past year and had, in effect, extinguished his remaining retinal function.

We remembered how Virgil had constantly complained of glare, even on relatively dull, overcast days—how glare seemed to blind him sometimes, so that he needed the darkest glasses. Was it possible (as my friend Kevin Halligan suggested) that with the removal of his cataracts—cataracts that had perhaps shielded his fragile retinas for decades—the ordinary light of day had proved lethal, burnt out his retinas? It is said that patients with other retinal problems, like macular degeneration, may be exceedingly intolerant of light—not merely ultraviolet but light of all wavelengths—and that light may hasten the degeneration of their retinas. Was this what had happened with Virgil? It was one possibility. Should we have foreseen it and rationed Virgil's sight, or the ambient light, in some way?

105 Another possibility—a likelier one—related to Virgil's continuing hypoxia, the fact that he had not had properly oxygenated blood for a year. We had clear accounts of his vision waxing and waning in the hospital as his blood gases went up and down. Could the repeated, or continuing, oxygen-starving of his retinas (and perhaps also of the visual areas of his cortex) have been the factor that did them in? It was wondered, at this point, whether raising blood oxygenation to 100 percent (which would have required sustained artificial respiration with pure oxygen) might restore some retinal or cerebral function. But it was decided that this procedure would be too risky, since it might cause long-term or permanent depression of the brain's respiratory center.

This, then, is Virgil's story, the story of a "miraculous" restoration of sight to a blind man, a story basically similar to that of Cheselden's young patient in 1728, and of a handful of others over the past three centuries—but with a bizarre and ironic twist at the end. Gregory's patient, so well adapted to blindness before his operation, was first delighted with seeing, but soon encountered intolerable stresses and difficulties, found the "gift" transformed to a curse, became deeply depressed, and soon after died. Almost all the earlier patients, indeed, after their initial euphoria, were overwhelmed by the enormous difficulties of adapting to a new sense, though a very few, as Valvo stresses, have adapted and done well. Could Virgil have surmounted these difficulties and adapted to seeing where so many others had foundered on the way?

We shall never know, for the business of adaptation—and, indeed, of life as he knew it—was suddenly cut across by a gratuitous blow of fate: an illness that, at a single stroke, deprived him of job, house, health, and independence, leaving him a gravely sick man, unable to fend for himself. For Amy, who incited the surgery in the first place, and who was so passionately invested in Virgil's seeing, it was a miracle that misfired, a calamity. Virgil, for his part, maintains philosophically, "These things happen." But he has been shattered by this blow, has given vent to outbursts of rage: rage at his helplessness and sickness; rage at the smashing of a promise and a dream; and beneath this, most fundamental of all, a rage that had been smoldering in him almost from the beginning—rage at being thrust into a battle he could neither renounce nor win. At the beginning, there was certainly amazement, wonder, and sometimes joy. There was also, of course, great courage. It was an adventure, an excursion into a new world, the like of which is given to few. But then came the problems, the conflicts, of seeing but not seeing, not being able to make a visual world, and at the same time being forced to give up his own. He found himself between two worlds, at home in neither—a torment from which no escape seemed possible. But then, paradoxically, a release was given, in the form of a second and now final blindness—a blindness he received as a gift. Now, at last, Virgil is allowed to not see, allowed to escape from the glaring, confusing world of sight and space, and to return to his own true being, the intimate, concentrated world of the other senses that had been his home for almost fifty years.

To See and Not See

The restoration of vision to those blinded early in life, though rare, has been documented with great care since Cheselden's report in 1728. All known cases up to 1930 are summarized in von Senden's encyclopedic book, *Space and Sight.* Many of these are analyzed by Hebb in his *Organization of Behaviour* and form, along with much other observational and experimental data he provides, crucial evidence that "seeing"—visual perception—must be learned.

The single richest and most detailed case study is that of Richard Gregory and Jean Wallace. This was subsequently reprinted, with further additions, including an exchange of letters with von Senden, in Gregory's *Concepts and Mechanisms of Perception.* The philosophical background to the Molyneux question and the impact of the Cheselden case are also well described by Gregory in his article "Recovery from Blindness," in *The Oxford Companion to the Mind.*

Alberto Valvo's deeply pondered cases of patients submitted to a new surgical procedure for corneal reconstruction are described in his *Sight Restoration after Long-Term Blindness.*

The effects of late blindness—most especially its effects on visual imagery and memory, orientations, and attitudes—have been masterfully described by John Hull in his autobiographical book, *Touching the Rock.* And the restoration of vision after late blindness is finely described in *Second Sight*, by Robert Hine.

One of the deepest, widest-ranging explorations of what it may mean in terms of identity to be blind, both to the individual and to those around him, was given by Diderot in his great *Letter on the Blind: For the Use of Those Who Can See* (he wrote a similar *Letter on the Deaf and Dumb: For the Use of Those Who Can Hear and Speak*). Von Feuerbach's account of Kaspar Hauser contains a remarkable description of his profound visual agnosia when first released into the daylight, after being kept in a lightless dungeon since infancy (pp. 64–5).

These themes have not only been the subject of philosophical discussions and case reports, but of fiction and dramatic reconstruction, ever since Diderot's imagination of Nicholas Saunderson's deathbed. In 1909 the novelist Wilkie

Collins based a novel, *Poor Miss Finch*, on such a subject, and the theme is also central in Gide's early novel *La Symphonie pastorale*. A more recent treatment is a brilliant reconstruction by Brian O'Doherty, *The Strange Case of Mademoiselle P.*, very closely based on Mesmer's original 1779 account. In Brian Friel's 1994 play, *Molly Sweeney*, the central character is, like Virgil, blind from early life with retinal damage and cataracts, and, following the removal of the cataracts in middle life, is plunged into a state of agnosic confusion and ambivalence, which is resolved only by a final reversion to blindness.

References

Berkeley, George. *A New Theory of Vision*. 1709. Everyman ed. New York: Dutton, 1910.

Borges, Jorge Luis. "Funes the Memorious." In *A Personal Anthology*. New York: Grove Press, 1967.

Cahan, David, ed. *Hermann von Helmholtz and the Foundations of Nineteenth-Century Science*. Berkeley: University of California Press, 1993.

Collins, Wilkie. *Poor Miss Finch*. New York: Harcourt, Brace & Co., 1925.

Diderot, Denis. *Lettre sur les aveugles*. Paris: Durand, 1749.

_____. *Lettre sur les sourds et muets*. Paris, 1751.

Feuerbach, Anselm von. *Kaspar Hauser: An Account of an Individual Kept in a Dungeon, Separated from all Communication with the World, from Early Childhood to about the Age of Seventeen*. 1832. English trans., London; Simpkin & Marshall, 1834.

Friel, Brian. *Molly Sweeney*. Old Castle, Co. Meath, Ireland: The Gallery Press, 1994.

Gide, André. *La Symphonie pastorale*. 1919. Reprint, London: Penguin Books, 1963.

Gregory, R. L., and Jean G. Wallace. "Recovery from Early Blindness: A Case Study." *Quarterly Journal of Psychology* (1963). Reprinted in *Concepts and Mechanisms of Perception*, by R. L. Gregory. London: Duckworth, 1974.

Gregory, Richard L. "Blindness, Recovery from." In Richard L. Gregory, ed., *The Oxford Companion to the Mind*, 94–96. Oxford: Oxford University Press, 1987.

Hebb, D. O. *The Organization of Behaviour*. New York: Wiley, 1949.

Helmholtz, Hermann von. *On Thought in Medicine (Das Denken in der Medizin)*, 1878. Reprint, Baltimore: Johns Hopkins Press, 1938.

_____. *Physiological Optics*. 1909. Ed. J. P. C. Southall. Optical Society of America, 1924.

Hull, John M. *Touching the Rock: An Experience of Blindness*. New York: Pantheon Books, 1990.

Lane, Harlan. *The Mask of Benevolence: Disabling the Deaf Community*. New York: Alfred A. Knopf, 1992.

Locke, John. *Essay Concerning Human Understanding*. 1690. Ed. P. H. Nidditch. Oxford: Oxford University Press, 1975.

O'Doherty, Brian. *The Strange Case of Mademoiselle P*. New York: Pantheon Books, 1992.

Pavlov, Ivan P. *Lectures on Conditioned Reflexes: Twenty-five Years of Objective Study of the Higher Nervous Activity (Behaviour) of Animals*. Trans. W. Horsley Gantt. New York: International Publishers, 1928.

Valvo, Alberto. *Sight Restoration after Long-Term Blindness: The Problems and Behavior Patterns of Visual Rehabilitation.* New York: American Foundation for the Blind, 1971.

von Senden, M. *Space and Sight: The Perception of Space and Shape in the Congenitally Blind Before and After Operation.* 1932. Reprint, Glencoe, Ill.: Free Press, 1960.

Zeki, Semir. *A Vision of the Brain.* Oxford: Blackwell Scientific Publications, 1993.

[1995]

1. How is this chapter different from a scientific article?
2. How are Virgil's experiences similar to those of Gregory and Wallace's subject S.B.?
3. The seventeenth-century philosopher William Molyneux posed the question of whether a blind person, suddenly enabled to see, could recognize merely by sight something he had formerly been able to recognize solely by touch. How do the experiences of S.B. and Virgil answer that question?

The Play and the Essays

1. In what ways are Molly Sweeney's experiences similar to those of S.B. and Virgil? How do they differ?
2. What other works in this section do the essays help interpret?

NONFICTION PROSE

ANNIE DILLARD

ANNIE DILLARD *(1945–), winner of a Pulitzer Prize for* Pilgrim at Tinker Creek, *which she wrote when she was twenty-nine, had a religious upbringing, rebelled against it, and was brought back to it by her priest with a well-thought-out argument based on the works of C.S. Lewis. She has since explored Sufism, Buddhism, and the religious systems of Eskimos and Hasidic Jews, and recently converted to Catholicism. She is an adjunct professor of English and writer-in-residence at Wesleyan University.*

Seeing*

When I was six or seven years old, growing up in Pittsburgh, I used to take a precious penny of my own and hide it for someone else to find. It was a curious compulsion; sadly, I've never been seized by it since. For some reason I always "hid" the penny along the same stretch of sidewalk up the street. I would cradle it at the roots of a sycamore, say, or in a hole left by a chipped-off piece of sidewalk. Then I would take a piece of chalk, and, starting at either end of the block, draw huge arrows leading up to the penny from both directions. After I learned to write I labeled the arrows: SURPRISE AHEAD or MONEY THIS WAY. I was greatly excited, during all this arrow-drawing, at the thought of the first lucky passer-by

*Annie Dillard, "Seeing," *Pilgrim at Tinker Creek* (Toronto, New York: Bantam Books, 1974).

who would receive in this way, regardless of merit, a free gift from the universe. But I never lurked about. I would go straight home and not give the matter another thought, until, some months later, I would be gripped again by the impulse to hide another penny.

It is still the first week in January, and I've got great plans. I've been thinking about seeing. There are lots of things to see, unwrapped gifts and free surprises. The world is fairly studded and strewn with pennies cast broadside from a generous hand. But—and this is the point—who gets excited by a mere penny? If you follow one arrow, if you crouch motionless on a bank to watch a tremulous ripple thrill on the water and are rewarded by the sight of a muskrat kit paddling from its den, will you count that sight a chip of copper only, and go your rueful way? It is dire poverty indeed when a man is so malnourished and fatigued that he won't stoop to pick up a penny. But if you cultivate a healthy poverty and simplicity, so that finding a penny will literally make your day, then, since the world is in fact planted in pennies, you have with your poverty bought a lifetime of days. It is that simple. What you see is what you get.

I used to be able to see flying insects in the air. I'd look ahead and see, not the row of hemlocks across the road, but the air in front of it. My eyes would focus along that column of air, picking out flying insects. But I lost interest, I guess, for I dropped the habit. Now I can see birds. Probably some people can look at the grass at their feet and discover all the crawling creatures. I would like to know grasses and sedges—and care. Then my least journey into the world would be a field trip, a series of happy recognitions. Thoreau, in an expansive mood, exulted, "What a rich book might be made about buds, including, perhaps, sprouts!" It would be nice to think so. I cherish mental images I have of three perfectly happy people. One collects stones. Another—an Englishman, say—watches clouds. The third lives on a coast and collects drops of seawater which he examines microscopically and mounts. But I don't see what the specialist sees, and so I cut myself off, not only from the total picture, but from the various forms of happiness.

Unfortunately, nature is very much a now-you-see-it, now-you-don't affair. A fish flashes, then dissolves in the water before my eyes like so much salt. Deer apparently ascend bodily into heaven; the brightest oriole fades into leaves. These disappearances stun me into stillness and concentration; they say of nature that it conceals with a grand nonchalance, and they say of vision that it is a deliberate gift, the revelation of a dancer who for my eyes only flings away her seven veils. For nature does reveal as well as conceal: now-you-don't-see-it, now-you-do. For a week last September migrating red-winged blackbirds were feeding heavily down by the creek at the back of the house. One day I went out to investigate the racket; I walked up to a tree, an Osage orange, and a hundred birds flew away. They simply materialized out of the tree. I saw a tree, then a whisk of color, then a tree again. I walked closer and another hundred blackbirds took flight. Not a branch, not a twig budged: the birds were apparently weightless as well as invisible. Or, it was as if the leaves of the Osage orange had been freed from a spell in the form of red-winged blackbirds; they flew from the tree, caught my eye in the sky, and vanished. When I looked again at the tree the leaves had reassembled as if nothing had happened. Finally I walked directly to the trunk of the tree and a final hundred, the real diehards, appeared, spread, and vanished. How could so many hide in the tree without my seeing them? The Osage orange, unruffled, looked just as it had looked from the house, when three hundred red-winged blackbirds cried from its crown. I looked downstream where they flew, and they were gone. Searching, I couldn't spot one. I wandered downstream to force them to play their hand, but they'd crossed the creek and scattered. One show to a customer. These appearances catch at my throat; they are the free gifts, the bright coppers at the roots of trees.

It's all a matter of keeping my eyes open. Nature is like one of those line drawings of a tree that are puzzles for children: Can you find hidden in the leaves a duck, a house, a boy, a bucket, a zebra, and a boot? Specialists can find the most incredibly well-hidden things. A book I read when I was young recommended an easy way to find caterpillars to rear: you simply find some fresh caterpillar droppings, look up, and there's your caterpillar. More recently an author advised me to set my mind at ease about those piles of cut stems on the ground in grassy fields. Field mice make them; they cut the grass down by degrees to reach the seeds at the head. It seems that when the grass is tightly packed, as in a field of ripe grain, the blade won't topple at a single cut through the stem; instead, the cut stem simply drops vertically, held in the crush of grain. The mouse severs the bottom again and again, the stem keeps dropping an inch at a time, and finally the head is low enough for the mouse to reach the seeds. Meanwhile, the mouse is positively littering the field with its little piles of cut stems into which, presumably, the author of the book is constantly stumbling.

If I can't see these minutiae, I still try to keep my eyes open. I'm always on the lookout for antlion traps in sandy soil, monarch pupae near milkweed, skipper larvae in locust leaves. These things are utterly common, and I've not seen one. I bang on hollow trees near water, but so far no flying squirrels have appeared. In flat country I watch every sunset in hopes of seeing the green ray. The green ray is a seldom-seen streak of light that rises from the sun like a spurting fountain at the moment of sunset; it throbs into the sky for two seconds and disappears. One more reason to keep my eyes open. A photography professor at the University of Florida just happened to see a bird die in midflight; it jerked, died, dropped, and smashed on the ground. I squint at the wind because I read Stewart Edward White: "I have always maintained that if you looked closely enough you could *see* the wind—the dim, hardly-made-out, fine débris fleeing high in the air." White was an excellent observer, and devoted an entire chapter of *The Mountains* to the subject of seeing deer: "As soon as you can forget the naturally obvious and construct an artificial obvious, then you too will see deer."

But the artificial obvious is hard to see. My eyes account for less than one percent of the weight of my head; I'm bony and dense; I see what I expect. I once spent a full three minutes looking at a bullfrog that was so unexpectedly large I couldn't see it even though a dozen enthusiastic campers were shouting directions. Finally I asked, "What color am I looking for?" and a fellow said,

"Green." When at last I picked out the frog, I saw what painters are up against: the thing wasn't green at all, but the color of wet hickory bark.

The lover can see, and the knowledgeable. I visited an aunt and uncle at a quarter-horse ranch in Cody, Wyoming. I couldn't do much of anything useful, but I could, I thought, draw. So, as we all sat around the kitchen table after supper, I produced a sheet of paper and drew a horse. "That's one lame horse," my aunt volunteered. The rest of the family joined in: "Only place to saddle that one is his neck"; "Looks like we better shoot the poor thing, on account of those terrible growths." Meekly, I slid the pencil and paper down the table. Everyone in that family, including my three young cousins, could draw a horse. Beautifully. When the paper came back it looked as though five shining, real quarter horses had been corralled by mistake with a papier-mâché moose; the real horses seemed to gaze at the monster with a steady, puzzled air. I stay away from horses now, but I can do a creditable goldfish. The point is that I just don't know what the lover knows; I just can't see the artificial obvious that those in the know construct. The herpetologist asks the native, "Are there snakes in that ravine?" "Nosir." And the herpetologist comes home with, yessir, three bags full. Are there butterflies on that mountain? Are the bluets in bloom, are there arrowheads here, or fossil shells in the shale?

Peeping through my keyhole I see within the range of only about thirty percent of the light that comes from the sun; the rest is infrared and some little ultraviolet, perfectly apparent to many animals, but invisible to me. A nightmare network of ganglia, charged and firing without my knowledge, cuts and splices what I do see, editing it for my brain. Donald E. Carr points out that the sense impressions of one-celled animals are *not* edited for the brain: "This is philosophically interesting in a rather mournful way, since it means that only the simplest animals perceive the universe as it is."

10   A fog that won't burn away drifts and flows across my field of vision. When you see fog move against a backdrop of deep pines, you don't see the fog itself, but streaks of clearness floating across the air in dark shreds. So I see only tatters of clearness through a pervading obscurity. I can't distinguish the fog from the overcast sky; I can't be sure if the light is direct or reflected. Everywhere darkness and the presence of the unseen appalls. We estimate now that only one atom dances alone in every cubic meter of intergalactic space. I blink and squint. What planet or power yanks Halley's Comet out of orbit? We haven't seen that force yet; it's a question of distance, density, and the pallor of reflected light. We rock, cradled in the swaddling band of darkness. Even the simple darkness of night whispers suggestions to the mind. Last summer, in August, I stayed at the creek too late.

Where Tinker Creek flows under the sycamore log bridge to the tear-shaped island, it is slow and shallow, fringed thinly in cattail marsh. At this spot an astonishing bloom of life supports vast breeding populations of insects, fish, reptiles, birds, and mammals. On windless summer evenings I stalk along the creek bank or straddle the sycamore log in absolute stillness, watching for muskrats. The night I stayed too late I was hunched on the log staring spellbound at spreading, reflected stains of lilac on the water. A cloud in the sky suddenly lighted as if turned on by a switch; its reflection just as suddenly materialized on the water upstream, flat and floating, so that I couldn't see the creek bottom, or life in the water under the cloud. Downstream, away from the cloud on the water, water turtles smooth as beans were gliding down with the current in a series of easy, weightless push-offs, as men bound on the moon. I didn't know whether to trace the progress of one turtle I was sure of, risking sticking my face in one of the bridge's spider webs made invisible by the gathering dark, or take a chance on seeing the carp, or scan the mudbank in hope of seeing a muskrat, or follow the last of the swallows who caught at my heart and trailed it after them like streamers as they appeared from directly below, under the log, flying upstream with their tails forked, so fast.

But shadows spread, and deepened, and stayed. After thousands of years we're still strangers to darkness, fearful aliens in an enemy camp with our arms crossed over our chests. I stirred. A land turtle on the bank, startled, hissed the air from its lungs and withdrew into its shell. An uneasy pink here, an unfathomable blue there, gave great suggestion of lurking beings. Things were going on. I couldn't see whether that sere rustle I heard was a distant rattlesnake, slit-eyed, or a nearby sparrow kicking in the dry flood debris slung at the foot of a willow. Tremendous action roiled the water everywhere I looked, big action, inexplicable. A tremor welled up beside a gaping muskrat burrow in the bank and I caught my breath, but no muskrat appeared. The ripples continued to fan upstream with a steady, powerful thrust. Night was knitting over my face an eyeless mask, and I still sat transfixed. A distant airplane, a delta wing out of nightmare, made a gliding shadow on the creek's bottom that looked like a stingray cruising upstream. At once a black fin slit the pink cloud on the water, shearing it in two. The two halves merged together and seemed to dissolve before my eyes. Darkness pooled in the cleft of the creek and rose, as water collects in a well. Untamed, dreaming lights flickered over the sky. I saw hints of hulking underwater shadows, two pale splashes out of the water, and round ripples rolling close together from a blackened center.

At last I stared upstream where only the deepest violet remained of the cloud, a cloud so high its underbelly still glowed feeble color reflected from a hidden sky lighted in turn by a sun halfway to China. And out of that violet, a sudden enormous black body arced over the water. I saw only a cylindrical sleekness. Head and tail, if there was a head and tail, were both submerged in cloud. I saw only one ebony fling, a headlong dive to darkness; then the waters closed, and the lights went out.

I walked home in a shivering daze, up hill and down. Later I lay open-mouthed in bed, my arms flung wide at my sides to steady the whirling darkness. At this latitude I'm spinning 836 miles an hour round the earth's axis; I often fancy I feel my sweeping fall as a breakneck arc like the dive of dolphins, and the hollow rushing of wind raises hair on my neck and the side of my face. In orbit around the sun I'm moving 64,800 miles an hour. The solar system as a whole, like a merry-go-round unhinged, spins, bobs, and blinks at the speed of 43,200 miles an hour along a course set east of Hercules. Someone has piped, and we are dancing a tarantella until the sweat pours. I open my eyes and I see dark, muscled forms curl out of water, with flapping gills and flattened eyes. I close my eyes and I see stars, deep stars giving way to deeper stars, deeper stars bowing to deepest stars at the crown of an infinite cone.

15   "Still," wrote van Gogh in a letter, "a great deal of light falls on everything." If we are blinded by darkness, we are also blinded by light. When too much light falls on everything, a special terror results. Peter Freuchen describes the notorious kayak sickness to which Greenland Eskimos are prone. "The Greenland fjords are peculiar for the spells of completely quiet weather, when there is not enough wind to blow out a match and the water is like a sheet of glass. The kayak hunter must sit in his boat without stirring a finger so as not to scare the shy seals away. . . . The sun, low in the sky, sends a glare into his eyes, and the landscape around moves into the realm of the unreal. The reflex from the mirror-like water hypnotizes him, he seems to be unable to move, and all of a sudden it is as if he were floating in a bottomless void, sinking, sinking, and sinking. . . . Horror-stricken, he tries to stir, to cry out, but he cannot, he is completely paralyzed, he just falls and falls." Some hunters are especially cursed with this panic, and bring ruin and sometimes starvation to their families.

    Sometimes here in Virginia at sunset low clouds on the southern or northern horizon are completely invisible in the lighted sky. I only know one is there because I can see its reflection in still water. The first time I discovered this mystery I looked from cloud to no-cloud in bewilderment, checking my bearings over and over, thinking maybe the ark of the covenant was just passing by south of Dead Man Mountain. Only much later did I read the explanation: polarized light from the sky is very much weakened by reflection, but the light in clouds isn't polarized. So invisible clouds pass among visible clouds, till all slide over the mountains; so a greater light extinguishes a lesser as though it didn't exist.

    In the great meteor shower of August, the Perseid, I wail all day for the shooting stars I miss. They're out there showering down, committing hara-kiri in a flame of fatal attraction, and hissing perhaps at last into the ocean. But at dawn what looks like a blue dome clamps down over me like a lid on a pot. The stars and planets could smash and I'd never know. Only a piece of ashen moon occasionally climbs up or down the inside of the dome, and our local star without surcease explodes on our heads. We have really only that one light, one source for all power, and yet we must turn away from it by universal decree. Nobody here on the planet seems aware of this strange, powerful taboo, that we all walk about carefully averting our faces, this way and that, lest our eyes be blasted forever.

    Darkness appalls and light dazzles; the scrap of visible light that doesn't hurt my eyes hurts my brain. What I see sets me swaying. Size and distance and the sudden swelling of meanings confuse me, bowl me over. I straddle the sycamore log bridge over Tinker Creek in the summer. I look at the lighted creek bottom: snail tracks tunnel the mud in quavering curves. A crayfish jerks, but by the time I absorb what has happened, he's gone in a billowing smokescreen of silt. I look at the water: minnows and shiners. If I'm thinking minnows, a carp will fill my brain till I scream. I look at the water's surface: skaters, bubbles, and leaves sliding down. Suddenly, my own face, reflected, startles me witless. Those snails have been tracking my face! Finally, with a shuddering wrench of the will, I see clouds, cirrus clouds. I'm dizzy, I fall in. This looking business is risky.

    Once I stood on a humped rock on nearby Purgatory Mountain, watching through binoculars the great autumn hawk migration below, until I discovered that I was in danger of joining the hawks on a vertical migration of my own. I was used to binoculars, but not, apparently, to balancing on humped rocks while looking through them. I staggered. Everything advanced and receded by turns; the world was full of unexplained foreshortenings and depths. A distant huge tan object, a hawk the size of an elephant, turned out to be the browned bough of a nearby loblolly pine. I followed a sharp-shinned hawk against a featureless sky, rotating my head unawares as it flew, and when I lowered the glass a glimpse of my own looming shoulder sent me staggering. What prevents the men on Palomar from falling, voiceless and blinded, from their tiny, vaulted chairs?

I reel in confusion; I don't understand what I see. With the naked eye I can see two million light-years to the Andromeda galaxy. Often I slop some creek water in a jar and when I get home I dump it in a white china bowl. After the silt settles I return and see tracings of minute snails on the bottom, a planarian or two winding round the rim of water, roundworms shimmying frantically, and finally, when my eyes have adjusted to these dimensions, amoebae. At first the amoebae look like muscae volitantes, those curled moving spots you seem to see in your eyes when you stare at a distant wall. Then I see the amoebae as drops of water congealed, bluish, translucent, like chips of sky in the bowl. At length I choose one individual and give myself over to its idea of an evening. I see it dribble a grainy foot before it on its wet, unfathomable way. Do its unedited sense impressions include the fierce focus of my eyes? Shall I take it outside and show it Andromeda, and blow its little endoplasm? I stir the water with a finger, in case it's running out of oxygen. Maybe I should get a tropical aquarium with motorized bubblers and lights, and keep this one for a pet. Yes, it would tell its fissioned descendants, the universe is two feet by five, and if you listen closely you can hear the buzzing music of the spheres.

Oh, it's mysterious lamplit evenings, here in the galaxy, one after the other. It's one of those nights when I wander from window to window, looking for a sign. But I can't see. Terror and a beauty insoluble are a ribband of blue woven into the fringes of garments of things both great and small. No culture explains, no bivouac offers real haven or rest. But it could be that we are not seeing something. Galileo thought comets were an optical illusion. This is fertile ground: since we are certain that they're not, we can look at what our scientists have been saying with fresh hope. What if there are *really* gleaming, castellated cities hung upsidedown over the desert sand? What limpid lakes and cool date palms have our caravans always passed untried? Until, one by one, by the blindest of leaps, we light on the road to these places, we must stumble in darkness and hunger. I turn from the window. I'm blind as a bat, sensing only from every direction the echo of my own thin cries.

I chanced on a wonderful book by Marius von Senden, called *Space and Sight*. When Western surgeons discovered how to perform safe cataract operations, they ranged across Europe and America operating on dozens of men and women of all ages who had been blinded by cataracts since birth. Von Senden collected accounts of such cases; the histories are fascinating. Many doctors had tested their patients' sense perceptions and ideas of space both before and after the operations. The vast majority of patients, of both sexes and all ages, had, in von Senden's opinion, no idea of space whatsoever. Form, distance, and size were so many meaningless syllables. A patient "had no idea of depth, confusing it with roundness." Before the operation a doctor would give a blind patient a cube and a sphere; the patient would tongue it or feel it with his hands, and name it correctly. After the operation the doctor would show the same objects to the patient without letting him touch them; now he had no clue whatsoever what he was seeing. One patient called lemonade "square" because it pricked on his tongue as a square shape pricked on the touch of his hands. Of another postoperative patient, the doctor writes, "I have found in her no notion of size, for example, not even within the narrow limits which she might have encompassed with the aid of touch. Thus when I asked her to show me how big her mother was, she did not stretch out her hands, but set her two index-fingers a few inches apart." Other doctors reported their patients' own statements to similar effect. "The room he was in . . . he knew to be but part of the house, yet he could not conceive that the whole house could look bigger"; "Those who are blind from birth . . . have no real conception of height or distance. A house that is a mile away is thought of as nearby, but requiring the taking of a lot of steps. . . . The elevator that whizzes him up and down gives no more sense of vertical distance than does the train of horizontal."

For the newly sighted, vision is pure sensation unencumbered by meaning: "The girl went through the experience that we all go through and forget, the moment we are born. She saw, but it did not mean anything but a lot of different kinds of brightness." Again, "I asked the patient what he could see; he answered that he saw an extensive field of light, in which everything appeared dull, confused, and in motion. He could not distinguish objects." Another patient saw "nothing but a confusion of forms and colours." When a newly sighted girl saw photographs and paintings, she asked, "'Why do they put those dark marks all over them?' 'Those aren't dark marks,' her mother explained, 'those are shadows. That is one of the ways the eye knows that things have shape. If it were not for shadows many things would look flat.' 'Well, that's how things do look,' Joan answered. 'Everything looks flat with dark patches.'"

But it is the patients' concepts of space that are most revealing. One patient, according to his doctor, "practiced his vision in a strange fashion; thus he takes off one of his boots, throws it some way off in front of him, and then attempts to gauge the distance at which it lies; he takes a few steps towards the boot and tries to grasp it; on failing to reach it, he moves on a step or two and gropes for the boot until he finally gets hold of it." "But even at this stage, after three weeks' experience of seeing," von Senden goes on, "'space,' as he conceives it, ends with visual space, i.e. with colour-patches that happen to bound his view. He does not yet have the notion that a larger object (a chair) can mask a smaller one (a dog), or that the latter can still be present even though it is not directly seen."

25   In general the newly sighted see the world as a dazzle of color-patches. They are pleased by the sensation of color, and learn quickly to name the colors, but the rest of seeing is tormentingly difficult. Soon after his operation a patient "generally bumps into one of these colour-patches and observes them to be substantial, since they resist him as tactual objects do. In walking about it also strikes him—or can if he pays attention—that he is continually passing in

between the colours he sees, that he can go past a visual object, that a part of it then steadily disappears from view; and that in spite of this, however he twists and turns—whether entering the room from the door, for example, or returning back to it—he always has a visual space in front of him. Thus he gradually comes to realize that there is also a space behind him, which he does not see."

The mental effort involved in these reasonings proves overwhelming for many patients. It oppresses them to realize, if they ever do at all, the tremendous size of the world, which they had previously conceived of as something touchingly manageable. It oppresses them to realize that they have been visible to people all along, perhaps unattractively so, without their knowledge or consent. A disheartening number of them refuse to use their new vision, continuing to go over objects with their tongues, and lapsing into apathy and despair. "The child can see, but will not make use of his sight. Only when pressed can he with difficulty be brought to look at objects in his neighbourhood; but more than a foot away it is impossible to bestir him to the necessary effort." Of a twenty-one-year-old girl, the doctor relates, "Her unfortunate father, who had hoped for so much from this operation, wrote that his daughter carefully shuts her eyes whenever she wishes to go about the house, especially when she comes to a staircase, and that she is never happier or more at ease than when, by closing her eyelids, she relapses into her former state of total blindness." A fifteen-year-old boy, who was also in love with a girl at the asylum for the blind, finally blurted out, "No, really, I can't stand it any more; I want to be sent back to the asylum again. If things aren't altered, I'll tear my eyes out."

Some do learn to see, especially the young ones. But it changes their lives. One doctor comments on "the rapid and complete loss of that striking and wonderful serenity which is characteristic only of those who have never yet seen." A blind man who learns to see is ashamed of his old habits. He dresses up, grooms himself, and tries to make a good impression. While he was blind he was indifferent to objects unless they were edible; now, "a sifting of values sets in . . . his thoughts and wishes are mightily stirred and some few of the patients are thereby led into dissimulation, envy, theft and fraud."

On the other hand, many newly sighted people speak well of the world, and teach us how dull is our own vision. To one patient, a human hand, unrecognized, is "something bright and then holes." Shown a bunch of grapes, a boy calls out, "It is dark, blue and shiny. . . . It isn't smooth, it has bumps and hollows." A little girl visits a garden. "She is greatly astonished, and can scarcely be persuaded to answer, stands speechless in front of the tree, which she only names on taking hold of it, and then as 'the tree with the lights in it.'" Some delight in their sight and give themselves over to the visual world. Of a patient just after her bandages were removed, her doctor writes, "The first things to attract her attention were her own hands; she looked at them very closely, moved them repeatedly to and fro, bent and stretched the fingers, and seemed greatly astonished at the sight." One girl was eager to tell her blind friend that "men do not really look like trees at all," and astounded to discover that her every visitor had an utterly different face. Finally, a twenty-two-year-old girl was dazzled by the world's brightness and kept her eyes shut for two weeks. When at the end of that time she opened her eyes again, she did not recognize any objects, but, "the more she now directed her gaze upon everything about her, the more it could be seen how an expression of gratification and astonishment overspread her features; she repeatedly exclaimed: 'Oh God! How beautiful!'"

I saw color-patches for weeks after I read this wonderful book. It was summer; the peaches were ripe in the valley orchards. When I woke in the morning, color-patches wrapped round my eyes, intricately, leaving not one unfilled spot. All day long I walked among shifting color-patches that parted before me like the Red Sea and closed again in silence, transfigured, wherever I looked back. Some patches swelled and loomed, while others vanished utterly, and dark marks flitted at random over the whole dazzling sweep. But I couldn't sustain the illusion of flatness. I've been around for too long. Form is condemned to an eternal danse macabre with meaning: I couldn't unpeach the peaches. Nor can I remember ever having seen without understanding; the color-patches of infancy are lost. My brain then must have been smooth as any balloon. I'm told I reached for the moon; many babies do. But the color-patches of infancy swelled as meaning filled them; they arrayed themselves in solemn ranks down distance which unrolled and stretched before me like a plain. The moon rocketed away. I live now in a world of shadows that shape and distance color, a world where space makes a kind of terrible sense. What gnosticism is this, and what physics? The fluttering patch I saw in my nursery window—silver and green and shape-shifting blue—is gone; a row of Lombardy poplars takes its place, mute, across the distant lawn. That humming oblong creature pale as light that stole along the walls of my room at night, stretching exhilaratingly around the corners, is gone, too, gone the night I ate of the bittersweet fruit, put two and two together and puckered forever my brain. Martin Buber tells this tale: "Rabbi Mendel once boasted to his teacher Rabbi Elimelekh that evenings he saw the angel who rolls away the light before the darkness, and mornings the angel who rolls away the darkness before the light. 'Yes,' said Rabbi Elimelekh, 'in my youth I saw that too. Later on you don't see these things any more.'"

30   Why didn't someone hand those newly sighted people paints and brushes from the start, when they still didn't know what anything was? Then maybe we all could see color-patches too, the world unraveled from reason, Eden before Adam gave names. The scales would drop from my eyes; I'd see trees like men walking; I'd run down the road against all orders, hallooing and leaping.

Seeing is of course very much a matter of verbalization. Unless I call my attention to what passes before my eyes, I simply won't see it. It is, as Ruskin says, "not merely unnoticed, but in the full, clear sense of the word, unseen." My eyes alone can't solve analogy tests using figures, the ones which show, with increasing elaborations, a big square, then a small square in a big square, then a big triangle, and expect me to find a small triangle in a big triangle. I have to say the words, describe what I'm seeing. If Tinker Mountain erupted, I'd be likely to notice. But if I want to notice the lesser cataclysms of valley life, I have to maintain in my head a running description of the present. It's not that I'm observant; it's just that I talk too much. Otherwise, especially in a strange place, I'll never know what's happening. Like a blind man at the ball game, I need a radio.

When I see this way I analyze and pry. I hurl over logs and roll away stones; I study the bank a square foot at a time, probing and tilting my head. Some days when a mist covers the mountains, when the muskrats won't show and the microscope's mirror shatters, I want to climb up the blank blue dome as a man would storm the inside of a circus tent, wildly, dangling, and with a steel knife claw a rent in the top, peep, and, if I must, fall.

But there is another kind of seeing that involves a letting go. When I see this way I sway transfixed and emptied. The difference between the two ways of see-ing is the difference between walking with and without a camera. When I walk with a camera I walk from shot to shot, reading the light on a calibrated meter. When I walk without a camera, my own shutter opens, and the moment's light prints on my own silver gut. When I see this second way I am above all an unscrupulous observer.

It was sunny one evening last summer at Tinker Creek; the sun was low in the sky, upstream. I was sitting on the sycamore log bridge with the sunset at my back, watching the shiners the size of minnows who were feeding over the muddy sand in skittery schools. Again and again, one fish, then another, turned for a split second across the current and flash! the sun shot out from its silver side. I couldn't watch for it. It was always just happening somewhere else, and it drew my vision just as it disappeared: flash, like a sudden dazzle of the thinnest blade, a sparking over a dun and olive ground at chance intervals from every direction. Then I noticed white specks, some sort of pale petals, small, floating from under my feet on the creek's surface, very slow and steady. So I blurred my eyes and gazed towards the brim of my hat and saw a new world. I saw the pale white circles roll up, roll up, like the world's turning, mute and perfect, and I saw the linear flashes, gleaming silver, like stars being born at random down a rolling scroll of time. Something broke and something opened. I filled up like a new wineskin. I breathed an air like light; I saw a light like water. I was the lip of a fountain the creek filled forever; I was ether, the leaf in the zephyr; I was flesh-flake, feather, bone.

When I see this way I see truly. As Thoreau says, I return to my senses. I am 35 the man who watches the baseball game in silence in an empty stadium. I see the game purely; I'm abstracted and dazed. When it's all over and the white-suited players lope off the green field to their shadowed dugouts, I leap to my feet; I cheer and cheer.

But I can't go out and try to see this way. I'll fail, I'll go mad. All I can do is try to gag the commentator, to hush the noise of useless interior babble that keeps me from seeing just as surely as a newspaper dangled before my eyes. The effort is really a discipline requiring a lifetime of dedicated struggle; it marks the literature of saints and monks of every order East and West, under every rule and no rule, discalced and shod. The world's spiritual geniuses seem to discover universally that the mind's muddy river, this ceaseless flow of trivia and trash, cannot be dammed, and that trying to dam it is a waste of effort that might lead to madness. Instead you must allow the muddy river to flow unheeded in the dim channels of consciousness; you raise your sights; you look along it, mildly, acknowledging its presence without interest and gazing beyond it into the realm of the real where subjects and objects act and rest purely, without utterance. "Launch into the deep," says Jacques Ellul, "and you shall see."

The secret of seeing is, then, the pearl of great price. If I thought he could teach me to find it and keep it forever I would stagger barefoot across a hundred deserts after any lunatic at all. But although the pearl may be found, it may not be sought. The literature of illumination reveals this above all: although it comes to those who wait for it, it is always, even to the most practiced and adept, a gift and a total surprise. I return from one walk knowing where the killdeer nests in the field by the creek and the hour the laurel blooms. I return from the same walk a day later scarcely knowing my own name. Litanies hum in my ears; my tongue flaps in my mouth Ailinon, alleluia! I cannot cause light; the most I can do is try to put myself in the path of its beam. It is possible, in deep space, to sail on solar wind. Light, be it particle or wave, has force: you rig a giant sail and go. The secret of seeing is to sail on solar wind. Hone and spread your spirit till you yourself are a sail, whetted, translucent, broadside to the merest puff.

When her doctor took her bandages off and led her into the garden, the girl who was no longer blind saw "the tree with the lights in it." It was for this tree I searched through the peach orchards of summer, in the forests of fall and down winter and spring for years. Then one day I was walking along Tinker Creek thinking of nothing at all and I saw the tree with the lights in it. I saw the back-yard cedar where the mourning doves roost charged and transfigured, each cell buzzing with flame. I stood on the grass with the lights in it, grass that was wholly fire, utterly focused and utterly dreamed. It was less like seeing than like being for the first time seen, knocked breathless by a powerful glance. The flood of fire abated, but I'm still spending the power. Gradually the lights went out in the cedar, the colors died, the cells unflamed and disappeared. I was still ringing. I had been my whole life a bell, and never knew it until at that moment I was lifted and struck. I have since only very rarely seen the tree with the lights in it. The vision comes and goes, mostly goes, but I live for it, for the moment when the mountains open and a new light roars in spate through the crack, and the mountains slam.

[1974]

1. Dillard uses some of the same sources that Sacks uses in his essay. What is Dillard's purpose? Does she use them in the same way that Sacks does or differently? With what other selections in the book does "Seeing" share concerns?
2. Characterize Dillard's style.

E. M. FORSTER

E[DWARD] M[ORGAN] FORSTER *(1879–1970) was a friend of Virginia Woolf and other members of the Bloomsbury group in England. Brought up by his mother and aunts after his father died when he was only two, Forster had a difficult time at school, but his years at Cambridge opened his mind to the influence of free-thinkers and literary lights, leading to his abandonment of his Christian faith and his subsequent development as a writer. Independent means, a legacy from a paternal great-aunt, allowed him to travel and to write the novels* The Longest Journey, A Room with a View, Howard's End, Maurice, *and his masterpiece,* A Passage to India; *all except the first have been used as the basis of films. The short stories collected in* The Celestial Omnibus *were mostly symbolic fantasies or fables. His published works also include letters, essays, and lectures.*

Art for Art's Sake*

An address delivered before the American Academy and the National Institute of Arts and Letters in New York

I believe in art for art's sake. It is an unfashionable belief, and some of my state-ments must be of the nature of an apology. Sixty years ago I should have faced you with more confidence. A writer or a speaker who chose "Art for Art's Sake" for his theme sixty years ago could be sure of being in the swim, and could feel so confident of success that he sometimes dressed himself in aesthetic costumes suitable to the occasion—in an embroidered dressing-gown, perhaps, or a blue velvet suit with a Lord Fauntleroy collar; or a toga, or a kimono, and carried a poppy or a lily or a long peacock's feather in his medieval hand. Times have changed. Not thus can I present either myself or my theme today. My aim rather is to ask you quietly to reconsider for a few minutes a phrase which has been much misused and much abused, but which has, I believe, great importance for us—has, indeed, eternal importance.

Now we can easily dismiss those peacock's feathers and other affectations—they are but trifles—but I want also to dismiss a more dangerous heresy, namely the silly idea that only art matters, an idea which has somehow got mixed up with the idea of art for art's sake, and has helped to discredit it. Many things, besides art, matter. It is merely one of the things that matter, and, high though the claims are that I make for it, I want to keep them in proportion. No one can spend his or her life entirely in the creation or the appreciation of masterpieces. Man lives, and ought to live, in a complex world, full of conflicting claims, and if we simplified them down into the aesthetic he would be sterilized. Art for art's sake does not mean that only art matters, and I would also like to rule out such phrases as "The Life of Art", "Living for Art" and "Art's High Mission". They confuse and mislead.

What does the phrase mean? Instead of generalizing, let us take a specific instance—Shakespeare's *Macbeth,* for example, and pronounce the words, "*Macbeth* for *Macbeth*'s sake". What does that mean? Well, the play has several aspects—it is educational, it teaches us something about legendary Scotland, something about Jacobean England, and a good deal about human nature and its perils. We can study its origins, and study and enjoy its dramatic technique and the music of its diction. All that is true. But *Macbeth* is furthermore a world

*E[dward] M[organ] Forster, "Art for Art's Sake," *Two Cheers for Democracy* (New York: Harcourt Brace, 1951).

of its own, created by Shakespeare and existing in virtue of its own poetry. It is in this aspect *Macbeth* for *Macbeth*'s sake, and that is what I intend by the phrase "art for art's sake". A work of art—whatever else it may be—is a self-contained entity, with a life of its own imposed on it by its creator. It has internal order. It may have external form. That is how we recognize it.

Take for another example that picture of Seurat's which I saw two years ago in Chicago—*La Grande Jatte*. Here again there is much to study and to enjoy: the pointillism, the charming face of the seated girl, the nineteenth-century Parisian Sunday sunlight, the sense of motion in immobility. But here again there is something more; *La Grande Jatte* forms a world of its own, created by Seurat and existing by virtue of its own poetry: *La Grande Jatte pour La Grande Jatte: l'art pour l'art*. Like *Macbeth* it has internal order and internal life.

5   It is to the conception of order that I would now turn. This is important to my argument, and I want to make a digression, and glance at order in daily life, before I come to order in art.

In the world of daily life, the world which we perforce inhabit, there is much talk about order, particularly from statesmen and politicians. They tend, however, to confuse order with orders, just as they confuse creation with regulations. Order, I suggest, is something evolved from within, not something imposed from without; it is an internal stability, a vital harmony, and in the social and political category it has never existed except for the convenience of historians. Viewed realistically, the past is really a series of *dis*orders, succeeding one another by discoverable laws, no doubt, and certainly marked by an increasing growth of human interference, but disorders all the same. So that, speaking as a writer, what I hope for today is a disorder which will be more favourable to artists than is the present one, and which will provide them with fuller inspirations and better material conditions. It will not last—nothing lasts—but there have been some advantageous disorders in the past—for instance, in ancient Athens, in Renaissance Italy, eighteenth-century France, periods in China and Persia—and we may do something to accelerate the next one. But let us not again fix our hearts where true joys are not to be found. We were promised a new order after the First World War through the League of Nations. It did not come, nor have I faith in present promises, by whomsoever endorsed. The implacable offensive of Science forbids. We cannot reach social and political stability, for the reason that we continue to make scientific discoveries and to apply them, and thus to destroy the arrangements which were based on more elementary discoveries. If Science would discover rather than apply—if, in other words, men were more interested in knowledge than in power—mankind would be in a far safer position, the stability statesmen talk about would be a possibility, there could be a new order based on vital harmony, and the earthly millennium might approach. But Science shows no signs of doing this: she gave us the internal combustion engine, and before we had digested and assimilated it with terrible pains into our social system she harnessed the atom, and destroyed any new order that seemed to be evolving. How can man get into harmony with his surroundings when he is constantly altering them? The future of our race is, in this direction, more unpleasant than we care to admit, and it has sometimes seemed to me that its best chance lies through apathy, uninventiveness and inertia. Universal exhaustion might promote that Change of Heart which is at present so briskly recommended from a thousand pulpits. Universal exhaustion would certainly be a new experience. The human race has never undergone it, and is still too perky to admit that it may be coming and might result in a sprouting of new growth through the decay.

I must not pursue these speculations any further—they lead me too far from my terms of reference and maybe from yours. But I do want to emphasize that order in daily life and in history, order in the social and political category, is unattainable under our present psychology.

Where is it attainable? Not in the astronomical category, where it was for many years enthroned. The heavens and the earth have become terribly alike since Einstein. No longer can we find a reassuring contrast to chaos in the night sky and look up with George Meredith to the stars, the army of unalterable law, or listen for the music of the spheres. Order is not there. In the entire universe there seem to be only two possibilities for it. The first of them—which again lies outside my terms of reference—is the divine order, the mystic harmony, which according to all religions is available for those who can contemplate it. We must admit its possibility, on the evidence of the adepts, and we must believe them when they say that it is attained, if attainable, by prayer. "O Thou, who changest not, abide with me," said one of its poets. "Ordena questo amore, tu che m'ami," said another: "Set love in order, thou who lovest me." The existence of a divine order, though it cannot be tested, has never been disproved.

The second possibility for order lies in the aesthetic category, which is my subject here: the order which an artist can create in his own work, and to that we must now return. A work of art, we are all agreed, is a unique product. But why? It is unique not because it is clever or noble or beautiful or enlightened or original or sincere or idealistic or useful or educational—it may embody any of those qualities—but because it is the only material object in the universe which may possess internal harmony. All the others have been pressed into shape from outside, and when their mould is removed they collapse. The work of art stands up by itself, and nothing else does. It achieves something which has often been promised by society, but always delusively. Ancient Athens made a mess—but the *Antigone* stands up. Renaissance Rome made a mess—but the ceiling of the Sistine got painted. James I made a mess—but there was *Macbeth*. Louis XIV— but there was *Phèdre*. Art for art's sake? I should just think so, and more so than ever at the present time. It is the one orderly product which our muddling race has produced. It is the cry of a thousand sentinels, the echo from a thousand labyrinths; it is the lighthouse which cannot be hidden; *c'est le meilleur témoignage que nous puissions donner de notre dignité. Antigone* for *Antigone*'s sake, *Macbeth* for *Macbeth*'s, *La Grande Jatte pour La Grande Jatte.*

If this line of argument is correct, it follows that the artist will tend to be an outsider in the society to which he has been born, and that the nineteenth-century conception of him as a bohemian was not inaccurate. The conception erred in three particulars: it postulated an economic system where art could be a full-time job, it introduced the fallacy that only art matters, and it overstressed

10

idiosyncrasy and waywardness—the peacock-feather aspect—rather than order. But it is a truer conception than the one which prevails in official circles on my side of the Atlantic—I don't know about yours: the conception which treats the artist as if he were a particularly bright government advertiser and encourages him to be friendly and matey with his fellow citizens, and not to give himself airs.

Estimable is mateyness, and the man who achieves it gives many a pleasant little drink to himself and to others. But it has no traceable connection with the creative impulse, and probably acts as an inhibition on it. The artist who is seduced by mateyness may stop himself from doing the one thing which he, and he alone, can do—the making of something out of words or sounds or paint or clay or marble or steel or film which has internal harmony and presents order to a permanently disarranged planet. This seems to be worth doing, even at the risk of being called uppish by journalists. I have in mind an article which was published some years ago in the London *Times,* an article called "The Eclipse of the Highbrow", in which the "Average Man" was exalted, and all contemporary literature was censured if it did not toe the line, the precise position of the line being naturally known to the writer of the article. Sir Kenneth Clark, who was at that time director of our National Gallery, commented on this pernicious doctrine in a letter which cannot be too often quoted. "The poet and the artist," wrote Clark, "are important precisely because they are not average men; because in sensibility, intelligence, and power of invention they far exceed the average." These memorable words, and particularly the words "power of invention", are the bohemian's passport. Furnished with it, he slinks about society, saluted now by a brickbat and now by a penny, and accepting either of them with equanimity. He does not consider too anxiously what his relations with society may be, for he is aware of something more important than that—namely the invitation to invent, to create order, and he believes he will be better placed for doing this if he attempts detachment. So round and round he slouches, with his hat pulled over his eyes, and maybe with a louse in his beard, and—if he really wants one—with a peacock's feather in his hand.

If our present society should disintegrate—and who dare prophesy that it won't?—this old-fashioned and démodé figure will become clearer: the bohemian, the outsider, the parasite, the rat—one of those figures which have at present no function either in a warring or a peaceful world. It may not be dignified to be a rat, but many of the ships are sinking, which is not dignified either—the officials did not build them properly. Myself, I would sooner be a swimming rat than a sinking ship—at all events I can look around me for a little longer—and I remember how one of us, a rat with particularly bright eyes called Shelley, squeaked out, "Poets are the unacknowledged legislators of the world," before he vanished into the waters of the Mediterranean.

What laws did Shelley propose to pass? None. The legislation of the artist is never formulated at the time, though it is sometimes discerned by future generations. He legislates through creating. And he creates through his sensitiveness and his power to impose form. Without form the sensitiveness vanishes. And form is as important today, when the human race is trying to ride the whirlwind, as it ever was in those less agitating days of the past, when the earth seemed solid and the stars fixed, and the discoveries of science were made slowly, slowly. Form is not tradition. It alters from generation to generation. Artists always seek a new technique, and will continue to do so as long as their work excites them. But form of some kind is imperative. It is the surface crust of the internal harmony, it is the outward evidence of order.

My remarks about society may have seemed too pessimistic, but I believe that society can only represent a fragment of the human spirit, and that another fragment can only get expressed through art. And I wanted to take this opportunity, this vantage-ground, to assert not only the existence of art, but its pertinacity. Looking back into the past, it seems to me that that is all there has ever been: vantage-grounds for discussion and creation, little vantage-grounds in the changing chaos, where bubbles have been blown and webs spun, and the desire to create order has found temporary gratification, and the sentinels have managed to utter their challenges, and the huntsmen, though lost individually, have heard each other's calls through the impenetrable wood, and the lighthouses have never ceased sweeping the thankless seas. In this pertinacity there seems to me, as I grow older, something more and more profound, something which does in fact concern people who do not care about art at all.

In conclusion, let me summarize the various categories that have laid claim to the possession of order. 15

(1) The social and political category. Claim disallowed on the evidence of history and of our own experience. If man altered psychologically, order here might be attainable; not otherwise.

(2) The astronomical category. Claim allowed up to the present century, but now disallowed on the evidence of the physicists.

(3) The religious category. Claim allowed on the evidence of the mystics.

(4) The aesthetic category. Claim allowed on the evidence of various works of art, and on the evidence of our own creative impulses, however weak these may be, or however imperfectly they may function. Works of art, in my opinion, are the only objects in the material universe to possess internal order, and that is why, though I don't believe that only art matters, I do believe in Art for Art's Sake. [1949]

1. What is the argument of this essay?
2. Forster begins by distinguishing his use of the phrase in his title from its use in the Aesthetic Movement in the late nineteenth century, when it was associated most strongly with poet and playwright Oscar Wilde and painter James Whistler, who tried to free art from demands that it be morally good, inspiring its audience to virtue. Their claim was thus that art had value in itself, not for its consequences, whether moral or immoral. Wilde, a flamboyant character of late nineteenth-century London, was parodied in Gilbert and Sullivan's operetta *Patience*, in which the main character Reginald Bunthorne is a poseur who claims to love art (especially medieval) and poetry, but doesn't. After the debut of the operetta, the same theatre company that sponsored it sponsored Wilde on a lecture tour in America, in which he dressed in velvet clothes and carried a lily (see paragraph 1).

How do the Aesthetic Movement, the parody of it, and Wilde's self-parody figure in Forster's essay?

3. What are Forster's strategies for supporting his claims?

4. What forms of art do you know that live up to Forster's claim that art creates order? Are there any that challenge his definition?

5. According to Forster, modern science produces a picture of the world more chaotic than the one we had before Einstein. Recently, chaos theory has found deep patterns in phenomena that look thoroughly random and the study of complex systems has found that nature can produce intricate patterns through repetitive operation of surprisingly simple rules. What might Forster say about such discoveries?

HELEN KELLER

HELEN KELLER *(1880–1968) lost her hearing and sight before she was two years old and, because she could not communicate with her parents except through screaming and grabbing things, became something of a "wild child." Inspired by the story of another deaf and blind child, Laura Bridgman (see p. 1453), her mother engaged Annie Sullivan, a gifted tutor who opened Helen's mind to knowledge of the world through language. Through her autobiography,* The Story of My Life, *which has been dramatized on the stage and in film as* The Miracle Worker, *millions of people have witnessed the dramatic moment of Keller's awakening. Her education at Radcliffe and her subsequent testimony on the abilities and rights of the disabled made her a symbol of what people can do when they are liberated by language and education. Received by royalty and applauded and listened to all over the world, Keller crusaded for the independence of the disabled and equal rights for women and for all races.*

Three Days to See*

I

All of us have read thrilling stories in which the hero had only a limited and specified time to live. Sometimes it was as long as a year; sometimes as short as twenty-four hours. But always we were interested in discovering just how the doomed man chose to spend his last days or his last hours. I speak, of course, of free men who have a choice, not condemned criminals whose sphere of activities is strictly delimited.

Such stories set us thinking, wondering what we should do under similar circumstances. What events, what experiences, what associations, should we crowd into those last hours as mortal beings? What happiness should we find in reviewing the past, what regrets?

Sometimes I have thought it would be an excellent rule to live each day as if we should die tomorrow. Such an attitude would emphasize sharply the values of life. We should live each day with a gentleness, a vigor, and a keenness of appreciation which are often lost when time stretches before us in the constant

*Helen Keller, "Three Days to See," *The Atlantic Monthly* 151.1 (January 1933).

panorama of more days and months and years to come. There are those, of course, who would adopt the epicurean motto of 'Eat, drink, and be merry,' but most people would be chastened by the certainty of impending death.

In stories, the doomed hero is usually saved at the last minute by some stroke of fortune, but almost always his sense of values is changed. He becomes more appreciative of the meaning of life and its permanent spiritual values. It has often been noted that those who live, or have lived, in the shadow of death bring a mellow sweetness to everything they do.

Most of us, however, take life for granted. We know that one day we must die, but usually we picture that day as far in the future. When we are in buoyant health, death is all but unimaginable. We seldom think of it. The days stretch out in an endless vista. So we go about our petty tasks, hardly aware of our listless attitude toward life.

The same lethargy, I am afraid, characterizes the use of all our faculties and senses. Only the deaf appreciate hearing, only the blind realize the manifold blessings that lie in sight. Particularly does this observation apply to those who have lost sight and hearing in adult life. But those who have never suffered impairment of sight or hearing seldom make the fullest use of these blessed faculties. Their eyes and ears take in all sights and sounds hazily, without concentration and with little appreciation. It is the same old story of not being grateful for what we have until we lose it, of not being conscious of health until we are ill.

I have often thought it would be a blessing if each human being were stricken blind and deaf for a few days at some time during his early adult life. Darkness would make him more appreciative of sight; silence would teach him the joys of sound.

Now and then I have tested my seeing friends to discover what they see. Recently I was visited by a very good friend who had just returned from a long walk in the woods, and I asked her what she had observed. "Nothing in particular," she replied. I might have been incredulous had I not been accustomed to such responses, for long ago I became convinced that the seeing see little.

How was it possible, I asked myself, to walk for an hour through the woods and see nothing worthy of note? I who cannot see find hundreds of things to interest me through mere touch. I feel the delicate symmetry of a leaf. I pass my hands lovingly about the smooth skin of a silver birch, or the rough, shaggy bark of a pine. In spring I touch the branches of trees hopefully in search of a bud, the first sign of awakening Nature after her winter's sleep. I feel the delightful, velvety texture of a flower, and discover its remarkable convolutions; and something of the miracle of Nature is revealed to me. Occasionally, if I am very fortunate, I place my hand gently on a small tree and feel the happy quiver of a bird in full song. I am delighted to have the cool waters of a brook rush through my open fingers. To me a lush carpet of pine needles or spongy grass is more welcome than the most luxurious Persian rug. To me the pageant of seasons is a thrilling and unending drama, the action of which streams through my finger tips. At times my heart cries out with longing to see all these things. If I can get so much pleasure from mere touch, how much more beauty must be revealed by sight. Yet, those who have eyes apparently see little. The panorama of color and action which fills the world is taken for granted. It is human, perhaps, to appreciate little that which we have and to long for that which we have not, but it is a great pity that in the world of light the gift of sight is used only as a mere convenience rather than as a means of adding fullness to life.

10   If I were the president of a university I should establish a compulsory course in "How to Use Your Eyes." The professor would try to show his pupils how they could add joy to their lives by really seeing what passes unnoticed before them. He would try to awake their dormant and sluggish faculties.

II

Perhaps I can best illustrate by imagining what I should most like to see if I were given the use of my eyes, say, for just three days. And while I am imagining, suppose you, too, set your mind to work on the problem of how you would use your own eyes if you had only three more days to see. If with the oncoming darkness of the third night you knew that the sun would never rise for you again, how would you spend those three precious intervening days? What would you most want to let your gaze rest upon?

I, naturally, should want most to see the things which have become dear to me through my years of darkness. You, too, would want to let your eyes rest long on the things that have become dear to you so that you could take the memory of them with you into the night that loomed before you.

If, by some miracle, I were granted three seeing days, to be followed by a relapse into darkness, I should divide the period into three parts.

On the first day, I should want to see the people whose kindness and gentleness and companionship have made my life worth living. First I should like to gaze long upon the face of my dear teacher, Mrs. Anne Sullivan Macy, who came to me when I was a child and opened the outer world to me. I should want not merely to see the outline of her face, so that I could cherish it in my memory, but to study that face and find in it the living evidence of the sympathetic tenderness and patience with which she accomplished the difficult task of my education. I should like to see in her eyes that strength of character which has enabled her to stand firm in the face of difficulties, and that compassion for all humanity which she has revealed to me so often.

15   I do not know what it is to see into the heart of a friend through that "window of the soul," the eye. I can only "see" through my finger tips the outline of a face. I can detect laughter, sorrow, and many other obvious emotions. I know my friends from the feel of their faces. But I cannot really picture their personalities by touch. I know their personalities, of course, through other means, through the thoughts they express to me, through whatever of their actions are revealed to me. But I am denied that deeper understanding of them which I am sure would come through sight of them, through watching their reactions to various expressed thoughts and circumstances, through noting the immediate and fleeting reactions of their eyes and countenance.

Friends who are near to me I know well, because through the months and years they reveal themselves to me in all their phases; but of casual friends I have only an incomplete impression, an impression gained from a handclasp, from spoken words which I take from their lips with my finger tips, or which they tap into the palm of my hand.

How much easier, how much more satisfying it is for you who can see to grasp quickly the essential qualities of another person by watching the subtleties of expression, the quiver of a muscle, the flutter of a hand. But does it ever occur to you to use your sight to see into the inner nature of a friend or acquaintance? Do not most of you seeing people grasp casually the outward features of a face and let it go at that?

For instance, can you describe accurately the faces of five good friends? Some of you can, but many cannot. As an experiment, I have questioned husbands of long standing about the color of their wives' eyes, and often they express embarrassed confusion and admit that they do not know. And, incidentally, it is a chronic complaint of wives that their husbands do not notice new dresses, new hats, and changes in household arrangements.

The eyes of seeing persons soon become accustomed to the routine of their surroundings, and they actually see only the startling and spectacular. But even in viewing the most spectacular sights the eyes are lazy. Court records reveal every day how inaccurately "eyewitnesses" see. A given event will be "seen" in several different ways by as many witnesses. Some see more than others, but few see everything that is within the range of their vision.

Oh, the things that I should see if I had the power of sight for just three days! 20

The first day would be a busy one. I should call to me all my dear friends and look long into their faces, imprinting upon my mind the outward evidences of the beauty that is within them. I should let my eyes rest, too, on the face of a baby, so that I could catch a vision of the eager, innocent beauty which precedes the individual's consciousness of the conflicts which life develops.

And I should like to look into the loyal, trusting eyes of my dogs—the grave, canny little Scottie, Darkie, and the stalwart, understanding Great Dane, Helga, whose warm, tender, and playful friendships are so comforting to me.

On that busy first day I should also view the small simple things of my home. I want to see the warm colors in the rugs under my feet, the pictures on the walls, the intimate trifles that transform a house into home. My eyes would rest respectfully on the books in raised type which I have read, but they would be more eagerly interested in the printed books which seeing people can read, for during the long night of my life the books I have read and those which have been read to me have built themselves into a great shining lighthouse, revealing to me the deepest channels of human life and the human spirit.

In the afternoon of that first seeing day, I should take a long walk in the woods and intoxicate my eyes on the beauties of the world of Nature, trying desperately to absorb in a few hours the vast splendor which is constantly unfolding itself to those who can see. On the way home from my woodland jaunt my path would lie near a farm so that I might see the patient horses ploughing in the field (perhaps I should see only a tractor!) and the serene content of men living close to the soil. And I should pray for the glory of a colorful sunset.

25   When dusk had fallen, I should experience the double delight of being able to see by artificial light, which the genius of man has created to extend the power of his sight when Nature decrees darkness.

    In the night of that first day of sight, I should not be able to sleep, so full would be my mind of the memories of the day.

III

The next day—the second day of sight—I should arise with the dawn and see the thrilling miracle by which night is transformed into day. I should behold with awe the magnificent panorama of light with which the sun awakens the sleeping earth.

    This day I should devote to a hasty glimpse of the world, past and present. I should want to see the pageant of man's progress, the kaleidoscope of the ages. How can so much be compressed into one day? Through the museums, of course. Often I have visited the New York Museum of Natural History to touch with my hands many of the objects there exhibited, but I have longed to see with my eyes the condensed history of the earth and its inhabitants displayed there—animals and the races of men pictured in their native environment; gigantic carcasses of dinosaurs and mastodons which roamed the earth long before man appeared, with his tiny stature and powerful brain, to conquer the animal kingdom; realistic presentations of the processes of evolution in animals, in man, and in the implements which man has used to fashion for himself a secure home on this planet; and a thousand and one other aspects of natural history.

    I wonder how many readers of this article have viewed this panorama of the face of living things as pictured in that inspiring museum. Many, of course, have not had the opportunity, but I am sure that many who *have* had the opportunity have not made use of it. There, indeed, is a place to use your eyes. You who see can spend many fruitful days there, but I, with my imaginary three days of sight, could only take a hasty glimpse, and pass on.

    My next stop would be the Metropolitan Museum of Art, for just as the Museum of Natural History reveals the material aspects of the world, so does the Metropolitan show the myriad facets of the human spirit. Throughout the history of humanity the urge to artistic expression has been almost as powerful as the urge for food, shelter, and procreation. And here, in the vast chambers of the Metropolitan Museum, is unfolded before me the spirit of Egypt, Greece, and Rome, as expressed in their art. I know well through my hands the sculptured gods and goddesses of the ancient Nile land. I have felt copies of Parthenon friezes, and I have sensed the rhythmic beauty of charging Athenian warriors. Apollos and Venuses and the Winged Victory of Samothrace are friends of my finger tips. The gnarled, bearded features of Homer are dear to me, for he, too, knew blindness.

30   My hands have lingered upon the living marble of Roman sculpture as well as that of later generations. I have passed my hands over a plaster cast of

Michelangelo's inspiring and heroic Moses; I have sensed the power of Rodin; I have been awed by the devoted spirit of Gothic wood carving. These arts which can be touched have meaning for me, but even they were meant to be seen rather than felt, and I can only guess at the beauty which remains hidden from me. I can admire the simple lines of a Greek vase, but its figured decorations are lost to me.

So on this, my second day of sight, I should try to probe into the soul of man through his art. The things I knew through touch I should now see. More splendid still, the whole magnificent world of painting would be opened to me, from the Italian Primitives, with their serene religious devotion, to the Moderns, with their feverish visions. I should look deep into the canvases of Raphael, Leonardo da Vinci, Titian, Rembrandt. I should want to feast my eyes upon the warm colors of Veronese, study the mysteries of El Greco, catch a new vision of Nature from Corot. Oh, there is so much rich meaning and beauty in the art of the ages for you who have eyes to see!

Upon my short visit to this temple of art I should not be able to review a fraction of that great world of art which is open to you. I should be able to get only a superficial impression. Artists tell me that for a deep and true appreciation of art one must educate the eye. One must learn through experience to weigh the merits of line, of composition, of form and color. If I had eyes, how happily would I embark upon so fascinating a study! Yet I am told that, to many of you who have eyes to see, the world of art is a dark night, unexplored and unilluminated.

It would be with extreme reluctance that I should leave the Metropolitan Museum, which contains the key to beauty—a beauty so neglected. Seeing persons, however, do not need a Metropolitan to find this key to beauty. The same key lies waiting in smaller museums, and in books on the shelves of even small libraries. But naturally, in my limited time of imaginary sight, I should choose the place where the key unlocks the greatest treasures in the shortest time.

The evening of my second day of sight I should spend at a theatre or at the movies. Even now I often attend theatrical performances of all sorts, but the action of the play must be spelled into my hand by a companion. But how I should like to see with my own eyes the fascinating figure of Hamlet, or the gusty Falstaff amid colorful Elizabethan trappings! How I should like to follow each movement of the graceful Hamlet, each strut of the hearty Falstaff! And since I could see only one play, I should be confronted by a many-horned dilemma, for there are scores of plays I should want to see. You who have eyes can see any you like. How many of you, I wonder, when you gaze at a play, a movie, or any spectacle, realize and give thanks for the miracle of sight which enables you to enjoy its color, grace, and movement?

I cannot enjoy the beauty of rhythmic movement except in a sphere restricted to the touch of my hands. I can vision only dimly the grace of a Pavlowa, although I know something of the delight of rhythm, for often I can sense the beat of music as it vibrates through the floor. I can well imagine that cadenced motion must be one of the most pleasing sights in the world. I have been able to gather something of this by tracing with my fingers the lines in sculptured

35

marble; if this static grace can be so lovely, how much more acute must be the thrill of seeing grace in motion.

One of my dearest memories is of the time when Joseph Jefferson allowed me to touch his face and hands as he went through some of the gestures and speeches of his beloved Rip Van Winkle. I was able to catch thus a meagre glimpse of the world of drama, and I shall never forget the delight of that moment. But, oh, how much I must miss, and how much pleasure you seeing ones can derive from watching and hearing the interplay of speech and movement in the unfolding of a dramatic performance! If I could see only one play, I should know how to picture in my mind the action of a hundred plays which I have read or had transferred to me through the medium of the manual alphabet.

So, through the evening of my second imaginary day of sight, the great figures of dramatic literature would crowd sleep from my eyes.

<h2 style="text-align:center">IV</h2>

The following morning, I should again greet the dawn, anxious to discover new delights, for I am sure that, for those who have eyes which really see, the dawn of each day must be a perpetually new revelation of beauty.

This, according to the terms of my imagined miracle, is to be my third and last day of sight. I shall have no time to waste in regrets or longings; there is too much to see. The first day I devoted to my friends, animate and inanimate. The second revealed to me the history of man and Nature. Today I shall spend in the workaday world of the present, amid the haunts of men going about the business of life. And where can one find so many activities and conditions of men as in New York? So the city becomes my destination.

40   I start from my home in the quiet little suburb of Forest Hills, Long Island. Here, surrounded by green lawns, trees, and flowers, are neat little houses, happy with the voices and movements of wives and children, havens of peaceful rest for men who toil in the city. I drive across the lacy structure of steel which spans the East River, and I get a new and startling vision of the power and ingenuity of the mind of man. Busy boats chug and scurry about the river—racy speed boats, stolid, snorting tugs. If I had long days of sight ahead, I should spend many of them watching the delightful activity upon the river.

I look ahead, and before me rise the fantastic towers of New York, a city that seems to have stepped from the pages of a fairy story. What an awe-inspiring sight, these glittering spires, these vast banks of stone and steel—structures such as the gods might build for themselves! This animated picture is a part of the lives of millions of people every day. How many, I wonder, give it so much as a second glance? Very few, I fear. Their eyes are blind to this magnificent sight because it is so familiar to them.

I hurry to the top of one of those gigantic structures, the Empire State Building, for there, a short time ago, I "saw" the city below through the eyes of my secretary. I am anxious to compare my fancy with reality. I am sure I should not be disappointed in the panorama spread out before me, for to me it would be a vision of another world.

Now I begin my rounds of the city. First, I stand at a busy corner, merely looking at people, trying by sight of them to understand something of their lives. I see smiles, and I am happy. I see serious determination, and I am proud. I see suffering, and I am compassionate.

I stroll down Fifth Avenue. I throw my eyes out of focus, so that I see no particular object but only a seething kaleidoscope of color. I am certain that the colors of women's dresses moving in a throng must be a gorgeous spectacle of which I should never tire. But perhaps if I had sight I should be like most other women—too interested in styles and the cut of individual dresses to give much attention to the splendor of color in the mass. And I am convinced, too, that I should become an inveterate window shopper, for it must be a delight to the eye to view the myriad articles of beauty on display.

From Fifth Avenue I make a tour of the city—to Park Avenue, to the slums, to factories, to parks where children play. I take a stay-at-home trip abroad by visiting the foreign quarters. Always my eyes are open wide to all the sights of both happiness and misery so that I may probe deep and add to my understanding of how people work and live. My heart is full of the images of people and things. My eye passes lightly over no single trifle; it strives to touch and hold closely each thing its gaze rests upon. Some sights are pleasant, filling the heart with happiness; but some are miserably pathetic. To these latter I do not shut my eyes, for they, too, are part of life. To close the eye on them is to close the heart and mind.

My third day of sight is drawing to an end. Perhaps there are many serious pursuits to which I should devote the few remaining hours, but I am afraid that on the evening of that last day I should again run away to the theatre, to a hilariously funny play, so that I might appreciate the overtones of comedy in the human spirit.

At midnight my temporary respite from blindness would cease, and permanent night would close in on me again. Naturally in those three short days I should not have seen all I wanted to see. Only when darkness had again descended upon me should I realize how much I had left unseen. But my mind would be so crowded with glorious memories that I should have little time for regrets. Thereafter the touch of every object would bring a glowing memory of how that object looked.

Perhaps this short outline of how I should spend three days of sight does not agree with the programme you would set for yourself if you knew that you were about to be stricken blind. I am, however, sure that if you actually faced that fate your eyes would open to things you had never seen before, storing up memories for the long night ahead. You would use your eyes as never before. Everything you saw would become dear to you. Your eyes would touch and embrace every object that came within your range of vision. Then, at last, you would really see, and a new world of beauty would open itself before you.

I who am blind can give one hint to those who see—one admonition to those who would make full use of the gift of sight: Use your eyes as if tomorrow you would be stricken blind. And the same method can be applied to the other senses. Hear the music of voices, the song of a bird, the mighty strains of an orchestra, as if you would be stricken deaf tomorrow. Touch each object you want to touch as if tomorrow your tactile sense would fail. Smell the perfume of flowers, taste with relish each morsel, as if tomorrow you could never smell and taste again. Make the most of every sense; glory in all the facets of pleasure and beauty which the world reveals to you through the several means of contact which Nature provides. But of all the senses, I am sure that sight must be the most delightful.   [1933]

1. Characterize Keller's style and tone in this essay.
2. What is Keller's strategy for the essay? Is it effective?
3. During Keller's lifetime she was several times accused of being a bookish fraud whose knowledge of the world was all secondhand. Charges of inauthenticity were leveled at her a number of times during her life by people who wanted her to stick to reporting what it was like to be unable to see rather than reporting so fully what the world is like. From this essay, do you think the criticisms are just? How would you answer them?
4. Whether you are sighted or visually impaired, you can perform Keller's experiment. Would your priorities be similar to hers or different? Whether or not you wish to share your results with your classmates, make notes on what you learn.

GEORGINA KLEEGE

GEORGINA KLEEGE *(1956–) lost most of her sight at the age of eleven as a result of macular degeneration. Her attempts at understanding her situation and the situations of others who are sightless are the material of her writing.*

From *In Oedipus' Shadow**

. . . If we believe Freud, we know that Oedipus' story stays with us because it enacts conflicts and desires we have all supposedly experienced, at least subconsciously. A man kills his father and marries his mother. But why does he have to blind himself? After all, his self-imposed sentence demands only exile. Of course when Oedipus decreed exile as punishment he was the last person he suspected to be guilty of those crimes. Once the truth is out it's understandable that he should want to toughen up the punishment, and dispel any suspicions of favoritism. Suicide is out of the question—the coward's way out. Clearly he must do something to show his outrage, horror, and shame. He must make an enduring spectacle of himself so that onlookers will have an example of what happens when taboos are violated. But gouging out his eyes seems histrionic excess. Couldn't he lop off some other organ or limb and make the same point? Of course it's not as if the act is exactly premeditated. Finding Jocasta's corpse, Oedipus lashes out at the last remaining person to blame for what has happened—himself—using the first weapon that comes to hand—the brooches on her robes. To stab himself in the leg, or even in the groin, would not have the desired effect. So he goes for his eyes.

*Georgina Kleege, "In Oedipus' Shadow," *Sight Unseen* (New Haven: Yale University Press, 1999).

It's only after the fact that the act becomes the one truly fitting punishment for his crimes. He deprives himself of the sense that not only gave him access to the world but also stimulated his desires and got him into trouble. Since he was "blind" to his own guilt, he must relinquish his sight.

It's the kind of justice the Olympians are famous for. The symmetry is perfect. 5 An almost unimaginable act of self-mutilation is the only appropriate response to crimes that are horrifyingly imaginable, at least as latent impulses. Though the imagined connection of blindness to sin probably predates his legend, Oedipus makes the sin distressingly and memorably specific. And the Oedipal image of blindness has had remarkable staying power. Even a random survey of nineteenth- and twentieth-century fiction written in English reveals the same notion, which links blindness to some sort of illicit sexual union, to a tragic reversal of fortune, and to the complete loss of personal, sexual, and political power.

For a mercilessly faithful retelling of the Oedipus story consider Anita Shreve's 1989 novel *Eden Close*.[1] Eden is blinded as a teenager in a mysterious incident in which an intruder (presumed but never proved to be her estranged boyfriend) sexually assaults her but is interrupted by her adoptive father, Jim. The two men scuffle over Jim's gun. The gun goes off, killing Jim and blinding Eden. Twenty years later other truths are revealed. It turns out that Jim is actually Eden's biological father. His secret lover left the infant on the Close family doorstep for Jim and his wife, Edith, to raise. On the fateful night, there was no intruder. The sexual act that was interrupted by gunfire was between father and daughter, and the assailant was the twice-betrayed wife. As with Oedipus, secrets about a child's origins lead to murder, and blindness punishes incest.

Other works borrow from the Oedipus story with less literal-minded fidelity. In Charlotte Brontë's *Jane Eyre* (1847), Mr. Rochester loses his sight when his house burns down.[2] We understand that his blindness is divine retribution for the sin of wishing to marry Jane when he already has a wife in the attic. The mighty man is brought low. Once all-powerful, and rather arrogant about it, he is left feeble and exiled from his ruined home. It's a reversal of fortune that readers find satisfying, in part because Rochester's blindness lasts only about three years. Permanent blindness would be too harsh a punishment for a Christian God who is supposed to temper justice with mercy. So Rochester loses only one eye, and the other one is left inflamed. The inflammation clears in time for him to see for himself that his first-born son "had inherited his own eyes, as they once were—large, brilliant and black" (457). Rochester's eyes, which were his most striking feature, and the emblem of his unruly spirit, are reproduced in his child. But now that Jane is there to keep an eye on things, there is little chance the child will repeat the mistakes of his father.

In Rudyard Kipling's novel *The Light That Failed* (1900), blindness punishes political rather than sexual sin.[3] The protagonist, Dick Heldar, goes blind as the delayed aftereffect of a blow to the head sustained during a stint as a war

[1] Anita Shreve, *Eden Close* (New York: Signet, 1989).
[2] Charlotte Brontë, *Jane Eyre*, ed. Margaret Smith (Oxford: Oxford University Press, 1975).
[3] Rudyard Kipling, *The Light That Failed* (New York: Carroll & Graf, 1986).

correspondent in the Sudan. Just before Dick receives the blow that blinds him, he kills an Arab who is scuffling with his friend Tropenhow. Significantly, during that scuffle, Tropenhow managed to gouge out the man's eye. At the end of the novel, Dick returns to the scene, this time taking a fatal bullet to the head. He pays for that fallen enemy, losing first his sight then his life. The novel has larger implications about the evils of one culture's exploitation of another. Dick's sketches for the illustrated newspapers are popular and help launch his career as a painter. Back in England, he discovers that art lovers can't get enough of his paintings of desert war scenes—the best of British soldiery suppressing the Arab heathen. Dick expresses his unease about the way his work caters to the "blind, brutal, British public's bestial thirst for blood" (70). Tempting the fates, Dick defines the public as not only bestial and brutish but also blind, dependent on artists like himself to show what they want to see—their own brutality projected onto the enemies of the Empire. Kipling seems to suggest that the blindness which ends Dick's career is retribution for having exploited people who resisted British domination.

When blindness comes as divine retribution for heinous crimes, its effects alter the lives of everyone around the blinded person. Blindness inverts, perverts, or thwarts all human relationships. The exiled Oedipus is utterly dependent on his daughters. As she pleads for her father, Antigone is obliged to expose herself to public view in ways that would have been considered not only unusual but unnatural for a woman of her time. His dependence and exile tears his daughters from conventional domestic life and makes marriage impossible.

10   For Jane Eyre, Rochester's blindness allows her to rise to power. When Jane returns to Rochester, she seems eager to establish that, though she has come back, it is under new terms. On their first evening together she becomes playfully maternal, fixing his supper, and combing his hair, grooming his eyebrows, which are still singed a year after the fire. With uncharacteristic coquettish skill, she entices him into a game of twenty questions about the time she's spent away from him. Although Jane asserts that all her teasing has the beneficial effect of "fretting him out of his melancholy" (444), it's hard not to sense that she enjoys her new power over him. In fact, his dependence on her makes him all the more attractive. She tells him, "I love you better now, when I can really be useful to you, than I did in your state of proud independence" (451). She even attributes the happiness of their marriage to the fact that he was blind for the first two years of it: "Perhaps it was that circumstance that drew us so very near—that knit us so very close, for I was then his vision, as I am still his right hand. Literally, I was (what he often called me) the apple of his eye" (456). Jane's lingering insecurities about her own appearance are erased when her husband must see the world (herself included) through her eyes.

In *The Light That Failed*, Dick's blindness not only ends his painting career but upsets the natural balance of all his relationships. Before blindness Dick enjoyed a remarkably intimate friendship with Tropenhow, his mentor and neighbor. He introduces Dick to dealers and nags him about his lack of discipline. When Dick starts leaving his studio to visit Maisie, his childhood sweetheart, Tropenhow worries that a woman's influence will spoil Dick's work. Dick is similarly preoccupied with protecting his friend from romantic entanglements. When he notices that his model Bessie is developing a romantic interest in Tropenhow, Dick separates them. But Dick's blindness disrupts this perfect male camaraderie. Tropenhow feels compelled to help dress and feed his newly blinded friend, and to tuck him into bed. He does this gladly at first, but as things heat up again in the Sudan, he becomes eager to return to the front. Dick's absolute helplessness makes him ask too much of the friendship. Dick's blindness threatens Tropenhow's masculinity, making him contemplate abandoning his manly pursuits to care for his friend. So Tropenhow must call in a woman. He tracks down Maisie, who is now studying painting in France, and persuades her to come back to take charge of Dick. When she learns of his blindness, she makes the journey, but she refuses to stay. Kipling intends her refusal to seem a betrayal, and her desire for independence to seem a childishly selfish denial of her true female nature. As a blind reader, I suppose I should have additional sympathy for Dick at this moment. But his moodiness and dependence compel me to deny any identification with him and make Maisie's rejection harder to condemn.

Only Bessie, an opportunistic former streetwalker, is willing to take on the burden of the blind man. Although she has no affection for him, she readily latches onto Dick as a meal ticket. And in a sense she is indirectly responsible for Maisie's flight. Dissatisfied with Dick's portrait of her, and angry at him for preventing her romance with Tropenhow, Bessie destroys the painting, scraping out her own face. When Dick shows Maisie his masterpiece, she is horrified, but not merely at the wanton destruction. Looking at the spoiled painting, Maisie is forced to see as blind Dick does. His vision has been blotted out, scraped away. Apparently everything he looks at is rubbed out, ruined like the portrait. Coming face to face with this graphic representation of Dick's blindness makes the prospect of living with it seem even more frightening to Maisie.

So while blindness brings Rochester and Jane closer, it drives Dick and Maisie apart. Without love, friendship, or career, Dick feels that he might as well be dead. Like Oedipus, he rejects suicide as a "weak-kneed confession of fear" (276). But being a man of action, he cannot sit alone and idle in London, waiting for his life to end. So he returns to the Sudan and makes himself an easy target for an enemy of the Empire.

These are the old stories of blindness. They make me weary and a little afraid. They take Oedipus at his word, and start from the assumption that blindness is both an outward sign of hidden sin and a punishment worse than death. They show no life after blindness, offer no hope to the blind, except that the condition might prove impermanent or that death might come quick. Oedipus does not adapt to his blindness. He could take his cue from Tiresias, who often bemoans the burden of his clairvoyance but seems comparatively unhampered by his lack of sight. But Oedipus never gets used to his condition. Time passes, but it seems that Oedipus still wakes each day shocked anew to discover he cannot see. And this is the whole point. If Oedipus got used to the idea of his lost sight, much less adopted new methods of getting around or recognizing people, then his blindness would be less of a punishment. He would cease to be the instructive and frightening spectacle he voluntarily made of himself.

15   When authors begin to entertain the notion that blindness may be something else, a character-testing physical hardship without moral implications, the Oedipal gloom brightens a bit. In his novel *Blindness* (1926), Henry Green suggests that loss of sight constitutes a change in life that evolves through stages.[4] And the titles of the novel's three sections—"Caterpillar," "Chrysalis," and "Butterfly"—imply that the result of this evolution is a fully matured life-form, natural, independent, even beautiful. The protagonist, John Haye, is a wealthy and rather callow adolescent, blinded in a random accident. A boy throws a rock that shatters the window of the railway carriage in which John is riding. His literary education has made him well versed in the standard tropes of blindness, and he finds them now both inadequate and stupid. He alludes self-consciously to the "traditional living tomb" metaphor for blindness (378), mocking the idea that blindness equals something less than living. At church he complains at the way the rector preaches "about blindness in the East, opthalmia in the Bible, spittle and sight, with a final outburst against pagans" (437). While a sighted reader may find these musings oversensitive, I find myself nodding my head. And I secretly applaud when he rebels, at least in imagination, against the stereotype of blind passivity. He imagines himself imprisoned for murdering the boy who threw the stone that blinded him: "He would make the warder read the papers to him every morning, he would be sure to have headlines: BLIND MAN MURDERS CHILD—no. TORTURES CHILD TO DEATH; And underneath that, if he was lucky, WOMAN JUROR VOMITS" (380). But for all his irritation at the unthinking assumptions and language of the sighted, there is nothing in his experience to tell him what blindness really is.

        The people around John have a much clearer image of blindness. They see it as infantile helplessness and a loss of sexuality. John's aging Nanny enjoys the chance to baby him, feeding and reading to him as she did when he was a child. Mrs. Haye, John's widowed stepmother, observes that a "girl would not want to marry a blind man" but holds out the hope that they might "still find some girl who had had a story, or who was unhappy at home" (387). Apparently only a girl made desperate by her own sullied reputation or an unsuitable home life could overlook a man's blindness. Mrs. Haye goes on to muse that "he could have a housekeeper. Yes, it was immoral, but he must have love, and someone to look after him" (388). Since, as she assumes, respectable marriage is now out of John's reach, he may have to settle for an unsanctioned liaison with a servant. At the same time, however, Mrs. Haye sees an advantage in keeping John dependent and isolated. If John stays single, she could stay on as the mistress of the estate she loves.

        John is conscious of all this speculation and has worries of his own about his prospects, especially those having to do with women. He takes up briefly with Joan Enwhistle, the daughter of the local defrocked rector. Having lost her mother at an early age, she lives in scandalous squalor with her embittered, alcoholic, and somewhat abusive father in a ramshackle cottage in the woods. Although Joan would seem to fit Mrs. Haye's requirements, both having "had a

[4]Henry Green, *Nothing, Doting, Blindness* (1926; rpt., New York: Penguin, 1993).

story" and being "unhappy at home," John's protectors see her as spectacularly unsuitable. This general disapproval makes Joan all the more attractive to John. Naturally John's courtship is inept at first. He worries that his missing eyes and unsightly scars will repel Joan. But soon he tries to use his blindness as a lure. Presumably he has read *Jane Eyre* and senses that his helplessness and utter dependency will seduce her. On their walks together he spouts gloomy complaints about darkness and solitude, and he stumbles against Joan on purpose so she will have to take his arm. Knowing that in the conventional language of love the eyes are always the focal point, he brings the discussion around to hers, which, as she points out, he has never seen. Undaunted, he responds:

> "Perhaps not. But I can feel them just the same."
> "Do you?"
> "Yes, they are so calm, so quiet. Such a lovely blue."
> "But they are dark brown."
> "Oh then your dress does not match?"
> "No, I suppose not."
> "But what does that matter? They are such lovely brown eyes. And sometimes, they light up and burn perhaps?"
> "How do you mean?"
> "Well . . . But have you ever been in love?"
> "I don't know."
> "Maybe they are burning now?"
> "N-no, I don't think so."
> "How sad. And mine, if they had not been removed, would have burned so ardently." (457)

As Green lampoons the eye-centered clichés of love he also demonstrates how mismatched this couple really is. But it is the gulf of class and education between them, rather than John's blindness, that makes union impossible. When John asks Joan to describe the landscape, she shows that she lacks the aesthetic sensibilities he longs for in a companion, saying, "I don't know what you see in views" (446). John tries to romanticize the squalor of her life, assuming that "it must be wonderful to be poor" while admitting, "Poor people are always much happier than rich people on the cinema. The cinema used to be the only way I had to see life" (458).

Joan is understandably insulted by his willful naiveté. And she finds John's juvenile musings on art and literature too reminiscent of her father's drunken rants to take seriously. So John must come to terms with his blindness on his own. He wants to be a writer and recognizes (citing Milton) that blindness need not hamper his art. In fact, it gives him what he lacked before—a subject. He now has something to show the world: "He would start a crusade against people with eyesight. It was the easiest thing in the world to see, and so many were content with only the superficial appearance of things" (502). Slowly, John learns to recognize blindness as a different way of perceiving. He becomes a connoisseur of voices and even learns to detect the presence of people without hearing them speak or move. More significantly, he learns that trying to translate every sound, taste, or sensation into visual terms is pointless and inaccurate. He even asserts that "sight was not really necessary; the values of things changed, that was all. There was so much in the wind, in the feel of the air, in the sounds that Nature lent one" (442).

20   Mrs. Haye and John move to London in the hope that the cultural energy of the city will help him begin his writing career. Understandably, John suffers a setback. The constant noise of the city torments his newly sensitized ears, and the unfamiliar surroundings and people challenge his newfound skills. He briefly regresses into helplessness and gloom. But at the end of the novel he undergoes the final phase in his transformation from sighted youth to blind man. He imagines "a white light that he would bathe in" (503) and then "a deeper blindness closed in upon him" (504). After this fit or hallucination passes, John writes to a school friend, "I have had a wonderful experience," and wonders, "Why am I so happy today?" (504). Green inverts the Christian trope that configures baptism as a washing away of unholy blindness, and salvation as an ascent into divine light. John has been reborn into a new sense of blindness. If the note of optimism at the end of the novel seems a bit shaky, still Green's reimagining of blindness is a radical departure from the Oedipal tradition in which blindness must be a life sentence of despair and dependency with no hope of respite or parole.

Of course Green is not simply writing about one young man's adaptation to blindness. He is using blindness to suggest all sorts of random accidents and quirks of fate that may force individuals to test their own resources and challenge the assumptions of their culture. Similarly, in his story "The Country of the Blind," H. G. Wells writes blindness into a parable about human intolerance.[5] At some unspecified time in the distant past, a small group of "Peruvian half-breeds fleeing from the lust and tyranny of an evil Spanish ruler" (439) settle in an upland valley in the Andes. The valley is cut off from the outside world by a landslide, but it offers sweet water, fertile spring-irrigated soil, and a mild climate. Then a strange disease afflicts an entire generation of children, who all go blind. After fifteen generations pass, the whole community is blind, but they have adapted their environment and habits to their sightlessness. They sleep in the warm daylight hours and work the fields at night. They pave their pathways with different textures and notched curbs so they can keep track of their location. Their non-visual senses are finely tuned: they learn to read intonation rather than expression and can hear gestures, even footsteps in grass. They favor soft-textured garments with raised stitching for tactile identification. They track their llamas by scent. Memory of the world beyond their valley has faded with their sight, and they believe that the world ends with the steep cliffs that surround the valley. But some scraps of belief from their Christian past are retained and reinterpreted in their philosophy and religion. For instance, they believe birds to be angels because they can hear them sing and flutter but can never lay hands upon them. Heaven for them is not the vast and awe-inspiring

[5]H. G. Wells, "The Country of the Blind," in *The Country of the Blind and Other Stories*, ed. Michael Sherborne (Oxford: Oxford University Press, 1996).

domed sky but a protective stone ceiling, exquisitely smooth to the touch but too high for anyone to reach. Theirs is a perfect and self-contained world, a "cosmic casserole" with a stone lid.

Into this blind paradise wanders a sighted traveler, Núñez, who falls off a mountain and slides into the valley on an avalanche. He's heard the legend of this place and goads himself into delusions of grandeur by repeating the proverb: "In the country of the blind the one-eyed man is king" (452). He assumes that his sight will give him a natural advantage over this race of mutants. But he is wrong. He underestimates their perfect adaptation. When he runs away from them, they track him with ease. When he tries to impress them with descriptions of what he sees, they ridicule him as a fool. Their language has no words for seeing. Because he stumbles, speaks nonsense, and lacks keen hearing, smell, and touch, they determine that he must be some sort of newly formed humanoid creature, a sort of full-grown baby, spontaneously generated from the rock. But they put up with him, keeping him around as a kind of jester and heavy lifter.

Then he falls in love. The girl, Medina-saroté, is beautiful by sighted standards, but within blind culture she falls short of the mark. Her voice is not soft enough, her features are too clear-cut, her long eyelashes are considered a disfigurement, and her skin lacks "that satisfying, glossy smoothness that is the blind man's ideal of feminine beauty" (459). Despite her shortcomings, her father is reluctant to throw her away on this unusual stranger. Others in the community fear that the union will corrupt the race. The elders determine that what makes Núñez act so strangely are the things he calls eyes. Clearly they act as a mental irritant, so if they were removed, he would become as normal as the rest of them. Medina-saroté urges Núñez to have the operation. He argues that it is his vision, his ability to see her, that makes him love her. But his desire, and the longing to be a normal citizen rather than a tamed freak, seem to persuade him. Finally, however, the sacrifice proves too great, and desperation drives him to scale the sheer walls of stone to escape.

In Wells's parable, the blind stand for human beings in general, prone to judge what's normal by their own experience, and ready to eradicate difference to achieve harmonious conformity. Wells startles readers out of complacency by subverting their expectations that blind people in the real world are in fact helpless, passive, and dependent. To imagine a world where sightlessness would be the norm, shaping every aspect of life, allows for the possibility that blindness might not be the dire disaster that Oedipus spends his life proclaiming.

In his novel *Waiting for the Barbarians* (1980), J. M. Coetzee also constructs an 25 allegorical narrative about human intolerance.[6] Set in an unspecified time and place, the novel recounts the struggle of the Magistrate, the civil administrator of a frontier outpost, who finds himself first in complicity then in conflict with an oppressive Empire waging war against the native people of the region, the Barbarians. And at the novel's center, there is a blind person. She is a young

[6]J. M. Coetzee, *Waiting for the Barbarians* (New York: Penguin, 1980).

Barbarian girl, maimed and blinded by the Empire's crack interrogator, Colonel
Joll. He blinds her by forcing her to stare at the prongs of a white-hot metal
fork until the intense light damages her retinas. Left behind when the other
Barbarian prisoners are set free, she serves as an instructive spectacle, ocular
proof of the Empire's power to alter a person's fundamental being without
leaving exterior marks. But her blindness also delivers a more personal message
to the Magistrate. During his first conversation with the Magistrate, Colonel Joll
explains why he wears dark glasses:

> "They protect one's eyes from the glare of the sun," he says. "You would find
> them useful out here in the desert. They save one from squinting all the time.
> One has fewer headaches. Look." He touches the corners of his eyes lightly. "No
> wrinkles." (1)

Joll, an expert manipulator of symbols, wears the traditional sign of blindness to
represent his own clear-sightedness. The desert sun is too illuminating and can
dazzle and even harm the eyes. Though the Magistrate disdains the "paltry theatrical mystery of dark shields hiding healthy eyes" (4) he still gets the message.
There is a danger, Joll says with his glasses, in looking too closely at the way the
Empire treats the Barbarians. Later, the Magistrate senses that, in blinding the
girl as he does, Joll has inscribed the same message for him and "until the marks
on this girl's body are deciphered and understood I cannot let go of her" (31). In
contemplating her literal blindness he is forced to confront his own figurative
blindness, his unthinking obliviousness to the Empire's oppressive practices.

But as the Magistrate questions the girl, he learns she is not completely
sightless:

> "I don't believe you can see," I say.
> "Yes, I can see. When I look straight, there is nothing, there is—" (she rubs the air
> in front of her like someone cleaning a window).
> "A blur," I say.
> "There is a blur. But I can see out of the sides of my eyes. The left eye is better
> than the right. How could I find my way if I could not see?" (29)

When I first read this passage it was with a shock of recognition unlike any
I'd known before. The girl's blindness is exactly like mine. That central blur
that will not wipe clean is before my eyes, too. In fact, until I read *Waiting
for the Barbarians* I had no language to describe my visual experience beyond
saying that I didn't see well. The simple analogy to the blur on a window both
gave me a way to describe my blindness and helped me see my blindness more
precisely.

I suspect my identification with this character exceeds what Coetzee intended
or wished. After all, one of the features of allegory is the way it forces readers to
perceive characters as representations of abstract concepts. So what does this
blind character represent? Significantly, she does not call herself blind, insisting
on the sight she has and the prospect of improvement. It is the Magistrate who
insists on calling her blind, and her blindness is part of the fascination she holds
for him. She is alien to him in every way, being not only Barbarian and female

but also blind. Her otherness at once attracts and repels him. He repeatedly tries to imagine her visual experience:

> Am I to believe that gazing back at me she sees nothing—my feet perhaps, parts of the room, a hazy circle of light, but at the center, where I am, only a blur, a blank? (31)
>
> I take her face between my hands and stare into the dead centers of her eyes, from which twin reflections of myself stare solemnly back. (41)

Since she cannot see the center, where he is, he calls her "blind" and discounts what she can see—the periphery. He knows that when she looks at him he is effaced. So when he looks at her he sees only an impenetrable and reflective surface. He is reminded of "the image of a face masked by two black glassy insect eyes from which there comes no reciprocal gaze but only my doubled image cast back at me" (44). When he looks at her, he sees Joll, Joll's handiwork, and more horrifying, his own unwitting complicity in that handiwork. Slowly he begins to recognize that his own paternalistic protection of her is only the inverted mirror image of Joll's torture. He is concerned with what the girl represents, but the girl herself eludes him. She remains a cipher, a vacancy, a blank.

What the Magistrate does not fully understand is that the Barbarians inhabit the periphery. They provide the outlines by which the center is defined. They are the "other" that gives the Empire its identity. When the Magistrate alters his vantage point and shifts his gaze off center, everything changes. He leads an expedition into uncharted Barbarian territory to return the girl to her people, and he begins to "see" the Barbarian girl as she really is. On the journey, her nomadic heritage shows, and her blindness does not hinder her. She sits on her horse with such ease that she can fall asleep in the saddle. The brackish water and rugged road food do not make her sick. When a storm comes up, she knows how to calm the horses. Then they meet a group of Barbarians, and the Magistrate tries to communicate what has happened to her. He discovers he does not know the Barbarian word for "blind." "Blind" is his word, from his context, bearing cultural associations that do not translate. In her language and context another word might be necessary. His words define only his experience of her and discount her own. He uses "blind" to mean "helpless victim of oppression" and "object of pity." When she refuses his labels she delineates the distance he still has to travel in order to understand both her and the complexities of his own situation.

In the real world, many blind people, like me, have some visual experience. Coetzee uses this fact to complicate and subvert the allegory he constructs. After all, he could have made the girl completely blind. When he does not, she slips free of the allegorical categories of his narrative. Facile binary oppositions— sight/blindness, civilization/barbarism, center/periphery, us/them—are for the Colonel Jolls of the world. For people like the Magistrate, who clings to abstract ideals about equality, responsibility, tolerance, and justice, simple categories and oppositions prove inadequate.

Certainly for Coetzee, as for Wells and Green, blindness begins to lose some of its Oedipal connotations. The meaning of blindness becomes harder to pin

30

down once authors put forward the idea that it could mean different things to different people. In his story "The Blind Man," D. H. Lawrence goes even further.[7] Maurice Pervin lost his eyes in the Great War and now lives in isolation with his wife, Isabel. Maurice is prone to bouts of brooding (what Lawrence hero is not?), and Isabel finds the isolation difficult. Still, as a couple they enjoy a "wonderful and unspeakable intimacy" and share a "whole world, rich and real and invisible" (347). Unlike Jane Eyre's marriage to Rochester, their happiness is not the result of the blind man's complete dependence on his wife. Maurice still manages his farm and performs many routine chores. And his blindness has not impaired his masculinity. He is a big man, massively built, taciturn and sensitive. He has a natural affinity for the animals in his care—the horses, the cattle, and a large, half-wild cat. His blindness seems to have heightened his physicality, instincts, and sensitivity. Like Henry Green's hero, John Haye, Maurice discovers that trying to re-create the world in remembered images does no good. Rather, he embraces his blindness as a new form of consciousness:

> He did not think much or trouble much. So long as he kept this sheer immediacy of blood-contact with the substantial world he was happy, he wanted no intervention of visual consciousness. In this state there was a certain rich positivity, bordering sometimes on rapture. Life seemed to move in him like a tide lapping, lapping, and advancing, enveloping all things darkly. It was a pleasure to stretch forth the hand and meet the unseen object, clasp it, and possess it in pure contact. He did not try to remember, to visualize. He did not want to. The new way of consciousness substituted itself in him. (355)

As if all this lapping and enveloping were not enough, he hints vaguely at certain compensations of blindness, but true to his nature, he cannot articulate what they are. Isabel attempts to explain it too: "I agree that it seems to put one's mind to sleep. But when we're alone I miss nothing: it seems awfully rich, almost splendid, you know" (361).

Into this connubial paradise wanders a sighted rival. Bertie Reid, a celebrated barrister and distant cousin of Isabel's, arrives for a visit. He is quicker, livelier, and more conversational than the blind man. But he is also, by his own definition, "neuter" (359) and, though capable of gallant adoration of women, wary of physical contact with them. Still, Isabel is glad to have him around. Apparently all that "unspeakable intimacy" gets a bit hard to take at times. Also, she has begun to worry that the child she is expecting will upset the careful balance of her marriage. So she is happy to have an old friend's advice and sympathy. She seems to hope that Maurice's blindness will have softened his distaste for Bertie or made Bertie more patient with Maurice. But the two men are such opposites that the tension between them seems insurmountable at first.

35   When they are alone together, Maurice disarms Bertie by letting down his guard. He questions Bertie about Isabel, hopeful that she may have confided

---

[7]D. H. Lawrence, "The Blind Man," in *The Complete Short Stories*, vol. 2 (London: William Heinemann, 1955).

secret concerns to her old friend. Then he asks the sighted man to describe the scars on his own face. Bertie defines them as a "disfigurement, more pitiable than shocking" (363), a distinction so subtle that it seems to assert the sighted man's superiority. Then Maurice asks permission to touch Bertie's face. But this touch is not the delicate flutter of braille-reading fingertips. Maurice wraps his beefy hands around the smaller man's head, knocks his hat off, then paws his shoulders, arms, and hands. Maurice envelops Bertie in pure contact, announcing that Bertie is not only shorter than he expected, but that his head and hands feel tender and young. As disconcerting as this manhandling is, Maurice then urges Bertie to touch his face, in particular his scarred brow and empty eyesockets. When Bertie reluctantly complies, Maurice presses Bertie's hands against his face. Maurice then trembles "in every fibre, rocking slightly, slowly, from side to side. He remained thus for a minute or more, whilst Bertie stood as if in a swoon, unconscious, imprisoned." This mutual laying on of hands leaves Maurice elated, exclaiming, "Oh my God . . . we shall know each other now shan't we?" (364). He announces to Isabel that he and Bertie are now friends. But Bertie is left feeling like a "mollusk whose shell is broken" (365). The encounter not only unmans him but unsights him. With a single, traditionally blind gesture, Maurice takes the measure of his rival and finds him lacking. Then, by forcing Bertie to experience his face as the blind do, through touch, Maurice forces him to recognize his own sensual deficiencies. Maurice triumphs in this physical intimacy while Bertie is shattered by it.

Lawrence uses blindness to explore a favorite theme about sensuality versus intellect. Deprived of one of his senses, Maurice revels in the four that remain. He defies the sense-privileged who would be foolish enough to pity him, or his wife. In "Cathedral" (1981), Raymond Carver retells Lawrence's story, presenting another rivalry between a sighted man and a blind man.[8] In Carver's version, the blind man, Robert, is the interloper. The sighted narrator's wife used to work for Robert, and since then they've kept in touch, exchanging taped letters in which the wife confides many secrets. The narrator is somewhat resentful about this correspondence, unsettled by the idea that the blind man may know more about his wife's true feelings than he does. Also, his wife admits that she once let the blind man touch her face, and the event was significant enough that she wrote a poem about it. So the narrator is apprehensive about Robert's pending visit: "My idea of blindness came from the movies. In the movies, the blind moved slowly and never laughed. Sometimes they were led by seeing-eye dogs. A blind man in my house was not something I looked forward to" (209). And he contemplates the plight of Robert's dead wife:

> I found myself thinking what a pitiful life this woman must have led. Imagine a woman who could never see herself as she was seen in the eyes of her loved one. A woman who could go on day after day and never receive the smallest compliment from her beloved. A woman whose husband could never read the expression on her face, be it misery or something better. (213)

---

[8]Raymond Carver, "Cathedral," in *Cathedral: Stories* (New York: Knopf, 1983), 209–228.

The stilted quality of his language reveals the hackneyed conventions to which he subscribes. Blind people cannot hope to enjoy a happy love life because they get no emotional or sexual stimulation from their eyes.

But Robert does not conform to the stereotypes. He's jovial and rather pushy, insisting on calling the narrator "Bub." Also he smokes and wears a beard, which the narrator believed are not things blind people do. Robert's failure to fit the narrator's image of blindness only irks the narrator more. But by the end of the evening, things change. As the wife dozes on the sofa between the two men, they watch (hear) a TV program about Gothic architecture. It occurs to the narrator that the blind man may not know what a cathedral is. But when he tries to translate the images he sees on the screen, he discovers he lacks the language to do justice to the task. In offering to help the blind man overcome his limitation, he confronts his own. So Robert suggests he draw a picture, and, as he draws, Robert takes hold of his hand to follow the motion of his drawing. Perhaps it's only the Scotch and dope they've consumed during the evening, but both men are satisfied with the experiment. They are even exhilarated. For a final twist, Robert tells the narrator to close his eyes. He does, and keeps drawing, with the blind man's hands still on his.

> Then he said, "I think that's it. I think you got it," he said.
> "Take a look. What do you think?"
> But I had my eyes closed. I thought I'd keep them that way for a little longer. I thought it was something I ought to do.
> "Well?" he said. "Are you looking?"
> My eyes were still closed. I was in my house. I knew that.
> But I didn't feel like I was inside anything.
> "It's really something," I said. (228)

It is significant that the collaborative sketch is of a cathedral rather than a supermarket or suspension bridge. This may remind the reader of all the biblical stories in which blindness occurs as a test of faith or in which sight is restored as a reward for conversion. But in Carver's story a different kind of enlightenment takes place. The sighted man feels an obligation to blind himself temporarily in order to experience another way of being. The touch of the blind man, and the effort they share, liberate him from the confines of the visible world and the limits of his own language, experience, and imagination.

Robert and Maurice, like Oedipus, still serve an instructive function. But their instruction is of a more active, hands-on variety. They invite sighted readers to experience the world with more than one sense, and to question the assumptions of their sight-centered culture.

40   In the century and a half since Brontë published *Jane Eyre*, the real lives of blind people have undergone radical improvements in terms of education, opportunity, and civil rights. So while this admittedly random sampling of English-language fiction from this period shows the tenacity of the Oedipal image, it also reveals this cultural evolution. Since Mr. Rochester would have been unable to learn braille or other techniques even if he had wanted to, it is understandable that he should equate blindness with helplessness. Carver's blind

man has received enough twentieth-century education and training to travel independently and hold down various jobs. Also, he is the only one of all these blind characters whose sight loss was not caused by injury or disease. For all we know, he has been blind since birth, so it seems only natural that he should be able to show the narrow-minded sighted man a thing or two. Still, there is something decidedly weird about even these latter-day blind people, something darkly mysterious, otherworldly, vaguely unnatural. They live lives apart, not quite as outcasts, but not exactly in the mainstream either. The Oedipal family resemblance is still there—something about the eyes.

As a blind reader, I am not so naive as to expect that fiction should provide me with role models, but it's hard not to cringe at traditional representations of blindness as a life-ending tragedy. And while the notion that a blind person can bring enlightenment to sighted peers shows progress, it still makes me weary and somewhat alarmed. So I admit a certain surge of triumph when Lawrence's blind man takes the annoying sighted man in hand, when Coetzee's blind Barbarian rejects sightist labels, when the citizens of Wells's country of the blind dismiss sight as a troublesome mental irritant. I like it when blind characters get uppity. It is in these moments that they begin to chip away at the lingering remnants of the Oedipal image. But I recognize that some sighted readers may shudder at these examples of blind assertiveness or shrug them off as far-fetched fictional invention. I could assert that when blind characters ask sighted characters to describe what they see, they remind readers that we are all blind when we read. The visions we "see" as we read are not what's before our eyes, but what's behind them. So blind characters serve as the reader's textual surrogate, asking the author's language to show us a vision of the world. But if this were true, any author with a self-reflexive bent would throw in a blind character to hold a mirror up to the reader, saying, "Look at me. I am you." And this would be merely another version of the old story—the blind man as instructive spectacle, useful to everyone but himself.   [1999]

1. What is Kleege's complaint about literary portrayals of blindness?
2. What are the assumptions of the "sight-centered culture" that Carver's Robert and Lawrence's Maurice invite us to question?

Critical Approaches

All of the approaches to or "schools" of literary criticism in this appendix offer ways to interpret imaginative literature. If you understand the image of a framework or lens that guides the way we see the objects and forces of the world, then you will understand that each of these methods guides our search for meaning in literature. Each approach highlights different aspects of the works. Therefore, as critics generate and refine their approaches, they can also reread all the works of literature that they have previously interpreted and refine their interpretations. They can also recover works that languished for lack of attention because no current critical approach valued them. Of course, the field of literary studies is constantly renewed and developed as new works of literature are written, but the invention and honing of critical tools mean that literature of the past, far from being interpreted for posterity, labeled with permanent ink, and filed away with dead documents, is continuously renewed, continuously reread with new eyes. The process is what keeps the discipline and the literary works it studies alive.

A traditional way of classifying different schools of criticism distinguishes between "intrinsic," which approaches works in themselves, isolated from the thoughts and feelings of writer and reader, isolated from the historical moments of creation and reception, and isolated from ideologies not arising from the work and "extrinsic" criticism, which, in contrast, is thought to integrate the work into one or more external contexts of the interpreter's choosing. But the distinction cannot really be maintained because when the intrinsic critic is deciding what features of a work are worthy of discussion, he or she is already guided by a theory not arising from the work of what is important in literary works. Such "extrinsic" norms shape even the "intrinsic" criticism.

As you can see from Chapters 8 through 10 of this book, the theories and concepts that are used as frameworks for interpretation do not necessarily "apply" perfectly to a particular literary work. Part of the critic's job is to decide which ones work well enough to be useful and to define the limits of the application. What doesn't fit can be as fruitful a part of the discussion as what does fit. In any case, the application of frameworks such as the ones described here can be ways of enriching our experiences and understandings of imaginative literature.

CLOSE READING AND NEW CRITICISM

Close reading is the technique of interpreting a text by paying very scrupulous attention to the details of its use of language. It is sometimes called "formalism," although its concern with form never obliterates its concern with meaning. In fact, it assumes that form and meaning are inextricably linked. Meaning is not something that can be extracted like juice from an orange, as if one could discard the rind and keep the essence. The challenge for the critic is then to say what a work means through, rather than apart from, the way it is expressed. The task is not to resort to mere paraphrase, as if the work were a fable with a "moral," but rather to explain how the parts of it function together. Critics using this approach like to be able to account for all the parts of the work and therefore value works that seem to have a coherent structure, with no extraneous parts. They look for the "organic unity" of the text, which implies that all the parts work together. Chapters 3–7 of this book outline the elements of texts in which formalist critics are most interested—e.g., word choice, word order, figures of speech, point of view, and tone of voice—and the sample student essays in these chapters are all examples (see Zak Owen's "Digging for Meaning" in Chapter 2, Derrick White's "How Do You See It?" in Chapter 5, and Kenji Takano's "Designing a Poem" in Chapter 7).

The technique of close reading is often applied to relatively short lyric poems but is used equally well for novels, plays, and essays. It usually proceeds with several assumptions: that texts worth reading carefully are complex and may include contradictory or opposing views, but that the oppositions and contradictions are ultimately resolvable and that works can be shown to be unified. For this reason, patterns, for instance in word choice and figures of speech, are particularly valuable. (See the section on "The Sequence of Images" in Chapter 6 and "Assumptions in Arguments about Literature" in Chapter 8.)

New Criticism attempts to detach a work from whatever intentions the writer had for it. While it is anchored to history through the meanings of words in the period of its composition, the author is not considered to be the final authority on what it means. Neither are readers in its own time. Nor are New Critics necessarily engaged by a work as a reflection of or reaction to its place in literary or social history. This method of interpretation tends to regard the literary work as an independent entity, "an object in itself,"[1] an idea captured in some of the titles of New Critical books such as

[1]Terry Eagleton, *Literary Theory: An Introduction* (Minneapolis: University of Minnesota Press, 1983).

Cleanth Brooks's *Well-Wrought Urn*.[2] It is particularly engaged by works that can be seen as ironic or paradoxical but ultimately organic and unified. In Zak Owen's essay in Chapter 2 on Seamus Heaney's poem "Digging," the narrator's contradictory feelings in reaction to his male relatives—admiring and yet hostile—are ultimately resolved when his pleasure in language helps turn memory into a sense of vocation.

STRUCTURALISM

Structuralism springs from the work of early twentieth-century French linguist Ferdinand de Saussure, who moved from the study of how a language has changed over time toward the study of how language functions as a system. He wanted to understand how languages refer to the nonlinguistic things of the world. Not by imitating them, he claimed. There is nothing rosy about the word *rose*. The reason that *rose* refers to a plant belonging to the genus *Rosa* or its flower is a result of historical accident; but what interests him is not the history leading to that accident, but rather the arbitrariness of the connection and the fact that the word functions only because it is different from its near neighbors: *rose* maintains its meaning because it is not *role* or *rote*, *nose* or *pose*.

With this insight, it is then possible to analyze much of culture as if it were language, that is, full of systems of signs that have meaning and can be read. For instance, as critic Roland Barthes points out, we can see clothing as a language, as if kinds of garments were words and people's outfits sentences. In March of 2001, Texas Technical University hired well-known basketball coach Bobby Knight. At a rally in the basketball arena, Knight was presented to the students by the athletic director, a man wearing a gray business suit, white shirt, and tie. Knight was wearing a red knit polo shirt with a large "T" on it. The "T" is a symbol of the school, of course, as is the color, but we can also interpret the business suit and the polo shirt. One says, "I am the authority who has the power to hire basketball coaches." The other says, "I am ready to join your school and go to work with your team."[3]

According to structuralism, we can "read" the meaning of these two "statements" primarily because they are different from each other. One can coach a basketball team in a suit (most coaches in the NBA do), but next to the business suit, the polo shirt made a statement. Its meaning depended

---

[2]Cleanth Brooks, *The Well-Wrought Urn; Studies in the Structure of Poetry* (New York: Harcourt, Brace, 1947); see also William K. Wimsatt, *The Verbal Icon: Studies in the Meaning of Poetry*, and two preliminary essays written in collaboration with Monroe C. Beardsley (New York: Noonday Press, 1954).

[3]During the course of the rally, the athletic director presented Knight with a red sweater vest, appropriately emblazoned with a "T." This garment has personal meaning, since Knight has been known for wearing sweaters on the sidelines of games. The gift might say, "We accept the way you do things," a meaningful statement given Knight's occasionally controversial behavior.

first on difference and then on the social convention that assigns meaning to differences. If someone arrived at a business meeting wearing sweat pants and a suit jacket, it would probably look odd to us. We wouldn't know how to "read" the message. Since there aren't any conventions that would recommend such an ensemble, the "statement" would seem like nonsense.[4] We might even question the wearer's mental health.

Since most categories of cultural objects can be interpreted as this kind of symbol system (why do we top pizza with pepperoni, for instance, but not caviar and not chopped liver?), the writers of imaginative literature can "write" meaningful statements by choosing carefully the "words" provided by these symbol systems. Both the clothes and the food in John Updike's story "A & P" (Chapter 3), for example, could be "read" for their significance to the culture and the characters.

But reading the material things that appear in literature isn't the only way to use the insights of structuralism for literary criticism. All the contrasts discussed in this book, such as that between metered and free verse in "When I Heard the Learn'd Astronomer" (Chapter 7), can be seen to have meaning insofar as they differ from each other. The discussion of diction in Chapter 6 draws on the powers of relative value when it claims that words have different levels of diction according to their origins. *Walk* has a special ring partly because words like *promenade* and *perambulate* exist. *Piss* gets its charge because the Latinate alternatives *urinate* and *micturate* are so formal.

The elements of narrative can be treated in the same way, as anthropologist Claude Lévi-Strauss showed by examining the structure of myths and finding similar actions in different myths of different peoples. If we looked at the elements of Tobias Wolff's story "Powder" (Chapter 1) in the most abstract way, we would find two kinds of characters, those who obey rules and those who break them. Structuralism would show that each one gets meaning by being different from the other, and the difference tests and can break their relationships with each other. Thus the rule-maintaining mother and rule-maintaining son distance themselves from the rule-breaking father. But the father's skill at breaking traffic rules—how *well* he drives on the forbidden snow-covered road—at least partially heals the relationship between father and son. Rule-breaking turns distance and disdain into admiration. To put it into more structuralist terms, the binary opposition (contrast between two opposing elements) gets mediated (is made less extreme).[5]

[4]Film director Woody Allen has been known to wear sneakers with a tuxedo. What message do you think that outfit is meant to convey?

[5]Good sources on structuralism are Jonathan Culler, *Structuralist Poetics: Structuralism, Linguistics and the Study of Literature* (London: Routledge & Kegan Paul, 1975); Frank Lentricchia, *After the New Criticism* (Chicago: University of Chicago Press, 1980); Christopher Norris, *The Deconstructive Turn: Essays in the Rhetoric of Philosophy* (New York: Methuen, 1983); Robert Scholes, *Structuralism in Literature: An Introduction* (New Haven: Yale University Press, 1974).

POST-STRUCTURALISM

The post-structuralist approach, also called "post-modernism" or "decon-struction," as the name implies, comes after structuralism and complicates it further. It seizes upon the importance of difference to symbol systems, structuralism's insight that business suits take on their cultural meaning in contrast with less formal and more formal attire. Exploiting the arbitrari-ness of the sign, deconstructive critics drive close reading to a new intensi-ty, reading so closely that they find ways in which an utterance not only makes but also unmakes its points. Unlike formalism, which values those literary works that contain paradox and contradiction, deconstruction contends that *all* works *necessarily* contain paradox and contradiction. In deconstructive critics' view, language by its very nature contradicts itself, constantly undermining its own claims. Whereas formalist critics usually produce and defend a reading of a work, an interpretive claim that has a particular meaning, deconstructionists' claims are usually multiple, that a work says one thing and its opposite at the same time. Thus deconstructive critics are not destroyers, as the name might seem to imply, but multipliers; they produce multiple and possibly contradictory interpretations.

What deconstructionists do challenge is the idea that there is a stable meaning "in" a text and that the author put it there. New Critics had already said that authors were not in control of a work's meaning—even if novelist J.R.R. Tolkien said that his monumental tale of a struggle between good and evil in the series, *The Lord of the Rings*, was not an allegory about the struggle against Nazism in the 1930s and '40s, readers who noticed when it was written might interpret it that way. But many New Critics treat the meaning they retrieve with their close reading of texts as something the author must have intended us to find there. Deconstructive critics show how language slips the knot of meaning that writers intend, always mean-ing more—and less—than the writer meant. Interpretations therefore can't give single, fixed readings of texts. Meaning is always multiple and undecidable. They produce these multiple readings partly by eroding the boundaries between the binary oppositions the structuralists lay out. Things treated as opposites like good and evil or illusion and reality turn out to be, in deconstructionists' hands, significantly alike. Since meaning is made by contrast, by the ways in which something is distinguished from its opposing partner, the stability of meaning crumbles.

Since, in theory, the impossibility of finding singular meaning infects all language, deconstructionists have been taken to task for trying to write about it, because in their own writing, they clearly intend to be understood. Most of them acknowledge that when you order a cup of coffee in a restau-rant, you are likely to get one, or at least are treated with dignity if a soft drink arrives instead and you send it back. Much language works, although even in so-called ordinary language, there are moments of incomprehensi-bility. If you ask someone the usual polite opening question and the answer is "I've been better," does that mean that the person was sick and is now recovering or that in comparison to a usual state of health, the person is currently suffering some unpleasant condition? Usually, if you're interested, a few more exchanges can clear things up.

Post-structuralism is really a theory of how language works, and it originated with the structuralism of linguist de Saussure and was developed by French philosophers like Jacques Derrida. But there are critics, especially in America, who apply it to interpret individual literary works. Again, one ought to be able to apply it to any work, but there are some that lend themselves especially well to the technique, especially those that can be seen to take undecidability as themes. This kind of interpretation reinstates the author as an agent of a work's meaning and has the same appeal as the New Critical reading of organic unity in a literary work. For instance, in Frost's poem, "Design," explored in the student essay in Chapter 7, you might look for the erosion of the opposing pairs, innocent/guilty, light/dark, and the theme of undecidability in ll. 11–14, as the poet poses a question, offers an unsettling answer, and then follows that with an even more unsettling one. The poem seems to be *about* undecidability, with two possible answers between which we can't decide, both being unpleasant—a world guided by a malevolent force or a world not guided at all:[6]

> What brought the kindred spider to that height,
> Then steered the white moth thither in the night?
> What but design of darkness to appall?—
> If design govern in a thing so small.

RECEPTION THEORY AND READER-RESPONSE CRITICISM

Both reception theory and reader-response criticism engage the relationships between literature and its audiences; both address the distance of time and the world-view that may come between them. That is, both take on the problem that writing produces for interpretation: Writing allows the separation of the sender and the receiver of a message. The message, put down on paper, gains its independence from the speaker and is able to travel across both time and space to receivers who don't know the situation that produced it or the reading practices or values of the audience an author was addressing. Since these change over time, an audience might misunderstand a work that was written to engage a very different kind of audience. Contrary to the principles of formalism and New Criticism, these kinds of criticism encourage the investigation of the reading practices of audiences.

To take an example from a different medium, if we could magically bring an audience from the early days of silent films into a twenty-first century

[6]Good sources on post-structuralism include Jonathan Culler, *On Deconstruction: Theory and Criticism after Structuralism* (Ithaca, NY: Cornell University Press, 1982); Christopher Norris, *Deconstruction: Theory and Practice* (London: Methuen, 1982).

multiplex, they might be confused by a number of habits of contemporary movies: several people talking at the same time, quick cuts from one scene to another without transitions or explanations, two scenes with the same characters in different places without visual explanation of their travel—all things that contemporary filmgoers readily accept. To interpret early twentieth-century film, then, it might be useful to think about how the audience "read" what they saw onscreen.

A reception theorist like Hans Robert Jauss[7] might recommend that one do similar research about the habits of readers of literature and their values in different times and places. To explore the nineteenth-century audience's scandalized response to Henrik Ibsen's play *A Doll's House* through contemporary reviews is to learn something about the roles women were expected to play in middle class families and to see the role of the play in its social context. If we ignore the impact of T.S. Eliot's poem "The Wasteland" on the audiences of 1922, we miss the first startled reactions to the literary fragmentation and "quick cuts" that perhaps helped prepare the way for our ability to read contemporary films.

The two different varieties of reader-response criticism encourage that kind of investigation of one's own reaction to a literary work. The first, especially as practiced by Stanley Fish in works like *Surprised by Sin: The Reader in Paradise Lost* and "Literature in the Reader," searches individual responses to discover how all readers are likely to respond.[8] The reader, not particularly individualized, represents all competent speakers of the language or all readers familiar with a genre, its conventions, and the conventions of reading. When we "know" that an interpretation of a literary work is implausible, that is partly because we belong to a community of interpreters and subscribe to its norms. The norms limit what we can say about works, but they are in the readers, not in the works themselves. Fish delights in demonstrating this by creating interpretations that we would all agree are absurd (a reading of a Faulkner story as a comment on the life of Eskimos) and then inventing a set of circumstances that would persuade us to change our minds (for instance, the discovery of a letter in which Faulkner records his interest in Eskimo culture).[9]

In the discussion of plot in Chapter 4 and narrative technique in Chapter 5, we saw that readers are often called upon to fill gaps left by language, which cannot reproduce the world point for point. The reader-response critic Wolfgang Iser is well known for his development of the

---

[7]Hans Robert Jauss, "Literary History as a Challenge to Literary Theory," *New Literary History* 2 (1970–71).

[8]Stanley Eugene Fish, *Surprised by Sin: The Reader in Paradise Lost* (Berkeley: University of California Press, 1971); Fish, "Literature in the Reader: Affective Stylistics," in *Influx: Essays on Literary Influence*, ed. Ronald Primeau (Port Washington, NY: Kennikat Press, 1977).

[9]Stanley Eugene Fish, "What Makes an Interpretation Acceptable," in *Is There a Text in This Class?* (Cambridge: Harvard University Press, 1980), 345–46.

observation of such gaps.[10] Another writer who is a presence in this book is Joseph Williams, whose ideas about syntax have influenced many literary critics and the discussion of word order in Chapter 6.[11] If these reader-response critics have a great deal in common, it is because all three are influenced by linguists, who try to investigate how readers construe meaning.

The second variety of reader-response critic is influenced more by psychologists than by linguists because such critics are more interested in the way a person's particular history interacts with a particular text. It thus starts with the very personal—as all reading must—as we respond sympathetically or critically to narrative voices, characters, and situations as they stir memories and associations from our own lives. They don't rest only in the subjective ("I like this guy because he reminds me of my Uncle Henry") but focus more narrowly on the factors in the text that give rise to these feelings. They use the techniques of close reading associated with formalism, but without trying to isolate the text from its various audiences.[12]

PSYCHOLOGICAL CRITICISM

Reader-response criticism is a kind of psychological criticism, with the psychological principles being applied to the audience of a work. Psychological criticism can also address the other points of the rhetorical triangle, applying the insights of the various branches of psychology (e.g., Freudian psychoanalysis, Jungianism, behaviorism, object relations theory, or existential or ego psychology) to the author or to the characters. One of the earliest author studies is Marie Bonaparte's *The Life and Works of Edgar Allan Poe: A Psychoanalytic Interpretation*.[13] One of the best-known character studies is Ernest Jones's psychoanalysis of Shakespeare's character, *Hamlet and Oedipus*.[14]

The problem that both of these raise is that the writers predate the theories. Since Poe isn't around to interview and Shakespeare couldn't possibly have known about the Oedipus complex, use of these frames might seem somewhat misguided or even unfair. If that fact were to constrain us, the

---

[10]Wolfgang Iser, *The Implied Reader: Patterns of Communication in Prose Fiction from Bunyan to Beckett* (Baltimore: Johns Hopkins University Press, 1974); Iser, *The Act of Reading: A Theory of Aesthetic Response* (Baltimore: Johns Hopkins University Press, 1978).

[11]Joseph Williams, *Style: Ten Lessons in Clarity and Grace*, 6th ed. (New York: Longman, 2000).

[12]David Bleich, *Subjective Criticism* (Baltimore: Johns Hopkins University Press, 1978); Louise Rosenblatt, *The Reader, the Text, the Poem* (Carbondale: Southern Illinois University Press, 1978); Jane P. Tompkins, ed., *Reader-Response Criticism* (Baltimore: Johns Hopkins University Press, 1980).

[13]Other good sources include Shoshana Feldman, *Literature and Psychoanalysis: The Question of Reading Otherwise* (Baltimore: Johns Hopkins University Press, 1981). Frederick Crews criticizes the method in *Out of My System* (New York: Oxford University Press, 1975).

[14]Ernest Jones, *Hamlet and Oedipus* (New York: Norton, 1949).

only good subjects of psychological interpretation of literary works would be those by authors whom we know to have known the theories; we would be limited to the works of writers like Eugene O'Neill, D.H. Lawrence, Sherwood Anderson, and Tennessee Williams, who were all acquainted with at least some of the ideas of Freud. Most critics are not troubled by the anachronism, since if the theories are good, it is not because they invented something that people adopted but because they can make valid observations about people's feelings and behavior. Besides, as the name of "the Oedipus complex" shows, Freud invented it partly through the insights he gained through literature. He generalized the pattern of the plot of Sophocles' play (see p. 1158 in the "Ethical Questions" section of the anthology) to say that as young children, males have the urge to displace their fathers (murder is an extreme version) and to monopolize their mothers (marriage is, again, an extreme way to accomplish this). The fear of the father's retaliation (castration anxiety) banishes the wish to the unconscious, but if it is not properly resolved, it can affect feelings and behavior in adult life, prompting the need for therapy.

The Oedipus complex is probably not as universal as Freud thought, but whether it works for the "created" people in literature is a separate question. Exploring the applicability of the theory to the figures of imaginative literature is the work of psychological literary criticism.

When working on Seamus Heaney's poem "Digging," for instance, Zak Owen noticed that while much of the poem is taken up with the narrator's admiration for his father and grandfather's skills with spades, it opens with an image of anger or at least aggression ("snug as a gun," l. 2; see Chapter 2). Ambivalent feelings about fathers are predictable in Freudian theory, and both pens and spades can be seen as phallic symbols, that is, symbols of the penis, not only because of their shape but because of their generative powers—his father and grandfather grow things or provide fuel and perhaps money with their tools. (In the context of Freud, words take on their bawdiest associations and it may not be irrelevant that the words *pen* and *penis* are almost anagrams.) "But I've no spade to follow men like them" (l. 28) could be seen as an expression of castration anxiety, and the fantasy of a gun as a wish to compensate for the loss of the phallus as compared to the father and grandfather's intimidating powers. The final lines of the poem make sense in Freudian terms, too, as the narrator's chosen instrument becomes, like the spade but with physical traits even closer to the penis, productive, and contributes to his sense of vocation.

Freud has no monopoly on psychological criticism, of course. You have already seen the ideas on adult attachment that R. Chris Fraley and Phillip R. Shaver reported in their *Journal of Personality and Social Psychology* article applied to Richard Wilbur's poem "For C" in Chapter 9; and in Chapter 10 you saw the ideas in the work of psychologists Martin L. Hoffman, Robert O. Hansson and his colleagues, and Rhoda Unger and Mary Crawford applied to David Kaplan's short story "Doe Season." The possibilities are as various as the many different threads in the discipline.

HISTORICAL AND SOCIOLOGICAL CRITICISM

Psychological criticism has historical issues embedded within it. Concerns about individual authors' lives automatically involve critics in the authors' times. There are a number of kinds of historical criticism, including biographical, linguistic, literary, and intellectual, as well as the social/political approaches like new historicism, Marxism, and cultural materialism.

Biographical criticism is obviously related to psychological criticism, but begins, not with applicable theories of the self, but with the facts and circumstances of a writer's life. All the biographical headnotes in this book assume that it might be useful to know when, where, and how writers lived. In the case of Robert Herrick, for instance, who wrote the poem "Delight in Disorder" (Chapter 6), knowing something about the poet's conflicts with the Puritan movement that took over the government during his lifetime highlights the word *precise* in the last line. It was used to satirize Puritans' religious zeal. Thus the biographical information turns the innocent-seeming little lyric into a poem of political protest. Although the poem is not obviously concerned with religion or politics, information about how Herrick earned his living through the Church and his collision with Puritanism reveals the struggle going on beneath the surface of that poem.

These hypotheses aren't personal enough to include details of the writers' upbringing and familial relationships. If you wanted to do a psychoanalytic reading of Poe's interest in insanity and murder, you would need a different kind of information, but there are sometimes payoffs for attending to a writer's place in history.

Literary history traces the development of genres, themes, and attitudes through time. One of its primary activities is defining commonalities and trends to characterize the literature of a specific period in a specific place. It thus distinguishes medieval from Renaissance literature, and within those periods, early from late medieval, and Tudor from Stuart and Jacobean. It also distinguishes British from American; and within those, English from Irish, and Southern from Western. The divisions are artificial, of course—just when did medieval literature end?[15] They are ignored when they seem irrelevant. We don't always remember that Oscar Wilde was born in Ireland or Richard Wilbur in New York. But it is hard to forget that Faulkner is a Southern writer or to take any of them out of their time periods. To "place" their work in literary history, critics would discuss its language, style, subjects, and form.

Intellectual history contextualizes literary works by connecting the ideas manifested in them to the ideas characteristic of their time periods. This means that, as in literary history, the critic is responsible for defining both the work and the age. Both definitions as well as their relationship are

---

[15]The most frequently used date, 1485, depends more on historical events than literary ones: The Wars of the Roses ended with Henry of Richmond's accession to the throne as Henry VII.

always arguable and must therefore be supported, but the dialogue between those who see Shakespeare as embodying the traits of the Renaissance and those who see him as universal is a valuable one. Even to define him as transcending his age, we have to know what he was transcending.

The basic insight that a literary work might be specifically related to its time has a corollary in sociological and anthropological approaches. The anthropologist Laura Bohannan showed the limitation on our ideas of "universal." In a 1966 article she recounted how some members of the Tiv tribe in Africa where she was living and doing research reacted to the plot of Shakespeare's *Hamlet*. She told it during the rainy season, a period of forced leisure when tribe members gather to tell and discuss stories. She quickly saw that her own interpretation of the story, or indeed any well-accepted interpretation that she knew, would not stand among the Tiv because the behavior of Hamlet's mother after the death of Hamlet's father, her speedy marriage to her dead husband's brother, earned instant approval among the Tiv. Although it produces in Hamlet the uneasiness that accounts for many of his subsequent actions, for the Tiv elders, it was exactly what she should have done. Hamlet's behavior, in contrast, is inappropriate because sons should never avenge the murder of their fathers all by themselves. The elders then pointed out to Bohannan all that was wrong with her interpretation of the play and recommended that, upon her return home, she share their wisdom with the elders of her own country.[16] The wisdom with which she returned includes the realization that the Western category of "universal" is probably not big enough.

The insights about literature's relationship to the time periods and cultures that produce literary works have generated much work in literary studies. *Historicism* puts literature into the context of the actual events of a time period, thus relating literature to social and political developments in the time in which it is written. The nature of government (both the individual leaders and the governing structures) and the issues that engage a society or that silently influence or change it all might appear in some way in the writing of the time. Historicists try to see what these factors are and how they relate to imaginative literature. One word used for a long time to name this relationship was *reflection*. The art of a culture was said to "reflect" its structure in some way.

But starting in the last decades of the twentieth century, a group of critics who came to be known as "new historicists" saw *reflection* as too passive a term and began talking about literature and the other arts as more active shapers of a society's norms and values. They weren't content to see literature as merely a mirror of a society created by other more powerful factors. The other factors—the government, the economy—are surely powerful, but do the arts just tag along? Where does a society get its ideas about itself?

[16]Laura Bohannan, "Shakespeare in the Bush," *Natural History* 75 (1966): 28–33. Reprinted in *Applying Cultural Anthropology: An Introductory Reader*, 5th ed., ed. Aaron Podolefsky and Peter J. Brown (Mountain View, CA: Mayfield, 2001), 35–40.

New historicists would say that the arts actively participate in a society's self-understanding.

One contemporary version of this discussion is the debate about whether the depiction of violence in the mass media is caused by the actual violence in society or causes it, or whether they reinforce each other. Other themes in which the mass media might be said to participate include individualism, the importance of the choice of commercial products for shaping an identity, and the centrality of romantic love to people's lives. Because of their pervasiveness in the media, themes of this sort can come to seem natural and obvious. The critics most likely to call attention to the way these themes in contemporary culture are *not* natural, that is, not the only way for humans to behave, are the *cultural materialists*, who try to examine the way a society's self-image is created.[17]

Like cultural materialists, new historicists are interested in all the texts that a society produces—not just imaginative literature—because history is by definition gone, now only present to us as the story of what happened. The partiality of narrative accounts has become evident in modern studies of memory that show that what we can sometimes feel certain we saw was really something different from what actually happened. Our views are partial in the sense that we see from only one angle and partial in the sense that we sometimes have a stake in how things occurred. So there is no single "history" that can provide certainty about past events or their meaning. Therefore, historicizing a literary text requires surrounding it with other texts from the period in which it was written—other texts of all kinds. Historicist interpretation of literature thus also requires "literary" interpretation of history.

In a way, historical issues are already present in biographical, intellectual, and psychological interpretation, as we saw above. When investigating the word *precise* in Robert Herrick's poem "Delight in Disorder," we were led to the Puritan movement in his time and its effect on his life. A fuller historicist interpretation would require more investigation into the language of Puritanism and the ways in which it permeated the discourse of seventeenth-century England—which is, of course, present to us only in the texts of the period.

Psychological criticism finds that the influence of Freud on literature is historical in a similar way, because some writers actually read Freud, and we may be able to discover that in their other works, especially if they wrote nonfiction or if their journals are published. These sources might provide evidence that the influence was direct. But we do not necessarily have to find the "smoking gun," explicit evidence of acquaintance with Freud's theories, because historicism brings in other kinds of texts to understand a period.

---

[17]E.g., Jonathan Dollimore and Alan Sinfield, "Culture and Textuality: Debating Cultural Materialism," *Textual Practice* 4.1 (1990): 91–100; *Political Shakespeare: New Essays in Cultural Materialism*, 2nd ed., ed. Dollimore and Sinfield (Manchester: Manchester University Press, 1994).

But more often than psychological issues, political ones engage new historicists. The first generation of new historicists, including Stephen Greenblatt[18] and Stephen Orgel,[19] study the way the dominant powers in Renaissance England controlled people's ideas and actions without exerting the most obvious kinds of military force—in other words, how people were coerced into policing themselves. In this view, literature becomes a way of shaping people's concepts of how society works and how individuals live and work within it, usually presenting practices that benefit the ruling or economic elite as if they are natural and of benefit to the majority. In this picture of how societies work, there is little room for resistance to the hegemonic power. Resistance is always folded back into the dominant structures.

The influence of the French theorist Michel Foucault (pronounced Mi shell' Fu koh') is evident here,[20] especially his interest in the way the dominant group's power is disseminated through all cultural forms and all social relationships. This is one of the new historicist ideas criticized by other commentators but also by some new historicists as well. The claustrophobic version of society—with no space outside the mainstream ideas—is not the only possible reading of Foucault himself. No ruling power can rule so completely that no resistance is possible for indefinite periods of time. Contemporary observers of China might draw the same conclusion.

New historicists' and cultural materialists' fascination with the relationship between literature and political and economic power structures also shows the influence of Karl Marx. *Marxist criticism* is both historical and sociological, taking interest in how the social and economic forces in a given society affect groups and their relationships to each other. The structure of modern Western society depends on the relations of different groups, or classes, to the means of production, the mechanisms by which goods are produced and distributed. The ruling class owns the means of production (for instance, factories), and the proletariat or working classes sell the owners their labor (work in the factories in exchange for wages). The different positions mean that classes have different amounts of power and authority, and Marxism sees social structure and historical change as the result of the conflicts among them.

[18]*Renaissance Self-Fashioning: From More to Shakespeare* (Chicago: University of Chicago Press, 1980); "Invisible Bullets: Renaissance Authority and Its Subversion," *Glyph* 8 (1981): 40–61; *Shakespearean Negotiations: The Circulation of Social Energy in Renaissance England* (Oxford: Oxford University Press, 1988).

[19]*The Illusion of Power: Political Theater in the English Renaissance* (Berkeley, CA: University of California Press, 1975).

[20]Particularly his *Archaeology of Knowledge*, trans. A.M. Sheridan Smith (London: Tavistock/Routledge, 1972); *The History of Sexuality, Vol. I: An Introduction*, trans. Robert Hurley (London: Penguin, 1981); and "What Is an Author?" in *Language, Counter-Memory, Practice: Selected Essays and Interviews by Michel Foucault*, ed. and intro. Donald F. Bouchard (Ithaca, NY: Cornell University Press, 1977), 113–38.

There are many different ways that Marxists can see the arts, including literature, as fitting into this picture of how society works. First, art can provide images that help make the unequal distribution of power seem natural and unchangeable. The groups with the most power have a vested interest in keeping things just as they are, and insofar as they have control of ideology, the beliefs that underpin the social structure, they want to present "the way things are" as "the way things must be." For instance, in most television situation comedies, all problems are individual. By focusing on the small scale, they steer their audiences far away from social analysis or political criticism in order to create a peaceful context in which to sell advertising time. A Marxist might see them as part of the ideological apparatus of capitalism.

But second, the arts can look at problems in a society, doing the social work not of reinforcing and validating the status quo, but rather of criticizing it or even attempting to change it.[21] For instance, Hô Xuân Hu'o'ng's "On Sharing a Husband" does not promote a specific plan for change, but the narrator's dissatisfaction constitutes a protest against the marriage system in eighteenth-century Vietnam that allows men to marry more than one wife. She presents the conditions of her life as a matter of fate (l. 1) and individual choice ("I think I would have lived alone," l. 8), but her specific complaints about her social and economic status ("You slave like a maid / but without pay" ll. 6–7) might be precise enough to rattle the system a little.

Many of the literary works included in this book describe social and economic relationships among groups. As interpreters, we can decide whether or not they seem to promote change, and if so, what kind and on what grounds.

Marxism is not the only kind of sociological criticism, of course. The work of many different kinds of sociologists can be used as interpretive frameworks for imaginative literature. We have seen this kind of pairing in Chapter 9 with Poe's "Cask of Amontillado" and Erving Goffman's *Presentation of Self in Everyday Life* in Chapter 9. A sociological analysis of Seamus Heaney's poem "Digging" (Chapter 2) might focus on the different kinds of labor that the different generations perform. The father and grandfather perform manual labor, the narrator intellectual/artistic. The exchange of spade for pen does not prompt protest, but is a pattern seen in many families. The poem seems to record some anxiety that comes along with the social shift.

Other kinds of sociological criticism are *feminist, gender,* and *gay and lesbian* criticism. We have already experimented with gender criticism in

[21]Pierre Marcherey, *A Theory of Literary Production,* translated from the French by Geoffrey Wall (London, Boston: Routledge & Kegan Paul, 1978). See also Terry Eagleton, *Marxism and Literary Criticism* (Berkeley: University of California Press, 1976), and Frederic Jameson, *Marxism and Form: Twentieth-Century Dialectical Theories of Literature* (Princeton, NJ: Princeton University Press, 1971).

Chapter 9 when applying the work of Friedl, Unger and Crawford, and others to the short story by David Kaplan. The focus there was the different roles of men and women in various societies and how boys and girls learn to fill them. The story wrestles with the question of whether those roles are natural and unavoidable, particularly urgent since the roles of both men and women are limited in most societies. Feminists all believe that males and females are equally important and ought to have equal political weight in society, but they are divided on the question of whether males and females are inherently different or (at least potentially) the same. How much of the difference in conventional male and female roles is determined by biology and how much by socialization?

Analogous questions can be asked about gays and lesbians in contrast to heterosexuals. However they answer these questions, critics concerned with gender and sexuality explore how these groups are portrayed in literature, how they write it, and how they read it. Critics seek out the work of little-known writers who have been neglected because of their gender or sexual orientation, and they interpret familiar works in new ways.[22] An interesting example of the latter that also combines cultural materialism with gay and lesbian points of view is Alan Sinfield's *Cultural Politics: Queer Reading*.[23]

DISCOVERING CRITICAL APPROACHES TO LITERATURE

There are, of course, more critical approaches than can be listed in a short appendix, but users of this book should have good tools for inventing them as they need them. A general description of psychological criticism will not be as usable an interpretive framework as a particular psychological insight made available by those working in the discipline of psychology. The skills of close reading developed in Chapters 4–7 should allow you to find, comprehend, and use varied approaches adaptable to your particular needs. Since all interpretations have to take careful account of the features of the literary work in question, these skills should help you read as closely as you care to. With this array of equipment, you should be a responsive, responsible, and versatile interpreter. I hope you also can find a great deal of pleasure in the process of reading and interpreting literature, and that it enriches your life.

---

[22]Among important works of feminist criticism are Sandra M. Gilbert and Susan Gubar, *Madwoman in the Attic: The Woman Writer and the Nineteenth-Century Literary Imagination* (New Haven: Yale University Press, 1979); Elaine Showalter, *A Literature of Their Own: British Women Novelists from Brontë to Lessing* (Princeton: Princeton University Press, 1977).

[23]Alan Sinfield, *Cultural Politics: Queer Reading* (London: Routledge, 1994).

Glossary of Terms

N.B. Italicized terms in bold type are defined elsewhere in the glossary.

Abstract: a compendium or summary; often the first section of an academic article, esp. in the sciences and social sciences, where it is likely to give the main claim(s) of the argument; the first stage in Labov's schematic map of anecdotes

Academe, academia (n.); academic (adj.): the environment, community, or life in educational institutions, particularly universities and colleges

Academic disciplines: fields of interest that are subjects for study in higher education; the rules and methods for study in an academic field, including the humanities, the social sciences, and the sciences

Academic discourse; academic genres: speech or writing produced by researchers in educational institutions, including such *genres* as primary research reports, review articles, textbooks, reviews, and books. Academics also sometimes write magazine and newspaper articles for non-specialist readers.

Academy: the school for advanced education founded by Plato or the philosophical matters associated with that school; higher education, used with *the*

Allegory: a painting or narrative in which characters, events, and material objects are used as symbols for ideas or principles. The word is derived from Greek roots meaning "other" and "speak," indicating the substitution involved in allegory. Spenser's *Faerie Queene* and Bunyan's *Pilgrim's Progress* are extended examples.

Alliteration: the repetition of usually initial sounds in two or more neighboring words or syllables, as *wild and wooly, threatening throngs;* also called *head rhyme, initial rhyme*

Allusion: an implied or indirect reference; the inclusion in one work of a piece of another, esp. when the audience might be expected to recognize (or be able to discover) the source for the included material. This technique is used in all kinds of writing, especially imaginative literature, as well as painting and music. It can bring associations from the source into the new text and stir audiences to consider the different meaning produced by the new context. In rap music, *sampling* is a form of allusion. In contexts where originality is highly prized, allusion can cause controversy, for instance, in academic writing, about plagiarism, and in the commercial arts, about copyright violations.

Anapest (n.), anapestic (adj.): a metrical foot consisting of two short syllables followed by one long syllable or of two unstressed syllables followed by one stressed syllable, as in the words *unabridged* and *unalloyed*

Anaphora: repetition of a word or expression at the beginning of successive phrases, clauses, sentences, or verses, especially for rhetorical or poetic effect (e.g., Lincoln's *Gettysburg Address*: "We cannot dedicate—we cannot consecrate—we cannot hallow—this ground.")

Antagonist: the chief opponent or adversary of the *protagonist* in a narrative

Argument: formal or informal reasoning in which a writer or speaker makes and defends *claims*; can refer to the structure of reasoning in any kind of discourse, from academic to poetic; may consist of *claim, reason, evidence, assumption, qualifiers, concessions,* and *refutations*

Assonance: resemblance of vowel sounds in the middle of words; repetition of vowels without repetition of consonants (as in *stony* and *holy* or the phrase *hot to trot*); often used in verse, especially as an alternative to *rhyme*

Assumption: the *warrant* of an argument; the principles or rules, often unstated, that link the reason to the claim, showing why the reason is appropriate for the particular claim; sometimes a claim that needs support of its own

Audience: the hearers of a play or the readers of a book; the readers to whom a piece of writing is addressed; anyone who reads it. See *implied author, implied audience.*

Author in the text: See *implied author.*

Character: one of the persons of a literary work; a person's qualities or traits

Chiasmus: an inverted relationship between the syntactic elements of parallel phrases, as in Goldsmith's "to stop too fearful, and too faint to go"

Civic discourse: the use of spoken or written language in the public realm, including such examples as letters to the editor, advertising, legal contracts. See *discourse.*

Claim: the part of an argument that makes an assertion that a statement is true; assertion that must be defended by reasons and evidence. Some claims define (claims of description), some evaluate (claims of evaluation), some compare (claims of resemblance), some address meaning (claims of interpretation), some recommend an action (claims of policy, proposals), and some assert causation (causal claims).

Climactic order: a series of things, events, or phrases arranged in order of importance or intensity leading to a *climax*

Climax: the point of highest dramatic tension or a major turning point in the action (as of a play); the point of supreme interest or intensity of any graded series of events or ideas, most commonly, the crisis or turning point of a story or play

Coda: the end of a composition, musical or verbal; The word comes from the Latin *cauda* meaning "tail," and a coda comes after the formal end or resolution of a piece

Colloquial: of or relating to conversation; used in or characteristic of familiar and informal conversation; using conversational style

Colloquialism: an informal expression; a local or regional *dialect* expression

Communications triangle: a schematization of the elements of communication, including a message and its subject matter (sometimes labeled *logos*, or reason), its sender (*ethos*), and the receiver (*pathos*). See Chapter 1, Figure 1.

Complicating action: in the analysis of plots in imaginative literature, a conflict or problem; in William Labov's pattern for anecdotes, the third element in the pattern

Concessions: the part of an argument that takes note of legitimate claims on the opposing side

Connotation: something suggested by a word or thing, apart from the thing it explicitly names or describes (contrasts with *denotation*)

Context: the parts of a *discourse* that surround a word or passage and throw light on its meaning; something outside of a *discourse* that throws light on its meaning; environment

Contextualize: to place something in a *context*; to provide an environment that reveals something about the meaning of a work or part of a work

Cumulative sentence: a sentence beginning with a complete syntactical unit that is followed by a number of modifiers

Dactyl (n.), dactylic (adj.): a metrical foot consisting of one long and two short syllables or of one stressed and two unstressed syllables, as in the words *citizen* and *tenderly*

Deduction, deductive reasoning, deductive argument: the thought process that leads the thinker to draw conclusions from premises; logic that moves from the general to the specific

Denotation: a direct, specific meaning as distinct from an implied or associated idea; often contrasted with *connotation*

Denouement: the final outcome of the main dramatic complication in a literary work; follows the resolution of the plot's conflict or problems

Dialect: a subset of a language that consistently follows rules that are somewhat different from the standard language (which can be thought of as a dialect spoken and written by a majority of speakers); used among a group defined, for instance, by region, class, or ethnic group; usually transmitted orally

Diction: word choice, especially with regard to correctness, clarity, or effectiveness. See *levels of diction.*

Dimeter: poetic meter in which a line of verse consists of two metrical feet

Discourse: connected speech or writing; a formal and orderly expression of thought on a subject; the verbal interchange of ideas. See *civic discourse* and *academic discourse.*

Documentation system: one of the methods for giving credit to the sources used in a scholarly work, such as books and articles (published and unpublished), websites, paintings and photographs, musical compositions, etc. Each system has its own rules for formatting and punctuating footnotes, endnotes, works cited lists, and bibliographies. Commonly used systems of acknowledgment are those of the MLA (Modern Language Association) system, the APA (American Psychological Association), and the CBE (Council of Biology Editors) system, all of which supply style sheets to inform writers of the conventions. See Appendix D.

Dummy slots: Stanley Fish's term for the missing parts of the sentence that competent readers or speakers of language learn to expect when a sentence begins. If a sentence begins with a subject, readers expect a verb to follow; if a subordinate clause, an independent one. Waiting for dummy slots to be filled becomes more pronounced when something intrudes between the element that has begun and the element that will finish a sentence, as when it contains *embedding.*

Embedding: a technique of word order in which an utterance begins with a subject for a clause but instead of supplying the verb quickly, it interrupts itself with other words, withholding the verb that completes the clause.
The next sentence contains an example of embedding: This technique, which sometimes makes sentences difficult to read, often has the effect of emphasizing whatever completes the grammatical structure, especially if it comes last in the sentence.

Enjambment: the completion in the following poetic line of a clause or other grammatical unit begun in the preceding line; the employment of "run-on": lines that carry the sense of a statement from one line to another without rhetorical pause at the end of the line. The term is also applied to the carrying over of meaning from one couplet or stanza to the next.

Ethos: the trustworthiness of a speaker or writer; often thought of as one corner of the *communications triangle*

Euphemism: the substitution of an agreeable or inoffensive expression for one that may offend or suggest something unpleasant, e.g., "let [an employee] go" for "fire" and "pass" or "pass on" for "die"

Evidence: the part of an *argument* that indicates the truth of the *reason*; can include examples, statistical data, expert testimony, and/or personal experience

Exposition: a setting forth in speech or writing of a meaning or purpose; discourse, or an example of it, designed to explain what is difficult to understand

Falling action: See *plot.*

Foot: the basic unit of verse meter consisting of any of the various fixed combinations or groups of stressed and unstressed or long and short syllables, sometimes expressed as a metrical foot; *anapest, dactyl, iamb, trochee,* and *pyrrhic* are examples

Foreshadowing: an indication at some point in a work of something that is going to happen later. It can consist of a tone or mood, a focus on a particular object or person, or direct prediction by a narrator. For interpreters, it raises the question of why an author wants the audience to have advance warning of an event or outcome.

Free verse: verse composed of unrhymed lines that do not conform to a fixed metrical pattern. The poet decides where to end each line, trying to make the break as meaningful as possible so that it does not seem to be determined merely by chance.

Genre (zhan'-ra): a type or class of artistic, musical, or literary composition characterized by a particular style, form, or content. The genres of civic discourse include any kind of writing meant for distribution to a wide non-specialist audience, such as the newspaper column or article, the magazine article, the editorial, and the letter to the editor. The genres of academic discourse include primary research reports, review articles, textbooks, reviews, and books, all written by specialists in particular fields and intended for specialized audiences. From the Latin *genus* and thus related to the word *kind.* See Chapter 3.

Iamb (n.), iambic (adj.): a metrical foot consisting of one short syllable followed by one long syllable, or of one unstressed syllable followed by one stressed syllable, as in the word *above*

Imaginative literature: writing such as stories, poems, plays, and creative nonfiction that does not depend on facts or literal truth for its subject matter, but offers images of and insights about human life through representation

Implied audience: hypothetical readers or listeners who would best understand and respond to a text; may not be directly represented within a text or identical with the actual audience; must be inferred from the characteristics of the text and its language

Implied author: the "author in the text," or narrator, sometimes the author him/herself, sometimes a combination of the author and a fictive narrator sharing some of the author's characteristics, or another persona altogether

IMRAD format (structure): a method of organizing primary research reports, especially in the sciences and social sciences; consisting of subsections called some variation of "Introduction," "Methods," "Results," and "Discussion," called IMRAD for short. The structure is not universal and it is regularly varied with further divisions given titles related to subject matter rather than function.

In medias res: the Latin phrase describes the beginning of narratives that start "in the middle of things" rather than starting with the initial stages of an action or event. The most common examples are epics like the *Aeneid* and the *Odyssey*, which traditionally avoid beginning with the birth of the hero or the initial causes of the war or journey that occupies them.

Induction, inductive argument, inductive reasoning: the thought process that leads the thinker to arrive at a generalized conclusion based on specific examples presented as evidence to support the conclusion

Inflection: change in pitch or loudness of voice; tone of voice, *intonation*; the change of form that words undergo to mark such distinctions as those of case, gender, number, tense, person, mood, or voice

Interjection: an ejaculatory utterance, usually lacking grammatical connection; a word or phrase used in an exclamation (as "Heavens! Dear me!")

Internal rhyme: rhyming words that appear in poetry other than at the ends of lines. See *rhyme*.

Intonation: manner of utterance of the tones of the voice in speaking; accent; specifically the rise and fall in pitch in speech; the action of reciting in a singing or chanting voice, as in the speech of the chorus in Greek drama, or poetry recitation; tone of voice, *inflection*

Jargon: the technical terminology or characteristic idiom of a special activity or group

Levels of diction: a term that describes the different degrees of formality and informality in speech or writing. See *diction*.

Literature: the body of written work in a given language; printed material; written work on a particular subject, particularly by academic scholars; imaginative or creative writing. See *imaginative literature*.

Logos: logic of the subject matter; often thought of as one corner of the *communications triangle*

Magic realism: a genre of literature that usually includes scenes and actions that are generally accepted as scientifically impossible or unreal and which ordinarily belong to the world of the imagination, dream, hallucination, religious experience, the supernatural; common in late twentieth century Latin American literature. See *realism*.

Metaphor: a figure of speech in which a word or place literally denoting one kind of object or idea is used in place of another to suggest a likeness or analogy between them (e.g., "drowning in money")

Meter: more or less regular poetic rhythm, determined by the alternation of stressed and unstressed syllables; the measurable rhythmical patterns manifested in verse. See individual entries for poetic meter, i.e., *iamb*, *trochee*, etc., and *stress*.

Narrator: the speaker of a piece of discourse, the teller of a tale, often assumed to be the author, but not always having the same characteristics as the author. See *implied author*. One who relates, recounts, gives an account of one or more incidents in a work of literature; the character in a story, either described or implied, who tells the tale, and may be considered to be or later found to be more or less reliable, but who may represent a particular point of view; thus, narrators may be **reliable** or **unreliable**, and **omniscient** (having infinite awareness, understanding and insight) or **limited omniscient** (having some of these but not necessarily all). The **objective narrator** does not report on characters' inner states at all, but just reports from an external point of view.

Null hypothesis: the theory that whatever differences seem to separate two or more groups are really just the results of normal variation. This is what statistical tests are testing. The null hypothesis bets that there is no significant difference between groups and experiments are designed to find out whether that's the winning bet.

Oxymoron: a combination of contradictory or incongruous words (as *cruel kindness*)

p (probability) value: the result of a *statistical test* that attempts to assess the role of chance in producing its outcome; expressed as a number equal to or less than a percentage that represents the likelihood that the outcome of the test could have been the result of chance. A p value equal to or less than .05 is in most cases accepted as *significant*.

Parallelism: similar ideas expressed in sequence using similar grammatical structures to produce emphasis (e.g., "I came, I saw, I conquered.")

Parody: a comic version of a serious work. The roots of the word mean "a song (ode) beside (para-)." That is, parody always imitates another work, usually following the original as closely as possible in form and style but substituting a less serious subject matter. In contrast, maintaining the subject matter but lowering the style produces burlesque or travesty. Matthew Arnold's poem "Dover Beach" (see p. 744 in Chapter 14), has been famously parodied by Anthony Hecht in "The Dover Bitch" (posted in several places on the Web, e.g., http://www.plagiarist.com/text/?wid=2409). Examples of parodic movies include *Monty Python and the Holy Grail* (1975),[1] Mel Brooks's *Blazing Saddles* (1976), and the parodic airplane disaster movie, *Airplane* (1980).

---

[1]Some of the expertise on matters medieval that makes the film such a good parody must come from Terry Jones, who engages in serious scholarship on Chaucer, for instance in his book *Chaucer's Knight: The Portrait of a Medieval Mercenary* (Baton Rouge: Louisiana State University Press, 1980).

Pathetic fallacy: the projection of human traits or feelings onto inanimate nature (e.g., *cruel sea*)

Pathos: in rhetoric, the values and feelings of the reader; often thought of as one corner of the *communications triangle*

Pentameter: a line of verse consisting of five metrical feet

Periodic sentence: a way of constructing a sentence so that it begins with modifiers and withholds its syntactical completeness until the end, creating *dummy slots* and making the reader wait to have them filled; creates emphasis. Front-end loaded with modifiers, withholding a complete syntactical unit, this sentence, an example of periodic structure, must be read to the end.

Persona, personae (pl.): identity or role assumed by a character in literary works such as novels or plays

Personification: attribution of personal qualities, especially representation of a thing or abstraction as a person or by the human form, e.g., "Miss Liberty"

Plot: the plan or main story of a literary work, often containing **rising action**, i.e., the separate events that advance the conflict to its crucial point, and that may include its crisis or *climax*, and **falling action**, i.e., the incidents and episodes in which the force destined to be victorious establishes its supremacy

Poetry: writing for which the writer, not the printer, determines the margin on the right side of the page; can be metrical writing or not; writing that formulates a concentrated, imaginative awareness of experience in language chosen and arranged to create a specific emotional response through meaning, sound, and rhythm

Point of view: a position from which something is considered or evaluated; standpoint

Profane, profanity: serving to debase or defile what is holy by a wrong, unworthy, or vulgar use

Prose: that form of writing for which the printer, not the writer, determines the margin at the right side of the page; a literary medium distinguished from poetry, especially by its closer correspondence to the patterns of everyday speech

Prosody: the study of versification, especially the systematic study of metrical structure

Protagonist: the principal character in a story; the chief personage in a drama

Pun: the usually humorous use of a word in such a way as to suggest two or more of its meanings or the meaning of another word similar in sound

Pyrrhic: a metrical foot consisting of two short or unaccented syllables

Qualifier: the part of an *argument* that limits the *claim*, including words like *most* instead of *all*, *somewhat* instead of *completely*, and *influences* instead of *determines*. In addition, *may* and *can* may indicate when outcomes are not guaranteed.

Realism: a kind of art concerned with giving a truthful impression of actuality as it appears to the normal human consciousness

Reason: the part of an argument that supplies the basis for a *claim*, explaining and justifying it; often supported by the evidence of examples, statistical data, or expert or personal testimony

Refutation: proof through argument that a point made by the opposition is false

Relationship to the opposition: the way an *argument* takes account of the claims and reasons of the other side, including concessions where its points are strong and relevant; counterarguments where they are not

Resolution: the part of a plot in which complications are untangled, problems solved or declared insoluble, and conflicts addressed, either successfully or unsuccessfully; in William Labov's pattern for anecdotes, the third element

Rhetoric: the art of using language effectively and persuasively; the discipline that studies how people use language

Rhetorical situation: the circumstances to which a speaker or writer directs a particular speech or text; defined by the relationships among all the elements of the *communications triangle*

Rhyme: two or more words or phrases with similar rhythms ending with the same letters or sounds; can involve a single echo, as in *roll* and *stole* (masculine or single rhyme) or more, as in *table* and *label* (feminine or double rhyme) or *statistical* and *mystical* (triple rhyme). In the twelfth and thirteenth centuries, it first supplemented then replaced alliteration as a way of marking the change from one line of poetry to another, an important function when poetry was heard more than read. Patterns of rhyme, *rhyme schemes*, create stanza structure. In the hands of masters such as George Gordon, Lord Byron, or Ogden Nash, rhyme has great comic potential.

Rhyme scheme: the pattern created by the variation of rhymes; can be schematized if each new rhyming sound is labeled by a letter of the alphabet, such as aabbccdd . . . for couplets

Rising action: See *plot*.

Rubric: This word comes from the Middle English word meaning red ocher, as in ruby, and means the heading in red letters of part of a book. The word now refers to that same function, but also means something under which a thing is classed, an authoritative rule, an explanatory or introductory commentary, a gloss, or editorial interpolation, an established rule, tradition, or custom.

Sampling: in statistics, the method of choosing individuals randomly so that they can represent a larger group; in rap music, the importation of a musical rhythm or melody from an earlier composition, usually synthesized, occasionally electronically modified, but still recognizable; a musical *allusion*

Scansion, to scan, scanning: the analysis of verse to show its meter by marking the patterns of stressed and unstressed syllables: ún strĕssed sýl lă blĕs

Setting: the time and place of the action of a literary work, whether in writing, on the stage, or in film

Significance (significant difference): a technical term meaning not "important" but rather reflecting actual differences between groups that vary in only a limited number of ways; a label given to acceptable results of statistical tests; expressed as *p values*

Simile: like *metaphor*, a comparison of one thing with another, but explicitly announced by the words *like* or *as*

Slam: A poetry slam is a competition in which individuals and teams perform original poetry for cash prizes. Each performance is a recitation, no more than three minutes long, sometimes accompanied by gesture and expressive motion, but never props. It tends to be more flamboyant than what is called, by contrast, academic poetry. Three judges chosen from the audience rate the performances the way professional judges give scores to figure skaters and competitive divers, holding the ratings up on placards. The audience is then free to respond not only to the performances but also to the judges' evaluations. Audiences sometimes register their disapproval of judges' judgments quite volubly. If there's no local slam venue in your area, you can get the flavor of slams from the documentary *Slam Nation* (which includes a clip from the Austin team's performance) or the film *Slam*, which stars several national winners, who wrote their own poems to fit into the plot of the film.

Slang: language peculiar to a particular group or an informal, nonstandard vocabulary composed typically of coinages, arbitrarily changed words, and extravagant or humorous figures of speech, sometimes short-lived but sometimes adopted by a wider community: e.g., *nifty, bad* meaning "good," "copacetic,"[2] "rock and roll" (originally black slang for sex), *cool* meaning acceptable because in sync with a group's latest values or "entire," as in "a cool million," *stash* (n.) meaning someone's secret hoard of money or drugs, *wired* meaning "in a state of excitement"

Sonnet: a lyric poem of fourteen iambic pentameter lines, usually characterized by either the Petrarchan or the Shakespearean (Elizabethan) rhyme scheme. The first consists of the rhyme scheme abba, abba, cdcdcd with the caesural pause or "turn" falling between the first eight lines (octave) and the second six (sestet), while the second consists of the rhyme scheme abab, cdcd, efef, gg, with the caesura after the twelfth line and before the final couplet. The pause or turn is often signaled at the beginning of a line (often l. 9 or l. 13) with a word like *But, Yet, Then,* or *For* (invoking the sense of a logical cause or consequence). The rhythm of thought (often point/counterpoint) usually parallels the stanza form.

Spondee (n.), spondaic (adj.): a metrical foot consisting of two long or stressed syllables

STAR criteria: the four criteria for descriptive argument proposed by Fulkerson consisting of **Sufficiency, Typicality, Accuracy, Relevance**. See Chapter 8.

Stasis point: a state of static balance or equilibrium; that place in a piece of writing that marks the move from one state of affairs or one side of an argument to another; often signaled by words or phrases such as *however, nevertheless, notwithstanding, despite,* or *without minimizing the importance of . . .*

Statistical test: a formula that operates on numerical data measuring one or more characteristics of groups that vary in known ways. Their purpose is to find out whether the apparent differences between the groups are actual or merely the result of chance; the results are often expressed as ***p values***.

Stress: the emphasis on a sound or syllable relative to those that surround it in a word or phrase; arises from the natural pronunciation of language. See ***scansion***.

Symbol: something that stands for or suggests something else because of similarity, relationship, or arbitrary convention; a visible sign of something invisible (e.g., the North Star as the symbol of constancy, the lion as the symbol of courage)

Synecdoche: a figure of speech by which a part is mentioned to stand in for the whole, or the whole for a part, e.g., "all hands on deck," "boots on the ground," "head of cattle," "tread the boards" for "act on stage"

Syntax (n.), syntactical (adj.): word order; the way in which words are put together, linked by grammar, to form phrases, clauses, or sentences

Tetrameter: a line of verse consisting of four metrical feet

---

[2]Not marked slang in the third edition of the *American Heritage Dictionary* but not understood by some electronic spell-checkers.

Theme: a subject or topic of discourse or of artistic representation; a specific or distinctive quality, characteristic, or concern

Tone of voice: the attitude implied by the way statements are said; that attitude as conveyed by writing. Word choice and syntax can give the reader insight as to the character of the speaker; they may include as many tones as the human vocal apparatus can express, such as irony, criticism, respect, intimidation, affection, etc. See *inflection; intonation*.

Trimeter: a line of verse consisting of three metrical feet

Trochee (n.), trochaic (adj.): a metrical foot consisting of one long or stressed syllable followed by one short or unstressed syllable, as in the words *apple* and *mandate*; the most common pattern in English words

Warrant: a guarantee; the main *assumption* of an argument that links the reasons with the *claim* explains why the particular reason is justification for a particular claim; the basis, often unstated, of an argument, to which the writer hopes the audience will consent. The audience, especially the opposition, scrutinizes the warrant, and, if need be, refutes or rejects it.

Zeugma: the use of a word to modify or govern two or more words usually in such a manner that it applies to each in a different sense or makes sense with only one (e.g., "he carried the letter and a grudge" or "she took heart and a taxi"). The effect of mixing material and nonmaterial is often a technique for irony.

Reading Nonliterary Texts[1]

Reading both literary and nonliterary texts can be blissful trips away from everyday reality, and I hope everyone can read in escape mode at will. If a book or article grabs us, that can be our experience on the first reading. But reading for school, reading to be able to use texts, must add another dimension: active, critical reading. Since this whole book is about strategies for reading literary texts, it might be good to offer a few strategies for reading ambitious nonliterary ones, as well. The key is to engage the text actively, joining the conversation of which it is part. Here are a few ways:

Read with a pen in hand:[2] Highlighters are very popular for indicating passages you think are important in a text and can be helpful (and fun to use), but that's all they indicate. They don't say *why* you think so, what part the passage is playing in the text, how it repeats, develops, or conflicts with other passages or other texts, or even what the passage is about. When I return to a highlighted text, all I find is a series of passages I once thought important lined up like identical beads on a string. They help me a little, but not much. Texts in which I've written with pen provide more substance, even if all I've done is made marginal notes about the subject under

---

[1]My list has been influenced by material created for the NC State Campus Writing and Speaking Program by its directors, Chris Anson and Deanna Dannels and by Lorraine Higgins' "Reading to Argue: Helping Students Transform Source Texts," in *Hearing Ourselves Think: Cognitive Research in the College Writing Classroom*, ed. Ann M. Penrose and Barbara M. Sitko (Oxford University Press, 1993), 71–101.

[2]Of course, this advice pertains only if you have "writing rights" over a text. If you need to be actively engaged with something from a library, photocopy it so that you can respond fully without intruding on the experience of later readers. If you own the book but plan to sell it at the end of the semester, ask your bookstore whether marginal notes decrease books' value. Mine says no, that physical damage to the cover and pages is more of a problem than annotation.

discussion. By putting it in my own words, I'm at least starting to map the terrain. Here are some things you can do with a pen:

In the margins:

- Note the subject under discussion in each section or even paragraph, depending on the density of the ideas.
- Note the claim being made and the evidence offered.
- Note your reaction—agreement, disagreement, surprise, delight, puzzlement, anger—and the questions the argument generates.
- Note the assumptions behind the claims. Since they're probably not stated, ask yourself what would have to be assumed to make a reasonable connection between the claims and the reasons.

In an endnote or on a separate sheet:

- Identify the important concepts. Make a list.
- Make notes on what arguments the writer seems to be trying to answer.
- Consolidate the questions in your marginal comments into a more compact list.
- Note any significant repetitions or contradictions within the piece itself.
- Note how the piece confirms or contradicts other things you have read. Is it an example of something else? In other words, can you see it differently by looking at it through a particular frame? Does it provide a frame for something else you know about?
- Make notes on how you would use or refute the writer's arguments.

Keep a reading journal: You can do any of the activities listed above in a separate notebook or computer file. If it is on paper, make it a "double entry" journal; divide the pages in half (or do this on facing pages) putting notes about content on one side and your questions and comments on the other. In a computer file, you can use different fonts to differentiate your descriptive notes from your evaluations and applications.

Make a map: Use a large sheet of paper or a regular size but unlined piece of paper, or rotate your notebook 90°—something that can help free your thinking. Write the major ideas *in* the piece with your ideas *about* the piece in no particular order (you might color code them). Then draw lines between the ones that are connected.

Make a chart: If you'd like some of the freedom of a map but still want to stay linear, try a chart with categories like this:

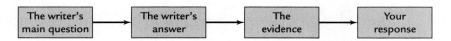

All of these techniques are also good strategies when you want to compare and contrast several pieces of writing. They can help synthesize multiple texts, exploring their relationships: what their approaches share and what they don't, how they agree and disagree. For this task, borrowing a technique from mathematics is sometimes useful:

Make a Venn diagram: Draw overlapping circles, one for each text (I find this works best for two or three. More than four makes the diagram too fussy. For large groups, you might categorize them and then work with the categories; or try a grid, the next strategy on this list). Place the different ideas in the appropriate areas of the diagram, depending on how many of the texts share them. Say we are exploring the relationships of three texts A, B, and C:

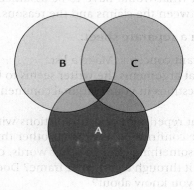

FIGURE 1 *Venn Diagram*

Even for the linear among us, those who tend to make vertical lists (perhaps especially for them), adding another dimension by breaking out into the horizontal can be useful. Visualizing relationships spatially can free your thinking.

Make a grid: Another way to get visual, especially when there are too many sources for a Venn diagram, is a grid. If a group of texts discusses common issues, you align the titles of the texts along one axis and topics, arguments, or specific claims along the other one, and fill in the boxes.

Texts	Claims:	A	B	C	D
Author A					
Author B					
Author C					
Author D					
Author E					

FIGURE 2

Different categories on the axes having to do with aspects of the subject matter can be very effective at showing you what's missing, either because one box doesn't apply or because something is missing and you need to do more research.

Make a deck of cards: It doesn't have to be a full deck, but a card for each author or for each claim, or both, allows you great freedom. You can arrange the cards and lay them out in different patterns on a large table or the floor, rearranging them as your understanding of the relationships among them changes.

Whatever technique you use, the idea is to join the conversation. Doing so will help you prepare to participate in your classes, prepare to write, and prepare for exams. You will be making texts your own, thus generating your own ideas about them. Once you have read actively and critically, you have something to say about complex and ambitious texts. You're on your way to creating your own.

ACTIVITY 1

The techniques listed in this appendix will work well and might be most useful with full-length articles and long excerpts from books. But you can get a sense of how they work by practicing some of them with these three abstracts. Since 1986, David Snowdon, an epidemiologist, has been studying, with researchers in various other specialties like neurology, psychology, and nutrition, an order of Catholic nuns. The papers emerging from the study investigate the factors in their earlier lives that seem to be correlated with health and mental alertness when they are old. Snowdon's book for general readers[3] is based on the academic papers he has written with his collaborators. Here are abstracts from three of the academic papers. Use any of the techniques for active reading to help you synthesize and respond fully to these short texts.

1. Positive Emotions in Early Life and Longevity: Findings from the Nun Study[4]

DEBORAH D. DANNER, DAVID A. SNOWDON, WALLACE V. FRIESEN

Handwritten autobiographies from 180 Catholic nuns, composed when participants were a mean age of 22 years, were scored for emotional content and related to survival during ages 75 to 95. A strong inverse association was found between positive emotional content in these writings and risk of mortality in late life ($p < .001$).[5] As the quartile ranking of

[3] *Aging with Grace: What the Nun Study Teaches Us About Leading Longer, Healthier, and More Meaningful Lives.* (New York: Bantam Books, 2001).

[4] *Journal of Personality and Social Psychology*, 80.5 (2001): 804–13.

[5] Editor's note: For p values, see pp. 156–57 and Appendix B.

positive emotion in early life increased, there was a stepwise decrease in risk of mortality resulting in a 2.5-fold difference between the lowest and highest quartiles. Positive emotional content in early-life autobiographies was strongly associated with longevity 6 decades later. Underlying mechanisms of balanced emotional states are discussed.

2. Linguistic Ability in Early Life and the Neuropathology of Alzheimer's Disease and Cerebrovascular Disease: Findings from the Nun Study[6]

DAVID A. SNOWDON, LYDIA H. GREINER, WILLIAM R. MARKESBERY

Findings from the Nun Study indicate that low linguistic ability in early life has a strong association with dementia and premature death in late life. In the present study, we investigated the relationship of linguistic ability in early life to the neuropathology of Alzheimer's disease and cerebrovascular disease. The analyses were done on a subset of 74 participants in the Nun Study for whom we had handwritten autobiographies completed some time between the ages of 19 and 37 (mean = 23). An average of 62 years after writing the autobiographies, when the participants were 78 to 97 years old, they died and their brains were removed for our neuropathologic studies. Linguistic ability in early life was measured by the idea (proposition) density of the autobiographies, i.e., a standard measure of the content of ideas in text samples. Idea density scores from early life had strong inverse correlations with the severity of Alzheimer's disease pathology in the neocortex: Correlation between idea density scores and neurofibrillary tangle counts were -0.59 for the frontal lobe, -0.48 for the temporal lobe, and -0.49 for the parietal lobe (all p-values < 0.0001). Idea density scores were unrelated to the severity of atherosclerosis of the major arteries at the base of the brain and to the presence of lacunar and large brain infarcts. Low linguistic ability in early life may reflect suboptimal neurological and cognitive development which might increase susceptibility to the development of Alzheimer's disease pathology in late life.

3. Language Decline Across the Life Span: Findings from the Nun Study[7]

SUSAN KEMPER, LYDIA H. GREINER, JANET G. MARQUIS, KATHERINE PRENOVOST, TRACY L. MITZNER

The present study examines language samples from the Nun Study. Measures of grammatical complexity and idea density were obtained from autobiographies written over a 60-year span. Participants who had met criteria

[6]*Vascular Factors in Alzheimer's Disease*, 903 (2000): 34–38.

[7]*Psychology and Aging*, 16.2 (2001): 227–39.

for dementia were contrasted with those who did not. Grammatical complexity initially averaged 4.78 (on a 0-to-7 point scale) for participants who did not meet criteria for dementia and declined .04 units per year; grammatical complexity for participants who met criteria for dementia initially averaged 3.86 and declined .03 units per year. Idea density averaged 5.35 propositions per 10 words initially for participants who did not meet criteria for dementia and declined an average of .03 units per year, whereas idea density averaged 4.34 propositions per 10 words initially for participants who met criteria for dementia and declined .02 units per year. Adult experiences, in general, did not moderate these declines.

MLA and APA Documentation

Whenever you write using ideas and words other than your own, you need to document the sources that you are drawing upon. Although you might hear interviews or read books that make interesting points and strong arguments, you cannot offer them to other people as your own. Doing so in a paper is plagiarism, which is really a form of theft and is a serious offense that can have serious consequences.

In particular, academic writing demands proper citations of the outside sources that you use in your writing. Documenting sources lends authority to your argument because it shows that you have considered what other people have thought and written and have come to your own conclusions. It also demonstrates to your readers that you are willing to share your information with them and therefore are confident of your conclusions. Documentation allows interested readers to follow your tracks.

Finding, evaluating, and incorporating sources are discussed in Chapter 10: Using Research to Write about Literature. This appendix deals with how to document sources properly using the styles of the Modern Language Association and the American Psychological Association, two of the most common styles used in college. Verify with your instructor which style to use before you begin drafting your paper.

MODERN LANGUAGE ASSOCIATION (MLA) DOCUMENTATION STYLE

Academics in English, world languages, and other disciplines in the humanities use Modern Language Association (MLA) style to document sources. The following examples illustrate how to cite a source in the body of your paper and how to list the works cited at the end of your paper. For more information about MLA style, consult the following:

Gibaldi, Joseph. *MLA Handbook for Writers of Research Papers,* 6th ed. New York: MLA, 2003.

The Purdue University Online Writing Lab <http://owl.english.purdue.edu/handouts/research/r_mla.html>

MLA Style for In-Text Citations

When you mention a source in your paper, the simplest way to cite it includes the author's last name and the page number that identifies exactly where the quotation or information is located. If the author's name is included in the text of the paper, it does not need to be repeated in the citation.

Page Number(s) for a Book

Postman states that "language is pure ideology" (123).

There is a difference between the extremes of people who are taken in by their own routine and by people who are cynical of the performance they play (Goffman 17–18).

Volume and Page Number(s) for One Volume of a Multivolume Work

Add the volume number, followed by a colon and the page number, after the author name.

A strong interest in this literature in the 1960s and 1970s inevitably led to a "significant reassessment of the aesthetic and humanistic achievements of black writers" (Inge, Duke, and Bryer 1: v).

Page Number(s) for an Article in a Journal or Magazine

Kaplan notes that United States foreign policy works best "not by intervening militarily on a grand scale but, rather, by placing a few quietly effective officers in key locations around the globe" (55).

Section and Page Number(s) for a Newspaper Article

A constitutional amendment banning same-sex marriage, according to Bob Herbert, would be nothing less than "enshrining bigotry into law" (A27).

Page Number(s) for a Work without an Author

```
Home schooling challenges a system in which "compulsory
mass education has been a hallmark of a civilized society"
("Secret Army" 32).
```

Page Number(s) for a Work by a Group or an Organization

```
The Commission on the Humanities has concluded that "the humani-
ties are inescapably bound to literacy" (69).
```

Page Number(s) for Several Works by One Author

Differentiate between the works by adding a shortened version of the title in the citation when the title of the work doesn't appear in the sentence.

```
In The Coming Fury, Catton identifies the "disquieting omens" (6)
which preceded the Civil War.
As Catton concludes his history of the Civil War, he notes that
"it began with one act of madness and it ended with another"
(Retreat 457.)
```

Page Number(s) for One Work Quoted in Another

```
Samuel Johnson praises She Stoops to Conquer because Goldsmith's
play achieves "the great end of comedy—making an audience merry"
(qtd. in Boswell 171).
```

Paragraph or Screen Number(s) for Internet and Nonprint Sources

Add paragraph (*par.* or *pars.*), section (*sec.*), or screen (*screen*) references when page numbers are unavailable.

```
Citing the struggle to allow interracial marriage, Andrew Sullivan
argues that historically marriage does not fall under the Full
Faith and Credit clause of the U.S. Constitution (screen 2).
```

MLA Style for Works Cited

Following your paper, list the references you have cited in alphabetical order on a separate page entitled "Works Cited." See the Works Cited page of the sample in Chapter 10 (p. 250) for an illustration of how you should prepare this page. Use the following sample entries and guidelines to help you format your reference in MLA style. Pay special attention to abbreviated names of publishers, full names of authors, details of publication, and other characteristic features of MLA citations.

General Guidelines for Books

When citing a book in your Works Cited page, place the information for the citation in the following order:

1. Author's last name, followed by the first name;
2. Full title of the book, including subtitle, underlined;
3. The original publication date, editor, translator, edition, and volume used (if these items are appropriate);
4. The place of publication;
5. Publisher's shortened name;
6. Most recent copyright date.

See the following samples for more specific rules for citing books.

Book by One Author

Ehrenreich, Barbara. <u>Nickel and Dimed: On (Not) Getting By in
America</u>. New York: Metropolitan, 2001.

Several Works by One Author

If you use several books or articles by one author, list the author's name in the first entry. In the next entry or entries, replace the name with three hyphens.

Schlosser, Eric. <u>Fast Food Nation: The Dark Side of the All-
American Meal</u>. Boston: Houghton Mifflin, 2001.
- - - . <u>Reefer Madness: Sex, Drugs, and Cheap Labor in the
American Black Market</u>. Boston: Houghton Mifflin, 2003.

Books with Two or Three Authors or Editors

List the names of the authors in the sequence in which they appear in the book or article. Begin with the last name of the author listed first because it is used to determine the alphabetical order for entries. Then identify the other authors by first and last names.

Yergin, Daniel, and Joseph Stanislaw. <u>The Commanding Heights:
The Battle for the World Economy</u>. New York: Touchstone, 2002.
Trueba, Henry T., Grace Pung Guthrie, and Kathryn Hu-Pei Au, eds.
<u>Culture and the Bilingual Classroom: Studies in Classroom
Ethnography</u>. Rowley: Newbury, 1981.

Books with More than Three Authors or Editors

Name all those involved, or list only the first author or editor with *et al.*, for "and others."

Nordhus, Inger, Gary R. VandenBos, Stig Berg, and Pia Fromholt,
    eds. <u>Clinical Geropsychology</u>. Washington: APA, 1998.

Nordhus, Inger, *et al*., eds. <u>Clinical Geropsychology</u>.
    Washington: APA, 1998.

Work with Group or an Organization as Author

National PTA. <u>National Standards for Parent/Family Involvement
    Programs</u>. Chicago: National PTA, 1997.

Work without an Author

<u>A Visual Dictionary of Art</u>. Greenwich, CT: New York Graphic
    Society, 1974.

Work in a Collection of Pieces All by the Same Author

Malamud, Bernard. "The Assistant." <u>A Malamud Reader</u>. New York:
    Farrar, 1967. 750–95.

Work in a Collection of Pieces by Different Authors

List the editor or editors after the title of the book, if applicable.

Sanneh, Kelefa. "Gettin' Paid: Jay-Z, Criminal Culture, and the
    Rise of Corporate Rap." <u>Da Capo Best Music Writing 2002: The
    Year's Finest Writing on Rock, Pop, Jazz, Country & More</u>.
    Ed. Jonathan Lethem and Paul Bresnick. Cambridge: Da Capo,
    2002.

Work in Several Volumes

Walther, Ingo F. <u>Art of the 20th Century</u>. 2 vols. Cologne:
    Taschen, 1998.

Book in Translation

Houellebecq, Michel. <u>Platform</u>. Trans. Frank Wynne. New York:
    Knopf, 2003.

Book Appearing as Part of a Series

Rohn, Suzanne. <u>The Wizard of Oz: Shaping an Imaginary World</u>.
    Twayne's Masterwork Studies 167. New York: Twayne-Simon,
    1998.

New Edition of an Older Book

Wharton, Edith. <u>The Custom of the Century</u>. 1913. NY Public

Library's Collector's Edition. New York: Doubleday, 1998.

General Guidelines for Articles in Periodicals

When citing an article from a periodical in your Works Cited list, place the information for the citation in the following order:

1. Author's last name, followed by the first name;
2. Title of the article in quotation marks;
3. Title of the publication, underlined;
4. Volume and issue number, if applicable;
5. Date listed by the day, month, and year;
6. Page numbers, if consecutive. If the article is not continuous, list the page on which it begins with a plus sign.

See the following samples for more specific rules for citing articles.

Article in a Journal with Pagination Continuing through Each Volume

Pistol, Todd A. "Unfinished Business: Letters from a Father to

His Son," <u>Journal of Men's Studies</u> 7 (1999): 215–31.

Article in a Journal with Pagination Continuing Only through Each Issue

Guyer, Jane I. "Traditions of Invention in Equatorial Africa."

<u>Africa Studies Review</u> 39.3 (1996): 1–28.

Article in a Monthly (or Bimonthly) Periodical

Cheney, Anne. "The Resurrection Men: Scenes from the Cadaver

Trade." <u>Harper's Magazine</u> Mar. 2004: 45–54.

Ivins, Molly. "Lone Star Strange." <u>Utne Reader</u> Mar.–Apr. 2004:

38–41.

Article in a Weekly (or Biweekly) Periodical

Thottam, Jyoti. "Is Your Job Going Abroad?" <u>Time</u> 1 Mar. 2004:

26–36.

Valby, Karen. "Just a Small Town Girl." <u>Entertainment Weekly</u>

27 Feb. 2004: 67–69.

Article in a Daily Newspaper

Gross, Jane. "Older Women Team Up to Face Future Together."

New York Times 27 Feb. 2004: A1+.

Article with No Author

"New Fuel for the Culture Wars." The Economist 28 Feb. 2004:

29–28.

Editorial in a Periodical

"Down and Dirty in the Gun Debate." New York Times 27 Feb. 2004:

A26.

Editorial Written to the Editor of Periodical

Campell-Orde, John. Letter. The Atlantic Mar. 2004: 14–16.

Review in a Periodical

Hitchens, Christopher. "Great Scot." Rev. of John Buchan: The

Presbyterian Cavalier. The Atlantic Mar. 2004: 104–107.

General Guidelines for Electronic Sources

When citing an electronic source in your Works Cited page, place the relevant information for the citation in the following order:

1. Author's last name, followed by the first name;
2. Title, either in quotation marks if you are citing an individual section or article or underlined if you are citing the entire site;
3. Publication information for the print version, if applicable;
4. Title of the site, if not already given;
5. Date the material was published or last updated;
6. Name of organization sponsoring the site, if applicable;
7. Date you accessed the information listed by the day, month, and year;
8. Electronic address or URL enclosed in angle brackets "< >".

For many Web pages, the URL might be unwieldy and too long to retype in your Works Cited. In those cases, cite the main page or search page URL. See the following samples for more specific rules for citing articles.

Work on a CD-ROM Database

Use "n.p." to indicate either "no place" or "no publisher" if such information is not available. Use "n.d." to indicate "no date."

"Landforms of the Earth: Cause, Course, Effect, Animation." <u>Phenomena of the Earth</u>. CD-ROM. N.p.: Springer Electronic Media/MMCD, 1998.

<u>Life in Tudor Times</u>. CD-ROM. Princeton Films for the Humanities and Sciences, 1996.

Work on a Nonperiodical CD-ROM

Poe, Edgar Allan. "The Raven." <u>ARIEL: A Reader's Interactive Exploration of Literature</u>. CD-ROM. New York: McGraw-Hill, 2003.

Internet Site

Page, Barbara. <u>Elizabeth Bishop at Vassar College</u>. 17 Dec. 2001. Vassar College. 5 Mar. 2004 <http://projects.vassar.edu/bishop/>.

Periodical Article Available Online

Markon, Jerry. "Va. Colleges May Bar Illegal Immigrants." <u>washingtonpost.com</u> 26 Feb. 2004. 27 Feb. 2004. <http://www.washingtonpost.com/wp-dyn/articles/A6936-2004Feb25.html>.

Article from an Online Scholarly Journal

Hsiung, Yuwen. "Kurosawa's Throne of Blood and East Asia's Macbeth." <u>CLCWeb: Comparative Literature and Culture: A WWWeb Journal</u>. 6.1 (2004). 3 Mar. 2004 <http://clcwebjournal.lib.purdue.edu/clcweb04-1/hsiung04.html>.

Review Available Online

Edelstein, David. "Lady and the Taliban." Rev. of <u>Osama</u>. <u>Slate</u>. 13 Feb. 2004. 16 Feb. 2004. <http://slate.msn.com/id/2095476>.

E-mail

After the subject line of the e-mail, indicate that the source is an "E-mail to the author."

Hadley, Destiny. "Re: Production Questions Arising." E-mail to the author. 1 Mar. 2004.

Posting to a Newsgroup

After the title of the post, indicate that the source is an "Online posting."

> Peter, Frank. "CFP Islam and the Dynamics of European National
>   Societies." Online posting. 26 Feb. 2004. 27 Feb. 2004.
>   <http://www.h-net.org/search>.

Other Sources

See the following samples of other types of sources that you might cite in your paper.

Film, Video, DVD

List the title, director, and key performer(s). For a DVD or videocassette, include the original release and medium before the distributor and date of distribution.

> Lost in Translation. Dir. Sofia Coppola. Perf. Bill Murray. Focus
>   Features: 2003.
>
> The Deer Hunter. Dir. Michael Cimino. Perf. Robert DeNiro,
>   Christopher Walken, and Meryl Streep. 1978. DVD. Universal:
>   2002.

Programs on Radio or Television

List the title of the show, any key people (such as producer, director, or actors), and the title of the series. Identify the network, local station with city, and date the show was broadcast.

> "The Invasion of Iraq." Prod. Eamonn Matthews. Frontline. PBS.
>   WNET, New York. 1 Mar. 2004.

CD or Other Recording

Only identify the format if it isn't a compact disc.

> Outkast. Speakerboxx/The Love Below. Arista, 2003.

Presentation at a Professional Meeting or Conference

> Sommers, Nancy. "The Undergraduate Writing Experience: A Longi-
>   tudinal Perspective." Conference on College Composition and
>   Communication. Sheraton Hotel, New York. 21 Mar. 2003.

Published or Personal Letter

> Ferster, Judith. Letter to the author. 1 Mar. 2004.

Thackeray, William Makepeace. "To George Henry Lewes." 6 Mar.

    1848. Letter 452 of <u>Letters and Private Papers of William</u>

    <u>Makepeace Thackeray</u>. Ed. Gordon N. Ray. Cambridge: Harvard

    UP, 1946. 335—354.

Published or Personal Interview

Raccuia, Lorraina. Telephone interview. 13 Feb. 2004.

Stameshkin, Anne. Personal interview. 20 Feb. 2004.

Previn, Andre. Interview. "A Knight at the Keyboard." By Jed

    Distler. <u>Piano and Keyboard</u>. Jan.—Feb. 1999: 24—29.

AMERICAN PSYCHOLOGICAL ASSOCIATION (APA) DOCUMENTATION STYLE

Academics in the social sciences use the American Psychological Association (APA) style to document sources. The following examples illustrate how to cite a source in the body of your paper and how to list the works cited at the end of your paper. For more information about APA style, consult the following:

American Psychological Association. *Publication Manual of the American Psychological Association.* 5th ed. Washington, DC: APA, 2001.
The Purdue University Online Writing Lab http://owl.english.purdue.edu/ handouts/research/r_apa.html

APA Style for In-text Citations

The basic APA in-text citation includes the author's last name and the date of publication, information generally sufficient to identify a source in the reference list. Although researchers in the social sciences often cite works as a whole, the page number can be added to identify exactly where a quotation or other specific information is located. If the author's name is included in the text, it does not need to be repeated in the citation.

Single Author

The city's most current traffic flow analysis (Dunlap, 2001) proposed two alternatives.

Nagle (2001) compared the costs and benefits of both designs.

Two Authors

Use both names each time a source is cited. Use the word *and* to join them in the text, but use an ampersand (&) when the names only appear in the citation.

```
Shultz and Feinstein (2000) outline the advantages of social
promotion.
```

```
An earlier study (Feldman & Johnson, 1996) was critical of the
proposed plan.
```

Three to Five Authors

Supply all the names the first time the source is cited. If it is cited again, use only the name of the first author and *et al.,* to mean "and others."

```
Whittaker, Brooke, and Harris (2002) maintain that mixed-use
real estate helps promote a more livable environment.
```

```
Whittaker et al. (2002) detail a set of steps that can be used
to revitalize most urban centers.
```

More than Five Authors

Use only the name of the first author with *et al.* In the list of references, supply the name of the first six authors.

```
Kao et al. (2001) continue to address the environmental
consequences of urban sprawl.
```

Group or Organization as Author

```
The Ford Foundation (1998) outlined several efforts to change
decision-making processes.
```

Work without an Author

```
"A Question of Justice?" (2004) identifies several of the prob-
lems in addressing global inequality.
```

Page Numbers for a Direct Quote

```
Impeding any rational understanding of terror is the suggestion
that terror "tends to magnify perceptions" (Mitchell, 2004,
p. 79).
```

Two or More Works in the Same Citation

If several citations are grouped in one pair of parentheses, arrange them alphabetically.

```
Recent reports about the quality of urban life (Chen & Hessenger,
2003; Kay, 1999; Walker & Moore, 2000) extol the benefits of
shared community space.
```

Letters, Telephone Calls, E-mail Messages, and Similar Communications

Communications that are personal are cited only in the text. Because no one else can retrieve or research them, they are not cited in the references.

```
Changes were made in order to maximize efficiency (J. Carter,

personal communication, January 3, 2004).
```

APA Style for List of References

As you examine the following examples, notice how capitalization, italics, punctuation, and other features change with the type of source noted. (If italics are unavailable to you, you may use underlining.) Although the entries in an APA reference list follow very specific patterns, references in your paper—to titles, for instance—should use standard capitalization. Similarly the word *and* should be spelled out in your paper (except in parenthetical citations) even though the ampersand (&) is used in the references.

General Guidelines for Books

When citing a book in your Works Cited page, place the information for the citation in the following order:

1. Author's last name, followed by the initials of first and middle name;
2. Most recent publication date;
3. Full title of the book, including subtitle, in italics and with only the first word and any proper nouns capitalized;
4. Edition number in parentheses;
5. The place of publication;
6. Publisher's shortened name.

See the following samples for more specific rules for citing books.

Books with One Author

```
Bryson, B. (2003). A short history of nearly everything. New

    York: Broadway.

Nuckalls, C. W. (1998). Culture: A problem that cannot be

    solved. Madison: University of Wisconsin Press.
```

Several Works by One Author

List the works in order of publication, starting with the earliest.

```
Schlosser, E. (2001). Fast food nation: The dark side of the

    all-American meal. Boston: Houghton Mifflin.

Schlosser, E. (2003). Reefer madness: Sex, drugs, and cheap

    labor in the American black market. Boston: Houghton Mifflin.
```

Books with Two or More Authors or Editors

List the names of the authors in the sequence in which they appear in the book or article. Use an ampersand (&) in place of the word *and*. Indicate an editor or editors by following their name with the abbreviation *Ed.* or *Eds.* in parentheses. Only use *et al.* in place of names after the first six authors or editors.

> Yergin, D., & Stanislaw, J. (2002). *The commanding heights: The*
> *battle for the world economy.* New York: Touchstone.

> Lieblich, A., McAdams, D., & Josselson, R. (Eds.). (2004).
> *Healing plots: The narrative basis for psychotherapy.*
> Washington: APA.

Work with Group or an Organization as Author

When the author is also the publisher, "Author" is used as the publisher's name.

> Amnesty International. (1998). *Children in South Asia: Securing*
> *their rights.* New York: Author.

Book without an Author

> *Ultimate visual dictionary of science.* (1998). New York: Dorling
> Kindersley.

Work in a Collection of Pieces by Different Authors

List the editor or editors after the title of the book, if applicable.

> Boehlert, E. (2001). Invisible man: Eminem. In N. Hornby &
> B. Schafer (Eds.), *Da Capo best music writing of 2001: The*
> *year's finest writing on rock, pop, jazz, country & more*
> (pp. 119—127). Cambridge: Da Capo Press.

New Edition of an Older Book

When you cite a reprinted book in your paper, include the original publication date at the end of the citation.

> Packard, F.A. (1969). *The daily public school in the United*
> *States.* New York: Arno Press. (Original work published 1866).

Book in Translation

When you cite a translation, include the name of the translator after the title. Also, cite the original publication date as you would with an older book.

Cervantes, M. (2003). *Don Quixote*. (E. Grossman, Trans.) New
   York: Ecco Press. (Original work published 1605.)

Article or Entry in a Reference Volume

Crystal, D. (Ed.). (1994). Breadfruit. In *The Cambridge
   encyclopedia* (2nd ed., p. 175). Cambridge: Cambridge
   University Press.

Work Issued by a Federal, State, or Other Government Agency

Nelson, R. E., Ziegler, A. A., Serino, D. F., & Basner, P. J.
   (1987). Radioactive waste processing apparatus. *Energy
   research abstracts* Vol. 12, (Abstract No. 34680.) Washington,
   DC: U.S. Department of Energy, Office of Scientific and
   Technical Information.

General Guidelines for Periodicals

When citing an article from a periodical in your list of references, place the information for the citation in the following order:

1. Author's last name, followed by the initials of first and middle name;
2. Year of publication, followed by month and day if applicable;
3. Article name, with only the first word and proper nouns capitalized;
4. Full title of the periodical, including subtitle in italics;
5. Volume in italics, if applicable;
6. Page numbers.

See the following samples for more specific rules for citing periodicals.

Article in a Journal with Pagination Continuing through Each Volume

Greene, J. O., Rucker, M. P., Zauss, E. S., & Harris, A. A.
   (1998). Communication anxiety and the acquisition of message-
   production skill. *Communication Education, 47*, 337–47.

Article in a Journal with Pagination Continuing Only through Each Issue

Brune, L. H. (1998). Recent scholarship and findings about the
   Korean War. *American Studies International, 36*(3), 4–16.

Article in a Monthly or Bimonthly Periodical

Werde, B. (2004, March). The war at home. *Wired*, 104–105.

Article in a Weekly or Biweekly Periodical

Hersh, S. M. (2004, March 8). The deal. *The New Yorker*, 32—37.

Article in a Daily Newspaper

Roig-Franzia, M. (2004, March 2). Weekend warriors go full time: National guard deployment is the biggest since World War II. *The Washington Post*, pp. A1, A16.

Article with No Author

More or less equal? (2004, March 13). *The Economist*, 69—71.

Review in a Periodical

Eagleton, T. (2004, March) I am, therefore I think [Review of the book *Flesh in the age of reason*]. *Harper's Magazine*, 87—90.

General Guidelines for Electronic Sources

When citing an electronic source in your list of references, place the relevant information for the citation in the following order:

1. Author's last name, followed by the first name;
2. Publication date in parentheses;
3. Title of document, including any journal information, if applicable;
4. The term "Retrieved" followed by the date the information was retrieved;
5. The electronic address or URL preceded with the term "from."

If the URL directs someone to the information rather than the material itself, use "Available from" in place of "Retrieved" and the date. For example, see the sample citation of a "Posting to a Newsgroup" on page A-47. See the following samples for more examples for citing electronic sources.

Work on a CD-ROM Database

Real facts about the sun. (2000). *The Dynamic Sun*. Retrieved October 27, 2001, from NASA Database.

Internet Site

Amnesty International. (2004). Syria: Punished for using the internet — Amnesty International calls for an end to the suppression of the right to freedom of expression. Retrieved March 18, 2004, from http://web.amnesty.org/library/index/engmde240172004

Periodical Article Available Online

> Booth, S. (2004, March 16). Teenage waist-land. *Salon*. Retrieved
>
> March 16, 2004, from http://www.salon.com/mwt/feature/2004/
>
> 03/16/gastric_bypass/index.html

Article from an Electronic Version of a Printed Journal

If you are citing the electronic version of an article that also appears in print, note that it is an electronic version after the title.

> Deangelis, T. (2002, March). Promising treatments for anorexia
>
> and bulimia [Electronic version]. *Monitor on Psychology*,
>
> *33*(3). Retrieved March 15, 2004, from
>
> http://www.apa.org/monitor/mar02/promising.html

Posting to a Newsgroup

> Sufian, S. (2004, February 14). Mental disability in Iraq.
>
> H-Disability Discussion Group. Available from
>
> http://www.h-net.org/~disabil/

Other Sources

See the following samples of other types of sources that you might cite in your paper.

Film, Video, DVD

> Ahlbreg, J. B. (Producer), & Morris, E. (Producer/Director).
>
> (2003). *The fog of war: The eleven lessons from the life of*
>
> *Robert S. McNamara* [Motion picture]. United States: Sony
>
> Pictures Classics.

Programs on Radio or Television

If you are citing the whole series,

> Glassman, G. (Writer/Director/Producer). (2004). Crash of flight
>
> 111 [Television series episode]. In P. Apsell (Executive
>
> Producer), *NOVA*. Boston: WGBH.

CD or Other Recording

Include the name of the performer if different than the writer.

> Marshall, C. (2003). Free [Recorded by Cat Power]. On *You are*
>
> *free* [CD]. New York: Matador.

Credits

1996, "Perceived Experiences of Racism as Stressful Life Events," *Community Mental Health Journal*, 32.3, pp. 223–233. Reprinted by permission of Kluwer Academic/Plenum Publishers. UPDIKE, JOHN, "A&P," from *Pigeon Feathers and Other Stories*, by John Updike. Copyright © 1962, renewed 1990 by John Updike. Used by permission of Alfred A. Knopf, a division of Random House, Inc. VALDEZ, LUIS, *Los Vendidos*. Copyright © Luis Valdez. Reprinted by permission of the author. WALKER, ALICE, "Everyday Use," from *In Love and Trouble: Stories of Black Women*. Copyright © 1973 by Alice Walker. Reprinted by permission of Harcourt, Inc. WALLING, HOBART, 1997, "Life's Brief Candle: A Shakespearean Guide to Death and Dying for Compassionate Physicians," *Western Journal of Medicine*, 166, pp. 280–284. Reprinted by permission of BMJ Publishing Group. WEBB, CHARLES HARPER, "Tone of Voice" from *Liver*. Copyright © 1999. Reprinted by permission of The University of Wisconsin Press. WELTY, EUDORA, "A Worn Path," from *A Curtain of Green and Other Stories*. Copyright © 1941 and renewed 1969 by Eudora Welty. Reprinted by permission of Harcourt, Inc. WEST, CORNEL, "Black Sexuality: The Taboo Subject," from *Race Matters*. Copyright © 1993, 2001 by Cornel West. Reprinted by permission of Beacon Press, Boston. WILBUR, RICHARD, "For C;" "Mayflies;" from *Mayflies: New Poems and Translations*. Copyright © 2000 by Richard Wilbur, reprinted by permission of Harcourt, Inc. WILBUR, RICHARD, "A Late Aubade," from *Walking to Sleep: New Poems and Translations*. Copyright © 1968 and renewed 1996 by Richard Wilbur. Reprinted by permission of Harcourt, Inc. Originally appeared in *The New Yorker*. WILLIAMS, WILLIAM CARLOS, "The Dance;" "Landscape with the Fall of Icarus;" from *Collected Poems 1939–1962, Volume II*. Copyright © 1953 by William Carlos Williams. Reprinted by permission of New Directions Publishing Corp. WILLIAM, WILLIAM CARLOS, "Poem," "The Yachts," from *Collected Poems 1909–1939, Volume I*. Copyright © 1938 by New Directions Publishing Corp. Reprinted by permission of New Directions Publishing Corp. WILSON, AUGUST, *Fences*. Copyright © 1986 by August Wilson. Used by permission of Dutton Signet, a division of Penguin Group (USA) Ltd. WILSON, EDWARD O., reprinted from *American Journal of Preventive Medicine*, 20 (3), "Nature Matters," pp. 234–240, 2001, with permission from American Journal of Preventive Medicine. WOLFF, TOBIAS, "Powder," from *Fish Stories or The Night in Question: Stories*, by Tobias Wolff. Copyright © 1996 by Tobias Wolff. Used by permission of Alfred A. Knopf, a division of Random House, Inc. WRIGHT, JAMES, "Lying in a Hammock at William Duffy's Farm in Pine Island, Minnesota," from *Above the River: The Complete Poems*. Copyright © by Anne Wright and reprinted by permission of Wesleyan University Press. Reprinted with permission. WRIGHT, RICHARD, "Big Black Good Man," from *Best American Stories of 1958*. London: Chatto and Windus. Reprinted with permission. YAMADA, MITSUYE, "To the Lady," *Camp Notes and Other Writings*. Copyright © 1992 by Mitsuye Yamada. Reprinted by permission of Rutgers University Press. YOUNG, NEIL, "Love Is a Rose." Copyright © 1975 (Renewed) Silver Fiddle Music. All Rights Reserved. Used by permission. Warner Brothers Publications, U.S., Inc., Miami, FL 33014. ZIMMER, PAUL, "The Day Zimmer Lost Religion," from *Crossing to Sunlight: Selected Poems*. Copyright © 1976 by Paul Zimmer. Reprinted by permission.

Index